DICTIONARY OF CANADIAN BIOGRAPHY

DICTIONARY OF CANADIAN BIOGRAPHY

DICTIONNAIRE BIOGRAPHIQUE DU CANADA

GENERAL EDITORS

GEORGE W. BROWN

1959–1963

DAVID M. HAYNE

1965–1969

FRANCESS G. HALPENNY

1969–

DIRECTEURS ADJOINTS

MARCEL TRUDEL

1961–1965

ANDRÉ VACHON

1965–1971

UNIVERSITY OF TORONTO PRESS

LES PRESSES DE L'UNIVERSITÉ LAVAL

DICTIONARY
OF CANADIAN
BIOGRAPHY

VOLUME III

1741 TO 1770

UNIVERSITY OF TORONTO PRESS

STAFF OF THE DICTIONARY

TORONTO

MARY McD. MAUDE textual editor

MARY P. BENTLEY, JANE E. GRAHAM, JOHN ST. JAMES manuscript editors

QUEBEC

GASTON TISDEL directeur des recherches

MARIE-CÉLINE BLAIS, MICHEL PAQUIN chargés de recherche

JEAN-PIERRE ASSELIN assistant à l'édition

TRANSLATOR J. F. FLINN

CONTENTS

INTRODUCTION

VOLUME III is the fourth volume of the *Dictionary of Canadian Biography/Dictionnaire biographique du Canada* to be published. Volume I, presenting persons who died between the years 1000 and 1700, appeared in 1966, and was followed in 1969 by volume II, based on death dates between 1701 and 1740. This numerical and chronological sequence was broken in 1972 with the publication of volume X, dealing with persons who died between 1871 and 1880. That volume, which had been inaugurated by means of a large grant from the Centennial Commission at the time of the celebration of Canada's 100 years of confederation, was the first venture of the DCB/DBC into the 19th century, and our staff and contributors have continued to work there as well as in the 18th century. Thus publication of volume IX (death dates 1861–1870) is expected to follow that of volume III.

The introductions to volumes I and II contain an account of the founding of the DCB by means of the generous bequest of James Nicholson (1861–1952), and of the establishment of the DBC with the support of Université Laval. The DCB/DBC has continued to develop the collaboration that has made execution of its immense bicultural and bilingual project possible, but at the same time has maintained the principles and standards of operation and selection set out in the preliminary pages of its first volumes. Acknowledgements of volume III record the gratitude of the DCB/DBC to the increased assistance of the Canada Council in 1973 which has especially supported its efforts to carry the project forward in the spirit and manner of its founders but at a faster pace.

The 170 contributors to volume III, writing in either English or French, have provided 550 biographies ranging in length from 300 to 10,000 words. They were invited to contribute because of their special knowledge of the period of the volume and the persons who figured in it, and all have been asked to write in accordance with the DCB/DBC's *Directives to Contributors*. It sets out a general aim for articles:

> Each biography should be an informative and stimulating treatment of its subject, presented in readable form. All factual information should be precise and accurate, and be based upon reliable (preferably primary) sources. Biographies should not, however, be mere catalogues of dates and events, or compilations of previous studies of the same subject. The biographer should try to give the reader an orderly account of the personality and achievements of the subject, against the background of the period in which the person lived and the events in which he or she participated.

After editorial preparation in the offices of the DCB/DBC and final approval by the author, each biography was translated into the other language, and then the printer's manuscript for the two parallel volumes in English and French was assembled.

The time span of volume III is 30 years, as compared with the 700 years of volume I and the 40 years of volume II. The contraction reflects the increased number of candidates for inclusion, with a larger population and a wider area that in volume III extends from Newfoundland to the western plains of the fur-traders, south into the Ohio and Mississippi country, and north to the upper reaches of Hudson Bay. The biographies present together a picture of developing societies in the areas of North America first occupied by Europeans and also of exploration beyond the great river systems of the east and the shores of Hudson Bay. Seigneurs and artisans, notaries and priests, governors, intendants, and bishops, surgeons and writers, criminals and heroes carry forward the story of the people of New France, and many biographies are of people in British colonies whose lives were connected with that story. The results of new documentary research undertaken on behalf of the DCB/DBC by our contributors are apparent in volume III as in other volumes. Of particular interest in this volume is the information provided about New France's merchants and entrepreneurs, those of the western fur trade but also those who established posts far up the Gulf coast towards the Labrador and those who carried on active trade with France and with the West Indies; at the end of the Seven Years' War most of these enterprises had to be abandoned. The explorers of volume III who make their way out into the western plains, with La Vérendrye and his sons at the forefront, introduce an enormous new area of endeavour, and the great trade rivalries that ensued will be especially important in the immediately succeeding volumes of the DCB/DBC. Native peoples are again represented in this volume to the extent documentation permits, and again they are caught up in the conflicts of Europeans in trade and war.

Volume III, of course, is much concerned with the repeated warfare that in the mid 18th century brought French and British into fierce combat for sovereignty and culminated in the Seven Years' War. The influence of these contests on the lives of the persons in volume III, and also many of those who will be in volume IV, has prompted the inclusion here of two introductory essays by Professors W.J. Eccles and C.P. Stacey, which describe the organization of the contending military forces. The sieges of Louisbourg, the border raids in New England, the skirmishes in the Ohio country, the battles at Carillon and on the Plains of Abraham all appear in a volume that inevitably brings together the two leaders linked by the fortunes of war: Montcalm and Wolfe.

The components of volume III in addition to the introductory essays and the biographies maintain the pattern established in earlier volumes. There is a glossary of Indian tribes, a general bibliography, and a full nominal index with cross-references to other volumes. An appendix contains three biographies which it was not possible to put in their proper place but to which readers will be referred by the indexes.

The members of staff who have been engaged upon volume III in Toronto and Quebec are listed on page iv. Their responsibilities in organizing the contents of the volume and in seeing the complicated text through every stage of editorial preparation and production into a printed book are many and significant. The DCB/DBC gratefully acknowledges their care and their concern in the carrying out of these responsibilities. In the autumn of 1973, M. Jean Hamelin was appointed directeur adjoint of the DCB/DBC. At the time of his appointment volume III had gone to press and so he has begun his participation in the project with volume IX.

It is with a sense of deep gratitude that the DCB/DBC makes a special acknowledgement here of its debt to André Vachon, who resigned as directeur adjoint in 1971, on his appointment as conservateur of the Archives nationales du Québec. M. Vachon came to the DCB/DBC as secrétaire général when the French edition was founded in 1961, and he became directeur adjoint with volume II. He participated in the planning and development of all aspects of the joint endeavours required for the DCB/DBC; his interest and knowledge as historian, editor, and, in the final years of his term, as director of Les Presses de l'université Laval were a constant support. We have benefited always from the vitality and imagination with which his appreciation of the history of New France has been put at the service of the DCB/DBC.

FRANCESS G. HALPENNY

ACKNOWLEDGEMENTS

THE *Dictionary of Canadian Biography/Dictionnaire biographique du Canada* receives assistance, advice, and encouragement from many institutions and individuals. They cannot all be named, nor can their kindness be acknowledged adequately, but we are always conscious of our debt to those who have supported our endeavours.

The DCB/DBC, which owes its founding to the generosity of the late James Nicholson, has been sustained over the years by its parent institutions, the University of Toronto and the University of Toronto Press and the Université Laval and Les Presses de l'université Laval. The Canada Council in 1973 announced a generous grant to the two university presses to help to accelerate the *Dictionary*'s publication programme. In this first volume to appear since the announcement we should like particularly to acknowledge our debt to the council.

Numerous individuals have assisted in the preparation of volume III. The largest group are our distinguished contributors, whose names will be found on pp. 723–29. We also have had the benefit of special consultation over several years with a number of persons, some of them also contributors. We should like to thank: Zilda Barker, Phyllis R. Blakeley, Michel Cauchon, Joseph P. Cossette, Joan Craig, T. A. Crowley, Antonio Dansereau, W. A. B. Douglas, W. J. Eccles, Micheline Fortin, Armand Gagné, Louis Garon, Marie Gérin-Lajoie, Michael Godfrey, Douglas Hay, Gilles Héon, Donald J. Horton, W. A. Hunter, André Juneau, James Lambert, Johane La Rochelle, Jean-Marie Leblanc, Jean-Jacques Lefebvre, T. J. A. Le Goff, Jacques Letarte, Jacques Mathieu, Dale B. Miquelon, Peter N. Moogk, Harold Naugler, Claude Poirier, Bernard Pothier, Honorius Provost, C. J. Russ, Denis Simard, Donald B. Smith, C. P. Stacey, S. Dale Standen, Alice R. Stewart, Étienne Taillemite, F. J. Thorpe, Glyndwr Williams, Yves F. Zoltvany.

Throughout the preparation of volume III we have again enjoyed the most willing cooperation from libraries and archives in Canada and elsewhere. We are particularly grateful to the administrators and staffs of those institutions to which we have most frequently appealed: in Toronto, the University of Toronto Library, the Metropolitan Toronto Central Library, the Ontario Legislative Library, and the Ontario Department of Public Records and Archives; in Quebec, the Bibliothèque générale de l'université Laval, the Bibliothèque and Archives du séminaire de Québec, the Bibliothèque de l'Assemblée nationale, the Archives nationales du Québec, and the Archives de l'archidiocèse de Québec; in Montreal, the Archives nationales du Québec; in Ottawa, the Public Archives of Canada, and the staff in its National Map Collection. The Public Archives of Nova Scotia in Halifax, and the

Fortress of Louisbourg Restoration Section at Louisbourg, Nova Scotia, were extremely helpful. We should like also to thank the staff of the *archives départementales* of France and of the Archives judiciaires du Québec, who answered our numerous requests for information so kindly.

In addition to the editors specifically working on volume III, other persons in, or associated with, the two offices helped with the preparation of the volume. In Toronto, editorial and research assistance have been given by Diane M. Barker, Henri Pilon, Phyllis Creighton, and Robert Brown; secretarial and administrative services have been provided by Paula Reynolds, Susan Dick, Anita Noel. In Quebec, Huguette Filteau was a constant help to the *chargés de recherche* during the last stages of the volume; Pierrette Desrosiers was in charge of the secretariat, assisted by Danielle Bourassa; Marika Cancelier, André Côté, Lucie Bouffard, Gérard Goyer, and Thérèse Pelletier-Lemay provided assistance to the editors at one stage or another of the volume. The translation into French of the biographies written in English has been done with the collaboration of Ethel C. de Léry, Louise Langlois, Claire Wells, and Suzanne Zay.

We should also like to recognize the guidance and encouragement we have received at all times from the two presses with which the DCB/DBC is associated, and in particular Marsh Jeanneret, Eleanor Harman, Harald Bohne, and H. Van Ierssel at University of Toronto Press; Claude Frémont, J.-Arthur Bédard, and Roch-André Rompré at Les Presses de l'université Laval.

DICTIONNAIRE BIOGRAPHIQUE DU CANADA   DICTIONARY OF CANADIAN BIOGRAPHY

Editorial Notes

PROPER NAMES

Persons have been entered under family name rather than title, pseudonym, popular name, nickname, or name in religion, an arrangement which has the advantage of bringing together prominent members of the same family [*see* BÉGON, GAULTIER, etc.]. Where possible the form of the surname is based on the signature (although contemporary spelling of names was often erratic) and is given in the language of origin. Commonly used variant spellings are included in parentheses. The spelling of the period is followed: for example, Beauharnois, which later became Beauharnais. Occasionally, research for a volume has suggested a change in spelling in a family name from that used in volumes published previously: for example, Mombeton (volume II) has been corrected in volume III to Monbeton, and Godé to Gaudé.

In the case of French names, "La," "Le," "Du," and "Des" (but not "de") are considered as part of the name and are capitalized. Compound French names and titles abound: Jean-Baptiste LE MOYNE de Bienville, Pierre GAULTIER de Varennes et de La Vérendrye, etc.; cross-references are made in the text from the compounds to the main entry, under the family name: from Bienville to Le Moyne, and from Varennes and La Vérendrye to Gaultier. First names generally appear in the modern form: Jean rather than Jehan; Noël rather than Noel.

Married women and *religieuses* have been entered under their maiden names, with cross-references to the entry from their husbands' names or their names in religion: Marie-Élisabeth ROCBERT de La Morandière (Bégon de La Cour), Marie-Andrée REGNARD Duplessis, *dite* de Sainte-Hélène.

Indian names have presented a particular problem, since an Indian might be known by his own name (spelled in a variety of ways by the French, English, or Dutch, unfamiliar with Indian languages), by a French or English nickname, and sometimes by a French baptismal name. Because it is impossible to establish an original spelling for an Indian name the form chosen is the one found in standard sources or the one linguists now regard as correct. An effort has been made to include major variants of the original name, as well as nicknames, with appropriate cross-references.

CROSS-REFERENCES WITHIN BIOGRAPHIES

The first time the name of a person who has a biography in volume III appears in another biography his family name is printed in capitals and level small capitals: e.g. Louis-Joseph de MONTCALM, James WOLFE.

ASTERISKS

An asterisk following a name indicates either that the person has a biography in a volume already published – Pierre Le Moyne* d'Iberville; Henry Kelsey* – or that he will receive a biography in a volume to be published:

François Bigot*; Guy Carleton*, Baron Dorchester. Birth and death (or floruit) dates for such persons are given in the index as an indication of the volume in which the biography will be found.

PLACE-NAMES

Place-names are generally given in the form used at the contemporary time of reference with the modern name included in parentheses. Complete consistency, however, has not been possible nor has it been thought desirable. In biographies which have both French and English protagonists, for example, the alternate place-names may be either the contemporary French or the contemporary English form: Oswego (Chouaguen), Lac Saint-Sacrament (Lake George). The English edition cites well-known place-names in their present-day English form: St Lawrence River, Quebec, Montreal, but uses Trois-Rivières rather than Three Rivers.

Many sources have been used as guides to establish 18th century place-names: Champagne, *Les La Vérendrye*; Clark, *Acadia*; Ganong, "Historic sites in New Brunswick," *RSCT*, 2nd ser., V (1899), sect.II, 213–357; *Johnson papers* (Sullivan *et al.*); W. A. Hunter, *Forts on the Pennsylvania frontier, 1753–1758* (Pennsylvania Historical and Museum Commission pub., Harrisburg, 1960); *Manitoba historical atlas . . .*, ed. John Warkentin and R. I. Ruggles (Historical and Scientific Society of Manitoba pub., Winnipeg, 1970); *Place-names of N.S.*; P.-G. Roy, *Inv. concessions*; G. R. Stewart, *American place-names . . .* (Oxford, 1970); Trudel, *Atlas de la Nouvelle-France*; Williams, *British search for the northwest passage*.

Modern names are based whenever possible on the Gazetteer of Canada Series issued by the Canadian Permanent Committee on Geographical Names, Ottawa, and on the *Répertoire géographique du Québec* (Ministère des terres et forêts du Québec, Études toponymiques, nouv. sér., 3, [Québec], 1969). European place-names are identified by county or department if not found in *The Canadian Oxford desk atlas of the world* (3rd ed., Toronto, 1972) and the *Atlas Larousse canadien* (Québec, Montréal, 1971).

QUOTATIONS

Quotations have been translated when the language of the original passage is different from that of the text of the biography. All passages quoted from works published in both languages are given in the accepted translations of these works. A name appearing within square brackets has been added or substituted for the original in order to provide a cross-reference to a biography within the volume or in another volume.

DATES

The discrepancy between Old Style (Julian calendar, used in England until 1752) and New Style (Gregorian calendar, used in Italy, Spain, Portugal, and France from 1582) affects many biographies in volume III. Most biographies, of course, present no problem: dates in those based entirely on English documents can be assumed to be Old Style; and in those based exclusively on French sources, New Style. But when an article draws on both English and continental or Quebec sources, authors have been asked to make the dates in the article uniformly Old or New Style and to indicate after the first date given (o.s.) or (n.s.). It should be noted that: (*a*) Old Style dates were 10 days behind New Style dates throughout the 17th century and 11 days behind in the 18th century; (*b*) the Old Style new year began 25 March and the New Style new year on 1 January (for Old Style dates between January and 25 March, the year is indicated as 1742/43).

BIBLIOGRAPHIES

Each biography is followed by a bibliography. Sources frequently used by authors and editors are cited in shortened form in individual bibliographies, and the general bibliography (pp. 689–722) gives these sources in full. Many abbreviations are used in the individual bibliographies, especially for archival sources; a list of these can be found on p.2.

The individual bibliographies are generally arranged alphabetically according to the five sections of the general bibliography: manuscript sources; primary printed sources (including contemporary newspapers); reference works; studies and theses; and journals. Wherever possible, references to manuscript material give the location of the original documents, rather than of copies. In general the items in individual bibliographies are the sources listed by the contributors, but these items have often been supplemented by bibliographic investigation in the DCB/DBC offices. Any special bibliographical comments by contributors are given with their initials, within square brackets.

TRANSLATION INTO ENGLISH (a note by the translator of French biographies)

The translator has been guided by the principles adopted by the translation committees in previous volumes. While striving to remain faithful to the original text, he has aimed at simplicity and clarity, particularly in translating passages from 18th century documents. The English equivalents for French words decided upon in earlier volumes have normally been used. At the same time it has frequently been necessary to seek new equivalents for terms used in new and different situations. Fields such as trade and commerce, which were becoming much more prominent in this period, present many terms not previously encountered, and even areas familiar from previous volumes reserve surprises. Thus, terms such as *castor gras*, *castor sec*, and *castor moscovite*, while setting new problems of translation, also remind us of the continued importance of the fur trade in New France, while others, such as *compagnon-voyageur* and *marchand-équipeur* or the increasing number of commercial terms, reflect the expanding economic activity and organization of the country in the middle of the 18th century. In addition, with the transfer of Acadia to the British crown and the conquest of Canada, many new and unfamiliar names and titles appear, for which it has been essential to determine the English originals.

The French forces in North America during the Seven Years' War

W. J. ECCLES

FROM 1713 TO 1744 France and England were at peace, the span of one generation. During those years French overseas trade steadily increased. Trade with the French colonies rose from 25,000,000 *livres* a year in 1710 to 140,000,000 by 1741. In the latter year the total of French overseas trade was valued at 300,000,000 *livres*, that is £12,500,000 sterling. Much of this trade was with the Spanish empire, one half to seven-ninths of the goods shipped from Cadiz being French in origin. France now supplied all continental Europe with sugar and coffee, and in addition French fishermen were garnering the lion's share of the fisheries on the Grand Banks and in the Gulf of St Lawrence. But while French trade had expanded during the 1730s, that of England had remained stationary. Moreover, a sizable proportion of England's overseas commerce consisted of contraband trade with the Spanish colonies. Thus, when Spain began taking effective measures to curb this illicit traffic the English commercial community became alarmed; half of the world's maritime commerce might still be under the British flag but were its trade to continue to stagnate while French industry and commerce kept on expanding, then England, its population less than half that of France, might well go the same way as the Netherlands, and eventually be reduced to the status of a fourth-rate power. It was to forfend this possibility that England went to war with Spain in 1739, and with France in 1744.

The British government did not pursue that war, the War of the Austrian Succession, known to the English colonies as King George's War, effectively. It chose to engage France on the continent where the poorly officered British army proved no match for the Maréchal de Saxe, the foremost soldier of his age. In North America a combined Anglo-American and British naval force captured Louisbourg in 1745 [see William PEPPERRELL and Peter WARREN], but it was not until 1747 that the Royal Navy gained the upper hand and succeeded in severing temporarily France's communications with her colonies. By 1748 the belligerents were exhausted and in October of that year the treaty of Aix-la-Chapelle

was signed, which merely restored the *status quo ante bellum*. France recuperated rapidly and her overseas trade quickly recovered. The English commercial community now became convinced that a better conducted spoiling war was essential to prevent the French overtaking them in the struggle for supremacy. The French, on the other hand, had no desire for a maritime war – they had too much to lose; nevertheless, they still had to prepare for it.

Although the West Indies were the great prize – by 1740 the exports of the French islands were valued at 100,000,000 *livres* a year and their imports, mainly slaves, at 75,000,000 – the north Atlantic fisheries were also extremely valuable, particularly since they were regarded as vital by both Britain and France for the training of seamen needed to man their fleets. In 1754, 444 ships from France fished in these waters, employing some 14,000 sailors. In addition the resident maritime population of Île Royale (Cape Breton Island), Îles de la Madeleine, and Gaspé provided a large number of mariners. It was estimated that the loss of these fisheries would cost France 15,000 experienced seamen, nearly a third of her total supply. Canada, on the other hand, produced little except furs, in good years some wheat for export to Louisbourg, and a few ships built at Quebec by the crown at great expense [see Pierre LUPIEN, *dit* Baron, and Louis-Pierre POULIN de Courval Cressé]. This colony was, in fact, an economic liability much of the time. Politically and militarily, however, Canada was regarded as valuable to curb the expansion of the English colonies, hence of England's commercial strength, and to protect Louisiana for whose resources great hopes were entertained. Moreover, it was calculated that in time of war the Canadians, with the aid of a few reinforcements from France, would be able to tie down a much larger British army and a sizable part of the Royal Navy, thus preventing their deployment elsewhere. The success enjoyed by the Canadians against the Anglo-Americans in the previous wars gave every reason for confidence in this policy.

The fortress of Louisbourg was therefore

strengthened to serve as a naval base for a fleet to protect the fisheries, guard the entrance to the St Lawrence, and prey on British shipping. When an influential group of Anglo-American land speculators began to implement their scheme to seize the Ohio valley, thereby threatening the French hold on the west, a Canadian force was dispatched, on orders of the minister of Marine, to drive the Americans out [see Paul MARIN de La Malgue]. Forts were then built in the region. In 1754 came the first clash of arms near Fort Duquesne (Pittsburgh, Pa.). Although war between England and France was not declared until 1756, this skirmish in the wilderness marked the beginning of the Seven Years' War [see Joseph COULON de Villiers de Jumonville].

Unfortunately for France the government, its personnel, and methods, were to prove inadequate to meet the challenge offered by Great Britain and her new-found ally, Prussia. Louis XV could rarely bring himself to make decisions and when he attended council meetings he concerned himself with trivia. Moreover, until 1761 when the Duc de Choiseul was given charge of the ministries of War, Marine, and Foreign Affairs, the ministers, all of them mediocrities or worse, did not remain long in office. During the course of the war there were four ministers of Foreign Affairs, four controllers-general of Finance, four ministers of War, and five ministers of Marine. Their ministries were grossly understaffed and overworked, which resulted in interminable delays and too often in non-decisions. To cap it all, the entire decision-making process was beset by intrigue of Byzantine proportions, the king being to the fore in this activity.

Nor were the instruments of government policy, the armed forces, in better condition. Under Louis XIV, and later under Napoleon, the French army was the best in Europe. Under Louis XV it sank to a low level of efficiency. After the demise of the Maréchal de Saxe its commanders were incompetent. Defence predominated over offence in their thinking. Here too intrigue was rife. Every general in the field knew that many about him, and at the court, were scheming to have him removed. At the regimental level also officers were not distinguished by competence, the military capacity of most of the colonels being virtually nil. Commissions were purchased; money and family connections, not merit, governed advancement.

As is always the case, military tactics were dominated by the principal weapon employed, in this instance the smooth-bore, flint-lock, muzzle-loading musket, mounted with a bayonet, making it both a fire and a shock weapon. Even well-trained soldiers could fire no more than two or three rounds a minute; loading and firing required some 12 movements executed to command and drum beat. At close range, under 80 paces, a musket volley could be murderous, but at that distance there was barely time to reload before the enemy's charge, if it were not checked, reached the line. In battle two basic formations were employed, the line and the column. The line, three ranks deep, depended on the fire power of the musket followed by a bayonet charge against the shattered foe. Attack by column depended on the shock effect of an attack on a narrow front to pierce and shatter the enemy's line. Deployment in line demanded the most rigorous discipline to make the men stand fast and deliver measured volleys against the charging foe. Attack by column also required discipline to have the men press on into the hail of fire. The swifter their advance, the fewer volleys they had to endure. The British army relied on the line; the French at this time still had a predilection for the column, believing that the charge with the *arme blanche* was better suited to their poorly trained troops with their impetuous temperament.

To manoeuvre the troops on the battlefield, and have them attack either in line or in column, required that they receive at least 18 months of basic training on the drill ground until they became virtually automatons. After that, five years' experience was deemed necessary to produce a good, dependable soldier. Iron discipline was the essence of it all, instilled by fear and by *esprit de corps*. The men had to be rendered more afraid of their own officers than of the enemy, and to be willing to stand and die rather than turn and run. Everything depended on the ability of the officers to manoeuvre their troops, and on the discipline and training of the men once battle was joined. Compared to other European armies the French army was deficient on both counts. Its officers lacked spirit and professional training, its men were badly instructed, poorly drilled, and wretchedly disciplined; its equipment, with the exception of the Charleville musket, was inferior. The supply system and the cannon were both antiquated, essentially the same as in the time of Louis XIV. All attempts at reform had been blocked by reactionary elements or vested interests.

The French navy was in a better state than the army. Its ships were superior to those of the Royal Navy. They could outsail and outgun the British ships. A French ship of 52 guns was a match for a British 72. The reverse was true of the officers of the two navies. The British officers were better trained and more aggressive. Although the Royal Navy was in poor shape at the onset of the war it had twice as many ships as the French and its reserve of seamen was much greater. To make matters worse for the French, before war was declared the Royal Navy seized 800 French merchant ships and 3,000 seamen. This was a crippling blow. Moreover, during the course of the war epidemics in the French ports took a heavy toll. At Brest alone, in 1757–58, 2,171 sailors died in a four-month period. Many others fled the ports to avoid the contagion. The navy was reduced to impressing landsmen who had never been afloat to work their ships. Yet despite the superiority of the Royal Navy supply ships reached Quebec every year until 1760 [*see* Jacques KANON], after the city had been taken by WOLFE's army.

When hostilities began the French had three distinct military forces at their disposal in North America: the colonial regular troops (*troupes de la Marine*), the militia, and the Indian allies. The colonial regulars were infantry units raised for guard duty in the naval ports of France and for service in the colonies. They were the creation of Louis XIV's great minister Jean-Baptiste Colbert and were under the control of the ministry of Marine, not of the ministry of War, hence were known as the *troupes franches de la Marine*. To obviate the abuses rampant in the regimental organization of the army Colbert had incorporated these marines in independent companies rather than in regiments. Commissions were not purchased but were obtained on merit and, of course, influence. A good reference was essential. Each company consisted of a captain, a lieutenant, a brevet ensign, a second ensign, two cadets, two sergeants, three corporals, two drummers and 41 soldiers. By 1758, 20 companies of these marines were stationed at Louisbourg and 21 in Louisiana. In Canada there were 30 companies in 1756. In that year their strength was increased to 65 non-commissioned ranks per company, and the following year their number was raised to 40 companies with a nominal strength of 2,760 officers and men.

During the half-century following the establishment of the colonial regulars, the officer corps became Canadian although the other ranks were nearly all recruited in France. By the 1740s commissions were reserved for the sons of serving officers, who were invariably seigneurs. Unlike the regiments of the French army the colonial regulars gave no direct entry into the commissioned ranks, except for such privileged persons as the son of a governor general [*see* JOSEPH-HYACINTHE and Louis-Philippe de RIGAUD de Vaudreuil]. With that notable exception, every

would-be officer had to serve in the ranks for several years as a cadet. Despite this arduous training, so eager were the Canadians for commissions that in 1728 the age for entry as cadets was lowered to 15, and the waiting list became ever longer. Promotion could not be accelerated by purchase, only by a display of exceptional valour in action, and even then, *only* when a vacancy occurred through death or retirement. This condition served to inculcate a very aggressive spirit in the corps.

When the Seven Years' War began most of the officers of the colonial regulars had had years of military experience at the western posts, in the Fox and Chickasaw campaigns, and in savage raids on the frontier settlements of the English colonies [*see* Louis COULON de Villiers, Jacques LEGARDEUR de Saint-Pierre, François-Marie LE MARCHAND de Lignery, Nicolas-Joseph NOYELLES de Fleurimont]. In addition to their training in the drill manoeuvres demanded in European style warfare these troops had had to master the art of guerilla fighting both against and alongside the Indian nations. They could travel long distances, winter or summer, living off the land if need be, strike swiftly, then disappear before the enemy could muster a force to counter attack. Against them the American provincial troops and militia were no match. Great mobility, deadly marksmanship, skilful use of surprise and forest cover, high morale and, like the Royal Navy, a tradition of victory, gave the colonial regulars their superiority. Just how effective they could be was demonstrated when, in 1755, 250 Canadians with some 600 Indian allies destroyed Edward Braddock's army of 1,500 [*see* Jean-Daniel Dumas*].

Supporting, and frequently serving alongside, the colonial regulars were the militia units. In 1669 Louis XIV had ordered the establishment of militia companies for colonial defence. Each company comprised all the able-bodied men between 15 and 60 in a parish and was commanded by a captain of militia (who also had important civil functions), with a lieutenant, one or two ensigns, and sergeants. They all served without pay. During the wars against the English colonies and hostile Indian nations the militia was called out for war parties, to repel invading forces, for corvées to supply the frontier fortresses, or for the building of military roads.

When properly utilized this Canadian militia was a formidable fighting force, but its men were of little use in European style warfare. Faced with regular army units in the open, firing massed volleys, they took cover or fled. They would not stand and be shot at while waiting for an order to fire back. There were other limits to the use that could be made of these habitant soldiers; many of them had to be released for work on the land in the spring and in late summer for the harvest; others had to serve in the canoe brigades to the western posts. A muster roll of 1750 lists 165 companies varying in number from 31 to 176, comprising 724 officers, 498 sergeants, 11,687 men; in all, 12,909. This total may well be too low, by as much as 25 per cent; it gives for one company a total strength of 55 whereas a separate muster roll of that particular company lists 76 names, half of whom are noted as fit to go on detachment. An important factor with these militiamen was their high morale. When they were ordered to Quebec in 1759 to help defend the city against Wolfe's army, MONTCALM and his staff were astounded by the number that appeared, boys of 12, old men of 85, all demanding muskets and the right to serve. The contrast with the militia of the English colonies could not be more marked.

In addition to the colonial regulars and the militia the French had the aid of a horde of Indian allies, Micmacs, Abenakis, Ottawas, Algonkins, Delawares, Shawnees, to mention a few. The British, significantly, had virtually none. The operative word here is "allies," for these nations would take orders from no one – indeed their own chiefs had no authority over the warriors. They did not regard themselves as an auxiliary force of the French, but as allies in a joint effort against a common foe. Another inducement was the liberal supplies of food, clothing, arms, and munitions provided by the French, as well as the bounties paid for scalps and prisoners. Although they proved to be highly effective in guerilla warfare, the Indians could never be relied on. They were subject to whims that appeared strange to Europeans. After being well supplied a war party would set out but, en route, suffer a change of heart and quietly disperse. Yet mixed war parties of Canadians and Indians did wreak havoc on the Anglo-American settlements and tied down enemy forces vastly superior in numbers. The enemy's supply lines were constantly threatened, his advanced bases frequently destroyed. The mere knowledge that a French force had Indians with it was sometimes enough to cause a large Anglo-American force to flee or surrender. As scouts and intelligence agents the Indians were particularly useful. Although their verbatim reports were, on occasion, imaginary tales of things not seen, they could take prisoners far behind the enemy's lines who revealed much when questioned by the French. By such means the French were usually better informed than

were the British of the opponent's dispositions and intentions.

When, in 1754, the British government decided to launch an all out assault on New France without the formality of a declaration of war, it detached two battalions of regular troops for service in America. France had to counter this threat by reinforcing its units at Louisbourg and in Canada. A serious military and administrative problem immediately emerged. The colonies were in the charge of the ministry of Marine but its colonial regular troops could not be expanded rapidly enough to meet the emergency. Recourse had to be had to the regiments of the French regular troops (*troupes de terre*, so called because most of them took their titles from the provinces of France where they were raised) under the ministry of War, and the mutual hostility of these two ministries was extreme. Moreover, the governor general of New France, always an officer in the Marine, was commander-in-chief of all the French forces in North America whether stationed at Louisbourg, in Canada, or Louisiana. The council of ministers, however, agreed that divided responsibility would be fatal, and that unity of command, at such a remove from the centre of authority, was essential. It was therefore concluded that the reinforcement of six army battalions from the regiments of La Reine, Artois, Bourgogne, Languedoc, Guyenne, and Béarn, 3,600 officers and men all told, would be placed under the orders of the ministry of Marine, which would be responsible for their pay and maintenance.

Two of the battalions, Artois and Bourgogne, went to Louisbourg. The other four went to Canada. In 1756 a battalion each from the La Sarre and Royal Roussillon regiments were shipped to Quebec, and in 1757 two more battalions from the Régiment de Berry were sent to Canada. Each battalion had an officer corps made up of a lieutenant-colonel in command, an adjutant (*aide-major*), and a surgeon major; a captain, a lieutenant, and a sub-lieutenant (*sous-lieutenant*) of grenadiers; 12 fusilier captains, 12 lieutenants, and two ensigns. The other ranks consisted of the grenadier company comprising two sergeants, two corporals, two lance-corporals, one drummer, 38 grenadiers; 24 fusilier sergeants, 24 corporals, 24 lance-corporals, 12 drummers, and 396 fusiliers; a total strength of 557. The grenadier company in each battalion was an élite group of shock troops, men chosen for their superior physique, martial appearance, and training. One of their functions was to stand directly behind the line in battle to prevent, with their bayonets, the fusiliers from turning tail – as occurred at Carillon in 1758 when some of the de Berry regiment made to bolt. If a section of the line reeled under an assault, the grenadiers stepped into the breach.

Separate from both the French regular troops and the colonial regulars were the engineers, represented by two French officers, Nicolas Sarrebource* de Pontleroy and Jean-Nicolas Desandrouins*, and a company of artillery. At this time the artillery was the weakest branch in the French army. The unit in Canada, commanded by François Le Mercier*, comprised eight officers, three of them Canadians, four sergeants, ten cadets, and 86 gunners. The engineers were mainly concerned with fortifications. Pontleroy agreed with Montcalm that all the fortifications in the colony, including Quebec, were worthless and could not resist an assault let alone bombardment. On some points, however, Pontleroy's testimony is palpably false, for example his statement that there was no dry moat beneath the walls of Quebec. After Quebec fell to the British the French officers, including Desandrouins, deemed its defences virtually impregnable. As for the frontier fortresses, in their criticisms the French officers ignored the fact that they had been built to fend off the feeble Anglo-American forces and hostile Indians, not a British army which, although its engineers were poor, had in the Royal Regiment of Artillery one of the finest artillery corps in the world.

At Louisbourg the four battalions from the regiments of Artois, Bourgogne, Cambis, and Volontaires Étrangers, along with 1,000 colonial regulars and 120 gunners, all came under the orders of the commandant, Augustin de BOSCHENRY de Drucour. For the battalions serving in Canada, however, a general staff had to be appointed. Baron Jean-Armand de DIESKAU accepted the appointment as commanding officer with the rank of major-general (maréchal de camp) – making him one of 170 holding that rank in the French army. He was given a staff consisting of a second in command, an adjutant (major), an aide-de-camp, a war commissary (commissaire des guerres) in charge of supplies, and two partisan officers for detached duties.

Great care was taken in the drafting of Dieskau's instructions to prevent any conflict or misunderstanding between him and the newly appointed Canadian-born governor general, Pierre de Rigaud*, Marquis de Vaudreuil. They carefully spelled out that the governor general was in full command of all the military forces. Dieskau was to take his orders from Vaudreuil, and whether he liked them or not he had no alternative but to obey them to the letter. The governor general was required to leave the details of

the command of the army battalions to Dieskau but the latter had to keep the commander-in-chief informed of their strength, deployment, and everything else needed to enable him to make the most effective use of them in any operations he chose to undertake. When, in 1756, the Marquis de Montcalm replaced Dieskau he received the same instructions and the same restricted authority. He and his officers were also subordinate to the governments at Montreal and Trois-Rivières, which consisted of a local governor, a king's lieutenant (lieutenant du roy), a town major, and an adjutant (aide-major). The army battalions were there for one main purpose, to defend the colony, and they had to take their orders from colonial authorities.

The council of ministers also decreed, not only that the French regular troops would, contrary to custom, be paid during the Atlantic voyage but that they would be paid over double the normal rate while serving in America. It was anticipated that the colonial regulars would protest, since the increase was not accorded them, but it was pointed out that they were defending their homeland. Their officers, and some of the men who had married in the colony, could enjoy the pleasures of their own homes and attend to their personal and business affairs when not campaigning. The French officers, on the other hand, had to face the prospect of years of exile from their families and friends in a colony where life was harder, and more expensive, than in France. Unfortunately, there was friction between the army and marine officers at the outset, and the pay differential aggravated the problem. More specifically it caused trouble when replacements for both corps were sent from France. The men all wanted to be incorporated into the higher paid French battalions.

Many of the French officers found campaigning in the North American wilderness not at all to their liking. The tedium of garrison duty at the remote frontier forts sapped their morale. Some of them were physically incapacitated and nearly driven out of their minds by the clouds of mosquitoes and stinging flies. Receiving news from home only once a year, and being unable to cope at such a remove with trouble that might arise, was hard to bear. Some of them were repelled by the seeming barbarism of the Indians and wanted nothing to do with them. The guerilla tactics of the Canadians, both regulars and militia, were remote from their concepts of how war should be waged. Even by European standards the French army was seriously deficient in reconnaissance and light infantry units trained for skirmishing and scouting duties. When army companies were detached to serve with the Canadians on their frontier raids their officers were disconcerted to discover that no mobile field hospitals or baggage trains went with them. Were they to be wounded they would have to make their way back to a French base as best they could before receiving medical attention. Their food supplies and equipment they had to carry on their backs like common soldiers. When rivers were encountered they had to wade or swim across. Resentful Canadians who were ordered to carry them a-cross on their backs had an unfortunate habit of tripping in mid-stream. Some of the French officers declared that this was not warfare at all, and they refused to have any part in it. For them military operations required a secure, comfortable base, with servants, camp followers, clean linen, well-prepared food, and wine, close by the chosen field of battle or fortified place, where all the paraphernalia of siege warfare could be brought into play.

The Canadians formed a low opinion of the French officers, and the latter thought that the Canadians had far too high an opinion of themselves. The Canadians thought the French troops displayed too great a reluctance to seek out the enemy, preferring to remain on the defensive and let the enemy come to them. The defeatist attitude of Montcalm and several of his officers did nothing to ease the situation. While the French troops were employed in garrison duty, taking part in a campaign each summer, then remaining in their dispersed quarters all winter, many of the Canadians were fighting on the enemy's frontiers all year round. Vaudreuil felt constrained to complain to the minister of Marine that the French officers were too loath to abandon their comforts for active campaigning. He also complained that some of these officers, including Montcalm, abused the Canadians shamefully, and that unless a stop were put to it there could be serious trouble. He stated bluntly that the moment hostilities ended he wanted the French troops shipped back to France. One cause of this problem, attested to in considerable detail by an official of the Marine recently arrived from France, may well have been that the French army in Europe, since the days of Louis XIV, had fought its wars on foreign soil and was accustomed to live largely off the land, treating the hostile population of the occupied territory with scant regard.

In this controversy one thing stands out clearly: the calibre of the French officers was much lower than that of the Canadians. Among the senior regimental officers physical and mental competence was not always in evidence. In 1758 Montcalm informed the minister of War that the commandants of the Béarn and Royal Roussillon battalions were *hors de combat* and ought to be retired. In fact, only one lieutenant-colonel, Étienne-Guillaume de SENEZERGUES de La Rodde of the La Sarre regiment was fit for active campaigning. After the battle of Carillon Montcalm had to ship nine officers back to France as quietly as possible. One, a knight of Malta and scion of an illustrious family, had been insane for some time and it had become impossible to conceal his condition; five others were sent back for displaying a want of courage – or as Montcalm put it, "pour avoir manqué à la première qualité nécessaire à un soldat et à un officier" – two for stealing from their fellow officers and one for having displayed considerable talent as a forger. Two other officers were allowed to resign their commissions, for good cause. Montcalm pleaded with the minister to see to it that replacements not be sent merely because their regiments, or their families, wanted to be rid of them. Meanwhile, he was obliged to fill the vacancies by granting the sons of Canadian officers lieutenants' commissions. Vaudreuil, although he sanctioned this solution, pointed out that it had established a bad precedent since these young officers entered the service with a higher rank than the Canadians in the colonial regular troops who had had several years of active campaigning. He added that too many of them could never have hoped to obtain commissions in the Canadian regulars.

Because the population of New France was only a fraction of that of the English colonies, some 75,000 compared to over 1,500,000, it is frequently assumed that the outcome of the war was a foregone conclusion. If numbers alone were what counted then Britain's ally, Prussia, also could not have escaped destruction. Such comparisons can be misleading since the size of the forces that either side could bring to bear was governed by the nature of the terrain, communications, and supply routes. The British had 23,000 regulars in America by 1758, but they were not able to make very effective use of their provincial levies. The largest force they could deploy in a campaign against Canada was 6,300 regulars and 9,000 provincials at Lake Champlain in 1758. That army was routed by Montcalm's 3,500 regulars. Similarly, at Quebec in 1759 Wolfe arrived with 8,500 troops, mostly British regulars. By September his force was reduced to 4,500 effectives. To oppose them the French had over 15,000 men – regulars, militia, and Indians. It was not numerical superiority that conquered Canada but poor generalship on the part of Montcalm that lost Quebec in one battle.

During the course of the war, however, the effectiveness of the British army improved, that of the French declined. On the British side the introduction of short term enlistments and the popularity of the war brought forth higher quality recruits for the regulars. Officers who proved to be too incompetent were weeded out; in some instances they were replaced by highly competent Swiss professional soldiers who, ironically, introduced the Canadian methods and tactics in the wilderness campaigns that the French officers sneered at. On the French side the quality of the reinforcements sent from France was low. They were mostly raw recruits, the sweepings of the streets. Some of them were even cripples who had to be shipped back. To make matters worse they brought disease with them that spread through the ranks and among the civilian population in epidemic proportions. In 1757, 500 troops were hospitalized and more than half of them died. Thus as the number of veteran trained soldiers dwindled through the wastage of war the quality of the regulars declined badly. By 1759 both the French battalions and the colonial regulars were not of the calibre they had been three years earlier. Among the French regulars discipline was not maintained; there were mutinies; morale sank to a low ebb. Thieving, looting, and other crimes became rampant. The war commissary was kept busy sending men before the council of war. He complained, "We spend our life having the rogues punished." The effectiveness of the French battalions was further reduced by Montcalm's decision to bring them up to strength by drafting Canadian militiamen into their ranks. It required more than the grey-white uniform of the French army to make regular soldiers out of them, capable of fighting in line. They did not receive the harsh, intensive, parade-ground training that that type of warfare demanded. The lack was to prove fatal on the Plains of Abraham.

Another frequently stated reason for the conquest of New France is inadequate supplies. The question requires more critical scrutiny than it has received to date. Far too much tainted subjective evidence has been accepted at face value. Owing to crop failures and the greatly increased number of mouths to feed, estimated to be 17 per cent, the colony could not produce enough food to supply its needs. It was dependent on supplies shipped from France, but the supply ships reached Quebec every year up to 1759. In 1757 Montcalm reported that a three years' supply of clothing for the troops had arrived and there was nothing to worry about on that score. Moreover, sizable quantities of food and other military supplies were captured by the

French; enough to maintain the army for months were captured at Oswego (Chouaguen) and Fort William Henry (Lake George, N.Y.). There is no viable evidence that military operations were curtailed by a shortage of supplies. Poor distribution and the habitants' distrust of inflated paper money obliged the urban population to tighten its belt and eat unpalatable food at times, such as horse meat, but no one starved.

Account also has to be taken of the fact that the British had supply problems. The chicanery of their colonial supply contractors and the provincial assemblies was notorious. At Quebec in 1759 over a quarter of Wolfe's army was on the noneffective list, suffering from the dietary diseases, dysentery and scurvy. Moreover, owing to the military ineptitude of the Anglo-Americans, the British had to import in far larger numbers than the French the most essential military commodity of all, fighting men. Had no regular troops been imported by either side, the Canadians would certainly not have been conquered.

In 1758 Vaudreuil had contrasted the attitude of the colonial regular troops towards the war with that of the French regulars. For the Canadians, he wrote, the colony was their homeland; it was there that they had their families, lands, resources, and aspirations for the future. The French troops on the other hand, being expatriates, wanted only to return home with their honour intact, without having suffered a defeat, caring little what wounds the enemy inflicted on the colony, not even about its total loss.

The events of 1759 and 1760 made all too plain that there was more than a little truth in these charges. After the *débâcle* on the Plains of Abraham the French officers refused to give battle again, despite the fact that they outnumbered the British three to one and still held Quebec. The following year their failure to recapture the city they had abandoned and to block the British drive up Lake Champlain, the arrival of three British armies at the portals of the colony, the failure of reinforcements to arrive from France, all meant that further resistance was completely hopeless. James Murray*, advancing up the river from Quebec, ravaged and burned the homes of the Canadians who had not laid down their arms. At one point his men got out of hand and some Canadian women were violated. Yet Lévis* and his staff still demanded that the British be resisted for the honour of the army, which meant their personal honour and future careers. When many of the Canadians deserted to protect their homes and families the French officers wanted them apprehended and shot. French troops were sent to seize at gun point the last remaining cattle of the habitants, who resisted vigorously since this was all that was left them to feed their families during the coming winter. Even when the British stood at the gates of Montreal in overwhelming strength, and although the sacking of the town might ensue, Lévis demanded that the capitulation terms be rejected because Jeffery Amherst* had churlishly refused to grant the French the honours of war. Vaudreuil would not heed him and capitulated to spare the colony further devastation. The king subsequently declared, in a savagely worded letter from the minister of Marine, that Vaudreuil should not have accepted the terms; that he should have heeded Lévis and continued to resist, come what may, for the honour of French arms. The missive made plain that the loss of the colony and the plight of the Canadians were of no consequence compared to the army's having surrendered without receiving the right to march out of Montreal bearing its arms, flags unfurled, and drums beating.

After the surrender arrangements had to be made for the transport of the regular troops, the civil officials, and the Canadians who chose to quit the colony rather than remain under the British, some 4,000 in all. Of the 2,200 French regular troops who remained on strength, 500 to 600 opted to stay in the colony; upwards of 800 had previously deserted to that end. Among them were 150 British deserters who had enlisted in the French forces. Vaudreuil and Lévis allowed these deserters to make themselves scarce before the capitulation, but most of them were subsequently rounded up by the British. Some French soldiers were persuaded to enlist in the British army, but one of their officers remarked that now they had discovered they were to be transported to serve elsewhere few would be tempted to follow their example.

The officer corps of the colonial regular troops, with the exception of those too severely wounded to make the voyage, crossed to France where they were retired from the service on half pay. With the conclusion of peace in 1763 21 officers returned to Canada to settle their affairs, then went back again to France hoping to receive appointments on the active list. Others quietly gave up and returned to Canada to eke out a living on their seigneurial lands. Those who held the cross of the order of Saint-Louis were in a difficult position as the oath of the order prevented them becoming subjects of His Britannic Majesty without the consent of the king of France. Several of those who chose to remain in France eventually received active appointments in the service, in Gorée, the West Indies, or Guiana. Louis-Thomas Jacau* de Fiedmont, for exam-

ple, the brave gunner captain who, at Jean-Baptiste-Nicolas-Roch de Ramezay*'s council of war that opted to surrender Quebec, declared that they should hold out until the ammunition was exhausted, eventually became governor of Guiana. Another, Gaspard-Joseph Chaussegros* de Léry, returned to Canada and became a member of the Legislative Council of Quebec but sent his young sons to France. One of them, François-Joseph, gained entry into the reformed and prestigious corps of engineers. He ultimately rose to be commander-in-chief of the engineers in Napoleon's Grande Armée. His name is engraved on the Arc de Triomphe along with those of Napoleon's other great generals. For some of these Canadian officers the career was all important; for others, it was their homeland that mattered. Some, at least, who chose the latter did so because, owing to age or lack of means and influential connections, they saw no future for themselves in the service of their king. Their cause was truly lost.

As for the soldiers of the colonial regular troops who returned to France, when an attempt was made to have them enlist in French regiments not one of them would do so. Their almost unanimous response was that they knew the route to Halifax and they could easily find their way back to Canada from there. The Maréchal de Senneterre commented: "All those who have returned from Quebec and Montreal appear to have a great love for that country."

Of printed source material on the 18th century wars in North America there is an abundance. Many of the leading participants wrote lengthy memoirs and journals during or after the events. Some of the material from the French side has been printed over the years in the APQ [AQ;ANQ] *Rapport*; it is listed under the headings *guerre*, *journaux*, *mémoires*, *capitulations*, and *siège de Québec* in *Table des matières des rapports des Archives du Québec, tomes 1 à 42 (1920–1964)* (AQ pub., Québec, 1965). The PAC *Report* for the years 1904, 1905, and 1929 contains correspondence by leading figures in the conflict. A major collection is *Collection des manuscrits du maréchal de Lévis* (Casgrain). Also useful is *Journal des campagnes au Canada de 1755 à 1760 par le comte de Maurès de Malartic . . . .*, Gabriel de Maurès de Malartic et Paul Gaffarel, édit. (Dijon, 1890). For the western theatre *Papiers Contrecœur* (Grenier) is a particularly well edited selection. *Anglo-French boundary disputes, 1749–63* (Pease) and *Illinois on eve of Seven Years' War* (Pease and Jenison) are also valuable. Doughty and Parmelee, *Siege of Quebec*, contains useful documents.

For the European diplomatic background to the struggle R. P. Waddington, *La guerre de Sept Ans: histoire diplomatique et militaire* (5v., Paris, [1899–1907]) and *Louis XV et le renversement des alliances: préliminaires de la guerre de Sept Ans, 1754–1756* (Paris, 1896), although dated are still useful. A succinct and valuable study of the period is W. L. Dorn, *Competition for empire, 1740–1763* (New York, 1940); unfortunately, the treatment of events in North America, of necessity based on the mediocre or worse secondary sources then extant, is poor. Parkman, *Half-century of conflict* and *Montcalm and Wolfe* are too dated and biased to have much merit. Equally partisan is Gipson, *British empire before the American revolution*, IV-VIII. H. H. Peckham, *The colonial wars, 1698–1762* (Chicago, London, 1964), is of no value; nor is G. M. Wrong, *The fall of Canada: a chapter in the history of the Seven Years' War* (Oxford, 1914).

Two sound modern studies are Frégault, *Canada: the war of the conquest*, and Stanley, *New France*. The best study to date of the campaigns of 1759 and 1760 is Stacey, *Quebec, 1759*. The article by W. J. Eccles, "The social, economic, and political significance of the military establishment in New France," *CHR*, LII (1971) treats of the dominance of the military in Canadian society. Lee Kennett, *The French armies in the Seven Years' War: a study in military organization and administration* (Durham, N.C., 1967), is a succinct and exceptionally valuable study. André Corvisier, *L'armée française de la fin du XVIIe siècle au ministère de Choiseul: le soldat* (Faculté des Lettres et des Sciences humaines de Paris, Série Recherches, XIV–XV, 2v., Paris, 1964), is sound and exhaustive. André Dussauge, *Études sur la guerre de Sept Ans: le ministère de Belle-Isle – Krefeld et Lütterberg, 1758* (Paris, 1914), is still valuable. On the French navy the best studies are still Joannès Tramond, *Manuel d'histoire maritime de la France, des origines à 1815 . . .* (Paris, 1947), and Lacour-Gayet, *La marine militaire sous Louis XV* (1910).

The British forces in North America during the Seven Years' War

C. P. STACEY

THE SEVEN YEARS' WAR inaugurated a new phase in the history of warfare in North America. It was characterized by the large-scale intervention of regular military forces from Europe. On the British side particularly there was a great deployment of military power in America, which for the first time was Britain's main theatre of operations. In the crucial year 1759 no fewer than 23 British regular infantry battalions were employed in continental North America, as compared with only six in Germany. In the course of the war a large and complex British military machine was created in the American theatre.

In earlier phases of the long duel with France the American colonies saw little of the British army. Its first appearance in them seems to have been occasioned by Nathaniel Bacon's rebellion in Virginia (1676), when a force including a mixed battalion of the Guards was sent from England to restore order. Subsequently certain colonies which were considered particularly important or exposed were given small and usually inefficient garrisons. New York was garrisoned throughout its history as a British province – for a long period by four independent companies which the British government shamefully neglected. In 1717 a number of independent companies in Nova Scotia and Newfoundland were formed into a regiment (later called the 40th Foot) which garrisoned Nova Scotia for many years. In general, however, it is clear that the British colonies were normally expected to provide for their own defence, apart from the contribution to their security made by the Royal Navy.

In 1746, after the New Englanders' capture of Louisbourg, the crown authorized the raising of two regular regiments (their colonels being William Shirley and Sir William PEPPERRELL) from among the provincial troops holding the fortress. These regiments were never completed to strength and were disbanded at the peace of Aix-la-Chapelle in 1748. Nevertheless, after the founding of Halifax in 1749 there were three regular regiments in garrison in Nova Scotia, the 40th, 45th, and 47th Foot.

The British army appeared more actively in North America in 1755. To counter Governor Duquesne*'s forward policy in the Ohio valley the British government, after much discussion, decided to send out a regular general officer to be commander-in-chief in America, to send with him an expeditionary force of two under-strength regiments (the 44th and 48th) from the Irish establishment (to be recruited up to strength in America), and to re-raise in America the Shirley and Pepperrell regiments (now numbered 50th and 51st). This was the beginning of a new British policy, which was to be persisted in despite the disaster to General Edward Braddock and his little army on the Monongahela in July 1755 at the hands of Jean-Daniel Dumas*. Recruiting in America for regular regiments was never a great success; but the regulars from Britain played the chief part in the British operations in America in the Seven Years' War.

The Royal Navy. The British triumph in North America was in the last analysis primarily due to command of the sea. The Royal Navy outnumbered the French roughly two to one in ships of the line. Its main strength was retained in the European theatre throughout the war. The French considered that their best strategy was a blow at Britain itself; such an invasion was specifically planned in 1759, and had always to be guarded against. In any case, British success in North America depended upon the maintenance of general naval superiority in the North Atlantic, and this was best assured by blockading the French fleet in its own ports and bringing it to action if it left them. Nevertheless, increasingly large British naval forces were dispatched to the American war zone season by season as the conflict proceeded: to protect troop convoys and supply ships on passage to North America, to intercept French vessels which had succeeded in leaving France on similar missions, to deal with the French naval squadrons on the American station, and to support the military expeditions sent against the French fortresses and islands. These operations were greatly facilitated by the possession of the new base at Halifax, with its splendid harbour and its dockyard [see Philip DURELL].

Generally speaking, the British enjoyed unquestionable naval superiority in American waters during the Seven Years' War. The most striking exception is the case of Louisbourg in 1757, when the French succeeded in concentrating there a squadron somewhat larger than that available to Rear-Admiral Francis Holburne* for the attack on the fortress then projected. This, and the lateness of the season, led to the abandonment of the enterprise. Next year Admiral Bos-CAWEN, supporting Jeffery Amherst*'s expedition against Louisbourg, had such a margin of superiority that the French squadron in the harbour did not venture to challenge him; it was destroyed piecemeal during the siege by bombardment and by boat attack. Boscawen provided covering fire for the army landings, many guns for use in the siege operations, some marines for shore duty, and a good deal of skilled labour.

The largest British naval force to operate against New France was that commanded by Charles Saunders* which conveyed and supported WOLFE's expedition against Quebec in 1759. This comprised, apart from large numbers of transports and storeships, 49 vessels of the Royal Navy, including 22 of 50 guns or more. Though it is evident that the smaller ships of the line were in general considered most suitable for operations up the St Lawrence, Saunders' fleet included three of the rather rare three-deckers which the navy used as flagships and as anchors for its lines of battle. As with Wolfe's army, the professional quality of Saunders' officers was exceptionally high. The fleet represented a tremendous reserve of gun-power and manpower for Wolfe. He was speaking of the fleet when he remarked in his last dispatch, "By the nature of the river, the most formidable part of this armament is deprived of the power of acting." Although there was much truth in this, and although Wolfe's journal is full of complaints and innuendoes against the navy, it seems clear that it served him well, in much the same ways in which it had served Amherst at Louisbourg. In addition, however, Saunders' almost total control of the St Lawrence conferred upon Wolfe a flexibility and ease of movement which were of the greatest advantage to him. With the help of wind and tide, the British could threaten a descent, or make an actual attack, at any point along the river; the French could counter these threats only by exhausting marches on foot. The feint made by the navy off the Beauport shore in the early hours of 13 September probably contributed to the success of the landing at the Anse au Foulon that morning. The navy's final service towards the capture of Quebec was four days after the battle

of the Plains of Abraham, when eight ships of the line moved up to threaten the Lower Town with bombardment. This action may well have helped to influence Jean-Baptiste-Nicolas-Roch de Ramezay* to hoist the white flag.

It is unnecessary to dwell upon the contribution of sea power to the last campaign in 1760. In this year – unlike 1759, when a large number of French supply ships reached Quebec – British ships were in the St Lawrence before the French. The appearance of Robert SWANTON's squadron at Quebec in May, and the destruction by it of the small French naval force that was supporting the Chevalier de Lévis*, instantly put an end to Lévis's siege of the city and finally sealed the fate of the colony. Commodore John Byron* intercepted the little squadron under François-Chenard Giraudais that was bringing the limited aid which the French court had decided to send to Canada that year; it took refuge in the Restigouche and was destroyed there in July.

The power of the ocean navies could not reach the inland waters of the continent; but control of these waterways, the best and often the only means of moving troops and supplies, was vital. Naval support, like water transport itself, had largely to be improvised. John Bradstreet*'s expedition against Fort Frontenac (Kingston, Ont.) in 1758 destroyed the vessels that had given France control of Lake Ontario. The following year Amherst, advancing on Canada by the Lake Champlain route, was assisted by a naval officer, Captain Joshua Loring*, who built and commanded a flotilla on the lake to support him. Loring was again present during Amherst's movement down the St Lawrence from Lake Ontario in 1760, with two vessels built at Niagara (near Youngstown, N.Y.) during the preceding winter. Their performance, however, was poor. The only affair that could be called a naval engagement was conducted on the British side by the Royal Artillery under Colonel George Williamson, manning the guns of five "row-galleys" (rowed by provincial troops) which on 17 August captured the French 10-gun brig *Outaouaise* at La Galette (near Ogdensburg, N.Y.).

Command on Land. The office of commander of the forces in North America, introduced with the arrival of Braddock in 1755, may be said to have had a virtually unbroken existence until the withdrawal of the imperial forces from Halifax and Esquimalt in 1905–6. It was held successively during the Seven Years' War by Braddock, Shirley (acting), Lord Loudoun, James Abercromby* and Jeffery Amherst. In addition to being military it had a political aspect. The commander-in-chief was the only central authority existing in the American colonies at this time. He was the mouthpiece and agent of the imperial government, and was constantly engaged in negotiations with the colonial governments, especially with respect to the local raising of troops. At the same time he was fully responsible for the direction of military operations. His commission made him (in the words of Loudoun's) "General and Commander in Chief of all and singular our Forces employed or to be employed in North America." His powers included appointment of officers to regular vacancies without purchase.

The appointment of the commander-in-chief's senior subordinates, as of the commander-in-chief himself, was a matter for the decision of the king as advised by his ministers. King and ministers might be influenced in turn by the advice of the commander-in-chief of the army in London. It is apparent that service in America was not particularly popular; Wolfe was presumably not being merely jocular when he wrote of his own appointment in 1759, "The backwardness of some of the older officers has in some measure forced the Government to come down so low." A natural and desirable tendency was for the government to employ and promote officers, often of relatively junior rank, who had already distinguished themselves in the American theatre. The case of Wolfe himself is typical. He became a colonel in 1757, and never held any higher substantive rank. He fought at Louisbourg in 1758 as "Brigadier in America"; he retained this local appointment for the Quebec expedition of 1759, plus the temporary rank of major-general (and the appointment of commander-in-chief) with respect to that expedition only. His instructions provided that when Quebec fell he would place himself under Amherst as brigadier in America. Amherst himself conducted the expedition against Louisbourg as colonel and "Major General in America"; he was given the substantive rank of major-general only in June 1759. Most officers in America above the regimental level held local rank. It is worth noting that an officer could hold a regimental rank and simultaneously a higher rank in the army at large. Thus George Scott was a lieutenant-colonel commanding light troops in Robert Monckton*'s expedition to Martinique in 1762 while retaining his "company" (that is, the rank of captain, presumably purchased) in the 40th Foot. It may be assumed that he drew the pay of both appointments.

Much has been written on the baneful effects of the system of purchasing commissions, and of those of family and political influence on military appointments. That these were grave evils there is no doubt. In spite of them there were a surprising number of active and efficient officers. General J. F. C. Fuller has written, perhaps without complete justification, that Wolfe in 1759 was "supported by probably the finest body of English officers which has ever taken the field." That the British officer corps was far superior in professional competence to the French is beyond question.

Armament. By the time of the Seven Years' War there was considerable uniformity in armament between European nations; and in America both British and French were almost entirely dependent upon weapons imported from the mother countries. There were however some respects in which the British seem to have had superiority.

The basic weapon of the foot soldier on both sides was the smooth-bore "firelock" (flint-lock) musket. Contrary to a fairly widespread belief, rifled weapons were little used in this war by the British colonial forces, even the rangers. The rifle was not unknown, however; Henry Bouquet obtained some rifled carbines for his battalion of the Royal Americans. The British musket commonly called "Brown Bess" underwent some modifications between its introduction in the 1720s and its official supersession in 1794. The French seem to have considered their own 1754 pattern musket quite satisfactory. Nevertheless, several references indicate that British officers felt that experience in the Quebec campaign showed that the British weapon was more effective. George Townshend* wrote later to General Amherst (26 June 1775), "I recollect that in our service at Quebec The superiority of our Musquets over the French Arms were generally acknowledged both as to the Distance they carried & the Frequency of the Fire."

The guns used by the French field artillery in this war were criticized as unduly heavy and awkward to move. On the British side the Royal Artillery had the advantage of having at least a small number of light brass guns which did good service in America; the two 6-pounders that played an important part on the Plains of Abraham afford perhaps the most striking example. As the war proceeded the British in America had an increasing superiority in the artillery arm. Wolfe's three artillery companies at Quebec had a most imposing "train" of guns. Twenty-nine guns and mortars bombarded the town from the Lévis heights across the St. Lawrence; some 50 pieces were emplaced to fire at the left flank of Montcalm's positions from the British camp at Montmorency; and in four days after the battle of the Plains the British brought 118 pieces up the cliff path at the Anse au Foulon.

The French lost most of their ordnance in North America with the fortresses of Louisbourg and Quebec. When Lévis tried to recover Quebec in the spring of 1760 he simply did not have the guns for a proper siege.

The Regular Army. The war in America was primarily an affair of infantry. Most foot regiments had only one battalion, though some had two or more. In practice the words "regiment" and "battalion" are virtually interchangeable. Each regiment normally had a colonel, frequently a general officer or a peer. Colonelcies of regiments, though still lucrative, were tending in other respects to become honorary, as they now are. It cannot be said that the colonel never exercised active command, but it was becoming increasingly exceptional for him to do so. When Wolfe was lieutenant-colonel of the 20th Foot (1750–57) he was *de facto* commanding officer, but the colonel occasionally visited the regiment and took command, and interfered constantly by correspondence. After Wolfe himself became colonel of the 67th Foot he had comparatively little to do directly with that regiment; it was not in America during his two campaigns there, but he visited it in England in the winter of 1758–59. The reform of 1751, by which regiments were designated by numbers instead of by their colonels' names, was a useful step away from the old system under which regiments were regarded virtually as their colonels' private properties; yet that tradition still affected even tactics in the Seven Years' War. In both the British and French armies, when it was necessary to detach a force from the main army in the field, the invariable practice was not to send a complete battalion or portion of a battalion, but to follow the militarily less efficient method of making the detachment a composite force drawn from a number of units, thus spreading the risk and presumably avoiding the possibility of a disaster to one regiment which would be embarrassing to its colonel.

A British infantry battalion of the Seven Years' War period was usually composed of ten companies, in most cases theoretically each 100 strong. In practice battalions, as always, tended to be considerably under strength. One company, made up of the tallest and strongest men, was designated the grenadier company. It was no longer armed with hand grenades, as it had been in Marlborough's day, but it was intended to take the lead in such operations as attacks on fortified positions. Frequently the grenadier companies of an army were "brigaded" together to form a special assault force. This was done by Wolfe in the battle of Montmorency.

On both sides the tactics of the period were based upon strict discipline, exacting drill and precise linear formations. It was the superiority of Wolfe's army in these European battlefield techniques that won the battle of the Plains, just as it was mainly European siege techniques that captured Louisbourg from Drucour [BOS-CHENRY]. Nevertheless it is far from true that the British army failed to adapt itself to American conditions. Its development of light infantry organization and tactics is a striking feature of its performance in this war. At a slightly later period every British infantry battalion had a light company, designed for scouting and skirmishing. In the Seven Years' War similar results were obtained by improvisation. Provisional units of light infantry were formed from the most active soldiers and best marksmen in the regular regiments of a force. At Louisbourg the light infantry were commanded by Major George Scott, at Quebec by Lieutenant-Colonel William Howe. In addition however an actual "Regiment of Light Armed Foot" was formed in the British army in America in 1758 on the suggestion of Thomas Gage*, who became its colonel. During its short life, which ended at the peace, it was known as the 80th Foot or, more commonly, Gage's Light Infantry. It was dressed in brown without ornament, carried no colours, and was armed with muskets shorter and lighter than those of ordinary infantry units. It was the first light infantry corps in the British army. The other "light" element in the British forces, the American rangers, is dealt with below.

Considerable recruiting for regular units was done in America, though the colonists in general were not enthusiastic about joining the regular army. One important regiment was raised in the colonies in 1756: the 62nd (shortly the 60th) or Royal American Regiment of Foot. It was of four battalions; the commander-in-chief in America for the time being was colonel-in-chief, and each battalion had a colonel commandant who was a senior officer serving in America (and who in most cases did not exercise actual command of the unit). Many of the officers were "foreign Protestants" appointed under a special act of parliament, and it was originally expected that the ranks would be filled with German settlers from Pennsylvania. In fact, the regiment's final composition was extremely mixed. Unlike Gage's Light Infantry, it survived the reduction of the army in 1763, and as the 60th Rifles (King's Royal Rifle Corps) became one of the most celebrated British regiments.

Other arms and services were engaged in the struggle for North America. In forest warfare there was little scope for mounted troops, and no British regular cavalry served in America in this war. The Royal Regiment of Artillery, however, played a great part in the American campaigns, though as late as 1757 its strength in North America was only 339 all ranks. Late in that year four of its 23 companies were in North America. Two years later the regiment had grown to 30 companies; nine were in North America, in addition to one at Guadeloupe. No attempt seems to have been made to use colonial units of this technical arm in the field. The engineer officers as a group (the Royal Engineers as such did not yet exist) were rather less professionalized than the artillery, and there was always a shortage of qualified officers for this work [*see* William EYRE]. There was a moderately efficient army medical service, consisting of a general hospital with branches at several points and surgeons and surgeon's mates with individual regiments. In the absence of any army supply and transport service the forces in America had to be fed in the main by English civil contractors, the supplies being moved within the theatre by means hired either by the contractors or (in more forward areas) by the commander-in-chief. The execution of contracts was checked and supervised by the commissariat, a civilian service. Enormous sums of money were spent for transport in the colonies. Much military labour was also used for transport. Cumbersome though the system was, the British forces in general seem to have been pretty adequately fed and supplied.

Provincial and Local Forces. Not only was the Seven Years' War particularly marked by the appearance in America of large British regular forces; in the main the war was won by these forces. But the British colonies, responding to the leadership and financial encouragement of William Pitt, made a greater military effort than ever before, placing large forces in the field.

From a very early period the various British provinces in America had militias based on universal service, every citizen of military age being liable to serve when required. These militias were called upon in the Seven Years' War only in emergency. British commanders would have been glad to make more use of them, for they represented the solid citizenry of the colonies. As it was, the provincial forces employed in the war were usually *ad hoc* units enlisted by the various colonial governments for the occasion and drawn from what may be called the floating population. This did not make for reliability or efficiency.

The conditions on which provincial units were raised varied from time to time. The two battalions raised in New England in 1755 for the attack on Beauséjour (near Sackville, N.B.) and commanded by John Winslow* and George Scott were authorized and paid from England. This was unusual. At the end of 1757 William Pitt made a new departure. He called on the northern colonies for 20,000 men for the coming campaign, and on the southern ones for as many as possible. He reckoned upon almost half of the troops employed in 1758 being colonials. The crown would furnish arms, equipment, and provisions; the colonial governments would have to pay and clothe the men. Pitt held out the hope, however, that parliament would compensate the colonies for their expense; and in 1759 it did in fact vote £200,000 for the purpose. Similar action was taken in subsequent years. In five campaigns after 1757 the total of such reimbursement was £866,666. G. L. Beer calculated that parliament repaid about two-fifths of the colonies' total outlay for military purposes.

The response to the requisitions for troops varied widely. Massachusetts, Connecticut, and New York always responded particularly well; the southern colonies did little. The northern colonies as a whole voted 17,480 men for 1758; the number actually enlisted was somewhat smaller. Roughly similar results were achieved in the next two years. Provincial regiments thus made up a considerable proportion of the British forces in America in 1758–60. Few Americans, and no provincial regiments, took part in the crucial campaigns against Louisbourg in 1758 and Quebec in 1759. On the other hand, Abercromby reported the strength of his army that advanced against Carillon (Ticonderoga) in July 1758 as "amounting to 6367 regulars, officers, light infantry, and rangers included, and 9024 provincials, including officers and batteau men." It was the regulars however who made the tragic and costly assault on the French entrenchments; Abercromby gives the losses in the operation as 464 regulars and 87 provincials killed. Generally speaking, the provincial regiments in this war have few striking feats of arms to their credit. (One success achieved largely by provincials was Bradstreet's capture of Fort Frontenac in 1758.) In the main these units acted as pioneers or labour battalions, working on defences or roads, or on transport work as waggoners or boatmen.

British officers made many complaints of the inefficiency of these amateur regiments and of their officers' lack of military knowledge. Ignorance of the rudiments of camp sanitation was a recurring charge. One of the most extreme comments was Wolfe's in a letter of 7 Aug. 1758: "The Americans are in general the dirtiest most contemptible cowardly dogs that you can conceive . . . They fall down dead in their own dirt and desert by battalions, officers and all." Wolfe himself can have had comparatively little contact with provincial troops, and he was doubtless repeating the snobbish gossip of the regular messes. There was considerable hostility between Englishmen and Americans, and particularly between those who wore the king's red coat and those who wore the provincial blue.

Relative rank was long a source of contention. In the beginning, under a regulation of 1754 made before the employment of large numbers of provincials was envisaged, provincial field officers (i.e., major and above) serving in conjunction with regulars were limited to the relative status of junior captains, that is, they were subject to the orders of all regular captains. In 1756 this was liberalized by giving provincial general and field officers in such circumstances rank as most senior captains. In other words, they outranked all regular captains, which made them subordinate only to a much smaller number of senior regulars, usually officers of experience. In 1757 Pitt, by a famous new regulation, gave all provincial officers rank immediately below regular officers of the same rank. This was duly appreciated by the colonists; but S. M. Pargellis has pointed out that its effect was reduced by a virtually simultaneous grant of local rank ("colonel in America") to all British lieutenant-colonels serving in the colonies.

When Lord Loudoun arrived in America as commander-in-chief in 1756 he found himself confronting the question of his authority over provincial troops in the field. A force raised entirely by the New England colonies on the initiative of Shirley, and commanded by John Winslow, was holding the forts facing Canada; and many of its officers were inclined to dispute Loudoun's right to control this army. There was a potential crisis, but Loudoun had a powerful weapon in the fact that the New Englanders needed ordnance and ammunition which he controlled. He acted tactfully, and Winslow finally agreed that he and his officers would "act in conjunction with His Majesty's troops and put themselves under the command of your Lordship who is commander in chief, so that the terms and conditions agreed upon and established by the several governments to whom they belong and upon which they were raised be not altered." No precisely similar confrontation seems to have arisen later in the war, though various difficulties with the colonial governments continued.

The British military authorities always recognized the need for experienced forest fighters, and one of their complaints against the provincial regiments was that few such men were found in their ranks. As we have seen, they sought to meet the need in part by developing regular units of "light" infantry fitted for woods warfare. They also relied upon special American light units, the ranger companies. These companies were on the whole the most effective colonial units on the British side.

Ranger companies are heard of from the beginning of the war. There was one such company in Nova Scotia in 1754. One, commanded by the celebrated if enigmatic Robert Rogers*, formed part of Winslow's provincial army referred to above. In 1756 Shirley, acting as commander-in-chief, formed three ranger companies, to be paid from imperial funds, and subsequently also took into service Robert Rogers' company which was still in existence. Loudoun continued and extended this policy, and by 1758 there were nine ranger companies serving. One (not perhaps technically considered rangers) was composed of Mohegan Indians. Some, if not all, of the other companies had Indians on their strength. It is worth noting that the Stockbridge Indians had earlier contributed a company, which though not called rangers certainly did the same work. The rangers were not provincial troops. They were armed, paid, clothed, and fed by the crown. They were not part of the British army, but their officers had British commissions. They have been defined as "independent companies attached to the British army, on an establishment of their own, a very expensive one, paid out of [imperial] contingencies." It is significant that Abercromby, in his account of his Ticonderoga army, reckons the rangers in with the regulars. One ranger officer, Robert Rogers, held the rank of major and apparently had some vague authority over the whole body. The army list shows that another ranger, Joseph Gorham*, was promoted major in 1760.

The rangers did much more fighting than the provincial regiments. Robert Rogers in particular was active in the no-man's-land around Lake Champlain, and groups of ranger companies served under Amherst at Louisbourg and under Wolfe at Quebec. The rangers have become the subject of something like a cult in the United States in recent years, the result in part perhaps of the writings of Kenneth Roberts. They were probably not quite so formidable as they have been made out to be. They were frequently but not invariably successful in their encounters with the French. As with the provincial units, their

xxix

discipline and general efficiency were criticized by British officers – Wolfe cheerfully called the six companies given him in 1759, four of which were newly raised, "the worst soldiers in the universe." The rangers had a rough reputation. That they regularly scalped their enemies is not surprising, since Shirley in 1756 had promised them £5 for every Indian scalp they brought in. But they made a larger contribution than any other American troops to winning the war.

Of great value is S. M. Pargellis, *Lord Loudoun in North America* (New Haven, Conn., and London, 1933), a scholarly account and analysis of colonial military problems before and during the Seven Years' War. See also *Military affairs in North America, 1748–1765* (Pargellis). Other items, of varying value, are: *Army list*, various dates. *Correspondence of William Pitt* (Kimball). Knox, *Historical journal* (Doughty). *Logs of the conquest* (Wood). *Battery records of the Royal Artillery, 1716–1859*, comp. M. E. S. Laws (Woolwich, Eng., 1952). G. L. Beer, *British colonial policy, 1754–1765* (New York, 1922). W. L. Clowes *et al.*, *The Royal Navy, a history from the earliest times to the present* (7v., London, 1897–1903), III. Corbett, *England in the Seven Years' War*. J. W.

Fortescue, *History of the British army* (13v., London, New York, 1899–1930), II. J. F. C. Fuller, *The decisive battles of the western world and their influence upon history* (3v., London, 1954–56). Gipson, *British empire before the American revolution*, VI, VII. Lee Kennett, *The French armies in the Seven Years' War: a study in military organization and administration* (Durham, N.C., 1967). A. T. Mahan, *The influence of sea power upon history, 1660–1783* (6th ed., Boston, 1894). H. L. Osgood, *The American colonies in the eighteenth century* (New York, 1924). S. M. Pargellis, "The four independent companies of New York," *Essays in colonial history presented to Charles McLean Andrews by his students* (New Haven, Conn., and London, 1931). Parkman, *Montcalm and Wolfe*. Stacey, *Quebec, 1759*; *Canada and the British army, 1846–1871: a study in the practice of responsible government* (London, 1936). Rex Whitworth, *Field Marshal Lord Ligonier; a story of the British army, 1702–70* (Oxford, 1958). Beckles Willson, *The life and letters of James Wolfe . . .* (London, 1909). Malcolm MacLeod, "Fight at the west gate, 1760," *Ontario History* (Toronto), LVIII (1966), 172–94. R. Scurfield, "British military smoothbore firearms," Society for Army Hist. Research (London) *Journal*, XXXIII (1955), 63–79. C. P. Stacey, "Halifax as an international strategic factor, 1749–1949," CHA *Report, 1949*, 46–56.

Glossary of Indian Tribal Names

THIS GLOSSARY INCLUDES the tribal names that appear most frequently in the biographies of volume III. It is designed to assist the reader in identifying and locating geographically those groups of native people involved in the development of New France or encountered by the French and the Hudson's Bay Company traders during western explorations. In their contacts with the indigenous population, Europeans frequently designated as tribes groups that would not be considered such by any modern ethnologist. These names appear in the documents of the 18th century, and they have therefore generally been used in volume III.

Full names of authors of the articles in this Glossary will be found in the list of contributors, pp. 723–29. Unsigned entries have been compiled by the staff of the Dictionary. The following published sources have been useful in the preparation of the glossary; shortened titles are listed in full in the general bibliography.

GENERAL WORKS

Découvertes et établissements des Français (Margry). *Ethnographic bibliography of North America*, ed. G. P. Murdock (5th ed., New Haven, Conn., 1960). *Handbook of American Indians* (Hodge). [The Smithsonian Institution is currently preparing a multivolume "Handbook of North American Indians" under the general editorship of W. C. Sturtevant; it will update and replace the original *Handbook.*] Jenness, *Indians of Canada. JR* (Thwaites). [C.-C. Le Roy] de Bacqueville de La Potherie, *Histoire de l'Amérique septentrionale . . .* (4v., Paris, 1722; [2e éd.], 1753). *North American Indians in historical perspective*, ed. E. B. Leacock and N. O. Lurie (New York, 1971).

EAST COAST

Gabriel Archer, "The relation of Captain Gosnold's voyage to the north part of Virginia, begun the six-and-twentieth of March . . . 1602," *Mass. Hist. Soc. Coll.*, 3rd ser., VIII (1843), 72–81. Charland, *Les Abénakis d'Odanak.* Charles Gill, *Notes sur de vieux manuscrits Abénakis* (Montréal, 1886). [Daniel Gookin], "An historical account of the doings and sufferings of the Christian Indians in New England in the years 1675, 1676, 1677," American Antiquarian Soc. *Trans. and Coll.* (Cambridge, Mass.), II (1836), 423–534. Daniel Gookin, "Historical collections of the Indians in New England," *Mass. Hist. Soc. Coll.*, 1st ser., I (1792), 141–232. William Hubbard, *The history of the Indian wars in New England from the first settlement to the termination of the war with King Philip, in 1677* (Boston, London, 1677; new ed., ed. S. G. Drake, 2v., Roxbury, Mass., 1865; repr., 2v. in 1, New York, 1969). R. H. Lord *et al., History of the archdiocese of Boston in the various stages of its development, 1604 to 1943 . . .* (3v., New York, 1944). J.-A. Maurault, *Histoire des Abénakis depuis 1605 jusqu'à nos jours* (Sorel, Qué.,

1866). F. G. Speck, "Native tribes and dialects of Connecticut, a Mohegan-Pequot diary," Smithsonian Institution, Bureau of American Ethnology *Annual Report, 1925–26* (Washington), 199–287; *Territorial subdivisions and boundaries of the Wampanoag, Massachusett, and Nauset Indians* (Museum of the American Indian *Indian notes and monographs*, [Misc. ser.], 44, New York, 1928).

GREAT LAKES AND OHIO VALLEY

Archives of Maryland, ed. W. H. Browne *et al.* (70v. to date, Maryland Hist. Soc. pub., Baltimore, Md., 1883–19   ). W. M. Beauchamp, *A history of the New York Iroquois . . .* (N.Y. State Museum *Bull.*, 78, Archeology, 9, Albany, 1905). [Henry Bouquet], *The papers of Col. Henry Bouquet*, ed. S. K. Stevens *et al.* (19v., Harrisburg, 1940–43). "Cadillac papers," *Michigan Pioneer Coll.*, XXXIII (1903), XXXIV (1904). R. C. Downes, *Council fires on the upper Ohio: a narrative of Indian affairs in the upper Ohio valley until 1795* (Pittsburgh, Pa., 1940). *French regime in Wis., 1727–48* (Thwaites). [Christopher Gist], *Christopher Gist's journals . . .* , ed. W. M. Darlington (Pittsburgh, Pa., 1893). C. A. Hanna, *The wilderness trail; or, the ventures and adventures of the Pennsylvania traders on the Allegheny path . . .* (2v., New York, London, 1911). Alexander Henry, *Travels and adventures in Canada and the Indian territories between the years 1760 and 1776*, ed. James Bain (Boston, 1901; repr. Edmonton, 1969). G. T. Hunt, *The wars of the Iroquois: a study in inter-tribal trade relations* (Madison, 1940). *The Indian tribes of the upper Mississippi valley and region of the Great Lakes, as described by Nicolas Perrot . . . Bacqueville de La Potherie . . . Morell Marston . . . and Thomas Forsyth . . .* , ed. and trans. E. H. Blair (2v., Cleveland, Ohio, 1911–12; repr., 2v. in 1, New York, 1969). *Johnson papers* (Sullivan *et al.*). W. V. Kinietz, *The Indians of the western Great Lakes* (Ann Arbor, Mich., 1940). *The Livingston Indian records, 1666–1723*, ed. L. H. Leder (Gettysburg, Pa., 1956). *NYCD* (O'Callaghan and Fernow). *The official records of Robert Dinwiddie, lieutenant-governor of the colony of Virginia, 1751–1758 . . .* , ed. R. A. Brock (2v., Virginia Hist. Soc. *Coll.*, new ser., III, IV, Richmond, 1883–84). *Papiers Contrecœur* (Grenier). A. C. Parker, *An analytical history of the Seneca Indians* (N.Y. State Archeol. Assoc. *Researches and trans.*, VI, Rochester, N.Y., 1926); *The constitution of the Five Nations* (N.Y. State Museum *Bull.*, 184, Albany, 1916). Peckham, *Pontiac.* Pennsylvania, *Colonial records*, III–IX. *Pennsylvania archives*, 1st ser., I–IV. F. G. Speck, *The Iroquois, a study in cultural evolution* (Cranbrook Institute of Science *Bull.*, 23, Bloomfield Hills, Mich., 1945). Virginia, *Calendar of Virginia state papers and other manuscripts . . .* , ed. W. P. Palmer *et al.* (11v. Richmond, 1875–93), I; *Executive journals of* the council of colonial Virginia, ed. H. R. McIlwaine et al. (6v., Virginia State Library pub., Richmond, 1925–66). N. B. Wainwright, George Croghan, wilderness diplomat (Chapel Hill, N.C., 1959). P. A. W. Wallace, The white roots of peace (Philadelphia, Pa., 1946). C. A. Weslager, The Delaware Indians, a history (New Brunswick, N.J., 1972). Peter Wraxall, An abridgement of the Indian affairs . . . from the year 1678 to the year 1751, ed. C. H. McIlwain (Harvard hist. studies, XXI, Cambridge, Mass., 1915).

WEST AND NORTH
[William Coats], The geography of Hudson's Bay: being the remarks of Captain W. Coats, in many voyages to that locality, between the years 1727 and 1751, ed. John Barrow (Hakluyt Soc., 1st ser., XI, London, 1852). Arthur Dobbs, An account of the countries adjoining to Hudson's Bay in the north-west part of America (London, 1744; repr. New York, 1967). Samuel Hearne, A journey from Prince of Wales's Fort in Hudson's Bay to the northern ocean, 1769, 1770, 1771, 1772, ed. Richard Glover (Toronto, 1958). HBRS, XII (Rich and Johnson). HBRS, XXV (Davies and Johnson). Journals and letters of La Vérendrye (Burpee). Alexander MacKenzie, Voyages from Montreal . . . through the continent of North America, to the Frozen and Pacific oceans, in the years 1789 and 1793 . . . (London, 1801). Christopher Middleton, A vindication of the conduct of Captain Christopher Middleton . . . (London, 1743), Joseph Robson, An account of six years residence in Hudson's Bay, from 1733 to 1736, and 1744 to 1747 . . . (London, 1752).

Abenakis; in French Abénaquis. A loose alliance of tribes in the area of what is now Maine and New Brunswick, which included, among others, the Malecites, Micmacs, Passamaquoddys, Penobscots, Norridgewocks, Pigwackets, and possibly the Sokokis. All these tribes spoke similar dialects. Hunting and fishing were important activities, but maize was grown for winter food, and by the 18th century the fur trade played an important part in tribal economies. In the 17th and 18th centuries the Abenakis were dependable allies of the French, and made many raids on New England during wars between the colonies [see GRAY LOCK]. The French considered them an important barrier to attack from the south, and maintained agents such as Joseph d'ABBADIE de Saint-Castin among them. In the wake of losses suffered in war many Abenakis moved to the French mission villages of Saint-François and Bécancour. See NORRIDGEWOCKS, PENOBSCOTS, SAINT-FRANÇOIS ABENAKIS.   D.H.

Agniers. See MOHAWKS

Algonkian (Algonquian); in French Algique, Algonkienne. The name refers to the family of languages spoken by numerous peoples in north central and northeastern parts of the United States and almost the entire eastern sub-Arctic of Canada. This family of languages was part of a larger family of dialects, languages, and language families, including Mus-

kogean, an important language family in the southeastern United States, whose member groups were distributed over about half of the occupied land of precontact North America. The term should not be confused with ALGONKIN.   H.H.

Algonkins (Algonquins). A congeries of closely related but politically separate tribes of the Ojibwa-Ottawa-Algonkin branch of the Algonkian language family occupying chiefly the Ottawa River valley and also a region north of Lake Huron where they merged with Ojibwas and Ottawas. To the north and east were other neighbours with a similar culture: the Montagnais, the Naskapis, and the Crees. The Algonkins were game hunters, fishermen, and wild food gatherers. They made extensive use of birch bark and participated energetically as trappers in the French fur trade. During the second half of the 17th century many of their settlements suffered from attacks by the Iroquois, resulting in wide dispersal north and northwest of their original locations in the Ottawa valley.   H.H.

Assiniboins; in French Assinipoil, etc.; also known as Stones or Stoneys. This was a large Dakota Siouan speaking congeries of woodland-prairie bands detached from one of the western Dakota divisions in the mid 17th century. The Assiniboins in the late 17th and early 18th centuries occupied the international boundary region around Lake of the Woods and Red River and lands northward an undetermined distance. Their settlements interpenetrated with those of closely allied Algonkian speaking Crees. Along with the Crees they were continuously at enmity with their Dakota congeners. It is probable that the fur trade was responsible for their fragmenting from their kinsmen. Because of their northerly position, they had access to the trade at Hudson Bay and elsewhere. During the last half of the 18th century, Assiniboins with western Crees gradually moved to the high plains. Anthony HENDAY encountered them in the Saskatchewan valley using horses to carry their baggage, and they also learned to hunt bison on horseback.   H.H.

Athapaskans. The tribes within the larger Athapaskan linguistic family of northwest North America who are in close cultural and linguistic relationship and inhabit the Arctic drainage and parts of the western drainage of Hudson Bay; frequently referred to as the Déné. This group includes the tribes known as the Beavers, Chipewyans, Dogribs, Hares, Yellowknives, and Slaveys.

For years after 1717, when Fort Prince of Wales was established at the mouth of the Churchill River, the only tribe that was in continuous contact was the Chipewyans, then known to the Hudson's Bay Company men only as the Northern Indians. In 1715 William Stuart*, accompanied by Thanadelthur*, a Chipewyan woman, and a number of Crees, had travelled northwest from York Factory to try to make peace between the Crees and the Chipewyans and thus to establish trade relations with the latter. Two years later the young Richard NORTON was sent inland from Churchill River in an attempt to bring Chipewyans down to the bay to trade, but he met no Indians. The aboriginal territorial limits of the Déné tribes cannot be defined exactly but the general areas can be described with a degree of certainty. The Chipewyans were exploiting the northern transitional forest zone north and west of Churchill almost to the mouth of the Coppermine River. They travelled by foot to Churchill for many years after they began trading; they did not follow the Churchill River route by canoes. There is archaeological and historical evidence that Algonkian speaking peoples, historically identified as the Crees, exploited the full boreal forest zone, which was south of Chipewyan lands, and which included the Churchill River basin. By the late 1700s the Chipewyans began to move into the boreal forest previously used only by the Crees. By the early 1800s the Chipewyans exploited a large expanse of territory from Churchill River west to Lake Athabasca and northward to the tundra, including the eastern end of Great Slave Lake and most of the Coppermine River.

The most easterly Chipewyan sub-group, later known as the Caribou Eaters (Mangeurs de Caribou), were probably the most frequent visitors to Churchill in the 18th century. The Copper Indians (Couteaux Jaunes), later known as the Yellowknives, were the only other group specifically identified in the first half of the 18th century. They were the Chipewyan sub-group that exploited the transitional forest from the eastern end of Great Slave Lake to near the mouth of the Coppermine River. Their designation as "Copper Indians" dates from 1714 when they were reported as Indians who made copper implements and who travelled in a distant area of rich copper deposits that the HBC attempted to locate several times in the 18th century. Occasionally some of these Indians travelled to Fort Churchill with other Chipewyans. Samuel Hearne*, who located the uneconomical copper deposits west of the Coppermine River, met the "Copper Indians" within their own territory in 1771. The Dogribs (Platscotés de Chiens) are also mentioned a few times in early accounts. Prior to Hearne these references must be considered a general designation, based on hearsay reports, for one or more tribes of the Déné group. Henry Kelsey*'s Dogsides (1691), Claude-Charles Le Roy* de La Potherie's Attimospiquaies (1753), and Arthur Dobbs' Platscotez de Chiens (1744) cannot be considered specific references to the Dogribs who inhabited the area between Great Slave Lake and Great Bear Lake in historic times. The Slaveys (Esclaves), are not specifically mentioned in 18th-century accounts. In this period "Slave" had no specific tribal attribution but was a term adopted by the traders from the Cree to refer to Déné groups bullied by the Crees. The Slavey tribe of more recent designation is located on the southwest end of Great Slave Lake, most of the Liard River, and along the Mackenzie River to the mouth of the Great Bear River. The Beaver Indians (Castors) were not identified as a tribe until the 1780s when Peter Pond* had a trading post on the Athabasca River. They inhabited the area between Lake Athabasca and the Rocky Mountains in the Peace River basin. The Hares (Peaux-de-Lièvres) were identified by Alexander Mackenzie* in 1789; they inhabit the area north and west of Great Bear Lake to the Mackenzie River.
B.C.G. and J.H.

Canibas. *See* NORRIDGEWOCKS

Cayugas; in French Goyogouins; their own term for themselves is variously interpreted as people of the swamp, great pipe people, and people where the locusts were taken out. One of the member tribes of the Iroquois Confederacy, the Cayugas lived between the Onondagas and Senecas in territory on either side of the present Cayuga Lake in west central New York state. Like all other league members, the Cayugas were agriculturalists, growing maize, beans, and squash. They also hunted deer and other woodland game. Together with the Oneidas they constituted the minor governing group in Confederacy politics known as the Younger Brothers. Following the American revolution the majority of Cayugas moved to a reservation on the Grand River (Ontario) where they reside today. Of all the member tribes of the Confederacy, they have tended to be the most conservative. *See* IROQUOIS, SIX NATIONS CONFEDERACY, MOHAWKS, ONONDAGAS, SENECAS.
H.H. and A.E.

Chaouanons. *See* SHAWNEES

Chickasaws; in French Chicachas. A leading Muskogean tribe, in the 18th century the Chickasaws lived in the area which is now Pontotoc and Union counties in northern Mississippi. They also claimed a much larger area, including the present state of Tennessee and northern Alabama. Warlike and independent, they dominated the region, and Chickasaw was the lingua franca of all the tribes on the lower Mississippi. The Chickasaws, always enemies of the French, especially resented French trade relations with their enemies the Choctaws. In the early 18th century the English, friendly with the Chickasaws, were attempting to enter the Mississippi valley, and this fact, and Chickasaw raids on Mississippi convoys, made the French determined to defeat the Chickasaws. In 1736 a force under Pierre d'Artaguiette attacked them in their home territory, but the result was a massacre of the French [*see* François-Marie Bissot* de Vinsenne]. The Chickasaws resisted successfully again when an expedition under Bienville [LE MOYNE] invaded their lands in 1739.

Chippewas. *See* OJIBWAS

Comanches; in French Padoucas. A nomadic plains tribe who hunted buffalo, they were known to be living in the western part of the present state of Kansas in 1719. That year Claude-Charles Dutisné* encountered them, and reported that they were mortal enemies of the Pawnees and had prevented the Spaniards from visiting that tribe. The Comanches' enmity towards other western tribes threatened the French system of alliances until Étienne de Véniard* de Bourgmond re-established good relations about 1723. PIERRE, a Comanche slave in Montreal, was the subject of a court case which raised the question of the legality of slavery in New France.

Crees; in French Cris, a shortened form of Kristinaux. (In English Cree is sometimes used to include the Maskegons (Swampy Crees), Naskapis, Montagnais-Naskapis, and Montagnais, but the French Cris is a more restrictive term.) An Algonkian speaking people closely related to the Montagnais-Naskapis, the Crees comprised a great number of related, but autonomous, villages and bands. At the height of their expansion in the late 18th century they occupied a region comprising most of the southern half of the Hudson Bay coast, extending westward to include large portions of what is now northern Ontario, Manitoba, Saskatchewan, and eastern Alberta. This expansion resulted in diversification into four main divisions: Swampy, Rocky, Woods, and Plains. The ancestral Crees were probably confined to the region contiguous to James Bay, including the inland lakes and waterways in the Shield. There they hunted wild fowl, moose, and woodland caribou, which with fish and wild plant products provided their subsistence. From the mid 17th century Crees were active in the French and British fur trade as trappers and as middlemen to far inland tribes, including the Blackfeet and northern Athapaskans. They traded at the HBC posts on James Bay, and the term Home Indians used by the HBC traders usually referred to them. They figured prominently in the explorations of Pierre GAULTIER de Varennes et de La Vérendrye. Close allies of the Siouan Assiniboins, they were at various periods bitter foes of the Dakota Sioux, Blackfeet, and Chipewyans. *See* MONSONIS.   H.H.

Delawares. English name for Algonkian speaking Indians of the middle and lower Delaware River and east to the seacoast; often applied also to the related Munsees on the upper Delaware. The French name Loups generally also included the Mahicans and smaller coastal groups. The Delawares styled themselves Lenape, men. Abandoning their homeland because of involvement in the fur trade, depletion of game, and pressure of white colonization, they resettled as Iroquois dependants on the Susquehanna and Allegheny rivers. In 1680 René-Robert Cavelier* de La Salle met a hunting party of 40 Loups near the southern end of Lake Michigan, and 12 years later a similar group escorted refugee Shawnees from the Ohio to the upper Delaware. Delaware settlement on the Ohio began about 1725. Despite grievances, Delaware relations with the English were close and generally friendly, though disrupted by French occupation of the upper Ohio, 1753–59, and strained by PONTIAC's War, 1763–64. Their westward movement accelerated by these hostilities, they established settlements on the Muskingum River by agreement with the Hurons; and a nativist revival in the 1750s gave impetus to a renewal of the "Delaware

nation" under Netwatwees, "King Newcomer" (d. 1776). Neutrality in the American revolution was only partially successful, and the steady influx of white settlers after the war completed the process of disruption and removal. Part of the Delawares (mostly Munsees) took refuge in southern Ontario and the rest moved beyond the Mississippi.   W.A.H.

Five Nations Confederacy. *See* SIX NATIONS CONFEDERACY

Flatheads, in French Têtes-plates, was a term applied to various groups of southern Indians with whom the Iroquois engaged in chronic warfare during the 18th century. Although referring to the deformation practised by some southern tribes, the name was applied somewhat more broadly. In the early part of the century the term Flatheads often referred to the Siouan speaking Catawbas of North Carolina, but it was later applied most frequently to the Muskogean peoples, Chickasaws and others, who with the Cherokees claimed the lands south of the Ohio. Generally speaking, the Iroquois were the aggressors in this warfare, but the southern Indians made effective counter-attacks, both sides using a series of north-south "warriors' paths," including the Tuscarora Path in the eastern Appalachian Mountains and the Catawba Path west of them. It was partly as a defence against attacks by these southern enemies that the Iroquois developed a practice of resettling dependent Indian groups such as the Shawnees along their borders, on the lower Susquehanna and the upper Ohio rivers.   W.A.H.

Foxes (Mesquakies, or Red Earth People); in French Renards, Outagamis. Originally located in the lower peninsula of Michigan, they migrated, probably under pressure from Iroquois, to the Baie des Puants (Green Bay, Lake Michigan) area where they were first met by French traders and missionaries in the 1660s. The Foxes spoke a central Algonkian language closely related to Sauk, Kickapoo, and Mascouten, the languages of the peoples with whom they were often allied and who had migrated with them. All these tribes lived in villages where they raised maize, beans, and squash; they held annual communal hunts for deer and bison. Drawn into the fur trade at an early date, they had a shortage of beaver in their own country, but occupying strategic positions on the important Fox-Wisconsin River trade route to the Mississippi, they demanded a share in the trade as middlemen or in the form of tolls. At the beginning of the 18th century the Foxes were on friendly terms with New France and her Indian allies [*see* Noro*], but after the Ojibwa massacre of a Fox village near Detroit in 1712 [*see* Pemoussa*] the Foxes became a major source of disruption. The nature of their raids was aggravated, in French eyes, by their attempts to ally themselves with the English. Temporarily subdued in 1716 [*see* Ouachala*], the Foxes finally suffered defeat in 1730 and 1731–32, when the French took prisoner their greatest war-chief, Kiala*. In 1733 many joined the Sauks and with them began a movement westward, first to the Mississippi, then across it into Iowa where some of the associated Sauk and Fox peoples continue to live today. *See* SAUKS.   H.H.

Goyogouins, *See* CAYUGAS
Huronne-iroquoise. *See* IROQUOIAN

Hurons (from the Old French hure, a bristly head). They were divided into four separate tribes: the Bear (Attignawantan), and the so-called Cord (Attingueenongnahac), Rock (Ahrendarrhonon), and Deer (Tahontaenrat). When Iroquois attacks led to the dispersal of the Huron confederacy early in 1649 [*see* Brébeuf*], many Hurons took refuge among the neighbouring Tionontatis (Petuns), who were closely allied to them in language and culture. Most of these refugees belonged to the Attignawantan tribe and came from the village of Ossossane, which by that time was largely Christian. After December 1649, however, the Tionontatis and their Huron guests were driven out of southern Ontario by the Iroquois, who did not wish to see the Huron trade fall into the hands of yet another tribe. About 800 Tionontatis and Hurons made an orderly retreat northward towards Lake Michigan. Although mostly Tionontatis, these people came to be known as the Wyandots, a corruption of Wendat, the old name the Hurons had applied to themselves. Between 1653 and 1670, the Wyandots wandered in the region of the upper Great Lakes, participating in the fur trade and living with and being influenced by the Ottawas and Potawatomis. In 1670 the Hurons founded a settlement at Mackinac. In 1701 the chief Kondiaronk* attended the peace conference convened at Montreal by Louis-Hector de Callière*, and the Hurons, among them MICHIPICHY, were persuaded to move to the vicinity of Fort Pontchartrain, which the French had just constructed at Detroit. About 1738 there was a division among the Wyandots. Some remained in the Detroit area, their descendants residing near present Sandwich, Ont.; the others, under war-chief ORONTONY, moved to Sandoské (Sandusky, Ohio). After many wanderings the latter group finally settled on the Wyandotte Reservation in Oklahoma. The Wyandot language died out in the first half of this century. *See* HURONS OF LORETTE, IROQUOIAN.   B.G.T.

Hurons of Lorette. After the overthrow of the Huron confederacy in 1649 [*see* Brébeuf*], a portion of the Huron people fled to Quebec and finally settled at Lorette, where they still reside.

In the spring of 1650, about 300 Christian Huron refugees, who had spent the winter living under French protection on Île Saint-Joseph (Christian Island) in Georgian Bay, asked to be taken to Quebec. In March 1651 they settled on Île d'Orléans. There they were joined by the Hurons who continued to arrive from what is now Ontario. By the end of the decade most of the Hurons at Quebec who belonged to the Ahrendarrhonon and Attignawantan tribes were forced to settle among the Onondaga and

Mohawk tribes respectively. The Hurons who remained at Quebec were mainly of the Attingueenongnahac tribe. The Hurons continued to reside close to the fort at Quebec until 1668, when they settled at Beauport. In 1669 they moved to Sainte-Foy, where they were joined by some Christian Iroquois. In 1673 the expanding population moved to Ancienne-Lorette and in 1697 to Jeune-Lorette (Loretteville). During the Anglo-French wars of the 18th century their warriors frequently assisted the French [*see* VINCENT]. For the past hundred years most of their income has been derived from the manufacture of snowshoes, moccasins, and baskets. The Hurons of Lorette are noted for their devotion to Christianity. Although they have retained their sense of ethnic identity, they have intermarried extensively with French Canadians and ceased to speak Huron in the early part of the 19th century. *See* HURONS.
                                                    B.G.T.

Illinois. Adapted by the French from Iliniwek, the people, a name which applied to some closely related tribes, chiefly the Kaskaskias, Cahokias, Peorias, Tamaroas, and Michigameas. The Illinois were distinct from Miami tribes who spoke different dialects of the same central Algonkian language. The Illinois were first met by Jacques Marquette* and Louis Jolliet* in 1673 on the Illinois and Mississippi rivers; throughout the French régime they lived in numerous agricultural villages on both banks of the Mississippi and its eastern tributaries in southern Iowa, northern Missouri, and Illinois. Maize, beans, and squash were staple foods, and communal bison hunts were conducted on foot west of the Mississippi during the summer. They traded furs to the French who from the 1680s established forts and, later, settlements in their country. Internecine warfare, first with the Iroquois, later with the Sioux, Foxes, and Chickasaws, combined with smallpox and other diseases, caused a severe reduction in their numbers; by the 19th century they were virtually extinct. Aboriginally the Illinois were probably organized in extended matrilocal families.   H.H.

Indiens des Missions. *See* MISSION INDIANS

Iroquoian; in French Huronne-iroquoise; generally refers to the linguistic family composed of the Hurons, Iroquois (League of Six Nations), Neutrals, Susquehannocks, Eries, Tuscaroras, Nottaways, Meherrins, Cherokees, Wenros, and the Laurentian "Iroquois" encountered by Jacques Cartier* in 1534. The member groups of this language family were largely concentrated in the eastern Great Lakes region of Canada and the United States; but small groups, as well as the numerous Cherokees, were distributed in the southeastern piedmont and tidewater regions of the middle Atlantic and southern United States. This family of languages was part of a larger group of distantly related language families, including Siouan and Caddoan, whose member groups were distributed over the western Great Lakes and Mississippi valley of early North America.

In specific usage the term might be used in reference to the league, or Six Nations Confederacy; it is also occasionally used as an adjective (i.e. Iroquoian costume, village). *See* IROQUOIS, SIX NATIONS CONFEDERACY. H.H. and A.E.

Iroquois; derived from the Algonkian word Irinakhoiw (literally, real adders, figuratively, rattlesnakes) with the French suffix-*ois*. The term is commonly used to refer to the five member nations of the Iroquois Confederacy: Mohawks, Oneidas, Onondagas, Cayugas, and Senecas. It is also applied formally to all the linguistic relatives of the above nations, such as the Hurons, Wyandots, Susquehannas, Tuscaroras, and Cherokees. *See* IROQUOIAN, SIX NATIONS CONFEDERACY. A.E.

Loups. *See* DELAWARES; MAHICANS

Mahicans (Mohicans); in French also called Loups. A powerful tribe to the east of the Iroquois Confederacy, the Mahicans inhabited the Hudson valley and extended into Massachusetts. They are related to but distinct from the Mohegans, an Algonkian tribe who lived in what is now Connecticut. They settled first at Schodac, on an island in the vicinity of Albany, New York, in 40 villages. After attacks by the Mohawks, they moved in 1664 to what is now Stockbridge, Mass. The French used the term Loups for the Schaghticokes, and for the Munsees and Delawares, as well as for the related Mahicans. In 1730 a large group of the Stockbridge Mahicans moved to the area of Wyoming, Pennsylvania, and later to Ohio.

Miamis. An Algonkian people closely related to the Illinois. The name derives from Omamey, applied by neighbouring tribes. English records usually called them Twightwees (one of their own names) or Naked Indians, though the latter term may have included other groups. The name Miamis was used in the 18th century both for a group of tribes, including the Weas and Piankeshaws, and for one tribe of this group, the Atchatchakangouens (Cranes). Miamis were first met in Wisconsin before 1670, but some were living south of Lake Michigan in 1680 and probably had been there earlier. They were among the Indians René-Robert Cavelier* de La Salle collected at Fort Saint-Louis (near LaSalle, Ill.) to oppose Iroquois attackers. From that time to about 1700, Miami parties ranged as far as the frontiers of the English colonies on retaliatory raids against the Iroquois or seeking trade. Virginia acted in 1699 to break off negotiations between resident Indians and the "Tawittawayes." New York tried without much success to reconcile the Iroquois and the western Indians; some "Twigh Twee Indians" came to Albany in 1719 to trade, but Louis-Thomas Chabert* de Joncaire's establishment of a French post at Niagara (near Youngstown, N.Y.) obstructed this commerce. By 1721 the Miamis occupied the three-river area of the present St Joseph (southeast of Lake Michigan), Maumee (west of Lake Erie), and upper Wabash. Following ORONTONY's lead in 1747, at least part of the Weas and the Piankeshaws formed an alliance with the English and moved to the Rivière à la Roche (Great Miami River), in present south-west Ohio. The Miamis were not conspicuous in the Seven Years' War. They joined PONTIAC in 1763 but accepted reasserted British authority in 1765. In the latter half of the century Shawnees replaced them on the Great Miami River and Potawatomis and Kickapoos occupied some of their Wabash lands. *See* PIANKESHAWS, WEAS. W.A.H.

Micmacs (etymologically the allies; Souriquois, Gaspesians, Miscouiens). A member tribe of the Abenaki Confederacy, which, at the time of its discovery, occupied what is now Nova Scotia, Cape Breton Island, the northern portion of New Brunswick, and Prince Edward Island. They are the Souriquois of the *Jesuit Relations* and the Gaspesians of Chrestien Le Clercq*. The tribe adopted agriculture, accepted the Christian teachings of the missionaries, intermarried freely with the French colonists, and, like their neighbours the Malecites, remained allies of the French throughout the wars of the 17th and 18th centuries. [*See* Étienne BÂTARD, Jean-Baptiste COPE, Paul LAURENT, Jacques PADANUQUES.]

Mingos (mengwe, treacherous), a term applied by the Delaware Indians to their Iroquoian speaking enemies. The term has been applied to specific groups in two historically unrelated situations. In the 17th century Dutch traders at the head of Delaware Bay identified the inland Indians with whom they traded as Minquas, and distinguished between Minquas specifically so called or White Minquas (Susquehannocks), seated on the Susquehanna River, and the Black Minquas (possibly also known as Eries or by other names) from the country west of the mountains. Similarity of name and locality notwithstanding, these Black Minquas were distinct from the Mingos of the following century. In the 18th century the term Mingo was conveniently applied by the English to those Iroquois, from the various nations, who settled on the upper Ohio. The French called them Tsonnontouans (Senecas), not distinguishing them from the most westerly of the Iroquois nations. Close trade relations with the neighbouring English colonies weakened the Mingos' ties with the parent Iroquois League. The French military occupation of the upper Ohio in 1753 drew protests from TANAGHRISSON, spokesman for the Mingos. When the French brushed the objections aside and proceeded with the occupation, many of these Iroquois migrants returned to New York; those who remained became further estranged from the league, and after the French withdrawal in 1759 they formed isolated groups such as "the Crow's band" and "Pluggy's gang." With the more numerous Delawares and the Shawnees, these Mingos were one of the three major Indian groups on the upper Ohio until after the American revolution. W.A.H.

Mission or **Praying Indians.** The Christianized Indians who lived in the missions of New France. The principal groups were the Iroquois of Sault-Saint-Louis (Caughnawaga); the Iroquois of the Mountain (at Lac des Deux-Montagnes, or Oka, after 1720); the Abenakis of Saint-François and Bécancour; and the Hurons of Lorette. After 1749 a number of Iroquois, particularly Oneidas and Onondagas, settled at François Picquet*'s mission of La Présentation at Oswegatchie (near Ogdensburg, N.Y.). *See* HURONS OF LORETTE, SAINT-FRANÇOIS ABENAKIS.

Mississaugas; in French Mississagués. The so-called Mississaugas are Ojibwas. In the Ojibwa language Mississaugas may signify either people who inhabit the country where there are many mouths of rivers, or people of a large lake. Their name probably is derived from the Mississagué (Mississagi) River on the north shore of Lake Huron. The French first encountered this group of Ojibwas in 1634 near the mouth of the Mississagué River and at Manitoulin Island. Nearly a century later the Mississaugas, together with other Ojibwas, advanced east and south into former Huron territory. In the mid 18th century the French referred to the Ojibwas newly established between lakes Huron, Erie, and Ontario as Mississagués. The English speaking settlers would continue to call Mississaugas those Ojibwas residing between Niagara, the Grand River, Lake Simcoe, Rice Lake, and Kingston, but the Mississaugas considered themselves Ojibwas. The Mississauga alliance with the French during the wars of mid century was less than firm. In 1756 they threatened to attack the French post at Toronto [*see* Pierre POUCHOT]. A certain division of sympathies apparently continued during PONTIAC's uprising of 1763: Mississauga warriors fought at Detroit by the side of the Ottawa chief but at least one Mississauga chief, WABBICOMMICOT, seems to have opposed their participation.

D.B.S. and B.J.

Mohawks; in French Agniers, in Dutch Maquaes. The English name for them is derived from the New England Algonkian word Mohowaùuck, figuratively, man-eaters. Their own designation is Kaniengehaga, meaning people of the place of flint. The Mohawks were the easternmost member of the Iroquois Confederacy; as the ritual keepers of the eastern door of the longhouse, they "defended" the eastern borders of Iroquois territory. The Mohawk language was for several centuries the lingua franca of the Confederacy and the official language of government. By the late 17th century the Mohawks had been greatly reduced in numbers, owing largely to disease and massive losses during intermittent clashes with the French and with surrounding Indian groups – particularly the Mahicans of the Hudson valley. For most of the 18th century the Mohawks were situated in three villages along the Mohawk River west of Schenectady, New York. Their alliance with the British was cultivated by Sir William Johnson*, the superintendent of northern Indians, who married among them and exerted tremendous influence. Mohawk war parties fought against the French during the War of the Austrian Succession and the Seven Years' War [*see*

THEYANOGUIN]. Following the American revolution the majority of Mohawks moved to the Grand River (Ontario) under the leadership of Thayendanegea* (Joseph Brant), and they reside there today with segments of all the Six Nations peoples. *See* IROQUOIS, MISSION INDIANS, SIX NATIONS CONFEDERACY.

A.E.

Monsonis (Algonkian for moose). The name may refer to a clan, or totemic affiliation, but it is more probably a reference to their moose hunting. The Monsonis were a division of the Woods or Swampy Crees with whom they eventually merged. During the French régime they inhabited the country adjacent to southwestern James Bay and also the international boundary region between Lake Superior and Lake Winnipeg. They were prominent partners of other Crees and Assiniboins in the accounts of Pierre GAULTIER de Varennes et de La Vérendrye. They were hunters, trappers, and fishermen, and participated to some extent in wars against the Sioux [*see* LA COLLE]. Like the rest of the Crees, their early social organization is not known, but they were probably less sedentary than the central Algonkians to the south. *See* CREES.

H.H.

Nipissings; in French Népissingues, Nipissiriniens. In Algonkian, people of the little water, so named from the location of their villages on Lake Nipissing. A central Algonkian speaking people of the Ojibwa-Ottawa-Algonkian language group, the Nipissings, like the others, were middlemen in the French fur trade, trading mainly with Crees to the north. They were also fishermen, hunters, and trappers. Although they grew little maize, they obtained ample supplies through trade with neighbouring and allied Hurons and others in exchange for hides. The Nipissings, like the Ojibwas, had exogamous patrilineal clans, or totems, and like other central Algonkians lived, when conditions permitted, in permanent villages, leaving them only seasonally to hunt, trap, and trade. Some Nipissings settled at the mission of Lac-des-Deux-Montagnes (Oka, Que.), and warriors like KISENSIK fought against the English during the Anglo-French wars of the 18th century. *See* OJIBWAS, OTTAWAS.

H.H.

Norridgewocks; in French Canibas. An important division of the Abenakis, the Norridgewocks usually lived at a village (now Old Point, Madison) on the Kennebec River in Maine. Led by chiefs such as Mog* and supported by Father Sébastien Rale*, their Jesuit missionary, they fought for the French during the War of the Spanish Succession, carrying scalps and prisoners to Quebec. The Penobscots, Pigwackets, and other Abenaki tribes also remained allied to the French. After the treaty of Utrecht in 1713, however, the Norridgewocks were the tribe principally affected by the spread of English settlement east of the Kennebec and up the river valley. Wowurna* and other chiefs protested and then harassed the English settlers, until Massachusetts declared war on the Abenakis in 1722. Rale was killed by the English in 1724, and most of the Norridgewocks moved to Saint-François in Canada. They joined the Penobscots in making peace in 1727, and many of the Norridgewocks returned to their native village at that time. Greatly reduced in numbers from the beginning of the century, they did not actively resist the quickening pace of English settlement. Their village was attacked again by the English in 1749, and most of them moved to Saint-François in 1754. Those who remained, such as NODOGAWERRIMET, suffered further depredations at the hands of the English. *See* ABENAKIS, PENOBSCOTS, SAINT-FRANÇOIS ABENAKIS.   D.H.

Ojibwas (Chippewas); now known in French as Ojibwé, but referred to in the 18th century as Sauteux. The meaning of Ojibwa has not been satisfactorily determined. The most popular explanation translates the word as to roast until puckered up. Canadian usage favours the spelling Ojibwa, or Ojibway. Chippewa, adopted by the Bureau of American Ethnology, is a corruption of the word. According to tribal tradition, the three Algonkian groups, the Ojibwas, Potawatomis, and Ottawas, were once united, and separated about the time of European contact. Linguistically and culturally they are very closely related. A loose confederacy, entitled the Council of the Three Fires, still existed early in the 20th century. The Jesuits met the Ojibwas near Sault Ste Marie in 1640. They translated their name Baourchitigouin (people of the rapids) literally to the French Saulteur (sometimes written Sauteur, Saulteux, or Sauteux). The Ojibwas who later occupied sections of northwestern Ontario, Manitoba, and Saskatchewan carried this name with them, and are known today as Saulteux. Their successful struggle with the Foxes expelled that group from the northern part of present Wisconsin at the beginning of the 18th century. In subsequent skirmishes with the Sioux, the Ojibwas gained most of what is now Minnesota and a part of North Dakota. In the southeast, approximately a century after European contact, some Ojibwas advanced into former Huron territory between lakes Huron and Ontario. These Ojibwas were called Mississaugas by the French and British, possibly because a number had come from the area around the Mississagué (Mississagi) River on the north shore of Lake Huron. By the end of the 18th century, the Ojibwas occupied a region stretching a thousand miles from the Saskatchewan River to the St Lawrence. They were active in the uprising against the British in the west in 1763–64. MINWEWEH led an attack on the garrison at Michilimackinac, and Ojibwa warriors fought by PONTIAC's side in the siege of Detroit.   D.B.S. and B.J.

Oneidas; in French Onneiouts. The name stems from the term Tiioeniote, figuratively, people of the upright stone. Members of the Iroquois Confederacy, the Oneidas were situated between the Mohawks on the east and the Onondagas on the west – that is, roughly between present Utica, N.Y., and Oneida Lake. In 1749 Father François Picquet* founded the mission of La Présentation at Oswegatchie (near Ogdensburg, N.Y.), and a number of Oneidas and Onondagas subsequently settled there. According to Sir William Johnson*, superintendent of northern Indians, during the early part of the Seven Years' War the Oneidas were "divided amongst themselves, and the greater part under the influence of those of their Nation whom the French have drawn off to live at Swegatchy. . . ." When John Bradstreet* raided Fort Frontenac (Kingston, Ont.) in 1758, no Oneidas would accompany him. As French power waned, however, the Oneidas became more willing to aid the British, and a party under GAWÈHE accompanied Jeffery Amherst*'s expedition against Montreal in 1760. Encouraged by Samuel Kirkland, a Congregationalist missionary, the Oneidas allied themselves with the Americans during the revolution, serving as scouts and aides to American officers. By the 1830s the majority of Oneidas had removed to Green Bay, Wisconsin, where they reside today. A smaller group came to the Thames River in Ontario, where they still live, near Strathroy. *See* IROQUOIS, SIX NATIONS CONFEDERACY.   A.E.

Onondagas; in French Onontagués; in their language Ononta ge, figuratively, people of the hills. Situated near present Syracuse, N.Y., the Onondagas were the most centrally located of the Iroquois nations, and the Confederacy's capital was consequently in their territory. During federal council deliberations involving representatives from all member nations, the Onondagas acted as mediators, or chairmen in council. Much of the action taken by this council was by unanimous decision. For most of the 18th century, the Onondaga capital was an active seat of international power in the constant negotiations conducted by the Confederacy both with New France and with the British colonies. Representatives and delegates, both Indian and European, were constantly travelling between Onondaga and the various colonial capitals. During the same era the federal council also administered Iroquois lands in Pennsylvania and Ohio, in addition to relocating and governing refugee Indian groups displaced from their coastal homes by white expansion. Supervisors such as SWATANA were appointed by the federal council to administer such tribes. At the beginning of the Seven Years' War the Onondagas opted for neutrality. They were few, they said, and their "Welfare & safety depended upon keeping all their Warriors together & ready at hand to defend themselves. . . ." In the later stages of the war they abandoned their neutrality: Onondaga warriors accompanied John Bradstreet* in his attack on Fort Frontenac (Kingston, Ont.) in 1758 [*see* ONONWAROGO] and took part in Jeffery Amherst*'s expedition against Montreal in 1760. The Onondagas took up the British cause during the American revolution, and a portion of them subsequently moved to the Grand River (Ontario). Another segment elected to remain in their homeland and they still maintain the Confederacy's capital on a reservation south of Syracuse. *See* IROQUOIS, SIX NATIONS CONFEDERACY.   A.E.

Ottawas, in French Outaouais, probably derived from the Ojibwa verb, to buy and sell, to trade. The French first applied the name Ottawa to all the upper Great Lakes Algonkian groups. In 1670, Father Claude Dablon* explained that as the Ottawas had been the first to reach the French settlements the others also were assumed to be Ottawas. Towards the start of the 18th century most commentators began to restrict use of the term Ottawa to four Algonkian groups: the Kiskakons, Sinagos, Sable, and Nassawaketons. In the mid 17th century, the Ottawas hunted around the shores of Lake Huron. After the Huron defeat at the hands of the Iroquois in 1649 the Ottawas were driven westward by the victors to the Baie des Puants (Green Bay, Lake Michigan). Later they returned to the eastern part of the upper Michigan peninsula. Shortly after the establishment of Detroit in 1701, some, including SAGUIMA, moved their homes there. Others remained at Michilimackinac until they moved to L'Arbre Croche (Cross Village, Mich.) in 1742. During the 1740s a Huron chief at Detroit, ORONTONY, set on foot a movement apparently intended to drive the French from the west. The Ottawas at Detroit were divided: those of KINOUSAKI's village remained favourable to the French whereas MIKINAK's people seem to have cooperated with Orontony to some extent. A more effective political organization was the Ottawa chief PONTIAC's coalition of Ottawas, Potawatomis, Ojibwas, and Hurons, which besieged the British garrison at Detroit throughout the summer of 1763. By the end of the 18th century, the Ottawas had spread out from L'Arbre Croche along the eastern shore of Lake Michigan as far south as the St Joseph River. In the north, Manitoulin Island was shared with the Ojibwas. To the east, along the southwestern shore of Lake Erie, their villages mingled with those of their old allies the Hurons.   D.B.S. and B.J.

Ouiatanons. See WEAS
Padoucas. See COMANCHES

Pawnees (Horn People); in French Panis. The Pawnees belonged to the Caddoan linguistic family and lived in the valley of the Platte River in what is now Nebraska. How their name also came to be given to any Indian slave is not known; when Claude-Charles Dutisné* visited them in 1719, however, they received him coldly because they had been told by the Osages that the Frenchman was looking for slaves.

Penobscots; in French Pentagouets. An important division of the Abenakis, they inhabited the land about Penobscot Bay and the Penobscot River in Maine. Their principal village was at Pentagouet (now Castine), and in language and customs they closely resembled the Norridgewocks. Like them, too, they fought the colonists during King Philip's War [see Benjamin Church*] and raided the New England frontier during King William's and Queen Anne's wars. Their allegiance to the French was maintained by common interest and by the influence of such men as Jean-Vincent* and Bernard-Anselme d'Abbadie* de Saint-Castin, and Father Pierre de LA CHASSE. After the treaty of Utrecht the Penobscots joined the Norridgewocks and other Abenakis in resisting the encroachment of English settlement on their lands, a resistance that culminated in war with Massachusetts. SAUGUAARAM was the chief Penobscot spokesman during the negotiations that culminated in the peace treaty of 1726 between that tribe and Massachusetts. Following the outbreak of the Anglo-French war of 1744–48, the Penobscots fled to Quebec, but they returned to New England once it was concluded and signed a treaty at Falmouth (Portland, Me.) in 1749. After that date they did not fight against the English again, and unlike the Norridgewocks did not join the Saint-François Abenakis near Quebec. They are now one of the most numerous remaining New England tribes, and still live on part of their ancestral lands at Oldtown, on the Penobscot River. See ABENAKIS, NORRIDGEWOCKS, SAINT-FRANÇOIS ABENAKIS.   D.H.

Piankeshaws; in French Peanquishas. One of the three most important of the Miami tribes, the others being the Weas and Atchatchakangouens (Miamis proper). A central Algonkian farming-hunting village people first encountered by the French in the 1670s, the Piankeshaws, during the last decades of the 17th century, separated from other Miamis, who were moving east. The Piankeshaws established villages, first on the Illinois River, later at the Fox-Wisconsin portage, on the west bank of the Mississippi nearly opposite the mouth of the Wisconsin, and in the Chicago region. In the early 18th century they too moved eastward, finally founding a village on the Ouabache (Wabash) River, a few miles south of present Lafayette, Ind. Except for a brief excursion in the 1730s to the area of what is now Vincennes, Ind., they remained near Lafayette until the 19th century. Like the other Miami tribes they trapped for the fur trade, and, as allies of the French, participated in the warfare which characterized intertribal relations in the Great Lakes region. See MIAMIS, WEAS.   H.H.

Potawatomis; in French Potéouatamis; meaning in Ojibwa, keepers of the fire. The French first contacted this Algonkian group, closely related to the Ojibwas and Ottawas, around the Baie des Puants (Green Bay, Lake Michigan). By the end of the 17th century, many Potawatomis had migrated southward into former Miami country on the St Joseph River. A few journeyed to Detroit after it was founded by Lamothe Cadillac [Laumet*] in 1701. By 1760 at least a hundred warriors resided there. The other principal bands remained in the St Joseph area. Steadfast in their French alliance, the Potawatomis fought with PONTIAC against the British in 1763. At the end of the 18th century, they controlled the country around the head of Lake Michigan. The Potawatomis practised agriculture in the summer and hunted in the winter months.   D.B.S. and B.J.

Renards. See FOXES

Saint-François Abenakis. The inhabitants of a mission village on the Saint-François River near its confluence with the St Lawrence, probably settled between 1660 and 1670. The first occupants were apparently Sokokis. There appear to have been Abenakis and "Loups" in the village before 1700. In 1705 or 1706, the mission of Saint-François-de-Sales moved from the lower falls of the Chaudière River to the Saint-François, bringing some Abenakis from Maine and many additional Sokokis and "Loups," so that in 1711 the village was estimated to contain 260 warriors, perhaps 1,300 persons. This population was reduced by epidemics and the colonial wars in which they were always allies of the French. Then, between the outbreak of the American revolution and 1800, Saint-François received numerous new inhabitants from the upper Connecticut River and from Missisquoi, at the mouth of the Missisquoi River on Lake Champlain. Until at least 1880, the band was known officially as the Abenakis and Sokokis of Saint-François. The present name conceals the Sokoki element but may nevertheless be accurate, since the Sokokis probably spoke an Abenaki dialect. The assertion, often repeated in the last 60 years, that the Abenakis of the Androscoggin River were the dominant group at Saint-François, remains to be proved and is probably incorrect. The idea seems to have originated in a fancied resemblance between place names on the Androscoggin River and the early Abenaki name for Saint-François, namely *Arsikantek8*, literally Empty Cabin River. Saint-François probably absorbed most of the fugitives from western New England – the Sokokis, Penacooks, Pigwackets, Piscataquas, Saco Indians, Nipmucs, and Schaghticokes – the Androscoggin Indians probably retiring to the nearby mission of Bécancour. *See* ABENAKIS.   G.M.D.

Sauks (Sacs); in French also Ousakis, Sakis. A central Algonkian tribe closely related in language and culture to the Foxes, Kickapoos, and Mascoutens, they had a village at the head of the Baie des Puants (Green Bay, Lake Michigan). The Sauks generally maintained an alliance with the Foxes, but did not participate as much in intertribal wars and wars against the French, perhaps because of their close proximity to French trading posts and missions at Baie-des-Puants. In 1733 the Sauks welcomed Fox refugees from their wars with the French, and from that date the history of the two tribes is indistinguishable. Gradual movement westward took them first to the Mississippi, then across it into Iowa. Like their kinsmen, the Sauks were village people who cultivated maize, beans, and squash, hunted large game during the summer, and trapped for the fur trade during the winter. *See* FOXES.   H.H.

Sauteux. *See* OJIBWAS

Senecas; in French Tsonnontouans, Djiionondo-wanen-a-ka being their own designation for themselves, literally, people of the big hill. The Senecas were the westernmost member of the Six Nations Confederacy; as the ritual keepers of the western door of the longhouse, they "defended" the western borders of Iroquois territory. In population the Senecas were, and still are, the most numerous of the member nations in the league. In the federal councils of the league they ranked with the Mohawks and Onondagas as members of the Elder Brothers, a legislative segment of the federal council. The Seneca chiefs Aouenano*, Cagenquarichten*, Tekanoet*, and Tonatakout* were involved in negotiations with the French during the late 17th and early 18th centuries. Louis-Thomas Chabert* de Joncaire was adopted by the Senecas and was one of a few Canadians who were able to influence the Iroquois during this period. Along with other members of the league, the Senecas were village farmers who raised maize, beans, and squash. They also depended on seasonal hunting, fishing, and gathering. Following the upheaval of the American revolution, the majority of the Senecas managed to remain in their traditional homeland in western New York State where they reside on reservations today. *See* IROQUOIS, SIX NATIONS CONFEDERACY.

H.H. and A.E.

Shawnees; in French Chaouanons, from an Algonkian word meaning southerners. They were an Algonkian people originally resident south of the Ohio on the Cumberland River (Rivière des Anciens Chouanons on a French map of 1764). Dispersed by Iroquois attacks, some moved toward Carolina; others who took refuge at René-Robert Cavelier* de La Salle's Fort Saint-Louis (near present La Salle, Ill.) provided a basis for a later French claim to the Ohio country. Paul MARIN de La Malgue would argue to Iroquois who protested the occupation of the region in 1753–54 that "M. de La Salle took possession of it when it was inhabited by the Shawnees, against whom the Iroquois made war incessantly, and who have always been our friends." A few years after their encounter with La Salle, however, in 1692, some of these Shawnees moved to the head of Chesapeake Bay and the upper Delaware River. The Iroquois maintained overseers like SWATANA and Scarroyady among them to supervise their affairs. After a minor disturbance in 1727, the Iroquois ordered the group to return to the Ohio. The retreat was a gradual one, covering more than 30 years, but by 1730 an appreciable number of Shawnees, possibly including some from the south, were living in western Pennsylvania, where they came once more under French influence. Their subsequent political role was ambiguous; receptive to French overtures, they retained close trade relations with the English. In 1745 a considerable part was persuaded to move to the upper Ouabache (Wabash), but the settlement was short-lived; part of the group soon returned to the Ohio and the remainder went to present-day Alabama. The Shawnees generally accommodated themselves to the French position in the Seven Years' War, and in spite of close relations with the Delawares they continued after the war to trouble the English on the Ohio frontier.   W.A.H.

Sioux; from Nadouessioux (French spelling of a central Algonkian term for little snakes, or enemies), also called Dakotas, which in Siouan means the people. Numerous bands and villages of this Dakota Siouan tribe were located in the Mississippi headwaters region, along the Minnesota River, and west to the eastern watershed of the Missouri below the Great Bend. The French referred to two divisions, Sioux of the Woods and Sioux of the Prairies. The former comprised those tribes known today as Santees, the latter, tribes from whom are descended the modern Yanktons, Yanktonais, and Tetons. The Santees, especially the Mdewakanton division, had most contact with the French, beginning about 1680 and, with interruptions due to intertribal warfare and distance, lasting throughout the French régime. The Santee Sioux were woodland village people cultivating a little maize, but relying chiefly on wild rice and other natural products including bison, which they hunted on foot in large communal parties on the prairies to the south and west. At first trading allies of the Ojibwas of Chequamegon peninsula, the Sioux began in 1736 to include them among their many Algonkian foes in warfare which lasted well into the 19th century.   H.H.

Six Nations Confederacy. Tradition credits the formation of the Confederacy (also called the Iroquois League) either to Dekanahwideh*, the Peacemaker, or to Hiawatha, his spokesman. This powerful political entity was apparently founded about 1570 and was composed of Mohawks, Oneidas, Onondagas, Cayugas, and Senecas. It was known to Europeans during the 17th and early 18th centuries as the Five Nations. Because of the pressure of white settlement, the Tuscaroras moved from their North Carolina homeland into Iroquois territory during the first two decades of the 18th century. Although this refugee group was never an equal voting member of the Confederacy, their presence gave rise to an impression among Europeans that a sixth nation had been added. The use of the term Six Nations was largely limited to the English and came about gradually, not becoming a common reference until about the time of the American revolution. The sign over the French trading fort at Niagara (near Youngstown, N.Y.) in 1726, *Porte des Cinq Nations* (Gateway of the Five Nations), indicates that the term was not then universally in use. The Confederacy maintained its political capital in the main village of the Onondaga nation, near present Syracuse, N.Y.; it is still located there and still functioning as a centre for rites and politics. The Iroquoian people who made up the Confederacy raised maize, beans, and other crops; they hunted and fished to supplement their diet. Their matrilineal clan structure vested considerable privileges and power in the women, who nominated the chiefs, who jointly owned the houses and fields, and from whom all children traced their descent and inheritance. In 1701 the Confederacy committed itself to neutrality in any future fighting between the French and English. The federal council could not enforce this policy on all individuals, however, and some Iroquois warriors were to be found on each side of the 18th century Anglo-French wars. In 1746 a meeting of Six Nations chiefs at Albany declared an end to neutrality and prepared to enter the war (the War of the Austrian Succession) on the side of the British. There is some question, however, as to whether the gathering was entitled to speak on behalf of the Confederacy. The Six Nations leaned to neutrality during the early stages of the Seven Years' War, although at one point there seemed to be some chance that they might declare against the British. As one Seneca explained, they resented British encroachment on their lands and were intimidated by the power of the French and of the western and northern Indians. British victories at Fort Frontenac (Kingston, Ont.) and Fort Duquesne (Pittsburgh, Pa.) in 1758 indicated a waning of French power, and the Six Nations became more friendly towards the British. In April 1759, at a conference with Sir William Johnson*, superintendent of northern Indians, members of the Confederacy claiming to represent their respective villages declared war against the French. Although this declaration may not have been an official decision of the federal council it was indicative of the direction in which events were forcing the Six Nations. That summer about a thousand Iroquois accompanied Johnson in his attack on Fort Niagara (near Youngstown, N.Y.), and in 1760 a large force representing all nations of the Confederacy accompanied Jeffery Amherst*'s expedition against Montreal. *See* IROQUOIAN, IROQUOIS, MOHAWKS, ONEIDAS, ONONDAGAS, CAYUGAS, SENECAS, MISSION INDIANS.   A.E.

Tamaroas; in French Tamarois. One of the tribal divisions of the historic Illinois, the Tamaroas shared a village with the Cahokias, another Illinois tribe, on the east bank of the Mississippi nearly opposite the present St Louis. In 1701 they broke off from the Cahokias and probably joined still another Illinois tribe, the Kaskaskias, who at the time were moving down to the Mississippi from Lake Peoria (Illinois River). Like other Illinois, they suffered heavy losses from warfare and disease throughout the French, British, and American periods. *See* ILLINOIS.   H.H.

Têtes-plates. *See* FLATHEADS
Tsonnontouans. *See* SENECAS and MINGOS

Weas; in French Ouiatanons, a Miami subdivision later regarded, like the related Piankeshaws, as a distinct group. French explorers first met them at the southern end of Lake Michigan, but their later home was on the upper Ouabache (Wabash) River. They are noted especially for their role in the 1747 uprising led by the Huron chief ORONTONY. In 1720 Governor Vaudreuil [Rigaud*] had built a post at Ouiatanon (near Lafayette, Ind.) to secure the French communication route with the Illinois country and to promote trade; but the English traders who influenced Orontony also affected the Miamis, who in October 1747 seized the fort and, assisted by the Shawnees and the Mingos, proposed a treaty with

Pennsylvania, which three Miami chiefs signed at Lancaster on 23 July 1748. The pro-British faction, apparently Weas and Piankeshaws, then moved to the Rivière à la Roche (Great Miami River) in present Ohio, where in 1749 Pierre-Joseph CÉLORON de Blainville found a small Miami town near present Cincinnati and a larger one, Pickawillany, where Piqua now stands. Headed by a chief known variously as Memeskia, La Demoiselle, or Old Britain, this place, also called the Pict Town, flourished as a centre for English trade until 1752, when it was destroyed by Charles-Michel Mouet* de Langlade, whose Indian followers boiled Old Britain and ate him.   W.A.H.

BIOGRAPHIES

List of Abbreviations

AAQ Archives de l'archidiocèse de Québec
ACAM Archives de la chancellerie de l'archevêché de Montréal
ACND Archives de la Congrégation de Notre-Dame, Montréal
AD Archives départementales, France
AHDQ Archives de l'Hôtel-Dieu de Québec
AHGQ Archives de l'Hôpital Général de Québec
AHSJ Archives générales des Religieuses hospitalières de Saint-Joseph, Montréal
AJM Archives judiciaires de Montréal
AJQ Archives judiciaires de Québec
AJTR Archives judiciaires de Trois-Rivières
AMUQ Archives du monastère des Ursulines de Québec
AN Archives nationales, Paris
ANDM Archives paroissiales de Notre-Dame de Montréal
ANDQ Archives paroissiales de Notre-Dame de Québec
ANQ Archives nationales du Québec
ANQ-M Archives nationales du Québec, dépôt de Montréal
APQ Archives de la province de Québec
AQ Archives du Québec
ARSI Archivum Romanum Societatis Iesu, Rome
ASGM Archives des sœurs Grises, Montréal
ASJCF Archives de la Compagnie de Jésus, province du Canada français
ASQ Archives du séminaire de Québec
ASSM Archives du séminaire de Saint-Sulpice, Montréal
BM British Museum, London
BN Bibliothèque nationale, Paris

BRH *Le Bulletin des recherches historiques*
CCHA Canadian Catholic Historical Association
CHA Canadian Historical Association
CHR *Canadian Historical Review*
CTG Comité technique du Génie, Paris
DAB *Dictionary of American biography*
DBF *Dictionnaire de biographie française*
DCB *Dictionary of Canadian biography*
DNB *Dictionary of national biography*
DPL Detroit Public Library
HBC Hudson's Bay Company
HBRS Hudson's Bay Record Society
IOA L'Inventaire des œuvres d'art, Québec
JR *Jesuit relations and allied documents*
NYCD *Documents relative to the colonial history of the state of New-York*
PAC Public Archives of Canada
PANL Public Archives of Newfoundland and Labrador
PANS Public Archives of Nova Scotia
PRO Public Record Office, London
RHAF *Revue d'histoire de l'Amérique française*
RSCT Royal Society of Canada *Proceedings and Transactions*
RUL *La Revue de l'université Laval*
SCHÉC Société canadienne d'histoire de l'Église catholique
SGCF Société généalogique canadienne-française
SHA Service historique de l'Armée, Paris
SHM Société historique de Montréal
SHQ Société historique de Québec
SHS Société historique du Saguenay
USPG United Society for the Propagation of the Gospel, London

BIOGRAPHIES

A

ABBADIE DE SAINT-CASTIN, JOSEPH D', **Baron de SAINT-CASTIN,** French officer and Abenaki chief; son of Jean-Vincent d'Abbadie* de Saint-Castin and Pidianske (Marie-Mathilde), an Abenaki woman; fl. 1720–46 in Acadia.

After the death of his brother Bernard-Anselme* in 1720, Joseph d'Abbadie inherited the title of Baron de Saint-Castin – he was the fifth of that name – but it appears that he did not attach much importance to it for he never went to France to assert his claims to his inheritance. He stayed among the Abenakis of Acadia with one of his brothers whose name we do not know. Having always lived in the tribe, Joseph was much more "Abenaki" than Bernard-Anselme, and the Indians conferred upon him the rank of great chief.

The Abenakis felt themselves in no way bound by the treaty of Utrecht, which France had signed in 1713 and which handed Acadia over to England. The governor of New France, Philippe de Rigaud* de Vaudreuil, secretly backed up the Abenakis. On 10 Nov. 1720 he asked the council of Marine to transfer the lieutenant's pay of the deceased Bernard-Anselme to the two Saint-Castin brothers, "who keep the Indians of this tribe faithful to French interests." Guerilla warfare was immediately intensified, and the English seized the baron by trickery. The captain of an English vessel invited Saint-Castin aboard to take some refreshment, then suddenly got under way and headed for Boston, Massachusetts. Saint-Castin was kept in prison in Boston from November 1721 till May 1722 and was released only in the hope of appeasing the Indians.

In 1726 Saint-Castin was in effect recognized as a French officer. During the next 20 years he and his brother continued to serve the king of France by keeping the Abenakis on the French side and by carrying on vigorous guerilla warfare against their New England neighbours, but during lulls in the fighting they and the Abenakis renewed their profitable trade with their erstwhile enemies.

On 25 Aug. 1746 Joseph's brother died of wounds received in a brawl. From that year on we lose track of Joseph too. Baron Jean-Vincent d'Abbadie de Saint-Castin's inheritance, which Joseph had not claimed, fell to Marie-Anselme, Bernard-Anselme's eldest daughter, and her descendants. Official correspondence mentions a nephew of Joseph whose services were acquired by the court of France and who waged war with the Abenakis. The name Saint-Castin or its English distortion Castine still survives in America.

GEORGES CERBELAUD SALAGNAC

AN, Col., B, 44, 45, 50, 54, 55, 57, 59, 63, 72, 74, 76, 78, 85; C¹¹ᴬ, 42, 43, 85, 124; C¹¹ᴰ, 8, f.72. *JR* (Thwaites), LXVII.

ABEL, OLIVIER. *See* OLIVIER

ABERGEMONT, JACQUES SIMONET D'. *See* SIMONET

ACARET. *See* DACCARRETTE

ADAMS, JOHN, merchant, member of the Nova Scotia Council; b. 1672 or 1673, son of John and Avis Adams of Boston; d. sometime after 1745.

A petty merchant in Boston, John Adams joined the New England regiment raised by Sir Charles Hobby* and was present at the capture of Port-Royal (Annapolis Royal, N.S.) in 1710. Shortly thereafter he returned to civilian life and, settling in Annapolis Royal, began an extensive trade, probably in manufactured goods, with the Acadians and Indians of Nova Scotia. He also acted as a real estate agent and contractor in Annapolis Royal. Adams' 20-year service on the governing council of that colony began on 28 April 1720 and the records show few who served as faithfully or as long. In 1725 he was appointed a notary public and deputy collector of customs for Annapolis Royal, and in March 1727 he was commissioned a justice of the peace. As deputy collector of customs, he was often involved in heated arguments with other traders such as William WINNIETT, and it appears that he occasionally used this advantageous position to obstruct the activities of his competitors.

By the mid 1720s Adams' eyesight had begun

Adhémar

to fail and he was almost completely blind by 1730. He became less active in community affairs and his trading seems to have declined. In several unsuccessful petitions to the king for a pension, he blamed his misfortune on over-exposure to the sun, "without hatt or wigg," during an Indian attack on Annapolis Royal in 1724. Adams remained an active councillor in spite of his infirmity, however, and in 1731 joined with other senior councillors, including Paul MASCARENE, in opposing the appointment of Alexander COSBY as president of the council.

Adams' desire for advancement was temporarily satisfied in December 1739, when the sudden death of Lieutenant Governor Lawrence Armstrong* and the absence of Major Mascarene elevated Adams to the position of president of the council and thus head of the civil government. Adams complained, however, that "now [that] Providence had put into my hands a Morsel of Bread Major Mascarene was come in all haste from Boston to take it from me." In a stormy meeting of council on 22 March 1740, both Mascarene and Adams claimed the right of presiding. After the councillors declared unanimously in favour of Mascarene, Adams retired to Boston in late August or early September 1740. In his unsuccessful petitions for redress, Adams pointed out that Mascarene had absented himself from the colony for years at a time, but Mascarene was able to account satisfactorily for these long absences and had managed to stay just within the rules governing council membership.

Adams seems to have spent the remainder of his life in Boston, poorly rewarded for his 20 years of service and greatly embittered by the supposed injustice done him.

BARRY M. MOODY

BM, Sloane MSS, 3607, pp.174–77. Mass., Archives, State papers, XVII, 776–79. PAC, MG 11, Nova Scotia A, 11, pp.108–9; 20, pp.94–97; 21, pp.1–3; 24, pp.228–29, 232–33; 25, pp.3–8, 9–13, 65–70, 175–78; Nova Scotia B, 2, pp.172–75. PANS, RG 1, 7, pp.213–16; 11, p.160; 14, p.203; 20, pp.9–10. *Nova Scotia Archives*, *I*; *II*; *III*; *IV*. New Eng. Hist. and Geneal. Register, XXXII (1878), 132–33. Brebner, *New England's outpost*; "Paul Mascarene of Annapolis Royal," *Dal. Rev.*, VIII (1928–29), 501–16. Murdoch, *History of Nova-Scotia*.

ADHÉMAR, JEAN-BAPTISTE, clerk of court, court officer, royal notary; baptized 16 March 1689 in Montreal, son of Antoine Adhémar* de Saint-Martin and Michelle Cusson; d. 19 Dec. 1754 in Montreal.

The son and grandson of royal notaries – his maternal grandfather Jean Cusson* had practised this profession – Jean-Baptiste Adhémar succeeded his father as clerk of court and royal notary. On 15 May 1714 Intendant Michel BÉGON granted him a commission as royal notary in the jurisdiction of Montreal. The following year, on 20 May, in Montreal, he married Catherine, the daughter of the notary Michel Lepailleur* de Laferté.

Soon, however, his reputation was tarnished, and in 1722 Intendant Bégon stated that Adhémar was "a bad lot." The notary had left town after having squandered the funds deposited with the registry of the jurisdiction of Montreal. The intendant added that Adhémar would not retain his situation if he returned. The following year Adhémar was back and had resumed practising his profession, having, it seems, reached an arrangement with the authorities. He also kept his office as clerk of court.

On 28 March 1729 the Conseil Supérieur ordered a "character investigation" of the notary Adhémar, formerly in practice, prior to his succeeding his father-in-law as court officer of that council in Montreal; on 17 April 1730 he was officially received. Meanwhile Adhémar had been acting since the previous year as deputy for the king's attorney in the royal jurisdiction of Montreal, and in 1731 he added to his other offices that of assessor for this court in various trials. But in 1737 he had to declare himself incompetent to judge in a lawsuit, and in 1740 a trial had to be started over again, at his cost. In 1734 Adhémar had asked the authorities for permission to retain his father's minute-book; the following year the king called upon him to deposit it with the registry of the provost court of Quebec, in conformity with the ordinance of 1717 and the recommendations of the attorney general Louis-Guillaume VERRIER.

Because he practised in Montreal, the centre of the fur trade, Jean-Baptiste Adhémar profited greatly by drawing up many enlistment contracts for the west. Like his father, Adhémar had an active career; it was cut off by his death on 19 Dec. 1754.

On 7 Jan. 1733 in Montreal, Adhémar had remarried; his second wife was Catherine Moreau. We know of only three children by this marriage, born between 1734 and 1740, and of none by his earlier marriage.

MICHEL PAQUIN

AN, Col., B, 61, f.530; 63, f.486. ANQ-M, Greffe de J.-B. Adhémar, 1714–54. "Liste des officiers de justice de la Nouvelle-France," *BRH*, XXXIV (1928), 45. É.-Z. Massicotte, "Les huissiers de Montréal sous le régime français,'' *BRH*, XXXII (1926), 85, 88; ''Les tribunaux et les officiers de justice de Montréal sous le régime français,'' *BRH*, XXXVII (1931), 188, 190, 191, 302, 303, 305. P.-G. Roy, *Inv. jug. et délib., 1717–1760*, I, III, V; *Inv. ord. int.*, I, 136; III, 42, 199. Tanguay, *Dictionnaire*. Vachon, ''Inv. critique des notaires royaux,'' *RHAF*, XI (1957–58), 94, 272.

ADHÉMAR DE LANTAGNAC, GASPARD (baptized **Gaspard-Balthazar**), officer in the colonial regular troops and king's lieutenant of Montreal; b. 3 March 1681 in Monaco, son of Antoine Adhémar de Lantagnac and Jeanne-Antoinette de Truchi (Truchy); d. 7 Nov. 1756 in Montreal.

The Adhémar family may be traced back to the time of the first crusade; in the 17th century, the Lantagnac branch was headed by Pierre Adhémar and his wife Anne, sister of Philippe de Rigaud* de Vaudreuil, who was appointed governor general of Canada in 1703. Their second son, Antoine, Gaspard's father, was named governor of Menton in 1701 for the prince of Monaco.

In 1702, at the age of 21, Gaspard, a tall youth, joined a regiment of the king's household. Unable to afford a captaincy, he sailed for Canada in 1712. He had to wait until 1715 for a vacant ensignship but nine months later was promoted lieutenant. In 1721 he became the subject of a dispute between Bishop Saint-Vallier [La Croix*] and his great-uncle, Governor Vaudreuil. The 39-year-old lieutenant was in love with Geneviève-Françoise, daughter of Mathieu-François Martin* de Lino, councillor. De Lino was prominent in Canadian society, but he and his wife were bourgeois, not noble. Consequently, Vaudreuil expressed his disapproval to the council of Marine and to the bishop. Nevertheless, the latter married the couple on 7 March 1720. Vaudreuil considered his grand-nephew's stubbornness and the bishop's concurrence an affront to his authority and transferred Adhémar to Île Royale (Cape Breton Island) in May 1721.

The following year Adhémar went to France on furlough, taking letters from Vaudreuil and the intendant, BÉGON, to the court. They recommended him for a captaincy but neither they nor the prince of Monaco were successful, although in 1726 the prince's efforts were a factor in the council's final approval of Adhémar's promotion.

In 1728 Adhémar requested the king's assistance for five years with a tile factory he had begun one league above Quebec on the north shore. The following year free passage was granted to two workers, but before the project became established Adhémar abandoned it to serve at Fort Chambly. Some of his material was used by Nicolas-Marie RENAUD d'Avène Des Méloizes in his own tile factory.

Adhémar's years as commandant at Chambly, although lucrative, were not entirely happy. His wife died leaving him in his late fifties with eight young children. He settled in Quebec, where, in 1742, he was invested with the cross of the order of Saint-Louis. On 6 March 1748, in his 68th year, Adhémar was appointed major of Montreal, and 14 months later king's lieutenant of the same town. In the latter capacity he was interim commandant for Charles LE MOYNE de Longueuil in 1752, but when Longueuil died in 1755 Adhémar was too old to replace him. On 17 March 1756 he retired with a pension of 2,000 *livres*.

The only son who lived beyond youth, Pierre-Gaspard-Antoine, served in the Louisiana colonial regular troops, was a captive of the Cherokees for nine years, and moved to France in 1765. Of Adhémar's seven living daughters, Anne married in 1741 Augustin-Antoine de La Barre, an officer in the colonial regular troops, and the other six devoted their lives to serving others through religious orders, with the Congregation of Notre-Dame, the Ursulines, at the Hôpital Général of Quebec or the Hôtel-Dieu of Montreal.

C. J. RUSS

AJQ, Registre d'état civil, Notre-Dame de Québec, 7 mars 1720. AN, Col., C¹¹A, 43, 63. ANQ, Greffe de J.-É. Dubreuil, 3 mai 1721. C.-J.-E. de Boisgelin, *Esquisses généalogiques sur les familles de Provence* (Draguignan, Aix-en-Provence, 1900). Caron, ''Inventaire de documents,'' APQ *Rapport*, 1941–42, 200. Fauteux, *Les chevaliers de Saint-Louis*, 137. Le Jeune, *Dictionnaire*. P.-G. Roy, *Les officiers d'état-major*, 119–23. Tanguay, *Dictionnaire*. Jules Villain, *La France moderne; grand dictionnaire généalogique, historique et biographique* (4v., Montpellier, France, 1906–13), I, 403–17.

J.-N. Fauteux, *Essai sur l'industrie*, I, 165–67. P.-G. Roy, *La famille Adhémar de Lantagnac* (Lévis, Qué., 1908); *La ville de Québec*, I, 482. Guy Frégault, ''Un cadet de Gascogne: Philippe de Rigaud de Vaudreuil,'' *RHAF*, V (1951–52), 40. P.-G. Roy, ''Les gouverneurs de Montréal,'' *BRH*, XI (1905), 171. Henri Têtu, ''Le chapitre de la cathédrale de Québec et ses délégués en France,'' *BRH*, XVI (1910), 263, 301.

AILLEBOUST, CHARLES-JOSEPH D', officer in the colonial regular troops, king's lieutenant; baptized 5 Dec. 1688 in Montreal, eldest son of Pierre d'Ailleboust* d'Argenteuil and Marie-Louise Denys de La Ronde; d. 13 Oct. 1761 in France.

Charles-Joseph d'Ailleboust began his military career as a cadet in the colonial regular troops in Acadia. During the winter of 1708–9 he accom-

Ailleboust

panied his father and his brother, Hector-Pierre d'Ailleboust de Saint-Vilmé, on the expedition led by Saint-Ovide [MONBETON] against the forts at St John's, Newfoundland. Then he returned to Acadia, where he was commissioned an ensign on 18 July 1710; he was present at the surrender of Port-Royal (Annapolis Royal, N.S.) to Francis Nicholson* in 1710. From Acadia he went to Rochefort, France, then to Quebec, where he arrived on 7 Oct. 1711. He was transferred to Île Royale (Cape Breton Island) in 1714, and he became a lieutenant there on 2 July 1720 and captain on 8 May 1730. During his early years of service on Île Royale he became familiar with garrison routine, both at Port-Toulouse (St Peters) and Louisbourg. In 1730 he received command of one of two companies of soldiers sent out from France.

In 1745 New England troops under the command of William PEPPERRELL laid siege to Louisbourg. At the time of their landing d'Ailleboust was posted with his company to the Island battery, which commanded the entrance to the harbour. On 6 June Samuel WALDO sent some 400 New England militiamen to seize this battery and thus allow the British fleet to enter the port; with about 180 men and 40 guns d'Ailleboust repulsed the assailants and forced them to give up any idea of an attack from that side. On 16 June his company was relieved by that commanded by Michel de GANNES de Falaise, whom d'Ailleboust replaced at the Grave battery, within the fortress itself. Some differences over the command of the militia brought him into conflict with Pierre MORPAIN, the port captain, who was dismissed from his command despite the protests of the gunners and militiamen. On 27 June d'Ailleboust went on board Admiral Peter WARREN's ship to hand over to him the act of surrender. He stayed at Louisbourg as the representative of the financial commissary, François Bigot*, to supervise the departure of the last inhabitants, and sailed on one of the last ships for Rochefort. There he received the cross of the order of Saint-Louis on 14 Sept. 1745.

Having been put in charge of the Île Royale troops, in 1747 he took command of them on board the ships in TAFFANEL de La Jonquière's squadron. The squadron had hardly left the coasts of France when it was forced to surrender on 14 May, after a desperate fight against the ships of Admiral George Anson and Admiral Warren; d'Ailleboust was taken to England as a prisoner, but he returned to France that same year. His stay there, however, was brief; he sailed for Canada the following year.

On 23 July 1749 he returned to Louisbourg – which had been handed back to France in 1748 – as king's lieutenant; on several occasions he acted as commandant in the governor's absence. In 1753 and 1754, after Jean-Louis de Raymond*'s departure and before Augustin de BOSCHENRY de Drucour's arrival, he assumed without difficulty the office of acting governor. Louisbourg had resumed its pattern of growth, which had been cut short abruptly from 1745 to 1749; things had returned to normal, and there remained only the everyday problems of administration.

D'Ailleboust was appointed king's lieutenant for Trois-Rivières on 1 April 1754, but he did not go there until the following year. On 31 March 1756 he accepted the same office in Montreal and stayed there until the capitulation on 8 Sept. 1760. At the end of that year or early in 1761 he returned to France with his family, which was left in mourning by his death on 13 Oct. 1761. His military career had been long and active; his experience and length of service had brought him to the rank of king's lieutenant, but his lack of originality and initiative perhaps explain why he had never become governor of Île Royale, an office which he had sought since 1748.

D'Ailleboust does not seem to have had too many financial worries. His pay as king's lieutenant had brought him an annual income of 1,888 *livres*; the king, who had already accorded him gratuities of 600 *livres* in 1746 and 1,500 in 1747, added an annuity of 800 *livres* from 1750 on and had increased it to 1,000 *livres* around 1756. In addition, he had secondary interests in fishing, in the hiring-out of a ship, and in the supply of building materials for the fortifications at Louisbourg and various articles for the troops. He also owned some properties in Louisbourg.

On 16 Jan. 1729, in Louisbourg, d'Ailleboust had married Marie-Josephte Bertrand, the widow of Gabriel Rousseau de Villejouin, by whom he had three children. She died sometime between 1745 and 1749, and on 23 Jan. 1758, in Trois-Rivières, he married the daughter of Charles ALAVOINE, Françoise-Charlotte, who gave birth to two sons.

H. PAUL THIBAULT

AN, Col., B, 36/6, pp. 48–60; 36/7, p.48; 42/2, pp. 334–41, 386; 54/2, p.524; 82/2, p.558; 84/2, p.354; 86/2, p.373; 91, p.292; 97, p.265; 99, pp.156, 215, 240 (PAC transcripts); C¹¹ᴮ, 2, ff.261–64; 5, ff.206–16; 14, ff.190v, 191; 17, ff.37v–38, 193; 23, ff.169–76; 26, ff.173–83v; 28, ff.48–52, 138–49; 29, ff.217–22; 33, ff.18–21v; 34, ff.3–4v, 9–10, 13–13v, 18–19v, 21–21v, 36–36v, 37–37v, 143–43v, 190–96; C¹¹ᴳ, 12, ff.85–85v, 106v; D²ᶜ, 2, ff.41–41v; 3, ff.19, 69–69v; E, 2 (dossier Ailleboust); F⁵ᴮ, art.56, ff.2/3; Section Outre-Mer, G¹,

406/2, ff.13v; 406/4, ff.22v, 27v, 46, 54v, 58, 70v; 407/1, f.5; 408/1, f.113; 466, pièces 69, 76 (recensements de l'île Royale), 83 (registre des actes de concessions à l'île Royale), [85] (registre pour servir à l'enregistrement des concessions de terrains à l'île Royale); G², 189, ff.270–360; 203, dossier 304, ff.60–60v; 207, dossier 474, ff.12–13, 34v–36; 209, dossier 500, ff.30v–31; G³, 2037 (14 mai 1728); 2038/2 (2 mars, 21 mai 1733); 2039/1 (22 déc. 1734, 17 sept. 1735); 2042 (12 janv. 1754); 2043 (8 nov. 1754); 2047/1 (31 juill. 1749, 20 sept. 1750); 2058 (3 déc. 1726); Dépôt des fortifications des colonies, Am. sept., no.216, ff.5v–6, 14, 14v, 15, 16v, 21–21v, 22, 25. Archives Maritimes, Port de Rochefort, 1E, 143, ff.269–75. Le Jeune, *Dictionnaire*. P.-G. Roy, *Les officiers d'état-major*. Ægidius Fauteux, *La famille d'Ailleboust* (Montréal, 1917).

AILLEBOUST DE PÉRIGNY, PAUL D', seigneur, officer of the colonial regular troops; baptized in Montreal on 31 March 1661, fifth child of Charles-Joseph d'Ailleboust* Des Muceaux and Catherine Legardeur de Repentigny; d. in Montreal on 25 Jan. 1746.

In his early twenties Paul d'Ailleboust de Périgny turned his attention to the west. For several years he invested in fur trade with the Ottawas, and on one occasion advanced money for the fortification of Detroit and Michilimackinac. In 1690, sent by Governor Frontenac [Buade*], he patrolled for Iroquois near Fort Frontenac (Kingston, Ont.) in the hope of extracting from them information about future Iroquois plans and the whereabouts of a captive, the Chevalier d'Au. At the age of 30 Périgny was commissioned half-pay lieutenant, and the following year, 1692, when his brother, Pierre d'Ailleboust* d'Argenteuil, was active in the west, he served in Acadia under Joseph Robinau* de Villebon. He had not been in Acadia more than a few months when he was accused of trading furs with an Englishman, probably John Alden*, for merchandise from Boston, but the charges were never substantiated. On 16 April 1693, Frontenac and Champigny [Bochart*] granted to Périgny the island of Grand Menane (Grand Manan) in Acadia, to hold as a seigneury.

On 11 Dec. 1698, two years after he was commissioned lieutenant, Périgny married in Montreal Madeleine-Louise, daughter of Séraphin Margane de Lavaltrie. Périgny and his wife probably lived on his land in Montreal (near the Place d'Armes) from 1699 until 1704, when he was appointed commandant of Chambly. In 1709 he voluntarily retired from this post, and with the help of a recommendation from the Marquise de Vaudreuil [Joybert*] was appointed captain in 1713. Périgny was awarded the cross of Saint-Louis in 1734. When he died 12 years later at the

age of 85 he was "first captain" (the captain with the longest service).

His wife died some time after retiring to the Sisters of Charity of the Hôpital Général of Montreal in 1761. The Pérignys seem to have had only three children; two died early and Thérèse married Pierre Hertel* de Moncours, a soldier, son of Joseph-François Hertel* de La Fresnière and Marguerite de Thavenet*.

C. J. Russ

AN, Col., C¹¹ᴬ, 10, ff.238–41; 11, f.29; 12, f.91v; 33, f.290; D²ᶜ, 57, ff.20, 60, 99v; 222/1, p.6 (PAC transcript). ANQ-M, Greffe d'Antoine Adhémar, 15 mai, 3 août 1688, 1ᵉʳ oct. 1689, 29 mars 1699; Greffe d'Hilaire Bourgine, 7 août 1685; Greffe de Claude Maugue, 7 avril 1683. *Coll. de manuscrits relatifs à la N.-F.*, I, 619. "Estat des employs vaquans ausquels Monsieur le comte de Frontenac … a pourvue en l'année 1691 en attendant les commissions de sa majesté," *BRH*, XIII (1907), 341. Fauteux, *Les chevaliers de Saint-Louis*, 129. P.-G. Roy, *Inv. concessions*, IV, 75. Tanguay, *Dictionnaire*. Ægidius Fauteux, *La famille d'Ailleboust* (Montréal, 1917), 116–20. P.-G. Roy, "Ce que le gouverneur de Callières pensait de nos officiers militaires en 1701," *BRH*, XXVI (1920), 329; "La famille Margane de Lavaltrie," *BRH*, XXIII (1917), 42.

ALAVOINE, CHARLES, surgeon; b. *c.* 1695 in France, son of Charles Alavoine, a merchant, and Marie-Thérèse Macard; d. 8 July 1764 at Trois-Rivières.

Charles Alavoine was less than five years of age when his father settled in Montreal sometime before 1699. Charles learned the rudiments of surgery there and subsequently seems to have had some difficulty in finding a permanent residence. On 27 April 1722 he married Marie-Anne Lefebvre, *dit* Laciseraye, who was to bear him 19 children; in May of that year he set himself up in Champlain, near Trois-Rivières, and stayed there for more than a year, since his first child was baptized in that parish on 24 May 1723. In August of the same year he bought a lot at Prairie-de-la-Madeleine (Laprairie). His second child was baptized at Montreal on 12 Aug. 1724, and on 4 Nov. 1725 his third son was baptized at Trois-Rivières. He finally settled there.

He was appointed surgeon to the Hôtel-Dieu and surgeon-major for the garrison; he received his official commission on 8 Oct. 1727, and his annual salary was 75 *livres*. In 1739 the governor, Charles de Beauharnois, and the intendant, Gilles Hocquart*, asked the minister of Marine to raise his salary to 300 *livres*, but he was awarded only 200 *livres*. He had therefore to count also upon fees paid by the sick who visited his office. But collection of accounts was not an easy matter

7

Aldridge

- on at least two occasions Alavoine had to appeal to the judicial authorities to obtain what was owing him [see Guillaume Baudry*, dit Des Butes]. The surgeon was himself, however, a bad debtor. Beginning in 1730 he experienced some particularly painful financial difficulties. Unbeknown to his wife he had contracted numerous debts, which he could not pay back. His house was even seized, and in 1743 his wife, who had left him to his fate several years before, harassed him in her turn. Then it was his own father who took legal action against him for a sum of 1,100 livres, owed since 1729.

Alavoine was apparently the only surgeon at Trois-Rivières until 1748, when François-Joseph Rembaud set up practice there. Alavoine enjoyed the confidence of the nuns of the hospital and the esteem of the general public. In 1754 he asked that his family be granted the use, free of charge, of a pew at church. For 20 years he had sung in the parish choir without any reward other than the rent for his pew. He was not able to obtain the favour requested, except that his children would pay a rent of 4 livres only and their pew would not be subject to being "auctioned off." In 1758 the minister of Marine informed the governor, Pierre de Rigaud* de Vaudreuil, and the intendant, François Bigot*, that Alavoine had obtained a warrant as king's surgeon, but it seems that because of the war he never received it. In 1759 came one of his finest achievements. Called to the home of Marguerite Chastelain and Marie-Josephte Boucher de Niverville, mother and daughter, whom their servant MARIE had tried to murder, Alavoine dressed the two women's wounds and succeeded, by chafing and bleeding, in reviving the servant, who had tried to hang herself. By an irony of fate the wretched woman was subsequently condemned to be hanged.

After the surrender of Canada Alavoine thought of returning to France. But the numerous entreaties of the nuns of the hospital and the habitants of Trois-Rivières, the possibility that his fellow citizens would be left without a French surgeon, and the hope that the colony would again come under Louis XV's authority and that he might receive his salary, persuaded him to remain in New France. So he said in a letter to the minister of Marine dated 3 Sept. 1761. Unfortunately New France remained under English sovereignty, and Alavoine never received the salary he had hoped for. He died on 8 July 1764 and was buried the following day at Trois-Rivières. According to the inventory made after his death his possessions were valued at 310 livres 5 sols.

RAYMOND DOUVILLE

AJTR, Greffe de J.-B. Badeau, 28 nov. 1771. Jug. et délib., IV, 307, 605, 612, 1068. É.-Z. Massicotte, "Chirurgiens, médecins et apothicaires sous le régime français," BRH, XXXVIII (1932), 516. P.-G. Roy, Inv. coll. pièces, jud. et not., I, 122; Inv. ord. int., II, 22; III, 128. Jouve, Les Franciscains et le Canada: aux Trois-Rivières, 145–48. Les Ursulines de Trois-Rivières depuis leur établissement jusqu'à nos jours (4v., Trois-Rivières, Qué., 1888–1911), I, 185, 229. C.-M. Boissonnault, "L'évolution de la santé publique; protection de la santé en Nouvelle-France," Revue de pharmacie pratique et professionnelle (Montréal), I (1950), no.6, 7–8. Raymond Douville, "Chirurgiens, barbiers-chirurgiens et charlatans de la région trifluvienne sous le régime français," Cahiers des Dix, XV (1950), 81–128. Gérard Malchelosse, "Un procès criminel aux Trois-Rivières en 1759," Cahiers des Dix, XVIII (1953), 207–26.

ALDRIDGE, CHRISTOPHER, Sr, military officer, member of the Nova Scotia Council; b.c. 1690; d. 15 March 1745/46 in Boston.

Christopher Aldridge Sr was commissioned a lieutenant in the British army in April 1706. He probably participated in the attack on Port-Royal (Annapolis Royal, N.S.) in 1710 [see Francis Nicholson*] and shortly became a captain in the independent company of foot stationed there. In October 1712 he was ordered to survey the "Works at Fort Annapolis Royal done by Major [John Livingston*]." Pay and provisions at this neglected outpost were inadequate, and by October 1715 he had personally spent over £700 "for necessaries" for his non-commissioned officers and men. He feared that the Acadians would desert Nova Scotia for Île Royale (Cape Breton Island), and wrote in May 1715 that they had reportedly built 40 or 50 sloops for that purpose and that "several of them slips away dayly." In 1717 the independent companies serving at Annapolis Royal and Placentia, Newfoundland, were formed into Philipps' Regiment of Foot (the 40th); Aldridge was a captain in the new unit. He remained at Annapolis Royal and in May 1727 was appointed to the Nova Scotia Council by Lieutenant Governor Lawrence Armstrong*. He was active on this body only until November 1727.

By 1732 Aldridge had assumed command of the company posted at Canso. That fall Edward How and other justices of the peace at Canso complained that Aldridge had licensed a "great number of taverns" and had misused his authority by taking "upon himself the entire management of civil as well as military affairs at Canso." Aldridge might have taken this action to protect his men from the civil authorities, who were upset at violence resulting from the seizure of firewood by the troops. Armstrong warned Aldridge that a military form of government would frighten prospective settlers but also urged the justices to respect Aldridge "both as a commandant and member of the Council." The aggressive conduct of Aldridge continued, however. In reply to a question from the Board of Trade in 1734 concerning officers trading out of Canso, his uncooperative response was that "he did not know that any Captn. of a ship of warr had any business with the officers there." To Aldridge's credit he was uneasy about the "defenceless Condition" of Canso and warned the council of the French menace to its fishery. In the summer of 1735 Armstrong visited Canso and was disturbed at what he saw: "I found that place in great confusion, and received and heard the complaints of the inhabitants and fishermen against Capt. Aldridge. . . ." Aldridge was removed from his command and given an eight-month leave of absence.

Aldridge retreated to England and appears to have spent most of the next eight years there. In November 1736 the London agent of Philipps' regiment, King Gould, reported: "Capt. Aldridge has been at Deaths Door this fall" and although now recovered had no "Intention of returning to Canso." In these years he won the support of both his regimental commander, Richard PHILIPPS, and the regimental agent, Gould, which was a useful counterweight to the humiliation suffered at the hands of Armstrong. Aldridge arranged that his son, CHRISTOPHER Jr, handle Gould's trade goods at Canso, which naturally endeared him to the regimental agent. In April 1742, while giving Aldridge his orders, Philipps promised that "I shall not be unmindfull of you when any thing offers." Aldridge was returned to "Duty at Canso" where "you will of Course have the Command of that Garrison." Apparently completely vindicated, Aldridge was slow, nevertheless, in taking up his post. He reached Boston only in the late fall of 1743 and postponed his return to Canso until the following spring. In the interval, as promised, Gould and Philipps had not neglected his interests, and in March 1743/44 Aldridge learned of his promotion to the rank of major.

Aldridge had probably passed the 1743/44 winter at Annapolis Royal for Paul MASCARENE, in command there, commented on his deteriorating health. Aldridge had suffered "a fitt of the palsie" and Mascarene gave him "leave to go to Boston." Unable to return to Canso, Aldridge was not present when the post fell to the French in May 1744. However, his wife and family were among the prisoners taken there when Captain Patrick HERON capitulated. In May 1745 the French threatened Annapolis Royal and Governor William Shirley of Massachusetts decided to send the former Canso garrison, now at Castle William (Boston), to its defence. He and Heron disagreed about whether the period of the garrison's commitment not to bear arms was over, and Shirley asked Aldridge, the senior officer on the spot, to order the troops to Annapolis. With some hesitation Aldridge did so and the troops sailed. The threat to Annapolis, however, had disappeared in the meantime.

At the time of this incident Shirley described Aldridge as "in a very weak Condition here," and his sickness culminated in death on 15 March 1745/46. Aldridge had at least one son, Christopher Jr, and at least three daughters.

WILLIAM G. GODFREY

National Library of Wales (Aberystwyth), Tredegar Park collection, 128/1730; MSS/262, pp.13, 14, 15; MSS/284, pp.53, 81, 186, 252; MSS/285, p.84; MSS/287, pp.97, 219. PAC, MG 11, Nova Scotia A, 6, pp.22–23; 21, p.63; 26, p.101. PANS, RG 1, 8, pp.112–14; 9, p.53; 12, no.38; 13, no.7. PRO, Adm. 1/3817; CO 217/4, ff.362, 363, 364, 372. *Correspondence of William Shirley* (Lincoln), I. *Documents relating to currency in Nova Scotia, 1675–1758* (Shortt), 63, 64, 70, 71, 78, 79, 93, 103–9, 147, 304. *N.S. Archives, II*; *III*. PRO, *CSP, Col., 1714–15*, 180; *1720–21*, 158, 159, 349; *1734–35*, 101, 397; *1735–36*, 64, 65. *English army lists* (Dalton), IV. Dalton, *George the first's army*, I.

ALDRIDGE, CHRISTOPHER, Jr, military officer; son of Christopher ALDRIDGE Sr; d. 1760 in England.

Christopher Aldridge Jr followed his father in a military career in the 40th regiment, serving in Nova Scotia and Newfoundland. In July 1734 as "Eldest Ensign" stationed in Nova Scotia, he was promoted lieutenant. A friend of the Pelhams had evidently been interested in the opening, and King Gould, the regimental agent in London, commented to the elder Aldridge: "Lucky was it for us that the Duke of Newcastle [Pelham-Holles] was out of Town!" After his father's departure from Canso in 1735, Christopher Jr continued to serve there. In March 1737/38 he was entrusted with the handling of King Gould's Canso trade goods, for which he was allowed "to Charge Commission for yr. trouble." In May 1744 he was among the English officers captured at Canso and taken to Louisbourg, Île Royale (Cape Breton Island). After his exchange, he reported, along with other officers, to Governor William Shirley* of Massachusetts the state of Louisbourg's garrison and fortifications. Shirley claimed Aldridge's information was a cause for his setting "on foot the late Expedition against the French settlement there." Armed with a letter of introduction from Shirley to Christopher Kilby, the London agent of the Massachusetts government, as well as a promise that Shirley would write the Duke of Newcastle on his behalf, Aldridge set out for England in 1745. Rewards were not long in coming: he received a captaincy in the 40th regiment in January 1745/46 and took command of his father's company upon Christopher Sr's death in March.

In the spring of 1746 he left England, depositing some regimental recruits at St John's, Newfoundland, and proceeding to Boston and then on to Annapolis Royal with clothing for the troops stationed there. The following year he served as intermediary in the abortive attempt made by his brother-in-law, John Bradstreet*, to purchase Sir William PEPPERRELL's military commission and regiment (the 51st). Shortly thereafter he began the Newfoundland service which was to consume the remaining years of his life. By 1749 Aldridge was serving with his company at St John's where he encountered the same problem as his father had at Canso – conflict between civil and military authorities. In 1753, for example, a private in Aldridge's company was arrested on the orders of Justice William KEEN for stealing three potatoes, held in jail for 20 days, and, though no one appeared against him, given 21 lashes. Aldridge then complained to Otho HAMILTON, lieutenant governor of Placentia, about Keen, "who Commits Soldiers when he thinks proper." Hamilton himself had often advocated controls over the civil authorities, particularly Newfoundland's justices of the peace.

A report to the Board of Trade in 1757 tells something about St John's during this period. The fortifications were in bad repair, with one of the batteries at the harbour entrance "being hardly able to support the Guns mounted, and totally exposed." Near Fort William were a number of huts, some erected by soldiers of the garrison who, considering them "their propertys," had signed several over "to the Merchants and Agents for Debts Contracted." A 1750 report says that St John's had "twelve Taverns or Publick Houses" – perhaps a cause of indebtedness.

In March 1758 Aldridge was promoted major. He requested leave that September to return to England to recover from sickness and was granted permission the following spring. He apparently did go back to England; General Jeffery Amherst* received word of his death in a letter sent from England in December 1760.

His will, proved in November 1760, named as his beneficiaries his wife Martha and son Christopher, a lieutenant in the 40th regiment.

WILLIAM G. GODFREY

Mass. Hist. Soc., Belknap papers, 61.A.130. National Library of Wales (Aberystwyth), Tredegar Park collection, MSS/262, p.14; MSS/284, pp.67, 79, 252; MSS/287. PAC, MG 11, Nova Scotia A, 26, p.101; MG 18, L4, pkt.6, p.43; pkt.9, p.118; N30; RG 22, B3, no.2 (William Shirley to Christopher Kilby, 20 Aug. 1745) (mfm B-3311). PRO, CO 194/12, ff.125, 126, 186; 194/13, ff.146, 219, 220, 221; WO 1/1, ff.272, 371. *Army list, 1757.* Usher Parsons, *The life of Sir William Pepperrell, bart. . . .* (1st ed., Boston, 1855; 2nd ed., Boston, London, 1856). Smythies, *Historical records of 40th regiment.*

ALLENOU DE LAVILLANGEVIN, RENÉ-JEAN, canon, vicar general, theologal, and official; b. 1685 or 1686 at Pordic (dept. of Côtes-du-Nord), France, in a small manor house called La Ville-Angevin; d. 16 Nov. 1753 in Quebec.

René-Jean Allenou de Lavillangevin, who, according to Bishop Pontbriand [DUBREIL], was a "man of good family," was ordained a priest in 1711. He had no degree in theology, even though he had studied it for four years with the Jesuits at the Collège Louis-le-Grand. He was doubtless a good preacher, since he was accorded the broadest powers to preach and hear confessions in the dioceses of Brittany. Later he became parish priest at Plérin, in the diocese of Saint-Brieuc, and took an interest in the community of the Filles du Saint-Esprit, founded by his uncle Jean Leuduger. He drew up definitive rules for the community and gave it such good care that in 1768 its annals would speak of Allenou de Lavillangevin as its "founding saint." When he decided in 1741 to go to "the distant missions" in Canada, thus giving up "a considerable living," the former parish priest of Plérin, as he liked to call himself, had 30 years of fruitful ministry in France to his credit.

On 29 Aug. 1741 the missionary arrived in Quebec with Bishop Pontbriand, who had asked him to accompany him. Bonds of friendship linked the former parish priest of Plérin, who was in his fifties, and the young bishop, in his thirties, and the bishop reserved some important tasks for his old friend. Indeed, two days after their arrival Allenou de Lavillangevin was made a canon of the cathedral of Quebec, then the bishop's vicar general and official of the diocese. The new canon let the bishop dispose of his Canadian benefices and lived on what he had brought from France, without entering into any "mad expenses"; until 1750 he resided in the episcopal palace with the bishop and had his entire confidence. Upon becoming theologal of the chapter in 1747 after the death of François-Elzéar VALLIER, who had been ecclesiastical councillor on the Conseil Supérieur and superior of the seminary, Allenou de Lavillangevin intended to take his role seriously; he wished to assume all the functions the law recognized for the theologal, especially the responsibility for teaching theology and Holy Scripture to the clergy and for preaching in the cathedral church. The new theologal's demands surprised many ecclesiastics. In Quebec the dignity of theologal had always been simply a title, for since Bishop Laval*'s episcopate the incumbent of the parish of Quebec had been chosen from among the directors of the seminary, who were also members of the chapter. According to custom, since the cathedral served as the parish church, the parish priest of Quebec acted as the regular preacher for the cathedral. In insisting on the theologal's right to be preacher, Allenou posed a problem for Pontbriand, who could not categorically refuse him. But, if he gave in to his demands the bishop would offend the seminary and the Jesuits, who had always been responsible for teaching theology, and also the new parish priest of Quebec, Jean-Félix RÉCHER. As was his habit in difficult circumstances, Pontbriand decided on a compromise, letting the theologal preach only on the 13 great feast days throughout the year and empowering him to give three theological lectures a week. The theologal could oblige the canons to attend them, but Pontbriand reserved the right to rule on the attendance of the ecclesiastics of the town and the seminarists. The theologal was compelled to hire at his own expense a hall big enough for his audience and to admit those who came to hear him free of charge. A.-H. Gosselin* claims it was Pontbriand's compromise that brought about the break or at least the beginning of the difficulties between the theologal and the bishop; the evidence, however, is that the two men remained on terms of confidence. Not until 1750, at the time of a dispute between the chapter and the seminary over the parish of Quebec [see Récher; Charles-Antoine GODEFROY de Tonnancour], did the two old friends have a difference of opinion and, at least as far as the bishop was concerned, come to a quarrel which was to mean the disgrace of the former parish priest of Plérin.

With the approval of the chapter, which was anxious to know its rights and duties concerning the parish of Quebec, the bishop gave Allenou de Lavillangevin the task of "putting into order and examining" the chapter's papers. Among other documents Clement X's bull of 1674 was discovered, which in addition to setting up the diocese of Quebec converted the parish church into the cathedral and gave the chapter the widest powers over its temporal affairs as well as the task of ministering to it. This discovery would lead the chapter, with Lavillangevin at its head, into a never-ending struggle with the seminary to assume its rights over temporal matters and the ministry of the cathedral church of Quebec. In the period from 12 January to 27 Feb. 1750 the chapter held five meetings under Lavillangevin's chairmanship. The latter decided to appeal to the Conseil Supérieur in order to assert the chapter's rights, despite a compromise suggested by the bishop, who would have liked to avoid so much fuss. Pontbriand suggested to the seminary's directors and the canons that they should either come to an understanding among themselves or rely on an arbitrator. But the dispute had a hearing and the canons lost their lawsuit as far as the conferring of the parish charge was concerned; on 16 Oct. 1750 they were sentenced to a fine and costs. The question of the ownership of the cathedral was then taken to France.

In the meantime Pontbriand had tried to make the theologal of the chapter, who lived in his palace, listen to reason, but the former parish priest of Plérin put the rights of the chapter ahead of the bishop's friendship, or to be more exact, he would not give up either. The bishop expelled him from the palace, as he considered the theologal the ringleader of the chapter in the continuing struggle. Allenou de Lavillangevin thus lost the bishop's friendship; despite the latter's opposition he found refuge with the Jesuits. He continued to go every day to the canons' office and to the meetings of the chapter on the appointed days. He upheld the chapter's interests vigorously and kept the esteem of the other canons. While protesting his friendship and submission towards the bishop, he declared that he had only done his duty: "I do not think that I have done anything against either my obligation or the respect that I owe your Grace, whom I still love and honour infinitely." In 1752 he thought of returning to France, but he was retained by illness in Canada where he died on 16 Nov. 1753. Pontbriand consented to give him the last rites and to attend his funeral, held on 17 November.

The canons of Quebec paid Lavillangevin the finest tribute: "We considered him rightly as our father," they said, "and we miss him as such." If it had not been for conflict between the chapter and the seminary, which was settled necessarily with the conquest, Pontbriand would himself have given witness to his merit. In any event, the historian can only recognize his honesty and sin-

Alquier

cerity, and the passage of time allows us to maintain that the quarrel in which the former parish priest of Plérin was engaged derived not so much from the people concerned as from the particular law governing the church of Canada at that time and the changes which had taken place since the institution of that law.

JEAN-GUY LAVALLÉE

AAQ, 10 B, Registre de délibérations. "Lettres et mémoires de l'abbé de L'Isle-Dieu," APQ *Rapport, 1935–36; 1936–37.*
[To our knowledge, there is no study specifically on René-Jean Allenou de Lavillangevin. Interesting material on him is found, however, in the following works: Paul-Marie Du Breil de Pontbriand, *Le dernier évêque du Canada français, Monseigneur de Pontbriand, 1740–1760* (Paris, 1910). Gosselin, *L'Église du Canada jusqu'à la conquête,* III. Henri Têtu, *Notices biographiques: les évêques de Québec* (Québec, 1889); "Le chapitre de la cathédrale de Québec et ses délégués en France," *BRH,* XIV (1908), 134, 200, 202, 259, 263; XV (1909), 68, 75–76; XVI (1910), 138; "M. Jean-Félix Récher, curé de Québec, et son journal, 1757–1760," *BRH,* IX (1903), 101; "Souvenirs d'un voyage en Bretagne," *BRH,* XVII (1911), 133, 138.   J.-G.L.]

ALQUIER (Dalquier) DE SERVIAN, JEAN D', officer in the French regular troops; fl. 1710–61.

Jean d'Alquier de Servian sailed from Brest for New France in April 1755 when he was more than 60 years of age. This officer already had behind him a career of many years in the army: he had been commissioned lieutenant in 1710, captain in 1734, and captain of grenadiers (an élite company in a battalion) in 1748. He bore the latter title upon his arrival in Canada, as a member of the second battalion of Béarn. He was in addition a knight of the order of Saint-Louis.

D'Alquier took part in several combats with his battalion. The Marquis de MONTCALM, who held him in high esteem, considered his ardour quite praiseworthy, although sometimes out of place in a man of his age. According to Lévis*, d'Alquier was one of the oldest soldiers in Canada at that period. On 4 Nov. 1757 he was promoted lieutenant-colonel and received command of the second battalion of Béarn. D'Alquier distinguished himself particularly in the battle on 13 Sept. 1759, in which he was wounded. On that same day he attended the council of war presided over by the governor general, Pierre de Rigaud* de Vaudreuil, which decided upon the strategy of withdrawal by the French army. D'Alquier renewed his exploits at the battle of Sainte-Foy on 28 April 1760. Succeeding BOURLAMAQUE he took command of the left flank and during the battle countermanded an order to retreat from Lévis. He succeeded in holding on to the Dumont mill, a strategic point on the Sainte-Foy road. After several hours of combat against Major John Dalling's soldiers, and after the opposing forces had in turn occupied the mill, d'Alquier's last counter-attack finally dislodged the Highlanders at bayonet point. D'Alquier was wounded once more and was taken to the Hôpital Général, outside the walls of Quebec. On 16 May Lévis raised the siege of the town, which had begun on 28 April, and d'Alquier remained at the Hôpital Général, where he was taken prisoner by the British, who took over the building. He regained his freedom after the capitulation of Montreal was signed on 8 Sept. 1760 and sailed for France on 20 October.

The king recognized the merits of this officer and on 10 Feb. 1761 granted him a supplementary pension of 400 *livres* to be paid from the royal treasury. D'Alquier had already obtained in 1757 a pension of 400 *livres* paid from the order of Saint-Louis, and on 12 Feb. 1760 he had received a gratuity of 600 *livres*. The date of his death is not known.

MICHEL PAQUIN

Knox, *Historical journal* (Doughty), III, 303. P.-B. Casgrain, "Le moulin de Dumont," *BRH,* XI (1905), 67. L.-P. Desrosiers, "Officiers de Montcalm," *RHAF,* III (1949–50), 367–70 (the author gives an excellent picture of this soldier's career). P.-G. Roy, "Le conseil de guerre du 13 septembre 1759," *BRH,* XXIX (1923), 116.

AMIOT, JEAN-BAPTISTE, blacksmith; m. Marie-Anne, a Sauk Indian, at Michilimackinac about 1720; d. after 1763 at La Baye (Green Bay, Wis.).

Sometime before 1724 Jean-Baptiste Amiot came to Michilimackinac, where he was employed as a blacksmith by the Jesuit priest. About 1737 he had a serious disagreement with the priest then in charge, probably Pierre Du Jaunay*, who consequently fired him, took all his tools, and hired another blacksmith. A broken gun could mean disaster in the west, and Pierre-Joseph CÉLORON de Blainville, the commandant, realizing that two smiths were needed for the rapidly growing community and the neighbouring Ottawas and Ojibwas, advanced Amiot the funds to continue working. The priest, citing the monopoly of blacksmithing granted to the mission by the king, insisted that Amiot pay him half his profits. Thus Amiot worked under the watchful eye of the priest in a shop adjoining the rectory.

Although he was training his oldest son Augustin in his craft, Amiot was barely able to eke out an existence on the profits he was allowed to keep. By 1742, with a family of eight children, he was reduced to begging at the lodges of the local Ottawas, and he was seriously considering moving to the Illinois country. The Ottawas complained of Amiot's plight to the governor, Charles de BEAUHARNOIS, and as a result of their intercession Amiot was permitted to retain all his profits.

Amiot did a considerable amount of work at the fort during the late 1740s, fixing guns, making axes, tomahawks, and picks, and doing other iron work. Apparently he practised his trade at Michilimackinac during the busy summer trading season and occasionally spent the winter with hunting Indian bands.

In 1758 his wife was buried in the cemetery at Michilimackinac. He continued working with the help of a slave or two and was residing at Michilimackinac when the English assumed control in 1761. Inspired by PONTIAC, the local Ojibwas attacked the fort and massacred most of the garrison on 2 June 1763. The commandant, George Etherington, who was ransomed by the Ottawas, rewarded them by having Amiot repair their guns [see GORRELL].

Amiot apparently moved to La Baye sometime after 1763. There he quarrelled with an Indian named Ishquaketa, who had left an axe to be repaired. When Amiot seized the Indian with a pair of hot tongs, the Indian knocked him senseless with the axe. While Amiot was recovering, another Indian paid him a visit and stabbed him to death as he lay in bed. The exact date of Amiot's death is unknown for the interment records of La Baye have not survived.

During his lifetime Amiot's skills as a blacksmith had contributed substantially to the local economy and the necessary maintenance of relations with the Indians.

DAVID A. ARMOUR

[Amiot's parentage is obscure. Information in Tanguay, *Dictionnaire*, is contradictory, and Godbout, "Nos ancêtres," APQ *Rapport, 1951–53*, and the *Dictionnaire national des Canadiens français (1608–1760)* (3v., Montréal, 1965), I, perpetuate the confusion. D.A.A.]

AN, Col., C¹¹A, 72, ff.125, 213; 117, ff.321–23, 329, 425, 448–49; 118, f.117; 119, ff.178, 278. Clements Library, Thomas Gage papers, Supplementary accounts, A state of houses and lands at Michilimackinac. Newberry Library (Chicago), MSS collection, George Etherington to Charles Langlade, 21 June 1763. *French regime in Wis., 1727–48* (Thwaites), 372–73, 375–76, 410, 423–24. Augustin Grignon, "Seventy-two years' recollections of Wisconsin," Wis. State Hist. Soc. *Coll.*, III (1857), 202–3. "Mackinac register of baptisms and interments – 1695–1821," ed. R. G. Thwaites, Wis.

State Hist. Soc. *Coll.*, XIX (1910), 2–6, 17, 22, 26, 31, 36, 40, 47–49, 64, 66, 153, 155. "The Mackinac register of marriages – 1725–1821," ed. R. G. Thwaites, Wis. State Hist. Soc. *Coll.*, XVIII (1908), 482–83. L. M. Stone, "Archaeological research at Fort Michilimackinac, an eighteenth century historic site in Emmet County, Michigan: 1959–1966 excavations" (unpublished PHD thesis, 2v., Michigan State University, East Lansing, Mich., 1970).

AMIOT (Amyot), JEAN-BAPTISTE (baptized **Jean**), merchant; b. 25 Nov. 1717 in Quebec, son of Pierre Amiot and Marie-Anne Cadet; d. 5 June 1769 in Quebec.

When he was 30 Jean-Baptiste Amiot was calling himself a merchant, which suggests that he was already in the import trade. In 1747, with the syndic and the other merchants of Quebec, he signed a report addressed to the minister of Marine, Maurepas, complaining of the excessively long terms for payment of bills of exchange drawn at Quebec on the royal treasury. In November of that year he sailed for France on the frigate *Martre*. After his return to the colony he was a supplier to the state, from which he received more than 90,000 *livres* in bills of exchange in 1751. He also did business with merchants in La Rochelle, France: on 1 Oct. 1751 he acted before the Conseil Supérieur "in the name and as the authorized agent of Jean-Baptiste Sombrun," who was probably a merchant in that city.

In 1759 Amiot was elected a church warden in the parish council of Notre-Dame de Québec. After the conquest he was occupied, with fellow bourgeois of the town, in re-establishing the religious institutions of the colony, which earned him the right to be buried in the chapel of the seminary of Quebec.

Jean-Baptiste Amiot married twice. On 26 Nov. 1749 he married at Quebec Louise Bazin, by whom he had eight children. Then, after her death, he married Catherine Mouet de Mora at Trois-Rivières on 19 March 1763. Amiot died six years later, leaving a considerable estate to his wife and children. It included two houses in the town of Quebec, a piece of land at Lorette, and negotiable instruments of considerable value. His daughter Marie-Anne married Jacques-Nicolas Perrault, the son of another Quebec merchant, Jacques Perrault*. It is difficult to determine exactly Amiot's place among the merchants of Quebec, for this group is not yet well known.

JOSÉ IGARTUA

AJQ, Registre d'état civil, Notre-Dame de Québec, 26 nov. 1717, 26 nov. 1749, 6 juin 1769. AN, Col., C¹¹A,

André

87, ff.286–91; 89, f.7; 116, ff.249, 255v, 257, 258, 290v; 119, ff.355v, 342v, 344–45. ANQ, Greffe de J.-C. Panet, 25 nov. 1749, 6 nov. 1756, 17, 26 juin 1769; AP, Coll. P.-G. Roy, Amyot. ASQ, Paroisse de Québec, 38a, 98. PAC, MG 8, A2, 37, ff.155–56v; 38, ff.51–52v; 40, ff.22–23. *Quebec Gazette*/*La Gazette de Québec*, 29 Sept. 1766, 23, 30 March, 10 Aug. 1769, 20 Feb., 11 June 1772. "Recensement de Québec, 1744" (APQ *Rapport*), 133. P.-G. Roy, *Inv. contrats de mariage*, I, 29; *Inv. jug. et délib., 1717–1760*, V, 164, 200; VI, 43. Tanguay, *Dictionnaire*. P.-G. Roy, *Fils de Québec*, II, 1–3.

ANDRÉ DE LEIGNE, LOUISE-CATHERINE (Hertel de Rouville), b. 1709 at Havre-de-Grâce (Le Havre, France), daughter of Pierre ANDRÉ de Leigne and Claude Fredin; d. 16 Jan. 1766 at Trois-Rivières.

Louise-Catherine André de Leigne was one of those women whose name has remained engraved upon people's memories, not because of warrior exploits against Indians or English, but rather for amorous adventures. She arrived in New France in 1718 and was a member of fashionable Quebec society, where she rapidly attracted attention. Her father held the important office of lieutenant general for civil and criminal affairs of the provost court of Quebec, and it seems the young girl had all the charms necessary for attracting penniless young officers, by whom she was continually courted. She much preferred their company to that of richer suitors whom her father favoured.

In 1734 M. de Leigne decided to deal rigorously with his daughter and forced her to give serious thought to her future. Through Governor BEAUHARNOIS and Intendant Hocquart* he had put her on board a ship sailing for France, where she would – so her father thought – quickly forget her impossible young suitors and acquire the good sense to accept a suitable marriage, one to her father's liking.

During the first night on board the *Renommée*, which was still in the port of Quebec, the lady disguised herself as a man and succeeded in fleeing, aided by two of her suitors. The next day the frivolous creature changed her mind and returned to the ship. Her absence lasted only a year; in 1735 she was back in Quebec, to her father's great despair, and she found refuge in the home of her brother-in-law, councillor Nicolas LANOULLIER de Boisclerc.

The beauteous Louise-Catherine did not bring herself to public notice again until 1741. She was now 32, and she was successful in winning the heart of a young officer, René-Ovide Hertel* de Rouville, 11 years her junior. They were married in Quebec on 20 May 1741, without having

obtained the consent of the groom's widowed mother. On 29 May the latter contested the validity of the marriage before the Conseil Supérieur, and on 12 June the court decided in her favour by declaring the marriage invalid. But four months later, when he had reached his majority, young Hertel was able to marry Louise-Catherine in all tranquillity. The wedding was held in the presence of the two families on 22 October.

The Hertels went to live at Trois-Rivières, and of their marriage five children were born. Because of ill health Mme Hertel was unable, after the capitulation of Montreal in 1760, to follow her husband to France where, almost ruined, he was looking for employment. In 1763 he returned to Trois-Rivières and carried on the small business which Mme Hertel had set up to make a living during the sombre years of her husband's absence. She lived for only three more years.

Louise-Catherine André de Leigne "was one of the prettiest women of her time . . . her manners, her upbringing, her virtues greatly surpassed the other advantages with which Nature had endowed her." It was in these terms that her son, Jean-Baptiste-Melchior Hertel* de Rouville, rendered homage to her in 1813.

MICHEL PAQUIN

AN, Col., C¹¹A, 61, ff.225, 259; 63, f.27. PAC *Report, 1886*, xxxiii. P.-G. Roy, *Inv. contrats de mariage* ; *Inv. jug. et délib., 1717–1760*, IV, 22, 24. Tanguay, *Dictionnaire*. Robert La Roque de Roquebrune, "Une canadienne du XVIIIᵉ siècle: mademoiselle de Leigne," *Nova Francia*, II (1926–27), 57–66.

ANDRÉ DE LEIGNE, PIERRE, king's counsellor; lieutenant general for civil and criminal affairs of the provost court of Quebec; b. 1663 at Tonnerre (dept. of Yonne), France, son of François André, a lawyer in the *parlement,* and Marie Turin; m. in 1694 Claude, daughter of Gabriel Fredin, king's counsellor, notary, and *grènetier* (judicial officer) of the salt warehouse in the town of Pontoise, France, and of Claude Robin; d. 7 March 1748 at Trois-Rivières.

Pierre André de Leigne descended from a family which, if not rich, was at least well-to-do. He himself had "properties and belongings" in his home town of Tonnerre. In 1683 he embarked upon a military career, and ten years later, on 15 April 1693, he obtained from Jacques-Henri de Durfort, Duc de Duras, a "final discharge" after "having done good service as a member of the King's bodyguard." The following year, on 15 Jan. 1694 when his marriage contract was signed, de Leigne had nothing more than the title of "bourgeois of Paris"; he was living there on Rue Saint-Jean-de-Beauvais. Some weeks later he sailed for Quebec to replace Jean Fredin, his wife's brother, as secretary to the intendant, Jean Bochart* de Champigny; his wife joined him in 1696. In 1702 he returned to France with the intendant and two years later bought the office of "provost general of the admiralty court and of the galleys," which he occupied at Le Havre until 1716. If his contemporaries are to be believed, however, he yearned after Canada, whose "tranquillity" delighted him. In April 1717 he obtained the office of lieutenant general for civil and criminal affairs of the provost court of Quebec, succeeding Denis Riverin*, who had never exercised his functions. De Leigne returned to Canada in 1718 and held the office from 1719 till 1744, when he resigned and was replaced by François DAINE. He also carried out for some time the duties of lieutenant general of the admiralty court in place of Jean-Baptiste Couillard* de Lespinay, and on occasion those of subdelegate of the intendant of Quebec.

Pierre André de Leigne ventured upon several undertakings in Canada which brought him, like many others, more worries than fine profits. He is mentioned in notarial contracts as "selling and delivering" wine and lending money. In 1721 he obtained a land grant in Labrador of four leagues by four, and signed an agreement in 1735 to develop it with his son-in-law, Nicolas LANOULLIER de Boisclerc. But "this perfect establishment for seal-fishing" brought him in little. An inventory made in July 1735 shows that the de Leignes were seriously burdened by debt. Movables, silver plate, and ready money – 153 *livres* in card money – were evaluated at 4,307 *livres*, their house at 3,239 *livres*; but 1,956 *livres* remained to be paid on the latter, bought from Nicolas Lanoullier in 1725. The de Leignes had, moreover, liabilities amounting to 6,142 *livres.* The greatest part of this sum consisted of a dowry of 3,000 *livres* promised on 26 Dec. 1720 in their daughter Jeanne's contract of marriage with Lanoullier. None of this had yet been paid in 1735, and with back interest the total was 4,082 *livres* 10 *sols*. To be convinced of the precariousness of their situation one has only to read through the letter of supplication which de Leigne sent the minister of Marine in 1745 with a view to obtaining a gratuity, however small it might be.

The de Leigne family had nevertheless good social connections and frequented the court. In France the elder daughter, Anne-Catherine, had pleased "Madame la Dauphine, who asked her parents for her, and as she was still too young to have a place in the service of this princess, Mme la Maréchale d'Estrée took her in and became attached to her as if she had been her own daughter." But when she returned to New France in 1718, Anne-Catherine, through associating with fashionable society, had acquired priggish manners which greatly displeased the society of Quebec. In 1741 her sister LOUISE-CATHERINE was a subject of conversation for the colony when she married a young man of quality, René-Ovide Hertel* de Rouville, a minor several years her junior. The lieutenant general had to intervene before the tribunal to defend the newly married couple against the excessive pretensions of Mme Hertel de Rouville, who undertook to have the marriage annulled and did indeed succeed.

The Sieur de Leigne's administration of justice seems to have been good and impartial. In 1731 Gilles Hocquart* wrote of him to the minister, Maurepas: "I have only good reports to give you of his application in dispensing justice and in making order respected in the town of Quebec, for which he is responsible." De Leigne had, however, been guilty of one error for which the minister severely blamed him. Intendant Hocquart took up his defence: "one cannot be," he wrote to the minister, "more keenly affected by the reprimand which you have given him on his conduct. . . . I ask you as a favour, *Monseigneur*, to overlook this officer's error, which he has openly admitted." The mistake Hocquart was talking about concerned the final episode in the long quarrel between Intendant Claude-Thomas Dupuy* and Governor Charles de BEAUHARNOIS. De Leigne got along well with Dupuy, and whenever there was a dispute between governor and intendant he invariably took the side of his immediate superior. Thus he had stood up to Beauharnois, in a way the latter considered flippant, over the question of lodgings for military personnel. In addition, when in March 1728 the governor suspended execution of all the ordinances issued by the intendant against Étienne Boullard* and the chapter of the cathedral of Quebec, de Leigne preferred, as did other officials, to follow the intendant, who defied the governor's injunction. When he was sure of being within his rights, he was inflexible, like his friend Dupuy.

Pierre André de Leigne carried out well his duty as lieutenant general for civil and criminal affairs until 1744, when he resigned and retired to live at his daughter Louise-Catherine's home in Trois-Rivières; he died there on 7 March 1748.

JEAN-CLAUDE DUBÉ

AN, Col., C¹¹ᴬ, 50, pp.126ff., 345–46; 55, p.114; E, 174, pp.1, 2–3, 5ff., 32–33 (PAC transcripts); Minutier central, Étude XI, 15 janv. 1694 (contrat de mariage de Pierre André de Leigne), 30 mars 1694 (procuration de Pierre André de Leigne), 24 mars 1695. ANQ, Greffe de Jacques Barbel, 20 déc. 1720; Greffe de J.-É. Dubreuil, 16 juill. 1724; Greffe d'Henry Hiché, 14 nov. 1733, 11, 12 nov. 1734, 13 janv., 28 juill. 1735. *Inv. de pièces du Labrador* (P.-G. Roy), I, 139. P.-G. Roy, *La famille André de Leigne* (Lévis, Qué., 1935).

ANGERS, *dite* **Saint-Simon, MARIE-ANGÉ-LIQUE LEFEBVRE.** *See* LEFEBVRE

ANVILLE, JEAN-BAPTISTE-LOUIS-FRÉDÉ-RIC DE LA ROCHEFOUCAULD DE ROYE, Marquis de ROUCY, Duc d'. *See* LA ROCHE-FOUCAULD

ARNAUD (Darnaud, Darnault), JEAN-CHARLES D', officer in the colonial regular troops; b. *c.* 1706 in France, youngest son of a lieutenant-commander in the navy; d. sometime after 1752 in France.

When at the early age of 16 Jean-Charles d'Arnaud arrived in Canada in 1722 as an ensign, the governor, Vaudreuil [Rigaud*], thought him sensible, spirited, and likely to make a good officer. Events bore out his judgement. Although a resident of Quebec, Arnaud spent many years in various western posts where he served competently and won the confidence of the Indians despite his short stature. After an apprenticeship as second in command at Fort Frontenac (Kingston, Ont.) in 1727 and 1728, he was stationed at Detroit in 1731. At this time the wars of the Fox Indians were jeopardizing the French alliances with the western tribes. The French were apprehensive about any contact between the Foxes and these tribes, and Arnaud persuaded the Hurons, allies of the French, to kill their Fox prisoners rather than keep them as slaves. For this diplomatic coup Arnaud received warm praise from Governor Charles de BEAUHARNOIS, who appointed him in 1732 commander of the post among the Miamis on the Maumee River (probably at or near present-day Fort Wayne, Ind.). It was likely also an important factor in his promotion to lieutenant the following year.

A smallpox epidemic in 1732 decimated the Miamis and their relatives, the Weas (Ouiatanons) and the Piankeshaws, causing most of them to disperse. The few that remained departed in 1733 to settle at Rivière Blanche (possibly the Scioto River, Ohio) nearer the English. The French were alarmed, but by 1734 Arnaud and a fellow officer, Nicolas-Joseph de NOYELLES de Fleurimont, had persuaded the scattered remnants of the Miami tribe to reunite at their old village, thus averting the collapse of an important alliance.

Immediately after, Arnaud led a force of French and Indians to put down an insurrection which had broken out in the Wea village over a dispute with a French trader, but the disturbance subsided before he reached the scene. Fearing the consequences of a general uprising against the French should the Weas receive support from their neighbours, Arnaud called off his detachment. Governor Beauharnois firmly supported his conciliatory behaviour as the only practical policy in view of the threat posed by the Fox and Chickasaw disturbances.

Arnaud's father was an old comrade of Beauharnois in the navy, so it is not surprising that the son enjoyed the governor's protection and praise while serving in Canada. His appointments to western posts were notable favours and Arnaud took full advantage of them by forming a company in 1733 to exploit the Indian trade at the Miami post.

The minister of Marine, Maurepas, allowed Arnaud to make three trips to France, each for two years, in 1733, 1738, and 1742, to look after family affairs in Brittany and Provence. The voyage of 1738 was apparently undertaken to marry the daughter of a M. Cugnet, probably Louise-Charlotte, daughter of François-Étienne CUGNET, but she fell seriously ill and there was no marriage.

Beginning in 1740 Arnaud commanded for two years at Fort Frontenac, his last major service in Canada. He was made captain on 17 May 1741. Illness prevented him from taking an active part in the War of the Austrian Succession, and was the reason for his retirement as captain on half-pay in 1746 with an annual pension of 300 *livres* and the cross of Saint-Louis. In addition to Beauharnois's protection, Arnaud enjoyed the constant influence of the Comtesse de Donge at court. It may explain why he alone won his retirement in 1746 while several officers much older, and at least as incapacitated, failed in their requests. He returned to his family's home in Quimper, France, where he drew his pension regularly for several years. Mme Bégon [ROCBERT] found him good company when passing through on her return to France in 1749. He was still alive in January 1752. Thereafter his name disappears from the records.

Jean-Charles d'Arnaud was an able military officer, without great ambition, who appears to have lived comfortably. On first departing for Canada he needed an advance on his salary; thenceforth he neither asked for gratuities from the king nor complained of any financial misery. Unlike many Canadian officers he seems not to have indulged immoderately in speculative commercial ventures, or spent lavishly beyond his means. He was a stranger to the courts and avoided the unhappy lot of many fellow officers who were hounded to their graves by irate creditors.

S. DALE STANDEN

AN, Col., B, 45, ff.85v–86; 55, f.500v; 64, ff.442, 434–35; 65, f.410; 69, f.79; 72, ff.396–96v; 83, f.263v; C¹¹A, 52, p.169 (PAC transcript); 57, ff.340, 348–50; 59, ff.18–19v, 37–38v; 61, ff.91–92, 299v–300; 64, ff.138–38v; 65, ff.49v–51v; 68, ff.153–55; 69, ff.136–36v; 70, ff.138–40; 74, ff.124–27; 75, ff.189–92; 77, f.296v; 83, ff.1, 124–28; 84, ff.218–21; 120/2, p.120 (PAC transcript); D²C, 18; 47/2, pt.3, p.150; 47/2, pt.4, pp.366, 398; 48/1, pp.3, 47; 222/1, p.14 (PAC transcripts); E, 8; Marine, C¹, 161/1, f.20. ANQ, Greffe de Nicolas Boisseau, 29 avril 1740, 21 août 1742. BN, MSS, Clairambault, 866, ff.343–444.

"Correspondance de Mme Bégon" (Bonnault), APQ *Rapport, 1934–35*, 79. *NYCD* (O'Callaghan and Fernow), IX, 1097. "Recensement de Québec, 1744" (APQ *Rapport*), 133. Fauteux, *Les chevaliers de Saint-Louis*, 142–43. Massicotte, "Répertoire des engagements pour l'Ouest," APQ *Rapport, 1929–30*, 296–97, 299–300. A. Roy, *Inv. greffes not.*, XV, 110. Tanguay, *Dictionnaire*. P.-G. Roy, "La famille du légiste François-Joseph Cugnet au Canada," *BRH*, XXI (1915), 236. "Le Sieur Darnaud," *BRH*, XXXIX (1933), 482. Henri Têtu, "Le chapitre de la cathédrale de Québec et ses délégués en France," *BRH*, XVI (1910), 263–64.

ARNAUD, MARIE-MARGUERITE-DANIEL, *dite* **Saint-Arsène** (incorrectly called Saint-Arnaud, the name of another family), nun of the Congregation of Notre-Dame; b. 15 Jan. 1699 in Montreal, daughter of Jean Arnaud, originally from Bordeaux, France, and Marie Truteau; d. 5 July 1764 in La Rochelle, France.

After having been a student in the Congregation of Notre-Dame in Montreal, Marie-Marguerite-Daniel Arnaud entered the noviciate on 31 Oct. 1717 and made her profession two years later under the name of Sister Saint-Arsène. She took part in the activities of her community in Montreal until 1733, when she was chosen to accompany Sister Saint-Joseph [Marguerite TROTTIER] to Louisbourg, Île Royale (Cape Breton Island). The idea was to give a fresh start to the distant mission on Île

Royale, which after five years of existence was proving to be a failure, attributed to the poor administration of the founder, Sister de la Conception [Marguerite ROY]. At Louisbourg Sister Saint-Arsène shared with her companions a life of hard work and continual deprivation. After Sister Saint-Joseph's departure in the autumn of 1744, she became superior of the mission.

The fall of Louisbourg in 1745 marked the beginning of a second period in the religious life of Sister Saint-Arsène and her three companions. "After losing their little house there and all their belongings," as Sister Saint-Arsène stated to the minister of Marine, Maurepas, on 18 March 1746, the nuns were deported with their boarders to the Rochefort coast. From there they went to live at the Hôpital Saint-Étienne in La Rochelle. Because the hospital was very poor, the nuns undertook to pay their own board and that of their students and to provide for all their needs. They were counting on their annual gratuity of 1,500 *livres* from the king [see Marguerite Roy]. But from 1743 to November 1748 they received only 1,040 of an expected 7,500 *livres*. They were able to cover their expenses of 4,085 *livres* between 24 Aug. 1745 and 26 Nov. 1748 but only because between 1743 and 1748 they received the equivalent of two years' allowance, at 1,600 *livres* per year, from the estate of Isaac-Louis de Forant* [see Marguerite Trottier]. When Île Royale was restored to France in 1748, the nuns were so poor that they could not contemplate returning there. In a report to Maurepas in November 1748 they said that they were "completely destitute" and asked the minister to note particularly that at Louisbourg "they would need allowances for six nuns and two servant girls whom they could not do without." The report received no reply until the following spring, when Maurepas, urged on by Abbé de L'Isle-Dieu, granted the nuns the price of their return voyage, plus 600 *livres* for their preparations, and promised that the gratuity they had always received at Louisbourg would again be granted them by the king.

Upon their return to Louisbourg Sister Saint-Arsène and her companions experienced only another series of deprivation, trial, and suffering. Financially incapable of rebuilding their convent, the nuns resigned themselves to renting a house, but it was so small that they could not assemble the children there to continue their teaching. Despite many entreaties and the pressing need in which they found themselves, they received no aid from the court for five years. Intent upon resuming their work, they decided in 1754 to rebuild their house at their own expense and to reopen their classes to boarders and day pupils,

17

Arnoux

to the great satisfaction of the inhabitants of the colony. In doing so, however, they placed themselves in a difficult financial position from which they were never able to extricate themselves. In 1757, no longer able to support themselves, they requested permission to return to Canada. The following year the commandant, Jean-Baptiste-Louis LE PRÉVOST Duquesnel, who wanted to keep them in Louisbourg, finally obtained a royal gratuity for them from the minister of Marine, Claude-Louis de Massiac.

In June 1758 the second siege of Louisbourg began; Sister Saint-Arsène wrote: "Never has there been so cruel a siege as that which we have undergone; I cannot think of it without still being frightened to death." After the fall of the fortress Sister Saint-Arsène was again deported to France with her companions. This time she was never again to see New France or her community in Montreal. She returned to the Hôpital Saint-Étienne in La Rochelle. During the six years she lived there she attended to the teaching of the few boarders whom she had brought with her from Louisbourg, which has led certain historians to say that she founded a convent in France. The sisters were able to subsist in their exile thanks to an annual pension of 250 *livres* per boarder which the court granted them and to M. de Forant's annuity.

Sister Saint-Arsène was still wanting to return to Montreal, or if not to Canada to the island of Miquelon, when death overtook her on 5 July 1764. In a letter on 9 June 1766 informing the superior of the Congregation of Notre-Dame in Montreal of the death of Sister Saint-Vincent-de-Paul, one of Sister Saint-Arsène's companions, Abbé de L'Isle-Dieu rendered this fine tribute to the last two sisters "of the little community in Louisbourg": "You have lost two good and excellent nuns in a short space of time; I regret them more than I can say, since both gave me all the satisfaction, contentment, and edification I could expect from them through their conduct until their final moments in the community where they had retired and whose esteem, veneration, and regrets they have taken with them."

ANDRÉE DÉSILETS

ACND, La Congrégation de Notre-Dame: son personnel, 1653–1768; Fichier général des sœurs de la Congrégation de Notre-Dame; Plans des lieux de sépulture depuis 1681-CND; Registre des sépultures des sœurs de la Congrégation de Notre-Dame; Registre général des sœurs de la Congrégation de Notre-Dame de Montréal. ANQ-M, Registre d'état civil, Notre-Dame de Montréal, 1699. Lemire-Marsolais et Lambert, *Histoire de la Congrégation de Notre-Dame*, II, 53; III, 281, 393–97; IV, 6, 29–35, 52, 90–101, 124–29, 141–57, 266–75, 277, 348, 354, 357, 361, 368–78, 408; V, 15, 17, 20, 87–98; VI, 23, 25. Tanguay, *Dictionnaire*.

ARNOUX, ANDRÉ, surgeon, surgeon-major; b. at Saint-Paul-de-Vence (dept. of Alpes-Maritimes), France, and baptized 22 Dec. 1720, son of Alexandre Arnoux, master-surgeon, and Lucresse Masson (Musson); d. 20 Aug. 1760 at Montreal.

André Arnoux was the son of a surgeon-major of the "king's hospitals," and took up the same career as his father. Until 1739 he worked in various hospitals; he then served as a surgeon on the king's ships, taking part in 12 campaigns at sea, during which he is believed to have made a small fortune buying drugs and medicaments and then reselling them at a good profit, a common practice at the time. On 17 June 1743 he married Suzanne Levret in the church of Saint-Louis de Toulon. In 1751, having been transferred from Rochefort and given an appointment in New France as assistant-surgeon, Arnoux settled in Quebec.

On 10 July 1755 he was attached to the Régiment de la Reine, stationed at Quebec. This regiment was scheduled to proceed by land to Montreal on 29 July; however, the accidental death of the surgeon-major of the troops, Jean-Baptiste Polemond, drowned in the Rivière du Chêne on 18 July, suddenly changed Arnoux's career. Arnoux, one of Polemond's assistants, succeeded him on 20 July, the same day the surgeon-major was buried at Deschambault. The commissary of wars, André DOREIL, justified this choice in a letter to Machault, the minister of Marine, saying that he had cast "his eyes on the Sieur Arnoux . . . whose talents and good sense . . . were not unknown to him." Along with his commission, signed by Doreil and countersigned by Intendant François Bigot*, Arnoux received an order to leave Quebec on 21 July and to proceed "with all possible dispatch to the place where the other surgeons were, and from there to Montreal to put himself at the disposal of M. le Baron de [DIESKAU]." He was instructed to set up mobile hospitals wherever there was a troop concentration. He took part in the battle at Lac Saint-Sacrement (Lake George) on 8 Sept. 1755 [see Dieskau], "having been, as it turned out, exposed to the same danger as the soldiers."

After the baron's army was defeated, Arnoux was stationed at Fort Saint-Frédéric (Crown Point, N.Y.), "where he finished treating the wounded" who could not be transported to Montreal. According to his instructions, he was to move with the troops; but it is rather difficult to follow the surgeon-major, since official documents are virtually silent about his activities. In a report dated October 1756 the surgeon tells us that his "talents have had less occasion to be used on the wounded, whose number does not exceed 50 . . . than on the maladies which the hardships, dirty food, and various encampments in the woods have caused in the small army." He added that "putrid fevers, scurvy, dysenteries and inflammations of the lower abdomen have caused the number of sick to reach 500 at one time." In 1758 Arnoux was at the battle at Fort Carillon (Ticonderoga, N.Y.). on 8 July. In 1759 he accompanied Bourlamaque, who had been instructed by Montcalm to carry out defensive works to bar the road to the enemy at three points, Carillon, Fort Saint-Frédéric, and on the Île aux Noix. It has been proven that at the time of General Montcalm's death on 13 Sept. 1759 Arnoux was at Île aux Noix. It was one of his two brothers, the surgeon Blaise or the apothecary Joseph, who attended Montcalm and assisted him at his death.

Having followed the regiments commanded by Bourlamaque to the outskirts of Quebec, Arnoux remained there until 28 July 1760. It was during this period that he suffered heavy financial losses. According to his contemporaries, after the battle at Sainte-Foy on 28 April 1760 [see Lévis*] the surgeon-major was ordered to stay at Quebec and to supply "medicaments and provisions" to all the wounded, "English as well as French," who were being treated at the Hôpital Général. "Sieur Arnoux provided not only for the subsistence and the necessary medicaments for the sick who were able to get into the aforementioned hospital, but he set up mobile hospitals at his own expense; made considerable puchases on all sides, at excessive cost, of all necessary and indispensable provisions; hired surgeons' assistants and hospital attendants; paid for expensive transport, and employed to this end much beyond his fortune to bring the sick the relief they needed." On 28 July Arnoux went to Montreal, where less than a month later, on 20 August, he died of an "inflammation of the lungs."

In a report dated 12 Sept. 1760 the commissary of wars, Benoît-François Bernier*, paid a posthumous tribute to the surgeon-major: "He died of the consequences and fatigues of the siege of Quebec, at which he exerted himself unstintingly, to the great admiration of everyone. He supported the sick with his own money and dies without resources, leaving a widow and young children. Public opinion is unanimous that the king should take an interest in this family. But Intendant Bigot is unwilling to do anything for them." Montcalm and Bourlamaque also spoke in high terms of Arnoux's career. The commissary of wars Doreil wrote: "He exceeded my expectations." Arnoux was a friend of Montcalm; the latter was even godfather to one of the surgeon's children, and he had complete confidence in Arnoux's skill. Out of this friendship grew the legend according to which the surgeon-major was present at Montcalm's last moments. Since Arnoux was also a friend of Bigot, who speedily forgot him, and of Joseph-Pierre Cadet* and Michel-Jean-Hugues Péan*, who refused to help his widow recover the sums advanced by her husband, it has been conjectured that if it had not been for his unexpected death the surgeon-major might have been incriminated in the Bigot affair. Pierre-Georges Roy* hints at this possibility on the sole evidence that in 1752 Arnoux is supposed to have paid in ready money 30,000 *livres* for Péan's house. According to the surgeon's contemporaries, Arnoux already had "a well-established fortune" when he arrived in New France. It was thanks to it that in 1759 he had been able to make considerable advances for the purchase, ordered by Bigot, of medicaments used for treating the wounded in an army of 18,000 men. These medicaments, stored in the vaulted cellars of Montcalm's house, were destroyed at the time of the capture of Quebec.

After her return to France in 1760 Arnoux's widow was justified, according to her contemporaries, in claiming more than "1,727,839 *livres*" to settle her husband's debts, which he had guaranteed by his personal fortune and the promise of repayment made by Intendant Bigot. For several years she vainly called upon the government to pay her husband's creditors. Louis XV deigned only to grant her and her six living children a pension of 3,000 *livres*, plus reimbursement of a quarter of the sum of 30,970 *livres* for which she was able to present some bills of exchange saved when the colony was lost. Sieur Arnoux had died without having had time to put his accounts in order.

RAYMOND DOUVILLE

AD, Alpes-Maritimes (Nice), État civil, Saint-Paul-de-Vence, 22 déc. 1720; Var (Draguignan), État civil, Saint-Louis de Toulon, 17 juin 1743. AN, Col., B, 125, f.32v; 127, f.223v; 152, f.74; E, 9 (dossier Arnoux) (copies at PAC). ANQ, "Inventaire analytique des Archives de la guerre concernant le Canada (1755–1760)," compilé par J.-É. Labignette et Louise Dechêne. *Journal du marquis de Montcalm* (Casgrain). "Lettres de Doreil," APQ *Rapport, 1944–45*, 25, 64, 67, 68, 83, 85, 124. *Lettres du marquis de Montcalm* (Casgrain). P.-G. Roy, *Inv. contrats de mariage*, I, 37;

Arrigrand

Bigot et sa bande, 304–8; *Hommes et choses du fort Saint-Frédéric*. "Biographies canadiennes," *BRH*, XX (1914), 373–74. P.-B. Casgrain, "La maison d'Arnoux où Montcalm est mort," *BRH*, IX (1903), 3–16, 33–48, 65–76. Gabriel Nadeau, "Les trois blessures de Montcalm," *Canada Français*, 2e sér., XXVII (1939–40), 639–42.

ARRIGRAND (Darrigrand), GRATIEN D', Sieur de La Majour, investor, concessionaire; b. 20 Jan. 1684 at Orthez, Béarn (dept. of Basses-Pyrénées), France, son of Jean-Jacques d'Arrigrand and Marguerite d'Auger de Subercase; d. after January 1754.

In 1703 Gratien d'Arrigrand accompanied his uncle, Daniel d'Auger* de Subercase, to Plaisance (Placentia, Nfld.), where he served until 1706 under Saint-Ovide [MONBETON]. While there he became a midshipman (1704) and took part in the raids on English posts at Bay Bulls (Baie des Taureaux), Petty Harbour (Petit Havre), and St John's. After further training at Rochefort, France, he joined the army (Régiment de Charolais) in Spain. Following his father's death in 1709, he left the army and spent nine years at his father's estate in Béarn, then lived in Paris until 1725. Having lost much of his large inheritance in the speculation attending John Law's "system," he was persuaded to try to recover some of it by investing in a colonial enterprise.

On 10 March 1725 d'Arrigrand became a private partner of François GANET, whom he had helped, through family connections, to obtain the fortification contract for Louisbourg, Île Royale (Cape Breton Island), and a partner, secretly, of Jacques d'Espiet* de Pensens. He went to Louisbourg in 1725, worked there with Ganet for two years, then returned to France, where his main task was to purchase materials and supplies for Ganet. Ganet became dissatisfied when in 1728 d'Arrigrand failed to send him what he needed; d'Arrigrand claimed that Ganet was concealing from him their profits and losses. In 1731 d'Arrigrand obtained a court order obliging Ganet to produce a financial statement, but no judgement could be carried out as long as Ganet was under a military construction contract with the crown outside metropolitan France. Despite d'Arrigrand's efforts to prevent it, Ganet obtained a new contract, running from 1731 to 1737. He refused to divide with d'Arrigrand the value of the equipment and materials which they jointly owned.

D'Arrigrand was anxious to recover moneys from the fortifications contract in order to reinvest them in Louisbourg. In April 1734 he was granted property at Plédien Creek; he proposed to transport timber from the nearby hills via the creek into Louisbourg harbour and to use water-power to operate sawmills and forge-hammers. On 8 Sept. 1735 he concluded an agreement with David-Bernard MUIRON, who was to undertake development of the site on d'Arrigrand's behalf. Unofficially, Muiron was also to try to win the fortifications contract from Ganet, forcing Ganet to return to France and the jurisdiction of the courts. Muiron, preoccupied with his tannery, did not even succeed in having d'Arrigrand's concession registered by the Conseil Supérieur of Île Royale. Though he did win the construction contract for the period 1737 to 1743, Muiron made a private deal with Ganet for the purchase of equipment and supplies instead of representing the interests of d'Arrigrand.

In 1739 Ganet, back in France, contested d'Arrigrand's suit against him. The conflict in the courts was long and confused; the case dragged on until 1745. That year d'Arrigrand was awarded two-fifths of the sums the crown owed Ganet, as well as 60,000 *livres* with which to pay his own debts. He also collected an additional 52,000 *livres* in a suit initiated by the estate of Pensens, and sued Muiron for further amounts. In 1753, his litigation finished, d'Arrigrand went to Louisbourg and finally had the Plédien Creek concession registered. He had mobilized financial and labour resources in France, and though the site had been neglected and misused he was ready to begin construction of facilities. There is no evidence, however, that he ever did so. A letter he wrote from Louisbourg in January 1754, when he was almost 70, is the last record of him that survives.

F. J. THORPE

AN, Col., B, 57, f.755; 71, ff.193–98v; C¹¹B, 18, ff.85–87; 22, ff.283–84; 23, ff.213–17v; 27, f.201; 33, f.10; C¹¹D, 5, ff.45–46; E, 9 (dossier d'Arrigrand); F¹ᴬ, 35, f.20; Marine, C¹, 161, f.21; Section Outre-Mer, Dépôt des fortifications des colonies, Am. sept., no.241; G², 183, f.430; 212, no.575. Robert Le Blant, *Histoire de la Nouvelle-France : les sources narratives du début du XVIIIe siècle et le Recueil de Gédéon de Catalogne* (1v. paru, Dax, France, [1948]), 254; "Un entrepreneur à l'île Royale, Gratien d'Arrigrand, 1684–1754," *La revue des questions historiques* (Paris), LXIV (1936) (offprint at PAC).

ARTIGNY, LOUIS ROUER D'. *See* ROUER

ATECOUANDO (Jérôme), chief and orator of the Abenaki tribe of Saint-François-de-Sales (Odanak, Que.); fl. 1749–57. There is no confirmation of the claim that he and the chief

Atecouando* who lived for some years (1706–14) at the same mission were related.

Atecouando was one of five chiefs who signed the letter written on 23 Sept. 1749 by Father Joseph AUBERY, the missionary at Saint-François-de-Sales, and sent to the canons of the cathedral of Chartres to renew the union of prayers entered into by the Abenakis nearly 60 years before [see Jacques and Vincent Bigot*].

As the recognized orator of his tribe, Atecouando played a leading role not only in urging it to attend to its internal affairs but also in expressing its views in dealings with other nations. Three of Atecouando's speeches have survived in French versions made by interpreters.

From 1748 to 1756, even though France and England were officially at peace, skirmishes continued on the frontier between the New England settlers and the Indians, and the Abenakis of Saint-François took an active part in these hostilities. In the summer of 1752 Captain Phineas Stevens came to New France on behalf of the governor of Boston to ransom English prisoners. On 5 July Atecouando addressed Stevens in the presence of Charles LE MOYNE de Longueuil, the acting governor, and the Iroquois of Sault-Saint-Louis (Caughnawaga, Que.) and Lac des Deux-Montagnes. Probably alluding to lands in present-day New Hampshire that the Abenakis claimed and the English were beginning to settle, the orator demanded who had authorized the English to have the Abenakis' lands surveyed. If the English wanted peace with the Abenakis, they would have to keep within the limits granted by former chiefs in previous treaties. "We forbid you very expressly," he said, "to kill a single beaver or to take a single stick of wood on the lands we live on. If you want wood, we will sell it to you, but you shall not have it without our permission."

In 1754 open conflict broke out between the French and English in the valley of the Ohio River, and by the following year the two nations were unofficially at war in North America. On 14 July 1755, when the new governor general of New France, Pierre de Rigaud* de Vaudreuil, was passing through Trois-Rivières, the Abenakis of Saint-François went to meet him and Atecouando addressed him in their name: "Tell us your command, give the order, we are ready to set out, if not by canoe then on foot. We can carry our belongings, beat all your enemies, who are our enemies, and then drive them as the wind scatters the dust." The Abenakis kept their word. About a hundred of them took the field the following month, and a detachment of French and Indians went under DIESKAU's command to repulse an English attack which, it was believed, would be directed against Fort Saint-Frédéric (Crown Point, N.Y.).

In 1757 one of Father Aubery's successors, Claude-François-Louis Virot, who apparently wanted to guard his flock from the temptations of European civilization, conceived the plan of going with his Abenakis to found a mission among the Delawares of the Ohio Valley. Having got word of this project, the chiefs from Saint-François and Bécancour went to Quebec to complain to Vaudreuil. Atecouando addressed the governor, setting forth his people's aversion to leaving the land where their ancestors were buried. In July Vaudreuil nevertheless allowed Virot to leave for the Ohio with a dozen "apostles"; but the Delawares, who had been hoping for trade goods and soldiers, proved rather unreceptive to the faith, and the Abenakis returned the following year.

Atecouando's speeches are good specimens of the frank and picturesque language of the Amerindian orators.

THOMAS-M. CHARLAND

Bougainville, "Journal" (Gosselin), APQ Rapport, 1923–24. Coll. de manuscrits relatifs à la N.-F., III, 509–12, 545–46. JR (Thwaites), LXIX. "Paroles des Abénakis de St-François au capitaine Stevens, député du gouverneur de Boston, en présence de M. le baron de Longueuil, gouverneur intérimaire du Canada, et des Iroquois du Sault-St-Louis et du lac des Deux-Montagnes (le 5 juillet 1752)," BRH, XXXIX (1933), 109–12, 546–49. Les vœux des Hurons et des Abnaquis à Notre-Dame de Chartres . . . , F.-J. Doublet de Boisthibault, édit. (Chartres, France, 1857), 50. Charland, Les Abénakis d'Odanak. Raymond Douville et J.-D. Casanova, La vie quotidienne des Indiens du Canada à l'époque de la colonisation française (Paris, 1967), 165. J.-A. Maurault, Histoire des Abénakis depuis 1605 jusqu'à nos jours (Sorel, Qué., 1866). Les Ursulines des Trois-Rivières depuis leur établissement jusqu'à nos jours (4v., Trois-Rivières, Qué., 1888–1911), I, 312–13.

AUBERT DE LA CHESNAYE, LOUIS, officer in the colonial regular troops; b. 8 July 1690 in Quebec, son of Charles Aubert* de La Chesnaye and his third wife Marie-Angélique Denys de La Ronde; d. 20 Oct. 1745 at the Hôtel-Dieu in Quebec.

The career of Louis Aubert de La Chesnaye has been confused with that of his half-brother, Louis Aubert Duforillon, 12 years his senior, and with that of Ignace-François Aubert de La Chesnaye, son of another half-brother. A résumé of the three careers is necessary for clarification.

Aubert

Louis Aubert Duforillon was born in La Rochelle in 1678, son of Charles Aubert de La Chesnaye and his second wife, Marie-Louise Juchereau de La Ferté. She died in March 1678 and two years later Charles Aubert married Marie-Angélique Denys de La Ronde. By 1700 he foresaw that difficulties might arise with his estates when he died because of his three marriages. A son from his first marriage was dead; to simplify his succession he gave 24,500 *livres* in property, merchandise, and *rentes* to each of the sons of his second marriage. Duforillon's share was the seigneuries of Kamouraska and of Sainte-Marguerite near Trois-Rivières, Île au Cochon and a piece of land called "marquisat du Sablé" near Trois-Rivières, a house in Trois-Rivières, as well as 2,500 *livres* in merchandise.

Duforillon shortly became engaged to Barbe, daughter of Montreal's town major Michel Leneuf* de La Vallière et de Beaubassin; his father disapproved and refused to sign their marriage contract. In November 1701 Duforillon gave all he had received from his father the previous year to his fiancée to show his sincerity, and in 1702, less than seven weeks after his father's death, he married Barbe.

On 15 May 1703 Duforillon and the Quebec merchant Joseph Riverin formed a partnership to share profits and losses in the exploitation of trade in cod, biscuits, peas, etc., with Plaisance (Placentia, Nfld.) via the ketch *Prospérité*. In 1703 and 1704 Louis travelled to Plaisance on business. The partnership was dissolved in October 1704, and Louis had to return to Plaisance in 1705 and 1706 to settle outstanding debts.

It is known that in 1710 Duforillon took the letters of the governor of Acadia, Daniel d'Auger* de Subercase, to France, but his activities thereafter are sketchy. He sold several properties he had received from his father, and drew 6,000 *livres* as his inheritance from Paul-Augustin Juchereau* de Maur. He was in France again in 1719, for Barbe Le Neuf was notified of his death by a letter from her cousin in Paris, dated 4 May 1720. Barbe renounced her rights to her husband's succession, and remained a widow until her death in Montreal on 14 Feb. 1733.

Documentation on the career of Louis Aubert de La Chesnaye is scant. His godparents were none other than Governor Frontenac [Buade*] and Intendant Bochart* de Champigny's wife, Marie-Madeleine de Chaspoux. Louis Aubert entered the colonial regular troops. He was a cadet in 1705 when Claude de Ramezay*, governor of Montreal, suggested that he be considered for an ensignship.

The career of an Aubert for 1707 to 1733 is detailed in the Archives des Colonies (AN, Col., E, 116) and appears to be that of Louis Aubert de La Chesnaye. This Aubert evidently served in Acadia where he was twice wounded in the English attack on Port-Royal (Annapolis Royal, N.S.) led by John March* in 1707. He sailed on the frigate *Vénus* under Louis DENYS de La Ronde, took part in the capture of a ship, and then fought with Saint-Ovide [MONBETON] in the taking of St John's, Newfoundland, in 1709, where he was again wounded. He travelled to Martinique and commanded a ship and 150 men in the capture of St Vincent (Lesser Antilles). He subsequently spent some time privateering against the English, and broke his leg. He later returned to Quebec where, in 1733, he was trying to establish the limits of the King's Domain in Canada. In 1741, after the death of Richard TESTU de La Richardière, port captain of Quebec, Aubert applied for the post but was passed over because of delicate health. Perhaps as compensation, the half-pay lieutenant was appointed captain of the governor's guards, a position he still held when he died a bachelor in 1745.

The third Aubert active in this period, Ignace-François Aubert de La Chesnaye, was born in 1699, son of François Aubert* de La Chesnaye and Anne-Ursule Denys de La Ronde. In 1730 he married Marie-Anne-Josette, daughter of Alexandre-Joseph Lestringant* de Saint-Martin. Ignace-François Aubert commanded ships taking supplies from Canada to Acadia. In the 1740s he served at Cap des Rosiers near Gaspé observing the movements of English ships and reporting to Quebec. La Galissonière [BARRIN] recommended him for the position of captain of the Quebec gates in 1748 and, the following year, La Jonquière [TAFFANEL] supported Aubert's candidacy, noting that he was a "poor gentleman." The position was not created until nine years later, however, when Pierre de Rigaud* de Vaudreuil stressed the importance of such a post and recommended Aubert who had served for a long time as a militia officer. On 1 Jan. 1758 Aubert was appointed captain of the Quebec gates at a salary of 800 *livres*. He died in Quebec in 1766.

C. J. RUSS

AHDQ, Registres des sépultures, 21 oct. 1745. AJQ, Registre d'état civil, Notre-Dame de Québec, 9 juill. 1690, 8 nov. 1702. AN, Col., B, 22, ff.97v–98; 32, f.128; C¹¹A, 20, pp.107, 109, 121; 22, pp.342–43 (PAC transcripts); E, 10, 116. ANQ, Greffe de Louis Chambalon, 18 oct. 1700, 7 nov. 1702, 16 janv. 1712, 20 juill. 1713; Greffe de Florent de La Cetière, 4 nov. 1712; Greffe de J.-C. Louet, 21 août 1720; NF, Coll. de pièces jud. et not., 612, 831, 3556, 3565, 3566. Bonnault, "Le Canada militaire," APQ *Rapport, 1949–51*, 300. P.-G. Roy, *Inv. ord. int.*, I, 99. Tanguay, *Dictionnaire*. P.-G. Roy, *La famille Juchereau Duchesnay* (Lévis, Qué., 1903), 49; "Les capitaines de port à Québec," *BRH*, XXXII (1926), 75–76.

AUBERY (Auberi, Aubry), JOSEPH (Jacques), Jesuit priest, missionary; b. 10 May 1673 at Gisors (dept. of Eure), France; d. 24 May 1756 at the Saint-François-de-Sales mission (Odanak, Que.).

Joseph Aubery at 17 years of age entered the Collège Louis-le-Grand in Paris, where he studied under the direction of Father Joseph Jouvency. He had the reputation of being a timid and frightened student. Yet he requested permission to continue his studies in Quebec, and he arrived there in 1694. While pursuing his theological studies he taught at the Jesuit college in Quebec for five years. Ordained a priest by Bishop Saint-Vallier [La Croix*] on 21 Sept. 1699, Aubery then devoted himself to studying the Abenaki language at the Sault de la Chaudière mission, and in 1701 he was entrusted with founding a mission for the Malecites, allies of the Abenakis, at Médoctec (Meductic, N.B.) on the Saint John River. From his arrival in this region of mainland Acadia, he championed a policy aimed at uniting all the Abenakis in the territory of New France, to shield them from English influence. It seems that Father Aubery travelled into every part of this hilly region and got to know it better than anyone else.

In 1709 Aubery had to replace Father Jean-Baptiste Loyard*, who had temporarily taken over the running of the Saint-François-de-Sales mission on the shores of the Rivière Saint-François, where the largest group of Abenakis "domiciled" in New France was located. In a letter to his former teacher, Father Jouvency, Aubery alluded to the difficulties of his ministry. He had to fight against "drunkenness, arrogance, and superstition." But the formerly timid student had greatly changed: he had become eloquent, and his vehemence as well as the rigour of his oratory had helped him persuade the elders to take responsibility for the practice of virtue in the mission. Thus Father Aubery rapidly acquired great influence over his flock, and he soon became a specialist in the Abenaki language.

In handing over to England Acadia "with its ancient boundaries," the treaty of Utrecht (1713) created a difficult situation for the Abenakis on the Atlantic coast, who were now on territory claimed by both crowns. Fully aware of the danger, that same year Aubery sent to the French court a report, accompanied by a map, which suggested clear boundaries between the English and French territories, in order not to allow "the English, in peacetime, to spread out, advance, and settle on our lands, and in that way become masters of Canada." "To be beyond dispute," he added, "these boundaries could only be the high grounds; but to set them there means giving away a great part of New France, since these high grounds are very near the St Lawrence River." Father Aubery therefore suggested: a definition of Acadia limiting it to the present-day peninsula of Nova Scotia; a post (the former fort of Pemaquid) to mark the boundary of New France and New England on the Atlantic; and the drawing of a line from this point, following the high grounds, to obtain "a fair and indisputable boundary between the lands which are considered to belong to one or the other." But this report and the map which Father Aubery had prepared with the help of Intendant Bégon made no lasting impression upon French policy, and mainland Acadia continued to be a disputed area.

It was at this point that in 1715 Father Aubery again took up his idea, formulated in 1703, of uniting all the Abenakis into a single village, and he proposed joining the Bécancour mission with that at Saint-François, "which is the most advantageous post in the colony in relation to the Iroquois in time of war and very appropriate for creating a strong settlement, since it has a great stretch of land which is very good and very suitable for the Indians." At the same time he tried to dissuade Atecouando*, an Abenaki chief who since the war had taken refuge with 60 warriors at Saint-François, from returning to re-establish his former village not far from New England, pointing out to him "the disadvantages which he himself will suffer from this re-establishment." In this way the missionary took an active part in the policy of the French government, which wanted at all costs to preserve the alliance with the Abenakis.

Like his superior, Father Pierre de LA CHASSE, Father Aubery probably had some part in the declaration of war which in 1718 opposed the Abenakis to the Anglo-Americans in New England. Indeed, in 1720 Aubery sent a second report to the court of France on the question of the boundaries of Acadia. In 1721 he received at his mission at Saint-François Governor Vaudreuil [Philippe de Rigaud*], who had come to meet the Abenaki warriors. He was, moreover, in close correspondence with Vaudreuil on all questions relating to the war. In 1725 he sent Father Louis d'Avaugour*, procurator in Paris of the Jesuit

Aubery

missions in New France, a report in which he stated: "The war is very necessary if we do not want to run the risk of losing as of now all the shore of the St Lawrence River." In 1726 the missionary wrote in the same vein to Father Jean-Baptiste DUPARC, Father La Chasse's successor; he told his correspondent specifically: "Religion has up till now been the only motive that has made the Abenakis French, and as soon as there are no more missionaries they will become English and will be capable by themselves of putting the English in possession of the whole country at the first war." We may, however, believe that the missionary endeavoured to the best of his ability to make this "just and necessary" war less harsh by receiving and ransoming the numerous prisoners brought back from the expeditions into New England. Since the mission records were destroyed in 1759, there is no evidence of the priest's having made any gestures of this sort; nevertheless we know that in 1720 he ransomed and converted young Dorothy Jeryan, who later joined the Ursulines of Quebec.

After peace between the English and the Abenakis was signed in 1726 and ratified in 1727, Father Aubery received at Saint-François the Indians who had survived the destruction of the villages of Narantsouak (Norridgewock, now Old Point, Madison, Maine) and Pentagöuet (Castine, Maine). But despite his desire to do so, he did not succeed in keeping all the refugees from New England. In 1733 a smallpox epidemic led to the departure of a number. Others tried to found a new village on Missisquoi Bay, where communications were much easier. In 1738, Father Aubery induced the governor of Trois-Rivières, Josué DUBOIS Berthelot de Beaucours, to forbid Jean-Baptiste Jutras, *dit* Desrosiers, seigneur of Lussaudière, "to allocate for settlement a part of his land grant which was adjacent to the Indians, on the plea that cleared lands would, by driving the game away, cause the Indians to go off elsewhere." The Abenaki village of Saint-François-de-Sales was in fact built on his lands. The seigneur of Lussaudière tried to have the ordinance annulled, but he was unsuccessful, because Versailles was trying to keep the Abenakis under French influence, and it was at Saint-François that they could best be kept under control.

In 1744, war having again broken out between the two crowns, Father Aubery tried to obtain from Governor Charles de BEAUHARNOIS permission for the arrest of an undesirable German who had been living in the village for two years, since he feared that he would return to live among the English and suspected him of being a "dangerous spy." Certainly there were grounds for fearing a leakage of information, as the Abenakis from Saint-François had since the beginning of the war been making "continual raids" on the territory of New England, sowing terror and destruction. The missionary kept abreast of all movements: in 1747 he was at Quebec to give a report on the activities of "his" warriors; in 1749 he was at Montreal to supervise the exchanges of prisoners.

After peace was signed in 1748, the missionary decided in 1749 to renew the Abenakis' vows to Notre-Dame de Chartres and wrote to this effect to the dean of the chapter of the cathedral of Chartres, France. This letter was countersigned by the five Abenaki chiefs of the village of Saint-François, one of whom was ATECOUANDO, and gave witness that in peace as in war the piety of the Abenakis was as ardent as at the time of Father Jacques Bigot*. In 1752 the Saint-François mission was visited by the engineer Louis FRANQUET, who was making a tour of inspection of the fortifications of New France, but Father Aubery was absent. The engineer's visit perhaps took place just at the time when the Jesuit was attending negotiations in July between the English and the Abenakis.

In 1756 Father Joseph Aubery died peacefully at Saint-François, at 83 years of age. He left behind him a well-organized mission endowed with a magnificently decorated church which possessed, along with other objects, a huge banner given to the missionary by Marie Leszczynska. He also left numerous works in Abenaki which he had written for the instruction of young missionaries. But above all he left the memory of a patriarch who had been completely devoted to the cause of his people. The reputation he enjoyed during his lifetime, his long years of apostolate, and especially the spelling of his name probably explain why in the 19th century some commentators identified him with Father Aubry, immortalized by Chateaubriand in *Atala*. As Thomas Charland has rightly shown, this opinion does not stand up to an analysis of the facts and the texts.

MICHELINE D. JOHNSON

[The museum at the Indian reserve at Odanak, Que., has held since 1966 the French-Abenaki and Abenaki-French dictionaries compiled by Father Aubery. M.D.J.].

AAQ, 12 A, Registres d'insinuations A, 805, 806, 807. AN, Col., B, 47, ff.1129, 1206; 48, ff.180–205, 855, 909; 50, ff.500–9, 531, 538v; 52, ff.516v, 547v, 586; 53, f.541v; 54, f.432v; 57, ff.652v–65; 58, ff.461v, 470v, 480; 64, ff.432v, 438v, 442; 65, ff.423v–27; 68, f.20; C¹¹A, 34, ff.8–9; 35, ff.15–51; 49, ff.124–28; 91, f.12; C¹¹E, 2, ff.63–69, 90–94; F³, 24, f.299. ASJCF, Fonds Roche-monteix, 4003, 108–11; 4006, 129, 130–33, 285–86; 4018, 57, 85–90, 105–6, 296, 363, 438; 4023, 229, 233. ASQ, Lettres, O, 28; Tiroir, 217, 14. Charlevoix, *History* (Shea). F.-A.-R. de Chateaubriand, *Atala*, Armand Weil, édit. (Paris, 1950). *Coll. de manuscrits relatifs à la N.-F.*, II, 405–6, 567; III, 23, 57–61, 78–91, 108–10, 132–33, 140, 146, 160, 161, 167, 169, 172–73, 182–85, 356, 359, 490, 505–6, 509–12, 515–18. ''Correspondance de Vaudreuil'', APQ *Rapport, 1938–39*, 12–24, 159–74; *1946–47*, 427–37; *1947–48*, 230–38. Franquet, *Voyages et mémoires sur le Canada*, 174–76. ''Le gouverneur de Vaudreuil et les Abénaquis; paroles des Abénaquis à monsieur le marquis de Vaudreuil,'' *BRH*, XXXVIII (1932), 569. *JR* (Thwaites). ''Lettre de M. de Rigaud de Vaudreuil au ministre (2 septembre 1749),'' *BRH*, XLIV (1938), 376–77. ''Lettre de MM. de Vaudreuil et Bégon au ministre au sujet des affaires des Abénakis (14 octobre 1723),'' *BRH*, XLI (1935), 624–29. ''Lettre des sauvages abénaquis au roi,'' *BRH*, XXXVII (1931), 368–40. [J.-F. Le Sueur], ''Histoire du calumet et de la dance,'' *Les soirées canadiennes; recueil de littérature nationale* (Québec), [IV] (1864), 114–35. *A narrative of Mrs. Johnson's captivity among the French and the Indians* (Boston, 1798). ''Paroles des Abénakis,'' *BRH*, XXXIX (1933), 546–49. ''Paroles des Abénakis à monsieur le marquis de Beauharnois,'' *BRH*, XXXIX (1933), 574–76.

[Melançon], *Liste des missionnaires jésuites*. Tanguay, *Répertoire* (hand-written annotated edition by the archivists of the Séminaire de Québec). Charland,

Les Abénakis d'Odanak. Coleman, *New England captives*, I, 28; II, 242–48, 293, 306, 389–90, 401. Charles Gill, *Notes sur de vieux manuscrits abénakis* (Montréal, 1886). J.-A. Maurault, *Histoire des Abénakis depuis 1605 jusqu'à nos jours* (Sorel, Qué., 1866). Luc Merlet, *Histoire des relations des Hurons et des Abnaquis du Canada avec Notre-Dame de Chartres, suivie de documents inédits sur la Sainte Chemise* (Chartres, France, 1858). Rochemonteix, *Les Jésuites et la N.-F. au XVIIᵉ siècle*, III, 367, 397–408; *Les Jésuites et la N.-F. au XVIIIᵉ siècle*, I, 25–28; II, 12–19. Benjamin Sulte, *Histoire de Saint-François-du-Lac* (Montréal, 1886). T.-M. Charland, ''Chateaubriand a-t-il immortalisé le père Aubery,'' *RHAF*, XVI (1962–63), 184–87. Désiré Girouard, ''L'étymologie du mot missisquoi,'' *BRH*, XI (1905), 270.

AUBUCHON, CATHERINE. *See* Jérémie, *dit* Lamontagne

AUDIN. *See* Daudin

AUREIL. *See* Doreil

AVÈNE DES MÉLOIZES, NICOLAS-MARIE RENAUD D'. *See* Renaud

AYRES. *See* Eyre

B

BARNARD, JOHN, Congregationalist minister; b. 6 Nov. 1681 at Boston, Massachusetts, son of John Barnard and Esther Travis; d. 24 Jan. 1770 at Marblehead, Massachusetts.

John Barnard's father, a housewright by trade, was elected in 1701 to the office of Boston selectman. Barnard received his AB from Harvard in 1700 and his MA in 1703. While at Harvard he also read theology under Cotton Mather. By 1707, however, his association with the Mather faction had come to an end.

In 1707 Barnard was appointed one of the five chaplains for the expedition against Port-Royal (Annapolis Royal, N.S.) which was led by Colonel John March* of Newbury. Barnard advocated a vigorous siege of Port-Royal, and on several occasions he himself came under enemy fire; the expedition was not, however, successful. An incident of ''scandalous conduct'' in the camp – namely, a game of cards – resulted in Barnard's confession and contrition upon his return to Boston. After this expedition, Barnard continued to lead a roaming and adventurous life for

a number of years. He spent about one year in England (1709–10), where he moved freely in both religious and commercial circles.

Barnard was ordained by the Marblehead church on 18 July 1716, and served that church for the rest of his life. On 18 Sept. 1718 he wed Anna Woodbury (Woodberry) of Ipswich; the marriage was without issue. At Marblehead Barnard was active in the stimulation of local commerce, and thereby the town achieved a certain economic autonomy. He also supported the education of several poor boys. In 1745 Barnard was offered a military chaplaincy with the expedition to Louisbourg, Île Royale (Cape Breton Island), but his congregation persuaded him to refuse on account of his age.

George E. Bates

[The best biographical sketch of John Barnard, along with a bibliography of his writings, can be found in Shipton, *Sibley's Harvard graduates*, IV, 501–14. Shipton states that several works attributed to the Reverend John Barnard should be credited to Deacon John Barnard of Andover, Mass. Barnard's manuscripts are in the library of the Massachusetts Historical Society. His "Autobiography," dated 14 Nov. 1766, is printed in Mass. Hist. Soc. *Coll.*, 3rd ser., V (1836), 177–243. See also: *DAB*. W. B. Sprague, *Annals of the American pulpit . . .* (9v., New York, 1857–69), I, 252–58. G.E.B.]

BAROLET, CLAUDE, merchant, writer in the Marine, royal notary; b. *c.* 1690 in France, son of Pierre Barolet and Marie Dauteuil, from the parish of Saint-Jacques de la Boucherie, Paris; d. 25 Jan. 1761 at Charlesbourg, near Quebec.

Claude Barolet arrived in New France around 1708 and settled in Quebec as a merchant. By 1710 he had developed an interest in legal affairs and became a clerk in the office of the notary Louis Chambalon*. Chambalon promised to supply his young clerk with "food and drink, a hearth and shelter," and an annual salary of 120 *livres*; Barolet for his part agreed to serve the notary faithfully. We do not know how long he stayed in the service of Chambalon, who died in June 1716. On 3 November of that year Barolet married Françoise Dumontier in Quebec. The Barolets moved into a house in Rue de Meulles, and the young bride was thus her mother's neighbour.

Barolet continued to be occupied in business, without, however, ceasing his legal activities. He practised as an attorney. On 28 June 1728 he obtained from Intendant Dupuy* a commission as royal notary to practise in Quebec, and 8 June 1731 Intendant Hocquart* extended Barolet's jurisdiction to the entire government of Quebec. Barolet, now living in Rue Saint-Pierre, was a busy notary during the 30 years or so of his practice. The colonial authorities had nothing but praise for him and commended particularly his work as writer in the Marine, an office he held for an undetermined period. Governor Charles de BEAUHARNOIS and Intendant Hocquart mentioned to the minister in 1740 that Barolet "writes well," and was hard-working. In his registry for the years 1743–47 are to be found most of the contracts for the granting of lands in Beauce.

After the capitulation of Montreal Barolet became on 29 Dec. 1760 the first notary to obtain from Governor James Murray* a commission in the government of Quebec. Unfortunately he made use of it for only a month; he died on 25 Jan. 1761.

Ten children were born of his marriage, including two daughters, Marie-Louise and Marie-Françoise. The first married the notary Jean-Claude Panet*, and the second Jean-Antoine Bedout. Claude Barolet lived to see a son born of

this marriage, who became the famous rear-admiral Jacques Bedout*.

MICHEL PAQUIN

AN, Col., B, 57, f.608; 58, f.492; C¹¹ᴬ, 73, f.299v. *Recensement de Québec, 1716* (Beaudet). "Recensement de Québec, 1744" (APQ *Rapport*). Létourneau et Labrèque, "Inventaire de pièces détachées de la Prévôté de Québec," ANQ *Rapport, 1971*, 120, 126, 149, 150, 156, 175, 184, 201, 257, 292, 405. P.-G. Roy, *Inv. contrats de mariage*, I, 77; *Inv. ins. Prév. Québec*, I, 36; *Inv. jug. et délib., 1717–1760*; *Inv. ord. int.*; *Inv. testaments*, I, 29. Tanguay, *Dictionnaire*. Vachon, "Inv. critique des notaires royaux," *RHAF*, IX (1955–56), 437. J.-E. Roy, *Histoire du notariat*, I, 355. "Le contre-amiral Jacques Bedout," *BRH*, XXXIV (1928), 641.

BARON, PIERRE LUPIEN, *dit. See* LUPIEN

BARRIN DE LA GALISSONIÈRE, ROLAND-MICHEL, Marquis de LA GALISSONIÈRE, naval officer, commandant general of New France; b. 10 Nov. 1693 at Rochefort, France, son of Roland Barrin de La Galissonière, lieutenant-general of the naval forces, and Catherine Bégon, sister of Intendant Michel BÉGON; m. in 1713 Marie-Catherine-Antoinette de Lauson, who was related to the family of the former governor of New France, Jean de Lauson*; d. 26 Oct. 1756 at Montereau (Montereau-fault-Yonne, dept. of Seine-et-Marne), France.

After a good course of study at the Collège de Beauvais in Paris under the direction of Charles Rollin, La Galissonière became a midshipman in Rochefort on 1 Nov. 1710; he had his first active service on the *Héros*, which carried supplies to Canada in 1711. He was promoted sub-lieutenant on 25 Nov. 1712; until 1736 he usually served at Rochefort, with, however, some sea postings which took him to Canada, Île Royale (Cape Breton Island), the West Indies, the Mediterranean, and along the coasts of Spain. On 7 May 1726 he was appointed assistant adjutant at Rochefort; on 17 March 1727 he opted for regular service as lieutenant-commander and took the *Dromadaire* in 1734 and 1735 on a campaign in the West Indies. In 1737 he received command of the *Héros* for transport duty to Canada. Powerful family influence, more than his own merits, was responsible for his promotion to captain on 1 April 1738 and his becoming a knight of the order of Saint-Louis on 13 May of that year. In 1739 he transported supplies to Louisbourg, Île Royale, on the *Rubis*, which he commanded. The following year he served in the Mediterranean on the ship of the line *Espérance*.

From 1741 to 1743 he commanded the *Tigre*,

part of the squadron led by the lieutenant-general of the naval forces, Court de La Bruyère, which almost never left the roadstead of Toulon. In 1744 La Galissonière returned to Brest to take command of the *Gloire*, one of the 19 ships of the line in the squadron of the Comte de Roquefeuil, lieutenant-general of the naval forces; this squadron was to support the attempts by Charles Edward, the Young Pretender, to land in England. On 1 Feb. 1745 La Galissonière was appointed commissary general of artillery at Rochefort, and in this capacity he was concerned with putting the coasts of Aunis and Saintonge into a state of defence.

In February 1746 La Galissonière received command of the *Juste*, which, together with the *Sérieux*, was to protect the establishments and ships of the Compagnie des Indes on the coasts of Africa. Following the instructions of the minister of Marine, the two ships left from Île de Groix on 27 April 1746, reached Senegal on 26 May, and left again on 28 June to meet three of the company's ships, two of which were coming from China, at Fernando de Noronha (Brazil) on 2 August. La Galissonière sailed again on 29 August for Grenada, West Indies, where he met the *Philibert*, another of the company's ships, and all the ships sailed for France on 3 October. But the *Juste* and the *Sérieux* arrived in Rochefort on 7 December alone, since bad weather east of the Grand Banks had caused them to lose sight of their convoy; it nevertheless succeeded in reaching Lorient without incident.

While he was thus engaged in protecting the company's interests, grave events had taken place in Canada. The Marquis de La Jonquière [TAFFANEL] had been appointed governor general on 15 March 1746, but his participation in the expedition against the British in Nova Scotia led by the Duc d'Anville [LA ROCHEFOUCAULD] had prevented him from taking up his post immediately, and, when he left for Quebec in May 1747, the convoy which he was protecting was attacked by a superior British squadron and he himself was taken prisoner. The minister of Marine, Maurepas, who obviously supported La Galissonière, thought of him for command of the colony during the governor's absence. Consequently on 1 May 1747 La Galissonière was entrusted with the functions of commandant general in New France. Maurepas wrote to him on 14 June: "As M. de La Jonquière has been appointed to the office of governor general, it is not possible at the present time to send you letters of appointment, but letters of command give you the same powers, the same rights, the same authority, the same honours as are attached to the office of lieutenant general, and you will receive the same salary."

La Galissonière accepted his new functions reluctantly; he would have preferred to continue serving in the navy, for he had just refused the office of governor general of Saint-Domingue (Hispaniola) after being posted to command the *Monarque* in the squadron under the Marquis de L'Étenduère, which was fitting out to sail for the West Indies. He agreed to leave for Quebec only "when it was pointed out to him that his presence there was necessary during the war." The court later recognized his devotion: his promotion to rear-admiral on 7 Feb. 1750 was "because of the promptness with which he sacrificed his repose, his inclinations and personal interests to the pressing needs of the service." La Galissonière, then, sailing on the *Northumberland*, reached Quebec on 19 Sept. 1747. He was not well acquainted with the situation in New France, for he knew only what a sailor making a short stay could have seen of it; but as a conscientious officer he immediately made every effort to learn by conferring with his predecessor, Charles de BEAUHARNOIS (with whom he had family connections), and with Intendant Hocquart*.

The general outlook was not encouraging; war had been going on for three years and had severely strained the already shaky finances of the colony, which was gravely threatened by the expansionist policy of the British. Far from being dismayed by these difficulties, La Galissonière sought energetically to resolve them, his whole policy being by force of circumstances a defensive one, but also wide-ranging in its concerns. Like his predecessors, he continually harassed the ministers to obtain reinforcements for his troops, which continued to be extremely reduced in numbers. Recourse had therefore to be had to recruiting habitants and Indians, a scheme that had the disadvantage of costing a great deal and of impeding farming; here he ran up against insurmountable obstacles. "There is no special fund for the expenses of the colonies," Maurepas explained to him on 6 March 1748, "they come out of the funds of the Marine, and it is far from receiving what would be necessary for its own needs." Consequently he was recommended to keep to a purely defensive strategy and to be self-sufficient. The minister had even refused him the guns that had been requested for the fortifications of Quebec and Montreal, whose construction had been decided in principle in 1745 after the fall of Louisbourg. La Galissonière favoured the fortifications project; in doing so he followed the ideas of his time and refused to understand that such works swallowed up enormous sums of money for a most debatable purpose, as the recent siege of Louisbourg had in fact just proved. At most, it was sufficient to build light entrenchments such as those at Fort Saint-Jean, which was intended to duplicate Fort Saint-Frédéric (Crown Point, N.Y.) and facilitate the settlement of the Lake Champlain region. This construction was begun in the spring of 1748 under the direction of the ensign Gaspard-Joseph Chaussegros* de Léry, who was the object of particular solicitude on the part of the commandant general.

La Galissonière attached, quite correctly, the greatest importance to Acadian affairs. The boundaries of this province had remained uncertain since 1715; consequently in 1749 the commandant general sent a detachment under the command of Charles Deschamps* de Boishébert to the Saint John River to check the British expansion towards the Gaspé peninsula and the valley of the lower St Lawrence, in regions to which the British crown claimed to have rights.

But a defensive policy could not rest entirely upon the military forces, and La Galissonière rapidly grasped the importance, on the one hand, of imitating his predecessors in gaining as much goodwill as possible from the Indians, and on the other of developing settlement to increase the indispensable demographic support. For that reason Indian policy was one of his vital concerns, and now this sailor, so prudent on the sea, conceived in New France an audacious plan, with great breadth of outlook, which aimed at joining Canada and Louisiana by a line of posts along the Ohio valley, a region that was to become one of the main theatres of Anglo-French rivalry. La Galissonière hoped that these posts would draw the Indians into the French orbit. He tried, therefore, as the minister's instructions to him laid down, to drive the British out of the Ohio valley by sending Pierre-Joseph CÉLORON de Blainville, who left Montreal on 15 June 1749, visited the regions of forts Frontenac (Kingston, Ont.), Niagara (near Youngstown, N.Y.), and the Ohio, returning to Montreal on 10 November. He had verified that the Indian tribes were falling more and more under British influence, because of the growing activity of the Ohio Company since its beginnings in November 1747. For lack of financial means Céloron could not act very effectively, and he remarked that the French traders had price lists that were much higher than those of their competitors.

With his objective always in mind, La Galissonière had construction started in June 1749 on Fort de La Présentation (Oswegatchie, now Ogdensburg, N.Y.), near Lake Ontario, and sent the Sulpician François Picquet* there to evangelize the Iroquois. At first glance La Galissonière had perceived the threat that the trading factories set up by British traders in the Great Lakes region, particularly at Fort Chouaguen (Fort Oswego), represented for the French colony. The destruction of this enclave was to be one of his obsessions, and it would have permitted all communication with the Iroquois tribes to be denied the enemy. In his great report of 1750 he came back to the point: "Nothing must be spared to destroy this dangerous post on the first occasion for reprisals, which the British will furnish by one of those hostile acts they are only too accustomed to committing in time of peace, supposing that we cannot have it ceded to us by mutual agreement in return for some equivalent."

As a good strategist the commandant general saw clearly the capital importance of Detroit, the key to communications with the Mississippi valley. He was unceasingly concerned to reinforce it and stimulate its development; he tried to send it settlers, but he succeeded in having only 45 people go there. He considered this post likely to become a great trading town. The Illinois country was also one of his preoccupations, but the weak reinforcements he proposed sending there – some 60 soldiers and a few families – could not play any serious role in stopping British expansion in that direction.

La Galissonière also saw clearly the problems in the management of the posts. He was anxious to have good interpreters, and suggested to the minister that gratuities be paid those officers who learned Indian languages. He criticized severely the system of farming out the posts to officers; the intention was that officers might obtain these posts cheaply "in order to place them in a situation where they could content the Indians." But the system produced the contrary effect: the posts were farmed out to the highest bidders, since "the idea people had of the profits to be made in them," he wrote on 23 Oct. 1748, "has caused these leases to reach prices much above what had previously been demanded from the officers. The purchasers have therefore thought that they have the right to draw as much profit from them as possible, without any regard for the disadvantages which might result." Prices of merchandise at the posts had risen enormously, with the result that those who had secured the contracts "have brought the Indians to the point of despair and reduced them to going to Chouaguen to seek goods that the British could not offer for a comparable price, if exclusive trade and the price of leases did not increase ours." La Galissonière consequently decided to give up this system and to return to the former one of licences (*congés*), hoping thereby to cause prices to drop and to bring the Indian clientele back to the French posts.

With the Indians in Acadia La Galissonière also followed a policy aimed at blocking the British expansion. After the loss of Île Royale, important elements of the Abenaki tribes had decided to leave their villages for the region around Quebec, away from the enemy's incursions. The commandant general endeavoured, however, to send them back to their homes, where they would be better able to contain the adversary. The minister approved and encouraged La Jonquière to continue this policy. It should be noted that La Galissonière was strongly opposed to marriages between Indians and French, claiming that they produced results exactly the opposite of those being sought.

Settlement of the colony was another of his main preoccupations. Struck by the high Canadian birthrate, La Galissonière thought at one time that the imbalance in population between the French and the British in North America would disappear as a result of the natural increase in the population of Canada. "France," he wrote on 1 Sept. 1748, "draws from herself and from her other colonies products of all sorts; this one will for a long time produce only men, but if we wish, it will produce in a fairly short period such a great quantity of them that, far from fearing the British colonies or the Indian tribes, it will be able to lay down the law to them." Did he retain this illusion? It is not certain, since in his major report of 1750 he insisted upon the necessity of sending settlers to Canada, without acknowledging that it was hardly possible to create such a trend without favourable public opinion in the mother country. For his part, La Galissonière did everything in his power to attract new settlers. Beginning in September 1748, he tried to encourage Acadians to move to Île Royale and Canada, and it was partly to this end that he sent Deschamps de Boishébert on a mission to that region. It must be noted, indeed, that he always showed the greatest solicitude towards the Acadians, and after his return to France continued to be interested in them and to intervene on their behalf, particularly at the time of the visit to Versailles in 1753 of the famous Abbé Jean-Louis Le Loutre*.

In requesting troop reinforcements he was also thinking of peopling the country. On 6 Sept. 1748 he asked the minister to send him recruits who would make it possible for him "to allow many marriages and give many discharges, which are as useful for the settling of this colony as they are necessary for getting some service from the troops in Canada, who, because of the great number of soldiers to be invalided out, were almost completely useless during the whole of the last war, and are becoming more and more so." He nevertheless remained selective in admitting new settlers. Thus he refused Maurepas's suggestion of settling Irishmen, Scots, and even Englishmen, on condition that they were Catholics, for he considered that they would be unsuitable subjects.

Economic activity was also among the commandant general's preoccupations. One might not go so far as to claim, as did the king's physician, Jean-François GAULTIER, in a letter of 21 Oct. 1752, that "the colony was almost nascent and that hardly anything had been done in it for 150 years," but the country, at the time of La Galissonière's arrival, was admittedly still little developed. This fact was recognized by the minister in the instructions he sent La Galissonière on 30 April 1749: "Although capable of supporting enterprises both solid and profitable, Canada has made but little progress in the course of a fair number of years. The first settlers, who were little concerned with these sorts of enterprises, concerned themselves solely with the fur trade they could manage to carry on with the Indians, and there are still a rather large number of them who, satisfied with what that trade brings them and attracted still more by the independence they enjoy in their travels, are not much interested in devoting themselves to farming."

La Galissonière endeavoured to remedy this state of affairs, as his uncle Bégon had tried to do some 30 years earlier, and sought to develop agriculture and livestock breeding to enable the colony to feed itself. His administration was too short, however, to produce appreciable results. He would also have liked to encourage certain industries, particularly woollen mills, but he ran up against the mercantilist ideas of the mother country, and on 6 March 1748 Maurepas reminded him "that they are to be tolerated only to the extent that they do not harm the market for those in France, and for this reason they must not be allowed to multiply." He was, however, allowed to support the Saint-Maurice ironworks, which were beginning to produce some guns, and the shipbuilding yards in Quebec, where at that time construction of the *Saint-Laurent* was being completed and work on the *Orignal* was beginning.

La Galissonière's intelligence, activity, and human qualities had caused him to be much appreciated by the Canadians. The physician Gaultier wrote, with some exaggeration: "M. le Marquis de La Galissonière is the only person to begin to put things on a good footing. In losing him Canada has suffered a great loss." Gaultier praised "the vast extent of his knowledge, combined with his great love for the public good and for everything that may profit the State." Mme Bégon [ROCBERT] – who was related to him – confirmed this enthusiasm and wrote to her son-in-law, Honoré MICHEL de Villebois: "I believe that Canada will suffer a great loss in losing him." Despite the favour he enjoyed, La Galissonière thought only of leaving Canada, and on 14 May 1749 the minister finally announced to him that he was sending him "the permission to return to France . . . requested so insistently," and added: "I am not unaware of the zeal with which you have devoted yourself to the purpose of your command in Canada and the success with which you have carried it out in all its details." Moreover, the king took advantage of his return to entrust to him a mission of inspection at Louisbourg, where he was "to ascertain the present state of the fortifications and the artillery," and to concern himself with regulations for the troops to prevent the renewal of the abuses which had provoked the disorders of 1745. He could also extend his investigations "as much as time will allow to the different parts of the administration of the colony."

After acquainting his successor, La Jonquière, with the state of affairs in New France, La Galissonière sailed from Quebec on board the *Léopard* on 24 Sept. 1749 and reached Louisbourg on 5 October. No time was lost in making his inspection, for he left again before 21 October. Together with the commandant, Charles DES HERBIERS de La Ralière he visited the forts, carried plans away with him, and gave the necessary instructions for improving the soldiers' material conditions by reforming the canteens and the distribution of rations.

Scarcely had he returned to France in December 1749 than La Galissonière received a confidential mission which was to keep him in touch with Canadian affairs. Along with Étienne de Silhouette, the Maître des Requêtes, he was appointed a commissioner "for the conferences which are to be held in Paris to settle the two nations' possessions in America and their boundaries as well as to wind up the matters concerning prizes taken at sea." William Mildmay and William Shirley, the governor of Massachusetts, represented the king of England.

This commission's labours produced the *Mémoirs des commissaires du roi et de ceux de Sa Majesté britannique sur les possessions & les droits respectifs des deux couronnes en Amérique – avec les actes publics & pièces justificatives* (4v., Paris, 1755–57). Included is a report on France's colonies in North America which seems clearly to be La Galissonière's work. In this report he puts forth his theory on colonization, after displaying remarkable lucidity about British policy and about the potential riches of Canada, of which he had caught a glimpse in the short time at his disposal. Broadly described, his recommendation was to combine the strength of the soldier with that of the plough and to display force in order not to have to use it. Thus, when François Picquet sent three Indians to France in 1754, La Galissonière, then counsellor to the ministry of Marine, recommended to the minister that he "take advantage of every opportunity to show them the different kinds of troops, which will give them an idea of France's might to spread among their people without there being any need of recommending that they do so."

His ideas were naturally coloured by the mercantilism of his period, but he was also an idealist and for him colonization could not be a purely economic matter. He might allude to the profitability of the colonies in the long term, but more lofty considerations kept him from envisaging abandoning them, and he wrote: "reasons of honour, glory, and religion do not permit the giving up of an established colony, the abandonment to their own resources or rather to a nation hostile by inclination, upbringing, and religious principles, of the French who have gone there at the government's urging, in the expectation of being protected by it, and who merit that protection through their loyalty and attachment." These are traditional ideas based upon principles scattered through his predecessors' correspondence, but he deserves credit for synthesizing them and expressing them forcibly.

La Galissonière's return to France was the occasion of new honours. On 7 Feb. 1750 he was promoted rear-admiral. On 1 January of that year he had been put in charge of the Dépôt des Cartes et Plans de la Marine (where were stored the plans and maps of the Marine), an office which allowed him to give free rein to his inclination towards the sciences. Indeed, he was one of the first sailors of his time to take part in the scientific movement. He had connections with numerous well-known scientists such as Henri-Louis Duhamel Du Monceau, Bernard de Jussieu, Pierre-Charles and Louis-Guillaume Lemonnier, and was particularly interested in botany, nautical astronomy, and hydrography. Not content to carry on a regular correspondence with a few great minds, he always found a way to benefit from his professional assignments and to gather unknown plants or seeds to be sent to the Jardin du Roi. He had also created a botanical garden for himself at his château of Monnières, near Nantes, France. His stay in Canada had obviously offered vast scope to his scientific activity. He made skilful use of the officers under his orders to collect a great deal of information; thus Daniel-Hyacinthe-Marie LIÉNARD de Beaujeu, the commandant at Fort Niagara, and Paul-Louis DAZEMARD de Lusignan at Fort Saint-Frédéric were commissioned to draw up natural history inventories according to a model prepared by Gaultier, while the engineers Gaspard-Joseph Chaussegros de Léry at Detroit and Michel Chartier* de Lotbinière at Michilimackinac kept logs of astronomical and geographical observations. Finally, when he sent Céloron de Blainville into the Ohio region, he gave him the Jesuit Joseph-Pierre de Bonnecamps* as an assistant, to gather scientific information of all sorts.

As a sailor La Galissonière was naturally interested in astronomy and nautical instruments. Already in 1737, during the voyage of the *Héros*, he had been commissioned to study a new instrument, probably a quadrant. While head of the Dépôt de la Marine he organized three scientific missions: one by Joseph-Bernard de Chabert along the coasts of North America (1750–51), in which Newfoundland, Acadia, and Île Royale were charted accurately, the results being published in 1753; one by Gabriel de Bory along the coasts of Spain, Portugal, and Madeira; and finally, the great astronomical mission by Abbé Nicolas-Louis de La Caille to the Cape of Good Hope and the Indian Ocean, which resulted in the publication of an excellent catalogue of the stars of the southern hemisphere.

Always precise and meticulous, La Galissonière drew up the instructions for the officers himself and demanded of them a rigorous system for presenting the results of their observations. He never ceased guiding and encouraging the sailors and scientists interested in the activities of his Dépôt. These activities were responsible for his unanimous election as an associate at large of the Académie de Marine on 29 April 1752 and for his reception in the same capacity into the Académie des Sciences on 1 May.

But he was not allowed to forget completely that he was, after all, a sailor. It seems that during his stay at the Dépôt he played a role as adviser to the minister of Marine, Rouillé, about which details are unfortunately lacking. At the beginning of 1754 he was given command of the *Sage* and a squadron of three ships of the line and six frigates, with which to protect merchant ships against the Barbary corsairs. From May to October the ships sailed off the coasts of Spain

and Portugal before returning to Toulon. This campaign earned him a gratuity of 4,000 *livres* and promotion on 25 Sept. 1755 to the rank of lieutenant-general of the naval forces. La Galissonière was in fact always well treated financially; thus, before his return from Canada, he received a gratuity of 6,000 *livres*, plus 13,400 *livres* in repayment for various items.

The rising tension between France and England was to furnish La Galissonière the occasion to direct a large-scale operation. At the beginning of 1756, when war had not yet been declared, the Maréchal de Richelieu had proposed seizing Minorca, which the British had occupied since the treaty of Utrecht. The navy's part of the expedition was entrusted to La Galissonière who, with 12 ships of the line and five frigates, escorted the 176 transport ships carrying the landing force of 12,000 men. The convoy left Toulon on 10 April and arrived before Ciudadela on 18 April. The landing was without incident, no resistance being offered. On 24 April La Galissonière proceeded to cruise off Port Mahón (Mahón, Minorca), and allowed the five British ships which were there to escape. On 18 May appeared a British squadron of 13 ships of the line and four frigates under Admiral John BYNG. After two days of manoeuvring, the two forces lined up against each other and the combat was begun with the greatest prudence on both sides. La Galissonière was not audacious enough to exploit confusion that arose in the enemy's line, and after three hours of gun-fire the British withdrew towards Gibraltar, without any attempt at pursuit by the French. With no support, Minorca surrendered on 29 June, and the squadron returned to Toulon on 18 July.

The very modest success of 20 May 1756 created a stir in France out of all proportion to its real importance. Obsessed with the idea of protecting the troops who had been landed, La Galissonière had carried out with regrettable timidity instructions that were too cautious. The historian O.-J. Troude wrote: "Issue cannot be taken with this general officer for having succeeded in the mission entrusted to him before Mahón, but this success cannot be considered the result of a skilful or daring plan, and circumstances aided the commander-in-chief greatly." In reality the success was brought about essentially by Byng's lack of vigour, and he paid for it with his life.

But La Galissonière was ill. On 24 September he received permission to land and left for Fontainebleau, where the king was waiting to give him, it was said, the baton of a *maréchal* of France. Death decided otherwise.

"An officer of great intelligence and well

informed, who knows his profession well and is devoted to the service," we read in the roll of officers. "He is well liked and esteemed by the whole Marine," adds a note kept in his file. Amiable, level-headed, extremely honest, a humane leader, religious and easily given to moralizing, knowing his men well and concerned for their well-being, La Galissonière was undeniably an engaging personality who was liked by many people, some of whom no doubt facilitated an advancement of surprising rapidity. He reached the rank of rear-admiral without ever having been engaged in combat, and if he showed himself to be an enterprising administrator, lucid and shrewd, and a subtle diplomat, his conduct at sea was much less brilliant; in the only one of his campaigns in which he commanded large forces and had to fight, he revealed himself to be extremely timid and gave no proof of possessing the qualities of a great leader. Was he really "the most remarkable of the governors of New France in the 18th century," as one historian maintains? During his stay on this side of the Atlantic he displayed intense and intelligent activity, but that stay seems too brief to this author to justify such a favourable opinion, particularly since the policy that he tried to implement shows less originality than has been claimed.

ÉTIENNE TAILLEMITE

AN, Col., B, 87, 88, 89; C¹¹A, 88–93, 96; C¹¹B, 28; Marine, B², 328, f.891; 329, f.468; 331, ff.282, 375, 387; 351, f.238; 352, f.81; 354; B³, 529, 530; B⁴, 39, ff.241–380; 54, ff.22–71; 56, ff.123–76; 59, ff.4–27; 67, ff.66–86; 69; 70; 71; C¹, 165; 166, p.27; C⁷, 159 (dossier La Galissonière); 1JJ, 1, 2. Bibliothèque du Muséum National d'Histoire naturelle (Paris), MSS 293. "Correspondance de Mme Bégon" (Bonnault), APQ *Rapport, 1934-35*, 1–227. R.-V.-P. Castex, *Les idées militaires de la Marine du XVIIIᵉ siècle; de Ruyter à Suffren* (Paris, [1911]), 229–30. Lionel Groulx, *Roland-Michel Barrin de La Galissonière, 1693–1756* (Études biographiques canadiennes, Québec, 1970). Lacour-Gayet, *La marine militaire sous Louis XV* (1910). Roland Lamontagne, *La Galissonière et le Canada* (Montréal, Paris, 1962). Jacques Levron, *Un libertin fastueux: le maréchal de Richelieu* (Paris, 1971). Moufle d'Angerville, *Vie privée de Louis XV, ou principaux événemens, particularités et anecdotes de son règne* (4v., London, 1781), III, 66. Troude, *Batailles navales de la France*, I, 330ff., 434.

BARRON. *See* LUPIEN

BASTIDE, JOHN HENRY, military engineer, army officer; b. *c.* 1700; parents and place of birth unknown; d. probably 1770.

While still a boy John Henry Bastide was commissioned an ensign, on 23 Aug. 1711 (o.s.), in Colonel John Hill's Regiment of Foot. His commission was renewed in 1715, and on 25 Feb. 1717/18 he purchased the rank of lieutenant in Hill's regiment. For well over 20 years he remained a lieutenant, probably in part because of his decision to serve as a military engineer. The status of engineers had never been properly defined in the British army and they frequently found that their appointments were not recognized as regular military appointments. They had therefore to secure commissions in regiments in addition to their engineering warrants. An officer such as Bastide, who placed engineering over regimental duties, could not expect, and probably would not seek, rapid promotion.

Bastide served in Scotland for a time and from 1726 to 1739 directed "the works and fortifications at Jersey and Guernsey." In 1740 he was appointed chief engineer at Annapolis Royal, Nova Scotia, and went to his new post there. The major portion of his career was spent thenceforward in North America; he was especially involved with Nova Scotia fortifications and, for almost three decades, the French fortress at Louisbourg, Île Royale (Cape Breton Island). He drew a plan of Louisbourg as it was in 1734 which was accurate enough to be employed by 20th-century historians in their reconstruction of the fortress' history. It is not known, however, when or how he came to draw this plan.

Before the outbreak of war between England and France in 1744, Bastide, probably on orders from the Board of Ordnance, assessed the measures necessary to rebuild and protect Fort William and Mary (New Castle, N.H.). In 1743 and 1744 he also aided Governor William Shirley of Massachusetts in the construction of fortifications at Castle William (Boston), Marblehead, Cape Ann, and Falmouth in Casco Bay. Fortifications for Nova Scotian outposts such as Annapolis Royal also grew in importance, and when war came Bastide was sent there to shore up its defences. By July 1744, Governor Shirley reported, Bastide had abandoned plans to erect new fortifications and was concentrating on putting "the old ones into the best repair they are capable of." The fortifications proved adequate, for Annapolis Royal withstood several French and Indian attacks in the following months. Bastide was promoted "Engineer in Ordinary" in 1744 and held the military rank of lieutenant in Sowles' regiment.

He was back in Boston for the winter of 1744–45 and helped Governor Shirley to organize the provisioning of stores and arms, and to formulate plans, for an attack on Louisbourg. By the time the expedition, under William PEPPERRELL, was launched in April 1745, Bastide had returned to Annapolis Royal. He did not join the Louisbourg force until June for the French and Indians besieged Annapolis Royal again and it was only on 24 May that they "struck their Standard & raised the Siege of that Place. . . ." On 27 May Bastide sailed to join Pepperrell, reaching Gabarus Bay early in June. He arrived at a critical time, when the attack on Louisbourg was in danger of faltering, in part because of the inadequacy with which the New England force was handling the siege operations. The extent of Bastide's contribution in the short time between his arrival and the fall of the fortress on 17 June is uncertain. After the Louisbourg triumph, Pepperrell expressed serious reservations concerning Bastide's engineering abilities, describing him to the Duke of Newcastle in November as not "equal to the care of the Works of this important Fortress."

To make Louisbourg defensible Bastide carried out limited repairs. By late October 1745 he provided the Board of Ordnance with "a plan of his projections" for the restoration of the defences, which would have required an expenditure of £9,000 8s. 6d. The board, however, claimed it was a hasty submission which had not properly assessed the cost of colonial labour or the availability of materials. Despite this rebuke Bastide was warranted as chief engineer of Louisbourg on 16 Oct. 1745. He also was given a company in a new regiment, to be raised under the command of Governor Shirley. Bastide was a friend of the Boston merchant, Thomas Hancock, and, no doubt through Bastide's influence, Hancock and Charles Apthorp of Boston were made joint agents and suppliers for the fortress in December 1746. Capping this phase of Bastide's career was his appointment as a director of the corps of engineers on 2 Jan. 1748/49.

The return of Louisbourg to French control in 1749 apparently resulted in Bastide's assuming the post of chief engineer at Annapolis Royal, for in 1750 he was receiving "20s/ a day as Director, 20s/ as Chief at Annapolis, and 10s/ in lieu of a clerk." He was in England from August 1751 to October 1754, when he went to Minorca to serve as chief engineer at Port Mahón (Mahón). This appointment was ill-fated from its beginning, with Bastide being chosen over the nominee of General William Blakeney, the governor of the colony. In April 1756 the French attacked Minorca and the defences proved woefully inadequate [see BARRIN]; Bastide, by now apparently "too old for his post, and crippled with gout," was unable to cope with the assault. The

British capitulation on 29 June ended a fiasco in which several other officers showed negligence and incompetence [see BYNG]. Bastide then returned to England.

In 1757 the military status of the corps of engineers was recognized and its officers received military rank. On 14 May Bastide was promoted lieutenant-colonel. The following year he was appointed chief engineer in Jeffery Amherst*'s expedition against Louisbourg and returned to familiar ground. In May 1758 he was at Halifax preparing for the assault and by the end of June was with the British force before Louisbourg. Bastide differed with his commanding officer over the best approach for the attack. Amherst wrote that on 17 June he, Bastide, and two other officers reconnoitred the ground around Louisbourg and "Colonel Bastide was determined in his opinion of making Approaches by the Green Hill. . . ." General WOLFE's rapid progress in the area northwest of Louisbourg, however, caused the major British pressure to be exerted from this direction instead of from Green Hill, southwest of the town. At a later stage General Wolfe made serious charges concerning "the ignorance and inexperience of the Engineers," asserting "It is impossible to conceive how poorly the engineering business was carried on here." Bastide was proceeding slowly and methodically with the siege operations and no doubt the impetuous Wolfe directed many of his barbs at the aging engineer. In any case on 8 July "Col Bastide got a Contusion by a Musket Ball on his Boot which lay him up in the Gout." Major Patrick Mackellar* then took over the direction of the engineering phase of the attack.

The siege was ended on 27 July. Though Bastide's role in the final fall of Louisbourg was limited because of his sickness and advancing age, he at least had the consolation, on 28 Nov. 1760, of reporting to Amherst that the demolition of its fortifications and harbour defences had been completed. William Pitt had ordered Amherst to take this action as it was no longer "expedient to maintain [the fortress], at so great an Expense."

Little is known concerning the last decade of Bastide's life. In February 1761 he was made a major-general and soon received orders to supervise the construction of fortifications at Halifax; he was engaged in this work until July 1762. At that time it was feared that Halifax was about to be attacked and Bastide took a major role in arranging emergency defence measures. The final result was a system of rough field works made of earth and sod. Bastide returned to England in October 1762. He was promoted

Bâtard

lieutenant-general in April 1770 and appears in the War Office list of officers for that year but not in 1771; in all probability he died in 1770. A memorial of 1766 says that he had three sons and two daughters.

WILLIAM G. GODFREY

Harvard University, Baker Library, Thomas Hancock papers (contain letters of Bastide); Harvard College Library, MS Can 62, bMS Can 3 (Bastide MSS). PAC, MG 11, Nova Scotia A, 27, pp.14–15; MG 18, L4, pkt.65, p.23; O9; MG 21, H10. PANS, RG 1, 12; 13; 19, nos.7, 8. PRO, CO 5/53, ff.176, 182–92v; 5/60, ff.25–25v, 141–41v, 143, 147–47v, 149, 151; 5/62, ff.282, 367 (copies in PAC, MG 11).

Amherst, *Journal* (Webster). *Army list, 1769*, 3; *1770*, 3, 176; *1771. Correspondence of William Pitt* (Kimball). *Correspondence of William Shirley* (Lincoln), I. Mass. Hist. Soc. *Coll.*, 6th ser., X (1899), 238, 239, 256, 302, 303. *N.S. Archives, I*, 702–6. [William Pote], *The journal of Captain William Pote, jr., during his captivity in the French and Indian war from May 1745, to August 1747*, ed. J. F. Hurst and Victor Paltsits (New York, 1896), xvi, 173. PRO, *Acts of P.C., Col., 1720–45*, 731–33; *JTP, 1741/42–1749*, 205. *English army lists* (Dalton), VI, 79, 80, 389. Dalton, *George the first's army*, I, 300.

W. T. Baxter, *The house of Hancock; business in Boston, 1724–1775* (New York, 1965). A. J. Kerry and W. A. McDill, *The history of the corps of Royal Canadian Engineers* (2v., Ottawa, 1962–66), I. J. C. Long, *Lord Jeffrey Amherst: a soldier of the king* (New York, 1933). McLennan, *Louisbourg*. Harry Piers, *The evolution of the Halifax fortress, 1749–1928*, ed. G. M. Self and P. R. Blakeley (PANS pub., 7, Halifax, 1947). Whitworth Porter, *History of the corps of Royal Engineers* (3v., London, New York, 1889–1915), I. Rawlyk, *Yankees at Louisbourg*. G. A. Wood, *William Shirley, governor of Massachusetts, 1741–56* (New York, 1920).

BÂTARD, ÉTIENNE (Anthony), Micmac from Miramichi (N.B.); d. probably in Nova Scotia sometime between 1754 and 1760.

Étienne Bâtard was a Micmac warrior who was involved in many adventures during the Anglo-Micmac war of 1749–53. Abbé Pierre MAILLARD's "Lettre . . . sur les missions micmaques" suggests that Bâtard had taken part around 1740 in a "theological" discussion at Port-Toulouse (St Peters, N.S.) between the merchant Edward How and a group of Micmacs. The Micmacs were said to have been shocked at that time by How's remarks, and the latter is supposed to have escaped rough treatment thanks only to the presence of mind of the interpreter Barthélemy PETITPAS.

In September 1750, when the French were trying to prevent the establishment of Fort Lawrence (near Amherst, N.S.) and were building

Fort Beauséjour not far away, the Micmacs from the various regions of Acadia gathered in the neighbourhood of Beauséjour and carried out raids against the English. On 15 October (N.S.) a group of Micmacs disguised as French officers called Edward How to a conference. This trap, organized by Étienne Bâtard, gave him the opportunity to wound How seriously, and How died five or six days later, according to Captain La Vallière (probably Louis Leneuf* de La Vallière), the only eye-witness.

On 15 July 1751, after a series of skirmishes, Saint-Ours (perhaps FRANÇOIS-XAVIER), the officer commanding the Indians' movements, sent them away from Beauséjour. But Bâtard and a few confederates remained near the fort, where they were surprised in discussions with some English officers who "received them very well, gave them gifts, and tried by all means to make peace with them." La Vallière then vainly suggested to his superiors that the traitors be arrested; Bâtard left Beauséjour in complete liberty on 27 July.

He reappears in 1753, as a participant in the punitive expedition led by Jean-Baptiste COPE, another Micmac, against some soldiers from Halifax. Bâtard succeeded in saving Anthony Casteel, the only survivor of the group, from the other Micmacs, who, having become drunk, were preparing to murder him. Bâtard is then lost from sight; his name is not on any of the peace treaties concluded after 1760 between the various Micmac tribes and the English authorities in Halifax. Presumably he died sometime between 1754 and 1760.

The accounts of How's death are far from agreeing: Albert David has called attention to no fewer than nine, which contain considerable contradiction. Numerous English-language historians, particularly Beamish Murdoch* and Francis Parkman*, maintain the possibility of Abbé Jean-Louis Le Loutre*'s involvement in the incident, but this interpretation has been vigorously criticized by Henri-Raymond Casgrain* and Édouard Richard. The historian David had two obvious aims in attempting to reconstruct Edward How's murder: to prove Le Loutre's innocence, and to minimize How's importance. Although it is strongly slanted, the analysis he makes of the nine accounts leads to the firm conclusion that Bâtard was indeed How's murderer. Since no document coming directly from the Micmacs exists, no valid suggestion of Bâtard's motives can be made. Nor can Abbé Le Loutre's participation, direct or indirect, in this affair be affirmed or denied.

MICHELINE D. JOHNSON

AN, Col., C^{11A}, 97, ff.16–34; C^{11B}, 29, ff.130–31. ASQ, Lettres, R, 190. [Anthony Casteel], "Anthony Casteel's journal," *Coll. doc. inédits Canada et Amérique*, II (1889), 111–26. [Louis Leneuf de La Vallière?], "Journal de ce qui s'est passé à Chicnitou et autres parties des frontières de l'Acadie depuis le 15 septembre 1750 jusqu'au 28 juillet 1751," PAC *Rapport, 1905*, II, pt.III, 324–30. [Pierre Maillard], "Lettre de M. l'abbé Maillard sur les missions de l'Acadie et particulièrement sur les missions micmaques," *Les soirées canadiennes; recueil de littérature nationale* (Québec), III (1863), 289–426 (*see* p.405). "Memoire du Canada," APQ *Rapport, 1924–25*, 103. *N.S. Archives, I*, 194–96, 210, 394. Pichon, *Lettres et mémoires*, 239–45. PAC *Report, 1894*, 181.

Casgrain, *Un pèlerinage au pays d'Évangéline*, 43, 505–7; *Une seconde Acadie*, 230–32. E. A. Hutton, "The Micmac Indians of Nova Scotia to 1834" (unpublished MA thesis, Dalhousie University, Halifax, 1961). Johnson, *Apôtres ou agitateurs*, 105–28. Murdoch, *History of Nova-Scotia*, II, 191–94. Parkman, *Montcalm and Wolfe* (1884), I, 123–24. Richard, *Acadie* (D'Arles), II, 85–121. J. C. Webster, *The forts of Chignecto; a study of the eighteenth century conflict between France and Great Britain in Acadia* (n.p., 1930), 32–33. H.-R. Casgrain, "Coup d'oeil sur l'Acadie avant la dispersion de la colonie française," *Canada-Français*, 1re sér., I (1888), 114–34. Albert David, "L'affaire How d'après les documents contemporains," *Revue de l'Université d'Ottawa*, VI (1936), 440–68. R. O. MacFarlane, "British Indian policy in Nova Scotia to 1760," *CHR*, XIX (1938), 154–57.

BAUDOIN, GERVAIS, surgeon; b. and baptized 3 Aug. 1686 at Quebec, son of Gervais Baudouin*, surgeon-major of Quebec, and Anne Auber; brother of Michel BAUDOUIN; d. 30 June 1752 and buried 2 July at Quebec.

Gervais Baudoin studied at the seminary of Quebec; then, following in his father's footsteps, he practised as a surgeon. In 1712 he vainly sought the position of surgeon-major of Quebec; his father had held this position from 1695 till his death in 1700. In 1716 Gervais was residing on Rue Sous-le-Fort, where he had been living since September 1714; indeed, a clause in his marriage contract, signed 2 Sept. 1714 before the notary Pierre Rivet* Cavelier and agreed to by his mother, called upon the latter to lodge and maintain the newly married couple until the following spring. In 1722 he was a churchwarden of the parish of Notre-Dame de Québec.

Baudoin occupied no other public office and devoted himself entirely, it seems, to his profession as a surgeon. He took a few cases to court, two of which were appealed to the Conseil Supérieur. His first lawsuit, from 1730 to 1732, was against his brother Louis and his sister Marie-Anne, widow of Jean-Baptiste Hertel* de Rouville, and concerned a house that had been a legacy from their father. From 1741 to 1744 he again went to court about the inheritance, this time with his sister Marie-Anne, against the claims of Henri Dusautoy who had married Marie-Anne Roussel, Louis Baudouin's widow. From 1744 till his death Gervais Baudoin lived on Rue de la Montagne, where his surgeon's consulting-room was located.

On 5 Sept. 1714 he had married Marie-Thérèse Guyon Fresnay, who bore him six daughters and five sons; one of his sons, Charles-Louis, became a priest, and three of his daughters entered religious orders. His second wife was Marthe Marcoux, by whom he had one daughter; when the marriage contract was drawn up before the notary Jacques-Nicolas PINGUET de Vaucour, 20 Nov. 1738, the wife declared she did not know how to sign her name.

Gervais Baudoin died 30 June 1752; on 5 July, three days after his burial, the notary Claude BAROLET began the inventory of their joint estate at the widow's request. Their possessions in furniture, dishes, linen, and other belongings, with the exception of "the bed and bedding belonging to the aforementioned deceased and his widow, which she has claimed by virtue of the clause inserted in her marriage contract," were appraised at about 1,100 *livres*. In addition there were two houses, on Rue Saint-Pierre and Rue de la Montagne, the dispensary and its books valued at 245 *livres* by the apothecary Jean-Jard BOIS-PINEAU, as well as "surgical instruments and equipment" valued at 259 *livres* by the surgeon André ARNOUX. The estate Gervais Baudoin left behind him was divided up on 25 Aug. 1752; it was a meagre fortune indeed that his profession as a surgeon, which he seems to have practised all his life, had enabled him to build up.

MICHEL PAQUIN

ANQ, Greffe de R.-C. Barolet, 2 janv. 1748, 5 juill., 25 août 1752; Greffe de J.-N. Pinguet de Vaucour, 20 nov. 1738; Greffe de Pierre Rivet Cavelier, 2 sept. 1714. "Correspondance de Vaudreuil," APQ *Rapport, 1947–48*, 137. Albertus Martin, "La famille Beaudoin," *BHR*, XL (1934), 693–700. *Recensement de Québec, 1716* (Beaudet), 54, 58. "Recensement de Québec, 1744" (APQ *Rapport*), 192. P.-V. Charland, "Notre-Dame de Québec : le nécrologe de la crypte," *BRH*, XX (1914), 214. Godbout, "Nos ancêtres," APQ *Rapport, 1953–54*, 507. P.-G. Roy, *Inv. contrats de mariage*, I; *Inv. jug. et délib., 1717–1760*, I, II, IV; *Inv. ord. int.*, II, 164; *Inv. testaments*, I, 34. Taillemite, *Inventaire analytique, série B*, I, 215. Ahern, *Notes pour l'histoire de la médecine*, 42–43. Amédée Gosselin, *L'instruction au Canada*, 413, 433.

Baudouin

BAUDOUIN (Baudoin), MICHEL, priest, Jesuit missionary; b. 16 March 1691 at Quebec to Gervais Baudouin* and Anne Auber; brother of Gervais BAUDOIN; d. 1768 at New Orleans.

Michel Baudouin entered the Jesuit noviciate at Bordeaux, France, in October or December 1713. By this time he had gone through college and had completed two years of philosophy. Whether he had done these studies in France or in his native Quebec is not known. In his early Jesuit years he made a fair impression as moderately capable. He had a good mind, common sense, and good health. Homesick perhaps for Canada, he seemed quiet and not over cheerful.

In 1715 he began teaching at Angoulême, and over the following two years advanced, according to the custom, with the same boys grade by grade. In the school years 1719–21 he taught the higher grades at Pau, and then spent a year each in the same work at La Rochelle and Fontenay-le-Comte (dept. of Vendée). He began his pre-ordination theological studies in 1722 at Poitiers and was ordained a priest in 1725. As 1726 drew to a close he was at Marennes, well into tertianship, the young Jesuit priest's year of spiritual renewal. After one more year of teaching, this time at Luçon (dept. of Vendée), he was assigned in 1728 to the missions in Louisiana. There, in 1731, he pronounced the final vows of a Jesuit spiritual coadjutor.

For two decades he ministered to the Choctaws, whom he came to know "perfectly," as Governor Bienville [LE MOYNE] wrote in praise of him. Baudouin, who annually accompanied the Choctaw leaders to Mobile (Ala.) to receive their gifts from the French, was a major source of information about the Choctaw nation. Drawn into the diplomacy of the enduring Franco-Choctaw confrontation with the English-Chickasaw alliance, Baudouin must have realized that his life was always in danger.

In 1751 he was named superior of all the Louisiana missions, and therefore took up residence in the colony's capital. He served in this role for almost a decade. Louisiana was in the diocese of Quebec and, against the will of the Jesuits and much to the displeasure of the Capuchins, Bishop Pontbriand [DUBREIL] of Quebec had since 1741 insisted that the Jesuit superior in New Orleans be diocesan vicar-general in Louisiana over Jesuit and Capuchin missionaries. Baudouin, a benevolent conciliator, had to suffer through years of quietly abrasive controversy that was settled only by the departure of the Jesuits from the colony.

When the Jesuits were suppressed in France, an imitation of the home-country court procedure was carried out in Louisiana in 1763 by the Conseil Supérieur. Then the missionaries among the the Indians were brought to New Orleans; all Jesuits in the colony were ordered to become secular priests and to return to France. The septuagenarian Baudouin was permitted to remain in New Orleans since by this time his native Canada was held by the English and he had no family to receive him in France. To him as to other former Jesuit missionaries, the French government accorded a pension drawn on confiscated Jesuit property. He lived for a time as a guest of planters Jean-Charles de Pradel and Étienne Boré, and also of the Capuchins. In July 1766, "indisposed of body, but sound of mind, memory and understanding," Baudouin was called forth from obscurity to give a deposition in New Orleans concerning former governor Louis Billouart de Kerlérec as part of the testimony in the interminable *affaire de la Louisiane*.

The date of Baudouin's death is unknown. Bishop Jean-Olivier Briand*, writing to Sébastien-Louis Meurin* in April 1767, seems to have erred in reporting Baudouin dead, for in France as late as the end of April 1768 his death was unknown at court and among the syndics handling Jesuit affairs, who were planning to write to him. In the light of an entry in the financial record book of St Louis parish, New Orleans, one can conclude that Baudouin died shortly before Easter 1768; he was buried in the old parish church.

According to a variety of witnesses testifying throughout his life, he was a dedicated, gentle man who served God, country, Frenchman, and Indian.

C. E. O'NEILL

AN, Col., C¹¹ᴬ, 99, f.476; C¹³ᴬ, 15, ff.9, 153v; 16, f.207; 17, ff.39–43; 44, ff.470, 739–49; D²ᴰ, 10. ANDQ, Registre des baptêmes, mariages et sépultures, 27 mars 1691. ARSI, Catalogi Aquitaniae (1714–30); Catalogi Franciae (1730–61). Louisiana State Museum Archives (New Orleans), 62/17, 3 Sept. 1763; 63/23, 17 Aug. 1763. St Louis Cathedral Archives (New Orleans), St Louis parish financial record book, 1756–1801, p.102. *New régime, 1765–67* (Alvord and Carter), 561. François-Philibert Watrin, "Banissement des Jésuites de la Louisiane," in *JR* (Thwaites), LXX, 212–301. Delanglez, *French Jesuits in Louisiana*. O'Neill, *Church and state in Louisiana*. Rochemonteix, *Les Jésuites et la N.-F. au XVIIIᵉ siècle*, I, 294, 331. A. E. Jones, "Le père jésuite Michel Baudouin," *BRH*, XXIV (1918), 30–32.

BAUDRY (Beaudry), *dit* **Saint-Martin (Baudry Desbuttes, Baudry Soulard), JEAN-BAPTISTE,** gunsmith; baptized 3 July 1684 at Trois-Rivières, son of Guillaume Baudry*, *dit* Des Butes, gunsmith and silversmith, and Jeanne Soullard; m. on 8 Oct. 1721 Marie-Louise, daughter of the armourer Nicolas Doyon, in Quebec; d. 20 Nov. 1755 at Detroit.

In using numerous surnames Jean-Baptiste Baudry, it seems, wanted to distinguish himself from a namesake who lived at the same period and who also practised the armourer's craft. Through his father, mother, and wife he belonged to three of the most important families of craftsmen in ironwork in Canada. His paternal grandfather, Urbain Baudry, *dit* La Marche, was a maker of edge tools and blacksmith at Trois-Rivières, and four of his brothers, Claude-Charles, Jean, Urbain, and René were also armourers.

Jean-Baptiste Baudry lived at a time when craftsmen formed an important social group in New France. From 1700 to 1750 there were numerous marriages among members of this group; the Baudry family did not escape this tendency, for Jean-Baptiste, his brothers, and his sisters chose their spouses from this milieu. Like all the other armourers, whose craft required frequent travel, Jean-Baptiste Baudry made several trips to work in the forts and trading posts. More particularly he travelled between Quebec and Detroit. It was at Detroit that in 1735 he acquired a piece of land, and it was there that he died on 20 Nov. 1755. His numerous descendants, who for a century continued to repair and make arms, are still known by the name of Des Buttes in Detroit and in Essex County, Ontario.

Although the craftsmen of the Baudry family had specialized above all in ironwork, they also left some pieces of silverware. Among the latter we are indebted to them for some consecrated vessels that are preserved in the Musée du Québec and in the church of Saint-Étienne de Beaumont (Que.).

JEAN-CLAUDE DUPONT

AJQ, Registre d'état civil, Notre-Dame de Québec, 23 août 1733. Godbout, "Nos ancêtres," APQ *Rapport*, 1953–55, 510–12. P.-G. Roy, *Inv. jug. et délib., 1717–1760*, IV, 101, 106; *Inv. ord. int.*, II, 212. Tanguay, *Dictionnaire*, I, 31; II, 152; III, 363. Télesphore St-Pierre, *Histoire des Canadiens du Michigan et du comté d'Essex, Ontario* (Montréal, 1895), 157. Traquair, *Old silver of Quebec*, 5, 26.

BAYNE, DANIEL, merchant, trader; b. *c.* 1730, possibly in Ross-shire, Scotland; d. 1769 in London, England.

Daniel Bayne was one of the British merchants who settled in Quebec City after the conquest. He entered into a partnership with another Scottish merchant, William Brymer, and on 26 April 1763 Governor James Murray* granted them for four years the fishing post of Cape Charles on the Labrador coast. Another Quebec Scot, William Lead, was given charge of the post, and a crew of French Canadians was sent up for the winter seal fishery.

In the meantime, however, the royal proclamation of 1763 placed the Labrador coast under the governor of Newfoundland and within the fishing laws of Newfoundland. In the interests of "an open and free fishery" fishing places could be held only from year to year, with preference given to fishers sending out ships annually from England.

Daniel Bayne and his partner felt the effects of the new régime only in the summer of 1765. In August the governor of Newfoundland, Hugh Palliser*, visited Chateau Bay, a few leagues southwest of Cape Charles. He was anxious to conciliate the Eskimos and to prevent illicit trade by the French in their old preserves. Hearing of the post at Cape Charles, the governor had Lead and his French Canadian helper seized, with their French goods and firearms. He ordered them to leave Labrador, and issued a proclamation barring colonials from the coast, under threat of dire punishment. William Lead set off for Quebec City, meeting at Mingan the sloop *Esquimaux* which Bayne and Brymer had just fitted out for the next winter's seal fishery "at very great expense." The master of the sloop turned back to Quebec City, where vessel and cargo were sold in October, at a considerable loss. The infuriated partners then went to England, determined upon indemnification "by the generous honest hearts of our peers."

Bayne and Brymer petitioned the Board of Trade for reinstatement and payment of damages of £5000. With other similarly aggrieved Quebec merchants, they declared their grants valid, and Palliser's actions "illegal, oppressive, and prejudicial to the rights and privileges which the inhabitants of Quebec are entitled to, as British subjects." They claimed exclusive land grants were necessary for the seal fishery, since the equipment had to be especially built for each locality.

An exasperated Palliser insisted that he had repeatedly told the merchants any losses from dispossession of lands would be made good. He justified his actions in 1765 by the proclamation of 1763 and his instructions to uphold the laws providing for an open and free fishery. The "illegal" grants of Murray would promote only the interests of a few "smuggling settlers," whereas his own regulations had opened up a new and extensive field, to the great increase of the fishery, trade, and seamen of Great Britain.

In the next four years, lengthy petitions and memorials passed back and forth between the Board of Trade, the Privy Council, and the Court of King's Bench. The government backed Palliser but eventually realized the legality of the merchants' grants could not be challenged successfully. In February 1770 the two parties settled privately: Palliser delivered £600 to the merchants, and was repaid by royal warrant.

For Daniel Bayne the settlement came too late: he died in London in the summer of 1769. A bachelor, he left his estate to the sons of his uncle John Bayne. William Brymer, now in business in Lombard Street, was an executor.

The persistence of Bayne and his partner in asserting their claims brought home to the British government the interest of the Quebec merchants in securing permanent rights of property and residence on the Labrador coast. In 1774 that coast was reunited with Quebec, a recognition that the interests of Canadians were not to be subordinated to "imperial" interests. Bayne and Brymer had demonstrated how determined protest could eventually bring to terms even a proud colonial governor, and exact compensation for injuries done to the rights of property.

WILLIAM H. WHITELEY

BM, Add. MSS, 35915 (Hardwick papers). PANL, Nfld., Dept. of Colonial Secretary, Letter books, III, 1759–65. PRO, CO 194/16, 194/18, 194/26, 194/27, 195/15; KB 122, roll 347, m.672: "Judgement roll," Easter, 8 Geo. III; PC 2/112–14; Prob. 11/951, p.301. *In the matter of the boundary between the Dominion of Canada and the colony of Newfoundland in the Labrador peninsula* (12v., London, 1926–27), III. Neatby, *Quebec*. G. O. Rothney, "The case of Bayne and Brymer, an incident in the early history of Labrador," *CHR*, XV (1934), 264–75. W. H. Whiteley, "The establishment of the Moravian mission in Labrador and British policy, 1763–83, " *CHR*, XLV (1964), 29–50.

BAZIL, LOUIS, merchant, militia officer; b. 1695 in La Rochelle, France, son of Louis Bazil and Marie-Madeleine Moreau; m. 13 Jan. 1721, at Quebec, Charlotte Duroy; buried 20 Feb. 1752 in Quebec.

At the time of his marriage Louis Bazil was engaged in the trade with La Rochelle. There is evidence from the later 1720s that he traded to Martinique and Île Royale (Cape Breton Island) and that he may have built and owned a small trading vessel.

In 1736, perhaps because of good connections, Bazil was granted the concession of a Labrador sealing station at Chateau Bay on the Strait of Belle Isle. Lacking the capital necessary to develop the post, he formed a partnership with three other merchants, François HAVY, Jean LEFEBVRE, and Louis FORNEL, who agreed, in exchange for a two-thirds interest in the post, to contribute all the needed investment, including Bazil's one-third share, which would eventually be repaid them from his portion of the profits. Because of high costs and the marginal success of the seal hunt, the company showed a deficit by 1744, and Bazil was unable to pay his share. The sympathetic governor and intendant, Charles de BEAUHARNOIS and Hocquart*, attempted to help Bazil salvage something from his affairs by working out a compromise between him and his partners. But Maurepas, minister of Marine, disdained this coddling, and in 1745 the concession was allowed to expire.

Other incidents suggest that in the 1740s Bazil's financial position was becoming increasingly precarious. In 1742 a creditor thought it wise to secure on the more solid basis of a mortgage a loan given Bazil the previous year for a promissory note. A small interest in a sealing station at Saint-Modet on the Labrador coast, which Bazil had already farmed out for ready cash, was ceded to the holder of another promissory note dating from 1729. In 1743 Bazil and his wife sold two pieces of land. Indeed, the much-beset merchant complained to the local authorities of his economic distress, which he described as "only too well known." His name often appears in judicial records, which would seem to bear out Louis Fornel's assertion that he was one who "besides being insolvent was prone to be litigious."

In 1749 or earlier, Louis Bazil was saved from indigence by the gift of a writership in the Quebec offices of the Domaine d'Occident. A widower since 1745, in 1751 he rented out part of his house in Rue de Meulles to a tavern-keeper; the following year, in February, he died in the apartment he had kept for himself. The house, which was the only item of value in his estate, was sold to pay his creditors. Through the career of this unsuccessful businessman we glimpse both the humanity and the encumbering favouritism inherent in the *Étatisme* of the old régime.

DALE MIQUELON

AN, Col., B, 81, f.271; C¹¹ᴬ, 81, ff.77, 82, 85; 83, f.261; 85, f.21; E, 21 (dossier Louis Bazil); Section Outre-Mer, G¹, 462 (mémoire pour la baye des Chateaux, 17 oct. 1742). ANQ, Greffe de Jacques Barbel, 5 janv. 1721; Greffe de C.-H. Du Laurent, 6 mars 1742, 18 sept. 1743, 12 oct. 1748, 26 avril 1749, 29 févr., 21 avril 1752,

3 avril 1753; Greffe de J.-C. Louet, 4 mai 1727, 25 nov. 1729; Greffe de J.-N. Pinguet de Vaucour, 15 sept. 1738, 8 nov. 1741; Greffe de François Rageot, 9 oct. 1742; NF, Coll. de pièces jud. et not., 1713. *Inv. de pièces du Labrador* (P.-G. Roy), I, 50, 51, 56, 60, 90, 151, 293; II, 201, 229. P.-G. Roy, *Inv. jug. et délib., 1717–1760*; *Inv. ord. int.* Tanguay, *Dictionnaire*.

BEAN, JOHN, HBC sailor and explorer; fl. 1751–57.

John Bean served as a second mate on the Hudson's Bay Company ship *Prince Rupert* for three voyages to Hudson Bay between 1751 and 1753, and was then appointed master of the *Churchill* sloop in the bay at an annual salary of £40. He reached Prince of Wales Fort (Churchill, Man.) at a time when interest in the possibility of finding a northwest passage along the west coast of the bay had revived with Indian reports of a great inlet, "Kish-Stack-Ewen," whose entrance reputedly lay in latitude 64° – about the same latitude as Chesterfield Inlet, discovered but never fully explored by the private expedition of 1746–47 under William Moor's command.

Since 1750 the London committee had instructed its sloopmaster at Churchill to explore the coast during his summer trading voyage north among the Eskimos, but not until Bean's first voyage in 1755 was any serious attempt made to carry out these orders. In 1755 and again in 1756 Bean made as thorough an examination of the Winchester Inlet and Daly Bay region as the short navigational season allowed, but he overlooked Chesterfield Inlet, which lay slightly south of the area where he began his search. By the end of the 1756 season Bean was convinced that "this fly away River Resembells old Brazill viz not to be seen but by some chimerical persons," and his final voyage in the company's employ in 1757 was a routine trading one. Though unsuccessful in his quest, Bean's detailed journals show him to have been a courageous seaman who carried out his exploration of a dangerous coast, often in bad weather, regardless of the fact that he sailed without a consort. At a time when the HBC was often criticized for its lethargy in exploration Bean's brief career showed that among its employees were men of resource and enterprise.

GLYNDWR WILLIAMS

[Bean's journals for 1755–57 are in HBC Arch. B.42/a/45, 47, and 49. Details of his service are in HBC Arch. A.1/38–39. The search for a passage north of Churchill is mentioned in HBC Arch. A.11/13, and in B.42/a/39–48. A brief description of Bean's voyages and their background is given in Williams, *British search for the northwest passage*. G.W.]

BEAUBOIS, NICOLAS-IGNACE DE, priest, Jesuit missionary; b. 15 Oct. 1689 at Orléans, France; d. 13 Jan. 1770 near Avignon, France.

Admitted to the Society of Jesus 29 Oct. 1706, Nicolas-Ignace de Beaubois made his noviciate in Paris. After two years he remained in Paris to add to the meagre philosophical studies he had begun before entering the order. Then he went to Rennes to teach in the fall school term of 1710; for three years he moved up a grade with the same group of boys, as was the custom. After another year of teaching, this time in Alençon, he began his pre-ordination theological studies at La Flèche. Ordained in 1717, he remained at La Flèche for the usual fourth year of theology. He was assigned to the Canadian mission in 1719, and seems to have spent a short while in Quebec before beginning his apostolate among the Illinois Indians in 1721. On 2 Feb. 1723, at Kaskaskia (Ill.), he pronounced the four solemn vows of the professed Jesuit.

After 1717 the Illinois country was no longer directly under the civil and military jurisdiction of Quebec, but rather lay within the territory of the newly named commandant of Louisiana, who would reside in New Orleans, seat not only of the government but also of the administration appointed by the proprietary Compagnie des Indes. The Jesuit order, recognizing the development of the Mississippi valley and its missions, designated the area as a distinct mission district – *Missio Ludovisiana* – within the diocese of Quebec.

Named superior of the new jurisdiction in 1724, Beaubois travelled to France to seek more men and greater support for his mission. He proved himself a tough negotiator in dealings with the Compagnie des Indes, which by charter was supposed to provide financially for parishes and missions in its monopoly colony. Typical of the brusquely vigorous debater that he was, Beaubois broke off negotiations with a resounding declaration that if the gentlemen of the Compagnie des Indes truly desired to have Jesuits in Louisiana they would not have made the propositions they had put forward.

Finally, the company administrators and Jesuit authorities (including Beaubois) agreed upon a contract on 20 Feb. 1726. The company pledged fixed sums *per annum*, and contributions for travel and supplies. The new contract authorized the Jesuits to open a house in New Orleans and to have a plantation near the city; however, they were to exercise no ministry in the city or surrounding area except with the consent of the Capuchins, whose field this was by contract with the company. Before leaving France, Beaubois arranged to have Ursuline nuns receive a pledge of financial aid from the Compagnie des Indes for the establishment of a girls' school in New Orleans, the first in the Mississippi valley.

Beaubois returned to Louisiana on the ship bringing the newly appointed commandant of Louisiana, Étienne de Périer. When they arrived in New Orleans in March 1727, they had established mutual respect and friendship that would develop through their years amid the colony's political factionalism. Louisiana's officialdom was perennially divided into Bienvillists and anti-Bienvillists. The former, the supporters of the Le Moyne brothers, were drawn frequently from the ranks of the *gens d'épée*. The latter, the officials of the Compagnie des Indes, were often from the bureaux of the *gens de plume*. The leader of the anti-Bienvillists was commissary Jacques de La Chaise, with whom Beaubois, an admirer of Bienville [LE MOYNE], clashed almost from their first meeting.

Périer keenly understood the tragic flaw in Beaubois's character. The Jesuit superior was, he judged, a dynamic, far-sighted leader, but he was "too frank," he lacked tact. Gilles-Bernard Raguet, the priest whom the Compagnie des Indes employed in its Paris office to supervise mission affairs, sketched this thumbnail portrait of Beaubois: "He has all the courage of his [Jesuit] Order; it's a pity he has not its prudence." Beaubois's fellow Jesuits likewise respected his enterprising intelligence but regretted his overconfident precipitousness.

Beaubois's zeal, looked at unsympathetically, seemed to be ambition. When he had passed through New Orleans in 1724, he had made disparaging remarks about the religious and educational situation in the town. His attitude implied that he could and would do better than the Capuchins. His prompt purchase of a house showed how cocksure he was that he would receive authorization to set up his Jesuit depot in New Orleans, whence he would send men and ship goods upriver to the Illinois country. Raphaël de Luxembourg, the Capuchin pastor of New Orleans, was apprehensive over possible friction between the two robes. Only the most discreet behaviour on Beaubois's part could have allayed the Capuchin's fears. Instead, when the newly arrived Ursulines elected Beaubois as their spiritual guide in 1727, he took it for granted that Father Raphaël must acquiesce.

Bishop Saint-Vallier [La Croix*] of Quebec named Beaubois a vicar general in 1727, but did the intended jurisdiction extend only over the Jesuits in the Louisiana missions? Death claimed Saint-Vallier in December before the question was settled. In any case, a tragic controversy had been launched, Capuchin fears of Jesuit domination were implanted, and the bumptious Beaubois was summarily recalled to France when Coadjutor Bishop Mornay, himself a Capuchin, succeeded Saint-Vallier as bishop of Quebec. The Compagnie des Indes was only too pleased to join the bishop in opposition to the strong-willed Jesuit negotiator tainted with Bienvillist ties. Beaubois, reacting with apparent nonchalance, took graceful leave of the colony, exchanging courteous farewells with La Chaise and the Capuchins.

Arriving in Paris in July 1728 Beaubois launched with tongue and pen a lengthy justification of his conduct, and looked forward to reinstatement. He disclaimed any canonical intrusion upon Capuchins. He proved the falsehood of a weak calumny against his character. He harped upon the antipathy of the directors of the Compagnie des Indes toward Bienville, which had led them to hate him also, "rendered criminal" because of his friendship for Bienville.

A reversal of fortunes followed the return of Louisiana to direct royal administration in January 1731. The company agents would go; its commissary would be replaced by a royal financial commissary. The commandant would be replaced by a full-fledged governor, and by mid-1732 none other than Bienville would be called to the governorship. In October 1731 Minister of Marine Maurepas informed Mornay of the government's intention to have Beaubois return to Louisiana as superior of the Jesuit missions "in a spirit of peace and reconciliation." Cardinal Fleury and Maurepas ignored the vigorous protest of Mornay, who threatened to interdict Beaubois if he should enter the diocese of Quebec.

The reinstated Jesuit superior arrived in Louisiana in March 1732 on his best behaviour. No conflict arose between him and Father Raphaël. Amid inter-order peace the few missionaries of each robe were busy about their apostolic work when in late 1732 Mornay sent out to Louisiana the threatened interdict. Reluctantly Raphaël notified Beaubois of the bishop's censure, whereby Beaubois and all Jesuits subject to his jurisdiction were forbidden to perform priestly functions as long as he remained in Louisiana. The angry complaints of Governor Bienville and commissary Edme-Gatien Salmon, annoyed at this disruption of peace, reached Versailles at a time (August 1733) when the court had little regard for the bishop who had never crossed the ocean to his diocese of Quebec. When Coadjutor Bishop Dosquet* came from Quebec for a visit in France, the court's pressure on Mornay increased. In September 1733 Mornay resigned. Out in the colony Vicar-General Raphaël, on his deathbed in February 1734, lifted the interdict. Subsequently, in the summer of 1734, Bishop Dosquet, ill disposed because of a dispute over whether Jesuits or Seminary priests should have the pastorate at Fort de Chartres (near Prairie du Rocher, Ill.), reconfirmed the interdict against Beaubois. Rather than continue in the paralysing tension, Beaubois concurred with his second (and final) recall by his Jesuit superiors. Maurepas, while acknowledging Beaubois's talent, judged that his removal would bring greater tranquillity to the church in Louisiana.

The Mississippi valley colony and missions owed much to the controversial Beaubois. He had promoted relations with the Indian nations. To secure the French position vis-à-vis the advancing English, he had written about the strategic importance of the Ohio River. To support the financially pressed missions, he had launched a model plantation which pioneered in sugar cane and experimented with indigo; he also tried to devise a new type of cotton gin. He obtained royal approval for the digging of a canal from the Rivière d'Orléans (Bayou St John) to the edge of New Orleans – later accomplished under the Spanish regime. He proposed the founding of a Jesuit college, but in vain, because the monarchy's mercantilist policy extended even to education. He was one of the most dynamic and far-sighted administrators to appear in Louisiana. Even his abrasive brashness seemed to be mellowing when others in their wounded sensitivity felt it was too late to forgive. Upon his return to France in 1735 he lived at the Jesuit college in Bourges while he worked as agent and fund-raiser for the American missions. In 1743 he took up the ministry he would exercise for the remainder of his life – the directing of retreats according to the spiritual exercises of St Ignatius. The college at Amiens was his residence from 1743 to 1750, and then the college at Vannes where he served as superior of the retreat apostolate from 1751 until the suppression of the Society of Jesus in France in 1762.

Where the septuagenarian then went and what he did remain unknown. He reappears only in a Jesuit death notice: he died "near Avignon" 13 Jan. 1770.

C. E. O'NEILL

AN, Col., B, 51, ff.89v–90; 55, f.238; 59, ff.482v–84; 61, ff.537v–38, 644v–46, 653v, 669, 674–74v; C², 23, f.192; C¹³ᴬ, 8, ff.407, 413–14, 421–21v, 426; 9, ff.126, 148–49; 10, ff.33–34, 47–48v, 60–65, 101–24, 296–300, 310–10v, 312–12v, 315–15v, 317–57 *passim*; 11, ff.5–5v, 12, 33–35v, 76–78, 191–216, 228–29, 232–37v, 239–39v, 241–41v, 243, 251–57v, 260–61, 272–82v, 328, 362v; 12, ff.3, 5–6v, 135–36, 138–38v, 195–201, 209–10, 212–12v, 214–67, 271–73, 276–77v, 278–78v, 280–81v, 283–84v; C¹³ᴮ, no.45, pp.1–4, 312–16v; C¹³ᶜ, 4, ff.45, 176–77; E, 22; F⁵ᴬ, 3, ff.170–235; Section Outre-Mer, Dépôt des fortifications des colonies, Louisiane, no.61; G¹, 412, ff.5–6v; 465 (dossiers Bienville, Diron). ARSI, Catalogi, Francia 17–28 (1711–62); Francia 49, f.443; Gallia 19, ff.482–83; Monumenta Historica Missionum Societatis Iesu, 53/a, p.147. ASQ, Évêques, 170, 170b.

Comptes rendus de l'Athénée louisianais (Nouvelle-Orléans), I (1887), 144–49. JR (Thwaites), LXVII, 268–74. Delanglez, *French Jesuits in Louisiana*. O'Neill, *Church and state in Louisiana*. Rochemonteix, *Les Jésuites et la N.-F. au XVIIIe siècle*, I, 281ff.

BEAUCOUR, PAUL MALLEPART DE GRAND MAISON, *dit. See* MALLEPART

BEAUCOURS, JOSUÉ DUBOIS BERTHELOT DE. *See* DUBOIS

BEAUDRY. *See* BAUDRY

BEAUFORT, *dit* L'AVOCAT, FRANÇOIS-CHARLES HAVARD DE. *See* HAVARD

BEAUHARNOIS DE LA BOISCHE, CHARLES DE, Marquis de BEAUHARNOIS, seigneur of Villechauve, naval officer, governor general of New France, lieutenant-general of naval forces; b. in the family château of La Chaussaye near Orléans and baptized 12 Oct. 1671, son of François de Beauharnois de La Boische and Marguerite-Françoise Pyvart (Pinard) de Chastullé; d. 12 July 1749 in the parish of Saint-Sauveur, Paris.

The Beauharnois were an old and notable family of Orléans, originally well-to-do merchants, then in successive generations holders of royal, ducal, and municipal offices. Under Henry IV, as magistrates of the lower courts of Orléans, they entered the *robe* nobility. Charles's father, a lawyer in the *parlement* and director general of finances and of the royal salt tax in Orléans, represented the cadet branch of the family and held modest seigneurial lands; his mother was the daughter of a *maître ordinaire* in the treasury court of Blois.

Significant among the notable marriages of the Beauharnois were those with the Phélypeaux of Blois. Louis Phélypeaux de Pontchartrain, grandson of one Beauharnois and brother-in-law of another, became secretary of state for the Marine in 1690. Prior to this date the two eldest

Beauharnois de La Boische

of Charles's six brothers had entered the army but after 1691 all the remaining Beauharnois sons entered the Marine where they could expect to enjoy favours from Pontchartrain, their cousin.

Charles de Beauharnois served at sea for 20 years, in the two longest wars of Louis XIV's reign – the League of Augsburg and the Spanish Succession. Beginning with La Hougue in 1692, the shattering engagement which turned French naval strategy from the *guerre d'escadre* to the *guerre de course,* he experienced fierce combat on eight different occasions. In 1698 he sailed with d'Iberville [Le Moyne*] to discover the mouth of the Mississippi, and the following year commanded a company of naval infantry against the pirates of Salé (Morocco). In 1703 Beauharnois was given his first ship command – the *Seine* destined for Quebec where his older brother FRANÇOIS had been appointed intendant by Pontchartrain. In 1707 he commanded the *Achille*, a corsair outfitted by René Duguay-Trouin, which caught fire in an attack on an English convoy off Cape Lizard. Though he lost his prizes both Duguay-Trouin and the Comte de Forbin praised the vigour with which he pressed his attack.

In 1710 Beauharnois transferred from Brest to Rochefort, probably hoping to benefit from the recent appointment of his brother François as intendant there. For the next 16 years, when the Marine had to retrench following the costly wars of Louis XIV, Beauharnois served in port.

In August 1716, at age 46, he married Renée Pays, wealthy widow of Pierre Hardouineau de Landianière, king's counsellor, receiver general for crown lands and forests in La Rochelle. This marriage made him master of an estate worth perhaps 600,000 *livres*, the most valuable portion consisting of sugar plantations in Saint-Domingue (Hispaniola). To this he added 66,000 *livres* of his own movables. Three years earlier his younger brother, Claude*, had married one of Renée Pays's daughters. Now Beauharnois became guardian of the three other minor stepchildren.

This childless marriage was not a happy one. In September 1719 Renée Pays launched a suit for separation of the *communauté de biens*, and her children by her previous marriage began legal action against her and Beauharnois to gain control of their inheritance. Beauharnois resisted successfully until 1725 when the courts ordered one-half of the *communauté* divided amongst the children. By this time his wife, after a brief truce in 1721, had refused to be reconciled, and had reopened her suit for separation. The only permissible grounds for dissolution of the *com-*

munauté were mismanagement of the wife's patrimony, and Renée, predictably in some measure, accused Beauharnois of ruinous gambling, plotting with his brother to dispossess her children, and letting the estate decline to a fraction of its former value. She embellished her plea with charges of physical and verbal abuse. The surviving evidence is not conclusive as to whether or not the value of the Hardouineau estate decreased owing to Beauharnois's alleged extravagance. Witnesses established that he gambled, but not that he gambled abnormally for a man of his class, nor that he lost by it. Hearsay evidence was presented that the plantations of Saint-Domingue were badly managed. There were extensive repairs needed to a *métairie* in France. But Beauharnois clung tenaciously to his rights as master of the *communauté*. Neither side displayed charity. Suits, appeals, and procedural irregularities filled the courts of La Rochelle and Niort in France, Léogane in Saint-Domingue, and even the *parlement* of Paris, almost until the death of Renée Pays in 1744. She never did win her separation. Beauharnois continued to enjoy some of the fruits of the *communauté*, particularly from Saint-Domingue, but his wife managed to extract a healthy living allowance as well as most revenues from France. The only certain victors were the lawyers.

In the heat of these disputes Beauharnois solicited the governorship of New France, left vacant by the death of Philippe de Rigaud* de Vaudreuil in October 1725. The king, having decided after Vaudreuil's administration that governors should have no close connections with Canadian families, rejected Charles Le Moyne* de Longueuil, governor of Montreal, and selected Beauharnois in February 1726. He arrived in Quebec in August. A naval captain since 1708, and knight of the order of Saint-Louis since 1718, he was the first naval officer to hold the position. His experience was not ill suited to the military situation of New France. In Canada, as at sea, French strategy was essentially defensive. Furthermore, forest warfare in Canada was similar to the naval *guerre de course* in that both involved small bands of marauders striking quickly wherever the enemy was at a disadvantage. Beauharnois's appointment is probably explained by the fact that his cousin, Jean-Frédéric Phélypeaux, Comte de Maurepas, had been minister of Marine since 1723. In addition to the customary title of marquis, Beauharnois procured letters of state, renewed subsequently, suspending all civil cases in which he was involved.

The overriding concern of New France during Beauharnois's government was English colonial expansion. By the treaty of Utrecht (1713) the French had been forced to concede to the English Hudson Bay, Acadia, and Newfoundland, and the right to trade directly with the western tribes. With cheaper trade goods the merchants of Albany, Pennsylvania, and Hudson Bay were well positioned to take over the western trade and the Indian alliances based upon it. Yet the Anglo-French alliance following Utrecht denied Canadian governors the use of military force. Beauharnois was faced with having to keep the Indian allies, upon whom the security of the French North American empire depended, hostile to the English while peace was imposed from Paris.

In Acadia the Abenaki Indians, disillusioned by the French refusal to join openly in their resistance to English settlement northeastward beyond Casco Bay, were entertaining attractive English peace proposals. Indeed before Beauharnois arrived the Penobscot Abenakis had already concluded an agreement with the governor of Massachusetts Bay, William Dummer [see SAUGUAARAM]. Beauharnois feared the worst: that the English would soon win over the Abenakis and pose a serious military threat to the east in the event of war. A number of precautions, however, prevented so harmful an outcome. Beauharnois persuaded the minister to maintain the war fund of 6,000 *livres* for the Abenakis to supplement the diplomacy of the Jesuit missionaries and the French half-breed brothers Saint-Castin [see Joseph d'ABBADIE]. He urged the Abenakis to join war parties against the Fox Indians in the west, thus keeping their alliance with the French active. He encouraged migration to the missions of Saint-François and Bécancour near Trois-Rivières, and discouraged the re-establishment of villages near the English settlements. But English trade and solicitations over the next 15 years did erode the French alliance, and as early as 1732 the English had established a fort and settlement at Pemaquid near Abenaki villages.

The English threat on Lake Ontario was especially critical. Governor William Burnet of New York, determined to destroy French trade in the west, began building Oswego in 1725 partly in response to the recent establishment of French posts at Niagara (near Youngstown, N.Y.), Toronto, and Kenté (Quinté). The Six Nations Iroquois, especially some of the Senecas, were openly hostile to the French countermeasure of fortifying Niagara, arguing that Le Moyne de Longueuil and Louis-Thomas Chabert* de Joncaire had tricked them into granting permission for the fort. But the Iroquois were also apprehensive about Burnet's aggressive policy which equally infringed upon their territory. The Iroquois, indeed, were now less able to defend either their middleman position in the Albany trade or their territorial claims in the face of increasing Anglo-French rivalry. Beauharnois, alarmed in the summer of 1727 by news that the English were fortifying Oswego with a garrison, sent Claude-Michel BÉGON with an ultimatum to withdraw within 15 days. He also called out the militia for a military expedition, but on second thought decided to consult the king before taking such a drastic step. The Iroquois made it clear they did not want blood spilled on their land. By insisting upon a strict balance of French and English strength, they assured the French possession of Niagara but also guaranteed that the English would not be removed from Oswego. This interpretation of Iroquois intentions became the basis of Beauharnois's policy for Lake Ontario. Henceforth this issue, like that of the Acadian boundary dispute, was left to diplomacy and the new status quo, which settled nothing, was confirmed at the congress of Soissons in 1728.

The French adjusted as best they could. A limited brandy trade had already been authorized to offset the attraction of unrestricted rum at Oswego. Beauharnois was instructed to reinstitute the practice of selling *congés*, or licences to trade at the western posts, in hopes of competing more effectively with the English. He issued regulations to prevent Frenchmen from going to Oswego, and recommended that the king's posts of Frontenac (Kingston, Ont.) and Niagara be well stocked with trade goods and that their trade be subsidized by the crown to compete with cheaper English goods across the lake. The minister refused to admit subsidization was necessary, but trade at these posts was soon being carried on at a loss. Clearly the presence of the English on Lake Ontario in direct contact with the western tribes would undermine French-Indian alliances.

The Fox wars were in some measure an expression of English influence in the west. Straddling the Wisconsin River west of the Baie des Puants (Green Bay, Lake Michigan), the Fox commanded the best trade route to the Sioux and other upper Mississippi tribes. They guarded their middleman position jealously, and exacted a heavy tribute from anyone, French or Indian, who wished to pass through their lands. Their rivals were the Ojibwas, who traded with the Canadians on Lake Superior, and the Illinois, who traded with the French from Louisiana on the Mississippi. Among the western tribes, even those related to them, they were known as untrustworthy troublemakers. The endless

Beauharnois de La Boische

intertribal wars disrupted French trade and threatened the delicate system of alliances.

The French government, in response to the English threat after Utrecht, had decided upon westward expansion and exploration. As a preliminary, Beauharnois was to establish a post and mission among the Sioux on the upper Mississippi, beyond the Fox Indians. The minister had hoped to shore up the fragile peace with the Fox and yet bypass them in the trade with the Sioux. Beauharnois attempted this unlikely policy by sending off an expedition in June 1727 under René BOUCHER de La Perrière and the Jesuit, Michel GUIGNAS. Alarming news soon arrived that the Fox had renewed their war against the Illinois, killing several Frenchmen. Worse, there were reports of English traders on the Ouabache (Wabash) River, and of invitations, through Indian intermediaries, to the Fox and other tribes to drive the French from the west. Having cancelled his plans against Oswego, Beauharnois, without awaiting approval from the minister, made secret preparations for a major campaign against the Foxes in 1728.

The force of 1,500 Canadians and Indians led by Constant Le Marchand* de Lignery failed dismally to bring the Foxes to heel, and the French lost prestige among the western tribes. Beauharnois, with some justification, blamed Lignery who turned the expedition into a personal trading venture. The minister expressed surprise at Beauharnois's precipitate decision to use force, but approved it – he was himself under pressure from the controller general of finance and the Compagnie des Indes to insist that Beauharnois end the Fox war against the Illinois. Officials in Louisiana (in fact, the Compagnie des Indes) suspected the new governor at Quebec of continuing Vaudreuil's policy of encouraging the Fox-Illinois war to prevent pelts from the northwestern tribes from going to New Orleans instead of to Canada. But even if this were so, events in 1727 had convinced Beauharnois that the Fox were too unreliable and he sought their destruction earnestly.

Meanwhile, Beauharnois's relationship with Intendant Dupuy* was rapidly deteriorating. When they first met in Paris in 1726 all appeared to be well. But despite the king's most insistent instructions that governor and intendant should ensure a perfect understanding between them, less than two months after arriving in the colony they had begun quarrelling. Beauharnois first complained in October that Dupuy was improperly attended at all public ceremonies by two armed archers, even in his pew at church. Disputes over precedence were not new in Canada, but this one forewarned of the intendant's insatiable appetite for the trappings, as well as the substance, of royal authority, and of the governor's determination to protect what he saw as his prerogatives.

Events from January to March 1727 widened the rift between them. On rather specious grounds Beauharnois steadfastly refused a request by Henry HICHÉ, king's attorney of the Quebec provost court, to authorize a drummer from the regular troops for the announcement of a court order. Dupuy rose to the bait, issued an ordinance proclaiming a civilian drummer, and forbade the publishing of ordinances without his, Dupuy's, express permission. There followed scenes reminiscent of the *mêlées* of Buade* de Frontenac's government. The ordinance was torn down: Dupuy accused the governor. Beauharnois summoned the intendant to the Château "for important business": Dupuy refused to go. Even the aging Bishop Saint-Vallier [La Croix*] could not persuade the intendant of the error of his challenge to the governor. Wisely refraining from the use of force, Beauharnois simply wrote a long account of the affair to Maurepas.

Defamatory verses, apparently all unfavourable to Dupuy, circulated in Quebec. Beauharnois reported that Dupuy brought ridicule upon himself by taking idle advice from rumour-mongers, such as his subdelegates Pierre ANDRÉ de Leigne and Pierre Raimbault*. Cooperation proved impossible. Whether settling a property dispute or leasing the fur trade at Toronto, Dupuy was always, so the governor charged, infringing upon his prerogatives. For his part, Dupuy accused the governor of abusing the sale of fur-trade licences, requiring money payments from western post commanders, and doing nothing to stop the illegal trade with Albany. He became convinced of a conspiracy against the king's authority, and it was finally clear that Dupuy had brought with him to Canada a constitutional view current in the sovereign courts of France, that the magistracy, not the old *noblesse de race*, was the rightful repository of royal authority. A social incompatability between the two officials could only aggravate their quarrels over prerogatives. Dupuy was a *parvenu* to the king's service: Beauharnois had been born into it. "It appears," wrote the governor on more than one occasion, "that he has played general and bishop as well as intendant." "He is a man totally exceeding his position."

The ultimate clash came in the winter of 1728. The occasion was a dispute over who was to exercise ecclesiastical authority in the colony following the death of Bishop Saint-Vallier in December

44

1727. Not for a moment questioning whether he and the Conseil Supérieur were competent to judge the dispute, Dupuy plunged in on the side of Eustache CHARTIER de Lotbinière, archdeacon appointed by the deceased bishop, against the defiant canons of the cathedral chapter and their elected capitular vicar, Étienne Boullard*. For two months Beauharnois officially remained aloof from the bizarre events which provided townsmen of Quebec with their principal winter's entertainment: the intendant secretly burying the bishop in the Hôpital Général, then unleashing impassioned diatribes against Boullard and an unrepentant chapter; the canons defying Dupuy's ordinances against them. Privately the governor encouraged Boullard and facilitated the sending of the chapter's complaints to court, via New England, at the end of January. On the basis of these Dupuy was recalled. In the meantime, when Dupuy showed no sign of relenting despite the scandal of public disorder, Beauharnois appeared personally in the Conseil Supérieur on 8 March to order the suspension of all deliberations upon the "delicate and dangerous" ecclesiastical disputes of the winter. The king was to decide. Then he left for Montreal. Dupuy refused to admit that the governor had any authority in matters of justice, and pressed the council to continue. Clear-thinking councillors balked at following Dupuy's defiant example, however, and only a rump council supported him. In May Beauharnois banished two of this group, Guillaume Gaillard* and Louis ROUER d'Artigny, to seigneuries outside Quebec, but they simply took refuge in the intendant's palace.

When news of Dupuy's disgrace arrived Beauharnois was publicly triumphant. Privately the minister took him to task for pettiness which contributed to the impasse. Beauharnois had claimed many prerogatives that were not his, particularly that of banishing councillors. Yet he had been no more sensitive about his prerogatives than others of his rank and social group would have been. On the essential point, that of the conduct expected of a governor when in disagreement with the intendant, he was perfectly correct. Not until matters had gotten quite out of hand – on this point the minister concurred – did he take the grave measure of intervening with his ultimate "authority." Learned in law though he was, Dupuy displayed an utter inability to comprehend the constitutional relationships worked out over half a century earlier between all the key Canadian institutions: the governorship, the intendancy, the council, the church. Beauharnois, an amateur in constitutional law, possessed political sense and understood the restraint with which he was expected to exercise his authority.

He was jubilant, and not very charitable in his victory. He did nothing to prevent the humiliating seizure of Dupuy's belongings as assurance for his sizable debts. His excuse was that the actions were a matter of justice. For many his apparent victory must have proved his influence with Maurepas.

The political tumult and frontier crises of his first two years of government subsided, but Beauharnois still faced chronic problems. He was alarmed at how vulnerable Canada's defences were. Peace, and financial retrenchment, placed colonial defence low on the scale of priorities. Most of Beauharnois's recommendations were rejected as too costly and unnecessary. He argued that the fortification of Quebec and the addition to the garrisons of at least 1,500 regular troops were essential. He bluntly dismissed the fortress of Louisbourg, Île Royale (Cape Breton Island) as useless to Canada: "I do not know, Your Excellency," he wrote the minister in 1727, "who could have led the court to believe that Île Royale was the rampart of this country; the entire English army could come to Quebec and nothing be known of it at Île Royale. Even if it were known there, what could they do about it?" Although the stone wall around Montreal, begun in 1716, was finally completed in 1741, the other recommendations were ignored.

He did persuade the minister to construct Fort Saint-Frédéric at the headwaters of Lake Champlain after learning of an English plan to settle on this, the major avenue from New York to the heart of the St Lawrence colony. First securing Iroquois neutrality, he built the fort and the English could only protest diplomatically. In a quick stroke Beauharnois had secured one of the most strategically important locations on the colonial frontier.

Beauharnois found himself increasingly drawn into the Ohio in proportion to the growth of English influence there, and in the 1730s had to keep a wary eye on tribes such as the Miamis, Weas, Piankeshaws [see Jean-Charles d'ARNAUD], and the migrating Shawnees on the Ouabache, and on the Iroquois and other eastern tribes who had migrated to Rivière Blanche. At Detroit, a vital post where a number of traditionally hostile tribes were gathered in uneasy alliance, Beauharnois was threatened constantly by tribal conspiracies. When in 1727 the Hurons complained bitterly of the high prices charged by the agents of Alphonse Tonty*, post commander and holder of the trade monopoly, Beauharnois recalled him, and issued several licences to different

Beauharnois de La Boische

traders to stimulate competition. But the Hurons, succumbing to the influence of the English and Senecas, made peace with the Flatheads to the south. A full-scale war involving all the Great Lakes tribes was narrowly averted in 1738 when the Ottawas, with good reason, accused the Hurons of treachery in an ambush of Ottawas on a raid against the Flatheads. Nicolas-Joseph de NOYELLES de Fleurimont, commander at Detroit, barricaded the French in the fort. With great difficulty Beauharnois and Noyelles negotiated an uneasy truce. They did not prevent a group of Hurons under ORONTONY moving to Sandoské (Sandusky) on the southwest shore of Lake Erie where they kept up a regular trade with Pennsylvania merchants.

Farther to the north the defiant Foxes were still disrupting French trade. Beauharnois worked tirelessly to isolate them diplomatically, and by 1730 the tribe sought refuge among the Senecas. They were intercepted en route and besieged by a combined force of 1,400 Louisianians, Canadians, and Indian allies [*see* Robert Groston* de Saint-Ange; Nicolas-Antoine Coulon* de Villiers; Noyelles; François-Marie Bissot* de Vinsenne]. Several hundred Foxes were killed when they attempted to escape and others were dispersed as slaves among the victorious tribes. Elated, Beauharnois re-established in 1731 the posts which had been abandoned at Baie-des-Puants (Green Bay, Wis.) and among the Sioux.

In dealing with the remnants of the Fox tribe, however, Beauharnois misjudged the reaction of the western tribes to recent events. Apparently he had no intention of negotiating in good faith with the Foxes who had earlier mocked his own efforts to make peace. Instead, he encouraged post commanders, western allies, and mission Indians to fall upon the remaining Foxes at every opportunity, until "that damned nation shall be entirely extinguished." In 1733 the principal Fox chief, Kiala*, begged for mercy. Beauharnois sent him to Martinique in slavery. If the remaining Foxes would not be dispersed among the missions within the colony, they were to be killed.

Many allies blanched before this ruthlessness and began openly to sympathize with the beleaguered tribe, even to the point of releasing their slaves. In September 1733, when Nicolas-Antoine Coulon de Villiers rashly demanded the surrender of some Foxes who had found refuge among the Sauks at the Baie des Puants he, his son, and several other Frenchmen were killed. Beauharnois sought to restore French prestige in 1735 through yet another military expedition, led by Noyelles de Fleurimont. It was a fiasco of bad

weather, poor planning, and lack of spirit among the Indian allies. The Foxes found refuge among the Sioux.

The expansion of the fur trade to the far northwest by Pierre GAULTIER de Varennes et de La Vérendrye, whose enterprise Beauharnois strongly supported, complicated the problem of stabilizing Indian relations in the west. The Ojibwas, Crees, and Assiniboins, whose friendship La Vérendrye required, were all traditional enemies of the Sioux. La Vérendrye was unable, or unwilling, to prevent the Crees from sending war parties against this numerous tribe. In 1736 a party of Sioux killed Jean-Baptiste Gaultier* de La Vérendrye, the Jesuit Jean-Pierre Aulneau* and 19 Canadians on Rainy Lake. LE GARDEUR de Saint-Pierre, whose position at the Sioux post was now untenable, withdrew in 1737. The Fox problem had given way to a Sioux problem farther west, which endangered the supply of half the beaver pelts exported from Canada. Beauharnois's attempt to exterminate the Foxes had failed. Now he was convinced that he could do little to "impose a law" upon the Indians. Conciliation was henceforth a necessity, even though it was impossible "to have a solid base given the inconstancy of the Indians." Lacking troops for the western garrisons, he increasingly relied upon lavish gifts and medals to cement his Indian alliances. Expenditures on gifts, which had been fixed at 22,000 *livres* annually, increased to 65,000 *livres* in 1741 and 76,600 *livres* in 1742 – to the anguish of the minister. Much success was due to the inspired diplomacy of Paul MARIN de La Malgue, whom Beauharnois had appointed to command at Baie-des-Puants in 1738. By 1743 an uneasy peace had been restored in the west. Had he employed conciliation in 1730 when the French and their western allies were united and victorious, Beauharnois might more easily have resisted the strains placed upon the French alliance system later.

Compared to his quarrels with Dupuy, Beauharnois's relations with other individuals appear tranquil indeed. There were reasons for tension in his favouring of the Ramezays, old rivals of the Vaudreuils. The latter he treated correctly, though not generously. The patronage attached to the governorship was considerable. Most governors engaged in the fur trade: Beauharnois was likely no exception. Dupuy accused him of it. The determination with which he established the Sioux post, and the protection he never ceased to give La Vérendrye in his monopoly of the *mer de l'Ouest*, may indicate a personal interest. The decision of the crown to expand the fur trade westward enhanced the governor's patronage.

Beauharnois also benefited from the decision in 1726 to reintroduce the selling of fur-trading licences for most of the Great Lakes posts. Twenty-five of these were to be issued at 250 *livres* apiece to impoverished families of repute in the colony. Instead, Beauharnois sold them to traders for whatever they would fetch – usually about 500 *livres* – and in some years issued as many as 50. He deposited 6,250 *livres* in the Marine account, and distributed 10,000 *livres* as pensions among widows of notable colonial families. The minister cautiously approved this innovation, which enhanced the governor's patronage. When in 1742 the crown, largely for fiscal reasons, drastically curtailed the licence system and undertook to lease most of the western posts to the highest bidder, Beauharnois, and the post commanders who thereby lost their trading privileges, naturally objected. The governor argued that a merchant with a lease would charge exorbitant prices for trade goods, driving the Indians to trade with the English.

On the whole, Beauharnois seems to have distributed his extensive patronage equitably. He had his favourites – La Vérendrye, Noyelles, d'Arnaud, Louis DENYS de La Ronde, Jacques de LAFONTAINE de Belcour, Marin, Gaspard-Joseph CHAUSSEGROS de Léry, his nephew Claude-Charles de Beauharnois – and there were a few complaints, but this was normal. He succeeded in lowering the age, and increasing the number, of cadets accepted into the colonial regular troops, and rigorously defended the interests of the officer class as a whole.

Committed to the Canadian trade system, Beauharnois did what he could to hinder trade through the rival colony of Louisiana. The Chickasaw Indians, allies of the Carolina English on the lower Mississippi, were reasonably effective in fulfilling the old role of the Foxes in disrupting the Louisiana trade. Beauharnois urged the Canadian Indians to send war parties against them. The capture in 1736 of some Louisiana Frenchmen under Pierre d'Artaguiette d'Itouralde intensified the war, but a concerted campaign in 1739, whose Canadian contingent was led by Charles LE MOYNE de Longueuil, accomplished little [see LE MOYNE de Bienville]. The Chickasaws did not keep their promise of peace. In fact, the continuing raids by Canadian Indians, encouraged by Beauharnois, served only to keep that tribe hostile to the French of Louisiana. Beauharnois opposed making peace with them or the Cherokees in 1746. When the Compagnie des Indes relinquished its government of Louisiana to the crown in 1732, he joined the chorus of Canadians in arguing that the Illinois country should revert to administration from Quebec. Unsuccessful in this bid, he continued to license Canadian traders for the Illinois on the grounds that Louisiana traders could not supply the needs of the Indians. In 1743 he protested strongly against the claim of Pierre de Rigaud* de Vaudreuil, newly appointed governor of Louisiana, to regulate the fur trade on the Missouri.

With one or two exceptions Beauharnois got on well with the clergy. Even when the coadjutor, Bishop Dosquet*, issued a pastoral letter in 1731 reviving some of Laval*'s old strictures against the brandy trade, Beauharnois admitted he was within his competence. He simply urged a lenient interpretation of the letter by missionaries at Montreal and the western posts. He firmly believed that, without an extension of the brandy trade, the Indians would trade with the English. Once they were engaging in regular commerce, "perhaps in the event of war we should have great difficulty in attracting them back." This old argument had gained validity since the establishment of Oswego on Lake Ontario.

Beauharnois showed a marked preference for the Sulpicians over the Jesuits. He praised the loyalty of the mission Indians at Lac des Deux-Montagnes under François Picquet*, and procured many favours for them. On the other hand, in 1741 he began scathing criticism of the mission Indians at Sault-Saint-Louis, and, by implication, of their Jesuit missionaries (especially Pierre de LAUZON) who had not used their proper influence to mediate an intertribal quarrel. He accused the Jesuits of conniving in the notorious illegal trade conducted by Marie-Anne Desauniers and her sisters Marguerite and Marie-Madeleine from their store at the Sault mission. "Everyone here," he wrote the minister, "affirms publicly that the college of Quebec was built upon fraudulent dealings in the English trade." Infuriated by what he saw as an independent Jesuit policy contrary to his own, he charged that "the Sault Saint-Louis has become a kind of Republic." This outburst coincided with a similar one against the Jesuit Armand de LA RICHARDIE, missionary among the Hurons of Detroit, whom Beauharnois accused of pursuing an independent policy in resettling that tribe, "which he calls his Indians, belonging to him alone, as absolute master." The Jesuits denied all these charges. The Sault Indians, they protested, did not have "an English heart" as the governor unjustly claimed. In 1742 Beauharnois suppressed the Desauniers' store, but relented somewhat in his attacks against the missionaries and their flock. War with England was threatening and the colony would need the support of all its

Beauharnois de La Boische

allies, however unreliable. He also knew that some illegal trade was necessary to supply French traders with the English merchandise demanded by the western tribes.

During these anxious years Beauharnois became involved in numerous disputes with Intendant Hocquart*. For some time they got on famously. After two trying years with Dupuy, Beauharnois expressed his relief to the minister: "Experience gives me a taste for peacefulness." Young, competent, and ambitious, Hocquart saw in his appointment as financial commissary to Canada in 1729 a step towards an eventual intendancy in France. But his hope to impress the minister with a brilliant success in restoring order to the colony's finances was sadly disappointed. Maurepas refused to admit that the Marine department and the treasurers general of the Marine owed the colony considerable sums for previous expenditures. Hocquart was expected to effect savings through regular retrenchment in current budgets. This expectation frustrated his quest for funds to support a number of ambitious projects, among them being the Saint-Maurice ironworks (*see* François-Étienne CUGNET) and the construction of naval vessels at Quebec. Hocquart decided that there must also be savings in military expenditures, and other areas where the governor had an interest. With persistence and circumspection he retrenched across a broad front: pensions for Indian interpreters, officers' uniforms, orders for gunpowder, claims by western post commanders for gifts distributed to Indian allies. He wanted to reduce costly garrisons at several forts, appoint a permanent commander at Detroit, and lease to the highest bidder the trade at each of the western posts. He claimed Beauharnois's expenditures on fortifications were excessive and often unnecessary.

Naturally, Beauharnois complained. And in 1740 he struck by exposing what he implied to be collusion between the intendant and Cugnet, farmer of the Tadoussac fur trade and leading partner in the Saint-Maurice ironworks, to misrepresent the true revenues of the Tadoussac post. The governor's protégé, Lafontaine de Belcour, offered twice what Cugnet was paying for the lease. This quarrel had developed partly out of a dispute about finding a gratuity for Nicolas LANOULLIER de Boisclerc, former agent of the treasurers general of the Marine. The war of patronage expanded to include an infinity of issues with the clients of each official lining up accordingly. The governor's claim that the intendant was at times encroaching upon his prerogatives echoed a familiar refrain from his quarrels with Dupuy. Yet the two episodes were significantly

different: despite their open conflict after 1739, Beauharnois and Hocquart were still able to cooperate on matters which required joint attention.

When news arrived in June 1744 that France and England were at war at last, much cooperation was necessary. The governor's tasks were clear: to assure the defence of the colony proper; to secure the Indian alliances and Iroquois neutrality; and to take offensive action against the English North American possessions. As early as the outbreak of the Anglo-Spanish war in 1739 Beauharnois began precautions. He repaired the fortifications and increased the garrisons at Saint-Frédéric, Niagara, and Frontenac. He ordered regular reconnaissance patrols on the Lake Champlain frontier. By 1742 the batteries of Quebec had platforms and mountings. With the declaration of war he constructed earthworks and a palisade along the Saint-Charles River, restored the stockade forts in the seigneuries, set up signal stations down the St Lawrence, and prepared fire boats at strategic locations.

The success with which Beauharnois had restored calm in the west was attested in 1744 when he and his post commanders encountered little difficulty bringing their allies to declare for the French. Aware, however, that inaction disgusted Indians, he ordered a quick raid in 1744 against English traders in the Ohio, followed by the *petite guerre* against the New England frontier. Parties of militia and Indians led by Canadian officers (Marin, François-Pierre de Rigaud* de Vaudreuil, Jean-Baptiste BOUCHER de Niverville, Luc de La Corne*, known as La Corne Saint-Luc, Le Gardeur de Saint-Pierre) fell upon outposts such as Saratoga (Schuylerville, N.Y.), Fort Massachusetts (Williamstown, Mass.), and Charlestown (N.H.), and laid the surrounding countrysides waste.

However, Beauharnois displayed extreme reluctance to undertake more substantial offensives, perhaps in part because of the defensive mentality in his naval background. But circumstances went far to justify it. The Iroquois had informed him their neutrality depended upon Oswego remaining unmolested, and though Maurepas might grumble the governor knew that while neutral the Iroquois would not support an English assault against Niagara. Thus the status quo on Lake Ontario remained undisturbed for the duration of the war.

More inhibiting was the dire shortage of provisions, munitions, and trade goods in the colony. Years before the declaration of war Beauharnois pleaded in a lengthy report for more troops to bolster the meagre 600 colonial regulars dispersed among the several garrisons, and the 12,000 militia in whom he had little confidence, "the long years of peace having moderated the fervour of the Canadians." One third of them were unarmed. First-hand experience in the navy having taught Beauharnois not to rely upon French shipping in wartime, he urged the stockpiling of more than a single year's supplies. But the minister, with some encouragement from a budget-conscious intendant, refused to admit these necessities. He rejected Beauharnois's plea for a wall around Quebec, because he thought the English, mindful of past failures, would not attempt to capture the capital. Beauharnois was under no such illusion: "The English will always have their sights on Quebec, which is the important objective, and will decide the fate of the rest." His position was further weakened by three successive poor harvests that left the colony dangerously short of provisions.

In these circumstances, large, prolonged campaigns were out of the question. In the spring of 1745 he scrapped an offensive against English posts on Hudson Bay, and reduced the *petite guerre* to the minimum needed to maintain the Indian alliances. He had grudgingly sent militia and Indians under Marin to support an attack against Annapolis Royal, Nova Scotia, but was reluctant to weaken his defences further for a campaign more logically conducted from Île Royale or France. It ended abruptly with the capture of Louisbourg on 28 June, by William PEPPERRELL and Commodore Peter WARREN.

Rumours of invasion by land and sea now abounded. There was a popular clamour in Quebec to fortify the town. Beauharnois seized the opportunity to begin, albeit without official approval, a project he had long favoured. The following year, 1746, Maurepas ordered it stopped unless the inhabitants were prepared to undertake the expense. Opinion was divided and a decision postponed, but much work had already been done.

Far more critical was the shortage of munitions and trade goods. Beauharnois's earlier scepticism of Louisbourg's effectiveness had seemed justified when English corsairs in the Gulf of St Lawrence had prevented many ships from arriving in 1744. The following spring Beauharnois sounded a prophetic alarm: "the scarcity and high price of merchandise has effected a reduction of trade. . . . There is reason to fear that the little merchandise which has been sent this year, be it to Niagara or the other posts, will disgust the Indians and encourage them to pass over to the English in order to satisfy their needs." But only a trickle of supplies arrived in 1745. Beauharnois

wrote pessimistically: "I will nonetheless seek the possible in the impossible. . . . It may not be within my means to guarantee the colony." He urged a determined campaign to recapture Louisbourg and Acadia, and establish naval security for French shipping in the north Atlantic. Such a plan was already under way in the Marine department, but the armada which set sail in June 1746 for Chebucto Bay under the Duc d'Anville [LA ROCHEFOUCAULD] met with complete disaster. The only achievement was the victory over a New England force at Grand-Pré by Nicolas-Antoine COULON de Villiers, second in command to Jean-Baptiste-Nicolas-Roch de Ramezay*, whom Beauharnois had sent with 1,800 Canadians and Indians to meet d'Anville. For the third year in a row sufficient munitions and trade goods failed to reach Quebec.

The result was what Beauharnois had predicted: the near-collapse of the French western alliance system. By spring 1747 the French posts were devoid of trade goods. To the Indians this made English tales of total French defeat credible. The Pennsylvanian trader and agent, George Croghan, incited the disgruntled Hurons of Sandoské to kill five French traders and invest the post of Detroit [see ORONTONY]. Ottawas, Potawatomis, Ojibwas all joined in. Settlements were burned and Paul-Joseph Le Moyne* de Longueuil, commander at the post, was completely helpless. The disturbance swept north to Michilimackinac and west to the Illinois country. Only when Beauharnois could dispatch a force from Montreal with newly arrived trade goods was the momentum of the uprising arrested. But the western tribes were no longer dependable.

Contributing to the general nature of the crisis was the ominous success of George CLINTON, governor of New York, and his brilliant Indian agent, William Johnson*, in persuading some Iroquois chiefs in the summer of 1746 to declare war upon the French. The western cantons, with the exception of some Senecas, remained essentially neutral, but the Mohawks, for the first time in 45 years, raided the outskirts of Montreal. To maintain French prestige in the eyes of his allies, Beauharnois declared war upon them in March 1747. Now even the supply of illegal trade goods from Albany was totally severed. The successful ambush of a Mohawk party in June 1747 near Châteauguay discouraged further raids [see KARAGHTADIE], but the impression of French isolation and weakness reverberated throughout the west. Upon departing for France in October 1747 Beauharnois left to his successor, BARRIN de La Galissonière, the task of reconstructing the French North American empire.

49

Beauharnois de La Boische

A decision in 1746 to recall Beauharnois had been postponed because of d'Anville's disaster. He was now 76 years old and the minister thought, as did Hocquart, that the demands of war required a younger general. His conduct was not seriously in question. There were rumours of mental weakness, but his alert dispatches to field lieutenants during the war discredit these. "The Marquis de Beauharnois has arrived in Paris in good health," wrote Pierre Hazeur* de L'Orme in February 1748. "Those who spread the rumour that he was senile have been greatly misled."

In recognition of his long service he was made lieutenant-general of naval forces in January 1748. He had already received the honours of commander and grand cross of the order of Saint-Louis in 1732 and 1738 and had been promoted rear-admiral on 1 May 1741. He survived all his brothers and spent the remaining two years of his life arranging their estates. As for his own estate, and that of his deceased wife, they were largely reunited when in 1751 his nephew François de Beauharnois de La Boische et de La Chaussée married Marie-Anne Pyvart de Chastullé, his cousin and rival claimant to the Hardouineau succession. Before this, however, on 12 July 1749, Charles de Beauharnois died in Paris and was buried at Saint-Sauveur.

Upon his arrival in Canada in 1726 the colony had been facing grave frontier crises in Acadia, on Lake Ontario, and beyond the Great Lakes. When he left in 1747 it had narrowly escaped the collapse of its Indian alliance system. It would be unfair to argue that Beauharnois was responsible for the state of affairs at his departure – if anything, he prevented it from being worse. His defensive, cautious strategy was essentially sound in the circumstances. If his policy toward the Fox Indians jeopardized the western alliances, he at least succeeded in restoring stability before the outbreak of war. In broad terms his policies were a continuation of those of Vaudreuil, reflecting a continuation of the problems facing the colony. That there was merit in Beauharnois's proposals is attested by their adoption after his departure: the fortification of Quebec; the increase of colonial regular troops; the buttressing of French power in the west.

Evidence relating to his character is sparse and perplexing. His legal embroilment with his wife and stepchildren raises more questions than answers. The pettiness displayed in his quarrels with Dupuy was balanced by restraint and reflection in almost all his decisions. Bishop Pontbriand [DUBREIL] commended his prudence during the heated debate over the continuation of the

Quebec wall in 1746. He impressed people as being refined and sensible. In his library were 38 titles representing a broad range of fashionable interests: history, geography, architecture, literature, the classics, as well as manuals on war, commerce, police, and genealogy. With a few pious works was a copy of Pierre Bayle's *Dictionnaire historique et critique*. Hocquart, despite his differences with him over policy, was not alone in describing Beauharnois as "kind, affable, and noble." The Indians knew him as "Peace." Many voiced their regrets at his departure.

On the other hand the Comte de Raymond* at Louisbourg several years later had the impression that Beauharnois was little respected at the end of his term of office. This may have been rumour. Yet, had he been widely popular, as was his predecessor Vaudreuil, one would expect to find more evidence of it. The absence of hostile opinions is understandable, given his influence with the minister. Apart from his unimproved seigneury of Villechauve, granted jointly to him and his brother Claude in 1729, he established no roots in the colony. Perhaps this, and fear of his influence, explain why he remained somewhat of an outsider in a community that was becoming increasingly provincial.

S. DALE STANDEN

[The documentation of Beauharnois's pre-Canadian career and personal life is scattered and spotty. Though many proprietary and civil records were destroyed in the war of 1939–45, the Archives départementales du Loiret (Orléans), and the *archives communales*, still contain much material on the Beauharnois family and estate. Valuable documents are also to be found in AN, 251 AP; in various *études* of the Minutier central; and in BN, MSS, Fr., 26726 (Pièces originales, 242). Hozier, *Armorial général de France*, is an indispensable genealogical reference work. The details of Beauharnois's naval career may be gleaned from AN, Col., D²C, E; Marine, B², B⁴, C¹, C², C⁷; and BN, MSS, Fr., 22770, 22771. Sources for his legal involvement with his wife and stepchildren are found largely in AD, Charente-Maritime (La Rochelle), séries B, E; in the Bibliothèque municipale, La Rochelle; and in AN, X¹ᵇ; Minutier central; Marine, C⁷.

The bulk of documentation for his public life in Canada is included in the well-known series of the AN, containing the official correspondence: Col., B, C¹¹ᴬ, C¹¹ᴱ, C¹³ᴬ, D²C, E, F³; Marine, B², B³. Transcripts or microfilm copies of most of these are available in PAC. There are also valuable, though scattered, documents in the ASQ. There is no published collection of Beauharnois's dispatches, though many translated ones pertaining to the New York frontier may be found in *NYCD* (O'Callaghan and Fernow).

The first biography of Beauharnois has yet to be written, though a few historians have touched upon aspects of his public life. Among these, Frégault, in *La civilisa-*

tion de la Nouvelle-France, gives a general commentary on the years of peace. On Beauharnois's handling of the Fox wars, Kellogg, *French régime*, is an early, if limited, attempt at analysis. His policy toward La Vérendrye and the far northwest is minutely documented in Champagne, *Les La Vérendrye*. On his quarrels with Dupuy, Dubé's *Claude-Thomas Dupuy* offers the most recent, and most thorough, analysis. s.d.s.]

BEAUHARNOIS DE LA CHAUSSAYE, FRANÇOIS DE, Baron de BEAUVILLE, financial commissary, intendant of New France, intendant of the Marine at Rochefort; baptized 19 Sept. 1665 in the parish of Saint-Laurent-des-Orgerils, Orléans, France, eldest son of François de Beauharnois de La Boische and Marguerite-Françoise Pyvart (Pinard) de Chastullé; d. 9 Sept. 1746 at Orléans.

The name Beauharnois, which was to become Beauharnais, acquired fame at the time of Napoleon, but the family had had a favourable reputation since the 14th century, particularly in the magistrature and administration. It had made brilliant marriages, such as that in 1605 between Anne de Beauharnois and Paul Phélypeaux de Pontchartrain. Towards the middle of the century the family began to turn towards the marine and the colonies; it supplied many colonial officials and naval officers and established further links through marriages; when Jeanne-Élisabeth de Beauharnois de La Boische, François's sister, married Michel BÉGON de La Picardière in 1711, she entered a family which had undergone an evolution similar to that of her own. Such family groups, veritable administrative clans, profited to the utmost from their relationship with the ministers; New France in the 18th century became familiar with the practice through the Bégons and the Beauharnois.

On 2 March 1691, François de Beauharnois had married Anne, the only daughter of François Desgrez and Anne Hugot. The dowry of 60,000 *livres* did not include any cash but a house worth 23,000 *livres* and Paris municipal bonds. When the Desgrez couple died in 1705, they left a fortune of 70,000 *livres*. Anne Desgrez, who died on 24 Sept. 1731, had no children by Beauharnois. She was not with him when he was in New France or serving in the ports of the mother country.

Beauharnois, who landed at Quebec as intendant on 29 Aug. 1702, was the protégé of the minister of Marine, Jérôme Phélypeaux, Comte de Pontchartrain; the latter had preferred him to M. de Villeboix, whom the priests of the Séminaire des Missions Étrangères in Paris wanted to send; "he is related to the minister by marriage," wrote Henri-Jean TREMBLAY, "and no one dares say anything." Pontchartrain, moreover, made no secret of it, since after Philippe de Rigaud* de Vaudreuil was appointed governor he wrote to him: "I hope that you will be further encouraged [to get along well with him] not only because of his good manners, but also because of the interest that I take in him." Was the minister thinking of promotion for him? It is possible. Perhaps he simply wanted to prepare François for succeeding Michel Bégon de La Picardière the elder in the important intendancy of Rochefort, where the experience François had already acquired as commissary of the Marine (at Toulon 1692–94, Rochefort 1694–95, Le Havre 1695–97, and Brest 1697–1702) and would acquire in the colonies would be of great value to him.

The New France that Pontchartrain was entrusting to Beauharnois as a means of proving his ability was, however, still only a small province, where in that very year 1702 the only important business, the fur trade, was in inextricable difficulties. As if to add to the confusion, war had just been declared between France and England. The new arrival's task was not the easiest.

According to the terms of his commission the intendant was first of all a judge, and as such his chief duty was to preside over the weekly meeting of the Conseil Supérieur. During Beauharnois's stay few important matters came to upset the council's routine. He got along well with the councillors and hastened to support their request for a salary increase. Similarly he recognized the necessity of providing a good legal library for these men who had little knowledge of the law. It was the "police" aspect of this role, however, that engrossed his attention the most. In this area, a large one, his activity was unfortunately not always beneficial to the colony.

On the council his only quarrel was with the attorney general, François-Madeleine-Fortuné Ruette* d'Auteuil, a turbulent and rather sly person. Beauharnois had to recognize in 1704 that the accusation of smuggling he made against d'Auteuil in 1702 was unfounded. Yet Beauharnois also had to maintain his rights; he succeeded in doing so against an upstart profiteer connected with Ruette, Lamothe Cadillac [Laumet*], who, having established himself at Detroit, refused to recognize the authority of governor and intendant.

In religious matters he gave complete satisfaction to the whole clergy, bearing out Tremblay's optimistic forecasts about him, but he refused a request from Bishop Saint-Vallier [La Croix*] to raise the tithe from one twenty-sixth to one thir-

Beauharnois de La Chaussaye

teenth. In the important and delicate question of setting food prices he brought upon himself accusations which were not unfounded, it seems. The meticulous regulation of the sale of beef which he introduced in August 1703 probably did not profit him, but it was the opposite with the wheat he sold "for the sustenance of the troops and the settlers" at three *livres* a bushel after paying 40 *sols* or less for it. Ruette d'Auteuil's testimony just quoted would be greatly suspect were it not for another source showing that Beauharnois was simultaneously speculating in salt. "He had it [the salt supply] allocated to two merchants," Tremblay wrote in 1705, "at 1 *écu* a bushel and sold it under their name for 15 or 16 *livres*. That was the audible rumour in the offices this year." Such speculation had also caused rather considerable "feeling" among the people of Montreal. There is every reason to believe that the mildness with which Vaudreuil repressed the rioters – and for which the court blamed him – was above all motivated by the part the intendant had had in causing the disturbance. A considerable share of the profits was also probably put aside for him in the sale of goods which his brother, Charles de BEAUHARNOIS, commanding the king's ship, brought in his cargo in 1703. But this operation was not continued and so there was little talk of it in the colony, especially since Beauharnois's main accuser, Ruette d'Auteuil (particularly in his report in 1712), was completely discredited shortly after.

In the execution of his economic plans, which were in fact fairly modest, the intendant encountered serious difficulties. The transport to France of wood – particularly for masts – was hampered by a shortage of suitable ships, which was worsened by the war. The growing of flax and hemp was promising; the intendant urged the settlers to cultivate them, and the crops were good, but the minister of Marine refused categorically to send weavers; the colony must not harm the industries in the mother country. As an encouragement to fishing, Beauharnois succeeded in obtaining a few hundred *livres* from the authorities – too little to ensure the prosperity of such a difficult and dangerous industry.

The great concern of his administration, however, even to the point of preoccupation, was the growing deficit of the Compagnie de la Colonie. Since 1700 the Canadians had been directing the trade in beaver pelts themselves. The court, which was expecting a great deal from this new company, had asked Beauharnois to encourage as many Canadians as possible to take part in it. On his arrival, however, Beauharnois noted that the shareholders were poor and unenthusiastic;

he soon learned the reason when he read through the report which Denis Riverin*, the company's representative in France, presented in 1702: in two years the company had contracted debts of nearly 1,000,000 *livres* and found itself forced to borrow 700,000 *livres* more in order to meet its "pressing needs." The revenues anticipated in the immediate future fell far short of this enormous total.

Beauharnois applied himself to discovering the causes of the difficulties; he saw two: first, the "small revenue from the king's tax farm," resulting from discontinuation by Versailles of the fur-trading licences because of an excess of beaver pelts; second "the excessive expenditures the directors have made, both from running their trading posts and for management expenses." Since the directors were "without money or credit," he had had to lend them the money necessary to pay "the expenses borne by the king's estate," which they had undertaken to meet in exchange for their privileges.

The minister had had much trouble in replacing the mercantile agents in Paris, who had withdrawn because of the absence of large profits, and he was angry at the Canadians' attitude: "The capital of this company is in reality a creation of the mind. No one has put a *sol* in it, and the private individuals only went into the partnership in the hope of sharing future profits." He announced tight restrictive measures against the company, limiting its production to "80 thousand dry and parchment beaver, excluding greasy beaver." According to the Canadians the restrictions ran the risk of ruining "all business in this colony." The directors of the company therefore sent a representative to France in 1704, Antoine Pascaud*, the choice being practically dictated by Beauharnois, to plead their cause with the minister. The intendant had to admit to the latter that the company's papers were badly kept; in fact, they were in complete disorder. He was once again obliged to advance the company the funds it needed to pay the "expenses borne by the king's estate"; in the autumn of 1704 he had to have "54,000 *livres* drawn in France in bills of exchange equivalent to two-thirds of the said estate [of the king] and ... playing-card money made at the king's discretion ... to pay off the remaining third of the said estate." This playing-card money was not sufficient; the intendant had to create more to finance the expedition the company had had to send to Hudson Bay. The minister protested; Beauharnois had made a great mistake in being so accommodating towards the Canadians. All his measures were vigorously criticized. Eventually the task of applying the necessary remedies and finally of liquidating the company – which was carried out in 1706 – was entrusted to Jacques Raudot*, Beauharnois's successor.

The financial role of the intendancy constituted the third of Beauharnois's tasks. In New France at the beginning of the 18th century there was a chronic deficit; to remedy it, the intendant had no other recourse but expedients; and, either through the irony of fate or by unavoidable mischance, the measures he took were always those the minister had forbidden. Thus in place of the defaulting company Beauharnois had paid the expenses of the king's domain; in the autumn of 1705 this loan amounted to nearly 200,000 *livres*. But to the minister this debt owed to the king by the company ought to have been avoided. The ordinary revenues of the colony were increased by the proceeds of the sale of goods deposited in the king's warehouses; in 1705 profits from them were said to have amounted to more than 50,000 *livres*. But there was a drop in profits in certain years for which two explanations may be offered: it is possible Beauharnois deducted a share in advance as personal profits; and when the king's ship did not arrive, as in 1704, only limited quantities of goods were sold.

The main source of the colony's funds continued to be, in spite of all efforts, "the money that is sent from France," on the king's ship. At the beginning of the 18th century this amounted to a little more than 300,000 *livres* a year. These annual remittances from the treasurer general of the Marine were systematically lower – by 87,000 *livres* in 1705 – than the estimates of the intendant, to whom the minister gave strict injunctions to reduce expenses. To settle accounts, therefore, it was necessary to issue bills of exchange and, inevitably, playing-card money. On this subject it should be noted that, faithful to the minister's orders, Beauharnois had refused in 1702 the 60,000 *livres* in playing-card money that governor Louis-Hector de Callière* demanded to "advance the fortifications." But in 1703 he had to give in, for questions of security were involved; indeed, there could be no further delay in "providing for the expenses of the fortifications and other supplementary war expenses." Pontchartrain was angered: "His Majesty has considered that it was unwise to restore playing-card money"; in only one situation would there be justification for making it, if the funds that had been granted were not received – exactly what happened in 1704. The vicious circle of inflation reappeared; in 1705 the cards were already beginning to be devalued.

François de Beauharnois remained barely three winters in Canada, leaving the colony in the autumn of 1705; he had perhaps not had time to show his capabilities fully. Above all he appears a practical man, a man of action, much more than a thinker. Certainly he was not lacking in intelligence, but he left no systematic report on the colony nor any brilliant or original views in his correspondence. He was, on the other hand, diplomatic and conciliatory, without being fooled by the turbulent elements in the colony, whose measure he took reasonably well.

Contrary to what often took place, Beauharnois's relations with his immediate superior, the governor general, were good; at least the available documents do not report any striking altercation, any serious clash. Perhaps the reason lies in the intendant's pleasant character and the brevity of his stay in Canada. But it also seems that Vaudreuil, a good politician, had taken seriously the warning the minister had given him to treat his cousin and protégé with respect. Besides, the two administrators may have been linked by common interests in the fur trade and commerce in Canada.

In the constant dilemma which administrators in Canada faced – whether to obey the minister's orders and make the population unhappy or to answer the people's needs and oppose the minister's directives if necessary – Beauharnois almost always chose the second policy. One has the impression that he was assured of immunity in high places. The harsh reproaches he received from the minister were not the cause of his recall and did not prevent him from pursuing his career in complete security, even after his protector's disgrace.

On his return to France Beauharnois held the office of intendant of the naval forces until 1710, when he was appointed intendant of the contingents enrolled for naval service. But he may never have actually exercised this function, for on 24 March 1710 he was appointed intendant of the Marine at Rochefort and was put in charge at the same time of the intendancy of the generality of La Rochelle. Now began his real career, which was to last 28 years. Unfortunately it has not yet been the subject of any full study, and only a few landmarks in it can be given here.

The task before Beauharnois was not the easiest: he was taking the place of an exceptional man, Michel Bégon, who by his authority and prestige had succeeded in maintaining good feeling among the population. Beauharnois was too complaisant with the naval officers, thus provoking some rather serious incidents. He also had to deal with the stagnation which the arrival of peace in 1713 brought to the port of Rochefort;

the shipbuilding yards were almost idle and the arsenal was reduced to virtually nothing. Beauharnois was still concerned with Canada, since nearly all supplies and other help destined for that colony left from Rochefort. He tried to remedy the inactivity and paid particular attention to assisting the poor. He also took an interest in the schools of anatomy and surgery which were founded around 1720 and depended upon the naval hospital. The port did not begin to prosper until after a visit made by the minister of Marine in 1727. Beauharnois seems to have carried out his duties honestly and conscientiously.

François de Beauharnois appears not to have had any financial difficulties; he was not able to enter into his inheritance until after his mother's death in 1721, but his marriage had been, at least financially, a fortunate one. Moreover, the various offices he held had provided him with many opportunities to make a fortune, and he had not let them go by, if we may believe his contemporaries. At his death he had a tidy fortune: 6,000 *livres* in movables, which was respectable without being luxurious; more interesting is the fact that his silverware was valued at 18,000 *livres*; still more remarkable, he had in his home 63,000 *livres* in cash, to which was added at the time of the inventory 16,000 *livres* owing in gratuities from the king or salary unpaid at his death. Debts due him amounted to 65,000 *livres* and there was no mention of any liabilities. Thus there were assets of 168,000 *livres*, to which must be added the land and château of La Chaussaye and the numerous pieces of land that he leased around Orléans.

François de Beauharnois was above all a man of the world; he was said to be "witty" and to have "liked his pleasure," but he was not wanting in a taste for letters. His library gives some indication of this taste: it included 87 titles, comprising 195 volumes, among which history and architecture predominated; there was also an interesting collection of prints and maps. His mind seems to have been open and curious; he owned the 1697 edition of Pierre Bayle's *Dictionnaire historique et critique* and several current publications, among them the 1731 edition of Louis Moreri's *Grand dictionnaire historique*.

He lived simply in the midst of these riches: his home was richly furnished but was far from lavish. He owned a collection of 19 "family paintings" and a finely decorated private chapel in which the bishop of Orléans had given him permission to have mass said. The Beauharnois were not indifferent to religion: François's mother had been a patroness of the Oratory in Orléans, and he himself asked in his will that on his tombstone be inscribed "Hic jacet Beauharnois peccator" (Here lies the sinner Beauharnois).

JEAN-CLAUDE DUBÉ

AD, Loiret (Orléans), État civil, Saint-Laurent des Orgerils; Greffe de Poullain; 3 juin 1694, 27 août 1700, 23 mai 1721, 7 oct. 1746, 1er sept. 1747. AN, Col., B, 25, p.181; C¹¹ᴬ, 20, pp.106ff., 124ff.; 22, pp.11ff., 68, 172–73; E, 22, pièce 8 (PAC transcripts); Marine, E,1, ff.339ff. ASQ, Lettres, N, 117, p.13; 123, p.17; O, 36, p.23. "Correspondance de Vaudreuil," APQ *Rapport, 1938–39*, 62, 84, 116. *Édits ord.*, II, 318. "Lettres et mémoires de François-Madeleine-Fortuné Ruette d'Auteuil, procureur général au Conseil souverain de la Nouvelle-France," APQ *Rapport, 1922–23*, 42. Le Jeune, *Dictionnaire*. Frégault, *Le XVIIIᵉ siècle canadien*, 242ff., 289ff., *passim*. Jacques Simard, "Un intendant au Canada, François de Beauharnois, 1702–1705" (unpublished MA thesis, University of Ottawa, 1967). J.-T. Viaud et E.-J. Fleury, *Histoire de la ville et du port de Rochefort* (2v., Rochefort, 1845).

BEAUJEU, DANIEL-HYACINTHE-MARIE LIÉNARD DE. See LIÉNARD

BEAUJEU, LOUIS LIÉNARD DE. See LIÉNARD

BEAUPRÉ, NOËL BONHOMME, *dit.* See BONHOMME

BEAUSOLEIL, JOSEPH BROSSARD (Broussard), *dit.* See BROSSARD

BEAUSSIER DE LISLE, LOUIS-JOSEPH, naval officer; baptized 15 March 1701 in Toulon, France, son of Louis Beaussier, port captain, and Claire Portanier; m. 10 Nov. 1757, at Brest, Louise-Françoise Jouenne de Lorière, by whom he had two daughters; d. 4 June 1765 at the château of Mollien near Brest.

Louis-Joseph Beaussier de Lisle belonged to one of the oldest families of Toulon. In 1716 he started sailing on merchant ships to the Levant and in 1724 he entered the king's service as a "junior pilot" on the *Solide* bound for Constantinople. After cruises off North Africa and in the eastern Mediterranean, he was appointed port ensign at Brest on 1 Jan. 1732. He served in European waters; then on 1 March 1739 he was promoted port lieutenant. In 1744–45, commanding the storeship *Chameau*, he led an expedition to Louisiana and Saint-Domingue (Hispaniola). In September 1746 he was given command of the frigate *Subtile*, with the task of escorting convoys along the coasts of Brittany and of meeting what remained of the squadron of the Duc d'Anville [LA ROCHEFOUCAULD] as it returned from

Acadia. On 29 November he encountered two English squadrons off Port-Louis (dept. of Morbihan), France; he escaped from one but was captured the next day after a gallant defence against a ship of the line and a frigate. He was back in Brest in January 1747.

Appointed naval captain and port captain on 1 Jan. 1749, on 30 May 1750 Beaussier was made a knight of the order of Saint-Louis. In 1755 he received command of the *Défenseur*, a ship of the line in the squadron commanded by the Comte Dubois de La Motte [CAHIDEUC], which took help to Canada and Louisbourg, Île Royale (Cape Breton Island). The following year he reached Quebec successfully with a squadron of six ships bringing the Marquis de MONTCALM and 1,300 reinforcements. Despite the efforts of the English squadron under Charles HOLMES he succeeded in entering Louisbourg harbour on 26 July. The next day he left again with the *Héros* to engage two English ships of the line; they had to retire after being badly damaged. The second-in-command of the ship, Luc-Urbain Du Boëxic de Guichen, wrote to Machault, the minister of Marine: "This combat did M. Beaussier boundless honour." Beaussier returned to Brest in September, once more eluding the English. The mission, which was carried out "in a praiseworthy manner," brought him a pension of 1,000 *livres*. His successes prompted the minister to entrust him with the same task at the end of 1757, but illness delayed him for some months. He then left, commanding the *Entreprenant* and accompanied by four other ships; he arrived at Louisbourg and joined with the governor, Drucour [BOSCHENRY], and the naval commander, Jean-Antoine Charry Desgouttes, in its defence. With the fall of the fortress on 27 July 1758, he was taken prisoner with the garrison.

After his return to France on 23 Feb. 1759, Beaussier was ordered to attack the coasts of Brazil, but the signing of peace preliminaries meant that the operation was cancelled. In April 1763 he was sent to repossess Martinique, Guadeloupe, and St Lucia, which had been returned to France by the peace treaty. He was promoted rear-admiral on 1 Oct. 1764. Endowed with "an extraordinary intelligence for everything concerning port works and an untiring diligence for such irksome routine," Beaussier also demonstrated at sea the most brilliant qualities as sailor and combatant.

ÉTIENNE TAILLEMITE

AN, Marine, B², 370, 371; B⁴, 58, 68, 73, 76, 80, 104, 105; C¹, 165; 166, f.156; C², 53, f.391; C⁶, 1203, ff.53, 281v; 1204, f.332v; C⁷, 22 (dossier Beaussier de Lisle); G, 38, f.72. Étienne Taillemite *et al.*, *Tables des noms de lieux, de personnes, de matières et de navires, sous-série B¹, B² et B³* (Paris, 1969), 34. Octave Teissier, *Armorial de la ville de Toulon: familles consulaires, officiers de marine, noblesse et bourgeoisie* (Toulon, 1900), 72. Lacour-Gayet, *La marine militaire sous Louis XV* (1910), 196, 254, 382, 394. Gustave Lambert, *Histoire de Toulon* (4v., Toulon, 1886–92), IV, 342. Troude, *Batailles navales de la France*, I, 327, 337, 369. Pierre Margry, "Une famille dans la marine au XVIIIᵉ s.: les Beaussier," *Revue maritime et coloniale* (Paris), 1879–81.

BEAUVAIS, RENÉ LEGARDEUR DE. *See* LEGARDEUR

BEAUVILLE, FRANÇOIS DE BEAUHARNOIS DE LA CHAUSSAYE, Baron de. *See* BEAUHARNOIS

BÉCART DE GRANVILLE ET DE FONVILLE, PAUL, officer in the colonial regular troops, seigneur; b. 18 Jan. 1695 at Quebec, son of Pierre Bécart de Granville and Marie-Anne Macard; d. 19 March 1754 at Quebec, a bachelor.

Bécart de Fonville, as he was generally called, was the son of a captain in the Régiment de Carignan-Salières; his brother Charles* was a king's attorney, 1700–3. Paul entered military service in 1712, became an ensign on 27 April 1716, lieutenant on 29 May 1725, and captain on 1 April 1737. He served as assistant garrison adjutant at Quebec from 1717 to 1737. On 3 Sept. 1733 he received the seigneury of Île aux Grues from his brother Pierre but does not seem to have spent much time there.

Recognized as a solid, dependable officer, Bécart de Fonville was for this reason made commandant of Fort Saint-Frédéric (Crown Point, N.Y.) in 1743, succeeding François-Antoine PÉCAUDY de Contrecœur. For years it had been a post that ambitious officers tried to avoid and no commandant had served there for much more than a year since its establishment in 1731. The intendant, Hocquart*, recognized that the western posts were more attractive because of their possibilities for profit in the fur trade. Fort Saint-Frédéric offered no such opportunities but because of its strategic location on Lake Champlain it could exercise military and diplomatic influence over the Iroquois and other Indians. It was also important as a barrier to the smuggling of furs into the English colonies and as an area where New France hoped to expand its agricultural production. Hocquart suggested, and Maurepas, the minister of Marine, concurred,

Bégon de La Cour

that to encourage longer service at Fort Saint-Frédéric by better officers special favours should be promised by the king.

Bécart de Fonville served at Fort Saint-Frédéric for about two years. When applying for the cross of Saint-Louis in 1747 he specifically mentioned the minister's letter of 1742 wherein special favours had been promised to the officers who served at Fort Saint-Frédéric. A copy of this letter, he remarked, was kept on hand by the commandants of that fort. In 1750 he was made a knight of the order of Saint-Louis. With the death of Paul Bécart de Granville et de Fonville this old family name of New France died out.

DAVID LEE

AN, Col., B, 65, f.420v; 74, f.39; 76, f.39; 78, f.45; C¹¹ᴬ, 75, pp.362–66; 77, pp.376–78; 79, pp.167–68; 80, pp.77–78; 81/1, pp.224–27; 83, pp.67–68; 89, pp.216–17; 120/1, pp.8, 294–95; 120/2, p.120 (PAC transcripts); D²ᶜ, 222/1; Marine, C⁷, 128. P.-V. Charland, "Notre-Dame de Québec: le nécrologe de la crypte," *BRH*, XX (1914), 215. Fauteux, *Les chevaliers de Saint-Louis*, 150. P.-G. Roy, *Inv. concessions*, I, 215–20; "Les commandants du fort Saint-Frédéric," *BRH*, LI (1945), 326–27; "La famille Bécard de Grandville," *BRH*, XXII (1916), 97–100.

BÉGON DE LA COUR, CLAUDE-MICHEL, officer in the colonial regular troops, governor of Trois-Rivières; b. 15 March 1683 at Martinique, son of Michel Bégon de La Picardière and Madeleine Druillon, and brother of Intendant Michel BÉGON; d. 30 April 1748 at Montreal, where he was buried on 1 May.

Descended from one of the most influential *robe* families in the Marine administration, Claude-Michel began his career in 1697 as a midshipman at Rochefort, where his father was intendant. He was promoted sub-lieutenant in the navy on 1 Jan. 1703. Nine years later he was appointed a half-pay captain in the colonial regular troops in Canada, to which he went with his brother Michel, the new intendant. In 1713 he became a full captain with a company of troops in the Montreal garrison and, in 1714, he was promoted naval lieutenant. Since there were no barracks at Montreal, he was billeted at the house of Étienne ROCBERT de La Morandière, the king's storekeeper. In classic story-book fashion, he fell in love with Rocbert's daughter, MARIE-ÉLISABETH. His brother and the Bégon family in France were horrified when he announced his intention to marry this low-born Canadian, whom they referred to as the "iroquoise." But despite their objections the marriage took place in

December 1718 and two children issued from it; Marie-Catherine-Élisabeth, who married Honoré MICHEL de Villebois de La Rouvillière, the commissary at Montreal, in 1737, and Claude-Michel-Jérôme, who became a naval officer in France. Claude-Michel was named a chevalier de Saint-Louis in 1718, and in 1722 Governor Philippe de Rigaud* de Vaudreuil described him as a "very good officer . . . extremely steady."

Although Bégon's career advanced, it did so only by Canadian standards, and there is reason to suspect that his marriage permanently prevented his having a career in France. If he chose to marry a Canadian, his powerful relatives may well have reasoned, then he could remain in Canada. It may be in recognition of this situation that he signed over certain of his assets in France to his brother Michel and to his other siblings prior to Michel's departure from Quebec in 1726. He was promoted that year to town major of Quebec and Governor BEAUHARNOIS selected him to head a detachment sent to expel the English from their new Fort Oswego (Chouaguen) on Lake Ontario. After a lengthy palaver with the English commander, Evert Banker (Bancker), and the Oswego Iroquois, he returned unsuccessful.

Bégon travelled to France in 1730, where he obtained an 800-*livre* pension as knight of the order of Saint-Louis. In 1731, after recommendations from Beauharnois and Intendant Hocquart* describing him as an excellent officer and drawing attention to his many battle wounds, he became king's lieutenant at Trois-Rivières. He held the same rank at Montreal as of 1 April 1733. In 1743, on the eve of the War of the Austrian Succession, he was named governor of Trois-Rivières. He served there throughout the war but was too old by then to take part in active campaigning. He died in 1748, and a year later Mme Bégon moved to Rochefort where she continued the fascinating correspondence with her son-in-law, Michel, that has given her a special place in Canadian history.

DONALD J. HORTON

AN, Col., B, 55–79; C¹¹ᴬ, 54–89; D²ᶜ, 222/1, p.46 (PAC transcripts). *Lettres au cher fils: correspondance d'Élisabeth Bégon avec son gendre (1748–1753)*, Nicole Deschamps, édit. (Coll. Reconnaissances, Montréal, 1972). Le Jeune, *Dictionnaire*, I, 151. Yvonne Bezard, *Fonctionnaires maritimes et coloniaux sous Louis XIV: les Bégon* (Paris, 1932). Benjamin Sulte, "Les gouverneurs des Trois-Rivières," *BRH*, II (1896), 71.

BÉGON DE LA COUR, MARIE-ÉLISABETH. *See* ROCBERT DE LA MORANDIÈRE

BÉGON DE LA PICARDIÈRE, MICHEL, commissary of the Marine, councillor in the *parlement* of Metz, France, inspector general of the Marine, intendant of New France, intendant of Le Havre, of the admiralty of Normandy, and of naval forces; b. 21 March 1667 at Blois, France; d. 18 Jan. 1747 at La Picardière.

The Bégons came from the region of Blois where they owned seigneuries – La Picardière was one of them – and served as fiscal and judicial officers until the mid-17th century. The marriage of Marie Charron, whose mother was a Bégon, to Jean-Baptiste Colbert on 14 Dec. 1648 transformed them into maritime and colonial administrators. Michel Bégon de La Picardière, the father of the intendant of New France and a cousin of Colbert, was intendant of Saint-Domingue (Hispaniola) from 1682 to 1685 (the very years when his brother-in-law Jacques de Meulles* was intendant of New France), intendant of the galleys at Marseilles from 1685 to 1688, and intendant of the port of Rochefort from 1688 until his death in 1710. He was one of the great intendants of the reign of Louis XIV and also one of the noted collectors and naturalists of his day. That decorative plant, the begonia, was named in his honour.

Three sons, Michel, Scipion-Jérôme, and CLAUDE-MICHEL, and five daughters were born of his marriage with Madeleine Druillon. One of the girls, Catherine, married the rear-admiral Roland Barrin de La Galissonière and their son, ROLAND-MICHEL, served as interim governor of New France from 1747 to 1749. Scipion-Jérôme entered the church and was bishop of Toul from 1721 to 1753.

Michel, the first born, remained in France to pursue his studies while his parents were in Saint-Domingue. His grooming in the affairs of the Marine began in 1686, soon after their return, when his father obtained for him a commission as chief writer at Toulon. In January 1690 he became a commissary of the Marine and on 30 June, while serving in that capacity, found himself at the battle of Beachy Head. Between voyages at sea and visits at court he studied law and in 1694 obtained his licentiate from Orléans. In 1697 his father purchased for him a councillor's commission in the *parlement* of Metz. In 1704 Michel must again have called upon his father's finances to purchase the post of inspector general of the Marine for the provinces of Aunis and Saintonge where Rochefort and La Rochelle were located. Thus by degrees he became solidly qualified for a senior administrative position in the department of Marine. He was a trained lawyer, was thoroughly schooled in the affairs of

the seaports, and must have been conversant with the situation in the North American colonies since royal supplies for Canada, Acadia, and Louisiana were shipped from Rochefort.

Bégon was appointed to succeed Jacques* and Antoine-Denis* Raudot as intendant of New France on 31 March 1710 but it was not until 1712 that he sailed for the colony. He was accompanied by his wife, Jeanne-Élisabeth de Beauharnois de La Boische, whom he had wed on 9 Jan. 1711. She was related to the Phélypeaux family, which gave France three ministers of Marine, and was the sister of FRANÇOIS, formerly intendant of New France and now intendant of Rochefort, and CHARLES, the future governor. As can be seen the Bégon-Beauharnois family establishment was an important force in the administrative history of New France, providing the colony with no less than three intendants and two governors general.

The War of the Spanish Succession was drawing to a close when Bégon landed at Quebec in the early autumn of 1712 [*see* Claude de Beauharnois* de Beaumont]. Governor Vaudreuil [Rigaud*], through skill and good fortune, had seen the colony safely through the war years but economically it had not yet found itself. The population of Canada in 1712 was 18,440; 52,965 acres of land were under cultivation. The wheat crop in that year amounted to 292,415 *minots*: 15.6 *minots* per capita. This was a better than average crop for it usually hovered just around the subsistence level of 12 *minots* per capita. The beaver trade had not yet recovered from the heavy overtrading of the late 17th century. The French firm of Aubert, Néret et Gayot, which held the monopoly on the purchase and sale of the pelts, was not accepting greasy beaver because of the backlog still on hand and was paying but 34 *sol* per *livre* weight for dry skins. Despite the crisis in the beaver trade, because of factors such as costs, distances, and inadequate shipping facilities, the colony had failed to diversify its economic base. The habitants grew little hemp although this product was in great demand in France. Only a few merchants were involving themselves in lumbering and the fisheries.

These problems paled beside the one of card money. With the War of the Spanish Succession devouring France's financial resources the sums sent out by the treasurer of the Marine beginning in 1702 repeatedly fell below actual expenditures [*see* François de Beauharnois]. The governor and intendant coped with this chronic shortage by issues of paper currency, actually money made out on ordinary playing cards. Initially these cards caused no problem, at least not for the pub-

lic who had confidence in them. Bearers knew
that in return for their cards they could obtain on
demand bills of exchange from the intendant and
that these would be redeemed in specie by the
treasurer of Marine in France. But in 1707 the latter failed to honour Canadian bills of exchange
and the whole financial structure began to crum-
ble. Confidence in card currency dropped and
prices soared by anywhere from 300 to 500 per
cent. New France was in the throes of runaway
inflation, ruinous for commerce and all those living on a fixed income. "We can no longer live,"
moaned Charles de Monseignat*, one of the latter. Clearly little could be undertaken in the
economic sphere until the problem caused by the
1,200,000 *livres* of cards in circulation – Ruette*
d'Auteuil's estimate – had been solved.

Bégon's stay in Canada began tragically. On 5
Jan. 1713 he and his wife were the dinner guests
of Governor Vaudreuil at the Château Saint-
Louis. On that day the winds blew fiercely from
the north and the cold was intense. Before going
to bed that night Bégon instructed a servant to ex-
tinguish all the fires. But one of the chimneys was
overlooked and in the middle of the night the
intendancy burst into flames. Clad only in
bathrobe and slippers the Bégons almost miracul-
ously managed to flee [*see* François de Lajoüe*].
The intendant lost three servants who perished in
the blaze, his secretary who found his way outside only to die a few days later of the effects of
frostbite, and personal possessions valued at
40,000 *livres*. To help himself recover from this
blow Bégon went into business with Jean Butler,
an important La Rochelle merchant. The intendant looked after the sale of merchandise which
his partner sent to Quebec and provided him with
lumber to build two vessels which traded
between New France, La Rochelle, and the West
Indies. Bégon professed to see nothing wrong
with these activities. On the contrary he claimed
that the country could only benefit from them.
But he was clearly treading on dangerous ground.

In his official capacity, the intendant first had
to deal with the card money. Several proposals
for its liquidation were under consideration by
1713. The minister of Marine, Pontchartrain,
favoured the conversion of cards into securities
bearing a fixed rate of interest but abandoned this
plan upon realizing that it would not satisfy the
colony's pressing need for an immediate supply
of money. Late in 1713 Bégon proposed the
redemption of the cards at half their face value
over a five-year period. Each year 320,000 *livres*
of cards would be called in for which 160,000
livres of bills of exchange redeemable in specie
would be issued. Reducing the value of the cards

by 50 per cent would cause no hardships, he
pointed out, since most of the holders had
acquired them at a fabulous rate of profit. The
court accepted the essence of the proposal. The
operation got under way in 1714 and despite
many difficulties was completed by 1720. It had
been a gigantic undertaking offering many opportunities for illicit gain. There is evidence to suggest that Bégon did not fail to profit from them.

The most important issue after card money in
the early years of Bégon's intendancy was that of
the beaver trade which was showing signs of
recovery by 1715. Aubert, Néret et Gayot's 12-
year monopoly on the purchase and sale of the
pelts would expire in 1718 [*see* Antoine Pascaud*]. Should the monopoly be continued in
either their or other hands after that date or
should there be free trade in beaver? This question caused a great debate in the colony with
Bégon emerging as the spokesman of those
favouring the second alternative. He maintained
that Canada was now sufficiently well established
to take charge of its own commercial affairs.
Furthermore, as a matter of principle, the intendant had little faith in companies. He felt that
commerce could be carried out more successfully
by individual merchants than by corporations
which, more often than not, were neglected by
their directors; and also could be carried out with
less danger since the failure of an individual
affected only a few persons while a whole country could suffer from the failure of a company.
The government was initially won to Bégon's
point of view, announcing in June 1716 that the
beaver trade would become free as soon as
Aubert, Néret et Gayot's contract expired. But it
soon reversed its stand. The monopoly was maintained and in 1717 granted to the newly founded
Compagnie d'Occident for 25 years.

Curiously Bégon, whose attitude towards companies makes him appear somewhat reactionary,
also believed in *laissez-faire*, an advanced theory
for his day. "Commerce," he wrote in 1714,
"must depend on neither the governor nor the
intendant who should enter into it only to prevent
disorder." In keeping with this philosophy he
proposed in that year a revolutionary free commercial system for the western hinterland.
Anyone wishing to trade there should be allowed
to do so. Bégon was confident that this liberty
would not result in an excessive growth in the
number of traders. Competition would keep it
down to what the commerce could bear. Nor
would it result in an overproduction of beaver
pelts. Merchants, who always regulate their
affairs judiciously when given the liberty to do so,
would not produce more than they could sell.

Even with these assurances the proposal was a little too radical for Pontchartrain, the minister of Marine, who could not yet bring himself to revive the 25 fur-trading licences (*congés*), and nothing came of it. But it remains interesting as a symptom of middle-class unrest with *dirigisme* at the end of the reign of Louis XIV.

By 1714 Bégon had arrived at some basic conclusions on the Canadian economy. It was of the low export type. Thus local merchants were obliged to buy in France more than they sold there and were kept perpetually in debt. Bégon therefore recommended the establishment of iron and glassworks in the colony. These industries would help right the commercial balance by reducing the dependency on French manufactures and would stimulate the vital industry of shipbuilding by making iron available at cheap rates. Pontchartrain with his narrow mercantilism – he wrote in 1704 that whatever competed with French products should not be manufactured in the colonies – must again have been startled by the unorthodoxy of his intendant. However, he could only agree with Bégon's diagnosis of the ultimate cause of Canada's problems. Indeed, he had independently arrived at much the same conclusion. "This country," wrote the intendant, "will become more and more miserable unless ways are found of sending people to it." The small number of workmen doomed to failure almost every economic undertaking. To fill the need for labour Bégon asked for soldiers whom he considered preferable to indentured employees (*engagés*). The latter often returned to France once they had served their time in the colony whereas soldiers got married and became habitants. But, he must soon have noticed, habitants were usually not available for labour off their farms and did not constitute a work force in the true sense of the word. This observation is probably what led him to ask in 1716 for a massive infusion of Negro slaves. They would, though he did not of course use the expression, constitute a permanent proletariat.

The request was turned down when Vaudreuil, to whom it had been referred for comment, remarked that the climate was too cold for Negroes and that the cost of clothing them during the long winters would be more than the habitants could bear. Still, the request marks out Bégon as a radical intendant. But he was not a very consistent one. The claim he made that Canada was poor by virtue of underpopulation and an unfavourable balance of commerce did not harmonize well with his other one that the country was sufficiently established to manage its own commercial affairs. And even as he was making

these conflicting statements he was up to his neck in activities that harmonized still less with his professed belief in *laissez-faire*. By 1716 these activities had nearly discredited him in the eyes of the home authorities.

On 24 Jan. 1714 Bégon issued an ordinance whose sweeping terms brought the wheat trade to a virtual standstill. It prohibited the shipment of wheat, flour, and biscuits outside the colony and even forbade transactions involving wheat within. Bégon claimed that this action was needed to avert the threat of famine, for the harvest of 1713 had not been good, but this contention was challenged by Claude de Bermen* de La Martinière, first councillor of the Conseil Supérieur. According to him the harvest of 1713 had been adequate and there was even wheat left over from the bumper crop of 1712. Famine, claimed La Martinière, was simply a pretext invented by Bégon to justify the gigantic wheat-grabbing operation upon which he had embarked. The January ordinance had placed the entire wheat supply at his disposal and his agents scoured the countryside buying up all available reserves as well as great quantities of pigs and cattle. Bégon was allegedly paying for his purchases with the cards the government had already redeemed and even churning out new ones! "All they cost him is the price of making them out," observed La Martinière. Some of this wheat was shipped aboard Butler's vessels to the West Indies, where it was in great demand because of crop failures in France. The rest was turned into bread at the king's bakery, bread which Bégon sold to the public at an excessive price.

How much truth there was in these accusations by La Martinière is difficult to say. The threat of famine was not something Bégon was making up. From 292,415 *minots* in 1712 the wheat crop plummeted to 251,460 *minots* in 1713 and to 236,049 *minots* in 1714. In a situation like this the intendant was duty-bound to protect the colony's food supply from depletion at the hands of hoarders and speculators. But it is also a fact that Bégon was in business with Butler. This was enough to arouse suspicions, perhaps not entirely unfounded, that the intendant was using the great powers of his office to further his own interests and those of his partner.

The complaints against Bégon did not leave Pontchartrain indifferent. "I am told that he is making himself the absolute master of the country's entire trade and that the people of Canada are lost unless we curb his greed and injustices," the minister wrote to Scipion-Jérôme upon learning that the latter's brother seemed

59

Bégon de La Picardière

well on the way to becoming Canada's leading baker, butcher, and shipowner. Scipion-Jérôme promptly wrote to Michel who attempted to refute these accusations. He admitted that he had been carrying out a private trade with Butler but attempted to minimize its scope. Naturally he vehemently denied that he had tried to seize control of the colony's food supply and did manage to offer some plausible explanations for even his most peculiar actions in 1714 and 1715. For instance, La Martinière had charged that individuals had been touring the countryside buying up livestock in the intendant's name. Bégon admitted that they had done so but rejected the motives imputed to him by the first councillor. He pointed out that a large supply of meat was needed to feed the troops. To obtain this supply he felt that it would be more economical to deal with someone who would buy directly from the habitants than to follow the usual practice of contracting with a butcher. Bégon could still be charged with appallingly bad judgement for not foreseeing how this totally irregular method of obtaining meat would be viewed in the colony; but he did succeed, if not in refuting the far more serious accusation that he was a food profiteer, at least in raising doubts about its veracity.

But he did not wax rich on his additional revenues, licit or illicit. The better part of them were probably used to replace the furniture and provisions lost in the fire of 1713, to entertain the colony's fashionable society – Monseignat described Bégon as the most lavish of the six intendants of New France he had known – and to help pay off the debts of his uncle François, grand master of waters and forests for the province of Berry. Finally, like Jean Talon* who also engaged in trade when he was intendant of New France, Bégon invested considerable sums in the country. In 1718, for 6,237 *livres monnaie de France*, he purchased from Françoise Duquet the *arrière-fief* of Grandpré on the seigneury of Notre-Dame-des-Anges on which he constructed sawmills and a tannery valued at 40,000 *livres*. Bégon could clearly not accomplish all these things on his official income. Including the annual gratuity of 3,000 *livres* paid to him in consideration of the losses he had sustained in the fire of 1713, it amounted to 15,000 *livres*, but its purchasing power must have been vastly inferior to that figure since it was remitted to him in depreciated cards. Even with the revenues from his trading activities he was unable to make ends meet. In 1719 he sold for 8,000 *livres* the Hôtel d'Alluye which he owned in France. Two years later he was searching for creditors.

Though the colony profited in many ways from Bégon's investments, the trade he was carrying on with Butler still met with the reprobation of the council of Marine, the committee which assumed the direction of maritime and colonial affairs soon after the death of Louis XIV on 1 Sept. 1715. "You recognize that you have engaged in commerce," it wrote the intendant. "You acted wrongly for you could not be unaware that this activity was not permitted and was in no way suitable in the position you occupied." Bégon was warned that any repetition of this offence would result in his immediate recall. But there was a second and still more bitter blow in store for him. During his leave of absence in France from 1714 to 1716, Governor Vaudreuil complained that Bégon had cramped his policy in 1712. He had not only vetoed his project for the reoccupation of Michilimackinac but also insisted on countersigning some orders issued to military personnel. Pontchartrain served Bégon with a sharp admonition; the council of Marine went much further. At Vaudreuil's request it decreed that his decision should prevail in case of future disagreements between him and the intendant. Bégon was being placed under the tutelage of the powerful governor.

He seems to have collapsed under these two blows, sinking into lethargy. An examination of the Canadian correspondence over the next few years discloses no significant proposals by him, no probing commentaries on social and economic questions. The intendant was confining himself to a purely administrative role, presiding over meetings of the Conseil Supérieur, managing royal supplies, and issuing routine royal ordinances. In 1717, as the result of a prolonged summer drought, the spectre of famine once more loomed over the colony. Bégon issued an ordinance prohibiting the export of flour and biscuits. Vaudreuil in Montreal and Jean Bouillet* de La Chassaigne, his delegate in Quebec, claimed that this move was inadequate but despite their frantic letters the intendant refused to take further action. You are the master, he in effect told the governor. Do whatever you think best. But ruling on this matter would have constituted such a blatant invasion of the intendant's jurisdiction that Vaudreuil held back.

In 1720 Bégon finally came to life. Since the death of Louis XIV France had been reassessing her attitude towards colonies and a new and more positive policy was gradually taking form. Where Canada was concerned the policy featured a more intensive effort to populate the country with *engagés* and soldiers and the making of greater sums of money available to help develop new enterprises. Bégon had long felt that the colony could perform a most useful service by acting as a supplier of hemp and he took it upon himself to offer 60 *livres* per quintal for this plant. This offer was more than three times the cost of the French product but even this incentive, he thought, would be inadequate unless the colony solved its labour problem. With far greater insistence than in 1716 he renewed his request for Negro slaves. For a start the Compagnie des Indes, which had a monopoly on the trade, should send 200 slaves to Canada. Bégon already claimed to have buyers for 100 of both sexes at 500 *livres* apiece. The council of Marine was favourably impressed but not the Compagnie des Indes, which did not act on the proposal. It was probably just as well for any large scale experimentation with Negro slavery would almost certainly have failed in Canada.

Encouraging the growing of hemp was only one of Bégon's activities during these years. In 1720 he inaugurated a system of mail delivery and public transportation between Montreal, Trois-Rivières, and Quebec, which followed water routes where the roads left off. The following year he began drawing up the colossal *papier terrier* (register of landed property) of New France, consisting of an exact description of the state of each seigneury in the colony. The intendant rightly felt that the edicts of Marly, calling for the forfeiture of uncleared seigneuries to the crown and of uncleared rotures to the seigneurial domain, could not be rationally applied until this information was available. Unfortunately, in the midst of these useful activities, Bégon became involved in a fresh cycle of difficulties with the home authorities, this time over finances. These difficulties probably convinced the council of Marine that he had outlived his usefulness as intendant of New France.

By 1720 card money had been totally withdrawn from circulation and Pierre-Nicolas Gaudion, the treasurer of Marine, began his final tabulation. To his astonishment he discovered that the fund set aside for the redemption of cards was overdrawn by 157,251 *livres*. "It appears that there is something in the case so extraordinary that the Council will not conceal from you that it has viewed it with much pain," Bégon was told. "It is willing however to suspend judgement until it has received the explanations it desires you to furnish on the point." The explanations he submitted made it appear that he had been erroneously charging some shipping expenditures to the card money fund. But hardly had this matter been cleared up, in a manner of speaking at least, than another complication arose. Now that card money had been abolished, much of the

funds required for government expenditures were sent to Canada in specie. In 1721 this cash remittance amounted to 188,000 *livres*. But within a month of the arrival of the ships the local treasurer of the Marine, Nicolas LANOULLIER de Boisclerc, announced that the funds were exhausted and closed his till. Most of the officers had not yet received their salary and little new specie had appeared in the colony. Vaudreuil sent a strong complaint to the council of Marine which promptly asked Bégon to explain where all the money had gone.

Perhaps the intendant was a victim of that negligence which marked so many of his actions in the 1720s. The state of the accounts of the royal stores in Montreal, Trois-Rivières, and Quebec, which were in arrears and total disarray, provide an example. Or perhaps he was a victim of a system which made him responsible for financial administration but placed the funds themselves under the control of an agent of the treasurers of the Marine. In principle the latter made no payment unless the intendant authorized it. In practice, however, it was difficult to prevent an unscrupulous treasurer from misappropriating funds, and Lanoullier was notorious for keeping loose accounts and indulging in sharp practices. Bégon, however, spoke well of Lanoullier and in 1721 granted him a 20-year exclusive franchise of the post and passenger system between Montreal and Quebec. This behaviour does nothing to dispel the suspicion that there was some collusion between the two men.

In 1723 the council of Marine was dissolved and the bureau of marine and colonies was once more entrusted to a minister. He was 22-year-old Jean-Frédéric Phélypeaux de Maurepas, the son of Pontchartrain. One of his first decisions was to appoint Bégon to the intendancy of Le Havre which had just become vacant. Maurepas was thereby disposing of a man who no longer gave satisfaction in the position he occupied and rendering a service to his relative, Jeanne-Élisabeth de Beauharnois, who was unhappy in Canada and yearned to return to France. Bégon was delighted by the news of his transfer. He thanked the minister profusely but claimed to be puzzled by his request to bring with him all the documents necessary to terminate the affair of card money. "The matter involves you too closely for me not to insist on it," wrote Maurepas. Bégon claimed not to see how it concerned him; it concerned rather the agents of the treasurers of the Marine. He did promise, however, to give an account of his stewardship which he hoped would satisfy his superior. "Saying more at present would serve no purpose," he concluded enigmatically.

Bégon de La Picardière

But two more years went by before Bégon left the colony. Edme-Nicolas Robert, who had been appointed to succeed him, died at sea in 1724, and Guillaume Chazel, who was appointed to succeed Robert, perished in the wreck of the *Chameau* off Île Royale (Cape Breton Island) in 1725. The time Bégon spent in the colony as a lame-duck intendant was costly. In December 1725, for the second time in 13 years, the intendant's palace was destroyed by fire. But the two years were not unproductive. In consultation with Bishop Saint-Vallier [La Croix*] and the parish priests he reduced the number of taverns to two per parish; reduction to one, it was felt, might expose consumers to being overcharged and served with spirits of inferior quality. As a means of raising revenue in the colony Bégon recommended that farming out the western posts was preferable to levying taxes on the refractory habitants. This was among the most important suggestions that Bégon ever made for before too long nearly all the western posts had been placed under a system of private leasehold. Finally, he strove mightily to maintain those cordial relations with Vaudreuil which had always prevailed despite many tense moments. They were gravely imperilled in April 1725 when the governor challenged his colleague's adjudication of the post of Témiscamingue to Joseph de FLEURY de La Gorgendière. The award had been made according to rules and on the order of the court. But Vaudreuil, who had a personal interest in the trade of the post, arbitrarily suspended Bégon's ordinance authorizing La Gorgendière to take possession of it. In the face of this provocation the intendant showed admirable restraint.

At length on 2 Sept. 1726 a new intendant, Claude-Thomas Dupuy*, arrived in the colony. Bégon could now depart. He took leave of Quebec on 18 October aboard the king's vessel, *Éléphant*. At 11 o'clock on the morning of 22 November after a rough but swift crossing the *Éléphant* entered the roadsteads of Rochefort. A few hours later, after an absence of 14 years, Bégon "with great joy" stepped down on the soil of France.

He served as intendant of Le Havre for approximately ten years. Situated at the mouth of the Seine, which led into the heartland of France, it was a busy seaport. A total of 893 vessels sailed from it in 1724. Towards 1736 Bégon was named intendant of the admiralty of Normandy with residence at Rouen. But both before 1736 and after he resided for long periods at La Picardière. According to Canon Pierre Hazeur* de L'Orme he did so to save money for his finances were gravely embarrassed. He owed an unspecified amount to Lanoullier, 30,000 *livres* to some La Rochelle merchants, and he suffered a severe blow in 1732 when a shipment of wine he was sending to Canada was lost at sea. But he did not meet with much sympathy from Claude-Michel in 1740 when he gave poverty as the reason why he had allowed the pension he was obliged to pay his younger brother by the terms of their father's will to fall in arrears. "[The pension] is a small sum for a man of your revenues," bitterly wrote Claude-Michel. But what he thought were revenues may in reality have been loans from Scipion-Jérôme and his two Carmelite sisters, Marie-Rose and Marie-Thérèse, to whom Michel could always turn in time of need. These loans were probably what enabled him to endow his daughters, Jeanne-Élisabeth and Catherine, handsomely at the time of their marriage and to afford himself the luxury of some exotic experiences. In 1743 he accompanied the Turkish ambassador, Sayde Pasha, who was returning to Constantinople. Among Bégon's activities in the Turkish capital was a visit, by extraordinary permission, to the Sultan's harem. Upon his return to France he wrote an account of his voyage.

Michel Bégon died at La Picardière on 18 Jan. 1747, only one year after having been named intendant of naval forces. Three of his eight children survived him: Catherine, Marie-Madeleine, an Ursuline nun at Blois, and Michel, who was intendant of Dunkerque from 1756 to 1761.

In the history of New France the period from 1712 to 1726 is one of gradual economic recovery. When Bégon arrived in the colony the economy was at a virtual standstill as a result of the collapse of the beaver trade and the financial system and the situation was further aggravated by bad harvests in 1713 and 1714. When he left the economy was rapidly reviving. The beaver trade had recovered from its prolonged slump and there were unmistakable signs of expansion in lumbering, shipbuilding, the fisheries, and the cultivation of hemp. For example, 47 sawmills were in operation in 1726, a category not even mentioned in the census of 1712. Unquestionably, the most fragile sector of the economy remained agriculture. Population stood at 29,396 in 1726 and the number of acres under cultivation at 96,202. But though land clearance had outstripped population growth 81 to 59 per cent since 1712 the colony was experiencing enormous difficulties in breaking out of the phase of subsistence agriculture. The wheat crop in 1726 amounted only to 14 *minots* per capita.

In this process of slow economic growth Bégon seems to have played but a marginal role. It is possible to speak of a Talon era and of a Hocquart* era in the history of New France but not of a Bégon era for, unlike the two other intendants, he did not sufficiently mark his period. He deserves credit for the decision to redeem card money at half value, for stimulating the cultivation of hemp, but not for much else. The fire of January 1713, after which he seems to have worked harder at private than at state affairs, and the paralytic effect of the reprimands of 1716 help to account for this unimpressive record but they do not explain it fully. Bégon also seems to have been prone to indolence and endowed with only an average mind. An example is the way he pinned his hopes for New France's economic recovery on Negro slavery. He had no alternative suggestion to make when the court twice failed to act on this unrealistic proposal.

But Bégon had many redeeming qualities. He was kind and generous. According to Hocquart, the money he spent in Canada on commercial establishments "turned less to his advantage than to that of the great number of unfortunates whom it provided with a living." In difficult moments, and he had many of them from 1713 to 1726, he never lost his serenity. Qualities like these made him perhaps the best liked intendant in the colony's history. "We are losing a perfect *honnête homme* and a worthy intendant in the person of M. Bégon," wrote Bishop Saint-Vallier, a man chary of compliments, in September 1726. In 1732, after describing Bégon's financial problems, Hazeur de L'Orme concluded sadly: "He did not deserve such a fate, being a kind and peaceable man who did nothing but good in Canada."

YVES F. ZOLTVANY

AN, Col., B, 33–50; C¹¹ᴬ, 33–48; Marine, B¹, 8; C⁷, 23 (dossier Bégon); Section Outre-Mer, G¹, 461. ANQ, Greffe de Florent de La Cetière, 28 oct. 1718; Greffe de Claude Louet, 12 oct. 1728. Archives du ministère des Affaires étrangères, Mém. et doc., Am., 7. ASQ, Lettres, O, 50, 51, 53; Séminaire, XIV, 4, no.7. BN, MSS, Fr., 29624. "Correspondance de Vaudreuil," APQ *Rapport, 1947-48*, 137–339. *Documents relating to Canadian currency during the French period* (Shortt), I, *passim*. "Lettres de Claude Bermen de La Martinière," *BRH*, XXXVIII (1932), 18–39.

[Although Guy Frégault remarked in 1944, in *La civilisation de la Nouvelle-France*, that "the career of Michel Bégon would deserve to be studied," little has been written on this intendant. The following works have been found to be the most useful: Yvonne Bezard, *Fonctionnaires maritimes et coloniaux sous Louis XIV: les Bégon* (Paris, 1932). (This is essentially a biographical study of the father of the intendant of New France, based largely on the family archives located at the Château de Gemeaux in France. There are letters of a personal nature by the Bégon of Canada but it was impossible to consult them in the preparation of this article.) Pierre Dardel, *Navires et marchandises dans les ports de Rouen et du Havre au XVIIIᵉ siècle* (École pratique des hautes études, Centre de recherches historiques, Ports-routes-trafics, [15], Paris, 1963); *Commerce, industrie et navigation à Rouen et au Havre au XVIIIème siècle; rivalité croissante entre ces deux ports; la conjoncture* (Rouen, 1966). (These two quantitative studies do not mention Bégon but give a general idea of the situation of Le Havre around the time of his intendancy.)

Dubé, *Claude-Thomas Dupuy*. J.-N. Fauteux, *Essai sur l'industrie*. Frégault, *La civilisation de la Nouvelle-France*; *Le XVIIIᵉ siècle canadien*, in particular, "Essai sur les finances canadiennes." Lanctot, *Histoire du Canada*, III. Trudel, *L'esclavage au Canada français*. J.F. Bosher, "Government and private interests in New France," *Canadian Public Administration* (Toronto), X (1967), 244–57. J.-E. Roy, "Notes sur l'intendant Bégon," *BRH*, IV (1898), 265–73. Régis Roy, "Michel Bégon," *BRH*, VIII (1902), 161–69. Henri Têtu, "Le chapitre de la cathédrale de Québec et ses délégués en France," *BRH*, XVI (1910), 229. Y.F.Z.]

BÉLAIR, JEAN-LOUIS PLESSY, *dit. See* PLESSY

BELCOUR (Bellecour, Bellecourt), JACQUES DE LAFONTAINE DE. *See* LAFONTAINE

BELLAIR, JOSEPH-NICOLAS GAUTIER, *dit. See* GAUTIER

BELLEFEUILLE, JEAN-FRANÇOIS LEFEBVRE DE. *See* LEFEBVRE

BELLE-HUMEUR, ALEXANDRE BOURG, *dit. See* BOURG

BELLEVILLE, JEAN-URBAIN MARTEL DE. *See* MARTEL

BELT OF WAMPUM. *See* KAGHSWAGHTANIUNT

BÉNARD (Besnard), MICHEL, receiving agent for the Domaine d'Occident, councillor of the Conseil Supérieur of New France; b. *c.* 1713 at Versailles, France, son of Louis Bénard, a soupcook in the king's kitchens, and Marie Guy; m. on 20 Nov. 1741 Marie-Germaine-Eustache Lanoullier de Boisclerc. After the conquest he returned to France, where he cannot be traced.

It is not known under what circumstances Michel Bénard arrived in Canada. On 19 Nov. 1733 he attended in Quebec the marriage of Thérèse Bouat and Louis-Jean POULIN de Courval, king's attorney at Trois-Rivières, in the

Bermen

home of Paul-Louis DAZEMARD de Lusignan, an officer in the colonial regular troops. Early in 1736 he was at Quebec, carrying out the duties of writer in the office of the Marine. By virtue of this office he was first secretary to Intendant Hocquart* until the latter's departure in 1748. He was then receiving 600 *livres* a year, an appreciable salary for the period. In the summer of 1752 Nicolas LANOULLIER de Boisclerc gave up his duties as controller for the Domaine du Roi in favour of his son-in-law, Bénard, who from 24 Dec. 1753 held this office along with that of assessor of the Conseil Supérieur. The king had established the office of assessor in 1741 "to create a spirit of competition among the young men of good family in the colony who have already made progress in the study of jurisprudence by means of the lectures on law which are being given by the king's attorney general [Louis-Guillaume VERRIER]." The assessor's work consisted essentially of preparing the documents in certain lawsuits for the councillors and of investigating and reporting to the council in certain civil suits. Only when reporting on a case was he entitled to speak and vote within the Conseil Supérieur. In all other instances he could act only in an advisory capacity. He enjoyed "the same honours, privileges, and prerogatives" as the members of the council, ranking after the last councillor within the council and in official ceremonies. On 24 April 1757 Michel Bénard was promoted councillor, succeeding his late father-in-law; he held this office until the conquest. From 1758 to 1760, Bénard was also commissary of the royal prisons in Quebec.

In the king's service from his arrival in the colony, married to the daughter of a councillor who was keeper of the seals of the Conseil Supérieur, Michel Bénard was a typical official of the old régime who through his work and diligence, and thanks to his marriage, succeeded in climbing the rungs of the administrative and social ladders in New France. In the course of his career Bénard struck up friendships with Jean-Victor Varin* de La Marre, commissary and controller of the Marine, Nicolas-Gaspard BOUCAULT, lieutenant general of the admiralty court, François DAINE, lieutenant general for civil and criminal affairs of the provost court of Quebec, and Charles-Denis REGNARD Duplessis de Morampont, an officer in the colonial regular troops and provost marshal, all members of the administrative élite in New France.

ANDRÉ LACHANCE

AN, Col., B, 66, f.244v; 95, ff.243–44; 97, f.271v; 105, f.198v; C¹¹A, 67, ff.114–15; 73, f.15; 114, ff.28–29, 50, 121, 292v, 384; 120, f.350v; F³, 11, f.33. ANQ, Greffe de C.-H. Du Laurent, 16 nov. 1741; NF, Coll. de pièces jud. et not., 2136, 2149; NF, Ins. Cons. sup., IX, 4v–6. "Recensement de Québec, 1744" (APQ *Rapport*). P.-G. Roy, *Inv. jug. et délib., 1717–1760*, IV, 76–77; V, 292; VI, 113, 114, 125, 298–99; "Les secrétaires des gouverneurs et intendants de la Nouvelle-France," *BRH*, XLI (1935), 103.

BERMEN DE LA MARTINIÈRE, CLAUDE-ANTOINE DE, officer in the colonial regular troops; b. 12 July 1700 at Quebec, son of Claude de Bermen* de La Martinière and Marie-Anne Cailleteau; d. 24 Dec. 1761 at Quebec.

Claude-Antoine de Bermen de La Martinière's father was a leading but impoverished citizen of Quebec, related, it seems, to the famous Duc de Saint-Simon. Shortly before his death in 1719, the father wrote to Saint-Simon asking him to arrange that Claude-Antoine, who was affected with the king's evil (scrofula), be sent to France to be cured, and to provide for his son's future, because he feared he was physically too weak to pursue any career. The letter does not seem to have received a response.

Claude-Antoine, however, managed on his own. He recovered sufficiently from his illness to take up a successful military career, rising to the rank of second ensign in 1722, ensign on the active list in 1727, lieutenant in 1734, and captain in 1743. In 1737 he commanded at Baie-des-Puants (Green Bay, Wis.). Made a knight of the order of Saint-Louis in 1751, he served as commander at Fort Beauséjour (near Sackville, N.B.) for several months in 1754. After enjoying a distinguished record of service, he was forced to retire with a pension of 600 *livres* a year in 1755 because of ill health, and died six years later.

He had married in Montreal in 1729 Hannah Parsons, by whom he had ten children. This Englishwoman was originally from Wells (Me.) and had been captured and brought to Canada at the age of two; on arrival there she was baptized Catherine. In 1763, not long after the death of her husband, she sold the only family property, the seigneury of La Martinière, adjoining the seigneury of Lauson, to Governor James Murray*, and went to live in France. The family name did not survive in Canada.

EDWARD H. BORINS

AN, Col., D²C, 57, f.116; 61, ff.35, 166; 222, f.499; E, 251 (dossier La Martinière). "Une lettre inédite du gouverneur Duquesne," *BRH*, XVIII (1912), 348. Fauteux, *Les chevaliers de Saint-Louis*, 151–52. Le Jeune, *Dictionnaire.* Tanguay, *Dictionnaire.* Coleman, *New England captives*, I, 410–13. J.-E. Roy, *Claude de Bermen de La Martinière (1636–1719)* (Lévis, Qué.,

1891), 90–100; *Histoire de la seigneurie de Lauzon* (5v., Lévis, Qué., 1897–1904). P.-G. Roy, *Fils de Québec*, I, 157–58; "Une supplique de M. de Bermen de La Martinière," *BRH*, XXXV (1929), 382–84 (contains part of a letter written by Claude de Bermen de La Martinière to the Duc de Saint-Simon).

BERTHELOT DE BEAUCOURS, JOSUÉ DUBOIS. *See* Dubois

BIENVILLE, JEAN-BAPTISTE LE MOYNE DE. *See* Le Moyne

BISAILLON (Bezellon, Bizaillon), **PETER** (baptized **Pierre**), coureur de bois; b. *c.* 1662 in Saint-Jean-d'Aubrigoux (dept. of Haute-Loire), France; m. 1727 in Pennsylvania to Martha Coombe; d. 18 July 1742 and buried in East Caln Township, Chester County, Pennsylvania.

Pierre Bisaillon was one of five brothers who came to New France and engaged in trade with the Indians, an occupation continued into the 19th century by their descendants. In 1686 Bisaillon contracted at Montreal to go with Henri Tonty*'s party in search of René-Robert Cavelier* de La Salle. At some time between 1687 and 1696 he entered into partnership for a trading voyage with Gédéon Petit and the Sieur de Salvaye, who had fled to Albany to escape Governor Brisay* de Denonville's accusation that they had been trafficking with the English. The voyage was unsuccessful, and the partnership dissolved.

About 1688 or 1689 Bisaillon went to Pennsylvania, "poor and miserable" but with invaluable knowledge of the best sources of peltry. There he joined the trading organization of Jacques Le Tort, an "eminent" Huguenot refugee from Bonnétable (dept. of Sarthe). This organization, based on the Schuylkill River near present Spring City, was in the employ of Dr Daniel Coxe, who planned to create an empire in the Indian trade on the south shore of Lake Erie through his New Mediterranean Sea Company.

Pursuing this goal, sometime between 1687 and 1692 three of Coxe's employees made a western voyage blazing new trails for the Indian trade that would soon make Pennsylvania a serious competitor of New York and New France. No document names these pioneers, and there is difference of opinion as to whether Bisaillon was among them or whether he came to Pennsylvania as a result of meeting them on their road; but it is known that they travelled up the Mississippi from the Ohio to a "great yellow river" which they ascended.

Coxe abandoned his schemes in 1692, but Bisaillon and other coureurs de bois went on trading from the "back parts" of Pennsylvania, distressing Philadelphia fur merchants who petitioned for controls over these Frenchmen "Tradeing in Remote and Obscure places ... and such some of them in Alliance with the ffrench and Indians in League with the ffrench." Bisaillon acquired protection by becoming chief factor, together with an associate named Louis Lemoisin, for the Pennsylvania Company and its manager Colonel Robert Quary, "the greatest Merchant or Factor in the Province." While so engaged, Bisaillon had to travel to Iroquoia to ransom one of his brothers who had been captured in Canada by the Mohawks in 1696.

He continued to add to his Indian contacts. While employed by Coxe he had traded actively with the nearby Delawares and Minisinks, as well as more distant tribes, and when bands of the Shawnees came into Pennsylvania in 1692, Bisaillon found among them an old Canadian acquaintance, Martin Chartier, who had been an associate of La Salle but had married a Shawnee and assimilated to her band. Peter, as he was now known, also kept in touch with his brothers Richard and Michel. The latter, who remained Canadian, became prominent and influential among the Illinois Indians. James Le Tort, the son of Peter's former employer, was known to have visited Canada in 1701, and was jailed in Philadelphia in 1704 because of suspicions about his purpose. A network of coureurs de bois thus apparently preserved close personal associations over a vast territory regardless of formal nationality or employment. While English colonials suspected their loyalty on the one side, French officials denounced their business enterprise on the other. In 1702 Henri-Louis Deschamps* de Boishébert complained from Michilimackinac of the willingness of coureurs de bois to trade with Albany or Philadelphia. Detroit has been called practically a satellite of New York's trading system, but Bisaillon and his associates seem to have diverted a share of Detroit's trade to Philadelphia.

William Penn, the proprietary of the province, was disturbed by rumours that this backwoods network was conspiring with the French, and he moved to "confine" Bisaillon. Bisaillon's loyalty was eventually cleared in England, but his wide-ranging activities disturbed Pennsylvania authorities, especially when France and England went to war. He was obliged to give security bonds from time to time between 1700 and 1711, and he was preventively jailed on at least one occasion.

These difficulties occurred when his competitors' patrons held power. In the intervals when controls were in the hands of the merchants with whom he dealt, Bisaillon was employed by the province as an interpreter of Indian languages. In 1712 he managed at last to find secure protection by coming under the wing of Pennsylvania's secretary, James Logan, who simultaneously established near-monopolies on political power and the Indian trade. Logan built a trading post at Conestoga on the Susquehanna River; and for six years Bisaillon, the Le Tort Family, and the Chartier. family formed the backbone of Logan's trading organization while Logan himself presided over the province's Indian treaty relationships. Though personnel changed and competitors arose, this organization provided the base from which Pennsylvania traders eventually challenged France's control over the Ohio country, a struggle which helped precipitate the Seven Years' War in America.

The Bisaillons were linked directly to the origins of that struggle through a policy of English expansion adopted by the Board of Trade in 1720. The board had been strongly persuaded by a long argument made by Pennsylvania's governor, Sir William Keith, on the basis of information about Canada and the Ohio country supplied by James Logan. He, in turn, had acquired it directly from Michel Bisaillon. Michel spoke with great authority. He had worked with Lamothe Cadillac [Laumet*] out of Detroit. In 1714 he had been denounced by Jean-Marie de Villes*, a Jesuit missionary, for planning to introduce the English "of Carolina" to the Illinois, and had extricated himself from this dangerous situation by zealously mobilizing hundreds of Illinois warriors in 1715 to aid Canada's attacks on the Fox Indians and allied tribes. The board moved aggressively through the governors of New York, Pennsylvania, and Virginia to challenge French domination of the tribes of the interior. Because of the complications of colonial politics, the expansionist policy temporarily failed, but it revived after the Pennsylvania traders established bases among the Indians of the Ohio region in the 1740s.

These traders were not French. James Logan had gradually replaced the Frenchmen in his organization with English colonials. Martin Chartier's son Peter broke so sharply with Logan that he led his Shawnee band into alliance with Canada. Peter Bisaillon, however, settled down in his old age. Unlike many of his brethren in the Indian trade, he had been astute and careful, and he not only acquired but kept sizeable estates in land in the Susquehanna valley, which he left intact to his widow.

FRANCIS JENNINGS

American Philosophical Soc. (Philadelphia, Pa.), Penn letters and ancient documents, III, 9. AN, Col., C^{IIA}, 20, ff.220–21; 34, f.356v; 35, ff.99–100v. Pennsylvania Hist. Soc. (Philadelphia, Pa.), Logan papers, X, 20; XI, 8, 9; Penn papers, additional miscellaneous letters, I, 23; Society miscellaneous collections, Indians, box 11c. PRO, CO 5/1261, no.87. *Archives of Maryland*, ed. W.H. Browne *et al.* (70v. to date, Baltimore, Md., 1883–19   ), VIII, 346, 517–18; XX, 406, 470–71. "Correspondance de Vaudreuil," APQ *Rapport, 1947–48*, 327–28. *The first explorations of the trans-Alleghany region by the Virginians, 1650–1674*, ed. C. W. Alvord and Lee Bidgood (Cleveland, Ohio, 1912), 231–49. Pennsylvania, *Colonial records*, I, 19 Dec. 1693; II, 17 May 1701, 17 Aug. 1703, 18 May 1704, 6 Aug. 1704, 18 March 1710, 28 May 1711, 22 Aug. 1711. PRO, *CSP, Col., 1719–20*, 31–37; *1720–21*, 436. Godbout, "Nos ancêtres," APQ *Rapport, 1955–57*, 474–75. Massicotte, "Répertoire des engagements pour l'Ouest," APQ *Rapport, 1929–30*. C. A. Hanna, *The wilderness trail...* (2v., New York, London, 1911), I. A. G. Zimmerman, "The Indian trade of colonial Pennsylvania" (unpublished PHD thesis, University of Delaware, Newark, 1966). E. A. Benson, "The Huguenot LeTorts: first Christian family on the Conestoga," Lancaster County Hist. Soc. *Journal* (Lancaster, Pa.), LXV (1961), 92–105. Francis Jennings, "The Indian trade of the Susquehanna valley," American Philosophical Soc. *Proc.* (Philadelphia, Pa.), CX (1966), 406–24. A. G. Zimmerman, "Daniel Coxe and the New Mediterranean Sea Company," *Pennsylvania Magazine of History and Biography* (Philadelphia, Pa.), LXXVI (1952), 86–96. Y. F. Zoltvany, "New France and the west, 1701–1713," *CHR*, XLVI (1965), 301–22.

BLAINVILLE, PIERRE-JOSEPH CÉLORON DE. *See* CÉLORON

BLANZY, LOUIS-CLAUDE DANRÉ DE. *See* DANRÉ

BOISCLERC, JEAN-EUSTACHE LANOULLIER DE. *See* LANOULLIER

BOISCLERC, NICOLAS LANOULLIER DE. *See* LANOULLIER

BOISPINEAU, JEAN-JARD (often called "Brother Jean the elder" or "Brother Boispineau the elder"), lay brother, Jesuit, apothecary; b. 11 Sept. 1689 at Lamothe (possibly La Mothe-Achard, dept. of Vendée), France; d. 10 Sept. 1744 in Quebec.

Jean-Jard Boispineau entered the noviciate of the Jesuits of the province of Aquitaine in Bordeaux on 10 Aug. 1711. He sailed for New France in 1713. On 4 November of that year he took his first vows as lay brother, and his final ones on 2 Feb. 1721. Generally the lay brothers who asked to enter the Society of Jesus had already acquired a certain competence in their profession. Often these brothers wanted to participate in missionary work but did not want to be priests or did not have the requisite education. It seems clear that Boispineau had acquired his training as an apothecary in France, and his reputation in Canada was excellent. He lavished his care not only upon the members of the Society of Jesus but also upon the other inhabitants of New France. Several statements confirm Boispineau's great activity and his numerous successes, as an apothecary and as a surgeon working with Michel Bertier* and Michel Sarrazin*.

Jean-Jard Boispineau died in Quebec on 10 Sept. 1744. His brother Charles, also a lay brother and apothecary, survived him, dying on 30 Jan. 1760. Charles, who had arrived in the colony in 1721, practised his profession competently, but his reputation as an apothecary never equalled Jean-Jard's.

C.-M. BOISSONNAULT

ASJCF, 499; 715. *JR* (Thwaites), LXIX, 131, 291; LXXI, 163. "Lettres du père Aulneau," APQ *Rapport, 1926–27,* 266, 271, 276. Ahern, *Notes pour l'histoire de la médecine,* 57–63.

BOLVIN, GILLES, wood-carver; baptized 30 Aug. 1710 in the parish of Saint-Nicolas d'Avesnes (Avesnes-sur-Helpe, dept. of Nord), France, illegitimate son of Jean-François Bolvin and Marie-Anne Isabeau; buried 31 Jan. 1766 at Trois-Rivières.

In all probability Gilles Bolvin came to Canada in 1729. Exactly when he settled at Trois-Rivières is not known but he was certainly there in 1731 already practising the wood-carver's craft, as we learn from a bill of sale drawn up before the notary Pierre Petit* on 19 November of that year.

Gilles Bolvin made his career principally in the region of Trois-Rivières. Like most artisans of the period, however, he moved about fairly regularly to practise his craft. Thus he worked at Lachenaie, Boucherville, La Pérade, Batiscan, L'Assomption, Berthier-en-Haut (Berthierville), Champlain, and Pointe-aux-Trembles (Neuville).

In 1734 he contracted for the interior decoration of the third parish church in Trois-Rivières. According to Gérard Morisset*, it was at the request of the Recollet, Father Augustin Quintal*, then the parish priest, that Bolvin carved the churchwardens' pew and the pulpit. These furnishings, which could still be admired at the beginning of the 20th century, were largely Louis XIV in inspiration, and until their destruction in 1908 constituted a fine example of Quebec art. It

may be that Bolvin executed these works from sketches furnished by Quintal, for, according to Morisset again, Quintal had some experience in architecture and the arts: he is believed to have been the architect responsible for the construction of some churches in the region, including that of Sainte-Anne-d'Yamachiche. Close collaboration between Bolvin and Father Quintal cannot, however, be affirmed, for no document confirms such a hypothesis.

Yet a contract from the parish archives of Saint-Charles-de-Lachenaie does suggest Quintal may have influenced Bolvin. In signing this document on 10 Feb. 1737 Bolvin undertook to carve for the church of Saint-Charles a tabernacle, a cross, and candlesticks, and to supply the crates necessary to transport them from Trois-Rivières. At the bottom of this document, besides the signatures of Bolvin, the parish priest, and the churchwardens, appears that of Augustin Quintal. There was, therefore, a certain amount of collaboration between the two men, even if it is not certain that Father Quintal signed the contract as the architect.

In 1739, according to a deed from the registry of Hyacinthe-Olivier PRESSÉ, Bolvin was churchwarden in charge of the church of Immaculée-Conception in Trois-Rivières. In the following years he executed a great number of carvings, among others the tabernacle of the church of Sainte-Famille in Boucherville, done sometime between 1745 and 1750, and the retable of the church of Sainte-Anne-de-la-Pérade, carved around the same period. In the 1750s, however, there was a drop in his artistic production. Perhaps because he was eager to increase his income, Bolvin began to be interested in business, but he soon became involved in unlawful activities. In fact, an ordinance issued by Intendant Hocquart* on 26 June 1748 forbade Bolvin to sell spirits, "on pain of a fine of 300 *livres* for the first infraction and a more severe penalty, including corporal punishment, in the event of a repetition of the offence."

Bolvin appears again in 1759, when he contracts to do carving for the church of Sainte-Geneviève in Berthier. A contract drawn up at Trois-Rivières before the notary Louis PILLARD indicates that this carving was to consist of "a retable in the Roman style," two statues representing St Peter and St John, some bas-reliefs, and a paschal candlestick. It seems that Bolvin never completed these works, which underwent numerous transformations during the 19th century. Shortly before working at Berthier, Bolvin had carved two retables for the church of Saint-Pierre-du-Portage in L'Assomption.

Bonfoy

Bolvin's wood-carving was not limited to these works, but it is difficult to estimate the whole of his production. Thanks, however, to the surviving pieces, it is possible to appreciate the value of his work. Bolvin's carving was characterized mainly by the superabundance of decorative motifs. The tabernacle in the church of Sainte-Famille in Boucherville is a good illustration of his style, with its multitude of floral motifs, tracery, and garlands.

Gilles Bolvin was married three times. On 24 May 1732, at Trois-Rivières, he married Marie-Marguerite Lamarque, by whom he had nine children. She died in 1748, and in May of the following year he took his second wife, Claire Jutras. According to Gérard Morisset it was of this marriage that Jean-Baptiste, the only one of Bolvin's sons to become a wood-carver, was born. Finally, on 26 Oct. 1761, seven years after the death of his second wife, Bolvin married Angélique Béland; she died in 1764, two years before her husband.

MICHEL CAUCHON and ANDRÉ JUNEAU

AJTR, Greffe de Louis Pillard, 28 févr. 1759; Greffe de H.-O. Pressé, 24 mai 1739; Registre d'état civil, Notre-Dame de Trois-Rivières, 24 mai 1732, 31 janv. 1766. Archives paroissiales de Saint-Charles (Lachenaie, Qué.), Livres de comptes, I, 1725–1739. Archives paroissiales de Sainte-Geneviève (Berthier, Qué.), Livres de comptes, I, II. IOA, Dossier Gilles Bolvin, sculpteur. P.-G. Roy, *Inv. ord. int.*, III, 107. Tanguay, *Dictionnaire*. Alan Gowans, *Church architecture in New France; Looking at architecture in Canada* (Toronto, 1958). R. H. Hubbard, *The development of Canadian art* (Ottawa, [1963]). Gérard Morisset, *L'architecture en Nouvelle-France* (Québec, 1949). Ramsay Traquair, *The old architecture of Quebec* (Toronto, 1947). Raymond Douville, "Sur deux retables de l'église de L'Assomption," *RHAF*, XII (1958–59), 30–35. Gérard Morisset, "Le sculpteur Gilles Bolvin," *Technique* (Montréal), XXVII (1952), 609–19; "Le sculpteur sur bois, Gilles Bolvin," *RUL*, III (1949), 684–94.

BONFOY, HUGH, naval officer, governor of Newfoundland; b. *c.* 1720; d. 12 March 1762.

Hugh Bonfoy entered the Royal Navy as a midshipman in the *Somerset* in 1739 and was promoted lieutenant in 1744. The following year he was commissioned captain in command of the *Greyhound*, and later commanded the *Augusta* and the *Berwick*, mostly in home waters.

In May 1753, commanding the *Penzance*, Bonfoy was commissioned governor of Newfoundland and received the usual Heads of Enquiry; he arrived at St John's on 24 July. The Board of Trade had for some time been concerned with the number of Irish "papists" in the country, and apparently asked Bonfoy to look into their conduct and make the first systematic enumeration of them. He estimated the number of residents in Newfoundland as 2,683 Irish and 1,816 English, the latter figure being based on an incomplete census. The number of Irish had grown rapidly since the early 1700s, when English fishing ships, stopping at Irish ports on their way to Newfoundland, had begun to take Irishmen on their crews; others soon came to seek employment with the resident fishermen. Many of these Irishmen stayed in the island after the fishing season ended. According to Bonfoy, the Irish who remained during the winter stole from the inhabitants and traders, having no other means of subsistence, and were the cause of many disorders. There had, however, been no cases for trial by the court of oyer and terminer. He encouraged the magistrates to restrict the activities of the Irish [*see* Richard DORRILL]. Concerning religious matters, Bonfoy stated that "Liberty of conscience is allowed to all Persons except Papists," and that "no ministers officiate in any Church or Chapel but such as are in Holy Orders sent as missionaries by the Society for Propagation of the Gospel." The Irish were also forbidden to take up a trade on their own account.

Bonfoy reported to the Board of Trade in February 1755 on his second tour as governor (1754). In addition to the usual statistical information on the fisheries and inhabitants, he enclosed the proceedings of three trials in the court of oyer and terminer, which he had convened in September 1754. They concerned one assault and two murder cases, one of them the killing of the chief magistrate, William KEEN, in the course of an attempted robbery on 9 September. Of the nine persons tried for this crime and condemned to death, four had been executed; the other five were respited by Bonfoy and later pardoned. Shortly after his return to England in 1754, Bonfoy had received a letter from the principal magistrate at St John's, Michael Gill, saying that thanks to his measures against the Irish everything was quiet, with only a few small thefts committed, and that "many of the Enemies of our Religion and Liberty are quitting the place" (probably for Ireland or New England).

Bonfoy next received a commission as captain of the *Dorset*, a yacht attending the lord lieutenant of Ireland. He died in this appointment, in 1762, and was survived by a daughter.

MICHAEL GODFREY

PRO, Adm. 6/16, 6/17; CO 194/9; 194/13, f.116v; 194/23; 195/8, pp.325, 327–28. PRO, *JTP*,

1749/50–1753; 1754–1758. Charnock, *Biographia navalis*, V. Lounsbury, *British fishery in Nfld*.

BONHOMME, *dit* **Beaupré, NOËL,** surveyor; b. 13 Nov. 1684 at Lorette (Ancienne-Lorette, Que.) and baptized the same day at Quebec, son of Ignace Bonhomme, *dit* Beaupré, and Agnès Morin; m. on 29 May 1709 Félicité Hamel at Ancienne-Lorette; d. there 29 May 1755.

It is difficult to know what Noël Beaupré's professional training was because his certificate of professional competency has not been found. This certificate was normally conferred by the king's hydrographer or the teacher of hydrography upon pupils who had followed the mathematics courses successfully, or by a recognized surveyor upon candidates who had completed their apprenticeship with good results. In any event, on 15 Dec. 1718 Noël Beaupré received official papers as surveyor and geometrician from the intendant, Michel BÉGON; he was 34 at the time. He styled himself royal surveyor in his deeds from 4 June 1731 until the end of his life but he does not seem to have received any official appointment confirming this title.

The surveyors' role, clearly defined in the official papers they received from the intendant, consisted of "surveying and measuring of every sort, [and] drawing up the written reports . . . as is the practice in the provost court and viscounty of Paris, for the allotted fees and emoluments." Surveyors were required to place plainly visible boundary marks and to use only compasses, lodestones, and other instruments that had been duly inspected by the king's hydrographer. Noël Beaupré mentions specifically in his reports that for his boundary marks he used stones, earthenware shards, or cinder blocks. In addition to measuring newly granted lands, the surveyors, thanks to their work of setting boundaries and making their reports, often put an end to the numerous lawsuits that arose over land boundaries between neighbours, even between seigneurs, and especially among heirs. They settled definitively disputes which had lasted for years.

Noël Beaupré's qualities and capabilities were speedily recognized, and people had recourse to his good offices on the Beaupré shore and Île d'Orléans, on the south as well as the north shore of the St Lawrence River, throughout the territory of the government of Quebec and even outside it. Between 1718 and 1752 he drew up close to 900 deeds and reports. Among the reports are two of special importance: one on the survey done in December 1737 and January 1738 on the lands in Nouvelle-Beauce recently granted to Thomas-Jacques TASCHEREAU, and another on the setting of the boundaries of the fiefs of Beaumont, Vincennes, and Saint-Gilles, done in 1743 at the request of Jacques-Hugues PÉAN de Livaudière, Charles-Marie Couillard de Beaumont, and Marguerite Forestier. The second report put an end to a difficult division of the seigneury of Beaumont after the sale of the seigneury by the heirs.

Noël Beaupré died at Ancienne-Lorette and was buried there on 29 May 1755. His reports demonstrate his attention to detail and accuracy, qualities that account for his great popularity everywhere in the government of Quebec.

ROLAND-J. AUGER

AJQ, Registre d'état civil, Notre-Dame de Québec, 13 nov. 1684. ANQ, Greffe de J.-É. Dubreuil, 12 juill. 1722; Greffe de Florent de La Cetière, 2 mai 1709; NF, Coll. de pièces jud. et not., 2975, 3125; NF, Ord. int., 15 déc. 1718; 31 mai 1730; 8 juin 1731; 13 août 1738; 16 mars, 26 août, 8 sept. 1743; 12 avril, 18 déc. 1745; 19 févr. 1746. ASQ, Fonds Verreau, XIII, 22; Polygraphie, III, 107c. Tanguay, *Dictionnaire*.

BONNAVENTURE (Bonaventure), CLAUDE-ÉLISABETH DENYS DE. *See* DENYS

BONNE DE MISSÈGLE (Misèle), LOUIS DE, officer in the colonial regular troops; b. *c.* 1717, probably at Saint-Martin de Lavaur (dept. of Tarn), France, son of Louis-Joseph de Bonne de Missègle and Marie de Villeneuve; d. 29 April 1760 at Quebec.

Louis de Bonne de Missègle was a half-pay captain in the Régiment de Condé when he came to Canada in August 1749 with Governor TAFFANEL de La Jonquière, a relative of his. He was first captain of the governor's guards, then was appointed captain of a company in 1751. La Jonquière had recommended him, without success, first in 1750 for the post of town major of Trois-Rivières, then in 1751 for the rank of garrison adjutant in the colonial regular troops. Louis de Bonne, who had been made a knight of the order of Saint-Louis on 1 Jan. 1759, was wounded at the battle of Sainte-Foy on 28 April 1760 [*see* Lévis*] and died the next day. He was buried on 30 April in the cemetery of the Hôpital Général of Quebec.

On 18 Oct. 1750 Louis de Bonne had obtained the grant of the fief of Sault-Sainte-Marie with Louis Legardeur* de Repentigny. The two partners built a small fort on their grant which served as a trading post. Louis de Bonne did not live at Sault-Sainte-Marie, leaving Legardeur de Repentigny the responsibility of looking after the post.

Boscawen

On 14 July 1751 Louis de Bonne had married Louise Prud'homme in Montreal. Their son, Pierre-Amable*, made a career for himself in the magistracy during the British régime.

JEAN-MARIE LEBLANC

AN, Col., B, 93, ff.8, 9, 15; 109, f.17; C¹¹ᴬ, 97, f.141. ANQ-M, Greffe de L.-C. Danré de Blanzy, 10 juill. 1751; Registre d'état civil, Notre-Dame de Montréal, 14 juill. 1751. "Les héros de 1759 et de 1760 inhumés au cimetière de l'Hôpital Général de Québec," APQ *Rapport, 1920–21*, 266. *Journal du chevalier de Lévis* (Casgrain), 272. P.-G. Roy, *Inv. concessions*, V, 72–73. Tanguay, *Dictionnaire*. Auguste Gosselin, "Les de La Jonquière au Canada," *BRH*, IV (1898), 275. Léonce Jore, "Un Canadien gouverneur du Sénégal, Louis Le Gardeur de Repentigny, 1721–1786," *RHAF*, XV (1961–62), 72–73.

BOSCAWEN, EDWARD, naval officer; sometimes called "Wry-necked Dick" from a habit of cocking his head to one side; more commonly known as "Old Dreadnought"; b. 19 Aug. 1711 to Hugh Boscawen, 1st Viscount Falmouth, and Charlotte Godfrey; m. 11 Dec. 1742 to Frances Evelyn-Glanville; d. 10 Jan. 1761 at Hatchland's Park, Surrey, England. The Boscawens, of ancient lineage, derived their name from the family seat in Cornwall, Boscawen Ros (or, the valley of the elder trees). Edward's maternal grandmother was Arabella Churchill, the Duke of Marlborough's remarkable sister.

Edward Boscawen entered the navy as a volunteer in the *Superbe* (60 guns) on 3 April 1726, and became a midshipman 19 months later while serving in the West Indies. Except for the two and a half years in the *Superbe* his training was in home waters and the Mediterranean. He was promoted lieutenant in 1732, and given command of the 20-gun *Leopard* on 12 March 1737.

He was commanding the *Shoreham* (20 guns) in the West Indies when war began in 1739. He immediately proved himself an offensively minded and courageous leader. After distinguishing himself during the sieges of the Spanish strongholds at Porto Bello (Portobelo, Panama) and Cartagena (Colombia), he was elevated to the command of the 60-gun *Prince Frederick*. In this ship he left the West Indies, never to return, in May 1742. On 15 July 1747 he was made rear-admiral of the blue for continuous distinguished service. He had been wounded in the victory over the French fleet off Cape Finisterre, Spain, on 3 May 1747, but he recovered in time to take up an extraordinary and demanding appointment that autumn as commander-in-chief of an expedition to the East Indies. The siege of the French fort at Pondicherry (India) in 1748, although a failure, provided important experience for his task at Louisbourg, Île Royale (Cape Breton Island), in 1758.

On 12 May 1749 Boscawen was promoted rear-admiral of the white. He returned from the East in April 1750 and remained in England for the next five years. Made a member of the board of admiralty in 1751, he was close to the centre of political and naval affairs. On 4 Feb. 1755 he was promoted vice-admiral of the blue and given command of a squadron with secret orders to intercept all French reinforcements "as may annoy & endanger the safety of our colonies" in America. Since a state of war did not formally exist, conscious provocation such as this could be expected to have explosive and unpredictable results. Boscawen faced the possibility under highly unfavourable conditions. His fleet had been hastily gathered, and a number of his ships were manned with the sweepings of the streets, the press gangs not having found enough trained seamen. In the unfamiliar waters off Louisbourg he was beset by fogs and "the dismal prospect of floating islands of ice sufficient to terrifie the most daring seaman." All but two of the French ships under Comte Dubois de La Motte [CAHIDEUC], slipped past the British squadron. So many men were dying from typhoid in Boscawen's ships and so many were totally incapacitated by the disease that he had to sail for Halifax.

Arriving there on 9 July 1755, he could not avoid playing a part in the removal of the Acadians from Nova Scotia. He and his second in command, Rear Admiral Savage Mostyn, attended the council meeting of 28 July 1755 at which Charles LAWRENCE won approval for the deportation of the French inhabitants from Nova Scotia. By his presence alone, as commander-in-chief and a lord commissioner of the admiralty with well-known high connections, Boscawen could not have failed to exert some influence on the deliberations. Once the decision was made, the physical removal of the Acadians became a naval and military responsibility, and several captains under Boscawen's command, including John ROUS, participated.

Despite this less than heroic prologue to the Seven Years' War, Boscawen was hailed on his return to England as "the Deliverer of America." In 1756 he was promoted vice-admiral of the white and in 1757 vice-admiral of the red. He was the only member of the board of admiralty to retain office when the Newcastle government resigned in 1756. As the commander-in-chief, Portsmouth, he had to sign the order for the execution of Admiral BYNG. He sailed in 1757 to command the blockading force off Brest, becoming second in command on the arrival of Admiral Edward Hawke.

In 1758 Pitt chose Boscawen to command the naval forces at the attack on Louisbourg. On 8 February he was promoted admiral of the blue and on 19 February sailed for Nova Scotia. Bad weather delayed the crossing, and the fleet did not reach Halifax until 9 May. Boscawen's activities with respect to the capture of Louisbourg have been dismissed as merely providing the covering forces for a purely military operation. In fact he did much more. With WOLFE and Lawrence he worked out the first plan of attack (which Jeffery Amherst*, the military commander, later changed); conducted valuable training exercises in the landing of troops; made the decision to land the British forces and supported them with gunfire from his ships. During the siege, as he had learned to do at Pondicherry in 1748, he provided men and equipment both to support the infantry and to relieve the land forces from burdensome tasks. He landed at least four 32-pounder guns, a dozen 24-pounders, and several 6-pounders to support land operations. Gunners, sappers, carpenters, and pioneers came off the ships to participate in the siege. Boscawen even found in his squadron 188 miners who volunteered to dig entrenchments.

On 25 July, under his orders, Captains John Laforey and George Balfour successfully cut out the last two French ships in Louisbourg harbour capable of giving battle. On 26 July he got Amherst to agree to a combined attack by sea and land, but on the same day Drucour [Boschenry], the commandant, capitulated. As in 1745, combined naval and military operations had defeated the French garrison.

Since it was too late in the season to attack Quebec, Boscawen returned to England, having appointed Philip DURELL to succeed him as senior officer at Halifax. For the rest of his naval career Boscawen was employed in the Mediterranean and in command of the Western squadron, which patrolled the "chops" of the English Channel. In 1759 he destroyed a French fleet in Lagos Bay, Portugal – the victory for which he is most often remembered. In 1760, despite abominable weather, he kept the Western squadron on its station. Worn out by continuous and trying sea service, in December 1760 he contracted a fever which proved fatal. He died in the home he had just built at Hatchland's Park, Surrey. He was survived by his wife, whose letters comprise a charming record of their married life, and by five children.

Boscawen inspired the loyalty of his subordinates, demonstrated a fertile imagination, and, particularly in the Pondicherry and Louisbourg campaigns, made full use of the knowledge of his juniors. Like Nelson he possessed an offensive spirit in war and a rare concern for the welfare of common seamen. As his wife's loving epitaph on his tomb at the church of St Michael Penkivel, Cornwall, claims, "with the highest exertions of military greatness he united the gentlest offices of humanity."

W. A. B. DOUGLAS

PRO, Adm. 1/480, ff.627, 663; 1/481, f.41; 1/482; 50/3, Boscawen's journals, 1755, 1758; CO 325. C. F. Aspinall Oglander, *Admiral's wife, being the life and letters of the Hon. Mrs. Edward Boscawen from 1719 to 1761* . . . (London, 1940). [Edward Boscawen], "Boscawen's letters to his wife, 1755–56," ed. P. K. Kemp, *The Naval Miscellany* (Navy Records Society pubs., XCII, London, 1952), IV. *N.S. Archives, I*. Charnock, *Biographia navalis*, IV. *DNB*. G.B., Adm., *Commissioned sea officers, 1660–1815*. J. S. Corbett, *England in the Seven Years' War: a study in combined strategy* (2nd ed., 2v., London, 1918), I. Gipson, *British empire before the American revolution*, VI. D. S. Graham, "British intervention in defence of the American colonies, 1748–1756" (unpublished PHD thesis, University of London, 1969), 309. G. S. Graham, *Empire of the north Atlantic: the maritime struggle for North America* (London, Toronto, 1950). McLennan, *Louisbourg*. H. W. Richmond, *The navy in the war of 1739–48* (3v., Cambridge, Eng., 1920), I, III. J. M. Hitsman with C. C. J. Bond, "The assault landing at Louisbourg, 1758," *CHR*, XXXV (1954), 314–30.

BOSCHENRY DE DRUCOUR (Drucourt), AUGUSTIN DE (he signed Chevalier de Drucour), naval officer, governor of Île Royale; baptized 27 March 1703 in Drucourt (dept. of Eure), France, son of Jean-Louis de Boschenry, Baron de Drucourt, and Marie-Louise Godard (Godart); d. 28 Aug. 1762 at Le Havre, France.

Augustin de Boschenry de Drucour was born without wealth of a Norman family, and entered the naval service at Toulon as a midshipman in 1719. His first sea duty was on a ship bound for Constantinople in 1723. During his career he made 16 major voyages to such places as Copenhagen, Stockholm, Martinique, and Saint-Domingue (Hispaniola). His promotions were steady: sub-lieutenant in 1731, lieutenant-commander in 1741, lieutenant of the "gardes du pavillon amiral" in 1743, and naval captain in 1751. In 1730–31, on one of the two voyages he made to Louisiana, Drucour participated in the campaign against the Natchez Indians. He also visited Acadia at least once, and in October 1746 was on the *Mars*, bound for Acadia, when that ship was captured by the British. Drucour was

Boschenry

taken to England, and was exchanged the following year. In 1749 he was created a knight of the order of Saint-Louis.

Drucour's appointment sometime in the late 1740s as commandant of the "gardes du pavillon amiral" at Brest was an honour he was said to have received without seeking. He seems to have been a capable administrator and a kindly figure to the guards. After several years in this post he was summoned to an interview with Machault, the minister of Marine, and offered the governorship of Île Royale. Drucour declined the office because of his lack of wealth, but he was persuaded to change his mind. His appointment was dated 1 Feb. 1754. After being delayed by an attack of sciatica, he sailed from Brest in June with his wife, Marie-Anne Aubert de Courserac, and eight domestics. They arrived in Louisbourg on 15 August.

Despite problems resulting from insufficient funds, troops, and supplies, Drucour did his best to promote the welfare of Île Royale. His honesty and moderation were evident, and Mme Drucour became known as a woman of intelligence and grace. The only criticism of Drucour as an administrator was that his judgement of men was not discriminating and that he allowed himself to be influenced by the financial commissary, Jacques Prévost* de La Croix.

Drucour's instructions had established three main goals: to maintain relations with the Indians, to encourage the settlement of Acadians in Île Royale, and to act in liaison with Governor Duquesne* of New France. Drucour and Prévost together were directed to increase the population of the island, develop agriculture and a measure of self-sufficiency within the colony, maintain the fisheries, and promote commerce with France and its dependencies by restricting trade with the English. The governor's efforts to carry out these instructions were hindered, then nullified, by the outbreak of war with England. In June 1755 Fort Beauséjour (near Sackville, N.B.) was captured after an ineffectual resistance by its commander, Louis Du Pont* Duchambon de Vergor. Two immediate results were the deportation of the Acadians by the British and an increase in military pressure against Île Royale.

Its dependence upon assistance from the French fleet made the garrison at Louisbourg unusually vulnerable to British sea power. An English squadron commanded by Edward BOSCAWEN appeared off the coast in June 1755, blockading Louisbourg harbour and disrupting commerce. In the following year the British began to raid outlying settlements; their captures of ships included the *Arc-en-Ciel*, trans-

porting recruits for the Louisbourg garrison and 6,000 *livres* of goods belonging to Drucour. The presence of Comte Dubois de La Motte [CAHIDEUC] and his fleet at Louisbourg in 1757 discouraged the expedition planned against Île Royale by Lord Loudoun [John Campbell], but British ships under Francis Holburne* blockaded the harbour until dispersed by a violent storm in September. The blockade and the embargoes on commerce reduced the colony to the verge of starvation, but with great effort Drucour and Prévost managed to fill the stores by 1758.

Early in 1758 a joint naval and military expedition against Louisbourg assembled in Halifax. The total British force under Jeffery Amherst* numbered 27,000 men in 157 warships, transports, and smaller vessels. Drucour had available some 3,500 soldiers, augmented by the militia, and approximately 3,800 crewmen on 11 vessels. On 8 June the British landed at Anse de la Cormorandière (Kennington Cove), a few miles west of Louisbourg. After a brief resistance the French defenders, led by Jean MASCLE de Saint-Julhien, withdrew into the fortress, leaving the besiegers free to establish camp and open batteries. No attempt was made to attack the British while they were landing their guns and supplies through a heavy surf, a critical operation which required a week. On 19 June WOLFE's cannoneers opened fire on the Island battery, and after that time the progress of the siege was inexorable until the surrender on 26 July. By then the French ships had been either sunk or burned, the walls had been breached in a dozen places, and the French cannon had been silenced so effectively that to Drucour they seemed "more like the minute guns at a funeral than a defence."

Even before the siege the fortifications at Louisbourg had been in ruinous condition, exposed on the land side and enfiladed throughout much of their length. The damage sustained in the siege of 1745 had not been fully repaired. Although Drucour personally despaired of the results, his garrison's defence was both more skilful and more vigorous than the resistance mounted in the earlier siege. There was an organized attempt to defend the coast and considerable activity outside the fortress during the siege, including one major sortie and several skirmishes by French pickets and volunteer companies. In 1758 the Royal battery was demolished to prevent its use by the besiegers; the failure to do this in 1745 had given a major advantage to the enemy. In 1745 there had been no French fleet in the harbour; the fleet in 1758, although it performed feebly under Jean-Antoine Charry Desgouttes, hindered the advance of the British batteries and discouraged any attempt to force British ships into the harbour after the Island battery had been silenced. The singular aggressiveness of Jean Vauquelin*, captain of the *Aréthuse*, demonstrated the effect a ship could have against enemy positions, for it forced the British to direct much of their fire against the fleet rather than the fortress. In the end, the length of the siege and the long exposure of the British fleet to the open sea, with the consequent need to refit, were significant factors in delaying the expedition against Quebec until 1759. As Drucour stated, "our main purpose was to resist and postpone our end as long as possible," and to that extent he was successful.

As governor during the siege Drucour had two main decisions to make. The first concerned the fleet. Although the naval officers were reluctant to risk their ships by staying in the harbour, and asked permission to leave in order to fight at sea or run for France, Drucour ordered them to stay. He worried that he had committed the ships mistakenly, but his action was supported by the council of war called to consider the matter on 9 June and also by the minister of Marine, Claude-Louis de Massiac, who observed that the request by the captains had been "premature" and "dangerous." Drucour was unable to force the captains to follow Vauquelin's example and turn the enormous firepower of their ships against the English batteries, although such action might have made the difference between winning or losing the siege.

Drucour's second major decision was when, and under what terms, to surrender. At a council of war held on 26 July some officers initially favoured surrender; others urged a continued defence, even to sustaining an assault against the town. Drucour asked the British for terms but when the harshness of these became known, the officers agreed to fight on. At this point Prévost spoke on behalf of the civilian population and urged capitulation. Persuaded by this plea, Drucour accepted the British terms; the garrison surrendered as prisoners and without the honours of war.

Despite the recent massacre of the British garrison of Fort William Henry (Fort George, now Lake George, N.Y.), which surrendered, according to Thomas Pichon*, "upon a more advantageous capitulation than that which we had but just concluded" [see Montcalm], the British seem to have acted honourably towards the Louisbourg garrison. It was embarked, Pichon claimed, "with as much tranquillity, as if it had been going upon a voyage of pleasure" and Drucour received "all the honours which a person of his rank deserved." Each day throughout the siege Mme Drucour had fired three guns to encourage the French troops, and after the surrender she assisted "all the unfortunate people that had recourse to her mediation." Amherst paid her compliments at parleys during the siege, and after the capitulation Boscawen granted every favour she asked. The Drucours sailed from Louisbourg on 15 Aug. 1758, exactly four years after their arrival.

Drucour's health had suffered at Louisbourg, and he had been obliged to borrow heavily to maintain himself in office. Having lost nearly all his possessions in the siege, he was destitute when he returned to France. Repatriated at Dunkerque, Drucour and 53 other officers from Île Royale were in such a wretched condition that they had to be given money to continue their journey home. Mme Drucour had already arrived from England, defending her husband's reputation to the ministry of Marine as she forwarded his journal of the siege. It is a restrained account which reveals the temperament of its author, "a man strong enough to be patient under the depression of fighting without hope, and yet not of the uncommon force which can impose his purpose on the unwilling and the backward." Such was the judgement of the historian J. S. McLennan.*

Drucour returned to the naval service briefly in 1759, then retired to Le Havre, where he existed on the charity of his brother. He died on 28 Aug. 1762, too soon to receive the pension that was granted to him. Mme Drucour died two months later.

JOHN FORTIER

Drucour's journal of the siege is to be found in AN, Col., C¹¹ᴮ, 38, ff.57–103v; C¹¹ᶜ, 10, ff.85–178.

AD, Eure (Évreux), État civil, Drucourt, 27 mars 1703; Seine-Maritime (Rouen), État civil, Saint-François du Havre, 29 août 1762. AN, Col., B, 99–113; C¹¹ᴮ, 34–38; C¹¹ᶜ, 10; D²ᶜ, 2, ff.27–29, 40–41, 142; 3; 4, f.107; F³, 50–51; Marine, C⁷, 89 (dossier Drucour); Section Outre-Mer, Dépôt des fortifications des colonies, Am. sept., no.236. CTG, Archives, art.15, pièces 4, 5, 7, 8. PAC, MG 30, D62, 11 (F. J. Audet's biographical notes on Drucour). SHA, A¹, 3540, no.74; 3544, no.33; Mémoires et reconnaissances, art.1105, pièce 21. Jeffery Amherst, "*Journal of the Siege of* Louisbourg," *Gentleman's Magazine*, XXVIII (1758), 384–89. Knox, *Historical journal* (Doughty), I, III. Le Courtois de Surlaville, *Derniers jours de l'Acadie* (Du Boscq de Beaumont). Pichon, *Lettres et mémoires*. Fauteux, *Les chevaliers de Saint-Louis*, 147–48. Le Jeune, *Dictionnaire*, I, 533–34.

Frégault, *Canada: the war of the conquest*. McLennan, *Louisbourg*. Stanley, *New France*. J. M. Hitsman and C. C. J. Bond, "Louisbourg: a foredoomed fortress," *Canadian Army Journal* (Ottawa), X (1956),

Boucault

78–87. J. M. Hitsman with C. C. J. Bond, "The assault landing at Louisbourg, 1758," *CHR*, XXXV (1954), 314–30. Régis Roy, "Drucourt," *BRH*, XLIV (1938), 187–88.

BOUCAULT, NICOLAS-GASPARD, king's counsellor, king's attorney, lieutenant general of the admiralty court, subdelegate of the intendant, merchant, and seigneur; b. *c.* 1689 in France, son of Nicolas-Gaspard Boucault, court officer for bankruptcy cases at the Châtelet in Paris, and Françoise-Anne Devene; d. 1755 or later, in France.

It was certainly not before the autumn of 1719 that Nicolas-Gaspard Boucault landed at Quebec to begin there a career as an official to which he was to devote the rest of his life. Nothing is known of his previous history, and in particular of his occupations before coming to the colony, but it can at least be assumed that he received legal training preparing him for the various functions entrusted to him during his 30 years in Canada.

Upon his arrival he entered Intendant BÉGON's service as secretary and held this post until Bégon finally left for France in October 1726. Had he not given satisfaction, he certainly would not have kept his position for such a long time, nor would he subsequently have received the support necessary to continue building a career. He was able, during the early years of his stay, to acquire valuable experience by becoming acquainted with the various administrative and legal questions the intendant had to settle. Circumstances were to give him a rather exceptional opportunity of adding to that experience direct knowledge of Canada and its inhabitants; from 4 February to 3 June 1721 he visited all the parishes on both shores of the St Lawrence to carry out an inquiry into the advantages and disadvantages – *de commodo et incommodo* – preparatory to a redistribution of parish districts. At that time he accompanied as clerk the attorney general, Mathieu-Benoît Collet*, who was responsible for the inquiry; as a reward for his services and indemnity for his travelling expenses Boucault received a gratuity of only 300 *livres*, whereas Collet received 1,200. In 1725 they were again commissioned to draw up new reports *de commodo et incommodo*, because of protests from several parish priests and habitants who were dissatisfied with the earlier delimitation of boundaries carried out in September 1721.

Shortly after Bégon's departure in the autumn of 1726 Boucault, without a job, decided to go to France. He remained there two years. During this first return to the mother country he married

Marguerite Buirette. Having decided to go back to the colony, he asked for and obtained the two offices left vacant by the departure of Jean-Baptiste-Julien Hamare* de La Borde, those of king's attorney for the provost court and for the admiralty court of Quebec. He was appointed to the first on 20 April 1728 and obtained the second on 18 May upon presentation by the Comte de Toulouse. Taking with him his letters of appointment, which promised new possibilities for him, he sailed on the *Éléphant*, with his wife and Louis-Guillaume VERRIER; the ship arrived at Quebec in the first half of September 1728. On 2 October the Conseil Supérieur ordered the character investigation, and two days later his reception as attorney. Scarcely had he been installed when Boucault had a raise in salary requested by Governor Charles de BEAU-HARNOIS and the acting intendant, François Clairambault* d'Aigremont, who wrote to the minister of Marine, Maurepas, on 6 Nov. 1728 to point out that "receiving only 300 *livres* as salary for his office, and having no other resources in Canada, it would not be possible for him to keep himself and his family here." The governor and the acting intendant also added: "He is a former resident of this country who served as secretary under M. Bégon with great impartiality and who always gave satisfaction."

Determined to take advantage of every opportunity to rise in his administrative career, Boucault requested in 1729 the office of chief road officer, left vacant by the death of Pierre Robinau* de Bécancour. But he was in competition with eight other candidates, and because he did not receive any support from the governor or the new financial commissary, Gilles Hocquart*, he failed to obtain the office to which Jean-Eustache LANOULLIER de Boisclerc was later appointed. On the other hand, on 30 Nov. 1729 Hocquart appointed him his subdelegate in Quebec, to judge all disputes involving sums not exceeding 100 *livres* and "to take cognizance of all other more important disputes and matters which we may refer to him." Boucault seems to have kept his title of subdelegate in Quebec and to have exercised the legal functions of this office at least until Jean-Victor de Varin* de La Marre was appointed subdelegate on 1 Oct. 1736. After 1731 Hocquart, now intendant, also entrusted him on a few occasions with the preliminary investigations of certain criminal affairs.

Jean-Baptiste Couillard* de Lespinay's death in March 1735 offered Boucault the opportunity for a new promotion. The offices of special lieutenant of the provost court and lieutenant general of the admiralty court became vacant. The experience he had acquired as attorney attached to these two courts marked Boucault out as the person to take over the offices. Beauharnois and Hocquart therefore recommended him, emphasizing that the candidate "combines with a great sense of honour and integrity all the competence required to occupy the positions." The king appointed him special lieutenant of the provost court on 27 March 1736 and lieutenant general of the admiralty court on 3 April of that year. The Conseil Supérieur ordered the investigation of character on 13 August and received Boucault into his new function on 20 August. Boucault was not to receive any further promotions until the end of his career. Like his predecessor, and his successor, Guillaume Guillimin*, he held the two offices at the same time, often presiding over hearings in the provost court, particularly from 1740 to 1743, because the lieutenant general, Pierre ANDRÉ de Leigne, was frequently ill.

In the autumn of 1747 Boucault sailed for France with the intention, it seems, of never returning to the colony. But once he had reached the mother country he changed his mind and asked for a two-year leave of absence, at the end of which he resigned as lieutenant general of the admiralty court, thinking that his brother GILBERT, a notary, would succeed him. Intendant Bigot*, who had got wind of the affair, thwarted these plans by writing to the minister that the notary was not "suitable . . . for any judicial office." Boucault returned to Canada before the end of September 1749 and took up only his duties in the provost court, exercising them until he left the colony for good in 1754 and returned to France. In a letter written from Saint-Germain-en-Laye, near Paris, on 14 March 1755 he no longer called himself anything but "former special lieutenant of the provost court," which suggests that he did not keep his office until 1757 as has been affirmed, but rather that he resigned soon after his arrival in France, although his successor was not appointed until April 1757.

An ambitious man, unable to content himself with his modest salary as an official, Boucault attempted, like many others, to make a fortune in business. In 1733 he set up a company with François FOUCAULT. The partners arranged the purchase of the schooner *Saint-Michel*, which they sent off on 27 May of that year with a crew of 17 under the command of captain Charles Chéron to look for a suitable place for hunting seals. The expedition set up its base on the Île du Grand Saint-Modet, Labrador, and did not return until the end of August 1734 with a cargo which, according to the partners, was far from meeting their expenses. Nevertheless they asked to be

granted the post, which was given to them on 27 April 1735 for nine years, with the exclusive right to hunt seals and trade with the Indians. On the following 12 May the two partners transferred to Chéron a third of the concession to be held jointly, on condition that he too contribute his third to the operation of the post. The size of the expeditions in 1735, 1736, and 1737 increased each year, as did the profits.

But the holders of neighbouring concessions were to create much trouble for them. With François MARTEL de Brouague, who was accused of frightening off seals by hunting them with firearms, the affair was rapidly settled in favour of Boucault and Foucault. The same was not true, however, of the case brought against them by Pierre CONSTANTIN, who claimed that the post on Grand Saint-Modet was within the concession he had received on 31 March 1716. Constantin, who had in vain challenged the concession to Boucault and Foucault, immediately took the dispute to Versailles. Four years of letters, reports, and petitions followed. Inquiries were held, witnesses were heard, maps were drawn, without any success in deciding accurately between the claims of the litigants. Constantin insinuated, with considerable likelihood, that Hocquart was prejudiced in favour of Boucault; the minister, Maurepas, tended rather to favour Constantin. On 18 April 1738 the governor and intendant suggested a temporary settlement; this Boucault and Foucault rejected, but they temporarily relinquished the running of the post to Constantin, though reserving their rights to it. Arbitrators were named to settle the amount of the indemnity that Constantin had to pay. Finally, unable to present any new proof to counter Constantin's claim, Boucault and Foucault gave up all their claims definitively; their title to Grand Saint-Modet was declared invalid, and Constantin was recognized as sole owner of the post by an ordinance of 28 Sept. 1740, which caused satisfaction in the ministry. Meanwhile, to compensate them for the unfortunate situation in which they had been put, Boucault and Foucault received on 1 May 1738 the concession of an area called Apetépy, on the Labrador coast, for ten years; this was ratified by the king on 26 April 1741. Immediately they began to operate it, but they were not able to retain the post beyond the date set, and in 1750 it was transferred to Jacques de LAFONTAINE de Belcour.

On 30 Sept. 1742 Boucault formed a trading company with Pierre Angers, "to share profits or losses equally" for a period of three years. Boucault supplied a ship, the *Saint-Antoine*,

Boucault

complete with rigging, as well as merchandise, all estimated at more than 9,700 *livres*. For his part Angers contracted to go to trade at Petit Degrat (Petit-de-Grat Island, N.S.). In mid-July of the following year, Boucault, worried at not receiving any news and fearing that his partner had been the victim of some accident, gave PHILIPPE and ANDRÉ CARREROT power of attorney to represent him at Petit Degrat and, should the occasion arise, "to claim all that [might] belong to the aforementioned company." But the disaster of which Boucault had a presentiment did not occur until later. Through Angers's agency the company seems to have entered into an agreement with Bigot, who was at that time financial commissary of Île Royale. Thus, in November 1744, it is supposed to have delivered more than 6,000 *livres* in supplies to aid Louisbourg, Île Royale (Cape Breton Island). Then in 1745 Angers signed a contract by which Bigot promised to repay 5,000 *livres* in the event of the company's ship *Marie* being captured by the English. The fall of Louisbourg was a terrible catastrophe for Boucault: he lost three ships, sunk in the port there, his partner was killed defending the town, and he did not receive his money for the accounts outstanding with Angers. He estimated that he had suffered a net loss of 25,000 *livres* in the venture. Moreover, Bigot refused to pay the indemnity of 5,000 *livres* that had been agreed upon, on the somewhat fallacious pretext that the ship had not been taken by the enemy but sunk in the port. It was because he had lost a great part of his fortune that Boucault resolved to go to France at the end of 1747, to try to obtain some compensation. He then sent the minister, Maurepas, two long reports in which he related his misfortune and pleaded his cause skilfully: "After such a catastrophe," he wrote, "can the law, even if it is written, be adhered to in all its rigour? Is it so narrowly defined that according to circumstances it does not allow of some interpretation and some favourable aid for him who has submitted to it, especially when it is apparent that there has been on his part no ill will nor any view of his own interest which prevented him from carrying out what he was obliged to do?"

Boucault's business enterprises often took him to the courts. There was scarcely a year that he did not plead before the provost court or the Conseil Supérieur. Moreover, on various occasions he seems to have acted as a lender of rather large sums, which indicates the fortune that he had accumulated. Furthermore, in 1728 Boucault was appointed attorney for the majority of the creditors of Louis TURC de Castelveyre, also known as Brother Chrétien, who had contracted large debts in France for his community. Boucault represented the interests of these creditors in the long lawsuit that did not end until April 1735.

On 15 April 1723 Boucault had obtained from Charles Le Moyne*, Baron de Longueuil, the grant of an *arrière fief* on the Rivière Chambly and depending upon the seigneury of Beloeil. On 20 Feb. 1732, some time after the baron's death, he took care to renew the oath of fealty and homage to his new seigneur, but he did not himself make any land grants. Finally, on 2 April 1743, he made his land over to Pierre-Antoine de La Corne de La Colombière.

In 1733 Boucault had had a luxurious three-storey stone house built on Rue Saint-Paul in Quebec, on a piece of land he had bought on 18 Oct. 1732. He lived there until 1747 with his wife, who was 15 years younger than he, and his three children. In the 1744 census he had three young servants in his employ. After the disappointments of his business affairs and before travelling to the mother country, he sold his house on 3 Aug. 1747 to Joseph-Pierre Cadet* for 10,000 *livres*, 8,000 of which were paid in cash.

In 1754 Boucault returned for good to France after having spent 30 years in Canada, during which he had performed conscientiously all the administrative and judiciary functions entrusted to him. Honest and competent, he always gave satisfaction to his superiors, who kept him in the same positions for long periods, while arranging advantageous promotions for him. He was certainly ambitious, and sought in various business activities a source of income that his salaries as a government official could not ensure him. But at the end of his career he saw the greater part of his fortune suddenly disappear, more through bad luck than bad management. He first sought a retirement pension, which was refused him "for lack of funds." Then he asked that he be granted half the post of Gros Mécatina (Que.); Governor Duquesne* and Intendant Bigot had just granted it to a Quebec merchant, Jean TACHÉ, who had, however, not yet received royal ratification. As this request probably met with certain reservations, Boucault tried a "more modest" approach by asking for only the 15th or 20th barrel of oil produced at the post, which was reputed, according to what he himself said, to bring in a yearly income of 20,000 *livres* net. He does not seem to have been any more fortunate in this last request, since the post of Gros Mécatina finally went to Hocquart; Taché had to be content with the one at Grand Saint-Modet that had caused Boucault so much trouble.

During the first months following his return to France, while he was endeavouring to obtain some support for a decent retirement, Boucault wrote a long report, accompanied by maps and entitled "Idée générale du Canada." Essentially it contains a description of the state of the colony which shows a broad knowledge of the country on the writer's part. New France, from Newfoundland to the *pays d'en haut*, receives detailed description; Canada itself, however, is treated more comprehensively. Boucault describes the general aspect of each region, its geographical situation and particularities, its inhabitants, its resources, its administration, both civil and ecclesiastical, throwing in numerous historical considerations and some miscellaneous facts. He also emphasizes the climate and its consequences for the Canadians' way of life, he compares the flora and fauna of Canada with those of France, and finally he outlines agricultural and industrial production. It is on the whole a well-documented report, with observations that are true and exact, the fruit of long acquaintance with the localities; it is disappointing nevertheless because of the absence of critical views and of any proposals for reform.

The work was finished at the end of December 1754. Boucault then presented it to some influential persons, seeking to acquire their favour for himself and their protection for two of his sons. One of his sons had already been serving for four years as port assistant at Brest under Hocquart; the other was in the service of Henri-Louis Duhamel Du Monceau, inspector general of the Marine.

ANDRÉ MOREL

AN, Col., C¹¹ᴬ, 50, ff.77–78; 51, ff.49–50; 59, ff.268–73; 93, ff.282–83; 109, ff.235–396; E, 43, ff.9–38. ANQ, Greffe de J.-É. Dubreuil, 29 juill. 1729; NF, Ins. Cons. sup., VI, 147–51, 455–61; VII, 431; VIII, 111–13 (copies at PAC). PAC, MG 18, J8. "Documents inédits," *RHAF*, II (1948–49), 583–89. *Documents relating to Canadian currency during the French period* (Shortt), II, 619. "État présent du Canada, dressé sur un nombre de mémoires et connaissances acquises sur les lieux, par le sieur Boucault (1754)," APQ *Rapport, 1920–21*, 11–50. *Inv. de pièces du Labrador* (P.-G. Roy), I, 29, 48, 62, 73, 103, 105, 113, 155, 162, 167, 171, 175, 183, 292; II, 46, 114, 116, 121–39, 144, 156, 161, 163, 168, 174, 181, 183, 184. "Loterie des demoiselles Rey-Gaillard (1730)," APQ *Rapport, 1923–24*, 147–48. "Loterie de Gaspard Chaussegros de Léry, ingénieur en chef de la Nouvelle-France (1732)," APQ *Rapport, 1923–24*, 153–54. É.-Z. Massicotte, "Nouvelles notes sur la foi et hommage," *BRH*, XXVI (1920), 300–3. "Procès-verbal de l'état des registres du greffe du siège de l'Amirauté de Québec dressé par Louis-Guillaume Verrier, procureur général du Conseil supérieur, les 2, 3, 6, 7, 10, 11, 12 septembre 1737," APQ *Rapport, 1920–21*, 111–31. "Procès-verbaux du procureur général Collet" (Caron), APQ *Rapport, 1921–22*, 262–380. PAC *Report, 1904; 1905*, I. "Recensement de Québec, 1744" (APQ *Rapport*).

Caron, "Inventaire de documents," APQ *Rapport, 1941–42*, 253. Gareau, "La Prévôté de Québec," APQ *Rapport, 1943–44*, 139–42. *Inv. greffes not.*, XXI, 104, 116, 121, 129, 157. Le Jeune, *Dictionnaire*. A. Roy, *Inv. greffes not.*, X, 161. P.-G. Roy, *Inv. coll. de pièces jud. et not.*, I, 84, 96, 126; II, 364; *Inv. concessions*, IV, 79–84; *Inv. jug. et délib., 1717–1760; Inv. ord. int.*, II, III. Tanguay, *Dictionnaire*. P.-G. Roy, *La ville de Québec*, II, 85–86, 239–40, 243–44. Benoît Robitaille, "L'habitation de Constantin et la possession du Grand Saint-Modet," *BRH*, LXI (1955), 163–68. J.-E. Roy, "Notes sur Mgr de Lauberivière," *BRH*, I (1895), 9.

BOUCAULT DE GODEFUS, GILBERT, merchant, royal notary; b. *c.* 1709 in the region of Paris, France, son of Nicolas-Gaspard Boucault, court officer for bankruptcy cases at the Châtelet in Paris, and Françoise-Anne Devene; d. probably in France, date of death unknown.

Gilbert Boucault de Godefus's career was far less lucrative than that of his brother, Nicolas-Gaspard BOUCAULT, who began as secretary to Intendant Michel BÉGON de La Picardière and became lieutenant general of the admiralty court of Quebec. We do not know when Gilbert Boucault arrived in New France. His brother, who had been in the colony since 1719, returned to France in 1726 and came back to Canada in 1728. It is quite possible that Gilbert, about 19 years old in the latter year, accompanied his brother to America, but nowhere does Nicolas-Gaspard mention that Gilbert travelled with him on the *Éléphant*, which arrived at Quebec in September 1728. Be that as it may, on 29 July 1729, before notary Jean-Étienne Dubreuil*, Gilbert Boucault signed his marriage contract, in which he declared that he was a writer in the Marine. On 7 Jan. 1730, at Sainte-Foy, he married Marie-Madeleine de Lajoüe, 12 years his senior and the widow of Pierre Frontigny.

At that period, in addition to holding his position in the office of the Marine in Quebec, Boucault was in business. The documents which mention this fact are not very informative, but Boucault's commercial activity seems to have been of some importance. In 1731 Intendant Hocquart* ordered him to hand over more than 1,169 *livres* in merchandise and 537 *livres* in cash to Nicolas LANOULLIER de Boisclerc. In 1734 he was living in a house on Rue Saint-Pierre; another house, on Rue Saint-Charles, belonged to him. He always seems to have had a certain interest in business, but subsequently he was more concerned with a legal career, in which, however, his success was limited.

On 27 Aug. 1736 Intendant Hocquart granted him a commission as royal notary, to replace Henry HICHÉ, who had been appointed attorney of the provost and admiralty courts of Quebec. On 17 Oct. 1739 he succeeded Jacques Barbel* as judge of the bailiff's court of the seigneury of Beaupré, which at that time belonged to the seminary of Quebec. In addition to these two offices Boucault practised law, replacing or aiding litigants before the courts. On occasion he occupied the office of assessor of the provost court of Quebec; he never held a more important judicial office in the colony.

In 1745 Boucault's family life was disturbed by the intrepidity of Catherine Frontigny, Mme Boucault's daughter by her first marriage. Mlle Frontigny, who was 27, applied to the lieutenant general of the provost court for permission "to issue a summons" to her stepfather and her mother in order to be able to marry. The latter were opposed to their daughter's marriage, alleging that she had "an unmanageable character" and that "far from following the precepts and upbringing that her mother and the aforementioned *Maître* Boucault have endeavoured to give her, through a whim and unheard-of stubbornness she wishes to acquire a condition and settlement through marriage." Despite her parents' opposition and maledictions, Catherine Frontigny appeared at the Boucaults' domicile and on 9, 10, and 11 September asked her parents in the form prescribed by law to consent to her marriage. Notwithstanding their refusal, Catherine Frontigny married Jacques Mourongeau in Quebec on 14 September.

Boucault also met with other reverses. The authorities considered that he was not sufficiently competent to hold important positions. In 1749 when Nicolas-Gaspard Boucault resigned as lieutenant general of the admiralty court in favour of his brother, Intendant Bigot* wrote to the minister of Marine, Maurepas, that the notary was not "suitable ... for any situation in the judicature," and Boucault remained royal notary and seigneurial judge.

In 1753 Gilbert Boucault lost his wife, and after that his financial situation deteriorated. At the beginning of 1756 his creditors seized one of his houses, and in the autumn of that year Boucault left New France. His career had had only mediocre success, and even if he had acquired some money in the beginning, he left for France penniless.

MICHEL PAQUIN

AN, Col., C¹¹ᴬ, 68, f.34; 93, f.259. ANQ, Greffe de Gilbert Boucault de Godefus, 1736–56; Greffe de J.-É. Dubreuil, 29 juill. 1729. "Recensement de Québec, 1744" (APQ *Rapport*). "Les 'sommations respectueuses' autrefois," APQ *Rapport, 1921–22*, 67ff. Lucille Labrèque, "Inventaire de pièces détachées de cours de justice de la Nouvelle-France (1638–1760)," ANQ *Rapport, 1971*, 5. Létourneau et Labrèque, "Inventaire de pièces détachées de la Prévôté de Québec," ANQ *Rapport, 1971*, 182, 203, 208, 269, 272, 300, 315, 331, 365, 367, 374, 393, 412. P.-G. Roy, *Inv. coll. pièces jud. et not.*, I, 126, 186, 188; II, 334, 355; *Inv. jug. et délib., 1717–1760*, III, IV, V, VI, *passim*; *Inv. ord. int.*, II, 98, 209. Tanguay, *Dictionnaire*. J.-E. Roy, *Histoire du notariat*, I, 357.

BOUCHEAU. *See* POUCHOT

BOUCHER, GENEVIÈVE, *dite* **de Saint-Pierre,** Ursuline, superior; b. 19 Aug. 1676 at Boucherville, Quebec, daughter of Pierre Boucher*, seigneur of Boucherville, and Jeanne Crevier; d. 30 May 1766 at Quebec.

Pierre Boucher was already 54 years of age when his last child, Geneviève, was born. Fearing that he would die before his daughter would be of an age to understand his last wishes, he composed a message for her, recommending that she seek the advice "of some worthy man" to "choose a condition in life," and he added: "But in whatever condition you are, try to attain perfection in it." Geneviève did not have to refer to this message, for her father was still living when she left the paternal roof in 1694 to enter the noviciate of the Ursulines of Quebec. Her mother, who accompanied her that day, obtained permission to enter the cloister and make a two-hour visit to the convent. On 14 Sept. 1694 Geneviève received the nun's habit from Bishop Saint-Vallier [La Croix*], and on 18 Sept. 1696 she made her profession. Her dowry was paid in money and in land.

During her long career Geneviève de Saint-Pierre held various offices in the order; she was in turn bursar, mistress of novices and boarders, zelatrice, and assistant superior. In 1750, when she was 74, she was elected superior and held this office for three years; she again became assistant superior and occupied the position for two terms, from 1753 to 1759. By then she was 83 years of age, and her physical disabilities forced her to retire to the infirmary. On 30 May 1766 she died in her 90th year, after 72 years as a nun; her father had died when he was more than 94.

The annals of the order, which called Geneviève de Saint-Pierre "the Methuselah of our history," praised this "perfect Ursuline" who worked for over 60 years for the welfare of her sisters.

GABRIELLE LAPOINTE

AMUQ, Actes d'élections des supérieures; Actes de professions et de sépultures, 1688–1781; Actes des assemblées capitulaires, 1686–1802; Annales; Entrées, vêtures, professions et décès des religieuses, 1647–1861; Lettre autographe de M. S.-Pierre, 18 juin 1699; Registre de l'examen canonique des novices, 1689–1807. Tanguay, *Dictionnaire. Glimpses of the monastery, scenes from the history of the Ursulines of Quebec during two hundred years, 1639–1839 . . .* (2nd ed., Quebec, 1897). *Les Ursulines de Québec* (1863–66).

BOUCHER, PIERRE-JÉRÔME, draftsman, cartographer, engineer; b. in Normandy, France, about 1688; d. 3 July 1753 at Louisbourg, Île Royale (Cape Breton Island).

After three years' apprenticeship at Rochefort, France (1709–12), Pierre-Jérôme Boucher, an ensign, served as draftsman and cartographer aboard the *Vénus* in East Indian waters. Following his return to France, he was sent to Louisbourg in 1717 as a draftsman for Jean-François de Verville*, the director of fortifications. He helped to build a relief model of Louisbourg. In 1720 he became an assistant-engineer and in 1721 a lieutenant. During Verville's tenure Boucher conducted parts of the construction work and from November until the opening of the construction season each year worked with Jean-Baptiste de Couagne* on plans and preparations. Under Étienne VERRIER, the engineer-in-chief, his planning, measuring, and cost-estimating responsibilities developed; in addition he did extensive mapping of the coasts and interior of Île Royale and instructed Verrier's son, Claude-Étienne*, in that art. For the governor and financial commissary, he prepared estimates for road and bridge construction. In 1740, on the death of Couagne, Boucher was promoted half-pay captain. First recommended for the cross of Saint-Louis in 1741, he was finally granted it in 1747.

Boucher was present at the siege of Louisbourg in 1745, during which he was slightly wounded, and was a member of the council of war which decided on capitulation to the Anglo-American forces. After some 18 months as a prisoner of war in England, he was repatriated to Rochefort, where he assisted in winding up the Louisbourg fortification accounts and signed them as the responsible engineer. Instead of sending Boucher to Canada to work under Gaspard-Joseph CHAUSSEGROS de Léry, in 1748 Maurepas, the minister of Marine, placed him in charge of works being done at Sables-d'Olonne

on the Poitou coast, and then at the port of Croix-de-Vie (both in the dept. of Vendée). After a few months it was decided that Boucher would join the group repossessing Louisbourg in 1749, since he was the available engineer most competent to assess the works required to restore Louisbourg to a state of defensive readiness. For a year, as engineer in charge, he prepared extensive reports on the state of the fortifications and public buildings, including those the Anglo-American troops had constructed or altered during their four years' occupation, and he drew up detailed estimates on the works required. In 1750, Louis FRANQUET was sent out as his superior and for the next three years Boucher worked under his direction, though with a considerable degree of autonomy, especially during Franquet's several absences in France and in Canada.

Boucher was allowed to return to France a few times during his 32 years at Louisbourg in order to attend to family matters. After 1749, his concern was primarily with his wife and children who had not returned to Louisbourg with him. During the winter of 1732–33, when he was about 45, he had married at Port-Dauphin (Englishtown, N.S.) Marguerite-Madeleine de Goutin (daughter of Mathieu* and sister of François-Marie de GOUTIN), said to be a lady of merit but of little fortune. She brought him two town lots in Louisbourg, which he combined with his own adjoining lots. He also had a concession at Petit Lorembec (Little Lorraine), scene of a small battle during the siege of 1745. Following his wife's death (apparently in France after 1750), Boucher had to arrange for the future of his four children, since his own health was failing. After being confined to his bed for four months by gout and a painful back ailment, he made his will on 8 June 1753. Paralysis developed, and he died less than a month later. Guardians were named, and in accordance with his will his movable goods were sold for the benefit of his heirs. They had little value: the largest item was a quantity of flour valued at 97 *livres*. Provision was also made for the disposal of his real property.

Boucher was the engineer with the longest continuous service at Louisbourg. Of all his superiors, only Saint-Ovide [MONBETON] wrote anything against him; that he was a "creature of Verville," continuing his former director's policies after the latter's departure. Verrier could not think of a better teacher of cartography for his son and recommended Boucher highly for the cross of Saint-Louis. Léry was delighted that he might have him in Canada. Jacques Prévost* de La Croix, the financial commissary, wrote that Boucher would be difficult to replace, to which

Boucher de Boucherville

Franquet added that there were few engineers who could survey and prepare plans with such accuracy.

Boucher was not only the author of excellent maps of Île Royale, and of plans and technical papers concerning fortifications, roads, bridges, and public buildings, but also the draftsman of others which bear the signatures of Verville, Verrier, and Franquet. To him goes a substantial share of the credit for planning and executing the public works of Louisbourg and the development of Cape Breton Island during the French régime.

F. J. THORPE

AN, Col., B, 52, 53, 54, 57, 65, 66, 68, 74, 91, 95, 97; C¹¹ᴬ, 126, pièce 62; C¹¹ᴮ, 6–23; C¹¹ᶜ, 13, 16; D²ᶜ, 222/1; D²ᴰ, 1; E 43; F¹ᴬ, 19, 20, 28, 30; F³, 50, ff.321–22; Marine, C⁷, 39; Section Outre-Mer, Dépôt des fortifications des colonies, Am. sept., nos. 208, 223, 224; G¹, 406; 407; 408; 466, no.69; G², 181, f.522; 202, dossier 287; G³, 2039, 2047. CTG, Bibliothèque, MSS in fol., 205ᵇ, ff.19, 134. BN, Cartes et plans, Portefeuille 131, div.6, no.6; div.7, no.5. PAC, Map div., H3/201, H3/239, M/210, M/310; MG 11, Nova Scotia A, 34, pp.156–65. *Inv. des papiers de Léry* (P.-G. Roy), II, 75–82. *Louisbourg in 1745* (Wrong), 52.

BOUCHER DE BOUCHERVILLE, PIERRE (baptized **François-Pierre**), officer in the colonial regular troops, seigneur; b. 9 June 1689 at Boucherville (Que.), son of Pierre Boucher de Boucherville and Charlotte Denys de La Trinité; buried 12 Sept. 1767 at Boucherville.

Following family tradition, Pierre Boucher de Boucherville had a military career. His grandfather, Pierre Boucher*, had been a soldier, and his father and several of his uncles were officers in the colonial regular troops. Boucher de Boucherville's career can easily be reconstructed by means of a report he wrote in 1748 for the minister of Marine, Maurepas, with a view to obtaining a promotion.

Boucher de Boucherville joined the colonial regular troops in 1702 as a cadet, and in 1707 he was sent to Detroit to serve under Lamothe Cadillac [Laumet*]. After returning from Detroit in 1710 he was appointed intelligence agent to the commandant of the garrison at Sault-Saint-Louis (Caughnawaga, Que.). Later he carried out several different missions, some of which were normally reserved for officers whereas he was only a cadet. On at least one occasion he acted as peacemaker with the Indians. In 1720 he went to France; he returned to the colony the following year with the rank of ensign and a post as commandant of the Îles de la Madeleine, where he

served for two years. In 1724 he was sent to Lake Champlain at the head of a detachment in order to prevent smuggling there.

In 1727, when it was decided to establish a post among the Sioux, Pierre Boucher de Boucherville was chosen second in command under his uncle, René BOUCHER de La Perrière, who led the expedition. They reached Lake Pepin (Wis.-Minn.) around the end of the summer and there they set up Fort Beauharnois. The following year Boucherville, on his way to Montreal, stopped at Michilimackinac, where he joined Constant Le Marchand* de Lignery's expedition against the Foxes. After this unsuccessful campaign Boucherville returned to Fort Beauharnois, where he assumed command in place of his uncle, who had had to return to Montreal because of illness. But in September 1728, on the advice of Lignery, who feared an attack by the Foxes, Boucherville left the fort by means of the Mississippi, which he believed the least dangerous route. He was nevertheless attacked, and was a prisoner of the Kickapoos and Mascoutens for over five months. He took advantage of his forced stay among these Indians to make friends with them; he offered to try to make peace with the Illinois for them and during the winter succeeded in concluding a treaty embracing the three tribes. According to Maximilien Bibaud*, Boucherville left an account of his stay in the Sioux country, "Relation des aventures de M. de Boucherville à son retour des Sioux en 1728 et 1729, suivie d'observations sur les mœurs des sauvages," but the whereabouts of this manuscript today is not known.

After returning to Montreal, probably during the summer of 1729, Boucherville was married there on 14 Sept. 1731 to Marguerite, Pierre Raimbault*'s daughter, by whom he had six children. In 1732 he obtained permission from the minister of Marine to go to France on private business, and in 1734 he was appointed to Fort Frontenac (Kingston, Ont.). The following year he was sent to Fort Niagara (near Youngstown, N.Y.), and in 1736, when the commandant of the fort, Nicolas Blaise* Des Bergères de Rigauville, was relieved of his post, Boucherville replaced him. That same year he was appointed a lieutenant in the colonial regular troops. Boucherville served as commandant at Niagara for three years, then returned to Montreal. In 1745 he received command of Fort Chambly, and the following year he was sent to Fort Saint-Frédéric (Crown Point, N.Y.), where he served as lieutenant and interpreter. He did garrison duty in Montreal again in 1748, and was appointed captain in March 1749.

On 1 Jan. 1758, after 56 years in the colonial

regular troops, Boucherville was retired with a pension and received the cross of the order of Saint-Louis in recognition of his services. He remained in Canada after the conquest; a note in his military record dated 25 Sept. 1766 mentions that his advanced age and infirmities had not permitted him to return to France and that from 1760 on he had not received the pension of 540 *livres* granted him in 1758. Pierre Boucher de Boucherville died in 1767 in the seigneury of Boucherville, of which he had been joint seigneur.

IN COLLABORATION

AN, Col., E, 43 (dossier Pierre Boucher), pièces 1–4; Marine, C⁷, 39 (dossier Boucher de Boucherville). PAC *Report, 1904*, app.K. Fauteux, *Les chevaliers de Saint-Louis*, 166. Tanguay, *Dictionnaire*. Maximilien Bibaud, *Le panthéon canadien* (Montréal, 1891), 33. P.-G. Roy, "Les commandants du fort Niagara," *BRH*, LIV (1948), 166–67.

BOUCHER DE LA PERRIÈRE, RENÉ, officer in the colonial regular troops, seigneur; b. 18 June 1668 in Montreal, tenth child of Pierre Boucher* and Jeanne Crevier; d. 12 Aug. 1742 in Boucherville (Que.).

René Boucher de La Perrière had learnt the languages and warfare of the Indians in his youth. On 2 Jan. 1694, with several years' military experience to his credit, he was commissioned ensign in the colonial regular troops. Two years later he went with a detachment of Canadians to assist Pierre Le Moyne* d'Iberville in his attack on the English settlements on the Newfoundland coast. With the fall of St John's on 30 Nov. 1696 Iberville instructed Jacques Testard* de Montigny and his Canadians to attack every village and hamlet on the island shores. La Perrière was prominent in these forays, operating as the leader of a small party of men that reduced settlements to ashes and invariably returned with both booty and captives.

La Perrière was wounded in 1704 while leading the Indian contingent in Jean-Baptiste Hertel* de Rouville's raid on Deerfield, Massachusetts. In 1708 he served as commandant at Sault-Saint-Louis (Caughnawaga), and two years later, recommended by Philippe de Rigaud* de Vaudreuil, Jacques Raudot*, and Claude de Ramezay*, he received a lieutenancy.

In 1712, when relations among the Indians in the west were tense and war broke out between the Foxes and the French allies, Vaudreuil sent small detachments of men to key points in the hinterland. It is probable that La Perrière went with

Constant Le Marchand* de Lignery to Michilimackinac, for in 1715, after a campaign to defeat the Foxes had failed, La Perrière returned to the colony with Lignery's letters. A second campaign was planned for 1716. This time Louis de La Porte* de Louvigny, with La Perrière as second-in-command, led an army of 800 coureurs de bois and Indians to Baie-des-Puants (Green Bay, Wis.) and forced the Foxes to sue for peace.

Ten years later, while Lignery and one de Liette [*see* Pierre-Charles de Liette*] were negotiating an end to hostilities among the French, Foxes, Sauks, Winnebagos, and Sioux in the west, the king of France gave approval to the establishment of a post among the Sioux, as CHARLEVOIX had recommended. On 6 June 1727 the Compagnie des Sioux was formed for the organization of commerce in the area, and La Perrière, promoted captain the previous year, was chosen to command an expedition to build a fort, mission house, and chapel. He and his party, which included his nephew Pierre BOUCHER de Boucherville and Jesuit fathers Nicolas Degonnor and Michel GUIGNAS, left Montreal on 16 June. Following a brief stop at Michilimackinac, the party – accompanied for a time by the Jesuit Jean-Baptiste CHARDON – moved out on 1 August and by the Fox, Wisconsin, and Mississippi rivers entered Lake Pepin on 17 Sept. 1727. Within four days La Perrière had built a small fort, named Beauharnois in honour of the new governor of Canada, Charles de BEAUHARNOIS. In the early summer of 1728 La Perrière was obliged to return to Montreal because of illness, and in September Fort Beauharnois was abandoned as a result of Lignery's unsuccessful campaign against the Foxes. La Perrière was appointed commandant of Fort Saint-Frédéric (Crown Point, N.Y.) in 1732, but gave it up after a year, again because of illness. His services did not pass unnoticed, however – on 26 April 1736 he was awarded the coveted cross of Saint-Louis.

On several occasions Pierre Boucher made land grants in the Boucherville seigneury to his son, which La Perrière subsequently sold. The one royal grant he received, in 1734 – six square leagues on Lake Champlain – reverted to the crown seven years later because it had been left undeveloped.

La Perrière died in Boucherville on 12 Aug. 1742. He had married Françoise Malhiot, sister of Jean-François MALHIOT, in Montreal on 15 Dec. 1705. Françoise bore La Perrière two children, Marie-Madeleine, who married in 1729 Claude-Pierre Pécaudy* de Contrecœur, and François-Clément who, like his father, entered military service. He received a captaincy in 1756 and dis-

Boucher de Montbrun

tinguished himself in the western campaigns of the Seven Years' War.

C. J. Russ

AN, Col., C^{11A}, 24, p.61; 28, p.17; 30, pp.69–70; 35, pp.37–38 (PAC transcripts). ANQ-M, Greffe d'Antoine Adhémar, 2 juill. 1693, 15 déc. 1705; Greffe de Michel Moreau, 23 juill. 1693; Greffe de Marien Tailhandier, dit La Beaume, 4 août, 30 oct. 1703, 8 févr. 1706, 14 déc. 1709, 7 déc. 1710, 3 févr. 1711, 5 oct. 1712, 10 janv. 1715. *Découvertes et établissements des Français* (Margry), VI, 537–63. Fauteux, *Les chevaliers de Saint-Louis*, 131. Le Jeune, *Dictionnaire*. Tanguay, *Dictionnaire*. Champagne, *Les La Vérendrye*, 89, 109. Martin Kavanagh, *La Vérendrye, his life and times, with many illustrations and maps; a biography and a social study of a folklore figure, soldier, fur trader, explorer* (Brandon, Man., 1967). Kellogg, *French régime*, 308–12. P.-G. Roy, *Hommes et choses du fort Saint-Frédéric*, 160–61, 340–41. Y. F. Zoltvany, "The frontier policy of Philippe de Rigaud de Vaudreuil, 1713–1725," *CHR*, XLVIII (1967), 227–50; "New France and the west, 1701–1713," *CHR*, XLVI (1965), 301–22.

BOUCHER DE MONTBRUN, JEAN, militia commandant, fur-trader, explorer; baptized 7 Feb. 1667 at Trois-Rivières, son of Pierre Boucher* and Jeanne Crevier; buried 20 Oct. 1742 at Boucherville, near Montreal.

In his youth Jean Boucher de Montbrun took part, probably as a militiaman, in several campaigns against the Iroquois, including the lamentable expedition led by La Barre [Le Febvre*] in 1684 to Anse de la Famine (Mexico Bay) on Lake Ontario. He also took part in the expeditions organized by Denonville [Brisay*] and Frontenac [Buade*] during the Iroquois wars. In 1692, at Pointe-Lévy (Lauzon, Que.), he married Françoise-Claire, the daughter of Étienne Charest Sr, seigneur of Lauson. The married couple seem to have lived for some time at Pointe-Lévy, since their first child was born there in 1693; then they settled at Boucherville, where Boucher helped his father manage his seigneury, being in charge of the flourmill and the roads. Moreover, in 1693 he had obtained from his father, jointly with his brother René BOUCHER de La Perrière, "a noble fief with justice reserved" in the seigneury of Boucherville, with a frontage of six *arpents* and a depth of two leagues.

From 1715 to 1729 Boucher is supposed to have been "commandant of the militia on the south shore," and it was in this capacity that in 1715 he attended to the distribution of the days of corvée among the habitants of the seigneury. At the same period Boucher took part in several trading or exploring expeditions in the west. In 1727 he was, it seems, at the post of Nipigon (near the mouth of the Nipigon River, Ont.), where he is believed to have met Pierre GAULTIER de Varennes et de La Vérendrye. He may have gone with his two sons, Jean-Baptiste and François, on La Perrière's expedition to found Fort Beauharnois on Lake Pepin (Wis.-Minn.) that same year.

Jean Boucher de Montbrun died in 1742 and was buried in the church of Sainte-Famille in Boucherville. He had been an active man, taking part in expeditions for war, trade, or exploration, at the same time attending to the Boucherville seigneury. He had a pleasant manner with those about him, particularly with his family: his domestic relations were indeed most cordial, as is shown by several notarial deeds.

Four years after the death of his first wife, who had borne him some 13 children, Boucher had on 10 Nov. 1729 married Françoise, the daughter of Jean-Amador Godefroy* de Saint-Paul, at Trois-Rivières. Boucher's death in 1742 gave rise to quarrels within his family. The succession was difficult to settle, and Boucher's widow had to come to arrangements with the heirs, all of whom were of her husband's first marriage, and in particular with René Boucher de Montbrun, who was both her stepson and brother-in-law. René, who had been the owner of half of his father's fief since 1740, had married in 1738 Madeleine Godefroy de Saint-Paul, his stepmother's sister. Even at Françoise Godefroy's death in 1770 the dispute may not have been settled. It was a far cry from the spirit of friendly understanding and cordiality which Jean Boucher de Montbrun had manifested all his life.

ROLAND-J. AUGER

Découvertes et établissements des Français (Margry), VI, 552. PAC *Report, 1899*, supp., 132. Bonnault, "Le Canada militaire," APQ *Rapport, 1949–51*, 289–90. Godbout, "Nos ancêtres," APQ *Rapport, 1959–60*, 304–5. Le Jeune, *Dictionnaire*. *Répertoire des mariages de Trois-Rivières, 1654–1900*, Dominique Campagna, compil. (Cap-de-la-Madeleine, Qué., [1963]), 198. A. Roy, *Inv. greffes not.*, IX, 148; XIII, 78; XVII, 121; XVIII, 32. P.-G. Roy, *Inv. coll. pièces jud. et not.*, I, 107, 136; II, 359; *Inv. concessions*, II, 296; *Inv. jug. et délib.*, *1717–1760*, V, 67, 103, 185; *Inv. ord. int.*, I, 131, 138, 167, 260; II, 70. Lemire-Marsolais et Lambert, *Histoire de la Congrégation de Notre-Dame*, IV, 157–64. Estelle Mitchell, *Messire Pierre Boucher (écuyer), seigneur de Boucherville, 1622–1717* (Montréal, 1967). J.-E. Roy, *Histoire de la seigneurie de Lauzon* (5v., Lévis, Qué., 1897–1904), I, 427; II, 69, 84. J.-J. Lefebvre, "La descendance de Pierre Boucher (1622–1717), fondateur de Boucherville," SGCF *Mémoires*, V (1952–53), 69–96.

BOUCHER DE NIVERVILLE, JEAN-BAPTISTE, officer in the colonial regular troops, seigneur; b. 6 Dec. 1673 at Boucherville (Que.), son of Pierre Boucher* and Jeanne Crevier; d. 1748 at Boucherville.

Jean-Baptiste Boucher de Niverville was initiated into a military career at an early age. He first was in the militia, then enlisted in the colonial regular troops. Around 1695 he was appointed an ensign, and in 1690 and 1696 he apparently took part in the expeditions organized by Frontenac [Buade*] against the English and Iroquois. In a letter to Pontchartrain, the minister of Marine, on 12 Nov. 1707, Governor Vaudreuil [Rigaud*] and Intendant Jacques Raudot* informed the minister that they were sending him "a bag full of mineral samples found at Lake Champlain by the Sieurs de Niverville, Graveline, and Destailly, as well as a map of Lake Champlain." It is not known, however, for what purpose they were at Lake Champlain. Boucher, who had been promoted lieutenant in 1705, was put on half pay in 1711.

In 1710 he married Marguerite-Thérèse, the daughter of Joseph-François Hertel* de La Fresnière and Marguerite de Thavenet*. Nine years earlier, in 1701, he had received from his father an *arrière-fief* of 60 acres in the seigneury of Boucherville, which he exchanged on 14 March 1719 for the rights and claims his brother-in-law, Zacharie-François HERTEL de La Fresnière, held in the seigneury of Chambly. On 28 September Boucher signed an agreement with the other members of the Hertel family, who held rights in that seigneury, to obtain a majority of the shares. In 1721, as seigneur of Chambly, he attended the meetings held by the attorney general, Mathieu-Benoît Collet*, on the redistribution of parish districts in New France. In this capacity also he rendered fealty and homage and drew up the recognition of sovereignty and census for the seigneury in 1723.

Boucher was interested in the settling and development of his domain. In 1721 he was successful in his request that Chambly be raised canonically to a parish, and in 1724 he made the Charon Brothers a land grant of 640 acres. He seems, however, to have had difficulty in interesting his *censitaires* in tending their land. On 27 July 1732 he had to restore to his domain of Chambly the lands of 19 who had not bothered to develop them or settle on them. On 10 March 1740 he had Intendant Gilles Hocquart* issue an ordinance to force five other habitants of the seigneury "to take up residence . . . otherwise proceedings will be taken to reunite their lands with the domain of Jean-Baptiste Boucher de Niverville."

Boucher died in 1748 at Boucherville. Of his 14 children, six at least survived him, including Joseph-Claude*, an officer in the colonial regular troops, who in 1754 became seigneur of Chambly after having bought out his father's other heirs.

ROLAND-J. AUGER

ANQ, NF, Aveux et dénombrements, I, 297; NF, Foi et hommage, I, 74; II, 119. ANQ-M, Greffe d'Antoine Adhémar, 20 août 1701, 10 févr. 1710. "Procès-verbaux du procureur général Collet" (Caron), APQ *Rapport*, *1921–22*, 308, 311. Le Jeune, *Dictionnaire*. P.-G. Roy, *Inv. concessions*, I, 243; II, 197–99, 298; IV, 96; *Inv. ord. int.*, I, 260; II, 70, 128, 156, 196, 287; III, 120. Tanguay, *Dictionnaire*. Séraphin Marion, *Pierre Boucher* (Québec, 1927). Estelle Mitchell, *Messire Pierre Boucher (écuyer), seigneur de Boucherville, 1622–1717* (Montréal, 1967). Montarville Boucher de Labruère, "La mort de Jacques Boucher de Montizambert," *BRH*, XXXIV (1928), 12–19.

BOUCHERVILLE, PIERRE BOUCHER DE. *See* BOUCHER

BOUMOIS, PIERRE GAULTIER DE LA VÉRENDRYE DE. *See* GAULTIER

BOURG, *dit* **Belle-Humeur, ALEXANDRE,** notary, king's attorney; b. 1671 at Port-Royal (Annapolis Royal, N.S.), son of François Bourg and Marguerite Boudrot; d. 1760 at Richibucto (N.B.).

Alexandre Bourg settled about 1694 at Grand Pré, Nova Scotia, where he married Marguerite Melanson, the daughter of Pierre Melanson, *dit* La Verdure, and Marguerite Mius d'Entremont; of this marriage at least 16 children were born. Immediately after the conquest of Acadia by the British in 1710 he was appointed notary for Minas Basin. On several occasions he was chosen to represent the Acadians of his region in dealing with the government at Annapolis Royal. Thus he was among the delegates sent by the Acadians of Minas to Annapolis in 1720 at the request of Governor Richard PHILIPPS after the latter had tried to have them take the oath of allegiance. After the same Acadians had refused to take the oath in 1727 Bourg was called to Annapolis to explain their conduct.

In December 1730 Governor Philipps granted Alexandre Bourg a commission as king's attorney for Minas, Pisiquid (Windsor, N.S.), Cobequid (near Truro, N.S.), and Chignecto, with authority to receive moneys due and annuities and to handle all cases of seizure of property and escheat. In 1731 he was accused of negligence in his accounts, and in September 1737 the lieutenant governor, Lawrence Armstrong*, dismissed him from his functions. He was replaced by François MANGEANT, *dit* Saint-Germain. On 27 May 1740, Paul MASCARENE, Armstrong's successor, who considered Bourg an old acquaintance, reinstated him as notary and tax-collector.

In 1742 Bourg and some settlers from Minas helped in finding belongings stolen by Indians from an English merchant vessel near Grand Pré. In 1744 Bourg was again accused of negligence in carrying out his duties and was even accused of having collaborated, along with his son-in-law Joseph LE BLANC, *dit* Le Maigre, with Joseph DU PONT Duvivier's troops during the invasion of Nova Scotia; on 17 December Bourg was suspended from office. He was taken to Annapolis Royal with Joseph Le Blanc and subjected to a close interrogation by Mascarene and the council. As punishment his office as notary at Minas was taken from him for good.

Bourg may have left Acadia at the beginning of the 1750s when several thousand Acadians emigrated to Île Royale (Cape Breton Island) and Île Saint-Jean (Prince Edward Island). In any event we meet him again in 1752 at Port-Toulouse (St Peters, N.S.), at the home of Joseph Le Blanc, who had been living there for three years. Bourg escaped the deportation of the Acadians in 1755 and the evacuation of Île Royale after the British capture of Louisbourg in 1758 [*see* WOLFE]. He seems to have taken refuge at Richibucto, where he died at 89 years of age.

C. J. D'ENTREMONT

AN, Col., E, 277, ff.17–20; Section Outre-Mer, G¹, 466, pièces 8, 13, 24, 25, 26, 27. Diocesan Archives (Baton Rouge, La.), Registres de St-Charles des Mines (Grand-Pré), 1707–1748 (baptêmes); 1709–1748 (mariages et sépultures) (copies at Diocesan Archives, Yarmouth, N.S., and PAC, MG 9, B8, 12). *Coll. doc. inédits Canada et Amérique*, II, 175. *Coll. de manuscrits relatifs à la N.-F.*, II, 260. *N.S. Archives, I*; *II*; *III*; *IV*. PAC *Report, 1905*, II, pt.I, 22. Murdoch, *History of Nova-Scotia*, I, 364, 405, 468, 478, 523; II, 4, 8, 10, 39, 71.

BOURLAMAQUE, FRANÇOIS-CHARLES DE, French army officer, governor of Guadeloupe; b. 1716, at Paris, France; d. "the night of 23–24 June 1764," at Guadeloupe.

François-Charles de Bourlamaque is said to have been of Italian descent. His father, whose name is given as Jean-François de Bourlamaque, was an officer in the French service who was killed in the battle of Parma, 1734, while serving as a captain of grenadiers in the Régiment du Dauphin. Bourlamaque himself entered the same regiment as a volunteer in 1739, and became a second lieutenant in 1740, lieutenant in 1742, adjutant in May 1745, and captain in December 1745. Though he is often described as a military engineer, it seems evident that he never belonged to the corps of engineers; he may however have been employed at times on engineering duties. He is reported to have seen much service in the War of the Austrian Succession, including the battles of Fontenoy (1745) and Raucoux (Rocourt, Belgium) (1746). In 1755 he was given a pecuniary award for two years' work devoted to improving the infantry drillbook.

In 1756 the court of Versailles reinforced New France and sent out new commanders for the troops there. The Marquis de MONTCALM was promoted major-general (*maréchal de camp*) and dispatched to take command of the regular force; the Chevalier de Lévis* was made brigadier and second in command. Bourlamaque, who was still at this time captain and adjutant (*capitaine aide-major*) in the Régiment du Dauphin, was commissioned as colonel of infantry in Canada (11 March 1756) and thus became third in command. At the same time he received the cross of Saint-Louis. He sailed from Brest in the *Sirène* in April 1756, and reached Quebec on 15 May.

Shortly after his arrival he was actively involved in the preparations for the attack on the three British forts at Oswego. In June he was sent to take command at Fort Frontenac (Kingston, Ont.), where a force for this enterprise was being assembled. On 5 August Montcalm, with Bourlamaque and most of the troops, left Frontenac for Niaouré Bay (now Sackets Harbor, N.Y.) en route to Oswego. On the night of 10–11 August Bourlamaque took a detachment forward to cover the engineers who were to reconnoitre Fort Ontario (Oswego, N.Y.). He was placed in charge of the siege works, and trenches were opened on the evening of the 12th. The following day, Montcalm's journal records, Bourlamaque received "a contusion to the head," but did not leave the trenches. That night the British abandoned Fort Ontario and retired across the river to the other forts; and on 14 August their whole force surrendered.

Bourlamaque played a prominent part in the campaign of 1757 on the Lac Saint-Sacrement (Lake George) front. In the spring he was placed in command on this frontier. When the main French army invested Fort William Henry (also called Fort George; now Lake George, N.Y.) in the first week of August he was again charged by Montcalm with the direction of the siege. The place surrendered on the 9th, the capitulation being followed by an Indian massacre of prisoners. Montcalm was unable to follow up the victory, and the season ended with Bourlamaque standing on the defensive at the head of Lake Champlain with two regular battalions, working on the fort at Carillon (Ticonderoga, N.Y.)

The summer of 1758 witnessed the disastrous attempt of General James Abercromby* to invade Canada by the Lake Champlain route. Bourlamaque had charge of the French advanced troops in front of Carillon and retired into the defences as the British moved forward. On 8 July Abercromby attacked the trench line and *abattis* which the French had thrown up before the fort. His army suffered a bloody repulse, successive charges being beaten back throughout the afternoon. Bourlamaque commanded the French left wing until about four o'clock, when he was "dangerously" wounded in the shoulder. The seriousness of the wound is indicated by the fact that he was able to leave Carillon to convalesce at Quebec only on 11 September.

In the crucial campaign of 1759 New France faced a double attack: by General WOLFE up the St Lawrence and by the new British commander-in-chief in America, General Jeffery Amherst*, following the line of Lac Saint-Sacrement and Lake Champlain. Montcalm, seconded by Lévis, opposed Wolfe at Quebec; it fell to Bourlamaque (who was promoted brigadier by a commission dated 10 February) to deal with Amherst. The latter had a force of over 11,000 men. Bourlamaque was given three of the eight French regular battalions in the country; colonial regular troops and militia brought the grand total of his command to some 4,000 men, of whom only roughly 3,000 were available for his main force. He had in addition a few Indians, whom he found to be of little use. He was in position at Carillon by the latter part of May, but Amherst did not advance until 21 July. To the surprise of the British, Bourlamaque did not attempt to defend the entrenched line in front of the fort on which they had been so badly defeated in 1758. To avoid the possibility of having his position turned and his whole force cut off, he withdrew from Fort Carillon on the night of 22–23 July. To delay the enemy he left a rearguard of 400 men under Captain d'Hébécourt (one of two officers of that name then serving in the Régiment de la Reine, and probably the senior, Louis-Philippe Le Dossu d'Hébécourt). Amherst brought up his artillery and began a siege of Carillon in form. D'Hébécourt made a spirited defence for four days; then on the evening of the 26th his force too slipped away by water and joined Bourlamaque, leaving a match burning in the magazine. The explosion did much damage to the fort. On 31 July Fort Saint-Frédéric (Crown Point, N.Y.) was likewise

blown up, and Bourlamaque pulled his little army back to Île aux Noix in the Richelieu, where he proposed to make a final defence.

The Île aux Noix position had been considerably strengthened during the summer, and Bourlamaque continued to improve it, among other things taking steps to flood the mainland nearby. He was worried by the possibility of the British outflanking him by a movement through the forest. Amherst, however, made no such attempt. He proceeded to build a great new fort at Crown Point and a naval squadron on Lake Champlain. On 11 September a British party attempted unsuccessfully to burn a sloop that the French had constructed at Île aux Noix. Finally on 11 October the British flotilla moved down the lake. Three of Bourlamaque's four armed vessels, cut off from entering the Richelieu, were put out of action on the 12th, two being sunk by their crews and the third run ashore. But on the 18th Amherst heard of the fall of Quebec and at once abandoned the campaign.

Bourlamaque's operations in 1759 must be accounted a successful example of delaying action, though they might not have been so successful against an adversary less cautious than Amherst. Bourlamaque himself told Lévis that the British general's campaign had been "stupid." The brigadier's own most severe critic was Pierre de Rigaud*, Marquis de Vaudreuil, who complained that d'Hébécourt might well have defended Carillon for a fortnight longer. He got no change out of Bourlamaque, who replied that Vaudreuil himself had sent him an order on 20 May, reinforced by another on 1 June, to the effect that Carillon should be evacuated as soon as the enemy had set up batteries against it, and that it was more important to preserve the garrison than to gain time. Bourlamaque's instruction to d'Hébécourt, he told the governor, had been copied word for word from Vaudreuil's own orders. Lévis, who had succeeded the dead Montcalm, was well pleased; he reported to France that Bourlamaque had performed his task of defending the frontier "with the greatest distinction."

As the 1759 campaign drew to its close, Bourlamaque was complaining of ill health, including "a return of asthma." He told Lévis that this made it impossible for him to carry out Vaudreuil's desire that he remain on the frontier for the winter. In fact, he probably spent the greater part of the winter at Montreal; but in February he was in the Quebec area investigating the possibility of an enterprise against the outposts of General James Murray*'s garrison there. Finding this impracticable he returned to Montreal. For

Bourlamaque

the 1760 campaign he did not go back to Lake Champlain. Lévis evidently wanted Bourlamaque with him for the stroke he was planning against Quebec, and it was Louis-Antoine de Bougainville* who was now sent to take command at Île aux Noix. Bourlamaque was thus second in command of the French army that attacked Quebec in April. He commanded the advanced guard during the approach to the city, and was wounded in the victory of Sainte-Foy, won over Murray on 28 April. In the early stages of the battle Lévis, fearing that his troops would not be able to form before Murray's attack came in, ordered a withdrawal of the left flank. While directing this Bourlamaque was hit in the right leg by a cannon-shot, his horse being killed under him. Subsequently Lieutenant-Colonel Jean d'ALQUIER, the officer now in command on the left, countermanded Lévis' order with excellent results for the French. Bourlamaque's injury was a flesh wound, and he recovered rapidly enough to play a part in the final stage of the year's campaign. In July he was sent to the Sorel area to prepare defences against a British advance up the St Lawrence from Quebec. On 10 August he was again dispatched there to oppose Murray's army. However, with the British in control of the water and his own militiamen deserting in large numbers, he was unable to offer any effective resistance and could only follow Murray's flotilla along the shore. On 2 September his attenuated detachment joined Lévis on the island of Montreal. Amherst had concentrated an overwhelming force against them – Murray from Quebec, William Haviland* by Lake Champlain, and Amherst's own army down the St Lawrence from Lake Ontario. There was no alternative, and Vaudreuil surrendered Montreal and Canada on 8–9 September.

Bourlamaque returned to France in accordance with the terms of the capitulation. His reputation had clearly been enhanced by the distinguished part he had played in the defence of the colony. He was promoted to the rank of commander in the order of Saint-Louis. In 1761 he led a military mission to Malta. On 1 Aug. 1762 he sent the Duc de Choiseul a striking "Mémoire sur le Canada" which argued that the country would be valuable to France if improvements were made in its administration. It would be well worth retaining, he said, even if the Great Lakes basin were lost; the colony had suffered through too much attention being paid to the fur trade and the establishment of distant posts, and not enough to developing the resources of the St Lawrence valley. Perhaps Bourlamaque hoped to be governor of Canada if the colony were returned to France

at the peace. This, however, was not to be. In February 1763 Bourlamaque (who had been promoted major-general) was appointed governor of the then important colony of Guadeloupe, and later that year he took it over from the British who had been in occupation of it. In 1764 he died in office.

No evidence has been found that Bourlamaque ever married. He was on friendly terms with Montcalm, and the general's intimate letters to him (which he preserved in spite of Montcalm's repeated injunctions to destroy them) are an important source of information about both Montcalm himself and the events in which he took part. Bourlamaque's own surviving letters – chiefly addressed to his military superiors – are in general severely professional in tone. What we know of him leaves us with the impression of a gallant soldier – in this respect his wounds seem to speak for him – and, rather less common in the French army of that era, a very competent officer. His memoir of 1762 suggests a keen and original mind. Beyond that there is little to be said. As a person, Bourlamaque largely eludes us.

C. P. STACEY

[Bourlamaque's letters to Lévis in 1759 and 1760 are in *Lettres de M. de Bourlamaque* (vol. V of the *Collection des manuscrits du maréchal de Lévis*, edited by H.-R. Casgrain). Montcalm's letters to Bourlamaque, published in the same volume, are not part of the Lévis manuscripts but are from the six-volume Bourlamaque collection, of which the originals, as in the case of the Lévis MSS, are now in PAC. Generally speaking, the Bourlamaque collection consists of letters addressed to him rather than written by him, though there are a number of unsigned campaign narratives and other papers which are probably by Bourlamaque. The collection is calendared in PAC *Report, 1923*, app.C. Bourlamaque's "Mémoire sur le Canada" is published in *BRH*, XXV (1919), 257–76, 289–305, and repeated in XXVI (1920), 193–209, 225–40. Many documents among the various volumes of the Lévis manuscripts provide details concerning Bourlamaque's career in Canada. A personal file in AN, Col., E, 48 (dossier Bourlamaque) (mfm in PAC) relates chiefly to Bourlamaque's connection with Guadeloupe. Another in SHA, Y^d, 2393 (also in microfilm in PAC) affords some details concerning promotions, family, etc., but little concerning Bourlamaque's campaigns. Jeffery Amherst, *Journal* (Webster) and [William Amherst], *Journal of William Amherst in America, 1758–1760*, ed. J. C. Webster (Frome, London, 1927) are useful sources for campaigns in which Bourlamaque took part.

No one has attempted to write a biography of Bourlamaque. The best account of him in print is in Le Jeune, *Dictionnaire*. There is a short article in *DBF*, VI. There are numerous references to Bourlamaque, and extended accounts of the operations in which he was involved, in Parkman, *Montcalm and Wolfe*; Gipson, *British empire before the American revolution*, VI, VII; R. P. Waddington, *La guerre de sept ans; histoire diplomatique et militaire* (5v., Paris, [1899–1907]); and Frégault, *La guerre de la conquête.* C.P.S.]

BOURVILLE, FRANÇOIS LE COUTRE DE. *See* LE COUTRE

BROSSARD (Broussard), *dit* **Beausoleil, JOSEPH,** settler, member of the militia; b. 1702 at Port-Royal (Annapolis Royal, N.S.), son of Jean-François Brossard* and Catherine Richard; d. 1765 in Louisiana.

Joseph Brossard is still revered today, particularly by the Acadians in Louisiana where he has become a legendary figure, for his bravery as leader of the resistance of the Acadians in the upper reaches of the Petitcodiac River at the time of the deportation. It must, however, be noted that not all of his exploits are recorded in the archives.

In September 1725, at Annapolis Royal, Brossard married Agnès, the daughter of Michel Thibodeau (Tibaudeau) and Agnès Dugas. Some years later he went to settle at Chipoudy (Shepody, N.B.), with his brother Alexandre. In this period Joseph was twice brought before the council of Annapolis. In 1724 he was accused of having treated an Acadian roughly, and in 1726 of being the father of an illegitimate child. Although he denied the latter accusation, he was imprisoned for some time for refusing to provide for the child's maintenance.

Brossard settled at Le Cran (Stoney Creek, south of Moncton, N.B.) about 1740. At the time of the battle of Minas at the beginning of 1747, Brossard gave assistance to Nicolas-Antoine COULON de Villiers's troops. On 21 October William Shirley, governor of Massachusetts, outlawed Brossard and 11 others for having provisioned the French troops.

In June 1755 the British, who were disputing possession of the Chignecto isthmus with the French, laid siege to Fort Beauséjour (near Sackville, N.B.). Brossard engaged in some skirmishes against the invaders and, in one outing, captured a British officer. In relating this incident the French officer Louis-Thomas Jacau* de Fiedmont testified that Brossard was recognized to be one of the bravest and most enterprising of the Acadians. On 16 June, the very day the fort capitulated, he was so bold as to attack the British camp with 60 men, French and Indians; he lost only one man. Two days later, provided with a safe conduct, he went to see Colonel Robert Monckton* for he proposed acting as mediator

between the British and Indians on condition that he be granted an amnesty. Monckton agreed to this arrangement, subject, however, to Charles LAWRENCE's approval.

Brossard and his family probably took to the woods at the time of the deportation of the Acadians. It is possible that he joined forces with Charles Deschamps* de Boishébert, along with the other heads of families in the region, to resist a British detachment which had come to devastate Chipoudy and Petitcodiac in September 1755. Shortly afterwards, Brossard, under orders from Governor Pierre de Rigaud* de Vaudreuil, fitted out a small privateer and was successful in capturing some prizes in the Bay of Fundy. Aided by his four sons and the Acadians who had taken refuge along the Petitcodiac River, he continued to harass the British forces. It was perhaps during an encounter with the troops commanded by George SCOTT which had come to lay waste the Petitcodiac region in November 1758 that he was wounded in the foot and obliged to go for a time to the other side of the Miramichi River.

A few Acadians were still resisting the British authorities in 1761 after the fall of Quebec and Louisbourg, Cape Breton Island. William Forster, a British colonel, wrote to General Jeffery Amherst* in August 1761: "These people are Spirited up in their obstiny by one BeauSoleil . . . and one or two others who have already rendered themselves so obnoxious to the English that they are conscious of the treatment they deserve at our hands." Brossard was reduced to a state of famine by November, and had no recourse but to surrender, along with a group of settlers, to Colonel Joseph Frye, the commandant of Fort Cumberland (formerly Fort Beauséjour). In October of the following year Brossard and his family were among the prisoners held in Fort Edward (Windsor, N.S.). Subsequently, they were sent to Halifax where they were confined until the treaty of Paris in 1763. Later in the year Brossard was arrested at Pisiquid (Windsor) and found to be in possession of a letter written by the ambassador of France in London in which the Acadians were urged to leave and go to France. Brought once more before the governor's council in Halifax, he was not released until the following year; it was then, it seems, that he chartered a schooner to sail to Saint-Domingue (Hispaniola) with some other Acadians. The climate overcame many of them, and Brossard is believed to have taken the survivors to Louisiana at the beginning of 1765.

On 8 April 1765, in New Orleans, Charles-Philippe Aubry, the commandant of Louisiana, appointed Joseph Brossard captain of the militia and commandant of the Acadians in the region of the Attackapas, which included the parishes of Saint-Landry, Saint-Martin, and Lafayette. He died a few months later and was buried on 20 October at Beausoleil, near the site of the present-day town of Broussard, a few miles south of Lafayette.

C. J. D'ENTREMONT

PAC, MG 9, B8, 24 (Registres de Saint-Jean-Baptiste du Port-Royal) (original of the volume for 1702–28 is at PANS and that for 1727–55 is at the Diocesan Archives, Yarmouth, N.S.), pt.I, p.222. [L.-T. Jacau de Fiedmont], *The siege of Beauséjour in 1755; a journal of the attack on Beauséjour, written by Jacau de Fiedmont ...*, ed. J. C. Webster (N.B. Museum, Historical Studies, no.1, Saint John, 1936), 41. Knox, *Historical journal* (Doughty), I, app., 3–4. *Mémoires sur le Canada, depuis 1749 jusqu'à 1760. Northcliffe coll. N.S. Archives, III.* "Les papiers Amherst," *La Société historique acadienne* (Moncton), 27e cahier (1970), 304, 307. Arsenault, *Hist. et généal. des Acadiens.* Antoine Bernard, *Histoire de la Louisiane de ses origines à nos jours* (Québec, [1953]), 157, 158, 410. D. J. Le Blanc, *The true story of the Acadians ...* ([Lafayette, La.], 1932), 65–67. Murdoch, *History of Nova-Scotia*, II, 117, 314, 431. J. C. Webster, *The forts of Chignecto; a study of the eighteenth century conflict between France and Great Britain in Acadia* (n.p., 1930), 55, 71, 87, 113.

BROUAGUE, FRANÇOIS MARTEL DE. *See* MARTEL

BROUILLAN, *dit* **Saint-Ovide, JOSEPH DE MONBETON DE.** *See* MONBETON

BRUNET (Brunel), *dit* **La Sablonnière, JEAN,** merchant butcher; b. 1687 in New France, son of Jean Brunet (Brunel), *dit* La Sablonnière, a farmer, and Marie-Madeleine Richaume; m. 23 Jan. 1719 at Montreal to Louise Maugue; buried 18 June 1753 at Montreal.

Jean Brunet, *dit* La Sablonnière, was an active and long-established butcher in Montreal. He began his trade as a young man and apparently received letters of emancipation in order to operate a business before the age of majority, 25. Brunet had already been a butcher for two or three years when an ordinance of the intendant, Antoine-Denis Raudot*, on 2 July 1710, listed him as one of the four authorized butchers in Montreal. Nine years later he married and in 1721 built a wooden house.

It is hard to estimate the scale of Brunet's trade. No record of meat sales remains except those that resulted in bad debts. Brunet's dealings in cattle and his credit are evidence that he was a successful butcher. In the early 1720s he obtained steers for his slaughter-house in exchange for draught-animals and other livestock. Later, he was able to buy fattened cattle and he had animals in pasturage and leased out a cow or two. From 1730 to 1734 Brunet acknowledged debts exceeding 3,000 *livres*, which he was able to repay.

Brunet was associated with several tanners but the degree of his involvement in tanning is uncertain. Butchers in New France often made annual contracts with tanners to supply them with the skins of all the cattle to be slaughtered in the coming year. From 1709 to 1736 Brunet made such agreements with Gérard and Jean-Baptiste Barsalou, Pierre Robreau, *dit* Leroux-Duplessis, Charles Delaunay*, and other tanners. In 1727 Brunet entered a five-year partnership with Nicolas-Auguste GUILLET de Chaumont, which was followed by a one-year partnership with Delaunay. In these partnerships Brunet, it seems, did not just supply skins for a half interest. A few accounts show that Brunet sold finished leather.

In the 1740s Brunet apparently lived in retirement in his house on Rue Saint-Vincent. He could probably afford to do so for he had sold several pieces of property, including his father's farm, and he rented out a house and a few lots in Montreal. Of his 11 children only three daughters married, and only one son lived to adulthood.

PETER N. MOOGK

ANQ, NF, Coll. de pièces jud. et not. 3538; NF, Documents de la juridiction de Montréal, IV, 129; VI, 12–14; XI, 43; NF, Ord. int., IV, 81f., 94–95. ANQ-M, Greffe de René Chorel de Saint-Romain, 27 nov. 1732; Greffe de Jacques David, 12 juin, 7 juill. 1720, 12 oct., 8 déc. 1721, 2 mars, 25 mai, 21 déc. 1722, 8 avril 1723, 20 juin 1724, 22 avril 1725, 8 juill., 24 août 1726; Greffe de C.-R. Gaudron de Chevrement, 29 nov. 1728, 10, 28 janv. 1729, 1er, 2 mai 1732; Greffe de Michel Lepailleur; Greffe de J.-C. Porlier, 9 sept. 1738, 22 mars 1744; Greffe de J.-C. Raimbault, 19 juill., 17 août 1727, 26 août 1730, 20 févr. 1732, 26 août 1734, 10 févr., 13 juin 1735, 20 mars, 21 août 1736, 4 juin, 11 juill. 1737; Registres des audiences, 7, ff.593v–94v, 603v, 642; 11, f.23; 12, ff.624, 671. "Recensement du Canada, 1681" (Sulte). "Recensement de Montréal, 1741" (Massicotte). P.-G. Roy, *Inv. jug. et délib., 1717–1760*, II, 41; IV, 293, 303; V, 101; VI, 124–25; *Inv. ord. int.*, I, 105–6, 140. Tanguay, *Dictionnaire*, I, 93; III, 493–94; V, 179.

BURTON, RALPH, military officer, lieutenant governor of the town of Quebec, of the Trois-Rivières district, and of the Montreal district, brigadier (commander-in-chief) of the Northern Department; d. in 1768 at Scarborough, Yorkshire, England.

Ralph Burton's origins are obscure, even the date and place of his birth being unknown. He is said to have been the son of a Yorkshire attorney, and his will makes a cousin, Robert Burton of Hotham, Yorkshire, his executor. He first came to prominence in the Seven Years' War in North America. In 1754 he was commissioned lieutenant-colonel in the 48th regiment and, serving under General Edward Braddock, was wounded in the expedition defeated on the Monongahela on 9 July 1755. In 1756–57 he served under Lord Loudoun [John Campbell] who commended him as "a diligent, sensible man." Burton commanded the 3rd brigade at Louisbourg, Île Royale (Cape Breton Island), in 1758, and in July 1759 he escorted WOLFE when he reconnoitred before Quebec. He was wounded at the end of July in the attack at Montmorency Falls, presumably not seriously for he commanded a reserve of the 48th on the Plains of Abraham and received Wolfe's dying command to cut off the retreating French at the Rivière Saint-Charles.

Burton spent the winter of 1759–60 as lieutenant governor, under James Murray*, military governor, at Quebec. On 28 April 1760 Murray led his forces to meet the French under Lévis* at Sainte-Foy, Burton commanding his right wing. During the battle the right wing retreated in disorder and Murray's force narrowly escaped disastrous defeat. At the time Murray did not hold Burton responsible; nor did two other officers, Captain John Knox* and Major Patrick Mackellar*, who left accounts of the battle. Later, after Murray and Burton had quarrelled, Murray stated that Burton had been to blame, and that he had mistakenly saved his junior from a court martial.

Shortly after the battle of Sainte-Foy British reinforcements arrived and Burton proceeded with Murray upriver to meet Jeffery Amherst* at Montreal where, on 8 Sept. 1760, the French army under Governor General Pierre de Rigaud* de Vaudreuil capitulated, surrendering the entire colony and the upper posts. Amherst, as commander-in-chief, made arrangements for the military administration of the colony before returning to New York. He retained the French administrative districts of Quebec, Trois-Rivières, and Montreal, appointed Thomas Gage* lieutenant governor of Montreal and Burton in the same capacity at Trois-Rivières, and confirmed Murray's governorship of Quebec. All three from both prudence and principle followed a conciliatory policy towards the Canadians, a policy approved by Amherst and practised by Murray during the previous winter in Quebec. The pledge of freedom of worship was scrupulously maintained, services from the habitants, though commandeered, were paid for, and efforts were made to check speculation in scarce food supplies and to send wheat from the upper districts to the town of Quebec, still suffering from the 1759 campaign. Justice was administered by military courts, with the help of the Canadian captains of militia, and according to local custom.

In 1762 Burton left Trois-Rivières for ten months' service in the West Indies. A few months after his return in 1763, Gage was sent to New York as acting commander-in-chief when Amherst went on leave, and Burton was transferred to Montreal from Trois-Rivières, being succeeded by Frederick Haldimand*.

According to Murray, Burton and Gage both hoped to be appointed civil governor of the new province of Quebec inaugurated in August 1764 and were resentful when Murray was chosen. Burton was offered instead the civilian post of lieutenant governor of Trois-Rivières. He refused, and requested to be allowed to go home to look after his private affairs and his health. It appears from Murray's letters, however, that Burton was rather gloomily contemplating retirement on half pay in England and that he was happy to be saved from this fate by new arrangements following Amherst's decision in 1764 not to return to North America. Gage remained at New York as commander-in-chief of the forces in America, and in October 1764 Burton learned from Gage that he was to be commissioned brigadier (commander-in-chief) of the Northern Department with headquarters at Montreal. Under Gage, he now commanded all troops in the newly defined province of Quebec and in the upper posts. He was therefore senior in military rank to Murray, under whom he had served in the Quebec campaign, and who was now, as civil governor, without a military command.

This awkward arrangement was most displeasing to Murray, who had assumed that he would also command the troops within the province. Murray argued that the tradition of New France where the governor had been commander-in-chief should have been followed. Not only did Murray's judgement condemn in the special circumstances of Quebec the usual American arrangement of separate military and civilian commands, but his vanity was deeply hurt and his warm friendship for Burton turned to suspicion and bitter dislike.

Burton's position in Montreal was a difficult one. As brigadier for the Northern Department he was charged with the defence of the whole province, and particularly of Michilimackinac, Detroit, and other posts on the Great Lakes.

Their commandants were ultimately responsible for the good conduct of fur-traders, for relations with the Indians, and, in general, for the security from the interior of the colony. While military rule lasted Burton could commandeer men, carts, and canoes for the transport of essential supplies to these up-country stations. Under civil government the practice was of doubtful legality and Murray, as governor, decided that it should be exercised only on his authority and through the justices of the peace.

The justices, however, constituted another of Burton's problems. Canadians as Roman Catholics being deemed ineligible, those appointed were retired officers or members of the small group of English merchants. These merchants had disliked the rule of military officers who, concerned to maintain good relations with the Canadians, had occasionally been careless of the rights and sensibilities of their fellow countrymen. One particular cause of resentment was the billeting of troops in Montreal. Until August 1764 billets had been found by the captains of militia, and any householder could be required to receive soldiers. Henceforth those merchants who were justices of the peace had to find the billets, but were themselves exempt from the never very welcome guests.

Thus in these two operations of government Burton had henceforth to secure the authority of Murray, and work through civilians who traditionally resented military authority and who might remember previous slights and hardships. Both the provision for transport duty and the finding of billets led to complex legal and jurisdictional disputes between Burton and Murray, disputes inflamed by their personal quarrel. Murray accused Burton of meddling in civil matters and of irritating the merchants; Burton retorted that Murray refused him the cooperation due to the commander of the troops in the performance of essential military duties.

It is difficult to judge this quarrel fairly as the chief source of information is Murray's letters to his superiors and friends. The few letters of Burton that survive are not revealing and any reconstruction of his character and conduct at this time must be largely based on speculation. In January 1765 the Earl of Halifax as secretary of state wrote to Burton ordering him not to meddle in civil affairs. In the colony, with its vociferous English and American merchants, the closest cooperation between governor and commander-in-chief was essential: there is no doubt that this was lacking. By 1766 Burton and Murray were barely on speaking terms and relations between the army and merchants so bad as to constitute a serious threat of disorder. In 1766 both men were recalled to Britain. This was the end of Burton's active career. He died at Scarborough in 1768. His will, dated 7 Feb. 1767, mentions a wife, Margaret, and a son and daughter; he appears to have been a good deal older than his wife. At this time he owned an estate in the parish of Cottingham, Yorkshire, and a house in London.

Burton seems to have won the confidence of officers under whom he served, with the possible exception of Murray at Sainte-Foy, but ten years of active service probably unfitted him for the difficult problems that he encountered in Quebec at the conclusion of the peace.

HILDA NEATBY

PAC, MG 23, GII, 1; RG 1, E1, 1–6; RG 4, A1, 2–16. PRO, CO 5; 42/1–42/26; Prob., 11/948, f.512. Knox, *Historical journal* (Doughty). Frégault, *La guerre de la conquête*, 138–40. Neatby, *Quebec*. S. M. Pargellis, *Lord Loudoun in North America* (New Haven, Conn., London, 1933).

BUSHELL (Bushel), JOHN, printer; b. probably 18 March 1715 in Boston, Massachusetts, son of John Bushel and Rebecca Parker; m. probably Elizabeth Strowbridge of Boston, by whom he had a son and a daughter; buried 22 Jan. 1761 in Halifax, Nova Scotia.

John Bushell served his apprenticeship in Boston and began a business in that city about 1734. He printed the *Boston Post-Boy* in 1735, and then worked in association with several Boston printers until 1749. In 1741 he had inherited various houses, tenements, and lands from his father. He printed on his own from 1749 to 1751, when he moved to Halifax and assumed control of the printing establishment begun by a former partner, Bartholomew GREEN.

On 23 March 1752 Bushell started publication of the *Halifax Gazette*. The enterprise seems to have been financed jointly by Otis LITTLE, king's attorney in Nova Scotia, and a Boston resident. The *Gazette* was first issued on a half-sheet of foolscap, printed in two columns on both sides. About a quarter of the paper contained material relating to Nova Scotia, such as information on ship arrivals, proclamations, and occasional notices on runaway slaves, stolen goods, and straying wives. The rest of the paper consisted mainly of excerpts from British newspapers on European politics and government, and news from the American and West Indian colonies. In addition to publishing the *Gazette*, Bushell printed proclamations and laws for the government and likely did job-work for local merchants.

He seems, however, gradually to have lost control of the *Gazette*. In 1754 Richard Bulkeley*, provincial secretary, assumed the editorship of the paper. In 1758 Anthony Henry* became Bushell's assistant and was soon doing much of the printing.

According to Isaiah Thomas, who worked in Henry's office, Bushell was a good workman, "but had not the art of acquiring property; nor did he make the most economical use of the little which fell into his hands." A number of 20th-century studies, probably stemming from an article by J. J. Stewart, suggest that Bushell drank excessively. Thomas, however, says nothing about Bushell's drinking habits although he knew Bushell's son and undoubtedly some of Bushell's acquaintances. Moreover, the records of the Inferior Court of Common Pleas of Halifax, which reveal that Bushell was frequently in debt while in that town, do not indicate that he owed excessive amounts for liquor. At various times Bushell owed money to his backers, his landlord, his assistant, Henry, and others. It is ironic that the earliest known piece of official printing by Bushell for the government of Nova Scotia was a six-page pamphlet containing "An act for the relief of debtors," dated 6 Dec. 1752.

Bushell's daughter is supposed to have remained in Halifax for some time after his death. His son was apprenticed to Daniel Fowle of Portsmouth, New Hampshire, and later was a printer at Philadelphia, where he is said to have run a tavern.

DONALD F. CHARD

PANS, RG 37, June 1757; March 1759; March, December 1760; June, September 1761. St Paul's Church (Halifax), Burial records, index B (mfm in PANS). Boston, Registry Dept., *Records* (Whitmore et al.), [24], 103; [28], 33, 195. *Checklist of Boston newspapers, 1704–1780, and bibliography* (Col. Soc. Mass. Pubs., IX, Boston, 1907), 470. Shipton, *Sibley's Harvard graduates*, IX, 64. Marie Tremaine, *A bibliography of Canadian imprints, 1751–1800* (Toronto, 1952), 661.

Brebner, *Neutral Yankees*, 136. *Canadian book of printing; how printing came to Canada and the story of the graphic arts, told mainly in pictures*, ed. Marie Tremaine (Toronto, 1940), 16, 19. Ægidius Fauteux, *The introduction of printing into Canada; a brief history* (Montreal, 1930), 44. D. C. McMurtrie, *The first printing in Nova Scotia* (Chicago, 1930), 6, 10. Isaiah Thomas, *The history of printing in America . . .* (2nd ed., 2v., Albany, N.Y., 1874), I, 127, 357. G. E. N. Tratt, "A survey and listing of Nova Scotian newspapers, with particular reference to the period before 1867" (unpublished MA thesis, Mount Allison University, Sackville, N.B., 1957), 135. Marie Tremaine, *Early printing in Canada* (Toronto, 1934), 2. J. J. Stewart, "Early journalism in Nova Scotia," N.S. Hist. Soc. *Coll.*, VI (1888), 93–101.

BYNG, JOHN, officer in the Royal Navy, governor of Newfoundland; baptized at Southill, Bedfordshire, England, 29 Oct. 1704, son of George Byng, 1st Viscount Torrington, and Margaret Masters; d. 14 March 1757.

John Byng entered the navy in 1718 in the *Superbe*, serving in the Mediterranean. He was commissioned lieutenant in 1724, and promoted captain of the frigate *Gibraltar* in 1727; he remained on the Mediterranean station until 1739. He saw little action during these years.

Early in 1742 Byng was commissioned governor of Newfoundland, and arrived at St John's on 18 June in command of the *Sunderland*. Seeking information on Newfoundland trade, he appointed William Keen Jr (*see* William KEEN) as "Navall Officer" to receive the records of imports and exports and watch for illicit trade. Several merchants, however, protested they would never allow the masters of their ships to make the required returns. In his report of February 1742/43 Byng told the Board of Trade that the whole island, particularly St. John's, was virtually a monopoly in the hands of three or four merchants who bought entire cargoes of ships as they arrived and sold the goods to the boat keepers and poor people at exorbitant prices. He had tried in vain to stop this practice and asked the board to devise some preventive measures.

As instructed Byng had collected statistical details on the cod and salmon fisheries and information on the living conditions of the local population. He reported there were many Irish "papists" on the island, mainly at Ferryland, who were peaceable and contented. The appointment of justices of the peace had been of great service in the island; the complaints of certain merchants in the west of England that the justices exceeded their powers seemed to be without foundation. He had heard of no murders or felonies. In general Byng seems to have been most conscientious in his administration of Newfoundland.

In August 1745, on the same day as Peter WARREN, he was promoted rear-admiral, and commanded a squadron sent to the east coast of Scotland to prevent help and supplies reaching the insurgents who were supporting the Young Pretender's attempt on the crown of England. He returned in 1747 to the Mediterranean, where he was made vice-admiral and commander-in-chief. In 1751 he was elected to parliament for Rochester.

Promoted admiral, Byng was sent in April 1756 with a weak and undermanned squadron to the Mediterranean to safeguard the British-held island of Minorca against a rumoured attack by the French. Byng had never led a fleet in a naval engagement or been part of an important action as commander of a vessel. On reaching Minorca he found Fort St Philip at Port Mahón besieged and a French squadron, under La Galissonière [Barrin], close at hand. His failure to relieve the fort, by not pressing home his attack on the French ships, led to his arrest and trial by court martial. Of several charges brought against him, including that of cowardice, only negligence was proved, and he was condemned to death. Despite efforts to save him by several prominent people, including Horace Walpole, he was executed by a firing squad on board the *Monarch* at Portsmouth on 14 March 1757.

Byng's trial excited the sympathy of Voltaire, who wrote to him, and who remarked in his *Candide* that the English thought it good "to kill an admiral from time to time to encourage the others."

MICHAEL GODFREY

PRO, Adm. 1/3878; CO 194/11, nos. 60, 62; 195/8, nos. 2–43. Charnock, *Biographia navalis*, IV. Sedgwick, *History of parliament,* I, 511. Dudley Pope, *At 12 Mr Byng was shot . . .* (London, 1962).

C

CACHOINTIONI (Caghswoughtiooni). *See* KA-K8ENTHIONY

CAFFIN, FRANÇOIS DE GALIFFET DE. *See* GALIFFET

CAHIDEUC, EMMANUEL-AUGUSTE DE, Comte DUBOIS DE LA MOTTE, naval officer; b. 1683 in Rennes, France, son of Jean-François de Cahideuc, Comte Dubois de La Motte, and Gilonne-Charlotte de Langan; m. Jeanne-Françoise d'Andigné de La Chaise, by whom he had two sons; d. 23 Oct. 1764 in Rennes.

Emmanuel-Auguste de Cahideuc joined the service as a midshipman at Brest on 8 Nov. 1698. After serving on several ships in the Atlantic and the Mediterranean, on 1 Nov. 1705 he was promoted sub-section leader in the midshipmen. He then served as a lieutenant in the grenadiers at the siege of Gibraltar, and later as adjutant of the coastal defence batteries at Saint-Malo. In 1706 he sailed on the *Dauphine* and campaigned brilliantly in the English Channel and the Atlantic. Having transferred to the *Achille* in René Duguay-Trouin's squadron in 1707, he took part in the engagement on 21 October which inflicted heavy losses on a large English convoy. The following year he took command of the privateer *Argonaute*, with which he conducted a new and profitable campaign at the entrance to the English Channel and in the Atlantic. On 10 Jan. 1708 he was promoted section leader in the midshipmen, and on 13 Feb. 1709 he received the rank of sub-lieutenant. Befriended by Duguay-Trouin, Dubois de La Motte accompanied him in the successful expedition against Rio de Janeiro in September 1711, and distinguished himself at the head of a grenadier company.

The peace which followed the treaty of Utrecht in 1713 caused a reduction in the number of ships in commission; as a result, Dubois de La Motte had a long period of service ashore at Brest. Promoted lieutenant-commander on 17 Aug. 1727, he was made captain on 1 April 1738. He cruised off Ireland in 1744 and conducted three successful campaigns in the West Indies in 1740–41, 1745, and 1746. In the last campaign his skilful manoeuvres ensured the safe arrival in France of the 163 merchant ships for which he was responsible. On 1 Jan. 1751 he was promoted rear-admiral and governor general of Saint-Domingue (Hispaniola). He remained there two years.

The Seven Years' War was to give Dubois de La Motte new opportunities to distinguish himself. In 1755 he received command of the *Entreprenant* and a squadron of 15 ships of the line and four frigates, with which he was instructed to take help to Canada. He sailed from Brest on 3 May and reached his destination, but on 10 June two of his ships, the *Alcide* and the *Lys*, which had been separated from the squadron by fog, had been attacked and captured by Edward BOSCAWEN's fleet, although war had not been declared. Dubois de La Motte left for France on 15 August, and to elude the enemy he daringly sailed all his vessels through the Strait of Belle Isle, a route which no king's ship had ever taken. Thanks to this adroit manoeuvre, the return voyage was without mishap.

On 25 Nov. 1755 he was promoted lieutenant-general of the naval forces, and at the beginning of 1757 he was given command of a squadron of nine ships of the line and two frigates with which to reinforce the defences of Louisbourg, Île Royale (Cape Breton Island). He arrived there on 19 June, and soon received additional strength in the form of five ships of the line and a frigate from Saint-Domingue under Joseph de Bauffremont, and four ships and two frigates from Toulon under Joseph-François de Noble Du Revest. Dubois de La Motte with this concentration of forces at his disposal was able to deploy before the citadel such an intimidating defence that the English squadron under Francis Holburne* did not dare attack, and on 24 September it was scattered by a gale. But lack of supplies and a typhus epidemic prevented Dubois de La Motte from pursuing the English fleet and forced him to return to France. He left Louisbourg on 30 October and reached Brest safely on 23 November, landing about 5,000 sick men there. His activity had delayed the fall of Île Royale by a year.

Dubois de La Motte's active naval career was ended, but in September 1758, when the English landed near Saint-Malo, he went there despite his 75 years and took part in the battle which repulsed the enemy. He had been made a knight of the order of Saint-Louis on 17 Dec. 1718, commander on 1 Sept. 1752, and knight grand cross on 4 July 1761. On 13 Dec. 1762 he was promoted vice-admiral. An expert seaman, a daring, methodical, and thoughtful leader, Dubois de La Motte was one of the finest figures in the French navy of his time.

ÉTIENNE TAILLEMITE

AN, Col., C⁹ᴬ, 90, 92, 94; Marine, B⁴, 27, 31, 32, 34, 35, 36, 42, 43, 50, 56, 57, 59, 61, 68, 74, 76, 78; C¹, 161; 165; 166, f.28; C⁷, 90 (dossier Dubois de La Motte); G, 38, f.10. *DBF*, VII, 830. Étienne Taillemite, *Dictionnaire de la marine* (Paris, 1962), 78. Étienne Taillemite *et al.*, *Tables des noms de lieux, de personnes, de matières et de navires, sous-série B¹, B² et B³* (Paris, 1969), 101. Lacour-Gayet, *La marine militaire sous Louis XV* (1910), 119, 200, 252, 383, 487, 530. Troude, *Batailles navales de la France*, I, 246, 249, 259, 271, 319, 326. Société historique et archéologique de l'arrondissement de Saint-Malo, *Annales* (Saint-Servan), 1940, 145–46.

CAILLY, FRANÇOIS-JOSEPH, officer in the Swiss Régiment de Karrer; baptized 16 Sept. 1700 in Sainte-Croix-en-Plaine (dept. of Haut-Rhin), France, son of Jean-Christophore Cailly and Marie-Salomé Duvallier; m. Anne-Marie Volant, niece of Colonel Louis-Ignaz Karrer, by whom he had five children; d. sometime after 1762.

François-Joseph Cailly joined the Karrer as a cadet in 1719 when the regiment was formed. An ensign in 1723, he was sent to Martinique; three years later he was promoted captain-lieutenant (the equivalent of captain in the colonial regulars) and given command of the half-company stationed in Saint-Domingue (Hispaniola). In 1730 he was involved in a quarrel there which resulted in the death of a fellow officer. Acquitted of murder, Cailly was sent to command the 100 Swiss in garrison at Louisbourg, Île Royale (Cape Breton Island), despite the protests of the governor, Saint-Ovide [MONBETON], who was a cousin of the dead officer. Cailly arrived in Louisbourg on 2 Sept. 1732.

Almost immediately Cailly clashed with Saint-Ovide; the issue was the drum roll to be used when the Swiss were on guard duty. As foreigners in the king's service, the Swiss were allowed to maintain many of their own customs and on this occasion Saint-Ovide was censured for trying to impose French procedure on them. During his stay in Louisbourg Cailly was assiduous in claiming all the rights and prerogatives of the Swiss, a policy which was to cause him many difficulties. For the rest of Saint-Ovide's period of command, however, there were no open conflicts, and before the governor left in 1738 he wrote a letter of recommendation for the Swiss commander. In the meantime Cailly had consolidated his personal position at Louisbourg. He had acquired two properties, one of which he rented to the crown as an officer's residence, and following the practice of most company commanders he established a canteen for his men from which he was said to make a considerable profit.

Soon after the arrival in 1740 of the new commandant, Jean-Baptiste-Louis LE PRÉVOST Duquesnel, Cailly felt he had to assert his own authority. He was determined to maintain his position with his troops and objected when they carried complaints to the civil authorities. In October 1741 he refused to allow his soldiers to assemble, in spite of a direct order from Duquesnel, and incriminated himself by writing out his refusal. Duquesnel sent a strong letter to Maurepas, the minister of Marine, enclosing a copy of Cailly's note; he listed a number of instances in which the Swiss commander had exceeded his authority and hinted at a spirit of revolt in these actions. Faced with this obvious case of disobedience, Maurepas had little choice. He informed Colonel Karrer that he had taken the matter up with the king and ordered Cailly's retirement as of 1 Jan. 1742. Cailly left Louisbourg late in 1741. In 1742, in response to a plea from Mme Cailly, who remained in Louisbourg

Callet

until the summer, Duquesnel requested that his former antagonist be reinstated. Cailly was allowed to re-enter the service in 1743 but was not permitted to return to Louisbourg. He took up duties in Rochefort, and for a time was acting commander of the regiment after Karrer's death in 1751. In that year he was awarded the cross of Saint-Louis; four years later he was promoted lieutenant-colonel. He was still active in 1762 but nothing is known of him after the regiment was disbanded in 1763.

Cailly seems not to have been an exceptional commander. His vigorous defence of Swiss rights at Louisbourg was carried to the extreme and by his opposition to Duquesnel he set an example of disobedience for his men, who mutinied against the French officials in 1744.

BLAINE ADAMS

AD, Haut-Rhin (Colmar), État civil, Sainte-Croix-en-Plaine, 16 sept. 1700. AN, Col., B, 56, f.178; 57, ff.768v–69; 59, ff.533–34; 74, ff.557–57v; 75, f.243; 76, ff.50–51v; 90, f.266; 94, f.56; C¹¹ᴮ, 12, ff.44–44v, 263–68; 13, ff.55–56; 23, ff.60–64, 82–83; 24, ff.47–47v, 49–50; C¹¹ᶜ, 11, f.144; Marine, C⁷, 50 (dossier Cailly); Section Outre-Mer, G¹, 406. SHA, X¹, cartons 31–33. *Louisbourg in 1745* (Wrong).

CALLET (Collet), LUC (baptized **Léonard-Philibert),** Recollet, military chaplain, missionary; b. 3 Nov. 1715 and baptized the following day in the parish of La Madeleine at Besançon, France, illegitimate son of Donat-Nicolas Callet and Marguerite Jandet; d. 5 Sept. 1767 in the parish of Sainte-Anne at Fort de Chartres (near Prairie du Rocher, Ill.).

Several historians have mistakenly claimed that Léonard-Philibert Callet (spelled Collet) was born in America; as a result, without any valid proof they have readily identified Father Luc as the brother of the Recollet Hippolyte Collet and of Canon Charles-Ange Collet. Nothing is known of Léonard-Philibert's youth until 20 March 1751, when he made his profession under the name of Brother Luc with the Recollets of the province of Saint-Denys. Shortly afterwards he arrived in Canada, where he received the minor orders and the diaconate on 23 and 24 Dec. 1752; he was ordained a priest on 24 Feb. 1753, without any of the difficulty which might have arisen because of his illegitimate birth. Since the documents in Canada concerning his ordination make no mention of any dispensation, it may be that Callet had been legitimized by the marriage of his father and mother, or that he had obtained a dispensation at the time of his profession in the Recollet order in 1751.

In the first year of his priesthood he served in the Quebec region and for a few months replaced Father Maurice IMBAULT, chaplain of the Hôpital Général of Quebec. Then he left the St Lawrence valley and went to the west, where the first engagements of the Seven Years' War were beginning; there he carried on his ministry as a military chaplain. In 1754 he was at the Chatacouin post (near Westfield, N.Y.) and returned to Quebec to spend the winter. At the end of the following spring he went to Fort Niagara (near Youngstown, N.Y.), then on to Fort de la Presqu'île (Erie, Pa.). At the beginning of July he left to go to Fort Duquesne (Pittsburgh, Pa.), where the commandant, Claude-Pierre Pécaudy* de Contrecœur, was begging for his services. After spending a month there he returned to the region of Fort de la Presqu'île and remained until 1760. He then took up residence at Fort Detroit. When the hostilities ceased he was no longer a military chaplain, and he went to the Illinois country, where he served the parishes of Sainte-Anne at Fort de Chartres, Saint-Philippe (Renault, Ill.), and L'Immaculée-Conception at Kaskaskia.

Despite various claims, Callet never served in Acadia, was never captured by the English, and certainly was never sent to captivity in England. It has been written, incorrectly, that he died 30 May 1765 in France. He died suddenly at Sainte-Anne, Fort de Chartres, on 5 Sept. 1767.

Callet's role during the Seven Years' War was limited to the duties of a military chaplain. He had to assure his ministry and his moral support to the soldiers stationed in the forts and at the same time to bring the succour of religion to combat victims. Antoine-Gabriel-François Benoist*, commandant of Fort de la Presqu'île, testified to the importance of Callet's role as a military chaplain when he expressed to Contrecœur his regrets at having to part with Father Luc for some weeks: "he [Callet] is extremely necessary here, this post being the collecting-station for all the sick, besides, the loss of a missionary would make this fort much more odious to me."

MICHEL PAQUIN

[Archives des Franciscains (Montréal), Dossier Luc Callet: the dossier contains copies of several documents, collected by Father Archange Godbout from Canadian, American, and European repositories, that have never been used by the historians who have worked on Léonard-Philibert Callet. The assertions of several of the historians who have written about Callet must consequently be treated cautiously. Some incorrect information concerning the places of birth and death, the spelling of the surname, and family relationships with the Collets, as well as the main events in Father Luc's life are contained in the following: ASQ, Fonds Casgrain, Acadie, p.67; *Papiers Contrecœur* (Grenier); Allaire, *Dictionnaire*; Tanguay, *Répertoire*; George Paré, *The Catholic Church in Detroit, 1701–1888* (Detroit, 1951); J. E. Rothensteiner, *History of the archdiocese of St. Louis . . .* (2v., St Louis, Mo., 1928); Amédée Gosselin, "Le père Luc Collet, récollet," *BRH*, XXX (1924), 397–400; F. M. Habig, "Fathers Luke and Hippolyte Collet," *Around the Province* (Teutopolis, Ill.), XX (1956), 399–400; "New light on Fr. Hippolyte Collet and Fr. Luke Callet pioneer Franciscans in the St. Louis area," *Around the Province*, XXI (1957), 292–97. The authors of the most recent works have copied their predecessors' statements without verifying them. M.P.]

CAMPBELL, DONALD, army officer; d. 4 July 1763 near Detroit.

Nothing definite is known of Donald Campbell's birth or early life, but he seems to have been a Scot. He had already had experience as an officer when in March 1756 he was commissioned lieutenant in the Royal American regiment. A few months later he was made quartermaster; he became captain-lieutenant on 17 April 1758 and captain on 29 Aug. 1759. Late in the fall of 1760, while at Fort Pitt (Pittsburgh, Pa.), he received orders to join Major Robert Rogers* on an expedition to receive the surrender of Detroit. Towards the end of December, Campbell became the second British commander of Detroit and the Upper Lakes posts, most of which the British had not yet occupied.

By modern standards Campbell would not have been considered fit for service, since he had poor eyesight and was "fat and unwieldy." Nonetheless he made a favourable impression on the ladies of Detroit, and they on him. "The Women surpasses our expectations," he reported. Every Sunday evening a convivial group of 20 gentlemen and ladies gathered at his house to play cards, and special occasions were celebrated with a grand ball.

Relations with the Indians, however, were a serious problem. Campbell mistrusted the native people and felt ineffective in his dealings with them. In the summer of 1761 a Seneca delegation led by Kayashoton* and Tahahaiadoris (a son of one of the Joncaires) arrived at Detroit apparently intending to make trouble. Their plan received a serious set-back when it was rebuffed by the local Hurons, Ottawas, Ojibwas, and Potawatomis and disclosed to Campbell. In September Sir William Johnson*, the superintendent of northern Indians, arrived to hold his first grand council with the western tribes. He promised better prices for furs and assured the Indians that

their lands would not be seized. In an attempt to strengthen the British presence in the west troops were sent to occupy some of the former French posts on the Upper Lakes, but the garrisons they established were too small for self-defence and the supply problem was critical. Two sailing vessels were being constructed on the Niagara River under the supervision of Charles ROBERTSON; they finally reached Detroit in the summer of 1762, but could not get past the sand bars in Lake St Clair. So the upper posts remained undermanned and short of provisions.

Having made many friends among the local traders, Campbell disapproved of building sailing vessels to supply the posts; he claimed the task could be accomplished more efficiently and economically by hiring civilians to transport goods by bateau. To him the idea of sending troops to the still-abandoned posts on Lake Superior simply meant "more Banishment for some unlucky fellows." There was at the same time a growing estrangement between Campbell and some of the French community, perhaps because they were becoming involved in PONTIAC's plans. "I begin to know the people too well," Campbell said in July 1762. "I do not think they improve on a long acquaintance." Being out of sympathy with the turn events were taking, he was pleased to surrender his command to Major Henry Gladwin* in August. He remained as second in command.

During this time the Indians were growing increasingly resentful of the British, who forbade the sale of rum and who were much less generous than the French. In May 1763 Detroit came under siege from Pontiac and his allies. Having failed to seize the fort by treachery, Pontiac invited the British to a council outside its gates on 10 May. Campbell and Lieutenant George McDougall volunteered to go and were almost immediately made hostage by the wily Ottawa chief, who probably told Gladwin they would be held until the fort and all its ordnance were surrendered. The easygoing Campbell seems to have had no fear for his own safety. One dark night, after being forced to ride in a fleet of canoes attempting to surprise and capture the sloop *Michigan*, he called a warning to the vessel's captain and thus thwarted Pontiac's plan. When McDougall escaped on 2 July, Campbell refused to go along, fearing that he could not run fast enough or see well enough to get away.

On 4 July 1763 a nephew of Ojibwa chief Wasson* was killed in a brief skirmish near the fort. On hearing the news, the enraged uncle seized Campbell, stripped him naked, and bludgeoned him to death with a tomahawk. The body was then scalped and cut to pieces; Wasson tore out the heart and ate it. Later Campbell's remains were thrown into the river; they floated down to the fort where they were recovered and buried.

HARRY KELSEY

PRO, WO 34/49, Amherst to Campbell, 27 May, 18 June 1761; Campbell to Amherst, 1 June 1762; Amherst to Gladwin, 24 Oct. 1762; Gladwin to Amherst, 26 Oct. 1762, 21 Feb. 1763; WO 34/71, pt.II, Barrington to Loudoun, 13 May 1757. "Bouquet papers," *Michigan Pioneer Coll.*, XIX (1891), 27–295, contains a report by James Macdonald to Bouquet, 12 July 1763, which appears in slightly altered form in PRO, WO 34/49, as "Journal of the siege of Detroit." *Diary of the siege of Detroit . . .* , ed. F. B. Hough (Albany, 1860), 129, 134–35. *Early western travels, 1748–1846 . . .* , ed. R. G. Thwaites (32v., Cleveland, Ohio, 1904–7), I, 100–25. *Johnson papers* (Sullivan et al.), III, 757–59; X, 743. *London Gazette*, 16–30 March 1756. [John Rutherford], "Rutherford's narrative – an episode in the Pontiac War, 1763 – an unpublished manuscript by Lieut. Rutherford of the 'Black Watch,' " Canadian Institute *Trans.* (Toronto), III (1891–92), 229–52. *British officers serving in America, 1754–1774*, comp. W. C. Ford (Boston, 1894), 4, 23. L. W. G. Butler and S. W. Hare, *The annals of the King's Royal Rifle Corps . . .* (5v., London, 1913–32), I, 20, 134–39. Thomas Mante, *The history of the late war in North America and the islands of the West Indies, including the campaigns of MDCCLXIII and MDCCLXIV against his majesty's Indian enemies* (London, 1772), 482–83, 514. Peckham, *Pontiac*. "An account of the disturbances in North America," *Gentleman's Magazine*, 1763, 455–56.

CAMPOT (Campau), JACQUES, trader, blacksmith, merchant; baptized 31 May 1677 at Montreal; son of Étienne Campot and Catherine Paulo; m. Jeanne-Cécile Catin 1 Dec. 1699 at Montreal; buried 14 May 1751 at Detroit.

Jacques Campot was one of the early arrivals in Detroit, travelling there for the Compagnie de la Colonie in 1703 and 1704. Apparently caught up in the internecine rivalries of the post, he falsely accused Pierre Rocquant, *dit* La Ville, a soldier from the garrison, of setting the fire which in 1703 destroyed the granary and nearly all the buildings of the fort. It had in fact been set by a Delaware Indian. The Conseil Supérieur ordered Campot to pay damages to Rocquant and a fine; it also condemned him to appear before the Quebec cathedral wearing only a tunic and there on his knees to proclaim the harm he had done and beg pardon.

In 1708 Campot brought his family to Detroit and the following year was granted a lot in the fort by Cadillac [Laumet*], the commandant. Although they later made several trips back to Montreal, the Campots settled permanently in Detroit. Jacques engaged in trade and also worked as a blacksmith, supplying the Detroit garrison and residents with metal work such as hinges and gun parts.

The decades after Cadillac's departure in 1710 were difficult for Detroit. Pontchartrain, the minister of Marine, hoped that the discredited settlement might collapse if neglected sufficiently. Alphonse Tonty*, commandant from 1717 to 1727, levied excessive rents and taxes. Campot appears in a petition of 1721 as one of the substantial residents aggrieved by his extortionate practices.

In 1734 Campot was granted a lot of four by 40 *arpents* east of the fort. By the 1740s he had, in addition to his blacksmithing, developed one of the best all-purpose merchant houses in Detroit, buying and selling wheat, corn, bread, and furs. Towards 1750 he became too ill to work, and died the next year. In the following century, his numerous descendants played leading roles in the commerce of the region.

DONALD CHAPUT

AN, Col., B, 29, f.311v; C¹¹A, 117, f.91ff.; 118, ff.51, 54, 60. DPL, Burton hist. coll., Macdonald papers, Extrait des registres d'intendance et du Conseil supérieur. "Cadillac papers," *Michigan Pioneer Coll.*, XXXIII (1903), 312, 378, 707. JR (Thwaites), LXIX, LXX. *The John Askin papers*, ed. M. M. Quaife (Burton Hist. Records, 2v., Detroit, 1928–31), I: *1747–1795*, 31–37. *Jug. et délib.*, V, 457–61, 510–12. *The siege of Detroit in 1763: the journal of Pontiac's conspiracy, and John Rutherfurd's narrative of a captivity*, ed. M. M. Quaife (Chicago, 1958). Massicotte, "Répertoire des engagements pour l'Ouest," APQ *Rapport*, 1929–30. *The city of Detroit, Michigan, 1701–1922*, ed. C. M. Burton (5v., Detroit, 1922), II, 1362–64. Télesphore St-Pierre, *Histoire des Canadiens du Michigan et du comté d'Essex, Ontario* (Montréal, 1895), 145–46.

CANNON (Canon). *See* KANON

CARCY, JACQUES PAGÉ, *dit. See* PAGÉ

CARDENEAU, BERNARD, merchant; b. probably 1723; d. after 1764.

Bernard Cardeneau first appears in the history of New France in 1751: on 24 November he married at Sainte-Foy Marie-Anne Guérin, widow of Nicolas JACQUIN, *dit* Philibert. His marriage contract, dated the month before, indicates that Cardeneau was 28 years old and that he had "formerly [been] provisions clerk on his majesty's ships" and that he possessed 25,000 *livres* in merchandise and currency. Cardeneau was active in commerce, and probably was among those merchants who dealt in goods and services supplied to the government of the colony [*see* Pierre CLAVERIE]. His signature appears on contracts that were presented in the *affaire du Canada* after the conquest [*see* François Bigot*], but little is known of his business. Cardeneau is significant, however, because of several memoirs he wrote after the loss of New France concerning the state of paper money in Canada and the problems associated with its liquidation.

In 1763, the minister of Marine, the Duc de Choiseul, had reversed the French government's policy of suspending payments on the paper money of New France. Reinforced by the loss of Canada, this policy had been undermining the credit of the French national treasury and leading to increased attacks on the administration of the government. Choiseul insisted on the need to restore the claims of colonial creditors like Cardeneau, so as to draw criticism away from the government and redirect it towards the malversations of the colonial officials who had returned from Canada after 1760. Choiseul now assured holders of colonial paper that interest of five per cent per annum would be added to the unpaid principal of government bills of exchange not yet redeemed, and replaced the old commission established in 1758 to examine the explosion of paper currency in New France with a special judicial commission to investigate and try those associated with the expenditure of funds in Canada during the recent hostilities.

The first of Cardeneau's reports is dated 30 April 1763, but probably was written the year before. It outlines concisely the different kinds of paper money in Canada, explains their different rates of depreciation, and justifies their redemption. Cardeneau clearly agreed with Choiseul's new policy of favouring colonial creditors. He claimed to have 20,000 *livres'* worth of ordinances and certificates, but implied that he had a much greater amount in bills of exchange. Towards the end of the year another memoir, unsigned, appeared whose author has been identified as Cardeneau; it presents a scheme to incite rebellion in Canada under cover of ascertaining the amount of Canadian paper still remaining in the colony. The author notes that an estimated three-quarters of the currency notes in circulation in Canada before the conquest still remained in the hands of habitants, and suggests that moving among the populace under pretext of discovering the amount would be a way of sounding out Canadian attitudes towards France. The details of the proposal concerned only the district of Montreal, and the plan may have been a ruse by the author to obtain government support to carry on his own affairs in Canada.

In the spring of 1764, after Canada had been ceded to Britain, another memoir appeared, also thought to have been written by Cardeneau, criticizing the plans instituted in France to liquidate the Canadian paper. In particular the author objected to the proposed appointment of Alexandre-Robert de Saint-Hilaire* de La Rochette, the last agent of the treasurers-general of the Marine in Canada, as agent in Paris to receive and arrange the declarations and claims of holders of paper money. The objections of Cardeneau notwithstanding, La Rochette obtained the appointment and by 1769 reported that he had redeemed 90 millions of Canadian paper, one half in specie and the other half in 4 per cent government bonds. Cardeneau, a frustrated colonial creditor whose proposals bore no fruit, disappeared from view as silently as he had arrived.

JAMES PRITCHARD

Documents relating to Canadian currency during the French period (Shortt), II, 946–50, 952–54, 956, 960, 962–64, 972–76. *NYCD* (O'Callaghan and Fernow), X, 1155–57. P.-G. Roy, *Inv. ins. Prév. Québec*, II, 54. Tanguay, *Dictionnaire*. Frégault, *François Bigot*, I, 382. P.-G. Roy, "L'histoire vraie du Chien d'Or," *Cahiers des Dix*, X (1945), 132.

CARREROT, ANDRÉ (Andres), merchant, commissary for naval conscription and for the colonial regular troops on Île Royale, councillor of the Conseil Supérieur of Île Royale; b. *c.* 1696 at Plaisance (Placentia, Nfld.), younger son of Pierre Carrerot*, storekeeper at Plaisance, and Marie Picq; m. *c.* 1725 Marie-Josèphte Chéron in France; d. 20 Nov. 1749 at Louisbourg, Île Royale (Cape Breton Island).

Upon his arrival at Île Royale André Carrerot was employed as inspector of fortifications, in 1716 at Port-Dauphin (Englishtown, N.S.), then in 1718 at Louisbourg. He succeeded his brother PHILIPPE as storekeeper at Louisbourg in 1724, and in 1735 he received, at the same time as his brother-in-law Guillaume DELORT, letters confirming his appointment as a councillor of the Conseil Supérieur of Île Royale. About this time he was also granted a commission as head writer in the Marine.

From 1718 on Carrerot worked a fishing room at La Baleine (Baleine Cove) near Louisbourg, where he employed a few sailors; he also operated trading vessels: first the *Saint-Jean*, whose home port was Bayonne, France, in partnership with François Boudrot and Joseph Dugas in 1725, and then the *Marguerite*, which was regularly in service to Quebec between 1734 and 1737. His name frequently appears in notaries' minutes and in statements of the colony's accounts in connection with various commercial transactions dealing with freighting of ships and supplying of wood, oil, and other merchandise. In 1729 he received a land grant at Louisbourg; in 1733 he bought two other pieces of land in the town and received rent from these properties.

After the fall of Louisbourg in 1745 the Carrerots took refuge in Saint-Jean-de-Luz, France, where their fourth child was born. In 1746 Carrerot sailed as a writer in the squadron of the Duc d'Anville [La Rochefoucauld] on the expedition to Acadia; he returned to France after losing all his belongings in the shipwreck of the *Borée*. He was back on Île Royale in 1749, but some months after his arrival he died, leaving his family penniless. Several of his children and grandchildren later bore the name Carrerot-Andres or Carrerot-Andresse.

Louise Dechêne

AN, M, 1031, no.81; Col., B, 35; C¹¹ᴮ, 1–29; E, 64 (dossiers de Marie Carrerot-Andresse, Pierre-Hyppolite Carrerot-Andresse, Thérèse Carrerot, fille de Philippe Carrerot, et André Carrerot le Cadet); Section Outre-Mer, G¹, 406–7; 462; 466, pièce 50; 467, pièces 1–19 (recensements de Plaisance, Terre-Neuve, 1671–1741); G³, 2056–58.

CARREROT, PHILIPPE, merchant, receiver of dues at the admiralty court of Île Royale; b. *c.* 1694 at Plaisance (Placentia, Nfld.), elder son of Pierre Carrerot* and Marie Picq; d. 1745 at Boston, Massachusetts.

Philippe Carrerot succeeded his father in 1713 as storekeeper when the colony at Plaisance moved to Île Royale (Cape Breton Island). In 1723 François Le Coutre de Bourville, the acting commandant of Île Royale, blamed him for neglecting his duties in favour of his own affairs; the following year, after a disagreement with the controller Antoine Sabatier, Carrerot handed over to his brother André the job as storekeeper, and the 500 *livres* salary that went with it, to devote himself to commerce. Philippe owned a schooner, the *Union*, and in 1726 he went into partnership with Jean Becquet of Quebec to sail this ship between Louisbourg and Canada. He also chartered his schooner to shipowners trading with the West Indies. He had been working a fishing concession at La Baleine (Baleine Cove) since 1717, and the census of 1734 shows that he employed five sailors there.

All these activities did not, however, make him wealthy. In 1728 Jacques-Ange Le Normant de Mézy, the financial commissary for Île Royale, asked him to account for the losses of provisions and clothing which had occurred while he had been storekeeper. Carrerot proved to Mézy's satisfaction that the losses were to be attributed to the wide dispersion of the warehouses and their poor condition. Mézy was able to write to the minister that there had not been any embezzlement. "This poor wretch," he added, "has no food for himself, his wife, and children, and is forced to navigate with a small schooner, which he charters to make a living." Around 1731, therefore, Carrerot appeared again on the payroll of the colony, being employed in the administrative services of the hospital, bakery, and artillery. Le Normant* de Mézy praised him and requested a commission for him as a writer in the Marine in 1736. In 1732 Carrerot had succeeded his father as receiver of dues at the admiralty court, and in 1738, after the death of Marc-Antoine de La Forest*, he even assumed the functions of acting attorney of the admiralty court.

In 1745, having rashly gone out of the fortress at Louisbourg, which was being besieged at the time by the Anglo-Americans under the command of William Pepperrell, Carrerot was captured and taken to Boston, where he died that same year of his wounds. He left a tangled succession, as his sudden death had prevented him from furnishing accounts for his various positions. The financial commissary of Louisbourg, François Bigot*, presumed that Carrerot might have sent part of the funds that could not be accounted for to Canada, where he had continued doing business.

Around 1721 Carrerot had married Marie-Thérèse, the daughter of Jean-Baptiste Gautier and Marie Guyon Desprez of Quebec, by whom he had 15 children. His wife, who had followed him to Boston, went to Rochefort, France, and later returned to Louisbourg, where she married Louis-Antoine Hertel de Rouville in 1754. She died in France in 1761.

Louise Dechêne

AN, Col., B, 35; C¹¹ᴮ, 1–29; E, 64 (dossiers de Marie Carrerot-Andresse, Pierre-Hyppolite Carrerot-Andresse, Thérèse Carrerot, fille de Philippe Carrerot, et André Carrerot le Cadet); Section Outre-Mer, G¹, 406–7; 462; 466, pièce 50; 467, pièces 1–19 (recensements de Plaisance, Terre-Neuve, 1671–1741); G³, 2042 (22 juillet 1754); 2056–58.

CARTIER, TOUSSAINT, called "the hermit of Saint-Barnabé"; b. *c.* 1707 in France; d. 30 Jan. 1767 and buried the next day in the church of Saint-Germain de Rimouski (Que.).

Information about Toussaint Cartier comes primarily from the burial register for the parish of

Saint-Germain de Rimouski and the account left by Archbishop Joseph Signay*. In July 1838, at the time of his second pastoral visit to the parish, the bishop of Quebec gathered the testimony of old people concerning this strange character. These people, of more than 80 years of age, remembered the hermit's story, told to them by their parents.

Toussaint Cartier was believed to have been born in France about 1707, and according to MONTCALM he came from "the region of Morlaix." Cartier arrived in Canada shortly before 1728 and obtained from Pierre Lepage de Saint-Barnabé, seigneur of Rimouski, a piece of land on the Île Saint-Barnabé; there he settled as the result of a vow he had made during the crossing. When he was about to perish, he had promised to live apart from the world in the first place on which he could land. He lived on the island until his death, subsisting on the fruits of his work and the generosity of the habitants, the seigneur of Rimouski, and Father Ambroise ROUILLARD, the local missionary. The latter regularly invited him to eat with him and often visited him in his hermitage on the island.

Cartier had frequent attacks of epilepsy and "as a result of this infirmity [according to the testimony gathered by Signay] one of his eyes seemed to start out of its socket, and to alleviate the severe pain which he suffered in this eye he used to have his dog lick it."

The hermit of Saint-Barnabé came to a sad end. In January 1767 he was found unconscious on the ice of the St Lawrence River; he had been trying to cross to Rimouski. He was carried to a house on the north shore of the Rimouski River, and there he died on 30 January.

The habitants of Rimouski long retained the memory of the hermit of Saint-Barnabé; oral tradition made of this illiterate person a descendant of the famous Jacques Cartier*, but it seems clear that the latter never had any children.

MICHEL PAQUIN

AAQ, 69 CD, Visites pastorales, XI, 116–19. Archives judiciaires de Rimouski (Rimouski, Qué.), Registre d'état civil, Saint-Germain, 30 janv. 1767. "L'hermite de Saint-Barnabé," *BRH*, XLIV (1938), 113–14. *Journal du marquis de Montcalm* (Casgrain), 52. Ivanhoë Caron, "Inventaire de la correspondance de Monseigneur Joseph Signay, archevêque de Québec, 1837–1840," APQ *Rapport, 1938–39*, 268. Tanguay, *Dictionnaire*, II, 570. J.-C. Taché, "L'île Saint-Barnabé," *Les soirées canadiennes; recueil de littérature nationale* (Québec), [V] (1865), 347–57.

CASSWETTUNE. *See* KAK8ENTHIONY

CASTELVEYRE, known as **Brother Chrétien, LOUIS TURC DE.** *See* TURC

CÉLORON DE BLAINVILLE, PIERRE-JOSEPH, officer in the colonial regular troops; b. 29 Dec. 1693 at Montreal, son of Jean-Baptiste Céloron* de Blainville and Hélène Picoté de Belestre; m. 30 Dec. 1724 at Montreal to Marie-Madeleine Blondeau; m. again 13 Oct. 1743 at Montreal to Catherine Eury de La Pérelle; d. at Montreal 12 April 1759.

Grandson of a member of the nobility of the robe and son of a captain in the colonial regulars, Pierre-Joseph Céloron de Blainville entered that force as a cadet in 1707, at the age of 13. He received the expectancy of a commission in 1712 and three years later was made first ensign. In 1731 he was promoted lieutenant and in 1738 captain. He received the latter rank a few months after his appointment to the command at Michilimackinac.

When in 1739–40 Governor Bienville [LE MOYNE] of Louisiana launched a full scale campaign against the Chickasaws, a tribe friendly to the English, Céloron commanded the western detachment of 200 Canadians and 300 Indians who travelled south to participate. A vigorous assault by his force was credited with preventing a French defeat and allowing a negotiated peace. In recognition he was awarded the cross of Saint-Louis in 1741. The following year he was transferred from Michilimackinac to command at Detroit. The Ottawa chiefs at Michilimackinac expressed a high regard for him and requested that his successor should be an officer of the same calibre. The merchant fur-traders at Detroit did not come to share this opinion. They claimed that he inhibited their commercial ventures. Their complaints were given credence by Governor Charles de BEAUHARNOIS and Intendant Gilles Hocquart*; Céloron was therefore removed from Detroit in 1744 and given command of Fort Niagara (near Youngstown, N.Y.). Similar objections were made by the traders there; as a result he was recalled late in 1745.

Beauharnois, nevertheless, had confidence in his military abilities for in the spring of 1747, with war raging, Céloron was appointed commandant at Fort Saint-Frédéric (Crown Point) on Lake Champlain, the forward bastion of the colony's defences. The following spring troop reinforcements and supplies had to be rushed to Detroit to quell an insurrection of western tribes that threatened to drive the French out of the west [*see* ORONTONY], and Céloron was placed in command. Beauharnois's successor, La Galissonière [BARRIN], later stated that the Indians

Céloron

had been cowed by Céloron's cool but tough attitude.

The situation in the west, however, was still dangerous. Traders from Pennsylvania and Virginia had begun to establish posts in the Ohio valley and had formed commercial alliances with the tribes of the region. The Indians who traded with the French were sorely tempted by cheaper English goods and liquor. Moreover, by the treaty of Utrecht (1713) the French had acknowledged the Iroquois to be British subjects, and the English now claimed title to the Ohio valley by virtue of its being Iroquois territory. Land speculators in Virginia and Pennsylvania were forming companies to open the Ohio valley to English settlement. Their activities posed a serious threat, not only to communications between Canada and Louisiana, but to the entire French position in the west. The French decided, therefore, to send an expedition through the Ohio valley to assert their claims to the region, to map the route, and to drive out the English traders. Céloron was given the command.

On 15 June 1749 he left Montreal with 213 men: regulars, militia, and a few Indians. Their route took them by way of Niagara to Lake Erie, along the south shore of that lake to the Chatacouin portage (near Westfield, N.Y.), then south to the Allegheny River, where Céloron buried the first of a series of engraved lead plates claiming the land for France and attached a plaque with the royal arms to a tree. Farther down the Ohio he encountered small groups of English traders whom he ordered to return whence they had come. To one such group he gave a letter addressed to the governor of Pennsylvania, protesting the trespass on French soil of men from his jurisdiction. Céloron also made the disturbing discovery that the Mingo, Shawnee, and Miami tribes were more strongly wedded to the English interest than had been feared. His blandishments and threats alike had little effect, and some of the tribesmen manifested open hostility.

At the end of August, with supplies running low, Céloron buried the last of his lead plates at the mouth of the Rivière à la Roche (Great Miami River), then turned north. On 13 September he reached the village of the Miami chief Memeskia (La Demoiselle) who made it plain that his tribe would not abandon its alliance with the English. After pausing briefly at Fort des Miamis (probably at or near Fort Wayne, Ind.), the French outpost south of Lake Erie, Céloron and his men began the return journey to Montreal, arriving on 9 November. It had required five months and 18 days to travel over 3,000 miles through unmapped and hostile territory. It is a tribute to Céloron's capacity as leader that only one man had been lost, drowned when his canoe tipped in a rapid. Joseph-Pierre de Bonne-camps*, the Jesuit chaplain and cartographer with the expedition, praised Céloron highly, declaring him "a man born to command." The disturbing intelligence Céloron had obtained revealed that the French would have to take determined action or lose the Ohio valley by default. He recommended that a fortified military route be constructed from Lake Erie to the upper Ohio. He also pointed out that the cost would be great.

Céloron barely had time to submit his report before he was sent back to the west as town-major of Detroit. In 1751 Governor General La Jonquière [TAFFANEL] ordered him to muster a force of Canadians and allied Indians and destroy the recalcitrant Miamis, but he demurred, claiming that should the campaign fail, the consequences would be disastrous and that 1,800 troops and militia would be needed to ensure success. La Jonquière was incensed at this refusal to carry out his orders and he made an adverse report to the minister of Marine. There had been other complaints of Céloron's conduct as commandant; although manifestly brave and intelligent, he was considered haughty and injudicious. Apparently he was better fitted for strictly military duties than for civil administration. In 1753, after Ange Duquesne* had become governor general, Céloron was recalled and given the less taxing post of town-major of Montreal. Duquesne stated that he was a very good officer but he was not suited for routine administration at Detroit.

Of Céloron's subsequent activities nothing is known. It seems unlikely that he succumbed to wounds received during the 1759 campaign, as has been claimed, since military operations did not begin until May that year and he is known to have died at Montreal on 12 April. He had not grown rich in the king's service. His son Pierre-Joseph, several times wounded, returned to France a captain in 1760, with nothing to his name but his 600 *livres* half pay. His widow joined the Grey Nuns and remained in Canada, thereby sacrificing the 300 *livres* pension the king had awarded her.

W. J. ECCLES

AN, Col., C¹¹ᴬ, 69, f.236; 71, ff.33, 36; 76, f.255; 77, ff.83, 90, 108, 179; D²ᶜ, 47, ff.5, 325, 382, 467, 531; 48, ff.15, 17, 37, 501; 49, ff.176, 204, 280, 282, 326, 341; 59, ff.10, 34; 61, ff.9, 105; 222, f.201; D²ᴰ, 1; F³, 13, ff.318–47. *Découvertes et établissements des Français* (Margry). *Documents relating to Canadian currency during the French period* (Shortt), II, 789–90. "Une expédition canadienne à la Louisiane en 1739–1740," APQ *Rapport, 1922–23*, 189. "French regime in Wis., 1743–60" (Thwaites), 36–58. *JR* (Thwaites), LXIX, 150–98. *Papiers Contrecœur* (Grenier). Gipson, *British empire before the American revolution*, VI. Parkman, *Montcalm and Wolfe*. P.-G. Roy, *La famille Céloron de Blainville* (Lévis, Qué., 1909). Stanley, *New France*.

CHABERT DE JONCAIRE, PHILIPPE-THOMAS, called **Nitachinon** by the Iroquois, trader, officer in the colonial regular troops, Indian agent, and interpreter; baptized 9 Jan. 1707 in Montreal; son of Louis-Thomas Chabert* de Joncaire and Marie-Madeleine Le Gay de Beaulieu; m. Madeleine Renaud Dubuisson 23 July 1731; d. *c.* 1766.

At the age of ten, Philippe-Thomas Chabert de Joncaire went to live among the Senecas, probably at Ganundasaga (near Geneva, N.Y.) where his father's trading post is said to have been located. From then until the fall of New France he spent most of his time in the west. He entered the colonial regular troops in 1726, became a second ensign in 1727, and rose to captain by 1751; but he had a diplomat's career, not a soldier's.

In 1735 he succeeded his father as principal agent for New France among the Iroquois. As such, he was hostage, trader, interpreter, and political agent. He had to supply the European trade goods on which the Indians had become dependent. He was obliged to pacify the Iroquois when the French or their Indian allies did something disquieting, and to mollify the French when young warriors, contrary to tribal policy, committed an aggression. Hostility towards Indian nations unfriendly to the French had to be maintained. British initiatives, such as the summoning to Chouaguen (Oswego, N.Y.) in December 1743 of one warrior from every village, required reporting to the governor. Some persuasion was needed to keep the Senecas supplying Fort Niagara (near Youngstown, N.Y.) with fresh game. So successful was Joncaire that by 1744 the British had offered a reward for him dead or alive. Governor George CLINTON of New York hopefully half-believed rumours that he might join the British service if good terms were offered.

Joncaire resigned his post in 1748, pleading ill health (and was succeeded by his brother, Daniel*). His wife had died two years before and he may have wished to stay in Montreal to look after their three young children, but he was soon recalled to the frontier. In 1749 he became interpreter and adviser for Pierre-Joseph CÉLORON de Blainville's expedition to the Ohio valley. Going ahead to establish first contact with the Shawnees, Delawares, and Mingos, Joncaire narrowly escaped death when he was seized at Sonioto (Portsmouth, Ohio) by some Shawnees who feared the French had come to destroy them. He was saved by the intervention of an Iroquois bystander.

When Céloron's forces withdrew in the autumn, Joncaire accompanied them. In 1750 he returned to the area and was stationed at Chiningué (Logstown, now Ambridge, Pa.) with 12 soldiers to prepare the ground for a more substantial French occupation. He reported that all the Indians favoured the traders from Pennsylvania and Virginia who ventured into the region, but with bribes, threats, and promises he struggled to win them over. When Paul MARIN de La Malgue arrived in 1753 to build a line of forts linking Lake Erie and the Ohio, many Delawares and Shawnees, overawed by the large French force and perhaps willing to see Iroquois influence in the area challenged, proclaimed themselves in favour of his presence. Moved to Venango (Franklin, Pa.), until 1755 Joncaire was in charge of the delicate diplomacy required to maintain the goodwill of the Delawares and Shawnees and to neutralize the opposition of TANAGHRISSON, spokesman for the Iroquois colonists on the Ohio, who protested the construction of forts.

The final crisis in Joncaire's 35-year rivalry with the British for Iroquois allegiance began in 1755. Replaced at Venango by Michel Maray* de La Chauvignerie, he returned to Niagara in the summer. In that tense season, when four separate enemy armies approached the borders of New France, Governor Pierre de Rigaud* de Vaudreuil was anxious to learn the sentiments of the Iroquois. "I sent my orders to M. Joncaire, the elder, to remain constantly with them. He has run from village to village, and met colonel [William Johnson's] and M. [William Shirley's] emissaries in each," he reported.

Though he dared not visit the Onondagas, Tuscaroras, or Oneidas for fear of British ambush, from his post with the Senecas Joncaire could learn of developments among all the Iroquois and promulgate French policy among them. He called on them to supply war parties to aid the French or, failing that, to observe strictly the neutrality they had officially prescribed for themselves; and he warned that if any of them were to heed Sir William Johnson*, the British superintendent of Indian affairs, and side with the enemy, their villages would be laid waste by the nations of the *pays d'en haut*. The destruction of Chouaguen by

Chapoton

MONTCALM in 1756 lent a temporary weight to Joncaire's words. At Niagara in February 1757, 60 warriors sang the war song, and by April Joncaire had paid them for 38 British scalps.

In 1758, as the Indians saw emerging evidence of British power, bad signs for the French cause began to appear. Some Senecas asked the British to send them a gunsmith (always a person in a position to exercise great political influence). Joncaire's network of informants failed to give the alarm that might have saved Fort Frontenac (Kingston, Ont.) from capture by John Bradstreet* in August. In June 1759 a party of Mohawks, traditional friends of the English, ventured into Seneca country and surprised Joncaire in his trading post. A leap through a window saved his life, but his son-in-law, Honoré Dubois de La Milletière, was taken prisoner and another companion killed.

Joncaire retreated to Niagara and was captured in July when the fort fell. British garrisons in the western posts, made permanent when Montreal capitulated in 1760, meant that his life's work had been ruined by causes outside his influence, and Canada's first tradition in diplomacy was ended. He went to France, where he was made a knight of the order of Saint-Louis. Whether he ever returned to Canada is uncertain, although a letter written 9 Nov. 1766 by Lieutenant Governor Guy Carleton* refers to him, saying he is "now dead."

MALCOLM MACLEOD

AN, Col., C¹¹A, 77, ff.204–6v; 79, ff.167–77v; 81, ff.210–10v; 101, ff.5–6v; 102, ff.9–11; 103, ff.111–12v; D²ᶜ, 222, f.325; F³, 14, ff.159v–60. Bougainville, *Journals* (Hamilton). *JR* (Thwaites), LXIX. *NYCD* (O'Callaghan and Fernow), VI–X. *Papiers Contrecœur* (Grenier). [Pierre] Pouchot, *Memoir upon the late war in North America, between the French and the English, 1756–60 . . .*, trans. from French ed. of 1781 by F. B. Hough (2v., Roxbury, Mass., 1866). Gipson, *British empire before the American revolution*, I–VII. W. A. Hunter, *Forts on the Pennsylvania frontier, 1753–1758* (Harrisburg, Pa., 1960). F. H. Severance, *An old frontier of France: the Niagara region and adjacent lakes under French control* (2v., New York, 1917).

CHAPOTON, JEAN-BAPTISTE, surgeon; b. *c.* 1690 in the parish of Saint-Jean-Baptiste, Bagnols (now Bagnols-sur-Cèze, dept. of Gard), France; son of André Chapoton and Anne Lassaigne; m. 16 July 1720 Marguerite Estève at Detroit; d. 11 Nov. 1760 at Detroit.

Jean-Baptiste Chapoton was assigned to Fort Pontchartrain (Detroit) as surgeon-major late in 1719. A description of him in the parish register for 1758 as "master surgeon of this town" suggests that his duties as post surgeon expanded over the years to encompass the care of the sick in the surrounding region.

Chapoton became an important landowner. In 1734 he received a grant on the recommendation of the commandant Jacques-Hugues PÉAN and the former commandant Henri-Louis Deschamps* de Boishébert. Nine years later he sold it because it was "too distant from the fort to enable him to care for the sick according to his duty as surgeon," and was granted another tract, four by 40 *arpents*, on which he had already erected buildings. The 1750 census shows that he was cultivating about 50 acres and raising wheat, oats, and livestock. In 1751 the size of his grant was doubled. He also owned a residence inside the fort.

Like most other prosperous frontiersmen, he bought, sold, and traded goods whenever he thought he could turn a profit. Father Armand de LA RICHARDIE's accounts for 1742 show that Chapoton borrowed 100 *livres* in furs from the Huron mission, agreeing to repay within a year. He sold grain, medicines, and building materials to the authorities at Detroit.

On retiring from his surgeon's post at the fort about 1752, he was succeeded by his son-in-law, Gabriel-Christophe Legrand de Sintré. Most of Chapoton's children married well, as befitted a leading family of the community.

HARRY KELSEY

AN, Col., C¹¹A, 118, ff.332, 347; 119, ff.165, 278, 298. DPL, Burton hist. coll., Chapoton papers, 7 July 1734; Moran papers, 18 June 1743; Macdonald papers, 18 June 1743; Registres des baptêmes, mariages et sépultures de Sainte-Anne, Détroit, 16 juill. 1720, 11 nov. 1760; F. J. Anderson, "Medicine at Fort Detroit in the colony of New France, 1701–60" (typescript, n.d.), 24–25; G. B. Catlin, "Early physicians of Detroit" (typescript, n.d.); Christian Denissen, [Genealogy of the French families of Detroit] (26v., typescript, n.d.), C/1, 2529. Clements Library, Thomas Gage papers, American series, John Campbell to Gage (encl.), 31 Oct. 1765.

"Cadillac papers," *Michigan Pioneer Coll.*, XXXIII (1903), 687–89; XXXIV (1904), 120–21. *The John Askin papers*, ed. M. M. Quaife (Burton Hist. Records, 2v., Detroit, 1928–31), I: *1747–1795*. *JR* (Thwaites), LXIX, 249, 308. *Michigan Pioneer Coll.*, VIII (1885), 454–56. *Some glimpses of life in ancient Detroit*, ed. M. M. Quaife (Burton hist. coll. leaflet, III, no.1, [Detroit], 1924), 1–6. *Windsor border region* (Lajeunesse). *Dictionnaire national des Canadiens français (1608–1760)* (2v., Montréal, 1958), I. Silas Farmer, *The history of Detroit and Michigan . . .*(Detroit, 1884). M. C. W. Hamlin, *Legends of le Détroit* (Detroit, 1884), 272–75, 281–84, 299–304. Télesphore St-Pierre, *Histoire des*

Canadiens du Michigan et du comté d'Essex, Ontario (Montreal, 1895), 150.

CHAPTES, *dite* **du Saint-Sacrement, MARIE-MADELEINE DE LA CORNE DE.** *See* LA CORNE.

CHARDON, JEAN-BAPTISTE, priest, Jesuit, missionary; b. 27 April 1671 in Bordeaux, France; d. 11 April 1743 in Quebec.

Jean-Baptiste Chardon was admitted into the Jesuit noviciate in Bordeaux on 7 Sept. 1687. He studied at Pau in 1689–90, taught the three classes, grammar, classics, and rhetoric, at the Jesuit college in La Rochelle from 1690 to 1695, and completed his studies at Poitiers in the period 1695–99. Subsequently he sailed for New France, arriving at Quebec in the summer of 1699. Chardon then undertook the study of Indian languages, for which he displayed "a rare talent," according to Pierre-Gabriel Marest*; he was to learn those of nearly all the tribes in the region of the Great Lakes and even mastered that of the Illinois, whom he was to encounter only occasionally.

In the spring of 1700 the new missionary was sent to the Saguenay country, and by the beginning of July he had been as far as Lac des Mistassins (Lac Mistassini), at that time almost unknown. Chardon perhaps returned to the Saguenay country before the winter; he was certainly there at the end of July 1701, for he officiated at a baptism on 24 July. Shortly afterwards, named a missionary to the Ottawas, he went to stay among them, at the time when peace with the Iroquois was being signed in Montreal [*see* Louis-Hector de Callière*]. Around 25 Sept. 1701 Chardon went to Michilimackinac on his way to the Baie-des-Puants (Green Bay, Wis.) region, where he was to help Father Henri Nouvel*, who was nearly 80. The closing of the Michilimackinac mission was already foreseen then. Missionary labours in these regions were considered to be sterile, as Bishop Pontbriand [DUBREIL] noted, not because of lack of zeal on the part of the missionaries, struggling against the Indian customs, but because of the demoralization of the neophytes by the coureurs de bois, soldiers, and fur-trading commandants, who supplied spirits to the Indians and let discipline become slack in the posts [*see* Joseph-Jacques Marest*; Koutaoiliboe*].

Chardon remained 32 years in the region, living as a rule at Baie-des-Puants until 1728. In turn he visited the Foxes, Menominees, Mascoutens, Kickapoos, Ottawas, Potawatomis, and Miamis. In 1711 he stopped at the post on the St Joseph River, temporarily replacing Father Claude Aveneau*, who was worn out through illness. In 1721 Father CHARLEVOIX encountered him at Baie-des-Puants.

In 1722 Chardon replaced Father Joseph-Jacques Marest as superior of the Ottawa mission. At this time New France had for some years been seeking in the west what it had lost by the treaty of Utrecht in the east and north [*see* Philippe de Rigaud* de Vaudreuil]. The French wanted to found a post in the Sioux country, counting upon the missionaries' support to obtain the right to pass through the territory of the Foxes, who opposed the plan; "the trade," they said, "which the French would carry on there would reduce considerably" what they themselves carried on with the Sioux. They had already killed several Frenchmen. Father Chardon was chosen to direct the founding of this mission, and from 1725 to 1727 he worked at making peace between the Indian tribes [*see* Charles de BEAUHARNOIS]; he even suggested a plan of action and in August 1727 accompanied for a time the first convoy led by René BOUCHER de La Perière.

In 1728 Chardon was no longer living permanently at the post at Baie-des-Puants, which was burned by Constant Le Marchand* de Lignery on his return from his expedition against the Foxes, and little is known about the missionary's activities until 1733. As the registers of the Society of Jesus mention, he was "among the Indians, in various places." During 1734 and 1735 Chardon lived in Montreal, and after that he retired to Quebec.

In 1740, when he was 69, Chardon went to the Saguenay country to initiate Father Jean-Baptiste Maurice into the life of a missionary. He spent the summer at Tadoussac, and from there he went to La Malbaie; he finally left his companion on 7 September to return to Quebec. He died there on 11 April 1743.

JOSEPH COSSETTE

ASJCF, 567; 579bis; 784; Fonds Rochemonteix, 4016; 4018; 4020. *Découvertes et établissements des Français* (Margry), VI, 543, 554–55. JR (Thwaites). Antonio Dragon, *Trente robes noires au Saguenay*, texte revu et corrigé par Adrien Pouliot (Publication de la SHS, 24, Chicoutimi, Qué., 1971). J. G. Shea, *History of the Catholic Church in the United States* (4v., New York, 1886–92), I, 622, 625, 627, 629.

CHARLEVOIX, PIERRE-FRANÇOIS-XAVIER DE, Jesuit priest, teacher, author of the *Histoire et description générale de la Nouvelle France . . .* (1744), procurator in Paris of the Jesuit missions

Charlevoix

and Ursuline convents in New France and Louisiana; b. 24 (al. 29) Oct. 1682 at Saint-Quentin, France, son of François de Charlevoix, deputy king's attorney, and Antoinette Forestier; d. 1 Feb. 1761 at La Flèche, France.

The Charlevoix family was of the old nobility; it had for centuries furnished legal officers, aldermen, and mayors to the town of Saint-Quentin. Pierre-François-Xavier de Charlevoix began his studies at the Collège des Bons-Enfants in his native town, later becoming a pupil of the Jesuits. On 15 Sept. 1698, when he was not quite 16, Charlevoix entered the Society of Jesus in Paris and began his two-year noviciate. At the end of the 17th century the Jesuits of the province of Paris were experimenting with a new program of studies to prepare future teachers for their colleges, and Charlevoix probably followed the new sequence: one year of rhetoric after the noviciate and then four years of philosophy at the Collège Louis-le-Grand in Paris. It may have been during his last year of philosophy that Charlevoix became a dormitory prefect responsible for younger pupils. Voltaire, who entered Louis-le-Grand in 1704, still remembered at the end of his long life "Father Charlevoix, who was my prefect, seventy-five years ago . . . and who was a bit long-winded."

Having been ordained deacon, Charlevoix was sent to New France to teach grammar at the Jesuit college there. He arrived at Quebec on 7 Sept. 1705 aboard the ship carrying the new intendant Jacques Raudot* and his sons Antoine-Denis* and Jacques-Denis and joined the little group of teachers in the dilapidated college building. There he was in daily contact with the veterans of the Canadian missions who were living in retirement at the college: Louis André*, who had spent 12 years in the Baie-des-Puants (Green Bay, Wis.) region, Pierre Millet*, missionary to the Oneidas, and Antoine Silvy* with his experience of Hudson Bay. Other residents of the college were still in mid-career; Sébastien Rale*, temporarily in the infirmary, Vincent Bigot*, superior general of the Canadian missions, and Pierre Raffeix*, the procurator. There too Charlevoix met "Monseigneur l'Ancien," François de Laval*, driven from his beloved seminary by the fire of 1 Oct. 1705. Nearby, at the Château Saint-Louis, Governor Philippe de Rigaud* de Vaudreuil was attempting to maintain the colony in an uneasy equilibrium; his eldest son, LOUIS-PHILIPPE, was a pupil of Charlevoix. The future historian of New France could not have asked for a more instructive setting.

We do not know whether Charlevoix saw much of the colony during this first stay. He sub-sequently wrote in his *Journal* that he "had earlier travelled through the country in all seasons"; in any event he was at Montreal in September 1708 when the raiding party led by Jean-Baptiste Hertel* de Rouville and Jean-Baptiste de SAINT-OURS Deschaillons returned from its attack on Haverhill [*see* Mary Silver*].

Back in France again, Charlevoix completed his four years of theology (1709–13) and was ordained priest. He was then assigned to Louis-le-Grand as a teacher of classics and philosophy. To this period belongs his first attempt at historiography: his three-volume *Histoire de l'établissement, des progrès et de la décadence du christianisme dans l'empire du Japon . . .*(1715), a revision and expansion of an out-of-print work published in 1689 by the Jesuit Jean Crasset.

Ten years after his return from Canada, Charlevoix was again drawn into its affairs when, in 1719, he was given the delicate task of recommending boundaries for Acadia, a constant subject of dispute between England and France after the treaty of Utrecht (1713) [*see* Jean-Baptiste Loyard*]. He worked ten months on this investigation and presented a report which has not been preserved, but which is summarized in a memoir by the former attorney general, François-Madeleine-Fortuné Ruette* d'Auteuil. Charlevoix maintained in his report that the Acadia ceded to the English in 1713 included only the Nova Scotian peninsula, and that the French should continue to support and trade with the Abenakis, a position which would be contested by the English until the end of the French régime [*see* Pierre de LA CHASSE].

While Charlevoix was still engaged in this inquiry, the regent, Philippe, Duc d'Orléans, charged him with a further task: to investigate the numerous rumours about the existence and location of a western sea between the New World and the Orient, a question that was of increasing commercial concern in those years. A thorough investigation by an impartial agent whose travels would appear to be visits to missions would, the French authorities hoped, avoid undue publicity and expensive exploratory expeditions.

Armed with a letter from the council of Marine authorizing him to "go up into the *pays d'en haut* with two canoes and eight voyageurs," Charlevoix left Paris in mid-June 1720 and on 1 July embarked at Rochefort on the royal flute *Le Chameau*, whose second in command was his former pupil at Quebec, Louis-Philippe de Rigaud. After a slow crossing and more than a month of violent seasickness, Charlevoix arrived at Quebec on 23 September and resigned himself to waiting out the winter there. He set about composing his final report on Acadia, which he sent off to the court on 19 October, urging a firm French stand against English infiltration into what is now New Brunswick. He also began making notes on Quebec and its inhabitants. These, together with other observations to be made during his travels, and enriched by his reading and conversations, would eventually find their way into his published *Journal*.

Eager to begin his investigations, Charlevoix waited impatiently for winter to come to an end. Early in March 1721, before the ice had broken up on the St Lawrence, he travelled by *carriole* to Trois-Rivières, visiting on the way Pierre Robinau* de Bécancour, whom he erroneously calls "baron de Bécancour." Leaving Trois-Rivières on 9 March he reached Montreal on the 14th and spent the next two months visiting Fort Chambly, commanded by his friend Jacques-Charles de Sabrevois*, Sault-Saint-Louis (Caughnawaga, Que.), and Fort Frontenac (Kingston, Ont). As he proceeded westward, guided by Jacques Hertel de Cournoyer, Charlevoix described his surroundings at every stage: Anse de la Famine (Mexico Bay, near Oswego, N.Y.) seemed to him "the worst place in the world"; he found the area around Niagara Falls, where Louis-Thomas Chabert* de Joncaire had built a new French post the previous year, infested with rattlesnakes; the region around Lake St Clair near the fort commanded by Alphonse Tonty* lived up to its reputation as "the most beautiful spot in Canada." During the long voyage by canoe through the Great Lakes, Charlevoix, compass in hand, made notes on the coastline and estimated distances, or verified latitudes; his observations and calculations, now lost, later enabled the hydrographer Jacques-Nicolas Bellin to publish greatly improved maps of the Great Lakes region.

By 28 June Charlevoix had reached Michilimackinac, where he met Jean-Paul Legardeur* de Saint-Pierre and Jacques Testard* de Montigny. The latter was on his way to take up his new appointment at Fort Saint-François on the Baie des Puants and Charlevoix seized the opportunity to accompany him there in order to question some Sioux camped at Baie des Noquets (Big Bay De Noc, Mich.). Having heard from them tales of "a great river that flows westward and empties into the southern sea," Charlevoix returned to Michilimackinac three weeks later, and questioned Zacharie Robutel* de La Noue, the commandant at Kaministiquia, and Father Joseph-Jacques Marest*, who had lived among the Sioux. On 27 July he wrote to the minister, Louis-Alexandre de Bourbon, Comte

de Toulouse, to report his intention to spend the winter making inquiries in Louisiana and then to return to visit the Lake Superior posts in the summer of 1722: he asked that all available accounts of the western sea be forwarded to him, and that Jean-Daniel-Marie Viennay-Pachot be assigned to guide him on his Lake Superior trip. In the meantime the council of Marine had written (6 July 1721) to the commissioners of the Compagnie de la Louisiane in New Orleans to issue instructions for Charlevoix to return to France when he reached that settlement. Unaware of this decision, Charlevoix set out from Michilimackinac (29 July) with Robert Groston* de Saint-Ange as his guide, and headed southward down the east side of Lake Michigan into the St Joseph River.

Delayed by illness and bad weather, Charlevoix stayed at Fort Saint-Joseph (probably Niles, Mich.) during August and early September; here he took advantage of his enforced leisure to study the Miami Indians. To avoid further delay, he rejected the Chicago portage route in favour of the Theakiti (Kankakee) River, which he descended in early October. He then followed the Illinois River to the Mississippi, reaching the mouth of the Missouri on 10 October. At the Cahokia mission (East St Louis, Ill.) he met two of his former students, Abbés Dominique-Antoine-René Thaumur* de La Source and Jean-Paul MERCIER. To regain his strength, Charlevoix rested for nearly a month at the Jesuit mission at Kaskaskia. Travel on the Mississippi was becoming difficult in the *pirogues* to which the party had transferred: the river was full of sandbanks and fallen trees, and the weather was surprisingly cold as December approached. Christmas Day was spent at Natchez, where Charlevoix could once more observe Indian customs. At Natchez he met the engineer Adrien de Pauger, with whom he descended the last stretch of the Mississippi as far as New Orleans. Arriving there 10 Jan. 1722, Charlevoix found the settlement so glowingly described in the *Nouveau Mercure* to consist merely of "a hundred or so shacks"; he could none the less foresee that it would one day become "an opulent city." He later accompanied Pauger to the mouth of the Mississippi, where the engineer carried out a series of soundings in the river channels. They reached Biloxi (Ocean Springs, Miss.) at the beginning of February, and there Charlevoix contracted jaundice. After six weeks' illness he decided he could not undertake the return voyage up the Mississippi, so, hoping to return to Quebec by sea, he sailed (24 March) on the *Adour,* a flute of 300 tons burden. On 14

Charlevoix

April the *Adour* ran on a reef off the Florida keys: all aboard were saved, but it took them 50 days to make their way in a skiff back along the Florida coast to Biloxi. Finally, on 22 June, Charlevoix embarked again from Biloxi, this time on the *Bellone*, and after a further delay set sail on 30 June for Saint-Domingue (Hispaniola); the voyage was to last more than two months.

Arriving at Cap (Cap Haïtien) only at the end of September 1722, Charlevoix concluded it was too late in the year to attempt to return to Quebec and instead sought passage to France, thus unwittingly carrying out the instructions of the council of Marine. He sailed on 25 September in the *Louis de Bourbon*, a merchantman from Le Havre, and after a slow crossing reached Plymouth on 2 December; delayed in England three weeks he finally landed at Le Havre on 26 December. Two days later, Charlevoix reports, the ship he had just left "rotted away in pieces."

Obliged to stop over in Rouen while waiting for a coach, Charlevoix had a long interview with René-Robert Cavelier* de La Salle's associate, Henri Joutel. Then, hastening on to Paris, he presented to the Comte de Toulouse a report of his travels and inquiries (20 Jan. 1723); a few months later he would be obliged to repeat the information for the new minister, Charles-Jean-Baptiste de Fleuriau, Comte de Morville. Charlevoix's tentative conclusions were that the western sea would likely be found between 40° and 50° latitude, that the Indian tribes west of the Sioux probably lived near the sea, that some Spaniards had already penetrated to that region, and that near the headwaters of the Missouri could be found rivers that flowed westward. Asked to make specific proposals, he stated that he could see only two courses of action to find the western sea: going up the Missouri River "whose source is certainly not far from the sea," or establishing a mission among the Sioux, by whom contact might be made with tribes farther west. The regent favoured the second proposal, but a shortage of missionaries delayed its implementation for some years. Although he favoured the Missouri alternative, Charlevoix nevertheless offered, despite his ignorance of the Sioux tongue, to be a missionary to that nation if no qualified priests could be assigned to the task, but his offer was not accepted.

The two and a half years Charlevoix had spent in North America had brought him little satisfaction. He had been plagued by illness and dogged by sheer bad luck at almost every stage of his laborious travels. His tireless inquiries had contributed little to the search for the western sea; indeed his conclusions about the proximity of that sea would prove to be erroneous. Fortunately, out of this unhappy journey came one of the most important journals of North American historical literature. This manuscript record of his trip was eventually to be reworked by Charlevoix in the form of 36 letters addressed to the Duchesse de Lesdiguières, Gabrielle-Victoire de Rochechouart de Mortemart, daughter of Mme de Montespan's brother, Louis-Victor de Rochechouart de Mortemart, Duc de Vivonne. Each letter recounts the events and sights of one stage of Charlevoix's round trip from France to Quebec, Michilimackinac, and Louisiana, and back to France. In addition to this narrative text, the letters contain instalments of a lengthy essay on the Indians of North America, which complements Joseph-François LAFITAU's *Mœurs des sauvages amériquains, comparées aux mœurs des premiers temps* (2v., Paris, 1724). By the detail of its observations and the precision of its references, Charlevoix's *Journal* is a unique document. "There is no other source," writes its editor, Louise Phelps Kellogg, "which approaches his journal either for accuracy or discrimination, and none which gives so good a description of the posts, the routes, the missions, the tribes, and the conditions in the Mississippi Valley during the first quarter of the eighteenth century."

Although Charlevoix, on his return from Louisiana, had already conceived the idea of publishing his journal together with a general history of the French colonies in North America, the actual publication was not to take place for more than 20 years. In the interval Charlevoix would publish three other works and serve as an editor of one of Europe's foremost literary and scientific reviews, a career which might have sufficed in itself to carry his name to posterity.

Charlevoix's first publication after his return to France was his life of Marie Guyart*, *dite* de l'Incarnation, dedicated to the daughter of the regent, Louise-Élisabeth d'Orléans, and published in 1724. If, as he claims in his preface, the biography was written in gratitude for his safe return from the New World, it must have been composed with great dispatch: the manuscript was approved by the ecclesiastical censor in November 1723, less than 11 months after Charlevoix's arrival in Paris. In attempting a new life of the foundress of the Ursulines of Quebec, Charlevoix hoped to give a more concise and less anecdotal portrait than Marie de l'Incarnation's son, Dom Claude Martin, had provided in 1677. Nevertheless Charlevoix's biography remains essentially hagiographical, intended for a devout public, and offering little of historical interest.

In 1725 Charlevoix went to Rome, perhaps in connection with the Italian translation of the *Vie de la mère Marie de l'Incarnation ...*, which was announced that year and appeared in 1727. When he returned to Paris in 1728 he resumed work on his history of French North America and took up again some memoirs he had received from his friend Jean-Baptiste Le Pers, a Jesuit missionary serving in Saint-Domingue since 1704. Finding that Father Le Pers's texts required extensive verification and expansion, Charlevoix applied to the minister, Maurepas [Phélypeaux], who granted him permission in April 1729 to consult documents and plans in the depository of the Marine. In gratitude, Charlevoix dedicated his two-volume *Histoire de l'isle Espagnole...* (1730–31) to Maurepas, and included in his foreword a discussion of the importance for historiography of making a critical study of the primary sources and of collating oral evidence and written documents. It is precisely this concern for documentation of all kinds – personal observation, oral testimony, and archival and bibliographical sources – that makes Charlevoix a remarkably modern historian.

As an authority on the western sea, Charlevoix was consulted early in 1730 about the western expedition being prepared by Pierre GAULTIER de Varennes et de La Vérendrye. Maurepas, seeking reassurance about La Vérendrye's program, sent the proposals to Charlevoix, who replied at length, more than a year later, in an unsigned text. He endorsed, with some reservations, La Vérendrye's general approach, but cautioned against delaying progress by constructing permanent posts along the way, and suggested certain economies. When Maurepas forwarded these comments to Quebec in the summer of 1731, the expedition was already under way, but Governor Charles de BEAUHARNOIS and Intendant Gilles Hocquart* nevertheless replied, point by point, in a long memoir of their own, dated 10 Oct. 1731.

Whenever he could, Charlevoix continued to work on his history of New France; in April 1732 Maurepas even authorized him to take to his room in the Collège Louis-le-Grand the archival documents he needed for his research, "except, however, acts or original documents referring to boundaries or to vital matters, which it is not appropriate for him to remove from the depository where he can have access to them."

By 1733, when his history of Saint-Domingue was being reprinted in Amsterdam, Charlevoix's three major published works had earned him a modest reputation in the learned world of Europe. In December of that year the respected Jesuit monthly review, *Mémoires pour servir à l'histoire des sciences et des beaux-arts* (subsequently called simply *Journal de Trévoux* from its original place of publication) underwent a reorganization and was moved to Paris, where Charlevoix became one of its new editors. During the score of years he seems to have held this appointment he published only one signed article in the *Journal de Trévoux*, his ambitious "Projet d'un corps d'histoire du Nouveau Monde" (January 1735), which was later reproduced with slight modifications in his histories of Japan and New France. In this important text Charlevoix, then 52 years of age, set down the pattern he was to follow in his great histories for the next 20 years. After defining the term "New World," by which he meant "all the countries that were not known to Europeans before the 14th century," he listed the components of a general history: an accurate annotated bibliography of all previous contributions to the subject, a complete description of the country and of its inhabitants, a chronological account of its entire history, including all significant events but excluding trivia, the whole accompanied by numerous maps and plans, and by illustrations of the flora and fauna.

The only other text in the *Journal de Trévoux* which is usually attributed to Charlevoix, although not signed by him, is the "Éloge historique de M. le cardinal de Polignac" (June 1742). Charlevoix's principal activity as an editor appears to have been the writing of anonymous reviews of new literary and historical works. The reviews of some books of North American interest, among them that of the *Aventures du s. C. Le Beau...* (1738) [*see* Claude Lebeau*] can be identified by internal evidence as being by Charlevoix.

In addition to his new duties with the *Journal de Trévoux,* Charlevoix was busy with the revision and expansion of his history of Christianity in Japan, which he republished in 1736 under the augmented title *Histoire et description générale du Japon.* This study became the second in his series of histories of the New World, and was introduced by his "Fastes chronologiques de la découverte du Nouveau Monde." After the publication of this huge work, Charlevoix returned to his manuscript on New France, which he completed in the spring of 1740.

While he was seeing the two editions of the latter through the press, Charlevoix received the news of his appointment in 1742 as procurator in Paris for the Jesuit missions and Ursuline convents in New France and Louisiana. In commenting on the appointment, Canon Pierre HAZEUR de

Charlevoix

L'Orme wrote drily (2 May 1742): "I doubt if he will be as well thought of as his late predecessor [Father Joseph DES LANDES]. . . . He is very quick-tempered for an administrator." Charlevoix himself was distressed to find that the procuracy was 40,000 *livres* in debt. "I waste all my time trying to borrow money," he wrote to the minister in July 1742, "and I can obtain it only on terms that would bring about the ruin of all the missions for which I am responsible." Charlevoix fulfilled these obligations until the year 1749, when he was replaced by Charles-Michel MÉSAIGER.

The appearance in August 1744 of the long delayed *Histoire et description générale de la Nouvelle France* . . ., dedicated to Louis-Jean-Marie de Bourbon, Duc de Penthièvre, son of the Comte de Toulouse, was the high point of Charlevoix's career as a historian. All his previous writings had been reworkings of histories published by others, or, in the case of *Histoire de l'isle Espagnole*, of material furnished by another. His history of New France, although it frequently drew on earlier works such as the *Description géographique et historique des Costes de l'Amérique septentrionale* . . . (1672) of Nicolas Denys* or the Jesuit *Relations*, was an original creation. Having visited most of the sites, and having developed his own theory of historiography, Charlevoix had consulted all available documents and had produced, after more than 20 years of research and reflection, the first general history of the French settlements in North America, together with the first annotated bibliography of Canadiana.

The chronological sequence of the history actually begins with the "Dissertation préliminaire sur l'origine des Amériquains," which reviews various theories about the origins and early migrations of North American Indians; it continues with revised "Fastes chronologiques du Nouveau Monde" which summarize early references to the existence and discovery of the New World. The history itself is presented in 22 books, covering the entire period from the first voyages of discovery to 1731, with a further page on the death of Pierre d'Artaguiette in 1736 [*see* François-Marie Bissot* de Vinsenne]. The *Journal historique d'un voyage fait par ordre du roi dans l'Amérique septentrionnale*, with a separate title-page, makes up the final third of the work, to which are appended numerous maps and plans, and a lavishly illustrated "Description des plantes principales de l'Amérique septentrionnale." Charlevoix had mentioned some 70 plants in the body of his text, but only about half of these are found in the botanical appendix, which sug-

gests that he was not the sole author of both lists. Charlevoix or his collaborator describes more than twice as many Canadian species as Jacques-Philippe Cornuti had done in his *Canadensium plantarum* (1635). Charlevoix identifies, for example, eight North American oaks, whereas the Swedish botanist Carolus Linnaeus was to list only five in his *Species plantarum* (1753). Yet the contribution made by Charlevoix's "Description des plantes . . ." has gone almost unnoticed.

The quarto (three-volume) and duodecimo (six-volume) editions of the *Histoire et description générale de la Nouvelle France* appeared simultaneously, each in five issues with the imprints of five different Parisian printers. Both editions are prized by collectors as handsome examples of 18th-century typography and engraving, with their two-colour title pages, their folding maps and plans by Bellin, and their 22 (4°) or 44 (12mo) folding plates.

The *Histoire et description générale* appears to have circulated widely and to have been of particular interest to English readers. *The importance and advantage of Cape Breton*, printed in London in 1746 and attributed to William Bollan, made extensive quotation from Charlevoix. In 1754, Thomas Jefferys, geographer to the Prince of Wales (the future George III), published a pamphlet entitled *The conduct of the French with regard to Nova Scotia* . . ., which was a detailed critique of Charlevoix's references to the Acadian boundary dispute; and in 1763 the second English translation of the *Journal* claimed "that it was from this Work in particular that our Ministers formed their Notions of the Importance of Canada."

Charlevoix's last published history, his *Histoire du Paraguay* (1756), became the most widely distributed of all his works, being eventually translated into English, Latin, German, and Spanish. Appearing at the precise time when the role of the Society of Jesus was being questioned in both Europe and America, it has remained the classic defence of the Jesuit administration in Paraguay.

Little is known of Charlevoix's last years, spent in retirement at the Jesuit college of La Flèche. He died there on 1 Feb. 1761, in his 79th year. The *Mercure de France* summed his career up tersely: "author of several valuable histories of different parts of the New World. . . ." And indeed, Charlevoix was, for his own and succeeding generations, the one unimpeachable historian of the New World. "A most veracious man," Voltaire said of him, and bought all his works. The Encyclopedists quoted him, as the ultimate authority on primitive peoples. When François-

René de Chateaubriand wrote *Les Natchez, Atala*, and his *Voyage en Amérique*, he paraphrased whole passages from the *Histoire et description générale de la Nouvelle France* and from the *Journal*.

In more recent years, Charlevoix's admirers have been less conspicuous and his critics more vocal, charging him with inaccuracy, bias, and tedium. The accusation of inaccuracy, levelled at each generation of historians by their successors, was to be expected; Charlevoix himself noted in old age that in his first book "I made mistakes in a number of places." Yet any just critic will be struck by the infrequency in Charlevoix's writings of serious misinformation. A wrong date (the defence of Quebec against Sir William Phips*), an undocumented event (Jean-François de La Rocque* de Roberval's second voyage), or a distorted episode (Jacques-René de Brisay* de Denonville's 1687 expedition) hardly outweighs his many pages of substantially accurate narrative, the result of continuous devotion to the Cartesian ideal of "sifting the true from the false." Nor can Charlevoix's relative impartiality in the context of his century be seriously questioned, despite his evident and freely acknowledged concern with missionary activities and sympathy for Christian principles.

Finally, Charlevoix, having assimilated over long years of study the great writers of antiquity and those of 17th-century France, and having been during his whole lifetime immersed in the humanistic and philological tradition of one of the most renowned Jesuit colleges of Europe, possesses an admirably balanced and elegantly varied French style which bears comparison with that of any but the best 18th-century writers. The undeniable literary qualities of his skilfully organized narrative, of his tasteful descriptions, and of his perceptive portraits of great figures are almost completely lost in the merely adequate English versions presented or reprinted by his modern editors. More than any other writer of the French régime, Charlevoix deserves to be re-edited in his original text.

By a curious irony, this master historian, who sought to make the past live for his readers, seemed destined to write only magnificent obituaries for dead or dying régimes. The New France he had chronicled was slipping out of French hands even as Charlevoix himself lay on his death-bed; the Jesuit empires in Japan and Paraguay were crumbling, and within a few months of his death the mighty Society of Jesus itself would be brought to its knees in France. It was as if Charlevoix, by writing his golden histories of the New World and its Jesuits, had brought the curse of Midas upon all that he had touched.

DAVID M. HAYNE

[P.-F.-X. de Charlevoix, *Histoire de l'établissement, des progrès et de la décadence du christianisme dans l'empire du Japon; où l'on voit les différentes révolutions qui ont agité cette monarchie pendant plus d'un siècle* (3v., Rouen, 1715); *La vie de la mère Marie de l'Incarnation, institutrice & première supérieure des Ursulines de la Nouvelle France* (Paris, 1724); *Histoire de l'isle Espagnole ou de S. Domingue, écrite particulièrement sur des mémoires manuscrits du P. Jean-Baptiste le Pers, Jésuite, missionnaire à Saint Domingue, & sur les pièces originales, qui se conservent au Dépôt de la marine* (2v., Paris, 1730–31); *Histoire et description générale du Japon; où l'on trouvera tout ce qu'on a pu apprendre de la nature & des productions du pays, du caractère & des coutumes des habitans, du gouvernement & du commerce, des révolutions arrivées dans l'empire & dans la religion; & l'examen de tous les auteurs, qui ont écrit sur le même sujet; avec les fastes chronologiques de la découverte du Nouveau Monde* (2v., Paris, 1736); *Histoire et description générale de la Nouvelle France, avec le Journal historique d'un voyage fait par ordre du roi dans l'Amérique septentrionnale* (3v., et 6v., Paris, 1744); *Histoire du Paraguay* (3v., Paris, 1756). Almost all of Charlevoix's works have passed through several editions and have been translated into various languages. None of them is available in a critical edition, although annotated English translations of the *Histoire et description générale de la Nouvelle France . . .* and of the *Journal . . .* appended to it have been published: *History and general description of New France*, trans. and ed., with notes, by J. G. Shea (6v., New York, 1866–72; New York, 1900; London, 1902; Chicago, 1962); *Journal of a voyage to North America*, trans. and ed., with historical introduction, notes, and index, by L. P. Kellogg (2v., Chicago, 1923). A complete collection of all works by Charlevoix is to be found in the John Carter Brown Library (Providence, R.I.). Some information was supplied by Dr Bernard Boivin, Research Branch, Dept. of Agriculture, Ottawa. D.M.H.]

AN, Col., B, 42, f.448; 44, f.62; 53, ff.33, 75v; 55, f.26; 56, f.28; 59, f.12; C¹¹D, 8, ff.163–64v; C¹¹E, 2, ff.63–68v; 3, ff.14–15v; 16, ff.96, 102–4v, 106–9; C¹³A, 7, f.4v; F¹A, 21, ff.277–78; 22, f.31; Marine, 3JJ, 388, 394. Archives du service hydrographique (Paris), 67–2, 11; 115–16, 4. BN, MSS, NAF 9287. *Découvertes et établissements des Français* (Margry), V, 632–39; VI, 521–80. "Jean Prat, correspondant de Bernard de Jussieu," Roland Lamontagne, édit., APQ *Rapport, 1960–61,* 146. *JR* (Thwaites), LXIX, 234, 303–4. *Journals and letters of La Vérendrye* (Burpee), 73–90. "Lettres et mémoires de l'abbé de L'Isle-Dieu," APQ *Rapport, 1935–36,* 279, 280. *Charlevoix (1682–1761),* Léon Pouliot, édit. (Collection classiques canadiens, 15, Montréal, 1959). Allaire, *Dictionnaire. Bibliothèque de la Compagnie de Jésus; Première partie: Bibliographie, par les pères Augustin et Aloys de Backer; Seconde partie: Histoire, par Auguste Carayon,* Carlos Sommervogel, édit. (11v., Bruxelles, Paris,

Charlotte de Sainte-Hélène

1890–1932), II, 1075–1079. *DAB*, IV, 23–24. *Biographie universelle* (Michaud et Desplaces), VII, 658–59.

C.-M.-J. Bédier, *Études critiques* (Paris, 1903), 125–294. Gustave Charlier, *De Ronsard à Victor Hugo* (Travaux de la faculté de Philosophie et Lettres de l'université de Bruxelles, Paris, [1931]), 221–34. Gilbert Chinard, *L'Amérique et le rêve exotique dans la littérature française au XVIIe et au XVIIIe siècle* (Paris, 1934), 333–39, *passim*. Delanglez, *French Jesuits in Louisiana*, 88–90, *passim*. Gustave Dupont-Ferrier, *Du collège de Clermont au lycée Louis-le-Grand (1563–1920)* (2v., Paris, 1921–22), I, 52–54. Rochemonteix, *Les Jésuites et la N.-F. au XVIIe siècle*, III, 367–68; *Les Jésuites et la N.-F. au XVIIIe siècle*, I, 176–81, 199–200, 206–8, 246–50. H.-A. Scott, *Nos anciens historiographes et autres études d'histoire canadienne* (Lévis, Qué., 1930), 167–81. Thérèse Ferron, "Essai sur un vieil historien de la Nouvelle-France," *Revue trimestrielle canadienne*, V (1919), 418–37. J. R. G. Hassard, "Shea's Charlevoix," *Catholic World* (New York), XVII (1873), 721–30. Velera Keller, "An early visitor to Michigan: Charlevoix," *Michigan History* (Lansing), XII (1928), 252–66. Albert Merchier, "Le Canada au siècle dernier d'après un Saint-Quentinoix," *Union géographique du Nord de la France* (Douai), VIII (1887), 36–57. W. F. E. Morley, "A bibliographical study of Charlevoix's *Histoire et description générale de la Nouvelle France*," Bibliographical Society of Canada *Papers*, II (1963), 21–45. Gilbert Chinard, "Les Michaux et leurs précurseurs," *Les botanistes français en Amérique du Nord avant 1850* (Colloques internationaux du C.N.R.S., LXIII, Paris, 1957), 267–68. Léon Pouliot, "François-Xavier de Charlevoix, s.j.," *Documents historiques* (Sudbury), 33 (1957), 5–29. J.-E. Roy, "Essai sur Charlevoix," *RSCT*, 3rd ser., I (1907), sect.I, 3–95. Jacques Rousseau, "Michel Sarrazin, Jean-François Gaultier et l'étude prélinnéenne de la flore canadienne," *Les botanistes français en Amérique du Nord avant 1850* (Colloques internationaux du C.N.R.S., LXIII, Paris, 1957), 152. William Sheppard, "Observations on the American plants described by Charlevoix," Lit. and Hist. Soc. of Quebec *Trans.*, 1st ser., I (1829), 218–30. Auguste Viatte, "Chateaubriand et ses précurseurs français d'Amérique," *Études françaises* (Montréal), IV (1968), 305–15.

CHARLOTTE DE SAINTE-HÉLÈNE. *See* DANEAU DE MUY

CHARLY SAINT-ANGE, LOUIS, merchant, fur-trader, entrepreneur, seigneur, syndic of Montreal merchants; b. 28 Feb. 1703, in Montreal, son of Jean-Baptiste Charly* Saint-Ange and Marie-Charlotte Le Conte Dupré; d. probably late 1767 or early 1768 in Saumur, France.

Louis Charly Saint-Ange and his older brother Jacques continued their father's Montreal merchandising and fur trade business after his death in 1728. They were soon in a legal dispute with their stepmother, Louise-Catherine d'Ailleboust de Manthet, who was acting for their infant half-brother Jean-Baptiste-François, over their father's estate of almost 74,000 *livres*, excluding real estate. Louise-Catherine claimed that capital invested in the western trade was part of her *communauté de biens*, and should belong to her son. In 1730–31 a preliminary agreement divided the assets equally among the three brothers. It took Louis and Jacques four years to sort out their accounts and propose an equitable sharing of the assets. Louise-Catherine's new husband, Pierre-Jacques Payen* de Noyan, disputed the division of interest charges, but the Montreal court generally upheld the fairness of the brothers' accounts.

Louis and Jacques separated in 1732 when both married into the colonial nobility. Louis Charly married Ursule, daughter of René Godefroy* de Tonnancour, on 22 Jan. 1732 at Trois-Rivières. The following year he lent 18,178 *livres* 4 *sols* to his brother-in-law, Jean-Baptiste-Nicolas-Roch de Ramezay*, commander at Chagouamigon (near Ashland, Wis.) on Lake Superior, one of the more lucrative trading posts in the west. The same year, 1733, Charly invested more than 25,000 *livres* in the copper mining venture on Lake Superior of Louis DENYS de La Ronde, successor to Ramezay as commander at Chagouamigon. This, the most substantial investment of Charly's life, attached him for 17 years to the fortunes of La Ronde and his inheritors.

Denys de La Ronde had been granted the fur trade monopoly at Chagouamigon in 1733 as a means of financing the copper mine. But after six years of optimistic reports the mother lode remained undiscovered and the scattered ore samples were impractical to exploit; in 1740 Maurepas, the minister of Marine, withdrew support. Charly's unredeemed investment stood at 30,000 *livres* in 1743. At the beginning he had doubtless hoped the venture would succeed, but had relied upon La Ronde's trade monopoly at Chagouamigon to cover his investment. Whether Charly lost heavily on the venture is not clear, but La Ronde's widow, Marie-Louise Chartier de Lotbinière, and son were granted an extension of their trade monopoly (this time paying for the privilege) until 1749 for the purpose of paying their debts. Charly's part in this new venture seems to have been that of financier. He continually lent money to the La Rondes during the 1730s and 1740s, and reaped interest regularly. If they had nothing to show for their efforts, Charly likely emerged unscathed.

On 27 Dec. 1734 Charly was elected churchwarden of the parish of Montreal. He refused to accept what was then an obligatory, burdensome honour on the grounds that he had too many pressing business affairs. After a year during which he failed to perform his duties the parish obtained a court order compelling him to do so. He had refused a similar nomination in 1729, and the parish priest and the Montreal judge must have felt that his excuses were no longer valid.

Until 1755, the year of his last recorded involvement in the western trade, Charly concentrated on the northern posts of Michilimackinac, Chagouamigon, Sault Ste Marie, Nipigon (near the mouth of the Nipigon River), and occasionally Kaministiquia (Thunder Bay, Ont.) and Michipicoton. Beginning in 1747, however, he also invested in the trade at Detroit, Rivière Blanche, and the Miami post (at or near Fort Wayne, Ind.). Initially, he may have done so to fulfil the trade obligations which his brother Jacques had assumed at these posts. Jacques had died in 1746 and Charly was executor of his estate and guardian of his two children. The colonial authorities, confronting an Indian uprising at Detroit aggravated by a shortage of trade goods, were anxious to find traders willing to exploit that post.

As syndic of the Montreal merchants in 1744 Charly signed a petition, along with the syndic of Quebec, Pierre TROTTIER Desauniers, complaining about the poor protection afforded Canadian maritime commerce by the French navy. In 1749–50 he was captain of militia in Montreal.

Louis Charly Saint-Ange, never having left the colony before, took his family to France after the conquest. Before departing in 1764 he sold his entire Canadian estate to William Grant for 100,000 *livres*, payable in four equal annual instalments. The estate included his house on Rue Saint-Paul, a garden plot outside Montreal, some land on Île Sainte-Thérèse, the small seigneury of Îles Bourdon (purchased in 1751), and Île aux Canards, all the islands being located near Montreal. Hard pressed financially, William Grant was late in some of his payments. In 1768 when he had paid only about two-thirds, Charly's widow, living in Saumur where Charly had died shortly before, launched a suit against him in the Court of Common Pleas in Montreal. The case quickly bogged down in the confusion enveloping the court system of Quebec in the 1760s. Grant defended himself by reneging on the contract, claiming that at the time of sale he was a minor under French law (under 25 years). Charly's widow retorted that he was of age under English law (21 years) and therefore the contract was valid. Grant also apparently accused Charly of

falsely representing the Île aux Canards as a seigneury, rather than as a simple roturial concession, and the case was held up in court over procedural technicalities. In 1772 Charly's widow implored the Duc d'Aiguillon, French minister of foreign affairs, to make official representations in London. As a result the Earl of Dartmouth requested Lieutenant Governor Hector-Théophilus Cramahé* in Quebec to investigate the affair. Cramahé was aware of the case but was pessimistic, and thought a settlement out of court would be the most practical resolution. This probably occurred as there is no further record of the case.

S. DALE STANDEN

AN, Col., B, 64, ff.439v–40; 65, ff.424v–25; 68, ff. 298, 303v; 70, ff.361v–62; 72, f.385; 81, ff.308–9; C¹¹ᴬ, 61, ff.75–78; 63, f.464v; 67, ff.66, 125v; 79, ff.92–93; 82, ff.338–43; C¹¹ᴱ, 13, pp.277–84 (PAC transcripts). ANQ, Greffe de Jacques Barbel, 30 oct. 1736; Greffe de C.-H. Du Laurent, 14 mai 1744, 26 jan. 1751, 27 août 1757; Greffe de J.-N. Pinguet de Vaucour, 21 oct. 1734; NF, Documents de la juridiction de Montréal, VI, 60f., 67v–69, 160–61; X, 16v–18; NF, Coll. de pièces jud. et not., 1437, 1481, 2442, 3619, 3866, 3909. PRO, CO 42/32, f.1; 42/35, f.157. Bonnault, "Le Canada militaire," APQ *Rapport, 1949–51*, 443–44. "Les congés de traite sous le régime français au Canada," APQ *Rapport, 1922–23*, 222, 224. Massicotte, "Répertoire des engagements pour l'Ouest," APQ *Rapport, 1929–30*; *1930–31*; *1931–32*. P.-G. Roy, *Inv. concessions*, II, 119, 265; *Inv. jug. et délib., 1717–1760*. Tanguay, *Dictionnaire*. J.-N. Fauteux, *Essai sur l'industrie*, I, 11, 33–34. P.-G. Roy, *La famille Charly Saint-Ange* (Lévis, Qué., 1945).

CHARTIER, MICHEL, seigneur; baptized 23 Oct. 1667 at Île d'Orléans, son of Michel Chartier and Marie Magné; buried 4 July 1750 at Berthier-en-Bas (Montmagny, Que.).

Michel Chartier married Catherine Chamberland at Saint-François, Île d'Orléans, on 11 July 1688; four children were born to them before 1695. It appears that Chartier went to Acadia in 1694 or early in 1695, for he is identified as an inhabitant of Acadia in a seigneurial grant of 8 July 1695. By this grant he acquired land on the site of present-day St Stephen, N.B. The seigneury was of one half league frontage on each side of the Descoudet (St Croix) River, adjacent to the property of Jean Serreau* de Saint-Aubin. In August 1696 Chartier arranged to lease the seigneury of Mathieu Damours* de Freneuse, on the Saint John River between the Jemseg and the Nashwaak rivers. The lease did not take effect, however, as the seigneury was destroyed by Benjamin Church*'s expedition of 1696.

Chartier returned to Quebec about 1698, and

Chartier de Lotbinière

two more children were born in 1699 and 1701. He and his wife sold the Descoudet seigneury to his brother Charles on 10 March 1701. Chartier seems to have returned to Acadia, for about 1703 he asked the French government to send supplies to the Indians on the Saint John River and to allow him to act as an intermediary with them. His wife Catherine died in 1703 and early in 1704 Michel married Anne Destroismaisons. Despite the earlier sale, Michel was residing on the Descoudet seigneury again in June 1704 with his new wife and the youngest child by his first marriage. At that time they were surprised by another expedition led by Church and fled to the woods. Church stated that "Madam Sharkee" left her silk clothes and fine linen behind her. Church also reported that "Sharkee" had been building a fort at Passamaquoddy (Pesmocadie), down river from the Descoudet seigneury. Chartier and his family returned to Quebec, where a daughter was born in November 1704. It is unlikely that he saw the St Croix River again.

Six more children were born to Chartier and his second wife before her death in 1721. Chartier was married twice more: to Jeanne Grondin (1722), who bore him a son, and to Jeanne Chartré (1734).

MAUD H. HODY

AN, Col, C¹¹ᴰ, 4, ff.328v–29. N.B. Museum, Webster coll., Manuscript contract for the lease of the seigneury of Mathieu Damours de Freneuse to Michel Chartier, 5 Aug. 1696 (shelf 40, pkt.40). Canada, Prov. of, Governor General, *Titles and documents relating to the seigniorial tenure, in return to an address of the Legislative Assembly, 1851* (Quebec, 1852), 154, 155. Thomas Church, *The history of Philip's war . . . of 1675 and 1676; also of the French and Indian wars at the eastward . . .* (2nd ed., Exeter, N.H., 1829), 260, 267, 269. P.-G. et A. Roy, *Inv. greffes not.*, II, 80; XVIII, 282. P.-G. Roy, *Inv. concessions*, IV, 116; *Inv. contrats de mariage*, II, 8, 24. Tanguay, *Dictionnaire*, I, 120, 121; III, 27, 28. Ganong, "Historic sites in New Brunswick," *RSCT*, 2nd ser., V (1899), sect.II, 308, 324.

CHARTIER DE LOTBINIÈRE, EUSTACHE, seigneur, councillor of the Conseil Supérieur, priest, vicar general, archdeacon and dean of the chapter of the cathedral of Quebec; b. 14 Dec. 1688 at Quebec, son of René-Louis Chartier* de Lotbinière and Marie-Madeleine Lambert; d. 14 Feb. 1749.

Eustache Chartier de Lotbinière's father, René-Louis, and his grandfather, Louis-Théandre*, for many years held the highest offices in the magistrature of New France. Eustache was the fifth and last son of a family of ten children, but it was he who perpetuated the Chartier de Lotbinière name before late in life he chose the ecclesiastical state. One of his sisters, Louise-Philippe, married François Mariauchau* d'Esgly, and he was the uncle of Louis-Philippe Mariauchau* d'Esgly, eighth bishop of Quebec.

At an early age Eustache was enrolled in the Jesuit college. At the time he does not seem to have thought of the priesthood despite the example of his two older brothers, Pierre-Alain and Antoine; the former later gave up studying theology and the latter became a Recollet under the name of Valentin. Also, his father, first councillor and reaching the end of his career, was visibly preparing him to be his successor. On 12 Nov. 1708, less than six months before his death, he had asked that his son, "22 years of age" (he was not even 20), be appointed by reversion to the post of first councillor of the Conseil Supérieur or to that of lieutenant general for civil and criminal affairs for the provost court of Quebec "which has been in his family for 48 years"; until his son could exercise one of these two offices he hoped that a seat as councillor of the Conseil Supérieur would be granted him "without his being entitled to speak and vote, in order to instruct him in the manner in which justice is dispensed there." The ministry's laconic reply, which simply refused Eustache the reversion, prompted the intendants Jacques* and Antoine-Denis* Raudot to request on 28 Oct. 1709 an ensign's commission for Eustache in the colonial regular troops, with a reference to him as first cousin by marriage to Governor Vaudreuil [Philippe de Rigaud*]. This precaution was quite unnecessary, for on 5 May 1710 the king appointed Chartier a councillor of the Conseil Supérieur and on 6 July 1711 sent him letters waiving the age limit in view of the fact that he was less than 25, the age of majority. The council admitted him on 23 November 1711, having already admitted him without right to speak and vote on 13 April. In 1716 Intendant BÉGON granted him a commission as keeper of the seals, confirmed by the king on 13 April 1717.

Chartier's advancement had been rapid, and the authorities in the mother country held out hopes that in future he might occupy the same posts as his father and grandfather. On 14 April 1711 he had married Marie-Françoise, daughter of François-Marie Renaud* d'Avène de Desmeloizes and Françoise-Thérèse Dupont de Neuville; her brother, NICOLAS-MARIE, was to marry Angélique Chartier de Lotbinière, Eustache's younger sister. In the marriage contract signed on 3 March in the presence of the highest dignitaries of the colony, Nicolas Dupont* de Neuville, Marie-Françoise's grandfather and guardian (her parents were dead), promised to pay the future husband the sum of 10,500 *livres* in settlement of her portion by anticipation. On his father's death in 1709 the seigneury of Lotbinière had fallen to Eustache in part, and in 1713 he became the sole owner, when his brother Pierre-Alain, who had been living in La Rochelle since 1711, and his three sisters, who were all married, made over to him their rights to the remainder. In 1714 he bought a piece of land measuring six *arpents* by 21 on the seigneury of Maure. Since his marriage he had been living in Rue Saint-Louis, in a house belonging to his wife. The 1716 census indicates that this house was inhabited by some ten persons. He stayed only intermittently on his seigneury of Lotbinière, for which he rendered fealty and homage on 2 Aug. 1724. His boldest undertaking on the seigneury, to which he devoted a great part of his income, was the building of a large stone church, 82 feet long and 38 feet wide, begun in 1717 and completed around 1725. He was helped in the construction by his brother, Father Valentin, parish priest at Lotbinière from 1717 to 1724.

Around the same time Chartier was preparing to enter the business world. On 28 March 1722 he became by a letter of instruction general agent at Quebec of the new Compagnie d'Occident, but it is clear that he had been acting as agent before that date. In a reference to an ordinance by Bégon on 12 Aug. 1718 Chartier de Lotbinière is described as general agent of the Compagnie d'Occident, and on 4 January of that year he is called "agent of the Compagnie du Castor" in a bill of exchange which his brother Pierre-Alain sent him from Bordeaux.

Within the Conseil Supérieur Chartier de Lotbinière had quickly distinguished himself by his competence, his integrity, and his innate sense of justice. In 1711 and on many other occasions he served temporarily as attorney general, and he was regularly chosen as reporter in important lawsuits. Consequently on 6 May 1719 Vaudreuil put forward his name as first councillor, to replace Claude de Bermen* de La Martinière, deceased. On this occasion the governor praised Chartier's honesty and competence: "He has won everyone's esteem and the reputation of being a well-informed and very honest judge." Vaudreuil pointed out, however, that Bégon had withdrawn his support, as Chartier had on more than one occasion firmly opposed attempts to interfere with decrees which the intendant wanted to have changed. Whether for this reason or because of his family relationship with the governor, or because others had precedence over him, Chartier did not get the promotion. Bégon's resentment was apparent again in 1722 in a report

to the minister on the officers of justice: "[Chartier] thinks that he knows as much as the most diligent. He is very fond of pleasure and not too fond of work."

Such a judgement seems to contrast, to say the least, with the important decision Chartier was soon to take after his wife's sudden death on 24 April 1723, following the birth of Michel*, her eighth child. Prompted by motives he seems never to have disclosed, he decided to become a priest. Burdened by professional as well as family obligations – his eldest child was only 11 – it was probably not possible for him to prepare for holy orders at the seminary of Quebec. It is more likely that he received his introduction to theology from his brother, Father Valentin, or from Bishop Saint-Vallier [La Croix*] himself, who held Chartier de Lotbinière in high esteem. Chartier's decision, moreover, reminded the old bishop of the calling under identical circumstances of his paternal ancestor, Jean de La Croix, who, having become a widower at 50 years of age, had shortly afterwards been consecrated bishop of Grenoble, France. Chartier received the tonsure and minor orders on 5 April 1726, the subdiaconate the next day, the diaconate on 7 April, and the priesthood on 14 April, the anniversary of his wedding 15 years earlier. Four days later Bishop Saint-Vallier appointed him simultaneously canon and archdeacon, a dignity of which he took possession the same day, and by June he had become vicar general to the bishop. In the latter capacity he made a pastoral visit to his seigneury on 20 June 1726. As was proper, he resigned his position as agent of the Compagnie d'Occident, but the king permitted him to continue to sit on the Conseil Supérieur as a lay councillor, on condition that he abstain from attending trials of criminal cases and relinquish his office as keeper of the seals.

In praising Chartier to the minister on 10 Sept. 1726, Bishop Saint-Vallier described him as "full of virtues and merits" and stated that "he deserved more than anyone else the dignity of dean" of the chapter. This appointment, like other high offices, was a privilege reserved solely for French priests. "If none is found, however," added the bishop, "as the aforementioned Sieur de Lotbinière surpasses all by his excellent qualities and his experience, he must be chosen in preference to the others. I have made him my vicar general because of the great services that he renders this diocese." Obviously Bishop Saint-Vallier had finally found among his clergy a man upon whom he could rely, and, obsessed by his own mortality, he was preparing to invest Chartier with the highest offices, to provide for all

Chartier de Lotbinière

contingencies that might arise in the church in Canada after his death.

Archdeacon and vicar general, Chartier de Lotbinière was at this time 38 years old. His capabilities and his experience justified his rapid ascension in office, but he was to pay dearly for the favours that Bishop Saint-Vallier had lavished upon him. Having been raised to the top rank of the cathedral chapter because the deanship was vacant, he took precedence over his colleagues, and in his capacity as pro-dean he presided over meetings. All these prerogatives, attained so rapidly, antagonized the other canons and roused the envy of some, who did not hesitate to humiliate him and cause him trouble in the exercise of his functions. On 26 Dec. 1727, when the bishop's death was announced, a splendid opportunity was offered the canons, who outdid themselves, removing him there and then from the office of capitular vicar in favour of Canon Étienne Boullard* and even depriving him of the honour of officiating at the bishop's funeral, a function that fell to him as archdeacon but was conferred upon Boullard. Unable in the circumstances to appeal either to the officiality of the diocese (it could not be re-organized in the interval since the bishop's death), or to the Conseil Supérieur (on holiday until the Monday after Epiphany), Chartier went the same day to the president of the council, Intendant Dupuy*, and insisted that his privileges as capitular vicar be upheld. Dupuy, who was also the bishop's executor, reacted quickly. Instead of instituting a temporizing measure – after all, the funeral had been set for 3 January – Dupuy, warned that the canons were thinking of burying the body in the cathedral, ordered that the burial take place immediately, and at his express demand on the afternoon of 2 January the archdeacon took charge of the funeral in the church of the Hôpital Général. The chapter excluded Canon Lotbinière for a time from its ranks, and the point of law of precedence took on sudden and unexpected importance, degenerating into a virulent jurisdictional dispute between the chapter and Boullard on the one hand and the Conseil Supérieur and the intendant on the other. The latter parties fiercely upheld Canon Lotbinière's jurisdiction as "born vicar general." Canon Lotbinière, however, quickly aware of the ambiguity of his situation in the dispute, since he was both canon and councillor, sensibly withdrew from the fray, leaving Dupuy and Boullard to rail against each other over the legality of his powers. The decision of the court, made known in September 1728, put an end to this growing conflict, which had already been moderated by the tardy but energetic intervention of Governor Charles de Beauharnois. The intendant was recalled immediately and all parties involved were censured, even the governor; the chapter was criticized severely for its conduct towards Canon Lotbinière, the only one to emerge from the crisis blameless.

The archdeacon's prestige does not seem to have suffered from this trial, since Bishop Saint-Vallier's successors continued to honour him with their confidence. In 1728 he took possession of the see in the name of Bishop Mornay, and in 1734 in the name of Bishop Dosquet*. Twice the latter chose him to make the episcopal visit of the diocese, but, with his prejudice against Canadian priests, he felt that he had to choose his vicar generals from among the French priests. He is even supposed to have offered the archdeacon a distant parish out in the countryside, in an attempt to eliminate all Canadians from the chapter.

As for the canons, they continued to harass M. de Lotbinière, and despite the regularity of his attendance at services, they relentlessly held back part of his stipend in his absences to attend meetings of the Conseil Supérieur. When, provided with a procuration from Bishop Mornay, he tried in September 1728 to take possession of the see, he was exposed to such puerile vexation on the part of Canon Joseph-Thierry Hazeur that in the autumn he went to France to escape from the unbearable atmosphere the chapter was creating. This trip was shortly after the crisis that had marked Bishop Saint-Vallier's death, and he had to make every effort in the mother country to convince Bishop Mornay, whose taking of possession had just been ratified by the king, that only the presence of a bishop could restore peace to the church in Canada. His attempt was unsuccessful, but it nevertheless speeded up the appointment of a coadjutor in the person of Bishop Dosquet. Returning to Quebec towards the end of July 1729, with a free passage, Chartier was able to take his place again in the chapter despite obstruction by his constant opponent Hazeur, thanks to letters which Bishop Mornay had sent him at La Rochelle on 10 May, giving him powers as vicar general until the coadjutor's arrival and requesting the chapter not to cause him any more difficulties. But action by the canons was only postponed, for upon Bishop Dosquet's arrival in August 1729 they prevented the archdeacon in the most insidious manner from presiding at the reception of the coadjutor.

Chartier became the senior member of the Conseil Supérieur in 1735. On 13 May 1738 the king also appointed him dean of the chapter of the cathedral to replace Canon Louis Bertrand* de

La Tour. He took possession of his dignity on 14 September, the first Canadian to hold this office. He owed this favour less to Bishop Dosquet's requests than to those of Governor Beauharnois and Intendant Gilles Hocquart*, who had recommended him in 1733 and 1735, each time in flattering terms. Was Canon Lotbinière ever sounded out about succeeding Bishop Dosquet in the see of Quebec, as some people have thought they could maintain? A letter from Canon Pierre Hazeur* de L'Orme, dated 1 July 1739 and which has never been quite clear, is the only evidence to support this affirmation.

Although chequered, M. de Lotbinière's double career was lacking neither in nobility nor in dignity. He entered holy orders just at the time when the church in Canada was about to experience a long period of instability and uncertainty, marked by intermittent crises and rivalries and vexations of which he was often the innocent victim. He was able to rise above his tribulations by incessant work and his dauntless convictions. In 1747 premature disabilities forced him to retire to the Hôpital Général, where he died on 14 Feb. 1749. He was buried the next day in the cathedral of Quebec, where his wife rested. The inventory of his possessions drawn up on 8 May shows that he owned nothing but the seigneury of Lotbinière and his house in Quebec.

Of the eight children born of his marriage, three sons and two daughters were still living in 1723. One of the daughters, Louise, became a nun in the Hôpital Général, and the other, Marie-Françoise, married Antoine Juchereau Duchesnay, seigneur of Beauport. The eldest of the sons, Eustache, was ordained a priest at Angers, France, on 18 March 1741, and François-Louis*, a Recollet, was ordained at Quebec on 23 Sept. 1741. The youngest son, Michel, continued the line; in 1747 he married Louise-Madeleine, daughter of Gaspard-Joseph CHAUSSEGROS de Léry, and was created a marquis by Louis XVI in 1784.

ARMAND GAGNÉ

AAQ, 12 A, Registres d'insinuations B, 266, 271–73, 291, 304; Registres d'insinuations C, 35f., 150, 155; 10 B, Registre du chapitre de la cathédrale, I, 82, 101–4, 425; 11B, Chapitre, II, 152f.; III, 9; IV, 40–42; IX, 68–84, 93; 91 CM, France, I, 4, 98. AHGQ, Annales, I. AN, Col., B, 32, f.33; 33, f.293; 34, f.301; 35, f.288; 36, f.408; 43, f.101; 50, f.487; 52, ff.516, 546, 554; 53, f.493; 54, f.403; 66, f.34; C¹¹ᴬ, 22, ff.235f.; 24, ff.214f.; 29, f.254; 40, f.166; 48, f.434; 60, f.154; 70, f.100; 107, f.392; C¹¹ᴳ, 4, ff.3, 97; 5, ff.54, 89; D²ᶜ, 222; E, 75 (dossier Chartier de Lotbinière); 363 (dossier Saint-Vallier) (copies at PAC). ANDQ, Registres des baptêmes, mariages et sépultures. ANQ, Greffe de Louis Chambalon, 3 oct. 1709, 3 mars 1711, 8 avril 1713, 16 janv., 30 mars 1714; Greffe de J.-B. Choret, 12 mai 1749; Greffe de Jacques de Hornay Laneuville, 6 juin 1718; Greffe de J.-N. Pinguet de Vaucour, 8 mai 1749; AP, Chartier de Lotbinière; AP, Seigneuries, Lotbinière; NF, Coll. de pièces jud. et not., 1323, 2040. Archives paroissiales de Saint-Louis (Lotbinière, Qué.). Harvard College Library, MS Can 39.

"Correspondance de Vaudreuil," APQ *Rapport*, *1938–39*, 94, 166–67; *1942–43*, 409, 437. *Documents relating to Canadian currency during the French period* (Shortt), I, 520–22. *Édit. ord.*, II, 322–29, 333. *Jug. et délib.*, VI, 201, 209–10, 267, 271. *Mandements des évêques de Québec* (Têtu et Gagnon), I, 533, 542. "Mémoire de M. Dupuy, intendant de la Nouvelle-France, sur les troubles arrivés à Québec en 1727 et 1728, après la mort de Mgr de Saint-Vallier, évêque de Québec," APQ *Rapport, 1920–21*, 78–105. *Recensement de Québec, 1716* (Beaudet). "Recensement de Québec, 1744" (APQ *Rapport*).

Le Jeune, *Dictionnaire*. Louis Moreri, *Le grand dictionnaire historique, ou le mélange curieux de l'histoire sacrée et profane* . . . (18ᵉ éd., 10v., Paris, 1759). P.-G. Roy, *Inv. concessions*, III, 80–81; *Inv. ins. Cons. souv.*, 146; *Inv. ins. Prév. Québec*, 134; *Inv. jug. et délib.*, *1717–1760*, I, 37, 340, 347; VI, 169, 248, 250–51; *Inv. ord. int.*, I, 159, 175, 286; II, 28–29, 31. Tanguay, *Dictionnaire*. François Daniel, *Histoire des grandes familles françaises du Canada* . . . (Montréal, 1867). Dubé, *Claude-Thomas Dupuy*. Gosselin, *L'Église du Canada jusqu'à la conquête*, I, II. *Mgr de Saint-Vallier et l'Hôpital Général*, 272–73, 612–13. L.-L. Paradis, *Les annales de Lotbinière, 1672–1933* (Québec, 1933). Ignotus [Thomas Chapais], "Eustache Chartier de Lotbinière," *BRH*, IX (1903), 238. Henri Têtu, "Le chapitre de la cathédrale de Québec et ses délégués en France," *BRH*, XIII (1907), 299–300, 305–6; XIV (1908), 33, 104, 201–2; XVI (1910), 198–99, 362. H. M. M. Thomas, "A Canadian Pooh-Bah," *Dal. Rev.*, VII (1927–28), 69–79.

CHASSIN DE THIERRY, FRANÇOIS-NICOLAS DE (he signed Thierry de Chassin), officer in the colonial regular troops; b. at Versailles, France, son of Nicolas de Chassin, billeting officer for the king's household, and Charlotte Thyerry; m. 26 Dec. 1734 at Louisbourg, Île Royale (Cape Breton Island), Marie-Josephe, daughter of Pierre Rousseau de Souvigny and Jeanne de Saint-Étienne de La Tour, by whom he had six children; d. 20 Oct. 1755 at Louisbourg.

François-Nicolas de Chassin de Thierry first came to Canada in 1717 as a cadet and returned to France the following year. In 1719 he was posted to Louisiana as a second lieutenant. Following a grave illness in 1725, he returned to France in the spring of 1726 to convalesce. He remained there until the spring of 1730 when he was appointed ensign at Île Royale. He was promoted lieutenant in 1737 and captain in 1744.

Chaumont

Thierry's service at Louisbourg apparently met with the approval of his superiors. In 1732 the governor of Île Royale, Saint-Ovide [MONBETON], charged him with supervising the annual assembly of the Indians of Nova Scotia and Île Royale; he was entrusted "with the presents for the savages and the goods with which to provide a feast." Of his performance Saint-Ovide reported: "one cannot be more satisfied than I was with the exactness, the devotion, and the care which this officer showed during the course of the journey."

Thierry is best remembered as the officer responsible for the hasty evacuation of Louisbourg's Royal battery on the night of 11 May 1745, shortly after New Englanders under the command of William PEPPERRELL landed at Gabarus Bay. In a terse note to the commandant, Louis Du Pont* Duchambon, Thierry had claimed that the battery was virtually impossible to defend against a landward assault and should therefore be evacuated and blown up. At a tumultuous meeting of the council of war, all the officers present, except Étienne VERRIER, the engineer, concurred with Thierry's recommendation. Finally a compromise was reached: the battery would be abandoned but not destroyed, its guns would be spiked and its stores of foodstuffs and munitions evacuated to Louisbourg. Once the order was transmitted, Thierry's men proceeded in uncontrolled panic, driving steel rods into the guns' touch holes, but neglecting to smash either trunnions or carriages, and leaving virtually all the stores behind in their flight into Louisbourg. On 12 May a detachment was sent out to carry away the foodstuffs and powder, but the shells and ball were left behind.

Meanwhile, detachments of New Englanders began pouring onto the high ground which dominated the walled fortress on three sides. Early on 13 May William VAUGHAN of New Hampshire discovered that the Royal battery had been abandoned and promptly proceeded, "with yͤ grace of God and yͤ courage of about thirteen men," to take possession. Within 24 hours New England armourers had unspiked the battery's guns and had them trained on Louisbourg. The anonymous "Habitant" noted in his *Journal*: "From the fourteenth, the enemy saluted us with our own guns and kept up a tremendous fire."

In this way Thierry provided "mighty Encouragement and Advantage" to the inexperienced New Englanders. The defenders eventually surrendered the fortress on 28 June and the French garrison was evacuated to France. It is perhaps amusing to note that as early as 1750 Thierry was posted once again to command a detachment at the scene of his first effort at soldiering in 1745. Four years later, with over 35 years in the service, he was received into the order of Saint-Louis. He died at Louisbourg a year later.

BERNARD POTHIER

AN, Col., B, 54, ff.503–3v; 65, ff.482–83; 78, f.410; 93, f.235; 98, f.178; 99, f.249; C¹¹B, 12, f.270v; 29, ff.39–44, 66–71v; F³, 50; Marine, C⁷, 320 (dossier Thierry de Chassaing); Section Outre-Mer, G¹, 406 (26 déc. 1734); 409 (7 sept., 20 oct. 1755, 5 févr. 1758). *Louisbourg in 1745* (Wrong), 39–41. "The Pepperrell papers," Mass. Hist. Soc. *Coll.*, 6th ser., X (1899). Thomas Prentice, *A sermon preached at Charlestown, on a general thanksgiving, July 18, 1745, for the reduction of Cape-Breton . . .* (Boston, 1745). Frégault, *François Bigot*, I. McLennan, *Louisbourg*, 150–52. Parkman, *Half-century of conflict*, II. Rawlyk, *Yankees at Louisbourg*, 89–97.

CHAUMONT, NICOLAS-AUGUSTE GUILLET DE. *See* GUILLET

CHAUSSEGROS DE LÉRY, GASPARD-JOSEPH (baptized **Gaspard**), army officer, engineer; b. 3 Oct. 1682 at Toulon, France, son of Gaspard Chaussegros, an engineer, and Anne Vidalle; m. 13 Oct. 1717 at Quebec, Marie-Renée, daughter of René LEGARDEUR de Beauvais, by whom he had at least ten children, including Gaspard-Joseph*; d. 23 March 1756 at Quebec.

Gaspard-Joseph Chaussegros de Léry was trained in military engineering, probably by his father. Although he was never admitted to the engineer corps, he appears to have done extensive drafting in his youth and to have served in an engineering capacity in the French army. He participated in the siege of Turin, Italy, in 1706 as aide-de-camp to the Marquis de Vibraye; took part in the abortive attempt to land James, the Old Pretender, in Scotland in 1708; and was subsequently commissioned infantry captain in the Régiment de Sault. In 1714 he finished a long manuscript, never published, entitled "Traité de fortification divisé en huit livres." In 1716, now in the department of Marine, he was sent to Canada to prepare plans of existing fortifications at Quebec and to recommend those required to protect the city from attack. Eventually his mission led to a permanent appointment as chief engineer, a post he held until his death 40 years later.

The public works for which Chaussegros was responsible included fortifications at Quebec and Montreal; the forts of Niagara (near Youngstown, N.Y.), Chambly, Saint-Frédéric (Crown

Point, N.Y.), and Sault-Saint-Louis (Caughnawaga, Que.); the governor's pavilion of the Château Saint-Louis at Quebec; design of the façade of Notre-Dame church at Montreal; repairs to the bishop's palace at Quebec; designs for a "palais de justice" at Trois-Rivières; studies of a canal from Lachine to Montreal; consultation with respect to the Saint-Maurice ironworks and the mines in the region of Baie Saint-Paul; and plans for shipyards and drydocks on the Rivière Saint-Charles at Quebec.

Any attempt to assess the quality of Chaussegros's achievements must take into account the attitude of the court at Versailles toward the work he was sent to do. The council of Marine in 1716 did not consider the resources of Canada vital enough to justify crown expenditures on their defence comparable to the moneys being spent on Île Royale (Cape Breton Island), for example, at the same time. The inhabitants, the wealthy religious orders, and the Domaine d'Occident should be prepared to share the cost. The policy changed little during the ministry of Maurepas from 1723 to 1749: the court was sparing in its contributions to the fortifications of Canada; and even in wartime, in 1746, Maurepas reasoned that to leave Quebec relatively unfortified would be a deterrent against Anglo-American invasion! The enemy would fear the consequences of having no winter refuge after the departure of the last naval vessels before freeze-up. In any event, between 1715 and 1752 the military engineers reputed to be the best in France – those who had been admitted to the corps according to standards laid down by its former head, Sébastien Le Prestre de Vauban – were not sent to Canada. The same council of Marine that dispatched Jean-François de Verville* to Île Royale was content to assign Chaussegros de Léry to a similar role in Canada. Nor could the connections that the latter apparently had with relatives of the king obtain for him an appointment in the engineer corps in France, which depended more on merit than did appointments in other branches of the French forces. He made unsuccessful overtures for such an appointment in 1729 and again in 1738.

Yet the evidence suggests that, although he may not have been outstanding as a military engineer, he was versatile and imaginative. During the years 1726–28 he proposed a rival French post close to Oswego on the south shore of Lake Ontario. He advised in 1733 against attempting a Lachine canal because the amount of rock which would have to be excavated by blasting would make the cost prohibitive. (His report does not indicate whether he was aware that Gédéon de Catalogne* had already discovered this difficulty in 1700.) He invented machinery and techniques for laying siege to Indian forts of a type encountered by troops from Louisiana. He analysed the potential productivity of the Saint-Maurice ironworks with particular reference to the use of waterpower for operating machinery. He offered suggestions regarding the location of shipbuilding yards at Quebec. He proposed a road from the Richelieu to Montreal to reduce the cost of freight, normally transported by water down the Richelieu and up the St Lawrence. He advocated a defensive strategy for Quebec which would have included not only a fairly large garrison inside the town, but a mobile force outside that could be rushed to trouble spots during a siege. He laid great emphasis on the use of fire-ships in order to repulse any British fleet that might venture up the river to attack the capital. He offered advice on retaking Louisbourg, Île Royale, and improving its defences.

The shortcomings of Quebec's fortifications about the time of his death cannot all be laid at the door of Chaussegros de Léry: he had inherited bad work and had had to follow indifferent policies. Nevertheless, and even if from 1752 the court was depending on the advice of Louis Franquet, the extensive works Chaussegros had constructed during the war years from 1746 to 1749 were quite defective. Exterior works, which would have protected the escarp from direct fire and from escalade, were almost non-existent. And there was no ditch. Although an analysis by Bernard Renau d'Éliçagaray, senior engineer at the department of Marine, had pointed out the need for one just before Chaussegros's departure for Canada in 1716, the latter told Charles de Beauharnois in 1745 that it was impossible to blast one out of the rock. Franquet, examining the site seven years later, said that on the contrary it could have been done. Of course, it would have had to be done before the escarp was constructed. Furthermore, Chaussegros had provided for few embrasures in the faces of the bastions overlooking the Plains of Abraham: in his "Traité" he had written that only sorties by the besieged could destroy attacking batteries; and he believed in using defensive artillery chiefly for flanking and enfilading fire. In spite of all this, Chaussegros reported proudly to the minister, Antoine-Louis Rouillé, in October 1749 that "this town is fortified in the modern style, the fortification is well flanked, it will be well equipped for war."

At Montreal, by virtue of a cost-sharing arrangement among the seigneurs (the Sulpicians), the inhabitants, the Domaine d'Occident, and the crown, the stockade was replaced during

Chaussegros

Chaussegros's time by a masonry *enceinte*. The most that can be said in its favour is that it presented an appearance of permanence which befitted the second town of the colony. In 1760, it was considered quite unfit to withstand bombardment. Chambly was a well-constructed fort, safe against everything but cannon, but the defences of Fort Saint-Frédéric were subsequently condemned for being badly laid out on the ground and consequently being badly constructed. Chaussegros had left most of the supervision of Saint-Frédéric to his eldest son, Gaspard-Joseph, whose engineering competence he had misjudged. The son resigned his post as an assistant engineer in 1748. Fort Niagara, however, proved its worth by withstanding a siege in 1759 for 20 days.

Most 18th-century French military engineers were trained in the basic principles and practices of civil architecture. With some exceptions, few of them were really creative architects. They could reproduce the barrack blocks, garrison churches, and military hospitals common to fortress towns in France, and these were by no means ugly. They could even design colonial "chateaux" and intendants' "palaces," provided little originality was demanded. According to Ramsay Traquair*, Chaussegros was no exception. Writing of his work on the old church of Notre-Dame in Montreal (1722–1830), Traquair says, "If the front of Nôtre Dame is to be taken as a good example of his quality as an architect, his knowledge and designing abilities were very slight indeed." Yet Chaussegros prepared all the plans, sections, and elevations for the second cathedral church at Quebec (built with little support from the court), as well as undertaking the work for the repairs on the Château Saint-Louis and renovating the intendancy after the departure of Claude-Thomas Dupuy*. He also designed jails and other utilitarian structures.

As a technical administrator, Chaussegros de Léry was variously regarded. Philippe de Rigaud*, Marquis de Vaudreuil, with whom he differed strongly over the renovations to the Château, condemned him, even implying that he was a liar; Dupuy ignored him; Beauharnois commended him and listened to his counsel; Gilles Hocquart* did the same until Chaussegros tried to point out the shortcomings of Hocquart's plans for the Quebec shipyards; Governor Duquesne* damned him by faint praise; and François Bigot*, drawing attention in 1748 to poor accounts relating to Fort Saint-Frédéric, complained that the chief engineer was not reporting to the intendant, adding that in any event he ought to be retired because of old age. On two occasions at least, the minister suspected Chaussegros of collusion with contractors for personal profit, in 1730–31 and again in 1748–49, and had investigations made; but nothing was proved. In any event, officialdom commonly suspected this of engineers, in France as well as in the colonies. On the other hand, there are instances of Chaussegros's seeking methods of saving costs for the crown: he refused to countersign the extravagant renovations instigated by the Marquise de Vaudreuil [Joybert*] in 1723–24; he sought ways of making the intendancy more fireproof by dismantling much of the woodwork installed by Dupuy, without wasting the materials; and he devoted considerable attention to the quality of a newly discovered Canadian slate which might have obviated the expense of importing French slate for the roofs of public buildings.

Chaussegros had a hot temper, which officials at court put down to his being a Provençal; and he was at least as conscious of status as his contemporaries were. His career problems may have stemmed from a failure to realize his own limitations. He importuned for 25 years before receiving the cross of Saint-Louis in 1741; he clamoured for recognition of what he considered to be his superior position as chief engineer. Before 1724 he was asking for the same title as Verville's in Île Royale. In 1749 he pointed out bitterly that he had been paid, over the years, little more than one-third of Étienne Verrier's salary in the same colony before its surrender in 1745. Not only did he oppose Franquet's plans for altering the fortifications of Quebec, but threatened to refuse to carry them out. Only his death in 1756 obviated his forced retirement. As late as 1754 he was asking for the special honour of being named first engineer of the department of Marine, by virtue of his long and faithful service. The Chaussegros de Léry papers at the Archives Nationales du Québec contain letters from the Comte de Toulouse, from Philippe, Duc d'Orléans, and from the Duc de Penthièvre, acknowledging receipt of his, expressing their affection for him and his family, and promising to do all they can to assist him in his career. As ministers changed, he sought assurance that he could depend on whatever patronage was available. Yet when Maurepas coldly told him in 1738 that for admission to the engineer corps Chaussegros would have to apply, himself, to the Marquis d'Asfeld – implying that he, Maurepas, could not help him – Chaussegros replied that he preferred to remain in the colony under those circumstances, and protested his personal loyalty to the minister.

Chaussegros de Léry made a good marriage and established himself among the leading families of the colony. In legal actions in 1747 he successfully defended his children's claims to the inheritance of their maternal grandfather, René Legardeur de Beauvais. He married one of his daughters, Louise-Madeleine, to Michel Chartier* de Lotbinière in 1747 and another, Marie-Madeleine-Régis, to Louis Legardeur* de Repentigny in 1750. Through his sons, he established a dynasty in Canada and in France that became distinguished in both the military and the civil fields.

Having raised a large family, he was not exceptionally wealthy, but at his death he possessed two lots in the town of Quebec, one in Rue Sainte-Famille purchased in 1726 from the seminary, on which his house was located, the other granted to him in 1732. Also, he possessed the seigneury on the Richelieu, granted in 1735, with a frontage of two leagues and a depth of three, extending from the limit of the seigneury of Longueuil northwest toward Lake Champlain. He owned a black slave, male, about 25 years of age, valued at 1,200 *livres*. The funeral expenses of Chaussegros de Léry amounted to 1,016 *livres*, 15 *sols*.

The historical legacy of Chaussegros de Léry consists of maps, plans, and papers concerning fortifications, public buildings, harbour facilities, and urban planning. His models of the fortifications of Quebec (1720) and of Montreal (1721), which long reposed in the Louvre, disintegrated in Paris during the 19th century. His "Traité de fortification" was recommended for publication in 1727 by Beauharnois, but Maurepas refused, ostensibly because of the cost, particularly of the illustrations. The real reason may have been that no senior officer of the engineer corps had a high opinion of its worth. Various manuals on fortifications were then appearing in print, some of them by distinguished French engineers, under their own names or under pseudonyms. Many other manuscripts on the subject may well have been refused.

The "Traité" has in common with some of its published contemporaries a tendency to condemn previous works on the subject; and it is curious that Chaussegros reproaches these predecessors for the very fault that Governor Duquesne found in him: a lack of practicality, too theoretical an approach. Duquesne appears to have been wrong to the extent that Chaussegros's theory was faulty too. Various manuals published before and after the completion of his manuscript emphasized the adaptation of fortifications to the peculiarities of the surrounding terrain – and appear to have done so more effectively. It was his particular method of adapting structures to the terrain that was defective.

Taken in balance, Gaspard-Joseph Chaussegros de Léry deserves an important place in the history of New France as the architect of the 18th-century public buildings and fortifications in its towns, as well as of the forts which constituted its outer defences. His name is indelibly stamped on such historical sites as Quebec and Fort Chambly in Canada, and Fort Niagara on the United States side of the border.

F. J. THORPE

Gaspard-Joseph Chaussegros de Léry's manuscript entitled "Traité de fortification divisé en huit livres" is in PAC, MG 18, K2. AN, Col., B, 38–99; C¹¹ᴬ, 36–100; D²ᶜ, 222/1 , p.142 (PAC transcript); Section Outre-Mer, Dépôt des fortifications des colonies, Am. sept., nos.285–308, 395–429, 462–63, 470–89, 499–501, 506–13, 519–21, 530–32, 540–42. ANQ, Greffe de R.-C. Barolet, 15 mai 1756. PAC, MG 8, G24. Archives municipales, Toulon, État civil, Sainte-Marie de la Seds, 3 oct. 1682. *Documents relating to Canadian currency during the French period* (Shortt). Franquet, *Voyages et mémoires sur le Canada*, 174–76. *Inv. des papiers de Léry* (P.-G. Roy). Fauteux, *Les chevaliers de Saint-Louis*, 136. Le Jeune, *Dictionnaire*. P.-G. Roy, *Inv. contrats de mariage*, II, 30; *Inv. ins. Prév. Québec*, I, 138; *Inv. jug. et délib., 1717–1760*, I, 232, 240–41, 266, 271, 297; II, 47, 158; III, 114; V, 30, 37, 39, 190, 263–64; *Inv. ord. int.*, I, 249, 286; II, 52, 55; III, 127; *Inv. testaments*, I, 116. Dubé, *Claude-Thomas Dupuy*, 153, 176, 277. Antoine Roy, *Les lettres, les sciences et les arts au Canada sous le régime français* (Paris, 1930), 140, 184. Stacey, *Quebec, 1759*. Stanley, *New France*. Ramsay Traquair, *The old architecture of Quebec* (Toronto, 1947).

CHAUVREULX (Chauvieux, Chevenaux, Chauvreuil, Le Chauvreulx), CLAUDE-JEAN-BAPTISTE, priest, Sulpician, missionary; b. *c.* 1706 at Orléans, France; d. *c.* 1760 in the same city.

Claude-Jean-Baptiste Chauvreulx arrived in Canada in 1728 as a simple subdeacon, after six years of study at the Sulpician seminary in Paris. The bishop of Quebec, Dosquet*, conferred the priesthood upon him on 23 Sept. 1730 and attached him to the parish of Notre-Dame de Montréal. After two years the young priest returned to France. At the request of M. Jean Couturier, superior of Saint-Sulpice, he agreed, however, to return to America in order to help the missions in Acadia. Chauvreulx went to Acadia in the autumn of 1735 to serve the parish at Pisiquid (Windsor, N.S.), whose two sister churches were L'Assomption and Sainte-Famille. He thus became the first resident priest in the thickly populated region of Minas Basin.

We are ill informed about the missionary's

Chauvreulx

career, for the only documents concerning him that have survived deal with rather brief episodes of his mission in Acadia. The dramatic character of those episodes might suggest that his ministry was an eventful one. In May 1736 the first dispute set Chauvreulx and his *confrère*, Claude de La Vernède de Saint-Poncy, the parish priest of Annapolis Royal (formerly Port-Royal), against the governor, Lawrence Armstrong*. The governor was trying to force the two priests to go to the south of the peninsula to persuade a group of Micmacs to repair the damage done to the *Baltimore*, a brigantine shipwrecked near Cape Sable which they had pillaged. The two missionaries refused to do so. It is difficult to know what really transpired in the council at Annapolis Royal on 18 May 1736 between the protagonists: words must have run high on both sides. Chauvreulx is even said to have claimed that he was not under the governor's jurisdiction. In June, Chauvreulx and Saint-Poncy were sent by Armstrong to Louisbourg, Île Royale (Cape Breton Island), but Chauvreulx succeeded in taking refuge at Pobomcoup (Pubnico region), with a group of Indians and French who were living on the seigneury of Entremont. The following year, upon being informed of these events by the governor of Île Royale, Saint-Ovide [MONBETON], the French minister of Marine, Maurepas, acknowledged that "these gentlemen have been lacking in politeness towards Armstrong and have laid themselves open to his vengeance." After Governor Armstrong's suicide on 6 Dec. 1739, Chauvreulx was able to return to his parish at Pisiquid.

In 1744, at the time of the War of the Austrian Succession, Chauvreulx was involved in a dispute between the Acadian missionaries and the French authorities. The missionaries were blamed collectively for having shown little enthusiasm at the arrival of the French troops which had come to lay siege to Annapolis Royal in the summer of 1744 [*see* Joseph DuPont Duvivier]. Maurepas reproached Chauvreulx for having pronounced "excommunications against those parishioners who took up arms in aid of the French"; on the other hand the bishop of Quebec, Pontbriand [DUBREIL], said in his favour: "I had nothing against M. Chauvreulx; on the contrary, I thought that he was a little too sharp against the English." In short, Chauvreulx was a victim of the ambiguous situation in which the missionaries in Acadia found themselves in the 18th century. Although they were French subjects, they had to guide subjects of his Britannic majesty. However irreproachable their conduct, it was inevitably subject to criticism from one side or the other. In this connection Paul

MASCARENE, the administrator of Annapolis Royal, wrote to London in December 1744: "The missionaries also writt to me and made their conduct appear to have been farr better than could have been expected from them." It is therefore legitimate to think that Chauvreulx had simply recommended neutrality to his flock throughout the war.

The last years Chauvreulx spent in Acadia were greatly affected by the Anglo-French struggle there. From 1749 on, after the departure of Charles de La GOUDALIE and Jean-Pierre de Miniac*, he was the only missionary in Minas Basin. He settled in the parish of Saint-Charles de Grand-Pré, which was more central and where he had the cure of more than 3,000 communicants. His situation became more awkward after the founding of Halifax, for the governor, Edward Cornwallis*, asked for a new oath of allegiance from the Acadian population and undertook to exercise tighter control over the missionaries. Chauvreulx was called to Halifax on 1 Aug. 1749 to have his powers regularized. Nevertheless his relations with the British authorities were good. In agreement with his *confrère* Jean-Baptiste de GAY Desenclaves, he advised his parishioners to take the oath to the king of England. Chauvreulx agreed moreover to swear the required oath himself. This gesture did not please Abbé de L'Isle-Dieu, the bishop of Quebec's vicar general in Paris. While acknowledging the excellent qualities of the two priests, the vicar general suggested that they were not "sufficiently well informed." Along with the minister and Jean-Louis Le Loutre*, the bishop of Quebec's vicar general in Acadia, Abbé de L'Isle-Dieu even thought that it would be wise to cut off any reinforcements to the two missionaries in English Acadia, in order to incite the Acadian population to emigrate in large numbers to the Chignecto isthmus and Île Saint-Jean (Prince Edward Island). It is noteworthy that from the parishes of these two priests emigrants had been fewest. In 1753, however, upon a complaint from Pontbriand, Abbé Henri DAUDIN was sent to help the two Sulpicians. In the autumn of that same year Chauvreulx had to lodge in his house Abbé Lemaire, a missionary on Île Saint-Jean, whose mind had become deranged and whose conduct was embarrassing his *confrères*.

On 4 Aug. 1755, a month before the deportation of the Acadians from Minas Basin began, Chauvreulx was arrested by Charles LAWRENCE's troops, imprisoned in Fort Edward (Windsor, N.S.) for a few days, and taken to Halifax along with Lemaire and Daudin in the middle of the month. Upon their arrival the missionaries were exposed in the market-place, then detained separately on ships of Boscawen's fleet. At the beginning of December 1755 they arrived in Portsmouth, England, where they were allowed to charter a ship to take them to France. They reached Saint-Malo on 8 Dec. 1755. From there Chauvreulx went to Orléans, where he was lodged with his family. It was there that he ended his days, ill, infirm, and incapable of resuming his apostolic tasks. A report by Abbé de L'Isle-Dieu, written soon after the capitulation of Montreal, tells us that he had died some time before. Despite the tragic character of the events that are known of Chauvreulx's stay in Acadia, we may believe that his long mission had for the most part been peaceful. Like the Acadians, this missionary was a victim of political conjuncture rather than a person openly involved in the Anglo-French conflict in Acadia.

MICHELINE D. JOHNSON

AAQ, 12 A, Registres d'insinuations, C, 216; 22 A, Copie de lettres expédiées, II, 519. AN, Col., B, 57, f.744; 58, ff.435, 616; 62, ff.16v, 38v; 65, ff.449, 452, 487; 72, f.16; 78, f.6; 81, f.64; 91, f.62; 104, f.44v; C¹¹A, 78, f.407; 82, f.326; 86, f.140; C¹¹B, 12, f.254; 13, f.103; 18, ff.20, 38, 73–78; 20, ff.35, 85; 21, f.21; 22, ff.116, 117; 33, ff.341, 343. ASQ, Fonds Casgrain, Acadie; Lettres, M, 113; S, 7i, 103; T, 59; Missions, I, 6; Polygraphie, VII, 114, 122; IX, 29. Coll. doc. inédits Canada et Amérique, I, 12–16, 41–46; II, 10–75; III, 60–80, 181–91. "Lettres et mémoires de l'abbé de L'Isle-Dieu," APQ Rapport, 1935–36, 301, 317, 321, 332, 383, 390; 1936–37, 404, 416, 421, 422, 424; 1937–38, 168, 169. N.S. Archives, I, 103–5, 146–50, 170, 188–92, 229f., 282–3; II, 99–111. PAC Report, 1894, 88–91, 94, 96, 139; 1905, II, pt.III, 346–56. Casgrain, Un pèlerinage au pays d'Évangéline, 53–144. Murdoch, History of Nova-Scotia, I, chap.LVII. Parkman, Half-century of conflict, II, chap.IX. Richard, Acadie (D'Arles), I, 274–96, 313, 342; II, 348–75.

CHEVAL, dit Saint-Jacques, and dit Chevalier, JACQUES-JOSEPH, wig-maker, tavern-keeper, "garde du port" (harbour-master or wharf-master) at Montreal, court officer; baptized 13 Dec. 1697 in the parish of Saint-Nicolas in Tournai, Belgium, son of Thomas Cheval and Gilette Nève; d. Dec. 1757 in Montreal.

Jacques-Joseph Cheval arrived in New France around 1720 and settled at Montreal, where for more than 20 years he was a wig-maker, then a tavern-keeper, undoubtedly a much more profitable trade. Around 1740 he obtained the office of "garde du port" at Montreal. Cheval's duty was to watch over the port and the roadstead, as well as the boats which anchored there, and to visit them to ensure that regulations were respected on them. He exercised this function until 1749; on 23 September of that year he was appointed court officer of the Conseil Supérieur, with residence in Montreal. He had acquired some experience with the machinery of justice through taking part in numerous lawsuits, either as plaintiff or as defendant. Cheval was still living in Montreal when his death occurred on 13 Dec. 1757.

On 3 Sept. 1725, at Saint-Laurent on Montreal Island, Jacques-Joseph Cheval had married Marie-Renée Cousineau, who bore him 12 children, seven of whom died in infancy. On 7 Jan. 1743 he became a widower, and on 27 May 1743, even before the notary Louis-Claude DANRÉ de Blanzy had made the inventory of the belongings from his first marriage, he was married again, this time to Geneviève Leduc, who bore him four children.

Even if he did not play a leading role, Jacques-Joseph Cheval managed nevertheless to accede gradually to functions of a certain importance.

ROLAND-J. AUGER

ANQ, NF, Coll. de pièces jud. et not., 2125; NF, Ins. Cons. sup.; NF, Ord. int., 9 juill. 1749; NF, Registres du Cons. sup. ANQ-M, Greffe de L.-C. Danré de Blanzy, 18 juin, 7 août 1743; Clôtures d'inventaires, 22 juin 1743; Registres des audiences, 1739, f.110; 1741, ff.43, 76; 1742, f.39; 1744, ff.400, 446; Registre d'état civil, Saint-Laurent, 3 sept. 1725. Archives de l'État (Tournai, Belgique), État civil, Saint-Nicolas, 13 déc. 1697. Tanguay, Dictionnaire. É.-Z. Massicotte, "Les huissiers de Montréal sous le régime français," BRH, XXXII (1926), 90. P.-G. Roy, "Les capitaines de port à Québec," BRH, XXXII (1926), 1–12, 65–78.

CHEVALIER, JEAN-BAPTISTE, voyageur, merchant; baptized 6 Aug. 1677 in Montreal; son of Joseph Chevalier and Françoise-Marthe Barton; m. 8 April 1709 to Marie-Françoise Alavoine in Montreal; d. late 1746 or early 1747, burial place unknown.

In 1718 Jean-Baptiste Chevalier moved his family to Michilimackinac from Montreal, and in the following years he established commercial and family ties throughout the west. As an engagé he made a number of trips from Montreal to the pays d'en haut, including one to the Saint-Joseph post (probably at or near Niles, Mich.) in 1730 and, for Pierre GAULTIER de Varennes et de La Vérendrye, one to Michilimackinac in 1735. He also became a leading merchant at the latter post. The business was probably tended in his absence by his wife and apparently continued by her after his death.

At least 12 of the 16 Chevalier children lived to maturity, and they also took part in the business.

Chevalier

(Jean-Baptiste, his wife, and several of the children were able to write – no common achievement at Michilimackinac.) The girls often accompanied the men of the family to the various outposts in spite of the rigorous travelling conditions in the *pays d'en haut*. They and their brothers intermarried with other important families in the region. Marie-Anne, for example, became the wife of Charles Chaboillez, a trader at Michilimackinac, and their five sons followed their father's occupation. Louis-Thérèse*, who married Marie-Madeleine Réaume, established another important branch of the family. Such alliances helped give the Chevaliers good trading connections at Nipigon (near the mouth of the Nipigon River, Ont.), Sault Ste Marie, the Saint-Joseph post, Michilimackinac, Cahokia (East St Louis, Ill.), and Detroit.

The exact date and place of Jean-Baptiste's death are uncertain. The most that can now be said is that he died sometime between 12 June 1746, when he signed a voucher for supplies at Michilimackinac, and 10 June 1747, when his widow submitted a similar claim. She later returned to Montreal, where she was buried on 20 March 1756.

HARRY KELSEY

AN, Col., C¹¹A, 117, f.91ff.; 118, ff.29, 30; 119, f.310. DPL, Burton hist. coll., Christian Denissen, [Genealogy of the French families of Detroit] (26v., typescript, n.d.), C/3, 2785–89. St Ann's Parish (Mackinac Island, Mich.), Registre des baptêmes, mariages et sépultures de Sainte-Anne-de-Michillimakinak, 1695–1821; an annotated version under the title "The Mackinac register" is in Wis. State Hist. Soc. *Coll.*, XVIII (1908), 469–513; XIX (1910), 1–149, but it contains some inaccuracies. *The John Askin papers*, ed. M. M. Quaife (2v., Detroit, 1928–31), I: *1747–1795*. "The St. Joseph baptismal register," ed. George Paré and M. M. Quaife, *Mississippi Valley Hist. Rev.*, XIII (1926–27), 213–15, 223, 227, 229–31, 239. *Dictionnaire national des Canadiens français (1608–1760)* (2v., Montréal, 1958), I, 258–71. Massicotte, "Répertoire des engagements pour l'Ouest," APQ *Rapport, 1929–30*.

CHEVALIER, JEAN-CHARLES (Jean-Baptiste), priest, Sulpician, subsequently priest at the seminary of Quebec; b. 1694 at Angers, France; d. 18 May 1760 at Montreal.

Jean-Charles Chevalier entered the Company of Saint-Sulpice at Angers on 25 June 1715 and went to its Paris seminary on 7 Nov. 1718. He was not ordained a priest until 1734, shortly before his departure for Canada. The circumstances of his coming to New France are puzzling. It was certainly the Séminaire des Missions Étrangères in

Paris which sent him to the seminary of Quebec, even paying for his personal belongings and his passage; the directors affirmed that they did not know him personally, but that Bishop Dosquet*, in France at the time, spoke highly of him and recommended him to take charge of the Petit Séminaire.

When he arrived in Canada on 6 July 1734, however, Chevalier placed himself under the direction of the Sulpicians, who made him assistant to the parish priest and seigneur of Terrebonne, Louis LEPAGE de Sainte-Claire; he filled this role from 1735 to 1738. Then he left the Sulpicians and joined the community of the seminary of Quebec. The act of admission has not been found, but documents dating from after Chevalier's death confirm it. His functions are not known, but Cyprien Tanguay* asserts that the grave scruples that led him to give up almost entirely the practice of the holy ministry did not prevent him in any way from rendering "good services to the seminary of Quebec over a period of several years." Indeed, the deliberations of the council of the seminary reveal that he was consulted just as were the directors and the other members of the community of priests. During the siege of Quebec he went with Bishop Pontbriand [DUBREIL] and other priests of the seminary to Montreal, where he died on 18 May 1760.

Jean-Charles Chevalier, who had entered holy orders late in life, seems to have been tormented by scruples, according to Abbé François Noiseux, the basis of whose assertion is not known. Noiseux wrote: "It was with great difficulty that he could be prevailed upon to say mass two or three times a year and . . . when he did say it he took more than an hour and a half to do so; . . . in fact he took half the day to say his ordinary breviary."

HONORIUS PROVOST

ASQ, Fonds Verreau, 0131 (Liste des prêtres de l'abbé Noiseux), 114; Lettres, M, 83, 120; Lettres, R, 15, 16; MSS, 437; Registre des délibérations. Allaire, *Dictionnaire*, I, 119. Gauthier, *Sulpitiana*, 182. Tanguay, *Répertoire*, 98.

CHEVENAUX. *See* CHAUVREULX

CHÉVIGNY, MÉDARD-GABRIEL VALLETTE DE. *See* VALLETTE

CHEVREMONT, CHARLES-RENÉ GAUDRON DE. *See* GAUDRON

CHRÉTIEN, LOUIS TURC DE CASTELVEYRE, known as Brother. *See* TURC

122

CLAPARÈDE (Claparet), JEAN, master lock-smith, blacksmith, merchant; son of Jacques Claparède and Marie Guy of Viols-le-Fort (dept. of Hérault), France; fl. 1714–58.

In December 1736 Jean Claparède was recorded as a member of a party inspecting bat-teries, bastions, and other of the king's buildings at Louisbourg, Île Royale (Cape Breton Island). Government accounts over the next 20 years indicate that Claparède was continually em-ployed as a smith on various royal buildings, government works, and fortifications at Louis-bourg. He assisted in arming a ship, the *Succès*, and in preparing artillery for the attacks made against the English at Canso and Annapolis Royal, Nova Scotia, in 1744 [*see* Joseph DU PONT Duvivier]. In that same year he fashioned ironwork for the "needs" of English prisoners held at Louisbourg.

In 1749 appears the first reference to Claparède's commercial ventures – the sale of a 27-ton schooner, the *Abigail*, on behalf of an Eng-lish merchant. After this date his commercial activities seemed as important as his smithing trade: 1749 is the year when "merchant" was first used to describe Claparède; it was used inter-changeably with locksmith during the rest of his life. In 1750 Claparède was purchaser at Île Royale of a 90-ton ship from the English. Throughout the 1750s he supplied the govern-ment with a variety of goods and services, the lat-ter including laundry for the troops and lodgings for certain officials at Louisbourg.

Claparède's financial status may be gauged from the fact that in 1750 he was paying 450 *livres* a year for a rented house with a forge at Louis-bourg. In 1753 he bought a house for 1,000 *livres*. The sale of Claparède's effects, arranged by a nephew in February 1758, realized 1,134 *livres* 1 *sol*.

From his first marriage, to Renée Grosse who died 10 Jan. 1753, there were two children. Claparède's second wife was a widow, Marie-Josephe Seigneur of Louisbourg; one daughter was born to them. A list drawn up in France in 1790 of former inhabitants of North America who were receiving a government subsidy includes Renée Claparède, daughter of a merchant, living at Viols-le-Fort near Montpellier.

BARBARA RILEY

AN, Col., C¹¹ᴮ, 18, ff.127, 131–32; 26, f.137v.; C¹¹ᶜ, 11–14; Section Outre-Mer, G¹, 407; 408, ff.322, 360; 409; 466, pièce 76 (recensement de l'île Royale, 1749), 79; G², 188, f.368; 206, dossier 462; G³, 2041/1 (23 juill. 1749); 2041/2 (4 oct. 1753); 2042 (19 janv. 1754); 2044 (23 déc. 1756); 2047 (24 sept. 1750).

CLARK, GEORGE, HBC carpenter; d. 17 Sept. 1759 at Henley House (at the junction of the Kenogami and Albany rivers).

George Clark's first service with the Hudson's Bay Company was from 1746 to 1748 as a car-penter and joiner at York Fort (York Factory, Man.). He returned to England in 1748 but was rehired on a five-year contract. He sailed in 1749 on board the *Success* sloop (Capt. Thomas MITCHELL), which in company with the *Mary* (Capt. William COATS) made a reconnaissance of Richmond Gulf (Lac Guillaume-Delisle, Que.) to decide on a site for a new post. On arriving at Albany (Fort Albany, Ont.), Mitchell reported that the trees at Richmond were too small for use in building, and Clark spent the winter at Albany cutting timbers, fitting them together, and mark-ing them for reassembly at Richmond. On 20 June 1750 he sailed with Mitchell for Richmond Gulf, but part of the wood had to be left behind because Robert PILGRIM, chief at Moose Factory, refused to allow the sloop attached to his post to take part in the expedition. Clark was chiefly responsible for the construction of Richmond Fort, which consisted of a square house built of the timber from Albany and four flankers made from the stunted local trees. In 1753 and 1754 he also con-structed a small outpost at Little Whale River.

Clark went to England in 1754. Returning to Albany in 1755 he found it upset because the mas-ter and men at its outpost, Henley House, had been killed by WAPPISIS and some other Indians. In the spring of 1757 Robert Temple, chief at Albany, tried to mount an expedition under the leadership of George Rushworth to resettle Hen-ley, but he could not persuade the men to go. They were afraid of being killed, provisions were poor and wages small, and Rushworth's fiery braggadocio alarmed them. In 1758 Temple asked Clark to be master at Henley. Clark agreed, and it is a measure of the respect he com-manded that there was little difficulty obtaining volunteers.

The party arrived at Henley on 1 June 1759 and decided to rebuild the post on the previous site. Clark erected a two-storey, square house and repaired the palisades, most of which were still standing. On 23 August he sent four men to Albany to assist in bringing up stores and provi-sions for the winter. It was an unfortunate deci-sion, for only four men were left at Henley. Early in the morning of 17 September Clark and John Spence walked toward the bank's edge, where some 20 men, probably French and Indians, lay in ambush. Clark was killed by the first volley of fire, but Spence, though wounded, managed to gain the house. The attackers kept up a steady fire

Claverie

until night, but Spence, John Cromartie, and James Inkster put up a stout defence and wounded several of them. Shortly after midnight the three defenders lowered themselves from a window and set out to walk to Albany. Spence was left at Fishing Creek in the care of some Indians, and his companions walked on until they met the boats on the way to Henley. Two Indians were sent to fetch Clark's body, which had been scalped. He was buried at Albany on 6 Oct. 1759.

The company found its men most reluctant to resettle Henley. In 1766 the post was finally re-established by William Richards at a somewhat safer location a few miles downstream from its original site.

GEORGE E. THORMAN

HBC Arch. A.1/38, p.78; A.5/1, f.34d; A.6/8, ff.10, 20, 134d; A.6/9, ff.5, 124d; A.6/10, f.13d; A.11/2, f.181; A.11/3, ff.24d, 28, 32, 33, 35d, 41, 43d, 51–51d; A.11/57, ff.7, 19d, 26d; A.11/114, ff.122d, 127, 128d. Morton, *History of the Canadian west*.

CLAVERIE (Clavery), PIERRE, naval officer, merchant, storekeeper, seigneur; b. 1719 at Susmiou (Oloron-Sainte-Marie, France), son of Jean Claverie, a merchant trader, and Jeanne La Barthe; buried 21 Aug. 1756 at Montreal.

Pierre Claverie arrived in Canada around 1745, probably as a naval officer. In 1746, while serving on board the *Andromède*, Claverie had to appear, along with the Sieur Fautoux, the ship's captain, before the admiralty court of Quebec because some of the cargo on their ship had been mixed up with the *Sultane*'s during unloading. Everything seems to indicate that this error was intentional and that Claverie had a hand in it. When examined in this light, the incident seems to prove that Claverie tended to get involved in doubtful operations. His attitude, combined with the credit which his uncle Drouillet, a French merchant trader doing business with the colony, extended him, explains in large measure how Claverie succeeded in climbing the social ladder rapidly.

As astute as he was ambitious, Claverie quickly realized that he could benefit financially from the inextricable chaos into which François Bigot* was deliberately plunging the administration of the colony. He struck up friendships, therefore, with members of the famous clique: Jacques-Michel Bréard*, controller of the Marine, Guillaume Estèbe*, king's storekeeper, and Jean-Victor Varin* de La Marre, financial commissary. As early as 1750 Claverie made an arrangement with Bigot to build a warehouse, part of which would encroach upon the king's land and which the king would buy "at cost price" if ever the need arose. As the Sieur de Courville* wrote: "They had an immense store built near the intendant's palace, with warehouses, and to avoid any appearance of mystery they sold by retail." Claverie, who was the owner of the establishment, and Guillaume Estèbe worked together, according to the Sieur de Courville again, to try "to attract all the business and above all to supply all the king's warehouses."

For three years thereafter, Bigot always asked the court for inadequate quantities of certain supplies; he took good care to inform Claverie beforehand, and Claverie would lose no time in obtaining goods, not only to sell to the state at top price, but also to "supply the king with the same goods several times over, and make him pay more each time." Exasperated at seeing their sales decline, the Quebec merchants nicknamed the establishment "La Friponne" ("the Rogue"). The ineffable Bigot was to pretend that "a servant-girl who had committed a theft there had first been responsible for the name." He later had to admit, however, that the merchant traders had kept the name and attributed quite a different meaning to it.

In view of the dissatisfaction, Bigot found himself obliged to buy "La Friponne" in 1753, paying 23,668 *livres* for it, and to close down the establishment. It was high time, moreover, for the abuses being committed in the colony were no longer unknown at court. On 1 June 1754 the minister of Marine, Antoine-Louis Rouillé, wrote a letter to Bigot in which he indicated clearly that he was well aware of the real activities of "La Friponne." He pointed out that "everything had been parcelled out," mentioning specifically that Bréard kept for himself all chartering of ships for the king, Michel-Jean-Hugues Péan* had a monopoly for supplying flour and vegetables, Joseph-Pierre Cadet* for meat supplies, and Claverie for all other supplies for the warehouse in Quebec. The former owner of "La Friponne," however, had had all the time he needed to make his fortune, and on 28 Oct. 1754 he bought the seigneury of Rivière-du-Loup-en-haut, on Lac Saint-Pierre, and some days later that of Madawaska.

During the winter of 1754–55 Bigot had to go to justify himself before the court. Having succeeded only too well, he returned to the colony the following spring. Because Estèbe was leaving for Europe, Bigot gave the position of storekeeper to Claverie as "a reward for having managed 'La Friponne' well." Claverie then lost no time in finding jobs for "his relatives."

124

However, he held the office for eight months only; he died in Montreal in August 1756, apparently of smallpox.

On 29 Jan. 1753, in Quebec, Pierre Claverie had married Marie-Anne, the 15-year-old daughter of Jean-Baptiste Dupéré, a Quebec merchant; of this marriage a daughter was born. After her husband's death Mme Claverie married on 9 May 1758, at Sainte-Foy, Nicolas-Antoine Dandane Danseville de L'Étendard, a lieutenant in the royal corps of artillery and engineering. At that time, in addition to her father's property and the two seigneuries, she owned 164,657 *livres* 12 *sols* "in bills of exchange on the treasury, promissory notes, money in coins and paper."

Contrary to what Cyprien Tanguay* claims, Claverie did not replace Estèbe on the Conseil Supérieur in 1755 or 1756. In fact, Estèbe did not relinquish his seat until 1 Feb. 1758, when Claverie was already dead. The fact that Claverie was a king's councillor, not a councillor of the Conseil Supérieur, likely explains this mistake.

ROBERT LAHAISE

ANQ, Greffe de R.-C. Barolet, 27 janv. 1753, 6 mai 1758; Greffe de J.-C. Panet, 18 déc. 1758. "Les malignités du sieur de Courville," *BRH*, L (1944), 65–86, 97–117. PAC *Report, 1905*, I, pt.VI, 193. *Dictionnaire national des Canadiens français (1608–1760)* (2v., Montréal, 1958). P.-G. Roy, *Inv. contrats de mariage*, II, 51; *Inv. jug. et délib., 1717–1760*. Tanguay, *Dictionnaire*. Frégault, *François Bigot*. P.-G. Roy, *Bigot et sa bande*, 258–61. Amédée Gosselin, "François-Joseph de Vienne et le journal du siège de Québec en 1759," *APQ Rapport, 1922–23*, 408. "Pierre Claverie a-t-il été membre du Conseil souverain?" *BRH*, XXIII (1917), 256. J.-E. Roy, "Les conseillers du Conseil souverain de la Nouvelle-France," *BRH*, I (1895), 177–88, P.-G. Roy, "Jean-Victor Varin de la Marre," *BRH*, XXII (1916), 176–82.

CLEVELAND (Cleaveland), AARON, Congregationalist minister and priest of the Church of England; b. 29 Oct. 1715, in Cambridge, Massachusetts, son of Aaron Cleveland, a building contractor, and Abigail Waters; d. 11 Aug. 1757 at Philadelphia, Pennsylvania.

Aaron Cleveland graduated in 1735 from Harvard College, where he was known as an outstanding wrestler, swimmer, and skater, "a large and powerful man." In 1739 he was ordained in the Congregational church at Haddam, Connecticut, and on 4 August of the same year he married Susannah Porter, an acknowledged belle and the daughter of the Reverend Aaron Porter of Medford, Massachusetts.

Cleveland's popularity waned within a few years, possibly because he was reflecting the influence of the celebrated revivalist, George Whitefield. In 1746 he "obtained dismission" from Haddam, and in April 1747 was called to Malden South (Everett, Mass.). He paid a visit to Halifax, Nova Scotia, in May 1749, and after preaching to a considerable assembly was urged to "make his settled abode" there. The Anglican community was already served by St Paul's church and a handsome meeting house was planned for the dissenters (Presbyterians, Congregationalists, Calvinists, etc.). February 1751 found Cleveland in his new charge. Pending completion of the meeting house, he preached in St Paul's every Sunday in the afternoon "to good Acceptance"; his colleague, William TUTTY of the Church of England, discoursed to his flock in the morning. This arrangement worked amicably, and Tutty could inform the Society for the Propagation of the Gospel of the perfect harmony existing between the two congregations. It had been otherwise the previous September, when Tutty had stigmatized the New Englanders as "a cheating designing people," dishonest and given to prevarication, "and all under the cloak of religion." Governor Edward Cornwallis*, who found Cleveland "well pleasing," granted him four lots of land in Halifax and area and took a keen interest in the new meeting house (later St Matthew's church), of which Cleveland was the first minister.

In a year or so Cleveland seems to have become restless; perhaps once more his popularity was lessening. He was veering towards the Church of England and left Halifax in late 1753 for Norwich, Connecticut, his widowed mother's home. As acceptance by the SPG demanded his presence in London, he settled his affairs in Halifax before sailing for England in June 1754; he left his wife and children in Boston. He was subsequently ordained and on 28 July 1755 was appointed a missionary of the SPG. The society offered him a post in Pennsylvania. The vessel in which he was returning to America was cast on the Nantucket shoals and Cleveland, who showed great bravery in assisting the sailors, received a severe head injury. Resuming this hazardous voyage he landed in Halifax in October 1755 and shortly afterwards continued to Norwich, still a sick man. The congregation in Lewes, Delaware, would not accept him as their new minister, but on the high recommendation of the Reverend William Smith he was transferred in 1757 to New Castle, Delaware. He then set out for New England to get his wife and ten children. In Philadelphia he stopped to rest in Benjamin Franklin's house and died there suddenly from "dropsey" on 11 Aug. 1757.

Clinton

Cleveland's widow received the remainder of his salary, plus £50, from the SPG and opened a shop in Salem, Massachusetts. Grover Cleveland, twice president of the United States, was a descendant of Aaron.

MAUD M. HUTCHESON

Essex Institute (Salem, Mass.), MS letter of Aaron Cleveland, [1751]. *The genealogy of the Cleveland and Cleaveland families*, comp. E. J. and H. G. Cleveland (3v., Hartford, Conn., 1899), I. *New Eng. Hist. and Geneal. Register*, XLII (1888), 73–78. Shipton, *Sibley's Harvard graduates*, IX, 493–500. [R. M. Hattie], *Looking backward over two centuries* (Halifax, 1949), 10–11. I. F. MacKinnon, *Settlements and churches in Nova Scotia, 1749–1776* (Halifax, [1930]). W. C. Murray, "History of St. Matthew's Church, Halifax, N.S.," N.S. Hist. Soc. *Coll.*, XVI (1912), 150–57.

CLINTON, GEORGE, officer in the Royal Navy, governor of Newfoundland and New York; b. *c.* 1686 in Oxfordshire, England, second son of Francis Fiennes Clinton, 6th Earl of Lincoln, and Susan Penniston; m. Anne Carle and had six children, of whom three survived infancy; d. 10 July 1761 in England.

George Clinton entered the navy in 1707 and was promoted captain in 1716. His first significant command came in 1731, when he was appointed governor of Newfoundland and commodore of the ships sent there, the first officer to hold both positions. Clinton was instructed to look into the conduct of the recently appointed local magistrates [*see* William KEEN], and in general he supported them in their jurisdictional disputes with the fishing admirals. He was careful, however, to ensure that they did not exceed their authority, for instance in their attempt to tax the wages of local labourers to help pay for the jail constructed at St John's. Though the admirals opposed his authority, Clinton showed himself a diligent and efficient administrator of the civil government established by his predecessors, Lord Vere Beauclerk and Henry Osborne*. In 1732 he was succeeded as governor by Edward FALKINGHAM.

In 1737, while still a captain, he was made commodore of the Mediterranean fleet. He held a command in the squadron being assembled in 1740 for service in the West Indies, but successfully petitioned to be relieved of the undesirable post. By this time Clinton was seriously in debt. He appealed to the Duke of Newcastle for more remunerative employment, and in 1741 was appointed governor of New York, though he did not arrive there until September 1743.

Following the declaration of war between England and France the next year, Governor Clinton took steps to protect New York's northern frontier and to participate in the conflict with the French. He strongly supported expeditions against the French garrison at Fort Saint-Frédéric (Crown Point, N.Y.) and urged that New York send troops for the siege of Louisbourg, Île Royale (Cape Breton Island) in 1745. His assembly, however, refused to raise troops for any offensive action, and in the end only artillery was sent to Louisbourg. Many assemblymen who were merchants wanted to protect their profitable trade with the French at Montreal and with the Indians under French influence. Thus Clinton also met opposition for his proposal to send aid to the Six Nations Indians to obtain their help against the French, for their neutrality was necessary to protect the trade. He and his representatives, however, held various meetings with the Six Nations, and from 1746 on Colonel William Johnson* worked diligently as Clinton's representative to encourage these Indians in the war.

In 1746 Clinton and the other colonial governors received instructions from England to raise volunteers for an expedition against Canada. About 1,400 men were raised in New York, and in 1746–47 the assembly approved funds to defray the initial costs of the expedition. Many assemblymen still opposed Clinton's support of the war, however, and his position became unenviable when the large and costly expedition was not carried through. Clinton's most serious opposition came from a faction led by James DeLancey. Clinton had early allied himself with DeLancey and had appointed him chief justice of the Supreme Court, but after 1746 DeLancey became his vehement foe. DeLancey's position was strengthened in 1747 when he was named lieutenant governor of New York. In a search for new allies Clinton gave control of Indian affairs to William Johnson and sought political advice from Cadwallader Colden, a veteran councillor. After the war he attempted to regain his authority and harden his dealings with the assembly, on the advice of Governor William Shirley of Massachusetts, but the DeLancey forces maintained the upper hand. Clinton begged the Board of Trade for assistance and asked to be relieved as his health was beginning to deteriorate. He also advised the board that in future the salaries of royal governors should be made independent of colonial legislatures. In 1753 he was finally replaced by Sir Danvers OSBORN.

Clinton seems to have been generally unfit by temperament, experienced, and political skill to manage the astute politicans of New York with their factional alignments. He worked diligently to carry out his instructions, but was largely unaided by the Board of Trade in his efforts to maintain the royal prerogative against the opposition of his assembly. His one success was in the area of Indian affairs, where his securing of an alliance with the Six Nations laid the basis of a permanent Anglo-Iroquois accord which survived the American War of Independence.

Clinton received various promotions in the Royal Navy while governor of New York, and rose to the rank of admiral in 1747, though he never served at sea again. His fortune upon returning to England seems to have been modest and he had financial problems for the rest of his life. In 1754 he was elected to parliament for Saltash, Cornwall, and became admiral of the fleet in 1757. He applied unsuccessfully to Newcastle for a pension, and died at age 75 in July 1761.

Clinton's daughter, Lucy Mary, married Captain, later Admiral, Robert Roddam; his son, Sir Henry Clinton, was commander of British forces in North America during part of the American Revolution.

DENNIS F. WALLE

Many original letters of George Clinton are in the Clements Library. See: *Guide to the manuscript collections in the William L. Clements Library*, comp. H. H. Peckham (Ann Arbor, Mich., 1942); 2nd ed., comp. W. S. Ewing (Ann Arbor, 1953).

BM, Add. MSS, 32856, f.225. *Johnson papers* (Sullivan *et al.*), I, IX. *NYCD* (O'Callaghan and Fernow). PRO, *Acts of P.C., Col., 1720–45*; *CSP, Col., 1731*; *JTP, 1728/29–1731, 1741/42–1749, 1749/50–1753*. William Smith, *The history of the late province of New-York, from its discovery, to the appointment of Governor Colden, in 1762* (2v., New York, 1830), II, 82–181. Peter Wraxall, *An abridgement of the Indian affairs contained in four folio volumes, transacted in the colony of New York, from the year 1678 to the year 1751*, ed. C. H. McIlwain (Harvard historical studies, XXI, Cambridge, Mass., 1915), 231–51.

Charnock, *Biographia navalis*, IV. Arthur Collins, *The peerage of England* (5th ed., 8v., London, 1779), II, 275–78. *DAB*. *The history of parliament: the House of Commons 1754–1790*, ed. Lewis Namier and John Brooke (3v., London, 1964), II, 222. P. U. Bonomi, *A factious people; politics and society in colonial New York* (New York, 1971), 150–51, 153–57. S. N. Katz, *Newcastle's New York; Anglo-American politics, 1732–1753* (Cambridge, Mass., 1968), 33–35, 179. M. M. Klein, "William Livingston's *A review of the military operations in North-America*," *The colonial legacy*, ed. L. H. Leder (2v., New York, 1971), II, 109–13. L. W. Labaree, *Royal government in America: a study of the British colonial system before 1783* (New Haven, Conn., 1930), 286–93. Lounsbury, *British fishery in Nfld*. W. B. Willcox, *Portrait of a general: Sir Henry Clinton in the War of Independence* (New York, 1964), 3–13.

COATS, WILLIAM, HBC captain and explorer; m. Mary McCliesh, daughter of Thomas McCliesh; d. January 1752.

William Coats entered the service of the Hudson's Bay Company in November 1726, and on his first voyage to the bay in 1727 lost his new command, the *Mary*, off Cape Farewell, Greenland. The misfortune was repeated nine years later when ice at the entrance to Hudson Strait beset the *Hudson's Bay* "and crush'd our sides in, and sunk her in twenty minutes." Despite these disasters, and accusations in 1742 that he had traded brandy with the garrison at Albany (Fort Albany, Ont.) (where, according to Joseph Isbister*, its factor, the captain "can in one day oversett a reformation of 2 years"), Coats retained the confidence of the London committee. He continued to sail one of the HBC ships to the bay each year and was awarded a gratuity of 50 guineas in 1744 for his "Services and fidelity for many years past." At about this time he began compiling a geography of the Hudson Bay region, since "no other person before my time ever collected so many notes, and but few have had more experience nor better opportunity to explain this geography."

In 1749 the HBC selected Coats to renew the exploration of the East Main (the eastern coasts of Hudson and James bays) begun five years earlier by Thomas MITCHELL and John LONGLAND, both of whom sailed on this later venture. Rumours in England that silver and furs were to be found along the East Main and that Richmond Gulf (Lac Guillaume-Delisle, Que.), discovered in 1744, perhaps led through the Labrador peninsula to the Atlantic coast made it essential for the company to complete its exploration of the coastal area. Although the official journals kept on the voyage have disappeared, Coats' private notes, his splendid manuscript maps, and his report to the HBC, show that he explored almost 500 miles of coastline from Cape Digges at the entrance of Hudson Strait to Richmond Gulf. In the sheltered waters of this gulf Coats was convinced he had found a suitable spot for a post, farther north than any other existing at this time; and the next year he was sent back to supervise the establishment of Richmond Fort, which he also visited with supplies in 1751. This was his last voyage for in November 1751 the London committee was informed that Coats had regularly engaged in illicit trade while in Hudson Bay, and after pleading guilty to this charge he was dismissed. He had been treated gener-

Cobb

ously by the company, with gratuities amounting to £180 over and above his normal salary in the previous two years, but he had abused his position in a systematic and cynical way.

Within a few weeks Coats was dead. No firm evidence of suicide has been found, and the parish register of his local church in East London, St Anne's, Limehouse, records his burial on 13 Jan. 1752 without comment. The parish registers and his will show that Coats was a family man of some substance. He had six children, a wife whose father had been an important HBC officer in the 1720s, and three houses – two in East London and one in Durham. His ownership of the latter, which had belonged to his mother, suggests that Coats' family home was on Teeside, a nursery of sailors from which three of his fellow captains came. Whatever the cause of death, William Coats' end was a singularly melancholy one. He died dismissed and disgraced. The notes painstakingly collected for his projected geography of Hudson Bay, and his maps of the East Main, lay unpublished and forgotten; and not until the rescue of his manuscript jottings by the Hakluyt Society in 1852 did this enterprising seaman begin to achieve recognition as an observer and explorer.

GLYNDWR WILLIAMS

[Coats' career with the HBC is outlined in HBC Arch. A.1/34–38, A.1/120–22. Personal information about him and his family is in his will at PRO, Prob. 11/792, and in St Anne's Parish (Limehouse, East London), Parish registers, 1734–52. Six of Coats' manuscript maps have survived: five in HBC Arch. G.1/14–18, and one in G.B., Admiralty, Hydrographic department (Taunton, Eng.), A/344, Ai/1. His notes came into the possession of the Arctic explorer Sir William Edward Parry*, who gave permission for their publication in 1852 as *The geography of Hudson's Bay: being the remarks of Captain W. Coats, in many voyages to that locality, between the years 1727 and 1751*, ed. John Barrow (Hakluyt Soc., 1st ser., XI, London); they then disappeared once more. Two of Coats' maps are reproduced in an article by Glyndwr Williams, "Captain Coats and exploration along the East Main," *Beaver* (Winnipeg), outfit 294 (winter 1963), 4–13. The nomenclature on the maps is analysed by the same writer in "East London names in Hudson Bay," *East London Papers: a journal of history, social studies and the arts* (London), VII (1964), 23–30. G.W.]

COBB, SILVANUS, mariner, military officer; b. 18 March 1709/10 at Plymouth, Massachusetts, son of Elisha Cobb and Lydia Rider; m. Elizabeth Rider 22 Oct. 1734 and had one daughter; d. probably at Havana, Cuba, in the summer of 1762.

Little is known of Silvanus Cobb's life before

1745, when he raised a company of soldiers in Plymouth for the New England expedition against Louisbourg, Île Royale (Cape Breton Island) [*see* William PEPPERRELL]; he was then a captain in the 7th Massachusetts Regiment. After the siege ended he served on garrison duty at Louisbourg. He was part of a committee chosen in July 1745 to "search for and secure all the plunder belonging to the army," and in March 1746 was ordered to inspect houses in the town and provide quarters for soldiers so that the barracks could be repaired.

In January 1746/47 Cobb was sent from Annapolis Royal, Nova Scotia, by Paul MASCARENE, the commanding officer, with reinforcements for Colonel Arthur NOBLE's garrison at Grand Pré; Cobb was not present when French forces attacked the garrison later that month. He commanded a detachment of Colonel Samuel WALDO's regiment sent to the Minas region in March to restore English authority and in April visited Chignecto as Mascarene's emissary to exchange some French prisoners. In 1748 he was master of a vessel carrying dispatches for Mascarene, and that August accompanied Charles Morris* and his soldiers on a reconnaissance up the Bay of Fundy.

Governor Edward Cornwallis* hired Cobb's sloop *York* for government service in January 1749/50 at a monthly rate of £22 10s., paying Cobb 10s. per day as master. Thus Cobb's vessel became part of Captain John ROUS's sea militia which helped keep open communications along the coast of Nova Scotia and with New England. Cornwallis described Cobb as a settler who "knows every Harbour and every Creek in the Bay [of Fundy], a man fit for any bold enterprise." He instructed Cobb to arm his vessel at Boston and recruit additional crew. Cobb was to sail secretly to Chignecto to capture Abbé Jean-Louis Le Loutre*, whom Cornwallis blamed for inciting Indian raids in Nova Scotia. The venture had to be abandoned after Spencer Phips, lieutenant governor of Massachusetts, allowed Cobb to advertise in Boston a "Cruise" against "the Enemy." In the summer of 1750 Cobb encountered French forces in a small fort at the mouth of the Saint John River, in territory which was claimed by both the French and the English. When the French commander, Charles Deschamps* de Boishébert, declared that he would remain until the boundaries were settled, Cobb told him "if he maintained the land, I would the sea."

For the next decade Cobb's vessel was employed in taking troops and supplies to Fort Anne (Annapolis Royal), Fort Edward (Windsor), Fort Lawrence (near Amherst), and the Saint John River, and in convoying transports which carried German settlers to found the town of Lunenburg in 1753 [*see* Patrick SUTHERLAND]. In the winters of 1753, 1754, 1755, and 1756 he was ordered to Chignecto with stores for the garrison and remained there each year till spring. Cobb had a house and farm near Fort Lawrence where he lived with his wife and daughter, and where, according to Jedediah Preble, he owned many cattle, sheep, swine, and a large supply of claret, the quality of which was highly approved by his friend Preble. Colonel John Winslow* stayed at Cobb's farm in the early days of the siege of Fort Beauséjour (near Sackville, N.B.) in June 1755. Cobb's vessel, the *York and Halifax* (80 tons), was active bringing supplies to the besiegers, and was attacked by French forces. On 28 August Cobb was sent with some of the soldiers of Major Joseph Frye to expel the Acadians from Chipoudy (Shepody, N.B.) and burn their houses. At Petitcodiac (near Hillsborough, N.B.) a party of Canadian troops and Indians attacked the New England soldiers, whose armed vessels operated with difficulty because of strong currents caused by the high Fundy tides.

Cobb was also active in 1754 and 1755 in the prevention of clandestine trade between the Acadians and the French and was the only master of a provincial vessel to bring prizes into the vice-admiralty court at Halifax. In April 1755, outside Halifax harbour, he seized the English schooner *Wolf* for conducting illegal trade. After the vessel was condemned, Cobb received £16 4s. 8d. as one-third share of the prize. Later that month, while searching for a wrecked vessel at Port La Tour, Cobb discovered the French schooner *Marguerite* (*Margarett*), laden with provisions, guns, and other military stores from Louisbourg destined for French troops on the Saint John River. He returned to Halifax with the news and was ordered by Governor Charles LAWRENCE to blockade the harbour until Captain William Kensey (MacKenzie?) arrived in the warship *Vulture*, and then to assist Kensey in capturing the French prize. A dispute arose later between Cobb and Kensey about their respective shares and each received £103 14s. 1d.

From 1755 to 1758 Cobb continued to cruise off the Nova Scotia coast. He is said to have conducted General WOLFE on a reconnaissance near the Louisbourg fortress in 1758 on board his vessel, and to have received high praise from Wolfe for his skilled seamanship and bravery. In the fall of that year, after the English captured Louisbourg, he accompanied the expedition under Robert Monckton* to the Saint John River to drive away the French and Acadians, and again displayed superior seamanship in these dangerous waters. Monckton had to rely on the smaller sloops and schooners to carry his forces and sailed upriver on board Cobb's vessel.

Cobb's sloop *York and Halifax* was engaged in many duties in connection with the movement of New England settlers to Nova Scotia. In July 1759 he transported their agents to view the lands available for settlement [*see* Robert DENISON], but after he reported to Governor Lawrence that a number of Acadians and Indians at Cape Sable had fired on them, the settlements were postponed. In April, June, and November 1760 he assisted a local committee in Plymouth in bringing settlers to Liverpool, and remained in Liverpool for the winter to protect the new township. In the grant of Liverpool Township, dated 1 Sept. 1759, Silvanus Cobb had received one share and his brother Jabez 1½ shares. The proprietors' committee gave permission on 1 July 1760 to Captain Cobb for a "Spot to build a Store, House & Wharf," and to Cobb and several others to dam the mill brook and flood four acres of land to provide water for a saw and grist mill. Tradition states that Captain Cobb demolished a house on Cape Cod and brought the materials on his own vessel to Liverpool where he built his home – the oldest house in Liverpool until it was burned in the 1940s. In April 1761 Cobb was sent to Boston to bring settlers to Truro and Onslow, and that autumn he was transporting Indian corn supplied by the government to the New England settlers in Cumberland and Kings counties, who had not been able to raise enough grain to feed themselves.

Cobb is said to have succumbed to sickness during the siege of Havana in the summer of 1762, expressing his chagrin that he had not died a soldier's death in battle. He may have gone there via New York with the rangers of Joseph Gorham*. A capable soldier and sailor, Cobb helped to protect the English possessions in Nova Scotia and was instrumental in extending the influence of New England in Nova Scotia. He cooperated with the English authorities to secure more effective control of the province and is remembered for his part in establishing settlements of New Englanders on lands formerly occupied by the Acadians in Nova Scotia.

PHYLLIS R. BLAKELEY

Halifax County Court of Probate, C85. Liverpool, N.S., Town Hall, Town clerk's office, N.S. Proprietors' records, 1 July 1760, 28 Aug. 1761, 12 Feb. 1762 (typescript in PAC, PANS). Plymouth, Mass., Town clerk's office, Town of Plymouth: births, deaths, mar-

Collet

riages and publishments, IA, 62, 181, 218, 303; Town records, III, 425. PAC, MG 11, Nova Scotia A, 30, pp.55–58, 145, 173–74, 187–88, 202–4; 38, pp.106–15. PANS, MG 1, 474, no.155; 824, Cobb family; RG 1, 21, pp.151–52, 172–73; 163/1, pp.24–25, 70; 163/2, pp.6, 14; 163/3, pp.3, 21, 26, 28, 29, 32, 40, 45, 49, 155, 164, 169; 164/1, p.78; 164/2, pp.29, 59; 165, pp.3, 19, 36, 52, 70, 80, 90, 127, 184, 185; 206, pp.61, 85, 115; 492, pp.204–9. PRO, CO 217/9, ff.188–93.

"The Pepperrell papers," Mass. Hist. Soc. *Coll.*, 6th ser., X (1899), 33, 56, 85, 195. *N. S. Archives, I; IV.* "Report of the proceedings of the troops on the expedition up St. John's River in the Bay of Fundy under the command of Colonel Monckton," PAC *Report, 1905,* II, app.A, pt. III, 236–41. Winslow, "Journal," N.S. Hist. Soc. *Coll.* III (1883), 151, 152; IV (1885), 145–48, 228, 241. Gipson, *British empire before the American revolution,* VII, 260–62, 264–68, 305–6. Murdoch, *History of Nova-Scotia,* II, 113, 172, 177, 183, 348. W. O. Raymond, *The river St John, its physical features, legends and history from 1604 to 1784* (Saint John, N.B., 1910), 197, 217, 226, 232, 252. F. E. Crowell, "Cobb family," *Yarmouth Herald,* 8 July 1930.

COLLET. *See* CALLET

COLLIER, JOHN, military officer, member of the Nova Scotia Council, judge in the Court of Vice-Admiralty, justice of the Supreme Court of Nova Scotia; b. in England; d. 14 April 1769 at Falmouth, Nova Scotia.

The founding of Halifax, Nova Scotia, in 1749 provided John Collier with an opportunity to launch a new career. He was then a retired army captain, and it is known that he was a protégé of the Earl of Halifax. According to Governor Edward Cornwallis*, Collier "belonged to the better sort of inhabitants," and thus was marked for appointment to office in the colony. On 18 July 1749 he was named a justice of the peace and on 27 Jan. 1752 was appointed to the Nova Scotia Council. He was given the key post of judge of the Court of Vice-Admiralty on 12 April 1753, succeeding Benjamin Green*.

Collier's outstanding contribution to the development of early Nova Scotia was made in the latter role. Particularly during the Seven Years' War the Court of Vice-Admiralty played an important part in the administration of justice in the colony. Collier, the presiding judge during this period, steadfastly refused to be swayed by local pressure. His unequivocal stand on judicial matters explains in part his unpopularity with Governor Charles LAWRENCE, who attempted on more than one occasion to tamper with decisions of the court. In August 1756, for example, Collier dealt with a petition concerning the French ship *Equito,* captured by a British squadron off Louisbourg, and declared it a lawful prize

as it had been taken after the declaration of war that spring; Lawrence ordered him to halt proceedings but Collier refused and eventually had his way. In April 1757 he ruled that a Dutch ship, *Patience,* captured by the Halifax-based privateer *Musketto,* was not a prize of war. Soon after he upheld a charge by five seamen of the *Patience* claiming "extreme cruelty and theft of goods" by the captain and crew of the *Musketto,* and ordered that restitution be made and damages paid to the Dutch owners.

In his capacity as a member of the Nova Scotia Council, Collier also opposed Lawrence. With fellow councillor Charles Morris* and Robert Grant – a Scottish merchant and later himself a councillor – Collier launched a complaint in January 1758 with the imperial authorities concerning the alleged dictatorial behaviour of Governor Lawrence. In a letter to his patron the Earl of Halifax, Collier suggested that the inhabitants of Halifax were "sufficiently alarmed . . . [that] in six months we shall see this province wholly under military government." Although an early advocate of representative government Collier also found himself at odds late in 1758 with the first Nova Scotia House of Assembly when, under the leadership of George Suckling, it requested that he furnish a schedule of fees for the Court of Vice-Admiralty. Collier's refusal on the ground that he held the office of judge through an imperial commission and consequently was not answerable to the assembly earned him a formal rebuke by the lower house. The incident was the first example of a financial dispute between the council and the assembly.

Collier possessed a strong personality and was a man of consistent views, qualities which stood him in good stead as judge of the Court of Vice-Admiralty, but also help to explain his running battle on the council with Chief Justice Jonathan Belcher*, lieutenant governor from 1761 to 1763 and a man of equally firm views. Collier worked against Belcher and followed the familiar pattern of petitioning imperial authorities regarding the "Unsteady and Irresolute Kind of Conduct (which indeed tinctures the whole of the Lt Governor's administration)." After June 1764, when Collier was appointed an assistant justice of the Supreme Court of Nova Scotia with Charles Morris, he continued to disagree with Belcher, but their disputes were of a more personal nature, arising from the latter's unwillingness to share responsibility with his fellow judges.

Collier played a prominent part in the civic life of early Halifax. He was named a trustee of St Paul's church in 1759 and acted on a commission to allocate government grants to the church. He

130

was also a captain in the militia and served on the board of trustees which established and maintained the Halifax Common.

In July 1768 he attended council for the last time. He died intestate the following April – probably a bachelor. He had acquired considerable land in the Falmouth area, but the entire estate was ordered sold to meet accumulated debts.

WILLIAM B. HAMILTON

PAC, MG 11, Nova Scotia A, 62, pp.51–52; 69, pp.174–91; 91, pp.218–52; MG 18, F20. PANS, RG 1, 164/2, pp.277, 302–4; 206; 215; 216; 492; 493. *Nova Scotia Chronicle and Weekly Advertiser*, 18 April, 10 May 1769. Brebner, *Neutral Yankees*. R. V. Harris, *The Church of Saint Paul in Halifax, Nova Scotia: 1749–1949* (Toronto, 1949). T. B. Akins, "History of Halifax City," N.S. Hist. Soc. *Coll.*, VIII (1895). D. G. L. Fraser, "The origin and function of the Court of Vice-Admiralty in Halifax 1749–1759," N.S. Hist. Soc. *Coll.*, XXXIII (1961), 57–80.

COLLIER PENDU, LE. *See* KAGHSWAGHTA-NIUNT

COLVILL (Colville), ALEXANDER, 7th Baron COLVILL of Culross, naval officer; b. 28 Feb. 1717 (o.s.), probably at Dundee, Scotland, eldest son of John Colvill, 6th Baron Colvill, and Elizabeth Johnston; m. 1 Oct. 1768 to Lady Elizabeth, daughter of Alexander Erskine, 5th Earl of Kellie, and widow of Walter Macfarlane; d. 21 May 1770 at Drumsheugh, near Edinburgh, Scotland.

Alexander Colvill's early career was unusual in that he entered the navy by procuring a king's letter and becoming a volunteer per order (roughly equivalent to a modern naval cadet) at a time (1732) when the system had practically disappeared. Most boys joined ships through "interest" with the captain, but the Colvill family apparently had little wealth and no connections in the service. Colvill left Dundee at the age of 15 and travelled to Bantry Bay (Republic of Ireland), where in April 1733 he joined HMS *Lime*, 20 guns. After two years as a volunteer in this ship he became a midshipman. In 1737 he joined the 20-gun *Phoenix* and in 1738 the *Rose*, 20 guns. On 25 Jan. 1739/40 he passed for lieutenant and after eight months' unemployment – a consequence, no doubt, of having no "interest" – was promoted on 31 Aug. 1739. Despite preparations for war with Spain he had difficulty finding a ship, but on 6 Sept. 1739 he joined the bomb vessel *Alderney*, sailing for the West Indies as tender to a ship under whose captain he had previously served.

Colvill took part in the sieges of Portobello (Portobelo, Panama) and Cartagena (Colombia). In 1740, for the first time since leaving home in 1732, he saw his father, whose regiment was in the West Indies. While they were both still there his father died, in 1741. Consequently, as Colvill later remembered, "my health was for some time visibly impaired." On 17 April he had joined the 70-gun *Hampton Court*; in September he returned to England in that ship, and was able to advance his interests by dispensing patronage on behalf of a relation of Daniel Finch, Lord Winchelsea, the first lord of the admiralty.

On 18 April 1742 as second lieutenant of *Russell*, 80 guns, he sailed for the Mediterranean. On 9 November he joined Admiral Thomas Mathews' flagship, the 90-gun *Namur*. He was placed in command first of the *Mercury* fireship and then the *Terrible*, bomb, and on 25 June 1743 he took command of the *Sutherland*, hospital ship. On 5 March 1743/44 he received post in command of the *Dursley* galley, 20 guns. On 24 July 1744 he took command of HMS *Leopard*, 20 guns. In this ship he distinguished himself, in the ensuing four years, by the capture and destruction of a large number of vessels, some of them under neutral flags. "Certain critical circumstances will sometimes occur," he recalled of these activities, "wherein a vigorous exertion of Powers may become necessary, without much consideration in point of Equity." He returned to England from the Mediterranean in the *Leopard* in 1748, paying off his ship on 19 December. His prize money amounted to about £5,000. With the death of his mother in 1748 he had become responsible for the support of two sisters and a younger brother.

From 1749 to 1752 he commanded the 20-gun *Success*, the station ship in New England, where by his efficient supervision of the annual convoy of the salt trade from the West Indies, he established an unusually harmonious relationship with the merchants of Boston. When he returned to England he won preferment "from a kind of negative merit" with the Board of Admiralty, his careering accounts having amounted to only half those of other station captains in America. On 10 Jan. 1753 he was given command of the 70-gun *Northumberland*, the beginning of a nine-year association with that ship. After a trooping assignment to Minorca, *Northumberland* reverted to the status of guardship in Plymouth until January 1755, when the fleet began to come to readiness for war.

In March 1755 Colvill sailed in *Northumberland* with Admiral BOSCAWEN, taking part in the attempt to intercept French reinforcements to

Colvill

North America, and returning with Boscawen's squadron in November. In the following year *Northumberland* cruised in home waters; in 1757 she sailed in Vice-Admiral Francis Holburne*'s squadron to Nova Scotia. After the attempt to capture Louisbourg, Île Royale (Cape Breton Island), that year had been given up, *Northumberland* was among the ships lying in wait off Louisbourg for the French fleet in the harbour, and she was caught in the disastrous hurricane of September 1757. She sailed then to Halifax, and when Holburne returned to England on 14 November he ordered Colvill to hoist a commodore's broad pendant and assume the duties of commander-in-chief, North America.

Holburne instructed Colvill to prepare a careening wharf in Halifax and to have the squadron ready for sea as early as possible for the Louisbourg expedition of 1758. Because it was a severe winter, it was not possible to prepare the wharf, but eight ships of the line were ready for sea, and another ship of the line and a sloop were cruising, when Sir Charles Hardy arrived from New York to assume command on 22 March. Colvill remained a commodore. The squadron sailed on 5 April and blockaded Louisbourg until 14 June, making an important contribution to the success of the expedition. Much to Colvill's indignation, the arrival of several captains senior to him resulted in the order to haul down his broad pendant in June. On completion of the campaign, he returned to England, having lost a third of his ship's company to scurvy.

In 1759 the ship returned to America, arriving at the Louisbourg rendezvous on 14 May for the expedition to Quebec. She was unable to play a large part in the campaign, being anchored with the other great ships under Rear-Admiral Philip DURELL east of the Île d'Orléans from 27 June to 22 September. After the surrender of Quebec the commander of the British naval forces during the operation, Vice-Admiral Charles Saunders*, ordered Colvill to take over as commander-in-chief, North America, for the winter. Colvill's task was to prepare the squadron at Halifax for a return to the St Lawrence at the first possible opportunity in the spring.

In 1760 a squadron sailing directly from England under Captain Robert SWANTON reached Quebec on 15 May, and raised the siege that had been mounted by Lévis*. Nevertheless, it has generally been considered that Colvill's ability to place his squadron, including five ships of the line, in the St Lawrence by 16 May was one of the decisive factors in the conquest of Canada. Only then did James Murray*, commanding at Quebec, gain full control of the river. Colvill's achievement was enhanced by the difficult ice conditions he had to overcome.

In the ensuing months, as the senior naval officer in North America, he armed and fitted sloops and schooners to search out small French privateers in the lower St Lawrence. A squadron under Captain John Byron*, sailing independently from Louisbourg, destroyed French warships and vessels that had taken refuge in the Restigouche River. To deal with the situation above Quebec, Colvill sent Captain Joseph Deane with HMS *Porcupine* and a fleet of vessels to support the army's advance on Montreal. After the capitulation of 8 Sept. 1760, Colvill arranged transportation for more than 4,000 French prisoners to La Rochelle, France, sending the rest to England in ships of Swanton's squadron. He established regulations for pilotage, appointed a master shipwright to maintain vessels required by the army, and supplied the Quebec garrison with wood from the Île d'Orléans, as well as coal from Louisbourg, to see them through the winter. He sailed for Halifax on 10 Oct. 1760, leaving Swanton to supervise the transportation of prisoners, and arrived in Halifax on 24 October. Admiralty orders for Swanton to relieve Colvill were received at Halifax, but by then Swanton was already on his way home.

In the next two years, plagued with "sore throats, swelled legs, innumerable pains all over me, sciatica, scurvy, rheumatism," Colvill devoted himself principally to improving the dockyard facilities at Halifax. With the outbreak of war against Spain in 1762 he diverted available forces for service in the Havana expedition. On 3 July 1762 he learned of Charles-Louis d'Arsac* de Ternay's capture of St John's, Newfoundland, with two ships of the line, a frigate, two ships *en flute* and 570 men. Colvill detained ships as they arrived at Halifax so that on 10 August he was able to sail with *Northumberland*, the 40-gun *Gosport* (Capt. John Jervis), and the Massachusetts provincial vessel *King George*, 20 guns, to join the 50-gun *Antelope* (Capt. Thomas Graves) and the 24-gun *Syren* (Capt. Charles Douglas*) at Placentia (Plaisance). He had tried without success to persuade the authorities in Nova Scotia to provide troops for an expedition to relieve St John's, but on 11 September Colonel William Amherst arrived from New York with 1,300 men, and on 13 September the force landed at Torbay. The French quietly withdrew two days later, easily eluding the English squadron under cover of night and fog. This escape would seem to reflect unfavourably on Colvill and the exceptionally distinguished captains under his command, but no repercussions followed. He had already been recalled to England, where he arrived on 26 October to find he had been promoted rear-admiral of the white on 21 October. The Newfoundland expedition had at least one consequence of importance: James Cook*, then master of the *Northumberland*, and Joseph Frederick Wallet DesBarres* had begun a survey of the Newfoundland coast on Colvill's orders.

The admiralty intended to give Colvill a command in the Mediterranean, but the signing of the preliminaries of peace resulted in cancellation of this commission. On 27 Jan. 1763, he relieved Durell as port admiral at Plymouth. In June, with much reluctance, he accepted the new North American command. He sailed on 31 August and arrived at Halifax on 13 October. There he established a "fixed Headquarters, or general Rendezvous," partly because of the excellent harbour and the proximity of the place to the new acquisitions of Cape Breton and Quebec, but mainly because it was "the best place in the whole extent of America for refitting the King's Ships," and offered fewer opportunities for desertion than more southerly ports. His ships were stationed from Quebec to Florida with a view to stamping out the notorious disregard in America of the trade and navigation laws. Attempts at enforcement met with various difficulties and Colvill's admitted hopes of financial advantage were disappointed. A royal proclamation of 1 June 1763 had led him to expect an unprecedented one-sixth of the proceeds from the sale of ships condemned for smuggling. But loopholes in the law, active interference by colonial officials, and the impossibility of keeping naval ships properly manned in North America tended to deprive Colvill of "an advantage, in the full assurance of which I undertook this voyage." Despite this disappointment his ships did curtail smuggling; he was instrumental in the success of surveys of Nova Scotia and the Gulf of St Lawrence; and he established Halifax as a naval base in time of peace. In August 1766 Philip Durell arrived to assume command in America but died shortly after coming ashore. Colvill therefore left Captain Joseph Deane in charge at Halifax before sailing for England. He was not employed again in the remaining four years of his life.

Colvill left no heirs by his brief marriage, but between 1750 and 1766 his naval "family" (which normally comprised his secretary and servants) had on three occasions included the mothers of his natural children. The first of these women was from New England, identified only by the initials "D.T." She died in 1752, but her son Charles, born near Boston in 1751, entered the navy and became a lieutenant. The second, "B.S.," came from Exeter, England. She joined Colvill in Plymouth in 1753 and died in England shortly before his return from Halifax in 1762. Her son, James Alexander, was born in 1760 and was living in Exeter in 1770. Finally, in 1765 Elizabeth Greene of Halifax gave Colvill a daughter, Sophia. He charged the Reverend John Breynton*, rector of St Paul's, Halifax, with the care of funds set aside for his Nova Scotian family. To his children – who "came into the World stigmatised with the name of Bastard thro' my Crime" – and their guardians, to his wife, and to the children of his two sisters, the admiral left his fortune, all of which was acquired "in the Service of my King and Country in the two last Wars." His younger brother, who had also entered the navy, had been lost at sea in 1761. A half-length portrait of Colvill remains in the possession of John Colville, the present Lord Colville of Culross, in Fifeshire.

W. A. B. DOUGLAS

PAC, MG 18, L1, Colvill's memoirs, 1732–64 (photostat). PRO, Adm. 1/480–82; Prob. 11/960, f.354. *Correspondence of William Pitt* (Kimball). *Despatches of Rear-Admiral Philip Durell, 1758–1759, and Rear-Admiral Lord Colville, 1759–1761*, ed. C. H. Little (Maritime Museum of Canada, *Occasional papers*, no.4, Halifax, 1958). *Despatches of Rear-Admiral Sir Charles Hardy, 1757–1758, and Vice-Admiral Francis Holburne, 1757*, ed. C. H. Little (Maritime Museum of Canada, *Occasional papers*, no.2, Halifax, 1958). *Despatches of Vice-Admiral Charles Saunders, 1759–1760: the naval side of the capture of Quebec*, ed. C. H. Little (Maritime Museum of Canada, *Occasional papers*, no.3, Halifax, 1958). *The recapture of Saint John's, Newfoundland: dispatches of Rear-Admiral, Lord Colville, 1761–1762*, ed. C. H. Little (Maritime Museum of Canada, *Occasional papers*, no.6, Halifax, 1959).

D. M. Clark, "The impressment of seamen in the American colonies," *Essays in colonial history presented to Charles McLean Andrews by his students* (New Haven, Conn., 1931), 198–224. J. S. Corbett, *England in the Seven Years' War; a study in combined strategy* (2nd ed., 2v., London, 1918). Carl Ubbelohde, *The vice-admiralty courts and the American revolution* (Chapel Hill, N.C., 1960). N. R. Stout, "The Royal Navy in American waters, 1760–1775" (unpubl. PHD thesis, University of Wisconsin, Madison, Wis., 1962).

COMBLES (Combes), JEAN-CLAUDE-HENRI DE LOMBARD DE. *See* LOMBARD

CONCEPTION, MARGUERITE ROY, *dite* **DE LA.** *See* ROY

CONSTANTIN, JUSTINIEN (baptized **Louis-Alexandre**), Recollet, missionary; b. 13 Nov.

Constantin

1716 at Quebec, son of Denis Constantin, a bourgeois, and Louise Bacon; d. 28 March 1760 at Saint-Joseph de la Nouvelle-Beauce (Saint-Joseph de Beauce, Que.).

Louis-Alexandre Constantin studied at the Jesuit college and on 4 Aug. 1734 he was admitted into the noviciate of the Recollets of Quebec under the name of Brother Justinien. He completed his training in 1739 but before he could be ordained had to wait two years for the arrival of a bishop in Quebec. Bishop Pontbriand [DUBREIL] conferred the minor orders and the diaconate upon him on 20 and 22 Sept. 1741 and the priesthood the following day.

The first 12 years of his ministry were spent at the convent in Quebec; on occasion he ministered to the parishes of Charlesbourg and Saint-Joseph (Lévis). Towards the end of 1751 or at the beginning of 1752 he went to the convent in Montreal. In 1753 he returned to Quebec and succeeded Father Bonaventure Cartier as missionary to the parishes of Saint-Joseph (Saint-Joseph-de-Beauce) and Sainte-Marie de la Nouvelle-Beauce. His ministry in this region lasted about six years. In 1753 he built a presbytery at Sainte-Marie; this saved him from having to live in the homes of parishioners, where missionaries serving parishes without a presbytery usually lodged. In addition he drew up a few contracts for marriages and land grants, there being no notary in this region.

But Father Justinien's most remarkable work was his active participation in the steps taken to obtain a suitable road between the Nouvelle-Beauce region and the St Lawrence River. This route, "following the trail which [had already been] opened by the settlers," was laid out in 1758 by Ignace-François-Pierre Martin* de Lino, the last chief road commissioner (*grand voyer*) of New France. It enabled the habitants of this region to escape from their isolation and to get to Quebec more easily. The road, "twenty-four feet wide, with a ditch three feet in width on each side," was about 30 miles long and began at the seigneury of Saint-Étienne, ending at the parish of Saint-Henri in the seigneury of Lauson. The inhabitants of Beauce wished to perpetuate the memory of the Recollet by naming this road the Route Justinienne. Today it is a section of the Route du Président-Kennedy.

Justinien Constantin, the last missionary to be stationed at Nouvelle-Beauce under the old régime, died at Saint-Joseph of "a violent illness that lasted two months" on 28 March 1760; he was buried in the parish church on 2 April.

MICHEL PAQUIN

Archives des Franciscains (Montréal), Dossier Justinien Constantin. P.-G. Roy, *Inv. coll. pièces jud. et not.*, I, 227, 228, 230; *Inv. procès-verbaux des grands voyers*, I, 174; IV, 221. Honorius Provost, *Sainte-Marie de la Nouvelle-Beauce; histoire religieuse* (Québec, 1967), 16–20; *Sainte-Marie de la Nouvelle-Beauce; histoire civile* (Québec, 1970), 362–64. Ivanhoë Caron, "Historique de la voirie dans la province de Québec," *BRH*, XXXIX (1933), 214.

CONSTANTIN, PIERRE (sometimes known as **Lavallée Constantin**), fisherman, trader, and militia officer; baptized 21 April 1666 at Sillery, son of Guillaume Constantin, and Jeanne Masse; d. *c.* 1750.

Nothing is known of Pierre Constantin before his marriage on 6 Nov. 1696 at Saint-Augustin near Quebec to Marguerite-Suzanne Guyon Durouvray. Soon afterwards he purchased a house at Quebec and was identified as a voyageur. In 1700 he was hired by Augustin Le Gardeur* de Courtemanche to travel to the Rivière des Esquimaux (St Paul River) to trade with the Indians and to erect a post, and was thus one of the first Canadians to explore this forbidding region of the north shore of the St Lawrence. The following spring he was hired by Mme Le Gardeur de Courtemanche to trade in the same region and to locate summer and winter trading sites. He was paid 600 *livres*, and a hogshead of wine, and was to receive half of the profits from any hunting.

Constantin continued to work for Courtemanche but approached François Hazeur*, entrepreneur and member of the Conseil Souverain, to try to obtain a concession on the northwest shore of Newfoundland. Finally in the spring of 1705 Hazeur was granted the seigneury of Portachoix. Constantin came to work for him in return for joint ownership and one-half of the profits from the inshore fishery, sealing, and trade with the Indians. The arrangement was renewed in May 1708, when they had four employees at Portachoix. When Hazeur died in June his creditors relinquished their half interest for 100 *livres* and Constantin found himself a seigneur. Two years later he signed an agreement with his brother-in-law, Jean Guyon Durouvray, to exploit the seigneury for five years: Guyon was to live in Newfoundland, establish a post, and fish and trade in the area. Constantin remained at Quebec to handle cargoes and supplies.

In November 1710 Constantin sold his Quebec property and moved to the seigneury of Maure. Perhaps as a mark of his increased position, he was appointed militia captain in the parish of Saint-Augustin (Saint-Augustin de Québec); later he became a churchwarden.

Constantin's interest shifted back to Labrador from Newfoundland and in May 1713 he obtained a ten-year grant on the Strait of Belle Isle, 30 leagues long and ten leagues deep, from an area not developed by Courtemanche. For the next four seasons he fished for cod and hunted seals at posts he established near the mouth of the Rivière des Français (Pinware River) and at Red Bay. The latter post was destroyed by Eskimos in 1719 and rebuilt two years later. In 1716 he received a grant for life, two leagues on either side of the Rivière des Français and four leagues deep, within the earlier concession. Constantin appeared to realize a profit from his ventures.

During the early 1720s Constantin was associated in the cod fishery with a merchant from Saint-Malo, Sieur Desferières Renaud, but in the summer of 1723 the latter broke their agreement, leaving Constantin with a 5,800 *livre* debt. In 1729 Constantin's request to have his grant extended was refused by Maurepas, minister of Marine, on the grounds that it was not fully exploited. Lack of capital may have been Constantin's difficulty; although he had obtained large land grants he had little to offer beyond shares in future returns.

In 1732 he leased his post at Red Bay and those in Newfoundland for seven years to his son-in-law, Pierre Hamel, and to François and Pierre Trefflé, *dit* Rottot, for 200 *livres* annually. Almost immediately his concession on the Rivière des Français was challenged by Nicolas-Gaspard BOUCAULT and François FOUCAULT, who outfitted a venture into the area that damaged the seal hunting of Constantin's lessees. In 1735 Boucault and Foucault were granted the island of Grand Saint-Modet which Constantin claimed was within the limits of his 1716 concession. The intendant ordered the three claimants to exploit the island jointly, but, despite the support of Governor Charles de BEAUHARNOIS and Intendant Gilles Hocquart* for Boucault and Foucault, Maurepas on appeal from Constantin found in his favour and in September 1740 their concession was revoked. The significance of the outcome is that it favoured a small entrepreneur of peasant background against two important individuals who were supported by the highest officials in the colony.

The exact death date of Pierre Constantin is not known; it is not given in the parish registers of Saint-Augustin. He was still living on 5 June 1750 when he initialled a notarial act. On the following 27 March, however, at the request of his widow, the joint estate was being inventoried.

JAMES S. PRITCHARD

ANQ, Greffe de J.-N. Pinguet de Vaucour, 20 août 1746; Greffe de Simon Sanguinet, 27 mars 1751. "Documents sur Pierre Constantin," P.-G. Roy, édit., *BRH*, XXXIV (1928), 257–63. *Inv. de pièces du Labrador* (P.-G. Roy), I, 16–17, 24–26, 29–30, 48–49, 167–74, 273–75, 287–89; II, 17–19, 114–29, 183–86. *Relation par lettres de l'Amérique septentrionale, années 1709 et 1710,* Camille de Rochemonteix, édit. (Paris, 1904). Bonnault, "Le Canada militaire," APQ *Rapport, 1949–51,* 372–73. A. Roy, *Inv. greffes not.,* XIX, 336. P.-G. Roy, *Inv. concessions,* IV, 180, 183–84. Tanguay, *Dictionnaire.* Benoît Robitaille, "L'habitation de Constantin et la possession du Grand Saint-Modet," *BRH,* LXI (1955), 163–68.

CONTRECŒUR, FRANÇOIS-ANTOINE PÉCAUDY DE. *See* PÉCAUDY

COPE, HENRY, military officer, merchant; b. *c.* 1688 in England; d. in Kingston, Jamaica, on 12 July 1742.

Henry Cope was commissioned ensign in General Webb's regiment in 1706 and served in Europe under the Duke of Marlborough. In 1715 he became a major in General Wetham's regiment, but soon after resigned his commission. He then went to New England and formed business interests in Boston which involved trade extending to Nova Scotia and Newfoundland. Like most men of the period who could afford to, he spent his winters in the comfort of Boston, where he was a member of the congregation of King's Chapel. In November 1725 he was appointed town major of Placentia (Plaisance) in Newfoundland. The duties of this appointment were not too strenuous, however, so that much of his time was spent travelling between New England, Nova Scotia, and Newfoundland.

On 29 Nov. 1729 Governor Richard PHILIPPS appointed Cope a member of the Nova Scotia Council at Annapolis Royal. He thereupon presented a proposal to the governor from the Reverend Andrew Le Mercier, pastor of the French congregation in Boston, for settling 100 or more French Protestant families in Nova Scotia. The proposal was approved by the council and 5,000 acres were granted for this purpose, but the plan did not materialize. In June 1732 Cope and his Boston associates petitioned council for permission to open a colliery at Chignecto, Nova Scotia. Permission was granted and the colliery operated for a few years before being abandoned.

Cope was appointed lieutenant governor of Placentia in 1736, but little is known of his activities there. In April 1737 he was one of five commissioners from Nova Scotia nominated by the crown to arbitrate a boundary dispute between Massachusetts and New Hampshire.

135

Cope

Cope was then resident in Newfoundland, however, and did not proceed on this mission. These same five commissioners were appointed in 1740 to arbitrate a similar dispute between Massachusetts and Rhode Island. Cope was absent again, for his regiment was preparing to proceed to the West Indies.

War with Spain had broken out in 1739 and Cope had been appointed lieutenant-colonel of His Majesty's American Regiment of Foot (26 December). This regiment was raised in New England for service in the West Indies in Admiral Edward Vernon's projected expeditions against the Spanish Caribbean possessions. In September 1740 Cope sailed with his regiment from New York for the general rendezvous in Jamaica, and arrived there early in November. He took part in the attack on Cartagena (Colombia) in April 1741 and in the expedition against Santiago de Cuba the following August. Both attacks were failures. In March 1742 another expedition left Jamaica to attack Panama, but severe sickness among the troops forced the ships to return to Jamaica in May. Colonel Cope survived every action, but finally died of fever in Kingston on 12 July 1742. By October his regiment had become so reduced by casualties and disease that it was disbanded in Kingston.

Governor Philipps described Cope as "a person of great honour, with a good understanding and zeal for His Majesty's service." Another described him as "a cleare cool headed determinate gallant man, well known in North America." Cope married Jane Patteshall, probably of Boston; they had one daughter.

C. E. THOMAS

Parish of Kingston (Jamaica), Burial registers, I, 13 July 1742. PANS, RG 1, 17, no.17. PRO, CO 5/41, f.13; 217/7, doc.212. [Cadwallader Colden], *The letters and papers of Cadwallader Colden* . . . (9v., N.Y. Hist. Soc. *Coll.*, L–LVI (1917–23), LXVII–LXVIII (1934–35), New York, 1918–37), II, 173. *N.S. Archives, III*, 169, 227. *NYCD* (O'Callaghan and Fernow), VI, 170–71. N.Y. Hist. Soc. *Coll.*, XXVII (1894), 400 (abstract of Cope's will). PRO, *CSP, Col., 1726–27; 1728–29; 1732; 1735–36. Records of the colony of Rhode Island and Providence plantations, in New England*, ed. J. R. Bartlett (10v., Providence, R.I., 1856–65), IV, 586. Dalton, *George the first's army*, II, 351. Murdoch, *History of Nova-Scotia*, I, 455, 519. W. Y. Baldry and A. S. White, "Gooch's American regiment of foot, 1739–42," Society for Army Hist. Research (London), *Journal*, XVI (1937), 235–39. Malcolm Storer, "Admiral Vernon's medals, 1739–42," Mass. Hist. Soc. *Proc.*, LII (1918–19).

COPE (Cop, Copt, Coptk), JEAN-BAPTISTE, also sometimes called **Major Cope,** chief of a Micmac tribe of Shubenacadie (N.S.); d. between 1758 and 1760, probably at Miramichi (N.B.).

Jean-Baptiste Cope was involved, along with some of his family, in the Anglo-Micmac war of 1749–53. Following the erroneous statement of the Chevalier de Johnstone*, a number of historians have believed that it was Cope who on 15 Oct. 1750 (N.S.) murdered Edward How on the Missaguash River, or they have confused him with How's real murderer, Étienne BÂTARD, alleging that these two names referred to the same person. It may, at most, be presumed that Cope, an Indian chief living at Abbé Jean-Louis Le Loutre*'s mission, took part in the ambush organized by Bâtard in the autumn of 1750, when all the Micmacs of Acadia were gathered around Fort Beauséjour (near Sackville, N.B.).

On 14 Sept. 1752 Cope appeared at Halifax to open peace negotiations with Governor Peregrine Thomas HOPSON. On 22 November a treaty was actually signed between the English and Cope, along with delegates from his tribe, on the principles of the treaty that had been negotiated at Boston in 1725 with SAUGUAARAM and other Penobscot chiefs. The news of the agreement with the Micmacs immediately reached Louisbourg, Île Royale (Cape Breton Island), and the governor, Jean-Louis de Raymond*, wrote to the minister of Marine on 24 Nov. 1752 that Cope was "a drunkard and a bad lot"; the governor reassured himself with the allegation that the other Micmacs had "disowned" Cope. On 12 May 1753 Raymond returned to the subject, this time calling Cope "a bad Micmac whose conduct has always been uncertain and suspect to both nations."

Raymond did not know how right he was. Indeed, at the time he was writing the treaty was already broken. In February 1753 an attack on a group of Micmacs by two English soldiers, James Grace and John Conner, had incited Cope to undertake an expedition to avenge his people. On 16 May 1753 he sent his son Joseph to Halifax to ask for a boat and an escort, supposedly to take provisions there. Captain Bannerman was sent, accompanied by seven men, one of whom was Anthony Casteel, to whom we owe the account of this expedition. On 19 May the crew was cut to pieces except for Casteel, who, knowing French, passed himself off for a Frenchman. Cope's expedition then continued in the direction of Cobequid (near Truro, N.S.), Baie-Verte (N.B.), and finally Louisbourg, where Casteel was freed on 28 June.

By examining the multiple incidents of this trip we can discover the real reasons behind the expedition. Cope wanted to reassert his prestige with his warriors: on 20 May he made a speech along these lines. He also wanted to terrorize his prisoner: on 22 May Casteel was freed from a woman who wanted to torture him, but the woman, together with Cope's daughter, "danced until froth, the size of one's fist, came out of their mouths, which caused tears to gush from his eyes." Cope was, however, above all intent on proving his loyalty to the French: on 23 May he burned the peace treaty which had been signed the previous year, and on 25 May he made a new speech in which he evoked Grace's and Conner's horrible crime and stated "that he was surprised to see that the English were the first to begin" hostilities. The peace signed by Cope had thus not lasted six months; the following summer the provincial secretary, William Cotterell, did not hesitate to write that it was Cope himself who had broken it.

According to Johnstone, Cope was in the neighbourhood of Miramichi after the fall of Louisbourg in 1758. This claim seems probable in view of the fact that many Micmacs, Acadians, missionaries, and soldiers took refuge south of the Baie des Chaleurs after the French defeat in Acadia. It is likely, therefore, that Cope died in this region before 1760, since his name does not appear on any of the peace treaties signed between the Micmacs and the English after that date.

MICHELINE D. JOHNSON

AN, Col., B, 89, f.10; 90, f.52; 97, ff.21–22, 30–31; C¹¹A 93, ff.169–72; 97, ff.16–34; C¹¹B, 28, ff.40, 75, 381–87; 29, ff.63, 130f.; 30, ff.110, 113, 117, 189–91; 31, ff.62, 116, 132–35; 32, ff.163, 280f.; 33, ff.22–23, 159–62, 181–83, 197. PAC, MG 11, Nova Scotia B, 4, pp.58, 62, 106; 5, pp.69, 112–20, 139, 152, 162, 164, 178, 234; 6, pp.118, 137, 141, 183f., 254f. [Anthony Casteel], "Anthony Casteel's journal," *Coll. doc. inédits Canada et Amérique*, II (1889), 111–26. *Derniers jours de l'Acadie* (Du Boscq de Beaumont), 72. *N.S. Archives*, I, 195, 671–74, 682–86, 694–98. PAC *Report, 1894*, 150, 195, 197f., 202; *Report, 1905*, II, pt.III, 281–356. Casgrain, *Un pèlerinage au pays d'Évangéline*, app.I; *Une seconde Acadie*, 231. Murdoch, *History of Nova-Scotia*, II, 193, 211, 213, 219–22. Parkman, *Montcalm and Wolfe* (1884), I, 106. Richard, *Acadie* (D'Arles), II, 85–121, 151–69. R. O. MacFarlane, "British Indian policy in Nova Scotia to 1760," *CHR*, XIX (1938), 154–67.

COQUART, CLAUDE-GODEFROY, priest, Jesuit, missionary; b. 2 Feb. 1706 at Melun, France; d. 4 July 1765 at the Chicoutimi mission, Quebec.

Claude-Godefroy Coquart entered the noviciate of the Society of Jesus in Paris on 14 May 1726. He arrived at the college in Quebec probably in 1739. The following year Pierre GAULTIER de Varennes et de La Vérendrye asked for a chaplain to replace Father Jean-Pierre Aulneau*, who had been massacred at Lake of the Woods in 1736; because of his youth Coquart was chosen over several other missionaries who applied for the post. On 26 June 1741 he left Montreal with La Vérendrye. But as a result of jealousies and intrigues on the part of adversaries not named by the explorer, and because the establishment of a permanent mission among the newly discovered tribes seemed risky, La Vérendrye was obliged to his great regret to leave Coquart at Michilimackinac. Coquart was there in August 1743, then rejoined La Vérendrye at Fort La Reine (Portage-la-Prairie, Man.). The missionary probably returned at the beginning of 1744 from this voyage with the explorer, who had been forced to give up his post as commandant. Coquart was the first missionary to go to present-day Manitoba and the first to reach a point so far west [*see* Charles-Michel MÉSAIGER].

Subsequently Coquart spent some time in the valley of the St Lawrence, and in 1746, on the death of Father Jean-Baptiste Maurice, he was assigned to the Saguenay mission. His first stay in this mission lasted 11 years. He was initially appointed to minister to the French in the posts along the north shore of the St Lawrence. He left Quebec on 13 May 1746 and at his return on 17 July he was re-directed to the Saguenay region. On 27 October he again left Quebec to winter at Chicoutimi, which he reached on 20 November. The following year he settled at Tadoussac, where, in keeping with his predecessor's vow, he undertook the construction of a chapel dedicated to St Anne. Begun on 16 May 1747, the work was completed on 24 June 1750, thanks to the generosity of intendants Hocquart*, who supplied the boards, beams, shingles, and nails, and Bigot*, who contributed in 1749 a gratuity of 200 *livres*.

In 1748 and 1749 Coquart spent the winter at Chicoutimi, making several trips, however, to Lac Saint-Jean. He admired the Indians' faith and their even temper in the midst of famine and trials which they endured "without complaining." At the request of Bishop Pontbriand [DUBREIL], the missionary conducted his ministry more regularly at Île aux Coudres from 1751 to 1757. He spent the winter there in order to spare the settlers from having to cross the St Lawrence by canoe to obtain a priest, and during the summer he made the round of his missions as far as Sept-Îles.

Corbin

In 1750, at Intendant Bigot's request, Father Coquart drew up a confidential report on the administration and the output of the posts of the Domaine du Roi. The missionary drew a detailed picture of the situation at the posts of La Malbaie, Tadoussac, the Îlets-Jérémie, Chicoutimi, and Sept-Îles, suggesting incidentally several improvements which would cost the king little and were prompted by his experience, observations, and common sense. According to his report the posts did not produce as much as they ought because the tax farmers lacked initiative and the employees, badly distributed among the posts, wasted their time, except for the girls, who worked "even beyond the limits of their strength." Coquart described La Malbaie as the Domaine's finest tax farm because of the "richness of the land" and the suitability for raising animals. He suggested that pitch be produced from the pine forests there and that salmon fishing be encouraged. The post of Tadoussac produced few peltries. Seal hunting was important, but hunters were scarce; he suggested that orphans from the post of Chicoutimi should be sent there. The Îlets-Jérémie produced a great quantity of seal oil, whereas the Chicoutimi post was outstanding for the quantity and quality of its peltries and the size of its sawmill on the Rivière Pepaouetiche. Finally, the post of Sept-Îles supplied the finest furs, but in limited quantity; salmon fishing, he said, ought to be encouraged there.

In 1757 Father Coquart returned to Quebec. He stayed at the Jesuit college, on occasion acting as confessor either at the Hôtel-Dieu or at the Hôpital Général. In the spring of 1759 the missionary went down the St Lawrence again, following the north shore and stopping at the various posts of the Domaine du Roi. He caught sight of the English fleet along the south shore. While he was on his missionary round, the British were attacking Quebec. In the autumn he returned to a town already occupied by the enemy and he had to find shelter with friends, since the college had been taken over by the British garrison; later he stayed at the Ursuline convent.

In April 1762 Father Coquart returned to Île aux Coudres and remained there until 28 August. After that he rejoined his Montagnais Indians, who were no longer as docile in listening to their missionary. Indeed, under the British régime the sale of liquor to the Indians made the ministry more difficult, and Father Coquart had to chastise his flock several times. But the missionary nevertheless defended the Montagnais when they were disturbed at seeing their lands occupied by the English and when the rumour spread that the

English intended to appropriate the lands for their own use. In 1765, some months before his death, Father Coquart sent Governor James Murray* a petition containing the grievances that his Indians had expressed orally to him.

Father Coquart died at Chicoutimi on 4 July 1765, at 59 years of age, without any of his *confrères* having been able to succour him. The French at the post buried him in the Montagnais cemetery. Before dying the missionary had expressed a wish to be buried in his chapel at Tadoussac, which was fulfilled in 1793.

JOSEPH COSSETTE

ASJCF, 637, ff.1–16; 638, ff.2–23; Fonds Rochemonteix, 4028bis, f.28. *JR* (Thwaites), LXIX, 80–126, 136–40. Antonio Dragon, *Trente robes noires au Saguenay*, texte revu et corrigé par Adrien Pouliot (Publication de la SHS, 24, Chicoutimi, Qué., 1971). L.-A. Prud'homme, "Le P. Claude-Godefroy Coquart, s.j., premier apôtre de la Rivière-Rouge," *Revue Canadienne*, XXXIII (1897), 81–92. Marcel Trudel, "Il y a Coquart et Cocquart," *BRH*, LX (1954), 9–10.

CORBIN, DAVID, king's master carpenter; b. *c.* 1684 in Canada, son of David Corbin, a butcher, and Marie Parent; m. first on 28 Feb. 1707 at Quebec to Marie-Jeanne Faveron, by whom he had seven children, and secondly on 12 Feb. 1719 at Quebec to Geneviève Gariépy; buried 2 Oct. 1755.

David Corbin and two of his sons, Étienne (1706?–68) and Joseph-Marie (1711–57), are best known for their role in the royal shipbuilding program of the 1730s and 1740s. Corbin had likely been trained as a carpenter by his stepfather, Joseph Rancour, and introduced to shipbuilding by Fabien Badeau, his brother-in-law.

Before his marriage in 1707, David Corbin had travelled in 1705 to the Detroit area for the Compagnie de la Colonie. He was still a young man when he came to the attention of the administration – a dispatch of 1744 refers to his "forty years" as "foreman carpenter in his majesty's service." He was made the king's master carpenter in January 1722 by Intendant BÉGON, "to work on the construction and refitting of the king's canoes and boats, to oversee the conduct of the said works . . . , to select and cut the necessary trees" for their construction, and to inspect the planks, masts, and other wood being sent in consignments by contractors to Rochefort, France. Corbin was paid 50 *livres* a month by the crown but had time to work also for himself.

In the official correspondence it is Corbin's work outside Quebec that is mentioned most often. In 1724 he went with an official party to

Baie Saint-Paul to test the suitability of its pine for masts. After 1730, with the crown actively promoting public and private shipbuilding in New France, these assignments increased. In 1733, 1735, and yearly from 1739 to 1745 he sought out stands of oak and pine around Montreal Island, Lake Champlain, and elsewhere. He had to select and mark trees, and in 1740, 1744, and 1746 to supervise the woodcutters and carpenters who prepared the timber for the shipyards. Specifications might be provided by the principal royal shipwright at Quebec, René-Nicolas Levasseur*, but it was the private contractors who were largely responsible for execution. Thus in 1740, for example, Corbin's instructions were to oversee the private contractor Pierre LUPIEN, *dit* Baron, who recruited, equipped, and fed his own woodcutters; Corbin was to have his recorder list the timber they produced and the supplies given by Baron, and to make weekly reports to the financial commissary at Montreal.

The Corbins' sensitivities were aroused in 1744 when a French carpenter, Chiquet, received a royal commission as a shipyard foreman in Canada. Étienne Corbin had been a foreman at the Quebec shipyard since 1740 and had greater seniority. The intendant, Gilles Hocquart*, appeased his jealousy by recommending for this "very good subject" a similar favour. David Corbin was recommended for a third "king's warrant": it would cost the king nothing and Corbin "would be greatly humiliated if he were denied it." The warrants were granted in 1745. The fidelity of this family was, according to Jacques Mathieu, rare among Canadians, and "only the Corbins, established in the shipyard from the beginning, became foremen."

Joseph-Marie gradually replaced his father as supervisor of woodcutting for the royal shipyard after 1742. Until 1750 he performed the same duties as his father in the forests, usually in autumn and winter. David, after his 62nd birthday, naturally enough remained in Quebec. Joseph-Marie was appointed king's master carpenter, probably after the death of his father in 1755, but died himself two years later.

In his history of industry in New France, Joseph-Noël Fauteux concluded that "the advances made in shipbuilding in Canada were owed to the tireless devotion of [René-Nicolas] Levasseur and his faithful master carpenters, the Corbins."

PETER N. MOOGK

AN, Col., B, 81, p.149; C¹¹ᴬ, 46, pp.210–18; 60, pp.188–91; 73, pp.65–68; 74, pp.206–11; 75, pp.353–55; 81, pp. 399, 401; 105, pp.288–89 (PAC transcripts).

ANQ, Greffe de Gilbert Boucault de Godefus, 30 janv. 1751; Greffe de Louis Chambalon, 28 avril 1705, 24 févr. 1707, 26 févr.–11 mars 1709; NF, Coll. de pièces jud. et not., 734¹/₄, 3037; NF, Ord. int. ANQ-M, Greffe de Cyr de Monmerqué, 14 févr. 1757. *Jug. et délib.*, III, V. "Recensement du Canada, 1681" (Sulte). *Recensement de Québec, 1716* (Beaudet). "Recensement de Québec, 1744" (APQ *Rapport*). P.-V. Charland, "Notre-Dame de Québec: le nécrologe de la crypte," *BRH*, XX (1914), 237. P.-G. Roy, *Inv. ins. Prév. Québec*, I, 166; II, 173; *Inv. jug. et délib., 1717–1760*, I, 190–91, 275, 295; *Inv. ord. int.*, I, II, III. Tanguay, *Dictionnaire*. J.-N. Fauteux, *Essai sur l'industrie*, I, 201, 251, 253, 259, 263, 266–67. Mathieu, *La construction navale*, 57–58. P.-G. Roy, "L'hon. René-Ovide Hertel de Rouville," *BRH*, XII (1906), 129–31.

COROLÈRE, JEAN, drummer in the grenadier and gunner company of the colonial regular troops, executioner for Canada; b. *c.* 1731 in the village of Kerquisinoir (?) in the diocese of Quimper, France, son of Christophe Corolère and Marie Dorollaire (?); it is not known when or in what circumstances he died.

Jean Corolère probably came to New France as a "recruit" in the colonial regular troops. He was one of the first drummers in the grenadier and gunner company, formed in Canada in the autumn of 1750.

On 26 Jan. 1751 Corolère, who was living in the barracks of the Saint-Jean gate, went "to have a drink" in Laforme's tavern. There he was insulted by some soldiers from his company, one of whom, a certain Coffre, he challenged to a duel. The combat took place the same evening in the suburb of Saint-Jean. The adversaries clashed swords for only a few minutes, for at the second exchange Corolère wounded Coffre in a finger of his right hand. As blood had been shed, the drummer's honour was saved; the duellists then put up their swords and went to drink together at Laforme's. The news of the duel reached the ears of the judicial authorities, who hastened to issue warrants for the arrest of the culprits. But only the drummer Corolère could be seized; the soldier Coffre had fled. On 30 Jan. 1751 the lieutenant general of the provost court of Quebec, François DAINE, opened the inquiry into the suit for duelling brought against Jean Corolère and the fugitive Coffre. On 6 March 1751 the lieutenant general declared that the charge of contumacy against Coffre had been thoroughly investigated and ordered that a further inquiry of one month's duration be carried out against him and Corolère, during which time Corolère "would remain in prison." But on

Coron

6 April the king's attorney general of the Conseil Supérieur, Joseph Perthuis*, appealed against the leniency of this judgement as being contrary to article VI of Louis XV's edict against duelling, which required that a decision be delivered against the duellist "only after further inquiry" which could not "be of less than one year." Finally, on 2 June 1751, the Conseil Supérieur revised the judgement of the provost court of Quebec and sentenced Coffre, as well as Corolère, to a year in prison, "during which time a further inquiry will be made."

During his imprisonment in the "royal prisons" in Quebec Corolère's cell was next to that of Françoise Laurent, daughter of the drum-major of Montreal, Guillaume-Antoine Laurent. On 26 Oct. 1750 the young servant, who was 20 years old, had been found guilty by the lieutenant general of the royal jurisdiction of Montreal, Jacques-Joseph GUITON de Monrepos, of stealing clothes from her employers, the Pommereaus, and had been sentenced to be hanged. This sentence had been confirmed on 12 March 1751 by the Conseil Supérieur, which had however "stayed the execution because of the lack of an executioner." The colony's hangman, Jean-Baptiste Duclos, *dit* Saint-Front, had in fact died on 28 Dec. 1750, and the authorities had not yet found a successor for him. It was thus that Françoise Laurent became acquainted with Corolère, who was to save her from the gallows. Except for letters of annulment, remission, or pardon, the only way at the time for someone under sentence of death to escape hanging was, for a man, to become a hangman, or, for a woman, to marry an executioner. The young criminal decided therefore to ensnare Corolère so completely that he would be ready to do anything to marry her, even serve as hangman, a role considered dishonourable at the period. After some months as his neighbour she had achieved her ends. Accordingly, on 17 Aug. 1751, Jean Corolère presented to the Conseil Supérieur "a written document" in which he entreated "the Court to accept him as executioner." The councillors granted his request and released him from the obligation of "remaining in prison" for the ten months or so that he had to complete. The very next day the new executioner presented a second request. He besought the councillors "to grant him in marriage the person named Françoise Laurent," so that he might "settle down solidly" in the colony. The wedding of Jean Corolère and Françoise Laurent was celebrated on 19 Aug. 1751 in the chapel of the intendant's palace.

The executioner Corolère exercised his functions for an unknown period of time; after 29 April 1752 all trace of him and his wife is lost.

ANDRÉ LACHANCE

AJQ, Registre d'état civil, Notre-Dame de Québec, 19 août 1751. AN, Col., C¹¹ᴬ, 95, ff.66–67. ANQ, NF, Coll. de pièces jud. et not., 1646; NF, Registres de la Prévôté de Québec, LXXXVI, 46v–47; NF, Registres du Cons. sup., registre criminel, 1730–1759, ff.107v, 120f., 122, 126v. Bornier, *Conférences des ord. de Louis XIV*, II, 416. Lachance, *Le bourreau au Canada*.

CORON, CHARLES-FRANÇOIS, organist (?), tailor, royal notary; b. 21 Dec. 1704 at Saint-François-de-Sales (Laval, Que.), Île Jésus, son of François Coron, royal notary, and Marie Cyr; buried 13 Feb. 1767 at Saint-François-de-Sales.

Several documents attest to the existence of a Charles-François Coron, organist, tailor, royal notary, and resident at Montreal, at Saint-François-de-Sales, and at Detroit. The difficulty of identifying the Charles-François Coron whose name appears in the available documents has led several historians into error; Cyprien Tanguay*, for instance, did not suspect the existence of more than one person of the same name.

The Sulpician archives at Montreal contain a reference to a Charles-François Coron who apparently held the post of organist at Notre-Dame church from 1722 to 1734. According to these documents, Coron received 83 *livres* 15 *sols* for 20 months' work. In 1725 and 1726 the organist's salary was a "hooded coat" and a "jacket from Mazamet" valued at 45 *livres*, and in 1727 he could choose between 45 *livres* in money or 50 *livres* in merchandise.

Other documents, dated 1728 and 1729, mention a Charles-François Coron, "master tailor," who is said to have bought a property, bordering on Notre-Dame square, Montreal, on which he built a house. Moreover, a marriage contract, signed on 27 Dec. 1730, between Charles-François Coron and Angélique-Françoise Roland clearly indicates that the husband is a "master tailor" and son of the royal notary François Coron and Marie Cyr. This tailor seems to have been the person who drew up, on 20 Jan. 1734, his first act as a notary, thus following in the steps of his father who practised this profession at Saint-François-de-Sales until his death in 1733. Charles-François Coron did not succeed his father at once: the documents give the immediate succession to Jean-Baptiste Dufresne. However, on 20 Sept. 1735 the intendant Hocquart* gave Coron a commission as royal notary and clerk of the court "for the whole of Île-Jésus and also the rest of the northern parts of the government of

Montreal, including the parish [Saint-Joseph-] de la Rivière-des-Prairies." A new commission, 23 June 1740, permitted him to practise in the whole of the government of Montreal, except for the town and its suburbs. After the surrender of Montreal, Coron was one of the first notaries to have his commission renewed by the military governor, Thomas Gage*, on 1 Oct. 1760, and he practised until 9 Feb. 1767. In March 1767, Antoine Foucher replaced the late Charles-François Coron as notary.

Coron had married Angélique-Françoise Roland in Montreal on 8 Jan. 1731; they seem to have had four children, but we know only a daughter, Victoire, who in January 1768 married Pierre Jendon. However, Tanguay, in his *Dictionnaire*, mentions the marriage of this Charles-François Coron in Detroit on 24 Oct. 1757 to Marie-Louise Binot; he is given as the "son of the late Charles-François Coron and the late Marie Cyr." Our man would then be a bigamist and ubiquitous, since Angélique-Françoise died only in 1768, and since on the same day in 1757 the notary Coron was recording an act in his office on Île Jésus while the bridegroom in Detroit declared himself unable to sign the parish marriage register.

Are the organist, the tailor, and the notary the same person? The spelling in a document in the organist's hand, dated 1729, is poor, which is not true for the acts of the notary. There seems to be no doubt that the tailor and the notary are the same person, but it is difficult to make a positive identification of this person with the organist. It is quite possible that the Charles-François Coron of Detroit simply had the same name as the notary of Île-Jésus, and that the former was the youngest son of François Coron and the latter was the oldest.

HELMUT KALLMANN

ANQ, NF, Ord. int., XXIII, 78. ANQ-M, Greffe de J.-B. Adhémar, 27 déc. 1730; Greffe de C.-F. Coron, 1734–1767; Greffe de J.-C. Raimbault, 9 oct. 1728; Registre d'état civil, Saint-François-de-Sales, île Jésus, 13 févr. 1767. ASSM, Catalogue historique et chronologique des prêtres du séminaire de Montréal. DPL, Burton hist. coll., Registres des baptêmes, mariages et sépultures de Sainte-Anne du Détroit, 24 oct. 1757. *Dictionnaire national des Canadiens français (1608–1760)* (3v., Montréal, 1965), I. A. Roy, *Inv. greffes not.*, XXI, 51. P.-G. Roy, *Inv. ord. int.*, II, 155, 189, 295. Tanguay, *Dictionnaire*. Vachon, "Inv. critique des notaires royaux," *RHAF*, XI (1957–58), 98–99. O.-M.-H. Lapalice, "Les organistes et maîtres de musique à Notre-Dame de Montréal," *BRH*, XXV (1919), 243–44. J.-J. Lefebvre, "François Coron et Charles Coron, notaires à l'île Jésus," *La Revue du notariat* (Montréal), 66 (1963–64), 252. É.-Z. Massicotte, "La justice seigneuriale de l'île Jésus," *BRH*, XXIX (1923), 275–76.

CORPRON, JEAN, merchant trader, assistant purveyor general of provisions in Quebec; b. *c.* 1729 at Pizanie (dept. of Charente-Maritime), France, son of Charles Corpron and Marie Gabriel; d. sometime after 1765, probably in France.

We do not know under what circumstances Jean Corpron arrived in Canada. He first worked as a clerk for different Quebec merchants, but his "rascally tricks" did not permit his remaining long in their service. A clever man with a real gift for trade, Corpron then set up on his own account. In September 1755, although by his own admission he had a lucrative business and "was on the point of forming with the Sieur [Pierre CLAVERIE] a company which was to have been heavily capitalized," he agreed to enter the service of Joseph-Pierre Cadet*, who at that time managed the king's slaughterhouse, who was carrying on "flour milling and a fairly large business in goods, wine, spirits, and other food supplies," and who "fitted out ships and imported them from France." Indeed, "everything suggested that he [Cadet] could not fail to carry on profitable operations." Corpron, an experienced businessman, was not content with a salary; he demanded and obtained from the king's butcher "the fifth part of the profits in all his trading." As Cadet's partner, Jean Corpron rapidly became his confidential agent; in 1756, when Cadet was put by Intendant François Bigot* in charge of supplying provisions in New France, Corpron received the responsibility of the "establishment" in Quebec [see François MAURIN]. Thus, within three years, while according to his own account taking "the precautions which prudence suggested to him to share only in legitimate profits," he was able to accumulate the tidy sum of 1,200,000 *livres*.

Having returned to France after the capitulation of Montreal, Jean Corpron was arrested and imprisoned in the Bastille in December 1761. He was accused of malversation and was tried at the Châtelet before a commission presided over by the lieutenant general of police, Antoine de Sartine. Finally, after 15 months of imprisonment, examinations, and cross-examinations, on 10 Dec. 1763 M. de Sartine and his 27 counsellors at the Châtelet found him guilty of the charges against him. By 19 to nine they sentenced him to be severely reprimanded in the chamber of the council, to pay six *livres* in alms, to make restitution to the king of the sum of 600,000 *livres*, and "to remain in the prison of the Bastille . . . until

Corriveau

payment of the said sum." As the commissioners refused to allow restitution to be made in bills of exchange from Canada, Corpron had to stay in prison. It was not until 21 Dec. 1764 that his lawyer obtained permission from the king to pay in Canadian bills of exchange. Therefore on 18 Jan. 1765 the lawyer delivered to the treasurer general of the colonies, Baudart de Vaudésir, 80 bills of exchange from Canada, to a value of 600,000 *livres*. But in addition to restitution the commissioners demanded payment "in specie" of the interest owing on the 600,000 *livres* from 10 Dec. 1763 to 10 Jan. 1765. Jean Corpron opposed this new demand on the part of the commissioners, alleging that the sentence of the Châtelet did not mention any payment of interest. Moreover, since he had made restitution in conformity with the sentence of 10 Dec. 1763, he demanded and on 21 May 1765 obtained his release from the Bastille. Despite his opposition to the commissioners' decision, at the end of November 1765 he had to pay to the treasurer general of the colonies the interest due; he was able, however, by permission of the minister, the Duc de Choiseul, to pay in Canadian bills of exchange. After this date he disappears from sight.

Because of his commercial activities Jean Corpron was able to form connections by marriage with the important merchant traders of the period. On 1 July 1754 he married Marie Roy, the widow of Joseph Lépine, *dit* Lalime, a Quebec trader, and the daughter of Joseph Roy, a well-to-do merchant in Beaumont. In 1755, when he was about to enter into partnership with Claverie, he preferred to enter the service of Cadet, who already appeared to him to be "an important personage." It was this knowledge of business and this flair for finding out men who could bring him money that enabled him to become a "millionaire" in the space of three years.

ANDRÉ LACHANCE

AJQ, Registre d'état civil, Notre-Dame de Québec, 1er juill. 1754. AN, Col., B, 122, ff.266, 375–76; E, 92 (dossier Corpron–Maurin–Penissault), 1–7. ANQ, Greffe de J.-C. Panet, 21 juin 1754. "Mémoire du Canada," APQ *Rapport, 1924–25*, 128, 197. *Mémoires sur le Canada, depuis 1749 à 1760*, 86. J.-E. Roy, *Rapport sur les archives de France*, 865ff. Tanguay, *Dictionnaire*. Frégault, *François Bigot*, II, 173, 176, 197–98, 216–17. P.-G. Roy, *Bigot et sa bande*, 91ff., 355–56.

CORRIVEAU (Corrivaux), MARIE-JOSEPHTE, known as **La Corriveau;** b. and baptized 14 May 1733 at Saint-Vallier, near Quebec, daughter of Joseph Corriveau, a farmer, and Marie-Fran-

çoise Bolduc; m. first on 17 Nov. 1749 Charles Bouchard, a farmer, who was buried on 27 April 1760 and by whom she had three children; and secondly on 20 July 1761 Louis Dodier, a farmer; died on the gallows at Quebec, probably on 18 April 1763.

There is scarcely any woman in all of Canadian history who has a worse reputation than Marie-Josephte Corriveau, generally called La Corriveau. This wretched woman died more than two centuries ago, but she continues to haunt the imagination. People still talk of her, of her crimes, real and fictitious. On 15 April 1763 she was condemned to death by a court martial for murdering Louis Dodier, her second husband, during the night of 26–27 Jan. 1763. This murder gave rise to two sensational trials before a military tribunal which met in one of the rooms of the Ursuline convent in Quebec and was composed of 12 English officers and presided over by Lieutenant-Colonel Roger Morris. The reports of these trials, discovered in London in 1947, allow us to establish the facts quite precisely and to separate them from the legend which grew up about them.

The first trial, which began on 29 March 1763, ended on 9 April with the death sentence for Joseph Corriveau, who was found guilty of the murder, and the sentencing of his daughter, Marie-Josephte, to be flogged and branded. But these sentences were not carried out because Joseph Corriveau's confession – made after sentence had been pronounced on the advice of his confessor, the Jesuit superior Augustin-Louis de Glapion* – revealed his daughter as the sole guilty person and indicated that the crown attorney, Hector-Théophilus Cramahé*, had erred in his charge and his interpretation of the facts. His error was due to the fact that he accepted the testimony, contradictory as it happened, of Joseph's niece, Élisabeth-Marguerite (Isabelle) Veau, *dit* Sylvain, that of a neighbour, Joseph Corriveau, the accused man's homonym, which was, at least on the surface, overwhelming, and finally that of another neighbour, the talkative and imaginative Claude Dion. It was the contradictions in the evidence that the defence lawyer, Jean-Antoine Saillant, had tried to bring out in his pleading.

The court met again on 15 April to hear Marie-Josephte's confession, in which she declared that she had killed her husband by hitting him on the head twice with an axe while he was sleeping. A new sentence, pronounced the same day, stipulated that Marie-Josephte would be hanged and that, in conformity with English law (Great Britain, *Statutes*, 25, Geo. II, 1752), her corpse

142

would be exposed in chains for an indefinite period. The execution took place on the Buttes-à-Nepveu, near the Plains of Abraham, probably on 18 April 1763, and the iron cage, which was set up at Pointe-Lévy (Lauzon), remained in sight of passers-by until at least 25 May, when an order from the governor, James Murray*, authorized its removal. As for Joseph Corriveau, he was discharged with a certificate of innocence, as was his niece, Isabelle Sylvain, who had been accused of perjury at the first trial. His pardon received royal assent from George III on 8 August of that year.

All these unusual facts and others still, such as the discovery of the iron cage in the cemetery of Lauzon around 1850, struck people's imaginations. They were transformed into deep-rooted legends that are still recounted in oral tradition and inspired several fantastic tales which have been cleverly used by some Canadian writers. In *Les Anciens Canadiens* (Quebec, 1863) Philippe-Joseph Aubert* de Gaspé brought out in particular the nocturnal appearances of La Corriveau in her cage, begging a belated habitant on the road to Beaumont to take her to the sabbath of the will-o'-the-wisps and witches on the Île d'Orléans. After Sir James MacPherson Le Moine* in his article "Marie-Josephte Corriveau, a Canadian Lafarge" in *Maple Leaves* (Quebec, 1863), William Kirby*, in his novel *The Golden Dog* (New York, 1877), made La Corriveau into a professional poisoner, a direct descendant of the famous Catherine Deshayes, called La Voisin, who was hanged in Paris in 1680. Several other writers and historians, among them Louis-Honoré Fréchette* in his article "Une Relique," in *Le Monde Illustré* (Montreal), 7 May 1898, and Pierre-Georges Roy* in "L'Histoire de La Corriveau," *Cahiers des Dix*, II (1937), 73–76, have told La Corriveau's story, without succeeding however in completely separating the true facts from anachronistic fantasies or legendary and romantic details. There is, for example, a lack of agreement on the number of murders – between two and seven – which are attributed to this wretched woman and on the different means which she used to carry them out. La Corriveau has also inspired artists: the sculptor Alfred Laliberté* made a remarkable bronze which is in the Musée du Québec portraying a haggard young woman bent under the weight of fatality and the cage in which she is imprisoned.

LUC LACOURCIÈRE

An exhaustive bibliography listing all manuscript and printed sources, reference works, and studies will be found in two articles by Luc Lacourcière: "Le triple destin de Marie-Josephte Corriveau," *Cahiers des Dix*, XXXIII (1968), 213–42; "Le destin posthume de la Corriveau," *Cahiers des Dix*, XXXIV (1969), 239–71.

COSBY, ALEXANDER, military officer, lieutenant governor of Annapolis Royal, Nova Scotia; b. *c.* 1685 in Ireland; m. Anne Winniett *c.* 1726; d. 1742.

Alexander Cosby was born on the family estate of Stradbally Hall, Queen's County (now Leix County, Republic of Ireland), the ninth son of Alexander Cosby and Elizabeth L'Estrange. When his younger sister, Elizabeth, married Richard PHILIPPS, governor of Nova Scotia and colonel of the 40th regiment, Cosby was appointed a major in this regiment and came to Nova Scotia, probably in 1721. At first he filled purely military functions, chiefly at Canso. In 1725 he sought appointment as lieutenant governor of Nova Scotia and was obviously bitter when the position went to Lawrence Armstrong*.

Trouble between these two men began almost at once and by 1727 Armstrong was complaining that Cosby refused to obey orders or remain in his post at Canso. That same year Philipps, who had been in England since 1722, greatly aggravated the situation by appointing Cosby to succeed John Doucett* as lieutenant governor of the fort and town of Annapolis Royal and by making him a member of the Nova Scotia Council. When both Cosby and Armstrong claimed command of the troops in the fort, a stalemate was reached, with neither one accepting orders from the other. Philipps returned from England in 1729 and resumed command of the troops, thus forcing an outward settlement; but, as Philipps himself observed, "the inward Leven may still remain."

Philipps added fuel to the quarrel when on 18 May 1730, taking advantage of Armstrong's absence, he appointed Cosby president of the council, thus ignoring the rights of Armstrong, Paul MASCARENE, John ADAMS, William Skene, and William Shirreff, all of whom occupied senior civil positions. When Philipps returned to England in 1731, these men made it quite clear that they would not sit on a council presided over by Cosby, and demanded redress from London. Their position was upheld by Whitehall but the difficulty had already been overcome in May 1732, when Cosby withdrew from the council because of quarrels with Armstrong.

Cosby refused to serve further under Armstrong's command and continued to stir up discontent and controversy, assisted by his father-in-law, William WINNIETT, an important merchant of Annapolis Royal. The differences

Coswentannea

between Cosby and Armstrong had grown so serious that the latter was unable to leave Annapolis Royal, for fear that Cosby would seize control in his absence. Armstrong ordered him to proceed to England to account for his actions, but Cosby refused to obey. A semblance of order appears to have been restored by 1737, when Cosby was sent to command the small garrison at Canso; there he soon quarrelled with the officers serving under him.

On the death of Armstrong in December 1739, the presidency of the council went automatically to Mascarene, but he was deliberately passed over when Cosby was appointed lieutenant-colonel of the regiment on 22 March 1739/40. Conflict between the two men became inevitable. As lieutenant-colonel, Cosby was in direct control of the regiment and thus Mascarene's superior officer. Mascarene, however, was not only in charge of civil affairs, but was also commander-in-chief of the British forces in Nova Scotia, and therefore could issue military orders to Cosby. Within three months unconfirmed rumours had spread in Annapolis Royal that Cosby would use his new military powers to order Mascarene to Canso, thus depriving him of his position as head of the civil government. By October 1740, Mascarene and Cosby were no longer speaking and the conflict continued unabated until Cosby's sudden death at Annapolis Royal on 27 Dec. 1742. He left a widow and six children, the second of whom, Philipps, later attained the rank of admiral of the white in the British navy and succeeded to the family estates at Stradbally Hall.

Cosby appears to have been habitually quarrelsome, lacking tact and good judgement in his dealings with others, and in many respects much like his brother William, who was governor of New York and New Jersey (1731–36) and has been described as "devoid of statesmanship, seeking money and preferment." In fairness to Alexander Cosby, however, it must be remembered that our view of him is based on the evidence of his detractors, as his own correspondence has apparently not survived.

BARRY M. MOODY

Mass. Hist. Soc., Mascarene family papers, Letter book, 1740–43. New Eng. Hist. Geneal. Soc., Lord Walter Fitzgerald, "Pedigree of the Cosbys of Stradbally from the 16th to the 18th century." PAC, MG 11, Nova Scotia, A, 20, pp.94–97, 101–11, 161–62, 163–64; 21, pp. 73–77; 23, pp.38–39, 40–41; 25, pp.58–59; Nova Scotia B, 3, p.27. PANS, RG 1, 9, pp.251–56, 262–66; 14, pp.186–87; 17, nos.12, 15, 23; 18, nos.39, 50, 52. *New Eng. Hist. and Geneal. Register*, X (1856), 143–47. *N.S. Archives, I; II; III; IV*. Smythies, *Historical records of 40th Regiment. DAB* (biography of William Cosby). *DNB* (biography of Phillips Cosby). S. C. W. Allen, *Our children's ancestry* ([Milledgeville, Ga.], 1935), 317–18. Brebner, *New England's outpost*; "Paul Mascarene of Annapolis Royal," *Dal. Rev.*, VIII (1928–29), 501–16. Calnek, *History of Annapolis* (Savary). Murdoch, *History of Nova-Scotia*.

COSWENTANNEA. *See* KAGHSWAGHTANIUNT

COTTON, MICHEL, shoemaker, silversmith; b. 1 July 1700 in Quebec, son of Barthélemy Cotton, merchant silversmith, and Jeanne Le Rouge; died sometime after 1747.

Craftsmen of the 18th century commonly had a variety of occupations, so that it is not surprising to discover that Michel Cotton was successively shoemaker and silversmith. Two contracts, signed before the notary Jean-Étienne Dubreuil*, reveal that master shoemaker Michel Cotton agreed to take Julien Ducharme as an apprentice on 16 March 1721, and François Potevin on 17 Nov. 1722. In 1724, however, Cotton wanted to learn a new specialty. This decision resulted in his being sued, since his new occupation did not permit him to continue any longer the apprenticeship in shoemaking that he was committed to offer to "a certain Dumoulin." Despite this obstacle Cotton became apprenticed to the master silversmith François Chambellan, as a contract signed on 31 March 1724 before the notary Dubreuil tells us.

In 1726 Cotton, still living in Quebec, styled himself "silversmith in this town." On 28 October of that year he signed a marriage contract with Françoise Gagnon from Château-Richer. He was not to remain in Quebec. It was probably the restricted clientele in his birthplace that forced him to move to Montreal in 1731. In 1732 he delivered a censer to the parish of Saint-Charles-de-Lachenaie, and the following year he signed a contract to teach the silversmith's craft to Jean-Baptiste Serré. This contract was annulled after a few weeks, but in 1734 Cotton took on a new apprentice for a period of three years. In 1737 he was still in Montreal and took a lease for a year on a house in Rue Saint-Paul. The end of this lease probably coincided with Cotton's return to Quebec, where he continued practising his craft. In the period 1739–47 a great number of documents describe him as "a silversmith, living in Quebec." After that period his activities are not known.

The Musée du Québec owns a goblet and a soup-spoon made by Cotton. Other articles, all in solid silver, are preserved in various places in Quebec and similarly bear Cotton's stamp consisting of the letters MC, his initials, crowned with a fleur-de-lis.

MICHEL CAUCHON and ANDRÉ JUNEAU

ANDQ, Registres des baptêmes, mariages et sépultures, 2 juill. 1700. ANQ, Greffe de J.-É. Dubreuil, 16 mars 1721, 17 nov. 1722, 31 mars 1724, 19 déc. 1726; Greffe de J.-N. Pinguet de Vaucour, 28 oct. 1726. ANQ-M, Greffe de J.-B. Adhémar, 7, 21 avril 1733; Greffe de F.-M. Lepailleur, 4 sept. 1734, 7 janv. 1735, 8 mai 1737. Archives paroissiales de Saint-Charles (Lachenaie, Qué.), Livres de comptes, I, 1725–1739. IOA, Dossier Cotton. P.-G. Roy, *Inv. coll. pièces jud. et not.*, I, 71, 135; II, 333; *Inv. jug. et délib., 1717–1760*, III, 213; IV, 127; V, 10. Tanguay, *Dictionnaire*. Marius Barbeau, *Maîtres artisans de chez-nous* (Montréal, [1942]), 34. Langdon, *Canadian silversmiths*. Gérard Morisset, *Le Cap-Santé, ses églises et son trésor* (Collection Champlain, Québec, 1944). Traquair, *Old silver of Quebec*. Gérard Morisset, "Un cordonnier orfèvre: Michel Cotton," *La Patrie* (Montréal), 26 févr. 1950; "L'orfèvrerie canadienne," *La Revue française de l'élite européenne* (Paris), 59 (août 1954), 60–64.

COUAGNE, RENÉ DE, merchant, colonel of militia, judge; baptized 30 Aug. 1690 in Montreal, son of Charles de Couagne* and Marie Gaudé; d. 23 Dec. 1767 in his birthplace.

René de Couagne was the son of a prominent Montreal merchant, and on 14 Oct. 1716 he married Louise Pothier, the daughter of another merchant, in the presence of several other businessmen. Through his marriage contract the husband received three pieces of land in Rue Saint-Paul, made over to him by his wife's brothers and valued at 1,500 *livres*. On 16 Oct. 1721 Couagne was commissioned as a surveyor, but he does not seem to have practised this profession, which perhaps required more thorough training than he had had. The only survey document discovered bearing his signature reveals that he was incapable of determining exactly the boundaries of a piece of land, even "after having measured the aforementioned piece of land three or four times."

René de Couagne's business activity is difficult to assess. It was he who was responsible in 1730 for collecting, in return for a five per cent commission, the tax to help the building of fortifications for Montreal. Intendant Hocquart* was satisfied with his work and asked the minister, Maurepas, to increase Couagne's gratuity because, he wrote, "He was loath to take on this task, which he considered might well bring public dislike and which, however, I urged upon him as a matter of honour." This request does not seem to have been favourably received by the minister. In 1731 Couagne was the assistant in Montreal of the chief road commissioner, Jean-Eustache LANOULLIER de Boisclerc. He was also involved in the fur trade, but as a supplier rather than a voyageur. In August 1724 permission was granted to him as well as to a certain Réaume to send a canoe with four men to the post of Baie-des-Puants (Green Bay, Wis.). He did not enter into any contracts for the west in his own name except in 1747, 1748, 1752, and 1756, but we may suppose that he also outfitted some expeditions with his cousin, Dominique Gaudé, who did so regularly.

In 1749 René de Couagne was host to the famous Swedish naturalist Pehr Kalm* during the latter's stay in Montreal. The traveller learned a great deal about the Canadians' way of doing business and their customs and had nothing but praise for the welcome he received from Couagne's family, who, he said, treated him as if he were one of them. As a matter of fact, this was not difficult, for Intendant Bigot* had decided to pay all of Kalm's expenses during his stay in New France, and Couagne made the necessary advances, which amounted to 1,404 *livres* 12 *sols* 6 *deniers* and which were promptly repaid. In addition, René de Couagne made deliveries of supplies to the government in 1750 and 1751, but for rather small amounts.

The Seven Years' War and the conquest brought the same difficulties to René de Couagne as to the other businessmen in the colony. Commodities that had been ordered from suppliers in La Rochelle, France, in 1757 remained in the warehouses of that city the following year and even later; in 1766 the merchant Denis Goguet, in La Rochelle, still had not disposed of some of these goods. Like the other Montreal merchants, Couagne signed various petitions in 1763 and 1764 requesting the favour of the British authorities when French paper currency was being liquidated, although in the registration of 1763 his name does not appear as a holder of any such assets.

In the final days of the French administration René de Couagne had served as colonel of militia in Montreal. On 6 Nov. 1760, two months after the surrender of the town, the new governor, Thomas Gage*, wishing to "maintain law and order" in his region, renewed Couagne's commission. Since the office of colonel of militia was directly linked with the administration of justice in Gage's government, Couagne consequently served from 1760 to 1763 as lower court judge in the militia court at Montreal.

René de Couagne died in December 1767 in Montreal at 77 years of age. His career should not be confused with that of Charles-René, his

Couagne

nephew, or those of René and Jean-Baptiste*, his two surviving sons.

JOSÉ IGARTUA

AN, Col., C¹¹A, 53, ff.52–60; 83, ff.65–69v; 89, ff.147–48; 93, ff.288v–92; 94, ff.59–63; 97, ff.165–70; 116, ff.294v, 299v, 305; 119, ff.267, 296, 334, 345–46. ANQ, NF, Registres du Cons. sup., 1728–1729, ff.29v–30; 1734–1735, ff.44, 60; 1741, ff.164v–66. ANQ-M, Greffe de Michel Lepailleur, 12 oct. 1716; Arpentage, 2 mai 1723; Registre d'état civil, Notre-Dame de Montréal, 30 août 1690, 14 oct. 1716, 24 déc. 1767. ASQ, Livres de comptes, C 8. PAC, MG 8, A2, 36, ff.167–68; E6, 1, 4, 5; MG 18, H28, 3; MG 18, O6; MG 24, L3, 3, pp.1610–13, 1619–20, 1692–94, 1706–10; 4, pp.2336–38; 38, pp.25285–86; 47, p.30459; 51, pp.33231–32.
Calendar of the Sir William Johnson manuscripts in the New York State Library, comp. R. E. Day (Albany, 1909), 104, 136, 146, 150, 171–72, 183, 186, 190–91, 198, 203, 223–24, 232, 234, 238, 297, 307. *Johnson papers* (Sullivan *et al.*). Pehr Kalm, *The America of 1750; Peter Kalm's travels in North America: the English version of 1770*, ed. A. B. Benson (2v., New York, 1966), II, 536, 553, 601. Robert Le Blant, *Histoire de la Nouvelle-France: les sources narratives du début du XVIIIᵉ siècle et le Recueil de Gédéon de Catalogne* (1v. paru, Dax, France [1948]), 135. "Les ordonnances et lettres de change du gouvernement de Montréal en 1759," APQ *Rapport, 1924–25*, 229–359. PAC *Report, 1918*, app. B, 34–35.
Bonnault, "Le Canada militaire," APQ *Rapport, 1949–51*, 426–27. Le Jeune, *Dictionnaire*. É.-Z. Massicotte, "Les arpenteurs de Montréal sous le régime français," *BRH*, XXIV (1918), 306; "Répertoire des engagements pour l'Ouest," APQ *Rapport, 1930–31*, 367–426; *1931–32*, 316–28. P.-G. Roy, *Inv. jug. et délib., 1717–1760*, I, 274, 280; II, 15; III, 20, 46, 51; IV, 40, 122, 150, 171, 177, 191, 282; V, 90, 92. Tanguay, *Dictionnaire*. Claude de Bonnault, "Les Coigne du Berry en Canada," *BRH*, XLVI (1940), 276–84. Philéas Gagnon, "Nos anciennes cours d'appel," *BRH*, XXVI (1920), 345–49.

COUAGNE, THÉRÈSE DE (Poulin de Francheville), b. 19 Jan. 1697 in Montreal, daughter of Charles de Couagne*, a merchant trader, and Marie Gaudé; d. 26 Feb. 1764 at the Hôtel-Dieu of Montreal.

Thérèse de Couagne, who was the daughter of one of the richest merchants in Montreal, married a young and active Montreal merchant trader, François Poulin* de Francheville, on 27 Nov. 1718. The previous day she had signed her marriage contract in the presence of the governor of Montreal, Claude de Ramezay*, and of several other members of Montreal society gathered in the home of her stepfather, Pierre Derivon de Budemon. To the communal estate, to which Poulin de Francheville contributed 8,000 *livres*,

she brought a dowry of 2,500 *livres* from the assets of the succession of Charles de Couagne, who had died in 1706.

Not until her husband's death on 28 Nov. 1733 did Thérèse de Couagne, who had always lived in a milieu of merchant traders, become interested herself in business. Being François Poulin de Francheville's sole heir, since their one child had lived only a month, she wanted to carry on her husband's work. He had left her all his fortune, including the family house in Rue Saint-Paul in Montreal and a 160-acre farm in the parish of Saint-Michel, which included 15 acres of land under cultivation, 15 acres in pasture, a stone house, a barn, a stable, and a cowshed; in addition he left her the shares he held in the Saint-Maurice ironworks. On 19 Dec. 1733 Mme Francheville undertook to respect the obligations which her husband had assumed towards the Saint-Maurice ironworks. Consequently she formed a new association with her husband's former partners, his brother Pierre POULIN, a merchant in Quebec, Ignace Gamelin* Jr, a Montreal merchant trader, François-Étienne CUGNET, the director of the Domaine d'Occident, and Louis-Frédéric de Bricault* de Valmur, Intendant Hocquart*'s secretary. But after a little less than two years of operation the partners returned their licence to work the iron mines to the king, since they had ascertained that they were not "able to continue working the aforementioned mines because of the considerable amounts of money that must be put up." In 1736 the ironworks passed into the hands of Cugnet and his partners. Mme Francheville also engaged in commercial activities, it seems, advancing money to merchants in need of funds.

Mme Francheville was not able to live for long in the two-storey stone house in Rue Saint-Paul on the shore of the St Lawrence; it was destroyed on 10 April 1734 in a fire that was set by her negro slave [see Marie-Joseph-Angélique*]. She apparently had her house rebuilt on the same site, since she was living in it in 1741, and in 1764, shortly before her death, she leased it for a yearly rent of 1,000 *livres*.

The day before her death, which occurred at the Hôtel-Dieu of Montreal on 26 Feb. 1764, she dictated her will to the notary Pierre Panet*, leaving 700 *livres* to two of her nieces, her silverware and linen to the community of the Hôtel-Dieu of Montreal "in consideration of the good care" that she had received. On 26 Feb. 1764, in accordance with the provisions of the will, Thérèse de Couagne was buried beside her husband in the chapel of Saint-Amable in the church of Notre-Dame de Montréal.

Like many other widows at that time [*see* Agathe de SAINT-PÈRE], Thérèse de Couagne played an active role in the economy of New France by taking in hand her deceased husband's business.

ANDRÉ LACHANCE

AN, Col., C11A, 61, ff.131ff.; 110, ff.93ff. ANQ, NF, Coll. de pièces jud. et not., 1036; NF, Dossiers du Cons. sup., Mat. crim., VIII, 237; NF, Registres du Cons. sup., registre criminel, 1730–1759, ff.24ff. ANQ-M, Greffe de François Comparet, 25 janv. 1747; Greffe de C.-R. Gaudron de Chevremont, 19 déc. 1733; Greffe de Michel Lepailleur, 26 nov. 1718; Greffe de Pierre Panet, 25 févr. 1764; Documents judiciares, 15 mai, 4, 21 juin 1734; Registre d'état civil, Notre-Dame de Montréal, 19 janv. 1697, 27 nov. 1718, 30 nov. 1733, 26 févr. 1764. "Aveu et dénombrement pour l'île de Montréal," APQ *Rapport, 1941–42*, 16, 146. "Recensement de Montréal, 1741" (Massicotte). P.-G. Roy, *Inv. jug. et délib., 1717–1760*, IV, 39–40; *Inv. ord. int.*, III, 44, 46.

COUC, ELIZABETH? (La Chenette, Techenet; Montour), daughter of Pierre Couc, *dit* Lafleur, and Marie Mite8ameg8k8e. The given name of this woman is not definitely known. If she was Elizabeth, as evidence suggests, she was born at Trois-Rivières in 1667. It has been claimed that she was married once in the church, but no record has been found and her husband's name is not known. Her several later marriages were probably according to Indian custom and cannot be dated exactly. She died about 1750 probably near Harris's Ferry (Harrisburg, Pa.).

Information on Elizabeth Couc's early life is vague and contradictory. She was captured by an Iroquois war party about 1695, just where is uncertain. According to one account she was only a child of ten and was seized by anti-French raiders; according to another she was already married and living among the English, and her captors were pro-French Iroquois. Ransomed by her brother-in-law Maurice Ménard, she accompanied him to Michilimackinac where he was an interpreter. While there, she apparently ran afoul of Cadillac [Laumet*], the commandant, who later reported that he had "sent her under guard to the Chevalier de [Callière*] who sent her down to Quebec to send her to France," but that she had been rescued by Outoutagan* who brought her back to Michilimackinac and married her.

Although it is not necessary to believe Cadillac's assertion that she had been "kept by more than a hundred men," her attitude to marriage was apparently somewhat casual. By 1704 she was living at Detroit and was known as Mme La Chenette or Mme Techenet. When in late 1706 Étienne de Véniard* de Bourgmond, a former acting commandant of Detroit, deserted the post to live in the woods, she went with him, and it was said that she had "for a long time led a scandalous life with the said Sieur de Bourgmont."

Her brother Louis Couc Montour left Detroit at about the same time and went to New York, where the governor engaged him to conduct the western Indians to Albany for trade, and she joined him in the English colony. After his death in 1709, Mme Montour (as she now called herself) was employed as an interpreter by the governor and became the wife of an Oneida chief, Carundawana (Robert Hunter), who was killed in 1729 when with an Indian war party in South Carolina.

In 1727 she and her husband attended an Indian conference in Philadelphia; and so far as is known she spent the remainder of her life in Pennsylvania, where she performed a few official services and was the centre of some attention. She was regarded as a Frenchwoman and was reported to have lived among the Miamis and as "having a Sister married to one of that Nation." Count von Zinzendorf, who met her in 1742, described her as an Indianized Frenchwoman from Quebec. The story of her early life as reported by Witham Marshe, who met her at Lancaster in 1744, is a mixture of fact and fiction: he understood that her father was a governor of Canada.

Mme Montour lived near the present site of Williamsport, Pa., about 1737–42 and at that of Sunbury about 1745. In the following year her son Andrew moved to the Ohio, travelling from Logstown (Ambridge, Pa.) to Venango (Franklin, Pa.) "in the Month of March, when his Mother who was blind rode on Horseback and he led the Horse on Foot all the Way." She was reported living with him near Harris's Ferry in October 1748, but seems to have died no great while afterward.

Andrew, also known as Henry, was employed in Indian affairs by Pennsylvania and Virginia; another son, Louis, is mentioned; her "daughters" included French Margaret, actually a niece, and even the latter's daughter Catherine, both of whom for a time made their home with her. A younger brother, Jean, traded at Albany in 1725 and is mentioned in Pennsylvania in 1728–34.

WILLIAM A. HUNTER

Moravian Church Archives (Bethlehem, Pa.), Indian missions, box 121, Shamokin. New York State Archives (Albany), Colonial manuscripts, 57, f.169a; 62, ff.1, 3. PAC, RG 10, A3, 1819, ff.55, 137a–38, 296–96a. "Cadillac papers," *Michigan Pioneer Coll.*,

Coulon de Villiers

XXXIII (1903), 237–38, 432–41; XXXIV (1904), 234–36. [Cadwallader Colden], *The letters and papers of Cadwallader Colden . . .* (9v., N.Y. Hist. Soc. *Coll.*, L–LVI (1917–23), LXVII–LXVIII (1934–35), New York, 1918–37), IX, 370–74; "Letters on Smith's history of New York,"N.Y. Hist. Soc. *Coll.*, I (1868), 200. *Information respecting the history, condition and prospects of the Indian tribes of the United States . . .* , ed. H. R. Schoolcraft (6v., Philadelphia, Pa., 1851–57), IV, 326–27. *NYCD* (O'Callaghan and Fernow), V, 64–65, 268, 273; IX, 830, 900, 902. Pennsylvania, *Colonial records*, III–IV. *Pennsylvania archives*, 1st ser., I; 2nd ser., VII, 146. "Witham Marshe's journal of the treaty held with the Six Nations . . . June 1744," Mass. Hist. Soc. *Coll.*, 1st ser., VII (1800), 189–91. Peter Wraxall, *An abridgement of the Indian affairs contained in four folio volumes, transacted in the colony of New York, from the year 1678 to the year 1751*, ed. C. H. McIlwain (Harvard historical studies, XXI, Cambridge, Mass., 1915), 50, 64–68. Benjamin Sulte, "The Montour family," *Notes and queries, historical, biographical and genealogical, relating chiefly to interior Pennsylvania* (4th ser., 2v., Harrisburg 1893–95), II, 19–21. Tanguay, *Dictionnaire*, I, 142, 440; III, 160.

COULON DE VILLIERS, LOUIS, officer in the colonial regular troops; b. 10 Aug. 1710 at Verchères, Que., son of Nicolas-Antoine Coulon* de Villiers and Angélique Jarret de Verchères; m. 29 Dec. 1753 to Marie-Amable Prud'homme at Montreal; d. 2 Nov. 1757 at Quebec.

Louis Coulon de Villiers began his career as a cadet in the colonial regulars, serving under his father's command at Fort Saint-Joseph (probably Niles, Mich.). In an attack on the Fox tribe some miles from the post at Baie-des-Puants (Green Bay, Wis.) in 1733 his father and one of his brothers were killed, and he himself was severely wounded. As recompense for his family's loss he was commissioned second ensign the following year. He continued to be stationed in the west where he won the respect of the Indian tribes and his superiors. He served in Louisiana on Le Moyne de Bienville's 1739 campaign against the Chickasaws; upon his return he was posted to Fort Saint-Frédéric (Crown Point) on Lake Champlain. In 1748 he was promoted lieutenant and two years later, because of his high reputation among the tribes of the region, he was appointed to command at Fort des Miamis (probably at or near Fort Wayne, Ind.). Anglo-American fur-traders had invaded the country and established close ties with the Miamis. His orders from Governor General Taffanel de La Jonquière required him to wean that tribe away from the English interest and restore French authority. He enjoyed little success but upon his return to Montreal in 1753 he was promoted captain.

When in 1754 tension mounted in the Ohio valley, with France determined to dispute the territorial claims of Virginia, Governor General Duquesne* rushed reinforcements to the forts recently built between Lake Erie and the fork of the Ohio River. Louis Coulon was given command of 600 Canadians and over 100 mission Indians. When he arrived at Fort Duquesne (Pittsburgh, Pa.) on 26 June he learned that although England and France were not at war a party of some 30 Canadians led by his brother, Jumonville [Coulon], had been ambushed by a detachment of Virginia militia under George Washington and some Indians led by Tanaghrisson. Jumonville and nine other Canadians had been killed; only one of the rest had escaped being taken prisoner. Claude-Pierre Pécaudy* de Contrecœur, commandant of the fort, had mustered 500 of his garrison to avenge this act and drive the Americans off the territory claimed by France. Louis Coulon's request that he be given command of the detachment was granted.

Two days later the party, accompanied by a number of allied Indians many of whom later defected, left Fort Duquesne. En route they came upon the site of the ambush of Jumonville's small party. Washington had left the scalped corpses unburied, a prey to wolves and crows. On 3 July the Canadians made contact with the enemy who had taken refuge in a crude log redoubt, aptly named Fort Necessity (near Farmington, Pa.). The morale and discipline of the American militia were low, their fear of the Canadians high. For nine hours, between intermittent rain squalls, the Canadian forces poured a withering fire on the enemy, inflicting a hundred casualties – about a quarter of the Americans' strength. By nightfall Louis Coulon's casualties were only three killed and 17 wounded, but his men were exhausted, powder and ball were running low, and there was reason to fear that American reinforcements were approaching. He therefore decided to parley. Washington quickly agreed. Coulon drew up articles of capitulation, declaring that the French had no desire to disturb the peace between the two kingdoms but wished only to "avenge the murder of one of our officers, bearer of a summons, and of his escort, and also to prevent any establishment being made on the lands of my King." The Americans were permitted to return to their country in safety with the honours of war, the condition being that they gave their word to abandon their establishments west of the Alleghenies for the ensuing 12 months. They also agreed to return to Fort Duquesne within two and a half months the prisoners they had taken in their attack on Jumonville's party. To ensure their compliance with these terms they handed over two hostages, Robert STOBO and their interpreter, Jacob Van Braam.

The next day the Americans fled back to their settlements so precipitately that Washington left his journal behind with the abandoned baggage. The French government made good use of its contents, and of the articles of capitulation, to label the English admitted murderers and aggressors. Washington denied that he had knowingly admitted guilt of murder. He and his fellow officers claimed that their interpreter, in translating the terms, had substituted either "death" or "loss of" for the incriminating word *assassin*. The Americans, however, subsequently made plain that they had no intention of honouring the document to which Washington had appended his signature. The French prisoners were not released, Stobo violated his parole and acted as a spy, and before the stipulated year was up Washington accompanied Major-General Edward Braddock's army in a full-scale assault on Fort Duquesne.

Although Governor Duquesne had serious misgivings concerning the clause in the terms of capitulation that barred the Americans from the Ohio valley for only one year, he was pleased with the outcome of the affair. French honour had been vindicated, and the American threat to the French position in the west removed. In his report to the minister of Marine he praised not only Coulon de Villiers's valour, but also his restraint in sparing the lives of the Americans despite the bitter resentment he must have felt at the killing of his brother.

The following year, 1755, when full scale hostilities began, Louis Coulon gained renown in the guerilla warfare on the Pennsylvania frontier. He subsequently distinguished himself at the capture of forts Oswego and William Henry (also called Fort George; now Lake George, N.Y.). In 1755 Governor General Pierre de Rigaud* de Vaudreuil had repeated the request of his predecessor in office that Louis Coulon de Villiers be awarded the cross of Saint-Louis, declaring that he had merited it long since for his valiant record, and adding that "The family of the Sieur de Villiers has always distinguished itself in the service. There is not one of them who has not died in action against the enemy." Ironically, that coveted award was received by Coulon de Villiers a few days before he was stricken by smallpox. On 2 Nov. 1757 Vaudreuil wrote to inform the minister that Louis Coulon had died. "It is

sad, My Lord," he wrote, "that such an excellent officer should succumb to that malady after having exposed himself to the greatest dangers."

W. J. ECCLES

[The eminent American historians Francis Parkman and L. H. Gipson strive to justify Washington's actions, to exonerate him from the charge of having murdered Jumonville and of admitting the crime. In discussing the aftermath of the affair both of them misconstrue some of the evidence and ignore certain pertinent facts. Both state that upon learning of Jumonville's death Governor General Duquesne dispatched Louis Coulon from Montreal with reinforcements. Duquesne did not receive word of the event until some time between 20 and 24 June, and Coulon de Villiers arrived at Fort Duquesne on 26 June. Quoting in translation (and giving the wrong provenance for the quotation), Parkman writes that the senior officers at Fort Duquesne agreed, "should the English have withdrawn to their side of the mountains, 'they should be followed to their settlements to destroy them and treat them as enemies, till that nation should give ample satisfaction and completely change its conduct.'" This translation might be taken to mean that Coulon de Villiers was ordered to destroy the English settlements, but the original French ["Si les Anglois s'étoient retirés de dessus nos terres qu'on iroit jusques dans leurs habitations pour les detruire et les traiter comme Ennemis jusqu'a ample satisfaction et changement de conduite de cette Nation"] allows of no such interpretation. It was Washington's force, not the English settlements, that was to be attacked. Using the same document, Gipson writes that Villiers was ordered that, should he discover the enemy had retired beyond the mountains, "he should nevertheless continue his march into the region of their settlements and proceed to destroy the habitations. . . . In other words, reprisals were to be made even to the extent of ravishing the English frontier settlements." In fact, war had not been declared and the French were being careful to give the English no grounds to declare it. Contrecœur's order of 28 June 1754 to Coulon specifically stated: "Despite their unheard of action, the Sr de Villiers is enjoined to avoid all cruelty so far as is within his power." W.J.E.]

See also: AE, Mém. et doc., Amérique, 10/1, ff.133–34. AN, Col., D²ᶜ, 47, ff.8, 689; 48, ff.41, 61, 216; 49, f.351; 57, ff.154, 164; 61, ff.8, 26, 47, 89, 116; E, 95; Marine, C⁷, 75. *Illinois on eve of Seven Years' War* (Pease and Jenison), xxxii–xxxiii. *Papiers Contrecœur* (Grenier). "Procès de Robert Stobo et de Jacob Wambram pour crime de haute trahison," APQ *Rapport, 1922–23*, 299–347. Eccles, *Canadian frontier*. Gipson, *British empire before the American revolution*, VI. Lanctot, *History of Canada*, III. Parkman, *Montcalm and Wolfe*. Stanley, *New France*.

COULON DE VILLIERS, NICOLAS-ANTOINE, captain in the colonial regular troops, major of Trois-Rivières; b. 25 June 1708 at Contrecœur, eldest son of Nicolas-Antoine Coulon* de Vil-

Coulon de Villiers de Jumonville

liers and Angélique Jarret de Verchères; d. 3 April 1750 in Montreal.

Nicolas-Antoine Coulon de Villiers was a member of a typical military family of the Canadian nobility. His father and at least two of his brothers, LOUIS and JOSEPH, had active military careers. A cadet in 1725, Nicolas-Antoine served under his father at Fort Saint-Joseph (probably Niles, Mich.). In 1730 he saw action against the Foxes. Two years later he was recommended for a commission as second ensign. In 1733, with his father, now commandant of Baie-des-Puants (Green Bay, Wis.), two brothers, and a brother-in-law, he was again in action against the Foxes; his father, brother-in-law, and one brother were killed, the other brother wounded. Nicolas-Antoine rallied the French forces, routed the enemy in a counter attack, then took over command of the post. In recognition of his valour and his family's loss he was given accelerated promotion to lieutenant in 1734 and succeeded to the command of his father's old post at Saint-Joseph.

About 1742, Nicolas-Antoine returned to Quebec where he married, on 7 Oct. 1743, Madeleine-Marie-Anne Tarieu de La Pérade, widow of Richard TESTU de La Richardière. In 1744 he received the commission of captain solicited for him by Governor BEAUHARNOIS. Two years later he was posted to Acadia and in February 1747, at Grand-Pré (N.S.), he led some 250 Canadians in an assault on over 500 New England troops commanded by Arthur NOBLE. His left arm was shattered by a musket ball but his force inflicted heavy losses on the enemy, forcing them to surrender. In October Coulon de Villiers went to France for treatment of his wound at a thermal spring [see Louis de LA CORNE]. In 1748 he was awarded the cross of the order of Saint-Louis with an 800-*livre* gratuity, and was appointed major of Trois-Rivières. After his return to Canada in 1749 he was obliged to have his wounded arm amputated. He did not survive the operation, and was buried at Montreal on 4 April 1750.

W. J. ECCLES

AJQ, Registre d'état civil, Notre-Dame de Québec, 7 oct. 1743. AN, Col., C¹¹D, 8, ff.130–34; D²C, 47, f.465; 48, ff.38, 176, 203, 279, 305, 320, 326. ANQ, Greffe de C.-H. Du Laurent, 4 oct. 1743. ASQ, Polygraphie, IV, 74; VII, 26. "Recensement de Québec, 1744" (APQ *Rapport*), 142. Fauteux, *Les chevaliers de Saint-Louis*, 144. P.-G. Roy, *Les officiers d'état-major*, 264–67. Amédée Gosselin, "Notes sur la famille Coulon de Villiers," *BRH*, XII (1906), 193–207.

COULON DE VILLIERS DE JUMONVILLE, JOSEPH, ensign in the colonial regular troops; b.

8 Sept. 1718 on the seigneury of Verchères, son of Nicolas-Antoine Coulon* de Villiers and Angélique Jarret de Verchères; d. 28 May 1754 near present Jumonville, Pa.

One of six brothers, all officers in the colonial regulars, Joseph Coulon de Villiers de Jumonville had a relatively undistinguished military career until 28 May 1754 when he was killed by what Horace Walpole described as "a volley fired by a young Virginian in the backwoods of America [that] set the world on fire." It proved to be the opening shot in the Seven Years' War.

In 1733 Jumonville, a 15-year-old cadet, was at the post of Baie-des-Puants (Green Bay, Wis.) when his father and one of his brothers were killed in an attack on the Foxes. In the ensuing decade, without major conflicts and their attendant casualties, promotion was slow in the colonial regulars; thus it was not until 1743, after serving in Louisiana on LE MOYNE de Bienville's 1739 campaign against the Chickasaws, that he received the expectancy of an ensign's commission. Two years later, however, with the onset of the War of the Austrian Succession, he was commissioned second ensign. His career now established, on 11 Oct. 1745 he married Marie-Anne-Marguerite Soumande at Montreal. During the following winter he served on the Acadian frontier and then saw action with war parties against the frontier outposts of New York.

No sooner had hostilities in Europe ended in 1748 than a conflict began in North America for the Ohio valley. Fur-traders from the English colonies had infiltrated the region and land speculators in Virginia claimed title to it. France disputed these claims, drove out the American traders, and in 1753 began constructing a chain of forts south of Lake Erie to the Ohio River. TANAGHRISSON and other Indian leaders of the region protested and the governor of Virginia sent an officer of the colonial militia, George Washington, to order the French to vacate this territory. He received a polite but firm refusal. The French then built Fort Duquesne, where Pittsburgh now stands, thereby gaining military control of the region. In the spring of 1754 Washington was again sent to the Ohio with a force of colonial militia to assert British sovereignty, by force if necessary, despite the fact that England and France were at peace.

The commandant at Fort Duquesne, Claude-Pierre Pécaudy* de Contrecœur, had strict orders to avoid hostilities with the Americans but to defend his position against attack. Learning of the approach of a reportedly large American force, on 23 May 1754 he dispatched Jumonville with some 30 men to discover if Washington had in fact invaded French-claimed territory. Were this to be the case he was to send word back to the fort, then deliver a formal summons to Washington calling on him to withdraw. His small force was an embassy, resembling Washington's to Jacques LEGARDEUR de Saint-Pierre the preceding year, and he neglected to post sentries around his encampment.

At daybreak on the 28th Washington with 40 men stole up on the French camp near present Jumonville, Pa. Some were still asleep, others preparing breakfast. Without warning Washington gave the order to fire. The Canadians who escaped the volley scrambled for their weapons but were swiftly overwhelmed. Jumonville, the French later claimed, was struck down while trying to proclaim his official summons. Ten of the Canadians were killed, one wounded, all but one of the rest taken prisoner. Washington and his men then retired, leaving the bodies of their victims for the wolves. A force of 500 Canadian regulars and militia sent to avenge the attack and drive the Americans out was led by Jumonville's brother, Louis COULON de Villiers.

W. J. ECCLES

ASQ, Polygraphie, VII, 26. *Papiers Contrecœur* (Grenier). Parkman, *Montcalm and Wolfe*. Stanley, *New France*. Marc de Villiers Du Terrage, *Les dernières années de la Louisiane française* . . . (Paris, 1905). Amédée Gosselin, "Notes sur la famille Coulon de Villiers," *BRH*, XII (1906), 207–18, 289–90.

COURVAL, FRANÇOIS-LOUIS POULIN DE. *See* POULIN

COURVAL, LOUIS-JEAN POULIN DE. *See* POULIN

COURVAL CRESSÉ, LOUIS-PIERRE POULIN DE. *See* POULIN

CROISILLE, CHARLES LEGARDEUR DE. *See* LEGARDEUR

CRUSOE, ROBINSON, Oupeshepow (Cree) hunter from Great Whale River; d. 9 Dec. 1755 at Richmond Fort.

Robinson Crusoe and his son Friday came to the Hudson's Bay Company's newly founded fort on Richmond Gulf (Lac Guillaume-Delisle, Que.) in 1750. For the next five years Crusoe was of inestimable assistance to the factor, John POTTS. Crusoe carried the annual packet to Eastmain House in 1751. The next year he was sent to Great Whale River with a captain's coat and hat for Shewescome, a chief there, to invite him

to bring his band to hunt whales at Little Whale River. Shewescome and his men came, accepted presents of brandy and tobacco, but did no hunting. Crusoe was a particularly effective killer of whales, and the smith at Richmond Fort made whaling instruments under his directions.

Crusoe's conduct of his domestic affairs brought him a brush with death in 1753. Several years before, he had taken his son-in-law's mother to wife. Then in 1753, when she was about 80, he turned her out and took another wife. Although other Indians supported his action, saying the woman and her relatives had given him much ill-usage, his son-in-law attacked him, inflicting six cuts on his head with a hatchet. Potts sent a sledge to bring him to the factory, as the death of "the best hunter, whale fisher, snowshoe maker, and best supplier of country provisions" would have been a serious blow to the settlement.

Crusoe recovered, and when in 1754 the Eskimos sacked the outpost at Little Whale River and carried off Matthew Warden, he supplied venison to the uneasy defenders of Richmond, who were afraid to leave their fort for fear of an Eskimo attack. When the two Eskimos whom Potts had captured as hostages for Warden were killed in trying to escape, Crusoe advised against hanging the bodies on a gibbet, English style, as doing so would be an invitation for the Eskimos to kill Warden if he were still alive. In March 1755 Potts sent Crusoe to Eastmain with letters for the forts at Albany (Fort Albany, Ont.) and Moose (Moose Factory, Ont.) describing the troubles at Richmond.

Crusoe was brought to the factory lame and ill in November, and he took a fever and died on 9 December. Henry Pollexfen Jr, who was in charge during Potts' absence, recorded: "This morning died Robinson Crusoe, an honest worthy Indian; a man that has been the greatest help if not the only one of real Service to the Factory, and on whome the Whale fishing chiefly depended which makes his death regreted by the Europeans here as well as by his own Countrymen."

GEORGE E. THORMAN

HBC Arch. B.182/a/1–8.

CUGNET, FRANÇOIS-ÉTIENNE, lawyer, merchant, entrepreneur, director of the Domaine d'Occident in New France, member of the Conseil Supérieur; b. in Paris in 1688, third and last child of Jean (Jean-Baptiste) Cugnet, and Madeleine Baudin; d. 19 Aug. 1751 in Quebec.

François-Étienne Cugnet's father was dean of

the faculty of law of the Université de Paris, an annual appointment, on four different occasions, and was particularly noted for his reform of the examination system. His older brother, Jean-Baptiste, like his father holding a doctorate-in-law, was dean of the faculty in 1734, 1740, and 1749. There was also an older sister. The two eldest children never married, and the French branch of the Cugnet family ended with their deaths. François-Étienne was married on or shortly after 23 Jan. 1717 to Louise-Madeleine Dusautoy (Dusaultoir), daughter of Charles Dusautoy, "a Paris bourgeois"; of this union five children would survive.

His marriage contract is the first positive evidence about François-Étienne as material pertaining to his childhood has disappeared. Documents concerning his father and mother and others dating after his arrival in New France nevertheless give some indication of the milieu in which he passed his childhood and reveal something of his education. He was born, raised, and educated within the shadows of the Sorbonne. His parents did not have great wealth or belong to the nobility but were among what have been called "the well-to-do Parisian families." A reference to him in 1730 as "lawyer in the *parlement* of Paris" indicates that he held a *license en droit* with a special field in either civil or commercial law, the former being the more logical area of study. But he made his career chiefly in commerce, finance, and administration rather than law, as his activities in the colony and his choice of a spouse demonstrate, even though he was to have judicial functions in New France. His wife's family belonged to the mercantile class; the provisions of their marriage contract illustrate a typical French bourgeois concern for the protection of a wife's inheritance within the family.

Cugnet, accompanied by his wife, a clerk, and a valet, arrived in New France on 1 Oct. 1719. They had been granted free passage and were seated at the captain's table on the ship. Cugnet's official post in the colony was that of representative of the lessee of the Domaine d'Occident; however, he sometimes describes himself, or is described by others, as director.

The Domaine d'Occident, in New France, was part of the Fermes Unies of France. Since 1674 the Domaine had been leased out, usually by subcontract, by the holders of the bail of the Fermes Unies. Prices for this lease varied from 350,000 to 550,000 *livres* per year. The privileges attached to the lease included the right to collect a tax of 25 per cent in kind on beaver pelts delivered to the lessee's counters, and a tax of 10 per cent on most other forms of pelts. The lessee could assess a

tariff of 10 per cent on wines and liquors and on tobacco imported into the colony, and could collect a tax on goods exported from it. The Domaine d'Occident had the right to revenues derived from seigneurial dues owed to the crown in the colony and from the estates of persons dying intestate and without heirs, and had also the trading rights in the Domaine du Roi. The latter privilege was usually sub-leased by the holder of the lease of the Domaine to a merchant-trader of New France.

This standard arrangement was complicated with the establishment of the Compagnie des Indes, as it became known, by the spectacular Scottish speculator, John Law. In 1717 his "System" was granted the fur trade monopoly of New France and Louisiana. After the collapse of the "System" in 1720, the fur trade monopoly in the colony remained in the hands of the company he had established, until the end of the French régime. The structure of the Domaine, and its privileges, were further complicated in 1732 when the French state took over the administration of the Domaine on its own account, but allowed the Compagnie des Indes to retain the fur trade monopoly. Thus from the time of Cugnet's arrival in 1719, the privileges and revenues of the Domaine d'Occident were divided into two: those derived from the trade in furs, the monopoly of which belonged to the Compagnie des Indes, and all other revenues, tariffs, seigneurial and succession rights, which belonged to the Domaine, under private lease till 1732 and controlled by the state after that date. But regardless who the lessee was, or to whom the revenues went, Cugnet was the effective administrator of the Domaine d'Occident from the time of his arrival till his death, with the exception of a trip to France in 1742–43.

Shortly after the Cugnets arrived in Quebec they rented a dwelling in the Rue Sault-au-Matelot at the fairly high annual rental of 400 *livres*, paid by the Domaine. A few years later Cugnet built a splendid house in the Rue Saint-Pierre, the élite merchant quarter of Quebec, at the high cost of 30,000 *livres*. Here he would reside until his death.

Cugnet's talents, administrative and legal, were quickly put to use. A series of ordinances were issued by the intendant at his request concerning the rights of the monopolists of the Domaine. Throughout the 1720s he was engaged in law cases on behalf of the Domaine regarding the estates of person dying intestate. Legal costs being high, the estates of the deceased were plucked for what the traffic would bear. In 1729, Cugnet, supporting the Domaine's right to collect duties on goods imported into the colony or exported from New France, associated himself with the representative of the Compagnie des Indes, Nicolas LANOULLIER de Boisclerc; together they would ensure respect for each other's monopolies. Cugnet's most important task, with the greatest return to the monopolist, was the administration of the Domaine du Roi: the north shore of the St Lawrence from the Île aux Coudres and Malbaie to Labrador and including the trading posts at Sept-Îles, the Moisie River, Chicoutimi, the Lac Saint-Jean area, and the dependent but ill-defined lands in the environs. In a report prepared by Cugnet, he claimed the Domaine du Roi had been viciously stripped of its resources by earlier sub-lessees such as Denis Riverin*, Charles Guillimin*, Pierre Soumande, and members of the Hazeur family. Indians living there had grown to suspect subcontractors to the point that trade in the area was reduced to nothing. Under his able administration Cugnet realized an annual profit for the monopolist of 3,800 *livres* per year between 1719 and 1732.

His administrative efforts and his energy were not without reward. His salary as administrator of the Domaine d'Occident was 3,000 *livres* per year, and he leased part of his home to it, at 1,000 *livres* per year. Moreover, in 1721, little more than a year after his arrival the intendant, Michel BÉGON, proposed him to the minister of Marine as worthy of consideration for a seat on the Conseil Supérieur. This proposal was refused on the ground of possible conflict of interest between Cugnet as administrator of the Domaine and Cugnet as a member of the superior court of New France. In 1727 Charles de BEAUHARNOIS, the governor, and the intendant Claude-Thomas Dupuy* proposed Cugnet as attorney general, again without result. Finally, in 1730, probably thanks to the influence of the new financial commissary, Hocquart*, Cugnet was appointed to the Conseil Supérieur in the place of Guillaume Gaillard* who had died the preceding year, but he still retained his administrative post in the Domaine. Within three years of his appointment to the council, he was named first councillor, an honour usually reserved for the senior member whereas Cugnet was a junior. The duties of New France's highest court were varied, but not onerous. The council, as a civil court of appeal, met between 45 and 50 times a year. Between the years 1730 and 1751, when Cugnet was a member, it sat as a criminal court 66 times. Cugnet was assiduous in his attendance and, in the absence of the intendant, he presided over council meetings. His services as an investigator and arbitrator were often called upon, an indication of the respect with which he was held in the community. These not too strenuous tasks brought him an annual stipend of 900 *livres* per year from 1733 till his death.

An astonishing range of economic activities also occupied this quick mind. Among his minor commercial endeavours was the raising and exporting of Canadian tobacco, little appreciated, let it be said, in France. Frenchmen much preferred the leaf produced in their West Indian holdings. He attempted the domestication of "bœufs illinois" for their hides but was unsuccessful in getting the scheme operative [*see* Jean-Baptiste GASTINEAU Duplessis]. A third small business was the manufacturing of glue.

One of his most important entrepreneurial endeavours was the Saint-Maurice ironworks. In 1729, François Poulin* de Francheville, a Montreal-based fur-trader and entrepreneur, had been granted rights to establish and exploit an iron industry that he proposed developing on the lands he owned at Saint-Maurice and in the environs. He soon realized that his project was beyond his personal financial capacities, and decided to associate several colonial notables in his enterprise, specifically Cugnet, Ignace Gamelin* Jr, a fellow fur-trader and Montreal cohort, his brother Pierre POULIN, and the intendant's secretary, Louis-Frédéric Bricault* de Valmur. This new association, with the active support of Intendant Hocquart, was granted a 10,000 *livres* loan by the French state. Francheville's death in November 1733 temporarily halted the establishment of the ironworks [*see* Thérèse de COUAGNE].

Between 1733 and 1735 Cugnet was the dominant figure in what would become the Compagnie des Forges du Saint-Maurice. As a result of letters written by Hocquart to Maurepas, it was decided in 1735 to send an experienced French forge master to assess the establishment made by the old associates and evaluate its potential. In the fall of 1735, Pierre-François Olivier* de Vézin arrived in the colony, and within a few months submitted an elaborate report on construction and establishment costs. The buildings and equipment, according to the forge master, would cost 36,000 *livres*; annual production costs would be 61,250 *livres*; expected annual profits might be 60,000 *livres*, almost double the establishment costs and equal to annual production expenditures.

On the basis of these high hopes, Cugnet formed a new company on 16 Oct. 1736 whose members were himself, Ignace Gamelin once again, Olivier de Vézin, Jacques SIMONET d'Abergemont, another forge master from

Cugnet

France (each of these four having a 4.25 share), Thomas-Jacques TASCHEREAU, the agent of the treasurer of the Marine in New France (two shares), and Hocquart (one share). All of them, as well as Maurepas (who, it should be noted, had requested *expert* opinion in France), placed a naïve faith in Vézin's cost projections. However, lack of capital and of savings, a common feature of colonial and underdeveloped societies, led to repeated demands for assistance from the French state. In addition to the 10,000 *livres* advanced to Francheville and associates, Cugnet and his associates initially received an advance of 100,000 *livres*, to be repaid out of production. Moreover, a guaranteed market for the ironworks' products was provided in the king's shipyards in Quebec, as well as those of Rochefort, France. If Vézin's estimates had been accurate, the associates would have found themselves in the enviable position of having capitalized their industry by state aid and without investing any of their own funds.

Vézin's visions were chimerical. By 1740 the 100,000 *livres* had been expended and also a further advance of about 83,000 *livres* made by the intendant without waiting for the prior consent of the minister. Cugnet borrowed, as Hocquart rather gently put it, 40,000 *livres* for the ironworks from the strong box of the Domaine d'Occident of which he was the administrator; he also obtained goods from the king's stores. Exhaustion of the state's advances also led Cugnet to assist the endeavour himself; he issued letters of credit, or assumed personally the obligation of paying for supplies required by the industry. Creditors were no longer willing to wait. Between 1735 and 1741 establishment and production costs had totalled 505,356 *livres*; receipts from sales and produce were 114,473 *livres*, and the ironworks – buildings, hammers, bellows, etc. – were valued a few years later at 141,000 *livres*. There was, obviously, a large deficit.

In spite of the fact that the articles of association had specified that each of the partners in the ironworks was responsible in proportion to his share in the enterprise, Cugnet was the only one pursued by the creditors. He declared personal bankruptcy in 1741, but through the intervention of the intendant, and with the support of the minister of Marine, he was permitted in 1742 to use sequestered goods for continued commercial activities. Despite his bankruptcy, the total value of his estate increased between 1741 and his death in 1751. The Saint-Maurice ironworks continued in operation until 1883.

In April 1737 Cugnet obtained the seigneury of Saint-Étienne which he had long wanted, thanks to Hocquart who was trying to encourage settlement of the south shore of the St Lawrence. Cugnet's most important, in the sense of most profitable, economic endeavour was the lease he held on the Tadoussac post from 1737 until 1749. He had administered this trade from his arrival in the colony as agent of the Domaine d'Occident and after 1732 as agent of the crown. Between 1732 and 1737 annual profits consistently went down. Nevertheless Cugnet leased the trade in 1737 for nine years at an annual lease price of 4,500 *livres*. In 1741, when the ironworks were in deep trouble, Beauharnois tried to have Cugnet's rights to the Tadoussac post annulled in favour of Jacques de LAFONTAINE de Belcour, but was not successful. In 1745 Cugnet submitted a report according to which his annual profits in eight years were 3,541 *livres* 10 *sols* 7 *deniers*. Gilles Hocquart, the intendant, under pressure from the minister who wanted the lease ended, questioned his figures; Cugnet revised them to indicate an annual profit of 6,000 *livres*. Even this figure was inaccurate for he consistently neglected to carry as a credit his initial outlay for stock and buildings, which would be, and was, returned to him when the lease was withdrawn from him in 1749 by François Bigot* who had no liking for him. His minimum annual profits during the tenure of his lease must have been 10,000 *livres* per year. Marie-Anne Barbel*, widow of Louis FORNEL, obtained the lease for the sum of 7,000 *livres* per year.

Cugnet's four sons pursued varied careers. The eldest, François-Joseph*, something of a scalawag, wrote several books on the legal system of New France after the conquest, and served as official translator during Guy Carleton*'s régime. Another son Jean-Baptiste, about whom little is known, died in the West Indies around 1748 or 1749. Thomas-Marie became a member of the Conseil Supérieur in 1757 after the death of Jean-François GAULTIER and an agent of the Compagnie des Indes. He retired to France after the conquest and died in Blois, France, in 1780. The last son, called, after the Intendant Hocquart, Gilles-Louis, became a priest and was a member of the chapter of Quebec; he returned to France after 1760 and died in Blois in 1767.

François-Étienne Cugnet, active citizen of New France, may, in spite of some failures, be considered to be "the very model" of a bourgeois-gentilhomme. In relatively restricted population areas, and in either colonies or countries in the process of development, exceptionally educated and active individuals assume

154

many functions within their society. Lack of trained personnel, and, most important, of entrepreneurial skills, allows them great social and economic mobility. In France, François-Étienne would have been one among thousands; in New France he was one among few. His activities in its society were political, legal, and economic. The extent of his library, and the continuous flow to it of reading materials from France, indicates, at the least, a curiosity and intellect well above the ordinary.

CAMERON NISH

[Because of his many activities, François-Étienne Cugnet is mentioned a number of times in various Canadian and European archives; a brief list would include: AJTR, Greffes de Joseph Caron, Pierre Petit, Louis Pillard, H.-O. Pressé, Joseph Rouillard. AN, Minutier central, Greffe de Savigny, 1690–1720; Greffe de Lemoyne, 1678–1728; MM, 1059–78, 1094–100; N, 88–101, 351–75; Y, 242–76, 14626; Col., B; C¹¹A; C¹¹G, 9; E, 101; F¹A; F³, 11–13. ANQ, Greffes de R.-C. Barolet, Nicolas Boisseau, C.-H. Du Laurent, Henry Hiché, Jean de Latour, J.-C. Panet, J.-N. Pinguet de Vaucour, François Rageot; NF, Ins. Cons. sup.; NF, Registres de la Prévôté de Québec. ANQ-M, Greffes de C.-R. Gaudron de Chevremont, J.-C. Porlier. "La banqueroute de François Étienne Cugnet, 1742," Cameron Nish, édit., L'Actualité économique (Montréal), 41 (1965–66), 146–202, 345–78, 762–810; 42 (1966–67), 161–208, 391–422, 704–27. Documents relating to Canadian currency during the French period (Shortt), I, 542. P.-G. Roy, Inv. jug. et délib., 1717–1760, passim; Inv. ord. int., passim. Raymond Du Bois Cahall, The sovereign council of New France: a study in Canadian constitutional history (Columbia University, Studies in history, economics and public law, LXV, no.1, New York, 1915). Adeline Daumard et François Furet, Structures et relations sociales à Paris au milieu du XVIIIe siècle (Cahiers des annales, 18, Paris, 1961). Dubé, Claude-Thomas Dupuy, passim. Frégault, François Bigot, I, 360–62. G. T. Matthews, The royal general farms in eighteenth-century France (New York, 1958). George Péries, La faculté de droit dans l'ancienne université de Paris (1160–1793) (Paris, 1890). Sulte, Mélanges historiques (Malchelosse), VI. Albert Tessier, Les forges Saint-Maurice, 1729–1883 (Trois-Rivières, Qué., 1952), 53–74. Marine Leland, "François-Joseph Cugnet, 1720–1789," RUL, XVI (1961–62), 3–13, 129–39, 205–14. Cameron Nish, "François Étienne Cugnet et les forges de Saint-Maurice: un type d'entrepreneur et d'entreprise en Nouvelle-France," L'Actualité économique, 42 (1966–67), 884–900. C.N.]

CUILLERIER, MARIE-ANNE-VÉRONIQUE, Nun Hospitaller of St Joseph, annalist; b. 13 Nov. 1680 in Montreal, daughter of René Cuillerier* and Marie Lucault; d. 21 Jan. 1751 in Montreal.

Marie-Anne-Véronique Cuillerier entered the order of the Nuns Hospitallers of St Joseph at Montreal in 1694 and made her profession in 1696. From 1725 to 1747 she held the office of secretary, which allowed her to communicate with the houses in France and brought her the task of continuing Sister Marie Morin*'s annals. Her letters and annals constitute documents of high quality. By her choice of details, her moving commentaries, her explanations of events, Sister Cuillerier furnishes first-hand information on the difficulties of daily life in New France and on the religious mentality of the inhabitants of Canada in the face of events.

In recalling the attack on the city of Quebec by Sir William Phips* in 1690, Sister Cuillerier set it in a great biblical perspective: "As Joshua was the only person to see the sun stand still in his favour, so this country may say that it is the only one which saw the ordinary ebb and flow of the sea stop for 24 hours to prevent its enemies from approaching Quebec before help coming from Montreal had arrived."

In speaking of the earthquake in 1732 she wrote: "It was on 16 September at a quarter past eleven that the first tremor was heard and felt: it knocked down 567 chimneys and cracked the walls of nearly all the houses . . . nothing can be more terrible than to see church towers and houses bending like reeds and swaying as badly as if they had been made of cards. . . . Public prayers did not move the Lord to pity, who was content to keep His whole people in a constant state of alarm for more than nine months. As rumblings had been heard constantly throughout this long period of time, the ladies made vows to give up hoop petticoats and frivolities, but there were some who, in accordance with the flightiness natural to the sex, when they no longer heard anything but a few small tremors, thought they were secure and resumed their adornments. God revenged Himself on the night of 25–26 October and caused a tremor like the first one to be heard."

With her attention to realistic and picturesque details, Sister Cuillerier was able to make little-known events tragic. For example, in 1746 she spoke of a "cloud of caterpillars sent by the Lord's justice or by some malicious acts of a bad Christian, as the settlers of Quebec say." When these "wretched creatures" died, she wrote, "they lay to the depth of half a foot in the countryside, and the froth that they had made while eating was so horrible that one stepped into it half way up to one's knees . . . that did not prevent them from getting into the houses and climbing on the children, whom they bit; people had to erect scaffoldings to save their innocent infants. They moved like famished creatures to look for people in their beds."

On reading the account of these misfortunes and many others, such as epidemics and fires, we understand why Sister Cuillerier wrote: "I should exhaust my stock of expressions, my dear Sisters, if I tried to tell you of the great suffering that we endured; we were no longer able to control ourselves, and night and day our tears sprinkled our bread and our beds." With a touch of irony she added: "As a crowning good fortune the crop has failed and nearly everyone is lacking bread; we are obliged to eat Indian corn twice a day."

In 1747 Sister Cuillerier was replaced in her office as secretary by Sister Catherine Porlier. The history of the community does not give us any information about her final years or her death, which occurred on 21 Jan. 1751.

HÉLÈNE BERNIER

AHSJ, Annales de sœur Marie Morin, 1697–1725; Annales de sœur Véronique Cuillerier, 1725–1747; Déclarations de nos anciennes Mères pour constater la profession religieuse et le décès de nos sœurs. Archives des religieuses hospitalières de Saint-Joseph (La Flèche, France), Lettres de sœur Véronique Cuillerier. Mondoux, *L'Hôtel-Dieu de Montréal*.

D

DACCARRETTE (Dacaret, d'Acaret), MICHEL or **Miguel** (he signed **Daccarrette le Jeune** (the younger)), ship captain, privateer, fishing entrepreneur, merchant; b. probably before 1690 at Hendaye, France, son of Jacques Daccarrette and probably Marie Gastaignol; d. in 1745 at the siege of Louisbourg, Île Royale (Cape Breton Island).

Michel Daccarrette apparently immigrated to the fishing station at Plaisance (Placentia, Nfld.) before 1704, when the census contains a reference to an elder brother Joannis and "two brothers," probably Michel and Jacques. Joannis ran a fishing enterprise, invested in privateers, and engaged in other mercantile activities. Michel's first recorded business venture is in 1709 as a shareholder in a privateer, the *Marie*. In 1712 he sailed as captain of a *charroi*, the *Trompeur*, a 15-ton privateer guaranteed for 15,000 *livres* by François Boschet de Saint-Martin, a prominent shipowner at Plaisance. In 1713 Daccarrette commanded the *Marianne*, a small ship bound for Cayenne, Guiana, and France. At Plaisance, Joannis and Michel Daccarrette were important members of what was apparently a close-knit group of influential merchants and fishing entrepreneurs, often bound by family ties, and with overseas connections, principally in the Bayonne region of France. After 1714 when the Plaisance colony moved to Île Royale this group was to occupy a considerable position at Louisbourg. Daccarrette married his first wife, Jeanne Gonillon, at Plaisance in 1713; she appears to have accompanied him to Louisbourg with one child, probably their daughter Catherine.

On Île Royale the Daccarrettes set up a fishing enterprise: Joannis established himself at Louisbourg; Jacques and Michel, at La Baleine (Baleine Cove), where Michel began with four shallops. By 1718 he had moved to Louisbourg where he bought a fishery; he had acquired additional fisheries at Niganiche (Ingonish), Saint-Esprit, and Fourché (Fouchu) by 1726, and was operating with a total of 34 shallops. Daccarrette pursued fishing with pertinacity; in 1721–22 he and Boschet de Saint-Martin, now established at Petit Degrat (Petit-de-Grat Island), succeeded in breaking the Comte de Saint-Pierre's fishing monopoly on Île Saint-Jean (Prince Edward Island) and neighbouring islands, and a long series of court battles on both sides of the Atlantic ensued [*see* Gotteville* de Belile]. Daccarrette also began trading fish on his own account; he had sent two ships to France by 1726 and by the late 1720s he had shipped fish to the West Indies as well. He was one of Île Royale's largest fishing entrepreneurs and this trade provided the basis for numerous other ventures.

Michel Daccarrette began some of these commercial operations with Joannis, but rapidly assumed the directing role. Paying 40 per cent above the French price, the brothers in 1718 imported salt, foodstuffs, clothing, hardware, and marine supplies from Saint-Malo; these goods were sold locally or exported to Quebec. In 1719 Michel and Blaise Cassaignolles imported foodstuffs from Joseph Cadet, a Quebec merchant. Apparently this trade continued through the 1720s and 1730s. Daccarrette was at one time suspected of being involved in illicit trade. In 1727 he was denounced by the minister of Marine for serving as a cover for the governor of Louisbourg, Saint-Ovide [MONBETON], who was accused of shipping New England products to the West Indies in French ships. This accusation was never proved, but it is known that in the same year Daccarrette rented a vessel to a Louisbourg merchant trading to Martinique. Between 1720 and 1740 Daccarrette was also involved in the sale of at least 17 vessels between 30 and 50 tons, valued at about 3,500 *livres* apiece, to owners on both sides of the Atlantic. Many of these ships seem to have been built at Île Royale.

Daccarrette made at least one voyage to Hendaye in the late 1720s and may have travelled to the West Indies and France on other occasions. In 1722 his widowed sister-in-law, Catherine Gonillon, entrusted him with the management of her affairs on Saint-Domingue (Hispaniola) and in La Rochelle. Perhaps it was on one of these trips that he gained his knowledge of the commercial techniques of his day, including the use of double-entry bookkeeping. In 1726, presumably after his wife's death, Daccarrette had a child by Catherine, out of wedlock. The following year they were married, having received a papal dispensation from the impediment of Daccarrette's first marriage. They had nine more children, of whom five died young.

Daccarrette's business relations with France appear to have been mostly with Saint-Jean-de-Luz and Bayonne. In the former port, his principal contacts were Bernard Damestoye, Joannis Darguinarat, and Joannis (Jean) de Saint-Martin for whom he acted as agent in 1725. Darguinarat and Damestoye provided bricks for Daccarrette which he sold to the king's storehouse in Louisbourg; in association with them and a Spanish merchant, Don Matheo Ilanos, he attempted to ship tobacco worth 50,626 *livres* to Saint-Jean-de-Luz in 1726. This venture was financed in part by the powerful Bayonne merchant Léon Brethous, who provided 10,000 *livres* at 24 per cent on a *prêt à la grosse* (an investment in which the ship is put up as security for a loan which need not be repaid if the voyage is not completed). In 1738 Joannis de Saint-Martin and Daccarrette sold 200 quintals of cod to Brethous in return for an advance of 16,000 *livres*. Daccarrette was to provide free transportation for the cod in his own or another's vessel. If he failed to deliver, a larger quantity was to be sent the next year at a lower price. He did fail to deliver but it is not known whether the recompense was made. Brethous became more deeply involved in Daccarrette's operations in 1738 by lending Saint-Martin 6,000 *livres à la grosse* at 18 per cent on Daccarrette's guarantee. Saint-Martin later defaulted. The fol-

lowing year Daccarrette failed to meet the payment for an advance of 6,000 *livres* from Brethous, and was condemned by the *bourse* of Bayonne in 1742. The result of all these operations was that Daccarrette had to agree to pay Brethous 30,000 *livres* in instalments by 1753.

These problems and the general decline of the sedentary fisheries in the period 1739–45 left Daccarrette in financial difficulties. In April 1743 he sold some of his Louisbourg property for 25,000 *livres*. At his death in 1745 he still owed 37,000 *livres*, 26,000 to Brethous. He retained a house and some land in Louisbourg, and houses and fishing establishments at La Baleine and Fourché. What happened to his other fishing establishments is not known. Additional assets consisted of debts owed to him, although many of these were never collected. In 1745 his property fell into the hands of the invaders but was later reclaimed by his son MICHEL and his other heirs.

T. J. A. LE GOFF

AN, Col., B, 45, 52; C¹¹C, 11, 12; E, 103 (dossier Daccarrette); Section Outre-Mer, G¹, 406–10, 466–67; G², 178–80, 183, 185, 211; G³, 7/175, 8/176, 2037–39, 2046–47, 2055–58. *Édits ord.*, II. P.-G. Roy, *Inv. jug. et délib.*, *1717–1760*. McLennan, *Louisbourg*. H. A. Innis, "Cape Breton and the French regime," *RSCT*, 3rd ser., XXIX (1935), sect.II, 51–87.

DACCARRETTE, MICHEL (sometimes written **Daccarrette, Dacaret, d'Acaret,** etc., but he signed **Daccarrette**), merchant, shipowner; b. 1730 at Louisbourg, Île Royale (Cape Breton Island), first and only surviving son of Michel DACCARRETTE (d. 1745) and Catherine Gonillon; d. in 1767 in Paris.

Michel Daccarrette, with the other members of his family, was evacuated from Louisbourg after the siege of 1745 during which his father died. In 1749 he returned to Louisbourg with the family of the merchant Philippe de Beaubassin, who had married his eldest sister Marie-Charlotte.

In 1753 Daccarrette married Marguerite, daughter of Jean La Borde*, treasurer of the Marine and royal notary at Louisbourg. By the marriage contract La Borde gave the couple 1,500 *livres* plus free lodgings for three years; Daccarrette contributed 4,000 *livres*. Perhaps it was no coincidence that in the same year he began to supply wood to the king's stores. He continued to supply the stores occasionally, usually with wood, but once with a shipment of rifles. In 1753 the tangled question of his father's succession was settled and Daccarrette received one-third of his father's stocks and equipment in return for concessions of land and houses to other relatives.

157

Dagneau

In 1754 Daccarrette moved to enter the fishing trade with the purchase of the Île Michaux (Michaud Ledges) in partnership with Pierre de La Forest, ensign of the troops in garrison at Louisbourg. In 1756 he owned a privateer, the *Heureux*, which captured a Rhode Island whaler, the *New Brunswick*; in 1758 he is known to have outfitted another privateer, the *Revanche*. During the siege of Louisbourg in 1758, the company of militia formed by the merchants of the town and commanded by Daccarrette performed with distinction and energy.

With the fall of the fortress Daccarrette moved to Bordeaux, France, where he set up as a merchant in 1759, outfitting one privateer sent to Martinique under Portuguese colours in 1759 and at least two others, under the Spanish flag, in 1762. In these ventures, as in the outfitting of a schooner for Saint-Domingue (Hispaniola) in 1763 and a 16-gun frigate, the *Vigilante*, he seems to have been using funds provided by his father-in-law who gave him credit facilities in Bordeaux and elsewhere after 1759. These operations appear to have been unsuccessful.

In March 1763, suspected of complicity in La Borde's fraudulent mismanagement of government funds at Louisbourg, Daccarrette was arrested and imprisoned in the Bastille. By August he had obtained Laborde's release by proposing to abandon all of the latter's possessions to the crown, but in December his house in Bordeaux burned to the ground, destroying all his effects, records, and commercial papers including those of his father-in-law. The charges against Daccarrette were dropped and he was released around February 1764. Undaunted, he began a third time to build up his fortunes, but he died on a trip to Paris in 1767, while attempting to obtain some relief from the ministry. According to his widow he left behind a family of seven, four known to have been born in Louisbourg and the rest probably after his return to France.

T. J. A. Le Goff

AD, Charente-Maritime (La Rochelle), B, 6122, nos.14–34; 6124, nos.1–2. AN, Col., B, 117, 120; C¹¹A, 14; E, 103 (dossier Daccarrette); Section Outre-Mer, G¹, 408, 409, 467/3; G³, 2041–43. McLennan, *Louisbourg*.

DAGNEAU DOUVILLE DE QUINDRE, LOUIS-CÉSAIRE, merchant, militia colonel; baptized 8 Oct. 1704 at Sorel (Que.), son of Michel Dagneau Douville and Marie Lamy; m. Françoise-Marie-Anne Picoté de Belestre in Montreal, 4 Dec. 1736; buried at Detroit 2 Feb. 1767.

As early as 1727 Louis-Césaire Dagneau Douville de Quindre was trading among the Miamis. The late 1730s found him sending canoes to Michilimackinac and, in partnership with Claude MARIN de La Perrière, leasing the lucrative Michipicoton post (near Michipicoten Harbour, Ont.) from Pierre GAULTIER de Varennes et de La Vérendrye. Between 1740 and 1742 he moved his wife and children from Montreal to Fort Saint-Joseph (probably Niles, Mich.) and there, with his partner Marin, carried on an extensive trade with the Miamis and Potawatomis.

The two associates transferred their operations to Michilimackinac in 1747 and became leading suppliers for the garrison at that strategic point. It was an uneasy year for the French posts as almost every Indian band in the west threatened and plotted their destruction, and de Quindre sent his wife back to the safety of Montreal. At Detroit there was open insurrection led by ORONTONY, but at Michilimackinac prompt, forceful action by the commandant, Jacques LEGARDEUR de Saint-Pierre, kept the peace with the neighbouring Ojibwas and Ottawas.

Probably in the early summer of 1749 de Quindre moved to Detroit, where settlement was being encouraged and the post reinforced. According to Mme Bégon [ROCBERT] the family was in financial difficulties and Mme de Quindre, now without resources, was obliged to leave Montreal to rejoin her husband. He began trading and became a major supplier to the Detroit garrison. In the next few years he provided it with many canoes, much clothing, and huge supplies of grain. The relationship he developed with the commandant, Pierre-Joseph CÉLORON de Blainville, probably led Céloron to arrange in 1752 for Île aux Cochons (Belle Isle) in the Detroit River to be ceded to him. Residents of Detroit, however, protested successfully, claiming that the island had always been common grazing ground. In 1753 the commandant was able to reward him with the largest of 12 land grants made on the west side of town.

Céloron was probably instrumental also in de Quindre's appointment as the colonel of the Detroit militia, a position of much local prestige. The role of the force, which in 1755 numbered 220, was to aid the few regular troops of the garrison at times of crisis. In 1759 a detachment headed by de Quindre joined François-Marie Le MARCHAND de Lignery in his unsuccessful attempt to relieve Fort Niagara (near Youngstown, N.Y.), which was under siege by Sir William Johnson* and a force of English and Indians.

De Quindre and his brother, Major Guillaume Dagneau Douville de Lamothe of the Detroit militia, were captured. (When Johnson visited Detroit in 1761, the two former prisoners were among his dinner guests.)

After the peace de Quindre adjusted to English rule and did not assist the Indians during PONTIAC's uprising of 1763. He is said to have aided the English cause, but evidence is slim. At his death in 1767, he was one of the settlement's wealthiest residents, with an estate valued at 5,000 *livres*. Although Detroit is often considered to have been a crude frontier community, the inventory of his goods indicates that he lived in considerable comfort. He was survived by several children, one of whom, Guillaume-François Dagneau de Quindre de La Picanier, is said to have become an officer in the British army.

DONALD CHAPUT

AN, Col., C¹¹ᴬ, 117, f.3; 118, f.142; 119, ff.236, 304v. ANQ, NF, Registres d'intendance, X. DPL, Burton hist. coll., Christian Denissen, [Genealogy of French families of Detroit] (26v., typescript, n.d.), D/1, 3288–89. St Ann's Parish (Mackinac Island, Mich.), Registre des baptêmes, mariages et sépultures de Sainte-Anne-de-Michillimakinak, 1695–1821; an annotated version under the title "The Mackinac register" is in Wis. State Hist. Soc. *Coll.*, XVIII (1908), 469–513; XIX (1910), 1–149, but it contains some inaccuracies. "The British regime in Wisconsin – 1760–1800," ed. R. G. Thwaites, Wis. State Hist. Soc. *Coll.*, XVIII (1908), 229–34. "Correspondance de Mme Bégon" (Bonnault), APQ *Rapport, 1934–35*, 68. *Johnson papers* (Sullivan *et al.*), XIII, 115, 251. "Petition of sundry inhabitants of Detroit," *Michigan Pioneer Coll.*, X (1886), 237. "The St. Joseph baptismal register," ed. George Paré and M. M. Quaife, *Mississippi Valley Hist. Rev.*, XIII (1926–27), 201–39.

Massicotte, "Répertoire des engagements pour l'Ouest," APQ *Rapport 1929–30; 1930–31*. Tanguay, *Dictionnaire*. Champagne, *Les La Vérendrye*. Silas Farmer, *The history of Detroit and Michigan . . .* (Detroit, 1884), 20. M. C. W. Hamlin, *Legends of le Détroit* (Detroit, 1884), 290–91. Télesphore St-Pierre, *Histoire des Canadiens du Michigan et du comté d'Essex, Ontario* (Montréal, 1895), 178.

DAINE, FRANÇOIS, lieutenant general for civil and criminal affairs of the provost court of Quebec, subdelegate of the intendant, controller of the Compagnie des Indes in New France, director of the Domaine du Roi; baptized 10 June 1695 in the parish of Saint-Rémi de Charlesville (Charleville-Mézières), France, son of Jacques Daine and Antoinette Pelletier; d. 1765 at Blois, France.

François Daine, who never made use in Canada of his birth, belonged to a family of administrators. His father was an inspector at the royal tobacco factory in Charlesville, then controller general of supplies in Champagne. His maternal grandfather was secretary to the commandants and presiding judge of the Duc de Mantoue, the sovereign of Charlesville, whilst his paternal grandfather, Nicolas, was inspector of the navy and of trade in Dunkerque. His paternal uncle, Marius-Basile, was financial commissary for the army of Flanders and was in charge of the negotiations which led to the treaty of Utrecht in 1713. In addition, his brother Jacques, who became an officer of the *parlement* and *maître des Requêtes*, was interested in Canadian affairs.

François Daine was married three times, to Canadians. On 5 Oct. 1721, in Quebec, he married Angélique Pagé, who died in August 1723 giving birth to their first child. The following year, on 20 August in Montreal, he married Louise-Jeanne, the daughter of François-Marie Bouat*; their marriage lasted 16 years. On 8 March 1742, at Boucherville, he was married again, his third wife being Louise, the daughter of François-Antoine PÉCAUDY de Contrecœur, who bore him four children, of whom only two daughters reached adulthood.

The exact date of Daine's arrival in Canada is not known. In 1715 he was clerk (king's writer) in the registry of the royal jurisdiction of Trois-Rivières. In 1719 he was in Quebec, as a witness at the marriage of Jean-Eustache LANOULLIER de Boisclerc. Daine himself married there on 5 Oct. 1721 and shortly thereafter went to France, probably to request a new position in the king's service. On 10 Feb. 1722, after energetic soliciting and thanks to his patrons, he was appointed chief clerk of the Conseil Supérieur of Quebec. On 20 May he obtained passage for Canada and on 12 October he registered his letters of appointment there.

Daine first lived in his friend Lanoullier's home, and in a short time he was able to make other friends and be admitted into the Canadian élite. There were only two witnesses at his first marriage in 1721, but 37 were at the second two years later, among them Governor Philippe de Rigaud* de Vaudreuil, Charles Le Moyne* de Longueuil, Intendant BÉGON, and François-Étienne CUGNET. Moreover, quite soon Daine was financially able to improve his living conditions. In 1726 he bought a house on Rue Saint-Pierre for 7,000 *livres*. In 1744 he occupied a house next door to Intendant Hocquart*'s, on Rue Saint-Nicolas, and in 1763 he was living on Rue Saint-Louis.

Daine

Daine devoted himself completely to his administrative duties, acquiring several offices at the same time to increase his revenues. His family milieu and his education – his library is evidence – had prepared him for such a career, but he served a stiff apprenticeship as he climbed the rungs one by one. From being king's writer at the beginning of his career, he became in 1722 chief clerk of the Conseil Supérieur. He even added to this title that of councillor and secretary. Several Canadian officials, seeking prestige, took on this honorary title which was reserved for a few high dignitaries and possession of which over 20 years permitted a person to be ennobled. In 1724 Daine also obtained the office of controller of the Compagnie des Indes in New France, and in 1728 he tried, without success, to obtain that of attorney general of the Conseil Supérieur. In 1736 Daine, as chief clerk, granted Christophe-Hilarion Du Laurent a commission as clerk of the registry. In addition to assisting the chief clerk, Du Laurent was to replace him during absences necessitated by his other duties. Daine did not accede to a higher office until 1744. On 25 March the king signed his letters of appointment to the office of lieutenant general for civil and criminal affairs of the provost court of Quebec, to succeed Pierre André de Leigne. He entered upon his duties on 12 October, without giving up his post as controller of the Compagnie des Indes. Daine had served unofficially as subdelegate of the intendant in the government of Montreal from 1739 on and in the government of Quebec from 1745 on, and he was granted on 10 Jan. 1748 an official commission as subdelegate, confirmed by Bigot* on 1 September of that year. When he was appointed director of the Domaine du Roi in 1752, he relinquished only his office of controller. In 1759, along with Guillaume Estèbe*, he received the rare honour of being appointed honorary councillor of the Conseil Supérieur, with the right of attending, speaking, and voting, and with all the honours pertaining to the rank, but without a stipend.

During the final days of French rule in Quebec, Daine was very active. With Jean Taché he headed a citizens' delegation which was the instigation of an expedition on 12 July 1759 against an English battery installed at Pointe-Lévy (Lauzon). On 19 July as lieutenant of the provost court he received from Intendant Bigot a special commission permitting him to execute thieves after summary trial. Shortly after 13 September, the day of the French defeat, Daine became the spokesman for the inhabitants, who asked the authorities to surrender the town in order to avoid the horrors of an assault; on this occasion he called himself "mayor" of the town. Immediately after the defeat, at his compatriots' request, he remained in the town to judge by French law "the disputes which might arise among them." He wrote: "I assured myself of the English generals' assent, until next year when I shall go to France." Daine left Canada on 20 Sept. 1764. There is no proof, however, that he really exercised any judicial function from the time of the surrender of Quebec until his departure for France.

Daine did not liquidate his assets in the colony until 1763, after the signature of the treaty of Paris. He sold his seigneury of Grand-Île on 22 September, and on 23 July 1764 he sold the fief of Saint-Joseph (Lespinay), which came from Pécaudy de Contrecœur's heritage. After his return to France in the autumn of 1764, Daine seems to have retired to Blois, where he died sometime in 1765. On 19 March of that year he had obtained from the king in recognition of his office as lieutenant general a pension of 2,000 livres, 1,000 of which could revert to his wife. The pension, double the amount asked for by Daine, was payable from 1 Jan. 1761.

Despite his supervision of trade and his family connections with a famous member of Bigot's clique, Michel-Jean-Hugues Péan*, his nephew, Daine did not dabble in any commercial activities, unless ownership of interests in the seigneuries can be so described. Besides, one of his seigneuries, Bois-Francs, granted in 1733, had been reunited with the royal domain in 1741. All his offices, however, brought him attractive annual revenues. One estimate of his annual income at 800 livres is far from the mark. By holding all the offices together – chief clerk of court and controller, lieutenant general and director of the domain, and subdelegate of the intendant – Daine was able to earn from 1724 on more than 2,500 livres a year; from 1752 on, his annual income exceeded 4,000 livres. The annual salary for the clerk of court was 800 livres, for the controller 800, the lieutenant general of the provost court 500, the director of the domain 3,000, and the subdelegate of the intendant 300. In addition the fees received for copies of deeds and for legal investigations, as well as the charges and costs from the Conseil Supérieur and the provost court, constituted an annual revenue of 1,500 to 3,000 livres. Thus the 60,000 livres in assets which he left behind at his death were the product of his 45 years in the administration and, according to Daine, of the dowries from his three marriages.

Daine's work was appreciated, and the testimonials from Governor Charles de Beau-

HARNOIS and Governor Pierre de Rigaud* de Vaudreuil, as well as from the intendants, Bégon, Hocquart, and Bigot, bear that out. He was an honest official whose integrity was recognized during the *affaire du Canada*.

JACQUES MATHIEU

AD, Ardennes (Charleville-Mézières), État civil, Saint-Rémi de Charlesville, 10 juin 1695. AN, Col., E, 104 (dossier Daine). ANQ, Greffe de Jacques Barbel; Greffe de Nicolas Boisseau; Greffe de C.-H. Du Laurent; Greffe de Florent de La Cetière; Greffe de J.-C. Panet; Greffe de J.-A. Saillant; NF, Documents de la juridiction des Trois-Rivières; NF, Ins. Cons. sup.; NF, Ord. int.; NF, Registres du Cons. sup., 1722–1760; NF, Taxes de dépens du Cons. sup. ANQ-M, Greffe de Pierre Raimbault, 20 août 1724. ASQ, Polygraphie, X, 37; XV, 27; XXIV, 29; Séminaire, I, 72; II, 6; XXIX, 71, 72. *Quebec Gazette/La Gazette de Québec*, 27 Sept. 1764. *Mémoire du sieur de Ramezay*, 27. Gareau, "La Prévôté de Québec," APQ *Rapport*, *1943–44*, 78–83. La Chesnaye-Desbois et Badier, *Dictionnaire de la noblesse* (3e éd.), VI, 697–98. "Liste des officiers de justice de la Nouvelle-France," *BRH*, XXXVI (1930), 151–57. "Liste des sujets qui composent le Conseil souverain et les juridictions royales de la colonie (1758)," *BRH*, XXXVI (1930), 464. Régis Roy, "M. Daine," *BRH*, XV (1909), 352.

DALQUIER. *See* ALQUIER

DAMOURS DE FRENEUSE, LOUISE. *See* GUYON [Appendix]

DANDIN. *See* DAUDIN

DANEAU DE MUY, CHARLOTTE, *dite* **de Sainte-Hélène,** Ursuline, annalist; b. 23 Nov. 1694 at Boucherville (Que.), daughter of Nicolas Daneau* de Muy and Marguerite Boucher; d. 14 Sept. 1759 at Quebec.

In September 1700, when she was six years of age, Charlotte Daneau de Muy entered the Ursulines' boarding-school at Quebec and stayed there for three years. On leaving she went to live with her grandfather, Pierre Boucher*, until she entered the noviciate of the Ursulines of Quebec on 21 Oct. 1716. On 21 Jan. 1717 she took the religious habit, having "received a dowry of 3,000 *livres*, her furniture, and her allowances"; she made her profession on 9 Feb. 1719.

The annals of the community remain silent about Charlotte de Sainte-Hélène's activities in the convent except to stress that she was a "witty and able sister" and that she did not "spare her talents in supporting . . . the choir with her fine voice, or her skill in making fine works to decorate the churches." In addition she had some literary gifts. But it was certainly not in her

"Abrégé de la vie de Mme la comtesse de Pontbriand [Angélique-Sylvie Marot de La Garaye]" that she showed herself to best advantage. Indeed, the work, which was written from memory and from the unpublished account by Dom Trottier, prior of the Benedictine abbey of Saint-Jacut-de-la-Mer (dept. of Côtes-du-Nord), France, belongs in the realm of old-fashioned hagiography, as unreal as it is boring. Her style was, however, of superior quality when she undertook to write the annals of the community during the Seven Years' War. She describes events in such a spontaneous and natural manner that it is difficult to believe this is the same author who wrote the insipid account of Mme de Pontbriand's life. In the annals her style is simple and correct; the account runs on without a stop for 24 pages and is sprinkled with sentences which convey the events vividly: "Never did God's hand appear more obviously to humble the pride of a new Holofernes, in the person of General [Edward] Brad[d]ock, who expected to have breakfast at La Belle-Rivière, dinner at Niagara, and supper at Montreal. He lost his life and the greater part of his army" [*see* Daniel-Hyacinthe LIÉNARD]. Shortly before the fall of Quebec the annalist added: "If the fact is certain, as there is reason to fear, the country is at a low ebb." Seven lines later the author stopped writing, death having kept her from continuing.

Charlotte de Sainte-Hélène died on 14 Sept. 1759, just as the burial of MONTCALM, whose victory at Carillon (Ticonderoga, N.Y.) she had celebrated, was taking place. She herself was buried in the Hôpital Général of Quebec, where from mid-July she had taken refuge with the Ursulines.

GABRIELLE LAPOINTE

[The AMUQ holds the "Abrégé de la vie de Mme la comtesse de Pontbriand," written by Charlotte Daneau de Muy, *dite* de Sainte-Hélène. The unsigned original of another biography of the Comtesse de Pontbriand is in the AD, Ille-et-Vilaine (Rennes), 1 H 5/31; a copy of it is kept in the ANQ and was published by P.-G. Roy in *BRH*, XVIII (1912), 202–10, 225–46, 257–80, 289–307, under the title "La vie de madame la comtesse de Pontbriand." There are several variants between the AMUQ and ANQ manuscripts. G.L.]
AMUQ, Actes des professions et des sépultures, 1688–1781; Annales; Entrées, vêtures, professions et décès des religieuses, 1647–1861; Livre des entrées et sorties des filles françaises et sauvages, 1641–1720; Registre de l'examen canonique des novices, 1689–1807. *Les Ursulines de Québec* (1863–66).

DANEAU DE MUY, JACQUES-PIERRE, army officer, seigneur; baptized 7 Oct. 1695 at

Daneau

Boucherville (Que.), son of Nicolas Daneau* de Muy and Marguerite Boucher; m. 30 Jan. 1725 to Louise-Geneviève Ruette d'Auteuil at Montreal; d. 18 May 1758 at Detroit.

Although Canadian-born, Jacques-Pierre Daneau de Muy received his first commission – an ensigncy – in the Louisiana troops in 1710. How he arrived in Louisiana at such an early age is not certain, but he may have been accompanying his father, who died en route to the colony from France in 1708. The next record of de Muy's career is in 1724, when at the unusually advanced age of 29 he was made a second ensign in the colonial regulars stationed in Canada.

During the 1730s de Muy commanded the tiny post of Saint-Joseph (probably Niles, Mich.), where he was responsible for the regulation of trade and the maintenance of good relations with the local Potawatomis and Miamis. He made a close study of the plants of the area, primarily seeking pharmaceutical knowledge, and apparently cured several Indians by means of local herbs. He sent back plant specimens for the intendant to see and the Jesuits to classify, and when he visited France in 1736–37 he took with him a memorandum on his findings.

De Muy had been promoted ensign in 1733. In 1741 he was made lieutenant. His whereabouts from 1737 to 1744 is not known, but in 1745 he undertook a mission characteristic of New France's Indian diplomacy at the time. English commercial influence on the Ohio valley Indians was growing, and the French were encouraging them to move farther west, away from English traders. De Muy left Detroit in May with a party of 15 Canadians in search of a band of Shawnees, who in response to French urging had deserted their village south of Atigué (Kittanning, Pa.). Their half-breed leader, Peter Chartier, had kept them together, and de Muy met them at the mouth of the Sonioto River (Scioto River, Ohio). He persuaded them to settle, for a while at least, on the lower Ohio River, promising that they would be as well supplied with trade goods as if they had remained in the English orbit.

In September 1745 de Muy travelled down to Montreal. The ensuing year was the most warlike of his career. To guard the southern approach to Montreal in a period of officially declared war with England, Governor Charles de BEAUHARNOIS sent a French and Indian squad of irregular troops to scout out of Fort Saint-Frédéric (Crown Point, N.Y.) during the winter of 1745–46. At first de Muy was second in command to Jacques LEGARDEUR de Saint-Pierre; by July 1746 he was in charge and the squad had grown to 60 French and 400–500 Indians, including many Hurons and Ottawas from the *pays d'en haut*. This force was preparing to raid a suspected British food dump at Saratoga (now Schuylerville, N.Y.) when news arrived that a British attack on Fort Saint-Frédéric was imminent. Gaspard-Joseph Chaussegros* de Léry came to take charge of blocking the water approach to the fort from the south, and 300 militia under François-Pierre de Rigaud* de Vaudreuil arrived as reinforcements. A scouting party led by de Muy was sent to the outskirts of Albany "to see if it is true that the Orange River is so covered with bateaux that the water cannot be seen." The alarm proved false – perhaps a fabrication by the British to prevent French raids while the harvest was being brought in. Rigaud then led the forces against Fort Massachusetts (Williamstown, Mass.), which capitulated late in August after a day's siege. It was burned, nearby farmsteads were ransacked and destroyed, and the captured garrison was taken back to Canada. De Muy had personal charge of the Reverend John Norton (and first claim upon the ransom); the clergyman's journal reveals de Muy as a humane, hospitable officer.

Throughout the fall of 1746 de Muy's detachment kept the American frontier uneasy. The year 1747 found him transferred to the Montreal region, where he commanded first at Prairie-de-la-Madeleine (Laprairie, Que.) then later in the year at Lac des Deux-Montagnes. In the following year he was promoted captain. From 1752 to 1754 he was commandant of Fort Chambly, during which time he was granted a seigneury on the east side of Lake Champlain.

He was eager, however, to return to the west. In 1753 he made several requests to accompany Paul MARIN de La Malgue in the occupation of the Ohio valley but was rejected because of poor health. In May 1754 he left Lachine for Niagara with a brigade of canoes and was told to expect further orders at Niagara. His new posting was to Detroit, relieving CÉLORON de Blainville as commandant. The position was a key one, since part of French strategy was to overawe the Iroquois and English with the strength of the western tribes, and the commandant of Detroit was largely responsible for the delicate diplomacy required to maintain the friendship of the Ottawas, Potawatomis, Ojibwas, and others. Governor Ange Duquesne* was delighted finally to have appointed de Muy to a post of real and sensitive importance; he praised his "integrity" and "ability," and called him "the best officer in this colony." De Muy was awarded the cross of the order of Saint-Louis on 1 April 1754.

Jacques-Pierre Daneau de Muy was typical of

many Canadian officer-seigneurs. The connections he maintained with Europe – especially the sometimes litigious correspondence with his d'Auteuil in-laws – were beyond the scope of the average *habitant*, whose Laurentian roots had become exclusive. His experience as a soldier, however, made him part of the Canadian military tradition of frontier war with its Indian alliances and winter campaigns. For him as for many others of his class, the long North American peace of 1713–44 meant a frustratingly slow climb up the ranks of officers. His family's brief annals reveal a commonplace tragedy: only two of his six children lived to adulthood.

De Muy did not see the end of the empire he had lived and fought to further, for he died at Detroit on 18 May 1758.

MALCOLM MACLEOD

AN, Col., C¹¹A, 99, ff.128–36v, 274–75, 282. ASQ, Fonds Verreau, X. "French regime in Wis., 1743–60" (Thwaites), 41. *NYCD* (O'Callaghan and Fernow). *Papiers Contrecœur* (Grenier). Tanguay, *Dictionnaire*. Parkman, *Half-century of conflict*, II. P.-G. Roy, *La famille Juchereau Duchesnay* (Lévis, Qué., 1903). N. W. Caldwell, "Shawneetown, a chapter in the Indian history of Illinois," Illinois State Hist. Soc. *Journal* (Springfield, Ill.), XXXII (1939), 193–205. W. J. Eccles, "The social, economic, and political significance of the military establishment in New France," *CHR*, LII (1971), 1–22. P.-G. Roy, "Nicolas Daneau de Muy et ses enfants," *Cahiers des Dix*, XVIII (1953), 157–70.

DANIÉLOU, JEAN-PIERRE, priest, Jesuit, missionary; b. at Brest, France, 15 July 1696; d. at Quebec 23 May 1744.

Jean-Pierre Daniélou entered the Jesuit order in Paris in 1713. He taught humanities at the Jesuit College in Quebec from 1715 to 1720, then at Arras, France (1720–22). He next studied philosophy at La Flèche (1722–23) and theology at Paris (1723–27), where he was ordained in 1727. By 1728 he had returned to Quebec and probably taught theology there for a few years. In the autumn of 1731 he was chosen to fill the duties of missionary to the Malecite Indians at Médoctec (Meductic, N.B.) on the Saint John River, replacing Father Jean-Baptiste Loyard* who had died there in June.

Médoctec, near the junction of the Médoctec (Eel) and Saint John rivers, had been a permanent fortified village, based on horticulture and hunting, since before the arrival of the white man. The French had missionaries posted there by the end of the 17th century and the Malecites became faithful allies of the French in war. For several reasons the system began to break down during the period of Daniélou's mission at Médoctec. The English in Nova Scotia were now beginning to push more vigorously their territorial claims in the area. Daniélou himself did not seem to have the leadership qualities which Fathers Loyard, Joseph AUBERY, and Simon Girard* de La Place had displayed before him. At about this time also the first Acadian settlers began to establish themselves in the upper Saint John River valley. With their arrival, the Indians became more interested in commerce. More time was spent away from the village hunting for furs to trade, and some Indians left Médoctec altogether to move closer to the Acadian settlement at Sainte-Anne (Fredericton). Daniélou conducted a census of the Saint John River Acadians for the French government in 1739 and counted 117 in the upper valley. Around 1740 he returned to Quebec, and during the wars of the 1740s his successor, Father Joseph-Charles Germain*, had to range over even wider territories to organize the Indians.

DAVID LEE

AN, Col., B, 59/1, f.462; 61, f.545; C¹¹A, 59, f.35ff.; Section Outre-Mer, G¹, 466/1, pp.264–66 (PAC transcript). ASQ, Polygraphie, XVIII, 59. PAC, MG 11, Nova Scotia A, 20, pp.139, 178.
JR (Thwaites), LXXI, 164. *NYCD* (O'Callaghan and Fernow), X, 13. *N.S. Archives*, II, 113, 188; III, 358–59. Allaire, *Dictionnaire*, I, 143. Rochemonteix, *Les Jésuites et la N.-F. au XVIIIe siècle*, II, 18. W. O. Raymond, "The old Meductic fort," N.B. Hist. Soc. *Coll.*, I (1894–98), 221–72.

DANRÉ DE BLANZY, LOUIS-CLAUDE, royal notary, seigneurial judge; b. 1710 in France, son of Charles Danré de Blanzy, a lawyer in the *parlement* of Paris, and Suzanne Morillon; d. in France, date of death unknown.

Louis-Claude Danré de Blanzy as a young man had a good position in society and was a lawyer in the *parlement* of Paris. He seems, however, to have led a wild existence, and his parents obtained a *lettre de cachet* to send him to New France. He arrived in 1736, and four other young ne'er-do-wells of good families came to the colony with him. Such recruits were always a problem for the colonial authorities. Too often these young men had no profession and lived at the expense of the colonial administration. Moreover, even if their parents thought they were sending them away from the mother country, it was easy for them to return to France, without, of course, advising the authorities. Such, however, was not the fate of all these newcomers.

Danré de Blanzy quickly settled down in Montreal, where on 25 Nov. 1737 he married

Dargent

Suzanne, daughter of the late Denis d'Estienne* Du Bourgué de Clérin. Some months later, on 20 March 1738, he obtained from Intendant Hocquart* a commission as royal notary to practise in the royal jurisdiction of Montreal, replacing the notary Joseph-Charles Raimbault* de Piedmont, who had died on the preceding 17 December. This commission was granted him, it seems, not so much because of his legal training but thanks to his family connections with the attorney general of the colony's Conseil Supérieur, Louis-Guillaume VERRIER.

In addition to his office as notary, Danré de Blanzy exercised other legal functions. In 1739 and 1740 he was judge of the seigneury of Boucherville, and on 13 Nov. 1744 he received a commission as clerk of court for the jurisdiction of Montreal, where on occasion he also served in the capacity of lieutenant general for civil and criminal affairs, king's attorney, assessor, and clerk of court of the courts martial judging deserters.

From 4 to 18 Sept. 1747 Danré de Blanzy was busy taking an inventory of the personal and real estate, papers and documents of the Hôpital Général of Montreal, which at that time was in a sorry state [see Jean JEANTOT; Marie-Marguerite Dufrost* de Lajemmerais]. The document he drew up at the time of this inventory gives in 90 pages of closely written text a detailed description of all the objects in the different rooms of the hospital and in the adjoining buildings.

Danré de Blanzy carried on his practice as a notary for 22 years, and his registry contains numerous contracts of indentures for the west. He signed his last deed on 29 April 1760 and shortly afterwards he sailed for France. In 1770 he was in Paris, where he disappears from sight.

MICHEL PAQUIN

AN, Col., E, 107 (dossier Danré de Blanzy). ANQ-M, Greffe de L.-C. Danré de Blanzy, 1738–1760. É.-Z. Massicotte, "Les tribunaux et les officiers de justice de Montréal sous le régime français," *BRH*, XXXVII (1931), 190, 303, 307. "Les notaires au Canada," *APQ Rapport, 1921–22*, 46. P.-G. Roy, *Inv. ord. int.*, II, 239; III, 63, 100. Tanguay, *Dictionnaire*. Vachon, "Inv. critique des notaires royaux," *RHAF*, XI (1957–58), 101. J.-E. Roy, *Histoire du notariat*, I. Gérard Malchelosse, "Les fils de bonne famille en Nouvelle-France, 1720–1750," *Cahiers des Dix*, XI (1946), 279, 284, 290, 292, 297–98. É.-Z. Massicotte, "La justice seigneuriale de Boucherville," *BRH*, XXVIII (1922), 75–76.

DARGENT, JOSEPH, Sulpician, parish priest; b. 4 July 1712 at Saint-Similien (dept. of Loire-Atlantique), France, son of François Dargent, a tanner and dealer in hides, and Renée Bernard; d. 22 Feb. 1747 at Pointe-aux-Trembles, Montreal Island.

Joseph Dargent joined the Society of Saint-Sulpice at the seminary in Nantes, France, on 31 Oct. 1731 and was ordained a priest in March 1737. Soon after, he sailed for New France, arriving at his destination, Montreal, on 13 August of that year. Thanks to his report entitled "Relation d'un voyage de Paris à Montréal en Canadas en 1737" we are fairly well informed of the circumstances surrounding his departure from France and his arrival in Canada. He left Paris on 5 May and went on board the *Jason* on 31 May, despite opposition from his family. Indeed, three of his brothers had caught up with him some days earlier at Rochefort and had tried to dissuade him from his plan; with the help of a canon in La Rochelle who had already lived at the seminary of Quebec, the Sulpician had resisted his brothers' "assault." The ship, which was carrying 437 passengers, among them the intendant, Hocquart*, was under command of M. Du Quesne, a person lacking in polish, a sort of "unlicked cub," who received Dargent on board and treated him during the whole voyage as he did everyone, "that is to say very roughly." Dargent was on the ship for ten days before it left France on 9 June, delayed by a fire which broke out and was quickly brought under control; the *Jason* was at that time in the roads two leagues from land.

On 2 August Joseph Dargent landed at Île aux Coudres, below Quebec, after a 54-day crossing which apparently was uneventful, since he says nothing of it in his account. His first remarks upon his arrival in New France are not devoid of interest, even if they are of unequal value. The capital made an excellent impression upon him; he considered it pleasing, and it impressed him with all its civil and religious institutions. Moreover he enjoyed the trip by boat from Quebec to Montreal, going up the river whose shores had houses at intervals of a league then of a quarter of a league, and even every 500 paces upon arriving at Montreal Island. Some of his remarks, however, are not original or accurate. Dargent had scarcely arrived when he was writing that the Canadian winter, with its seven long months, seemed endless to him, and he asserted unreflectingly that all the habitants, men and women, were vain, improvident, and spendthrifty.

We have little information about his ministry during his ten years in Canada. Upon his arrival in Montreal his superior, Louis NORMANT Du Faradon, appointed him curate to the parish of

Notre-Dame. Dargent held this office until 1739, when M. Normant put him in charge of the parish of Pointe-aux-Trembles. He was apparently an excellent architect, but we know little about his works. In 1741 he enlarged his church, adding a choir and two side chapels. Joseph Dargent had been working for some weeks on the building of the retable for the main altar when he died on 22 Feb. 1747.

Antonio Dansereau

AD, Loire-Atlantique (Nantes), État civil, Saint-Similien, 5 juill. 1712. ASSM, Section des biographies. Joseph Dargent, "Relation d'un voyage de Paris à Montréal en Canadas en 1737," *APQ Rapport, 1947–48*, 7–17. Allaire, *Dictionnaire*. Gauthier, *Sulpitiana*. A.-L. Bertrand, *Bibliothèque sulpicienne ou histoire de la Compagnie de Saint-Sulpice* (3v., Paris, 1900), I. Olivier Maurault, "Trois Français du Canada au XVIIIᵉ siècle," *Cahiers des Dix*, XII (1947), 32–52. "Paroisse de l'Enfant-Jésus-de-la-Pointe-aux-Trembles (île de Montréal)," *Annuaire de Ville-Marie* (Montréal, 1867), 209–56.

DARNAUD (Darnault). *See* Arnaud

DARRIGRAND. *See* Arrigrand

DASILVA, *dit* **Portugais, NICOLAS** (practically the only one of the family to sign **Dassilva**), master mason and stone-cutter, masonry contractor at Quebec; b. 1698 in Canada, son of Pedro Dasilva of Lisbon, Portugal, and Jeanne Greslon La Violette; m. 12 April 1722 at Quebec Élisabeth Laisné by whom he had 13 children, and 8 Jan. 1759 at Quebec Marie-Gabrielle La Roche, a widow; d. 4 May 1761 at Quebec.

Nicolas Dasilva was the 15th and last child born to a Portuguese farmer in the seigneury of Beauport. Like the sons of many other poor farmers, Nicolas became a mason's apprentice in his adolescence. Since masonry work was looked upon as mean and servile, the terms offered to apprentices to attract them were generous. Admission to apprenticeship was easy and the master usually provided all living costs.

Nicolas and his brother Dominique became master masons but their brothers in Quebec did not rise above the level of carters and day-labourers. Though his master was the architect and builder Jean-Baptiste Maillou, *dit* Desmoulins, it is unlikely that Nicolas received more than a mason's and stone-cutter's training. After five years' apprenticeship, Nicolas hired himself out to the mason Jacques Danguel Lamarche in 1720. By the late 1720s Dasilva was hiring his own journeymen.

Dasilva was a small contractor who specialized in the construction of private dwellings. He built houses in Quebec for Guillaume Dupont (1728), Pierre Chanmazart (1729), Michel Berthier (1735), Guillaume Estèbe* (1752), and Joseph Charest (1757). When in 1751 Dasilva contracted to build the Estèbe house, which still stands on Rue Saint-Pierre, he was in partnership with René Paquet and Pierre Delestre, *dit* Beaujour. Delestre was evidently Dasilva's associate and friend for the rest of the 1750s. He and, it seĕms, the noted builder Dominique Janson, *dit* Lapalme, witnessed Dasilva's marriage contract in 1759.

The early poverty or ill health of Dasilva's family is suggested by the death of seven of his 13 children before the age of four – more than double the average death rate for infants in New France. Dasilva was, it appears, unable to write more than his name and yet he rose to the rank of an independent contractor who owned his own home on Rue du Sault-au-Matelot. A complaint by one of his tenants in 1735 suggests that he was a grasping man by nature. At the end of his life Dasilva was styled "master masonry builder" of Quebec.

Peter N. Moogk

ANQ, Greffe de R.-C. Barolet, 12 mars 1732; 13, 17 juin 1735; 21 juill., 2 nov. 1738; 17 juill., 31 oct. 1742; 16 avril, 27 déc. 1747; Greffe de Louis Chambalon, 26 nov. 1715; Greffe de J.-É. Dubreuil, 22 oct. 1720; 7 avril 1722; 2 mai 1724; 1ᵉʳ mars, 10 juin, 1ᵉʳ déc. 1726; 15 févr., 18 oct., 17 nov. 1728; 21 févr., 17, 27 mars, 11 déc. 1729; 24 mai 1730; 15 avril 1731; Greffe d'Henry Hiché, 30 avril, 18 juin 1731; Greffe de J.-C. Panet, 7 sept. 1757, 7 janv. 1759; NF, Coll. de pièces jud. et not., 1195, 1955, 3783, 4026. *Recensement de Québec, 1716* (Beaudet), 26. "Recensement de Québec, 1744" (APQ *Rapport*), 92. P.-V. Charland, "Notre-Dame de Québec: le nécrologe de la crypte," *BRH*, XX (1914), 238. P.-G. Roy, *Inv. jug. et délib., 1717–1760*, III, 268.

DASSEMAT. *See* Dazemard

DAUDIN (d'Audin, Dandin, Daudier), HENRI, priest, missionary; b. *c.* 1709 in the diocese of Blois, France; d. August 1756 in Paris.

Henri Daudin was a French worker of the 11th hour in English Acadia. In April 1753 the French government was looking for an astute priest, one who was capable of carrying out the delicate mission of persuading the Acadians to emigrate to French Acadia, the region around present-day Moncton, without upsetting the Nova Scotia authorities. On the recommendation of Jean-Louis Le Loutre*, with whom Daudin had studied at the Séminaire du Saint-Esprit in Paris, Abbé de L'Isle-Dieu, vicar general of the French colonies, chose Daudin, whom he described as a "mature person . . . possessed of prudence, intelligence, and experience." For this mission Daudin had to leave a rich parish in the diocese of Sens.

In October 1753 Daudin arrived in Nova Scotia where Governor Peregrine Thomas HOPSON received him cordially. The missionary had barely settled into his parish of Pisiquid (Windsor, N.S.) when he gave his attention to the question of Acadian emigration. In order to bring this about he urged the Acadians to ask leave to make "visits" in the Chignecto isthmus. At the same time he informed the authorities at Louisbourg, Île Royale (Cape Breton Island) and the Abbé de L'Isle-Dieu that the British "will go to any expense . . . not to let the Acadians be lacking in priests," and that "they will apply to the Pope." This plan, aimed at keeping the Acadians in Nova Scotia, worried him greatly. He therefore sought to obtain the recall of Jean-Baptiste de GAY Desenclaves, the parish priest of Annapolis Royal, whom he considered too favourable to the policy of the British. After Desenclaves's departure in April 1754 for Pobomcoup (in the region of Yarmouth and Pubnico), Daudin became parish priest at Annapolis. In keeping with his instructions he remained in correspondence with Le Loutre, who continued to be the soul of the Acadian resistance. Some of his letters were intercepted and made known in Halifax. In fact, a junior clerk at Fort Beauséjour (near Sackville, N.B.), Thomas Pichon*, was spying for the British and was transmitting much information to the authorities. Daudin became suspect and was arrested early in October 1754, along with four of his parishioners. Upon giving his solemn promise to change his conduct, he succeeded in obtaining his liberty and returned to his post at Annapolis on 21 October.

In 1755 the Abbé de L'Isle-Dieu tried to have Daudin appointed vicar general for Nova Scotia. But events were moving fast in Acadia; in July 1755 the decision was taken to deport the Acadians (see Charles LAWRENCE), and on 6 August Daudin was arrested while he was saying mass. He was imprisoned in Fort Edward (Windsor), then a few days later taken to Halifax, along with his confrères CHAUVREULX and Lemaire, amid a great display of arms and soldiers. Upon their arrival in the capital the missionaries were exposed to the population for three-quarters of an hour. The details of these events have apparently come down to us through an account by Daudin himself. An allusion by Abbé de L'Isle-Dieu in a letter dated 28 March 1756 supports the existence of such an account, which would be the one H.-R.

Casgrain* published in *Un pèlerinage au pays d'Évangéline*. The three missionaries were deported from Halifax to Portsmouth, England, where they were allowed to charter a ship which took them to France.

After his return to France on 8 Dec. 1755, Daudin took Chauvreulx to Orléans and then returned to Paris, where he made preparations to return to Acadia. In March 1756 the Abbé de L'Isle-Dieu presented him to the archbishop of Paris. He died suddenly in August of that same year, just as he was about to sail for Acadia. His death altered the plans of the Abbé de L'Isle-Dieu who, not having any other candidate for the missions in America, was obliged to give up a policy of resistance in Acadia.

MICHELINE D. JOHNSON

AN, Col., B, 104, ff.172v, 333. C¹¹B, 33, ff.242, 341–43. ASQ, Polygraphie, VII, 5. PAC, MG 18, F12. *Coll. doc. inédits Canada et Amérique*, I, 12–16, 41–46; II, 10–75; III, 60–80, 181–91. Knox, *Historical journal* (Doughty), III, 341–48. *Derniers jours de l'Acadie* (Du Boscq de Beaumont), 73, 132. "Lettres et mémoires de l'abbé de L'Isle-Dieu," APQ *Rapport, 1935–36*, 378–79, 381, 383; *1936–37*, 357, 404–5, 416, 421–22, 425, 453; *1937–38*, 168–69, 172–73, 185. *N.S. Archives*, I, 202, 210, 221–23, 226–27, 229, 235, 239, 282–83. PAC *Report, 1905*, I, pt.III, 346–56, Le Jeune, *Dictionnaire*. Tanguay, *Répertoire*, 109 [Tanguay is mistaken in the identity of Daudin and confuses him with another unidentified missionary. M.D.J.]. Casgrain, *Un pèlerinage au pays d'Évangéline*, 137–44; *Les Sulpiciens en Acadie*, 410–17. Gosselin, *L'Église du Canada jusqu'à la conquête*, III, 361, 366, 375, 431. Richard, *Acadie* (D'Arles), II, 349, 369–75. Albert David, "Les Spiritains en Acadie," *BRH*, XXXV (1929), 461–63.

DAVERS, Sir ROBERT, 5th baronet of Rushbrook, tourist; b. *c.* 1735, probably at Rushbrook, near Bury St Edmunds, England, to Sir Jermyn Davers and Margaretta Green; d. 6 May 1763, on the St Clair River near Lake St Clair.

Upon the death of his father in February 1742, Robert Davers inherited the title. The following July he entered Bury Grammar School. In the spring of 1756, armed with a recommendation from Horace Walpole, he began his travels on the Continent, stopping in Rome long enough to have his portrait painted by Pompeo Batoni. Possibly travel was a way for Davers to escape unpleasant conditions at home. His mother was a melancholy person, and two of his three brothers took their own lives while still in their twenties. In 1759 he left home, leasing the estate for seven years. He apparently travelled through Europe at least once again and completed his studies at Lausanne. In 1761 he came to America, where his brother Charles was serving in the 44th Regiment, and embarked on a lengthy tour of the Great Lakes. One writer says he "left England in a pique careless what his fate might be, and visited America seeking the most savage and uncultivated spots."

By September 1761, Davers was apparently in New York introducing himself to Major-General Jeffery Amherst* and discussing a plan to visit the Upper Lakes. Carrying dispatches from Amherst for Captain Donald CAMPBELL, he arrived at Detroit on 1 Dec. 1761. Davers planned to stay a month or so, then return to Fort Niagara (near Youngstown, N.Y.), by land. Whether he actually made the trip to Niagara or not, he was in Detroit again shortly and passed the winter there studying the language and culture of the neighbouring Indians. Campbell considered Davers "a very accomplished young Gentleman," "an excellent companion," and "a great addition to our small society."

Late in April 1762, Davers began touring the Upper Lakes, probably alone or with a small party. John Rutherford* reported that Davers and his Pawnee slave travelled about in a canoe, which was "so easily navigated that he and his boy were sufficient to cross the lakes and go up the creeks among the Indian villages." Since the Indian boy could speak a little English, and Davers knew a few Indian words, they kept each other company during their long journey. Before the end of June Davers was at Sault Ste Marie, having completed a voyage on Lake Superior. Here he met Alexander Henry*, who travelled with him back to Fort Michilimackinac. Probably Davers and his Pawnee companion then went at least part of the way down Lake Michigan before returning to Detroit, which they reached by 23 Sept. 1762. During his journey he had made some useful discoveries on both Lake Huron and Lake Michigan.

About this time Davers prepared a petition to the Privy Council for a grant of title to Grosse Île, several surrounding islands in the Detroit River, and some land along the south bank. Early in May Davers accompanied Lieutenant Charles ROBERTSON on a short trip from Detroit to the upper end of Lake St Clair to sound the entrance of the St Clair River in an attempt to take Robertson's six-gun schooner into Lake Huron. Robertson, young John Rutherford, and six or eight men were in a large bateau, Davers and his Indian boy in a small canoe. Although French settlers warned them about PONTIAC's plan for a surprise attack on the British, the party proceeded and

was confronted at a narrows by hostile-looking Indians. Davers stopped and "smoked a pipe of friendship" with the tribesmen, advising his companions to move upstream to a wider part of the channel where they might be able to make the far shore. His efforts failed, and a crowd of warriors began firing on the party. Davers, Robertson, and two others were killed instantly; the rest were taken prisoner.

Early published reports said Davers' body was boiled and eaten, but Rutherford, who was there, reported that although Davers' body was mutilated, he was given a proper burial near the Ojibwa village at the mouth of the St Clair River. Robertson, however, was roasted and eaten, his remains being buried later alongside those of Davers; the other dead soldiers were fed to the dogs. The Pawnee boy was eventually bought by an Albany merchant and sent to the Davers family in England.

HARRY KELSEY

BM, Add. MSS, 21662, ff.78–79v, Gage to Haldimand, 18 Nov. 1762. Bury St Edmunds and West Suffolk Record Office (Bury St Edmunds, Eng.), MSS 941/63/6. Clements Library, Thomas Gage papers, American series, Gage to Campbell, 17 Aug. 1765, 1 March 1766. DPL, Burton hist. coll., Silas Farmer MSS, Z A 515, Gladwin to Amherst, 14 May 1763 (transcript); Porteous papers, John Porteous to his father, 20 Nov. 1763. PRO, WO 34/49, Campbell to Amherst, 10 Jan., 20 April 1762; Gladwin to Amherst, 5 Sept., 23 Nov. 1762; MacDonald, Journal of the siege of Detroit. *Diary of the siege of Detroit . . . ,* ed. F. B. Hough (Albany, 1860). *Johnson papers* (Sullivan *et al.*), III, 757–59. *Journal of Pontiac's conspiracy, 1763,* ed. M.A. Burton (Detroit, 1912). *Michigan Pioneer Coll.,* VIII (1885), XIX (1891), XXVII (1896). *Rushbrook parish registers, 1567 to 1850 with Jermyn and Davers annals,* ed. S. H. A. Hervey ([Woodbridge, Eng.], 1903). [John Rutherford], "Rutherford's narrative – an episode in the Pontiac War, 1763 – an unpublished manuscript by Lieut. Rutherford of the 'Black Watch,'" Canadian Institute *Trans.* (Toronto), III (1891–92), 229–52. *County of Suffolk; its history as disclosed by existing records and other documents, being materials for the history of Suffolk . . . ,* ed. W. A. Copinger (5v., London, 1904–5), II, 210. Peckham, *Pontiac.* "An account of the disturbances in North America," *Gentleman's Magazine,* 1763, 455–56. "American news," *Gentleman's Magazine,* 1763, 413.

DAVIS (Device), MARIE-ANNE, *dite* de Saint-Benoît, English captive, Ursuline; d. 2 March 1749 at Quebec.

Little is yet known about the origins of the Ursuline Marie-Anne de Saint-Benoît. Only by examining together a few documents can the important dates in her life until her entry into the

Dazemard

Ursuline convent of Quebec be traced with some probability. It seems that her given name was Sarah, that she was born at Casco (Portland, Me.) in 1679, and that she was the daughter of Isaac Davis and Lydia Black. She was captured in June 1690, at the time of the attack against Casco by René Robinau* de Portneuf and his Abenakis, and is said to have been taken as a prisoner to the Abenaki village at the Saint-François-de-Sales mission on the Chaudière River; Father Jacques Bigot* is supposed to have ransomed her and taken her to Quebec in the late summer or early autumn of 1691. She was baptized 23 March 1692, receiving the name Marie-Anne. She is believed to have lived with different Quebec families, among others with Marie Mars, François Rivière's widow and Paul Berry's wife, and to have been a boarder at the Ursulines' school from February 1696 to February 1697.

On 29 Nov. 1698 Bishop Saint-Vallier [La Croix*] asked that "Marie-Anne Device" be admitted into the convent, and the chapter of the community agreed to "try her out." On 19 March 1699 she entered the noviciate, and on 24 May the chapter decided to give her six months more in order to "be able to determine whether she could learn to read and what progress she will make there." Marie-Anne must have satisfied the chapter's requirements, for she took the habit on 14 September of the same year. On 5 Sept. 1701 Charles de Glandelet* certified that she had been "examined according to the Holy Council of Trent and approved as being acceptable for admission to profession"; she made her profession on the following 15 September.

The annals of the convent emphasize that "she was very clean, careful, tidy, and thrifty ... [and] was very zealous in adorning the altars, so that she was several times vestry nun, to the satisfaction of the people without [the convent] as well as those within." Marie-Anne de Saint-Benoît died 2 March 1749, at about 70 years of age and in her 50th year of religion. She was the first Ursuline of English origin to make her profession at the convent of Quebec.

GABRIELLE LAPOINTE

[The author would like to thank Mr Gerald Kelly of New York who provided her with the results of his research on the origins of Marie-Anne Davis, *dite* de Saint-Benoît. G.L.]

AJQ, Registre d'état civil, Notre-Dame de Québec, 23 mars 1692. AMUQ, Actes des assemblées capitulaires, 1686–1802; Actes des professions et des sépultures, 1688–1781; Annales; Cahier du P. Ragueneau, copié par Jacques Bigot, s.j., et dédié à M. S.-Benoît Davis; Entrées, vêtures, professions et décès des religieuses, 1647–1861; Livre des entrées et sorties des filles françaises et sauvages, 1641–1720; Registre de l'examen canonique des novices, 1689–1807. ANDQ, Registre des baptêmes, mariages et sépultures, 23 mars 1692. *JR* (Thwaites), LXI-LXXI. *Genealogical dictionary of Maine and New Hampshire*, ed. Sybil Noyes *et al.* (Portland, Maine, 1928–39). Tanguay, *Dictionnaire*. Coleman, *New England captives*.

DAZEMARD (Dassemat, Dazmard, Dazmat) DE LUSIGNAN, PAUL-LOUIS, captain in the colonial regular troops, commandant; b. at Champlain (Que.) 19 Nov. 1691, only child of Paul-Louis Dazemard de Lusignan and Jeanne Babie; d. 2 Sept. 1764 at Quebec.

Paul-Louis Dazemard de Lusignan's career followed a familiar pattern: cadet in 1705; ensign, 1712; second lieutenant, 1721; lieutenant, 1734; captain, 1744. In 1734 Lusignan was assistant adjutant at Fort Niagara (near Youngstown, N.Y.). The following year he was appointed commandant of Fort Saint-Joseph (probably Niles, Mich.), a post he held until 1743. According to his service record, compiled in 1766 at the request of his widow who was seeking a pension, he may have been instrumental in 1736 in negotiating and securing a definitive peace with the Sauks and Foxes, thereby ending an expensive war. From 1743 to 1747, Lusignan was commandant at Baie-des-Puants (Green Bay, Wis.). His most important command was Fort Saint-Frédéric (Crown Point, N.Y), which he held from 1749 (officially from 1751) until 1758. During the war years 1755–60 Lusignan served variously at Saint-Frédéric, Carillon (Ticonderoga, N. Y.), Île aux Noix, Saint-Jean, and finally Chambly in 1760, but he apparently did not take part in any major engagements, rather acting as a garrison commander who sent supplies and reinforcements to the fighting troops.

His career of 53 years as an officer was long, but others matched it. Lusignan was, however, more than normally competent, judging by the comments of the authorities. In 1732 Intendant Hocquart* spoke well of him: a "prudent man, who likes his duty and who is able to bring honour to the service." The following year Hocquart defended him against a charge of private trading, pointing out that it was permissible "for gentlemen in this country" according to the edict of 1685. It is probable, then, that Lusignan, like other post commandants, eked out his meagre pay as a private trader with the Indians, while keeping a watchful eye on the activities of other traders, legal and illegal, passing by his post. In 1744, for example, he was commended by Governor Charles de BEAUHARNOIS for dealing with "disorders" in the trade at the Baie des Puants (Green Bay, Lake Michigan).

In 1749 Lusignan requested appointment as permanent commander at Saint-Frédéric, at that time the most advanced French outpost on Lake Champlain. The appointment was strongly recommended by both Governor La Jonquière [TAFFANEL] and Intendant François Bigot*, the latter pointing out that Lusignan could form an agricultural community around the post thereby lessening the burden of supplying it. The normal function of Saint-Frédéric, which the French government considered of great importance, was to prevent or at least restrain the illegal passage of goods between New France and Albany. The appointment, then, was one of considerable responsibility and the choice of Lusignan open to at least two interpretations. The most charitable is that Lusignan was an experienced officer of proven probity, given the post as a sinecure in his declining years. The other, borne out by the warmth of Bigot's recommendation, is that Lusignan may have been an agent of the *grande société* and connived at smuggling, but this interpretation must remain only a suspicion.

In July 1749 Lusignan welcomed to Fort Saint-Frédéric Pehr Kalm*, a prominent Swedish naturalist, en route to Montreal and Quebec from Albany. Kalm found his host to be a man "about fifty years old, well acquainted with polite literature and [who] had made several journeys into this country, by which he had acquired an exact knowledge of several things relative to it." Other comments confirm that the eminent *savant* found the Canadian-born and Canadian-educated officer a person of some refinement.

Lusignan was made a knight of the order of Saint-Louis in 1752 as a reward for long and faithful service. Severe illness apparently prevented his departure for France with the troops in 1760. He convalesced in Canada until 1764 and, when on the point of embarkation, died 2 September of a sudden illness. His widow returned to France. Lusignan had married at Montreal, on 8 Jan. 1722, Madeleine-Marguerite, daughter of François-Marie Bouat*. Ten children were born of the marriage; the eldest, Louis-Antoine*, had a distinguished military career.

J. R. TURNBULL

AN, Col., D²ᶜ, 222/4, f.136; 59, f.21; Marine, C⁷, 190. Pehr Kalm, *The America of 1750; Peter Kalm's travels in North America: the English version of 1770*, ed. A. B. Benson (2v., New York, 1966), II, 4. Fauteux, *Les chevaliers de Saint-Louis*, 152. Le Jeune, *Dictionnaire*. Tanguay, *Dictionnaire*. P.-G. Roy, "La famille Dazemard de Lusignan," *BRH*, XXXVII (1931), 579–85; "Les commandants du fort Saint-Frédéric," *BRH*, LI (1945), 330.

DEANAGHRISON. *See* TANAGHRISSON

DÉAT, ANTOINE, Sulpician, parish priest of Notre-Dame de Montréal, vicar general; b. 16 April 1696 at Riom, France, son of Antoine Déat, a dealer in spices, and Catherine Metayer; d. 23 March 1761 in Montreal.

Antoine Déat entered the seminary of Saint-Sulpice in Clermont-Ferrand on 31 Oct. 1718 and arrived in Montreal on 19 Oct. 1722, two years after his ordination. He was first a curate in the parish of Notre-Dame de Montréal, and later chaplain to the Congregation of Notre Dame from 1723 to 1730. At the nuns' request he undertook to draw up the *Coutumier* of the congregation, which was intended to serve as a commentary on the rules of the community, but he soon gave up this work for fear of causing trouble among the nuns. In 1730, after the resignation of the parish priest of Notre-Dame de Montréal, Jean-Gabriel-Marie Le Pape* Du Lescöat, Déat held this office. Little information is available about his activities as parish priest. In 1731 Bishop Dosquet* named him in addition vicar general for the Montreal region. The following year Déat introduced into Montreal the devotion to St Amable, patron saint of his native parish in Riom whom he held in great veneration. In honour of this saint he had a chapel built in the church of Notre-Dame; it became the seat of the Confrérie de la Bonne Mort, which he founded that same year.

Antoine Déat left a reputation as an eloquent and moving preacher; 150 extant sermons written in his hand allow us to a certain extent to judge his talent. They are pieces of oratory composed with great care according to the rules for the genre in force at the period. These sermons, delivered on the occasion of the chief liturgical feast-days, are varied and cover practically all the great truths of Christian doctrine. Among them are panegyrics, particularly of St Anne, St Louis [Louis IX], St Augustine, St Ignatius of Loyola, St Francis Xavier, and two Lenten addresses, one on the Passion, the other on the sacrament of penance which was delivered in 1742 and in 1746.

About a third of these sermons deal with questions of morality, such as false piety, false penance, sin, relapses, evil example, unchastity, dancing, false worldly pleasures, and the keeping of the Sabbath. They furnish valuable information on the morals of our ancestors in the 18th century. Echoes of them are found in the correspondence of the period: Mme Bégon

Decous

[ROCBERT] refers to the sermon given on 26 Jan. 1749, in which the preacher condemned dances indiscriminately and unsparingly. She had not heard the sermon, and in speaking of it in her letter of 26 January deforms and exaggerates it. The passage which she quotes does not exist in the text, and she borrowed from here and there in the address words and phrases which, taken out of context and stripped of their nuances, assume a meaning and an importance that the preacher never intended.

Antoine Déat's oratorical talent does not seem to have suffered any eclipse throughout his ministry. He submitted his resignation in 1760, after more than 37 years of service in the parish of Notre-Dame, and on 23 March 1761, at 65 years of age, he died at the seminary of Montreal. He was entitled to a public funeral in the chapel of the Confrérie de la Bonne Mort.

ANTONIO DANSEREAU

AD, Puy-de-Dôme (Clermont-Ferrand), État civil, prieuré Saint-Jean, 16 avril 1696. ASSM, Section des associations et des communautés; Section des biographies; Section prédication. "Correspondance de Mme Bégon" (Bonnault), APQ *Rapport, 1934–35*, 31, 199–200. Allaire, *Dictionnaire*. Gauthier, *Sulpitiana*. [É.-M. Faillon], *Vie de la sœur Bourgeoys, fondatrice de la Congrégation de Notre-Dame de Villemarie en Canada, suivie de l'histoire de cet institut jusqu'à ce jour* (2v., Villemarie [Montréal], 1853), II, 290, 296, 327; *Vie de Mme d'Youville, fondatrice des Sœurs de la Charité de Villemarie dans l'île de Montréal, en Canada* (Villemarie [Montréal], 1852), 62. Lemire-Marsolais et Lambert, *Histoire de la Congrégation de Notre-Dame*, III, IV. Olivier Maurault, *L'œuvre et fabrique de Notre-Dame de Montréal* (Montréal, 1959).

DECOUS (Decoust). *See* DESCOUTS

DEGAWEHE. *See* GAWÈHE

DEGOUTIN. *See* GOUTIN

DEGUISE, *dit* **Flamand (Flamant), GIRARD-GUILLAUME** (known as **Guillaume Flamand**), mason and master builder; baptized 8 Sept. 1694 at Quebec, son of Guillaume Deguise, *dit* Flamand, mason, and Marie-Anne Morin; m. 7 Jan. 1717 at Lorette, near Quebec, to Marie-Anne Rouillard; buried 22 March 1752 at Quebec.

The Deguise, *dit* Flamand, family formed a modest but not unimportant craft dynasty in New France. The founder was Guillaume Deguise, the elder, a mason who had immigrated in the late 17th century. Because he had come from Dunkerque in French Flanders, he and his descendants were nicknamed "Flamand." Guillaume lived in the Quebec suburb of Petite-Rivière. He fathered four sons but was unable to train them completely in his craft before he died in 1711.

In that year, Girard-Guillaume, his oldest son, was apprenticed by his widow to Jean-Baptiste MAILLOU, *dit* Desmoulins, the Quebec architect and builder. Young Guillaume was to receive four years of training as a mason and stonecutter, with food, lodging, laundry, and clothes provided by his master. Legal and administrative records show that Guillaume followed the conventional life of a masonry builder: contracting with suppliers of lime, rubble, and stonework; hiring workers; training apprentices in building chimneys, gables, walls, and houses; going to court with creditors and debtors.

In 1716 Guillaume Deguise was living with his wife-to-be on Rue Champlain in Quebec's Lower Town. They were at Lorette in the early 1730s and back in Quebec in the 1740s when Guillaume was employed as an expert estimator for the intendant. Just before his death he worked on the counterscarp of the Saint-Louis gate. In these years Guillaume lived in the Upper Town, on Rue Saint-Louis and then on Rue Saint-Jean in a small stone house acquired in 1749. Deguise's only other assets in 1756 amounted to some 600 *livres*.

Guillaume's brother, Jacques Deguise, *dit* Flamand, a masonry contractor in Quebec, perpetuated the family tradition; he built houses for Nicolas LANOULLIER de Boisclerc which still stand on Rue des Remparts. Guillaume's oldest son François was a mason and two of his daughters married into a family equally renowned in this craft, that of Michel Jourdain.

PETER N. MOOGK

ANQ, Greffe de Jacques Barbel, 28 juin 1734; Greffe de Louis Chambalon, 26 déc. 1711; Greffe de J.-É. Dubreuil, 28 déc. 1716, 3 déc. 1723, 2 avril 1724, 5 août 1725, 11 mars, 27 avril 1728; Greffe de C.-H. Du Laurent, 21 févr. 1754, 18 janv. 1755, 23 déc. 1756; Greffe de P.-A.-F. Lanoullier Des Granges, 8 sept. 1750; Greffe de J.-C. Louet, 29 juill. 1725; Greffe de J.-N. Pinguet de Vaucour, 12 janv. 1748, 19 juin 1749; NF, Coll. de pièces jud. et not., 998, 1389, 1829, 2615, 4229. PAC, MG 8, B1, 20/2. *Recensement de Québec, 1716* (Beaudet). "Recensement de Québec, 1744" (APQ *Rapport*). P.-G. Roy, *Inv. jug. et délib., 1717–1760*, V, VI; *Inv. ord. int.*, I, II, III. Tanguay, *Dictionnaire*.

DEJORDY (Desjordy) DE VILLEBON, CHARLES-RENÉ (he signed **Dejordy Villebon** and sometimes **Vilbon**; the name Villebon came from his uncle, Joseph Robinau* de Villebon), military officer; b. at Îles Bouchard and baptized

12 June 1715 at Saint-Sulpice (Que.), son of François Desjordy* Moreau de Cabanac and Louise-Catherine Robinau de Bécancour; married Catherine Trottier Desrivières in Montreal (the marriage contract is dated 11 Feb. 1741); d. 15 Nov. 1761 in the shipwreck of the *Auguste*.

Charles-René Dejordy de Villebon joined the colonial regular troops as a cadet and in 1749 was promoted second ensign. He was sent as second in command to Baie-des-Puants (Green Bay, Wis.), with the mention "a very steady fellow"; he conducted himself there to everyone's satisfaction from 1750 to 1754 or 1755, under the orders of Joseph Marin* de La Malgue. In 1756 he received the rank of ensign on the active list and in the course of that year took part in two expeditions against Chouaguen (Oswego), first with Gaspard-Joseph Chaussegros* de Léry in the early spring, then with Montcalm in August.

After that we find him in the west as partner to Louis-Joseph Gaultier de La Vérendrye in 1757 and commandant of the *poste de l'Ouest* from 1758 to 1760. He was the last of the commandants of that post, which consisted of eight establishments of varying importance situated in the region of Lac Ounipigon (Lake Winnipeg) and the Rivière Paskoya (Saskatchewan River). In 1756 the minister of Marine, Machault, had established in the west a state monopoly or the system of the highest bidder, which was already in effect in the less distant posts but was difficult to apply in the far west because of the distances. According to this system the post was put up for auction, and the state kept for itself the commerce in furs, which was entrusted to the commandant. Like his predecessor La Vérendrye, for three years Villebon had to pay 8,000 *livres* and three quarters of the revenues; he and his partners shared the remaining quarter.

While one Henri Janot, *dit* Bourguignon, served as his clerk at Fort Dauphin (Winnipegosis, Man.) and on the Paskoya, Villebon took up residence at Fort La Reine (Portage-la-Prairie) and carried out his role as best he could. Given the circumstances, there was no longer any question of making discoveries; it was wartime, and all that could be done was keep the Indians well occupied in the fur trade, the only means of maintaining peace in that region.

But how could business be carried on when trade goods were no longer arriving and everything was scarce throughout the colony? Consequently the furs took the route to Hudson Bay, all the more so since the employees of the Hudson's Bay Company, such as Anthony Henday and Joseph Smith, were promoting this change during their voyages in the interior of the country. Urged on by the English – as was normal in time of war – the Indians destroyed the forts one after another. Fort des Prairies or Fort Saint-Louis (near Fort à la Corne, Sask.), the one farthest west, was the first to fall, in 1757. In the next few years the others were destroyed by the Indians or abandoned by the French. Only Fort Dauphin and Fort La Reine, the two main centres, were to remain, under new masters after 1760. They were first occupied by Villebon's former employees or by coureurs de bois, then after the conquest by the British.

Villebon had been promoted lieutenant in 1759. A new appointment which was supposed to extend to 1762 or 1763 had apparently been given to him for the *poste de l'Ouest*, but in fact he returned to Montreal before the end of his term. He left the west with his belongings and a load of furs at the beginning of the summer of 1760. He could not reach his destination until the end of September or early October. As Montreal had capitulated on 8 September, he did not have the opportunity of taking up arms to defend his country. With Charles-René Dejordy de Villebon's departure the *poste de l'Ouest* had ceased to exist.

On 26 Sept. 1761 Villebon was at Montreal, preparing to leave for France with his family. He perished with his sister, his wife, and his three children in the wreck of the *Auguste* on the coast of Cape Breton Island on 15 Nov. 1761. In the confusion which followed the conquest of Canada, Villebon was accused of having amassed money unlawfully through dealing in brandy or otherwise. On 10 Dec. 1763 the court of the Châtelet in Paris gave its decision concerning the dishonest acts committed in New France. Villebon was found "absent and contumacious." At the date mentioned he had been dead for more than two years, which the court was not aware of, and proof of his guilt was never established. There is reason to believe that he was innocent and that, like many others, he was accused without any grounds; even if he had wanted to, he could not have found the trade goods, above all brandy, at a time when everything was in short supply in New France and only the powerful succeeded in getting any for themselves.

Antoine Champagne

[G.-J. Chaussegros de Léry], "Les journaux de M. de Léry," APQ *Rapport, 1926–27*, 334–48. "Journal de Marin, fils, 1753–1754," Antoine Champagne, édit., AQ *Rapport, 1960–61*, 237–308. E.-J. Auclair, *Les de Jordy de Cabanac, histoire d'une ancienne famille noble du Canada* (Montréal, 1930). Champagne, *Les La Vérendrye*.

Delaborde

DELABORDE (de la Borde, La Borde) JEAN, king's attorney; b. 1700 or 1701 in the parish of Saint-Germain-le-Vieux, Paris, France; d. 1754 at Louisbourg, Île Royale (Cape Breton Island).

Jean Delaborde issued from a bourgeois family. From his uncle, Jean de La Borde, who had bought the office of billeting officer for the king's household in 1687, he inherited 21,000 *livres* in 1719. Little else is known of him before he arrived in Louisbourg in 1739 to assume the posts of king's attorney at the bailiff's and the admiralty courts. At the bailiff's court he replaced Claude-Joseph Le Roy* Desmarest and at the admiralty, Philippe CARREROT, a temporary appointee. The duties for both positions were the same; to hold the admiralty office, which pertained solely to maritime affairs, one had first to be nominated by the admiral of France and then commissioned by the king. The offices were ones of trust, the holders representing the interests of both king and public in seeing that laws were obeyed and justice rendered impartially. The king's attorney was responsible for investigating and presenting civil and criminal cases to the court for its decision. Before being permitted to exercise his duties Delaborde was required to present to the Conseil Supérieur his commissions and certificates of baptism and good character, and to swear before it an oath of office. He held his posts until the fall of Louisbourg to New England troops in 1745. Four years later Île Royale was restored to France, and in 1750 Delaborde resumed his functions.

Delaborde appears to have been a kind and unobtrusive person. In 1749 he became guardian to the three daughters of Louis LEVASSEUR, lieutenant general of the admiralty court, and at his own expense sent two of them to school at Quebec under the care of the notary Paul-Antoine-François Lanoullier Des Granges. The third, Thérèse, stayed with him in Louisbourg where he appears to have attended to her every need, including lessons from the dancing master, Ducourday Feuillet.

After nearly a year of insanity Delaborde died, and was buried at Louisbourg on 17 Nov. 1754. He had married early in life, but his wife's name is not known and there is no indication that she ever lived in Louisbourg. His career should not be confused with that of Jean La Borde*, notary, agent of the treasurers-general of the Marine in Île Royale, and attorney general of the Conseil Supérieur of Louisbourg.

T. A. CROWLEY

AD, Charente-Maritime (La Rochelle), B, 270, f.67. AN, Col., B, 68, f.355; C¹¹ᴮ, 34, f.60; E, 238 (dossiers Jean Delaborde, Jean La Borde); F³, 50, f.233; Section Outre-Mer, G¹, 409/1, f.39; G², 185, f.488; 192/3, ff.12, 17v; 212, dossier 573. C.-J. Ferrière, *Dictionnaire de droit et de pratique, contenant l'explication des termes de droit, d'ordonnances, de coutumes et de pratique* (3ᵉ éd., 2v., Paris, 1749), 598–600. [Most authors, such as J.-E. Roy, *Histoire du notariat*, I, 373, have confused Jean Delaborde and Jean La Borde. T.A.C.]

DeLAUNE, WILLIAM, army officer; place and date of birth unknown; apparently unmarried; d. 18 Feb. 1761 in England.

William DeLaune may have been a son or connection of Henry DeLaune, a captain in Harrison's Regiment of Foot according to the 1740 army list. William became a lieutenant in the 20th Foot as of 24 July 1754 and a captain 1 Sept. 1756. At this time James WOLFE was lieutenant-colonel in the regiment. When in 1758 the 2nd battalion was converted into a new regiment, the 67th Foot, with Wolfe as its colonel, DeLaune became a captain in it.

Wolfe evidently thought highly of him as a potential commander of light infantry. On 11 Feb. 1758, when about to sail for Louisbourg, Île Royale (Cape Breton Island), Wolfe wrote that DeLaune was "formed by nature for the American war"; after the fall of Louisbourg he wrote again, "If his Majesty had thought proper to let [Guy Carleton*] come with us as engineer and Delaune and 2 or 3 more for the light Foot, it would have cut the matter much shorter. . . ." Wolfe was allowed to take DeLaune with him in the expedition against Quebec in 1759. During the passage to Quebec DeLaune witnessed Wolfe's will. He was one of six officers to whom the general left "each a hundred guineas, to buy swords & rings in remembrance of their Friend."

DeLaune was apparently appointed to the provisional battalion of light infantry, commanded by Lieutenant-Colonel William Howe. He was presumably a company commander; there is at least one casual reference to him as a major, but if he was given this local rank it is not reflected in the army list. When Wolfe was planning the landing that took place at the Anse au Foulon (Wolfe's Cove) on 13 Sept. 1759, he selected DeLaune to command the detachment of 24 light infantry volunteers, carried in the leading boat, which was to rush the famous path up the cliff. The ebbing tide took the boats below the spot planned for the landing, and the most vital role was apparently played by Howe. According to Brigadier George Townshend*'s notes, Howe ordered DeLaune to move along the beach and assault the path as planned, while he himself and the leading companies of his battalion "very gallantly scrambled up the rocky height in his front" – an action which seems to have been no part of Wolfe's plan. Howe's attack took the defenders of the path in rear and "most happily facilitated ye success" of DeLaune's party.

After the battle DeLaune, along with Captain Thomas Bell*, one of Wolfe's aides-de-camp, took Wolfe's body back to England and, in Bell's words, "accompanyed our noble master to the Grave." He then presumably returned to regimental duty with the 67th in England, and died little more than a year later, still a captain. His will, dated 1755, left all his possessions to his mother Lucy.

C. P. STACEY

PAC, MG 18, M3, 24 (Thomas Bell's journals). PRO, Prob. 11/864, f.99. *Army list, 1740; 1756; 1757; 1759; 1761.* C. T. Atkinson and D. S. Daniell, *Regimental history: the Royal Hampshire Regiment . . .* (3v., Glasgow and Aldershot, Eng., 1950–55), I. Stacey, *Quebec, 1759.* Beckles Willson, *The life and letters of James Wolfe . . .* (London, 1909).

DELIETTE. *See* TONTY

DELONGRAIS. *See* DESLONGRAIS

DELORT (Delord, de Lord, de Lort), GUIL-LAUME, merchant, councillor of the Conseil Supérieur of Île Royale (Cape Breton Island); b. at Auch, France, son of Jacques Delort and Suzanne Despenan; d. before August 1749, place unknown.

Guillaume Delort is first mentioned in November 1706 at Plaisance (Placentia, Nfld.). Both here and later at Louisbourg he played a varied role in the commercial life of the colonies, and his career illustrates the different ways in which an entrepreneur could prosper in French colonial America. Much of his activity was as a broker, buying and selling goods and ships on his own account and on behalf of merchants in other ports, such as Quebec and Saint-Jean-de-Luz, France. An example is Delort's purchase, with permission of Saint-Ovide [MONBETON], the governor of Île Royale, of the *Joly Bachelier* and its cargo from an English captain for 6,000 *livres* on 19 Oct. 1729. Two weeks later he sold the ship to a merchant of Saint-Domingue (Hispaniola) for 6,400 *livres*. In 1733 Delort obtained a schooner, the *Margot*, for debts owing him to the value of 2,500 *livres* and resold it for 2,800 *livres*.

The extent of Delort's business dealings is evident in the many legal actions in which he was involved, often with shipowners or merchants in La Rochelle, France. Delort was frequently named as the inheritor of an estate because of debts owed him by the deceased. Many of those with whom he dealt were probably engaged in the commercial fishery since Delort was in the business of equipping and provisioning fishing ships. In 1738, for example, Gervais Brisset, a navigator of Port-Toulouse (St Peters, N.S.), stated that he owed Delort 2,008 *livres* for supplying his ship the *Saint-Jean-Baptiste.* In 1740 Michel Richard, *dit* Lafond, a merchant, owed Delort 1,687 *livres* for merchandise, for which sum he would forfeit all his goods. Delort also engaged in the fishery himself. In 1721 in partnership with a merchant and ship captain from Saint-Jean-de-Luz he had land on Île Royale cleared for drying fish, rented three schooners, and paid the wages of a crew to fish on them for a period of four years.

Beginning in 1730 Delort provided a wide variety of merchandise for the government. Goods supplied included tools, firewood, nails and planks, tobacco, candles, glass, and foodstuffs. On at least one occasion the supplies were brought in from New York. Delort also rented residence accommodation to government officials at Louisbourg.

In May 1723 Delort was serving as churchwarden of the parish of Louisbourg, and he was reported as acting as king's attorney of the admiralty court in July 1724. In September 1735 Delort was appointed a councillor of the Conseil Supérieur of Île Royale to replace Jacques d'Espiet* de Pensens. His brother-in-law André CARREROT was also appointed at the same time. Because of their relationship special dispensation was required from Versailles though they were allowed to sit on the council until approval arrived the following year. At the time of his death Delort was keeper of the seals of the Conseil Supérieur.

Delort had first married, on 10 Jan. 1711, Françoise-Ovide Carrerot, daughter of Pierre Carrerot* and Marie Picq. One son, Louis, was baptized on 6 May 1713. On 24 Jan. 1717 he married his second wife, Marie-Charlotte Gautier, daughter of Jean-Baptiste Gautier, bourgeois of Quebec, and Marie Guyon Desprez. They had three sons, Philippe, Michel, and Guillaume, and two daughters. Delort's children contracted marriages with many of the prominent families of Louisbourg including the Leneuf de La Vallière and the Espiet de Pensens families. Delort's eldest son, Louis, was supplying goods to the government in 1735 and in 1743 Philippe was engaged in the same occupation. During the 1750s the Delort brothers continued their father's business activities as merchants and dealers in ships. At least two of Delort's sons were named

Denis

to the Conseil Supérieur: Louis in 1750 and Guillaume, as councillor and assessor, in 1754.

Guillaume Delort's business success, his family connections, and his status in the community indicate that he was among those wealthy citizens in the higher economic, social, and administrative circles of Louisbourg.

BARBARA RILEY

AN, Col., C¹¹C, 11–13; Section Outre-Mer, G¹, 406–8, 466; G², 178, ff.323, 364; 180, f.114; 181, ff.437–40; 182, ff.1044–50; 183, ff.414–16, 431; 190/1, ff.4, 17, 19; 190/2, f.14; 190/3, f.27; 190/4, f.30; 191, ff.94–95, 118; 192/4, ff.9, 21; 212, nos.558, 577; G³, 7/175; 8/176; 2037; 2039 (16 oct. 1734); 2046 (26, 27 août 1737, 26 oct. 1738, 26 juin 1740, 29 avril 1741); 2055; 2056, 1717, nos.1, 26, 31–32; 2057 (24 nov. 1721); 2058 (18, 31 mai, 3, 18 sept. 1733). McLennan, *Louisbourg*, 359, 386–87.

DENIS. *See* DENYS

DENISON, ROBERT, soldier, settler, member of the Nova Scotia assembly; b. 1697 in Mohegan (now Montville, Conn.), son of Robert Denison and Joanna Stanton; d. at Horton (now Hortonville, N.S.), probably in late June 1765.

For most of his life Robert Denison served as a militia officer in New England's campaigns against the French and Indians. In October 1728 he was commissioned ensign in the North Company in New London, Connecticut, and was promoted captain in October 1731. He was elected to the Connecticut general assembly in 1737 and 1742. In March 1745 he became captain of a company for the expedition against Île Royale (Cape Breton Island) [*see* Sir William PEPPERRELL] and served at the capture of Louisbourg that June.

Denison was elected to the general assembly again in 1751, and in March 1755 commissioned a major in the 1st Regiment of Connecticut. In August he attended a war council held by William Johnson* near the south end of Lac Saint-Sacrement (Lake George), and early in September took part in the battle of Lake George against French forces under DIESKAU. He was discharged on 3 Oct. 1755; he served again in the general assembly the following year.

Governor Charles LAWRENCE's proclamations of 1758 and 1759 offering free lands to immigrants attracted land-hungry planters from southeastern Connecticut to the fertile shores of the Bay of Fundy, vacant since the expulsion of the Acadians in 1755. Major Denison was one of the agents for the Connecticut grantees who appeared before the Nova Scotia Council in April 1759 to make arrangements for 200 families. The agents were sent with Surveyor General Charles

Morris* to view the lands and they selected a township of 100,000 acres at Minas (near Wolfville), which was granted under the name of Horton on 21 May. The council was to provide transportation for the settlers and their stock, farming equipment, and household goods, and to supply grain for needy families. Robert Denison heads the list of proprietors of Horton Township and he received 750 acres. On 4 June 1760 the main flotilla of 22 ships arrived and the settlers disembarked at Horton Landing. Denison was commissioned lieutenant-colonel of the militia of Horton Township that same day. Committees distributed the land so that each proprietor received a town lot and a portion of marshland, upland, and woodland. Horton became an agricultural community, trading farm products and some lumber with Connecticut for manufactured goods.

In 1760 Denison was commissioned a justice of the peace for Kings County. He became a justice of the Inferior Court of Common Pleas for Horton Township in August 1761. He faithfully attended from 1760 to May 1765 the Court of Quarter Sessions held at Horton which administered the local government of the township and tried minor criminal offences. In 1762 he was the first to sign a protest by 63 "New Eng'd Settlers of King's County . . . the Magistrates, Representatives, and other principal Inhabitants" blaming Lieutenant Governor Jonathan Belcher* for breaking promises made by the late Governor Lawrence, especially that the settlers would have their own township government and "all our civil and Religious Rights and Liberties, as we enjoyed them in the Governments from whence we Came." The Court of Quarter Sessions, however, remained the principal municipal governing body until 1879.

Denison was one of the first New England planters elected to the Nova Scotia assembly, taking his seat on 1 July 1761. He supported Benjamin* and Joseph Gerrish* against Belcher, who was trying to repeal laws protecting debtors from their creditors in England. In August 1762 Denison was dismissed from his "employments both civil and military" (his commission in the militia and probably his appointment to the Court of Common Pleas) for his opposition to Belcher; he was reappointed a justice of the Court of Common Pleas for all of Kings County in February 1764. He resigned from the assembly in April 1764 "on account of his age and infirmities."

Denison signed his will on 25 June 1765 and seems to have died soon afterwards. He had been married on 19 Oct. 1721 to Deborah Griswold and on 4 April 1733 to Prudence Sherman, and had 15 children; several of them died young. He left to his eldest son his "Cape Britton Gun and Silver Hilted Sword." Three other sons inherited his property in Nova Scotia.

PHYLLIS R. BLAKELEY

Hants County Court of Probate (Windsor, N.S.), Will book, I, 16–21. PANS, MG 1, 181, I; MG 34, 26; RG 1, 164/2, pp.109, 146, 170, 237; 359, nos.1, 2, 4; 361, nos.3a, 3b, 3c, 17–22. *The Fitch papers: correspondence and documents during Thomas Fitch's governorship of the colony of Connecticut, 1754–1766* (2v., Conn. Hist. Soc. *Coll.*, XVII, XVIII, Hartford, 1918–20), I, 129–30. *Johnson papers* (Sullivan *et al.*), XIII, 50. Nova Scotia, *Votes of the House of Assembly, Province of Nova-Scotia* ([Halifax, 1761]), 1 July 1761; *Votes and journals of the House of Assembly* ([Halifax, 1764]), 3 April 1764. *The Pitkin papers: correspondence and documents during William Pitkin's governorship of the colony of Connecticut, 1766–1769, with some of earlier date* (Conn. Hist. Soc. *Coll.*, XIX, Hartford, 1921), 11, 262. *Rolls of Connecticut men in the French and Indian War, 1755–1762* (Conn. Hist. Soc. *Coll.*, IX, Hartford, 1903). E. G. Denison, *Denison genealogy; ancestors and descendants of Captain George Denison* (Stonington, Conn., [1963]), 12–13.

Brebner, *Neutral Yankees*. A. W. H. Eaton, *The history of Kings County, Nova Scotia, heart of the Acadian land, giving a sketch of the French and their expulsion; and a history of the New England planters who came in their stead, with many genealogies, 1604–1710* (Salem, Mass., 1910). D. C. Harvey, "The struggle for the New England form of township government in Nova Scotia," CHA *Report, 1933*, 15–22. R. S. Longley, "The coming of the New England planters to the Annapolis Valley," N.S. Hist. Soc. *Coll.*, XXXIII (1961), 81–101. Jean Stephenson, "The Connecticut settlement of Nova Scotia prior to the revolution," National Geneal. Soc. *Quarterly* (Washington), XLII (1954), 53–60.

DENYS DE BONNAVENTURE (Bonnaventure), CLAUDE-ÉLISABETH (he signed both Denys de Bonnaventure and **Denis de Bonnaventure**), officer in the colonial regular troops; b. 22 June 1701 at La Rochelle, France, son of Simon-Pierre Denys* de Bonnaventure and Jeanne Jannière; m. 25 Nov. 1748 at Quebec his cousin Louise, daughter of Louis DENYS de La Ronde and Louise Chartier de Lotbinière; d. May 1760 at Rochefort, France.

Commissioned an ensign at Louisbourg, Île Royale (Cape Breton Island) on 2 July 1720, Claude-Élisabeth Denys de Bonnaventure was almost immediately posted to the garrison at Île Saint-Jean (Prince Edward Island), commanded by his uncle, Louis Denys de La Ronde. Its function was to protect the colonists sent there by the Comte de Saint-Pierre, who had been granted the island and its fisheries in 1719. But by 1724 the colonization venture had failed, and Bonnaventure returned to Île Royale that year.

For several years his career in Louisbourg was uneventful. Like many officers he acquired land in the town; on 20 March 1730 he was promoted lieutenant. When in late 1733 the colony ran short of supplies – a not infrequent occurrence, for Île Royale was never self-sufficient – Bonnaventure and Michel de GANNES de Falaise were dispatched in two ships to seek supplies at New York. But bad weather on the return journey forced Bonnaventure to Martinique where he sold his cargo and, apparently, contracted a malady which later plagued him. On 1 April 1737, some years after his return to Louisbourg, he was promoted assistant garrison adjutant with a captain's commission. Illness prevented him from carrying out his heavy duties and he was eventually relieved of the appointment. On 1 April 1738 he assumed formal command of his own company.

Shortly after the outbreak of the War of the Austrian Succession in North America in 1744, the governor of Île Royale, Jean-Baptiste-Louis LE PRÉVOST Duquesnel, vigorously attacked the English in Acadia, sending Joseph DU PONT Duvivier first on a successful mission against Canso, and later against Annapolis Royal. The second venture was to be undertaken by a combined land and sea force, the latter under Bonnaventure's command. When his three ships arrived at Annapolis Royal on 25 October, however, Bonnaventure discovered that Duvivier, at de Gannes's instigation, had withdrawn his troops, dispersed his Micmac allies, and returned to Louisbourg – despite the weak, almost mutinous condition of the English garrison. Although unable to mount a land attack, Bonnaventure had some success at sea, capturing two New England ships. This partial success was short-lived; eight months later, when Louisbourg fell to the New England militia, it was Bonnaventure who delivered the documents of capitulation to William PEPPERRELL.

After his repatriation to France, Bonnaventure busied himself with plans to secure naval assistance for Canada, but these were rejected by Maurepas, the minister of Marine. As the war drew to a close Bonnaventure was appointed, on 7 Feb. 1748, acting major of the Île Royale companies in Canada. In the same month he received the cross of Saint-Louis. It is not known when he reached Canada, nor – aside from his marriage at Quebec – what happened to him there. Île Royale was restored to France in 1748 and Bonnaventure and his wife moved there the following year. In August he was designated acting major and com-

Denys de La Ronde

mandant of Île Saint-Jean, perhaps the most demanding appointment of his career.

Before the war Île Saint-Jean had not received particular attention from France, but Britain's expanding presence in Nova Scotia, heralded by the founding of Halifax, gave the island a new importance in French policy. The Acadians were encouraged to take up farms there, for the successful colonization of the island would end Louisbourg's dependence on European and New England food sources. To encourage migration France promised the prospective immigrants free equipment and supplies, provided transport to the island, and played upon the Acadians' fear of losing their religion under British rule.

Bonnaventure had expected to be at Île Saint-Jean only temporarily, but he was promoted full major commanding on 1 April 1751 after Duvivier, nominated king's lieutenant for the island the previous year, was discovered in Paris in the compromising company of the English commissioners to the Boundaries Disputes Commission. The settlement of the island and the organization of its agriculture were difficult tasks. The French government gave little direction and only limited financial encouragement to the colony; the land system was unsuited to the island and to the agricultural methods of the Acadians who were expected to live there. From the beginning, moreover, the crops were afflicted with insects and blight and there were frequent shortages of food and supplies. It is not surprising that the Acadians showed slight interest in settling on the island. "There was little to choose," they said, "between starving at home or on Île Saint-Jean." Weighed down by his responsibilities and in ill health, Bonnaventure constantly asked to be relieved of his duties, but not until 1754 did Gabriel Rousseau* de Villejouin replace him.

On 1 April 1754 Bonnaventure was made king's lieutenant at Louisbourg. In this office he was officially second in command and would normally replace the governor in the governor's absence. But because of his physical incapacities and his inexperience in warfare, in August 1755 he was relieved of this particular responsibility of office, should it occur in war time. He retained the usual day to day functions of the position.

He continued thus, complaining of his poor pay and poor health, until the fall of Louisbourg in 1758. On his return to France he was made inspector of the colonial troops at Rochefort but, weakened by war wounds and general ill health, he died there in the spring of 1760.

ANDREW RODGER

AN, Col., B, 54, ff.503–3v; 59, ff.530–32, 547; 61, ff.605v–6v; 63, ff.541–41v; 64, f.473; 82, f.127; 87, p.196; 88/2, p.280; 91, pp.180, 361ff.; 92/2, p.480; 93, pp.200, 235; 94, p.91; 95, pp.250, 302, f.380v; 99, p.221, f.249; 108/2, p.587; C^{11A}, 93, p.313; 96, p.3; C^{11B}, 6, ff.76–95; 7, ff.73, 78–78v; 8, ff.78–93; 14, f.187; 15, ff.43, 187–87v; 18, ff.26, 52v, 69, 384; 19, f.10v; 20, f.317v; 25, ff.43–45; 26, ff.79–88; 28, ff.10–13v, 156; 30, pp.13, 17, 21, 23, 31, 35, 40, ff.13–13v, 294–301v; 33, f.95; 34, ff.18–19v; 35, ff.139–40, 345; 36, ff.49–50v, 77; 37, ff.40, 44; 38, ff.88, 92v–93, 245v; C^{11C}, 16, pièces 26, 35 (2e sér.); D^{2C}, 2, f.p.64; 3, pp.43, 66; 47; 48; 60, ff.14v, 121v; 61, f.83; 222; Section Outre-Mer, G^1, 408, p.6; 411 (paginated references are to PAC transcripts). PAC, MG 18, H13. Fauteux, *Les chevaliers de Saint-Louis*. Archange Godbout et R.-J. Auger, "Familles venues de La Rochelle en Canada," ANQ *Rapport, 1970*, 113–377. Casgrain, *Une seconde Acadie*. Harvey, *French régime in P.E.I.*

DENYS DE LA RONDE, LOUIS (he signed La Ronde Denys), officer in the navy and in the colonial regular troops; b. 2 Aug. 1675 at Quebec, son of Pierre Denys* de La Ronde and Catherine Leneuf de La Poterie; m. 20 July 1709 at Quebec, Marie-Louise, daughter of René-Louis Chartier* de Lotbinière, and first cousin of Louise-Élisabeth Joybert*, wife of the governor-general of New France, Philippe de Rigaud* de Vaudreuil; had three sons and three daughters; buried 25 March 1741 at Quebec.

Louis Denys de La Ronde entered the naval service as a midshipman at Rochefort, France, in 1687. For the next 20 years he served in a wide variety of campaigns: he accompanied the deposed English king James II to Ireland in 1689, and saw action there at Bantry Bay and again off Beachy Head, England; in eight campaigns to New France between 1692 and 1705, serving several times under his older brother, Simon-Pierre Denys* de Bonaventure, he came to know the New England coastline well; in 1697 he accompanied Pierre Le Moyne* d'Iberville on his final and most dramatic campaign to Hudson Bay; and in 1699–1700 and 1701, at the specific request of d'Iberville, he served in the Mississippi expeditions. He was given his first command in November 1701, when d'Iberville entrusted him with the *Enflammé* for the return voyage to France. The following year, on his way to Quebec, he suffered a serious shoulder wound in an action against an English vessel. Twice, in 1695 and 1704, he was taken prisoner by the English on the high seas.

La Ronde began his colonial service in 1705 when he was given command of a small frigate to be used against English shipping in Acadian and New England waters. To counter France's increasing inability to meet the wartime requirements of the colony, the governor of Acadia, Jacques-François Monbeton* de Brouillan, had decided to have the *Biche*, 18 to 20 guns, built at Port-Royal (Annapolis Royal, N.S.). Finding the vessel unfinished when he arrived, La Ronde took charge of a brig and began privateering and reconnoitring English strength along the New England seaboard. In 1706 he went so far as to put in at Boston "on the pretext of making inquiries about developments . . . regarding exchanges [of prisoners]." It may have been on this occasion that he made contacts which later would be useful to him.

Just as the *Biche*, with a crew of 60 Canadians under Charles-Joseph Amiot* de Vincelotte, was ready to sail from Port-Royal in the spring of 1707, a force of New England provincials under John March* arrived before the town. The energy of the new governor, Daniel d'Auger* de Subercase, aided substantially by La Ronde and his men, compelled the New Englanders to withdraw; La Ronde carried news of the successful defence to the court. While in France he had the *Biche* replaced by a larger frigate, the *Vénus*, and after an arduous crossing he returned to Port-Royal on Easter Sunday 1708. Anticipating a new English attack, Subercase ordered him to take up his command of the infantry company awarded him in 1707 following the resignation of Louis-Simon Le Poupet* de La Boularderie.

It was only late in August therefore – and despite the desertion of the greater part of his crew – that La Ronde was able to resume his privateering. Taking on 40 men recently arrived from the West Indies, he set out from Port-Royal on the *Vénus* and promptly captured two prizes worth more than 115,000 *livres*. But contrary winds forced him to put in at Plaisance (Placentia, Nfld.), where the governor, Philippe Pastour* de Costebelle, persuaded him to join an expedition against the English forts at St John's. Leaving Port-Royal to its fate, La Ronde carried munitions and supplies to St John's by sea, while troops under Saint-Ovide [MONBETON] proceeded overland. On New Year's Day 1709, barely hours after the French arrived, the English under Thomas Lloyd* surrendered. When the station was abandoned by the French in the spring and the forts destroyed, La Ronde carried the artillery back to Plaisance aboard the *Vénus*. He then agreed to transport the English garrison of St John's to Quebec and, once there, stood by in anticipation of the massive British invasion expected for 1709. It was on this occasion that he married Marie-Louise Chartier de Lotbinière. When it became apparent that Canada would

enjoy a respite in 1709, La Ronde returned with his bride to Plaisance in October.

As early as 1708 Subercase had complained bitterly not only of La Ronde's insubordination in not returning to Port-Royal but of his mistreatment of minor officials who had opposed his attempts that year to undervalue his captured prizes, thereby cheating the government, which was owed taxes on the vessels, as well as the outfitters of his ship. Although he agreed that La Ronde ought to be severely punished, the minister of Marine, Pontchartrain, faced a dilemma: "I really do not know how to deal with him," he remarked, "since he acquitted himself so well at St John's." La Ronde returned to France in 1710 to account for his conduct. Though at first glance he appears to have withstood the wrath of authorities, the balance of his career was adversely affected by his indiscipline. Despite his advancement at the normal rate (section leader of a detachment of midshipmen at 26, sub-lieutenant in the navy at 27, captain in the colonial regulars at 32), and despite a truly impressive record of service, he never rose beyond the rank of captain. He did, however, receive the honour of the cross of Saint-Louis in 1721.

In 1710 La Ronde sailed for Port-Royal only to learn before arriving of its surrender to Francis Nicholson* in October. He therefore stayed at Plaisance, much to the delight of his patron Costebelle, by whom he was soon to be dispatched on his most spectacular adventure. The following spring La Ronde, who, Costebelle claimed, "knows enough English to understand it and to make himself understood without an interpreter," went to Boston under a flag of truce, ostensibly to negotiate an exchange of prisoners. In reality he was to make careful military observations, seeking at the same time, surreptitiously and with "great caution," to subvert the fighting spirit of the New Englanders. He was to suggest "in conversation" that by subscribing to the cause of Old England in America, the colonists were in effect using "their own weapons for the destruction of the freedom of their republics."

There was apparently no opposition to La Ronde's presence in Boston, in spite of the fact that preparations were being made for a massive invasion of Canada. He may already have had contacts there, and in any case he was a personable man who made a favourable impression despite his uneasiness in his role. Sir Hovenden Walker* must have thought him amenable for he suggested that he aid the British cause by piloting a vessel to the St Lawrence – an offer La Ronde was probably not above accepting for a price. It was not long, however, before a copy of his

Denys de La Ronde

instructions was discovered. Markedly less welcome now and anxious, as he later claimed, to get his news to the French, La Ronde made a dash by night for the safety of the open sea. In the first of many difficulties which "endangered his life several times," he was stopped and thrown into the dungeon of Castle William. Although he had had the foresight to swallow the original text of his instructions, the General Court of Massachusetts summarily condemned him to hang. In the meantime, however, news of Walker's disaster had reached Boston. Out of compassion, or influenced perhaps by La Ronde's colourful personality, Governor Joseph Dudley intervened and gave the Frenchman the opportunity to make his escape. Otherwise he would have paid dearly for his rash plunge into the vagaries of international diplomacy in wartime. Late in 1711, having been "tossed about on the sea like a latterday Telemachus," he drifted into Martinique. He returned to Plaisance in July 1712.

By the spring of 1713 the peace of Utrecht had ceded Acadia and Newfoundland to England, and in an effort to counter the loss France decided upon a new venture on Île Royale (Cape Breton Island). Serving under Saint-Ovide, La Ronde reconnoitred the island, making recommendations for settlement and preparing charts and reports of his observations. It is perhaps significant that he noted with some emotion the vestiges of the pioneering efforts of his grandfather, Simon Denys* de La Trinité, who more than 60 years previously had built a trading post at Sainte-Anne (Englishtown). In the summer of the following year La Ronde joined Jacques d'Espiet* de Pensens on an unsuccessful journey to Nova Scotia to encourage the Acadians to leave the province and immigrate to Île Royale.

La Ronde carried the colony's dispatches to France in January 1715. Upon his return he commanded the detachment at Port-Toulouse (St Peters) intermittently from November 1715 to the spring of 1720. In 1719, at the request of Governor General Philippe de Rigaud de Vaudreuil and seemingly against his own wishes, he was appointed to the garrison in Canada. By procrastinating, however, he missed the last vessel to Quebec in 1719. In 1720 Robert-David Gotteville* de Belile, sent by the Comte de Saint-Pierre to command at Île Saint-Jean (Prince Edward Island), secured from Saint-Ovide, now governor of Île Royale, the services of an unenthusiastic La Ronde to assist in the founding of the colony. In November 1721 La Ronde prepared a detailed *mémoire* on their progress. Its reliability is highly suspect, however, for it seems that La Ronde was more interested in promoting himself as a colonizer than in reporting accurately. In 1722 he took advantage of some administrative confusion at Versailles to leave Île Saint-Jean and take up the Canadian post Vaudreuil had held for him since 1719.

La Ronde, with his knowledge of English and his contacts in New England, proved especially useful to Vaudreuil as a plenipotentiary. In 1723, for example, the governor sent him overland to Boston on a diplomatic mission, the precise purpose of which is unclear. He also impressed Vaudreuil's successor, Charles de BEAUHARNOIS, who appointed him, on 6 June 1727, commandant of Chagouamigon (near Ashland, Wis.), a key post on the route to the far west. Even though his appointment included the right to trade for furs, for unknown reasons La Ronde did not immediately depart from Quebec.

In 1728 he became embroiled in the power struggle between Beauharnois and the intendant, Claude-Thomas Dupuy*. Dupuy charged that La Ronde was involved in illegal fur trade, presumably with his merchant acquaintances in Boston, and Beauharnois, forced to admit that the charge was true, refused him permission to go to Chagouamigon. The rare concurrence of the governor and intendant was apparently taken as proof of La Ronde's guilt. After raising the possibility of dismissing him, in 1729 the minister of Marine, Maurepas, ordered Beauharnois to keep La Ronde at Quebec: "I cannot have any confidence in him," he wrote. For La Ronde the possibility of further promotion was finally eliminated, but he was able, thanks chiefly to his friendship with Dupuy's successor, Gilles Hocquart*, to take up his command at Chagouamigon in 1731.

There a new chapter in his spectacular career unfolded. Having learned from the area's Indians and from Jacques LEGARDEUR de Saint-Pierre, a veteran officer in the region, that several islands in Lake Superior held rich copper deposits, he began to gather samples and to lay plans for a major industry. In 1732 he wrote to Beauharnois and Hocquart with a proposal to construct two ships on lakes Superior and Huron to carry ore to Niagara (near Youngstown, N.Y.); there it would be loaded on barges for the voyage to Montreal. In return he asked for a free nine-year lease on the fur trade at Chagouamigon to help him finance the venture. After Maurepas approved the plan in 1733 La Ronde formed a partnership with Saint-Pierre and Louis-Mathieu Damours de Clignancour, agreeing to put up half the capital. Since he apparently did not have it, he borrowed 25,411 *livres* in merchandise from the Montreal merchant Louis CHARLY Saint-Ange. In 1734 he drew another merchant, Simon Guillory, into the partnership. Meanwhile, Beauharnois and Hocquart modified the terms of his monopoly, allowing him to forgo the construction of the Lake Huron vessel until 1735 and to use the king's barque on Lake Ontario.

The Lake Superior vessel was constructed by La Ronde and Guillory in 1734. The ore samples they sent to France were assayed at the royal mint in Paris as more than 90 per cent pure copper and led Maurepas to believe that "the venture could become quite important." La Ronde, who, as Hocquart observed, possessed only "ordinary resourcefulness, which is not supported by any practical knowledge," realized that expert artisans would be needed to select the best location for the mine and to set up the smelting furnace. In 1735 he petitioned Maurepas to send help from France at his expense. Maurepas chose instead to send two German miners, John Adam and Christopher Henry Forster, with instructions merely to assess the venture's feasibility. The Forsters arrived in Canada in the late summer of 1737 but, as a result of various mishaps, did not reach Lake Superior until June 1738. After investigating the copper deposits and taking ore samples, they returned to Quebec in the early summer of 1739 where they also examined copper deposits at Baie Saint-Paul before sailing for France. Their report on La Ronde's venture confirmed the existence of at least three rich copper deposits on Lake Superior but declared that the cost of exploiting them would be prohibitive.

La Ronde anticipated the effect of this report in France. In 1739 he wrote to Maurepas painting a bright picture of the mining enterprise and requesting a number of artisans, but his dispatch was couched in defensive terms. It sought to justify all his actions since 1736 and contained a lengthy account of his services since 1687. But Maurepas replied in 1740 that the enterprise was dead and angrily ordered La Ronde to reimburse the king for the sums advanced to the Forsters, more than 6,000 *livres*. He apparently did so, and Beauharnois and Hocquart requested that he be permitted to exploit the fur trade at Chagouamigon for two or three years so that he could also pay his private creditors. The certainty of the Forsters' report cast doubt upon La Ronde's sincerity about the mining venture; that the costs of labour and transportation would be prohibitive was so clear to them that La Ronde, even with his limited expertise, might have been expected to be aware of the problem. Moreover, in the seven years that he led the authorities to believe in the enterprise he achieved little, aside from building a ship on Lake Superior which would transport furs and trade goods as readily as ore. That his

private financial support came from fur merchants who were all linked with the far western trade is also suspicious. Official documents suggest that La Ronde took the venture seriously, that he suffered losses, and that he was finally defeated by Canada's geography, but it is worth noting that they can be given a different interpretation. It is at least a possibility that La Ronde used the mining venture as a means of obtaining a free lease on the fur trade.

After the failure of the mining enterprise, La Ronde sought promotion to commandant of the colonial regular troops in New France, as well as promotions for two of his sons, Philippe and Pierre-François-Paul, both of whom were officers. Philippe had served at Chagouamigon during his father's absences and took over permanently when La Ronde died in 1741. In 1743 Mme de La Ronde went to France to ask for a further extension of her husband's lease so that she and her sons could pay Charly the 30,000 *livres* she maintained were still owed him. This request may have sounded disingenuous since she and her children had earlier renounced their inheritance to avoid paying a 1,100 *livres* debt to the Canadian treasury agent, Thomas-Jacques TASCHEREAU. Even so she was granted the fur *ferme* at Chagouamigon from 1744 to 1748 at 3,000 *livres*, and one-third of its product from 1748 to 1751.

It is difficult to assess La Ronde's career. He was without doubt a daring soldier of fortune whose exploits covered the French Atlantic empire and ranged from heroic military feats to diplomacy, exploration, and entrepreneurship. On the other hand he was guilty of insubordination, apparently guided by self-interest, and often suspected, at least, of treachery. The many mysteries that surround him, concerning not only his motives for the mining venture but his contacts in New England and his alleged collusion with them, only add to the fascination of his career.

BERNARD POTHIER and DONALD J. HORTON

AJQ, Registre d'état civil, Notre-Dame de Québec, 4 août 1675. AN, Col., B, 21, 29, 30, 32, 35, 37, 41, 42, 56–75; C¹¹A, 53–87; C¹¹B, 1–5, 12; C¹¹C, 4, 6, 7, 11, 15; C¹¹D, 4–7; C¹¹G, 2–3; D²C, 222/2; E, 119, 189. BN, MSS, Clairambault, 875, ff.245–47. "Mass. Archives," II, V, XXXVIIIA. PRO, CO 218/1. *Édits ord.*, II, 373–74. Fauteux, *Les chevaliers de Saint-Louis*. "Genealogy of the de la Ronde family," J. E. Ducros, comp. (typescript, Mandeville, La., 1938), 14–15. Le Jeune, *Dictionnaire*, I, 79–81. A. Roy, *Inv. greffes not.*, IV, 31–32; XVIII, 170; XIX, 208, 282. P.-G. Roy, *Inv. concessions*, IV, 263–64; *Inv. jug. et délib., 1717–1760*, II, 60, 128, 215, 225; III, 138–39. Dubé, *Claude-Thomas Dupuy*, 269. J.-N. Fauteux, *Essai sur l'industrie*, II,

Denys de Saint-Simon

10–20. Frégault, *La civilisation de la Nouvelle-France*. Harvey, *French régime in P.E.I.*, 43–50. Kellogg, *French régime*, 351. La Morandière, *Hist. de la pêche française*, II, 646, 695ff. Robert Le Blant, *Un colonial sous Louis XIV: Philippe de Pastour de Costebelle, gouverneur de Terre-Neuve puis de l'île Royale, 1661–1717* (Paris, Dax, 1935), 125, 149. McLennan, *Louisbourg*, 11–17, 32, 37. Nish, *Les bourgeois-gentilshommes*, 90, 111. H.-R. Casgrain, "Éclaircissements sur la question acadienne," *RSCT*, 1st ser., VI (1888), sect.I, 23–75. Henri Têtu, "Le chapitre de la cathédrale de Québec et ses délégués en France," *BRH*, XVI (1910), 321.

DENYS DE SAINT-SIMON, CHARLES-PAUL, provost marshal; b. 31 Jan. 1688 at Quebec, son of Paul Denys* de Saint-Simon, provost of the marshalsea, and Marie-Madeleine de Peiras; d. 7 Sept. 1748 at Quebec.

On 3 Sept. 1714 Charles-Paul Denys de Saint-Simon officially succeeded his father as provost of the marshalsea; his father had resigned in his favour upon the king's promise that he would receive the first empty seat in the Conseil Supérieur.

Charles-Paul's letters of appointment conferred upon him the power "to conduct investigations of all prisoners accused of crime, to issue warrants against and to judge the same without appeal," as well as competency to judge "all thefts, premeditated murders, homicide committed by persons without fixed domicile, and in general all crimes which the provosts of our said cousins the marshals of France deal with." In reality the provost of the marshalsea in Canada never exercised these judicial functions, restricting himself to searching for criminals and deserters from the army with the help of his four archers or sometimes soldiers, seeing that the king's carpenter built the instruments of torture necessary for executions, and accompanying criminals to their place of execution. Under these conditions the office of provost of the marshalsea was on the whole a sinecure in the 17th century. But in the 18th century, with the increase in population, the sending to Canada of soldiers, habitual offenders, and ne'er-do-well sons of good families, crime increased. The provost, who might formerly have been considered a "sort of pensioner," saw his office grow in importance. As provost marshal he had to hunt criminals in all seasons, over a country covered with forests and intersected by several rivers. It was not easy to lay his hand on the guilty in this immense territory, especially since the habitants preferred to hide them rather than hand them over to the law.

The office of provost thus took up all the Sieur de Saint-Simon's time and excluded him from other remunerative occupations, from which several members of the Conseil Supérieur, for example, profited. Nevertheless, in 1742, "being in a state of extreme poverty" and needing help "to subsist with his family," Denys de Saint-Simon sought a seat on the Conseil Supérieur. Maurepas, the minister of Marine, refused him one, alleging that Intendant Gilles Hocquart*'s candidate, Jean-François GAULTIER, king's physician, was more cultivated and intelligent and that the office of provost marshal could not go with that of councillor. The colonial authorities might consider him a devoted man who carried out his functions well, but it seems, according to Hocquart, that Charles-Paul Denys de Saint-Simon was not sufficiently acquainted with "customary law and procedure" to be able to perform other judicial duties. He was therefore obliged to go on making do with the 500 *livres* that went with his office and with an annual sum of 200 *livres* for his "travelling expenses." But these revenues were not sufficient "to maintain the honour and condition of his office." In 1744 Maurepas granted him an exceptional royal gratuity of 400 *livres*.

Towards the end of his life Denys de Saint-Simon had gone through all the wealth he had acquired and was considered by the authorities of the colony as a man "of limited means." On 17 Oct. 1713 he had married at Quebec Marie-Joseph Prat, daughter of the port captain Louis Prat*, and he was the father of a numerous family – 16 children, four of whom were still dependent upon him in 1744. At his death in Quebec on 7 Sept. 1748 he left little behind him. To be able to subsist, his widow had to ask Maurepas for help.

ANDRÉ LACHANCE

AJQ, Registre d'état civil, Notre-Dame de Québec, 31 janv. 1688, 17 oct. 1713, 8 sept. 1748. AN, Col., B, 36, f.403; 78, ff.337, 348v; 89, f.260v; C^{11A}, 50, ff.348–48v; 52, f.84v; 56, ff.159–60v; 70, f.217v; 76, f.259; 77, f.106v; 79, f.343v; 89, ff.231v–33. ANQ, NF, Ins. Cons. sup., IV, 5v–6; NF, Ord. int., VI, 299vff.; IX, 15v–16. *Recensement de Québec, 1716* (Beaudet). "Recensement de Québec, 1744" (APQ *Rapport*). Tanguay, *Dictionnaire*, III, 343.

DEPÉRET, ÉLIE, Sulpician, missionary, parish priest; b. 28 July 1691 in Limoges, France, son of Jean Depéret, a merchant, and Valère Limousin; d. 17 April 1757 at Sainte-Anne-du-Bout-de-l'Île (Sainte-Anne-de-Bellevue, Que.).

Élie Depéret joined the Society of Saint-Sulpice on 27 May 1712. When he arrived in Montreal on 22 Aug. 1714 he was not yet a priest, and Bishop Saint-Vallier [La Croix*] ordained him on 21 Sept. 1715. Only with difficulty can this Sulpician be followed in the exercise of his ministry, among either the French or the Indians, because of his many and various moves. François Vachon* de Belmont, his superior, first sent him to assist René-Charles de Breslay*, parish priest of the new parish of Sainte-Anne-du-Bout-de-l'Île. De Breslay also directed the Indian mission at Île aux Tourtres which he had founded in 1704 for the Nipissings from Baie d'Urfé and for passing Algonkins. This mission was shut down in 1721, shortly after de Breslay's departure, and the Indians of Île aux Tourtres were joined with the Iroquois of the mission at Lac-des-Deux-Montagnes (Oka, Que.); Depéret became the parish priest at Sainte-Anne-du-Bout-de-l'Île.

In 1727 he left this parish to serve in the mission at Oka among the Nipissings and Algonkins, his former neophytes of Île aux Tourtres, whose languages he knew fluently. He took advantage of this ministry to learn Iroquois and succeeded in acquiring it as easily as he had the other languages. His numerous manuscripts are evidence: a dictionary and sermons in Iroquois, a grammar, a catechism, some canticles, and instructions in Algonkin.

Depéret left this mission in 1734 to devote himself to the parochial ministry. His knowledge of Indian languages – according to tradition he was master of all of them – enabled him, however, to return on two occasions among the Indians. In 1746 he went as chaplain with the Indians who took part in the expedition led by François-Pierre de Rigaud* de Vaudreuil against the English colonies. In addition, from 1753 to 1754, during the voyage to France of François Picquet*, founder of the mission to the Iroquois at La Présentation (Ogdensburg, N.Y.), Depéret ran this mission.

During his lifetime Depéret was parish priest of different parishes in the Montreal region: Longue-Pointe (1735–36, 1743–44), Île-Dupas (1737–39), Sainte-Anne-du-Bout-de-l'Île (1721–27, 1734–35, 1740–42, 1747–53, 1755–57). It was at Sainte-Anne-du-Bout-de-l'Île that he died on 17 April 1757.

Antonio Dansereau

ASSM, Section de la seigneurie du Lac-des-Deux-Montagnes; Section des biographies; Section des manuscrits indiens: Depéret, œuvres en langue algonquine, 2v. Bibliothèque municipale de Limoges (France), État civil, Limoges, 28 juill. 1691. Allaire, *Dictionnaire*. Gauthier, *Sulpitiana*; *Le diocèse de Montréal à la fin du XIXᵉ siècle* (Montréal, 1900). André Chagny, *Un défenseur de la « Nouvelle France » ...* (Montreal, 1913), 78, 197. Olivier Maurault, *Marges d'histoire* (3v., Montréal, 1929–30), III. J.-A. Cuoq, "Anotc kekon," *RSCT*, 1st ser., XI (1893), sect.1, 171–72. Olivier Maurault, "Quand Saint-Sulpice allait en guerre," *Cahiers des Dix*, V (1940), 11–30.

DESAUNIERS, PIERRE TROTTIER. *See* Trottier

DESBUTTES. *See* Baudry

DESCHAILLONS, JEAN-BAPTISTE DE SAINT-OURS. *See* Saint-Ours

DESCHEVERY, *dit* **Maisonbasse, JEAN-BAPTISTE** (he often signed **Meson Basse**), silversmith and merchant; b. *c.* 1695, son of Jean Deschevery and Jeanne Damboise who probably came originally from the parish of Notre-Dame in Bayonne, France; m. on 24 Jan. 1718 Louise-Élisabeth Couteron; d. *c.* 1745 in Quebec.

Little is known about Jean-Baptiste Deschevery's origins and education. He was probably born in France; the earliest document confirming his presence in Canada is his marriage certificate, dated 1718, in which he is said to be 23 years old. How he acquired his training as a silversmith cannot be ascertained; perhaps he did his apprenticeship in France before coming to Canada.

After his arrival in the colony Deschevery seems to have struck up friendships with the other silversmiths in Canada. Despite the absence in New France of a guild of silversmiths such as existed in the mother country, business and personal relations among the artisans engaged in the silversmith's trade seem to have been fairly good. Thus the silversmith Jacques Gadois, *dit* Mauger, signed Deschevery's wedding certificate in Montreal on 24 Jan. 1718. Similarly, on 2 May 1721, again in Montreal, Deschevery put his signature to the wedding certificate of the master silversmith, François Chambellan, with whom Michel Cotton did his apprenticeship in 1724. Towards 1725 Deschevery left Montreal and went to set up a business in Quebec, where he made friends among the people in his craft. Indeed, on 20 Nov. 1727 in the church of Notre-Dame de Québec, the silversmith Jean-François Landron acted as godfather to Marie-Françoise Deschevery, Jean-Baptiste's daughter.

Like most artists of his time, Deschevery did not confine himself solely to his art. He had to attend to the marketing of his works, and perhaps even to the sale of imported objects related to his trade, whence the designation "merchant silversmith" which is sometimes found. He was also an appraiser for lotteries and inventories. Appointed an expert by the civil authorities, in

Descombes

1728 he was commissioned to weigh, with the help of Jacques PAGÉ, *dit* Carcy, Claude-Thomas Dupuy*'s silver plate. In 1730 he was asked to appraise, among other things, the articles being raffled off by the silversmith and merchant Jean-François Landron. In 1734, after Jean Crespin's death, he appraised, for the inventory of goods made on 13 January, "the deceased's handsome silverware."

The exact date of Deschevery's death cannot be determined; it can, however, be placed around the years 1744 and 1745. The 1744 census of Quebec mentions "Jean Baptiste Maison Basse, silversmith," 49 years of age, living in Rue Sous-le-Fort. In a document dated 6 Oct. 1745 the artist's wife is indicated as being "Demoiselle Elisabeth Coutron, widow of the Sieur Jean Baptiste Maison Basse in his lifetime the said silversmith."

This silversmith's work is not well known. Only a few examples have been found: a goblet, a chalice, and a porringer in solid silver. All these items can be identified by the stamp formed of the letters M.B. on a five-pointed star, the whole crowned by a fleur-de-lis.

MICHEL CAUCHON and ANDRÉ JUNEAU

AJQ, Registre d'état civil, Notre-Dame de Québec, 6 nov. 1725, 20 nov. 1727. ANQ, Greffe de Nicolas Boisseau, 13 janv. 1734; Greffe de J.-C. Panet, 6 oct. 1745. ANQ-M, Greffe de Michel Lepailleur, 6 déc. 1718, 30 avril 1721; Registre d'état civil, Notre-Dame de Montréal, 24 janv. 1718, 2 mai 1721. IOA, Dossier Jean-Baptiste Deschevery, dit Maisonbasse, orfèvre. "Les loteries sous le régime français au Canada," APQ *Rapport, 1923–24*, 144–47. "Recensement de Québec, 1744" (APQ *Rapport*). P.-G. Roy, *Inv. ord. int.*, II, 151, 158. Langdon, *Canadian silversmiths*. Traquair, *Old silver of Quebec*.

DESCOMBES. *See* LOMBARD

DESCOUTS (Decous, Decoust), MARTIN, surgeon; originally from Salies (Salies-de-Béarn), France; fl. 1682–1745.

Martin Descouts arrived at Plaisance (Placentia, Nfld.) around 1700 as a surgeon with a fishing company. He himself engaged in commercial fishing at Plaisance until 1714. After the treaty of Utrecht, by which Plaisance passed into the hands of the British, Descouts went to fish at Canso, Nova Scotia. In 1715 he employed ten fishermen and curers as well as a clerk. He claimed that he lost 10,000 *écus* in 1718, probably as a result of the British expedition led by Thomas Smart* which seized the French fisheries at Canso that year. Descouts had diffi-

culty in liquidating this bankruptcy, and he even had to sell properties in France to pay his debts.

In 1726 the French settled on Île Saint-Jean (Prince Edward Island), and Descouts was enlisted as a surgeon for the troops. According to the census of Port-La-Joie (Fort Amherst) in 1734 he was a bachelor and was still practising his profession as a surgeon. He owned 19 cattle and had a servant. Because of his age and infirmities he asked to be put on half pay in 1743 in order to retire. François Bigot* and Jean-Baptiste-Louis LE PRÉVOST Duquesnel, the financial commissary and the commandant of Île Royale, communicated this demand to Maurepas, the minister of Marine, praising Descouts, whom they described as "a man who has carried out his duties to the satisfaction of his superiors." He was still on Île Saint-Jean in 1744, but disappears from sight after the British occupation in 1745.

HERVÉ BÉLANGER

AN, Col., C[11B], 8, pp.134–35; 25, p.8; C[11C], 12, pp.147–81; Section Outre-Mer, G[1], 466/1, p.585; 466/2, pp.244–45 (PAC transcripts); G[3], 2046/2, 2057, 2058. Harvey, *French régime in P.E.I.*, 202. McLennan, *Louisbourg*, 9, 60.

DESENCLAVES, JEAN-BAPTISTE DE GAY. *See* GAY

DESGOUTINS. *See* GOUTIN

DES HERBIERS DE LA RALIÈRE (La Ratière), CHARLES, naval officer; b. *c.* 1700, only son of Armand Des Herbiers of Poitou, France; d. 18 April 1752.

Charles Des Herbiers was born into a prominent family of naval officers. After the death in 1710 of his father, a naval captain, he was raised and tutored by his uncle Henri-François Des Herbiers de L'Étenduère, a rear-admiral who had himself been raised from the age of ten by Charles's father. Charles became a midshipman in 1716; his first assignment at sea was in 1719 on the *Chameau*. He later made several voyages to New France on ships commanded by his uncle, including missions to map the area around Louisbourg, Île Royale (Cape Breton Island) and to survey, sound, and chart the St Lawrence River. Charles was made sub-lieutenant in the navy in 1727 and lieutenant-commander in 1738. Following both promotions, in 1728–29 and in 1738–39, he was posted with the colonial regular troops at Port-Louis, France; on the second occasion he had charge of a company. He received the cross of Saint-Louis in 1742, and from that year to 1745, during the War of the Austrian Succession, commanded the artillery of the Marine in Flanders. He carried out this assignment "with distinction" and in 1748 was promoted naval captain. When Île Royale was returned to France by the treaty of Aix-la-Chapelle (1748), Des Herbiers, "one of the most capable officers," was chosen as king's commissioner to reoccupy the colony.

He sailed from Rochefort in May 1749 with the first of several warships and transports carrying soldiers, provisions, and inhabitants for the colony. He reached Louisbourg on 29 June and immediately entered into negotiations with the commander, Peregrine Thomas HOPSON, for the removal of the British garrison. The formalities were concluded on 23 July 1749, and Des Herbiers remained as commandant of the colony. As instructed, he provided some of his own ships to help transport the British garrison to Halifax, Nova Scotia.

French policy toward the colony of Île Royale – made up of that island and Île Saint-Jean (Prince Edward Island) – was concerned primarily with its resettlement and its development as a base from which to protect the lucrative cod-fishery, guard the gulf of the St Lawrence, and check British power in Nova Scotia. The appointment of senior officers, such as the engineer Louis FRANQUET, and the assignment of regular troops and more warships to reinforce the garrison, indicate France's concern with the colony's strategic importance.

Des Herbiers was active in reviving the colony. After the original inhabitants had been resettled, he had unclaimed properties surveyed in order to award them to new occupants. He began the repair of the fortifications and buildings in Louisbourg, which were in a ruinous condition as a result of the siege of 1745. Despite a scarcity of boats he re-established both the fishing industry and trade with other North American colonies, including New England, and furthered large-scale mining of the island's enormous coal deposits. He also suppressed the troublesome officers' canteens and improved the condition of the artillery.

The new commandant was actively engaged in affairs beyond Louisbourg. Immediately after his arrival he sent a garrison under Claude-Élisabeth DENYS de Bonnaventure to Port-La-Joie (Fort Amherst, P.E.I.); less than a month later he began to settle refugee Acadians in the ports around Île Royale and Île Saint-Jean. Under the protection of the garrison, the population of Île Saint-Jean grew from some 735 in 1749 to more than 2,200 in 1752. Des Herbiers provisioned the refugees – 3,000 throughout the colony by 1751 – and offered them every possible assistance in leaving British territory. In accordance with his instructions to resist British encroachments by all means short of force, he gave clandestine support to Pierre MAILLARD and Jean-Louis Le Loutre*, encouraging the latter to menace the new settlements around Halifax.

Des Herbiers was in communication with La Jonquière [TAFFANEL] in Quebec over mutual support for the French outposts under Charles Deschamps* de Boishébert on the Saint John River and under Louis de LA CORNE at Fort Beauséjour (near Sackville, N.B.) and Pierre-Roch de Saint-Ours* Deschaillons at Fort Gaspereau (near Port Elgin, N.B.). He was also in close contact with these local commanders, sending troops to reinforce Fort Beauséjour and ships to guard the passage to Île Saint-Jean at Baie-Verte. The attention given these political and strategic pressure points by the administrations of Quebec and Île Royale – and their willingness to exploit vague boundaries and allegiances while dissimulating to the British their intentions – exacerbated international antagonisms and roused the Duke of Newcastle to complain about "the wild French governors in America."

Although Des Herbiers had orders to avoid compromising the government in any way by his dealings with the British, he was not one to avoid a confrontation. In 1750, off Cape Sable, the British seized two French ships carrying supplies to the outposts of the Saint John River on charges that they were smuggling goods to Nova Scotia. In response the king instructed Des Herbiers to order his naval commanders to seize the first English frigate they met, and La Jonquière directed him to confiscate three or four of the next English ships into Louisbourg, adding that his captains should act, if necessary, as though a state of war existed. Des Herbiers seized four ships, reporting that he had done so "with regret," since they had brought necessary cargoes at the request of the French.

The court was well pleased with Des Herbiers's conduct as commissioner but he asked repeatedly to be relieved of his duties as commandant, which he had accepted only with reluctance. In 1751 he was replaced by Jean-Louis de Raymond*; Des Herbiers reached France in October and died six months later. In 1740 he had married Marie-Olive, daughter of his uncle Henri-François. They had four sons; two died at an early age but Antoine-Auguste succeeded to the title of Marquis de L'Étenduère.

JOHN FORTIER

183

Desjordy

AN, Col., B, 89–93; C¹¹B, 27–31; D²C, 2–3; Marine, C¹, 153/1, p.325 (PAC transcript); C⁷, 85 (dossiers Des Herbiers, Des Herbiers de L'Étenduère). PAC, MG 30, D62, 10, pp.606–9. Placide Gaudet, "Acadian genealogy and notes," PAC *Report, 1905*, II, pt.III, 281–356. Fauteux, *Les chevaliers de Saint-Louis*, 213. Le Jeune, *Dictionnaire*, 1, 504–5. Clark, *Acadia*. Frégault, *Canada: the war of the conquest*. McLennan, *Louisbourg*. MacNutt, *Atlantic provinces*. Stanley, *New France*. Régis Roy, "Les Desherbiers de l'Étenduère," *BRH*, XXIII (1917), 93–94.

DESJORDY. *See* DEJORDY

DES LANDES, JOSEPH, Jesuit, professor of hydrography; b. 10 Nov. 1691 in India; d. 25 Jan. 1742 in Paris, France.

Nothing is known of Joseph Des Landes's early life until he entered the noviciate of the Jesuits of the province of France in Paris on 10 Sept. 1710. He studied theology in Paris in the period 1722–26, and in 1727 he landed at Quebec. His special aptitude for mathematics enabled him to take responsibility for the teaching of mathematics and hydrography at the Jesuit college in Quebec until 1732. The courses included arithmetic, geometry, physics, as well as the use of the rule and dividers. Practical exercises had an important place in the teaching: pupils learned the use of essential astronomical instruments, map-reading, and map-making so that they would be able "to survey newly discovered regions." The aim of this instruction was above all to prepare pilots and surveyors, but the latter could also obtain their certificate of proficiency by apprenticeship to a recognized surveyor, without having to follow the courses. The apprentice pilots received theoretical courses during the winter; when fine weather returned they embarked under the orders of the second in command of the port for practical training in the pilot's profession. After 1717, the hydrography teacher issued certificates to his pupils attesting to their qualifications and authorizing them to call themselves pilots.

From about 1661 instruction had been given in New France by the king's hydrographer [*see* Boutet* de Saint-Martin; Franquelin*; Louis Jolliet*; Deshayes*]; in 1708, however, the teaching of hydrography was entrusted definitively to the Jesuits, who assumed it until the end of the French régime [*see* Silvy*; GUIGNAS; LAUZON; MESAIGER; Bonnecamps*].

From 1732 to 1735 Des Landes probably "looked after the boarders" at the college and again taught hydrography during the academic year 1735–36. Nothing is known of his activities from then till the beginning of 1741, when his provincial, Father Jean Lavaud, chose him to succeed Father Joseph-François LAFITAU as procurator in Paris of the Jesuit missions in Canada. He sailed for France in the autumn of 1741 and on 25 Jan. 1742, "about one or two months after his arrival in Paris," he died of "an inflammation of the lungs," despite "all the care possible" that he received from Claude-Michel Sarrazin [*see* Michel Sarrazin*]. Des Landes was succeeded as procurator by CHARLEVOIX, who wrongly believed that this post "would only be a slight and necessary distraction" for him from his literary work.

LOUIS-PHILIPPE AUDET

AN, Col., B, 73, f.69. ASJCF, Fonds Rochemonteix, 4018, f.184. [Melançon], *Liste des missionnaires jésuites.* P.-G. Roy, *Inv. jug. et délib., 1717–1760,* II, 26. L.-P. Audet, *Histoire de l'enseignement au Québec, 1608–1971* (2v., Montréal, 1971). Amédée Gosselin, *L'instruction au Canada.* Léon Pouliot, *Charlevoix (1682–1761)* (Classiques canadiens, 15, Montréal, Paris, 1959), 9. Rochemonteix, *Les Jésuites et la N.-F. au XVIIᵉ siècle,* I, 213–15. L.-P. Audet, "Hydrographes du roi et cours d'hydrographie au collège de Québec, 1671–1759," *Cahiers des Dix,* XXXV (1970), 13–37. J.-E. Roy, "La cartographie et l'arpentage sous le régime français," *BRH,* I (1895), 49–56. Henri Têtu, "Le chapitre de la cathédrale de Québec et ses délégués en France," *BRH,* XVI (1910), 231, 295, 329.

DESLIETTES. *See* TONTY

DESLONGRAIS (Delongrais, Des Longraye), NICOLAS, merchant trader, storekeeper; originally from Saint-Malo, France; fl. 1734–58.

The 1734 census of Louisbourg, Île Royale (Cape Breton Island), reveals that Nicolas Deslongrais was unmarried and childless and had no servants or employees. He supplied certain manufactured goods to the administration there. In addition he maintained good relations with at least one high official of the Conseil Supérieur of Louisbourg, François-Marie de GOUTIN. After the restoration of Île Royale to France in 1749 Goutin was sent to Île Saint-Jean (Prince Edward Island) as keeper of the king's warehouse. He hired Deslongrais as his book-keeper. Goutin, however, fell ill shortly afterwards and in fact Deslongrais carried out the duties of storekeeper from 1749 to 1752. When Goutin died in 1752, Deslongrais replaced him officially, and at that time Jacques Prévost* de La Croix, the financial commissary for Île Royale, recommended him to Rouillé, the minister of Marine, as "a sensible and diligent young man." But according to the

184

historian H.-R. Casgrain*, Prévost's testimony is more compromising than flattering for Deslongrais, for Prévost was not in the least trustworthy and it is possible that Deslongrais was one of the individuals who served to cover up his exactions; he infers that Deslongrais was probably in part responsible for the poverty and famine from which the population of Île Saint-Jean suffered around 1750. Certain complaints from the missionaries against the storekeeper tend to confirm this supposition.

In 1754 Deslongrais witnessed a profession of faith; after that date the archives provide little information about him. We know, however, that he left Île Saint-Jean when the inhabitants were deported in the fall of 1758. He landed at La Rochelle, France, in 1759 and left for Paris.

HERVÉ BÉLANGER

AN, Col., C¹¹B, 38, p.401; C¹¹C, 11, p.118; Section Outre-Mer, G¹, 411/1, p.124; 466/3A, p.414 (PAC transcripts). Casgrain, *Une seconde Acadie*, 284. Harvey, *French régime in P.E.I.*, 202.

DES MÉLOIZES, NICOLAS-MARIE RENAUD D'AVÈNE. *See* RENAUD

DESMOULINS, JEAN-BAPTISTE MAILLOU, *dit. See* MAILLOU

DESPEROUX (Despeiroux), PIERRE DE LESTAGE. *See* LESTAGE

DEVICE. *See* DAVIS

DIESKAU, JEAN-ARMAND (Johan Herman?), Baron de DIESKAU, army officer, governor of Brest, commander of the French regular troops in Canada; b. 1701, in Saxony; d. 1767, at Suresnes (dept. of Hauts-de-Seine), France.

Jean-Armand Dieskau, a Saxon in the French service, was the protégé of the Maréchal de Saxe, the finest general of French armies between Turenne and Napoleon. Dieskau was brought to France by his compatriot as an aide-de-camp in 1720 and served with him in various campaigns from 1733 to 1744. He became a colonel of cavalry, and apparently fought as such at Fontenoy (Belgium); in 1747 he was made major-general, and military governor of Brest, the chief French naval base on the Atlantic.

On 1 March 1755 he was appointed commander of the battalions of French regulars being sent as reinforcements to Canada, and arrived in Quebec in June on the *Entreprenant*. His authority, while great, was scarcely absolute, for his instructions specifically made him subordinate to Governor General Pierre de Rigaud* de Vaudreuil. Baron Dieskau's role, therefore, was that of a battlefield commander with control of tactics but not of strategy.

By the summer of 1755, largely through the capture of Edward Braddock's papers at the battle of the Monongahela in July, the French knew of British plans for an attack on Fort Frontenac (Kingston, Ont.) and Fort Niagara (near Youngstown, N.Y.) as well as on Fort Saint-Frédéric (Crown Point, N.Y.) on Lake Champlain. Vaudreuil considered the former operation a greater danger and planned a countermove against Oswego to deprive the British of their base of operations on the Great Lakes. Dieskau was to direct it with a force of some 4,000 men.

While his force was assembling at Fort Frontenac, reports came in from Lake Champlain that the British expedition against Saint-Frédéric, commanded by Colonel William Johnson*, was already under way, threatening to ravage the country up to Montreal. Dieskau was called back by August 1755 and sent down the Richelieu against Johnson's colonial militia, now at the head of Lac Saint-Sacrement (Lake George). The French were encamped on the future site of Fort Carillon (Ticonderoga, N.Y.) by 1 September. Some of Dieskau's soldiers had been left at Fort Frontenac, so that his force was now smaller: 1,500 regulars, 1,000 militia, five to six hundred Indians. Johnson could muster some 3,000 colonial militia and 300 Indians, mostly Mohawks commanded by their chief THEYANOGUIN.

When word of the French arrival at the Ticonderoga site reached Johnson, he decided to build a fort at the head of Lake George, at the site of the future Fort William Henry (also called Fort George, now Lake George, N.Y.), 14 miles northwest of his first base, Fort Edward, on the Hudson River. Dieskau became aware of this division of enemy forces on 3 September through a prisoner. But he was led to believe that the British army had retired to Albany, leaving only 500 men at Fort Edward, and that Johnson's expected reinforcements – some 2,400 militia – would ignore this fort on their way to Lake George.

Dieskau saw in this news a marvellous opportunity to destroy the 500 colonials at Fort Edward and thus cut off the rest of Johnson's army at Lake George. This strategy would have been sound, if his intelligence had been accurate and he had moved with all his men. But he divided his forces and set off for Fort Edward with an élite corps of 1,500 men: some 200 regulars, 600 militia, and about 700 Indians including 300 Mohawks from Sault-Saint-Louis (Caughnawaga,

Dieskau

Que.). He left behind at Ticonderoga 1,300 regulars and 400 militia as defence against any British attack. In dividing his strength, he not only disobeyed orders, but displayed a fatal overconfidence against mere colonials.

By 7 September his detachment had reached the Hudson River. At this point, however, the Indians refused to attack Fort Edward. Had Dieskau been more familiar with Indian warfare, he could have predicted their reluctance to assault fortified positions equipped with cannon. At the prospect of attacking with drastically reduced forces, Dieskau chose to divert his attack to the head of Lake George where the enemy were less solidly entrenched and had fewer cannon. The Indians agreed to support him.

On 8 September, he led his regulars along the wagon road to Lake George, with Indians and militia flanking them on the difficult terrain. On this march the French became aware that Johnson was sending 1,000 men to relieve Fort Edward, which he assumed was under attack. Dieskau laid plans for an ambush; he posted his disciplined regulars in formation on the road, his Indians and militia in advance on both forest flanks with instructions to hold their fire until the regulars fired. Into a similar trap Braddock had fallen. Success depended upon both militia and Indians keeping silent until the last moment. Whether by accident or because the Indians wished to warn their Mohawk cousins – Dieskau, of course, believed the latter – the trap was sprung prematurely. Both Colonel Ephraim Williams and Theyanoguin were killed, but their troops were able to retreat though in confusion.

Dieskau's pursuit of the terrified mob was hampered by the near exhaustion of his Indians and militia. Thus only his 200 regulars reached the British camp at Lake George on the heels of the defeated detachment. Johnson had fortified his position with anything available – carts, tree trunks, overturned boats – and had mounted cannon. Dieskau was confronted with the classic military problem of frontal assault on a prepared position. His regulars, with parade ground precision, marched to the assault; the militia, when they caught up, fired on the British from the flanks, as did some Indians. After several hours the battle ended in a stalemate. Dieskau himself was wounded three times in the legs and propped against a tree by his second in command, Pierre-André de Montreuil*. Even when the French finally retreated, Dieskau refused to be moved, allegedly stating he might as well die there as in bed. Later a British soldier (according to Dieskau a renegade Frenchman) shot him through the groin.

The British colonials claimed a major victory, not merely a tactical one. It was, in fact, a strategic stalemate: the British remained at what became Fort William Henry; the French constructed Fort Carillon. The British thrust of 1755 was stopped, and the French would capture William Henry before the final British victory.

Baron Dieskau survived his wounds. He was taken to New York, then to London, and then for treatment of his still unhealed wound in the groin to Bath, whence he dispatched letters to the French government, outlining his medical condition in graphic detail, emphasizing his lack of funds, and justifying his conduct, usually in that order. With peace in 1763, he was repatriated to France.

Contemporaries were, on the whole, condemnatory. Vaudreuil was vehement: Dieskau, by contravening orders not to divide his forces, had lost a chance to "massacre" the British. Montreuil, anxious to refute any accusation of abandoning his chief on the battlefield, was almost equally accusatory. André DOREIL, the war commissary, noted that Dieskau was too rash for top command. But Dieskau had gambled, and lost. Aware that French regulars in Canada could not easily be replaced, he decided, understandably, to risk only 200 of them on a wilderness march. He showed adaptability to North American warfare in his attempt at ambush and also personal bravery at Lake George. With accurate intelligence, his actions might well have proved successful; at the least he stopped an invasion, and inflicted casualties as severe as those he received.

J. R. TURNBULL

[Primary sources for a biography of Dieskau are fairly extensive: AN, Col., B, C^{11A} and F^3, all contain material. His "dossier personnel" in AN, Col., E, 134, is also useful, as is material in the SHA. The "Lettres de Doreil," APQ *Rapport, 1944–45*, contains an assessment of Dieskau, and the *Johnson papers* (Sullivan *et al.*) also includes material. The NYCD (O'Callaghan and Fernow), X, gives a full account in English of the French records, including the famous dialogue between Dieskau and the Maréchal de Saxe – an apologia for Dieskau's conduct of the battle. Secondary sources that give more than cursory mention are reasonably numerous. Gipson, *British empire before the American revolution*, VI, throws light on British strategy and makes good use of the *Johnson papers*. Frégault, *Canada: the war of the conquest*, is indispensable for the French side. I. K. Steele, *Guerillas and grenadiers, the struggle for Canada, 1689–1760* (Frontenac Library, 3, Toronto, 1969), briefly but succinctly sums up the military situation, and Stanley, *New France*, provides a somewhat fuller treatment. J.R.T.]

DIZY (Disy) DE MONTPLAISIR, PIERRE, farmer, seigneurial judge, militia colonel, subdelegate of the intendant; b. *c.* 1675, probably at Champlain (Que.), youngest child of Pierre Dizy, *dit* Montplaisir, and Marie Drouillet (or Drouillard); buried on 14 March 1761 at Champlain.

Like his brother, Michel-Ignace*, Pierre Dizy de Montplaisir married a daughter of René Baudouin. His wife, Marie-Madeleine, was the widow of François Lucas Dontigny and the mother of three children. The marriage took place on 11 Nov. 1700 at Champlain. There Pierre Dizy settled, on a part of his father's land and on his wife's domain, which was later the subject of vigorous dispute with the Dontigny children.

As the father of a large family and apparently possessing an enviable fortune, Pierre Dizy seems to have entertained some social ambitions. He married four of his daughters to seigneurs and a fifth to the son of a seigneur; Marguerite, the youngest, entered the order of the Nuns Hospitallers of the Hôtel-Dieu of Quebec as a choir nun, and Dizy promised in a written contract to pay the required dowry, "whatever the said dowry may amount to." Considered one of the leading inhabitants of Champlain and highly regarded by the colonial authorities, he was acknowledged to be "an honourable man," an "upright man, with whose conduct one can find no fault," at the 1725 inquiry which preceded his admission to the magistrature.

In 1733 his property still comprised only six acres of cultivated land, but in 1738 it amounted to 25, with eight acres of meadow, a house, a barn, a cowshed, and a stable; he ran it himself until he was about 80. On 2 June 1725 he was appointed judge of the seigneury of Champlain. It is not known whether he occupied this office without a break until the end of his life, or was invested with it a second time. What is certain is that he delivered sentences as judge of Champlain in the years 1754, 1755, and 1758. Moreover, from 1750 to 1755 he acted as judge at Batiscan, and he exercised the same function for the seigneury of Cap-de-la-Madeleine from 1753 to 1755.

Dizy had become a militia officer at least 20 years before he reached the magistrature. In 1705, when he was barely 30, he was a militia lieutenant at Champlain and a militia captain at Batiscan. He was also young when he joined the higher ranks of the militia. Although none of his officer's commissions has been found, it can be stated that he was already an adjutant in 1714, adjutant general in 1721, and colonel of the militia troops of the government of Trois-Rivières in 1724; he still held this last rank when he died in 1761. On 12 March 1754 he had been appointed subdelegate of the intendant, a function he exercised for some months.

Pierre Dizy's activity extended far beyond his property and the seigneury of Champlain. He divided his time between the clearing and farming of his land, the exercise of several magistracies, and service in the militia of the government of Trois-Rivières.

MAURICE FLEURENT

AJTR, Greffe de Nicolas Duclos, 25 mars 1752, 8 mai, 18 nov. 1754, 19, 23 avril 1755; several uncatalogued acts should also be consulted: 12, 28 déc. 1750, 12 août 1751, 26, 30 mars, 27, 29 avril, 23, 29 juill. 1754, 5 déc. 1755, 7 juill. 1758; Greffe de Daniel Normandin, 16 mars 1714, 31 oct. 1720, 28 juill. 1722, 3 sept. 1723; Greffe d'A.-B. Pollet, 27 mars 1742, 31 mai 1745; Greffe de J.-B. Pottier, 1er avril 1705; Greffe de Pierre Poulain, 1er mars 1719; Greffe de François Trotain de Saint-Surain, 25 avril 1705, 31 mai 1718; Grand voyer: registre des procès-verbaux de chemins, 1708–1781; Registre d'état civil, Champlain, 18 nov. 1699–13 déc. 1729 (pp.188, 191, 205, 207, 212, 223, 230, 238, 246, 254, 258, 272, 277, 279, 322, 353, 380), 9 mars 1734, 1er juill. 1736, 26 mars 1741, 14 févr. 1746, 14 mars 1761. ANQ, Greffe de Louis Chambalon, 30 oct. 1714; Greffe de J.-N. Pinguet de Vaucour, 6 août 1743; NF, Coll. de pièces jud. et not., 1445, 2050½, 2235, 2629, 2687, 2777; NF, Cours seigneuriales, Batiscan, 29 juin 1753; NF, Documents de la juridiction des Trois-Rivières, 2 juin 1725; NF, Procès-verbaux des grands voyers, I, 1, 53; V, 28, 29, 54v, 117v; NF, Registres du Cons. sup., 2 juill. 1742, 7 janv. 1743, 30 juin 1752.

"Les congés de traite accordés en 1717," *BRH*, XXIX (1923), 273. *Édits ord.*, II, 342. *Jug. et délib.*, V, 571; VI, 260, 917. "Procès-verbaux du procureur général Collet" (Caron), APQ *Rapport, 1921–22*, 279. Bonnault, "Le Canada militaire," APQ *Rapport, 1949–51*, 498–99, 505. P.-G. Roy, *Inv. ins. Prév. Québec*, I, 220; II, 224; *Inv. jug. et délib., 1717–1760*, I, 121, 128; IV, 84, 113; V, 233; *Inv. ord. int.*, II, 94; *Inv. procès-verbaux des grands voyers*, I, 12, 30, 33, 38, 68, 80, 91; II, 62, 63; *Inv. testaments*, I, 169. Tanguay, *Dictionnaire*. [Prosper Cloutier], *Histoire de la paroisse de Champlain* (2v., Trois-Rivières, 1915–17), I, 87, 93, 111, 113, 410, 419; II, 77, 97, 106. Oscar de Poli, *Inventaire des titres de la maison de Billy* (Paris, 1894), 212.

DOREIL (d'Aureil, d'Oreil), ANDRÉ (Jean-Baptiste), financial commissary of wars in New France; son of Philippe Doreil and Jeanne-Catherine Blancheteau; fl. 1749–59.

It is from his marriage act and reports to superiors in France that certain biographical details about André Doreil can be ascertained. He probably came from the west of France, from Niort where his mother lived. He settled in Provence in 1749, when he was appointed provincial commissary of wars of the department of Toulon.

Doreil

Before this date he lived in Paris. On 22 April 1750 he married at Aix-en-Provence Marguerite-Charlotte-Baptistine, daughter of the Marquis de Pontevès. Mme Doreil died on 19 April 1754, leaving her husband with three young children. The following year he was named commissary of wars in New France.

Doreil was both ambitious and competent. The first quality is implicit (and explicit) in his acceptance of a commission in Canada as commissary of wars at a time when his personal affairs were in some disorder. He came reluctantly on the understanding that he would receive immediate promotion and would have to serve no more than two years in the colony. His competence kept him there well over three, despite repeated pleas for recall on the grounds of ill health and his children's needs.

His role as commissary of wars was roughly that of a deputy quartermaster-general in charge of the care and maintenance of all the French regular troops in Canada, attending to their billeting, equipment, clothing, rations, and hospital care. Doreil stated that Intendant Bigot* did not interfere in any way with the military functions or with the hospitals. The commissary of wars also commented that the intendant ''honoured me with his friendship and with kindnesses to me in personal matters.'' In 1756 he was promoted financial commissary of wars and could then authorize expenditures.

Doreil's letters show genuine concern for his men. They are filled with details concerning the soldiers' billeting (often with the habitants), their pay (he is not at all happy with paper money and the resultant loss in exchange for the troops), their clothing (they require more shoes and those of better quality), their rations (including a ration of wine for those in hospital). He set up field hospitals for the first time, harassed the minister for more, and better, surgeons and surgical instruments, and carried on a running feud with the financial commissary and commissary of wars at Louisbourg, Île Royale (Cape Breton Island), Jacques Prévost* de La Croix, whose apparent indifference to the needs of the regular battalions stationed there was a constant worry to Doreil.

He was courageous; in 1757 when the newly arrived soldiers of the Régiment de Berry were dying like flies of ship-fever (typhus?) in the Hôpital Général of Quebec and passing this disease on to the nuns and chaplains, Doreil visited the hospital twice a day to make sure all was in order. He praised the unstinting and expert care given his soldiers by the religious nursing orders, procuring for those at Quebec and at Montreal substantial grants from the crown.

In his letters Doreil also betrays the sycophancy and self-praise characteristic of 18th century officials. By repeatedly pointing out to the minister how hard and competently he was working, he managed to get promotion to financial commissary of wars after one year in Canada. He also obtained 12,000 *livres* compensation for the loss of his household effects captured by the British in 1755 on the *Alcide*, although this sum was twice their current value in France. He even asked for the cross of Saint-Louis, a military honour to which he was not entitled. An indication of his solid reputation, however, is that the request was at least considered.

On a different level, his comments on leading figures in the colony are interesting. He noted in 1755 Governor Pierre de Rigaud* de Vaudreuil's reluctance to deal with corruption inside Intendant Bigot's sphere of influence and characterized Baron de DIESKAU as a courageous officer better fitted for subordinate than supreme command. He made the sensible suggestion, after Dieskau had been taken prisoner in September 1755, that the new general should be ''a good-natured and mild-mannered man,'' who would then be able to ''govern the governor''; apparently with Vaudreuil's approval, he suggested a replacement – Jean-François de Gantès, ''Brigadier Commandant des volontaires de Dauphiné'' and his own brother-in-law. As the war went on, Doreil's cautious insinuations that all was not well within the colonial administration became more outspoken and, at times, almost incoherent. He was, naturally, strongly identified with the French regulars and with MONTCALM after the latter's arrival in May 1756, so that his later letters, filled with pessimism over the fate of the colony and contempt for the Canadian officials, must be seen in the light of this sympathy.

Doreil's work in Canada was rewarded, finally, by his recall to France in the autumn of 1758; he was replaced by Benoît-François Bernier*. After a harrowing crossing, mainly because of English corsairs in the Bay of Biscay, Doreil landed in Spain and went overland to Versailles. He is last heard of in Vannes in November 1759, serving as financial commissary, and then fades into oblivion.

Perhaps the real value of Doreil's correspondence is its depiction of the underside of 18th century warfare – the squalor, misery, and appalling death rates from disease in contrast to the fife and drum of battle. It shows, too, the humanitarian concern intimately connected with the idea of paternalism.

J. R. TURNBULL

[The main sources for the life of Doreil are found in the AD, Bouches-du-Rhône (Marseille), État civil, Saint-Sauveur d'Aix-en-Provence, 22 avril 1750, and in the "Lettres de Doreil," APQ *Rapport, 1944–45*, 1–171. Some of his letters are in AN, Col., C¹¹ᴬ, 100–3, but his service record seems to have been lost. La Chesnaye-Desbois et Badier, *Dictionnaire de la noblesse* (3ᵉ éd.), VIII, 938–40, and XVI, 138–39, gives some biographical information, but Doreil is called there Jean-Baptiste. Some historians have attributed to Doreil the "Éloge historique du marquis de Montcalm," published in the *Mercure de France*, in January 1760. Modern scholarship has dismissed this attribution on the basis of internal evidence and style. J.R.T.]

DORRILL, RICHARD, officer in the Royal Navy, governor of Newfoundland; b. *c.* 1719; d. 1762.

Richard Dorrill entered the navy in 1732. He was promoted lieutenant in the *Royal Oak* in 1739, and was present at the action against the combined French and Spanish fleets off Toulon in 1744. In 1746 he was given command of the sloop *Jamaica*.

Commanding the *Penzance*, Dorrill was commissioned governor of Newfoundland in May 1755, and arrived at St John's on 5 August. The Heads of Enquiry he was given were similar to those issued to his predecessor, Hugh BONFOY. Dorrill did not provide full replies to them "as I was a single ship there this year," though he did collect complete statistics on the fisheries and on the number of inhabitants. He also reported on the strength of the various military garrisons, and included inventories of ordnance and ordnance stores.

Like Bonfoy, Dorrill had been instructed to look into the conduct of the Irish settlers on the island. During his relatively short stay he encouraged the local magistrates to enforce more vigorously the restrictions initiated by Bonfoy against the practice of Catholicism. He had a Roman Catholic priest at Harbour Grace arrested for celebrating mass. At Harbour Main fines were assessed against the owners of 18 dwellings where mass had been said; some of the buildings were burned to the ground. Dorrill ordered magistrates at St John's to prohibit Irishmen, or persons employing them, to retail liquor; violation of this order entailed the destruction of dwellings built by the Irish and the seizure of their lands.

The Irish, like most of the migrant fishermen and settlers, were poor; low wages were not enough to pay their passage home or to support them after the fishing season ended. They were held responsible for most of the disorders committed during the winters. With their rapidly growing numbers – according to Dorrill they formed one third of the population – they were more and more feared by the Protestant settlers. Dorrill ordered all ship masters to carry home at the end of the fishing season "the whole Number and same Passengers they Bring here, except such as may have my Order to remain in the Land"; after his departure, however, this order was not strictly enforced. It should be noted that Dorrill's actions were not unlike measures against Catholics enacted elsewhere under the British penal laws. Yet other than religious motives were involved: many Irish served in the French military forces, and, with the threat of war with France, the Irish in Newfoundland were distrusted by the British as a large group of disaffected subjects.

On returning to England Dorrill was commissioned captain in the *Royal George* at Deptford (now part of London) in February 1756, and in May he was given command of the *Lowestoft* on the Channel station. His health began to fail, and in a letter to the admiralty from Plymouth Sound, dated 2 April 1757, he asked to be relieved, complaining of "swimming in the head, so that he could hardly stand." He was placed on half-pay and died at Bath on 1 Jan. 1762. He was survived by his wife Elizabeth.

MICHAEL GODFREY

[It has been wrongly stated in some works that Dorrill was governor in 1756. There was no governor that year, but Captain George Darby commanded the convoy. M.G.]

PANL, Nfld., Dept. of Colonial Secretary, Letter books, I/2, p.236. PRO, Adm. 1/1700, sect.8, 13; 25/62; 80/121, pp.10, 14; CO 194/13; 195/8, pp.333–35. PRO, *JTP, 1754–1758*. Charnock, *Biographia navalis*, VI. M. F. Howley, *Ecclesiastical history of Newfoundland* (Boston, 1888), 172–74. Lounsbury, *British fishery in Nfld.*

DOUVILLE DE QUINDRE, LOUIS-CÉSAIRE DAGNEAU. *See* DAGNEAU

DRUCOUR (Drucourt), AUGUSTIN DE BOSCHENRY DE. *See* BOSCHENRY

DUBOIS BERTHELOT DE BEAUCOURS, JOSUÉ (Jean-Maurice-Josué), naval officer and officer in the colonial regular troops, chief engineer of Canada, governor of Trois-Rivières and Montreal; b. *c.* 1662, probably in France, son of Jacques-Hyacinthe Dubois Berthelot and Péronelle de Magnan; d. 9 May 1750 in Montreal.

Josué Dubois Berthelot de Beaucours began a career of service to the king at 20 years of age when he enlisted in the French navy. On 15 April

189

Dubois Berthelot

1684 he was appointed to the rank of midshipman at Brest, where he probably studied the techniques of engineer Sébastien Le Prestre de Vauban who had directed the fortification of the port since 1680. Beaucours served in several naval campaigns in these early years, but on 26 June 1687 the king ordered him discharged from the service. The cause of his dismissal is unknown. Did he then volunteer for service in the colonies as atonement for his error, or was he ordered abroad as punishment? Whatever the case, on 1 March 1688 Beaucours was commissioned a lieutenant in the colonial regular troops of Canada, and later that year arrived in the colony.

By 1690 guerilla warfare with the Iroquois had reached the point that even Quebec, Trois-Rivières, and Montreal were deemed vulnerable. Since engineer Robert de Villeneuve* had returned to France in 1689, Governor Claude de Ramezay* of Trois-Rivières set Beaucours to work on the town's defences. In 1691 Frontenac [Buade*] visited the town and, impressed with the young officer's work, promoted him half-pay captain. Early in 1692 Beaucours took over the command of an expedition, originally headed by Claude Guillouet* d'Orvilliers, against the Iroquois to the west. His successful encounter with an Iroquois band on the island of Toniata (near present-day Brockville, Ont.), was commended by both Frontenac and Champigny [Bochart*], and the following year the king confirmed him in the rank of half-pay captain.

By the fall of 1692 Villeneuve's successor still had not been chosen and Frontenac, believing an English attack to be imminent, commissioned Beaucours to draw up plans for the fortification of Quebec. Working under pressure, Beaucours laid out new walls that were easier to defend and required fewer soldiers. He designed the Saint-Jean and Saint-Louis gates, the Cap-Diamant redoubt, and the Royal, Dauphine, and Saint-Roch strongholds. That winter Champigny wrote that Beaucours's work was better and cheaper than Villeneuve's, and in 1693 Frontenac recommended him for the post of engineer.

From April 1693 until July 1694, when he left for France to settle some domestic affairs, Beaucours drew the engineer's salary of 100 *livres* per month. Two assistants at 40 *livres* per month each helped supervise the work of 500 troops in Quebec. Again Frontenac and Champigny praised Beaucours and requested a promotion for him.

In 1696 Beaucours was named to command Claude-Sébastien de Villieu*'s company in Acadia and to improve that colony's defences during Villieu's detention in Boston, but he never took up this post. He sailed to Canada in 1698 where his presence was required during engineer Jacques Levasseur* de Neré's absence in France.

On 31 May 1701 Beaucours was commissioned captain, and the following year set to work on the forts in the Montreal area. By 1703 he was working in Quebec under Levasseur who had returned to Canada in 1700. Probably irked by this subordination Beaucours sought an opportunity to distinguish himself in the hope of further promotion. In 1704, therefore, he led a party of about 800 men into New England, but the expedition returned to Montreal after a soldier deserted and warned the English. Later that year, however, Beaucours commanded 120 men sent by Governor Rigaud* de Vaudreuil to join Daniel d'Auger* de Subercase in his attack on English settlements in Newfoundland. Beaucours was back in Quebec in October 1705.

An attack on Quebec by the English was feared in the summer of 1707, and Beaucours, acting as chief engineer in Levasseur's absence, was instructed to set up an alarm system of fires from Bic to Quebec, and to complete the town's defence works as quickly as possible. Although only Acadia was attacked [*see* John March*], Beaucours's diligence and efficiency were such that Vaudreuil and Jacques Raudot* recommended him, without success, for the cross of the order of Saint-Louis.

Between 1707 and 1709 Beaucours worked in Montreal and Quebec. He strengthened the Montreal ramparts, and designed a new prison and court house on Rue Notre-Dame. In the past land had been granted and houses built in such a haphazard fashion that planning had become a necessity in both towns, and Beaucours worked on the alignment of roads. In Quebec he improved the walls and restored parts of the redoubts. Then in 1709 Levasseur, who had begun work on a stone fort at Chambly, returned to France leaving Beaucours to direct its construction.

On 25 Oct. 1710 Beaucours submitted a proposal for the fortifications of Quebec, complete with a detailed estimate. This proposal was less expensive and grandiose than Levasseur's and was accepted. Undoubtedly pleased by this decision, Beaucours returned to Chambly to supervise the fort's construction, which was finished by September 1711. During this year, however, new rumours of a British attack brought Beaucours back to Quebec [*see* Sir Hovenden Walker*]. Under his direction, the defence of the capital improved daily, and the Beauport shore was made safe from landing parties. Beaucours's ability to convince the habitants to work contentedly and in excess of the corvée was stressed in a letter written by Vaudreuil and Raudot in which they again requested the cross of Saint-Louis for him.

Not everyone in Quebec was impressed with Beaucours's work, however. The religious orders which held most of the land in the upper town tried to protect their privacy by imposing restrictions on buildings when they sold land bordering on their property. The Ursulines complained that Beaucours had built a high terrace close to their house for the sole purpose of annoying them.

Despite such complaints, the following year Beaucours was awarded the cross of Saint-Louis and appointed chief engineer of Canada. He was to direct two deputy engineers: Gédéon de Catalogne* in Montreal and ensign Claude-Dorothée Laguer de Morville in Quebec. After 24 years' work in the colony, during which time he had drawn plans and directed fortifications for Quebec, Trois-Rivières, Montreal, and Chambly, 50-year-old Beaucours had received the formal recognition he had earned.

On 1 July 1713 Beaucours was sent instructions to rebuild in Quebec on its original location the intendant's palace, which had burned [see Michel Bégon]. The palace was to contain the intendant's lodgings, the king's stores, the armoury, the chambers of the Conseil Supérieur and the provost court, a chapel, and a prison. The finished product, which stood three storeys high, was a finer looking and more comfortable structure than the residences of the governor and the bishop.

On 10 March 1715 Beaucours was appointed engineer to the new French colony on Île Royale (Cape Breton Island), with the title of second king's lieutenant [see Philippe Pastour* de Costebelle]. The following year Jean-François de Verville* was named director of Île Royale fortifications, and Beaucours was transferred from Port-Dauphin (Englishtown, N.S.), where he had originally been sent, to Port-Toulouse (St Peters) with instructions to build adequate defences and to encourage the Acadians to settle there. On 13 June 1716 he received orders to command Île Royale in the absence of the governor; in February 1717 he was moved back to Port-Dauphin. Eight months later he was named king's lieutenant of Île Royale. On 3 Feb. 1722 Beaucours was appointed to succeed Robert-David Gotteville* de Belile as commandant of Île Saint-Jean (Prince Edward Island) for a two-year period. He was expected to use his engineering talents to put the colony's three settlements in a state of defen-sive readiness, and to encourage Acadians to settle there with the island's 300 residents. However, the next year Beaucours was returned to his previous post on Île Royale.

In 1724 it was decided that a resident chief engineer should be appointed for Île Royale, but although governor Saint-Ovide [MONBETON] recommended Beaucours, the position was awarded to Étienne VERRIER of the engineers' corps. The next year Beaucours learned that he had been refused the governorship of Montreal, and the following year the governorship of Trois-Rivières. But on 16 Jan. 1730, after a 15-year absence from Canada, he was at last appointed governor of Trois-Rivières. This appointment must have led Beaucours to reflect on his long life of public service. It was in Trois-Rivières that he had begun his career in Canada; now, 40 years later, he returned to the town as its senior official. During his brief governorship his chief contribution to the town was several fire prevention regulations. Amongst these was an order forbidding the covering of houses with straw and requiring all chimneys built of mud and interlaced branches to be dismantled.

On 1 April 1733 Beaucours was appointed to replace Jean Bouillet* de La Chassaigne as governor of Montreal. As might be expected, his prime interest was the physical lay-out of the town. By 1738 Gaspard-Joseph CHAUSSEGROS de Léry had completed the wall, with eight large gates for carts and other vehicles and eight small gates for the townsfolk. The river side of Montreal had five large and five small gates because it was from the river that much of the traffic came, and the settlers needed easy access to the water as fires were frequent in the town. In 1743 Beaucours decided that the daily opening and closing of 16 gates was not only a nuisance but a hazard if the town were attacked, and he considered walling-in some of the gates.

Shortly after he took up his post in Montreal a problem arose concerning a property in Louis-bourg which he had sold in 1730 for 15,000 *livres* to Sister Marguerite ROY de la Conception of the Congregation of Notre-Dame. By 1734 Sister de la Conception had been discredited and recalled and the order was unable to make the annual 1,000 *livres* payment to which she had agreed, even though the purchase price had been reduced to 10,000 *livres*. A further debt of 5,000 *livres* to Beaucours which Sister de la Conception had contracted in 1733 was repudiated altogether.

On 15 Feb. 1748, aged 86, Beaucours retired with a pension of 3,000 *livres* and a gratuity of 600 *livres*. By 1749 he had overspent his allow-ances by 1,800 *livres* and was selling his furniture

Du Boisdecourt

to subsist. He died in Montreal on 9 May 1750, and was buried two days later in the church of Notre-Dame. He was survived by his wife, Françoise, daughter of Charles Aubert* de La Chesnaye and Marie-Angélique Denys de La Ronde, and widow of Paul Le Moyne* de Maricourt. They had married in Quebec on 15 Nov. 1713 and had only one child, Georges-François.

Beaucours's greatest assets were undoubtedly his ability to work efficiently under pressure, and with others, and to satisfy a succession of colonial administrators. His fortifications were functional, and were therefore less expensive and more acceptable than the flamboyant projects of some other engineers from France. Moreover, his talent was not confined to military installations, for in addition to the Montreal prison and the intendant's palace he designed a church for Sainte-Anne-de-Bellevue and added the finishing touches to the gates of Montreal's church of Notre-Dame. He was a truly devoted servant of his king and country.

C. J. RUSS

AN, Col., B, 17–22, 27, 29, 34–36, 45, 48–50, 57, 64, 69, 71, 76, 78, 81; C¹¹ᴬ, 6, 9–13, 15–17, 19, 24, 27–30, 32, 60; D²ᶜ, 47; E, 22; Marine, B², 60, 169; Section Outre-Mer, Dépôt des fortifications des colonies, Am. sept., nos.3, 7, 9. ANQ, Greffe de Louis Chambalon, 1ᵉʳ, 24 sept. 1694; Greffe d'Hilaire Bernard de La Rivière, 10 juin 1714; Greffe de Florent de La Cetière, 13 nov. 1713. ANQ-M, Greffe de J.-C. Porlier, 12 sept. 1737, 9 juin 1742. ACAM, 525.101, 733-1, 733-2, 734-1, 734-2, 735-1, 742-1. "Correspondance échangée entre la cour de France et le gouverneur de Frontenac, pendant sa seconde administration (1689–1699)," APQ *Rapport, 1928–29.* "Correspondance de Vaudreuil," APQ *Rapport, 1938–39 ; 1939–40 ; 1947–48.* Fauteux, *Les chevaliers de Saint-Louis.* McLennan, *Louisbourg,* I, 129–30. É.-Z. Massicotte, "Madame Boisberthelot de Beaucours," *BRH,* XXI (1915,) 239–42. Gérard Morisset, "Boisberthelot de Beaucours," *BRH,* LIX (1953), 11–21. L.-A. Vigneras, "Documents inédits: l'Isle Royale en 1716," *RHAF,* XIII (1959–60), 422–34.

DU BOISDECOURT, Marquis de LA MAISONFORT, ALEXANDRE DE LA MAISONFORT. *See* LA MAISONFORT

DUBOIS DE LA MOTTE, EMMANUEL-AUGUSTE DE CAHIDEUC, Comte. *See* CAHIDEUC

DUBREIL DE PONTBRIAND, HENRI-MARIE, sixth bishop of Quebec; b. in Vannes, France, probably in January 1708, son of Joseph-Yves Dubreil, Comte de Pontbriand, captain of coast-guards in the bishopric of Saint-Malo, and Angélique-Sylvie Marot de La Garaye; d. 8 June 1760 in Montreal.

Henri-Marie Dubreil de Pontbriand spent his childhood at Pleurtuit (dept. of Ille-et-Vilaine), where the château of Pontbriand was located. He was the youngest of nine children. His three sisters became nuns in the convent of the Visitation in Rennes, and three of his brothers took up military careers, one of them being the Comte de Nevet, with whom the bishop of Quebec carried on a close correspondence. The other two brothers adopted the ecclesiastical state: one was a canon in Rennes, and the other lived in Paris, where he was occupied with charitable work on behalf of young Savoyards and took an interest in the bishop of Quebec's dealings with the court. The latter brother sometimes clashed with Pierre de La Rue, Abbé de L'Isle-Dieu, who was specifically responsible for this liaison.

The future bishop of Quebec did his classical studies with the Jesuits at the famous college in La Flèche. He then went to Paris, where he continued his philosophical and theological studies at the Sulpician seminary. He spent ten years in Paris, where he was ordained in 1731 and was given his doctor's degree from the Sorbonne. Upon his return to Brittany, his native province, he put himself at the service of the bishop of Saint-Malo, who lost no time in making him his vicar general. He held this office in 1740, when at the suggestion of Jean Couturier, the superior general of Saint-Sulpice in Paris, and of the Comte de La Garaye, his maternal uncle, Cardinal Fleury had him named bishop of Quebec by Louis XV. He learned of his appointment officially through a letter from the president of the council of Marine dated 19 Dec. 1740. On 6 March 1741 Benedict XIV gave him his bulls; he was consecrated on 7 April and took the oath of loyalty to the king ten days later.

Since he was unacquainted with the immense country over which his jurisdiction extended, Pontbriand went to live at the Sulpician seminary in Paris before sailing for Quebec and obtained information from Abbé de L'Isle-Dieu, who was probably the best-informed person about the various colonies which made up New France, especially those parts farthest from the see of Quebec, and from Pierre Hazeur* de L'Orme, who represented the interests of the chapter of Quebec in France. A few months later he sailed on the *Rubis,* with François-Elzéar VALLIER, the superior of the seminary of Quebec, who had just spent two years in the mother country to recover his health. All these associations enabled the new bishop of Quebec to become acquainted with his diocese before reaching it. He landed at Quebec on 29 Aug. 1741 and took possession of his see the following day.

At that time the diocese of Quebec had been in existence for more than 60 years. The first incumbent of the see, Bishop Laval*, had given the new-born church of Canada its main institutions. His successor, Bishop Saint-Vallier [La Croix*], had endowed it with an ecclesiastical discipline strongly marked by the spirit of reform of the Council of Trent. Between those two episcopates, which covered some 50 years, and Pontbriand's, the office had been assumed successively by three bishops: Mornay, who never set foot in Canada, Dosquet*, who spent about two years here, and Lauberivière [Pourroy*], who died upon his arrival. Pontbriand showed himself determined to amend the institutions of the church of Canada as they had been set up by Laval because he was hampered by them, to end the abuses resulting from the absenteeism of his immediate predecessors, and to continue Saint-Vallier's work of reform, although with more flexibility. "He appears to have much initiative," wrote Hazeur de L'Orme quite rightly, "and to want to bring about a good number of reforms in Canada, to hold synods, and to organize assemblies of the parish priests." But his episcopate was of necessity marked by the difficult conditions which prevailed in the various colonies under his jurisdiction. In addition to hard times resulting from the years of bad crops, the greater part of his episcopate was overshadowed by war and the abuses to which the people were subjected by Bigot*'s administration.

Upon his arrival Pontbriand filled the vacancies in the chapter by naming to it Jean-Baptiste GOSSELIN and two Bretons who had arrived with him: René-Jean ALLENOU de Lavillangevin, the former parish priest of Plérin (dept. of Côtes-du-Nord), and the young priest Jean-Olivier Briand*. He made Allenou de Lavillangevin his vicar general for Quebec, and Louis NORMANT Du Faradon, from whom the chapter had previously taken away the title, for Montreal. He allowed Étienne Marchand* to retain the title for Montreal also, probably in order not to displease the chapter. Then, with the consent of the council of Marine, he required parish priests holding appointment for life, who had been named by the chapter while the office of bishop was vacant, to hand their titles over to him. Neither the parish priests concerned nor the chapter complained, although one canon pointed out in a letter to Hazeur de L'Orme: "He is determined to be master in his church." Not until 1750 did his relations with the members of the chapter

deteriorate, when the latter found out what their rights in temporal matters and over the ministry of the Quebec cathedral were and demanded that these rights be respected.

On friendly terms with the "gentlemen of the chapter," as he liked to call them, Pontbriand likewise maintained good relations with the Jesuits, in whose convent the bishop and the chapter went from time to time to say the office, on New Year's Day or on the feast days of St Ignatius or St Francis Xavier. But the rapport between the bishop and the Jesuits also ended in 1750, when against the bishop's wishes the Jesuits took into their house Allenou de Lavillangevin, who had been expelled by Pontbriand from the bishop's palace, and threatened to write to Paris and Rome about the matter.

But although he was an enterprising administrator, Pontbriand was first of all a pastor. So he lost no time in making his pastoral visit to the parishes and his canonical visit to the religious communities. On 9 Dec. 1741 he issued a pastoral letter announcing his visit to the parish of Quebec for the following 8 January. This letter was inspired by the decrees of the Council of Trent concerning a bishop's visits to the parishes in his diocese. After this visit Pontbriand was on the whole satisfied, but he nonetheless made some remarks to the chapter on its relations with the parish council; he likewise drew attention to the fact that too many ne'er-do-wells were being sent to the colony and obtained the recall of two. He pointed out at the same time to the council of Marine that there should be no Protestants in the colony: "The spiritual welfare of my diocese," he wrote, "requires that none should be accepted. . . . I even believe I can add that the good of the state is consistent with this view." The bishop also made his canonical visit to the religious communities in the episcopal town: he met the Ursulines at the end of January 1742 and again at the end of December. Meanwhile he had visited the Nuns Hospitallers of the Hôtel-Dieu in the spring and those of the Hôpital Général in the autumn. According to the annals of these communities the prelate made an excellent impression everywhere.

During the summer of 1742 Pontbriand continued his visit of his diocese, going to the parishes and missions between Quebec and Montreal. In a pastoral letter on 22 June 1742 he had given the clergy and faithful of those regions notice both of his visit and of the reasons for it. On 25 June he was in Montreal. In 1743 he visited the Beaupré shore and the Île d'Orléans, and a little later that year he was at Bécancour. The south shore was visited in 1744. Thus ended

Dubreil

Pontbriand's first episcopal visit. The second one did not take place until 1749 and lasted several years. This time the bishop went as far as Fort de La Présentation (Ogdensburg, N.Y.) and Île Lamothe (Isle La Motte, Vt.). They were the only two posts outside Canada that Pontbriand visited. As for the other colonies under his jurisdiction, he had to be content with the information supplied by Abbé de L'Isle-Dieu.

At the time of his arrival in Quebec Pontbriand went to live temporarily at the seminary, since the bishop's palace, which had been built by Saint-Vallier, was in bad condition and it was not known exactly to whom it belonged. Before his departure for Quebec the court had promised Pontbriand to have "the bishop's residence" repaired at its expense. The king confirmed this promise in three decrees, the last of them, dated 30 May 1742, donating the building, which had been repaired according to Gaspard-Joseph CHAUSSEGROS de Léry's plans, to the bishop and his successors. But once the royal subsidies had been spent, there remained the chapel, the sacristy, the stables, and the rough-cast of part of the building which had not been touched. Intendant Hocquart* maintained that a room could be for a chapel, as had been done under Dosquet. However the bishop took possession of the building on 26 Oct. 1743, though without prejudice concerning what had not been repaired. The intendant offered to give the bishop 1,200 *livres* for what remained to be done. On 30 Oct. 1744 the bishop accepted, and the king ratified the arrangement on 26 April 1745. But the following autumn, in the presence of the notaries Claude BAROLET and Christophe-Hilarion Du LAURENT, the bishop handed back the sum that had been received and decided to let the chapel and sacristy fall into ruin.

There remained the cathedral. At the time of his first visit the bishop had found it in bad condition. It had to be repaired and enlarged, since the population was growing. Pontbriand entrusted this task to Chaussegros de Léry, and the work, begun in 1745, was completed in 1748; during that time the Recollets had put their church at the disposal of the bishop, the chapter, and the parish. Through Abbé de L'Isle-Dieu, Pontbriand sought the aid of the court, which refused it to him, and he had to turn to his faithful, to whom he sent a pastoral letter to this end on 22 Jan. 1748. The collection brought in 10,000 *livres*, and as the sum was insufficient – the expenses had amounted to 80,000 *livres* – the bishop asked his congregation in a pastoral letter dated 16 July 1748 to endow masses. From the very beginning the chapter had offered 200 *livres*, and now it

added 672 *livres*. In a letter to the president of the council of Marine on 9 Oct. 1748 Pontbriand wrote: "I have gone considerably into debt to finish the cathedral and parish church of Quebec." And he was right. But the council of Marine was not wrong in blaming him for an undertaking of this sort at such a time. Yet, despite the hard times, Pontbriand had been successful, with or without the king's aid, in restoring the bishop's palace and enlarging the cathedral.

Because of its dependence upon the Missions Étrangères in Paris, the seminary of Quebec had always tended to consider itself independent of the bishop of Quebec. Until 1747 this situation did not create any problems in the colony. But upon the death of Vallier, the superior of the seminary and a friend of Pontbriand, Joseph-André-Mathurin Jacrau*, who was old and tactless, succeeded to the office and would not hear of an episcopal or diocesan seminary. For him the seminary in Paris was master of the one in Quebec, which had not been established as an episcopal seminary. Pontbriand, who held a contrary view, took over the running of the seminary personally. To redress the situation the seminary in Paris sent a conciliator, Christophe de Lalane, who arrived in Quebec in the summer of 1748. The bishop gave him the title of superior of the seminary and was so well satisfied with his services that he made him his vicar general. M. de Lalane was also able to please his fellow religious by rebuilding the outer chapel of the seminary, which had burned down in 1701.

The good relations between the bishop and the seminary were not to last long. The parish of Quebec had not had a titular priest since Charles PLANTE's death in the spring of 1744. The ministry was maintained by priests from the seminary until 1749, at which time the seminary decided to name Jean-Félix RÉCHER titular parish priest. The deed of appointment and presentation, drawn up before notaries and bearing the date 1 Oct. 1749, stated categorically that this presentation and appointment rested with the seminary of Quebec. On 3 November Pontbriand appointed Récher parish priest of Quebec, without, however, taking into account the presentation and appointment of the seminary, for according to him the seminary had overstepped its rights. This was the beginning of a new dispute [see Récher; Allenou de Lavillangevin], marking the end of the era of peace which had characterized the beginning of Pontbriand's episcopate.

In the meantime the bishop continued to look after his diocese. The burning of the Ursuline convent at Trois-Rivières in 1752 was one of the incidents which delayed his second episcopal visit, begun in 1749. The bishop had intended to preach a mission at Trois-Rivières, but he had to take in hand the rebuilding of the Ursuline house. He spent several months at Trois-Rivières, and succeeded in finding the necessary money by having "the nuns borrow." On 7 June 1755, when the bishop was on a visit to Montreal, the Hôtel-Dieu was a prey of flames [see Marie-Catherine TIBIERGE, *dite* de Saint-Joachim]. Pontbriand then organized a collection in Montreal, in Quebec, and in the rural regions "for this good work." The community was nevertheless forced to go into debt. Two years later the bishop blessed the new hospital.

Pontbriand was not, however, equally solicitous towards all the communities. Knowing that the court did not want to see communities multiply in Canada, he accepted the idea of uniting the Hôpital Général of Montreal, which was run by the Brothers Hospitallers of the Cross and of St Joseph, with the sisters of the Congregation of Notre-Dame or the Nuns Hospitallers of St Joseph; he was suspicious of Mme d'Youville [Dufrost*] and her companions, to whom certain people were thinking of entrusting the hospital, which was on the brink of ruin [see Jean JEANTOT]. On 27 Aug. 1747 the bishop consented, not without some reluctance, to entrust the institution "temporarily" to Mme d'Youville and her companions. With the money they received from various individuals the latter undertook to pay off the hospital's debts and to take in as many destitute persons as possible. On 15 Oct. 1750, however, Bigot issued an ordinance joining the Hôpital Général of Montreal with that of Quebec, and Pontbriand was one of the signatories to this ordinance. It provoked dissatisfaction in Montreal, and Normant Du Faradon, along with some Montreal citizens, sent a petition to the court, which gave them a favourable reply, reversing the ordinance of October 1750. On 14 Dec. 1751 a new ordinance handed the Hôpital Général over to Mme d'Youville, and the matter was settled for good on 3 June 1753. Pontbriand recognized that he had committed a serious error and endeavoured to make amends for it, writing to Mme d'Youville: "You are too fair to doubt the feelings of affection and respect which I pride myself in having for you." In 1755 he visited the Hôpital Général of Montreal in person, approved the rules which Normant Du Faradon had given Madame d'Youville and the habit of her pious women.

While lavishing his attention upon the religious communities, in the course of his pastoral visits the bishop also concerned himself with the service offered the faithful. He established, in fact, a score of parishes, not to mention missions. During his episcopate he always refused to institute permanent parish charges, which the court was constantly demanding. He did not acknowledge the king's right to set up parishes and respectfully submitted: "It appears that it is the bishop's responsibility to set up parishes, and to expand or restrict them according to the need, which changes with an increase or decrease in the numbers of the settlers." This precise statement turned out to be necessary, for the court was apparently entertaining claims in this area.

The sixth bishop of Quebec has been blamed wrongly for not having worked enough at formulating a system of ecclesiastical discipline in his church. Here he simply followed Saint-Vallier who during the 40 odd years of his episcopate had endowed his diocese with a reasonable system of ecclesiastical discipline. In his initial pastoral letter Pontbriand approved and continued this discipline. He had only to complete it, and on many occasions to adapt it to the difficult circumstances the colony was experiencing. He did indeed complete it by instituting retreats for priests and ecclesiastical conferences. On 1 May 1753 he urged his priests to make a retreat every two years at the seminary, taking upon himself to pay their board or to have it paid for. As for ecclesiastical conferences, it was out of the question to bring his priests together often. He decided to send out to his priests subjects for study and their further development every six months. They were to send their work back to the bishop who, after examining it, would make a synthesis of it, adding his own reflections, which he would transmit on the occasion of the ecclesiastical retreat.

The privilege of the retreat was even extended to the people in certain places, for instance in the parish of Notre-Dame de Québec during Lent in 1746. Like his predecessors Pontbriand followed up his pastoral visits with instructions and pastoral letters aimed at correcting the deplorable situations which he had observed or to which his attention had been drawn [see Normant Du Faradon]. Again, faced with the difficult situation in the colony, the bishop adapted the ecclesiastical discipline which Saint-Vallier had worked out for better times, drawing his inspiration from the practice followed in the dioceses of the mother country, but without taking account sufficiently of the particular conditions in the various colonies that made up New France. For example, although all the credit does not go to him, after his first pastoral visit Pontbriand reduced by 19 the number of public holidays, an action which dissatisfied part of the population for some years. During the most difficult years of the war he appreciably relaxed the laws concerning fasting and abstinence. These relaxations did not, however, prevent him from insisting upon the importance of prayer and returning often to the subject of the spirit of sacrifice and the necessity of doing penance.

Like his predecessors and the bishops of France, Pontbriand, who had been appointed by the king, had taken an oath of loyalty to the sovereign which made him in reality a royal official. As long as possible he was a good and loyal servant of the king. He tried to get along well with the succession of governors and intendants during his episcopate. With the exception of Bigot he was successful with the intendants, even if he did not always share their opinions. At the beginning of his episcopate he was well thought of by the court and the council of Marine. In addition to the 9,000 *livres* he received as bishop of Quebec, Cardinal Fleury had another allowance made to him of 3,000 *livres* out of funds at the king's disposal from vacant benefices. But he was soon considered a poor bishop, because of the needs of the colony and his great generosity.

The correspondence file between Bishop Pontbriand and the president of the council of Marine proves the subordination of the church of Canada to royal authority. There was scarcely a year in which the bishop did not have recourse two or three times to the council, either directly or through the Abbé de L'Isle-Dieu. Generally the president of the council replied to the bishop once a year in a letter in which he announced the king's decisions to him. What he expressed as desires constituted in effect orders for the bishop. Often he went through his ordinary agents, the governor and the intendant, to address himself to Pontbriand. Through this correspondence the church shows up as highly dependent upon royal authority throughout Pontbriand's episcopate. The poverty of the colonies and of the church that assured their spiritual government only increased the power of the state.

Pontbriand did not have jurisdiction over Canada only. The immense expanse of his diocese, within which communications were difficult, forced him from the beginning of his episcopate to govern different parts of his diocese, like his predecessors, through vicars general. Moreover, the distance from the mother country, where all important decisions were made, forced the new bishop of Quebec to imitate Dosquet in naming Abbé de L'Isle-Dieu vicar general of New France in Paris. The latter played a considerable role in the administration of the immense diocese of Quebec under Pontbriand's episcopate. Indeed, in addition to representing the bishop of Quebec with the council of Marine and watching over the interests of the church of Quebec in France, he had to act as intermediary between the vicars general of various colonies and the bishop of Quebec, since communications, though always slow and relatively difficult, were in fact easier between those colonies and the mother country. Abbé de L'Isle-Dieu was thus much better acquainted with the affairs of the diocese, Canada excepted, than the bishop himself. And this situation was inevitable. As his voluminous correspondence reveals, this vicar general nevertheless did not misuse his powers, nor did he take advantage of the favourable conditions in which he found himself with the bishop of Quebec. It is nonetheless true that Pontbriand's jurisdiction over the immense diocese of Quebec was exercised directly only within the narrow limits of Canada, and that the rest of the diocese was administered by the vicars general.

After 1713 it was difficult to distinguish between French and English Acadia. At the beginning of Pontbriand's episcopate the ministry in English Acadia was under the direction of Abbé Jean-Pierre de Miniac* [*see* Jean-Baptiste de GAY Desenclaves; Charles de LA GOUDALIE; Claude-Jean-Baptiste CHAUVREULX], while that of French Acadia was assigned to Jean-Louis Le Loutre*. The Jesuits ministered to the Abenaki missions on the Saint John River, and the Recollets were responsible for Louisbourg, Île Royale (Cape Breton Island) [*see* Pierre MAILLARD]. Pontbriand was much concerned about Acadia and wrote: "In the situation in which Acadia and a great part of Île-Royale find themselves today, the rule of caution is to be observed more than ever." In 1755, speaking of the English, he noted: "Their conduct towards the populations in Acadia foretells what we would have to fear if they were victorious." And he described the English as enemies "on whose word it would be imprudent to rely."

In the immense region of Louisiana the Jesuits were in charge of all the Indian missions except that to the Tamaroas, who were the responsibility of the Missions Étrangères; the Capuchins ministered to all the French posts on the lower Mississippi. While in France Pontbriand had issued letters of appointment as vicar general for the Jesuit superior and for the superior of the Capuchins, both of whom had their residence in New Orleans, and for the superior of the Missions Étrangères. But a little later he wrote to Abbé de L'Isle-Dieu, telling him to give the letters only to the superior of the Jesuits, because he proposed placing both the upper and the lower regions of Louisiana under his jurisdiction. For the sake of order the bishop wanted a single vicar general [*see* Michel BAUDOUIN]. He had nothing but acts of insubordination to attribute to the Capuchins, who for their part considered themselves exempt from his authority. The Tamaroa mission, under the authority of the Missions Étrangères, was in a difficult situation, and disappeared with the conquest [*see* Jacques-François FORGET Duverger; Jean-Paul MERCIER]. To the north of Louisiana, the Indian missions around Lake Michigan and the French posts in the *pays d'en haut* were entrusted to the superior of the Jesuits at Michilimackinac, who was Pontbriand's vicar general and in the bishop's name sent missionaries where they were needed [*see* Jean-Baptiste CHARDON]. Closer to Canada was the Saguenay mission, of which Father Claude-Godefroy COQUART was the missionary during nearly all of Pontbriand's episcopate.

As the military situation became more and more favourable to England, it appeared evident that an English victory was inevitable. Pontbriand, who in keeping with his oath of office had always been a faithful servant of French interests, was no longer concerned with anything but the preservation of his church. His last pastoral letters, his circulars, as well as the correspondence he exchanged with his vicar general Briand and with General Murray*, must be interpreted in this light. In his actions Pontbriand was not repudiating anything of his past, any more than he was being disloyal to his most solemn promises; he was conforming to a situation that he would have wished different but which he accepted as God's will.

In October 1758, when he was already ill, Pontbriand wrote to his sisters in the convent of the Visitation about his intention to leave the colony, but he added immediately: "I should not leave until peace had returned." He already believed that the colony was lost but was not in the least thinking of leaving his church without a bishop. Already in 1758 considering the eventuality of an English victory, he wrote: "If these gentlemen [the English] are willing to leave me amidst my flock, I shall remain; if they force me to leave, I shall have to yield to force." The same worry tormented him in 1759: "This year must inevitably decide our fate." By "our fate" the bishop meant of course the fate of the colony and also, probably, of the church he was governing. But the two seemed to him to be necessarily linked. As long as the French ruled the colony, the church would be assured of survival. If the situation were to change and England were to

become master of the country, the church would be endangered and no one could foresee what would be its fate. On Bishop Pontbriand's part only one attitude was possible: conciliation and submission; under compulsion he adopted it.

At the beginning of June 1759 Pontbriand thought it advisable to issue a circular letter to all the priests of the parishes into which the enemy might penetrate and gain control. Some of the terms in these instructions demonstrate the conciliatory and submissive attitude the bishop had decided to adopt. The priest, of course, "will not be armed, any more than military chaplains are." If the enemy were to take possession of a parish, "the parish priest will greet him as courteously as possible and will ask him to spare human lives and the churches." If the enemy demanded it, the parish priest could even take an oath of loyalty and promise to do nothing "directly or indirectly against the conqueror," with the proviso, however, that these engagements were valid only for the time during which the enemy was in control. Should the occasion arise, the enemy could hold his religious services in the parish and have first choice of a suitable time. The Catholic service would take place afterwards. And the bishop added: "In sermons and even in conversation everything that might irritate the new government will be avoided." These instructions were only the beginning of Bishop Pontbriand's conciliatory attitude towards the enemy. When English arms had overcome Quebec, he was to maintain it.

In December 1759 Pontbriand wrote to Briand, his vicar general in Quebec and his friend of many years' standing: "You must avoid falling out with the governor [Murray], to avoid greater troubles." He enjoined him to advise the parish priests "to act with all possible prudence," and in February 1760 confirmed: "Only spiritual matters must concern us." Governor Murray had insisted to the bishop that religion not be spoken of to English who were sick. The bishop therefore ordered his vicar general in Quebec to be "careful that neither priests nor nuns speak of religion to English who are ill." In his anxiety he added: "They might take it badly." Writing another time to Briand, in November 1759, Pontbriand had said: "I am writing to the governor of Quebec and I am recommending you to him. I am convinced that you will conduct yourself in such a way that you will not deserve any censure from him." He went on: "As the king of England is now through right of conquest sovereign of Quebec, we owe him all the sentiments of which the apostle Paul speaks." And the bishop was ready to submit to English authority himself. He had written to Murray on 13 Nov. 1759: "If my health allowed me to do so, I should have the honour of going to assure you of my very humble respects." Of the religious communities in Quebec he said: "I hope that they will conduct themselves in such a way that they will not merit any blame. I am recommending that to them explicitly, as well as to all the clergy." In the same letter to Murray Pontbriand left no doubt about his own attitude: "For my part, I shall always act according to the principles of the Christian religion and as do all bishops who have diocesans who are subject to two sovereigns." He also declared that he was ready to deal severely with any priests who departed from these principles. He especially recommended his vicar general to the governor, assuring him that his views would coincide with his own.

According to the diary of the parish priest, Récher, Pontbriand had retired on 1 July, during the siege of Quebec, to Charlesbourg, not far from his episcopal town. After the signing of the capitulation of Quebec on 17 Sept. 1759, the bishop, in order to remain on French territory, withdrew to Montreal, where he enjoyed the hospitality of the Sulpician seminary until his death. We do not know the exact date of his departure for Montreal. Nor do we know whether he visited Quebec before leaving. It is true that some precise details on the condition of the town after the capitulation given in his "Description imparfaite de la misère au Canada" would lead us to believe that he had. But the bishop may have received these details from other witnesses. In any event, from the end of October 1759 on – a pastoral letter is dated 28 October – Pontbriand issued his last pastoral letters and other items of official correspondence from the Sulpician seminary in Montreal. It was from there that he corresponded with the court, his vicars general, and the English governor in Quebec. It was there that he voiced his last wishes, which are included in his testament, and gave his final instructions to his canons concerning the administration of the diocese after his death.

In the first pastoral letter he issued from Montreal, on 28 Oct. 1759, Pontbriand spoke of "the sad situation of this colony": "Blessed are those who, without attributing it wrongly and rashly to secondary causes, recognize in it the avenging arm of the Lord and submit to it." Indeed, for this bishop the misfortunes of the colony were simply the consequence of sin, as he had already insisted in a previous letter. Thus he regretted that "disorders and injustices have not ceased" and that "the ignominious passion of drunkenness, even when the enemy was within

sight and was threatening on all sides, has caused great ravages." The bishop mentioned also the "insulting talk," the "continual grumbling," the "little fidelity in the observance of feast-days and the Sabbath." From the bishop's point of view this pastoral letter was not unjustified. One has only to think of Bigot and his friends. Moreover drunkenness was a plague in the colony affecting not only the lower classes. The conduct of "the better people" was such as to fuel the habitants' grumbling and excuse them for not obeying orders. Pontbriand had tried to denounce the abuses of the régime through Abbé de L'Isle-Dieu. The latter's correspondence bears this attempt out. But these abuses were already well known in France. After some discreet allusions to them in this pastoral letter of 28 Oct. 1759, the bishop ordered public prayers for the late General MONTCALM, the officers, soldiers, and militiamen, and for the return of peace. The litany of the Blessed Virgin was to be recited at the end of all low masses, and the psalm *Miserere* at all benedictions of the Blessed Sacrament.

In a letter to the council of Marine on 9 Nov. 1759 Pontbriand made a point of defending the reputation of Governor Vaudreuil [Rigaud*], and in his famous "Description imparfaite de la misère du Canada," dated 5 November of the same year, he described the habitants' distress. Of Vaudreuil Pontbriand wrote: "There is much argument here about the events which have taken place; blame is easily distributed. I have followed them closely. . . . I cannot refrain from saying that it is utterly wrong to attribute all our misfortunes to him." He added that "simple truth" led him to furnish this testimony. It said enough for the authorities in the mother country to be able to understand what he meant.

On 19 May 1760, a little less than a month before his death, Pontbriand addressed to the canons, who had been "scattered with his permission and through circumstances," his final recommendations with a view to assuring the good administration of his diocese after his death. According to his own words he addressed himself to his chapter as bishop, father, and friend. He said that he was stricken with a fatal illness. He recognized that, "in accordance with the privileges granted by the pope," he had given his vicars general powers they could exercise even after his death. He recommended, however, that they meet as soon as his death was known, to "fill the vacancy in the see by appointing vicars general." "For the well-being of this poor diocese" – he was aware of the precarious state of his church, as were the canons – Pontbriand recommended strongly that they "maintain his vicars general in office" because of their knowledge of the situation. He also asked them not to multiply the offices in the chapter. In short, he wanted to see his church fall into expert hands and in that way to assure its survival beyond his episcopate.

Pontbriand died on 8 June 1760, after asking for and receiving the last rites from the Sulpician superior, his friend Étienne Montgolfier*, as the latter certified. His funeral had to be held quickly, since the scarcity of spices did not permit the embalming of his body. A more formal funeral service was held on 25 June in the church of Notre-Dame de Montréal, and on that occasion his funeral oration was delivered by Louis Jollivet, a Sulpician priest. Father Récher's diary informs us that another service was held on 15 July at the Hôtel-Dieu of Quebec. In the autumn, by a letter dated 13 Sept. 1760, Montgolfier made known to the Comte de Nevet the death of his "illustrious brother" and at the same time the victory of the English in Canada, which had been confirmed by the signing of the act of surrender of Montreal a few days earlier.

Although he spent 19 years in Canada without interruption, Pontbriand's episcopate did not have the significance of Laval's and Saint-Vallier's. Nevertheless it was third in importance under the French régime and also one of the most delicate, difficult, and painful in this period of Canadian history.

The almost permanent absence of a bishop from Quebec from 1727 to 1741 resulted in many problems remaining unsolved, while difficulties multiplied. Over the years the state had strengthened its authority over the church of Quebec, thus making local administration more difficult and complex; yet the weakness of the authorities in the mother country also made for an unsettled atmosphere because of the almost general dissatisfaction it engendered. Finally the Seven Years' War came along to increase hardships and multiply administrative difficulties. The surrender of Quebec, and before that the conquest of Acadia, placed Pontbriand between two countries: France, which he had to keep on satisfying, and England, which he had to avoid displeasing. In the face of the colony's troubles, whether those of the religious communities, of the clergy, or of his diocesans in general, his behaviour sprang entirely from the generosity of a warm heart and an eager soul. His actions demonstrate these motives beyond any doubt. After exhausting his own resources, he multiplied his requests to the council of Marine, which replied usually with promises and repeated affirmation of its good intentions, though sometimes with concrete acts.

But if the problems of the Canadian church were the object of the constant preoccupation of the sixth bishop of Canada, he did not always show the determination that was necessary. Pontbriand had the defect of not wanting to displease anyone, especially where his superiors were concerned. Problems dragged on because the bishop refused to intervene directly. The quarrel between the chapter and the seminary illustrates well this characteristic of Pontbriand.

When confronted with the abuses of the régime under Bigot, he intervened only through Abbé de L'Isle-Dieu. It must be admitted that in his dealings with the authorities in Canada and the mother country Pontbriand never displayed the determination Laval and Saint-Vallier had shown. In his correspondence with the council he did not denounce Bigot. At the height of the crisis his pastoral letters made only timid allusions to the abuses of the régime. Tolerant, perhaps too much so, Pontbriand was in no way an accomplice of the régime, but through his attitude he probably harmed the interests of the colony and the church at a time when France was perhaps still capable of doing something for Canada.

After the capture of Quebec, however, Pontbriand's conciliatory attitude towards Governor Murray, an attitude he imposed upon his clergy, unquestionably served the interests of the church in Canada and perhaps the material interests of the population at the same time. Always well informed, certain of an English victory, a bishop before being a French subject, he had to think first of the survival of the church, and this objective inspired all his important acts until his death. His directives to his vicar general Briand guided his successor's entire activity as bishop. His influence would thus survive him, a fact which his humility had probably prevented him from foreseeing.

JEAN-GUY LAVALLÉE

AAQ, 20 A, Lettres manuscrites, I; 22 A, Copies de lettres, II; 10 B, Registre des délibérations; CD, Diocèse de Québec, II, VI; 1 W, Église du Canada, I. AN, Col., B, 70–112; C[11A], 74–112 (PAC transcripts). "Lettres et mémoires de l'abbé de L'Isle-Dieu," APQ *Rapport, 1935–36; 1936–37. Mandements des évêques de Québec* (Têtu et Gagnon), II, 5–184. Paul-Marie Du Breil de Pontbriand, *Le dernier évêque du Canada français, Monseigneur de Pontbriand, 1740–1760* (Paris, 1910). Gosselin, *L'Église du Canada jusqu'à la conquête*, III. Claudette Lacelle, "Monseigneur Henry-Marie Dubreuil de Pontbriand: ses mandements et circulaires" (unpublished MA thesis, University of Ottawa, 1971). Henri Têtu, *Notices biographiques: les évêques de Québec* (Québec, 1889), 219–57.

Dubreuil

DUBREUIL, FRANÇOIS-JOSUÉ DE LA CORNE. *See* LA CORNE

DUBUISSON, LOUIS-JACQUES-CHARLES RENAUD. *See* RENAUD

DUBUISSON, ROBERT POTIER. *See* POTIER

DUCHESNAY, *dite* de l'Enfant-Jésus, **MARIE-JOSEPH JUCHEREAU.** *See* JUCHEREAU

DUDLEY, WILLIAM, military officer, legislator; b. 20 Oct. 1686 at Roxbury (now part of Boston, Mass.), son of Joseph Dudley, governor of Massachusetts, and Rebecca Tyng; m. 10 March 1721 Elizabeth Davenport, daughter of Judge Addington Davenport; d. 5 Aug. 1743 at Roxbury; survived by eight children.

William Dudley graduated from Harvard College in 1704 and made his first venture into public life in 1705, when he travelled with Samuel Vetch* and others to Quebec to arrange with Governor Philippe de Rigaud* de Vaudreuil an exchange of prisoners, particularly of those taken in the Deerfield massacre of 1704. Dudley had been sent by his father to gain experience and to prove himself worthy of his name. The mission lasted six months (two and a half months in Quebec), but only a few prisoners were brought back, one being the son of the Reverend John Williams* of Deerfield. Following this mission, Governor Dudley was accused of countenancing illegal trade, and Vetch was convicted of trading with the enemy. The governor and his son, however, escaped from the controversy unscathed. In New France, Governor Vaudreuil received a mild reprimand from the colonial minister, Pontchartrain, because of the dangers of spying and illegal trade inherent in the mission. In 1710 Joseph Dudley wrote to the secretary of state, St John, that the mission had indeed been used for the purpose of spying.

William Dudley participated in Colonel John March*'s expedition to Port-Royal (Annapolis Royal, N.S.) in 1707. Appointed by his father as the expedition's secretary of war, Dudley wrote a penetrating description of the dissension in New England ranks on this abortive campaign against Acadia. In 1710, holding a major's commission from his father, he served in William Tailer's regiment under Vetch and Francis Nicholson* in the capture of Port-Royal. As lieutenant-colonel he accompanied Vetch on the ill-fated expedition of Sir Hovenden Walker* against Quebec in August 1711. By 1713 he was a colonel in command of the 1st regiment in Suffolk County, Massachusetts.

With the end of Queen Anne's War, the northeastern Indians (Abenakis of the Penobscot, Saint John, and Kennebec rivers) sued for peace with New England, and signed articles of submission at Portsmouth, New Hampshire, on 13 July 1713 [*see* Mog*]. This was the first of several such peace conferences in which Dudley participated as witness or commissioner. Others occurred in 1717, 1720, 1722, and after the Indian war of 1722–25 [*see* Sébastien Rale*]. Early in 1725 Lieutenant Governor William Dummer sent Dudley and Samuel Thaxter to Montreal to seek an end to French assistance to the Indians and to obtain a release of prisoners. The French denied giving the Indians military aid, but did grant the release of 26 individuals.

Dudley held various public offices during his life. In 1713 he was appointed a justice of the peace, and was a sheriff about the same time. He served in the Massachusetts house of representatives from 1718 to 1729 and was speaker of the house (1724–29). From 1729 until his death he sat on the Massachusetts Council. In his legislative career Dudley, whom Shipton has called a "gentleman woodsman," proved useful to the colony because of his knowledge of the back country. He served on every important boundary commission dealing with Massachusetts' disputes with her neighbours and on many committees concerned with military and Indian affairs. Dr William Douglass, a contemporary, commented that he was the most knowledgeable legislator on land value and other provincial matters. Fellow councillor Thomas Hutchinson wrote that he was "deservedly esteemed and constantly employed in the most important services of government."

Dudley died suddenly on 5 Aug. 1743, at his home in Roxbury. The *Boston Weekly News-Letter*, 11 Aug. 1743, stated that his passing was much lamented and that he was buried with great honour and respect.

DENNIS F. WALLE

Mass. Hist. Soc., Misc. Large coll., William Dudley commission, 1710. PAC, MG 18, N8 (Massachusetts muster rolls, 1710). *The acts and resolves, public and private, of the province of the Massachusetts Bay* (21v., Boston, 1869–1922), II, VIII–XIII. [John Barnard], "Autobiography of the Rev. John Barnard," Mass. Hist. Soc. *Coll.*, 3rd ser., V (1836), 177–243. Boston, Registry Dept., *Records* (Whitmore *et al.*), [6], [12], [13], [15], [24]. *Boston Weekly News-Letter*, 11 Aug. 1743. *Documentary history of Maine*, IX, X, XXIII. William Douglass, *A summary, historical and political, of the first planting, progressive improvements, and present state of the British settlements in North-America*... (2v., Boston, 1747–52; London, 1755; London, 1760). Hutchinson, *History of Mass.-Bay* (Mayo),

II. *Journals of the House of Representatives of Massachusetts* (40v., in progress, Mass. Hist. Soc. pub., Boston, 1919–), II–XX. "Papers connected with the administration of Governor Vetch," ed. George Patterson, N.S. Hist. Soc. *Coll.*, IV (1885), 64–112. PRO, *CSP, Col., 1704–5; 1706–8; 1711–12; 1724–25.* [Samuel Sewall], "Diary of Samuel Sewall," Mass. Hist. Soc., *Coll.*, 5th ser., V–VII (1878–1882); [ ], "Letter book of Samuel Sewall," Mass. Hist. Soc. *Coll.*, 6th ser., II (1888), III (1889), V (1892). *Vital records of Roxbury, Massachusetts, to the end of the year 1849* (Essex Institute pub., Salem, Mass., 1925). *Walker expedition* (Graham).

Shipton, *Sibley's Harvard graduates*, V. J. P. Baxter, *The pioneers of New France in New England, with contemporary letters and documents* (Albany, 1894). Dean Dudley, *History of the Dudley family, with genealogical tables . . .* (2v., with supplements, Wakefield, Mass., 1886–1901) [contains biographical sketch of Dudley with many errors. D.F.W.]; *Memorial of the reunion of the descendants of Governor Thomas Dudley* (Wakefield, Mass., 1893) [gives some corrections to the *History* and a reproduction of a portrait of William Dudley. D.F.W.]. *New Eng. Hist. and Geneal. Register*, I (1847), X (1856), XXI (1867), XLI (1887), XLVI (1892).

DU FARADON, LOUIS NORMANT. *See* NORMANT

DUFOURNEL, LOUIS-GASPARD, parish priest; b. 15 Sept. 1662 at Lyons, France, son of Guillaume Dufournel, a lawyer in the *parlement* and at the court of justice of Lyons; d. 30 March 1757 at L'Ange-Gardien (Que.).

Louis-Gaspard Dufournel was ordained a priest in 1687 and shortly afterwards obtained the canonical benefice of the church of "Notre-Dame de Trevolse," in the principality of Dombes (now in the dept. of Ain, France), which he resigned 3 Nov. 1693. He had come to New France in 1688 and first served the parishes of Champlain and Batiscan until October 1694, when Bishop Saint-Vallier [La Croix*] appointed him parish priest of L'Ange-Gardien; he spent the rest of his life there. From his 63 years as priest of this parish there remain only the records of baptisms, marriages, and burials, which he drew up himself without a break until June 1749, and a few notarial deeds, which are listed in the inventory made after his death, on 5 April 1757. The archives of the seminary of Quebec, however, preserve several documents written by Father Dufournel, when he, in conjunction with the parish priest of Beauport, Étienne Boullard*, decided in 1705 and 1706 to exact tithes on all products of the soil.

At the founding of his seminary at Quebec on 26 March 1663, Bishop Laval* had assigned to the upkeep of his institution "all tithes of any sort whatever and as they will be levied in all the parishes and localities of the said country." On 10 October of that year the Conseil Souverain registered this deed of foundation which allowed the institution of tithes. In April 1663 letters patent from the king for the foundation of the seminary stipulated: "All tithes of any nature whatsoever, whether arising from what is produced by men's work or from what the soil produces itself, will be paid at the rate of only one in thirteen"; they would be allocated forever "to the founding and upkeep of this Seminary and Clergy." All products of "all the lands of the said country of New France" would be tithed. The settlers' protests forced Bishop Laval to restrict the scope of these measures. On 26 Oct. 1663 he declared that in view of the present state of the country he had deemed it fitting to concede to the settlers that tithes be paid "only at the rate of one-twentieth for a period of six years." On 1 Feb. 1664 he had to concede that tithes would be levied at the rate of one-twentieth during his lifetime. Finally, on 10 March 1664, to clarify the expression "arising from what is produced by men's work," which the settlers feared would be held to apply to an unlimited variety of products, Bishop Laval specified that it did not signify "anything other than the tilling of land" and consequently that it could apply only to cereals.

Bishop Laval was nevertheless not willing to let the rights which the letters patent of 1663 accorded him be lost by limitation, and on 23 Aug. 1667 he is supposed to have obtained from Tracy [Prouville*], Courcelle [Rémy*], and Jean Talon* an ordinance by virtue of which "tithes of any nature whatsoever, whether from what is produced in Canada by men's work . . . or from what the soil produces by itself, will be levied on behalf of the Ecclesiastics who will serve the Parishes, at the rate of the twenty-sixth part, provisionally and for the present, without prejudice to the Edict mentioned above or for the future." This document, preserved in the archives of the seminary of Quebec, is a copy which the notary Claude Auber* said he collated on 22 Oct. 1671 "with the original on paper . . . the said original having been given back." The copy consequently bears no signature, and the Conseil Supérieur later refused to recognize its authenticity because of flaws, doubtful omissions, lack of registration, and other irregularities which the king's attorney general, François-Madeleine-Fortuné Ruette* d'Auteuil, set forth at length in his conclusions on 20 Jan. 1706 and in his report of 30 May 1707 on the difficulty that had arisen over the question of tithes.

It was on the ordinance of 1667 that the two

Dufournel

parish priests, Boullard and Dufournel, took their stand in insisting upon the tithe "not only on cereals, as has been practised up until now, but also on everything that the soil produces through cultivation or without cultivation." For its part the council took its stand on a king's edict of May 1679 which stipulated that tithes would be levied in accordance with a regulation of 4 Sept. 1667, that is to say "on cereals only at the rate of the twenty-sixth bushel, taking into account the fact that the settlers would be required to harvest, thrash, winnow, and bring it to the presbytery." As this regulation existed neither in its original form nor in a copy, the two parish priests denied its authenticity. The council maintained that it had been deposited with Intendant Talon's secretariat, "and although it does not appear there, because the greater part of this secretariat has been dispersed . . . it has been carried out in good faith on both sides." In short it was alleged that the usage followed since 1667 could not be otherwise than in conformity with this regulation.

According to the "replies" the two priests, Boullard and Dufournel, made to the Conseil Supérieur on 22 Dec. 1705 – following the council's decree of 18 November summoning them to explain the new tithe exacted and instructing other parish priests to maintain the old one – Boullard would seem to have insisted only upon the tithe on flax, which the settlers had begun to cultivate two years earlier. For him, as for the legal experts in France, "the substance of the soil not having changed, although the surface or the nature of the produce that is sown upon it changes, *remanet eadem causa debendi*, and the tithe imposed on the soil still being due and remaining in existence as long as the soil exists, the produce which grows there is subject to the tithe." The parish priests pointed out that the tithe on cereals was going to diminish gradually, for experience showed them "that a great part of the lands which formerly grew grain crops are now left in pasture, that others are going to be taken over for hemp and flax, and others for large orchards which are already being prepared in several places."

In his own reply Father Dufournel went further than Father Boullard. He maintained not only that "wheat, peas, and all other cereals, flax, hemp, pumpkins, tobacco, garden produce, particularly that which is for trade, apples, and all other fruits and products of the soil . . . are the result of men's work and consequently are subject to the tithe," but also that hay and other products "that the soil produces by itself," are likewise tithable, "the king by his edict [of 1663] excepting no product and no ground." He observed too that the settlers, having little sale

for their cereals, "endeavour to raise as much live-stock as they can and consequently turn the greatest part of their lands into pasture, a practice which is general throughout the country."

After examining the decree of 18 Nov. 1705, the replies of 22 December by the two parish priests, and the conclusions of the attorney general on 20 Jan. 1706, the Conseil Supérieur announced its decision on 1 Feb. 1706, ordering that tithes be levied and paid "according to the usage that has been followed until now . . . until the matter is settled by the king." Boullard and Dufournel replied with a long indictment, signed 6 April 1706, in which they refuted in 40 points the decrees of 18 Nov. 1705 and 1 Feb. 1706 and even expressed displeasure that the party opposing them, "which is interested in the matter inasmuch as it owns several pieces of land and domains subject to the tithe, should be admitted to give its findings against them."

When the council failed to take this indictment into consideration, the "parish priests of Canada" presented a petition to the king, "as to the protector of the Church in New France," asking him to annul the decrees of 1705 and 1706 and to allow them "to collect the tithe in the fields at the rate of one part in thirteen," or else to receive it "pure and clean" at their presbyteries, but "at some other quota more advantageous to the parish priests than 1 in 26." This was all in vain, for on 12 July 1707 the Conseil d'État pronounced a judgement, in conformity with the views of the attorney general, Ruette d'Auteuil, that the decisions of the Conseil Supérieur of Quebec be carried out, reserving the right for the parish priests and missionaries to provide themselves with the supplement, in pursuance of the edict of May 1679.

It seems clear that in this whole affair Boullard and Dufournel were not supported, at least officially, by their superiors, for nowhere can the intervention of Saint-Vallier or of his vicars general be detected; the attorney general's task was thus eased. Bishop Laval, though often cited by the two parish priests as confirmation that there had never been any ordinance concerning tithes other than that of 23 Aug. 1667, maintained the silence which his great age and his long retirement enjoined on him.

The decree of 1707 was therefore adhered to. Only in 1737 was the question raised again by the parish priests of Canada in a request to Bishop Dosquet*, Governor Charles de BEAUHARNOIS, and Intendant Hocquart*. In it they requested permission "to levy the tithe at the field," as well as continuation of the supplement of 6,000 *livres* "which His Majesty has distributed to the poor parish priests of Canada." When this request remained unanswered, they presented another in 1738 asking that "tithes be paid to the priests at the field thus and in the manner prescribed by the custom of Paris," and "that lands that have once been sown in grain always be tithable . . . even if they were converted from arable lands to meadows, pastures, or bore products not subject to the tithe such as tobacco, flax, hemp." This new request was no more successful, and the following year the vicar general, Jean-Pierre de Miniac*, repeated these requests vainly to the minister Maurepas.

It is not known whether Father Dufournel took part in the latter proceedings. Whether he did or not, there is no more mention of him concerning tithes. He continued to attend to his duties as parish priest faithfully until his death, on 30 March 1757, at the age of 94 years, 6 months, and 15 days, as his burial certificate specifies; he was buried in the sanctuary of his church on 1 April. On 12 Feb. 1753 he had made his will before the notary Antoine Crespin, and on 5 April 1757 the same notary drew up the inventory of his belongings at the request of Colomban-Sébastien Pressart*, superior of the seminary of Quebec. On 22 April 1757 the habitants of L'Ange-Gardien divided up at auction the few belongings that remained after their parish priest's specific legacies had been taken care of.

RAYMOND GARIÉPY

ANQ, Greffe de Jacques Barbel, 5 oct. 1736, 10 oct. 1737; Greffe de Gilbert Boucault de Godefus, 3 avril 1752; Greffe d'Antoine Crespin, 12 févr. 1753, 5 avril 1757; Greffe de François Genaple de Bellefonds, 3 nov. 1693. ASQ, Polygraphie, V, 3–26; Séminaire, III, 54–54H. Édits ord., I, 231–33, 305–11; II, 133–35, 139. Jug. et délib., V, 184–86, 230–31. "Lettres et mémoires de François-Madeleine-Fortuné Ruette d'Auteuil, procureur général du Conseil souverain de la Nouvelle-France," APQ Rapport, 1922–23, 22–29, 32–36. Mandements des évêques de Québec (Têtu et Gagnon), I, 160–61. Provost, Le séminaire de Québec: documents et biographies, 1–3, 8–10. Ivanhoë Caron, "Liste des prêtres séculiers et religieux qui ont exercé le saint ministère en Nouvelle-France (1680–1690)," BRH, XLVII (1941), 264. R.-É. Casgrain, Histoire de la paroisse de L'Ange-Gardien (Québec, 1903). Auguste Gosselin, Vie de Mgr de Laval, premier évêque de Québec et apôtre du Canada, 1622–1708 (2v., Québec, 1890), I, 395–414. Émile Chartier, "Notre droit ecclésiastique sous le régime français," BRH, XXX (1924), 360–63. Auguste Gosselin, "Un épisode de l'histoire de la dîme au Canada," RSCT, 2nd ser., IX (1903), sect.I, 45–63.

DUHAGET, ROBERT TARRIDE. See TARRIDE

DU LAURENT, CHRISTOPHE-HILARION, registry clerk of the Conseil Supérieur of Quebec, royal notary; b. c. 1695 in France; d. 13 April 1760 in Quebec.

The year of Christophe-Hilarion Du Laurent's arrival in the colony is unknown. He was a resident in 1722, when his name appears on the list of court clerks in the royal jurisdiction of Montreal. Until 1728 he held on occasion the office of acting clerk of court. During that year he may have left Montreal for Quebec to join Louis-Guillaume VERRIER, the new attorney general of the Conseil Supérieur, who arrived from France in September. Verrier was to be Du Laurent's patron throughout his career.

On 25 March 1730 the minister of Marine, Maurepas, requested Attorney General Verrier to examine the minute-books of the notaries of the provost court of Quebec. Verrier chose Du Laurent as his recording clerk, and Du Laurent was to receive 50 livres a month. This work kept him busy for two years. His subsequent activities are unknown until 11 Aug. 1734, when he was commissioned royal notary for the government of Quebec. He held this position until 1760.

At the end of 1732 Attorney General Verrier had been commissioned to compile a register of landed property in the colony. Three years later, on 10 Jan. 1736, Intendant Hocquart*, in keeping with the king's desire to speed up the compilation of this register, commissioned Du Laurent to gather declarations from the seigneurs of the colony about their title-deeds and all other information "favourable to the rendering of the aforementioned oaths of fealty and homage, recognitions of sovereignty and census." In 1740 Verrier delivered the final volume of the register of landed property to the intendant. In the meanwhile Du Laurent became, on 6 Dec. 1736, registry clerk of the Conseil Supérieur, acting as the deputy of the chief clerk of court, François DAINE. On behalf of the council he was "to serve as secretary, draw up decrees, and even sign copies of them . . . [and] generally carry out as registry clerk what we [Daine] as chief clerk of court might do."

On 28 Jan. 1745 the governor, Charles de BEAUHARNOIS, and Intendant Gilles Hocquart entrusted Du Laurent with another mission for which his work on the register of landed property had prepared him. The colonial authorities granted him a commission to compile "the separate census for each parish or seigneury" in the three governments of the colony. Ten years later he was entrusted with the census of the Domaine du Roi, but, confined to bed by illness, he could not undertake it.

Duparc

Du Laurent died, a bachelor, at Quebec on 13 April 1760; the census of 1744 informs us that he boarded with a shoemaker on Rue Saint-Jean. He seems to have been a conscientious man, as the missions with which the colonial authorities entrusted him bear out. On 13 Feb. 1752 he had the signal honour of drawing up Governor TAFFANEL de La Jonquière's will.

MICHEL PAQUIN

ANQ, Greffe de C.-H. Du Laurent, 1734–1760. *Édits ord.*, II, 390, 537. "Recensement de Québec, 1744" (APQ *Rapport*). P.-G. Roy, *Inv. coll. de pièces jud. et not.*; *Inv. ins. Cons. sup.*, 216–17; *Inv. jug. et délib., 1717–1760*; *Inv. ord. int.*, II, III. Tanguay, *Dictionnaire*. Vachon, "Inv. critique des notaires royaux," *RHAF*, IX (1955–56), 547. J.-E. Roy, *Histoire du notariat*, I, 305, 356–57.

DUPARC, JEAN-BAPTISTE, Jesuit, superior of the Jesuit missions in New France; b. 18 June 1676 in the diocese of Chartres, France, son of Claude Duparc de Tenanguer, and Jeanne de Meur; d. 31 Jan. 1742 at Quebec.

Jean-Baptiste Duparc descended from an old noble family which had an estate at Saint-Jacut-du-Mené (dept. of Côtes-du-Nord), France. He entered the Jesuit noviciate in Paris on 28 Sept. 1695; previously he had done three years of philosophical and one of theological studies. From 1697 to 1702 he taught in succession the classes in grammar, classics, and rhetoric at the Jesuit college in Tours, then from 1702 to 1706 he again studied theology at the Collège Louis-le-Grand in Paris.

In 1707 he sailed for New France and came to live at the Jesuit college in Quebec, where he taught philosophy and theology until 1715. At the same time Father Duparc preached in the church of the college and acquired a reputation for his sermons. He did not leave the college except to visit the sick, the hospitals, and the prisons. His apostolic zeal found a unique opportunity among the English prisoners at Quebec, most of whom were Protestants. Soon he was studying their language, and he mastered it so well after a few months that he was able in 1709 to invite them to weekly, then daily meetings. He had much success and the converts to Catholicism were numerous. "Nearly all of them have been converted," wrote Father Antoine Silvy* to the general of the Jesuits in Rome on 24 Oct. 1710. In 1715 Duparc's activities as preacher, confessor at the Jesuits' church, director of the Congrégation des Hommes, and minister (assistant to the superior) of the college of Quebec obliged him to give up his teaching, which was taken over by Father Louis-Bertrand Gérard. In 1714 he had become confessor to Bishop Saint-Vallier [La Croix*]. Even if he had wanted to devote himself to the missions to the Indians, his health would not have permitted him to do so. His whole career as a priest was spent at Quebec and Montreal.

In 1726 he took on a new responsibility, that of superior of the Jesuit missions in New France and rector of the college of Quebec. Problems were not lacking: the field for missionary activities was growing with the expansion of the French empire in America, but the number of missionaries was decreasing, for the more promising missions in the Far East had a greater attraction for the young missionaries. In addition the mission to the Abenakis in Acadia was threatened by the English, and within the colony itself the traditional esteem the Jesuits enjoyed was declining because of the quarrels over Jansenism in Europe and over the Chinese rites, quarrels which had repercussions as far as Quebec. The dispute at the time of Bishop Saint-Vallier's funeral gave certain members of the clergy the opportunity to display their sentiments against the Jesuits: some of them were dismissed from their duties as confessor to the nuns in the capital; the procession which for 68 years had been made to the Jesuits' church in tribute to the services rendered the church in Canada by the priests of the society was abolished. During this quarrel, which went on for eight months between the canons [*see* Boullard*] and the intendant, Dupuy*, the Jesuits endeavoured to keep peace.

In September 1732 Father Duparc again assumed his office as confessor and preacher at the Jesuits' church in Quebec; then in 1733 he went to Montreal, where he carried out the same duties. In 1741 he returned to Quebec, and on 31 Jan. 1742, just as he was finishing a sermon, he died suddenly. In the letter announcing his death Father Jean-Baptiste de SAINT-PÉ emphasized the dead man's great charity, his fondness for mortification, and the regularity of his religious life, which he carried to the point of doubt and mental struggle.

JOSEPH COSSETTE

ASJCF, 579bis; Fonds Rochemonteix, 4018. Melançon, *Liste des missionnaires jésuites.* Dubé, *Claude-Thomas Dupuy*, 235 [The author of this work asserts that the Jesuits of Montreal blamed their Quebec *confrères* for taking sides in the 1728 quarrel between the chapter and Intendant Dupuy and states that the reproof is supposed to have been presented by a Jesuit named Cabrara. This name does not appear on any list of Jesuits in New France. J.C.]. Rochemonteix, *Les Jésuites et la N.-F. au XVIIIᵉ siècle*, I, 135–45.

Henri Têtu, *Notices biographiques: les évêques de Québec* (Québec, 1889), 178–79.

DUPLESSIS, JEAN-BAPTISTE GASTINEAU. *See* GASTINEAU

DUPLESSIS (Gastineau Duplessis; Radisson, *dit* **Duplessis), MARGUERITE (Marie-Marguerite),** Indian woman of the Pawnee tribe, slave; b. *c.* 1718; date of death unknown.

Marguerite Duplessis, a member of the Pawnee tribe, became René Bourassa's slave in 1726. Bourassa, partner of François-Antoine Lefebvre Duplessis Faber at Baie-des-Puants (Green Bay, Wis.), offered her to the latter's wife, who lived in Montreal in the home of the merchant Étienne Volant* de Radisson. After Duplessis Faber's death in 1733, Marguerite remained in the Volants' home until the merchant's death in 1735. Then she was sold to the merchant Louis FORNEL, who in turn let Marc-Antoine Huart Dormicourt have her in 1740. According to the latter's testimony, Marguerite Duplessis was addicted to vice, libertinage, and theft, and consequently, regretting his purchase, he decided to deport her to the West Indies to be sold there.

Before being put on a ship bound for the West Indies, Marguerite Duplessis was locked up in the prison of Quebec, where she succeeded in getting some quixotic souls interested in her sad fate, one of them being the legal practitioner Jacques Nouette. On 1 Oct. 1740 or a few days earlier Marguerite Duplessis presented a petition to Intendant Gilles Hocquart* in which she claimed that she was the natural daughter of Duplessis Faber and that since she had always lived on the territories of the king of France and was baptized, she was a free woman. This was a tendentious interpretation of the *Code Noir* of 1685, the royal edict of 1716, tinction between contin onies, Jacques Raudo legalizing slavery in the bault*'s decision of 17 a baptized slave [*see* PIERRE]. The intendant referred the litigants to the provost court of Quebec, and on 4 Oct. 1740 this court accepted Huart Dormicourt's arguments which demolished the slave's petition, and ordered the practitioner Nouette to produce his client's certificate of baptism. This document was not to the advantage of the applicant, who asked the intendant four days later for permission to appeal to the Conseil Supérieur of Quebec. On 17 October the council received the litigants and referred them to the intendant. But the sailing season was already far advanced, and Huart Dormicourt was afraid that he would have to supply food and shelter for the slave until the following autumn. He would have been ready to give Marguerite Duplessis her freedom, if the worthy souls who had upheld the slave's cause had been willing to give him the amount he had paid for his servant.

On 20 October the intendant delivered an ordinance which recognized Marguerite Duplessis as Huart Dormicourt's slave and rejected the appeal, sentencing her at the same time to pay costs. She was the first slave who succeeded in setting in action the whole judicial apparatus of New France.

After that we lose trace of Marguerite Duplessis. A slave with the same name took her first communion at Montreal on 13 June 1767; however, it seems more likely that after the intendant's ordinance the slave, who through petitions, postponements, and summoning of witnesses had succeeded in delaying her departure, did in fact leave New France for the West Indies at the end of October 1740, when the sailing season was coming to an end.

MICHEL PAQUIN

[As for the biography of the Comanche PIERRE, the reader should look at *L'esclavage au Canada français*, in which Marcel Trudel has analyzed fully the case of the Pawnee Marguerite Duplessis. M.P.]

DUPLESSIS, *dite* **de Sainte-Hélène, MARIE-ANDRÉE REGNARD.** *See* REGNARD

DUPLESSIS DE MORAMPONT, CHARLES-DENIS REGNARD. *See* REGNARD

DUPLESSIS FABER, FRANÇOIS LEFEBVRE. *See* LEFEBVRE

DU PONT DUVIVIER, JOSEPH
A problem relating to identification of this figure and of his brother François* is discussed in the latter's biography in Volume IV, scheduled for publication in 1977.

DU PONT DUVIVIER, JOSEPH, officer in the ... aptized 12 Nov. 1707 at ...oyal, N.S.), second son ...vivier and Marie Mius ...oup; d. 1760.

Following a brief interlude in France after the surrender of Port-Royal to Francis Nicholson* in 1710, François Du Pont Duvivier was posted to the new colony of Île Royale (Cape Breton Island) in 1714. The hardship imposed on his family by his premature death in November of that year appears to have hastened the advancement of his sons: Joseph and Michel became cadets in the garrison in 1717. The following year Joseph was made a midshipman and in 1719 he was granted an ensigncy. Little is known of his early military career, but he apparently enjoyed the favour of the governor of Île Royale, Saint-Ovide

Du Pont

[MONBETON], who constantly sought his advancement in the service. In 1730 he was promoted lieutenant, and in 1732 assistant town major with a captain's commission.

By the late 1720s Duvivier had demonstrated a greater propensity for trade than for military detail. In this regard he was not unlike his commanding officer and patron, and indeed other members of the garrison who, buttressed by the authority of their military posts, sought to dominate all aspects of commerce in the colony. Duvivier himself was an unusually frequent visitor to France, ostensibly to attend to family matters or because he was "threatened by palsy," but in reality to see to the details of his increasingly lucrative business interests. It was inevitable that Louisbourg's merchant community should react with vigour. In November 1728 the most influential merchants (including Michel DACCARRETTE (d. 1745) and François MILLY) complained bitterly of the extent to which Duvivier and his brothers sought to monopolize, overtly or through their agents, the greater part of the trade in fishing supplies and foodstuffs, as well as the sale not only of Île Royale's fish, but that of the English station at Canso, Nova Scotia, as well. Duvivier's most notable client was Peter Faneuil, the leading Boston merchant of his time. Although there is no record of the reaction of the ministry of Marine to Duvivier's activities, he was probably severely rebuked, like Saint-Ovide himself, who was replaced in 1739.

Duvivier is best remembered for his part in the attempt to recover Acadia from the British during the War of the Austrian Succession. In May 1744, when Jean-Baptiste-Louis LE PRÉVOST Duquesnel, the commandant of Île Royale, received first word of the outbreak of war, he appointed Duvivier to lead an expedition of 140 colonial regulars against the English fishing station at Canso. There was no resistance from the defenders and at dawn on 24 May their commander, Patrick HERON, surrendered. This attack had been the first formal venture into warfare not only for Duvivier but for the Louisbourg garrison as well.

The easy victory at Canso persuaded Duquesnel to attempt the capture of Annapolis Royal. The missionary Jean-Louis Le Loutre* agreed to lead 300 Nova Scotia Micmacs against the English fort in mid-July on the understanding that they would be joined shortly by a detachment of colonial regular troops under Duvivier and a small naval squadron. The warships failed to arrive, and the Micmacs withdrew in disgust. Nothing daunted, on 29 July Duquesnel dispatched Duvivier to Nova Scotia with 50 colonial regulars and an undetermined number of Île Royale Micmacs, and the expectancy that the warships would soon appear.

Having landed at Baie Verte on 8 August, Duvivier cast himself as the Acadian liberator back among his own, but despite strong emotional appeals along the route to Annapolis Royal he succeeded in detaching no more than a dozen Acadians from the strict neutrality which by this time had become the practical expedient of government and governed in Nova Scotia. Keenly disappointed, he retaliated with threats which served only to alienate the Acadian community. He fared little better with the Indians; after the miserable fiasco of July, only 300 Micmacs and Malecites rallied to his side on 7 September, the day he invested the British fort.

The siege lasted a full four weeks. Despite decided tactical and psychological advantages, the French effort was compromised from the start by Duvivier's singular lack of offensive spirit. Aided not a little by the ailing Duquesnel's ambiguous, even contradictory, communications from Louisbourg (instructing him to attack if a favourable occasion presented itself, but not to take unnecessary risks), he adamantly refused to seize the opportunity afforded by the decrepit state of the English fort and the low morale of its garrison. "My position did not permit me to take chances . . .," he wrote, "I had no right to jeopardize a sure thing."

The garrison at Annapolis Royal, which consisted of no more than 75 able-bodied soldiers, was commanded by Lieutenant Governor Paul MASCARENE. Shrewd, practical, and courageous, Mascarene inspired an effective and confident defence. His efforts were considerably assisted by the arrival on 26 September of two vessels bringing reinforcements and supplies from Boston. Although the morale of his detachment was shaken, Duvivier refused to withdraw. The fate of the French effort was, however, sealed abruptly on 2 October with the arrival from Louisbourg of Michel de GANNES de Falaise bearing the news that the naval squadron had not sailed and the order to withdraw to winter quarters at Minas. Duvivier feigned disgust at the prospect of retreat, "la fourche au cul," at a time when an assault on the English fort would have been warranted, but Duquesnel's order was in reality fortunate for him since it enabled him to divert attention from his own indecisiveness.

With the Acadians refusing even to supply foodstuffs for the detachment, the French declined to winter at Minas and withdrew precipitately from Nova Scotia on 4 October: "it is flight, not retreat," Duvivier wrote, "the soldiers, even the officers, obey no order." When he arrived back in Louisbourg, Duvivier found in command not Duquesnel, who had died on 9 October, but his own uncle, Louis Du Pont* Duchambon. Thinking that he might be blamed for not having upheld "the honour of the king's arms" before Annapolis, he immediately requested a council of war to hear his version of events. When de Gannes arrived the next day he found the entire town and garrison against him, for Duvivier had led them to believe that Annapolis could have been taken had the siege been continued.

Duvivier carried the colony's dispatches to Versailles in late November. There is no doubt he welcomed the opportunity to relate the story of the Acadian expedition to the ministry of Marine himself. The exercise proved to be a fruitful one for "in consideration above all of Canso and Acadia," he was received into the order of Saint-Louis on 17 May 1745 at Brest where he had reported for embarkation.

The fall of Louisbourg to New England troops under the command of William PEPPERRELL in the summer of 1745 thwarted Duvivier's plans to return to his post. In 1747, rather abruptly it would seem, he retired from the service. He rejoined as a half-pay captain in 1749 when Île Royale was restored to France and returned there either in 1749 or in 1750. In 1750 he was appointed king's lieutenant commanding at Île Saint-Jean (Prince Edward Island), but he did not take up the post. Perhaps it was denied him after he was discovered in Paris in the company of the English boundary disputes commissioners. In any case the prospect of exile from Louisbourg caused him to solicit with considerable vigour the governorship of Île Royale. In Quebec the governor general, La Jonquière [TAFFANEL], reacted with righteous scorn to Duvivier's rash pretension to a governorship: "They will never convince me that M. Duvivier should be governor of Île Royale . . . to speak frankly, Duvivier would do much better to enjoy his profits from trade in France than to aspire to positions which he does not merit, especially to the prejudice of a number of deserving officers in your government who have served the king well, while M. Duvivier was busy enriching himself." Duvivier was of course unsuccessful in his quest, and in 1753, pleading ill health, he retired finally from the service with a pension of 1,200 *livres*. He apparently continued to reside at Louisbourg where, on 24 Oct. 1750, he had contracted a most advantageous marriage with his cousin, Marie-Josephe Le Borgne de Belle-Isle, the widow of Jacques-Philippe-Urbain RONDEAU, the former agent of the treasurer-general of the Marine; only one of their two children survived infancy. Nothing is known of the circumstances of Duvivier's death.

BERNARD POTHIER

AN, Col., B, 36, f.164v; 39, f.292v; 54, f.503; 57, f.743; 62, ff.161v–62; 64, f.129v; 65, ff.482v–83; 81, f.146; 92, p.253 (PAC transcript); 98, f.178; C11B, 9, f.77v; 12, f.29; 15, ff.112–14; 18, ff.59v, 322v; 20, ff.18v, 96, 304–6v; 26, ff.40v, 48–52v, 68, 194–94v, 196, 205, 230–30v; 30, ff.58v–59, 102–20v; C11D, 8, ff.87–114v; D2C, 4, f.106; E, 169 (dossier Du Pont Duvivier); Section Outre-Mer, G1, 408/1, ff.121–22, 318–19; 408/2, ff.65–66; 409/1, f.42; G2, 183, f.195; 188, ff.288–303v; G3, 2042 (21 juin 1754); 2056 (1 sept. 1715). PANS, RG 1, 26, p.6. *N.S. Archives*, *IV*, 57–67, 80–84. Brebner, *New England's outpost*, 104–14. Clark, *Acadia*, 192. McLennan, *Louisbourg*, 109–18. Rawlyk, *Yankees at Louisbourg*, 1–15.

DUPRÉ, JEAN-BAPTISTE LE COMTE. *See* LE COMTE

DUQUESNEL, JEAN-BAPTISTE-LOUIS LE PRÉVOST. *See* LE PRÉVOST

DURAND, JUSTINIEN, priest, Recollet, missionary, provincial commissioner of the Recollets in Quebec; b. *c.* 1667 in France; d. in Quebec on 1 Aug. 1746, according to the "Nécrologe des Récollets," or early in 1748, according to the chronicler of the Hôpital Général of Quebec.

No information is available about Justinien Durand's life before his arrival at Port-Royal (Annapolis Royal, N.S.) in October 1704 as vicar general of the bishop of Quebec and parish priest of Port-Royal. Because his predecessor, Abel Maudoux, had had numerous differences with the governor of Acadia, Jacques-François de Monbeton* de Brouillan, Durand had been instructed to improve the clergy's relations with the civil authorities. He seems to have been successful. Brouillan's death in September 1705 undoubtedly helped to improve the atmosphere, but so did Durand's attitude, which was characterized by prudence and discretion, particularly in the Louise GUYON affair. Brouillan's successor, Daniel d'Auger* de Subercase, had every reason to be satisfied with the Recollets' presence at Port-Royal.

After the surrender of Port-Royal to Francis Nicholson* on 13 Oct. 1710, Durand sought to reunite the settlers "in the upper region of the river [Annapolis River]," in order to shield them from the terms of the capitulation, which required an oath of allegiance on the part of the Acadians from "the outskirts of Port-Royal." His conduct was considered seditious by Samuel Vetch*; he was taken prisoner in January 1711 and escorted to Boston. Louis Denys de La Ronde succeeded in bringing him back at the end of the year in an exchange of prisoners.

After the treaty of Utrecht in 1713 Durand and other missionaries in Acadia tried, at the request of the French government, to encourage the Acadian population to emigrate to the territories that had remained French. At first Durand was optimistic about his parishioners' desire to leave. But the British authorities increased the obstacles, and the French authorities showed little inclination to respect the wonderful promises made by their agents. In reality the Acadians did not want to leave their land if freedom of religion and property rights were guaranteed them.

Neither did they want to take the oath of allegiance to the British king. None of the early administrators of Nova Scotia, Francis Nicholson, Samuel Vetch, John Doucett*, Thomas Caulfeild*, had succeeded in obtaining it. When a new governor, Richard Philipps, arrived in April 1720, he was firmly resolved to settle the question. Three days after his arrival Durand took the initiative and led a delegation of Acadians to the governor to explain why they could not take the oath. Durand was told by Philipps to publish the proclamation requiring everyone to take the oath on pain of having to leave the province within four months. He yielded to the governor's demands and at this juncture went to Louisbourg to seek on behalf of the Acadians the advice of Saint-Ovide [Monbeton], the governor of Île Royale. On his departure the missionary wrote to Philipps that he had left his parishioners "entirely free to take whatever decision they considered advantageous"; he asked permission to retire to Île Royale (Cape Breton Island) "in order," he said, "that any troubles that arise will not be imputed to me." Durand's action seems to have contributed to Philipps' failure to obtain the oath of allegiance from the Acadians in 1720. He was not to be successful until 1730.

Father Durand was at Quebec in 1726, when he was appointed provincial commissioner of the Recollets in New France, an office he seems to have exercised at intervals until around 1734. His term of office was uneventful, except for the episode linked with the soldiers' mutiny in July 1730 against the commandant at Fort Niagara (near Youngstown, N.Y.), Nicolas Blaise* Des Bergères de Rigauville. Two Recollet friars, Brothers Césarée and Charpentier, succeeded in freeing the instigators of the revolt on the eve of their execution in Montreal and took refuge with them in the Recollet monastery in Quebec. Father Durand refused to hand the guilty persons

over to the law, although he recognized the complicity of the two friars. The civil authorities took advantage of this incident to obtain from the king the "declaration of 1732," an ordinance that deprived the church in New France of the right of asylum. Those who violated the ordinance were denied the right to be tried by ecclesiastical courts. It appears, however, that the ordinance was never observed.

Justinien Durand spent the final years of his life at the Recollet monastery in Quebec. If we are to believe the chronicler of the Hôpital Général of Quebec, he was appointed confessor of the nuns there on two occasions, from 1731 to 1733 and from 1747 to 1748. During his ministry to nuns who were ill he succumbed to an epidemic which raged in Quebec in early 1748. The "Nécrologe des Récollets" attributes his death to this cause, but sets the date at 1 Aug. 1746. Its date is questionable, since the epidemic did not break out until November 1746.

MICHELINE D. JOHNSON

AAQ, 12A, Registres d'insinuations, C, 130. AN, Col., B, 35, ff.11–12; 36, f.447; 48, f.887; 49, f.666; 57, ff.650, 664, 672v; 64, f.444; 68, f.51v; C¹¹ᴬ, 35, ff.106–30; 52, ff.118–26; 55, f.295; 56, ff.141–42, 204; 58, ff.18–19, 214–16; 62, ff.279–80; C¹¹ᴮ, 1, ff.411–12; C¹¹ᴰ, 5, ff.197, 221, 248–58; 6, ff.159–211; 7, f.182; 8, ff.49–54. ANQ, NF, Registres du Cons. sup., 1727–1728, 18 févr. 1728. Archives des Franciscains (Montréal), Dossier Justinien Durand. ASQ, Fonds Amédée Gosselin, XLIX. *Coll. de manuscrits relatifs à la N.-F.*, III, 538–39, 547–48. *Coll. doc. inédits Canada et Amérique*, I, 110–11, 120–30, 151–52, 193–96; II, 6–10. *Édits ord.*, I, 528. *Lettres de noblesse* (P.-G. Roy), II, 84, 167–89. *N.S. Archives*, I, 21–35; II, 57–59, 166. Gosselin, *L'Église du Canada jusqu'à la conquête*, II, 98–99, 158–73, 431. Jouve, *Les Franciscains et le Canada: aux Trois-Rivières*, 160, 285. *Mgr de Saint-Vallier et l'Hôpital Général*, 317–19, 712. Murdoch, *History of Nova-Scotia*, II, 278–386. Rochemonteix, *Les Jésuites et la N.-F. au XVIIIᵉ siècle*, I, 111–33. P.-P. Gaudet, "Les premiers missionnaires et curés de Port-Royal," *BRH*, XIV (1908), 375–79. Auguste Gosselin, "Le clergé canadien et la déclaration de 1732," *RSCT*, 2nd ser., VI (1900), sect.i, 23–52.

DURELL, PHILIP, naval officer; b. 1707 at St Helier, Jersey, and baptized there 25 May 1707; son of John Durell, solicitor general of Jersey, and Elizabeth Corbet; m. his first cousin Madeline Saumarez, secondly a Bristol lady named Skey, thirdly the widow of Captain Wittewronge Taylor; d. 26 Aug. 1766 at Halifax, Nova Scotia, "from eating dolphins."

After receiving his early education from an aunt, Philip Durell entered the navy through the offices of his uncle, Captain Thomas Durell. He joined the latter's ship, the 20-gun *Sea Horse*, as ordinary seaman in 1721. Three years later, as able seaman, he joined the *Ludlow Castle* (40 guns). During his formative years from 14 to 19 he served on the Newfoundland, Nova Scotia, and New England stations in these two ships. He was commissioned lieutenant in 1731, and while in the West Indies was appointed to the 40-gun *Eltham* as post captain on 6 Feb. 1742/43 (o.s.).

After returning to England for a refit in 1743, the *Eltham* sailed in July 1744 for Boston (by way of Antigua) to convoy the mast ships from the Piscataqua River (Me.-N.H.) to England. Before that task could be undertaken, however, Durell's instructions were changed: in the spring of 1745 he was to join Commodore Peter WARREN and William PEPPERRELL in attacking Louisbourg, Île Royale (Cape Breton Island). Through his local knowledge and surveying skills Durell played an important part in the expedition. While his ship was wintering in Nantasket Roads, Massachusetts, he assisted in formulating Pepperrell's instructions, and the *Eltham* was the first ship to join Pepperrell at Canso (Canseau). During the siege Durell assisted in the capture of the *Vigilant* (Capt. Alexandre de LA MAISONFORT Du Boisdecourt), which was laden with supplies for the fortress, and, as captain of the *Chester*, he helped take two French East Indiamen, prizes of enormous value. In October 1745 he returned to England armed with dispatches and a survey of Louisbourg harbour which, according to Warren, "he had been at great pains to make."

As captain of the *Gloucester* (50 guns) Durell took part in Rear-Admiral Edward Hawke's decisive defeat of a French squadron off Cape Ortegal, Spain, on 14 Oct. 1747. He remained in European waters until 1755, when as captain of the *Terrible* (74 guns) he sailed with Rear-Admiral Francis Holburne*'s squadron to reinforce Vice-Admiral BOSCAWEN off Louisbourg and Newfoundland. After returning to England with Boscawen's fleet in November, Durell took command of the *Trident* (64 guns) and under Vice-Admiral John BYNG participated in the fateful action of 20 May 1756 off Minorca that ended in Byng's failure to engage the enemy.

On 15 Jan. 1758 Durell hoisted his commodore's broad pendant in the frigate *Diana* to be Boscawen's third in command for the slated attack on Louisbourg. Finding himself senior naval officer on his arrival at New York on 7 March, Durell organized the transportation and convoy to Halifax of the troops. Sailing on 4 May, he arrived at Halifax on 17 May, shifted his broad pendant to the *Princess Amelia* (80 guns), and sailed for Louisbourg as soon as weather permitted, on 28 May. He played an important part in the capture of the fortress through his advice regarding the place and time of the landing in Gabarus Bay. Surf conditions made this a critical decision. Durell advised postponement twice, on 5 and 7 June. In the small hours of 8 June he took his barge within pistol shot of the breastworks "and found there was a Surf on the Shore, but not such as to prevent Boats landing." Just after sunrise, having confirmed his opinion, he advised Major-General Jeffery Amherst* accordingly, and the disembarkation began.

On 8 July 1758 Durell was promoted rear-admiral of the blue, and remained in North America as commander-in-chief for the winter months. During this time he carried out instructions "to fix on a proper place here for building a Careening Wharf and erecting a Convenioncior [*sic*] for refitting his Majesty's Ships." Boscawen had hired a wharf at Halifax in 1755, and Charles HOLMES had appointed a storekeeper in 1756, but these had been temporary measures. In 1757 the admiralty had finally recognized a need for permanent facilities, but neither Holburne nor Lord COLVILL could spare the time and effort needed to prepare a proper site. Durell examined the alternatives and in December 1758 selected land at Gorham's Point in present Halifax. Additional land was acquired in February 1759, and by mid-March two storehouses and a storekeeper's office were built, and contracts were drawn up for the careening wharf, capstan house, and adjoining storehouses.

Boscawen and Pitt had instructed Durell to get his squadron ready for sea as early as possible in the spring and to prevent French reinforcements from reaching Quebec. Despite a hard winter all his ships were ready by 8 April 1759, but when Major-General WOLFE and Vice-Admiral Charles Saunders* arrived in Halifax on 30 April they found Durell still in port. Even though the ships were at single anchor, awaiting only a favourable wind, Wolfe was displeased. Durell's peers in the naval service, however, did not in the end find fault with him. Ice conditions that spring had been particularly severe, and ships were unable to get into the Gulf of St Lawrence or Louisbourg harbour as late as mid-April. Durell had postponed sailing until there was a reasonable chance of getting into the gulf. In the interim he had sent John ROUS, who had more local knowledge than any other captain in his squadron, to Canso to watch for French ships and for the improvement of ice conditions. But while an overwhelming British naval strength was concentrating in Halifax a small French squadron was sailing unmolested through leads in the pack ice that still pervaded the gulf; yet there is nothing to substantiate a modern suggestion that Durell had a superstitious fear of the ice. He simply knew too well the difficulties of ice navigation. He had been with Boscawen in 1755 on a vain search for the French fleet in these same waters, and had seen him incur such a loss of men through sickness that the squadron could not remain at sea. In 1759 Durell saved his ships and men to lead the British fleet up the St Lawrence. His judgement had been that of a prudent seaman with far better knowledge of North American waters than most of his contemporaries. Perhaps he did not possess the decisive qualities of a great commander-in-chief, but it is difficult to fault his course of action as a subordinate commander.

One of the officers who sailed from Halifax with Durell on 5 May was James Cook*, master of the *Pembroke* (Capt. John Simcoe). Assisted by charts which the *Alcide* (Capt. James Douglas*) had captured, Cook surveyed the Traverse, the passage south-east of the Île d'Orléans, and thus removed the last obstacle to reaching Quebec – one the French had deemed impossible to overcome. As Saunders' second in command, Durell remained between Île d'Orléans and Île Madame to guard the Traverse during the siege.

After the capture of Quebec in September 1759 he returned to England. He had been promoted rear-admiral of the red on 14 Feb. 1759, and on 14 June 1761 he was appointed port admiral of Plymouth. On 21 Oct. 1762 he was promoted vice-admiral of the blue and in 1766 was named commander-in-chief of the North America station in succession to Colvill. During his passage to Halifax he fell ill, and he died four days after his arrival. He was buried on 27 Aug. 1766 from St Paul's Church, Halifax, where his hatchment is still to be seen.

W. A. B. DOUGLAS

Portraits of Durell are in the Saumarez Manor, Jersey, the City Museum and Art Gallery in Plymouth, England, and St Paul's Church, Halifax. Several photographs of paintings are in the PANS.

BM, K. Top., CXIX, 87, 88(2) (copies in PAC). Priaulx Library (St Peter Port, Guernsey, C.I.), MS Coll. PRO, Adm. 1/480; 1/481, ff.41, 140, 530–31, 597–98; 1/482, f.530; 1/1694; 1/1701; 1/2453; 1/2654–55; 8/14–15; 50/3; 50/7, ff.185–227; 51/309; 51/4147. [Philip Durell], "An accurate plan of the River St. Lawrence . . . drawn from the original by Wm. Roberts," *RSCT*, 3rd ser., XIX (1925), sect.II, 152; *A particular account of the taking cape Breton . . .* (London, 1745). *Logs of the conquest* (Wood). G. R. Balleine, *A biographical dictionary of Jersey* (London, New York, [1948]). Charnock, *Biographia navalis*, V, 167–70. G. B., Adm., *Commissioned sea officers, 1660–1815*.

Corbett, *England in the Seven Years' War*, I. Gipson, *British empire before the American revolution*, VI. G. S. Graham, *Empire of the north Atlantic: the maritime struggle for North America* (London, Toronto, 1950). R. V. Harris, *The Church of Saint Paul in Halifax, Nova Scotia: 1749–1949* (Toronto, 1949). Rawlyk, *Yankees at Louisbourg*. Robin Reilly, *The rest to fortune: the life of Major-General James Wolfe* (London, 1960). *The Royal Navy: a history from the earliest times to the present*, ed. W. L. Clowes (7v., London, 1897–1903), III. C. B. Fergusson, "Durells in eighteenth century Canadian history," *Dal. Rev.*, XXXV (1955–56), 16–30. E. A. Smillie, "The achievement of Durell in 1759 (facts relating to Admiral Philip Durell and the St. Lawrence expedition)," *RSCT*, 3rd ser., XIX (1925), sect.II, 131–51.

DUROCHER, JOSEPH (baptized **René-Joseph**), merchant, tailor; b. 2 July 1706 in Angers, France, son of Joseph Durocher, a tailor, and Marguerite Le Roy; d. sometime before 15 Sept. 1756.

Joseph Durocher's name appears for the first time in Canadian documents in 1730. On 6 May that year he married Marie-Louise-Catherine Juillet at Batiscan. In his marriage contract, signed on the preceding 19 February before the notary Nicolas-Auguste GUILLET de Chaumont, it is stated that Durocher gave his wife the sum of "three thousand *livres* as stipulated jointure." On 24 June 1743, shortly after the death of his wife, who had borne him nine children in 13 years, Durocher remarried in Montreal; his second wife was Marguerite Gaudé, the widow of Jean-Baptiste Jarry, a "merchant and voyageur" in Montreal. Having married with joint estate, Durocher brought his new wife "fifteen hundred *livres* as stipulated jointure." One child was born of this marriage, but did not live.

Durocher was both a tailor and a merchant for a great part of his life. Only his commercial activities, however, are known to us. He had apparently an expansive business and multiplied his purchases of houses, land, and farms. He was also interested in the fur trade; it was in this connection that he hired five men in 1745 for the post at Michilimackinac. Two years later his business was, it seems, prosperous enough to allow him to hire for a year Jean-Baptiste Dumontet, *dit* Lagrandeur, and his wife "to serve him in all lawful and honest matters which will be ordered them." In the 1750s Durocher had dealings with the Quebec merchants François HAVY and Jean LEFEBVRE; on 15 Jan. 1753 we find him before the Conseil Supérieur in a lawsuit with the two men over three building sites.

The "merchant and tailor" had, however, over-reached himself; he was sued by his numerous creditors, who forced him to settle his accounts. The balance sheet of his personal fortune showed income in excess of expenditures by 35,408 *livres* 18 *sols* 3 *deniers*; but since he owed 60,398 *livres* 16 *sols* 7 *deniers*, he was judged to be bankrupt. Each of his creditors received 58 5/8 per cent of what was owing him.

Joseph Durocher probably died in Montreal in 1756: on 15 September that year his wife was called a widow in the contract for the auction of his belongings drawn up by the notary Louis-Claude DANRÉ de Blanzy.

ROBERT LAHAISE

ANQ, Greffe de J.-A. Saillant, 29 sept. 1757 (acte de L.-C. Danré de Blanzy, 15 sept. 1756). ANQ-M, Greffe de N.-A. Guillet de Chaumont, 19 févr., 27 juill. 1730, 24 janv. 1732; Greffe de J.-C. Raimbault, 1er août 1733, 24 oct. 1734, 21 juill., 4 sept. 1735; Greffe de Simon Sanguinet, 24 juin, 18 juill., 1er août 1747; Greffe de François Simonnet, 20 juin 1743. *Dictionnaire national des Canadiens français (1608–1760)* (2v., Montréal, 1958). Massicotte, "Répertoire des engagements pour l'Ouest," APQ *Rapport, 1929–30*, 457, 459, 460, 462, 465. P.-G. Roy, *Inv. jug. et délib., 1717–1760*, III, 110, 114; V, 5, 15, 259. Tanguay, *Dictionnaire*. J.-J. Lefebvre, "Les familles Durocher de Montréal et de Saint-Antoine-sur-Richelieu," *BRH*, LXV (1959), 67–82.

DUVERGER, JACQUES-FRANÇOIS FORGET. *See* FORGET

DUVIVIER, JOSEPH DU PONT. *See* DU PONT

E

EHRHARD. *See* ERAD

ELLIOT (Elliott), ROBERT, army officer; probably b. *c.* 1715; married (his wife's name is unknown); *fl.* 1740–65.

Robert Elliot purchased a lieutenancy in the 43rd regiment on 27 Jan. 1740 and a captaincy on 26 May 1746. In 1754 he was quartered with the regiment at Athlone (Republic of Ireland). He was promoted major on 2 Feb. 1757. He probably arrived in North America with the regiment in June that year and wintered in Nova Scotia, since in the following May he went by boat from Fort Cumberland (formerly Fort Beauséjour, near Sackville, N.B.) to command at Annapolis Royal, where he remained throughout the summer. After he had returned with his detachment to Fort Cumberland on 6 Dec. 1758, he and other officers of the 43rd petitioned the regimental commander for employment in the campaign against the French planned for the following year.

On 24 May 1759 Elliot and his regiment joined the force assembling at Louisbourg, Cape Breton Island, for WOLFE's assault on Quebec, and by 27 June they had landed on the Île d'Orléans. Elliot and a party of 200 men made an abortive attempt on 11 August to join the British troops already above Quebec by working upstream in boats past the city, but they were beaten back by fire from its batteries. On the 27th they succeeded in reaching a point on the south shore immediately across from the Anse au Foulon. The regiment took part in the storming of the heights of Abraham on the night of 12 September, and under Elliot's command occupied a position in the centre of the British line in the subsequent battle. Following the capitulation of Quebec, on 18 September Elliot was sent with a detachment to dislodge the French from a strong entrenchment north of the Saint-Charles River and to disarm the inhabitants of Beauport – two operations he performed with few losses. The 43rd wintered at Quebec and took part in the battle at Sainte-Foy against the forces of Lévis* on 28 April 1760, and in Jeffery Amherst*'s attack on Montreal that summer.

After the capture of Montreal the regiment moved to winter quarters at Quebec, but on 23 September Elliot sailed from Quebec with a detachment of over 100 men to receive the capitulation of the French garrison at Restigouche, on the Baie des Chaleurs. He accepted the surrender of the French commander, Gabriel-François d'Angeac*, on 21 October and sailed for New York on 5 November. Nine days later his ship was wrecked on Sable Island. He and his crew built shelters using the yards and sails of the vessel, thatched with sedge; they subsisted on the few provisions they had been able to save and on the cattle and horses they discovered on the island. On 20 Jan. 1761 a New England schooner rescued them and took them to Halifax. Being in "no very good condition for a voyage" Elliot remained there with his men.

On 23 March he was promoted lieutenant-colonel of the 55th regiment. Amherst intended him to command at Crown Point, New York, and Elliot arrived at New York on 2 July 1761 en route to this post, but he was "extreamly ill" and did not join his new regiment until 21 November. At

Crown Point Elliot spent his time repairing the fortifications, recruiting provincials into the regular forces, and facilitating communications between Montreal and Albany. He was transferred to command at Albany in October 1763. In a letter of April 1764 he mentions returning to England and had in fact done so by the following January, having left the regiment the previous month.

Elliot appears to have been a competent career soldier, whose services at Quebec led Major-General James Murray* to consider naming a Canadian county after him.

JOHN HUMPHREYS

PRO, CO 5/51, f.102; Ind. 5436, f.115; 5438, f.343; 5441, f.82; 5444, f.18; 5449, f.113; 5455, f.109; WO 1/1, ff.354v–55; 12/6470, ff.42, 52, 82, 112; 34/12, ff.84–85, 42–49v; 34/13, f.44; 34/51, ff.152, 218, 339–39v; 34/52, ff.132, 233, 239, 316. Knox, *Historical journal* (Doughty). *Army list, 1765*, 109. *Johnson papers* (Sullivan *et al.*). H. J. Newbolt, *The story of the Oxfordshire and Buckinghamshire light infantry, the old 43rd and 52nd regiments* (London, 1915), 4, 17, 20, 25–26.

ENFANT-JÉSUS, MARIE-JOSEPH JUCHEREAU DUCHESNAY, *dite* DE L'. See JUCHEREAU

ERAD (originally Ehrhard), JOHANN BURGHARD, surgeon; b. *c.* 1695 in Eutingen (near Pforzheim, Federal Republic of Germany), son of a pastor; buried at Lunenburg, Nova Scotia, 24 March 1757.

Aboard the *Pearl*, a ship carrying "foreign Protestants" to Halifax in 1751, were two former officers whom the British emigration agent, John Dick, described as mere "adventuriers," in spite of recommendations they possessed from the margrave of Baden-Durlach. Both Johann Erad, 56, and Leonard Christian Rudolf*, 40, seem to have had diversified and adventurous careers in various parts of Europe; Erad had been a surgeon in the French service for a long time. These two friends, who were amongst the handful able to pay their own passage, had agreed to emigrate together and were to become two of the outstanding personages of the community begun at Lunenburg in 1753.

Erad was appointed surgeon in Lunenburg that year by Governor Peregrine Thomas HOPSON, as was Leonard LOCKMAN who had come over with Governor Edward Cornwallis* in 1749. Erad was the senior of the two and the more highly paid. The territory was divided between them until Erad's death in 1757 when his work was carried on by a young surgeon named John Phillips, who

had been assisting Erad without salary or appointment.

Perhaps because of his military experience Erad was commissioned a captain in the Lunenburg militia regiment in 1753. At the time of the Lunenburg insurrection in December 1753 [*see* PETTREQUIN] he remained loyal to the government side and was one of two officers singled out by Charles LAWRENCE for having "distinguished themselves by their good behaviour in every particular during the Riot." One of his daughters married another distinguished immigrant, Joseph Pernette*, on whose behalf Erad superintended a merchandise business in Lunenburg, from 1754 to 1755.

RONALD ROMPKEY

PANS, MG 1, 109, p.110; 583–85; RG 1, 134, p.67; 382, no.4; RG 3, Minutes of Nova Scotia Council, 28 June 1759. PRO, CO 217/12. Bell, *Foreign Protestants*.

ERHARDT, JOHN CHRISTIAN, Moravian trading agent on the Labrador coast; b. *c.* 1720 at the Baltic seaport of Wismar, then in Swedish territory (now German Democratic Republic); d. 1752, on the Labrador coast.

John Christian Erhardt, a German sailor, joined the Moravian Brethren after coming under the influence of their missionaries on the island of St Thomas in the West Indies. Subsequently Erhardt sailed in the supply ship serving the Moravian mission stations in Greenland. There he picked up some Eskimo words and talked with the missionaries, especially with the veteran Matthew Stach, who told him that the Eskimos on the opposite side of Davis Strait probably were similar to the Greenlanders in their language and customs. Erhardt wrote to Bishop Johannes [John de Watteville] in 1750 offering his services in establishing a Labrador mission, saying that as "an old Greenland traveller," he had "an amazing affection for these countries, Indians and other barbarians, and it would be a source of the greatest joy if the Saviour would discover to me that he had chosen me and would make me fit for this service."

In 1752 three merchants of the London Moravian congregation fitted out the vessel *Hope* to trade with the Labrador Eskimos as a means of financing a voyage of reconnaissance along the then virtually unknown coast. Erhardt was appointed second in command of the ship and was to be in charge of the trade. Four Moravian Brethren went out in the ship as missionaries: George Golkowsky, John Christian Krum, Christian Frederick Post, and Matthew Kunz.

The Moravians left London on 18 May 1752

and first met Labrador Eskimos on 29 July, north of Hamilton Inlet. On 31 July they picked out a suitable site for a mission post, called it Nisbet's Harbour, and took possession of the land in the name of King George III. Nisbet's Harbour was probably in the region of modern Hopedale, about ten leagues south of Davis Inlet.

Erhardt immediately began a brisk barter trade with apparently friendly Eskimos for whalebone and seal skins. He found himself hampered by his limited knowledge of Eskimo and lamented: "I often wish I had the Stachs with me, for my little bit of Greenlandish does not go far." Meanwhile the ship's crew laboured to set up a prefabricated house brought from Europe, in case the missionaries should decide to winter in Labrador.

In early September, with the missionaries in their new home, the *Hope* sailed north to Davis Inlet for more trading before returning to England. At the mouth of the inlet Erhardt, with Captain John Madgshon and five crew members, left the ship with a boatload of goods to trade among the islands. The boat was never seen again. After waiting for two days, the remaining crew sailed the *Hope* back, reaching Nisbet's Harbour on 14 September. A search party set out in the missionaries' yawl, but was driven back by high winds. The missionaries now decided to return home since their help was needed to man the ship. They left supplies behind in case Erhardt and his companions somehow survived and should reach Nisbet's Harbour.

The following summer, the chief mate of the *Hope*, Elijah Goffe, went again to Labrador, found the mission house destroyed, and located the bodies of the missing men on a nearby island. After they left the ship, Erhardt and his party may have been delayed or detained by the Eskimos; they made their way back to Nisbet's Harbour, and were later murdered in the vicinity. There can be little doubt that they were killed by Eskimos: some of the murderers were actually pointed out to later missionaries. At this time the Eskimos made summer voyages to southern Labrador to trade with or plunder Europeans, as opportunity afforded. Erhardt's slight knowledge of Eskimo was probably insufficient for him to make clear to the natives the ultimate purpose of his mission. When the Eskimos encountered Erhardt's trading party in an isolated position, they simply took advantage of it as they had done with French and English traders in the past.

The idea of a Labrador mission did not die with Erhardt. A Moravian carpenter, Jens Haven*, was stirred by a strong desire to carry the Gospel to Erhardt's murderers. He took a leading part in the Moravian expeditions of the 1760s which led to the establishment of the first mission post in 1771. Haven and others of his colleagues were fluent in Eskimo and had nothing to do with the trade themselves. They were thus able to demonstrate convincingly that they were not as other Europeans, and so gain the confidence of the Eskimo people.

WILLIAM H. WHITELEY

Memorial University Library (St John's), Moravian missions, Labrador, Papers relating to the exploratory voyages, 1752–70 (mfm reel 4), pp.1–13. PAC, MG 17, D1, Diary of Kunz, Post, Krum and Golkowsky, May–November, 1752 (mfm 4–548). David Cranz, *The history of Greenland: including an account of the mission carried on by the United Brethren in that country, from the German of David Crantz; with a continuation to the present time, illustrative notes, and an appendix containing a sketch of the mission of the Brethren in Labrador* . . . (2v., London, 1820); *The Moravians in Labrador* (Edinburgh, 1833). J. W. Davey, *The fall of Torngak; or the Moravian mission on the coast of Labrador* (London, 1905). W. G. Gosling, *Labrador: its discovery, exploration, and development* (London, 1910). J. K. Hiller, "The foundation and the early years of the Moravian mission in Labrador, 1752–1805" (unpublished MA thesis, Memorial University of Newfoundland, St John's, 1967).

ESPAGNOLI. See SPAGNIOLINI

ESTOURMEL, CONSTANTIN-LOUIS D', naval officer; b. 1691, son of Louis d'Estourmel and Marie-Aimée de Hautefort de Montignac; d. 6 April 1765 in Paris, France.

Constantin-Louis d'Estourmel, who was a knight, then a commander of the order of Malta, belonged to an old family from Picardy. He joined the Marine as a midshipman at Brest on 30 April 1707 and enjoyed rapid advancement; he was promoted sub-lieutenant on 13 Feb. 1709 and lieutenant-commander on 1 Nov. 1712. Six years later he became a knight of the order of Saint-Louis, and on 17 March 1727 he was promoted captain. He participated in the two campaigns against the Barbary pirates in 1728 and in 1736–37. In 1740–41, commanding the *Parfaite* in the squadron sent to the West Indies, he took an active part in the combat with an English squadron off Cap Tiburon, Saint-Domingue (Hispaniola), on 18–19 Jan. 1741.

Promoted rear-admiral on 1 Jan. 1746, d'Estourmel was given command of the *Trident* in the squadron led by the Duc d'Anville [LA ROCHEFOUCAULD], which was outfitted at Brest that year to undertake offensive operations against the British possessions in Acadia and Newfoundland. After reaching the coasts of

Evison

Acadia in September 1746, the squadron was scattered by a strong gale. D'Estourmel gathered together five warships and most of the transports and entered the port of Chebucto (Halifax, N.S.) on 27 September, where he learned of the Duc d'Anville's death. On 29 September a council of war made him commander-in-chief; it also decided to attack Annapolis Royal. But, "either incapable of great deeds, or fearing failure, or because a misplaced delicacy kept him from asking someone to share with him a task for which he considered himself unsuited, finally despair, anxiety, and rage so possessed M. d'Estourmel, that during the night he attempted suicide . . . he was seized by a burning fever which quickly developed into a frenzy." Believing himself surrounded by enemies, he seriously wounded himself with his sword. On 30 September he handed his command over to rear-admiral La Jonquière [TAFFANEL] and returned to France. On 1 March 1747 the king permitted him to retire from the service, but to retain his pay. The only information we have about him after his retirement is that he died in Paris in 1765.

ÉTIENNE TAILLEMITE

AN, Marine, B², 302, f.197; B³, 255, f.394; B⁴, 43; 44; 50, ff.218–44; 59, ff.117–54; C¹, 161; C⁷, 101 (dossier Estourmel). La Chesnaye-Desbois et Badier, *Diction-naire de la noblesse* (3ᵉ éd.), VII, 556. Lacour-Gayet, *La marine militaire sous Louis XV* (1910), 140, 194–95. Troude, *Batailles navales de la France*, I, 289, 309.

EVISON (Everson, Eveson, Evinson), ROBERT, engineer at Fort Prince of Wales, Churchill (Man.); fl. 1746–49.

Robert Evison joined the Hudson's Bay Company on 26 March 1746 as "Chief Engineer" for three years at £100 *per annum*. He was sent to Churchill where his duties, under Governor Robert PILGRIM, were connected with the defence of the recently completed stone fort against attack from the French and with the training of the men in military discipline, "the use of small arms and also of great Guns." On his arrival in the summer of 1746 Captain Evison examined the powder magazine and, according to Pilgrim, pronounced it "a Compleat Pece of work & not much unlike the magazine in the Famous City of Tournay." The governor added, "I Sopose he has seen that having been as he says in Flanders." Evison inspected the battery that had been positioned on Cape Merry to protect the entrance to the Churchill River and he reported to London that the guns could be pointed against the fort. His recommendation to move the battery to the side of the river on which the fort stood was dis-

missed, however, and in 1747 he was sent exact instructions for correcting and improving the site.

Like Joseph ROBSON, who had been transferred to Churchill in 1746, Evison was a member of the council there. He can be identified as the engineer who according to Robson "knew very little of the theory of military architecture" and who became involved in Robson's disagreements with Pilgrim in 1746 and 1747. Before Robson left the country in 1747, however, Evison had become reconciled with the governor. Evison returned to England in 1749 and nothing further is known of him.

ALICE M. JOHNSON

[HBC Arch. A.1/37; A.6/7; A.11/13; A.16/10, Officers' and servants' ledger (Churchill) for 1749–69 (the previous ledger is missing). Evison's "Draught of the battery at Cape Merry" and "Draught of Prince of Wales's Fort," both dated 4 Oct. 1749, are in G.1/94 and 95 respectively. *See also*: Joseph Robson, *An account of six years residence in Hudson's-Bay, from 1733 to 1736, and 1744 to 1747 . . .* (London, 1752), 35–36. A.M.J.]

EYRE (Eyres, Ayres), WILLIAM, army officer, engineer; d. 1765.

Nothing is known of the early life of William Eyre except that he had considerable military experience in Europe before coming to North America. A practitioner engineer in 1744, Eyre fought in Scotland with the government forces against the Jacobite uprising of 1745. In 1747 he worked as engineer in ordinary defending Bergen op Zoom, Netherlands, and the next year was ranked as sub-engineer.

Eyre came to Virginia with Major-General Edward Braddock early in 1755 as captain in the 44th regiment, but was posted to the colony of New York before Braddock launched his ill-fated expedition against Fort Duquesne (Pittsburgh, Pa.). That same year Eyre acted as engineer and quartermaster in William Johnson*'s march against Fort Saint-Frédéric (Crown Point, N.Y.). He built palisaded Fort Edward (N.Y.), then joined Johnson's main force in time to fortify a campsite at the head of Lake George (Lac Saint-Sacrement) before General DIESKAU's forces attacked. Eyre's success in commanding the artillery in the ensuing battle won commendation from his superior, thanks from colonial governments, and a promotion to major. His professional influence upon colonial officers can be seen in his instructions to commandants of his forts. These were introductions to siege warfare and descriptions of the "honours of war" which the officer was to insist upon if he were defeated.

214

Eyre designed and supervised the building of Fort William Henry (also known as Fort George) at the head of Lake George in 1756. In March 1757 he successfully commanded its 500-man garrison against a force three times as large attacking under François-Pierre de Rigaud* de Vaudreuil. Governor Pierre de Rigaud* de Vaudreuil referred to Eyre as "an officer of consummate experience in the art of war."

Eyre was commissioned lieutenant-colonel 17 July 1758, nine days after he had been wounded while commanding the 44th at Fort Carillon (Ticonderoga, N.Y.). A year later he was made acting chief engineer and began building the new Fort Ticonderoga. General Jeffery Amherst* ordered Eyre to Fort Niagara (near Youngstown, N.Y.) that autumn "as I thought it the best thing I could do, for effectually securing that place." In the summer of 1760 Eyre rejoined Amherst's force in time to help with the taking of Fort Lévis (east of Prescott, Ont.) and the march on Montreal, where he spent the winter.

As the military focus shifted westward, Eyre returned to Fort Niagara in July 1761, where he participated in a conference with WABBICOM-MICOT and some other Mississaugas. The winter of 1761–62 he surveyed the flood damage at Fort Pitt, which had been built on the site of Fort Duquesne. As he was about to go to Niagara again in the fall of 1763, Eyre confessed "I am tired of the War in this Country." Even with eight years of continuous service, he could not obtain

leave. It was finally granted in the autumn of 1764, but Eyre was drowned near the English coast on his way home in 1765.

For all his European professionalism, Eyre was not oblivious to the realities of the frontier. One of the few British officers to criticize Amherst's Indian policy, Eyre described it as "Chastize them if they misbehave," an approach "so obviously Romantic and Contrary to common Reason." Eyre suggested withdrawal from the posts west of Niagara to reduce provocation, to enable the remaining posts to give one another better support in emergencies, and to weaken such Indian attacks as did occur by lengthening their routes. He argued that small trading parties, led by men bonded to trade fairly, would deal more equitably with the Indians than the forts did, and that any harm done to traders could be countered by an embargo against the offending tribe. Yet Eyre's real contribution was as a part of that military professionalism which triumphed in both contending armies, and then in the contest for Canada itself.

I. K. STEELE

PRO, WO 34/76, 34/85. *Correspondence of William Shirley* (Lincoln). *Johnson papers* (Sullivan *et al.*). Knox, *Historical journal* (Doughty). *Military affairs in North America, 1748–1765: selected documents from the Cumberland papers in Windsor Castle*, ed. S. M. Pargellis (New York, London, 1936). *NYCD* (O'Callaghan and Fernow), X.

F

FABER (Fabert), FRANÇOIS LEFEBVRE DUPLESSIS. *See* LEFEBVRE

FALAISE, MICHEL DE GANNES DE. *See* GANNES

FALKINGHAM, EDWARD, officer in the Royal Navy, governor of Newfoundland; b. *c.* 1683 in England; d. 18 Sept. 1757.

Edward Falkingham was promoted lieutenant in 1703 and received his first commission as captain in 1713. He commanded several ships on operations in the Baltic and Mediterranean, and, in command of the *Orford*, distinguished himself at the battle of Cape Passero, Sicily, in 1718.

In April 1732, with the command of the *Salisbury*, Falkingham received a commission as governor and commander-in-chief in Newfoundland. Arriving at Placentia on 13 July, he inspected the

garrison and noted, in a favourable report, that the soldiers did not meddle with the fishing industry. He found only one prison, at St John's, so that in winter the conveyance of prisoners was difficult, and he ordered the construction of prisons at Ferryland, Bonavista, and Carbonear, with smaller "roundhouses" in other parts. Falkingham demanded the enforcement of the laws relating to throwing ballast overboard, as disregard of them was causing serious damage in the harbours of Bonavista, Trinity, and Carbonear. He remarked that the fishing admirals were more concerned with furthering their own interests than with carrying out their duties efficiently. Most districts seemed to be well regulated since the appointment a few years before of local magistrates [*see* William KEEN].

On his return to England Falkingham commanded other ships but his career was uneventful. He left sea service in 1742 and was appointed resident commissioner of the navy at Port Mahón, Minorca. In 1745 he was moved to a similar post at Woolwich dockyard, London. His health began to fail in 1755 and he retired on a pension of £600 *per annum*; he died in 1757. His son Edward also became a captain in the navy.

MICHAEL GODFREY

PRO, Adm. 7/638, 107/2; CO 194/9, 0.136–47; 194/24, pp.63–74; 195/7, pp.266, 269–77; *CSP, Col.*, *1716–17*; *1732*; *1733*; *JTP*, *1728/29–1734*. Charnock, *Biographia navalis*, IV. D. A. Baugh, *British naval administration in the age of Walpole* (Princeton, N.J., 1965), 133. Lounsbury, *British fishery at Nfld*.

FAUTOUX, LÉON, merchant; b. in Bayonne, France, date unknown, to Georges Fautoux and Marie Meyracq (Mayrac); m. on 16 Jan. 1738 in Louisbourg, Île Royale (Cape Breton Island), Marie-Madeleine Lartigue, daughter of Joseph LARTIGUE; three of their children survived infancy; d. 14 Sept. 1748.

It was perhaps the long-standing interest of the town of Bayonne in the Atlantic fishery that brought Léon Fautoux to Louisbourg, where he was engaged in commerce as early as 1730. Fautoux was a commission agent, the typical merchant of an *entrepôt* such as Louisbourg, handling the cargoes of others and even buying and selling ships for them. The commission agent aspired to build up his capital and one day trade on his own account. Fautoux's alliance by marriage with an important local family in 1738 indicates that he had by then become a merchant of some consequence. This indication is confirmed by his establishing relations in November with Robert Dugard et Cie of Rouen, the firm which had placed François HAVY in Quebec in 1732.

Although it was not Fautoux's only business, he acted as a commission agent for his Rouen correspondents for the next six years. He received 13 major company cargoes and provided as many returns, their total value being more than 500,000 *livres*. French and Canadian cargoes supplied the local market; Canadian primary products together with the region's dried cod were exchanged for Caribbean cargoes. The company's trade at Louisbourg ended with the town's capture by New England forces in 1745 [*see* PEPPERRELL]. In an agreement signed at Rouen on 13 November the company gave a small settlement in money and merchandise to Fautoux, then a refugee in France, and abandoned to him all their debts at Louisbourg. "I would be delighted

if he could get something out of it," wrote one member. "This man is worthy of pity."

Fautoux returned to Île Royale where he is said to have been killed by the explosion of a bomb while he was on militia duty. His widow was a merchant at Louisbourg until its second capture by British forces in 1758. The family fortune twice destroyed, she and her daughter retired to France and were given pensions by the crown.

DALE MIQUELON

AN, 62 AQ, 35 (G. France à Robert Dugard, Paris, n.d.; G. France à R. Dugard, 3 déc. 1745); 41, 15e cargaison en retour, pièce 66 (Robert Dugard, son compte courant avec Fautoux, 1739–45); Section Outre-Mer, G¹, 407–9, 458–59, 466; G², 180, ff.374–81; 181, f.502; 202, no. 275; G³, 2037 (11 avril, 17 mai 1730); 2039/1 (26 juin, 21 oct. 1734); 2046/2 (9 sept. 1741, 28 juin, 17 juill., 7 oct., 21 nov., 7 déc. 1742); 2047 (18 oct. 1743). [Sources cited in the bibliography of François HAVY were also used in preparing this entry. D.M.]

FLAMAND (Flamant), GIRARD-GUILLAUME DEGUISE, *dit*. *See* DEGUISE

FLAME (Flemme). *See* PHLEM

FLEURIMONT, NICOLAS-JOSEPH DE NOYELLES DE. *See* NOYELLES

FLEURY, JEAN-BAPTISTE GUYART DE. *See* GUYART

FLEURY DE LA GORGENDIÈRE, JOSEPH DE, merchant, seigneur, agent-general in Canada for the Compagnie des Indes; b. 9 April 1676 at Quebec, son of Jacques-Alexis de Fleury* Deschambault and Marguerite de Chavigny de Berchereau; m. 11 May 1702, Claire, daughter of Louis Jolliet*; seven of their children lived to adulthood; d. 1 May 1755 at Quebec.

Although nothing is known of La Gorgendière's youth, in 1701 he was appointed by the Compagnie de la Colonie for a five-year term as fur-trader at Fort Frontenac (Kingston, Ont.), indicating early, and perhaps substantial, experience in the trade. Evidently his business was successful, for when the company abandoned the post he was appointed, on 23 Jan. 1706, as chief trader on the government's account, with an annual wage of 900 *livres*; in September of that year he was made subdelegate of the intendant at the fort. But, apparently wishing to make a greater fortune than his wages and place of residence allowed, he returned the following year to Quebec to become a merchant.

La Gorgendière at first dealt in seal oil, probably because his wife had inherited part of the seal fishery at Mingan. Despite altercations with Jacques de LAFONTAINE de Belcour and others, he continued to exploit this fishery during his entire active career. Soon, however, he acquired ships and developed trade connections with France and the West Indies, importing cloth and other necessities, and exporting furs, fish, and oil. These developments were undoubtedly aided by his family, for his elder brother Charles, later a director of the ill-fated Compagnie de l'Île St-Jean [see Robert-David Gotteville* de Belile], was already established as a banker and merchant at La Rochelle, Canada's chief port in France; another brother, Simon-Thomas de Fleury de La Janière, lived in Martinique. But extensive and varied as were La Gorgendière's mercantile activities – he may even have engaged in the Guinea slave trade – they depended on Canada's fur-based economy.

The government commonly auctioned the rights to the fur trade in certain areas, and because such concessions were often obtained by merchants, they would in turn be sub-let to one or more voyageurs who did the actual trading. In October 1724 La Gorgendière acquired a five-year concession to the post of Témiscamingue; however, only five months previously the governor, Philippe de Rigaud* de Vaudreuil, had granted part of this area to one Paul Guillet in return for a percentage of Guillet's trade. Conflict was inevitable. In the spring of 1725 Vaudreuil issued an ordinance preventing La Gorgendière and his associates from sending off their voyageurs. La Gorgendière in retaliation seized Guillet's furs. Only then did Vaudreuil permit their voyageurs to leave Montreal, but just for the limited area Guillet had traded in.

Thus hindered in his trade, La Gorgendière not only refused to pay his first year's rental, but demanded restitution of his losses. After Vaudreuil's death in October the intendant, Michel BÉGON, had Charles Le Moyne* de Longueuil, interim governor, rescind Vaudreuil's prohibitions and demand that La Gorgendière pay. When he refused, a new auction was held at which he agreed to pay 2,000 *livres* for the first year; because the fur market was glutted, he was granted the four remaining years of his concession at the reduced annual rent of 4,150 *livres*. His troubles were not, however, finished. In 1727 the Témiscamingue concession was annulled by royal decree, and subsequently granted through fur-trading licences (*congés*). Although La Gorgendière obtained two of these and illicitly arranged for a third, he again complained to the government of his losses and repeatedly asked

for indemnification. Not until 1731 was the matter closed, when he was discharged of 2,000 *livres* rent; but he still owed the government some 1,400 *livres* for trade goods.

On 25 May 1731, La Gorgendière was appointed agent-general in Canada for the Compagnie des Indes. The company's financial situation was precarious: a depressed market, which left too many poor quality furs rotting in Paris warehouses, and illicit trading with the English and Dutch had combined to undermine its economic strength. Earlier in the year the company had had to surrender all its trading privileges, save those with Canada. La Gorgendière, chosen, said the company's directors, for his "integrity, ability, competence, and experience," was given succinct instructions: cut costs, improve fur quality, stop illicit and illegal trading, and increase the company's trade. The directors' confidence was not misplaced: by 1734 the company moved to newly constructed quarters in Montreal and in 1745, having outgrown these, was relocated in the Château de Ramezay. La Gorgendière may have remained as agent-general as late as 1753; about this time his son Joseph de Fleury Deschambault, previously chief trader at Montreal, assumed the position.

Despite his position in the Compagnie des Indes, La Gorgendière continued to pursue his own ventures, including those in the fur trade. In common with many merchants, he also sold merchandise, munitions, and food to the government; indeed, in the 1730s, he was a principal cloth supplier. Again in common with many merchants, he acquired land.

On his father's death in 1715, La Gorgendière inherited a part of the seigneury at Deschambault. By 1720 he had purchased the remainder from his relatives, and he apparently then embarked on a series of efforts to attract settlers, beginning in 1721 when he asked for the creation of a parish in the seigneury and the appointment of a permanent parish priest. Not, however, until 1736 did he obtain another seigneury, when he was given a concession three leagues long by two deep on both sides of the Rivière Chaudière in the Nouvelle-Beauce region, contiguous with grants made simultaneously to his sons-in-law Thomas-Jacques TASCHEREAU and François-Pierre de Rigaud* de Vaudreuil. Their grants were conditional on their building, by 1739, a cart-road from the St Lawrence up the valley to the end of La Gorgendière's seigneury. Again, as with Deschambault, he seems to have energetically undertaken the seigneury's development; but in 1747 he exchanged it for Vaudreuil's concession, which was nearer the St Lawrence.

Fonville

Advancing age and the War of the Austrian Succession brought a decline in La Gorgendière's activities and fortunes; towards the end of his life he claimed he would have been a millionaire but for his losses during the war. His standing in the community is evident, however, in his holding of the positon of colonel of militia for about 20 years. La Gorgendière died 1 May 1755 at Quebec, and was buried there in the cathedral.

ANDREW RODGER

AN, Col., B, 43, ff.921–29, 930; 45, f.835; 48, ff.891–94, 908–9; 53, ff.507–8v; 54, f.409v; 65, f.413v; 66, f.249; C¹¹ᴬ, 45, pp.79–82, 185–86; 46, pp.189–90, 197–202; 47, pp.21, 37–48, 78–82, 100–2, 103–4, 105–6, 123–24, 130–32, 142–54, 238–43, 275–77; 49/2, pp.372–79, 384–86; 50, pp.110–14, 166–68; 52, pp.54–57; 56, pp.30, 52 (PAC transcripts); D²ᶜ, 57, f.37; E, 185 (dossier La Gorgendière). ANQ, Greffe de R.-C. Barolet, 5 janv. 1747, 28 mai 1757; Greffe de François Genaple de Bellefonds, 30 juill. 1707, 10 nov. 1708, 20 avril 1709; Greffe de Florent de La Cetière, 10 sept. 1716, 30 juill. 1719; NF, Coll. de pièces jud. et not., 497 1/2, 551 7/8, 581, 937, 2303, 2324, 3528; NF, Ord. int., 23 janv. 1706, 6 juill. 1710, 20 mai 1715, 1ᵉʳ avril 1730, 12 janv. 1735. "Procès-verbaux du procureur général Collet" (Caron), APQ *Rapport, 1921–22*, 361, 364. Bonnault, "Le Canada militaire," APQ *Rapport, 1949–51*, 269–71, 286. Le Jeune, *Dictionnaire*. Massicotte, "Répertoire des engagements pour l'Ouest," APQ *Rapport, 1929–30*, 207. François Daniel, *Histoire des grandes familles françaises du Canada . . .* (Montréal, 1867), 371–96. Nish, *Les bourgeois-gentilshommes*, 68, 164. Honorius Provost, *Sainte-Marie de la Nouvelle-Beauce; histoire religieuse* (Québec, 1967), 4–6. Trudel, *L'esclavage au Canada français, passim*. J.-B. Caouette, "Documents inédits sur Claire-Françoise Bissot, veuve de Louis Jolliet," *BRH*, XXII (1916), 336–38. Guy Frégault, "Un cadet de Gascogne: Philippe de Rigaud de Vaudreuil," *RHAF*, V (1950–51), 39–40. Marc Gaucher *et al.*, "Les engagés pour le Canada au XVIIIᵉ siècle," *RHAF*, XIII (1959–60), 249, 255, 420; XIV (1960–61), 101, 102, 107. J.-J. Lefebvre, "La famille Fleury d'Eschambault, de la Gorgendière," SGCF *Mémoires*, III (1948), 152–74. Victor Morin, "Les Ramezay et leur château," *Cahiers des Dix*, III (1938), 42–43. Cameron Nish, "La bourgeoisie et les mariages, 1729–1748," *RHAF*, XIX (1965–66), 594–95. P.-G. Roy, "Père de trente-deux enfants!" *BRH*, XLIX (1943), 244–50.

FONVILLE, PAUL BÉCART DE GRANVILLE ET DE. *See* BÉCART

FORBES (fforbes), JOHN, army officer; b. 5 Sept. 1707 (o.s.) in Edinburgh, Scotland, son of Elizabeth Graham and posthumous son of Lieutenant-Colonel John Forbes of Pittencrief, Fifeshire; d. unmarried 11 March 1759 in Philadelphia, Pennsylvania.

John Forbes began his military career, after abandoning a medical one, by purchasing a cornet's commission in the Scots Greys, dated 16 July 1735. At the battle of Fontenoy (Belgium) in May 1745 he served as captain and aide-de-camp to Sir James Campbell, commander of the British cavalry. The same year he was promoted major and lieutenant-colonel in the army, and saw service in the suppression of the 1745 rising in Scotland, including action at Culloden. Again in Flanders, he served as aide-de-camp to Sir John Ligonier in the disastrous defeat at Laffeldt, 2 July 1747. The following year he became quartermaster-general on the Duke of Cumberland's own staff, and in 1750 was made lieutenant-colonel in the Scots Greys.

Forbes came to Halifax in the summer of 1757, as colonel of the 17th Regiment of Foot and adjutant-general to Lord Loudoun [John Campbell], in which capacity he supervised the arrest of Lord Charles HAY. Forbes was promoted brigadier-general 28 December, and the following March, probably on Ligonier's recommendation, was given his first independent command, the expedition against Fort Duquesne (Pittsburgh, Pa.). This same assignment had lured a 2,500-man army under veteran Major-General Edward Braddock to disaster three years earlier.

Much of the spring and summer of 1758 Forbes spent in Philadelphia, gathering men and means for the expedition. Difficulties in obtaining colonial troops, supplies, and wagons, together with the onset of his own fatal illness, brought irritating delays. Intercolonial trade and land rivalries flared over the route: should Forbes follow Braddock's road, as favoured by the Virginians, or cut a new road west from Raystown (Bedford), Pennsylvania, as that colony urged? Distance, forage and supply considerations, and dangers of flooding at several points on Braddock's road led Forbes to choose the new road, and hold firmly to his decision. When finally gathered, his force consisted of about 5,000 colonial militia, 1,400 Montgomery's Highlanders, 400 Royal Americans, and 40 artillerymen.

Convinced that Braddock's supply system in 1755 had been so weak that a withdrawal would have been necessary even after victory, Forbes was determined to build a supply road marked by defensible stockades and forts no more than 40 miles apart. He claimed to have learned this strategy from Turpin de Crissé's *Essai sur l'art de la guerre* but must have come to appreciate it from experience in Scotland and as quartermaster-general in Flanders. Forbes' fortified road was a clear and eminently successful application of the theory. His attack was not to be a raid but a permanent conquest, and, as the Virginians feared, the road proved to be an enduring route to the Ohio country from Pennsylvania.

Supervision of road construction and forward positions fell to the able Colonel Henry Bouquet, as Forbes' "bloody flux" continued. By September, when he reported that his health was improved, Forbes could travel only in a litter slung between two horses. Without his order, first contact was made with the defenders of Fort Duquesne on 14 September when an 800-man advance party under Major James Grant was defeated. For ten weeks this victory seemed to the French to have secured the fort, and the garrison under François-Marie LE MARCHAND de Lignery was reduced for the winter.

Harassed by bad weather and the unending claims that Braddock's road would have been quicker, Forbes nevertheless made good use of time. Aside from Grant's adventure, no contact with Fort Duquesne was made until a conference between colonial officials and Indians at Easton, Pennsylvania, in October 1758, encouraged by Forbes, had won the neutrality of the Delawares, Shawnees, and Mingos. Although late autumn brought problems for the advancing English, it weakened the French by reducing cover for raiding parties and urging their remaining Indian allies to their winter hunting grounds. By outwaiting his opponents, Forbes achieved a bloodless conquest. On 24 November, when his force was within a day's march of the fort, the garrison blew it up and retreated. Forbes took possession of the smouldering site, which he renamed Pittsburgh, 193 miles and five months from the beginning of his road, and five days before the expiry of service of his colonial troops.

In fortifying his road, Forbes intended it to be defensible against Indian and Canadian raiding parties, and the raids attempted the following winter all failed. The road was safe, and so were the frontier settlements that had been terrorized by incursions from Fort Duquesne since Braddock's defeat. The Indians of the upper Ohio had made their peace with the victors. Forbes' caution, thoroughness, and tenacity had succeeded; he had delivered the upper Ohio to British control.

Forbes returned to Philadelphia in January 1759, bearing visible evidence of the progress of his illness. He died on 11 March, aged 51, and the colony afforded him a funeral befitting one of their own heroes. He was buried in the chancel of Christ Church, Philadelphia.

I. K. STEELE

BM, Add. MSS, 21630–60 (Bouquet papers). Henry E. Huntington Library (San Marino, Calif.), Abercromby papers, Loudoun papers. PRO, CO 5/50; WO 34/44, 34/76. Scottish Record Office (Edinburgh), Dalhousie Muniments, GD 45/2. [Henry Bouquet], *The papers of Col. Henry Bouquet, II: the Forbes expedition*, ed. S. K. Stevens *et al.* (Harrisburg, 1951). [John Forbes], *Writings of General John Forbes*, ed. A. P. James (Menasha, Wis., 1938). Knox, *Historical journal* (Doughty). *Pennsylvania Gazette* (Philadelphia), 15 March 1759. *DAB. DNB.* J. W. Fortescue, *History of the British army* (13v., London, 1899–1930), II. D. S. Freeman, *George Washington: a biography* (7v., New York, 1948–57), II. Gipson, *British empire before the American revolution*, VII. A. B. Hulbert, *Historic highways of America* (16v., Cleveland, Ohio, 1902–5), V. Parkman, *Montcalm and Wolfe*, II. Lancelot Turpin de Crissé, *Essai sur l'art de la guerre* (2v., Paris, 1754).

FORDYCE, JOHN, priest of the Church of England, missionary at St John's, Newfoundland; d. 1751 at Prince Frederick (Georgetown), South Carolina.

John Fordyce was ordained by the bishop of St David's, Pembrokeshire, Wales, in 1730. He was then sent to St John's, Newfoundland, where he was warmly welcomed by the residents, who had been without a missionary since the death of Jacob Rice* in 1728 and had petitioned the Society for the Propagation of the Gospel for a replacement. In September 1731 Fordyce obtained from the leading churchmen of St John's a certificate that he had behaved well and given attention to his duty, and handed this document to Governor Henry Osborn* to be forwarded to the bishop of London.

Within a month, however, Fordyce informed the bishop that he was having to contend with some "capricious and fractious people.". His situation was rendered uncomfortable by the failure of the residents to fulfil their promise to the SPG to provide him with a subscription of £45 and a quintal of merchantable fish for every shallop fishing from St John's Harbour. In November 1735 Fordyce appealed for assistance to the SPG, which decided to increase his grant "if the Lord Bishop of London is satisfied in his character." After some persuasion from the SPG, the defaulting residents agreed to carry out their promise if Fordyce would have a gallery built for them in the church. Fordyce had the gallery erected in 1734 at a cost of £30 10s. 6d. to himself, but "after all that, they paid him in such miserable fish as they would never have dared to give to anyone else." Their cash dues remained unpaid.

In 1735 Fordyce asked to be transferred to South Carolina, and the society agreed. He arrived in New York in July 1736 and took up residence soon afterwards in his new parish of Prince Frederick, South Carolina. Three years later his parishioners sent a testimonial to the SPG thanking it for sending him as their missionary. This happy relationship was not to last, however, for in 1741 Fordyce decided to "quit his ungrateful parish," when the vestry raised objections about his character. He moved for a while to the neighbouring parish of Prince George's (Winyaw). The parishioners of Prince Frederick, however, complained bitterly that they were without a missionary, and when they promised to elect Fordyce their minister, despite the vestry's objections, he returned to them. By October 1744 his health was failing and he asked to be allowed to return to England. Though permission was given the following spring he did not return, probably because of a serious outbreak of yellow fever around Prince Frederick. His wife died of consumption in 1748, and in October 1751 the wardens and vestry of Prince Frederick notified the bishop of London of Fordyce's death.

Fordyce seems to have been a deserving minister who was treated harshly in the two colonies in which he served. The bishop of London and the SPG dealt cautiously with his complaints, however; and his letters from St John's and Prince Frederick suggest that life might have been a bit easier for him if nature had endowed him with a greater degree of tact.

F. M. Buffett

USPG, A, 25, p.348; 26, pp.280–81; B, 7–2, p.249; 10, pp.146–48; 12, p.90, 92–93; 13, p.351; 16, p.134; 19, p.147; Journal of SPG, 6, pp.223–38. *The Fulham papers in the Lambeth palace library*, ed. W. W. Manross (Oxford, 1965), 5. Prowse, *History of Nfld*.

FORESTIER (Foretier, Fortier), **ANTOINE-BERTRAND**, master surgeon; b. 30 Aug. 1687 at Montreal, son of Antoine Forestier* and Marie-Madeleine Le Cavelier; m. 7 April 1712 at La Rochelle, France, to Élisabeth-Charlotte Camoin; buried 25 June 1742 at Montreal.

Antoine-Bertrand Forestier's father was surgeon to the Hôtel-Dieu after 1681, a churchwarden, a medical adviser to the courts, and surgeon-major to the colonial regular troops. Intendant Jacques Raudot* appointed him surgeon-major in 1708 "upon the good report . . . given by the superior of the Montreal hospital [Charlotte Gallard*], . . . Sieur [François Clairambault*] d'Aigremont, the naval commissary . . . and several other persons" and because Forestier was "the most experienced surgeon." Antoine-Bertrand and his brother Jean-Baptiste were also surgeons though they do not appear to

have enjoyed the same high reputation as their father. Even though Antoine-Bertrand served, like his father, as an expert for the court at Montreal, the authors of *Notes pour l'histoire de la médecine* exaggerate in saying that "he was the foremost surgeon in Montreal in his time." Pierre Puibareau and Joseph Istre were equally favoured.

A house brought Antoine-Bertrand Forestier to grief. In 1729 he began construction of a 26 by 34 foot, one-storey, stone house on Rue Notre-Dame, on a lot purchased from his sister Élisabeth and her husband Joseph Istre. While Forestier was in Quebec pursuing a debtor his wife made arrangements with various contractors. The Forestiers incurred a debt of 1,480 *livres* with Jean-Baptiste Boucher, *dit* Belleville to begin construction, another of 3,600 *livres* with Jacques and Louis Charly for building materials, and a further 600 with François Montfort and company to complete the house. Forestier's liabilities even exceeded these three accounts, and from 1731 to 1741 he was continually sued for debt. He often failed to answer the summons of the Conseil Supérieur when an appeal was being heard at Quebec. While fending off his creditors, Forestier sought recovery of small debts to himself for medicines and treatment but to no avail. His property was seized and the 5,500 *livres* realized from the judicial sale of his house in 1735 were divided among six creditors.

There were few heirs for what remained of his property when Forestier was buried seven years later in Montreal on 25 June 1742. Except for a daughter, whose history is not known, all his children had died young.

Peter N. Moogk

[Since Forestier used Antoine in preference to his baptismal name Bertrand, he is easily confused with his father and a number of other persons who bore the name Antoine Forestier (Fortier). The bibliography contains references to Antoine-Bertrand as well as to his father. p.n.m.]

AD, Charente-Maritime (La Rochelle), État civil, Notre-Dame de La Rochelle, 7 avril 1712. AN, Col., C¹¹ᴳ, 3, pp.491–92, 493–96, 499–501; 4, pp.62–63 (PAC transcripts). ANQ, NF, Coll. de pièces jud. et not., 328, 882; NF, Documents de la juridiction de Montréal, III, 4, 39v–40; VI, 113–14; VIII, 34v; X, 1ᵉʳ–8 oct. 1735. ANQ-M, Greffe de Bénigne Basset Des Lauriers, 3 nov. 1670; Greffe de Jacques David, 7 janv. 1720, 16 juill. 1723; Greffe de N.-A. Guillet de Chaumont, 24 avril 1732; Greffe de Claude Maugue, 6 oct. 1679, 16 juill. 1681; Greffe de J.-C. Raimbault, 10, 11 août, 21 sept., 6, 21 oct. 1729, 16 mars 1730; Documents divers, 2 janv., 13 juin 1728; 10 mars, 18, 23 juill. 1729; Registres des audiences, VII, 517, 531–32, 683v, 745,

752; XII, 932; Registre du bailliage, 1682–1687, f. 58. *Jug. et délib.*, III, 567–68; IV, 830, 893, 900. *L'île de Montréal en 1731* (A. Roy), 38, 75. P.-G. Roy, *Inv. jug. et délib., 1717–1760*, II, 85–86, 260, 315; III, 3, 34, 223–24; IV, 28, 47. Tanguay, *Dictionnaire*. M. E. Abbott, *History of medicine in the province of Quebec* (Toronto, 1931; McGill University pubs., VIII, no. 63, Montreal, 1932), 20. Ahern, *Notes pour l'histoire de la médecine*, 226–30.

FORGET, ANTOINE, tonsured cleric, schoolmaster; b. 19 Nov. 1672 at Reuilly (dept. of Indre), France; d. 21 Oct. 1749 at the seminary of Angers, France.

We know little of Antoine Forget's childhood and early studies. Living at Reuilly, where the Sulpicians enjoyed seigneurial rights, Forget probably benefited from the schools which the seigneurs put at the disposal of their *censitaires*. The same policy was observed by the Sulpicians of Montreal, who at the end of the 17th century urged their *confrères* in Paris to send them qualified teachers for the primary schools ("petites écoles") in Montreal. The seminary of Paris then decided to grant "a six-month bursary" to a candidate who would go to train, according to the methods advocated by Jean-Baptiste de La Salle, at the seminary for schoolmasters in the parish of Saint-Hippolyte in Paris. This seminary was run by Brother Nicolas Vuyart, one of the leading members of the new order of Brothers of the Christian Schools. Forget probably arrived at the seminary in October 1700 to correct certain faults and to aquire practices suitable for his role as an educator, in accordance with La Salle's recommendations in his *Conduite des Écoles chrétiennes*.

In April 1701 Antoine Forget was ready to leave for Canada; François Lechassier, superior of the seminary in Paris, then informed François Dollier* de Casson, superior in Montreal, that Forget was "capable of teaching children well and that he is known of long date to be of good morals." Armand Donay, who was to travel to New France with Forget, stated that the latter "taught school well and besides reading and writing he was good in arithmetic." Before his departure it was agreed that the schoolmaster should neither wear the cassock nor direct himself towards the priesthood; in addition he would not receive any salary and would be content with "being fed and clothed."

Forget arrived in Montreal in July 1701 and was soon after permitted by Dollier de Casson to wear the cassock. In February 1702 he asked Paris to send him books and school supplies such as a spelling-book, La Salle's *Instructions et prières pour la Sainte-Messe*, a handwritten collection of letters, a *civilité* (a manual of etiquette for children), a catechism, a psalter, etc. Thanks to these books, and by drawing inspiration from his training in Paris, Forget reformed the archaic methods of teaching used in Montreal's primary schools.

In 1703 he received, it seems, the minor orders, but he was still refused permission to receive the priesthood, on the pretext that he had not "enough education." He pursued his career thus until 1715, when, tired and ill, he returned to France to seek care and rest. The following year Forget tried to return to Montreal – Jacques TALBOT seems to have replaced him then – but the Sulpicians of Paris were opposed and sent him to Issy-les-Moulineaux (dept. of Hauts-de-Seine) to try him out. Two months later, on 17 May 1716, he was offered the direction of the school at Villeneuve-le-Roi (dept. of Val-de-Marne), but Forget refused stubbornly and the Sulpicians tried to get rid of him by offering him 300 *livres* and even suggesting to him that he "go into trade" to make a living. Forget replied that he "was not apt for that."

It cannot be stated with certainty that Antoine Forget ever lived at Villeneuve-le-Roi, but it is known that he left the seminary at Issy before 29 July 1718 for the seminary of Angers, where he was bursar. He died there on 21 Oct. 1749. Although he had received no salary he left the sum of 339 *livres*, which was distributed among his heirs, as much to ease their poverty as in recognition of the services rendered the seminary of Angers by Antoine Forget.

LOUIS-PHILIPPE AUDET

Archives du grand séminaire d'Angers (France), Registre des sépultures du séminaire, MSS, 8²⁹, f.2. Archives de la Compagnie de Saint-Sulpice (Paris), Lettres de M. de Tronson, XIV, 221, 240, 244, 252, 282f., 288, 291, 318, 355, 376, 410; Registre des assemblées du séminaire de Paris, I, 415, 683, 684, 685, 689, 693, 694, 704, 740; II, 524. Jean-Baptiste de La Salle, *Conduite des Écoles chrétiennes* (Avignon, 1720). Gauthier, *Sulpitiana*. Frère Maximin, *Les Écoles normales de saint Jean-Baptiste de La Salle* (Brussels, 1922), 34–39. Olivier Maurault, "Les origines de l'enseignement secondaire à Montréal," *Cahiers des Dix*, I (1936), 95–105. Yves Poutet, "Une institution franco-canadienne au XVIIIᵉ siècle : les écoles populaires de garçons à Montréal," *Revue d'histoire ecclésiastique* (Louvain), LIX (1964), 52–88 (this article provides some biographical information on Antoine Forget).

FORGET DUVERGER, JACQUES-FRANÇOIS, priest, missionary; originally from the diocese of Angers (dept. of Maine-et-Loire), France; d. after 1764 in France.

Fornel

Jacques-François Forget Duverger was ordained a priest in the spring of 1753. Shortly afterwards he was sent to the seminary of Quebec by the Séminaire des Missions Étrangères in Paris, which was intending to post him to the Sainte-Famille mission among the Tamaroas at Cahokia (East St Louis, Ill.). The superiors in Quebec were well satisfied with the new recruit, their colleagues in Paris writing the following year: "We are quite delighted that his character is agreeable to you and we bless the Lord for having preserved him in his favourable sentiments towards the missions; we are firmly convinced that they will be strengthened in his contact with you. Our kindest regards to this dear gentleman." When the letter, dated 28 April 1754, reached Quebec, Forget had already set out to join the Tamaroas. He had left on 22 April with Lieutenant Gaspard-Joseph Chaussegros* de Léry, who had been detailed to take a detachment of troops to Fort Detroit. The expedition reached its destination on 6 August, and Forget set off again on 3 September for his own post.

The Sainte-Famille mission consisted at that time of an Indian village and a small French establishment called Cahokia or Kaokia. Two missionaries were there already: Nicolas Laurent, the superior and the bishop of Quebec's vicar general, and Joseph Gagnon. Both died in 1759, and Forget was left alone. When the news of the cession of Canada reached him at the end of 1763, the unhappy missionary was panic-stricken. Convinced that the British would confiscate church property, he took it upon himself to sell to two traders in the region, Jean-Baptiste Lagrange and Pierre-Étienne Marafret Layssard, all the mission's belongings – the house, four square leagues of land, two mills, and even 12 black slaves – for 32,500 *livres*, a sum much below their real value. The contracts, which were signed on 5 Nov. 1763, stipulated that the buyers would pay in six annual instalments, due not to the Quebec seminary but to the seminary in Paris, for which the missionary claimed to have power of attorney. After this splendid achievement Forget fled to New Orleans, whence he sailed for France on 6 Feb. 1764.

Jacques-François Forget Duverger was severely condemned by his superiors, who quite rightly refused to ratify a sale made without authorization of any sort. In the autumn of 1764 Forget retired to Candé (dept. of Maine-et-Loire), France, and what became of him after that is not known. As for the buyers of the belongings of the Tamaroa mission, Lagrange and Layssard, the former died insolvent some time later and the other disappeared without leaving any

trace. Needless to say the seminaries of Quebec and Paris never received the least payment for the property disposed of by Forget. Steps were taken to obtain annulment of the transaction of 5 Nov. 1763, but they produced no results.

NOËL BAILLARGEON

ASQ, Lettres, M, 122–26; P, 122, 123; Missions, 20, 23, 25, 26, 30, 32–40; Polygraphie, XIX, 54; XXVI, 42; Séminaire, VIII, 28, 38; XI, 23–23b. [G.-J. Chaussegros de Léry], "Journal de Joseph-Gaspard Chaussegros de Léry, lieutenant des troupes, 1754–1755," APQ *Rapport, 1927–28*, 355–429. *JR* (Thwaites), LXX, 292; LXXI, 37. *Old Cahokia: a narrative and documents illustrating the first century of its history*, ed. J. F. McDermott (St Louis, Mo., 1949).

FORNEL, JOACHIM, priest, canon, promoter and then judge of the Officiality; b. 17 March 1697 at Quebec, son of Jean Fornel, merchant, and Anne-Thérèse Levasseur; d. sometime after 1753 in France.

Joachim, the older brother of the merchant Louis FORNEL, entered the Petit Séminaire of Quebec on 14 July 1712, "at 15 years of age," say the annals of the institution, as "a student in the fourth form." He received the tonsure from Bishop Saint-Vallier [La Croix*] on 4 Oct. 1717 and was ordained a priest on 18 Aug. 1720. On the day after his ordination Abbé Fornel was named parish priest at Ancienne-Lorette. He returned to Quebec in 1724 to join the chapter on 4 January, and on 14 October he became promoter of the Officiality of the diocese.

In 1726 Bishop Saint-Vallier, who obviously appreciated his abilities, gave him the task of restoring order in the parish of Louisbourg, Île Royale (Cape Breton Island), which was served by the Recollets of the province of Brittany [*see* Bénin Le Dorz*]. Although Fornel was invested with a vicar general's powers, the governor, Saint-Ovide [MONBETON], refused to receive him, since he was satisfied with the Recollets and considered the accusations against them unfounded. The bishop's delegate did not insist, but instead of returning to Quebec he decided to go to France. At the Séminaire des Missions Étrangères in Paris, where he stayed, Joachim Fornel made an excellent impression. The superiors consequently recommended to their *confrères* of the seminary of Quebec that they make use of him, as of other equally gifted Canadians, "to give lectures on religion" to the seminarists. "It is altogether likely," wrote the directors in Paris, "that they would be delighted to do so, since they retain a store of affection and gratitude for a house that has educated them and brought them up."

Joachim Fornel did indeed return to the seminary of Quebec in 1727, but it was to support a faction there against the new superior, Jean LYON de Saint-Ferréol. From that time on, until his final departure for France in 1742, the irrepressible canon would be involved in all the disputes which were to trouble the church of Quebec. He had, moreover, early given signs of his taste for wrangling. In 1719, when he was still only a minor cleric, he had ventured to send a letter to the Jansenist monk Georges-François Poulet*, whom the bishop had had expelled from the diocese the preceding year. In it he denounced and railed at the Jesuits: for their relentless opposition to the secular clergy (which they accused "of not declaring in favour of the constitution [*Unigenitus*]"), for the ethics "of the most abominable sort" which they allowed to be taught in their Quebec college, and for the little zeal they showed in "condemning after the Pope their Chinese superstitions." At the time of the redistribution of the parish districts in 1721 Fornel, who had just taken charge of Ancienne-Lorette, protested in a petition to the council of Marine the boundaries assigned to his parish. Indeed he had some reason to complain, and in 1727 his successor, Louis Chevalier, had the ruling modified.

Fornel's opposition to Lyon de Saint-Ferréol's superiorship as well as certain addresses he made to nuns against the bull *Unigenitus*, decidedly his pet aversion, attracted the attention of the authorities to him again. Governor Charles de BEAUHARNOIS, whom his early conduct had strongly antagonized, did not hesitate to write to the minister of Marine, Maurepas, that such a man was "a plague in a country as sound as this one." His was not, however, the feeling of the members of the chapter, for in 1728 they trusted Fornel to go to France and make known Bishop Saint-Vallier's death and the circumstances surrounding his burial [*see* Étienne Boullard*; Claude-Thomas Dupuy*; Eustache CHARTIER de Lotbinière], and also justify the chapter's conduct. Upon his return to Canada in 1729 Joachim Fornel threw himself anew into controversies, to the great despair of the coadjutor, Dosquet*. Together with his colleague Joseph-Thierry HAZEUR, he upheld the cause of the parish priests named for life by the chapter during the vacancy of the see of Quebec, whom the bishop was asking to resign; he rebelled against the dean, Louis Bertrand* de Latour, whose chief fault, in his eyes, was not being a Canadian. Fornel succeeded, however, only in bringing upon himself

from the minister a *lettre de cachet* in 1730 authorizing the coadjutor to send him to France to explain his actions. The threat produced an effect, and Bishop Dosquet esteemed it preferable not to use the court's order. "I am not surprised," noted the representative of the chapter in France, Pierre Hazeur* de L'Orme, to his brother Joseph-Thierry, "that M. Fornel is not as ardent as in the past. . . . He is careful of what he does and says. He is intelligent and will always do well when he wants to." Furthermore, at Maurepas's suggestion the bishop offered Fornel in 1732 the office of parish priest of Saint-Pierre-de-la-Rivière-du-Sud (Saint-Pierre-Montmagny), which he accepted. Two years later he was also serving as parish priest of Saint-Thomas (Montmagny). Fornel held these two offices until 1736, although he returned regularly to Quebec to attend the meetings of the chapter. His *confrères* still esteemed him and appointed him secretary of the chapter on 2 Sept. 1740 and judge of the Officiality on 28 November. They also seem to have had particular appreciation for his oratorical gift, since they had asked him to pronounce Bishop Saint-Vallier's funeral oration in January 1728, and he gave one for Bishop Lauberivière [Pourroy*] on 26 Aug. 1740. But a reading of these two laborious exercises tempts one, like Abbé de L'Isle-Dieu, to consider their author a "great talker" and "a man who writes volumes to say trifling things."

In 1742 three canons, Pierre de Gannes de Falaise, Jean-Baptiste GOSSELIN, and Joachim Fornel, asked permission of the chapter to go to France to recover their health. Fornel sailed in October of the following year, but without having taken leave of the dean or having obtained his exeat from Bishop Pontbriand [DUBREIL]. Deprived of his stipend, he was continually obliged to seek employment. In his discouragement he thought several times of returning to Canada, but each time sickness or war postponed his departure. Finally, at Bishop Pontbriand's request, he resigned himself to relinquishing his canonry on 24 April 1752; he was replaced by Pierre-Joseph RESCHE, against whom he had 11 years earlier led an intrigue over the succession to the office of parish priest of Château-Richer. In return he asked the chapter to grant him the title of honorary canon "as a veteran priest and a former canon of more than 25 years' standing." When the canons of Quebec had approved his request and decided "that it would be entered in the registry," Joachim Fornel thanked them for this gesture of kindness towards him in a letter of 13 April 1753. He never returned to Canada.

NOËL BAILLARGEON

Fornel

AAQ, 12 A, Registres d'insinuations B; 12 A, Registres d'insinuations C; 10 B, Registre des délibérations; 11 B, Correspondance, VIII, 42, 43; 1 CB, Vicaires généraux, I, 105; 1 W, Église du Canada, I. ASQ, Lettres, M, 52, 60; T, 60; MSS 2; Polygraphie, II, 24, 29; Registre B, 122–31; Séminaire, XIV, 5, no.7. BN, MSS, Fr., 20973, ff.133ff. "Lettres et mémoires de l'abbé de L'Isle-Dieu," APQ Rapport, 1935–36, 330, 331, 338, 339, 340, 370. Caron, "Inventaire de documents," APQ Rapport, 1940–41, 472; 1941–42. P.-G Roy, Inv. jug. et délib., 1717–1760, I, IV. Tanguay, Dictionnaire, I, 239. Gosselin, L'Église du Canada jusqu'à la conquête. P.-G. Roy, Toutes petites choses du régime français (2 sér., Québec, 1944) 2e sér., 58f. (Roy writes that Fornel died in France on 14 May 1769 but provides no source for the statement). Henri Têtu, "Le chapitre de la cathédrale de Québec et ses délégués en France," BRH, XIII (1907), 301, 302, 304; XIV (1908), 13, 14, 15, 19, 80, 145, 173, 174, 202; XV (1909), 14, 42, 69; XVI (1910), 141, 162, 324, 361.

FORNEL (Fournel), LOUIS (Jean-Louis), merchant and entrepreneur at Quebec, explorer, seigneur; baptized 20 Aug. 1698 at Quebec, son of Jean Fornel, merchant, and Anne-Thérèse Levasseur; m. 31 Dec. 1723 Marie-Anne Barbel*; seven of the 14 children born of their marriage survived infancy; d. 30 May 1745 at Quebec.

Judging from his position as an administrator of the Hôpital Général of Quebec, the elder Fornel had been a respected member of the community. The status of the family may further be measured by Louis Fornel's marriage to the daughter of Jacques Barbel*, a seigneur and the holder of important judicial appointments. Signatories to the marriage contract included Governor Rigaud* de Vaudreuil, Intendant Michel BÉGON, and many lesser government officials.

The colony's judicial records contain scattered references to Fornel's disputes with ship's captains and merchants concerning bills of exchange, items of cargo, and freight payments: evidence of his involvement to an indeterminable extent in maritime commerce. As did many Quebec City merchants, in the 1730s he turned his attention to the sealing industry of the Labrador coast, then a new and promising field of enterprise.

In 1737 he, François HAVY, and Jean LEFEBVRE acquired a two-thirds interest in an undeveloped sealing station at Chateau Bay on the Strait of Belle Isle from its concessionaire, Louis BAZIL, husband of his maternal cousin, Charlotte Duroy. Fornel, Havy, and Lefebvre provided the capital, including Bazil's one-third share, for what proved to be an unprofitable undertaking. As early as 1742, considering Bazil a drone, Fornel was beseeching the local authorities and Maurepas, minister of Marine, to

grant him the post upon expiration of Bazil's concession in 1745. He argued that using the post as an advance base "in order to attract the Eskimos, as a depot and place of refuge in case of need," he could explore and eventually develop the more remote Baie des Esquimaux (probably Hamilton Inlet). This development would help extend French trade to the Eskimos, whom he claimed he had already done much "to humanize" at Chateau Bay.

In 1744 the solvent partners offered alternately to surrender the post to Bazil in return for full payment of the sums owed them or to write off his debt in exchange for title to the concession. The intendant, Hocquart*, who favoured arbitration, temporized; and the colony's involvement in war in 1745 postponed decision indefinitely. In any case the lease expired in 1745.

Exploration of the Baie des Esquimaux, however, could not be put off. Louis Fornel was not the only Canadian to have designs on the bay, and with the spur of competition he undertook in 1743 the expedition he had hitherto declared impossible without the concession of Chateau Bay. Beyond Cape Charles, the last French outpost on the Labrador coast, waited the broad and promising estuary (Hamilton Inlet) of the Kessessakiou (Churchill) River.

Fornel left Quebec on 16 May 1743 as a passenger aboard the Expérience, owned by himself, Havy, and Lefebvre, on its regular run to Chateau Bay, and continued in a fishing schooner rented at Tierpon in Newfoundland. He landed at Baie des Esquimaux, which he renamed Baie Saint-Louis, on 11 July, taking possession of it, as he wrote, "in the name of the king, and the French nation." In fact, Intendant Hocquart thought in 1740 that the site was identical with the fief of Saint-Paul, conceded to Jean-Amador Godefroy* de Saint-Paul in 1706 and long since reunited to the king's domain.

On 25 August, Fornel arrived back at Quebec on the Expérience. His "Relation de la découverte . . . ." is a minor classic in Canadian exploration literature, combining an engaging adventure story with much close observation of the Eskimos. It includes a description of Fornel's experiment to disprove the myth that Eskimos subsisted on raw meat and salt water.

Fornel's request for the concession of Baie Saint-Louis, backed up by his claim of exploration, alarmed the leaseholder of the king's posts, François-Étienne CUGNET, and Hocquart. Both feared that a post at the bay would draw off the Indian trade of the domain; with good reason Fornel had avoided mention of Indians in his supplications, concentrating on the prospects of the seal hunt and development of trade with the Eskimos.

In 1749 a new intendant, François Bigot*, finally came to a decision regarding Chateau Bay and Baie Saint-Louis. The former was granted to a new concessionaire; and, Fornel having died in 1745, the latter was conceded to his widow, who had formed a company with Havy and Lefebvre.

Fornel was also interested in acquiring real estate, an almost invariably safe investment in the uncertain business world of the 18th century. In the 1740s he purchased suburban land, on La Canoterie road and in the seigneury of Notre-Dame-des-Anges, and a lot near his own house on the square in Lower Town. On 14 May 1741 he was granted a seigneury directly behind the seigneury of Neuville, not far from the city. He immediately began to develop this concession, which he named Bourg-Louis. With it came the title of seigneur and a social rank that the successful merchant coveted, indeed merited, but that only the ownership of land conferred.

Louis Fornel fell ill in March 1745 and died on 30 May at only 47 years of age. His commerce was continued for many years by his widow, who, a typical merchant's wife of her time, was well versed in business affairs. Fornel's life and career are not only the manifestation of a unique and dynamic personality, but also a recognizable reflection of his class, his country, and his era.

DALE MIQUELON

The "Relation de la découverte qu'a faite le sieur Louis Fornel en 1743 de la baie des Eskimaux nommée par les Sauvages Kessessakiou" is found in AN, Col., C¹¹ᴬ, 109, ff.272–86, and is published in APQ *Rapport*, *1920–21*, 60–75, and *Inv. de pièces du Labrador* (P.-G. Roy), II, 204–29.

AJQ, Registre d'état civil, Notre-Dame de Québec, 31 mai 1745. AN, Col., B, 81, f.271; C¹¹ᴬ, 81, ff.77, 85–89; 83, f.261; 85,f.21; 92, f.359; 96, f.101; 100, f.337; 101, f.398; E, 189 (dossier Fornel); Section Outre-Mer, G¹, 462, ff.339–40, 344, 346–49. ANQ, Greffe de C.-H. Du Laurent, 10 sept., 3 oct. 1736, 1ᵉʳ mai 1740, 21 juin, 3 oct. 1742, 15 mai, 27 sept. 1743; Greffe de J.-C. Louet, 26 août, 31 déc. 1723; AP, J.-L. Fournel, 1725–1742. PAC, MG 24, L3, pp.571, 602–3, 608–10. *Inv. de pièces du Labrador* (P.-G. Roy), I, 50, 51, 56, 60, 99, 151, 293; II, 88, 176, 181, 201, 229, 234, 235, 244, 249, 255, 256, 258, 259, 260. P.-G. Roy, *Inv. concessions*; *Inv. ins. Cons. souv.*; *Inv. ord. int.*

FORTIER. *See* FORESTIER

FOUCAULT, FRANÇOIS, seigneur, merchant, member of the Conseil Supérieur; b. 1690 in the diocese of Bayonne, France, son of Eusèbe

Foucault and Catherine Catalon; d. 19 July 1766 at Quebec.

Although he has been described as a distant relation of the Gascon counts of Foucault, François Foucault was probably from less illustrious ancestry. He was sent to New France in 1715, at age 25, to serve under the intendant, Michel BÉGON. On 11 Aug. 1715, Bégon appointed him king's storekeeper at Quebec, a post he held for the next 25 years. Indeed, in an administrative system characterized by the clientage of its high officials, he managed to retain the confidence of four successive intendants. He became a close friend of Bégon, who left him in charge of his extensive private interests when he returned to France in 1726. Claude-Thomas Dupuy*, Bégon's successor, prized his friendship only slightly less than his generous credit. In fact, when Dupuy departed from New France in 1728, he owed Foucault 27,082 *livres*. Gilles Hocquart*, intendant from 1729 to 1748, relied heavily on Foucault's administrative abilities and, in contrast to Dupuy, did much to extend the storekeeper's private interests. Although Foucault was not one of François Bigot*'s inner circle, Bigot did recommend his appointment, in 1752, as first councillor and keeper of the seals of the Conseil Supérieur, a promotion which afforded him the dubious honour of presiding over that body's final session on 28 April 1760.

It was Hocquart, however, who exerted the greatest influence on Foucault's career. Because Hocquart regarded him as one of the most trustworthy and capable officials in New France, his functions were gradually extended into several branches of the civil administration. For example, on 18 April 1733, he was appointed to the Conseil Supérieur. While conceding that Foucault possessed no legal training, Hocquart assured the minister that he would study law under the attorney general Louis-Guillaume VERRIER. In 1737 Foucault was named principal writer in reward for his frequent assistance in the financial affairs of the intendancy. He was also employed from time to time to investigate natural resources and agricultural conditions. Although he retired as king's storekeeper in October 1740, he took charge, almost immediately, of the financial management of the royal shipbuilding industry. In 1740 and again in 1747 he served in place of Jean-Victor Varin* de La Marre as controller of the Marine. For these heavy responsibilities he received the modest salary of 600 *livres* until 1742 and 900 *livres* thereafter, in addition to his stipend as a councillor and occasional bonuses. Hocquart's repeated attempts to increase his salary failed.

225

Foucault

Foucault's private affairs prospered, however, in other ways. For example, he operated his own store at Quebec conjointly with the king's store. It catered to the dry goods requirements of the town populace and involved him in the agricultural trade of the countryside. He also owned at least one small fishing vessel, the *Manoir*, and he chartered others in partnership with various Quebec merchants. He bought and sold land at Quebec and he even tried to manufacture fish glue for export to France. Like many other Quebec merchants, moreover, he consigned and sold imported goods to fur-traders, a branch of his commerce that was definitely enhanced by his marriage on 3 June 1718 to Catherine Sabourin, *dit* Chauniers (d. 1731), daughter of a Montreal merchant. His ties to the colony's economic élite were strengthened, moreover, by the marriage, in 1744, of his daughter Marie-Claude-Geneviève to Guillaume Guillimin*, a Quebec merchant and, like Foucault, a councillor. In 1747, two other daughters, Marie-Thérèse and Louise-Catherine married respectively Jean-André Lamaltie, a Quebec merchant whose father was a prominent Bordeaux merchant, and Joseph-Étienne NOUCHET, assessor to the Conseil Supérieur whose father JOSEPH was director of the Domaine d'Occident in Canada.

Foucault also benefited during the 1730s from Hocquart's policy of developing New France's industrial-agricultural economy by encouraging selective private initiatives. On 3 April 1733 he was granted a large seigneury, with two leagues of river frontage, on the Richelieu. He did little to improve it, however, and it was withdrawn in the massive reunification of undeveloped seigneuries in 1741, only to be returned to him, with an extra league of frontage added, on 1 May 1743. Another league of frontage was added on 1 Nov. 1744, making his one of the largest seigneuries in the colony. Foucault sold his house at Quebec for 2,650 *livres* to build a grist mill on his seigneury, and by 1746 he had settled six habitants on his land. By 1747 a presbytery had been constructed and, with Hocquart's assistance, Foucault persuaded Maurepas to pay for the establishment of a parish priest.

On 27 April 1735, Foucault had been granted the lower St Lawrence fishing post of Saint-Modet, in partnership with Nicolas-Gaspard BOUCAULT. They established a sedentary fishery, and in 1736 they obtained 200 barrels of porpoise oil. Although they were forced to withdraw in 1737, following a dispute with Pierre CONSTANTIN over legal title to Saint-Modet, they were granted a second post, Apetépy, on the Labrador coast, on 1 May 1738. Foucault also obtained Maurepas's approval, in 1739, to join François DAINE and Louis FORNEL in exploiting the fisheries of the remote Baie des Esquimaux (probably Hamilton Inlet).

Given these extensive private interests and the quasi-private nature of the financial administration in New France, it was almost inevitable that Foucault's affairs would become enmeshed with the king's. The revenues from both went into his private cash-box, and the accounting system in New France was notoriously inadequate. It was not always clear, for example, whether the large credits Foucault extended were from his own or from the king's revenues. Consequently, when a creditor proved insolvent, he could shift the loss from his own to the king's ledger. In Dupuy's case, however, the king refused to accept any liability and Foucault was forced to absorb a loss of more than 11,000 *livres*.

Other conflicts arose over Foucault's purchases of supplies at Quebec for the king's service. In 1740 Maurepas learned that he had paid two *livres* more than the market rate for wheat dispatched on the king's account to Martinique the previous year. He suspected that Foucault was favouring some friend or relative, but Hocquart's investigation revealed that he had actually purchased the wheat from himself under the fictitious name of Lemieux. Dealings like these may have played a part in Maurepas's decision to send a special agent, Jean de LAPORTE de Lalanne, to investigate New France's financial administration in 1740, and revelations about them may also have had something to do with Foucault's rather sudden retirement as king's storekeeper in 1740. Even so, he seems to have profited personally thereafter in his function as a buyer for the king's shipyard.

But despite his successful administrative career and extensive private interests, Foucault ended his days in post-conquest Canada as an enfeebled and poverty-stricken old man. The tenants had long since been driven from his seigneury on the Richelieu and his fishing enterprises had ceased altogether. In addition, the French defeat cut him off from the 600-*livre* pension he had enjoyed since his retirement as principal writer in April 1751, and his salary as first councillor was discontinued in January 1761. He was left with his store at Quebec and 875 *livres* per year from the sale of his house in 1758. Though anxious to join his daughter Marie-Thérèse in France, he was unable to sell his store to an Englishman, even after borrowing 5,100 *livres* to refit it as a house. Obliged to remain in Canada, he received infrequent news of his son Nicolas-Denis, who acted as a controller of the

Marine in Louisiana after 1763. In 1764 he made a final futile request for the restoration of his pension, describing "the most dismal situation to which I am reduced; at 75 years of age with no resources and burdened by infirmities which put me in dire need. . . ." He died two years later, a pathetic victim of France's expulsion from North America.

DONALD J. HORTON

AN, Col., B, 61–74; C[11A], 51–85; E, 190 (dossier Foucault), 253 (dossier Lanoullier de Boisclerc); F[1A], 28, 30, 31 (PAC transcripts). ANQ, AP, Perrault, l'aîné. ASQ, Lettres, P, 97, 97[b]. *Documents relating to Canadian currency during the French period* (Shortt), II, 755, 855. Le Jeune, *Dictionnaire*, I, 642–43. A. Roy, *Inv. greffes not.*, X, 171, 173; XII, 88; XVI, 148; XVIII, 90, 313, 326. P.-G. Roy, *Inv. concessions*, IV, 247–49; *Inv. jug. et délib.*, *1717–1760*, I–V. Dubé, *Claude-Thomas Dupuy*, 273, 276, 293, 296–300. J.-N. Fauteux, *Essai sur l'industrie*, II, 147–48, 433–34, 495. Nish, *Les bourgeois-gentilshommes*, 68, 110, 140, 163, 177. P.-G. Roy "La famille Foucault," *BRH*, XXI (1915), 369–79.

FOUCAULT, SIMON (baptized **Pierre**), Recollet, missionary; b. and baptized 3 March 1699 at Quebec, son of François Foucault, a merchant, and Catherine Nafrechoux; d. 6 July 1744 at Montreal.

Pierre Foucault entered the Petit Séminaire of Quebec in 1712, when he was 13. He left it two years later and continued his studies at the Jesuit college. Around 1719 he took his vows with the Recollets of Quebec under the name of Brother Simon, and on 18 Dec. 1723 he was ordained a priest by Bishop Saint-Vallier [La Croix*]; he had received the tonsure, minor orders, and the subdiaconate on the preceding 30 November, and the diaconate on 5 December.

In the autumn of 1724 Father Simon began serving the parishes of Notre-Dame-de-Bon-Secours (L'Islet) and Cap-Saint-Ignace; on occasion he exercised his ministry at Île aux Grues and Saint-Thomas-de-Montmagny. He remained in this region until 1741. In the first year of his ministry a conflict arose between him and his parishioners: the latter refused to finish the presbytery at Cap-Saint-Ignace. The intendant, BÉGON, therefore issued an order on 1 Aug. 1725, constraining the parishioners to sheathe the walls and roof of the presbytery with solid boards.

During the 17 years he spent on the south shore of the St Lawrence Father Simon acted as notary and the intendant's delegate in addition to carrying out his religious duties. In the absence of a notary he drew up several marriage contracts, which were ratified by the provost court of Quebec. Moreover, the intendants delegated him to arbitrate conflicts which arose among his parishioners. By his ordinance of 6 April 1740 Gilles Hocquart* confirmed the Recollet's good judgement in the lawsuit between Philippe Bernier and François Caron, habitants of the parish of Saint-Ignace.

In 1741 Father Simon was recalled to Quebec and was replaced by Abbé Joseph-Romain Dolbec, who had been ordained not long before. The following year he went to the Montreal convent; he served on occasion the parishes of Saint-Antoine, Longueuil, and Sainte-Famille, Boucherville, and carried on his ministry at the Hôpital Général of Montreal. He died at the Hôtel-Dieu of Montreal on 6 July 1744 and was buried the same day in his convent.

MICHEL PAQUIN

Archives des Franciscains (Montréal), Dossier Simon Foucault. Caron, "Inventaire de documents," APQ *Rapport, 1941–42*, 223, 238. P.-G. Roy, *Inv. coll. pièces jud. et not.*, I, 214, 216; *Inv. ins. Prév. Québec*, I, 125, 149, 272, 278; II, 5, 57; *Inv. ord. int.*, I, 277; II, 58, 290, 298; III, 96; "La famille Foucault," *BRH*, XXI (1915), 369–79.

FOUCHER, FRANÇOIS, merchant, king's attorney; b. 1699 in the marquisate of Maillebois, diocese of Chartres, France; son of Jacques Foucher, a king's councillor and salt-tax collector, and Charlotte-Élisabeth Goubert; d. 1770 in France.

François Foucher came to Canada in 1722. In 1723 he was housed in the intendant's palace where he was employed as Michel BÉGON's secretary. A document dated 1724 describes him as also a "writer in the office of the intendant." During the 1720s, moreover, he invested privately in the fur trade and in the lower St Lawrence fisheries. These investments were no doubt enhanced by his marriage, in 1724, to Marie-Bernadine Lebé, daughter of a prominent Montreal merchant and fur-trader. On 29 April 1727, Foucher received *lettres de provisions* for the post of king's attorney at Montreal and the Conseil Supérieur registered them on 15 Sept. 1727. He did go to Montreal in 1728, but he soon returned to Quebec where he took advantage of the confusion created by Claude-Thomas Dupuy*'s recall to France to treat his position as a sinecure. When Dupuy's successor, Gilles Hocquart*, ordered him in 1729 to take up his duties, he stated that he would rather lose his salary and remain at Quebec where his private affairs required his presence. He changed his mind, however, when Hocquart informed him that he would lose his office as well as the salary attached to it. After delaying for as long as he could, he went finally to live at Montreal in 1731.

It is easy to understand why Foucher was reluctant to perform the functions of king's attorney. They were demanding, especially at Montreal where there was only one judge in 1731 and where the scarcity of seigneurial courts in the surrounding countryside threw even more of a burden on the king's court. In addition to preparing civil cases, the king's attorney was responsible for the elaborate investigative and interrogative procedures that were a key feature of the inquisitorial criminal law system. He was also charged, as numerous notarial entries testify, with locating good homes for and overseeing the care of illegitimate children, who were treated as wards of the state in New France until the age of 18. In a frontier town, this in itself could be a burdensome task.

Foucher, furthermore, possessed little or no legal training, a fact too often apparent, according to Hocquart, in the inaccurate and unprofessional legal processes drawn up at Montreal during the 1730s. Hocquart had his enthusiasm well in hand, therefore, when he described Foucher, on 27 Oct. 1732, as "30 years of age, a mediocre individual . . . will become really useful if he continues to apply himself." He applied himself too well, however, for the comfort of the councillors who reprimanded him on several occasions for overstepping his authority. Hocquart was obliged to do the same in 1742, after the judge at Montreal, Jacques-Joseph GUITON de Monrepos, accused Foucher of encroaching on his prerogatives. On balance, Foucher seems to have been a hard working, but poorly trained and overly aggressive crown official.

The evidence pertaining to his private affairs at Montreal suggests that he was also an unbending and, at times, unscrupulous businessman. During the 1730s and 1740s he sold and advanced merchandise on credit to Montreal merchants and hired voyageurs to trade for him in the west. Contracts involving sums up to 9,500 *livres* appear under his name in the notarial records. He obtained his trade goods from merchants at La Rochelle. In 1734, Jean Butler, a merchant of that port, sent an agent to Canada to collect a large debt owed him by Foucher. The latter refused to pay, however, on the rather shabby pretext that their contract had not been properly registered. When Maurepas, the minister of Marine, heard about this refusal, he wrote Hocquart demanding that he collect the debt and adding that "if the Sr Foucher is no fairer in matters that affect the public than in this one it appears it would not do

to keep him in his position." Had this view been popularly known, Maurepas would undoubtedly have received strong support for it from the Canadian merchants, officers, and even close relatives with whom Foucher had numerous and bitter court battles.

Foucher retained his post, however, for some 31 years, and in 1753 he persuaded Intendant Bigot* to appoint his son François, who had studied law under the attorney general, Louis-Guillaume VERRIER, as his substitute whenever he was away from Montreal. Although the danger of a backlog of legal business accumulating was the reason he gave, it was also true that much of his energy from that time on was devoted to the preservation of his children's inheritance in the Labrador fisheries. That inheritance stemmed from his second marriage, in 1728, to Marie-Joseph, daughter of Augustin Le Gardeur* de Courtemanche, who bore him 13 children, five of whom survived her death in 1753. Through her they were entitled to a one-sixth share in the fishery of the Baie de Phélypeaux (Baie de Brador, Que.), one of the richest in New France, but legal entanglements involving their co-proprietor, François MARTEL de Brouague, led to their receiving a cash settlement instead. Soon after, in 1758, Foucher elected to return to France, leaving François as king's attorney at Montreal and another son, Charles, known as Foucher de Labrador, an officer in the colonial regular troops. Both sons fled the colony after the conquest and continued their career in Martinique. Nothing is known of Foucher's final years in France except that he died there in 1770.

DONALD J. HORTON

AN, Col., B, 61; C¹¹ᴬ, 53, 81, 84; E, 43 (dossier Bouat), 190 (dossier Foucher). A. Roy, *Inv. greffes not.*, X, 166, 172, 173, 177; XII, 6, 17, 28; XVI, 144, 159, 161, 166, 171. P.-G. Roy, *Inv. jug. et délib., 1717–1760*, I, 332; II, 121, 238, 244–45, 259; III, 19, 21, 22, 81, 129, 137, 178; IV, 151–52, 193, 204, 246; V, 223, 282. "La famille Foucher de Labrador," *BRH*, XL (1934), 250–52. P.-G. Roy, "Les secrétaires des gouverneurs et intendants de la Nouvelle-France," *BRH*, XLI (1935), 99.

FOURNEL. *See* FORNEL

FRANCHEVILLE, THÉRÈSE POULIN DE. *See* COUAGNE

FRANQUET, LOUIS, army officer, military engineer; baptized 11 June 1697 at Condé (Condé-sur-l'Escaut, dept. of Nord), France, son of Jean-Baptiste Franquet and Marie-Marguerite de Romby; d. 12 April 1768 at Condé.

Louis Franquet was commissioned in the army at the age of 12, and from 1709 to 1720 he served in the infantry regiments of Franclieu, Miroménil, and Piémont. In 1720 he was admitted into the engineer corps, serving in it with distinction in Europe for the next 30 years. After participating in the Italian campaigns of the War of the Polish Succession from 1733 to 1736, he was made chief engineer at Condé in 1738. Three years later he was awarded the cross of Saint-Louis, and from 1742 to 1748 he took part in campaigns of the War of the Austrian Succession in Germany and the Netherlands. Promoted lieutenant-colonel in 1747, he was wounded the same year at the siege of Bergen op Zoom. In 1750, when he was chief engineer at Saint-Omer, the director of the Bureau of Fortifications, Noël de Régemortes, asked him to go to Île Royale (Cape Breton Island) to examine the defences of the colony and recommend the works necessary to put Louisbourg and other places in a state of readiness against attack. He was then almost 53 years of age.

Although Franquet came out that year aboard the *Mutine* on the understanding he would observe, report, and then return to his duties in France, he actually remained for eight years. Arriving at Louisbourg on 9 Aug. 1750, Franquet examined buildings and fortifications; prepared maps, plans, and sections; and undertook experiments to determine the causes of structural deterioration. He began sending preliminary reports to France in October. In 1751 he toured the remainder of Île Royale, as well as Île Saint-Jean (Prince Edward Island), and Baie-Verte and Fort Beauséjour (N.B.); completed many plans and detailed reports on the Louisbourg fortifications; and recommended required works. In the same year he was promoted colonel. In 1752 and 1753, his original assignment modified, he toured Canada in summer and winter, examining fortifications and buildings in Quebec, Trois-Rivières, Montreal, and other towns and forts, and, incidentally, observing virtually every facet of Canadian life. He sailed for France in the autumn of 1753, and returned to Louisbourg the following spring, not as commandant as he had requested, but with the rank of army brigadier, the title of director of fortifications for the whole of New France, and a special pension for his services in the colony.

The next four years were spent in preparing for the expected British attack on Louisbourg: sending plans to France for approval, repairing and rebuilding the fortifications, housing the battalions of regular troops dispatched from France to strengthen the garrison, and directing the work of the various engineers who were sent to assist him. Until 1753, Franquet had the services of Pierre-Jérôme BOUCHER, whose death that year was a great loss to him. In 1752 the court had sent him de Breçon, a member of the engineer corps with little experience but with some influence in high places. He and the sons who assisted him returned to France in 1754, leaving behind them an impression of mediocrity. Two able and experienced officers came out in 1755: François-Claude-Victor GRILLOT de Poilly and Nicolas Sarrebource* de Pontleroy. In 1757, on Franquet's recommendation, the latter succeeded Gaspard-Joseph CHAUSSEGROS de Léry as chief engineer for Canada and left Louisbourg in September of that year. The former remained with Franquet until the surrender of Louisbourg in 1758, along with Michel de Couagne* (son of Jean-Baptiste de Couagne*) and two other engineers.

The most important of Franquet's responsibilities was the defence of Louisbourg. It is not easy to assess the value of the measures he recommended and undertook, since the issue was decided finally, not by the classic defence of permanent fortifications in the European manner, but by naval power. Jean-Louis de Raymond*, governor of Île Royale from 1751 to 1753, favoured a large number of coastal redoubts. It is curious that a career officer of the regular army with no colonial experience should have advocated great reliance upon field works, which were more common in North America than permanent masonry structures, but Raymond feared a British landing might come at any convenient point on the island and he wished to meet it where it occurred, keeping the enemy away from the fortress as long as possible. Franquet vigorously opposed the scheme as an undesirable dispersal of funds, labour, and military force. He insisted on strengthening the fortress (with some field works nearby), and it was his views which prevailed. Raymond, after his recall, continued to "lobby" at court, but to no avail. It is distinctly possible, however, that some modified form of his proposal would have favoured the French defence more than Franquet's did, and at less cost.

Franquet has been accused by J. S. McLennan* of lethargy in construction before 1755. But it had little to do with his failure to accomplish much actual work. Only in 1754 did the court decide not to let a construction contract but to conduct work through its own officers. Franquet had been travelling since 1751 and until 1755 he faced a shortage of competent assistance. The illness cited by McLennan for this period is one

Franquet

which afflicted the engineer in 1758, not necessarily earlier. Certainly the British blockades from 1755 on provided an added spur to activity, but about 108,500 *livres* had already been spent in 1754 on construction, compared to only 38,000 in the previous year. In 1755 the court approved 120,000 *livres* for fortifications. It sent two battalions of regulars, who were available to Franquet as labour, but left to him the task of housing them. Officers expected the sort of barrack furniture they had had in France; battalion commanders were to have houses. For months Franquet tried to satisfy the demands of these officers, who had been promised "they would lack nothing." He provided them with over 8,000 *livres'* worth of furnishings but they constantly clamoured for more and their relations with Franquet deteriorated. These problems diverted attention from the fortifications, with the result that emergency work, such as gun-platforms, took priority over new construction of permanent features. Nevertheless, Machault, the minister of Marine, was satisfied with the work done in 1755. In 1756 about 267,000 *livres* were devoted to construction; in 1757, some 207,000. Repairs and alterations were effected to most parts of the fortifications and virtually every public building. It is worth noting that when the British besieged Louisbourg in 1758, the defenders were starved into submission before the fortress was taken, in spite of the breaches in the walls.

Franquet expected in November 1757 that the British attack would come the following spring. His requests for reinforcements were only partially filled. He and his engineers had devoted much of their time and resources to the field defences designed to repel landings. To the east and west of Louisbourg, along the coast, batteries and trenches were built: at Pointe à la Croix (Lighthouse Point), at Anse à Gautier (Landing Cove), at Anse du Grand Lorembec (Big Lorraine), at Pointe Platte (Simon Point), and at Anse de la Cormorandière (Kennington Cove). These fieldworks were not especially effective in delaying the British advance in 1758, but the fault was not so much in their construction as in the conduct of the defence. When the siege was upon him, Franquet's health was "upset by scurvy and a threat of dropsy accompanied by double tertian ague, for more than two months. . . ." His legs were so swollen that he could hardly move; however, he wrote, "I go . . . with every alert to the covert-way and on the rampart, and I direct the engineers from my room, on all the works devised every day for the defence of the place." According to others, the illness was more debilitating than Franquet allowed. As Grillot de

Poilly wrote, "the chief engineer was a man of war, loving good (all his actions were directed to that end), a gentleman and a good citizen; but unfortunately an illness which undermined his health had so weakened the body that the spirit of the man was lost, he only had moments."

The state of the Louisbourg defences was such by 24 July 1758 that some officers favoured an honourable surrender. Others were for resistance to the end. The fortifications were inspected that day by the governor, Drucour [BOSCHENRY], Franquet, and Mathieu-Henri Marchant* de La Houlière, the commander of the land forces. Franquet alone refused to consider that the breaching of the walls had reached a stage where a full-scale assault was possible. In a report to the governor the following day he insisted that the covered way must be taken before there should be any surrender and, following his advice, Drucour decided on continued resistance. By the evening of the 25th, however, a breach in the covered way had been made, and the effectiveness of the fortifications continued to deteriorate. At a council of war on the 26th, therefore, it was decided to ask the British for terms. The harshness of Jeffery Amherst*'s demands – that the garrison should surrender without the honours of war – persuaded the council to fight on. But after an impassioned appeal by the financial commissary, Jacques Prévost* de La Croix, on behalf of the bombarded and starved civilian population, Drucour decided to surrender. Angry officers said resistance should have been continued to the end, once it had been decided not to seek a conditional surrender on the 24th. Some of them blamed Franquet, because it had been his views that had forestalled the earlier settlement on more honourable terms. Franquet replied that he had followed the directives of the court in constant cooperation with Drucour, and that whenever he had gained respite from his painful ailments he had studied the problems and offered the governor his advice.

Returning to France in October, Franquet appears to have remained on the payroll of the engineer corps at least for another two years, but not to have been very active during that time. He was concerned that criticisms of his work, particularly by Jean MASCLE de Saint-Julhien, lieutenant-colonel in the Régiment d'Artois at Louisbourg, might have damaged his reputation at court. In 1759 he appealed for the continuance of a pension of 1,500 *livres* paid him since 1754 by the ministry of Marine, pointing out that his zeal in its service, as well as in that of the war ministry, had always exceeded the normal call of duty, in spite of what his "enemies" had been saying.

In 1761 he was still justifying his conduct in the siege of Louisbourg. It is likely that he lived in retirement at the family home in Condé until his death at the age of 70.

Franquet is remembered today chiefly for his reports of 1751, 1752, and 1753, his many maps and plans, and his contribution to the building of the original Louisbourg. Valuable also are his frequent letters to Régemortes, in whom he confided a great deal, and his accounts of the second siege of Louisbourg. The reports have been published: on his travels of 1751 in the Gulf of St Lawrence region (1924) and on his tour of Canada during 1752 and 1753 (1889). Franquet was an astute observer not only of fortifications but also of economic conditions, natural resources, demography, and human character. His writings serve as a useful introduction to Canadian society in the 1750s. They are so voluminous that only a few of his observations can be mentioned here.

Franquet believed that Île Saint-Jean and Canada were capable of much greater agricultural productivity. The soil was fertile and some areas had been occupied for almost 150 years. Settlement on agricultural land must be stimulated by greater government incentives; dishonest marketing practices must be eradicated by strict government controls; prices must be regulated; accurate records of yield and productivity must be kept at the parish level; the government must in good years withhold emergency stocks of grain for the years of famine.

He thought the Saint-Maurice ironworks, where he said the iron was superior in quality to that of Spain (one of France's chief suppliers), required an experienced specialist from France as director. He also recommended improved accounting practices. In his own field of construction, Franquet sought to bring to Louisbourg Flemish brickmakers and limeburners who would know how to use Cape Breton coal (hitherto unexploited in those trades), as well as miners who knew how to use specialized tools for extracting hard stone from quarries.

Franquet was particularly interested in the manners and customs of the Indians, Acadians, and Canadians. His descriptions of Indians were confined chiefly to the acculturated families living in villages near the Canadian settlements. He comments at some length on appearance (including dress) and on feasts, dances, and musical instruments. Acadians, he wrote, were strong and healthy enough for hard work on the land, but lazy, since subsistence farming satisfied them. In religion they were zealous to the point of superstition. Canadians were distinguished by their independent spirit and their stubbornness.

Almost everyone was married (wrote the 55-year-old bachelor) whether he could afford it or not, and almost everyone had a horse of his own – something unknown in France. Entertaining tended to be lavish, and not only at the table of François Bigot*; even the governor of Trois-Rivières could entertain in a manner worthy of "the best provinces of France." The education that girls were receiving from the nuns gave them "airs" entirely unsuited to the "peasant" existence they would be required to lead. It was shocking that officers generally put their business interests ahead of their service to the king.

Although these reflections are of historical interest, the court of the 1750s paid little attention to them. It deferred to Franquet, however, in matters related to his specialty, military engineering. He was once overruled on a matter of detail by the strategists BARRIN de La Galissonière and Adrien-Maurice de Noailles, but his views always prevailed over such persons as the Comte de Raymond and Chaussegros de Léry. The last two, along with Saint-Julhien and some other officers who took part in the second siege of Louisbourg, seem to have disliked Franquet, but Drucour and Prévost had nothing but praise for his spirit of cooperation. Drucour wrote in 1755, "It gives me great satisfaction to see in charge of the works of this place a person who combines as he does the talents of his profession and the harmony which must prevail if they are to be pushed forward." Franquet was politically astute and carefully cultivated people at court. In his frequent letters to Régemortes, he always asked to be remembered to members of his chief's family, to whom he often sent exotic gifts; he was always ready, too, with notes of congratulation for prominent officials who had received new appointments. He understood the extent to which influence was the politics of the 18th-century French monarchy.

F. J. THORPE

[The manuscript version of Franquet's account of his 1751 voyage is in AN, Col., C¹¹C, 9, ff.143–74. It has been published under the title "Le voyage de Franquet aux îles Royale et Saint-Jean," APQ *Rapport, 1923–24*, 111–40. The 1752–53 journal has been published as "Voyages et mémoires sur le Canada par Franquet," Institut Canadien de Québec, *Annuaire*, 13 (1889), 31–240. The majority of Franquet's original maps and plans are to be found in AN, Col., C¹¹A, 126; Section Outre-Mer, Dépôt des fortifications des colonies, Am. Sept., nos.225–37; CTG, Archives, art.14. Copies of many of these maps may be found in PAC, National Map Collection. F.J.T.]

AD, Nord (Lille), État civil, Condé-sur-l'Escaut, 11 juin 1697, 12 avril 1768. AN, Col., B, 91, 93, 95, 97, 99,

100, 101, 103, 105, 107; C¹¹ᴬ, 98, 99, 126; C¹¹ᴮ, 29–38; C¹¹ᶜ, 13, 14, 16; E, 194 (dossier Franquet); F²ᶜ, 5; F³, 50; Marine, B⁴, 76, f.76; 80, f.164; Section Outre-Mer, Dépôt des fortifications des colonies, Am. Sept., nos.225–37. CTG, Archives, arts.3, 8, 14, 15; Bibliothèque, mss in 4°, 66; mss in fol., 205ᵇ, 208ᶜ, 210ᶠ. SHA, Xᵉ, 4; Yᵃ, 183; Y⁴ᵈ. *Inv. des papiers de Léry* (P.-G. Roy), II, 120, 122–26. A.-M. Augoyat, *Aperçu historique sur les fortifications, les ingénieurs et sur le corps du génie en France* ... (3v., Paris, 1860–64), II,

375, 378, 386, 417, 431. Frégault, *La civilisation de la Nouvelle-France*; *François Bigot*, II, 13, 19–21, 60–61. McLennan, *Louisbourg*, 189, 191, 197–98, 234, 245, 283, 285. F.-J. Audet, "Louis Franquet," *RSCT*, 3rd ser., XXV (1932), sect.ɪ, 69–80. Association for Preservation Technology *Bull.* ([Ottawa]), IV (1972).

FRENEUSE, LOUISE DAMOURS DE. *See* Guyon [Appendix]

G

GADOIS, *dit* **Mauger, JACQUES** (he often signed **J. Gadois Mogé),** silversmith and merchant; baptized 22 Aug. 1686 at Montreal, son of Pierre Gadois*, armourer, and Jeanne Besnard; m. on 21 Sept. 1714 in Montreal Marie-Madeleine Chorel de Saint-Romain, *dit* d'Orvilliers; buried 24 Nov. 1750 in his birthplace.

Jacques Gadois adopted the surname Mauger, probably in memory of his grandmother Louise Mauger, wife of Pierre Gadoys*, who was the first settler to receive a land grant at Montreal. At the time of his wedding in 1714, Gadois was already a silversmith, as his marriage contract and wedding certificate, signed the same day, attest. These two documents, however, constitute the only proofs that Gadois practised that craft. Several pieces of work are attributed to him, among them a cup and a goblet in solid silver which are preserved in the convent of the nuns of the Congregation of Notre-Dame in Montreal and which bear the stamp M.G. Some other pieces of silverware bear a similar stamp: MG/fleur-de-lis/MG/fleur-de-lis; but there is nothing to indicate with certainty that these stamps really correspond to Gadois's mark. It is not rare to encounter such problems in studying silver work of the 18th century. Indeed, no document has preserved a registry of the silversmiths' stamps, a gap which a professional guild in New France could probably have prevented.

Gadois spent his whole life in Montreal. According to É.-Z. Massicotte*, he is believed to have lived until the 1721 fire in a house in Rue Capitale, in the busiest commercial district of the period. Towards 1741, according to a census taken that year by the Compagnie des Indes, he was living in Rue Saint-Paul. Several documents from Montreal notarial registries, and deliberations and decisions of the Conseil Supérieur, show not only that Gadois spent his life in the Montreal region but that he was a merchant there for more than 27 years. Between 1721 and 1748,

in fact, Gadois signed a great number of contracts in which he is always described as being a merchant, dealer, or bourgeois of Ville-Marie. The same is true for all the lawsuits in which he was involved during this period. This activity would in large measure explain why only scanty information can be found about his career as a silversmith. It is quite possible that Gadois forsook his art early to concern himself solely with business. A document taken from the account books of the church of Notre-Dame de Montréal for 1729 could, however, cause doubts: it is a list of pieces of silverware (a cross, a crucifix, and a censer are mentioned), and it bears Gadois's signature. Despite some views to the contrary, it is not obvious that the person signing was the creator of the pieces: the person signing is described in the document as "churchwarden in charge of the fabric fund and parish council of the parish church of Ville-Marie," and it was probably in his capacity as churchwarden rather than silversmith that Gadois, *dit* Mauger, signed.

Even if Gadois's artistic career was short, it must not be overlooked, for only a few people were adept in the silversmith's craft in New France. The Musée du Québec owns a silver soup-spoon which bears the stamp attributed to the silversmith and also the monogram C.H.L.B. and the arms of the Chevalier Le Borgne.

Michel Cauchon and André Juneau

ANDM, Livres de comptes, 1724–1735. ANQ-M, Greffe de Michel Lepailleur, 21 sept. 1714; Registre d'état civil, Notre-Dame de Montréal, 21 sept. 1714. IOA, Dossier Jacques Gadois, dit Mauger, orfèvre. "Recensement de Montréal, 1741" (Massicotte). Tanguay, *Dictionnaire*. Langdon, *Canadian silversmiths*. Gérard Morisset, *Évolution d'une pièce d'argenterie* (Collection Champlain, Québec, 1943). Traquair, *Old silver of Quebec*. Marius Barbeau, "Deux cents ans d'orfèvrerie chez-nous," *RSCT*, 3rd ser., XXXIII (1939), sect.ɪ, 183–89. É.-Z. Massicotte, "A propos de congés," *BRH*, XXXII (1926), 296–300; "L'incendie du vieux Montréal en 1721," *BRH*, XXXII (1926), 583–608; "Orfèvres et bijoutiers du régime français," *BRH*, XXXVI (1930), 31. Gérard Morisset, "La tasse à quêter," *RSCT*, 3rd ser., XLI (1947), sect.ɪ, 65.

GAGHSWAGHTANIUNT. *See* KAGHSWAGH-TANIUNT

GALIFFET DE CAFFIN, FRANÇOIS DE, military officer; governor of Trois-Rivières; b. 1666 in Provence, son of Pierre de Galiffet, seigneur of Honon, and Marguerite de Bonfils; d. in 1746, possibly at Avignon, France.

François de Galiffet came to New France in 1688 as an officer in the colonial regular troops, and the following year he was appointed commandant at Trois-Rivières. In 1692, in a memorandum to Governor Frontenac [Buade*] and Intendant Champigny [Bochart*], the king appointed Galiffet town major of Quebec. The young officer was threatened with dismissal two years later because of "his lack of discretion, his imprudence, and the misuse of his office to the point of impropriety." He mended his ways, for in 1695 he was given command of the troops in Philippe de Rigaud* de Vaudreuil's absence.

In the spring of 1699 he received his letters of appointment as king's lieutenant at Montreal. Of the ten years he held this commission, Galiffet spent at least three in France, from 1706 to 1708, with the result that Pierre de Saint-Ours* was almost appointed king's lieutenant in his stead. In 1708 the minister, Pontchartrain, extended his leave for another year to allow him to settle the estate of his brother, Joseph d'Honon de Galiffet, the former governor of Saint-Domingue (Hispaniola).

Galiffet returned to Canada in 1709 and was appointed governor of Trois-Rivières. In this capacity, in 1711 he re-established the garrison, which had been done away with four years earlier, and in 1712 he recommended giving the secular clergy charge of the parish there, which was held by the Recollets. This suggestion brought a severe reprimand from the minister, who told Galiffet that he knew "that he was not on good terms with the Recollets and that he was creating scandal with his habits." Indeed, the parish priest, Father Joseph Denys*, accused him of keeping Marie-Anne Le Boulanger with him; in his own defence Galiffet replied "that this girl was of very good conduct and that she was necessary to him for the upbringing of his daughter and for taking care of his house." Yielding to pressure from the civil and religious authorities,

he finally had to send her back to her family. Scarcely was this affair settled than another scandal sullied the governor's reputation: he was accused of having made pregnant the daughter of Jacques Hertel de Cournoyer, an ensign in the troops. Governor Vaudreuil intervened and on 2 Nov. 1716 he wrote to the council of Marine: "The Sieur Hertel de Cournoyer has assured me that he had no reason to complain of M. de Galiffet and that these complaints came from his father, who had been induced to make them through the solicitations of His Excellency the bishop." The latter, in this case Bishop Saint-Vallier [La Croix*], did not, apparently, think much of Galiffet's conduct during his stay at Trois-Rivières.

François de Galiffet retired from the service in 1720 and returned to France. On 14 Jan. 1697, in Quebec, he had married Catherine, daughter of Charles Aubert* de La Chesnaye and Marie-Angélique Denys de La Ronde. She had died of smallpox in 1703, leaving a son and daughter. He himself died in 1746, probably in Avignon, where he had been living in retirement for many years.

In 1706 Governor Vaudreuil and Intendant Jacques Raudot* had written to the minister that the Sieur de Galiffet "was an honourable man." Theirs was the finest tribute he had ever merited. His sense of morality might have been poor, but he had a sense of honour, which, indeed, had earned him the cross of the order of Saint-Louis in 1705.

ROLAND-J. AUGER

AN, Col., B, 17, f.144v; 20, f.227v; 22, ff.271, 273v; 27, ff.31, 62v; 30, f.35; 33, f.123v; 34, f.32; 35, f.58; 36, ff.355v, 359v; 37, ff.166, 195v; 38, f.202v (copies at ANQ); C¹¹ᴬ, 3, f.54; 4, f.97 (copies at PAC). Fauteux, *Les chevaliers de Saint-Louis*, 93. P.-G. Roy, *Inv. coll. pièces jud. et not.*, I, 55, 294. Taillemite, *Inventaire analytique, série B, I*. P.-G. Roy, *La famille de Galliffet* (Lévis, Qué., 1917). Antoine Roy, "Visiteurs français de marque à Québec (1850–1885)," *Cahiers des Dix*, XXII (1957), 219–20.

GAMELIN MAUGRAS, PIERRE, merchant, king's interpreter; b. 1697 at Saint-François-du-Lac (Que.), son of Pierre Gamelin and Marie-Jeanne Maugras; d. 2 July 1757 in Montreal.

When he reached adult age, Pierre Gamelin added to his patronymic the surname Maugras, by which he is often referred to in notarial acts, perhaps to distinguish him from his father whose career overlapped his own. On 16 May 1724 he entered into partnership with Alexis LEMOINE, *dit* Monière, a "merchant-outfitter" in Montreal, and Louis-Mathieu Damours de Clignancour, for

Ganet

the fur trade in the *pays d'en haut*. Gamelin Maugras went a few times to the trading post at Baie-des-Puants (Green Bay, Wis.); the partnership lasted four years.

In 1728, after the partnership had been dissolved, Gamelin Maugras continued in the fur trade on his own account before settling permanently as a merchant in Montreal. On 15 Nov. 1735, in Montreal, at the signing of his marriage contract, he declared that he was worth 25,000 *livres*; the next day he married Marie-Clémence Dufrost de La Gemerais, daughter of François-Christophe Dufrost de La Gemerais and Marie-Renée Gaultier de Varennes, thus joining the Dufrost and Gaultier family circle. In 1740 he agreed to be procurator for Pierre GAULTIER de Varennes et de La Vérendrye, and in 1742 for Philippe Leduc, the explorer's partner. Louis-Joseph GAULTIER de La Vérendrye appointed him administrator of his property in 1745, and his agent with power of attorney on 31 Dec. 1749, at the time of the inventory of the estate of La Vérendrye Sr. Gamelin Maugras was already the "merchant-outfitter" of Louis-Joseph Gaultier and his partners, who in 1748 undertook not to dispose of their peltries until they had settled their debts with Gamelin Maugras, he having just advanced them funds for the next three years.

Pierre Gamelin Maugras, having travelled in the west over a period of several years, had learned several Indian languages in the course of his journeys; he consequently often served as interpreter. In recognition of his many valuable services, Governor Charles de BEAUHARNOIS appointed him king's interpreter on 30 May 1743. This office, to which no remuneration was attached, allowed the holder to receive certain honours and to enjoy certain rights, prerogatives, and exemptions.

Gamelin Maugras died in Montreal on 2 July 1757, survived by his wife, who died in 1768. His was a family of merchants, of which his uncle and his cousin, Ignace Gamelin* Sr and Ignace Gamelin* Jr, were the most famous representatives.

YVES QUESNEL

ANQ-M, Greffe de J.-B. Adhémar, 16 mars 1724; Greffe de L.-C. Danré de Blanzy, 31 oct. 1740, 22 août 1745, 14 juin 1748; Registre d'état civil, Notre-Dame de Montréal, 16 nov. 1735, 3 juill. 1757; Registre d'état civil, Varennes, 26 janv. 1704. *Jug. et délib.*, V, 102. "Recensement de Montréal, 1741" (Massicotte). Massicotte, "Répertoire des engagements pour l'Ouest," APQ *Rapport, 1929–30*, includes a number of Gamelin Maugras's contracts. "Marguilliers de la paroisse Notre-Dame-de-Ville-Marie de 1657 à 1913," *BRH*, XIX (1913), 279. Tanguay, *Dictionnaire*. É.-Z. Massicotte, "Les interprètes à Montréal sous le régime français," *BRH*, XXXIV (1928), 149.

GANET, FRANÇOIS, contractor of fortifications and public buildings; b. *c.* 1675 in Burgundy, France; d. 14 Oct. 1747 at Paris.

In 1724 the Comte de Maurepas, minister of Marine, decided to implement plans for building the Royal battery and the Island battery at Louisbourg, Île Royale (Cape Breton Island). Bidders for the construction contract included Jean-Baptiste MAILLOU, *dit* Desmoulins (backed by Gédéon de Catalogne*) and Jean-Baptiste Boucher, *dit* Belleville, both of Quebec; but in France, Jacques Raudot*, former intendant of New France, and Jean-François de Verville*, the director of fortifications for Île Royale, recommended François Ganet, a successful builder with European experience in fortifications, whose rates were well below those of the previous contractor, Michel-Philippe Isabeau*. The contract was signed on 24 Feb. 1725. On 10 March, Gratien d'ARRIGRAND, a nephew of Daniel d'Auger* de Subercase, became Ganet's business partner, without being a signatory to the contract with the king. D'Arrigrand came to Louisbourg in 1725 and spent two years with Ganet.

Isabeau's death had created an emergency: the masonry of the King's bastion and its garrison quarters had to be finished in order to protect it from the climate, and most of the officers and troops had to be housed in a central citadel. Ganet, fancying that this additional work would be profitable, persuaded Arnoud Isabeau, his predecessor's father and chief heir, to let him assume all risks and profits. After arriving at Louisbourg in June, Ganet made an agreement to that effect with Antoinette Isabeau Planton, the late contractor's widowed sister. Within a few months he regretted it. He complained that the younger Isabeau had realized large profits in the coarse work of the early stages, and that his own responsibility comprised the slow, fine, expensive work of finishing. On a legal technicality, Ganet cancelled his agreement with Isabeau's heirs; he was to be paid by them for the work he had already done.

During his stay at Louisbourg from 1725 to 1737 Ganet built, in addition to the two batteries, the Dauphin demi-bastion, the main storehouse, the careening wharf, the hospital, and the lighthouse; he helped to finish the garrison quarters of the King's bastion; and he carried out a number of repairs. In general there was little cause for dissatisfaction with the quality of his work (the value of which was estimated at some 1,700,000 *livres*), but he himself frequently complained of delayed payments, unforeseen expenses, shortages of building materials, and low valuations by the chief engineer, Étienne VERRIER. His relations with Verrier, and with most of the other officials, were nevertheless harmonious.

There is no reason to believe that Ganet suffered any losses in the long run. Those due to "acts of God" were assumed by the king, and the minister made some effort to facilitate Ganet's work. The settling of accounts between Ganet and Isabeau's heirs took several years. It proved necessary first to finish work on the citadel in order to measure the total contribution in labour and materials of each party, then to adjust these figures in accordance with their earlier bilateral transactions. Mme Planton died in 1729, but it was 1731 before the final accounting was made.

A dispute between Ganet and d'Arrigrand lasted about 20 years. In 1728 the latter failed to send Ganet certain building materials for which public funds had been ear-marked in France. Two years later Ganet refused to provide his partner with a first statement of profits and losses for their firm, in which d'Arrigrand had a 60 per cent share, whereupon the latter obtained a court order obliging him to do so. Before the work under his first contract was finished, Ganet won his second in 1731, underbidding an associate of d'Arrigrand, and ending his own partnership with the latter. D'Arrigrand wished to draw lots for the equipment and materials which they jointly owned, but Ganet declined, although he had offered d'Arrigrand a judicial estimate of their assets, or an inventory, which he had refused. Ganet continued to use the equipment as his own.

In 1735 d'Arrigrand sent David-Bernard MUIRON to Louisbourg, ostensibly to work on a private project, but really to challenge Ganet's monopoly. Upon the expiration of the second contract, Muiron in 1737 underbid Ganet. The latter wound up his work at Louisbourg during that year, still refusing to share the equipment and supplies. D'Arrigrand began an action in Paris in 1739 seeking to oblige Ganet to render a full accounting of all the assets and liabilities of the former partnership, and to make a substantial interim payment. After a long series of motions by both parties, the matter was taken to the royal council in 1740. That body decreed in February that three experts in fortifications and construction should examine the thousands of documents in the case and render a decision. Because of difficulties among the arbiters, the council decided in May to rely on one of them alone: Jacques Gabriel, first architect to the king. D'Arrigrand was not convinced of the impartiality either of Gabriel or of his son who succeeded him as arbiter in 1742. The judgement, three years later, apparently favoured Ganet in the long run, but he lived only two years to enjoy his profits.

F. J. THORPE

AN, Col., B, 48, ff.398, 925, 929, 950; 49, ff.697–97v, 703, 707–11; 50, ff.570, 577, 594v–99; 52, ff.588–93, 602v; 53, ff.66v, 67v, 587v–88v, 593v–95v, 602v–6, 607v–8, 617–17v; 54, ff.27, 496, 499v, 501–3; 57, f.755; 59, ff.534v, 540, 551v–58; 61, ff.614v, 616; 63, ff.537v–39v, 543v, 548v, 550; 64, ff.486, 490v; 65, ff.49v, 477–79, 481; 71, ff.193–96v, 198; C¹¹B, 7, ff.185–90, 194–97v, 261–66v, 324, 328–32, 342, 348–51, 352–55v, 357–60, 363, 366–72; 8, ff.111–21v, 157–59v, 161–74, 215, 219, 221–22, 225–28v; 9, ff.93–99, 127–32, 141–47v, 153–79v, 193–206, 210–50v; 10, ff.81–84, 104–8, 166–73; 242–45; 11, ff.45–49, 55–57, 83, 90; 12, ff.122–43, 145, 166–69v; 13, ff.206, 261, 298–309, 310–17v, 329, 408–11v; 15, ff.72–74, 149–52, 180–80v; 16, ff.182–93, 221–22; 17, ff.94–96, 154; 18, ff.85–87, 133–36, 145–48, 271–87, 301–2; 19, ff.232–40; 21, ff.290–91v, 293; 23, ff.213–17v; 27, ff.315–18; E, 9 (dossier d'Arrigrand), ff.2, 4, 6–8, 11, 17; Section Outre-Mer, G¹, 466, no.69. Archives Maritimes, Port de Rochefort, 1E, 105, f.531. Robert Le Blant, "Un entrepreneur à l'île Royale, Gratien d'Arrigrand, 1684–1754," *La Revue des questions historiques* (Paris), LXIV (1936) (offprint at PAC). Pierre Mayrand, "La renaissance de Louisbourg," *Vie des arts* (Montréal), XLVI (1967), 32–35.

GANNES DE FALAISE, MICHEL DE, officer in the colonial regular troops; baptized 2 May 1702 at Port-Royal (Annapolis Royal, N.S.), son of Louis de Gannes* de Falaise and Marguerite Leneuf de La Vallière et de Beaubassin; d. 23 Oct. 1752 at Louisbourg, Île Royale (Cape Breton Island).

In 1719 Michel de Gannes de Falaise was appointed an ensign at Île Royale, but he did not go there until three years later. On 29 May 1725 he was made lieutenant, then on 8 May 1730 captain. His military career involved few heroic acts. In 1726 he was posted to Port-Toulouse (St Peters, N.S.), and returned to Louisbourg shortly afterwards. Garrison routine was broken only by a voyage in 1730 to France, where he was responsible for recruiting soldiers for Île Royale.

On 21 Nov. 1730 de Gannes married Élisabeth, the daughter of Gédéon de Catalogne*. The marriage almost failed to take place. On 21 May 1729 Marie-Anne Carrerot, his mistress, had given birth to a daughter who, de Gannes admitted, might well be "of his doing." Despite this incident he appeared at the parish church of Louisbourg on 14 Nov. 1730 to marry Élisabeth de Catalogne. But his mistress objected publicly to the marriage, and the ceremony was postponed;

the dispute was settled amicably, however, and the marriage took place a week later. Of this union seven children, five daughters and two sons, were born, all at Louisbourg. De Gannes's wife died on 12 Aug. 1750.

In 1744 the commandant of Île Royale, Jean-Baptiste-Louis LE PRÉVOST Duquesnel, decided to retake Port-Royal, which had been captured by the English in 1710 and renamed Annapolis Royal. To this end he dispatched a detachment of soldiers under the command of Joseph DU PONT Duvivier; they were to be supported by a small number of ships. At the beginning of the siege Duvivier obtained from the English commandant, Paul MASCARENE, a promise of surrender as soon as the French ships arrived. On 2 October de Gannes relieved Duvivier. Two days later, when the ships still had not appeared, de Gannes decided to withdraw the troops, despite Duvivier's objections. Alleging the lack of supplies, the impatience of the Indians to return to their families, and the numerical superiority of the English, de Gannes withdrew to Minas (Grand Pré region) on 10 October, then to Beaubassin (near Amherst) on 19 October. There he received the reprimands of Louis Du Pont* Duchambon, who had assumed command of Île Royale after Duquesnel's death. On his way through Port-Toulouse de Gannes learned that Claude-Élisabeth DENYS de Bonnaventure had left Louisbourg for Annapolis Royal, where he arrived the night of 25–26 October with 50 soldiers on board a merchant vessel and a privateer brigantine. He set off again for Louisbourg three days later, without getting in touch with de Gannes, whom he believed still to be at Minas. Although de Gannes had not been ordered to continue the siege of Annapolis Royal, he was criticized for not having waited longer for the French vessels and for not having attempted an assault. At two meetings of officers assembled to investigate the attitude of those responsible for the expedition, he was not able to justify his conduct, and on 19 November he admitted his error to the financial commissary François Bigot*, but insisted on his good intentions.

His courage during the siege of Louisbourg in 1745 succeeded, however, in dispelling the unfavourable opinion of his superiors. When the militia from the English colonies landed, he was stationed at the Grave battery inside the fortress; later he relieved Charles-Joseph d'AILLEBOUST at the Island battery, which commanded the harbour. It was with reluctance that he had to hand over the island to the English colonists on 27 June, not understanding why the fortress had been surrendered. He then attended to the transfer of the inhabitants, under d'Ailleboust's orders, and sailed on one of the last ships to leave the port.

Created a knight of the order of Saint-Louis in September 1746, de Gannes returned to Île Royale in 1749 as town major of Louisbourg. He was concerned with his personal affairs until his death. During his career his social and economic activities seem to have taken precedence over his military activities. His financial situation appears to have been brighter than that of the majority of the officers at Louisbourg. He profited by three inheritances: from his father-in-law, his brother Louis-François, and his brother-in-law Jean-Baptiste de Couagne*. Some properties at Louisbourg and elsewhere on Île Royale brought him certain revenues, as did his partnership with Antoine Rodrigue, Michel Rodrigue*'s brother, with whom he was joint owner of the schooner *Salamandre*. In 1752 he established for one of his daughters a dowry of 10,000 *livres*, of which he had time to pay 8,000. The sale of his furnishings brought in the sum of 4,862 *livres* 2 *sols*. This relative prosperity was certainly not due to his slender officer's pay; even a king's lieutenant received only 1,800 *livres* a year.

On 1 April 1752 the king appointed de Gannes king's lieutenant at Trois-Rivières, but he never took up the post. He died on 23 October. At his burial two days later in the chapel of the barracks of the King's bastion the governor honoured him with a nine-gun salute.

H. PAUL THIBAULT

AN, Col., C¹¹B, 26, ff.48–52v, 79–88, 204–7v; 32, ff.191–91v; C¹¹C, 16, 2ᵉ sér., ff.26ff.; D²C, 2, f.64v; 3, ff.19, 49v; 4, f.123v; E, 65 (dossier Gédéon de Catalogne); F²C, 3, ff.289–92; F³, 50, ff.301–1v, 344; F⁵B, 56, ff.2/3; Section Outre-Mer, Dépôt des fortifications des colonies, Am. sept., no.216, ff.14v–15, 21, 25; G¹, 406/4, ff.11v, 24v, 30v, 46v, 65; 408/1, ff.113, 143, 155v; 408/2, f.69; 466, pièce 68, f.12 ; pièce 69, f.17; pièce 76 (recensements de l'île Royale, 1724, 1726, 1749); G², 180, ff.873, 875–76; 184, ff.19–20, 64v–65v; 190/4, ff.64v–83v; 196, dossier 124, ff.42v–43; 197, dossier 129; dossier 153 *bis*, ff.27v–31, 31–33v, 35–35v, 36–36v, 41–42, 45–46v; dossier 154, ff.1–2; 200, dossier 202, f.4v; 201, dossier 254; G³, 2041/1 (17 juin, 25 nov., 11 déc. 1752); 2046/1 (15 mars 1740); 2047/1 (18 oct. 1749); 2047/2 (26 janv., 6 oct. 1752). Archives Maritimes, Port de Rochefort, 1E, 99, f.489. BN, Service hydrographique de la Marine, Dépôt des cartes et plans, portefeuille 131, div. 10, nos.4, 5. Le Jeune, *Dictionnaire*. Ægidius Fauteux, "La famille de Gannes," *BRH*, XXXI (1925), 271–85.

GASCHET, RENÉ, surgeon, seigneurial notary, seigneurial judge; b. *c.* 1665 in France, son of

Pierre Gaschet and Hélène Bourgina from Poitiers; m. on 22 Aug. 1694 Françoise Phélypeaux in Quebec; d. 9 March 1744 at Saint-Vallier (Que.).

We do not know the year of René Gaschet's arrival in the colony. In 1693 he had been living in Quebec for some time, for on 5 Feb. 1694 the provost court of Quebec rendered a judgement in his favour which freed him from his contract as "journeyman-surgeon" with the surgeon Timothée Roussel*. The court sentenced the surgeon to pay Gaschet 25 *livres* for three months' services. Subsequently Gaschet himself practised as a surgeon. On 7 Sept. 1694, however, Gervais Baudouin*, lieutenant to the chief surgeon Félix de Tassy, contested Gaschet's competence before the provost court. Gaschet had to sit for an examination, which he passed, it seems, since he continued to practise his profession.

After his wife's death in 1698 Gaschet left Quebec for Montreal. He stayed there several years; in 1711 he was back in the Quebec region. On 11 January of that year Olivier Morel* appointed him notary and judge in his seigneury of La Durantaye. The seigneurs of Beaumont and Bellechasse in turn appointed Gaschet notary in their seigneuries, one on 20 February and the other on 14 March. The new notary immediately found himself in competition with the royal notary Abel Michon, commissioned on 1 April of that year to practise from Pointe-Lévy (Lauzon) to Kamouraska, a territory which covered the three seigneuries. In the next two years Gaschet succeeded in entering 23 deeds in his minute-book, but his competitor drew up 62 deeds. On the other hand, Gaschet held a power of attorney for the seigneurs of La Durantaye and received nearly all the contracts for land grants for the seigneury of Beaumont. He registered his last act on 29 Dec. 1743 and died at Saint-Vallier on 9 March 1744.

Like many other notaries of the French régime, René Gaschet had practised another occupation before exercising the profession of notary. He had been penniless when he gave up surgery; at his death in 1744, after more than 30 years as notary, his situation had scarcely improved.

MICHEL PAQUIN

ANQ, Greffe de Louis Chambalon, 18 déc. 1696; Greffe de René Gaschet, 1711–1743; Greffe de Guillaume Roger, 18 août 1694. É.-Z. Massicotte, "Les chirurgiens de Montréal au XVIIᵉ siècle," *BRH*, XXVII (1921), 46. A. Roy, *Inv. greffes not.*, XVI, 10–95. P.-G. Roy, *Inv. coll. pièces jud. et not.*, I; *Inv. ord. int.*, I, 117, 173, 250; II, 240. Tanguay, *Dictionnaire*. Ahern, *Notes pour l'histoire de la médecine*, 243–48. J.-E. Roy, *Histoire du notariat*, I, 176–78.

GASTINEAU DUPLESSIS, JEAN-BAPTISTE,

"voyageur-associate," fur-trader, militia officer, merchant; b.1671 in the Trois-Rivières region, son of Nicolas Gastineau Duplessis and Marie Crevier; buried 9 Feb. 1750 at Trois-Rivières.

Between 1694 and 1702 Jean-Baptiste Gastineau Duplessis went on several trading expeditions to the west as a "voyageur-associate." On 9 June 1694 Daniel Greysolon* Dulhut hired him and some other men to go on a trading expedition to Michilimackinac. In 1701 he went to Detroit with his younger brother Louis and some 40 men, all of whom had been hired in the king's name by Intendant Jean Bochart* de Champigny. The following year Gastineau Duplessis and his brother were employed by the Compagnie de la Colonie to go to Detroit with an expedition that was fully as large as the preceding one.

After these voyages Jean-Baptiste Gastineau Duplessis settled at Trois-Rivières where, it seems, he became lieutenant of the militia. We do not know at what moment he went into business, but around 1730 he entered into partnership with François-Étienne CUGNET to try to introduce buffalo into Canada; this enterprise was not, however, successful. Some years later Gastineau Duplessis had new business dealings with Cugnet, who in 1736 had become the chief shareholder in the Saint-Maurice ironworks company. Gastineau Duplessis furnished the ironworks with supplies valued at 7,071 *livres* 2 *sols* 6 *deniers*. He had trouble, however, in obtaining payment and, when Cugnet's business began to fail, had to present a petition to Intendant Hocquart* in June 1741. In 1750, shortly after Gastineau Duplessis's death, his wife encountered the same difficulties: this time Cugnet was sentenced in an ordinance from Intendant Bigot* dated 1 April to pay 2,722 *livres* 3 *sols* to Mme Gastineau Duplessis for the goods she had sold to the employees of the ironworks.

On 19 Nov. 1711 Jean-Baptiste Gastineau Duplessis had married Charlotte Le Boulanger at Cap-de-la-Madeleine. Three children were born of this marriage, including a daughter, Marie-Joseph, who in 1749 married Pierre-François Olivier* de Vézin.

ROLAND-J. AUGER

AN, Col., C¹¹ᴬ, 53, ff.228–30. ANQ, NF, Ord. int., 1ᵉʳ avril 1750. ANQ-M, Greffe d'Antoine Adhémar, 9 juin 1694. PAC *Report, 1904*, app.K. Bonnault, "Le Canada militaire," APQ *Rapport, 1949–51*, 522. Massicotte, "Répertoire des engagements pour l'Ouest,"

Gastineau

APQ *Rapport, 1929–30*, 202, 206–7. P.-G. Roy, *Inv. ord. int.*, III, 164. Tanguay, *Dictionnaire*. Albert Tessier, *Les forges Saint-Maurice, 1729–1883* (Trois-Rivières, Qué., 1952). Edgar Le Noblet Du Plessis, "Nicolas Gatineau, sieur du Plessis," SGCF *Mémoires*, IV (1950–51), 23–39 P.-G. Roy, "Les bœufs illinois," *BRH*, XXIII (1917), 275–84.

GASTINEAU DUPLESSIS, MARGUERITE. *See* DUPLESSIS

GAUDÉ (Godé, Gaudet), FRANÇOISE, nun, Religious Hospitaller of Saint-Joseph, superior; b. 16 April 1671 in Montreal, daughter of Nicolas Gaudé, a carpenter, and of Marguerite Picard; d. 15 Jan. 1751 in Montreal.

Françoise Gaudé entered the noviciate of the Nuns Hospitallers of Saint-Joseph in Montreal in 1690 and made her profession there in 1692. After the death of the superior, Charlotte Gallard*, in 1725, Françoise Gaudé, who had been her assistant, was entrusted with the destinies of the community and the responsibility for the hospital work. She took over this office at a critical moment: the reconstruction of the buildings of the Hôtel-Dieu of Montreal, destroyed by fire in 1721, had not yet been completed, expenses kept increasing steadily, and revenues were diminishing. Sister Gaudé carried out her duties energetically until 1731, when she was replaced by Geneviève Levasseur. In 1733 she was again elected superior. During this second term of office a third fire devastated the Hôtel-Dieu of Montreal [*see* Marie-Joseph-Angélique*] during the night of 10–11 April 1734. The convent and the church were destroyed and the nuns found themselves once more without shelter. The losses were enormous: the furniture, the vestry linen, the articles for sale (the money from which was to be used to provide for the needs of the sick and the nuns), the supplies on hand, the register of minutes and of persons taking the veil or making their profession, all were destroyed in the fire. The consecrated vessels of the church were saved, however, and the damage to the hospital, particularly to the pharmacy, was less serious. As Sister Marie-Anne-Véronique CUILLERIER wrote, Sister Gaudé "took vigorous action to seek relief for us, but what could she do, since she had nothing ?" This declaration by the annalist shows clearly the wretched state in which the Nuns Hospitallers found themselves at the time. On the second day after the fire they separated into three groups, for that, it seems, was the only way to find temporary lodgings. A number of the sisters took up their abode in the old bakery of the hospital, others, who were invalids, had to go to a house in the country belonging to the sick – that is to say, forming part of the property of the Hôtel-Dieu separate from that of the community – and the third group sought shelter at the Saint-Joachim farm. Several months after their separation the Hospitallers came together again in a new dwelling belonging to Jacques Testard* de Montigny and located near the chapel of Notre-Dame-de-Bonsecours.

Misfortune, however, again struck the Nuns Hospitallers in 1734. One of the king's ships, on which were soldiers who had been stricken with a malignant and contagious fever, had berthed at Quebec. Those passengers who were considered to be "out of danger" were sent on to Montreal. But upon arriving in Montreal on 11 November a soldier fell ill and was taken to the Hôtel-Dieu. This was the beginning of an epidemic, and nine Nuns Hospitallers died of it. The community thus went through trying times, and Sister Cuillerier has left this touching account: "I should exhaust all my stock of expressions, my dear Sisters, if I tried to describe to you the great grief in which we found ourselves . . . our tears sprinkled our bread and our beds night and day at having lost such good members . . . it was impossible to sing any of the offices. The gentlemen of the seminary did us this kind service and buried all our sisters in the chapel of Bon Secours, which belongs to them. All the coffins were sealed so that no one would catch the infection, and such precautions were taken in town that no one passed by the street where we were; people simply asked from a distance if sisters were still dying, and were told in reply how things were."

Throughout these trials Sister Gaudé continued seeing to the efficient functioning of her community and the hospital and received new novices. As a result of a report favouring increased aid for the Hôtel-Dieu sent by Governor Charles de BEAUHARNOIS and Intendant Gilles Hocquart*, the king allowed, in addition to a gratuity of 10,000 *livres*, an annual grant of 1,500 *livres* to be made until the work of rebuilding was completed. On 28 Sept. 1735, 18 months after the fire, the nuns and the sick returned to the Hôtel-Dieu.

In 1739 Sister Françoise Gaudé was replaced in her office by Anne-Françoise LEDUC, *dite* Saint-Joseph. She died on 15 Jan. 1751. She had directed the community in difficult periods, and her courage, her initiative, and her sense of responsibility led to her being called " a heroine of the Institution" in the annals of the Hôtel-Dieu.

HÉLÈNE BERNIER

AHSJ, Annales de sœur Marie Morin, 1697–1725; Annales de sœur Véronique Cuillerier, 1725–1747; Déclaration de nos anciennes Mères pour constater la profession et le décès de nos sœurs. Mondoux, *L'Hôtel-Dieu de Montréal*.

GAUDRON DE CHEVREMONT, CHARLES-RENÉ, clerk in the office of the Marine, royal notary, judge; b. 5 July 1702 at Linas (dept. of Essonne), France, son of Nicolas Gaudron, postmaster, and Marie Gohel; m. 7 Jan. 1730 Marie-Bénigne Derome who bore him ten children; d. in France sometime before April 1745.

Charles-René Gaudron de Chevremont came to Canada in 1726 as one of Governor Charles de BEAUHARNOIS's secretaries. He pursued a career in the civil service, enjoying the governor's protection in all his endeavours. When Gilles Hocquart* arrived in the colony in 1729 he employed Gaudron as writer in the office of the Marine. Three years later, on 27 July 1732, Hocquart gave him a commission as royal notary in Montreal and on the same day added to the office of writer that of clerk. Although these appointments were necessary, Beauharnois was probably responsible for Gaudron's being chosen. Settled in Montreal, Gaudron was appointed judge of the newly created seigneurial court of Île Jésus on 16 April 1734 by the directors of the seminary of Quebec; he apparently held this position for two years.

Soon after arriving in Canada Gaudron began to run up debts in France and Canada. He appears to have dabbled in commerce of one form or another. His financial situation is not documented but his marriage contract of 1729 suggests modest means. In 1733 he turned down the opportunity to become special lieutenant of the royal jurisdiction of Montreal, preferring his emoluments as notary to the poorly paid job of judge.

A fire in Montreal in 1734 [*see* Marie-Joseph-Angélique*] destroyed the house he was renting from the widow of François Poulin* de Francheville, but he managed to save his official papers. His moving appeal for compensation for a loss of 6,000 *livres* and a request for a brevet of writer got a flattering recommendation from Beauharnois and Hocquart, but the minister of Marine, Maurepas, firmly refused this request and similar later ones. Maurepas did not want to increase the number of offices in Canada, or to compensate individuals for losses in the fire for fear of establishing an expensive precedent.

As royal notary in Montreal Gaudron de Chevremont counted among his clientele the most respectable families of the town. Many indentures for the west are in Gaudron's register. As clerk in the office of the Marine Gaudron's tasks included keeping a register of receipts and expenditures at the king's store, overseeing receipt, delivery, preservation and quality of the king's munitions and supplies, and recording precisely shipments made to the king's posts. More frustrating, perhaps, was his obligation to pursue individuals for their debts to the crown.

In the spring of 1738 Hocquart sent Gaudron to audit the accounts of the king's storekeepers at the forts of Niagara (near Youngstown, N.Y.) and Frontenac (Kingston, Ont.). The king reserved their trade for his own account, and the profits had declined so rapidly that the minister suspected abuses by Pierre Pépin, *dit* Laforce, storekeeper at Niagara. Gaudron analysed the accounts for the preceding ten years and made an inventory of merchandise. Hocquart concluded from this report that Pépin was a man of probity, guilty only of negligence, and attributed decline in profits to increased competition by the English based at Chouaguen (Oswego) who offered unlimited quantities of rum to the Indians. To compete, Pépin was compelled to sell his trade goods at a loss. Gaudron's investigation underscored the shortage of educated, experienced men for the civil service in Canada, and may also have been a major factor in the decision taken in 1742 to abandon royal exploitation of the trade at forts Niagara and Frontenac and to farm it out to the highest bidder.

A year after this assignment, in 1739, Gaudron de Chevremont returned to France apparently hoping to remain there. Just before he came back in 1740, he visited Pierre Hazeur* de L'Orme, canon and Parisian agent of the cathedral chapter of Quebec, who found him an amiable and intelligent fellow with differing opinions of Beauharnois and of Hocquart. The intendant may have had some dissatisfaction with Gaudron's report on the Niagara trade; in any case in his report on civil employees in the colony in 1740 he charged that Gaudron performed his functions as clerk in the office of the Marine only superficially and busied himself with other affairs unrelated to his various official duties. He intended to dismiss him as soon as he could find a more useful subject, and did so in 1741, but in the meantime employed him as inspector of commerce.

Gaudron de Chevremont, protesting to Maurepas, requested a half-pay pension to support his numerous family. Despite Beauharnois's support, Maurepas accepted Hocquart's decision, refusing Gaudron the pension on the grounds that these were given only to employees forced to retire owing to age or infirmities. Fortunately for Gaudron the governor proved himself a protector in deed as well as in word: in 1742 Beauharnois employed him as his attorney, sending him to France to look after private affairs. His wife and two of his children joined him in France in 1744.

In a letter to Beauharnois of April 1745 Maurepas comments that he thought Charles-René Gaudron de Chevremont had died some time before.

S. DALE STANDEN

AD, Yvelines (Versailles), État civil, Linas, 11 déc. 1695, 5 juill. 1702. AN, Col., B, 63, ff.474v–75v; 64, ff.420vf.; 72, ff.364f.; 74, ff.434f.; 76, ff.421f.; 81, ff.280f.; C¹¹A, 53, pp.206, 213 (PAC transcripts); 60, f.38v; 61, ff.250–51, 252–53; 73, ff.300, 306–9v; 75, f.167v; 77, ff.106v, 117f.; 79, f.138v; 81, ff.134–35v, 178–79v; 82, f.275; D²ᴰ, 1; E, 81. ANQ, Greffe de Jacques Barbel, 21 oct. 1733; Greffe de J.-É. Dubreuil, 20 nov. 1739; NF, Documents de la juridiction de Montréal, X, 7–8. ANQ-M, Greffe de C.-R. Gaudron de Chevremont, 1732–1739 (see A. Roy, Inv. greffes not., XII, 5–55). ASQ, Séminaire, XXV, 14. P.-G. Roy, Inv. ord. int., II, 87, 127–28, 218–19, 220, 244–45. Tanguay, Dictionnaire. P.-G. Roy, "Les secrétaires des gouverneurs et intendants de la Nouvelle-France," BRH, XLI (1935), 87–88.

GAUFIN, VALÉRIEN (baptized **Jean-Philippe**), Recollet, provincial commissioner; b. 16 Feb. 1699 in Douai, France, the son of Jean-Philippe Gaufin and Marie-Joseph Moreau; d. 5 April 1759 in Paris, France.

Valérien Gaufin entered the Recollet order of the province of Saint-Denys in 1722 and was ordained a priest about 1725. In 1727 this worthy Recollet arrived in Quebec and lost no time in becoming involved in the political and social life of New France. Not long after the death of Bishop Saint-Vallier [La Croix*] Gaufin took sides in the famous quarrel over the direction of the diocese while the episcopal seat was vacant, which set Canon Étienne Boullard* and the chapter against Intendant Dupuy*, Eustache CHARTIER de Lotbinière, and the Conseil Supérieur. He preached several sermons in which he attacked the council, comparing the members of this tribunal to the tyrants and persecutors of the early Christians. On 2 Feb. 1728 he preached a final sermon, and the next day he was summoned before the council, to which he went in the company of his superior, Father Étienne Piscot, and the provincial commissioner, Father Justinien DURAND. The council demanded that the Recollet not preach other than God's word and that within three months he retract his last sermon. Instead of a retraction the Recollet presented on

16 February a text justifying his position in the conflict and approving Boullard's election by the Quebec chapter.

Like many other members of the clergy and society in New France, Gaufin had openly adopted a position in this conflict, which had rapidly turned into a tragi-comedy; it was Louis XV who settled the question by recalling one of the protagonists [see Dupuy] and lecturing the others.

Father Valérien remained in New France until 1742; he then went to France on the Canada as chaplain. He returned the following year as provincial commissioner. His active participation in the social life of the colony earned Gaufin several mentions in the correspondence of Mme Bégon [ROCBERT] with her son-in-law, Honoré MICHEL de Villebois de La Rouvillière. We learn that he was the spiritual director of young Marie-Catherine-Élisabeth Michel, Mme Bégon's granddaughter, and that in 1749 he was interdicted from his clerical functions for having absolved ladies who had attended a ball in Montreal. Again according to Mme Bégon, in this same year the provincial commissioner received a reply to a letter he had sent to Jean-Michel HOUDIN, who had been unfrocked in 1744 and was living in New England. Gaufin had tried to persuade the ex-Recollet to return to the bosom of the Roman Church. In his reply Houdin cast accusations against all and sundry and called Gaufin a "scoundrel"; "he pities him greatly for having to live with a gang of libertines who are capable of every sort of crime."

Father Valérien exercised his ministry in the Trois-Rivières area in 1750 and left Canada in 1752. He died in Paris on 5 April 1759, at which time he was definitor and novice master.

This somewhat quarrelsome and open-minded friar offers a faithful portrait of the Recollet who lived in New France in the 18th century: even while exercising his ministry all over the colony and fulfilling various functions in his order, he took an active part in Canadian social life.

MICHEL PAQUIN

Archives des Franciscains (Montréal), Dossier Valérien Gaufin. AN, Col., C¹¹A, 72, f.293. "Correspondance de Mme Bégon" (Bonnault), APQ Rapport, 1934–35, 22, 49, 56, 65, 176, 177. "Mémoire de M. Dupuy, intendant de la Nouvelle-France, sur les troubles arrivés à Québec en 1727 et 1728, après la mort de Mgr de Saint-Vallier, évêque de Québec," APQ Rapport, 1920–21, 78–105. Caron, "Inventaire de documents," APQ Rapport, 1941–42, 287, 288. P.-G. Roy, Inv. jug. et délib., 1717–1760, I, 343–44; II, 146. Dubé, Claude-Thomas Dupuy, 236–37. Henri Têtu, "Le chapitre de la cathédrale de Québec et ses délégués en France," *BRH*, XVI (1910), 356.

GAULTIER (Gautier, Gauthier, or **Gaulthier,** but he signed Gaultier), **JEAN-FRANÇOIS,** physician, naturalist; b. 6 Oct. 1708 at La Croix-Avranchin (dept. of Manche, France), son of René Gaultier and Françoise Colin; d. 10 July 1756 in Quebec. He has sometimes been confused with a contemporary of the same name who lived in Acadia and with a French botanist of the second half of the 17th century. *See* Appendix.

GAULTIER DE LA VÉRENDRYE, LOUIS-JOSEPH (most often he used the name Joseph, and he was called the Chevalier from 1736 on), explorer, fur-trader, military officer; b. 9 Nov. 1717 at Île aux Vaches on Lac Saint-Pierre (Que.), fourth son of Pierre GAULTIER de Varennes et de La Vérendrye and Marie-Anne Dandonneau Du Sablé; perished in the shipwreck of the *Auguste* on 15 Nov. 1761.

Little is known of Louis-Joseph Gaultier de La Vérendrye's childhood, but he probably received the usual elementary education. In October 1734 his father sent him to spend the winter in Quebec "to learn mathematics and drawing, so that he will be able to map accurately the regions to be explored." His letters and reports reveal a fairly good literary education.

Louis-Joseph's scientific training was of little more than six months' duration. On 18 April 1735 he was in Montreal, busy preparing his departure for the west and enlisting men with that end in view. He left on 21 June; his father and the Jesuit Jean-Pierre Aulneau* were among the party. The group reached Fort Saint-Charles on Lake of the Woods (Ont.) and settled there for the winter.

Louis-Joseph's first year in the west was marked by two trials: first, the death of his cousin, Christophe Dufrost* de La Jemerais, in May 1736; then, a month later, the death of his older brother, Jean-Baptiste Gaultier* de La Vérendrye, killed by a band of Sioux at Lake of the Woods. On 14 September Louis-Joseph was sent by his father to re-establish Fort Maurepas, which had been abandoned after La Jemerais's death. It was on this occasion that Louis-Joseph received from his father the title of chevalier, with precedence over his brothers. Louis-Joseph was joined by his father at Fort Maurepas on 27 Feb. 1737 and was present at the great council held on 4 March with the Cree and Assiniboin chiefs. The map of the west dating from 1737 which incorporates information obtained on this occasion was probably drawn by the Chevalier

and subsequently redone by the engineer Gaspard-Joseph CHAUSSEGROS de Léry.

Some days later Louis-Joseph was sent on an exploration trip to Lake Winnipeg; but smallpox among the Crees in that region forced him to return to Fort Saint-Charles; he was there on 28 May. Thanks to his good treatment and his advice about hygiene, however, none of the Crees accompanying him was seriously affected by the malady, whereas all those who were at Fort Maurepas died of it.

Louis-Joseph took over acting command of Fort Saint-Charles when his father left for Montreal at the beginning of June 1737. On the latter's return in August 1738 the two explorers set out for the Mandan country, a region which corresponds approximately to present-day North Dakota. They hoped during this voyage to discover the way to the western sea [*see* Pierre Gaultier de Varennes et de La Vérendrye]. When the expedition reached the Mandan country in early December, Louis-Joseph left for a short exploratory trip as far as the Missouri, which his father believed to be the famous River of the West. Having achieved the goal of their expedition, the La Vérendryes decided to return to Fort La Reine (Portage-la-Prairie, Man.), which they had built the preceding October.

In April 1739 Louis-Joseph was entrusted by his father with resuming the expedition around Lake Winnipeg which had been cut short in 1737. He was to seek a site north of Lac des Prairies (lakes Manitoba and Winnipegosis) for the fort which the Crees in the region had been requesting; then he was to explore the periphery of Lake Winnipeg and enter the Rivière Blanche (the lower stretch of the Saskatchewan River). The Chevalier carried out his mission and went up the river as far as the fork at which the Crees used to meet every spring, probably some miles to the northwest of Cedar Lake (Man.). Louis-Joseph then returned to Fort La Reine via the southern end of Cedar Lake and the Red and Assiniboine rivers.

When his father left for Montreal in June 1740, Louis-Joseph took over command of Fort Saint-Charles. He held it until September of the following year, then he went to spend the winter of 1741–42 at Fort La Reine. There he prepared to resume the expedition into the southwest which his older brother, Pierre GAULTIER de La Vérendrye, had not been able to complete the previous year for lack of a guide.

Louis-Joseph left on 29 April 1742, accompanied by his brother, François Gaultier Du Tremblay, two Frenchmen, and some Indian guides. The group first went to the country of the

Gaultier de La Vérendrye

Mandans, who were to lead them to a tribe called the Gens des Chevaux. In August they had reached the "Montagne des Gens des Chevaux," probably in the northwest of present-day Wyoming, but they found no one. Shortly afterwards the Chevalier and his companions met a group of Beaux-Hommes, then some Petits-Renards and "Pioyas." The expedition finally reached a village of Gens des Chevaux, whom they found in a state of indescribable devastation as a result of an attack by Gens du Serpent (Shoshonis), who had partially annihilated them. The Gens des Chevaux advised the Chevalier to go to see the Gens de l'Arc, who could better inform them about the route to the western sea. In mid-November the explorers arrived among the Gens de l'Arc, who were organizing a coalition of tribes and clans to make war against their formidable enemy, the Gens du Serpent. Louis-Joseph was well received by them, to the point that despite his own wishes he had to follow them in their war venture. On 8 Jan. 1743 a large group of the allied tribes was approaching the mountains; scouts were sent in the direction of the enemy, and after several days of searching they brought back word that the Gens du Serpent had fled. Fearing an attack against their villages, which they had left unprotected, the panic stricken warriors left the mountains in a general rout, to the great despair of the chief of the Gens de l'Arc, who could not keep them back, and the Chevalier, who was hoping to find the sea on the other side of the mountains. Everyone went home, and the Chevalier accompanied the Gens de l'Arc as far as their village. At the beginning of March 1743 the French left the Indians, after promising to come back to them the following spring. Not far from the village the Chevalier and his men found a camp of the Gens de la Petite-Cerise, a clan of the Pawnee-Arikaras. They followed these Indians to their fort at the juncture of the Bad and Missouri rivers, opposite present-day Pierre, the capital of South Dakota. They reached this fort on 19 March 1743 and stayed a fortnight there.

To mark his passage, the Chevalier de La Vérendrye buried at this spot, unknown to the Indians, a lead plaque bearing on one side a Latin inscription: "The 26th year of the reign of Louis XV. For the king, our very illustrious lord. By Monsieur le Marquis de Beauharnois [Charles de BEAUHARNOIS], 1741. Placed here by Pierre Gaultier de Laverendrie." The other side, which was engraved on the spot with a knife or awl, bore the following words: "Placed by the Chevalyer de Lave. – tblt [Tremblet or Tremblay, François Gaultier's official form of address] – Louy La

Londette [perhaps Louis Lalonde] – Amiotte [Amiot or Amyot]. 30 March 1743." It is not possible to identify positively the last two persons. This plaque, which was discovered in 1913, is one of the most valuable monuments of the history of the west.

On 2 April 1743 the Chevalier left the fort of the Gens de la Petite-Cerise to proceed to Fort La Reine, which the party did not reach until three months later, after stopping several times in the prairies among the Assiniboins and the Sioux. Louis-Joseph, who had been away more than 14 months, did not return with the precise information which his father would have liked about the western sea. Despite that, his expedition had positive results: it added considerably to the geographical knowledge of the period, it ensured for the Canadians and French the friendship and loyalty of a great number of Indian tribes until then unknown, and it consequently laid the bases for commercial operations which might turn out to be useful later. Moreover, as a result of this expedition it became increasingly clear to La Vérendrye Sr that the route to the western sea was not to be sought to the southwest, but to the northwest, where another route, the Saskatchewan River, was available.

In the autumn of 1743 La Vérendrye, under the pressure of unfortunate circumstances, had to present his resignation to Beauharnois for the following year as commandant of the *poste de l'Ouest* [see Pierre Gaultier de Varennes et de La Vérendrye]. Nicolas-Joseph de NOYELLES de Fleurimont, the explorer's nephew by marriage, succeeded him in 1744. La Vérendrye's sons retained their posts for the time being, and the Chevalier apparently acted as commandant until Noyelles's arrival in the west the following year.

In 1747 Louis-Joseph returned to the colony on business in company with Noyelles, who had resigned his command. The War of the Austrian Succession was in full swing: the Chevalier was entrusted by Charles-Joseph de Noyelles de Fleurimont, the acting commandant of Michilimackinac, with letters intended for Governor Beauharnois concerning the military operations in that region. Shortly afterwards the governor sent Louis-Joseph back to Michilimackinac as his messenger. Louis-Joseph expected to continue farther west, as is indicated by a power of attorney that he left his cousin by marriage, Pierre GAMELIN Maugras, but he had to return to Montreal where he spent part of the winter.

From January to March 1748 he took part in a military expedition against the Mohawks, then he prepared to return to the west. His father had been recalled the previous year to resume the

Gaultier de La Vérendrye

post of commandant, but it was in fact the Chevalier who was to fulfil this function, though unofficially. He left on 20 June 1748, after hostilities had ceased, and reached the west that autumn. In 1749 he returned to Montreal, where he learned that the king had accorded him on 1 May a well-deserved promotion to the modest rank of second ensign. That year was, however, marked by a sad event: his father's death, which occurred on 5 December after a "bad fever." The Chevalier also fell ill but recovered fairly quickly. At the end of December he attended to the formalities concerning his father's succession and had a posthumous inventory made.

The Chevalier expected to succeed his father in the west, but François Bigot* and his gang had begun their dealings, to which Governor La Jonquière [TAFFANEL] was no stranger, and the La Vérendryes were eliminated from the west with the appointment of Jacques LEGARDEUR de Saint-Pierre as commandant. On 17 April 1750 Louis-Joseph obtained permission, with difficulty, to go to Michilimackinac, then to Grand Portage (near present-day Grand Portage, Minn.), to meet the canoes coming from the west, in order to settle his father's business. To be able to pay the most pressing debts he had to resign himself on 15 July 1750 to selling the last piece of land his mother owned at Île Dupas, in Lac Saint-Pierre. In a moving report to the minister of Marine on 30 September he asked for reparations for what he considered to be injustices and oulined his sad situation and that of his brothers, but he waited in vain for a reply.

At the beginning of 1752 the Chevalier again launched into the trade in furs: on 18 February he entered into partnership with Luc de La Corne*, dit La Corne Saint-Luc, to run for a period of three years the post of Chagouamigon (Ashland, Wis.). La Corne was the "outfitter," Louis-Joseph the post commandant, and his younger brother, François Gaultier Du Tremblay, signed on to work for them as an interpreter. During his stay at Chagouamigon the Chevalier had a rather sharp dispute with Joseph Marin* de La Malgue, the commandant at Baie-des-Puants (Green Bay, Wis.). Marin had jurisdiction over the former Sioux post, which took in the upper Mississippi. But the Chevalier de La Vérendrye went into this region during the winter of 1752–53, as well as the following winter, to trade with the Indians. He claimed that he received orders from Governor Duquesne* to do so. He even set up two small posts in the territories which Marin claimed as his, and he dared confiscate possessions belonging to the latter's men, threatening to put them in irons. This bitter dispute lasted until 1754 and

was brought before Duquesne. Unfortunately the conclusion of the affair is not known. It seems that the governor had indeed given Louis-Joseph a licence for trading in the Sioux territory, to the detriment of Marin, to whom this right in fact belonged, and who had not been warned; but it is impossible to say what inspired Duquesne's action.

On 1 April 1753 the Chevalier had received his commission as ensign on the active list. When he returned to Montreal in 1755 he resumed his place in the garrison in that capacity. On 17 November of that year he married Marie-Amable, the daughter of Jacques Testard* de Montigny, thus becoming a member of one of the most important families in the colony. Of this marriage a daughter was born on 7 Nov. 1756, but she lived only a few days; the mother died a short time afterwards.

The year 1756 was fertile in transactions of all kinds for Louis-Joseph. He had to obtain ready cash and settle some business affairs; but the great event was the Chevalier's appointment as commandant of the *poste de l'Ouest* for a three-year term, on condition that he put up 8,000 *livres*. Trade in the west had in fact become free in 1756, and the post went to the highest bidder. In the period from 2 April to 14 June 1756 the Chevalier hired the men he would need. On 13 June he gave power of attorney to his wife to run his affairs during his absence. Nevertheless, despite all these measures he remained in Montreal, perhaps because of the necessities of the war. In any event, Louis-Joseph kept his post as commandant, operating from a distance for two years. On 1 May 1757 the Chevalier was promoted lieutenant; he remained in Montreal and on 31 Jan. 1758 he married again, his second wife being Louise-Antoinette de Mézières de Lépervanche.

In that year he left his post in the west to Charles-René DEJORDY de Villebon and was again given command of Chagouamigon, which he entrusted to Jacques-Marie Nolan Lamarque while he himself attended to Kaministiquia and Michipicoton (located respectively on the northwest and northeast shores of Lake Superior) in place of Joseph de Fleury Deschambault. The Chevalier was useful on Lake Superior because of his great hold on the Indian tribes. But precisely for that reason he did not complete his term of command at Chagouamigon: his services were required in another theatre. At the end of June and the beginning of July 1759 he took to Montreal from Michilimackinac groups from eight Indian tribes who were to aid in the defence of Lake Champlain. In August Louis-Joseph sent BOURLAMAQUE a plan of the military posts to be

Gaultier de La Vérendrye

set up in that region which was recognized by the authorities to be appropriate. We do not know, however, whether his suggestions were put into practice.

After the cessation of hostilities the Chevalier made known his intention of remaining in Canada, as we learn from several military rolls of 1760. He made preparations, however, for a trip to France, apparently to settle some business matters. He sailed from Quebec on 15 Oct. 1761 on board the *Auguste*; a month later, on 15 November, the ship was dashed to pieces on the shores of Cape Breton Island during a gale. The Chevalier perished, as did most of the passengers and crew members. Louis-Joseph's widow lived in great poverty, it seems, and died in Montreal on 3 March 1825.

Louis-Joseph Gaultier de La Vérendrye was certainly the most remarkable of the great discoverer's children. Energetic and strong-willed like his father, he was less idealistic and perhaps more practical, having a better education and more ability in handling men and affairs. A man of great integrity, he succeeded in winning the esteem and confidence of all his relatives, friends, and partners. Except for the two years of difference with Joseph Marin de La Malgue, he never had any interminable disputes with anyone. He even carried honesty to the point of repaying, when he had the means to do so, his father's old debts, some of which went back 40 or even 60 years. The Chevalier's commercial relations with his partners, his two marriages with important Montreal families, the praises he received from the military authorities, and the missions entrusted to him from 1747 on, without counting the years spent in the west, all suggest general recognition of a combination of qualities. It is a pity that the outcome of the Seven Years' War and this man's tragic end should have cut short such a fine career.

ANTOINE CHAMPAGNE

AN, Col., C^IIA, 87, 91; C^IIE, 16, ff.308–13; D²C, 59, f.32. ANQ-M, Greffe de L.-C. Danré de Blanzy, 15 févr. 1756; Greffe d'Antoine Foucher, 18 févr. 1752; Greffe de Marien Tailhandier, dit La Beaume, 2 juill. 1718. *Découvertes et établissements des Français* (Margry), VI, 598–611. "Documents sur Pierre Gaultier de La Vérendrye," J.-J. Lefebvre, édit., APQ *Rapport, 1949–51*, 33–67. "Journal de Marin, fils, 1753–1754," Antoine Champagne, édit., AQ *Rapport, 1960–61*. *Journals and letters of La Vérendrye* (Burpee), 406–32. "Mémoire du Canada," APQ *Rapport, 1924–25*, 154. PAC *Report, 1923*, app.C, 48, 49. L. J. Burpee, *The search for the western sea* (London, 1908; 2nd ed., Toronto, 1935). Champagne, *Les La Vérendrye*; *Nouvelles études sur les La Vérendrye*.

GAULTIER DE LA VÉRENDRYE DE BOUMOIS, PIERRE (he signed La Vérendrye *l'aîné* (the elder) after the death in 1736 of his brother Jean-Baptiste Gaultier* de La Vérendrye), explorer; b. 1 Dec. 1714 at Île aux Vaches on Lac Saint-Pierre (Que.), second son of Pierre GAULTIER de Varennes et de La Vérendrye and Marie-Anne Dandonneau Du Sablé; d. 13 Sept. 1755 in Quebec.

In 1728 Pierre Gaultier de La Vérendrye joined the colonial regular troops as a cadet and for two years did garrison duty in Montreal. In 1731, when he was barely 16, he left for the west with his father and spent the winter with him at the post of Kaministiquia (Thunder Bay, Ont.). In 1732 he accompanied him to Lake of the Woods (Ont.), where they built Fort Saint-Charles. In the spring of 1734, after his father had left for Montreal, Pierre took command of Fort Saint-Charles. He was relieved of this command by his cousin, Christophe Dufrost* de La Jemerais, towards the end of the summer and was ordered to build Fort Maurepas on the Red River. His brother Jean-Baptiste, who had previously been given this task, had, however, returned earlier than foreseen from an expedition into the Sioux country in the region of the upper Mississippi; consequently it was he who went to the Red River. In February 1737 Pierre accompanied his father to Fort Maurepas, and in June the two men left the west for Montreal and Quebec.

Upon their return to Fort Saint-Charles in August 1738 the explorer entrusted command of the fort to his son for the period of his voyage into the Mandan country, in present-day North Dakota. Pierre remained in command until November 1739. The following summer his father, who was on his way to Montreal, sent him from Michilimackinac the goods necessary for an exploratory voyage into the Mandan and Pawnee country. Pierre went to Fort La Reine (Portage-la-Prairie, Man.), on the Assiniboine River, and there he was forced to stay until the spring of 1741. Accompanied by two Frenchmen, he then continued south "as far as two Spanish forts," probably in present-day Nebraska; for lack of a guide, however, he had to turn back. He returned from his expedition with two horses and some articles of Spanish make. Pierre was already at Fort La Reine when his father, returning from the east, reached it in October 1741. The explorer immediately sent his son to build Fort Dauphin (Winnipegosis, Man.), north of Dauphin Lake. His mission completed, Pierre invited the Crees and Assiniboins to bring their furs from then on to the new fort, then he returned to Fort La Reine where he spent the entire year of 1742. He remained in the west after his father, who was replaced as commandant of the *poste de l'Ouest* by Nicolas-Joseph de NOYELLES de Fleurimont, had left for good in 1744.

Pierre went back to Montreal in 1745, but did not stay there long. He left again that same year for New England, where he fought under the orders of Jacques LEGARDEUR de Saint-Pierre. In May 1746 he followed Legardeur to Acadia, and in the spring of the following year, still under the same command, he fought against the Mohawks. He was then "detached to go to run the *postes de l'Ouest*," and made his preparations accordingly. The necessities of the war, however, changed his plans and the expedition was not able to set out for Michilimackinac until 10 Aug. 1747. Upon their arrival at the post the voyageurs were detained by Charles-Joseph de Noyelles de Fleurimont, the acting commandant, who feared what might result from the Indians' illwill. But Pierre "took it upon himself to go with great difficulty to the posts" and succeeded in winning the Indians over to the French cause again. In the spring of 1748 Pierre came back to Michilimackinac, then went on to the west, where he rebuilt the Fort Maurepas situated on the Winnipeg River, which had been burned by the Indians, and Fort La Reine, which was falling into ruin. On 1 May 1749 he received the rank of second ensign; although he was suggested as a lieutenant for service in the West Indies, he preferred to remain in Canada with his lower rank, which he was to keep until his death. Pierre was at Michilimackinac when he learned in December 1749 of his father's death. He returned to Montreal at the end of the summer of 1750.

During 1751 Pierre was occupied with several military operations at Quebec and Montreal. The following year he was sent to Fort Beauséjour (near Sackville, N.B.), where he served until its surrender to the British in 1755. At the beginning of his stay there, in 1752, he had sent Rouillé, the minister of Marine, a report in which he summed up his services and asked for the aid and protection of the court, but he does not seem to have received a reply. Pierre returned to Canada in the summer of 1755 and died, a bachelor, in the month of September.

An excellent soldier and a good explorer, Pierre Gaultier de La Vérendrye seems to have been endowed with the same qualities as his cousin La Jemerais and his brothers Jean-Baptiste and LOUIS-JOSEPH, but not with the latter's breadth of vision. He might perhaps have done significant work if circumstances had furnished him the opportunity for leadership.

ANTOINE CHAMPAGNE

AN, Col., C¹¹ᴬ, 87, f.81; 93, f.97; D²ᶜ, 48, f.178. ANQ-M, Greffe de François Simonnet, 15 juill. 1750. *Découvertes et établissements des Français* (Margry), VI, 628–31. Champagne, *Les La Vérendrye*; *Nouvelles études sur les La Vérendrye*.

GAULTIER DE VARENNES, JACQUES-RENÉ (he signed **DeVarennes**), officer in the colonial regular troops; baptized 2 Oct. 1677, second son of René Gaultier* de Varennes, governor of Trois-Rivières, and Marie Boucher; m. 7 Aug. 1712 Marie-Jeanne, daughter of Jacques Le Moyne* de Sainte-Hélène; buried 28 July 1757 at Montreal.

Jacques-René Gaultier de Varennes began his military career as a cadet at the age of 13 in the defence of Quebec against William Phips* in 1690. Thereafter he served with distinction in Canada during the wars of the League of Augsburg and the Spanish Succession; he was appointed ensign in 1704, and lieutenant in 1710. In 1726 his wife's uncle, Charles Le Moyne*, Baron de Longueuil, interim governor of New France, appointed him to command at Kaministiquia (Thunder Bay, Ont.) for three years. While there, at the age of 51, he took part in his last military campaign – under Constant Le Marchand* de Lignery against the Foxes in 1728.

In 1709 Varennes had promised to marry Marie-Marguerite-Renée Robinau de Bécancour "when his affairs permit and conditional upon the permission of his mother and the governor general," and failing marriage to pay her 6,000 *livres*. The following year he retracted his promise, citing the refusal of his mother and Governor Philippe de Rigaud* de Vaudreuil to give their consent. Pierre Robinau* de Bécancour, Marguerite's father, won a court order in Montreal holding him to his original promise. Appealing to the Conseil Supérieur in 1712, on the grounds that the engagement had not been reciprocal, Jacques-René won a reduced sentence and had to pay Robinau only 3,000 *livres*. A few days after this judgement he married Marie-Jeanne Le Moyne de Sainte-Hélène.

Jacques-René, who became eldest son on the death of his brother Louis in 1706 or 1707, accepted responsibility with his other brothers for part of his widowed mother's debt. She was obliged to support three widowed daughters and her grandchildren. The family seigneurial holdings were small, and although Jacques-René inherited the largest portion it likely produced only a modest income even by the end of the French régime.

Probably much more lucrative was his exploitation of the fur trade at Kaministiquia. It was a

Gaultier de Varennes

post commander's unofficial prerogative to control the trade in his area, and Jacques-René formed partnerships with several prominent merchants of Montreal from 1726 to 1728. That he had to borrow money to finance his enterprise indicates he was not wealthy, but the trade seems to have been normal during the three years he was in command. In 1727 a rearrangement of the partnership brought in his younger brother, Pierre GAULTIER de Varennes et de La Vérendrye, to begin his life of enterprise and exploration in the west.

From Kaministiquia Jacques-René came back to the garrison of Montreal. He was appointed captain in 1736 at the age of 60. A nobleman with an enviable military record, including praise for his moral conduct and devotion to the king's service, Jacques-René might have looked forward to an honourable retirement. Instead he was stripped of his command when in 1743 as captain of the guard in Montreal he refused to supply troops at the request of the court ushers to arrest his brother-in-law, Timothy SULLIVAN, known as Timothée Silvain, king's doctor, at the suit of Jacques-Joseph GUITON de Monrepos, lieutenant general of Montreal. Monrepos, whose haughtiness in claiming certain honours for himself since his arrival two years earlier had inflamed a traditional animosity between military and civil officials, had earned the scorn of the local officer corps. Jacques-René's obstruction of the normal course of justice in this instance received support from many officers of the garrison and likely reflected their common resentment against Monrepos.

The importance of Sullivan's relationship to Jacques-René is more difficult to estimate. There is evidence that the Varennes family disapproved of Sullivan's marriage to Marie-Renée Gaultier de Varennes. Wife-beating figured among his several outrages, and in 1738 the Varennes launched a suit against him for legal separation. But in 1743 Jacques-René may have acted to protect Sullivan out of loyalty to the family. The intendant, Gilles Hocquart*, thought Monrepos foolish to have pursued a man whose wife was so well connected throughout the colony.

The minister of Marine, Maurepas, was determined to make an example of Jacques-René to check what he believed to be widespread insubordination among Canadian military officers. In vain did Governor BEAUHARNOIS, Intendant Hocquart, and Bishop Pontbriand [DUBREIL] plead extenuating circumstances on Jacques-René's behalf. The principle of punishment to set an example assumed that the more illustrious the example the more effective it would be. Even under a new governor, La Jonquière [TAFFANEL], and a new minister, Rouillé, Jacques-René failed to win reinstatement. He endured poverty and misery, though he himself seemed more concerned with his disgrace, which lowered him "to the level of ordinary individuals in the colony." He died on 27 July 1757 and was followed ten days later by his wife.

Two of Jacques-René's sons served in the colonial regular troops. Jean-Hippolyte (b. 7 Sept. 1717) married Charlotte-Louise-Angélique Sarrazin in 1746, fought in Canada during the Seven Years' War, and died en route to France in the shipwreck of the *Auguste*, 15 Nov. 1761. René was born 27 April 1720, served as ensign at Île Royale (Cape Breton Island) from 1750 to 1757, then returned to Canada. He was wounded in the battle of Sainte-Foy and died the following day, 29 April 1760.

S. DALE STANDEN

AN, Col., B, 78, ff.313–14, 319–19v, 344–44v; 81, ff.281–81v, 293–93v, 300, 307; C¹¹A, 79, ff.222–23v, 296v–98; 80, f.293; 81, ff.329v–39v; 82, ff.326–26v; 93, ff.121–22, 124–25; 120/2, p.117 (PAC transcript); D²ᶜ, 47/2, pt.4, pp.365, 395 (PAC transcripts); D²ᴰ, 1; Section Outre-Mer, G², 213, no. 21. ANQ, Greffe de C.-H. Du Laurent, 1ᵉʳ févr. 1746; AP, René Gaultier de Varennes (fils). PAC, MG 7, IA, 3, 9286, f.38; MG 8, A14. "Correspondance de Vaudreuil," APQ *Rapport*, 1946–47, 417. *Jug. et délib.*, VI, 451–55. "La « foi et hommage » sous le régime seigneurial," APQ *Rapport*, 1925–26, 342. Le Jeune, *Dictionnaire*. É.-Z. Massicotte, "Congés et permis déposés ou enregistrés à Montréal sous le régime français," APQ *Rapport*, 1921–22, 214. Antoine Roy, *Inv. greffes not.*, XIX, 402; XXI, 32. Tanguay, *Dictionnaire*. Champagne, *Les La Vérendrye*. Harris, *Seigneurial system*, 47–50. Ivanhoë Caron, "La famille Gaultier de Varennes," BRH, XXVI (1920), 14–21, 78–89.

GAULTIER DE VARENNES ET DE LA VÉRENDRYE, PIERRE (also called Boumois), officer, fur-trader, explorer; b. 17 Nov. 1685 at Trois-Rivières, son of René Gaultier* de Varennes and Marie Boucher; d. 5 Dec. 1749 at Montreal.

The Gaultiers came from the district of Angers, France, where their name is mentioned for the first time in the mid-16th century. Apparently they were prominent members of their community. They were substantial landowners – Varennes and La Vérendrye were the names of two of their estates – and held positions in the army, the judiciary, and the government. Although they were members of the third estate they were affecting a coat of arms by 1600.

René Gaultier de Varennes, the father of Pierre, came to Canada in September 1665 as a lieutenant in the Régiment de Carignan-Salières. His company was stationed in the Trois-Rivières district during the winter following his arrival. Undoubtedly, this is when he became acquainted with the local governor, Pierre Boucher*, whose 12-year-old daughter, Marie, he married in September 1667. René thus became connected with one of New France's most prominent families and, as he had no doubt anticipated, his own fortunes soared as a result. He became governor of Trois-Rivières when Boucher resigned this office in 1668 and was granted seigneuries by Talon* and Frontenac [Buade*]. He thus acquired status but, despite involvement in the fur trade, not a great deal of wealth. He left his family destitute when he died in 1689.

Thirteen children were born of the marriage, eight of whom – four sons and four daughters – reached maturity. Pierre was the youngest and the only one to achieve prominence in Canadian affairs. Other children, however, also deserve mention. Louis, the eldest, was the original bearer of the name La Vérendrye (during Louis's lifetime Pierre was called Boumois). Louis left Canada for France, entered the army, and was killed in action during the war of the Spanish Succession, either in 1706 or 1707. JACQUES-RENÉ was an officer in the colonial regular troops. Marie-Renée, born in 1682, first married François-Christophe Dufrost de La Gemerais. One of their sons, Christophe*, was Pierre's "second in command" in the west from 1731 to 1736.

Pierre received a little formal education at the seminary of Quebec where he was a student from 1696 to 1699. Already, however, he had chosen a military career. He received a cadet's commission in the colonial regular troops in 1696 and saw considerable action during the War of the Spanish Succession. He was a member of the French and Indian unit commanded by Jean-Baptiste Hertel* de Rouville which attacked Deerfield, Massachusetts, in 1704, and he campaigned in Newfoundland under Daniel d'Auger* de Subercase the following year. Shortly afterwards he was promoted ensign. This, however, was a minor rank and Pierre decided to pursue his career in France where he expected better chances of advancement. He arrived in the mother country early in 1708 and was attached to the Régiment de Bretagne, the one in which Louis had served until his death, with the rank of second lieutenant. At the battle of Malplaquet, on 11 Sept. 1709, he was seriously wounded by gunshot and eight sabre cuts and taken prisoner by the enemy. Following his release in 1710 he was promoted lieutenant.

A lieutenant had costly social obligations which consumed more than his salary. La Vérendrye found that he could not support himself and asked the court for permission to return to Canada. His request was granted on 24 May 1712. He sailed from France in July, no more advanced than when he had arrived four years before. His lieutenancy in the French army had been cancelled and he had forfeited his ensign's commission in the Canadian troops when he left the colony. Fortunately he was able to regain the latter rank through the influence of Mme de Vaudreuil [Joybert*] who was then residing at the court and who interceded on his behalf.

On 24 Oct. 1712, shortly after landing in Canada, La Vérendrye wed Marie-Anne, daughter of Louis Dandonneau Du Sablé, to whom he had become engaged shortly before his departure for France. Dandonneau was one of Trois-Rivières's substantial landowners and he endowed his daughter with 2,000 *livres* as well as land on Île Dupas and Île aux Vaches, located in Lac Saint-Pierre. The couple made their residence on Île aux Vaches, where they lived obscurely for the next 15 years. They had six children – four sons and two daughters – and cleared a 38-acre farm. To round out the slender income derived from this property, La Vérendrye had the revenue of the fief of Tremblay, inherited from his family, his ensign's pay, and the fur-trading post of La Gabelle founded by his father on the Rivière Saint-Maurice. In 1715, Claude de Ramezay*, acting governor of New France, granted La Vérendrye permission to go there to trade with the Indians a few weeks every year. Even with these additional sources of revenue he was far from affluent. Only by borrowing and selling portions of his properties was he able to make ends meet.

By the mid-1720s La Vérendrye was fast approaching middle age and his life thus far had been anything but successful. His military career had fizzled out in 1712 and since that time he had done little more than eke out a subsistence as a farmer and occasional fur-trader. But the third and most important period of his life was about to open. In 1726 his brother Jacques-René received command of the *poste du Nord*, embracing a vast area north of Lake Superior. The main post was located at Kaministiquia (Thunder Bay, Ont.), with secondary ones at Nipigon (near the mouth of the Nipigon River) and Michipicoton, north of Sault Ste Marie. Over the next year Jacques-René formed a partnership to carry out the fur trade in the area, hired *engagés* (inden-

Gaultier de Varennes

tured employees), and borrowed money from various merchants for the purchase of trade goods. La Vérendrye was taken into the partnership to act as second in command and became commander-in-chief in 1728 when his brother left the post to participate in the war against the Foxes. As far as one can judge it was at this time that the idea of discovering the western sea began to germinate in his mind. As late as 1726 his face was turned towards France, not the Canadian plains, for he was contemplating a trip to the mother country to recover the lieutenancy lost 14 years before.

The search for the western sea, which now began to engage La Vérendrye's attention, goes back to the dawn of the French presence in North America. Since the days of Verrazzano* and Cartier*, explorer after explorer had tried to find this supposed short route to the Far East. Nebulous at first, the concept of the western sea became quite precise by the end of the 17th century when the French had acquired a clearer picture of the geography of North America. They had ascertained that the land mass was indented on the north and south by great gulfs: the Gulf of Mexico to the southeast, the Gulf of California (*mer Vermeille*) to the southwest, and Hudson Bay (*mer glaciale*) to the north. The Gulf of California was known to connect with the Pacific and it was strongly suspected that Hudson Bay did so too. Partly from this geographical pattern, partly from the information obtained from Indians, the French deduced the existence in the middle latitudes of the American continent of a gulf-like western sea (*mer du couchant*) which opened on the Pacific. La Vérendrye, in brief, was chasing a mirage.

The discovery of these non-existent waters became a matter of some urgency following the death of Louis XIV in 1715. The regent, Philippe, Duc d'Orléans, who governed the kingdom in the name of the young Louis XV, was keenly interested in the geographical and scientific aspects of the problem as were some important members of his entourage such as the cartographers Claude and Guillaume Delisle and the Abbé Jean Bobé. Canadians were also interested in this discovery but for more practical reasons. Executing the project, they anticipated, would require the establishment of a chain of posts in the northwest which would help reconstruct a fur-trading network severely injured by the cession of Hudson Bay to the British in 1713.

In the 1720s the French still knew little about the Canadian interior – their point of farthest recorded penetration was Rainy Lake (or Tekamamiouen), reached by Jacques de NOYON

in 1688 – but a concept of the west was firmly established among those interested in questions of discovery and exploration. It postulated the existence, somewhere in the interior, of a height of land or divide which could be reached via an eastward-flowing stream and which any explorer must eventually climb. There he would find the source of another river flowing into the western sea. This conceptualization of the interior was approximately correct, if one reads Pacific Ocean instead of western sea, and was the one held by La Vérendrye, but the French had no inkling whatever of the enormity of the distances. Data obtained by Noyon from Indian informants indicated that the Western Sea lay in the latitudes of Lake Winnipeg (Ouinipigon), that the watershed was in the vicinity of Lake of the Woods, and that the westward-flowing stream was the Winnipeg (Ouinipigon) River.

It thus seemed that the western sea lay within easy distance of the border lakes (the Rainy Lake–Lake of the Woods complex). In 1717 an expedition commanded by Zacharie Robutel* de La Noue set out for the area with instructions from Governor Vaudreuil [Rigaud*] to establish a chain of three posts terminating at Lake of the Woods. From this advanced position some of his men could strike out for the western sea. La Noue erected a post at Kaministiquia but advanced no farther. Indian hostility held him back. Disappointed by his failure, the court, acting on the recommendation of Father CHARLEVOIX, whom it had sent to America to make a personal study of the situation, decided to abandon the attempt to reach the western sea by way of the border lakes and to proceed instead from a base on the upper Mississippi. As a preliminary measure a mission was established on Lake Pepin in Sioux country in 1727 for the purpose, among other things, of gathering information from the Indians on possible westward routes [*see* René BOUCHER de La Perrière; Michel GUIGNAS].

La Vérendrye changed this orientation. While commanding at the *poste du nord* he questioned the Indians who came to trade about the land to the west and their answers convinced him that the route to the sea lay indeed through the border lakes and not the Mississippi valley country. A Cree chief named Pako, who had journeyed far into the unknown land, told him something about Lake Ouinipigon and the river system surrounding it. The slave of an elderly chief named Vieux Crapaud described in sketchy fashion the land of the Mandans. Another Indian named Auchagah* drew for him on a piece of bark a map of the western country. From this information La Vérendrye composed his own picture of the

Canadian interior. Its chief improvement over previous ones was the location of the western sea, which no longer appears in the area of the Manitoba lakes but an undetermined distance to the west. Its chief weakness was the representation of Lake Ouinipigon not as the nub of a complex set of waterways but merely as an enlargement of the River of the West (as the waterway the explorer sought came to be called). Its chief riddle was the identity (was it the Saskatchewan or the Nelson River?) of the river flowing out of Lake Ouinipigon on which the ebb and flow of the tide reportedly became noticeable after a ten-day journey. In any event La Vérendrye concluded, not wrongly, that the key to the problem of the discovery lay in the region of Lake Ouinipigon. Once the French had a post on those waters they would be strategically located for their dash to the western sea.

The next step was for him to win the French officials over to his plan. In 1728, at Michilimackinac, he met the Jesuit Nicolas Degonnor who was on his way from the Sioux mission to Quebec. The missionary was greatly interested by the data La Vérendrye was gathering and agreed to carry his reports and maps to the governor. Then, in 1730, La Vérendrye himself went down to Quebec and out of his meetings with Governor Charles de BEAUHARNOIS the project emerged in its definitive form. Its nature is described in the joint dispatch of Beauharnois and Hocquart* to Maurepas, minister of Marine, of October 1730. The two officials announced that they planned to send La Vérendrye west the following spring to build a post on Lake Ouinipigon. This establishment would not only facilitate the discovery of the western sea but also greatly benefit French commerce since the area was rich in peltries, peltries which were at present going to the English on Hudson Bay through the Crees. La Vérendrye, moreover, would carry out this undertaking without expense to the king except for a modest sum of 2,000 *livres* to buy presents for the Indians. The minister sanctioned the project although Charlevoix, to whom he referred it for comment, opposed the establishment of permanent posts which, he feared, would enable commerce to get the better of exploration.

The manner in which the expedition was organized did indeed greatly enlarge its commercial dimension. With the court providing only token support, La Vérendrye was obliged to turn to Canadian merchants to find the capital he needed to finance his undertaking. Between March and June 1731 a nine-man partnership made up of four distinct sub-partnerships was formed. It included La Vérendrye, his eldest son

Jean-Baptiste*, his nephew Christophe Dufrost de La Jemerais, and the merchants Louis Hamelin, Laurent-Eustache Gamelin Châteauvieux, and Ignace Gamelin* Jr. A ruling issued by Beauharnois appointed La Vérendrye commandant of the post to be built on Lake Ouinipigon and stipulated that he and his associates would hold a monopoly of the area's fur trade for a three-year period. Nothing was said in this nine-clause document about the discovery of the western sea.

On 8 June 1731 La Vérendrye, accompanied by his sons Jean-Baptiste, PIERRE, François, and some 50 *engagés*, set out from Montreal. They were joined at Michilimackinac by the Jesuit missionary Charles-Michel MÉSAIGER and arrived at the Grand Portage, at the western extremity of Lake Superior, on 26 Aug. 1731. Here the *engagés*, worn out by the rigours of the journey and discouraged by the difficulties of the road ahead, refused to advance any farther. However, La Vérendrye and Mésaiger prevailed upon the bolder ones to push on into the interior with Jean-Baptiste and La Jemerais. In the autumn this advance party, moving by an intricate and broken chain of lakes and streams, reached Rainy Lake where it built Fort Saint-Pierre, the first of eight posts eventually established by the La Vérendrye expedition in the northwest. Meantime the commandant and his main body of people had retraced their steps to Kaministiquia where they settled for the winter. In the spring of 1732 the two groups rejoined and, accompanied by some 50 canoes of Crees and Assiniboins, moved on to Lake of the Woods from which the river of the west allegedly sprang. Here they built Fort Saint-Charles which served as La Vérendrye's headquarters for the next several years.

By means of these two forts La Vérendrye now controlled the border lake country. In the spring of 1733 he sent La Jemerais and Jean-Baptiste on to Lake Ouinipigon to find a suitable location for the post he intended building there. Unfortunately his two lieutenants started out too soon from Fort Saint-Charles. Ice stalled their advance after they had descended the Ouinipigon River to within 15 or 20 leagues of the lake. The younger La Vérendrye remained where he was and La Jemerais returned to Fort Saint-Charles. Almost immediately he was sent to Quebec by the commandant to present a report to Beauharnois on what had been accomplished to date.

He reached Montreal on 20 September and from there went on to Quebec. He discussed with the governor the financial condition of his uncle's enterprise; 43,000 *livres* had thus far been spent and returns were inadequate to cover this outlay. Would the crown help finance the expedition by

Gaultier de Varennes

granting the partners 10,000 *livres per annum* during three years? This request was passed on to Maurepas for consideration. But when he turned from finance to other matters La Jemerais fairly brimmed with optimism. Prevailing winds on Lake of the Woods were westerly and since they brought copious showers the sea could not be far off. Encouraged by this phenomenon he planned to start off in quest of this sea the following spring. By leaving Quebec as soon as the ice broke in 1734 he hoped to reach the land of the "Sioux who go underground," or the Mandans, some time in 1735. The description of the Mandans which he had obtained from the Crees suggested that they had marked affinities with the Europeans. Their hair was light and their language and their dwellings resembled those of the French. These people reportedly dwelt on the River of the West (in fact they lived on the Missouri), 300 leagues from Lake of the Woods.

Two basic points must be noted from this report. First, the supposition about the proximity of the western sea strengthened Maurepas in his conviction that reaching these waters was a relatively simple matter and did not prepare him to look with understanding upon the delays La Vérendrye was to encounter. Second, solely on the basis of Indian reports and without any prior exploration of Lake Ouinipigon, the search for the River of the West was being diverted from the Canadian plains to the Mississippi basin. This diversion was a fundamental error. It took eight years and two expeditions for the La Vérendryes to realize that the Missouri flowed southeast to the Mississippi and the Gulf of Mexico rather than to the western sea. At this point, belatedly, the search returned to the Canadian plains.

While his lieutenants were exploring advanced locations, meeting Indian groups, and surveying the land for the best strategic sites for posts, La Vérendrye was spending much of his time at Fort Saint-Charles supervising Indian affairs and organizing the fur trade. The pattern of tribal relations which he found west of the Great Lakes bore some similarity to the one which had prevailed in the St Lawrence valley in the 1600s. When Quebec was founded in 1608 the Algonquins and Montagnais were at war with the Iroquois. Since Quebec was situated on the territory of the Algonquins and Montagnais, Champlain* had to extend military assistance to these Indians in order to win their friendship and their commerce. West of the Great Lakes, in the 18th century, a chronic state of war pitted the Assiniboins, Crees, and Monsonis against the Sioux and the Ojibwas. La Vérendrye's chain of posts being located on the land of the Assiniboins and

Crees, he had to side with these Indians in their quarrel; but he could not afford Champlain's recklessness, for the Sioux and Ojibwas, unlike the Iroquois, were French allies. By openly espousing the quarrels of the Crees and Assiniboins he might well wreck a large segment of New France's Indian alliances and render untenable French positions on Lake Superior, home of the Ojibwas, and on the upper Mississippi, home of the Sioux.

Thus La Vérendrye had to proceed with extreme caution in his conduct of Indian affairs. Initially his diplomacy met with much success for he was able to prevent a major conflict from breaking out on the Canadian plains. By May 1734, however, the Crees and Assiniboins could no longer be restrained. Seeing this La Vérendrye gave his assent to a military expedition on condition that it be carried out not against the Sioux of the River, who could threaten Fort Beauharnois on Lake Pepin, but against the Sioux of the prairies. At a meeting at Fort Saint-Charles he exhorted his allies to fight well, provided them with ammunition, and allowed Jean-Baptiste to go along as a councillor who would have a voice in deliberations without engaging in actual combat. The commandant would later pay dearly for this rash gesture, even though Jean-Baptiste abandoned the war party when it decided to march against the Sioux of the River.

On 27 May 1734, a few days after his meeting with the Indians, La Vérendrye started out for Montreal. Pressing business called him there. The trading system which he was in the process of organizing was not yet functioning smoothly and some members of the association formed in 1731 to finance the expedition were becoming disenchanted. La Vérendrye himself, for some unstated reason, was unhappy with Louis Hamelin, to whom he owed 7,768 *livres*, and wished to terminate the agreement with him which still had two years to run. The commandant, furthermore, was anxious both to find out how Maurepas had responded to his appeal for financial aid and to inform Beauharnois that the fort on Lake Ouinipigon, which he had been commissioned to build in 1731, was about to become a reality. On 11 May two of his men had returned to Fort Saint-Charles after exploring the lake and selecting for the fort a site on the Red River a few miles above its mouth. On his way to Montreal La Vérendrye met Joseph Cartier, one of his associates, and instructed him to proceed forthwith to this location to begin the construction. Jean-Baptiste got there first, however, and completed the work by June 1734. The fort was called Maurepas, in honour of the minister.

The news which greeted La Vérendrye when he arrived in the colony was not encouraging. In Montreal he learned that his associates would advance nothing more on credit. In Quebec the governor informed him that the king was unwilling to contribute anything to his enterprise; it must finance itself from the revenues of the fur trade. Although the situation was disheartening, Beauharnois had no intention of abandoning La Vérendrye. On the contrary, he was determined to find a formula that would enable him to press forward with the discovery, thus satisfying Maurepas who was unhappy with the results so far achieved, and also enable the colony to expand its network of posts on the Canadian plains, thus satisfying its need for fur. The solution he hit upon called for La Vérendrye to farm out his posts to his business associates for a three-year period in return for an annual salary of 3,000 *livres*. These associates would concern themselves with the commercial aspect of the venture while La Vérendrye devoted himself entirely to the discovery. On 18 May 1735 a new association was formed, dominated by Jean-Baptiste Legras and Jean-Marie Nolan. The latter was a younger brother of Charles NOLAN Lamarque, one of Montreal's most important merchants, who was reputed to have sent the most voyageurs to the west and to have sent them the farthest.

On 21 June 1735 La Vérendrye departed once more for the west accompanied by LOUIS-JOSEPH, the youngest and perhaps the ablest of his sons, and the Jesuit Jean-Pierre Aulneau*, who was replacing Mésaiger. They arrived at Fort Saint-Charles on 23 October, and almost immediately the worst series of setbacks of the commandant's career began. First came the death of La Jemerais. He was stricken ill while commanding at Fort Maurepas and died on 10 May 1736 as he was being brought back to Fort Saint-Charles. Then it became evident that the arrangements of 1735 had not improved but impaired the efficiency of operations. The merchants traded where they pleased and left the forts unprovided for. Their negligence in provisioning the posts made it necessary in the spring of 1736 for La Vérendrye to send a 19-man emergency expedition under the command of Jean-Baptiste to Kaministiquia and Michilimackinac for supplies. And now he paid the penalty for having armed the Indians of his command against the Sioux in 1734. A band of the latter Indians on 8 June 1736 attacked the expedition on an island in Lake of the Woods and massacred them to the last man. "In that calamity," lamented La Vérendrye, "I lost my son, the Reverend Father [Aulneau], and all my Frenchmen to my lifelong regret." Yet he did not retaliate, knowing full well what the consequences might be.

Despite this tragedy, he was determined to push on to Lake Ouinipigon. Louis-Joseph had gone there in the autumn of 1736 with the intention of starting out for the Mandans but had been obliged to abandon the project when the supplies he required failed to arrive. After cooling the warlike ardour of the Crees, Assiniboins, and Monsonis who wanted to avenge the French blood, his father too left for Fort Maurepas where he arrived in February 1737, five years and eight months after initially setting out for the west. The time was propitious for him to continue on to the Mandans. It was still early in the season and the Indians offered to guide him. Unfortunately, his own men refused to follow him. These two missed opportunities left La Vérendrye with no alternative. He would have to go east to recruit fresh personnel and complain to the governor about the failure of the merchants to support him.

The voyage to Lake Ouinipigon had not been totally wasted, however. It enabled the La Vérendryes to gain a fresh understanding of the complicated Manitoba lakes system and how it related to the western sea. A map drawn in 1737, probably by Louis-Joseph, indicates two major possibilities for reaching that ocean. One, which would be attempted first, was to pass southwest to the Mandan country. The other was to utilize the Saskatchewan River, referred to on the map as the Rivière Blanche. According to Indian reports, this Rivière Blanche connected with a westward flowing river by means of a lake lying on a height of land. This is the first expression of interest in the Saskatchewan as a potential westward route. For the moment La Vérendrye stored in his mind the information about the river, to be used in case the Mandan route proved to be a blind lead.

La Vérendrye received a cool reception when he reached Quebec in the fall of 1737. Maurepas, nearing the end of his patience, had flatly informed Beauharnois in April "that the beaver trade had more to do than anything else with the Sieur de la Veranderye's western Sea expedition." The governor may have substantially agreed with this diagnosis but, unlike his superior at Versailles, he attached great importance to the commercial aspect of La Vérendrye's enterprise. The posts established west of Lake Superior had proved their worth in spectacular fashion in 1735 by producing, jointly with Fort Beauharnois, 100,000 *livres* weight of beaver, over half the total crop for that year. Still, something had to be done to mollify Maurepas. The governor therefore extracted from La Vérendrye a promise that he

Gaultier de Varennes

would reach the Mandans in 1738 and warned him that he would be recalled if he did not keep his word. He must also have dealt sternly with the merchants for they cooperated closely with La Vérendrye over the next year. Indeed, the Nolan brothers accompanied him on his trek to the Mandans.

La Vérendrye was not only gathering peltries in the west but also a substantial number of Indian slaves. In a dispatch of 26 May 1742 to Beauharnois, Father Claude-Godefroy COQUART reported that a war party of Crees and Assiniboins had recently routed the Sioux of the prairies in a four-day battle, killed 70 men besides women and children, and captured such a large number of slaves that they made a line four *arpents* long. In his memoir of 1744 to Maurepas, La Vérendrye himself stated that the colony had benefited from his western activities in three chief ways. "Do the great number of people my enterprise provides with a living, the slaves it procures to the colony and the pelts which had previously gone to the English count for nothing?" This statement provides some indication of the magnitude of the slave trade. Most historians, however, for reasons which are not too difficult to understand, have preferred to ignore this aspect of his career.

After his interview with Beauharnois in 1737, La Vérendrye realized that his future was at stake. Now, at last, he displayed the true manner of an explorer. Passing rapidly from post to post he reached Fort Maurepas on 22 Sept. 1738. On 3 October he was on the site of present-day Portage-la-Prairie where he built Fort La Reine "on the road by which the Assiniboins go to the English." On 16 October, accompanied by 20 picked men, his sons Louis-Joseph and François, the Nolan brothers, and 25 Assiniboins, he set off again on the final leg of his journey. It came to a triumphant end on 3 December when, his Indian escort swelled to 600 Assiniboins and 30 Mandans, he entered the main Mandan village with drums beating and colours flying. This village was located in present-day North Dakota, near the upper waters of either the Little Knife River or Shell Creek, about 20 miles from the modern town of Sanish. At last La Vérendrye stood, he thought, within a few miles of the famous River of the West. The most significant comment on him as an explorer is that, after having journeyed some 1,500 miles, he did not trouble himself to move the short remaining distance to view the river but sent Louis-Joseph to do it in his place. The latter took his bearings at Old Crossings, where the meandering Missouri turns sharply to the southwest. Had high bluffs not blocked his view downstream he could have seen the Missouri resuming its normal southeast flow and probably lost any illusion about its being the River of the West.

The journey to the Mandans had left La Vérendrye physically exhausted and burdened with debt. He struggled back to Fort La Reine in January 1739 and never afterwards displayed the stamina and fortitude which had characterized his early years on the Canadian plains. In June 1740 he made a third voyage to the colony, hoping to straighten out his finances in preparation for another and yet deeper thrust into the Missouri River country. Upon reaching Montreal he learned that his wife Marie-Anne, who had ably served him as attorney and procurator during his long absences, had died the previous September and lay buried in Sainte-Anne's chapel of Notre-Dame church. In Quebec, however, Beauharnois received him graciously, lodged him in his residence during the winter, and tried to place his finances on a sounder basis by granting him, beginning in June 1741 when the arrangements concluded in 1735 expired, the fur-trading monopoly of the posts he had founded. In June 1741, accompanied by Father Coquart, he set out on his fourth and last voyage to the west.

In his headquarters at Fort La Reine he seems to have had two main preoccupations. His first was to determine once and for all if the western sea could be reached by a southwesterly route. With this end in view he sent Louis-Joseph on the memorable journey that took him in 1742–43 as far as the Big Horn mountains of Wyoming. His second concern was to consolidate his control of the Manitoba lakes as he had done previously of the border lakes. This task was delegated to Pierre. Between 1741 and 1743 Pierre built Fort Dauphin (Winnipegosis, Man.); others, probably members of his party, built Fort Bourbon, to the northwest of Lake Winnipeg, and Fort Paskoya, to the northwest of Cedar Lake. These posts were located in the country of the Crees who had long been asking for them so as to be spared the lengthy journey to the counters of the Hudson's Bay Company. With the exception of Fort Paskoya, their purpose was clearly trade, not exploration, and they probably further discredited La Vérendrye in the eyes of Maurepas who by now regarded his every gesture with suspicion. In 1742 he informed Beauharnois that La Vérendrye's enterprise might show better results if some suitable officer – to whom the commandant himself would pay an annual salary of 3,000 *livres*! – were associated with him and if one of his sons were replaced by another officer. Although Beauharnois protested such an arrangement, the handwriting on the wall was clear: Maurepas was intent upon squeezing the La Vérendrye clan out of the west. La Vérendrye did not misread it. Alleging ill health, but in reality to avoid the humiliation in store for him, he handed in his resignation in 1743, to take effect the following year.

He resigned but, thanks to Beauharnois's unflagging loyalty, his links with the west were not severed. Nicolas-Joseph de NOYELLES de Fleurimont who succeeded him as commandant was married to one of his nieces, his sons remained at their posts, and he himself carried on a sizeable trade in the area thanks to permits issued to him by Beauharnois and his successor La Galissonière [BARRIN]. In 1744, thanks again to Beauharnois, Maurepas grudgingly granted him a captain's commission and shortly afterwards Beauharnois named him captain of his guards. La Vérendrye now settled down to the good life, entertaining and being entertained by the colony's fashionable society and courting Esther Sayward (Sayer), widow of Pierre de LESTAGE, one of New France's great merchants. In 1746 Noyelles resigned his command. La Vérendrye was appointed to succeed him and began planning yet another western expedition, this time up the Saskatchewan River, which, he belatedly realized, was the most convenient route by which to pursue the discovery of the western sea. He planned to leave for the west himself in 1750 but died on 5 Dec. 1749, not, however, before having received the greatest honour of his career, the cross of Saint-Louis, bestowed upon him by Antoine-Louis Rouillé, successor of Maurepas. He left a small estate worth perhaps 4,000 *livres*, much of it consisting of articles of clothing and adornment, the estate, in brief, of an impecunious nobleman.

And this is what La Vérendrye had essentially been. After unsuccessful attempts to pursue a military career in France and, following his return to Canada, to make a living from agriculture and the fur trade near Trois-Rivières – he once referred to this latter period as his forgotten years – he turned to the west. Why? To perform deeds which, by contributing to the glory of the king, would also contribute to his own. But glory in his eyes did not consist exclusively or even essentially in the discovery of the sea of the west. "I am only seeking," he informed Maurepas in 1731, "to carry the name and arms of His Majesty into a vast stretch of countries hitherto unknown, to enlarge the colony and increase its commerce." Thirteen years later, writing this time in the past tense, he made almost exactly the same statement.

How successful was he? As a discoverer, the most important aspect of his mission in the eyes of Maurepas if not in his own, he was a failure, and this for many reasons. The ocean was far away and the intervening area completely uncharted. With the crown refusing to subsidize his venture he was obliged to rely on local merchants. Unfortunately, these merchants were grouped in small partnerships that could not generate the capital required to sustain an expedition so far away from the St Lawrence valley. Their repeated failures to provision the posts prove it clearly. Furthermore, La Vérendrye had neither the tastes nor the qualifications of an explorer. It took him five years and eight months to reach Lake Winnipeg. Without any prior exploration of these waters he allowed his expedition to veer towards the blind alley of the American plains. When, after seven and a half years, he finally stood within a half-day's journey of the Missouri River, he did not bother to move this short distance to view the alleged River of the West. Significant incuriosity! All these incidents help to explain the weakness of his westward thrust.

But this is the debit side of the ledger. When all is said and done, one must recognize that La Vérendrye pushed back the frontiers of New France as far as Manitoba; that in countless meetings with the Indians he enshrined loyalty to the French monarchy among important new tribes; that the posts he built west of the Great Lakes transformed Rainy Lake, Lake of the Woods, and Lake Winnipeg into French inland seas and diverted much of the fur of the Saskatchewan and Assiniboine areas from Hudson Bay to the St Lawrence. He did all this quietly, without fuss and fanfare, in the face of personal tragedies and unusual adversities. Had he only been more articulate and outspoken in his dispatches, perhaps Maurepas, like Beauharnois, would have recognized the great merits of this valiant son of New France.

YVES F. ZOLTVANY

[Correspondence, memoirs, maps, and the journals kept by La Vérendrye are found in AN, Col., B; C¹¹ᴬ; C¹¹ᴱ E; F³; Section Outre-Mer, Dépôt des fortifications des colonies. Important items will also be found in Archives du ministère des Affaires étrangères (Paris), Mém. et doc., Amérique, 8; BN, NAF 9286 (Margry). A convenient starting point for the study of La Vérendrye is AN, Col., C¹¹ᴱ, 16, in which considerable documentation on him has been gathered, and AN, Col., E, 263, his personal dossier. Many of these documents have been published in *Découvertes et établissements des Français* (Margry), VI; *Journals and letters of La Vérendrye* (Burpee). The latter is the more widely used of the two. The journal of the expedition of

Gautier

1738–39 to the Mandans is published in PAC *Report, 1889*, A, 1–14; the inventory of his belongings taken after his death is in "Documents sur Pierre Gaultier de La Vérendrye," J.-J. Lefebvre, édit., APQ *Rapport, 1949–51*, 33–67. Notarial archives are indispensable for an understanding of the organization and financing of the La Vérendrye expeditions. *See* in particular, ANQ-M, Greffe de J.-B. Adhémar; Greffe de F.-M. Lepailleur; Greffe de Michel Lepailleur de Laferté; Greffe de J.-C. Porlier; Greffe de Pierre Raimbault.

Early historians, such as William Smith* and François-Xavier Garneau*, barely mentioned La Vérendrye and what they wrote was far from favourable. This is not surprising. The principal source available on him until the mid-19th century was *Mémoires sur le Canada, depuis 1749 jusqu'à 1760*. La Vérendrye is therein depicted as a man who was motivated by selfish interests and who, because of lack of education and natural aptitudes, was unsuited for the career of discoverer.

The basis for a reassessment was laid by Pierre Margry, the French archivist, who discovered in the papers entrusted to his care a large quantity of documents concerning La Vérendrye. In 1852 he published a short revisionist article, "Les Varennes de La Vérendrye," in *Le Moniteur universel* (Paris). This article, and more particularly the documents which he later published, enabled La Vérendrye to blossom into one of the major figures of the French régime.

Since that time he has fared quite well at the hands of historians. He is traditionally represented as an explorer first and foremost, one who is misunderstood by the government in France. This is the point of view put forward by his two major biographers, Champagne, *Les La Vérendrye*, and N. M. Crouse, *La Vérendrye, fur trader and explorer* (Ithaca, N.Y., Toronto, [1956]). The chief dissenting voice has been that of A. S. Morton in *History of the Canadian west* and "La Vérendrye: commandant, fur-trader, and explorer," *CHR*, IX (1928). He does not question La Vérendrye's importance and merit but maintains that his real preoccupation was the establishment of posts on the Canadian plains and the organization of the fur trade.

Although somewhat traditional in its approach, Champagne's *Les La Vérendrye* is the basic work on the subject. It reassesses, among other things, the nature of La Vérendrye's personality and of his financial problems. Also important is Rich, *History of the HBC*, I, which examines the impact of La Vérendrye's activities on the Hudson's Bay Company. R. I. Ruggles, "The historical geography and cartography of the Canadian west, 1670–1795" (unpublished PHD thesis, University of London, 1958) is indispensable for the geographical aspects of the La Vérendrye expeditions. Jean Delanglez, "A mirage: the sea of the west," *RHAF*, I (1947–48), 346–81, 541–68, studies the evolution of the concept of the western sea from the 1500s to 1720.

The problems raised by La Vérendrye's itineraries and the location of some of his forts are dealt with in a large body of periodical literature. See for instance N. M. Crouse, "The location of Fort Maurepas," *CHR*,

IX (1928) 206–22. O. G. Libby, "La Verendrye's visit to the Mandans in 1738–39," North Dakota State Hist. Soc. *Coll.* (Bismarck), II (1908), 502–8, and "Some Verendrye enigmas," *Mississippi Valley Hist. Rev.*, III (1916–17), 143–60. C. P. Wilson, "La Vérendrye reaches the Saskatchewan," *CHR*, XXXIII (1952), 39–50. Y.F.Z.]

GAUTIER, *dit* **Bellair, JOSEPH-NICOLAS,** farmer, merchant, navigator; b. 1689 at Rochefort, France, son of Nicolas-Gabriel Gautier, a native of Aix-en-Provence; m. 4 March 1715 at Annapolis Royal, Nova Scotia, Marie, daughter of Louis Allain (d. 1737), a merchant of consequence, and Marguerite Bourg; d. 1752 at Port-La-Joie (Fort Amherst, P.E.I.).

Joseph-Nicolas Gautier, *dit* Bellair, apparently settled in Acadia in 1710 but there is no evidence for an exact date. His prominence as a merchant in the Acadian community resulted in large part from his marriage and subsequent inheritance of his father-in-law's estates. As late as 1720 the Nova Scotia Council rejected him as one of six deputies for the Annapolis region, "not proveing that he was a freeholder of this province; only a transient person." During the 1730s, however, he appears to have joined the ranks of the "ancientest and most considerable in Lands & possessions"; his nomination as one of the deputies of his region was accepted by the Annapolis authorities at least as early as 1732.

There is no doubt that Gautier was an exceptionally wealthy Acadian. He amassed a considerable fortune in land, both at Bellair, his estate on the south bank of the Annapolis River, and at Annapolis Royal. He operated a sawmill and a gristmill, and his vessels were engaged in trade with France, the West Indies, New England, and Louisbourg, Île Royale (Cape Breton Island). In Acadian terms at least, he was, according to A. H. Clark, "a veritable tycoon." By the mid-1740s he claimed assets valued at 85,000 *livres*.

With the spread of the War of the Austrian Succession to North America in 1744, France determined to recover Acadia from the British. Four expeditions were sent to Nova Scotia between 1744 and 1747. On each of these occasions Nicolas Gautier and his two eldest sons, Joseph and Pierre, were among the handful of Acadians who actively supported the French effort. The fact that Gautier had spent his youth in France undoubtedly influenced his determination to eschew the strict neutrality of virtually the entire Acadian community in the 1740s. He supplied intelligence on British defences and troop movements; transported foodstuffs, materials, munitions, and troops; and piloted French vessels along the coastal waters of the province on behalf of Joseph Du Pont Duvivier in 1744, Paul Marin de La Malgue in 1745, La Jonquière [Taffanel] in 1746, and Jean-Baptiste-Nicolas-Roch de Ramezay* in the winter of 1746–47.

Gautier's partisanship was at great personal cost; in 1744 the British seized his 40-ton vessel and its cargo, valued together at 6,000 *livres*, and in the following year destroyed his habitation at Bellair, which had served as Duvivier's headquarters during the siege of Annapolis Royal. Although from 1744 there was a price on his head, Gautier managed to keep one step ahead of the British. His wife and one of his children were less fortunate; they were incarcerated at Annapolis Royal for ten months, "their feet in irons," before making good their escape in February 1746 by forcing the bars of their prison and scaling the walls of the fort.

In 1746 when Ramezay withdrew his detachment north of the Missaguash River, Gautier abandoned his remaining assets in the Annapolis region and sought refuge with his family at Beaubassin (near Amherst, N.S.). He was apparently given some compensation by the French government for the loss of his estates; in April 1748 Maurepas, the minister of Marine, referred to a "new additional grant of 500 *livres* to enable him to establish himself [on French territory]." Certainly he was not entirely destitute: in September 1749 he contracted to supply 16 head of live cattle to the Acadian refugees recently arrived at Port-Toulouse (St Peters, N.S.).

In 1749 Gautier and other Acadian collaborators determined to settle on Île Saint-Jean (Prince Edward Island). François Bigot*, the financial commissary at Louisbourg, reported that to encourage them he had "treated them very well and had them supplied with all they wanted, whether for their ships and buildings or for their subsistence and they will be assisted in whatever they can undertake." This assistance was not altogether altruistic on the part of the authorities. Earlier, Maurepas had suggested that Gautier's influence and stature among the Acadians might help to attract even greater Acadian immigration to Île Royale and Île Saint-Jean.

On Île Saint-Jean the Gautiers settled by the Rivière du Nord-Est (Hillsborough River), on the site of present-day Scotchfort, close to the administrative capital of the island at Port-La-Joie. In August 1751 they were visited by the engineer, Louis Franquet, who was impressed by their efforts and believed they would soon find "the means of recouping themselves for the pos-

sessions they had left behind [in Acadia]." The following year, however, far removed now from the prosperity he had known a decade before, Gautier could lay claim to but 18 head of cattle, four sheep, 80 fowl, and seven *arpents* by 40 of land. His death occurred on the evening of 10 April 1752 and he was buried the following day at Bellair, as he had nostalgically christened his new habitation. At least two of his sons continued in the service of the French cause beyond 1760. Joseph-Nicolas married the daughter of Joseph Leblanc, *dit* Le Maigre, another hapless Acadian supporter of France in the 1740s; both he and his brother, Pierre, eventually settled at Miquelon.

BERNARD POTHIER

AN, Col., B, 89, f.229; C¹¹ᴮ, 28, ff.12v–13, 124, 359–66; E, 169, f.3 (Du Pont Duvivier journal, 1744); 200 (dossiers Nicolas Gautier, Pierre Gautier); Section Outre-Mer, G¹, 411/2, p.27; 413/A, pp.60, 65; 466/1, pp.169–206, 215–31 (recensements de l'Acadie, 1671–1752) (PAC transcripts); G², 212, dossier 560; G³, 2046 (26 juillet 1737). [Louis Franquet], "Le voyage de Franquet aux îles Royale et Saint-Jean," APQ *Rapport, 1923–24*, 117. *N.S. Archives*, I, 24–25; II, 59–85; III, 7, 156, 261; IV, 65, 68–69, 94, 98. PAC *Report, 1905*, II, pt.1, 87–88. Arsenault, *Hist. et généal. des Acadiens*, I, 335. Brebner, *New England's outpost*. Clark, *Acadia*. [F.-E.] Rameau de Saint-Père, *Une colonie féodale en Amérique: l'Acadie (1604–1881)* (2v., Paris, Montréal, 1889), II, 79–81.

GAWÈHE (Degawehe, Gawickie, Goweaaey, Goweah, Koé, Kouée, Koweahe, baptized **Pierre),** chief councillor of the Wolf clan of the Oneidas. His official title in the Iroquois federal council may have been Deyo'ha'gwen de', meaning Through the Opening or Open Voice; d. *c.* 1 June 1766 at Fort Stanwix (near Rome, N.Y.).

Gawèhe took an active part in the Seven Years' War. He is first recorded in 1756 as an intelligence courier for Sir William Johnson*, the superintendent of northern Indians. During the abortive campaign against the French fort at Niagara (near Youngstown, N.Y.), he was commissioned lieutenant by Major-General William Shirley.

In the early stages of the war a majority of Iroquois doubted an English victory, and the Oneidas feared a French attack. Although Gawèhe professed continued allegiance to England, he took the precaution of keeping communications open with Canada. Encouraged by Johnson to pass a war belt through the Confederacy, the Oneida chief instead accepted a French invitation to a conference at Montreal with Governor Pierre de Rigaud* de Vaudreuil, where he declared his fidelity to the French. In 1757 he made frequent trips to François Picquet*'s mission of La Présentation (Oswegatchie, now Ogdensburg, N.Y.) and to Montreal, once delivering to Vaudreuil an offer of an alliance from dissident German settlers in the colony of New York. A possibility exists that Gawèhe was secretly acting in the English interest, for Johnson continued to pay him for services rendered; more likely he was assessing for the Iroquois the military strength of both European powers.

By 1760 England was completing its conquest of Canada, and Gawèhe joined Major-General Jeffery Amherst*'s drive on Montreal. He continued working for the English during the unrest inspired by PONTIAC in 1763 and 1764, supplying Johnson with intelligence on the western Indians. When he died in 1766, possibly of a bayonet wound received in a drinking brawl, Johnson accepted responsibility for his family and provided presents for the condolence ritual.

ARTHUR EINHORN

Inv. des papiers de Léry (P.-G. Roy), III, 8, 10. *Johnson papers* (Sullivan et al.) *NYCD* (O'Callaghan and Fernow), VII, 151–52, 232; VIII, 240; X, 461–65, 499–518. W. N. Fenton, *The roll call of the Iroquois chiefs; a study of a mnemonic cane from the Six Nations reserve* (Washington, 1950), 60.

GAY DESENCLAVES, JEAN-BAPTISTE DE, priest, Sulpician, missionary; b. 29 Jan. 1702 in Limoges, France; d. sometime after 1764 in unknown circumstances.

Jean-Baptiste de Gay Desenclaves joined the Society of Saint-Sulpice some months after his ordination on 15 June 1726. The authorities intended to send him to the missions in Canada, where he arrived in July 1728. He exercised his ministry in several parishes in the government of Montreal: at Notre-Dame in 1728; Sainte-Anne-du-Bout-de-l'Île (Sainte-Anne-de-Belle-vue), 1729–31; Repentigny, 1732–34; Longue-Pointe, 1734–35; and Sault-au-Récollet in 1736. It appears that he then returned to France. In June 1739, at the request of Abbé Jean Couturier, superior of Saint-Sulpice, he agreed to go to Acadia. On 9 September he arrived at Louisbourg, Île Royale (Cape Breton Island), at the same time as François Bigot* and Isaac-Louis de Forant*.

Among the missionaries who worked in Acadia in the 18th century, Desenclaves is distinguished by the fact that his relations with the British authorities in Nova Scotia were always cordial; his conduct consequently laid him open to criticism by the French authorities, religious as well as political. Desenclaves first went to Minas Basin, which was without its parish priest, Abbé Claude-Jean-Baptiste CHAUVREULX, who was at the time in disgrace with the governor, Lawrence Armstrong*. After Chauvreulx's return in December 1739, Desenclaves took charge of the parish of Rivière-aux-Canards, at Minas. From there he carried on an exchange of letters with the English administrator, Paul MASCARENE, concerning the difficulties which the ecclesiastical jurisdiction might create for civil justice, and vice versa. Several historians, in particular Henri-Raymond Casgrain* and Francis Parkman*, concluded from this correspondence either that Mascarene interfered in the administering of the sacraments or that the missionaries exercised undue influence in civil affairs. In reality this exchange amounted to the working out between Mascarene and Desenclaves of their respective jurisdictions and of the missionaries' delicate situation in Nova Scotia.

In June 1742 the bishop of Quebec, Pontbriand [DUBREIL] appointed Desenclaves parish priest of Annapolis Royal. Since the treaty of Utrecht in 1713 this office had always engendered strife between the governors and the parish priests. With Desenclaves's arrival began an era of good feeling between the two sides, with the result that a British officer had occasion to complain that the soldiers had had their children baptized there by the Roman Catholic priests.

In 1744, when troops from Île Royale were trying to take possession of Annapolis Royal and were besieging the town [see Joseph DU PONT Duvivier], the conduct of some missionaries, among them Desenclaves, was severely criticized by the French authorities: "The Sieur Desenclaves," wrote Maurepas, minister of Marine, to the bishop of Quebec, "informed the English governor exactly of all that he could learn of the proceedings of the French and exhorted his parishioners to be loyal to the king of England." The bishop of Quebec could only admit the validity of these criticisms.

It is understandable that Mascarene praised the missionaries' conduct. In May, June, and November 1747, however, Desenclaves agreed to pass on information about the activities of the English to the officers of the expedition from Canada led by Jean-Baptiste-Nicolas-Roch de Ramezay*, but it seems that his chief reason was to hasten the retreat of the French troops. Indeed, in agreement with Mascarene, he wrote a letter at this time to the habitants at Minas "to reassure them and to urge them not to take sides," indicating clearly that he hoped that the Canadians had already withdrawn.

On 1 Aug. 1749, at the time of the founding of Halifax, Desenclaves was called to the new capital to put his affairs in order with the authorities and to receive new instructions concerning the policy of the British government towards the Acadians. The missionary continued to have good relations with the government. He advised his parishioners to take the oath of allegiance to the king of England but succeeded nevertheless in eluding the oath for himself; his colleague Chauvreulx, on the other hand, took it. In 1752, after Abbé Jacques Girard*'s departure for Île Saint-Jean (Prince Edward Island), Desenclaves was left alone with Chauvreulx to carry on his work in English Acadia. Although Abbé de L'Isle-Dieu, the bishop of Quebec's vicar general in Paris, increased the number of missionaries in all the posts in French Acadia, he refused to send reinforcements for the two Sulpicians, who did not share the views of the French government sufficiently for his liking. In 1753, however, the vicar general acceded to the bishop of Quebec's request and sent Abbé Henri DAUDIN with instructions aimed at inciting the population of English Acadia to remain under French allegiance.

Either because he "was obsessed with jealousy of Abbé Daudin," as the Abbé de L'Isle-Dieu believed, or because he was in disagreement with French policy, which is more likely, Desenclaves gave up the parish of Annapolis in the spring of 1754 to withdraw to the seigneury of Entremont at Pobomcoup (Pubnico) in the south of the peninsula. He thus escaped deportation in 1755; in April 1756 he was present, helpless, at Jedediah Preble's raid on the Pobomcoup region, an incident of which he was the sole eye witness. He succeeded in escaping this new deportation, and with a score of persons he took to the woods, where he was confident that "the English will have difficulty in finding me." Nevertheless, he was captured in 1758 by Captain Joseph Gorham* and was imprisoned in Halifax. He was deported to France and reached Le Havre in February 1759. Abbé de L'Isle-Dieu succeeded in getting a pension of 400 *livres* for him. It was at this period that the missionary sent the minister, Nicolas-René Berryer, an extremely curious letter in which he set forth his views on France's policy in America. He indicated that he was more aware of the objectives of British policy than of those of the French; among other things he was an advocate of the project of having the Canadians transmigrate to Louisiana in the event that Canada was lost.

From Honfleur, where he wrote this letter, Desenclaves went to Limoges, probably in 1759, where family matters had been requiring his presence for nearly five years. Since 1746 he had suffered from a pulmonary illness, and he was exhausted by the final years of his mission. A certificate dated 1764 informs us that he was at Saint-Iriex-la-Pérèche, near Limoges, but nothing is known about his death.

Desenclaves has been in particularly high favour with English-language historians. The opinion expressed by one of them, A. G. Doughty*, in 1916 sums up fairly well that of the others: "If the Acadians had had more advisers of the type of the Abbé Desenclaves, they might have been spared much of the suffering which fell to their lot." This statement implies that Desenclaves was the only missionary in English Acadia who did not play a political role in France's favour among the Acadian population. In any case, it seems difficult to maintain that the Acadians' fate would have been different if all their missionaries had acted as had Abbé Desenclaves.

MICHELINE D. JOHNSON

AAQ, 312 CN, Nouvelle-Écosse, II, 2ff; IW, Église du Canada, II, 519, 791. AN, Col., B, 69, ff.55, 77v; 78, f.6; 81, f.64; 110, ff.60, 119, 214; C¹¹ᴬ, 78, f.407; 82, f.306; 86, f.140; 87, f.365; 93, f.80; 95, ff.150–54; 100, f.130; C¹¹ᴮ, 20, f.85; 21, f.21; 22, f.116. ASQ, Lettres, S, 7 i, 103; T, 59; Polygraphie, VII, 5, 114, 122; IX, 29; Séminaire, XIV, 6, no.14, p.6. "Acadiens: certificats concernant l'état civil, 1764," *Nova Francia*, IV (1929), 183–87. *Coll. doc. inédits Canada et Amérique*, I, 12–16, 41–46; II, 10–75; III, 60–80, 181–91. *Coll. de manuscrits relatifs à la N.-F.*, III, 343, 346, 369, 438. Knox, *Historical journal* (Doughty), I, 275; III, 341–48. "Lettres et mémoires de l'abbé de L'Isle-Dieu," APQ *Rapport, 1935–36*, 301–6, 317, 321, 332, 383; *1936–37*, 404, 405, 416, 422; *1937–38*, 169, 185. *N.S. Archives, I*, 111–13, 118, 122–26, 146–50, 170, 211, 305; *II*, 135, 144, 149, 153, 155, 160. PAC *Report, 1894*, 124, 137, 153, 179, 195, 209; *1905*, II, pt.III, 346–56. Casgrain, *Un pèlerinage au pays d'Évangéline*, 419–32; *Les Sulpiciens en Acadie*, 281–87. Parkman, *Half-century of conflict* (1892), I, 194. Richard, *Acadie* (D'Arles), I, 402–6; III, 285–91.

GEANNEAU. *See* JEANNEAU

GENEVIÈVE DE SAINT-PIERRE. *See* BOUCHER

GERVAISE, LOUIS (later the final e of the surname was dropped), sawmill-owner, militia captain; b. 12 April 1708 at Montreal to Charles Gervaise and Marie Boyer; m. 18 Feb. 1737 to Marie-Madeleine Langlois; d. 5 Feb. 1763 at Detroit.

Louis Gervaise, formerly a voyageur, moved from Montreal to Detroit in 1740 and entered the lumber business. His sawmill was at the pinery

Giard

up the St Clair River, in the vicinity of the present city of Port Huron, Mich. From there the planks and joists were floated downstream 25 leagues on timber rafts to the fort at Detroit.

In 1749, Gervaise, Louis Plichon, *dit* Saint-Louis, and Pierre Dinan, *dit* Saint-Étienne, were among settlers granted lots of three *arpents* frontage on the so-called south shore by the commandant, Charles de Sabrevois*. Gervaise's land was just below the mouth of the now-vanished Ruisseau de la Vieille Reine (about two miles below the Windsor end of the present Ambassador Bridge). He immediately erected a better-than-average dwelling and outbuildings, and soon the stream became known as Rivière à Gervais. A 1760 census of Detroit listed Gervaise as a well-to-do inhabitant having two slaves and one hired man.

Gervaise was captain of the militia company formed among the inhabitants of the new agricultural settlement on the south shore. Besides training and commanding the militia, as captain he was responsible for civil administration in his locality. During the Seven Years' War the company remained at home for defensive purposes and saw no action.

After the British occupation of Detroit in late November 1760, Louis Gervaise was reappointed militia captain, probably by Donald CAMPBELL. Two years and two months later he died at his home and was buried at Detroit. His widow died in October the same year. In 1766 their two sons moved from Detroit to the parish of Saint-Antoine-de-Padoue (Sainte-Antoine-sur-Richelieu, Que.).

E. J. LAJEUNESSE

Library of Congress (Washington), Peter Force collection, census of Detroit, 1760 C. [G.-J. Chaussegros de Léry], "Les journaux de M. de Léry," APQ *Rapport, 1926–27*, 334–48. *Windsor border region* (Lajeunesse). Tanguay, *Dictionnaire.*

GIARD (Girard, Gyart) ANTOINE, farmer, militia officer; b. 28 Mar. 1682 at Montreal to Nicolas Giard and Claude Prat; d. 1746 or 1747 at Kaskaskia (Ill.).

Antoine Giard's first trip to the west may have been in 1705, when he and his elder brother Gabriel were employed by the Compagnie de la Colonie to go to Detroit. Two years later he travelled to the same post for Cadillac [Laumet*]. By 1726 Giard had made his way to Kaskaskia. There, on 12 Oct. 1734, he married Marianne Martin, *née* Lafontaine, a sister-in-law of Jean-François MERCIER, and there he spent the rest of his life.

The Illinois economy was based on agriculture and the Indian trade. The original land holdings were grants made by the commandants in the king's name, without seigneurial obligations. The established homes and farms were allowed to pass from one person to another by contract, often with payment in furs and produce since currency was scarce. Information on Giard derived from such contracts shows him to have been one of the more enterprising settlers. He had a house in Kaskaskia village, several farm strips in its commons, and another farm above Fort de Chartres (near Prairie du Rocher). At times he rented out farm-land to others, and agreements with *engagés* indicate that he did some fur-trading as well. His civic activities included service as militia officer, church warden, and administrator of estates for friends and neighbours.

A quiet, steady citizen, he went to court only once – to have nullified the gambling debts contracted by his ward, Étienne Lalande. His reputation for responsibility led to his selection in 1744 as guardian of the two daughters of François-Marie Bissot* de Vinsenne. As a guardian he looked after the leasing of his wards' farms.

Antoine died in 1746 or 1747. His estate was settled in 1752, and the census of that year shows seven children, two of them male, in his widow's household. One was likely the Antoine Giard who signed a document in 1750, then disappears from the records. Three daughters inherited the Fort de Chartres property, and their children married into the Saucier-Louvière, Cerré, Morrison, and Chouteau families – all prominent names in the early statehood of Illinois and Missouri and notable in the Rocky Mountain fur empire.

KATHRINE WAGNER SEINEKE

ANDM, Registres des baptêmes, mariages et sépultures. ANQ-M, Greffe d'Antoine Adhémar, 30 mai 1705, 5 juin 1707. Chicago Historical Society, Kaskaskia oversize papers. Randolph County Courthouse (Chester, Ill.), Office of the circuit clerk, Private papers, I, 14 Jan. 1746; Kaskaskia manuscript record book, II, "Copie des repertoire des actes laissér au greffe des Illinois," 1734, 1744. St Louis University Library (St Louis, Mo.), Archives paroissiales de Notre-Dame de l'Immaculée-Conception des Cascaskias (Kaskaskia, Ill.). Alvord, *Illinois country*. Belting, *Kaskaskia.*

GODÉ. *See* GAUDÉ

GODEFROY DE TONNANCOUR, CHARLES-ANTOINE, priest, theologal of the chapter of the cathedral of Quebec; b. 13 May 1698 at Trois-Rivières, eldest son of René Godefroy* de Tonnancour, seigneur of La Pointe-du-Lac, and Marguerite Ameau; d. 30 Sept. 1757 at Quebec.

Charles-Antoine Godefroy de Tonnancour spent his childhood at Trois-Rivières. During this period, according to his mother, he was believed to have been cured, through the intercession of Brother Didace Pelletier*, of a throat ailment due to "a fleshy growth on both sides, the size of a pigeon egg, which threatened to choke him and impeded his speech." At the age of 15 he entered the Petit Séminaire of Quebec, "having some slight rudiments of knowledge." When his schooling was finished he was admitted into the seminary, on 29 Sept. 1719, where he completed his four years of theology. On 18 Dec. 1723 he was ordained a priest by Bishop Saint-Vallier [La Croix*], who on 4 Jan. 1724 gave him a canonry in the cathedral chapter.

Godefroy de Tonnancour was thereafter concerned with the ceremonies and singing at the seminary and taught catechism to the children at the cathedral. In 1740 he took over the office of ecclesiastical superior of the Hôtel-Dieu of Quebec, and in 1748 Bishop Pontbriand [DUBREIL] thought of appointing him dean of the chapter. In applying to the minister, Maurepas, concerning the choice of a new dean, the prelate, however, had Abbé René-Jean ALLENOU de Lavillangevin, a Frenchman, much more in mind than Godefroy de Tonnancour. Nevertheless he proposed that the latter be appointed, if the minister thought of thus "favouring the Canadians." The bishop of Quebec pointed out that, of the canons then living at Quebec, M. de Tonnancour had most seniority, "even though he is only about 50"; he regarded him as "a man of rank, who works zealously at his ministry and is rather free of the shortcomings which the Canadians are charged with." The prelate added: "He has wealth and can live in a respectable manner." In the end Tonnancour had to be content with the title of theologal of the chapter, which he received on 1 Nov. 1753.

In November 1749 his seniority was responsible for his being chosen as syndic by his colleagues in the jurisdictional dispute which developed with the appointment by the seminary directors of Abbé Jean-Félix RÉCHER, a priest from the seminary, as parish priest of the cathedral. On 6 November M. de Tonnancour first opposed the installation of the parish priest as an honorary canon; later, in the chapter's name, he registered with the Conseil Supérieur a motion of appeal "for abuse of the act of creation of the new parish in the cathedral of Quebec and of the union which is made between it and the seminary of the Missions Étrangères." His

appeal was dismissed on 16 Oct. 1750. It was Godefroy de Tonnancour who, at Quebec, received from the hand of BOURLAMAQUE two of the five flags which were taken at the battle of Fort Chouaguen (Fort Oswego) on 14 August 1756 and which the governor, Pierre de Rigaud* de Vaudreuil, had deposited in the churches of Montreal, Trois-Rivières, and Quebec.

After devoting himself, as had the other canons, to taking care of victims of an epidemic at the Hôpital Général of Quebec, Godefroy de Tonnancour fell victim to the infection himself and died on 30 Sept. 1757. He was buried the next day in the crypt of the church of Notre-Dame de Québec.

HONORIUS PROVOST

AAQ, 10 B, Registre des délibérations. ASQ, MSS, 2; Polygraphie, XXIX, 16. "Actes du très dévot frère Didace Pelletier, récollet, mort en odeur de sainteté en 1699," Canada-français, 1re sér., IV (1891), 277. P.-G. Roy, Inv. jug. et délib., 1717–1760, V, 151, 156, 163; La famille Godefroy de Tonnancour (Lévis, Qué. 1904). Sulte, Mélanges historiques (Malchelosse), XI. O.-M. [Jouve], "Étude historique et critique sur les actes du frère Didace Pelletier, récollet," BRH, XVII (1911), 209. P.-G. Roy, "Les drapeaux de Chouaguen," BRH, V (1899), 350. Henri Têtu, "Le chapitre de la cathédrale de Québec et ses délégués en France," BRH, XIV (1908), 203, 260; "M. Jean-Félix Récher, curé de Québec, et son journal, 1757–1760," BRH, IX (1903), 101.

GODEFUS, GILBERT BOUCAULT DE. *See* BOUCAULT

GOLDTHWAIT, BENJAMIN, military officer; b. in Boston, Massachusetts, 25 Nov. 1704 (o.s.), son of John Goldthwait and Sarah Hopkins; m. 10 Oct. 1726 to Charity Edwards; d. 10 May 1761.

Benjamin Goldthwait began his varied career as a saddler and then a chaise-maker. He was first elected to civic office in 1735 when he was sworn in as a town constable of Boston; in 1742–43 he held the office of clerk of the market. When the government of Massachusetts decided to launch an expedition against Louisbourg, Île Royale (Cape Breton Island), Goldthwait enlisted and on 9 Feb. 1744/45 was commissioned a captain in Samuel WALDO's 2nd Massachusetts Regiment. He was placed in command of the 4th Company and served in that capacity during the siege of Louisbourg. By 1746 he had been appointed commissary agent for Waldo's regiment, a position he held for at least two years.

In the fall of 1746 Goldthwait was sent to Annapolis Royal as part of a New England reinforcement for Nova Scotia. That winter the New

Gorham

Englanders were dispatched to the Minas area under the command of Arthur NOBLE, in an attempt to rout the French forces in that region. Goldthwait was present at Grand Pré on 31 Jan. 1746/47 when the French launched a surprise attack against the New England forces. On the death of Noble, Goldthwait assumed command of the troops, but seeing the hopelessness of their situation, he agreed to surrender to the French commander, Nicolas-Antoine COULON de Villiers, and formal terms of capitulation were drawn up and signed. Goldthwait then returned with his men to Annapolis Royal, where he apparently remained as a company commander until 1748.

In 1755 Goldthwait was once again on active service, as a major in the company raised by Colonel John Winslow* to attack Fort Beauséjour (near Sackville, N.B.). He was an active participant in the siege of that fort and was present at the council of 16 June 1755 which deliberated on the terms of surrender. He later assisted in the deportation of Acadians from the Chignecto region to the American colonies.

In 1756–57 Goldthwait was actively engaged in military service in Massachusetts and New York and in 1758 he served as a major in the second Louisbourg expedition. He died in Medford, Massachusetts, in 1761; he was declared insolvent, and his estate was divided among his creditors. He had at least five children.

BARRY M. MOODY

AN, Col., C¹¹A, 87, ff.314–61; C¹¹D, 8, ff.130–34. BM, Add. MSS, 19071. Mass., Archives, Military records, 73, f.474; 75, ff.405–6; 77, ff.52–53. Mass. Hist. Soc., Winslow papers, 61.E¹. 88; 61.E¹.103; 61.E².9. PAC, MG 18, F10. PANS, RG 1, 13, nos.38, 39; 13¹/₂, nos.19, 23, 24; 357, pp.1–247 (Winslow's journal at Beauséjour; printed in N.S. Hist. Soc.*Coll.*, IV (1884), 113–246; see especially pp.119, 124, 137, 143, 157). Boston, Registry Dept., *Records* (Whitmore *et al.*), [12], [19]. *Boston Evening-Post*, February, March 1747. Charlotte Goldthwaite, *Goldthwaite genealogy: descendants of Thomas Goldthwaite, an early settler of Salem, Mass.* . . . (Hartford, Conn., 1899), 78–81. *New Eng. Hist. and Geneal. Register*, XXIV (1870), 370; XXV (1871), 253.

GORHAM (Goreham, Gorum), JOHN, merchant, military officer, member of the Nova Scotia Council; b. 12 Dec. 1709 (o.s.) in Barnstable, Massachusetts, son of Colonel Shobal (Shubael) Gorham and Mary Thacter; m. Elizabeth Allyn (Allen) 9 March 1731/32 and had 15 children; d. in London, December 1751.

John Gorham began his career as a merchant, trading at various ports in Newfoundland and speculating in land. In 1738 he sought a grant of land on Sable Island, Nova Scotia, and in 1743 was granted 400 acres at Gorham (Maine). He seems to have entered military service in Massachusetts about 1741; by 1744 he had attained the rank of captain. In September of that year, with his company of 50 "picked Indians and other men fit for ranging the woods," he arrived at Annapolis Royal, Nova Scotia, to reinforce the undermanned garrison which had been besieged for about three weeks by French and Indian forces commanded by Joseph DU PONT Duvivier. According to Massachusetts Governor William Shirley, Gorham used his Indian rangers, consisting mostly of full blood Mohawks, so "that the garrison is now entirely free from alarms." Early in the next year, however, "as that fort was then in great danger of falling into the hands of the enemy," Paul MASCARENE sent Gorham to Boston to recruit additional troops for its defence.

In Boston, Shirley and William PEPPERRELL induced Gorham to raise troops for the expedition "then in embryo" against Louisbourg, Île Royale (Cape Breton Island). He was appointed lieutenant-colonel in the 7th Massachusetts Regiment, under the command of his father, and led the successful landing at Gabarus Bay on 30 April 1745. With Colonel Arthur NOBLE he was selected to lead the volunteer assault on the Island battery on 23 May "which fail'd of being put in execution." Because of numerous complaints of cowardice and dereliction of duty made by the raw, obstreperous, hard-drinking volunteers, a council of war was convened to investigate their officers' actions in the assault. The council decided that "it did not appear that Col. Noble or Col. Gorham were chargeable with misbehaviour in the affair." Upon his father's death, on 20 Feb. 1745/46, John Gorham was promoted colonel and succeeded to the command of his father's regiment. He attended meetings of the council of war at Louisbourg until mid-April 1746.

Despite the English victory, the Louisbourg campaign was not a particularly rewarding engagement for Gorham and he was no doubt happy to return to Nova Scotia in the summer of 1746. His spirited efforts in its defence were his most significant contribution to the English war effort. As a result of his activities, he became "well Acquainted with the Country in general, and with the Temper and Dispositions of the Inhabitants in particular" and was called upon to perform a variety of duties. Highly mobile and "far more terrible than European soldiers," Gorham and his Indians ranged the province during 1746 and 1747. In the summer of 1746 he built blockhouses at such strategic points as Cobequid (near Truro) and Chignecto. In November he reported to Shirley that "our Expedition up the Bay [of Fundy] by Water is over for this year" and recommended that it was "of the Utmost Consequence to get possession of Minas this Winter or in the Spring. . . ." Forces under Arthur Noble were dispatched and Gorham met him at Grand Pré in January 1747. Two days after Gorham left for Annapolis Royal, a French force surprised the English at Grand Pré, killing Noble and forcing the garrison's surrender.

Gorham returned to New England where he discussed the problem of Nova Scotia with Shirley who, in turn, sent him in April 1747 to England to explain the situation to the Duke of Newcastle. The rejection of Shirley's proposal that the English government meet the costs of "raising 2,000 Men out of the Massachusetts bay" made Gorham and his rangers, as the Duke of Bedford informed Newcastle, "more than ever absolutely necessary for the immediate preservation of the Province of Nova Scotia." As a result, Gorham received a commission to command a company of 100 men for the defence of the province. Newcastle ordered Shirley to assist Gorham in every way possible, for "the case of this gentleman is so particular and the service he has and may render so great, that no inconvenience can arise from this mark of favour to him."

Upon his return to Nova Scotia, Gorham assumed sole responsibility for its defence. With the cessation of hostilities, but before a peace had been concluded, Mascarene ordered Gorham and his rangers in October 1748 to exact submission from the French settlers along the Saint John River, an area claimed by both France and England. Gorham had orders "not to commit any hostility," unless provoked. When unknown assailants killed some of his men, Gorham seized two Abenakis to give the Indians, according to Mascarene, an opportunity "to clear themselves of having a share in that outrage and to bring to light the Offenders." Despite the strenuous protest of the Marquis de La Galissonière [BARRIN], Governor Shirley backed Gorham in this matter.

With the arrival of Edward Cornwallis*, newly appointed governor of Nova Scotia, in July 1749, Gorham was appointed to the Nova Scotia Council. Despite occasional disagreements with the governor, he held his position until his departure from Nova Scotia two years later. He remained active in the defence of the province, establishing Fort Sackville at the head of Bedford Basin for the protection of the new settlement at Halifax and engaging in numerous skirmishes with hostile Indians. In August 1751 Gorham left Nova Scotia

for England aboard his ship, the *Osborne*, the first ship built in Halifax. He died in London of smallpox in December 1751.

Governor Shirley wrote in February 1746 that "the great Service which Lieut. Colonel Gorham's Company of Rangers has been of to the Garrison at Annapolis Royal, is a demonstration of the Usefulness of such a Corps." Gorham and his company of brutal rangers seem to have been a necessary ingredient in maintaining the English presence in Nova Scotia.

JOHN DAVID KRUGLER

"Barnstable, Mass., Vital records," *Mayflower Descendant* (Boston), XXXIII (1935), 119. 126. "Col. John Gorham's 'Wast Book,'" ed. F. W. Sprague, *New Eng. Hist. and Geneal. Register*, LII (1898), 186–92. "Col. John Gorham's 'Wast Book' and his 'Dayly Journal,'" *Mayflower Descendant*, V (1903), 172–80. "Col. John Gorham's 'Wast Book' and the Gorham family," *N.Y. Geneal. and Biog. Record* (New York), XXVIII (1897), 133–36, 197–201. *Correspondence of William Shirley* (Lincoln), I, 135. *Documentary history of Maine*, XI, 315, 341, 344, 387–89, 465; XII, 60, 71, 74. *Documents relating to currency in Nova Scotia, 1675–1758* (Shortt), 274, 281, 294, 304, 335, 338, 342. "Gorham letters, with facsimiles," *Mayflower Descendant*, IV (1904), 181–84. *NYCD* (O'Callaghan and Fernow). *N.S. Archives*, I. "The Pepperrell papers," Mass. Hist. Soc. *Coll.*, 6th ser., X (1899). *The Wyllys papers: correspondence and documents chiefly of descendants of Gov. George Wyllys of Connnecticut, 1590–1796* (Conn. Hist. Soc. *Coll.*, XXI, Hartford, 1924), 427–28. Murdoch, *History of Nova-Scotia*, II, 36, 104–5, 124, 139, 166. J. G. Palfrey, *History of New England* (5v., Boston, 1858–90), V, 59, 242. T. B. Akins, "The first council," N.S. Hist. Soc. *Coll.*, II (1881), 26–27. G. T. Bates, "John Gorham, 1709–1751: an outline of his activities in Nova Scotia, 1744–1751," N.S. Hist. Soc. *Coll.*, XXX (1954), 27–77. F. W. Sprague, "Barnstable Gorhams," *New Eng. Hist. and Geneal. Register*, L (1896), 32–34.

GORRELL, JAMES, army officer; b. *c.* 1735, probably in Maryland; d. *c.* 1769 in the West Indies.

James Gorrell apparently lived on the western frontier in Frederick County, Maryland. By October 1757 he was an ensign in Joshua Beall's company of the Maryland militia. On 29 June 1758 he joined John Dagworthy's company and was promoted second lieutenant on 9 Nov. 1758. His militia unit was active on the Pennsylvania frontier and was with the forces under John FORBES that took Fort Duquesne (Pittsburgh, Pa.) from the French on 25 Nov. 1758. Gorrell became an ensign in the 1st battalion of the Royal American Regiment on 30 May 1759 and was transferred to the New York frontier. By 1761 he had been sent to Detroit, where he earned the respect of his superiors for his work in conducting bateaux with supplies from Niagara to that post.

In September of that year he accompanied Captain Henry Balfour's expedition, which established the British presence at the various posts on the Upper Lakes. On 12 October they reached La Baye (Green Bay, Wis.), where Gorrell was placed in command of 17 soldiers as a garrison for the rotting fort, renamed Edward Augustus. While stationed there Gorrell purchased a lieutenant's commission, dated 2 March 1762. Besides protecting the British traders and maintaining a semblance of law and order at this frail outpost of empire, Gorrell's main function was to try to secure good relations with the Menominees, Foxes, Sauks, Winnebagos, and Sioux in the region. Despite a lack of funds to disperse adequate presents to the 39,100 warriors for whom he estimated he had responsibility, Gorrell won the Indians' respect. When in 1763 the western tribes, inspired by PONTIAC, attacked the English garrisons, those around Green Bay did not join the uprising.

On 15 June 1763 Gorrell was shocked to receive a letter from Captain George Etherington, commanding officer of Michilimackinac, informing him that the fort had been captured by the Ojibwas and that the remnant of the garrison was under the protection of the Ottawas at L'Arbre Croche (Cross Village, Mich.). Gorrell was ordered to join Etherington at once. He immediately called together the neighbouring Indians and gave them lavish presents, which he borrowed from the local English traders. Accompanied by an escort of 90 Menominee, Fox, Sauk, and Winnebago warriors, Gorrell, his garrison, and a few English traders crossed Lake Michigan and joined Etherington. The Indians from La Baye then negotiated with MINWEWEH and the Ojibwas for safe passage to Montreal for all the British troops. After more than two weeks, permission was secured. On 18 July the troops, escorted by some Ottawa warriors, set out, arriving at Montreal nearly a month later.

Almost immediately Gorrell left Montreal for Albany, New York, to get his expenses approved. He was ordered, however, to join Major John Wilkins' expedition to relieve Detroit, which was being besieged by Pontiac's forces. After the disaster of 7 November, which wrecked the expedition on the north shore of Lake Erie, Gorrell returned to Albany. There he discussed with Sir William Johnson* the payment of his expenditures for Indian presents. From 1764 to 1767 Gorrell was on half pay and

spent considerable time in New York seeking payment for these presents. The debts were finally cleared during the summer of 1765, over three years after some of them had been contracted.

Eager for active duty, Gorrell received a lieutenancy in the 70th regiment on 18 March 1767, and was assigned to the West Indies. He is mentioned in the army list of 1769 but is absent from the 1770 list and presumably died of disease.

DAVID A. ARMOUR

PRO, WO 34/49, MacDonald, Journal of the siege of Detroit; returns of soldiers, 18 Sept., 8 Nov. 1761; Balfour to Amherst, 24 Nov. 1761; returns of soldiers, 10 Jan., 18 Feb., 20 April 1762; Campbell to Amherst, 8 June 1762; returns of soldiers, 22 June, 5 Sept. 1762; returns of troops, 23 Nov. 1762; returns of soldiers, 7 Jan. 1763; list of Indian nations; Moran to [Gladwin?], 18 May 1763; Etherington to Gladwin, 18 July 1763; Amherst to Gladwin, 28 Aug. 1763. Clements Library, Thomas Gage papers, American series, Gorrell to Gage, 24 Dec. 1763; Gage to Gorrell, 1 Jan. 1764; British series, petition of Gorrell enclosed in Barrington to Gage, 14 June 1767; Supplementary accounts, Accounts relating to expenses at Green Bay, 1761–63, James Gorrell's journal. This journal has been published in: *Johnson papers* (Sullivan *et al.*), X, 697–714, and in Wis. State Hist. Soc. *Coll.*, I, 24–48.

Army list, 1759, 111; *1760*, 115; *1761*, 117; *1763*, 117; *1765*, 6; *1766*, 193; *1767*, 125; *1769*, 125. "Bouquet papers," *Michigan Pioneer Coll.*, XIX (1891), 67, 70, 72–73, 77, 130, 136, 142. "The British regime in Wisconsin – 1760–1800," ed. R. G. Thwaites, Wis. State Hist. Soc. *Coll.*, XVIII (1908), 245–46, 255, 264. *Calendar of the Sir William Johnson manuscripts in the New York State Library*, comp. R. E. Day (Albany, 1909), 170, 176, 208, 214, 254, 263, 266, 278, 302, 308, 322. [James Gorrell], "Lieut. James Gorrell's journall from Montreal on the expedition commanded by Major Wilkins with some account of that expedition &c.," *Maryland Hist. Mag.* (Baltimore), IV (1909), 183–87. "Green Bay and the frontiers, 1763–65," Wis. State Hist. Soc. *Coll.*, VIII (1879), 232–38. Augustin Grignon, "Seventy-two years' recollections of Wisconsin," Wis. State Hist. Soc. *Coll.*, III (1857), 226–27. *Johnson papers* (Sullivan *et al.*), III, 525, 756; IV, 123, 192, 383, 643, 851; V, 139–40, 344; X, 450, 546, 559; XI, 274, 930; XII, 1072; XIII, 258. "Langlade papers, 1737–1800," Wis. State Hist. Soc. *Coll.*, VIII (1879), 218. T. J. C. Williams and Folger McKinsey, *History of Frederick county, Maryland . . .* (2v., [Frederick, Md.], 1910; repr., Baltimore, 1967), I, 661, 664.

GOSSELIN, JEAN-BAPTISTE, priest of the Séminaire des Missions Étrangères, parish priest, canon, plant collector; b. in France, probably in 1712; d. in September 1749 in the diocese of Amiens, France.

Jean-Baptiste Gosselin completed his studies

in Amiens in 1728 and then entered the Séminaire des Missions Étrangères in Paris; the following year, when the seminary of Quebec requested an assistant for their bursar, the directors in Paris decided to send him to fill this office. He sailed from La Rochelle on 22 May 1729, on the same ship as the coadjutor of Quebec, Pierre-Herman Dosquet*, and the financial commissary, Gilles Hocquart*.

Upon his arrival in Quebec Gosselin worked under the direction of Abbé Charles PLANTE and became bursar by appointment on 23 August 1730. But it seems clear that he had little aptitude for his task, for in 1733 François de MONTIGNY, who was at the time procurator of the seminary of Quebec in Paris, reproached him with being "little suited to keeping books and accounts." On 15 Oct. 1732 he sailed for France, where he spent two years, attending to family matters after his father's death and studying for one year at the seminary of Laon. The directors of the seminary in Paris were planning to send him as a missionary to Île Royale (Cape Breton Island) if he attained the priesthood. During his stay in Laon Gosselin received only the tonsure and minor orders. In August 1734 he was back in Quebec, where he received the subdiaconate, the diaconate, and the priesthood in succession on 8, 12, and 18 September. He is believed to have been appointed to the parish of Saint-Joseph-de-Lanoraie shortly afterwards; however, on 19 Oct. 1735, when Bishop Dosquet granted him an *arrière fief* in the seigneury of Bourgchemin, he was living in the seminary of Quebec. On 12 Oct. 1748 Gosselin gave this grant to François Lemaître.

In the autumn of 1736 he again left Canada for a two-year stay in France. The seminary of Quebec had refused to pay him an allowance in Paris, where he hoped to live as a pensioner. He seems to have resided in the diocese of Amiens, where he served as a curate. In May 1738 he was back in Canada. Before his departure he had wanted to be appointed to the seminary of Quebec, but in Paris he was considered unsuitable for teaching and the directors in Quebec were advised, in view of his quick and difficult disposition, not to accept him as a life member of the community. Consequently, in the summer of 1738 he was appointed as auxiliary to the parish priest of Notre-Dame de Québec, and in the autumn he exercised his ministry in the parish of Saint-Michel-de-Yamaska, at the same time serving the missions along the Rivière Chambly. In September 1740, when he had just been appointed irremovable parish priest of Yamaska, he resigned, claiming that this parish was not able to support him. He was then put in charge of the parishes of Saint-Louis (Saint-Joseph de Chambly) and Saint-Charles (Saint-Charles-sur-Richelieu); he was the first parish priest of Saint-Charles.

In the summer of 1740 Gosselin was at Quebec when the ship carrying Bishop Lauberivière [Pourroy*] arrived, laden with carriers of pestilence. Gosselin devoted himself body and soul to these people, and in recognition of his devotion Hocquart obtained a canonry for him. Gosselin assumed his charge officially on 31 Aug. 1741. He remained in Quebec, where in addition he fulfilled the functions of curate at Notre-Dame and chaplain at the intendant's palace. In September 1742 he requested permission of the chapter to return to France for a period of two years in order to take care of his health. But since he could not justify his request with a doctor's certificate, the chapter refused it. On 16 April the following year the members of the chapter elected him treasurer; he gave this office up on 13 Oct. 1744. In 1748 he repeated the request that he had made in 1742, this time accompanying it with a doctor's certificate, and the chapter consented to his returning to France. During this same year Bishop Pontbriand [DUBREIL] had suggested to the minister, Maurepas, that Gosselin not be considered as a replacement for the dean of the chapter. Indeed, the bishop of Quebec little appreciated the canon's independent and irresolute character. Gosselin left Canada in the autumn of 1748 and probably went to the Séminaire des Missions Étrangères in Paris, and then to the diocese of Amiens, since he died there in September of the following year.

At the period when Gosselin lived in Canada Intendant Hocquart was sending to France to the naturalist Buffon, director of the Jardin du Roi, plants, seeds, medicinal roots, and minerals in order to make known the natural products peculiar to Canada. On several occasions Gosselin supplied numerous specimens of plants for these shipments. As early as 1739 Gosselin, a parish priest at the time, had sent to Rochefort through Intendant Hocquart's agency "a small bundle containing a herbarium." In 1742 he even made a voyage on the north shore of the St Lawrence River estuary to gather new specimens, and in 1744 the intendant accorded him 150 *livres* as encouragement. Although certain historians have called Gosselin "a renowned botanist of the period," he deserves rather the title of plant collector.

CATHERINE FORTIN-MORISSET

AAQ, 12 A, Registres d'insinuations C, 54; 10 B, Registre des délibérations, 118, 142, 144, 147–47v, 150,

Goutin

160–60v, 172v. ASQ, Lettres, M, 67, 79–80, 81, 82, 83, 85, 89, 90, 93, 99; P, 120; Livres de comptes, C 10, pp. lf.; Polygraphie, VII, 2; XLII, 11, 12; Séminaire, VIII, 9, 16, 18, 19, 35; LVII, 25; LXXVIII, 23. PAC *Report, 1905*, I, pt.vi, 6, 12, 20, 26, 29, 36, 59. Allaire, *Dictionnaire*. P.-G. Roy, *Inv. concessions*, IV, 114. Gosselin, *L'Église du Canada jusqu'à la conquête*, II, 42, 218, 266, 383, 384; III, 4, 24.

GOUTIN (Degoutin, Desgoutins; he signed **de Goutin), FRANÇOIS-MARIE DE,** officer in the colonial regular troops, subdelegate of the financial commissary on Île Royale (Cape Breton Island) and Île Saint-Jean (Prince Edward Island); b. *c.* 1690, probably at Port-Royal (Annapolis Royal, N.S.), son of Mathieu de Goutin* and Jeanne Tibaudeau; m. 20 May 1719 in Louisbourg, Île Royale, Marie-Angélique Aubert de La Chesnaye (d. 1729), by whom he had one daughter and four sons; m. 9 April 1736, in Louisbourg, Marie-Angélique Puyperoux de La Fosse, by whom he had three daughters and three sons; d. 5 Jan. 1752 on Île Saint-Jean.

The date of François-Marie de Goutin's entry into the colonial regular troops is uncertain. As a cadet he took part in the struggle against the Anglo-Americans in Acadia and Governor Daniel d'Auger* de Subercase considered recommending his promotion to second ensign. But the capture of Port-Royal by Francis Nicholson* in 1710 ended his career in Acadia. He went to France with his family and later moved to Île Royale, sometime after the establishment of the French colony there in 1714. Little is known of his military career on the island; he is referred to as an adjutant in 1717 and served in that capacity at Port-Dauphin (Englishtown).

By 5 June 1717 Goutin had been appointed agent of the treasurer-general of the Marine at Île Royale, a position which involved responsibility for the payment of bills approved by the financial commissary and for the preparation of an annual accounting to the ministry of the Marine for the receipts and expenditures of royal funds. Later, following a joint recommendation by the governor, Saint-Ovide [MONBETON], and the financial commissary, Pierre-Auguste de Soubras*, he received a titular appointment, at 300 *livres* a year, to the recently established Conseil Supérieur of Louisbourg.

In 1727 an investigation begun by Saint-Ovide led to a controversy which threatened Goutin's career and nearly terminated that of the financial commissary, Jacques-Ange LE NORMANT de Mézy. Ignoring warnings given in 1718 and 1724 to keep fortification funds separate from those for other projects and to employ them only

for their stated purpose, Mézy had borrowed from them illegally and had otherwise allowed the colony's finances to fall into disorder. The inquiry into his accounting practices also revealed that Goutin was badly in debt. Treasury agents frequently invested royal funds for their own benefit, and the practice was tolerated. But Goutin appears to have invested unwisely. By 1727 he had allowed the shortage in the fortifications account to reach 48,936 *livres,* highly imprudent at a time when the ministry was concerned about their cost. As a result, in 1730 he was dismissed from his post by the treasurer-general and ordered to make restitution. Maurepas, the minister of Marine, believed Mézy's disorderly administration to be largely responsible for the trouble, however, and Goutin was somewhat vindicated by the minister's reprimand to Mézy. He continued to sit on the Conseil Supérieur. In 1733 he claimed that he was head of the council; in 1739 he was referred to as senior councillor and in 1740 as first councillor.

Goutin enjoyed the favour of Mézy's son and successor as financial commissary, Sébastien-François-Ange Le Normant* de Mézy. Appointed subdelegate of the financial commissary, he often visited such outposts as La Baleine (Baleine Cove) and Lorembec (Lorraine) to uphold the prolific ordinances of the commissary. He was responsible for enforcing the fishing regulations and fining those who contravened them, and he ruled on lawsuits and arguments between merchants, partners, and inhabitants.

From his various appointments Goutin enjoyed an annual income of 1,200 *livres*. He acquired two properties in Louisbourg, and took an early interest in the coastal trade. In 1729 he made a mortgage payment on the 24-ton *Union* and by 1730 he had acquired half-ownership of the 35-ton *Meriane Charlotte*. But after Louisbourg fell to Anglo-American troops under William PEPPERRELL in 1745, Goutin landed, apparently poverty stricken, at the refugee port of Saint-Malo, France. In 1746, burdened by his large family, he was granted a gratuity of 300 *livres*.

On 12 Aug. 1749 Goutin received a commission as subdelegate of the financial commissary and storekeeper on Île Saint-Jean. For the general responsibility of enforcing the civil regulations of the island he received a salary of 600 *livres*. Though he was no longer a member of the Conseil Supérieur of Louisbourg, Goutin's new role was still attractive and important; working with the commandant, Claude-Élisabeth DENYS de Bonnaventure, he was to help create an agricultural colony. After taking stock of the storehouse, he was to make a census of the inhabitants and provide for their welfare. He was also to protect former land grants and to encourage farming in the fertile areas. Pasture was to be made available to settlers, but codfishing discouraged so as to safeguard the new agricultural base. He was ordered especially to promote settlement by the Acadians.

Goutin took up his new residence at Port-La-Joie (Fort Amherst) in poorly constructed quarters. The severity of the winter of 1750–51 was aggravated by a shortage of meat; Goutin fell ill in November 1751 and died the following January.

ERIC R. KRAUSE

AN, Col., B, 39, ff.134v–35; 41, f.584; 42, f.474v; 48, f.953; 50, f.575; 52, ff.566–68, 579v; 53, ff.593v–95v; 54, ff.509v–12, 514–14v; 57, f.774; 84, f.170; 86, f.200; 91, ff.331, 357–58v; 95, f.281v; C¹¹ᴬ, 126, pièce 111; C¹¹ᴮ, 1, f.439; 2, ff.254–54v; 3, ff.10v–11, 90, 129; 4, ff.25v, 129v; 5, ff.37v, 70v–71, 173v–74; 6, ff.182–82v, 220v–21; 7, ff.42v, 62; 9, ff.80–83, 98–98v, 122v; 10, ff.89–91v, 96–97, 104–8v, 138–39, 168, 169–69v; 11, ff.45v–49, 70–72, 87–87v; 12, f.98v; 13, ff.4–6; 14, f.262; 15, ff.32, 36v–37v, 64; 17, ff.21, 22v; 18, f.114; 20, ff.147v–48v; 25, f.167; 28, ff.155–55v, 164v, 291–92, 367–69v; 29, ff.217v–18; 30. ff.29v–30, 35v, 37, 101, 289v, 298v, 299v–300; 32, ff.220, 285–85v; C¹¹ᶜ, 11, ff.23, 28; 15, pièces 15, 123, 131, 177; 16, 1ʳᵉ sér., pièce 6; 2ᵉ sér., pièces 17, 18, 19; C¹¹ᴰ, 6, f.93v; E, 10 (dossier Aubert), 114 (dossier de Goutin), 124 (dossier de Goutin); Marine, A¹, art.54, pièces 60, 61; art.56, pièce 44; Section Outre-Mer, Dépôt des fortifications des colonies, Am. sept., no.153; G¹, 406/4, ff.1, 19v, 30, 38; 407/1–2; 466, pièces 51 (recensement de Louisbourg, 1715), 56 (recensement du Port-Dauphin, 1717), 62, 76 (recensements de l'île Royale, 1720, 1749), 81a (recensement de l'île Royale et de l'île Saint-Jean, 1752); G², 180, ff.463–86v; 181, f.477; 182, ff.1106–7; 208, dossier 479; 212, dossier 542, f.75v; G³, 2037 (24 mai 1729, 3 sept. 1730); 2038/1 (3 août, 27, 29 nov. 1731); 2038/2 (25 juill. 1733); 2039/1 (4 déc. 1735); 2041/2 (28 sept. 1730); 2046/2 (5 août 1742); 2047/1 (19 nov. 1750); 2056 (1 janv., 12 sept. 1715); 2057 (6 juill. 1722); 2058 (20 nov. 1724).

GOWEAAEY (Goweah). *See* **GAWÈHE**

GRAND MAISON, *dit* **BEAUCOUR, PAUL MALLEPART DE.** *See* MALLEPART

GRANDMESNIL, ÉTIENNE VÉRON DE. *See* VÉRON

GRAND SAUTEUX, LE. *See* MINWEWEH

GRANVILLE ET DE FONVILLE, PAUL BÉCART DE. *See* BÉCART

GRAY LOCK (La Tête Blanche, The Whitehead, Wawenorrawot, Wewonorawed, Wawanolewat), an Indian chief at Missisquoi (near Swanton, Vt.); apparently fl. 1675–1740.

The bearer of the name Gray Lock seems to have belonged originally to the Waranoke tribe from the Westfield River region of Massachusetts; under this name are recorded activities spanning such a length of time that there may even be a father and son involved. The name Wawenorrawot first appears in a letter of 28 April 1727 from John GYLES to the governor of Massachusetts and is obviously the Abenaki name wawánolewát, meaning "he who fools the others or puts someone off the track." It is so descriptive of Gray Lock's exploits during Dummer's War (1722–27) that it seems likely to have been bestowed at that time, replacing whatever Indian name he had previously borne.

Gray Lock (the name is said to have come from a streak of prematurely white hair) is reported to have been active in King Philip's War (1675–76) against the Massachusetts colonists and to have fled to Mohawk country upon Philip's defeat. More probably he was one of the refugees who fled after the war to the Hudson River region and were settled at Schaghticoke (near the mouth of the Hoosic River) in Mahican country during 1676 and 1677. The loss of his territory in the war has been assumed to account for his hostility towards the English.

The name Gray Lock reappears in the records some 35 years later. In 1712 this Indian attacked Northampton, Massachusetts, in one of the last raids of the War of the Spanish Succession. He was said to have come "from Montroyall" – possibly Sault-Saint-Louis (Caughnawaga, Que.) or Chambly, although even Missisquoi or Saint-François-de-Sales (Odanak) might have been considered as Montreal by the southern New Englanders.

During Dummer's War an Indian by the name of Gray Lock achieved renown for his daring raids against Massachusetts and his elusive tactics. In the course of this war, Albany officials frequently served as intermediaries between Massachusetts and Gray Lock, since New York was not engaged in the war and since it maintained relations with the Schaghticokes, from whom Gray Lock had recruited much of his band. In the spring of 1723, Lieutenant Governor William Dummer of Massachusetts attempted to conciliate Gray Lock, who was living at Missisquoi, with a wampum belt and presents offered through Colonel Johannes SCHUYLER of Albany. Dummer's overture apparently did not reach Gray Lock, who in August fell upon Northfield and

Gray Lock

Rutland, Massachusetts, and escaped with captives. Scouts and cavalry were called out, but in October Gray Lock attacked Northfield again and again escaped safely. More troops were sent, and early in 1724 a blockhouse, Fort Dummer, was erected above Northfield near present Brattleboro, Vt., to guard against future attacks. The forts at Northfield were also strengthened.

In June 1724 Gray Lock left Missisquoi, and although the Albany government warned the Massachusetts frontier villages only two days after his departure, he made another successful raid. Scouts from Hatfield pursued him as far as Otter Creek (in present Vermont), but he eluded them and doubled back to spend the summer lurking west of the Connecticut River settlements and raiding Deerfield, Northampton, and Westfield. Haying and harvesting at Northfield that summer were done by large parties under arms, and scouting expeditions continued to probe northward even after Gray Lock had returned to Missisquoi early in November.

The last of these parties was out in March and April 1725, and as soon as it withdrew Gray Lock left his winter quarters and threw the settlements into a state of alarm. Intending retaliation, Captain Benjamin Wright recruited some men and set out in July for Missisquoi but was forced to turn back by lack of provisions. Gray Lock followed Wright to Northfield, and alarms and skirmishes continued around Fort Dummer and Deerfield the rest of the summer.

In the autumn of 1725, the Penobscot Abenakis brought word to Boston that a great council of tribes had taken place the previous summer at Saint-François and that all were in favour of peace. Word from Albany confirmed that the Canadian Abenakis were tired of the war and revealed that only two war parties – one of them Gray Lock's – were out. In December 1725 the Penobscots negotiated a tentative peace treaty [*see* SAUGUAARAM], but the agreement did not include the other Abenakis, and in March 1725/26 Dummer learned that Gray Lock was mustering yet another war party at Otter Creek. Dummer asked the Penobscots to persuade Gray Lock to make peace and directed the Massachusetts frontier towns to encourage him to come in to parley. In January 1726/27 the Albany authorities sent Gray Lock's brother Malalamet, who was apparently still at Schaghticoke, to invite the war chief to Albany to negotiate, but Malalamet reported that he had missed him. When the Canadian Abenakis sent word through the Penobscots that they wanted peace, some 20 warriors, including Gray Lock, Amaraguened, and Onedahauet (Comhommon), sent a separate belt and

a letter stating that they were undecided. They were said to have been encouraged in their stand by Joseph AUBERY, the missionary at Saint-François. It is not clear if their message ever reached Dummer.

In April 1727 a large group of Canadian Abenakis assembled at Ticonic (Winslow, Me.) to await conclusion of a treaty. In May a runner brought word that the dissenting warriors had set out against the English. Those who wished peace sent a party after the warriors and forced them to return. Peace with Massachusetts was finally established by the Penobscot and Canadian Abenakis together at Falmouth (Portland, Me.) in July 1727. None of Gray Lock's party appears in reports of the transactions.

English accounts of Gray Lock stop in 1727. In the registers of Fort Saint-Frédéric (Crown Point, N.Y.) there is a baptismal entry dated 19 April 1740 for Jean-Baptiste, son of Pierre-Jean, *dit* La Tête Blanche, and his wife Hélène. Pierre-Jean was presumably Gray Lock himself. Nicolas Ouaouënouroué, one of the five chiefs at Saint-François in 1750, was probably a son of Gray Lock. Captain Louis, or Louis Wahawanulet, possibly a grandson, was known in the Lac Memphrémagog region and was killed at Châteauguay in 1813. Wawanolet is now one of the more common family names among the Abenakis of Saint-François.

Neither the death date nor the grave of Gray Lock is definitely known. His monument is Mount Greylock, the highest peak in the Berkshire Hills of Massachusetts, named for him by the descendants of his old enemies.

GORDON M. DAY

[Much of Gray Lock's early career is known only through traditions preserved in New England town histories, and it deserves further research. French accounts take surprisingly little note of this important Indian leader, even during Dummer's War. One reason may be that Missisquoi did not have a French mission until 1743 and then only for a year or two. Such ministrations as the Missisquoi Indians received came from the chaplains at Fort Saint-Frédéric, and therefore we lack the detailed vital records which would have been kept by a resident missionary. The loss by fire of the mission records of Saint-François-de-Sales in 1759 and again in 1819 has made it impossible to be certain that Louis Wahawanulet was a grandson of Gray Lock. G.M.D.]

"Mass. Archives," XXXI, 520; XXXIIIA, 111. Private archives, A. G. Styan (Saint-Lambert, Qué.), E. Harrington, Notes made at St. Francis Indian village in 1869, 9, 21–22. H. S. Burrage, "Capt. John Wilson and some military matters in Maine in the war of 1812–15," *Maine Hist. Soc. Coll.*, 2nd ser., X (1907), 403–8. *Documentary history of Maine*, XXIII, 186–202.

William Hubbard, *The history of the Indian wars in New England* ... (Boston, London, 1677; new ed., 2v., Roxbury, Mass., 1865), II, 94, 98, 188. "Indian treaties," Maine Hist. Soc. *Coll.*, 1st ser., III (1853), 377, 407–47. *JR* (Thwaites), LXIX, 72–73. *NYCD* (O'Callaghan and Fernow), III, 561; IV, 575–77, 715, 743–44, 902–4, 990–92. J. H. Lockwood, *Westfield and its historic influences, 1669–1919* ... (Springfield, Mass., 1922), 342–49. P.-G. Roy, *Hommes et choses du fort Saint-Frédéric*, 271. J. H. Temple and George Sheldon, *History of the town of Northfield, Massachusetts, for 150 years* ... (Albany, 1875), 191–215. J. R. Trumbull, *History of Northampton, Massachusetts, from its settlement in 1654* (2v., Northampton, Mass., 1898–1902), I, 513. *The Vermont historical gazetteer* ..., ed. A. M. Hemenway (5v., Burlington, Vt., 1868–91), IV, 962–63, 998–1000. T.-M. Charland, "Un village d'Abénakis sur la rivière Missisquoi," *RHAF*, XV (1961–62), 319–32. Nathan Goold, "Col. James Scamman's 30th regiment of foot, 1775," Maine Hist. Soc. *Coll.*, 2nd ser., X (1907), 337, 358–59, 371–73, 376–80, 385–87, 391–92, 400. M. A. Safford, "Annual field day, 1897," Maine Hist. Soc. *Coll.*, 2nd ser., IX (1907), 321.

GREEN, BARTHOLOMEW, printer; b. 1699 in Cambridge, Massachusetts, son of Bartholomew Green, printer of the *Boston News-Letter*, and Maria (Mary) Mather; m. Hannah Hammond, 19 Nov. 1724, by whom he had five children; d. 29 Oct. 1751 at Halifax, Nova Scotia.

After serving his apprenticeship with his father, Bartholomew Green set up for himself in 1725. From then until 1751 he printed occasionally on his own and sometimes with other printers, including his brother-in-law, John Draper, and John BUSHELL. Green printed the *Boston Gazette* from 1725 or 1726 until 1732. The quality of the work done by one firm with which he was associated, that of Bushell, Allen and Green, seems to have been high. Isaiah Thomas, in *The history of printing in America*, remarked that "they used handsome types, and printed on good paper."

In February 1744/45 Green was commissioned a second lieutenant in the train of artillery to be sent to Louisbourg, Île Royale (Cape Breton Island), in the expedition commanded by William PEPPERRELL. According to Green, "a disposition to Serve His Majesty and [my] Native Country ... put [me] out of good Business," which he could not regain. In 1748 he therefore petitioned the General Court of Massachusetts to take his case under consideration and appoint him doorkeeper of the General Court.

In 1751 Green moved to Halifax, arriving there in September aboard the sloop *Endeavor*. He proceeded to erect on Grafton St (north of Duke St) the first printing office in what is now Canada, but died sometime in October. In the meantime

he may have issued a prospectus concerning the publication of a newspaper, which was actually initiated by John Bushell as the *Halifax Gazette*. Green had two sons who were printers, but apparently they never went to Halifax.

Donald F. Chard

"Mass. Archives," LXXIII, 294. St Paul's Church (Halifax), Burial records, p.67 (mfm in PANS). PRO, *CSP, Col., 1730*, 388. *Checklist of Boston newspapers, 1704–1780, and bibliography* (Col. Soc. Mass. *Pubs.*, IX, Boston, 1907), 447–48. *New Eng. Hist. and Geneal. Register*, XIV (1860), 376. Marie Tremaine, *A bibliography of Canadian imprints, 1751–1800* (Toronto, 1952), 661. H. A. Hill and G. F. Bigelow, *An historical catalogue of the Old South Church, Boston* (Boston, 1883), 348–49. *The memorial history of Boston, including Suffolk County, Massachusetts, 1630–1880*, ed. Justin Winsor (4v., Boston, 1880–81), II, 392, 400. Isaiah Thomas, *The history of printing in America* (2nd ed., 2v., Albany, 1874), I, 121.

GRILLOT DE POILLY, FRANÇOIS-CLAUDE-VICTOR, army officer, military engineer; b.15 March 1726 at Fort Barraux, near Grenoble, France, son of Claude-Victor, also a military engineer; d. 24 Feb. 1761 at Göttingen, in the Electorate of Hanover (Federal Republic of Germany).

François-Claude-Victor Grillot de Poilly served in the artillery from 1740 to 1743, when he was admitted to the engineer corps. After three years of siege warfare in Italy (1745–48), during which he was for a time a prisoner of war, he had seven years of duty at the fortresses of Grenoble, Perpignan, and Bayonne. Having asked for a colonial assignment, he was sent in 1755 to Île Royale (Cape Breton Island) to serve under Louis FRANQUET. He participated at Louisbourg in directing the repair and reconstruction of the fortifications and public buildings. Franquet, who valued him highly, recommended him twice for the cross of Saint-Louis.

During February and March 1757, Poilly was sent on a survey of Île Royale for the purpose of updating existing maps, suggesting road improvements, and proposing repairs to fortifications and public buildings. Travelling mainly on snowshoes, he and his party covered most of the island, with the exception of the north cape. His 12-page diary of the trip provides a good general view of topographical detail, resources and their use, roads, buildings, and the scattered inhabitants, both French and Micmac. His observations persuaded him that the agricultural, game, and timber resources of the island could be much better developed. The valley of the Rivière de

Guen

Miré (Mira River) must have more labour for its agriculture; the peninsula between the Bras du Nord-Est (East Bay) on the south and the Petit Lac de La Brador (Great Bras d'Or) and Petite Brador (St Andrew's Channel) on the north must have oxen to pull ploughs and to provide fertilizer if it was to produce certain types of grain; new farms near Port-Dauphin (Englishtown) must be equipped with ploughs and supplied with cattle. The Micmac hunted fur-bearing game but a possible market in pelts was unexploited; the forests abounded in a wide variety of usable timber but there were not enough sawmills. Roads and trails must be improved for both economic and military reasons. The defences of Port-Toulouse (St Peters) and Port-Dauphin must be strengthened, and the harbours of the Grand Lac de La Brador (Bras d'Or Lake) and the Petit Lac de La Brador, an excellent avenue for internal trade, could provide fine shelters for ships fleeing British raiders. Poilly's observations give an indication of the French government's attitude toward the economic development of Île Royale. Although the raison d'être of the colony was the fishery, the government would have liked to see greater diversification of the economy. The condition was that it should cost the crown nothing.

Poilly also kept his own diary of the events of 1758, from New Year's Day to the surrender of Louisbourg to Jeffery Amherst* and Edward Boscawen in July. After the siege, he added to it his assessment of the defence. Running to 127 folios, and accompanied by a map, the document deals primarily with the siege, during which Poilly was kept busy directing repairs, building defensive works, and reconnoitring the siege works of the attackers. It also mentions the main activities of the winter months. The Louisbourg garrison and citizens enjoyed themselves at several balls and wedding receptions while preliminary skirmishes were taking place at sea. When the Prudent, commanded by Jean-Antoine Charry Desgouttes, entered the harbour on 24 April, two-thirds of her crew were found to be ill; the 50 recruits she had brought from France were, in Poilly's opinion, the dregs of humanity. Prayers in expectation of an imminent British attempt to land included a procession on 1 June in which the Blessed Sacrament was carried through the town. When the siege came, Poilly felt, the defenders were quite unprepared, both in plans and in materials. This unreadiness was inexcusable, since for two years an attack had been fully expected. The governor, Drucour [Boschenry], was a fine, loyal officer quite unsuited to commanding a colony under siege; Franquet was a sick man; Jean Mascle de Saint-Julhien was selfish and jealous, and made little use of his wide experience; Claude-Élisabeth Denys de Bonnaventure, the king's lieutenant, was "corpulent ... [and] scarcely able to walk, a man with great zeal for the service, but rash, obtuse and brawling." As for Desgouttes, he could have covered himself in immortal glory by sacrificing his squadron in order to destroy the invasion fleet in Gabarus Bay; instead, he chose to preserve his ships at all cost. Poilly had little good, in fact, to say of any naval officer.

Taken prisoner at the capitulation, Poilly was later released and returned to duty in France, where he became engineer at Thionville in 1759. In 1760, he received the cross of Saint-Louis. He died on active service.

F. J. Thorpe

Grillot de Poilly's 1757 diary is found in CTG, Bibliothèque, mss in fol., 210f; that for 1758 is in mss in 4°, 66, ff.3–129. AN, Col., C¹¹ᴮ, 35, ff.282–83; 36, ff.262, 268–70; 38, ff.169–70. CTG, Archives, arts. 3, 15; Bibliothèque, mss in fol., 208. SHA, Xᵉ, 4, 5; Yᵃ, 183. Léon Jacob, "Un journal inédit du siège de Louisbourg (Île du Cap-Breton) en 1758," in Mélanges d'histoire offerts à M. Charles Bémont ... (Paris, 1913), 619–52. McLennan, Louisbourg, 259–60, 284–85, 287, 301.

GUEN, HAMON, priest, Sulpician, missionary; b. 1687 in the diocese of Saint-Pol-de-Léon (dept. of Finistère), France; d. 15 April 1761 at the mission at Lac des Deux-Montagnes (Oka, Que.).

Hamon Guen entered the Sulpician community in 1711. He arrived in Canada on 22 Aug. 1714 and was ordained on 21 Sept. 1715. Immediately after he was appointed to the mission at Sault-au-Récollet to learn Indian languages and to be initiated into the ministry under the direction of his fellow priests Robert-Michel Gay* and Maurice Quéré de Tréguron. He succeeded in mastering Iroquois and in speaking Huron respectably; he is supposed to have left some writings in Iroquois: sermons, instructions, and meditations. He is also supposed to have written canticles, hymns, anthems, and other church songs in the two languages he knew, for at that time the Indian languages were used in the liturgical offices [see Luc-François Nau].

In 1721 he went with the Indians when the mission at Sault-au-Récollet was moved to Lac des Deux-Montagnes [see Gay; Quéré de Tréguron]. He is credited with founding for the Indians the pilgrimage of the Calvary, situated on the mountain nearest to the mission, where he had seven stations built in stone with the help of his fellow priest François Picquet*, who agreed to take on the task of carrying out the ornamentation. This place of pilgrimage still exists.

In 1749, when Picquet undertook to establish the mission to the Iroquois at La Présentation (Oswegatchie, now Ogdensburg, N.Y.), Guen lost no time in following to assist him in his labours and particularly to devote himself to the conversion of the Iroquois. After two years of intense labour he returned to the mission at Lac des Deux-Montagnes. In 1754 he succeeded Quéré de Tréguron as superior of the mission, and he held this office until 1760. He died at the mission on 15 April 1761, at 74 years of age.

ANTONIO DANSEREAU

ASSM, Section des biographies, 78; Section de la seigneurie du Lac-des-Deux-Montagnes, 308; Section des manuscrits indiens; Joseph-Vincent Quiblier, "Notes sur le séminaire de Montréal, 1847" (typescript). *Lettres édifiantes et curieuses escrites des missions étrangères* (14v., Lyon, 1819), XIV, 262–301. Allaire, *Dictionnaire*. Gauthier, *Sulpitiana*. C.-P. Beaubien, *Le Sault-au-Récollet; ses rapports avec les premiers temps de la colonie; mission-paroisse* (Montréal, 1898). *Petit manuel des pèlerins au Calvaire du lac des Deux-Montagnes* (nouv. éd., Montréal, 1926). Pierre Rousseau, *Saint-Sulpice et les missions catholiques* (Montréal, 1930). J.-A. Cuoq, "Anotc kekon," *RSCT*, 1st ser., XI (1893), sect. I, 137–79. Olivier Maurault, "Les vicissitudes d'une mission sauvage," *Revue trimestrielle canadienne* (Montréal), XVI (1930), 121–49.

GUIGNAS, MICHEL, Jesuit, missionary, professor of hydrography; b. 12 Jan. 1681 at Condom (dept. of Gers), France; d. 6 Feb. 1752 in Quebec.

Michel Guignas entered the noviciate of the Jesuits of the province of Aquitaine in Bordeaux, France, on 9 Dec. 1702 after having studied philosophy for two years. When his two noviciate years were completed, and after a year of literary studies, he taught in turn grammar, classics, and rhetoric classes at the Jesuit college in Pau from 1705 to 1710 and subsequently studied philosophy and theology in Poitiers. He left France for Canada in June 1716. He probably spent several months at the Saint-François-Xavier mission near Bécancour before leaving the St Lawrence valley for his first stay of five years in the western missions, particularly among the Ottawas. On 2 Feb. 1718, in the church of the Saint-Ignace mission at Michilimackinac, he took his four perpetual vows between the hands of Father Joseph-Jacques Marest*. In 1720 and 1721 he was a missionary at Saint-Joseph (near St Joseph, Mich.). He returned to Quebec in 1722 to replace Father Pierre de LAUZON as professor of hydrography at the college of Quebec [*see* Joseph DES LANDES].

After four years of teaching Guignas went once more to the western missions. He asked to be allowed to take part, along with Father Nicolas Degonnor, in the expedition to the Sioux country commanded by René BOUCHER de La Perrière; he left Montreal on 16 June 1727. At the beginning of 1728, however, illness forced Boucher to leave Fort Beauharnois, which he had just built on Lake Pepin (Wis.-Minn.). His nephew Pierre BOUCHER de Boucherville succeeded him. In September Boucher de Boucherville left the fort and Guignas accompanied him. During the return voyage, on 16 Oct. 1728, they were captured by the Kickapoos and Mascoutens and held for five months. Thanks to their adoption by a member of one of the tribes, their lives were spared. During the winter of 1729 Guignas went to the Illinois country and lived among the Mascoutens. In 1730 he was back at the Michilimackinac mission, and the following year he accompanied René Godefroy de Linctot, the newly appointed commandant in the Sioux country. There was then no news of the Jesuit until 1735, when it was learned that he was still alive.

In 1737 Guignas left the Sioux missions and went to Michilimackinac, and from there to Quebec in 1738. He exercised his ministry in the Saguenay region until 1740; then he retired to Quebec and died there on 6 Feb. 1752.

Father Guignas, a Gascon, was of a zealous and jovial disposition and possessed a quick and open mind; he was robust, original, at times eccentric in his manners and in expressing his opinions. He liked to suggest, for example, that after all there was some good in brandy, which he called jokingly "the radical humour."

LOUIS-PHILIPPE AUDET

ASJCF, 528; 608; Fonds Rochemonteix, 4012, 1; 4017, 304–16; 4018, 117, 123, 126, 133, 149, 161. ASJ, France (Chantilly), Liste des pères et des frères jésuites. *Découvertes et établissements des Français* (Margry), VI, 577–79. "Lettres du père Aulneau," APQ *Rapport, 1926–27,* 269, 278, 281, 285, 286. Melançon, *Liste des missionnaires jésuites.* Charland, *Les Abénakis d'Odanak,* 42. Rochemonteix, *Les Jésuites et la N.-F. au XVIIe siècle,* I, 204–31; *Les Jésuites et la N.-F. au XVIIIe siècle,* I, 180–202, 447–63. L.-P. Audet, "Hydrographes du roi et cours d'hydrographie au collège de Québec, 1671–1759," *Cahiers des Dix,* XXXV (1970), 13–37.

GUILLET DE CHAUMONT, NICOLAS-AUGUSTE, soldier, royal notary; b. *c.* 1695 in Paris, France, son of Antoine Guillet de Chaumont and Marie-Louise Esprit; buried 3 April 1765 at Terrebonne (Que.).

Nicolas-Auguste Guillet de Chaumont came to Canada as a soldier. When he arrived is unknown, but in 1721, at the time of his first marriage, he was a sergeant in the colonial regular troops. Since he arrived in the colony without an officer's commission, the nobility of his family must have been of small consequence. After only a short time with the military he joined the legal circle of Montreal. He began practising law, representing his fellow citizens before the courts. In this capacity he entered the first two deeds in his minute book in 1727, but not until 6 Nov. 1728 did he sign his first document as a notary. We do not know when he obtained his commission as a royal notary, since the document confirming this appointment has not been found.

Guillet de Chaumont, like many other notaries in the colony, exercised other legal and administrative functions. He was writer in the office of Marine, dealing particularly with administrative detail concerning the troops and occasionally he served as court clerk, king's attorney, assessor, and lieutenant-general of the jurisdiction of Montreal.

He was not one of the most active notaries in this jurisdiction. His minute book contains only 465 deeds, 440 of which were drawn up before 1736; his last two deeds were entered in 1748 and 1752. Guillet de Chaumont gave up his office during 1752 and retired to Terrebonne. In a letter to the minister of Marine, Maurepas, in 1740 Intendant Hocquart* criticized the notary severely, calling him a "very dull man."

On 6 Nov. 1721, in Montreal, Guillet de Chaumont had married Marie-Catherine Legras, the widow of Antoine Barsalou. Not only did she saddle him with 11 children, "big and small," and with a "poorly organized tannery," but she also brought many vexations upon him. On 14 June 1735, after 14 years of childless marriage, Guillet de Chaumont unsuccessfully demanded a judicial separation, based on the troubles he had put up with during these years. He accused his wife and the Barsalou children of stealing from him continually, taking sums of money belonging to his clients from his cash box. In addition, he claimed that one son, Jean-Baptiste Barsalou, had tried to murder him. His wife died on 6 Feb. 1737. Four months later, on 27 June, the notary married Félicité, daughter of Jean-Baptiste d'Ailleboust* Des Muceaux, and finally enjoyed the peace of family life. Eight children were born of the marriage, and the descendants bear the name Chaumont today.

MICHEL PAQUIN

AN, Col., C¹¹ᴬ, 73, f.300. ANQ-M, Greffe de N.-A. Guillet de Chaumont, 1727–1752 (inventoried in A. Roy, *Inv. greffes not.*, XVI, 90–175). É.-Z. Massicotte, "Les tribunaux et les officiers de justice de Montréal sous le régime français," *BRH*, XXXVII (1931), 188, 189, 192, 303, 306, 312. P.-G. Roy, *Inv. jug. et délib., 1717-1760*, III, 308; IV, 297; V, *passim*. Tanguay, *Dictionnaire*. Vachon, "Inv. critique des notaires royaux," *RHAF*, XI (1957–58), 402. J.-J. Lefebvre, "Nicolas Auguste Guillet de Chaumont (1695–1765), notaire, 1727–1752," *La Revue du notariat* (Montréal), 66 (1963–64), 361–66. É.-Z. Massicotte, "Un notaire dans une ménagerie," *BRH*, XLII (1936), 132–35.

GUITON DE MONREPOS, JACQUES-JOSEPH, lieutenant general for civil and criminal affairs in the royal jurisdiction of Montreal; a native of the former province of Guyenne, France; fl. 1740–64.

On 16 Oct. 1740 Pierre Raimbault*, lieutenant general for civil and criminal affairs in the royal jurisdiction, died in Montreal. There was no question of replacing him by the special lieutenant Jean-François MALHIOT: in the summer of 1740, after numerous procedural irregularities committed by Malhiot, it had been necessary to appoint the councillor Jacques de LAFONTAINE de Belcour interim lieutenant general. In view of Malhiot's incompetence in judicial matters and the impossibility of finding someone in the colony to discharge the office satisfactorily, the colonial authorities asked the minister of Marine, Maurepas, "to find in the provinces" a judge who would combine honesty with "experience in questions of judicature." On 1 Feb. 1741 the minister accorded the office of lieutenant general for civil and criminal affairs in the royal jurisdiction of Montreal to Jacques-Joseph Guiton de Monrepos, a lawyer in the *parlements* of Bordeaux and Paris. Guiton de Monrepos sailed in May 1741 on board the king's vessel the *Rubis*, and arrived in the colony in the summer. He was received formally into his office on 18 Sept. 1741 and began officially to exercise his duties as a judge on 13 November.

Being a nobleman, and having just arrived from the mother country "full of his own importance," he thought that by virtue of his office he took precedence over all the other officials in Montreal. He demanded of them a deference that made him ridiculous in the eyes of the people of Montreal. The financial commissary and subdelegate of the intendant in Montreal, Honoré MICHEL de Villebois, would not admit that Guiton de Monrepos took precedence in public ceremonies. A dispute resulted between the two men which Louis XV was obliged to settle by drawing up a regulation defining the powers and prerogatives of each of them. He quite naturally granted precedence in public ceremonies to the financial commissary, with the judge subordinate to him.

A Tartuffe with a haughty manner, Guiton de Monrepos made an enemy of almost everyone when in 1743 he haled Timothy SULLIVAN, known as Timothée Sylvain, king's physician in Montreal, into court for having "overtaxed his patience by menacing him with his cane." Jean-Baptiste ADHÉMAR, acting judge in the court of Montreal, sentenced Sullivan to two years in prison, but when the case was appealed the Conseil Supérieur "dismissed the parties," considering that there was not "sufficient ground" to constitute a case. Once more Guiton de Monrepos made himself ridiculous by his intransigent attitude during this lawsuit. The people of Montreal composed satirical poems and songs about him on this occasion.

Although he had an annual salary of 450 *livres* and fees varying between 700 and 800 *livres* a year, Guiton de Monrepos considered he was "unable to keep himself with some semblance of respect in his situation with the modest salary and fees that go with it." He therefore frequently asked the authorities in the mother country for an increase in pay. Thanks to his backers at the court, he received a gratuity of 400 *livres* on a few occasions.

He returned to France after the surrender of Montreal, and on 12 July 1761 he expressed the desire to retire to live with his family in Guyenne. The king, however, needed him to testify at the trial of François Bigot* and "his band," and kept him in Paris. He provided a special gratuity of 1,000 *livres* for him. Having been a diligent and honest judge, once the *affaire du Canada* was finished Guiton de Monrepos was awarded by the king on 28 Nov. 1764 a pension of 600 *livres* because of his services in Canada as lieutenant general for civil and criminal affairs in the royal jurisdiction of Montreal. Afterwards he disappears from view.

ANDRÉ LACHANCE

AN, Col., B, 72, f.38v; 73, f.428v; 78, ff.22f.; 81, ff.293v, 304f.; 82, f.94; 85, ff.201f.; 91, f.259v; 109, f.341; 113, f.202; 115, ff.187v, 211v; 117, f.155v; 120, f.354; C¹¹A, 73, ff.15v-16, 40-40v; 75, ff.16v-17; 78, ff.56-56v; 79, ff.296v-98; 81, ff.329v-39v; 85, ff.270-79; 93, f.299v; 99, ff.409-9v; 100, f.127; 101, ff.131-31v; 115, f.53v; 120, f.351; F³, 11, ff.2-2v, 173-74v, 244-45v. ANQ, NF, Arrêts du Conseil d'État du Roi, V, 51v; NF, Coll. de pièces jud. et not., 2098; NF, Ins. Cons. sup., VIII, 65v-66. ANQ-M, Documents judiciaires, 13 nov., 13 déc. 1741, 31 déc. 1742, 2, 3, 4 janv., 9, 11, 12, 14, 15, 16 févr. 1743. *Documents relating to Canadian currency during the French period* (Shortt), II, 636, 638. P.-G. Roy, *Inv. jug. et délib., 1717–1760*, IV, 44, 127-28, 131-32, 196.

GUY, PIERRE, merchant, militia officer at Montreal; b. 5 May 1701 in Paris, France, son of Nicolas Guy and Élisabeth Leduc; d. 14 April 1748 in Montreal.

The date of Pierre Guy's arrival in New France is not known. In 1725 he was in Montreal, where on 18 November he married Élisabeth Garreau, the widow of Jean Lalande. The *aveu et dénombrement* of Montreal in 1731 mentions one "S. Guy" who owned a two-storey stone house in Rue Saint-Joseph. This was perhaps Pierre Guy; in any case it seems certain that it was he who in 1730 received the commission as ensign in the militia granted to "Sieur Guy, a merchant." The following year Guy became a lieutenant in the militia, and in 1738 he received a commission as second captain.

On 29 Sept. 1734, some months after the death of his wife, by whom he had had eight children in nine years of marriage, Pierre Guy remarried, this time with Jeanne Truillier, *dit* Lacombe. Of this second marriage were born five children, including Pierre*, who played an important role in Montreal after the conquest.

Pierre Guy may well have been known as a merchant in Montreal even in 1730, but it is only with the 1740s that one discovers useful information about his business career. He had, however, already become reasonably well-off, for in 1741 he owned four pieces of land at Montreal, the last of which had been bought for 1,600 *livres*. His accounts, which are still available though incomplete, indicate a fairly high level of business. Guy imported general merchandise, wine, and spirits, and he exported peltries to France through the agency of François HAVY and Jean LEFEBVRE, his principal correspondents in Quebec. Guy sometimes had recourse to other merchants in that town and occasionally was directly in touch with his suppliers in the mother country, but the bulk of his trade was done with Havy and Lefebvre, from whom he sometimes bought for considerable amounts. For example, a current account dated 18 Oct. 1743 lists numerous shipments of cloth, lead, wine, and paper, the total of which amounted to 19,857 *livres* 5 *sols* 7 *deniers*. Guy paid his suppliers fairly promptly with furs or bills of exchange and sometimes raised difficulties about the quality of the merchandise he received.

Trade was not always an easy matter for Pierre Guy. At times he made errors of judgement which caused Havy and Lefebvre to step in. In 1745, when war was hindering transportation between the colony and the mother country and imports were becoming scarcer, Havy and Lefebvre wrote to Guy: "We see that you are selling as much as you can; we cannot say that you are acting entirely wisely, you are selling for small profit and to all appearances you will pay very dearly for your purchases.''

In August 1745, when it was feared that New France would be invaded by British troops, Guy came down to Quebec with militia officers from Montreal to repulse a possible attack. He was soon back in Montreal, but one may believe that the fear of an English invasion continued to be a preoccupation, for in 1745 and 1746 he transferred to France considerable funds which he did not intend to use in his business until peace had returned. It may be supposed that he anticipated returning to France if the colony came into the hands of the English, for certain Canadians already had a presentiment of the colony's fall.

JOSÉ IGARTUA

AN, Col., B, 46, f.101; 47, f.1219; C¹¹ᴬ, 85, ff.72–81. ANQ-M, Greffe de F.-M. Lepailleur, 28 sept. 1734; Greffe de Michel Lepailleur, 18 nov. 1725; Registre d'état civil, Notre-Dame de Montréal, 18 nov. 1725, 29 sept. 1734, 15 avril 1748. PAC, MG 8, C3, 38, 15 juin 1748; MG 18, H28, III, Liste des habitants de Montréal, 1640–1800; MG 23, GIII, 25, Pierre Guy, Grand Livre no.4, 1735–1740, Livre de comptes, 1742–1745 [These two account books contain retail sales and did not provide any important information for this biography. J.I.]; 28, Pierre Guy, 1739–1749; MG 24, L3, 2, pp.543–55, 558–63, 566–79, 582–89, 592–633, 637–63, 670–71, 677–718, 722–26, 730–75, 776–1130, 1131–35, 1139–50; 28, pp.17756–61; 35, pp.22417–35, 22469–76; 39, p.25147; 40, pp.25537–46; 43, pp.28127–29; 46, pp.29617–20, 29622–23. "Aveu et dénombrement pour l'île de Montréal," APQ *Rapport, 1941–42*, 25–26. Bonnault, "Le Canada militaire," APQ *Rapport, 1949–51*, 441. Tanguay, *Dictionnaire*.

GUYART DE FLEURY, JEAN-BAPTISTE, soldier, court officer, royal notary; b. *c.* 1719 at Seignelay (dept. of Yonne), France, son of Jean-Baptiste Guyart and Anne Gigou; date and place of death unknown.

Jean-Baptiste Guyart came to New France as a soldier; on 7 Jan. 1740 he married Élisabeth Jobin in Montreal. On 20 Feb. 1741 he presented a petition to obtain the post of court officer; later he was an applicant for the office of attorney. In 1745 he was compromised, along with Jean Eymard, king's writer, in an obscure matter involving the destruction of a judicial file; his career in Montreal thus came to an abrupt end.

On 29 April 1746 Guyart, who had been living in Quebec for some time, asked François DAINE, lieutenant general for civil and criminal affairs of the provost court of Quebec, for recognition of his commission as a court officer, "wishing to enjoy the prerogatives attached to the said office,

which he cannot do without having first of all been installed and put in possession of the said office.'' The next day, in the investigation into his character, he was acknowledged to be an honest man, without any mention of the matter in 1745. He was then granted the office and was admitted to it on 3 May 1746.

Some months later Guyart was accused of counterfeiting orders for payment: in the night of 15/16 September the authorities went to his domicile in Rue Couillard in Quebec to arrest him. At five o'clock in the morning he gave himself up. During the questioning in the ensuing trial much attention was given to a trip made without permission to Montreal – to receive payment of a debt, said Guyart. About ten witnesses were called and gave evidence in this affair, which had no effect upon the accused's career.

A few years later, on 8 Jan. 1754, Guyart obtained from Intendant François Bigot* a notary's commission to practise in the parishes on the north shore in the government of Quebec, from Pointe-aux-Trembles (Neuville) to the seigneury of Sainte-Anne-de-la-Pérade; some weeks later, on 20 February, he was appointed seigneurial judge of Sainte-Anne-de-la-Pérade. At almost the same time Guyart asked for a broader territory, pleading that the one assigned him on 8 January was too limited and the clientele too small to allow him to make a living for himself and his family. He then received permission to draw up deeds on the south shore from Saint-Nicolas to Lotbinière, replacing the notary Jean-Baptiste Chorest, deceased. Furthermore, on 12 April 1758 he was given permission to practise at Saint-Augustin (Saint-Augustin-de-Québec).

In 1761 Guyart left the colony, shortly after receiving from James Murray*, on 29 Dec. 1760, a commission to practise as a notary from Cap-Santé to Les Grondines and on the south shore opposite Cap-Santé. We then lose track of him. Jean-Baptiste Guyart had six children, five of whom died in infancy.

LOUIS-PHILIPPE AUDET

ANQ, Greffe de J.-B. Guyart de Fleury, 1754–1761; NF, Coll. de pièces jud. et not., 1446, 2116; NF, Ord. int., XL, XLII. P.-G. Roy, *Inv. ins. Prév. Québec*, II, 61; *Inv. ord. int.*, III, 42, 80, 83, 182, 194, 207. Tanguay, *Dictionnaire*. É.-Z. Massicotte, "Les huissiers de Montréal sous le régime français," *BRH*, XXXII (1926), 89–90.

GUYON, LOUISE. *See* Appendix

GYART. *See* GIARD

GYLES, JOHN, interpreter, soldier; b. *c.* 1680 at

Pemaquid (Me.); m. Ruth True (1703) and Hannah Heath (1722); d. at Roxbury (now part of Boston, Mass.), 1755. It is not known how many children he had.

John Gyles is the author of the most authentic and remarkable account in English of the Malecites (Etchemins) of the Saint John River. In 1689, when he was nine years of age, he was living with his family at Fort Charles (Pemaquid). On 2 August of that year (o.s.), while labouring with his father Thomas in the vicinity of the new fort, he was taken prisoner by Malecites in one of the bloody forays that characterized the period. John's father was killed, one brother was captured and later killed, and another brother escaped. John was conveyed up the Penobscot River, across portages to the Chiputneticook Lakes, and on to the confluence of the Médoctec (Eel) River with the Saint John, ten miles below present-day Woodstock, N.B.

For six years Gyles was slave to the Malecites. His graphic story of his adventures describes the customs of the Malecites, their techniques in the chase, their social order, the tortures inflicted on captives, and the impact made on them by the relatively few French on the Saint John before 1700. The account gives a striking impression of the extremities endured by the Malecites in good and bad times, their gluttony when rewarded by hunting, and their misery in the winter season when game was scarce. They could live only by dispersal from the fort at Médoctec (Meductic), where they were ministered to by the Recollet priest Simon Girard* de La Place. John Gyles was forced to serve as drudge to one of the many small hunting parties which moved as far north as Gaspésie. Starvation for seven or eight days on end was not unusual.

His fortunes greatly improved in the summer of 1695 when he was sold to Louis Damours* de Chauffours, who had a seigneury at Jemseg. John hunted and traded for Damours and worked in his store. In October 1696 English invaders came up the Saint John River to attack Governor Joseph Robinau* de Villebon's fort at the Naxouat (Nashwaak) River. Damours was in France at the time, but Gyles helped to save his master's house from destruction. He posted on the door a statement, written by Damours's wife, that English captives had been treated kindly there. After the peace of Ryswick Gyles was delivered to the captain of an English vessel at the mouth of the Saint John and sailed for Boston, where he arrived on 19 June 1698. His account of the French inhabitants of the Saint John is sympathetic.

Gyles' facility in the Indian dialects of Acadia made him invaluable to the governing authorities of New England when war broke out again in 1701. He served as an interpreter under many flags of truce, sailed with Major Benjamin Church* in 1704, and fought with Colonel John March* at Port-Royal (Annapolis Royal, N.S.) in 1707. Most of his later life was given to military service and to liaison with the Indians. In 1715 he helped construct Fort George at Pejepscot (Brunswick, Me.); he remained to command the fort until 1725. He finished his military career as commander of the New England garrison on the St George's River.

In 1736 Gyles published his memoirs of his adventures. He said that he had collected them from his "minutes" some years before, at the request of his second wife, Hannah, "for the use of our family, that we might have a memento ever ready at hand, to excite in ourselves gratitude and thankfulness to God." When the memoirs were read by some of his friends, Gyles was "pressed for a copy for the public."

W. S. MacNutt

Gyles' account of his captivity is entitled *Memoirs of odd adventures, strange deliverances, etc. in the captivity of John Gyles, esq., commander of the garrison on Saint George River, in the district of Maine*. First printed in Boston in 1736, it was reprinted in S. G. Drake, *Indian captivities, or life in the wigwam* (Buffalo, 1853), 73–108, and, as a separate volume, in Cincinnati (1869) and Saint John, N.B. (1875). For a "semifictional" account, *see* Stuart Trueman, *The ordeal of John Gyles . . .* (Toronto, [1966]).

Documentary history of Maine, IX, X, XXIII–XXIV. "Indian treaties," Maine Hist. Soc. *Coll.*, 1st ser., III (1853), 362, 381, 420. "John Gyles's statement of the number of Indians," Maine Hist. Soc. *Coll.*, 1st ser., III (1853), 356–57. Coleman, *New England captives*. J. A. Vinton, *Thomas Gyles and his neighbors, 1669–1689 . . .* (Boston, 1867). John McKeen, "Some account of the early settlements at Sagadahock and on the Androscoggin River . . . ," Maine Hist. Soc. *Coll.*, 1st ser., III (1853), 314–15.

H

HALDIMAND, PETER FREDERICK, military officer, surveyor; b. 1741 or 1742, probably in Switzerland, son of Jean-Abraham Haldimand; d. 16 Dec. 1765 off Cape Breton Island.

Hale

When less than 15 years old, Peter Frederick Haldimand left Switzerland to join his uncle, Sir Frederick Haldimand*, and was commissioned an ensign in the Royal American Regiment by General James Abercromby*, who commented on his small size. He served throughout the Seven Years' War in America and took part in the capture of Montreal in 1760. Promoted lieutenant, he was engaged on survey work in 1762 and 1763, with instructions to prepare sectional maps of the province of Canada. He was also to draw up historical accounts of the towns of Montreal and Trois-Rivières and collect details of their present administration. In a letter to his uncle in June 1762 Peter Haldimand mentioned the difficulties of this task and his determination to elicit an "exact description" from local officials. He is described at this time as a young man of no vices but expensive tastes, to whom General James Murray* had given a year's pay in advance to settle his debts.

After the war Peter Haldimand became an assistant to Captain Samuel Holland*, who had been appointed to survey the northern district in the great survey of British possessions in North America. In October 1764 Haldimand was landed with a week's provisions on the Island of St John (Prince Edward Island), in charge of an exploring party. So little appreciated were the distances and the obstacles of the terrain that the party had to be rescued after three days without food. The following summer Haldimand surveyed the Magdalen Islands and also wrote for the Board of Trade a valuable account of the "sea-cow" (walrus) fisheries. In December 1765, while making soundings off Cape Breton, he fell through breaking ice and was drowned. Captain Holland, like many others, had a high opinion of Peter Haldimand's abilities and described him, young though he was, as a most accomplished mathematician and his principal assistant in astronomy.

A. T. MILNE

BM,Add. MSS, 21661, 21679, 21687, 21728 (calendared in PAC *Report, 1884; 1885; 1886*). *Holland's description of Cape Breton Island and other documents*, ed. D. C. Harvey (PANS pub., no.2, Halifax, 1935). J. N. McIlwraith, *Sir Frederick Haldimand* (2nd ed., London, Toronto, 1926). Willis Chipman, "The life and times of Major Samuel Holland, surveyor-general, 1764–1801," Ontario Hist. Soc., *Papers and records* (Toronto), XXI (1924), 11–90. "Place-names on Magdalen Islands, Que.," comp. R. Douglas, Canadian Geographic Board *17th Report* (Ottawa, 1922), 66–67.

HALE, ROBERT, doctor, politician, military officer; b. 12 Feb. 1702 (o.s.) in Beverly, Massa-

chusetts, son of Dr Robert Hale and Elizabeth Clark; d. 20 March 1767 in Beverly.

As a youth of 16, Hale kept the Beverly grammar school and began his studies at Harvard College, where he received his degree in 1721. After teaching for a time at Exeter, New Hampshire, he undertook the study of medicine with Joseph Manning of Ipswich, Massachusetts. In 1723 he completed his apprenticeship and married Elizabeth Gilman (11 December). He and his new bride settled in Beverly, where he resumed the position of head master at the grammar school as a supplement to his medical practice. In the summer of 1731 Hale made a trading voyage to Nova Scotia aboard the schooner *Cupid*, in which he had part interest, and visited Annapolis Royal and settlements in the Chignecto area. He was an interested, though not unprejudiced, observer of Acadian customs. His journal notes the use of wooden shoes, the mining of coal, and the baleful effects of swarms of "Muskettoes." The local priest appeared to him as "Habited like a Fool in Petticoats," and women's fashions, which looked "as if they were pitched on with pitchforks, & very often yr Stockings are down about their heels," did not impress him.

Dr Hale, who was to hold every important local office in Beverly, was in 1733 appointed justice of the peace. In the same year he was first elected to the Massachusetts House of Representatives. He was married again on 21 Dec. 1737, to Elizabeth Clark. In 1740 he was one of the organizers and directors of the Massachusetts land bank, a scheme meant to alleviate a shortage of currency in the colony. When Governor Jonathan Belcher opposed the scheme, the Massachusetts Council ordered its directors removed from all elective offices, but the house stood by Hale. He later received several posts, including one as manager of the provincial lottery.

Hale was involved in the planning of the 1745 expedition to Louisbourg, Île Royale (Cape Breton Island), as a member of the committee on transportation. When the expedition sailed, Hale found himself colonel of the 5th New England Regiment, a position granted him by Governor William Shirley in return for his political support and intended to help him recoup his losses – about £125 – suffered in the collapse of the land bank scheme. At Louisbourg his regiment was posted on guard duty, and he served on the council of war from 14 April to 6 July. He became ill and feuded with William PEPPERRELL, alleging that the latter refused to provide medical aid for the regiment. Pepperrell pointed out that Hale had illegally detached "about two companys which he kept . . . principally to waite on him-selfe." Apparently Hale's illness was not serious, for he found ample time to begin a farm at Louisbourg, known to Yankee fishermen for over a century as "Col. Hale's garden." Upon his return to Massachusetts late in the summer of 1745, Hale was rewarded for his services with an appointment as sheriff of Essex County. In this capacity he supervised in 1756 the distribution of 36 Acadian exiles among the towns of the county.

Hale represented the province of Massachusetts at a congress with the Iroquois at Albany in 1747. He was defeated in an election for the house in 1749, and was not re-elected until 1754. In 1755 he was chosen by Governor Shirley to persuade New Hampshire to participate in the expedition against Fort Saint-Frédéric (Crown Point) on Lake Champlain. Through his efforts, and his promise of free provisions for its troops, New Hampshire raised her quota from 400 to 500 men. Hale offered a set of plans for the expedition and was considered eligible for its command. When John Winslow*, a more experienced soldier, was given the post instead, Hale refused to serve in a medical role.

Little is known of Hale's life after this time. In the spring of 1766, after a third of a century of steady, and occasionally distinguished, public service, Dr Hale "was strangely seized with an almost total loss of his Limbs and Reason, in which state he continued till his Death" on 20 March 1767.

ROBERT L. WAGNER

American Antiquarian Soc. (Worcester, Mass.), Hale papers; Additional MSS on French and Indian war, Robert Hale, "Chronicle relating [to] some remarkable transactions respecting the disputes between the english & french [1755–62]"; Curwin papers, IV. Mass. Hist. Soc., Gilman papers. [Benjamin Cleaves], "Benjamin Cleaves's journal of the expedition to Louisbourg in 1745," *New Eng. Hist. and Geneal. Register*, LXVI (1912), 113–24. *Correspondence of William Shirley* (Lincoln), II, 131–32. [Robert Hale], "Journal of a voyage to Nova Scotia made in 1731 by Robert Hale of Beverly," Essex Institute (Salem, Mass.), *Hist. Coll.*, XLII (1906), 217–44. Massachusetts, *Journals of the House of Representatives . . .* (40v., in progress, Mass. Hist. Soc. pub., Boston, 1919–), XXII, 20–23, 118. New Hampshire, *Provincial and state papers, published by the authority of the legislature of New Hampshire*, ed. I. W. Hammond et al. (40v., Manchester, Concord, N.H., 1867–1943), VI, 361–63, 439–40. "The Pepperrell papers," Mass. Hist. Soc. *Coll.*, 6th ser., X (1899), 4, 33, 331–32, 354–55, 389, 504. [William Pepperrell], "The Sir William Pepperrell journal," American Antiquarian Soc. *Proc.* (Worcester, Mass.), new ser., XX (1909–10), 139–76. *Vital records of Beverly, Massachusetts, to the end of the year 1849* (2v., Topsfield, Mass., 1906–7), I, 161; II, 145. G. B. Billias, *The Massachusetts land bankers of 1740* (University of

Maine studies, 2nd ser., no.74, Orono, 1959). McLennan, *Louisbourg.* J. A. Schutz, *William Shirley: king's governor of Massachusetts* (Chapel Hill, N.C., 1961). Shipton, *Sibley's Harvard graduates*, VI, 483–87. E. M. Stone, *History of Beverly, civil and ecclesiastical, from its settlement in 1630 to 1842* (Boston, 1843), 44.

HALEVEAR. *See* OLIVIER

HALHEAD, EDWARD, schoolmaster; fl. 1749–52.

On 6 April 1749, in London, a letter was forwarded by the Lords of Trade and Plantations to the Society for the Propagation of the Gospel recommending that clergymen and schoolmasters be named to serve in the settlements and townships to be established in Nova Scotia. The society accepted the proposal and appointed Edward Halhead "schoolmaster to Nova Scotia with a salary of £15 per year to commence from Lady Day last [25 March 1749]" and ordered "that a gratuity of £10 be immediately paid to him." Halhead, having learned of the British government's plan to settle the province, had already volunteered for such service. Highly recommended by Bishop Richard Trevor of St David's, Pembrokeshire, Wales, as "a proper person for that purpose being well skilled in accounts, mathematics and mensuration," Halhead arrived in Halifax in September 1749. From the beginning he was appalled by the primitive conditions in the new colony. The first winter was particularly difficult as numerous settlers died from the cold. Halhead along with many others fell ill and mere survival rather than education became his primary objective. According to William TUTTY, the SPG missionary at Halifax, construction of a schoolhouse was delayed "owing to the fortification of the town against the Indians and the building of a hospital and other government works." Eventually, Halhead was assigned a room in the orphanage; however, this proved unsatisfactory and on 12 Oct. 1752 he tendered his resignation. Once described by Tutty as "a very regular and sober man" Halhead lacked the drive and initiative required to establish a school effectively under the primitive conditions of early Halifax. Nothing is known of Halhead's career following his departure from Nova Scotia in the autumn of 1752.

WILLIAM B. HAMILTON

[Halhead's career in Nova Scotia was traced through his letters in USPG, B (mfm in PAC, MG 17, B1). Further information on conditions in early Halifax was gleaned from PAC, MG 11, Nova Scotia A, 33. Unfor-

Hamilton

tunately, the SPG did not keep records on lay missionaries in the 18th century. Consequently the USPG archives contains information only on Halhead's three-year sojourn in Halifax. *See also*: James Bingay, *Public education in Nova Scotia; a history and commentary* (Kingston, Ont., 1919). P. W. Thibeau, *Education in Nova Scotia before 1811* (Washington, 1922). T. B. Akins, "History of Halifax City," N.S. Hist. Soc. *Coll.*, VIII (1895). w.b.h.]

HAMILTON, OTHO, military officer, secretary and member of the Nova Scotia Council, lieutenant governor of Placentia, Newfoundland; b. *c*. 1690 in Edinburgh, Scotland, one of 12 children of Thomas and Grizel Hamilton; d. 26 Feb. 1770 at Waterford (Republic of Ireland).

The Edinburgh family of Otho Hamilton had a tradition of military service, which was probably a factor in his choice of a career. On 16 June 1710 he was commissioned an ensign in the Earl of Portmore's (2nd Queen's) Regiment of Foot, and the same year he was among the recruits arriving at Boston to serve in the planned attack on Port-Royal (Annapolis Royal, N.S.) under Francis Nicholson* and Samuel Vetch*. It is not known, however, whether Hamilton went to Port-Royal at this time. He next appears as an ensign in the garrison at Annapolis Royal in October 1714; by this time he had left Portmore's regiment. In 1717 he was absorbed into the newly created regiment of Colonel Richard PHILIPPS (later the 40th Regiment of Foot), which supplanted the independent companies serving in Nova Scotia and Newfoundland. Hamilton became a lieutenant on 9 Aug. 1718. In June 1729 Robert Wroth* resigned his commission as adjutant of Philipps' regiment "in favour of Lt. Otho Hamilton." The latter continued his career in this regiment, rising to captain on 3 Sept. 1739 and major in January 1745/46. There is limited evidence that on his retirement from the regiment in 1761 he received the rank of lieutenant-colonel.

Like other officers stationed in Nova Scotia during this period, Hamilton soon found himself involved in the government of the colony. When William Shirreff resigned as secretary of the Nova Scotia Council in July 1727, Lieutenant Governor Lawrence Armstrong* was "obliged . . . to employ a Lieut. of the Garrison who acts now in that office," and thus Hamilton temporarily became provincial secretary. The departure of Paul MASCARENE for Boston in 1731 necessitated a new appointment to the council to meet the required quorum, and in October Hamilton, whom Armstrong described as "a gentleman of an untainted charracter," was chosen to fill the vacancy. For about 14 years he was an active member of the council. In 1736 he again accepted the job of secretary temporarily when Shirreff was on leave in England.

Hamilton received another civil role in 1737, when the Lords of Trade and Plantations appointed him, along with William Skene and Erasmus James PHILIPPS, to a colonial commission to resolve the boundary difficulties between Massachusetts and New Hampshire. He was chosen again in 1740 as a Nova Scotia representative for a similar commission concerning the boundaries between Rhode Island and Massachusetts.

On 25 Dec. 1744 Hamilton's diligent fulfilment of his various duties was rewarded by his appointment as lieutenant governor of Placentia, Newfoundland. He went to Newfoundland shortly afterwards and served first at St John's, before moving on to Placentia in the summer of 1747. Hamilton apparently regarded this post as more than a sinecure, for on several occasions he made an honest attempt to improve the conditions of the colony. Charles Knowles*, English governor of Louisbourg, Cape Breton Island, wrote to the Duke of Newcastle late in 1746 concerning the report he had received from Hamilton of "the miserable condition of the Soldiers of that Garrison [Placentia] are in both for want of Bedding Pay and Cloathing. . . ." In the fall of 1747 Hamilton wrote to the Board of Trade and Plantations "complaining of the want of civil officers" at Placentia, particularly justices of the peace. He was also troubled that he had no authority over the justices, as they were responsible solely to the official governor of the island, the commodore of the Newfoundland squadron, who was resident there for only a few months each year. In general, Hamilton carried out his duties at Placentia capably and conscientiously. He may also have been involved in the fishery there as he vigorously defended the involvement of some of the men under his command.

Hamilton remained at Placentia until at least 1764. Little is known of his activities after 1760 and the fact that one of his sons bore the same name makes it difficult to pursue his career at this period. Otho Hamilton Jr followed his father in the 40th regiment, joining as an ensign in 1744 and purchasing the rank of major in 1761. The elder Hamilton had two other children, John and Grizel. By 1768 he had taken up permanent residence at Waterford, Ireland. There he drafted his will in August of that year, and there he died on 26 Feb. 1770.

WILLIAM G. GODFREY

PRO, CO 194/12, ff.51–52, 79v–91, 167–68; 194/13, ff.5,

32–33v, 135, 146–48v, 220, 240–41; 194/14, f.11; 194/15, ff.28–29v, 67; 194/16, f.28; WO 1/1. *Documents relating to currency in Nova Scotia, 1675–1758* (Shortt), 64, 70, 78, 201, 202, 252. *N.S. Archives, III; IV.* PRO, *Acts of P.C., Col., 1720–45*, 439, 666; *1745–66*, 55; *CSP, Col., 1726–27*, 396; *1728–29*, 412; *1732*, 146; *JTP, 1734/35–1741*, 262; *1741/42–1749*, 271; *1759–1763*, 242; *1764–1767*, 388, 390, 392. Calnek, *History of Annapolis* (Savary). *English army lists* (Dalton), VI, 65–66. Dalton, *George the first's army*, I, 240, 312–13. A.W.H. Eaton, *Lt.-Col. Otho Hamilton of Olivestob: Lieutenant-governor of Placentia, lieutenant-colonel in the army, major of the 40th Regiment of Foot, member of the Nova Scotia Council from 1731 to 1744* (Halifax, 1899). Lounsbury, *British fishery at Nfld.* Murdoch, *History of Nova-Scotia.* Harry Piers, "The fortieth regiment, raised at Annapolis Royal in 1717; and five regiments subsequently raised in Nova Scotia," N.S. Hist. Soc. *Coll.*, XXI (1927), 120–21. Smythies, *Historical records of 40th regiment.*

HANDFIELD, JOHN, military officer, member of the Nova Scotia Council; m. Elizabeth Winniett; d. *c.* 1763.

Little is known of John Handfield's early life. Commissioned an ensign in Philipps' regiment (the 40th Regiment of Foot) in February 1719/20, he spent his entire military career in Nova Scotia. In 1721 he was among the officers signing an indictment of Lieutenant John Washington*'s behaviour and in the winter of 1729/30 he witnessed the oath obtained by the governor of Nova Scotia, Richard PHILIPPS, from the Acadians of the Annapolis River area. By 1731 he had built a home at Annapolis Royal (formerly Port-Royal) "at a Considerable Charge for the Conveniency of his ffamily. . . ." Mention of his family would indicate that his marriage to the daughter of William WINNIETT had taken place by this time.

Promoted lieutenant in April 1731, he was appointed to the council, along with his brother-in-law, Lieutenant Edward Amhurst, and Ensign John Slater, in November 1736. Lieutenant Governor Lawrence Armstrong* described the new members as "Men of Sense & Merit. . . ." For 13 years Handfield regularly attended council meetings, contributing to the discussions and serving on committees. In 1740 he was promoted captain. He was still at Annapolis Royal in 1744 when French troops under the command of Joseph DU PONT Duvivier unsuccessfully besieged the fort.

A break in his Annapolis service came in 1749 when Paul MASCARENE, the commanding officer of the garrison there, was instructed to send 100 men to Minas to meet the French and Indian threat in the area. Handfield was in charge of the contingent and, in one skirmish with the Indians, his son, Lieutenant John Handfield, was taken prisoner. By the early 1750s Handfield was back in Annapolis Royal commanding the troops there. He was granted a commission as justice of the peace in July 1751 and, because there was no clergyman present at the time, he received permission to perform the marriage ceremony between his daughter and John, son of Otho HAMILTON, in August 1752. As commandant of Annapolis Royal, Handfield was ordered to threaten with severe punishment "such Inhabitants as Communicate too much with the French" and to try to prevent the Acadians and the English traders on the Bay of Fundy from supplying the French and Indians with corn. These instructions were embarrassing for him since one of the individuals suspected by Governor Charles LAWRENCE of trading with the enemy was his brother-in-law, Joseph Winniett*.

The Acadian deportation provided another occasion when Handfield was torn between personal relationships and his duty as a British officer. In August 1755 he received instructions that the Acadians were to be "dispersed among his Majesty's Colonies upon the Continent of America" and that he was to be responsible for the embarkation of the inhabitants of the Annapolis district. He carried out his orders methodically and on 8 Dec. 1755 seven transport ships left Annapolis Basin carrying their cargoes of exiled Acadians to the New England colonies and the Carolinas. In correspondence with Colonel John Winslow*, who was carrying out the same task at Minas, Handfield revealed his dislike of his duties: "I heartily join with You in wishing that we were both of us got over this most disagreeable and troublesome part of the Service. . . ." He had good reason for finding the deportation "most disagreeable." His wife's mother had been Marie-Madeleine MAISONNAT, and among the victims of the deportation were Elizabeth's "sister-in-law, nephews and nieces, uncles, aunts and cousins." In at least one instance he intervened, delaying a relative's departure and writing on his behalf to New England.

Promoted major on 15 Oct. 1754, Handfield became lieutenant-colonel in March 1758. In the same year he participated in the capture of Louisbourg, Île Royale (Cape Breton Island). According to the *Army lists* he retired from the regiment in 1760. He apparently took up residence in Boston, and his death date has been suggested as around 1763. In addition to his son John and his daughter Mary there was at least one other child, Thomas, who "became the ancestor of the Handfields of Montreal."

WILLIAM G. GODFREY

Havard

Boston Public Library, Mellen Chamberlain autograph coll., Ch.F.1.65. PANS, RG 1, 21, pp.29, 150; 35, nos.5, 11; 134, pp.2, 6, 7, 74, 75, 86, 87, 88, 107, 201, 202, 246, 247, 248, 287, 288, 302, 303, 321, 322, 323, 324, 325, 326; 164/1, p.68. *Army list, 1760*, 91. *Documents relating to currency in Nova Scotia, 1675–1758* (Shortt), 147. Knox, *Historical Journal* (Doughty), I, 214. *N.S. Archives*, I, 274–76, 580; *III*, 182, 183, 185, 186, 232, 233, 234, 239, 243, 249, 254; *IV*, 6, 10, 11, 14, 18, 22, 25–27, 29–33, 40, 42, 49–53, 55–56, 86, 88, 90, 93, 95–97. Winslow, "Journal," N.S. Hist. Soc. *Coll.*, III (1883), 103, 134, 137, 138, 142, 164, 168. Calnek, *History of Annapolis* (Savary). Dalton, *George the first's army*, II. C. J. d'Entremont and H.-J. Hébert, "Parkman's diary and the Acadian exiles in Massachusetts," *French Canadian and Acadian Geneal. Rev.* (Quebec), I (1968), 241–94. A. W. H. Eaton, *Lt.-Col. Otho Hamilton of Olivestob: lieutenant-governor of Placentia, lieutenant-colonel in the army, major of the 40th Regiment of Foot, member of the Nova Scotia Council from 1731 to 1744* (Halifax, 1899). Harry Piers, "The fortieth regiment, raised at Annapolis Royal in 1717; and five regiments subsequently raised in Nova Scotia," N.S. Hist. Soc. *Coll.* XXI (1927), 115–83. Smythies, *Historical records of 40th regiment*.

HAVARD DE BEAUFORT, FRANÇOIS-CHARLES, known as **L'Avocat**, soldier, "sorcerer"; b. *c.* 1715 in Paris; returned to France in the autumn of 1742, date and circumstances of death unknown.

François-Charles Havard de Beaufort was known in the Montreal region as a public entertainer and "sorcerer." But, having an ingenious mind and a superior education for the period, he tried, as he himself admitted, to make use of his card and knife tricks not only to divert and amuse spectators but also to "intimidate ordinary people in serious matters."

The judicial annals of New France relate certain facts concerning Havard de Beaufort that merit some description because they throw light in several respects on the social history of Canada during the French régime. In 1737 Havard de Beaufort tried "by some craftiness and card tricks" to discover the thief of a "valuable ring" which the wife of Jacques Testard* de Montigny, Marie de La Porte de Louvigny, had lost. He was not able, however, to identify the robber. Despite this lack of success Havard de Beaufort tried his skill again five years later. On 28 June 1742, when stationed at Montreal, he learned that the shoemaker Charles Robidoux, from the suburb of Saint-Joseph, had been robbed of 300 *livres* and that the search for the guilty person had been vain. Havard de Beaufort then made an offer to the shoemaker, for the sum of 20 *livres*, to conjure up the thief's

face in a mirror. Prepared to go to any lengths to get his money back, Robidoux agreed to the bargain and immediately paid Havard de Beaufort six *livres*. The seance of catoptromancy was held that same evening in Robidoux's home in the presence of a dozen persons, all of them relatives, neighbours, or friends of the shoemaker.

Havard de Beaufort first tried to create an atmosphere that would impress his spectators. He set on a table near the fireplace a white table-cloth, a little bottle of olive oil, three packages – one white, one yellow, one black – of gunpowder and powdered rosin, two candles, and a mirror. He turned the mirror upside-down on the table and placed it between the two lighted candles. The "sorcerer" held a book of prayers, the *Verba Jesu Christi ex Evangeliis*, in his hands and read aloud some verses, spreading pinches of powder on the back of the mirror after each verse. On the powder he placed the crucifix that René-Charles Laigu, *dit* Lanoue, had brought him, poured on each end a mixture of olive oil, gunpowder, and powdered rosin called "viper oil," and without losing any time dried the oil up with the candle flames. When this rite was ended he prepared three slips of paper into which he poured a little gunpowder. He had the candles extinguished and the fire covered up in the fireplace, seized the moment when the room was plunged into darkness to pick up the mirror, and, holding the crucifix, muttered some Latin prayers. At that instant the thief's face was supposed to appear in the mirror. Nothing happened, and Havard de Beaufort ordered the fire in the fireplace to be uncovered and threw into it, one after the other, the three small packages of powder he had just prepared, each time taking care first to read a verse from the Gospel. This new ceremony was just as ineffectual.

It seems clear that the dread which the sorcerer created among his spectators was not sufficient to lead the thief to reveal himself. After an hour of "divinations and prognostications" he had to admit that he was incapable of identifying the thief. But he did not admit that he was completely vanquished and wanted to prove to his spectators that he was indeed a diviner. Therefore he had the candles lit again and drew three black lines on the mantel of the fireplace, using the edge of the cross and a piece of charcoal. Then he invited his spectators to touch the black lines, stating that he would name all those who did so without seeing them. In fact, having withdrawn to the vestibule of the house, he succeeded in identifying everyone who touched the lines. They amused themselves with this little game for some time more.

Of course, the news of this sorcery seance rapidly spread about Montreal and reached the ears of the law. The next day, 29 June 1742, the judicial authorities had Havard de Beaufort imprisoned, along with Charles Lanoue, Charles Robidoux, and the latter's wife Anne Lehoux, all three on the accusation of being accomplices. The case was investigated by the lieutenant general for civil and criminal affairs in the jurisdiction of Montreal, Jacques-Joseph GUITON de Monrepos. Havard de Beaufort was accused of "having profaned the text of the New Testament as well as the representation of Jesus Christ crucified, by using them both for prognostications and other profane and unlawful uses." He declared that his intention had not been "to profane his God" but rather to intimidate his spectators and thus lead the thief to give himself up. On 13 Aug. 1742, after a trial that lasted a month and a half, the accused was found guilty of "profanations of holy objects" and was sentenced to serve five years on the king's galleys and to make the *amende honorable* on a market day before the main door of the church of Notre-Dame de Montréal, where he would be taken by the hangman, Mathieu LÉVEILLÉ. His crime would be described on two signs which he would carry on his back and chest. Robidoux, who was convicted of having had recourse to François-Charles Havard de Beaufort's "prognostications and divinations" and of "having permitted" these acts in his home, was sentenced to stay outside the government and town of Montreal for three years and to be present on his knees, "dressed only in his tunic," at the *amende honorable* which Havard de Beaufort would pronounce in front of the parish church of Montreal. The Montreal court gave the same punishment to Charles Lanoue, convicted of having supplied Havard de Beaufort with the prayer book and the crucifix. But it acquitted Anne Lehoux, since the preliminary investigation had revealed her complete innocence.

Since Havard de Beaufort, Robidoux, and Lanoue had been sentenced to corporal punishment, the deputy king's attorney, François FOUCHER, presented himself before the judge immediately after the sentences had been read to the accused to constitute himself an appellant before the Conseil Supérieur of Quebec against the condemnations, in compliance with chapter XXVI, article VI of the criminal ordinance of 1670, according to which any sentence to the galleys, corporal punishment, banishment for life, or the *amende honorable* had to be sent in appeal before a superior court. On 17 Sept. 1742 the court of appeal upheld the guilty verdicts reached by the Montreal tribunal but, as frequently happened, reduced the severity of the sentences. It modified Havard de Beaufort's punishment by reducing the time to be served on the king's galleys from five to three years but added flogging to the sentence handed down by the royal jurisdiction of Montreal. Instead of being sentenced to banishment, Lanoue had to appear before the councillors to receive a reprimand and pay a fine of three *livres* to the king. Robidoux was simply admonished by the councillors and given a fine of three *livres* which was intended to serve for the upkeep of prisoners. On 5 Oct. 1742 the executioner, Mathieu Léveillé, carried out in Montreal the sentences of the Conseil Supérieur.

Informed of this "sacrilege," Bishop Pontbriand [DUBREIL] of Quebec issued on 10 Sept. 1742 a pastoral order addressed to the clergy and population of Montreal. He ordered an adoration of the cross during a general procession of the faithful from the church of Notre-Dame de Montréal to the Bonsecours chapel. Later on, the bishop had the "desecrated crucifix" handed over to him. On 1 March 1744 he decided to entrust it to the Nuns Hospitallers of the Hôtel-Dieu of Quebec, who had made an *amende honorable* and taken general communion at the time of the desecration to make atonement for the "sacrilege." The crucifix later became the subject of special veneration on the first Friday of October, and after 1782 the faithful, as well as the nuns, could obtain plenary indulgence by visiting the chapel of the Hôtel-Dieu where the crucifix was exposed.

In the autumn of 1742 François-Charles Havard de Beaufort, *dit* L'Avocat, went on the king's ship to France to be sent to the king's galleys. After that no more is heard of him. In the history of sorcery in New France he was only a "false sorcerer," of a kind to be found in France at the time. He used his talents as a good talker and public entertainer to take advantage of the credulity of simple and naïve people and to make ill-acquired gains at their expense.

ANDRÉ LACHANCE

AN, Col., B, 76, f.376 (copy at PAC). ANQ, NF, Documents de la juridiction de Montréal, XVII, août 1742; NF, Registres du Cons. sup., registre criminel, 1730–1759, ff.72v–75v. ANQ-M, Procès fameux 1734–1756, affaire Havard de Beaufort, 30 juin–13 août 1742. Bornier, *Conférences des ord. de Louis XIV*, II, 369–72. *Mandements des évêques de Québec* (Têtu et Gagnon), II, 19–21, 33–34. Raymond Boyer, *Les crimes et les châtiments au Canada français du XVIIe au XXe siècle* (L'Encyclopédie du Canada français, V, Montréal, 1966), 303–5.

Havy

HAVY, FRANÇOIS, merchant and entrepreneur; b. 1709 in the Pays de Caux, France; d. at Bordeaux, France, on 12 Dec. 1766.

François Havy, a Huguenot, first came to Canada in 1730 as supercargo aboard the *Louis Dauphin*, a ship owned by the newly formed Robert Dugard et Cie of Rouen, France. From Quebec, the *Louis Dauphin* carried a cargo of Canadian produce and forest products to Martinique and then sailed to its home port of Le Havre with a cargo of sugar. The following year, the ship again visited Quebec, returning directly to Le Havre. These two trial voyages convinced Dugard et Cie that the Canada trade was sufficiently profitable to merit long-term investment. Thus when Havy returned to Quebec for the third time in 1732, he came as a permanent factor to establish a warehouse and office. He and his assistant and cousin, Jean LEFEBVRE, found quarters on Rue Saint-Pierre in the merchant district of Lower Town. In 1735 they rented part of the house of Louis FORNEL on the adjacent market square and from there conducted their business for more than 20 years.

François Havy and Jean Lefebvre formed a partnership in 1734 in which Havy was the senior. It is difficult to separate their activities. As Lefebvre wrote to a business correspondent, "When our Sieur Havy or myself write you, our letters are in common. Our signatures show that there is no difference of opinion between us." Havy and Lefebvre conducted some business for their own account as permitted by the custom of the time, but they were still the employees of Dugard et Cie, which paid them salary, board, and lodging. Their position in the merchant community depended primarily upon the volume of trade they managed for the company. The trial cargoes had been small; but from 1732 to 1743 annual sales at Quebec totalled around 200,000 *livres*, except for 1740 and 1741 when receipts rose to well over 300,000 *livres*. Comparison of these figures with the rough estimates of the annual value of French imports sold in Canada prepared by the intendant reveals the relative importance of the trade Havy managed. From 1733 on it usually accounted for an eighth or a tenth of the colony's import trade, climbing to a sixth in 1738, a seventh in 1740, and a fifth in 1741. Not surprisingly, François Havy was one of the acknowledged "principal traders" of Quebec City, who in 1740 numbered only 17.

From the time of establishing the Quebec factory, Havy handled 13 company cargoes. The merchants' busy season was framed by the arrival and departure of ships from France, the West Indies, and Louisbourg, Île Royale (Cape Breton Island). Arrivals began in July and continued steadily through October. No matter how late the ships arrived, with rare exception they departed in November. When the ships dropped anchor before Quebec, they delivered their cargoes to small lightering craft. Bales, cases, and barrels for Havy's and Lefebvre's warehouse were left on the beach to be picked up by carters. Havy and Lefebvre supervised this trans-shipment, ascertained the condition of the merchandise, and declared imports of Brazil tobacco, wine, and spirits.

When the harbour was filled with ships unloading, Havy and the other merchants alerted their Montreal correspondents [*see* Pierre GUY]. The inland merchants soon arrived; money and merchandise began to change hands; and in a classic manner prices would find their level in response to the market. Rapidly, Havy and Lefebvre's warehouse began to fill with return cargo, the most important item being fur. The practical necessity of the Canadian trader's selling his furs in bales to one buyer, rather than hawking individual skins, and his need to arrange terms of credit for his purchases made it desirable that he be able to satisfy all his needs at one warehouse. Like the modern department store, Havy and Lefebvre and their competitors therefore each offered a wide assortment of merchandise. Those who could not provide this facility had to accept a smaller profit on their sales.

Bills of exchange were another important export. A large number of these were given to Canadian traders in exchange for beaver pelts by the Compagnie des Indes, which held a monopoly on their export. These bills thus represented purchasing power gained in return for a commodity export. Other bills of exchange drawn on the French government and received in exchange for Canadian paper money were employed because Canada could not provide sufficient exports to balance its foreign trade. As their continued use was a measure of Canadian economic underdevelopment, it is significant that in the 1730s and 1740s the proportion of Havy and Lefebvre's return cargoes constituted by bills of exchange declined from between 37 and 44 per cent in the years 1730–32 to 4 to 13 per cent in 1741–43. As the Canadian economy reacted favourably to a long era of peace, the quantity and range of export items were increasing.

Receiving and sending cargoes imposed a considerable burden on the Quebec factors. Goods were distributed and collected. Crew rolls were registered with the admiralty and permits and passports obtained for outgoing ships. The enormous bulk of invoices, bills of lading, accounts, and letters were prepared in triplicate. When the last ships had left, thousands of entries in daybooks had to be transferred meticulously to the ledger and then condensed into current accounts to be sent to all business correspondents. Final disposal of the cargo and the time-consuming paperwork meant that accounts were not closed until the following summer. But by the middle of November the feverish activity was over. "I wish it was never autumn at Quebec," an exhausted François Havy complained to a friend, "and I would be in better health."

Havy and Lefebvre also traded with Louisbourg, where Dugard et Cie maintained permanent relations with Léon FAUTOUX, a commission agent. The soldiers and fishermen of Louisbourg depended to a considerable extent upon Canadian provisions, and most company ships stopped at the fortified harbour on their return voyages from Quebec to France. Canadian cargoes of wood and grain were also suitable for the West Indian market when increased in value by dried cod available at Louisbourg. The sugar island trade remained marginal, however, as Canada could surrender its major export of fur only in exchange for French manufactures to supply the fur trade and could neither absorb a large quantity of Caribbean produce nor provide a sufficiently large and dependable supply of provisions and forest products in return. Thus of the 68 voyages to Canada and the West Indies undertaken by the ships of Dugard et Cie between 1730 and 1755, only ten were triangular.

Company activities in Canada under Havy's direction also included shipbuilding. Between 1736 and 1745 Havy and Lefebvre launched six ships for the company having a combined value of almost 300,000 *livres*. The *Alcion* was begun in 1734, the year after a revised system of royal bounties for Canadian-built ships was established. Although bounties could not fully offset the high cost of labour in an underpopulated country, the Rouen company persevered because ships were yet another export, a means of repatriating profits made in Canada. Thus Intendant Gilles Hocquart* was correct in interpreting Havy's building of so many ships as "certain proof that he found profit in the first." Havy and Lefebvre also built many smaller ships for their exploitation of sealing concessions on the north shore of the St Lawrence and Labrador, enterprises apparently undertaken on their own account.

From 1737 to 1748 they held a lease on a post at Mingan, the value of the rent being deducted annually from debts owed them by the post's owner, Charles Jolliet d'Anticosti. In 1737 they also began exploiting a post at Chateau Bay on the Strait of Belle Isle for a one-third share along with Louis Fornel and the post's concessionaire, Louis BAZIL. Havy and Lefebvre appear to have maintained an interest in Chateau Bay until 1754, when the post's ship and sealing equipment, described as belonging to them, were sold at public auction at Quebec. In 1740 Havy and Lefebvre also sublet a two-thirds interest in the concession of Grand Saint-Modet. The original lease ended in 1747, but they apparently sent a ship to the post in 1758, their last known sealing venture.

In 1745 war between France and Great Britain reached the Gulf of St Lawrence. In July Abel OLIVIER, captain of a Dugard et Cie schooner, sent word to Quebec that Louisbourg had fallen to the Anglo-Americans. The Quebec merchants were cut off from the gulf and their sealing stations; buildings, equipment, and barrels of oil were a total loss. Although Louis Bazil had made no financial contribution to the post at Chateau Bay, Havy and Lefebvre and Fornel had invested over 100,000 *livres*. The enterprise had returned less than two-thirds of this investment.

After 1748 the sealing industry quickly recuperated, unlike the trade with Dugard et Cie. Because of the near famine in Canada resulting from a succession of crop failures, and the derangement of the fur trade and of ocean traffic by the war, Robert Dugard sent a much smaller cargo to Canada in 1744. The following year he sent nothing, English control of the Atlantic being complete. Havy decided to launch the *Astrée*, which had lain on the stocks for several years because of poor economic conditions, and to send it to Le Havre laden with seal oil and furs for which there was no other transportation.

Sales plummeted to about 100,000 *livres* in 1744 and 1745 and then to 19,000 in 1746 and 32,000 in 1747. After 1744 the company sent none of its own ships to Quebec although small amounts of cargo were sent aboard those of La Rochelle. Tempest and war combined to destroy most of the company fleet. In 1743, for instance, the *Alcion* and the *Louis Dauphin* sank in storms while returning from the West Indies, and by 1747 five more ships were lost or captured. The company was on its knees, and in October 1747 Havy and Lefebvre received word that it would cease all its trade with Canada. Since 1730 Havy had handled incoming and outgoing cargoes for his Rouen employers valued at almost 6,000,000 *livres*.

Havy and Lefebvre still had their interest in the Labrador sealing industry. Their associate Louis Fornel had died on 30 May 1745, but they maintained a close business relationship with his

Havy

widow, Marie-Anne Barbel*. Before the war intervened, Fornel had explored the Labrador coast beyond Chateau Bay and had discovered and laid claim to an excellent site for sealing and trade, the Baie des Esquimaux (probably Hamilton Inlet), which he named Baie Saint-Louis. With access to the coast again free, Widow Fornel claimed the concession of the post for herself and her associates, Havy and Lefebvre. On 20 Sept. 1749 they were given the concession for 12 years. At the same time, under the name Veuve Fornel et Cie, they also received a six-year lease on the scattered trading posts east of Quebec and north of the St Lawrence known collectively as the King's Posts. In 1755 they relinquished the lease, fearing war losses. They were the last lessees under the old régime.

Havy's interest in the import-export trade also remained. With other Quebec City merchants, he and Lefebvre owned a few small ships which they sent to Martinique. As general commission agents, they handled cargoes for Garisson of Bordeaux and Gardère of Bayonne. In 1750 the *Astrée* stopped at Quebec on its way to Martinique, leaving some cargo in their care. For a few years in the 1750s they owned a ship named the *Parfaite Union* in company with Robert Dugard and a fourth associate, probably Jean-François Jacquelin of Quebec.

François Havy, as a Huguenot, was free neither to marry in the colony nor to bring a family to it; though prosperous he could not think of remaining in Canada permanently. The occasion of his final departure was yet another war. Havy and Lefebvre apparently decided that under hazardous but potentially profitable war-time conditions, one of them should return to France to supervise their export of merchandise to Canada and to prepare for eventual transfer of their business from the colony. In January 1756 Havy arrived at La Rochelle, having "escaped the clutches of the English." The following year he visited Rouen to accelerate the closing of his accounts with Dugard et Cie and then returned to La Rochelle, where in 1758 he declared himself resolved to stay. But trade there was at a standstill, the English once again having control of the sea route to Canada.

It was probably in 1758 that Havy married for the first time. His wife was of the François family of Bordeaux, said to be "a family both Rich and highly Respectable." In January 1759 their first child was born. But domestic happiness came too late for François Havy. The British conquest of Quebec in September 1759 destroyed the business he had built up over 30 years. Considerable assets in sealing stations and mortgages on houses in Quebec were lost. A fortune in Canadian paper money and bills of exchange was rendered almost worthless by governmental repudiation. Not without cause did he think, "The life of man is short and still it is naught but sorrow and labour."

For the last six months of 1760 Havy suffered from a severe illness. When he had sufficiently recovered, he was told of the accidental death of Jean Lefebvre some months before. He had lost his fortune, his associate and oldest friend, and his health. He was involved in more than a dozen bankruptcies. The heirs of his dead partner and other creditors were hounding him. In 1762 or 1763 the Havys moved to Bordeaux, probably to be near Mme Havy's family. In the autumn of 1766 François Havy died at Bordeaux, aged 57.

The connection between the old firm of Havy and Lefebvre and Canada did not end with the conquest. In their later years at Quebec, Havy and Lefebvre had been joined by another, younger, cousin, François Levesque. It was Levesque who settled their affairs at Quebec, and he remained in Canada to establish his own commerce under the British flag.

In 1763 the commission of the Châtelet acquitted François Havy of any malversation in his furnishings to the king in Canada. He had been an honest merchant. Backed by Rouen businessmen of expansive ideas, he and his partner were at the forefront of the Canadian economic advance. Could a Protestant have lived his life in New France, perhaps Havy would have been absorbed into the Canadian community, bringing with him mercantile knowledge and attitudes rare in the colony and precious in the aftermath of conquest.

François Havy's career in Canada and his relation to the colony might best be summarized by two sentences drawn from his own correspondence. "There is no metropolitan trader who worked as hard as I," he once wrote to Robert Dugard. Again, in one of his last letters to a Canadian, he expressed the privation he felt at his separation from New France: "I have always loved your Country and its people."

DALE MIQUELON

AN, 62 AQ, 30–45; Col., B, 53–96; C⁸ᴬ, 55; C¹¹ᴬ, 51–109, 125. ANQ, Greffe de R.-C. Barolet, 30 sept. 1733, 8 sept. 1734, 8, 9 oct. 1736, 2 avril 1738, 30 oct. 1741; Greffe de C.-H. Du Laurent, 3 oct. 1736, 23 oct. 1742, 15 sept., 26 oct. 1743, 18 oct. 1744, 10 nov. 1746, 13 août 1747, 18 mai, 4 juin, 7 nov. 1748, 27 janv., 15 déc. 1750, 8 oct., 6 nov. 1751, 6 avril 1759; Greffe de J.-C. Louet, 11 oct. 1735; Greffe de J.-C. Panet, 9 sept. 1745, 19 août, 23 nov. 1751, 21 oct. 1753, 22 nov. 1758,

10 oct. 1760, 10 oct. 1764, 5 avril 1769; Greffe de J.-N. Pinguet de Vaucour, 5 sept. 1743; Greffe de J.-A. Saillant, 7 févr. 1751, 4 janv., 7 oct. 1752, 18 sept., 25 oct., 6 nov. 1753, 5 avril, 17, 18 sept. 1754; NF, Coll. de pièces jud. et not., 1242, 1290, 1296, 1316, 1410, 1456; NF, Registres de l'Amirauté de Québec, 1741–1760. Archives municipales de Bordeaux, France, État civil, 12 déc. 1766. Bibliothèque de l'Arsenal (Paris), MSS, 12144, 12145, 12148. PAC, MG 23, GIII, 28; MG 24, L3, pp.580–2447. *Édits ord.*, II, 554–55. *Inv. de pièces du Labrador* (P.-G. Roy). "Recensement de Québec, 1744" (APQ *Rapport*). P.-G. Roy. *Inv. jug. et délib., 1717–1760*; *Inv. ord. int.* A. J. E. Lunn, "Economic development in New France, 1713–1760" (unpublished PHD thesis, McGill University, Montreal, 1943).

[The reader will find a comparison of the activities of the Quebec factor with those of his counterparts in other places very illuminating. *See*, for example, Ralph Davis' study of English trade in Turkey, *Aleppo and Devonshire Square: English traders in the Levant in the eighteenth century* (London, 1967). D.M.]

HAY, Lord CHARLES, army officer, member of parliament; b. *c.* 1705, possibly at Linplum, East Lothian, Scotland, to Charles Hay, 3rd Marquess of Tweeddale, and Susannah Cochrane, Countess of Dundonald, *née* Hamilton; d. unmarried, 1 May 1760, in London, England.

Charles Hay was gazetted ensign in the Coldstream Guards on 18 May 1722 and made captain in the 33rd Foot on 14 Sept. 1727 during the siege of Gibraltar. In 1741 he entered parliament for Haddingtonshire as an opponent of Sir Robert Walpole. He adhered first to the administration of John, Lord Carteret, and, after 1744, to that of the Pelhams.

On 7 April 1743 Hay had become captain of King's company in the Grenadier Guards, with rank of lieutenant-colonel in the army. He commanded this company at the battles of Dettingen (Federal Republic of Germany) in 1743 and Fontenoy (Belgium) in 1745. At Fontenoy he was involved in an incident made famous by Voltaire. When leading his men over the crest of a hill through murderous artillery fire Hay suddenly found himself confronted by the massed French and Swiss Guards. He later reported that taking his flask he drank the health of the enemy and called to them, "I hope, gentlemen, that you are going to wait for us today, and not now swim the Scheldt as you swam the Main at Dettingen." According to Voltaire, the French commander replied to Hay's challenge to fire with "Gentlemen, we never fire first; fire yourselves." Shortly afterwards Hay was severely wounded and at first reported dead. In 1746 he was said to be in an asylum, and he did not stand in the

general election of 1747. In 1749, however, he was named aide-de-camp to George II.

Hay became colonel of the 33rd Foot on 20 Nov. 1753 and major-general on 22 Feb. 1757, when he was sent to Nova Scotia as second in command of the troops under Major-General Peregrine Thomas HOPSON who were dispatched to join the Earl of Loudoun [John Campbell] at Halifax for the projected attack on Louisbourg, Île Royale (Cape Breton Island). Because of large-scale French naval reinforcements there, no attempt was made and the British expeditionary force spent the summer at Halifax. Hay, who after a lengthy passage had reached the town on 9 July, found the inaction galling. He was not part of Loudoun's council of war, which he suspected of not being seriously committed to the enterprise. Irritated by the lack of vigorous leadership, he was overheard by Colonel John FORBES to exclaim while the troops were engaged in a simulated attack on a mock fortification: "by God, difficult as it may be, I shall find a method of letting the mother country know what is doing here, that we are taken up in building sham forts and making approaches to them, when we should be employed in real attacks. The fleet should sail up the bason, and have a sham fight there; and then we might write home that we had a sea fight and taken a fort." Loudoun had him arrested but did not charge him, merely suggesting to the government that "the voyage, climate and season of the year have been prejudicial to his Lordship's health." Hay's fellow officers thought him mad, and he was closely confined for seven months. Though he had been ordered home, no ship was offered him. In desperation he entered as a volunteer on the *Dublin* (Capt. George Brydges Rodney), which put into Halifax late in May 1758, having carried Major-General Jeffery Amherst* from England to command at Louisbourg. From the *Dublin* Hay witnessed the siege of the fortress before returning to England in the *Shannon*.

In England he demanded a court martial to clear his name. His wish was granted in 1759; he was charged with endeavouring "to bring into contempt the conduct and authority of the commanders of the fleet and land forces in America," and with behaving "in a manner evidently tending to excite mutiny and sedition amongst the troops." The trial, at which all the principal Louisbourg officers then in England appeared, lasted for more than a month in February and March 1760. The matter was then referred to the king, who had taken no decision when Hay died suddenly on 1 May 1760. He had had a distinguished army career, and it seems doubtful that

Hazeur

the first charge would have stuck; the second, from evidence advanced by the crown, was absurd.

JULIAN GWYN

PRO, CO 5/212, f.43. National Library of Scotland (Edinburgh), Hay papers, Hay to 4th Marquis of Tweeddale, 20 May 1745, MS 7087. *Gentleman's Magazine*, 1745, 247, 251, 276. W. H. H. Scott, *Report on the manuscripts of Lord Polwarth preserved at Mertoun House, Berwickshire* (Historical Manuscripts Commission, no.67, 5v., London, 1911–61), V, 187. Cokayne, *Complete peerage. DNB.* Sedgwick, *History of parliament*, II, 117–18. Dalton, *George the first's army*, II, 269, 271. Voltaire [François-Marie Arouet], *Précis du siècle de Louis XV* (*Œuvres*, 70v., [Kehl, Germany], 1785), XXII.

HAZEUR, JOSEPH-THIERRY, parish priest, grand penitentiary of the chapter of the cathedral of Quebec, vicar general; b. 25 June 1680 at Quebec, son of François Hazeur*, a merchant, and Anne Soumande; d. 1 April 1757 at the Hôpital Général of Quebec.

Joseph-Thierry Hazeur entered the Petit Séminaire of Quebec on 11 Sept. 1691. He left it on 22 May 1696, "being in the first year of philosophy," say the annals of the Petit Séminaire, "not having much aptitude or bent for study or inclination for the church." This judgement by his superiors was indeed severe towards a schoolboy who, at 15 years of age and after only four years of study, was already in the philosophy class. Furthermore, it was at the least premature, since Thierry Hazeur persevered in his vocation. He was tonsured 9 Aug. 1699 by Bishop Saint-Vallier [La Croix*], and received the minor orders on 11 November. In the absence of the bishop of Quebec, Bishop Laval* conferred the subdiaconate upon him 24 July 1701, the diaconate 27 April 1704, and on 25 April 1706, at the same time as his younger brother, Pierre Hazeur* de L'Orme received it, the priesthood.

Abbé Joseph-Thierry Hazeur first exercised his ministry at Saint-François, on Île d'Orléans, from 1707 to 1712. In 1715 Bishop Saint-Vallier offered him a canonry, left vacant by the death of Abbé Jean Pinguet of the seminary of Quebec. The new canon received his letters of appointment on 21 March and was installed on 4 May. At the end of that year the bishop sent him to the parish of Saint-François-de-Sales at Pointe-aux-Trembles (Neuville); Jean Basset*, the parish priest there, had died on 20 November. Canon Hazeur went to Pointe-aux-Trembles on 5 December, intending, however, as he himself specified both in the parish register and in the account book of the parish council, to "carry out

the functions of parish priest for the space of one whole year." His stay was to extend nevertheless to September 1725. He seems to have carried out his task conscientiously; his records were carefully kept and attest to his faithfulness in maintaining residence.

Once more in Quebec, Thierry Hazeur, whom the bishop had appointed grand penitentiary of the chapter on 24 May 1723, lived henceforth on his prebend. He also drew interest on a sum of 10,000 *livres* that he had lent on 2 Nov. 1724 to the Quebec seminary at a rate of 1 in 20 (5 per cent). Almost always ill, complaining in particular of a continual perspiration, the grand penitentiary rarely attended the cathedral services. In 1730 Bishop Dosquet* asserted that he had "been reprimanded for being absent more than 1,300 times this year." However, the coadjutor added, "He claims his right to receive the remunerations as if he had been present." After 1744 he appeared at no more meetings of the chapter.

Whether real or imaginary, Thierry Hazeur's infirmities did not prevent him from living to the age of 77, or, in particular, from taking an active part in the incessant quarrels which rocked the chapter of Quebec after Bishop Saint-Vallier's death. On 3 Jan. 1728 he was elected vicar general by his colleagues, and, urged on by his friend Joachim FORNEL, he undertook to support the claims of the chapter to direct the diocese. In a letter dated 31 May 1728 Bishop Mornay [Duplessis], Bishop Saint-Vallier's successor, in vain ordered the vicar general and his partisans to wait for the orders which his coadjutor, Dosquet, would bring to New France. They did not do so and on 12 September signed an order intimating to the faithful that they were to recognize the chapter's authority during "the vacancy of the see." As soon as he had landed Bishop Dosquet reacted firmly against the spirit of insubordination which reigned in the Quebec church and unsparingly denounced the guilty to the minister, Maurepas. The canons, he wrote, "think of nothing but quibbling and sowing discord among themselves as well as among the laity and will not recognize rules, or statutes, or superiors. They treat the dean as an inferior and the bishop as their equal, making it a point to oppose everything he desires. This applies principally to Messieurs Fornel and Hazeur, who enjoy discord and attract the others to their side." The minister's reply was not long in coming. He sent Governor Charles de BEAUHARNOIS and Intendant Gilles Hocquart* a *lettre de cachet* authorizing the coadjutor to send Fornel back to France if he considered it advisable. As for

Canon Hazeur, the minister charged them to warn him that if he did not conduct himself better in future, the king would give "orders to bring him into line."

Somewhat chastened by the reprimand he had received, Thierry Hazeur prudently remained in the background until 1740 when, at the request of Hazeur de L'Orme, Bishop Lauberivière [Pourroy*] chose him to preside in his absence at the official taking of possession of his episcopal see. This time the grand penitentiary felt sufficiently strong to preside over the official ceremony, on 20 June. After the bishop's untimely death on 20 August the canons again took over the administration of the diocese. On 7 November they entrusted Thierry Hazeur with the office of vicar general, which Canon Jean-Pierre de Miniac* had just given up to return to France. Thierry Hazeur remained in office until Bishop Pontbriand [DUBREIL] arrived on 9 Aug. 1741. This short period was nonetheless sufficient for him to bring two condemnations upon himself from the Conseil Supérieur: the first arose from a lawsuit brought against him by none other than Joachim Fornel, and the other from the authorization he had incautiously given for the marriage of René-Ovide Hertel* de Rouville and Louise-Catherine ANDRÉ de Leigne, despite the opposition of the bridegroom's family.

The grand penitentiary does not seem to have been any more fortunate in the conduct of his own affairs. In 1734, shortly before dying, the doctor Michel Sarrazin*, the canon's brother-in-law, had chosen him as guardian of his children and heirs. From then until 1747 Hazeur had to suffer several lawsuits brought by the dead man's creditors, which cost him much worry and money. Towards 1748, exhausted and at the end of his resources, he sought refuge with his friend Abbé Louis LEPAGE de Sainte-Claire, the seigneur of Terrebonne. In 1751 Joseph-Thierry Hazeur returned to Quebec and retired to the Hôpital Général. There he died on 1 April 1757 and was buried two days later in the cathedral choir.

NOËL BAILLARGEON

AAQ, 12A, Registres d'insinuations A; 12 A, Registres d'insinuations B; 10 B, Registre des délibérations; 1 W, Église du Canada, I, II. AN, Col., C¹¹A, 53, f.373v; 56, ff.75–76. Archives paroissiales de Saint-François-de-Sales (Saint-François, Île d'Orléans, Qué.), Registres des baptêmes, mariages et sépultures, 1706–1712 (copies at ANQ). Archives paroissiales de Saint-François-de-Sales (Neuville, Qué.), Registres des baptêmes, mariages et sépultures; Livres de comptes, I. ASQ, MSS, 2, 18; MSS, 12, 208f, 488f; Registre A, 28f.; Séminaire, XCII, 20, p.42. P.-G. Roy, Inv. jug. et délib., 1717–1760, V. Gosselin, L'Église du Canada jusqu'à la conquête, I, II. Henri Têtu, "Le chapitre de la cathédrale de Québec et ses délégués en France," BRH, XIII (1907), 238, 240; XIV (1908), 79, 98; XV (1909), 75; XVI (1910), 138, 160.

HENDAY (Hendey, Hendry), ANTHONY, HBC labourer and net-maker, explorer; fl.1750–62.

Anthony Henday was one of the first white men to probe the vast distances of the Canadian west. There had been journeys to the interior before his time: Henry Kelsey* had travelled to the prairies in 1690–92; William Stuart* had crossed the Barrens to the country southeast of Great Slave Lake in 1715–16; but generally the Hudson's Bay Company had not taken much interest in the all-but-unknown lands beyond Hudson Bay. As Pierre GAULTIER de Varennes et de La Vérendrye and his successors began to tap the western trade during the 1740s, however, the HBC became more concerned with what was occurring out in the vast territory its charter claimed for it. So when James ISHAM, chief at York Fort (York Factory, Man.), suggested that "if a proper Person were sent a great way up into the Country with presents to the Indians it may be a means of drawing down many of the Natives to Trade," the company's London committee agreed.

Henday volunteered to undertake the expedition. A native of the Isle of Wight, he had been a fisherman before joining the HBC in 1750 as a net-maker and labourer. According to Andrew Graham*, who knew him at York, he had been outlawed as a smuggler in 1748, a fact unknown to the HBC officials who hired him. After coming to the bay Henday had gained some experience in inland travel, having journeyed with a party of Indians as far as Split Lake in February and March 1754 to collect information on distances from York.

On 26 June 1754 he set out with some Plains Crees who were returning to the interior. Following a route several miles north of the one that was to be used by the York-boat brigades of the 19th century, they left the Hayes River at the mouth of the Fox and travelled through Utik and Moose lakes to the Paskoya (Saskatchewan) River. Having been informed that in three days' time they would pass a French post, Henday recorded apprehensively, "I dont very well like it, having nothing to Satisfy Them on what account I am going up the Country and Very possably they may expect Me to be a Spy. . . ." When the party reached Paskoya (The Pas, Man.) on 22 July the French traders (one of whom may have been Louis de LA CORNE) did threaten to seize Hen-

Henday

day and send him to France, but awed perhaps by the number of Indians with whom he was travelling they allowed him to proceed.

He and his companions soon abandoned their canoes and struck out on foot over the immense prairies. After a few miles the Indians joined company with the members of their families who had not made the long journey by water to the bay. Henday was already travelling with a Cree woman whose assistance as food-gatherer, cook, and interpreter was invaluable. He does not mention her name in his journal, calling her only his "bed-fellow." Reference to his relationship with her is excluded from the official version of the journal that Isham sent to London, for the committee's disapproval of such arrangements was well known.

The augmented party continued westwards, crossing the South Saskatchewan River north of present Saskatoon and passing south of the future site of Battleford. Its route, especially after it left the Battleford area, is a matter of some controversy. Henday's original journal is not extant, and there are serious contradictions among the four copies that have survived. In any case, his brief entries lend themselves to various interpretations and, as the London committee later observed, "We apprehend Henday is not very expert in making Drafts with Accuracy or keeping a just Reckoning of distance other than by guess. . . ." The most recent and convincing attempt to trace his wanderings is in J. G. MacGregor, *Behold the Shining Mountains*. According to MacGregor, the travellers continued northwest and west along the southern edge of the Battle River valley.

On 6 September they met a group of Eagle Indians, an Assiniboin band who had never traded with white men. Henday's diplomacy was apparently effective, for thereafter groups of Eagles went down to York annually. The Indians whom Henday had come seeking, however, were those the HBC men knew vaguely as the "Archithinues" – either Atsinas (Gros Ventres) or Siksikas (Blackfeet). Attickasish, the Cree leader of Henday's party, had met two Archithinues on 4 September, but the others were farther west following the main buffalo herds. On 15 September Henday recorded, "the Buffalo so numerous obliged to make them sheer out of our way." As he and his companions proceeded they encountered numerous groups of Assiniboins hunting buffalo. On 14 October, when they were about 18 miles southeast of present Red Deer, Alta., they finally came to the great camp of the Archithinues – some 200 teepees pitched in two rows. At one end stood the

buffalo-hide lodge of the head chief, capable of seating about 50 people. Attended by 20 elders, the chief received Henday, seating the visitor at his right hand on a newly dressed buffalo hide. Several pipes were lit and passed around without a word to break the silence; then boiled buffalo meat was circulated in baskets of woven grass, and the honoured guest was presented with 12 tongues – the greatest delicacy known to the Archithinues.

The next day Henday met the chief again and, in keeping with the company's instructions, requested that some of the young men be allowed to return to York with him. The chief replied that they could not live without buffalo meat or leave their horses, and that they did not know how to use canoes. He had heard, moreover, that the people who went down to the settlements on the bay often starved on the journey. "Such remarks I thought exceeding true," noted Henday, who had only half-completed the gruelling journey after 16 weeks of travel by river, lake, and prairie.

Henday and some of the Crees moved along to the area west of present Innisfail and Red Deer, where they spent the early winter. In this region they were within sight of the Rocky Mountains, but there is no clearly identifiable mention of this imposing range in the surviving versions of Henday's journal. In mid-January they began making their way north-northeast, past the present Sylvan Lake towards the point where the Sturgeon River empties into the North Saskatchewan River (about 20 miles downstream from modern Edmonton). There they camped from 5 March to 28 April, building canoes for the long journey east.

As they paddled down the North Saskatchewan they were met by bands of Indians who joined them or traded their furs to the Crees for English goods. Henday's companions had promised him that they would try to persuade the Archithinues to come down to the bay, but although they encountered many of that tribe the shrewd Crees made no attempt to keep their word. Instead, as Henday observed, "there are scarce a Gun, Kettle, Hatchet, or Knife amongst us, having traded them with the Archithinue Natives." It became clear to him that the Indian economy was more complex than the HBC had realized. Many of the Indians who traded at Hudson Bay had given up trapping and hunting, and had become middlemen for the rest of their own tribe or for the tribes of the interior who did not use canoes.

When the flotilla, by then numbering 60 canoes, arrived at Fort Saint-Louis, some ten miles below the forks of the Saskatchewan, the

French traders there began by offering their customers brandy and then traded from them about a thousand prime skins. The process was repeated farther down the river at Paskoya, and Henday reported "The French talk several Languages to perfection: they have the advantage of us in every shape; and if they had Brazile tobacco . . . would entirely cut off our trade." After four days at Paskoya, with only the heavy skins remaining, Henday and the Crees started once more for Hudson Bay, following the same route as on their outward trip. On 23 June their astonishing journey ended at York. They had been absent nearly a full year. Henday had been farther into the western interior than any other European, and he had made valuable discoveries about the Indian economy and the nature of the company's French competition. Some of his tales seemed so strange to the stay-at-homes at the bay that they were met with considerable disbelief. His claim that the Archithinues rode horses provoked particular scepticism and much laughter.

After less than a week at York, Henday went inland again, accompanied this time by William Grover. Grover, however, was unable to stand the strain of the journey, and by 2 July they had returned to the bay. Henday had also apparently been affected by the hardships of his trips, for when Isham sent him inland in 1756 "to take a true and Exact acct. of the place he entemates, for a Settlement, computed 500 miles up," ill-health obliged him to return to York without completing the mission. In 1758 he wintered at Ship River, an outpost of York, but became so ill "of a cold" that a party was sent out in March to bring him back to the main factory. He recovered and in June 1759 went to the Archithinue country once more. No journal of this trip exists. He travelled with a few Archithinues who had come to trade at Hudson Bay as a result of his previous expedition, and with Joseph SMITH, who had already made several long inland journeys. Henday, Smith, and 61 canoes of Indians reappeared at York in June 1760.

In 1762 Henday left the company's service. According to Andrew Graham, who was at York at the time, he was disappointed at not being promoted and angry at being abused by the supply-ships' companies for not buying luxuries from them. Thus ended the career of a "bold and enterprising" explorer who had contributed so much to the company's knowledge of the lands it claimed and the people who inhabited them.

CLIFFORD WILSON

[Henday's original journal is not extant, and the four different copies that survive in the HBC Archives seriously contradict one another on some points. B.239/a/40 contains the copy sent from York by James Isham in 1755, inaccurate in some respects but ending with a powerful plea for inland expansion. In the manuscripts composing Andrew Graham's "Observations" are three copies: E.2/4, ff.35–60, misdated 1755–56 and actually made about 1768–69; E.2/6, ff.10d–38d, written about 1767–69; and E.2/11, ff.1–40d, possibly written as late as 1790 and including some valuable annotations by Graham. This version, the only one that has been published, appears as "York Factory to the Blackfeet country – the journal of Anthony Hendry, 1754–55," ed. L. J. Burpee, in *RSCT*, 3rd ser., I (1907), sect.II, 307–64.

Other sources of information on Henday are: Morton, *History of the Canadian west*. J. G. MacGregor, *Behold the Shining Mountains, being an account of the travels of Anthony Henday, 1754–55, the first white man to enter Alberta* (Edmonton, 1954). Glyndwr Williams, "Highlights in the history of the first two hundred years of the Hudson's Bay Company," *Beaver* (Winnipeg), outfit 301 (autumn 1970), 4–63. C. P. Wilson, "Across the prairies two centuries ago," CHA *Report, 1954*, 29–35. C.W.]

HENDRICK. *See* THEYANOGUIN

HERON, PATRICK, soldier, commanding officer at Canso, Nova Scotia; fl. 1709–52.

The dates of Heron's birth and death are not known. In 1709 he received a lieutenant's commission and in 1711 was appointed captain in Lord Lovelace's Regiment of Foot. Two years later Heron was placed on half pay. In 1730 he received a captain's commission in Governor Richard PHILIPPS' regiment (later the 40th Foot) and was stationed at the fishing outpost of Canso. On 3 Dec. 1738 (O.S.) Heron was arrested and charged with being "indebted to some of the men of his company for their subsistence, by giving them notes and afterwards refusing to pay." Heron's court martial took place at Annapolis Royal, Nova Scotia, in April 1739. Since there was a great deal of conflicting oral evidence, the lieutenant governor of Nova Scotia, Lawrence Armstrong*, decided that the commanding officer of Canso, Captain James Mitford, should immediately organize another court martial to ascertain the actual facts of the case. Heron must have been completely exonerated for he was the commanding officer at Canso in 1744 when war broke out between France and Britain.

On 13 May 1744, soon after word reached Île Royale (Cape Breton Island) of the declaration of war, a French force of some 350 men from Louisbourg, led by Joseph DU PONT Duvivier, arrived to attack Canso, which was defended by 87 Brit-

Hertel de La Fresnière

ish soldiers. In preparation for the French landing, two Louisbourg privateers began to bombard the Canso blockhouse with cannon-shot. When the first shot sailed through the thin blockhouse walls, Heron rushed out with a flag of truce, thinking "it advisable to capitulate in time to obtain the better terms."

The Canso troops were taken to Louisbourg where they were to remain as prisoners of war for a period of 12 months. But because of the serious scarcity of food supplies in the French fortress and also because some of his men were defecting to the enemy, Heron reacted sympathetically to the suggestion of Governor Duquesnel [Le Prévost] that new capitulation terms be drawn up. According to these terms, Heron's troops were to be sent immediately to Boston in exchange for some French prisoners held there. Moreover, Heron promised that his men would not serve in any capacity against the French until September of the following year. After signing the new capitulation terms, Heron and his troops, together with other British prisoners, were sent to Boston early in September 1744. The British government and Governor William Shirley of Massachusetts refused to accept the revised terms of the capitulation, and so the Canso troops were ordered to Annapolis Royal in the early summer of 1745.

Heron and his men brought with them to Massachusetts valuable intelligence concerning what they conceived to be Louisbourg's surprising military weaknesses. By providing detailed information concerning the French fortress and by emphasizing its vulnerability to a surprise assault, the Canso soldiers played a key role in encouraging William Shirley and the Massachusetts General Court to organize an expedition in 1745 against Louisbourg.

Heron apparently returned later to Nova Scotia. There is some evidence to suggest that in 1750–51, while at Fort Lawrence on the Chignecto Isthmus, Heron may have once again been court-martialed – this time for habitual drunkenness and "conduct unbecoming a gentleman." Since his name was removed from the regimental roll for 1752, he either died that year or else was dismissed from the service.

G. A. Rawlyk

PAC, MG 11, Nova Scotia A, 26, pp.97–98, 172–76. *Correspondence of William Shirley* (Lincoln), I, 146–47. *N.S. Archives*, II, 122, 225.

English army lists (Dalton), V, 171, 244–45. McLennan, *Louisbourg*, 110–13. B. M. Moody, "Paul Mascarene, William Shirley and the defence of Nova Scotia, 1744–1748" (unpublished MA thesis, Queen's University, Kingston, Ont., 1969), 50–51, 159–60.

Harry Piers, "The fortieth regiment, raised at Annapolis Royal in 1717; and five regiments subsequently raised in Nova Scotia," N.S. Hist. Soc. *Coll.*, XXI (1927), 127–29. Rawlyk, *Yankees at Louisbourg*, 4–6. Smythies, *Historical records of 40th regiment*, 7–12, 17.

HERTEL DE LA FRESNIÈRE, ZACHARIE-FRANÇOIS, seigneur, officer in the colonial regular troops; b. *c.* 1665, probably in Trois-Rivières, oldest son of Joseph-François Hertel* de La Fresnière and Marguerite de Thavenet*; buried in Montreal, 20 June 1752.

Members of the Hertel family are often confused: several, in active military service at the same time, were referred to by the family name. This confusion is most evident with Zacharie-François, who carried his father's title of "de La Fresnière." Only incidents that can definitely be related to the son's career have been included here.

Zacharie-François was wounded in a raid on Salmon Falls, New Hampshire, led by his father in 1690, but he participated in an attack on the Iroquois the following year and was taken prisoner. He returned to Trois-Rivières after three years of captivity and married Marie-Charlotte, daughter of half-pay captain Michel Godefroy* de Lintot, on 17 Jan. 1695. In October he was officially commissioned half-pay lieutenant, and served as storekeeper at Fort Chambly, south of Montreal, for the next two years. In 1708 he replaced Alphonse Tonty* as commandant of Fort Frontenac (Kingston, Ont.), where his knowledge of several Indian languages was frequently exercised. He left the command of Fort Frontenac in 1712 with the rank of lieutenant. Appointed a captain on 5 Feb. 1731, he was given the important task of supervising the construction of Fort Saint-Frédéric (Crown Point, N.Y.) on Lake Champlain.

Zacharie-François inherited one-half of the fief and seigneury of Chambly, but exchanged it in 1719 for an *arrière-fief* of 60 square *arpents* in the seigneury of Boucherville. During the next 25 years he renounced or conceded more than 500 square *arpents* of land in the Richelieu River area which were his by right of inheritance.

On 2 March 1745, Zacharie-François was invested with the cross of the order of Saint-Louis. He retired from military service on 17 Feb. 1748, and died four years later in Montreal. Although he left no wealth, Zacharie-François had carried arms in his country's name for 60 years, and had served satisfactorily in three different military roles.

C. J. Russ

[Despite what is said in the biographies of Joseph-François Hertel de La Fresnière and Alphonse Tonty (*DCB*, II), it was Zacharie-François Hertel de La Fresnière, and not his father, who was commandant at Fort Frontenac from 1708 to 1712. Several reasons justify this statement. First, the commandant during this period is referred to as "Hertel de La Fresnière" (AN, Col., C¹¹ᴬ, 29, f.243); and Zacharie-François's father was generally called "Hertel the elder." In 1708 the latter was 66 years of age while his son was 43. Finally the commandant, who was a second lieutenant in 1708, asked that year to be promoted lieutenant on the grounds that his position merited a rank of greater importance (AN, Col., C¹¹ᴬ, 29, f.243; 31, f.178v). Both father and son were half-pay lieutenants at this time. However, a "Hertel de La Fresnière" was promoted lieutenant by Vaudreuil* in 1711 (AN, Col., C¹¹ᴬ, 32, f.236) and confirmed in this position by the king the following year (AN, Col., D²ᶜ, 222/1, p.304). Was this the father or the son? According to Laffilard, the father was still a half-pay lieutenant when he died in 1722 (AN, Col., D²ᶜ, 222/1, p.303); and we know that the Hertel at Fort Frontenac was promoted lieutenant and that Zacharie-François was a lieutenant in 1719 (ANQ-M, Greffe de Michel Lepailleur, 14 mars 1719). c.j.r.]

AJTR, Greffe de J.-B. Pottier, 2, 10 août 1710. AN, Col., B, 16; C¹¹ᴬ, 11, 13, 28, 29, 30, 31, 32, 113; Marine, C⁷, 142. ANQ-M, Greffe d'Antoine Adhémar, 12 mars 1704; Greffe de J.-C. Porlier, 13 juill. 1741, 14 févr. 1742, 16 mars 1744; Greffe de Marien Tailhandier, dit La Beaume, 7 mars 1714; Greffe de J.-B. Tétro, 16 mars 1728. Fauteux, *Les chevaliers de Saint-Louis*, 139. Le Jeune, *Dictionnaire*. [Le Jeune is in error in stating that Zacharie-François Hertel de La Fresnière died in 1730. c.j.r.] P.-G. Roy, *Inv. concessions*, II, 197–98. Tanguay, *Dictionnaire*. P.-G. Roy, *Hommes et choses du fort Saint-Frédéric*, 14–15. Henri Têtu, "Le chapitre de la cathédrale de Québec et ses délégués en France," *BRH*, XVI (1910), 194.

HERTEL DE ROUVILLE, LOUISE-CATHERINE. *See* André de Leigne

HERTEL DE SAINT-FRANÇOIS, ÉTIENNE (after the death of his older brother Joseph in 1748, Étienne was referred to as Hertel the elder), officer in the colonial regular troops; b. 8 Nov. 1734 at Saint-François-du-Lac (Que.), son of Joseph Hertel de Saint-François and Suzanne Blondeau; d. 18 July 1760.

Étienne Hertel de Saint-François's short life was an active one. True to the Hertel tradition he entered military service early. At the age of 14 he was a cadet with the colonial regular troops at Fort Saint-Frédéric (Crown Point, N.Y.) on Lake Champlain. On 23 Oct. 1749, Governor La Jonquière [Taffanel] transferred him to Louisbourg, Île Royale (Cape Breton Island), where he was promoted second ensign in 1751, and full-pay ensign in 1755. After eight years' service at

Louisbourg he was recalled by Governor Pierre de Rigaud* de Vaudreuil to Michilimackinac.

On 1 Jan. 1759, Vaudreuil's recommendation of Hertel for a full-pay lieutenancy was approved by the king. Hertel played an active part in that year's Quebec campaign. On 26 July a reconnaissance by Wolfe of the Montmorency fords produced a bloody skirmish. Hertel led 200 Indians and 30 Canadians across the river and drove back part of the British force, only to be driven back himself when the British were reinforced. The affair seems to have led Wolfe to conclude that an attack directed at the Montmorency fords was unlikely to succeed. Three weeks later Hertel was with another party of Canadians and Indians, under Pierre-Jean-Baptiste-François-Xavier Legardeur* de Repentigny, who made a surprise attack across the Montmorency. Without properly scouting the area beforehand, Hertel led the Indians against some light infantrymen; English reinforcements appeared almost immediately and scattered Hertel's men into the woods.

After the capitulation of Quebec on 18 Sept. 1759, Hertel retired with the remnants of Montcalm's army to a camp near Cap-Santé at the mouth of the Rivière Jacques-Cartier. In the early months of 1760 Vaudreuil was concerned with the safe convoy of food to French military headquarters. To help to stop the progress of the English and to conserve food, Hertel was sent to the rural parishes leading a detachment of 150 men which he established at Saint-Michel-de-Bellechasse. General James Murray*, believing Hertel had a force of 400 to 500 men, thought it necessary in March to establish a stronghold and a battery of 22 cannon at Pointe-Lévy (Lauzon). But Hertel's appeal for reinforcements produced only ten men, and he was advised to escape by the woods if attacked by superior numbers. His Indian allies returned to their villages shortly thereafter, but Hertel took the offensive by attacking two enemy strongholds at Pointe-Lévy on 27 April. Unable to maintain their positions, the 80 English defenders fired the strongholds and retired to Quebec.

In June, two French detachments were sent to the south shore to bolster the habitants' morale and to ensure that they would be able to protect themselves. Hertel led the party responsible for the area above Lotbinière. Less than one month later, Murray left Quebec for Montreal with 2,500 men, disarming civilians and forcing the oath of neutrality *en route*. On 18 July a detachment of 100 of Murray's men encountered Hertel's party of 40 at Lotbinière. After the first volley, Hertel's men fled to the woods, leaving their commander and several other seriously wounded men to be

Hervieux

taken prisoner. Later that night, aboard the British frigate *Diana*, Hertel de Saint-François died of his wounds at the age of 25. The following day, Murray, aware of Hertel's contributions in the previous 12 months, sent his body to Deschambault on the north shore to receive proper honours. He was buried at Cap-Santé on 19 July.

Because he was at ease among the Indians and at home in the woods young Hertel was able to serve his country well when detached from the main body of troops and left to his own initiative. The return of his body to Cap-Santé was fitting tribute to his stature among seasoned soldiers.

C. J. RUSS

AN, Col., C¹¹ᴬ, 104, f.439; D²ᶜ, 3; F³, 16, ff.24–25, 101–3. Chicago Historical Society, Oversize documents, La Jonquière à Hertel, 23 oct. 1749. *Coll. de manuscrits relatifs à la N.-F.*, IV, 285. *Journal du marquis de Montcalm* (Casgrain), 590–91. "Journal du siège de Québec" (Fauteux), APQ *Rapport, 1920–21*, 179, 233, 257. Knox, *Historical journal* (Doughty), I, 412; II, 34. "Les 'papiers' La Pause," APQ *Rapport, 1933–34*, 105–6. *Lettres du chevalier de Lévis* (Casgrain), 223. Henri Têtu, "M. Jean-Félix Récher, curé de Québec, et son journal, 1757–1760," *BRH*, IX (1903), 143. PAC *Rapport, 1905*, I, pt.ɪᴠ. P.-G. Roy, *Hommes et choses du fort Saint-Frédéric*, 146. Thomas Charland, "Les neveux de Madame de Beaubassin," *RHAF*, XXIII (1969–70), 72–78.

HERVIEUX, LOUIS-FRANÇOIS, merchant; b. 15 May 1711 in Montreal, son of Léonard-Jean-Baptiste Hervieux, a merchant, and Catherine Magnan; d. 5 June 1748 at his birthplace.

During the first half of the 18th century kinship ties in a community as small as that of the "town" of Montreal were one of the main bases of social interaction. Thanks to his family ties Louis-François Hervieux occupied a rather important position within the group of Montreal businessmen. Through his mother, brothers, and sisters, he was linked with several families of merchants: the Magnans, the Marins de La Malgue, the Pothiers, the Le Contes Dupré, and the La Cornes. On 8 Jan. 1742 Hervieux married Louise Quesnel, daughter of another Montreal merchant. Of this marriage was born a daughter who was to marry the son of Pierre GUY in 1764. On 21 Nov. 1747 Hervieux was remarried, this time to Angélique Gamelin, also the daughter of a merchant. The large number of witnesses who signed the marriage contracts suggests that these ceremonies were important social gatherings.

Louis-François Hervieux carried on a large part of his business, it seems, with his brother Jacques and his fathers-in-law, Jacques Quesnel

and Joseph-Jacques Gamelin. His business activity reflects that of most Montreal merchants during the French régime. An examination of the book-keeping documents that remain shows the great variety and the small volume of most of Hervieux's operations. The merchant bought dry goods and sold them to the craftsmen or habitants of Montreal and the surrounding area. In partnership with his brother he fitted out voyageurs and shipped furs (except beaver) to France to the brothers Antoine and Joseph-Marie Pascaud in La Rochelle who acted as his correspondents and suppliers. Payments between merchants and correspondents were usually in bills of exchange and sometimes in *récipissés de castor*, whose value was more certain. The absence of metallic currency does not seem to have hindered retail trade, which in Hervieux's book-keeping was much like barter and had to be estimated in money of account for the requirements of the account books. From this point of view the merchants' economic activity may seem rather rudimentary, but there was actually a rather remarkable complexity in the circulation of bills of exchange within the system which linked the merchants of the colony and extended to their correspondents in the mother country.

It is difficult to give precise details about Louis-François Hervieux's fortune. The debts recovered for his succession by his wife and brother in the period from his death in June 1748 to February 1751 amounted to nearly 40,000 *livres*. His brother carried on his business.

JOSÉ IGARTUA

AN, Col., C¹¹ᴬ, 84, f.202; 114, ff.36–59. ANQ-M, Greffe de J.-B. Adhémar, 28 déc. 1741; Greffe de L.-C. Danré de Blanzy, 20 nov. 1747; Registre d'état civil, Notre-Dame de Montréal, 15 mai 1711, 8 janv. 1742, 21 nov. 1747, 7 juin 1748. PAC, MG 8, C3, 5, ff.52–53; 38, 15 juin 1748; MG 23, GIII, 25 (Brouillard de Louis-François Hervieux, 1746–1751); MG 24, L3, 12, pp.1018–19, 1022, 1136–38. Tanguay, *Dictionnaire*.

HICHÉ, HENRY, merchant, seigneur, royal notary, king's attorney, subdelegate of the intendant, councillor of the Conseil Supérieur of Quebec; b. *c.* 1672 in Paris, France, son of Bernard Hiché, a bourgeois, and Marie-Catherine Masson; d. 14 July 1758 at Quebec.

The circumstances of Henry Hiché's arrival in Canada around 1700 are unknown. In 1704 he was clerk in the king's warehouse in Quebec. In 1707 he went to Acadia as secretary to the new governor of that colony, Daniel d'Auger* de Subercase. After the surrender of Port-Royal (Annapolis Royal, N.S.) to the English in 1710, Hiché returned to Quebec. As a trader he had business relations not only with Canadian merchants but also with merchants in Martinique. It appears that his commercial activities brought him large profits, since at the time of the signing of his marriage contract on 20 July 1713 at Quebec, he declared to notary Louis Chambalon* that he owned personal property and real estate to a value of 60,000 *livres*. In this amount was included the seigneury of Kamouraska, "valued and estimated" at 15,000 *livres*, which Louis Aubert Duforillon and Barbe Leneuf de La Vallière had just given him that same day on condition that he marry their niece Marguerite, daughter of Jean-Paul Legardeur* de Saint-Pierre. The wedding took place on 24 July 1713 in the church of Notre-Dame de Québec. Hiché kept this seigneury until 15 Sept. 1723, when he sold it to Louis-Joseph Morel de La Durantaye for the sum of 15,000 *livres*.

On 28 Sept. 1726 the newly arrived intendant, Claude-Thomas Dupuy*, appointed Hiché deputy for Jean-Baptiste-Julien Hamare* de La Borde, king's attorney of the provost and admiralty courts of Quebec, who was leaving to go to France. On the intendant's orders Hiché had to give up temporarily his duties as royal notary, which he had been exercising since 25 June 1725, to devote himself entirely to his new offices; he held them until 20 April 1728. At that time the king appointed Nicolas-Gaspard BOUCAULT the attorney, Hamare having decided not to return to New France. Hiché resumed his practice as notary. Competent, experienced, and well acquainted with legal customs in Canada, he was often called upon to represent private persons before the civil courts of Quebec. For instance, in 1730 he served as attorney for the former intendant Dupuy, recalled to France two years earlier.

In the spring of 1736 Intendant Hocquart* proposed Hiché to the minister of Marine, Maurepas, for the offices of king's attorney of the provost and admiralty courts of Quebec in place of Boucault, who had been called to other duties. Hocquart was satisfied with the work carried out by Hiché; he had continued fulfilling unofficially the duties of deputy for the king's attorney in certain lawsuits judged by the intendant. Hiché was appointed to the provost court on 27 March 1736, and to the admiralty court on 3 April of the same year. He then gave up his practice as a notary.

On 4 April 1739 Intendant Hocquart, who, it seems, had complete confidence in Hiché, made him his subdelegate for the town and government of Quebec. In this capacity he was required "to take cognizance of all personal and summary proceedings between the inhabitants of the town and government of Quebec." Like his predecessor, Intendant François Bigot* had confidence in Henry Hiché, since on 1 Sept. 1748, shortly after his arrival in the colony, he granted him, as well as the lieutenant general of the provost court of Quebec, François DAINE, a warrant as subdelegate for the town and government of Quebec. Hiché, already 76 years of age, seems to have carried out these duties more or less assiduously. On 23 Nov. 1753 he put forward his great age (81) to obtain from Bigot permission for his son-in-law, Jean-Baptiste-Ignace PERTHUIS, to be deputy for the king's attorney of the provost court of Quebec. Finally, on 15 May 1754, Louis XV appointed him, at 82 years of age, councillor of the Conseil Supérieur of Quebec. This appointment crowned a career of nearly 30 years in the service of the king. His son-in-law succeeded him in the offices of king's attorney of the provost and admiralty courts of Quebec. Henry Hiché sat on the Conseil Supérieur of Quebec until his death at Quebec on 14 July 1758. A member of the élite of Quebec, he received the outstanding privilege of being buried, the next day, in the church of Notre-Dame de Québec.

His long career in the king's service did not prevent him from attending to his personal affairs. Intendant Hocquart was able to write to Maurepas on 12 Oct. 1735 that Hiché had an income which could "support him honourably." By a decision of the provost court of Quebec adjudicating the property of Louis Aubert Duforillon, deceased, his wife's uncle, Henry Hiché became the owner of the "Maison Blanche," located on Rue Saint-Vallier, as well as of all the pieces of land belonging to it, and was able to speculate with these properties. He made grants of several of them, and the region adjoining the "Maison Blanche" finally was called the Faubourg Saint-Henry or Faubourg Hiché. As a rich landowner he was able to give his daughter Marie-Josephte-Madeleine a large dowry when she married Perthuis in 1742. She received the stone house and ground next to her father's home, which were valued at 3,000 *livres*. In addition he gave her an annual income of 502 *livres*. He also bestowed respectable dowries on three of his daughters who became nuns in the Hôpital Général of Quebec. For each of them he had to pay a dowry varying from 2,500 to 3,000 *livres*.

Well off, a member of the administrative and commercial élite of Canadian society, at his death Henry Hiché was worth 3,219 *livres* 15 *sols* 6 *deniers* in personal property, 696 *livres* 11 sols 6 *deniers* of it in ready money, 609 *livres* 2 *sols* 6 *deniers* in silver plate, 496 *livres* in clothing, and

Hodiesne

791 *livres* 10 *sols* in furniture for his bedroom and study. These two rooms contained some articles of luxury, including a clock, a mirror five feet high and two feet wide, and two pictures representing the king and queen.

Ten children were born of his marriage with Marguerite Legardeur, three of whom survived him: Mme Perthuis, Marguerite-Françoise de Saint-Henri, and François-Gaspard. François-Gaspard was wounded at the battle of Sainte-Foy on 28 April 1760 and shortly afterwards went to France, where he died; his widow, Charlotte Soupiran, married Joseph Arnoux in Quebec on 10 Dec. 1764.

ANDRÉ LACHANCE

AN, Col., B, 29, ff.2, 4v; 45, ff.799, 948; C¹¹ᴬ, 120, ff.230, 254v–55, 283v; D²ᶜ, 222/1, p.305; E, 43, ff.7, 8; 221 (dossier Henry Hiché) (copies at PAC). ANQ, Greffe de R.-C. Barolet, 18 juill. 1758; Greffe de Nicolas Boisseau, 16 sept. 1742; Greffe de Louis Chambalon, 20 juill. 1713 (donation et contrat de mariage); Greffe de François Genaple de Bellefonds, 4 nov. 1704; Greffe d'Henry Hiché, 1725–1736; Greffe de J.-C. Louet, 23 août 1727; NF, Coll. de pièces jud. et not., 755v, 861, 948, 1675, 2052v, 2079, 2140, 2409, 3954. "Recensement de Québec, 1744" (APQ *Rapport*), 52. Gareau, "La Prévôté de Québec," APQ *Rapport, 1943–44*, 109ff. P.-G. Roy, *Inv. ins. Cons. souv.*, 185, 216, 267; *Inv. jug. et délib.*, *1717–1760*, II, 95, 96; III, 148, 149; VI, 175; VII, 2–3; *Inv. ord. int.*, I, II, III. Tanguay, *Dictionnaire*. D'Allaire, *L'Hôpital Général de Québec*, 114–15. "La famille Hiché," *BRH*, XLI (1935), 577–606. P.-G. Roy, "Henry Hiché, conseiller au Conseil supérieur," *BRH*, XXXIII (1927), 193ff.

HISPANIOLI. *See* SPAGNIOLINI

HODIESNE, GERVAIS, Brother Hospitaller of the Cross and of St Joseph, tonsured cleric, royal notary; b. 1692 in France, son of Julien Hodiesne and Renée Hubert; d. 27 May 1764 in Montreal.

We know virtually nothing about Gervais Hodiesne's life before 2 April 1721, when his presence at the Hôpital Général of Montreal is recorded. He probably came to Canada after the recruiting trip made to France in 1719 by the founder of the Hôpital Général, François Charon* de La Barre. Hodiesne took his vows in the presence of the superior, Louis TURC de Castelveyre, on 2 Oct. 1722. Subsequently he held in succession the offices of bursar and procurator of the community, but it is difficult to determine exactly when. He was bursar in 1728 and 1729, and shortly afterwards procurator. As procurator he made a trip to France at the end of 1733. The minister, Maurepas, had approved Hodiesne's voyage to the mother country in order to associate the hospitallers of Montreal with one of the French teaching communities. On 23 March 1734 Hodiesne obtained free passage on the *Rubis* for his return to New France.

His trip seems to have had happy results, since in 1737 Brothers Denis and Pacifique, of the Brothers of the Christian Schools, arrived in the colony. But they came too late; in 1735 the hospitallers had had a disastrous year [*see* Jean JEANTOT], and in the same year Gervais Hodiesne had left the Hôpital Général of Montreal for the seminary of Quebec. On 15 Sept. 1735 he received the tonsure, and on 12 October Bishop Dosquet* made him a land grant in the seigneuries of Bourgchemin or Saint-Herman, to be taken up "at his choice or option and at the moment he will consider proper." During his years at the seminary, Hodiesne seems to have held the office of secretary to the bishop.

In July 1739 Gervais Hodiesne left the seminary and settled in the seigneury of Chambly. On 12 December he obtained a commission to practise as a royal notary in that seigneury. At Chambly sometime between 25 and 29 November, he had married Marguerite Lareau, the widow of Charles Campagna. Four children were to be born of this marriage. Some years later, on 18 July 1747, Hodiesne obtained from Intendant François Bigot* a second commission as royal notary to practise in the entire government of Montreal except the town and suburb of Ville-Marie. He could not practise in the town of Montreal until 26 May 1752, when he received a new commission. From 1750 to 1759 he acted occasionally as assessor.

The capitulation of Montreal brought little change to Gervais Hodiesne's life, since on 1 Oct. 1760 Governor Thomas Gage* confirmed him as notary for the town and government of Montreal. Hodiesne practised for four more years and died in Montreal on 27 May 1764.

MICHEL PAQUIN

AN, Col., B, 58, f.398; 60/1, f.174v; 63, f.491. PAC *Report, 1918*, 23. É.-Z. Massicotte, "Inventaire des documents concernant les frères Charon," APQ *Rapport, 1923–24*, 181, 184, 186, 195, 201; "Les tribunaux et les officiers de justice de Montréal sous le régime français," *BRH*, XXXVII (1931), 303. P.-G. Roy, *Inv. concessions*, IV, 115; *Inv. jug. et délib., 1717–1760*, III, 88; *Inv. ord. int.*, II, 284; III, 95–96, 171. Tanguay, *Dictionnaire*. Vachon, "Inv. critique des notaires royaux," *RHAF*, XI (1957–58), 101. *L'Hôpital Général de Montréal*, I, 65. É.-Z. Massicotte, "Hospitalier, ecclésiastique, notaire et père de famille," *BRH*, XLII (1936), 304–9; "Le mariage du notaire Hodiesne," *BRH*, XLII (1936), 599.

HOLMES, CHARLES, naval officer; baptized 19 Sept. 1711 at Yarmouth, Isle of Wight, son of the governor of the Isle, Henry Holmes, and Mary Holmes, his cousin; d. 21 Nov. 1761 at Jamaica.

In 1727 Charles Holmes joined the *Captain* (70 guns) as an ordinary seaman. Promoted lieutenant on 18 June 1734, he served in the Home station and the Mediterranean, and in 1740 went to the West Indies. In 1741 he received his first command, the *Strombolo* fireship, and then was given the *Success* fireship, in which he returned to England. On 20 Feb. 1741/42, when he assumed command of the *Sapphire* (24 guns), he was confirmed in the rank of post captain. In June 1743 he took command of the *Enterprise* (44 guns) and went to the West Indies. There he became captain of the 70-gun *Lennox* in May 1747.

He was involved in Sir Charles Knowles*' engagement with the Spanish fleet near Cuba in the fall of 1748. This indecisive action led to a controversy in which Knowles accused several captains, including Holmes, of negligence. A court martial not only acquitted Holmes but praised his conduct.

From 1748 to 1754 Holmes served in home waters. In 1755 he came to North America apparently for the first time when, as captain of the *Grafton* (74 guns), he sailed in Rear Admiral Francis Holburne*'s squadron to reinforce Vice-Admiral BOSCAWEN. The following year he returned to North America as commodore of the squadron charged with preventing French reinforcements from reaching Louisbourg, Île Royale (Cape Breton Island). Two imponderables of 18th century naval warfare – the weather and the health of the seamen – kept his more than adequate force from success. Captain Richard Spry, who commanded the part of the squadron that had wintered in Halifax, was off Louisbourg by May, but was forced off station late in June by the number of seamen disabled and dying from scurvy and dysentery. Holmes reached Nova Scotia on 26 June and, missing Spry in the foggy weather, cruised off Louisbourg until he encountered four French ships under Louis-Joseph BEAUSSIER de Lisle on 26 July. Holmes was outmanœuvred by Beaussier, who entered Louisbourg harbour to land supplies desperately needed by the fortress. After a protracted and indecisive engagement when the French came out to seek battle the following day, Holmes retired to Halifax for repairs. On 10 August Beaussier's ships sailed safely for France. For the remainder of the season, Holmes' ships terrorized the French fishery of the Gulf of St Lawrence and Newfoundland.

During his command Holmes had to rely on the limited facilities of Halifax to support his squadron's insatiable demands. In 1756 naval stores worth over £16,000 were sent to Halifax from England, and between them Holmes and Spry drew on bills of exchange to the value of more than £1,600. Because of the Newcastle administration's reluctance to pursue an offensive strategy in North America, Holmes was not given authority to create dockyard facilities, and Halifax was little improved as a naval base during his command. As a sop to Governor Charles LAWRENCE, when Holmes returned to England in October 1756 he left a ship of the line among the warships remaining behind to defend the harbour.

During the winter Holmes was a member of the court martial that convicted Admiral John BYNG. He returned to North America with the *Grafton* in 1757. The ship was among those severely damaged by a hurricane while cruising off Louisbourg on 24 September. Although she had lost her masts and rudder, Holmes, in a superb demonstration of seamanship, sailed her to England with a jury-rudder made of a spare topmast. In 1758 he was employed in home waters and was promoted rear admiral of the blue.

A further promotion, to rear admiral of the white, came to him in 1758 or 1759, possibly on his appointment as third in command under Charles Saunders* for the attack on Quebec. He arrived at Île aux Coudres on 27 June 1759. On 21 July he went above Quebec by land and took command of the ships that under Captain John ROUS had slipped past the fortress a few days before. With the *Sutherland* (50 guns), the *Squirrel* (20 guns), and a few smaller vessels, Holmes and Brigadier-General James Murray* were able to carry out an extended raid up river from 8 to 25 August, forcing Colonel Bougainville* to maintain an exhausting patrol along the north shore. Although Holmes himself returned down river on 25 August, the threat from the squadron continued until the eve of the final landings and helped deprive MONTCALM of Bougainville's assistance when it was so desperately needed on the Plains of Abraham. On 6 September Holmes accompanied WOLFE up river to prepare for the final assault. The choice of the Anse au Foulon as a landing place compounded the difficulties facing Holmes: he had to guarantee a safe landing in darkness, on a narrow beach, in a tidal current of four knots on the ebbing tide. It was "the most hazardous and difficult task I was ever engaged in," he wrote. "The failing in any part of my Disposition, as it might overset the Generals plan, would have brought upon me an imputation of being the Cause of the Miscarriage of the Attack...." As it happened, his dispositions were masterly, and his seamen played their part well, although the tide carried their boats a little farther to the east than intended. The enterprise was, according to C. P. Stacey, "a classic of combined operations . . . a professional triumph."

Late in September Holmes returned to England. In 1760 he was appointed commander-in-chief at Jamaica, where he pursued a lucrative campaign against French commerce until his death the following year.

W. A. B. DOUGLAS

PRO, Adm. 1/480, f.728; 1/481, ff.173–80, 210, 223, 229; 1/482; 1/1892; 3/64, f.191. Doughty and Parmelee, *Siege of Quebec*, II, IV. *Logs of the conquest* (Wood). Charnock, *Biographia navalis*, V. J. J. Colledge, *Ships of the Royal Navy: an historical index* (1v. to date, New York and Newton Abbott, Eng., 1969), I. *DNB*. G. B., Adm., *Commissioned sea officers, 1660–1815*. Corbett, *England in the Seven Years' War*, I. Christopher Lloyd, *The capture of Quebec* (London, 1959). H. W. Richmond, *The navy in the War of 1739–48* (3v., Cambridge, Eng., 1920), III. Stacey, *Quebec, 1759*.

HOPSON, PEREGRINE THOMAS, military officer, governor of Louisbourg, Cape Breton Island, and Nova Scotia; b. probably in England, possibly a son of Admiral Sir Thomas Hopsonn; d. 27 Feb. 1759 at Basse-Terre, Guadeloupe.

Peregrine Thomas Hopson was a career officer; little is known about his private life. His first recorded appointment was as a lieutenant in Lord Shannon's marines in 1703, and by 1738 he was a major in Clayton's regiment (14th Foot). He was promoted lieutenant-colonel in Chomondeley's regiment (48th Foot) in January 1740/41. He went to Gibraltar during the siege of 1727 and, except for a brief stay in England from 1741 to 1743, was with regiments stationed there until 1745. Seeking promotion in 1746 he claimed, in a letter to the Duke of Newcastle, more than 35 years of actual duty in the army.

In the spring of 1746 Hopson arrived at Louisbourg from Gibraltar, as senior officer in Fuller's regiment (29th Foot), which had been sent to reinforce the garrison. Louisbourg had been captured from the French the previous year by a joint New England and British force under William PEPPERRELL and Peter WARREN. Likely through Newcastle's patronage, Hopson took command of the colony in September 1747 as lieutenant governor, succeeding Governor Charles Knowles*, and later became governor. By 1747 the English position at Louisbourg was a caretaking opera-

tion, punctuated by minor French and Indian raids on the outlying areas and worries about the threat they posed to the fuel supply of the colony. In June 1748, for example, a party led by Joseph Marin* de La Malgue captured boats and a detachment of men loading coal at the Table Head colliery (near Glace Bay, N.S.), and threatened to destroy the incomplete blockhouse there.

Hopson was promoted colonel of his regiment on 6 June 1748. In October the treaty of Aix-la-Chapelle returned Louisbourg and Cape Breton Island to France. Late in June 1749 Hopson and the French commissary, Charles DES HERBIERS de La Ralière, began negotiations for the restoration of Louisbourg to the French, and concluded the transfer by the end of July. Hopson took the British troops and supplies to the new English settlement at Halifax (Chebucto) and then returned to England.

In 1752 he was welcomed back to Halifax as governor of Nova Scotia, taking office on 3 August. He admitted to the Board of Trade that he had no effective jurisdiction over much of the area he nominally commanded from Halifax, and saw the Acadians and Indians, encouraged from Quebec and Louisbourg, as tools of an active French policy of encroachment on the English. He believed the Acadians were essential to his colony as the only established farmers and so he secured the consent of his superiors to avoid for the moment the issue of the oath of allegiance, and argued successfully against settling "foreign Protestants" among them. He also ordered that Acadians supplying military posts with wood and provisions be paid a fair price. If military control were maintained, he hoped, the Acadians might eventually accept British rule and even take the oath. His one opportunity to follow a similar policy with the Indians was provided by a short-lived treaty concluded in November 1752 with Jean-Baptiste COPE, leader of a small band of Micmacs on the east coast of Nova Scotia.

Rivalry between English and North American factions in the colony was growing at this time. For example, there were disputes over whether English or New England law practices would be observed in the courts [see James MONK]. Hopson tried to reconcile the opposing sides, for he believed the passage of time and the regularizing of the affairs of the colony would ultimately dispel the "spirit of party." In the meantime he sought to keep the peace "by the most moderate measures, and carrying myself as equally as possible on both sides." His most effective positive action in office, however, was the settlement of many of the German- and French-speaking Protestants who had been congregating in Halifax in increasing misery since 1750. Although his instructions contained no special orders concerning their relocation, Hopson made vigorous efforts to obtain necessary supplies from the British government so that they could be moved to a new settlement during the summer of 1753. The site chosen for the new colony was Mirligueche, which was renamed Lunenburg, probably after one of the titles of George I as Elector of Hanover. Hopson chose Lieutenant-Colonel Charles LAWRENCE and Captain Patrick SUTHERLAND to direct the founding of the settlement in June 1753. This colonizing venture occurred during a lull in acts of hostility by the French and Indians, perhaps caused by the absence of Abbé Jean-Louis Le Loutre* from the province. Hopson himself believed that the French were simply gathering their forces for a more decisive offensive.

Severe eye trouble forced Hopson to hand over the government of Nova Scotia to Lawrence and he left for England on 1 Nov. 1753. He finally resigned the governorship in 1755. He was promoted major-general in February 1757, and in July he arrived back in Halifax, with reinforcements for the army commanded by the Earl of Loudoun [John Campbell]; Loudoun had reached Halifax from New York at the end of June and was to lead an expedition against Louisbourg that summer. As a former governor of Louisbourg, Hopson served partly as an adviser, and he fully concurred in Loudoun's decision to abandon the expedition because of the late arrival of the British troops and the strength of the French fleet at Louisbourg. Loudoun returned to New York in August, leaving Hopson in command of the troops in Nova Scotia and having designated him to lead a new expedition against Louisbourg in 1758. Hopson was recalled to England, however, before the 1758 campaign, on grounds that the government feared for his health.

On 10 Nov. 1758 he sailed as commander of the land forces in an expedition against the French sugar islands, Martinique and Guadeloupe. After an initial landing in Martinique, its first objective, the expedition withdrew and took up a position at Basse-Terre, Guadeloupe. Hopson was already seriously ill and died a month later. John Barrington, his second in command, completed the conquest of the island. Hopson's age and health, as well as the different qualities required in the two situations, seem to explain the differences in his performance as governor of Nova Scotia and as leader of this expedition.

The main beneficiaries of his will, drawn up a month before he left for Martinique, were Lydia Goodall, a niece then living with him at Berry, near Gosport, Hampshire, and two sisters, Grace Hopson and Anne Bennett.

WENDY CAMERON

BM, Add. MSS, 23830, ff.168–69v; 32709, ff.194–94v; 32713, ff.507–8v; 32716, f.299; 32733, ff.93–93v. PRO, CO 5/44; 5/45; 5/48; 110/1; 217/13; 217/15, ff.15–16; 217/17, ff.46–50; 217/33; 217/40; Ind. 5432, 5433, 5435, 5436, 5437, 5438–39; Prob. 11/847, f.204 (will of Peregrine Hopson, October 1758); WO 34/44, 34/71, 34/101. *Army list, 1754; 1755; 1756; 1757; 1758; 1759.* Robert Beatson, *Naval and military memoirs of Great Britain, from 1727 to 1783* (6v., London, 1804), II, III. *Coll. de manuscrits relatifs à la N.-F.,* III, 426, 430, 447. Knox, *Historical journal* (Doughty). *Military affairs in North America, 1748–1765: selected documents from the Cumberland papers in Windsor Castle,* ed. S. M. Pargellis (New York, London, 1936). *N.S. Archives, I.* PAC *Report, 1905,* II, pt.III, 282–83. Bell, *Foreign Protestants.* Brebner, *New England's outpost. English army lists* (Dalton), V, 135; VI, 129. Dalton, *George the first's army,* II, 298. McLennan, *Louisbourg.* Marshall Smelser, *The campaign for the sugar islands, 1759: a study of amphibious warfare* (Chapel Hill, N.C., 1955). W. P. Ward, "The Acadian response to the growth of British power in Nova Scotia, 1749–1755," *Dal. Rev.,* LI (1971), 173.

HOUDIN, JEAN-MICHEL (called Father Potentien), Recollet, later Church of England clergyman; b. January 1706 in France; d. *c.* 1766 at New Rochelle, New York.

We know little about Jean-Michel Houdin's youth except that on 25 May 1725, at the age of 19 years and four months, he made his profession with the Recollets under the name of Brother Potentien. On 4 March 1730 he was ordained at Trèves (Trier, Federal Republic of Germany) and was sent to Canada shortly afterwards; he was at Quebec in 1734. Nine years later he was appointed superior and parish priest of Trois-Rivières, and in 1744 he went to the convent in Montreal. In that year Houdin cast off the frock and, accompanied by Catherine Thunay, *dit* Dufresne, widow of François Demers Monfort, fled to the Huguenots in New England. The gossip written by Mme Bégon [ROCBERT] on 17 May 1749 to her son-in-law, Honoré MICHEL de Villebois de La Rouvillière, tells us of a missive sent by "that rogue Potenssien" to the superior of the Recollets, Valérien GAUFIN. In it Houdin accused Gaufin of having stolen about 500 *livres* "to give to prostitutes in their quarter with whom he amuses himself." According to the letter-writer, Houdin stated that he was not interested in the Pope's pardon and "that he no more believes in the Holy Father's relics than do those with whom

Houdin

he is living; that moreover, the Pope has enough to do distributing pardons and indulgences to the Spaniards." Finally Houdin is supposed to have said that he was "content with his condition and convinced that God blesses him, since he gives him a fine family; that he would consider he would be doing greater wrong in abandoning it [his family] than he does in remaining as he is, and a thousand other things equally extravagant and horrifying"; and Mme Bégon added: "Best of all, he does not speak at all of his companions in debauchery."

On 29 June 1744 Houdin was in the city of New York, where the provincial council authorized him to live at Jamaica (N.Y.C.) until August. After that he seems to have returned to New York; in 1749, on Easter Sunday, he was received into the Church of England, and some time later accepted as a clergyman. In 1753 the new pastor was a missionary at Trenton, New Jersey, and on 29 Aug. 1757 he was named military chaplain for the 48th regiment. In this capacity he took part in the capture of Quebec and the battle of Sainte-Foy, which led to the military conquest of New France by the British armies.

Did Houdin have some responsibility in the capture of Quebec? General WOLFE could probably have made use of his knowledge of the region, since Houdin had lived there some years earlier. Did he really point out the Chemin du Foulon, or was he only an interpreter? Whatever the truth may be, Houdin, after Wolfe's death, claimed the reward the general had promised for his services.

Houdin spent the winter of 1759–60 in Quebec, where he ministered among the Huguenots, and in the spring he was replaced as missionary by the clergyman John Brooke*. Houdin went to New Rochelle that same year and returned to Montreal early in 1761 to plead on his wife's behalf. During this few months' stay Houdin seems to have been received coldly by his former compatriots. The talk his presence caused forced the vicar general, Étienne Montgolfier*, to intervene. In February the Sulpician wrote him, urging him to leave his wife, do penance, and return to the Church of Rome. Houdin lost no time in handing this letter over to James Murray*, who used it in 1763 to belittle the vicar general to Lord Shelburne and to diminish the Sulpician's chances of succeeding Bishop Pontbriand [DUBREIL] in the see of Quebec.

The annalist of the Hôtel-Dieu of Montreal enlightens us about an attitude which was perhaps general among the inhabitants of New France at that time towards a person such as Houdin: she describes the visit to the hospital wards of an unhappy apostate monk who some years earlier had said mass in their church; the circumstances suggest that she referred to the former Recollet Houdin. The presence of the English Protestant soldiers, and the sight of this monk "who had become the minister of those sectarians," filled the hospitaller's soul with bitterness. "Under the pretence of zeal," she wrote, "he remained constantly in the wards, to blaspheme against religion and to ridicule our most venerable mysteries and sacraments; equipped with a potful of disgusting grease, he visited, one after the other, the sick heretics, to give them, he said, the last Sacrament." And the annalist added: "We were not allowed to make any reply to all these harangues."

Jean-Michel Houdin left Canada in 1761 and was replaced as chaplain of the 48th regiment by Richard Griffith. After his departure the Huguenots in New France – their presence there was tolerated in the final decades of the French régime – found themselves without a French-speaking pastor. Indeed, John Brooke, Houdin's replacement in Quebec after 1760, neither spoke nor understood French; the French Protestants had to wait for David Chabran* to arrive from Lille in 1766 to enjoy again regular religious services in French.

Houdin subsequently settled for good with his family in New Rochelle. It seems certain that he had married Catherine Thunay, dit Dufresne shortly after his flight from Montreal in 1744. A petition by the French community of New Rochelle signed on 1 Feb. 1762 informs us that they had at least three children, John, Kitty, and Elizabeth.

Jean-Michel Houdin's case resembles somewhat those of Pierre-Joseph-Antoine Roubaud* and Emmanuel Veyssère*. The Jesuit Roubaud, however, was a schemer and left his church ostentatiously; the Recollet Veyssère broke with the Catholic community of Quebec without friction or fuss. As for Jean-Michel Houdin, he left his order and his church furtively, and apparently was extremely bitter in his relations with his former compatriots.

MICHEL PAQUIN

AAQ, 1 CB, Vicaires généraux, 3. ANQ, QBC, Cours de justice, Chambre des milices, 1761. New York State Library (Albany), Council minutes, XIX, 262, 273, 276. "Church and state papers" (Kelley), APQ *Rapport, 1948–49*, 297, 301, 303. "Correspondance de Mme Bégon" (Bonnault), APQ *Rapport, 1934–35*, 65–66, 216–17. Desrosiers, "Correspondance de cinq vicaires généraux," APQ *Rapport, 1947–48*, 79. *Documentary history of New-York* (O'Callaghan), III, 577–78. "Historical records of the Church of England" (Kelley),

APQ *Rapport, 1946–47*, 187. Knox, *Historical journal* (Doughty), III, 28, 496. PAC *Report, 1921*, app.D, 1. *Quebec Gazette / La Gazette de Québec*, 27 Oct. 1766, 8 Oct. 1767. P.-G. Roy, *Inv. jug. et délib., 1717–1760*, V, 248. Tanguay, *Dictionnaire*, III, 528. Philip Carrington, *The Anglican Church in Canada; a history* (Toronto, 1963), 35–36. Mondoux, *L'Hôtel-Dieu de Montréal*, 307. Jouve, *Les Franciscains et le Canada: aux Trois-Rivières*, 165–66. H. C. Stuart, *The Church of England in Canada, 1759–1793; from the conquest to the establishment of the see of Quebec* (Montreal, 1893), 7–8. Trudel, *L'Église canadienne*. É.-Z. Massicotte, "La veuve du pasteur Houdin," *BRH*, XXXIX (1933), 550–51.

HOW, EDWARD, justice of the peace, militia officer, member of the Nova Scotia Council; b. possibly *c*. 1702 in New England, perhaps the son of David How and Elizabeth D'Eath; d. near the Missaguash River (N.S.-N.B.), October 1750.

Nothing is known of Edward How's life before 1722, when his presence at Canso, Nova Scotia, is first noted. Troops were sent there in 1720 to protect the New England fishery from French marauders and soon a permanent population, almost entirely from New England, was established. How began his career at Canso as a merchant and was prominent enough by 1725 to be recommended by Lieutenant Governor Lawrence Armstrong* for a seat on the Nova Scotia council; he was not, however, appointed on this occasion. That same year he received a grant of 12.6 acres on an island in Canso harbour – now called How's Island – as part of a plan for a permanent settlement. Indeed Armstrong had requested permission to move the seat of government from Annapolis Royal to Canso that year, but the Board of Trade took no action. How may have been nominated for the council so that Canso could be represented at Annapolis Royal. He often went to parley with the Indians in the Canso area and likely learned the Micmac tongue. This might explain his commission in 1725 as captain in the local militia, though he always considered himself a civilian.

In 1728 he paid for the building of barracks and a guardhouse at Canso. He also owned a schooner which was sometimes used for local government business. In 1730 he was appointed justice of the peace at Canso and, about the same time, sheriff. A crisis arose in 1732 between How and his associate justices and Christopher ALDRIDGE Sr, the garrison commander, when Aldridge tried to preside over the meetings of the local justices to protect the interests of his troops. The New England residents at Canso were furious over Aldridge's arbitrary action and the justices appealed to Annapolis; Aldridge was reprimanded.

How was appointed commissary of musters for the British forces in Nova Scotia in March 1736 and in August was sworn in as a member of the provincial council at Annapolis Royal. At this time the council authorized the erection of a 50,000-acre township of Norwich in the Chignecto area, and How was one of the 36 grantees; but the township was never established. How was sent to England, probably in September 1736, to report on the state of affairs at Canso, but was unable to obtain help to improve the fortifications there. In 1735 he himself had financed construction of a blockhouse. He built two storehouses for the king's provisions in 1737 and repaired the barracks in 1739. The Canso fishery had begun to decline after 1735, however, and by 1738 the population had greatly diminished, with fewer than ten families remaining. How had spent much on the Canso defences – likely upwards of £800 in view of the large sums owed him by the crown at his death. Possibly to salvage their own operations and provide a bulwark against a French attack on Canso from Île Royale (Cape Breton Island), How and his associates proposed in 1739 that lands adjacent to Canso be laid out as a township. The local military officers opposed this suggestion, fearing their interests would be hampered by the presence of a civil power at Canso. The council finally approved the plan in April 1744, but shortly afterwards a French force under Joseph Du Pont Duvivier destroyed the settlement and carried off the garrison to Louisbourg. How's business there was completely wiped out.

How was summoned to Annapolis Royal in 1743 by Paul MASCARENE, president of the council, in view of the worsening relations between the French and the English. He seems to have been respected by the Acadians and for this reason Mascarene sent him in May 1744 to visit French settlements on the Saint John River and at Minas to try to secure their allegiance or ensure at least a strict neutrality. In June, at Annapolis, How married Marie-Madeleine Winniett, his second wife, daughter of William WINNIETT and Marie-Madeleine MAISONNAT. Family papers indicate that he had at least three sons and one daughter by a previous marriage. That summer Annapolis Royal itself was under siege and How was prominent in helping to save the lower part of the town from being burned by pro-French Indians.

As commissary of musters, How was obliged to remain at Annapolis Royal during the colonial expedition against Louisbourg in 1745. In August

Imbault

1746 he was sent up the Bay of Fundy with a small force to obtain intelligence of French movements and managed to gain news of a sizable French fleet which was sailing for Nova Scotia [see LA ROCHEFOUCAULD]. How later reported that he had also kept "the inhabitants in Due Allegiance punishing some offenders and reducing the Cattle and Grain, In order to render the Approaches of the Enemy less formidable than before." The following winter at Grand Pré he was commissary for the garrison and a commissioner in charge of civil affairs, along with Erasmus James PHILIPPS. On the night of 31 Jan. 1746/47, the French attacked the English garrison, and How was so badly wounded in the battle that he lost the use of his left arm. He was taken prisoner and was later exchanged for six Frenchmen – an indication of his importance to the colony. Later that year he was made a judge of the vice-admiralty court.

In July 1749 How was appointed to the new provincial council at Halifax and was immediately sent by Governor Edward Cornwallis* to renew and ratify a peace treaty with Indians in the Saint John River area. Because of his lack of professional military experience he was bypassed in favour of Charles LAWRENCE in 1750 when Cornwallis chose a new lieutenant governor. How accompanied Lawrence as commissary to the Missaguash River on the Chignecto isthmus of Nova Scotia in August 1750 and shortly thereafter the British began to build a fort – later named after Lawrence – to offset French forces on the other side of the river. How knew the region and many of the inhabitants and was chosen to meet with the French under a flag of truce on the banks of the Missaguash, mainly to secure the release of some English prisoners. On 4 October, after several meetings, How was returning from a parley at the river when a shot rang out and he fell, seriously wounded. He died either that day or within several days of the attack.

Accounts of the murder differ. Some say it was an ambush, others that an Indian named Jean-Baptiste COPE or, more likely, Étienne BÂTARD killed How. Many writers have put the real responsibility on the Abbé Jean-Louis Le Loutre*, but his role has not been proved conclusively. Whoever the guilty party might have been, How's death certainly made conditions throughout Acadia more tense.

Governor Cornwallis noted in a memorial on How that he "always behaved . . . with the greatest Fidelity & Care in everything I required of him." How's widow sought compensation for the funds he had devoted to public construction at Canso and a claim for £1,320 was approved in 1769; it was paid as an annuity of £100 per annum, which came into force two years later. The number of children surviving How from his two marriages is not known.

C. ALEXANDER PINCOMBE

PANS, MG 1, 472, nos.10, 13; 473, no. 5. [The warrant for How's marriage (item no. 13) names his wife as "Mrs. Magdelene Winniett," but the available evidence and family tradition indicate that he married Winniett's daughter, not his widow.] *The building of Fort Lawrence in Chignecto; a journal recently found in the Gates Collection, New York Historical Society*, ed. J. C. Webster (Saint John, N.B., 1941), 9, 10, 12. [Louis Leneuf de La Vallière ?], "Journal de ce qui s'est passé à Chicnitou et autres parties des frontières de l'Acadie depuis le 15 septembre 1750 jusqu'au 28 juillet 1751," PAC *Report, 1905*, II, pt.III, 325–26. *N.S. Archives, I*; *II*; *IV*. PRO, *CSP, Col.*, 1732. Calnek, *History of Annapolis* (Savary), 115–16, 527–30.

W. S. MacNutt, *The Atlantic provinces: the emergence of colonial society, 1712–1857* (Toronto, 1965), 21–24. Murdoch, *History of Nova-Scotia*, II, 193–94. J. C. Webster, *The career of the Abbe Le Loutre in Nova Scotia with a translation of his autobiography* (Shediac, N.B., 1933), 21–24; *The forts of Chignecto; a study of the eighteenth century conflict between France and Great Britain in Acadia* (n.p., 1930), 91–92. G. T. Bates, "Your most obedient humble servant Edward How," N.S. Hist. Soc. *Coll.*, XXXIII (1961), 1–19. Albert David, "L'affaire How d'après les documents contemporains," *Revue de l'Université d'Ottawa*, VI (1936), 440–68.

I

IMBAULT, MAURICE (baptized **Jean-Jacques**), Recollet, missionary, superior; b. 1686 in Paris, France; d. in New France sometime after 1759.

Little information is available about Father Maurice Imbault's life before his arrival in New France. All that the Recollets' archives says is that he made his profession in that order in the province of Saint-Denys under the name of Maurice on 14 April 1714, at the age of 27 years and 8 months, and that he came from Paris. When he was ordained is not known, and the date of his arrival in Canada is uncertain. He seems to have crossed on board the *Chameau* in 1719. If he did, he arrived at Quebec with Mathieu-Benoît Collet* and during the crossing must have been present at the death of François Charon* de La Barre, the founder of the Brothers Hospitallers of the Cross and of St Joseph.

Father Maurice began his service in November 1719 in the parishes of Saint-Roch-des-Aulnets in the seigneury of Les Aulnets, Notre-Dame-de-Liesse (Rivière-Ouelle) in the seigneury of La Bouteillerie, and Sainte-Anne-de-la-Pocatière in the seigneury of La Pocatière. On 23 March 1721, "towards evening," Father Maurice received in his presbytery at Sainte-Anne the inquirers Mathieu-Benoît Collet and Nicolas-Gaspard BOUCAULT, bearing a commission from Governor Philippe de Rigaud* de Vaudreuil and Intendant Michel BÉGON, "His Majesty's intention being that the parish districts of this colony shall be established according to the same formalities as those which are observed in France." Starting the next day Collet, attorney general to the Conseil Supérieur, and his clerk of court Boucault received 32 of the 69 heads of families in the three parishes served by the Recollet. After describing the size of their respective parishes the delegates from Saint-Roch and Notre-Dame-de-Liesse called for the disappearance of the parish of Sainte-Anne, despite the protests of its representatives, and asked that half of Sainte-Anne be joined to the parish of Saint-Roch and the other half to Notre-Dame-de-Liesse. In addition they requested the appointment of two parish priests, "in view of the fact that the great size of the three parishes, which the said Reverend Father Maurice serves, very often prevents them from being able to attend divine service and from being succoured in case of sickness." A report of this meeting was drawn up, and when it had been read the inquirers, Father Maurice, and 12 delegates signed it, the other 20 "having declared that they do not know how to write or sign their names." This inquiry had only limited results in New France; despite a decree of 3 March 1722 stipulating that half of the parishioners of Saint-Anne were to be united with the parish of Notre-Dame-de-Liesse and the other half with Saint-Roch, Father Maurice kept on serving the three parishes until 1731.

In addition to his ministry the Recollet also carried out the duties of notary and arbiter delegated by the intendant, as did many other missionaries whose territory was far away from Quebec. On 14 May 1724 Imbault drew up a bill of sale, one of the parties to it being the notary Étienne JEANNEAU. The latter could not apply to anyone other than Father Maurice: Jeanneau was in fact the only notary in the region. The intendants Bégon and Dupuy* entrusted Father Imbault

with the settlement of several disputes among the habitants of the three parishes he served.

After 1731 and until 1756 Father Maurice lived in Quebec. The documents reveal little about his activities during this period. It is known that for three years he was superior of the Recollet convent. Subsequently he was in turn or simultaneously confessor to the Ursulines and confessor and chaplain to the nuns of the Hôpital Général. By the end of 1757 Father Imbault was in Trois-Rivières, and there he drops from sight after 8 Feb. 1759. His death certificate cannot be found.

MICHEL PAQUIN

Archives des Franciscains (Montréal), Dossier Maurice Imbault. "Procès-verbaux du procureur général Collet" (Caron), APQ *Rapport, 1921–22*, 346–49. "Témoignages de liberté au mariage," APQ *Rapport, 1951–53*, 35. A. Roy, *Inv. greffes not.*, XIV, 30. P.-G. Roy, *Inv. ord. int.*, I, 256, 282, 292, 294; II, 4. Caron, "Inventaire de documents," APQ *Rapport, 1941–42*, 229. Jouve, *Les Franciscains et le Canada: aux Trois-Rivières*, 166, 202, 212. *Mgr de Saint-Vallier et l'Hôpital Général*, 713. Trudel, *L'Église canadienne*, I, 89–90, 341. *Les Ursulines de Québec* (1863–66), II, 147.

IMBERT, JACQUES, royal notary, merchant trader, agent of the treasurers-general of the Marine, councillor of the Conseil Supérieur; b. *c.* 1708 in France, son of Jean Imbert, police officer of the town of Montargis, and Edmée Chambrois; m. Agathe Trefflé, *dit* Rottot, in Quebec on 12 Aug. 1743; d. 8 Sept. 1765 at Branches, in the diocese of Sens, France.

Jacques Imbert came to Canada sometime between 1737 and 1740, under unknown circumstances. Around this time he served as writer in the office of the administration (office of the Marine) in Quebec. Having decided that he possessed "the necessary knowledge and ability," Gilles Hocquart* appointed him to replace the royal notary Jacques Barbel* upon the latter's death in July 1740. As notary Imbert was not particularly active; according to his register he signed only some 50 acts during his ten years in this profession. His office as notary would not alone have permitted him to live decently. For that reason, from 1740 to 1745 he filled at the same time the offices of writer, notary, and purveyor to the state. In the latter capacity he sold the colonial government in 1744 and 1745 more than 15,000 *livres* of merchandise for the shipbuilding yard in Quebec; in 1743 he had entered into partnership with three other Quebec merchants and had furnished the state at that time with more than 17,000 *livres* of merchandise for the construction of the ship *Caribou*.

After 1745 he left the office of the Marine to become assistant to Thomas-Jacques TASCHE-REAU, agent of the treasurers-general of the Marine in Canada. When Taschereau died on 25 Sept. 1749 Imbert succeeded him, first on a temporary basis, then officially from 1750 on by commission of the treasurers-general of the Marine. The post of agent in Canada did not leave him sufficient time to continue as notary, and on 17 Nov. 1750 he was replaced by François Moreau. As agent Imbert was responsible for settling the warrants for payment and promissory notes issued by the intendant. He also had to administer for the treasurers-general of the Marine in his personal capacity funds over which the intendant had no control; he kept his books as if they were for private accounts. This office thus left the agent a great deal of latitude in the use of the funds in his account, and he could borrow from them as he wished for his personal affairs, for unless there was a scandal it was only upon his death that the true state of his account could be determined exactly [*see* Georges Regnard* Duplessis; Nicolas LANOULLIER de Boisclerc].

The office of agent was no sinecure, particularly towards the end of the French régime, when the mother country was sending more and more soldiers every year. In 1754 Imbert received "permission to go to France to improve his knowledge of his office and to receive new instructions," in order to run in a more orderly fashion financial operations that were continually made more complicated by the increasing number of soldiers. In the report he presented to the minister of Marine, Machault, in Paris on 2 Feb. 1755 he stressed his need for an assistant capable of helping to keep accounts of the treasury of Canada up to date, in view of the mass of paper money in circulation which came back every year to the treasurer's office for conversion into bills of exchange. In the spring of 1758 the treasurers-general of the Marine complied with his request and assigned him as his assistant Alexandre-Robert de Saint-Hilaire* de La Rochette, in Canada since 1755 as secretary to the commissary of wars André DOREIL. Imbert had returned to Canada in the spring of 1755 on the frigate *Fidèle*, along with Intendant François Bigot* and the assistant town major of Quebec, Michel-Jean-Hugues Péan*.

Jacques Imbert occupied one of the most important posts in the administration of New France; it was therefore quite normal that on 15 May 1754 the king should appoint him, as he had his predecessor Taschereau, councillor of the Conseil Supérieur. Being well acquainted with protocol, he was delegated, along with the councillors François FOUCAULT, Guillaume Estèbe*, and Jean-Antoine Bedout, to go to "compliment" the Marquis de Vaudreuil [Pierre de Rigaud*] on his "safe arrival" in Canada on 23 June 1755. Another time the council put him in charge of the ceremonies for the *Te Deum* of thanksgiving, sung in the cathedral of Quebec on 22 Aug. 1756, for "the capture from the English of Fort de l'Étoile and the surrender of Chouaguen [Fort Oswego] on 13 and 14 Aug. 1756." In addition, from 15 Nov. 1756 to 20 Nov. 1758 Imbert was the commissary in charge of administering the royal prisons, having been appointed by his colleagues of the Conseil Supérieur.

After the conquest Jacques Imbert returned to France, and was at Nemours in July 1761. On 9 July 1764 he was commissioned by the minister of Marine, Choiseul, to supply certain information to aid in the redemption of the paper money for the years 1756, 1757, and 1758; on 29 Oct. 1758 documents concerning the expenses and receipts of the Domaine du Roi for these years had been put on board the *Sauvage*, which was captured by the English. Imbert died at Branches on 8 Sept. 1765.

Through hard work, intelligence, and a sense of order, Jacques Imbert was able to climb the various ranks of the financial administration of New France. During his career he associated with people in this field as important as Jean-Victor Varin* de La Marre, commissary and controller of the Marine, Joseph de FLEURY de La Gorgendière, agent of the Compagnie des Indes, and Thomas-Jacques Taschereau, agent of the treasurers-general.

ANDRÉ LACHANCE

AN, Col., B, 66, f.244v; 99, f.183; 102, f.202v; 107, f.22; 116, ff.140–40v; 122, ff.232–32v, 336v; 144, f.519; C¹¹ᴬ, 115, ff.34ff., 105v; 120, ff.333, 350v; E, 227 (dossier Jacques Imbert) (copies at PAC). ANQ, Greffe de Jacques Imbert, 1740–1749; Greffe de J.-C. Louet, 10 août 1743; NF, Coll. de pièces jud. et not., 2096, 2144; NF, Ord. int., XXVIII, 72v–73. *Documents relating to Canadian currency during the French period* (Shortt), II. P.-G. Roy, *Inv. jug. et délib., 1717–1760*, VI; VII, 4–5; *Inv. ord. int.*, III, 134, 152, 160. Tanguay, *Dictionnaire*. Nish, *Les bourgeois-gentilshommes*, 67–68. P.-G. Roy, *Bigot et sa bande*, 278–81.

ISBISTER, WILLIAM, HBC sailor, carpenter, fl. 1739–51.

A William Isbister, labourer, was sent home from York Fort (York Factory, Man.) in 1735; he appears to have been a different person from the subject of this biography, who was hired as a sailor by the Hudson's Bay Company in 1739. Isbister the sailor served on the *Eastmain* sloop out of Fort Albany (Ont.) for three years. During the 1742–43 season he was at Moose Fort (Moose Factory, Ont.) repairing the *Beaver* sloop. In July 1743 he was recalled to Albany by his brother Joseph*, who on his own initiative had decided to found the company's first inland post.

The spring trade at Albany in 1743 had been a disaster. Some French traders had established a camp near the junction of the Kenogami and Albany rivers and had intercepted the Indians on their way to the bay. Even the Home Indians (Crees), who lived nearest the bay, arrived dressed in French cloth. They reported that the traders intended to return to build a permanent post. Should they do so, wrote Joseph Isbister, "then may we Shut up Shop and go home." So on the north side of the junction he began constructing Henley House.

On 16 July 1743 William was appointed master of Henley and dispatched upriver to finish the project. The London committee issued strict instructions that the post's function was to stop the French from intercepting Indians on their way to Albany. Trading was to be kept to a minimum – to be done only in winter and to be in nothing but necessities such as powder and shot. For their part the Indians could never understand why they should make the long journey to Albany.

The loneliness of the site and the fear of an Indian or French attack on the little garrison may have contributed to William's attack of delirium tremens in the fall of 1745. Joseph reported that his brother was "taken ill with light-headedness and a sort of frenzy . . . got a fright." In fact, through continual drinking William had lost his senses and threatened to blow up Henley with gunpowder. His men had overpowered him and brought him handcuffed to Albany, where he talked like a madman all night. When he recovered, Joseph sent him back to Henley.

William kept his drinking under control for the next few years, although the situation at the post was difficult. In 1745–46 some French traders wintered upriver and carried off the trade of the upland Indians. During June and July 1746 the men were kept indoors at Henley in anticipation of an attack which never came. William had a relapse in 1749, when he stove in a barge loaded with goods for the post because he fell into a drunken stupor at the helm. Optimistically, he had requested a raise in pay to begin in 1750, but the HBC refused. In June 1750 he was reported to be mad drunk with brandy, and the men at

Henley stated they would rather go back to England than stay with him another year. He voluntarily returned home in 1751. Had he not done so, the London committee was prepared to order him back because of his "sottishness and ill Conduct."

GEORGE E. THORMAN

HBC Arch. A.6/6, f.33d; A.6/7, ff.16, 34, 70d, 76, 103d–5, 155, 161; A.6/8, f.63d; A.11/2, ff.111d, 116, 121, 124d, 128, 132d, 136, 140–41, 146, 148–48d; B.3/a/29–43, B.3/b/1, B.3/d/48–58, B.59/a/4–6, B.86/a/1–7. HBRS, XXV (Davies and Johnson), 326. Rich, *History of the HBC*, I.

ISHAM, JAMES, HBC factor, naturalist; b. *c.* 1716 in St Andrew's parish, Holborn, London, England, to Whitby Isham and Ann Skrimshire; m. 1748 in London to Catherine Mindham; d. 13 April 1761 at York Fort (York Factory, Man.).

James Isham began his career with the Hudson's Bay Company in 1732 and served at the bay continuously, with brief visits to England in 1737, 1745, 1748, and 1758, until his death. Although his English style, grammar, and spelling are always eccentric, his writings stand out as essential source-material for any approach to the fur trade of the 18th century, for an understanding of the problems of the HBC as it faced challenge and opposition, and for a study of the flora and fauna of Rupert's Land. Isham was at once a skilled and understanding trader, a perceptive planner and strategist, and a conscientious and observant natural historian.

He had received enough education to be employed at the HBC in 1732 as a "writer" and was sent to York Fort, there to be instructed in book-keeping. Later in his career Isham was to be accused of arbitrary rule, both in directing the trade of his post and in disciplining his men. Early reports, however, contain nothing but praise of his sober conduct, his industry, and the progress he made. In 1736, when he was only 20, he was appointed to be chief at York if Thomas WHITE should insist on going home; and in 1737, when White departed, Isham took command. He himself was anxious to go back to England, and initially he was appointed only till a replacement could arrive from home; but he stayed on until 1741, gaining in competence as a trader and acquiring knowledge of the "French Indians" who came down from the posts which Pierre GAULTIER de Varennes et de La Vérendrye was then establishing near Lac Ouinipigon (Lake Winnipeg). During this period Isham showed a shrewd independence of mind in his comments on the trade goods sent to him and in his answers

Isham

to the many inquiries addressed to him. He revealed a subtle understanding of Indian character, he increased the trade of his post, he began systematic reports on the men under his command, and he started to develop his interest in the natural history of the region.

The record of Isham's first serious contribution to this study comes from the naturalist George Edwards, who in 1750, in his *Natural history of uncommon birds*, pt.III, said he was indebted to Isham for more than 30 species of birds; eight of Isham's birds had never previously been described. Isham's "commendable curiosity," said Edwards, had led him to make a collection of birds, beasts, and fishes, as well as of the habits, toys, and utensils of the Indians. Isham brought the stuffed birds and beasts to London in good state in 1745. But his interest had been aroused earlier; he had done much of the work at York before 1741, and there he enjoyed the company of Alexander Light, shipwright, whose interest in natural history was equally deep and who also helped George Edwards in his publications.

Except that he had been overruled in his view that the old site of York Fort was too marshy to stand the weight of a stone building, everything was in Isham's favour when he was transferred to Churchill (Man.) in 1741; and the move was an act of confidence since it was the company's policy to concentrate trade behind the stone fortifications which were being erected at Churchill. York, though remaining to some extent the centre of an approach to the "Western Indians" and of a drive against French "encroachment," was to be subordinate to Churchill. But earlier ideas for using Churchill as the spring-board for a search for the rumoured Coppermine River and for developing trade with the Eskimos and Northern Indians were in abeyance. They had been frowned on since Arthur Dobbs had persuaded Sir Bibye Lake, governor of the HBC, to send Captain James Napper* on a voyage north from Churchill to Rankin Inlet in 1737. Dobbs and Captain Christopher MIDDLETON were not content to accept Napper's inconclusive voyage as the end of the search for a northwest passage, and in 1741 they got two naval vessels on loan for a further expedition under Middleton's command. As Isham went to Churchill in 1741 his orders from London were to give assistance to Middleton if he were in real distress or in danger of losing his ship. A supplementary order told Isham to give the best assistance in his power, and some more detailed instructions were given him verbally by Thomas White, freshly arrived from London to take over at York before Isham went to Churchill. Nevertheless Isham's precise course of conduct was not laid down, and he was somewhat at a loss on his arrival at Churchill in mid-August 1741 to find the two naval vessels already anchored and their crews preparing to spend the winter there.

Isham and Middleton were, however, well known to each other and they had much in common in their scientific curiosity and in their contempt for charlatans. Middleton's men, living in the old fort, suffered through the winter from frostbite, scurvy, idleness, and alcohol; 10 men died before spring. Isham found the explorers a distraction, a responsibility, and an annoyance; five of his men went with Middleton when he set forth in spring 1742, and he had to resort to thrashing and imprisonment to maintain his control over the remainder. But the two commanders appreciated each other, and while Middleton prevented his crews from trading furs Isham allowed his men to work for the expedition and accorded such fresh provisions and other amenities as he could afford. This sensible behaviour brought both men into disrepute, for Dobbs maintained that Middleton had been bribed to protect the company's trade and the company suspected that Isham had been too complaisant for the wrong reasons.

On the departure of the expedition Isham settled down to develop the trade of Churchill, to supervise the building of the fort (on which he made some caustic but sound comments which showed his independence of judgement), and to endure the ill health that always plagued him there. He apparently suffered from a bronchial complaint and was lame from gout and a strained groin from 1741 to 1743; in the latter year he asked to come home on account of his health. He was recalled only in 1745, after he had renewed his contract for a further three years in 1744, and not for health reasons but to be questioned about his conduct towards Middleton. He brought not only his birds and beasts with him, but writings he had put together in 1743: a "Vocabulary of English and Indian," an "Account of goods traded with discourses upon different subjects," "Observations upon Hudson's Bay," and a "Small account of the Northward Indian language, with a description of that part of the country towards the copper mines." In London he put these writings to the governor and committee. There is no evidence that they paid any attention to them, and the writings certainly did nothing to dispel the general ignorance about Hudson Bay since they were not published until 1949 [in HBRS, XII (Rich and Johnson)]. But the shrewd observation, wide knowledge, and naïvely attractive style entitle Isham to a high place in the literary history of Canada. His "Discourses" and his "Vocabulary of English and Indian" set out the essential phrases for the conduct of trade with the Crees, and his descriptions of the fur posts are invaluable. His notes on the flora and fauna, though sometimes fanciful, are a pioneer contribution to knowledge.

These are matters on which Isham's writings were to gather significance; of more immediate importance were his views on rivalry with French traders, on exploration-cum-trading expeditions, and on the possibility of reaching the rumoured copper mine. His "Observations" clearly set out his view that the English ought to go inland, to the country west of Churchill and south of the Hayes River and also to "the head of Port Nelson River" (somewhere in the region of the later Cumberland House, Sask.); and he advocated that a few good men should be sent to travel with Indians to ascertain the locality of the copper mine. He thought this "might sooner be Discover'd by Land then by Sea" and thereby he anticipated the plan which took Samuel Hearne* to the mouth of the Coppermine River in 1771. Although he referred to Middleton's attempts at astronomical observations and to a paper on "The effects of cold . . ." which Middleton had published, Isham did not, in his "Observations," directly refer to the explorers except to say that "it's not unlikely if a passage had been Discov'd in 1741 but the ships wou'd have fell in with the Copper Indians Country."

There can, however, be no doubt that Isham was closely questioned about the explorers; for Dobbs had openly parted from Middleton and was preparing an attack on the charter and trading privileges of the HBC. In March 1745 Dobbs had pushed through the House of Commons a report on the "Discovery of a north west passage, through Hudson's Straits" and a bill to reward any discoverer of the passage with £20,000. He and his backers then equipped two ships, the *Dobbs Galley* (Capt. William Moor) and the *California* (Capt. Francis Smith), for a voyage. It was to plan against this intervention that Isham had been called home, and it was in company with the *Dobbs Galley* and the *California* that he sailed to York again, to arrive late in August 1746.

Having come under suspicion for his conduct towards Middleton, and with strong instructions from his employers, Isham tried to avoid contact when the explorers decided to winter with him at York. Later, his conduct was called into question, and he was stung to write his "Notes on a voyage to Hudson's Bay" in answer to the "things which is neither consistant with truth, Justice, nor honour" that had been published in *A voyage to Hudson's-Bay* . . . by Henry Ellis, agent for the proprietors aboard the *Dobbs Galley*. Isham's journal, submitted to the governor and committee, leaves no doubt that he was as unhelpful as possible to the discoverers, that they were obstinate and ignorant, and that it was a dangerously uncomfortable winter for all concerned.

The voyage of the *Dobbs Galley* and the *California* in 1747 proved as inconclusive as Middleton's had been; but again Dobbs refused to accept the evidence. He challenged the company's charter before the privy council, the law officers of the crown, and ultimately before parliament. In March 1749 he secured the appointment of a parliamentary committee "to enquire into the state and condition of the countries adjoining to Hudson's Bay and of the trade carried on there." Isham would obviously be a key witness, and as pressure mounted the governor and committee ordered him home. He arrived in October 1748, and he gave valuable evidence before the parliamentary committee – evidence consistent with his long-held views that settlement by the shores of the bay was impossible since food crops could not be grown there, that inland posts were needed even at uneconomic costs in transportation, and that no practicable northwest passage existed.

The parliamentary inquiry vindicated the HBC, but when Isham was sent out again to York in 1750 it was not yet certain that opposition was over. He was therefore not appointed to York itself but to a small outpost, Flamborough House, planned to fight off interlopers from the sea. Isham took command at York on his arrival, however, since chief factor John Newton had drowned. He remained in command there until his death, with a brief return home for health and family reasons during 1758 and 1759.

At York during this last period Isham gave constant thought to French opposition, and he set the pattern that took English traders inland, to Lac Ouinipigon, to the Paskoya (Saskatchewan) River and the prairies, and even to the Rockies, in the next generation. He supported the building of a post at Severn River and the maintenance of Henley House (at the junction of the Albany and Kenogami rivers) as means of luring Indians away from the French, and he began a policy of sending adventurous men inland to make peace between warring Indians, to counteract French enticement, and to draw the Indians down the rivers past the French to trade at the bay. In 1754 he sent Anthony Henday in company with a band of Crees on an epic journey which took him to the Saskatchewan River, the prairies, the buffalo-hunts, and the horsed Siksika (Blackfoot) Indians, and in subsequent years sent him inland again several times. Isham's trade at York improved greatly as a result of such voyages, and he fostered a notable group of inland travellers (Joseph SMITH, Joseph Waggoner, William Grover, Isaac Batt*, and George Potts); he instilled his ideas into two later masters, Andrew Graham* and Humphrey Marten*, who always acknowledged their debt to him as the "beloved Friend" and "worthy Master" of their generation. Indeed, Isham's ideas were in advance of the governor and committee, for in 1756 he ordered Henday to choose a site for a post about 500 miles up-country. This was the thinking which went into the ultimate plan to establish Cumberland House.

Isham's detailed knowledge was unrivalled, but it did not obstruct perception. An acclaimed master to the traders, he was mourned at his death as "the Idol of the Indians." His comments and proposals were sound and shrewd; though they were not always adopted, they were never resented by his employers. But one thing was held against him – his Indian family. He had relations in England, and a daughter and his wife figure in his correspondence until the latter died in 1760, but on his death at York, 13 April 1761, he left all his property to his halfbreed son

Charles Thomas Price Isham*, himself destined to become a redoubtable traveller and trader in the service of the HBC.

E. E. RICH

HBC Arch. A.6; A.11/2, A.11/13, A.11/114; B.42/a; B.239/a; Arthur Dobbs folder. [William Coats], *The geography of Hudson's Bay: being the remarks of Captain W. Coats, in many voyages to that locality, between the years 1727 and 1751*, ed. John Barrow (Hakluyt Soc., 1st ser., XI, London, 1852). Arthur Dobbs, *An account of the countries adjoining to Hudson's Bay in the north-west part of America* (London, 1744; repr. New York, 1967); *Remarks upon Middleton's defence*. George Edwards, *A natural history of uncommon birds, and of some other rare and undescribed animals* . . . (4pt., London, 1743–51), pt.III. Henry Ellis, *A voyage to Hudson's-Bay by the Dobbs Galley and California, in the years 1746 and 1747, for discovering a north west passage* . . . (London, 1748). G.B., Parl., *Report from the committee on Hudson's Bay*. HBRS, XII (Rich and Johnson), XXV (Davies and Johnson), XXVII (Williams). Christopher Middleton, "The effects of cold; together with observations of the longitude, latitude, and declination of the magnetic needle, at Prince of Wales's fort, upon Churchill-River in Hudson's Bay . . . ," Royal Society *Philosophical Transactions* (London), XIII (1742–43), 157–71; *A vindication of the conduct of Captain Christopher Middleton* . . . (London, 1743). [Charles Swaine (T. S. Drage)], *An account of a voyage for the discovery of a north-west passage* . . . (2v., London, 1748–49). Morton, *History of the Canadian west*. Rich, *History of the HBC*, I.

J

JACQUIN, *dit* Philibert, NICOLAS, merchant trader, hero of the legend of the Golden Dog; b. 1700 in the small market-town of Martigny (Martigny-les-Bains, dept. of Vosges, France), son of Jean-Claude Jacquin, a merchant, and Anne Perrot; d. 21 Jan. 1748 in Quebec.

We do not know when Nicolas Jacquin, *dit* Philibert, came to live in New France. In 1733 he was already in business in Quebec; there on 23 November he married Marie-Anne Guérin, daughter of the tailor Louis Guérin. Of this marriage four children were born, the eldest of whom, Pierre-Nicolas, became one of the characters in William Kirby*'s famous novel, *The Golden Dog*. As a well-to-do merchant – he had eight domestic servants – Nicolas Jacquin seems to have been rather well known among the ruling class; he was purveyor to the troops for several years, and according to certain documents he is believed to have been king's purveyor. But it was

first and foremost through the legend about his name that he passed into history.

On 20 Jan. 1748 the bourgeois Philibert had a violent altercation with Pierre-Jean-Baptiste-François-Xavier Legardeur* de Repentigny, an officer in the colonial regular troops, over a billeting order the latter had received, authorizing him to be lodged by Philibert. Being unwilling to take him, Philibert is supposed to have gone to the home of a certain Mme Lapalme (perhaps Marie-Geneviève Pelletier, the widow of Pierre Janson, *dit* Lapalme), where the officer was already living, and to have asked her to keep the Sieur de Repentigny in her home. Having been unable to come to an agreement over the price of the room, he is supposed to have told the woman that he was going to have the order changed. Thereupon the officer intervened and told the merchant, among other things, "that he was a fool to want to make this change." Philibert was much offended, and "not content with uttering the most vulgar insults . . . struck him with his cane." Losing his temper, the officer is supposed to have "drawn his sword and wounded the aforementioned Philibert, who died as a result some time later." That is the version that can be read in the reprieve given the assailant by the king the following year. Another version, to be found in a letter sent by the merchants François HAVY and Jean LEFEBVRE to a correspondent in Montreal a week after the incident, gives a quite different account. According to these witnesses, the Sieur de Repentigny had begun heaping insults upon the merchant, and the discussion had continued on a very sharp note. Finally, it was said, the officer shoved the merchant out of the house, then went to his room to get his sword and ran after Philibert to inflict the sword thrust of which he died the following day. When the law proceeded against the Sieur de Repentigny, he fled to Fort Saint-Frédéric (Crown Point, N.Y.); on 20 March 1748 he was condemned by default to be decapitated. In April 1749, after his family had paid the victim's widow 8,675 *livres* 10 *sols* in damages and interest, he obtained his reprieve.

It was this incident, later related to an inscription on the façade of his house bearing the date 1736, that is, 12 years before Philibert's death, that gave rise to the legend of the Golden Dog. This inscription, which was accompanied by a bas-relief representing a dog holding a bone between its paws, read as follows:

JE SVIS VN CHIEN QVI RONGE LO
EN LE RONGEANT JE PREND MON REPOS
VN TEMS VIENDRA QVI NEST PAS VENV
QVE JE MORDERAY QVI MAVRA MORDV

and it is translated in Kirby's novel:

I am a dog that gnaws his bone,
I couch and gnaw it all alone –
A time will come, which is not yet,
When I'll bite him by whom I'm bit.

In 1759 the British officer John Knox* made the first allusion to the enigmatic inscription in his *Historical Journal*. Having been unable to obtain any information about its origins, he ventured an explanation that was, to say the least, fanciful: the dog was supposed to be the symbol of the colony's faithfulness in defending the country against the Indians. In 1829 the clergyman George Bourne* published a first account of the legend, which was repeated, with variants, by James Pattison Cockburn* in 1831 and Alfred Hawkins* in 1834. According to this account Philibert had put this inscription on the façade of his house for Intendant BÉGON's benefit, according to Hawkins, or for that of Bigot*, according to Bourne and Cockburn. The angry intendant is supposed to have had Philibert murdered by the Sieur de Repentigny, then allowed the officer to flee to India. Later, one of the victim's brothers is supposed to have caught up with the murderer in Pondicherry (India) and killed him in a duel.

In his novel, published in 1877, William Kirby took up the main elements of the legend, which he incorporated into his huge fresco and to which he added certain details borrowed from James MacPherson Le Moine*. Because of the many editions it has gone through, the work has certainly contributed to popularizing the legend of the Golden Dog.

As for the sign, which until this day decorates the façade of the post office located at the corner of Côte de la Montagne and Rue Buade (where Philibert's house stood), the best explanation of its origin is probably that offered by Benjamin Sulte*. Before 1700 the house in question was lived in by the surgeon Timothée Roussel*, who originally came from Montpellier in France. According to Sulte, some 40 kilometres from there, at Pézenas, was an inscription bearing the date 1561 which was nearly identical with the one in Quebec. It may fairly reasonably be supposed that the surgeon had wanted to reproduce the sign he had seen in his childhood and thus keep a memento of his native region. Again according to Sulte, the date 1736 was probably inscribed by Philibert when he made an addition to his new house.

JEAN-CLAUDE DUPONT

Knox, *Historical journal* (Doughty), 206–7. "Recensement de Québec, 1744" (APQ *Rapport*), 22, 29. Tanguay, *Dictionnaire*. George Bourne, *The picture of Quebec* (Quebec, 1829). [J. P. Cockburn], *Quebec and its environs; being a picturesque guide to the stranger* (Quebec, 1831). Alfred Hawkins, *Picture of Quebec with historical recollections* (Quebec, 1834). William Kirby, *The Golden Dog* (Rouses Point, N.Y., 1877). P.-G. Roy, *Toutes petites choses du régime français* (2 sér., Québec, 1944), 2e sér., 79–81. Léonce Jore, "Pierre, Jean-Baptiste, François-Xavier Le Gardeur de Repentigny," *RHAF*, XV (1961–62), 556–71. "L'origine du 'Chien d'Or'," *BRH*, XXII (1916), 15. P.-G. Roy, "L'histoire vraie du Chien d'Or," *Cahiers des Dix*, X (1945), 103–68. Benjamin Sulte, "Le Chien d'Or," *BRH*, XXI (1915), 270–73.

JAMET, JOHN, army officer; d. 2 June 1763 at Michilimackinac. His origins, like most of the rest of his life, are shrouded in obscurity.

Janson

Following Edward Braddock's defeat near Fort Duquesne (Pittsburgh, Pa.) in 1755, a new regiment, the Royal Americans, was raised to serve on the frontier. Since most recruits were Pennsylvania Dutch and could not speak English, it was necessary to appoint officers who could command them in their own language. John Jamet was one of these new officers.

He received a commission as ensign on 30 March 1758, and doubtless soon saw service at a frontier fort. He apparently served with some distinction with the regimental artillery. In the summer of 1761, when he was promoted lieutenant, he was the only experienced artillery officer in the Île Perrot (Montreal) garrison.

In the summer of 1762 Jamet arrived at Detroit with a detachment under Major Henry Gladwin*, the post's new commandant. On 3 September he was a member of a three-man court of inquiry appointed to determine whether any dereliction of duty was involved in Lieutenant Charles ROBERTSON's failure to locate a route for deep-draft vessels over the sand bars in Lake St Clair. When Captain George Etherington was dispatched to assume command of Michilimackinac a day or so later, Jamet and a small party of soldiers went along to take charge of the sub-post at Sault Ste Marie.

On 21 December a disastrous fire destroyed the soldiers' lodgings at the Sault, and Jamet, badly burned, barely escaped with his life. His little garrison retired to Fort Michilimackinac for the winter, Jamet being transported overland on an Indian sledge because he was too seriously injured to make the trip by boat.

Inspired by PONTIAC's siege of Detroit, some Ojibwas and Sauks distracted the guard detail at Michilimackinac with a game of lacrosse on 2 June 1763 and staged a surprise attack on the fort. Captain Etherington and another officer were seized at the outset. Jamet, by some accounts the only officer to offer any resistance, drew his sword and fought off several of the attackers before being struck down himself. The Indians then cut off his head and dispatched several other soldiers who had already surrendered. Father Pierre Du Jaunay*, the Jesuit priest at Michilimackinac, intervened to stop the slaughter, and it seems likely that he also had Jamet and the other fallen British soldiers buried in the graveyard at the post.

HARRY KELSEY

BM, Add. mss, 21661, f.178, Haldimand to Amherst, 21 Sept. 1761. DPL, Burton hist. coll., Porteous papers, John Porteous to his father, 20 Nov. 1763. Mackinac Island State Park Commission (Lansing, Mich.), Journals of the travels of Jonathan Carver in the year 1766 and 1767 (typescript copy), p.4. PRO, WO 34/49, return of the detachment of the Royal American Regiment, 23 Nov. 1762. *Army list, 1758,* 110; *1761,* 117. "Bouquet papers," *Michigan Pioneer Coll.,* XIX (1891), 161–62, 177, 182–83. Jonathan Carver, *Three years travels through the interior parts of North America . . .* (Glasgow, 1805), 32–33. *Diary of the siege of Detroit . . .,* ed. F. B. Hough (Albany, 1860), 30–31. Great Britain, *Statutes,* 29 George II, c.5. [James Gorrell], "Lieut. James Gorrell's journal," Wis. State Hist. Soc. *Coll.,* I ([1854]), 24–48. Alexander Henry, *Travels and adventures in Canada and the Indian territories between the years 1760 and 1776,* ed. James Bain (Boston, 1901; repr. Edmonton, 1969), 78–79. *JR* (Thwaites), LXX, 250–54. "Memoir of Charles Langlade," Wis. State Hist. Soc. *Coll.,* VII (1876), 156. R. W. Hale, *The Royal Americans* (William L. Clements Library *Bull.,* XLI, Ann Arbor, Mich., 1944). Francis Parkman, *The conspiracy of Pontiac and the Indian war after the conquest of Canada* (10th ed., 2v., Boston, 1886; repr. New York, 1962). Peckham, *Pontiac.*

JANSON (Jeanson), *dit* **Lapalme, DOMINIQUE,** architect, land surveyor; b. 2 April 1701 at Quebec, son of Pierre Janson, *dit* Lapalme, and Madeleine-Ursule Rancin; d. 27 May 1762 at Quebec.

The Janson, *dit* Lapalme, family had a strong craft tradition. The progenitor of this clan was Pierre Janson, *dit* Lapalme, a Parisian stonemason who was brought to Canada in 1688 by Bishop Saint-Vallier [La Croix*]. Pierre Janson was indentured to the Quebec seminary and during his term of service worked on the parish church of Quebec. He later became a partner of Jean Le Rouge*, a masonry contractor, and one of their works was the Saint-Louis gate of Quebec. In 1708 Janson received a land surveyor's commission, and he went to Montreal soon after, his family following in 1710.

Pierre Janson, *dit* Lapalme, evidently had a reputation for fine stonework. In 1710 he was engaged to complete the lower façade of Notre-Dame de Montréal and in 1712 and 1719 he undertook work on the façade of the Recollet chapel and the body of the Jesuit church in Montreal. He was also the builder and architect of the second church at Varennes in 1718. None of his major works has survived to the present day.

Pierre was thrice married and he fathered 22 children. Of the seven sons who reached adulthood, Christophe, Louis, Dominique, Charles, and Philippe became stonemasons. Such trade solidarity was common in France but it was rare in the freer society of New France. Dominique was the most successful son. He was probably trained as a mason and stone-cutter by his father, and was, to judge from subsequent crown contracts and appointments, a competent draughts-

306

man. The Quebec seminary possesses two books by Augustin-Charles Daviler, *L'architecture de Vignole avec les commentaires du Sr Daviler* (Paris, 1720) and *Explication des termes d'architecture* (Paris, 1720) that Dominique used.

At the age of 25, Dominique was already an independent stonemason and contractor in Montreal. In July 1726 he promised to build a two-storey stone house for Pierre de LESTAGE "following the plan and drawings that will be given to him." On 12 February of that year, Janson, who styled himself "architect and masonry contractor," had married Marie-Joseph, the 17-year-old daughter of the Montreal builder Pierre Couturier*, *dit* Le Bourguignon. His brother Louis had married in 1722 another daughter of Couturier, Jeanne-Charlotte.

Janson's fortune was favoured by a program of military construction in the 1730s. He was a capable builder but private contracts usually offered only limited profits. In 1731 he won the crown contracts for three of the four major gates into Montreal and parts of the town wall. Intendant Gilles Hocquart* wrote on 18 Oct. 1731 that he "granted the undertaking [for the gates] to Sieur LaPalme who will complete it in accordance with the estimate of Sieur [Gaspard-Joseph CHAUSSEGROS de Léry]. . . . Sieur LaPalme is a very good worker."

Work on the fortifications continued into 1734 when Lapalme received a primary contract for Fort Saint-Frédéric (Crown Point, N.Y.). In late 1734 and early 1735 Janson hired masons and stone-cutters in Quebec and Montreal. He also contracted with quarrymen, lime-burners, draymen, and a man to mix mortar for the great project. Although he still lived in Montreal, he was a frequent visitor at Fort Saint-Frédéric in the period 1735–42. In 1742 he was entrusted with work on the side chapels of Notre-Dame de Montréal church.

His major undertaking as a masonry contractor was for the gates and watch towers (*guérites*) of Quebec. The capture of Louisbourg, Île Royale (Cape Breton Island), in 1745 led to the decision to complete Quebec's defences, and the work there lasted until 1749. Dominique took on Michel Denis and his own brothers, Philippe and Charles, as partners. The partners disagreed over the sharing of the profits and Charles went his own way after 1746.

Dominique received official recognition from the crown in 1751. On 10 September he was given the title of "king's architect" with a commission "to serve under our [the intendant's] orders or for the convenience of private citizens who are building houses." This post did not, it seems, involve any novel duties. Dominique had already served the crown and public as a builder and architect and he continued to act, but with greater frequency, as a surveyor and legal estimator. Quebec was now to be Janson's permanent home. His wife, who had borne him no children, died a few weeks after they had moved into their new home on Rue de la Fabrique.

Janson's appointment as king's architect prepared him for the higher post of acting chief road commissioner (*grand voyer*). In 1757 he was performing the duties of a deputy road commissioner in Quebec, that is, establishing property alignments and severances. He first appears as acting chief road commissioner in November 1758 and he continued to exercise this office until his death in 1762. He left no descendants. His second marriage, to Madeleine Trefflé, *dit* Rottot, young widow of the merchant Luc Schmid, was also childless.

Janson's career was produced by a mixture of talent and good luck. Like Jean-Baptiste MAILLOU, *dit* Desmoulins, an earlier king's architect in New France, Dominique Janson had a chance to show his ability in the execution of military building contracts. Thus he came to the attention of the government and became a candidate for an official appointment.

Both Pierre and Dominique Janson, *dit* Lapalme, planned many of the private structures that they built, but their major undertakings usually followed the plans of others. Their careers show that an architect in New France was not necessarily the designer of a building. The term "architect" was given to a builder who understood the terminology of architecture and who was capable of superintending construction according to another's design.

PETER N. MOOGK

AJQ, Registre d'état civil, Notre-Dame de Québec, 9 nov. 1751, 15 avril 1761, 29 mai 1762; Registre d'état civil, fort Beauharnois de la Pointe-à-la-Chevelure, 24 juill. 1735, 7 oct. 1742. AN, Col., C¹¹ᴬ, 55, pp.183–84; Section Outre-Mer, G³ [many original, notarized contracts for the crown were taken to France after the conquest and may now be found in this series which also contains Chaussegros de Léry's specifications for the fortifications at Montreal and Saint-Frédéric. P.N.M.] (copies at PAC). ANQ, Greffe de R.-C. Barolet, 27 oct. 1734, 10 oct. 1747, 24 sept. 1751, 15 mai 1755; Greffe de Louis Chambalon, 18 déc. 1701, 28 févr. 1703, 10 juin 1704; Greffe de François Genaple de Bellefonds, 3 juin 1693; Greffe de J.-C. Panet, 24 août 1752, 12 avril 1761; Greffe de Simon Sanguinet, 26 oct. 1751, 20 juin 1755; AP, Dominique Janson-Lapalme; NF, Coll. de pièces jud. et not., 1325, 1836, 1895, 1924. ANQ-M, Greffe de J.-B. Adhémar, 12, 14, 22 nov. 1734, 3 mai 1735; Greffe de N.-A. Guillet de Chaumont, 8, 9, sept. 1732; Greffe

Jarret

de Michel Lepailleur, 11 févr. 1726, *passim*; Greffe de J.-C. Raimbault, 27 févr. 1729, 9 mai 1731, 18 sept. 1732, 26 mars 1735; Greffe de Pierre Raimbault, 7 juill. 1726. ASQ, Seigneuries, VIII, 20, 20A; Séminaire, XXXVII, 88, 89; CCII, 122. PAC, MG 24, L3, pp.22253–58, 22409–16, 22460–64, 25714–17, 25910–13 (sales of property made to and by Pierre and Dominique Janson Lapalme before Montreal notaries in the period 1715–18).

L'île de Montréal en 1731 (A. Roy), 43. *Inv. des papiers de Léry* (P.-G. Roy), II, 89. É.-Z. Massicotte, "Maçons, entrepreneurs, architectes," *BRH*, XXXV (1929), 139–40. P.-G. Roy, *Inv. jug. et délib., 1717–1760*, IV, 302; V, 189; *Inv. ord. int.*, II, 232; III, 87, 159. Pierre Mayrand, *Sources de l'art en Nouvelle-France* (Québec, 1963). Gowans, *Church architecture in New France*. Gérard Morisset, *L'architecture en Nouvelle-France* (Québec, 1949), 133.

JARRET DE VERCHÈRES, MARIE-MADE-LEINE (more often called **Madeleine**, and sometimes **Madelon**) (**Tarieu de La Pérade**), b. 3 March 1678 at Verchères (Que.) and baptized 17 April, fourth of the 12 children of François Jarret de Verchères and Marie Perrot; buried 8 Aug. 1747 at Sainte-Anne-de-la-Pérade (Que.).

Madeleine's father, François Jarret, originally came from Saint-Chef (dept. of Isère), France. Born around 1641, he was about 24 when he landed at Quebec in August 1665 with the company commanded by his uncle, Antoine Pécaudy* de Contrecœur, in the Régiment de Carignan. Once the Iroquois had been subdued he decided to settle in Canada, following his uncle's example. On 17 Sept. 1669 he married a peasant girl of twelve and a half years of age, Marie Perrot, at Sainte-Famille, Île d'Orléans. Jarret himself was not "of noble birth" as has been said: in 1672 and 1674 Frontenac [Buade*] sought letters of nobility for him, without success, in recognition of his continuing services.

His title as an ensign in the Carignan regiment, however, and probably his uncle's support brought him the grant by Intendant Talon* on 29 Oct. 1672 of land with a frontage and a depth of a league, on the south shore of the St Lawrence. The new seigneury, called Verchères, was enlarged in August 1673 by two islands directly in front of it, the Île aux Prunes and the Île Longue, and in October 1678 – the year of Madeleine's birth – another league was added to the back of the original grant.

Although M. de Verchères campaigned occasionally, he did not neglect his seigneury. In 1681 he had 11 *censitaires* at least, and some 120 acres of land were under tillage. The seigneur himself had 20 acres, and, according to the census, 13 cattle and five muskets. The firearms – there were 15 in the seigneury – were necessary; the

Iroquois were beginning to maraud again in the region, the most exposed in Canada because of the proximity of the Richelieu River (or "Rivière des Iroquois") which this redoubtable enemy used to penetrate the colony. Verchères and the neighbouring lands of Contrecœur and Saint-Ours were to be threatened still more in the terrible years to come for the Iroquois used them as short cuts to avoid the fort at Sorel.

Like many other seigneurs, M. de Verchères had a fort built for the protection of his family and *censitaires*: a rough, rectangular stockade 12 to 15 feet high, with a bastion at each corner; it had no moats, and a single gate, on the river side. Inside were the seigneur's manor-house, a redoubt which served as guard-house and magazine, and probably some temporary building which could shelter the women, children, and animals in case of danger. One or two guns, probably just swivel guns intended to sound the alarm rather than repulse the enemy, completed this modest defensive system.

The years went by, and the seigneur's children grew rapidly, at least those who survived. In 1692, when Madeleine was nearing 14 years of age, she had already lost her older brother Antoine, who had died in 1686; two brothers-in-law, both of whom had been married to Marie-Jeanne and had been killed by the Iroquois, one in 1687, the other in 1691; her brother François-Michel, also killed by the Iroquois in 1691 at 16 years of age. Six brothers and sisters came after her, their ages varying from 12 to two (two boys had not yet been born). A fine family, which seemed to attract the fury of the Iroquois.

One day in 1690 the alert had been close at the manor-house, and the little group had been in great danger. Knowing that it was almost defenceless, the Iroquois tried to scale the stockade; a few musket shots made them fall back at first. Mme de Verchères, who was 33 at that time, had only three or four men with her. She took command and repulsed the attackers several times. Did she sustain the attack in the fort, as CHARLEVOIX maintains, or in a redoubt more than 50 paces outside the stockade, as La Potherie [Le Roy*] claims? It does not much matter. According to Madeleine the redoubt was within the walls of the fort: it would have served as a reduit if the Iroquois had breached the stockade. The siege lasted two days, and with the bearing of a veteran Mme de Verchères finally forced the enemy to retire. She had lost only one combatant, whose name was L'Espérance.

The same scene and the same peril were to be repeated two years later. Mme de Verchères would be absent this time, in Montreal, as was her husband, called to Quebec. It was Madeleine who in her 15th year would have to play the role her mother had played so well in 1690. Had she perhaps helped her at that time? Instinctively she assumed the same attitude and carried out the same actions, adding, it appears, a dash of boldness befitting her age if not her sex.

There are five accounts of the siege of 1692: two by Madeleine herself, two by La Potherie (in the same work, the second correcting in part the first), and one by Charlevoix. They were all composed after the event, Madeleine's first one being the closest to it, although it was not made until 15 Oct. 1699; her second was not made before 1722; La Potherie's and Charlevoix's date respectively from about 1700 and 1721. The heroine's original narration, contained in a letter to the Comtesse de Maurepas, was attested to by Intendant Champigny [Bochart*]. It agrees fairly well with those by La Potherie and Charlevoix, since Charlevoix had followed La Potherie and La Potherie, who knew Madeleine, had certainly seen her letter, if indeed he had not suggested it to her himself, dictating it to her word by word.

On 22 Oct. 1692 then, at eight o'clock in the morning, with only one soldier on duty at the fort of Verchères, some Iroquois, who had been hidden in the thickets nearby, suddenly seized some 20 settlers working in the fields. Madeleine, who was 400 paces from the stockade, was pursued and quickly overtaken by an Iroquois who seized her by the kerchief she was wearing around her neck; she loosened it and rushed into the fort, closing the gate behind her. Calling to arms and without stopping to listen to the cries of some women who were distressed at seeing their husbands carried off, she wrote, "I went up on the bastion where the sentry was. . . . I then transformed myself, putting the soldier's hat on my head, and with some small gestures tried to make it seem that there were many people, although there was only this soldier." She fired a round from the gun against the attackers, which "fortunately had all the success I could hope for in warning the neighbouring forts to be on their guard, lest the Iroquois do the same to them."

According to La Potherie the noise of the cannon "struck [the Iroquois] with terror, upset all their calculations and at the same time signalled all the forts on the north and south shores of the river from Saint-Ours as far as Montreal to be on their guard. With each fort passing the word on to the next after the first signal from Verchères, up to Montreal a hundred men were sent to bring it help, which arrived shortly after the Iroquois had disappeared into the woods."

Charlevoix, the least exact of the three narrators, puts Madeleine 200 paces from the fort when the Iroquois appeared, agreeing on this point with La Potherie, but he simply states that all the settlers were taken by the Iroquois, who pursued Madeleine until one of them had seized her by her neckerchief. La Potherie, on the contrary, gives more details than Madeleine does, saying that 40 to 50 Iroquois surrounded the fort after seizing 22 settlers, 20 of whom were burned, and that two Iroquois fired on the girl during the pursuit (first account); that (second account) 40 Iroquois, after taking a score of settlers threatened the fort and fired four or five rounds with their muskets at Madeleine, without wounding her. For the rest, the narratives agree; in the end the heroine's first account, simple and plausible, seems the one most deserving of belief.

Up to this point there is nothing astonishing and nothing to make the daughter's resistance more noteworthy than the mother's – unless it were Madeleine's age; but in New France many girls of 14 were married and had children, or, like Marie-Jeanne de Verchères, were already widowed. As for the 20 settlers burned by the enemy, La Potherie himself set the facts straight by telling later how a party of friendly Indians freed these unfortunates in the region of Lake Champlain. The absence of civil records and the silence of the authorities prevent us from knowing how many victims there were. They could not have been numerous, since of the 11 tenants in 1681, eight died before or after this affair – and the other three need not have perished in it. In her second account Madeleine speaks of only two deaths.

About Madeleine's first account there is a disturbing fact which historians have not noted, namely the perfect concordance between her narration and La Potherie's second one, the correspondence often being word for word:

Madeleine: "Comme je conservé, dans ce fatal moment, le peux dasseurance Dont une fille est Capable et peut être armée, Je luy Laissay entre Les mains mon mouchoir de Col et Je fermay la porte sur moy en Criant aux armes et sans marrester aux gemissement de plusieurs femmes désolées de voir enlever leurs Maris, Je monté sur le bastion où estoit le sentinelle."

La Potherie: "mais elle conserva dans le moment plus d'assurance que n'en pouvait avoir une Fille de quatorze ans, elle lui laissa entre les mains son mouchoir de col se jettant dans son Fort, dont elle ferma la porte sur elle en criant aux armes, & sans s'arrêter aux gémissements de plusieurs femmes désolées de voir enlever leurs maris, elle monta sur un Bastion où était la Sentinelle."

And so on, except for some details.

Jarret

Is it possible that Madeleine was not the author of the account attributed to her, having simply copied the text composed by La Potherie? In that event her testimony would not be as spontaneous or as naïve as has been believed. Or was it the terrible La Potherie who plagiarized Madeleine? As a consequence one would have to deduce that the details given by him and taken up in part by Charlevoix, all of them tending to dramatize the action, had been rejected by Madeleine as not being in keeping with the truth or had been invented outright by La Potherie after the event, which amounts to the same thing. – Or had Madeleine not wanted to scare the Comtesse? An oratorical preamble at the beginning of her letter might suggest it: "Although my sex does not permit me to have inclinations other than those it demands of me, allow me nevertheless, Madame, to tell you that, like many men, I have feelings which incline me to glory." – On balance, and since we are in doubt, we must keep to the account signed by the heroine and witnessed by Champigny.

It is not the first account that is perplexing but the second one, which was first published in 1901 and which launched the "legend" of Madeleine. Much more detailed and dramatic, it constantly puts the heroine in the forefront. It differs from the first on several points and sometimes completes it: there are now 45 Iroquois pursuing her, who give up trying to catch her and fire on her: the shots from 45 muskets whistle about her ears, she writes; the episode of the kerchief, which is no longer believable, disappears from the story; once she is inside the fort she no longer rushes to the bastion; rather, she inspects the stockade and repairs the holes in it, setting the stakes up again herself with the help of the people present, more numerous than one would have thought; in addition to the women and children, whom she tries to quiet, there are her servant Laviolette, her two young brothers, Pierre* and Alexandre, 12 and 10 years old, an 80-year-old man, and two soldiers, Labonté and Galhet, whom she finds in the redoubt, terrified and ready to set fire to the stocks of powder; all these people shoot at the enemy, even firing the cannon under the direction of Madeleine, her hair in disorder and a man's hat on her head; this combat goes on for a week, before M. de La Monnerie comes to the rescue with a detachment sent from Montreal by Louis-Hector de Callière*.

Gone are the sobriety, the moderation, and the plausibility of the earlier account! Who will believe that a 14-year-old girl outran 45 Iroquois over a distance of 5 *arpents* (1,000 feet), when no white man could compete with these Indians? Or

that 45 muskets all missed her, when the Iroquois, half a century earlier, had been using them "with skill and daring," according to the Jesuit Barthélemy Vimont*? How was she able, without any accident, to repair the holes in a wall surrounded by the enemy, with her men busy fixing the heavy stakes in place instead of keeping the attackers at bay? Finally, is it conceivable that the siege lasted a week if, as all versions say, she gave the alarm by firing the gun at the very beginning? The distance between Montreal and Verchères (about 12 leagues) was not so great that it took a week to cover it, sailing down the river. Did not help reach her mother in less than two days in 1690? If the siege had lasted so long, Madeleine would have said so in her first account, and La Potherie would have expressed himself quite differently in the text quoted above.

The Indians, moreover, were not acquainted with siege techniques and never lingered when, the first moment of surprise being past, a reception was prepared for them. As they had no defensive arms and did not like costly victories, they did not expose themselves, counting only on ruse to win. Madeleine knew this: on the first night cattle which had escaped being massacred came to low at the gate of the fort; immediately she thought of a "trick" by the enemy, whom she imagined coming behind the animals, covered with skins. In addition, the cannon terrified the Indians: according to La Potherie the first shot Madeleine fired from it "upset all their calculations." Finally, it was customary for the Indians as soon as they had taken some prisoners – they held 20 odd in this case – to give up and go home. This is certainly what they did here, as a passage by La Potherie appears to confirm: the alarm was spread with cannon from one fort to another as far as Montreal – certainly the same day, since the siege began at eight in the morning; "scarcely was this news known than the Chevalier de Crizafi [Thomas Crisafy*] was sent by water with one hundred men . . . while fifty Indians hastened by land. . . . Monsieur de Crizafi arrived an hour after the Iroquois had withdrawn, but our Indians caught up with them on Lake Champlain after a six-day march." Must we not take this to mean that six or seven days after the beginning of the siege the Iroquois were already at Lake Champlain, having covered about the same distance as the Indians from Montreal, and consequently taken the same amount of time?

As in 1690 then, the Iroquois probably withdrew on the second day, shortly before the arrival of La Monnerie or Crisafy, and with all the more reason since, if we are to believe Madeleine, she had succeeded in giving them the impression that the fort was swarming with soldiers. She probably exaggerated a little in writing that for the first 48 hours she went without eating or sleeping and without going into her father's house. Otherwise, she talks only of what took place on the first day, which she calls the day of the great battle, and on the first night, during which the Indians did not show themselves – probably a sign that nothing happened on the second day or on the following ones.

On the first day, according to her second account, Madeleine is supposed to have made three sorties, one, by herself, to cover the landing of Pierre Fontaine, *dit* Bienvenu, and his family, who arrived by canoe, and two others, with her young brothers, to pick up three bags of laundry and some blankets that she had left on the shore. Each sortie had to cover five *arpents* in each direction, while, according to her, the Indians surrounded the fort. "That is enough," she wrote "to give you an idea of my assurance and calm." In all then, she is supposed that day to have covered 35 *arpents* (a mile and a quarter) without a scratch, in the face of or within musket shot of 45 Iroquois! Let us speak no more of temerity, but of invulnerability and miracles, and let us keep to the first account, in which the daughter proves herself worthy of her mother, without putting her in the shade.

After the prisoners' return, life went on as usual in the seigneury. For the Jarrets de Verchères two more births in 1693 and 1695 came to complete the family. The father, a half-pay lieutenant since 1694, died on 26 Feb. 1700. The pension of 150 *livres* he received as a former officer in the Régiment Carignan was then transferred to Madeleine in consideration of her exploit in 1692 and on condition that she provide for her mother's needs. (Mme de Verchères was buried on her seigneury on 30 Sept. 1728.) Madeleine, who had an "agreeable personality and an energetic air, but also the modesty of her sex," and who was a "sensible" girl, had to put off her marriage until she was 28, probably to manage the seigneury and to keep her family from falling into "the deepest poverty." Perhaps she spent her spare time hunting, since, according to La Potherie, there was "no Canadian or officer who was a better musket shot" than she. She was married in September 1706 to Pierre-Thomas Tarieu de La Pérade, a lieutenant in a company of the colonial regular troops. In the marriage contract Madeleine declared that she was bringing a dowry of 500 *livres* "accumulated through her savings and care." The couple went to live on the north shore, at Sainte-Anne-de-la-Pérade, of which Tarieu was in part seigneur.

The Sieur de La Pérade's father, Thomas de Lanouguère*, who was born around 1644 in Mirande (dept. of Gers), France, of an old noble family, had arrived in Canada with the Régiment de Carignan. On 29 Sept. 1670 Edmond de Suève and he bought the seigneury of Sainte-Anne, near Batiscan, from Michel Gamelain* de La Fontaine. Talon confirmed their rights to this land on 29 Oct. 1672. The co-seigneurs soon divided the seigneury between them, Lanouguère keeping the western part and Suève the eastern. In 1707 the latter part was willed to Edmond Chorel de Saint-Romain, who made it over on 14 March 1714 to his brother, François Chorel de Saint-Romain, *dit* d'Orvilliers (whence the name of the fief of Dorvilliers). M. de Lanouguère, who had married Marguerite-Renée Denys de La Ronde at Quebec on 16 Oct. 1672, probably died in May 1678; he left a daughter, Louise-Rose, who became an Ursuline, and two sons, Louis, who died around 1692, and Pierre-Thomas, who was born on 11 September and baptized in Quebec on 12 Nov. 1677, Madeleine de Verchères's future husband. On 4 March 1697 Frontenac and Champigny made a grant to Mme de Lanouguère of three more leagues to the rear of her seigneury, across its whole width, and on 6 April of that year they confirmed her property rights to the islands in front of her land; Mme de Lanouguère received a new grant of these islands on 30 Oct. 1700. Finally, on 4 Nov. 1704, she made over all her rights to the seigneury of Sainte-Anne to her son, Pierre-Thomas, who was owner through a grant made on 30 Oct. 1700 of the fief of Tarieu (measuring two leagues by one and a half) located to the north of his mother's seigneury. Mme de Lanouguère was married again in 1708, her second husband being Jacques-Alexis Fleury* Deschambault, and went to Montreal to live. In 1721 Pierre-Thomas's patrimony was further enlarged by a share in the seigneury of Verchères which fell to Madeleine, and on 20 April 1735 by the addition of three more leagues of land to the fief of Tarieu across its entire width.

These lands and the relations of the habitants with their seigneurs gave rise to many lawsuits, with the result that it has been possible to write articles entitled "Madeleine de Verchères, plaideuse" ("Madeleine de Verchères, litigant") and "Madeleine de Verchères et Chicaneau" ("Madeleine de Verchères and Chicaneau"). Historians have made Madeleine responsible for nearly all these quarrels (too numerous and varied to be related here), but a closer study of each case reveals that traditional affirmations require some modification. In speaking of the first "lawsuit" for example (1708), Pierre-Georges

Jarret

Roy* wrote that Messrs de Suève and de La Pérade, "neighbours for 20 years, had never had words." "Scarcely had Madeleine de Verchères entered the manor-house of La Pérade," he added, "than quarrelling began between the two neighbours over the boundaries of their land grants." In fact there was no discussion with M. de Suève, since he had been dead for a year, but with his heir, Edmond Chorel de Saint-Romain; and it was the latter who claimed a certain piece of land from M. de La Pérade, who simply asked the intendant to appoint a surveyor, promising to respect the dividing line to be traced at that time. There was thus no lawsuit, no quarrel, and in any case Madeleine had nothing to do with the matter. Pierre-Georges Roy's account of the second "lawsuit" contains a similar error; as for the third, he blamed Madeleine for some acts of violence for which her mother-in-law, Mme de Lanouguère, was responsible. The same can be said of many of the "lawsuits" in Madeleine's career. In about half the litigations the seigneurs of La Pérade did not start the contestation, and most often their rights were upheld; in the other cases they usually appear to have been justified in resorting to the courts of justice, which were generally favourable to them.

One does not, however, need to exonerate the seigneur of La Pérade and his wife entirely. Certainly the two of them were ill tempered, and on occasion they threatened and terrorized their *censitaires* and even committed serious acts of violence against them. M. de La Pérade in particular sometimes lost his head. A *censitaire* who had had to snatch a musket from his hands declared that the settlers' lives were "in very great danger, since they are dealing with a furious man who is out of his mind, as he frequently is to everyone's knowledge." The seigneur's fits of anger, and sometimes those of his wife, who strongly supported him, explain why they were not loved by those about them. Their tenants tried to avoid them, and perhaps even to do them harm: for instance, they went to have their grain ground in a neighbouring seigneury rather than at the banal mill of Sainte-Anne, and one farmer asked for the cancellation of a farm lease immediately after signing it because of the Sieur de La Pérade's rages, which he considered a constant threat to his life. (Would these bad relations with his employees and farmers explain his recourse to slaves for the work around his house?) The parish priest himself, Joseph Voyer, did not refrain on occasion from enraging the seigneurs, who showed a little too clearly their preference for his *confrère*, Gervais Lefebvre from Batiscan.

For years Abbé Lefebvre acted as "director" for the La Pérade family. Suddenly in 1730 he had the two Tarieus summoned before the provost court of Quebec, complaining that Madeleine in particular had accused him in public of having composed and sung some burlesque rigmaroles full of impious, obscene, and defamatory terms, of having made insulting and salacious remarks about the La Pérade family, and having incited a woman to take a false oath by promising her absolution. The witnesses were heard, the lawyers' addresses prepared, the speech for the prosecution delivered, and the parish priest was sentenced in a judgement rendered on 29 Aug. 1730 to pay 200 *livres* in damages and interest to the seigneurs of La Pérade. M. Lefebvre appealed his case to the Conseil Supérieur; he defended himself there so well that the curious judgement of the provost court was upset on 23 Dec. 1730. Madeleine, who did not like defeats, could not resign herself to this one. In 1732 she sailed for France to put her case before the king's council. She was admitted into the ministries, but the appeal was refused. Did she have time to search, as her brothers and sisters had asked her to do, for property that might belong to them in the mother country as a consequence of their father's death? She sailed again in the spring of 1733 on the king's ship. At the suggestion of the minister of Marine, Maurepas, however, and with the intervention of the colonial authorities the lawsuit was settled out of court by notarial deed on 21 Oct. 1733. According to the arrangement Abbé Lefebvre released M. and Mme de La Pérade from the convictions they had incurred on condition that there was no more talk of this scandalous affair on either side. Madeleine, who signed the deed in her own name and as her husband's representative, had won the day.

Many other judicial or military exploits have been attributed to her. But legend is generous towards those who have once brought themselves to the attention of posterity. Of the three or four feats of arms claimed for her in addition to the siege of 1692, it seems that only one in 1722 must be retained, when she saved her husband's life after he was attacked by two colossal Indians, disabling one while the other was being subdued. Immediately she was surrounded by four enraged Indian women who would have killed her if her 12-year-old son, Charles-François, the worthy offspring of this "Amazon," had not freed her from them. Madeleine recounted this action herself, and Charles de BEAUHARNOIS later verified it personally. (It was in this account that she declared she had never shed a tear.)

Madeleine died at Sainte-Anne-de-la-Pérade

and was buried on 8 Aug. 1747 underneath her pew in the parish church. She was 69 years of age. A surprising number of priests were present at her funeral: the parish priests of Sainte-Anne-de-la-Pérade, Saint-Joseph (Deschambault), Sainte-Geneviève (Batiscan), Saint-Charles-des-Roches (Saint-Charles-des-Grondines), Saint-Pierre-les-Becquets (Les Becquets), and perhaps some others, had been anxious to pay her a final homage.

Pierre-Thomas Tarieu de La Pérade outlived her by nearly ten years. He was buried at Sainte-Anne-de-la-Pérade on 26 Jan. 1757, at 79 years of age.

ANDRÉ VACHON

AJTR, Greffe de Jean Cusson, 5 juin 1695; Greffe de Daniel Normandin, 14 mars 1714; Greffe d'A.-B. Pollet, 5 mars 1746. AN, Col., C¹¹ᴬ, 18, p.69 (PAC transcript). ANQ, Greffe de Louis Chambalon, 31 août 1711; Greffe de Pierre Duquet, 7 sept. 1669, 29 sept. 1670, 27 oct. 1676; Greffe de François Genaple de Bellefonds, 4 nov. 1704; Greffe d'Henry Hiché, 21 oct. 1733; AP, Coll. P.-G. Roy, Verchères et Jarret de Verchères; AP, Madame de Maurepas; NF, Coll. de pièces jud. et not., 550½, 886, 2426, 2675; NF, Foi et hommage, *passim*; NF, Ins. Cons. sup., *passim*; NF, Ord. int., *passim*; NF, Registres de la Prévôté de Québec, *passim*; NF, Registres d'intendance, *passim*; NF, Registres du Cons. sup., *passim*. ANQ-M, Greffe d'Antoine Adhémar, 29 mars, 22 oct. 1710; Greffe de René Chorel de Saint-Romain, 6 juill. 1732; Greffe de Michel Lepailleur, 8 sept. 1706. Charlevoix, *Histoire de la N.-F.* (1744), III, 123–25. "Correspondance de Vaudreuil," APQ *Rapport, 1939–40, passim*. "Correspondance échangée entre la cour de France et le gouverneur de Frontenac, pendant sa seconde administration (1689–1699)," APQ *Rapport, 1926–27, passim*; *1927–28, passim. Édits ord.*, II, III, *passim. Jug. et délib.*, *passim*. [C.-C. Le Roy] de Bacqueville de La Potherie, *Histoire de l'Amérique septentrionale* . . . ([2ᵉ éd.], 4v., Paris, 1753), I, 313, 324–28; III, 150–55. PAC *Report*, 1899, supp., 5–12. "Recensement du Canada, 1681" (Sulte). Le Jeune, *Dictionnaire*. Tanguay, *Dictionnaire*. F.-A. Baillairgé, *Marie-Madeleine de Verchères et les siens* (Verchères, Qué., 1913). François Daniel, *Histoire des grandes familles françaises du Canada* . . . (Montréal, 1867), 447–80. A. G. Doughty, *A daughter of New France; being a story of the life and times of Magdelaine de Verchères, 1665–1692* (Ottawa, 1916). Raymond Douville, *Les premiers seigneurs et colons de Sainte-Anne de la Pérade, 1667–1681* (Trois-Rivières, 1946). E. T. Raymond, *Madeleine de Verchères* (Ryerson Canadian history readers, Toronto, [1928]). [L.-S. Rheault], *Autrefois et aujourd'hui à Sainte-Anne de la Pérade*; [2ᵉ partie] *Jubilé sacerdotal de Mgr des Trois-Rivières* (1v. en 2 parties, Trois-Rivières, 1895). P.-G. Roy, *La famille Jarret de Verchères* (Lévis, Qué., 1908); *La famille Tarieu de Lanaudière* (Lévis, Qué., 1922); *Toutes petites choses du régime français* (2 sér., Québec, 1944), 2ᵉ sér., 37–40. Jean Bruchési, "Madeleine de Verchères et Chicaneau," *Cahiers des Dix*, XI (1946),
25–51. Philéas Gagnon, "Le curé Lefebvre et l'héroïne de Verchères," *BRH*, VI (1900), 340–45. Henri Morisseau, "Pierre Fontaine dit Bienvenu: lieutenant de Madeleine de Verchères dans la défense du fort le 22 octobre 1692," *Revue de l'université d'Ottawa*, XIII (1943), 163–78. P.-G. Roy, "Madeleine de Verchères, plaideuse," *RSCT*, 3rd ser., XV (1921), sect. I, 63–71.

JEANNEAU (Geanneau, Janot), ÉTIENNE, merchant, court officer and notary, militia officer; b. *c*. 1668, probably at "La Tardière" in Poitou, France, son of Étienne Jeanneau, a merchant, and Jacquette Clément (Vincent); m. on 16 Aug. 1694 Catherine Perrot at Sainte-Famille, Île d'Orléans; d. 8 May 1743 at Rivière-Ouelle, on the south shore of the St Lawrence.

Étienne Jeanneau was in Quebec by 1686; he is described as a merchant, without any indication being given of what kind of commerce he conducted. We know only that he had business dealings with merchant traders in La Rochelle. He remained in business until about 1702, although he had left Quebec in 1698 to settle on land he had bought that year in the seigneury of Rivière-Ouelle.

Some years later, on 14 June 1709, Étienne Jeanneau obtained a commission as court officer and notary to practise in the seigneuries of Grande-Anse, Rivière-Ouelle, Kamouraska, Rivière-du-Loup, and Port-Joli. This immense territory on the south shore of the St Lawrence was without a notary, and before Jeanneau's appointment the habitants of these seigneuries had to request the missionaries or militia captains to draw up their articles of sale and other legal deeds; these are in part to be found in the notary Jeanneau's minute book. Jeanneau also exercised the functions of subdelegate of the intendant, since there were no "judges in office" in the seigneuries of Grande-Anse, Rivière-Ouelle, and Kamouraska. Intendant BÉGON gave him authority to draw up deeds of guardianship and to preside over the taking of property inventories. In 1721 Jeanneau was a lieutenant of militia.

Jeanneau may have carried out his duties to the satisfaction of the habitants in his territory, but his nearest neighbours quarrelled with him on several occasions, and Jeanneau had to appear before the Conseil Supérieur to obtain justice. The location of a fence, a right of way or a right to cut wood was often the cause of these disputes, which as a rule were verbal; in 1706, however, one of them ended in fisticuffs, and Jeanneau obtained 100 *livres* in damages for the blows he had received.

Jeanneau's career as a notary lasted more than 30 years. He is typical of the travelling notary

313

Jeantot

who had to cover a vast territory and had often, without any preparation, to exercise more than one judicial and administrative function, while at the same time farming his land to feed his family.

MICHEL PAQUIN

ANQ, Greffe de Louis Chambalon, 5 août 1694; Greffe d'Étienne Jeanneau, 1674–1743; Greffe de Guillaume Roger, 6 août 1698. *Édits ord.*, II, 453. *Jug. et délib.*, III, IV, V, VI, *passim*. Bonnault, "Le Canada militaire," APQ *Rapport, 1949–51*, 356. P.-G. Roy, *Inv. coll. pièces jud. et not.*, I, 40, 149, 181; *Inv. ord. int.*, I, II, *passim*. Tanguay, *Dictionnaire*. Vachon, "Inv. critique des notaires royaux," *RHAF*, X (1956–57), 101. J.-E. Roy, *Histoire du notariat*, I, 185–89.

JEANTOT (Jantot), JEAN, Brother Hospitaller of the Cross and of St Joseph, schoolmaster, superior; b. *c.* 1666; d. 12 Aug. 1748 in the Hôpital Général of Montreal.

Although he was not one of the founders, Jean Jeantot took part from its beginning in the work of the Hôpital Général of Montreal and in the founding of the community of the Brothers Hospitallers of the Cross and of St Joseph. From 1695 he worked in the hospital, which in fact had only received its letters patent on 15 April 1694. On 25 April 1701, at the same time as François Charon* de La Barre, the founder of the two institutions, he assumed "the habit of the Brothers Hospitallers."

Together with François Charon, Jean Jeantot pronounced his simple vows on 17 May 1702 and his oaths of stability on 27 July 1704. A few days later, on 6 August, he was elected counsellor for a year; the next year his term of office was renewed for another year. At the end of this second term of office, in 1706, Jeantot went to Pointe-aux-Trembles on Montreal Island as a schoolmaster, for according to their founding letters patent the hospitallers were to attend to the teaching of boys. Brother Jeantot was back at the Hôpital Général in 1721 when on 16 September he was re-elected counsellor. In 1718 he had acquired 63 acres of land at Pointe-aux-Trembles, and four years later he donated it to the parish priest there so that the priest and his successors would sing four low masses each year for souls in purgatory and two for him.

On 17 April 1731 the members of the community entrusted to Brother Jeantot the office of superior, which he held until 13 July 1745, when he was replaced as a result of the strong opposition he had shown to a decision by Bishop Pontbriand [DUBREIL]. The bishop had expelled Brother Pierre Martel from the community because of the bad company he kept.

During the 14 years that Jeantot was superior the community was unable to solve its financial difficulties due on the one hand to the financial commitments entered into by the founder, and on the other to the hospitallers themselves, who in 1735 were recognized to be responsible for the bad situation in which the community found itself [*see* Louis TURC de Castelveyre]. But these difficulties were also to be attributed to the overall economic situation, to the loss of the royal subsidies for the upkeep of schools, the economic slump of 1737–38, and the lack of new members. Jeantot worked to ensure the financing of the hospitallers' work by selling school equipment, increasing the production of beer, and trying to draw as much revenue as possible from the "store," from hiring out horses, and from tending animals. Despite all efforts to restore the institution's finances the Hôpital Général, along with the community, fell into bankruptcy. The hospitallers had to give up the administration of the hospital, which was handed over to Marie-Marguerite Dufrost* de Lajemmerais on 27 Aug. 1747.

Jean Jeantot, who after 1745 held no further office, was lodged in the Hôpital Général where he had laboured selflessly almost his entire life. There he died on 12 Aug. 1748, and there he was buried the same day. Of all who were engaged in it from the start, Jeantot was the only one to witness the sad ending to François Charon's work.

JACQUES GRIMARD

AN, Col., B, 54, ff.433–34; C¹¹A, 107, ff.93–222; F³, 5, ff.421–22 (copies at ANQ). ANQ-M, Greffe de Pierre Raimbault, 24 janv. 1722. ASGM, Recette et dépense de juin 1718 à septembre 1746; Registre des sépultures, 1725–1759; Registre des vêtures, professions, etc., des Frères Charon, 1701–1748. ASSM, Cahiers Faillon. *Édits ord.*, II, 391. Amédée Gosselin, *L'instruction au Canada*, 100. Hamelin, *Économie et société en Nouvelle-France*, 64.

JÉRÉMIE, *dit* **Lamontagne, CATHERINE (Aubuchon; Lepailleur de Laferté),** midwife, botanizer; baptized 22 Sept. 1664 at Quebec, daughter of Noël Jérémie*, *dit* Lamontagne, a trader, and Jeanne Pelletier; buried 1 July 1744 at Montreal.

There are few documents that enable us to retrace Catherine Jérémie's life. On 28 Jan. 1681, at 16 years of age, she was married near Trois-Rivières, at Champlain, to Jacques Aubuchon, by whom she had a daughter. On 3 Nov. 1688 she was married again, this time to Michel Lepailleur* de Laferté, at Batiscan; they were to have 10 or 11 children. In 1690 the Lepailleurs were living in Quebec, and in the autumn of 1702 they settled in Montreal, where Lepailleur received a commission as a royal notary. It was at Montreal particularly that Catherine Jérémie practised her profession as a midwife and established her reputation as a botanizer.

In the 18th century French naturalists, supported by the intendants of New France, were trying to discover the medicinal and practical properties of the flora of Canada. Every year the intendants encouraged plant collecting and the dispatch of living or dried specimens to France on the king's vessels. Catherine Jérémie was not as important as someone like Pehr Kalm* or even Jean-François GAULTIER and Michel Sarrazin*, who played a great role in making the flora of Canada known, but she has her place among amateur botanists such as Jean-Baptiste GOSSELIN, Hubert-Joseph de LA CROIX, Joseph-François LAFITAU, and Pierre-François-Xavier de CHARLEVOIX. She distinguished herself not only in collecting plants but particularly in attaching to her shipments notes explaining the properties and effects of the medicinal herbs. According to the testimony of Intendant Hocquart* in 1740, Mme Lepailleur, who had been widowed in 1733, had "long striven to discover the secrets of Indian medicine."

Catherine Jérémie died in 1744 at Montreal. We know nothing of the nature, scope, and interest of the notes which accompanied her shipments and which should be in the Muséum National d'Histoire Naturelle in Paris.

CATHERINE FORTIN-MORISSET

AN, Col., C¹¹A, 65, f.140; 70, ff.113, 129; 72, f.63; 80, f.69. PAC *Report, 1905*, I, pt.vi, 20, 59. "Recensement de Montréal, 1741" (Massicotte). Tanguay, *Dictionnaire*. Gosselin, *L'Église du Canada jusqu'à la conquête*, II, 384.

JÉRÔME. *See* ATECOUANDO

JOHONERISSA. *See* TANAGHRISSON

JOLLIET DE MONTIGNY, FRANÇOIS. *See* MONTIGNY

JONCAIRE, PHILIPPE-THOMAS CHABERT DE. *See* CHABERT

JONES, HENRY, priest of the Church of England, missionary; fl. 1725–50.

Henry Jones' presence at Bonavista, Newfoundland, is first recorded in November 1725. Soon after he was compelled to return to England because of ill health. While in London, in Feb-

ruary 1726/27, he wrote the Society for the Propagation of the Gospel to express his "most humble and hearty thanks" for an "acceptable Present of Books," and also for "their goodness in ordering me so handsome a sum." He had "raised by Subscription 8£" for his educational work, and was promised more. Encouraged by this response to his efforts he had "ordered a Schoolmistress." At the end of May 1727 he returned with his wife and family to Bonavista. That November he assured the society that the people of Bonavista "truly are willing to provide a Maintenance & Habitation for the Minister, to rebuild the Church, to set up a Charity School, to build a Schoolhouse, and to provide all things necessary to be used in Divine Service (as a Communion Table & Font etc.)."

In 1729 Captain Henry Osborn*, the newly commissioned governor of Newfoundland, appointed Jones a justice of the peace at Bonavista. Jones informed the SPG in November 1730 that "the Case of the Church is near finished," and that "a gentleman of London hath given a neat set of vessels for the Communion, and a handsome stone font." By 1735 there were two schools in Bonavista, supported by Jones' "utmost Endeavours and Encouragement." The promise of the residents to provide a "Maintenance" for him was not easily fulfilled. In 1740 Jones informed the archbishop of Canterbury, president of the SPG, that he was suffering great hardship "through ye poverty, removal, or decease of many of ye inhabitants, & ye extraordinary Charge of Provisions wch arise now to about one-third more than usual."

In 1742 he succeeded Robert KILPATRICK as missionary at Trinity, Newfoundland, which had by then become "ye centre of Trade, not only for this Bay, but all ye Northern Harbours." The summer population of Trinity was approximately 600, "all of whom sometimes attend Church." Though he lived "in good Harmony" with the people in his mission, Jones wrote in 1744 that he was forced to protest frequently at the "Considerable obstruction" caused by "certain unauthorised persons [non-conformists] taking upon them to Marry, Baptize, and Church Women (as they term it)." The reluctance of some people to pay the subscriptions they had promised was overcome by a letter from the SPG in April 1747 which "caused them immediately to chuse Churchwardens, and to set about repairing the Church, and to collect what was due to him."

The society gave Jones leave to return "with the Fleet" to London in 1747. Jones next asked to be sent as the society's missionary to the Mosquito Indians in Jamaica. His application was accepted, and shortly after his return to Newfoundland in 1749, he sailed with his wife for Jamaica, *via* Barbados. The society had been careful to prepare a welcome for him in Jamaica: when he arrived there on 1 March 1749/50 Jones presented to Governor Edward Trelawny a letter of commendation from the secretary of the society, describing him as "venerable in his person and of tried Virtue and abilities." The governor noted that Jones had "a wife who is come with him, & it would be a miserable living for a woman on the Mosquito Shore," and offered him the charge of the parish of St Anne's, Jamaica. Jones accepted the offer, with the SPG's approval, and arrived in his new parish in April 1750. After suffering privations for more than a quarter century, Jones was relieved to be the incumbent of a benefice worth approximately £300 a year.

Nothing is known of his career after 1750.

F. M. BUFFETT

USPG, A, 19, pp.285–87; 20, p.268; 25, p.67; B, 7/2, p.67; 10, p.58; 11, p.104; 13, p.195; 15, pp.1–2; 16, p.4; 18, pp.81–83, 87–88. *The Fulham papers in the Lambeth palace library*, ed. W. W. Manross (Oxford, 1965). F. M. Buffett, *The story of the church in Newfoundland* (Toronto, [1939]). Prowse, *History of Nfld.*

JOURDAIN, dit Labrosse, PAUL-RAYMOND, organ builder, master carpenter, wood-carver; baptized 20 Sept. 1697 in Montreal, son of Denis Jourdain, *dit* Labrosse, master carpenter, and Marie-Madeleine Fagot; d. 8 June 1769 in his birthplace.

Paul-Raymond Jourdain, *dit* Labrosse, practised the wood-carver's craft for a great part of his life, a craft which produced a large number of artists in New France. Their professional training was based above all on apprenticeship but was also given at the beginning of the 18th century by the school at Saint-Joachim, near Quebec [*see* Louis Soumande*]. Whether Jourdain attended this school or became an apprentice in his father's shop is not known, but he certainly spent five or six years, as was customary, learning his craft under the surveillance of a master.

Curiously enough, Jourdain seems to have been an organ builder before turning to carving. How or where he learned this craft is unknown, but he was practising it in 1721. A contract drawn up on 31 July of that year in Montreal before the notary Jacques David* required "Paul Jourdain *dit* LaBrosse organ builder at Ville-Marie" to make for the cathedral of Quebec "an organ with 7 stops, including the *vox humana*, in consideration of the sum of 800 *livres* payable upon delivery of the said instrument." This contract, however,

seems to be the only one that Jourdain carried out as an organ builder.

Towards 1725 he was practising the carpenter's trade. Then from 1730 to 1741 he worked as a wood-carver at Pointe-Claire, Lachenaie, Prairie-de-la-Madeleine (Laprairie), and Varennes, sometimes helped by the carpenters Augustin Gauthier and Vincent Lenoir; he also worked at Montreal with his brother Denis. During this period he carried out his major work: the retable of the church of Sainte-Anne de Varennes. In 1741 he undertook to carve a tabernacle and retable for the church of Saint-François-Xavier de Verchères, and the following year he did some work for the church of Sainte-Geneviève de Pierrefonds. Later, between 1753 and 1755, he made a paschal candlestick and a tabernacle for the church of Saint-Antoine-de-Padoue (Saint-Antoine-sur-Richelieu). Finally, in 1756 he carved "the frame for the great picture" in the church of Saint-Pierre-du-Portage at L'Assomption.

The wood-carver's craft in the 18th century was not limited to the slavish execution of works conceived by an architect. Sometimes the artisan himself conceived the whole of the interior decoration of a church and participated in the exterior decoration by doing statues for the niches on the façade. On the other hand, in different circumstances he only carried out works destined to complete an *ensemble* or had to content himself with restoring works.

On 16 July 1725, in Montreal, Paul-Raymond Jourdain, *dit* Labrosse, had married Françoise Gaudé. One of his sons, Dominique, was interested in carving; another, Paul, was a surveyor and clerk of the chief road officer in Montreal at the time of the conquest and at the beginning of the English régime.

Jourdain died on 8 June 1769 in Montreal at 71 years of age. He was buried two days later in the chapel of Saint-Amable in the church of Notre-Dame de Montréal. His carving is not well known. But thanks to some pieces that have survived, he can easily be included among the most important artisans of the 18th century. This opinion is confirmed in a letter from Mme Bégon [ROCBERT], who stated in 1750 that in Rochefort, France, she had never found "a workman equal to Labrosse."

MICHEL CAUCHON and ANDRÉ JUNEAU

ANQ-M, Greffe de Guillaume Barette, 6 mai 1736; Greffe de Jacques David, 31 juill. 1721; Greffe de N.-A. Guillet de Chaumont, 11 sept. 1732; Greffe de Michel Lepailleur, 15 juill. 1725; Registre d'état civil, Notre-Dame de Montréal, 20 sept. 1697, 10 juin 1769. Archives paroissiales de Sainte-Geneviève (Pierrefonds, Qué.), Livres de comptes, I. Archives paroissiales de Saint-François-Xavier (Verchères, Qué.), Livres de comptes, I. IOA, Dossier Paul-Raymond Jourdain, dit Labrosse, sculpteur. "Correspondance de Mme Bégon" (Bonnault), APQ *Rapport, 1934–35*, 126–27. P.-G. Roy, *Inv. procès-verbaux des grands voyers*, III, 1. Tanguay, *Dictionnaire*. É.-Z. Massicotte, *Faits curieux de l'histoire de Montréal* (Montréal, 1922), 58. Morisset, *Coup d'œil sur les arts*, 111; *Les églises et le trésor de Varennes* (Québec, 1943), 11. Ramsay Traquair, *The old architecture of Quebec* (Toronto, 1947), 256. Henri Têtu, "Le chapitre de la cathédrale de Québec et ses délégués en France," *BRH*, XIV (1908), 359.

JUCHEREAU DE SAINT-DENIS, LOUIS, explorer, trader, officer in the colonial regular troops; b. 17 Sept. 1676 in Quebec, son of Nicolas Juchereau* de Saint-Denis and Marie-Thérèse Giffard; m. late 1715 or early 1716 to Emanuela Ramón de Navarro; d. 11 June 1744 at Natchitoches, Louisiana.

Little is known about the early life of Louis Juchereau de Saint-Denis. The story that he was educated in Paris cannot be documented, but, as he was a member of a network of important Canadian families, it is not unlikely. In 1699 he accompanied Pierre Le Moyne* d'Iberville, to whom he was related by marriage, on Iberville's second voyage to Louisiana. He remained there and with Bienville [LE MOYNE] in 1700 and 1701 made some explorations in the region between the Red and Ouachita rivers. In 1702 or 1703 he received command of the Fort du Mississipi (18 leagues from the river's mouth), a position he held until the abandonment of the fort in 1707. During these years he is said to have been as far north as the mouth of the Ohio, where he briefly took charge of a tannery established by his brother Charles*. He also made a number of journeys westward into the present state of Texas, trading and exploring.

At some time after 1707 he settled on the Rivière d'Orléans (Bayou St John) as a landowner and trader. In 1713 the new governor of Louisiana, Lamothe Cadillac [Laumet*], appointed him leader of an expedition to seek a trade route to New Spain. The choice was a good one, for Saint-Denis was an experienced traveller in the often hostile lands west of the Mississippi and a talented diplomat who spoke the Indian languages of the area. He went up the Red River to the vicinity of present Natchitoches, Louisiana, where he established the post of Saint-Jean-Baptiste des Natchitoches on an island. Continuing across Texas he stopped to trade with Hasinai Indians (the Caddo confederacy) and may even have returned to Louisiana for more

goods. He arrived at the Spanish garrison town of San Juan Bautista (Piedras Negras, Mex.) in July 1714. The commandant, Diego Ramón, detained the party while he awaited instructions from his superiors. Saint-Denis used the time to court Ramón's granddaughter, Emanuela. In the spring of 1715 he was taken from San Juan Bautista and sent to prison in Mexico City. During the time of his imprisonment the Spanish authorities decided to occupy Texas and they accepted his offer to guide a party being sent to that region to establish missions. On the way, Saint-Denis stopped at San Juan Bautista late in 1715 or early in 1716 to marry Emanuela. Then, leaving her behind, he set out eastward with the priests and soldiers (including several of the Ramón family). Four missions were founded, the easternmost in the neighbourhood of Nacogdoches (Tex.), less than 100 miles from Natchitoches.

By August 1716 Saint-Denis was back in Mobile (Ala.). Although the Spaniards were not prepared to countenance trade between Louisiana and New Spain, Saint-Denis apparently foresaw a profitable future in smuggling. He raised all the money he could and, with several associates and his goods on a mule-train, set out for the Rivière du Nord (Rio Grande). Word of this bare-faced contravention of Spanish law leaked out, however; when the party arrived at San Juan Bautista, Ramón was obliged to impound the merchandise. Saint-Denis went to Mexico City to try to arrange to get it back. By July 1717 he was in prison again. After several months he was released, with permission to sell his goods but with orders never to return to Texas. He arrived back in Natchitoches in February 1719. His wife either accompanied him or came soon after.

When France and Spain went to war in 1719 he fought at the defence of Mobile that year and in the second French capture of Pensacola (Fla.). He had resigned from the colonial regular troops some years before; on 3 Mar. 1720 he re-entered them with a lieutenant's commission and a few months later he was given command of the Natchitoches area. During the winter of 1720–21 Spanish sources reported that he was organizing Indians west of the Hasinais. In the spring of 1721 the Compagnie des Indes, now responsible for Louisiana, granted him a five per cent commission on goods sold to foreigners, since it was eager to promote trade with the Spaniards in Texas. France and Spain were at peace after May 1721 and this trade was contrary to Spanish law, but the Spaniards had established Los Adayes (near Robeline, La.), just 15 miles west of Natchitoches, as the capital of Texas. It was far from

Juchereau Duchesnay

a legal source of supply and business flourished. Saint-Denis found time apart from his military and commercial activities to manage his estate – he claimed local vines would produce wine as good as that of France – and to conduct the delicate diplomacy with the Indians that was necessary to keep the peace on the frontier.

Not all the French were as tactful as Saint-Denis. The commandant at Fort Rosalie (Natchez, Miss.), having tried to dispossess the local Natchez village of its land, provoked the tribe into an uprising against the French in 1729. The Natchez captured that post in 1731. Those of the tribe who had moved to the neighbourhood of Natchitoches were massacred by Saint-Denis's garrison with the help of some Spaniards.

Saint-Denis lived at Natchitoches in considerable luxury, but in 1741 financial difficulties dating in part from his journeys to New Spain began to plague him. He was obliged to acknowledge a debt of 18,361 *livres* to the former Compagnie des Indes. He was reduced to straitened circumstances, and a mood of disappointment, quite unlike the ebullient optimism that had previously governed his life, settled on him. "Happy is the person who can leave [Louisiana], and happier is he who never came here," he wrote in April 1741. In January 1744 he requested relief from his command and permission to move with his family to New Spain, but in June he died. He was buried in the Natchitoches church.

Despite his colourful career Saint-Denis seems to have been little involved in the bitter internal political controversies of Louisiana. He gained the respect of the French, the Indians, and the Spanish missionaries in Texas. Spanish officials breathed a sigh of relief at his demise; their reaction is perhaps the best measure of his contribution to French Louisiana.

IN COLLABORATION WITH WINSTON DE VILLE

Cathedral of the Immaculate Conception (Natchitoches, La.), Registres des baptêmes, mariages et décès de la paroisse des Natchitoches. [André Pénicaut], *Fleur de lys and calumet: being the Pénicaut narrative of French adventure in Louisiana*, ed. and trans. R. G. McWilliams (Baton Rouge, 1953). "Natchitoches and the trail to the Rio Grande, two early eighteenth-century accounts by the Sieur Derbanne," trans. and ed. Katherine Bridges and Winston De Ville, *Louisiana History* (Baton Rouge), VIII (1967), 241–42. *DAB.* J. F. Bannon, *The Spanish borderlands frontier, 1513–1821* (New York, 1970). Ross Phares, *Cavalier in the wilderness, the story of the explorer and trader Louis Juchereau de St Denis* (Baton Rouge, 1952). P.-G. Roy, *La famille Juchereau Duchesnay* (Lévis, Qué., 1903).

JUCHEREAU DUCHESNAY, MARIE-JOSEPH, *dite* **de l'Enfant-Jésus,** Hospitaller of the Hôpital

Général of Quebec, superior; b. 20 Feb. 1699 at Beauport (Que.), daughter of Ignace Juchereau* Duchesnay, seigneur of Beauport, and Marie-Catherine Peuvret Demesnu; d. 20 Nov. 1760 at Quebec.

Marie-Joseph Juchereau Duchesnay entered the convent of the Hôpital Général of Quebec on 3 Nov. 1713 and made her profession on 23 April 1715. In view of her youth – she was 14 and a half years old – the Juchereaus offered a dowry of 3,500 *livres* in local currency to facilitate her admission; they had agreed to give only 2,500 *livres* for her sister, Geneviève de Saint-Augustin, who had entered the convent four years earlier. When a novice made her profession she undertook in writing to give a certain sum in money or in property which would serve for her keep and, if necessary, help the order out of financial difficulties. Under this system of dowries the state played a role in setting the amount; except during the period 1722–32, the dowry required in New France was 3,000 *livres*. However, because of the country's poverty, it sometimes happened that this requirement was waived at the Hôpital Général, as with the other orders in Quebec. Again, in place of hard cash the candidates often offered a fur-trading licence, a piece of land, lumber, or wheat.

In 1716 Bishop Saint-Vallier [La Croix*] sent Marie-Joseph de l'Enfant-Jésus to study leaf gilding and embroidery with gold and silver thread with the Ursulines of Quebec, who excelled in this sort of work. Five years later, in 1721, Marie-Joseph was helping her sister in running the house: she was elected assistant superior to Geneviève de Saint-Augustin, superior since 1717. From 1724 to 1729 Marie-Joseph appears to have held the position of senior Hospitaller. Then in 1729, in the triennial elections, she was chosen, along with Angélique Hayot, *dite* de Saint-Joseph, depositary (bursar) and discreet (counsellor). She did not hold these offices long, for in 1730, immediately after the death of her sister Geneviève, the dean of the chapter, Louis Bertrand* de Latour, decided to appoint Marie-Thérèse LANGLOIS, *dite* de Saint-Jean-Baptiste, superior; this arbitrary act brought about a sharp division within the community. As one of the group of recalcitrant nuns, Marie-Joseph Juchereau remained for some time out of the important offices in the community. In 1732, following canonical elections, Marie-Thérèse de Saint-Jean-Baptiste yielded the direction to Marie-Joseph Juchereau, who was elected superior a second time in 1735.

During this period from 1732 to 1738 Marie-Joseph de l'Enfant-Jésus, with the permission of the court, tried more or less successfully to set up a sort of "hôtel des invalides" or army pensioners' hospital. The plan was to attract to the Hôpital Général soldiers unfit for service, who were lodged here and there in the country with habitants or who were in hospitals in Montreal or Quebec. Since the king made an annual payment to the habitant or the hospital equivalent to half-pay for the disabled soldier, it is easy to understand that the undertaking appeared interesting to the nuns of the Hôpital Général as a means of supporting their work.

With the 1738 elections Marie-Joseph Juchereau relinquished her office as superior, as was normal after two consecutive three-year terms, but she continued to carry out important functions in the community, since she was elected depositary and discreet, along with Marie-Thérèse Langlois. Once more eligible in 1741, Marie-Joseph Juchereau was re-elected superior, replacing Marie-Charlotte de RAMEZAY, *dite* de Saint-Claude de la Croix. Once more she remained at the head of the community for two three-year periods.

The affair of the episcopal palace was definitively settled during her administration. As Saint-Vallier's sole legatees the nuns laid claim, from 1728 on, to the episcopal palace, which, according to Bishop Dosquet* and Bishop Mornay [Duplessis], had belonged to the late bishop. In her capacity as superior Marie-Joseph de l'Enfant-Jésus intervened directly in the conflict in 1737, setting forth her point of view to Maurepas, the minister of Marine. She pointed out the injustice of making the nuns pay for repairs to the abbeys which were attached to the episcopal seat and asked for repayment of 10,000 *livres*. She defended herself so well that the minister decided in favour of the community, which claimed ownership only of the palace.

Nevertheless, in 1743, after indemnifying the Hôpital Général, the court reunited the palace to the king's domain.

Marie-Joseph Juchereau assumed the office of depositary and discreet again in 1747, leaving the administration of the house to Marie-Joseph Legardeur de Repentigny, *dite* de la Visitation. The latter resigned her office at the end of her three-year term, and Marie-Joseph de l'Enfant-Jésus was again elected in 1750 and 1753. At the end of this last term of office she handed the direction of the community over to Marie-Charlotte de Ramezay and became assistant superior. Finally, in 1759, she was re-elected superior for the seventh and last time. Marie-Joseph had little opportunity to carry out her duties, for she died on 20 Nov. 1760, at 61 years of age, when the Hôpital Général of Quebec was suffering the painful consequences of the Seven Years' War.

Of all the nuns of the Hôpital Général of Quebec during the whole of the 18th century, it was Marie-Joseph Juchereau Duchesnay who held the office of superior for the longest period, for 19 of her 45 years of religious life, beginning with her profession.

MICHELINE D'ALLAIRE

AHGQ, Actes capitulaires, 12, 16; "Annales"; Registre des entrées et des dots. AJQ, Registre d'état civil, Notre-Dame-de-Miséricorde de Beauport, 20 févr. 1699. AN, Col., B, 66, f.35; 76, ff.101, 104; C¹¹A, 54, f.36; 107, ff.397, 404. *Mgr de Saint-Vallier et l'Hôpital Général*, 301–3.

JUGON, FRANÇOIS LEMAÎTRE, *dit. See* LEMAÎTRE

JUMONVILLE, JOSEPH COULON DE VILLIERS DE. *See* COULON

K

KAGHSWAGHTANIUNT(Coswentannea,Gaghswaghtaniunt, Kachshwuchdanionty, Tohaswuchdoniunty, Belt of Wampum, Old Belt, Le Collier Pendu, White Thunder), a Seneca Indian living on the upper Ohio River by 1750; d. *c.* 1762.

As Cadsedan-hiunt he was identified in 1750 as one of the "Chiefs of the Seneca Nations settled at Ohio"; as Kachshwuchdanionty, he appeared in 1753 as one of "the Chiefs now entrusted with the Conduct of Publick affairs among the Six Nations" on the Ohio; and in 1755 he was described as "Belt of Wampum or White Thunder [who] keeps the wampum." His English and French designations apparently attempt to translate his Seneca name; compare Zeisberger*'s form, *gaschwechtonni*, of the Onondaga word meaning to make a belt of wampum.

Kaghswaghtaniunt was closely associated with TANAGHRISSON from 1749 to 1754, during the rising conflict between English and French over the Ohio country. In 1753 he was one of the delegation that confronted Paul MARIN de La Malgue at

Kak8enthiony

Fort de la Rivière au Bœuf (Waterford, Pa.) with a protest against the French military advance toward the Ohio. Suffering some hurt, Kaghswaghtaniunt made the return trip to Logstown (Chiningué, now Ambridge, Pa.) by canoe, arriving in mid-January 1754. He was accompanied by Tanaghrisson and a French party under Michel Maray* de La Chauvignerie. Soon afterward he was accused by an associate, Jeskakake, of conspiring to betray the French officer to the English.

Kaghswaghtaniunt was among the 80 to 100 Mingos who later in 1754 joined Lieutenant-Colonel George Washington near present Uniontown, Pa., on his march toward Fort Duquesne (Pittsburgh, Pa.). With Washington's defeat by Louis COULON de Villiers, the group of Mingos took refuge at Aughwick (Shirleysburg, Pa.). Kaghswaghtaniunt was one of the Indians who joined Major-General Edward Braddock's campaign against Fort Duquesne in 1755 and after the British defeat retired to the vicinity of Harris's Ferry (Harrisburg, Pa.).

After Tanaghrisson's death in October 1754, Scarroyady had succeeded him as "half king" or spokesman for the Iroquois of the Ohio; but Scarroyady's absences in New York left the leadership unsettled, and in January 1756 Kaghswaghtaniunt and another Seneca, the White Mingo, were reported to be at odds about the succession to Tanaghrisson.

Later in 1756 the Mingo refugees moved from Pennsylvania to New York under the protection of Sir William Johnson*, the superintendent of Indian affairs. In June of that year Johnson sent Kaghswaghtaniunt with a message to the Senecas, and advised him and his family to settle among them. The western (Geneseo) division of the tribe, encouraged by Louis-Thomas Chabert* de Joncaire and his sons, had traditionally been favourable to the French, but Kaghswaghtaniunt continued to attend Johnson's councils and in April 1759 announced to him the Geneseo decision (said to have been made the previous winter) to take the British side. He was one of the Seneca chiefs who conferred with Johnson at Oswego (Chouaguen) in August 1759 after the British capture of Fort Niagara (near Youngstown, N.Y.); a year later he headed a party that with 600 other Iroquois accompanied Major-General Jeffery Amherst*'s army to Montreal, which fell on 8 Sept. 1760.

In 1761 Donald CAMPBELL, commandant of Detroit, sent Johnson word of Seneca activity against the English in the west. When Kaghswaghtaniunt met Johnson at Niagara in August, however, he assured Johnson that "he

was invested with the direction of the affairs of the nation where he lived" and that "all [was] well and very peaceable." Kaghswaghtaniunt visited Fort Niagara again during the winter, and William Walters, the commandant, wrote of him on 5 April 1762: "He is a good old fellow & I always Receive him Kindly and give him a Little Ammunition & provision." Not long after this, Kaghswaghtaniunt seems to have died.

Not much is known of his family. His wife and three grown daughters were with him at a council in Philadelphia in April 1756, and also at Fort Johnson, New York, in November 1759. A stepson, Aroas or Silver Heels, prominent in his own right, appears in documents of 1755 and later. A reference to "the Old Belts Daughter" in June 1763 gives the impression that her father was then dead, and in subsequent documents the daughters are identified as Silvers Heels' sisters.

WILLIAM A. HUNTER

The diaries of George Washington, 1748–1799, ed. J. C. Fitzpatrick (4v., Boston, New York, 1925), I, 54, 62–63. The history of an expedition against Fort Du Quesne in 1755, under Major-General Edward Braddock, ed. Winthrop Sargent (Philadelphia, 1855), 378. Johnson papers (Sullivan et al.). NYCD (O'Callaghan and Fernow), VII, 141–47, 197, 325–28, 391. Papiers Contrecœur (Grenier). Pennsylvania, Colonial records, V–VI. Pennsylvania archives, 1st ser., II. David Zeisberger, Zeisberger's Indian dictionary . . . (Cambridge, Mass., 1887).

KAK8ENTHIONY (Cachointioni, Caghswoughtiooni, Casswettune, Kaghswoughtioony, Kaghswughtioni, Red Head), an important member of the Onondaga council, and official speaker of the Onondagas; d. c. June 1756 at the Onondaga castle (near Syracuse, N.Y.). His son ONONWAROGO was usually called the young Red Head by the British and gradually became known as Red Head after the death of Kak8enthiony.

Kak8enthiony first appears in historical records in 1748, when he spoke at a conference of Iroquois with Governor La Galissonière [BARRIN] in Montreal. On behalf of the Confederacy he denied British claims that the Six Nations were vassals of the British crown. The Iroquois "had not ceded to any one their lands, which they hold only of heaven," he was reported to have said.

In July 1751 Kak8enthiony and numerous other Onondaga chiefs attended a conference with Governor La Jonquière [TAFFANEL]. Claiming to represent the Six Nations Council, they apparently intended to sell the portage at

Kanon

Oneida Lake (N.Y.) to the French. Some Oneidas, however, rejected the delegation's claim to speak for the Six Nations. The sale would have been a blow to the British, since the land was on the route from Albany to Oswego, the only British post on the Great Lakes. After considerable dissension within the Confederacy, the land was instead deeded to William Johnson*.

Since 1701, when Teganissorens* and other Iroquois leaders had concluded a treaty with New France, the official policy of the Confederacy had been neutrality in the struggle between the French and British. In the early 1750s Kak8enthiony was apparently still attempting to maintain this stand, but efforts to keep on good terms with both sides failed to prevent the Iroquois from being increasingly weakened by the expansion of the European powers. He lamented to Johnson in 1753 that "we dont know what you Christians French, and English together intend we are so hemm'd in by both, that we have hardly a Hunting place left, in a little while, if we find a Bear in a Tree, there will immediately Appear an Owner for the Land to Challenge the Property, and hinder us from killing it which is our livelyhood, we are so Perplexed, between both, that we hardly know what to say or to think."

By the early stages of the Seven Years' War in America, Kak8enthiony appears to have been won to a policy of cooperation with the British. On behalf of Johnson, who had been appointed superintendent of northern Indians, he delivered a speech on 21 June 1755 to a thousand Indians assembled at Mount Johnson (near Amsterdam, N.Y.). In February 1756 at another major conference Kak8enthiony, as speaker, presented Johnson with an immense belt of wampum "as a pledge of our inviolable attachment to you, and of our unshaken resolution, of joining you in all your measures. . . ." Although this commitment did not mark the end of neutralist and pro-French sentiment among the Six Nations, it foreshadowed their eventual decision to join the British side in the war.

By June 1756 Kak8enthiony was dead, and Johnson along with the Six Nations chiefs mourned his passing in a condolence ceremony at the Oneida castle (near Oneida, N.Y.).

ARTHUR EINHORN

[The identification of Red Head with Sequaresera in the index of the *Johnson papers* is an error deriving from an editorial misreading of a letter in the collection. The name Kaghswoughdioony appears in the *Johnson papers* for a Mohawk who accompanied the British forces to Montreal in 1760; he is not the same person as the subject of this biography. A.E.]

Johnson papers (Sullivan *et al.*), I, 365, 925–27; II, 579; IX, 80, 82, 110–20, 366–75. *NYCD* (O'Callaghan and Fernow), VI, 812, 964–88; VII, 55, 61, 67, 133–34; X, 232, 234. W. N. Fenton, *The roll call of the Iroquois chiefs; a study of a mnemonic cane from the Six Nations reserve* (Washington, 1950), 56–57.

KALOGG. *See* KELLOGG

KANAGHKWASE. *See* KARAGHTADIE

KANON (Canon, Cannon), JACQUES, privateer, officer in the navy; fl. 1756–61.

The first known record of Jacques Kanon is for the fall of 1756 when he was in command of a privately outfitted privateer from Dunkerque, France. On a cruise in the English Channel he took several prizes including a much larger enemy vessel, and subsequently received a commission as lieutenant in the navy. In January 1758, in command of the frigate *Valeur* (20 guns), he captured an English privateer. In April, under orders to escort three vessels carrying rice, wheat, and flour to New France, he left Dunkerque with a smaller frigate *Mignonne*. During the crossing the ships took a prize north of the Strait of Belle Isle, but otherwise had an uneventful passage.

Kanon may or may not have known François Bigot* and Joseph-Pierre Cadet* before his arrival in Quebec. He quickly gained their confidence afterwards. In August, Cadet hired Kanon and gave him instructions for his agents at Bordeaux concerning supplies he needed for the next year. In return for services to Cadet, Kanon was to receive 200 *livres* per month, 50 tons of free cargo space, and 2½ per cent of the net profit from the sale of any prizes taken en route. Late in August, Kanon sailed without convoy from Quebec to Bordeaux where Cadet's agents began to purchase several ships and to charter others. Difficulties prevented an early departure for New France. But finally, on 25 March 1759, 17 heavily laden merchantmen left Bordeaux under the over-all command of Kanon in the newly acquired 26-gun *Machault*, of 550 tons burden and with a crew of 166 men. Again Kanon's crossing was uneventful and unobserved. By the last week in May all Cadet's ships had reached Quebec safely. These ships and two navy frigates and a flute under the command of Jean Vauquelin* were the only ships to reach Quebec in 1759.

Vauquelin, who had distinguished himself the year before at Louisbourg, Île Royale (Cape Breton Island), was Kanon's senior in rank, but the

321

Karaghtadie

latter, as Cadet's chief captain, was not without influence in the councils held at Quebec. During the attack by the English Kanon resisted serving under Vauquelin and at times appeared to operate quasi-independently, thus frustrating some of the operations against the English in the river. These included an attempt to capture a 50-gun ship and three frigates above the city.

After the fall of Quebec, the French retained their naval vessels in the upper St Lawrence and Kanon was ordered to lead the merchant ships to France. Several ran aground during departure, but on 25 November Kanon sailed past Quebec and down river with five ships. Their crossing to France was unopposed and on 23 December Kanon anchored at Brest. Kanon was apparently under Cadet's orders to command a second convoy to New France but, no doubt after learning how unpromising the naval situation was for the French, he abandoned the venture. Instead, he returned to Dunkerque where outfitters readied two privateers for him to sail to Saint-Domingue (Hispaniola). He is last heard of in 1761, in command of yet another privateer on a four month cruise.

Jacques Kanon was first and foremost a privateer. His association with New France had been in his own interest, which was directed elsewhere with the fall of Quebec.

JAMES S. PRITCHARD

[The most detailed sketch of Kanon's antecedents and career is in the text and notes of Jean de Maupassant, "Les deux expéditions de Pierre Desclaux au Canada (1759 et 1760)," *Revue historique de Bordeaux,* VIII (1915), 225–40, 313–30. J.S.P.]

Journal du marquis de Montcalm (Casgrain), 431, 557, 595. "Journal du siège de Québec" (Fauteaux), APQ *Rapport, 1920–21,* 140, 146, 203, 239. *Lettres de divers particuliers* (Casgrain), 100, 218. *Lettres de l'intendant Bigot* (Casgrain), 52, 82, 100. *Lettres du marquis de Vaudreuil* (Casgrain), 89, 171. *Mémoires sur le Canada, depuis 1749 jusqu'à 1760,* 126–27. "Le sieur Canon ou Kanon," *BRH,* XXV (1919), 206–9.

KARAGHTADIE (Karaghiagdatie, Kanaghkwase, Kuriahtaaty, Nicholas, Nickus), sachem of the Wolf clan of the Mohawks; probably born in the early 1700s at Canajoharie (Indian Castle, Herkimer County, N.Y.) and probably died there in March 1759.

Like most Mohawks, Karaghtadie sided with the British against the French during the last two colonial wars. On 21 March 1747 he received from William Johnson*, who was in charge of Indian participation in these conflicts, provisions to take out a war party. On 7 May 1747 Karagh-

tadie accompanied some 38 warriors headed by THEYANOGUIN. This expedition ended in disaster when it was ambushed near Montreal in mid-June by French forces under Louis de LA CORNE and Jacques LEGARDEUR de Saint-Pierre. Karaghtadie and some 14 others were captured. He remained a prisoner in Canada, first with the French and then with the Indians, probably the Hurons of Lorette, until August 1750.

While a captive, Karaghtadie, hoping to get his release, invited his Mohawk friends to come to Canada to confer with the French authorities about an exchange of prisoners. The French wished to negotiate a separate peace with the Indians, as they had formerly done. The British, however, insisted on negotiating for all prisoners, white and Indian, claiming in effect that the Indians were their subjects. Johnson managed to prevent a delegation of several chiefs and Karaghtadie's wife and family from leaving for Canada in 1749. Their going, he said, would have been all that the French governor (BARRIN de La Galissonière) could have desired. When Karaghtadie returned home in August 1750, after the French and English had finally reached agreement on the exchange of prisoners, he was angry and upset at having been allowed to languish in captivity, and it took three days of hard work by Johnson to restore his good humour.

Though winning considerable respect from his white neighbours in his many dealings with them, Karaghtadie made a grave mistake when in 1754 he was lured by John Hendricks Lÿdius* into signing a deed for land in the Wyoming valley of Pennsylvania. This rash act, done without the consent of the Six Nations council, set off years of strife in the valley.

Karaghtadie's wife, Sarah, appears to have been head woman of the Mohawks, for their son Hans became the Tekarihoken or head chief, an office which descends through the female line. Sarah was not a woman to be taken lightly, even by her husband. In the summer of 1755, when Karaghtadie was being urged by an agent of Major-General William Shirley to join an expedition against Fort Niagara (near Youngstown, N.Y.), he hesitated. Finally he said, pointing to Sarah, "There is my wife . . . ask her Consent."

The expedition against Niagara was cancelled, but on 8 Sept. 1755 many Mohawks, probably including Karaghtadie, took part in the battle against DIESKAU's forces at Lake George (Lac Saint-Sacrement), and a son of Karaghtadie was killed there.

In 1758 Karaghtadie journeyed to Pennsylvania where, with other deputies of the Six Nations, he helped put down the pretensions of

Teedyuscung, a Delaware chief. Teedyuscung had denied the authority of the Iroquois over his tribe and at least twice had seemed to turn to the French in order to advance his cause. In Easton, at a conference culminating on 23 October, the Six Nations deputies made peace with Pennsylvania over the heads of their Delaware dependants, thus paving the way for the fall of Fort Duquesne (Pittsburgh, Pa.) and British conquest of the west.

Karaghtadie was a Christian, and at least one of his children was baptized by an Anglican missionary, Henry Barclay. A daughter married George Croghan, the Pennsylvania trader and Indian agent, and their daughter became the third wife of Joseph Brant [Thayendanegea*].

ISABEL T. KELSAY

N.Y. Hist. Soc. (New York), Henry Barclay, Register book, Fort Hunter 1734/35–[1745/46], 25 June 1741. *Johnson papers* (Sullivan *et al.*), I, 738; III, 162; IX, 18, 22–23, 39, 62–65, 600, 767; X, 43–48, 57–58; XIII, 113. *NYCD* (O'Callaghan and Fernow), VI, 527; X, 108–10. Pennsylvania, *Colonial records*, VIII, 175, 218. *Pennsylvania archives*, 1st ser., II, 174–76. [Charles Thomson], *An enquiry into the causes of the alienation of the Delaware and Shawanese Indians from the British interest, and into the measures taken for recovering their friendship . . .* (London, 1759), 178. P. A. W. Wallace, *Conrad Weiser, 1696–1760, friend of colonist and Mohawk* (Philadelphia, London, 1945), 350–63, 520–52.

KEEN, WILLIAM, merchant, justice of the peace; d. 29 Sept. 1754 at St John's, Nfld.

A native of Boston, Massachusetts, William Keen went to Newfoundland in 1704 to act as agent for New England merchants involved in the supply trade. After 1713 he commenced trading on his own account. As one of the first men to exploit the salmon fishery along the old French shore north of Cape Bonavista, he was a powerful force in the extension of English settlement into that area. By 1740 he was carrying on a considerable trade to New England, Britain, and southern Europe, exchanging fish – and possibly furs – for provisions and manufactured goods. At the time of his death he possessed extensive property in St John's, Harbour Grace, and Greenspond.

Keen is remembered, however, not for commercial acumen, but as a key figure in the development of justice in Newfoundland. By 1699 the British government had decided to allow limited settlement in Newfoundland, without encouraging its expansion. A rudimentary legal system was created which vested all power in the "fishing Admirals," who migrated annually to Newfoundland during the fishing season, with a power of appeal to the equally transitory naval convoy commanders who escorted the fishing fleet from Europe. The theory behind this system was that fixed government would inevitably encourage an increase in fixed settlement and destroy the migratory "nursery of seamen" so vital to England's Royal Navy. This rudimentary justice was probably inefficient and corrupt even when the fishing admirals were visiting Newfoundland, but when convoy and fishing ships left the island at the end of the fishing season, there was no established judiciary for the winter inhabitants. Under the system, all men accused of capital crimes were to be transported, with two witnesses, to England for trial. Not surprisingly, few men were ever accused of capital crime, and from 1715 onwards the "respectable" portion of the Newfoundland residents began to agitate for a judicial system that would protect their lives and property from lawless servants and "masterless men" during the winter.

Many naval convoy commanders, distrusting the fishing admirals and detesting lawlessness, sympathized with the need for a more permanent judicial system, and in 1718 one of them, Commodore Thomas Scott, recommended that "winter justices" be appointed annually to serve until the fleet returned the following year. His first suggestion for magistrate was William Keen who "tho a native of New England seem[s] concerned for the prosperity of the fishery . . . and has spirit enough." The Board of Trade refused to change their policy but in 1720 the murder of a prominent planter, Thomas Ford, created a new crisis. Keen apprehended the suspects, and sent them with witnesses to England in one of his ships, at his own expense, but pointed out that the cost discouraged "respectable" inhabitants from apprehending criminals. A petition of the planters of Petty Harbour asked that winter justices be appointed and that "encouragement be given to such usefull and able men as Mr. Keen." The Board of Trade again refused to take action. In the winter of 1723–24 the planters of St John's, in some desperation, formed themselves, for their mutual protection, into a Lockian "society" [see John Jago*] which, though it soon collapsed, once more demonstrated to the authorities that a growing population would inevitably require a formal year-round legal system. Keen sent a capital criminal for trial in England again in 1728, and noted that malcontents, knowing their chances of conviction were remote, were growing daily more insolent and the "sober inhabitants" would soon be forced to leave the country.

Keen's attempts were now greatly aided by the reports and arguments of Lord Vere Beauclerk,

Kellogg

the convoy commander in 1728, who was distressed by lawlessness in St John's and by the inefficiency of the fishing admirals. Above all he felt that only permanent civilian magistrates could control the depredations committed by Samuel Gledhill*, garrison commander at Placentia. When he left Newfoundland in the fall Beauclerk appointed Keen to report on any lawless occurrences. Keen duly wrote several letters urging that magistrates be appointed, and offering himself as a candidate. In 1729 the English government admitted the need for justice by issuing an order in council which turned the naval convoy commander into a "governor" (though still migratory) and by sanctioning the establishment of "winter" justices of the peace who were to act only when the fishing admirals were absent and hear only petty criminal offences. William Keen was one of the first magistrates appointed, and he retained the position almost annually until his death.

In fact the first "governor," Captain Henry Osborn*, encouraged the magistrates to hear cases on a year-round basis, and also to settle civil disputes. Until 1732 there were many conflicts between the new justices and the fishing admirals. The latter had legality on their side, but the magistrates had the active support of the governors, such as George CLINTON, and the passive acquiescence of the English authorities. By 1735 the migratory merchants, some of whom were staying on through the winter, either themselves became the magistrates, or controlled those who were appointed, and they ceased to oppose the innovation. Keen, as the leader of those who had urged a magistracy, now became the leading figure in Newfoundland. Successive governors, appointed only for a year or two and spending only a few months on the island, relied heavily upon him for advice and assistance, and Keen was able to monopolize whatever meagre official positions were created during his lifetime, becoming commissary of the vice-admiralty court in 1736, naval officer for St John's in 1742, and Newfoundland prize officer in 1744. He was often criticized for his conduct as a magistrate, as in 1753 when Christopher ALDRIDGE Jr, commander of the St John's garrison, charged that Keen had jailed some of his soldiers without trial. His mercantile contemporaries characterized him as a man who used his official influence for private advancement and gain and was "carefull to keep in with the Commodores." Though there is little doubt that he took whatever advantages came from his position, it is difficult to see that any man of this age would have acted differently.

The order in council of 1729 had created a resi-

dent judiciary in Newfoundland, but the trial of capital crimes was still reserved for English courts. During the 1730s successive governors, such as Fitzroy Henry LEE, urged that a court of oyer and terminer be established in Newfoundland, and in 1737 the Board of Trade almost decided to initiate one. No action was taken, however, and the war of 1740–48 forced both naval governors and English authorities to turn their attention elsewhere. In 1750 another order in council provided that the justices of the peace in St John's might act as commissioners of oyer and terminer in all cases except treason, although they could only sit during the presence of the governor. William Keen was the first commissioner to be appointed.

Ironically one of the first cases of murder to be tried by the new court was that of Keen himself, committed by soldiers and fishermen in the course of robbery in September 1754. Four of the nine persons implicated in the murder were subsequently hanged; the remainder were reprieved. Keen's son, William, inherited his father's business and his position as a magistrate, but was eclipsed in political influence by another New England immigrant, Michael Gill*. By 1760 he had moved to Teignmouth, Devonshire, England, and the centre of his Newfoundland commerce shifted north to Greenspond. The Keen plantations in St John's and Harbour Grace remained, however, in the family's possession until 1839.

KEITH MATTHEWS

Dorset County Record Office (Dorchester, Eng.), doc. 2694 (account of the life of John Masters, 1687–1755, n.d. [probably between 1755 and 1770]). PAC, MG 18, F23, F24. PRO, Adm. 1/3738, 1/3881; CO 194/7, ff.21–23; 194/8; 194/9; 194/12; 194/13, ff.164–68; *CSP, Col., 1717–18; 1728–29; 1730; JTP, 1708/9–1714/15; 1754–1758. Coll. de manuscrits relatifs à la N.-F.,* II, 538–39. *Newfoundlander* (St John's), June 1839.

KELLOGG (Kellug, Kalogg), JOSEPH, militiaman, Indian agent, interpreter, trader; b. 8 Nov. 1691 at Hadley, Massachusetts, eldest son of Martin Kellogg and Sarah Lane, *née* Dickinson; d. summer of 1756, at Schenectady, New York.

Joseph Kellogg moved with his family to Deerfield, Massachusetts, about 1692 and was taken captive by Indians in February 1704 in the infamous Deerfield raid led by Jean-Baptiste Hertel* de Rouville. His younger brother, Jonathan, was killed on the spot. His parents and elder half-brother, Martin, escaped within a short time, but Joseph and his sisters, Joanna and Rebecca, were held prisoner in Canada. His sisters subsequently married Indians, and Joanna refused to return to Massachusetts. Joseph was held at the Caughnawaga mission at Sault-Saint-Louis (near Montreal) for a year. He learned the Mohawk language readily and proved to be such a good linguist that he was delivered to the French, who naturalized him in May 1710, and employed him as an interpreter on trading expeditions. He later reported that he travelled about freely, learned the languages of all the Indians with whom he traded, and made a considerable amount of money.

Interest in Joseph Kellogg probably springs chiefly from a manuscript in the archives of the Royal Society of London: "A short account of a trading voyage performed by Joseph Kellug . . . to Missasippi in the year 1710. . . ." The account was written in 1721, after Kellogg's return to Massachusetts, by Paul Dudley, at the time a judge of the Superior Court of Massachusetts as well as an amateur scientist long in correspondence with the Royal Society of London. In March 1721 Dudley wrote: "The Journall is what I took from his own mouth and then digested into the method you see, and tho' he be not a man of Letters, yet has so much probity and ingenuity that you may depend upon the truth of what he says." The report excited much interest in the Royal Society, especially because it contained materials which corrected geographical details of the Illinois country recently portrayed in John Senex's map of North America (1710) and confirmed some of the information in Father Louis Hennepin*'s *Description de la Louisiane* (1683).

It appears that Kellogg was the first Englishman to penetrate the Illinois country. His party of "Six French Men of Canada" went from Montreal *via* Lake Nipissing to Lake Huron, and wintered at Michilimackinac. They then proceeded along Lake Michigan to "Chigaquea" (Chicago) and portaged to the Illinois River, which they followed to the Mississippi and southward to the mouth of the Ohio. Here, in 1711, "Mr. Kellug's Company ended their trading Voyage and so returned back to Canada." In addition to geographical features, Kellogg commented upon the flora and fauna of Illinois with some remarks about the French settlements along the route.

Kellogg's half-brother, Martin, accompanying a Massachusetts commission to recover captives from Canada, brought him back to Massachusetts in 1714. Joseph returned to his family, now settled at Suffield, Connecticut. On 20 June 1716 the Massachusetts government appointed him an interpreter to the Indians and sergeant of the guard at Northfield, Connecticut. Thus he entered upon a career to which he devoted most of his life. He rose to lieutenant and second in command at Northfield in 1721, to captain in 1723, and, after Fort Dummer (south of Brattleboro, Vt.) was constructed in 1724, he served as commander there from December 1726 until June 1740. On 26 December of that year, he was appointed "an established interpreter for this province [of Massachusetts]," a post he held until 1749.

Kellogg had set up a trading post at Fort Dummer, to which he was appointed "truck master" in 1728. He made at least two visits to Canada (1721 and 1727–28) to seek the release of captives held there. He also served repeatedly both as agent and as interpreter in Indian negotiations, and died in this service in 1756 at Schenectady, where he had accompanied Governor William Shirley of Massachusetts. He was rewarded with lands and several gifts of money by the provincial government and held in high regard as a dutiful, fearless, judicious, and vigilant Indian agent, the best interpreter of his day. He had married Rachel Devotion of Suffield in 1720 and had five children.

RAYMOND P. STEARNS

[Dudley's account of Kellogg's voyage is in the Royal Society of London, Archives, Classified papers (1660–1740), VII/2, no.1, and is entitled: "A short account of a trading voyage performed by Joseph Kellug an English man of New England in company with six French men of Canada to Missasippi in the year 1710 in two cannoos made of birch bark, with some general remarks made by the said Kellug." A copy is in the Register book, XI (1722–24), pp.132–36. It has been published by R. P. Stearns: "Joseph Kellogg's observations on Senex's map of North America (1710)," *Mississippi Valley Hist. Rev.*, XXIII (1936), 345–54. Dudley's letter concerning the account is also in the Royal Society Archives, Guard-book, D/1, no.73 (copy in Letter-book, XVI, pp.195–96). Quotations from these materials are with the permission of the president and fellows of the Royal Society of London. Senex's map is found in BM, K. Top., 148.e.3. R.P.S.]

Mass., Archives, Council records, VI, VII; Court records, XIV; "Mass. Archives," XXXI, XXXII, LXXII. *The acts and resolves, public and private, of the province of the Massachusetts Bay* (21v., Boston, 1869–1922), XII. "Belcher papers," Mass. Hist. Soc. *Coll.*, 6th ser., VI (1893), VII (1894). "Indian treaties," Maine Hist. Soc. *Coll.*, 1st ser., IV (1856), 124–25, 129, 131. Massachusetts, *Journals of the House of Representatives . . .* (40v., in progress, Mass Hist. Soc. pub., Boston, 1919–), I, IV–VI, VIII–XVII, XXXI, XXXII. Mass. Hist. Soc. *Coll.*, 1st ser., IV (1795); X (1809). *New Eng. Hist. and Geneal. Register*, IV (1850), IX (1855). *New-England Courant* (Boston),

Kilby

from 26 Nov. 1722 onwards, contains occasional notices concerning Kellogg.

Coleman, *New England captives*. Dean Dudley, *History of the Dudley family, with genealogical tables . . .* (2v., with supplements, Wakefield, Mass., 1886–1901). Timothy Hopkins, *The Kelloggs in the old world and the new* (San Francisco, Calif., 1903). [This work contains an inaccurate copy of the "Short account" of Kellogg's voyage. R.P.S.] Sylvester Judd, *History of Hadley, including the early history of Hatfield, South Hadley, Amherst, and Granby, Mass. . . .* (Springfield, Mass., 1905). J. P. Kellogg, *A supplement to notes on Joseph Kellogg of Hadley* ([Geneva, Switzerland], 1899). Kellogg, *French régime*. J. H. Temple and George Sheldon, *History of the town of Northfield, Massachusetts, for 150 years . . .* (Albany, 1875).

KILBY, THOMAS, merchant, justice of the peace, commissary at Louisbourg, Île Royale (Cape Breton Island); b. 1699 in Boston, Massachusetts, son of Christopher Kilby and Sarah Sempkins; m. Sarah Ellis 18 Aug. 1726; seven of their nine children died young; d. 23 Aug. 1746 at Louisbourg.

Thomas Kilby entered Harvard in 1722, and after four quiet years at Cambridge, Massachusetts, completed the requirements for his AM in 1726. He was married that year in the New North (Congregational) Church in Boston; he became a member of the Boston Episcopal Charitable Society within a few months. He was apparently inactive in the Episcopal Church, but his dislike of the revivalist Great Awakening in the Congregational Church is shown in his support of a pamphlet critical of its excesses. Kilby was an active mason, and was master of St John's Lodge, in Boston, from December 1744 to December 1745. He was known as a wit among his contemporaries, and may have been a contributor to the *New England Weekly Journal*, but it is no longer possible to identify his contributions. However, a satirical poem he wrote on the land bank scheme [*see* HALE], in which he seems to have lost money, was still enjoyed early in the 19th century.

Upon his graduation from Harvard, Kilby set up as a merchant in Boston. His business endeavours took him to Canso, Nova Scotia, where he was granted land sometime prior to 1729 and was likely engaged in buying fish and selling supplies to fishermen. In 1729 Kilby and three associates petitioned Governor Richard PHILIPPS to resolve the "many petty differences which dayly arise in the Fishery" by establishing a civil magistracy at Canso, and to confirm land grants formerly made to them. Philipps agreed to confirm the grants, and in addition, in August 1730, appointed Kilby, Edward How, and four others as justices of the peace at Canso.

Kilby's activities for the next few years are obscure, but from 1737 to 1739 he was the agent at Canso for the Boston merchant Peter Faneuil. According to Shipton, Kilby had retired to "the northern wilderness" in the late 1730s after failing in business. He wrote a humorous will which included a bequest of his sins to a certain clergyman without any, and the choice of his legs to crippled Peter Faneuil. The latter is supposed to have been so amused that he rewarded Kilby with the agency at Canso. This position involved Kilby in trade with Louisbourg in various goods, including meat, flour, lumber, rum, and sugar. It is probable, therefore, that Thomas Kilby was the "kinsman" whom Christopher Kilby, colonial agent in London for Massachusetts, sent to Louisbourg about 1741 to investigate the strength of the fortress. Thomas Kilby's report likely provided the basis for his cousin's detailed proposal for the capture of Louisbourg submitted to the Board of Trade in April 1744. The report described the extent of the Louisbourg fortifications and emphasized their poor condition. About this time Thomas Kilby also wrote an account of the French fishery in North America, to which William Bollan, another Massachusetts agent, referred in a memorial to the king.

Kilby vigorously assisted William Shirley in promoting the Louisbourg expedition of 1745, and as a result he was recommended by Shirley in November 1745 to be keeper of the ordnance stores at Louisbourg or to receive some equivalent post. He was appointed commissary of the royal stores at Louisbourg, but he was unable to assume his duties immediately because of a severe fever. He was also hampered by gout at this time, an affliction which seems to have bothered him from at least 1740. He requested that his brother-in-law, Edward Ellis, be allowed to administer the position for him. The death of his wife and of Ellis shortly thereafter left Kilby with two children of his own, his brother-in-law's family, and several other orphaned relatives to provide for. Kilby probably did not arrive at Louisbourg until late spring 1746; he died there shortly afterwards.

Although Kilby does not seem to have profited greatly from his connections with Nova Scotia, he is representative of the many lesser known New Englanders who were gradually extending New England's sway over Nova Scotia before the American Revolution.

DONALD F. CHARD

"Mass. Archives," XX, 675. Mass. Hist. Soc., Joseph Green, "A supplement to Tom Kilby's Drollery"; Pepperrell papers, Thomas Kilby to Pepperrell, 3 Nov. 1745. PAC, MG 11, Nova Scotia A, 26, pp.186–97. PRO, Adm 1/2655, "Description of Lewisburg in the Island of Cape Breton, 1741." *Correspondence of William Shirley* (Lincoln), I, 289. *Harvard College records* ... (3v., Col. Soc. Mass. *Pubs.*, XV–XVI, XXXI, Boston, 1925, 1935), II, 540. "Land-bank and silver-bank papers . . . ," Col. Soc. Mass. *Pubs.* (Boston), IV (1910), 88. PRO, *CSP, Col., 1728–29; 1732.* Shipton, *Sibley's Harvard graduates*, VII, 193–96. A. E. Brown, *Faneuil Hall and Faneuil Hall Market; or, Peter Faneuil and his gift* (Boston, 1900), 45. S. L. Knapp, *Biographical sketches of eminent lawyers, statesmen and men of letters* (Boston, 1821), 146. Rawlyk, *Yankees at Louisbourg*, 32. L. M. Sargent, *Dealings with the dead* (2v., Boston, 1856), II, 567. H. N. Shepard, *History of Saint John's Lodge of Boston* (Boston, 1917), 18. W. B. Weeden, *Economic and social history of New England, 1620–1789* (2v., New York, 1890; repr., 1963), II, 614–15.

KILPATRICK, ROBERT, priest of the Church of England, missionary; b. in England; d. 19 Aug. 1741 at Trinity, Newfoundland.

Robert Kilpatrick's mission at Trinity was one of several started along the east coast of Newfoundland in the early 18th century. Trinity was settled by fishermen from the English west country, and in 1729 the inhabitants petitioned the Society for the Propagation of the Gospel for a missionary. The settlers promised £30 per annum for a minister's support and the SPG thereupon sent Kilpatrick.

He arrived in 1730, but before 16 months had passed was complaining to the society. He had received no letters from home, the cost of living was high, provisions were scarce and his parishioners "difficult and disagreeable." Few or no contributions towards his support were made by the people, some of whom treated him cruelly, and he was faced with starvation. He asked the SPG for "removal from this unpleasant corner of the earth." The majority of the inhabitants, however, headed by the justices of the peace, testified on Kilpatrick's departure that he had been diligent and had worked a moral reformation. He had toiled among a people ignorant and unbaptized, had built a church, and had distributed prayer books and tracts. Many people regretted his going.

In July 1732 the SPG sent Kilpatrick to New Windsor, New York, where promises similar to those made by the people of Trinity had indicated the desire for a missionary. But there he found no house, no subscriptions, and a hostile reception. He lodged with a family so ill natured that they often threatened to throw him out in the depths of winter. He therefore appealed to the SPG in

October to send him back to Newfoundland, with a possible addition to his salary. The SPG agreed to his requests and he landed at Placentia en route for Trinity in June 1734. At Placentia he preached, baptized, and visited. He had a large congregation and felt they needed a missionary. By September 1734 he was back at Trinity.

His congregation during the summer fishing season was large, but in winter most of the remaining families went away to trap or hunt seals. He instructed his parishioners carefully in their religion and ordered books from England on the New Testament and the Book of Common Prayer. Children and adults were baptized and tracts distributed. At about this time he married and began to father a family.

In 1737 Kilpatrick visited England and the SPG headquarters in London, to which his congregation had sent a petition thanking the society for his work and asking that he be given more money. George CLINTON, a former governor, supported their request, describing Kilpatrick as "a good Christian." Aided by a grant of £10, Kilpatrick returned to Trinity, where he worked until his death in August 1741. He left a wife and five children who were granted £25 by the society. Henry JONES of Bonavista, at his own request, was transferred to Kilpatrick's mission.

Kilpatrick was like many pious and hardworking 18th century clergymen who volunteered for missionary work, presumably because of lack of employment in England. He was promised financial support, but such promises, given by a community dependent upon the uncertain yield of the fisheries, were not worth much. In practice he had to depend upon the SPG. Newfoundlanders, like colonists everywhere, would not pay for clergy whom missionary societies would provide free of charge. Kilpatrick's initial efforts at reform seem to have met with opposition from men unaccustomed to the influence of the church, but he persisted in his efforts to bring elements of civilization to a rough and uneducated community. He was a typical missionary, receiving a typical colonial welcome.

FREDERICK JONES

USPG, A, 22, pp.226–27; 23, pp.33–36, 38–39, 250; 24, pp.250, 254, 479; 25, pp.148, 319; B, 7, p.249; 9/2, p.54; Journal of SPG, 5–6; 7, pp.202–4; 8, pp.293–94; 9. [C. F. Pascoe], *Classified digest of the records of the Society for the Propagation of the Gospel in Foreign Parts, 1701–1892* (5th ed., London, 1895). F. M. Buffett, *The story of the church in Newfoundland* (Toronto, [1939]). Prowse, *History of Nfld.*

KING HENDRICK. *See* THEYANOGUIN

Kinousaki

KINOUSAKI (Qinousaki; Quinousaquy?), an Ottawa chief at Detroit; fl. 1700?; d. 1752.

Kinousaki was apparently one of the speakers at the war council that Charles Le Moyne* de Longueuil held at Detroit in 1700. Longueuil's aim was to encourage the Indians to attack English traders who had penetrated the Ohio country. On behalf of the Potawatomis, Ojibwas, and Ottawas, a chief named "Quinousaquy" spoke in favour of the project to the Hurons.

Nothing more is known of Kinousaki until, as an "aged man," he represented one of the two bands of Detroit Ottawas at a conference in Montreal in 1742. There he requested and received a new canoe. He assured Governor Charles de BEAUHARNOIS of his loyalty to the French and of his constant efforts to persuade his people not to trade with the English. Either then or within the next few years the French gratefully presented to him a fine scarlet coat with silver trimmings.

By early 1747, the Huron chief ORONTONY had successfully encouraged many of his tribe to abandon their French alliance and was apparently organizing a movement to drive the French from the western Great Lakes. The unrest spread to the Ojibwas, Potawatomis, and MIKINAK's band of Ottawas at Detroit. Of all the Indian groups in the area, only Kinousaki's remained firmly allied to the French.

Working against his own people, Kinousaki won few friends among the other Detroit Ottawas. His attempt to bring back the Ottawas who had fled to join the dissident Hurons at Sandoské (Sandusky) was unsuccessful. During one phase of the crisis in late 1747 he and his followers appear to have been totally dependent on the French for protection and supplies. Fortunately for both the French and Kinousaki, the crisis eased with the arrival of troop reinforcements in late September 1747, and especially with the halving of the price of French trade goods in 1748.

In early 1752 smallpox carried away 40 persons in the Ottawa village at Detroit. Old Kinousaki died at this time, presumably of the same disease.

DONALD B. SMITH

AN, Col., C¹¹ᴬ, 18, ff.133–36v; 77, ff.199–201; 87, ff.98–103, 175–225. *French regime in Wis., 1727–48* (Thwaites), 387–93. *NYCD* (O'Callaghan and Fernow).

KISENSIK, chief of the Nipissings of the Lac des Deux-Montagnes (Que.); fl. 1756–58.

The father of Kisensik, whose name is unknown, was apparently a celebrated Indian, having been to France and to the court, where Louis XIV personally presented him with an inscribed silver gorget.

Kisensik fought the English on several occasions during the early part of the Seven Years' War. He was the leader of an advance guard of Indians on MONTCALM's successful expedition against Chouaguen (Oswego) in August 1756. Early in July the following year he spoke for the Nipissings at a conference and war feast held when Montcalm visited the Indian settlement at Lac des Deux-Montagnes to rally support for an attack on Fort William Henry (also called Fort George; now Lake George, N.Y.). He asked Montcalm for permission to give advice on the war when the occasion offered and he informed the French general of his tribe's requests and the number of warriors it could furnish.

Both Kisensik and his son took part in the expedition, which left Montreal about 12 July. A great many Indian nations were represented in the force and shortly before the attack on the fort an assembly was held to unite them in the common cause. Kisensik spoke, saying to the Indians of the *pays d'en haut*, "We domiciliated Indians thank you for having come to help us defend our lands against the English who wish to usurp them." Of Montcalm he said, "It is not his cause he has come to defend, it is the great King who has said to him: 'Go, cross the great ocean and go to defend my children.' He will reunite you my brothers, and bind you with the most solemn of ties."

In May 1758 Kisensik set out again for the Lake Champlain frontier, determined "to redden with English blood the ashes of his father," who had died the previous autumn, and to prove himself worthy of wearing the silver gorget. Near the end of the month he and his war party encountered a force of English and Indians on the Rivière du Chicot (Wood Creek) south of Lake Champlain and took four scalps and nine prisoners whom they brought back to Montreal.

There is no further mention of Kisensik in Bougainville*'s journals, our only source of information on this Nipissing chief. Bougainville called him "famous" and referred to him as "a rare bird in the world" for his willingness to sacrifice his personal interests in the larger cause.

KENNETH E. KIDD

Bougainville, "Journal" (Gosselin), APQ *Rapport, 1923–24*.

KOÉ (Kouée, Koweahe). *See* GAWÈHE

KURIAHTAATY. *See* KARAGHTADIE

L

LA BOISCHE, Marquis de BEAUHARNOIS, CHARLES DE BEAUHARNOIS DE. *See* BEAUHARNOIS

LA BORDE. *See* DELABORDE

LA BRETONNIÈRE. *See* NEVEU

LA BRETONNIÈRE, JACQUES-QUINTIN DE, priest, Jesuit, missionary; b. 5 May 1689 in Bayeux, France; d. 1 Aug. 1754 in Quebec.

Jacques-Quintin de La Bretonnière entered the noviciate of the Jesuits of the province of France in Paris on 20 Sept. 1710, after having done two years of philosophy. He taught the third and fourth forms at Eu, studied philosophy for a year at La Flèche, taught the third form and classics at Blois, did four years of philosophy, and left for Canada in 1721. He was sent immediately to the Sault-Saint-Louis (Caughnawaga, Que.) mission, where he was to spend several years.

In the spring of 1728 La Bretonnière accompanied the Iroquois from his mission who had joined the military expedition that Constant Le Marchand* de Lignery was leading against the Fox tribe. Four years later he was appointed superior of the Sault-Saint-Louis mission, succeeding Father Pierre de LAUZON, who was taking over as superior of the Jesuit missions in New France. In 1739 he again went with his warriors in the expedition against the formidable Chickasaws [*see* Pierre-Joseph CÉLORON de Blainville; Charles LE MOYNE de Longueuil]. After that it is difficult to determine exactly where he carried on his ministry. In October 1740 he had not yet returned to the Sault-Saint-Louis mission; a document dated 1749 tells us that he was "among the Iroquois." In 1750 Governor La Jonquière [TAFFANEL] mentioned him as the possible successor to Father Jean-Baptiste TOURNOIS at the Sault-Saint-Louis mission, after the famous Desauniers-Tournois affair. Two years later La Bretonnière went to the Jesuit college in Quebec, where he served as confessor until his death on 1 Aug. 1754.

Father La Bretonnière did not leave any documents which might provide information concerning his ministry. Like a great number of missionaries, he knew how to devote himself zeal- ously to evangelizing and teaching the "settled" Indians.

ANDRÉ COTÉ

ASJCF, A-7-5, 8; Fonds Rochemonteix, 4018, 457, 461. *JR* (Thwaites), LXVIII, 233, 271–73, 277, 331; LXIX, 35, 39, 49, 77, 237. "Lettres du père Aulneau," *APQ Rapport, 1926–27,* 268, 283, 285, 302, 306, 307, 314. Allaire, *Dictionnaire.* François de Dainville, *La naissance de l'humanisme moderne* (2v., Paris, 1940), I. E. J. Devine, *Historic Caughnawaga* (Montreal, 1922), 219–51. Rochemonteix, *Les Jésuites et la N.-F. au XVIIIe siècle,* I, 190–91; II, 17–50. J.-G. Forbes, "Saint-François-Xavier de Caughnawaga," *BRH,* V (1899), 131–36. C. M. Lewis, "French priests in Western Pennsylvania, 1739–1759," *Mid-America* (Chicago), XXIX (1947; new ser., XVIII), 92–98.

LABROSSE, PAUL-RAYMOND JOURDAIN, *dit. See* JOURDAIN

LA CHASSE, PIERRE DE, priest, Jesuit, missionary, superior of the Jesuit missions in New France; baptized 7 May 1670 in the parish of Saint-Pierre-en-Château at Auxerre, France, son of Joseph de La Chasse, king's counsellor at the bailiff's court and presidial bench of Auxerre, and of Edmée Roussol; d. 27 Sept. 1749 in Quebec.

Pierre de La Chasse entered the noviciate of the Jesuits of the province of France in Paris on 14 Oct. 1687. When his noviciate was completed, he taught at Rennes for six academic years and in 1695 entered upon his four years of theology at the Collège Louis-le-Grand in Paris. In 1700, when his final probationary year was ended, he sailed for Canada, and in 1701 he replaced Father Vincent Bigot* at Naurakamig (probably on the Androscoggin River, near Canton, Me.). In November 1708 La Chasse had a census made of all the Abenakis in the Kennebec region. He remained in that region until 1709, and his presence on the frontiers of the English and French colonies led him to play a very real role in the military events which marked the War of the Spanish Succession in North America. His correspondence with the civil authorities is proof of that: he served at one and the same time as a liaison officer, informant, and counsellor, and he was particularly zealous in stimulating the "patriotism" of the Abenakis. His conduct came to

La Chasse

the attention of Governor Philippe de Rigaud* de Vaudreuil, who saw in him an efficient emissary. In instructions to the Baron de Saint-Castin [Bernard-Anselme d'Abbadie*] the governor recommended that he "consult [the missionary] when occasion arises on matters concerning the greatest good to his Majesty's service." After the treaty of Utrecht in 1713 La Chasse was the principal instigator of the policy of "gifts to the Indians," which was intended to keep the Abenakis allied with the French.

On 15 July 1719 La Chasse was named superior of the Jesuit missions in New France, replacing Julien Garnier*. The religious and civil authorities were in agreement in recognizing in him an exceptional man, gifted with numerous and "admirable" talents. His new functions allowed him to play a more efficacious role in French-Abenaki relations. In 1719, indeed, the authorities of New France promised to protect the Abenakis and to join them "if, to retain their country, they were forced to resort to war." In his report on the boundaries of Acadia dated 29 Oct. 1720 and sent to the Duc d'Orléans, Father CHARLEVOIX says explicitly that it was Father La Chasse himself who advanced this policy. "This counsel," the report adds, "given by a man who knew the Abenakis better than anyone ... was considered wise and was adopted." Subsequently, in 1721 and 1724, the Jesuit superior twice made the round of visits to the Abenaki missions in French Acadia, to keep them in the French allegiance. At the time of the negotiations between the English and Abenakis in 1721, Father La Chasse was chosen by the Abenakis, in accord with the authorities in Quebec, to accompany the Abenaki delegation [see Sébastien Rale*] during the meeting with the representatives from Boston. In 1724 he immortalized in a famous letter the "martyrdom" of Father Rale, who had died on 23 Aug. 1724 during what was called Dummer's or Lovewell's War.

His superiorship was distinguished by some notable events. In 1727 at the time of their exhumation he was called upon to draw up the minutes attesting to the state of preservation of the bodies of the first three nuns of the Hôpital Général of Quebec, one of whom was the first superior, Louise Soumande*, dite de Saint-Augustin, as well as to the miraculous cures which took place on that occasion. He was successful in increasing the personnel of the missions in America: in 1720 he entrusted to Pierre-Michel Laure* the re-establishment of the Saguenay mission, which had been shut down for 18 years [see François de Crespieul*], and in 1723 he was in favour of setting up the "Louisiana mission" [see Nicolas-

Ignace de BEAUBOIS]. In 1726 in a discussion on the brandy trade, he expressed the opinion, which he later rejected, "that the use of Brandy was necessary for the preservation and domination of the King and the Catholic religion."

On 6 Aug. 1726 La Chasse quit his post as superior, leaving it to Jean-Baptiste DUPARC, to devote himself exclusively to the nuns of the Hôpital Général of Quebec, whose confessor he had been since 1720. He was also the confessor and an intimate friend of Bishop Saint-Vallier [La Croix*]. Because of this he was associated in 1727–28 with the painful events which accompanied the death of the bishop of Quebec. He was involved, despite himself, it seems, in the quarrel between Intendant Dupuy* and the chapter of Quebec. He delivered the prelate's funeral oration at the Hôpital Général; the role that he played in these circumstances presumably brought about his interdiction for some months by Canon Étienne Boullard*.

Pierre de La Chasse spent the last 20 years of his life at the Jesuit college in Quebec, dividing his time between prayer, poetry, and the task of acting as spiritual father of the community. During his final years he suffered from sciatica and could no longer "exercise his ministry publicly." When he was more than 70 he learned English to try to convert some prisoners who were being held in Quebec. He died in that town on 27 Sept. 1749, leaving behind him the memory of a man of "great talents for preaching the work of God and for administration."

MICHELINE D. JOHNSON

AD, Yonne (Auxerre), État civil, Saint-Pierre-en-Château d'Auxerre, 7 mai 1670. AN, Col., B, 47, ff.1129, 1206; 48, f.855; 49, f.678; 50, f.500; 53, ff.450v, 541v; C¹¹ᴬ, 22, f.32; 36, f.124; 43, f.372; 44, f.131; 45, ff.11, 12, 118; 46, ff.19, 27, 144, 307; 47, ff.60, 121, 301; 48, ff.106, 140; 49, ff.124, 561, 576; 50, f.23. ASJCF, 588; 588 bis; 2220; 2221; Fonds Rochemonteix, 4006, 143, 168, 276; 4018, 38. ASQ, MSS, 176; Polygraphie, II, 24A. Newberry Library (Chicago), Ayer Coll., Lachasse census (1708). Coll. de manuscrits relatifs à la N.-F., II, 497, 530–31, 534–36, 567–68; III, 5, 49–54, 57–63, 68–70, 93, 108–10. "Éloge funèbre de Mgr de Saint-Vallier," BRH, XIII (1907), 66–80, 97–118. JR (Thwaites). Martyrs de la Nouvelle-France; extraits des relations et lettres des missionnaires jésuites, Georges Rigault et Georges Goyau, édit. (Bibliothèque des missions; mémoires et documents, 1, Paris, 1925), 215–72. Melançon, Liste des missionnaires jésuites. Tanguay, Répertoire (hand-written annotated edition by the archivists of the seminary of Quebec).

F. G. Bressani, Les jésuites-martyrs du Canada, Félix Martin, trad. (Montréal, 1877), 243–49. Charland, Les Abénakis d'Odanak, 42, 63, 91. Dubé, Claude-Thomas Dupuy, 187, 237, 245. Johnson, Apôtres ou *agitateurs*, 79, 91, 98, 100, 139, 143. J.-A. Maurault, *Histoire des Abénaquis depuis 1605 jusqu'à nos jours* (Sorel, Qué., 1866), 378–407. *Mgr de Saint-Vallier et l'Hôpital Général*, 250–93, 712. Rochemonteix, *Les Jésuites et la N.-F. au XVIIᵉ siècle*, III, 442–78; *Les Jésuites et la N.-F. au XVIIIᵉ siècle*, I, 145–61; "Le père Sébastien Rasle," *BRH*, V (1899), 229. P.-G. Roy, "Un poème héroï-comique," *BRH*, III (1897), 114–16. Henri Têtu, "Le chapitre de la cathédrale de Québec et ses délégués en France," *BRH*, XVI (1910), 329.

LA CHAUSSAYE, Baron de BEAUVILLE, FRANÇOIS DE BEAUHARNOIS DE. *See* BEAUHARNOIS

LA CHENETTE, MME. *See* COUC, ELIZABETH

LA CHESNAYE, LOUIS AUBERT DE. *See* AUBERT

LA COLLE, Cree chief; fl. 1736–42.

La Colle was a civil and war chief of the Monsoni division of the Woods or Swampy Crees, with its main village at Rainy Lake in the vicinity of Fort Saint-Pierre built by Pierre GAULTIER de Varennes et de La Vérendrye in 1732. He enters and leaves history in the portions of the journals and letters of La Vérendrye covering the period 1736–42. La Colle was described by La Vérendrye as the "principal chief of the Monsoni; and in high repute also with the Cree and Assiniboin, acquired through his intelligence and his bravery. . . ." La Colle's influence, not only with the Monsonis, but with allied Crees and Assiniboins as well, was noted by La Vérendrye on at least three occasions. He was the chief go-between in diplomacy between La Vérendrye and the allied tribes. On several occasions La Colle was able to forestall war expeditions against the Sioux on behalf of the explorer. Despite La Vérendrye's asserted policy to the contrary, however, La Colle in September 1741 led a war party of over 200 men, mostly Crees and Assiniboins, against the Sioux of the Prairies, killing at least 70 of the enemy while losing but six men. All in all, La Colle played a major role in aiding La Vérendrye's exploration and trade westward.

HAROLD HICKERSON

Journals and letters of La Vérendrye (Burpee).

LA CORNE, LOUIS (Jean-Louis, Pierre, Louis-Luc, Louis-François) DE, known as the **Chevalier de La Corne**, officer in the colonial regular troops; b. 6 June 1703 at Fort Frontenac (Kingston, Ont.) (he received the public ceremonies of baptism in Montreal on 21 June 1704), son of Jean-Louis de

La Corne* de Chaptes and Marie Pécaudy de Contrecœur; d. 15 Nov. 1761 in the sinking of the *Auguste*.

Confusion about the identity of Louis de La Corne has arisen because of the variety of names given to him. He is referred to in his 1703 private baptism and 1728 marriage contract as "Louis," in a 1733 notarial deed as "Jean-Louis," in an official act of 1748 as "Pierre," in most contemporary sources as simply the "Chevalier de La Corne." Secondary sources also use "Louis-Luc" and "Louis-François."

La Corne entered the colonial regulars and was appointed second ensign in 1722 and full ensign in 1727. On 21 Jan. 1728 he married Marie-Anne Hubert de Lacroix. During his first three years of marriage La Corne showed an inclination for commerce, advancing more than 21,500 *livres* to traders travelling to Detroit, to the Lake Michigan area, and to Louisiana. In 1731 he was directing his fur-trading interests from his Montreal home on Rue Saint-Paul, and serving as assistant garrison adjutant. He was not yet 30 years of age.

La Corne became lieutenant in 1738 and was promoted captain six years later. His first combat experience was in Acadia in February 1747 when he served as second in command of a party of some 300 Canadians and Indians led in a winter attack by Nicolas-Antoine COULON de Villiers against Colonel Arthur NOBLE and 500 men in Grand Pré. Villiers was wounded almost immediately, but under La Corne's leadership Colonel Noble and a large number of the enemy were killed, wounded, or taken prisoner. La Corne's part in this action won him the cross of Saint-Louis, awarded in May 1749. In the meantime he had returned to Montreal. On 15 June 1747 the governor of Montreal, Josué DUBOIS Berthelot de Beaucours, gave him command of a detachment being sent to intercept an Indian raiding party said to be in the area. A group of Mohawks, Senecas, and Oneidas, along with some English and Dutch companions, was ambushed at the Cascades (near Île des Cascades, Que.) by a force under Jacques LEGARDEUR de Saint-Pierre which La Corne had posted to watch the river during the night. The Mohawk leader, THEYANOGUIN, escaped, but KARAGHTADIE and some other warriors were captured by Saint-Pierre's men and La Corne's party, which rushed to the scene.

In mid-October 1749 La Corne left for French Acadia to take oaths of allegiance from the habitants coming to reside in French territory; he was also to organize militia companies and fortifications at Chipoudy (Shepody, N.B.), Mem-

La Corne de Chaptes

ramcook, and Petitcodiac (near Hillsborough). La Corne arrived in November, and began strengthening the Beauséjour area (near Sackville) while Jean-Louis Le Loutre* endeavoured to persuade French Acadians to move under La Corne's protection west of the Missaguash River, the accepted temporary boundary. In April 1750 Major Charles LAWRENCE appeared before Beaubassin (near Amherst, N.S.), which Le Loutre and his Indian allies had burned to the ground. In the face of La Corne's firmness Lawrence had little alternative but to withdraw. He returned again in September with a larger force and began to dig in east of the Missaguash River while La Corne watched from the west bank. La Corne maintained this deliberate stalemate for a month before he was recalled from Acadia and replaced by Pierre-Roch de Saint-Ours* Deschaillons.

In 1752, probably, La Corne was appointed to a three-year term as commandant of the *poste de l'Ouest*, succeeding Jacques Legardeur de Saint-Pierre. He engaged 57 men for the west before setting out in June 1753, leaving his younger brother Luc de La Corne*, known as La Corne Saint-Luc, to hire the other men needed. On 7 August he was briefed on the west by Saint-Pierre at Les Petites Écores to the north of Lake Superior. During his term in the west La Corne improved Fort Paskoya (Le Pas, Man.). He travelled farther west than his predecessors, built Fort Saint-Louis (Fort-à-la-Corne, Sask.) near the forks of the Saskatchewan River, seeded several acres of grain, and explored the Carotte (Carrot) River valley. Anthony HENDAY records meetings with French traders in this area but identification is difficult.

In July 1755 La Corne was back in the colony at the head of a party of 500 men harassing the British at the portage between Lake Champlain and Lac Saint-Sacrement (Lake George). For the next five years he led a mobile patrol varying between 1,000 and 2,000 men along the Montreal to Lake Ontario waterway. In 1757 Governor Rigaud* de Vaudreuil suggested that the position of battalion commander of the colonial regular troops, with the same rank, honours, and salary as army battalion commanders in France, be created and awarded to La Corne, but nothing came of this proposal.

By 1759 the British pincer movement was well under way from east and west. In June La Corne was given the important assignment of dislodging the British force under Colonel Frederick Haldimand* which had just begun to fortify Oswego (Chouaguen). He surprised it but did not follow up his advantage strongly, and his lack of success

helped to open the St Lawrence for the British; there was now only La Présentation (Oswegatchie, now Ogdensburg, N.Y.) between the enemy and Montreal. In April 1760 La Corne was wounded while leading a battalion of troops in Lévis*'s offensive at the battle of Sainte-Foy. Four months later he was on the St Lawrence observing the advance of Jeffery Amherst* down the river; when Fort Lévis on Île aux Galops (east of Prescott, Ont.) fell in August La Corne had to retreat toward the Cèdres rapids. Surrender of the colony was now only a matter of time. On 8 Sept. 1760 Montreal capitulated.

La Corne decided to leave for France. He sailed from Quebec on 15 Oct. 1761, but drowned with three of his relatives when the *Auguste* sank the following month off the coast of Cape Breton. Louis's branch of the La Corne family came to an end with the death of his wife at Repentigny (Que.) in 1768 at the age of 91.

C. J. RUSS

AN, Col., D²ᶜ, 222/1, p. 165 (PAC transcript); E, 242, 243; Marine, C⁷, 175. ANQ-M, Greffe de C.-R. Gaudron de Chevremont, 3 avril 1733; Greffe de Michel Lepailleur, 17 janv. 1728; Greffe de J.-C. Raimbault, 2, 17 sept. 1728, 31 juill. 1730, 31 mars, 14 juin 1731; Registre d'état civil, Notre-Dame de Montréal, 21 juin 1704. La Corne's precise movements between 1755 and 1760 may be found in *Collection des manuscrits du maréchal de Lévis* (Casgrain), I, II, V, VI, VII, VIII, X, XI. *See also:* "Les 'Mémoires' du chevalier de La Pause," APQ *Rapport, 1932–33*, 333–38, 373–91. Fauteux, *Les chevaliers de Saint-Louis*, 148–49. Le Jeune, *Dictionnaire*. Tanguay, *Dictionnaire*. Champagne, *Les La Vérendrye, passim*. J.-N. Fauteux, *Essai sur l'industrie*, II, 301–4. Frégault, *Canada: the war of the conquest*, 167–68, 170–71, 258–59. Gosselin, *L'Église du Canada jusqu'à la conquête*, III, 118–20, 179–80, 504–5. Stanley, *New France*.

LA CORNE DE CHAPTES, MARIE-MADELEINE DE, *dite* **du Saint-Sacrement,** sister of the Congregation of Notre-Dame; b. 1700 in France, daughter of Jean-Louis de La Corne* de Chaptes and Marie Pécaudy de Contrecœur; d.13 March 1762 in Montreal.

Marie-Madeleine de La Corne de Chaptes was born in France in 1700, while her father, a soldier, was on leave in his native land. Within four years the La Corne family had returned to New France, and in 1718 Marie-Madeleine requested admittance to the Congregation of Notre-Dame of Montreal. Since she had been born in the year of Marguerite Bourgeoys*'s death, she received the name in religion that had been taken by the founder of the congregation, "Sœur du Saint-Sacrement." In 1720 she took her simple vows of religion. From then on she shared in the apostolic activities of the sisters in Montreal and in the parish of Sainte-Famille on Île d'Orléans.

The life that Sœur du Saint-Sacrement led for 44 years in the Congregation of Notre-Dame was uneventful. It was only after her death on 13 March 1762 that she attracted attention in the annals of her community because of a dispute between her family and the congregation concerning the succession of her brother Louis de LA CORNE, known as Chevalier de La Corne, who had died in the shipwreck of the *Auguste* on 15 Nov. 1761. As he had died childless, his succession had legally been allotted to all his surviving brothers and sisters, including Marie-Madeleine. Consequently the community claimed from Luc de La Corne*, known as La Corne Saint-Luc, the share of the inheritance due his sister. The nuns had a legitimate claim to it: when Marie-Madeleine had joined the congregation, her father, who was burdened with a large family and whose only resource was his salary of 400 *livres*, was unable to pay his daughter's dowry in cash and had had her accepted by means of her future rights. In a letter to the superior of the congregation on 18 June 1718 Bishop Saint-Vallier [La Croix*] had personally approved the arrangement reached between M. de La Corne and the community. But La Corne Saint-Luc flatly refused to give the nuns the share of the succession due his sister, alleging that there was neither a written contract nor a will in their favour at the time of her death on 13 March 1762. The matter was then taken to the Chamber of Militia. In a declaration on 16 Nov. 1762 the court decided in favour of the community. But the five other heirs to the succession appealed the decision to the governor of Montreal, Thomas Gage*. The sisters also made representations to Gage, who "condemned M. de La Corne [Luc de La Corne] to give the congregation 2,000 *livres* for his sister's dowry and in addition to pay interest on this sum from the date of her profession."

ANDRÉE DÉSILETS

ACND, La Congrégation de Notre-Dame : son personnel, 1653–1768 ; Fichier général des sœurs de la Congrégation de Notre-Dame; Plan des lieux de sépulture depuis 1681–CND; Registre des sépultures des sœurs de la Congrégation de Notre-Dame; Registre général des sœurs de la Congrégation de Notre-Dame. Desrosiers, "Correspondance de cinq vicaires généraux," APQ *Rapport, 1947–48*, 88, 94. J.-J. Lefebvre, "Inventaire des biens de Luc Lacorne de Saint-Luc," APQ *Rapport, 1947–48*, 29–70. Tanguay, *Dictionnaire*. Lemire-Marsolais et Lambert, *Histoire de la Congrégation de Notre-Dame*, III, 287, 299; IV, 101, 102, 177, 428–35.

LA CORNE DUBREUIL, FRANÇOIS-JOSUÉ DE, officer in the colonial regular troops; b. 7 Oct. 1710, son of Jean-Louis de La Corne* de Chaptes and Marie Pécaudy de Contrecœur; d. in Quebec on 17 Oct. 1753.

François-Josué de La Corne Dubreuil, like his older brothers, was involved in the military and commercial life of the interior of the colony in the 1740s and 1750s. In 1739 he served as second in command at Michilimackinac while François de Couagne looked after his financial affairs in Montreal. Two years later he was commandant at Fort Kaministiquia (Thunder Bay, Ont.) on the northwest shore of Lake Superior. Dubreuil evidently exercised his permission to trade at this post, for in 1741 alone he borrowed over 2,000 *livres*' worth of powder and cloth from Joseph de FLEURY de La Gorgendière, agent-general for the Compagnie des Indes.

That same year friction among western Indians led to indecisive intertribal warfare, and in the fall of 1742 Dubreuil had to use diplomacy to convince the Ojibwas in the Kaministiquia area not to attack their enemies. His rhetoric was so persuasive that in the winter of 1742–43 the Ojibwas hunted peacefully alongside their enemies, the Sioux and the Sauks, in the Snake River region west of Lake Superior.

In Montreal on 28 Dec. 1745 Ensign Dubreuil married Michelle Hervieux, daughter of a family involved in the western trade. He remained in Montreal for five or six years and then returned to the west where, with the rank of lieutenant, he pursued his career in the Ohio country. In June 1753 he contracted a serious illness while surveying the portage at Fort de la Rivière au Boeuf (Waterford, Pa.). His condition rapidly deteriorated, forcing him to leave the Ohio valley and return to Quebec. He died in the capital on 17 Oct. 1753. Dubreuil was survived by his wife and their only child, François-Michel, who was probably the cadet "La Corne Dubreuil" drowned with his uncle Louis de LA CORNE in the sinking of the *Auguste* in November 1761.

C. J. RUSS

AN, Col., C¹¹ᴬ, 79, pp.157–59 (PAC transcripts). ANQ-M, Greffe de J.-C. Porlier, 12 juin 1741. "Les congés de traite sous le régime français au Canada," APQ *Rapport, 1922–23*, 196. Le Jeune, *Dictionnaire*. Tanguay, *Dictionnaire*. Champagne, *Les La Vérendrye*, 262, 298–301. Nish, *Les bourgeois-gentilshommes*.

LA CORRIVEAU, MARIE-JOSEPHTE CORRIVEAU, dite. See CORRIVEAU

LA COUR, CLAUDE-MICHEL BÉGON DE. See BÉGON

La Cour

LA COUR, MARIE-ÉLISABETH BÉGON DE.
See ROCBERT DE LA MORANDIÈRE

LA CROIX, HUBERT-JOSEPH DE, doctor, botanizer; b. 1703, son of Dominique de La Croix and Catherine Clément, both from Liège (Belgium); d. 5 Jan. 1760 at Beaumont (Que.).

Nothing is known about Hubert-Joseph de La Croix's activities prior to his marriage, which took place in Quebec on 4 Feb. 1732. He married Anne-Madeleine Dontaille, who bore him 16 children, 9 of whom died in infancy. The newly married couple seem to have settled at Montmagny, where La Croix practised medicine. Around 1735 the La Croixs came to live in Quebec, Hubert-Joseph hoping to succeed Michel Sarrazin* as king's physician. The appointment went to Jean-François GAULTIER, who was probably better qualified.

La Croix presumably practised his profession at the Hôtel-Dieu of Quebec, where he was, moreover, hospitalized in 1740. Little is known about his career as a doctor, but his interest in botany is better documented, thanks to his shipments of plants to enrich the Jardin du Roi (Muséum National d'Histoire Naturelle) in Paris. On at least two occasions La Croix sent living or dried specimens from the region around Quebec or even Montmagny. In 1739 Intendant Hocquart* dispatched to Buffon, the intendant of the Jardin du Roi, "a case of plants" collected by La Croix. The following year the intendant of New France mentioned to Maurepas, the minister of Marine, that "an excess of plants [had] been collected by the Sieur La Croix, a surgeon at Quebec"; the intendant emphasized that he had even awarded him a gratuity. This financial aid [*see* Jean-Baptiste GOSSELIN] and the encouragement given to the study of the natural sciences by the Académie des Sciences of Paris allowed new botanizers to be recruited more easily to take the place of the conscientious botanist and observer Michel Sarrazin.

Hubert-Joseph de La Croix died at Beaumont on 5 Jan. 1760. One of his sons, also Hubert-Joseph, was a member of the first House of Assembly of Lower Canada in 1792. La Croix did not have Sarrazin's talent and great ability; his contribution to the advancement of Canadian botany is minimal or else unknown; but he belongs to the group of doctor-naturalists whose scientific activity deserves to be emphasized.

CATHERINE FORTIN-MORISSET

AHDQ, Registres des malades. PAC *Report, 1905*, I, pt.vi, 20, 36, 59. P.-G. Roy, *Inv. contrats de mariage*, III, 287. Tanguay, *Dictionnaire*. Ahern, *Notes pour l'histoire de la médecine*, 124–27. Gosselin, *L'Église du Canada jusqu'à la conquête*, II, 384. Arthur Vallée, *Un biologiste canadien: Michel Sarrazin, 1659–1735, sa vie, ses travaux et son temps* (Québec, 1927), 195 Jacques Rousseau, "Michel Sarrazin, Jean-François Gaultier et l'étude prélinnéenne de la flore canadienne," *Les botanistes français en Amérique du Nord avant 1850* (Colloques internationaux du C.N.R.S., LXIII, Paris, 1957), 155.

LAFERTÉ, CATHERINE LEPAILLEUR DE.
See JÉRÉMIE, *dit* Lamontagne

LAFITAU, JOSEPH-FRANÇOIS, priest, Jesuit, missionary, discoverer of ginseng in North America, author of *Mœurs des sauvages amériquains* ...; baptized 31 May 1681 at Bordeaux, France, son of Jean Lafitau, wine merchant and banker, and Catherine Berchenbos; d. 3 July 1746 at Bordeaux.

The Lafitau family gave two sons to the Jesuits: Joseph-François and Pierre-François (1685–1764). The latter became bishop of Sisteron, France, and was much respected in Rome; he defended his older brother's literary activities, and helped get his books published. The family's resources meant ready access to books, and its commercial activities in a busy port, harbouring vessels from New France, the Antilles, South America, and Africa, afforded opportunities to hear strange tongues and witness diverse manners. Exhibits of captives from the New World were a tradition at Bordeaux festivals. Besides the wines of Gironde, Bordeaux could boast the eminence of Montaigne, and would also claim Montesquieu.

Joining the Jesuits of his native city in the autumn of his 15th year, Joseph-François Lafitau thereafter received a typical Jesuit education. After finishing his noviciate in 1698, he studied philosophy for two years and rhetoric for a year at Pau (1698–1701), before teaching grammar for a year at Limoges (1702); then he read and taught humanities at Saintes for three years (1703–5), and taught rhetoric for a year back at Pau (1706). He completed his studies at Poitiers with a year of philosophy and two years of theology (1706–9), passing his last year at La Flèche and finally going to the Collège Louis-le-Grand in Paris, where he completed the course in theology in 1711. This was a fair sample of centres of learning in France. During these years he must have read works on the customs of ancient peoples and the New World which would later provide background when he was studying the customs of the Iroquois.

On 10 April 1711, from Paris, he petitioned the general of the Society of Jesus, Michelangelo

Tamburini, at Rome, to go to the missions of New France, and was granted permission to leave at the end of the year. Arrangements for his third probationary year in the field and his voyage would be made with the procurator in Paris, Father Jean de Lamberville*. Meanwhile, an ordained priest, he had returned home to be professor of rhetoric at the college of Bordeaux.

Lafitau arrived in New France just before the treaty of Utrecht (1713) and toward the end of a period of intense hostility with the Five Nations. Reporting at Quebec, he was soon ordered to Sault-Saint-Louis (Caughnawaga), on the south shore of the St Lawrence opposite Montreal. Here he remained nearly six years (1712–1717) as missionary. To this settlement founded by Pierre Raffeix*, Jacques Frémin*, and Jean de Lamberville, Iroquois converts had been drawn, especially from the Mohawks. By 1682 it had a winter population of some 600 residents in 60 lodges, and a transient summer population half again as large. Kinship ties with the Iroquois confederacy remained strong. At the time of CHARLEVOIX's visit in 1708, and before Lafitau arrived in 1712, the community was declining because intensive cultivation of maize had depleted the soil, firewood was scarce, and the brandy traffic was debauching both longhouse and chapel. But Sault-Saint-Louis still had a great tradition among the Jesuits and Iroquois. There were experienced Jesuits at the mission who could help Lafitau in the studies he soon undertook. Jacques Bruyas* had reduced Iroquois verbs to a system during a long residence at Oneida (N.Y.). Most important was Julien Garnier*, then quite aged and a veteran of 50 years among the Iroquois, who became his tutor, and before whom Lafitau pronounced his vows in the Jesuit church at Montreal on 25 Aug. 1716. On 12 September both men were in Quebec to sign the *Cahier des vœux*, which afforded Lafitau an opportunity to consult books not at the mission.

There are few clues as to how Lafitau gathered information from his Indian subjects; he names no sources among them. Rather his interests ran to topics, and his scientific bent was soon directed not only to discovery but also to publication. He afterward wrote that five of his six years in Canada were spent among the Indians, that he read the *Relations* of previous missionaries, and that he was not content simply to know the practices of the Indians but wanted to erect a science of customs by comparing their manners with those of the peoples of antiquity. He was a keen observer himself, and his writing is salted with penetrating insights which combine theory and verification.

We can infer how he worked from his report on the discovery of ginseng (1718), which made him famous in the academies of Europe. In a letter dated 12 April 1711 to the procurator of the missions in India and China, afterwards widely published in Europe, Father Pierre Jartoux first reported the ginseng of Tartary. This letter Lafitau chanced to see on a visit to Quebec in October 1715. For reasons relating to climate and surroundings Jartoux concluded that the plant ought to occur in Canada, and Lafitau set out to find it. Knowing that the Iroquois valued medicinal knowledge above all else, he thought they might know it, and if so he would have partial proof of their own Asiatic origin. The plant was indeed native to North America and that it had not been discovered up to then was a comment on the low regard of the French for Indian medicine and the failure of his colleagues who knew the languages to extract information. Lafitau soon discovered that a little respect for the ability and learning of Indians would weaken their opposition to divulging private knowledge. The Iroquois herbalists encouraged him to continue the hunt, and one day he chanced to see the plant growing by a house. Amazingly a Mohawk woman whom he had hired to hunt for it herself recognized it as one of the common remedies of the Iroquois, and, acting on his description of the Chinese respect for it, she cured herself of a chronic fever. He promptly sent to Quebec for Jartoux's publication and his informants readily identified the plant from the plate. Lafitau was thus the first to employ botanical plates in the field to elicit information from native informants. Ginseng was reputed as an aphrodisiac in Asia and a proven febrifuge in the New World; the published report of his 1716 discovery was to set off a hunt by market collectors that well nigh eradicated the species from the St Lawrence valley and prompted attempts to grow the species commercially both there and in France. His 1718 memoir further comments on related species of the Araliaceae – notably Spikenard and Sarsaparilla – which Mohawk herbalists still employ.

Three other examples from his work on the Indians document his powers of observation and illustrate his ability to make theoretical inferences from field data and reading. In treating the topic of housing he probed the Iroquois term for themselves – Builders of Lodges – and observed so carefully how longhouses were erected that his detailed description can readily be translated into an architectural rendering, and compares favourably with later accounts by John Bartram (1751) and Lewis Henry Morgan (1851). Second, by noting the actual composition of a household he

Lafitau

worked out what are recognized as the basic rules of Iroquois kinship and exogamy. Thirdly, he perceived how the village council of elders functions as the basic unit of Iroquois political structure and how status is equated with age-grading. Finally, noting the inferior workmanship and crankiness of the Iroquois' elm bark canoes, which were inventions of necessity when they could not purchase birchbark canoes of superior workmanship from peoples living within the range of the canoe birch, he developed what is an argument of cultural speciality and ecological fit: the Algonkians were artists in birchbark and the Iroquois perforce workers in elm bark; like the discovery of ginseng, this presentation shows a nice use of theory and fact.

Lafitau returned to France in 1717 to present a memorial at court in person opposing the sale of brandy to the Indians; he was also to secure permission for removal of the mission village of Sault-Saint-Louis from the rapids to its present site where the soil is better and the strategic location more advantageous. In the former undertaking he was partially successful; in the latter completely.

The urgent appeal of Julien Garnier, Lafitau's superior in Canada, for his early return, on the grounds that he uniquely appreciated the language and culture of the Iroquois, was evidently denied. Why was Lafitau kept in France? Incomplete records of correspondence in the Jesuit archives in Rome have recently provided further information about his activities in Europe. Presumably Joseph-François went to Rome in 1718, personally to hand the second of his petitions to Tamburini on behalf of the mission, including an appeal for his return. His brother had gone to Rome earlier. They were there together on business sometime in 1719–20, just when is not certain; in the spring of 1720 Joseph-François was ill and his arrival in Rome was still anticipated in late October, when the general congratulated him on settling some controversy within the Canada mission in the manner of his distinguished brother. In March 1721 Tamburini wrote to Joseph-François: "It is not a small obligation that I owe for what you have accomplished in Paris; and what your brother has accomplished in Rome." Tamburini evidently held the Lafitau brothers in high esteem, especially Pierre-François, a gifted diplomat and soon to be elevated to monsignor; he respected Joseph-François's scientific accomplishments, and he needed someone at court in France who could get things done with the regent, Philippe, Duc d'Orléans. The administrative needs of the order thus apparently took precedence over the

Canada mission; Joseph-François was kept in France, and became procurator in Paris of the Jesuit missions in New France in 1722. He shared this office with Father Louis d'Avaugour* from 1723 to 1732, then held it alone until 1741; this arrangement explains how Lafitau found time to write. After publishing his great work, Lafitau actually returned to Canada for a year between 1727 and 1729, when he is listed as superior of the Sault-Saint-Louis mission.

The *Mémoire . . . concernant la précieuse plante du gin-seng . . .* had been presented to the regent in 1718, and Lafitau wrote his two-volume *Mœurs des sauvages amériquains . . .* between 1722 and 1724. This work of comparative ethnology, again dedicated to the regent, was an immediate success and went through two printings in 1724, the first in two quarto volumes and the second in four octavo. It was soon available in Dutch (1751) and later in German. The two original volumes are of disproportionate length and emphasis. Written hastily, the work evidently got out of hand: the first volume contains a book-length chapter on religion, but only two chapters on ethnographic topics. Later Lafitau decided to issue the chapter on religion separately, and his brother, now bishop, guaranteed the printing; but after Joseph-François had secured the necessary permissions from his order and other church authorities, oddly enough the civil censor frustrated his plans. Apparently Lafitau had let some of his colleagues see the second version of the chapter; later he accused one of them of pirating his ideas, without giving a name. At one point he had entrusted the manuscript to Father Antoine Gaubil of the China mission who kept it until after Lafitau's death, when he wrote: "I failed at the time to read it because of other occupations. I intended to send him my views, especially with regard to China, when I was apprised of his death . . . without knowing whether his manuscript, full of citations of every kind, had been printed. . . ."

Lafitau published two other works. One, *Histoire de Jean de Brienne, Roy de Jérusalem et Empereur de Constantinople* (Paris, 1727), was released before he returned to Canada; it is little known and seldom seen. A two-volume *Histoire des découvertes et conquestes des Portugais dans le Nouveau Monde . . .* (1733) appeared after he came home to France. Frequently found in libraries, it is not just a compilation of original sources but an attempt to make available to French readers a story of exploration and adventure otherwise denied to them; in the chronicles he sees a long development of customs hitherto unnoticed, such as he had reported in the *Mœurs*;

from them, understood only, he says, in the original languages of the people who practise them, he builds his "system" or philosophy of history, and once more he is concerned too with the relation between custom and natural history, or ecology.

Lafitau is of special interest today to historians of anthropology. What sets him apart from his immediate predecessors and contemporaries is, indeed, his explicit formulation of a method for recovering the past; without reference to dates, places, or persons, and putting himself outside of events, he uses his observations in America by a kind of evolutionary inference to illuminate the customs and practices of antiquity. Lafitau's concept of the method of reciprocal illumination came from two kinds of sources: the literature of exploration of the New World – writers such as André Thevet*, Marc Lescarbot*, and José de Acosta – which compared peoples of the new and ancient worlds; and second, the literature on heathen conformities written by contemporaries and predecessors about religions of the Orient. But where Lafitau departs from all the grand comparators is in his stress on the importance of describing cultures in terms of themselves. In his view the savages of the New World were men, the Iroquois were people in their own right, and their customary ways were worthy of study. This was a new kind of primitivism that would transform generic savages into specific Indians.

Although many of his comparisons seem far-fetched today, and his inferences from them unjustified, he was more competent than his contemporaries and more mature because of his unique way of utilizing field observations to criticize earlier sources on the Iroquoian peoples and of employing their customs as a means of understanding the nature of antique society and culture. The extent to which his work exceeded expectations for historiography and belonged to another genre prompted his colleague Charlevoix, himself an historian, to remark of the *Mœurs*, ". . . we have nothing more exact on this subject. The parallel between ancient nations and the Americans is very ingenious, and shows a great familiarity with antiquity." Indeed it is possible that Charlevoix, who had returned to France in 1722 and was assigned to the editorial staff of the Jesuit journal, the *Mémoires*, at the moment when Lafitau was writing the *Mœurs*, was responsible for the extensive review articles which began to appear while Lafitau's book was still in manuscript and alerted the learned world to its scope and importance (and price) while it was in press.

Largely ignored by the great minds of the Enlightenment, Lafitau's reputation has been rehabilitated by historians of ideas in the present century. In Paris on the eve of World War I, Arnold Van Gennep critically appraised Lafitau and his period, applauding his systematic sense and pointing to him as an inspiration for modern French ethnology. Similarly Gilbert Chinard (1913) discovered and placed him in the history of French thought. Recently, Alfred Métraux has compared the outline of Lafitau's work to a modern anthropological textbook; but M. T. Hodgen has demonstrated that the arrangement of his table of contents reflects the concerns of the Reformation, and that cultural classifications based on these concerns had become the accepted way to organize such a work. After a "Design and Plan" in two preliminary chapters, Lafitau gives an Asiatic origin for the peoples of America, considers the "Idea and Character of Savages in General," whom he finds quite human, and then plunges into the troublesome morass of "Religion," at last emerging to finish volume one with "Political Government" and "Marriage and Education." Volume two opens with paired chapters on the division of labour by sex – "Occupations of Men in the Village" and "Occupations of Women," the latter being crucial in a kinship state based on matriliny; then follow appropriately major chapters on "War" and on "Embassies and Trade" – chief activities of Iroquois men; "Hunting and Fishing" get short shrift to our impoverishment, although "Games," of perennial interest to the court of Versailles, rate 20 pages; there are two balanced chapters on "Sickness and Medicine" and "Death, Burial and Mourning," representing pervasive concerns of the Iroquois even today. The final chapter on "Language" falls short of the mark attained by his predecessors, particularly Pierre-Joseph-Marie Chaumonot* and Bruyas, and belies Garnier's claim for Lafitau's abilities.

But "Lafitau . . . took the first step toward ethnological research for its own sake," as K. Birket-Smith has remarked. And his contributions were not inconsiderable. He brought forward the empirical evidence for exploding the notion then prevalent in Europe that stone implements similar to celts that he observed Indians grinding were "thunder stones." In social organization, he discovered matriliny, and outlined the classificatory kinship system of the Iroquois, which L. H. Morgan, who never read Lafitau, was to rediscover a century later; he related residence to social structure; and he indicated the importance of age-grading in differentiating the status and role of warriors and chiefs. This last contribution marked him for the social anthro-

Lafontaine

pologists who from Sir John Myers to A. R. Radcliffe-Brown would claim him as a pioneer in their discipline. In his treatment of the boundaries of local government – the importance of the old men in decision-making – he anticipated the present interest in political anthropology.

No prophet, Lafitau had his eye on the contemporary scene. That a matron had the power to make peace or war would certainly be news in Europe. And he had learned as a citizen of France under Louis XV that war is but one face of politics and of the state. He probed the subtleties of Iroquois "cold war" tactics and diplomacy. He described warrior bands travelling enormous distances through sombre forests to strike a blow, lift a few scalps, take prisoners, and then fade into the wilderness. He knew the need of replenishing dwindling numbers by adopting captives rather than burning them, a choice in which women could influence the council of elders. He observed that the Iroquois old men had learned the advantage of federation in contending with their neighbours, and with the whites; but he nowhere describes the League of the Five Nations as such or lists the composition of tribal delegations to the Grand Council at Onondaga (near Syracuse, N.Y.). Today we should like more historical depth on surviving Iroquois political institutions; but in the area of local politics at the village level, Lafitau's empirical observations are unexcelled.

At various points Lafitau discusses the Condoling Council and its attendant customs, which he compares with those of the ancients. The guarantee of continuity for Iroquois society and polity even now is their custom of resuscitating the dead by symbolically passing on the name or title to a living person, who assumes the personality and duties of the deceased. This perpetuation is the purpose of the Condoling Council for installing chiefs, whose ritual roots we can trace to the treaty-making process and alliance systems of the first third of the 17th century.

In his own day Lafitau was a man of the past; but in his scientific contributions he belongs to the 18th century, for he was a voyageur in the mainstream of empirical ethnography.

WILLIAM N. FENTON

Joseph-François Lafitau, *Mémoire présenté à S.A.R. Mgr le duc d'Orléans . . . concernant la précieuse plante du gin-seng de Tartarie, découverte en Canada* (Paris, 1718; Hospice Verreau, édit., Montréal, 1855); *Mœurs des sauvages amériquains, comparées aux mœurs des premiers temps* (2v., Paris, 1724; 4v., Paris, 1724); *Histoire des découvertes et conquestes des Portugais dans le Nouveau Monde . . .* (2v., Paris, 1733); *De Zeden der Wilden van Amerika . . .* (Amsterdam,

1751); "Mémoire du P. Lafitau: sur la boisson [vendue] aux sauvages," *JR* (Thwaites), LXVII, 38–46.

AD, Gironde (Bordeaux), État civil, Bordeaux, 31 mai 1681. ARSI, Aquitaine 7, f.261; 12, f.318; Epist. Gen. ad diversos, 1719–1726, VI, 46; Epp. NN.; Francia 49, 79/133–34, 116, 209ff.; Gallia 65; Gallia 110, ff.133, 331–33. *Bibliothèque de la Compagnie de Jésus, première partie: bibliographie par les pères Augustin et Aloys de Backer; seconde partie: histoire, par Augustin Carayon*, Carlos Sommervogel, édit. (11v., Bruxelles, Paris, 1890–1932). John Bartram, *Observations on the inhabitants, climate, soil, rivers, productions, animals, and other matters worthy of notice, made by Mr. John Bartram, in his travels from Pensilvania to Onondago, Oswego and the Lake Ontario, in Canada; to which is annex'd a curious account of the cataracts at Niagara, by Mr. Peter Kalm, a Swedish gentleman who travelled there* (London, 1751). Kaj Birket-Smith, *The paths of culture: a general ethnology*, trans. Karin Fennow (Madison, Milwaukee, 1965). Gilbert Chinard, *L'Amérique et le rêve exotique dans la littérature française au XVIIe et au XVIIIe siècle* (Paris, 1913). J. M. Cooper, "Joseph-François Lafitau (1681–1746)," *Encyclopaedia of the social sciences*, ed. E. R. A. Seligman (15v., New York, 1930–35). M. T. Hodgen, *Early anthropology in the sixteenth and seventeenth centuries* (Philadelphia, 1964). F. E. Manuel, *The eighteenth century confronts the gods* (Cambridge, Mass., 1959). L. H. Morgan, *League of the Ho-dé-no-sau-nee, or Iroquois* (Rochester, N.Y., 1851). A. R. Radcliffe-Brown, *Method in social anthropology: selected essays*, ed. M. N. Srinivas (Chicago, 1958). Rochemonteix, *Les Jésuites et la N.-F. au XVIIIe siècle*, III, 384–86.

Kaj Birket-Smith, "The history of ethnology in Denmark: Huxley memorial lecture for 1952," Royal Anthropological Institute of Great Britain and Ireland *Journal* (London), LXXXII (1952), 115–28. W. N. Fenton, "Contacts between Iroquois herbalism and colonial medicine," Smithsonian Institution *Annual Report, 1940–41*, 503–26; "J.-F. Lafitau (1681–1746), precursor of scientific anthropology," *Southwestern Journal of Anthropology* (Albuquerque, N. Mex.), XXV (1969), 173–87. Alfred Métraux, "Les précurseurs de l'ethnologie en France du XVIe au XVIIIe siècle," *Cahiers d'histoire mondiale/Journal of World History/Cuadernos de Historia mundial* (Neuchâtel), VII (1962–63), 721–38. Léon Pouliot, "Les procureurs parisiens de la mission de la Nouvelle-France," *Lettres du Bas-Canada* (Saint-Jérôme, Qué.), XXII (1968), 38–52. Arnold Van Gennep, "Contributions à l'histoire de la méthode ethnographique," *Revue de l'histoire des religions* (Paris), LXVII (1913), 321–38.

LAFONTAINE DE BELCOUR (Bellecour, Bellecourt), JACQUES DE (he signed **Delafontaine**), member of the Conseil Supérieur, attorney general and commissary for the south shore of the St Lawrence River (Quebec district); b. 22 Sept. 1704 and baptized on 24 September in the parish of Notre-Dame, Versailles, France, son of Jean-Baptiste de Lafontaine, ordinary of the king's music at Versailles, and Bernardine Jouin; m. at Quebec, on 24 Oct. 1728, Charlotte Bissot by whom he had 12 children, and secondly Geneviève Lambert on 7 Aug. 1751 by whom he had three children; d. at Quebec 18 June 1765.

Jacques de Lafontaine arrived in Canada in 1726 as Charles de BEAUHARNOIS's secretary and protégé, and from then on schemed to make a fortune. Apart from a dowry of 4,000 *livres* and whatever charms Charlotte Bissot may have possessed, he was attracted to marry her in 1728 by a ten-year partnership with her father, François-Joseph Bissot*, to exploit the seal fisheries and Indian trade at his seigneury of Mingan on the Labrador coast (now part of Quebec). The venture failed, and Lafontaine withdrew in 1732 after Bissot agreed to pay him 2,000 *livres* compensation for his losses.

Thinking he could do better on his own, Lafontaine leased Mingan from Bissot in 1733, but withdrew the following year to exploit the more valuable concession recently granted him by Beauharnois and Gilles Hocquart*, the intendant: a nine-year monopoly of the seal fishery and Indian trade between the rivers Itamamion (Étamamiou) and Nontagamion (Nétagamiou) on the north shore of the St Lawrence River. Immediately he plunged into a dispute with the owners of the islands opposite the post of Mingan which were crucial for seal fishing. In the fall and spring the migrating seals passed through the narrow channels between the islands and the mainland; there hunters stretched nets to trap them. The inheritance from Lafontaine's father-in-law (who died in 1737) was limited to the mainland concession of Mingan, the islands being part of a seigneury conceded to Jacques de Lalande de Gayon and Louis Jolliet* jointly in 1679, extending a great length along the Labrador coast from Mingan to Spanish Cove (Baie des Esquimaux, Que.). The families of Bissot, Lalande, and Jolliet were, however, related by marriage so that the inheritors of the Mingan islands were the cousins and uncle of Lafontaine's wife.

The vagueness of the original concessions explains some of the litigation among the numerous inheritors, but greed probably counted for much; as early as 1734 the owners of the islands complained that Lafontaine was encroaching on their rights and trying to engross all the profits. They also accused him of illegal trade. Selling brandy to the Indians, trading with the English, and shipping beaver pelts directly to France instead of to the receiving offices of the Compagnie des Indes at Quebec were all illegal but commonly engaged in by the owners of Labrador concessions. Lafontaine was probably no exception. In 1733 Hocquart ordered him to enforce the laws that forbade selling liquor to the Indians and in 1736 wrote Maurepas, minister of Marine, that although Lafontaine was then behaving himself he had formerly displayed "some irregularity in his conduct."

Joseph de FLEURY de La Gorgendière, spokesman for the Jolliet inheritors, claimed the islands opposite Lafontaine's post of Nontagamion as belonging to the Mingan islands. Lafontaine denied the claim as implying too vast an original grant. In 1737 he asked that his concession include these islands, and subsequently that it be prolonged, first for life, then in perpetuity. In spite of Beauharnois's support, Maurepas rejected a perpetual concession. The governor and intendant recommended a lifetime grant but without the offshore islands in view of the claim of the Jolliet inheritors. They recommended also that the owners of these islands concede their use to mainland concession-holders at some prescribed compensation. In 1743, after years of bickering, three per cent of the total product of the seal fisheries was agreed on as proper rent.

Lafontaine's quarrel with his wife's cousins changed abruptly in 1739 when her uncle, Jacques de Lalande, owner of one half the Mingan islands, donated the use of his share to Lafontaine. The latter now did an about-face on the question of how far the Mingan islands extended, suddenly discovered that his wife had had a claim to the islands since her father's death and joined the Jolliet inheritors in exacting compensation from other holders of mainland concessions, notably Claire-Françoise Boucher de Boucherville, widow of Jean-Baptiste POMMEREAU. No sooner did they win this case than La Gorgendière and Lafontaine resumed their family quarrel, which Lafontaine won by virtue of Lalande's donation.

Ambitious, intelligent, and capable, Lafontaine not surprisingly sought royal office as a means of social and material advancement. In 1732, when his commercial fortunes were low, he proposed to the minister that to prevent errors in notarial acts a central repository be established for their registration, requesting that he be given the job of registrar. The minister had been working on the problem for some years, in utmost secrecy to avoid a panic of litigation had the public suspected their property or investments to be in jeopardy. As secretary to Beauharnois, Lafontaine had access to the governor's correspondence and thus tried to take advantage of his inside information. It is not known whether

339

Lafontaine

Lafontaine influenced subsequent reforms of notarial procedures.

In 1734, the year that the four junior councillors of the Conseil Supérieur were granted a salary of 300 *livres*, Lafontaine asked to be given one of the vacant positions. With a recommendation from Beauharnois and Hocquart, he was appointed in 1735. An application to become also a principal writer was refused by Hocquart. In November 1740 he was appointed interim lieutenant general for civil and criminal affairs in the royal jurisdiction at Montreal upon the death of Pierre Raimbault* and served until the new judge, Jacques-Joseph GUITON de Monrepos, took office in September 1741. His request for a gratuity from the king, with Beauharnois's persistent support, was refused by Maurepas on the grounds that Lafontaine's salary and emoluments while at Montreal were more than adequate to cover all his expenses.

Lafontaine and François DAINE, head clerk of the Conseil Supérieur, were contenders for two posts: in 1743 to succeed Pierre ANDRÉ de Leigne as lieutenant general for civil and criminal affairs of the provost court of Quebec, and in 1751 the lucrative office of director of the Domaine du Roi. Both times Daine won the appointment, the loser pouring invective upon him on the second occasion. Although Beauharnois and Hocquart had suggested both men in 1743, privately Hocquart supported Daine and Beauharnois Lafontaine. Once again Lafontaine found limits to the governor's influence.

On still other occasions Lafontaine sought to exploit quarrels between governor and intendant. In 1737, on Hocquart's recommendation, the Tadoussac post was farmed out to François-Étienne CUGNET. In 1740 Lafontaine offered to pay a much higher rent, whereupon Beauharnois implied to Maurepas that the profitability of the lease had been misrepresented by Cugnet. Hocquart made a masterful defence of Cugnet, perhaps his most effective argument being his comment on Lafontaine's offer: "this farm could not fall into worse hands and . . . at the expiration of the lease accorded to him the basis of the trade would be in total ruin."

Lafontaine applied himself only slightly to his duties as councillor, devoting most of his time to his commercial enterprises. From the 1740s he appeared in court more often as plaintiff or defendant than as judge. He lost more cases than he won.

Despite increasing seal-oil production at his concession of Nontagamion, renewed in 1745, and a substantial inheritance from his sister-in-law in 1747, Lafontaine was sinking into debt.

Yet he bought land on the *côte* Saint-Jean worth 4,600 *livres* and took on a whale-fishing concession at Apetépy on the Labrador coast and a sawmill on the Rivière Chaudière, financing them, however, by borrowing money and forming partnerships, notably with Gilles William STROUDS. In 1754 Lafontaine went bankrupt and his creditors, headed by Jean TACHÉ, took over his Labrador operations.

Lafontaine acquired three seigneuries, apparently for their prestige or speculative value rather than for income: in 1733 a new concession on the Richelieu River, the seigneury of Belcour, reunited to the king's domain in 1741 when nothing had been done to improve it; an *arrière-fief* on the seigneury of Plaines, reunited in 1749; and third, the seigneury Lafontaine de Belcour, granted in 1736. The third one was, however, claimed by Jacques-Hugues PÉAN de Livaudière, who accused Lafontaine of duping the governor and intendant when he knew the land belonged to Péan's wife. Lafontaine was probably gambling that the minister, in his present unsympathetic mood toward seigneurs who did nothing to settle their land, would favour him if he gave evidence of putting the land into production. In the summer of 1740 he made several roturial concessions to habitants, but his title was revoked, though with 948 *livres* compensation for improvements made since 1736.

The higher French officials who commented on Lafontaine agreed upon his exceptional ability and intelligence, but all, except Beauharnois whose defence of his secretary was unfailing, agreed with Hocquart that he was untrustworthy. Two reports, dating from the end of the régime and likely part of the official investigation into the *affaire du Canada*, record damning opinions of Lafontaine.

Perhaps because he guessed he had no future in France, Lafontaine remained in Canada after the conquest. General James Murray*, as part of his policy of gaining the confidence of Canadians, appointed him in the fall of 1760 commissary and attorney general for the south shore (Quebec district). Murray soon reached the same opinion of Lafontaine as Hocquart. The storm broke in October 1763, when Lafontaine wrote the Earl of Halifax that Murray had despoiled him of his property, prevented him from exploiting his post of Mingan in 1761, vindictively deprived two of his daughters of their royal pension, and abused him verbally when he submitted his humble remonstrances. The Lords of Trade ordered a full public investigation so as to assure Canadians of the equity of British justice. In fact, Lafontaine's case was largely an audacious fabrication.

The property in question was the Labrador

post of Gros Mecatina (Île du Gros Mécatina, Que.), which Lafontaine interpreted as the island itself, and therefore part of the Mingan islands, which could not be conceded to someone else. But at no time during the French régime had he or any of his co-inheritors established proprietorship of the post of Gros Mecatina. They had only been guaranteed the three per cent compensation for use of the offshore islands, and Murray offered witnesses to prove this was paid. As for the post of Mingan, Murray maintained, with the support of witnesses and documents, that the owners had not the resources to exploit their post in 1761 and that they were perfectly content with the lease to Joseph Isbister*. Lafontaine's daughters had never had a royal pension. The assistance they were receiving came out of Murray's own pocket, because they were left destitute by Lafontaine himself who had deceptively mortgaged their estates to pay off his own debts. Subsequently, part of his estate was sold and the remainder sequestered to satisfy his creditors, who were never fully repaid. It was in an assembly of Lafontaine and his creditors, after Lafontaine had publicly denied the equity of British justice, that Murray upbraided him for his financial sharp practice and his maltreatment of his daughters, pronouncing him a "wicked man, whose conduct is monstrous and shocking to humanity."

There were other reasons why Murray distrusted Lafontaine, including evidence of disloyalty and misuse of his position as attorney general. Lafontaine may have struck out at Murray in 1763 because of his inability to resist fishing in troubled waters, and the mounting dissatisfaction of English merchants with Murray's policies may have led him to gamble on Murray's recall. The Lafontaine affair was included among the merchants' grievances in their petition to the king in 1765. Murray, of course, was exonerated of all accusations against him.

Lafontaine died at Quebec on 18 June 1765. Despite his intelligence, his considerable influence with Governor Beauharnois, and his advantageous first marriage, Jacques de Lafontaine squandered a fortune, mismanaged what should have been a profitable enterprise, and earned the distrust of most people with whom he had dealings.

S. DALE STANDEN

AD, Yvelines (Versailles), État civil, Notre-Dame, Versailles, 24 sept. 1704. AN, Col., B, 57, ff.694v–96; 61, f.567; 63, f.473v; 64, f.428v; 65, f.407; 66, ff.241v–42; 68, ff.278, 293v–94v; 70, ff.320f., 321f., 329f., 334f.; 74, ff.430, 440f., 460v; 76, ff.364, 369f., 410–11v; 78, f.316v; 87, ff.183f.; 89, ff.261f.; 91, ff.257f.; 93, f.196; C¹¹A, 57, ff.247–51; 58, ff.167–72v;

61, ff.231–32, 276–77v; 65, ff.33–34; 66, ff.88–89, 114, 131–32v; 67, ff.6v–7, 119f.; 69, ff.46f.; 70, f.9; 71, ff.12–13, 14–15v, 80f.; 73, ff.40f., 42f.; 74, ff.31, 93–95, 131–32; 75, ff.217v–18; 76, ff.8–13; 77, ff.86f., 352–54, 365–67; 79, ff.61v, 148f., 209f., 343–45v; 80, f.271v; 83, f.261; C¹¹B, 32, pp.335–37 (PAC transcripts); D²ᴰ, 1; E, 114, pp.2–11, 12–14, 17f.; 246 (PAC transcripts); Section Outre-Mer, G¹, 462, ff.325–31. ANQ, Greffe de Jacques Barbel, 18 oct. 1728; Greffe de R.-C. Barolet, 5 avril 1732, 22 août 1753, 11, 15 août 1737, 11 sept. 1738, 10, 28 juill., 20 août 1740, 10 janv. 1744, 16 oct. 1747, 4 sept. 1752; Greffe de Nicolas Boisseau, 19 oct. 1740; Greffe de C.-H. Du Laurent, 15 déc. 1748, 3 mars, 24 mai, 31 août 1751; Greffe de J.-C. Panet, 25 août 1746, 21 mars, 1ᵉʳ oct., 2 nov. 1747; Greffe de J.-N. Pinguet de Vaucour, 15 oct. 1744, 15 févr., 13 mars 1745; AP, Charlotte Bissot; NF, Coll. de pièces jud. et not., 1204, 1267, 1279, 1455, 1634, 1831, 1855, 4127. PAC, MG 23, GII, 1, 2, pp.92f.; MG 30, D58, 1, pp.1–48.

Édits ord., II, 354–58, 550–51, 567–72; III, 315, 470. *Inv. de pièces du Labrador* (P.-G. Roy), I, 5, 46, 55, 103, 138, 147, 149, 193, 196, 198. "Les 'papiers' La Pause." APQ *Rapport, 1933–34*, 218–19. Le Jeune, *Dictionnaire*, I, 152. P.-G. Roy, *Inv. jug. et délib., 1717–1760*, IV, 50, 176; VI, 2, 3, 21, 44. Tanguay, *Dictionnaire*. P.-G. Roy, "Les secrétaires des gouverneurs et intendants de la Nouvelle-France," *BRH*, XLI (1935), 74–107.

LA FRANCE, JOSEPH, fur-trader; b. *c.* 1707 at Michilimackinac, the son of a French fur-trader and an Ojibwa woman; d. between 1742 and 1749.

When Joseph La France was about five his father took him to Quebec to spend the winter learning French. La France left the *pays d'en haut* for a second time when he took a cargo of furs to Montreal about 1723. After some nine more years of hunting and trading in the Michilimackinac area, he travelled down the Mississippi as far as the mouth of the Missouri River. The next year he set out from Michilimackinac with a load of furs and made his way to the vicinity of the English post at Oswego (Chouaguen), where some Iroquois sold the furs for him. About 1736 he went to Montreal seeking a licence to trade, which was refused him on the grounds that he had been selling brandy to the Indians.

In danger of arrest as an unlicensed trader, La France determined to deal instead with the English on Hudson Bay. Setting out in 1739, he followed the Rainy Lake, Lake of the Woods, Winnipeg River route to Lac Ouinipigon (Lake Winnipeg). (Whether he was aware of the explorations of Pierre GAULTIER de Varennes et de La Vérendrye in this country during the 1730s is not known.) La France spent the winter of 1740–41 with the Crees of the Lac Ouinipigon area and that of 1741–42 in the region of Lac des Prairies

La Fresnière

(lakes Manitoba and Winnipegosis) and the lower Paskoya (Saskatchewan) River. Travelling by way of the Hayes River, he reached York Factory (Man.) on Hudson Bay in June 1742 with a large band of Indians and a cargo of furs.

Since Hudson's Bay Company posts were forbidden to harbour French traders and since La France refused to return to Michilimackinac, he was sent to England, probably by the factor, Thomas WHITE. He was apparently maintained there at the expense of the admiralty "on Prospect of his being of Service on the Discovery of the North-West Passage." In London about 1742 he met Arthur Dobbs, a leading critic of the HBC; the only source of biographical information on La France is Dobbs' book, *An account of the countries adjoining to Hudson's Bay . . .* , a compilation of narratives relating to the exploration of Hudson Bay and trade in the company's territories. Dobbs was attempting to prove that the HBC had not fulfilled its obligations under its charter and that the fur trade should be thrown open to all merchants. He made use of statements by La France in his charges that the HBC was hindering the development of a vastly rich land to the west and south of the bay. By 1749, when a parliamentary committee investigated Dobbs' accusations, La France was dead.

His trip, though discounted at the time because Dobbs' evidence was suspect, is ranked today as an important step in the exploration of the northwest. The map Dobbs based on La France's evidence was primitive, but it pointed out a water route between Lake Superior and Hudson Bay in the years immediately after the La Vérendryes had reached the Lake Winnipeg basin. The description of his journey provides details of climate, game, and vegetation, of the nature of the trade between the interior and York Factory, and of the geographical distribution of the Indian people at the time when white explorers were first approaching the region.

La France had advised the HBC that it could meet growing French competition in the west by establishing posts in the interior and lowering the standard of trade, but the company ignored his advice at the time. In the 1750s, however, it began to send out men like Anthony HENDAY to encourage the Indians to bring their furs down to the bay, and in 1774 it built Cumberland House (Sask.), the first of many posts deep in the western interior.

HARTWELL BOWSFIELD

Arthur Dobbs, *An account of the countries adjoining to Hudson's Bay in the north-west part of America* (London, 1744; repr. New York, 1967). G.B., Parl., *Report from the committee on Hudson's Bay.*

LA FRESNIÈRE, ZACHARIE-FRANÇOIS HERTEL DE. *See* HERTEL

LA GALISSONIÈRE, ROLAND-MICHEL BARRIN DE LA GALISSONIÈRE, Marquis de. *See* BARRIN

LA GAUCHETIÈRE, DANIEL MIGEON DE. *See* MIGEON

LA GORGENDIÈRE, JOSEPH DE FLEURY DE. *See* FLEURY

LA GOUDALIE (La Gondalie), CHARLES DE, priest, Sulpician, missionary; b. *c.* 1678 at Rodez, France; d. *c.* 1753 in Nantes, France.

Charles de La Goudalie received his ecclesiastical training at the seminary of Saint-Sulpice in Paris and was ordained a priest in 1705. He was not, however, immediately admitted as a member of the society. He came from the Massif Central, and it appears that he had the sturdy build of the French peasant; his superior, M. François Lechassier, described him: "He is very robust, hard-working, self-disciplined; his manner is not engaging. However, his charity and zeal give him the ability to win over his fellow-men and make himself liked." La Goudalie arrived in New France in 1707 and took charge of four parishes in turn in the Montreal region: Prairie-de-la-Madeleine (Laprairie) from 1707 to 1708; Sorel, 1708 to 1718; Pointe-aux-Trembles, 1718 to 1727; and Sainte-Anne-du-Bout-de-l'Île (Sainte-Anne-de-Bellevue), 1727 to 1728. In 1728 he had to return to France to be admitted into the society of Saint-Sulpice. He was nominated a missionary in "English Acadia" (Nova Scotia) and was put in charge of the parish of Saint-Charles, which at that time took in the two villages of Grand Pré and Rivière-aux-Canards (near Wolfville). He arrived there in 1729.

In 1730, in conjunction with Noël-Alexandre de Noinville, the parish priest of Pisiquid (Windsor), La Goudalie was successful in negotiating with Richard PHILIPPS, governor of Nova Scotia, the conditions of an oath of allegiance which would suit both the British authorities and the population of Minas Basin. The oath signed by the people of Minas stipulated simply that they would be "completely loyal" to the king of England, who was recognized as "the Sovereign Lord of Nova Scotia and Acadia." On 25 April La Goudalie and Noinville drew up a certificate which declared that Philipps had exempted the

Acadians "from the war against the French and Indians and [that] the aforementioned inhabitants … have promised never to take up arms in the event of war against the kingdom of England and its government." From that date the Acadians were referred to by the British authorities as "French Neutrals," and until the founding of Halifax in 1749 they were not asked to take any other oath. This settlement ended 20 years of discussion on the oath of allegiance and ensured nearly 20 years of relative calm in the internal affairs of Nova Scotia.

In 1731 La Goudalie was appointed the bishop of Quebec's vicar general for English Acadia. He contented himself with increasing the number of missionaries, thus satisfying the religious and political authorities. For their part, the religious authorities wrote: "The missionaries are of great importance to Acadia, the English clergymen [are] insinuating, and simple peoples easily become accustomed to a less confining religion." On the the other hand, except for a few disputes with the lieutenant-governor, Lawrence Armstrong*, La Goudalie maintained excellent relations with the authorities in Annapolis Royal. In 1740, "being of rather advanced age," he returned to France, but as the court had granted him a pension of 800 *livres*, payable to the bishopric of Laon, he agreed to return to Acadia in 1741. He ministered temporarily at Annapolis Royal until Jean-Baptiste de GAY Desenclaves arrived in June 1742, then returned to his former parish.

La Goudalie's return can be explained by the international situation. The Austrian succession had just become open, and a conflict between France and England seemed inevitable; for the first time the Acadians' neutrality was to be tested. At Versailles, as at Annapolis Royal, it seems that people were counting upon La Goudalie's experience to govern the Acadians' conduct under these circumstances. According to Maurepas, the minister of Marine, La Goudalie "offered to procure help for the French" when they attempted to take possession of Annapolis Royal in 1744. In February 1747, however, with his *confrère* Jean-Pierre de Miniac* he obtained the release of a certain Mr Newton, an English officer taken prisoner by the French at Grand Pré [*see* Arthur NOBLE]. Newton's uncle, "a councillor at Port Royal, had rendered [services] to the missionaries on several occasions." These two incidents illustrate the missionaries' difficulties. The small number of Acadians who did in fact take part in the fighting suggests that the missionaries preached and practised neutrality. Certainly compared to a partisan spirit such as Abbé Jacques Girard*, the parish

priest of Cobequid (near Truro), La Goudalie gives the impression of being a moderate.

After the treaty of Aix-la-Chapelle in 1748 La Goudalie asked to be allowed to return to France. In 1749 the new governor, Edward Cornwallis*, intended to demand an unconditional oath of allegiance from the Acadians, and when they refused to comply the authorities in Halifax carried La Goudalie off and "forced him to return to France." Fundamentally, the negotiator of 1730 was considered a nuisance. In 1750 the president of the council of Marine decided to send the old man to Île Saint-Jean (Prince Edward Island), to which the French government hoped to attract Acadians. La Goudalie left it soon after his arrival and went to Louisbourg, Île Royale (Cape Breton Island), perhaps at the beginning of 1751. In 1752 he was at the fort on the Saint John River as garrison chaplain, but he was still vicar general of Acadia. Abbé de L'Isle-Dieu, the bishop of Quebec's vicar general in Paris, considered him "a very good man, but a great talker who does not think much and makes decisions without reflection."

We do not know when La Goudalie returned to France. After 1754 his name is no longer encountered in correspondence. A report dated 1761 informs us that he was dead.

MICHELINE D. JOHNSON

AAQ, 12 A, Registres d'insinuation, C, 170; 1 W, Église du Canada, I, 240. AN, Col., B, 55, f.563; 57, f.744; 62, f.16; 72, ff.16, 32v; 73, f.43v; 74, f.23; 75, f.47v; 76, f.73; 81, f.64; 85, f.38v; C¹¹ᴬ, 78, f.407; 82, f.326; 86, f.140; 87, f.365; 93, f.80. ASQ, Lettres, M, 99; S, 7 j; Polygraphie, IX, 29; Séminaire, XIV, 6, nos.3, 6. *Coll. doc. inédits Canada et Amérique*, I, II. *Derniers jours de l'Acadie* (Du Boscq de Beaumont), 257. "Lettres et mémoires de l'abbé de L'Isle-Dieu," APQ *Rapport, 1935–36. N.S. Archives*, I, 95, 96, 113, 118, 119; II, 82, 85, 89, 115, 116, 132. PAC *Report, 1905*, II, pt.III, 21 n., 283.

Brebner, *New England's outpost*. Casgrain, *Un pèlerinage au pays d'Évangéline*, chap. II; *Les Sulpiciens en Acadie*, 343–88. A. G. Doughty, *The Acadian exiles; a chronicle of the land of Evangeline* (Chronicles of Canada ser., 9, Toronto, Glasgow, 1916), chap. III. Gipson, *British empire before the American revolution*, V, chap. VI. N. E. S. Griffiths, *The Acadian deportation: deliberate perfidy or cruel necessity?* (Toronto, 1969), pt.II. James Hannay, *The history of Acadia, from its first discovery to its surrender to England, by the treaty of Paris* (Saint John, N.B., 1879). Johnson, *Apôtres au agitateurs*. Lauvière, *La tragédie d'un peuple* (1924), I. Parkman, *Half-century of conflict* (1892), chap. VII, IX, XXII. [F.-E.] Rameau de Saint-Père, *Une colonie féodale en Amérique: l'Acadie (1604–1881)* (2v., Paris, Montréal, 1889), II. Richard, *Acadie* (D'Arles), I, chap. IV, V, VI, VII. Robert Rumilly, *Histoire des Acadiens* (2v., Montréal, [1955]), I.

La Jonquière

LA JONQUIÈRE, JACQUES-PIERRE DE TAFFANEL DE LA JONQUIÈRE, Marquis de. *See* TAFFANEL

LAJUS, JORDAIN, surgeon, representative of the first surgeon to the king; b. 4 Feb. 1673 in the parish of Saint-Vincent de Nay, France, son of Jean Lajus and Anne Vigneau; buried 12 March 1742 in the chapel of the Quebec Recollets, reburied in Notre-Dame, Quebec, in 1796.

Jordain Lajus was a provincial surgeon who came to Quebec in 1694 and worked at the Hôtel-Dieu. In 1696 he was first surgeon to the militia during the campaign directed by Frontenac [Buade*] against the Iroquois. For most of his life, he lived in Quebec's Lower Town.

Lajus commended himself to the populace and the clergy as a responsible and Christian individual. He joined the religious confraternity of Sainte-Anne in 1702 and from 1710 to 1713 was a warden of Notre-Dame de Québec parish. Although employed by the seminary and other religious houses in Quebec, Lajus was most closely associated with the Recollets. He was their regular surgeon from about 1706 onward and by 1708 he was their trustee, responsible for the management of their property and the representation of their material interests.

Lajus had sufficient legal knowledge to act as an attorney before the courts and this with his experience as a surgeon favoured his appointment as an expert for the courts. Under the criminal ordinance of 1670, judges appointed surgeons to investigate cases involving death or physical injury, and from 1701 Lajus gave expert testimony before the provost court of Quebec, the seigneurial court of Notre-Dame-des-Anges, and the Conseil Supérieur. He also estimated the cost of medicines.

Service to the courts was a prelude to the appointment of Lajus by letters patent dated 2 March 1709 as representative of the first surgeon to the king, Georges Mareschal, to replace the late Gervais Baudouin*. The commission, registered at Quebec in October 1710, directed Lajus to uphold all laws governing surgery "with the duty also not to license any surgeon whose capacity is not proven." The regulatory powers of this post were, it seems, gradually assumed by the first physician to the king and the post was allowed to disappear after the death of Lajus.

As the first surgeon's representative, Lajus presented a petition from Quebec's four surgeons to the Conseil Supérieur in April 1712. The surgeons had obtained an intendant's ordinance in 1710 forbidding ships' surgeons to treat anyone in the colony, and now the Quebec surgeons tried to invoke the same argument to deny other Canadian surgeons the right to practise within the town. The issue was no longer the maintenance of standards but simply self-interest. The Conseil Supérieur dismissed the request.

There are scattered references to Lajus in the following 25 years. He continued to perform his duties as surgeon, court expert, estimator, and trustee. His clientele now included the notables of Quebec. In 1717 Lajus testified to a miraculous cure obtained through Didace Pelletier*, a dead Recollet lay brother. From 1717 to 1725 he was surgeon to the Hôpital Général. In 1734 he answered the call for a surgeon to treat smallpox victims on board *Le Rubis*. He went twice, without being paid, to care for the fever-stricken officers and soldiers before they were taken to the Hôtel-Dieu. In August 1740 the same ship arrived at Quebec with fever on board, and Lajus attended Bishop de Lauberivière [Pourroy*] before he died. The surgeon Lajus received 20 *livres* for his services.

In 1738 Jordain Lajus petitioned the minister of Marine, Maurepas, for a commission as "surgeon-clerk for all legal reports," a post not yet established in Canada. Lajus had feared that his 1709 commission would be invalidated by the death of the first surgeon to the king in 1736 and he was anxious to retain his exemption from billeting troops. Lajus claimed that he had worked for more than 30 years under the physician Michel Sarrazin*, from whom he had learned something of internal medicine. In an accompanying letter, Intendant Gilles Hocquart* stated that the new post would be superfluous and that Lajus, as trustee of the Recollets, was already exempt from billeting. "Sieur Lajus," wrote Hocquart, "is indifferently versed in the art of surgery; major operations are always performed at the Hôtel-Dieu ... he is liked by the public for his attentive care of the sick and even for his selflessness."

Lajus attained eminence in Canada by devoted service to the public, the church, and the crown. The respect earned by his selflessness is evident in a letter written by Pierre Hazeur* de L'Orme. When he heard that Lajus had died in 1742 after a visit to France, Canon de L'Orme wrote "I am very upset by the death of poor M. de Lajus, he assuredly deserves the sorrow of all who knew him."

Lajus married in Quebec on 21 Nov. 1697 Marie-Louise, daughter of Guillaume Roger*, principal court officer of the Conseil Souverain; they had 14 children. His first wife died in 1716, and on 8 Sept. 1717 he was married again, to Louise-Élisabeth Moreau, *dit* Lataupine. Ten children were born of the second marriage, but only five of all Lajus's children reached adulthood. His two daughters, Marguerite-Ursule and Élisabeth-Simone, married into the mercantile and seigneurial gentry of the colony. His oldest son, Jean-François, entered the Recollet order in 1727, under the name Jean-Baptiste. After many years as a military chaplain, he became the superior of the order in 1761. Another son, François-Michel, became a ship's captain, and Louis-François-Xavier* was his father's successor in surgery and one of the most distinguished surgeons of his day.

PETER N. MOOGK

AD, Pyrennées-Atlantiques (Pau), État civil, Saint-Vincent de Nay, 6 févr. 1673. AN, Col., C¹¹ᴬ, 71, pp.134–35, 139–42; E, 249 (dossier Lajus) (PAC transcripts). ANQ, Greffe de Louis Chambalon, 14 mars 1710, 17 mars 1713; Greffe de J.-C. Louet, 8 mars 1732; NF, Coll. de pièces jud. et not., 309, 509, 611, 651, 753, 803, 830, 1089, 1205, 1206, 2006, 2800. PAC, MG 8, B1, 9, pp.199–200, 227–28; 10, pp.185–86; 12, pp.149–50, 154–55, 225; 20/3, pp.739–40; 35/3, pp.1071–72. *Coll. de manuscrits relatifs à la N.-F.*, III, 463. *Jug. et délib.*, IV, V, VI. J.-F. Perrault, *Extraits ou précédents des arrests tirés des registres du Conseil supérieur de Québec* (Québec, 1824), 29. *Recensement de Québec, 1716* (Beaudet), 41. "Recensement de Québec, 1744" (APQ *Rapport*), 68. P.-G. Roy, *Inv. jug. et délib., 1717–1760*, I, III; *Inv. ord. int.*, I. Tanguay, *Dictionnaire*. Ahern, *Notes pour l'histoire de la médecine*. P.-G. Roy, *La ville de Québec*, I, 252; II, 166, 192. Arthur Vallée, *Un biologiste canadien: Michel Sarrazin, 1659–1735, sa vie, ses travaux et son temps* (Québec, 1927), 66–72. O.-M. [Jouve], "Étude historique et critique sur les actes du frère Didace Pelletier, récollet," *BRH*, XVII (1911), 91, 206. P.-G. Roy, "La famille Lajus," *BRH*, XL (1934), 243–47. Henri Têtu, "Le chapitre de la cathédrale de Québec et ses délégués en France," *BRH*, XVI (1910), 356.

LALANNE, JEAN DE LAPORTE DE. *See* LAPORTE

LA MAISONFORT DU BOISDECOURT, ALEXANDRE DE, Marquis de LA MAISONFORT, naval officer; m. Catherine Chicoyneau, daughter of the king's chief physician, who bore him a son; fl. 1699–1752.

Alexandre de La Maisonfort Du Boisdecourt entered the service as a page to the Comte de Toulouse, the admiral of France. He was accepted as a midshipman at Brest, France, on 8 March 1699 and immediately was assigned to an expedition against corsairs from Salé (Morocco). After cruises to the East Indies and West Indies, he was promoted sub-lieutenant and campaigned

in the Mediterranean and again in the East Indies. In 1706 he took part in the siege of Barcelona, Spain. The following year he was given the important mission of escorting Spanish galleons between Veracruz (Mexico) and Cadiz. This mission, which lasted three years, was brilliantly executed. On 25 Nov. 1712 he was promoted lieutenant-commander, and that same year he sailed for a new campaign in the East Indies.

Upon his return to Europe in 1716 La Maisonfort was inactive for a long period as a result of the small number of ships in commission. On 28 June 1718 he was made a knight of the order of Saint-Louis. He served ashore at Brest until 1727, when he set sail again on the *Brillant*. On 1 Oct. 1731 he was promoted captain. As second in command on the *Fleuron* in 1732, he spent a season on the Newfoundland Banks and at Louisbourg, Île Royale (Cape Breton Island), then returned to cruise off the coasts of Spain in pursuit of corsairs from Salé. From 1734 to 1744 he served as second in command or as commandant on several ships, most of them belonging to the Brest squadron.

In 1745 La Maisonfort, now commanding the *Vigilant*, was given the task of transporting munitions and supplies to Louisbourg. When in May he arrived in sight of the port, already besieged by troops from the English colonies under the command of William PEPPERRELL, he fell into a trap set for him by an English privateer. Challenged by the privateer, the *Vigilant* pursued it and found itself confronted by Peter WARREN's English squadron. After a long fight, La Maisonfort had to surrender. In a report he claimed that he had surrendered "only at the last moment, after losing many men and when he could no longer defend himself." Other accounts are less favourable to him. At the ministry of Marine he was blamed for not having fought more vigorously and for having surrendered too quickly. The loss of the *Vigilant* had a double result: a material one in that it deprived the defenders of Louisbourg of the help intended for them, and a psychological one in that it showed England's supremacy on the seas, which would destroy for the besieged fortress any possibility of relief.

Having been taken prisoner, La Maisonfort did not return to France until March 1746. After the affair of the *Vigilant* he received no further command and served until the end of the war with the coastal batteries at Le Conquet. He retired on 1 July 1752 with a pension of 3,000 *livres*.

ÉTIENNE TAILLEMITE

AN, Marine, B⁴, 50, ff.270–76; C¹, 165, f.38; C⁷, 161 (dossier La Maisonfort). Lacour-Gayet, *La marine*

La Majour

militaire sous Louis XV (1910), 192–93. Troude, *Batailles navales de la France*, I, 299.

LA MAJOUR. *See* ARRIGRAND

LA MALGUE, CLAUDE MARIN DE. *See* MARIN DE LA PERRIÈRE

LA MALGUE, PAUL MARIN DE. *See* MARIN

LA MARQUE. *See* MARIN

LAMARQUE, CHARLES NOLAN. *See* NOLAN

LA MARTINIÈRE, CLAUDE-ANTOINE DE BERMEN DE. *See* BERMEN

LAMBERT, *dit* **Saint-Paul, PAUL,** silversmith; b. 1691, son of Paul Lambert and Thérèse Huard, of the parish of Sainte-Catherine, Arras, France; d. 25 Nov. 1749 in Quebec.

Lambert was the outstanding worker in precious metals in Quebec City during the first half of the 18th century. Though there are extensive records of his activities, they do not reveal his birthplace or where and with whom he served his apprenticeship as a silversmith. Ramsay Traquair* subscribes to the view that Lambert was born in Quebec City, but Gérard Morisset* favours France. It is significant that Lambert is not mentioned in the census of 1716 and the earliest Quebec documentary reference to him dates from 30 Aug. 1729 when, at nearly 40 years of age, he married Marie-Françoise, daughter of François Laberge, widower, of Château-Richer. Following the death of Marie-Françoise on 28 Nov. 1747, Lambert married on 19 Feb. 1748, Marguerite, the eldest daughter of Jean-Baptiste MAILLOU, *dit* Desmoulins, and Marguerite Caron. Maillou's second son, Joseph, was apprenticed to Lambert, then living on Rue Sault-au-Matelot.

Some confusion has arisen from the fact that around 1730 Lambert adopted the name of Saint-Paul. References are made to a silversmith named "Saint-Paul" in the account books of the parish churches of Sainte-Anne-de-Beaupré in 1732, of Les Écureuils in 1744, and of Saint-Pierre, Île d'Orléans, in 1746. An écuelle bearing the accepted punchmark of Paul Lambert – P L surmounted by a fleur-de-lis with a small decorative mark under the initials – together with a somewhat similar punch with the letters S P on the same piece, is given by Traquair as supporting evidence of an interlocking relationship between Paul Lambert and Saint-Paul, though he points out the second punch could be that of Samuel Payne*, a contemporary New France silversmith. The change in name is recorded by Tanguay, and Morisset states that it was common practice in the early part of the 18th century to "sanctify" the Christian name: Paul Lambert, *dit* Saint-Paul. Examination of a receipt for work done and signed by Saint-Paul, dated 20 April 1745, does not suggest any association with Paul Lambert. Morisset quotes from the church records of Notre-Dame de Québec to the effect that Paul Lambert and Saint-Paul were one and the same person. With the exception of the écuelle mentioned by Traquair, the known pieces of silver fashioned by Lambert only carry the punchmark incorporating the letters P L.

Though there were other silversmiths working in New France – Jean-Baptiste DESCHEVERY, *dit* Maisonbasse, Michel COTTON, Jean-François LANDRON, and François Lefebvre to mention a few – the amount of Lambert's work which has survived leads to the conclusion that he was the most important. His skill and artistry compare favourably with those of fellow craftsmen in France and the American colonies. The quality of his work set a standard that was to influence those who followed him, notably François Ranvoyzé*, Pierre Huguet*, *dit* Latour, Laurent Amiot*, and other Quebec silversmiths. Silver fashioned by Lambert is outstanding not only for its fine design but for the manner in which it is decorated. He favoured a combination of flat chasing in the form of an open acanthus leaf, gadrooning, the crimping of edges to give the effect of "beading," and repoussé work. These decorative features are illustrated in an *instrument de paix* in the Henry G. Birks collection in Montreal. After the close of the French régime, the English type of silver, featuring line rather than decoration, set the style for silversmiths in Quebec until the commencement of the Victorian era when elaborate and over-decorated pieces of silver became the fashion.

Examples of Lambert's work are to be seen in the Musée du Québec, the chapel of the Ursulines and Hôtel-Dieu in Quebec City, the Huron chapel at Ancienne-Lorette, the Royal Ontario Museum in Toronto, the Detroit Institute of Arts, and a number of private collections. There are also pieces in the parish churches of Saint-Michel de Sillery, Montmagny, Saint-Augustin-de-Québec, Saint-Charles-Borromée in Charlesbourg, Sainte-Famille, Île d'Orléans, and Saint-Michel-de-Bellechasse.

JOHN LANGDON

AJQ, Registre d'état civil, Notre-Dame de Québec, 1748–1752, f.102v. ANQ, Greffe de J.-É. Dubreuil, 29 août 1729; Greffe de C.-H. Du Laurent, 23, 28 nov. 1749; Greffe de J.-C. Panet, 23 nov. 1747, 13 févr. 1748, 28 nov. 1749. Tanguay, *Dictionnaire*. Langdon, *Canadian silversmiths*. Gérard Morisset, *Coup d'œil sur les arts*, 95–96; *Paul Lambert dit Saint-Paul* (Collection Champlain, Québec, 1945). Traquair, *Old silver of Quebec*. Marius Barbeau, "Deux cents ans d'orfèvrerie chez-nous," *RSCT*, 3rd ser., XXXIII (1939), sect.I, 183–92. E. A. Jones, "Old church silver in Canada," *RSCT*, 3rd ser., XII (1918), sect.II, 150.

LAMONTAGNE, CATHERINE JÉRÉMIE, *dit.* *See* JÉRÉMIE

LA MORANDIÈRE, ÉTIENNE ROCBERT DE. *See* ROCBERT

LA MORANDIÈRE, MARIE-ÉLISABETH ROCBERT DE. *See* ROCBERT

LAMORINIE (La Morénerie, Morimé), JEAN-BAPTISTE DE, priest, Jesuit, missionary; b. 24 Dec. 1704 or 1705 in Périgueux, France; d. after 1764, presumably in France.

Jean-Baptiste de Lamorinie became a Jesuit novice at the age of 18, and on 6 Oct. 1725 made his final vows. He sailed for Canada in 1736 and, after spending a little time in Quebec or Montreal, left for the west to begin 25 years of missionary work there. He passed the 1738–39 winter season at Detroit before moving to Michilimackinac. In 1741, under the instruction of Pierre Du Jaunay*, Jesuit superior at Michilimackinac, Lamorinie studied the language of the Ottawas. Although he would serve briefly in other areas – among the Miamis at Fort Saint-Joseph (probably Niles, Mich.) in 1746 and 1749, and among the Assiniboins at Fort La Reine (Portage la Prairie, Man.) from 1750 to 1751 – Michilimackinac was to be his home base for the next two decades.

In the summer of 1750 Lamorinie set out with Jacques LEGARDEUR de Saint-Pierre for Fort La Reine. He found life with Saint-Pierre unbearable and work among the Assiniboins fruitless, for the Indians instantly disliked the new commandant and consequently refused to cooperate with the missionary. Dejected, Lamorinie left the fort on 22 June 1751 and returned to Michilimackinac. In his journal Saint-Pierre condemned him for not having mathematical instruments to make scientific observations. He was too old, added Saint-Pierre, for the rigours of missionary work, and his inability to speak any Indian languages would have made evangelizing "barbarians hardened

in their blindness" impossible, despite his eloquence and piety. These criticisms were somewhat unfair, since the Assiniboins spoke a Dakota Siouan language, whereas the Ottawa language, which Lamorinie had studied, was Algonkian. The missionary's age, moreover, did not hinder him from 14 more years of work in North America.

By 1760 the effects of the Seven Years' War were being felt in the west, even where no fighting had occurred. In that year Lamorinie left Fort Saint-Joseph for the Illinois country, to be joined the following year by Jean-Baptiste de Salleneuve from Detroit. The two missionaries worked at the French village of Ste Genevieve (Mo.), where, with the assistance of Salleneuve, Lamorinie tended the religious needs of the French and Miamis. With the formal conclusion of the war, the Jesuit order, which had been suppressed in France in 1762, was expelled from Louisiana. Lamorinie, Salleneuve, and Jesuits from Kaskaskia (Ill.) and Vincennes (Ind.) returned to France *via* New Orleans in the spring of 1764.

C. J. RUSS

JR (Thwaites), LXX, 87, 277; LXXI, 172. Jacques Legardeur de Saint-Pierre, "Mémoire ou journal sommaire du voyage ...," in *Découvertes et établissements des Français* (Margry), VI, 637–52. Champagne, *Les La Vérendrye*, 409. Gosselin, *L'Eglise du Canada jusqu'à la conquête*, III, 329, 335, 339. A.-G. Morice, *Histoire de l'Église catholique dans l'Ouest canadien du lac Supérieur au Pacifique (1659–1905)* (3v., Winnipeg, Montréal, 1912), I, 58–59. Trudel, *L'Église canadienne*, I, 338; II, 139, 158.

LA MOTTE, EMMANUEL-AUGUSTE DE CAHIDEUC, Comte DUBOIS DE. *See* CAHIDEUC

LANDRON, JEAN-FRANÇOIS, silversmith, merchant; b. 27 Dec. 1686 in Quebec, son of Étienne Landron, a merchant, and Élisabeth de Chavigny; d. probably in 1760.

Nothing is known of Jean-François Landron's childhood and education. On 10 Nov. 1719 he signed a marriage contract with Marie-Anne Bergeron in Montreal before the notary Michel Lepailleur*; the wedding took place on 22 November. Born in Quebec and married in Montreal, he was referred to in 1724 as a silversmith in the account books of the church of Notre-Dame de Québec. For making a censer he received that year from the churchwarden in charge the sum of 138 *livres* 12 *sols* 6 *deniers*, which represented half the total cost, the difference to be paid by the canons of the chapter. The silversmith's craft, however, does not seem to have been his only activity. Like the silversmith Michel COTTON, who was also a shoemaker, Jean-François Landron had to engage in other activities to be assured of a decent income. This diversity of occupation is encountered not only among the silversmiths, but also among painters and sculptors.

A document dated 17 July 1728 mentions that Landron, silversmith, bought from Pierre Trefflé, *dit* Rottot, "50 barrels of green peas at nine *livres* per barrel," and in return he promised "to supply and deliver to the aforementioned Sieur Rotot four casks of spirits, four casks of tafia, eight casks of Bordeaux wine, a hundred bushels of salt." This document illustrates the importance of Landron's commercial activities, although his official occupation continued to be that of silversmith, according to this notarial deed. From 1730 on, it seems, Landron devoted himself more and more to trade. At least that is what the judgements and deliberations of the Conseil Supérieur at this time lead us to believe. The lawsuits in which Landron was involved deal in general with trade, and he himself is hardly referred to any more as a silversmith, but rather as a merchant, bourgeois, or trader. If a document of the period is to be believed, he apparently organized in 1730 a lottery, the articles in which were evaluated at a little more than 2,025 *livres*. In 1731 he bought at Île Jésus for 1,800 *livres* a boat named the *Saint-Guillaume*. According to the intendants' ordinances for 1744 and 1747 he is supposed to have owned in addition two other boats, the *Heureux Retour* and the *Saint-François*, for his trade on the Labrador coast.

It seems therefore that Landron was a merchant more than a silversmith for a great part of his life. Despite that, he does not seem to have neglected the silversmith's craft completely, since in 1742, at the time of the inventory after the death of Jacques PAGÉ, *dit* Carcy, he was appointed the expert for appraising the deceased man's silversmith and clockmaker's tools. Some examples of Landron's work remain today. The Musée du Québec owns three pieces of plate bearing his stamp: on them can be read his initials I.F. above L crowned with a fleur-de-lis.

The place and date of Jean-François Landron's death cannot be stated with certainty. He died sometime between 26 July 1756, the date when he became godfather to Françoise Poisset, and 7 Nov. 1760, when his widow lent some money. A document from the judicial archives of Beauce (Saint-Joseph-de-Beauce) mentions that a certain François-Xavier Landron, "in his lifetime a trader at Quebec," was buried on 24 Jan. 1760 in the parish of Saint-Joseph. Only the slight difference in given names prevents a positive assertion that this death certificate is that of Jean-François Landron.

IN COLLABORATION WITH MICHEL
CAUCHON AND ANDRÉ JUNEAU

AJQ, Registre d'état civil, Notre-Dame de Québec, 27 déc. 1686, 26 juill. 1756. ANQ, Greffe de Jacques Barbel, 17 juill. 1728; Greffe de R.-C. Barolet, 7 nov. 1760; Greffe de J.-N. Pinguet de Vaucour, 18 juin, 17 août 1742. ANQ-M, Greffe de François Coron, 17 mai 1731; Greffe de Michel Lepailleur, 10 nov. 1717. Archives judiciaires de Beauce (Saint-Joseph-de-Beauce, Qué.), Registre d'état civil, Saint-Joseph-de-Beauce, 24 janv. 1760. IOA, Dossier Jean-François Landron, orfèvre. P.-G. Roy, *Inv. coll. pièces jud. et not.*, I, 83. Tanguay, *Dictionnaire*. Gérard Morisset, *Évolution d'une pièce d'argenterie* (Collection Champlain, Québec, 1943), 8–9. Marius Barbeau, "Indian trade silver," *RSCT*, 3rd ser., XXXIV (1940), sect.II, 27–41; "Old Canadian silver," *Canadian Geographical Journal* (Ottawa), XXII (1941), 150–62.

LANGIS (Langy) MONTEGRON, JEAN-BAPTISTE LEVRAULT DE. *See* LEVRAULT

LANGLOIS, MARIE-THÉRÈSE, *dite* **de Saint-Jean-Baptiste,** Nun Hospitaller of the Hôpital Général of Quebec, superior; b. 20 Jan. 1684 in Quebec, daughter of Jacques Langlois, a tailor and then a baker in Quebec, and Marie-Thérèse de Lessard; d. 26 Feb. 1743 in Quebec.

Marie-Thérèse Langlois entered the convent of the Hôpital Général of Quebec on 29 Dec. 1706 and made her profession on 30 April 1708. Her father could promise a dowry of 1,000 *livres* only, on which he would pay the income; to guarantee this obligation he had to mortgage two houses he owned in Quebec. Since she could not make up the amount of 3,000 *livres* required as a dowry, Marie-Thérèse Langlois was admitted thanks to the foundation dowry, a donation made by Bishop Saint-Vallier [La Croix*] to the Hôpital Général through which he allocated 1,100 *livres* as annual income to be used in perpetuity as provision for a nun.

The annals of the community do not say a great deal about Marie-Thérèse Langlois. That she held the offices of depositary, assistant superior, mistress of novices, and superior is known, but her activities from 1717 to 1723 and from 1726 to 1729 are a mystery. Marie-Thérèse de Saint-Jean-Baptiste was superior first from 1723 to 1726, and the annalist barely mentions the superiorship which devolved upon her in 1730. The author of *Mgr de Saint-Vallier et l'Hôpital Général*, who knew nothing about Marie

Thérèse's superiority from 1730 to 1732, asserted instead that Marie-Joseph JUCHEREAU Duchesnay, *dite* de l'Enfant-Jésus, sister of Geneviève Juchereau Duchesnay, *dite* de Saint-Augustin, who had died, was chosen superior to succeed her sister in this office. However, in 1730, upon the death of Geneviève de Saint-Augustin, Marie-Thérèse de Saint-Jean-Baptiste, who had been assistant superior since 1729, served as superior until the end of the three-year term.

It is appropriate to recall briefly this troubled period in the 1730s, when Marie-Thérèse Langlois became superior. The nuns had chosen sides in the conflict which began between the civil and religious authorities upon Saint-Vallier's death in 1728 [*see* Étienne Boullard*; Claude-Thomas Dupuy*]; conflicts of personalities and dissensions within the community resulted, and the coadjutor, Pierre-Herman Dosquet*, only aggravated them. However, everything that Dosquet said cannot be taken literally; he had little sympathy for the nuns of the Hôpital Général, who had been specially protected by his predecessor, Saint-Vallier. According to the coadjutor a spirit of independence and liberty, of individualism and discord, reigned in the community. He went so far as to state that several nuns of the Hôpital Général were admitted to make their profession without doing their noviciate – an allegation which is certainly not confirmed by a serious study of the registry of admissions and professions. To complete his picture of indiscipline Dosquet added that these "rebellious nuns come rather sharply to blows."

Behind Dosquet was the dean of the chapter, Louis Bertrand* de Latour, who had been appointed superior of the religious communities. By his provocative attitude he antagonized a good many of the nuns of the Hôpital Général. In 1730 Latour had the election for a new superior held on 28 March, the day after the death of the superior, Geneviève de Saint-Augustin, despite the opposition of 17 nuns who wanted the ceremony held after the Forty Hours' Devotion, as the regulations of the community stipulated. Latour, like Dosquet, seemed to favour nuns of humble condition rather than those from great families, in reaction against Saint-Vallier, who was inclined to support the latter when important offices were in question. Thus, according to Charles de BEAUHARNOIS and Gilles Hocquart*, it was Latour himself who decided to appoint a superior for two years, in this case Marie-Thérèse Langlois, the daughter of a craftsman. After this arbitrary appointment the nuns were truly divided within the community, and the group opposed to Latour went so far as to remove the ropes from the bells before the end of the ceremony. However, the seriousness of such events should not be exaggerated: the strife that followed the pseudo-election of 1730 was not in the least unusual; reactions of this kind were common in the communities of women in Canada, as in France.

Nevertheless it cannot be denied that around 1730 there was a certain slackening of discipline with respect to the rules of the cloister among these nuns. Again it was Dosquet who deplored the fact that before his arrival "the nuns used to go to the Château Saint-Louis or the intendant's palace for dinner or supper parties, to the great indignation of the public." Henceforth, under his authority, the governor and intendant would no longer be permitted to enter the convents. But this sort of irregularity was encountered also in the other two communities of women in Quebec.

It was in this tense atmosphere, then, that Marie-Thérèse de Saint-Jean-Baptiste had to carry out her duties as superior. The election in 1732, which took place according to canonical rules, gave the superiorship to Marie-Joseph Juchereau Duchesnay. After that date Marie-Thérèse held the office of mistress of novices for two three-year terms, and in 1738 she was elected depositary and discreet. She held these offices until her death, on 26 Feb. 1743 in the convent of the Hôpital Général.

MICHELINE D'ALLAIRE

AAQ, 1 W, Église du Canada, II, 285–87, 349. AHGQ, "Annales"; Cahiers divers, notices, éloges funèbres, circulaires, notes diverses; Divers extraits de nos annales et autres notes diverses; Registre des entrées et des dots. AJQ, Registre d'état civil, Notre-Dame de Québec, 20 janv. 1684. AN, Col., B, 57/1, ff.106–108; C¹¹ᴬ, 54, f.36; 56, ff.66, 174, 186. *Mgr de Saint-Vallier et l'Hôpital Général*, 301, 718. Léon Roy, "Jacques Langlois et Marie-Thérèse de Lessard," *BRH*, L (1944), 119–26.

LANNELONGUE, JEAN-BAPTISTE (baptized **Jean**, but referred to as Jean-Baptiste; he signed Lannelongue or Lannelongue *aîné*), fishing entrepreneur, merchant, privateer; b. 1712 at Bayonne, France, apparently the eldest son of Armand Lannelongue, merchant and bourgeois, and Marie Barrière; d. 1768 at Bayonne.

The first possible mention of Jean-Baptiste Lannelongue in North America is in 1735 when a Sieur Lannelongue is recorded in Louisbourg, Île Royale (Cape Breton Island), as a supplier to the crown of various materials of small value. We do know that Jean-Baptiste was resident in Louisbourg from 1743 when he began providing miscellaneous goods to the government storehouse. Most of his transactions were for inconsequential amounts, but a Sieur Lannelongue did provide one large order of flour and peas worth 55,893 *livres* in 1743. Sometime after this year Lannelongue disappears from Louisbourg; he may well have returned to France either before or at the time of its occupation by the forces of William PEPPERRELL in 1745. After the return of the fortress to the French, he reappears; he continued to trade with the government, but the sums involved were trifling and his principal activities lay elsewhere.

By 1750, Lannelongue had formed a company with Bertrand Imbert, another Louisbourg merchant, and made some attempts to enter the fishing trade. Although we do not know the scale of their operations, we have evidence that they engaged fishermen and beachworkers in 1749 and 1750, and were still active in this trade in 1757. They bought four schooners before the Seven Years' War, and seem to have shipped goods – probably cod – to Martinique and Bayonne in 1756.

After the outbreak of the war the two partners outfitted a series of privateering expeditions. The first was the voyage of a schooner, the *Tourterelle*, sent out in July 1756, commanded by Maurice Simonin. Two English ships were captured; however, total expenses of 4,870 *livres*, plus the crew's share of the gross profits (1,350 *livres*), resulted in a loss of about 3,400 *livres*. Later that year the *Victory* brought in a 50-ton New England schooner, but there is no record whether the partners gained or lost in this venture. Their next expedition, that of the schooner *Capricieuse* in 1757–58, resulted in considerable losses – 14,711 *livres*, after the crew's share was paid. A fourth ship, the *Junon*, brought in a 50-ton Virginia ship.

Lannelongue was back in Bayonne by the end of 1759, and continued to carry on the same activities with Imbert. By the end of the war, they had outfitted no less than six more privateers, some of them prize ships, some built for the purpose. These ships took more than a dozen prizes. With the return of peace, the partners took up the fishing trade again, outfitting about three ships a year, which they dispatched either with trading goods for the fishermen at Saint-Pierre and Miquelon or on the Grand Banks, or as fishing expeditions. These ships may have been involved in some coasting trade as well. In 1767–68 Lannelongue and his partner also shipped grain to Spain.

In 1743, at Louisbourg, Lannelongue married Anne Richard, the widow of Jean-Baptiste Lascoret (probably the former clerk of Michel DACCARRETTE (d. 1745)). They had at least six children at Louisbourg, and another five after leaving in 1758, the last of these being born in 1765. His younger brother, Pierre, was also at Louisbourg, acting as clerk (*greffier commis* and *greffier*) of the bailiff's court.

T. J. A. LE GOFF

AD, Charente-Maritime (La Rochelle), B, 6119; 6122, nos.1–13; 6124. AN, Col., C¹¹ᴬ, 11–13; Section Outre-Mer, G¹, 407–9, 431, 459; G³, 2044–45, 2047. Archives communales, Bayonne, EE, 65, 69, 71–73; FF, 329–31, 361; GG, 56, 102, 104–5, 127. Archives de la Chambre de Commerce de Bayonne, regs.32–33, 39–48. Musée basque de Bayonne, manuscript notes of M. René Godinot on Bayonne privateers.

LANOULLIER DE BOISCLERC, JEAN-EUSTACHE, controller of the Marine, chief road commissioner (*grand voyer*); b. 1689 or 1694 in Paris, son of Jean Lanoullier, bourgeois, and Marie-Reine Grasse of Saint-Nicolas-du-Chardonnet parish, Paris; d. 25 Nov. 1750 in the Hôtel-Dieu at Quebec.

Details of Jean-Eustache Lanoullier de Boisclerc's early life are sketchy and are often confused with those of his step-brother NICOLAS, with whom he travelled to New France in 1712. He probably came to seek a brighter future than his father, a Paris bourgeois who eventually went bankrupt, could provide for him in France. Like Nicolas, he may have counted on using the influence at the French court of a sister-in-law, Mme Mercier, who had been a nurse to Louis XV, to obtain an advantageous colonial position. In 1719 he was appointed controller of the Marine; on 21 December of that year he married Marie-Marguerite Duroy, widow of Claude Chasle. Ten years later the arrival of Gilles Hocquart* at Quebec as acting intendant signalled a major change in his career. On 14 June 1729 the chief road commissioner in New France, Pierre Robinau* de Bécancour, died and Hocquart, who complained that the holders of this office had treated it hitherto as a mere sinecure, sought an energetic replacement who would develop the road system as a catalyst for internal commerce and colonization. On 26 Oct. 1730 he recommended Jean-Eustache Lanoullier, pointing out that he had manifested both energy and organizational skill in handling the goods salvaged from the shipwrecked royal vessel *Éléphant* in 1729. On 10 April 1731 Lanoullier was given letters-of-appointment as chief road commissioner, and these were registered in the Conseil Supérieur on

20 August. He held the post until his death in 1750.

He was the first chief road commissioner to give serious attention to his duties, which encompassed inspecting, constructing, and maintaining all roads and bridges in the towns as well as in the countryside. He drew up hundreds of *procès verbaux*, 34 in 1731 alone, outlining improvements to the existing road system, and he persuaded Hocquart to pass dozens of ordinances regulating the maintenance and use of the roads. Although he and his assistant at Montreal, René de COUAGNE, always came to some agreement with interested parties – seigneurs, parish priests, churchwardens, farmers – before launching any project, they were often forced to threaten fines of up to 20 *livres*, provided for in the ordinances, to persuade the habitants to perform the royal *corvées* which were the primary source of labour. In 1732 Hocquart stated that Lanoullier was educating many habitants in their obligations in that regard and, by so doing, was helping to extend royal authority into the countryside. By the late 1740s the roads and bridges of virtually every parish in New France had been upgraded.

But Lanoullier's greatest accomplishment was the construction of two royal roads which, by 1750, spanned the length and breadth of the central part of the colony. The first and most impressive of these was the Quebec–Montreal route which ran along the north shore of the St Lawrence for almost 200 miles. He began work on it at the Rivière Maskinongé in July 1732 and he built virgin stretches 24 feet wide across 23 seigneuries, while improving the 14 seigneurial roads with which these new sections linked up. In 1733, when he spent 45 days on horseback, the difficult section around Lac Saint-Pierre was complete; ten of the 13 bridges required between the Maskinongé and Rivière du Loup were in place; and ferries, operated according to a toll schedule set by the intendant, had been launched on the unbridgeable rivers. A year later a carriage could travel from Quebec to Trois-Rivières in four days, and, when the road was finished in 1737, a rider who was unconcerned with a little mud could reach Montreal in four and a half. Lanoullier spent ten more years on improvements to this road. In 1739, he had begun work on a north–south route that ran from Montreal east along the south shore of the St Lawrence to Fort Chambly on the upper Richelieu, then extended down the Richelieu to Fort Saint-Jean where it linked up with a ferry, a flat-bottomed boat built in 1741 to navigate on Lake Champlain as far as Fort Saint-Frédéric (Crown Point, N.Y.). In 1747 this road was extended farther south from Fort Saint-Jean until it eventually reached Fort Saint-Frédéric.

Considering the obstacles, these roads were reasonably well built. Hocquart thought them excellent and he outlined their benefits to the colony. ''These roads provide easier communications from one place to another than ever before,'' he stated in 1735, adding that they also made it easier for habitants to bring their produce to the town markets. Finally, they opened new areas to settlement. Hocquart claimed that the rapid development of the Lac Saint-Pierre region during the 1730s was due entirely to Lanoullier's roads and that the settlement of the Richelieu valley was greatly facilitated by them. Without doubt they constituted one of the great practical achievements of the French régime.

Lanoullier's familiarity with New France's geography and his daily contacts with the countryside's inhabitants made him valuable for other tasks as well. Hocquart employed him as his special agent for everything from assessing the condition of the crops to participating in the biennial census-taking. Then too, whenever new reports of rich mineral deposits reached Quebec, Lanoullier was sent to investigate them. In 1734, for example, he passed several months at Portage des Chats on the Ottawa River sampling lead deposits and, in 1740, he went with Jacques SIMONET of the Saint-Maurice ironworks to search for iron ore at Pointe-du-Lac. In fact, he was Hocquart's unofficial watchdog at Saint-Maurice, having been present when Pierre-François Olivier* de Vézin drew up plans for the ironworks in 1735. On all of these excursions he prepared reports on the suitability of the lands he passed through for cultivation, and in 1739 he was sent to Fort Saint-Frédéric to mark off 90 concessions for future settlement. During the crop failures of 1736–37 and 1742–43, Hocquart dispatched him to soothe the superstitious fears of the habitants and to convince them to sell rather than hoard their surplus wheat. During the second crisis, Lanoullier used force to empty all the barns on the Île d'Orléans. Indeed, as the enforcer of the royal *corvée* and the agent of central authority, the inhabitants must have regarded him with the aversion reserved by French peasants for the tax collector.

He was rewarded, however, by Hocquart. In addition to his annual salary of 600 *livres*, he received a 500-*livre* bonus almost every year and he was compensated for expenses incurred on his many journeys. In 1734, moreover, Hocquart and Governor Charles de BEAUHARNOIS recommended him for a seigneurial grant behind the Jesuit mission at Sault Saint-Louis. Although approved in 1735, it was withdrawn a year later after a spirited protest by the Jesuits who maintained that it would block the mission Indians from their hunting grounds. This setback to his hopes of establishing a large patrimony for the six of his 15 children who survived infancy, was eased somewhat by Hocquart's willingness to employ his sons in the intendancy. All in all, Lanoullier benefited deservedly from his years of strenuous efforts to open the countryside of New France to settlement and trade. His contribution to the economic expansion of the colony during the 1730s was significant.

DONALD J. HORTON

[The best sources on Lanoullier's background and career are P.-G. Roy, "Les grand voyers de 1667 à 1842," *BRH*, XXXVII (1931), 449–50 and *La famille Lanoullier* (Lévis, Qué., 1935). *See also*: AN, Col., C¹¹ᴬ, 57–80; this series, along with P.-G. Roy, *Inv. procès-verbaux des grands voyers*, V, and *Inv. ord. int.*, III, is the best primary source on his road-building activities. Roland Sanfaçon, "La construction du premier chemin Québec-Montréal et le problème des corvées (1706–1737)," *RHAF*, XII (1958–59), 3–29, and G. P. de T. Glazebrook, "Roads in New France and the policy of expansion," CHA *Report, 1934*, 48–56, contain the best secondary description of the Quebec to Montreal road. Lanctot, *History of Canada*, III, and Émile Salone, *La colonisation de la Nouvelle-France: étude sur les origines de la nation canadienne française* (Paris, 1906; réimp. Trois-Rivières, Qué., 1970), give short accounts of the general impact of road-building on the economy. D.J.H.]

LANOULLIER DE BOISCLERC, NICOLAS, agent for the Compagnie du Castor and the Compagnie des Indes, agent in Quebec for the treasurers general of the Marine, controller of the Domaine du Roi, and councillor in the Conseil Supérieur; b. *c.* 1679 in Paris, France, son of Jean Lanoullier, bourgeois, and Marie Tollet (Taudet), of Saint-Nicolas-du-Chardonnet parish in Paris; d. 6 Jan. 1756 in Quebec.

Nicolas Lanoullier de Boisclerc, barrister of the *parlement* of Paris, arrived in Quebec in 1712 as the agent of Louis-François Aubert, Jean-Baptiste Néret, and Jean-Baptiste Gayot, directors of the Compagnie du Castor which held the beaver trade monopoly in Canada. He was to inspect its Canadian operation, reduce costs, and make any necessary changes in personnel. In 1716, Jean-François Martin* de Lino claimed unsuccessfully to be the agent of the Compagnie du Castor; the colonial officials would not recognize his commission because of a mistake in its form, and Lanoullier continued in this position until 1717. In 1715 the Compagnie du Castor had

been unable to honour its letters of exchange and the following spring defaulted on all payments. In 1716 it contracted to receive all Canadian beaver through Antoine Pascaud* and Jacques Le Clerc, merchants in La Rochelle, and to honour its Canadian letters of exchange as sale of pelts permitted. The Canadian merchants saw a conspiracy between Pascaud, Le Clerc, and the company at their expense, and refused, in spite of their contract of 1706, to deliver their pelts to the company's warehouses in Quebec without assurances of full payment. Lanoullier had to try to compel the colonists, knowing that on some of its payments the company would probably default. Néret and Gayot's monopoly expired in 1717, and with it Lanoullier's position. Later, 1726–32, he was agent of the Compagnie des Indes, administering their affairs in Canada.

The 1720s, active years for Lanoullier, began with his appointment in 1720 as agent for the treasurers general of the Marine in Quebec, succeeding Jean Petit*. Secure for the moment, he married, on 4 Jan. 1721, Jeanne, daughter of Pierre ANDRÉ de Leigne, lieutenant general for civil and criminal affairs of the Quebec provost court. She died on 12 March 1722, six days after giving birth to a daughter, Marie-Germaine-Eustache. On 23 Feb. 1726 while in Paris for a year on business and family affairs, he married Marie-Jeanne Bocquet.

In 1721 Lanoullier was granted for 20 years the monopoly for mail service between Quebec, Trois-Rivières, and Montreal, but never even registered his brevet with the Conseil Supérieur. The next year he obtained a monopoly for floating tide-mills for grinding flour in the vicinity of Quebec, but this project too was stillborn.

The first of Lanoullier's royal offices in Canada began on 10 Feb. 1722 with his appointment as councillor to the Conseil Supérieur. When the attorney general, Mathieu-Benoît Collet*, died in March 1727 Intendant Dupuy* appointed Lanoullier as interim successor. During his tenure Dupuy and the council plunged into their mêlée with the cathedral chapter and Governor Charles de BEAUHARNOIS over the funeral of Bishop Saint-Vallier [La Croix*] and the question of episcopal authority [*see* Étienne Boullard*; Eustache CHARTIER de Lotbinière]. As attorney general, Lanoullier had to follow the orders of his superior, the intendant. Furthermore, Lanoullier's former father-in-law, Pierre André de Leigne, was one of Dupuy's most ardent supporters. With the intendant's recall in disgrace in 1728, Lanoullier was vulnerable but apparently convinced Beauharnois he had acted only on Dupuy's orders. Perhaps Beauharnois was favourably impressed by the ruthless seizure of Dupuy's personal belongings by Lanoullier's step-brother, JEAN-EUSTACHE, controller of the Marine, as security for his debts in the colony. Another step-brother, Paul-Antoine-François Lanoullier Des Granges, was employed in the governor's household.

This tumult was still reverberating when in 1729 the king ordered an investigation into Lanoullier's management as agent of the treasurers general [see Georges Regnard* Duplessis; Jacques IMBERT]. Complaints had begun shortly after he took office in 1720. He was lending merchandise at Quebec retail prices to numerous Canadian officials, claiming that these loans were official advances against their salaries. The royal funds authorized for these salaries he then sent to Paris as letters of exchange drawn against the treasurers general, with which his father purchased merchandise wholesale for Lanoullier in Quebec. Employing the king's funds for personal profit was common practice, and the treasurers general themselves engaged in it. This group of financiers contracted to manage the revenues of the ministry of Marine, and as their agent Lanoullier was not a royal official; rather he was akin to a private banker who looked after the king's account. He accepted deposits on the king's behalf, but he was supposed to make expenditures, for which he was accountable, only when authorized by the intendant. His error was to extend too much credit to too many bad risks, at a time when the treasurers general and the minister of Marine expected there to be ample funds in the king's account for expenditures.

The intendants BÉGON and Dupuy were among Lanoullier's greatest debtors, owing 69,000 livres and 11,000 livres respectively. It is not surprising to find them rushing to his defence. But even Gilles Hocquart*, who authorized Lanoullier's arrest and the seizure of his property in 1730, concluded that at most he was guilty of too much generosity in giving advances on salaries. Lanoullier spent only three days in jail, but was under house arrest for a year until he and Montreal merchant Pierre de LESTAGE put up 55,000 livres for his security. He spent the rest of his life trying to pay off his debts, which to the king were personal debts to be settled between him and the treasurers general. In 1730 the deficit in Lanoullier's books stood at 300,000 livres, but the following year Maurepas estimated it to be 180,000 livres. Much of this reduced figure still represented legitimate deficits in the colony's budget which had been accumulating since 1716. After Lanoullier went to France in 1732 and 1736 to negotiate, and after concessions to him such as

a retroactive increase in salary, he still owed the treasurers general 45,000 livres and finally settled by turning over the 44,000-livre debt then owing him by Bégon.

Lanoullier, however, still had a crushing private debt to metropolitan merchants. As early as 1731 Maurepas had agreed with Bégon, Dupuy, and Hocquart that Lanoullier had not been guilty of bad faith. Beauharnois also appealed to the minister on his behalf. In 1732 he was replaced as agent for the treasurers general by Thomas-Jacques TASCHEREAU and the next year he was appointed controller of the Domaine du Roi at a salary of 1,800 livres – a post he held until 1752 when his son-in-law, Michel BÉNARD, succeeded him. In 1735 he succeeded Michel Sarrazin* as keeper of seals of the Conseil Supérieur, and in 1736 the king awarded him a gratuity of 3,900 livres as compensation for irrecoverable loans to officers. More helpful were special favours which Maurepas, Beauharnois, and Hocquart worked out. In 1733 and 1736 Lanoullier asked for the privilege of exploiting the Tadoussac trade. But Hocquart wished the post for François-Étienne CUGNET and suggested giving Lanoullier, free of charge, the farm of the post of Témiscamingue. This was a delicate matter. Témiscamingue and the other western posts were the patronage of the governor, and Beauharnois struck back at Hocquart by suggesting to Maurepas that Cugnet and the intendant had misrepresented the Tadoussac trade in order to increase Cugnet's profits. But Beauharnois accorded Lanoullier 3,000 livres from the fur-trading licence (congé) receipts, and beginning in 1741 for five years granted him the 3,000 livres annually received from the lease of the Témiscamingue post. In 1747 he was given a final 1,500 livres. His sister-in-law, Mme Mercier, had been Louis XV's nurse. Her influence probably helped procure these special favours.

Yet in 1747 Lanoullier still owed metropolitan merchants more than 27,000 livres, and again travelled to France to try to settle his debts. There his second wife died. His possessions included a house on Rue des Remparts in Quebec worth 14,500 livres, the uncleared seigneury of Lac-Métis, some land at Saint-Roch, small plots near Quebec, a fishing concession at Cape Charles on the Labrador coast worth 200 livres annually, and a few small annuities. Almost all these assets he had acquired in the 1720s.

He died in debt on 6 Jan. 1756 in the house of his son-in-law in Quebec, having had to sell his own house and much of his land.

S. DALE STANDEN

Lantagnac

AN, Col., B, 34, f.78v; 45, ff.810–24, 859–60; 48, ff.824–26, 877, 880–83; 49, ff.632–33v, 691v–92; 50, ff.527–28; 53, ff.34v, 491–92, 495f., 498–504v; 54, ff.410–11; 55, ff.476, 528v–31; 57, f.603v; 61, ff.553v–54; 64, ff.448–49; 68, f.273v; 70, ff.347f.; 72, f.339; 74, f.457; 81, ff.302f.; 85, ff.208f.; 95, ff.46f.; C¹¹ᴬ, 36, pp.316–41, 342–53 (PAC transcripts); 47, ff.49–57; 49, ff.45–47v, 365–70v, 412–23v; 50, ff.291–303; 51, ff.221–24; 53, ff.130–49, 198v, 234–71, 275–78; 55, ff.101–4, 159–63; 58, f.92; 59, ff.41f.; 60, ff.62–67v; 61, ff.235–36, 270–75v; 62, ff.300–1v; 66, ff.119–20v; 74, ff.40–41; 75, ff.182–86v; 89, ff.305–7; D²ᴰ, 1; E, 253; F³, 11, ff.333–34, 335–37; Section Outre-Mer, G², 213, pp.38–84; 215, pp.1–62 (PAC transcripts). ANQ, Greffe de Jacques Barbel, 26 déc. 1720; Greffe de Louis Chambalon, 11 nov. 1712; Greffe de J.-B. Decharny, 28 janv. 1756; Greffe de C.-H. Du Laurent, 16 nov. 1741, 20 sept. 1747; Greffe d'Henry Hiché, 19 oct. 1730, 13 janv. 1735; Greffe de J.-C. Louet, 1ᵉʳ oct. 1726; NF, Coll. de pièces jud. et not., 1115, 1547, 1846. ASQ, Lettres, O, 102, 103, 104; Registre B, pp.30–33, 35–39; Seigneuries, VII, 8; Séminaire, XXIX, 64. *Documents relating to Canadian currency during the French period* (Shortt), I, 357–59, 507–9, *passim*. Le Jeune, *Dictionnaire*. P.-G. Roy, *Inv. concessions*, IV, 63–64; *La famille Lanoullier* (Lévis, Qué., 1935). J. F. Bosher, "Government and private interests in New France," *Canadian Public Administration* (Toronto), X (1967), 244–57.

LANTAGNAC, GASPARD ADHÉMAR DE. *See* Aᴅʜᴇ́ᴍᴀʀ

LAPALME, DOMINIQUE JANSON, *dit. See* Jᴀɴsᴏɴ

LA PÉRADE, MARIE-MADELEINE TARIEU DE. *See* Jᴀʀʀᴇᴛ ᴅᴇ Vᴇʀᴄʜᴇ̀ʀᴇs

LA PERRIÈRE, CLAUDE MARIN DE. *See* Mᴀʀɪɴ

LA PERRIÈRE, RENÉ BOUCHER DE. *See* Bᴏᴜᴄʜᴇʀ

LA PICARDIÈRE, MICHEL BÉGON DE. *See* Bᴇ́ɢᴏɴ

LAPORTE DE LALANNE, JEAN DE (sometimes referred to as **Armand**), commissary of the Marine, special investigator in Canada, 1740–41; fl. 1720–58.

Originally from Bayonne, France, Jean de Laporte de Lalanne moved to Paris in the 1720s with his brother Arnaud. He entered the Marine in the office of the colonies in the wake of Arnaud's meteoric rise from a minor functionary in 1731 to first clerk in 1738. Within a few years Jean had himself risen to the rank of commissary. In 1740 he was sent to Canada to study the opera-

tions of the civil government and to investigate, in particular, the administration of crown finances. In a letter to Governor Bᴇᴀᴜʜᴀʀɴᴏɪs and Intendant Hocquart*, the minister of Marine, Maurepas, stated that Laporte was on a tour of the colonies as a way of educating him for important future posts. Pierre Hazeur* de L'Orme, representative of the chapter of Quebec at Paris, informed his brother, Joseph-Thierry Hᴀᴢᴇᴜʀ, at Quebec of Laporte's mission, adding that everyone in Canada, "important or unimportant," should pay court to Jean for "he could well one day come to hold a high position." It also seems likely that Maurepas wanted Laporte to investigate irregularities in the organization of finances in Canada that had come to light in 1739 as a consequence of the deteriorating relations between Beauharnois and Hocquart. For his part, Laporte had an eye out for lucrative colonial enterprises in which he might wish to acquire an interest.

Laporte arrived at Quebec in the early autumn of 1740, in time to help Hocquart prepare the annual financial dispatches. Hocquart reported that "he has begun to go into much of the routine. I think that he will certainly profit from his time in Canada. He is fortunate to have been born with great natural ability. . . ." Whether he accepted Hocquart's advice to visit the Saint-Maurice ironworks that winter is not clear, but he did inspect them on his way to Montreal the following summer. None of his views on the colonial administration has survived, but the very absence of serious repercussions for Canadian officials following his return to France in 1741 may indicate that he was reasonably satisfied. Then too, Hocquart, who left nothing to chance, was careful to send him off bathed in praise.

Hocquart's opinion changed, however, when it became apparent that Laporte was using his recently acquired familiarity with the Canadian economy for private benefit. On 17 April 1744, Maurepas informed the Canadian officials that Laporte was to be given the fur *ferme* of Lac Alemipigon (Lake Nipigon, Ont.) from that year forward as a reward for his services in New France. In a letter dated a week later, Maurepas confirmed that the Laporte brothers had received a warrant granting them five-sixths of the fishery of Baie de Phélypeaux (Baie de Brador, Que.) on the death of the proprietor, François Mᴀʀᴛᴇʟ de Brouague; revenues from the whole concession had been more than 55,000 *livres* in 1741. Both Beauharnois and Hocquart resisted these metropolitan intrusions, asserting that the colonial inhabitants who developed such enterprises should reap the benefits. But Hocquart's successor, François Bigot*, proved more cooperative. Arnaud de Laporte became a key figure in the *grande société*, acting as Bigot's protector in the office of the colonies. Jean was also involved, as evidence at Bigot's trial confirmed, but his role was peripheral after his posting, sometime prior to 1750, as commissary at Saint-Domingue (Hispaniola), where the Laportes had extensive private investments. Jean's son, Arnaud, later entered the Marine and succeeded him as commissary.

DONALD J. HORTON

AN, Col., B, 70/1, 78/1; C¹¹ᴬ, 73, 75, 77, 81; E, 177 (dossier Favry Duponceau) (PAC transcripts). *Documents relating to Canadian currency during the French period* (Shortt), II, 698. *Inv. de pièces du Labrador* (P.-G. Roy), I, 79–80; II, 241–43. M.-A. Deschard, *Notice sur l'organisation du corps du commissariat de la marine française depuis l'origine jusqu'à nos jours, suivie d'une liste chronologique des anciens intendants de marine et des colonies* (Paris, 1879), 78. L.-E. Dussieux, *Le Canada sous la domination française d'après les archives de la Marine et de la Guerre* (3ᵉ éd., Paris, 1883), 128, 130. Frégault, *François Bigot*, I, 97, 133–34, 290–93; *Le grand marquis*, 418–20. P.-G. Roy, "Armand Laporte de Lalanne," *BRH*, L (1944), 161–69. Henri Têtu, "Le chapitre de la cathédrale de Québec et ses délégués en France," *BRH*, XVI (1910), 291, 296.

LA RALIÈRE (La Ratière), CHARLES DES HERBIERS DE. *See* DES HERBIERS

LA RICHARDIE, ARMAND DE (the name also appears as **Richardie**), priest, Jesuit missionary; b. 4 Jan. 1686 at Périgueux, France; d. 17 March 1758 at Quebec.

Armand de La Richardie entered the Society of Jesus at Bordeaux on 4 Oct. 1703. He studied at various centres in France and taught at La Rochelle, Luçon, and Saintes (dept. of Charente-Maritime). Following his ordination in 1719, he was an instructor at Angoulême until his departure for Canada six years later.

After his arrival in the colony in 1725, he spent some time at the mission of Lorette (near Quebec) learning the Huron language. Then in 1728 he journeyed to Detroit to establish the mission of Notre-Dame-de-l'Assomption among the Hurons. The governor, Charles de BEAUHARNOIS, called him well fitted to carry on the mission, but La Richardie's initial apostolic labours were frustrating.

In 1702–3, despite the opposition of Father Étienne de Carheil*, the Hurons had accepted the invitation of Cadillac [Laumet*] to leave the Jesuit mission on the Straits of Mackinac and settle at Detroit. There for a quarter of a century

their spiritual needs had been attended to, if at all, by the Recollet chaplain Constantin Delhalle* and his successors at the nearby fort. The Indians had drifted away from Christianity. Eventually, however, La Richardie's patient devotion was rewarded. Hoosiens, a chief, was converted and his kindred followed his example until by 1735 there were 600 neophyte Christians.

The progress of the mission was set back when the Hurons incurred the wrath of the Ottawas, Potawatomis, and Ojibwas of Detroit by warning their enemies the Flatheads of an impending raid. Fearing retaliation, a large number of La Richardie's converts remained at their winter hunting quarters near Sandoské (Sandusky) and made only occasional visits to Detroit. They begged Beauharnois to move them near Montreal, but La Richardie opposed the move, partly from fear that they would be settled at the Sulpician mission of Lac-des-Deux-Montagnes. Attempting to reunite his flock, in 1742 he transferred the mission some 20 miles downstream from the fort to Bois Blanc Island at the mouth of the Detroit River. The change was accepted by all except one faction led by ORONTONY (Nicolas).

The strain of his life led the weary Jesuit to ask for relief from his responsibilities. In the summer of 1743 Nicolas Degonnor came to replace him, but sickness forced Degonnor to return to Quebec the next year. In September 1744, Pierre Potier* arrived to understudy the mission's founder. His coming proved timely, for in the spring of 1746 La Richardie suffered a stroke and at the end of July returned to Canada for a rest cure.

His retirement was short. The following May some disaffected Hurons and other Indians from Sandoské, inspired by the English it was said, destroyed the mission. The Christian Hurons appealed for the return of the missionary whom they had learned to love and revere as a father, and in October La Richardie arrived in Detroit. With the aid of a grant of 5,000 *livres* from the government, in 1748 he re-established the mission at La Pointe de Montréal (in the present city of Windsor). Having completed the reconstruction and made renewed efforts to bring back to the fold the scattered remnants around Sandoské, La Richardie returned to Quebec in summer 1751.

During his retirement he became vice-superior of the Jesuit college (1755) and spiritual director and confessor at the Hôtel-Dieu monastery (1756). He also served as a confessor at the college until his death in 1758.

E. J. LAJEUNESSE

355

La Richardière

ARSI, Gallia 110/II, ff.348–49. ASJCF, MSS Potier, La gazette du père Potier. DPL, Burton hist. coll., Potier papers, Livre de compte de la mission des Hurons du Détroit, 1733–91. "Cadillac papers," *Michigan Pioneer Coll.*, XXXIV (1904), 49–51, 63. *JR* (Thwaites), LXVIII, LXIX. *Windsor border region* (Lajeunesse). Casgrain, *Histoire de l'Hôtel-Dieu de Québec*, 574. George Paré, *The Catholic Church in Detroit, 1701–1888* (Detroit, 1951). Rochemonteix, *Les Jésuites et la N.-F. au XVIIIᵉ siècle*, II, 36, 56. W. E. Shiels, "The Jesuits in Ohio in the eighteenth century," *Mid-America* (Chicago), XVIII (1936; new ser., VII), 27–47.

LA RICHARDIÈRE, RICHARD TESTU DE. *See* TESTU

LA RIVIÈRE, CLAUDE-NICOLAS DE LORIMIER DE. *See* LORIMIER

LA ROCHEFOUCAULD DE ROYE, JEAN-BAPTISTE-LOUIS-FRÉDÉRIC DE, Marquis de ROUCY, Duc d'ANVILLE, naval officer; b. 17 Aug. 1709, son of Louis de La Rochefoucauld, Marquis de Roye, lieutenant-general of the galleys, and Marthe Ducasse; m. 28 Feb. 1732 Marie-Louise-Nicole de La Rochefoucauld, by whom he had a son and two daughters; d. 27 Sept. 1746 at Chebucto (Halifax, N.S.), and buried on George Island in the port of Halifax, then at Louisbourg, Île Royale (Cape Breton Island), and finally in France.

Jean-Baptiste-Louis-Frédéric de La Rochefoucauld de Roye was invested on 7 Dec. 1720 with the reversion of the office held by his father, but as his father did not die until 1751, he never actually held it. He was made Duc d'Anville by letters patent from the king on 15 Feb. 1732. In 1734 he was serving on board a galley, but because the corps of officers for service on the galleys was about to be abolished, d'Anville was transferred to the sailing-ship component of the Marine, retaining his rank. In January 1745 he was appointed lieutenant general of naval forces. He does not seem ever to have received proper naval training, and he was in no way qualified to lead the expedition which he commanded the following year.

After Louisbourg fell to William PEPPERRELL and Peter WARREN in June 1745, the Duc d'Anville was given the mission of trying to retake the citadel, defend Canada against a possible English attack, and undertake operations as far as possible against the English settlements in Acadia and Newfoundland. To carry out this ambitious program, a squadron of 54 ships had been planned; d'Anville was supported by the rear-admirals La Jonquière [TAFFANEL] and Constantin-Louis d'ESTOURMEL. The fitting-out of this fleet was slow and difficult, and it did not set sail until 22 June 1746. Wind-bound, the squadron did not sight the coasts of Acadia until 10 September. Three days later it was scattered by a violent gale that seriously damaged some ships, which were consequently forced to return to France. D'Estourmel entered Chebucto harbour on 27 September, only to learn that d'Anville had died at three o'clock that morning "of an attack of apoplexy, which had seized him on the morning of the 25th while walking on his forecastle deck." D'Estourmel then took command, but on 30 September he wounded himself seriously while trying to commit suicide and handed his powers over to La Jonquière. The sorry state of the squadron, with its ships battered by the elements, and their crews reduced by an epidemic, led La Jonquière to give up any attack on Annapolis Royal, Nova Scotia. A return of losses as of 15 October listed 587 dead and 2,274 sick out of a total complement of 7,006 sailors and soldiers. Four transport ships left for Canada on 10 October, escorted by the *Renommée* under the command of Guy-François de Coëtnempren de Kersaint; the others set sail for France two weeks later.

The expedition was a complete failure, which can be explained by several factors, bad luck being not the least important. The failure emphasized forcefully the weakness of the French navy and also the difficulties of assisting the French colonies in North America. These were the logical consequences of the neglect of the French navy since the death of Louis XIV: the ships were insufficient in number, and, since they had done little sailing for years, the officers as well as the crews were inadequately trained.

ÉTIENNE TAILLEMITE

AN, Marine, B², 328; B⁴, 59; C¹, 161. La Chesnaye-Desbois et Badier, *Dictionnaire de la noblesse* (3ᵉ éd.), VII, 336. Lacour-Gayet, *La marine militaire sous Louis XV* (1910), 177, 194–96, 200–2. Troude, *Batailles navales de la France*, I, 309.

LA RODDE, ÉTIENNE-GUILLAUME DE SENEZERGUES DE. *See* SENEZERGUES

LARON. *See* SAUGUAARAM

LA RONDE, LOUIS DENYS DE. *See* DENYS

LA ROUVILLIÈRE, HONORÉ MICHEL DE VILLEBOIS DE. *See* MICHEL

LARTIGUE, JOSEPH, fisherman, merchant, councillor, judge; b. *c.* 1683 in the province of

Armagnac, France; d. 28 May 1743 at Louisbourg, Île Royale (Cape Breton Island). He married Jeanne Dhiarse (d'Hiarse, Dihars), the daughter of a fisherman from Plaisance (Placentia, Nfld.), and they had four sons and five daughters. One of his daughters married Léon FAUTOUX and another, Michel Rodrigue*.

We do not know when Joseph Lartigue immigrated to Plaisance, perhaps as a hired hand. His name appears for the first time in the records of the colony in 1708, the year he was awarded the contract for supplying the expedition led by Saint-Ovide [MONBETON] against the English forts at St John's, Newfoundland. Securing payment involved Lartigue in many years of painful litigation, and although he eventually received a substantial sum from the crown, as late as 1752 his widow was trying to recover 2,800 *livres* apparently still owing from Saint-Ovide.

Lartigue claimed to have been ''without doubt one of the best established [settlers at Plaisance].'' His situation at Île Royale, where he went with the Plaisance colony in 1714, confirms his prominence. His principal property in Louisbourg was in a choice location at the foot of the interior glacis of the King's bastion and was considered to be ''the finest in the town.'' With six shallops and 20 men in his employ in 1719, he figured among the town's most important fishermen, but from the early 1720s he appears to have abandoned the fishery in favour of trade. In 1726 he employed 12 men and two vessels in trade. He also rented two warehouses to the crown, as well as space for the admiralty court.

After acquiring some legal experience as a clerk from 1715, he was appointed a councillor in the Conseil Supérieur in 1723 and keeper of the colony's seals in 1731. In 1734 he became the first (and only) judge of the Louisbourg bailiff court on the recommendation of the governor, Saint-Ovide, and the financial commissary, Sébastien-François-Ange Le Normant* de Mézy, who described him, perhaps a little flatteringly, as a ''very steady fellow, honest and straightforward.'' Throughout his Louisbourg career Lartigue showed a remarkable propensity for building in areas about to be expropriated in the interests of the king's service. Although the crown replaced his expropriated property with comparable land in other areas, he nevertheless complained of losses and it may be that his offices were given him in partial compensation. Indeed, most of the source material we have on Lartigue is his voluminous correspondence with the ministry of Marine seeking redress for his grievances in connection with these expropriations and complaining of his victimization at the hands of Saint-

Ovide and Philippe Pastour* de Costebelle at the time of the St John's expedition in 1709.

BERNARD POTHIER

AN, Col., B, 55, f.557v; 61, ff.602–2v; 89, f.320; C¹¹ᴮ, 1, ff.514–17; 6, f.158; 14, ff.398–99v, 400–1v; 15, ff.52–59; 17, ff.289–90; 18, ff.332–35; 19, ff.64–66v, 265–68; 20, ff.288–89; E, 258 (dossier Lartigue); Section Outre-Mer, G¹, 407 (29 mai 1743); G³, 2038, 2039, 2041, 2043, 2046, 2055–58. Robert Le Blant, *Un colonial sous Louis XIV: Philippe de Pastour de Costebelle, gouverneur de Terre-Neuve puis de l'île Royale, 1661–1717* (Paris, Dax, 1935), 227–30.

LA SABLONNIÈRE, JEAN BRUNET, *dit. See* BRUNET

LA TÊTE BLANCHE. *See* GRAY LOCK

LATOUCHE MacCARTHY, CHARLES, naval officer; b. 1706 at Brest, France, son of Timothée Latouche MacCarthy and Hélène Shee; d. 24 Jan. 1765 in Paris, France.

Charles Latouche MacCarthy's family, Irish in origin, sought refuge in France around 1690 and gave the army and the Marine a great number of officers. Latouche MacCarthy began sailing in the merchant marine about 1730, and he was probably in command of a merchant ship when he came to Canada. In 1737 he was at Quebec, and there, on 7 October, he married Angélique-Jeanne, daughter of Charles Guillimin*, a councillor of the Conseil Supérieur. On 1 April 1745 Latouche received a commission as a naval lieutenant and was appointed port captain and harbour master at Quebec in succession to the late René Legardeur de Beauvais (the younger), but he was never to occupy that post. In fact, while he was on board the *Gironde* to sail to Canada, he was ordered to go to Dunkerque to superintend the embarking of the troops who were to cross to England to support the endeavours of Charles Edward Stuart, the Young Pretender.

In 1746 he sailed on the *Léopard* in the squadron of the Duc d'Anville [LA ROCHEFOUCAULD] and took part in the ill-starred campaign in Acadia. The following year he received command of the *Rubis* in the squadron commanded by the Marquis de La Jonquière [TAFFANEL], which was bound for Canada, and he took part in the combat of 14 May, during which ''he conducted himself with very great distinction. . . . The Sieur Macarthy, whose ship carried only 22 guns, fought for 4 hours against 2 and 3 vessels of 50 and 60 guns and surrendered only because his ship was completely disabled, riddled with

357

Laurent

shots, and had 6 feet of water in the hold." For this fine action he received on 1 April 1748 the rank of fireship captain, an "intermediate" rank granted officers of the merchant marine who had entered the king's service. In 1749 he was in command of the *Pie*, bound for Cayenne.

On 1 March 1751 he was promoted lieutenant-commander and was created a knight of the order of Saint-Louis. That same year he received command of the frigate *Fidèle*, bound for Louisbourg, Île Royale (Cape Breton Island). In 1755 he served on board the *Entreprenant* in the squadron commanded by Dubois de La Motte [CAHIDEUC]; it sailed for Canada, but illness prevented MacCarthy from taking part in the campaign. The following year he commanded the frigate *Valeur*, which was being sent on a new mission to Louisbourg. On 17 April 1757 MacCarthy was promoted captain and commanded the frigate *Abénaquise* in Dubois de La Motte's squadron, which had orders to go to the defence of Île Royale. On the return trip the frigate was separated by a squall from the rest of the squadron and had to fight a vessel of 70 guns and a frigate. MacCarthy, wounded in the head, had to surrender and was taken to England, where he remained a prisoner until May 1758.

In 1760 he was given command of the *Sirène*, *Flore*, and *Valeur*, ships that had been fitted out by private individuals with Saint-Domingue (Hispaniola) as their destination. He reached that colony safely, but on the return voyage the three ships were attacked by three English vessels as they sailed out of Cap (Cap Haïtien or Le Cap). The combat lasted two days, and the accidental explosion of a cannon and a fire on board ship forced MacCarthy to surrender. He returned to France on 31 Aug. 1761 and afterwards served at the port of Rochefort.

MacCarthy had two daughters and also a son who served in the Marine and perished in the shipwreck of the *Bayonnaise* off Martinique in August 1765.

ÉTIENNE TAILLEMITE

AN, Marine, B³, 549, ff.34–41; B⁴, 61, 64, 73, 76, 80, 98; C¹, 160; 165; 166, p.362; C⁷, 191; G, 38, p. 140. Taillemite, *Inventaire analytique, série B, I.* Fauteux, *Les chevaliers de Saint-Louis*, 152. Lacour-Gayet, *La marine militaire sous Louis XV* (1910), 182, 496. Troude, *Batailles navales de la France*, I, 344, 347, 423. "Le capitaine Macarty," *BRH*, XIV (1908), 61–62.

LAURENT, PAUL, Micmac warrior; d. probably at La Hève (La Have, N.S.), sometime after 1763.

Since Paul Laurent spoke English, it may be supposed that he had shared his father's captivity in Boston, Massachusetts, where the latter was hanged at an unknown date. Nothing is known about his return to Acadia, but between 1753 and 1763 he turns up in different places all over Nova Scotia. He seems to have been connected with Abbé Jean-Louis Le Loutre*'s mission at Shubenacadie.

One of the earliest mentions of Paul Laurent occurs in the diary of Anthony Casteel, an English prisoner. On 12 June 1753 (o.s.), at Baie-Verte (N.B.), Laurent offered to pay Casteel's ransom, which had been set at 300 *livres*, intending to scalp him and thus avenge his father's death. Casteel was saved by a French officer and was finally ransomed by an Acadian named James Morrice (Jacques Maurice). Then, adds Casteel, the other Micmacs "went out of the house and shoved Paul Laurent out before them and used him very ill."

In January 1755 Laurent was at the Chignecto isthmus, where he was involved in the peace negotiations in which Le Loutre engaged with Captain John Hussey, the commandant of Fort Lawrence (near Amherst, N.S.). Laurent was sent on a mission to Halifax with the chief Algimou, but on the way he was stopped at Cobequid (near Truro, N.S.) by Abbé Jean MANACH, who detained Algimou and sent Laurent on alone to Halifax, apparently with special instructions. On 12 Feb. 1755 the Nova Scotia Council declared that the Micmacs' demands were exorbitant, and no agreement was signed. The previous summer the council had refused Le Loutre almost identical peace conditions.

After the fall of Fort Beauséjour (near Sackville, N.B.) in July 1755, Laurent apparently joined Abbé Manach's group of Micmacs and took part in the Acadians' resistance, under Charles Deschamps* de Boishébert's command. Early in 1760, after a capitulation had been signed by Manach, Laurent accompanied the missionary to Fort Cumberland (previously Fort Beauséjour). The commandant of the fort then sent him to Halifax, probably to take the announcement of peace.

In 1762 Paul Laurent was captain of the Micmacs from La Hève, whose chief, Francis Mius, had signed a peace treaty with the English on 9 Nov. 1761. One event suggests that Laurent probably enjoyed great prestige among his people: in July 1762 Abbé Pierre MAILLARD, whom the English had appointed the government agent to the Indians, arranged for negotiations with the Micmacs from La Hève and Cape Sable, Nova Scotia. But illness prevented him from being present; during the talks an Indian woman committed a theft, and in the missionary's

358

absence the authorities immediately turned to Paul Laurent to dispense justice in this delicate situation. After this date the documents say nothing directly concerning Laurent. He may have accompanied the chiefs from La Hève, including Francis Mius, when they appeared before the governor and council on 22 Aug. 1763 to obtain the appointment of a successor to Maillard, who had died the previous year. If this is so, Laurent must have died sometime after 1763 among his tribe.

Laurent, who had been a fierce enemy of the English, became peaceful to an exemplary degree after the missionaries advised the Micmacs in the autumn of 1759 to make peace. For this reason his career is particularly interesting.

MICHELINE D. JOHNSON

PAC, MG 11, Nova Scotia B, 7, pp.57, 64; 8, pp.2–7; 9, pp.47, 166–67; 10, pp.2, 13–20, 26–42, 49, 148, 160, 166, 171, 182, 184–85, 217, 220, 230, 236, 278, 282, 288; 12, pp.6, 47, 129, 134, 139, 145, 153, 158, 176, 178, 188, 189, 198–99, 209; 13, pp.95, 188, 216; 14, pp.13, 15, 107, 170, 181. [Anthony Casteel], "Anthony Casteel's journal," *Coll. doc. inédits Canada et Amérique*, II (1889), 111–26. E. A. Hutton, "The Micmac Indians of Nova Scotia to 1834" (unpublished MA thesis, Dalhousie University, Halifax, 1961). "Indians in Acadie, A.D. 1760," *Mass. Hist. Soc. Coll.*, 1st ser., X (1809), 115–16. *N.S. Archives*, I, 210, 215–19, 237, 694–98. Murdoch, *History of Nova-Scotia*, II, 222, 257, 407, 419, 431. Albert David, "L'apôtre des Micmacs," *Revue de l'université d'Ottawa*, V (1935), 49–82, 425–52; VI (1936), 22–40. R. O. MacFarlane, "British Indian policy in Nova Scotia to 1760," *CHR*, XIX (1938), 154–67.

LAUVERJAT, ÉTIENNE, priest, Jesuit, missionary; b. 25 Jan. 1679 at Bourges, France; d. 16 Nov. 1761 at Quebec.

Étienne Lauverjat entered the noviciate of the Society of Jesus in Paris on 8 Nov. 1700. As soon as he had been ordained a priest he left for Canada, probably in 1710, for the records of Saint-François-du-Lac attest to his presence in that parish on 14 February and on 18 and 30 March 1711. His superior, Joseph-Louis Germain*, who intended to send him to the Abenaki missions in Acadia, had sent him to the one at Saint-François to learn the Abenaki language there under Joseph AUBERY. After a stay in the missions at Sault-Saint-Louis (Caughnawaga) and Bécancour, he went to replace Pierre de LA CHASSE at Pannawambskek (Panaouamské), a village located a few miles north of the present-day city of Bangor, Maine. He was there in the autumn of 1718. In spite of his efforts the Abenakis of Panna-wambskek let the English settle in the vicinity of Pemaquid in 1720.

In March 1723, during the first year of the war between Massachusetts and the Abenakis of Maine, Colonel Thomas Westbrook, coming from Boston with a troop of 230 men, burned the village and the Jesuit's chapel to avenge the Abenakis' attack the previous year against a small English fort on the St George's River. Around 1728 Lauverjat quarrelled with Joseph d'ABBADIE de Saint-Castin and his younger brother. Among other things the missionary accused them of having regularly thwarted his warlike undertakings.

Like his *confrère* Aubery, Lauverjat believed that the Abenakis of Acadia had to resist, even by force of arms, the encroachments of the English on their lands. He thought that, once masters of the country, the English would chase out the Catholic missionaries and that that would spell the end of their flocks' religious fidelity. He was encouraged in his attitude by the governors and intendants of New France in whose opinion the surrender of their lands by the Abenakis of Acadia would open the door to Canada for the English. The Jesuit received financial aid from the authorities of New France secretly, since it could not be given openly because of the treaty of Utrecht (1713).

In 1732, after his dispute with the Saint-Castin brothers, Lauverjat left Pannawambskek to go to Médoctec (Meductic) on the Saint John River. In 1734 he returned to Canada, and from 1735 to 1738 he served the parish and mission of Bécancour, then from 1738 to 1740 the parish of Sainte-Geneviève-de-Batiscan. After another two years at Pannawambskek and a stay at the Jesuit residence in Montreal in 1742, he took charge of a new mission created for the Abenakis of Saint-François and Bécancour at the mouth of the Missisquoi River (in present-day Vermont). The authorities counted upon him to detach the Abenakis from the English and to keep them informed of the Indians' attitude. Governor Charles de BEAUHARNOIS and Intendant Gilles Hocquart* had a house built and furnished for him. At the same time the Jesuit served "as a mission" the parish of Saint-Denis, which was at that time planned for the seigneury of Foucault, on Missisquoi Bay.

In 1747 Lauverjat left Missisquoi for Saint-Michel-de-Bellechasse (Que.). In 1749 he went to Pointe-à-la-Caille (Montmagny) to bring spiritual succour to the hundreds of Indians from Acadia who had sought refuge there at the beginning of the War of the Austrian Succession in 1744. The war being over, he returned to their country with them in 1749 and served the mission at Norridgewock (Narantsouak; today Old Point, Madison, Maine), then that at Médoctec until 1754. Later he lived in retirement at the Jesuit college in Quebec, applying himself to confessing the Indians. Marcel Trudel believes that Lauverjat was the aged religious arrested by Lieutenant John Knox* after the fall of Quebec because he was suspected of having urged English soldiers to desert. He died at Quebec in 1761.

THOMAS-M. CHARLAND

AJTR, Registre d'état civil, Bécancour et Sainte-Geneviève-de-Batiscan. AN, Col., B, 45, f.801; 78, f.25; 81, f.42; C¹¹ᴬ, 49, f.124; 81, f.12; 93, f.181; F³, 2, f.457. ANQ-M, Registre d'état civil, Chambly, 12 nov. 1745. ASJCF, Extraits des catalogues. *Coll. de manuscrits relatifs à la N.-F.*, III, 31, 54, 61, 134, 136, 143, 161, 166. *JR* (Thwaites), LXVI, 204, 206, 345; LXIX, 78; LXX, 80; LXXI, 163, 399. Knox, *Historical journal* (Doughty), II, 277–78. Mass. Hist. Soc. *Coll.*, 2nd ser., VIII (1826), 264. [Thomas Westbrook *et al.*], *Letters of Colonel Thomas Westbrook and others relative to Indian affairs in Maine, 1722–26*, ed. W. B. Trask (Boston, 1901), 76–77.

J.-D. Brosseau, *Essai de monographie paroissiale: Saint-Georges d'Henryville et la seigneurie de Noyan* ([Saint-Hyacinthe, Qué.], 1913), 35, 64, 227. Charland, *Les Abénakis d'Odanak*, 66, 77, 79, 80, 98, 99. Pierre Daviault, *Le baron de Saint-Castin, chef abénaquis* (Montréal, 1939), 182–83. E. J. Devine, *Historic Caughnawaga* (Montreal, 1922), 169. M. C. Leger, *The Catholic Indian missions in Maine, 1611–1820* (Catholic Univ. of America studies in American church history, VII, Washington, 1929), 89. É.-Z. Massicotte, *Sainte-Geneviève de Batiscan* (Pages trifluviennes, sér. A, no.18, Trois-Rivières, 1936), 56. Parkman, *Half-century of conflict*, chap.X. Honorius Provost, *Les Abénakis sur la Chaudière* (Saint-Joseph-de-Beauce, Qué. 1948), 14. [F.-E.] Rameau de Saint-Père, *Une colonie féodale en Amérique; l'Acadie (1604–1881)* (2v., Paris, Montréal, 1889), II, 379. Rochemonteix, *Les Jésuites et la N.-F. au XVIIᵉ siècle*, III, 440, 443, 467; *Les Jésuites et la N.-F. au XVIIIᵉ siècle*, I, 147; II, 13, 16, 202. Marie-Antoine [Roy], *Saint-Michel de la Durantaye [notes et souvenirs]: 1678–1929* (Québec, 1929), 68, 69. Trudel, *L'Église canadienne*, I, 31.

LAUZON, PIERRE DE, priest, Jesuit, missionary, superior of the Jesuit missions in New France; baptized 13 Sept. 1687 at Leignes-sur-Fontaine (dept. of Vienne) France, son of Pierre de Lauzon, a lawyer, and Marguerite Riot; d. 5 Sept. 1742 at Quebec.

After classical studies in France at the Jesuit college in Poitiers, Pierre de Lauzon entered the noviciate of the Jesuits of the province of Aquitaine in Bordeaux on 26 Nov. 1703 and pronounced his first vows on 27 Nov. 1705. From 1705 to 1707 he studied logic and physics at Limoges and he taught from 1707 to 1710. After a third year of philosophy at Limoges, he taught rhetoric there until 1712; then he started on his theology at Bordeaux and was ordained a priest four years later.

Lauzon sailed for Canada in 1716; shortly after arriving in Quebec he went to the mission at Lorette to help Father Pierre-Daniel Richer and to learn the Huron and Iroquois languages. In 1718 he was sent as a missionary to Sault-Saint-Louis (Caughnawaga), where he pronounced his vows on 2 Feb. 1721. After three years at this mission he returned to Quebec, where he taught hydrography [*see* Joseph DES LANDES] during the school year of 1721–22. He was probably replacing Father François Le Brun, who had just died, but the assignment was probably also to allow him to recover his strength, for his labours among the Iroquois had undermined his health. His rest period was short, because the Indians at Sault-Saint-Louis urged his return. In 1721 there had in fact been some trouble at Sault-Saint-Louis and the Iroquois had set forth their grievances in a petition to Governor Philippe de Rigaud* de Vaudreuil and Intendant BÉGON, maintaining that the 'disorders at the mission had originally been caused by the too frequent changing of the missionaries; therefore they requested the return of Gannenrontié (Father Lauzon's Indian name). Furthermore they considered that the plan to re-establish a French garrison in the village was an insult to their loyalty; it would be a source of bad examples for their young people, a danger for their wives and daughters, and a waste of money which would be better employed helping the widows and orphans of the numerous warriors who had died defending the interests of the French against "both their own brothers and the English."

There was great danger that the inhabitants of Sault-Saint-Louis would leave the locality to withdraw to the Iroquois country or reach an agreement with the English. The governor and the intendant therefore thought it necessary to ask that Father Lauzon return to Sault-Saint-Louis, since he had already succeeded in warding off a similar threat during his first stay at that mission and since the Iroquois were very much attached to him. Lauzon returned in 1722, and the following year was appointed the superior at the mission, succeeding Father Julien Garnier*. He retained this office until 1732, at which time the ability he showed at the head of the Sault-Saint-Louis mission for nine consecutive years led Father François Retz, the general of the Society of Jesus, to name him superior of the Jesuit missions in New France. This appointment also included that of rector of the college of Quebec. He took up his functions in September, succeeding Father Jean-Baptiste DUPARC.

In 1733, during his superiorship, he went to France to seek reinforcements, particularly for the western missions. He returned in 1734, bringing with him Fathers Jean-Pierre Aulneau* and Luc-François NAU. The three Jesuits made the return voyage with Bishop Dosquet* on board the warship *Rubis*. On the 80-day crossing there were gales and epidemics, and 20 people died. Father Lauzon acted as boatswain's mate, for all the passengers had to share in the ship's duties.

When Jean-Baptiste de SAINT-PÉ succeeded him as superior of the Jesuit missions in New France in 1739, Lauzon returned to Sault-Saint-Louis and resumed the direction of his former mission [*see* Nau]. A painful experience was in store for him there: he had to defend his flock against accusations of disloyalty to France and illegal trade with the English. In a report dated 1741 and addressed to Pierre de Rigaud* de Vaudreuil de Cavagnial, then governor of Trois-Rivières, with the request that he see that it reached the minister, Maurepas, Lauzon recalled the services the Iroquois of Sault-Saint-Louis had rendered France in the struggles against other Indians and the English, and he drew attention to the suspicion and unfair treatment they had received in return from the French. He also rejected the accusation brought against the Jesuits at this mission of engaging in trade. This was the beginning of the Tournois-Desauniers affair: the Jesuit Jean-Baptiste TOURNOIS was accused of being in business partnership with the Misses Desauniers and encouraging the Indians to patronize the store that the women ran. Lauzon's report did not get to the minister soon enough, and on 12 April 1742 the minister ordered that the Desauniers' store be closed and had a request sent to Father Lauzon asking him to prevent the Indians from moving to English territory.

Pierre de Lauzon was sensitive to the suspicion; it touched his honour as a missionary and a Frenchman. Exhausted by illness and affected by the merchants' accusations, he was recalled to Quebec in 1741. The pain caused him by these accusations even hastened his death, which occurred on 5 Sept. 1742, after a few days' illness.

JOSEPH COSSETTE

AD, Vienne (Poitiers), État civil, Leignes-sur-Fontaine, 13 sept. 1687. ASJCF, 555; Cahier des vœux; Fonds Rochemonteix, 4006, 227, 259; 4018, 18. *JR* (Thwaites), LXVII, 66, 72–78; LXIX, 45–47, 57. Melançon, *Liste des missionnaires jésuites*, 46.
Rochemonteix, *Les Jésuites et la N.-F. aux XVIIIᵉ siècle*, I, 211; II, 20, 21, 23, 52, 245, 256.

LAVALLÉE CONSTANTIN, PIERRE. *See* CONSTANTIN

LAVALTRIE, FRANÇOIS MARGANE DE. *See* MARGANE

LA VÉRENDRYE, LOUIS-JOSEPH GAULTIER DE. *See* GAULTIER

LA VÉRENDRYE, PIERRE GAULTIER DE VARENNES ET DE. *See* GAULTIER

LA VÉRENDRYE DE BOUMOIS, PIERRE GAULTIER DE. *See* GAULTIER

LAVILLANGEVIN, RENÉ-JEAN ALLENOU DE. *See* ALLENOU

L'AVOCAT, FRANÇOIS-CHARLES HAVARD DE BEAUFORT, *dit. See* HAVARD

LAWRENCE, CHARLES, military officer, governor of Nova Scotia; b. *c.* 1709 in England, son of Herbert Lawrence; d. Halifax, Nova Scotia, 19 Oct. 1760.

Charles Lawrence's life before his arrival in Nova Scotia in July 1749 is obscure, and existing accounts of it are inaccurate. It seems that he was commissioned in the 11th Regiment of Foot in 1727, was in the West Indies from 1733 to 1737, and then served in the War Office. He was promoted lieutenant in 1741 and captain in 1742, and fought with the 54th regiment in 1745 at Fontenoy (Belgium) where he was wounded. He was gazetted major with the 45th regiment (Warburton's), and joined it at Louisbourg, Île Royale (Cape Breton Island), in 1747. His family was related to the Montagus, which partly explains why he enjoyed the patronage of George Montagu Dunk, 2nd Earl of Halifax, president of the Board of Trade. This connection was his only source of influence, however, and he was without private means. He was popular in the army and was known to be strong, energetic, and direct in his methods.

Lawrence became a company commander in the 40th regiment in Nova Scotia in December 1749. The following April Governor Edward Cornwallis* sent him with a small force to establish British authority in the isthmus of Chignecto. On the north bank of the Missaguash River Lawrence found French forces under Louis de LA CORNE, who had orders to prevent British

Lawrence

penetration beyond that point and who had had the village of Beaubassin, near the south bank of the river, burned. Rather than fight the French, with whom the British were not at war, or admit to any territorial limitation, Lawrence withdrew.

Authorities in London were divided on the question of how far their troops in Nova Scotia should proceed in peace time in establishing British claims to the whole of Acadia. The Duke of Bedford, secretary of state for the Southern Department, had refused to reinforce Cornwallis so that he could implement these claims. But the Duke of Newcastle, prompted by Lord Halifax, intervened and despite royal opposition ensured that the 47th regiment was sent to Cornwallis in June 1750. Lawrence was promoted lieutenant-colonel about this time, and in August he left for the Missaguash River with a stronger force and routed a group of Indians led by the Abbé Jean-Louis Le Loutre*. Captain John Rous, the naval commander supporting the landing of troops in this engagement, was full of praise for Lawrence's coolness and leadership under fire. Cornwallis, in dispatches to London, commended his tactics. In the fall of 1750 Lawrence built Fort Lawrence on the south bank of the river. He remained there through the following year, and returned to Halifax in 1752, about the time that Peregrine Thomas Hopson succeeded Cornwallis as governor.

In the summer of 1753 Governor Hopson chose Lawrence to direct the settlement of the European Protestants who had waited vainly since their arrival in Halifax in 1751 and 1752 for the land promised them. Hopson decided to settle them on the coast south of Halifax at Mirligueche, renamed Lunenburg. There the French would not be able to stir up trouble for them, although Indian raids were to be expected. Lawrence accompanied the settlers to Lunenburg in June and supervised the establishment of the colony.

The settlers found cleared land, but most of the work remained to be done. Soured by months or years of waiting in squalid huts in Halifax, they were impatient to stake their claims and to start cultivation. Lawrence had seen the effects of Indian raids in different parts of the province and had to persuade the settlers to build defences before anything else. It was human to ignore a danger which few of them had experienced and it required artifice on Lawrence's part to make them do communal work. "Decent people," he noted, had to be cajoled into sleeping in communal shelters for protection and sharing them with those who were "dirty [and] full of Vermin." Building supplies were pilfered and fights

over favoured sites were frequent. But little by little this "inconceivably turbulent" crew was brought to see that they must either "proceed in another manner, or have [their] throats cut." By a mixture of bribery, bullying, and verbal persuasion, Lawrence gained their affection – "not only their hats but their hearts," as he described it – and retained it, to his political advantage, after his return to Halifax in August 1753. By then Hopson was preparing to return to England and had summoned Lawrence back as president of the council.

In 1754 Governor William Shirley of Massachusetts approached Lawrence with a plan to drive the French troops out of their Chignecto forts. Both men were sure of Lord Halifax's support and took advantage of an ill-advised letter from Thomas Robinson, the new secretary of state, ordering them to cooperate to throw the French out of Acadia. Robinson later repudiated the letter, but Shirley used it as authority to plan an operation. Late in the fall of 1754 he and Lawrence raised two battalions in Massachusetts, giving the command to Lieutenant-Colonel Robert Monckton*, assisted by the New Englander John Winslow*. This force was to attack Fort Beauséjour (near Sackville, N.B.), which the French had built on the north shore of the Missaguash River, opposite Fort Lawrence. Without authority, Lawrence paid for the force with the annual parliamentary grant for Nova Scotia. Early in 1755 General Edward Braddock, commander-in-chief in North America, sailed for America with flexible orders for the removal of French "encroachments" given him by the Duke of Cumberland, commander-in-chief of the army. Braddock was permitted to undertake several operations against the French simultaneously if he had sufficient troops. He authorized Monckton's expedition and it sailed from Boston on 19 May 1755. Fort Beauséjour fell to Monckton on 16 June.

The capture of Beauséjour was the only British success that year, but Lawrence had no orders for exploiting it. Braddock was killed near Fort Duquesne (Pittsburgh, Pa.) early in July [see Daniel-Hyacinthe-Marie Liénard de Beaujeu], while Shirley, his second in command, was proceeding towards Fort Oswego (Chouaguen) for operations against the French. In June, off Louisbourg, Vice-Admiral Boscawen let most of the French fleet escape with reinforcements for Louisbourg, Quebec, and Montreal. In an atmosphere of doubt about his superiors' activities and intentions and of apprehension about the enemy's, the defence of what he had gained became Lawrence's main concern.

As early as 1 May the Nova Scotia Council had

considered how to deal with the Acadians north of the Missaguash once Beauséjour had fallen. Those who had deserted to the French under the blandishments of Le Loutre could be punished for breaking their limited oath of allegiance to George II [*see* Richard PHILIPPS] if they had taken up arms or assisted the French. The other Acadians in this area could be required to depart to whatever destination the defeated garrison chose. The decision to expel all these Acadians was formally taken by the council on 25 June. The council planned to put settlers from New England on the vacated Acadian lands of the Chignecto isthmus as a barrier between the French in Île Royale and Île Saint-Jean (Prince Edward Island) and the Acadians remaining on the Nova Scotia peninsula. A military force in Chignecto would raid northwards and eventually enable the rest of Acadia beyond the Missaguash (present-day New Brunswick) to be settled. This was also Lord Halifax's conception.

John Winslow was the linchpin of the plan to obtain New England settlers. But owing to Lawrence's uncertainty about how to exploit his victory, Winslow was not permitted enough time to survey the land around Chignecto after the fall of Beauséjour. Inactivity caused the discipline of Winslow's troops to collapse and he quarrelled with Monckton, who had been ordered to recruit New Englanders for the regular battalions. Shirley also raided their ranks for his own use on the American continent. Winslow became embittered and lost interest in settlement. Short of troops and under the impression that the French were going to counter-attack, Lawrence turned his attention to securing his communications with Chignecto and was thus forced to deal with the issue of the loyalty of the Acadians of the peninsula. The scene was set for the tragedy.

Lawrence learned from the correspondence of previous governors, such as Richard Philipps and Peregrine Thomas Hopson, that although he should not drive the Acadians into the arms of the French, he should not grant them tenure unless they took an oath of allegiance which included the promise to bear arms for the English king. There was to be no compromise with the principle that before receiving the rights of subjects, they must accept their duties, and that Acadians who had left the country could not return without taking the oath. Hopson had been told to demand the oath when the circumstances of the province allowed. It had been an assumption of Lord Halifax's policy since 1749 that that moment would arrive when the French military presence had been removed from Nova Scotia. A change in the attitude of Acadian leaders after the French

surrender at Beauséjour seemed to bear out this assumption.

Early in July 1755 a group of 15 delegates from Minas (Grand Pré region) came before the council to present a petition concerning the confiscation of their boats and arms that spring by Alexander MURRAY at Fort Edward (Windsor). Lawrence took advantage of their presence to demand of them an unqualified oath of allegiance. The Acadians were reluctant to believe that the English would at last enforce the oath or protect them from Indian and French reprisals if they now took it. Consequently they refused the unqualified oath without a general consultation with the populace of Minas. Lawrence and his council insisted that each man decide on the oath himself, and when they still refused to do so they were imprisoned. Exasperated by the Acadians' intransigence the English became legalistic and felt compelled to pursue their course to the end. New Acadian delegates were summoned from Annapolis Royal and Minas to meet with Lawrence and the council, which included John Rous, John COLLIER, and Jonathan Belcher*. On 25 July the Annapolis delegates were told "they must now resolve either to take the Oath without any Reserve or else quit their lands, for that Affairs were now at such a Crisis in America that no delay could be admitted." They and the Minas delegates refused the oath and on 28 July were "ordered into confinement." The council, having resolved to expel all Acadians who rejected the oath, agreed that "it would be most proper to send them to be distributed amongst the Several Colonies on the Continent." Admiral Boscawen and Vice-Admiral Savage Mostyn attended this meeting and assented to the council's decision. Over the next few months most of the Acadian population of Nova Scotia was rounded up and transported to the American colonies, from Massachusetts to South Carolina.

The expulsion proved to have been as unnecessary on military grounds – with the subsequent capture of Louisbourg and Quebec – as it was later judged inhumane. Lawrence was not a cruel man, however, even if he lacked imagination. It is too simple to explain the decision as simply a matter of greed; legalism, deference to precedent, and over reliance on the collective responsibility of councils – marks of the age – provided an umbrella for it. The policies of the Board of Trade over the years, ambiguous in many respects, were specific in demanding the oath when the occasion arose. The unauthorized operation against Beauséjour provided the occasion. No military plan existed in London for the Nova Scotia operation, but after the expulsion

Lawrence

Lawrence received no reprimand for acting without orders. His decision was made in that "motly state neither peace nor war" (Lord Holdernesse) which Nova Scotia had experienced since 1749. The chief elements in the affair were confusion, misunderstanding, and fear. Each step towards the tragedy created the facts which pointed to the next. At no time did those who had the power also have the information to decide aright. They planned in a vacuum. Indeed, the only note of irritation appearing in letters from London in the months after the expulsion was caused by the complaints of the American governors on whom the Acadians had been foisted with little or no notice. Lawrence had overlooked the administrative and social implications of what he had considered a military operation.

In July 1756 Lawrence became governor of Nova Scotia. He saw as his most important task the settlement of the Acadian lands. But by 1757 merchants who were opposed to his personal rule, such as Joshua Mauger* and Ephraim Cook, had convinced the Board of Trade that settlers would not come unless they had an elected assembly. They also tried to show that Lawrence had favoured his friends with contracts and offices and would not call an assembly for fear of exposure.

In October 1754 the Board of Trade had instructed Jonathan Belcher, on his arrival as chief justice, to inquire into the legality of enactments made without an assembly. He reported that the governor's instructions did not make an assembly mandatory and pointed out that only one township would qualify for representation at that time. In fact, he added, an assembly would be a hindrance to the administration of the province. Both the attorney-general and solicitor-general of Great Britain, however, advised that without an assembly Lawrence's acts as governor could be illegal. The board then instructed Lawrence to prepare a scheme for setting up an assembly, although it was aware that undue representation might be given to "dram-sellers" and contraband runners in Halifax, and that the Lunenburg settlers, who were not yet naturalized, could not be represented until 1757. The board also knew that an assembly might be a forum for the struggle which had broken out in Hopson's time between the New England and British elements in the population. The correspondence about various schemes dragged on through 1755 and 1756.

The council finally hammered out a plan by which an assembly could be convened in April 1757. But Lawrence, who was stalling until he could get the Lunenburg votes, instigated a memorial, with only 11 signatures, demanding that the plan first be submitted to London. He then departed for Boston early in 1757 to meet Lord Loudoun [John Campbell], commander-in-chief of British forces in America, giving instructions that Monckton, president of the council in his absence, should issue writs for elections only if "he found the people pressing." Monckton received a memorial but would not issue the writs. Angered, Belcher, Charles Morris*, and two others in the council petitioned the Board of Trade in March. In May the board also received a petition from the grand jury of Halifax and was finally persuaded that the issue had shifted from recognizing the rights of Englishmen to cleansing the administration. The petition accused Lawrence of bias against merchants and failure to advertise contracts, of preventing the council from examining his accounts and allowing offices to accumulate in a few hands. These accusations were familiar enough to the board, but they indicated that Lawrence was losing support.

Lawrence might have prevented the alliance between members of the council and the Halifax merchants simply by issuing the writs after his return from Boston in May 1757. But he claimed that Loudoun did not approve of assemblies and that he could not attend to the matter himself that summer because he would be involved in preparations for an expedition against Louisbourg. He went off to Chignecto in the fall, on Loudoun's orders, to strengthen its defences. He was determined not to submit to pressure, lest he lose control of his government. In February 1758 the board finally ordered Lawrence to convene an assembly. When he received this order in May, he told the council he would issue writs for the autumn. He intended to fill council vacancies with his supporters, and hoped that the Louisbourg campaign, in which he was about to take part, would prove victorious and thereby restore his popularity.

Lawrence, with the temporary rank of "brigadier in America," commanded a brigade under General Jeffery Amherst* in the successful expedition against Louisbourg. He returned to Halifax in September to help prepare the British forces for operations against Quebec in 1759. Stores were scarce but he improvised. Thousands of pairs of shoes were made, arms repaired, and light infantry units formed and trained. Lawrence paid special attention to feeding the troops and thanks to fresh meat, milk, spruce beer, and "our climate in spite of the opinions of the C.O.s," the sick recovered. When James WOLFE, the commander of the Quebec expedition, returned in the spring, that critical young man had nothing but praise for Lawrence and his subordinates. Lawrence had hoped to command a brigade at Quebec; in the end the commands went to Monckton, James Murray*, and George Townshend*, that of the latter through political influence. It was a "mortifying situation" to be left behind, but Lawrence threw off his disappointment and turned to the problems of settlement and politics in Nova Scotia, which were less glamorous, but in the long run more important, than commanding a brigade on the Plains of Abraham.

The first meeting of the new assembly had taken place on 2 Oct. 1758, with 20 assemblymen present, and its business was conducted with surprisingly little trouble. Lawrence's support on the council grew in August 1759 with the appointment of Richard Bulkeley*, Thomas SAUL, and Joseph Gerrish*, to the seats left vacant by the absence of William Cotterell, Robert Grant, and Montagu WILMOT. In December the first Lunenburg representatives entered the assembly, and Lawrence received an address of praise from that body for his achievements in the province.

Lawrence's aggressive policy for finding settlers had much to do with his success. He was supported by Charles Morris, the surveyor and council member, who was involved deeply in the settlement plans. Lawrence began the drive to settle the Acadian lands in October 1758 with a proclamation seeking proposals for settlement. In January 1759 a second proclamation informed would-be settlers of the actual terms they could expect. Each grant would combine cultivated land and wild woodland. One thousand acres was the maximum initial grant for each family, with further grants available when the terms of the first one had been complied with. The proclamations were directed mainly at New Englanders.

Settlers were reluctant to break new forest land while the marsh land of Chignecto and the cleared areas of the Annapolis valley were vacant. To resolve this difficulty, Lawrence preferred to combine old land with new in each grant and thus offered favourable conditions usually permitted only to those breaking in new lands. He had been instructed to submit proposals for settling the old lands to the Board of Trade, but he disregarded this directive and informed the board of his policies after the fact, as was his custom. The board was angry, but by the time it had explained that the good lands were intended as rewards for the army and navy, Morris had surveyed lots with representatives of "some hundreds of associated substantial families" from New England and had promised them advantageous conditions. The

board could not cancel the arrangements and had to be satisfied with Lawrence's assurances that new land taken by Monckton's expedition up the Saint John River in the fall of 1758 and land on the Miramichi River would be kept for the military. Lawrence wrote privately to Lord Halifax, however, to point out that servicemen were bad settlers. Their "drunken, dissolute and abandoned" habits, "particularly that most unhappy one," idleness, made them quite unsuitable. Lord Halifax's influence ensured that when the commissioners for Trade and Plantations received copies of the grants in 13 townships at the end of 1759 under conditions which they had earlier condemned, they wrote that it was a great satisfaction "to us . . . to express to you our approbation." From the Board of Trade, which seldom had anything good to say about its governors, that was praise indeed.

Lawrence's death on 19 Oct. 1760 took everyone by surprise. "I should have taken an annuity on his life as soon as anyone I knew," wrote Amherst to General James Murray. It was a shock to his friends that this enormous, bluff, and competent man could have been struck down so quickly after catching a chill. His many friends grieved for him, though relief may have been uppermost in the minds of the New Englanders and publicans of Halifax. After his death the Board of Trade ordered an investigation of charges against him of "partiality, profusion and private understanding" in relation to provision contracts for the Nova Scotia settlements, and of maintaining his own vessels at the expense of the colony. It was also charged that he had assumed illegal powers in intervening on behalf of soldiers who were being tried for civil offences in the courts. The board declared that he had granted lands in larger amounts to single persons than was permitted, and that he had concealed the real cost of his land policy. It later complained that he had placed all trade with the Indians in the hands of a government agency. Jonathan Belcher investigated the charges against Lawrence and reported, in January 1762, that "upon the best examination in the severest charges" the accusations were unfounded.

The prosecution of the war against the French had been the first duty of the North American governors in these years. Shirley was the only one among them who had persuaded his assembly to act vigorously in this cause; the others were at one with Whitehall in considering that their assemblies were a nuisance. In this light, Lawrence's policy concerning the assembly was justified. His land policy was in the best interests of the province, and Lord Halifax himself had

Leblanc

advised the establishment of a government agency for Indian trade for the whole North American frontier region. It is true, however, that Lawrence favoured his friends with contracts and on occasion protected soldiers from the civil courts. Yet he did not grow rich as Governor George CLINTON of New York was reputed to have done. In fact, the charges against him might not have been pressed had Lord Halifax not left the Board of Trade in 1761 to be lord lieutenant of Ireland.

Referring to the monument raised to Lawrence's memory in St Paul's Church, Halifax, to indicate the late governor's popularity, Belcher wrote, "In a grateful sense of his affection and services the last tribute that could be paid to his memory was unanimously voted by the General Assembly at their first meeting after the late Governor's universally lamented decease." These sympathetic remarks by a contemporary with whom Lawrence had sometimes been at odds and the considerations mentioned above should be placed in the scales against the views of historians who condemn him for his inhumanity to the Acadians.

DOMINICK GRAHAM

BM, Add. MSS. 32736, p.259; 35870, pp.161, 163, 166, 175; 35909, f.139; Egerton MSS. 3401–97 (Holdernesse papers). Nottingham University Library, Newcastle papers (Henry Pelham), Ne C 971, 1002, 1203a. PAC, MG 11, Nova Scotia B, 8, pp.183–84; MG 18, F13; F20; M1, 4, 5, 8, 11, 20; N15; N16. PANS, RG 3, Minutes of Nova Scotia Council, 16 Aug. 1759. PRO, CO 5/13–19; 5/21, ff.4, 59, 76–78; 5/46; 5/47; 5/52; 5/212; 217/10; 217/14–18; 218/2; 218/3; 218/4, f.425; 218/5; 218/6; 324/12–15; 325/1–2; WO 34/13; 34/46; 34/46B.
Coll. doc. inédits Canada et Amérique, I, 142, 148; II, 146. *Correspondence of William Pitt* (Kimball), I, 140. [Charles Lawrence], *Journal and letters of Colonel Charles Lawrence* (PANS *Bull.*, 10, Halifax, 1953). *Military affairs in North America, 1748–1765: selected documents from the Cumberland papers in Windsor Castle*, ed. S. M. Pargellis (New York, London, 1936). *Northcliffe coll. N.S. Archives*, I. PAC *Report, 1894; 1905*, II, pt.III. *Royal instructions to British colonial governors, 1670–1776*, ed. L. W. Labaree (New York, 1935). [Abijah Willard], "The journal of Abijah Willard, an officer in the expedition which captured Fort Beauséjour in 1755," N.B. Hist. Soc. *Coll.*, 13 (1930). Winslow, "Journal," N.S. Hist. Soc. *Coll.*, III (1883); IV (1885), 113–246.
Bell, *Foreign Protestants*. Brebner, *Neutral Yankees; New England's outpost*. D. S. Graham, "British intervention in defence of the American colonies, 1748–1756" (unpublished PHD thesis, University of London, 1969); "The making of a colonial governor: Charles Lawrence in Nova Scotia, 1749–60" (unpublished MA thesis, University of New Brunswick, Fredericton, 1963). S. M. Pargellis, *Lord Loudoun in North America* (New Haven, Conn., London, 1933).

J. C. Webster, *The forts of Chignecto; a study of the eighteenth century conflict between France and Great Britain in Acadia* (n.p., 1930), app.II, 28–29, 36. D. S. Graham, "The planning of the Beauséjour operation and the approaches to war in 1755," *New Eng. Q.*, XLI (1968), 551–66. J. F. Kenney, "The genealogy of Charles Lawrence, governor of Nova Scotia," CHA *Report, 1932*, 81–86. W. P. Ward, "The Acadian response to the growth of British power in Nova Scotia, 1749–1755," *Dal. Rev.*, LI (1971), 165–75.

LEBLANC, dit Le Maigre, JOSEPH, farmer, trader, Acadian patriot; b. 12 March 1697 at Les Mines (Minas, N.S.), son of Antoine Leblanc and Marie Bourgeois; m. 13 Feb. 1719 Anne, daughter of Alexandre BOURG, dit Belle-Humeur, and Marguerite Melanson, dit La Verdure; d. sometime after February 1767.

So little is known of Joseph Leblanc's early life that it is difficult to explain what prompted him to side with successive French efforts to reconquer Acadia in the 1740s. He was one of only a dozen patriots who actively supported the French at this time, and the pattern of his collaboration closely follows that of his contemporary, Joseph-Nicolas GAUTIER, dit Bellair.

Leblanc made a notable contribution to the expedition led by Joseph Du PONT Duvivier against Annapolis Royal, Nova Scotia, in the late summer of 1744. For Leblanc this expedition was primarily a commercial venture: in a petition, drafted some years later, he claimed that it had cost him 4,500 *livres* though the extant accounts total only 1,200 *livres*. Leblanc's figures may well have been inflated to include expenses incurred in carrying Duvivier's dispatches to Louisbourg, Île Royale (Cape Breton Island), during the siege of Annapolis Royal in September. On the 22nd of that month Duvivier ordered him to go to Louisbourg post-haste, " on pain of being handed over to the mercy of the savages." It was 18 October before Leblanc reported back, and by that time Duvivier was at Beaubassin (near Amherst, N.S.), having lifted the siege. Duvivier's threat notwithstanding, Leblanc had seized the opportunity to take a number of sheep and black cattle to sell in Louisbourg.

In the aftermath of the expedition, the Nova Scotia authorities sought out those Acadians who had collaborated with the French. Leblanc at first refused to appear before the Nova Scotia Council, "as so many things were falsely Imputed to him which made him afraid." When he was finally persuaded to come forth he pleaded ignorance of any wrongdoing, "not being enlightened enough to distinguish between a time of war and a time of untroubled peace." However implausible, his explanations appear to have satisfied the council for he was asked to do nothing more than post £100 as a bond of good behaviour.

Within months, in the summer of 1745, Leblanc was busily engaged in assisting a new French effort led by Paul MARIN de La Malgue. He was captured, charged, convicted, and incarcerated for six months at Annapolis Royal " in a frightful dungeon, laden with chains." In February 1746 he managed to escape, just in time to assist the huge French fleet commanded by the Duc d'Anville [LA ROCHEFOUCAULD] which had been sent to recapture both Acadia and Île Royale. At Minas Leblanc assembled 230 head of livestock to provision the fleet. By the time his herds arrived at Annapolis Royal, however, the ill-fated expedition had come to its inauspicious end. Having lost 2,000 *livres* in his abortive speculation, and now at the mercy of the British authorities, Leblanc abandoned his assets at Minas and fled to the remote Beaubassin region.

When Île Royale was restored to France in 1749, Leblanc settled with his family at Port-Toulouse (St Peters). Late in 1750, Jacques Prévost* de La Croix, the financial commissary of the colony, described him as being "reduced to begging." He was given crown rations for three years; in 1752 he could claim only one small boat, 25 cattle, and 16 fowl.

After the fall of Louisbourg in 1758 Leblanc fled to Miquelon. Shortly after his wife died on 13 July 1766 he moved to Belle-Île-en-Mer (dept. of Morbihan), France, settling with his family among other Acadian refugees in the village of Kervaux. He last figures in the documents in February 1767; it is likely that he remained in France until his death.

BERNARD POTHIER

AN, Col., C¹¹ᴮ, 29, ff.211–12v, 180v; C¹¹ᴰ, 8, ff.109–11v, 283–84; E, 169 (dossier Du Pont Duvivier); Section Outre-Mer, G¹, 413/A (4 juill. 1766). PAC, MG 9, B8, 12 (13 févr. 1719). *Coll. doc. inédits Canada et Amérique*, II, 170, 175. *N.S. Archives*, IV, 50, 52, 55, 56–60, 62–64, 76, 78. PAC *Report, 1905*, II, pt. ɪ, 22. Arsenault, *Hist. et généal. des Acadiens*, 673.

LE CHAUVREULX. *See* CHAUVREULX

LE COLLIER PENDU. *See* KAGHSWAGHTANIUNT

LE COMTE DUPRÉ, JEAN-BAPTISTE, merchant and trader, militia captain; baptized 4 Aug. 1689 in Montreal, son of Louis Le Conte* Dupré, a merchant, and Marie-Catherine de Saint-Georges; d. 24 May 1765 in Montreal.

Upon his father's death in 1715, and under his mother's direction, Jean-Baptiste Le Comte Dupré took over the family business, which was based upon the fur trade. On several occasions he went to the *pays d'en haut*; in the 1720s he apparently gave up being a "voyageur" to devote himself entirely to the role of "merchant-outfitter." He signed several contracts of partnership, among them one in 1726 with Jean-Baptiste Jarret de Verchères and another in 1730 and 1731 with Charles LEGARDEUR de Croisille. In addition to promising "boatmen" for the trip to the *pays d'en haut*, Le Comte Dupré supplied funds and merchandise to the traders.

In 1733 Le Comte Dupré was elected churchwarden for the parish of Notre-Dame de Montréal, and in 1749 he was entrusted with the post of militia captain for the *côte* of La Visitation (government of Montreal), a post he held until 1760. After the signing of the treaty of Paris, Le Comte Dupré was one of the prominent Canadians who sent a petition to George III on 12 Feb. 1763, requesting him to recognize Canadian paper money and to authorize the importation of French goods bought a long time before. In an ordinance of 22 May 1763 Governor Thomas Gage* requested that the Canadians present their bills of exchange, card money, and certificates to the notary Pierre Panet* so that two detailed statements could be drawn up from them. Subsequently these claims were to be sent to England and from there to the French government for compensation. Le Comte Dupré entered the sum of 74,857 *livres* 10 *sols*.

Jean-Baptiste Le Comte Dupré died on 24 May 1765 in Montreal, where on 30 Jan. 1727 he had married Marie-Anne Hervieux, sister of the merchant Louis-François HERVIEUX. Two of their sons, Jean-Baptiste* and Georges-Hippolyte, were also merchants.

YVES QUESNEL

ANQ-M, Greffe de Michel Lepailleur, 17 janv. 1727; Registre d'état civil, Notre-Dame de Montréal, 4 août 1689, 25 mai 1756. *Documents relating to Canadian currency during the French period* (Shortt), II, 969–71. "Les ordonnances et lettres de change du gouvernement de Montréal en 1759," APQ *Rapport, 1924–25*, 232, 256. Bonnault, "Le Canada militaire," APQ *Rapport, 1949–51*, 442. "Marguilliers de la paroisse Notre-Dame de Ville-Marie de 1657 à 1913," *BRH*, XIX (1913), 278. Massicotte, "Répertoire des engagements pour l'Ouest," APQ *Rapport, 1929–30*, 229, 237, 238, 256, 275, 283, 284, 295. P.-G. Roy, *Inv. jug. et délib., 1717–1760*, I, 167; III, 108. Tanguay, *Dictionnaire*.

LE COUTRE DE BOURVILLE, FRANÇOIS, naval officer, king's lieutenant; b. *c.* 1670 near Rouen, France, son of François Le Coutre de Bourville and Élisabeth Faustin; m. January 1729

Le Coutre

at Louisbourg, Île Royale (Cape Breton Island), Marie-Anne, daughter of Gabriel Rousseau de Villejouin and Marie-Josephte Bertrand, by whom he had two daughters; d. before April 1758 in France.

François Le Coutre de Bourville began his naval service as a midshipman at Brest, France, in 1690. For many years his responsibilities included the training of midshipmen there. Appointed leader of a detachment in 1706, he was promoted sub-lieutenant in the navy late in 1712. In 28 years he participated in 21 expeditions, 16 in wartime, and took part in a total of 11 actions, including the siege and capture of Rio de Janeiro in 1711. In 1695 he suffered a serious wound which incapacitated him for five years. He was cited for gallantry in 1703; his ship, the frigate *Aurore*, having come upon a Dutch privateer, Bourville dashed onto the enemy vessel's bowsprit and secured her to her captor. This exploit earned him a congratulatory note from the minister of Marine, Pontchartrain, who referred to the incident as an "action of distinction."

In 1718 Bourville was appointed garrison adjutant of Île Royale (Cape Breton Island), replacing the cantankerous Jean Ligondès de Linars. Although he had been warmly recommended by his superiors in France as a "steady fellow, a good administrator, courageous and resolute," his appointment was coldly received in the colony. In a strong protest, the local officers complained of vacancies being awarded to "foreign officers" when appointments from among their own number would have helped to alleviate the demoralizing garrison life at Louisbourg.

After borrowing 139 *livres* for the voyage from France, Bourville reported to Île Royale in the summer of 1719 to take up his first and only land appointment. In contrast to his impressive record of service to 1718, his career at Louisbourg for a quarter-century was rather toneless in character. After being received into the order of Saint-Louis in 1725 (he had been appointed as early as 1721), Bourville succeeded, almost as a matter of course, to the king's lieutenancy of Île Royale in 1730.

On four occasions he commanded at Île Royale in the absence of the governor: for six months in 1722–23 and from late 1729 to the summer of 1731 during the governorship of Saint-Ovide [MONBETON]; from November 1737 to the arrival of Governor Isaac-Louis de Forant* in September 1739; and, finally, for six months from the latter's death in May 1740 to the arrival of his successor, Jean-Baptiste-Louis LE PRÉVOST Duquesnel. The experience was costly, for Bourville had no means save his salary with which to sustain the honour of his rank. After each interim command, "heavily in debt," he pleaded for a gratuity to offset what he termed extraordinary expenses incurred "mainly at the time of royal celebrations." In 1742 Duquesnel confirmed Bourville's abject circumstances, adding that, though an honest man, he had too often fallen victim to the evil counsel of his intimates.

Interim commanders did not usually take the initiative in government, although they frequently sought to enhance their temporary status by subjecting their subordinates to undue marks of deference. Bourville was no exception on either count. In 1732 he was rebuked by the minister, Maurepas, for his pretensions at the Conseil Supérieur. Like other interim officials Bourville was reluctant to send in a report which might disturb his superiors. In January 1738 he reported to the ministry that "the garrison enjoyed good health and did its duty with great precision" when exactly the opposite was the well-known reality at Louisbourg.

The circumstances surrounding Bourville's retirement from the service in 1744 are of some interest because they reflect so well the fate of aged colonial officials without means. Though he was nearly 70 when Forant died, Bourville solicited the governorship of Île Royale. He was turned down in favour of Duquesnel who, more out of compassion for his subordinate's age and deprivation than respect for his merits, interceded on Bourville's behalf in October 1742 and requested that he be given a post "where he would have nothing to do, such as the governorship of Trois-Rivières." It was at this point that the ministry wondered, apparently for the first time, whether Bourville was indeed fit to continue in the service: "Would it not be better, from all points of view, if he decided to retire?" With characteristic delicacy, Duquesnel, aided by Bourville's wife, apprised him of the intention of the authorities and of their willingness to provide him with an "easy retirement." Bourville concurred, and on 1 April 1744 he retired with a pension of 1,200 *livres*, succeeded by Louis Du Pont* Duchambon as king's lieutenant.

François Le Coutre de Bourville returned to France in the summer of 1744. He intended to shun Normandy in favour of Niort, "where prices are lower." He reconsidered, however, and settled at Fécamp. In 1758 his widow was still domiciled there; in the 1770s both his single daughters lived in Sens.

BERNARD POTHIER

AN, Col., B, 40, ff.32v–33v, 514–17v, 538–39v; 41, ff.164–66, 592–96v; 49, f.245; 54, f.496v; 57, ff.748–51;

65, ff.484–84v; 68, ff.353–55v; 76, ff.498–98v; 78, ff.410–10v; C¹¹ᴮ, 4, ff.164–66; 5, ff.35–40v; 6, ff.99, 283; 7, ff.204–9; 10, ff.216–16v; 11, ff.26–27; 14, ff.373–73v; 15, ff.26–50; 17, f.264; 18, ff.16–18; 20, ff.79–82, 108–8v; 22, ff.105–5v, 136–37v; 23, ff.208–9; 24, ff.61–61v; 25, ff.72–73v, 212–12v; 27, f.41; D²ᶜ, 222/1, p.94 (PAC transcript); E, 49 (dossier Bourville), 1ʳᵉ série, 2, 5, 6, 7; 2ᵉ série, 7, 9; 4ᵉ série, 1, 2; Section Outre-Mer, G¹, 406; G³, 2037 (15 janv. 1729); 2045 (22 avril 1758). Fauteux, *Les chevaliers de Saint-Louis*. Le Jeune, *Dictionnaire*, I. McLennan, *Louisbourg*.

LEDUC, ANNE-FRANÇOISE, *dite* **Saint-Joseph,** nun, Religious Hospitaller of Saint-Joseph, superior; b. 14 March 1664 at Montreal, daughter of Jean Leduc and Marie Soulinié (Souligny); d. 22 Oct. 1750 at Montreal.

Anne-Françoise Leduc entered the order of the Hospitallers of Saint-Joseph of Montreal in 1694 and made her profession in 1696. She was one of the first Canadian women to enter the Hôtel-Dieu of Montreal, and her sister Marie, who preceded her in the community, was the first Hospitaller born in Montreal.

Sister Saint-Joseph was mistress of novices in 1714 when she fell gravely ill, stricken with an epithelial neoplasm for which, it seems, there was only one solution, an operation. According to Mother Jeanne-Françoise Juchereau* de La Ferté, Sister Saint-Joseph wrote to the superior of the Hôtel-Dieu of Quebec, Marie-Charlotte Aubert de La Chesnaye, *dite* de Saint-Michel, asking her "to approve of her coming" to Quebec "to have herself cured of a breast cancer, since she could not entrust herself for such a painful operation to anyone but Monsieur [Michel Sarrazin*]." In May, therefore, she went to Quebec, where she was operated on by the famous surgeon. The operation was a success for at the end of July, after a brief convalescence, she was sufficiently recovered to visit the Ursulines, the priests of the seminary, the Jesuit fathers, and the Recollets. A short time later she returned to Montreal.

In 1717 she was appointed superior of the Hôtel-Dieu, an office she held until 1720. In 1721 a fire (the second one) devastated the hospital, and the rebuilding did not begin until two years later. It proceeded slowly, for Sister Saint-Joseph, the depositary at the time, did not have the necessary funds to carry it out. "My Sister Saint-Joseph for her part uses all her ability, which is not slight," Sister Marie Morin* wrote in her annals, "to gather materials during this winter in order to make a new start on having work done when God has given us the wherewithal." The civil and religious authorities, in particular Bishop Saint-Vallier [La Croix*], were disturbed by the slowness of the work. From time to time the bishop wrote to the superior, Charlotte Gallard*, urging her to hasten the rebuilding of the hospital. But what could Sister Saint-Joseph do to speed it up, "finding herself without means and without hope of having any until after the arrival of the king's ship, which ordinarily does not arrive from France until about 15 September at the earliest"? Saint-Vallier wanted to finish the work despite the scarcity. Sister Saint-Joseph claimed that it was impossible to do so and suggested renting for another year part of the house of the Brothers Hospitallers of the Cross and of St Joseph. The bishop rejected this solution and, believing that the depositary was dilatory, replaced her by Sister Marie-Clémence Guénet in the summer of 1724. At the request of Father François, a Recollet and a friend of Sister Saint-Joseph, however, Saint-Vallier reinstated her soon afterwards.

In 1739, five years after the Hôtel-Dieu had burned for the third time, Sister Saint-Joseph was called upon to replace the superior, Françoise GAUDÉ, and therefore to concern herself once more with its reconstruction, although resources were almost non-existent. In 1742 a new present from the king and some private gifts, among them 2,000 *livres* from the Sulpician Pierre LE SUEUR, enabled reconstruction to begin on all the buildings, which were completed two years later.

After finishing her term as superior in 1745 Anne-Françoise Leduc retired; she died on 22 Oct. 1750, at 86 years of age, after 54 years in religion.

HÉLÈNE BERNIER

AHSJ, Annales de sœur Marie Morin, 1697–1725; Annales de sœur Véronique Cuillerier, 1725–1747. Juchereau, *Annales* (Jamet). *Premier registre de l'église de Notre-Dame de Montréal* (Montréal, 1961). Mondoux, *L'Hôtel-Dieu de Montréal*.

LEE, FITZROY HENRY, officer in the Royal Navy, governor of Newfoundland; b. 2 Jan. 1698/99, probably at Ditchley, Oxfordshire, England, son of Sir Edward Henry Lee, 1st Earl of Lichfield, and Lady Charlotte Fitzroy, natural daughter of Charles II and the Duchess of Cleveland; d. 14 April 1750.

Fitzroy Henry Lee entered the Royal Navy as a volunteer in the *Launceston* in 1716 and was promoted lieutenant in 1722. Appointed captain of the *Falkland* in February 1734/35, he received a commission as governor of Newfoundland in May of that year, and carried out three tours as governor in the summer months of 1735, 1736, and 1737. In his reports to the Board of Trade he suggested that persons charged with capital

369

Lefebvre

offences should not be sent to England to stand trial, but that powers should be given to local authorities to try such cases. He also recommended that a vice-admiralty court be established at St John's. Replying to an inquiry about Irish Catholic settlers, Lee seemed to have no complaints and reported that "the poor Irish papists were happy because they had no priests."

After commanding the *Pembroke* on the Mediterreanean station from 1738 to 1742, Lee joined the *Suffolk* in 1746 as commodore of a small squadron in the West Indies. He was unpopular with his crew, and when many inhabitants of the islands complained of his drunkenness, incivility, and neglect of duty, he was relieved of his command. The council and assembly of Antigua complained further that the island's trade was "almost ruined" by his negligence, but as no evidence was produced for these charges, Lee was not brought to trial. His promotion to rear-admiral was delayed, however, and though he was advanced to vice-admiral in 1748 he did not serve again at sea. He died of palsy.

Lee seems to have served well in Newfoundland, but gained a reputation as a "free liver" and "a man of debauched habits." It has been suggested that Tobias Smollett, who may have heard of Lee while serving in the navy in the early 1740s, used him as the model for Commodore Trunnion in *The adventures of Peregrine Pickle*.

MICHAEL GODFREY

PRO, Adm. 1/305; CO 194/10, 195/7; *CSP, Col., 1734–35, 1735–36, 1737; JTP, 1734/35–1741.* Charnock, *Biographia navalis*, IV. *DNB.* G.B., Adm., *Commissioned sea officers, 1660–1815.* D. A. Baugh, *British naval administration in the age of Walpole* (Princeton, N.J., 1965), 101n, 134, 143, 143n. Lounsbury, *British fishery at Nfld.*

LEFEBVRE, JEAN, merchant and entrepreneur; b. 1714 in the Pays de Caux, France; d. 1760.

Jean Lefebvre first set foot in Canada in 1732. He was only 18 and had come to act as assistant to his cousin François HAVY, who was to be Quebec factor for Robert Dugard et Cie of Rouen, France. Like his cousin, Lefebvre was a Huguenot; the law forbade his settling in Canada with wife and family. But few metropolitan agents, Protestant or Catholic, ever expected to stay at Quebec for very long, so this restriction could not have weighed on his mind. A young, aspiring merchant submitted to the exile of colonial life to learn his trade and earn enough money to set up business in one of the French Atlantic ports. Lefebvre was no doubt resigned to passing some nine or ten years at Quebec, but he could

not have imagined that it would be 28 long years before he would leave it for the last time or that he would then look at it, a heap of rubble, from the rail of an English warship.

In 1734 Lefebvre became the junior member in a partnership with François Havy. Henceforth they shared a collective responsibility in business and signed their accounts jointly, "Havy et Lefebvre." Their primary interest was their annual trade for Dugard et Cie, for whom they handled 13 major incoming cargoes and 14 return cargoes. They also built the company six ships, making a significant contribution to the growth of Canadian industry. But between 1743 and 1748 Atlantic storms and English privateers combined to destroy most of the company's fleet, forcing it to abandon the Canada trade.

Havy and Lefebvre were left to their own not inconsiderable resources. Beginning in 1737, they had acquired interests in sealing stations on the north shore of the St Lawrence at Mingan and on the coast of Labrador at Grand Saint Modet, Chateau Bay, and Baie des Esquimaux (probably Hamilton Inlet). They also became directly involved in the fur trade by joining a company that leased the King's Posts from 1749 to 1755. Their import-export trade with France and the West Indies was continued, and Havy and Lefebvre became money-lenders as well.

The Seven Years' War separated the two partners. Under war-time conditions, the successful continuation of their business necessitated Havy's removal to La Rochelle, France, while Lefebvre remained at Quebec with yet another cousin, François Levesque. In 1758 the invasion of Canada began; Jean Lefebvre wrote his will, "considering that Nothing is more Certain than death and Nothing more Uncertain than its hour." The massive destructions of the war and the collapse of the French empire in America destroyed what he and Havy had built up over 30 years.

Jean Lefebvre spent the difficult winter of 1759–60 in Quebec. In the spring he left the ruined town, seeking refuge on the Île d'Orléans, where he learned of the surrender of the colony in September 1760. As so many merchants did, Lefebvre then made arrangements to return to France. He wrote of "my projected voyage to Europe which I have desired for a Long Time, particularly since the Calamity which has happened in this country and of which I see a sad end."

Sometime in October 1760, leaving the Canadian business in the hands of his agent Levesque, Lefebvre boarded the *Trident* bound for Portsmouth, England; from there he would make his way to La Rochelle to join Havy. An unexplained accident intervened, however; and he did not live to see his partner again. Lefebvre was only 46 when he died and he had never married. He had made a valuable contribution to the struggling colonial economy, which had repaid him with a measure of wealth and status. That war and accident should so cut short his enjoyment of them must give to his life, in retrospect, the appearance of a long preparation for a future that never happened.

DALE MIQUELON

[The sources for this biography are the same as those cited under François HAVY. A few items of particular interest may be singled out. Lefebvre's last will and testament is in ANQ, Greffe de J.-C. Panet, 22 nov. 1758. The only extant letter identified by his own signature rather than the corporate one of "Havy et Lefebvre" is in PAC, MG 24, L3 (Lefebvre à Dargenteuil, Québec, 13 oct. 1760). His death is mentioned in AN, 62 AQ, 36 (François Havy à Robert Dugard, La Rochelle, 17 janv. 1761). D.M.]

LEFEBVRE ANGERS, MARIE-ANGÉLIQUE, *dite* **Saint-Simon,** sister of the Congregation of Notre-Dame, superior of the community (superior general); b. 25 Oct. 1710 in Montreal, daughter of Jean-Baptiste Lefebvre Angers and Geneviève-Françoise Faucher; d. 28 April 1766 in Montreal.

Marie-Angélique's grandfather, Simon Lefebvre Angers, emigrated to Quebec from Picardy in the second half of the 17th century. On 30 Aug. 1700 at Pointe-aux-Trembles (Neuville) his son Jean-Baptiste married Geneviève-Françoise Faucher and moved to Montreal around 1705.

When she was 16 Marie-Angélique entered the boarding-school of the Congregation of Notre-Dame, then in 1728 asked to be admitted into the community. On 20 Nov. 1730 her father undertook in writing to give the sisters the sum of 2,000 *livres* (800 were paid in 1730 and 1,200 in 1733). The next day Marie-Angélique took the nuns' simple vows of poverty, chastity, obedience, and the vow to teach girls. In religion she received her grandfather's name and became Sister Saint-Simon.

After participating in the apostolic activities of the congregation in Montreal, Sister Saint-Simon held important offices in her community. She was mistress of novices twice, from 1750 to 1756 and from 1763 to 1765. In between these two terms of office she assumed the office of superior general of the congregation.

Sister Saint-Simon's superiorship took place during the Seven Years' War. Her task was consequently made heavier by the hardships that befell the colony at this time and by the tragic events that the annals of the community record for the years 1757–63: the deportation to France of the sisters at Louisbourg, Île Royale (Cape Breton Island); the flight of the sisters from Quebec to Ville-Marie; the burning of the convents in the Lower Town of Quebec, at Château-Richer, and at Sainte-Famille (Île d'Orléans); the dangers incurred by the sisters on Montreal Island, especially at Lachine and Pointe-Saint-Charles. Sister Saint-Simon was in addition concerned, with good reason, about the fate that the conqueror, English and Protestant, had in store for her community. Under her direction, however, the congregation adopted a positive attitude towards the occupying forces. The sisters, it seems, believed in the régime of cooperation which Jeffery Amherst* claimed in his poster to want to set up. In any event, in the spirit of the church, for whom all authority was of divine right, they showed only submission and respect to the country's new masters.

Six years as superior under such conditions exhausted Sister Saint-Simon. After serving the community for two more years as mistress of novices, she had to retire and died a few months later, on 28 April 1766; she was buried the next day. Marie-Angélique Lefebvre Angers was only 55, but she had given 38 years of her life, and all her resources of intellect and heart, to the educational work of the Congregation of Notre-Dame.

ANDRÉE DÉSILETS

ACND, La Congrégation de Notre-Dame: son personnel, 1653–1768; Fichier général des sœurs de la Congrégation de Notre-Dame; Plans des lieux de sépulture depuis 1681-CND; Registre des sépultures des sœurs de la Congrégation de Notre-Dame; Registre général des sœurs de la Congrégation de Notre-Dame de Montréal. ANDM, Registres des baptêmes, mariages et sépultures, 26 oct. 1710. ANQ-M, Greffe de J.-C. Raimbault, 20 nov. 1730. Archives paroissiales de Saint-François-de-Sales (Neuville, Qué.), Registres des baptêmes, mariages et sépultures, 30 août 1700. Sister Saint Ignatius [Catherine Jane] Doyle, *Marguerite Bourgeoys and her congregation* (Gardenvale, Que., 1940). Lemire-Marsolais et Lambert, *Histoire de la Congrégation de Notre-Dame.*

LEFEBVRE DE BELLEFEUILLE, JEAN-FRANÇOIS, seigneur; b. probably 27 Aug. 1670 at Sillery (Que.), son of Thomas Lefebvre* and Geneviève Pelletier (Peltier); d. *c.* 1744 at Pabos in the Gaspé region (Que.).

Jean-François Lefebvre de Bellefeuille settled in Newfoundland around the beginning of the 18th century and operated a small dry-cod fishing establishment near Plaisance (Placentia). In 1706

Lefebvre Duplessis

he was reported as employing six fishermen and two boys. He married, probably in 1703 or 1704, Anne Baudry, daughter of another local fisherman; they had three sons and two daughters.

Lefebvre de Bellefeuille left Plaisance after the English took control in 1713 and probably went to Île Royale (Cape Breton Island). In 1729 his brother Pierre bought the seigneury of Grand-Pabos from the heirs of René Hubert. Pierre Lefebvre de Bellefeuille appears never to have resided on the seigneury and it was Jean-François who, in effect, became the seigneur. Grand-Pabos was located a few leagues south of Île Percée.

Lefebvre de Bellefeuille was the only seigneur who established himself permanently on a Gaspé seigneury during the French régime. With his sons Georges and François* he developed a successful dry-cod fishery without any government assistance and virtually independent of government control. In 1730 he apparently had at his fishery about 30 men whom he armed and deployed to prevent a crew of Basque fishermen from landing on the beach at Pabos where they had traditionally dried their fish. Subsequently Lefebvre de Bellefeuille allowed visiting fishermen to establish their drying operations on his beaches if they paid a fee, sometimes a year in advance, based on the number of shallops they brought. There were complaints that Lefebvre de Bellefeuille and his sons tried to extend their authority beyond the limits of their seigneury; the government warned them but it had little effective control in this area. In fact, in 1737 the government relinquished some of its control by appointing Georges Lefebvre de Bellefeuille as subdelegate of the intendant for the Gaspé coast. After his death Lefebvre de Bellefeuille's sons carried on the fishery until it was wiped out by WOLFE's raiding expedition on the Gaspé coast in the autumn of 1758.

DAVID LEE

AN, Col., B, 74, f.17; 76, f.35; C¹¹ᶜ, 5, pp.50ff. (PAC transcripts); F²ᴮ, 11; Marine, B³, 415, ff.31–37. ANQ, Greffe de J.-N. Pinguet de Vaucour, 22 oct. 1729; NF, Ord. int., XXVI, 3v–4; XXVIII, 26 août 1740. PRO, CO 194/5, f.355. "Recensement de Terre-Neuve et de Plaisance, 1704" (SGCF *Mémoires*). P.-G. Roy, *Inv. concessions*, IV, 127–29; *Inv. ord. int.*, II, 150, 292. La Morandière, *Hist. de la pêche française de la morue*, II, 601–3. A.C. de Léry Macdonald, "La famille Le Febure de Bellefeuille," *Revue canadienne*, 2ᵉ sér., XX (1884), 168–76, 235–47, 291–302.

LEFEBVRE DUPLESSIS FABER (Fabert), FRANÇOIS, seigneur, officer in the colonial regular troops; b. 9 Nov. 1689 in Champlain, near Trois-Rivières, oldest son of François Lefebvre Duplessis Faber and Madeleine Chorel de Saint-Romain, *dit* d'Orvilliers; d. 20 July 1762 in Rochefort, France.

Because the early years of François's career were determined in part by his father's activities, the life of François Sr merits some attention. François Sr may have been helped by his father Pierre Lefebvre Duplessis Faber, *maître d'hôtel du roi*, to rise rapidly to a full captaincy in the Régiment de Saint-Vallier at the age of 24. In 1687, aged 40, François Sr sailed for Canada to assume command of a company of colonial regular troops. On 7 Jan. 1689, he married Madeleine Chorel de Saint-Romain in Champlain, where he made his home for the next seven or eight years. In July 1689 he wounded Captain Raymond Blaise* Des Bergères de Rigauville in a sword-fight, and was obliged to pay him 600 *livres* in damages. During the next 20 years he applied for the governorships of Acadia and of Plaisance (Placentia, Nfld.) and the positions of commander of the troops, king's lieutenant of Trois-Rivières, commandant of Chambly, and road surveyor. On 5 May 1700 the minister of Marine, Pontchartrain, wrote to the intendant, Champigny [Bochart*], that "the Sieur Duplessis . . . having been recommended to me by persons of whom I think highly, I would be pleased if you would be of service to him if the occasion arises." But François Sr's liking for wine made his promotion to the general staff unwise. As compensation, however, his son was commissioned ensign at the age of 11. François Sr died on 12 April 1712; in June he was awarded the cross of Saint-Louis, an honour he had requested since 1700.

On 31 Dec. 1713, his son François married at Montreal Catherine-Geneviève, daughter of Jean-François-Xavier Pelletier. During that year he had received an expectancy of a commission as lieutenant which he obtained in 1714. François was interested in serving in Louisiana in 1717, but remained in Montreal where, in 1722, he became assistant town major, a position with status but without salary. While serving in this capacity he sold Île Ronde, near Sorel, and three islands in the St Lawrence River which had been given to him by Étienne Volant* de Radisson, step-father of his wife, and Montreal agent of the Compagnie des Indes. His appointment to a full captaincy in April 1727 – he was then commandant at Baie-des-Puants (Green Bay, Wis.) – came as a direct result of the recommendation of Mme de Vaudreuil [Joybert*].

In 1732 François again applied for a transfer to Louisiana, this time to serve as garrison adjutant. Upon rejection he asked for the cross of Saint-

372

Louis, but this was also denied him. In 1739 he was appointed commandant of Fort Saint-Frédéric (Crown Point, N.Y.), but his interest in trade and commerce and a bitter dispute with the storekeeper, Médard-Gabriel VALLETTE de Chévigny, led to his recall in 1741. He was not in total disgrace, however, for in April 1742 he was awarded the cross of Saint-Louis. In 1744 the king suspended him for three months for refusing to arrest Timothy SULLIVAN, known as Timothée Silvain, but he was not out of favour long. In 1745 he was appointed commandant of Fort Niagara (near Youngstown, N.Y.) to replace Pierre-Joseph CÉLORON de Blainville. His talents were exercised maintaining the dubious loyalty of the Senecas.

Duplessis was not long at Niagara; in 1747 he was obliged by illness to ask to be relieved of his command. He was succeeded by Claude-Pierre Pécaudy* de Contrecœur. Two years later, Duplessis was appointed commandant at Michilimackinac, and on 17 March 1756 he was appointed town major of Montreal. In August 1758, from Fort Frontenac (Kingston, Ont.), Pierre-Jacques Payen* de Noyan, anticipating an attack by Lieutenant-Colonel John Bradstreet* with 3,000 men, appealed for help, and Pierre de Rigaud* de Vaudreuil ordered Duplessis to lead 1,500 militiamen to Noyan's assistance. But the preparations at Lachine took so long that news of the fort's loss arrived shortly after Duplessis's party had set out. He subsequently visited the Indians in the Fort Frontenac area, and returned to Montreal. After the fall of Canada, Duplessis returned to France with a pension of 300 *livres*, and he died in Rochefort on 20 July 1762.

Twelve children were born of his marriage to Catherine-Geneviève Pelletier, of whom six lived to adulthood; one son, François-Hippolyte, served in the colonial regular troops and retired a half-pay captain in 1760, and another, Joseph-Alphonse, was an officer in Canada, Île Royale (Cape Breton Island), and Rochefort, retiring in 1764 with the rank of lieutenant.

The career of Duplessis Faber is difficult to assess because he was promoted in the military hierarchy through connections at court, but he seems to have shown himself able and conscientious while serving as assistant town major of Montreal and commandant of Niagara.

C. J. RUSS

AJTR, Registre d'état civil, Immaculée-Conception de Trois-Rivières, 11 nov. 1689. AN, Col., B, 22, ff.122v, 124v; 27, ff.89v, 270; 29, f.373v; 33, f.140v; 34, f.34v; C¹¹ᴬ, 17, ff.335–38; 18, f.69; D²ᶜ, 47, f.3v; 222/2, p.167 (PAC transcript). ANQ-M, Greffe d'Antoine Adhémar, 30 déc. 1713; Greffe de Guillaume Barette, 28 avril 1726; Greffe de Jacques David, 17 mars 1725; Greffe de Michel Lepailleur, 29 janv. 1722; Greffe de J.-C. Raimbault, 30, 31 août, 3 sept. 1727.
Royal Fort Frontenac (Preston and Lamontagne). Fauteux, *Les chevaliers de Saint-Louis*, 138. Le Jeune, *Dictionnaire*, I, 557 [Le Jeune confused the two François Lefebvre Duplessis Fabers and erred in the date of François Jr's appointment as commandant of Fort Saint-Frédéric. c.J.R.]. P.-G. Roy, *Inv. ord. int.*, I, 275; II, 241; *Les officiers d'état-major*, 80–85. Tanguay, *Dictionnaire*, I, 367; III, 544 [In vol. III Tanguay incorrectly dated François Sr's birth as 1637 instead of 1647. c.J.R.]. P.-G. Roy, *La famille Lefebvre Duplessis Faber* (Lévis, Qué., 1937); *Hommes et choses du fort Saint-Frédéric*, 49–57, 168–70. Stanley, *New France*, 184, 186. P.-G. Roy, "Les commandants du fort Niagara," *BRH*, LIV (1948), 168–70.

LE FÈNE. *See* PHLEM

LEGARDEUR DE BEAUVAIS, RENÉ, midshipman, officer in the colonial regular troops; baptized in Quebec on 3 Oct. 1660, son of Charles Legardeur* de Tilly and Geneviève Juchereau de Maur; d. 26 Dec. 1742 in Montreal.

René Legardeur de Beauvais spent the greater part of his young adult years in the west, combining fur-trading with military service. In August 1683 he set out from Michilimackinac to trade in the Illinois country, but was pillaged *en route* by the Iroquois and returned empty-handed. The following year he led the Batiscan militia in Le Febvre* de La Barre's ill-fated campaign against the Iroquois. In 1686–87, while serving as Daniel Greysolon* Dulhut's lieutenant at Fort Saint-Joseph (on the west shore of the St Clair River), he was present when Olivier Morel* de La Durantaye claimed the area bounded by lakes Erie and Huron in the king's name. In addition, he helped the western post commandants rally the Indians for Brisay* de Denonville's 1687 campaign against the Iroquois. He subsequently returned to Montreal, and directed his fur-trading interests from there.

Beauvais was commissioned half-pay lieutenant in 1688, lieutenant in 1690, and received the *brevet* of midshipman in 1694. He headed westward again two years later, this time leading the La Montagne and Lorette mission Indians in Buade* de Frontenac's expedition against the Iroquois. In 1714, with recommendations from several superiors, he was commissioned captain. He served briefly at Fort Saint-Joseph (probably Niles, Mich.) in the 1720s, and held the post of commandant of Fort Frontenac (Kingston, Ont.) from 1728 to 1736. He was awarded the coveted cross of the order of Saint-Louis in 1733.

Legardeur de Croisille

Beauvais was married three times. His first wife, Marie-Barbe, daughter of Pierre de Saint-Ours*, whom he married on 19 Sept. 1694 in Montreal, died in 1705 after bearing 11 children. He married Madeleine Marchand, widow of Jean Malhiot, in Montreal in 1715. She died in 1722, and three years later he took his third wife – Louise Lamy, widow of Charles-Paul de Marin* de La Malgue, in Montreal. Beauvais died in 1742 at the age of 82.

C. J. RUSS

AN, Col., C¹¹ᴬ, 6, 9, 10, 11, 14, 21, 22, 34; D²ᶜ, 47; 222/2, p.44 [in the Alphabet Laffilard, the date of his promotion to a lieutenancy and his date of death are wrong. C.J.R.]; Marine, B², 96, ff.9–9v; C⁷ (dossier Legardeur de Beauvais). ANQ-M, Greffe d'Antoine Adhémar. "Correspondance de Vaudreuil," APQ *Rapport, 1947–48*, 237. *Royal Fort Frontenac* (Preston and Lamontagne). Fauteux, *Les chevaliers de Saint-Louis*, 128. Le Jeune, *Dictionnaire*. Tanguay, *Dictionnaire*. Kellogg, *French régime*, 227–28. Gérard Malchelosse, "Le poste de la Rivière Saint-Joseph (Mich.) (1691–1781)," *Cahiers des Dix*, XXIII (1958), 139–86.

LEGARDEUR DE CROISILLE, CHARLES, seigneur, officer in the colonial regular troops; b. 23 April 1677 in Boucherville (Que.), son of Jean-Baptiste Legardeur* de Repentigny and Marguerite Nicollet de Belleborne; d. 3 Dec. 1749 in Trois-Rivières.

The earliest reference to Charles Legardeur de Croisille is dated 20 Sept. 1702, when his father granted him a tract of land. On 4 Feb. 1709, in Cap-de-la-Madeleine, Croisille married Marie-Anne-Geneviève, daughter of Pierre Robinau* de Bécancour, Baron de Portneuf, and Marie-Charlotte Legardeur de Villiers. By this marriage Croisille became seigneur of part of the barony of Portneuf, a substantial property on the north shore of the St Lawrence River. One month after the wedding Croisille's father added another land grant to his son's holdings. Croisille was involved in the fishing industry; in 1723 he was confirmed in his rights to fish off the barony of Portneuf, and he developed his interest in seal fishing. In 1729 he received another land grant – this time 80 acres of land on the Rivière L'Assomption. He sold the barony of Portneuf to Eustache Lambert Dumont the younger in 1741 for 12,000 *livres*.

Croisille served in the colonial regular troops, and there his advancement was slow. In 1710, at the age of 33, he was commissioned ensign, and he was not raised to a lieutenancy until 1728. In 1729, when Pierre Robinau died, Croisille considered retiring from the colonial regulars with the aim of taking over his father-in-law's position as

chief road commissioner (*grand-voyer*) of New France; however, Jean-Eustache LANOULLIER de Boisclerc was awarded the position. On 17 May 1741 Croisille was promoted captain; the following year he was sent to Fort Saint-Frédéric (Crown Point, N.Y.) and four years later he replaced Paul BÉCART de Grandville et de Fonville as post commandant. He served in this position for one year. He received the cross of Saint-Louis on 15 Feb. 1748, and the following year, on 3 December, Croisille died in Trois-Rivières.

C. J. RUSS

ANQ-M, Greffe d'Antoine Adhémar, 20 sept. 1702, 17 avril 1709; Greffe de J.-C. Raimbault, 24 mai 1728. Fauteux, *Les chevaliers de Saint-Louis*, 144–45. Le Jeune, *Dictionnaire*. P.-G. Roy, *Inv. concessions*, I, 240–41. Tanguay, *Dictionnaire*. Nish, *Les bourgeois-gentilshommes*, 107, 119–20. P.-G. Roy, *Hommes et choses du fort Saint-Frédéric*, 146, 172. J.-E. Roy, "Le patronage dans l'armée," *BRH*, II (1896), 117.

LEGARDEUR DE REPENTIGNY, AGATHE. *See* SAINT-PÈRE

LEGARDEUR DE SAINT-PIERRE, JACQUES, officer in the colonial regular troops, explorer, interpreter; b. 24 Oct. 1701 at Montreal, son of Jean-Paul Legardeur* de Saint-Pierre and Marie-Josette Leneuf de La Vallière; killed in the battle of Lac Saint-Sacrement (Lake George), 1755.

Jacques Legardeur de Saint-Pierre was a descendant of several prominent families of New France; he was a grandson of Jean-Baptiste Legardeur* de Repentigny and great-grandson of Jean Nicollet* de Belleborne. His father, Jean-Paul, spent many years in the *pays d'en haut* and in 1718 founded the post at Chagouamigon (near Ashland, Wis.). There is some evidence that while he was still in his teens Jacques joined his father at the post. Several accounts from Montreal praised Jacques early in his career for his knowledge of Indian languages and life; for example, in 1732 Governor Charles de BEAUHARNOIS claimed that Jacques had been in the west for nine years and "Knows the savage language better than the savages, as they themselves admit." Jacques was to be one of the foremost advisers on Indian affairs in New France.

Like his father, he took up military service and was appointed second ensign in 1724; in 1729 he had a key mission to enlist support from Ojibwas, Crees, and Sioux for one of the many abortive campaigns against the Foxes. In 1733 he was an ensign on the active list. At this time Louis DENYS de La Ronde, commandant at Chagouamigon, was engaged in a search for the Lake

Superior copper fields. He made use of Legardeur as his assistant in this venture, because he had "much wisdom and intelligence."

A frustrating experience for the talented Legardeur was his period as commandant at Fort Beauharnois (on Lake Pepin, Wis.-Minn.), 1734–37. In its brief career the fort had to be moved several times, but Montreal merchants continued to hope the area would develop into a major fur trade zone. Indian rivalries prevented this result. Legardeur was a master at strong-arm diplomacy, but even his method did not work in this no-man's-land: the fort was theoretically in Sioux country, but there were several factions of Sioux constantly quarrelling; the notorious Sauks and Foxes were nearby, and they always meant problems for the French; also in the vicinity were Crees, Assiniboins, and Ojibwas. This last group and the Sioux were traditionally bitter enemies, and Legardeur finally found his position as referee untenable. Fearing that the garrison would be slaughtered by the Sioux, Legardeur abandoned and burned the fort on 30 May 1737.

Legardeur next figured in the French attempt to control the Mississippi River valley. From 1737 through 1740 he campaigned against the Chickasaws, going as far south as what is now Alabama. Legardeur even served as a hostage among the Chickasaws. Governor Beauharnois's assessment of his service on this campaign is typical of the praise Legardeur received throughout his career: "this is an excellent officer who will be very useful in the future, and he is equally feared and loved by the Indians."

Legardeur was promoted lieutenant in 1741. After a short stint about 1742 as commandant of the Miami post (probably at or near Fort Wayne, Ind.), Legardeur returned to Montreal, where he carried out many assignments during 1745–47. In December 1745 he led a contingent to the relief of Fort Saint-Frédéric (Crown Point, N.Y.), under threat from the British; in July 1746 he took a detachment of Abenakis to Acadia to help prepare for battle against the English; in the spring of 1747 he led an attack in Mohawk country. This last effort must be called a failure, because Legardeur's Indian allies were over-eager and fired so early that the Mohawks were warned. Legardeur did, though, take some Mohawk prisoners back to Montreal. In June 1747, with militia and Indians, he and Louis de LA CORNE rushed to the Lachine area and warded off an attack from a party of Indians and English.

Indian troubles erupted in the *pays d'en haut* in 1747, and for some time it seemed that the French were losing their allies [*see* ORONTONY]. Several Frenchmen were murdered and trade was disrupted. Because of his talent and experience Legardeur was sent to command at the strategic post of Michilimackinac, where he could influence events in the entire Upper Lakes area. According to Governor La Galissonière [BARRIN], most of the French officials were ineffective in resolving problems with the Indians, but Legardeur showed "good management," and forced the Indians to deliver the murderers and ask for peace. In 1748, still serving at Michilimackinac, he was promoted captain. A fragile peace was arranged in the region, and in the spring of 1749 Legardeur asked to be relieved. On 26 July of that year he was replaced by François LEFEBVRE Duplessis Faber and returned to Montreal.

Legardeur's interests and talents were still associated with the *pays d'en haut*, and in 1750 Governor La Jonquière [TAFFANEL] appointed him to lead in the search for the western sea, a project that had been hindered by the death of Pierre GAULTIER de Varennes et de La Vérendrye. However he was soon involved in a quarrel with LOUIS-JOSEPH and PIERRE GAULTIER de La Vérendrye, who insisted on some role in the search and glory. Legardeur eventually realized that the La Vérendrye family had cause to feel slighted, and he apologized. On 5 June 1750 Legardeur left Montreal. After several weeks at Michilimackinac in July, he set off again for Fort La Reine (Portage la Prairie, Man.) where he arrived that fall. During the two years he spent at this post, Legardeur, despite what some historians say, travelled several times to the area of the Red and Winnipeg rivers and Lake of the Woods. He was constantly forced to calm Indian rivalries; it seems that in 1752 he handled major negotiations alone between Cree and Sioux warriors. The search for the western sea was of course fruitless, but under Legardeur's orders and directions a party, led by Joseph-Claude Boucher* de Niverville, did in 1751 establish Fort La Jonquière (probably in the Nipawin, Sask., area).

Returning to Montreal, likely in 1753, Legardeur was at once sent to the Ohio country, where the French were establishing possessory rights, to the growing resentment of the English. That year Paul MARIN de La Malgue founded in the region two forts, one being Fort de la Rivière au Bœuf (Waterford, Pa.). After Marin's death in October, Legardeur was sent to command at the fort. The presence of the French military upset the Virginia colony, and Governor Robert Dinwiddie sent a young major, George Washington, with a party of seven to order Legardeur out of the country at once. After a difficult journey

Legardeur de Tilly

Washington arrived at Fort de la Rivière au Bœuf on 11 December and delivered Dinwiddie's written order to Legardeur. In what has become a celebrated communication, Legardeur wrote to Dinwiddie and suggested that Washington was wasting his time by trying international diplomacy with him. He suggested that Quebec, not Fort de la Rivière au Bœuf, was the reasonable place to submit such messages. Legardeur's position was firm but courteous: "As to the summons you send me to retire, I do not think myself obliged to obey it." This affair has received much more attention from some historians than it merits, simply because it was Washington's introduction to great military-political events. The historians of New France have had a clearer understanding of the event than most, seeing in this encounter a seasoned military professional being polite, firm, and probably amused at the "threat" from the Virginia militia major. Washington seems to have been favourably impressed by Legardeur: "He is an elderly Gentleman, and has much the Air of a Soldier."

Washington returned to the region in 1754, was involved in the notorious assault on the party of Joseph Coulon de Villiers de Jumonville, and was eventually defeated, captured, and released by the French at Fort Necessity (near Farmington, Pa.). Diplomacy was forgotten, and the French and English once again battled for control of the Ohio country and all of North America. In 1754 Legardeur was recalled to Montreal to help in gathering forces for the coming actions. The Baron de Dieskau, a German in the French service, prepared a major offensive in the vicinity of Lac Saint-Sacrement and on 4 Sept. 1755 Legardeur was sent with a force of Canadian militia and hundreds of Indians to accompany him. The battle of Lac Saint-Sacrement occurred on 8 September, actually a series of three major conflicts. In the first, shortly after 10:00 A.M., Legardeur, leading his Indian warriors, was killed at once. His loss affected the Indians deeply, and Governor Vaudreuil [Rigaud*], other French leaders, and even the British commented that the loss of Legardeur could be a major factor in the coming battles.

During the French régime few professional military men could match Legardeur's combination of bravery, intelligence, and dedication. For most of his career he was in far-flung outposts, where his knowledge of frontier life and Indian languages made him indispensable to a series of Quebec officials. He was frequently sent on trouble-shooting missions; he was a logical successor to La Vérendrye; he performed well in the Ohio country; he was awarded the cross of Saint-Louis; and he died in action. Although his highest rank was that of captain, his services to France were significant and well recognized.

On 27 Oct. 1738 he had married Marie-Joseph, daughter of Charles Guillimin*, in Quebec; they had no children. His widow remarried in 1757, to Luc de La Corne*, dit La Corne Saint-Luc.

DONALD CHAPUT

AN, Col., C^IIA, 53, p.296; 73, p.166; 76, pp.186, 255, 307; 117, pp.3, 227, 259, 305; 118, pp.154, 216, 236, 248, 275, 276, 293, 298, 303, 334, 354; 119, pp.35–38, 39–49, 56–57, 63, 168, 182, 364; D^2C, 222/2, p.161 (PAC transcripts). St Ann's Parish (Mackinac Island, Mich.), Registre des baptêmes, mariages et sépultures de Sainte-Anne-de-Michillimakinak, 1695–1821. "Correspondance de Mme Bégon" (Bonnault), APQ Rapport, 1934–35, 53, 178. Découvertes et établissements des Français (Margry), VI, 637–52. Extraits des archives de la Marine et de la Guerre (Casgrain), 38–41, 97–98. French regime in Wis., 1727–48 (Thwaites), 165–66, 187, 255–59, 262–74, 478–79, 505–12. "French regime in Wis., 1743–60" (Thwaites), 19–22, 76–79, 133f. "Lettres et mémoires de l'abbé de L'Isle-Dieu," APQ Rapport, 1936–37, 446. NYCD (O'Callaghan and Fernow), VI, 1006–7; X, 81, 105, 258–59, 318–22. PAC Report, 1886, clvii–clxiii. Fauteux, Les chevaliers de Saint-Louis, 150–51. Le Jeune, Dictionnaire. Massicotte, "Répertoire des engagements pour l'Ouest," APQ Rapport, 1929–30, 315; 1930–31, 395, 396. A.-G. Morice, Dictionnaire historique des Canadiens et des Métis français de l'Ouest (Québec, 1908), 273–75. Champagne, Les La Vérendrye; Nouvelles études sur les La Vérendrye. H. H. Peckham, The colonial wars, 1689–1762 (Chicago, London, 1964), 130–31, 150–51. G. M. Wrong, Conquest of New France; a chronicle of the colonial wars (Toronto, Glasgow, 1921), 130–35, 150–55. Edmond Mallet, "Jacques Le Gardeur de Saint-Pierre," BRH, V (1899), 233–36. E. D. Neill, "Last French post in the Mississippi Valley," Magazine of Western History (Cleveland), VII (1887), 17–29. P.-G. Roy, "La famille Legardeur de Repentigny," BRH, LIII (1947), 201–4.

LEGARDEUR DE TILLY, JEAN-BAPTISTE (also known as Legardeur de Moncarville et de Tilly), officer in the French navy; b. 30 Oct. 1698 at Rochefort, France, son of Jean-Baptiste Legardeur de La Mothe-Tilly and Jeanne-Élisabeth Girard; d. 3 March 1757 at sea.

Jean-Baptiste Legardeur de Tilly entered the French navy as a midshipman in 1713. He made several voyages to Île Royale (Cape Breton Island), Louisiana, Saint-Domingue (Hispaniola), and Martinique before accompanying his father to New France in 1724 on a mission to survey its potential for ship masts and timber. Two years later on 8 June he married at Montreal Anne-Geneviève Rocbert de La Morandière, sister of Mme Bégon [Rocbert]. In 1727 he returned to

France. Legardeur de Tilly continued to serve at sea and rose slowly in the officer ranks. He often sailed to Quebec. He did not receive his first independent command until 1742, the same year that he was received into the order of Saint-Louis.

In 1745, during the War of the Austrian Succession, Legardeur de Tilly was ordered to Quebec with supplies and munitions, but the season was advanced when he left Rochefort in September and he turned back before the end of the month. At the conclusion of the war he returned to New France and took command of the newly constructed third-rate ship-of-the-line *Saint-Laurent* during her maiden voyage to France. Following the outbreak of the Seven Years' War, in 1757, he received command of another third-rate, the *Inflexible*, but he died a few days after departing from Brest.

Legardeur de Tilly's 44 years of service were undistinguished. He was more than 40 years old when he received his first command, and the minister of Marine was unhappy with the lack of zeal he displayed in 1745. Indeed Legardeur de Tilly's career illustrates the malaise affecting the French navy during the middle of the 18th century: over-aged junior officers, too long passed by for promotion and inhibited from vigorous action by their own cautious careers.

Legardeur de Tilly left five children. Each of three girls received royal pensions of 300 *livres* following their father's death. The eldest, Marie-Anne, ill and crippled, was entrusted from birth to her aunt, Mme Bégon, who sheltered and cared for her for 23 years. In 1757 the two sons were already ensigns in the French navy. One, known only as the Chevalier Legardeur de Tilly, died on 21 Aug. 1778 on the *Concorde* in action off Saint-Domingue against the English frigate *Minerva*. The other, Armand, rose to the rank of vice-admiral under the old régime and spent some time in prison during the Terror.

JAMES S. PRITCHARD

[Claude de Bonnault, "Saintonge et Canada: les Tilly," *BRH*, XLI (1935), 238–56, 296–313; Le Jeune, *Dictionnaire*, II, 719; and P.-G. Roy, "La famille Le Gardeur de Tilly," *BRH*, LIII (1947), 99–123, 133–46 all confuse the careers of Jean-Baptiste Legardeur de Tilly, father and son. The clearest brief account, which contains information not found elsewhere, is in Fauteux, *Les chevaliers de Saint-Louis*, 137. None of the above appears to have used the full account of Legardeur de Tilly's service record in AN, Marine, C⁷, which also includes one for his father. Other manuscript sources were found in AN, Marine, B⁴, 62, f.81; 4JJ, 12, 38. J.S.P.]

LE GRAND SAUTEUX. *See* MINWEWEH

LEIGNE, LOUISE-CATHERINE ANDRÉ DE. *See* ANDRÉ

LEIGNE, PIERRE ANDRÉ DE. *See* ANDRÉ

LE MAIGRE, JOSEPH LEBLANC, *dit*. *See* LEBLANC

LEMAÎTRE, *dit* **Jugon, FRANÇOIS,** sailor, merchant, ship outfitter; b. 1707, son of François Lemaître and Bertrane Michelle of "Lequouet" (Les Couettes, dept. of Ille-et-Vilaine), France; d. before 22 Nov. 1751.

Little is known about François Lemaître, *dit* Jugon, including when or where he became a sailor. He may have served on local Canadian ships that began to sail to the West Indies during the 1730s, or, just as likely, he came to Canada from the West Indies. He apparently brought his wife, Marie Collet, born in Guadeloupe, to live in New France before 1744 for he was then residing with her on Rue Sainte-Famille in Quebec. At that time he had a servant and two Negro slaves living with him. He probably was already co-owner with a Sieur Saint-Germain, apparently located in Martinique, of the 130-ton brigantine *Saint Esprit*, which left Quebec in the autumn of 1745 for Martinique with a cargo of cod, flour, and planks. The next year this ship returned to Quebec *via* La Rochelle. In October 1746 Gilles Hocquart* freighted the ship, armed with four guns and a crew of 18, and identified as belonging to Jugon et Cie; he sent it to Baie-Verte (N.B.) under the command of Michel de SALLABERRY. Unfortunately the vessel ran aground below Quebec. The following season Hocquart made use of the ship to send 81 English prisoners to Louisbourg, Île Royale (Cape Breton Island). The ship probably sailed on to Martinique, whence it returned in the summer of 1748 with a cargo of tafia and syrup. The last mention of Jugon and his ship is in 1750 when the *Saint Esprit* left Martinique for Quebec with a mixed cargo of French wine, syrup, tafia, coffee, and sugar. He must have died not long after for on 22 Nov. 1751 Marie Collet married Jean-Louis Frémont, merchant and ship captain.

François Lemaître, *dit* Jugon, left no descendants. His younger brother Jean was at one time a servant of the cooper Simon Touchet, later became a cooper himself, and died at Quebec in 1781.

Louis Poulard, a metropolitan merchant who died at Jugon's residence in 1746, apparently considered Jugon to be his confidential agent in Canada, which suggests that he had business connections in France as well as in the West Indies.

Le Marchand

Perhaps the significance of Jugon's career lies in its brief indication of the degree of social mobility in the French colonies which permitted an illiterate member of the lower class to rise to modest circumstances as a merchant and shipowner.

JAMES S. PRITCHARD

AN, Col., C⁸ᴮ, 20, 22; C¹¹ᴬ, 83, f.263; 86, ff.160–63; 88, f.192v; 121, ff.175v–77. ANQ, Greffe de R.-C. Barolet, 22 nov., 3 oct. 1751; Greffe de J.-N. Pinguet de Vaucour, 19 déc. 1746. "Recensement de Québec, 1744" (APQ *Rapport*). P.-G. Roy, *Inv. ins. Prév. Québec*, II, 152. Tanguay, *Dictionnaire*.

LE MARCHAND DE LIGNERY, FRANÇOIS-MARIE, officer in the colonial regular troops; b. 24 Aug. 1703 in Montreal, son of Constant Le Marchand* de Lignery and Anne Robutel de La Noue; d. 28 July 1759.

Lignery joined the colonial regular troops at the age of 14 as a cadet, but did not see active service until 1728 when he participated as aide-de-camp in a campaign led by his father against the Fox Indians. He was promoted second ensign in 1733, and during the winter of 1734–35 accompanied Nicolas-Joseph de NOYELLES de Fleurimont in another campaign against the Foxes. In 1739 Lignery served as major of Charles LE MOYNE de Longueuil's detachment against the Chickasaws. Longueuil's subsequent recommendation of Lignery led to his promotion to ensign on 17 May 1741. Later that year Lignery was appointed assistant town major of Montreal, and in 1744 received a commission as lieutenant.

Lignery's foe changed from Indian to English in 1744 with the spread of the War of the Austrian Succession to North America. In April 1745 he acted as major and second in command under Paul MARIN de La Malgue in an attack on Annapolis Royal, Nova Scotia. Lignery served in two further campaigns in Acadia – a 22-day blockade of Annapolis in October 1746 under Jean-Baptiste-Nicolas-Roch de Ramezay*, and a raid led by Nicolas-Antoine COULON de Villiers on an English detachment at Grand Pré four months later. On 1 April 1751, with a total of 12 separate campaigns to his credit and a glowing recommendation from Governor La Jonquière [TAFFANEL], Lignery was promoted captain.

He now returned to the west, where on 9 July 1755 he played an important role with Jean-Daniel Dumas* in the defeat of General Edward Braddock's army in the battle of Monongahela; he was awarded the cross of Saint-Louis. Eight months later he was appointed commander on the Ohio, in succession to Dumas, with orders to maintain the loyalty of the western tribes and to harass the English with frequent war parties. During the next two years, from his base at Fort Duquesne (Pittsburgh, Pa.), Lignery sent several raiding parties into Virginia and Pennsylvania. The raids were so successful that they greatly affected Anglo-American morale. In March 1758 General John FORBES was given command of operations to be carried out against Fort Duquesne, and proceeded towards it slowly, creating defended supply stations as he went. Lignery's harassment of this expedition was effective. On 14 and 15 Sept. 1758 he easily defeated an advance party of 800 troops led by Major James Grant of the Scottish 77th regiment and continued the hit-and-run raiding tactics.

Fort Frontenac (Kingston, Ont.) had fallen in August, however, food supplies were low, Indian allies were deserting, the season was late, and Forbes' main army was increasing in size daily. In November a council of war agreed that Fort Duquesne should be abandoned. Lignery decided to send the bulk of his forces to Montreal, Detroit, and the Illinois country; he delayed the destruction of the fort until 23 November, when Forbes' army was only 12 miles away, and then retired to Fort Machault at Venango (Franklin, Pa.) on the Ohio.

From Fort Machault, where his force began to build up again in 1759, he continued sending parties on raids against the English. On 6 July however, Pierre POUCHOT, the commandant of Fort Niagara (near Youngstown, N.Y.), was besieged by the English, and he appealed to Lignery for help. The latter abandoned his plans for a major attack on Fort Pitt, which the English had built to replace Fort Duquesne, and advanced to Niagara. On 24 July Lignery and his force of French and Indians were ambushed and he was captured. The fort fell on the 25th, and Lignery died of his wounds on the 28th.

On 27 Jan. 1738 Lignery had married Marie-Thérèse, daughter of Daniel MIGEON de La Gauchetière, in Montreal; seven children were born of this marriage, two of whom died young. The sons served as officers in the colonial regular troops; Lignery's widow and two daughters retired to France with government pensions.

C. J. RUSS

AN, Col., E, 125; F³, 15, ff.225–30. *Journal du chevalier de Lévis* (Casgrain), 155, 161–64, 166. *Journal du marquis de Montcalm* (Casgrain), 110–11, 149–51, 192, 245, 462–63, 473–75, 493. *Lettres de M. de Bourlamaque* (Casgrain), 23, 26, 152, 193, 280–81. *Lettres du chevalier de Lévis* (Casgrain), 217–18. *Lettres et pièces militaires* (Casgrain), 153. "Une expédition canadienne à la Louisiane en 1739–1740," APQ *Rapport, 1922–23*,

Le Moyne de Bienville

157, 181, 184–89. Fauteux, *Les chevaliers de Saint-Louis*, 161–62. Le Jeune, *Dictionnaire*. Frégault, *La guerre de la conquête*, 310–11, 332–33, 350–51. Gosselin, *L'Église du Canada jusqu'à la conquête*, III, 410–12, 491. Kellogg, *French régime*, 425–26, 434. McLennan, *Louisbourg*, 148–49. Stanley, *New France*, 99, 149, 186–91, 214–21.

LEMOINE, *dit* **Monière, ALEXIS (Jean-Alexis),** merchant; b. 14 April 1680 at Sainte-Anne-de-la-Pérade, son of Jean Lemoine and Madeleine de Chavigny de Berchereau; d. 23 June 1754 at Montreal.

The career of Alexis Lemoine, *dit* Monière, is fairly representative of that of the average Canadian "merchant-outfitter" in the first half of the 18th century. His father, a shareholder in the Compagnie de la Colonie, was a small trader in the region of Trois-Rivières. The family had few means, and when the sons reached manhood the trading networks formerly about Lac Saint-Pierre had shifted towards the interior; trade had become more structured and less easy of access. Like his older brother, René-Alexandre, *dit* Despain, Alexis had to leave for Montreal, whence the convoys for the west set off. He spent his entire youth as a voyageur and fur-trader on behalf of others, particularly for Cadillac [Laumet*]. Towards 1712 he began financing his own voyages to Michilimackinac and those of some "voyageur-associates."

At this time Alexis adopted the name "Monière," perhaps devised from an anagram of Lemoine. In doing so he followed the custom of the voyageurs, which in turn was copied from a peculiarity of the military, and this name became better known than his patronymic.

He was almost 35 years old when he married Marie-Louise Zemballe in Quebec on 22 March 1715 and opened a shop in Montreal. It took him several years more to establish a credit rating capable of sustaining large annual loans, to acquire and keep a regular clientele of voyageurs and officers garrisoned in the posts, and, finally, to expand his small local trade so that he could stabilize receipts. Except for a few rare occasions when he was a supplier to the troops, he is not known to have engaged in any activities other than this trade in furs, which he seems to have conducted successfully until an advanced age. It is true that he carried out certain property deals, in particular the acquisition of a piece of land on the *côte* Notre-Dame-des-Vertus, the management of which he oversaw attentively; but these are interests which go with growing old, which indicate stabilization and then recession of capital assets in business undertakings.

Rare were the young indentured employees (*engagés*) in the fur trade who succeeded in climbing to the rank of "merchant-outfitter." Monière had talent, a prudence which enabled him to save part of his wages, and above all influential friends. Through his mother, daughter of François de Chavigny de Berchereau, one of the members of the Conseil Souverain [*see* Éléonore de Grandmaison*], he was related to people in high business and administrative offices. His sisters married "merchant-voyageurs," and this family circle supplied the initial nucleus of his clientele. Monière's first marriage, with an Englishwoman, had perhaps not furthered his establishment in business, but the second one, in 1726, with Marie-Josephte, daughter of Charles de Couagne*, who was in his lifetime an important Montreal merchant and who was related to several officers, could only have helped in putting his business on a sound footing. Monière's children married into the same privileged circle, and his son, Pierre-Alexis, carried on his father's business undertaking even after 1760.

An annual turnover of 10–15,000 *livres* was not enough to build up a fortune, but it ensured a comfortable living and in the most favourable conditions enabled the saving of some 30–50,000 *livres*. In a sector which had reached its ceiling and was dangerously competitive, Monière is an example of respectable success.

LOUISE DECHÊNE

ANQ-M, Greffe de J.-B. Adhémar; Greffe de Jacques David; Greffe de F.-M. Lepailleur; Greffe de J.-C. Raimbault; Greffe de Nicolas Senet; Registre d'état civil, Notre-Dame de Montréal, 12 août 1726. PAC, MG 23, GIII, 25, A. "Correspondance de Mme Bégon" (Bonnault), APQ *Rapport, 1934–35*, 9. Bonnault, "Le Canada militaire," APQ *Rapport, 1949–51*, 444. Massicotte, "Répertoire des engagements pour l'Ouest," APQ *Rapport, 1930–31; 1931–32*. Tanguay, *Dictionnaire*. Nish, *Les bourgeois-gentilshommes*.

LE MOYNE DE BIENVILLE, JEAN-BAPTISTE, officer, explorer, governor of Louisiana; baptized as an infant 23 Feb. 1680 in Montreal; son of Charles Le Moyne* de Longueuil et de Châteauguay and Catherine Thierry (Primot); d. 7 March 1767 in Paris, France.

Jean-Baptiste Le Moyne belonged to a family many of whose members left their mark on the history of Canada and Louisiana. His parents died when he was young, but fraternal solidarity compensated for the loss. When his brother François, Sieur de Bienville, died in 1691, Jean-Baptiste received the landed title by which he would be known to history.

In 1692 Bienville began his naval service as a

Le Moyne de Bienville

midshipman. He served under his elder brother Pierre Le Moyne* d'Iberville near Newfoundland, along the New England coast, and in Hudson Bay; wounded in action in 1697, he accompanied Iberville to France. The War of the League of Augsburg had just ended; France and England were now ready to race each other to colonize the Mississippi valley, which had been opened to exploration by Jacques Marquette* and Louis Jolliet*, René-Robert Cavelier* de La Salle and Henri Tonty* shortly before the war. Iberville, fresh from spectacular exploits against the English, was chosen to lead the French search for the mouth of the Mississippi. Bienville sailed with his brother from Brest, 24 Oct. 1698. After hailing the Spanish outpost at Pensacola (Fla.), the French headed westward along the coast; finding a strong current of fresh water that flowed between piles of driftwood, they made their way into the great river on 2 March 1699. They were the first Europeans to enter the Mississippi from the open sea.

When in May 1699 Iberville sailed back to France, he left Ensign Sauvole in command at Biloxi (at a site now within Ocean Springs, Miss.) over a garrison of some 70 men. Bienville was second in command. While exploring the lower Mississippi with five men in two canoes, Bienville met the English naval officer Bond, whose corvette was part of the English enterprise to occupy the Mississippi. With a bluffing threat to call for support, Bienville ordered Bond out of the French king's river. Bienville was to recall this incident two decades later in his representations to the king: "I obliged them [the English] to abandon their enterprise." The event left a place name on the river: English Turn.

Iberville returned in January 1700 and departed again for France in late May. Meanwhile, Bienville, after exploring the lower Red and Ouachita rivers, had been given command of the small Fort de Mississipi, on the left bank, 18 leagues from the river's mouth. When Sauvole died in August 1701, Bienville succeeded him as commandant. At a mere 21 years of age, he began administering Louisiana for a decade of its leanest years. Iberville, during a four-month sojourn in the colony in 1702, confirmed Bienville in his role, and then sailed for France in April, never to return to Louisiana. The War of the Spanish Succession had broken out; Iberville led an expedition to the West Indies, and took the island of Nevis, only to die of fever in Havana on 9 July 1706. Bienville, Iberville's junior by 19 years, would now be the leading Le Moyne in the colonizing of Louisiana.

A decade of war (1701–13) left Louisiana poorly supplied and constantly menaced. Bien-

ville's diplomacy with the Indians, based on his knowledge of their language and customs, was a key factor in the survival of the infant colony. In spite of the promise young Bienville showed, the minister of Marine, Pontchartrain, passed over him and, in the spring of 1707, named Nicolas Daneau* de Muy governor of the colony. The Le Moynes were under a cloud because of charges that Iberville had used his official position and goods to increase his and the family's fortunes. Bienville himself was accused of authoritarianism toward his countrymen and of cruelty toward Indian prisoners. A steady stream of charges against him was sent to France by Nicolas de La Salle*, the acting commissary of the colony, and Henri Roulleaux de La Vente, pastor of the parish in Mobile (Ala.). (In 1702 Bienville had transferred his headquarters to Fort Louis on the Mobile River; in 1711 fort and town were relocated some 25 miles downriver at the present site of Mobile.) La Salle, jealous of the Le Moynes, complained of the commandant's encroachment upon his prerogatives. La Vente denounced Bienville for weakness in the face of the Koroas when members of the tribe hacked to death a party of Frenchmen including Nicolas Foucault*, a missioner from the Quebec seminary; he also blamed Bienville for not halting debauchery with Indian slave girls. Jealous of the Jesuit Jacques Gravier* whom Bienville had befriended and named chaplain, La Vente complained that Bienville was interfering with parish worship, was giving a bad example by not practising his religion, and was involved in an affair with an unnamed woman. Both La Salle and La Vente accused Bienville of harassment and of intercepting their correspondence with Versailles.

Pontchartrain's nominee, de Muy, died in Havana en route to Louisiana. The home government then entrusted the investigation of Bienville's public and private life to Jean-Baptiste-Martin d'Artaguiette Diron, who was to serve as co-commissary with La Salle. The investigator never substantiated the charges. Whatever may have been the reality in the drawn-out case of Iberville's profiteering, Bienville went for years without receiving payment of his salary. No example of torture or of cowardice was proven. Food was scarce for all, not just for the commandant's political enemies who blamed him for their wartime hunger. The unnamed woman was reportedly dead when d'Artaguiette arrived, and Bienville claimed that La Vente had retracted the charge; subsequently the archives record no charges of debauchery against the lifelong bachelor. The accusation of intercepting letters proved also to be a canard.

Le Moyne de Bienville

The decade of charges and counter-charges is an example of the traditional hostility between the *gens de plume* such as La Salle and the *gens d'épée* such as Bienville. This factionalism in the bicephalous administration of Louisiana was doubled by the ecclesiastical allies each political leader befriended. Bienville continued the Le Moyne friendship with the Jesuits. La Salle needed the aid of La Vente, a member of the Séminaire des Missions Étrangères, which in Europe and Asia was debating with the Society of Jesus the momentous Chinese rites question.

Louis XIV, unable to provide the capital needed to develop Louisiana, contracted the colony over to the wealthy Antoine Crozat in 1712. The new proprietor linked to himself in financial cooperation the new governor Cadillac [Laumet*], who, appointed in May 1710, made his way *via* France from Canada to Louisiana, arriving in June 1712. Bienville had again been passed over. The loquacious Gascon governor pursued the investigation into Bienville's behaviour without results other than the humiliation and alienation of Bienville, whom he would brand a caballing political intriguer. Bienville reported to Pontchartrain a further reason for Cadillac's hostility: he had refused to marry Cadillac's daughter. Louisiana's bifactionalism continued, but now with Bienville in a weak position as king's lieutenant serving under Governor Cadillac.

Nonetheless, Pontchartrain, feeling somewhat more favourable toward Bienville in 1714, provided him with the military command of the Mississippi River from the Ohio to the gulf. Cadillac proved inept at dealing with the natives, and Bienville was called upon to repair the ties of alliance and friendship. No thanks were given him for the braggart governor was annoyed at his military commandant's initiatives. Yet when a crisis developed, a band of Natchez having killed four French voyageurs, Cadillac ordered Bienville into action, with only 34 men at his disposal, to demand justice from a tribe that had 800 warriors. Recruiting several Canadians to advance with him, Bienville went into Natchez territory, where, by ruse and kidnapping, he obliged the chiefs to condemn to death the six murderers. The tension subsided without a shot being fired. At Bienville's insistence, the Natchez worked with the French and Canadians to erect Fort Rosalie (Natchez, Miss.).

Meanwhile in France the newly empowered council of Marine removed Cadillac from office; although less suspicious of the Le Moynes than Pontchartrain had been, the council passed over Bienville and named as governor Jean-Michel de Lespinay*. In the interim prior to Lespinay's arrival (October 1716 to March 1717) Bienville was acting head of the colony. The king rewarded Bienville in October 1716 with the grant of Horn Island on the Gulf coast, not *en seigneurie* as Bienville had requested, but *en roture*, a commoner's tenure. Bienville intensely desired the honour of being named a knight of the order of Saint-Louis; this royal recognition was accorded him on 20 Sept. 1717.

When in 1717 the regent of France entrusted Louisiana to John Law's Compagnie d'Occident – soon to be called the Compagnie des Indes – the office of royal governor ceased. The new role of commandant general, with responsibility for royal defence of the company's colony, was given to Bienville. The Illinois country was attached to Louisiana, and thereby came under his military jurisdiction. Company affairs were in the hands of the civilian administrator, Marc-Antoine Hubert. The company brought Bienville further into its administration by naming him one of the directors, and by having him preside over the meetings of the governing council.

In the spring of 1718, at a place he had recommended – a portage between the Mississippi River and Lake Pontchartrain – Bienville was in charge of establishing a company post and a town to be known as New Orleans. He knew that silting passes at the mouth of the Mississippi River would be a problem, but he favoured dredging to maintain needed depth rather than abandoning the advantages of a river and sea port. He recognized the need of levees as a protection against flooding and proposed a canal that would link river and lake.

In general, Bienville was guardedly cooperative with the Spaniards to the east and to the west, and dreamed of commerce with Veracruz. Yet as the Spaniards extended their colonial reach to Los Adayes (near Robeline, La.), Bienville fortified Natchitoches and thereby fixed the eastern line of Texas. Vainly he hoped to occupy the upper Arkansas River. In 1719, when war broke out between the two Bourbon monarchies, he had the advantage of earlier news, and seized Pensacola; after a turnabout counter-offensive by the Spaniards, he led the recapture of Pensacola.

Bankruptcy brought an end to John Law's dreams and to his company. Early in 1722 Bienville learned that the reorganized Compagnie des Indes was retaining him as commandant general. (It prescribed New Orleans as his ordinary residence rather than Nouveau-Biloxi (Biloxi, Miss.), headquarters since 1720.) Yet not for long. Within two years he was recalled to France "for consultation." Being of the *gens d'épée*, this

Le Moyne de Bienville

Le Moyne was not attractive to the new commercial managers who were sending out *gens de plume* and company men to control the colony. Always tempted to feel a paternal or proprietary right over Louisiana, Bienville was obliged to sail in the summer of 1725 for the mother country he hardly knew; the company judged that "it was not suitable to its interests" to retain him in office in Louisiana.

Controller General Charles-Gaspard Dodun, head of the Conseil des Indes, understood the company's position, and explained to Maurepas that Bienville was "a man of courage and a good officer; [and that] although it would not be good for him to go back as commandant, there is in this position no attack on his honour or honesty, and he could indeed be capable of serving well in all other posts to which you might name him." To replace Bienville, Étienne de Périer was commissioned in August 1726 as commandant general of Louisiana. During the rest of the year the company secured the removal of several Bienvillists from Louisiana offices. The Le Moyne era in Louisiana had come, it seemed, to a definitive end.

The new administration performed its functions satisfactorily until the local commandant at Fort Rosalie provoked the Natchez into rising up against the French. The killing of settlers and soldiers struck fear into all the colonists, undermined confidence in the leadership, and brought the Compagnie des Indes, which foresaw no gains for itself in this poor colony, to beg the king to reassume the administration of Louisiana. The change was effected in the summer of 1731. The court was in contact with Bienville in the spring of that year, and in the summer of 1732 the king commissioned him as governor of Louisiana because "Sieur de Bienville, by the services which he has already rendered, has given evidence of his experience and capability, and His Majesty is all the more willingly led to this decision, for knowing that Sieur de Bienville has the confidence both of settlers and of natives."

In the first days of March 1733, as the governorship changed hands in New Orleans, Périer complained of the shabby treatment Bienville gave him even though he had befriended the Le Moynes and their supporters. On his part Bienville reported the colony "in a worse state than expected"; he referred to the dwindling population, the shortage of food and goods, and especially the Indians' attitude toward the French. Strong in the belief that "the colony was grounding all its hope on [his] return," he pleaded repeatedly for troops, munitions, manufactured goods, and food supplies.

The questions and problems Bienville faced during the 1730s concerned trade – legitimate and contraband – with France, England, and Mexico; importation of Negro slaves; land grants for retired soldiers; experimentation with crops; processing and shipping of tobacco; search for a better cotton gin; value of paper money; fortifications and barracks; desertions from his troops; hurricanes and floods; and, of course, the annual budget.

Bienville warmly endorsed the work of his old friend Nicolas-Ignace de BEAUBOIS, recently renamed superior of the Jesuit missions in Louisiana. The governor showed interest in the royal hospital and praised the care given the sick and wounded servicemen by the nuns. During the administration of Bienville and Commissary Edme-Gatien Salmon, a bequest by sailor-merchant Jean Louis launched the charity hospital of Louisiana for civilians. An admiring officer had written years before that Bienville was "charitable. I have seen him give the last morsel of [wheat] bread and the last drop of wine for the sick, and reduce his own diet to corn bread and often to sagamité."

In administration Bienville collaborated for years with Salmon in that "good understanding" often recommended by the home government to its Louisiana officials. Although the colonial bicephalism brought the two to mutual countercharges by 1740, they were reconciled in early 1742. Bienville praised his nephew Gilles-Augustin Payen de Noyan and promoted his interests, thus leaving himself open to the old charge against the Le Moynes of nepotism and partisanship. From New Orleans Bienville petitioned the king for revalidation of his Mississippi River land grants that had been annulled by the Compagnie des Indes.

In diplomacy with the Indians Bienville ever gave them that first courtesy of learning their languages. He acquired and practised the tribes' ways of greeting and of holding councils, and sent French or Canadian youths to live for a time in the native villages in order to learn language and etiquette. His main policy throughout his administration was to sustain the Choctaws in their warring with the Chickasaws, who were supported by the English. He fostered friendly cooperation with the smaller tribes; he had welcomed the Apalachee refugees fleeing from their Florida villages destroyed by the English. A major handicap, which his personal diplomacy had to counterbalance, was the French inability to provide cheap trade goods to rival the English supplies and prices on the frontier.

The condition for peace between the French

and the Chickasaws, Bienville insisted, was for the latter to hand over as slaves the Natchez to whom they had given asylum after that tribe's defeat by the forces of Louis JUCHEREAU de Saint-Denis in 1731; the Chickasaws refused and continued to harbour these political refugees. From the time of his return in 1733 Bienville sought to bring the Chickasaws to cooperation or to submission. To sustain the morale of the Choctaws and other allies, he himself led an offensive in 1736 even though "such a campaign was painful at [his] age." His army included unreliable French troops, Canadians (whom he called "naturally a bit unruly"), and Indians. The timing was faulty, the manoeuvres were inconclusive, and he had to withdraw from the Chickasaw country. Young Bernard d'Artaguiette Diron bitterly complained that Bienville's failure to arrive earlier at a rendezvous point had cost the life of his brother Pierre. Diron further complained that Bienville favoured Canadians "shamefully, to the extreme, as if only they were capable."

Means were lacking to mount an offensive in 1737 and 1738. But men and munitions, even artillery, were dispatched from France. The minister of Marine wanted more than a "doubtful success." During the winter of 1737–38 Bienville was often confined to his bed by "very painful sciatica," but he nonetheless continued preparations.

Before launching his campaign he sought new officers for his troops. They and the civilians were hard to govern. The troops were tempted to desert because of the hard life in the frontier outposts. The civilians were often former coureurs de bois. His ideal was to have (and be) "a commandant who knows how to make himself esteemed and respected without trying to make himself feared." A split among the Choctaws developed when those "of the east" made peace with the Chickasaws and accepted trade with the English. Bienville countered the English move by strengthening his alliance with the Choctaws " of the west," and with friendly elements among those "of the east."

The long-prepared offensive got under way in the fall of 1739 after all the Choctaws rallied to the side of the French. Canada sent troops and Indian allies under Charles LE MOYNE de Longueuil and Pierre-Joseph CÉLORON de Blainville. The outcome of this impressive expedition fell short of complete victory. Unable to transport to the enemy villages the artillery that would have destroyed them, Bienville decided to come to terms with the Chickasaws when they sued for peace in the face of such a large, well-provisioned

force. They surrendered some Natchez refugees to him and pledged peaceful cooperation.

In June 1740, the sexagenarian, who had first complained "of the bad state of [his] health" to Maurepas's father in 1707, begged the minister for leave to go to France for his health. He proposed the summer of 1742 as departure time, for he was confident that by then he would have solidified the newly made armistice into stable peace. Maurepas in October 1741 granted the requested retirement, but almost a year elapsed before a successor was named.

Pathetically, in March 1742 Bienville reflected that "a sort of fatality [has been] set for some time upon wrecking most of my best-planned projects." Learning that he would soon be replaced, he pledged to spend his time smoothing out all he could for his successor who, he hoped, would have better fortune. The new governor, Pierre de Rigaud* de Vaudreuil, arriving in May 1743, questioned the solidity of Bienville's peace, and reported a need for reforms and greater military discipline.

Weary of the burden of leadership which he had borne intermittently for four decades, Bienville bade a final farewell to Louisiana on 17 Aug. 1743. His ship reached Rochefort, France, on 19 October, and he took up residence in Paris where he was to live in relative obscurity for more than two decades of retirement.

The aging retiree was comfortable financially – with a pension from the king in recognition of his services, with revenues from the municipality of Paris on certificates he had purchased, with a small annuity from the Compagnie des Indes, and with an annuity from the Jesuits for leased acreage adjoining the land he had sold them outside New Orleans. Served by a valet and a lackey, a cook and a kitchen maid, Bienville had also a coachman for his carriage and horses. One might picture him strolling from his Rue Vivienne residence – marked since 1968 by a plaque – to the nearby gardens of the Palais Royal where he would recount the deeds of yesteryear. Meanwhile, in faraway Louisiana he was remembered not only by the French but also by the Indians, who "always mention[ed] him in their speeches. His name [was] so deeply rooted in the hearts of these good people that his memory will always be dear to them," noted one traveller. He lived to see his Louisiana pass under Spanish rule in 1766 despite petitions to Versailles by its French inhabitants.

He died in 1767 in his 88th year. His will, redolent of piety toward God, made provisions for his servants and divided his estate among his nephews, great-nephews, and great-nieces. The

Le Moyne de Longueuil

funeral was held in his parish church of Saint-Eustache, but, if he was interred within its walls, the record has through pillage and fire been lost.

His mortal remains are thus deprived of honoured recognition – just as in his lifetime he was never fully rewarded by king or nation for the intrepid leadership that nurtured a sickly outpost into an enduring centre of French culture. He even had to wait two centuries for New Orleans, the largest city he founded, to erect a splendid statue in honour of the father of Louisiana.

C. E. O'NEILL

AN, Col., B, 25, ff.15–23v; 27, ff.193–94; 29, ff.269–94v; 32, ff.321–24v, 477–78v; 38, ff.288–89v, 326v–27, 338; 39, ff.449v–53; 42 bis, ff.83–86, 188; 43, pp.342–43, 363, 408–9; 57, ff.796–863v; 59, ff.571–620; 61, ff.644v–705; 63, ff.591–633; 64, ff.500–30v; 65, ff.495–532; 66, ff.341–73v; 68, ff.401–26v; 70, ff.453–73v; 72, ff.470–98v; 74, ff.609–26v; C¹³ᴬ, 1–27; C¹³ᴮ, pièces 6, 8, 9, 10; C¹³ᶜ, 1, f.406; 2, ff.43–45; 4, ff.45–48, 93; E, 277; F³, 24, ff.341–57; Marine, B¹, 9, ff.263–93; Minutier central, II, 621, 622; Section Outre-Mer, G¹, 465 (dossier Bienville). ANDM, Registres des baptêmes, mariages et sépultures, 23 févr. 1680. Archives du séminaire des Missions étrangères (Paris), 344, p.62. ASQ, Lettres, M, 35, 38; R, 79, 83. Louisiana State Museum Archives (New Orleans), 63/68, 3 Sept. 1763; 2196, 20 July 1767.

Bénard de La Harpe, *Journal historique de l'établissement des Français à la Louisiane* (Nouvelle-Orléans, 1831). "Bienville's claims against the Company of the Indies for back salary, etc., 1737," ed. H. P. Dart, *Louisiana Historical Quarterly* (New Orleans), IX (1926), 210–20. [J.-B. Bossu], *Travels in the interior of North America, 1751–1762*, trans. and ed. Seymour Feiler (Norman, Okla., 1962). Charlevoix, *Histoire de la N.-F.* (1744), II. *Découvertes et établissements des Français* (Margry), IV, V, VI. "Documents concerning Bienville's lands in Louisiana . . . ," ed. H. P. Dart, *Louisiana Historical Quarterly*, X (1927), 5–24, 161–84, 364–80, 538–61; XI (1928), 87–110, 209–32, 463–65. "The first state trial in Louisiana," ed. H. P. Dart, *Louisiana Historical Quarterly*, XIV (1931), 5–35. *JR* (Thwaites), LXVI, 128–40. Le Page Du Pratz, *Histoire de la Louisiane* (3v., Paris, 1758). [André Pénicaut], *Fleur de lys and calumet: being the Pénicaut narrative of French adventure in Louisiana*, ed. and trans. R. G. McWilliams (Baton Rouge, 1953). Tanguay, *Dictionnaire*.

Frégault, *Le grand marquis*. Giraud, *Histoire de la Louisiane française*. G. E. King, *Jean Baptiste Le Moyne, Sieur de Bienville* (New York, 1892). O'Neill, *Church and state in Louisiana*. Marc de Villiers Du Terrage, *Histoire de la fondation de la Nouvelle-Orléans, 1717–1722* (Paris, 1917). C. E. O'Neill, "The death of Bienville," *Louisiana History* (Baton Rouge), VIII (1967), 362–69.

LE MOYNE DE LONGUEUIL, CHARLES, Baron de LONGUEUIL, the second to hold the title, officer in the colonial regular troops, governor of Montreal, acting administrator of New France; b. 18 Oct. 1687 at Longueuil (Que.), son of Charles Le Moyne* de Longueuil, Baron de Longueuil, and Claude-Élisabeth Souart d'Adoucourt; d. 17 Jan. 1755 in Montreal.

Charles Le Moyne de Longueuil early embraced a career in arms. Following the example of his father and several other members of the Le Moyne family, he went to learn the military profession in France, and was at Rochefort in December 1705, serving as a midshipman. He returned to Canada and on 18 June 1712 he obtained the expectancy of an appointment as lieutenant. A year later the king granted him his commission. A diligent officer and "very steady in his conduct," he was promoted captain on 13 May 1719, after six years as a lieutenant. On 28 April 1726 his father, at the time acting administrator of New France, appointed him commandant of Fort Niagara (near Youngstown, N.Y.), a post much sought after by Canadian military officers, as were all the posts in the *pays d'en haut* at the period, for the supplementary income that the fur trade brought them. In 1729, after his father's death on 7 June of that year, he inherited the title of Baron de Longueuil. Finally, after 14 years as a captain, Charles Le Moyne was promoted on 1 April 1733 town major of the government of Montreal, replacing François de Gannes de Falaise. The following year, 1734, Louis XV made him a knight of the order of Saint-Louis as a reward for his 31 years of "good and loyal services."

In June 1739 the town major of Montreal was sent by Governor Charles de BEAUHARNOIS to Louisiana to aid the governor of that colony, Bienville [LE MOYNE], the Baron de Longueuil's uncle, in his struggle against the Chickasaw tribe. The expedition, consisting of a detachment of 442 men, 319 of them Indians, was successful in pacifying the Chickasaws, thanks to Captain Pierre-Joseph CÉLORON de Blainville, who on 22 Feb. 1740 intimidated them sufficiently through a bold attack to make them seek peace.

Charles Le Moyne was back in Montreal in the summer of 1740 and remained there until May 1743, when he took over as king's lieutenant at Trois-Rivières in place of Louis LIÉNARD de Beaujeu, who was incapacitated by illness. In March 1748 he returned to Montreal as king's lieutenant, and was responsible for the government of Montreal until a governor was appointed to succeed Josué DUBOIS Berthelot de Beaucours, who had been retired because of his advanced age. On 23 May 1749 the king informed him of his appointment to the important post of

Le Moyne de Sainte-Marie

governor of Montreal, an office which in the military hierarchy of Canada at that period came after that of governor general. In addition, Montreal was the centre of the fur trade, the gateway to the *pays d'en haut*, and nerve centre for all the military expeditions towards the *pays d'en haut* and Louisiana.

On 25 March 1752, after the death of the governor general, La Jonquière [TAFFANEL], Charles Le Moyne, as governor of Montreal and as the senior officer on the general staff, was put in charge of the administration of New France by Intendant Bigot* until a new governor was appointed. He seized the occasion to ask the king to confirm him in this function, just as his father had done 27 years earlier, but the king could not accede to this request, for on 1 Jan. 1752, even before La Jonquière's death, he had appointed the Marquis Duquesne* to the office. During the four months of his interim government, Le Moyne succeeded, with the help of the inhabitants of Montreal, in convincing the minister, Rouillé, to give up the project of suppressing the Hôpital-Général of Montreal, which Mother d'Youville [Dufrost*] had just taken in hand. On Duquesne's arrival in August 1752 Le Moyne resumed his functions as governor of Montreal, exercising them until his death on 17 Jan. 1755.

On 29 April 1730, at Saint-Ours, in the presence of many representatives of the Canadian nobility, Charles Le Moyne de Longueuil had married Catherine-Charlotte, the daughter of Marguerite Legardeur de Tilly and the late Louis-Joseph Le Goüès de Grais, a captain in the colonial regular troops, and the step-daughter of Pierre de Saint-Ours* and Charles Le Moyne de Longueuil, first Baron de Longueuil, both deceased. Between 1721 and 1739 18 children were born of this marriage, six of whom survived their father: two sons, who were officers in the colonial regular troops, and four daughters. At his death Charles Le Moyne left a large inheritance consisting of a house on Rue Saint-Paul in Montreal, a farm on Île Sainte-Hélène, 11,681 *livres* 10 *sols* in personal goods, including 5,103 *livres* 10 *sols* in silverware, 1,104 *livres* 5 *sols* in "solid gold," 1,075 *livres* in furniture, 566 *livres* in linen, and 284 *livres* in clothing, 34 animals valued at 436 *livres*, and two black slaves "valued" at 500 *livres* each.

Charles Le Moyne de Longueuil, a rich man, a member of the nobility and the military élite of New France, was a typical example of the sons of great Canadian families who were able to accede to the highest offices in New France and indirectly to wealth, thanks to their rank, the prestige of their "noble name," and the patronage which, in New France as in the mother country, played a prominent role in the distribution of vacant offices in the king's service.

ANDRÉ LACHANCE

AN, Col., B, 87, ff.32ff., 40v; 89, f.78; 103, f.21v; C¹¹A, 98, ff.86, 345, 350; 101, f.125; D²C, 222/2, f.25; E, 203 (dossier Germain), 290 (dossier Le Moyne de Longueuil, Charles II). ANQ-M, Greffe L.-C. Danré de Blanzy, 12 mars 1755; Greffe de Pierre Raimbault, 29 avril 1720; Registre d'état civil, Notre-Dame de Montréal, 20 oct. 1687, 19 janv. 1755. "Une expédition canadienne à la Louisiane en 1739–1740," APQ *Rapport, 1922–23*, 156ff. Tanguay, *Dictionnaire*. Frégault, *François Bigot*, II, 53ff. A. Jodoin et J.-L. Vincent, *Histoire de Longueuil et la famille de Longueuil* (Montréal, 1889), 231ff. P.-G. Roy, "Les gouverneurs de Montréal (1642–1760)," *Cahiers des Dix*, VII (1942), 116–17.

LE MOYNE DE SAINTE-MARIE, MARGUERITE, *dite* **du Saint-Esprit,** sister of the Congregation of Notre-Dame, superior of the community (superior general); b. 3 Feb. 1664 in Montreal, daughter of Jacques Le Moyne de Sainte-Marie and Mathurine Godé; d. 21 Feb. 1746 at Montreal.

Through her father and mother Marguerite Le Moyne de Sainte-Marie belonged to two of the founding families of Ville-Marie. She was the fifth child in the family, and with her sisters she was a pupil of the Congregation of Notre-Dame. When she was 16 she asked to be received into the community; her sister Françoise, five years her senior, had already been admitted.

After making her profession in 1682, Marguerite Le Moyne taught at Ville-Marie, then at the La Montagne mission. She was only 24 when she was appointed probation mistress, with the responsibility of receiving new arrivals to the congregation and preparing them for the religious life. She carried out this office intelligently and zealously for ten years. In 1698 she participated with the Montreal community in the ceremonies accompanying the granting of official approval of the rules and the solemn pronouncement of the religious vows [*see* Marie Barbier*]. In the elections which immediately followed, Marguerite Le Moyne, *dite* du Saint-Esprit, was chosen superior of the congregation, succeeding Sister Marie Barbier. She was the third superior of the institution founded by Marguerite Bourgeoys*, and she held the office four times, from 1698 to 1708, 1711 to 1717, 1719 to 1722, and 1729 to 1732. Thus the annalist of the community remarked in her conclusion: "To be elected so many times to this office is a proof of my Sister Lemoyne's rare qualities and of the sincere esteem she enjoyed in the minds of all the Sisters."

Le Normant

Numerous events marked the life and work within the congregation during Sister Le Moyne's long superiorship. The most important of these events concerned Bishop Saint-Vallier [La Croix*], who, moved by the spirit of reform of the Council of Trent, tried by every means to transform the congregation into a regular, cloistered religious community. One of Sister Le Moyne's early actions after her first election was to reject a proposal to found a noviciate at Quebec. Bishop Saint-Vallier was repeating in 1702 a request he had made in 1698, when Mother Bourgeoys was alive and to which she had given no support. Sister Le Moyne wanted thus to remain faithful to the spirit of the foundress, especially as she was afraid of dividing forces still young and few in number between two institutions.

In 1720 the superior was more favourable to the bishop's recommendations concerning the liturgical life of the community. As nuns associated with the parish, the sisters up till then had had no sung service in their chapel other than that of the Visitation, which was the feast-day of their order, and the evening services on the main feast-days of the Virgin. At Saint-Vallier's invitation the sisters borrowed "the practices of the most holy communities": they commenced the custom of singing motets accompanied by music on the great religious feast-days and hymns on other occasions, such as the feast-day of their superior.

Another time when Bishop Saint-Vallier interfered, Sister Le Moyne opposed him. In a letter dated 15 Feb. 1722 the bishop forbade the sisters to accept anyone into the community without his "especial and written" permission and without a dowry of 2,000 *livres*. Such instructions were contrary to the spirit of the foundress, who had wanted her congregation to be autonomous, poor, and open to all classes of society. But the superior had to comply with the bishop's wishes.

It was again Sister Le Moyne who in 1729 received Bishop Dosquet*'s strict recommendations concerning the sisters' conduct towards the parish priests and missionaries. Designed to keep "regularity and good order" in the missions, these recommendations were the source of an attitude that has often divided the craftsmen of a common evangelical work.

While attentive to the internal life of the community she directed, Sister Le Moyne was also occupied with the teaching work of the congregation. Under her administration three houses were founded: Boucherville in 1703, Prairie-de-la-Madeleine (Laprairie) in 1705, and Pointe-aux-Trembles (Neuville) in 1716. Two former missions were taken over again: Lachine in 1701,

and Champlain in 1702. The mission at La Montagne was moved to Sault-au-Récollet in 1701, then in 1721 from Montreal Island to Lac des Deux-Montagnes. Finally, it was during Sister Le Moyne's term of office that the congregation acquired in 1707 the fief of La Noue on Île Saint-Paul, the first third of what was to become the famous "Île des Soeurs."

After she gave up the government of the congregation in 1732 Sister Le Moyne lived for 14 more years in the community. Descended from a family which had seen the birth and growth of Ville-Marie, imbued with the spirit of Mother Bourgeoys, whom she had known well, she became for the colony and her community a veritable living legend. Her death, on 21 Feb. 1746, was consequently felt as a great loss by her sisters and the population of Ville-Marie.

ANDRÉE DÉSILETS

ACND, La Congrégation de Notre-Dame: son personnel, 1653–1768; Fichier général des sœurs de la Congrégation de Notre-Dame; Plans des lieux de sépulture depuis 1681–CND; Registre des sépultures des sœurs de la Congrégation de Notre-Dame; Registre général des sœurs de la Congrégation de Notre-Dame de Montréal. Tanguay, *Dictionnaire*. Sister Saint Ignatius [Catherine Jane] Doyle, *Marguerite Bourgeoys and her congregation* (Gardenvale, Que., 1940). Lemire-Marsolais et Lambert, *Histoire de la Congrégation de Notre-Dame*. É.-Z. Massicotte, "Le Moyne de Sainte-Marie et Le Moyne de Martigny," *BRH*, XXIII (1917), 125–27.

LE NORMANT DE MÉZY, JACQUES-ANGE (he signed **Lenormant Demesi**), financial commissary (*commissaire ordonnateur*) of Île Royale; b. probably in France, son of Ange Le Normant, king's secretary and chief clerk of the king's great council, and Claude-Madeleine Gourdan; m. Anne-Marie Debrier; d. 23 Oct. 1741 in Paris, France.

Excavations for the fortifications at Louisbourg, Île Royale (Cape Breton Island), had not long been under way when Jacques-Ange Le Normant de Mézy arrived late in the summer of 1719. To this son of an important French administrative family on his first voyage across the Atlantic, the nascent New World fortress stood in stark contrast to the established might of Dunkerque where he had been financial commissary since 1701. He brought traditions from both sides of his family with him: his conflict with Governor Saint-Ovide [MONBETON], which would nearly paralyse the government of the colony in 1719 and 1720, stemmed to a great extent from the old feud between the nobility of the pen and that of the sword. It was aggravated, however, by the imbalance and overlapping jurisdictions inherent in the colonial administrative system, a system only partially implemented at Plaisance (Placentia, Nfld.) and not completely understood by Saint-Ovide.

Although the governor's position was the more prestigious, he had little real influence in routine administration outside the military sphere. Mézy, by virtue of his commission as *commissaire ordinaire* on 15 April 1718, was responsible for all regular commissariat functions: the supply of stores and material, particularly for the military and the construction of the fortress. To these duties were added, on 23 April, the powers of *ordonnateur* which were inherent in the commission of intendant but not that of *commissaire ordinaire*, and which involved control of finances, including the preparation of annual budgets, the authorization of all types of expenditure, and the payment of Marine personnel. By his commissions as subdelegate of the intendant of New France and first councillor of the Conseil Supérieur (both dated 19 June 1718), Mézy exercised the same broad authority over the administration of justice as did his theoretical superior at Quebec. He was, moreover, responsible for taking censuses of population, trade, and fishing, making all contracts for the king, and administering various royal ordinances such as those pertaining to maritime conscription (*les classes*).

To administer the numerous areas under his authority the financial commissary was assisted by several types of officials. His principal subordinates were the scriveners or writers (general, principal, and ordinary), to whom he assigned specific tasks such as the accounts of the stores of the hospital. Below them were the clerks, copyists, and the storekeeper. Two other officials, essential to the civil administration, were not directly subordinate to him. Funds sent from France were deposited with the agent of the treasurer-general of the Marine, who was responsible for payment of salaries and bills for goods authorized by the financial commissary. The treasury agent's accounts were private and he was personally responsible for them. Somewhat closer to the financial commissary, particularly at Louisbourg where he also generally held the rank of scrivener, was the controller. Responsible to both the controller-general in France and to the ministry of Marine, this official was expected to prevent the misuse of royal funds by verifying all receipts and expenditures approved by the financial commissary and by assisting at the calling of public tenders to ensure that the lowest bidder obtained the contract.

A working relationship between governor and financial commissary was possible within the administrative system at Louisbourg but was prevented by a clash of personalities. Saint-Ovide and Mézy were forceful men, jealous of their own prerogatives and lacking any spirit of compromise. Their first dispute arose in the fall of 1719 when Mézy opposed an attempt by Saint-Ovide to intervene in financial affairs; during the winter they came into conflict again over Mézy's interference in matters pertaining to military justice, properly within the jurisdiction of the council of war. At a meeting of the Conseil Supérieur on 14 March 1720 the two men openly confronted each other over which of them should preside. After a stormy session a compromise was struck whereby, pending the king's decision, the financial commissary would act as president of the chamber but the two officials would jointly sign all judgements. Mézy, however, did not let the matter rest. In subsequent months he publicly aired his views on his proper functions and openly defied the governor's authority. Angered, the council of Marine repudiated the pretensions of both men and threatened punitive measures if their quarrels continued. Although Mézy's position as president of the Conseil Supérieur was confirmed, he was reprimanded for his acts of defiance. The extreme tone of rebuke in the council's dispatches shocked both officials and thereafter their relations were more civil, but never friendly.

In the area of judicial administration Mézy exhibited the same independence. Here he was at a considerable advantage for not only were his powers as subdelegate of the intendant extensive and ill defined, but the inexperienced attorney general of the Conseil Supérieur, Antoine Sabatier, was mild-mannered and his direct subordinate in the civil administration. "He is extremely rash . . .," wrote Sabatier. "He would like to do everything; that involves him occasionally in errors and it's the very devil to get out of them." Mézy used the Conseil Supérieur to extend his own influence and that of the civil authority. As early as 1719 he urged that the representational basis of the court be broadened, with fewer military men and more representatives of commercial interests. After Saint-Ovide had secured the appointment of Joseph Lartigue to the council in 1723, Mézy recommended one of his own favourites, Pierre Carrerot*, in 1724. His request was refused, but the following year his only son, Sébastien-François-Ange*, gained a seat at the tender age of 23. Mézy's judgements, it should be noted, were not always impartial, as a case in 1724 involving the governor's friend Lartigue showed.

Le Normant

Mézy and Saint-Ovide were particularly concerned with the social and economic problems resulting from the rapid growth of Louisbourg in the 1720s. In a community with less than 2,000 inhabitants, including the garrison, the administration was not far removed from the daily concerns of its residents. Business and government were in close communication, and in their ordinances pertaining to fishing and trade the two men always favoured business over labour, and local as opposed to metropolitan interests. Particular problems arose with the fishery, the island's primary economic activity and one of the main reasons for the establishment of the colony in 1713. In 1720 Saint-Ovide and Mézy tried to stabilize credit arrangements between outfitters and suppliers by instituting written agreements, already introduced in 1718 for contracts between fishermen and employers. Partly to alleviate the severe manpower shortage, they forbad French merchants to engage crews on the island for the fall fishing. Since the sale of liquor to fishermen had become an instrument in the fierce competition among employers for labour, they made several attempts to regulate the trade in it. In order to place the local commercial community on an equal footing with merchants from France, where fish could be sold for nearly twice as much as on Île Royale, the price of cod was fixed at 12 *livres* the quintal in 1724. Further, to ensure that the resident merchants had a steady supply of fish, Saint-Ovide and Mézy decreed a first option for them on the catches which their crews received as salary. Aside from his attempts to rationalize the fishing industry, Mézy made some limited initiatives in other economic spheres, such as coal mining and the timber trade, but these efforts were without result.

The authority of the governor and the financial commissary in the area of public regulation was broad. Ordinances ranged from establishing Paris weights and measures as the standard for the colony to ordering that pigs which roamed the streets and threatened the lives of children be penned, or forbidding partridge shooting during the construction season so that soldier-workers would not wander off in search of game. Enforcement of their legislation and of royal decrees, however, was exceedingly lax. Decrees regulating both the cabarets, Louisbourg's favourite pastime, and the consumption of alcoholic beverages were issued or reissued every year from 1719 to 1722 and again in 1727 and 1728. Yet by 1726 there were 15 taverns, excluding canteens for the soldiers, for a resident population of slightly less than a thousand, a situation explained by Mézy's attitude that "soldiers and sailors must be able to drink [since] they work only for that."

More difficult to comprehend is the negligence of both Saint-Ovide and Mézy in other areas. The town grew haphazardly at first since neither official bothered to see that the zoning regulations issued in 1721 were obeyed. A new royal ordinance was issued two years later which prohibited private dwellings in designated public areas, and the governor and financial commissary were ordered to expropriate, with compensation, those settled in reserved areas. Although his house was in an ideal location near the quay, Mézy did not provide close surveillance of trade or effectively prevent smuggling. But unlike Saint-Ovide he was not directly implicated in the charges of favouritism and pecuniary interest brought against the administration in 1727 and 1728 for its tolerance of trade with the English colonies. He was reprimanded, however, for his failure to insist on the enforcement of laws which were the cornerstone of imperial trade policy and for his failure to inform the ministry of what had transpired.

Mézy felt a particular responsibility for the erection of public and social facilities. He noted that the people who lived in the colonies or came there to trade lacked the public spirit evident in France. They had been motivated to leave the mother country, he felt, by "extreme avarice [and] the disorder of their business affairs; some come here as punishment for their crimes, and all want to acquire wealth in order to return to France." In 1720, therefore, he suggested that a church, public school, and court house be constructed through taxes imposed on cod, wine, and brandy. Although only the tax on cod was levied, it was hotly contested by the local merchants and suspended in 1723 after one year of operation. Mézy also attempted to protect the interests of the crown against clerical pretensions and opposed the Recollets, who were established in the colony, on a number of occasions. He thought that secular priests would better serve the interests of church and state, but Louisbourg was considered too poor to support a secular clergy.

Mézy's greatest deficiencies as financial commissary were in precisely those areas of bookkeeping and finances which were essential to his position. In the early years of his administration he neglected to submit his records to the ministry of Marine in the prescribed manner or to send to France annual censuses of trade and fishing. Ministerial criticism forced him to improve his performance after 1724, but he never succeeded in putting the colony's financial records in order.

When he was commissioned in 1718 he had been warned to pay particular attention to this responsibility, for there had been irregularities in the accounts of one of the former storekeepers. Ignoring this sound advice, Mézy signed bills on stores and the treasury unthinkingly, prepared his accounts hastily, and did not keep accurate records. Contrary to orders, he sold provisions intended for the troops. When Philippe CARREROT resigned as storekeeper in 1724, Mézy replaced him, despite opposition from Saint-Ovide, with Carrerot's brother, ANDRÉ; he then departed from normal procedure by neglecting to make an inventory of the stores. Years later it was charged that he had concealed fraud on the part of Philippe Carrerot, an accusation to which his deviation from standard practice and the arrears in Carrerot's accounts lend credence.

His failure to organize the colony's financial accounts proved to be Mézy's undoing. In 1720 the director of fortifications, Jean-François de Verville*, accused Saint-Ovide and Mézy of misusing funds which had been earmarked for fortifications although they had not been separated from funds for regular expenses. The agent of the treasurer-general of the Marine, François-Marie de GOUTIN (described by Verville as Mézy's "weak-willed creature"), refused to show the engineer his accounts. At the same time discrepancies were discovered in France between Mézy's financial statements and those submitted by Verville. Verville's suggestion that a clerk of the treasurers-general of fortifications be appointed was rejected as a solution, but the budgets for the fortifications account and for regular expenses were thereafter kept strictly separate. To guard against further irregularities Louis LEVASSEUR was appointed controller in 1720.

Year after year, however, the ministry continued to find errors and omissions in the Louisbourg accounts. In 1724 and 1727 Mézy sent his son to France with his excuses. Finally, in 1728, his negligence and incompetence caught up with him. Having exceeded his budget he borrowed from the fortifications fund. When the engineer Étienne VERRIER came to make payments from it, the treasury agent's strongbox was found empty. Mézy admitted to some failings but tried to cover himself by blaming the treasury agent, his limited staff, and the confusion which had resulted from Verville's failure to submit annual accounts. Although Goutin was indeed later found to be over 48,000 *livres* in arrears, Maurepas, the minister of Marine, refused to accept Mézy's rationalizations. "I must tell you," he wrote in 1729, "that such an administration is inexcusable and if I had informed the king

you would be severely punished for it." Closing his accounts for 1722–28, Mézy went to France in 1729 to justify his behaviour. The following year he asked permission to resign but he returned to Louisbourg one more time before the ministry recalled him in 1731. His official date of retirement was given as 1733 and he was accorded a pension of 2,400 *livres*. Nothing is known of his life after his return to France.

Lacking the administrative ability of Jacques Prévost* de La Croix, the initiative of Pierre-Auguste de Soubras*, and the imagination of François Bigot*, Le Normant de Mézy was the least competent of Louisbourg's financial commissaries. His administration was chaotic and lacking in substantive innovation. Pugnacious and irascible, convinced that "men act only through rivalry," he not only interfered with the work of others but never effectively organized his own staff. Instead he relied on a few favourites such as the Carrerots, Levasseur, and Jacques-Philippe-Urbain RONDEAU. Over the years Mézy's son began to assume greater responsibilities and in 1729 replaced his father temporarily. The ministry realized, however, that a more thorough change was needed and on 21 Feb. 1731 it appointed Pierre de Belamy, an experienced civil administrator who was then financial commissary at La Rochelle, to replace Mézy. For unknown reasons Belamy did not come to Île Royale. It was only slowly and hesitantly that Maurepas permitted Sébastien-François-Ange Le Normant de Mézy to replace his father, the beginning of a career which would reach its summit when he was appointed deputy minister of Marine in 1758.

T. A. CROWLEY

AD, Nord (Lille), État civil, Dunkerque, 28 nov. 1702. AN, Col., B, 40–55; C[11B], 4–13; 20, ff.311–12v; C[11C], 15, ff.23, 177, 210, 212, 234; D[2C], 60, p.7; 222/2, p.117 (PAC transcripts); F[2C], 3, ff.88, 155; F[3], 59, ff.75, 86–87, 167; Marine, C[2], 55, p.6 (PAC transcript); C[7], 180 (dossier Le Normant de Mézy); Section Outre-Mer, G[1], 466, pièce 67 (recensement général de l'île Royale, 1724); G[2], 190/1, ff.55–56; 192/1, f.5; G[3], 2038/2 (1 sept. 1733); 2057 (23 mai 1721); 2058 (18 oct. 1721); Minutier central, Étude XV, pqt.377. *Select documents in Canadian economic history, 1497–1783*, ed. H. A. Innis (Toronto, 1929), 81, 88, 98–99, 104–6, 117 [The originals must be checked as the editor does not always indicate when he has not transcribed the complete document. T.A.C.]. Édouard Le Normant Des Varannes [Édouard Burton], *Généalogie de la famille Le Normant* (Orléans, France, 1853), 57–59. T. A. Crowley, "French colonial administration at Louisbourg, 1713–1744" (unpublished MA thesis, Duke University, Durham, N.C., 1970). La Morandière, *Hist. de la pêche française de la morue*, II, 659–60, 671, 673–74. McLennan, *Louisbourg*, 45, 50, 54, 59, 78–80, 87, 92.

Lepage

LEPAGE DE SAINTE-CLAIRE, LOUIS, priest, canon, seigneur; b. 22 Aug. 1690 at Saint-François, Île d'Orléans, son of René Lepage de Sainte-Claire, the first seigneur of Rimouski, and Marie-Madeleine Gagnon; d. 3 Dec. 1762 at Terrebonne (Que.).

Louis Lepage de Sainte-Claire belonged to a family that had been in New France since 1663. He entered the seminary of Quebec, and on 8 Oct. 1713 he received the minor orders from Bishop Saint-Vallier [La Croix*]. On 6 April 1715 he was ordained a priest in the cathedral of Quebec. As soon as he had been ordained, he was appointed priest of the parish of Saint-François-de-Sales on Île Jésus. Some years after his installation he bought some pieces of land, and in January 1719 he obtained his first land grant from the seminary of Quebec, the owner of Île Jésus; he acquired other properties in February and March 1720. In addition, he had a project for developing the immense domains situated on the other side of the Rivière des Mille-Îles. Indeed, the seigneury of Terrebonne, which had been first granted in 1673, had scarcely been developed. The successive owners, André Daulier Deslandes, Louis Le Conte* Dupré, and François-Marie Bouat*, had settled only a small number of *censitaires*, and no banal mill or seigneurial manor had been built. On 2 Sept. 1720, following financial reverses, Bouat made the seigneury of Terrebonne over to Lepage for the sum of 10,000 *livres*, while keeping the mortgage on the lands. The seigneury then consisted of a territory of two leagues by two.

Lepage de Sainte-Claire, who had been named a canon of the chapter on 9 June 1721, received permission from his bishop to reside on his domain. He began making land grants in 1723 and in a single day signed 24 contracts. The recognition of sovereignty and the census of his seigneury in 1736 show that the number of *censitaires* had reached 81. Even though the authorities of the colony forbad its establishment, Lepage de Sainte-Claire created a proper village on the Rivière des Mille-Îles. On his domain he had built a stone church, a presbytery which served as the seigneurial dwelling, four flour mills, and a sawmill. According to Intendant Hocquart*, such industry was unparalleled in the colony.

The development of his seigneury had, however, left him scarcely any time to carry out his duties as a canon. He was not the only one in this situation, and in a letter to Maurepas on 19 Oct. 1728 Canon Charles PLANTE complained of the canons' negligence in attending services and mentioned particularly "M. Louis Lepage [who] has his land and mills to develop." When asked by Bishop Dosquet* to comply with the residence requirement, Lepage de Sainte-Claire resigned in 1729.

In 1731 the seigneur of Terrebonne obtained a grant of a piece of land two leagues deep adjoining his seigneury, in order to increase the reserves of wood he needed. That same year he contracted to supply ship yards in the colony and the mother country with pine and oak boards and planking, and to obtain more raw materials he worked oak stands in the seigneuries of Berthier-en-Haut and Dautré. On 20 Oct. 1730 Lepage de Sainte-Claire had sent the minister a long report in which he emphasized that the difficulties "in succeeding in the different undertakings ... simply come from the scarcity of money and men." To cope with these two difficulties he proposed that a greater number of ships be built, which "would cause an influx of money into the colony" and "would promote competition." His argument was not, however, considered.

At this period Lepage de Sainte-Claire, whose health was delicate, was constantly contending with financial worries. He wanted to retrieve his position, and 12 July 1738 he signed a deed of partnership with the d'Ailleboust brothers of Montreal for the establishment of ironworks on his seigneury. But he had overlooked an essential step, obtaining the king's permission, and despite Canon Pierre Hazeur* de L'Orme's support he received a royal order not to go ahead with the project. The king was afraid that this new enterprise might injure the Saint-Maurice ironworks, which at that time were in great financial difficulties. Lepage de Sainte-Claire was in an awkward position, as his partners had on 29 Sept. 1739 obtained annulment of the contract. Lepage was consequently under the obligation of repaying the sums advanced by his partners and of handing over to them possession of his sawmill for eight years. He again tried, but without success, to interest the authorities in his enterprise. In a final attempt he asked permission to operate the Saint-Maurice ironworks, which were in a bad way, but when he could not put up guarantees his proposal was rejected.

As his financial situation did not improve he sold his seigneury on 15 Jan. 1745 to Louis de La Corne, known as La Corne *l'aîné*, for 60,000 *livres*, to which was added an annual payment of 1,000 *livres* that was to cease at his death. The statement of his debts attached to the bill of sale showed the sum of 55,268 *livres*; according to contemporary estimates the seigneury was worth at least 150,000 *livres*. In a final effort in 1749 Abbé Lepage built a sawmill on the Rivière des Mille-Îles, but the business rapidly declined.

The following year he retired to the presbytery of Saint-Louis-de-Terrebonne, where he died on 3 Dec. 1762 at 72 years of age. Like many other builders who could rely only upon themselves, Lepage de Sainte-Claire ran several enterprises without worrying too much about the debts he might contract. His activities on his seigneury and the running of his numerous enterprises did not prevent him from exercising his ministry in his seigneury and neighbouring parishes that were without a priest. He had also been titular parish priest or the serving priest at Saint-François-de-Sales, Lachenaie, and Sainte-Rose, Île Jésus. The numerous gifts he made to these different churches still bear witness to his devotion and activity.

AIMÉ DESPATIE

AAQ, 12 A, Registres d'insinuations B, 245, 246; Registres d'insinuations C, 7; 11 B, Correspondance, II, 150; 1 W, Église du Canada, I, 69–75. AJQ, Registre d'état civil, Saint-François, île d'Orléans, 22 août 1690. AN, Col., C¹¹ᴬ, 53, pp.116–23; 57, pp.123–28; 58, pp.52f; 74, pp.27–31; E, 278 (dossier Lepage) (PAC transcripts). ANQ, Greffe de Pierre Duquet, 26 oct. 1681; NF, Aveux et dénombrements; NF, Ord. int., I, 115. ANQ-M, Greffe de C.-F. Coron, 10 juill. 1749; Greffe de L.-C. Danré de Blanzy, 15 janv. 1745; Greffe de Pierre Raimbault, 1ᵉʳ oct. 1718, 2 sept. 1720; Greffe de Nicolas Senet, 24 janv. 1719, 24 avril 1723, 26 mars 1730, 12 juill. 1738. PAC, MG 8, A7, 5; MG 24, L3, 7, 37, 44. "Procès-verbaux du procureur général Collet" (Caron), APQ Rapport, 1921–22, 291, 369.

LEPAILLEUR DE LAFERTÉ, CATHERINE.
See JÉRÉMIE, *dit* Lamontagne

LE PRÉVOST, PIERRE-GABRIEL, parish priest; b. *c.* 1674; buried 18 Nov. 1756 at Sainte-Foy.

Pierre-Gabriel Le Prévost's origins are obscure. According to Cyprien Tanguay* he may have been the son of Jacques Le Prévost and Jeanne Fauvault, whose marriage took place on 25 Nov. 1669 in the church of Notre-Dame de Québec. Yet the couple, of whom there is no record after this date, do not seem to have had any children, at least in the colony. Le Prévost's certificates for the tonsure and priesthood tell us nothing about his origins. His year of birth can, however, be set around 1674, as his burial certificate mentions that he died at 82 years of age.

Le Prévost was ordained a priest in the cathedral of Quebec on 7 Oct. 1714, 13 years after receiving the tonsure. On 13 Jan. 1715 he was appointed parish priest of Notre-Dame-de-Foy de Sainte-Foy. A few weeks later, on 5 February, Le Prévost took possession officially of this parish; he had already been tending it for some time, having entered certificates in the parish registry since 28 Sept. 1714, when he was only a deacon. On 8 Nov. 1756, after a ministry of more than 41 years, he entered his last certificate in the registry as priest of this parish. He died soon after, leaving a will dated 15 Nov. 1756 which he was unable to sign having been overwhelmed by great weakness. He was buried on 18 November 1756 in the old church of Sainte-Foy.

Despite the lack of information about his life and career, Pierre-Gabriel Le Prévost has attracted the attention of several researchers, who thought that in him they recognized the author of a statue of Notre-Dame de Foy, preserved today in the church of the parent parish of Sainte-Foy. This supposition rests upon too fragile a base not to raise certain doubts. It would indeed be risky to translate without reservation the inscription on the statue, "L.P.S. 1716" by "Le Prévost Sculpsit 1716." This inscription has been the source of hypotheses, for the most part impossible to verify, concerning the alleged artistic training of the parish priest of Sainte-Foy. The experts are in agreement in recognizing that the author of the statue found his inspiration in the wood-carving techniques characteristic of Canadian art, and certain investigators have deduced further that Le Prévost had learned his craft from the teachers at the École des Arts et Métiers at Saint-Joachim, but no document justifies this assertion.

In short, nothing allows us to assert that Le Prévost was really an artist. Perhaps we shall never know who carved the little statue of Notre-Dame de Foy, but this work is no less important for the study of Canadian art at the beginning of the 18th century.

IN COLLABORATION WITH MICHEL CAUCHON
AND ANDRÉ JUNEAU

AAQ, 12 A, Registres d'insinuations A, 809. AJQ, Registre d'état civil, Notre-Dame de Québec, 25 nov. 1669. ANQ, Greffe de P.-A.-F. Lanoullier Des Granges, 15 nov. 1756; Greffe de J.-N. Pinguet de Vaucour, 7 juin 1734, 8 janv. 1747; AP, Pierre-Gabriel Le Prévost. Archives paroissiales de Notre-Dame-de-Foy (Sainte-Foy, Qué.), Registres des baptêmes, mariages et sépultures, 28 sept. 1714, 8, 18 nov. 1756. ASQ, Polygraphie, XXIII, 53g; XLVI, 9ᵉ; Séminaire, XCII, 22A, p.1f. IOA, Dossier Pierre-Gabriel Le Prévost, sculpteur.

"Procès-verbaux du procureur général Collet" (Caron), APQ Rapport, 1921–22, 264–66. Caron, "Inventaire de documents," APQ Rapport, 1940–41, 346, 407, 445, 446; 1941–42, 188, 251. P.-G. Roy, Inv. ord. int., II, 10; Inv. testaments, II, 57–58. Tanguay, Dictionnaire; Répertoire. Marius Barbeau, J'ai vu Québec (Québec, 1957). Amédée Gosselin, L'instruction au

Le Prévost Duquesnel

Canada. Morisset, *Coup d'œil sur les arts.* Antoine Roy, *Les lettres, les sciences et les arts au Canada sous le régime français* (Paris, 1930), 230. H.-A. Scott, "Notre-Dame de Sainte-Foy," *BRH*, VI (1900), 67–75.

LE PRÉVOST DUQUESNEL (Du Quesnel), JEAN-BAPTISTE-LOUIS, naval officer, fourth commander of Île Royale; b. probably in the mid-1680s; m. in Martinique in the 1730s Marguerite Girault Du Poyet, by whom he had two daughters and a son; d. 9 Oct. 1744 in Louisbourg, Île Royale (Cape Breton Island).

Jean-Baptiste-Louis Le Prévost Duquesnel was a career naval officer who served on the French flagship in the battle of Málaga off southern Spain in 1704. He was severely wounded in the fighting and lost his left leg. From 1708 he was a fire-ship captain (a rank equal to that of a lieutenant-commander) and had charge of a series of small vessels. In 1731 he was promoted naval captain. Six years later, after serving as second on the *Achille* in northern European waters, he received his first full command as captain of the *Jason*, which was sent to carry supplies to Quebec and to guard fishing vessels on the Grand Banks. On 1 Sept. 1740 he was appointed commandant of Île Royale. He enjoyed all the rights of governor but, perhaps because he was not in line for such high office, he was not given the title.

Duquesnel was delighted with his promotion and hastily secured an advance of 5,000 *livres* to prepare himself for life in Louisbourg. But his enthusiasm soon waned; within a year he had applied for a transfer to the first vacant governorship. An inspection of the town after he landed on 3 Nov. 1740 revealed an understaffed and under-equipped garrison, further weakened by indiscipline and drunkenness. With regard to the officers, Duquesnel faced much the same problem as his predecessor, Isaac-Louis de Forant*. Over the years they had established an independence which the new governor considered inconsistent with the welfare of the colony. Although he realized that their salaries were inadequate, he felt that personal interests should not work to the detriment of the garrison, and he therefore sought to limit their exploitation of their troops. His chief endeavour was his attempt to suppress the officers' canteens through which soldiers frequently became considerably indebted to their superiors; however, he allowed officers to supply their soldiers with wine on non-working days. Problems of a different kind arose with the commander of the Swiss troops in Louisbourg, François-Joseph CAILLY, whose vigorous defence of the rights and privileges of his men led to charges of insubordination. Duquesnel accused him of fostering an atmosphere of revolt and eventually Cailly was forced to retire. Later, persuaded by the pleas of Cailly's wife, Duquesnel was instrumental in having the Swiss commander reinstated.

Although Duquesnel found the fortifications generally to be in a good state on his arrival, he was not entirely satisfied with them. The alterations he effected to the Princess demi-bastion and the Royal battery, however, were not only expensive and unnecessary, but left unfinished; his proposals to neutralize the high ground outside the walls of the fortress were, on the other hand, never approved because of cost. Duquesnel also faced serious problems in supplying the garrison; there were constant shortages of food, especially during the winter of 1742. But the financial commissary, François Bigot*, was an able administrator and Duquesnel worked well with him. Such cooperation between Louisbourg officials was rare.

Duquesnel's instructions had charged him specifically with ensuring the colony's safety in anticipation of war with England, but he was also urged not to neglect the offensive. He consulted the plans made by his predecessors for attacks on Annapolis Royal, Nova Scotia, and Placentia, Newfoundland, and, when war was declared on 18 March 1744, he immediately launched an offensive, although he had complained annually of a lack of troops and artillery. The first objective was the small English fort on Canso Island (Grassy Island, N.S.) which, after a negligible resistance, was surrendered by its commander Patrick HERON to Joseph DU PONT Duvivier on 24 May 1744. Emboldened by this victory Duquesnel moved against the more substantial garrison at Annapolis Royal. Ignoring his earlier reservations about sending out just such an expedition without aid from France, he dispatched in mid-July a company of 50 men, also under Duvivier. He hoped that ships expected from France would be able to support the attack, but when the *Ardent* docked a month later, her captain, Jérémie de Meschin*, was reluctant to venture into unknown waters late in the season. About the same time Duquesnel received instructions from France stating that it was too late in the year for an attack and requesting that plans be submitted before any initiative was taken. Encouraged by his earlier success, however, Duquesnel ignored these instructions and attempted to arm two private ships for the expedition. He died before they could be made ready. Even though they were eventually sent, the expedition failed.

Virtually all opinion of Duquesnel is influenced by the anonymous author of the *Lettre d'un habitant* who accused him of having a violent temper, of harbouring all forms of excess, of alienating officers from their soldiers, and of being largely responsible for the capture of Louisbourg in 1745 by provoking the English. His bad temper can be explained by his physical condition. When his body was exhumed from the chapel of the Louisbourg barracks in 1964, an autopsy revealed that in addition to his leg wounds Duquesnel suffered from severe dental problems, arthritis, and extensive arteriosclerosis. His confrontation with the officers probably contributed to any difficulties they had with their troops, but his opposition to them was well founded. In attacking the English he was simply, if not prudently, following his original orders. The author of the *Lettre* also claimed that Duquesnel had been ruined financially and sent to Louisbourg to re-establish his fortune. Although the inventory of Duquesnel's effects revealed many debts, it also brought to light a number of commercial interests, including shares in at least two ships. He was, in fact, able to leave his family over 13,000 *livres*. It may well be, however, that his commercial interests were acquired during his visits to Quebec in the mid-1730s.

Duquesnel showed little imagination in his administration but he used a firm hand; he would almost certainly have prevented the mutiny which occurred two months after his death and his determination might have served the colony better during the siege of the following year than the indecisiveness of the acting governor, Louis Du Pont* Duchambon.

BLAINE ADAMS

AN, Col., B, 70–78; C¹¹B, 22–27; Marine, C⁷, 50, 181; Section Outre-Mer, G¹, 407/2, f.42; G², 199, dossier 189; Dépôt des fortifications des colonies, Am. sept., nos.209, 210. Archives Maritimes, Port de Rochefort, 1E, 133–39. *Louisbourg in 1745* (Wrong). Le Jeune, *Dictionnaire*, I, 563. Frégault, *François Bigot*, I, 103–57. McLennan, *Louisbourg*, 98–127. Parkman, *Half-century of conflict* (1922), II, 59–64. Rawlyk, *Yankees at Louisbourg*, 1–15.

LÉRY, GASPARD-JOSEPH CHAUSSEGROS DE. *See* CHAUSSEGROS

LESTAGE, PIERRE DE (in the early years of the 18th century he referred to himself as **Pierre de Lestage Desperoux** or **Despeiroux**), merchant, seigneur, militia officer; b. 8 Feb. 1682 in Notre-Dame de Bayonne, son of Jean de Lestage, merchant, and Saubade de Noliboise; m. on 5 Jan. 1712 at Montreal Esther Sayward (Sayer); none of their children lived to adulthood; buried 22 Dec. 1743 in Montreal.

When Pierre de Lestage and his brother Jean immigrated to Canada, Jean established himself as a merchant at Quebec and Pierre proceeded to Montreal, where he became chiefly concerned with the outfitting of fur-traders. Both men signed the agreement of October 1700 founding the Compagnie de la Colonie, which for six years controlled the Canadian fur trade. A Monsieur de Lestage served as secretary to the company, but this was almost certainly Jean, who had subscribed a capital of 1,200 *livres*, and not Pierre, subscribed for a modest 560 *livres* and listed in a cryptic reference of 1708 as having "abandoned the country."

Whatever his whereabouts in that year, his participation in the Montreal fur trade from 1709 to 1743 is proven by the compilations of fur trade indentures and licences (*congés*). These records, however, cite Lestage's name for only 25 of the more than 40 years that he participated in the trade. The lacunae probably, but not certainly, result more from the loss of notarial documents and from the use of promissory notes under private signature than from a discontinuous pattern of investment.

A substantial number of the documents calendared under the heading of "Engagements" (indentures) are not the contracts of voyageurs, but obligations of record by which traders whom Lestage had financed pledge to him as security the product of their year's trade. These reveal the size of Lestage's investment for certain years, and it is frequently considerable: for example, 25,066 *livres* in 1718 and 33,247 *livres* in 1726.

After the collapse of the Compagnie de la Colonie, two of Lestage's acquaintances in the Montreal merchant community, Antoine* and Marguerite Pascaud, transferred the seat of their business to France, at La Rochelle; as metropolitan exporters they were now at the most powerful position in the structure of colonial trade. In order to assure themselves of good trade connections with Canada, on 29 June 1710 the Pascauds formed a partnership with Lestage and Jean-François Martin* de Lino. By such trans-Atlantic arrangements the complementary flows of furs and trade goods were most efficiently maintained. In 1713 Martin de Lino left the company. But it was not until 1739, long after the death of Antoine Pascaud, that Lestage and Marguerite Pascaud dissolved their partnership, Lestage agreeing to pay 15,000 *livres* for their Canadian assets.

Lestage did not confine himself to legitimate

Le Sueur

channels of trade. His furs passed up the Richelieu as well as down the St Lawrence, and there is extant a receipt to him for 443 pounds of beaver, dated 22 Sept. 1717 and signed by Stephen DeLancey of New York.

The fur trade did not account for all of Lestage's business. He was a purveyor of general merchandise; there is record of his buying up large quantities of flour locally, probably for resale in the colony; and on one occasion he lent money for the building and outfitting of a ship. For an unspecified number of years after 1710 Lestage also acted as agent for the treasurer of the Marine, having the care of the treasurer's money in Montreal and paying the troops stationed there. This arrangement was in some way related to his partnership with the Pascauds, who posted bond for him; it would seem that the arrangement was profitable to their company. They may have enjoyed interest-free use of the Marine fund.

The security and prestige of landed wealth exercised no less attraction on Pierre de Lestage than on any other aspiring bourgeois of the 18th-century Atlantic world. On 26 April 1718 he purchased from Nicolas Blaise* Des Bergères de Rigauville the seigneury of Berthier-en-Haut for 6,000 *livres*. He intended this to be a profitable investment. In 1721 he explained that, "having already spent much to provide his habitants with needed sawmills and grist mills," the addition of a church would suffice to attract a full complement of settlers to his lands. Whatever meaning may be imputed to this typical diversion of commercial capital to land, it did not represent any dampening of the acquisitive instinct or abandonment of business principles. In this regard it is significant that until his death in 1743 Lestage remained active in the fur trade and continued to live in Montreal. There he owned two stone houses, two urban lots, and two small farms.

Mme de Lestage was New England born, but when only seven had been captured by Abenakis with her mother and her sister Mary Sayward* and ransomed in Canada. Three years after her husband's death, she formed a business partnership with her nephew, Pierre-Noel Courthiau, but this was dissolved in 1750. At a later date she became a boarder at the Congregation of Notre-Dame, where she had been raised as a child. She died there in 1770 at the age of 86. Courthiau left Montreal after the conquest, settling at Bayonne in France, the home of Pierre de Lestage's sister and only heir, Marie. It was from this town that Pierre and Jean had set out in search of fortune in the last years of the 17th century.

DALE MIQUELON

[AN, Col., C¹¹ᴬ, 125, pp.365–70 (PAC transcripts). ANQ, Greffe de Nicolas Boisseau, 22 oct. 1741; Greffe de Louis Chambalon, 9 nov. 1708, 24 oct. 1710, 14, 18 nov. 1713; Greffe de J.-É. Dubreuil, 24 oct. 1729; Greffe de C.-H. Du Laurent, 13 nov. 1742, 10 juill. 1747; Greffe de Jean de Latour, 28 oct. 1739; AP, Pierre de Lestage, 1717. Bibliothèque municipale de Bayonne, France, État civil, Notre-Dame de Bayonne, 8 févr. 1682. PAC, MG 24, L3, pp.19740–62.

"Correspondance de Mme Bégon" (Bonnault), APQ *Rapport, 1934–35*, 37, 42. *Documents relating to Canadian currency during the French period* (Shortt), I, 452. (Shortt incorrectly identifies Lestage as a notary on the grounds that he frequently represented persons before the courts. In this he confuses Pierre with his brother Jean de Lestage, who in his capacity as Quebec businessman, and not as a notary, frequently represented Montreal businessmen in suits. The ordinance signed "Lestage" and published by Shortt, was probably signed by Jean in his capacity as king's writer. *See also*: Philéas Gagnon, "Noms propres au Canada-français," *BRH*, XV (1909), 47, and P.-V. Charland, "Notre-Dame de Québec: le nécrologe de la crypte," *BRH*, XX (1914), 180.)

Édits ord., I, 280–84; II, 581–83. *L'île de Montréal en 1731* (A. Roy). *Jug. et délib*. Bonnault, "Le Canada militaire," APQ *Rapport, 1949–51*. "Marguilliers de la paroisse de Notre-Dame de Ville-Marie de 1657 à 1913," *BRH*, XIX (1913), 278. É.-Z. Massicotte, "Congés et permis déposés ou enregistrés à Montréal sous le régime français," APQ *Rapport, 1921–22*, 189–225; "Inventaire des documents concernant les frères Charon," APQ *Rapport, 1923–24*, 164–92; "Répertoire des engagements pour l'Ouest," APQ *Rapport, 1929–30*, 191–466. P.-G. Roy, "Congés de traite conservés aux Archives de la province de Québec," APQ *Rapport, 1922–23*, 192–265; *Inv. concessions*; *Inv. jug. et délib., 1717–1760*; *Inv. ord. int.*; "Les ordonnances et lettres de change du gouvernement de Montréal en 1759," APQ *Rapport, 1924–25*, 229–359. Tanguay, *Dictionnaire*, I, 174; III, 314; V, 373. (Tanguay attributes to the Lestages one son who lived to adulthood, identifies him with a Pierre de Lestage of La Prairie who married Marie-Madeleine Rivet in 1737, and gives this latter Lestage the title of seigneur de Berthier. In all three instances he is in error. Lestage of La Prairie was probably a simple cultivator and appears frequently as an *engagé* in the lists of indentures and fur-trading licences drawn up by Massicotte and P.-G. Roy.) Frégault, *Le XVIIIᵉ siècle canadien*. Lemire-Marsolais et Lambert, *Histoire de la Congrégation de Notre-Dame*, III, 274–77; V, 73–75. D.M.]

LE SUEUR, JACQUES-FRANÇOIS, priest, Jesuit, missionary; b. 22 July 1685 or 24 Aug. 1686, probably in the diocese of Coutances, France; d. 28 April 1760 in Montreal.

Jacques-François Le Sueur entered the Society of Jesus in Paris on 7 Sept. 1705. After his noviciate, completed in 1707, he taught until 1713, and then completed his philosophy and did two years of theology. He was ordained a priest in 1716 and sailed for Canada, bound for the Illinois country and from there to the Arkansas country. But he stayed in New France, "having learned at Quebec that difficulties had arisen concerning the setting-up of an establishment."

After studying the Abenaki language for some months he was put in charge of the Saint-François-Xavier mission, near Bécancour. In 1721 Father Le Sueur received a visit from his fellow Jesuit, Father CHARLEVOIX. He confided to the historian that his flock no longer had its original fervour and that he was often reduced to bemoaning before God the disorders caused by the spirits brought in by whites. While he ministered among the Abenakis, Le Sueur served as priest for the seigneury of Bécancour from 1718 to 1725 and from 1749 to 1753, "although he was not obliged to do so"; he also brought divine service to the parishioners of Sainte-Geneviève, in the seigneury of Batiscan, from 1727 to 1732 and from 1740 to 1741. Between times he called upon the Abenakis of the mission at Narantsouak (Norridgewock, now Old Point, Madison, Me.). Around 1734 he spent some time at the Abenaki mission of Saint-François-de-Sales (Odanak, Que.), according to the information contained in his short treatise, "Histoire du calumet et de la dance." In this little work the missionary told of the attempts made to introduce among the Abenakis a dance that was practised by the Foxes and nearly all the Indian tribes of the *pays d'en haut*. He wondered whether he could honestly allow this idolatrous worship, since this dance was accompanied by a song the words of which constituted an invocation to the guardian spirit to keep away all sorts of evils and bestow all sorts of benefits.

In 1742 he was at the Jesuits' residence in Montreal, serving as prefect of the congregation; in 1749 he held the office of missionary there. In 1756 he was again at the college in Quebec, where he held the post of confessor to the Indians and the religious of the community; it would appear that he had been living there since 1755. In July 1759, like many others, he left this besieged city to go to Montreal, where he died 28 April 1760.

THOMAS-M. CHARLAND

[J.-F. Le Sueur's manuscript, which also contains sermons and instructions in Abenaki, is preserved in the Museum of the American Indian (New York) and was published in French under its original title, "Histoire du calumet et de la dance," in *Les soirées canadiennes, recueil de littérature nationale* (Québec), [IV] (1864), 114–35, and in English in a translation by R. P. Breaden under the title *History of the calumet and of the dance*

(Contributions from the Museum of the American Indian, 12, no.5, New York, 1952). J.-A. Maurault in *Histoire des Abénakis depuis 1605 jusqu'à nos jours* (Sorel, Qué., 1866), 503–4, and others after him, such as J. C. Pilling, *Bibliography of Algonquian languages* (Washington, 1891), have incorrectly attributed to Le Sueur a dictionary of the roots of the Abenaki language. Charles Gill, in *Notes sur de vieux manuscrits abénakis* (Montréal, 1886), 16–19, has proven that Joseph AUBERY was the author of this dictionary. The ASQ, MSS, 71-a-1, contain Father Le Sueur's "Catechismus prolixus de Baptismo et dissertatio christiana de justificatione ... apud Uanbanakaeos Nanransuakos," 1730. T.-M.C.]

AN, Col., B, 47, f.1206. Charlevoix, *Histoire de la N.-F.* (1744), III, 111–12. *JR* (Thwaites). Fernand Ouellet, "Inventaire de la Saberdache de Jacques Viger," APQ *Rapport, 1955–57*, 78. É.-Z. Massicotte, *Sainte-Geneviève de Batiscan* (Pages trifluviennes, sér. A, 18, Trois-Rivières, Qué., 1936). Honorius Provost, *Les Abénakis sur la Chaudière* (Saint-Joseph-de-Beauce, Qué., 1948), 13–14. Rochemonteix, *Les Jésuites et la N.-F. au XVIIᵉ siècle*, III, 397–99; *Les Jésuites et la N.-F. au XVIIIᵉ siècle*, I, 263. Olivier Maurault, "1742," *Cahiers des Dix*, VII (1942), 171.

LE SUEUR, PIERRE, priest, Sulpician, founder of the town of L'Assomption (Que.); b. 28 Feb. 1684 at Saint-Éloi(?), diocese of Amiens, France; d. 12 May 1752 in Montreal.

After philosophical and theological studies at the Sulpician Grand Seminary in Le Puy, France, Pierre Le Sueur was ordained a priest on 15 March 1710 and in July sailed for Canada. He arrived in Montreal on 8 October. He spent his whole life in the parochial ministry. He was first curate for three years in Notre-Dame de Montréal parish, then for two years he was parish priest of Saint-Joachim-de-la-Pointe-Claire on Montreal Island. In 1715 he became the first parish priest in residence at Saint-Sulpice, at the time the only parish in the seigneury of that name.

In these years colonization of this territory was still in its early stages. This seigneury had been granted in 1640 to Pierre Chevrier, Baron de Fancamp, and Jérôme Le Royer de La Dauversière; in 1663 it was given to the Sulpician seminary in Paris along with the seigneury of Montreal Island. Lack of monetary and human resources and wars had delayed its development, to such a degree that at the time of Pierre Le Sueur's arrival land grants scarcely extended beyond the *côte* Saint-Sulpice on the shore of the St Lawrence.

As the sole representative of the Sulpicians, seigneurs of the region, Le Sueur thought he should explore the seigneury completely, following the waterways. Upon seeing a certain portage situated on the Rivière L'Assomption upstream

Levasseur

from Repentigny, he had the idea of establishing a centre for colonization there. He sketched out the first plan for it, which included king's road, seigneurial domain, land grants, church, and presbytery. He even began to clear the land that he had reserved for the future chapel. The clearing took place in January 1717, and the settlers began to arrive the following spring. Thomas Goulet and his sons were the first to receive land grants, after a verbal agreement with the seigneurs' representative. In 1723 there were about 20 families, and according to Le Sueur that was enough to justify the building of a chapel. The following year the centre for colonization was raised to a parish, and Pierre Le Sueur became its first pastor. So, on this Sulpician's initiative, the present town of L'Assomption – for a long time called Saint-Pierre-du-Portage – was born. Le Sueur remained as parish priest for 18 years, becoming identified with his parishioners and participating in their labours and privations. He distinguished himself by his humility, his austerity, and the simplicity of his life.

In 1742, worn out with fatigue, he had to retire to the seminary of Montreal. Moved by the wretched state in which the Nuns Hospitallers of the Hôtel-Dieu of Montreal were living, and wishing to help them reconstruct the hospital and particularly the chapel [see Anne-Françoise LEDUC, dite Saint-Joseph], Pierre Le Sueur made them a gift of 2,000 livres from his savings. He died at the seminary of Montreal on 12 May 1752.

ANTONIO DANSEREAU

ASSM, Section des biographies. Allaire, Dictionnaire. Gauthier, Sulpitiana. Mondoux, L'Hôtel-Dieu de Montréal. Christian Roy, Histoire de L'Assomption (L'Assomption, Qué., 1967).

LEVASSEUR, LOUIS, scrivener, lieutenant general of the admiralty court of Île Royale; b. 27 Dec. 1671 at L'Ange-Gardien (Que.), son of Louis Levasseur and Marguerite Bélanger; m. 6 Jan. 1736 at Louisbourg, Île Royale (Cape Breton Island), Marie-Anne, daughter of Jean-François Lorant and Marie-Suzanne de La Bazanière, by whom he had three daughters; d. 3 June 1748 at Saint-Malo, France.

Born into the bourgeoisie, Louis Levasseur early served as secretary to Intendant Jean Bochart* de Champigny at Quebec. He later moved to Marseilles, France, where in 1695 he was appointed scrivener. At the request of the financial commissary Pierre-Auguste de Soubras* he came to Île Royale as scrivener in 1716;

he was made responsible for daily accounts and stores and was appointed clerk to the financial commissary. His advancement at Louisbourg was in large part a result of the protection of Soubras and of his successor, Jacques-Ange LE NORMANT de Mézy, with whom Levasseur lodged in the 1720s.

In 1718 Levasseur was appointed lieutenant general of the admiralty court at Louisbourg. As the chief official and judge of this court he was responsible for a wide variety of administrative and judicial matters pertaining to maritime commerce. His regulation of such actions as smuggling was lax, but one of his reports on this subject contributed to the replacement of the governor, Saint-Ovide [MONBETON], in 1739. Although he had no legal training, Levasseur appears to have been a competent and impartial judge.

A suggestion in 1719 that Levasseur be appointed clerk of the Conseil Supérieur was vetoed by the ministry of Marine, but in 1720 the function of controller was added to his regular duties. The ministry's decision to appoint an inspector of finances was the result of the misuse of funds earmarked for the fortifications at Louisbourg [see Le Normant de Mézy]. Levasseur was made responsible for certifying treasury receipts, verifying expenditures authorized by the financial commissary, preparing quarterly accounts of both, and assisting at the calling of official tenders. Saint-Ovide, who had originally been jointly responsible with the financial commissary for signing accounts and whose duties were therefore restricted by the appointment, complained to the ministry about the number of positions Levasseur held. He claimed that "the public is strongly ill-disposed towards the Controller . . . and he suits neither the interests of the king nor those of the country." As a result Levasseur was replaced by Antoine SABATIER in 1723, but he continued to act as scrivener until 1730. Mézy appointed him his judicial subdelegate during his absence in France in 1723.

From his position as lieutenant general Levasseur earned approximately 4,000 livres annually, augmented by the pension of 300 livres granted him in 1734. He supplemented his income by the sale of cod in partnership with his wife's stepfather, Claude-Joseph Le Roy* Desmarest, and one Morel, a Louisbourg merchant. He also rented his house on the Rue d'Orléans to Desmarest and built an addition to it where he himself lived in the 1730s.

Levasseur remained lieutenant general of the Admiralty court until 1745 when Louisbourg was captured by Anglo-American troops under William PEPPERRELL. He returned to France, probably that year, but nothing is known of his activities there. He died at Saint-Malo on 3 June 1748.

T. A. CROWLEY

[I should like to thank M. Adrien Levasseur of Longueuil, Que., for providing the date and place of Levasseur's birth. T.A.C.]
AD, Charente-Maritime (La Rochelle), B, 6110, ff.8, 13, 32, 42. AN, Col., B, 38, f.196; 54, f.509; C¹¹ᴮ, 1–25, especially 1, f.176; 4, f.133; 5, ff.224, 235, 407; 10, f.253; 14, f.368; 17, f.337; 18, f.343; 19, ff.276, 285; 20, ff.321, 330; C¹¹ᶜ, 15, ff.15, 23, 177; C¹¹ᴳ, 12, f.116; E, 238 (dossier Jean Delaborde); F³, 50, f.245; Marine, C², 55, f.28; C⁷, 184 (dossier Louis Levasseur); Section Outre-Mer, G¹, 407/1–2; G², 192/1, f.13v; 208, dossier 479; G³, 2041/2 (5 janv. 1736). J.-M. Pardessus, *Collection de lois maritimes antérieures au XVIIIᵉ siècle* (6v., Paris, 1828–45; repr. Torino, Italy, 1968). Tanguay, *Dictionnaire*, V, 390 [Tanguay's identification of Levasseur's wife as Marie-Anne Desmarest is inexact since she issued from her mother's first marriage and not the second to Claude-Joseph Le Roy Desmarest. T.A.C.]. Jacques de Chastenet d'Esterre, *Histoire de l'amirauté en France* (Paris, 1906).

LEVASSEUR, PIERRE-NOËL, wood-carver, surveyor; b. 28 Nov. 1690 at Quebec, son of Pierre Levasseur, a master carpenter, and Madeleine Chapeau; d. 12 Aug. 1770 at Quebec.

Pierre-Noël Levasseur belonged to the great family of craftsmen in wood which left its particular stamp on artistic production in Canada in the 18th century. Two great lines, descended from the brothers Jean* and Pierre Levasseur*, constituted this dynasty. Pierre-Noël Levasseur, a grandson of Pierre, was one of its principal representatives. On the other side, Jean Levasseur's descendants included famous people such as Noël Levasseur* and his two sons, François-Noël Levasseur* and Jean-Baptiste-Antoine Levasseur*, *dit* Delort.

No apprentice's diploma in the name of Pierre-Noël Levasseur has been discovered. He probably learned the basic elements of his craft working either with his father or with Noël, a distant cousin, who was already a master-carver in Quebec when Pierre-Noël reached the age of apprenticeship. On the other hand towards 1705 the École des Arts et Métiers at Saint-Joachim was enjoying a profitable period under the administration of Abbé Louis Soumande*. It is therefore possible that Pierre-Noël received some instruction at that school.

Several parish archives furnish information about this wood-carver's career. The references, however, too often are concerned with pieces of work that have been destroyed or misplaced, and it is difficult to get an over-all picture of Levasseur's production. In 1723 he was living in the Montreal region – on 3 March of that year he had his son Charles baptized in the church of L'Enfant-Jésus-de-Pointe-aux-Trembles. In addition, the account books of the church of Sainte-Famille-de-Boucherville permit us to date Levasseur's earliest piece of work from 1723: on 18 July he signed a contract before the notary Marien Tailhandier* to make a retable for that church. A little later he did some work at Varennes for the church of Sainte-Anne, including "the main door."

Absent from Quebec in the 1720s, Levasseur returned to the region around 1730. At that time he is believed to have given up carving religious subjects for a few years to devote himself to secular works. His name is mentioned on 7 March 1746 in the deliberations and decisions of the Conseil Supérieur in connection with a lawsuit concerning various wood-carving jobs on ships: "the council has reduced the Sieur Levasseur's memorandum of costs to the sum of 1,362 *livres* for the works done by him for the ships *Imprévue*, *Saint-Louis*, *Union*, *Centaure*, *Expérience*, *Astrée*." The date of this lawsuit and the time required for building each of these ships permit the placing of these works in the period 1730–44. On 31 May 1737, thanks to his "talent and experience," he obtained a commission as royal surveyor and geometrician in the government of Quebec. Unfortunately nothing is known about Levasseur's career as a surveyor, but it is certain that after the conquest he was still practising this profession.

Towards 1742 he completed pieces of carving for parish councils in the Quebec region. His name is mentioned in 1742 and 1743 in the account books of the parish of Saint-Charles-de-Charlesbourg, where he carved two statues representing St Peter and St Paul. The last known reference of importance to his artistic production comes from the registry of the notary Jean-Antoine Saillant in Quebec. It concerns a contract drawn up on 29 Nov. 1750 engaging Pierre-Noël Levasseur to carve and have gilded a tabernacle, a retable, and a baldachin for a confraternity called the Congrégation de l'Immaculée-Conception de Notre-Dame.

Of all the works completed by Levasseur during his long career as a wood-carver, there are today only a few vestiges. The parish of Saint-Charles de Charlesbourg still has its two carvings of St Peter and St Paul, which are typical of traditional Quebec wood-carving. The curved line, an important characteristic of baroque art, is evident, with a certain vigour in the draping of the garments and the movement of the subjects.

Léveillé

These carvings give an impression of strength and lightness of touch worthy of the best Quebec tradition.

On 7 Jan. 1719, in Quebec, Pierre-Noël Levasseur had married Marie-Agnès de Lajoüe, daughter of François de Lajoüe, architect, contractor, and engineer. The marriage contract had been signed in Quebec on 21 Nov. 1718 before the notary Florent de La Cetière*. Three of their sons carried on this line of wood-carvers: the eldest, Pierre-Noël, studied wood-carving in France at Rochefort; Charles and Stanislas worked with their father, one at the church of Charlesbourg, the other at the former church of Saint-Vallier.

MICHEL CAUCHON and ANDRÉ JUNEAU

AJQ, Registre d'état civil, Notre-Dame de Québec, 28 nov. 1690, 13 août 1770. ANQ, Greffe de Florent de La Cetière, 21 nov. 1718; Greffe de J.-A. Saillant, 29 nov. 1750; NF, Ord. int., 31 mai 1737; NF, Registres du Cons. sup., 7 mars 1746; QBC, Cours de justice, Conseil militaire de Québec, 6 juin 1761. ANQ-M, Greffe de Marien Tailhandier, dit La Beaume, 18 juill. 1723. Archives paroissiales de Saint-Charles (Charlesbourg, Qué.), Livres de comptes, I, 1675–1749. Archives paroissiales de Sainte-Anne (Varennes, Qué.), Livres de comptes, I, 1725–1729. IOA, Dossier Pierre-Noël Levasseur, sculpteur. "Pour servir à l'histoire de la sculpture religieuse au Canada," *BRH*, XXXIII (1927), 367–68. "Recensement de Québec, 1744" (APQ *Rapport*). Tanguay, *Dictionnaire*.

Marius Barbeau, *J'ai vu Québec* (Québec, 1957). Gérard Morisset, *L'architecture en Nouvelle-France* (Québec, 1949); *Coup d'œil sur les arts*. Musée du Québec, *Sculpture traditionnelle du Québec* (Québec, 1967), 64. Charles Trudelle, *Paroisse de Charlesbourg* (Québec, 1887). Marius Barbeau, "Les Le Vasseur, maîtres menuisiers, sculpteurs et statuaires (Québec, *circa* 1648–1818)," *Les Archives de Folklore* (Québec), III (1948), 35–49. Gérard Morisset, "Une dynastie d'artisans: les Levasseur," *La Patrie* (Montréal), 8 janv. 1950; "Pierre-Noël Levasseur (1690–1770)," *La Patrie*, 9 nov. 1952.

LÉVEILLÉ, MATHIEU, Negro slave, executioner in Canada from 1733 to 1743; b. *c.* 1709 in Martinique; d. 9 Sept. 1743 at the Hôtel-Dieu of Quebec.

After the death of the executioner Pierre Rattier [*see* Jean Rattier*] on 21 Aug. 1723, the colonial authorities searched the colony in vain for a successor to him. Three years later they asked the minister of the Marine, Maurepas, to find a hangman for Canada in France. In reply Maurepas recommended that they buy a Negro from Martinique, but quickly thought better of this idea and sent them a certain Gilles Lenoir, *dit* Le Comte, an inmate of the Hôpital Général of Paris. Gilles Lenoir was a confirmed drunkard,

"so violent when he had been drinking and so disorderly in his conduct" that he had to be kept in prison all year long. He proved useless as an executioner and was sent back to France in the autumn of 1730. Guillaume Langlais, originally from London, England, replaced him. But he was so "old [about 51], feeble, and addicted to wine," that he was no better than his predecessor. Finally, on 12 Oct. 1731, the colonial authorities decided to take "the necessary measures to obtain a Negro from Martinique to act as executioner." On 24 March 1733 Maurepas asked Jacques Pannier d'Orgeville, a royal official in Martinique, to send to Quebec the Negro slave requested by New France. On 1 Aug. 1735 the treasurer general of the Marine, Barthélemy Moufle de La Tuillerie, paid 800 *livres*, drawn from the funds remitted by the farmer-general of taxes of the Domaine d'Occident, to a certain Sieur Sarreau, who lived in Martinique, "as the price for a Negro sent to Quebec to serve as executioner."

Léveillé, the Negro hangman, had scarcely arrived in Quebec when he was hospitalized at the Hôtel-Dieu on 31 July 1733. He had lived until he was 24 in the hot climate of the West Indies, and he had great difficulty adapting himself to the sudden changes of temperature in Canada. He had to be hospitalized at the Hôtel-Dieu of Quebec many times.

The hangman was very poor, if we are to judge by the facts recorded in the judicial documents of the period. On 28 Nov. 1740 he received a visit from François Mouïsset, a young ne'er-do-well of good family, to whom he had offered hospitality at Quebec around 1736. With the help of two other vagabonds, Nicolas Contant, *dit* Lafranchise, a day-labourer from Montreal, and the latter's sister, Élisabeth, the wife of Antoine Tranchant of Cap à l'Arbre (Cap à la Roche, near Deschaillons), Mouïsset got Léveillé drunk and proceeded to steal his belongings: a pot, a jacket, and a blanket. The thieves were arrested almost immediately and were first tried before Pierre ANDRÉ de Leigne, lieutenant general of the provost court of Quebec. They were sentenced to be put in the market-place pillory in Lower Town, Quebec, by the hangman Léveillé and to carry on their backs and chests signboards on which was written: "Vagabonds, vagrants who live a scandalous life." The lieutenant general also sentenced them to be banished from the government of Quebec for three years and to pay to the king a fine of 3 *livres* each. But the king's attorney, Henry HICHÉ, appealed this sentence to the Conseil Supérieur in conformity with title XXVI, article VI, of the great criminal ordinance of 1670.

This tribunal finally modified the sentence and condemned François Mouïsset and Nicolas Contant, *dit* Lafranchise, to two months in prison on bread and water. As for Élisabeth, the council ordered her to return to her husband, and to furnish the king's attorney general with a certificate that she had indeed returned and was living with him.

Léveillé suffered from "melancholy," as the executioner's profession did not take up a great deal of time at that period. Intendant Hocquart* thought he would cure the slave's morbid ennui by buying a West Indian wife for him. When she arrived in Canada in 1742, Leveillé was ill again. For fear of infecting the *fiancée*, the intendant wanted to wait for the executioner to recover before giving permission for their marriage. Léveillé's condition, however, grew worse; on 5 Sept. 1743 the hangman was again hospitalized, and four days later he died, a bachelor, at the Hôtel-Dieu. He was buried in the hospital cemetery on 10 September.

The colonial authorities then decided to have the Negress baptized Angélique-Denise – this was done on 23 Dec. 1743 at Notre-Dame de Québec by the parish priest, Joseph-André-Mathurin Jacrau* – and to put her up for sale, probably at a price of 700 or 800 *livres*, if we are to judge by the sum paid by the authorities for Léveillé and the prices for the purchase of slaves proposed in 1737 by a La Rochelle merchant to settlers in Louisiana. Intendant Hocquart must have succeeded in selling her, for after 10 May 1744 Angélique-Denise is no longer mentioned in the documents consulted.

Mathieu Léveillé's case brings into relief two facts in the social history of New France. After his death it seemed obvious that it was difficult for a Negro from the West Indies to adapt to Canada's harsh climate. Maurepas therefore advised Hocquart to replace "the Negro executioner who had died" with a white man. This policy was followed until 1760. The impasse which had led to bringing Léveillé to Canada also illustrates the constant difficulty in finding an executioner locally. In Canadian society as in French society under the old régime the position of executioner was a dishonourable one. According to the legislation of the period a condemnation was all the more ignominious in that it had to be carried out by the hangman, and indirectly the infamy associated in the public's mind with the penalty itself was cast upon the executioner.

ANDRÉ LACHANCE

AHDQ, Registres des malades, 5 août 1723, 31 juill. 1733, 5 sept. 1743; Registres des sépultures, 10 sept. 1743. AJQ, Registre d'état civil, Notre-Dame de Québec, 23 déc. 1743. AN, Col., B, 52, ff.516, 549; 58, f.410; 78, f.145; F¹ᴬ, 32, f.177; F³, 11, f.176. ANQ, NF, Coll. de pièces jud. et not., 1234; NF, Registres de la Prévôté de Québec, LXVI, 44v–45; NF, Registres du Cons. sup., registre criminel, 1730–1759, ff.65v–67; Manuscrits relatifs à l'histoire de la N.-F., 3ᵉ sér., IX, 411; XII, 15, 25, 28 oct. 1730, 12 oct. 1731 [sans folio]. Bornier, *Conférences des ord. de Louis XIV*, II, 336–37, 348. [J.-N.] Guyot, *Répertoire universel et raisonné de jurisprudence civile, criminelle, canonique et bénéficiale; ouvrage de plusieurs jurisconsultes...* (17v., Paris, 1784–85), VII, 156. Lachance, *Le bourreau au Canada*, 78–81. Trudel, *L'esclavage au Canada français*, 116–17.

LEVRAULT DE LANGIS (Langy) MONTE-GRON, JEAN-BAPTISTE, officer in the colonial regular troops; baptized 8 Oct. 1723 in Batiscan (Que.), son of Léon-Joseph Levrault de Langis and his second wife Marguerite-Gabrielle Jarret de Verchères; d. 1760.

Jean-Baptiste Levrault de Langis Montegron followed in the footsteps of his father and three older brothers by choosing a career in the colonial regular troops. He began military service in Île Royale (Cape Breton Island) in the early 1750s. In 1755 with the rank of ensign he commanded an observation post of ten or 12 soldiers three-quarters of a mile from Fort Beauséjour (near Sackville, N.B.). After the fort was captured by the British in June 1755, Langis left for New France where, in Verchères the following year, he married Madeleine d'Ailleboust de Manthet, widow of Jean Jarret de Verchères.

During the Seven Years' War, Langis and his older brother Alexis were employed scouting, taking prisoners, and gathering information on the enemy's strategy in the Lake Champlain–Lac Saint-Sacrement (Lake George) area. In June 1756 Langis took a prisoner in the vicinity of Fort Oswego (Chouaguen); he returned to the neighbourhood of the fort the following month to help draw up plans for a full-scale attack on it. Early in August Langis and one Richerville led reconnaissance parties, and one week later, on 14 Aug. 1756, Oswego fell – the first victory for French arms [*see* MONTCALM].

Following this success, scouting parties continually struck deep into English territory, leaving the enemy uneasy and uncertain where the French and their allies would appear next. In October 1756, for instance, Langis penetrated well into New York with a party of Nipissings and Potawatomis. The following spring, while patrolling the area of Fort Lydius (also called Fort Edward; now Fort Edward, N.Y.) with about 100

Liénard

Indians, Langis fell upon a group of 50 Englishmen who were chopping trees, killed about 20, and captured half a dozen.

For the next few months Langis patrolled the area of Fort George (also called Fort William Henry; now Lake George, N.Y.). In July 1757 Lévis* sent him from Carillon (Ticonderoga, N.Y.) with some Iroquois and Ottawas to scout a land route between Carillon and the British Fort George. On this assignment Langis surprised two separate enemy parties. Later in July Joseph Marin* de La Malgue led 400 Canadians and Indians to see whether the enemy had built in the vicinity of Rivière du Chicot (Wood Creek, N.Y.), and then to try to intercept convoys between Fort George and Fort Lydius; Langis, with his brother Alexis serving under his orders, was responsible for the Indian contingent.

On 4 July 1758, Montcalm sent a detachment of 130 volunteers from Carillon to the area of Fort George. This expedition was novel in that Montcalm entrusted command of the party to Ensign Langis, and then asked for officers to volunteer to serve under his orders. The young ensign's stature was such that the number of volunteers had to be restricted. Langis returned to Carillon the following night, reporting that he had sighted the enemy. Defensive positions were taken up, and in the resulting battle on 8 July a numerically superior British force was successfully repelled by Montcalm. Although Langis was wounded, he was able two months later to lead a scouting party from La Présentation (Oswegatchie, near Ogdensburg, N.Y.) to Niagara (near Youngstown, N.Y.) and Oswego.

In the spring of 1760, while participating in the defence of Montreal, Langis drowned near Île Saint-Paul (Île des Soeurs, near Montreal). He was buried at Longueuil on 1 June. Described in contemporary military journals as an excellent and extremely brave officer, Langis had served his country well. His rank was still ensign at the age of 37, though men of his calibre and talents were vital to New France's defence.

C. J. RUSS

Journal du chevalier de Lévis (Casgrain), 89. *Lettres de la cour de Versailles* (Casgrain), 67. *Lettres de l'intendant Bigot* (Casgrain), 12. *Lettres du chevalier de Lévis* (Casgrain), 120–27. *Lettres du marquis de Montcalm* (Casgrain), 35, 79–80, 84, 91, 452–53. *Relations et journaux* (Casgrain), 14, 17, 30, 67, 69, 70, 78, 82, 151–52, 160. Le Jeune, *Dictionnaire*. Tanguay, *Dictionnaire*. Frégault, *Canada: the war of the conquest*, 60–61. Stanley, *New France,* 110–11, 159. "La famille Jarret de Verchères," *BRH*, XIV (1908), 248–49, 253–54. Henri Têtu, "M. Jean-Félix Récher, curé de Québec, et son journal, 1757–1760," *BRH*, IX (1903), 305.

LIÉNARD DE BEAUJEU, DANIEL-HYA-CINTHE-MARIE, officer in the colonial regular troops, seigneur, entrepreneur; b. 9 Aug. 1711 at Montreal, son of Louis LIÉNARD de Beaujeu and Thérèse-Denise Migeon de Branssat; killed in action near Fort Duquesne (Pittsburgh, Pa.), 9 July 1755.

Daniel-Hyacinthe-Marie Liénard de Beaujeu grew up in Montreal and, like his father, joined the armed forces as an officer candidate while still in his teens. He may have spent some of his boyhood in the west, his father having been at posts such as Michilimackinac. The locations of his early service and the dates of his promotions are not recorded. At age 25, in Quebec, he married Michelle-Élisabeth, the daughter of François FOUCAULT (4 March 1737). Of their nine children only two daughters survived into adulthood.

In June 1746 Lieutenant Beaujeu was among the leaders of a 700-man Canadian army dispatched to Nova Scotia to link up with forces expected from France for the capture of Louisbourg and Annapolis Royal [*see* LA ROCHEFOUCAULD]. His 28,000-word journal of the 10-month campaign includes a detailed account of their greatest exploit. After a 150-mile march in bitter mid-winter, 300 Canadians and Indians attacked 500 New Englanders billeted in Grand Pré and forced their surrender after bloody fighting (11 Feb. 1747) [*see* Arthur NOBLE]. In several separate columns, they made a stealthy approach in the middle of the night. "A sentry who spotted us cried Who goes there? . . . We saw the watchkeeper come at once to the door. But the night was so dark, and we were hugging the ground so carefully, making no noise, that although we were within thirty paces, he considered it a false alarm and went back inside again. . . . In less than ten minutes we took the guardhouse . . . . All around we could hear musket fire. In every direction we could see men moving without being able to distinguish if they were our people or the enemy . . . . We had almost all lost our snowshoes and the amount of snow prevented us from moving smartly . . . . We would have been more gratified with our achievements if we had been able to learn that the other detachments had had as good success."

With 20 years' service, and recently promoted captain, Beaujeu was named commanding officer at Fort Niagara (near Youngstown, N.Y.) in 1749. He arrived there to take charge on 5 July. Niagara was the most strategic post in the *pays d'en haut* and Beaujeu apparently filled his role efficiently; still, he did not relish it. He knew sites farther west would yield more profit from furs. In December he reminded La Jonquière [TAF-

Liénard

FANEL] that his predecessor as governor, La Galissonière [BARRIN], had pledged, "in detaching me for Niagara, to station me the next spring in an advantageous post. . . ." He was full of complaints: his fort was crumbling into Lake Ontario, the garrison consisted of "veteran drunkards from Montreal," he lacked skilled workers and vital materials for simple maintenance. Reaching a shrill pitch of eloquence, he likened his post to a "cattle pen." Nevertheless, he was commandant of Niagara for the next several years.

In addition to directing military affairs he enforced trade regulations and tried to improve the portage road, but relations with Indians were his major concern. He had to try to preserve peace in the Great Lakes basin, on one occasion restraining some 40 Senecas who had decided to go on the warpath. Oswego was the most consistently troublesome problem. Beaujeu could not stop Indians who came down the Niagara portage from going on to trade their choicest furs at that New York outpost. To sustain French commerce, either Oswego had to be destroyed, he advised, or French prices for brandy and textiles had to come down to English levels.

Beaujeu's last big assignment, in 1755, was to replace Claude-Pierre Pécaudy* de Contrecœur as commanding officer of newly built Fort Duquesne. His group left Lachine for the disputed Ohio country at the opening of navigation, 20 April, and arrived at Fort Frontenac (Kingston, Ont.) at the month's end. Embarking in two sailing vessels, they reached Niagara in the second week of May.

The 500-mile supply line from Montreal to Fort Duquesne was complicated and still experimental. For his passage along the route, Beaujeu came armed with authority – in association with Pierre Landriève – to decide all arrangements necessary for supporting Canada's southward expansion. Everyone seemed to be waiting for him, requesting orders, approval, solutions. Correspondence among the western posts mentioned, as a matter of high moment, that Beaujeu had just left or was expected. At Niagara he decreed where extraordinary reinforcements he might be needing were to come from, looked to his men's health, bullied tons of supplies up the steep hill around the falls, dispatched 13 boats to row to Fort de la Presqu'île (now Erie, Pa.) and a gang of men to drive horses there through the woods, and still found composure enough to get down on paper proposals for making portage operations more efficient and for improving French bateaux. On 1 June he himself embarked on Lake Erie with 16 more boats. From Presqu'île

Beaujeu sent orders back to Niagara to hasten 14 dozen muskets, and ahead to Ohio to muster all available craft up towards the headwaters. On 17 June, from Fort de la Rivière au Bœuf (Waterford, Pa.), he sent ahead wheat, bullets, and gunpowder. At Venango (Franklin, Pa.) he pressed into the reluctant hands of Michel Maray* de La Chauvignerie a commission to build a regular fort there whether materials were available or not, along with a plan of what it should look like.

En route, Beaujeu was receiving urgent messages from the man he was coming to replace. Bring your men quickly, Contrecœur wrote in mid-May, let Philippe-Thomas CHABERT de Joncaire expedite the supplies. Three weeks later ominous details were learned from an enemy deserter: 3,000 English and American soldiers, under Edward Braddock, were pushing towards Duquesne with over a dozen 18-pounder cannon.

His progress to the fort was the peak of Beaujeu's career. Forty-four years old, active and incisive, he now assumed a leading role at the centre of continent-shaping affairs. Promotions had come rapidly. The Ohio valley was just such a fur-rich land as he had long yearned to win. He had business interests on the Labrador coast, had recently assembled three linked fiefs, and was angling for a fourth, which would make him seigneur of a 250-square-mile estate in the Richelieu valley (Lacolle).

At the end of June he arrived at the forks of the Ohio. Contrecœur remained commandant until the crisis cooled. The tempo of preparations increased as Fort Duquesne's leaders weighed information about the enemy's approach, wooed tribes whose manpower was needed to strengthen the French, and hammered out a strategy to keep the Ohio a link between Canada and Louisiana. They decided to fight the first battle well beyond the walls. At 8.00 A.M. on 9 July, Beaujeu led off a squad to ambush the British advance force of 1,500. He had 637 Indians, 146 Canadian militia, and 108 officers and men from the colonial regulars. As at Grand Pré, they would attack the enemy with inferior numbers. The French would have had to reconsider risking this initiative had not Beaujeu harangued the Indians – local Ottawas and Delawares, along with Hurons and Abenakis from the St Lawrence valley – into forgetting their fears of British numbers and cannon: "I am determined to go ahead and meet the enemy. What! Will you let your father go by himself? I am sure to beat them."

About 1.00 P.M., before the ambush was prepared, Beaujeu's party unexpectedly met the British in the woods. Contrecœur reported: "The enemy's artillery caused our people to fall back

Liénard

twice, M. De Beaujeu was killed by the third discharge . . . just as our French and Indians were beginning to hold their own. This accident instead of discouraging our men only reanimated them. . . . '' Rallied by Jean-Daniel Dumas*, the French and Indians put the English and Americans to rout – a victory that made the Ohio safe for French interests for another few years.

Beaujeu's body was carried back to Fort Duquesne and buried there 12 July. His career had been one of ever greater success; he never knew defeat, old age, or failure. The geographical dispersion of his major battles – the Bay of Fundy and the Ohio valley – reveals him as an agent of an ambitious French empire in New France. But in the mid-1750s that empire was about to disappear.

MALCOLM MACLEOD

ANQ, Greffe de R.-C. Barolet, 3 mars 1737; NF, Ins. Cons. sup., IX, 82–83; X, 6. Archives du Collège Bourget (Rigaud, Qué.), Famille Beaujeu, papiers de famille et notes par le Père Alphonse Gauthier. PAC, MG 8, F50. Coll. doc. inédits Canada et Amérique, II. Inv. de pièces du Labrador (P.-G. Roy). ''Lettres de Daniel-Hyacinthe Liénard de Beaujeu, commandant au fort Niagara,'' BRH, XXXVII (1931), 355–72. NYCD (O'Callaghan and Fernow), XI, 303–4. Papiers Contrecoeur (Grenier). Le Jeune, Dictionnaire. P.-G. Roy, Inv. concessions, IV, 263–67. Monongahéla de Beaujeu, Le héros de la Monongahéla: esquisse historique (Montréal, 1892), 3–4, 10–21. François Daniel, Histoire des grandes familles françaises du Canada… (Montréal, 1867), 255, 261–62. P.-G. Roy, Les petites choses de notre histoire (7 sér., Lévis, Québec, 1919–44), 3ᵉ sér., 239–42. Stanley, New France. C.-F. Bouthillier, ''La bataille du 9 juillet 1755,'' BRH, XIV (1908), 222–23.

LIÉNARD DE BEAUJEU, LOUIS, officer in the colonial regular troops; b. in Paris, France, 16 April 1683, son of Philippe Liénard de Beaujeu, officer in charge of the king's cellar and pantry and standard bearer in the company of light horse of the king's guard, and Catherine Gobert; d. 27 Dec. 1750.

Born into a noble family with access to the court, Louis Liénard de Beaujeu was on 11 June 1691, at the age of eight, appointed to succeed his father as officer in charge of the king's cellar and pantry. He occupied this position until 1697, when he went to New France to seek his fortune, but continued to draw the salary attached to it until 1706. He sought advancement through the military and proved a competent officer, though his connections at court were of utmost importance. He was commissioned ensign in a detachment of the colonial regular troops on 1 April 1702, lieutenant in 1704, and captain on 30 June

1711. On 6 Sept. 1706 Beaujeu married Thérèse-Denise, daughter of Jean-Baptiste Migeon* de Branssat, and widow of Charles Juchereau* de Saint-Denys, lieutenant general of the royal jurisdiction of Montreal and prominent fur-trader. Eleven children were born of the marriage.

Beaujeu went to France in 1712 on family business and was also entrusted with the official dispatches by Philippe de Rigaud* de Vaudreuil, who considered him a judicious officer, ''exact in carrying out orders,'' and strongly ''attached to the service and very zealous to maintain good order. . . .'' A few years later Beaujeu went to the western Great Lakes with Constant Le Marchand* de Lignery, and by 1719 had replaced his superior as commandant at the newly constructed fort at Michilimackinac. He served there until 1722. He attempted to curtail the trade in brandy which was so devastating to the Indian culture. Like other officers at the western posts, Beaujeu engaged in the fur trade, occasionally importing merchandise from François Poulin* de Francheville. His ill health was a problem at this post, and indeed throughout his life.

He left Michilimackinac in 1722 and returned to Montreal to try to restore his health. At this time he requested the cross of Saint-Louis, an honour he received in 1726. In June 1728 Beaujeu returned to the upper lakes as second in command of Le Marchand de Lignery's ill-fated expedition against the Foxes in Wisconsin. Lignery was sick much of the time, yet refused to turn command of the 450 French and 1,000 Indians over to Beaujeu. The Foxes eluded pursuit, and the large French force returned in September having accomplished nothing except to earn recriminations.

Nevertheless Beaujeu was not discredited, and the following year he was promoted. No openings were available until April 1733 when he succeeded Pierre de Rigaud* de Vaudreuil as garrison adjutant of New France and took his place on the council of war. At this time he was also given a seigneury on Lake Champlain. This was an eventful year for in October his daughter Charlotte married Jean-Victor Varin* de La Marre, member of the Conseil Supérieur.

In 1742 Beaujeu again went to France. He was appointed on 31 May 1743 as king's lieutenant at Trois-Rivières. Because of ill health he remained in France and in 1746 asked for retirement. He was refused, and returned to New France, where war was in progress. At a meeting in July at the Château Saint-Louis he voted to continue strengthening the fortifications of Quebec.

Retirement with a pension of 2,000 *livres* per year was finally granted to Beaujeu in March

1748. He died on 27 Dec. 1750. Three sons survived him: the scholarly Louis-Joseph*, the officer DANIEL-HYACINTHE-MARIE, and Louis Liénard* de Beaujeu de Villemomble, the last French commandant at Michilimackinac, who distinguished himself during the American revolution.

DAVID A. ARMOUR

AN, Col, B, 44, f.521; C¹¹A, 44, ff.45, 46; Marine, C⁷, 20. "Cadillac papers," *Michigan Pioneer Coll.*, XXXIII (1903), 482, 534, 567, 704; XXXIV (1904), 13, 186. "Canadian documents," Wis. State Hist. Soc. *Coll.*, V, 92–95. "Correspondance de Vaudreuil," APQ *Rapport, 1946–47*, 373, 403, 417; *1947–48*, 172, 186, 211. *French regime in Wis., 1634–1727* (Thwaites), 386. *French regime in Wis., 1727–48* (Thwaites), 71–72. "Liste des officiers de guerre qui servent en Canada (octobre 1722) dressée par le gouverneur de Vaudreuil," *BRH*, XXXVI (1930), 209. PAC *Report, 1899*, supp., 143, 156; *1904*, app.K; *1905*, I, pt.VI, 13, 14, 48, 71, 77, 104, 106. *Dictionnaire national des Canadiens français (1608–1760)* (2v., Montréal, 1958). Le Jeune, *Dictionnaire*. É.-Z. Massicotte, "Congés et permis déposés ou enregistrés à Montréal sous le régime français," APQ *Rapport, 1921–22*, 193, 194, 198, 199, 203. P.-G. Roy, *Les officiers d'état-major*, 28–30. Tanguay, *Dictionnaire*. Emmanuel de Cathelineau, "Les Liénard Sieurs de Beaujeu, Saveuse et Villemomble," *Nova Francia*, III (1927–28), 327–54.

LIETTE, CHARLES-HENRI-JOSEPH DE TONTY DE. *See* TONTY

LIGNERY, FRANÇOIS-MARIE LE MARCHAND DE. *See* LE MARCHAND

LISLE, LOUIS-JOSEPH BEAUSSIER DE. *See* BEAUSSIER

LITTLE, OTIS, lawyer, politician, military officer, king's attorney; b. 29 Jan. 1711/12 at Marshfield, Massachusetts, son of Captain Isaac and Mary (Otis) Little; d. possibly 1754.

Otis Little's parents came from two of the most important and rising families in southeastern Massachusetts. It was almost inevitable that he should attend Harvard College – an advantage his father had not enjoyed – and he received his AB in 1731 and his MA in 1734.

Little settled in Pembroke (near Marshfield) to practise law and married Elizabeth Howland of Bristol, Massachusetts (later Rhode Island), on 3 Oct. 1733. His wife's family was Church of England, and Little joined St Michael's Church in Bristol on Christmas Day, 1735, thus breaking with his family's Pilgrim heritage. In 1736 he apparently visited Nova Scotia, for he was commissioned a justice of the peace for Annapolis

Royal on 22 November of that year. Little was not a terribly successful lawyer, but he undoubtedly received some clients in Massachusetts on the strength of connections with his uncle James Otis Sr, considered by many the best trial lawyer in the province. These connections were probably necessary, since Little was sufficiently slapdash to be forced on one occasion to petition the Massachusetts General Court for re-entry of a suit in which he had failed to perform the paperwork properly.

Returning to Marshfield, Little won a seat in the General Court in the election of 1740, fought over the Massachusetts land bank. A subscriber to the bank – a private venture proposing to issue currency backed by mortgages on land – Little was part of a political upheaval in which rural voters turned out of office most opponents of the bank. In the General Court, where he served for five years, Little acted as liaison between the legislative leaders and the rural backbenchers. In return for his efforts in keeping the backbenchers in line, he eagerly sought and received patronage appointments from both the legislature and Governor William Shirley, the most remunerative being as deputy judge of the admiralty for the counties of Bristol and Plymouth in June 1740. In one legislative job, he displayed a venality that would later destroy him, submitting an outrageously high expense account which the governor and council had to cut drastically. He was clearly a man out to make his living from public life and connections, a practice less common and less acceptable in America than in England.

When trouble with France over Nova Scotia loomed in 1744, Little quickly recognized the possibilities for advancement. He was commissioned a major and at his own expense collected a company of volunteers in the summer of 1744 to help defend the beleaguered garrison at Annapolis Royal. As he was entering Annapolis Basin, Little was captured by the French. He was sent to Boston on parole in December and was exchanged in July 1745, a few weeks after the reduction of Louisbourg, Île Royale (Cape Breton Island). He and his company were engaged in clean-up operations and the occupation of the Annapolis fortress until relieved in May 1746. He then left for London with official papers from Governor Shirley and letters of introduction to important people in England – the one from merchant Thomas Hancock warning, "As to Mr. Little's circumstances they are unknown to me, be cautious not to go too far."

Little was seeking employment in London, as well as the permanent rank of major and reimbursement for military expenditures made by

403

Little

himself and the New England colonies. His principal efforts were devoted to two projects: one to put British North America on a hard money basis, and the other the settlement of Nova Scotia. Despite previous support for the land bank and his connections with Governor Shirley, who sought compromise on the currency issue, Little lobbied in England for the most fiscally conservative of New England merchants. In 1748 he submitted a memorial to the Lords of the Treasury which not only asked that any reimbursement for the Louisbourg expedition be used to retire paper money, but sought parliamentary action both to end future colonial currency emissions and to provide the Louisbourg funds in special coinage which would become a distinctive American currency.

About the same time, Little produced a tract promoting Nova Scotia settlement, *The state of trade in the northern colonies considered.* (Despite frequent attributions, Little is not the author of another work of 1748, *A geographical history of Nova Scotia.*) In *The state of trade*, he countered the argument that northern colonies were least useful to the mother country since they were least profitable, insisting that further settlement with the British and foreign Protestants in the north would enlarge the market for British goods and better enable the colonists to pay for them. He also denied vigorously that the colonies might become independent, concluding: "Upon the whole, nothing can, nor ever will, prevail upon them to attempt, or think of a State of Independence, whilst they enjoy the Freedom of *English* Subjects under so happy a Constitution." Little's was the only tract of this period which attempted to relate the settlement of Nova Scotia to the larger questions of colonial economic patterns and British imperial policy. As for Nova Scotia, Little waxed lyrical about its resources: "It is obvious from this Account, which is far from being exaggerated, that no Country is better calculated to yield an early Support to its infant Colonies, with more Certainty and less labour, and affording them in the mean time, a comfortable subsistence." He warned of the danger of "French Bigots" (the Acadians) living in Nova Scotia, but believed that Protestant immigration, not expulsion of the Acadians, would deal with this problem. As he admitted himself later, he regarded Cape Breton as a lost cause since it was soon to be restored to the French. But Nova Scotia might provide a "chance to get some Employment: if not I shall (like many other faithful Servants of the Government) have my Labor for my pains."

Nova Scotia did provide employment. Little headed there in April 1749 with the fleet of Gover-

nor Edward Cornwallis*; he was listed as captain in an independent company and was accompanied by ten male and six female servants as befitted the "Surveyor-General of Nova Scotia." To that appointment Little soon added others. On 15 July 1749 he was appointed commissary of the stores and provisions of the new Halifax settlement. After admission to the bar of Nova Scotia on 3 Feb. 1749/50, he became advocate general in the Vice-Admiralty Court and by 11 Oct. 1750 was "acting as Kings Attorney." Unfortunately, his style of living apparently exceeded his income, and he began to take chances. Though his venality was not excessive by 18th-century standards, an overbearing and pretentious manner probably did not help make him popular with the administration of the province. He was suspended from his commissary position in 1751 for irregularities in the books, and possibly for selling supplies directly to settlers on his own account. On 3 April 1753 he was charged before the governor and council with accepting money (£5 in advance and £5 later) as an attorney from the wife of a man he was prosecuting as king's attorney. The council found the charge "as fully proved as the nature of the case would admit," stripped Little of his positions and forbad him "to plead in General Court except in such cases which shall be appealed from the judgement of the Inferior Court in which he was concerned." Unable to support himself and pressed by creditors, Little liquidated his assets (including a share in John BUSHELL's "Press and printing business" which produced the *Halifax Gazette*) and in 1754 disappeared into the West Indies; he died there or on the way.

Otis Little's problem was that his pretensions and ambitions outstripped his capabilities. He was too obviously self-serving and apparently incapable of rendering sufficient real value to permit his failings to be overlooked or excused by those who employed him.

J. M. BUMSTED

John Carter Brown Library (Providence, R.I.), Otis Little, "Proposals for a new currency in America" (autographed MS copy). "Mass. Archives," VI, 572a, 573, 575; XVIII, 189; XX, 321, 344, 357; XXXI, 408, 447; XLI, 595; XLII, 88, 89; XLVI, 123, CXIV, 444. Mass. Hist. Soc., John Davis coll., Winslow papers, Mascarene family papers. PANS, RG 1, 164/1, p.21; RG 3, Minutes of Nova Scotia Council, 11, 15 Oct. 1750; 4, 5, 6 Dec. 1752; Vertical MS file, Otis Little documents. Suffolk County Court House (Boston, Mass.), Court files, no.66530.

Boston Post-Boy, 10 Dec. 1744. *Boston Weekly News-Letter*, 7 July 1743, 1 June 1749. *The Law papers: correspondence and documents during Jonathan Law's governorship of the colony of Connecticut,*

1741–1750 (3v., Conn. Hist. Soc. *Coll.*, XI, XIII, XV, Hartford, 1907–14), III, 186. Otis Little, *The state of trade in the northern colonies considered; with an account of their produce, and a particular description of Nova Scotia* (London, 1748; repr., Boston, 1749). *N.S. Archives*, I, 539; II, 177. PRO, *Acts of P.C., Col., unbound papers*, 273. Shipton, *Sibley's Harvard graduates*, IX, 60–64. John Doull, *Sketches of attorney generals of Nova Scotia, 1750–1926* (Halifax, 1964), 1–3. Robert Zemsky, *Merchants, farmers, and river gods; an essay on eighteenth-century American politics* (Boston, 1971), 190–91, 282–83.

LIVAUDIÈRE, JACQUES-HUGUES PÉAN DE. *See* PÉAN

LOCKMAN, LEONARD, surgeon; b. *c.* 1697 at Hanover (Federal Republic of Germany), son of John Lockman; d. 2 May 1769 at Halifax, Nova Scotia.

Leonard Lockman's father was a page of the future King George II of England and "had the honour to teach His Majesty French and Italian." Upon the completion of his training in anatomy and surgery in Germany and France, Leonard was a surgeon to the guards of George I of England at Hanover and at a hospital in Mecklenburg (German Democratic Republic). He was in England briefly in 1722 and late that year sailed for Barbados with the new governor, Henry Worsley. In Barbados Lockman volunteered to care for the crew of a naval ship infected with fever, and as a reward was appointed inspector general of health. He held this post until 1733 when ill health caused by the climate forced him to move his family to New England.

Nothing is known of his activities until 1742, when he returned to England. That year he persuaded his patrons, Earl Granville and the Duke of Richmond, to obtain for him appointment as judge of the Vice-Admiralty Court and naval officer of Rhode Island. He went to Rhode Island in 1743, but the general assembly of the colony refused to accept his appointment to the post and chose their own judge instead. Lockman remained in Rhode Island and in 1746 he volunteered for the proposed expedition against Quebec [*see* WARREN]. He was commissioned a captain after he succeeded in being the first to raise a company of men, and was promoted major the following year. After many delays, however, the expedition was finally called off.

He returned to England in 1748 and petitioned for another position in compensation for the loss of the Rhode Island post. He was appointed a surgeon, at ten shillings a day, in Governor Edward Cornwallis*' expedition to found Halifax in 1749, but was disappointed when he learned he had to share the post and salary with John Steele. Lockman brought several apprentices with him to Nova Scotia. When an epidemic broke out in 1750 in Halifax among German settlers from the ship *Ann*, Cornwallis ordered the sick to be moved to Lockman's house "where there are chimneys [fireplaces]." In June 1753 Governor Peregrine Thomas HOPSON sent Lockman and Johann Burghard ERAD to care for the Germans who were going to the new settlement at Lunenburg.

Lockman did not stay long at Lunenburg. He had been partially disabled by a groin injury he received late in 1749 and was unable to travel by horseback or carriage to do his work. Also, when he found his pay was set at five shillings a day, he regarded this "as only half pay and that he was to do no duty." He returned to Halifax and left as his deputy one of his "journeymen," who worked at 18 pence a day. In 1759 he was relieved of his duties at Lunenburg when they were officially taken over by Erad's assistant and successor, John Phillips. Lockman continued to receive his regular allowance as a pension. In April 1761 he received additional income when he was appointed "Interpreter in the Courts of Law and Equity . . . of the German and French Languages." When the post of Lunenburg surgeon was abolished in 1768 and Lockman lost his pension, he petitioned the crown for a small allowance for himself and his wife, Tanalia. One daughter, Carolina, is mentioned in his will.

PHYLLIS R. BLAKELEY

Halifax County Court of Probate, 1769, L68a. PANS, MG 1, 109–11; MG 5, Halifax City, "Old Dutch" [St George's Anglican] cemetery inscriptions; RG 1, 37, nos.66, 67; 163/3, p.132; 164/1, 29; 164/2, p.310; 165, p.125; 167, p.29; 342, no.25; RG 3, Minutes of Nova Scotia Council, 28 June 1759; RG 36, 1751–70, p.83, bundle 11. Rhode Island State Archives (Providence, R.I.), Letters, L-1, 2, pp.1, 27, 29, 35, 39, 45, 54, 63, 66; L-2, 1, pp.28, 86. *The correspondence of the colonial governors of Rhode Island, 1732–1775*, ed. G. S. Kimball (2v., Boston, New York, 1902–3), I. *Nova Scotia Chronicle and Weekly Advertiser* (Halifax), 9 May 1769, p.151. PRO, *JTP, 1741/42–1749*, 397, 405, 408. *Records of the colony of Rhode Island and Providence plantations, in New England*, ed. J. R. Bartlett (10v., Providence, R.I., 1856–65), V, 70–71, 96, 271. Bell, *Foreign Protestants*. T. B. Akins, "History of Halifax City," *N.S. Hist. Soc. Coll.*, VIII (1895), 6, 72, 203–4, 234–35, 253n.

LOISEAU. *See* LOZEAU

LOMBARD DE COMBLES (de Combes, Descombes), JEAN-CLAUDE-HENRI DE, officer in the French regular troops, engineer; b. 10 Dec. 1719 at Combles (dept. of Meuse), France, son of Jean-Adrian de Lombard, seigneur of Combles and king's engineer, who died 11 Dec. 1733 from wounds suffered at the siege of Kehl (Federal Republic of Germany), and of Antoinette Hilaire; m. 24 Dec. 1744 in Palais, Belle-Île-en-Mer, France, Marie-Rose Périn by whom he had three daughters and four sons; d. accidentally in Canada 12 Aug. 1756.

Jean-Claude-Henri de Lombard de Combles was admitted to the engineer corps in 1743 and promoted captain in 1751, retaining his commission in the Régiment de Champagne, as was the custom. As king's engineer of the fortress of Belle-Île-en-Mer in 1749, he established a plan for repair of the batteries, erection of walls to protect beaches that were too easily accessible, and building of massive walls able to support cannon. In 1752 and 1753 he drew up plans for the citadel of Belle-Île-en-Mer, and in 1755 he took part in the reconstruction of the quay of the town of Palais; during the latter year his wife died.

In 1756 Lombard de Combles and the engineer Jean-Nicolas Desandrouins* were sent to New France, to replace three engineers who the year before had been captured at sea by the British while on their way to Canada. As part of the staff of the Marquis de Montcalm, Lombard sailed from Brest in the frigate *Sauvage*, which carried Lévis*, and reached Quebec on 31 May.

He went two days later to Montreal, then on to Fort Frontenac (Kingston, Ont.), where he arrived on 24 June to take part in the operations against Fort Chouaguen (Fort Oswego). On 11 July he led 200 men to reconnoitre the British forts there, camping at Niaouré (Sackets Harbor, N.Y.). He completed his reconnaissance by 25 July, questioning also two British deserters about the strength of the garrison. On 28 July he returned exhausted to Fort Frontenac where he prepared a report for Montcalm and a sketch of Oswego showing the topography, the fort's defences, and the possible routes for a French attack. On 4 August he and Desandrouins accompanied Montcalm's force to the region, and on 10 August the two engineers were sent to reconnoitre Fort Ontario, one of the defences of Oswego. Lombard instructed Desandrouins not to accompany him to the forward area; when he himself was within some 240 feet of the fort, in fairly thick forest, a Nipissing ally, a chief named Hotchig (Aouschik), mistook him for a British officer in the dark and shot him. Desandrouins had his superior officer carried to his tent, but he died within half an hour.

Although he was in the country a short time,

the loss of this engineer was evidently strongly felt by the French commanders. Lombard de Combles left "in poverty" six dependent young children and a brother and sister who lived in France. The king granted to the children an annual gratuity in recognition of the loyal services of their father.

F. J. Thorpe

AD, Meuse (Bar-le-Duc), État civil, Combles, 10 déc. 1719; Bas-Rhin (Strasbourg), État civil, Saint-Étienne de Strasbourg, 11 nov. 1733; Morbihan (Vannes), État civil, Le Palais, 24 déc. 1744. AN, Col., C^{11A}, 101, f.350; C^{11B}, 36, ff.268–70; Section Outre-Mer, Dépôt des fortifications des colonies, Am. sept., nos. 536–37. Archives de la mairie du Palais (dép. du Morbihan), État civil, 2 nov. 1745, 16 janv. 1747, 5 nov. 1748, 16 janv. 1750, 14 janv. 1752, 27 sept. 1753, 20 févr., 13 mars 1755. Archives du port de Lorient, 1E^4 46, ff.123–57; 1E^5 50, f.381; 4S^2 27 C. CTG, Archives, art. 3; art. 8, carton 1; art. 15, sect. 3, pièce 3; Bibliothèque, ba 8^0 25; mss in 4^0, 121; mss in fol., 208^b, no.40; 208e, no.1. SHA, A^1, 3417, pièces 22, 93, 95, 160, 209. *Lettres du chevalier de Lévis* (Casgrain), 9–12. *NYCD* (O'Callaghan and Fernow), X, 560, 564. A. M. Augoyat, *Aperçu historique sur les fortifications, les ingénieurs et sur le Corps du Génie en France ...* (3v., Paris, 1860–64), II, 90, 503. C.-N. Gabriel, *Le maréchal de camp Desandrouins* (Verdun, 1887), 26–47.

LONGLAND, JOHN, HBC sloopmaster and explorer; d. 16 June 1757 at Eastmain House (on James Bay at the mouth of the Eastmain River).

John Longland's career with the Hudson's Bay Company was closely associated with that of Thomas Mitchell. Longland was appointed master of a trading sloop at Moose Factory (Ont.) in May 1742, and in the summer of 1744 took the sloop *Phœnix* north in company with Mitchell in the *Success* on a discovery voyage along the East Main (the eastern coast of Hudson and James bays). His journal contains no maps, is less informative than Mitchell's, and breaks into articulate comment only when it expresses suspicions of Mitchell's actions. This dislike was reciprocated, and Mitchell complained of Longland's *Phœnix*: "I cannot see what service it can be to the Honble. Company having this vessel to take care of to tow at my stern or otherwise she goes broadside foremost." With his cranky vessel and beset by fears that Mitchell's insistence on pressing northward through thick fog would run them on the rocks, Longland was an unadventurous second in command, always more ready to turn back than to advance.

Nor was his later career with the HBC more distinguished. In 1744 complaints were made of his habitual drunkenness at the bay posts, in 1748 he returned to England without the company's leave, and in 1749 during the parliamentary inquiry into the trade of Hudson Bay he was taken into custody by the sergeant-at-arms for prevarication. He sailed with Captain William COATS later that year and again in 1750 and 1751, as first mate and linguist on ventures to explore the East Main and to establish and supply a post there. He finished his service with the HBC as he had begun it – master of a sloop along the East Main. He died at Eastmain House in June 1757, having apparently had some premonition of death since one of the company journals noted that Longland had been buried "in a Spot of Ground he made choice of himself about a month before, he was not Sick at all went of[f] very suddenly."

GLYNDWR WILLIAMS

[Longland's log of the *Phœnix* during the discovery expedition of 1744 is in HBC Arch. B. 59/a/11. References to his service with the HBC are in HBC Arch. A. 1/36–40; the note on his conduct during the parliamentary inquiry of 1749 is in HBC Arch. E.18/1, f.181. Entries relating to his death are in HBC Arch. B.3/a/49. A brief account of the discovery voyage of 1744 is given in Glyndwr Williams, "Captain Coats and exploration along the East Main," *Beaver* (Winnipeg), outfit 294 (winter 1963), 4–13. G.W.]

LONGLEY, LYDIA (later baptized **Lydia-Madeleine**), *dite* **Sainte-Madeleine,** English captive, sister of the Congregation of Notre-Dame; b. 12 April 1674 at Groton, Massachusetts, daughter of William Longley; baptized according to the rites of the Roman Catholic Church on 24 April 1696 at Montreal; d. 20 July 1758 in Montreal.

Lydia's grandfather, William Longley, came to America from England around 1650 with a group of Puritans who settled at Groton, near Boston. Her father was also called William Longley, but her mother's name is not known. Lydia was 11 in 1685 when her father remarried with the widow Delivrance Crisp.

At the age of 20 Lydia was unexpectedly separated from her family when Abenakis, allies of the French in the war against the English colonies, attacked Groton on 27 July 1694. After killing the Longleys and five of their children, they carried off Lydia, John, and Betty into captivity in New France. Betty died during the difficult journey, which was done on foot; John was kept a prisoner in the Abenaki village of Saint-François-de-Sales (Odanak), on the Rivière Saint-François. Lydia was taken to Ville-Marie, where the French immediately bought her and placed her in the charge of Jacques Le Ber*, the father of Jeanne* and Pierre*. In her new family the young captive discovered a way of life which ran counter to her Puritan faith and upbringing. But she was surrounded with so much affection that she refused to return to Groton when exchanges of prisoners were arranged.

Influences that were discreet but decisive led Lydia Longley from Presbyterianism to Catholicism, then to the religious life: on 5 Aug. 1695 Jeanne Le Ber became a voluntary recluse in the Congregation of Notre-Dame, and Lydia was struck by the young woman's generosity and by the ceremony of retirement; Pierre Le Ber was preparing to join the Brothers Hospitallers of the Cross and of St Joseph, of which he had been a cofounder, along with François Charon* de La Barre and Jean Fredin; in addition Mary Sayward*, another English captive with whom Lydia had struck up a friendship, had already been converted to Catholicism on 8 Dec. 1693. When Lydia expressed her desire to become a Catholic, she was entrusted to Marguerite Bourgeoys* for her religious instruction. On 24 April 1696 the young girl solemnly abjured her religion in the chapel of the Congregation of Notre-Dame. On the same day she received baptism and was named Lydia-Madeleine after her godmother, Marie-Madeleine Dupont de Neuville, wife of Paul Le Moyne* de Maricourt and Jeanne Le Ber's cousin.

Lydia-Madeleine joined the congregation in December 1696. She was the second English captive to be received by Mother Bourgeoys, since Mary Sayward, *dite* Marie des Anges, had preceded her by two years. But, it seems, she was the first to make her profession in the congregation. As her name in religion she received that of her baptism and pronounced her simple vows on 16 Sept. 1699.

Sister Sainte-Madeleine lived in the community for 62 years, mainly in Montreal, then at Sainte-Famille, Île d'Orléans, where she was the superior of the mission. She died on 20 July 1758 at 84 years of age and was buried the next day in the Enfant-Jésus chapel in the former church of Notre-Dame de Montréal. Lydia Longley had attained a place in history in accord with the title Helen A. McCarthy gave to her in a romantic biographical novel, "the first American nun."

ANDRÉE DÉSILETS

ACND, La Congrégation de Notre-Dame: son personnel, 1653–1768; Fichier général des sœurs de la Congrégation de Notre-Dame; Plans des lieux de sépulture depuis 1681–CND; Registre des sépultures de sœurs de la Congrégation de Notre-Dame; Registre général des sœurs de la Congrégation de Notre-Dame de Montréal. Coleman, *New England captives*. Sister Saint Ignatius [Catherine Jane] Doyle, *Marguerite Bourgeoys and her congregation* (Gardenvale, Que., 1940). Lemire-

Longueuil

Marsolais et Lambert, *Histoire de la Congrégation de Notre-Dame*. H. A. McCarthy, *Lydia Longley, the first American nun* (New York, London, 1958).

LONGUEUIL, CHARLES LE MOYNE DE LONGUEUIL, Baron de. *See* LE MOYNE

LORIMIER DE LA RIVIÈRE, CLAUDE-NICOLAS DE, officer in the colonial regular troops; baptized 22 May 1705 at Lachine, near Montreal, son of Guillaume de Lorimier* de La Rivière and of Marie-Marguerite Chorel de Saint-Romain, *dit* d'Orvilliers; buried 15 Dec. 1770 at Lachine.

Claude-Nicolas de Lorimier de La Rivière had a military career similar to that of his father, who died when he was four years old: second ensign in 1726; ensign, 1733; lieutenant, 1741; and captain, 1749. On 7 Jan. 1730 he married Marie-Louise, daughter of Michel Lepailleur* de Laferté and Catherine JÉRÉMIE, *dit* Lamontagne – over the next 21 years they had ten children of whom eight survived into adulthood, the boys in their turn following their father into the army.

Lorimier probably spent a good part of his first 30 years' service in the west. In 1757, as liaison officer with Indian auxiliaries accompanying MONTCALM's army, he had particular responsibility for the Ojibwa warriors. Such a role seems to indicate a familiarity with that nation gained through being stationed at Michilimackinac or one of its dependencies. In 1749 he had been touted for a command in that lucrative country, but his posting on promotion to captain apparently put him in charge of the garrison at Lac-des-Deux-Montagnes (Oka, Que.) instead. When large-scale hostilities against the Anglo-Americans began in 1755, he was made commandant of Fort La Présentation (Oswegatchie, now Ogdensburg, N.Y.).

La Présentation was a Six Nations mission village and recruiting office; it provided a listening post among the Iroquois; it was a way-station, storehouse, and defensive position halfway between Montreal and Fort Frontenac (Kingston, Ont.); and it was a base for incursions against targets in the Albany-Oswego area. The establishment – its Indian population was about 500 in 1756 – had been inaugurated only six years previously by Father François Picquet*, an energetic Sulpician who brooked assistance with no greater grace than he did interference.

Although his command was small – between 20 and 30 men – Lorimier was involved in sensitive operations. For example, in 1756 he expedited the passage of the force under Gaspard-Joseph Chaussegros* de Léry that blew up Fort Bull

(Oneida Lake, N.Y.) with its supplies; in the reconnaissance force that kept up pressure on Oswego during the spring and summer of 1756, he seems to have commanded the left column's rearguard. Information affecting the security of Canada's western empire often arrived first at La Présentation, where Lorimier would make initial evaluation and response, and transmit it to higher authority.

The commandant's sharing of authority with Abbé Picquet was uncomfortable. According to Bougainville*, it was Picquet who drilled the Indians in military exercises: "There is in the fort a captain of colonial troops as commander, but both inside and out all real authority is ecclesiastical." In 1757, serious jurisdictional disputes having estranged the two men, Picquet was withdrawn. However, the Indians at La Présentation petitioned for the priest's return in February 1758, and complained about having Lorimier as their official contact with the French. Bougainville put the question: "Is it necessary to put French garrisons in the Indian missions, or leave their conduct solely to the missionaries?" "Altercations between the missionary and the commandant," wrote Montcalm, had been "detrimental to the King's service . . . the best thing to do would be to have neither commandant nor garrison. Should the English come there in force, the little garrison will be no defence, and the Indians will be sure to keep out of the way. If the English should come with only a small raiding party, the Indians are enough. This would be the advice of Abbé Picquet and he is right; but the Marquis de Vaudreuil [Pierre de Rigaud*] thinks differently."

Fort Frontenac's destruction in August 1758 brought for the first time a strong possibility that the enemy would move down the St Lawrence River towards Montreal. Picquet was sent back to La Présentation. "It is certain that he himself formed this establishment, [and] that since his departure affairs have gone badly there," wrote Bougainville. Lorimier was recalled and replaced as military commander by Antoine-Gabriel-François Benoist*.

Recall terminated the most independent and important appointment Lorimier ever held. The blow was softened when he received the cross of the order of Saint-Louis in January 1759. His participation in the last of New France's great battles was honourable too, his name appearing among the wounded at Sainte-Foy.

Lorimier was part of a genteel yet active military tradition that reached back from his sons to their grandfather. The fact that his main business was soldiering did not prevent him from dabbling in other business as well. Accused of complicity in Intendant Bigot*'s ring of swindlers, he was acquitted; his certified claim of 1,716 *livres* against the French government was put forward in 1763, and ignored like all the others. The ill wind of conquest, which demolished traditions, hurt creditors, and destroyed careers, had affected his fortunes also. He may have survived to concentrate on trading activities and seems to have been in the Ohio country about 1769.

MALCOLM MACLEOD

PAC, MG 24, L3, 3. PRO, WO 34 (copies at PAC). Bougainville, *Journals* (Hamilton); "Journal" (Gosselin), APQ *Rapport, 1923–24*, 202–393. "Correspondance de Vaudreuil," APQ *Rapport, 1939–40*, 436. *Journal du marquis de Montcalm* (Casgrain). *Lettres du marquis de Vaudreuil* (Casgrain). "Mémoire sur les postes du Canada adressé à M. de Surlaville, en 1754, par le chevalier de Raymond," APQ *Rapport, 1927–28*, 324, 339, 347–48. *Papiers Contrecoeur* (Grenier). É.-Z. Massicotte, "La famille de Lorimier," *BRH*, XXI (1915), 10–16. Louvigny [Testard] de Montigny, "Le Lorimier et le Montigny des Cèdres," *BRH*, XLVII (1941), 33–47.

LORON (Loring). *See* SAUGUAARAM

LORT (Lord). *See* DELORT

LOTBINIÈRE, EUSTACHE CHARTIER DE. *See* CHARTIER

LOTTRIDGE (Loteridge), JOHN, Indian agent; brother of Thomas Lottridge of Albany, New York; possibly a son of Richard Lottridge of that town; d. 1763 in the Lake Champlain area.

John Lottridge is first mentioned as a second lieutenant in Edmond Mathews' company of the New York militia. He was present at Lake George (Lac Saint-Sacrement) in September 1755 when French forces under DIESKAU halted a British army marching toward Fort Saint-Frédéric (Crown Point, N.Y.). By 1757 Lottridge was in command of a militia company, but early in 1758 he volunteered to join the Indian service. He was, according to the superintendent of northern Indians, Sir William Johnson*, "a Young Man who had shown Resolution, was a good Woods-man, known to & liked by many of the Indians."

As an Indian agent with the rank of lieutenant he took part in Lieutenant-Colonel John Bradstreet*'s expedition which captured and destroyed Fort Frontenac (Kingston, Ont.) in August 1758; he was subsequently recommended by Bradstreet and Johnson for a captaincy, a promotion confirmed in October. Until the spring of 1759 he accompanied Indian scouting expeditions on the northern frontier of New York. He was apparently present at the siege of Fort Niagara (near Youngstown, N.Y.) in July 1759. After its capitulation he returned to Oswego (Chouaguen), where he was in charge of Indian affairs during the winter and spring of 1759–60. While there he had a disagreement with Colonel Frederick Haldimand*, the commandant, over the problem of Iroquois who came from Oswegatchie (La Présentation, now Ogdensburg, N.Y.) to trade. Haldimand, thinking them spies, wanted to send them away. Lottridge intervened because he accepted their claim to be on the British side and believed that dismissing them would offend the Six Nations. The dispute illustrates the delicacy of relations with the Indians during the war; it also suggests the impatience with which many British military authorities were inclined to regard the Indian service. They seemed to believe that undue attention was paid to the Indians' feelings and rather disliked the independence that the Indian agents, who were responsible to Johnson, enjoyed.

By 1760 many Iroquois had allied themselves with the English, and a number of them accompanied Major-General Jeffery Amherst* in the late summer as he headed down the St Lawrence to attack Montreal. Lottridge was with the expedition, scouting in advance of the main force with parties of Indians. After the capitulation of Montreal in September, Lottridge was based there as a subordinate to Daniel Claus*, Johnson's deputy. Lottridge spent that winter and the following one with the Indians from the area on their annual hunt in the vicinity of Lake Champlain.

In the summer of 1762 Claus reported that Lottridge was "uneasy abt his Situation in Case I should leave this Country as he wont pretend to take the Care of the Indns upon him alone," but by the autumn Lottridge had taken on that responsibility temporarily and apparently discharged it capably. Yet, although he was doing well in the Indian service, he was concerned for his future since the authorities believed that with the establishment of peace it was safe to make drastic cuts in that department. He considered entering the regular army but was pleased when he was retained in the Indian service, the field he preferred.

Late in 1762 Lottridge travelled into the *pays d'en haut* and spent the winter "in the trading way" with the "Indians at Millacky," that is, in southeastern Wisconsin. Either by actually visiting the Sioux or by contact with their neighbours, he gained an impression of the great strength of

Lozeau

that nation, about whom the English knew little; and he acquired some buffalo robes and Sioux artifacts to send to Johnson. By the summer of 1763 Lottridge was back in Montreal. On 9 August he attended a conference between General Thomas Gage*, the military administrator there, and the Ottawas of L'Arbre Croche (Cross Village, Mich.), who had escorted James GORRELL and the surviving soldiers from the Michilimackinac region to the safety of Montreal after violence inspired by PONTIAC broke out in the *pays d'en haut*.

Lottridge set out again for the Lake Champlain region in the autumn of 1763. In October word reached Montreal "that Captain Lutteridge is lost in the Bay de Mischisque [Missisquoi], going to explore that Country."

JANE E. GRAHAM

BM, Add. MSS, 21661, ff.36, 107; 21670, f.14. PAC, MG 19, F1, 1, pp.16, 20, 58, 74, 89; 14, p.37. *Johnson papers* (Sullivan *et al.*).

LOZEAU (Loiseau, Lozaus), JEAN-BAPTISTE (Jean) (he has been confused, by Cyprien Tanguay* and others, with Jean Loiseau, labourer of Quebec), master locksmith and tinsmith; b. *c.* 1694, son of François Lozeau and Marguerite Gauron of Rochefort, France; m. 28 Nov. 1713 at Quebec to Marguerite Mercier, without issue, and 7 May 1729 at Quebec to Catherine Gautier; d. probably 7 Feb. 1745.

At the time of his marriage to the daughter of Quebec locksmith Louis Mercier, Jean-Baptiste Lozeau was described as "a soldier of d'Alogny." He had likely served in a detachment of colonial regular troops under Captain Charles-Henri d'Aloigny* de La Groye. About 19 when he married, he may have been one of those undersized or unhealthy recruits frequently sent to Canada only to be discharged. As a civilian, Lozeau lived on Quebec's Rue de la Montagne among the town's metalworkers.

Like most Canadian craftsmen Lozeau performed several trades. He was a blacksmith, a locksmith, and a tinsmith as occasion demanded, but not at the expense of quality. He was employed by Governor Philippe de Rigaud* de Vaudreuil and by the widow of Michel Sarrazin*. In 1727 Lozeau complained to Intendant Dupuy* that "having acquired some fame for the quality of his work . . . several masters and journeymen in this town . . . wishing to profit from the high opinion held of him, conceal their name from those seeking Lozeau . . . and present themselves as the one being sought, and they use his name and his trademarks." The intendant authorized

Lozeau to advertise himself as a locksmith and tinsmith, using whatever symbol he chose for his sign. Other metalworkers were forbidden to copy Lozeau's trademark, and the imitation of one tradesman's "signs, ceilings and shop paintings" by another was outlawed.

The year 1729 was a dark one for Lozeau. His wife died childless in April, after 16 years of marriage; the following month he married again. He was still liable, however, for the debts of Louis Mercier, his first father-in-law. Later in the year Lozeau's apprentice, Jean-Charles Le Guettier, ran away after serving only half of his three-year term. An intendant's ordinance was issued against any who might harbour the fugitive.

In the summer of 1730 Jean Lozeau asked the Quebec provost court if he could raise money by a lottery. The prizes were a fully harnessed horse, a new *calèche*, a gilded and engraved snuffbox "of the latest fashion," and a watch. Henri Solo, a Quebec watchmaker, testified that the watch alone was worth 150 *livres*, "being the work of Pierre Rousseau in Paris and not from Geneva like so many others." The court seems to have permitted the lottery after being assured that the prizes were in good condition and of high value.

The few references to Jean Lozeau in the notarial and court records are indicative of an honest and peaceful life. In disputes, such as one with Ruette* d'Auteuil in 1725 over a property encroachment, he was often a passive participant. Lozeau trained over six apprentices and he was frequently employed as an expert estimator. His skill and knowledge in metalworking were evidently respected.

It is difficult to be certain of the death date of this artisan. On 28 Sept. 1744 he was present at the baptism of his last child, Pierre-Louis, and some months later, in the Quebec city census for 1744, Mme Lozeau declared herself to be a widow and her son Pierre-Louis to be three months old. However the register of the parish of Notre-Dame de Québec on 8 Feb. 1745 has a brief reference to the burial of a Jean Loiseau, "ironmonger," aged about 50, who had died the night before.

PETER N. MOOGK

AJQ, Registre d'état civil, Notre-Dame de Québec, 28 sept. 1744, 8 févr. 1745. ANQ, Greffe de R.-C. Barolet, 9 avril 1753; Greffe de J.-É. Dubreuil, 10 août 1715, 14 févr. 1719, 24 févr. 1722, 11 mai 1724, 19 oct. 1731; Greffe de Florent de La Cetière, 15 avril 1728; Greffe de J.-C. Louet, 7 mai 1729, 11 juin 1731; NF, Coll. de pièces jud. et not., 850, 860, 1044, 1045, 3617, 3646, 3692; NF, Ord. Int., XIIA, 92. PAC, MG 8, B1, 20/1, pp. 464–66. "L'ameublement d'un seigneur canadien

sous l'ancien régime," APQ *Rapport, 1921–22*, 261.
"Loterie de Jean-Baptiste Lozeau, maître-serrurier,"
APQ *Rapport, 1923–24*, 144–45. "Loterie de Joachim
Girard, maître-cordonnier," APQ *Rapport, 1923–24*,
159. "Permis d'enseigne à Jean Lozeau," *BRH*,
XXXIII (1927), 147. "Un inventaire de l'année 1743,"
APQ *Rapport, 1943–44*, 30. *Recensement de Québec,
1716* (Beaudet). "Recensement de Québec, 1744"
(APQ *Rapport*). P.-G. Roy, *Inv. jug. et délib.,
1717–1760*, I, II, III, IV; *Inv. ord. int.*, II, 11–12, 40;
III, 18. Tanguay, *Dictionnaire*.

LUCAS, FRANCIS, naval officer, merchant
trader; b. *c.* 1741 at Clontibret, Co. Monaghan
(Republic of Ireland); d. 1770, at sea.

Francis Lucas began his naval career as an able
seaman, then master's mate, serving from 1764 to
1766 in HMS *Niger* (commander Sir Thomas
Adams), which patrolled the fisheries on the
northern coast of Newfoundland and southern
coast of Labrador. In 1765 the *Niger* brought to
Chateau Bay, the chief port on the southern Labrador coast, four Moravian missionaries seeking
a suitable place along the almost unknown shore
for a mission to the Eskimos. Two of them, Jens
Haven* and Christian Andrew Schloezer, were
transferred to the schooner *Hope* for a reconnaissance. Governor Hugh Palliser*, who was at
Chateau Bay that summer, sent Lucas along to
help make "the needful observations." During
August the schooner explored Davis Inlet and
adjacent coasts, as well as the surrounding country, where the men observed much timber and
wildlife, but no Eskimos. Lucas' report to Palliser in St John's left the governor more than ever
sure that the Labrador coast, "under proper regulations," would prove valuable for its fisheries
and trade.

Lucas transferred to Palliser's flagship, HMS
Guernsey, in March 1767 and again spent the
summer at Chateau Bay. York Fort had been
built at Chateau the previous year to protect English fishing ships from the Eskimos and the "far
more mischievous plundering crews from the
[New England] plantations"; Palliser now made
Lucas second in command of the year-round garrison, with special responsibility for the fort's
boats. In November 1767 an Eskimo band
attacked Nicholas Darby's fishing premises at
Cape Charles, northeast of Chateau, stealing
boats and killing three men. The Eskimos seem
to have been seeking revenge for harsh treatment
by some New England whalers. Lucas pursued
the Eskimos, killed 20 or more, and captured
some women and children. He was able to establish friendly relations with the prisoners, especially with an intelligent woman called Mikak*,
and, during the long winter, learned something of
the Eskimo language. Palliser decided to bring
some Eskimos to England to impress them with
the greatness of his nation, and Lucas escorted
Mikak and two of the children to London in the
fall of 1768. The following spring Lucas, now a
lieutenant, was charged with returning Mikak.
Early in August he landed her and the other
Eskimos who had survived captivity on an island
northwest of Byron Bay (north of Hamilton
Inlet). Back at Portsmouth, England, in November, he wrote the secretary of state, Lord
Hillsborough, reporting the success of the voyage, and promising to call at his London home in
a few days.

Lucas now decided to go into business for himself on the Labrador coast, and apparently left
active naval service. On 30 March 1770 he
entered into a partnership with Thomas Perkins
and Jeremiah Coghlan, merchants of Bristol,
England, and Fogo, Newfoundland, and George
Cartwright*, a former army captain with private
means. Cartwright was to oversee trade in fish
and fur on the Labrador; Lucas, put in command
of a schooner, the *Enterprize*, was to trade with
the Eskimos. They did not reach Chateau Bay
until almost the end of July; Cartwright settled
then at Charles River and Lucas went north in the
Enterprize in quest of the Eskimos and Mikak in
particular.

The Moravians, however, had also been looking for Mikak, hoping that she would help them
set up a mission post. They had taken the precaution of leaving England early in the season, and
found her in Byron Bay on 16 July. Having no
news of Lucas, she and her husband agreed to
travel with the missionary ship to northern Labrador to find a site. Thus Mikak and most of the
Eskimos were far to the north when Lucas
searched the coast in August. He was able to
purchase only a little whalebone and a few seal
skins before returning to Cape Charles in early
October. However he had persuaded an Eskimo
family to return with him to pass the winter at
Cartwright's post. Lucas went next to Fogo, and
late in October set out for Portugal with a cargo
of dry fish. According to the Moravians, he was
in some haste and "gave out that he had great
business to do with the King, . . . but probably he
will scarce know how to pass the winter without
Mikak." The *Enterprize*, however, foundered at
sea. Cartwright continued to fish, seal, and trade
with the Eskimos at Cape Charles.

Lucas contributed to the security of English
enterprises in southern Labrador by fostering
friendly relations with the natives. The missionaries distrusted him as being rash in temperament and "fleshly" in his tastes, but he was

Lupien

regarded as a "man of honour" by his partner Jeremiah Coghlan. Given positions of responsibility by Governor Palliser, he was obviously capable and enterprising. He seems to have been reasonably well educated and certainly was intelligent and quick-witted enough to learn the rudiments of the Eskimo language and to try to profit from his knowledge of the Labrador coast. By 1769 he was doubtless regarded as something of an authority on the Eskimos and had the ear of even the secretary of state. Whatever his plans for the future, however, they vanished with him into an Atlantic grave.

WILLIAM H. WHITELEY

PANL, Nfld., Dept. of Colonial Secretary, Letter books, IV. PAC, MG 17, D1. PRO, Adm. 36/7104, 36/7384–85, 36/7446–47, 50/19, 51/629, 51/636, 51/4210, 51/4220, 52/1288; CO 194/16, 194/27, 194/28. George Cartwright, *A journal of transactions and events, during a residence of nearly sixteen years (on the coast of Labrador); containing many interesting particulars, both of the country and its inhabitants, not hitherto known* (3v., Newark, Eng., 1792). *Joseph Banks in Newfoundland and Labrador, 1766*, ed. A. M. Lysaght (London, 1971). *London Chronicle*, 6 June 1769. W. G. Gosling, *Labrador: its discovery, exploration and development* (London, 1910). J. K. Hiller, "The foundation and the early years of the Moravian mission in Labrador, 1752–1805" (unpublished MA thesis, Memorial University of Newfoundland, 1967). H. W. Jannasch, "Reunion with Mikak," *Canadian Geographical Journal* (Ottawa), LVII (1958), 84–85.

LUPIEN, *dit* **Baron, PIERRE** (often referred to as Sieur **Baron**, or **Barron**), master carpenter, timber supplier to the royal shipyards; baptized 10 Oct. 1683 at Montreal, son of Nicolas Lupien, *dit* Baron, and Marie-Marthe Chauvin; d. 1744 in New France.

Until he was 50 years old Pierre Lupien, *dit* Baron, followed the trade of carpenter. His father raised animals and farmed at Montreal and later at Longue-Pointe; he also was a butcher and dabbled in the lumber trade. No doubt the latter activity later led Pierre into house-building. In 1734 while living in Montreal Pierre received a grant of three acres from Governor Charles de BEAUHARNOIS in the seigneury of Villechauve. Soon afterwards he expanded his activities from house carpentry to supplying timber to the small shipbuilding industry in the colony.

In the fall of 1736 or the following spring he agreed to supply timber and masts for a 300-ton merchantman to be built at Quebec. In 1738 the ship was completed, christened the *Fier*, and sailed to Bordeaux, France. At that time Baron was cutting ship timber along the Richelieu River around Sorel where he had gathered 22,000 running feet of oak boards. He already had sent a similar quantity of pine to Quebec. Clearly he was in a position to attract the notice of Gilles Hocquart* when the intendant began to search for individuals to supply timber to the newly established royal shipyards. In 1738 Baron and Clément de Sabrevois de Bleury jointly signed an agreement with Hocquart to cut timber and ship it to Quebec.

On 18 Nov. 1705 at Montreal Pierre had married Angélique Courault, *dit* La Coste, who gave him ten children. His two eldest sons, Antoine and Jean-Marie, worked with their father as timber suppliers to the government.

From 1738 until his death in 1744 Baron and his sons searched the forests of southwestern New France for suitable ship timber, as far west along the St Lawrence as Châteauguay and Long Sault and south along the shores of Lake Champlain. During that period he supplied material for the first three naval vessels to be built at Quebec, the flutes *Canada* and *Caribou* and the frigate *Castor*. He was unable to find any large stands of big trees, however, an indication of the major difficulty in building naval vessels in New France. Canadian forests simply were not able to supply easily the material needed for large warships. This fallacy in the government's policy may well have been known to contemporary merchants of greater experience. It appears significant that wealthier men in the colony, who frequently obtained government contracts and possessed influential connections with colonial officials, did not enter the ship timber business. In 1742 Hocquart referred to Baron as the "sole timber entrepreneur" in New France, and drew attention to his age and lack of financial resources. Apparently the intendant was counting on Baron's sons to do better, but meanwhile Hocquart was desperate. Widely dispersed resources and increased costs made the timber enterprise unattractive and later forced the government to carry out its own exploitation.

Sometime in 1744, while searching for more timber, Baron died, whether by accident is unknown. His estate was probably paltry. Hocquart agreed to pay his widow at the rate of 26 *sols* per board foot, 2 *sols* more than the agreed price, but the intendant reported that the poor woman was nevertheless reduced to beggary. His sons Antoine and Jean-Marie apparently continued in the timber trade, and in June 1744 his widow apprenticed a younger son to a sculptor-joiner. Baron might be considered an entrepreneur although the severe limitations on exploiting the forest resources of Canada for large ship construction ruined him. A self-made craftsman, his lack of experience and his ambition had led him into a highly dubious business venture.

JAMES S. PRITCHARD

AN, Col., C¹¹ᴬ, 74, pp.206–11; 75, pp.351–52, 353–60; 79, pp.357–65; 80, pp.85–88, 91–93; 82/2, pp.383–84; 83, pp.332–34; 84/2, pp.21–24; 114, p.129 (PAC transcripts). ANQ-M, Greffe de Michel Lepailleur, 15 nov. 1705. "Recensement du Canada, 1681" (Sulte). Godbout, "Nos ancêtres," APQ *Rapport, 1953–55*, 489. P.-G. Roy, *Inv. coll. pièces jud. et not.*, I, 97; *Inv. ord. int.*, II, 230, 231, 301; III, 37, 47. Tanguay, *Dictionnaire*. J.-N. Fauteux, *Essai sur l'industrie*, I, 213–14. Mathieu, *La construction navale*, 33, 36, 47–51.

LUSIGNAN, PAUL-LOUIS DAZEMARD DE. *See* DAZEMARD

LYON DE SAINT-FERRÉOL, JEAN, priest, a director of the Séminaire des Missions Étrangères in Paris, France, superior of the seminary of Quebec, parish priest of Quebec, and vicar general; b. 1692 in the diocese of Sisteron, France; d. sometime after 1744 in France.

Jean Lyon de Saint-Ferréol studied theology at the Sulpician seminary in Paris and apparently was still living there when he was admitted into the Séminaire des Missions Étrangères in 1726. He was immediately elected one of the directors of the seminary in Paris and was appointed superior of the seminary of Quebec. The directors of the Missions Étrangères felt, however, that there was a risk in choosing someone whom no one in Canada knew and who knew nothing of the customs there. Therefore, to reassure their Quebec colleagues, they endeavoured in their letter of 31 May 1726 to draw a most flattering portrait of M. de Saint-Ferréol: "He is in his prime, being 34 years of age," they pointed out, "serious-minded, naturally discreet, of good morals, sound in doctrine, a doctor of the Sorbonne, a man of rank, full of piety and detachment from all worldly things. . . . We have appointed him in the proper manner, and it will be for you to present him to His Excellency your bishop; there is every reason to believe that he and you will be pleased with him later on."

Contrary to the expectations of the directors in Paris, the superior was badly received when he presented himself at the seminary of Quebec on 28 Aug. 1726. For some years the Canadian-born clergy had been complaining, not without reason, of being systematically kept out of the important offices, both by Bishop Saint-Vallier [La Croix*] and by the authorities in the mother country [*see* Jean-Baptiste Gaultier* de Varennes]. The ap-

pointment of Abbé Lyon de Saint-Ferréol was naturally interpreted as further proof of the policy of discrimination of which the Canadians were victims. Moreover, the new superior made a few blunders, such as becoming friendly with Abbé Clément Robert*, visitor from the Sulpician seminary, who advocated openly the union of the seminaries of Quebec and Montreal. It did not require anything more for the superior to be accused of favouring the Sulpicians' plans. Luckily this crisis did not last long, and by dint of patience and tact Jean Lyon de Saint-Ferréol succeeded in getting himself accepted. The following year the seminary in Paris noted with satisfaction that "the slight troubles" in Quebec were disappearing. The directors recommended to the superior and his assistants, however, that they "administer the seminary of Quebec as formerly, without changing anything for the time being, always taking care not to offend the Canadian ecclesiastics and making use of them as much as possible." In 1730 the same officials referred in a letter to the order which they saw prevailing in the seminary, the application to studies, and the increased piety among the seminarists and the pupils: "all that taken together is a very great matter of comfort for you and for us."

The prejudice against M. de Saint-Ferréol, however, had not entirely disappeared, particularly among certain members of the chapter. This was quite evident in 1731 when Bishop Dosquet*, who did not hide his own preference for the French clergy, proposed conferring upon the superior of the seminary the dignity of theologal. The canons, mostly Canadians, were opposed, and the bishop had to give up his plan. This persistent ill will distressed Abbé Saint-Ferréol considerably, to the extent that for a moment he thought of going as a simple missionary somewhere in Acadia. Moreover, from the letters that Abbé Henri-Jean TREMBLAY wrote him, Lyon de Saint-Ferréol seems to have been a rather poor administrator. The directors of the Missions Étrangères consequently decided that it was better to find a replacement for him. In 1734, although Bishop Dosquet had chosen him to be vicar general, they appointed him parish priest of Quebec and named François-Elzéar VALLIER to be superior of the seminary in his stead. At first M. de Saint-Ferréol seemed to submit to his lot; but the following spring he sailed for France with the firm intention of never again setting foot in Canada. On 6 May 1737, indeed, Jean Lyon de Saint-Ferréol, who had become canon and treasurer of the "royal and venerable chapter of Sainte-Marthe de Tarascon," sent the seminary his resignation as parish priest of Quebec. In 1744 the former superior was still living at Aix-en-Provence, where since 1739 he had been fulfilling the duties of vicar general. The place and date of his death are unknown.

NOËL BAILLARGEON

AAQ, 12 A, Registres d'insinuations B. AN, Col., C¹¹ᴬ, 53, f.371. ASQ, Documents Faribault, 184; Lettres, M, 48ff.; Paroisse de Québec, 5, 6; Polygraphie, XXII, 46; Séminaire, V, 51; VIII, 7. Gosselin, *L'Église du Canada jusqu'à la conquête*, II.

M

MacCARTHY, CHARLES LATOUCHE. *See* LATOUCHE

McCLIESH, THOMAS (sometimes written **Macklish, Maclish, Mack Leish,** and **Mack Clish),** carpenter, overseas governor of the HBC; described as of Limehouse (now part of London), England, in 1734; fl. 1698–1746.

Nothing is known about Thomas McCliesh's early life except that he was a carpenter like his uncle, also named Thomas McCliesh and a former Hudson's Bay Company employee. According to his account in the London grand ledger the younger McCliesh began his career in the HBC in 1698 at Fort Albany (Ont.), which was then the only fort in the possession of the English, York Fort (York Factory, Man.) having been captured by Pierre Le Moyne* d'Iberville the preceding year. McCliesh served under governors James Knight* (1698–1700), John Fullartine* (1700–5), and Anthony Beale* (1705–7), working ashore and afloat. His "Extraordinary Service in Traveling to Gilpins Island [off the East Main] and back" early in the winter of 1702–3 to obtain news of the delayed supply-ship from London was rewarded by a gratuity of £10 about six months before he returned to England in the autumn of 1707.

By January 1708 McCliesh had agreed to go back to James Bay. Until sailing time in June he was employed aboard the *Hudson's Bay* [II] and, because England was at war with France and Spain, protection against his possible impressment into the navy was obtained from the admiralty. Once at the bay he probably wintered with Henry Kelsey* off the East Main (the eastern coast of Hudson and James bays) in 1708–9. He served again under governors Fullartine (1708–11) and Beale (1711–14). When Kelsey began a short spell as governor in August 1711 McCliesh became master of the *Eastmain* sloop, and in 1712 Beale persuaded him "to continue one year as master of the sloop and trader to the East Main." The next year (as in 1710 when his

contract was first extended) no ships sailed from Albany, and he was unable to return to England until 1714.

McCliesh was re-engaged in the spring of 1715. After superintending the building of the *Hudson's Bay* [III] he sailed in the *Port Nelson* (Capt. James Belcher) to Albany, where he succeeded Richard STAUNTON as chief factor. McCliesh was subordinate to governors-in-chief Knight (1715–18) and Kelsey (1718–21); their headquarters, except during 1717–18, were at York, which had been returned to the HBC by the French in 1714. McCliesh succeeded Kelsey as deputy governor in 1718, but was still stationed at Albany. His surviving reports to London during this third phase of his career indicate his chief concerns at Albany. The trade at that post was threatened by increased French competition in its hinterland. Zacharie Robutel* de La Noue had re-established a post at Kaministiquia (Thunder Bay, Ont.) in 1717, and in 1719 one was built near the mouth of the Nipigon River. Albany also suffered from Knight's attempt to rehabilitate business at York by ordering that all "northward Indians and Christeens [Crees]" who had been coming to trade at Albany while York was in French hands should now deal at the more northerly post. As one means of offsetting these liabilities McCliesh tried to keep annual contact with the Indians of the East Main, who hunted the most valuable "small furs." All his tasks were made more difficult by the indiscipline that had developed among the company's servants during the war when labour was scarce. By the time McCliesh returned to England in 1721, the factory at Albany had been almost rebuilt and a permanent post established on Eastmain River.

In 1722 McCliesh succeeded Kelsey as governor-in-chief. He spent one trading season at York, which stood on "bogs worse than the bogs of Allen," and where he lived "in a Scotch or Irish hut in comparison of new Fort Albany"; he was, however, "mighty well satisfied in all respects" because he commanded "a place of greater profit." But he maintained that the subordinate post of Churchill (Man.), built to attract the distant Northern or Chipewyan Indians, gained its fur trade at the expense of York. He returned to England in 1726, leaving Anthony Beale in charge. After superintending the building of the *Mary* [II], of which his son-in-law William Coats was given command, McCliesh again sailed for Hudson Bay in 1727. The *Mary* was wrecked off Cape Farewell, Greenland, and crew and passengers reached Churchill and York in the *Hannah* (Capt. Christopher Middleton). McCliesh resumed his command at York, but in 1731 Churchill was made independent under another son-in-law Richard Norton. By 1734, when McCliesh returned to England, business at York was declining because of stiff rivalry from the posts established by the La Vérendrye family on the route from Lake Superior to Lake Winnipeg, and from the activities of coureurs de bois trading among the Indians. McCliesh had tried to meet this competition by requesting better quality trading goods from London and adequate supplies of "that cursed bewitching weed," Brazil tobacco, but the French saved the Indians great inconvenience by taking goods inland and threatened force if necessary to wrest the trade from the English.

McCliesh was re-engaged in 1735 as "Governor in Hudson Bay" and sailed to Albany, where he was to have succeeded chief factor Joseph Adams* and to have supervised the business of Moose Fort (Moose Factory, Ont.), but severe illness made it necessary for him to return home. The following year he went out again, but once more ill-health obliged him to leave. Although he was again re-engaged in 1737 his contract was cancelled before the ships sailed. Some time later he left Limehouse, where his wife Mary and their numerous children had lived during his absence in Hudson Bay, and in 1746 he was living in "low Circumstances" at Woodbridge, Suffolk.

The course of McCliesh's career in Hudson Bay was not altogether unusual during the early 18th century. Many HBC tradesmen, of course, remained just that, but McCliesh demonstrated his skills as a carpenter and seaman and because of his energy, reliability, and shrewdness earned promotion. His final qualification for command at Albany came with his initiation by Kelsey into the methods of trading with the Indians. So began his rise in the company.

Alice M. Johnson

[McCliesh's surviving letters to the London governor and committee are printed in HBRS, XXV (Davies and Johnson), which also lists the pertinent sources in the HBC Archives. For background information, *see* Rich, *History of the HBC*, I. a.m.j.]

MAILHIOT. *See* Malhiot

MAILLARD (Maillart, Mayard, Mayar), PIERRE (sometimes called Pierre-Antoine-Simon), priest of the Missions Étrangères and missionary; b. *c.* 1710 in France, in the diocese of Chartres; d. 12 Aug. 1762 in Halifax, Nova Scotia.

Pierre Maillard received his ecclesiastical training at the Séminaire de Saint-Esprit in Paris. He was there in 1734 when the Abbé de L'Isle-Dieu chose some seminarists to lend to the Séminaire des Missions Étrangères which was short of personnel. Maillard spent eight months in the latter institution, then was selected for the Micmac missions on Île Royale (Cape Breton Island) in the spring of 1735. His superiors wrote of him: "He is a young priest who has greatly edified us . . . full of zeal and piety."

Maillard arrived at Louisbourg, Île Royale, on 13 Aug. 1735 on the *Rubis* and began to study the Micmac language under the guidance of his predecessor, the Abbé de Saint-Vincent. Having a remarkable talent for languages, Maillard succeeded within a few months not only in mastering Micmac, despite the difficulties in pronunciation, but also in perfecting a system of "hieroglyphics" to transcribe Micmac words. He was thus able to write down in note-books the formulas for the principal prayers and the responses of the catechism so that the Indians might learn them more easily. This system was worked out during the winter of 1737–38, according to the Abbé Jean-Louis Le Loutre*, who had come to help Maillard in the Micmac missions. For his part Maillard mentioned that the winter he had spent with Le Loutre had furnished him with "an excellent opportunity to learn through teaching his fellow religious." In fact, the two missionaries spurred each other on in their apprenticeship, but the master, without any doubt, was Maillard, who "is a naturalized Indian as regards language." Indeed, he even succeeded in acquiring the gift of rhyming at each member of a sentence, which was the genius of that tribe, so that he reached the point of "speaking Micmac with as much ease and purity as do their women who are the most skilled in this style." It is therefore not surprising that he was used by the officials at Louisbourg to train officers as interpreters.

Did Maillard really invent the sign method which facilitated his linguistic work? The ques-

Maillard

tion has not been resolved. In 1691 Father Chrestien Le Clercq* mentioned that he had devised a similar method to catechize the Micmacs of the Gaspé Peninsula. If we accept William Francis Ganong*'s learned deductions, we can accept that in the 17th century Le Clercq had systematized and expanded a custom that the Micmacs had of setting down short messages by means of diagrams. Maillard would seem simply to have taken up and perfected the same procedure, and done so all the more easily because its usage had become widespread since Le Clercq's time. It is possible, however, that the missionary did not know that he had been preceded in this matter. In any event, it must be acknowledged that Maillard was the great specialist in the Micmac language; the numerous works that he left behind him bear this out.

At the same time as he was absorbed in linguistic studies, Maillard was devoting himself to his apostolic task. Every year he had to visit all the settlements on Île Royale, Île Saint-Jean (Prince Edward Island), and, until Le Loutre arrived, those in English Acadia (Nova Scotia). His intermittent presence among the Indians made missionary work difficult. Consequently Maillard kept asking the authorities for a church and presbytery in order to set up a regular mission which would prevent "the Indians on this island [from being] wanderers or vagabonds." His wish kept being deferred so that he himself assumed the cost of the buildings that he constructed after 1754 on Île de la Sainte-Famille (today Chapel Island) in the south of Grand Lac de La Brador (Bras d'Or Lake), where his main mission was located. Nevertheless, he received reimbursement of 3,000 *livres* in March 1757. It was probably during these years, when he was establishing his missionary work, that he wrote his long "Lettre . . . sur les missions micmaques" of unquestionable historical value. In it he sets out in detail his views on the Indians' customs and the missionary's work. His remarks on the Micmac language, his models for sermons, his reflections on the problem of alcohol and the torturing of prisoners, and above all the interpretation that he gave of the murder by the Micmacs of Edward How deserve to be mentioned in particular.

The political and religious authorities were not long in recognizing in Maillard an exceptional person: the minister of the Marine, Maurepas, Abbé de L'Isle-Dieu, and Bishop Pontbriand [DUBREIL] did not conceal their esteem for him. It is not surprising, therefore, that in 1740 he was appointed the bishop of Quebec's vicar general for Île Royale. In 1742 the provincial of the Recollets of Brittany, who were responsible for the

ministry at Louisbourg, asked that the new men he was sending there be independent of the vicar general of Île Royale. This request brought about a quarrel between Maillard and the Recollets. Scandalized by the conciliatory attitude of the Recollets towards "the disorders and dissoluteness in the colony," the missionary lost no opportunity to criticize them. His severity led Duquesnel [LE PRÉVOST] and François Bigot* to demand Maillard's recall. Bishop Pontbriand, however, was not ready to approve this recall, for he considered it an attempt "to escape his episcopal jurisdiction." His opinion commanded all the more respect since in the mother country Maillard's presence among the Micmacs was considered indispensable. In 1744 the bishop was obliged, nevertheless, to divide the vicar general's powers between Maillard and the superior of the Recollets in Louisbourg.

The conflict died down momentarily during the War of the Austrian Succession, particularly after the capture of Louisbourg, but it flared up again after 1750, when the chief protagonists returned to Île Royale. This time Maillard had even fewer qualms about being severe, since he now had a protector in the person of the Abbé de L'Isle-Dieu. Indeed, the latter had received many complaints about the canonical irregularities and the delinquencies of the Recollets, and he was actually thinking of replacing them, for, he claimed, "six secular priests would do more work than nine Recollets." In 1751 he took the initiative of sending Maillard the bull announcing Benedict XIV's jubilee, together with instructions which left no doubt about what he thought of the Recollets' authority. The following year Maillard formally organized the celebration of the Holy Year, with ceremonies, sermons, and processions, and thus asserted his authority over all the clergy on Île Royale. In 1754 Bishop Pontbriand confirmed him in his functions as vicar general, which he exercised henceforth alone. The bishop also authorized Maillard to force the Recollets to submit to his jurisdiction, a solution which is proof both of Maillard's prestige at Louisbourg and of the influence which the Abbé de L'Isle-Dieu was acquiring in running the affairs of the church of Canada.

Even more than with his ecclesiastical administration, Maillard's name is associated with the important political role which he played on Île Royale and in Acadia during the final years of the French régime. This role seems to have fallen to him quite naturally at the opening of hostilities between France and England in 1744, for Maillard was needed to direct the Micmacs' movements in the military campaigns. He was present at the siege of Annapolis Royal in 1744, and some time after the fall of Louisbourg, in June 1745, he encouraged his Micmacs to make raids against the British occupation forces. At the end of 1745 he was taken prisoner, probably through treachery. He was sent to Boston, and from there to France. In 1746 he returned to Acadia with the fleet commanded by the Duc d'Anville [LA ROCHEFOUCAULD] and took an active part in the military campaigns during the winter of 1746–47 directed by Jean-Baptiste-Nicolas-Roch de Ramezay*. He saw to it that some Micmacs took part in them and sought supplies from the Acadians for the Canadian troops. On 11 Feb. 1747 it was he who gave general absolution at three o'clock in the morning before the famous battle of Minas which was to put the British garrison to flight [see Arthur NOBLE].

Maillard was then particularly conscious of the ambiguity of his role in the war. This comes out clearly in his correspondence with British officers, such as Peregrine Thomas HOPSON and Edward How, whom he met and to whom he tried to justify the conduct of the Acadians and Micmacs. But he did not even think of discussing his own participation in the French cause: "There is no reason to fear any slackening of ardour on this missionary's part," wrote the president of the council of Marine, "but rather that he will carry it too far in some respects."

The founding of Halifax in the summer of 1749 involved Maillard even more directly in political matters. On 23 Sept. 1749 the Micmacs declared war on the British who had settled on Chebucto Bay. In transcribing the Micmac text of this declaration of war, along with its translation, for the Abbé Du Fau, one of the directors of the Séminaire des Missions Étrangères, Maillard commented: "The Indians are really forced to defend themselves as they can and to prevent the British from becoming entirely the masters of the interior of Acadia." It is clear that the true aims of this war were to put obstacles in the way of British settlement and that Maillard was the intermediary between the officials at Louisbourg and the Micmacs. It has, moreover, been shown that the anonymous report entitled "Motifs des sauvages mikmaques et marichites de continuer la guerre contre les Anglais depuis la dernière paix" ("Motives of the Micmac and Marichite Indians for continuing the war against the English since the last peace"), which was sent by the Comte de Raymond*, governor of Louisbourg, had been prepared and written by Maillard himself.

Edward Cornwallis*, the governor of Halifax, was so firmly convinced of Maillard's role in the war that he made the missionary "the most

advantageous offers, both by word of mouth and in writing . . . to have him go to live at Minas." It is worth noting that the pension for Maillard that had been sought from the king of France for nearly two years was thereupon granted him. In August 1750 the missionary was awarded a pension of 800 *livres* from the Abbaye de Chaux. Moreover, Maillard and Jean-Louis Le Loutre also obtained an assistant, whom they had been requesting for several years. The new arrival was the Abbé Jean MANACH, whom Maillard hastened to initiate into the difficulties of the Micmac language. "In the circumstances in which the Indians are at present," Maillard wrote to the Abbé Du Fau in 1751, "it is not possible for any one of us to abandon them without exposing them to the opportunity of going over unfailingly to the British, who are only watching for the right moment." From his mission on Île de la Sainte-Famille Maillard kept the Micmacs in a state of war, and continued to do so until 1758.

Five days after the beginning of the second siege of Louisbourg, Maillard, at the request of Governor Drucour [BOSCHENRY], tried vainly to persuade Charles Deschamps* de Boishébert, a Canadian officer, to march on the town with a force of Indians and Acadians in order to try to run the blockade. Maillard always remained convinced that this strategy could have changed the course of events. After the fall of the fortress the missionary took refuge with his Micmacs at Miramichi Bay where a large number of Acadians who had escaped deportation in 1755 were gathered. "Here I see only the greatest distress and poverty," he wrote to the Abbé Du Fau. "All the families who have come over to us are starving." Earlier he had made a short stay on Île Saint-Jean, where the settlers were hoping that they would not be disturbed by the British. But, in 1758, the deportation of the Acadians from Île Saint-Jean only added to the number of refugees south of the Baie des Chaleurs. Maillard then decided to settle at Malagomich (Merigomish, N.S.), to spend the winter "in a cove which the British do not know," and to bring together there all the Micmacs from the east coast. He also planned to go to Quebec to ask for help, but it is not known whether he was able to make this trip.

On 26 Nov. 1759 Maillard was still at Malagomich, where he accepted from Major Henry [Alexander?] Schomberg peace conditions which he considered "good and reasonable." Other missionaries, such as Manach and Joseph-Charles Germain*, did the same. These initiatives led the French officer Jean-François Bourdon de Dombourg to compile an incriminating dossier against the missionaries, which he sent to

Maillard

Pierre de Rigaud* de Vaudreuil. The governor of Canada reacted violently against the missionaries, accusing them of treason, and in the spring of 1760 he sent an officer, Gabriel-François d'Angeac*, to Restigouche to investigate this affair. It was probably to this officer that Maillard wrote in 1760 an impassioned letter in which he declared that he had been slandered and that he hoped that he would have the opportunity to reestablish himself in Vaudreuil's presence "by summing up 23 years . . . spent in this country in the service of our Religion and our Prince." He had indeed treated for peace with Schomberg, not treasonably, as Vaudreuil claimed, but because of his powerlessness and because he realized that the Acadians, the Micmacs, and their missionaries had been completely abandoned. Nothing can better illustrate the missionary's moral distress at this time than a letter that he wrote to a British officer to advise him to be tolerant toward the Acadians; he ended the letter thus: "If through the misfortunes of the times and the fortunes of war I am now enchained, I love my chains because you have made them seem agreeable to me, to the point that I wish that you will not break them for a good while." This letter probably coincided with Maillard's decision to accept the invitation of the governor of Nova Scotia, Charles LAWRENCE, to go to Halifax to cooperate with the British authorities in the pacification of the Micmacs.

That he should have been approached for this difficult mission is certainly revealing. We do not know when he arrived in Halifax, but it was likely at the beginning of the autumn of 1760, before Lawrence's death, which occurred on 19 October of that year. Maillard became a British official with the title of government agent to the Indians and a salary of £150. He received permission to maintain an oratory at a battery in Halifax, where he was able to hold Catholic services for the Acadians and Micmacs in the area "with great freedom." Many Acadians had followed him to Halifax, in particular the family of Louis Petitpas, his daily companion and confidential agent since 1749, in whose home he lived and whom he made his sole legatee. Maillard did in fact mediate with the different tribal chiefs and was in most instances successful in persuading them to sign peace treaties with the British in Halifax. Thus Joseph Argimault signed for the Micmacs of the Mesigash (Missaguash) River on 8 July 1761 and Francis Mius for those at La Hève (La Have) on 9 November of that year. Eloquent testimonials confirm these deeds: "Thanks to him," wrote Thomas Wood*, "many Englishmen were saved from being massacred."

In the upheaval of 1760 Maillard had been confirmed in his functions as vicar general for all the territory of Nova Scotia, since Acadia no longer existed. From Halifax he tried to communicate with the Acadians who were dispersed about the surrounding territories. In 1761 he even corresponded with the Acadian colony at Salem, Massachusetts, and gave Louis Robichaud*, the son of Prudent Robichaud and leader of the little community, permission to receive "the mutual consent . . . of all those men and women who may wish to be joined in marriage." This letter shows that Maillard considered himself at that time to be the spiritual leader of all the dispersed Acadians. Although they were without news of the missionary, the French religious authorities tried vainly in July 1762 to impose him upon James Murray* as superior of the seminary of Quebec. Everything indicates that Maillard was not aware of this final honour which it was desired to confer upon him.

In July 1762 Maillard fell seriously ill. He was cared for by his faithful followers as well as by Thomas Wood, a former surgeon-major who in 1759 had become chaplain to the House of Assembly at Halifax. On 12 Aug. 1762 Pierre Maillard died in Petitpas's home, attended at his own request by the Anglican clergyman, Thomas Wood, who gave an account of his death and added that he had recited the office of the visitation of the sick in French. He received a state funeral organized by the government of Nova Scotia. The pall-bearers included Jonathan Belcher*, the president of the council, and William Nesbitt*, the speaker of the assembly. The government thus recognized the great services that Maillard had rendered in the pacification of the Indians as well as the respect he had earned because of his strong personality. According to the Reverend Mr Wood, "He was a very sensible, polite, well bred man, an excellent scholar and a good sociable companion, and was much respected by the better sort of people here as it appeared." With him disappeared the last missionary to Acadia.

The historians who have written about Acadia in the 18th century are unanimous in their favourable opinion of Pierre Maillard, and this unanimity about a person from Acadian history seems exceptional. They try to outdo one another in praising his talents as a linguist, his missionary zeal, his devotion to the Micmacs' cause, his loyalty to France, and his collaboration with the British after the fall of Louisbourg. Maillard represents beyond a doubt the true missionary, enlightened, particularly lucid in complicated situations, always sure of where he stands, and passionate in expressing his opinions. He was probably one of the best ambassadors of the French cause in America in the 18th century.

MICHELINE D. JOHNSON

AAQ, 12 A, Registres d'insinuations, B, 324; Registres d'insinuations, C, 170–70v, 220; 22 A, Copies de lettres expédiées, I, 51; II, 516, 579, 681, 686, 795; 10 B, Registre des délibérations, 110, 113, 236v; T, Manuscrits Maillard; 1 W, Église du Canada, I, 235–37. ASJCF, Abbé Maillard, "Livre de prières en langue micmaque avec traduction française en regard." ASQ, Carton Laverdière, 11–20, 117a; Fonds Casgrain, Acadie; Fonds Verreau, "Ma saberdache", X, 26; Grand livre de délibération, 1734–1736 ff.30, 31; Lettres, M, 85, 91, 113, 118; P, 60–75, 77–79, 120; R, 87–93, 190; MSS, 196; Polygraphie, VII, 5, 112; XI, 3; XIII, 66; Séminaire, IV, 91; IX, 1; XIV, 6, nos.3–4, 6, 14; XV, 66. AN, Col., B, 70, f.393; 74, f.554; 76, ff.350, 352, 500; 77, f.64; 78, f.392; 81, f.307; 83, f.265v; 86, ff.106, 233v; 90, f.209; 91, ff.352, 363; 92, f.171v; 95, f.294; 105, f.227; 112, f.498v; 115, f.349; C¹¹ᴬ, 78, f.407; 82, f.326; 83, ff.3–36; 86, ff.260–69; 87, ff.314–61, 365; 89, f.266; 93, ff.80–86; 105, ff.31–42, 71–73; 107, ff.76–77; C¹¹ᴮ, 20, f.85; 26, ff.38, 48–54; 28, ff.60–62; 29, f.81; 31, ff.51, 116; 37, f.39; C¹¹ᶜ, 9, ff.100–1.

Coll. de manuscrits relatifs à la N.-F., III, 359, 369, 410, 439. *Coll. doc. inédits Canada et Amérique*, I, 5–39, 47–52, 55–69; II, 58–75. Le Clercq, *New relation of Gaspesia* (Ganong). *Derniers jours de l'Acadie* (Du Boscq de Beaumont). "Lettres et mémoires de l'abbé de L'Isle-Dieu," APQ *Rapport, 1935–36; 1936–37; 1937–38.* [Pierre Maillard], *Grammaire de la langue micmaque*, J. M. Bellenger, édit. (New York, 1864); "Lettre de M. l'abbé Maillard sur les missions de l'Acadie et particulièrement sur les missions micmaques," *Les soirées canadiennes; recueil de littérature nationale* (Québec), III (1863), 289–426. N. S. *Archives, I*, 184–85. Pichon, *Lettres et mémoires.* PAC *Report, 1894*, 101–2, 120, 132–33, 147–48, 154–56, 237; *1905*, II, pt.III, 186–95, 206–7. Le Jeune, *Dictionnaire*. Casgrain, *Un pèlerinage au pays d'Évangéline*, app. I; *Une seconde Acadie*, 160, 205, 334, 336, 347; *Les Sulpiciens en Acadie*, 21, 181, 215, 366–67, app. Gosselin, *L'Église du Canada après la conquête*, III, 306–8, 349, 361, 365, 375–90. Johnson, *Apôtres ou agitateurs.*

J. E. Burns, "The Abbé Maillard and Halifax," CCHA *Report, 1936–37*, 13–22. N. M. Rogers, "Apostle to the Micmacs," *Dal. Rev.*, VI (1926–27), 166–76. Albert David, "L'apôtre des Micmacs," *Revue de l'université d'Ottawa*, V (1935), 49–82, 425–52; VI (1936), 22–40; "Une autobiographie de l'abbé Le Loutre," *Nova Francia*, VI (1931), 1–34; "Messire Pierre Maillard, apôtre des Micmacs," *BRH*, XXXV (1929), 365–75; "Les missionnaires du séminaire du Saint-Esprit à Québec et en Acadie au XVIIIᵉ siècle," *Nova Francia*, I (1925–26), 9–14, 52–56, 99–105, 152–59, 200–7; "A propos du testament de l'abbé Maillard," *Nova Francia*, II (1926–27), 99–109, 149–63.

MAILLET (Mailhet, Malet). *See* MALLET

MAILLOU (Mailloux), *dit* **Desmoulins, JEAN-BAPTISTE,** mason, master builder, king's architect, clerk of the chief road commissioner (*grand voyer*), land surveyor; b. 21 Sept. 1668 at Quebec, son of Pierre Maillou, *dit* Desmoulins, a maker of wooden shoes, and Anne Delaunay; buried 18 Sept. 1753 in the crypt of Notre-Dame de Québec church.

Jean-Baptiste Maillou's success was due in part to his older brother Joseph. Both worked independently as masons, Jean-Baptiste on Saint-Charles church at Charlesbourg (1695), and his brother on the intendant's palace (1697); about 1697 they became partners in the construction business. The partners were well patronized by merchants and officials in Quebec. Their knowledge of formal architecture and decoration might explain this appeal: their library included Marcus Vitruvius Pollio, *Architecture, ou art de bien bastir . . .* (Paris, 1572), Philibert Delorme, *Le premier tome de l'architecture . . .* (Paris, 1567), Giacomo Barozzi, known as Il Vignola, *Règles des cinq ordres d'architecture . . .* (Paris, 1632), Blaise-François de Pagan, Comte de Merveilles, *Les fortifications . . .* (Paris, 1624), Louis Savot, *L'architecture françoise des bastimens particuliers . . .* (Paris, 1624), as well as 17 architectural engravings.

Some of these books may have come from the library of the builder-architect Claude Baillif* for the inventory of his estate listed similar titles. The Maillou brothers had been his employees and Baillif witnessed Jean-Baptiste Maillou's first wedding contract. Jean-Baptiste bought Baillif's house on Rue Sault-au-Matelot in 1701 and even though he moved to Upper Town about 1720 it remained his business address. Maillou was, in a sense, a successor of Claude Baillif.

The premature death of Joseph Maillou in December 1702 left Jean-Baptiste in command of their flourishing concern. His talents were not confined to domestic architecture. He acted as a builder-contractor for several ecclesiastical buildings: the friary of the Recollets at Quebec, the church at Saint-Laurent, Île d'Orléans (1702, 1708), the Hôpital Général at Quebec (1717), and the church of Saint-Étienne-de-Beaumont (*c.* 1727). In December 1720 an ordinance of the intendant, Michel BÉGON, called for a new church and presbytery at Saint-Nicolas, in the seigneury of Lauzon, following the plans of Maillou, "builder of the King's works." A signed but otherwise unidentified plan by Maillou for a typical parish church exists in the ASQ. Alan Gowans suggests it might be the plan "for a new standard type of Quebec parish church" commissioned by Bishop Saint-Vallier [La Croix*].

Maillou

Jean-Baptiste Maillou quickly gained the confidence of the royal government. In 1726 he rebuilt the upper storey of the intendant's palace and in 1731 was the contractor for the stone vaults of the Château Saint-Louis. Most of his crown contracts were for military structures: the restoration of the Lower Town battery called "la grande plateforme" (1702), the Saint-Louis bastion (1705–7), and other parts of Quebec's fortifications (1711), as well as similar work at Fort Saint-Frédéric (Crown Point, N.Y.) in the 1730s. In 1724 Maillou submitted an unsuccessful tender for the fortifications at Louisbourg, Île Royale (Cape Breton Island) [see Gédéon de Catalogne*].

Maillou was suitably rewarded by the government though his accounts were not always acceptable. By 1719 he had received the honorific title of king's architect. On 6 Nov. 1728 Pierre Robinau* de Bécancour, the chief road commissioner, gave Maillou a commission to perform his duties in the jurisdiction of Quebec: Maillou was to act "in our absence" but the road commissioner actually left matters in the Quebec area entirely to his delegate. Maillou was empowered "to grant house alignments along the streets; to keep the streets clear in accordance with the highway ordinances; to prevent any protrusion, projections or encroachment on the streets without our permission or that of our delegate; and . . . to regulate, inspect and ensure maintenance of the royal roads of the said town." In 1735 Maillou's son-in-law Michel Petrimoulx was also made a clerk of the road commissioner, possibly to assist or replace Maillou.

From 1702 until the last years of his life Maillou was frequently called upon by the courts and private individuals to measure and appraise land, houses, and masonrywork and to draw up plans. He also worked as a land surveyor even though no surveyor's commission had been registered in his name. He marked out country roads in 1717 and 1729. He was an occasional assistant to the chief royal engineer Gaspard-Joseph CHAUSSEGROS de Léry. In 1728, 1730, and 1742 Maillou was one of the experts who assessed the necessary repairs and possible modifications to the bishop's palace. After the publication of Intendant Dupuy*'s ordinance of 1727 on construction, Maillou helped to enforce those sections dealing with shingle roofs and fireproof chimneys.

A variety of sources testify to the rise of Jean-Baptiste Maillou in the society of New France. He was of humble origins; his first wife, Louise Phélippeaux, whom he married at Quebec on 4 Feb. 1695, was a tailor's daughter, and his second wife, Marguerite Caron, was the child of a merchant seaman; they were married at Quebec on 2 July 1703. On 30 Oct. 1720 the intendant, Bégon, and his wife attended the signing of the wedding contract between Jean Maillou and his third wife, Marie-Catherine Amiot, dit Villeneuve, a merchant's daughter. From 1723 on Maillou rented a pew in the cathedral of Quebec, and in July 1746 he was one of four representative "merchants and townsmen" of Quebec consulted by the authorities about the town's defences.

Several factors might account for Maillou's rapid advancement. He was a competent masonry contractor and he had learned draughting and surveying. Jean-Baptiste and Joseph Maillou were uncommonly literate for masons: both owned copies of the Bible, small collections of sacred and profane histories, and books of devotion. Jean-Baptiste's last home was decorated with a variety of prints and paintings. He was public-spirited as well as intelligent. He and his brother Pierre volunteered for training in gunnery from 1725 to 1727 for the defence of the town.

Maillou also had a sound but not venturesome business instinct. He bought real estate in Quebec and a few farms in the region, investments which showed a preference for security and a regular revenue. One of his biggest acquisitions was the former home of René-Louis Chartier* de Lotbinière. It was a large, two-storey, mansard-roofed house on Rue Saint-Louis in Quebec's Upper Town, which he obtained in 1713 in a legal auction for a bid of 10,000 livres. It was later rented to the crown as a residence for Chaussegros de Léry. The house Maillou built for himself on the adjoining lot in 1736 was a relatively modest, one-storey, stone dwelling. In this house he died in 1753, and it still stands, much enlarged in height and breadth.

None of Jean-Baptiste Maillou's sons seems to have shown enthusiasm for his trade. Vital was a mason for some years and then became a tavern-keeper; Louis-Marie was "in the pays d'en haut for the king's service" when his father died. Joseph (1708–94) achieved some distinction as a silversmith and merchant; in 1723 his father had had to pay 500 livres in restitution to the parents of a girl whom he had accidentally killed. Two of Jean-Baptiste's daughters married well and he provided a handsome dowry for Marie-Joseph when she became a nun of the Hôtel-Dieu. From 1707 to 1723 Jean-Baptiste had trained six apprentices in masonry, including Girard-Guillaume DEGUISE, dit Flamand, Nicolas DASILVA, dit Portugais, and an Englishman called Charles-Étienne Camanne. These apprentices and not Maillou's children followed in his footsteps.

PETER N. MOOGK

[AHGQ, Livres de comptes, I, 90v. AN, Col., B, 47, ff.1247–59; C¹¹A, 59, ff.67–70; F³, 11, ff.224–25; G³, 2040 (here we find two original acts drafted by Claude Louet and the specifications for Maillou's work at Fort Saint-Frédéric). ANQ, Greffe de Jacques Barbel; Greffe de R.-C. Barolet, 21 sept. 1753, *passim*; Greffe de Louis Chambalon, 30 janv. 1695, 12 avril 1704, 21 déc. 1705, 26 déc. 1711, 26 nov. 1715, *passim*; Greffe de J.-É. Dubreuil, 22 nov. 1723, *passim*; Greffe de François Genaple de Bellefonds, 16 juin 1683, 9 janv. 1700, 5 juill. 1702, 26, 29 juin, 29 août 1703, 19 avril 1707, *passim*; Greffe de Florent de La Cetière; Greffe de Jean de Latour; Greffe de Claude Louet; Greffe de J.-C. Louet, 30 oct. 1720, *passim*; Greffe de J.-N. Pinguet de Vaucour; Greffe de Gilles Rageot; Greffe de Pierre Rivet Cavelier, 8 avril, 6 nov. 1713, 21 nov. 1717, *passim* (since the quantity of notarial acts involving Maillou as a party or expert assessor is immense, one can only cite the most important deeds and indicate where the others might be found); NF, Coll. de pièces jud. et not., 69, no.2, *passim*. P.N.M.]

Archives paroissiales de Saint-Étienne (Beaumont, Qué.), Livres de comptes, I. ASQ, Polygraphie, II, 77; Seigneuries, VI, IX; Séminaire, XX. PAC, MG 8, B1, 20/1, pp.245–54; 25/3, pp.1113–14, *passim*. "Correspondance de Vaudreuil," APQ *Rapport, 1947–48*, 309, 326. *Édits ord.*, III, 100. *Jug. et délib.*, IV, V, VI. *Recensement de Québec, 1716* (Beaudet). "Recensement de Québec, 1744" (APQ *Rapport*). P.-V. Charland, "Notre-Dame de Québec: le nécrologe de la crypte," *BRH*, XX (1914), 215, 237, 238. Godbout, "Nos ancêtres," APQ *Rapport, 1951–53*, 462, 490. P.-G. Roy, *Inv. ins. Cons. souv.*, 185; *Inv. jug. et délib., 1717–1760*, I, II, III, IV, V; *Inv. ord. int.*, I, II, IiI. Tanguay, *Dictionnaire*. Alan Gowans, *Church architecture in New France*. P.-B. Casgrain, "Le Kent-House, rectification historique," *BRH*, XIX (1913), 11.

MAISONBASSE, JEAN-BAPTISTE DES-CHEVERY, *dit*. *See* DESCHEVERY

MAISONNAT, MARIE-MADELEINE (Winniett), b. 1695 at Port-Royal (Annapolis Royal, N.S.), daughter of Pierre Maisonnat*, *dit* Baptiste, and Madeleine Bourg (sister of Alexandre BOURG); d. sometime after 1770.

Marie-Madeleine Maisonnat's father, Pierre, the renowned corsair, is listed in the 1693 census of Port-Royal as being married to Madeleine Bourg, aged 16. The couple had a comfortable estate with numerous livestock and an arsenal of 15 guns. By the time of the 1698 census, however, Pierre had been reunited with Judith Soubiron, a former wife – he was reputed to have many. Madeleine Bourg had married a widower, Pierre Le Blanc, by this time and was living in his house-

hold with her three-year-old daughter, Marie-Madeleine.

In 1710, at 15 years of age, Marie-Madeleine witnessed the capture and occupation of Port-Royal (renamed Annapolis Royal) by British forces. The next year, before John Harrison*, the Protestant chaplain of the garrison, she married Lieutenant William WINNIETT, one of Francis Nicholson*'s colonial troops, who had volunteered to remain at Annapolis on garrison duty. Winniett soon abandoned his military status to pursue a successful career as a merchant and shipowner, and was later a member of the Nova Scotia Council. The couple had 13 children. When Winniett died in 1741, Marie-Madeleine and her family were left impoverished, "a particular concern to everybody here," according to Paul MASCARENE, the administrator of the province. Mascarene urged Winniett's debtors to settle their accounts as soon as possible.

Three of Marie-Madeleine's daughters were married to prominent members of the British establishment in Nova Scotia: Anne (b. 1712) to Alexander COSBY, Elizabeth (b. 1714) to Lieutenant John HANDFIELD, and Marie-Madeleine (b. 1718) to Captain Edward HOW. There are indications that Marie-Madeleine Maisonnat and her daughters had some influence among the garrison and officials at Annapolis Royal. Captain John Knox* speaks in 1757 of "an old French gentlewoman . . . of the Romish persuasion" – undoubtedly Marie-Madeleine – "whose daughters, grand-daughters, and other relations, have . . . intermarried with Officers, and other gentlemen of this garrison . . . ; the ladies soon acquired an influence, the spirit of the soldier and the characteristic of a good Officer were gradually changed, and succeeded by rusticity." According to Knox, some soldiers were persuaded to do work for the inhabitants of the town and neglected their own duties. If any soldier was confined for his negligence, however, "the old gentlewoman ordered him to be released by her own authority, which was deemed sufficient. . . . I am also assured that this good lady has actually presided at councils of war in the fort, when measures have been concerting to distress the common enemy, her good kindred and countrymen."

Marie-Madeleine Maisonnat was still alive in 1770, as she is mentioned in the census of Annapolis Royal.

HECTOR J. HÉBERT

AN, Col., C¹¹A, 12, f.225; 13, f.322; Section Outre-Mer, G¹, 407, 466 (recensements de l'Acadie, 1693, 1698, 1700). "Mass. Archives," V, 452. PAC, MG 9, B8, 24 (registres de Saint-Jean-Baptiste du Port Royal)

Malhiot

(original of the volume for 1702–28 is at PANS, and that for 1727–55 is at the Diocesan Archives, Yarmouth, N.S.); MG 23, C16. Knox, *Historical journal* (Doughty). Shipton, *Sibley's Harvard graduates*, VI, 423, 511–27. Calnek, *History of Annapolis* (Savary), 95–96, 119–21, 152–56, 631–32. Savary, *Supplement to history of Annapolis*, 92–93, 97. C. J. d'Entremont and H.-J. Hébert, "Parkman's diary and the Acadian exiles in Massachusetts," *French Canadian and Acadian Geneal. Rev.* (Quebec), I (1968), 241–94.

MALHIOT (Mailhiot), JEAN-FRANÇOIS, merchant, special lieutenant of the royal jurisdiction of Montreal; b. 4 Nov. 1692 in Montreal, son of Jean Malhiot, a merchant, and Madeleine Marchand; m. on 18 Dec. 1724 Charlotte, daughter of the merchant Ignace Gamelin* (1663–1739), in Montreal; d. 28 Jan. 1756 and was buried the next day in Montreal.

By 1719 Jean-François Malhiot, like his father, was a merchant with a shop in Montreal. Montreal at that period was the centre of the fur trade and the gateway to the *pays d'en haut*, and Malhiot's business consisted mainly of outfitting voyageurs who were on their way west. In March 1730, when he had become a prominent merchant, he was chosen with 12 of his fellow citizens to present to Governor Charles de BEAUHARNOIS the remonstrances of the citizens of Montreal, on whom the king intended to levy a tax for the construction of the town's fortifications.

Because Malhiot enjoyed "the esteem of all honest people," the colonial officials appointed him special lieutenant of the jurisdiction of Montreal on 19 Feb. 1740. With no legal training and no knowledge of procedure, Malhiot proved incapable of adequately replacing the lieutenant general for civil and criminal affairs, Pierre Raimbault*. In the summer of 1740 he perpetrated so many irregularities in the trial of the soldiers Jean Bontemps and Jean Dupont, *dit* Printemps, who were accused of counterfeiting orders for payment, that the Conseil Supérieur, after ordering that the trial be begun again, decided "for the sake of justice" to appoint the councillor Jacques de LAFONTAINE de Belcour acting lieutenant general of Montreal. Jean-François Malhiot nevertheless remained special lieutenant of Montreal until his death. On a few occasions he judged certain civil cases, carrying on his business at the same time.

In April 1742 Malhiot fell dangerously ill, to the point that "no hope was held out for his life." He recovered, according to the Sulpician Mathieu Falcoz, thanks to the intervention of "a pious person" who fastened to the sick man's chest "a small part of the clothes" that had belonged to Bishop Lauberivière [Pourroy*]. Malhiot lived on until 28 Jan. 1756, when he died in his house on Rue Saint-Paul, Montreal. He left two stores, and his fortune amounted to 15,814 *livres* 17 *sols* 10 *deniers*.

ANDRÉ LACHANCE

AN, Col., C¹¹ᴬ, 73, ff.15v, 40f., 296–97; 116, f.283; F³, 9, ff.257–58; 10, ff.366–67 (copies at PAC). ANQ, NF, Arrêts du Conseil d'état du roi, V, 48; NF, Coll. de pièces jud. et not., 958, 1217, 2095; NF, Registres du Cons. sup., 1730–1759, ff.67–69. ANQ-M, Greffe de L.-C. Danré de Blanzy, 3 juin 1756; Greffe de Pierre Raimbault, 17 déc. 1724; Documents judiciaires, 17 juill.–22 août, 24 sept., 22–24 nov. 1740; Registre d'état civil, Notre-Dame de Montréal, 4 nov. 1692, 18 déc. 1724, 29 janv. 1756. Massicotte, "Répertoire des engagements pour l'Ouest," APQ *Rapport, 1929–30*, 264, 276, 278, 281, 282, 352. A. Roy, *Inv. greffes not.*, XII, 45, 46, 77, 129, 136, 167, 168; XV, 48, 49, 69, 124, 127, 134, 135, 185. Tanguay, *Dictionnaire*; *Monseigneur de Lauberivière, cinquième évêque de Québec, 1739–1740* (Montréal, 1885), 127–28.

MALLEPART DE GRAND MAISON, *dit* **Beaucour, PAUL** (he generally signed **Paul Beaucour** or **Paul de Beaucour**), soldier, painter; baptized in 1700 in the parish of Saint-Eustache in Paris, France; m. on 25 June 1737 Marguerite Haguenier in Montreal; d. 15 July 1756 in Quebec.

The scarcity of documents concerning painters in the first half of the 18th century restricts considerably research on the life and work of Paul Beaucour. According to Gérard Morisset*, Beaucour is believed to have come to New France around 1720 in the colonial regular troops. The only information we have on his activities until his marriage in 1737 is that he served in the army. In his wedding certificate he is described as "sergeant in the troops of the company of M. de Beaujeu [Louis LIÉNARD]." In the Montreal census of 1741 he is listed as "one of Beaujeu's sergeants," on Rue Saint-Paul. On 25 February of the previous year he had had his son François* baptized at Laprairie; François was to become the first painter of Canadian origin to study in Europe.

Beaucour's life from 1740 to 1746 is unknown, but everything suggests that during this period he gave up his military career to become a painter. In 1746 he was in the region of Quebec. In the "inventory of the furnishings and belongings of the church" drawn up at Cap-Santé in 1747 are mentioned "two gilded frames, in one the portrait of the Virgin Mary, in the other that of Saint Joseph." Gérard Morisset, who was able to examine these two paintings closely around 1934, states that they represent the "Virgin and Child" and "St Joseph and the Infant Jesus"; "they bear the almost illegible signature of Paul Beaucours and the date 1746." Another piece of evidence of Paul Beaucour's artistic production is furnished by the account books for 1751 of the parish of Saint-Pierre, Île d'Orléans: in them mention is made of a payment "to the Sieur Beaucourt for different paintings, to wit three baldachins and their supporting columns, and for having repaired the picture of the high altar and some others, all at the rate of four *livres* per day for 40 days, 160 *livres*." It seems certain, moreover, that Beaucour continued to work as a painter at Quebec until his death. Indeed, the baptismal registers of the parish of Notre-Dame de Québec for the years 1747 to 1756, the period in which four of his children were baptized, always describe him as a painter. It was in the cemetery of this parish that Paul Beaucour was buried on 16 July 1756, the day after his death.

MICHEL CAUCHON and ANDRÉ JUNEAU

ANQ-M, Registre d'état civil, Laprairie, 25 févr. 1740; Notre-Dame de Montréal, 25 juin 1737. AJQ, Registre d'état civil, Notre-Dame de Québec, 11 nov. 1747, 5 nov. 1749, 30 sept. 1751, 14 nov. 1753. Archives paroissiales de Saint-Pierre (île d'Orléans), Livres de comptes pour 1751. IOA, Dossier Paul Beaucour, peintre. "Recensement de Montréal, 1741" (Massicotte), 31. Morisset, *Coup d'œil sur les arts*. Antoine Roy, *Les lettres, les sciences et les arts au Canada sous le régime français* (Paris, 1930), 241–55. Gérard Morisset, "Généalogie et petite histoire, le peintre François Beaucourt," SGCF *Mémoires*, XVI (1965), 195–99; "Paul Beaucourt (1700–1756)," *Vie des arts* (Montréal), I, no.4 (1956), 20–21; "Paul Malepart de Beaucours (1700–1756)," *L'Événement* (Québec), 5 déc. 1934.

MALLET (Maillet, Mailhet, Malet), PIERRE-ANTOINE, trader, explorer; b. 20 June 1700 in Montreal, son of Pierre Mallet and Madeleine Thunay, *dit* Dufresne; m. Louisa Deupet at a date and place unknown; d. after June 1751, possibly in Spain.

Pierre-Antoine Mallet belonged to a family that had been interested in the western trade as early as 1694. At some time between 1700 and 1706 his parents moved to Detroit. Paul, his brother and future travelling companion, was baptized there in 1711. Like many Canadian traders the two young men eventually drifted to the Illinois country, probably arriving in 1734.

The French had long wished to reach Spanish territory through the unknown west. At least twice during the second decade of the 18th century Louis JUCHEREAU de Saint-Denis had crossed the present state of Texas to the presidio of San Juan Bautista (near Piedras Negras, Mex.), but his attempts at establishing trade had been blocked by the Spanish viceroy. During the 1730s, however, the Spanish outposts in East Texas were through necessity largely supplied by the French. The possibility of the Missouri as an alternative route to the more distant Spanish settlements had been imagined, for the river, with whose lower reaches French traders were familiar, was thought to originate in the southwest.

In 1739 the Mallets and a small party of whom at least five others were Canadians set out from Fort de Chartres (near Prairie du Rocher, Ill.). At some point on the upper Missouri the local Indians persuaded the traders that they were taking the wrong direction to reach the Spaniards. So they retraced some of their way and then crossed by land to the Platte River, which they ascended. Leaving the south fork of this river, they continued southward overland, guided by an Indian slave. They arrived at the Spanish mission of Picuries (south of Taos, N.Mex.) and on 22 July entered Santa Fe. The success of the journey was a credit to their diplomatic skills in dealing with the various Indian nations, for although a tribe might welcome European traders bringing guns and ammunition, it would often be reluctant to let them proceed lest they arm the tribes beyond.

At Santa Fe the travellers were detained by the chief civilian official, but they could not be accused of attempting illegal trade since they had lost their goods in fording a river. While they awaited the decision of the viceroy in Mexico City as to their fate they were treated with more gentleness than was prescribed for such intruders. After nine months the decision arrived: they were ordered to quit Spanish territory and not to return without official permission. On 1 May 1740 seven of the original party (one or two, who had married Spanish women, decided to remain) left Santa Fe and travelled eastward *via* Pecos (N.Mex.). On 13 May three members of the group struck out northeastward and returned to the Illinois by the present Pawnee and Osage rivers. The other four, including the Mallets, continued east to the Arkansas post (near the junction of the Arkansas and Mississippi rivers) and south to New Orleans.

The Mallets reported their experiences to Governor Bienville [LE MOYNE] and to the financial commissary, who praised them for their findings. The route to the western sea might yet be found, and despite the Spanish ban on commerce with foreigners a profitable exchange of French products for gold and silver might yet be estab-

Manach

lished with Santa Fe. French hopes for trade must have been further encouraged by a letter carried by the Mallets. In it the chaplain of Santa Fe asked the Jesuit superior in New Orleans to send certain specified merchandise, for which payment in silver would be made.

The Mallets' achievement prompted André Fabry de La Bruyère, king's writer in the Marine and a former secretary of Bienville, to offer to lead another expedition to Santa Fe if the Mallets would serve as guides. The new party, which was to go by way of the Arkansas River, was outfitted by Bienville at considerable cost. It turned out to be an expensive failure. Fabry, the Mallets, Philippe Robitaille, and Michel Belleau, *dit* La Rose, left New Orleans at the end of August 1741. Difficulties arose between the Mallets and Fabry. The water in a fork of the Canadian River proved too shallow for travel, and the Mallets were unsuccessful in obtaining horses from the Mentos. While Fabry went back to buy horses at the Arkansas post the Mallets set out on foot for Santa Fe, but they appear not to have reached it.

The brothers asserted in 1743 that they were going to make another attempt to get to the Spanish town, but not until 1750 did one of them, Pierre, take part in a third expedition. In the meantime they settled near the Arkansas post. The 1749 census reveals that Paul farmed and traded; he had a wife, three daughters, one slave, an ox, and a cow. Pierre, who may have been a widower (his wife had died by 1751 at least), traded upriver.

Talk of the Mallets' travels certainly had some effect. During the 1740s a number of French soldiers deserted and reached Santa Fe. The commandant of the Arkansas post, Louis-Xavier Martin de Lino de Chalmette, formed a project of commerce between that place and Santa Fe. He took Pierre Mallet to New Orleans with him in 1750, and Mallet received permission from Governor Pierre de Rigaud* de Vaudreuil to make the journey. No official funds were available, but Vaudreuil and Lino may have invested privately in the expedition.

With letters from Vaudreuil and the merchants of New Orleans, Mallet and three companions set out. They travelled slowly, taking about two months to reach Natchitoches (La.) where they stayed some time. They proceeded as far as the Caddodacho post (probably somewhere near Texarkana, Tex.-Ark.) by canoe, and then went overland to Pecos. The journey from Natchitoches took about three months, and during the course of it the Comanches seized most of their merchandise. When they arrived at Pecos in November 1750 they were arrested and taken first to Santa Fe and subsequently to El Paso (Tex.), where Governor Tómas Vélez Cachupín was at the time. The governor sold their remaining goods at auction and used the money obtained to send the former owners under guard to Chihuahua (Mex.) and, in February 1751, to Mexico City. The viceroy had them interrogated again and ordered them sent to Spain to the jurisdiction of the Casa de Contratación, which was in charge of the economic administration of the colonies. He also reaffirmed the ban on illicit commerce. Further information on Pierre Mallet is lacking, most likely buried in Spanish archives, for this Canadian pioneer in the western trade was probably imprisoned in Spain.

A. P. NASATIR

ANDM, Registres des baptêmes, mariages et sépultures, 20 juin 1700. *Before Lewis and Clark: documents illustrating the history of the Missouri, 1785–1804*, ed. A. P. Nasatir (2v., St Louis, 1952), I, 27–43. *Découvertes et établissements des Français* (Margry), VI. J. A. Pichardo, *Pichardo's treatise on the limits of Louisiana and Texas . . .*, ed. and trans. C. W. Hackett (4v., Austin, Tex., 1931–46), III, 299–370. *The Plains Indians and New Mexico, 1751–1778 . . .*, ed. A. B. Thomas (Albuquerque, N.Mex., 1940).

J. F. Bannon, *The Spanish borderlands frontier, 1513–1821* (New York, 1970). H. E. Bolton, "French intrusions into New Mexico, 1749–1752," in *The Pacific Ocean in history*, ed. H. E. Bolton and H. M. Stephens (New York, 1917), 389–407; repr. in *Bolton and the Spanish borderlands*, ed. J. F. Bannon (Norman, Okla., 1964), 150–71. Henry Folmer, *Franco-Spanish rivalry in North America 1524–1763* (Glendale, Calif., 1953), 297–303. N. M. Loomis and A. P. Nasatir, *Pedro Vial and the roads to Santa Fe* (Norman, Okla., 1967). Stanley Faye, "The Arkansas post of Louisiana: French domination," *Louisiana Historical Quarterly* (New Orleans), XXVI (1943), 633–721. Henry Folmer, "The Mallet expedition of 1739 through Nebraska, Kansas, and Colorado to Santa Fe," *Colorado Magazine* (Denver), XVI (1939), 163–73.

MANACH (Manack, Manachs), JEAN (Jacques), priest of the Missions Étrangères, missionary; b. probably *c.* 1727 in France; ordained a priest in Paris in 1750; d. 22 Jan. 1766 at sea.

Jean Manach received his ecclesiastical training at the Séminaire des Missions Étrangères in Paris. Upon his ordination his superiors planned to send him to the Micmac missions in Acadia, but he was first to make a brief stay at the seminary of Quebec "to become stronger in the moral sciences and the other branches of knowledge which are necessary to him." The ship which was carrying him called at Louisbourg, Île Royale

(Cape Breton Island); Manach yielded to Pierre MAILLARD's entreaties and went immediately to his Acadian mission in October 1750. Although this act of disobedience "mortified" his superiors, Manach stayed in Acadia. There he became an indispensable assistant to Jean-Louis Le Loutre*, whom he often replaced in his work among the Micmacs at the Shubenacadie mission, and by 1752 he had mastered the Micmac language despite its reputation of being "primitive and barbarous."

Manach was closely involved in the border incidents which began in September 1750 while forts Beauséjour and Lawrence were being constructed on the Chignecto Isthmus. We know that he intervened in the deliberations over the exchange of deserters in April 1753, that he reprimanded the Acadian women who had gone to hang about Fort Lawrence in August of that year, and that he acted as liaison between the officers at Fort Beauséjour and the Micmacs at his mission. His attitude, in short, was that of the majority of the French priests in Acadia in the 18th century, that of a man who openly supported the cause of France. Manach's servant at this time was a certain Daniel, a Swiss in origin, who, after acting as a double agent, went over to the English at the beginning of 1756. This man attributed to his master subversive utterances: "Every Englishman that you kill will be a step on the ladder to paradise," the missionary was supposed to have told his Micmacs. In reporting these remarks, Abbé François Le Guerne stated specifically that they were nothing but lies. However, when we consider that the Micmacs did not accept the English peace proposals until Manach had set an example, we may presume that he had encouraged his flock to take an active part in the skirmishing on the frontiers of Acadia. When Fort Beauséjour was taken in July 1755, Manach had to flee to the region of Miramichi, along with the people who had survived Robert Monckton*'s raids. For nearly four years he remained hidden in the woods, the only priest among the Acadian and Micmac fugitives. His superiors said at that time how moved they were by his attachment to his Indians, but they were conspicuously unaware of the conditions in which he lived. Like the civil authorities, they believed that he was being well supplied by Intendant Bigot*, whereas the little group was surviving in the most wretched conditions. After 1760 Abbé Manach's testimony was in fact added to the file on the bad administration of Canada.

On 26 Oct. 1759, when the capture of Quebec became known, Manach accepted in the name of the Acadians at Richibucto (N.B.) and Baie des Ouines (Bay du Vin) the peace proposals put forward by "Commandant Henry [Alexander?] Schomberg." Other missionaries, such as Maillard and Joseph-Charles Germain*, likewise agreed to local capitulations. These initiatives were severely criticized by Jean-François Bourdon de Dombourg, a French officer at the camp on the Restigouche, and led him to prepare a file on the missionaries, whom he accused of treason. Informed of the file, Governor Pierre de Rigaud* de Vaudreuil contemplated having them "arrested" but decided to follow "the wisest and most prudent course on account of the importance of their position." As early as July 1760 Manach collaborated with Maillard in pacifying the Micmacs, but in March 1761 he was arrested by the authorities in Halifax who accused him of "creating unrest among the Indians." He was taken to New York and from there to England, where he remained a prisoner for some months in the roadstead of Portsmouth, without knowing "the reason for his detention."

He was freed in August 1761 and went to Paris, where he was ill received at the seminary. The directors of the seminary claimed, in fact, that he had left his mission without permission, and agreed to lodge him only if he paid board. Consequently he had to obtain, through the influence of the Abbé de L'Isle-Dieu, two benefices from the court to ensure his subsistence. Manach wanted, however, to return to Acadia and increased his endeavours to this end. The Abbé de L'Isle-Dieu approached Lord Stanley, a British diplomat, in order to obtain permission for Manach to return to Acadia. Yet the directors of the Séminaire des Missions Étrangères were really contemplating placing the former missionary as a curate in a parish in Paris.

Faced with these vexations, Manach then undertook, together with Jacques Girard* who had also been a missionary in Acadia, to bring an action against the superior and directors of the Séminaire des Missions Étrangères, "appealing by writ of error or for excess of power" against the rules of the community and demanding the participation of the missionaries in the running of the seminary. According to them the directors had failed in their missionary ideal in laying down the secret regulation of 1716 which virtually relieved the directors of any obligation towards the missionaries. The results of such a regulation were inevitable: in 1762 there were 11 directors to train two young ecclesiastics. In other words the Séminaire des Missions Étrangères had become a source of benefices rather than a centre of missionary expansion. The group of missionaries, who were joined by Le Loutre, some

Mangeant

former vicars apostolic to the East and West Indies, and some bishops, including Dosquet*, produced a number of interesting reports in the course of this affair. The directors were able, however, to interpret to their advantage the original acts of the seminary. Above all they were successful in transforming the grounds of the challenge by asking "whether the bishops, the vicars apostolic, and the missionaries who were their fellow-workers, being outside the kingdom, could form a congregation within it and be a member of any legal body within it." The Abbé de L'Isle-Dieu considered that the directors' position bore the stamp of "absurdity" and "irreligion." The case was brought before the civil courts of the upper chamber of the *parlement* of Paris. The directors of the seminary won the case on 6 Sept. 1764, through a decree which maintained "the Superior and directors of the Séminaire des Missions Étrangères established in Paris in possession of the aforementioned seminary."

"Wishing to do justice to oppressed virtue and innocence," the Abbé de L'Isle-Dieu took the missionaries under his protection. On 7 June 1765 he obtained for Girard and Manach the offices of "prefect and vice-prefect in the new apostolic prefecture of the islands of Saint-Pierre and Miquelon," where many Acadian refugees were living. This appointment gave proof of the regard which was shown the two missionaries, who were being entrusted in this way with some of the powers of a bishop. The ship which was carrying Manach and Girard was shipwrecked and ran aground in Martinique. Manach died on 22 Jan. 1766 during the voyage taking him back from Martinique to the mother country.

MICHELINE D. JOHNSON

AAQ, 11 B, Correspondance, III, 277; 1 W, Église du Canada, VII, 101–8, 133–36, 209–26, 229–49, 273–83. ASQ, Chapitre, 147; Lettres, M, 113, 115, 118, 120–21; P, 67; Polygraphie, V, 40; VII, 5; XI, 2–4; Séminaire, XIV, 6, no.14. AN, Col., B, 113, ff.229, 231; 115, f.242; 120, f.431; 121, f.654; 122, ff.223, 265, 586, 588; C¹¹ᴬ, 105, ff.82–108. PAC, MG 17, A3, 26/1–2.
Coll. doc. inédits Canada et Amérique, I, 47–52; II, 142–45; III, 60–87, 181–91. Placide Gaudet, "Acadian genealogy and notes," PAC *Report, 1905*, II, pt.III, 186–97, 345–56. Knox, *Historical journal* (Doughty), III, 353–421. *Derniers jours de l'Acadie* (Du Boscq de Beaumont). "Lettres et mémoires de l'abbé de L'Isle-Dieu," APQ *Rapport, 1935–36*, 275–410; *1936–37*, 331–459; *1937–38*, 147–95. *N.S. Archives, I*. Johnson, *Apôtres ou agitateurs*. Albert David, "Les missionnaires du séminaire du Saint-Esprit à Québec et en Acadie au XVIIIe siècle," *Nova Francia*, I (1925–26), 9–14, 52–56, 99–105, 152–59, 200–7.

MANGEANT (Maugean), *dit* **Saint-Germain, FRANÇOIS (Louis-François),** merchant, ship owner, rent gatherer; b. 1686 or 1687 in the parish of Saint-Paul, Paris, France, son of Louis Mangeant and Anne Deschamps; d. after September 1744.

François Mangeant's presence in the new world is first recorded on 24 April 1713 (N.S.), when he married Marguerite Caissy (Keissis), daughter of Jean Caissy, *dit* Roger, and Anne Bourgeois, at Beaubassin (near Amherst, N.S.). He appears to have left Nova Scotia shortly thereafter for Quebec, where he was evidently a ship owner and probably a trader; in a 1716 census he is called a "scribe." By 1726 his vessels were valued at 2,000 *livres*. That year, in a heated quarrel with Joseph-Alphonse Lestage, of Quebec, who "Did most Basely and Heinously Insult, Affront and provock" him, Mangeant attacked and wounded Lestage so seriously that he died two days later. This, at least, was the story which Mangeant told in Nova Scotia, where he fled after the murder. According to evidence submitted to the admiralty court at Quebec, the quarrel took place in the Gaspé region, on board a ship owned by Mangeant and commanded by Lestage. Mangeant was pardoned by the king of France in 1732.

Mangeant presented himself to the council at Annapolis Royal in September 1726 and requested permission to settle, with his family, in the Chignecto region. He was even willing to swear allegiance to the British crown, a step few Acadians would take. Mangeant soon found a firm supporter and friend in the lieutenant governor, Lawrence Armstrong*, and was often employed by the government in its dealings with the Acadians [*see* René-Charles de Breslay*]. Unfortunately for Mangeant, by accepting Armstrong's patronage he incurred the hatred of his enemies as well. In June 1729, while reading a government proclamation to the Acadians at Annapolis Royal, Mangeant came close to blows with Major Alexander Cosby, one of Armstrong's more outspoken critics. The cause of the conflict is not clear, as we have only Armstrong's account, but Armstrong considered it serious enough to call an assembly of officers to examine the incident.

Governor Richard Philipps returned to Nova Scotia in 1729, and in 1730 Armstrong and Mangeant sailed for England to seek redress for grievances against the governor. Writing to the Duke of Newcastle, Philipps said of Mangeant that his "character is very bad, but is allowed to have a Genius, and would make an excellent Minister to an arbitrary Prince." He reported that the Acadians disliked Mangeant intensely because of the advice he gave Armstrong about governing the colony. Philipps, however, probably disliked Mangeant mainly because of his friendship with Armstrong.

In mid-July 1731 Armstrong returned to Annapolis Royal, triumphant, with orders for Philipps to return to England. Mangeant likely returned with Armstrong; in the next few years he lived at Minas (Grand Pré region) and was employed to supervise land transactions, examine new settlers, and oversee the implementation of wills. He was frequently entrusted with official government missions. In November 1736, for example, he was instructed to organize a search in the Minas region for two men wanted for a recent robbery. He was asked in December to investigate the delinquency in payment of quitrents by Acadians at Grand Pré, which had plagued the government for years. By December 1737 Alexandre BOURG had been removed from his position of rent gatherer at Minas and Mangeant was appointed in his place. Mangeant's job, and possibly his temperament, seem to have made him unpopular with the Acadians among whom he lived. Armstrong felt it necessary on one occasion to caution him "to Guard Agst all violent and Disagreeable Proceedings and treat ... all others [with] whom you may have any Dealings with Decency and Mildness." The sudden death of Armstrong in December 1739 removed Mangeant's chief support in the government. With his position greatly undermined, he resigned his official post early in 1740, ending his public role in Nova Scotia.

In the spring of 1742 Mangeant and the two deputies of Minas, Alexandre Bourg and Amand Bujeau, were instrumental in recovering a trading vessel seized near Grand Pré by Indians. Paul MASCARENE, the new head of government, promised to do all in his power to advance Mangeant's position in the colony for his part in the affair. Shortly thereafter Mangeant moved to Canso, where he had "found a way to employ himself in a more advantageous way than he would at Menis," as Mascarene phrased it. It would appear that he was taken prisoner during the French seizure of Canso on 24 May 1744 [see Patrick HERON]. In July he helped convey some of the prisoners from Louisbourg, Île Royale (Cape Breton Island), to Boston and in September was still acting as a liaison between the governments at Louisbourg and Boston. No other mention of François Mangeant is to be found in the records of Nova Scotia, and the dispersal of the Acadians a decade later may have been a factor in his disappearance from sight. He had three daughters and one son who survived infancy.

BARRY M. MOODY

AN, Col., B, 57, ff.677v, 730 (calendared in PAC *Report, 1904*); Marine, C⁷, 205. Mass. Hist. Soc., Mascarene family papers, Mascarene to Dr Douglass, 28 April 1742. PAC, MG 6, A2, E, État civil de la paroisse Notre-Dame de Beaubassin (mfm copy at PANS); MG 11, Nova Scotia B, 2, pp.233–34; 3, pp.16–19. PANS, RG 1, 12, nos.24, 34; 14, pp.101, 103, 169–70, 177–78, 180–82, 187–88, 207, 210–12, 258; 17, nos.18, 19; 18, no.39; 21, ff.3–4. *N.S. Archives, II; III; IV.* PAC *Report, 1905*, II, pt.III, 71. *Recensement de Québec, 1716* (Beaudet), 29. P.-G. Roy, *Inv. jug. et délib., 1716–1760*, I, 257, 283. Tanguay, *Dictionnaire*, I, 174; V, 482. Arsenault, *Hist. et généal. des Acadiens*.

MARCOL, GABRIEL, priest, Jesuit, missionary, superior of the Jesuit missions in New France; b. 14 April 1692 at Saint-Sébastien de Nancy, in the duchy of Lorraine, son of Pascal Marcol, provost of Nancy, and Catherine Lorson; d. 17 Oct. 1755 at Quebec.

Gabriel Marcol received the tonsure 17 Sept. 1706 and entered the noviciate of the Jesuits of the province of Champagne at Nancy 8 Sept. 1708. After two years of noviciate he taught the first and second forms at Reims (1710–12), studied philosophy at Pont-à-Mousson (1712–14), taught the fourth form and the classics class at Reims (1714–16), classics at Pont-à-Mousson (1716–17), and the senior class at Nancy (1718–19); then he studied theology at the Collège Louis-le-Grand in Paris (1719–23). After a final year of spiritual instruction he left Nancy for the Canadian missions on 3 June 1724, without saying farewell to his family in order, he wrote his brother, a member of the Society of Jesus, to avoid the objections to his vocation which he feared he would encounter from them. On 5 July he sailed from La Rochelle on board the *Chameau*, but contrary winds kept the ship in the roads until 24 July. On that day the intendant Edme-Nicolas Robert, who was going to take up his office at Quebec, suddenly died on board the vessel. On 9 Oct. 1724, after a 78-day crossing, the vessel reached Quebec.

On 6 Oct. 1725 Marcol wrote from Bécancour: "I am at present the only missionary in a village of Abenaki Indians 30 leagues from Quebec; I am beginning to understand these poor savages ... in matters concerning religion." On 5 Oct. 1727, at Quebec, he made his solemn profession before Father Jean-Baptiste DUPARC. But his health suffered from the harsh Canadian winter, and during the winter of 1730 he was gravely ill with smallpox; he was taken to Quebec, where he was

Mareuil

delirious for 16 or 17 days. The following year he fractured his arm in a fall on the ice. In 1733 he was again very ill. The glare of the snow and the smoke in the lodges damaged his sight and he became almost incapable of reading. In 1735 he was recalled to Quebec to teach philosophy, but he yearned after his mission.

From 1737 to 1740 he was the superior at Montreal, then at his own request he returned in 1741 to the Saint-François-Xavier mission near Bécancour. He remained there until October 1748, when he was appointed rector of the college of Quebec and superior general of the Jesuit missions in New France. He held this office for six years; few details are known about this period of his life. The most unpleasant matter he had to deal with was undoubtedly the ukase in May 1750 from Governor La Jonquière [TAFFANEL], which ordered Father Jean-Baptiste TOURNOIS to leave the mission of Sault-Saint-Louis (Caughnawaga); Marcol defended his fellow priest before the governor. In October 1754 Jean-Baptiste de SAINT-PÉ succeeded him as superior of the Jesuit missions in New France. Marcol died at Quebec a year later, on 17 Oct. 1755.

Gabriel Marcol's correspondence reveals a man of energetic character, full of affection for his family and friends, whom he kept informed of the temporal and spiritual progress of the colony. The author of these letters appears as a perfect religious, completely engaged in God's business.

JOSEPH COSSETTE

Archives municipales de Nancy (France), État civil, Saint-Sébastien de Nancy, 14 avril 1692. ASJCF, 582; 607; 695; 759; 760; Fonds Rochemonteix, 4018. ASJ, Gallo-Belge (Lille), Lettres de Gabriel Marcol (38 pièces). Rochemonteix, Les Jésuites et la N.-F. aux XVIIIᵉ siècle, II, 35–65.

MAREUIL, PIERRE DE, priest, Jesuit, missionary; b. 29 June 1672 at Bourges, France; d. 19 April 1742 in Paris.

After studying at the Jesuit college in Bourges, Pierre de Mareuil entered the noviciate of the Jesuits of the province of France in Paris on 8 Sept. 1692. He finished his education in letters at the Collège Louis-le-Grand in Paris, then taught classes in grammar and humanities at the Jesuit college in Caen from 1695 to 1701. After teaching classics at the Collège Louis-le-Grand for a year, he began his four years of theology there. When his last probationary year was finished, in 1707, he sailed for Quebec.

Pierre de Mareuil spent about six years in New France, and one in captivity at Albany, New York. On arrival he was sent among the Onon-dagas to help Father Jacques de Lamberville*. The Jesuits were still in the Iroquois territory, in spite of New York's claim to exclusive control of the area and despite the laws passed by the New York legislature against Catholic propaganda among the Indians. This colony did not, however, feel the same hostility towards the French to the north as did New England in its entirety. The English colony, the former apanage of James II, in which the Dutch mercantile families still had a powerful influence, as yet recognized Queen Anne's authority only with some hesitation. The Iroquois, whose territory was a buffer zone for the English and French, did not want to be dominated by the colony of New York and were using their alliance with New France to preserve their independence.

In 1709 the English colonies decided to conquer the St Lawrence valley and a fleet was to set out from Boston and sail up the river, while an army would go up the Hudson and attack Montreal. In May Abraham Schuyler, a relative of Peter Schuyler*, was sent to the Onondagas to win them over to the English cause. He began by frightening Father Lamberville, who went north to warn Governor Philippe de Rigaud* de Vaudreuil. Thus rid of the Jesuit's influence, the English agent was successful in winning over the Onondagas and persuaded Father Mareuil to take refuge at Albany, without mentioning, of course, that he had been ordered to take him prisoner. The missionary followed Schuyler and spent a year in New York settlements – a prisoner, but well treated by his guardians. During this time the English army gave up its attempt at invasion [see Francis Nicholson*; Claude de Ramezay*; Samuel Vetch*]. Once freed in May 1710 in exchange for Barent Staats, a nephew of Peter Schuyler and a French prisoner, Father Mareuil explained that Nicholson's failure was due to the Iroquois, who had contaminated the drinking water in Peter Schuyler's camp and had thus reduced the English force to impotence.

It is possible that upon returning to the St Lawrence valley Father Mareuil lived for some time at the Sault-Saint-Louis mission (Caughnawaga) while waiting to go back among the Onondagas. But since the Iroquois mission could not be re-established, he stayed at the Saint-François-de-Sales mission (Odanak) from May to August 1711; then he went to the Jesuit college in Quebec to teach philosophy. He was a victim of the epidemic of fever and purpura which ravaged the colony in 1713 and had to sail back to France in the autumn of that year. It is said that the ship on which he was travelling was captured by the English and that he had to spend a year as a prisoner in England; his return to France is in any case mentioned only in 1715, at the time when he took up his abode at La Flèche. Subsequently he was for 13 years prefect of studies in Jesuit colleges in France. He died at the Collège Louis-le-Grand on 19 April 1742, having given up all activity two years before.

After his return to France, Pierre de Mareuil acquired a reputation as a Latinist by publishing religious poems and translating religious or patristic works. In addition his knowledge of English enabled him to translate and publish, among other works, Milton's *Paradise regained.* Finally, he wrote and published some works in French, one of which, a life of St Jeanne de Valois, was translated into Italian.

LUCIEN CAMPEAU

For more extensive information on the works of Pierre de Mareuil as author and translator see: *Bibliothèque de la Compagnie de Jésus, première partie: bibliographie, par les pères Augustin et Aloys de Backer; seconde partie: histoire, par Auguste Carayon*, Carlos Sommervogel, édit. (11v., Bruxelles, Paris, 1890–1932), V, 538–41, and the *Catalogue général des livres imprimés de la Bibliothèque nationale: auteurs* (206v. to date, Paris, 1924–   ), CVI, 478–79.

ASJCF, 479; 487; 784; 891. Charlevoix, *Histoire de la N.-F.* (1744), II, 334, 338–39. *NYCD* (O'Callaghan and Fernow), IX, 836, 842, 845, 847, 856.

MARGANE DE LAVALTRIE, FRANÇOIS, seigneur, trader, priest; b. 9 Sept. 1685 at Lavaltrie (Que.) on the north shore of the St Lawrence, son of Séraphin Margane de Lavaltrie and Louise Bissot; m. on 9 May 1712 Angélique Guyon Després at Beauport; d. 6 March 1750 at the Hôtel-Dieu of Quebec.

François Margane de Lavaltrie belonged to a family of soldiers. His father had come to New France with the Régiment de Carignan, and his brother, François-Marie Margane* de Batilly, died in the raid on Deerfield, Massachusetts, in February 1704 (10 March N.S.). François probably acquired a taste for adventure from them, and early began trading on the Labrador coast. It is difficult to tell when he first went there, but it seems that from 1701 on he took part in the earliest expeditions to Labrador, organized by Augustin Le Gardeur* de Courtemanche and his wife, Marie-Charlotte Charest. Later Margane served under Le Gardeur at Fort Pontchartrain, built in 1705 on Baie de Phélypeaux (Baie de Brador).

On 13 Aug. 1711 Margane de Lavaltrie was ordered by Le Gardeur to deliver to Governor Philippe de Rigaud* de Vaudreuil in Quebec a message he had received from the minister of Marine, Pontchartrain, warning the governor that an English fleet was preparing to sail up the river to attack Quebec. His mission completed, Margane left Quebec on 18 September for Fort Pontchartrain, having received instructions from Vaudreuil to return to Quebec if he encountered the enemy. Margane reached Île aux Oeufs on 1 October and discovered the wreckage of part of Admiral Hovenden Walker*'s fleet which had been shipwrecked during the night of 22–23 August. Margane returned to Quebec with news of the shipwreck, and on 17 October declared before the admiralty court that Vital Caron, a sea captain, and his men had pillaged the wreckage and that he himself, "giving up the profits that he could have made, like the others," had immediately returned to Quebec to make his declaration and to lay claim to "the rights which belong to the denunciator."

Margane de Lavaltrie returned to Fort Pontchartrain to assist Le Gardeur de Courtemanche. But the latter died in 1717 and was replaced by his stepson, François MARTEL de Brouague. Then began a conflict over trade with the Indians and Eskimos between Margane and the new commandant of Labrador, who was backed by his mother, Le Gardeur's widow. If we are to judge by the declarations of the antagonists, it seems that Mme Le Gardeur wanted to retain a certain monopoly for herself and her son; yet the former commandant, Le Gardeur, had allowed Margane to carry on trade, although he did not have a concession on the coast. The dispute was ended by Governor Vaudreuil's mediation, Margane obtaining the concession to the post of the Rivière Saint-Augustin on 26 May 1720.

In the years that followed Margane, by himself or in partnership, operated this concession, which allowed him to engage in cod fishing, seal hunting, and fur trading with the Indians and Eskimos "without obligation to pay His Majesty . . . any money or compensation." In 1737 he leased his concession for three years to Michel Pétrimoulx, Charles Chéron, and Nicolas Caron for an annual rent of 250 *livres*. Margane had decided to retire to Beauport, where he had settled his family. Two years later, on 29 Dec. 1739, his wife died. From then on he lived alone; his only son, Louis-François, had been married on 22 January of that year.

On 9 Dec. 1741 Margane de Lavaltrie leased his concession to Jean-Baptiste POMMEREAU for ten years. Shortly before or after he was admitted into the seminary of Quebec and on 22 Sept. 1742 was ordained a priest. He remained at the seminary for some years, and from January 1746 to

Marie

September 1747 he was parish priest of Cap-Saint-Ignace. Upon his return to Quebec he was appointed chaplain of the Hôtel-Dieu; he died there on 6 March 1750 and was buried the next day in the hospital cemetery. For a man of his stamp, the end of his life was a peaceful one, in marked contrast with the adventurous beginning of his career.

In his will, drawn up on 28 Feb. 1750 when he was very ill, François Margane de Lavaltrie left all his property to his grandchildren, since his son had died in 1743. The heirs had only the post of the Rivière Saint-Augustin to divide; Margane had given up his rights to the family seigneury of Lavaltrie in 1735. But in fact the heirs were not able to enjoy this inheritance, for in accordance with the deed of concession the post of Saint-Augustin became the property of the crown on Margane de Lavaltrie's death.

MICHEL PAQUIN

AN, Col., B, 44, f.506v; 61/2, f.525; 68, f.46; C¹¹B, 4; E, 262 (dossier Lavaltrie). ANQ, Greffe de J.-R. Duparc, 8 mai 1712; Greffe de P.-A.-F. Lanoullier Des Granges, 28 févr., 16 juin 1750. *Inv. de pièces du Labrador* (P.-G. Roy), I, 33, 45, 278–80; II, 3. Juchereau, *Annales* (Jamet), 365. Le Jeune, *Dictionnaire*. P.-G. Roy, *Inv. concessions*, I, 39; II, 245; *Inv. ord. int.*, III, 46. Tanguay, *Dictionnaire*; *Répertoire*. P.-G. Roy, "La famille Margane de Lavaltrie," *BRH*, XXIII (1917), 33–53, 65–69. "Saint-Ignace du cap Saint-Ignace," *BRH*, VI (1900), 293.

MARIE, Indian slave; date of birth unknown; tried in Trois-Rivières for attempted murder and suicide and sentenced on 29 Dec. 1759 to be hanged.

The little information we possess about this slave, who belonged to Joseph-Claude Boucher* de Niverville of Trois-Rivières, is concerned especially with the criminal acts of which she was accused during the final months of French domination in Canada. On 20 Aug. 1759, towards half-past one in the afternoon, Marie-Josephte Chastelain, Boucher de Niverville's wife, and her mother Marguerite asked the slave, who was sharpening a kitchen knife on a stone, to perform some task or other; the slave, who hated her two mistresses, then threw herself upon them, striking them with the knife. Marguerite Cardin was wounded in the upper chest and in the left shoulder; the young Mme de Niverville – she was only 22 – was wounded in the right shoulder and received a scratch on the left shoulder. Blood flowed, the ladies cried "Murder!" and neighbours arrived; the slave fled to the attic and hanged herself with a rope.

While the wounds were being dressed, the king's lieutenant, Nicolas-Joseph de NOYELLES de Fleurimont, arrived on the scene with four soldiers. He discovered the woman hanging in the attic and asked Théodore Panneton to cut the rope. The surgeon Charles ALAVOINE was sent for and had the slave carried to a bed. Discerning some signs of life, he gave her a good bleeding. A half hour later Marie had regained consciousness and the ladies were recovering from their wounds, which were only superficial.

The inquiry started the same day in the presence of the notary Jean Le Proust, who in the absence of René-Ovide Hertel* de Rouville, the lieutenant general for civil and criminal affairs, was the judge in the affair. That day and on the following days numerous witnesses appeared before the court. The slave, knowing only the Ottawa language, spoke through an interpreter appointed by the court, the armourer Joseph Chevalier. According to the accused's version, the wounds were inflicted not to kill but only to frighten; she did not believe that she deserved to be punished for harming her mistresses, and if she had tried to commit suicide, it was not from regret or from fear.

On 11 Sept. 1759 the surrogate judge declared the slave guilty "of having inflicted knife wounds mentioned in the procedure and then of having hanged herself"; she was to be "beaten and flogged naked with rods by the executioner of *haute justice* at the crossroads and customary places in this town"; at one of the crossroads she was to be "branded on the right shoulder with a hot iron stamped with a fleur-de-lis"; she was then to be banished for ever from the jurisdiction of Trois-Rivières after having paid a fine of three *livres*.

Considering this sentence too mild, the king's attorney, Louis-Joseph Godefroy* de Tonnancour, appealed it to the Conseil Supérieur of the colony. The Conseil Supérieur sat in Montreal on 29 December and sentenced "the said Marie, Indian, to be hanged and strangled until death do ensue on a gallows erected for that purpose in the marketplace of this town"; it then ordered "that her dead body be exposed for two hours" before being thrown on the refuse dump.

This trial reveals the severity of criminal justice in New France; it also indicates that the slave and the free person appeared before the same tribunal and suffered their punishment under the same conditions.

ANDRÉ CÔTÉ

ANQ, NF, Dossiers du Cons. sup., Mat. crim., VI, 397; NF, Registres du Cons. sup., registre criminel,

1730–1759, ff.195f. Trudel, *L'esclavage au Canada français*. Gérard Malchelosse, "Un procès criminel aux Trois-Rivières en 1759," *Cahiers des Dix*, XVIII (1953), 207–26.

MARIE-ANDRÉE DE SAINTE-HÉLÈNE. *See* Regnard Duplessis

MARIE-ANNE DE SAINT-BENOÎT. *See* Davis

MARIE-CATHERINE DE SAINT-JOACHIM. *See* Tibierge

MARIE-CHARLOTTE DE SAINT-CLAUDE DE LA CROIX. *See* Ramezay

MARIE-JOSEPH DE L'ENFANT-JÉSUS. *See* Juchereau Duchesnay

MARIE-THÉRÈSE DE SAINT-JEAN-BAPTISTE. *See* Langlois

MARIN DE LA MALGUE (La Marque), PAUL, officer in the colonial regular troops; baptized 19 March 1692 at Montreal, eldest son of Charles-Paul de Marin* de La Malgue and Catherine Niquet; d. 29 Oct. 1753.

Paul Marin de La Malgue, son of an officer in the colonial regular troops, married Marie-Joseph Guyon Desprez on 21 March 1718, at Montreal. Several children were born of the marriage, including a son Joseph* who had a military career.

In 1720 Marin was serving in the west where he was to spend most of his life. He was commissioned an ensign in the colonial regular troops on 26 May 1722. That year he was given command of Chagouamigon (near Ashland, Wis.), with the customary monopoly of the region's fur trade to defray the expenses of maintaining the post. His chief responsibility was to retain the Indian nations in the French interest, and at peace with one another. He earned the confidence of Governor General Philippe de Rigaud* de Vaudreuil, and of his successor, Charles de Beauharnois, who declared that Marin was feared and respected by the Indians and always ready to risk his life for the French cause. After serving as first ensign for seven years he was promoted lieutenant in 1741. The minister of Marine, however, had informants who persuaded him that Marin was a poor officer, more interested in fur trade profits than in maintaining the Sioux, Fox, and Sauk tribes at peace. He therefore ordered him recalled. Beauharnois took it upon himself to disregard that order. He explained, in 1741, that Marin had succeeded in pacifying the warring tribes and had persuaded delegates from the Sioux and five other nations to accompany him to Quebec to ratify a general peace settlement, and that the king's interest required he be kept at the Sioux post.

Two years later Marin crossed to France on family business, returning to Canada at the onset of King George's War. He campaigned in Acadia and on the New York frontier. In 1746 he commanded the war party that destroyed Saratoga (Schuylerville, N.Y.) and ravaged the outlying settlements. In these campaigns he gained a reputation for bravery and ruthlessness. In 1748 he was promoted captain.

At the termination of hostilities he was sent back to the west to command at Baie-des-Puants (Green Bay, Wis.), the most lucrative of all the western posts and the one most eagerly sought after by officers of the colonial regular troops. He appears to have made the best of his opportunities. During his previous command in the west, down to 1738 he had employed not more than six voyageurs each year to transport goods to his post; in 1739 he engaged 11, in 1740 23, in 1741 29, and in 1742 31, but for the years 1750–52 he engaged at least 190. He may well have made considerable profits, but the high costs of the trade and the limitations of the market make it unlikely they were as astronomical as unsubstantiated rumours claimed. In his defence it could be said that it was a fundamental aim of French policy to retain the allegiance of the western nations and prevent their having dealings with the Anglo-Americans. This required that the French supply them with the goods they demanded and accept their furs in exchange. If the exchange could be done at a profit, so much the better. Since the political aim was achieved, the king's service clearly did not suffer during Marin's tenure at Baie-des-Puants.

Significantly, when Governor Duquesne*, immediately upon his arrival at Quebec in 1752, decided to dispatch a large force of troops and militia the following year to wrest control of the Ohio valley from the Americans, he chose Marin to command it. Marin's orders were to establish a fortified post on the south shore of Lake Erie, construct a road to the head-waters of the Allegheny River, make the Rivière au Bœuf (French Creek) navigable, then establish a chain of forts to the Ohio River, and garrison them. Marin, now 61 years old, drove himself and his 1,500 men unmercifully all through the summer and fall of 1753. He allowed nothing to stand in his way. Junior officers who showed a lack of zeal for the task were threatened with instant dismissal from the service. When the Iroquois protested the invasion of their lands they were bluntly told that if they opposed it they would be crushed [see TANAGHRISSON]. American fur-traders caught in the region were sent to Montreal in chains as a warning to others. Hundreds of the Canadian labour force sickened from poor food and over exertion; many of them perished and the wraith-like appearance of those who survived made Duquesne blanch when they arrived back at Montreal. Marin himself fell sick and, although instructed to return to convalesce, he refused. In September Duquesne sent him the cross of Saint-Louis, awarded in that year's honours list. It arrived too late. Marin died on 29 October at Fort de la Rivière au Bœuf (Waterford, Pa.). He had deliberately chosen to die on active service rather than relinquish his command.

Marin had not succeeded in clearing the route through to the Ohio but he had paved the way. The following year the task was completed and Fort Duquesne (Pittsburgh, Pa.) built, giving France control of the region [see Claude-Pierre Pécaudy* de Contrecœur]. Duquesne, when he received word of Marin's death, wrote that he was deeply moved: "the King loses an excellent subject who was made for war. . . . I had formed the highest opinion of that officer."

W. J. ECCLES

AN, Col., C¹¹A, 71, p.35; 77, pp.102, 113–14; D²C, 47, pp.12, 17, 402; 48, pp.39, 70; 49, pp.257, 320, 326 (PAC transcripts). "Journal de Marin, fils, 1753–1754," Antoine Champagne, édit., APQ Rapport, 1960–61, 240–41. Mémoires sur le Canada, depuis 1749 jusqu'à 1760. Papiers Contrecœur (Grenier). Fauteux, Les chevaliers de Saint-Louis, 154. Massicotte, "Répertoire des engagements pour l'Ouest," APQ Rapport, 1929–30; 1930–31. Stanley, New France. Régis Roy, "Les capitaines de Marin, sieurs de la Malgue, chevaliers de Saint-Louis, officiers canadiens, etc., en la Nouvelle-France, de 1680 à 1762," RSCT, 2nd ser., X (1904), sect.I, 25–34.

MARIN DE LA PERRIÈRE, CLAUDE (occasionally called **Marin de La Malgue**), trader; baptized 28 Oct. 1705 at Montreal, son of Charles-Paul de Marin* de La Malgue and Louise Lamy; d. before 28 Sept. 1752.

By 1727 Claude Marin de La Perrière was trading to the pays d'en haut, occasionally in partnership with Louis Hamelin. In 1733 his trade focused on the Nipigon post (near the mouth of the Nipigon River), and from 1738 to 1741 he and his maternal cousin Louis-Césaire DAGNEAU Douville de Quindre leased the Michipicoton post (near Michipicoten Harbour, Ont.) from Pierre GAULTIER de Varennes et de La Vérendrye.

His trade shifted in 1741 to the Saint-Joseph post (probably Niles, Mich.). Marriage on 30 Dec. 1737 to Marie-Madeleine Regnard Duplessis, née Coulon de Villiers, had given him connections with that location. She had lived there for a number of years when her father Nicolas-Antoine Coulon* de Villiers was the commandant, and in 1745 her brother NICOLAS-ANTOINE was in charge of the post. Following his marriage, Marin apparently resided during at least part of the year at Saint-Joseph. He and de Quindre, often as partners, carried on business there and also began trading heavily from Montreal to Michilimackinac. The company was particularly active in 1743 and 1744; for example, in March 1743 it provided supplies for 60 Ojibwas and Ottawas who were going southward from Michilimackinac to fight the Chickasaws. Business declined during 1745–48 as a result of the War of the Austrian Succession. During the summer of 1747 Marin served as temporary commandant at Saint-Joseph. By negotiating with the local Potawatomis he foiled an Iroquois attempt to lure them away to the English interest.

By September 1747 Marin and de Quindre had moved to Michilimackinac, probably for business reasons. Their partnership apparently ended when de Quindre went to settle at Detroit in 1749. Marin did little trading in the two following years, but in 1752 he hired several engagés to go to Michilimackinac. He died that summer. Since an inventory of goods belonging to him at Michilimackinac includes no household articles, it appears he was residing elsewhere at the time of his death. No children survived him. His wife, who had outlived two husbands, married Joseph Damours Des Plaines in 1754.

DAVID A. ARMOUR

AN, Col., C¹¹A, 117, ff.3, 13–14, 434, 437, 438, 439, 442, 444, 457, 461, 463; 118, ff.142, 230. Chicago Historical Society, Otto L. Schmidt coll., II, 311. French regime in Wis., 1727–48 (Thwaites), 483. Illinois on the eve of Seven Years' War (Pease and Jenison), xxiv. "Mackinac register of baptisms and interments — 1695–1821," ed. R. G. Thwaites, Wis. State Hist. Soc. Coll., XIX (1910), 22. NYCD (O'Callaghan and Fernow), X, 139. "The St. Joseph baptismal register," ed. George Paré and M. M. Quaife, Mississippi Valley Hist. Rev., XIII (1926–27), 209, 220–22. Dictionnaire national des Canadiens français (1608–1760) (3v., Montréal, 1965), I, II. Massicotte, "Répertoire des engagements pour l'Ouest," APQ Rapport, 1929–30; 1930–31. Tanguay, Dictionnaire.

MARTEL DE BELLEVILLE, JEAN-URBAIN, clerk, merchant, director of the Saint-Maurice ironworks; b. 8 Jan. 1708 in Quebec, son of Jean

Martel* de Magos and Marie-Anne Robinau; m. 3 Aug. 1747 at Quebec to Élisabeth Gatin, who died the next year shortly after the birth of their only child; d. in Saint-Domingue (Hispaniola) in or before 1764.

Jean-Urbain Martel de Belleville began his career as a civil servant – which, in one way or another, he would remain throughout his life – under the tutelage of the intendant of New France, Gilles Hocquart*. The date of his entry into this career is uncertain, for he had brothers who were in the civil service too and there is no positive indication that the post granted to a "Sieur Martel" in 1739 was necessarily his. More certain is the fact that, while employed by the government, he also engaged in commercial activities on his own account, and, as well, acted as a procurator for the Rouen merchant, Pierre Le Vieux, in several cases, especially those in appeal before the Conseil Supérieur. In 1741, the year he began his association with the troubled affairs of the Saint-Maurice ironworks near Trois-Rivières, he was still designated as a "merchant trader at Quebec."

Martel appears in a report on the activities of the ironworks for the period 1 Oct. 1741 to 1 Aug. 1742 as a clerk. His salary dated from 1 July 1742 and from that time most of his career in New France would be intimately linked to the ironworks. There has been some confusion about his official position. In 1741 he is a clerk, and the ironworks are under the direction of Guillaume Estèbe*. In 1742 Claude Poulin de Courval Cressé is designated as forge master, and Hocquart, writing on 26 Oct. 1742 to the minister of Marine, Maurepas, gives to Martel de Belleville, as of August of that year, the title of "director of the enterprise." In effect, Martel was the senior administrative officer or civil servant, a function quite separate from that of forge master. Since the industry was run by the state from the fall of 1741 until the conquest, this division is not at all surprising. It has been claimed that Martel continued to hold his position after 1750, but there is evidence that he was replaced as director in that year by René-Ovide Hertel* de Rouville. Martel's signature does not appear on documents concerning the ironworks after 1750.

During his, and the state's, administration, a relatively small profit was realized in most years. Losses were due to breakdowns of equipment, inability to replace production equipment, or unexpectedly cold weather. Notable during Martel's administration was the diversification of the production of the ironworks: stoves, armaments, ammunition, as well as the more usual bar and plate.

We know little of Martel personally. He appears to have been well thought of by Hocquart; yet François Bigot* replaced him almost as soon as he reached the colony as intendant. The action may, however, have resulted from Bigot's desire to make sweeping changes rather than from a lack of ability on the part of Martel de Belleville.

It was only after the conquest, it seems, that Martel went to France where he obtained the post of clerk of the Conseil Supérieur of Saint-Domingue. However he cannot have held this position long since according to a notarial act he was dead by 1764. His appointment at Saint-Domingue indicates a degree of status, although after his death his daughter, living in France, was refused a pension from the French government because her father's contribution had not been such that it deserved greater award.

CAMERON NISH and CLAUDE RICHARD

AN, Col., B, 66, 68, 74, 81; C¹¹ᴬ, 80, 88, 96, 111, 112. *Dictionnaire national des Canadiens français (1608–1760)* (2v., Montréal, 1958), II. P.-G. Roy, *Inv. jug. et délib., 1717–1760*, III, IV. Tanguay, *Dictionnaire* [Tanguay is mistaken in giving the date of the marriage of Jean-Urbain Martel de Belleville and Élisabeth Gatin as 7 Aug. 1747. c.n.]. "La famille Martel de Magesse," *BRH*, XL (1934), 711–13.

MARTEL DE BROUAGUE, FRANÇOIS, commandant of the Labrador coast, merchant, shipowner; b. 30 April 1692 in Quebec, son of Pierre-Gratien Martel de Brouague and Marie-Charlotte Charest; d. probably in 1761.

Thanks to his family background it was quite likely that François Martel de Brouague would succeed in a business career. Upon their arrival in the colony his father and his uncle Raymond Martel* had rapidly acquired good contacts. His father had become associated with the Charests and the Bissots, with whom he had business interests in Labrador; he even married the daughter of one of his partners, Étienne Charest. For his part, Raymond went into partnership with Augustin Le Gardeur* de Courtemanche, with whom he had interests in the Labrador trade and with whom he bought the seigneury of Lachenaie.

After the death of his father François's mother married Courtemanche. In 1702 Courtemanche obtained from Governor Callière* and Intendant François de BEAUHARNOIS a land grant in Labrador for a period of ten years, and in 1714 the king granted him the Baie de Phélypeaux (Brador Bay) and appointed him commandant of the Labrador coast. Courtemanche, whom François

Martel de Brouague

Martel de Brouague had been helping for some years, died in 1717, and François took his place as commandant in January 1718. At the same time he took on the management of the post at Baie de Phélypeaux in the name of his mother and half-sisters. The exploitation of this grant was the only compensation he received for his obligations as commandant: the representative of royal authority on the north coast, he had to dispense justice and defend the post of Baie de Phélypeaux and all the temporary settlements of French fishermen on the coast against raids by the Eskimos, whom he attempted, more or less successfully, to pacify [see Acoutsina*]. In 1725 François Martel de Brouague went to France to see to business matters; there, on 25 Dec. 1725, he obtained from the king a commission which granted him for his lifetime his mother's rights to the Baie de Phélypeaux.

On 21 Feb. 1726, at Versailles, Martel de Brouague married Anne-Marie Favry Du Ponceau, and the following day another royal commission ensured him and his new wife of the succession to the rights of Mme de Courtemanche and her daughters to the post in Labrador. From this first marriage Martel de Brouague had a daughter, who lived in France with her maternal uncles until her death in 1740 at 14 years of age. His wife died around 1730 in Labrador, and on 15 Sept. 1732 Martel de Brouague married Louise, daughter of François Mariauchau* d'Esgly, who had been king's lieutenant at Trois-Rivières, and sister of Louis-Philippe*, the future bishop of Quebec. Their marriage contract, concluded a few days earlier in Quebec, was signed by Governor Charles de BEAUHARNOIS, Intendant Gilles Hocquart*, and several members of the military and social élite of the colony.

Martel de Brouague enjoyed a certain prestige as commandant of Labrador, but he did not have the financial means to develop fully his grant on the Baie de Phélypeaux. For that reason he entered into partnership with his first cousin, Pierre TROTTIER Desauniers, a Quebec merchant, for exploitation of the Labrador fishery in a more profitable manner. An initial agreement, signed in 1732 before the notary Henry HICHÉ, gave Desauniers the exclusive rights for supplying Martel de Brouague's post and made him responsible for marketing the products of the fishery, in return for a commission of five per cent. The deed mentions in addition that Martel de Brouague owned a ship plying between Quebec and Labrador. Three years later the two partners formed a company: Desauniers put up 100,000 *livres* in merchandise, and Martel de Brouague brought his land grant as well as 38,000

livres he had already invested. Profits and losses would be shared equally. In five years the agreement brought Martel de Brouague nearly 28,000 *livres* in profits, which he sent to France. The partnership was less profitable to Desauniers than to his cousin. At the time of the dissolution of the company in 1746 Martel de Brouague took back his initial investment of 38,000 *livres*, as well as 93,999 *livres* 7 *sols* for his share of the profits, an equal amount going to Desauniers.

During his long term in command of Labrador, Martel de Brouague concerned himself perhaps more with business than with military affairs. In 1739, in fact, the minister of Marine, Maurepas, asked Governor Beauharnois and Intendant Hocquart to warn Martel de Brouague to stop neglecting his post; if he were "the object of new complaints, the king would attend to the matter." In addition to his exploitation of the Labrador fishery, Martel de Brouague acquired pieces of land, including the fief of Argentenay, which he first owned jointly with Desauniers. When the latter was preparing to retire to France in 1746, Martel de Brouague became sole owner of the fief, for which he had to render fealty and homage three years later.

François Martel de Brouague had with the years arrived at a comfortable situation. Although all his sons died in infancy, his daughters made good matches, one of them, Louise, marrying Gaspard-Joseph Chaussegros* de Léry. According to Pierre-Georges Roy*, Martel de Brouague died at Quebec on 15 March 1761. Three years before his death there had been some talk of relieving him of his command in Labrador on the pretext that he was "old and infirm," but he was spared this indignity.

JOSÉ IGARTUA

AD, Yvelines (Versailles), État civil, Versailles, 21 févr. 1726. AJQ, Registre d'état civil, Notre-Dame de Québec, 30 avril 1692, 15 sept. 1732. AN, Col., B, 49, f.687v; 65, f.45v; 68, ff.282–83; 109, f.344; C¹¹ᴬ, 41, ff.57–63v; 43, ff.149–61v, 314–17v; 44, ff.168–69; 51, ff.29–31; 54, f.185; 65, ff.33–34; 71, ff.7–8v; 74, f.58; 109, ff.9–32, 49–59, 64–65, 65–122v, 171–84v, 200, 261, 272–309; D²ᶜ, 222, f.161; E, 177 (dossier Brouague), ff.1–9. ANQ, Greffe de Jacques Barbel, 29 déc. 1735; Greffe de Gilbert Boucault de Godefus, 20, 23 mai 1741, 7, 9 nov. 1746; Greffe d'Henry Hiché, 6 sept. 1732; AP, François Martel de Brouague; NF, Registres du Cons. sup., 1735–1736, ff.67–71; 1738–1739, ff.31–32v. PAC, MG 8, A2, 36, ff.158–59; 37, ff.54–55, 157, 167v–69; 39, ff.5–7, 109v–10, 172–73, 177v, 178v–79; B3; B6, Greffe de J.-C. Panet, 12 mars, 16 mai 1749.

"François Martel de Berhouage, Brouague ou Brouage, commandant au Labrador," APQ *Rapport, 1922–23*, 356–406. [In presenting these documents the author made an error concerning Martel de Brouague's first daughter. J.I.] *Inv. de pièces du Labrador* (P.-G. Roy), I, 16–17, 31–32, 37–38, 42–44, 124, 125, 153–55, 239–41; II, 68–87, 187–88, 192–93, 196. "Les 'papiers' La Pause," APQ *Rapport, 1933–34*, 218. "Recensement de Québec, 1744" (APQ *Rapport*), 104. Le Jeune, *Dictionnaire*. *Répertoire des mariages de l'Hôpital Général de Québec (paroisse Notre-Dame-des-Anges) (1693–1961)*, Benoît Pontbriand, compil. (Société canadienne de généalogie, 2, Québec, 1962). *Répertoire des mariages de Notre-Dame de Québec*, Benoît Pontbriand, compil. (6v., Sillery, Qué., n.d.), II, 180. P.-G. Roy, *Inv. contrats de mariage*, IV, 224; *Inv. jug. et délib., 1717–1760*, III, 114, 116, 126, 129, 250; V, 10, 51, 87, 122, 123, 165, 169, 223, 282; VI, 20, 24, 25. Tanguay, *Dictionnaire*. La Morandière, *Hist. de la pêche française de la morue*, II, 669, 714–30. P.-G. Roy, *Fils de Québec*, I, 136–39; "La famille Margane de Lavaltrie," *BRH*, XXIII (1917), 48–52; "La famille Martel de Brouage," *BRH*, XL (1934), 513–49.

MARTIN, BARTHÉLEMY, merchant; b. *c.* 1713, son of Vincent Martin and Hélène Guilhermy of the parish of Saint-Ferréol de Marseille, France; d. sometime after 1765.

Barthélemy Martin set up one of the most important trading companies in Quebec towards the end of the French régime and seems to have been involved in the activites of the "Grand Société." The name of the "Sieur Martin" appears for the first time in the accounts of the colony for 1749, when more than 14,000 *livres* of supplies were bought from him. The following year he received some 15,000 *livres* in bills of exchange for various supplies. In 1751 Rouillé, the minister of Marine, sent Governor La Jonquière [TAFFANEL] and Intendant Bigot* a letter of recommendation for "the Sieur Troppez Martin," probably Barthélemy's brother: "You will do me a favour," he wrote, "if you render him service whenever the occasion may arise, if he does not cause any obstacle through his conduct." On 4 October of that year the Conseil Supérieur in Quebec gave its decision in a lawsuit between "the Sieurs Tropez and Barthélemy Martin, merchants in this town," and Joseph-Pierre Cadet*, a merchant butcher, who was to become the purveyor-general of the colony. Cadet had not fulfilled the terms of a contract with the Martin brothers for the sale of cod and the latter were demanding compensation. The account of the council's sitting leads us to believe that the Martins were intending to send this cod to the Martinique market; this incident would indicate that they traded with the West Indies, which implies that they conducted a substantial business. Only a systematic study of notarial deeds and lawsuits heard by the provost's court and the admiralty court of Quebec would provide evidence for an appreciation of the scale of the Mar-

tins' trade. Documents more easily available lead us to suspect, however, that Barthélemy Martin was a considerable merchant.

In 1752 Martin suggested to the president of the council of Marine that "magasins d'abondance" ("stockpiles") be set up in the three towns of the colony for the storing of provisions and the prevention of scarcities. Too grandiose and above all too costly, the scheme was rejected, but at the same time Governor Duquesne* and Intendant Bigot were instructed to help Martin in his plan for exporting Canadian timber.

In the spring of 1760, when the French armies were making a last effort to recapture Quebec, Martin made a deal with Bigot to supply spirits to the troops; it was a big contract which was ultimately not very profitable to him. Martin had to get 250 casks of spirits out of Quebec without the British troops' knowledge. He brought them near Montreal and sold them to the king at a price lower than the current Montreal price. Martin's invoice amounted to more than 500,000 *livres* and was paid in bills of exchange on the treasury of France. In 1765 Martin, who had returned to France after the surrender of Canada, was still awaiting payment of his bills of exchange; it had been forgotten in the contentions arising from the *affaire du Canada*. We do not know whether he was ever paid.

On 31 Aug. 1752, in Quebec, Martin had married Marie-Françoise-Renée, daughter of René-Nicolas Levasseur*; among those who signed his marriage contract as witnesses were Governor Duquesne, Intendant Bigot, and Bishop Pontbriand [DUBREIL] of Quebec.

JOSÉ IGARTUA

AJQ, Registre d'état civil, Notre-Dame de Québec, 31 août 1752. AN, Col., B, 93, f.1v; 95, ff.27, 29f.; 97, ff.23–25v, 53v, 97v; 113, f.262v; C¹¹A, 105, ff.116–32, 387f.; 108, ff.1–90; 116, ff.251v, 252, 254, 255, 290v, 291v, 296f., 298; 119, ff.341v, 342v, 343, 344v, 347. ANQ, Greffe de J.-C. Panet, 24 août 1752. PAC, MG 7, II, 12142, ff.76–77v, 164, 378; MG 8, A2, 38, ff.52v–54v; 39, ff.37v–38, 106v–7; 40, ff.107–9. ASQ, Polygraphie, XXIV, 32B, 37J, 37K, 37L; Séminaire, XI, 28. *Documents relating to Canadian currency during the French period* (Shortt), II, 984–86, 988. P.-G. Roy, *Inv. jug. et délib., 1717–1760*, V, 200–1, 242, 280; VI, 85. Tanguay, *Dictionnaire*.

MASCARENE, PAUL (born **Jean-Paul**), military officer, administrator of Nova Scotia; b. 1684 or 1685 in the province of Languedoc, France, probably at Castres, son of Jean Mascarene and Margaret de Salavy; m. Elizabeth Perry of Boston, Massachusetts (d. *c.* 1729) by whom he had four children; d. at Boston 22 Jan. 1760.

Mascarene

Paul Mascarene's Huguenot father was banished from France after the revocation of the edict of Nantes in 1685, and Paul was cared for by relatives who in 1696 smuggled him to Geneva. He was educated there, and after moving to England about 1706 received an ensigncy in the Regiment of French Foot, raised among the Huguenot immigrants. He was commissioned a lieutenant in April 1706 and was at Portsmouth in 1708 when he received orders to join a force being assembled in New England for an expedition against Canada. The British contribution to this force, along with Samuel Vetch* and Francis Nicholson*, arrived in Boston in April 1709. The expedition being abandoned for that year, Mascarene spent the winter drilling the colonial troops in artillery exercises. Word came in the spring of 1710 that the Canada scheme was being replaced by an attempt against Port-Royal (Annapolis Royal, N.S.). Mascarene was promoted captain and put in charge of a grenadier company; and when Daniel d'Auger* de Subercase surrendered Port-Royal to Nicholson in October, the young captain "had the honour to take possession of it in mounting the first guard."

Mascarene's first years in the new province of Nova Scotia involved a thorough initiation into the challenges and frustrations he was to face in the future, and illustrate his knack for making himself useful in matters requiring diplomacy, attention to detail, and a capacity for analysis. In November Governor Vetch, partly to show the inhabitants that they were under a new and masterful authority, and partly because he thought it only his due, decided to exact "a verry good present" from the Acadians. He sent Mascarene, "having the advantage of the French language," to Minas (Grand Pré region) with a detachment of troops, charging him to be courteous but to collect a tribute worth 6,000 *livres*. Mascarene could assemble only a small portion, the Acadians pleading poverty, but his week at Minas afforded his first experience in dealing with the Acadians. Vetch later appointed him and three other officers, together with two Acadians, to hear and settle disputes between the inhabitants. By his own account, much of his time was occupied in translating Vetch's letters and proclamations into French.

Mascarene went to Boston with Vetch in October 1711, and remained there until early 1714. In August of that year he and Captain Joseph Bennett were sent to Minas to discuss with Louis DENYS de La Ronde and Jacques d'Espiet* de Pensens the terms under which the Acadians would be allowed to move to Île Royale (Cape Breton Island). During the next five years

Mascarene divided his time between Boston, where he seems to have married and set up house, and Placentia, Newfoundland, where he was in charge of an infantry company. In August 1717 he was commissioned a captain in the newly formed 40th regiment. Whether by formal education or breadth of interests, he was considered an engineer as well as a regular officer and artilleryman, and a visit to England during this period resulted in his appointment as engineer to the Board of Ordnance. By 1719 he was back in Boston preparing to embark for Annapolis with orders to report on the state of the fortifications there.

The sudden interest of the Board of Ordnance in Nova Scotia was a small reflection of the British government's new resolve to improve its housekeeping in the neglected province. Colonel Richard PHILIPPS was sent out as governor in 1719 and spent his first winter in Boston, where he presumably gained his favourable opinion of Mascarene. Both arrived at Annapolis Royal in April 1720, and when Philipps chose his council from among the officers and local merchants, he nominated Mascarene third on the list as "Chief Engineer, and a Person of great prudence and Capacity." Mascarene was subsequently employed at various engineering tasks, including a survey of the coast in 1721, improving the jerry-built defences at Canso, and trying to salvage the crumbling fort at Annapolis while not seeming to disobey the unrealistic but positive orders of the Board of Ordnance to avoid expense. Mascarene's life was so consistently riddled with the problems of divided command and conflicting orders from home that his frequent visits to Boston must have been a great relief. His orders as engineer came from the niggardly and jealous Board of Ordnance; as an army officer he was responsible to his regimental superiors, Philipps and John Doucett*. The Board of Trade and Plantations thought that the pleas of the Annapolis officers for support made sense, but could make little impression on the Ordnance office.

During this period Mascarene's participation in civil affairs was confined to his attendance at council, where he observed the failure of Philipps' attempt in 1720 to exact an unqualified oath of allegiance from the Acadians. Philipps' undermanned regiment, confined at Annapolis Royal in a dilapidated fort, clearly could not convince a scattered population of Acadians that British authority or protection should be taken seriously. Though Mascarene cannot be credited with any particular prescience in his recognition of the weakness of the British position in Nova

Scotia, he was one of the first to give this fact clear and cogent analysis. His "Description of Nova Scotia," written for the Board of Trade in 1720 at Philipps' behest, is an informative essay on the state of the province and its French-speaking inhabitants. He recommended a stronger military force, to be divided among the major settlements, and the administration, once this force was sent, of an unqualified oath, with those who still demurred being moved to French territory. English-speaking Protestant settlers should be introduced in any event. He noted that the French authorities were themselves not anxious to receive the Acadians, since it was to their advantage to have a self-sufficient population on the mainland, accessible to influence from Île Royale through their priests. Though little in the paper is original, it is a good summary of the problems faced by the Annapolis government, and for several years seems to have been passed around in London whenever officials there considered the continuing question of Nova Scotia.

In 1725 Mascarene was sent to New England to represent Nova Scotia in peace negotiations with the Indians of the New England seaboard. By the time he returned in 1729, the first problem-ridden residence of Lawrence Armstrong* as lieutenant governor was over, and the Acadians were more determined than ever not to take an unqualified oath. Petty feuds between the officers and councillors were making a mockery of the government and interfering with garrison discipline. Philipps, who had left Annapolis in 1722, returned in November determined to set things in order again, but added fuel to the conflicts among his councillors when he appointed his own brother-in-law, Major Alexander COSBY, as president of the council, despite Cosby's lack of seniority. Mascarene objected strenuously, to Philipps' surprise and annoyance.

Philipps was recalled to England in 1731 and Armstrong returned to Annapolis. After wintering in Boston, Mascarene resumed his duties at Annapolis in the spring of 1732, but returned to Boston in the fall with orders from Armstrong to encourage New Englanders to move to Nova Scotia. He was to seek the support of Governor Jonathan Belcher, who seems to have been a personal friend, "taking Especial Care not to transact anything that may seem to make this province . . . Subordinate to, or Dependent on that of New England. . . ." Mascarene had no success, the New Englanders having a low opinion of both the government and the safety of Nova Scotia. Except for a year at Annapolis in 1735–36, and possibly 1738 as well, he remained in Boston until 1740, building his "Great Brick house" and look-ing after his now motherless family of four, to whom he was intensely devoted.

He hurried back when word came that Armstrong had committed suicide in December 1739. Armstrong had earlier sought a ruling from home at Mascarene's request on the question of precedence among the councillors, and the ruling confirmed that the senior councillor must become president of the council and head of the government in the absence of the governor and his deputy. When Mascarene arrived late in March 1739/40, the elderly John ADAMS unsuccessfully contested his right to sit as president, claiming that Mascarene's long absence invalidated his claim. It is a measure of the state into which the neglected capital had fallen that Adams in his subsequent appeals to Westminster hinted darkly that Nova Scotia was in peril so long as a French-born officer was in charge. About the time of Mascarene's return Alexander Cosby was made lieutenant-colonel in the 40th regiment, becoming Mascarene's superior officer. The conflict between them was finally resolved with Cosby's death in 1742, after which Mascarene became lieutenant-colonel.

Even if his experience and abilities fitted him for it, the situation facing Mascarene in 1740 was a murky one. The Acadians were equipped with the firm memory of Philipps' promise ten years before of exemption from military service if they took the oath, and Mascarene, who was nothing if not a pragmatist, saw that there was now no hope of administering a new and proper oath. The garrison was as poorly maintained as ever, the fort at Annapolis had never been properly repaired, and the isolated detachment stationed at Canso to protect the vital fishery there had scarcely a roof over its head. With the current war between Great Britain and Spain making an Anglo-French conflict almost certain, he decided that his province's security depended largely on the continued neutrality, if not the loyalty, of the Acadians. He set out, therefore, to "make these french Inhabitants sensible of the difference there is between the Brittish and french Governments by administering impartial justice . . . and treating them with lenity and humanity, without yielding anything. . . ." In the early months of 1740 he notified the Acadian deputies of his position and goodwill, then reminded them of their rent-gathering duties and their obligation to keep in touch with the government. They were warned that if war came they should not give reason to be suspected of disloyalty. Great Britain had been lax in asserting her sovereignty, but common sense dictated that this would not always be so. The day of reckoning would come, and affairs

Mascarene

might not allow time for distinguishing between the guilty and the innocent.

What particularly worried Mascarene, and at the same time gave him hope, were the priests, whom he had described in 1720 as having sufficient influence over the Acadians to "guide and direct them as they please in temporal as well as spiritual affairs." His practical approach to the problem was characteristic. He began a regular correspondence with several of the priests, including Charles de LA GOUDALIE, Claude de La Vernède de Saint-Poncy, Jean-Baptiste de GAY Desenclaves, and the Abbé Jean-Louis Le Loutre*, meeting them personally and cultivating a reserved friendship when he could. He assured them he was "of that temper as not to wish ill to any person whose Persuasion differs" from his own, and exhorted each not to do anything to the "prejudice of himself and of the inhabitants." His subsequent relations with the priests were cordial on the whole.

Mascarene received no reply to his dispatches to England during his first two years as administrator; if he wanted support, he would have to find it elsewhere. In 1741 he wrote to Governor William Shirley of Massachusetts, pleading New England's interest in the safety of Nova Scotia and expressing the hope that in the event of war with France the governor would send help to defend the province. Shirley's sympathetic replies could be used to impress the Acadians, but Mascarene feared that in an actual war "assistance . . . may not be too much relied on. . . ."

Shirley's control over the Massachusetts assemblymen was, however, better than that. News of war with France reached Mascarene and his 150 officers and men at Annapolis in May 1744, along with the intelligence that Canso had fallen. The troops and Ordnance men set to work repairing the worst breaches in the Annapolis fort. Mascarene reminded the Acadian deputies that their people would be watched closely for disaffection and committed the women and children of the garrison to Shirley's care in Boston. The first attack came on 1 July when a force of about 300 Indians led by Le Loutre, with whom Mascarene had thought himself on good terms, advanced against the patched-up fort. Mascarene's cannon and a couple of vigorous sorties held the enemy at a distance until 5 July when 70 soldiers arrived from Boston, with the news that more soldiers were coming, and the attackers retreated. Joseph DU PONT Duvivier made a much more determined attempt in August with a mixed body of Indians and French soldiers, but the arrival in September of Colonel John GORHAM with 60 Indian rangers led Duvivier to abandon his goal.

That August Mascarene had been appointed lieutenant governor of the town and fort of Annapolis Royal. During the winter New England prepared for an attack on Louisbourg, Île Royale. Mascarene, expecting more assaults against his little fort in 1745, could only look on wistfully at the events that were passing him by in Boston and at Louisbourg, which was captured in June. The reinforcements remained at Annapolis at Mascarene's request, so that Paul MARIN de La Malgue found the fort too strongly garrisoned when he came from Quebec to attack it with a small force the following May. By October 1746, when Jean-Baptiste-Nicolas-Roch de Ramezay* invested the fort, the garrison was more seasoned, and Ramezay's hopes that part of the armada of the Duc d'Anville [LA ROCHEFOUCAULD] would join with his land force were dashed when the hapless fleet was dispersed by a storm. On 3 November the arrival of yet another reinforcement from Boston discouraged him completely, and he withdrew to Minas and Beaubassin (near Amherst, N.S.).

Mascarene gave full credit to Shirley for help during the crises of 1744–46, but his own role had been significant. Until late 1744 he still had less than 300 men, of whom nearly half had come without weapons. New England individualists and the jaded veterans of Philipps' regiment did not make a harmonious command for an officer who had been so long without routine orders from home that his authority to carry out sentences of courts martial was in doubt. Discipline was not apparently Mascarene's strong point as an officer, and fresh recruits from England, "the Refuse & Dregs of the Jayls," who arrived in the spring of 1746, taxed him to the limit by their numerous desertions and particularly their drunkenness, in which they were abetted by bootlegging subalterns. Yet it was Mascarene, pressed by dispirited officers to accept Duvivier's preliminary terms of surrender in 1744, who had convinced them that Duvivier had "no other intention ... than sowing division" in the beleaguered garrison. To the aggressive military mind Mascarene's preference for defence may be exasperating, but coolheadedness was the quality best suited to the situation. Gorham's rangers were adept at sorties, but the New England troops were no more skilled in bush fighting than Mascarene's raw recruits, and when they straggled outside the fort they fell prey to ambushes just as easily.

Mascarene was always convinced, however, that his Acadian policy was as important as Shirley's help. If his statements that the province owed its safety to a general Acadian refusal to assist the invaders sound a bit defensive, it is because his belief in their basic neutrality and desire to be left alone was severely challenged by his officers and council. There had certainly been some voluntary connivance with the enemy at Minas and even Annapolis. Mascarene had no illusions about the inhabitants, and had been more hopeful than trusting. He knew that there was a faction at Minas sympathetic to the French, and he questioned the deputies and suspected offenders rigorously. Nevertheless his view was that general neutrality was the best he could have expected, and this was what he got. Pressed by the majority on the council, however, he signed and forwarded home in December 1745 their representation on the history of Acadian allegiance, recounting incidents of suspected collaboration and raising the question of a general expulsion. At the same time he enclosed his own summary, admitting that the substitution of a Protestant population had clear advantages, but explaining his more measured policy for leading the Acadians "by time and good care. . . first to become Subjects and after that good Subjects. . . ." Shirley noted the split opinion at Annapolis, and worried that there was "danger of too much tenderness . . . on [Mascarene's] part and perhaps vigour on theirs. . . ." Yet Shirley too saw the need to handle the Acadians gingerly, and at Mascarene's urging assured them by proclamation in 1746 not to credit the rumours that Bostonians were coming to seize their estates.

The rest of the 1740s were easier years for Annapolis, which was not attacked again. Ordnance supplies began to come frequently, so that by 1750 the fort was more defensible than it had been since 1710. In 1748 Île Royale was returned to France, arousing Great Britain's interest in overseas empire and a determination to take a firm hold on Nova Scotia. In July 1749 Mascarene received an order from the new governor, Edward Cornwallis,* to join him at Halifax for the swearing in of a new council. The first meeting was on 14 July and the first item of discussion was the oath of allegiance. Mascarene reviewed the history of the question, including Philipps' exemption. The ensuing council resolution that an unqualified oath be administered, the subsequent refusal of the Acadians to take it, their threat to leave the province, and Cornwallis' vain imposition of a deadline for compliance must have seemed terribly familiar to Mascarene the ageing pragmatist. He returned to Annapolis in August while these events were unfolding, doubtless feeling very much an anachronism. In

1750 he disposed of his lieutenant-colonelcy in the 40th regiment and received a brevet colonel's rank. Cornwallis sent Mascarene to New England in 1751 to renew the 1726 treaty with the eastern Indians (Norridgewocks, Penobscots, Malecites), and although he corresponded with his Annapolis friends for several years, he did not return to Nova Scotia. He was content to settle in Boston – reading, playing chess, and cutting the modest figure of a comfortably retired officer, who had at last arrived "thanks to Almighty God in my own house amongst my Children and . . . grandchildren."

Mascarene was in some ways an odd fish in the imperial backwater of Annapolis Royal. Like those who preceded him, he was caught up in the tedious and unrewarding business of guarding an imperial possession before the crown had decided to take its imperial role seriously. Even if one credits him with the preservation of Acadian neutrality and the retention of the province in 1744, events on the larger scale were as much outside his control as they were for Philipps or Armstrong. But though he may have worn himself out, as Thomas Caulfeild* and Armstrong did, and petitioned in vain for the official post of lieutenant governor of the province, his life was hardly tragic or pathetic as theirs were. The reasons for his survival lay in his temperament and background. He was educated in the classics and was a devotee of them. In fact, Mascarene was somewhat of a patrician in his attitudes, and it may not be too much to suggest that his actions as a servant of the state were classical in inspiration. Early historians were quick to perceive this, crediting him with a respect for moderation, justice, learning, public service, and family. The reasonable assumption that he was guided by these ideals, together with the personality that emerges from his official and family letters, in contrast to his less documented contemporaries, help to explain why he became a minor hero of Canadian history in the mid-19th century. These classical qualities were ones which Victorians admired, and such writers as Beamish Murdoch*, Duncan Campbell*, and James Hannay* turned with discernible relief from the recitation of the tangled Nova Scotia chronicle before 1739 to the approbation of one in whom they detected a capitoline serenity. The image is not, perhaps, a satisfactory reflection of an 18th-century British career officer who was educated in Geneva and founded a thoroughly New England family, but probably he would have been immensely flattered.

MAXWELL SUTHERLAND

Mascle

BM, Add. MSS, 19071, ff.55–67 (transcript in PAC, MG 21, E 5, 42). PAC, MG 11, Nova Scotia A, 4, pp.215–16; 5, pp.4, 92; 20, pp.94–95; 25, pp.3–5, 9–11, 33–36, 80, 223–29, 260; 26, pp.107–10, 117. PRO, CO 5/901; 217/3, pp.184–94 (mfm in PAC, MG 11).
The army list of 1740 . . . (Soc. for Army Hist. Research, Special no., III, Sheffield, Eng., 1931). *Coll. doc. inédits Canada et Amérique*, II, 40–49. *N.S. Archives, I; II; III; IV.* [William Pote], *The journal of Captain William Pote, jr., during his captivity in the French and Indian war from May 1745, to August 1747*, ed. J. F. Hurst and Victor Paltsits (New York, 1896), 24, 27. *PAC Report, 1894; 1905*, II, pt.III. *English army lists* (Dalton), VI, 196. *DNB. New Eng. Hist. and Geneal. Register*, IX (1855), 239; X (1856), 143–48. Brebner, *New England's outpost*; "Paul Mascarene of Annapolis Royal," *Dal. Rev.*, VIII (1928–29), 501–16. Smythies, *Historical records of 40th regiment*, 527–44. George Patterson, "Hon. Samuel Vetch, first English governor of Nova Scotia," *N.S. Hist. Soc. Coll.*, IV (1885), 70, 81.

MASCLE DE SAINT-JULHIEN, JEAN (the name usually appears as **St. Julien,** but he signed St. Julhien; his baptismal certificate gives the surname as **Masclé**), officer in the French regular troops; b. 7 July 1693 in Lunel, France, son of Jean Mascle, attorney, and Suzanne Courtade; d.1759.

Jean Mascle de Saint-Julhien came to Louisbourg (Cape Breton Island) in 1755, as senior officer in command of the second battalions of the Artois and Bourgogne regiments, two units of the French regular army sent to assist the colonial regular troops in the defence of Île Royale during the Seven Years' War. He was a veteran of long experience in the Artois. Beginning as a sub-lieutenant in 1709 he had fought in a dozen sieges and numerous battles. During the War of the Austrian Succession he was severely wounded at Dettingen (Federal Republic of Germany) in 1743 and four years later at Assiette (Italy), where he commanded the regiment. He had received the cross of Saint-Louis in 1737 and on 19 Feb. 1755 he was appointed lieutenant-colonel. In his service record he is cited as a "good officer," a "man of war," and a firm disciplinarian who had the bearing and talents to be an effective lieutenant-colonel.

During his stay at Louisbourg, however, Saint-Julhien proved to be a difficult and troublesome figure. He quarrelled repeatedly, especially with the financial commissary, Jacques Prévost* de La Croix, over the prerogatives of his command and the administration of his troops. The administrative responsibilities which Prévost, as financial commissary, exercised over the colonial regular troops had been extended, by virtue of his appointment as commissary of wars in April 1755, to the French regulars. Saint-Julhien nevertheless insisted upon the independence and the special privileges of the French regulars. Besides creating difficulties with Prévost, his attitude and that of his fellow officers antagonized the colonial officer corps. The engineer François-Claude-Victor GRILLOT de Poilly described Saint-Julhien as "the most dangerous person I know, full of jealousy and presumption" and said that he was "incapable of desiring any good which does not originate with him."

At the request of the governor, BOSCHENRY de Drucour, Saint-Julhien had been appointed on 1 Sept. 1755 to act as commander of the colony in the governor's absence. But his relationship with Drucour deteriorated and he was eventually replaced as potential commandant by the chief engineer, Louis FRANQUET. His position as senior officer commanding the French regular troops was altered with the arrival of other battalions from France in 1757 and 1758. In 1758 Mathieu-Henri Marchant* de La Houlière assumed command of all the land forces at Louisbourg and Saint-Julhien was left in command only of the Artois.

Saint-Julhien's battalion, reinforced by the grenadier company of the Bourgogne regiment and some colonial regulars, Acadians, and Indians, was stationed at the Anse de la Cormorandière (Kennington Cove) on 8 June 1758 when the British landed to begin the second siege of Louisbourg. The assault began about 4:00 A.M. and under cover of a naval bombardment three divisions of boats rowed for shore. The left division, led by James WOLFE, was being repulsed when three of its boats drifted to the right and their crews found a landing place which had been left unguarded. Saint-Julhien finally sent his two grenadier companies to check the British move, but he had hesitated too long. After a sharp skirmish the French line was flanked; Saint-Julhien's soldiers abandoned their position and the other divisions of the landing force followed Wolfe ashore. Saint-Julhien seems not to have been censured for his failure to post lookouts at the landing spot.

Saint-Julhien was in command of his battalion throughout the siege and participated in the councils of war held on 9 June and 26 July. Otherwise his role was undistinguished. After the surrender he was sent with his battalion to England and was exchanged at Calais in December. He died in 1759.

JOHN FORTIER

AN, Col., B, 99–113; C¹¹B, 34–38; C¹¹C, 10, 15; D²C, 1–4; F³, 50–51; Section Outre-Mer, Dépôt des fortifications des colonies, Am. sept., no.236. Archives municipales,

Lunel (France), GG (Actes paroissiaux, culte Catholique), 4, f.492v. CTG, Archives, art. 15, pièces 4, 5, 7, 8; Bibliothèque, mss in 4⁰, 66. SHA, A¹, 3417, 3457, 3499; X^b, 61; Y^a, 97; 470, ff.25–26, 183–84; Y^b, 122, f.198; Travail du roi, art.91. Jeffery Amherst, "*Journal of the siege of* Louisbourg," *Gentleman's Magazine*, XXVIII (1758), 384–89. [James Johnstone], *Memoirs of the Chevalier de Johnstone*, trans. Charles Winchester (3v., Aberdeen, 1870–71). Knox, *Historical journal* (Doughty). *Derniers jours de l'Acadie* (Du Boscq de Beaumont). Pichon, *Lettres et mémoires*. Le Jeune, *Dictionnaire*, II, 591–92. McLennan, *Louisbourg*. Stanley, *New France*. J. M. Hitsman with C. C. J. Bond, "The assault landing at Louisbourg, 1758," *CHR*, XXXV (1954), 314–30.

MAUGEAN. *See* MANGEANT

MAUGER, JACQUES GADOIS, *dit*. *See* GADOIS

MAUGRAS, PIERRE GAMELIN. *See* GAMELIN

MAUPAS, PIERRE POUCHOT DE. *See* POUCHOT

MAURIN, FRANÇOIS, clerk, assistant purveyor-general; b. *c.* 1726 at "Jarnac in Saintonge," France, son of Philippe Maurin, a merchant, and Marguerite-Geneviève Mounier; d. sometime after 1765, probably in France.

François Maurin arrived in Canada in circumstances unknown to us. Intelligent and well educated, he worked at first as a clerk for some Montreal merchants. In the spring of 1756 Joseph-Pierre Cadet*, whom Intendant Bigot* had just appointed purveyor-general of supplies in New France, went to Montreal, where he chose Maurin to be his head clerk. François Maurin received from Cadet the task of managing the "establishment" in Montreal, "under the direction of the Sieur [Michel-Jean-Hugues Péan*], the chief partner" of the purveyor-general. François Maurin was to furnish supplies to the soldiers and settlers in the Montreal region, as well as to those at the forts and trading posts in the *pays d'en haut*. In this affair he was associated with a Montreal merchant, Louis Pénissault*, whose work was limited to the purely material operations. The latter had entered into partnership in 1754 with Brouilhet, the receiver general of finances in Paris, and the La Ferté brothers, merchants, who sent him merchandise from France.

Maurin and Pénissault, eager to make a fortune rapidly, paid particular attention to placing "people who were devoted to them" in the forts and posts in the *pays d'en haut*. Thus, "hand in hand with several storekeepers and ... post commandants," they quickly became rich. For example, they quadrupled the number of monthly rations for the posts and forts in the west; they sold wheat, bought for 6 *livres* a bushel, for 24 *livres*; they inflated the figures in victualling books, adding zeroes, multiplying by a hundred and even a thousand the figure of what was really consumed by the garrison and posts. It was hardly surprising, therefore, that at the time of the signing of his marriage contract, on 19 Dec. 1758, François Maurin could declare to the notary Pierre Panet* that he owned 200,000 *livres* "in ready money, personal property, merchandise, and negotiable instruments." Thus although he was thought to be "the most misshapen man in the colony," being "hunch-backed and pigeon-chested" and having "a face like a snail," he was able on 21 Dec. 1758 to marry Archange, the under-age daughter of Louis-Césaire DAGNEAU Douville de Quindre, who brought to the matrimonial estate, held jointly, 15,000 *livres* in cash and personal property.

One of the principal witnesses at Maurin's marriage was Pierre Landrière, the chief writer of the colony. From the beginning of the 1750s part of his task, given him by Bigot, was to inspect the book-keeping, buildings, and records of the forts in the *pays d'en haut*. He was a valuable friend.

François Maurin continued his misappropriations as assistant purveyor in Montreal until 1759. According to MONTCALM he was able "to spend more on carriages, sets of harness, horses, than a conceited and harebrained young farmer general." But in 1759 the affairs of the purveyor-general, Cadet, began to "decline." A prudent man, Maurin decided to retire from business and to put his wealth in a safe place. In the autumn of 1760 he and his wife, along with his partner Louis Pénissault and the Chevalier de Lévis*, sailed on board the *Marie*, a ship which Pénissault had bought back from the English for the sum of 21,000 *livres*. Maurin took with him the pretty sum of 1,900,000 *livres* which he had succeeded in accumulating in the space of three years.

Maurin arrived in France at the beginning of 1761. In December of that year he was arrested and imprisoned in the Bastille. He was accused of "having committed malversations and breaches of trust detrimental to the interests of the King" in the government of Montreal and in the posts and forts of the *pays d'en haut*. He was tried at the Châtelet before a commission composed of 28 members, 27 of whom were counsellors at the Châtelet, and presided over by the lieutenant general of police, Antoine de Sartine. The inquiry lasted 15 months. Maurin, who remained in the Bastille all that time, was able to enjoy preferential treatment, like most of his Canadian colleagues. Thanks to the goodwill and forbearance of the officers of the guard at the Bastille, it was possible for Maurin to have brought in shirts, stockings, dressing gowns, books, tobacco, wine, and delicacies which made his months of imprisonment less disagreeable. Finally, on 10 Dec. 1763, M. de Sartine and the commissioners found him guilty of the charges against him; according to them Maurin had knowingly participated in "the unlawful profit from the enterprise" of the purveyor-general, since he was "a partner in it at the rate of one and two-thirds thirteenths [8 per cent] or thereabouts." The court sentenced François Maurin to be banished from Paris for nine years, to pay the king a fine of 500 *livres* in addition to the trial costs, and to return to him the sum of 600,000 *livres*. The sentence added that the guilty person had to "remain in prison in the Bastille . . . until payment of the said sum [600,000 *livres*]." The next day after sentence was pronounced Maurin wanted to make the restitution specified in the sentence with bills of exchange from Canada. The commissioners objected and demanded that restitution be made in specie. Maurin could not satisfy their demands and remained in prison. But after 13 months of negotiations his lawyer obtained on 10 Jan. 1765 permission for him to make restitution with bills of exchange from Canada. It was not, however, until May 1765 that the former assistant purveyor for Montreal was "set at liberty from the prisons of the Bastille," after having deposited with the treasurer general for the colonies, Baudart de Vaudésir, 600,000 *livres* in bills of exchange from Canada. The commissioners further required Maurin to pay interest owing on the 600,000 *livres* from 10 Dec. 1763 to 10 Jan. 1765. On 24 Nov. 1765 Maurin received from the minister, the Duc de Choiseul, permission to pay this interest in bills of exchange from Canada.

During his stay in Canada François Maurin had been able to strike up friendships with people in good positions, such as Pénissault and Pierre Landrière. He was a war profiteer who took advantage of the situation existing in Canada in the last years of the French régime to become a "millionaire."

ANDRÉ LACHANCE

AN, Col., B, 120, f.178v; 122, ff.266, 375–76; E, 92 (dossiers Corpron, Maurin, Penissault). ANQ-M, Greffe de Pierre Panet, 19 déc. 1758; Registre d'état civil, Notre-Dame de Montréal, 21 déc. 1758. "Dossier Charles-François Pichot de Querdisien Trémais," APQ *Rapport, 1959–60*, 1–22. *Journal du marquis de Montcalm* (Casgrain), 489. *Mémoires sur le Canada, depuis 1749 jusqu'à 1760*, 87. J.-E. Roy, *Rapport sur les archives de France*, 866ff. Frégault, *François Bigot*. P.-G. Roy, *Bigot et sa bande*.

MAYAR (Mayard). *See* MAILLARD

MECKINAC (Mequinac). *See* MIKINAK

MENEHWEHNA. *See* MINWEWEH

MERCIER, JEAN-FRANÇOIS, farmer, merchant, and perhaps blacksmith; b. 23 March 1699 at Quebec to Louis Mercier and Anne Jacquereau; d. 1769 or 1770 at Cahokia (East St Louis, Ill.).

In 1725 Jean-François Mercier first visited Illinois, where he had relatives in the various villages. At Fort de Chartres (near Prairie du Rocher, Ill.) he purchased the Canadian inheritance of one of them, and, as a young man of property, returned to his father's Quebec home. On 17 Feb. 1726 he married Catherine Lafontaine at Sainte-Foy. Soon after, his elderly father turned over his home and blacksmith shop to him and to a son-in-law, and for a few years Jean-François apparently practised the trade of blacksmith in Quebec.

The memory of the fertile lands of the Illinois remained with him, however, and some time between 1732 and 1735 he went to Cahokia to stay. He was one of the first to bring a wife to the mission settlement. His brother JEAN-PAUL had been serving there since 1718, when he and another priest accompanied their superior, Goulven Calvarin*, to the Sainte-Famille mission to the Tamaroas. By 1735 Jean-Paul was in charge, and his plan of the mission seigneury, made in that year, shows the house and barn of Jean-François on the mission property. By 1752, except for the mission itself, his was the largest single property in Cahokia. That he was the only head of a household called "Sieur" in the 1752 census indicates the social status he had achieved. He resided on three acres with his wife and three children, and with two hired workers and four slaves cultivated about 70 acres of land. Documents which refer to him as a *voyageur-négociant* reveal that he was also active in trade.

Jean-Paul Mercier died in 1753; his successor, Jacques-François FORGET Duverger, fled when the region was ceded to Britain in 1763, and the mission was left without its own priest. Sébastien-Louis Meurin* of Prairie du Rocher, who visited Cahokia at intervals to officiate, wrote in 1769: "I usually have living with me there the brother of Monsieur Mercier, the very worthy deceased missionary. . . . It is he who cares for the church in my absence." Jean-François Mercier, bereft of immediate family, apparently spent his last days serving his late brother's church. By June 1770 he was dead. His will, naming his sister-in-law Marianne Dornon, *née* Lafontaine (the widow of Antoine GIARD), as his heir, was contested by Joseph-Marie Mercier, his half-brother, who had moved to Illinois about 1743.

KATHRINE WAGNER SEINEKE

ANQ, Greffe de J.-É. Dubreuil, 17 févr. 1726; Greffe de François Rageot, 9 janv. 1728. Henry E. Huntington Library (San Marino, Calif.), LO 426. Randolph County Courthouse (Chester, Ill.), Office of the circuit clerk, Kaskaskia MSS, Commercial papers, VII, VIII; Private papers, I, V; Public papers, I. St Louis University Library (St Louis, Mo.), Archives paroissiales de Notre-Dame de l'Immaculée-Conception des Cascaskias (Kaskaskia, Ill.). *Old Cahokia: a narrative and documents illustrating the first century of its history*, ed. J. F. McDermott (St Louis, Mo., 1949). *Recensement de Québec, 1716* (Beaudet). *Trade and politics, 1767–69* (Alvord and Carter). Belting, *Kaskaskia*.

MERCIER, JEAN-PAUL, priest, missionary; b. and baptized 1 Aug. 1694 at Quebec, son of Louis Mercier, a locksmith, and Anne Jacquereau; d. 30 March 1753 at the Tamaroa mission (at Cahokia, now East St Louis, Ill.).

Jean-Paul Mercier entered the Petit Séminaire of Quebec on 23 June 1710. He was ordained a priest by Bishop Saint-Vallier [La Croix*] on 8 May 1718, after only two years at the seminary. Two days later the young priest left with two *confrères*, Goulven Calvarin* and Dominique-Antoine-René Thaumur* de La Source, to go to the Sainte-Famille mission which the seminary of Quebec maintained among the Indians of the Tamaroa tribe. These Illinois Indians lived on the banks of a small, eastern tributary of the Mississippi, some five leagues below its juncture with the Missouri. At that time the missionaries from the seminary of Quebec also ministered to the garrison of Fort de Chartres, 15 leagues farther south, as well as to the nearby French parish of Sainte-Anne. The apostolate in these out-of-the-way places was most arduous. The superior of the mission, Calvarin, quickly wore himself out at the task and died in 1719. CHARLEVOIX, who visited the Tamaroa mission in 1721, has rendered in the account of his journey an emotional tribute to the zeal of the other two missionaries, who had remained at their post, "formerly my disciples," he wrote, "and who today would be my masters." In speaking of Mercier in particular he noted: "I found him as he had been described to

me, hard on himself, full of charity for others, and through his own person making virtue attractive. But his health is so poor that I do not think he can long endure the kind of life one must lead in these missions."

On 1 Sept. 1728 Thaumur de La Source left for Quebec, where he died on 4 April 1731. Two young priests from the seminary of Quebec, Joseph Courier and Joseph Gagnon, left on 8 May 1730 to take his place alongside Mercier. In 1739 Courier was in turn replaced by Nicolas Laurent, who was sent from Paris by the Séminaire des Missions Étrangères.

By 1735 the material situation of the mission at Cahokia had improved greatly, as a map and report sent to Quebec by Mercier and Courier indicate. The missionaries were by then no longer alone, since seven French settlers had come to join them. The two priests lived in a house 84 feet long. Close by were a barn, stable, and some cabins for the slaves. There was also a garden, an orchard, and six acres under cultivation. But evangelization was progressing only slowly: the Tamaroas still resisted the missionaries' preaching, and conversions were rare. Faced with these Indians' obduracy, it is not surprising that Mercier sometimes felt discouraged. "I must admit to you," he wrote to his superiors in 1732, "that I have been on the point of giving them up and returning to Canada with our two gentlemen." Only the fond hope of being able "to baptize some children and even of winning over a few adults" kept this courageous apostle from leaving. Jean-Bernard Bossu, who visited the Illinois country in 1752, drew attention to his admirable intelligence and his fluency in the Indians' language. Mercier died at his post in 1753, after 35 years of labour.

One of Mercier's brothers, JEAN-FRANCOIS, went to settle at Cahokia sometime between 1732 and 1735. Two other brothers also entered the orders: Louis, the eldest, who was born of his father's first marriage and who died as parish priest of Beaumont in 1715, and the youngest, Jean-Auguste, who was born of a third marriage and died in 1752 as parish priest of Ange-Gardien.

NOËL BAILLARGEON

[Allaire, *Dictionnaire*, and Tanguay, *Répertoire*, list the names of the two Merciers who were parish priests, but they unfortunately omit that of the apostle to the Tamaroas. Information on him can be found in: AAQ, 12A, Registres d'insinuations C, 16–18. ANDQ, Registres des baptêmes, mariages et sépultures, 1 août 1694. ASQ, Lettres, M, 82, p.8; 95, p.2; P, 123; MSS, 2, 38; 12, 22–26; Missions, 30, 43, 43a-c; Polygraphie, IX, 15, 18, 19, 26, 42. Charlevoix, "Journal d'un voyage fait par ordre du roi dans l'Amérique septentrionale ..."

Mésaiger

in *Histoire de la N.-F.* (1744), III. Noël Baillargeon, "La vocation et les réalisations missionnaires du séminaire des Missions-étrangères de Québec aux XVIIᵉ et XVIIIᵉ siècles," SCHÉC *Rapport, 1963*, 35–52. N.B.]

MÉSAIGER, CHARLES-MICHEL, priest, Jesuit missionary, hydrography teacher, procurator of the Jesuit missions in New France; b. 7 March 1689 (or 1690) in Paris, France; d. 7 Aug. 1766 in Rouen, France.

Charles-Michel Mésaiger entered the noviciate of the Jesuits of the province of France in Paris on 9 (or 19) Sept. 1706. From 1710 to 1715 he taught grammar and humanities classes at the Collège Louis-le-Grand; then he studied theology there until 1720. After teaching rhetoric at the Jesuit college in Eu (dept. of Seine-Maritime) for a year, he sailed in 1722 for Canada, arriving in the summer. The following year he was sent to the mission to the Ottawas, which was centred at Michilimackinac. He took charge of the Saint-Joseph mission (probably Niles, Mich.), where he made great efforts to reconcile the Foxes with the Illinois and other western tribes. He took his final vows at Michilimackinac on 25 July 1723.

As chaplain to the French and missionary to the Mandans, Mésaiger accompanied Pierre GAULTIER de Varennes et de La Vérendrye in 1731 on his voyage of exploration towards the west. At the end of August the men mutinied at Grand Portage (near the western end of Lake Superior) and forced La Vérendrye to return to Kaministiquia (Thunder Bay, Ont.) for the winter. The Jesuit used his influence to persuade some men to go as scouts to Rainy Lake and build Fort Saint-Pierre there. These men returned to Kaministiquia shortly before the end of May 1732, and the entire expedition set off again on 8 June; that year it reached Lake of the Woods, where La Vérendrye built Fort Saint-Charles. Mésaiger's health had not stood up to the hardships of the voyage, and he had to set off for Montreal in 1733 with Christophe Dufrost* de La Jemerais. On 9 August, during a halt at Michilimackinac, the Jesuit drew up, in the absence of a notary, a new agreement between La Jemerais, La Vérendrye's representative, and the latter's partners. Then he continued on his way.

In 1735 we encounter him again, ill, at the Jesuit college in Quebec. The following year he was teaching hydrography [*see* Joseph DES LANDES], and in 1740 he fulfilled in addition the functions of minister (bursar). In 1741 he became procurator of the college in Quebec and of the Canadian mission, and he held this office until 1749. At that time he went to France to succeed CHARLEVOIX as procurator in Paris of the Jesuit missions in Canada. At the same time he looked after the interests of the Ursulines of Quebec, and in this capacity he left a few business letters in which he reveals himself to be a man endowed with good sense, a clear mind, and a cheerful disposition. Towards 1754 his health failed again; Father Alain de Launay succeeded him as procurator in 1755. We have no information concerning Father Mésaiger's final years other than that he ended his days at Rouen after the suppression of the Society of Jesus in France in 1762. He died on 7 Aug. 1766.

LUCIEN CAMPEAU

AMUQ, Fonds des pères jésuites, Lettres du père Charles-Michel Mésaiger. ASJCF, 580; 581; 635; 855; Cahier des vœux, 33v; Fonds Rochemonteix, 4018, 67, 74, 159, 489. *Découvertes et établissements des Français* (Margry), VI, 586–87. Champagne, *Les La Vérendrye*, 119–35, *passim*; *Nouvelles études sur les La Vérendrye*, 113–17. Rochemonteix, *Les Jésuites et la N.-F. au XVIIIᵉ siècle*, I, 205, 211.

MÉZY, JACQUES-ANGE LE NORMANT DE. *See* LE NORMANT

MICHEL DE VILLEBOIS DE LA ROUVILLIÈRE, HONORÉ, king's councillor, commissary of the Marine and subdelegate of the intendant, general commissary and *ordonnateur* in Louisiana; b. 1702 near Toulon, France, son of Jean-Baptiste Michel de Villebois, financial commissary, and Anne de Rostan; d. 18 Dec. 1752 in New Orleans.

Honoré Michel de Villebois's ancestors were of the *robe*, and his family was deeply involved in the administration of the Marine. His father was a commissary at Bordeaux during the 1720s, where his uncle, Henri de Rostan, later served as financial commissary. Two of his brothers were also in the navy commissariat. He began his career at Brest, in 1719, as a writer in ordinary and was promoted, on 1 Jan. 1727, chief clerk at Toulon. He remained there until 25 March 1730, when he was chosen to replace Jean-Baptiste de Silly*, who was retiring, as commissary at Montreal. Gilles Hocquart*, the acting intendant in New France, was disconcerted by his appointment. Though Michel was intelligent and "very willing," he remarked in 1730, his inexperience and lack of familiarity with Canadian affairs were serious handicaps, particularly since the backlog of business at Montreal precluded retaining him at Quebec for a winter of thorough instruction. To maintain closer control of Michel, Hocquart also appointed him, in October 1730, as his subdelegate at Montreal.

Michel, however, rapidly overcame Hocquart's misgivings. Various accounts describe him during the 1730s and 1740s as an efficient bureaucrat with a taste for hard work, a penchant for detail, and a passion for power. Certainly he displayed all of these qualities in performing his onerous duties. Briefly summarized, these entailed directing the commercial and financial transactions of the crown at Montreal, paying and provisioning the troops garrisoned there as well as in the western posts, and maintaining order in the jurisdiction through the exercise of "police" powers delegated to him by the intendant. His many ordinances regulating cabarets, enforcing *corvées*, improving sanitation, etc., testify to his energy in this last sphere. Moreover, as Hocquart's confidence in him grew he was able to extend his authority. In 1733, for example, he obtained a rank in the Conseil Supérieur, which also empowered him to preside when the intendant was absent. In 1736 he was named acting intendant while Hocquart was in France for a year. Following Michel's return to Montreal in 1737, Hocquart relied entirely on his judgement for the administration of that jurisdiction.

Although Michel apparently failed to make his fortune in Canada, his private affairs did prosper. In 1734, for instance, his salary was raised from 1,800 to 2,400 *livres* and he was granted freight privileges on the king's vessel. He also received over 9,500 *livres* in special bonuses between 1731 and 1747 including 3,000 *livres* for his brief service as intendant. Moreover, 500 *livres* were paid annually to the commissary at Montreal by the Compagnie des Indes. In 1737 Michel married Marie-Catherine-Élisabeth Bégon, daughter of Claude-Michel BÉGON de La Cour who was a brother of the former intendant in New France, Michel BÉGON, and who was serving then as governor of Trois-Rivières. Besides gaining him the support of the powerful Bégon family in France, this alliance helped to reinforce his influence at Montreal, for his wife was related, through her mother, Marie-Élisabeth ROCBERT de La Morandière, to many prominent persons there including ÉTIENNE and Louis-Joseph Rocbert, the king's storekeepers. Between them, Michel and the Rocberts conducted most of the crown's business at Montreal and the evidence indicates that they did so with a sharp eye to their own interests as well as to those of their relatives and intimates.

This self-interest was undoubtedly why the latter years of Michel's administration were scarred by controversy. During the early 1740s, for example, several complaints about his patronage practices, especially his methods of purchasing goods locally for the king's service, reached beyond Hocquart, his patron, to the French court. In addition, he antagonized Governor Josué DUBOIS Berthelot de Beaucours and the Montreal military élite in a dispute over payments due to officers for those of their troops stationed in the far west. By far the most damaging confrontations stemmed from his bitter power struggle with Jacques-Joseph GUITON de Monrepos who was sent to New France in 1741 to serve as lieutenant general for civil and criminal affairs at Montreal. They quarrelled in public for several years over their respective powers and honours and, after fruitless attempts by Hocquart to resolve their differences, the king was forced to sign a ruling spelling out their functions in detail. Perhaps because of this long dispute Michel was passed over in the large-scale promotion of commissaries in 1743. It was only after his relatives in France, particularly the Bégons, delivered "strong recommendations" to Maurepas on his behalf that he was finally promoted, on 1 Jan. 1747, commissary general and *ordonnateur* in Louisiana. Because of the heavy wartime work-load at Montreal, Hocquart delayed Michel's departure until the autumn of 1747 and he did not actually arrive at New Orleans until May 1749.

Michel's brief administration in Louisiana was undermined by his numerous disputes with Governor Pierre de Rigaud* de Vaudreuil. It is of interest in the Canadian context chiefly because of the fascinating correspondence addressed to him by his mother-in-law, Mme Bégon, beginning in 1748. It seems that she had fallen in love with him sometime after the death of his wife, her daughter, in 1740. Mme Bégon moved to Rochefort, France, in 1749 with Michel's two children, Honoré-Henri-Michel-Étienne and Marie-Catherine-Élisabeth, and she continued to write to him from there with all the news from New France. She also endeavoured to use her family's influence in the ministry of Marine to offset the poor impression his disputes with Vaudreuil created. Michel, however, did not appreciate her efforts and he answered her affectionate letters sarcastically, threatening to remove his children from her custody. Indeed he ended his days in Louisiana in a pitiable state of distemper, lashing out at both friend and foe. As one historian concludes, he was a talented and efficient functionary who lacked the personal qualities needed to survive in a government system that turned on patronage, not efficiency.

DONALD J. HORTON

445

Michipichy

AN, Col., B, 54–58; C¹¹A, 55–87, 113–15; C¹³A, 35–36; D²C, 222/2, p.74; D²D, 10; F¹, 34; F³, 11–12; Marine, C², 55, ff.36v, 232v, 323v. ANQ-M, Registre d'état civil, Notre-Dame de Montréal, 25 oct. 1738, 23 oct. 1739. "Correspondance de Mme Bégon" (Bonnault), APQ *Rapport, 1934–35*, 1–277. *Documents relating to Canadian currency during the French period* (Shortt), II, 634 n.2, 636 n.3. *Lettres au cher fils: correspondance d'Élisabeth Bégon avec son gendre (1748–1753)*, Nicole Deschamps, édit. (Coll. Reconnaissances, Montréal, 1972), 18–19, *passim*. A. Roy, *Inv. greffes not.*, XVI, 148, 171–72. P.-G. Roy, *Inv. ord. int.*, III. Frégault, *Le grand marquis*. Gipson, *British empire before the American revolution*, IV, 1201–3. Nish, *Les bourgeois-gentilshommes*. Isabels Landels, "La correspondance de madame Bégon" (unpublished doctoral thesis, Université Laval, Québec, 1947). P.-G. Roy, *La famille Rocbert de La Morandière* (Lévis, Qué., 1905). N.M.M. Surrey, *The commerce of Louisiana during the French regime, 1699–1763* (New York, 1916).

MICHIPICHY (Quarante Sols), Huron chief; fl. 1695–1706 (or possibly 1748) in the Detroit region.

Nothing is known of Michipichy's origins. By the end of the 17th century his band of Hurons lived among the Miamis in what is now Indiana and lower Michigan, but frequently travelled to the Saginaw valley and to Michilimackinac. In 1695 Michipichy was a prisoner of the Iroquois, having been captured during one of the frequent Huron-Iroquois clashes. His personal bravery was proved during this captivity when, at considerable risk to himself, he warned his fellow tribesmen to be wary of Iroquois requests for a favourable peace settlement.

The French for the most part were suspicious of this determined Huron chief, probably because he had already undertaken a policy of playing the French, the British, the Miamis, the Ottawas, and the Iroquois against one another. Frontenac [Buade*] told the Miamis in 1697 that Michipichy and another Huron chief, Le Baron, had prodded the Iroquois "to go and devour the Miami, and then to promenade in your prairies." When in 1701 Cadillac [Laumet*] undertook the establishment of Detroit as the major western outpost of New France, he persuaded Michipichy and his people to settle nearby. Cadillac then hired the chief to convince the Miamis and other Hurons, including those at Michilimackinac, to move to Detroit also. Michipichy's effectiveness in the negotiations was diminished because he could not get along with Étienne de Carheil*, the Jesuit missionary at Michilimackinac. Moreover, Michipichy began negotiating on his own with the English through the Iroquois in an attempt to attract both English and French traders and thus force prices down.

Michipichy was only partly successful in reaching his objective. Many Indians moved to Detroit, but by 1703 it was apparent that Cadillac did not intend to make the attractive trade arrangements that he had promised in 1701. Relations between the two men then quickly deteriorated. Cadillac began to speak of the chief's treachery, made vague references to "a drunken savage," and callously suggested that the authorities might "hang him if they like. . . ." Although the quarrel was eventually smoothed over, Michipichy seems not to have trusted Cadillac afterwards.

In 1706 the Huron chief was accused of complicity in the Ottawa-Miami troubles at Detroit, but the facts are not clear. Miscouaky*, an Ottawa chief, claimed that Michipichy called on the Miamis to fall upon the Ottawa villages while the Ottawa warriors were off fighting the Sioux. According to another report, Michipichy had told the Miamis that the Ottawa war party was in fact directed against them. Cadillac made a half-hearted defence of his former emissary, but Michipichy thereafter disappears from the record. His dozen years of work to improve the position of the Hurons had accomplished little.

There was at least one other Huron in the region who was called Quarante Sols by the French. He lived with the Hurons at Michilimackinac, and even the French officials had difficulty distinguishing between the two. In January 1748 a chief named Quarante Sols appeared at Detroit with a band of Hurons from Sandoské (Sandusky). This could have been Michipichy reappearing after 40 years, but it is impossible now to be certain.

HARRY KELSEY

Charlevoix, *History* (Shea), V. "Correspondance de Vaudreuil," APQ *Rapport, 1938–39*, 46. *Découvertes et établissements des Français* (Margry), English MS translation, V. *French regime in Wis., 1634–1727* (Thwaites), 206, 211–13, 217–18, 220–21, 223–25, 238–39. *JR* (Thwaites), LXV, 189–253. "Cadillac papers," *Michigan Pioneer Coll.*, XXXIII (1903), 106, 114–15, 118–19, 126–27, 159–60, 198–270, 288–94, 296–97, 319–24, 424–52. *NYCD* (O'Callaghan and Fernow), IX, 594–606, 664–77, 743–44, 752–53; X, 137–79. Jean Delanglez, "Cadillac, proprietor of Detroit," *Mid-America* (Chicago), XXXII (1950; new ser., XXI), 155–88, 226–58.

MIDDLETON, CHRISTOPHER, HBC captain, Royal Navy officer, explorer; b. late 17th century at Newton Bewley, near Billingham, England; d. 12 Feb. 1770.

By his own account Christopher Middleton served on board privateers during Queen Anne's War (1701–13) and gained experience of the

Spanish and Spanish American trades. Then in 1721 he joined the Hudson's Bay Company to sail as second mate on the *Hannah* to York Factory (Man.). Contrary to the usual practice of HBC sailors, he spent the winter in the bay; John Scroggs*, master of the *Whalebone* sloop at Churchill (Man.), was intending to sail north the next summer to search for traces of James Knight*'s lost expedition, and Middleton owned himself eager to participate in the hope of discovering information about the elusive northwest passage. Middleton must already have been a proficient navigator, since he taught the elements of the art to several of Scroggs' crew during the winter months at Churchill – only to find that Scroggs refused to take him on the expedition in the summer of 1722.

In 1723 and 1724 Middleton made further voyages to Hudson Bay, and in January 1724/25 was appointed commander of the *Hannah*. He sailed his new command to York and Churchill that summer. In total he made 16 annual voyages, during which he visited all the company's main posts in the bay. In 1726 came proof of his enthusiasm for scientific observation when the Royal Society published in its *Philosophical Transactions* Middleton's "New and exact table collected from several observations, taken in four voyages to Hudson's Bay . . . shewing the variation of the magnetical needle . . . from the years 1721, to 1725."

This paper was to exercise a fateful influence on Middleton's career for it attracted the attention of Arthur Dobbs, an Ulster landowner and an influential member of the Irish House of Commons, whose long-standing interest in trading matters was after 1731 directed towards the finding of a northwest passage. When in 1735 Dobbs decided to approach one of the company's captains for information about the west coast of Hudson Bay and the possibility of a northwest passage there, he chose Middleton because he had noted his observations in the *Philosophical Transactions*. Middleton was by this time firmly established as one of the company's senior captains, and in 1734 had been given command of its newest and largest ship, the 170-ton *Seahorse*. Middleton's early interest in the northwest passage was evidently revived by his contact with Dobbs; he passed on what he knew about the voyages of Knight and Scroggs, and promised to seek further information about the passage during his visits to the bay posts. In 1737, under pressure from Dobbs, the HBC sent two sloops north from Churchill along the west coast of the bay and its governor, Sir Bibye Lake, tried to convince Dobbs that after a hazardous voyage not "the

least Appearance of a Passage" had been found. But Middleton had been at Churchill when the sloops returned, and he revealed to Dobbs that their crews, "not duly qualified for such an Undertaking," had sailed only as far as latitude 62°15′N and had made little attempt at serious exploration.

Dobbs in reply to the HBC made it clear that he would now look for support for a discovery expedition from those "who I believe will undertake it chearfully, as they are convinced it will be a national Benefit," and during the winter of 1737–38 he made the first of a series of approaches to the admiralty with this end in view. In Middleton he seemed to have the ideal commander for the great undertaking: a believer in the northwest passage, a seaman experienced in ice-navigation, and one who in 1737 achieved a rare distinction when he was elected a fellow of the Royal Society in recognition of the contributions to the theory and practice of navigation. Already he was making use of Hadley's quadrant, and his later publications show that he was continually experimenting to find a practical method of ascertaining longitude at sea.

For three years little progress was made. Middleton's friendship with Dobbs strained relations between him and the London committee. As he told Dobbs in February 1738, "they keep every Thing a Secret; and from some Questions I have been lately asked, I found they seem suspicious of my corresponding with you." In 1739 Middleton was at Churchill again, where the factor Richard NORTON recalled that while with Scroggs in 1722 he had observed the tide to rise five fathoms in Roes Welcome Sound (near the west coast of Hudson Bay) and had seen the land fall away to the west. Indian reports of trading with Europeans on the Pacific coast of America were further proof to Middleton "that the two seas must unite," and during the winter of 1739–40 he spent tedious hours waiting at the court and great houses of London in hope of interesting two of Dobbs' correspondents, the first minister, Sir Robert Walpole, and the first lord of the admiralty, Sir Charles Wager, in an expedition to find a passage. In May 1740, just before sailing to Hudson Bay on what was to be his last voyage in the company's employ, he wrote to Dobbs with heartening news: George II had been approached by Wager and had given his blessing to the venture. The following year a naval expedition would sail in search of the northwest passage, and the understanding was that it would be commanded by Middleton.

On 5 March 1740/41 Middleton received his long-awaited commission in the navy, and four

Middleton

days later was formally appointed commander of the Arctic discovery expedition. The same day the deputy-governor of the HBC informed the committee that Middleton had resigned, and in April the governor warned shareholders that the forthcoming expedition "might affect their Property and be Prejudicial to the Company in their Trade." The company's attitude was one of vital concern to Middleton, who was experiencing frustrating difficulties in his efforts to get the expedition to sea in time to pass through Hudson Strait as the ice broke up. His command, the bomb-vessel *Furnace*, had to be converted to a sloop and altered in order to provide more storage space; her consort, the *Discovery*, was a collier which was not bought by the admiralty until late April; and above all there were the crew problems familiar to the wartime navy. Middleton had persuaded a few old HBC hands to sail with him, including his cousin and former chief mate, William MOOR, who was to command the *Discovery*; but for the rest he had to rely on the press-gang to make up his complement. Of the men already on the *Furnace* most "looked ailing, having scarce any Cloths," an admiralty report noted, and they were kept under close guard to prevent desertion. Middleton knew that there was little possibility of returning to England that year; so it was essential for him to obtain permission from the HBC for his crews of ragamuffins and pressed men to winter at one of its posts. After a brisk exchange of acrimonious letters with various government departments the HBC capitulated and ordered its factors in the bay to give Middleton "the best Assistance in your Power." During these arduous weeks Middleton was further distracted by the death of his wife, which brought on him "a great many Family Fatigues."

At last, on 8 June 1741, Middleton's two vessels sailed from the Nore on their historic voyage – the first naval expedition to leave England in search of the northwest passage. Middleton's instructions, largely drawn up by Dobbs, directed him to look for a passage on the west coast of Hudson Bay near latitude 65°N, Scroggs' most northerly point on his voyage of 1722. Once through the passage Middleton was to make a rapid survey and then return, so that a more powerful expedition could be sent out to secure his discoveries. The vision of a short trade route to the east, which had lured so many English seamen to the ice-choked bays and inlets of northeast America, was still a glittering one, but for the moment Middleton had more immediate problems. Delay in leaving England (six weeks later than the HBC ships) meant that the expedition

did not reach the west coast of Hudson Bay until late July, and amid thick fog and with the threat of gathering ice always imminent, Middleton decided to winter at Churchill and attempt the discovery the next summer.

The winter at Churchill, farthest north and coldest of the HBC posts, with most of Middleton's men miserably housed in the semi-derelict "old fort," was an ordeal which (in the words of Dobbs' later allegation) "broke the Spirits of the Men." There was more truth in this than in most of Dobbs' accusations, for ten men died of scurvy, and many others were ill or had toes amputated after frost-bite. On 1 July 1742, however, Middleton's vessels set sail, watched with some relief by the factor James ISHAM, who reported to the London committee that Middleton had been "a Very Troublesome Guess [guest]." By 12 July Middleton had passed Scroggs' Whalebone Point (Whale Point), the farthest north of previous explorers. On the other side of a headland in latitude 65°10′N, named Cape Dobbs by Middleton, an inlet opened out which he called after Sir Charles Wager. For three weeks masses of ice driving into the Wager trapped the ships and so gave Middleton time to send four boat expeditions to explore the area. Their reports convinced him that he was anchored in an inlet or river, nothing more, and as the ice cleared in early August the ships worked their way out of the Wager to continue their voyage north through Roes Welcome. A flood tide so strong that the ships could hardly steer gave rise to excited speculation that they were in the entrance of the passage, but on 6 August Middleton entered in his journal "to our great Disappointment we saw the Land from the Low Beach quite round to the Westward of the North which met the Western Shore and makes a very deep Bay. Thus our Hopes of a Passage that way were all over." The Welcome was a closed inlet, whose northern extremity Middleton named Repulse Bay, and the flood tide swirling down it came not from the Pacific but through an ice-choked strait in the northeast corner of the Welcome, which Middleton termed Frozen Strait. To all intents and purposes the expedition was over. A perfunctory examination was made of the west coast of the bay on the way home, and Middleton – like his predecessors – mistook the entrance of Chesterfield Inlet for a deep bay. At times on the grim homeward voyage only two men on the *Furnace* could take the wheel, and the officers did the work of seamen in order to keep the sloop afloat.

It says much for Middleton's own stamina that within a month of the expedition's return he was ready to read before the Royal Society a paper on climatic conditions at Churchill, together with some observations on latitude, longitude, and the magnetic variation, which won for him the society's Copley prize medal. Of the results of his exploration Middleton had no doubt, but in the spring of 1743 Dobbs claimed that the Wager was in fact a strait, and crew members, notably Edward THOMPSON, John WIGATE, and John RANKIN, came forward to swear that Middleton had deliberately concealed the passage. Thus began a prolonged and vituperative dispute which continued with an inconclusive investigation by the admiralty in May 1743, and with the publication of five books and pamphlets by Middleton and three by Dobbs. The key to Dobbs' conduct is to be found in his initial plea to Middleton in January 1743 that if he would admit the continued possibility of a passage, then "the Presumption will be a great Inducement to open the Trade to the Bay." From this time forward the passage was part of a more ambitious scheme to abolish the trading monopoly of the HBC, and Middleton's blunt refusal to agree that a passage might still be found meant that his conduct of the expedition had to be discredited. On all but one of the points at issue Middleton was correct: the Wager was a closed inlet (as Moor was to discover in 1747); the Frozen Strait existed, and the tide and whales passed through it into Roes Welcome (as Edward Parry* noted in 1821). Middleton's only lapse was that on the homeward voyage with his sickly and dispirited crew he had missed Chesterfield Inlet. In every other way his achievement was a praiseworthy one. His map of the expedition's discoveries, published in 1743, contains the first recognizable outline of the west coast of Hudson Bay, and included all its main features except Chesterfield Inlet.

During the wearisome pamphlet war Middleton was not offered another command by the admiralty, and he was forced to live on his capital until in May 1745 he was given command of the tiny *Shark* sloop. Even then, Middleton continued to bombard the admiralty with petitions for "the command of a Ship of Force, by which I may hope to retrieve the fortune I ruin'd, In my former attempt to be of Service to my Country," but his pleas met with no response. In 1747 he was involved in an incident during which he struck his boatswain and, concluded the investigating officer, "I fear . . . he is passionate, which I have given him a Caution of." When peace came in 1748 it was no surprise that Middleton was placed on the half-pay list at 4s. a day, in company with hundreds of other officers. The minute books of

the HBC record the receipt of two letters from him in December 1751 and February 1752, shortly after the dismissal of Captain William COATS, but if Middleton was seeking re-employment with the company he was disappointed. He remained on the half-pay list until his death on 12 Feb. 1770, a skilled navigator and enterprising explorer whose career was wrecked by a malicious campaign of denigration.

About the circumstances of Middleton's last years there is some uncertainty. The *Monthly Review* for 1784 has a melancholy passage on Middleton: "He died, some years ago, near Guisborough, in Yorkshire, in the utmost penury and distress: having, long before, been drove to the necessity of parting with Sir Godfrey Copley's gold medal. . . . His children, four daughters, brought up in ease and elegance by the produce of his labours in the early part of his life, all died, if we remember right, before him: some of them, at least, in a more wretched situation than himself." This account is belied by local reports that Middleton died and was buried at Norton, county Durham (certainly his home since the days of his HBC service), and by his will, drawn up in December 1769. It referred to a daughter Judith by his first marriage, his second wife Jane (originally his servant according to local sources) who was to receive £40, and two girls and a boy by his second marriage. The Copley medal was bequeathed to the boy, and his books, instruments, and an unspecified sum in South Sea annuities were left to the three children jointly. The values involved seem small, but the will indicates that although Middleton may have lived in straitened circumstances during his enforced retirement at least he did not die a pauper.

GLYNDWR WILLIAMS

[References to Middleton's service with the HBC are in HBC Arch. A.1/34–35, A.1/120–22; a note of his letters to the company in 1751 and 1752 in A.1/39. Middleton's log and journal of the *Furnace*, 1741–42, are in PRO, Adm. 51/379, pt.i-iii. Details of the fitting out of the expedition are in PRO, Adm. 1/2099; 2/57, 2/202, 2/473; 3/45; SP 42/81, 43/103; and in HBC Arch. A.1/35, A.2/1. The admiralty investigations into Middleton's conduct are in PRO, Adm. 1/2099, 2/479, 3/47. References to his service between 1745 and 1748 are in 1/2105–6; to his years on the half-pay list and his death in 25/35–78. Middleton's will is in PRO, Prob. 11/963. Of contemporary printed sources the most important are the books published by Middleton and Dobbs between 1743 and 1745, which give full if repetitious details of events after their first meetings in 1735. A list of these books can be found in Williams, *British search for the northwest passage*. Middleton's scientific papers are in Royal Society, *Philosophical Transactions* (London), XXXIV (1726–27), 73–76, and XLII (1742–43), 157–71. His map

Migeon

was published in 1743 with the title *Chart of Hudson's Bay and Straits, Baffin's Bay, Strait Davis and Labrador Coast* (London).

Some local evidence on Middleton's last years is retailed in John Brewster, *The parochial history and antiquities of Stockton upon Tees* ... (2nd ed., London, 1829), 374–80. See also, *Monthly Review or Literary Journal* (London), LXX (1784), 469. A short biographical sketch is contained in HBRS, XII (Rich and Johnson), 325–34.

For differing views by two modern writers on the Middleton-Dobbs controversy see Desmond Clarke, *Arthur Dobbs, esquire, 1689–1765; surveyor-general of Ireland, prospector and governor of North Carolina* (London, 1958), and Williams, *British search for the northwest passage*. G.W.]

MIGEON DE LA GAUCHETIÈRE, DANIEL, seigneur, officer in the colonial regular troops; baptized 6 Aug. 1671 in Montreal, son of Jean-Baptiste Migeon* de Branssat and Catherine Gauchet de Belleville; m. 31 Jan. 1712 in Montreal Marie Le Gay de Beaulieu, by whom he had two daughters; drowned 3 May 1746 near Pointe-aux-Trembles, Montreal Island.

As a young man Daniel Migeon de La Gauchetière lived in France and at the age of 21 he was appointed midshipman to serve in Rochefort. He was assigned to Pierre Le Moyne* d'Iberville's crew for both the 1694 voyage to Hudson Bay and the journey to the mouth of the Mississippi four years later but did not participate in either venture. He began military service in 1694 as an ensign in the colonial regular troops of Canada. From about 1701 he was acting as assistant garrison adjutant in Montreal.

Migeon applied for the position of lieutenant general for civil and criminal affairs for Montreal in 1704, in the hope of using the legal training he had received from his father. His application was rejected, no doubt because of his fight with Lieutenant Frédéric-Louis Herbin outside a parish church the previous year. In 1707 he pledged homage and fealty to the seigneurs of Montreal Island "for the fief called La Gauchetière," inherited from his father who had died in 1693. He acted as adjutant in the 1708 campaign of Jean-Baptiste de SAINT-OURS Deschaillons and Jean-Baptiste Hertel* de Rouville against New England, and received a commission as lieutenant two years later. In 1712 he was formally appointed assistant garrison adjutant in Montreal and in 1726 he became a captain. Governor Charles de BEAUHARNOIS sent him in 1730 to Fort Niagara (near Youngstown, N.Y.) to inquire into the causes of the garrison's mutiny in July of that year against the discipline imposed by

the fort's commandant, Nicolas Blaise* Des Bergères de Rigauville.

In 1733 Migeon was involved in a dispute with Philippe You de La Découverte over a debt of 3,500 *livres*. To ensure that he would be repaid this sum, Migeon had had La Découverte's slave, the Comanche PIERRE, seized, and this action was approved in December 1732 by the lieutenant general for civil and criminal affairs of Montreal, Pierre Raimbault*. The proceeds from the sale of the slave to Charles NOLAN Lamarque went to Migeon, and there the matter rested despite the protests of La Découverte who, in defending his case, brought before the Conseil Supérieur the question of the legality of slavery in New France.

Migeon was appointed commandant at Fort Saint-Frédéric (Crown Point, N.Y.) in 1735 to replace Pierre-Jacques Payen* de Noyan, and left the post the following year with the cross of Saint-Louis. He was granted in 1735 a seigneury on Lake Champlain which he did not develop and therefore forfeited six years later. Finally, at the age of 71, Migeon was appointed to assist Jacques-Joseph GUITON de Monrepos, lieutenant general for civil and criminal affairs in the royal jurisdiction of Montreal. On the morning of 3 May 1746 he fell from a bridge into Rivière des Prairies and drowned.

C. J. RUSS

AN, Col., C¹¹A, 12, 22, 23, 26, 28, 29, 30, 32, 34; D²C, 222/2, p.76 (PAC transcript); Marine, B², 88, 96, 130. ANQ, Greffe de Louis Chambalon, 26 oct. 1710. ANQ-M, Greffe d'Antoine Adhémar, 28 sept., 2, 22 oct. 1707, 16 oct. 1708, 23 oct. 1709, 29 janv. 1712; Registre d'état civil, Notre-Dame de Montréal, 1ᵉʳ sept. 1694. *Découvertes et établissements des Français* (Margry), IV, 50–51, 61, 64. Fauteux, *Les chevaliers de Saint-Louis*, 131. Le Jeune, *Dictionnaire*. P.-G. Roy, *Inv. concessions*, I, 191; IV, 270–71; *Inv. ord. int.*, I, 48. Tanguay, *Dictionnaire*. Gosselin, *L'Église du Canada jusqu'à la conquête*, III, 81–82. P.-G. Roy, *Hommes et choses du fort Saint-Frédéric*, 164–65, 336. Trudel, *L'esclavage au Canada français*, 44–45. Ægidius Fauteux, "Mort de M. de la Gauchetière," *BRH*, XXXVII (1931), 680–82. P.-G. Roy, "Nicolas-Blaise des Bergères de Rigauville," *BRH*, XXII (1916), 261–62; "Le sieur de Sauvolles," *BRH*, XIV (1908), 90.

MIKINAK (Meckinac, Mequinac, "The Turtle"), Ottawa chief; d. 1755 at Detroit.

Mikinak is first reported in 1695 or 1696 as a leader of an Ottawa-Potawatomi expedition from Michilimakinac against the Iroquois. The Iroquois had been actively seeking alliance with the tribes of the *pays d'en haut*. Their aim, had it been achieved, would have been disastrous for

French interests, since trade would then have drained through Iroquois middlemen to the English. Prompted by Cadillac [Laumet*], the commandant of Michilimackinac, Mikinak and his party attacked some Iroquois who had been hunting around Detroit, and thus effectively disrupted chances for peace between their nations.

After Cadillac established a post at Detroit in 1701, Mikinak frequently carried messages between him and Joseph-Jacques Marest*, the Jesuit missionary among the Michilimackinac Ottawas. Commandant and missionary struggled bitterly over where the Indians should settle, and in 1702 Mikinak was still unwilling to move to Detroit. By 1737 he was certainly living there and was described as a "great chief of the Ottawas."

He made several trips to Montreal, including one in 1742 when he presented his son to the governor, Charles de BEAUHARNOIS. Although on this occasion and almost certainly on the others Mikinak made polite assurances of support and promised to discourage all trade with the English, he apparently had an independent view of Ottawa interests. When ORONTONY and a group of Hurons from Sandoské (near Sandusky, Ohio) revolted against the French in the summer of 1747, Mikinak was said to sympathize with them. Years later PONTIAC told the French that Mikinak had declared he "would carry the head of your commander to his village, and devour his heart, and drink his blood. . . ." Whatever the foundation of such accusations, after the arrival of more troops at Detroit in the fall of 1747 Mikinak appeared more friendly toward the French. He offered to use his influence to get the dissident Hurons to move back to Detroit from Sandoské, and suggested that the French bring in reinforcements to use against them should they remain defiant. In return for his good offices he demanded to have his prestige restored by being given equal treatment with KINOUSAKI, an Ottawa chief opposed to the revolt, who had been sent a scarlet coat with silver lacings. Paul-Joseph Le Moyne* de Longueuil, the commandant at Detroit, advised that Mikinak could provoke considerable trouble if his request were refused.

Although a coat was sent, Mikinak continued his somewhat independent course. In 1751 KAK8ENTHIONY reported to Governor La Jonquière [TAFFANEL] that Mikinak had been to the English post at Chouaguen (Oswego) and he hinted that the Ottawa chief had also had dealings with the English in the Ohio country.

When Gaspard-Joseph Chaussegros* de Léry visited Detroit in the winter of 1754–55, he noted that Mikinak was discontented at being obliged to cede the land around Presqu'île (Erie, Pa.) to the French for a fort, and that he was to have gone to Montreal in the spring. On 26 February, however, the old chief died.

In contemporary documents and in later accounts, Mikinak is usually described as a vacillator, one whose "loyalty to the French weakened." Such an interpretation does an injustice to an Ottawa chief whose territory was occupied by one European power and threatened by another. No one ever questioned Mikinak's fighting ability or his qualities as a leader. Only after his death was Pontiac able to gain ascendancy among the Detroit Ottawas.

DONALD CHAPUT

AN, Col., C¹¹A, 67, f.139v; 75, f.91; 77, f.199. "Cadillac papers," *Michigan Pioneer Coll.*, XXXIII (1903), 113–14, 121–22, 126–29; XXXIV (1904), 288. Charlevoix, *History* (Shea), IV, 278. [G.-J. Chaussegros de Léry], "Journal de Joseph-Gaspard Chaussegros de Léry, lieutenant des troupes, 1754–1755," APQ *Rapport, 1927–28*, 411, 413, 414, 418. *French regime in Wis., 1727–48* (Thwaites), 262–64, 456–68, 478–92; "French regime in Wis., 1743–60" (Thwaites), 104–8. *NYCD* (O'Callaghan and Fernow). *The siege of Detroit in 1763: the journal of Pontiac's conspiracy, and John Rutherfurd's narrative of a captivity*, ed. M. M. Quaife (Chicago, 1958), 99–100.

MILLY, FRANÇOIS, fishing entrepreneur and merchant; b. before 1691 at Plaisance (Placentia, Nfld.), eldest of the four surviving sons of Jean Milly and Marie Aubert; d. before 1749.

François Milly immigrated with his brothers, Jean, *dit* La Croix, Thomas, and Gaspard, to Louisbourg, Île Royale (Cape Breton Island), around 1714. In 1719 he married Catherine Baudry, daughter of the late Pierre Baudry of Pointe Verte (Pointe Verde, Nfld.) and Jeanne Mechin. The couple were to have at least 11 children before Catherine died in 1744. As no dowry was specified in the marriage contract, we can presume that they had relatively modest means.

In 1719 François and his brothers held their property in common; it consisted of fishing establishments on the north side of Louisbourg harbour, on the Rue du Quay and the Rue Dauphin in Louisbourg, and at Saint-Esprit. François Milly seems to have achieved a modest prosperity in the fishing trade. Until about 1726 he apparently lived and worked with his brother, Thomas, as a habitant fisherman. As early as 1724 he had four shallops of his own. In 1727 the brothers divided their property among themselves with François retaining the establishment to the north of Louisbourg. He built up his fishing enterprise to the extent that by 1734 he employed 67 sailor-fishermen, about 40 servants, and some 14 shallops, working two fishing establishments at Louisbourg and Saint-Esprit. In 1742 he also acquired some further (unspecified) property and possessions, probably at Port-Toulouse (St Peters, N.S.), from a friend, Jean Baptiste, a ship's captain residing in Louisbourg.

Unlike the larger sort of merchant at Louisbourg, such as Michel DACCARRETTE (d. 1745), Milly does not seem to have taken much initiative in overseas trade. He may have attempted to set up a slaughter-house with one or more of his brothers in 1737. He sold a small quantity of pine to the government in 1741, and he is known to have sold one ship, a 30-ton shallop, for 1,900 *livres* in 1724 and to have rented out two schooners in 1741. His nephew, whose name was also François Milly and who carried on local fishing and business activities between 1749 and the fall of Louisbourg in 1758, appears to have had better success than his uncle. Perhaps because his stepfather was Jean La Borde*, treasurer of the Marine, he was able to obtain several government supply contracts for food and equipment.

During the siege of Louisbourg by the Anglo-Americans under William PEPPERRELL in 1745, Milly signed the petition of the inhabitants asking for the surrender of the fortress. He appears to have died en route to France or after landing, since he is reported dead in 1749. At least three of his daughters were recorded as still living at Marcombe, near Agen, and subsequently at La Rochelle in 1789.

T. J. A. LE GOFF

AD, Charente-Maritime (La Rochelle), B, 6117, 6120–21. AN, Col., B, 65; C¹¹ᶜ, 12–14; F³, 50; Section Outre-Mer, G¹, 406–7, 467; G², 202; G³, 2041, 2043, 2046–47, 2056, 2058.

MINWEWEH ("the one with the silver tongue," **Menehwehna, Minavavana, Ninākon**), Ojibwa chief, also known as **Le Grand Sauteux** because of his six-foot height; b. *c*. 1710; d. 1770.

Nothing is known of Minweweh's early life. By 1761 he had emerged as a war chief of the Ojibwas on Mackinac Island (Mich.). During the Seven Years' War he had been a firm ally of the French, and after their defeat he refused to accept English domination. When Alexander Henry*, one of the first English traders to come to the region, arrived at Fort Michilimackinac in 1761, Minweweh and 60 warriors confronted him. Minweweh declared that "the French king is our father," and that

"although you have conquered the French, you have not yet conquered us. We are not your slaves. These lakes, these woods and mountains were left us by our ancestors. They are our inheritance; and we will part with them to none." Although the Ojibwa chief permitted Henry to remain unmolested because the Englishman was a trader, he never changed his view of the English and actively resisted them for the rest of his life.

On 2 June 1763, encouraged by PONTIAC's siege of Detroit, Minweweh organized a surprise attack on Fort Michilimackinac under the guise of a lacrosse game. The 35 English soldiers of the garrison, including John JAMET, were killed or captured. Only one of the the four English traders was killed, but all were plundered. In the days following the attack other unsuspecting traders arrived and were robbed. One of these victims was William Bruce, who developed a passionate hatred for Minweweh.

When the British army reoccupied Fort Michilimackinac in 1764, Minweweh did not resist but moved his band westward. In 1765 he travelled through the Illinois country and the region around Fort Saint-Joseph (probably Niles, Mich.), planning with the Potawatomis, Ottawas, and Miamis to renew the war that Pontiac had begun. Indians friendly to the English reported the scheme to their anxious allies. Despite attempts by Sir William Johnson*, the superintendent of northern Indians, to win his friendship, Minweweh remained hostile.

The Ojibwa band then migrated to the Wisconsin country, where they met several parties of the expedition that Major Robert Rogers* had dispatched in 1767 to search for the elusive northwest passage. Minweweh confronted Captain James Tute with an "insolent" speech at Prairie du Chien (Wis.) and greeted Captain Jonathan Carver in an unfriendly manner at Lake Pepin. He worked actively with French traders from Louisiana to lure the Indians southward to trade. In doing so he was competing with the English who were trading in the Wisconsin area. William Bruce, who had married a Fox woman and had been made a chief of the tribe, was put in serious financial trouble by this rivalry. An attack against the Foxes by an Ojibwa scalping party worsened matters. In the fall of 1770, Bruce led a war party that attacked Minweweh's band of 15 to 20 warriors encamped near Michilimackinac. Minweweh died in his tent – the victim of a well-placed knife. Upon learning of his death Daniel Claus*, the deputy Indian superintendent, commented, "I think his being out of the way avails us as much as the Death of Pondiac or Akaasdarax [Gaustrax] as many Machinations among the Illinois Ind[ns] will thereby be quashed & the white people live undisturbed. ...''

DAVID A. ARMOUR

Clements Library, Thomas Gage papers, American series, Turnbull to Gage, 29 May 1771, 27 June 1771. Jonathan Carver, *Travels through the interior parts of North America, in the years 1766, 1767, and 1768* (London, 1781; repr. Minneapolis, Minn., 1956), 95–99. Alexander Henry, *Travels and adventures in Canada and the Indian territories, between the years 1760 and 1766* (New York, 1809); repr. as *Attack at Michilimackinac*, ed. D. A. Armour (Mackinac Island, Mich., 1971). *Johnson papers* (Sullivan et al.). *NYCD* (O'Callaghan and Fernow), VII, 785.

MISSÈGLE (Misèle), LOUIS DE BONNE DE.
See BONNE

MITCHELL, GEORGE, surveyor; date of birth unknown; d. 20 March 1755.

George Mitchell came to Nova Scotia in September 1732 as deputy to David Dunbar, surveyor of his majesty's woods in America. Dunbar had been commissioned to enforce the White Pine Acts of 1711, 1712, and 1729, which prohibited the cutting of white pine, reserved for mast-making, on government lands. Following the instructions of Dunbar and the provincial lieutenant governor, Lawrence Armstrong*, Mitchell surveyed lands from Passamaquoddy to Cape Sable for stands of pine and mapped the Annapolis River basin. He also helped to oversee the construction of a road from Annapolis Royal to Minas, where he and several others had been granted a patent to recently discovered mines.

In 1737 Mitchell left Nova Scotia and subsequently served as surveyor with the commissioners from that province assigned to arbitrate a boundary dispute between Massachusetts and New Hampshire. Erasmus James PHILIPPS, an acquaintance of his in Nova Scotia, was one of the commissioners. Mitchell settled in Portsmouth, New Hampshire, married Sarah Taylor, raised a large family, served as master of the local Masonic lodge, and continued his surveying. Well connected with New Hampshire's governing aristocracy – Governor Benning Wentworth was an old political associate of Dunbar's – Mitchell became a justice of the Superior Court and received several land grants. But keeping up with the Wentworths proved too much for Mitchell. When he died suddenly in 1755, he was found to be insolvent.

JERE DANIELL

New Hampshire Hist. Soc., St John's Church (Portsmouth, N.H.), Records, 1738–73. New Hampshire State Archives (Concord), Court records, nos.8883, 22144, 27893, 27896; Probate records, XVI, 444–46; XIX, 413–17; XX, 474–75; XXI, 262. New Hampshire State Library (Concord), Portsmouth tax records, XIV, XVI (mfm copy). St John's Lodge no. 1 (Portsmouth, N.H.), Minute books, 1739–55; W. S. Adams, "George Mitchell, Esquire, first known master of a masonic lodge in the province of New Hampshire."

New Hampshire, *Provincial and state papers, published by the authority of the legislature of New Hampshire*, ed. I. W. Hammond et al. (40v., Manchester, Concord, N.H., 1867–1943), XVII, XIX, XXIV, XXV, XXVIII, XXIX, XXXV. *N.S. Archives*, II; III. Bell, *Foreign Protestants*. Clark, *Acadia*. A map based on a 1733 survey of the Annapolis River basin, probably Mitchell's, can be found as an appendix to Knox, *Historical journal* (Doughty), I.

MITCHELL, THOMAS, HBC sloopmaster and explorer; fl. 1743–51.

Thomas Mitchell was appointed master of the Hudson's Bay Company's new trading sloop *Eastmain* in February 1743, and sailed from London to Hudson Bay that summer. His age is not known, but he was described the next year in one of the HBC journals as "a young Trader." Normally Mitchell's work would have been confined to routine slooping voyages between the company's bay posts, but within a month of his appointment the London committee had made it clear that he was to sail north along the East Main (the little-known eastern coast of Hudson and James bays) on discovery. Reports from Indians of the interior suggested that in about latitude 60°N three great lakes occupied "the greatest part of the Labradore," and the committee felt that the possibility of trade with Indians (and perhaps Eskimos) should be investigated.

In accordance with his instructions Mitchell headed north in the *Eastmain* in the summer of 1744, accompanied by John LONGLAND in the *Phoenix* sloop. Mitchell's log, which describes a perilous voyage in thick, squally weather along an uncharted coast, bears the mark of an inexpert navigator – as one despairing entry put it, "Where we are Now it is past ye art of man to take a true acc[t] of his Course and dis[t]." Despite his lack of surveying skill and drawing materials ("haveing Nothing But a Black Lead Pencill"), Mitchell managed to include in his log rough maps of the entrances of Big River (Fort George River), Great Whale River, and Little Whale River. At the latter he collected some ore, "and amongst it several Christal stones which may be Dimonds for what I know for they are ye same form." A few miles farther north, in latitude 56°15'N, the sloops were whirled through a narrow cleft in the shoreline into the unexpected

Monbeton

haven of Richmond Gulf (Lac Guillaume-Delisle), shown on Mitchell's map as "S! Atwls lake" (after a member of the London committee) but mentioned in his log as "ye Muskeetay Gulph." From here the sloops returned to Moose Factory (Ont.), without attempting to reach their official objective of latitude 60°N. Mitchell and Longland had explored 500 miles of coastline, and their logs and Mitchell's sketch-maps provide the earliest documentary evidence of exploration along the more northerly stretches of the East Main coast.

After several years of routine slooping, Mitchell had leave in England in 1748–49, during which time he appeared before the parliamentary committee inquiring into the trade of Hudson Bay. In 1749 he took part under William COATS in the renewed exploration of the East Main. He was entrusted in 1750 with the establishment of a new post at Richmond Gulf and the supervision of a lead-working at Little Whale River. Reports of his illegal trading led to his dismissal in the late summer, and the wisdom of the company's decision was borne out when the London committee heard that his unenthusiastic attitude towards the new project – summed up in his comment "that the Mine is a Chimera and the Settlement a Joke" – had demoralized the little garrison at Richmond. Mitchell appeared for the last time in HBC records when he wrote in June 1751 from Philadelphia, Pennsylvania, probably to request re-employment, for in its reply the London committee was at pains to remind him of his past transgressions.

GLYNDWR WILLIAMS

[Mitchell's sloop logs are in HBC Arch. B.59/a/8–15. His log for the discovery expedition of 1744 is in B.59/a/9. Other references to his career with the company are in HBC Arch. A.1/36–39; A.6/8, ff.22–24d, 34; A.11/57, f.7; and B.3/a/35–54. His evidence before the parliamentary committee of 1749 is in G.B., Parl., *Report from the committee on Hudson's Bay*, 227–28. Extracts from his log of 1744 and a photograph of his map of Richmond Gulf are in Glyndwr Williams, "Captain Coats and exploration along the East Main," *Beaver* (Winnipeg), outfit 294 (winter 1963), 4–13. G.W.]

MONBETON DE BROUILLAN, *dit* Saint-Ovide, JOSEPH DE, officer in the colonial regular troops, governor of Île Royale; b. 1676 at Bourrouillan (dept. of Gers), France; d. 4 April 1755 at Saint-Sever (dept. of Landes), France.

The father of Joseph de Monbeton de Brouillan, *dit* Saint-Ovide, was a brother of Jacques-François de Monbeton* de Brouillan; his mother was Charlotte Des Roches Duplesy. Although Saint-Ovide never married, he braved at least one adventure of the heart. At Plaisance (Placentia, Nfld.) about 1705 he divested one Renée Bertrand, aged 15, "[of] what is more sacred than anything in religion." He seems not to have been held accountable for the child. Renée Bertrand later married the younger Michel Leneuf* de La Vallière de Beaubassin, who served under Saint-Ovide at Île Royale (Cape Breton Island).

After entering the Marine as a midshipman in 1689, Saint-Ovide followed his uncle to Plaisance as an ensign in the colonial regulars in 1692. He was promoted lieutenant in 1694 and captain in 1696. His period of service at Plaisance witnessed the most significant military accomplishments of his career in America. In 1696 he was introduced to the hit-and-run warfare characteristic of Anglo-French relations in Newfoundland; in an operation commanded by his uncle he led a detachment ashore at Bay Bulls in September and captured two English positions. From November of that year he participated in the massive five-month campaign which, under the direction of his uncle and Pierre Le Moyne* d'Iberville, devastated nearly every English settlement on the island. He also accompanied André de Nesmond's squadron to St John's in 1697. In the years that followed he enjoyed a respite from warlike activity. At Plaisance, however, he, like other French officials, fell victim to the irascible interim commander, Joseph de Monic*. He was twice incarcerated in 1701, but when his eyesight began to suffer in prison he was transferred to house arrest.

Saint-Ovide took leave in France in the autumn of 1705, returning to Plaisance as king's lieutenant in 1707. The trust he inspired in his new superior, Philippe Pastour* de Costebelle, was soon to result in the most distinguished action of his career: the attack on St John's in 1709. In the autumn of 1708, Saint-Ovide, who had initiated the plan, gathered together a motley band of 164 volunteers and set out overland for the English stronghold. Supplied by Joseph LARTIGUE, the expedition was supported by the frigate *Vénus* under Louis DENYS de La Ronde and 50 men carrying artillery, munitions, and supplies. The party arrived before the English forts at St John's in the early hours of New Year's Day 1709. Completely undetected under cover of darkness, it took up positions around Fort William and awaited Saint-Ovide's signal. What ensued, if we may credit the commander's own account, was an action of unusual efficiency, the irresolute English defence under Thomas Lloyd* notwithstanding. "I shouted long live the king. . . . I

454

reached the covert way with 15 or 16 men and crossed the trench, [and] in spite of the gunfire from the two forts I set up the two ladders which I brought and ordered six men to climb up. . . . when the inhabitants saw that I controlled the ramparts [they] asked for quarter. . . ." The entire action, in which the French lost three killed and 11 wounded, was over in little more than an hour, and Saint-Ovide was rewarded with the cross of Saint-Louis. Costebelle realized, however, that his resources would not allow him to retain this conquest for long, and in April he ordered St John's abandoned. Saint-Ovide complied reluctantly, the forts were destroyed, and English artillery and munitions worth more than 50,000 *livres* were carried off.

Saint-Ovide next embarked upon a brief career in privateering, taking command of the frigate *Valeur* which he, Costebelle, and one Lasson (probably Georges de Lasson) outfitted in 1710. Costebelle's misgivings about his lieutenant's abilities as a mariner ("He should not pride himself on being an expert seaman") were borne out, for *Valeur* was promptly captured, and captain and crew were imprisoned in England.

The treaty of Utrecht having awarded Acadia and Newfoundland to Great Britain, France determined to re-establish the lucrative cod-fishery on neighbouring Île Royale. Back in France by the spring of 1713, Saint-Ovide was given command of the storeship *Semslack* with orders to sail from Rochefort to assist in the evacuation of Plaisance. Upon his arrival at Plaisance he led a party to Île Royale to reconnoitre a site in advance of permanent settlement. He remained there as king's lieutenant until the autumn when he returned directly to France, "in order to get for himself all the credit at court" according to Costebelle. Promoted lieutenant-commander, Saint-Ovide returned to Île Royale as king's lieutenant in 1714 and from late 1716 he served as administrator of the colony. Following Costebelle's death in the autumn of 1717, he was made governor in April 1718. Saint-Ovide himself seems to have had no doubts about his destiny: as early as January 1715 he had subdued an antagonist with the terse reminder "that he would be in charge one day and he would make me regret it."

The relative success with which Saint-Ovide faced the problems of the Île Royale colony in its early years is frequently overshadowed by the scandals of the latter part of his administration. Despite the influx of 3,000 settlers by 1716 – and chronic shortages of food, building materials, transport, and labour – Saint-Ovide managed somehow to organize the colony. There is no doubt that he was an able officer, albeit inclined to laxity and self-indulgence. Years before, Costebelle had described him as "a great help and very hard-working." In 1715 he had reported: "He has all the talents of a man of the sword and a man of letters and his eloquence enhances the beauty of the objects he wishes to praise."

For many years Saint-Ovide's eloquence served him best in avoiding the consequences of his acrimonious relations with senior Louisbourg officials: the financial commissaries, Jacques-Ange LE NORMANT de Mézy and his son, Sébastien-François-Ange*, and the engineers Jean-François de Verville* and Étienne VERRIER. Although his differences with the Mézys were frequently only petty in substance and characterized by quarrels over precedence and rank, the resulting absence of harmony and administrative solidarity caused more damage to the welfare of the colony than the divisions between the governor and the engineers. Saint-Ovide's disagreements with Verville arose from their opposing views on the practical defence of Louisbourg. Saint-Ovide's reasoning, though sound ("we should not be looked at in this country in the same way as a town in Europe"), was no match for the prestige enjoyed by the Corps du Génie. As a result, Louisbourg received, at enormous cost in time and money, classical European fortifications when "a good, well flanked *enceinte* . . . to give protection from a surprise attack" would have been amply sufficient.

There can be little doubt that the defence of the French interest in North America in the crucial period between the wars of the Spanish and the Austrian successions presented Saint-Ovide with the most significant opportunity of his 45 years there. His instructions were, essentially, to foster the loyalty of the Acadians and the Micmacs to the French and to encourage their active hostility towards Nova Scotia's new masters. Secrecy was, of course, important. "Your steps in this regard should be taken very cautiously," warned Maurepas, the minister of Marine, "so that they [the English] do not suspect that we know of them. . . ." It is difficult to appraise Saint-Ovide's contribution in this area. His reports to his superiors and his instructions to the missionaries (his agents in fact) in Nova Scotia all indicate vigour and determination. Similarly energetic were his harangues to the assemblies of Micmacs who gathered annually at Port-Toulouse (St Peters, N.S.) and Île Saint-Jean (Prince Edward Island) to receive the wages of their loyalty to the French king in the form of powder and ball, muskets and utensils. But the record of Saint-Ovide's performance in diplomatic incidents, in particular the

Monbeton

claims on Canso made by Thomas Smart* in 1718, suggests a degree of irresolution.

Other aspects of Saint-Ovide's administration were less attractive as well. By the mid-1730s his involvement in trade at Louisbourg had so compromised his position that his governorship became untenable. The earliest evidence of his commercial pursuits dates from his first leave back to France in 1705 when he carried with him aboard the king's vessel 108½ quintals of marketable cod. Such activities were apparently not unusual among Plaisance officials, 13 of whom employed 92 men in the fishery in 1706. Saint-Ovide employed 14. The outfitting of the *Valeur* in 1710 was similarly a private venture. It was, moreover, with a view as much to his personal interest as to the glory of French arms that Saint-Ovide had sought to command the expedition against St John's in 1709. The council of Marine later received complaints about the amount of his gains. Soon after his arrival at Louisbourg in 1714 Saint-Ovide, anticipating Louisbourg's role as a clearing house for the trade of France, England, and their respective colonies in America, "purchased for himself" the entire contents of four Boston merchantmen. There is ample evidence as well pointing to an elaborate network of local commercial patronage involving Saint-Ovide and his military subordinates (such as Joseph Du Pont Duvivier) in the fishery, in the local carrying trade, and in the protection of contraband trade with New England. Another allegation, seemingly well founded, went so far as to link him with a quarter interest in the contract for the king's works obtained by François Ganet and Gratien d'Arrigrand in 1725.

By the late 1720s complaints against Saint-Ovide's high-handed control of the trade of Île Royale had reached such proportions that Maurepas was moved to warn, "It is to your interest that there should be no more complaints on this score." Saint-Ovide for his part dismissed the accusations as "slander which some low and evil person has invented against me," and indeed the controversy ebbed for a time, aided not a little by the governor's return to France from late 1729 to mid-1731. He was, in fact, promoted naval captain at this time. Not long after his return to the colony, however, complaints against him resumed. In 1733, for example, Intendant Hocquart* claimed that Saint-Ovide and Le Normant, in league with the Louisbourg merchants, were manipulating food prices to the prejudice of Quebec merchants.

Saint-Ovide returned to France in November 1737 to see to family affairs at Bourrouillan. Although he was now 62, he reported to La Rochelle the following June, "waiting only for a good wind to get back to Île Royale." By September, however, he was back at Bourrouillan, and during the ensuing winter Maurepas apparently had second thoughts about continuing him at Louisbourg. A successor, Isaac-Louis de Forant*, was appointed third governor of Île Royale on 1 April 1739. There is no doubt that the colonial authorities had valid cause for dissatisfaction: the commercial policies of Versailles had been virtually ignored for almost a generation, and years later François Bigot* continued to encounter "evidence of the sacrifice of the king's interests made by Saint-Ovide for his own benefit and for the benefit of his creatures." With the advance defences of New France, Forant inherited, by his own admission, the worst set of officers and men he had ever known and a liquor problem which had long been out of control.

Saint-Ovide retired to Saint-Sever, whence he maintained some communication with Île Royale. Between 1739 and 1753 he made a leisurely disposal of his holdings there: a town lot, a warehouse, some livestock at Louisbourg, and modestly stocked pasture lands at the head of Louisbourg harbour and along the Rivière de Miré (Mira River). When he died at Saint-Sever in 1755, he was almost 80 years of age. His career, especially at Île Royale, is best epitomized by the observation made by Lahontan [Lom* d'Arce] on the Plaisance garrison: "Each of them [the officers] regards his position only as a gateway to money or wishes to stay only as long as is necessary to become rich."

BERNARD POTHIER

AD, Landes (Mont-de-Marsan), État civil, Saint-Sever, 5 avril 1755. AN, Col., B, 40, ff.514–17v; 51, ff.62v–63v; 52, ff.581v–86, 586–88; 53, ff.590–92v; 54, ff.498, 506–7v; C¹¹ᴬ, 60, ff.280–84v; 69, ff.243–46; C¹¹ᴮ, 1, ff.11–11v, 82–85, 149–64v, 211–11v, 462–64v; 2, ff.163–84v; 3, ff.76–86, 179v–80; 5, ff.100–4, 340ff.; 10, ff.85–87; 18, ff.28–29; 19, ff.51v–52; 20, ff.37–37v, 39–39v; 21, ff.290–91v; 22, ff.149–51v, 158–63; 32, ff.64–65; C¹¹ᶜ, 3, ff.192–215; 5, ff.214v–15, 300–1, 335v; 6, ff.4–10, 137–86v, 276–83, 294–99; 7, ff.42–50, 263–69v; D²ᶜ, 222/1, pp.102–3 (PAC transcript); E, 53 (dossier Brouillan), 59 (dossier Cailly); Marine, C⁷, 295 (dossier Saint-Ovide de Brouillan); Section Outre-Mer, G², 178, f.279; G³, 2038 (16 octobre 1733); 2041 (22 mai 1752, 27 mars, 4 juillet 1753).

Charlevoix, *Histoire de la N.-F.* (1744), II, 188, 331–34, 399–400. *Coll. de manuscrits relatifs à la N.-F.*, II, 145, 559–68; III, 27–168. *Journal de l'expédition de d'Iberville en Acadie et à Terre-Neuve, par l'abbé Beaudoin; lettres de d'Iberville*, Auguste Gosselin, édit. (Les Normands au Canada, Évreux, France, 1900). *N.S. Archives*, I, 4–105; II, 59–107; IV, 8–9. *DBF*, VII, 446. Le Jeune, *Dictionnaire*, II, 600–2.

Brebner, *New England's outpost*, 57–103. J.-M. Cazauran, *La baronnie de Bourrouillan . . .* (Paris, 1887). Robert Le Blant, *Un colonial sous Louis XIV: Philippe de Pastour de Costebelle, gouverneur de Terre-Neuve puis de l'île Royale, 1661–1717* (Paris, Dax, 1935), 78–227. McLennan, *Louisbourg*, 10–191. Parkman, *Half-century of conflict*, II. "Pastour de Costebelle et les officiers de la garnison de l'île Royale," *Nova Francia*, II (1926–27), 177–80.

MONCHARVAUX, JEAN-BAPTISTE-FRANÇOIS TISSERANT DE. *See* Tisserant

MONIÈRE, ALEXIS LEMOINE, *dit*. *See* Lemoine

MONK, JAMES, merchant, surveyor, justice, solicitor general of Nova Scotia; b. *c*. 1717 in Wales; m. Ann Deering at Boston, Massachusetts, 20 Jan. 1739/40; d. 6 May 1768 at Halifax, Nova Scotia.

James Monk was educated at Eton College and by 1736 had emigrated to Boston where he was set up as a shopkeeper and merchant. He enjoyed prosperity for many years, but eventually was "unfortunate in trade & oppressed by his creditors." In June 1745 he was commissioned an aide-de-camp to General William Pepperrell and was present at the siege of Louisbourg, Île Royale (Cape Breton Island). He may have remained there during the English occupation of the fortress from 1745 to 1749. In August 1749 he was in Halifax and that September was appointed the assistant surveyor of Nova Scotia. His financial position became more secure in February 1750/51 when the Nova Scotia Council passed a debtors' act, protecting provincial residents from debts contracted in England or her other colonies before their arrival in Nova Scotia. Monk had been appointed a justice of the peace by Governor Edward Cornwallis* in December 1750 and became a justice of the newly established Inferior Court of Common Pleas in March 1752. He may have had some legal training, for among his papers was found a notebook on law cases which he began in 1735. Lawyers and justices in Nova Scotia at this time, however, were generally untrained in law.

Conflicts soon arose in the colony between English and New England attitudes towards law and judicial procedure. In 1752 Ephraim Cook, an Englishman, lost his commissions as justice of the peace and of the Inferior Court, and, when he continued to act as a justice, was indicted by the Inferior Court justices for issuing a warrant without authority. A group of citizens, headed by Joshua Mauger*, complained in January 1753 that the Inferior Court judges frequently favoured "the Laws and Practice of the Massachusetts" in preference to English legal practice. They also accused Monk and Charles Morris*, the chief surveyor, of "labouring with the evidence and Grand Jury to support the Bill of Indictment against him [Cook]." The Nova Scotia Council acquitted Monk and the other judges of the charges. In April 1753, however, Monk was accused of attempting to defraud a settler of his land and was reprimanded by the council for actions "very unworthy the character a Magistrate ought to support."

Little is known of Monk's life over the next few years. In the fall of 1759 he and the other justices applied for land grants on the Bay of Fundy. According to Monk, the distribution by Charles Morris of some 25,000 acres of land around the Pisiquid (Avon) River was unfair, favouring council members over other applicants. (The grant established this area as a centre of country estates for Halifax councillors and officials.) Monk also charged that because of his complaints against the chief surveyor's conduct, Morris refused him the support to maintain "chainmen" for his surveying work. Monk claimed he was finally forced to sell his office to Morris's son in December 1759. The following March the council recommended that Governor Charles Lawrence withdraw Monk's commissions as justice because of non-attendance at court. Monk had then to fall back on "the Practice of the Law, as the only resource for a Subsistence for his Family." In July 1760 Lawrence appointed him solicitor general of Nova Scotia, though without regular salary.

Monk retired in 1767, "Malancholly, dejected and distressed," to his estate near Windsor, called "Monkville." Some books in the inventory of his estate indicate that he was interested in scientific farming, which he may have applied there. He died in May 1768 in Halifax, where he had gone to attend court. Five children survived him, including James*, who became attorney general of the province of Quebec, and George Henry*, who became a chief justice of the Supreme Court of Nova Scotia.

Phyllis R. Blakeley

Halifax County Court of Probate, 1768, James Monk, M135. PAC, MG 23, GII, 19 (Monk family papers; copies in PANS, Vertical mss file). PANS, MG 1, 701A; RG 1, 29, no.19, p.5; 37, no.23; 164/1, pp.33, 58, 73; 164/2, pp.85, 113, 201; 166A; RG 3, Minutes of Nova Scotia Council, 29 Dec. 1752–5 March 1753; 3, 5, 7, 9 April 1753; 10 March 1760; 27 Feb. 1762. Boston, Registry Dept., *Records* (Whitmore *et al.*), [28], 215. "The Pepperrell papers," Mass. Hist. Soc. *Coll.*, 6th ser., X

(1899), 288. R. A. Austen-Leigh, *The Eton College register, 1698–1752, alphabetically arranged and edited with biographical notes* (Eton, Eng., 1927), 237. A. W. H. Eaton, "The Deering or Dering family of Boston, Mass., and Shelter Island, N.Y.," *N.Y. Geneal. and Biog. Record*, LII (1921), 47–49. Brebner, *Neutral Yankees* (1937), 35–36, 75, 138, 241n, 249n; *New England's outpost*, 245–47.

MONREPOS, JACQUES-JOSEPH GUITON DE. *See* GUITON

MONTBRUN, JEAN BOUCHER DE. *See* BOUCHER

MONTCALM, LOUIS-JOSEPH DE, Marquis de MONTCALM, seigneur of Saint-Veran, Candiac, Tournemine, Vestric, Saint-Julien, and Arpaon, Baron de Gabriac, lieutenant-general; b. at Candiac, France, 28 Feb. 1712, son of Louis-Daniel de Montcalm and Marie-Thérèse-Charlotte de Lauris de Castellane; d. at Quebec 14 Sept. 1759.

The Montcalms were an old and distinguished family of the nobility of the robe. In 1628 Louis de Montcalm had married Marthe de Gozon who brought her family's lands to the marriage on condition that her husband and their male children bear the name and arms of Gozon. In the 17th century the family turned to military service and its members won distinction. At the age of nine, on 16 Aug. 1721, Louis-Joseph de Montcalm was commissioned an ensign in the Régiment d'Hainaut. Eight years later he obtained a captaincy, no doubt by purchase, in the same regiment. Not until 1732, however, did he begin his active military career. Prior to that he was educated, in the usual manner of the aristocracy, by a despairing private tutor who came to regard him as altogether too opinionated and stubborn. During the War of the Polish Succession Montcalm served in the Rhineland with armies commanded by the Maréchal de Saxe and the Maréchal Duke of Berwick. In 1736, on 3 October, he married Angélique-Louise Talon de Boulay. Of their progeny, two sons and three daughters survived childhood. Mme la Marquise de Montcalm was a daughter of Omer Talon, Marquis de Boulay, colonel of the Régiment d'Orléans, and of Marie-Louise Molé. Her parents were both members of old and powerful families of the robe, which may help to account for her husband's subsequent rapid rise in the military hierarchy.

At the outbreak of the War of the Austrian Succession Montcalm obtained the post of aide-de-camp to lieutenant-general the Marquis de La Fare and was wounded while besieged with the army of the Maréchal de Belle-Isle in Prague. During the famous retreat from Bohemia he served with the rearguard. On 6 March 1743 he acquired the colonelcy of the Régiment d'Auxerrois, valued at 40,000 *livres*, and for the remainder of the war campaigned in Italy. In April of the following year he was made a knight of Saint-Louis. According to his own accounts he had served with distinction and was always in the thick of the fighting. This last was certainly true at Piacenza (Italy) in June 1746 when the Austrians won a crushing victory over the Franco-Spanish armies. Montcalm's regiment was destroyed; he was severely wounded and taken prisoner. When he had recovered sufficiently to travel he went to Paris on parole and on 20 March 1747 was appointed to the functional post of brigadier. As soon as an exchange of prisoners released him from his parole he returned to the army of Italy and was again wounded at yet another disastrous defeat, the battle of Assiette (near Fenestrelle in the Italian Alps). In 1748 peace was declared and on 10 Feb. 1749 the Régiment d'Auxerrois was incorporated into that of Flandres. Montcalm thereby lost his investment but a month later he was commissioned *mestre-de-camp* to raise a regiment of cavalry bearing his own name.

Peace-time soldiering, however, proved expensive. On 6 Oct. 1752 he petitioned the Comte d'Argenson, minister of war, for a pension on the grounds of long service (31 years, 11 campaigns, five wounds), the good opinion held of him by his superior officers, and his mediocre private fortune, which he declared he had never stinted while at the head of his regiment. His plea was heard. On 11 July 1753 he was accorded a pension of 2,000 *livres*. During the seven years of peace Montcalm enjoyed the tranquil life of the provincial nobleman, dividing his time between the provincial society of Montpellier and his *château* at Candiac, supervising his children's education, disputing with a neighbour over property in the courts, and making periodic visits of inspection to his regiment.

Meanwhile hostilities between the French and the English had begun in North America. In one engagement, on 8 Sept. 1755, Baron de DIESKAU, commander of the regulars drawn from the French army, had been captured. A replacement had to be found. With war looming in Europe experienced general officers were loath to serve in such a remote theatre. Recourse had to be had to the lower echelons and the choice fell on Montcalm. On 11 March 1756 he was appointed major-general (*maréchal de camp*), receiving the same rank and pay and allowances as Dieskau – 25,000 *livres* salary, 12,000 *livres* to cover his expenses in moving to Canada, 16,224 *livres* living allowance – plus a pension of 6,000 *livres* payable upon his return to France with the reversion of half of it to his wife should she survive him.

Montcalm's commission and instructions explicitly stated that the governor general of New France, Pierre de Rigaud* de Vaudreuil, had command of all the armed forces in the colony and that Montcalm was subordinate to him in everything. Montcalm was responsible only for the discipline, administration, and internal ordering of the army battalions. He was merely the commander in the field, had to obey any orders he received, and was strictly enjoined to keep on good terms with the governor general. These instructions had been carefully drafted and revised several times to avoid conflicts between the two senior officers.

On 14 March 1756 Montcalm took leave of the king and set off for Brest, accompanied by Colonel Bougainville*, a member of his staff of whom he thought highly. At Brest he met the other members of his staff: his second in command, the Chevalier de Lévis*, and Colonel BOURLAMAQUE. The latter he did not regard with much favour; Lévis he thought to be sound but unimaginative. Also in the convoy were two battalions of regulars from the La Sarre and Royal-Roussillon regiments. Five weeks after setting sail on 3 April the ships were safely in the St Lawrence. Weary of shipboard life, Montcalm disembarked at Cap Tourmente and proceeded to Quebec by road, arriving there on 13 May. He remained in the city for a week, garnering all the information he could on, as he put it, "a country and a war where everything is so different from European practice." He then proceeded to Montreal to report to the governor general who was preparing to launch an assault against Fort Oswego (Fort Chouaguen).

Their meeting was amicable enough, but in his first reports to Argenson, minister of War, Montcalm voiced reservations, declaring that Vaudreuil had little use for anyone but colonials and, although well intentioned, was irresolute. In appearance, background, character, and temperament, these two men were very different. Vaudreuil, Canadian born, was a big man, courteous and affable, lacking self-confidence but not given to intrigue, obsessed by a need to issue a constant stream of directives to junior officers and officials, anxious to impress his superiors in the ministry of Marine, but always motivated by a genuine concern for the people he governed. To him the French regulars served but one function,

the protection of New France from Anglo-American assaults. Montcalm, by contrast, was physically small and rather portly, vivacious, extremely vain, determined to have his own way in all things, critical of everything that did not conform to his preconceived ideas and of anyone who failed to agree with him completely, and possessed of a savage tongue that he could not curb.

Anticipating a renewed Anglo-American assault on Lake Ontario, in February 1756 Vaudreuil had sent, under the command of Gaspard-Joseph Chaussegros* de Léry, 360 Canadians and Indians to harass communications between Fort Oswego and Schenectady (N.Y.). They succeeded admirably, taking Fort Bull (on Oneida Lake, N.Y.) by assault, destroying the fort and a vast amount of stores. The garrison received no quarter. Other Canadian war parties harassed Oswego all spring and early summer, preventing supplies getting through and putting the fear of God into the garrison. By July Vaudreuil believed the time had come for the destruction of the fort itself. He sent Montcalm to Fort Carillon (Ticonderoga, N.Y.) to inspect the new fort there, and deceive the enemy as to his intentions, then he massed 3,000 men at Fort Frontenac (Kingston, Ont.). Montcalm joined them on 29 July. Before leaving Montreal he had expressed grave misgivings about the expedition, but the main problem proved to be nothing more than the building of a road to bring up the siege guns. After a short bombardment, and with the Canadians and Indians commanded by Vaudreuil's brother, François-Pierre de Rigaud* de Vaudreuil, swarming within musket range, the garrison surrendered. Seventeen hundred prisoners were taken, several armed ships, a large number of cannon, munitions and supplies of all sorts, and a war chest containing funds to the value of 18,000 *livres*. Montcalm stated that the cost of the expedition had been 11,862 *livres*. All told a profitable enterprise, but strategically it was worth far more than that. French control of Lake Ontario was now assured, the northwestern flank of New York was open to attack, and the danger of an assault on either Fort Frontenac or Niagara (near Youngstown, N.Y.) dissipated.

Vaudreuil was pleased with what he referred to as "my victory." Montcalm still had reservations. In a dispatch to the minister of War he admitted that the audacity of the assault would have been regarded as foolhardy in Europe. He assured the minister that were he to be given a command in Europe he would conduct himself differently and that, even on this occasion, had things gone wrong he would have retreated, and saved the guns and the honour of the army by sac-

Montcalm

rificing perhaps two to three hundred men. The nature of the terrain, the timidity of the Anglo-Americans, their fear of the Indians had, he declared, given him victory. Vaudreuil, too, had misgivings, but not over the manner in which victory had been achieved. He was gravely concerned at the attitude of the French regulars towards campaigning in America, and towards the Canadians. Trouble that was to plague the colony for the ensuing four years was just beginning. Montcalm was critical of the strategy and tactics that Vaudreuil was employing. Whereas Vaudreuil believed in spoiling attacks to frustrate enemy offensives, in the form of raids on the English frontier settlements, to cut their communications, destroy their supply depots, and keep them continually off balance, Montcalm was convinced that against British regular troops the only hope lay in a static defence. He had nothing but contempt for guerilla warfare and insisted that the only sane way to fight the war was the way that war was fought in Europe. He quickly came to nurture considerable antipathy towards Vaudreuil and also towards all things Canadian. He considered that the Canadian regulars had an inflated opinion of themselves and that the militia were an undisciplined rabble of little or no military value. As for the Indians, he regarded them with contempt, declaring that their only merit was to be a good thing not to have against one. Yet at the same time he claimed that he had won the esteem and confidence of the Canadians and that the affection with which he had come to be held by the Indians had astonished Vaudreuil who was not a little jealous of it.

For a general to hold a low opinion of his superior, and give voice to it, was quite normal in the French army of the day. A senior officer had to devote much of his time to countering the intrigue and chicanery of other general officers and their supporters at court who sought his dismissal. In Montcalm's case the minister of War encouraged intrigue by providing him with a special cipher and a private address to enable him to express himself more freely than his normal dispatches through regular channels would allow. Montcalm, however, carried this propensity to excess; before his officers and servants he would make what was, at times, slanderous criticism of Vaudreuil. Needless to say, the governor general was quickly informed.

Early in 1757, while the British were preparing to besiege Louisbourg, Île Royale (Cape Breton Island), Vaudreuil made plans for an attack on the English bases south of Lake Champlain. Were they to be destroyed the feared invasion by that route would be disrupted. In July, after the supply ships had arrived from France, Montcalm mustered 6,200 men, regulars and militia, at Carillon. With them were 1800 Indians. Vaudreuil's orders were to destroy Fort William Henry (also called Fort George) at the southern tip of Lac Saint-Sacrement (Lake George, N.Y.), then to destroy Fort Edward, a few miles south. These orders contained the escape clause that Montcalm was to use his own discretion if a push beyond Fort William Henry would endanger the army, but Vaudreuil made it clear that nothing less than this manifest danger should deter Montcalm from marching on Fort Edward.

By 3 Aug. 1757 Montcalm had his forces massed around Fort William Henry with its garrison of some 2,500 men. The commander, Lieutenant-Colonel George Monro, rejected a call to surrender. Montcalm therefore, in deliberate European siege style, had a road, entrenchments, and gun emplacements built. On 6 August eight cannon opened fire. Three days later the garrison offered to surrender on terms. These were quickly arranged. The garrison was allowed to retire with the honours of war and their baggage, but could not serve against the French for 18 months; within three months all prisoners held by the British, taken in North America, were to be returned to Canada; all cannon, munitions, and stores in the fort were to be left intact. For their part, the French agreed to escort the garrison to Fort Edward to protect them against the Indians.

The responsibility for what ensued has been much disputed. As the garrison was marching off it was attacked by the Indians; a number were killed and some five or six hundred were dragged off to the Indian encampment. Montcalm and his officers, after the trouble had started, did all they could to stop it and about 400 of the prisoners were recovered. Vaudreuil later ransomed most of the remainder but several were killed and some eaten. Montcalm made light of the incident. He wrote to generals Daniel Webb and John Campbell, Earl of Loudoun, warning them that the unfortunate event did not provide them with an excuse to fail to abide by the terms of the surrender. The British thought otherwise; the garrison of Fort William Henry was released from its parole, and the Canadian prisoners were not returned. But the 44 pieces of artillery, large stocks of ammunition, and enough food to sustain 6,000 men for six weeks were welcome additions to the French stores.

The enemy had been dealt a sharp blow but its effect was to a degree nullified by the breach in the surrender terms and by Montcalm's failure to follow up the victory by destroying Fort Edward. The British were thoroughly demoralized, Fort

Edward was only 16 miles away, a day's march, and in New York there was near panic as word was expected any hour that the French had taken, not only Fort Edward, but Albany as well. Montcalm, however, refused to go farther. He claimed that the road to Fort Edward was in too bad a condition to move his heavy guns, that the garrison of the fort had been reinforced by four to five thousand militia, that the consumption of food supplies would be too great, and that he had to send back the Canadian militia to bring in the harvest. Vaudreuil was irate over Montcalm's decision. He regarded the reasons advanced as inadequate, as mere excuses in fact, and François Bigot* reported to the minister that several senior French officers agreed with him.

Montcalm was, however, well pleased with what he had accomplished. In his dispatch to the minister of War he had great praise for his own conduct, declared that he was doing everything he could to please Vaudreuil, and submitted a plea for promotion to lieutenant-general on the grounds of his length of service, that he was the only major-general in command of an army 1,500 leagues removed from France, and that he had already gained two victories. He may have been encouraged to press his case upon receiving word, in a letter dated 11 March 1757, that he had been appointed a commander of the order of Saint-Louis. He also requested that in the event of Vaudreuil's demise the post of acting governor general should go to him rather than, in the customary succession, to the governor of Montreal, who happened to be Vaudreuil's brother, François-Pierre, and a man recognized to be of meagre talents under whom Montcalm could not be expected to serve. His point was well taken, but Machault, minister of Marine, had already seen to it. The previous year a sealed packet had been sent to Bigot to be opened in the event of Vaudreuil's death, containing letters patent delegating the governor general's authority to Montcalm, and, in the event of his death, to Lévis.

Another serious problem, inflation, was not so easily solved. The influx of French regulars, the Acadian refugees, the horde of allied Indians who had to be fed and supplied during campaigns, resulted in a shortage of goods of all kinds. In addition, money poured into the colony, over a million *livres* a year for the army battalions alone; thus too much money and too few goods caused prices to soar. Montcalm complained continually, and bitterly, that he and his officers could not live on their pay, even though they were paid twice as much as the Canadian regulars. His own situation, he claimed, was particularly bad since he had to keep an open table. He declared in 1757 that he had already overdrawn his pay by 12,000 *livres* and was consuming his children's patrimony to maintain the dignity of his position.

During the winter of 1757–58 complaints over the food supply became more and more vociferous. Rations of the staples, bread and meat, were reduced severely. In Montreal there were protests from both soldiers and civilians. When horse meat was issued instead of beef the authorities had to take stern measures. Montcalm thought they had not been stern enough. The urban dwellers certainly had to tighten their belts but there is no evidence that anyone starved. A main cause of the trouble was crop failures in 1757 and again in 1758. The colony was therefore heavily dependent on supplies from France. But the needed supplies were sent and the bulk of them reached the colony.

This situation offered Montcalm an opportunity to attack Vaudreuil and the entire Canadian administration, which he labelled as totally corrupt and hopelessly inefficient. Montcalm also began declaring over and over again to his officers, and to the ministers of War and Marine, that defeat was inevitable, that the colony was doomed despite his own efforts and the valour of his troops. The two factors, corruption in the administration and defeat, were linked as cause and effect. Vaudreuil was the main target of Montcalm's hostility, but Bigot, although Montcalm was openly on good terms with him, was also the subject of detailed accusations. These charges had a telling effect, for the minister of Marine was already alarmed by the soaring cost of military operations in America. He became convinced that the main cause was the huge profits that Bigot and his associates were making by devious means. The Canadian administration appeared in a bad light and the minister of Marine now tended to give greater credence to Montcalm than to Vaudreuil, who was not always his own best advocate.

Vaudreuil's position was further weakened by Montcalm's reports of the excessive gambling, the lavish banquets, that were indulged in by Vaudreuil's and Bigot's entourage. Montcalm, although critical of these activities, felt obliged to take part in them. He also entertained some of the Canadian notables and found their society agreeable. He was particularly appreciative of the charm and wit of the Canadian ladies but he appears not to have enjoyed the same success in the boudoir as did Lévis, and he was rather disgruntled about it.

In 1758 Vaudreuil hoped to block a British drive on Lake Champlain with the French reg-

Montcalm

ulars at Carillon under Montcalm while Lévis, with 1,600 men, mainly Canadians, led a diversionary attack on Schenectady by way of the Mohawk Valley. When Montcalm received his orders he refused to comply with them and demanded that they be revised. To avoid a public scandal and the disruption of the campaign Vaudreuil complied, but he was outraged when Montcalm made the incident public. After Montcalm had departed for Carillon, in June, word was received that the British army at Lac Saint-Sacrement was much larger than anticipated. Lévis's diversionary force was immediately recalled and ordered to Carillon post-haste.

At the southern end of Lac Saint-Sacrement Major-General James Abercromby* had massed the largest army ever assembled in North America, over 6,000 British regulars and 9,000 provincial troops. On 5 July they started north down the lake. Montcalm meanwhile was trying to decide where, or even if, to make a stand. The fort at Carillon he regarded as unable to withstand an assault, let alone a siege. At one point he contemplated blowing it up and retreating to Fort Saint-Frédéric (Crown Point, N.Y.) but he was persuaded to hold fast. The killing of Brigadier George Augustus Howe, Abercromby's popular and competent second in command, in a skirmish at the portage between the two lakes on 6 July disheartened the British and delayed their advance 24 hours. This delay alone allowed Montcalm to complete his defence works. On the evening of the 7th Lévis arrived with 400 Canadian regulars and militia, bringing Montcalm's total force to over 3,600.

Next day, 8 July, Abercromby made a hasty inspection of the site and, believing that Montcalm was shortly to receive 3,000 reinforcements, decided to attack at once without waiting to bring up his guns. Had he brought his cannon into play Montcalm's log wall would quickly have been smashed to kindling, and his troops with it. In fact, there was no need even to do this. Had Abercromby surveyed the terrain more closely he could not have failed to see that to the right of and below Montcalm's defence work, which stretched across the crest of the rising ground, half a mile of level, open land extended to the lake and back to the fort. All he had to do was use part of his force to hold Montcalm, then march the remainder round on the north flank and take the French in the rear. The British would then have been between Montcalm's force and the fort. Abercromby would have had the French pinned against their own barricade. All that Montcalm placed on that plain was the 400 Canadians behind another short and hastily constructed log

wall at the foot of the slope. They could easily have been outflanked or overwhelmed, and indubitably would have been blamed for the ensuing disaster. Fortunately for the French, Abercromby ignored that glaring flaw in the French position. (After the battle Montcalm extended this defence line to the lake.)

Shortly after noon on 8 July the British regulars formed up in four columns, provincial skirmishers between them, and the attack went in against the French abatis. Their formations were quickly broken up as they scrambled through the tangle of felled trees. Before they reached the French line they were shot to pieces by steady musket fire. They re-formed and attacked but were beaten back with heavy loss every time. By seven o'clock they could take no more. The French then vaulted their barricade and drove off the remaining skirmishers. At that the whole British army turned and fled in wild disorder, abandoning their arms, their equipment, and their wounded. For them it was a stunning defeat. For Montcalm and the French a glorious victory. The British had suffered 1,944 casualties, 1,610 of them regulars, the French only 377.

Three days after the battle Montcalm sent a brief account of it to the minister of War, which on certain points was not in accord with the facts. In it he declared that Vaudreuil had deliberately held back the 1,200 Canadians and a large force of Indians that he had promised to send to Carillon. He stated that his small army had been attacked by 20,000 British – he subsequently raised this estimate to 25,000, then 27,000, and eventually to 30,000 – from eight in the morning until eight that night. The British casualties he placed at 5,000. But what he found most gratifying was that he had saved the colony without the French regulars' having to share the glory; there had been only some 400 Canadians and a handful of Indians present at the battle. On 20 July, however, he stated that without necessity, without a specific objective, he had been sent a large body of Canadians and Indians that he had neither wanted nor requested, and who, arriving too late to take part in the action, had merely consumed precious supplies. He declared that he had no doubt they had been sent to reap profit from his victory. He also stated that had he had 200 Indians at the battle the British could have been destroyed in their retreat. Only the lack of these Indians had prevented him from following up his victory. He then went on to accuse the officials of the ministry of Marine of holding back his dispatches, and concluded by requesting his recall, declaring that his health and his finances were ruined; by the end of the year he would have overdrawn his pay by 30,000 *livres*. But most of all, the unpleasantness and contradictions that he had to endure, the impossibility of doing things properly or of preventing abuses, determined him to ask for his release.

In a subsequent account of the battle written for publication he praised all who had taken part, including the Canadians, but this was accompanied by a private dispatch to the minister of War, sent in cipher on 28 July by André DOREIL, the war commissary. In this last Montcalm told a different story. He declared he was in no doubt the ministry of Marine would seek to enhance the glory of the Canadians at the battle and diminish that of the French troops, but in truth the Canadians had performed badly. They had refused to attack the enemy when ordered and had had to be fired on when they tried to abandon their post. Montcalm claimed that he had had to silence the officers and men of the French battalions who swore that Vaudreuil had sought to have them slaughtered by sending such a small force against a large army. Doreil added there could be no doubt that Vaudreuil, jealous of the glory previously gained by Montcalm, had sought to deny him the means to establish a sound defence.

It did not take long for word of Montcalm's accusations to reach Vaudreuil and he was, of course, furious. On 4 Aug. 1758 he responded by criticizing, in a dispatch to the minister of Marine, Montcalm's entire conduct of the campaign and exalting the part played by the Canadians, who had been placed in such a dangerous position on the day of the battle. He was sure that Montcalm would fail to give them their due. He stated that the Indian allies had returned to Montreal and stated publicly that they would never serve with Montcalm again. He also informed the minister that to prevent an open conflict he had chosen to ignore all the personal insults and slurs emanating from, or sanctioned by, Montcalm, but things had now gone too far; he therefore requested the minister to accept Montcalm's request for his recall. He stated that Montcalm possessed many estimable qualities and deserved to be promoted lieutenant-general, for service in Europe, but he most certainly did not have the capacity to command the forces in Canada. The Chevalier de Lévis, he declared, did. Vaudreuil therefore requested that Lévis be appointed to succeed Montcalm.

Between Montcalm and Vaudreuil an angry exchange of letters took place in August and September 1758. Montcalm retorted to Vaudreuil's querying his failure to pursue the defeated foe by stating that it would have served no useful purpose, that Vaudreuil had had no military experi-

ence, and that had he visited the region he would have realized pursuit had been impossible. As for the complaints of the Indians, they had behaved badly and he had scolded them. He denied vehemently that he had ever spoken ill of Vaudreuil, or allowed others to do so in his presence. He declared that he had always been at pains to write nothing unfavourable concerning Vaudreuil or his brother, this despite the fact that he knew he was constantly criticized in Vaudreuil's entourage. (His letters, dispatches, and journal are, however, replete with savage comments on both Vaudreuil and his brother.) He concluded by requesting Vaudreuil to solicit his recall on the grounds of health and his debts. If the minister concluded that the real reason was Montcalm's discontent with Vaudreuil, no matter.

Although Montcalm's victory at Carillon and the long drawn out siege of Louisbourg, Île Royale (Cape Breton Island), had saved Canada from a full scale assault in 1758, there was no doubt in anyone's mind that it would be renewed the next year. The question was, how best to meet it? Here again Montcalm and Vaudreuil were in violent disagreement. Montcalm was convinced that the colony could not be successfully defended, but the attempt had to be made and the inevitable end delayed as long as possible, for the honour of the army. The British, he stated to the minister of Marine, could put 50,000 men in the field, not counting those employed at Louisbourg, against the 7,400 regulars and militia available in Canada. In fact, the British had 23,000 regulars in America, plus some provincial troops and the militia who were of dubious value. Moreover, Montcalm grossly underestimated both the number and the effectiveness, when properly employed, of the Canadian militia. Thus the odds were nowhere near as disadvantageous as Montcalm claimed. He maintained that only if peace were to be declared before the British launched a triple assault, or he were to receive several thousand additional regular troops with supplies, could defeat be averted, and given the weakness of the French navy he regarded it as impracticable for France to risk sending such a force across the Atlantic.

Although he hoped to be removed from the scene a year thence, Montcalm in early autumn 1758 submitted proposals to Vaudreuil for the colony's defence against the expected onslaught. He called for the abandonment of the Ohio valley and the outer defences on Lakes Ontario and Champlain; the guerilla warfare on the English colony's frontiers had to cease and 3,000 of the Canadian militia be incorporated into the regular troops; the colony's entire forces then had to be

Montcalm

concentrated on the inner defences on the St Lawrence and Richelieu rivers. He maintained that the nature of the war had changed, that it had now to be fought on European, not Canadian lines. Vaudreuil rejected Montcalm's recommendations. He refused to abandon the outer defence lines, declaring that the enemy had to be made to fight every foot of the way and worn down before he reached the central colony.

To impress on the French government the urgent need for troop reinforcements and supplies Vaudreuil in August sent a Canadian officer, Major Michel-Jean-Hugues Péan*, to the court. Doreil promptly arranged with the captain of the ship he was to cross on to open the mail pouch and have copies made of Vaudreuil's dispatches. He also wrote to warn the officials in the ministry of War that Péan was a base character who was being sent to France for sinister reasons. To counter whatever it was that Vaudreuil had instructed Péan to do, Montcalm obtained Vaudreuil's consent, at the beginning of November, to send Bougainville and Doreil to the court to make clear his view of the situation.

In his dispatches Vaudreuil, in an attempt to impress on the minister of Marine the urgency of the situation, made it appear bleak. Bougainville went much farther; he described it as utterly hopeless. In two memoirs, and doubtless several interviews, he reiterated Montcalm's expressed opinion that Canada could not be defended against the forces the British were prepared to throw against it. None of the fortified places was defensible, least of all Quebec, therefore it would be futile to send reinforcements to Canada. In any event the Royal Navy would surely intercept them. He failed to mention that supply convoys had eluded the British and reached Quebec every year of the war. Following Montcalm's dictates he recommended that the outer defences of the colony be abandoned, the available forces concentrated in the inner colony, and the inevitable defeat delayed as long as possible. He also asked that instructions be sent on the capitulation terms the French should request, and orders given empowering Montcalm, 24 hours before the capitulation took effect, to muster what remained of the regular troops and embark in a fleet of canoes for Louisiana. This move, it was claimed, would prevent the loss of a sizeable body of men and preserve the honour of French arms by a feat rivalling the retreat of the Ten Thousand that had immortalized the Greeks. A second proposal, even more bizarre, was that Canada could be saved were France to send an expeditionary force to invade North Carolina. The British would be taken by surprise, their forces being concentrated in the north; the southern colonies abounded in supplies; the large slave population could be made use of in one way or another; and if the invading army were unable to maintain itself in the Carolinas it could retire to Louisiana.

Given these wild proposals and the fact that they were postulated on one premise, defeat, the wonder is that the council of ministers took seriously anything recommended by Montcalm and Bougainville. Yet their views carried more weight than did those of Vaudreuil. The government, pinning its hopes on the plan for an invasion of England, decided that neither ships nor men could be spared for Canada, or for a diversionary assault on the Carolinas. Montcalm's request for his recall was given serious consideration, then denied. Instead, on 20 Oct. 1758, he was promoted lieutenant-general, the second highest rank in the French army, and his salary was increased to 48,000 *livres*. Since a lieutenant-general ranked much higher than a colonial governor general, Montcalm was given command of all the military forces in Canada and Vaudreuil was instructed to defer to him in all things, even routine administrative matters. They were both instructed that little in the way of reinforcements could be spared, therefore they were to remain strictly on the defensive and strive to retain a foothold in Canada; then the territory given up to the enemy could be recovered at the peace table. In short, the strategy recommended by Montcalm had to be adopted. The ministers of Marine and of War both expressed confidence that the general, who with only 4,000 men had won such a resounding victory over greatly superior forces at Carillon, would find a way to frustrate the enemy's coming offensive, and that Montcalm and Vaudreuil would establish a close union to achieve this end.

Early in May 1759 over 20 supply ships reached Quebec. On one of them was Bougainville, accompanied by 331 recruits and a handful of officers. Close behind them was the Royal Navy escorting Major-General James WOLFE at the head of 8,500 troops, the bulk of them well trained British regulars. This fleet was able to sail up to Quebec and put the troops ashore on the Île d'Orléans without hindrance. Montcalm, accompanied by an engineer and a naval officer, Nicolas Sarrebource* de Pontleroy and Gabriel Pellegrin*, had, the year before, surveyed the river from Quebec to Cap Tourmente and had subsequently suggested to Vaudreuil where batteries might be sited. As early as 1753 an engineer officer, Dubois, had made the same survey and declared that a battery on Cap Corbeau, opposite

Île aux Coudres, would wreak havoc on any fleet coming up the narrow channel, where it could not manœuvre or bring its guns to bear; but nothing had been done. For this Vaudreuil has to be held responsible. As late as March 1759, however, Montcalm had declared that there was little cause to fear for Quebec, because the difficulties of river navigation would render it virtually impossible for the British to bring a fleet up the river. The real threat, he believed, would be on the Lake Champlain front. Vaudreuil agreed with him, being sure that the British could not bring ships of the line to Quebec without Canadian pilots. It did not cross his mind that the British would make use of captured pilots. In any event, when word was received that the British fleet was approaching, frantic efforts began, under Montcalm's directions, to fortify the shoreline from the Rivière Saint-Charles to the Montmorency. All told, Montcalm had some 15,000 to 16,000 men under his command, and the advantage of a fortified position that the enemy would have to assail. Moreover, time was on his side. The British had to defeat his army and take Quebec before the end of the summer. Montcalm had only to hold them off for not more than three months, then they would be forced to sail away or be destroyed by the onset of the winter. He did not have to defeat them in a set battle, merely make sure that they did not defeat him. The British, however, did have one advantage – command of the river. This advantage was greatly enhanced by Montcalm's decision to establish his main supply base at Batiscan, some 50 miles above Quebec, while he massed his army at Beauport, on the other side of the city.

Another grave mistake was the failure to fortify Pointe-Lévy across from Quebec. At the behest of Admiral Charles Saunders* the British landed 3,000 men and quickly dug in. The Canadians, fearing that the British would establish batteries to bombard the city, were greatly perturbed but Montcalm and his officers were of the opinion that the range was too great for much damage to be done. Not until 11 July did Montcalm consent to an attack on the British position. By then they were well entrenched [see Robert Monckton*]. Instead of using his regulars Montcalm authorized a night attack by 1,400 volunteers led by Jean-Daniel Dumas* – including a detachment of schoolboys who had never been in action before – and only 100 regulars. Against more than double their number of British regulars in a fortified position the attempt had no hope of success. It was a fiasco and Montcalm voiced his disdain for military operations conducted by amateurs. The next day the bombardment of

Quebec began. It was to continue for two months and reduce the city to rubble.

Fortunately for the French, Wolfe was a poor tactician. Instead of making use of the fleet's mobility to attack above Quebec where the French were most vulnerable, he was determined to smash through Montcalm's lines below the city, then attack across the Rivière Saint-Charles which could be forded at low tide. On 9 July he landed a brigade at Montmorency which Montcalm declined to oppose, fearing to commit his forces lest it prove to be a feint; then Wolfe quickly brought in reinforcements and made the position impregnable. Wolfe also sent diversionary forces up river to make surprise landings and threaten Montcalm's supply line. This move forced Montcalm to establish mobile detachments to follow the ships' movements and counter the raids.

On 31 July Wolfe launched an assault on the Montmorency-Beauport lines. It was beaten back with heavy losses. This result convinced Vaudreuil that Wolfe would not attack there again. He was gravely concerned lest Wolfe should attack above the city and wanted that flank strengthened but Montcalm refused to believe that the danger there was real. He was convinced that Wolfe would continue to hammer at the Beauport lines.

Montcalm did not know it, but Wolfe too had begun to despair and his health had deteriorated seriously. Frustrated at every turn, he gave orders to lay the Canadian settlements waste. He was determined that if he could not take Quebec, he would destroy as much of the colony as possible. All through August into September this destruction persisted until some of the British officers were sickened by it [see George Scott]. As the days slipped by and the nights became cooler the navy became anxious. Admiral Saunders declared that the fleet would have to sail by 20 September at the latest.

Before admitting defeat and departing, Wolfe had to launch a final assault, although he had little confidence of success. He wanted to attack the Beauport lines again but when he proposed this plan to his brigadiers they rejected it. They submitted proposals for an attack above Quebec, to cut Montcalm's supply route and his communications with Montreal. This action, they claimed, would force him to come out of his lines and give battle. Wolfe gave way and made preparations to shift his army up river. Vaudreuil, seeing the British abandon their base at Montmorency and the army transported upstream, became more concerned than ever about that flank and wanted the forces above Quebec strengthened. His urging

Montcalm

alone was enough to cause Montcalm to regard such a move as ill advised and to persist in holding his main force below Quebec. He insisted that Bougainville, based at Cap Rouge, with 3,000 élite troops and Canadian volunteers, had an adequate force to repel any attempt to land astride the Montreal road, or at least to hold the enemy until the main force could come up from Beauport.

At the last minute Wolfe made a vital change in the brigadiers' plan. Instead of landing well above Quebec to cut the Montreal road he chose to land within two miles of the city walls, thus placing his army between Quebec and Bougainville's force. By this time the French were congratulating themselves that the campaign was virtually over; that the British would shortly be forced to sail ignominiously away.

Then, in the early hours of 13 September, a series of errors on the part of the French, and incredible luck for the British, allowed Wolfe's men to effect a landing at Anse au Foulon. Within hours, to the great surprise of even Wolfe, the British had some 4,500 men on the Plains of Abraham, less than a mile from the city. At daybreak Montcalm was informed but he refused to believe it. Only a small force was sent to bolster the outposts on the cliff. A few hours later he decided to see for himself. When he reached the heights beyond the city walls and saw the British army drawn up he was staggered and immediately ordered the army to come up at the double. There was, however, no need for Montcalm to oblige Wolfe by giving battle immediately; in fact, no need for him to give battle at all. As the Maréchal de Saxe had observed, more was to be gained by manœuvre than by giving battle. All that Montcalm had to do was avoid a major engagement for a few days, then Wolfe would have been forced to attempt to withdraw his army down the steep cliff to the narrow beach to be taken off by ships' boats. Given the forces at Montcalm's disposal, withdrawal could have been made a costly operation. In fact, Wolfe had placed his army in terrible jeopardy.

With the enemy virtually at his mercy, Montcalm chose the one course of action that ensured his defeat. He decided to attack at once with the troops he had at hand, not wait for Bougainville to come up with his force. He failed even to notify Bougainville that the enemy had landed, relying on the outposts to do that. It was, in fact, Vaudreuil who sent word to Bougainville. While the Canadian militia and Indians were galling the British lines from cover, Montcalm mustered his troops in three units, some 4,500 in all, approximately the same number as the British and less

than half the force he could have put in the field. Wolfe's regulars were well disciplined and trained. Montcalm's were not. He had recently incorporated a large number of untrained militia into their ranks. Some of the regulars, come from the Beauport lines at the double, hardly had time to catch their breath before Montcalm gave the order to abandon the high ground and advance down the thicket-strewn slope towards the foe. The result was predictable. The French formations quickly became disorganized. At extreme musket range they halted to fire ragged volleys, then many of the men dropped to the ground to reload. The British held their fire until the range closed, replied with rapid platoon fire, advanced through the smoke, then gave crashing volleys by battalion all down the line. Great gaps were torn in the French ranks, the survivors turned and ran, the British in hot pursuit. The French were saved from complete destruction only by the deadly fire of the Canadian militia from the flanks. It was they who forced the British to halt and regroup. The French regulars, in a disordered mass, poured through the city streets, Montcalm, on horseback, bringing up the rear. Just as he was about to enter the Saint-Louis gate he received a mortal wound. Wolfe, wounded earlier, was already dead. For both generals in an 18th-century battle to be killed is indication enough that the tactics employed left something to be desired. After the battle was over Bougainville arrived with his force, then quickly withdrew to Cap Rouge.

At Beauport Vaudreuil sought to reorganize the demoralized army. He sent a courier to Montcalm, who was being given medical aid in the city, requesting his advice on what should be done. The reply was that Vaudreuil had a choice of three courses of action: give battle again, retreat to Jacques Cartier, or capitulate for the entire colony. He left it to Vaudreuil to decide. But, without informing the governor general, he wrote to Brigadier-General George Townshend*, who had succeeded Wolfe, surrendering the city to him. This missive, if received, was without immediate effect. Vaudreuil meanwhile held a council of war attended by Bigot and the principal officers of the French regulars. Both he and Bigot urged that another attack be made, since they could still put twice as many men in the field as the British and still held the city, but the French officers had no stomach for it. They demanded that the army retire to Jacques Cartier, join forces with Bougainville, and regroup. In the face of this opposition Vaudreuil gave way and ordered the retreat to begin that night. At 6:00 P.M. he wrote to Montcalm informing him of the decision and also that he had provided the officer commanding in Quebec, Jean-Baptiste-Nicolas-Roch de Ramezay*, with a copy of the terms of the capitulation that were to be asked of the British. These terms had been drawn up by Montcalm weeks earlier and concurred in by Vaudreuil. The tone of Vaudreuil's letter was calm and gentle. He expressed his deep concern at Montcalm's condition, his hope that he would quickly recover, and urged him to care for himself, to think only of his restoration to health. Montcalm's aide-de-camp, Marcel, sent word back that Montcalm approved of Vaudreuil's decisions, that he had read the terms of capitulation, and that they had been handed over to Ramezay. In a postscript Marcel added that Montcalm's condition had not improved as of ten o'clock but that his pulse was a little better. Later that night he received the last sacraments, then he instructed his aide-de-camp to write to his family conveying his last farewell. His papers he ordered turned over to Lévis. At five in the morning, as dawn was breaking over the shattered city, his defeated army in full retreat, Montcalm expired. He was buried in a shell crater under the floor of the Ursulines' chapel.

The Chevalier de Lévis came post-haste from Montreal when he received word of the defeat, assumed command, and set about restoring order. He was livid with fury. In his dispatch to the minister of War he declared: "One must admit that we have been very unfortunate; just when we could hope to see the campaign end with glory, everything turned against us. A battle lost, a retreat as precipitous as it was shameful, has reduced us to our present condition, all caused by attacking the enemy too soon without mustering all the forces at his [Montcalm's] disposal. I owe it to his memory to vouch for the honesty of his intentions, . . . he believed he was acting for the best, but unfortunately, the general who is defeated is always wrong." And Bourlamaque, at Lake Champlain, cynically remarked that the only satisfaction to be derived from the disaster was to have had no part in it.

Despite the valiant efforts of Lévis and the reorganized forces he now commanded, Vaudreuil, over the protests of Lévis, was obliged to capitulate the following September to General Jeffery Amherst* at Montreal. The French officers, including Lévis, sought desperately to ensure that Montcalm's defeat and its consequences would not rub off on them. This attempt placed them in a dilemma; to blame Montcalm meant that the army had to accept responsibility for the loss of Canada, and they feared that they would have to share in that blame. Nevertheless, several of them admitted that Montcalm's precipitate action on the day of the battle had been fatal.

When Louis XV and his ministers received word of the capitulation they were far more disturbed over the fact that the army had surrendered without being accorded the honours of war than they were over the loss of the colony. They showed no concern whatsoever for the plight of the Canadians. Someone had to be held responsible for the disaster, and it could not be Montcalm. He was not there to defend himself and he had to be exonerated to spare the reputation of the army. It clearly could not be Lévis, who had protested the terms of the capitulation. The obvious choice was Vaudreuil. For the preceding four years Montcalm and his entourage had predicted the outcome, defeat, and held that the corrupt colonial administration would be to blame – it was now even held accountable for the outcome of the battle of 13 September. Montcalm's predictions, and the body of evidence amassed against Bigot, made Vaudreuil an easy mark. The loss of Canada was therefore blamed, not on Montcalm's poor generalship, not on the superiority of a small army of British regulars over the French battalions in one brief battle that should not have been fought, but on Vaudreuil and the colonial officials. In the letter of condemnation written to Vaudreuil by Berryer, minister of Marine, on orders of the king, Montcalm's name was not mentioned.

Given these circumstances, it is not surprising that when the Marquise de Montcalm requested compensation for her grievous loss, the government was sympathetic. One thing the Marquise specifically requested was that, in consideration of her husband's services and the short time he had enjoyed the perquisites of his lieutenant-general's appointment, the crown would assume the debts he had been obliged to incur while serving in Canada. He had declared that by the end of 1758 they would amount to over 30,000 *livres*, and they must have increased during the ensuing eight months. The minister thereupon wrote to Vaudreuil and Bigot to discover the exact amount that Montcalm had overdrawn his pay and allowances. The reply may well have caused eyebrows to lift. Far from having incurred debts in Canada, as he had so vociferously claimed, Montcalm had amassed a small fortune. In January of each year he had drawn his pay for the ensuing 12 months. The sale of his personal effects, household furnishings, wine cellar, and provisions, had realized enough to reimburse the treasury the amount he had drawn as major-general on 1 Jan. 1759. His estate was thus owed, by the ministry

Montcalm

of Marine, his pay as lieutenant-general from 1 Jan. until his death. It amounted to 38,269 *livres* 8 *sols* 10 2/3 *deniers*. Also, among his papers had been found 34,717 *livres* in treasury notes (*billets de caisse*) and seven to eight thousand *livres* in letters of exchange dated 1757 and 1758. In addition Bigot had provided him every year with several other letters of exchange to enable him to transfer funds to France. He had thus put aside, over a three year period, after paying all his living expenses, an amount in excess of 80,000 *livres*. How he had contrived to do it is a mystery.

Historians have long been at odds in their assessment of Montcalm. Some have depicted him as does the plaque on the Plains of Abraham:

Montcalm
Quatre fois victorieux
Une fois vaincu
Toujours au grand honneur de la France
Blessé à mort ici le 13 septembre 1759

The gallant, good, and great Montcalm
Four times deservingly victorious
and
at last defeated through no fault of his own

Others can find little good to say of him and hold him mainly responsible for the conquest of Canada. The former assessment requires that virtually everything he wrote be accepted at face value. A critical assessment of the evidence makes plain that to do so would be a mistake – the matter of his debts is sufficient indication of that. He was a brave officer, of this there can be no doubt, but serious defects in his character made him unfit to command an army. His intrigues to undermine the authority of his superior, the governor general, his open and at times slanderous criticism of Vaudreuil and the Canadians, his refusal to admit that tactics other than those employed in Europe had any merit, his chronic defeatism, all caused trouble and undermined the morale of the forces. Yet he had won some notable victories. But in his final campaign, when he was presented with an opportunity to destroy Wolfe's army, or at least avoid his own defeat, he threw it away and suffered one of the most disastrous defeats in history.

It was not, however, Montcalm alone who was responsible for that defeat and the ensuing loss of the French colonial empire in North America. He was merely a product of a military system that was long overdue for the reforms soon to come. As a contemporary military expert, Jacques-Antoine-Hippolyte de Guibert, remarked of the French army in the Seven Years' War: "The machine is so worn out that even a man of genius could only touch it with trepidation. His genius would not suffice to guarantee success." Montcalm was a product of that system. Indeed, he personified it.

W. J. ECCLES

[The manuscript source material touching on the career of Montcalm is quite extensive, but the great bulk of it dates from his appointment as commander of the French battalions in Canada. Prior to that he was only one of some 900 colonels in the French army, and the ministry of War, a rather slipshod organization at this time, obliged to work in temporary quarters in rented houses, dealt only with officers of general rank who, by the end of 1757, numbered 753. Some of Montcalm's early correspondence with his family is cited in Emmanuel Grellet de La Deyte, *Une sœur de Montcalm, la présidente de Lunas* (Nevers, France, 1900), but his importance as a historical figure dates from his Canadian appointment. Details on his family origins are to be found in Pinard, *Chronologie historique-militaire* ... (8v., Paris, 1760–78), V, and in La Chesnaye-Desbois et Badier, *Dictionnaire de la noblesse* (2ᵉ éd.), X. Most of the pertinent documents dealing with his later career are to be found in SHA, A¹, and AN, Col., B, C¹¹ᴬ, D²ᶜ, F³. There is also some important manuscript material in the ASQ, and the valuable collection of Lévis papers, which include Montcalm's journal and his letters to the Chevalier de Lévis, is in the PAC, MG 18, K7 and K8.

A goodly proportion of this primary source material has been published, including the *Collection des manuscrits du maréchal de Lévis* (Casgrain). The Abbé Casgrain* also edited a selection of documents from the AN, Col., C¹¹ᴬ, 100: *Extraits des archives de la Marine et de la Guerre*. Many pertinent documents have been published over the years in the APQ (AQ; ANQ) annual *Rapport*; the *Table des matières des rapports des archives du Québec, tomes 1 à 42 (1920–1964)* (Québec, 1965) should be consulted under the headings Guerre, Journaux, Mémoires, Capitulations, Siège de Québec. A select list of English manuscript and published sources will be found under the biography of James WOLFE.

Most of the secondary sources dealing with the Seven Years' War in general, and Montcalm in particular, leave much to be desired. Exceptions are the sound, concise, and valuable study by Lee Kennett, *The French armies in the Seven Years' War: a study in military organization and administration* (Durham, N.C., 1967), and the serious study by André Corvisier, *L'armée française de la fin du XVIIᵉ siècle au ministère de Choiseul: le soldat* (Faculté des Lettres et des Sciences humaines de Paris, Série Recherches, XIV–XV, 2v., Paris, 1964). On the European background R. P. Waddington, *La guerre de Sept Ans; histoire diplomatique et militaire* (5v., Paris, [1899–1907]), and *Histoire de France, depuis les origines jusqu'à la révolution*, Ernest Lavisse, édit. (9v., Paris, 1903–11), VIII, pt.2: Henri Carré, *Le règne de Louis XV (1715–1774)*, are dated but still useful. W. L. Dorn, *Competition for* empire, 1740–1763 (New York, 1940), is excellent on the European aspects, poor on events in North America – reflecting the paucity of good monographs at the time of writing.

Of works dealing more specifically with the war in North America, Francis Parkman, *Montcalm and Wolfe* (Boston, 1884), is vitiated by the author's partisan view of events and his cavalier treatment of evidence. Unfortunately, too many subsequent Anglo-Canadian, British, and American historians have slavishly accepted his interpretations and value judgements. A case in point is Gipson, *The British empire before the American revolution*, IV–VIII. G. M. Wrong, *The fall of Canada: a chapter in the history of the Seven Years' War* (Oxford, 1914) has little value. H. H. Peckham, *The colonial wars, 1689–1762* (Chicago, 1964), is riddled with errors. Frégault, *La guerre de la conquête*, trans. by M. M. Cameron as *Canada: the war of the conquest* (Toronto, 1969), views the conflict with exemplary detachment but is highly critical of Montcalm. Stanley, *New France*, is also detached but the work is based on secondary sources and tends to be superficial. Of the spate of books commissioned by publishers prior to 1959 for the bicentenary of the crucial battle of Quebec, Stacey, *Quebec, 1759* is the best.

The biography of Montcalm by Thomas Chapais, *Le marquis de Montcalm (1712–1759)* (Québec, 1911), is dated, overwritten, and biased, striving to extol, or justify, Montcalm in all things. Conversely H.-R. Casgrain, *Guerre du Canada, 1756–1760; Montcalm et Lévis* (2v., Québec, 1891; Tours, France, 1899) is hostile to Montcalm and seeks to extol Vaudreuil and Lévis. Neither work has much merit. W.J.E.]

MONTCHERVAUX. *See* TISSERANT

MONTEGRON, JEAN-BAPTISTE LEVRAULT DE LANGIS. *See* LEVRAULT

MONTIGNY, FRANÇOIS DE (sometimes called **François Jolliet de Montigny,** though incorrectly), parish priest, vicar general, missionary, director of the Séminaire des Missions Étrangères, procurator of the seminary of Quebec in Paris, France; b. 1669 in Paris; d. there 19 Dec. 1742.

François de Montigny came to Canada at the invitation of Bishop Saint-Vallier [La Croix*]. Montigny had entered the Sulpician seminary in Paris on 15 July 1687, and although not a Sulpician himself he was apparently still living there in 1692 when the bishop of Quebec asked him to join him. The young abbé, who had simply received the tonsure, landed at Quebec on 15 August. He received the subdiaconate on 19 December, the diaconate on 1 Feb. 1693, and the priesthood on 8 March. In October of that year Abbé Montigny was appointed parish priest of L'Ange-Gardien, where he served for a year. In 1694 Bishop Saint-Vallier, about to sail for

France, recalled him to Quebec to entrust the administration of the diocese to him in conjunction with François Dollier* de Casson, vicar general at Montreal. On his return in 1697, the bishop, satisfied with his protégé's conduct, bestowed upon him letters in due form, appointing him vicar general for the whole colony.

The year 1698 was to bring a radical change in François de Montigny's career. The directors of the seminary of Quebec had asked for permission to set up missions among the tribes living on the banks of the Mississippi, and Bishop Saint-Vallier deferred to their wishes, granting them letters patent to this effect on 30 April. But the prelate wanted as head of the undertaking and superior of the future establishments none other than his vicar general. The latter received his appointment on 12 May and immediately started making elaborate preparations for the hazardous journey.

On 12 July François de Montigny and the two priests whom the seminary of Quebec had chosen, Jean-François Buisson* de Saint-Cosme (1667–1706) and Albert Davion*, left Quebec for Montreal. The group set out from Lachine on 24 July; besides the three missionaries it included 12 men, voyageurs and servants, divided among four birch-bark canoes. The travellers followed the traditional route up the Ottawa and reached Michilimackinac on 8 September. There they had the good luck to meet René-Robert Cavelier* de La Salle's former lieutenant, Henri Tonty*, who agreed to take them as far as the Arkansas River. Under this intrepid explorer's guidance Abbé Montigny and his group went up the west shore of Lake Michigan as far as the portage at Chicago (Ill.), then descended the Des Plaines and Illinois rivers and finally the Mississippi. The expedition reached the Arkansas Indian country without mishap on 27 Dec. 1698. After pushing farther south and leaving Davion among the Tunica Indians at the beginning of 1699, Abbé Montigny returned to the portage at Chicago to get provisions he had left there. He took advantage of the trip to lay the foundations for the mission to the Tamaroas, where Abbé Buisson de Saint-Cosme settled in April.

Having found out, probably at Fort Saint-Louis-des-Illinois (near present-day La Salle, Ill.), that Pierre Le Moyne* d'Iberville was at the mouth of the Mississippi, the indefatigable Montigny decided to go to ask the famous sailor about the court's plans concerning the founding of a colony in the region. The missionary and his escort, along with Davion whom they had picked up on the way, reached Fort Maurepas (Ocean Springs, Miss.) on Biloxi Bay on 2 July 1699.

Montour

When he was again on the banks of the Mississippi after his exhausting trip, François de Montigny settled among the Taensas and their neighbours the Natchez. But his stay did not last a year: the immeasurable distances to cover, the cruelty of the Indians, and their incessant roaming deprived him after a few months of all hope of accomplishing any fruitful work. On 28 May 1700 he sailed on Iberville's ship, never to return.

François de Montigny had nevertheless not given up the missionary apostolate. At his proposal the superiors of the Missions Étrangères agreed to send him to China. He set off in February 1701. Montigny spent six years in China and left the country only after an order for his expulsion had been issued by the emperor K'ang-Hsi.

Abbé Montigny returned to the seminary in Paris at the end of 1709 or the beginning of the following year; on 10 July 1711 he was elected director, and in 1712 he became assistant to Henri-Jean TREMBLAY. In 1714 he was appointed procurator general of the Société des Missions Étrangères in Rome. He held this office until 1726, when he was replaced by Pierre-Herman Dosquet*, the future bishop of Quebec. In 1728 Montigny succeeded the procurator of the seminary of Quebec in Paris, Henri-Jean Tremblay, who had become almost blind. From then on he was "the support of all Canada," but particularly of the seminary of Quebec, whose interests he served, with as much intelligence as devotion, until his death on 19 Dec. 1742 at the seminary of Paris. The memorialist of the Société des Missions Étrangères recorded his last words: "I die as I always thought it fitted a priest to die: without debts and without possessions."

NOËL BAILLARGEON

AAQ, 12 A, Registres d'insinuations A. ANQ-M, Greffe d'Antoine Adhémar, 30 mai, 22 juill. 1698. ASQ, Lettres, M, 22, 23, 41, 44, 52, 68, 95; Lettres, N, 115; Lettres, O, 12, 27, 31, 34, 50; Lettres, R, 26–30, 143; Missions, 41, 61, 82, 107; Polygraphie, IX, 3, 4, 10, 17, 24; Séminaire, VIII, 15. "Les missions du séminaire de Québec dans la vallée du Mississipi, 1698–1699," Noël Baillargeon, édit., AQ Rapport, 1965, 13–70; [Louis Tronson], Correspondance de M. Louis Tronson, troisième supérieur de la Compagnie de Saint-Sulpice: lettres choisies [16 juillet 1676–15 janvier 1700], A.-L. Bertrand, édit. (3v., Paris, 1904), II, 354, 377. Adrien Launay, Mémorial de la Société des Missions étrangères (2v., Paris, 1912–16), II, 457. Noël Baillargeon, "The seminary of Quebec: resources for the history of the French in the Mississippi valley," in The French in the Mississippi valley, ed. J. F. McDermott (Urbana, Ill., 1965), 197–207. Amédée Gosselin, "M. de Montigny," BRH, XXXI (1925), 171–76.

MONTOUR, Mme. See COUC, ELIZABETH

MONTPLAISIR, PIERRE DIZY (Disy) DE. See DIZY

MOODY (Moodey), SAMUEL, minister of the Congregational Church; b. at Newbury, Massachusetts, 4 Jan. 1675/76 (o.s.), son of Caleb Moody and Judith Bradbury; d. 13 Nov. 1747 at York (Maine).

Samuel Moody was a grandson of William Moody who migrated to New England from Wales in 1633. His father Caleb represented Newbury in the General Court of the colony (1677–78) and was imprisoned for five weeks under the tyrannical regime of Edmund Andros for daring to speak and act as a freeman. Samuel Moody's first wife, Hannah Sewall (m. 15 July 1698), was a niece of Chief Justice Samuel Sewall and a relation of the wife of William PEPPERRELL.

Moody attended Harvard College, where he experienced conversion from reading Joseph Alleine's An alarm to unconverted sinners. He graduated in 1697 and the following year accepted the chaplaincy of York in northeastern Massachusetts (now Maine). Only a man inured to the prospect of hardship and possessed of exceptional courage would have agreed to go to a place where the previous minister and a number of inhabitants had lately been murdered by Indians. Moody declined a regular salary, believing that the Lord would provide. Once he gave away his wife's shoes to a poor woman, but a neighbour gave her a new pair before the day was out. Anxious to divest himself of the love of created things, he gave away his most prized possession, his horse, saying, "He goes right up with me into the pulpit, and I cannot have him there . . . ." Although he never failed in the performance of compassionate acts on behalf of the unfortunate, he nevertheless was a man of violent temper, as he showed when he visited the alehouses, driving home the tosspots whom he found idling there. Many of the tales told of him throughout New England and his strange utterances found their way into Agamenticus, a work of fiction.

Ministering to a people who knew the horrors of the petite guerre waged by the French and their Indian allies, Moody volunteered as a chaplain to John March*'s ill-fated expedition to Port-Royal (Annapolis Royal, N.S.) in 1707. In 1712 York was attacked by Indians and some of Parson Moody's parishioners were killed. The following year, however, he signed a treaty with the Abenakis, which gave some temporary respite [see Mog*]. The year before he died, the members of his congregation still found it necessary to go to church under arms.

Moody was a powerful preacher and took part in the religious revivals of his time, including the Great Awakening, which helped to give the expedition to Louisbourg, Île Royale (Cape Breton Island), in 1745 something of the character of a crusade. The fishery in which Maine settlers were so much engaged was threatened by the destruction of their station at Canso, Nova Scotia, and the attack on Annapolis Royal in 1744 by detachments from Louisbourg [see Joseph Du Pont Duvivier]. Thus a third of the Massachusetts contingent sent to reduce that fortress in 1745 was drawn from Maine, the whole force being placed under the command of Moody's neighbour, William Pepperrell.

Moody joined the expedition as senior chaplain, and when he boarded the transport at Boston he seized an axe and exclaimed, "The Sword of the Lord and of Gideon," predicting that Louisbourg would be taken and that he would cut down the objects of papal worship. "O that I could be with you and dear Mr. Moodey in that single church," wrote Deacon John Gray to Pepperrell, "to destroy ye images their sett up, and hear ye true Gospel of our Lord and Saviour Jesus Christ their preached." It is said that following the siege Moody did attack the altar and images in the French church with his axe. He subsequently gave the first Protestant sermon preached within the precincts of Louisbourg. Though he had always been a long-winded and extemporaneous speaker, at the banquet tendered by Pepperrell to the British naval forces he astonished all present by the brevity of his thanksgiving.

Moody was over 70 at the time of the capture of Louisbourg, the oldest man in the army. He died two years later at York in the arms of his son, the Reverend Joseph Moody. His first wife, Hannah, had died in 1728; he married Ruth Newman, née Plummer, in 1732 or 1733. The other surviving child by Moody's first marriage, Mary, was the great-grandmother of Ralph Waldo Emerson.

ALFRED G. BAILEY

University of New Brunswick Library, Archives and Special Collections Dept., Bailey family papers, Genealogical notes on the family of Loring Woart Bailey. *Documentary history of Maine*, IX. "The Pepperrell papers," Mass. Hist. Soc. *Coll.*, 6th ser., X (1899), 106. *New Eng. Hist. and Geneal. Register*, CXIV (1960), 125. [Samuel Sewall], "Diary of Samuel Sewall," Mass. Hist. Soc. *Coll.*, 5th ser., V–VII (1878–82). Shipton, *Sibley's Harvard graduates*, IV, 356–65. Ralph Emerson, *Life of Reverend Joseph Emerson* . . . (Boston, 1834), 444. C. C. P. Moody, *Bio-* graphical sketches of the Moody family . . . from 1633 to 1842 (Boston, 1847), 54–94. Parkman, *Half-century of conflict* (1893), II, 96–98, 109, 153. E. P. Tenney, *Agamenticus* (Boston, 1878). W. D. Williamson, "Sketches of the lives of early Maine ministers," Maine Hist. Soc. *Coll.*, 2nd ser., IV (1893), 199–205.

MOOR, WILLIAM, HBC sailor, explorer; m. 1757 to Mary Bradley at Greatham, Co. Durham, England; d. there 1765.

William Moor was a County Durham man who served on Hudson's Bay Company ships on their annual voyages to the bay from about 1730 to 1741. Under the guidance of his cousin, Christopher MIDDLETON, he advanced from ship's boy to first mate on vessels in Middleton's command. With his cousin he left the company's employ in 1741, and he was given the command of the 150-ton converted collier, *Discovery*, which the admiralty had purchased to accompany Middleton in the *Furnace* on an expedition to search for the northwest passage. On the voyage Moor played a secondary role, and his terse and uninformative journal adds little to the fuller record kept by Middleton. The poor quality of the crew recruited in London, and sickness during the expedition's wintering at Prince of Wales Fort (Churchill, Man.) [see THOMPSON], hampered Moor in his efforts to assist Middleton in the survey of the shoreline and tides of the west side of Hudson Bay. As he lamented in his journal in early July 1742, "we cannot spare time to Sound . . . What with Making and Short^{ng} Sail for the Furnace, and then being so badly Mann'd." The *Discovery* usually kept close company with the *Furnace*, and as the ships left for home in mid-August 1742 Moor firmly observed in his journal, "There is no Passage into the other Ocean between Churchill and the Latit^d 67°N."

Moor was not at first involved in the attack on Middleton launched by Arthur Dobbs and some of the *Furnace*'s crew after their return to England. In correspondence with Middleton in May and June 1743 he denied that there was a passage through the Wager, a large inlet discovered by the expedition the previous July, and was sceptical about the "Cock-and-Bull Story" to that effect being put about by Middleton's accusers. But by 1745 Moor was publicly repeating the arguments of Dobbs on this issue, and the reason for his belated change of allegiance is not hard to find. In March 1744 Dobbs had written that Moor was to be given command of the proposed private discovery expedition to Hudson Bay as he was "very sober and carefull and will also be an Adventurer [subscriber] himself." This expedition, financed by £100 shares, sailed in May 1746 to discover the northwest passage, claim the £20,000 reward offered by an act of parliament the previous year, and pave the way for a dramatic expansion of British trade in North America and the Pacific. Moor commanded the *Dobbs Galley*; another former HBC seaman, Francis SMITH, the smaller *California*.

The expedition spent a month struggling through the ice of Hudson Strait, and explored for only a few days before deciding to winter at the HBC post at York Factory (Man.). The winter was notable for acerbic disputes between Moor and Smith, carefully recorded by the factor James ISHAM, and for outbreaks of scurvy which killed seven of the crew and weakened many others. The panic that accompanied a fire on the *Dobbs Galley* on the outward voyage, the quarrels at York between the officers of the two ships, and the hard drinking which contributed to the attacks of scurvy, say little for Moor's competence as a commander; and the explorations of the 1747 summer season confirm the impression that weakness and uncertainty afflicted the whole expedition. The two ships usually explored independently, with little apparent attempt by Moor to coordinate the surveys made. Most of the close coastal work was carried out by the *Resolution*, the longboat of the *Dobbs Galley* which had been converted into a small schooner, and by the *California*'s longboat. Separately or in company with each other they explored most of the west coast of the bay between latitudes 61°N and 65°N, discovered Chesterfield Inlet but did not follow it to its end, and pushed up the Wager until 150 miles from the entrance "we had the Mortification to see clearly, that our hitherto imagined Strait ended in two small unnavigable Rivers. . . ." Amid confusion and dissension, with Moor facing a threat of mutiny, and one-third of his crew too ill to come on deck, the decision was taken to sail for home.

On the expedition's return to England the organizing North West Committee expressed its dissatisfaction with Moor's conduct, including his creditable reluctance to engage in illegal trade while at York. This frosty reception may explain the fact that Moor's evidence before the parliamentary committee of 1749 inquiring into the trade of Hudson Bay did little to help Dobbs' cause. In particular, he asserted that if a northwest passage existed it was farther north than he had once thought, and was perhaps unnavigable. There are no further references to Moor in HBC records or Dobbs' papers. He appears to have retired at about this time to Greatham, where he married a local woman and where he died in 1765.

GLYNDWR WILLIAMS

[There are references to Moor's service with the company in HBC Arch., particularly in A.1/34. His log of the *Discovery* on the 1741–42 voyage is in PRO, Adm. 51/290, pt.ix. References to his role on the voyage and to his career in general are scattered throughout the voluminous pamphlet literature produced during the Middleton–Dobbs controversy (and listed in Williams, *British search for the northwest passage*) and among the Dobbs correspondence in Castle Ward (Downpatrick, N.I.), Castle Ward papers, VI. No log kept by Moor has been found for the 1746–47 expedition, but Henry Ellis, Dobbs' agent on board the *Dobbs Galley*, published *A voyage to Hudson's-Bay by the Dobbs Galley and California, in the years 1746 and 1747, for discovering a north west passage* . . . (London, 1748). More critical references to Moor are to be found in the rival version by the "Clerk of the California" [Charles Swaine (T. S. Drage)], *An account of a voyage for the discovery of a north-west passage* . . . (2v., London, 1748–49), and in Isham's notes printed in HBRS, XII (Rich and Johnson). Moor's evidence before the 1749 parliamentary committee is in G.B., Parl., *Report from the committee on Hudson's Bay*, 228–29. Some details of his last years are in John Brewster, *The parochial history and antiquities of Stockton upon Tees* . . . (2nd ed., London, 1829). A short biographical sketch of Moor is given in HBRS, XII (Rich and Johnson), 334–36, and Moor's part in the discovery voyages is discussed in Williams, *British search for the northwest passage*. G.W.]

MORAMPONT, CHARLES-DENIS REGNARD DUPLESSIS DE. *See* REGNARD

MOREAU, EDME, shoemaker; b. in the parish of Saint-Césaire, diocese of Troyes, France, son of Jacques Moreau, shoemaker in Chaource (dept. of Aube), France, and Marguerite Germain; fl. 1706–47.

The first reference to Edme Moreau is in his marriage contract of 24 Aug. 1706 with Françoise, daughter of the Montreal baker, Étienne Fortier (Forestier). Two tanners and two shoemakers, including Jean Ridday, *dit* Beauceron, "his friend and fellow worker," were Moreau's witnesses to the contract.

In the first quarter of the 18th century, the shoemakers were the most active craft group in Montreal, and Edme Moreau typified this energy. Moreau is known to have trained a son and nine apprentices. He was one of the few craft masters known to have had an Indian apprentice, the Pawnee servant of a tanner. Another apprentice was a foster-child placed in Moreau's care by an ailing labourer overburdened with children.

About 1712–13 a friend taught Edme how to sign his name phonetically (he signed em moreau), and thus gave him a valuable skill for business transactions. Moreau possessed little property and he lived in various rented lodgings for most of his life. He spent a great deal of time in and out of court pursuing or being pursued for debts. He also did some speculating in town lots.

The vitality and solidarity of the Montreal shoemakers and cobblers were expressed in the 1720s by the formation of the Confrérie de Saint-Crépin et Saint-Crépinien, for which Moreau, Jean Ridday, and Jacques Viger acted as spokesmen. Each year, on the day of saints Simon and Jude (28 October), a high mass was celebrated in honour of the confraternity's patron saints. At the end of the mass, blessed bread contributed by one of the shoemakers was distributed. In Montreal, the organization went beyond a religious confraternity. The shoemakers banded together to defend their material interests. On 19 Aug. 1729 a group of 21 shoemakers led by Moreau and Ridday appeared in the Montreal royal court and requested that, in accordance with the intendant's ordinance of 20 July 1706, the tanner Joseph Guyon Després be ordered to close his shoemaking shop. Limited shoemaking by the employees of certain tanners was countenanced, but extension of the practice would be detrimental to the free marketing of leather and would create unfair competition for independent shoemakers.

The deputy to the king's attorney, Michel Lepailleur* de Laferté, referred the case to the intendant, Hocquart*. There is no evidence that the latter received or judged the appeal. The costs of carrying the case to Quebec may have discouraged the shoemakers. In any case the administration of New France was hostile to unauthorized assemblies and independent group initiatives from the lower orders of society.

There is an air of tragedy about Moreau's family life. Nine of his 13 children died in infancy. His oldest living son, François-Urbain Moreau, who was trained as his father's successor and who rose to the position of court usher, died at 28. Another son, Georges, was accused of robbing the church at Lévis in 1731. The last reference we have to Edme Moreau is his signature in 1747 on his granddaughter's marriage act.

PETER N. MOOGK

ANQ, NF, Coll. de pièces jud. et not., 893. ANQ-M, Greffe d'Antoine Adhémar, 21 sept. 1708, 23 févr., 10 oct. 1710; Greffe de J.-B. Adhémar, 14 sept. 1735; Greffe de Jacques David, 23 juill. 1724, 24 août 1726; Greffe de C.-R. Gaudron de Chevremont, 9 mars 1738; Greffe de N.-A. Guillet de Chaumont, 31 déc. 1728, 8 févr., 21 mars 1729; Greffe de Michel Lepailleur, 24 août 1706, 2 mars 1713, 15 nov. 1716, 8 sept. 1717, *passim*; Greffe de C.-J. Porlier, 19 févr., 18 mai 1735; Greffe de J.-C. Raimbault, 30 janv. 1729, 14 févr. 1730, 6 août 1733, 3 mai 1734, 4 sept., 4 déc. 1735, 1er juill. 1736, 22 juill. 1737; Greffe de François Simonnet, 22 mars 1743, 21 févr. 1744, 6 mai 1746; Documents divers, 17 août, 2 sept. 1729; Juridiction de Montréal, 9 avril 1710, 17 août, 2 sept. 1729 (feuillets séparés); Registre d'état civil, Notre-Dame de Montréal, 1747, ff.317, 456; Registres des audiences, VII, 501, 503f., 507v, 642, 772v–73.

Édits ord., II, 265. *L'île de Montréal en 1731* (A. Roy), 52, 132, 146. "Recensement de Montréal, 1741" (Massicotte). *Les origines de Montréal* (SHM Mémoires, XI, Montréal, 1917), 86, 97, 227, 238. P.-É. Renaud, *Les origines économiques du Canada; l'œuvre de la France* (Mamers, France, 1928), 390–91. É.-Z. Massicotte, "La communauté des cordonniers à Montréal," *BRH*, XXIV, (1918), 126–27.

MOREAU, JEAN-BAPTISTE, missionary of the Church of England; b. Dijon, France, probably between 1707 and 1711; d. at Lunenburg, Nova Scotia, 25 Feb. 1770.

According to William TUTTY, the Anglican missionary at Halifax, Nova Scotia, Jean-Baptiste Moreau was a French priest and prior of the abbey of Saint-Mathieu near Brest before he left the Catholic Church and emigrated to England. By 1749, when Moreau and his wife embarked for Nova Scotia with the settlers of Edward Cornwallis*, he had become an adherent of the Church of England. Moreau's motive for settling in Nova Scotia, says Tutty, was to pursue "honest undertakings in a mercantile way," and he was described in the list of settlers as a gentleman and schoolmaster. Soon after his arrival in Halifax, however, the Society for the Propagation of the Gospel adopted him as an Anglican missionary on Tutty's recommendation.

From 1749 to 1753 Moreau resided in Halifax and served chiefly as missionary to the French-speaking Protestants amongst the new settlers, most of whom had come from Montbéliard and were among the group known as the "foreign Protestants." Moreau visited New Jersey in the summer of 1752 with an eye to an alternative mission, but unlike so many settlers who left Nova Scotia for the American colonies in these years he returned to Halifax.

In June 1753 he accompanied a group of about 1,600 German- and French-speaking individuals to their new settlement at Lunenburg; about 30 per cent of the settlers spoke French. Moreau likely enjoyed more comfortable living conditions than most of the settlers; he at least had the advantage of his annual missionary stipend and a government allowance for his rent. He supervised the construction of St John's Church, which was being used in good weather by the mid-1750s. Because of a shortage of funds, however, the building remained in an incomplete state until

Morimé

the early 1760s. It was cold and leaky, and winter services often had to be cancelled. Moreau found such conditions a severe strain on his health. About 1761 he reported "mine eyes have grown weak and my constitution entirely broke by the great cold."

He does not seem to have been a particularly prominent or talented clergyman, though the fact that he persisted in the pioneering conditions of Lunenburg indicates his tenacity and probable success as a community leader. His claim to have reconciled the foreign settlers – mostly Lutherans – to the Church of England does not emerge as a significant achievement at a time when no services other than Anglican were available. His primary ambition was to proselytize amongst the Catholic and French-speaking Indians, and he frequently remarked on the "pains he [had] taken to bring over the Savages to embrace our holy Religion." But he received little encouragement in this task from the government, the SPG, or his own flock. His major drawback as a clergyman at Lunenburg was his inability to speak fluent German. Though he claimed to have ministered to his multilingual congregation principally in English and French, even his facility in the English language was apparently deficient. His English reports to the SPG were in the hand of another, and by the mid-1760s he had resumed his earlier habit of writing his own correspondence in French.

Moreau was the only clergyman of any persuasion in Lunenburg until 1761. His sole assistance during that period came from Georges-Frédéric Bailly, a Montbéliard settler who was the SPG schoolmaster in Lunenburg. In 1761 Moreau's burden appeared to be lightened when a second Anglican clergyman, Robert VINCENT, who spoke only English, was appointed missionary to the German inhabitants. A personal antagonism developed between the two men, however, and it was not until 1767, when Paulus Bryzelius, a German-speaking replacement for Vincent, arrived, that a fruitful partnership was established.

Little is known of the last years of Moreau's life. He was survived by at least two sons and one daughter.

JUDITH FINGARD

PAC, MG 9, B9, 10 (will of Moreau). PANS, MG 1, 109–11; RG 1, 163. USPG, B, 25, no.28; Journals of SPG, 11, pp.187–88; 12, pp.102, 357; 15, pp.335, 387–88; 16, pp.326–27. *An abstract of the charter, and of the proceedings of the Society for the Propagation of the Gospel in Foreign Parts, from the 16th day of February 1770, to the 15th day of February 1771* (London, 1771). Bell, *Foreign Protestants*.

MORIMÉ. *See* LAMORINIE

MORPAIN, PIERRE, privateer, port captain, naval and militia officer; b. *c.* 1686 in Blaye, France, son of Jacques Morpain, a businessman and local dignitary of modest means, and Marguerite Audoire; m. 13 Aug. 1709 at Port-Royal (Annapolis Royal, N.S.) Marie-Joseph (d. 1726), daughter of Louis Damours* de Chauffours and Marguerite Guyon; d. 20 Aug. 1749 in Rochefort, France.

Following the premature death of both his parents, Pierre Morpain went to sea in 1703. In Saint-Domingue (Hispaniola) in 1706 he obtained his first command, the *Intrépide*, and a commission to cruise against British shipping in the Caribbean. During his career Morpain recorded amazing successes as a privateer. In 1706, on his own initiative, he sailed north to the coast of New England where he promptly took two important prizes, a slave-ship and a frigate laden with foodstuffs. Making for the closest French harbour, Morpain sailed into Port-Royal, his prizes in tow, in August 1707.

The arrival of the foodstuffs was viewed locally as a manifestation of Providence; in June Port-Royal had been besieged by 1,600 New Englanders under John March* and food supplies were depleted. Just a week after Morpain's arrival a larger force renewed the attack, but it too was forced to withdraw. In a report to Pontchartrain, the minister of Marine, Governor Daniel d'Auger* de Subercase stated that Morpain and his freebooters "helped us to fight them off and left us 700 barrels of flour without which we would certainly have been in difficult straits."

Morpain returned to Saint-Domingue with his captive slaves, but in 1709, in command of the *Marquis de Choiseul*, a vessel belonging to the governor of that colony, François-Joseph de Choiseul de Beaupré, he sailed north again to cruise out of Port-Royal. He had probably been encouraged to do so by Subercase. In a single ten-day outing he sank four British vessels and brought in nine prizes. Morpain's activities were vital to Port-Royal; preoccupied with the war in Europe, France had not sent any supplies there since 1706. Mindful of his past services and anticipating another attack on Port-Royal, Subercase sought every means to keep Morpain and his men close by. He reported to Pontchartrain that he had "persuaded M. Morpain . . . to stay here with us and even to take a wife, by leading him to hope that you would take into account his service to the colony. . . ."

When it became apparent that there would be no attack on Port-Royal in 1709, Morpain left some of his men there and returned to Saint-Domingue. There he faced the wrath of his employer, Choiseul, who strongly disapproved of the use of Saint-Domingue's resources for the benefit of Port-Royal. Shortly afterwards Morpain left the Caribbean for good. In 1711 he was domiciled at Plaisance (Placentia, Nfld.), where his wife joined him. That summer, while he was in command of a small privateer running munitions and supplies to Acadian and Micmac resisters around Port-Royal (which had fallen to the British the previous year and been renamed Annapolis Royal), Morpain was captured by a British frigate following a three-hour engagement. Taken to St John's, Nfld., as a prisoner, he was sent back to Plaisance in 1712.

After attending to the large number of privateering ventures in which he held an interest at Plaisance, Morpain returned to France later in 1712 and stayed in Blaye for a year. With the return of peace in 1713 he appears to have sought a formal naval appointment. But in June 1715 he was named port captain at Île Royale (Cape Breton Island) and he reported to Louisbourg a year later. He supervised all the details relating to the maritime interests of the crown in Île Royale: the construction of facilities; the building, maintenance, and outfitting of ships; and the conduct of navigation. He also piloted the larger storeships into the various harbours of the colony and oversaw their loading and unloading.

Although Morpain carried out his duties well, his performance on at least one occasion contrasted markedly with the swagger of the buccaneer of the first decade of the century. In October 1717 he reluctantly agreed to pilot a detachment of officers and troops in bad weather along the rugged coast between Louisbourg and Port-Toulouse (St Peters, N.S.). The journey took nine days during the whole of which Morpain allegedly gave unabashed vent to his fear, made a series of erroneous navigational readings, saw reefs where there were none, and finally, in mid-journey, left the helm altogether. When the detachment reached Port-Toulouse, he was severely dealt with, being insulted and incarcerated by Louis DENYS de La Ronde. In their report to the court the governor and the financial commissary, Saint-Ovide [MONBETON] and Pierre-Auguste de Soubras*, concluded that "Morpain . . . belied his reputation on that occasion. . . ."

Morpain regained the confidence of his superiors; in 1721 he received his first naval commission, storeship captain. His principal duties continued to be the details of local crown navigation including, in 1725–27, salvage operations in connection with the storeship *Chameau* which had

gone down off Louisbourg in 1725. In the 1740s he taught navigation to the young mariners of the colony.

The resumption of hostilities between France and Great Britain in March 1744 gave Morpain, despite his 58 years, the opportunity to ply the trade which had earned him notoriety. A fire-ship captain now, he was ordered out on coastal patrol and, despite wholly inadequate equipment, had considerable success against New England shipping in April. In May he participated in Joseph DU PONT Duvivier's attack on Canso (N.S.). The late war had established his reputation in New England where the merchants and inhabitants now kept their ships in harbour in fear of the dreaded "Morepang."

It was the events of 1745, however, which were to mark the zenith of Morpain's career. Although Louisbourg had been founded as France's key stronghold in the new world, New England troops commanded by William PEPPERRELL were able to land on Île Royale and lay siege to the fortress in May 1745. By that time Morpain, who had been patrolling the coast in command of the frigate *Castor*, had returned to his base. The Louisbourg garrison was completely demoralized; the entire officer corps lacked the energy and boldness required to meet the occasion. In these circumstances, Louis Du Pont* Duchambon, the acting governor, was forced to rely on Morpain rather than the regular officers to direct the French defence. His performance between 11 May and mid June 1745 (when he was relieved of his command because of differences with the regular officers) shows that the 60-year-old privateer, however rash and unorthodox some of his manœuvres, possessed a better military mind than any in Louisbourg's officer corps.

Morpain and Antoine Le Poupet* de La Boularderie were the only persons in Louisbourg who advocated taking the offensive in order to oppose the enemy landing at Gabarus Bay on 11 May. Morpain requested 300 to 400 men for the task but Duchambon, inept and paralysed by fear, procrastinated until the bridgehead had been secured. He belatedly allocated 80 men to march on the Anglo-American position, but the force was inadequate and too long delayed. When the detachment arrived at Gabarus Bay the New Englanders were already well established on shore. La Boularderie wished to retreat immediately in the face of brisk enemy musketry, but Morpain ordered the column to press on. It was only when his men were threatened with annihilation that he gave the order to withdraw, every man for himself.

The following day Morpain made his way back

Moulton

to Louisbourg and promptly took charge of the entire defence of the fortress. His tireless devotion to the task was an inspiration not only to the combatants but to the inhabitants as well. His popularity in Louisbourg was matched by the awe in which he was held outside its walls. He found his way into the victory lore of the New Englanders in 1745 and that in itself was a significant tribute to his energetic defence of New France.

Following the surrender of Louisbourg, Morpain returned to France. He went on at least one campaign to Louisiana in 1748, and when Île Royale was restored to France that year he was invited to return to his post. Whatever his intentions were, his death intervened at Rochefort in August 1749.

BERNARD POTHIER

AN, G⁵, 253, 258; Col., B, 42, f.559; 82, ff.85, 315; 90, f.300v; C¹¹ᴮ, 2, ff.176, 283–85; 7, ff.375–75v, 377; 9, f.44v; 20, ff.280–81; 23, f.85; 25, ff.25–26; 26, f.66v; 27, ff.191–92v; C¹¹ᶜ, 7, ff.12, 98–98v, 121–121v, 372; C¹¹ᴰ, 6, f.48; 7, ff.34–36, 179; D²ᶜ, 4; 222/2, p.101 (PAC transcript); Marine, C⁷, 221 (dossier Morpain); Section Outre-Mer, Dépôt des fortifications des colonies, Am. sept., no.216; G¹, 406 (23 sept. 1726); G³, 2055 (14 avril, 6 juillet 1712). *Boston Weekly News-Letter*, 29 June 1744. *Derniers jours de l'Acadie* (Du Boscq de Beaumont), 288–89. *Louisbourg journals* (De Forest), 130. *Pennsylvania Journal, or Weekly Advertiser* (Philadelphia), 4 July 1744. J. R. Dunn, *The militia in Île Royale* (Canada, National Historic Sites Service Manuscript Report, 31, [Ottawa, n.d.]). McLennan, *Louisbourg*. Rawlyk, *Yankees at Louisbourg*. Robert Le Blant, "Un corsaire de Saint-Domingue en Acadie: Pierre Morpain, 1707–1711," *Nova Francia*, VI (1931), 193–208.

MOULTON, JEREMIAH, militia officer, member of the Massachusetts Council; b. York, Massachusetts (now in Maine), 1688, youngest son of Joseph Moulton and Hannah (?) Littlefield; d. York, 20 July 1765.

Jeremiah Moulton's father was a tavernkeeper and prominent citizen of York, which by 1692 was one of the last southern Maine settlements to survive repeated French and Indian attacks. Early in that year a sizeable band of Penobscots, some of them converts of Father Louis-Pierre Thury*, encouraged by the promises of Acadia's Governor Joseph Robinau* de Villebon to give them presents, arms, and ammunition, joined Indians from the Kennebec River in a winter raid on the remaining Maine towns. On 25 January (o.s.) they surprised York and overran all but its fortified garrison houses. They killed or made captive about half its people;

one of the dead was York's first minister, the noted Shubael Dummer. Joseph Moulton, his wife, and a number of his guests were killed and some of his children were captured. Among them was the four-year-old Jeremiah, a determined youngster who struggled, managed briefly to get away from his captors, and was finally allowed to take refuge in one of the garrison houses.

Over the next few years Jeremiah grew up in a relative's home in York, learned the trade of surveying, and married Hannah Ballard (?) of Portsmouth, New Hampshire; they were to have eight children. He also served in the militia, advancing from sergeant to captain, and gaining a reputation as an energetic, capable, and popular leader of colonial scouting expeditions during Lovewell's or Dummer's War (1722–1725). A central enterprise of that war was the colonial effort to capture the controversial Father Sébastien Rale*, French missionary to the Norridgewock Indians of the Kennebec River. A hero and martyr to most French Canadian historians, he was the evil genius of the Maine Indians to contemporary and many later English writers. His influence with the Indians made him an inevitable target for English colonists angered by attacks on their frontier settlements. Between 1721 and 1724 there were four attempts to capture the missionary; Captain Jeremiah Moulton played a prominent role in at least two of these, including the last, which succeeded.

In August 1724 a carefully planned expedition of over 200 colonial soldiers headed up the Kennebec from Fort Richmond (Richmond, Maine). After stopping briefly at Ticonic (Winslow), where they left their whaleboats and a guard of 40 men, they continued north on foot towards Norridgewock (Narantsouak; today Old Point, Madison). Captain Johnson Harmon led the raid, with Moulton as second in command. Among the raiders were many York soldiers who, like Harmon, Moulton, and some other officers, had been present, had had relatives killed or captured, or had been made captives themselves in the raid on York in 1692. Coming within striking distance of Norridgewock about noon on 12 August, the raiding force was divided into two sections of some 80 men each. Captain Harmon, who chose to attack through the tribe's cornfields, found no Indians and missed the whole fight. Captain Moulton led his men directly into the village. They were warned to silence and were under strict orders not to fire until the enemy had emptied their guns. The surprised warriors, about 50 or 60 in number, rushed out of their homes shooting wildly at the attackers, withstood a disciplined return volley, fired again, then retreated to join the women and children whose earlier flight they had been trying to cover. They were pursued by most of Moulton's men, who cut them down in the river and in the forest. The old chief Mog* and Father Rale held out in the village. As he was firing from a cabin, Rale was killed by Lieutenant Richard Jaques, Harmon's son-in-law, against orders from Moulton that he be captured alive. Norridgewock was looted and later burned, and the dead were scalped.

After this attack, Captain Moulton continued to take part in scouting expeditions. When the war was over, he remained a militia officer, but resumed his civil career. He became a judge, sheriff of York County, member of the Massachusetts Council, and holder of various other offices. He also developed farms and mills, and helped to found the town which later became Sanford, Maine. During King George's War, Moulton, now a colonel and one of New England's most experienced soldiers, once more saw active service; he commanded one of the three Massachusetts regiments in the expedition against Louisbourg, Île Royale (Cape Breton Island) in 1745. In April of that year he landed with the New England troops at Canso and went from there, leading a detached force of New Hampshire men, to capture and destroy Port-Toulouse (St Peters, N.S.) in early May. He sat regularly with the council of war at Louisbourg and stayed on after the fall of the town to help with its occupation. He did not return to Maine until December 1745; shortly thereafter he was appointed judge of probate for York County.

In 1760 Moulton's first wife died; in 1762 he married Mrs Mary Lord. He remained an active and respected citizen of York until his death in 1765. In the words of a Maine historian, "few men of this age and this Province, had a greater share of public confidence, or were called to fill so many places of official trust and responsibility .... [He was] a man of sound judgment possessing a character of uncommon excellence."

ALICE R. STEWART

[The account of the Norridgewock attack given in this biography is based largely on New England sources which, with some exceptions, seem much more accurate than the French sources, however biased they might be against Father Rale. The principal French source is a letter of Father Pierre de LA CHASSE of October 1724, which is printed in *JR* (Thwaites), LXVI, 231–47. Among the main New England sources are two newspaper stories: *New-England Courant* (Boston), 17–24 August 1724, and *Boston News-Letter*, 20–27 August 1724. These stories reflect Captain Harmon's sworn testimony before the Massachusetts Council and give him the credit for the success of the

raid. Moulton's story is embodied in Thomas Hutchinson, *History of Mass.-Bay* (Mayo), II, 234–38. Hutchinson, a careful historian, interviewed Moulton at some length about the incident. For another contemporary account, *see* Penhallow, *History of wars with eastern Indians* (1726), 102–4.

See also: Charlevoix, *History* (Shea), IV, V. *Documentary history of Maine*, X, XI, XII. Cotton Mather, "Decennium luctuosum, 1699," in *Narratives of the Indian wars, 1675–1699*, ed. C. H. Lincoln (New York, 1913). *New Eng. Hist. and Geneal. Register*, LV (1901), 314. J. C. Webster, *Acadia at the end of the seventeenth century: letters, journals and memoirs of Joseph Robineau de Villebon, commandant in Acadia, 1690–1700, and other contemporary documents* (N.B. Museum, Monographic ser., I, Saint John, N.B., 1934), 36. [Thomas Westbrook *et al.*], *Letters of Colonel Thomas Westbrook and others relative to Indian affairs in Maine, 1722–26*, ed. W. B. Trask (Boston, 1901), 26, 46, 78–79, 91–92, 104, 109, 154–56, 173. C. E. Banks, *History of York, Maine . . .* (2v., Boston, 1931–35), I, 296–97, 322–25, 328. J. P. Baxter, *The pioneers of New France in New England, with contemporary letters and documents* (Albany, 1894). Coleman, *New England captives*. F. H. Eckstorm, "The attack on Norridgewock, 1724," *New Eng. Q.*, VII (1934), 541–78. George Ernst, *New England miniature: a history of York, Maine* (Freeport, Maine, 1961), 36, 118–21. G. T. Little, *Genealogical and family history of the state of Maine* (4v., New York, 1909), I, 413–14. K. M. Morrison, "Sebastien Rale vs. New England: a case study of frontier conflict" (unpublished MA thesis, University of Maine, Orono, 1970). Parkman, *Count Frontenac and New France* (1891), 348–51; *Half-century of conflict*, I. W. D. Williamson, *The history of the state of Maine; from its first discovery, A.D. 1602, to the separation, A.D. 1820 inclusive* (2v., Hallowell, Maine, 1832; repr. [1966]), I, 628–30; II, 102, 350–51. A.R.S.]

MOUNIER, FRANÇOIS, merchant, member of James Murray*'s council, judge; b. at La Rochelle, France; d. 17 June 1769 in Quebec.

François Mounier, a Huguenot merchant trader, came to Canada shortly before the conquest, probably towards the end of the 1740s. Two of his brothers were merchants in La Rochelle; one of them, Henry, lived for a time in Quebec.

François Mounier opened a business in Quebec. In the 1750s he was in partnership with one Sieur Grelleau, a merchant in that town. They are mentioned in 1753 in the account books of the Montreal merchants Alexis LEMOINE, *dit* Monière, and his son Pierre-Alexis. The two men still had business connections in 1756, since on 23 August of that year they sold a ship and some wine to the purveyor general Joseph-Pierre Cadet*. Two years later Mounier acted as the commission agent for the sale of another ship to Cadet. In 1762 Mounier had John Lee as a

Muiron

partner. On 17 Sept. 1763 he bought from Joseph Perthuis* de La Salle the seigneury of Perthuis (near Quebec), for which he paid 300 *livres*; ten months later, on 23 July 1764, he sold it in his turn to Antoine and François Germain for 600 *livres*. In partnership with another Quebec merchant trader, Jean Marteilhe, he bought Grosse Île and Île aux Ruaux from Charles Vallée on 1 Oct. 1764. On several occasions between 1763 and 1767 he petitioned the governor to obtain grants of large tracts of land (from 10,000 to 20,000 acres) but nothing seems to have come of his requests.

On 13 Aug. 1764 Governor Murray appointed him to the newly created council, which was made up exclusively of Protestants; François Mounier was the only French-speaking member. Murray thought that this appointment might encourage the Canadians to embrace Protestantism. At least that is the explanation he gave in a letter to the Board of Trade on 23 Aug. 1764. Moreover, a remark by Murray's successor, Guy Carleton*, leaves few illusions about the role that this French-speaking member was to play in the council; Carleton wrote to the secretary of state, Shelburne, in a dispatch dated 25 Oct. 1766: "M\u02b3 Mounier, an honest quiet Trader, who knows very little of our Language or Manners, like most of the Canadians, will sign, without Examination whatever their Acquaintance urge them to. . . ."

Mounier was appointed examiner in the Court of Chancery (the governor and council) on 13 Nov. 1764. The following May he was commissioned justice of the peace for the districts of Quebec and Montreal, and about the same time he is referred to as judge of the Court of Common Pleas.

He died on 17 June 1769 and was buried the next day in "the chapel of the bishop's palace," where Protestants had been able to be buried since 1759. Like other French or Swiss Huguenots, Mounier had suddenly been given important offices after the treaty of Paris, whereas his presence had barely been tolerated under the preceding régime.

JEAN-MARIE LEBLANC

ANQ, Greffe de J.-C. Panet, 23 août 1756, 17 oct. 1758. PAC, MG 23, GIII, 25, A. *Documents relating to constitutional history, 1759–91* (Shortt and Doughty), I, 193. P.-G. Roy, *Inv. concessions*, I, 170, 220; V, 84; *Les juges de la province de Québec* (Québec, 1933), 389. Brunet, *Les Canadiens après la conquête*, 95, 99–100. Neatby, *Quebec*. Trudel, *L'Église canadienne*, passim. F.-J. Audet, "François Mounier," *BRH*, II (1896), 62; "Les législateurs de la province de Québec, 1764–1791," *BRH*, XXXI (1925), 482–83. É.-Z. Massicotte, "Les tribunaux de police de Montréal," *BRH*, XXVI (1920), 181.

MUIRON, DAVID-BERNARD, businessman and architect, contractor for the fortifications of Île Royale (Cape Breton Island); b. 8 Sept. 1684 at Bar-sur-Seine, France, son of François Muiron, the town's commissary-inspector (a civilian agent of the war department) and of Marie Champion; m. 18 Jan. 1723 at Dijon, France, Claudine Seroin, by whom he had five children, including at least two sons; d. 27 Nov. 1761 at Arcenant (dept. of Côte d'Or), France.

By 1723 David-Bernard Muiron was king's architect at Dijon, and subsequently became roads and bridges contractor for the provinces of Burgundy and Champagne. In 1736 he came to Île Royale for three reasons: ostensibly, under an agreement of 8 Sept. 1735, to develop Gratien d'ARRIGRAND's logging and sawmill concession on the Plédien Creek near Louisbourg; to establish his own tannery; and to try to underbid François GANET for the fortifications contract when it was renewed in 1737. Muiron refused, however, to be an instrument of furthering d'Arrigrand's interests in the latter's long-standing dispute with Ganet; after winning the contract in 1737 he negotiated a separate settlement with Ganet concerning materials and equipment in Ganet's hands, to which d'Arrigrand laid claim. Furthermore, following an initial reconnaissance of the Plédien Creek and an unsuccessful attempt to have d'Arrigrand's concession there registered by the Conseil Supérieur at Louisbourg, Muiron did nothing to develop it. Instead, he devoted his energies to his tannery and to the fortifications.

From 1736 to 1738 Muiron hired skilled tanners (who were scarce) and helpers; established a workshop, equipped with a water-mill, on the north side of the harbour; and tanned a quantity of cow-hide, sheepskin, sealskin, and walrus hide. By 1740 he had invested 4,500 *livres* in plant and 6,000 in labour and materials. He had no success in obtaining a monopoly, however, the only basis upon which he felt he could continue. The minister's reason for refusing was that Muiron appeared to have overextended himself financially, and he wished him to concentrate on the fortifications.

Muiron did experience difficulty with his financial affairs. Under the contract he concluded with the king on 10 May 1737 after underbidding Ganet by 20 per cent, Muiron's chief task was to construct Étienne VERRIER's new works completing the Louisbourg *enceinte*. Like his predecessors, he paid current bills with promissory notes. Caught, with few liquid assets, between a tardy debtor (policy was always to have the crown in debt to him, rather than the reverse) and impatient creditors, Muiron found his notes being discounted at 10 per cent or even refused. The government, fearing a threat to local business, would redeem the notes (or at least most of their value) and deduct the amounts from the payments to Muiron.

When setting the rate for his services, Muiron had counted on paying the soldier labourers in part with necessities and luxuries obtained at wholesale prices, and in part with money. Here his interests clashed with those of the officers of the garrison, who were used to supplementing their incomes by selling such goods to the troops at retail prices. As permanent residents, said to require the additional income, they received official sympathy. Consequently, when Muiron bid for the renewal of his contract in 1743, the government did not accept a condition that the men be paid partly in kind.

Muiron's difficulties continued during this second contract. Though under the possible threat of military attack, the government reduced construction of the fortifications in 1744 in order to permit him to pay off his notes. In France, following the siege of 1745, Muiron faced pressing debts of 35,000 to 36,000 *livres* while claiming 104,500 *livres* from the crown. It was not until 1747, however, that authorization was given to pay him in full. On the other hand, d'Arrigrand appears to have been unsuccessful in his attempt to recover the value of materials and equipment provided by Ganet in 1737, although in March 1752 he was still trying in the courts to obtain 100,000 *livres* from Muiron.

In general, one suspects that Muiron's nine years at Louisbourg were by no means unprofitable, even though his construction contract may have been rather less lucrative for him than speculation in the *entrepôt* trade of that port. In 1751 he purchased the hereditary office of court officer of the treasury court for Dijon. This suggests he was well off (since venal offices were usually expensive) and that he provided well for his heirs.

F. J. THORPE

AD, Côte d'Or (Dijon), B, 65, ff.556–57 (Chambre des comptes de Dijon, enregistrement); C, 8993 (Bureau du contrôle des actes de Dijon); État civil, Saint-Jean de Dijon, 18 janv. 1723; État civil, Arcenant. AN, Col., B, 65, 66, 68, 70, 72, 74, 76, 78, 84, 86; C¹¹ᴮ, 19–27; C¹¹ᶜ, 11, ff.128, 148, 164, 176; 12, ff.52, 73, 101, 141, 150, 168; E, 9 (dossier d'Arrigrand); F¹ᴬ, 34, ff.205–12, 223; Section Outre-Mer, G², 183, pièce 234, f.430; G³, 2039, 2047.

J.-N. Fauteux, *Essai sur l'industrie*, II, 440–41. Frégault, *François Bigot*, I, 128–31. McLennan, *Louisbourg*, 101. Robert Le Blant, "Un entrepreneur à l'île Royale, Gratien d'Arrigrand, 1684–1754," *La revue des questions historiques* (Paris), LXIV (1936) (offprint at PAC). Pierre Mayrand, "La renaissance de Louisbourg," *Vie des arts* (Montréal), XLVI (1967), 35.

MURRAY, ALEXANDER, army officer; probably b. *c*. 1715 at Cringletie, Peeblesshire, Scotland, eldest son of Alexander Murray; d. 19 March 1762 at Martinique. By his wife Marianne, whom he married in 1749, he had three children, the youngest of whom he named James Wolfe Murray.

Alexander Murray was commissioned ensign in the 17th Foot on 17 July 1739 and was promoted lieutenant in the 6th Foot on 19 Jan. 1740. He joined the 45th Foot on 19 April 1742 as a captain and was with the regiment when it arrived in Gibraltar on 17 June to take up garrison duties.

Murray came to Louisbourg, Cape Breton Island (Île Royale), with the regiment in April 1746. When it was moved to Halifax in July 1749 he was in England, but he had rejoined it in Nova Scotia by December. He remained with it in the colony for almost ten years, during which time he built a house at Halifax and succeeded to the family estates at Cringletie on his father's death in September 1755. At first he commanded at Fort Sackville (at the head of Bedford Basin), but in September 1751 he was given command of Fort Edward (Windsor, N.S.), where he remained for most of the ensuing seven years, except for a tour of duty at Halifax in 1753. In the spring of 1755 he impounded the boats belonging to the Acadians of the Minas Basin, whom he suspected of violating Charles LAWRENCE's embargo on the export of wheat. On orders from Lawrence, in June he confiscated their guns in case they might hinder Robert Monckton*'s planned seizure of Fort Beauséjour (near Sackville, N.B.). Following the decision of Lawrence and his council to expel the Acadians from Nova Scotia Murray supervised the deportations from the immediate area of Fort Edward. During October 1755 he sent off 1,100 persons in four ships.

Murray was promoted major in the 45th on 1 Oct. 1755. The regiment took part in Jeffery Amherst*'s expedition against Louisbourg in June 1758, and during the initial landings at the Anse de La Cormorandière (Kennington Cove) Murray had joint command of the four grenadier companies which formed the left wing of the attacking force. He continued to command grenadier companies throughout the siege.

He remained at Louisbourg until May 1759 when, with the local rank of lieutenant-colonel, he left at the head of three companies of "Grenadiers of Louisbourg" to take part in

Muy

WOLFE's campaign against Quebec. During the siege he led the grenadiers in an unsuccessful attack against French positions near the Montmorency River on 31 July. He subsequently commanded on the Île d'Orléans. The Louisbourg grenadiers under Murray fought on the British right flank during the battle of the Plains of Abraham (13 September), and according to a family tradition the keys of the city were formally surrendered to him.

After wintering at Louisbourg Murray was transferred on 25 Feb. 1760 to the 55th regiment and by August he was encamped with it on Staten Island, New York. He was with the 48th when it sailed from New York on 19 Nov. 1761 to take part in a campaign against Martinique. He suffered from an attack of yellow fever shortly after his arrival on the island, but he had apparently recovered completely when he died suddenly on 19 March 1762.

Murray, who liked to be "thought a good soldier," won Wolfe's "great regard" and was considered by Amherst to be "a very good and useful officer." When during the siege of Quebec dissension among the officers was beginning to grow bitter, Murray reported to his wife, "I meddle with no politicks or party, am well with all, and, I am told, a Favourite of the whole Army; I go by the name of 'the old Soldier.' " From the many letters that he wrote to his wife and family while at his various posts he emerges as a conscientious professional soldier, a keen observer, and a deeply religious and affectionate husband and father.

JOHN HUMPHREYS

A portrait of Murray can be found in Sherwood Foresters *Regimental Annual, 1924* (London, 1925). PRO, Ind. 5436, f.120; 5438, ff.355–56; WO 1/1, ff.354v–55; 1/5, ff.15, 209–10; 12/5718, f.32; 12/6470, f.22; 34/3, ff.17–19; 34/19, ff.17–18, 34–34v; 34/55, ff.114–14v. [Alexander Murray], "Letters of Colonel Alexander Murray," Sherwood Foresters *Regimental Annual, 1926* (London, 1927), 181–220; *1927* (London, 1928), 240–68. *Army list, 1740*, 30. Knox, *Historical journal* (Doughty). Brebner, *New England's outpost*. Russell Gurney, *History of the Northamptonshire regiment, 1742–1934* (Aldershot, Eng., 1935), 53–54. H. C. Wylly, *History of the 1st & 2nd battalions the Sherwood Foresters, Nottinghamshire and Derbyshire regiment, 1740–1914* (2v., London, Frome, Eng., 1929), I, 5, 8–9, 16, 20, 34, 40–42, 45–46, 48. "Colonel Alexander Murray," Sherwood Foresters *Regimental Annual, 1925* (London, 1926), 117–22.

MUY, JACQUES-PIERRE DANEAU DE. *See* DANEAU

MUY, *dite* **de Sainte-Hélène, CHARLOTTE DANEAU DE.** *See* DANEAU

N

NAU, LUC-FRANÇOIS, priest, Jesuit missionary, superior of the Sault-Saint-Louis mission (Caughnawaga, Que.); b. 17 Jan. 1703 at Noirmoutier-en-l'Île, France, son of Lucas Nau, a skipper, and Françoise Lorin; d. 5 Sept. 1753 at Luçon (dept. of Vendée), France.

After his studies at the Jesuit college in Poitiers, Luc-François Nau was admitted into the noviciate of the Jesuits of the province of Aquitaine in Bordeaux on 12 Dec. 1720. He was a teacher of grammar at Tulle from 1722 to 1724, and completed his philosophical studies at Poitiers in two years. He taught grammar and humanities at the Jesuit College in Luçon from 1726 to 1730 and did his theology in Bordeaux from 1730 to 1734. He then left for Canada, sailing on the *Rubis* along with the new bishop of Quebec, Dosquet*, and the superior of the Canadian mission, Father Pierre de LAUZON. They embarked at La Rochelle on 29 May 1734, and landed at Quebec on 16 August after a difficult 80-day crossing.

Lauzon decided immediately to send the missionary to the Sault-Saint-Louis mission to help Father Jacques-Quintin de LA BRETONNIÈRE. Nau went there the following November. The Indian village of "some 1,200 Christians" was made up mainly of Iroquois and Hurons, who were continually being joined by prisoners of war from other tribes. Nau learned Iroquois and Huron. Huron was, however, spoken more than anything else, and religious services were conducted solely in that language. Some time after his arrival the new missionary submitted to the Indian custom of adoption and the bestowing of a surname. This cost him "an ox, some bread, two bushels of peas, and some tobacco." Adopted by the Bear clan, he received the name Hatériate, the great-hearted man.

In 1738 Nau went to Quebec, and on 2 February he took his final vows. In the summer of 1739 La Bretonnière, who was accompanying "300 Iroquois warriors" on an expedition against the Chickasaws, handed direction of the Sault-

Saint-Louis mission over to Nau. He fulfilled this function for some months, until the arrival of Lauzon, who had finished his term of office as superior general and came to take over the running of his former mission. Lauzon was not of much help to the missionary, since he was continually ill and confined to bed. After Lauzon's death in 1742, Nau, aided by Father Jean-Baptiste TOURNOIS, ran the mission again until 1744, at which time he left the colony. When he left for France he was hoping to find a cure for his gout, from which he suffered well before his departure for Canada, and to return to his Canadian mission. But he never again saw New France, and from 1749 on his name no longer appears on the rolls of the province of France. He had probably returned to his original province of Aquitaine; he died at the Jesuit college in Luçon on 5 Sept. 1753.

LUCIEN CAMPEAU

AD, Vendée (La Roche-sur-Yon), État civil, Noirmoutier-en-l'Île, 17 janv. 1703. ASJCF, 566; 572; 616; BO 80, 16, 18; Fonds Rochemonteix, 4008, 1–324; 4018, 290, 363, 365. *JR* (Thwaites), LXVIII, LXIX. Rochemonteix, *Les Jésuites et la N.-F. au XVIIIe siècle*, II, 23–29.

NAVIÈRES, JOSEPH, parish priest; b. and baptized 12 June 1709 in the parish of Saint-Michel-des-Lions in Limoges, France, son of Jean Navières, a merchant, and Madeleine Sicot; d. 25 Dec. 1756 at Saint-Paul d'Eyjeaux, Limousin, France.

Joseph Navières was ordained a priest on 14 Dec. 1733 and at the end of June 1734 he left France for Canada, sailing on the ship which was carrying Bishop Dosquet*. He landed at Saint-Joachim on 13 August, reached Quebec by land the next day and was appointed parish priest of Sainte-Anne-de-Beaupré, where he went on 25 August. Shortly after he wrote a letter to his friend, M. Veyssière, curate of the collegiate church of Saint-Martial de Limoges. In this letter he gave a picturesque and sometimes humorous account of the voyage from Newfoundland to Quebec. Then he described Lower Town, "where all the merchants live," and Upper Town, "which is inhabited by what we commonly call the bourgeois." All the houses were built of stone "and except for three or four which are roofed with slate, the others have roofs made of wood shaped like slates, which nevertheless is not disagreeable in appearance." The town was well situated and "it is not less well fortified than the fortress towns of France." The population was dense, and "the people there are gracious,

courteous, decent, kind, everything in the manner of Paris, which they pride themselves on following."

At the end of August Navières went to his parish of Sainte-Anne; he explained to his friend Veyssière that it was "located not quite seven leagues from Quebec on the shore of the St Lawrence River, in a broad plain about ten leagues in length which is fertile and pleasant." His church, he wrote, was "one of the most beautiful and most finely embellished in Canada. . . . The country churches in France are not comparable to that in the region where I live." He praised the variety of liturgical ornaments, "all of them clean and beautiful; the consecrated vessels, costly and in silver gilt; the immense church, decorated with pictures given as votive offerings. . . . The high altar is architecturally exceptional, and the retable surpasses in richness and magnificence everything that I have seen." He observed that "relics in the church are very popular and are held in great veneration; the main one, although it is the smallest, is a well-authenticated part of the hand of St Anne." Pilgrims flocked there, "which causes me no small inconvenience." Joseph Navières emphasized that he had "in abundance everything necessary to live well"; he lacked only a good cook, and he regretted that he was not familiar with "this science, so necessary for a parish priest, particularly in Canada, where good cooks are as rare as wine."

The following year, in a letter addressed to M. Romanet de Briderie and dated 28 Sept. 1735, he pointed out among other things that there were "almost no poor in Canada; the least favoured with fortune do not lack good wheaten bread." In October 1737, however, he confided to his sister that his income was scanty, despite the great numbers of pilgrims, and that he found it hard to put up with the solitude in which he was confined for long months each year and with the lack of books "in this country where there is neither a printing press nor a bookshop."

Joseph Navières left his parish 3 Sept. 1740 and returned to France. On his arrival he announced the death of Bishop Lauberivière [Pourroy*] to Canon Pierre Hazeur* de L'Orme, at that time the delegate in France of the chapter of the cathedral of Quebec. His return had not been without difficulty. Indeed he had to make a stay in the port of Flushing (Neth.), for the ship on which he was travelling was captured. He was able to resume his journey immediately, however, since France was not at war.

Shortly after his return Joseph Navières was appointed parish priest of Saint-Sylvestre de Grandmont, Marche, then on 15 May 1755

Neveu

archpriest of Saint-Paul d'Eyjeaux, where he died on Christmas day, 1756.

RAYMOND GARIÉPY

AD, Haute-Vienne (Limoges), G 689, 14 déc. 1733. Bibliothèque municipale de Limoges (France), État civil, Saint-Michel-des-Lions, 12 juin 1709. "Un voyage à la Nouvelle-France (Canada) sous Louis XV (1734); relation inédite," Ludovic Drapeyron, édit., *Revue de géographie* (Paris), X, no.1 (1882), 81–105. "Un voyage à la Nouvelle-France en 1734," Benjamin Sulte, édit., *Revue canadienne*, 2ᵉ sér., VI (1886), 15–25. "Sainte-Anne de Beaupré," *Annales de la Bonne Sainte Anne de Beaupré* (Québec), XXXIV (1906), 102–6, 133–37. Henri Têtu, "Le chapitre de la cathédrale de Québec et ses délégués en France," *BRH*, XIV (1908), 103–4; XVI (1910), 294–95.

NEVEU, JEAN-BAPTISTE (also written **Nepveu**; he is sometimes called **Sieur de La Bretonnière**), merchant and trader, seigneur; baptized Jean on 20 Dec. 1676 in Quebec, son of Philippe Neveu, a tailor, and Marie-Denise Sevestre; d. 24 June 1754 in Montreal.

Jean-Baptiste Neveu left his birthplace to settle in Montreal, where in January 1701 he appeared as a merchant. His business enterprise, located on Rue Saint-Paul, brought him large profits which enabled him to finance numerous fur-trading trips throughout the *pays d'en haut* and to organize for himself several of these lucrative expeditions. In 1709 he acquired from his brother Jacques for 200 *livres* a slave named Marie, who was 11 years old and of the Pawnee tribe.

His financial situation soon enabled him to diversify his investments, and on 28 Nov. 1710 he bought the seigneury of Dautré, situated on the St Lawrence. Five years later, on 21 Sept. 1715, he purchased from the Sulpicians a piece of land situated on Rue Saint-Paul where he had a two-storey stone house built for himself. Then from 1717 on he increased his investments in land; he bought from different owners the seigneury of Lanoraie, which belonged to him in its entirety in 1721. In that year his house on Rue Saint-Paul was destroyed by fire; the recognition of sovereignty and census of Montreal Island in 1731 tells us that at that date it had been rebuilt on the same site and to almost identical dimensions. On 4 July 1739 Governor Charles de BEAUHARNOIS and Intendant Hocquart* granted him the land at the back of his two seigneuries, extending to the Rivière L'Assomption. This piece of land and his two seigneuries were incorporated into a single seigneury which was called Lanoraie.

Neveu developed his vast domain wisely and encouraged settlement. He had a tar kiln, sawmill, and flour mill built on his lands. He also had built, at his own expense, the first chapel and the presbytery of Lanoraie. In 1744 he gave the site for the building of the first stone church, then in 1752 he made over to the council of the parish, free of charge, a piece of land of 120 acres.

Like many other merchants, Jean-Baptiste Neveu was a churchwarden of the parish of Notre-Dame de Montréal; he exercised this responsibility from 1706 to 1709. He was also a member of the militia of the government of Montreal. In 1720 he was a captain, and in 1737 and 1741 he held the rank of colonel, which he seems to have retained until his death in 1754.

On 24 Jan. 1702, in Montreal, he had married Marie-Jeanne Passard; of this marriage a daughter was born. Having lost his wife on 3 Feb. 1703, he married Françoise-Élisabeth Legras in Montreal on 27 July 1704; of his second marriage 14 children were born. His wife survived him, dying in 1771.

YVES QUESNEL

ANQ-M, Greffe d'Antoine Adhémar, 21 janv. 1702, 11 juill. 1704, 14 oct. 1708, 19 oct. 1709, 5 mars 1713; Greffe de L.-C. Danré de Blanzy, 15 déc. 1745; Greffe de J.-C. Porlier, 25 sept. 1740; Registre d'état civil, Notre-Dame de Montréal, 24 janv. 1702, 27 juill. 1704. "Aveu et dénombrement pour l'île de Montréal," APQ *Rapport, 1941–42*, 118. *Édits ord.*, I, 456; II, 515; III, 178–82. *Jug. et délib.*, IV, 917. "Procès-verbaux du procureur général Collet" (Caron), APQ *Rapport, 1921–22*, 302, 307, 308, 368. "Recensement de Montréal, 1741" (Massicotte). Bonnault, "Le Canada militaire," APQ *Rapport, 1949–51*, 423, 425, 439. "Marguilliers de la paroisse Notre-Dame de Ville-Marie de 1657 à 1913," *BRH*, XIX (1913), 277. Massicotte, "Répertoire des engagements pour l'Ouest," APQ *Rapport, 1929–30*, 219, 225, 232, 240, 257, 260. Tanguay, *Dictionnaire*.

NEWTON, JOHN, shipmaster, HBC chief at York Fort (York Factory, Man.); d. there 28 June 1750. By his first wife he was the father of John Newton, the theologian; by his second wife, Thomasina, whom he married *c*. 1733, he had three children.

John Newton was master of a ship in the Mediterranean trade until his retirement in 1742; during the next six years he apparently lived in Aveley, Essex, and in Rotherhithe, Surrey, England. In 1748 the Hudson's Bay Company called James ISHAM home from York to help defend the company's monopoly against attacks by Arthur Dobbs and other critics. Contrary to its usual practice of giving command of its posts to men experienced in its service, it appointed Newton to replace Isham at York. Newton arrived there in August 1748 by the *Prince Rupert* (Capt. George SPURRELL). The next year, on the instruction of the London committee, he superintended the construction of Cumberland Fort (soon renamed Flamborough House). Located on the estuary of the Nelson River, the post was designed to confront any interlopers from England who, inspired by Dobbs, might try to go up the river and intercept Indians coming to trade at York.

On 28 June 1750 Samuel SKRIMSHER recorded in the York journals: "the water being Clear and Smooth he [Newton] had a mind to Treat his Selfe with a Swim." His men soon saw him in distress and rushed to his assistance "but pore Gentel Man Never apering the Second time Renderd our Indeavers on Servesable. . . ."

Newton's tenure at York must have been difficult. His air of distance and severity, attributed by his son John to his Spanish education, cannot have endeared the new recruit to his more experienced subordinates. The London committee also regretted his appointment to York, which they had described to him as their "best Factory." In 1751 they complained to Isham of Newton's inattention to the fabric of the fort and of the decrease in trade brought on "by the Indians not being prevented from going to Warr & other Mismanagemt."

JOAN CRAIG

HBC Arch. A.1/130, ff.7d, 38; A.6/7, pp.276, 281, 342; A.6/8, ff.15–15d, 44–45, 131; A.11/114, ff.128d, 134–35d; B.239/a/32–33. HBRS, XXVII (Williams). John Newton, *An authentic narrative of some remarkable and interesting particulars in the early life of the Reverend John Newton . . .* (Bristol, Eng., 1824); *The works of the Reverend John Newton . . .* (4v., Aberdeen, Scot., 1836), I. *DNB*, biography of John Newton (1725–1807). Rich, *History of the HBC*, I.

NICHOLAS (Nickus). *See* KARAGHTADIE

NICOLAS. *See* ORONTONY

NINĀKON. *See* MINWEWEH

NITACHINON. *See* CHABERT DE JONCAIRE

NIVERVILLE, JEAN-BAPTISTE BOUCHER DE. *See* BOUCHER

NOBLE, ARTHUR, merchant, military officer; date of birth unknown; killed at Grand Pré, Nova Scotia, 31 Jan. 1746/47 (o.s.).

Family tradition recounts that Arthur Noble was born at Enniskillen, Co. Fermanagh (Northern Ireland), and that he came to North America about 1720 with his brothers Francis and James. He settled on the Kennebec River (Maine), where he maintained a trading post on Arrowsic Island and a farm at Pleasant Cove (Winnegance). It is probable that he also ran a tannery and manufactured shoes. His business ventures evidently prospered as he left an estate in excess of £8,000 (old tenor). He married Sarah Macklin(?), possibly in 1725, and had at least three children. By 1744 Noble was acting as military commander in his district, serving under Samuel WALDO, and also as commissary agent for the garrisons in the Falmouth-Kennebec region.

When the government of Massachusetts decided in January 1744/45 to undertake an expedition against the French fortress at Louisbourg, Île Royale (Cape Breton Island), Arthur Noble was appointed lieutenant-colonel in Samuel Waldo's 2nd Massachusetts Regiment and captain of the 2nd company (5 Feb. 1744/45). He sailed with the expedition in April of that year and took part in the capture of Louisbourg. After a series of unsuccessful attempts to capture the Island battery which guarded Louisbourg harbour, an assault was planned for the evening of 23 May, with approximately 800 New England troops under the joint command of Noble and Lieutenant-Colonel John GORHAM. As the men in their whale-boats neared the battery that night, it was discovered that neither Noble nor Gorham was in his position of command; the attack disintegrated in confusion and frustration. An inquiry the next day, however, absolved both men of all blame, and Noble was commended for his bravery by Waldo.

Noble returned to his home in 1746 and in the fall of that year was ordered to Nova Scotia as commander of the New England troops sent to reinforce the British garrison at Annapolis Royal. Probably in response to the prodding of Governor William Shirley of Massachusetts, Paul MASCARENE, the civil and military commander of Nova Scotia, decided to undertake a winter offensive in the hope of driving the French forces out of the Minas (Grand Pré) region. A 500-man expedition was to attack the French, if they were still in the Grand Pré area, and then take up winter quarters in the midst of the Acadian population. The whole campaign was placed under the command of Noble. A first detachment set out for Grand Pré on 5 Dec. 1746, and Noble himself arrived there on 1 Jan. 1746/47. The French forces under Jean-Baptiste-Nicolas-Roch de Ramezay* had already withdrawn to the Chignecto region where they intended to winter, so

Nodogawerrimet

the New England troops encountered no opposition. During the winter some of the Acadians kept the French informed of English military movements.

Heavy snowfalls and the long distance from Chignecto to Minas lulled the New Englanders into a false sense of security and caused them to grow careless. No serious notice was taken of warnings from the Acadians that Ramezay planned an offensive against Minas. The French, however, under Ramezay's second-in-command, Captain Nicolas-Antoine COULON de Villiers, had decided on just such a venture and on 12 January 240 Canadians and about 60 Indians set out from Chignecto for Minas.

About three o'clock on the morning of 31 January, in a raging snow-storm, the French launched their attack on the ill-prepared and unsuspecting New Englanders. In spite of later attempts to gloss over their inefficiency, it is obvious that Noble and his officers were tragically neglectful of ordinary precautions and that the New Englanders were taken completely by surprise. According to English sources, about 70 of the 500 New England troops were killed, some of them still in their beds. Noble's quarters were attacked first and the commander was wounded twice before a bullet penetrated his forehead. Ensign Francis Noble died defending his brother's quarters. Within a few hours of the attack, the New England forces, now under the command of Benjamin GOLDTHWAIT, capitulated and were allowed to return to Annapolis Royal after agreeing not to serve in the Minas-Chignecto area for six months. Arthur Noble and the men who fell with him were buried at Grand Pré.

BARRY M. MOODY

AN, Col., C¹¹ᴬ, 87, ff.314–61; C¹¹ᴰ, 8, ff.130–34. Mass. Hist. Soc., Belknap papers, 61.B.41; Waldo papers, Burns to Noble (19 May 1744); Noble to Waldo (28 June, 6 July 1744). PAC, MG 18, F10. PANS, RG 1, 13, nos.37, 39; 13¹/₂, nos.19, 23, 24; 21, p.90.
Boston Evening-Post, February and March 1747. *Louisbourg journals* (De Forest), 77, 87. "The Pepperrell papers," Mass. Hist. Soc. *Coll.*, 6th ser., X (1899), 21. *NYCD* (O'Callaghan and Fernow), X, 78, 89–93.
Grand Pré tragedy, 1745–55; the Noble memorial (n.p., n.d.) [A badly researched and written pamphlet, available at the PANS; gives Noble's wife's name as Macklin. B.M.M.]. McLennan, *Louisbourg*. B. M. Moody, "Paul Mascarene, William Shirley and the defence of Nova Scotia, 1744–1748" (unpublished MA thesis, Queen's University, Kingston, Ont., 1969), pp.219–24. *New Eng. Hist. and Geneal. Register*, XXIV (1870), 370. Rawlyk, *Yankees at Louisbourg*, 126–27. William Goold, "Col. Arthur Noble, of Georgetown: his military services at Cape Breton and Nova Scotia, and his death at Minas," Maine Hist. Soc. *Coll.*, 1st ser., VIII (1881), 109–53.

NODOGAWERRIMET (Noodogawirramet, Nov dogg aw wer imet), Norridgewock Abenaki sachem and orator; d. November 1765 at Cobbosseecontee Lake, Massachusetts (now Maine).

The renewal of Dummer's treaty of 1727 by the Norridgewock, Penobscot, and Canadian Abenakis on 16 Oct. 1749 closed five years of hostilities between the Indians and Massachusetts. Soon after, however, one Norridgewock was killed and two others wounded by Englishmen at Wiscasset, Massachusetts (now Maine). Despite her promises to the Indians, the colony delayed the trials of the accused murderers. Frustrated by this, by the trespassing of English hunters, and by a proposal to establish English settlements on the Kennebec River, the Abenakis resorted to raids on frontier outposts.

Unlike the Canadian Abenakis who, with the strong encouragement of Governor La Jonquière [TAFFANEL], rejected English peace overtures, the Norridgewocks were genuinely eager to end this new fighting. Nodogawerrimet was one of the sachems leading their continued attempts to reach agreement with Massachusetts. In November 1751 he and two other chiefs asked to negotiate with commissioners from Massachusetts in hopes of breaking the impasse but were told that it was too late in the year. The following September Nodogawerrimet was among those who again urged a meeting.

At the conference, which was finally held at Fort St George (now Thomaston, Maine) in October 1752, the Indians declared their opposition to the proposed settlements on the Kennebec and to English hunting on tribal territory. The commissioners replied vaguely, and Nodogawerrimet was given two wampum belts: one for the Norridgewocks and the other for the Abenakis of Saint-François and Bécancour, who had not attended, as a symbol of Massachusetts' good intentions.

The Norridgewocks carried their belt to another conference in June 1753. "We Do not want to Brack it," they said, but they warned that they would not tolerate any settlements above Fort Richmond (now Richmond, Maine) on the Kennebec. Their continued opposition led to a declaration of war against them by Massachusetts on 13 June 1755.

There was no formal peace between the Abenakis and Massachusetts after the Seven Years' War, and all the old issues continued to irritate the Indians. After repeated requests had been ignored by the governor, the Norridgewocks finally sent Nodogawerrimet to Boston in August 1765. The sachem explained that the Indians were upset because they had "found the Beaver mostly killed up" when they returned to their village after the war. But the Norridgewocks' complaints were relatively few. Nodogawerrimet insisted that the law barring English fur-trappers from Norridgewock lands was being laxly enforced. He asked that his tribe receive payment in money for their skins so that they could pay their debts at Quebec. Finally, he begged the governor to replace the Jesuit at Bécancour, who had died.

Nodogawerrimet's death in November 1765 showed the frail basis of English-Abenaki relations and the problems created by ever increasing numbers of settlers. Little had he realized that in August he had pleaded for his own life. He and his wife were neither the first nor the last Indians to be killed and robbed by marauding English hunters. The Norridgewocks were upset by the crime. The truck master at Ticonic (Fort Halifax, now Winslow, Me.) reported that "if ye English hunters is Determined to steel their Lives away by peace meals, for ye sake of Hunting, they say it's better for them to Die lick men, then to be kill'd lick Dogs. . . ." Nevertheless, Massachusetts found the Norridgewocks below regard. A £100 reward was offered for the murderers, but they were not apprehended, and the demands Nodogawerrimet had made were ignored.

KENNETH M. MORRISON

Mass., Archives, Council records, XII. *Documentary history of Maine*, XII, XIII, XXIII, XXIV. "Indian treaties," Maine Hist. Soc. *Coll.*, 1st ser., IV (1854), 168–84. "Materials for a history of Fort Halifax: being copies and abridgements of documents . . . ," Maine Hist. Soc. *Coll.*, 1st ser., VII (1876), 165–98. *NYCD* (O'Callaghan and Fernow), X. R. H. Lord *et al.*, *History of the archdiocese of Boston in the various stages of its development, 1604 to 1943* . . . (3v., New York, 1944), II. H. O. Thayer, "The Indian's administration of justice: the sequel to the Wiscasset tragedy," Maine Hist. Soc. *Coll.*, 2nd ser., X (1899), 185–211; "A page of Indian history: the Wiscasset tragedy," Maine Hist. Soc. *Coll.*, 2nd ser., X (1899), 81–103.

NOLAN LAMARQUE, CHARLES, merchant; b. 25 Nov. 1694 in Montreal, son of Jean-Baptiste Nolan, a merchant, and Marie-Anne de La Marque; d. 5 Oct. 1754 in Montreal.

Like many other men enlisted to go to the west, Charles Nolan added to his patronymic his mother's name, which he wrote in a single word and without the nobiliary particle. In 1717 Nolan Lamarque was enlisted by Alphonse Tonty*, whose second wife was Nolan's mother, and

went to Fort Pontchartrain (Detroit) for three years. Once his enlistment was over, he in turn launched into the fur trade and equipped numerous traders with articles of trade. He also hired for himself or his partners more than 100 "boatmen-voyageurs" for the west during his career.

Nolan Lamarque wanted to ensure solid foundations for his commercial enterprise and went into partnership on 28 Sept. 1726 with Antoine Pascaud Jr [*see* Antoine Pascaud*] of La Rochelle; on 28 May 1732 he renewed this agreement. Each partner invested in the company a sum of 32,600 *livres*. But Nolan Lamarque neglected to present a balance sheet and to pay in the revenues from the company's operations, and on 4 June 1735 his partner named Denis Goguet, a Quebec merchant, as his special procurator to annul the deed of partnership and to draw up a financial report. The inquiry, conducted by Goguet, revealed that a profit of 107,004 *livres* 14 *sols* had been realized and that the sum of 82,102 *livres* 7 *sols* was due Pascaud. In order to settle the matter out of court and to compensate Nolan Lamarque for the difficulties he had incurred, Goguet consented to reduce the debt by 11,102 *livres* 7 *sols*. A balance remained due of 71,000 *livres*, payable in four unequal instalments.

In the desire once more to put his business, which had become mediocre, on a sound footing, Nolan Lamarque founded a new company on 21 April 1738 with his brother, Jean-Marie Nolan, Jean-Baptiste Legras, and Ignace Gamelin* Jr. The company obtained from Pierre GAULTIER de Varennes et de La Vérendrye "all the trade in the west," in return for 1,000 *livres* in cash per year. On 9 Oct. 1738 Nolan Lamarque joined La Vérendrye at Fort La Reine (Portage la Prairie, Man.), and on 16 October he went with the explorer into the Mandan country. At the beginning of February Nolan Lamarque was back at Fort La Reine, and at the end of the month he reached Fort Maurepas, on the Red River, where he waited in vain until 23 April for a party of Indians in several canoes laden with furs; he then went to the Rivière Ouinipigon (Winnipeg River) to intercept them and prevent them from going to Hudson Bay to sell their peltries to the English. Not having succeeded as he had hoped, Nolan Lamarque returned to Montreal. The company was dissolved in 1741.

The following year his wife, Marie-Anne Legardeur de Saint-Pierre, whom he had married in Montreal on 28 Jan. 1727, died. He did not remarry, and continued his activities as a "merchant-outfitter" and silent partner until his death, which occurred on 5 Oct. 1754 in his house

Normant

built in 1730 on Rue Saint-Paul. Nolan Lamarque still owed Antoine Pascaud the sum of 59,644 *livres* 14 *sols.*

YVES QUESNEL

ANQ-M, Greffe de C.-R. Gaudron de Chevremont, 6 juill. 1736; Greffe de Michel Lepailleur, 27 janv. 1727; Greffe de J.-C. Porlier, 21 avril 1738; Greffe de J.-C. Raimbault, 9 mai 1730; Registre d'état civil, Notre-Dame de Montréal, 25 nov. 1694, 28 janv. 1727, 6 oct. 1754. "Aveu et dénombrement pour l'île de Montréal," APQ *Rapport, 1941–42,* 89. PAC *Report, 1905,* I, xxxix. Massicotte, "Répertoire des engagements pour l'Ouest," APQ *Rapport, 1929–30.* Tanguay, *Dictionnaire.* Champagne, *Les La Vérendrye.* Antoine d'Eschambault, "Le voyage de La Vérendrye au pays des Mandannes," *RHAF,* II (1948–49), 424–31.

NORMANT DU FARADON, LOUIS, priest, Sulpician, bursar, director, and superior of the Sulpician seminary in Montreal, vicar general; b. 18 May 1681 at Châteaubriant, France, son of Charles Normant, a doctor, and Marie Legrand, Dame Du Faradon; d. 18 June 1759 in Montreal.

After completing his secondary education in Nantes, France, Louis Normant Du Faradon studied theology at the Sulpician seminary in Angers and was admitted into the Society of Saint-Sulpice in Paris on 2 Nov. 1706. At first he was entrusted with various important posts in the administration of the order, including the office of bursar of the seminary of Paris. In 1722 Normant insisted on going to Canada, and the superior general, François Lechassier, consented all the more willingly because François Vachon* de Belmont, the superior in Montreal, was elderly and Normant possessed the qualities required to assist him. Consequently, shortly after his arrival in Montreal, he was appointed bursar and director (vice-superior) of the Society of Saint-Sulpice in Canada.

The new bursar's early years in Montreal were distinguished by two events. On 25 Feb. 1725, provided with a procuration from the Sulpician seminary in Paris, the seigneur and owner of Montreal Island and Saint-Sulpice, Normant Du Faradon took the oath of fealty and homage to the governor general, Philippe de Rigaud* de Vaudreuil, in Quebec. Later, on 1 Sept. 1731, he appeared before the intendant, Hocquart*, to present the recognition of sovereignty and census for these two seigneuries, an important document for the history of Montreal Island.

Upon Vachon de Belmont's death on 22 May 1732, Normant Du Faradon became superior of the seminary of Montreal. Shortly afterwards he had to take up the difficult problem of the efficient operation and upkeep of the Hôpital Général of Montreal, founded in 1692 by the Brothers Hos-

pitallers of the Cross and of St Joseph [*see* François Charon* de La Barre]. Around 1735 this community, with serious financial difficulties and short of personnel, was in danger of disappearing. In 1747 the Charon Brothers ran out of money and gave their resignation [*see* Jean JEANTOT]. The superior of the Sulpicians had long foreseen this outcome and in anticipation had already prepared successors for the Charon Brothers. He suggested to the authorities of the colony that they be replaced by the Grey Nuns.

M. Normant had taken an active part in the founding of this new institution by Marie-Marguerite d'Youville, *née* Dufrost* de Lajemmerais, in 1738. He had encouraged the foundress to devote herself to the service of the poor and the ill. After the sisters had settled into a house near the church of Notre-Dame with a few poor persons, he visited them frequently, encouraged them to persevere, even drew up for them a set of rules which form the basis of the constitutions of the Grey Nuns. The superior believed that the new community offered sufficient guarantees to enable it to take over management of the Hôpital Général. But Governor Charles de BEAUHARNOIS, Bishop Pontbriand [DUBREIL], and Intendant Hocquart were less convinced. At first they opposed the superior's project, but subsequently they were obliged by circumstances to agree in 1747 to entrust the management of the hospital temporarily to Mme d'Youville and her nuns.

The experiment was, however, short-lived, for in 1750 Intendant Bigot*, with Bishop Pontbriand and Governor La Jonquière [TAFFANEL], issued an ordinance suppressing the institution and transferring all its belongings to the nuns of the Hôpital Général of Quebec. The Sulpician then began to intervene more frequently and more insistently. Foreseeing even before the ordinance appeared a disadvantageous resolution, Normant Du Faradon had drawn up a petition, signed by the Grey Nuns, in which he pointed out to the authorities the considerable harm that the suppression of the Hôpital Général would cause the inhabitants of Montreal. After Bigot's ordinance, Normant, in view of the citizens' increasing discontent, took the initiative of sending in their name a supplication to Rouillé, the minister of Marine. At the same time he made the whole affair known to the superior general of the Society of Saint-Sulpice, Jean Couturier, who had great influence at the court of France. Thanks to these several measures Normant finally obtained the most favourable solution that could be hoped for. In 1753 Louis XV put Mme d'Youville by letters patent back in possession of the Hôpital

Général and gave final approval to the community that she had founded.

Normant Du Faradon's activity was not limited to the town of Montreal. As representative of the superior general in Paris, he was responsible for the administration of all domains owned by the seminary of Saint-Sulpice in Canada, which included three seigneuries: Montreal Island, Saint-Sulpice, and Lac-des-Deux-Montagnes. In 1735 the Sulpicians obtained at M. Normant's request an increase in the last-named seigneury by more than half, so that the Indians at Lac-des-Deux-Montagnes would have a larger hunting region. In that same year the Sulpicians increased their domain by accepting half of the fiefs of Saint-Herman and Bourgchemin, which Bishop Dosquet*, a former Sulpician, had given them before his final departure for France. These fiefs were located south of the seigneury of Sorel, on both sides of the Rivière Yamaska. The wars at the end of the French régime prevented settlers from being established on these lands and those at Lac-des-Deux-Montagnes, but Normant Du Faradon did succeed in developing almost the whole of the seigneuries of Saint-Sulpice and Montreal Island.

In 1726 Bishop Saint-Vallier [La Croix*] had appointed Normant Du Faradon vicar general for the region of Montreal; Bishop Dosquet had confirmed him in this office in 1729 and named him administrator of the diocese of Quebec during his long absences, from 1732 to 1733 and from 1735 to 1739. During the second period the Sulpician carried out certain functions that normally rested with the bishop. Thus in 1738 and 1739 he made canonical visits in the parishes of Saint-Pierre-de-Sorel and La Visitation-de-l'île-Dupas, in Saint-Charles-de-Lachenaie, where he arranged a rebuilding of the presbytery, in Sainte-Trinité-de-Contrecœur and in Saint-Joseph-de-Chambly, where he ordered that the churches be rebuilt, and in Pointe-Olivier (Saint-Mathias), where he had a chapel built.

On 20 Aug. 1740, the day of Bishop Pourroy* de Lauberivière's death, the chapter of Quebec took upon itself not to renew Normant Du Faradon's appointment as vicar general. But a year later Bishop Pontbriand re-established him in his functions, which he exercised until 1759. During this second term of office Normant Du Faradon gave his attention especially to building churches. The religious edifices in the Montreal region needed to be renovated as a result of the increase in population and the progress in colonization over 30 years. The number of settlers and the area of cleared land had more than doubled. Old buildings that had become inadequate had to

be enlarged or demolished and replaced with larger ones. Moreover, the newly cleared lands were generally in the rear of the old seigneuries, far from the churches, which were usually at the opposite end, on the waterways; the churches had become virtually inaccessible to the settlers, who asked that new parishes be created. Bishop Pontbriand noted this problem at the time of his first pastoral visit in 1742, and he issued several ordinances calling upon the parishioners to renovate or enlarge their churches. Afterwards it was the vicar general's job to carry out the ordinances, if necessary choose the sites of the new buildings, approve the architects' plans, find means of providing for the upkeep of the parish priests, and dedicate the new places of worship.

This was no new task for the Sulpician. In the period 1729–40 he had superintended the building of several churches: Notre-Dame-de-Lorette at Lac des Deux-Montagnes, Saint-Louis-de-Terrebonne at Saint-Laurent, Montreal Island, Saint-Denis (Saint-Denis-sur-Richelieu), Saint-Joseph-de-Chambly, Pointe-Olivier, and the presbytery and chapel of Sainte-Geneviève-de-Pierrefonds. In 1742 the vicar general superintended the building of two churches on Île Jésus: Saint-Vincent-de-Paul and Sainte-Rose. In 1744 the parishes of Saint-Constant and Saint-Philippe were created deep in the seigneury of Laprairie, and Bishop Pontbriand directed the parishioners to obtain the approval of his vicar general for two churches, which were built in 1749 and 1751. Finally, during the pastoral visit of 1749, the bishop ordered four churches to be rebuilt in stone, all of them situated on the domain of the seminary of Saint-Sulpice: Saint-Joachim-de-la-Pointe-Claire, La Visitation du Sault-au-Récollet, Saint-Pierre-du-Portage-de-L'Assomption, and Sainte-Geneviève-de-Pierrefonds. These many and varied works, carried out under the ultimate direction of Louis Normant Du Faradon, suffice to justify his title of church-builder.

In 1753 the superior was stricken with a serious illness from which he never recovered fully and which forced him to give up some of his occupations. To help him he called upon Étienne Montgolfier*, whom he had already begun to initiate into the affairs of the seigneuries, and on 21 Jan. 1759, some months before his death on 18 June, he entrusted all the administration to him, resigning in his favour.

With Louis Normant Du Faradon the seminary of Montreal lost one of its most remarkable superiors. A man of learning and virtue, endowed with sound judgement, he distinguished himself above all by the extent of his knowledge of civil and ecclesiastical law, which enabled him to direct the temporal affairs of Saint-Sulpice most efficiently.

ANTONIO DANSEREAU

AD, Loire-Atlantique (Nantes), État civil, Château-briant, 20 mai 1681. ASSM, Catalogue historique et chronologique des prêtres du séminaire de Montréal; Section des biographies; Section des concessions de terre et d'emplacement de l'île de Montréal; Section des titres de propriété du séminaire de Montréal. "Aveu et dénombrement pour l'île de Montréal," APQ Rapport, 1941–42, 3–163. Allaire, Dictionnaire. Le diocèse de Montréal à la fin du dix-neuvième siècle (Montréal, 1900). Gauthier, Sulpitiana. P.-G. Roy, Inv. concessions.

É.-J. Auclair, Sainte-Rose-de-Laval; notice historique sur les origines de la paroisse (Montréal, 1940). C.-P. Beaubien, Le Sault-au-Récollet; ses rapports avec les premiers temps de la colonie; mission-paroisse (Montréal, 1898). A.-L. Bertrand, Bibliothèque sulpicienne, ou histoire de la Compagnie de Saint-Sulpice (3v., Paris, 1900). Azarie Couillard-Després, Histoire de la seigneurie de Saint-Ours (2v., Montréal, 1915); Histoire de Sorel de ses origines à nos jours (Montréal, 1926). J.-U.-A. Demers, Histoire de Sainte-Rose, 1740–1947 (Montréal, 1947). René Desrochers, "Précis historique, deuxième centenaire de la paroisse Saint-Mathias," Souvenir des fêtes du deuxième centenaire de la paroisse Saint-Mathias (Montréal, 1939). [É.-M. Faillon], Vie de Mme d'Youville, fondatrice des Sœurs de la Charité de Villemarie dans l'île de Montréal, en Canada (Villemarie [Montréal], 1852). Gosselin, L'Église du Canada jusqu'à la conquête. Lemire-Marsolais et Lambert, Histoire de la Congrégation de Notre-Dame, III, IV, V. L.-P. Phaneuf, Historique de Saint-Mathias (Cahiers de la Société historique de la Vallée du Richelieu, V, Saint-Jean, Qué., 1955). Christian Roy, Histoire de L'Assomption (L'Assomption, Qué., 1967). Robert Rumilly, Histoire de Saint-Laurent (Montréal, 1969). Émile Salone, La colonisation de la Nouvelle-France; étude sur les origines de la nation canadienne française (Paris, 1906; réimp. Trois-Rivières, Qué., 1970). Trudel, L'Église canadienne. Jacques Viger, Archéologie religieuse du diocèse de Montréal, 1850 (Montréal, 1850). J.-J. Lefebvre, "Saint-Constant et Saint-Philippe de Laprairie, 1744–1946," SCHÉC Rapport, 1945–46, 125–58.

NORRIS, Sir JOHN, officer in the Royal Navy; b. 1670 or 1671; d. 13 or 14 June 1749, probably at Hemsted Park, Kent, England.

John Norris' parentage is unknown; he may have been of Irish ancestry. He entered the Royal Navy in 1680 as a captain's servant, and by August 1689 had been appointed a lieutenant in the *Edgar*, commanded by Admiral Sir Cloudesley Shovell, who had been his patron for several years and with whom he established a firm friendship. He was promoted post captain in 1690 and in May 1692 was present at the battle of La Hougue off the Pointe de Barfleur (dept. of Manche), France.

In April 1697, in command of the *Monk*, Norris was commissioned commander-in-chief in Newfoundland and commodore of a small squadron which was to embark the regiment of Colonel John Gibsone* from England and recapture the Newfoundland territories seized the previous winter by a French force led by Pierre Le Moyne* d'Iberville and Jacques Testard* de Montigny. On his arrival at St John's, Norris found the town abandoned by the French and laid waste. He landed seamen and soldiers to repair the fortifications. In July he received news of the presence off the Grand Banks of a powerful French fleet under Jean-Bernard-Louis Desjean de Pointis. Norris was eager to engage the French but the council – which would have included Gibsone and the engineer, Michael Richards* – overruled him and decided to remain on the defensive. His inaction brought him some criticism on his return to England in October, but he was absolved of all blame.

The peace of Ryswick was concluded in September 1697. Norris commanded the Newfoundland convoy again in 1698 and was able to report to the Board of Trade that good progress had been made in rebuilding the fortifications at St John's and that the fishing industry there was rapidly recovering. In May 1699 he married Elizabeth Aylmer, daughter of Admiral Matthew Aylmer.

Norris' subsequent career, greatly aided by Admiral Aylmer, was distinguished. He was knighted in 1705 and made admiral in 1709. "Foul-weather Jack," as he came to be called, commanded the Baltic squadron in 1715–16, 1719–21, and 1727, went to St Petersburg (Leningrad), Russia, in 1717 as a special envoy, and was a lord of the admiralty between 1718 and 1730. In 1735 he led a large squadron to Lisbon to support the Portuguese during a minor dispute between Portugal and Spain. From 1739 on he commanded the Channel fleet. In February 1744, shortly before the outbreak of war with France, he nearly caught the Brest squadron becalmed off Dungeness. He retired from active service in March, in part because of his disappointment over this failure.

Norris was a member of parliament, representing Rye and Portsmouth, from 1708 to 1749, and generally voted against government measures. He had 11 children, five of whom seem to have survived infancy. Two sons followed him in the naval service.

MICHAEL GODFREY

BM, Add. MSS, 28126–57 (Norris papers). PRO, Adm. 2/23. *Gentleman's Magazine*, 1749, p.284. G.B., Privy Council, *In the matter of the boundary between the*

Dominion of Canada and the colony of Newfoundland in the Labrador peninsula ... (12v., London, 1926–27), IV, 1800–6. PRO, *CSP, Col., 1696–97; 1697–98. The registers of St Paul's Church, Covent Garden, London*, ed. W. H. Hunt (5v., Pubs. of the Harleian Soc., [Registers], XXXIII–XXXVII, London, 1906–9), I, 112–81, *passim*. Charnock, *Biographia navalis*, II, 341–62. *DNB*. Sedgwick, *History of parliament*, II, 298. D. D. Aldridge, "Admiral Sir John Norris 1670 (or 1671)–1749: his birth and early service, his marriage and his death," *Mariner's Mirror* (Cambridge, Eng.), LI (1965), 173–83. G. Hinchliffe, "Some letters of Sir John Norris," *Mariner's Mirror*, LVI (1970), 77–84.

NORTON, RICHARD, overseas governor of the HBC; b. 1701; m. *c*. 1730 to Elizabeth McCliesh; d. October or November 1741. In his will, dated 17 Jan. 1734, Norton described himself as of Limehouse (now part of London), England, and gave his mother's name as Sarah.

Apprenticed to the HBC for seven years, Richard Norton arrived at York Fort (Fort Bourbon; now York Factory, Man.) in September 1714 and must have witnessed its restoration to the English by the French governor, Nicolas Jérémie*. Norton was with the advance party that left York in June 1717 for Churchill River, where governor James Knight* intended to establish a new post for trading with the distant Chipewyan or Northern Indians. A party of these Indians had already arrived to trade however and had turned homewards disappointed. Norton, an active, hardy lad, who much preferred outdoor life and Indian company to the study of writing and accounts, was sent after them on 18 July with orders to go, if necessary, "into thare own Country." Travelling with a Northern man and woman, he went north along the coast by canoe before going inland on foot. He caught up with about 12 or more of the tribe (including one who was later rewarded for caring for "the Boy Norton . . . when he was froze"), and they arrived back at Churchill during the winter of 1717–18 in a starving condition. Exactly where and how far he had travelled remains unknown. William Coats, who later questioned him about the journey, recorded during the 1740s that "I did not find anything remained on his memory, but the danger and terrour he underwent." In 1749, eight years after Norton's death, it was claimed that he had reached the Coppermine River, but the limited time he was absent from Churchill makes the assertion impossible. Arthur Dobbs' account of the journey, published in 1744, is nearer the truth in relating that Norton went north no farther than latitude 60°, and then struck inland to the southwest.

Norton served at Churchill under Richard Staunton (1718–22) and Nathaniel Bishop* (1722–23). His knowledge of the Northern Indian language was put to use in the fall of 1718 when Staunton sent him to Seal River, north of Churchill, to keep the peace between local Chipewyans and a hunting-party of Crees from Hayes River. In the spring of 1721 Norton made a trip inland, and later that year he and a Chipewyan accompanied Henry Kelsey* on a voyage to the north, their object being to find the source of the copper seen in the possession of the more distant Northern Indians who traded at Churchill. Norton went on a similar voyage with John Scroggs* the following year. Both voyages were unsuccessful, and evidence was found that Knight's ships, which had sailed from London in 1719 in search of copper and gold, had been wrecked.

When Bishop died in June 1723 Norton and Thomas Bird*, acting under instructions from Thomas McCliesh at York, took joint charge at Churchill. Later that year, on learning that the HBC had intended Norton to be chief trader under Bishop, McCliesh appointed him to the command of Fort Prince of Wales, the name given to the post on Churchill River in 1719. As a trader Norton was unsuccessful. He was unwilling to relinquish old, and less profitable, terms of barter previously used at Churchill, thereby causing McCliesh to write to London in 1725, "I wish that Mr Norton had more discretion in him in the management of your affairs." As the profits from Churchill remained unsatisfactory the HBC transferred Norton in 1727 to York where, as "second" to McCliesh, he could learn more about trading methods and accounts. In the following year he applied for reinstatement at Churchill, but his request was refused because Anthony Beale* was successfully putting affairs there into a better condition. So Norton remained at York, where he "behaved himself with honesty and fidelity" until he sailed for England in 1730. There he married McCliesh's daughter Elizabeth.

Norton returned to Hudson Bay in 1731 as chief factor and commander at Fort Prince of Wales, which was now independent "of the Governour of any other Factory." Thomas Bird, acting chief there following Beale's death earlier in the year, became Norton's deputy. Immediately on arrival Norton began preparatory work at Eskimo Point (about six miles below the existing wooden fort), where he had been ordered to build a stone fort "both for the advantage of the Compies. Trade as well as Defence" in the event of a war with France. Although the construction of this stone fort (originally designed by Captain

Nouchet

Christopher MIDDLETON and later modified by Captain George SPURRELL) occupied much of Norton's attention, the work was unfinished at the end of his career, and a great deal had to be rebuilt in the following decade. Norton, as the London committee knew, was without experience of such specialized work; nevertheless his unbounded self-confidence and eagerness to please his employers led him to reject the advice of the knowledgeable but arrogant stonemason Joseph ROBSON, and to use unsuitable materials as a means of expediting the building. Yet Norton's letters reporting the progress of operations show that during the season when outdoor work was possible there were never enough labourers or animals to assist the masons; and some of the latter, according to Robson, were without skill in, or experience of, the type of construction required of them.

By 1739 the London committee members had become critical of Norton's behaviour towards themselves and of his management of their affairs. In particular he was reprimanded for disregarding their orders and for flatly refusing to disclose his method of obtaining the "overplus," or profit, on the furs and other produce he traded. He angrily requested return home in 1740. The committee, obviously using his own expressions, replied, "We do assure you we had not no thoughts of Embracing the Service of Birds raired to pluck out your eyes, or of depriving you of your dependence by Employing those at Considerable less Wages who thought they were Equally Capable of Serving the Company," but reminded him that he would suffer financially if he broke his contract. So he remained at Churchill until 1741 when he was succeeded by James ISHAM. Norton, now a sick man, arrived in the Thames early in October and died before 9 November, when his will was proved. A half-breed son Moses* later commanded at Churchill.

ALICE M. JOHNSON

[Norton's surviving letters to the London governor and committee are printed in HBRS, XXV (Davies and Johnson), which also lists the pertinent sources in the HBC Archives. Brief extracts from correspondence between the governor and committee and Norton are printed in G.B., Parl., *Report from the committee on Hudson's Bay*, 271–72. For background information *see* Rich, *History of the HBC*, I.

The only contemporary references to Norton's journey of 1717 are in [James Knight], *The founding of Churchill* . . . , ed. J. F. Kenney (London, 1932), and in the Churchill account book for trading season 1717–18, HBC Arch. B.42/d/1, f.2d. Arthur Dobbs' account of the journey is in his *Remarks upon Middleton's defence*, 25.

Norton's part in the 1721 voyage to the north of Churchill is briefly referred to by Henry Kelsey in *The Kelsey papers*, ed. A. G. Doughty and Chester Martin (Ottawa, 1929), 116. The Churchill journal entry for 19 June 1722 (HBC Arch. B.42/a/2) states that Norton accompanied Scroggs on the 1722 voyage northwards. For background information on these and later voyages northwards of Churchill, *see* Williams, *British search for the northwest passage*.

Norton's "plan of The Work That was Done att The New Fort on Askimay Point att Churchill River . . ." dated 18 Aug. 1735 is in HBC Arch. G.1/88. As Norton was in England in 1735 and 1736 and had retired in 1741, all mentions of "the governor" in Joseph Robson's *An account of six years residence in Hudson's-Bay, from 1733 to 1736, and 1744 to 1747* . . . (London, 1752) should not be taken as references to Norton.

Norton's will dated 17 Jan. 1734 and proved 9 Nov. 1741 is in PRO, Prob. 11/713, f.314. Moses Norton's will is in Prob. 11/994, f.374. A.M.J.]

NOUCHET, JOSEPH, controller and later director of the Domaine d'Occident in Canada, merchant; b. 1690 in the parish of Saint-Vincent du Lude (dept. of Sarthe), France, son of Julien Nouchet and Barbe Barrat; d. 27 Sept. 1750 in Quebec.

The circumstances of Joseph Nouchet's arrival in Canada are not known; in August 1723 he was exercising there the functions of controller of the farms of the Domaine du Roi (Domaine d'Occident). His reputation as a "diligent man, assiduous in his work" caused him to be chosen on 16 Aug. 1742 by the intendant, Hocquart*, to replace his friend François-Étienne CUGNET as receiver of dues (director) for the Domaine d'Occident. The latter had been relieved of his duties for having borrowed from the funds of the Domaine to finance his operation of the Saint-Maurice ironworks. The receiver's duties consisted of "receiving import and export duties, domanial and seigneurial dues, and other taxes payable to the Domaine"; he was then required to enter them in one of the six registers of receipts which were entrusted to him for this purpose. To carry out these functions Nouchet received the considerable salary of 2,000 *livres* annually. As a member of the administrative élite, one of the highly placed officials of the time, and a merchant, Joseph Nouchet carried on business dealings with the ruling group in Quebec society. He was also the churchwarden in charge of the parish council of Notre-Dame de Québec in 1743.

On 7 Aug. 1723 Joseph Nouchet had married Geneviève, "a minor 15 years of age," whose father, a Quebec merchant, was Jean Gatin. By this marriage he had a son, JOSEPH-ÉTIENNE.

ANDRÉ LACHANCE

AN, Col., C[11A], 114, ff.144v, 233, 234; 115, ff.105v, 216; 120, f.230; 122, ff.225v–26. ANQ, Greffe de Jacques Barbel, 7 août 1723; Greffe de J.-C. Louet, 23 déc. 1728; AP, Timothée Provost, 14 mai 1743. *Documents relating to Canadian currency during the French régime* (Shortt), I, 544, 546, 566, 568. P.-G. Roy, *Inv. jug. et délib., 1717–1760*, III, 203; V, 48–49, 238–39; VI, 56, 79, 90. Tanguay, *Dictionnaire*, VI, 165.

NOUCHET, JOSEPH-ÉTIENNE, councillor of the Conseil Supérieur, director of the Domaine d'Occident, commissary of prisons; b. 7 July 1724 at Quebec, son of Joseph NOUCHET and Geneviève Gatin; d. 3 Feb. 1758 in Quebec.

Like his father, Joseph-Étienne Nouchet chose a career in the administration. Even while attending the law lectures given by the king's attorney general, Louis-Guillaume VERRIER, he was writer in the office of the administration in Quebec in 1744 and 1745. His assiduity at Verrier's lectures resulted in his appointment on 3 Dec. 1746 by the colonial authorities as assessor to the Conseil Supérieur. For three and a half years he prepared the documents on certain lawsuits for the councillors and investigated and reported on other cases. After the death of Eustache CHARTIER de Lotbinière the king promoted Joseph-Étienne councillor on 1 June 1750. On 27 September of the same year, the day his father died, he took his place as director of the Domaine d'Occident. Because he was well informed about the rules of protocol, he was on a few occasions "delegated" by his colleagues of the Conseil Supérieur to congratulate the new governor general "on his safe arrival in New France" or to lead the delegation of the council at an official meeting. On 26 Jan. 1756 Nouchet was appointed by the Conseil Supérieur commissary of the king's prisons in succession to Joseph Perthuis* de La Salle; on 15 November of that year, when his commission came to an end, he was replaced by Jacques IMBERT.

On 8 Feb. 1747 Joseph-Étienne Nouchet had married Louise-Catherine, daughter of François FOUCAULT, chief writer in the Marine and a member of the Conseil Supérieur. Nouchet died 3 Feb. 1758 and was buried the next day in the crypt of the church of Notre-Dame de Québec, which was a signal privilege for the period.

ANDRÉ LACHANCE

AN, Col., C[11A], 114, ff.144v, 233, 234; 115, ff.105v, 216; 120, f.230; 122, ff.225v–26. ANQ, Greffe de R.-C. Barolet, 1er févr. 1747; NF, Coll. de pièces jud. et not., 2114. P.-V. Charland, "Notre-Dame de Québec: le nécrologe de la crypte," *BRH*, XX (1914), 238. P.-G. Roy, *Inv. jug. et délib., 1717–1760*, VI, 289–92. Tanguay, *Dictionnaire*, VI, 165. P.-G. Roy, "La bibliothèque de Joseph-Étienne Nouchet, conseiller au Conseil supérieur," *BRH*, XXIV (1918), 285–88.

NOV DOGG AW WER IMET. *See* NODOGA-WERRIMET

NOYAN, PIERRE-BENOÎT PAYEN DE. *See* PAYEN

NOYELLES DE FLEURIMONT, NICOLAS-JOSEPH DE, officer in the colonial regular troops in Canada; b. 13 Oct. 1695 in Quimper, France, son of Pierre-Philippe de Noyelles, Baron de Fleurimont, and Marie Bridou; d. 16 Aug. 1761 at Rochefort, France.

Nicolas-Joseph de Noyelles was born into a cadet branch of an old and illustrious noble house of Artois. His father was a colonel in a French cavalry regiment and knight of the ancient order of Saint-Esprit de Montpellier. The Noyelles were related to Henri-François d'Aguesseau, the powerful chancellor, who took a lively interest in their fortunes in Canada. Perhaps this helps explain Governor Charles de BEAUHARNOIS's favours to Nicolas-Joseph and his sons.

The controversial military career of Nicolas-Joseph in Canada began when he arrived as ensign in 1710, not yet 15 years of age. Posted to Montreal, where he made his home, in 1718 he married Marie-Charlotte, daughter of Charles Petit* de Levilliers, and related to many of the colonial nobility. After serving as interim commander of Detroit in 1720, Noyelles was promoted lieutenant in 1721. In 1725 he was second in command under Jacques-Charles Renaud* Dubuisson at a post among the Miamis (at or near Fort Wayne, Ind.), and after that year commanded it until 1732. He entered into the fur trade there in partnership with Louis Marin, borrowing over 14,000 *livres* from a Montreal merchant, Pierre de LESTAGE, in 1726 and 1727.

In 1730, leading 40 French and some 600 Miamis, Weas, and Piankeshaws, Noyelles joined Nicolas-Antoine Coulon* de Villiers, commander at Fort Saint-Joseph (probably Niles, Mich.), and Robert Groston* de Saint-Ange, commander of Fort de Chartres (near Prairie du Rocher, Ill.), in a campaign against the Foxes who were continuing war against the French allies in the west. Heavy losses in killed and captured were inflicted on the Foxes, who were thus foiled in their attempt to seek asylum among the Iroquois. For his contribution to the expedition, described by Beauharnois as until then "the most complete military engagement" in New France under Louis XV, Nicolas-Joseph was awarded an expectancy of a captaincy, which

Noyelles

he obtained in 1733. In 1734 he assisted his successor at the Miami post, Jean-Charles d'ARNAUD, to resettle Miamis who had migrated closer to the English.

Immediately after this assignment Nicolas-Joseph was given charge of the last major campaign against the irrepressible Foxes. Leaving Montreal in October 1734, he led his party *via* Detroit and the Miamis from whom he hoped to muster reinforcements. After delays and fruitless wandering through the snow-bound forests, without adequate food supplies, he stumbled upon the Fox villages only to find them far stronger than anticipated. His force had also been reduced by the defection of many Hurons and mission Iroquois, who had taken exception to Beauharnois's orders to pardon the Sauks if they would abandon their Fox allies. After a chaotic engagement Noyelles had to come to terms. With a weak promise from the Sauks to abandon the Foxes and settle at Baie-des-Puants (Green Bay, Wis.), he withdrew. The governor blamed the fiasco on the fickleness of the Indian allies and argued that more French troops would obviate dependence upon them. The minister, Maurepas, however, listened to other reports blaming Noyelles for inept management of the Indian allies.

The minister therefore greeted with sharp disapproval Beauharnois's choice of Noyelles to command at Detroit beginning in 1736. It was the Hurons of Detroit that he had found so difficult to manage on the Fox campaign. But the governor persisted, and the minister grudgingly assented. His own candidate had been Pierre-Jacques Payen* de Noyan, whom Beauharnois passed over.

At Detroit Noyelles was confronted with an Ottawa-Huron feud which threatened to ignite an Indian war in the west. English trade and diplomacy had wooed the Hurons into alliance with the Senecas and a peace treaty with the Flatheads to the south. In the spring of 1738 a raiding party of Ottawas from Detroit were ambushed by Flatheads, forewarned by Hurons [*see* Armand de LA RICHARDIE]. Incensed, the Ottawas laid accusations at Detroit against the Hurons, who sought aid from the Iroquois and the Canadian missions. The Ottawas turned to their allies of the west. At Detroit, Noyelles forbade trade in arms to all Indians, and with generous gifts he managed to establish an uneasy truce. But the Hurons no longer felt safe at Detroit, and, after considering joining the mission Indians at Sault-Saint-Louis (Caughnawaga, Que.) or at Lac-des-Deux-Montagnes (Oka, Que.), some of them finally settled at Sandoské (Sandusky) on the southwest shore of Lake Erie. When Noyelles left Detroit in 1740 it was calm, though the seed of future conflict had been planted. The minister, perhaps influenced by Payen de Noyan's complaints, put this crisis down to lack of respect for Noyelles among the tribes.

Beauharnois's favours seemed limitless. When in 1744 Pierre GAULTIER de Varennes et de La Vérendrye, uncle of Mme de Noyelles, lost the privilege to exploit the fur trade while exploring a route to the western sea, the governor granted it to Noyelles. The latter too soon learned with his associates the hindrances to trade: warfare between the far western tribes and the Sioux, scarcity and high cost of trade goods during the War of the Austrian Succession, and high overhead in transporting furs and merchandise over long distances. He concluded that further search for the western sea was futile. In 1746 Noyelles submitted his resignation; it was accepted the following year by the minister, who was convinced that Noyelles had neglected exploration for trade even more single-mindedly than his predecessor.

Noyelles had returned to Quebec in 1747, the year Beauharnois declared war against the Mohawks who were raiding the outlying settlements of Montreal to take advantage of New France's weakness during the war. Noyelles led a force of French and Indians to Lac Saint-François in an attempt to intercept their raiding parties. He seems to have served on no other campaigns, and was awarded the cross of Saint-Louis in 1749 after repeated recommendations by Beauharnois. He was promoted town major of Trois-Rivières in 1751 and king's lieutenant in 1759. After the conquest he returned to France with his family, except for one son, and died in Rochefort, 16 Aug. 1761. His widow, who claimed to be destitute and unable even to bury him, received a pension of 600 *livres*. His death seems to have ended an inquiry into his integrity which for some reason had been begun in 1760.

Nicolas-Joseph had eight children. The eldest son, Charles-Joseph, served in the colonial regular troops; he fought against the Chickasaws in 1739 and at Michilimackinac, 1745–47, and commanded at Fort Rouillé (Toronto), 1754–57. A younger son, Pierre-Philippe, also served in the regular troops in Canada. A report to the minister dated June 1763 refers to a "Sieur Noyelles Fleurimont" convicted of stealing military funds. If this is Pierre-Philippe, the incident may explain why he alone remained in Canada after the conquest.

S. DALE STANDEN

AN, Col., B, 63, f.466v; 64, ff.430–30v, 441v–42, 446v; 65, ff.407–8, 415v; 70, f.342v; C¹¹A, 61, ff.86–89; 63, ff.226–32v, 236–45v; 64, ff.162v–66; 65, ff.142–49; 66, ff.150v–53v; 67, f.171; 69, ff.125–30v; 70, ff.117–19, 188–95; 71, ff.103–4; 74, ff.3v, 81v–84; D²ᶜ, 49/5, pt.3, p.437; 49/6, pt.3, pp.480–85; 59, p.4 (PAC transcripts); Marine, C⁷, 228. ANQ, AP, Famille de Noyelles. Champagne, *Les La Vérendrye*, 319–23. Kellogg, *French régime*, 314–41. L.-A. Prud'homme, "Les successeurs de La Vérendrye sous la domination française," *RSCT*, 2nd ser., XII (1906), sect.I, 65–68.

NOYON, JACQUES DE, voyageur, coureur de bois, sergeant in the colonial regular troops; b. 12 Feb. 1668 in Trois-Rivières, second son of Jean de Noyon, master edge-tool maker, and Marie Chauvin; m. 1704 to Abigail Stebbins at Deerfield, Massachusetts; d. 12 May 1745 in Boucherville (Que.).

Jacques de Noyon first comes to our attention at age 20. In 1688 he led a trading party from Fort Nipigon (built on the lake of that name by Daniel Greysolon* Dulhut four years before) up the Kaministikwia River and across Dog Lake to Rainy Lake where he wintered among the Assiniboins. He had penetrated farther west than any previous Frenchman. His trip home in 1689 was marred by the accidental drowning of a man named Lacroix and two other men in a lake later called Lac Sainte-Croix.

In 1690 Noyon was hired by François Charon* de La Barre to travel west with Gilles Papin, Charon's *commis*, to collect a debt from Nicolas Perrot*. Noyon earned 200 *livres* a year for the duration of this assignment, and was allowed to trade on his own account. In 1693, with an outstanding bill of 118*livres* at Louis Marchand's inn in Quebec and a loan of almost 200 *livres* from Charles Macard*, he left for the Ottawa country (probably the Michigan peninsula) in a party of voyageurs headed by Pierre-Charles Le Sueur*. Noyon went west again two years later, this time with 150 *livres* credit from Charles Aubert* de La Chesnaye.

On 2 Jan. 1698, perhaps still celebrating the arrival of the new year, the slightly drunk Noyon exchanged insults in Boucherville with Gilles Papin, now a merchant. In the ensuing *mêlée* Papin drew his sword. The outcome of Noyon's complaint to the Montreal tribunal the following day was that certain goods belonging to Noyon were removed from Papin's house by Charles de Couagne*, probably to settle Noyon's unpaid 1688 account.

Most western traders established a credit rating with one merchant and patronized him year after year, but Noyon's mismanagement of credit had been such that he was unable to borrow from the same merchant twice. By 1700 he appears to have been swamped with debts. In that year,

Noyon and Louis Gosselin offered their services to the governor of New York, Lord Bellomont, promising that 52 comrades, 10 or 12 Ottawa chiefs, and furs would be brought to Albany within one year. All they wished in return was permission to live and trade in Albany. Although Noyon did settle in New England, his evasion did not last long. In 1704, the Reverend John Williams* married him to Abigail Stebbins in Deerfield. Two weeks later Williams, the entire Stebbins family, and the bride and groom were among the captives taken by Jean-Baptiste Hertel* de Rouville in a raid against Deerfield.

This all-expenses-paid honeymoon was an event Noyon would have gladly missed. He returned to Canada to face unpaid bills with a wife to support. Abigail, referred to in Montreal notarial deeds as "Marguerite Stebens," had greater cause for disappointment, however; not only was she in a foreign country with which her people were at war, but her husband had described himself to her family as the owner of substantial property and a man of considerable means.

When back in Canada Noyon may have written a narrative about his 1688 westward journey which is mentioned in several documents, for while in New England he had learned to write. Within a few months of his return to the colony he borrowed over 100 *livres* from a new creditor, Jean-Baptiste Crevier Duvernay, and set out for Fort Pontchartain (Detroit) in a party of 64 *engagés*. Noyon apparently made a sincere effort to mend his ways, for by 1708 he had found more stable employment. He had become a sergeant – the highest non-commissioned rank in the colonial regular troops – in the company of Alphonse Tonty* with a net monthly salary of 15 *livres* 2 *sols* 5 *deniers*. This was insufficient, however, to placate his creditors and support a family. His total movable property in 1708 was less than 400 *livres*, and Marguerite had to rely on charity for assistance in raising her children. As a result the Noyons were declared separate as to property in July, and in August Marguerite bought a modest house and property in Boucherville. In 1719 she was able to visit her relatives in England.

The Noyons had at least 13 children between 1704 and 1726. The Danio families in Massachusetts today may trace their ancestry to Jacques-René de Noyon (spelt "Danio" in the registration of his parents' marriage), eldest son of Jacques and Marguerite, who was sent to his grandparents in Deerfield in 1714.

On 26 April 1742, 17 months after the death of his wife, Jacques de Noyon bequeathed his few resources to his children since he was no longer able to work his land. He moved in with his daughter Marie and son-in-law Louis Renaud, and here he spent his last three years, supported by a 200-*livre* life annuity from his children.

Was Noyon's indebtedness typical of most voyageurs? Were the coureurs de bois who transferred their allegiance to Louisiana or New England simply adventurers, were they greedy, or were they hopelessly in debt? These and other questions raised by Noyon's experiences may remain unanswered because of inadequate documentation.

C. J. RUSS

AN, Col., C^{11A}, 6, f.301. ANQ-M, Greffe d'Antoine Adhémar, 13 mai 1688, 21 janv., 12 sept. 1693, 31 juill. 1704; Greffe de Marien Tailhandier, dit La Beaume, 10 juill. 1708, 10 avril 1713, 11 avril 1716, 30 nov. 1717, 20 août 1719. ANQ, Greffe de Louis Chambalon, 29 oct. 1695. *NYCD* (O'Callaghan and Fernow), IV, 782, 797. Tanguay, *Dictionnaire*. Champagne, *Les La Vérendrye*, 21, 40. Coleman, *New England captives*. N. M. Crouse, *La Verendrye, fur trader and explorer* (Toronto and Ithaca, N.Y., 1956). C. J. Russ, "Les troupes de la marine, 1683–1713" (unpublished MA thesis, McGill University, Montreal, 1971). Jean Delanglez, "A mirage: the sea of the west," *RHAF*, I (1947–48), 346–81. É.-Z. Massicotte, "Jacques de Noyon: nouveaux détails sur sa carrière," *BRH*, XLVIII (1942), 121–25. Benjamin Sulte, "Jacques de Noyon," *BRH*, XIV (1908), 183–85; "Le lac Lacroix," *BRH*, XXII (1916), 350.

O

OLD BELT. *See* KAGHSWAGHTANIUNT

OLIVIER (Ollivier, Halevear), ABEL (sometimes identified as **Olivier Abel)**, navigator; b. probably in 1683, perhaps in London, England; d. 29 May 1768 at Quebec.

An Englishman, Abel Olivier may have been among the many prisoners who were carried into New France during the War of the Spanish Succession and elected to remain. In 1731 he was described as an English gentleman from Boston and a good Catholic, and credited with 19 years' residence in the colony. Soon after the war, around 1717, Olivier had begun sailing in colonial ships between Quebec, the West Indies, and Bordeaux. During the 1720s he became involved in several suits for unpaid wages owed by local shipowners. As late as 1750 he appears as a ship's captain in command of a colonial vessel.

On 14 Nov. 1718, Olivier had married at Quebec a widow, Marie-Madeleine Lefebvre; their one child died before reaching maturity. In his marriage contract, dated 6 November, Olivier described himself as the son of François Olivier, merchant, and Marie Castille, "of the city of London in old England." Ten years later he acquired land along the Rivière Saint-Charles in the seigneury of Saint-Ignace and in 1730 a lot at Pointe-aux-Lièvres on Rue Saint-Roch. Although his name continued to appear in the records as a ship's captain, thereafter Olivier seems to have settled into semi-retirement. He received his naturalization papers in 1732, and in 1744 was still living on Rue Saint-Roch.

After the conquest, he was named in the *affaire du Canada* owing to an agreement that he had once made with François Bigot*, but Olivier, who was nearly 75 when it was made, had been merely a front for others. He died on 29 May 1768, aged 85 years, predeceasing his 91-year-old wife by a single day. Both were buried on 31 May. By his will he had left his belongings to his wife's daughter, Marie-Madeleine Minet, in return for moneys advanced and the care given to him and his spouse in their old age.

Abel Olivier's career reflects, perhaps, the kind of social mobility in New France that permitted a foreign sailor to end his days as a modest landowner.

JAMES S. PRITCHARD

AD, Gironde (Bordeaux), 6B, 92, ff.56v, 88v; 313; 373. AN, Col., C^{8A}, 35, f.6; C^{8B}, 20, 21; C^{11A}, 52, ff.301–3v, 304–6v; 54, f.140; 60, f.96v; 61, f.73v; 73, f.410; 76, ff.122–23; 114, f.251; F^{2B}, 11. "Recensement de Québec, 1744" (APQ *Rapport*). "Recensement du gouvernement de Québec, 1762" (APQ *Rapport*). P.-G. Roy, *Inv. contrats de mariage*, IV, 89–90; *Inv. ins. Cons. souv.*, 194; *Inv. ins. Prév. Québec*, II, 246; *Inv. jug. et délib., 1717–1760*, I, 187, 323; II, 111, 290; III, 8, 218, 231. Tanguay, *Dictionnaire*, I, 1; VI, 167. P.-G. Roy, *Bigot et sa bande*, 244–45; "Le sieur Abel Olivier," *BRH*, XL (1934), 224–26.

ONKISWATHETAMI. *See* SWATANA

ONONWAROGO (Red Head), a chief warrior of the Onondagas; son of KAKꙞENTHIONY, who was also known as Red Head; d. 24 June 1764 at Oswego (Chouaguen).

Historical records first mention Ononwarogo in 1751, when he instigated the migration of a number of Onondagas to François Picquet*'s mission of La Présentation (Oswegatchie, now Ogdensburg, N.Y.). Ononwarogo seems to have been an active French partisan until the early stages of the Seven Years' War in America. About 1755 he threw in his lot with the British, but he was for some time suspected of being a French agent. By 1757, however, he was carrying regular intelligence reports on French movements to Sir William Johnson*, the British superintendent of northern Indians, and was apparently trusted enough to be dispatched on missions important to British interests.

Ononwarogo recruited Indians to accompany Lieutenant-Colonel John Bradstreet* against Fort Frontenac (now Kingston, Ont.) in the summer of 1758, and distinguished himself by his bravery during the attack. Later in the summer he took part in scouting expeditions around La Présentation, which was still held by the French, and as a delegate from Onondaga he attended a conference at Easton, Pennsylvania, in the fall.

The fact that Johnson provided him with clothing, money, and numerous weapons during the latter stages of the war suggests that Ononwarogo was active in the conflict. When in 1759 Johnson and Brigadier-General Thomas Gage* were planning an offensive against Montreal, Ononwarogo drew a detailed map of the French fortifications along the upper St Lawrence River. In late August 1759 Johnson attempted to dispatch him to La Présentation in an effort to induce the Indians of that mission to abandon the French. The Six Nations Council objected vigorously, however. They may have believed that Ononwarogo would be viewed as a traitor by those he had previously converted to the French interest. Rather than have his presence inflame matters, they persuaded Johnson to send others. Ononwarogo was dispatched instead to Cayuga country to recruit warriors for the campaign against Montreal, scheduled for the spring of 1760.

During and after PONTIAC's uprising, Ononwarogo frequently brought Johnson intelligence regarding the western Indians and on several occasions acted as a mediator between those Indians and the English. He died on 24 June 1764, apparently from overdrinking, while trading at Oswego. Johnson, who attended the condolence ceremony, described him as "a very ready fellow and much esteemed."

ARTHUR EINHORN

Johnson papers (Sullivan *et al.*), II, 889; III, 161, 166, 175, 177; IV, 454; IX, 80, 618, 803; X, 43, 57; XI, 96, 105–6, 246, 253–54; XIII, 113, 124, 132–34, 136.

OREIL. *See* DOREIL

ORONTONY (Orontondi, Rondoenie, Wanduny, Nicolas), a Huron chief, reportedly a member of a sept of the Turtle clan; fl. 1739–50.

Driven by the Iroquois from their original homes in the Ontario peninsula in the mid-17th century, parts of the Huron and Tionontati tribes (commonly known afterwards as Wyandots) resettled in the vicinity of Detroit. Dissension between them and the nearby Ottawas led in 1739 to a request by Orontony and two other Huron chiefs that their people be settled nearer the centre of New France. The following year Orontony went in person to press their wish on Governor Charles de BEAUHARNOIS. The Hurons feared for their lives at Detroit, and when the French authorities failed to act promptly, some of the tribe left Detroit and established themselves at the village of Etionnontout (Ayonontout, Junundat) near Sandoské (Sandusky) Bay, where they came under the influence of British traders and of a mixed Indian population, partly Iroquois, settled on the Cuyahoga River (near present Cleveland, Ohio).

To strengthen these relations, three "Janondides," headed by Orontony, appeared at Albany, New York, on 30 July 1743 with a wampum treaty belt given to the Hurons 40 years earlier, at the time when MICHIPICHY was attempting to bring English traders into the Detroit region. The Hurons' new request for trading privileges was readily granted.

Traders, especially those from Pennsylvania, were moving into the region south of Lake Erie. French countermoves had limited success, since the price of their trade goods remained high. Orontony and some other chiefs also complained that the French "wou'd always get their [the Indians'] Young Men to go to War against their Enemies and wou'd use them as their own People, that is like Slaves. . . ." The outbreak of King George's War in 1744 led to acts of open hostility. In the spring of 1747 five French traders returning to Detroit were killed near Cuyahoga. Orontony's people were implicated, and the commander at Detroit, Paul-Joseph Le Moyne* de Longueuil, weighing the significance of the episode, saw the whole French position in the region imperilled.

George Croghan, the chief British trader at Cuyahoga, called upon Pennsylvania in May 1747 to support the Indians' further endeavours. In November ten Iroquois warriors from the Ohio, undoubtedly encouraged by Croghan and alert to personal advantage, appeared at Philadelphia professing their eagerness to strike the French. The province voted a present of £150 for the Ohio Indians and one of £50 for those of Cuyahoga.

Osborn

The Iroquois had not in fact declared war on the French, but Detroit was uneasy. The Ottawas of MIKINAK's band and the Potawatomis and Ojibwas in the neighbourhood of the fort were in sympathy with Orontony, and normal Indian trade and diplomatic relations with the French were disrupted. Orontony continued to be visited by English traders in his fortified village at Sandoské, and about August 1747 he persuaded the Miamis to destroy a French trading post in the Miami country. He appeared at Detroit professing to seek peace, but while he was there a party of Indians killed three Frenchmen near the fort and then took refuge on nearby Bois Blanc Island.

Late in September 1747 a convoy of French reinforcements reached Detroit and on 7 April 1748 Longueuil learned that Orontony had burned his fort and town and had set off for the Ohio valley with 119 warriors. The Hurons' retreat had the support of the Indians in the Ohio country, and about 70 of the warriors and their families settled at Conchaké (Coshocton, Ohio). The remainder went farther east to build a new town at Kuskusky (near New Castle, Pa.).

Conrad Weiser, Pennsylvania's Indian agent, arrived at Logstown (Chiningué, now Ambridge, Pa.) near the end of August 1748 with a present of some £700 worth of goods. Conspicuous in the impressive aggregation of Indians who met Weiser were Orontony and four other Hurons from Kuskusky, who "behav'd like People of good Sense & Sincerity; the most of them were grey headed. . . ." They displayed again the treaty belt that Orontony had carried to Albany five years earlier; and a Six Nations spokesman, on behalf of the other Indians and of Pennsylvania, received them to the council fire as allies.

Unknown to these treaty makers, Anglo-French hostilities had ceased; and by October 1750 Orontony was dead, probably the victim of an epidemic that decimated his band. Trade rivalry continued unabated, however. An English trader who visited Conchaké in December 1750 described it as consisting of a hundred families of Hurons, and he found English flags flying at "the King's House" and at Croghan's store.

Writing on 10 Aug. 1751 the governor of New France, La Jonquière [TAFFANEL] reported the arrest of John PATTIN and some other English traders south of Lake Erie, whom he accused of trying to revive the projects of Orontony. The defiant Indians and associated English traders suffered a second blow when on 21 June 1752 a group of Miamis who had made peace with the English and had settled at Pickawillany (Piqua,

Ohio) were routed and their chief killed by Charles-Michel Mouet* de Langlade and a party of pro-French Indians.

At some time before 1755 Orontony's people abandoned their villages in the Ohio valley and apparently returned to Etionnontout. In August 1755 a Huron delegation visited Philadelphia in response to an invitation. Its embassy coincided inopportunely with Jean-Daniel Dumas*'s defeat of Major-General Edward Braddock, of which the Indians learned on their way. They found the Pennsylvania governor hospitable but militarily powerless. Taking leave at the end of their visit, the Hurons thanked the officials for their kind treatment, assured them of their friendship, and added somewhat drily that "We live on this side Lake Erie, at a place called Deonandady. If you should get the better of the French and come into our parts you will find us your Friends and we will join you."

WILLIAM A. HUNTER

Bibliothèque municipale de Montréal, Fonds Gagnon, père Potier, Vocabulaire huron-français, 195, 200, 212. Moravian Church Archives (Bethlehem, Pa.), Conrad Weiser's Reise Diarium 1748. PAC, RG 10, A3, 1820, 253–54. [G.-J. Chaussegros de Léry], "Journal de Joseph-Gaspard Chaussegros de Léry, lieutenant des troupes, 1754–1755," APQ Rapport, 1927–28, 404–5, 425–28. [Christopher Gist], Christopher Gist's journals . . . , ed. W. M. Darlington (Pittsburgh, Pa., 1893), 37–41. Early western travels, ed. R. G. Thwaites (32v., Cleveland, Ohio, 1904–7), I, 29. French regime in Wis., 1727–48 (Thwaites), 279–88. "French regime in Wis., 1743–60" (Thwaites), 74–75. NYCD (O'Callaghan and Fernow), VI, IX, X. Pennsylvania, Colonial records, V, VI. Pennsylvania archives, 1st ser., I, II.

OSBORN, Sir DANVERS, member of the Nova Scotia Council, governor of New York; b. in England 17 Nov. 1715; d. in New York 12 Oct. 1753.

Danvers Osborn of Chicksands, Bedfordshire, was the son of John Osborn and Sarah Byng, daughter of George Byng, 1st Viscount Torrington, and sister of Admiral John BYNG. Danvers' grandfather was Sir John Osborn, 2nd baronet, and from him he inherited the title in 1720, as his father had already died. On 25 Sept. 1740 Danvers married Lady Mary Montagu, sister of George Montagu Dunk, 2nd Earl of Halifax, president of the Board of Trade from 1748 to 1761. Lady Mary died on 23 July 1743, after giving birth to their second son. Sir Danvers was greatly affected by her death and never seemed to recover his spirit afterwards.

For several years he led a restless life, and spent some of his time at Horton, Northamptonshire, with his brother-in-law, the Earl of

Halifax. In 1745, during the rebellion of Charles Edward, the Young Pretender, Osborn raised and led a troop of men in support of the king. He was elected to parliament for Bedfordshire in 1747. In 1750, possibly through the influence of the Earl of Halifax, he went to Halifax, Nova Scotia, where he became a member of the Nova Scotia Council on 29 August.

During his attendance at council meetings in the next month, Osborn and his associates were faced with such problems as the victualling of new settlers, the suppression of "the scandalous practice of selling meat and other things publicly on the Lord's Day," and the payment of wages to labourers employed on the king's works. After being in Halifax for six weeks, Sir Danvers returned to England, and on 18 December he discussed the financial affairs of Nova Scotia with the commissioners for Trade and Plantations.

In May 1753 the Board of Trade recommended the appointment of Osborn as governor of New York, and his commission to that office was approved in July. He was officially welcomed on 10 October by the mayor, aldermen, and people of the city of New York. On the morning of 12 October, however, he was found in the garden of the house where he was lodging "strangled in his Handkercheif." In reporting Osborn's death to the Board of Trade, Lieutenant Governor James DeLancey observed that although Osborn "expressed his sense of the peoples joy upon his accession to the Government in the most engaging manner, yet he never shewed any cheerfulness, but appeared with a sedate and melancholy Countenance, complaining of a great indisposition of body and disturbance of mind, which could not be diverted." It was later said that Osborn had made two previous attempts at suicide.

Osborn's body was at first interred in a vault in the chancel of Trinity Church, New York, and was taken to England in 1754.

CHARLES BRUCE FERGUSSON

PANS, RG 3, Minutes of Nova Scotia Council, 1750; Unpub. papers of N.S. Hist. Soc., Danvers Osborn, "Sir Danvers Osborn and his services in connection with the founding of Halifax" (paper read at N.S. Hist. Soc. meeting, 8 March 1918). PRO, Prob. 11/696, f.105; 11/807, f.53. "The burghers of New Amsterdam and the freemen of New York, 1675–1866," N.Y. Hist. Soc. *Coll.*, XVIII (1885). [Cadwallader Colden], *The letters and papers of Cadwallader Colden . . .* (9v., N.Y. Hist. Soc. *Coll.*, L–LVI (1917–23), LXVII–LXVIII (1934–35), New York, 1918–37), IX. *Documentary history of New York* (O'Callaghan), IV, 1057–58. *NYCD* (O'Callaghan and Fernow), VI. N.Y. Hist. Soc. *Coll.*, III (1870). *N.S. Archives, I.* PRO, *JTP, 1749/50–1753; 1754–1758.* T. C. Banks, *The dormant and extinct baronage of England . . .* (4v., London, 1807–37), III, 335–37. Bernard and A. P. Burke, *A genealogical and heraldic history of the peerage and baronetage, the privy council, knightage and companionage,* ed. A. W. Thorpe (80th ed., London, 1921). *Debrett's baronetage, knightage and companionage* (London, 1895). *Herald* (Halifax), 1 July 1899. *The Victoria history of the county of Northampton,* ed. L. F. Salzman (Victoria history of the counties of England, London, 1900–   ), IV (1937), 259, 261.

P

PADANUQUES, JACQUES, chief of the Micmacs of Île Royale (Cape Breton Island) in the middle of the 18th century; killed by the English in Boston, Massachusetts, in May 1744.

Jacques Padanuques's name appears in an important document concerning the war between the English and the Micmacs in Nova Scotia: "Motifs des sauvages mikmaques et marichites de continuer la guerre contre les Anglais depuis la dernière paix" ("Motives of the Micmac and Marichite Indians for continuing the war against the English since the last peace"). This document, written by Pierre MAILLARD, missionary to the Micmacs of Île Royale, states that in May 1744 "a certain Danao or David, an English privateer, having craftily hoisted the French flag in the Fronsac channel [Canso Strait], through a French turncoat whom he had as an interpreter induced the chief of the Indians of Île Royale, called Jacques Padanuques, to board his ship with all his family; he took him to Boston, where Padanuques was thrown into a dungeon as soon as he was set ashore; he was withdrawn from it only to be smothered on the ship on which they said that they had had him put solely to return him to Île Royale." The document adds that Padanuques's son was kept as a hostage, despite the fact that the Micmacs handed over prisoners for his liberation. In 1750 this son was still a prisoner, and subsequently nothing more was heard of him.

Jacques Padanuques's existence is not confirmed by any other document. Moreover the American historian Samuel Drake casts doubt

Pagé

upon the authenticity of the events reported in Maillard's document, since he could find no trace of the persons mentioned in it. It is true that the capture of an Indian chief by Bostonians at the opening of Anglo-French hostilities in the War of the Austrian Succession was in itself commonplace, considering the long tradition of Indian raids in the region about Boston and the exasperation they created in the Anglo-American colonies, whose leaders awarded bounties for Indian scalps. It is possible therefore that this particular seizure was remembered in Boston only as the capture of some unknown Indian. In fact the propagandistic intention behind the document in which Padanuques's name appears is of greater historical interest than the list of outrages enumerated in it. Indeed, the "Motives . . . for continuing the war" constitutes a typical example of the attitude which excuses the atrocities of one's own side by evoking the crimes committed by the adversary.

The document in question also mentions a crime that was, to say the least, spectacular: the infecting by contaminated blankets of more than 200 Micmacs during 1746. No other record of this criminal act is to be found anywhere, but Beamish Murdoch* wrote in the 19th century that in this same year of 1746, at the time of the disaster which struck the expedition led by the Duc d'Anville [LA ROCHEFOUCAULD], the French soldiers "were stricken with scorbutic fevers and dysentery; upon coming into contact with them the Indians contracted these maladies and died in great numbers." The coincidence is disturbing.

Must one conclude that both Padanuques's murder and the epidemic were products of Maillard's imagination? Only one thing is certain: his contemporaries (Thomas Pichon*, Jean-Louis de Raymond*, Michel Le Courtois* de Surlaville) are unanimous in not questioning them. These authors also agree that the war between the English and the Micmacs was brought about more or less directly by the French government.

MICHELINE D. JOHNSON

Derniers jours de l'Acadie (Du Boscq de Beaumont), 248–62. Pichon, Lettres et mémoires. Casgrain, Les Sulpiciens en Acadie, 435–44. S. G. Drake, A particular history of the five years' French and Indian war in New England and parts adjacent . . . (Albany, 1870), 41–44, 132. Johnson, Apôtres ou agitateurs, 105–28. McLennan, Louisbourg (1918), 65–67, 424–25. Murdoch, History of Nova-Scotia, II, 27–125. E. A. Hutton, "The Micmac Indians of Nova Scotia to 1834" (unpublished MA thesis, Dalhousie University, Halifax, 1961).

PAGÉ, dit Carcy, JACQUES, silversmith, watch-maker; b. 11 Dec. 1682 in Quebec, son of Guillaume Pagé, dit Carcy, a maker of edge tools, and Élisabeth Letartre; m. 9 Sept. 1715 in Quebec Marie-Louise Roussel; d. 2 May 1742 in his birthplace.

Jacques Pagé, dit Carcy, apprenticed as a silversmith in rather special circumstances. It was, in fact, thanks to an ordinance issued by the intendant, Jacques Raudot*, on 2 May 1708 that Pagé was able to apprentice to the master silversmith Michel Levasseur*. Since his arrival in Canada around 1699 Levasseur had taught the "mysteries" of his craft to a single apprentice, Pierre Gauvreau. Now Levasseur intended to leave Canada in 1708, without training any other silversmiths, in keeping with his agreement with Gauvreau to "teach his craft to no one but him." Informed of the terms of this contract and of the master silversmith's decision to leave Canada, the intendant decided that it was "contrary to the public good, which requires, at least for a craft such as this one, that there be two persons practising it." Thus, knowing Jacques Pagé's talent "through several objects that he has already made with his own hands and his natural ability," Raudot made Levasseur take Pagé as an apprentice until the silversmith left for France. On the same day as Raudot issued the ordinance Levasseur signed before the notary Jacques Barbel* a contract with Pagé, according to the intendant's requirements.

A few years later, in 1712, Pagé went to France, where he wanted to practise the silversmith's craft. But despite his request in 1713 to the minister of Marine, Pontchartrain, to be allowed to set up in business in Paris, he ran up against the opposition of the corporation of silversmiths of the capital. This refusal should not be attributed to Pagé's Canadian origins, but to his lack of experience in his craft. In 1664, to promote emigration to New France, the authorities in the mother country had decided to grant the privilege of masterhood in all the towns of the kingdom to those artisans who had "exercised their art and crafts in America for ten years." Jacques Pagé was not entitled to this privilege, even if he claimed he was, for he had been a silversmith only since 1708. Realizing the futility of his application, he returned to the colony and set himself up in business permanently there.

He was already back in Quebec by 1714; his name is mentioned that year in the account books of the church of Notre-Dame. In September 1715 he married Marie-Louise Roussel, and the following year, according to the census of Quebec, he was living with his wife in a house on Rue de la Montagne. This same census tells us that Pagé was not only a silversmith but also a watch-maker. Where or how he learned this other craft is not known, but he was probably already practising it when he was taken on as an apprentice by Levasseur in 1708. It is, moreover, possible, considering the scarcity of watch-makers in New France, that Pagé worked all his life at repairing watches and clocks. According to the inventory of his belongings made by Jacques-Nicolas PINGUET de Vaucour in 1742, at the time of his death, Pagé was still in possession of "the tools used in the watch-maker's craft." The same document also mentions that among Pagé's books was a "treatise on clocks and watches."

In the period 1718–28 Jacques Pagé made several pieces of silver for the religious communities and churches in Quebec and the surrounding region. An ordinance by François Clairambault* d'Aigremont, the acting intendant, in 1728, informs us that Pagé was still exercising his silversmith's craft, since he was asked, along with the silversmith Jean-Baptiste DESCHEVERY, *dit* Maisonbasse, to weigh "the silver plate of Monsieur [Claude-Thomas Dupuy*]." After that date little is known of Pagé's activities. A great number of documents refer to him as a merchant silversmith or simply "a bourgeois, of Quebec." Through several petitions that he made in 1730 to the Conseil Supérieur we know that he was for some time "churchwarden in charge of Notre-Dame de Québec." But he had perhaps not given up his craft entirely, since the inventory after his death mentions a great number of silversmithing tools and pieces of silver plate that Pagé kept in his home.

Jacques Pagé, *dit* Carcy, died in Quebec on 2 May 1742, without leaving any descendants. This silversmith had acquired a good reputation, if we are to judge by the numerous references to him in the account books of the religious communities and parishes in the region. Several objects in various collections in the province are attributed to him, among which are some forks and spoons, a cup, some salvers, and a ciborium. The Musée du Québec owns four pieces of Pagé's work, two soup spoons, a fork, and a salver with the stamp I P above reversed C, crowned with a fleur-de-lis.

IN COLLABORATION WITH
MICHEL CAUCHON AND ANDRÉ JUNEAU

AJQ, Registre d'état civil, Notre-Dame de Québec, 11 déc. 1682, 9 sept. 1715, 3 mai 1742. AN, Col., B, 35, ff.101, 134, 180. ANDQ, Livres de comptes, 1709–1724. ANQ, Greffe d'Antoine Adhémar de Saint-Martin, 18 mars 1712; Greffe de Jacques Barbel, 2 mai 1708; Greffe de J.-N. Pinguet de Vaucour, 18 juin, 17 août 1742. IOA, Dossier Jacques Pagé, dit Carcy, orfèvre. *Recensement de Québec, 1716* (Beaudet). P.-G. Roy, *Inv. coll. pièces jud. et not.*, I, 62; II, 320; *Inv. jug. et délib., 1717–1760*, I, 12; II, 94, 121; IV, 51. Tanguay, *Dictionnaire.* Langdon, *Canadian silversmiths.* Morisset, *Coup d'œil sur les arts.* É.-Z. Massicotte, "Orfèvres et bijoutiers du régime français," *BRH*, XXXVI (1930), 31. Gérard Morisset, "Jacques Pagé dit Quercy (1682–1742)," *Technique* (Montréal), XXV (1950), 589–600.

PAIN, FÉLIX, priest, Recollet, missionary; b. 1668 at Paris, France, son of "a successful merchant"; d. 27 Nov. 1741 at Quebec.

Félix Pain joined the Recollets of the Saint-Denys province in Paris and was ordained about 1692. From 1694 to 1701 he served as garrison chaplain at Plaisance (Placentia, Nfld.). Governors Philippe Pastour* de Costebelle and Joseph de Monic* complained of his conduct which, Monic claimed, provided "much cause for reproach and dissatisfaction." On one occasion Monic was driven to eject Pain from his house. Pain left Plaisance in 1701 when his community was replaced by Recollets of the province of Brittany.

The Paris Recollets were invited to found a convent at Port-Royal (Annapolis Royal, N.S.) that year, and Félix Pain was appointed garrison chaplain. In 1702 the parish priest at Port-Royal, Abel Maudoux of the Séminaire des Missions Étrangères, was recalled after a decade of involvement in the petty contentions characteristic of Acadia at this time. Pain himself was not long removed from the local discord: his most noteworthy clash with local authorities occurred in January 1705 when, clandestinely and against the orders of the interim commander at Port-Royal, Simon-Pierre Denys* de Bonaventure, he celebrated the marriage of an officer of the garrison, François Du Pont* Duvivier, to Marie Mius d'Entremont, who was six months pregnant. Bonaventure had been sniped at in the preceding year by the local Recollets for his illicit alliance with Mme de Freneuse [Louise GUYON], and used Pain's insubordination as an opportunity to take vengeance. According to Bonaventure, Pain had said that "he [Pain] took about as much notice of me as the mud on his shoes." Pain's defiance was mitigated by the fact that, although an officer required his commander's formal permission to marry, marriages such as Duvivier's were expedited to avoid an illegitimate birth. A routine forced marriage, unlikely to be noticed outside the gossipy confines of Port-Royal, was now transformed into a celebrated affair; it earned Pain severe reprimands from the minister

Paradis

of Marine and his own order, and also severely injured Bonaventure's career.

Pain continued to serve at Port-Royal until its capture in 1710 by English forces under Francis Nicholson*. He then became missionary for the Minas (Wolfville) and Beaubassin (Amherst) regions. As early as 1721 he is referred to as "superior of the Recollets of Acadia." Pain seems to have served his charges well, guiding the Acadian community as best he could through the perilous diplomatic morass into which they were thrown by the treaty of Utrecht. On the one hand he protected the Acadians from the excesses of the French policy of having them remain loyal to faith and flag, journeying many times to Louisbourg in his efforts to prevent wholesale removal of the Acadians to Île Royale (Cape Breton Island), a notoriously inhospitable land. On the other hand, he stoutly resisted the British insistence on unconditional allegiance to the crown by the Acadians remaining in Nova Scotia.

In 1725 Pain left Nova Scotia and began ministering to the Acadians of Île Saint-Jean (Prince Edward Island), undoubtedly as much because of difficulties with Governor Lawrence Armstrong* as because no missionary had yet been assigned to the island. Pain's presence is recorded at Île Saint-Jean at various times between July 1725 and July 1731. In 1727 the governor of Île Royale, Saint-Ovide [MONBETON], expressed the hope that Pain's good offices would help attract more Acadian emigrants.

When Félix Pain left the Île Saint-Jean mission in July 1731, he went to serve at Louisbourg and retired from the active ministry in 1733. Though he might have preferred to live out his life in France, his advanced age and his fear of travel on the high seas compelled him to retire to Quebec. He served there from age 65 to his death in 1741 in the less arduous post of superior of the Recollets of New France.

BERNARD POTHIER

AN, Col., B, 27, ff.3v–4; C¹¹ᴮ, 6, ff.8, 102–3; 9, f.52; 13, f.26; C¹¹ᶜ, 2, f.170v; 3, f.154; 5, f.154; 7, ff.223v–24; C¹¹ᴰ, 4, ff.165–65v, 258; 5, ff.105–6v, 221–21v, p.313 (PAC transcript); Section Outre-Mer, G¹, 411. Archives des Franciscains (Montréal), Table générale de tous les religieux morts depuis l'érection de la province. PAC, MG 11, Nova Scotia A, 17, p.159. PANS, RG 1, 26. *Coll. doc. inédits Canada et Amérique*, I, 116–18. *N. S. Archives, III*, 69–73, 89–90. Allaire, *Dictionnaire*, I, 408. Ivanhoë Caron, "Liste des prêtres séculiers et religieux qui ont exercé le saint ministère en Nouvelle-France (1680–1690)," *BRH*, XLVII (1941), 264–65. Johnson, *Apôtres ou agitateurs*, 143. Harvey, *French régime in P.E.I.*, 240. Robert Le Blant, *Un colonial sous Louis XIV: Philippe de Pastour de Costebelle, gouverneur de Terre-Neuve puis de l'île Royale, 1661–1717* (Paris, Dax, 1935), 93–94, 171, 186. *Mgr de Saint-Vallier et l'Hôpital Général*, 712. "Profiles franciscains; le Père Félix Pain," *Revue Franciscaine* (Montréal), XLIII (1927); XLIV (1928). [F.-E.] Rameau de Saint-Père, *Une colonie féodale en Amérique: l'Acadie (1604–1881)* (2v., Paris, Montréal, 1889), I, 403–11.

PARADIS, ROLAND, silversmith; b. c. 1696, son of Claude Paradis and Geneviève Cussy of the parish of Saint-Jacques-de-la-Boucherie, Paris; m. 3 Feb. 1728, in the church of Notre-Dame de Québec, Marie-Angélique Boivin; d. 28 April 1754 in Montreal.

It is not known when Roland Paradis came to Canada, but at the time of his marriage in 1728 he evidently had been here for some years, since the kind of marriage licence that persons newly arrived had to present has not been found in his name. Paradis probably acquired his taste for the silversmith's craft and did his apprenticeship in Paris with his father, a merchant silversmith.

In 1728 he was in business in Quebec but did not stay there long, for on 25 June 1736, before the notary François-Michel Lepailleur in Montreal, he signed a "farming lease for three full years for a farm of two acres . . . back of Ville-Marie." The same document also refers to Paradis as a "silversmith in Ville-Marie." The earliest information about Roland Paradis's silversmithing works comes from the account books for 1739 of the parish of Saint-Charles-de-Lachenaie, where it is mentioned that he received the sum of 145 *livres* 10 *sols* from the parish council in payment of "the material and workmanship for a ciborium for the Eucharist." He also did various pieces of work for the churches of Sainte-Anne-de-Varennes in 1742 and Saint-François-de-Sales on Île Jésus in 1745. The seminary of Trois-Rivières possesses a silver chalice engraved with the inscription "1748 Paradis Fesite." According to a contract signed before the notary Gilbert BOUCAULT de Godefus, Paradis was still a merchant silversmith in Montreal in 1749.

The Musée du Québec owns a few pieces of Paradis's silverware: five silver soup spoons with plain handles and upturned bowls, a goblet ornamented with fillets, a pyx in the shape of a miniature ciborium with silver gilt on the inside, and finally a monstrance from the church of Saint-François-de-Sales on Île Jésus. Several other objects by Paradis are preserved in various parts of the province, particularly at the archbishopric, the Hôpital Général, and the

Pattin

Hôtel-Dieu of Montreal, and in the museum of the basilica of Sainte-Anne de Beaupré. All these objects are in silver and bear the stamp RP surmounted by a crown.

MICHEL CAUCHON and ANDRÉ JUNEAU

AJQ, Registre d'état civil, Notre-Dame de Québec, 3 févr. 1728. ANQ, Greffe de Gilbert Boucault de Godefus, 10 sept. 1749; Greffe de Florent de La Cetière, 22 janv. 1728. ANQ-M, Greffe de F.-M. Lepailleur, 25 juin 1736; Registre d'état civil, Notre-Dame de Montréal, 29 avril 1754. Archives paroissiales de Saint-Charles (Lachenaie, Qué.), Livres de comptes, I, 1725–1739. Archives paroissiales de Sainte-Anne (Varennes, Qué.), Livres de comptes, I, 1725–1729. Archives paroissiales de Saint-François-de-Sales (Laval, Qué.), Livres de comptes, I. IOA, Dossier Roland Paradis, orfèvre. Tanguay, *Dictionnaire*. Langdon, *Canadian silversmiths*. Morisset, *Coup d'œil sur les arts*. Traquair, *Old silver of Quebec*. Gérard Morisset, "L'orfèvre Roland Paradis," *Technique* (Montréal), XXXIV (1959), 437–42.

PARIS, BERNARD, ship's captain; b. 1708 in Plaisance (Placentia, Nfld.), the eldest child of Antoine Paris and Renée Boucher; m. 25 May 1758 in Louisbourg, Île Royale (Cape Breton Island), to Marie-Anne Le Blanc; d. April 1760 in La Rochelle, France.

The Paris family was among those that retired from Placentia after its cession to Great Britain in 1713 to form the nucleus of settlement at Louisbourg. At the age of 19 Bernard was already working for his father and his father's Quebec partner Perrault – perhaps François PERRAULT. He commanded their bateau the *Saint-Pierre*, which carried the peas, wheat, flour, and wood of Canada to Louisbourg where they were exchanged for return cargoes of West Indian rum, molasses, sugar, and fruits. But Antoine had more ambitious plans for his business and for his son. In 1729 he launched a 90-ton schooner, the *Marie-Magdelaine*. Bernard became its captain, sailing between Louisbourg, the West Indies, and Bordeaux. The letters of Antoine's Bordeaux correspondent, Jean Jung, attest to Bernard's good character and intelligence, complain of his youthful extravagance (at Bordeaux he had the schooner rerigged as a snow, "the prettiest ship in the river and the best equipped"), and comment on his lack of experience. Bernard brought the ship home from its third voyage in 1731; it was sold following his father's death on 3 November.

Bernard next claims our attention as a ship's captain for Robert Dugard et Cie of Rouen for whom he made several voyages between 1738 and 1744. He commanded the company's *Ville de Québec*, which sailed between Canada and France *via* Louisbourg in 1738, and its *Saint-Louis* and *Imprévû* in 1739 and 1740 respectively, on their maiden voyages from Quebec to Louisbourg and Le Havre. In 1742 he took the *Imprévû* to Martinique. The following year he captained the *Trois Maries* from Honfleur to Quebec and Louisbourg; it was sunk under him on the return voyage after a collision with the *Brillant* belonging to the Compagnie des Indes. Thus it was not impossible for a colonial to find employment with a large metropolitan company.

Although Bernard's connection with Dugard ceased after the War of the Austrian Succession, when the company abandoned the North American trade [*see* HAVY], he was thereafter employed by other French shipowners. His name recurs from time to time in notarial and port records, as in 1751, for example, when he is described as a resident of La Rochelle and captain of the *Saint-Sebastien*. The record of his marriage in 1758 describes him as still a resident of Louisbourg and still a ship's captain. After a second capture of the town by British forces, this time under Jeffery Amherst*, he and his wife moved to La Rochelle where he died two years later.

DALE MIQUELON

[AN, 62 AQ, 31 (François Havy à Robert Dugard, 7 juin 1760, La Rochelle); Section Outre-Mer, G¹, 406, f.55v; 409, f.44; G², 180, ff.560–98 (includes letters to Antoine Paris from Perrault, almost certainly the well-known merchant François Perrault, but after the custom of the time signed only by the surname); 181, ff.45–393 (févr. 1732 à 1736, succession Antoine Paris, négociant); G³, 2041/1 (4 mai 1751).

Voyages for Dugard et Cie. have been pieced together from the following sources: AD, Gironde (Bordeaux), 6B, 96, f.98; 387. AN, 62 AQ, 40 (Havy et Lefebvre, Québec, compte courant, 1738; Havy et Lefebvre, Québec, compte général de balance); 41 (Robert Dugard, compte courant avec Fautoux de Louisbourg; papiers de cargaison, *Trois Maries*, 1744); 43 (papiers de cargaison, *Imprévû* et *Imprévû*, compte courant avec Renault); 45 (Robert Dugard, compte courant avec Leukens, 1741–1742; prêt à la grosse avanture, 3 avril 1742); Col., B, 73, f.133; 75, f.127; C⁸ᴮ, 20; C¹¹ᴬ, 70, f.167; 71, f.182; 72, f.78; 73, f.411; 75, f.83; 76, f.322; 81, f.260; F²ᴮ, 11. ANQ, NF, Ord. int., XXIX, 3 avril, 16 juin 1741.

Sources cited in the bibliographies for François HAVY and Léon FAUTOUX were also used in preparing this entry. D.M.]

PATTIN, JOHN, trader, map maker, explorer; b. *c.* 1725 in Wilmington, Pennsylvania (now Delaware); d. 1754, probably on the Labrador coast.

The name of John Pattin is first known in 1750,

when he was trading in the Ohio country under a licence from Pennsylvania. In November he was arrested near Fort des Miamis (probably at or near Fort Wayne, Ind.) by the commandant, Louis COULON de Villiers, and charged with encroachment on French territory and "endeavoring to debauch our Indians." A brief detention at Detroit was Pattin's initiation into a series of imprisonments, as he was moved in turn to forts Niagara (near Youngstown, N.Y.), Toronto, and Frontenac (Kingston, Ont.), then to Montreal and Quebec. In Montreal on 19 June 1751 he was examined by Governor La Jonquière [TAFFANEL], who found him "mutinous and threatening" and passed him on to Quebec. During these peregrinations Pattin kept a journal describing the forts and settlements through which he had passed.

In November 1751 he and two other traders were sent from Quebec to a prison in La Rochelle, France. They boldly appealed to the British ambassador in Paris, who swiftly demanded that the men be freed and given restitution for their trading goods, which had been confiscated. He arranged that they receive funds to come to Paris and, after talking with them, paid their way to London so that they might report what they had seen in North America to Lord Holderness, secretary of state for the southern department. After returning to Philadelphia, Pattin made a verbal statement on his experiences to the assembly on 17 Oct. 1752 and later drew a map to accompany his account.

Adventure by sea then cast its spell over him. He joined the *Argo* (Capt. Charles Swaine [Drage*]) as "draughtsman and mineralist" on a commercial venture that was also authorized to search for a northwest passage. The expedition sailed from Philadelphia on 4 March 1753. Despite repeated attempts, they got no farther into Hudson Strait than Resolution Island because of heavy ice. Early in August they made for the Labrador coast, which they "discover'd . . . perfectly from [latitude] 56 to 55, finding no less than 6 Inlets . . . of which they [Pattin?] have made a very good Chart." They also noted a fine fishing bank and acquired some samples of copper.

Shortly after Pattin's return late in 1753, Governor James Hamilton of Pennsylvania approached him to undertake a clandestine mission to the Ohio country for the purpose of investigating French military preparations and mapping the area. He was to work in conjunction with George Croghan, the trader, and Andrew Montour, the interpreter, joining them *en route*. They were apparently not a harmonious team, for Croghan found Pattin "Bigotted of himself" and

noted that "he and Androw Montour dose nott agree well." They completed their task, however, and early in March 1754 Pattin presented the Pennsylvania legislature with his diary of the mission and a map. For his services he received £50.

In the spring of 1754, Pattin sailed again with Captain Swaine on another *Argo* expedition to the arctic. Little is known of the undertaking, but the sad report was brought back that "poor Mr. John Patten, . . . with two of the sailors, were killed by the Indians, being on an Island some distance from the Schooner fishing." According to another report, they had met their deaths after slipping away from the ship to search for a copper mine.

MAUD M. HUTCHESON

[Two manuscripts by Pattin are held by the Mass. Hist. Soc. in its Misc. Large coll.: John Pattin's acct. of distances computed by Indian traders; A journal or account of the capture of John Pattin. They have been published by H. N. Eavenson in "Who made the 'Trader's map'?" *Pennsylvania Magazine of History and Biography* (Philadelphia), LXV (1941), 420–38, and in *Map maker and Indian traders: an account of John Patten, trader, Arctic explorer, and map maker; Charles Swaine, author, trader, public official, and Arctic explorer; Theodorus Swaine Drage, clerk, trader, and Anglican priest* (Pittsburgh, 1949). The latter work is particularly valuable since its appendices contain many other documents relating to Pattin's career. An extract from the journal has been published in "French regime in Wis., 1743–60" (Thwaites), 112–14. M.M.H.]

Other sources and studies are: Pennsylvania, *Colonial records*, V. *Pennsylvania archives*, 1st ser., II, 118, 240. E. S. Balch, "Arctic expeditions sent from the American colonies," *Pennsylvania Magazine of History and Biography*, XXXI (1907), 419–28. H. N. Eavenson, "Patten's map of the road to Shannopintown," *Western Pennsylvania Historical Magazine* (Pittsburgh), XXVII (1944), 21–28. Bertha Solis-Cohen, "An American search for the northwest passage: an account of the little known expeditions which set sail from Philadelphia in 1753 and 1754," *Beaver* (Winnipeg), outfit 274 (autumn 1943), 24–27.

PAUMEREAU. *See* POMMEREAU

PAYEN DE NOYAN, PIERRE-BENOÎT, officer in the colonial regular troops; b. *c.* 1700 in Normandy, France, son of Pierre Payen* de Noyan and Catherine-Jeanne Le Moyne de Longueuil et de Châteauguay; m. Marie Faucon Dumanoir on 14 March 1739 in New Orleans, Louisiana; d. 1765 in Avranches, France.

After Pierre Payen de Noyan's death in 1707 the king granted his widow an annual pension of 500 *livres* for the support of her four sons, among them Pierre-Jacques*, who became king's lieutenant of Trois-Rivières, Gilles-Augustin, who became king's lieutenant of New Orleans, and Pierre-Benoît.

The latter arrived in Louisiana in 1722 as half-pay ensign because of the "good reports about him and the man's value." He came to join his brother, Gilles-Augustin, who had held a post there since 1717, and his uncle, Bienville [Le Moyne], commandant general of the colony. His first stay in Louisiana was short, since he returned to France in 1726 after a new administration's purge of Bienvillists. On 8 May 1730 Noyan was appointed ensign on the active list on Île Royale (Cape Breton Island). He served in Charles de Saint-Étienne* de La Tour's company until the latter's death in 1731 and for some years after that.

In 1732 Bienville was appointed governor of Louisiana, and in 1735 Noyan obtained permission to return there as a lieutenant. The following year he was appointed assistant adjutant of Fort Condé (Mobile, Ala.). As a soldier he concentrated his activity upon the struggles between the French and the Indians. He took part in several expeditions against the Chickasaws and the Natchez and was even slightly wounded. In 1739 he was sent to map a route to the Chickasaw country for an impending French attack. He was at that time commandant of Fort de l'Assomption (Memphis, Tenn.).

On 1 Oct. 1740 the king recognized his services by promoting him captain. Although the documents make no mention of him, Noyan may have distinguished himself on a few occasions, since he was appointed town major of New Orleans around 1750. He received the cross of the order of Saint-Louis in 1752.

Noyan returned to France in 1760 and died in 1765 in Avranches. His military career was uneventful. His different ranks and posts were probably often obtained through his family relationship with Bienville.

JEAN-PIERRE PROULX

Archives du ministère des Affaires étrangères (Paris), Mém. et doc., Amérique, 1/1–2, 7/2. AN, Col., B, 43, ff.124, 629; 64, f.464; 78/1; 96, f.171; C¹¹ᴮ, 12, 15, 16, 21; C¹¹ᶜ, 11–15; C¹¹ᴳ, 12; D²ᶜ, 2; 222/2, p.121 (PAC transcript); F³, 24, f.270; 50/1; Marine, C⁷, 238, f.30. Bénard de La Harpe, *Journal historique de l'établissement des Français à la Louisiane* (Nouvelle-Orléans, 1831). L. Lindsay, "Souvenirs de Quiberon," *La Nouvelle-France* (Québec), V (1906), 20–32. Fauteux, *Les chevaliers de Saint-Louis*. Le Jeune, *Dictionnaire*. [François Daniel], *Nos gloires nationales, ou histoire des principales familles du Canada . . .* (2v., Montréal, 1867).

PÉAN DE LIVAUDIÈRE, JACQUES-HUGUES, seigneur, officer in the colonial regular troops; b. in Paris, France, in 1682, son of Jean-Pierre Péan and Anne de Corbarboineau; d. in Quebec on 25 Jan. 1747.

At the age of 16, Jacques-Hugues Péan joined the colonial regular troops of New France as a cadet, drawing a regular soldier's annual pay of 108 *livres*. In his 30th year he was raised to an ensignship, and in 1714 left the colony to serve on Île Royale (Cape Breton Island). Three years later he was promoted lieutenant and returned to Canada; on 11 Feb. 1721 he received command of a company with a salary of 1,080 *livres*. The following year, on 25 June, he married Marie-Françoise, daughter of François-Antoine Pécaudy de Contrecœur and Jeanne de Saint-Ours, in Montreal. By his marriage Péan became an integral part of the colony's élite.

In September 1722 Vaudreuil [Rigaud*] sent Péan to command at Fort Frontenac (Kingston, Ont.), where he served until 1725. Two years later he was named commandant of Fort Chambly (south of Montreal) where his father-in-law succeeded him in 1729. On 4 April 1730 he was made a knight of the order of Saint-Louis, with a minimum pension of 800 *livres* per year. Péan was appointed to the command of Detroit in 1733, but on 1 April he was made town major of Quebec and did not leave for Detroit until 1735. In the meantime Ignace Gamelin* the younger handled Péan's affairs at the post.

From 1733 until his death, Péan acquired, by grant and by purchase, a financial interest in a number of seigneuries in New France. On 10 April 1733 he was granted a fief of six square leagues, called Livaudière, on Lake Champlain, but the undeveloped property reverted to the crown in 1741. In 1735 Péan and his wife bought the Saint-Joseph or Lespinay fief, which they kept until 1744. On 14 April 1736, the Péans were awarded the fief of Saint-Michel, which covered half of the seigneury of La Durantaye. Péan, between 1741 and 1744, bought a large number of the shares and rights to the seigneury of Beaumont, adjoining the Saint-Michel fief, and on 20 Sept. 1744 he had himself granted a piece of land, which he called the Livaudière fief, situated west of the seigneuries of Beaumont and La Durantaye. The following year he rendered homage and fealty for the fiefs of Saint-Michel and Livaudière which formed one seigneury. Despite the fact that he acquired all these properties, it seems that Péan, like many seigneurs at the time, was more interested in speculation and in the prestige his seigneuries gave him than in improving them.

Jacques-Hugues Péan died on 25 Jan. 1747 and

was buried in the crypt of Notre-Dame de Québec. He had served himself and the colony well. He had risen from cadet to commandant, received the highest military award, and had been town major of Quebec. Of his four children only two lived beyond infancy; it is unfortunate that the career of Jacques-Hugues was eclipsed by that of one of his surviving children, the infamous Michel-Jean-Hugues Péan*.

C. J. RUSS

AN, Col., D²ᶜ, 47. ANQ, Greffe de R.-C. Barolet, 21 déc. 1735; Greffe de C.-H. Du Laurent, 29 févr. 1744. ANQ-M, Greffe de C.-R. Gaudron de Chevremont, 27 mai 1733; Greffe de J.-C. Raimbault, 1ᵉʳ août 1728. *Royal Fort Frontenac* (Preston and Lamontagne). P.-V. Charland, "Notre-Dame de Québec, le nécrologe de la crypte," *BRH*, XX (1914), 212, 216. Fauteux, *Les chevaliers de Saint-Louis*, 125. Le Jeune, *Dictionnaire*. A. Roy, *Inv. greffes not.*, IV, 268, 269; V, 58–59. P.-G. Roy, *Inv. concessions*; *Les officiers d'état-major*, 200–2. C. J. Russ, "Les troupes de la marine, 1683–1713" (unpublished MA thesis, McGill University, Montreal, 1971).

PEASELEY, WILLIAM, priest of the Church of England, missionary; b. 1714 in Dublin (Republic of Ireland); d. after 1756.

William Peaseley was educated at Dr Quigg's school, Dublin, and at Dublin University, where he received his BA in 1737. Lacking employment at home, he was accepted as a missionary by the Society for the Propagation of the Gospel, and was ordained by the bishop of London in September 1742.

At this time several missions in Newfoundland were without clergymen because of the difficulty of ensuring adequate financial support. Since 1736, when John FORDYCE had left it in disgust, St John's had been without a missionary. Bonavista had lost its pastor when Henry JONES, who had served there since he founded the mission, moved to Trinity in search of a higher stipend in 1742. Peaseley was sent to succeed Jones at Bonavista, and arrived in June 1743, after spending several months in St John's waiting for transportation.

His report on St John's, in which he spoke of being kindly treated, coupled with a letter of 1742 from Thomas Walbank, chaplain to HMS *Sutherland*, led the SPG to consider whether a missionary should be sent there. Walbank had spoken of 200 families who had built a wooden church, "with a decent altar, font, and pulpit, and Ten Commandments and Lord's Prayer handsomely written over the Communion Table," and of a "well disposed fisherman" who "hath lately given to it a silver patten and chalice." He had also been impressed by the resistance of the inhabitants to New England traders who wished to convert them to Presbyterianism. Consequently when the SPG received a petition from some inhabitants of St John's asking for a missionary and promising £40 a year for his support, it ordered Peaseley to move there from Bonavista.

Peaseley arrived in October 1744, was greeted warmly, and given a house. One of his first objects was to provide a school so that Protestant children, who had been attending a Roman Catholic school – the only one available – could have an appropriate religious education. The SPG granted him £10 a year for this purpose. In 1745 he reported that his congregation was increasing and his church was full. He extended his mission by visiting Petty Harbour. The SPG helped his work with another £10 a year, but his financial difficulties continued, as he did not receive enough money in subscriptions. It was only by securing the position of garrison chaplain that he could manage to survive. Though his school and mission were still flourishing in 1747, a series of fires led to a doubling of rents and a halving of subscriptions, and he had to appeal to the SPG for money and books; he received £10 and a box of books.

Despite this aid Peaseley felt that he could not continue in St John's. In 1749 he begged to be moved elsewhere "out of the many difficulties he had laboured under for six years in that miserable island." Besides a lack of funds there was violent opposition from some parishioners to his appeals for money and his efforts to curb work on Sunday, excessive drinking, and sexual immorality. On returning to England, he secured the parish of St Helena, South Carolina. He laboured there until 1756, when he retired because of bad health and competition from the Methodists. No further trace of him can be found.

Peaseley's career illustrates the plight of 18th-century clergymen in Newfoundland. Though he firmly re-established the presence of the Church of England in St John's and began its educational work there, he was forced to leave for want of money and support from his congregation.

FREDERICK JONES

USPG, B, 11, 13–17, 19; Journal of SPG, 9, pp.78–79, 121–22, 203, 250; 10, pp.15, 95, 225–26; 11, pp.89, 158; 12, p.352; 13, p.207. [C. F. Pascoe], *Classified digest of the records of the Society for the Propagation of the Gospel in Foreign Parts, 1701–1892* (5th ed., London, 1895). T. T. Sadleir and G. D. Burtchaell, *Alumni Dublinenses . . . 1593–1860* (new ed., Dublin, 1935), 658. Prowse, *History of Nfld.* (1896), 580.

PÉCAUDY DE CONTRECŒUR, FRANÇOIS-ANTOINE,

PÉCAUDY DE CONTRECŒUR, FRANÇOIS-ANTOINE, commandant, seigneur; b. *c.* 1676, son of Antoine Pécaudy* de Contrecœur, seigneur and officer in the Régiment de Carignan-Salières, and Barbe Denys de La Trinité; d. 2 July 1743 at Montreal.

Like several seigneurs of the time, François-Antoine Pécaudy de Contrecœur was to have a long military career. He was a member of the expedition which Governor Frontenac [Buade*] led against the Onondagas and Oneidas in the summer of 1696. Right after this campaign he was in the contingent which Nicolas Daneau* de Muy led against the English settlements in Newfoundland. In 1704 he was appointed an ensign on the active list, and four years later he took part in the destruction of the village of Haverhill, New Hampshire [*see* Jean-Baptiste Hertel* de Rouville]. In 1710 he was sent to Port-Royal (Annapolis Royal, N.S.) with Nescambiouit*, Jacques Testard* de Montigny, and a score of seasoned soldiers to bring help to the governor of Acadia, Daniel d'Auger* de Subercase, who was expecting the English to attack.

From 1711 to 1728 Pécaudy de Contrecœur took part in campaigns in which he often won his superiors' praise. He was appointed lieutenant on 1 July 1715 and captain on 11 April 1727. In October 1729 he was in command of Fort Chambly, on the Richelieu River, succeeding his son-in-law Jacques-Hugues PÉAN de Livaudière; he retained command until 1732.

Pécaudy de Contrecœur became a knight of the order of Saint-Louis on 25 March 1738, and that same year he prepared a map of Lake Champlain. In October 1741 he was in command of Fort Saint-Frédéric (Crown Point), south of Lake Champlain, replacing François LEFEBVRE Duplessis Faber; he kept this important post until the spring of 1743, when he had to return to Montreal after an illness which he was never to get over.

His military service did not prevent him from developing the seigneury of Contrecœur which he had inherited from his father in 1688. In 1712, according to Gédéon de Catalogne*'s report, the land in this domain was very good and produced all kinds of cereals and vegetables. The number of habitants, 69 in 1681, sank to 44 in 1695, to rise to 138 in 1706 and 283 in 1739. His seigneury of Pancalon (Grand Isle, Vt.), located on Lake Champlain, was not as successful and in 1741, since it had not been developed, was reunited to the king's domain.

On 2 July 1743 François-Antoine Pécaudy de Contrecœur was buried at Montreal, "at about the age of 67." On 15 Nov. 1701, before the notary Antoine Adhémar*, he had signed a marriage contract with Jeanne, daughter of Pierre de Saint-Ours* and Marie Mullois. Seven children were born of this marriage. Two daughters made good marriages, and the two sons were active soldiers: Marie-Françoise married Jacques-Hugues Péan de Livaudière, and Louise married François DAINE; Antoine was killed at 26 years of age in Louisiana by the redoubtable Chickasaws, and Claude-Pierre*, who carried on the line, distinguished himself in the Ohio valley during the Seven Years' War.

ANDRÉ CÔTÉ

AN, Col., B, 33, f.181; 37, f.191v; 49, f.647; 50, f.492v; 53, f.552; 66, f.27v; 68, f.34; 74, f.68; 76, f.87; 78, ff.45, 69; D²ᶜ, 222/1, f.163; E, 90 (dossier Contrecœur), pièces 1–15. ANDM, Registres des baptêmes, mariages et sépultures. ANQ, Seigneuries, Contrecœur. ANQ-M, Greffe d'Antoine Adhémar, 15 nov. 1701. ASQ, Fonds Verreau, Ma Saberdache; Polygraphie, XXVII, 49. *Documents relating to seigniorial tenure* (Munro), 115. *Papiers Contrecœur* (Grenier). Fauteux, *Les chevaliers de Saint-Louis*, 133. Le Jeune, *Dictionnaire*. P.-G. Roy, *Inv. concessions*, II, 155–57, 163–66; III, 125; IV, 276–77; *Inv. ord. int.*, II, 123, 165–66, 193, 233, 295; III, 9, 11, 20. F.-J. Audet, *Contrecœur, famille, seigneurie, paroisse, village* (Montréal, 1940). P.-J.-U. Baudry, "Un vieux fort français," *RSCT*, 1st ser., V (1887), sect.ı, 93–99. É.-Z. Massicotte, "Les commandants du fort Chambly," *BRH*, XXXI (1925), 456–57. J.-E. Roy, "Le patronage dans l'armée," *BRH*, II (1896), 117. P.-G. Roy, "Les commandants du fort Saint-Frédéric," *BRH*, LI (1945), 325–26.

PEPPERRELL, Sir WILLIAM,

PEPPERRELL, Sir WILLIAM, merchant-shipowner, commander of the colonial forces that took Louisbourg, Île Royale (Cape Breton Island), in 1745; b. 27 June 1696 (o.s.) at Kittery Point, Massachusetts (now in Maine), son of William Pepperrell* and Margery Bray; m. 1723 to Mary Hirst, daughter of a wealthy Boston merchant and granddaughter of Judge Samuel Sewall, the diarist; they had four children, two of whom died in infancy; d. 6 July 1759 at Kittery Point.

Entering his father's counting-house at an early age, the young William Pepperrell was forced by the death of his older brother in 1713 to assume much of the burden of the family business. By about 1730 the entire direction of the firm of "Messrs. William Pepperrell" was in his care. At that time the firm had 30 or 35 vessels under its management, and had a minor share in the ownership of a number of others. They ranged in size from small sloops to a brigantine of 110 tons and the ship *Eagle*, 180 tons. For the most part, the Pepperrell vessels shuttled back

Pepperrell

and forth from Kittery, northeast to Newfoundland, south to Virginia and Maryland and to the sugar islands – usually Antigua or Barbados – and across the Atlantic to Lisbon, Cadiz, the Canary Islands, Madeira, and England, in a pattern resembling the ribs of a Chinese fan. Unlike the vessels, the commodities in which the Pepperrells dealt followed labyrinthine lines that crossed and criss-crossed in a variety of geometric patterns.

Basic to the Pepperrells' trade were two native products – lumber and fish – that were in brisk and widespread demand. Newfoundland, where they traded with William KEEN and others, offered a ready market for pine boards and planks, oak staves and hoops, for rum, molasses, and sugar brought from the West Indies, and for tobacco, naval stores, livestock, and provisions that had come from North Carolina and the Chesapeake region. The return cargoes from Newfoundland consisted of English goods – textiles, cutlery, ironware, clothing and shoes, luxury goods such as silks, wines and brandy (which hinted at an illicit trade between Newfoundland and the Continent), and finally marine supplies for the New England shipping industry. Noncommodity returns – namely, money, bills of exchange, and passengers – were an important item in the Pepperrell ledger. Not all the passengers were emigrants deserting the Newfoundland fishing settlements; many of them were masters and crews of New England vessels that had been sold at the island. The same type of lumber cargoes that were shipped to Newfoundland comprised, with the addition of fish (cod, mackerel, and haddock), the outbound cargoes to the West Indies and to Spain and Portugal. For a number of years William Pepperrell owned an interest in fishing boats operating out of Canso, Nova Scotia, and Port-Toulouse (St Peters) on Île Royale. Later, the firm purchased its fish cargoes at Marblehead and Newburyport, Massachusetts, nearer home. It was not unusual for the Pepperrells to switch the direction of their trade back and forth according to the circumstances of the moment. If one general characteristic typified Pepperrell's business activities, it was diversification and flexibility, made possible by the many vessels in which he held a controlling share.

Much of the surplus capital that came to the Pepperrells from their mercantile pursuits was invested in England, left on deposit with their London bankers. Surplus profits accumulated in New England were invested in loans and real estate. The Pepperrells became the neighbourhood bankers. William inherited from his father most of the harbourside land at Kittery Point and sizeable holdings in York and Saco. Later he acquired the larger part of present-day Saco and Scarborough, Maine, and eventually his landholdings, although·by no means the largest in New England, lay scattered along the coast from Kittery to what is now Portland.

In Kittery, as elsewhere in coastal New England, shipping was a source of wealth, but landownership represented gentility and status, which in turn brought responsibility in the shape of public office and military command. In Kittery, the Pepperrells were one of nine families who constituted the "better sort" and among whom town and provincial offices were passed around and handed down from father to son and grandson. It was natural, therefore, that William Pepperrell in 1720, at the age of 24, should be chosen to represent Kittery in the provincial assembly. In 1724 and 1726 he was again chosen, to represent the town in Boston. Then, in 1727, at the age of 31, he was appointed by Governor William Dummer to a place on the Massachusetts Council board. It speaks well for Pepperrell's prudence and tact that he retained his seat on the council throughout the turbulent politics of the next 32 years, under five different governors. For 18 of these years he presided over the council, where he soon established a reputation as an expert on military and Indian affairs. He also attended all the treaty conferences with the eastern Indians for almost 30 years. When Indians complained against the prices charged by the truckmasters at the forts or when settlers charged the Indians with depredations, Pepperrell was generally on the investigating committee.

In 1725 Pepperrell was appointed a judge on the York County Court and five years later he was elevated to chief justice. Like his colleagues on the bench, he was untrained in the law, but, from the point of view of the times, his qualifications were outstanding. His business experience gave him the competence to sit in judgement on many of the matters that came before the court; his fairness and personal integrity were unquestioned; and his rank and standing in the community brought respect and deference that gave added weight to his judicial decisions. Most of the cases were simple matters, but an ordinary action of trespass that came before Pepperrell in 1734 ended as one of the most celebrated legal battles of colonial times, *Frost* v. *Leighton*, a landmark in defiance against royal authority over the colonial timberlands.

Sometime in the 1720s William Pepperrell succeeded his father as colonel of the York County regiment of militia, in command of the entire region from the Piscataqua River to the Canadian border. Until the spring of 1744 the frontiers were nominally at peace and Pepperrell's military duties were not too exacting, although there were alarms and incidents that kept the eastern outposts in an almost constant state of readiness. When war broke out in 1739 between England and Spain, Pepperrell summoned all the militia officers to a meeting at Falmouth (present-day Portland, Maine) to discuss problems of organization, discipline, and equipment. Vacancies in the ranks were filled, new companies were added to the regiment, and a new regiment was formed out of the militia from Falmouth eastward. Adopting a report of the council drafted by Pepperrell, the Massachusetts assembly voted funds to strengthen the harbour defences of Boston, Salem, Marblehead, and the other coastal towns. In the fall of 1743, when the situation became more threatening, Governor William Shirley notified Pepperrell that word of an imminent break with France had arrived from England. He directed Pepperrell "forthwith" to warn and secure the exposed frontier settlements against any sudden assault. Seven months later, on 12 May 1744, as a merchantman from Glasgow was entering Boston harbour with the long-expected news that France had declared war, a small French flotilla commanded by Joseph Du Pont Duvivier sailed from Louisbourg to attack the English settlement at Canso, which quickly fell to the superior French force. In August the French and their Indian allies attacked – this time unsuccessfully – the important English defence outpost at Annapolis Royal. Before the year was out, Governor Shirley had become convinced that the defence of Annapolis Royal, indeed the security of all New England, required the reduction of the French stronghold at Louisbourg.

On several past occasions when war had threatened, a number of colonials and a few Englishmen – among them William Pepperrell and Commodore Peter Warren – had set forth the idea of an assault on Louisbourg, but all the advocates had visualized an expedition from England with the colonies taking a minor role. Now Governor Shirley was audaciously proposing that it be a colonial undertaking, financed, directed, and carried out by the colonies alone, with perhaps some support from the British naval units stationed in American waters. Initially, the Massachusetts General Court had no more enthusiasm for a colonial expedition than there had been in England for an English expedition, but thanks to the influence and efforts of Pepperrell and other zealots such as William Vaughan and John Bradstreet*, the General Court eventu-

ally voted to enlist 3,000 volunteers and to provide whatever was necessary for the expedition. As chairman of the joint committee of the house and council that drew up the resolution for the expedition, Pepperrell helped to influence the General Court's decision.

William Pepperrell was the logical choice to command the forces. The task of raising an army, keeping it intact, maintaining a respectable standard of discipline, and keeping relations with the Royal Navy on an even keel demanded those personal qualities for which he was noted. Pepperrell at first declined Shirley's offer to command the expedition, but within a day or two he accepted the appointment. His long career as colonel of militia had made him thoroughly familiar with the problems of military administration and command, but Pepperrell (and more particularly his battalion majors) would have been in considerable difficulty if it had become necessary to put the troops through the intricate manoeuvres by which an 18th-century army was deployed into line of battle. But they were not counting on meeting the French in the open field; the problem was to assault a fortress. The plan of assault which Pepperrell took with him to Louisbourg had been drafted by Shirley, possibly with the aid of Philip Durell and John Henry Bastide. It called for a surprise attack on the fortress, but authorized Pepperrell to act at his discretion should unforeseen circumstances arise.

On 24 March 1744/45 the Massachusetts forces sailed from Boston for Canso, where they arrived on 4 April. They were joined there by smaller contingents from New Hampshire and Connecticut and by a naval squadron from the West Indies under the command of Commodore Peter Warren. Estimates of the total number of New Englanders who eventually faced the French at Louisbourg range up to some 4,300 men; probably the effective strength at any one time amounted to half that figure. After stopping at Canso for some three weeks, the New England forces arrived off Louisbourg early on 30 April. With the help of good luck, good weather, and good boatmanship, nearly 2,000 men gained the beach at the head of Gabarus Bay within the space of eight or ten hours. No opposition was met until the first troops were on shore, when a small French detachment under the command of Pierre Morpain made an ineffective sortie. By this time, Pepperrell had shelved the original plan and adopted as an alternative a formal siege, a highly standardized process of advancing guns and men up to the walls in a series of parallel trenches connected by zigzag approaches. The New Englanders, however, astounded the

Pepperrell

French by dragging their heavy cannon through a marsh considered impassable, and then moving the guns into position under cover of night and fog instead of first digging trenches to protect the advance. The second morning after the landing, a small party under William Vaughan discovered that one of the key points of the defences – the Grand (Royal) battery – had been abandoned. Vaughan occupied it, and soon the guns of the battery were brought into action against the town.

Although the New England army had its share of chronic grumblers and malcontents, during most of the siege the men faced the dangers and hardships bravely and light-heartedly. Plundering in the countryside around Louisbourg was a troublesome problem for the New England commanders, however, particularly during the early days. Several unsuccessful and costly attacks against the Island battery, which commanded the harbour entrance [see WALDO], brought matters to a standstill, and as the siege went into its fourth week the morale of the New Englanders sank very low. But at a certain point, according to the formula of 18th-century siege warfare, the defenders of a fortress would know whether they must capitulate. When the New England forces established a battery on Lighthouse Point, overlooking the Island battery, the French position became untenable. The harbour lay open to Warren's fleet and on 15 June the acting governor Louis Du Pont* Duchambon decided to ask for terms. Negotiations ended on the afternoon of 17 June when, after a siege of seven weeks, Louisbourg surrendered. The terms of the capitulation [see Warren] included permission for the officers and townspeople to remain in their homes and to enjoy the free exercise of their religion until they could sail for France, and a guarantee that no personal property would be disturbed.

The reduction of the French stronghold set all the church bells in Boston ringing, produced applause in London, and brought fame and honour to William Pepperrell. As a reward for merit, King George II commissioned Pepperrell colonel in command of a regiment in the regular army – the 66th Regiment of Foot – and conferred on him a baronetcy. But to the rank and file of the army at Louisbourg, the surrender presented no great cause for rejoicing. Disgruntled at being denied plunder – especially since the fleet had taken several rich prizes – and discouraged at the prospect of having to remain on garrison duty, some of the troops threatened to lay down their arms. Moreover, relations between the land and sea forces deteriorated. Minor differences between Pepperrell and Warren during the siege and at the

time of surrender were magnified in camp rumours into an attempt by Warren to claim chief credit for the victory, and were further exaggerated in Boston. The troops were not appeased until a large pay increase was promised them and reinforcements began to arrive. Sir William Pepperrell, as he now was, remained in Louisbourg until late May 1746. He served jointly with Warren in administering the affairs of the town and garrison, and spent much of his time on matters relating to his regiment. The major problem during the winter and spring was disease among the troops. Estimates of the number of deaths range from 1,200 to 2,000.

On his return to New England, Sir William resumed his seat on the council board and prepared to live the life of a country squire at Kittery. When the provincial government appealed to the Privy Council for reimbursement of the costs of the expedition, Pepperrell and Warren were called upon to examine and verify all the accounts. In the fall of 1749 Sir William went to England, where for a year he was something of a lion. His old comrade-in-arms, Peter Warren, welcomed him cordially; the city of London presented him with a handsome silver service, and he made his appearance at court. By this time, however, the treaty of Aix-la-Chapelle (1748) had undone his great achievement by returning Louisbourg to the French. Colonials, including Pepperrell, were bitter.

His regiment disbanded, Pepperrell returned to New England in October 1750, and settled down in his mansion overlooking the harbour at Kittery. He had no intention of resuming his mercantile career, but the death in 1751 of his son Andrew, who had been managing the business for some years, forced Sir William to take the helm again. In 1754, when a frontier incident on the western slopes of the Allegheny Mountains [see Joseph COULON de Villiers] ushered in the Seven Years' War in America, Pepperrell's regiment was restored to the army list as the 51st; but for Sir William the war was an anticlimax. Although plagued by ill health, he had hoped to lead his regiment against the French at Fort Niagara (near Youngstown, N.Y.), but his promotion to major-general in June 1755 meant, according to General Edward Braddock, the British commander in North America, that he could not "with any propriety" take the field as colonel of his regiment.

Pepperrell returned to Boston from his regimental headquarters in New York and resumed his seat on the Massachusetts Council. After the death of Lieutenant Governor Spencer Phips in the spring of 1757, Sir William served as acting governor of Massachusetts for four months until the arrival of the new governor, Thomas Pownall. The aging conqueror of Louisbourg lived to see Jeffery Amherst* and James WOLFE, with 9,000 British regulars and 40 ships of war, duplicate his feat in 1758. The following year Pepperrell became the only native American to receive a commission as lieutenant-general in the British army. The honour came almost too late, for by May he was dangerously ill. He lingered on for two months more, and then on Friday, 6 July 1759, Sir William Pepperrell died, greatly lamented.

Although Amherst and Wolfe won a measure of acclaim from colonials for their exploits at Louisbourg and Quebec, Sir William Pepperrell was, to the post-1745 generation of Americans, the foremost military figure of the colonies. For 30 years his fame endured, until a famous musket shot on Lexington Green created a whole new set of heroes.

BYRON FAIRCHILD

The principal manuscript collections of Pepperrell papers are those of the Harvard College Library, the New England Historic Genealogical Society, the Massachusetts Historical Society, and the privately held collection of Joseph W. P. Frost, Kittery Point, Maine. Other valuable documentary sources are the town records of Kittery (Maine), Books I–II (1648–1799), and the Warren papers and Louisbourg papers of the Clements Library.

See also: *Correspondence of William Shirley* (Lincoln). *Louisbourg journals* (De Forest). Mass. Hist. Soc. *Coll.*, 1st ser., I (1792). "The Pepperrell papers," Mass. Hist. Soc. *Coll.*, 6th ser., X (1899). *Province and court records of Maine*, IV, V. R. G. Albion, *Forests and sea power; the timber problem of the Royal Navy, 1652–1862* (Harvard economic studies, XXIX, Cambridge, Mass., 1926). Byron Fairchild, *Messrs. William Pepperrell: merchants at Piscataqua* (Ithaca, N.Y., 1954). J. W. P. Frost, *Sir William Pepperrell, bart., 1696–1759, his Britannic majesty's obedient servant of Piscataqua* (Newcomen Soc. in North America pub., New York, 1951). J. J. Malone, *Pine trees and politics; the naval stores and forest policy in colonial New England, 1691–1775* (Seattle, 1964). McLennan, *Louisbourg*. Parkman, *Half-century of conflict*. Usher Parsons, *The life of Sir William Pepperrell, bart. . . . .* (1st ed., Boston, 1855; 2nd ed., Boston, London, 1856). Rawlyk, *Yankees at Louisbourg*. W. G. Saltonstall, *Ports of Piscataqua; soundings in the maritime history of the Portsmouth, N.H., customs district . . .* (Cambridge, Mass., 1941). J. A. Schutz, *William Shirley: king's governor of Massachusetts* (Chapel Hill, N.C., 1961). E. S. Stackpole, *Old Kittery and her families* (Lewiston, Maine, 1903).

PÉRIGNY, PAUL D'AILLEBOUST DE. *See* AILLEBOUST

PERRAULT, FRANÇOIS, merchant; b. *c.* 1694 in the parish of Saint-Jacques in Cosnesur-Loire, France, son of Jacques Perrault, a surgeon, and Marguerite Caché; d. 7 Aug. 1745 at Trois-Rivières.

François Perrault perhaps came to Canada with his brother Jacques. In 1715 François was settled in Quebec, where on 26 November he married Suzanne Pagé, sister of the silversmith Jacques PAGÉ, *dit* Carcy. Jacques, for his part, married the daughter of a surgeon in 1724 and settled at Lachenaie, where he practised the same profession as his father and father-in-law.

François Perrault was an ambitious man and displayed great initiative in increasing his dry goods business. In 1719, in partnership with Louis Dunière, he signed a trading lease for three years for the seigneuries of Restigouche, Miramichi, and Nipisiguit, situated on Baie des Chaleurs and belonging to the commissary of artillery, Pierre Rey Gaillard. Gaillard tried to have the lease broken before its expiry date, but the two partners had no difficulty in obtaining a judgement in their favour.

In 1732 Perrault bought at auction an immense house on Rue Sault-au-Matelot in Quebec. At that time he had a large family, of which he soon had to take sole charge, since his wife died the following year. In 1737 he took over the management of the trading post on the Nontagamion (Nétagamiou) River in Labrador (Que.), in partnership with Jacques de LAFONTAINE de Belcour, a merchant and councillor of the Conseil Supérieur who some years earlier had obtained an exclusive privilege to operate the fisheries in that region. In 1740, in partnership with his son Jacques* and Charles Levreau, Perrault took a trading lease on the same post. Thanks to these new interests Perrault added profits from fishing, hunting, and especially trade in peltries to his already prosperous business. In 1741 the three partners were accused by the merchant Pierre TROTTIER Desauniers, syndic of the Quebec merchants, of having misappropriated certain funds coming from the post, but no proof could be brought against them.

In addition to his store in Quebec François Perrault owned branches at Trois-Rivières, at the Saint-Maurice ironworks, and in the parish of Saint-Sulpice near Montreal. In them were a great variety of materials, from the finest linen to the loveliest lace – serge, cotton, pulled wool, basan, and even tanned sealskin. Perrault also sold handkerchiefs, sheets, blankets, gloves, stockings, necklaces, pewter knives and spoons, needles, thread, nails, and fishhooks. He supplied his stores by a schooner, the *Marie*

Perrault

Angélique, which he owned with his son Jacques. His clientele was found particularly on the north shore of the St Lawrence, between Quebec and Saint-Sulpice, but also on the south shore.

It was during one of his business trips that this active man died, on 7 Aug. 1745 at Trois-Rivières, where he was buried the next day. On 2 November following, Jacques was appointed guardian for his under-age brothers and sisters; the inventory of Perrault's possessions was drawn up on 8 June 1746.

François Perrault left a large inheritance to his children, thanks to the wealth that he had been able to acquire by hard daily work. Besides Jacques, certain of his descendants played an important role in the society of their times, among them his son Joseph-François* (1719–74), who was the bishop of Quebec's vicar general at Trois-Rivières and provost of the chapter, and Joseph-François* (1753–1844), a grandson, who became one of the most eminent organizers of elementary teaching in Canada.

ROLAND-J. AUGER

ANQ, Greffe de Florent de La Cetière, 22 nov. 1715; Greffe de J.-C. Panet, 8 juin 1746. *Inv. de pièces du Labrador* (P.-G. Roy), I, 46–47. *Recensement de Québec, 1716* (Beaudet), 51. Le Jeune, *Dictionnaire.* P.-G. Roy, *Inv. coll. pièces jud. et not.*, I, 90–99; *Inv. jug et délib., 1717–1760*, I, 58, 145, 273, 334; II, 96; IV, 42, 65, 90; *Inv. ord. int.*, II, 150–51, 160, 226, 285. Tanguay, *Dictionnaire; Répertoire.* Jacques Mathieu, "Un négociant de Québec à l'époque de la conquête: Jacques Perrault l'aîné," ANQ *Rapport, 1970*, 27–34.

PERRAULT (Perrot, Perreault), PAUL, adjutant-general of militia in Canada; baptized at Deschambault (Que.) on 4 April 1725, son of Jacques Perrault and Marie-Madeleine Paquin; d. at Kourou, French Guiana, 29 Jan. 1765.

Son of a farmer and a farmer himself, Paul Perrault also apparently engaged in trade and transportation ventures, and was successful enough to buy extra land. An early testimony to his ambition and ability was his appointment to head his community's militia. As captain for the *côte* he was a sergeant, inspecting drills and equipment; a sheriff, enforcing the decrees of Intendant Bigot*; and a social symbol with a special pew in church. He directed statute labour (*corvée*) for the upkeep of roads and bridges and could even act as a minor magistrate.

With the coming of war in 1755 Perrault assigned the men of Deschambault to serve chiefly as bateau crews to convey troops and war materials to Lake Champlain. Military supplies were kept under armed guard in a storehouse on

Perrault's property, and he billeted passing officers, for example the Chevalier de La Pause [Plantavit*], in his home.

Perrault received a new appointment on 3 June 1759, with a rise in status. Governor Pierre de Rigaud* de Vaudreuil, having been refused permission to fill the vacant post of adjutant-general of militia with his first choice, his nephew, named Perrault. Though a simple habitant, he was perhaps marked for promotion because of his record as militia captain. Moreover, his wife – Marie-Joseph Rivard, *dit* Lanouette, whom he married at Sainte-Anne-de-la-Pérade on 3 Aug. 1750 – may have been related to Joseph-Pierre Cadet*, Bigot's associate. To one onlooker Perrault's outstanding characteristics were his zeal and his fondness for intrigue.

As adjutant-general of militia Perrault coordinated the employment of all Canada's able-bodied men (16,000). They were required as bateaumen, soldiers, and farmers: all of these needs were simultaneous and all were urgent. He was stationed at Montreal, his work being primarily as administrator and inspector, although he might occasionally advise the strategy-makers when he had particular knowledge. In 1759 one of his tasks was to select the militiamen to be incorporated into French regular and colonial regular units, in accordance with MONTCALM's favourite scheme for increasing the usefulness of colonial manpower. Writing to Lévis* about the importance of efficient supply convoys from Montreal to Quebec, Île aux Noix, and La Présentation (Oswegatchie, now Ogdensburg, N.Y.), Vaudreuil stressed that for planning "Perrot can be useful to you in this matter; you know just as well as I do how keen he is."

Vaudreuil's continued confidence was shown in his proposal (9 Nov. 1759) that Perrault should become assistant town major of Quebec: previous incumbents had all been officers in the colonial regular troops. Early in 1760 Perrault toured the parishes of non-occupied Canada to review the militia and to bolster the habitants' determination to recapture Quebec in the spring, a difficult task after five years of war.

Perrault, his wife, and his three daughters (a son was born later) survived the war unscathed. Their homestead burned in August 1759, however, when an enemy raiding party blew up the military storehouse behind it. He was offered the chance to stay on as adjutant-general of militia under the British but refused. Instead, he aspired to serve the king of France further, and in 1761, without his family, went to Paris. By April 1762 he found himself in prison, charged with graft in the *affaire du Canada*. He was released on 10

Dec. 1763, and given the type of post he sought. "I have the anguish of seeing swindlers given 2,000 *livres*, 1,600 *livres*," wrote Jean-Baptiste-Nicolas-Roch de Ramezay* to his wife in April 1764. "Even one of our Canadian peasants is to have 1,600 *livres*, namely that inconsequential Perrot from Deschambault, who is going to Cayenne [French Guiana] as adjutant of militia."

In the summer of 1764 Perrault came to Canada to fetch his family. They sailed from Quebec during August in the *Nourice*, calling at Saint-Pierre and Miquelon on the way south. Perrault was charged by the French government to persuade about 300 miserable Acadians there to accept an offer of three years' initial support if they would emigrate to French Guiana. The refugees were afraid of its hot unhealthy climate, which, Perrault argued in writing, was exaggerated; moreover, he added, Miquelon might be attacked by the British: "You, and myself too – we're like the Israelites seeking the promised land. . . . In St-Pierre and Miquelon there are no streams flowing with milk and honey, on the contrary. . . . I am on my way to settle at Cayenne. Do you think that my family and my health are less dear to me than yours?" He could not move the Acadians, and in the middle of September carried on to South America.

Within three months of his arrival in French Guiana heat or a tropical plague brought him down, at Kourou. His family returned to France. Talent, tact, good luck, and good connections carried an ordinary habitant into association with the powerful men who ran the French administration. He was only 39 when he died – the price of ambition.

MALCOLM MacLEOD

AN, Col., D²ᶜ, 48, f.334. "Le chevalier de la Pause," APQ *Rapport, 1931–32*, 11. Bougainville, "Journal" (Gosselin), APQ *Rapport, 1923–24*, 388. *Édits ord.*, II, 343. "Journal du siège de Québec" (Æ. Fauteux), APQ *Rapport, 1920–21*, 137–241. Knox, *Historical journal* (Doughty). *Lettres de l'intendant Bigot* (Casgrain), 77. *Lettres du marquis de Vaudreuil* (Casgrain), 99, 106. "Mémoire du Canada," APQ *Rapport, 1924–25*, 160. PAC *Rapport, 1905*, II, pt.III, 215–20. "Les 'papiers' La Pause," APQ *Rapport, 1933–34*, 208. Bonnault, "Le Canada militaire," APQ *Rapport, 1949–51*, 272–74. P.-G. Roy, *Inv. procès-verbaux des grands voyers*, IV, 137. Tanguay, *Dictionnaire*. P.-G. Roy, *Bigot et sa bande*, 150–51; *Les petites choses de notre histoire* (7 sér., Lévis, Québec, 1919–44), 3ᵉ sér.; "M. de Ramesay, lieutenant de roi à Québec, après 1759," *BRH*, XXII (1916), 359–60.

PERTHUIS, JEAN-BAPTISTE-IGNACE, merchant, last king's attorney for the provost and admiralty courts of Quebec; b. 13 April 1716 at Quebec, son of Charles Perthuis* and Marie-Madeleine Roberge; d. sometime after 1767 in France.

The son of a rich Quebec merchant, Jean-Baptiste-Ignace Perthuis followed his father and made a career in business. On 16 Sept. 1742, on the eve of his marriage in the church of Notre-Dame de Québec and in the presence of the administrative, business, and military élite of the capital of New France, he signed a marriage contract with Marie-Josephte-Madeleine, daughter of Henry HICHÉ, king's attorney and rich Quebec merchant. His wife brought him as her dowry a piece of land and a stone house worth 3,000 *livres*, plus an annual income of 502 *livres* and a trousseau valued at 1,000 *livres*. Having made such a rich marriage, Perthuis acquired more and more importance in Quebec society. He became at this time one of the contractors to the state; in 1744 he sold it more than 8,000 *livres* of merchandise intended for the construction of the *Caribou*; in 1747 he was one of five Quebec merchants who supplied the state with munitions and general merchandise to a value of 61,740 *livres*.

While he was doing business with the government, Ignace Perthuis was following the lectures in law given by the attorney general, Louis-Guillaume VERRIER. He nourished the ambition of one day filling a position in the judicature. His father-in-law enabled him to realize this ambition. Not being able, at 81 years of age, to carry out with all the assiduity desired the functions of king's attorney for the provost court of Quebec, Henry Hiché obtained on 23 Nov. 1753 from the intendant, Bigot*, permission for his son-in-law to act as his deputy in case of illness, absence, or challenge. On 15 May 1754, when Hiché was named a councillor of the Conseil Supérieur of Quebec, Perthuis succeeded him in the offices of king's attorney for the provost and admiralty courts of Quebec. He fulfilled these two functions zealously until 1760. After the conquest he went to France with three of his five children. He took up residence in Paris and was still living there in November 1767. After that no more is heard of him.

Jean-Baptiste-Ignace was the son of an important Quebec merchant. But his rank as the youngest son in the family hardly favoured him, since in New France the customary law of Paris was followed as regards the transmission of the father's estate. Thanks to his marriage, however, he succeeded in climbing the social ladder and in becoming wealthy.

ANDRÉ LACHANCE

Peters

AN, Col., B, 99, f.4; C¹¹A, 120, f.351. ANQ, Greffe de Nicolas Boisseau, 16 sept. 1742; NF, Coll. de pièces jud. et not., 1866, 2137, 2139, 4050; NF, Documents de la Prévôté de Québec, 8 janv. 1742. PAC *Report, 1886*, clxxxi; *1888*, 47. "Recensement de Québec, 1744" (APQ *Rapport*), 52. Gareau, "La Prévôté de Québec," APQ *Rapport, 1943–44*, 111. P.-G. Roy, *Inv. concessions*, I, 16–17; *Inv. jug. et délib., 1717–1760*, V, 284, 286; VI, 100, 110; *Inv. ins. Cons. souv.*, 270–71. Tanguay, *Dictionnaire*. Nish, *Les bourgeois-gentilshommes*, 68, 75, 114. P.-G. Roy, *Fils de Québec*, I, 187–88.

PETERS, HENDRICK. *See* THEYANOGUIN

PETITPAS, BARTHÉLEMY, navigator, agent to the Micmac Indians, interpreter; b. 1687, probably at Mouscoudabouet (Musquodoboit Harbour, N.S.), son of Claude Petitpas* and a Micmac woman named Marie-Thérèse; m. Madeleine Coste *c*.1715 and had six sons and two daughters; d. January 1747 at Boston, Massachusetts.

From childhood Barthélemy Petitpas's mores and habitat were those of the Micmacs. He spoke the Micmac tongue even before he spoke French, and, through sustained associations with New Englanders trading and fishing in Acadia, he became fluent in English as well. Petitpas's knowledge of all three languages made him an invaluable instrument of the rival diplomacies of England and France in Acadia, not only among his own people, the Micmacs, but likely also among the Acadians. It is part of the irony of Barthélemy Petitpas's career that he could be branded by a Frenchman as a "bad [type capable] of doing things that are most prejudicial to our interests" (Pierre-Auguste de Soubras*, 1717), and at about the same time be accused by an English official of doing "great damage to my master's subjects by incensing the savages against them" (John Doucett*, 1718).

When he assisted Captain Thomas Smart* in the expulsion of a group of French fishermen from Canso in 1718 Petitpas was firmly in the British camp. He spent the next three years as a guest of the English in Boston, perfecting his English, and returned late in 1721 to become the official British agent among the Micmacs in Nova Scotia. Philippe de Rigaud* de Vaudreuil and Michel BÉGON reported that the intention was for Petitpas to return as a Protestant missionary among the Micmacs, "to win over this nation and make it change its religion."

Petitpas's return caused grave concern at Île Royale (Cape Breton Island). Knowing he was fast becoming more dangerous even than his father, who had also helped the English, Governor Saint-Ovide [MONBETON] contrived to have Barthélemy captured, probably in November 1721 when his 18-ton schooner was confiscated at Louisbourg for trading in contraband goods from Canso. In 1722 Saint-Ovide sent him to the seminary of Quebec in the hope that after years of study Petitpas's ardours would be channelled to the French missionary effort. In Quebec, however, Petitpas confided to Bishop Saint-Vallier [La Croix*] that he desired only to learn navigation. Late in 1722, therefore, he was sent to Rochefort, France, where he was maintained and trained by a competent hydrographer at crown expense. He nevertheless remained intractable, and by the summer of 1723 the intendant at Rochefort, François de BEAUHARNOIS, requested that Petitpas be sent to Martinique as a soldier, as he "won't stick at anything, and has been ruined by wine and women." His conduct was no better in Martinique, however, and the authorities so feared he would lead his comrades to desert that he was eventually sent back to France and imprisoned at Le Havre.

He was released from prison in June 1730, still proscribed from returning to New France. It is surprising, therefore, to find him back at Île Royale as early as the summer of 1731, being warmly recommended by the financial commissary, Jacques-Ange LE NORMANT de Mézy, for the post of Indian interpreter. His father in fact received the appointment, but after Claude's death the following summer the position, with an annual stipend of 300 *livres*, devolved in course upon Barthélemy.

Petitpas appears to have been restored to favour at Île Royale in the interests of the colony. Beauharnois had readily admitted his intelligence, and Saint-Ovide and Le Normant were quick to recognize there was "no other person here" fit to act as interpreter. His abilities were appreciated: after being dispatched early in 1734 to pilot a vessel to New York to purchase sorely needed supplies of food for the colony, he reminded the authorities that he could be earning more than 1000 *livres* in the coastal trade. His stipend was immediately doubled to 600 *livres*.

The final 12 years of Barthélemy Petitpas's life remain obscure. We know nothing of the direction of his influence among the Micmacs, nor of his relations with the colonial authorities. We do know that he was serving as a pilot in 1745, the year the New Englanders captured Louisbourg [*see* William PEPPERRELL]. Petitpas himself was captured and imprisoned in Boston. Governor William Shirley maintained his right to detain him even after the exchange of prisoners because, he claimed, Petitpas "had no right to throw off his allegiance and go into the french King's service.'' Petitpas died in January 1747, still in prison in Boston. His widow was reported in a 1752 census as living with six of their children at L'Ardoise, Île Royale.

BERNARD POTHIER

AD, Charente-Maritime (La Rochelle), B, 265, ff.20–21 (Amirauté de Louisbourg). AN, Col., B, 45, ff.200, 205; 54, f.42; 59, f.516; 63, ff.535–37; C¹¹ᴮ, 2, f.38v; 5, f.43; 6, ff.107–8; 12, ff.53–53v; 14, ff.3–7; 15, ff.12–14, 90v, 139; F²ᶜ, 3, ff.556–57, 576; Marine, C⁷, 244; Section Outre-Mer, G³, 2041, f.52; 2047/1, f.90. PRO, CO 217/2, f.215. Coll. de manuscrits relatifs à la N.-F., III, 379. PAC Report, 1905, II, pt. ɪ, 12. Arsenault, Hist. et généal. des Acadiens, I, 477–78. Coleman, New England captives, I, 97–98.

PETTREQUIN (Petrequin), JEAN, joiner; b. c. 1724 in Montbéliard, France; buried Lunenburg, Nova Scotia, 19 Dec. 1764.

Jean Pettrequin arrived in Nova Scotia from Montbéliard in July 1752 aboard the *Betty*, a ship carrying European Protestant settlers. These "foreign Protestants," as they were called, had been arriving in Halifax since 1750, and were part of a British plan to populate Nova Scotia without drawing off badly needed agricultural workers from Britain. For the most part the new settlers were Germans and Swiss. They were offered an initial grant of 50 acres of land free of quit rents and taxes for ten years, with additional grants as their families increased. Free subsistence was granted them for a year upon arrival, as well as any necessary arms, and materials and utensils for clearing and cultivating land and erecting dwellings. Non-British immigrants were not granted free passage to America, however, and so most of these settlers had to indenture themselves to the government and work on public projects in Halifax for a time. By the fall of 1752 about 1,500 of them were crowded together in Halifax in inadequate conditions. In the summer of 1753 Governor Peregrine Thomas HOPSON was able to settle them on the south coast at Mirligueche (Lunenburg).

Jean Pettrequin was among those who settled at Lunenburg and achieved some notoriety the first winter as an important figure in the December "insurrection" there. He claimed to have received through a sailor a letter from a cousin in England connected with government stores, who asked how the Lunenburg settlers were being treated and whether they were receiving the supplies ordered for them. Rumours about the kinds of supplies mentioned in the letter began to circulate in Lunenburg, and the list

began to appear more extensive than the goods the settlers had actually received. A faction of the Germans, disenchanted with their treatment in Nova Scotia, became angry when Pettrequin claimed that the sailor had forbidden him to show the letter to anyone, and finally, on 15 December, they seized Pettrequin and confined him to the militia blockhouse. He was released briefly by Colonel Patrick SUTHERLAND but was taken again by a mob and returned to the blockhouse. That evening he was tortured by members of the guard to find the letter's whereabouts. He finally confessed to one current rumour, namely, that he had sold the letter to the magistrate, Sebastian Zouberbuhler*.

The next morning the settlers visited Colonel Sutherland demanding that Zouberbuhler hand over the letter, but the magistrate denied that he had ever seen it. That evening 150 armed settlers attempted to take the lower blockhouse and two attackers were wounded in an exchange of fire. Sutherland immediately dispatched an officer to Halifax for reinforcements. The next day the settlers demanded a vessel to carry 20 deputies to England, "to make their complaints to the Parliament. . . ." A force arrived from Halifax under Robert Monckton* on 22 December and within a few days the settlers had been disarmed.

Pettrequin confessed at a hearing that another settler, John William Hoffman*, had read him a letter which he claimed he had received on Pettrequin's behalf from a sailor in Halifax, and had urged Pettrequin to send a reply and let the contents be known to the rest of the settlement. Hoffman was taken to Halifax where he was subsequently found guilty of "false and scandalous libel" and of inciting the settlers to riot. Pettrequin's testimony was the only positive feature of the crown's case.

Whoever the ringleaders had been, someone had used an illiterate newcomer to foment opposition to the administrators of the colony, with not surprising success. From the time of their arrival the settlers had generally felt cheated of the promises made to them by the government, frustrated during the long delay at Halifax, and handicapped by the shortage of supplies at Lunenburg.

Nothing is known of Pettrequin's life after 1754.

RONALD ROMPKEY

PANS, MG 1, 110, p.149; RG 1, 134, 342, 382, 474. PRO, CO 217/13, ff.190, 200; 217/15. Bell, *Foreign Protestants.*

PHILIBERT, NICOLAS JACQUIN, *dit.* See JACQUIN

513

Philipps

PHILIPPS, ERASMUS JAMES, military officer, member of the Nova Scotia Council and Nova Scotia House of Assembly; b. 23 April 1705, possibly the son of Erasmus Philipps, the brother of Richard PHILIPPS; d. 26 Sept. 1760 at Halifax, Nova Scotia.

Little is known of the early years of Erasmus James Philipps' life. He appears first in Nova Scotia as an ensign in the 40th Regiment of Foot. In the autumn of 1726 he was ordered by Lieutenant Governor Lawrence Armstrong* to proceed from Annapolis Royal to Beaubassin (near Amherst, N.S.) to administer the oath of loyalty to the Acadian inhabitants in that region. Because of bad weather at Annapolis the mission was postponed until the spring of the following year, and then it was totally unsuccessful. Philipps reported that "the inhabitants of Beau Bassin . . . resolutely refused to take the oath I tendered them." They threatened to withdraw to Île Saint-Jean (Prince Edward Island) rather than sign the oath and felt free "to dispose of their goods to the first that would pay for them, whether French or English."

Despite this inauspicious beginning, Philipps received several important appointments and quickly became a significant figure in Nova Scotia. In 1729 he was commissioned king's advocate for a vice-admiralty court which Governor Richard Philipps was intending to establish in Nova Scotia. The governor does not seem to have carried through his plan, and it is uncertain how often Philipps functioned in the capacity of king's advocate. In December 1730 he was appointed to the Nova Scotia Council, and by 1734 he seems to have attained the rank of major.

In addition to his council and military duties Philipps was assigned other responsibilities which were to make him a frequent visitor to New England. An appointment, with William Skene and Otho HAMILTON, as a Nova Scotia representative on a commission for settling a boundary dispute between New Hampshire and Massachusetts, took him to Hampton (N.H.) in August 1737 and then on to Boston for a lengthy visit. While in Boston, in November 1737, Philipps was initiated into the masonic order. He attended a number of lodge meetings in Boston and was likely encouraged to extend the order into Nova Scotia. In March 1738 he was appointed provincial grand master of the Ancient Free and Accepted Masons in Nova Scotia, and in June he became the founder and first master of the first masonic lodge in Canada, at Annapolis Royal. Thus he has been considered the founder of freemasonry in Nova Scotia. In the spring of 1741 he served on a commission concerning the boundaries of Rhode Island and Massachusetts which met in Providence (R.I.).

At the outbreak of war between France and England in 1744, Philipps was still serving at Annapolis Royal. He was commissary of provisions there in April 1746 and in October of that year he was ordered, along with Edward How, to accompany the British forces being sent to the Grand Pré area under the command of Arthur NOBLE. As commissioners in charge of the administration of civil affairs in the area, Philipps and How were to inquire into the loyalty of the Acadians to the British government and to confiscate any arms, foodstuffs, or vessels that might be intended for use by the French. Philipps also functioned as virtual quartermaster for the English troops, arranging for their accommodation and food. On 29 Jan. 1746/47 Philipps was recalled to Annapolis Royal; two days later the French attacked Grand Pré and overran the garrison.

The arrival of Governor Edward Cornwallis* in 1749 brought major changes in Nova Scotia, such as the replacement of the old council, but Philipps made the transition well and was appointed to the new council in August. At the same time he resigned his commission as a vice-admiralty advocate. He continued to reside at Annapolis, serving as commissary of musters. In his last years several further honours came to Philipps. He received a vote of thanks from the Nova Scotia Council for capturing in 1757 a number of Acadians who had fled two years before, at the time of the expulsion, and formed a temporary settlement on St Mary's Bay. In 1759 Governor Charles LAWRENCE appointed him commander of the forces at Annapolis. That same year the people of the Annapolis area honoured one of their better known residents by electing Philipps to the Nova Scotia House of Assembly. He died of apoplexy while visiting Halifax in September 1760.

Erasmus James Philipps was married to Ann Dyson; they had one son and three daughters.

WILLIAM G. GODFREY

PRO, CO 217/5, ff.31–32v. *Documents relating to currency in Nova Scotia, 1675–1758* (Shortt), 240–41. *N.S. Archives, I; III; IV.* PRO, *Acts of P.C., Col., 1720–45; CSP, Col., 1726–27, 1734–35; JTP, 1734/35–1741.* G. T. Bates, "John Gorham, 1709–1751: an outline of his activities in Nova Scotia, 1744–1751," *N.S. Hist. Soc. Coll.,* XXX (1954), 41. Brebner, *New England's outpost.* Calnek, *History of Annapolis* (Savary). D. G. L. Fraser, "The origin and function of the Court of Vice-Admiralty in Halifax 1749–1759," *N.S. Hist. Soc. Coll.,* XXXIII (1961), 66. J. R. Robertson, *The history of freemasonry in Canada, from its introduction in 1749*

(2v., Toronto, 1899), I. Savary, *Supplement to history of Annapolis.* ''The Erasmus James Philipps medallion'' (pamphlet published by the Grand Lodge of A.F. and A.M. of Nova Scotia, Halifax).

PHILIPPS, RICHARD, military officer, governor of Nova Scotia; b. *c.* 1661 in Pembrokeshire, Wales (according to a plaque marking his burial place), son of Richard Philipps and Frances Noel; d. at London 14 Oct. 1750.

Richard Philipps came from a Pembrokeshire family with political and mercantile connections – none of them outstanding, but all of them useful in an England where the continued prosperity of a landed family often depended on its ability to follow the turns of politics and the royal succession. A younger son with no prospects of inheriting the family baronetcy, Richard entered the army as a lieutenant about 1678. His chance for preferment and a basis for his later career came in 1688 when William of Orange set sail for England and he was employed to circulate printed announcements of the prince's intentions among the Jacobite troops in advance of William's landing at Torbay. Philipps was arrested near Dartmouth, and, though accounts differ on the details, it is known that he was about to be hanged when the news of William's arrival came and his captors hurriedly released him. He was awarded a captaincy, and with his good service at the Battle of the Boyne was launched on an army career that took him to Flanders and Spain. In 1712 he purchased the colonelcy of the 12th Regiment of Foot (Bretton's).

Philipps' first official connection with Canada came on 17 Aug. 1717, the effective date of his formal commission as ''Governor of Placentia in Newfoundland and Captain General and Governor in Chief of the Province of Nova Scotia.'' He was given an additional commission on 25 August as colonel of a new regiment that was to be formed from the independent companies of foot then garrisoning the posts at Placentia and Annapolis Royal (formerly Port-Royal), Nova Scotia. The governorship was apparently only an appointment by letter at first, for the commission was not issued until June or July of 1719.

The selection of a governor for Nova Scotia to succeed Samuel Vetch* was part of the British government's plan to regulate the untidy affairs of the province. Since the capture of Port Royal in 1710 and the ratification of the treaty of Utrecht in 1713, British control of Nova Scotia had been erratic and ineffectual, betraying the home authorities' lack of real interest and a seeming absence of policy. The senior officer at Annapolis Royal – the only British-occupied part of the province – was expected to govern the colony, extract a binding oath of allegiance from the resident Acadian population, and maintain authority with four infantry companies who had no regimental affiliation. The French were securing Île Royale (Cape Breton Island) by building a fortified settlement at Louisbourg, and were testing British resolve in Nova Scotia by claiming the rich fishery at Canso. The difficulties of governing the scattered Acadians effectively from a crumbling fort at Annapolis were balanced by British fears that the French strength in Cape Breton would be increased if the Acadians were allowed to take advantage of a clause in the 1713 treaty and leave the mainland.

The members of the Board of Trade and Plantations in London, spurred by the activities of the French and by the tangled financial affairs of the troops at Annapolis, convinced the government of the need for a change in the methods of running the colony. They seem, however, to have thought little about details. If Philipps had gone to Nova Scotia when his appointment was announced, it is doubtful whether much difference would have been noticed in the province, for the changes would have been limited to the appointment of a new governor, the creation of a regiment on the army establishment, and a set of vague instructions. Whatever might be said about Philipps' subsequent efforts to earn his salary, or the disparity between official intentions and effective action, his astuteness in seeking a formal commission and more specific instructions gave the province what limited benefit it did receive from this brief flurry of interest at Westminster. He pointed out that his appointment would be valueless unless a form of civil government were provided. Since it was now the British government's intention to encourage settlement and trade, he requested instructions ''. . . proper for laying the foundations of a Civill Government . . . necessary for settling a Colony.'' He was kept informed of developments in Nova Scotia by Captain John Doucett*, who had been sent out as lieutenant governor of the town and garrison of Annapolis Royal in the fall of 1717. Armed with Doucett's lucid reports, and able to wait upon the Board of Trade in person, Philipps advocated settling the colony, retaining the Acadians for the time being, and vigorously promoting the fisheries.

The final instructions issued in June 1719 reflected Philipps' views, and included a copy of the instructions given to the governors of Virginia to guide him in setting up a civil government. He arrived in Nova Scotia in April 1720 after wintering in Boston, and wasted no time in meeting the most pressing local problems. He appointed a council for the province, consisting of himself and 11 townsmen and officers, and spread the news of his arrival among the Acadians to prepare the ground for the administration of an oath of allegiance. Like Thomas Caulfeild* and Francis Nicholson* before him, he quickly found that the appearance of power without the substance was of little value in overawing the Acadians. He partially lost the initiative three days after his arrival, when Father Justinien DURAND came to the fort with 150 Acadians ". . . as if he meant to appear formidable." Philipps informed them that his instructions were to invite them to take the oath; Durand replied that in accordance with the choice given them by the 1713 treaty they had previously "in General Nicholson's time . . . sett their hands unanimously to an obligation of continuing Subjects of France & retireing to Cape Breton. . . ." They were not, therefore, free to swear allegiance. Philipps stalled by persuading the Annapolis Acadians to choose six deputies to represent them in discussions on the issue, but by the end of May the people had signed only a submission that they would behave as good subjects if not required to bear arms. They showed no intention of leaving the mainland, however, and this attitude more than anything underlined the impotence of the new council.

Philipps wrote home for instructions, and informed the Acadians that he had unilaterally extended the royal deadline of four months for the imposition of the oath. This announcement removed the tension from the issue, but by autumn the only action that Philipps and the baffled council could think of was to petition the king for 600 new troops to enforce the government's authority. The question of the oath was left in abeyance for the rest of Philipps' first residence. In spite of this setback, Philipps had managed to establish a working relationship with the Acadians, at least in the Annapolis area. His extension of the deadline for the oath without seeming to lose face, his promptness in appointing a provincial council, and his willingness to let matters ride when new instructions were not forthcoming, seem to have convinced the people that the new governor was a man of some authority and prestige, and that they could reach an accommodation with him.

Powerless though he was with a small force, Philipps acted vigorously whenever the chance afforded. In 1720 he tried to induce the inhabitants of Newfoundland to move to Nova Scotia, but Lieutenant Governor Samuel Gledhill*, who resented Philipps' authority, refused to circulate the governor's proclamations. He was particularly interested in the Canso fishery, and quickly realized that the French threat in Île Royale could neither be watched nor contained from a seat of government at the opposite end of the province. The plundering of New England fishermen at Canso by Indians on 8 Aug. 1720 provoked quick action. Philipps sent Major Lawrence Armstrong* with troops to help the fishermen build a small fort, and in 1721 moved to Canso himself. When the Indians continued to harass the fishermen he first tried diplomacy, opening discussions with them in 1722 and distributing presents; but when in July of that year they turned pirates and showed alarming competence in preying on local shipping, he organized the New Englanders at Canso, put his own troops to work as marines, and in three weeks had dispersed or killed the marauders.

Philipps returned to England in the fall of 1722, and for the next six years the council at Annapolis and the senior officers, Doucett and Armstrong, were left to govern by what J. B. Brebner has aptly called "analogy and rule of thumb." The question of whether Philipps was more neglectful of his duties than other absentee governors is fruitless, since it is difficult to find parallels to Nova Scotia's condition. Certainly the province was to suffer in his absence, but, in the light of his second residence (1729–31), it would be gratuitous to claim that his presence would have saved the province from a neglect that originated with British priorities rather than with any apathy on his part. While in England he seems not to have bothered to reply with any frequency to the correspondence of his distraught deputies at Annapolis, but kept himself informed through consultations with the Board of Trade. In reply to the board's queries as to what should be done, he reiterated in precise and patient memorials the same problems and solutions that he had identified with Doucett's help before ever setting foot in the province. It was a mistake, he claimed, to think that an effective government could operate from Annapolis so long as there were insufficient troops, no Protestant settlers, no provincial revenue, and no fortifications at the principal Acadian settlements. He wanted a fort at Chignecto (near Amherst, N.S.), where the most independent Acadians lived, and a more substantial protection for Canso, as well as a road between the settlements at Chignecto, Cobequid (Truro), Pisiquid (Windsor), Minas (Wolfville), and those along the Annapolis River.

The Board of Trade managed to interest the king's Privy Council in Nova Scotia in 1728, and Philipps was directed to return there. He could not have been too optimistic about the support of a government that in 1722 had refused to allow his expenses for a small vessel to enable him to inspect his province occasionally; but he offered his thanks, ventured to express the hope that his majesty would reread his earlier recommendations, and left for Nova Scotia in the spring of 1729.

After spending the summer at Canso keeping order among the fishermen, he arrived at Annapolis on 20 November. While at Canso he had received word of Acadian discontent, caused by Lieutenant Governor Armstrong's harsh treatment of Father René-Charles de Breslay* at Annapolis, and his blunt attempts to administer the oath. Philipps' policy now was to capitalize on Armstrong's heavy-handedness and administer the oath after placating the inhabitants. By the end of the year he had reinstated Breslay in his parish and assured the Acadians that the government would take steps to confirm them in possession of their lands. On 3 Jan. 1729/30 he sent home an oath of allegiance signed by 194 Annapolis Acadians, obtained without "threats or compulsion, nor . . . a scandalous capitulation" – a reference to Ensign Robert Wroth*, who in 1727 had modified the oath to overcome Acadian reservations against bearing arms. Philipps spent the early spring of 1729/30 visiting the settlements at Minas and Chignecto, and capped his earlier success by returning to Annapolis in May with "the entire submission of all those so long obstinate People." Curiously, and perhaps significantly, the council minutes take only perfunctory note of Philipps' return, and Philipps did not report his success to the Duke of Newcastle until 2 September. He made another exhausting trip in the fall to obtain the signatures of the few who had not subscribed to the oath in the spring.

It is generally conceded that Philipps gave the Acadians at Minas and Chignecto – the more intractable inhabitants – a verbal promise exempting them from the normal subject's duty to bear arms, and that he told a spectacular and portentous lie by simply not giving Newcastle the whole truth. A lengthy list of events and documents have been cited in proof, including a notarial declaration attesting to the verbal promise, recorded by the Minas people days after the oath was taken [see LA GOUDALIE]. Moreover, it was the unquestioning assumption of later administrators, including Governor Edward Cornwallis*, that Philipps had temporized and "did not do his duty." The reason why Philipps granted the qualified oath may lie less in his hopes of official approval than in a cynical, if realistic, belief that the difference did not matter so long as the British authorities could not enforce an unqualified oath. He had a low opinion of the Acadians, calling them "a pest and encumbrance," and this, rather than any understanding of their position, may have convinced him that the best to be expected was their neutrality. He was not, of course, the first to retreat from the unqualified oath. In 1726 Armstrong had agreed to write a marginal note concerning the exemption on the copy of the oath he read to the Annapolis Acadians. The difference between Armstrong's verbal concession and Philipps' is important, however, for the Acadians took no particular reassurance from the former and placed their faith in the latter. Philipps' compromise was to haunt the masters of Nova Scotia for 25 years and contribute significantly to the tragic elements of the expulsion of 1755.

Philipps' final months in Nova Scotia were devoid of accomplishments. The loss of his authority over Placentia, occasioned by the appointment of Captain Henry Osborn* in 1729 as governor of Newfoundland, affected him little, since he had been unable to exercise control over Samuel Gledhill, the lieutenant-governor, because of distance and the political nature of Gledhill's position. He could not have been surprised when the colonization schemes advanced by the Board of Trade in 1728 came to nothing. His recall in 1731 was due directly to the complaints of his officers over non-payment of the debts they had incurred to supply and feed their soldiers in his absence. The tangled treasury accounts at Annapolis led to an inquiry in England and Philipps, as the 40th regiment's colonel, was abruptly summoned home in July to explain. He left his council with the legacy of Acadian neutrality and a host of jurisdictional jealousies. Major Alexander COSBY, who had been appointed lieutenant governor of the town and garrison after Doucett's death, was Philipps' brother-in-law; and his further appointment in 1730 as president of the council over more senior members, such as Paul MASCARENE and John ADAMS, ensured that the tendency of this isolated garrison to petty disputes would flourish long after Philipps' departure. Philipps' relations with Mascarene seem to have cooled after the latter's objections to Cosby's appointment as council president. Armstrong and Philipps were barely civil to each other; Philipps had earlier refused to support Armstrong's claims for financial losses.

During his long tenure as governor Philipps took great pains to avoid expense, for the treasury officials were notoriously picayune about money matters; but he seems not to have even

517

Phlem

risked displeasure by insisting on extra expenditures for the province. He kept a particularly watchful eye over anything that would be chargeable to his governor's allowance. Though he escaped censure in the matter of his regiment's victualling debts, there is little doubt that he skimped on the legitimate needs of his troops and the salaries of such government officers as Arthur Savage*, William Shirreff, Doucett, and Mascarene. Philipps deprived Mascarene of his pay as acting administrator in his absence by persuading the authorities that the lieutenant governorship of the province was an unnecessary position. At best he can be charged with miserliness; at worst he falls under a suspicion of building a personal fortune at the expense of his troops and council.

Philipps remained governor of Nova Scotia until 1749, making occasional appearances before the Board of Trade to give advice when requested. He could suggest nothing new, because the fundamental problems remained the same. Nothing is known of his later years, or whether he was consulted when the government decided to establish a settlement at Chebucto (Halifax). He became a lieutenant-general in 1743, and in 1749 or 1750 he exchanged his regiment, which became Cornwallis', for the 38th (Dalzell's). His last days were spent in Great Queen Street in fashionable Westminster, where several of his kinsmen apparently lived, and he died there 14 Oct. 1750. The death notice in the *Gentleman's Magazine* was a garbled reference to "Lieut.-Gen Philips of horse, formerly Col. of a Regt. of Foot in the Leeward Islands, aged near 100." He was buried in the north transept of Westminster Abbey, appropriately in the corner occupied by the dukes of Newcastle.

Philipps was married twice: to Elizabeth Cosby (d. *c.* 1739), sister of Alexander, and to Catherina Bagshawe, *née* Stratham. He had two daughters and possibly a son by the first marriage.

MAXWELL SUTHERLAND

PAC, MG 11, Nova Scotia A, 8, p.214; 9, pp.27, 128; 10, pp.85–97; 15, pp.198–207, 252–65; 17, pp.230–31; 19, pp.3, 39; 20, pp.94–96; MG 21, E5, 42. *Gentleman's Magazine*, October 1750. *N.S. Archives*, *I*; *II*; *III*; *IV*. J. B. Burke, *A genealogical and heraldic dictionary of the peerage and baronetage of the British Empire* (34th ed., London, 1872), 905. *English army lists* (Dalton), VI, 65. *DNB*. Brebner, *New England's outpost*. Smythies, *Historical records of 40th regiment*, 496–97.

PHLEM (Flame, Flemme, Le Fène), *dit* **Yvon, YVES,** healer; b. at Morlaix, France, son of Guil-

laume Phlem and Marguerite Péroine; d. 26 Sept. 1749 at Sainte-Anne-de-la-Pérade (Que.).

According to his own testimony Yves Phlem grew up at Morlaix, where presumably he learned the rudiments of the art of healing as then known: bleeding, dressing wounds, and using "several remedies for curing different maladies." When Phlem arrived in Canada is not known, but he was there in 1724, since on 8 April of that year he married Marie Levreau (L'Heureux) at Sainte-Famille, Île d'Orléans. The couple was living at Saint-Nicolas when their first child was born the following year, and in 1727 they were at Sainte-Anne-de-la-Pérade. It was in that parish that Phlem put into practice, for more than 20 years, his healing knowledge.

It is difficult, however, to determine what his activities as a surgeon were, particularly at the beginning of his career. A great number of documents refer to him by that title, but few tell us anything about his patients and the treatment he gave them. He was above all renowned for curing cancer, and in this field he achieved, it seems, "remarkable cures." The sick sometimes came from a considerable distance to be treated by him. But Phlem's treatment was not always efficacious, as is shown by the case of Michel Desmarais, a habitant from Saint-Sulpice who died in 1729 at Sainte-Anne-de-la-Pérade "in the home of the Sieur Yves Phlem, surgeon."

Nevertheless nothing seems to have disturbed the healer's peaceful existence until 1735, when what could be called the Bilodeau affair began. Phlem could not have suspected difficulties when he agreed in September 1735 to treat Jean Bilodeau, who was afflicted with a sort of cancer which had "eaten away his lower lip and almost all of his chin." Before having recourse to Phlem, the sick man, who lived at Saint-François, Île d'Orléans, had already been treated by the surgeon Jean Mauvide of Île d'Orléans. As the latter had been unable to check the malady, Bilodeau had gone to Quebec to consult Michel Bertier*, king's surgeon, and the Jesuit Jean-Jard BOISPINEAU, both of whom considered the malady incurable. Phlem was much more optimistic: in an agreement signed in the presence of Joseph Voyer, the parish priest of Sainte-Anne, he undertook to treat Bilodeau "to the best of his ability for a period of six consecutive months . . . unless the aforementioned Bilodeau is completely cured before the said period of six months." Phlem promised in addition to supply his patient with board, lodging, and laundry, to dress his wound twice a day, and to give him all necessary care. For his part Bilodeau promised to give the surgeon "for his pains, treatment, and supplies" the sum of 500 *livres*, payable in three instalments.

Unfortunately the six months went by without the over-confident Phlem curing his patient, or the over-trusting Bilodeau paying his doctor. On 25 March 1736 the two men ratified their previous agreement before the notary Arnould-Balthazar POLLET. Bilodeau, who still owed Phlem 400 *livres*, mortgaged all his belongings in favour of the latter. It was to no avail, for the patient, suffering more and more, died on the following 10 May in Phlem's house.

This death was to have unpleasant consequences for Phlem. Marie Turgeon, Jean Bilodeau's widow, refused to make the payments which the surgeon demanded according to his agreement with the patient. On 14 Oct. 1736, therefore, Phlem presented a request concerning this matter before the provost court of Quebec. He had cause to regret it. On 15 March 1737 the lieutenant general for civil and criminal affairs, Pierre ANDRÉ de Leigne, not only declared the agreement between Yves Phlem and Jean Bilodeau null and void, "whereas the aforementioned appellant has no qualifications as a surgeon and cannot be recognized as such," but strictly forbad him to "assume in the future the profession of surgeon and to exercise its functions," on pain of a severe fine. The decision did, however, award Phlem the sum of 120 *livres*, since he had lodged and boarded the deceased for eight months.

Phlem was greatly discontented with this decision and appealed to the Conseil Supérieur, to whom he presented a long memorial dated 22 March containing his complaints. In it he explained, in much detail, that this healer's talents could not be questioned and that it was his duty to utilize them, "otherwise one could apply the parable of the Saviour of the world, and what He said against him who had hidden what had been given him. . . . When the master asked him for an account of it, he was punished for having done so." Imbued with these pious sentiments, Phlem had up till then carried out the functions of a surgeon publicly and had earned the approbation of his fellow-citizens. He had, he said, even obtained the protection of the authorities; for example, Intendant Hocquart*, whose great "exactness . . . in correcting abuses" no one could question, had never forbidden him to practise his profession, although he was perfectly well aware of his activities. In his memorial Phlem also stressed his agreement with Bilodeau which the provost court had refused to recognize. The agreement in question could not be annulled, he maintained, since it had been ratified by a deed signed before a notary. He asked the Conseil Supérieur therefore to enforce the clauses in the deed and make the widow Bilodeau pay him his due. To back up his argument Phlem presented, along with his memorial, the minutes of a protest meeting held at Sainte-Anne-de-la-Pérade on 22 March 1737. They had been written up by the notary Pollet and signed by the parish priest, the local seigneur, Pierre-Thomas Tarieu de La Pérade, and a great number of habitants. All bore witness to the surgeon's good reputation and asked the Conseil Supérieur to overrule the judgement of the provost court and allow Phlem to continue practising his profession.

The Conseil Supérieur submitted the case to the surgeon Jourdain LAJUS, who declared that Phlem had no choice but to obtain letters of qualification if he wanted to practise his profession. When it met on 13 April 1737 to render its verdict, the Conseil Supérieur took this opinion into consideration. It dismissed Phlem's appeal and called upon him to take out surgeon's papers. On the other hand, the court sentenced the widow Bilodeau to pay the appellant the sum of 180 *livres*, 60 more than the provost court had awarded the healer.

Despite its severity this judgement does not seem to have unduly impressed Phlem, who took no steps to obtain letters patent and continued to treat the sick. It is true that any request on his part would probably have been refused, since his surgical knowledge was much more empirical than theoretical, and this he surely realized. Moreover, he was not unaware that as long as no one lodged any new complaints against him, he could continue to practise as a surgeon without being disturbed.

The years following the Bilodeau affair were quiet. It seems that Phlem's reputation had remained intact in the eyes of his fellow-citizens. As in the past, the healer continued receiving sick persons in his home. No complaint was brought against him, even if there might have been some occasions to do so. Indeed, according to the parish records of Sainte-Anne-de-la-Pérade, three of his patients died in his home: Nicolas Marion in 1738; Paul Desmarais, from Verchères, who was suffering from dropsy, in 1739; and Gabriel Desmaisons, a Saint-Maurice ironworks employee who also had dropsy, in 1742. But there were certainly many who found relief thanks to him.

Yves Phlem died at Sainte-Anne-de-la-Pérade on 26 Sept. 1749 and was buried the next day "in the presence of the greater part of the said parish." The inventory of the deceased's belongings was drawn up on the following 3 October by the notary Pollet. Strangely enough, he makes no

Pierre

mention either of remedies or of surgical instruments!

MARIE-CÉLINE BLAIS

AJTR, Greffe d'A.-B. Pollet, 25 mars 1736, 3 oct. 1749. ANQ, NF, Coll. de pièces jud. et not., 1145, 2406. Archives paroissiales de Sainte-Anne (La Pérade, Qué.), Registres des baptêmes, mariages et sépultures, 10 mai 1736, 22 juill. 1738, 12 déc. 1739, 22 févr. 1742, 27 sept. 1749. P.-G. Roy, *Inv. coll. pièces jud. et not.*, I, 217; *Inv. jug. et délib., 1717–1760*, III, 170, 172. Tanguay, *Dictionnaire.* Ahern, *Notes pour l'histoire de la médecine.* Raymond Douville, "Chirurgiens, barbiers-chirurgiens et charlatans de la région trifluvienne sous le régime français," *Cahiers des Dix*, XV (1950), 114–18. Sylvio Leblond, "La médecine dans la province de Québec avant 1847," *Cahiers des Dix*, XXXV (1970), 69–74. Victor Morin, "L'évolution de la médecine au Canada français," *Cahiers des Dix*, XXV (1960), 64–71.

PIERRE. *See* GAWÈHE

PIERRE, Comanche Indian, slave; b. *c.* 1707; baptized 11 Sept. 1723 in Montreal; buried there 5 Aug. 1747.

This slave, a Comanche, was probably born in the central prairies of the present United States. The tribe was the relentless enemy of its neighbours, the Pawnees, who were found in great numbers as slaves in the St Lawrence valley and whose name in French, "Panis," came to be used to mean any Indian slave.

In 1732 Pierre, as he had been baptized, was the subject of a legal struggle which obliged the authorities of New France to pronounce more definitively on the legality of slavery in the colony than had Intendant Jacques Raudot* in his ordinance of 1709. Philippe You de La Découverte, the slave's owner, was the object of a distraint upon this piece of property as security for a debt of 3,500 *livres* that he owed Daniel MIGEON de La Gauchetière. In December 1732 Pierre Raimbault*, the lieutenant general for civil and criminal affairs in the jurisdiction of Montreal, approved the distraint and ordered the slave to be sold for the benefit of Migeon de La Gauchetière. The merchant Charles NOLAN Lamarque purchased him for 351 *livres*.

You de La Découverte appealed the decision of the Montreal judge to the Conseil Supérieur of New France. He alleged that the sale should be declared "invalid and harmful to religion," and that the Indian, "being a Christian," should recover his liberty. In addition, he claimed that Migeon de La Gauchetière should return the purchase price of 351 *livres* to Nolan Lamarque and Raimbault should be summoned before the council for having ordered "the sale of a Christian on the marketplace."

The Conseil Supérieur referred the litigants to Intendant Gilles Hocquart*, who, basing his decision on Raudot's ordinance which had legalized the enslavement of Negroes and Pawnees, confirmed the judgement handed down by Raimbault in the case of the Comanche Pierre. The affair might have been the occasion for the king to issue a regulation concerning slavery, but he preferred that the judges respect Canadian custom. Pierre Raimbault had created a precedent.

When he was buried in Montreal on 5 Aug. 1747, Pierre was still the property of Charles Nolan Lamarque.

MICHEL PAQUIN

[In his work *L'esclavage au Canada français* Professor Marcel Trudel has studied exhaustively the cases of Pierre the Comanche and many other slaves in Canada. The writer has used his work, every statement in which is based on primary sources. M.P.]

PILGRIM, ROBERT, HBC mariner and chief factor; buried 1 Dec. 1750 at Hackney (now in London), England.

Robert Pilgrim was first employed by the Hudson's Bay Company in 1730 as a steward aboard the *Hudson's Bay* (Capt. Christopher MIDDLETON). For the next five years he was aboard company ships making the annual supply trips from London to the James Bay factories. In 1735 he became master of the sloop attached to Moose Fort (Moose Factory, Ont.), a position he held until 1738 when he returned to the trans-Atlantic voyages.

In 1740 Pilgrim contracted for five years' employ in Hudson Bay and was appointed to the governing council of Prince of Wales Fort (Churchill, Man.). There he served grudgingly under Richard NORTON (1740–41) and James ISHAM. When Isham went to England in 1745 Pilgrim was given charge. In 1748 he was transferred to the command of Moose.

Badly afflicted with rheumatism, Pilgrim, accompanied by his Indian wife Ruehegan (Thu a higon) and a son, returned to England by the *Seahorse* in 1750. Shortly after, he died. His will expressed the wish that his son be placed under a guardian in England and Ruehegan be allowed to rejoin her family at Churchill. The HBC afforded facilities for her to return to the bay but ordered its captains to refuse in future to bring any natives as passengers to Britain.

The HBC's trust of important charges to Pilgrim had been unwise. He was soon at odds with neighbouring factors and with Joseph ROBSON, Robert EVISON, and others of his subordinates. He traded unfairly with the Indians and neglected the maintenance of fort buildings. To a query about him from the London committee, Thomas WHITE, who took charge at Moose in 1751, replied, "Mr Pilgrim being dead having very little to say of his general good Character We beg to be excus'd entring into his bad one."

JOAN CRAIG

Greater London Record Office, St John-at-Hackney parish register, 1737–69. HBC Arch. A.1/34, pp.227, 292; A.1/35, p.9; A.6/5, pp.222–25; A.6/6, pp.39–40, 154, 156; A.6/7, pp.15, 50, 91, 152–53, 157, 222–23, 287; A.6/8, pp.130, 135; A.11/13, ff.96–99d; A.11/43, ff.49d, 51, 54d, 58–58d, 60; A.15/9, pp.49, 72–73, 128, 283–84, 336, 387–88, 444; A.15/10, pp.18, 72, 129, 191, 245, 314, 324; B.3/a/41; B.42/a/23; B.42/a/38; B.135/a/6; B.135/a/7; B.135/a/20b; B.239/b/7, f.3; B.239/b/8, f.3d; C.2/1, ff.25, 30, 35, 41; C.2/2, ff.50, 59, 61. PRO, Prob. 11/784, f.396ff. G.B., Parl., *Report from the committee on Hudson's Bay*. HBRS, XXV (Davies and Johnson). Christopher Middleton, *A reply to the remarks of Arthur Dobbs esq.* . . . (London, 1744); *A vindication of the conduct of Captain Christopher Middleton* . . . (London, 1743). Joseph Robson, *An account of six years residence in Hudson's-Bay, from 1733 to 1736, and 1744 to 1747* . . . (London, 1752). Morton, *History of the Canadian west*. Rich, *History of the HBC*, I.

PILLARD, LOUIS, Brother Hospitaller of the Cross and of St Joseph, royal notary, royal court officer and court clerk; b. *c*. 1700, son of Pierre Pillard and Anne Parisette, originally from the parish of Saint-Sulpice in Paris, France; buried 12 Jan. 1768 at Trois-Rivières.

Louis Pillard was a Brother Hospitaller of the Cross and of St Joseph by 1719, and he continued as such until 1735. He devoted himself particularly to teaching, was bursar of the Hôpital Général of Montreal in 1733 and bursar of his community in 1734. Then he settled at Pointe-aux-Trembles, in the seigneury of Neuville. There, on 24 Dec. 1735, he received a commission as royal notary for the north shore of the government of Quebec, between the outskirts of the town of Quebec and Sainte-Anne-de-la-Pérade. The investigation into his character took place on 7 Jan. 1736. On 10 March 1740 Pillard was appointed royal court officer for the region.

He carried out his duties for ten years in the government of Quebec, then went to that of Trois-Rivières. On 15 March 1746 he had received letters of appointment as court clerk for this jurisdiction, "as well as notary and court officer for the same." In 1748 he was acting judge at Trois-Rivières, and from 1758 to 1767 he was

bursar for the Ursulines of that town. He kept his offices as court clerk and notary after the conquest.

On 12 Aug. 1737 at Pointe-aux-Trembles he had married Marie-Angélique Dubuc, who died in December 1752. On 26 June 1753 at Trois-Rivières he remarried, his second wife being Marguerite Beaudry, who survived him. His son Louis tried in vain to succeed him as notary.

ANDRÉ VACHON

AJTR, Greffe de Louis Pillard, 1736–1767. ANQ, Greffe de J.-N. Pinguet de Vaucour, 11 août 1737; NF, Coll. de pièces jud. et not., 2084, 2097; NF, Ins. Prévôté de Québec, VI, 487; VII, 47; VIII, 49; NF, Ord. int., XXIII, 72; XXXIV, 22; NF, Registres du Cons. sup., 1741–1749, ff.376ff. Massicotte, "Inventaire des documents concernant les frères Charon," APQ *Rapport, 1923–24*, 181, 185, 194, 196, 200. "Les notaires au Canada," APQ *Rapport, 1921–22*, 45. J.-E. Roy, *Histoire du notariat*, I, II. Gérard Malchelosse, "Un procès criminel aux Trois-Rivières en 1759," *Cahiers des Dix*, XVIII (1953), 219–20.

PINGUET DE VAUCOUR, JACQUES-NICO-LAS, royal notary and seigneurial judge; b. 10 Aug. 1692 in Quebec, son of Jacques Pinguet de Vaucour, seigneurial judge, and Marie-Anne Morin; d. 7 April 1749 in Quebec.

Jacques-Nicolas Pinguet de Vaucour belonged to a family whose members have been more than once mistaken for one another. His career was uneventful. On 18 July 1726 Intendant BÉGON granted him a commission as royal notary to practise in the area of the provost court of Quebec. Four years later, on 20 Jan. 1730, he succeeded his father, who had died the previous year, as judge for the seigneuries of Notre-Dame-des-Anges, Saint-Gabriel, and Sillery. He continued in these offices until 1748, when illness forced him to resign. He died in Quebec on 7 April 1749.

Pinguet belonged to the fourth generation of this family, which had settled in New France in 1634. His father, Jacques, who married twice, had 22 children, several of whom died in infancy. But enough survived to cause confusion when it comes to describing the career of each member of the family. When Jacques Pinguet's 14th child was born, Jacques-Nicolas was old enough to be its father, and at the birth of the 22nd he was 36 years old. Since he was the eldest of the family, he had to watch over the interests of his brothers and sisters after his father's death, and a too hasty reading of the documents has sometimes led to Jacques-Nicolas's becoming the father of this progeny. Moreover, his Christian name was

Plante

similar to his father's, and often in documents the distinguishing element, Nicolas, was left off; much more frequently still, no Christian name is given. Confusion has also occurred with Jacques-Nicolas's uncle, Charles Pinguet, and his brother, Joseph-Régis, who were sailors, and with another brother, Nicolas-Charles Pinguet de Bellevue, who was judge at Beauport.

Jacques-Nicolas and Nicolas-Charles were bachelors and lived in their father's house on Rue Desjardins. Nicolas-Charles was thus able to act as notary for a time in place of his brother, who was kept at home by his infirmities. The provost court of Quebec objected to this in a verdict delivered on 2 April 1748. On 20 September of that year Jacques-Nicolas resigned as notary and was replaced by Simon Sanguinet. Nicolas-Charles was, however, able to practise officially as a notary when he obtained his commission on 22 March 1749, two weeks before Jacques-Nicolas's death.

MICHEL PAQUIN

ANDQ, Registres des baptêmes, mariages et sépultures, 10 août 1692, 7 avril 1749. ANQ, Greffe de N.-C. Pinguet de Bellevue, 1749–1751; Greffe de J.-N. Pinguet de Vaucour, 1726–1748. P.-G. Roy, *Inv. coll. pièces jud. et not.*; *Inv. ins. Prév. Québec*; *Inv. jug. et délib., 1717–1760*; *Inv. ord. int.*; *Inv. testaments*. Tanguay, *Dictionnaire*. J.-E. Roy, *Histoire du notariat*, I, 353. P.-G. Roy, "La famille Pinguet de Vaucour," *BRH*, XL (1934), 257–90.

PLANTE, CHARLES, priest, canon, director of the seminary of Quebec, vicar general, parish priest of Quebec, ecclesiastical superior of the Hôpital Général of Quebec; b. 18 Dec. 1680 at Sainte-Famille, Île d'Orléans, son of Claude Plante and Marie Patenotre; d. 20 March 1744 in Quebec.

Charles Plante had already begun studying Latin when he entered the Petit Séminaire of Quebec on 20 Oct 1696. On 24 July 1701 he received the tonsure from Bishop Laval*, who ordained him a priest on 22 Dec. 1703, having conferred the other orders on him in the course of the year 1702.

Sounded out in 1702 by Abbé Jean-François Buisson* de Saint-Cosme (1667–1706) about going to the missions in the Mississippi country, Plante was instead sent to Beaumont in September 1704, to replace Jean Pinguet, who had become old and infirm. Besides Saint-Michel (Saint-Michel-de-Bellechasse) he served Berthier-en-Bas (Montmagny), of which he was the founding parish priest. His name appears among the 13 signers of an important report on the tithe, presented to the court by the parish priests of

Canada and dated 27 April 1706 [*see* Étienne Boullard*; DUFOURNEL]. He is again found at Beaumont from 1715 to 1718 after being parish priest of Saint-François-de-Sales, Île Jésus, from November 1711 to October 1715. On 26 Nov. 1712 Plante was appointed a canon; he served as secretary of the chapter of the cathedral of Quebec from 1718 to 1725 and as treasurer from 1733 on. Although he was reputed to have "a gentle disposition," he was a dutiful and exact person, and he protested to the court against Canon Louis LEPAGE de Sainte-Claire's repeated absences from the services and meetings of the chapter on the plea that he "has his land and mills to put into production." Plante's function as secretary had obliged him to return to Quebec, and from 1718 to 1739 he served the parish as curate. On 31 Dec. 1727 the chapter designated him vicar general of the diocese; his letters of appointment are dated 3 Jan. 1728. He had first been elected on 26 Dec. 1727 to the assembly of the chapter, which had been hurriedly called together immediately after the death of Bishop Saint-Vallier [La Croix*], but so great had been the canons' agitation that nothing had been recorded and his election was declared null and void. Despite his hopes Abbé Plante does not appear to have been attached to the seminary of Quebec until the spring of 1728, when he was chosen as a director, notwithstanding his title of canon, which could have been an obstacle.

It was only after he had spent many years ministering to the parish of Quebec, that on 25 April 1739 a decision was made to appoint him titular priest of the parish. He was the ninth parish priest of Quebec, and since M. Boullard's death in 1733 three of his predecessors had followed one another in the office in rapid succession. Only Jean LYON de Saint-Ferréol had taken possession of the parish, but he had remained there less than a year. In other words, during nearly this whole time Abbé Plante carried out the duties of the parish priest, and he should have been given this benefice by 1733. Now it was feared that his age and infirmities might prevent him from accepting the office. Nevertheless he had been carrying out the "duties of curate" sufficiently long "to deserve to be the incumbent of the benefice," and it was felt this appointment would "make it known that Canadians are capable of something." Abbé Plante was indeed the first Canadian to become parish priest of Quebec. Although exhausted and ill, he kept this charge for five years until his death, and the taking of possession, delayed until 18 Oct. 1739, brought him in addition the worries of a dispute with the chapter [*see* Pierre-Joseph RESCHE]. As he preferred to keep his charge as parish priest, he resigned his canonry on 15 Oct. 1740. A month earlier he had accepted the office of ecclesiastical superior of the Hôpital Général of Quebec. He was also confessor to the Nuns Hospitallers of the Hôtel-Dieu from 1736 to 1742.

An ascetic despite his infirmities and a talented orator, he was said to "show great zeal for the destruction of vice, which was increasing day by day." In 1717, at the urging of Bishop Saint-Vallier, he had had a house fitted out near the Hôpital Général to take in the unfortunate victims of prostitution who wanted to be converted. In his will made on 20 Feb. 1744 he made a recommendation: "I have a great desire that my successors in charge of the parish of Quebec keep up the work which I have begun with the cells or houses of correction to detain dissolute women and to prevent offence against God and scandal, and in order that it may be strong and may endure this house must be demolished and rebuilt on the end of the house where are lodged the ladies who are paying guests of the Hôpital Général. The house in its present location is too much in danger of being entered by force by libertines, who have several times broken in to release the women shut up in it; therefore, it can be raised by a storey and cells can be built to the number of six or more on the top storey, with small windows, in such a way that no one can speak to them or get them out." The rebuilding of the house was compromised because of the constant poverty which soon after beset the Hôpital Général, and the alms the parish priests of Quebec continued to supply were barely sufficient, with other aid, for the upkeep of this charitable work.

After more than 40 years in the priesthood Charles Plante died of a malignant fever at the Hôtel-Dieu of Quebec on 20 March 1744. He was buried in the cathedral the next day.

ARMAND GAGNÉ

AAQ, 1 W, Église du Canada, I, 49; 12 A, Registres d'insinuations A, 810–18; 12 A, Registres d'insinuations B, 198, 273, 315; 12 A, Registres d'insinuations C, 142; 10 B, Registre des délibérations; 11 B, Correspondance, II. AHGQ, "Vie de Mgr de Saint-Vallier," 223. ANQ, Greffe d'Abel Michon, 1ᵉʳ août 1730. ASQ, Brouillard, 1732–51; Lettres, M, 56, 57, 62, 95; Lettres, R, 35; MSS, 2; Paroisse de Québec, 7–9; Séminaire, IV, 99–104. Provost, *Le séminaire de Québec: documents et biographies*, 437–38. P.-V. Charland, "Notre-Dame de Québec: le nécrologe de la crypte," *BRH*, XX (1914), 211. Tanguay, *Dictionnaire*. Gosselin, *L'Église du Canada jusqu'à la conquête*. *Mgr de Saint-Vallier et l'Hôpital Général*, 305, 710. J.-E. Roy, "Saint-Étienne de Beaumont," *BRH*, XIX (1913), 222–24.

PLESSY (Plessis), *dit* **Bélair, JEAN-LOUIS,** merchant tanner of Montreal; b. 1678, son of Jean Plessy, *dit* Bélair, a master tanner, and Françoise Mathusson of Metz in Lorraine (France); m. 27 Feb. 1713 at Montreal to Marie-Anne Petit Boismorel; they had 20 children of whom 13 died young; buried 21 March 1743 at Montreal.

Jean-Louis Plessy's nickname "Bélair" can only have described his appearance for tanneries were so malodorous that they were kept well outside the towns. The low repute of tanning was, however, sweetened by the smell of money. Though it took considerable capital to establish a tannery, many in New France tried their hand at it and the inferior leather produced by the inexperienced forced the intendant in the early 18th century to restrict the trade to a few proven tanners. In Montreal Charles Delaunay* and Gérard Barsalou enjoyed a near monopoly of the lucrative craft. To foster greater competition and productivity Intendant Jacques Raudot* gave Jean-Louis Plessy permission in 1710 to operate a tannery in the same town and warned the other two not "to trouble him [Plessy] in the exercise of his trade."

Plessy had come to Canada as a recruit in the colonial regular troops and had been discharged in his twenties. The son and grandson of master tanners at Metz, he had worked in France before enlisting. The records and testimony given to the intendant in 1710 also bore witness that Plessy "had for two years managed Jean [L'Archevêque]'s tannery, one of the largest in this country, and that he had even worked in all the other tanneries." Plessy, however, lacked the means to establish his own business. He went into partnership with a butcher, Joseph Guyon Després, who agreed to erect and equip a tannery and to finance its first year of operation. Plessy's relations with his backer's family were evidently good for in 1713 he married Després's sister-in-law. His part of the marriage settlement was 1,000 *livres* earned as a tanner. Jacques Thibierge, the king's gunsmith at Montreal and a friend, acted as his witness to the contract.

In 1714 Plessy felt that he could now run his own tannery. With savings and loans amounting to 2,200 *livres*, he bought land upon which he had a carpenter build a 37 by 21 ft tannery, a tanbark mill, a house, and outbuildings. Plessy enjoyed a modest prosperity; he erected other buildings, leased a house, and bought a Pawnee slave whom he apprenticed to a shoemaker. Contracts were made with butchers for raw skins, and Plessy's leather found a ready market with shoemakers of the region.

After Jean-Louis Plessy, *dit* Bélair, died in

Poilly

1743 his eldest son Charles carried on in his trade until 1749. Another son, Joseph-Amable, became a blacksmith and fathered Plessy's most illustrious descendant: Bishop Joseph-Octave Plessis*.

PETER N. MOOGK

ANQ, Greffe de François Genaple de Bellefonds, 8 févr. 1707; NF, Documents de la juridiction de Montréal, VI, 193–95; XI, 67–68; XII, 40–43; NF, Ord. int., IV, 27–28. ANQ-M, Greffe de Jacques David, 31 oct. 1721, 13 sept. 1722, 4 avril 1723; Greffe de Michel Lepailleur, 24 févr. 1713, 21 mai 1716, *passim*; Greffe de J.-C. Raimbault, 19 oct. 1727; Greffe de Pierre Raimbault, 27 mars 1710; Documents judiciaires, 2 juill. 1728; Registres des audiences, VII, 793, 835. *Édits ord.*, II, 265–66. *L'île de Montréal en 1731* (A. Roy), 43. P.-G. Roy, *Inv. jug. et délib., 1717–1760*, I, 101, 126, 128, 235; II, 25; *Inv. ord. int.*, I, 17, 48, 96. Tanguay, *Dictionnaire*, I, 478; VI, 390. J.-N. Fauteux, *Essai sur l'industrie*, 419–21, 426, 436, 443.

POILLY, FRANÇOIS-CLAUDE-VICTOR GRILLOT DE. *See* GRILLOT

POLLET, ARNOULD-BALTHAZAR, royal notary; b. 1702 in France, son of Germain Pollet and Marguerite Harry, of the parish of Saint-Nicolas-des-Champs in Paris; d. and buried 17 Jan. 1756 at Batiscan in the government of Trois-Rivières.

We have little information about Arnould-Balthazar Pollet prior to his marriage with Angélique Hamelin on 10 May 1729 at Les Grondines, in the government of Quebec. He was living there on 6 Jan. 1730 when he was appointed notary and clerk of court for Batiscan, a seigneury which at that time belonged to the Jesuits. Some months later, on 12 September, he received from Gilles Hocquart*, the financial commissary, a commission as royal notary for the region covering the seigneuries of Batiscan, Champlain, and Les Grondines. On 24 March 1732 Intendant Hocquart granted him a new commission as notary for the seigneuries of La Chevrotière, Deschambault, Les Becquets, and Saint-Ours as well. To exercise his office, which he held for 23 years, Pollet had to go into the governments of Montreal, Trois-Rivières, and Quebec; his jurisdiction extended from Saint-Ours on the west to Deschambault on the east, a distance of more than 80 miles.

On 3 Jan. 1753 Pollet was forbidden to exercise his functions. In the ordinance concerning this affair Intendant Bigot* mentions, without giving any details, that it was the itinerant notary's bad conduct that had warranted this interdiction. Pol-

let died three years later and was buried at Batiscan.

MICHEL PAQUIN

AJTR, Greffe d'A.-B. Pollet, 1730–1753. ANQ, NF, Coll. de pièces jud. et not., 2068; NF, Ord. int., 12 sept. 1730, 24 mars 1732, 3 janv. 1753. Tanguay, *Dictionnaire*. Vachon, "Inv. critique des notaires royaux," *RHAF*, IX (1955–56), 438. J.-E. Roy, *Histoire du notariat*, I, 204–5.

POMMEREAU (Paumereau), JEAN-BAPTISTE, storekeeper, king's writer, entrepreneur in the fishery; b. in Montreal, 15 April 1702, son of Pierre-Jacques Pommereau and Françoise Nafrechoux; d. in Quebec, 26 March 1742.

Jean-Baptiste Pommereau's father was a merchant and militia captain at Montreal. Apparently he filled supply contracts for the colonial government, and his contacts with colonial officials probably enabled Jean-Baptiste to obtain positions in the king's storehouses and in the office of the Marine.

On 2 May 1738 Jean-Baptiste Pommereau acquired a ten-year concession, for the seal fishery, to a four-league frontage on the Labrador shore running northeast from Cap du Gros Mécatina. In the fall the right to use some offshore islands was added; a ship and shallop were outfitted at a cost of 9,000 *livres* but got only as far as Gaspé. In the spring of 1739 he surrendered a half-interest to Guillaume Estèbe* and Daniel-Hyacinthe-Marie LIÉNARD de Beaujeu. Estèbe inspected the grant, and in September the concession was extended three or four leagues to Rivière Thekaapoin.

In 1740 a considerable establishment was formed at Gros Mécatina. At least 14 men including two coopers were hired to work under Charles Lecourt, a ship's master, and during the two succeeding years 16 and 22 men were hired. Also, the bateau used during the first year was abandoned and the schooner *Louise* entered into service. Each fall the ship left Quebec with men and supplies, wintered in Labrador, and returned the following spring with the harvest. In December 1741, Pommereau leased from François MARGANE de Lavaltrie an additional post at the Rivière Saint-Augustin for 250 *livres* annually. Some evidence suggests that his father participated with him in his undertakings. There can be little doubt Pommereau's sealing ventures were profitable. During the six years following 1740, 2,730 hogsheads of seal and oil were harvested at Gros Mécatina; in the last three years more than 10,000 seal pelts, nearly half the production between Cape Charles and Mingan, were taken there. Pommereau appears to have been on the point of becoming an important Canadian merchant on the eve of his death in 1742.

Pommereau was undoubtedly assisted by his alliance with a great seigneurial family of Canada. On 11 March 1736 he married Claire-Françoise, daughter of Pierre Boucher de Boucherville. From this marriage there were five children whose godparents, François FOUCAULT, member of the Conseil Supérieur, Intendant Hocquart*, and military officers Michel-Jean-Hugues Péan* and François Pécaudy de Contrecœur, indicated, along with Pommereau's business associates, the social élite with which he identified. Later, his sons moved in this society, Jean-François serving as an officer in the colonial militia during the Seven Years' War and the American invasion, Gilles-François becoming paymaster of the Saint-Maurice ironworks. Two of his three daughters, Catherine-Élisabeth and Françoise-Renée, married English officers: John Bruyeres*, secretary to governor Ralph BURTON, and John Gough, military officer. During the next generation the influence Pommereau and his children had enjoyed disappeared.

Jean-Baptiste Pommereau predeceased his father who apparently remained well-to-do. In 1745 Pommereau's widow married Joseph-Michel Legardeur* de Croisille et de Montesson who joined Estèbe and Beaujeu in the exploitation of the sealing grounds at Gros Mécatina.

JAMES S. PRITCHARD

Inv. de pièces du Labrador (P.-G. Roy), I, 66–68, 71, 179; II, 11, 20–45, 50–53, 54–57. "La chasse des loups-marins autrefois," *BRH*, XXXIV (1928), 734. Gérard Malchelosse, "La famille Pommereau et ses alliances," *Cahiers des Dix*, XXIX (1964), 193–222 [This article provides manuscript sources for the Pommereau family.].

PONTBRIAND, HENRI-MARIE DUBREIL DE. *See* DUBREIL

PONTIAC (also spelled Pontiak, Ponteack, or Pontiague by the English in the 18th century, and **Pondiac**, Pondiak, or Pondiag by the French; called **Obwandiyag** in the Ottawa tradition of the 19th century), war chief of the Ottawas from Detroit; b. sometime between 1712 and 1725; murdered 20 April 1769 at Cahokia (East St Louis, Ill.).

The exact place and date of Pontiac's birth are not known, and the 19th century sources disagree about his parents' tribal affiliation. One of Pontiac's supposed widows, Kan tuck ee gun, was still alive in 1807. He is believed to have had at least two sons. Pontiac's personality seems to have made a greater impression upon his contemporaries than did his external appearance, which has been described in vague, subjective, and contradictory ways. All those who spoke of Pontiac saw him as a commanding, respected, and highly intelligent leader. To the author of the *Journal of Pontiac's conspiracy* (probably Robert Navarre*, a Detroit notary), he appeared "proud, vindictive, warlike, and very easily offended." In 1765 Major Robert Rogers* wrote: "I had several conferences with him, in which he discovered great strength of judgment, and a thirst after knowledge." That same year Lieutenant Alexander Fraser met the famous chief at Fort de Chartres (near Prairie du Rocher, Ill.) and noted: "He is in a manner Ador'd by all the Nations hereabouts, and He is more remarkable for His integrity & humanity than either French Man or Indian in the Colony."

We know nothing of the first 30 years or so of Pontiac's life, for French documents rarely note what happened in the Ottawa villages from 1720 to 1740. In 1736, 200 Ottawa warriors are believed to have been settled in the neighbourhood of Detroit. Since 1732 they had not lived near the French fort, but rather across from it, on the other side of the river, in a community of 800 to 1,000 inhabitants. The governors of Canada and the commandants of Fort Pontchartrain and Fort Michilimackinac without exception asserted that the Ottawas remained attached to the French and useful to them until 1744.

Then came war between France and England. In 1745, 60 Ottawas and Ojibwas asked to be taken "to Montreal to fight the English." Pontiac was perhaps one of them. In 1747 he was a witness to the conspiracy of ORONTONY, the Huron chief at Sandoské (in the vicinity of Sandusky, Ohio). An increase in the prices of goods for the Indians had created great discontent. The Iroquois stirred up a revolt, which was joined by some Ottawas. Detroit itself was in danger, but the plan was discovered. Did Pontiac take part in it? He is said to have denied it in a speech delivered in 1763 protesting his faultless loyalty to the French, but he must have gained experience of sedition; and he was beginning to work his way up to the office of war chief in his village, if he did not hold it already.

Forced to make peace and discontented, Orontony and his group emigrated to the Ohio valley to move closer to the English. Memeskia (La Demoiselle, Old Britain) and the pro-English Miamis went off to Rivière à la Roche (Great

Pontiac

Miami River) and founded Pickawillany (Piqua, Ohio). The French wanted to counter these lost Indian alliances and the settling of the English in their territory. In June 1749 Pierre-Joseph CÉLORON de Blainville warned the English to leave the area, but the trader George Croghan nevertheless visited Pickawillany in 1752. Shortly afterwards the village was wiped out by Charles-Michel Mouet* de Langlade at the head of 240 Canadians and Ottawas, one of whom was perhaps Pontiac. In 1754 the French, under Claude-Pierre Pécaudy* de Contrecœur, seized a trading post being built by the English and enlarged it as Fort Duquesne (on the site of present-day Pittsburgh, Pa.). Thus began the hostilities leading up to the Seven Years' War, which the Anglo-Americans called the French and Indian War because the Indians took such an active part in it.

In 1755 a British army commanded by Edward Braddock set out to capture Fort Duquesne. Pontiac may have been among the Indians, some 800 to 1,000 strong, who, with Jean-Daniel Dumas* and the French garrison, inflicted a terrible defeat on the British not far from the threatened fort. Some 300 Ottawas from Detroit and 700 from Michilimackinac remained at Fort Duquesne until 1756. They were vigilant scouts and multiplied their raids into the British colonies. A year later MONTCALM brought a certain number of these Algonkians to Montreal and took them on an expedition against Fort William Henry (or Fort George, now Lake George, N.Y.). Among his forces were 30 Ottawas from Pontiac's village.

In 1757 Pontiac delivered a speech before Pécaudy de Contrecœur at Fort Duquesne. He maintained that George Croghan had just tried to deceive him by claiming that Quebec had fallen and had called upon him to become an ally of the British. Pontiac said that he had resisted his advances and recalled the advantageous promises made to the friends of the French. In 1758 some Ottawas from Detroit were still fighting for France not far from Fort Duquesne, which the French abandoned to John FORBES on 24 November. In the colonial period many Algonkians often changed European allies. They scorned the vanquished and frequently went over to the side of the strongest and most generous. Would Pontiac and his men break their long-standing alliance with the French? After the capture of Louisbourg, Île Royale (Cape Breton Island), and forts Duquesne, Carillon (Ticonderoga, N.Y.), and Niagara (near Youngstown, N.Y.) in 1758–59, the victory of the British became a predictable certainty. Croghan, who

had been appointed deputy superintendent of western Indians, did not fail to point out to the Algonkians the inevitability of an eventual British victory in order to draw them to trade with him. At a meeting he held in August 1759, two of the leading Ottawas are reported to have been present and to have given proof of their goodwill towards the English. Pontiac was not there. In November 1759 his village was so divided that the pro-English faction and its chief moved to the region south of Lake Erie. About 200 Ottawas remained near Detroit. The following year, when the capitulation of the French was imminent, Croghan prepared the western Indians for the coming of British rule. He promised a much more liberal system of trade. In August 1760, along with other chiefs from Detroit, Pontiac may have gone to see him to find out how he would be treated. He was perhaps playing for time, trying to evaluate the eventual relations between the Indians and the English.

Montreal surrendered on 8 Sept. 1760. Major Rogers and his 200 rangers were immediately sent to take possession of Detroit. It seems that they met Pontiac on the way at the mouth of the Detroit River, on 27 November. He is supposed to have come to welcome the detachment with a group of Ottawas, Hurons, and Potawatomis. He is said to have shown, in complete sincerity, a peaceful attitude and one that was favourable to the arrival in his country of people who quite recently had been his enemies – a typical change in response to promises of full and free trade.

The French supplied the Indians with munitions and heaped presents and free services upon them. The English did not intend to continue the custom. Nevertheless, while waiting for regulations establishing new commercial relations, the commandant of Detroit, Donald CAMPBELL, tried, more or less successfully, to maintain the bartering customs that had been followed up till that time by the French. Sir William Johnson*, the superintendent of northern Indians, advised General Jeffery Amherst*, the commander-in-chief, to continue allowing supplies and munitions to be given to the Indians. General Amherst agreed, but noted: "When the Intended Trade is once Established they will be able to supply themselves with these, from the Traders. . . ." The British régime brought other changes in the west: trade was to be carried on only at the posts, and the rum trade was to be completely done away with. The Indians were deeply disappointed and lost no time in protesting. In June 1761, according to Campbell, they incited "all the Nations from Nova Scotia to the Illinois to take the Hatchet against the English." Johnson was

Pontiac

alarmed and called a great peace conference at Detroit in September 1761. A strong contingent of troops, under the orders of Henry Gladwin*, joined him there. This contingent was to complete the occupation of all the newly conquered posts. Just before arriving at Detroit, Johnson received from Amherst a letter forbidding the custom of buying the Indians' good conduct with presents; he considered this decision so unwise that he said not a word about it to the Indians at the meeting and even offered them presents. Instead of Pontiac, another chief spoke in the name of the Ottawas. It is not possible to say whether Pontiac had simply wanted to let the civil chief Mécatépilésis, who was older, speak, or chose to remain silent because he already no longer believed in the possibility of a *modus vivendi* with the British. A short time after the meeting the Indians became bitterly aware that Amherst's secret orders had been put into force. In the spring of 1762, at the end of the hunting season, they were suffering from a serious scarcity of rum, powder, and lead. Johnson urged Amherst to return to French trading practices, but the general rejected his advice.

The rumour then spread of an eventual recapture of Quebec which encouraged the Indians to revolt. In the summer of 1762 a council met secretly in the village at Detroit. Ottawa, Ojibwa, Huron, Potawatomi, and other chiefs from Lake Superior were present, along with two Canadians. The motives for the meeting are not precisely known, but presumably they were warlike and Pontiac instigated the gathering, for he was on his own territory and he was a war chief.

Like his neighbours, he was perhaps impressed by the words of Neolin, an Abenaki or Delaware, who claimed divine inspiration and loudly declared the necessity of returning to the values recognized before the arrival of the Europeans. The prophet urged his listeners to abstain completely from contact with whites. He praised "all the northern tribes," particularly their warriors, according to Jean-Jacques-Blaise d'Abbadie, the general commissary and *ordonnateur* in Louisiana, who spoke of him in the following terms: " . . . Among the Abenakis a man of that tribe had no difficulty in convincing all his people and in turn all the Red men that God had appeared to him and had said to him ' . . . I warn you that if you allow the English among you, you are dead, maladies, smallpox, and their poison will destroy you totally, you must pray to me and do only my will.' " Pontiac must have listened to the prophet, and whether or not he was still loyal to France, he must have understood the ultility of such preaching in justifying the annihilation of the English. A

speech he made in 1763 at Rivière à l'Écorce (some miles south of Detroit) gave evidence of that.

Like the Weas in the west, the Senecas stirred up a centre of rebellion in the east in 1762. They intended to promote an uprising of all the Indians. To their neighbours the Delawares they sent an "underground belt," which then reached the Shawnees. The Miamis of the upper Ouabache (Wabash) River received it in March 1763. At the beginning of the year the Senecas also sent the Hurons a war message. But the conflict they were trying to instigate did not come about. Robert Holmes, the commandant of Fort des Miamis (Fort Wayne, Ind., or nearby), intercepted their first wampum belt. The second one provoked no reaction from its recipients.

Upon his return from the hunt in the spring of 1763 Pontiac wanted to launch an armed uprising. Having been assured of the support and the arrival of the Potawatomis of Ninivois's band and Také's Hurons, two communities that were neighbours of his, he convoked the first of a number of secret councils at the Rivière à l'Écorce on 27 April. About 460 warriors came, including those from his own village. A plan of attack was worked out. Three days later, 40 to 60 Indians got into Fort Detroit on the pretext of wanting to "dance the Calumet" for the occupants, and they took advantage of their visit to observe the state of the garrison and locate the magazines. Before launching the attack, Pontiac is supposed to have tried to bring in other Algonkian groups with messages he sent to them: the Ojibwas from the Baie de Saguinam (Saginaw Bay), the Ottawas from L'Arbre Croche (Cross Village, Mich.), and the Mississaugas from the Rivière à la Tranche (Thames River).

A second conference was held on the Potawatomis' territory, but the Algonkians who had been invited did not attend. The plan took form. The Indians were to ask Gladwin, the commandant at Detroit since 23 Aug. 1762, to bring together a great council. They were to make their way into the fort, hiding their arms under their clothes; a certain number of arms would be distributed to the French residents, and the conspirators would go into action on a signal from Pontiac. The Ottawa chief claimed that François-Marie Picoté* de Belestre, the former commandant of Detroit, had sent him a war belt.

An informer – his name is a matter for conjecture – had warned Gladwin of the plot. On 7 May Gladwin nevertheless let some 300 of the factious Indians into the fort, but he had doubled the guard. He and his officers wore their swords at the assembly on the parade ground, and the whole garrison surrounded the intruders. Pontiac

Pontiac

then realized that his scheme was known. He did not give the order to fight. After this failure he went next day with three Ottawa chiefs to parley with Gladwin, in order to alleviate his suspicions; he claimed that there had been a misunderstanding about his men's attitude, and announced that he would come back to the fort with them shortly "to smoke the pipe of peace." In the meantime he invited the Hurons, Potawatomis, and Canadians from round about to play lacrosse in his village, to display their peaceful intentions. On 9 May he returned to Detroit with 65 canoes to make a second attempt. This time Gladwin did not open the gates. Annoyed, and wishing moreover to preserve his influence, the Ottawa chief rapidly changed his tactics. He decided to besiege the fort and to set ambushes around it. There were soon victims among the farmers, and upstream the Ojibwas attacked Charles RO-BERTSON's detachment; they killed Robertson as well as Sir Robert DAVERS and two soldiers.

On 10 May Pontiac said that he was ready to propose a truce to Gladwin. He brought some Indian and French followers together at the home of Antoine Cuillerier, *dit* Beaubien. Among them were Jacques Godfroy, who later took part in the insurrection, and Pierre Chesne, *dit* Labutte, an interpreter. They sent for delegates from the other side to talk about peace. Two officers, Donald Campbell and George McDougall, arrived and were taken prisoner. Immediately the Potawatomis and Hurons were advised. They captured two Englishmen at Fort Saint-Joseph (probably Niles, Mich.) and took them to Cuillerier's house, where they were put to death. Pontiac, who still had two hostages, called on the commandant, Gladwin, to surrender, but met with a refusal. The next day Pontiac, with the Potawatomi chiefs, forced some farmers to hand over provisions to him. This action scarcely encouraged them to collaborate with him. The Christian Hurons of Téata's band were also reluctant to follow him. Father Pierre Potier* advised them to remain neutral, but Pontiac used intimidation to bring 60 warriors over to his side. Other groups put themselves directly under his authority, in particular 250 Ojibwas from the Baie de Saguinam and the Rivière à la Tranche. On 18 May he called a conference of all the habitants and demanded that they write to Pierre-Joseph Neyon de Villiers, the commandant of Fort de Chartres, to ask him for help. They did so, but unwillingly, it seems, for the signatories added a note to the letter: "We are forced to submit to what the Indians demand of us; the English are shut up, and all passages are cut off; we cannot express our perplexity to you. . . . "

So far, few Canadians had collaborated actively with Pontiac. Towards the end of May 1763 a dozen of them went to see him to complain of pillaging and to make clear their intention of remaining neutral. The Indian chief promised to put an end to the depredations and in return asked them to bring provisions and to let the Indian women grow corn in their fields.

The uprising spread for a month throughout the *pays d'en haut*, and signal victories give an indication of its extent. At the end of May Lieutenant Abraham Cuyler, unaware of the disturbances raging west of Lake Erie, left Niagara with 96 men and 139 barrels of provisions. Ten boats took them towards the imperilled fort at Detroit. A party of Ottawas surprised them at Point Pelee; 46 of the English were taken prisoner and two boats were captured. On 26 May forts Saint-Joseph and Miami fell into the hands of the Miamis and Illinois. The Weas, Kickapoos, and Mascoutens seized Fort Ouiatanon (near Lafayette, Ind.) on 1 June, and the next day the Ojibwas took Michilimackinac. Lieutenant James GORRELL and his troops then abandoned Fort Edward Augustus (Green Bay, Wis.). In Pennsylvania the Delawares and Senecas occupied William Chapman's store on 27 May, then laid siege to Fort Pitt (formerly Fort Duquesne). Early in June the Shawnees joined the Delawares. The Senecas burned Venango (Franklin, Pa.) around 16 June and a few days later they took possession of Fort de la Rivière au Boeuf (Waterford, Pa.). On 21 June, together with 200 Ottawas, Hurons, and Ojibwas from Detroit, they seized Fort de la Presqu'île (Erie, Pa.).

Progressively the highest authorities in the colonies were informed of the agitation that reigned among the Indians. Amherst was ill acquainted with the Indians, and in his incredulity underestimated the gravity of the situation. On 16 June he was informed of the losses that had been inflicted upon Cuyler's convoy. He then sent his aide-de-camp, James Dalyell, to Albany with orders to pick up troops and take them to Fort Niagara, and as far as Detroit if the uprising had not already been crushed. For its part, the Pennsylvania assembly decided to recruit 700 soldiers to defend the colony. The surrender of the various English posts considerably heightened Pontiac's prestige west of the Appalachians. More than anyone else he had set off the resistance of the Indians, but, though he was recognized at least theoretically by all the insurgents, he had under his immediate command only those besieging Detroit, that is, about 870 warriors, according to the figure given by the author of the *Journal of Pontiac's conspiracy*. When he estab-

528

lished that figure on 9 June, this witness was perhaps not counting the 200 Ottawas, Hurons, and Ojibwas who had been sent to Fort de la Presqu'île and a smaller number of Potawatomis who had already gone to Saint-Joseph.

The groups gathered about Detroit for a common cause slowly began to disintegrate, however. During a drinking bout some Ottawas tortured several prisoners and threw them into the river. Angered, the Potawatomis went to see Gladwin to tell him that they had been forced into the war by the Ottawas. Téata's Hurons met the commandant to negotiate an understanding. Kinonchamek, the son of a highly respected Ojibwa chief, blamed Pontiac for having violated the rules of war, to which charge the Ottawa chief gave no reply. Pontiac made one final attempt to win over the Canadians who had remained out of the action; Zacharie Chiquot and possibly 300 young men agreed to follow him. Other Frenchmen, however, took sides with the English and formed a company to reinforce the garrison of the fort. Meanwhile Cuyler reached Detroit, bearing the text of the treaty of Paris. Subsequently, on 6 July, the Potawatomis dissociated themselves from Pontiac; Také's Hurons likewise broke their alliance. On 25 July Jacques Godfroy returned from Fort de Chartres with the news that Neyon would not send the reinforcements that had been hoped for.

The British reinforcements, consisting of 260 soldiers under Dalyell, arrived under cover of fog on 29 July. No sooner had he reached Detroit than, against Gladwin's advice, the young and ambitious Dalyell rushed into a risky and spectacular expedition. In the night of 1 August he set out with a contingent of 247 men to surprise the besiegers' camp. Some Canadians had warned the Indians the day before of the manoeuvre. Pontiac hoped through a practice rather uncommon among Indians to encircle the enemy, but he only half succeeded: a bloody encounter ensued on the bridge across Parent's Creek (later called Bloody Run), and the British, cut to pieces, hurried back to the fort. Among the numerous dead was Dalyell.

Farther east, in Pennsylvania, Colonel Henry Bouquet received instructions to leave Carlisle on 18 July for Pittsburgh. He was to lead 460 soldiers to defend the fort, which was under siege. The besiegers, Delawares, Shawnees, and Senecas, were tiring of the fight. On 1 August they tried to take the fort, but in vain. Shortly afterwards they ambushed Bouquet's columns at Edge Hill (26 miles east of Pittsburgh), but were repulsed. At New York, however, Amherst had received nothing but crushing news since June.

On 7 July he learned of the loss of Venango, Rivière au Boeuf, and Presqu'île. Furious, he suggested to Bouquet: "Could it not be contrived to send the small pox among the disaffected tribes of Indians? We must on this occasion use every stratagem in our power to reduce them."

At Detroit the defenders were still resisting. It was already September, and Pontiac could not prevent the schooner *Huron* and the sloop *Michigan* from bringing provisions and ammunition to the besieged. He would have had to change his strategy, that is to say, risk a massed charge against the fort. For Algonkians, divided up in small bands, warriors – even a few – were not thought to be expendable, and a concerted offensive could entail considerable losses. Despite the news – false, at it turned out – of the impending arrival of Louis Liénard* de Beaujeu de Villemomble's forces, and despite a final appeal by Pontiac, little by little most of his Ojibwa and Ottawa followers deserted him in October and scattered to their winter hunting grounds.

On 29 October a messenger from Fort de Chartres confirmed the news that France and England had made peace. He brought letters from the commandant Neyon urging the Indians to bury the hatchet and advising the habitants to submit to the British or withdraw to the region west of the Mississippi. Subsequently the Canadians agreed to sell 8,000 pounds of wheat to the Detroit garrison who were in great need. On 31 October Pontiac wrote to Gladwin: "My Brother, the word that my father has sent to make peace I accept; all of my young men have buried their hatchets. I think that you will forget the bad things that have happened this past while. For my part I shall forget, which you can show me how to do, in order to think only of good things. I, the Ojibwas, the Hurons, we must go to speak to you when you will ask us. Reply to us. I am sending you the adviser so that you may see him. If you are indeed like me you will give me a reply. I send you greetings."

Having lost credit among his followers, Pontiac decided to go himself to see Neyon, to win him over to collaboration in his plan. On the way he stopped among the Hurons at Sandoské, who were not yet pacified, and made an encampment for the winter with several Ottawa families on the Rivière des Miamis (Maumee River). Some Frenchmen who had fought with him and were fleeing Detroit joined him. The group started out again in the early spring of 1764 and in March arrived among the Illinois, whom Pontiac stirred up. On 15 April Pontiac was received by Neyon and asked him to reinforce his "army at Detroit, where it continues the war against the English

Pontiac

and will not stop until there are no more Red men." Neyon declared that he no longer wanted to fight, since the English and French had become brothers and were living in peace. The chief did not accept his argument and did not want to hear more; he returned to sow discontent among the Illinois. In July 1764 he was back at his encampment on the Rivière des Miamis. The Delawares and the Hurons at Sandoské were remaining at peace, and in his absence the chief Manitou, his rival, had undertaken to pacify Pontiac's last partisans, and had consequently brought about a split in the village. In the summer of 1764 Pontiac did not attend Sir William Johnson's conference at Niagara, where only those groups which had taken no part in the uprising were represented. Pontiac avoided punishment by two expeditions under John Bradstreet* and Bouquet, who had been sent to put down the last resisters. He was not present at the meeting of the Indians that was held at Detroit on 5–7 September.

Little is known of Pontiac's activities during the autumn of 1764; the following winter he kept fomenting disturbances along with MINWEWEH, some habitants, and a Shawnee chief, Charlot Kaské. Pontiac may have sought to bring the northern and southern Indians into a confederation. But if he did not try this, he at least urged the Arkansas to rise in rebellion. For his part, Charlot Kaské sought vainly on 27 Aug. 1764 the military support of Louis Groston* de Saint-Ange et de Bellerive, the commandant at Vincennes (Ind.). The "Shawnee chief and another from the Illinois who had been delegated by more than 40 villages which are at war with the English" appealed to the French authorities in New Orleans in December 1764 and February 1765, but they obtained no assistance. The Illinois did not, however, lay down their arms, and Pontiac encouraged them to prevent the English from occupying their land. The English sent them two peace missions. The first came to nothing, but the second, which met with Pontiac on 18 April 1765, succeeded in making him give in for good. Saint-Ange and Lieutenant Alexander Fraser finally convinced him that the only two reasons he had for continuing to stir up conflicts were no longer valid: the Shawnees and Delawares had been pacified and the Illinois territory no longer belonged to the French. George Croghan conferred with Pontiac at Ouiatanon in July 1765, and a preliminary agreement was signed. Pontiac stipulated as one condition for peace that the British should not consider that the surrender of the French forts gave them the right to own the whole country and to colonize it: the French had settled among the Indians only as tenants, and not as owners. Pontiac and Croghan went to Detroit to have the agreement ratified by a gathering of Ottawas, Ojibwas, Hurons, and Potawatomis. The French had not conquered them and had not bought their lands, the chiefs from the Ouabache River repeated to Croghan, and therefore their territory could not be handed over to the English. In the spring of 1766 the Algonkian chiefs went to Fort Ontario (Oswego, N.Y.) to sign a final treaty. Sir William Johnson presided over the ceremony in July. Previously the rumour had spread that Pontiac would receive a captain's pay from the British authorities, which roused the jealousy of the other chiefs. Their envy increased at the conference when Johnson had Pontiac speak in the name of all of them and showed him exceptional deference, thus winning his allegiance.

In the autumn of 1766 and the summer of 1767 dissatisfied groups sought Pontiac's complicity to continue the struggle against the English. He continued nevertheless to declare his loyalty to England, thus setting his former allies against him; his village even decided to banish him. Subsequently he appears to have alienated the Illinois for some reason. When he reappeared at Kaskaskia (Ill.) a year later, with a group of relatives and friends, he caused some anxiety, as the Kaskaskias were afraid of him; they spread the report that he had an army and was going to attack the Illinois confederacy. He was there, however, only to sell his peltries. On 30 March 1769 he went to Cahokia. Nearby there was a village of Peorias, well known for their vindictive murders, who met in council in April and decided that one of them, the nephew of the chief Makatachinga, would execute Pontiac. The sinister plan was carried out on 20 April, just as the famous Ottawa, accompanied by the murderer, was leaving the Baynton, Wharton, and Morgan store in Cahokia. Without delay, and to demonstrate the innocence of the English in the affair, the commandant of Fort Cavendish (as Fort de Chartres had been renamed), John Wilkins, ordered a local businessman to bury the victim. The merchant is believed to have let the French carry the body to the other side of the Mississippi, and they are supposed to have buried it, not without honours, at St Louis (Mo.). The exact burial place is still unknown. Only Minweweh tried to avenge the foul deed. He killed two employees of Baynton, Wharton, and Morgan.

Throughout the uprising the French authorities in Louisiana and the Illinois country had acted correctly. In August 1763 the English went up the Mississippi and occupied the territory as far as the Illinois country. The French authorities were aware that the Indians were angry, but they did not seek to inflame their feelings. On the contrary, they complied with their new diplomatic instructions from Versailles, for fear of falling into disfavour. "As for all the reactions on the part of the Indians that I have hinted at to you, Your Excellency, I shall do everything in my power to prevent them," wrote the governor of Louisiana, Louis Billouart de Kerlérac, to the minister of Marine in the summer of 1763. Once the treaty of Paris had been signed, no Frenchman in a position of authority had any interest in stirring up the Indians in Louisiana. "Convinced as I am," wrote Charles-Philippe Aubry, the commandant of the troops at New Orleans, "of the little trust one can put in men without laws and that their armed rising will bring no change in the arrangements between the two Crowns, [I believe] it will be necessary to evacuate this post [Fort de Chartres], that is the only way of putting an end to their enterprise."

"Pontiac [is] forever famous in the annals of North America," someone wrote as early as 1765, and history has retained his name, even if his actions did not achieve the result he anticipated. He was able to persuade a great number of Indians from the "old west" to join him, but he convinced too few Frenchmen, and was therefore prevented from carrying out his plan. He was unable to set on foot an army which through its numbers and tactics could have equalled that of his opponents. Pontiac did not lack stature and fought with exceptional discernment and tenacity. His nation had transmitted to him the rules for his strategy, and generally he followed them. From this point of view we cannot judge him by our criteria. His speeches at the beginning of his activity demonstrate his down-to-earth preoccupation with subsistence; prompted by it he compared two conceptions of trade to try to choose the less enslaving. But he also perceived with great acuteness the problems that would afflict the Indians for generations to come: the threat of assimilation and the slow taking-over of their lands by a European population constantly implanting its frontier and its culture farther west.

LOUIS CHEVRETTE

AN, Col., C¹¹A, 33–47, 75–105; C¹³A, 42–51. [Henry Bouquet], *The papers of Col. Henry Bouquet*, ed. S. K. Stevens *et al*. (19v., Harrisburg, 1940–43). *Critical period, 1763–65* (Alvord and Carter). "The Gladwin manuscripts," ed. Charles Moore, *Michigan Pioneer Coll.*, XXVII (1896), 605–80. D. E. Heineman, "The startling experience of a Jewish trader during Pontiac's siege of Detroit in 1763," *American Jewish Hist. Soc.* *Pub.* (Baltimore, Md.), no.23 (1915), 31–35. [Thomas Morris], *Journal of Captain Thomas Morris, from Miscellanies in prose and verse* (London, 1791; repr. Ann Arbor, Mich., 1966). [Robert Navarre?], *Journal of Pontiac's conspiracy, 1763*, ed. C. M. and M. A. Burton, trans. R. C. Ford (Detroit, 1912). *New régime, 1765–67* (Alvord and Carter). Robert Rogers, *A concise account of North America* (London, 1765; repr. New York, 1966); *Journals . . .* (London, 1765). *The siege of Detroit in 1763: the journal of Pontiac's conspiracy, and John Rutherfurd's narrative of a captivity*, ed. M. M. Quaife (Chicago, 1958). William Smith, *An historical account of the expedition against the Ohio Indians in the year 1764 under the command of Henry Bouquet . . .* (Philadelphia, 1765); repr. as *Expedition against the Ohio Indians* (Ann Arbor, Mich., 1966). *DAB*.

A. J. Blackbird, *History of the Ottawa and Chippewa Indians of Michigan, a grammar of their language, and personal and family history of the author* (Ypsilanti, Mich., 1887). Lewis Cass, "Discourse delivered before the historical society of Michigan," in *Historical and scientific sketches of Michigan* (Detroit, 1834). Francis Parkman, *The conspiracy of Pontiac and the Indian war after the conquest of Canada* (10th ed., 2v., Boston, 1886; repr. New York, 1962). Peckham, *Pontiac* [This study is thoroughly researched and the author's interpretations are well-founded. L.C.]. H. R. Schoolcraft, *Algic researches, comprising inquiries respecting the mental characteristics of the North American Indians* (2v., New York, 1839). C. E. Slocum, *History of the Maumee river basin from the earliest account to its organization into counties* (Indianapolis, Ind., Toledo, Ohio, 1905). C.-M. Boissonnault, "Les Canadiens et la révolte de Pontiac," *RUL*, II (1947–48), 778–87. Louis Chevrette, "Un modèle psychologique de processus du changement social et un concept d'idéologie y intégré," *Culture* (Québec, Montréal), March 1971, 405–14 [The case of Pontiac's uprising confirms this cognitive model set forth without any normative proposition. L.C.]. O. W. Collet, "Notes on Parkman's 'Conspiracy of Pontiac'," *United States Catholic Hist. Magazine* (New York), II (1888), 35–48. C. E. Hunter, "The Delaware nativist revival of the mid-eighteenth century," *Ethnohistory* (Tucson, Ariz.), XVIII (1971), 39–49. "Potier's connection with Pontiac's conspiracy," *Detroit Evening News*, 18 Feb. 1899.

PORTNEUF, PHILIPPE-RENÉ ROBINAU DE. *See* ROBINAU

PORTNEUF, PIERRE ROBINEAU DE. *See* ROBINEAU

PORTUGAIS, NICOLAS DASILVA, *dit*. *See* DASILVA

POTE, WILLIAM, surveyor, ship captain; b. 15 Dec. 1718 at Marblehead, Massachusetts, son of Captain William Pote and Dorothy Gatchell; date of death unknown, but dead by October 1755.

Potier

William Pote became a sailor and by 1745 held command of the merchant vessel *Montague*. In that year John Henry BASTIDE, chief engineer at Annapolis Royal, Nova Scotia, engaged him to carry supplies there. Pote's vessel was boarded at Annapolis on 17 May by a mixed party of French and Indians, part of a force headed by Paul MARIN de La Malgue. Pote was captured with five of his crew, and was later allocated to a group of Hurons from Lorette, near Quebec. He was taken to Quebec *via* Chignecto, and the Petitcodiac, Saint John, and St Lawrence rivers. Along the way he was badly beaten at different camps by the Indians. At Aucpac (near Springhill, N.B.) on the Saint John River, some Malecites wanted to kill Pote and other captives in retaliation for the slaying of members of their tribe by Captain John GORHAM's rangers the year before.

After four months of travel Pote reached Quebec, where he was kept in confinement and had little freedom of movement over the next two years. During the voyage to Quebec and throughout his imprisonment Pote kept a journal of his experiences which includes first hand accounts from fellow prisoners of events in King George's War. There was much sickness among the prisoners and Pote's journal is full of notices of their deaths; over 75 prisoners died during his stay in Quebec. Pote also described in part the defences of Quebec and commented on the mood of the French settlers, who were "Under Continual aprehensions of ye English paying them a Vissite both By Land and Sea. . . . Several farmers have made no Scruple to Let us know they would turn to ye English In Case they Should Come against ym Rather then Loose their Estats as they have no Intrest In old france nor are their Indians much to be Depended on for they have often told me in Case ye English Should Come they would be on ye Strongest Side."

Early in June 1747 Pote and some of his companions learned that they would soon be sent home. Before departing he gave his journal to a woman prisoner to carry to Louisbourg, Cape Breton Island (Île Royale) "Under her peticoats," lest it be confiscated. Pote left Quebec on 30 July 1747 aboard the *Saint-Esprit* and in mid-August reached Louisbourg, where he reported to Bastide for employment. He continued his life at sea, commanding a merchant vessel as late as 1752. Neither the place nor the circumstance of his death is known.

GEORGE MacBEATH

N.B. Museum, Webster coll., pkt.242. [William Pote], *The journal of Captain William Pote, jr., during his captivity in the French and Indian war from May 1745, to August 1747*, ed. J. F. Hurst and Victor Paltsits (New York, 1896). *New Eng. Hist. and Geneal. Register*, XIV (1860), 146. W. O. Raymond, *The River St John, its physical features, legends and history from 1604 to 1784*, ed. J. C. Webster (Sackville, N.B., 1943). G. T. Bates, "John Gorham, 1709–1751: an outline of his activities in Nova Scotia, 1744–1751," N.S. Hist. Soc. *Coll.*, XXX (1954), 49.

POTIER DUBUISSON, ROBERT, subdelegate of the intendant on Île Saint-Jean (Prince Edward Island); b. 14 Dec. 1682 on Staten Island, New York, but not baptized until June 1683; son of Jean-Baptiste Poitiers Du Buisson and Élisabeth Jossard; d. 25 March 1744 at Port-La-Joie (Fort Amherst, P.E.I.).

Robert Potier Dubuisson spent his childhood and youth in New England with his family, and evidently learned to speak both Dutch and English. His parents moved back to New France around 1699 and settled in Montreal where his father was organist of Notre-Dame for some years. Robert was employed there by the crown from 1703; in 1707 he was a clerk in the office of the Marine and by 1719 he was controller of the king's stores. He also acted from time to time as an interpreter.

On 10 March 1722 Potier Dubuisson was commissioned subdelegate of the intendant of New France for Île Saint-Jean with power to hear civil and criminal cases. The island was still held by the Comte de Saint-Pierre, and Dubuisson had been appointed to help avoid the involved legal disputes which had arisen when Michel DACCARRETTE (d. 1745) and others had attempted to break Saint-Pierre's monopoly of the fishing industry [*see* Robert-David Gotteville* de Belile]. In 1725 Saint-Pierre's exclusive fishing rights were revoked, and Jacques d'Espiet* de Pensens, a captain in the colonial regular troops stationed at Louisbourg, Île Royale (Cape Breton Island), arrived the following year to take possession of the island, now to be administered from Louisbourg. Dubuisson had evidently returned to Canada but in the fall of 1726 he was back on the island where, the governor of Île Royale, Saint-Ovide [MONBETON], reported, he was needed to settle "a host of disputes" of the kind that regularly arose at the end of the fishing season. Saint-Ovide thought him "a very honest man who carries out the duties he is entrusted with most judiciously." Maurepas, minister of Marine, thought his position unnecessary, however, and it was not until 1728 that Jacques-Ange LE NORMANT de Mézy, financial commissary at Louisbourg, included in his statement of expenses 600 *livres* for Dubuisson, described as a "man of good birth and merit." From this time on Dubuisson also acted as king's storekeeper on the island. He was now secure in his position as subdelegate of the intendant, which he held until his death by virtue of his original commission although he reported to the financial commissary at Louisbourg. His successor, François-Marie de GOUTIN, was commissioned subdelegate of the financial commissary.

Dubuisson was responsible during the next 15 years for compiling censuses of the inhabitants and reporting to the financial commissary on the state of agriculture and fishing. He also distributed supplies to newly arrived settlers – few in number during these years – and to all habitants in times of shortage due to failed harvests. He assisted the commandants of the island – Pensens, Robert TARRIDE Duhaget, and Louis Du Pont* Duchambon – in marking off concessions. His most important function, however, was to settle disputes which arose during the fishing season. In 1732, for example, he reported that he had spent two months at Havre Saint-Pierre (St Peters Bay), the location of the largest fishing community on the island, resolving problems both among the habitants and between them and Jean-Pierre ROMA, "according to the customs of Newfoundland, followed in Île Royale."

Dubuisson had married Marie-Charlotte Arnaud in Montreal in 1707; she died the following year, two weeks after the birth of their daughter. His household on Île Saint-Jean included his daughter and one of his sisters, and the respect in which they were held in the community is shown by the number of times they acted as godparents. Dubuisson often complained that his salary did not cover his expenses and asked for an increase, but his appeals were not granted. Nor was his request to be commissioned principal king's writer and to be allowed to return to Canada. He died on the island in his 62nd year.

MARY McD. MAUDE

AN, Col., B, 45/2, pp.915–20; 50/2, pp.583–84v (PAC transcripts); C¹¹B, 6, ff.7, 137v–38; 7, ff.96–97; 8, ff.66–70 (printed in *BRH*, XXX (1924), 88–90); 10, ff.80–80v, 114, 118v–19, 160–61; 13, ff.195–96v, 197–98v; 16, ff.215–16; 18, ff.310–10v; 20, ff.16–19v, 122–23v, 195–200; 21, ff.314–15; 25, ff.23–24v; 27, ff.177–81; Section Outre-Mer, G¹, 411, ff.9, 14v, 22, 24v, 26, 41v; 466 (recensements de l'île Saint-Jean). A. Roy, *Inv. greffes not.*, XII, 83; XXI, 189. Tanguay, *Dictionnaire*. Harvey, *French régime in P.E.I.* O. Lapalice, "Les organistes et maitres de musique à Notre-Dame de Montréal," *BRH*, XXV (1919), 243–49. É.-Z. Massicotte, "Les interprètes à Montréal sous le régime français," *BRH*, XXXIV (1928), 147;

"Notes sur les familles Freté, Ferté, Forté et Poitiers Dubuisson," *BRH*, XXII (1916), 275–77.

POTTS, JOHN, HBC surgeon and post factor; d. 28 June 1764 at Prince of Wales Fort (Churchill, Man.).

John Potts was one of several "surgeons" (their formal medical qualifications were often sketchy) sent to Hudson Bay in the 18th century who became factors at Hudson's Bay Company posts. First engaged in 1738 to serve as surgeon for three years at York Factory (Man.), he went back to the bay in 1745, this time as surgeon at Moose Factory (Ont.). In the season 1747–48 he took command of the latter post when the factor returned to England because of ill health; and in 1750 he replaced the disgraced Thomas MITCHELL as factor of the new trading post at Richmond Gulf (Lac Guillaume-Delisle, Que.), far to the north along the East Main coast.

Potts was set three main objectives: to complete the building of the post, to develop the fur trade among the Indians of the interior, and to supervise the three miners hopefully sent out to work mineral deposits just south of Richmond Gulf. His years at the post were ones of frustration and failure. In 1751 he sent home the trio of "disorderly and intolerably idle" miners, whose efforts had produced only some sulphur and low-grade brass; the next year he declared of the fur trade that "we Really think (having now had Experience) that it never will turn out to Your Honours Satisfaction." Attempts to persuade servants to venture inland to make contact with the elusive Naskapi Indians of the Labrador interior failed, and although a few Naskapis and some of the coastal Crees [*see* CRUSOE] came to the post they brought little trade. The Indians to the south generally continued to trade with Eastmain House (at the mouth of the Eastmain River) or the other established HBC posts towards James Bay, and as Potts' deputy pointed out, "Richmond Fort can never rise but on the ruins of Eastmain." The company had hoped that the post's northerly situation would attract Eskimos, but after a clash in 1754 which resulted in the deaths, first of a young HBC servant and subsequently of two Eskimo hostages, Eskimos avoided the area. The incident, together with Potts' commercial ineffectiveness and the suspicion that he was engaged in private trade, brought a heavy reproof from the London committee, which told him, "We are greatly displeased with your management." With the post receiving only the derisory total of £100 worth of furs in six years, the HBC decided in 1756, apparently on Potts' recommendation, to move it southward to

Pouchot

Little Whale River, where it would be better placed for the white whale fishery.

Potts met with no more success here, and in 1759 the company abandoned the post, since "no Trade of any sort can possibly be Obtained in that part of Hudsons Bay the least beneficial to the Company or Advantageous to the Nation." Lack of country provisions, mutual fears and antagonisms among the Indians and Eskimos, and the reluctance of the garrison to journey inland, all made the factor's task an unenviable one; but his gloomy journals and letters give little indication that Potts was the right man for this difficult post.

After a year's leave in England Potts returned in 1761 to the less strenuous position of surgeon at Prince of Wales, and there he served until his death three years later. Most of his clothes he had already given to his son John, also serving at the post; his feather bed and a cloth banyan were sent home to his wife Elizabeth. His only obituary was written by Moses Norton* in the Churchill post journal for 30 June 1764: "We also Buried Mr. Potts in as Decent a manner as I possibly Could, and as he had been Hon^rd with ye Command of one of your Hon^rs Forts and has always Beheaved well Ever Since he has been here, and on those Considerations I fired 7 of our 1 lb. Guns at his Funeral."

GLYNDWR WILLIAMS

[Potts' Richmond Fort journals, more detailed than most kept by post factors, are in HBC Arch. B.182/a/1–4 and 6–11. His letters home are in A.11/57, and the company's outward letters to Richmond are scattered through A.5/1 and A.6/8–9. Potts is mentioned in A.1/34, p.86; A.1/36, p.286; and occasionally in A.1/37–42. His service at Moose is referred to in A.6/7, f.72d. Details of his last illness and death are given in B.42/a/60. Brief studies of Richmond Fort in the 1750s will be found in Rich, *History of the HBC*, I, 619–24, and in HBRS, XXIV (Davies and Johnson), xxi– xxiv. G.W.]

POUCHOT (Pouchot de Maupas, Pouchat, Pourchaut, Boucheau), PIERRE, military engineer, officer in the French regular troops, author of *Mémoires sur la dernière guerre de l'Amérique septentrionale . . .* ; b. 8 April 1712 at Grenoble, France, son of an impecunious merchant; d. 8 May 1769 on Corsica.

At the age of 21 Pierre Pouchot joined the regular army as a volunteer engineer, and on 1 May 1734 was appointed second lieutenant in the Régiment de Béarn. He had an aptitude for military engineering and studied the standard works on fortification; in the late 1730s he gained practical experience in Corsica. He later served in Italy, Flanders, and Germany and was an assistant adjutant within ten years. In the War of the Austrian Succession his engineering service won distinction; he received the cross of the order of Saint-Louis and, in September 1749, a captain's command.

With the resumption of war in North America in 1754 Pouchot's regiment was chosen for service in Canada, and was sent to Fort Frontenac (Kingston, Ont.), arriving in July 1755. The quality of the entrenchments he laid out there induced Governor Pierre de Rigaud* de Vaudreuil to send him on detached service to improve Niagara's defences with the advice of the king's engineer Gaspard-Joseph CHAUSSEGROS de Léry.

At Fort Niagara (near Youngstown, N.Y.) Pouchot soon began reconstruction of the stone building surrounded by a "rotten stockade, with no defensive works" save four wooden bastions. His plan was to protect the fort with substantial earthworks on the landward side. Vaudreuil approved it and left Pouchot with 200 regulars and several colonials for labour on the earthworks in the winter of 1755–56.

On 22 July 1756 Pouchot, reunited with his regiment, joined the French forces converging on Fort Oswego (Chouaguen). Arriving on 12 August, he was ordered to assist MONTCALM's inexperienced engineer, Jean-Nicolas Desandrouins*, in laying out the siege works. The French trenches and batteries were advanced with speed and secrecy, and Oswego, in an indefensible situation, surrendered on 15 August. Vaudreuil singled out Pouchot as one of his best officers and asked that he be given a lieutenant colonel's commission with pension.

After some construction in the Montreal area and minor additions to forts Carillon (Ticonderoga, N.Y.) and Frontenac, Pouchot took up in mid-October his appointment as commandant of Fort Niagara. This appointment had been made by Vaudreuil in August on Montcalm's advice, with orders to complete the fortifications. Pouchot was the first officer in the French regular army to enjoy this post, which officers of the colonial regular troops looked upon as theirs by custom. It was commonly believed that only a Canadian could deal with the Indians, but Pouchot attracted large numbers of Iroquois to the French cause. Many had been impressed by the victory at Chouaguen, and were drawn to Fort Niagara by Pouchot's liberality and trade on good terms. The Senecas, on whose lands Fort Niagara stood, also responded to Pouchot's appeal for military aid as did some Cayugas and Onondagas. They flattered him with the name Sategariouaen or Sategayogen, meaning "the centre of good transactions." He also equipped war parties of

Delawares, Shawnees, and Mississaugas which brought back scalps, prisoners, and information from the English colonies to be passed on to Vaudreuil. Pouchot's influence, however, depended on French victories and trading goods. Thus in June 1757 the Mississaugas, hearing a rumour of French defeat, prepared to seize the French post at Toronto and had to be dispersed by a force from Niagara. In the winter of 1756–57 the garrison under Pouchot had completed the main earthworks and various buildings; Niagara was now regarded as a major French stronghold.

Although Pouchot's *Mémoires* suggest he was at the siege of Fort William Henry (Fort George; now Lake George, N.Y.) in August 1757, other records indicate that he remained at Niagara. In that month he was told he had received a 200-*livre* pension but not a lieutenant-colonel's commission, perhaps because of his social origins.

A second disappointment followed: in October 1757 Captain Jean-Baptiste Mutigny de Vassan of the colonial regular troops took over the command of Fort Niagara. Pouchot blamed his removal on the jealousy of the colonial officers who had influenced Vaudreuil. Bougainville* was explicit: "why, by the rebound of backlane intrigues among junior officers, did they replace M. de Pouchot, whom the Indians adored, with a man whose Spanish haughtiness had no affinity with their temperament?" Pouchot rejoined his regiment at Montreal. The following summer his company was ordered to aid in the defence of Fort Carillon against James Abercromby* [*see* Montcalm]. The Béarn defended the right flank of the French breastworks, and Pouchot later claimed he had averted a costly error. In a moment of bravado a French officer goaded the advancing Highlanders with a red handkerchief. The attackers mistook it for a sign of French surrender and ran forward, arms held high. The French troops, confused, mounted the parapet. Pouchot wrote that he alone kept the French firing.

The French victory at Carillon coincided with a rise in Pouchot's fortunes. In April 1758 he had received two more 200-*livre* pensions, in place, apparently, of a promotion. He acted as a geographer for Governor Vaudreuil and his maps were sent to the ministry of Marine. After the battle of Carillon he and Lévis* advised Montcalm on the defence of Canada. With the loss of Fort Frontenac in the summer and the growing disaffection of the Iroquois, French control of the Great Lakes was endangered, and someone with influence among the Iroquois was needed at Niagara. If that post were attacked Pouchot would be best qualified to defend it. But Vau-

dreuil, though he promised Pouchot the post, delayed in releasing him. He was finally dispatched about 22 March 1759.

Pouchot was to take provisional command of Pointe-au-Baril (Maitland, Ont.) and La Présentation (Oswegatchie; now Ogdensburg, N.Y.) until two armed corvettes being constructed there were finished. These ships would then convey him with 450 men to Niagara. This contingent and the men at all the upper posts were expected to give Pouchot an army of 3,000. If he felt secure at Fort Niagara and Oswego remained deserted, he was to send most of his force southward to François-Marie Le Marchand de Lignery for an attack on Fort Pitt (Pittsburgh, Pa.). Montcalm pronounced this an impossible scheme and complained to Bourlamaque, "never did France have more confidence in Maréchal de Saxe than the Marquis de Vaudreuil has in Pouchot, who has become a Canadian saying amen. . . . If he gains credit among that group, he loses it with us."

Pouchot arrived at Pointe-au-Baril on 4 April and entrenched the post. He embarked for Niagara on 25 April, and set to work restoring the fort and conciliating the Iroquois. Early in June Montcalm noted that "it is greatly to be feared that M. Pouchot, caressed in the study of the Marquis de Vaudreuil, has not gained caution by it." Indeed Pouchot's conduct that spring betrays a blind confidence. Early in June he sent over 2,500 men to Lignery with precious arms and supplies.

This reckless dispersal of forces was encouraged by Vaudreuil and by faulty intelligence. The English had been expected to attack in early spring when Fort Niagara was undermanned; they did not. The Ohio campaign was thought necessary to preserve the loyalty of the western tribes. Pouchot accepted the assurance of some Iroquois chiefs that they would remain neutral and forewarn him of any English attack, and ignored reports that supporters of the English were assuming leadership of the Iroquois nations and preparing for an attack on Niagara. Only in late June after mistreatment of French agents among the Iroquois and news of an army descending the Oswego River did he think of his own protection. Well might he reflect in later years that the Indians "knew very well the advantage of being on the strongest side."

The corvette *Iroquoise*, watching off Oswego for the British army, missed it and Pouchot was taken by surprise on 6 July when some of his men were ambushed outside Fort Niagara. The British were already disembarking at Petit Marais a few miles to the east. He recalled the forces in the

Pouchot

Ohio valley and withdrew his outposts. The guns of the fort and the corvette harassed the British, who methodically burrowed toward the Flag or Lake bastion, which faced inland and lacked a parapet. Pouchot had not yet finished his grand design for the Niagara fortifications. British bombardment of the fort began on 13 July and on the 17th a battery across the river opened up on the lightly protected flank. Pouchot had neglected Vaudreuil's advice to safeguard the opposite shore.

The garrison of about 500 was sustained by anticipation of Le Marchand de Lignery's relief force. That force was engaged within view of the fort on 24 July but was defeated. Pouchot "could scarcely keep the soldiers and militia at their posts. . . ." He surrendered to Sir William Johnson* on 25 July 1759 and was granted the honours of war. The loss of Fort Niagara, believed by many to be impregnable, meant that the French had lost control of the vital portage linking Lake Ontario with the posts of the upper lakes and the Mississippi valley. The canoe routes to the north were useless for the transport of heavy supplies.

Pouchot had received the officer bearing the first summons for surrender with brave words, a bottle of claret, and a glass of liquor. Before his departure for New York on 26 July he gave a supper for the British officers. His conduct was a contrast to the pillage by the victors and their Indian allies. The French officers were otherwise treated with kindness and generosity in captivity. There was an exchange of prisoners in November, and Pouchot and his men struggled back to Montreal.

Early in March 1760 Pouchot was named commandant of Fort Lévis (east of Prescott, Ont.) to relieve Desandrouins who was needed for the siege of British-held Quebec. Pouchot reached the fort by the end of the month and set to work with characteristic zeal. The 250-man garrison rebuilt the fort, which covered two thirds of Île Royale (Galop Island, near Ogdensburg, N.Y.). He negotiated with the Mississaugas and Iroquois but as the British army assembled at Oswego even the loyal mission Indians of La Présentation lost heart. Some Canadian militiamen deserted. With the crews of the two corvettes under his command, Pouchot had in June a fighting force of 316 with a few more reinforcements before August.

He must have had no illusions about his mission. It was to delay the British army's descent of the St Lawrence River for as long as possible. Jeffery Amherst*'s force encamped at Pointe-au-Baril on 16 August, and on the 17th the cor-

vette *Outaouaise* was captured. On the 18th the enemy barges filed past Fort Lévis; those British officers who knew Pouchot braved his fire and "bade him good morning in passing." On the 21st a cannonade from islands and ships began, preceding an attempt by British landing parties. The French gunners holed two assault vessels and forced the third to strike its colours. The British were badly stung, and Pouchot only surrendered on 25 August, when his guns could no longer fire and the fort was a wreck. Amherst and his staff treated Pouchot with respect. In the end his heroic stand cost them 13 days.

Pouchot was again conveyed to New York, and after the fall of Montreal was repatriated to France. He landed on 8 March 1761, six years after he had embarked for Canada. According to the eulogy appended to his published memoirs, he was denounced as having shared in the corruption that contributed to Canada's downfall. Vaudreuil's favour could not protect him and *lettres de cachet* were issued. He hastened to defend himself but was told evasively that he was wanted as a witness against the embezzlers and would be rewarded later for his services.

Pouchot retired to Grenoble smarting from these calumnies. In his fifties, his ambitions frustrated, he apparently saw the war in Corsica as a chance to prove himself once more. He was employed as a military engineer there, and was killed on 8 May 1769 when reconnoitring a post.

Pouchot began writing his memoirs three months before he went to Corsica. "This short space of time," wrote his eulogist, "did not permit him to arrange them with care, nor to use his materials properly." Though the text refers to Pouchot in the third person, the work is substantially his own and seems to be based on fragmentary journals and memory. One such journal, chronicling the events at Niagara in the summer of 1757, is contained in the Lévis manuscripts.

Pouchot's memoirs are especially valuable for the sieges of forts Niagara and Lévis. They reflect the dismay of the French regular troops at being consigned piecemeal to the colonies and their disdain for the Canadians. Pouchot was amused by the colonial veneration for military ranks and honours and noted the relative emancipation of the women. Like many Europeans he was fascinated by the American Indians. The maps and memorials annexed to his history reveal his interest in geography. The *Mémoires* are, nonetheless, the product of a man anxious to vindicate himself. Pouchot exaggerated his role in events; much that he did before 1758 under orders is attributed to his own initiative. Contrary to the records of the time, he said that he took leave of Montcalm in 1759 knowing that Niagara must fall. Yet he attempted to divest himself of responsibility for surrendering.

The rumour of malfeasance was the most painful to Pouchot. He not only declared his innocence in the *Mémoires*; he portrayed himself as the active enemy of corruption and described the sins of François Bigot*, Joseph-Pierre Cadet*, François Le Mercier* and Michel-Jean-Hugues Péan*. A letter he wrote in 1757 indicates he tacitly accepted the activities of Bigot's *Grande Société*.

Pierre Pouchot was a professional soldier whose abilities were superior to those of most officers in the colony. He executed his duties with intelligence, zeal, and imagination. He had a genial manner and a natural courtesy. The neatest summation of his character was written in French by Walter Rutherford, a British officer who had visited him during the siege of Fort Niagara: "bon soldat et homme d'esprit."

PETER N. MOOGK

[American authors customarily refer to François Pouchot, following the precedent of the noted historian F. H. Severance, author of *An old frontier of France: the Niagara region and adjacent lakes under French control* (2v., New York, 1917). French sources speak only of a Pierre Pouchot and an entry dated 28 March 1758 in the ANDM identifies him as Pierre Pouchot de Maupas. He signed simply Pouchot. P.N.M.]

Pierre Pouchot, *Mémoires sur la dernière guerre de l'Amérique septentrionale entre la France et l'Angleterre, suivis d'observations, dont plusieurs sont relatives au théâtre actuel de la guerre, et de nouveaux détails sur les mœurs et les usages des sauvages, avec des cartes topographiques* (3v., Yverdon, 1781); translated from the French by F. B. Hough under the title *Memoir upon the late war in North America, between the French and the English, 1756–60* . . . (2v., Roxbury, Mass., 1866).

AN, Col., B, 105, f.31; CIIA, 101, pp. 7–8, 67–68, 165–66, 442; 102, pp.134, 147, 151; 103, pp.203–4, 466; 105, pp.38, 171–78, 319–20; F³, 15, pp.54–55, 97; 15/2, pp.519–28; 16/1, pp.207–9, 215–16 (PAC transcripts). PAC, MG 24, L3, 3. SHA, A¹, 3404, nos.46, 111; 3457, nos.57, 81; Yᵇ, 121, f.120 (dossier Pouchot). Bougainville, "Journal" (Gosselin), APQ *Rapport, 1923–24*, 221, 253, 261, 266, 278–79, 313, 326, 327. "Le chevalier de la Pause," APQ *Rapport, 1931–32*, 21, 24, 32, 35, 60, 87–90, 92, 94. *Coll. de manuscrits relatifs à la N.-F.*, IV, 25, 53, 90, 105, 151, 155, 198, 227, 244, 300, 303, 307. *Guerre du Canada: relations et journaux* (Casgrain), 72–73, 87–116, 182. *Inv. des papiers de Léry* (P.-G. Roy), II, 192. *Johnson papers* (Sullivan et al.), II, 511; III, 110; X, 124; XIII, 114, 170. *Journal du chevalier de Lévis* (Casgrain), 63, 171–74, 177, 182, 188–91, 241. *Journal du marquis de Montcalm* (Casgrain), 87, 95, 110, 122, 129, 150–51, 168–69, 193, 195, 197, 213, 244–45, 312, 350. *Lettres de divers particuliers* (Casgrain), 119–22, 202. *Lettres de la cour de Versailles* (Casgrain), 73, 117. *Lettres de M. de Bourlamaque* (Casgrain), 138, 152, 200, 237, 293, 302–3, 306–8, 310. *Lettres du chevalier de Lévis* (Casgrain), 363. *Lettres du marquis de Montcalm* (Casgrain), 84, 118, 153, 156–57, 190. *Lettres du marquis de Vaudreuil* (Casgrain). *Lettres et pièces militaires* (Casgrain), 52, 147, 149–50, 153–56. "Les malignités du sieur de Courville," *BRH*, L (1944), 99. "Mémoire du Canada," APQ *Rapport, 1924–25*, 148, 157, 159. "Les 'mémoires' du chevalier de La Pause," APQ *Rapport, 1932–33*, 353, 373–77. *Mémoires sur le Canada, depuis 1749 jusqu'à 1760*. "La mission de M. de Bougainville en France en 1758–1759," APQ *Rapport, 1923–24*, 53. "Pour avoir pris part au siège de Chouaguen," *BRH*, L (1944), 159.

H.-R. Casgrain, *Guerre du Canada, 1756–1760: Montcalm et Lévis* (2v., Québec, 1891; Tours, France, 1899). Frégault, *La guerre de la conquête*. L.-P. Desrosiers, "Officiers de Montcalm," *RHAF*, III (1949–50), 371–72. *Nova Francia*, IV (1929), 190. P.-G. Roy, "Les commandants du fort Niagara," *BRH*, LIV (1948), 199–201.

POULIN, PIERRE, royal notary, clerk of court; b. 10 March 1684 at Trois-Rivières, son of Michel Poulin, seigneur of the fief of Saint-Maurice, and Marie Jutra; m. on 19 Nov. 1717 Madeleine-Louise Le Boulanger at Cap-de-la-Madeleine; d. sometime after 1744.

Unlike his younger brothers, François Poulin* de Francheville and Abbé Michel Poulin de Courval, Pierre Poulin never added a title to his family name. In 1711 he obtained a commission as royal notary and clerk of court for Trois-Rivières, succeeding Jean-Baptiste Pottier*, whom he also replaced as keeper of the prison on 16 June 1713. He resigned from the last two posts in 1722.

On 4 April 1725 Pierre Poulin rendered fealty and homage for the fief of Saint-Maurice located on the Rivière Saint-Maurice. He thus became principal owner of the land on which the Saint-Maurice ironworks were to be operated from 1730 on. Half of this property belonged to him, while the other half was held by his brothers François and Michel. In the act of fealty and homage Pierre is referred to as royal notary and deputy king's attorney.

Pierre Poulin was a member of the association formed on 16 April 1733 by François Poulin de Francheville with a view to accelerating the working of the iron deposits on the Saint-Maurice. When François died in November of that year, his widow, Thérèse de COUAGNE, carried on his work; a new association was set up and Pierre was again a member of it. The enterprise, however, made little headway, despite subsidies from the court and the arrival from France of trained workmen. In 1735 the partners gave up

Poulin de Courval

their operating licence. On 16 Oct. 1736 François-Étienne CUGNET formed a new association; Pierre Poulin then sold his interest in the business.

Subsequently Pierre Poulin went to live in Quebec. The census of 1744 mentions him as a merchant trader, the father of five daughters and a son. We do not know what became of him in later years.

HERVÉ BIRON

AJTR, Greffe de Pierre Poulin, 1711–1720. "Procès verbaux du procureur général Collet" (Caron), APQ Rapport, 1921–22, 281–83. Nish, Les bourgeois-gentilshommes. Sulte, Mélanges historiques (Malchelosse), VI. Albert Tessier, Les forges Saint-Maurice, 1729–1883 (Trois-Rivières, Qué., 1952).

POULIN DE COURVAL, FRANÇOIS-LOUIS, naval officer; b. 30 Oct. 1728 in Quebec, son of Louis-Jean POULIN de Courval and Françoise Foucault; d. in the autumn of 1769 at La Rochelle, France.

François-Louis, only son of Louis-Jean Poulin de Courval, studied at the Jesuit college in Quebec. Bishop Pontbriand [DUBREIL] planned that he enter the priesthood, but by his own admission the young man had a much greater inclination for a military career. In 1746 he succeeded in convincing his uncle and guardian, Claude Poulin de Courval Cressé, to let him take part in the expedition which Jean-Baptiste-Nicolas-Roch de Ramezay* was mounting to besiege Annapolis Royal, Nova Scotia. Upon his return to Quebec in November 1746, his guardian had Poulin de Courval follow the courses in pilotage which the Jesuit Joseph-Pierre de Bonnecamps* was giving at the college in Quebec. The following spring he began sailing between Canada, Île Royale (Cape Breton Island), France, and the West Indies as a naval officer. He wanted to be freed from his uncle's guardianship, and on 30 Sept. 1748 obtained from the Conseil Supérieur letters of emancipation and benefit of age.

In 1752 Poulin de Courval became a captain in command of a merchant-ship and sailed the seas for some years. In the spring of 1756 his ship ran aground in the St Lawrence. He then entered the service of the king of France, who had just declared war on England. An experienced captain, Poulin de Courval made several crossings between Canada and France. During one of these crossings his ship, the *Diamant*, was captured; the wounded Poulin was taken prisoner to England, where he spent eight months. After being freed towards the end of 1758 he took the ship

Bienfaisant, with a cargo of supplies and munitions, to Canada. He reached Quebec on 17 May 1759 and took part in the defence of the town. On 28 July he made an unsuccessful attempt to set fire to the English fleet by means of rafts used as fire-ships. A month later, while at Saint-Augustin (Saint-Augustin-de-Québec), he was the victim of an unlucky accident; a French soldier, taking him for an Englishman, fired upon him, hitting him in the thigh. Consequently Poulin de Courval was unable to take part in the final combats which were to decide the fate of the colony.

In the autumn of 1760 he arrived in La Rochelle, where he stayed for several months; from there he went to "take the waters" nearby to cure his bad leg. His stay at the spa put him 4,000 *livres* in debt. Anxious to pay these debts, he fitted out a privateer towards the end of 1761. Just as he was to sail, he received an order to go to Brest, where he was appointed a fire-ship captain in the Marine. In the spring of 1762 he sailed for Newfoundland with Charles-Louis d'Arsac* de Ternay in the expedition to destroy the English settlements there.

Poulin returned to France in the summer of 1762 to seek help for the expedition, and received command of the frigate *Zéphir*. Just as he was leaving the port of Brest to sail to Newfoundland, he was attacked by three English ships and forced to surrender. He was imprisoned in England for a month, then returned to France, thanks to the peace. As a consequence of this battle the Duc de Choiseul awarded him the cross of the order of Saint-Louis and a gratuity of 3,000 *livres*.

In 1763 Poulin de Courval received command of the flute *Garonne* and was commissioned to take the new governor, Gabriel-François d'Angeac*, and his officers to the islands of Saint-Pierre and Miquelon. He returned there in 1764 with a cargo of provisions. Apparently during one of these voyages he made a survey of the possibilities for fishing, agriculture, and lumbering on Saint-Pierre and Miquelon. But the supplying of these islands was always a precarious matter. During the winter of 1765–66 the situation at Saint-Pierre became critical, and Versailles asked the port authorities of Rochefort to send help, despite the difficulties of navigation in that season. This perilous mission was entrusted to Poulin de Courval, who knew the waters well. He successfully carried it out, reaching Saint-Pierre at the end of the winter of 1766. This final exploit earned him the rank of lieutenant-commander in the Marine and a gratuity of 600 *livres*.

Worn out by his numerous sea voyages, his military campaigns, and his wounds, François-Louis Poulin de Courval died at La Rochelle in

October 1769. A few years earlier at Saint-Pierre and Miquelon he had married Marguerite Leneuf de Beaubassin, who in May 1769 bore him a son in La Rochelle.

ANDRÉ LACHANCE

AJQ, Registre d'état civil, Notre-Dame de Québec, 30 oct. 1728. AN, Col., B, 108, f.1; 114, ff.1, 203; 115, ff.23, 85; 118, ff.56, 229; 122, f.9; 125, f.78; 149, f.259; C¹¹A, 104, f.117; E, 96 (dossier Courval); Marine, C⁷, 257. ANQ, Greffe de R.-C. Barolet, 25 juin, 13 oct. 1754; NF, Coll. de pièces jud. et not., 3952. "Journal du siège du Québec" (Fauteux), APQ *Rapport, 1920–21*, 137–241. Henri Têtu, "M. Jean-Félix Récher, curé de Québec, et son journal, 1757–1760," *BRH*, IX (1903), 134. "Précis de la vie et des aventures de Poulin de Courval chevalier de l'ordre royal et militaire de Saint-Louis capitaine de brulot; première partie, depuis 1746 jusqu'à 1765" [The author of this biography has a copy of this manuscript; the original belonged in 1939 to Sir Bruce Ingram of the *Illustrated London News*. A.L.]. Fauteux, *Les chevaliers de Saint-Louis*, 215–16. P.-G. Roy, *Inv. jug. et délib., 1717–1760*, IV, 287–88; V, 85. La Morandière, *Hist. de la pêche française de la morue*, II, 734, 737–38. P.-G. Roy, *Fils de Québec*, II, 45–48.

POULIN DE COURVAL, LOUIS-JEAN, merchant, seigneur, king's attorney and later lieutenant general for civil and criminal affairs for the royal jurisdiction of Trois-Rivières; b. 15 Nov. 1696 at Trois-Rivières, eldest son of Jean-Baptiste Poulin* de Courval, king's attorney at Trois-Rivières, and of Louise Cressé; d. 19 Feb. 1743 in his home town.

In 1724 Louis-Jean Poulin de Courval was living in Quebec, where he was known as a merchant. After his father's death on 15 Feb. 1727 at Trois-Rivières, he inherited his title of seigneur of Nicolet and succeeded him as king's attorney for the royal jurisdiction of Trois-Rivières. As "guardian of public vindication," he was required to investigate in the king's name all crimes and offences made known to him by denunciation, complaint, or "public outcry." But since judicial affairs in the royal jurisdiction of Trois-Rivières were not sufficiently numerous to allow him to keep his family there decently, he continued living in the capital on Rue Sault-au-Matelot, devoting his attention to business. During the autumn of 1738, however, he went to settle permanently at Trois-Rivières, after the death of the lieutenant general for civil and criminal affairs for Trois-Rivières, René Godefroy* de Tonnancour. This decision on Poulin de Courval's part was to be a profitable one. The following year, on 24 Sept. 1739, the colonial authorities suggested to the minister of Marine, Maurepas, that he fill the office left vacant by the death of the

Sieur de Tonnancour. They preferred him to Louis-Joseph Godefroy* de Tonnancour, René's son, because although he was "barely conversant with jurisprudence" Poulin de Courval had "a little more experience in legal affairs." On 1 April 1740 the king consequently made the appointment, which Poulin held until his death on 19 Feb. 1743.

On 18 Dec. 1724, in the church of Notre-Dame de Québec, Poulin de Courval had married Françoise, daughter of François FOUCAULT, a Quebec "bourgeois and merchant." On 25 April 1730 he was widowed, and on 22 Nov. 1733, in Quebec, he was remarried, this time to Thérèse, the "emancipated" daughter of the deceased lieutenant general for civil and criminal affairs for the royal jurisdiction of Montreal, François-Marie Bouat*. By his first marriage Poulin de Courval had three children, two daughters who died in infancy, and a son, FRANÇOIS-LOUIS, who survived him. There were no children of the second marriage.

Poulin de Courval chose his wives from the *milieu* which he frequented at the period. Thus, being a merchant in 1724, he married the daughter of a merchant, and being king's attorney in 1733, he married the daughter of an officer of the law. Marriage became for him a means of social advancement.

ANDRÉ LACHANCE

AN, Col., C¹¹A, 73, f.14v; 75, ff.77f.; 79, ff.58v–59v; 120, ff.230v, 267f., 348v–49; D²C, 222/1, f.181. ANQ, Greffe de Nicolas Boisseau, 19 nov. 1733; Greffe de Florent de La Cetière, 17 déc. 1724; NF, Coll. de pièces jud. et not., 1003, 1147, 2062, 3592; NF, Documents de la Prévôté de Québec, 8 janv. 1742. Bornier, *Conférences des ord. de Louis XIV*, II, 66–67. P.-G. Roy, *Inv. concessions*, II, 239. Tanguay, *Dictionnaire*.

POULIN DE COURVAL CRESSÉ (Cressé de Courval), LOUIS-PIERRE, assistant builder in the royal shipyards, seigneur; b. 8 April 1728 in Quebec, eldest son of Claude Poulin de Courval Cressé, merchant and shipbuilder, and Marie-Anne Lefebvre; d. 29 June 1764 at Trois-Rivières.

Louis-Pierre Poulin de Courval Cressé followed in a family tradition: both his father and his grandfather, Jean-Baptiste Poulin* de Courval, were shipbuilders in New France. At an early age Louis-Pierre was placed in one of the offices of Intendant Hocquart* in Quebec. There in 1746 he came to the attention of the superintendent of the royal shipyards, René-Nicolas Levasseur*, who had been instructed to find a young Canadian of good family to train as his understudy. Cressé

Poulin de Francheville

was taken on by Levasseur and by the end of 1746 was reported to be receiving instruction from the master of hydrography, Joseph-Pierre de Bonnecamps*, and to have taken quickly to drafting and design. In the winter Cressé accompanied Levasseur in a search for ship timber and, in March 1747, he was appointed deputy builder at 30 *livres* per month. Thereafter Levasseur became Cressé's strongest advocate in New France, teaching him all he knew about naval construction and organizing a shipyard.

By the end of 1747 Cressé was reported able to manage a shipyard under some supervision. His salary was scarcely adequate, and for several years had to be augmented by sums sent by his father. Levasseur was tireless in his efforts to obtain a raise in emoluments for him, but in 1754 Cressé was receiving only 480 *livres* per year although he was supervising master shipwrights being paid 900 *livres*.

By that date the royal shipyards were experiencing serious difficulties. Levasseur believed that François Bigot* was deliberately hampering progress and in the fall of 1753 had gone to France to present his complaints in person to the minister of Marine, Rouillé. Cressé was left in charge of the yards with the newly laid keel of the frigate *Abénaquise* on the stocks. Probably owing to his father's influence, on 25 Sept. 1754 Cressé received one of the last seigneurial grants to be made under the French régime: that of Courval, located south of Baie-du-Febvre (Baieville, Que.) and adjoining the seigneury of Nicolet. Not long after, on 7 January, Cressé married in Quebec Charlotte-Louise, daughter of Eustache Lambert Dumont, the younger, seigneur of Mille-Îles, by whom he was to have three children.

Cressé continued to work on ship construction. In July 1755 the Marine decided to lay down no new ships in Canada until those on the stocks were completed and sent to France for inspection, but the outbreak of hostilities between France and England led to immediate demands for small warships to sail Lake Champlain and Lake Ontario. During the winter of 1755–56, Cressé was sent with a work party to Fort Frontenac (Kingston, Ont.) where he began building two ships, a schooner of ten guns (probably the *Louise*) and a larger vessel (either the 12-gun *Hurault* or the 16-gun *Marquise de Vaudreuil*). In the summer of 1756 the ships were ready.

Cressé's subsequent activities remain uncertain. In 1757 Governor Pierre de Rigaud* de Vaudreuil recommended that he and Levasseur be sent to France to continue naval ship construction. Following the loss of Fort Frontenac in

1758, however, Cressé was sent to Pointe-au-Baril (Maitland, Ont.) near La Présentation (Oswegatchie; now Ogdensburg, N.Y.) where he began to build two or three corvettes for the planned campaign on Lake Ontario in 1759. These vessels were substantial: one, the *Outaouaise*, was 160 tons burden and mounted ten 12-pounder guns. Cressé remained at La Présentation through 1759, and after the capitulation of Montreal the next year he went to Trois-Rivières.

Seigneur of Courval and heir to Nicolet since his father had acquired the whole of this seigneury in 1747, Cressé appeared about to take up residence on the land after the conquest. In 1764, in return for one quarter of the revenues, his father granted him the banal rights over Nicolet on condition that he build a grist mill. Construction was begun, but on 29 June, at age 36, Louis-Pierre died at Trois-Rivières. His widow probably moved to Nicolet and completed the work. There in any case she raised her family and built the seigneurial manor. In 1785 Cressé's son Pierre-Michel inherited from his grandfather two-thirds of Nicolet and became the first seigneur in a century to reside there.

JAMES S. PRITCHARD

AN, Col., C¹¹A, 85, 86, 89, 99, 100, 103. *Journal des campagnes au Canada de 1755 à 1760 par le comte de Maurès de Malartic . . .* , Gabriel de Maurès de Malartic et Paul Gaffarel, édit. (Dijon, 1890), 59. *Royal Fort Frontenac* (Preston and Lamontagne). P.-G. Roy, *Inv. concessions*, II, 239–41; III, 281; V, 85–86. J.-E. Bellemare, *Histoire de Nicolet, 1669–1924* (Arthabaska, Qué., 1924), 117–32. J.-N. Fauteux, *Essai sur l'industrie*, I, 272–74. Mathieu, *La construction navale*, 15, 58, 80, 103. P.-G. Roy, "Le sous-constructeur Cressé," *BRH*, LII (1946), 131–35.

POULIN DE FRANCHEVILLE, THÉRÈSE. *See* COUAGNE

POURCHAUT. *See* POUCHOT

PRESSÉ, HYACINTHE-OLIVIER, clerk of court, court officer, and royal notary; fl. 1735–46.

Nothing is known about Hyacinthe-Olivier Pressé's birth or death. His stay in New France lasted about 12 years, during which he held various judicial offices. On 1 Oct. 1735 Pressé obtained from Intendant Hocquart* a commission as clerk of court, court officer, and royal notary, for the royal jurisdiction of Trois-Rivières. He succeeded Pierre Petit*, who was giving up these three offices because of age and infirmities. The inquiry into the new notary's character took place on 7 Nov. 1735.

Pressé exercised the three functions for eight

years, and on 31 Oct. 1743 he gave up his office as clerk of court. The following year, on 30 June 1744, he lost the right to exercise his other two functions; the Conseil Supérieur had suspended him for three months, alleging that certain irregularities had been committed in a trial presided over by Jean-Baptiste Fafard de La Framboise, the deputy king's attorney.

Some years later Pressé was himself the victim of dubious legal procedures. On 1 March 1746 Joseph Heu, *dit* Millet, received a mortal sword wound during a trip from Sorel to the Chenal du Moine with Pressé, Pierre-François Rigault, and Louis Lavallée. The deputy king's attorney, Fafard de La Frambroise, began his investigation on 3 March and rapidly became convinced that the sword thrust had been delivered by Pressé. Pressé was arrested during the night of 4/5 March, and shortly afterwards Rigault was imprisoned as an accomplice. Fafard ordered a trial, which began on 17 March in Trois-Rivières. Lavallée's vague evidence incriminated neither Pressé nor Rigault. And the other witnesses could only relate what happened after the murder: before he died the victim had not been able to identify his aggressor, and Pressé and Rigault had each accused the other of being responsible for his death. On the basis of this unconvincing evidence the king's attorney demanded on 12 April the death sentence for Pressé and banishment from the jurisdiction for Rigault. The next day the court sentenced Pressé to the galleys. Rigault was found innocent and was released.

The notary immediately appealed his case to the Conseil Supérieur. In the second trial a new version of the affair was admitted as evidence. After a trifling quarrel between Pressé and Rigault, both of whom were drunk, Pressé was said to have drawn his sword to frighten his companion, but slipped on the snow; in trying to avoid the sword, Rigault was supposed to have deflected the blade, which struck Joseph Heu in the side, wounding him mortally. The council accepted this version, and on 26 April it suspended judgement on Pressé while awaiting a reprieve from the king. At the same time Rigault was found innocent.

On 9 November of that year Intendant Hocquart pleaded Pressé's cause when he sent the trial documents to the minister of Marine, Maurepas. We do not know whether the king granted him a reprieve, and after this date no trace of him in New France is found.

MICHEL PAQUIN

AJTR, Greffe de H.-O. Pressé, 1735–1746. AN, Col., C¹¹A, 86, ff.91–154 (copy of the documents of the trial of Pressé and Rigault). P.-G. Roy, *Inv. coll. pièces jud. et not.*, I, 186; II, 358; *Inv. jug. et délib., 1717–1760*, II, 164; IV, 191, 194; *Inv. ord. int.*, II, 190; III, 50, 80. J.-E. Roy, *Histoire du notariat*, I, 194–97. [Raymond Douville in "La tragédie du chenal du Moine," *Cahiers des Dix*, XXXV (1970), 55–67, gives a résumé of the testimony heard during the trial at Trois-Rivières. M.P.]

PRICE, BENJAMIN, merchant, member of James Murray*'s council, master in chancery; d. between September 1768 and May 1769.

Benjamin Price was a merchant of postconquest Quebec, sufficiently reliable and prominent to be given important commissions by Governor Murray. Unfortunately the only information available about him consists of brief references in the minutes and papers of the Legislative Council, which include a complaint lodged by him in 1767 against his confidential clerk giving all that has been found about his origins.

He was, apparently, an Englishman. In March 1761 he sent a ship from Plymouth for Quebec, chiefly loaded with his own goods under the charge of a supercargo. In 1762 he himself followed with more goods. He settled at Quebec and also did business through a confidential clerk in Montreal. By some authorities he has been mistakenly identified with the merchant James Price of Montreal.

In the autumn of 1764 he was appointed by Governor Murray to his newly formed council and was commissioned a justice of the peace. He was also commissioned, with Thomas Dunn*, a master in the Court of Chancery, Adam Mabane* and François MOUNIER being examiners, and the governor being the chancellor.

Price's chief service to the government was in connection with the disastrous fire which occurred in Montreal in May 1765, destroying 121 houses and much goods as well as exposing the merchants' warehouses to looting. There was no senior civil official in Montreal and merchants complained to the council that the measures taken by Ralph BURTON, the brigadier of the Northern Department who had his headquarters there, were inadequate. The council agreed to send Adam Mabane with Price to report on the whole situation and to spend £300, later increased to £400 by a gift from Murray, to assist the most needy.

Mabane and Price presented their report at the end of June. They were very critical of some of the local justices of the peace who, through "pride and obstinacy in consequence of former disputes with the military," had not even asked for guards to prevent the looting. Mabane and Price in conjunction with the army and the jus-

541

tices took measures for the restoration of stolen goods, and made immediate arrangements to give help to charitable institutions and to relieve the needy. Their report to the council emphasized the need for more help, and for a stronger civil administration to cope with incompetence and even some corruption on the part of junior officials.

Almost immediately after the presentation of the report Benjamin Price went to London, presumably on private business, but with a commission from the council to secure subscriptions from the authorities and from private individuals for the relief of the victims of the fire. He apparently returned in the summer of 1766 but was not present as a council member to welcome Guy Carleton* as governor in September. Nor did he attend the meetings during the crisis of the autumn which culminated in Carleton's dismissal of Colonel Paulus Æmilius Irving* and Adam

Mabane. He appeared again in council in January 1767. During that year he was engaged in litigation with his confidential clerk whom he accused of incompetence and fraud. He was also, with Daniel Robertson of Montreal, the subject of a petition to Carleton from Samuel MacKay, deputy surveyor for the navy. MacKay had claimed for the navy 200 trees in the Lake Champlain area, cut them, and floated them to Quebec where they had been seized by Robertson and Price as having been cut on their land.

Benjamin Price is shown as present at council meetings as late as September 1768. He probably died during the following winter for in May 1769 the furniture of "the late Mr. Price" was sold at auction.

HILDA NEATBY

PAC, RG 1, E1, 1–6; RG 4, A1, 2–18. Neatby, *Quebec*. F.-J. Audet, "Les législateurs de la province de Québec, 1764–1791," *BRH*, XXXI (1925), 485.

Q

QINOUSAKI. *See* KINOUSAKI

QUARANTE SOLS. *See* MICHIPICHY

QUÉRÉ DE TRÉGURON, MAURICE, priest, Sulpician, missionary; b. probably 23 Sept. 1663 at Châteauneuf-du-Faou (dept. of Finistère), France; d. 7 Aug. 1754 at Montreal.

Maurice Quéré de Tréguron was ordained a priest on 9 Sept. 1689, but he did not enter the Society of Saint-Sulpice in Paris until 20 Feb. 1692, after having received his licentiate in theology. According to Louis Tronson, superior general of the Society of Saint-Sulpice, Quéré de Tréguron presumably arrived in Montreal in the autumn of 1692. On the superior general's recommendation François Dollier* de Casson, superior of the seminary of Montreal, granted him a few months' rest, then in the autumn of 1693 entrusted him with the office of bursar and secretary of the seigneurs of Montreal Island. He exercised this function until February 1695, when he became a missionary to the Indians residing in the vicinity of Montreal.

Quéré de Tréguron began his ministry at the La Montagne mission, just when it was entering a period of instability which was to last more than 30 years, and which he became acquainted with in all its phases. This instability took the form of successive moves, the first of which was caused

by the burning of the fort at La Montagne and all the mission's installations, fired in the autumn of 1694 by a drunk Indian. It was then decided to move the Indians farther from the town, where they could too easily obtain intoxicants, and to set up the new mission on the bank of the Rivière des Prairies, at the foot of the Sault au Récollet, in a wild site separated on all sides from the French habitations by a wood that was four to five miles wide. Ground had to be cleared, then a chapel, fort, seigneurial manor, and residences for the nuns and the Indians had to be built. The move to this site began in 1696 and was not completed until 1704. During those years Quéré de Tréguron participated in all the work of building and moving, under the direction of his *confrère* Robert-Michel Gay*, the superior of the mission.

In 1720, to protect the Indians against drunkenness, it was deemed necessary to move them still farther from the whites, who in the intervening years had acquired lands in the vicinity of the mission, both on Île Jésus and Montreal Island. This time, however, because of his age and infirmities, the mission superior entrusted to M. Quéré the work of setting up new installations and moving, which took place in February 1721.

The Sulpicians had chosen as their site an isolated spot 35 miles from Montreal, on the shore of Lac des Deux-Montagnes in the seigneury of the same name which the seminary of Saint-Sulpice in Paris had obtained in 1717. In 1720 a start was made on clearing an immense area intended for the Indians; later a temporary chapel and a temporary residence for the missionaries were built. Excavations carried out in 1876 revealed that these buildings, situated about 300 feet from the lake, were made of wood and that the chapel measured 100 feet by 40 and the residence 40 by 60.

In 1725, upon Robert-Michel Gay's death, Quéré de Tréguron became superior of the mission and therewith acquired the task of watching over the spiritual and temporal needs of his neophytes. It may be presumed that he personally chose the final site for the mission and concerned himself with all the details of the new establishment, three-quarters of a mile to the west of the old site, on a headland jutting out into the lake, where the presbytery of the parish of L'Annonciation d'Oka is situated today. Work began in 1728 with the building of a church and a manor house in stone, as was required by the deed of grant of the seigneury of Lac-des-Deux-Montagnes; the fort, also to be in stone, was not built until 1741. By 1734 the Indians were all installed near the new church, the Iroquois to the west and the Algonkins to the east, each group having its own organization.

In 1754, after 59 years of missionary work, characterized by great charity and rare patience, Quéré de Tréguron submitted his resignation and was replaced by Hamon GUEN. He retired to the seminary of Montreal, where he died on 7 August of that same year, nearly 91 years of age.

ANTONIO DANSEREAU

ASSM, Section de la correspondance générale; Section de la seigneurie du Lac-des-Deux-Montagnes; Section des biographies; Section des cartes et plans; Section des concessions de terre et d'emplacement de l'île de Montréal. Allaire, *Dictionnaire*. Gauthier, *Sulpitiana*. C.-P. Beaubien, *Le Sault-au-Récollet; ses rapports avec les premiers temps de la colonie; mission-paroisse* (Montréal, 1898), 155–56, 274–80. [É.-M. Faillon], *Vie de la sœur Bourgeoys, fondatrice de la Congrégation de Notre-Dame de Villemarie en Canada, suivie de l'histoire de cet institut jusqu'à ce jour* (2v., Villemarie [Montréal], 1853), II, 168, 264–67. Olivier Maurault, *Marges d'histoire* (3v., Montréal, 1929–30), III. Pierre Rousseau, *Saint-Sulpice et les missions catholiques* (Montréal, 1930). J.-A. Cuoq, "Anotc kekon," *RSCT*, 1st ser., XI (1893), sect. I, 137–79. Olivier Maurault, "Les vicissitudes d'une mission sauvage," *Revue trimestrielle canadienne*, XVI (1930), 121–49.

QUINDRE, LOUIS-CÉSAIRE DAGNEAU DOUVILLE DE. *See* DAGNEAU

QUINOUSAQUY. *See* KINOUSAKI

R

RADISSON, *dit* **Duplessis, MARGUERITE.** *See* DUPLESSIS

RAMEZAY, MARIE-CHARLOTTE DE, *dite de* **Saint-Claude de la Croix,** Nun Hospitaller of the Hôpital Général of Quebec, superior; b. and baptized 31 July 1697 at Trois-Rivières, daughter of Claude de Ramezay*, governor of Trois-Rivières and Montreal, and Marie-Charlotte Denys de La Ronde; d. 15 Nov. 1767 in Quebec.

Marie-Charlotte was first a boarder with the Ursulines of Quebec, as were her five sisters. On 18 Nov. 1716 she entered the convent of the Hôpital Général of Quebec, and on 30 May 1718 she made her profession. The dowry offered by her parents was rather unusual. After having promised to give 3,000 *livres* in money of France, her father began by paying 1,000 *livres* and suggested to the superior that he pay the remaining 2,000 *livres* in boards and planks, to which he would add the sum of 200 *livres* coming to him each year from the Ursulines of Trois-Rivières.

It was after 1730 that Marie-Charlotte de Ramezay exercised her most important offices; from then on she helped Marie-Joseph JUCHEREAU Duchesnay, *dite* de l'Enfant-Jésus, in the administration of the convent. Immediately after the death in 1730 of the superior, Geneviève Juchereau Duchesnay, *dite* de Saint-Augustin, the dean of the chapter, Louis Bertrand* de Latour, arbitrarily appointed Marie-Thérèse LANGLOIS, *dite* de Saint-Jean-Baptiste, as superior. Marie-Charlotte de Ramezay and Marie-Joseph Juchereau sided with the nuns who opposed his disregard of the community's constitution. But the canonical elections in 1732 delivered the office of superior to Marie-Joseph Juchereau, with Marie-Charlotte de Ramezay accepting the charge of depositary (bursar) and discreet (counsellor). In 49 years of religious life,

Rankin

beginning with her profession, Marie-Charlotte held the office of depositary for 26 years, from 1732 to 1738, 1741 to 1747, 1750 to 1756, and from 1759 till her death, on 15 Nov. 1767, when she was 70 years old. In between she was assistant superior to Marie-Joseph Legardeur de Repentigny, *dite* de la Visitation, from 1747 to 1750, and superior from 1738 to 1741 and 1756 to 1759, replacing Marie-Joseph Juchereau in this office each time.

Marie-Charlotte de Ramezay came from a family of soldiers and was particularly affected by the misfortunes which the French troops suffered during the Seven Years' War; her sympathy led her after the capture of Quebec to try to demoralize the English soldiers who were hospitalized in the Hôpital Général by making a false announcement of an English defeat. Yet this feeling for her compatriots did not prevent her before September 1759 from treating the English patients well, who were moreover grateful to her. It is reported that Captain David Ochterloney "was cared for most tenderly by Madame de Ramezay, directress of the hospital, 'who wept when he died.' " Upon Ochterloney's death General WOLFE hastened to write to Marie-Charlotte de Ramezay to thank her for her kindness to this officer and to assure her that he would protect the convent if fortune favoured him.

MICHELINE D'ALLAIRE

AHGQ, Actes capitulaires, 35f.; Actes de profession et contrats de dot, 1; "Annales"; Registre des entrées et des dots. AJTR, Registre d'état civil, Immaculée-Conception de Trois-Rivières, 31 juill. 1697. AMUQ, Registre des entrées des pensionnaires. AN, Col., C¹¹ᴬ, 54, f.80. Knox, *Historical journal* (Doughty), II, 20–21, 367–68. *Mgr de Saint-Vallier et l'Hôpital Général.*

RANKIN, JOHN, naval officer; fl. 1741–48.

In the spring of 1741 John Rankin was appointed lieutenant on the sloop *Furnace* (commander Christopher MIDDLETON), which was bound on a voyage to Hudson Bay to find the northwest passage. Rankin headed three of the four boat expeditions that explored Wager Bay in July 1742. When the *Furnace* returned to England that autumn Arthur Dobbs, one of the chief advocates of a search for the elusive northerly route, provoked a controversy by accusing Middleton of concealing evidence that the entrance to the passage lay in the Wager. Having investigated that inlet, Rankin became a central figure in the dispute. At hearings before the admiralty in May 1743 he joined two other members of the *Furnace*'s crew, Edward THOMPSON

and John WIGATE, in testifying against Middleton.

A scrutiny of the available evidence does not inspire confidence in Rankin's veracity. His log of the boat expeditions in the Wager refers to it only as a river, and contains no mention of the flood tide coming through it from the west upon which Dobbs laid such stress. A report signed by him after the final exploration stated that he had turned back when he sighted "a great Run or Fall of Water" about a league distant. Equally damaging is evidence of Rankin's attitude after his return to England but before Dobbs had attacked Middleton's findings. This includes a letter of 12 Feb. 1742/43 to Middleton which concludes, "I shall for Ever Think My Self bound to pray for your good health, and prosperity, If Ever it should be in my pour to Serve you by Night or day, I shall allways Think my self in Duty bound to do it." Middleton's own journal – soon alleged by Dobbs to be a forgery – was signed by Rankin on 19 April 1743 as being "a true Coppy from the Original Logbook kept on Board his Majestys Sloop Furnace."

Rankin continued in the navy and at the end of the War of the Austrian Succession in 1748 was placed on the half-pay list. The name Rankin Inlet, given by Middleton to an opening on the west coast of Hudson Bay explored by Rankin in the summer of 1742, is an ill-deserved memorial to an officer whose mendacity helped to wreck the career of his former commander.

GLYNDWR WILLIAMS

[Rankin's log of the *Furnace* is at the National Maritime Museum (Greenwich, Eng.), Adm. L/F 109. His letter to Middleton of February 1743 is in PRO, Adm. 1/2099; his testifying signature is on the first page of Middleton's log in PRO, Adm. 51/379, pt.ɪ. The part Rankin played in the attack on Middleton is outlined in the various books written at the time of the controversy, notably Christopher Middleton, *A vindication of the conduct of Captain Christopher Middleton . . .* (London, 1743), and Arthur Dobbs, *Remarks upon Middleton's defence.* The Middleton voyage is examined in Williams, *British search for the northwest passage.* G.W.]

RANSONNET, SYLVESTRE-FRANÇOIS-MICHEL, priest of the Missions Étrangères; originally from the bishopric of Liège, Austrian Netherlands (Belgium); d. sometime after 1743, probably in his native land.

Sylvestre-François-Michel Ransonnet was a member of the seminary of the Missions Étrangères in Paris when he dwelt temporarily in Rome to assist Bishop Dosquet*, who had become procurator of the Missions Étrangères at the Holy

See at the end of 1726. It was probably during this stay, and thanks to his "close relative" Bishop Dosquet that Ransonnet received the title of apostolic protonotary that he was later reputed to hold. He returned to Paris in 1728 and was appointed a director of the seminary of the Missions Étrangères on 27 May 1729, even though he was not yet ordained. As the act of reception mentions, the directors of the seminary had received beforehand assurance that Ransonnet intended "never to leave the ecclesiastic state," but that if this were to happen, "he would immediately cease to be a director of the seminary." Meanwhile, at Dosquet's request he had had *La vie de la sœur Bourgeois . . .* printed in Avignon. This biography must have been drawn either from notes by Dosquet, who had been chaplain of the Congregation of Notre-Dame in Montreal from 1721 to 1723, or from another biography written by Abbé Charles de Glandelet*.

Ransonnet left for Canada at the end of May 1734 with Dosquet, who had become bishop of Quebec in 1733 after the resignation of Bishop Mornay. Scarcely had Ransonnet arrived than he was ordained a priest on 18 Sept. 1734. Shortly afterwards, in October, the bishop of Quebec asked the minister, Maurepas, to grant his relative letters of naturalization, free of charge, with the right to enjoy ecclesiastical benefices. Ransonnet did not receive these letters until April 1738.

Since he had held office as a director of the seminary of the Missions Étrangères in Paris, it was natural that Ransonnet should exercise some function at the seminary of Quebec, where he went to live. We have no indication as to his occupation at the beginning except the recommendation from the directors in Paris "that it was requisite to put him in charge of the office of bursar of temporalities" of the seminary of Quebec, because he had held this office at the seminary of Paris. Be that as it may, not only was Ransonnet admitted as a member of the community of priests, but as soon as he arrived he was one of the directors of the house, signing the deliberations of the council in this capacity. In addition he was ecclesiastical superior of the Hôtel-Dieu of Quebec for five years, beginning in 1735. There is no evidence, however, that he was titular bursar of the seminary. Rather, he deputized for the superior, François-Elzéar VALLIER, who remained in France from the autumn of 1739 till the summer of 1741. Fearing that Vallier, who was suffering from a serious illness, might die, the directors of the seminary in Paris had on 10 May 1739 already recommended that he be replaced by Ransonnet. Their action probably explains the fact that Bishop Laubervière [Pourroy*], successor to Bishop Dosquet, who had resigned, wrote Ransonnet that he was counting on living at the seminary upon his arrival and asked him to prepare a room for him. After the young bishop's premature death Ransonnet was present with the bursar of the seminary, Balthazar André, at the inventory of his belongings.

In 1740 relations between the seminary and the chapter of Quebec were extremely strained over their respective rights and privileges in the cathedral. Ransonnet had received in rather cavalier fashion two canons who had interrupted him during vespers with a request that the pupils of the seminary be allowed to serve as choir boys when the body of Bishop Laubervière was removed for the funeral. The chapter dealt severely with this offence, and Ransonnet submitted readily to the penitence that was imposed upon him. Was he himself a canon, or was he still replacing Abbé Vallier, who was the theologal of the chapter? The answer to this question has not been found. Nevertheless it was in this same year that, having discovered in the back of the bursar's office of the seminary a bundle of documents concerning the chapter, he took it upon himself simply to hand them over to the canons. Later the canons were to use them to institute proceedings against the seminary and the bishop [*see* Charles-Antoine GODEFROY de Tonnancour; Jean-Félix RÉCHER].

Ransonnet, whose health was delicate, had to reduce his activities shortly before he left Canada in the autumn of 1743, partly at his father's request; he returned to the Austrian Netherlands and subsequently disappears from the record.

HONORIUS PROVOST

ASQ, Chapitre, 129, 202; Évêques, 202; Grand livre de délibération, 1734–1736; Lettres, M, 85, 102; Paroisses de Québec, 6; Polygraphie, XXIII, 27; Séminaire, XIV, 4; LXXVIII, 18. P.-G. Roy, *Inv. jug. et délib., 1717–1760*, III, 253. Gosselin, *L'Église du Canada jusqu'à la conquête*, II. Albert Jamet, *Marguerite Bourgeoys, 1620–1700* (2v., Montréal, 1942). Adrien Launay, *Mémorial de la Société des Missions étrangères* (2v., Paris, 1912–16), II, 543. J.-E. Roy, "Notes sur Mgr de Laubervière," *BRH*, I (1895), 6–7. Henri Têtu, "Le chapitre de la cathédrale de Québec et ses délégués en France," *BRH*, XV (1909), 205.

RÊCHE. *See* RESCHE

RÉCHER, JEAN-FÉLIX, parish priest, author of a diary of events at Quebec from 1757 to 1760;

Récher

b. 1724, probably in the diocese of Rouen, France; d. 16 March 1768 in Quebec.

Jean-Félix Récher was already a priest when he landed at Quebec in the summer of 1747. He had been sent by the Missions Étrangères in Paris to become one of the directors of the seminary of Quebec. According to his superiors he was a man of sound mind, diligent, and conscientious about his duties. Two years later, on 1 Oct. 1749, the directors of the seminary of Quebec chose him to become parish priest of Notre-Dame de Québec, a signal honour for a priest 25 years of age. The parish had been without a priest since the death of Abbé Charles PLANTE in 1744. The presentation and appointment of a candidate for it depended upon the seminary by virtue of the union between it and Bishop Laval*. Until then no one had questioned this procedure, but Récher's arrival on the scene set off a quarrel in which the parish priest of Quebec, the bishop, the directors of the seminary, and the canons of the chapter would be involved for a score of years.

Once the presentation had been made by the seminary, everything seemed to be for the best: Bishop Pontbriand [DUBREIL], as bishop of Quebec, appointed Récher parish priest of Notre-Dame, adding, however, that he could not take into consideration the presentation that had been made, "suspecting some error in the union of the parish with the seminary." On 4 November, the day after the appointment, the priest took formal possession of the parish, though protesting against the bishop's remark. Two days later Abbé Récher asked the chapter to receive him as an honorary canon, putting forward the custom observed up until that time. This favour was granted him, but after some hesitation, which disappeared after it was discovered in the archives that the parish priest François Dupré* had been accorded the same honour in 1687. Everything seemed to be calm again, but scarcely a month and a half later the affair revived in an unexpected manner: the canon René-Jean ALLENOU de Lavillangevin, who had been chosen by the bishop and the chapter to examine the archives and put its papers in order, discovered the bull by Pope Clement X, dated 1 Oct. 1674, which set up the bishopric and chapter of Quebec. Among other things it stated that the church of Quebec would become the cathedral church, that the chapter would have the broadest powers over the temporal matters of the church and was to have charge of the ministry of the parish. Armed with this document and regretting their past ignorance, the canons undertook to claim their rights. They had not taken into account the energetic parish priest, who had no intention of surrendering so easily. Discussions, reports, lawsuits, incidents deliberately provoked: the parish priest, like the good Norman he was, overlooked nothing in asserting his rights. He had been appointed parish priest of Quebec without opposition from anyone, and he intended to remain parish priest.

The affair was taken before the Conseil Supérieur, which sentenced the canons to pay a fine and costs in 1750, at the same time maintaining the parish priest in possession of his office. The bishops and canons, as was to be expected, had recourse to the king, but before judgement was rendered a great deal of water was to flow down the St Lawrence. In the meantime both sides stood their ground, presenting the spectacle of a series of exchanges in which, to say the least, charity was not always present. Anything was a pretext for winning. When a seminarist died in 1753, the chapter claimed that it had the right to offer him a funeral, because the young man had rendered service to the canons. Naturally the parish priest objected to the canons' interference, as he did at every opportunity, firmly convinced that he was in the right. The matter was in fact settled only after his death.

Meanwhile war had been declared, and the civil and ecclesiastical authorities had many other things to do than to question the legitimacy of Father Récher's election. The war did not prevent him from exercising his ministry steadily. Well before the British siege of Quebec began in the summer of 1759, he had started a diary relating day by day the events he had seen or heard of. This diary, first published by Henri Têtu* in 1903 in the *Bulletin des recherches historiques*, is one of the most valuable extant documents of the period. In it came to light a mass of hitherto unknown details, not so much about the course of military operations as about the everyday life of the inhabitants of Quebec, victims of restrictions caused by the hostilities and of a war that could be called total. A reader of the priest's manuscript relives the anguish and sufferings of a population which was on the verge of disaster, but which would not face up to it. When the bombardment of the town began on 12 July, the inhabitants were seized with terror; the women "formed platoons to tell their beads." Then there were fires, deaths, desertions, summary executions, massacres, which the priest recounts without any commentary. One feels more and more weariness in his account as the end of the siege draws near. The battle of the Plains of Abraham is told, under date of 13 September, in three disappointingly curt lines: "The British land a little below the Foulon at 3 hours past midnight, take

M. de Vergor [Louis Du Pont* Duchambon] prisoner, and at half past ten rout our army.'' After that the diary, which continues until the autumn of 1760, is so laconic that it loses its interest.

At the beginning of the siege the parish priest had had to take refuge outside the walls, close by; later he sought shelter in the home of the tanner Joachim Primault, near the Hôpital Général. When Quebec fell he returned to the seminary. But on 8 Nov. 1759, after being robbed and wounded by a British soldier, he took refuge in the Ursuline convent. He remained there until 24 Dec. 1764, holding services in the sisters' chapel. He then returned to live at the seminary.

In 1767 the churchwardens of the parish of Quebec decided to rebuild the cathedral. Taking advantage of the fact that the episcopal seat was vacant and believing, wrongly, that Abbé Jean-Olivier Briand* would come back from London with only the title of vicar apostolic, Récher, as parish priest, had become accustomed to running everything in the parish church himself. Since Bishop Pontbriand's death in 1760 he had stated in public several times that he did not want a titular bishop to be appointed, that a bishop *in partibus* would suffice, and that he intended to maintain his church as a parish. As long as the parish priest lived, Briand was patient, contenting himself with offering to finance the rebuilding of a cathedral church. After Récher's death he proceeded to deal with the churchwardens and the British and Roman authorities so that Notre-Dame would become his cathedral church, and he finally won out in 1774. In the bishop's memoirs the parish priest appears as the main enemy, who never missed an opportunity to oppose his superior. The latter had, however, written a month after M. Récher's death: ''The parish priest's death has grieved me greatly. Despite the vexations he caused me, I liked and esteemed him. He was a worthy worker.'' Which goes to show that certain quarrels among ecclesiastics under the *ancien régime* must not be taken too seriously.

JEAN-PIERRE ASSELIN

AAQ, 22 A, Copies de lettres expédiées, 10 mars 1774; 10 B, Registre des délibérations, 183, 191v, 196, 207v, 208, 262; 11 B, Correspondance, VI, 13; X, 31, 40. Gosselin, *L'Église du Canada jusqu'à la conquête*, III, *passim*. Henri Têtu, *Notices biographiques: les évêques de Québec* (Québec, 1889); ''M. Jean-Félix Récher, curé de Québec, et son journal, 1757–1760,'' *BRH*, IX (1903), 97–122, 129–47, 161–74, 289–307, 321–46, 353–73.

RED HEAD. *See* KAK8ENTHIONY

RED HEAD. *See* ONONWAROGO

REGNARD DUPLESSIS, MARIE-ANDRÉE, *dite* **de Sainte-Hélène,** Nun Hospitaller of the Hôtel-Dieu of Quebec, annalist, letter-writer, superior; b. 28 March 1687 in Paris, France, daughter of Georges Regnard* Duplessis and Marie Le Roy; d. 23 Jan. 1760 at the Hôtel-Dieu of Quebec.

Marie-Andrée Regnard Duplessis was two years old when her parents decided to emigrate to New France. She was therefore left in the care of her maternal grandmother, who lived at Chevreuse, near Paris. All that is known of her upbringing is that at 13 years of age she was sent to the convent of the Filles de la Croix in Rue Saint-Antoine in Paris, where ''a good number of ladies and young girls of all conditions and even some duchesses resided.'' Judging from her writings, she must have received a rather thorough education there, which later permitted her to hold important offices in the Hôtel-Dieu of Quebec.

In 1702, when she was 15, she joined her parents in Quebec, and there she frequented fashionable society, in which, it seems, her appearance made a sensation. The report is believable since, according to a witness, she had ''a fine figure and an excellent wit.'' Her obituary mentioned that she was ''sought after in marriage by several persons of rank.''

The year 1707 marked a turning-point in Marie-Andrée Regnard Duplessis's life. On 27 July she entered the community of the Nuns Hospitallers of the Hôtel-Dieu of Quebec. She was 20, and contrary to what one might think she was considered to be rather old, since the average age of nuns at the time of their entry to the noviciate was at that period 14 to 16. Two years later, on 27 July 1709, she made her profession under the name of Sainte-Hélène.

We have little information about her early years of religious life. In 1713 her sister Geneviève came to join her at the Hôtel-Dieu. Marie-Andrée later wrote: ''We are very fond of each other and are closely linked in our feelings.'' Her sister's presence would have helped relieve the austerity of the cloister and the bitterness of seeing her family reduced almost to poverty after having held a most honourable position.

In 1718 Mother Sainte-Hélène was named mistress of novices (a little later she was to become depositary for the poor), an office that she exercised until 1721. It was during this period that she wrote *Les annales de l'Hôtel-Dieu de Québec, 1636–1716*, in collaboration with Mother Jeanne-Françoise Juchereau* de La Ferté, *dite* de Saint-Ignace. The latter supplied Mother Sainte-Hélène with the material but relied on her col-

Regnard Duplessis

laborator "for the style, order, economy, and piety." The work, which remained in manuscript form until 1751, chiefly recounts the history of the Hôtel-Dieu of Quebec from its beginnings, but through the narration the entire history of New France lives again, with its ups and downs, its social and political problems, its immense spaces peopled with Indians and wild animals, all seen from the point of view of a cloistered nun, whose horizons were, despite her culture, necessarily limited.

As for the history of the Hôtel-Dieu, the work presents an accurate picture, indeed even a meticulous one, of the sisters' daily life, of their preoccupations as nuns and hospitallers. The modern reader may consider tedious, if not naïve, certain "miraculous" happenings, such as that of the "barrel of peas, from which several bushels were taken every day [and which] lasted more than three months." One is free to believe moreover that providence did not intervene each time that fire – always to be feared then when nearly all dwellings were in wood – was successfully brought under control or went out by itself. The fact remains that the work is full of extremely interesting information on the life of an important religious community in Canada over a period of 80 years, on medical techniques used at the time, and on the handicrafts of the sisters. The descriptions or accounts dealing with the life of the Canadian colony often give first-rate information which is found nowhere else and which no historian of the period can overlook. The opinions expressed about certain persons must be taken with a grain of salt, especially when those persons, such as Mme d'Ailleboust [Boullongne*], Intendant Jean Talon*, or Governor Denonville [Brisay*], happen to have been benefactors of the community.

It must be kept in mind when reading the *Annales* that it was intended to be read by the community, which explains some voluntary omissions, certain gaps, that would otherwise seem to be unpardonable weaknesses. The reader must not be astonished, therefore, when every sister receives after her death an eulogy leading us to believe she had hardly any faults, or such slight ones that they were scarcely hateful. Certainly one must trust the annalist when she speaks of the nuns' devotion to the sick and the poor, French or Indian. The *Annales* gives evidence of a real talent for writing, both in the quality of the expression and in the liveliness of the account. It is clearly one of the important Canadian works of the period.

While she was writing the *Annales*, Mother Sainte-Hélène started a correspondence (which lasted until 1758) with Mme Hecquet de La Cloche, who lived in Abbeville in France. Only Mother Sainte-Hélène's letters, 32 in number, have been preserved. They can be considered an extension of the *Annales* in that they contain a mass of information concerning life at the Hôtel-Dieu and events in the colony. In them the writer is much more at her ease in making judgements, sometimes, it is true, debatable, about people and things. For example, she entertained the same prejudices about Canadians in general that certain French people had at the period. Her opinion of them was not very flattering. She considered Canadian products mediocre. As for the Indians, according to her "they are very unpleasant people, they are savages, I need not say anything more." She attributed the little progress made in evangelizing them to the bad example set by the French. Not as important as the *Annales*, these letters nevertheless constitute an interesting and not unimportant documentation for the period. Their literary form is on the whole poor, compared to that of the *Annales*. It must be said that they were written in haste. What is rather astonishing is that Mother Sainte-Hélène's correspondent was a strict Jansenist who at 47 years of age wrote a profession of faith in which she rejected definitively the bull *Unigenitus* and admitted that she was a heretic, unyielding and unamenable to the church. Either Mother Sainte-Hélène showed indulgence, or else she knew nothing at all of her correspondent's beliefs, which seems more probable from an examination of the letters. Nowhere, indeed, does one find in them any allusion to Mme La Cloche's ideas.

Mother Sainte-Hélène held the office of superior several times. In all she occupied the post for nearly 16 years, 1732–38, 1744–50, and 1756–60, the year of her death. In between she carried out the duties of assistant superior.

Her last term as superior was marked by cruel trials for the community. Scarcely had they recovered from a disastrous fire which entirely destroyed the Hôtel-Dieu on 7 June 1755, when the hospitallers had to suffer the repercussions of war. In the space of five years, from 1754 to 1759, more than 15 nuns died, most of them of illnesses contracted at the bedside of the sick, the majority of whom were soldiers. Then there came the invasion and capture of Quebec, when the community was forced to move to the Hôpital Général, whence it returned after the battle of the Plains of Abraham almost completely ruined, to such a degree that Mother Sainte-Hélène even considered its suppression. Overwhelmed by grief and trials, during the night of 17 Jan. 1760 the superior was taken by a fit of shivering, along with a pain in her side. Although she was attended by a French doctor and an English one sent by James Murray*, she died on 23 January, after having received the last sacraments from the vicar general, Jean-Olivier Briand*.

With her disappeared the last nun of the Hôtel-Dieu born in France and one of the most remarkable superiors of that institution. In the letter of condolence written to the community two days after Mother Saint-Hélène's death the vicar general praised "her gentleness, good nature, prudence, modesty, humility, love of prayer, her mortification, her regularity and entire fidelity to everything, even in the smallest matters." Unfortunately there remains no portrait of Mother Duplessis de Sainte-Hélène.

JEAN-PIERRE ASSELIN

"La correspondance de la mère Sainte-Hélène avec Mme Hecquet de La Cloche," A.-L. Leymarie, édit., *Nova Francia*, II (1926–27), 66–78; III (1927–28), 35–56, 94–110, 162–82, 220–37, 279–300, 355–61; IV (1928–29), 33–58, 110–23. Juchereau, *Annales* (Jamet); this work was published at Montauban, France, in 1751 by Louis Bertrand* de Latour as *Histoire de l'Hôtel-Dieu de Québec*. Casgrain, *Histoire de l'Hôtel-Dieu de Québec*. M. L. Gies, "Mère Duplessis de Sainte-Hélène, annaliste et épistolière" (unpublished doctoral thesis, Université Laval, Québec, 1949). Juliette Rémillard, "Mère Marie-Andrée Duplessis de Sainte-Hélène," *RHAF*, XVI (1962–63), 388–408.

REGNARD DUPLESSIS DE MORAMPONT, CHARLES-DENIS, officer in the colonial regular troops in Canada, provost marshal; b. 22 June 1704 at Quebec, son of Georges Regnard* Duplessis, treasurer of Marine, and Marie Le Roy; brother of the Jesuit François-Xavier* and of Mother MARIE-ANDRÉE de Sainte-Hélène; m. on 29 May 1742, at Quebec, Geneviève-Élisabeth, daughter of Charles Guillimin*; d. in France sometime after 1759 in unknown circumstances.

Charles-Denis Regnard Duplessis de Morampont began his studies in Quebec and from 1719 to 1723 continued them at the Jesuit college in La Flèche, France, under the supervision of his older brother François-Xavier, who for three years had been doing his noviciate in the Society of Jesus. The following year he began to study philosophy in Paris, but soon tired of it and returned to Canada in 1725 where, against his brother's advice, he took up a military career.

A cadet in the colonial regular troops, he went to France in the autumn of 1733 to settle "the accounts which his late father . . . had" with Pierre-Nicolas Gaudion, treasurer general of the Marine, and "to obtain a posting." On 13 April 1734 he received the expectancy of a posting as second ensign and immediately returned to Canada, where he obtained the promised promotion on 1 April 1735. Eight years later, on 31 May 1743, the king appointed him ensign on the active list. Finally on 1 May 1749, thanks to his older brother and despite the colonial authorities, who had put forward the name of Antoine Juchereau* Duchesnay, Charles-Denis succeeded Charles-Paul DENYS de Saint-Simon, who had died the previous year, as provost of the marshalsea in Canada. He held this office in the colony for only a short time, however; difficulties with his wife – her family threatened him with a request for a separation for her – led him to decide to go to France in the autumn of 1751. Subsequently he refused to return to the colony, even though the king granted him free passage on the royal flute *Outarde* in 1756 and Governor Vaudreuil [Rigaud*] was clamouring for his presence. He lived in Paris until about 1759, at which time we lose track of him.

Son of a noble family, "a very pretty child," the darling of the "ladies of Canada," Charles-Denis Regnard Duplessis de Morampont moved in the best society of his time. He led the life of a son of a great family, and his only thought was to seek pleasure and spend money; he and his wife even treated themselves to the luxury of having as many as three slaves in their service. He lived so much beyond his means that his numerous creditors had to take proceedings for seizure of his land and barn in 1757 and his money in 1758.

ANDRÉ LACHANCE

AN, Col., B, 59, f.453v; 61, f.529v; 76, f.449; 94, f.96; 104, f.505; 149, ff.560f.; C¹¹A, 91, ff.95f.; 101, ff.143f.; 120, ff.251v–52; 121, f.333; D²C, 222/2, f.132 (copies at PAC). ANQ, Greffe de C.-H. Du Laurent, 16 nov. 1741; NF, Coll. de pièces jud. et not., 1369, 1681; NF, Documents de la Prévôté de Québec, 24 oct., 5, 7 nov. 1743; NF, Ins. Cons. sup., IX, 76f. "Lettres de la révérende mère Marie-Andrée Regnard Duplessis de Ste. Hélène," H.-A. Verreau, édit., *Revue canadienne*, XII (1875), 54, 190. *Lettres du P. F.-X. Duplessis de la Compagnie de Jésus*, J.-E. Roy, édit. (Lévis, Qué., 1892).

REICHE (Reische). *See* RESCHE

RENAUD D'AVÈNE DES MÉLOIZES, NICOLAS-MARIE, officer in the colonial regular troops, seigneur; b. 21 Jan. 1696 at Quebec, son of François-Marie Renaud d'Avène* de Des-

Renaud d'Avène

meloizes and Françoise-Thérèse Dupont de Neuville; d. 4 July 1743 at Quebec.

Nicolas-Marie Renaud d'Avène Des Méloizes's father, who had come to New France in 1685, was from a distinguished *épée* family in Nivernais (France). His mother was the eldest daughter of Nicolas Dupont* de Neuville, a councillor and seigneur. Through her he inherited the seigneury of Neuville near Montreal, which his son Nicolas* sold in the 1760s for 45,000 *livres*. It was his grandfather, Dupont, moreover, who helped launch his military career in 1714 by petitioning Governor Rigaud* de Vaudreuil on his behalf for a commission in the troops. On 1 July 1715 he received the expectancy of an ensigncy and on 27 April 1716 he was appointed ensign on the active list. His marriage, on 19 April 1722, to Angélique, daughter of René-Louis Chartier* de Lotbinière and widow of Jean-François Martin* de Lino, helped to solidify his position in the colonial élite. He used his position, moreover, to obtain leaves of absence from the colonial governors to travel to the French court in search of greater honours. In 1724 he returned after one such junket with the rank of lieutenant, and after carrying the Canadian dispatches to France in 1732 he was promoted captain on 1 April 1733.

During this latter stay in France, Des Méloizes became interested in the manufacture of roofing tile. He was aware of the great need in the towns of New France, where fire was a serious hazard, for a fireproof covering to replace the cedar boards normally employed for roofing. He was probably aware, too, that a recent attempt to solve the problem by quarrying slate at Grand Étang in the Gaspé had failed miserably [*see* Michel Sarrazin*]. In 1732 he presented a memoir to the minister of Marine, Maurepas, which argued that tile would be an ideal alternative to slate, for both technical and economic reasons. In the memoir he offered to begin manufacturing tile provided the king would lend him 6,000 *livres*. Maurepas, recalling perhaps that another officer, Gaspard ADHÉMAR de Lantagnac, had established a tile furnace one league below Quebec in 1728 only to abandon it a year later, refused to involve the king until the enterprise showed some initial success. When Governor BEAUHARNOIS and Intendant Hocquart* heard of the project, however, they gave Des Méloizes strong support. In fact, Hocquart took the unusual step of recommending him for a seat on the Conseil Supérieur, pointing out that he possessed rare business talents. Maurepas refused to appoint a military officer to the council, but he did authorize Hocquart, on 27 April 1734,

to advance Des Méloizes the 6,000 *livres* in Canadian card money.

Even with this loan, however, Des Méloizes faced formidable obstacles. Because there were no skilled tile workers in New France, he was forced to arrange in 1733 for several to be sent from France the following year. When they did not arrive, he contracted with Jean Le Brun, a tile-maker from Dieppe, to come on a merchant vessel in 1735. But when Le Brun also failed to appear, he used a worker from among the indentured servants arriving at Quebec in 1735 to supervise the baking. Two years had been lost and he still did not have the skilled labour he required.

In 1735 Hocquart placed 3,500 of the 4,000 tiles produced that year on a government warehouse for a two-year test of their durability under winter conditions. He reported that Des Méloizes had only borrowed 2,500 *livres* of the authorized loan since he did not wish to incur the expense of re-establishing Lantagnac's furnace until the results of the test were known. An inspection in 1736 revealed that only one per cent of the tiles had broken and this failure was apparently caused by a minor error in baking. By 1737, however, ice had destroyed over 200 tiles and Des Méloizes, thoroughly discouraged, offered to pay back his loan and abandon the enterprise. Hocquart's insistence that the problem lay with the mortar used to put on the tile and that it could be solved by using nails instead finally persuaded him to make a second two-year trial. Although it proved successful, Des Méloizes had lost his resolve. After obtaining a three-year extension for the repayment of his loan in 1740, he withdrew from the business. The tile works were taken over, in 1741, by Barthélemy Cotton*, receiver of the Compagnie des Indes, but he was forced to close it down during the crop failure of 1743. When Des Méloizes died on 4 July 1743, his loan was still unpaid.

In many ways Des Méloizes's failure typified the problems of industrial entrepreneurship in New France. He was clearly no bourgeois, lacking both the financial resources and the speculative spirit to succeed in an ambitious industrial undertaking. More important, however, the colony lacked the capital, labour, and technical and climatic conditions to operate such an industry profitably. The prospect of a large local market, the king's financial assistance, the cooperation of colonial officials, and his own ties to the merchant community were not enough to overcome these basic drawbacks. In the end, Des Méloizes's name was distinguished in Canadian history not for his entrepreneurship but because his daughter, Angélique*, who married Michel-Jean-Hugues Péan* on 3 Jan. 1746, became the paramour of François Bigot*.

DONALD J. HORTON

AN, Col., D²ᶜ, 222/2; E, 126. ANQ, Greffe de Jacques Barbel, 18 avril 1722. *Documents relating to Canadian currency during the French period* (Shortt), I, 680, 682, 684, 686. PAC *Report, 1886*, cxiv, cxxiv, cxxvii; *1904*, app.K. Le Jeune, *Dictionnaire*. P.-G. Roy, *Inv. concessions*, II, 24–27; *Inv. jug. et délib., 1717–1760*. J.-N. Fauteux, *Essai sur l'industrie*, I, 160–69. Nish, *Les bourgeois-gentilshommes*. P.-É. Renaud, *Les origines économiques du Canada; l'œuvre de la France* (Mamers, France, 1928), 187. P.-G. Roy, "La famille Renaud d'Avène des Méloizes, *BRH*, XIII (1907), 171–78.

RENAUD DUBUISSON, LOUIS-JACQUES-CHARLES, officer in the colonial regular troops; b. 22 July 1709 at Quebec, son of Jacques-Charles Renaud* Dubuisson and Gabrielle Pinet (Desmarest); d. in France, probably in 1765.

Louis-Jacques-Charles Renaud Dubuisson followed in the footsteps of his father, town major of Trois-Rivières, and embarked upon a military career at an early age. After being a gentleman cadet for several years, he was about to be promoted second ensign when, on 12 Jan. 1736, he fought a duel at Trois-Rivières with another cadet in the colonial regular troops, Charles Hertel de Chambly. Hertel had challenged Dubuisson after an exchange of "sharp words" when they were drunk. Hertel received a sword wound in the lower part of the abdomen and died two days later.

As the affair had been between two soldiers, the court martial of the government of Trois-Rivières dealt with it first. On 17 Feb. 1736 it sentenced Dubuisson in his absence and the "remembrance" of his companion Hertel to be shot. This sentence was, however, only "read and posted before the troops" in the three governments of Canada, since Dubuisson had fled before he could be arrested. He first took refuge at Fort Orange (Albany, N.Y.), where the authorities kept him in prison for 11 months, believing him to be a spy. Then he went to the French West Indies, where he begged the authorities in the colony and in the mother country for a pardon. The king would not grant him anything before the final judgement.

The Conseil Supérieur, being authorized in certain circumstances to judge duelling cases in the first instance, and supporting its right by the small number of judicial officers in the jurisdiction of Trois-Rivières, had taken up this affair on 26 Jan. 1736, two weeks after the duel. The tribunal of Trois-Rivières had not then examined the case. On the one hand the lieutenant general for civil and criminal affairs of Trois-Rivières, René Godefroy* de Tonnancour, had refrained from instituting legal proceedings in the matter, for fear of seeing his whole investigation annulled by challenge. There was, in fact, a family relationship between him and the duellists: he was Hertel de Chambly's cousin, and a cousin by marriage of Dubuisson. On the other hand the provost of the marshalsea, Charles-Paul DENYS de Saint-Simon, had not yet proceeded with an investigation, though it was his duty to do so "at the very moment" he learned that fights which might be duels had taken place.

Although the Conseil Supérieur published a monitory in certain parishes of the government of Trois-Rivières in the autumn of 1737, it could not obtain "revelation of the facts and circumstances of the duel." Therefore on 28 March 1738 it ordered that "a further investigation be carried out for a year." In the meantime Dubuisson, still in the West Indies, continued bombarding the authorities in the mother country with requests for a pardon. He finally was successful and hastened to return to Canada. On 3 Sept. 1740 the court martial of Trois-Rivières ratified the pardon. And the Conseil Supérieur of Quebec, finding "no matter for conviction of the crime of duelling in the investigation," acquitted Dubuisson on 19 Sept. 1740.

Dubuisson then resumed his military career and in 1741 was promoted second ensign, the appointment the king had promised him in the spring of 1736. His subsequent career was the usual one in the colonial regular troops; he became ensign on the active list in 1745, lieutenant in 1750, and captain in 1759. It was as a captain that he distinguished himself during the siege of Quebec and particularly in the battle of Sainte-Foy on 28 April 1760, when he was seriously wounded in the shoulder. As a reward he was decorated with the cross of the order of Saint-Louis on 2 Feb. 1762. Having gone to the mother country in the autumn of 1761 on the *Molineux*, probably with one of his daughters and his two sons, Dubuisson died in France sometime before 5 Jan. 1766, the date on which the king granted a pension to his three children living in France.

On 3 Aug. 1741, in Montreal, he had married Thérèse Godefroy, who was buried in Montreal on 24 May 1778. All his life Dubuisson seems to have been in straitened circumstances. In 1740, according to Governor Charles de BEAUHARNOIS, he was reduced "to men's charity," and in 1760, according to the Chevalier de Lévis*, he was "poor."

Duels between soldiers were frequent under the French régime. Not all duellists, however, were prosecuted, particularly during the last years of French rule when with the arrival of French regulars duels became a common occurrence. Dubuisson's case was thus not unique in New France. Louis XIV's edict of 14 Dec. 1679 against duelling was applied more or less strictly according to the "quality" of the person who had committed the offence. Military officers most often benefited from the leniency either of the court or of the Conseil Supérieur which invoked certain extenuating circumstances such as legitimate defence and drunkenness; ordinary soldiers were often sentenced to death, for their civil status and lack of financial means gave them no hope of obtaining a pardon from the king.

ANDRÉ LACHANCE

AN, Col., B, 64, f.435v; 65, f.404; 66, f.11v; 68, f.52; 71, f.29; 81, f.68; 91, f.55; 125, f.7; C¹¹A, 71, ff.78v–79; 74, ff.36f.; 75, f.182; 76, ff.31f.; 104, f.117; 115, f.16v; D²C, 222/1, f.108 (copies at PAC). ANQ, NF, Dossiers du Cons. sup., Mat. crim., IV, 317–44v, 390–99; NF, Registres du Cons. sup., 1730–1759, ff.37v–49, 59v–63. ANQ-M, Registre d'état civil, Notre-Dame de Montréal, 3 août 1741. Bornier, *Conférences des ord. de Louis XIV*, II, 130, 393ff. *Journal du chevalier de Lévis* (Casgrain), 271, 457. PAC *Report, 1886*, clxxxiii. *Relations et journaux* (Casgrain), 239. Fauteux, *Les chevaliers de Saint-Louis*. Tanguay, *Dictionnaire*. Ægidius Fauteux, *Le duel au Canada* (Montréal, 1934); "La famille Renaud Dubuisson," *BRH*, XXXVII (1931), 673–76. P.-G. Roy, "Le duel sous le régime français," *BRH*, XIII (1907), 136–38.

RENÉ, PATRICE, priest, Recollet, missionary; b. 1667 in France; d. 1742 in Paris.

Patrice René joined the Recollets in Paris in 1682 and made his profession the following year. He came to Canada around 1690, and on 30 June 1693 he signed a baptismal certificate at Beaumont, near Quebec. In 1703 he arrived in Port-Royal (Annapolis Royal, N.S.), joining his *confrère*, Father Félix PAIN, who had been chaplain at the fort since 1701. René became the first superior of the convent which his order founded at Port-Royal, and in 1708 he was appointed the bishop of Quebec's vicar general in Acadia. In addition to ministering to the parish and visiting the missions near Port-Royal, Patrice René gave his attention to education and opened a school for boys in Port-Royal, probably for whites only; Sister Marie-Élisabeth Chausson, of the Congrégation des Filles de la Croix, had been running a school for girls there since 1701.

Several differences arose between the Recollets – René, Pain, Justinien DURAND – and certain officers whose conduct seems to have been unsatisfactory. When Marie Mius d'Entremont became pregnant by the officer François Du Pont* Duvivier, the Recollets made the couple get married in January 1705, even though the king's lieutenant in Acadia, Simon-Pierre Denys* de Bonaventure, forbad the marriage. Patrice René wrote that the Sieur de Bonaventure had scandalous relations with Louise GUYON, Mathieu Damours* de Freneuse's widow, and that he had had several children by her. Bonaventure continued to keep this lady at Port-Royal despite the king's orders to send her away.

Patrice René went to France in 1707 to request of the minister of Marine, Pontchartrain, that these scandals be made to cease. He reached La Rochelle in August 1707. In October, replying to his request, the minister urged him to return to his mission – he hoped that Mme de Bonaventure, Jeanne Jannière, who had just been sent there, would succeed in improving her husband's conduct.

Patrice René came back to Acadia, but during the summer of 1707 the English, under the orders of John March*, had attacked Port-Royal and burned several houses, including the Recollets'. René entered his last act in the parish records on 25 Sept. 1708. He returned to France that same year, never to come back. In speaking of Father René's ministry Daniel d'Auger* de Subercase, the governor of Acadia, wrote that the missionary had restored the settlers "with great difficulty to obedience and has succeeded in making himself feared by the most wicked and loved by the others."

His later duties and activities in France are not known. He died in 1742 in Paris.

ANSELME CHIASSON

Archives acadiennes, Université de Moncton, Fonds de Placide Gaudet, "Missionnaires de l'Acadie." Archives des Franciscains (Montréal), Dossier Patrice René. AN, Col., B, 22, ff. 155v, 174v; 29, ff.238v, 247v; C¹¹D, 4, f.316v; 5, ff.95, 103, 195v, 221, 259; 6, ff.104v–5v. PAC, MG 9, B8, 24 (registres de Saint-Jean-Baptiste du Port-Royal) (original of the volume for 1702–28 is at PANS and that for 1727–55 is at the Diocesan Archives, Yarmouth, N.S.). Arsenault, *Hist. et généal. des Acadiens*, I, 83–84. Lauvrière, *La tragédie d'un peuple* (1924), I, 189. Omer Le Gresley, *L'enseignement du français en Acadie (1604–1926)* (Bathurst, N.B., 1926), 52.

REPENTIGNY, AGATHE LEGARDEUR DE.
See SAINT-PÈRE

RESCHE (Rèche, Reiche, Reische), PIERRE-JOSEPH, parish priest, organist of the cathedral of Quebec, canon; b. 12 June 1695 at Quebec, son of François Resche and Marguerite Pinard; d. 2 April 1770 at Quebec.

Pierre-Joseph Resche entered the third form at the Petit Séminaire of Quebec on 20 Oct. 1711, when he was 16. He was admitted into the seminary in 1716 and received the tonsure on 4 Oct. 1717, the minor orders and subdiaconate in 1719. On 16 March 1720 he was made a deacon, and on 18 August he was ordained a priest in the cathedral of Quebec.

In October 1720 he was entrusted with the ministry to the mission of Saint-Nicolas, near Quebec, a charge he kept even when he became parish priest for Saint-Antoine de Tilly in November 1720. He had to deal with large administrative problems, since it had become necessary either to restore or to rebuild the church and the presbytery in both parishes; consequently in February 1721 he stopped serving Saint-Nicolas. The annexation of part of the neighbouring fiefs to the parish district of Saint-Antoine, decreed by the Conseil d'État on 3 March 1722, was the source of repeated litigation between the habitants of these fiefs and Abbé Resche, whom the habitants refused to recognize as parish priest. From 1721 to 1727 intendants BÉGON and Dupuy* issued no fewer than four ordinances to force the parishioners to pay the parish priest the tithes and other sums due him for administering the sacraments.

After the death in 1733 of the parish priest of Quebec, Étienne Boullard*, Abbé Resche was sent to assist the curate, Charles PLANTE, in administering the parish. He spent eight years there. A few months before he left Quebec he was the object, with his *confrère* Roger-Chrétien Le Chasseur, of an appointment which until then had been unknown in the religious history of Canada. On 7 Nov. 1740 the chapter, which had no intention of giving up what it considered to be its rights and privileges, appointed both of them titular or perpetual curates of the parish of Quebec. Only the complete legal union of the parish of Quebec with the chapter would have justified such a decision. Consequently these appointments appeared unacceptable to Charles Plante, who had been titular parish priest of Quebec since April 1739. He affirmed in writing the invalidity of the appointment and forbade the two ecclesiastics, who had become almost his equals and whom the chapter had imposed upon him, to exercise the functions of curate in his parish. The two interdicted priests delivered their riposte before the provost court of Quebec, and Abbé Resche had

in addition the impertinence to call himself titular curate in a baptismal certificate which he signed 11 Feb. 1741. Plante, the parish priest, immediately had the word "titular" stroked out.

The chapter itself, however, seemed to change its mind, for on 20 Feb. 1741 it appointed Abbé Resche parish priest of Château-Richer. The act of taking possession of the charge was delayed until 9 April as a result of the scheming of Canon Joachim FORNEL, secretary of the chapter, who refused to issue Resche's letters of appointment because he had wanted his friend Le Chasseur nominated. The dispute, however, constantly stirred up by Fornel, degenerated into a quarrel over tithes between Abbé Resche and his predecessor, Louis-François Soupiran; the litigation was taken by Fornel to the Conseil Supérieur, which rejected his claim. The sketch of the first plan for the village of Château-Richer, made around 1752, is attributed to Resche. Three years earlier he had had a presbytery built, thus bringing into question the ownership of the seigneurial manor-house, which had served as the presbytery until then. He carried on unsuccessfully the lawsuit that ensued between the parish council and the seminary of Quebec.

To replace Fornel, who had resigned his canonry, not without reason, Abbé Resche was appointed canon on 28 Sept. 1752 and moved to Quebec. His skill as a musician had perhaps induced the chapter to accept him into its ranks, since it saw in him an honourable incumbent for the majestic organ which the canons had ordered from Paris and which was installed in the cathedral in 1753. According to the historian Auguste-Honoré Gosselin*, Canon Resche was one of the foremost musicians in Quebec. He had, moreover, been organist at the cathedral while he was a curate in Quebec, from 1733 to 1741.

In 1755 he became chaplain at the Ursuline convent, where his musical accomplishments were also recognized and appreciated. On the occasion of great celebrations by the community, it was said, he was invited to play the organ. At the convent he occupied the parlour of the Holy Family, previously reserved for noble ladies who were staying there; after the siege of Quebec these apartments served on more than one occasion as chapter room for the serious deliberations which administration of the church of Quebec made necessary. At the height of the siege of Quebec Resche refused to leave the convent, although most of the community had had to seek refuge at the Hôpital Général. Canon Charles-Ange Collet had come to join him. The historian Henri-Raymond Casgrain*, confusing the spelling of names as well as persons, wrote that the parish priest of Quebec, Abbé Resche, officiated at MONTCALM's burial on the evening of 14 Sept. 1759. Leaving aside the fact that the parish priest of Quebec at that time was M. Jean-Félix RÉCHER, the chronicles of the period do not mention explicitly, any more than do the other remaining documents, the circumstances surrounding the burial. Nevertheless the burial certificate, which indicates that Montcalm had received the succour of religion before his death, bears the name of Canon Resche as principal signer. It is therefore reasonable to believe that he assisted the dying man and officiated at his funeral.

After being chaplain to the Ursulines for 12 years Canon Resche retired in 1767 to the home of his nephew Charles Berthelot. The chapter, which he had in turn served as syndic and treasurer, had been paying him a pension since 1766. In 1769, stricken with paralysis, he was taken to the Hôpital Général of Quebec where, after 50 years in the priesthood, he died on 2 April 1770. He was buried the following day in the church of the convent.

ARMAND GAGNÉ

AAQ, 12 A, Registres d'insinuations B, 336–37; 12 A, Registres d'insinuations C, 16–23, 83; 10 B, Registre des délibérations; 61 CD, Notre-Dame de Québec, I, 7. ASQ, MSS, 2; Polygraphie, XXV, 5; Séminaire, XXXVI, 14–29. Tanguay, *Dictionnaire*. H.-R. Casgrain, *Guerre du Canada, 1756–1760: Montcalm et Lévis* (2v., Québec, 1891), II, 274. Raymond Gariépy, *Le village du Château-Richer* (SHQ Cahiers d'histoire, XXI, Québec, 1969), 115–17. Gosselin, *L'Église du Canada jusqu'à la conquête*, II, III; *L'Église du Canada après la conquête*, I. P.-G. Roy, *Fils de Québec*, I, 149–50; *La ville de Québec*, II. *Les Ursulines de Québec* (1866–1878), II, 323; III, 10, 44–46. Archange Godbout, "Les prêtres Resche," *BRH*, XLIX (1943), 170–72.

RÉVOL, PIERRE, salt smuggler, trader, merchant; b. *c.* 1714 in France, son of Jacques Révol, a lawyer in the *parlement* of Grenoble, and Hélène Bastard; d. February 1759 at Gaspé.

Pierre Révol, banished from the kingdom of France, arrived in Canada on the king's ship in 1739. He had received this punishment for having broken the law of the salt tax. The *gabelle*, a term which originally referred to any sort of tax, was soon reserved for the tax on salt. Philippe VI made this tax general by his ordinances of 1331 and 1343. Subsequently basic legislation on the salt tax, which varied throughout the kingdom, was established by the great ordinance of Louis XIV in May 1680. The kingdom was divided into six regions, each with a different tax rate on salt. This situation, which had in fact existed before Louis XIV's ordinance, caused the price of salt to vary from one region to another and thus offered an irresistible temptation to smugglers. The illicit salt trade was truly the "great national industry" in all regions bordering the territories exempt from the tax and the *pays de grande gabelle*, even though the salt smugglers risked a fine of 200 *livres* for a first offence and banishment or death for a subsequent offence.

Révol must therefore have been convicted more than once when he arrived in Quebec. He was neither the first nor the last salt smuggler to land in New France; from 1730 to 1743 the colony received nearly 600 who had been banished for the same crime. Little is known of Révol's early years in Canada; his career as a trader and merchant does not take definite shape until he contracted a marriage at Beaumont, near Québec, on 17 Feb. 1744. His wife was Marie-Charlotte, the daughter of Joseph Roy, who seems to have been successful in the Labrador trade at that time. Révol took part in his father-in-law's activities and quickly proved to be a skilful though sometimes imprudent trader. The partnership between the two men lasted only a year, during which they clashed before the provost court of Quebec. Mme Roy's death on 14 April 1745 brought about the final break. The dead woman's succession was contested by Joseph Roy's sons-in-law; Roy did not want to make over the property held in joint estate until after his own death. Révol and his brothers-in-law then took legal action before the provost court against their father-in-law, who won the case in 1747. But Révol obstinately appealed to the Conseil Supérieur. At the time of Joseph Roy's death in 1756 nothing had been settled. Révol never knew how the 14-year lawsuit ended, for he himself died a month before the final settlement.

This legal affair was not Révol's only adventure. His finances were soon such that he was able to acquire a ship in the 1740s, the *Comte de Saxe*, so that he might extend his business to the West Indies; but his status as a deportee did not allow him to leave the colony. Early in 1748 Governor La Galissonière [BARRIN] sent the king a request for repeal of Révol's condemnation, and in the autumn, without waiting for the royal reply, Révol sailed for Martinique. His evasion was quickly known, and the governor sent a detachment of soldiers after him. The *Comte de Saxe* was overtaken at Île aux Coudres, but the soldiers were not able to approach the ship, as Révol threatened to sink their boat with gunfire.

Révol seems to have spent the winter at Martinique; he was arrested there and brought back to Canada in June 1749. On 24 December of that year he was sentenced to six months in prison, and the captain of the ship suffered the same punishment, in addition to a fine of 500 *livres*.

His activities as a trader and businessman brought Révol more than once before the courts of the colony. He came several times before the Conseil Supérieur after first appearing before the provost court; he was much more frequently defendant than plaintiff; as plaintiff, he most often lost beforehand. From 1744 to 1756 the Conseil Supérieur refused more than six times to hear his appeals and condemned him some eight times for non-appearance. In 1752 Révol was even accused of selling bread weighing less than the stated amount.

His greatest financial adventure, equalled only by his matrimonial tribulations, was the leasing of the trading post of Gros Mécatina on the Labrador coast, which led to total bankruptcy for himself and for his friends. On 1 April 1756, before the notary Jean-Claude Panet*, Révol agreed to the terms of a trading lease for the post of Gros Mécatina, of which the former intendant, Hocquart*, had become the owner the preceding year. Révol undertook for ten years to pay annually three per cent of the proceeds from fishing to the Jolliet and Lalande heirs [*see* Louis Jolliet*], and 5,000 *livres* a year to Hocquart. But at that time Révol was in serious financial difficulties. Only six months later he was completely insolvent. Even on 10 April 1756 he had to pay creditors 13,168 *livres*, and on 30 October he had to meet financial obligations exceeding 50,000 *livres*. Révol was partially successful in getting out of this impasse, thanks to the brothers Jean and Alexandre Dumas, who offered the creditors payment of half their claims, plus interest and court costs, in two instalments, one in April 1757 and the other in May 1758. The creditors accepted, and Révol had no choice but to seek his fortune elsewhere.

An opportunity presented itself, but it did not bring him wealth. In 1757 Governor Pierre de Rigaud* de Vaudreuil appointed Révol lookout at Gaspé, a post fully justified by the threat of a British invasion *via* the St Lawrence. But instead of watching the British, Révol would have done better to keep an eye on his wife. Indeed, when he returned to Quebec at the end of the autumn, after the sailing season was ended, he learned that his wife had been unfaithful to him with Alexandre Dumas; he was paying dearly for his bankruptcy of 1756!

Révol decided to take the guilty lovers to court,

as French law permitted him to do. This decision furnished MONTCALM with an occasion to write to Lévis*: "We are going to have a lawsuit for cuckoldry . . . which, if it were argued by skilful lawyers at the *parlement* of Paris, would add to the number of celebrated cases." But Révol changed his mind, and the interested parties settled privately on 11 Jan. 1758 before the notary Panet. Mme Révol was to retire to a convent and give up all the rights her marriage contract granted her. Alexandre Dumas was to leave Quebec until Révol's departure for Gaspé, and after that he was to sail for France in the autumn of 1758 at the latest. In addition, Dumas was to pay Mme Révol a yearly income of 400 *livres*.

At the opening of the sailing season Révol returned to Gaspé, where he died in February 1759. On 10 March his relatives met to elect a guardian for his three underage children. Mme Révol's name is not mentioned in the account of the meeting.

MICHEL PAQUIN

AN, Col., B, 89, ff.71, 84; 90, ff.96, 121; C¹¹ᴬ, 91, ff.264–67; 93, f.49; Marine, C⁷, 273. PAC *Report, 1899*, supp., 154. Létourneau et Labrèque, "Inventaire de pièces détachées de la Prévôté de Québec," ANQ *Rapport, 1971*, 323, 325, 346, 386. Marion, *Dictionnaire des institutions*. P.-G. Roy, *Inv. coll. pièces jud. et not.*, I, 150, 156, 166, 168, 172, 224; *Inv. contrats mariage*; *Inv. jug. et délib., 1717–1760*, IV, V, VI; *Inv. ord. int.*, III, 75. Tanguay, *Dictionnaire*. Gérard Malchelosse, "Faux sauniers, prisonniers et fils de famille en Nouvelle-France au XVIIIᵉ siècle," *Cahiers des Dix*, IX (1944), 161ff. P.-G. Roy, "Le faux-saunier Pierre Revol," *BRH*, L (1944), 193–201, 225–35.

RICHARDIE. *See* LA RICHARDIE

RIGAUD DE VAUDREUIL, JOSEPH-HYACINTHE DE, officer in the colonial regular troops, governor general of the French part of the Île de Saint-Domingue (Hispaniola); b. 21 June 1706 at Quebec, son of Philippe de Rigaud* de Vaudreuil and Louise-Élisabeth de Joybert* de Soulanges et de Marson; d. 17 Nov. 1764 in Paris, France.

Joseph-Hyacinthe de Rigaud de Vaudreuil entered the colonial regular troops in Canada as an ensign on 2 June 1715, when he was nine years old, and on 7 May 1720 he was promoted lieutenant. He went to France and in 1723 was accepted into the French guards as an ensign, but, unable "to support himself in the service in France," he was appointed captain in the French colony on the Île de Saint-Domingue on 17 Jan. 1726; it was in this colony that a career leading

Rigaud

him to the highest offices unfolded. On 8 May 1730 he became town major of Petit-Goâve; on 1 Nov. 1734 he went in the same capacity to the district of Île à Vache, in the southern part of the island. Then on 15 Jan. 1740 he became king's lieutenant, before assuming the same duties at Le Cap (Cap-Haïtien) on 20 Nov. 1743. On 1 Nov. 1749 he was promoted governor of the western and southern parts of the colony, and the following year, with the honorary rank of naval captain, he carried out the duties of lieutenant general in the government of the colony, with the responsibility of taking command in the event of the governor general's absence. In May 1753 he was appointed governor general of the French part of the Île de Saint-Domingue. In March 1757 he retired, and he returned to France in June 1764. Thanks to the protection of Adrien-Maurice de Noailles, Comte d'Ayen, and later of Louis de Noailles, Duc d'Ayen, he had been made a knight of the order of Saint-Louis in 1739.

Vaudreuil's activity in Saint-Domingue was intense and many-sided. As commandant of the district of Le Cap during the War of the Austrian Succession (1740–48), he concerned himself with the coastal defences to prevent any attempt at landing by the enemy. On two occasions, in 1748 and 1756, he proposed, though unsuccessfully, that a corps of Negro gunners be created which would be responsible for manning the coastal batteries. Vaudreuil also had to settle various frontier incidents with the Spanish, particularly concerning the Turks Islands. He encouraged the beginnings of the new town of L'Hôpital (Port-au-Prince), where he resided and whose defences he organized, as he did those of the regions of Léogane and Les Cayes. His activity also extended to two fields which were particularly important for the economic life of the colony: the building of roads linking the western and northern parts and the construction of agricultural hydraulic works, mainly in the valley of the Artibonite and in the district of Torbeck where he owned a large plantation.

Vaudreuil's career was marked in 1750 by a sharp conflict with the governor general, Henri de Brienne, Comte de Conflans. Their relations had begun most auspiciously; in a letter dated 23 March 1750 Conflans, speaking of Rigaud, praised "his fine qualities, his good intentions, the superiority of his character, and the particular talents which he has for governing well"; on 25 March, in a letter to the minister, Rouillé, he acknowledged Vaudreuil's "incomparable sagacity, superior character, thorough instruction . . . his zeal knows no limits, the king's service absorbs him completely." This good feeling did

not last long. On 3 and 12 Oct. 1750 Conflans poured out vehement abuse against Vaudreuil. He accused him of misuse of authority, of arrogance, vanity, insubordination, ingratitude, insatiable ambition, and called him "a greedy underling who does not know how to do his job." Vaudreuil, he wrote, "did not have an *écu* when he came to serve as a captain in this colony, and by his own admission he is today worth three million and has run through as much again." On 3 Oct. 1750 Vaudreuil was suspended from his functions by Conflans for "very serious offences against the king's authority, the obedience that he owes us, and the duties which have been entrusted to him." These grievances seem to have been exaggerated and inspired above all by personal rivalry. The suspension was lifted by the king in April 1751, and Conflans was recalled to France. Vaudreuil's administration seems to have been much appreciated by the people, who regretted his departure and gave his name to a street in the town of Le Cap. Judging with a certain perspective, Médéric-Louis-Élie Moreau de Saint-Méry wrote in 1785: "serving in the colony for 21 years . . . he displayed rare talents, untiring zeal, great affection for the colony."

Vaudreuil had married Marie-Claire-Françoise Guyot de Lamirande, by whom he had a son, Joseph-Hyacinthe-François de Paule, born 2 March 1740 at Torbeck. His son became grand falconer of France and was a deputy from Saint-Domingue to the National Constituent Assembly of 1789.

ÉTIENNE TAILLEMITE

AN, Col., C⁹ᴬ, 74, 85, 93, 94, 96, 97, 99, 104; Marine, C⁷, 340 (dossier Vaudreuil). [M.-L.-É.] Moreau de Saint-Méry, *Description topographique, physique, civile, politique et historique de la partie française de l'isle de Saint-Domingue*, Blanche Maurel et Étienne Taillemite, édit. (Bibliothèque d'histoire coloniale, nouv. sér., 3v., Paris, 1958).

RIGAUD DE VAUDREUIL, LOUIS-PHILIPPE DE, Marquis de VAUDREUIL, naval officer; b. 26 Sept. 1691 in Quebec, eldest son of Philippe de Rigaud* de Vaudreuil and Louise-Élisabeth de Joybert* de Soulanges et de Marson; d. in France probably in 1763.

Louis-Philippe de Rigaud de Vaudreuil joined the service on 8 May 1695 when still a child, with an expectancy of an ensigncy in the colonial regular troops in Canada. On 20 May 1698 he received a commission as ensign on the active list and midshipman. He was promoted lieutenant on 15 June 1705. He embarked in 1707 upon the *Héros* and took part in the fight in which this ship was engaged off the Azores. On 5 May 1710 he was promoted captain and took part in action on the *Africain*. The following year he was sent to the court by his father to report the disaster which had befallen an English squadron *en route* to attack Quebec [*see* Sir Hovenden Walker*]. On that occasion he was presented to Louis XIV and to Pontchartrain, the minister of Marine, who on 5 July 1711 granted him a commission as naval sublieutenant. On 28 June 1713 he was promoted lieutenant-commander and served in turn on the *François* (1716), the *Éléphant* (1718), the *Chameau* (1720 and 1723), and the *Dromadaire* (1722 and 1725), carrying out transport missions between France and Canada.

In 1727 he was on the *Ardent* in the Mediterranean, then in 1729 in command of the *Éléphant*. This ship, which sailed for Quebec with the new financial commissary, Hocquart*, the coadjutor, Dosquet*, and Louis-Philippe's two brothers Pierre* and François-Pierre*, was lost on 1 Sept. 1729 on a rock near Cap Brûlé, some 30 miles from its destination [*see* Claude Lebeau*; Richard TESTU de La Richardière]. All those on board were saved, and Vaudreuil was absolved from blame by the court martial held on 7 March 1730 in Rochefort, France, under the presidency of the naval officer commanding the port. That same year he served in Canada as second in command of the *Rubis*. In 1731 he took part in action in the West Indies on the *François*, and in 1734–35 he commanded the *Charente* when it sailed for Île Royale (Cape Breton Island). On 1 April 1738 he was promoted naval captain. The following year he took command of the *Jason* and carried Isaac-Louis de Forant* and François Bigot* to Louisbourg, where they were governor and financial commissary.

Vaudreuil received command of the *Victoire* in 1741. In 1744 he assumed command of the *Aquilon*, then of the *Heureux* in the Mediterranean squadron and took part in the battle fought off Toulon by Claude-Élisée de Court de La Bruyère against the squadron of the English admiral Thomas Mathews. Then he escorted convoys between Toulon and the island of Malta. In 1747 he distinguished himself particularly while commanding the *Intrépide*, one of the squadron of eight vessels commanded by Henri-François Des Herbiers de L'Étenduère which had the task of protecting a huge convoy of 252 merchant ships en route from France to the West Indies. On 25 October the formation was attacked by the 14 vessels led by the English admiral Edward Hawke. Quickly caught in crossfire thanks to a skilful manoeuvre on the part of the enemy, the French squadron defended itself with the utmost determination, and the combat was extremely violent. Brilliantly supporting his commander, who was on the *Tonnant*, Vaudreuil saved the ship from certain loss, wresting it by main force from capture by three enemy vessels, and towed it as far as Brest. Thanks to the energetic defence the convoy was able to escape, and the disabled English vessels were unable to pursue it. His brilliant conduct earned Vaudreuil a promotion on 1 April 1748 to the rank of rear-admiral. On 25 Aug. 1753 he was named vice-admiral, and he ended his career as naval officer in command at Rochefort.

Vaudreuil had been named a knight of the order of Saint-Louis on 23 Dec. 1721, and was promoted commander of the order on 1 July 1754 and knight grand cross on 14 Nov. 1756. On 22 Dec. 1723 he had married Élisabeth-Catherine, daughter of Joseph Le Moyne* de Serigny et de Loire, governor of the port of Rochefort, and Marie-Élisabeth Héron. Of this marriage were born three sons who served in the Marine. Two of them, Louis-Philippe and Jean-Louis, reached the rank of vice-admiral and distinguished themselves during the American revolution.

ÉTIENNE TAILLEMITE

AN, Col., B, 17, f.244v; 20, f.71v; 29, f.390; 35, f.337; C¹¹A, 51; Marine, B⁴, 40, ff.368–76; 56, ff.53–122; 61, ff.177–250; C¹, 165; 166, p.26; C⁷, 340 (dossier Louis-Philippe de Vaudreuil); G, 38, p. 7. Taillemite, *Inventaire analytique, série B, I,* 296; *Dictionnaire de la Marine* (Paris, 1962), 266. R.-V.-P. Castex, *Les idées militaires de la Marine du XVIIIᵉ siècle; de Ruyter à Suffren* (Paris, [1911]), 223ff. Lacour-Gayet, *La marine militaire sous Louis XV* (1910), 157, 187, 388, 498. Troude, *Batailles navales de la France*, I, 316. N.-E. Dionne, "Le naufrage de l'*Éléphant*," *BRH*, XI (1905), 119–21.

RIVERIN, JOSEPH (baptized **Jean-Joseph**), merchant, militia officer; b. 5 Aug. 1699 in Quebec, son of Joseph Riverin, a merchant, and of Michelle Mars; d. 23 Oct. 1756 in Quebec.

Jean-Joseph Riverin came from a prominent merchant family and consequently had every advantage in going into business. He profited not only from the fortune left him by his father, who had died around 1716, but also from the prestige enjoyed by his uncle, Denis Riverin*, the representative in France of the Compagnie de la Colonie from 1702 until his death in 1717. In addition, his maternal grandfather, Simon Mars, had been a merchant in La Rochelle, France, and then in Quebec.

Like many other merchants of the time, Jean-Joseph Riverin had a varied business. In a store

Robertson

located in Lower Town, Quebec, at the end of Rue Sault-au-Matelot he sold silver plate, fabrics, and other dry goods. He also dealt in wood, hay, animals, and food supplies such as beef, pork, mutton, milk, butter, flour, and eggs. The dry goods came from France, but the other items were amply supplied by his farms at Ancienne-Lorette, on Île d'Orléans, and on Île aux Grues. A number of clerks, tenant farmers, and servants were in his employ.

Firmly established in the business world through family ties, Riverin chose a wife from the same milieu. On 20 June 1724, in Quebec, he married Marie-Joseph Perthuis, daughter of the merchant Charles Perthuis*. Widowed, on 27 July 1740 he married Marie-Charlotte Guillimin, daughter of another rich merchant, Charles Guillimin*. Riverin had by his two wives at least 17 children, of whom only four outlived him.

Riverin was a dedicated and highly esteemed citizen as well as a prosperous merchant. In 1737 he is mentioned as a churchwarden of Notre-Dame de Québec. In 1746, at a meeting in the Château Saint-Louis to decide on "the advisability or not of continuing [the construction of the] fortifications" of Quebec, Riverin, along with a score of other merchants of the town, sided with the minister of Marine, Maurepas, in considering these works useless. Some years later, with the English threatening, Riverin did not hesitate to enrol in the Canadian militia for the better defence of his town; he became a colonel in the militia of the government of Quebec.

On his death at Quebec in 1756, Jean-Joseph Riverin left more than 45,000 *livres* in assets, including 18,000 *livres* in bills of exchange, nearly 3,000 *livres* in playing-card money, and as much in cash. In his Quebec house, on the corner of Rue Notre-Dame and Rue Sous-le-Fort, he had among other things a great number of pieces of silver and silver cutlery bearing Parisian stamps, and a library consisting of 32 works, most of them religious. The sum of 45,000 *livres* did not include the real estate in his succession – the property on Rue Notre-Dame, the store and warehouse in Lower Town, the houses and lands at Ancienne-Lorette and Île aux Grues – nor his cattle and other such possessions.

Joseph Riverin had acquired a small fortune during his lifetime, and, although he did not play a prominent role in New France, his multiple activities contributed to its economic growth at the end of the French régime.

ROLAND-J. AUGER

AJQ, Registre d'état civil, Notre-Dame de Québec, 6 août 1699, 20 juin 1724, 27 juill. 1740, 25 oct. 1756.

ANQ, Greffe de J.-É. Dubreuil, 21 févr., 17 mars 1725; Greffe de Florent de La Cetière, 18 janv. 1724; Greffe de J.-N. Pinguet de Vaucour, 23 juill. 1740; Greffe de J.-A. Saillant, 28, 29 nov. 1756; AP, Famille Riverin. PAC *Report, 1899*, supp., 156. "Recensement de Québec, 1744" (APQ *Rapport*), 133. Bonnault, "Le Canada militaire," APQ *Rapport, 1949–51*, 286, 301. P.-G. Roy, *Inv. concessions*, I, 106, 169; *Inv. jug. et délib., 1717–1760*, III, 88, 239; V, 108, 189, 194; *Inv. ord. int.*, II, 226. Tanguay, *Dictionnaire*.

ROBERTSON, CHARLES, army officer; d. 6 May 1763 at Lake St Clair.

Nothing is known of Charles Robertson's life until his service with the British forces in North America during the Seven Years' War. He was commissioned lieutenant in the 77th regiment on 15 Sept. 1758 and may have been among the troops under John FORBES who occupied Fort Duquesne (Pittsburgh, Pa.) later that year. At Carillon (Ticonderoga, N.Y.) in March 1760, Robertson led a party that discovered more than a hundred bateaux and whaleboats abandoned by the French in their evacuation of the fort the previous summer.

Perhaps Robertson's work in reassembling this fleet led Major-General Jeffery Amherst* to consider him an expert on naval matters. In 1761 Amherst placed him in charge of building two armed sailing vessels in a shipyard on the Niagara River. Assuming that the task would be quickly finished, Amherst dispatched Major Henry Gladwin* and 300 men of the 80th regiment with orders to explore lakes Huron and Michigan on Robertson's ships, examining the former French outposts and estimating the size of garrison each would require. The ships would then be used to maintain communications among the posts. Robertson, however, failed to start the construction early in the season and did not anticipate the difficulty of navigating the Niagara River. He finished only the *Huron*, a six-gun schooner, in the summer of 1761 and then could not get her through the rapids at the head of the river. In the following summer he had more success. The *Huron* became the first British sailing vessel on Lake Erie and was probably the first such ship in those waters since René-Robert Cavelier* de La Salle's *Griffon* had passed through in 1679. By midsummer Robertson had finished the second ship, the sloop *Michigan*, and taken both vessels to Detroit. Only then did he discover sand bars blocking the passage through Lake St Clair. Gladwin, in Detroit with a second expedition, convened a court of inquiry to take official note of the added delay, and the ships were laid up for another winter.

Accompanied by Sir Robert DAVERS, in the spring of 1763 "Captain" Robertson (as he was popularly dubbed) took a party to look for a channel through Lake St Clair. Although warned that PONTIAC planned hostilities, they pressed on to the mouth of the St Clair River but were overwhelmed there in a clash with some Indians. Robertson's body was roasted and eaten in a savage conclusion to the slaughter. His remains, along with those of Davers, were buried near the Indian camp.

Robertson's ship-building career had important consequences for the British in the west. During the Pontiac uprising Detroit might have fallen to the Indians if the *Huron* and the *Michigan* had not been available to bring in men and supplies. The delay in getting ships into the Upper Lakes, however, had made impossible the proper garrisoning and supplying of the forts beyond Detroit, and every one of them fell in the opening days of the war. Some of the delays had been beyond Robertson's control but others had not, and this military ship captain must bear part of the blame for the early success of the Indian uprising in the Upper Lakes region.

HARRY KELSEY

DPL, Burton hist. coll., Porteous papers, John Porteous to his father, 20 Nov. 1763. PRO, WO 34/49, Amherst to Campbell, 27 May 1761; Amherst to Gladwin, 22 June 1761; court of inquiry, 3 Sept. 1762; MacDonald, Journal of the siege of Detroit. Clements Library, Gage papers, American series, Robertson to Gage, 3 March 1760; Sterling letter book, James Sterling to John Duncan, 25 Oct. 1762. *Army list, 1759*, 131. *Johnson papers* (Sullivan *et al.*). [John Rutherford], "Rutherford's narrative – an episode in the Pontiac War, 1763 – an unpublished manuscript by Lieut. Rutherford of the 'Black Watch,'" Canadian Institute *Trans.* (Toronto), III (1891–92), 229–52. *British officers serving in America, 1754–1774*, comp. W. C. Ford (Boston, 1894), 86. Thomas Mante, *The history of the late war in North America and the islands of the West Indies, including the campaigns of MDCCLXIII and MDCCLXIV against His Majesty's Indian enemies* (London, 1772), 482–83. M. M. Quaife, *The Royal Navy of the upper lakes* (Burton hist. coll. Leaflet, II, [Detroit], 1924), 52.

ROBINAU DE PORTNEUF, PHILIPPE-RENÉ (better known under the name **René Portneuf**), parish priest; baptized 13 Aug. 1707 in Montreal, son of René Robinau* de Portneuf and Marguerite Daneau de Muy; killed by the British at Saint-Joachim, near Quebec, on 23 Aug. 1759, with a group of his parishioners.

If it were not for his part in the war of the conquest, Abbé Philippe-René Robinau de Portneuf would probably have escaped notice. He was ordained a priest in Quebec on 21 Oct. 1731, and the following year he was appointed parish priest of Saint-Jean, in Île d'Orléans. This charge he held until 1735. Except for the routine acts of his ministry, the parish registers reveal nothing concerning him except an occasion, which was to say the least piquant, when he declared on 12 April 1734 that he "had designated himself as godfather after having refused Simon Campagna because of his crass and obvious ignorance" when he had "questioned him on the shorter catechism." In the course of the next 24 years he was parish priest at Saint-Joachim, a few leagues downstream from Quebec on the north shore of the St Lawrence opposite the northeast corner of the Île d'Orléans. This spot was well situated to observe the movements of the British ships at the beginning of the final campaign which was to decide the fate of Quebec.

In the spring of 1759 the British sailed up the St Lawrence with the firm intention of taking possession of Quebec. They easily made themselves masters of the river up to the outskirts of the town, destroying on their way a good number of farms and some churches. On the latter point, however, orders were strict: they were to respect churches if the French did not make use of them for defensive operations. On the French side, as far as the population is concerned a distinction must be made between the attitude of the civil and military authorities and that of the religious authorities. For the former this war was developing into a movement of general resistance in which the whole population was invited to take part. Cooperation with the military forces, wherever it came from, was well received and even encouraged, and this despite the laws of war which forbad civilians to have a hand in military operations. WOLFE was well aware of this situation, and he did not fail to remind the habitants of the risk they were taking in being captured under arms; from threats he proceeded to reprisals on several occasions when his warnings had been flouted. As for the religious authorities, they confined themselves to a position of prudent reserve, contenting themselves with giving directives to the pastors that reminded them of the interdiction against carrying arms on pain of excommunication and of their duty to watch over the spiritual interests of their flocks. "If by chance the enemy come into a parish," wrote Bishop Pontbriand [DUBREIL] in a pastoral letter dated 5 June 1759, "the parish priest will greet them as courteously as possible, asking them to spare human lives and the churches." It can be said that a great majority of the clergy kept to that

Robinau

line of conduct. Of the 194 priests who comprised the Canadian church at that time, the historian Marcel Trudel has been able to count only about 15 who were "more or less engaged in the conflict," leaving aside, of course, the military chaplains. Of these 15, only two became victims of their ill-timed ardour: the ecclesiastic Joseph Couillard, who served under Bougainville*'s orders and was killed in a skirmish while returning home after the defeat on the Plains of Abraham, and Abbé Portneuf.

Certainly Abbé Portneuf did not take part in military operations before August 1759, which was only a few weeks before his death. In that month he sent three letters to Governor Vaudreuil [Rigaud*] with information about the movements of the British fleet. On 20 August the governor replied, instructing the parish priest to act in such a way that "the habitants be united, that they be constantly on the watch and able to put up the most vigorous resistance to the British." At this time the British were engaging in devastating raids on the Beaupré shore and elsewhere in the vicinity of Quebec as reprisals and a means of dissuading the habitants from harassing their troops or aiding the French forces.

It is difficult to determine exactly the circumstances of Father Portneuf's death, since the English as well as the French accounts are contradictory or strewn with improbable details. On the English side there is a tendency to exaggerate the importance of the parish priest's participation in the military operations: the number of partisans fluctuates between 20 and 150. These associates are described to us as being entrenched in an imposing house, defying the British troops; they even disguise themselves as Indians. In the French accounts the figures are much smaller. The number of participants does not exceed some 50, and the victims a score. But no words are too strong to describe the inhumanity of the English towards the "poor" parish priest and his habitants. After having overcome the priest and his parishioners, these "cruel enemies" in cold blood had "his throat cut . . . in his own church." Another account speaks of the priest "whose head was split wide open and completely scalped," without explaining how these two operations could be combined. In still another, the priest, after being killed, is blamed by the British "for having abandoned his priestly role and roused some habitants to insult them." By way of adding some spice, one author specifies that the priest and his parishioners were "on their knees crying for quarter. . . ." It was then only a short step to making a martyr of Father Portneuf. Abbé Auguste-Honoré Gosselin* took

it easily when he wrote that "having withdrawn into the woods with some parishioners, in accordance with the bishop's instructions . . . to administer to them in case of need the succour of his ministry," the priest was surrounded and murdered.

There is good reason to be puzzled by this accumulation of accounts, all of them, let us note, based on hearsay. Only one document can help clear up the matter. This is the burial certificate, in which it is stated that the parish priest was "massacred by the British on the 23rd, being at the head of his parish to defend it against the incursions and hostilities which the enemy was carrying on against it." Then come the names of seven parishioners killed at the same time. This document, drawn up by Jean-Louis-Laurent Parent, priest of the parish of Sainte-Anne-du-Petit-Cap (Sainte-Anne de Beaupré), three days after the incident, brings the affair back to more reasonable proportions. The priest had well and truly taken part in resisting with a group of parishioners, thus justifying the action of the British. Was he shot, or did he die "hacked to pieces by sabres"? Either is equally possible. As for the place, the incident seems to have happened not far from the church and the presbytery of Saint-Joachim, since the two buildings were destroyed on the same occasion – the reason, moreover, that the bodies were buried in the neighbouring parish.

The affair of Abbé Portneuf was, in summary, a minor incident of the sort that happens in every war, but one that struck the imagination, probably because it was unusual at the period to see a parish priest die while participating in a military operation. Although it was doomed to failure in advance, Father Portneuf's gesture may possibly be considered as a courageous attempt to put up a dignified resistance against the invader before final defeat.

JEAN-PIERRE ASSELIN

Archives paroissiales de Sainte-Anne (Beaupré, Qué.), Registres des baptêmes, mariages et sépultures, 26 août 1759. Gosselin, L'Église du Canada jusqu'à la conquête, III, 511. Trudel, L'Église canadienne, II, 1–65 [Trudel gives a full bibliography for a study of the life of Robinau de Portneuf. J.-P.A.].

ROBINAU DE PORTNEUF, PIERRE, officer in the colonial regular troops; b. 9 Aug. 1708 in Montreal, second son of René Robinau* de Portneuf and Marguerite Daneau de Muy; m. on 22 April 1748 Marie-Louise Dandonneau Du Sablé; d. 15 Nov. 1761 in the shipwreck of the *Auguste* off Cape Breton Island.

Pierre Robinau de Portneuf is mentioned in 1729 as a cadet in the colonial regular troops at Michilimackinac. On 1 April 1733 he was promoted second ensign, and on 1 Oct. 1740 he was made an ensign on the active list in Louisiana. On 15 April 1750 the minister of Marine, Rouillé, consenting to a request made by Governor La Jonquière [TAFFANEL] and Intendant Bigot*, granted permission to build a small fortified post at Toronto on the shore of Lake Ontario. The authorities of the colony hoped by this means to attract the Indians in the region, probably the Mississaugas, to trade with the French and thus dissuade them from taking their furs to the English at Fort Oswego (Chouaguen). Pierre Robinau de Portneuf, who was an ensign at Fort Frontenac (Kingston, Ont.) at this time, was designated to carry out the project.

The Sieur de Portneuf set out on 20 May 1750 and reached Toronto some time later. While the necessary provisions and articles for trade were being forwarded from Montreal, he began to build the fort that was planned on the east bank of the Rivière Toronto (Humber River), near its mouth. Within two months a warehouse and a stockade were put up. Trade with the Indians at Fort Toronto proved successful, and by 17 July a shipment of furs worth 18,000 *livres* had been sent to Montreal. This result surpassed expectations. On 20 August the governor wrote to the minister to acquaint him of the success and to inform him that he intended to build a new and larger fort "at the point of the peninsula called La Baye" (about a league to the east of the Humber River). He recommended the Sieur de Portneuf for this new project. Recalling the reasons for building the first post, he noted that they were more than ever valid. Moreover, he suggested the possibility of persuading the Indians to destroy Oswego. Finally, as a good strategist, he asked the minister's permission to give the name Rouillé to the new fort. Work was begun in the autumn of 1750 and went ahead throughout the winter. The fort was virtually finished in April 1751, when the Sieur de Portneuf returned from Fort Frontenac, where, it seems, he had spent the winter. He was in command at Fort Toronto, as it was still called, during the 1751 trading season and returned to Fort Frontenac in the autumn. Early in 1752 he was replaced as commandant of Fort Toronto by Thomas Robutel de La Noue.

After that the Sieur de Portneuf fades somewhat from the scene. In 1756 he was appointed commandant of Fort de la Presqu'île (Erie, Pa.). The following year he was promoted captain. He played an active role in the engagements in the Ohio valley during the Seven Years' War. When Fort Niagara (near Youngstown, N.Y.) was under attack in 1759, he was busy at Fort de la Presqu'île rallying the Indians of the west. After Fort Niagara surrendered, he sent an emissary under a flag of truce to William Johnson*, set fire to Fort de la Presqu'île, and went to Detroit, where he surrendered to the English. In October 1761 he sailed from Quebec on the *Auguste* for France, perhaps with the hope of making a new career for himself there. A vain hope: one month later he was among the 113 passengers and crew members who perished when the ship sank off Cape Breton Island.

JEAN-PIERRE ASSELIN

AN, Col., D²C, 222/2, p.177 (PAC transcript). É.-J. Auclair, *Les de Jordy de Cabanac, histoire d'une ancienne famille noble du Canada* (Montréal, 1930), *passim*. Frégault, *François Bigot*, II, 22. P. J. Robinson, *Toronto during the French régime* . . . (Toronto, 1933), *passim*. Désiré Girouard, "Le fort de Toronto," *BRH*, V (1899), 137–40. É.-Z. Massicotte, "Les Montréalais et les deux forts de Toronto," *BRH*, XXXIX (1933), 259–66.

ROBSON, JOSEPH, stonemason, surveyor, engineer, critic of the HBC; fl. 1733–63.

Joseph Robson entered the service of the Hudson's Bay Company in 1733, and was engaged as a stonemason for three years at an annual salary of £25 to help build the massive stone Prince of Wales Fort (Churchill, Man.). He returned to the bay in 1744 for another three-year period at a salary of £32, this time as "Surveyor and Supervisor of the Buildings," first at York Factory (Man.), and then during his last year at Churchill again. One of the reasons for the dual nature of his second appointment was probably the desire of the HBC to obtain more precise information about the country near its bayside posts, since the lack of such knowledge brought it under attack from Arthur Dobbs and other critics. Robson's published maps and the HBC records show that he took his surveying duties seriously. Equipped with a box of surveying instruments he explored 40 or 50 miles up the Nelson River and produced charts of its course and soundings, as well as a plan of York Factory. At Prince of Wales Fort he similarly drew a plan of the post and a map of the lower reaches of the Churchill River.

This final year at Churchill, where he had been sent after quarrelling with other servants at York, was a turbulent one. Within a few days of arrival he was involved in disputes with the factor, Robert PILGRIM, about the construction of the fort, and these, together with the rumour that

Rocbert

"the Govr was an odd sort of a man," determined Robson to keep a journal of his experiences. This has survived, and reveals continual quarrelling between Pilgrim and Robson which reached a climax just before Robson left for England in August 1747, when he was accused with others of near-mutiny. In his letter to the London committee that autumn Pilgrim commented that Robson and two others had "Declar'd themselves Your Honrs. Enemys."

With this history behind him, it is not surprising that after his return to England Robson became involved in the campaign mounted by Dobbs against the HBC, and he gave evidence before the parliamentary committee of 1749 investigating the trade of Hudson Bay. His statements were moderately critical of the company, which he thought adopted too harsh a trade standard with the Indians, and whose servants were reluctant to expand inland; but on the whole his evidence, which comes to life only when he is castigating the factors at York and Churchill for their amateurish interference with construction work at the forts, must have been a disappointment to Dobbs. This impression is confirmed by Robson himself in his book, *An account of six years residence in Hudson's-Bay*, published in 1752, when he refers to his appearance before the parliamentary committee: "for want of confidence, and an ability to express myself clearly, the account I then gave was far from being so exact and full as that which I intended to have given."

Robson's book was of prime importance, since it was the earliest to reflect first-hand knowledge of service with the HBC, and was written by someone who had spent six years in Hudson Bay. (Other authors such as Henry Ellis had spent only one winter there.) Displaying maps of the Nelson, Hayes, and Churchill rivers, tables of winds and tides, and statistics of the costs incurred in building Prince of Wales Fort, it had an authentic ring, "honest and just" as one reviewer described it. Its criticisms of the HBC were consequently the more telling, with stories of oppressive behaviour by the company factors, their refusal to explore the interior, and their incompetence in building work. In one vigorous sentence Robson summarized the case of the company's critics: "The Company have for eighty years slept at the edge of a frozen sea; they have shewn no curiosity to penetrate farther themselves, and have exerted all their art and power to crush that spirit in others." This general allegation was supported by a 64-page appendix which scutinized the company's history and the evidence produced by its spokesmen before the parliamentary committee of 1749. Recent investigations have shown that Dobbs, not Robson, wrote this long and polemic appendix, that he also revised Robson's text, and that he intended the book to "further expose the management of the Company." In brief, although on certain technical points connected with the construction of the forts Robson's evidence is probably reliable, his more general comments on the company's policies must be regarded as those of a biased and partial critic.

After 1752 Robson slips from sight, to emerge again briefly in 1763 when his second book, *The British Mars*, was published. It was a work devoted in the main to techniques of coastal warfare and the art of fortifications, but contained a short section which repeated the allegations Robson had made against the HBC many years earlier, and suggested yet another attempt to find a northwest passage through Hudson Bay. In the preface Robson referred to his "Practice and Experience of above Thirty Years, in almost all kinds of Foundations and Walls, both in the Sea and on dry Land"; no other evidence has been discovered about his later career.

GLYNDWR WILLIAMS

[References to Robson's career with the company are in HBC Arch. A.1/36, p.145; A.1/122, p.83; A.6/7, ff.92d, 95; A.11/13, ff.24d, 101, 102; A.11/114, f.121. His Churchill journal of 1746–47 is in B.42/a/30 and his statements before the parliamentary committee of 1749 in G.B., Parl., *Report from the committee on Hudson's Bay*, 215–17. Evidence of Dobbs' co-authorship of *An account of six years residence in Hudson's-Bay, from 1733 to 1736, and 1744 to 1747 . . .* (London, 1752) is in the Public Record Office of Northern Ireland, D.162/62, and has been examined by Glyndwr Williams in "Arthur Dobbs and Joseph Robson: new light on the relationship between two early critics of the Hudson's Bay Company," *CHR*, XL (1959), 132–36. For some contemporary comments on Robson's book, see *Gentleman's Magazine*, 1752, 290; *Monthly Review (or Literary Journal)* (London), VII (1752), 75–76; Jacques Savary Des Bruslons, *The universal dictionary of trade and commerce, by Malachy Postlethwayt* (2v., London, 1751–55), I, 961. Robson's second book was *The British Mars: containing several schemes and inventions, to be practised by land or sea against the enemies of Great-Britain . . .* (London, 1763). G.W.]

ROCBERT DE LA MORANDIÈRE, ÉTIENNE,

king's storekeeper, subdelegate of the intendant; b. 1668 at Saint-Étienne-d'Étréchy, bishopric of Sens, France, son of Abel Rocbert, notary and lieutenant of the provost court of Étréchy, and Marie Pothier; d. at Rochefort in 1753 or 1754.

Étienne Rocbert de La Morandière began his

career as a king's attorney at Le Havre, but in 1690 he came to New France with his brother Urbain. He was secretary to the commissary of the Marine in Canada, Louis Tantouin* de La Touche, until 1692 when Intendant Champigny [Bochart*] named him king's storekeeper at Montreal. Although he was destined to remain in that post for 39 years, a bizarre incident in 1705 nearly cut short his career. While strolling with his brother Urbain in the crowded Montreal streets, early in September, he encountered Claude de Ramezay*'s valet on horseback. A quarrel ensued over who should give way, and after insults had led to blows a soldier in Ramezay's company intervened on the valet's side. He was killed accidentally by Étienne. Both Rocberts were thrown into jail, where they remained until Governor Rigaud* de Vaudreuil obtained letters of clemency from the king on 17 March 1706. Notwithstanding Vaudreuil's assistance, however, Étienne supported the intendants Jacques* and Antoine-Denis Raudot* in their bitter disputes with the governor between 1707 and 1711. Jacques Raudot rewarded him in 1709 with a full commission as king's storekeeper.

Over the next two decades, Étienne built up a handsome private establishment at Montreal. Although he failed in numerous attempts to have his salary increased from 600 *livres* per year, he did get permission to operate the king's store side-by-side with his own in the 2,400 square-foot building constructed for him on Rue Saint-Louis in 1700. This arrangement was advantageous in an administrative system that functioned by the long-term accountability of its financial officers more than by day-to-day distinctions between public and private transactions. Unfortunately, it is impossible to determine which of the many creditors mentioned in the notarial records were his own and which were the king's. Nevertheless he was obviously involved privately in a number of fur-trading ventures and he bought and sold small plots of land at Montreal. One sign of his respected position was his election as a church warden of Notre-Dame parish in 1711. During the 1720s, moreover, he served as syndic of the Recollet fathers.

Marriage alliances also played a big part in enhancing Rocbert's social standing. On 25 Sept. 1695 he married Élisabeth Duverger, daughter of a Montreal merchant and a relative of the prestigious Saint-Ours family. Several of their six offspring also married into influential Canadian families such as the Petit de Levilliers, Gaultier de Varennes, and Puygibaults. But the most significant marriage alliance was struck *à la gaumine* in 1718 between Marie-Élisabeth Rocbert and Claude-Michel Bégon, a military officer and brother of Intendant Michel Bégon. Their romance developed during Bégon's billeting at the Rocbert home in 1712 and continued despite the opposition of the intendant and of the Bégon family in France. In 1737, Marie-Élisabeth's daughter, Marie-Catherine-Élisabeth, married Honoré Michel de Villebois de La Rouvillière, the commissary of the Marine at Montreal.

This tie proved beneficial to both Étienne and Louis-Joseph Rocbert (b. 6 Aug. 1697); Louis-Joseph had served as a clerk in the Montreal commissariat and in 1731 succeeded his father as king's storekeeper. Michel periodically employed Étienne throughout the 1730s, adding small bonuses to his pension of 300 *livres* per year. In 1737 he named him subdelegate of the intendant at Montreal during his own brief tenure as acting intendant at Quebec. At that time, moreover, he and Governor Beauharnois granted Louis-Joseph a large seigneury, called Rocbert, on Lake Champlain. It was reunited to the king's domain in 1741, but was returned to him on 9 July 1742. Michel also permitted Louis-Joseph to advance huge credits on the king's account and, when the latter died in 1743, his books showed large deficits. Six years later the Rocbert home was rented to François Bigot* for 1,500 *livres* per year and Étienne, accompanied by Mme Bégon, went to Rochefort. His son Étienne (b. 22 Feb. 1701) remained in Canada and rose to the rank of captain in the colonial regular troops.

Donald J. Horton

AN, Col., B, 55–85, C^{11A}, 51–85, 113/2; F³, 12. *Documents relating to Canadian currency during the French period* (Shortt), I, 359. *Jug. et délib.*, V, 465–71. *Lettres au cher fils: correspondance d'Élisabeth Bégon avec son gendre (1748–1753)*, Nicole Deschamps, édit. (Coll. Reconnaissances, Montréal, 1972). Le Jeune, *Dictionnaire*. A. Roy, *Inv. greffes not.*, XII, 42; XVI, 120, 171–72. P.-G. Roy, *Inv. concessions*, V, 47–49; *Inv. jug. et délib., 1717–1760*, IV, 85, 125, 153, 174, 181, 196; V, 45, 110. Frégault, *La civilisation de la Nouvelle-France*, 158; *François Bigot*, I, 344–45. P.-G. Roy, *La famille Rocbert de La Morandière* (Lévis, Qué., 1905); "Les secrétaires des gouverneurs et intendants de la Nouvelle-France," *BRH*, XLI (1935), 98.

ROCBERT DE LA MORANDIÈRE, MARIE-ÉLISABETH (Marie-Isabelle) (Bégon de La Cour) (usually called **Élisabeth**), letter-writer; b. 27 July 1696 in Montreal, daughter of Étienne Rocbert de La Morandière and Élisabeth Duverger; d. 1 Nov. 1755 at Rochefort, France.

Rocbert

Marie-Élisabeth was the eldest of the Rocbert family; her father held the office of king's storekeeper in Montreal. In 1711, at the time of his first voyage to Canada, the sublieutenant Claude-Michel BÉGON de La Cour, who was to be Élisabeth's husband, became acquainted with Étienne Rocbert. Bégon returned to the colony the following year to continue his career there on land, and since there were no barracks in Montreal he lived with the Rocbert family. His many and varied war wounds, including the loss of one eye and some missing fingers, had not deprived him of all charm: he soon won Élisabeth's heart, and the couple decided to get married as soon as possible.

The intendant of New France, Michel BÉGON, however, considered the young Mlle Rocbert to be of too modest an origin and for several years opposed his younger brother's marriage. In addition, military men could not marry without the governor's permission, and Philippe de Rigaud* de Vaudreuil officially refused it to the young Bégon, as he did to all officers who wanted to marry persons of lower rank, even though he secretly encouraged Bégon's passion to vex the intendant, with whom the governor did not get along well. But the lovers resisted all pressure. They even ended up by marrying *à la gaumine*, in keeping with a custom that was vigorously condemned by Bishop Saint-Vallier [La Croix*]. In the face of such obstinacy the intendant gave in, and the pseudo-marriage was regularized in Montreal on 19 Dec. 1718.

In 1719 Mme Bégon gave birth to Marie-Catherine-Élisabeth. When she was 18 this girl married Honoré MICHEL de Villebois de La Rouvillière, then commissary and subdelegate of the intendant in Montreal. The young woman died in 1740, leaving a little boy and girl to be raised by her mother. Claude-Michel-Jérôme, born in 1732, was the only one of Mme Bégon's four or five children to survive her.

The Chevalier Bégon had been appointed successively town major of Quebec (1726), king's lieutenant for Trois-Rivières (1731) and Montreal (1733), then governor of Trois-Rivières (1743), and so his wife no doubt had the opportunity to become well acquainted not only with the small Montreal community but also with the society of the other two "governments" of the Canada which she was later to chronicle. When she was widowed in 1748, Mme Bégon moved back to the family house in Montreal, on Rue Saint-Paul, at the site where the Bonsecours market is located today. Before renting this house to François Bigot*, who was to make it into an intendant's palace famous for dissipation, Mme Bégon spent her last year in New France in it, "preoccupied with grief and study," to use her own words. During this period she wrote the first five of the nine quires that are still extant of her correspondence with her son-in-law, Michel de La Rouvillière, then the financial commissary of Louisiana. Élisabeth Bégon's only consolation was to converse with her "dear son": this widower, almost her own age, seems to have inspired in her a genuine amorous passion which she disguised, consciously or not, as maternal affection. In the seclusion to which mourning confined her, Mme Bégon observed ironically the comportment of her fellow citizens. Daily she noted and commented on their behaviour and the events of the day, or simply recorded the pattern of family activities. The letter-writer was well informed: many visitors frequented her salon, who were often as much self-seeking as they were importunate, for Mme Bégon's influence on the acting governor general of the colony, La Galissonière [BARRIN], was known.

It was, indeed, under the protection of La Galissonière, her nephew by marriage and her faithful friend, that she travelled to France with her household in the autumn of 1749. She went to Rochefort to live, hoping for her son-in-law's return to the mother country. There she knew only disappointment and sadness, finding her chief consolation in the journal she continued to send to Michel. In it she made interesting comparisons between the French provinces and Canada, to the latter's advantage. News from the colony was always plentiful in this correspondence, for Mme Bégon heard it from people arriving from her native land and through the incredible number of letters she exchanged with her friends in New France.

Élisabeth Bégon passed away at Rochefort on 1 Nov. 1755. She had never again seen her beloved, who had died at New Orleans three years earlier having sent his mother-in-law letters full of "harsh words."

Élisabeth Bégon's correspondence – the reason she is remembered by posterity – is certainly not a literary masterpiece. Written in a familiar if witty and colourful style, it constitutes nevertheless an extremely lively account of the final years of the French régime in Canada. As Claude de Bonnault has so correctly written, it is "a precious and invaluable collection which could be entitled 'The 18th-century Canadians described by themselves.'"

CÉLINE DUPRÉ

[Mme Bégon's correspondence is preserved at the ANQ and includes 9 quires and 38 separate items covering the years 1749–53. The various letters are dated from Montreal and then from Rochefort, with occasional ones from Brest, Blois, La Rochelle, and Bordeaux. This correspondence was published under the titles "Correspondance de Mme Bégon" (Bonnault), APQ *Rapport, 1934–35*, 5–186 (modernized text), 187–277 (original text), and *Lettres au cher fils: correspondance d'Élisabeth Bégon avec son gendre (1748–1753)*, Nicole Deschamps, édit. (Coll. Reconnaissances, Montréal, 1972); selected letters were published by Céline Dupré as *Élisabeth Bégon (1696–1755)* (Collection classiques canadiens, 19, Montréal, 1961). c.d.]

Yvonne Bezard, *Fonctionnaires maritimes et coloniaux sous Louis XIV: les Bégon* (Paris, 1932). Frégault, *François Bigot*; *Le grand marquis*. Isabels Landels, "La correspondance de madame Bégon" (unpublished doctoral thesis, Université Laval, Québec, 1947). P.-G. Roy, *La famille Rocbert de La Morandière* (Lévis, Qué., 1905). Claude de Bonnault, "Saintonge et Canada: les Tilly," *BRH*, XLI (1935), 238–56, 296–313. É.-Z. Massicotte, "Quelques maisons du vieux Montréal," *Cahiers des Dix*, X (1945), 254–62. P.-G. Roy, "Honoré Michel de La Rouvillière," *BRH*, XXII (1916), 151–56.

ROLLO, ANDREW, 5th Baron ROLLO in the peerage of Scotland, army officer; b. 18 Nov. 1703 at Duncrub, Perthshire, Scotland, the eldest son of Robert, 4th Baron Rollo, and Mary Rollo; m. 22 April 1727 to Catharine Murray; m. 16 Feb. 1765 to Elizabeth Moray; d. 2 June 1765 in Leicester, England.

Andrew Rollo entered the army at the age of 40 and so distinguished himself at the battle of Dettingen (Bavaria) in 1743 that he was given a captaincy in the 22nd regiment. He became major in the same regiment on 1 June 1750 and succeeded to the title of Rollo on his father's death the following year. A promotion gave him the rank of lieutenant-colonel on 22 Nov. 1756.

The year 1757 found Rollo in North America, fighting in the Seven Years' War. He participated in operations in the Albany and Schenectady areas of New York that autumn. On 20 Jan. 1758, while the 22nd regiment under his command was wintering at Halifax, Nova Scotia, he was made colonel "in America." In May 1758 his regiment joined the forces preparing to besiege Louisbourg, Île Royale (Cape Breton Island), and during the siege he led one of the brigades ordered to the Lorembec (Lorraine) area. Following the capture of Louisbourg, Rollo was sent to Île Saint-Jean (Prince Edward Island) to arrange for the capitulation of that island and the removal of its inhabitants and to erect a fort. By the time of his departure for Louisbourg in November he had embarked 2,200 islanders for France and had built Fort Amherst at Port-La-Joie.

Rollo remained with his regiment at Louisbourg until 1 July 1760, when he sailed with the 22nd and the 40th regiments to join General James Murray*'s campaign in Canada. During its journey up the St Lawrence Rollo's detachment disarmed and administered an oath of neutrality to Canadians living on its banks, finally joining the main British force at Lac Saint-Pierre on 18 August. The following day Rollo was given the local rank of brigadier-general and command of the reserve in Murray's order of battle. On 22 August he led his regiments in a raid on Sorel that "laid waste the greatest part of the parish," many of whose inhabitants were still in arms. "I pray God this example may suffice," wrote Murray, who had ordered the action, "for my nature revolts, when this becomes a necessary part of my duty." The parish was doubly unfortunate since BOURLAMAQUE, who was in charge of the French defences at Sorel, was having houses burned to prevent desertions from his forces.

After the capture of Montreal on 8 Sept. 1760 Rollo commanded temporarily at "the island of Teresa" (Île Sainte-Thérèse); he was then ordered to assist in the fortification of Crown Point (formerly the site of Fort Saint-Frédéric) before proceeding with his regiment to Albany, where he arrived on 24 November. On 3 May 1761 he sailed from New York to the West Indies to take part in the successful British attack on Dominique (Dominica). He was subsequently made commander-in-chief on the island. He became full colonel on 19 Feb. 1762 and took a prominent part in the capture of Martinique that month and in the campaign against Havana the ensuing spring and summer. In July 1762 the lingering sickness that was to cause his death some three years later forced him to leave for England.

Lord Rollo, although joining the army relatively late in life, proved himself a competent commander and during his service in North America gained the confidence of the commander-in-chief, General Jeffery Amherst*. He was buried with full military honours at St Margaret's Church, Leicester. His son John, who served with him in the St Lawrence and on Martinique, predeceased him.

JOHN HUMPHREYS

PRO, CO 5/53, ff.154–55; Ind. 5442, f.115; 5444, f.14; WO 1/1, ff.102, 354v–55; 34/7, ff.225–25v, 232; 34/17, ff.2–3, 81–82v; 34/46b, ff.165, 175–76, 191; 34/55, ff.37–39. Knox, *Historical journal* (Doughty). *DNB*. *The Scots peerage, founded on Wood's edition of Sir Robert Douglas's peerage of Scotland*, ed. J. B. Paul (9v., Edinburgh, 1904–14), VII, 180–211. Harvey, *French régime in P.E.I.*, 189–97. Stanley, *New France*.

Roma

ROMA, JEAN-PIERRE, director of a sedentary fishing venture; b. at Bordeaux, France; m. Marie-Madeleine Moreau of Paris, and had two daughters and two sons; fl. 1715–57.

Jean-Pierre Roma is chiefly remembered for his activities in Île Saint-Jean (Prince Edward Island); little is known of his life elsewhere. He wrote in 1741 to the minister of Marine that in 1715 his fortune had been ruined by one M. Desmarets, that the Duc d'Orléans had then frustrated his attempts to re-establish this fortune by reuniting to the royal domain a concession he had had on the south coast of Saint-Domingue (Hispaniola), and that in 1726 the French ambassador at Turin had prevented him from entering the employ of the king of Sardinia.

On 17 July 1731 a grant signed by Louis XV of France and his minister of Marine, Maurepas, was made to Sieurs Claude Cottard, Joseph Du Boccage, Joseph-Philippe Narcis, and Jean-Pierre Roma, who was described as a merchant of Paris. These four men formed the Compagnie de l'Est de l'Île Saint-Jean. Their concession, of 3,500 *arpents* frontage and 40 *arpents* depth on the eastern coast of Île Saint-Jean, included the lands drained by the modern Brudenell, Montague, and Cardigan rivers; the site was known as Trois-Rivières, and occasionally "La Rommanie." The grant was to be held "en franc aleu noble," with no royal dues, but homage was to be paid at Louisbourg, Île Royale (Cape Breton Island), and justice was reserved for the king. To establish a sedentary fishing operation, the company was to settle 80 persons in 1732 and 30 annually thereafter; these settlers were to clear land and construct buildings. Fish-drying stations and storehouses could be established on the north coast, where land would be granted in proportion to the number of boats used there.

Roma, who was appointed director of the company, arrived at Trois-Rivières in June 1732. He envisaged the colony becoming not only a fishing venture trading with France but also the centre of trade between Quebec, Île Saint-Jean, and the West Indies. In the West Indies he would sell cod, planks, and beer from Trois-Rivières in exchange for molasses and rum which he would then sell in Quebec in return for supplies such as flour.

In April 1733 Roma was named commandant in the concession, under the administration at Louisbourg. Almost immediately, however, he encountered difficulties. Relations with the priest, Abbé Bierne (Byrne), deteriorated rapidly as the two quarrelled over the boundaries of temporal and ecclesiastical power. Equally stormy were Roma's relations with his partners in

France. They complained of his management, his independent spirit, and his ambitious plans; and when no profits were derived from the company's first year of operation, they refused further financial assistance. Roma defended himself, pointing out that expense had been unavoidable in establishing the colony, disclaiming responsibility for financial losses, indicating that he had accomplished a great deal considering his financial backing, and warning of the deterrent effect his failure would have on others contemplating similar ventures. To demonstrate his industry, he made a detailed report of every project undertaken, its purpose, and the manner in which it had been accomplished.

By August 1734 Roma had levelled the cape at Trois-Rivières, built two piers, cleared an area of about 1,700 by 1,200 feet, and constructed nine buildings. Five were houses and the remaining four were a storehouse, a bakery, a forge, and a stable. Wells were dug and an ice house was built. Gardens were set out, and fields of wheat and peas planted. A large cellar was made for storing food, and two water reservoirs and several small boats were constructed. Roads were cut to Saint-Pierre (St Peters) to the north, to Rivière des Esturgeons (Sturgeon River), to the Rivière du Nord-Est (Cardigan River), Souris, and Port-La-Joie (Fort Amherst). At Saint-Pierre houses and drying platforms were built for the 55 people involved in operations there.

Despite favourable accounts of his activities from Jacques d'Espiet* de Pensens and Saint-Ovide [MONBETON], officials in Île Saint-Jean and Louisbourg, Roma was unable to convince his associates of the value of the enterprise. He negotiated with them in France during the winter of 1736–37, and the next May became sole proprietor of the concession. His problems, however, continued. In 1737 he complained that the father superior of the Recollets at Louisbourg had helped lure away two girls he had brought from France, and that these girls had in turn enticed away three of his men and a badly needed cooper. In 1738 a plague of mice ruined the crops. Because settlers could take up free land elsewhere from the crown, Roma found them difficult to attract and he was forced to bring in several convicted salt smugglers. In January 1740 fire destroyed some buildings and cattle, and in 1741 Roma lost a ship and its cargo in a wreck. By September 1741 he was forced to ask the minister for an advance of 500 *livres*.

Roma's venture in Île Saint-Jean ended on 20 June 1745, when New England troops, sent by William PEPPERRELL from the victorious expedition to Louisbourg, destroyed his establishment.

Roma, his son, daughter, and five servants escaped first to the woods, then to Quebec. At Quebec Roma was employed in the magazines but his records were kept in such an unorthodox fashion that many had to be redone. In 1752 he was considered for, but not appointed to, the post of subdelegate of the intendant in Île Saint-Jean, once again in French hands. From Quebec Roma went to Martinique where, in 1757, he was director of the domain of Guadeloupe.

Roma's venture was the second attempt by a chartered company to establish a settlement in Île Saint-Jean, and, like that of the Comte de Saint-Pierre, it failed [see Gotteville* de Belile]. Roma was widely regarded as headstrong and partial, and his explanations of his problems frequently suggest a persecution complex; nevertheless one must admire his perseverance and acknowledge that many of his misfortunes and his final failure were the result of factors largely beyond his control.

Few signs of Roma's efforts remain; much of the shoreline has washed away, and when, in 1968 and 1969, archaeological investigations at the site were conducted by the National Historic Sites Service, only a few bits of foundation and masonry were found to remind us of the ambitious project Roma began there.

MARGARET COLEMAN

AN, Col., B, 55, ff.59v, 569, 585; 57, ff.602, 740; 58, ff.518v, 565; 59/1, f.434v; 61, ff.616v, 617–17v; 62, ff.9, 45v, 54v; 63, f.563; 64, f.466; 65, ff.53, 455, 480v–81; 66, f.304; C^11B, 13, ff.53, 79, 195, 197; 14, ff.22, 379, 387, 403, 405; 15, ff.84, 211; 16, ff.161, 165, 169, 173, 224, 252; 19, ff.35, 67, 76, 248; 20, ff.52, 122, 271; 23, ff.220, 222; 28, f.10; 29, ff.356–84, 400–27; 30, f.294; 32, f.220; Section Outre-Mer, G^1, 466/2 (recensements de l'île Saint-Jean, sept. 1734, 1735); G^2, 190/2/D, f.2; G^3, 2038/1 (8 juin 1732); 2045 (28 juin 1757). Harvey, *French régime in P.E.I.*, 73–89 [This is the fullest secondary account available, and it seems to be accurate. M.C.].

RONDEAU, JACQUES-PHILIPPE-URBAIN, scrivener, agent of the treasurer general of the Marine, notary; b. 1695 or 1699 at Trois-Rivières, son of Jacques Rondeau and Françoise Baudry; m. in 1733 Marie-Josephe, daughter of Alexandre Le Borgne de Belle-Isle and Marie-Josephe d'Abbadie de Saint-Castin; d. c. 1749.

Jacques-Philippe-Urbain Rondeau came to Louisbourg, Île Royale (Cape Breton Island), in the early 1720s. He lived there with the financial commissary, Jacques-Ange LE NORMANT de Mézy, served as his secretary, and was appointed scrivener in the Marine. It was his connection with Mézy and with the financial commissary's son and successor, Sébastien-François-Ange*, that allowed Rondeau to rise within the civil administration of the island. On their recommendation the treasurer general of the Marine, Pierre-Nicolas Gaudion, named Rondeau to replace François-Marie de GOUTIN as his agent in Île Royale in 1730. He was thus made responsible for all money dispensed directly in the colony. But to ensure that there would be no further irregularities like those with Goutin, three separate locks were placed on the treasury strongbox and Rondeau was given but one key; the other two were held by the financial commissary, who initiated and authorized expenditures, and the controller, who inspected the management of funds on behalf of the ministry of Marine and the controller general.

In the 1730s Sébastien-François-Ange Le Normant de Mézy assigned Rondeau responsibility for the upkeep of the newly constructed Louisbourg lighthouse. He was also entrusted with the functions of *Invalides* treasurer; in conjunction with the governor, king's lieutenant, financial commissary, and controller he collected the required six *deniers* per *livre* from all Marine salaries and administered the half-pay accorded wounded soldiers. In addition he was made responsible for clerical duties related to maritime conscription (*les classes*). It was thus with some justification that in 1733 Governor Saint-Ovide [MONBETON] complained that Rondeau occupied enough positions to keep three men busy. But in 1736 Le Normant appointed Rondeau notary as well.

Rondeau was an excellent example of a colonial placeman. It was particularly easy in the colonies to give one man close to the highest officials a number of responsibilities which, in the larger French ports, would normally have been separated into distinct offices. There is no evidence, however, to suggest that Rondeau abused his position. His commercial activities were circumscribed and the inventory of his effects taken on 30 Oct. 1750 shows that his assets only slightly outweighed his debts.

Rondeau had presumably gone to France after the fall of Louisbourg in 1745 but it is not known whether he died there or whether he returned to Louisbourg, as his wife did, after the restoration of Île Royale to France in 1749. He had died by the time the 1749 census of the island was compiled. Jean La Borde* succeeded him as agent of the treasurer general of the Marine. Rondeau's widow later married Joseph DU PONT Duvivier.

T. A. CROWLEY

Rondoenie

[The registers of the parish of Trois-Rivières indicate that Jacques Rondeau and Françoise Baudry had, among other children, a son Jacques (baptized 31 May 1695) and a son Urbain (baptized 28 June 1699). It is impossible to tell which of these was Jacques-Philippe-Urbain. T.A.C.]

AN, Col., B, 54, ff.509, 514; 61, f.602v; C¹¹ᴮ, 14, ff.126, 156; 17, f.87; 18, f.157; 20, f.124; Section Outre-Mer, G¹, 407; G³, 2038/1 (25 nov. 1731), 2038/2 (16 avril 1733), 2039/2 (17 déc. 1736), 2042 (21 juin 1754), 2047/1 (30 oct. 1750). R.-J. Valin, *Nouveau commentaire sur l'ordonnance de la Marine du mois d'août 1681 . . .* (2v., La Rochelle, France, 1766), I, 692–702. Eugene Asher, *The resistance to the maritime classes: the survival of feudalism in the France of Colbert* (University of California pubs. in history, 66, Berkeley, Los Angeles, 1960). Henri Legohérel, *Les trésoriers généraux de la Marine, 1517–1788* (Paris, 1965).

RONDOENIE. *See* ORONTONY

ROSEBOOM (Rooseboom), JOHANNES, trader; b *c.* 1661 at Albany, New York, to Hendrick Roseboom and Gysbertje Lansing; m. Gerritje Coster 18 Nov. 1688; buried 25 Jan. 1745 at Albany.

Johannes Roseboom early followed the trade of his father, who had become a fur-trader at Albany before 1660. Johannes was occasionally over-aggressive in attracting customers and was fined in 1678 and 1685 for breaking the law that forbade the soliciting of business from Indians in the city. He became moderately prosperous.

Prior to 1723 all fur trade in the colony of New York was restricted by law to within the walls of Albany. By 1685 traders were eager to establish firmer trade connections with the Hurons and Ottawas from the Upper Lakes who occasionally came to trade. Governor Thomas Dongan of New York supported their desires, and in August 1685 he granted Johannes Roseboom a pass to live among the Indians and later a licence to travel, trade, and hunt among the Hurons and Ottawas. Directed by a French deserter, Roseboom led an expedition of 11 canoes as far as Michilimackinac, which it reached about June 1686. The Indians were pleased with the high prices they received from these first English traders on the Upper Lakes, and the Albany trading community was elated on their return late that summer. The French, who had been unable to prevent this intrusion, lamented, "Missilimakinac is theirs."

Eager to repeat his success, Roseboom secured another commission from Governor Dongan. Leaving in the fall of 1686, Roseboom's men wintered with the Senecas and in the spring of 1687 were to join forces with a second party headed by Major Patrick Magregory. Wishing to be the first to reach Michilimackinac, however, Roseboom's party pushed ahead. When they were within a day and a half's journey of the Straits of Mackinac, they met a force of 120 French and Indians led by Olivier Morel* de La Durantaye. Outnumbered, Roseboom's men were seized and escorted eastward. The French expedition, augmented by hundreds of additional Indians, encountered Magregory's party on Lake Erie, swiftly captured the English, and plundered their canoes.

Roseboom and the other prisoners were taken to Niagara (near Youngstown, N.Y.); there Abel Marion, *dit* La Fontaine, one of their guides, was executed. They were then removed to Montreal and Quebec, where they were held until October, when Governor Dongan negotiated their release. The failure of the Roseboom and Magregory expedition demonstrated that the French still held sway on the Upper Lakes and would tolerate no interlopers. Not until 1760 did English traders again penetrate this area. Johannes Roseboom's chance to take revenge on the French came in 1711, during Queen Anne's War, when he accompanied Peter Schuyler* on an expedition which destroyed the trading post being built at Onondaga (near Syracuse, N.Y.) by Charles Le Moyne* de Longueuil.

Roseboom remained active in the fur trade throughout his life, purchasing furs from Indians who brought them to Albany and selling them in Europe. As late as 1723, he took an oath that he had not sold Indian trade goods directly to the French. He was also active in civic affairs. He served several terms as alderman, and held appointments as lieutenant in the militia and justice of the peace. In 1710–12 and 1728–30 he was a commissioner of Indian affairs. His later years passed in relative quiet and, upon his death in 1745, he was honoured with burial under the Albany Dutch Reformed Church, in which he had served as an elder.

DAVID A. ARMOUR

Charlevoix, *History* (Shea). *The Livingston Indian records, 1666–1723*, ed. L. H. Leder (Gettysburg, Pa., 1956), 106–7, 146. *Minutes of the court of Albany, Rensselaerswyck, and Schenectady, 1668–1685*, ed. and trans. A. J. F. Van Laer (3v., Albany, 1926–32), II, 345, 396; III, 327, 418, 538, 545. Joel Munsell, *The annals of Albany* (10v., Albany, 1850–59), I, 108, 138, 302; II, 18; III, 24, 33–34; IV, 104, 119, 130, 137, 144, 162, 184, 195; V, 125, 141, 173, 187, 288; VII, 21, 37, 59, 68, 81, 238. *NYCD* (O'Callaghan and Fernow), III, IV, V, IX. D. A. Armour, "The merchants of Albany, New York: 1686–1760" (unpublished PHD thesis, Northwestern University, Evanston, Ill., 1965). A. W. Trelease, *Indian affairs in colonial New York: the seventeenth century* (Ithaca, N.Y., [1960]), 269–71. Helen Broshar, "The first push westward of the Albany traders," *Mississippi Valley Hist. Rev.*, VII (1920–21), 228–41. A. H. Buffinton, "The policy of Albany and English westward expansion," *Mississippi Valley Hist. Rev.*, VIII (1922), 327–66.

ROUCY, Duc d'ANVILLE, JEAN-BAPTISTE-LOUIS-FRÉDÉRIC DE LA ROCHEFOUCAULD DE ROYE, Marquis de. *See* LA ROCHEFOUCAULD

ROUER D'ARTIGNY, LOUIS, seigneur, merchant, special lieutenant of the provost court of Quebec, councillor of the Conseil Supérieur; b. 9 Feb. 1667 at Quebec, son of Louis Rouer* de Villeray and Catherine Sevestre; d. 5 July 1744, a bachelor, at Quebec.

Thanks to his father's influence, Louis Rouer d'Artigny had on 27 Aug. 1684 obtained the seigneury of Île Verte, which he held jointly with his brother Augustin Rouer* de Villeray et de La Cardonnière until 1688, when it devolved upon him completely. He was even successful in having it enlarged in 1689. On May 1701 he sold this seigneury to Pierre de Niort de La Minotière.

The Sieur d'Artigny had some difficulty in obtaining office in the colony. He could not get himself appointed to the Conseil Supérieur in 1709, or in 1711 upon his brother's death. In 1712, however, he managed to get an appointment to deputize as special lieutenant of the provost court of Quebec, a function he exercised until 1716, when Jean-Baptiste Couillard* de Lespinay was appointed permanently. In 1717, at 50 years of age, he became a councillor of the Conseil Supérieur, an office he held until the end of his life. "He is honest and diligent," Intendant BÉGON said of him, "well acquainted with judicial matters." Probably because of his competence, he acted on occasion as attorney general.

His term on the council would have been uneventful, had he not compromised himself in the quarrel between Intendant Dupuy* and Governor Charles de BEAUHARNOIS in 1728. For having declared himself in favour of the intendant's cause he was excluded from the council on the governor's order and even exiled to Beaumont, near Quebec [*see* Guillaume Gaillard*]. He tried, but in vain, to defy this order of exclusion. Certainly the governor had exceeded his rights, but the recalcitrant councillor, though reinstated in his functions, received from the intendant, on the king's order, a reprimand aimed at reminding him of the respect due the first personage in the colony.

Notarial minutes enable us to have some idea of the fortune and the economic activities of this member of the colonial aristocracy who bore the title of esquire and belonged to the Conseil Supérieur. His father, who had died in 1700, had left him properties in the town of Quebec and lands outside the walls between the Chemin de la Grande Allée and the river, on the way to Sillery. The Sieur d'Artigny's most numerous transactions were in land and the agreement generally was to pay him in the form of "cens et rente." For the lands he sold he was rarely paid in ready money: redeemable annuities were established in his favour. Thus in 1701 an annuity of 240 *livres* had been established for him in payment of the 4,800-*livre* sale price for his seigneury of Île Verte. He made other deals that were still larger, such as the sale to the Ursulines, completed on 30 April 1727, of several pieces of land for the sum of 8,000 *livres*; of this amount 2,250 *livres* went to pay off an old debt, contracted by the Sieur d'Artigny's father. For the remaining 5,750 *livres* the nuns set up an annuity of 287 *livres* 10 *sols*. In 1734 he sold his windmill situated on his piece of land called "la Cardonnière," "the said mill turning well and making good flour"; the sale price amounted to 2,410 *livres*, payable by "a redeemable annuity." It has been possible to discover only one house rental, at 200 *livres* a year for a house on Rue Saint-Pierre in Lower Town.

Louis Rouer d'Artigny sometimes lent money, but not in large amounts: 233 *livres* to his brother, 100 *livres* and 50 *livres* to two individuals. He rarely dealt in annuities apart from land sales: in 1713 he sold the merchant Jean Fournel an annuity of 240 *livres* on a capital of 4,800 *livres*, and in 1733 he bought one for 37 *livres* 10 *sols* on a capital of 750 *livres*.

But d'Artigny's activities did not stop there. In 1707 the seigneur of Île Verte, the Sieur de La Minotière, recognized a debt to the Sieur d'Artigny of 1,520 *livres* "for goods . . furnished to equip him for trading in peltries and fishing." Rouer d'Artigny delivered goods to even more distant points, since he traded with Plaisance (Placentia, Nfld.), where he had a factor. He also sold livestock: on 7 Aug. 1703 the butcher Michel Cadet bought 80 sheep from him at 15 *livres* each. He had an interest in fishing as well: for 300 *livres* a year he hired for nine years from François Gauvin the "porpoise, herring, and salmon fishing ground located at the cape and outlet of the aforementioned river [Rivière Ouelle]." And one last item, in 1699 he signed an agreement with Nicolas Pinaud*, a bourgeois of Quebec, to share with him the "tackle, utensils, and other effects that were discovered on the *Aymable*, shipwrecked at Cacouna."

Rouer de Villeray

In the present state of research it is impossible to give exactly the total amount of this councillor's fortune, but it was relatively large. His commercial activities were varied, but they did not include retail trade, and because of that Intendant Jacques Raudot* declared to the king in 1709 that the Sieur d'Artigny was not engaged "in any business." His life enlightens us greatly on the economic activities of that Canadian "nobility" whose way of life was so different from that of the nobility in the mother country.

JEAN-CLAUDE DUBÉ

AN, Col., D²ᶜ, 222/2, p.232 (PAC transcript). ANQ, Greffe de Louis Chambalon, 17 avril 1701, 24 oct. 1702, 23 avril, 7 août 1703, 29 oct. 1704; Greffe de J.-É. Dubreuil, 1ᵉʳ févr. 1734; Greffe de François Genaple de Bellefonds, 31 oct. 1708; Greffe de Florent de La Cetière, 27 oct. 1707, 17 janv. 1709, 2 janv. 1712, 2 sept. 1713; Greffe de J.-N. Pinguet de Vaucour, 28 avril 1733; Greffe de François Rageot, 30 avril 1727; Greffe de Guillaume Roger, 20 sept. 1699. P.-G. Roy, *Inv. jug. et délib., 1717–1760*, VII, 20. Frégault, *Le XVIIIᵉ siècle canadien*, 187. P.-G. Roy, *Diverses familles* (3v., Lévis, Qué., 1920), I, 46ff.

ROUER DE VILLERAY, BENJAMIN (he signed Villeray), officer in the colonial regular troops; b. 1701, son of Augustin Rouer* de Villeray et de La Cardonnière and Marie-Louise Legardeur de Tilly; d. 30 Nov. 1760 in Rochefort, France.

Little is known of Benjamin Rouer de Villeray's youth, and his military career is difficult to trace before 1733. In February of that year it was proposed that he be made second ensign; he was already a cadet, and it was remarked that he had served well. Governor Charles de BEAUHARNOIS did not, however, support the suggestion, for he hoped that Villeray would receive an appointment in Louisiana. Villeray nonetheless became second ensign in Canada on 1 April 1733. Six years later, with Beauharnois's recommendation, Villeray was made an ensign on the active list; he was considered a good officer who had a great deal of authority and enthusiasm for the service. In 1743 Beauharnois put his name forward for a vacant lieutenancy. Villeray did garrison duty in Montreal in 1747 and 1748; we know nothing about his activities between 1733 and 1747, except that he was married in Montreal in 1735.

Villeray arrived at Louisbourg, Île Royale (Cape Breton Island), on 20 Sept. 1749 on the *Léopard*; at that time he was "acting as lieutenant by an order from Mʳ La Jonquière [TAFFANEL] of 16 Sept. 1749." On 11 Oct. 1749 La Galissonière [BARRIN] and Charles DES

HERBIERS suggested granting him a post as lieutenant in the Louisbourg garrison, and on 15 April 1750 Villeray was promoted lieutenant; he served in Captain Michel Du Pont Duvivier de Gourville's company in 1750 and 1751. Although he had not yet received his lieutenant's commission, he became a captain on 1 May 1751.

In 1753 Villeray was given command of Fort Gaspereau, which had been built in 1750 and 1751 on the north coast of Baie Verte (in what is now part of New Brunswick) to serve as a depot. On 17 June 1755 he surrendered to a British force under Robert Monckton* without any shots being fired. Villeray and his men were taken to Louisbourg by sea. The governor of Île Royale, Drucour [BOSCHENRY], criticized Villeray's conduct severely; he considered it "more a fault of the head than of the heart" and proposed to take his company away from him. Villeray appeared before the court martial at Quebec on 22 and 24 Oct. 1757. He justified his conduct by the fact that Fort Beauséjour (near Sackville, N.B.) had been surrendered by Louis Du Pont* Duchambon de Vergor after only three days' resistance; he had sent the greater part of his troops there, keeping only a score of men for himself. In addition he had considered that the condition of the fort did not permit him to resist an artillery attack. Finally he alleged that the Acadians had refused to obey him. Not being able to rely on either the garrison at Beauséjour or the Acadians, he had decided to surrender without offering any resistance. MONTCALM remarked about Villeray: "He is the less guilty of the two commandants; but they wanted to sacrifice him . . . concerning Gaspereau the only mistake was not to withdraw and burn it." Villeray was acquitted on 28 October. Immediately afterwards Governor Pierre de Rigaud* de Vaudreuil ordered him to resume command of his company at Louisbourg. He took part in the defence of the fortress in June and July 1758.

The documents do not allow us to retrace exactly Villeray's activities after the capture of Louisbourg. In July 1760 he was living in Rochefort, but a list of the officers and soldiers who had come back from England on 1 Oct. 1760 mentions that at Drucour's order he was in Canada. He died on 30 November in Rochefort, after being made a knight of the order of Saint-Louis on 8 Feb. 1760.

Villeray's financial situation is difficult to determine: he engaged in few transactions, preferring to devote himself to his military career. In 1748 he sold two pieces of land that he had inherited; they were located in Quebec, at the foot of Cap Diamant. The two articles of sale stipulated that if the purchasers were dispossessed of their land by the establishment of a ship-building yard, the sale would be annulled. When the yard was built, Villeray lost both the land and the profits from their sale; he then tried to obtain compensation. His marriage in Montreal on 16 Aug. 1735 with Marie-Joseph, the daughter of Pierre Pépin, *dit* Laforce, king's storekeeper at Niagara (near Youngstown, N.Y.), and Michelle Lebert, denotes a certain affluence; Marie-Joseph was assured of a dowry of 3,000 *livres*. Of this marriage nine children were born, most of whom died in infancy.

YVON DESLOGES

AN, Col., B, 47, 65, 66, 68, 91, 103, 107, 112, 144; C¹¹ᴬ, 67, 75, 79, 91, 93–95, 103; C¹¹ᴮ, 28–29, 31–33, 35, 37; D²ᶜ, 4, 7, 17, 18, 48, 49, 53, 57–59, 61, 222; Section Outre-Mer, G³, 2051. PAC, MG 8, B3, C3, C4; MG 18, M1, 7. PAC *Report, 1904*, app.G. Fauteux, *Les chevaliers de Saint-Louis*. Thomas Chapais, *Le marquis de Montcalm (1712–1759)* (Québec, 1911). Pierre Margry, *Familles de la France coloniale: les Rouer de Villeroy* (Paris, 1851). P.-G. Roy, "La famille Rouer de Villeray," *BRH*, XXVI (1920).

ROUFFIO, JOSEPH, merchant; b. 31 Oct. 1730 at Montauban, France, son of Jean-Jacques Rouffio and Marquèze Nègre; d. sometime after 1764.

Little is known about the Rouffio family's business career in New France. The Rouffio brothers, Jean, Dominique, Pierre, François, Étienne, and Joseph, along with their brother-in-law François Romagnac, probably arrived in the colony in 1752, and there they formed a partnership. In 1755 Joseph Rouffio withdrew from the partnership after a quarrel with his family over his marriage to Louise Cadet.

The Rouffio family's differences with Louise Cadet and Augustin Cadet, her father, began in 1753. Pierre Rouffio, who was not yet 20 years of age, fell in love with Louise Cadet and prepared to renounce Protestantism in order to marry her. Jean, the eldest member of the Rouffio family, was opposed to this marriage. To force his hand Pierre abducted Louise Cadet. The girl's father brought action against the abductor before the provost court of Quebec, which condemned the young man to the galleys. A few weeks later the Conseil Supérieur modified the sentence: it ordered Pierre Rouffio to pay 10,000 *livres* in damages and to leave the colony unless he preferred to marry Louise Cadet. Rouffio chose to pay the money, but it is not known whether he had to leave Canada.

Louise Cadet was consequently provided with a considerable dowry. It was probably with the idea of bringing this money back into his family that Joseph Rouffio, Pierre's brother, took it into his head to marry Louise Cadet. But he encountered his older brother Jean's frenzied opposition, for this project meant, among other things, that a second member of the Rouffio family would abjure his faith, Pierre having already done so. In February 1755 Jean Rouffio endeavoured to obtain from the provost court of Quebec, then from the Conseil Supérieur, an order forbidding his brother, who was still under age, from entering into this marriage. The council, however, ordered "a new assembly of neighbours or friends in the absence of parents in this country . . . to give . . . their opinion and assent" to the marriage. On 20 March 1755 the engaged couple contracted a marriage with community of property according to the customary law of Paris: Rouffio paid 3,333 *livres* 6 *sols* 8 *deniers* into the joint estate out of the 8,000 *livres* that he declared he owned in the partnership to which he belonged. For her part Louise Cadet brought her indemnification of 10,000 *livres*. The wedding took place on 8 April of that year.

In July Joseph Rouffio withdrew from his brothers' partnership; he received his share of 8,000 *livres* in the partnership, his share in his father's estate and that of a brother who had died in France, likewise amounting to 8,000 *livres*, and in addition 2,000 *livres* as compensation. Joseph Rouffio's debts to the partnership were cancelled, but those of the partnership to Joseph Rouffio were paid off. The interests of the Rouffio family were thus separated, but Joseph was the only one who profited from it. In his will, dated August 1755, Jean Rouffio disinherited his brother Joseph.

Shortly after the conquest Joseph Rouffio is believed to have gone back to France and to have settled in Tours. He returned to the colony in 1764, probably to attend to the registration and clearing off of his French bills, for he registered more than 85,000 *livres* in bills of exchange at the clearing of accounts carried out in 1763. After 1764 he disappears from sight.

JOSÉ IGARTUA

AAQ, 42 CD, Abjurations, A, 63, 145; 65, 147. AD, Tarn-et-Garonne (Montauban), État civil, Saint-Jean-Villenouvelle, 31 oct. 1730. AJQ, Registre d'état civil, Notre-Dame de Québec, 8 avril 1755. AN, Col., C¹¹ᴬ, 108, ff.1–90. ANQ, Greffe de R.-C. Barolet, 20 mars 1755; Greffe de J.-C. Panet, 6 août, 29 sept., 17 oct. 1753, 18 juill., 18 août 1755, 26 oct. 1764; NF, Registres du Cons. sup., registre criminel, 1730–1759, ff.140v–41; 1752–1755, ff.175–75v. PAC, MG 7, II, 12147, ff.118–19, 247. P.-G. Roy, *Inv. contrats de*

Rouillard

mariage, V, 241; *Inv. ins. Prév. Québec*, III, 31; *Inv. jug. et délib., 1717–1760*, II, 191; V, 186; VI, 22, 66. Tanguay, *Dictionnaire*. P.-G. Roy, *La ville de Québec*, II, 231–32 [P.-G. Roy wrongly attributes to Joseph Rouffio the abduction of Louise Cadet in 1753. J.I.].

Archives des Franciscains (Montréal), Dossier Ambroise Rouillard. Caron, "Inventaire de documents," APQ *Rapport, 1941–42*, 223. Jouve, *Les Franciscains et le Canada: aux Trois-Rivières*, 220. Trudel, *L'Église canadienne*. J.-C. Taché, "Le gobelet d'argent du père Ambroise," *BRH*, IV (1898), 52–54.

ROUILLARD, AMBROISE (baptized **Louis-Joseph**), Recollet, missionary; b. 28 March 1693 at Quebec, son of Jean Rouillard and Jeanne Levasseur; d. in an accident in 1768.

Louis-Joseph Rouillard entered the Recollet order in 1718 and was ordained a priest in the chapel of the Hôpital Général of Quebec on 18 Dec. 1723. Subsequently his ministry took him over a great part of the south shore of the St Lawrence. First he served the parish of Rimouski until 1735, when he was appointed missionary at Restigouche on the Baie des Chaleurs. After 1741 we find him in different parishes between Sorel and Sainte-Croix; in 1745 he again took up his abode at Rimouski and served the region until 1759; he was then appointed military chaplain at Restigouche and styled himself "chaplain of the *Machaud*." He remained at Restigouche until 1761, when he returned for good to Rimouski. In January 1767 he assisted the hermit of Saint-Barnabé, Toussaint CARTIER, on his deathbed.

Legend has it that Father Ambroise regularly stayed at the home of the seigneur of Trois-Pistoles, Nicolas Rioux, during his trips in the region. The last time he went there the Recollet consented to have his portrait painted by an itinerant artist, at the request of the seigneur and other parishioners. When the portrait was completed, Father Ambroise is supposed to have made a single remark: "I look like a drowned man." On the eve of his departure for Rimouski Rouillard asked Rioux to lend him a tin goblet, because he had lost his own. The seigneur chose a silver goblet and offered it to the Recollet, who would not take such a precious gift. The master of the house insisted, and finally Father Ambroise accepted it, saying to the seigneur that if he were to die during one of his trips the goblet would be returned to the donor. Next morning the mistress of the house found the famous goblet in the place from which her husband had taken it the day before. Father Ambroise had been drowned while returning to Rimouski. These events took place, the legend tells us, in the year 1768.

Father Ambroise Rouillard's career resembles that of all the Recollets in New France except that it ended in a tragic death, and the legend of the silver goblet.

MICHEL PAQUIN

ROUS, JOHN, privateer, naval officer, member of the Nova Scotia Council; b. between 1700 and 1710; d. at Portsmouth, England, 3 April 1760.

John Rous was foremost among New England's privateer captains in the War of the Austrian Succession (1740–48). According to some authorities, he made extensive raids on the French fishing fleets and ports on the north shore of Newfoundland in 1744. The following year he was second in command of the Massachusetts naval forces at the siege of Louisbourg, Île Royale (Cape Breton Island). He was the first to come to the assistance of the *Mermaid* in the engagement that resulted in the capture on 20 June (O.S.) of the French 64-gun *Vigilant* [*see* Alexandre de LA MAISONFORT]. Commodore Peter WARREN, realizing that this "brisk, gallant man" could be useful "in future schemes of this kind," made Rous third lieutenant of the *Vigilant*, though he left him in command of the 20-gun snow *Shirley*. The *Shirley* sailed for England with dispatches early in July and, on its return in September, Warren purchased the vessel, with Rous as captain, for use in North America. The *Shirley* was rated a frigate and Rous became a post captain in the Royal Navy.

Rous was stationed at Annapolis Royal, Nova Scotia, in 1746. The *Shirley* was damaged by a hurricane in September, and Rous was unable to sail out of Annapolis; he thus could not assist the English garrison at Grand Pré, which was attacked by the French early the next year [*see* Arthur NOBLE]. In March he led an expedition of 100 men under John Winslow* and Silvanus COBB to reassert British authority at Minas. The *Shirley* was paid off in June 1747 and Rous then served briefly under Admiral Charles Knowles*. That winter Governor William Shirley of Massachusetts sent Rous to England as an emissary and to seek employment; he arrived in April 1748, near the end of the war. Armed with Shirley's and Knowles' dispatches, and favoured with their recommendations, Rous was consulted about the plan for settling Nova Scotia and was given command of the 14-gun sloop *Albany*. On 7 May 1749 he received orders to convoy settlers from the Nore (east of London) to Nova Scotia. He put down some early disorders with a firm hand, then shepherded the settlers from Portsmouth to Halifax, where he arrived on 29 June.

Between 1749 and 1755 Rous was the senior naval officer on the Nova Scotia station and made a notable contribution to the preservation of the new colony. As the admiralty did not provide effective naval forces for the defence of Nova Scotia, Rous had to improvise the protection essential to the survival of the settlements at Halifax, Canso, Lunenburg, Annapolis Royal, and Chignecto. He had at his disposal three 14-gun sloops of the Royal Navy, the occasional man-of-war from England, and several New England coasting vessels. He was active against the French at this time, as in 1749 when he carried a letter from Governor Edward Cornwallis* to Charles Deschamps* de Boishébert at the Saint John River, claiming the mouth of the river for the British. By force of his personality Rous made the French commander strike his colours and acknowledge that the territory was at best disputed. Rous accompanied the expeditions under Charles LAWRENCE against the French at Chignecto in April and September 1750. He provided vital naval support for the landing of troops and gave Lawrence shrewd counsel, including the advice that English forces should spend the summer at Minas to prevent a general uprising.

Late in 1753 Rous took command of the 24-gun frigate *Success*. The following year he was appointed to the Executive Council of Nova Scotia. In the spring of 1755 he commanded the naval force – three 24-gun frigates and a sloop – that accompanied the 33 transports and 2,100 men sent to capture Fort Beauséjour (near Sackville, N.B.). With the surrender of the French fort on 17 June, Rous sailed for the Saint John River to destroy the fortifications there. When he arrived, however, the French fired their forts and burst their guns. In July he took part in the decision by the Nova Scotia Council to deport the Acadians. He was in charge of the convoy that sailed in October with the French inhabitants of Chignecto, "who have always been the most rebellious." Late that month he was able to get the transports clear of the Bay of Fundy and send them on their way to Georgia and the Carolinas. On his return to Halifax, he had to undergo a court martial, in which he was cleared of some malicious, though perhaps not absolutely groundless, charges of abusing his authority in Halifax.

Rous was to convoy the mast ships to England late in 1756, but he was ordered back to Halifax to become senior naval officer again. He spent much of that winter in Boston meeting with Lord Loudoun [John Campbell], commander-in-chief of British forces in North America, and Charles Lawrence concerning the offensive strategy to be followed in North America. In February 1757 he relinquished command of the *Success* and was subsequently sent to sea in command of other ships and squadrons. He took a leading part in the preparations for an attack on Louisbourg in 1757, but the expedition was abandoned. When it was resumed the following year Rous sailed in command of the *Sutherland* (50 guns) and was active in the landings at Gabarus Bay. In the spring of 1759 he was sent to Canso by Admiral Philip DURELL to survey the ice conditions there and watch for French ships. He sailed against Quebec in June with the *Sutherland*. Admiral Charles Saunders* chose him to lead a small squadron of ships up river, above the town, and on the night of 18–19 July the *Sutherland* and other ships passed Quebec, under furious fire from the city batteries, without losing a man. This manoeuvre eventually sealed the fate of the city. And when, on 13 September, British troops landed for the assault on Quebec it was from the *Sutherland* that their landing barges dropped down on the Anse au Foulon.

Rous convoyed the mast fleet to England that fall, arriving on 26 December. He died at Portsmouth on 3 April 1760 and was buried from St Thomas's Church (now Portsmouth Cathedral). He was survived by his widow Rachel, his second wife; by two sons and three daughters, one of whom was married to Richard Bulkeley*, secretary of the province of Nova Scotia; and by his brother Joseph, who was the first keeper of the lighthouse at Sambro, Nova Scotia.

There are no known portraits of Rous, although the occasional place-name in Nova Scotia preserves his memory. The most lasting epitaph to John Rous is that by the Nova Scotia historian, Beamish Murdoch*: "On all occasions he was active, skilful and fully relied on."

W. A. B. DOUGLAS

City Records Office, Portsmouth, Eng., St Thomas's Church parish records. New York Public Library, Rare book div., Great Britain, Prize Causes, Lords Commissioners of Appeals in (189 pamphlets, [London, 1736–58], bound in two vols.), *Notre-Dame de Délivrance* (1747). PAC, MG 11, Nova Scotia A, 27, f.80; 30, ff.1–106; 34, ff.148, 234; 35, f.4; 36, ff.209–69; 38; MG 18, M1, 6, 8. PANS, RG 1, 163, 164, 491, 492; Vertical ms file, Halifax, Earl of, Plan for settlement of Nova Scotia, 1749. PRO, Adm. 1/234, 1/480–82, 1/1892, 1/2109, 1/2381–86, 1/2471, 1/2472, 1/2654, 1/2655, 1/3818; 8; 50/3; 50/7, ff.272–76; 51/820, f.385; Prob. 11/855, f.385; WO 71/180. St Paul's Church (Halifax), Marriage records, 1750.

Rouville

Journals of Beauséjour: diary of John Thomas, journal of Louis de Courville, ed. J. C. Webster ([Sackville, N.B.], 1937). Knox, *Historical journal* (Doughty). *Logs of the conquest* (Wood), 321. *N.S. Archives, I.* [William Pepperrell], "The Sir William Pepperrell journal," American Antiquarian Soc. *Proc.* (Worcester, Mass.), new ser., XX (1909–10), 135–78. Charnock, *Biographia navalis*, V, 412–14 [There appears to be no substantiation for Charnock's statement that Rous, having entered the navy previously, quit the royal service for a time and "took the command of a private ship of war fitted out from New England." W.A.B.D.]. G.B., Adm., *List of sea officers, 1660–1815*. H. M. Chapin, *Privateering in King George's War, 1739–48* (Providence, 1928). Corbett, *England in the Seven Years' War*. S. G. Drake, *A particular history of the five years' French and Indian war in New England and parts adjacent* (Albany, 1870). McLennan, *Louisbourg*. Murdoch, *History of Nova-Scotia*, II. S. M. Pargellis, *Lord Loudoun in North America* (New Haven, Conn., London, 1933). Rawlyk, *Yankees at Louisbourg*. Stanley, *New France*. W. A. B. Douglas, "Halifax as an element of sea power, 1749–1766" (unpublished MA thesis, Dalhousie University, Halifax, [1962]); "The sea militia of Nova Scotia, 1749–1755: a comment on naval policy," *CHR*, XLVII (1966), 22–37.

ROUVILLE, LOUISE-CATHERINE HERTEL DE. *See* ANDRÉ DE LEIGNE

ROY, MARGUERITE, *dite* **de la Conception** (incorrectly called Le Roy), nun of the Congregation of Notre-Dame of Montreal; b. 4 July 1674 at Prairie-de-la-Madeleine (Laprairie, Qué.), daughter of Pierre Roy and Catherine Ducharme; d. 13 Dec. 1749 in Montreal.

The sisters of the Congregation of Notre-Dame did not establish a convent at Prairie-de-la-Madeleine until 1705. But during the 17th century they usually conducted itinerant missions there, and it was undoubtedly on these occasions that Marguerite Roy made the acquaintance of the nuns. At the age of 15 she joined the community in Montreal. She was one of the sisters who on 25 June 1698 officially accepted the rules prescribed by Bishop Saint-Vallier [La Croix*], took the three simple vows of poverty, chastity, obedience, and the vow to teach girls, and on 1 July made their perpetual profession.

Sister Marguerite Roy de la Conception was employed in several missions, but it seems that she was the cause of numerous difficulties. She was therefore quickly recalled to the community in Montreal. She was there when Bishop Saint-Vallier, feeling his end draw near, decided to realize a part of the dream that he had had since 1685: the establishment of teaching houses in the farthest reaches of his immense diocese, in Louisiana and Acadia. In 1724 he had made an official request to the superior of the community, Sister Saint-Joseph [Marguerite TROTTIER], to send some nuns on a mission to Louisbourg, Île Royale (Cape Breton Island), but the superior asked him to find the means of providing for the nuns' subsistence. Moreover, the rule of the community required spiritual direction by a secular priest, and there were only Recollets at Louisbourg. The bishop thought to obviate these difficulties by asking the court to assume support of the foundation. But the court replied that it could not "grant new favours to the religious communities."

In 1727, after a dispute with the confessor of the community, who did not attach much importance to her visions, Sister de la Conception put herself under the spiritual direction of the bishop himself. Since she could not find in the nuns' activities in Montreal work corresponding to her high aspirations and her excessive inclination towards the miraculous, she offered her services to the bishop to realize his desire for an institution in Louisbourg. The bishop accepted, despite the opposition of the officials of the community who maintained that the congregation had neither the means nor the personnel necessary for such an institution. Sister de la Conception was therefore obliged to bring two lay sisters into the undertaking. In these exceptional circumstances and with Bishop Saint-Vallier's blessing, she left Quebec in May 1727, to the great relief, it seems, of her community. In 1733 Dosquet*, the bishop of Quebec, wrote that in 1727 the community "had been very pleased to be rid of her because she caused trouble when she lived there and no priest wanted her in his parish."

Bishop Saint-Vallier had to act with great dexterity in dealing with the civil authorities of Île Royale, who were aware of the court's opposition to the project in question. In a letter to the governor, Saint-Ovide [MONBETON], and the financial commissary at Louisbourg, Jacques-Ange LE NORMANT de Mézy, he did not hesitate to introduce the founder as "the most capable [nun] in her community." In addition he stated that her mission was "to become acquainted with the place and its condition and to consider the advisability of the proposed work." It may be confidently stated that the establishment of the Louisbourg mission was due both to Bishop Saint-Vallier's authoritarianism and to the intemperate zeal of the woman under his direction.

According to her obituary notice the founder of the Louisbourg mission was "endowed with a quick and penetrating mind, and a rare talent and skill in teaching pupils." She was consequently much appreciated as an educator and won general esteem. In its first year the mission had 22 boarders and "in a short while the number of its pupils became so great that it was unable to cope with everything." In the spring of 1728 Saint-Ovide and Mézy asked the minister of Marine, Maurepas, for a gratuity for the mission. In April 1730 the king authorized an allowance of 1,500 *livres* for the upkeep of the three nuns who were employed there.

To cope with their task, and above all to meet the king's requirements, Sister de la Conception asked her community in Montreal for reinforcements. But the circumstances surrounding her departure for Louisbourg had already created a rift between her and her community. In addition, the Louisbourg mission was in a difficult financial situation: the founder, who had no aptitude for temporal matters and was much inclined to extravagance, had bought for the mission, under very onerous conditions of payment (1,000 *livres* a year), a piece of land and a house that were not worth the 15,000 *livres* that Josué DUBOIS Berthelot de Beaucours had demanded for them. The officials of the community were therefore hesitant to send nuns to heal the rift at Louisbourg. They decided to do so in the summer of 1732, but Bishop Dosquet did not give his permission for the departure of Sister Saint-Joseph and her two companions until the autumn of 1733, when he was sure that the founder would return immediately to Montreal, as he had ordered.

Back in Montreal, Sister de la Conception followed from afar what was called "the re-establishment of the Louisbourg mission." Physically spent, morally exhausted by the numerous accusations brought against her and by the consciousness that she was considered a useless burden to her community, she lived until her death in humility, obscurity, and silence. In the *Histoire de la Congrégation de Notre-Dame de Montréal* Sister de la Conception appears as an unique case. To her obituary notice is appended a long appeal in her defence: "Coup d'œil sur les accusations portées contre Sœur de la Conception avec objections." The author seems to have wanted to refute Bishop Dosquet, who wrote, for example, to Abbé de L'Isle-Dieu on 25 March 1733 these surprisingly harsh and slanderous words: "She is the most deceitful, the most scheming nun, and the one most filled with illusions that I know." This defence would lead us to conclude that if Sister de la Conception, a person who was very free in her aspirations and actions, was an outsider in her community, she was also, with the backing if not the irresistible stimulus of Bishop Saint-Vallier, the tenacious and courageous woman who started the work of the Congregation of Notre-Dame on Île Royale.

ANDRÉE DÉSILETS

ACND, La Congrégation de Notre-Dame: son personnel, 1653–1768; Fichier général des sœurs de la Congrégation de Notre-Dame; Plans des lieux de sépulture depuis 1681-CND; Registre des sépultures des sœurs de la Congrégation de Notre-Dame; Registre général des sœurs de la Congrégation de Notre-Dame de Montréal. AN, Col., B, 54, ff.433–34. ANQ-M, Registre d'état civil, Laprairie, 1674. PAC *Report, 1904*, app.K, 49. Lemire-Marsolais et Lambert, *Histoire de la Congrégation de Notre-Dame*, II, 115; III, 166, 348–55, 393–97; IV, 6, 14–16, 29–35, 124–26, 201–11, 241. Tanguay, *Dictionnaire*.

ROYE, Marquis de ROUCY, Duc d'ANVILLE, JEAN-BAPTISTE-LOUIS-FRÉDÉRIC DE LA ROCHEFOUCAULD DE. *See* LA ROCHEFOUCAULD

S

SABATIER, ANTOINE, principal scrivener, controller, attorney general of the Conseil Supérieur of Île Royale; b. probably in Toulon, France, son of Joseph Sabatier and Madeleine Arnauld; d. 22 Sept. 1747 at Rochefort, France.

Issuing from a bourgeois family of Toulon, Antoine Sabatier entered the Marine service there as scrivener in 1703. He requested a transfer to Île Royale (Cape Breton Island) in 1717 where he became clerk of the fortifications, responsible for stores and work records. As Pierre-Jérôme BOUCHER came to assume more clerical duties, the director of fortifications, Jean-François de Verville*, found he no longer had need of Sabatier, and the financial commissary, Jacques-Ange LE NORMANT de Mézy, recommended him as scrivener in 1721. To this position was added that of controller in 1723 when Governor Saint-Ovide [MONBETON] complained to the ministry about the performance of Louis LEVASSEUR. Sabatier was inadequately prepared to assume this function and, although he wrote officials at Rochefort for instructions, it was not until a number of years later that he fully understood what the job entailed.

Sabatier had found himself in a similar situation in 1719 when he was appointed attorney general of the Conseil Supérieur at Louisbourg upon the recommendation of Pierre-Auguste de Soubras*. In addition to the difficulties naturally encountered in launching a new judicial body, Sabatier had to contend with quarrels between the governor and the financial commissary as well as attempts by Mézy to usurp legal functions properly within the jurisdiction of the Conseil Supérieur. Lacking legal training, he sought the advice of his counterpart in Quebec, Mathieu-Benoît Collet*, who informed him at length about practices and procedures in that city. Throughout his years of service Sabatier was a steadying and humane influence on the administration of justice at Île Royale.

Sabatier was a hard-working second rank civil servant, a man who attempted to do his best but who never stepped on the toes of his superiors if he could avoid it. Saint-Ovide perhaps best characterized him in 1723 as "an honest man, agreeable to the officers and residents, and [one] who knows how to work." For helping Mézy bring the colony's accounts into order he was made principal scrivener in 1730. In 1734–35 and 1738–39 he replaced Sébastien-François-Ange Le Normant* de Mézy as financial commissary when the latter was in France, but he was passed over in favour of François Bigot* when the position fell vacant in 1739. Like his predecessors, Bigot found him a trustworthy subordinate and in 1743 at last secured for him his commission as controller as well as an annual bonus of 300 *livres*.

Sabatier saw to the advancement of his brother, François de Paule Sabatier, within the Louisbourg civil administration after 1725. Although he was married it appears that neither his wife nor his daughter ever left France; they received a pension of 500 *livres* after his death.

T. A. CROWLEY

AN, Col., B, 44, f.572; 48, f.438; 49, f.728v; 54, f.509; 61, f.615v; 76, f.476; 88, f.358; C^{11B}, 1–26, especially 2, f.75; 3, f.76; 4, ff.25, 39, 232; 5, f.349; 7, f.292v; 9, f.135; 17, ff.164–98v; 20, f.243; 21, ff.137, 180; D^{2C}, 60, f.16; 222/2, p.239 (PAC transcript); E, 17 (dossier Perrotin de Barmont); F^{2C}, 5, f.89; F^3, 50, f. 147; 51, f. 135; Marine, C^2, 55, p.24 (PAC transcript); C^7, 184 (dossier Louis Levasseur); Section Outre-Mer, G^1, 466, pièce 69 (recensement général de l'île Royale, 1734); G^2, 178, f.831; 181, f.570; 190/1, f.24v; G^3, 2038/1 (3 mars 1731), 2038/2 (1er août, 23 déc. 1733). Frégault, *François Bigot*, I, 100. McLennan, *Louisbourg*, 73, 74, 83, 100. J.-B. Torchet de Boismêlé, *Histoire générale de la marine, contenant son origine chez tous les peuples du monde, ses progrès, son état actuel et les expéditions maritimes anciennes et modernes . . .* (3v., Paris, Amsterdam, 1744–58) [Vol. III contains the ordinance of 1689 which outlined the organization of the Marine department. T.A.C.]. François de Veillechèze de La Mardière, *L'évolution historique du contrôle de la marine . . .* (Poitiers, 1912).

SAGOUARRAB (Sagouarrat, Saguaarum). *See* SAUGUAARAM

SAGUIMA (Saguina, Sakima, Saquima and possibly **Saquin),** Ottawa chief; fl. 1707?–44? Since the name is an Ottawa word for medicine man, it is impossible to be certain that all references in documents are to the same individual.

Saguima, an Ottawa chief from Michilimackinac regarded by the French as a loyal ally, attended councils at Montreal and Quebec in 1707. He and Koutaoiliboe* reported to Governor Philippe de Rigaud* de Vaudreuil on events at Detroit and Michilimackinac, claiming much of the credit for the surrender of Le Pesant*, an Ottawa chief involved in the killing of two Frenchmen. At the same time Saguima apologized to Vaudreuil for not fulfilling a promise to bring slaves for the French to give the Iroquois.

By 1712 Saguima had moved to Detroit, and he became a key figure in the early stages of the Fox war, which troubled the west until 1737. Apparently provoked by the taunts of a group of Mascoutens who were hunting close to his village, Saguima planned their destruction. In April 1712 he and a Potawatomi chief named Makisabi headed a party of a hundred warriors who attacked the Mascoutens near the St Joseph River and after a three-day battle slaughtered 200 of the survivors. The remainder of the Mascouten band fled to Detroit.

As soon as the Foxes living at Detroit learned of the massacre of their Mascouten allies, they prepared to attack the French, whom they regarded as indirectly responsible. Then Saguima, Makisabi, and 600 warriors – Ottawas, Potawatomis, Illinois, Osages, Sauks, and Menominees – arrived at Detroit in pursuit of the fleeing Mascoutens. A deep-seated resentment towards the Foxes and Mascoutens by the other tribes probably explains why Saguima was able to mobilize so large a force so quickly and why he was joined shortly by Mississaugas, Ojibwas, and Hurons.

The Detroit garrison under Jacques-Charles Renaud* Dubuisson allied itself with Saguima's coalition and attacked the fortified Fox village, blockading it for 19 days. Before the attack Saguima's wife and two other women from his village had been taken prisoner by the Foxes, and by a ruse the allies secured their release. Many Foxes and Mascoutens died from hunger, thirst, and disease, and terms of surrender were offered several times by the Fox chief Pemoussa* but were rejected by the allies. Finally under cover of darkness the besieged Indians escaped from their fort, but they were pursued, surrounded, and slaughtered. Dubuisson estimated their losses at a thousand men, women, and children.

After the battle Saguima abandoned his village and returned to Michilimackinac. Joseph-Jacques Marest*, the Jesuit missionary there, welcomed Saguima's presence, believing that the Foxes and Mascoutens feared him and would be deterred from attacking the settlement.

In Marest's opinion Saguima had more influence over the Ottawas than anyone else, but his power, like that of most Algonkian chiefs, was not great. When, for example, he requested in the summer of 1712 that the French send him one or two red blankets and a *justaucorps*, he specified that the gifts should not be delivered by any of his own people. They would steal them.

In 1744 there are documentary references to a "Saquin," who was much respected by the Indians, but it seems unlikely that this was the same person.

Donald B. Smith

AN, Col., C¹¹A, 33, ff.71–76, 85–90, 160–78; 35, f.222; 81, ff.38–42. "Cadillac papers," *Michigan Pioneer Coll.*, XXXIII (1903), 320, 335, 347, 350, 354, 362, 365–67, 384–86, 537–57. Charlevoix, *Histoire de la N.-F.* (1744), IV, 95–102. "Correspondance de Vaudreuil," APQ *Rapport, 1947–48*, 162–66. *French regime in Wis., 1634–1727* (Thwaites), 267–82, 288–90. Y. F. Zoltvany, "New France and the west, 1701–1713," *CHR*, XLVI (1965), 301–22.

SAINT-ANGE, LOUIS CHARLY. *See* Charly

SAINT-ARSÈNE, MARIE-MARGUERITE-DANIEL ARNAUD, *dite. See* Arnaud

SAINT-BENOÎT, MARIE-ANNE DAVIS, *dite* **DE.** *See* Davis

SAINT-CASTIN, JOSEPH D'ABBADIE DE SAINT-CASTIN, Baron de. *See* Abbadie

SAINT-CLAUDE DE LA CROIX, MARIE-CHARLOTTE DE RAMEZAY, *dite* **DE.** *See* Ramezay.

SAINT-DENIS, LOUIS JUCHEREAU DE. *See* Juchereau

SAINTE-CLAIRE, LOUIS LEPAGE DE. *See* Lepage

SAINTE-HÉLÈNE, CHARLOTTE DANEAU DE MUY, *dite* **DE.** *See* Daneau

SAINTE-HÉLÈNE, MARIE-ANDRÉE REGNARD DUPLESSIS, *dite* **DE.** *See* Regnard

SAINTE-MADELEINE, LYDIA LONGLEY, *dite. See* Longley

SAINT-ESPRIT, MARGUERITE LE MOYNE DE SAINTE-MARIE, *dite* **DU.** *See* Le Moyne

SAINT-FERRÉOL, JEAN LYON DE. *See* Lyon

SAINT-FRANÇOIS, ÉTIENNE HERTEL DE. *See* Hertel

SAINT-GERMAIN, FRANÇOIS MANGEANT, *dit. See* Mangeant

SAINT-JACQUES, JACQUES-JOSEPH CHEVAL, *dit. See* Cheval

SAINT-JEAN-BAPTISTE, MARIE-THÉRÈSE LANGLOIS, *dite* **DE.** *See* Langlois

SAINT-JOACHIM, MARIE-CATHERINE TIBIERGE, *dite* **DE.** *See* Tibierge

SAINT-JOSEPH, ANNE-FRANÇOISE LEDUC, *dite. See* Leduc

SAINT-JOSEPH, MARGUERITE TROTTIER, *dite. See* Trottier

SAINT-JULHIEN (Saint-Julien), JEAN MASCLE DE. *See* Mascle

SAINT-MARTIN, JEAN-BAPTISTE BAUDRY, *dit. See* Baudry

SAINT-OURS, FRANÇOIS-XAVIER DE, officer in the colonial regular troops; b. 12 Dec. 1717 at Montreal, fourth child of Pierre de Saint-Ours the younger and Hélène Céloron de Blainville; m. 1 May 1747 at Montreal to Thérèse Hertel de Cournoyer, by whom he had at least three surviving children; d. of wounds on the Plains of Abraham, 13 Sept. 1759.

François-Xavier de Saint-Ours came of a military family of some distinction; both his grandfather, Pierre de Saint-Ours*, and his father received the cross of the order of Saint-Louis as officers in the colonial regular troops. His father

Saint-Ours Deschaillons

ended his career as king's lieutenant at Trois-Rivières; his uncle, Jean-Baptiste de SAINT-OURS Deschaillons, as king's lieutenant at Quebec. His brothers and cousins appear to have chosen military careers as well.

His own career, outlined in a memoir to Rouillé, minister of Marine, in 1750, reads as follows: cadet in 1732, second ensign in 1742, and ensign in 1748. He served in the west in 1732, on the New York frontier under Paul MARIN de La Malgue in 1745, in Acadia under Jean-Baptiste-Nicolas-Roch de Ramezay* in 1746, and in upper New York under François-Pierre de Rigaud* de Vaudreuil in 1747. He had therefore seen considerable active service by the end of the War of the Austrian Succession in 1748. In 1749 and again in 1750 he was sent to the Ohio country and Detroit at the head of detachments of 50 to 100 men. In 1751 he received his lieutenancy and appears to have spent the following years in the west, returning to the colony during the winter months. His career, until 1757 at least, seems like that of many others: slow promotion and service in various outposts of France's American empire.

According to his widow, Saint-Ours fought in 17 campaigns, distinguishing himself particularly at Lac Saint-Sacrement (Lake George, N.Y.) in the summer of 1757 while serving under Lévis*. In March 1757 Saint-Ours had commanded one of the columns of Pierre de Rigaud* de Vaudreuil's raid on Fort William Henry (Fort George; now Lake George). The action which brought him to the attention of his superiors, however, took place below Fort Carillon (Ticonderoga, N.Y.) in September 1757 when, with only ten to 12 men, he repulsed 120 British troops three times before retiring in good order. Both Governor Vaudreuil and Captain Jean-Daniel Dumas* praised this action highly, noting that Saint-Ours had been slightly wounded and recommending a pension and promotion to a captaincy. Both were granted 1 Jan. 1759.

It was traditionally held that Saint-Ours commanded the right wing of the French army on the Plains of Abraham. Vaudreuil, though, assigns that role to Dumas. More probably Saint-Ours had tactical command of the militia under Dumas. There is no question, however, but that he was killed on the battlefield.

His widow, with their children, departed for France in 1760, taking up residence at Blois, where she died in 1785. Two sons, recommended by Lévis, received commissions in the colonial troops in recognition of their father's services to the crown.

The product of a military family, François-Xavier de Saint-Ours became, practically as a matter of course, an officer in the colonial regular troops. The responsibility given him in 1759, however, indicates more than normal competence as a soldier.

J.R. TURNBULL

[The occasional reference to Saint-Ours can be found in AN, Col., C¹¹ᴬ, and in the *Journal du marquis de Montcalm* (Casgrain). The most interesting and informative material is to be found, however, in his personal dossier in AN, Col., E, 363, where his own summary of his service up to 1750, his official record of service, and his widow's letters requesting pensions, etc., give a clearer picture of the man. Saint-Ours' birth and marriage certficates can be found in ANQ-M, Registre d'état civil, Notre-Dame de Montréal, 12 déc. 1717, 1ᵉʳ mai 1747. Both Le Jeune, *Dictionnaire,* and Tanguay, *Dictionnaire,* mention him, the latter assigning him nine children. His widow, however, mentions only three; and the others listed in Tanguay, if in fact they were Saint-Ours' children, would have been still young in 1760. J.R.T.]

SAINT-OURS DESCHAILLONS, JEAN-BAPTISTE DE, officer in the colonial regular troops, king's lieutenant; b. 1669 in the Saint-Ours manor-house and baptized in Sorel (Que.) in October 1670, son of Pierre de Saint-Ours* and Marie Mullois; d. 8 June 1747 in Quebec.

Jean-Baptiste de Saint-Ours Deschaillons's father was a prominent noble and military figure in the colony, but like many of the nobility in Canada was not prosperous. In the status-oriented society of Canada, solvency was not as important as the maintaining of appearances, and in this respect, as in others, Deschaillons would be like his father.

Deschaillons began his military service in 1688, and two years later received a commission as ensign with an annual salary of 360 *livres*. Aided by a steady flow of requests and recommendations from his father, and from his father's cousin, he was promoted half-pay lieutenant in 1693, full lieutenant in 1702, and captain on 9 June 1708. However, these promotions were not unmerited. In 1695, Governor Frontenac [Buade*] sent Deschaillons, then 25 years old, and 15 Indians in the direction of Albany to scout for Iroquois and white traders and to take prisoners if possible. Deschaillons's mission was successful, for when he returned he brought four captives, three Mohawks and a Dutchman.

In June 1703 Deschaillons was commissioned midshipman, a title which carried social status but did not entail any naval responsibilities. Two years later, on 25 November, Deschaillons and his 19-year-old *fiancée*, Marguerite, daughter of

Pierre Legardeur* de Repentigny and Agathe de SAINT-PÈRE, signed a marriage contract. The wedding, well attended by his fellow officers, took place later that day. Deschaillons was now linked to one of the oldest noble families in the colony.

In 1708, after a council of war with the Mission Indians in Montreal, another raiding expedition was sent against New England. Deschaillons and Jean-Baptiste Hertel* de Rouville, entrusted with the command of this expedition, left Montreal on 26 July with a party of 100 soldiers and habitants, and a number of Indians. The party sacked Haverhill on the Merrimack River and returned to Montreal with a loss of 10 dead and 19 wounded.

The following year Montrealers were alerted that their town would be attacked by Colonel Francis Nicholson* and his army, invading the colony *via* Lake Champlain. Deschaillons was put in command of one of the five companies of Canadians led by Montreal Governor Claude de Ramezay* to head off the invasion. The Canadians left Montreal on 28 July but returned shortly thereafter because Nicholson's army had, among other mishaps, fallen prey to a contagious disease and turned back.

In the autumn of 1717, Deschaillons set out for the Ottawa country (the Michigan peninsula), leaving his wife in charge of his business affairs in the colony. From 1721 to 1723, Deschaillons commanded at Fort Kaministiquia (Thunder Bay, Ont.); Jacques Le Ber de Senneville, in Montreal, hired voyageurs on his behalf to take merchandise to the hinterland and to return with furs. Deschaillons's fur-trading interests continued in the 1720s through his association with a merchant, perhaps Jean-Louis Volant d'Haudebourg. In 1728 he was appointed commandant of Detroit where he served for two years.

Deschaillons was awarded in 1730 the cross of the order of Saint-Louis, which carried a minimum pension of 800 *livres*. He applied for the vacant king's lieutenancy of Trois-Rivières, but the position was awarded to Claude-Michel BÉGON, whom Deschaillons replaced in February 1731 as town major of Quebec. His interest now turned from the fur trade to real estate. He already received 400 *livres* per year from his inheritance of half of the Saint-Ours seigneury. On 20 Aug. 1732 he bought a small house in Montreal on a piece of land 22 feet by 30 feet, which he subsequently leased. After two years as major of Quebec he replaced François Le Verrier* de Rousson as king's lieutenant, with a salary of 1,800 *livres*. However, his sources of income were drastically reduced by the Montreal

fire of 1734, in which two houses producing an annual revenue of 800 to 1,000 *livres* were burned. Deschaillons was obliged to call in an outstanding loan of 1,000 *livres*, owed to him by his relative, Pierre Legardeur de Repentigny. Both Governor Charles de BEAUHARNOIS and Intendant Gilles Hocquart* requested a pension for Deschaillons from the order of Saint-Louis or the *Invalides* funds in recognition of his services. Accordingly, in 1735, 1737, 1738, 1739, and 1743, Deschaillons received bonuses of 400 *livres*. In 1742, when Governor Pierre de Rigaud* de Vaudreuil of Trois-Rivières was appointed governor of Louisiana, Deschaillons applied for the Trois-Rivières post. This promotion was refused him.

On 14 March 1741 an ordinance of Intendant Hocquart had obliged Deschaillons to inhabit and develop the *arrière-fief* of Saint-Ours Deschaillons on Île Jésus which had been granted to him in 1719 by the seminary of Quebec. He disregarded the ordinance, and on 2 August of the following year the land reverted to the seminary.

During his long service to the king, Deschaillons was promoted from cadet to king's lieutenant of Quebec, held two post commands, and was awarded the cross of Saint-Louis. His investments in the fur trade and in real estate, combined with his military income and assistance from the state, enabled him to live in the style of a noble. He had nine children – five daughters and four sons; two of his sons, one being Pierre-Roch*, pursued careers in the colonial regular troops.

C. J. RUSS

AN, Col., C¹¹A, 11–14, 18–19, 22, 30, 79; D²C, 47; E, 120 (dossier Saint-Ours Deschaillons). ANQ-M, Greffe d'Antoine Adhémar, 25 nov. 1705; Greffe de Jacques David, 15 mai 1722; Greffe de C.-R. Gaudron de Chevremont, 7 avril 1735; Greffe de J.-C. Raimbault, 20 août 1732. Fauteux, *Les chevaliers de Saint-Louis*, 126. P.-G. Roy, *Inv. concessions*, I, 140–41; II, 172; *Les officiers d'état-major*, 231–35. Tanguay, *Dictionnaire*. Kellogg, *French régime*, 298, 326. Nish, *Les bourgeois-gentilshommes*, 92, 150. C. J. Russ, "Les troupes de la marine, 1683–1713" (unpublished MA thesis, McGill University, Montreal, 1971).

SAINT-OVIDE, JOSEPH DE MONBETON DE BROUILLAN, *dit. See* MONBETON

SAINT-PAUL, PAUL LAMBERT, *dit. See* LAMBERT

SAINT-PÉ, JEAN-BAPTISTE DE, priest, Jesuit, missionary, superior of the Jesuit missions in New France; b. 10 Oct. 1686 in Pau, France; d. 8 July 1770 in Quebec.

Jean-Baptiste de Saint-Pé was admitted into

Saint-Père

the noviciate of the Jesuits of the province of Aquitaine in Bordeaux on 13 Oct. 1703. When his noviciate was ended, he did two years of philosophy at Limoges (1705–7), after which he taught grammar for a year at La Rochelle. During the academic year of 1708–9 he returned to his studies at Poitiers, and taught grammar and humanities at Périgueux from 1709 to 1712 and rhetoric at Agen until 1714. He then embarked upon his four years of theology at Bordeaux and completed his final year of religious training at Marennes.

Father Saint-Pé sailed for Canada, where he is found in 1720. Immediately on his arrival his superior, Pierre de LA CHASSE, sent him to the mission to the Ottawas. Did he, at the beginning, stay at Michilimackinac? It is possible, for he took his final vows there, between the hands of Father Joseph-Jacques Marest* on 2 Feb. 1721. The following October he was at the Saint-Joseph mission (probably Niles, Mich.), and on 23 Aug. 1724 he took part in a council held at Baie-des-Puants (Green Bay, Wis.) with a view to restoring peace between the Foxes and the tribes allied to the French. It was he who was designated to accompany Pierre GAULTIER de Varennes et de La Vérendrye in his explorations into the west, but he was replaced by Charles-Michel MÉSAIGER. On 10 Oct. 1733 he was at Michilimackinac, where he certified a statement of accounts by Nicolas Rose, and in September of the following year he again visited the Saint-Joseph mission, without our knowing just where he usually lived. In 1737 he was back at Quebec. In the summer of 1739 he served the Montagnais missions at Tadoussac and La Malbaie; on 21 September he succeeded Pierre de LAUZON as superior of the Jesuit missions in New France, assuming thereby the office of rector of the Jesuit college in Quebec.

During his superiorship the most disagreeable matter that he had to deal with was probably the accusation of complicity in the contraband trade with the English colonies which was brought against the Jesuit missionaries at Sault-Saint-Louis (Caughnawaga) [see Pierre de Lauzon] and maintained by the intendant, Hocquart*. In the autumn of 1742 Saint-Pé sailed for France, leaving Father Mésaiger to look after the college and the mission. The following year he returned on the *Rubis*, which took 96 days to make the crossing.

In October 1748 Saint-Pé was replaced as superior by Gabriel MARCOL, and shortly afterwards became superior of the residence in Montreal, where the Jesuits, who had already in 1727 and 1731 hoped to open a college there,

maintained a church and offered hospitality to their missionaries who passed through. His stay in Montreal lasted until October 1754; then he returned to Quebec, having again been appointed superior of the missions. In addition to his administrative work he carried out the functions of extraordinary confessor to the Hôtel-Dieu of Quebec.

On 30 March 1759 Saint-Pé, along with the procurator, Father Augustin-Louis de Glapion*, signed the official papers appointing Mathieu Hianveu notary for the seigneuries of Notre-Dame-des-Anges, Saint-Gabriel, Sillery, and Bélair. This was probably the Jesuits' last seigneurial act under French rule. A short time later the superior followed the example of Bishop Pontbriand [DUBREIL] and took refuge at Montreal, to remain in touch with the missions. He was already 73 years old, and the superiorship was a heavy burden for him. But it was difficult to replace him, because of the English government's determination to expel the Jesuits from the former French colony. In 1762, through Alain de Launay, procurator in Paris of the Jesuit missions in New France, Saint-Pé requested the general of the society, Lorenzo Ricci, to appoint a new superior; the following year he was replaced by Father Glapion. Jean-Baptiste de Saint-Pé remained in Quebec, where he died on 8 July 1770 at nearly 84 years of age.

LUCIEN CAMPEAU

ASJCF, 525, 575, 586, 653, 705; Fonds Rochemonteix, 4018, pp.66, 223, 268, 275, 461; 4021, p.18. Rochemonteix, *Les Jésuites et la N.-F. au XVIIIe siècle*, II, 181.

SAINT-PÈRE, AGATHE DE (Legardeur de Repentigny), manufacturer; b. 25 Feb. 1657 in Montreal, daughter of Jean de Saint-Père*, a notary, and Mathurine Godé; d. in 1747 or 1748 in Quebec.

Agathe de Saint-Père belonged to a family of renowned colonists of Ville-Marie. Her father, her grandfather Nicolas Godé, and her godfather Raphaël-Lambert Closse*, were killed by the Iroquois. In 1658 her mother, some months after she had been widowed, married the merchant Jacques Le Moyne de Sainte-Marie; Agathe de Saint-Père thus entered a family whose name was made famous by the exploits of Charles Le Moyne* de Longueuil et de Châteauguay, brother of Jacques, and his sons.

Agathe de Saint-Père probably attended Marguerite Bourgeoys*'s school, as her Le Moyne half-sisters did. In 1672, after her mother's death,

Agathe, who was barely 15, took over the raising of the ten Le Moyne children, the youngest of whom was a new-born baby. She seems to have brought these children up firmly and to have retained responsibility for them even after her marriage, on 28 Nov. 1685, with the ensign Pierre Legardeur* de Repentigny. A son and seven daughters were to be born of her marriage.

Legardeur's easy-going nature allowed the dynamic Agathe de Saint-Père to outshine her husband frequently. She signed contracts, made profits on fur-trading licences, bought and sold land, made loans, and settled her accounts as well as the debts of her husband and her brothers-in-law. In 1701 she opposed the marriage of her half-brother, Nicolas Le Moyne de Leau, with a commoner. Together with Catherine Le Moyne de Sainte-Marie, her half-sister, she successfully took legal action to prevent the marriage. Nicolas left the colony for the Mississippi country, never to return; he had given Agathe power of attorney.

At the beginning of the 18th century the economic situation forced the colony periodically to manage on its own resources; such an economy was, indeed, a return to the ideas Intendant Jean Talon* had advanced during his two periods of service in New France. To make up for the shortage of linen and wool, Mme de Repentigny experimented widely, especially with nettles and bark fibres, cottonweed, and the woolly hair of the buffalo. The king considered that her samples of cloth were successes and enjoyed the maple-sugar candy of her own making that she sent him. In 1705, when news arrived of the shipwreck of the *Seine*, which was bringing supplies for a whole year, the daring woman set up in her house "a factory to make linen, drugget, twilled and covert-coating serge." She ransomed nine English weavers who were prisoners of the Indians, hired them, and assigned Canadian apprentices to assist them. She put at their disposal and distributed about Montreal looms that she had had made from the sole model to be found on the island. Several inhabitants of the island learned the techniques and soon there were more than 20 looms, which turned out daily 120 ells of coarse cloth and canvas both hard-wearing and cheap.

Continuing her experiments, the indefatigable and hard-working Mme de Repentigny discovered, with the help of a blue stone and native tinctorial plants, a number of dyes and new processes for fixing colours. She even succeeded in dyeing deerskins without treating them with oil. In 1707, when the inhabitants of Boston ransomed the nine English weavers, Mme de Repentigny's workshop could continue on its own.

Until 1713, or as long as she was the owner, it kept up its rate of production. In 1712 the king was still granting her an annual gratuity of 200 *livres* in recognition of her services. Having come out of the clothing crisis triumphantly, and having completely achieved her aim, Mme de Repentigny decided to hand over her industry on 9 Oct. 1713 to Pierre Thuot Duval, a master baker.

A few years earlier she had paid the ransom for young Warham Williams, who was four years of age and whom the Indians had brought to Canada as a captive in 1704 after the expedition against Deerfield, Massachusetts. Later she refused to exchange this child for an English weaver who was offered her and whom she needed badly.

We lose sight of this exceptional woman for some time after 1713. After her husband's death in Montreal in 1736, she chose to finish her days at the Hôpital Général of Quebec. She rejoined her daughter, Marie-Joseph de la Visitation, who was to be superior there for nine years, and she was also living nearer to another daughter, Marie-Jeanne-Madeleine de Sainte-Agathe*, who had been a nun in the Ursuline convent since 1717.

In the will she signed on 6 Feb. 1746 she indicated that she wanted to be buried at the Hôpital Général. Although her death certificate has not yet been found, it is likely that she passed away in her 91st year: in 1748, the annalist of the institution inscribed under the heading of receipts at the end of the year the sum of 400 *livres*, the "first legacy from Madame de Repentigny."

MADELEINE DOYON-FERLAND

AHGQ, "Annales." AN, Col., B, 34, ff.92v, 193; C¹¹ᴬ, 22, f.188; 23, f.35 (copies at ANQ). ANQ, Greffe de C.-H. Du Laurent, 7 févr. 1746. ANQ-M, Greffe d'Hilaire Bourgine, 24 juill. 1685; Registre d'état civil, Notre-Dame de Montréal, 25 févr. 1657. Tanguay, *Dictionnaire*. J.-N. Fauteux, *Essai sur l'industrie*, II, 465–69. Lemire-Marsolais et Lambert, *Histoire de la Congrégation de Notre-Dame*, II, 131, 134; IV, 420. Marine Leland, "Madame de Repentigny," *BRH*, LX (1954), 75–79. É.-Z. Massicotte, "Agathe de Saint-Père, Dame Legardeur de Repentigny," *BRH*, L (1944), 202–7.

SAINT-PIERRE, GENEVIÈVE BOUCHER, *dite* **DE.** *See* BOUCHER

SAINT-PIERRE, JACQUES LEGARDEUR DE. *See* LEGARDEUR

SAINT-SACREMENT, MARIE-MADELEINE DE LA CORNE DE CHAPTES, *dite* **DU.** *See* LA CORNE

Saint-Simon

SAINT-SIMON, CHARLES-PAUL DENYS DE. *See* DENYS

SAINT-SIMON, MARIE-ANGÉLIQUE LE-FEBVRE ANGERS, *dite. See* LEFEBVRE

SAKIMA. *See* SAGUIMA

SALLABERRY (Salaberry), MICHEL DE, naval officer, shipowner; b. 4 July 1704 in the parish of Saint-Vincent, Ciboure (dept. of Pyrénées-Atlantiques), France, son of Marsans de Sallaberry and Marie de Michelance; d. 27 Nov. 1768 at Salles near La Rochelle, France.

Michel de Sallaberry was descended from a branch of the noble house of Irumberry in French Navarre. The details of his early life remain unknown, but he may have accompanied his father to Quebec in 1733. Two years later Sallaberry was identified as a ship's captain and had established a residence at Quebec. In 1736 he launched his own ship, the *Saint-Michel*, a 68-ton brigantine, and began to carry cargoes to Île Royale (Cape Breton Island). Soon he was sailing larger ships to Martinique, Saint-Domingue (Hispaniola), La Rochelle, and Bordeaux. In 1741 he launched a second, larger ship. Until the outbreak of war with England, Sallaberry was an active member of New France's commercial maritime community, voyaging to all parts of the French American empire.

In 1745 he was to have sailed a large merchantman from La Rochelle to Quebec but owing to the War of the Austrian Succession the ship's owners cancelled the voyage. In mid-November, after a naval frigate commanded by Jean-Baptiste LEGARDEUR de Tilly had failed to reach Quebec, Sallaberry offered to outfit and command the small schooner *Marie* to carry dispatches and munitions to New France. Sallaberry encountered severe storms during the crossing and early in January, after reaching the French island of Saint-Pierre off the south coast of Newfoundland with his ship badly damaged, he saw no alternative but to make for the West Indies for the winter. In the spring, at Martinique, Sallaberry refitted his ship and left for New France escorted by a French privateer. He reached Quebec on 6 June 1746. During the summer he patrolled the mouth of the St Lawrence River off Cap Chat watching for an English invasion fleet that was rumoured to be heading for Quebec. Towards the end of the year along with several other ship's captains he was to have transported military supplies to Baie-Verte in Acadia, but he ran aground only 15 leagues from Quebec.

On 20 May 1748, Sallaberry was commissioned flute captain for his services and abandoned maritime trade in favour of a career in the navy. In 1750 he was serving in the frigate *Anglesea* when it called at Quebec. Two years later he obtained command of the armed transport *Chariot Royal* on a voyage to Louisbourg, Île Royale. In November 1755 this ship was captured by the English and he was taken to London. As France and England were still technically at peace he was soon released and returned to France. On 20 Nov. 1757, he was promoted to the regular naval rank of lieutenant-commander and given command of the frigate *Fidèle*. The following summer he cruised off Louisbourg and during the siege his ship was sunk in the mouth of the harbour. After the Seven Years' War, Sallaberry retired to Salles near La Rochelle where he lived with his daughter Angélique. In 1766, only two years before his death, he was made a knight of the order of Saint-Louis and a year later was awarded a pension of 1,000 *livres*.

On 17 May 1735 Sallaberry had married Marie-Catherine Rouer de Villeray, a widow with several children. She died five years later leaving him with only a daughter. A decade later, 30 July 1750, he remarried, at Quebec, Madeleine-Louise Juchereau Duchesnay de Saint-Denis. The one son from this marriage inherited land from his mother and remained in Canada to become founder of the family of Irumberry de Sallaberry. Michel de Sallaberry did not own land in New France. His marriages had provided his major ties with the colony. His marine and naval careers reveal him as a participant in the French empire rather than as a resident of New France.

JAMES S. PRITCHARD

[Both P.-G. Roy, *La famille d'Irumberry de Salaberry* (Lévis, Qué., 1905), and Le Jeune, *Dictionnaire*, II, 608–9, ignore Sallaberry's own signature in spelling his name and incorrectly identify his father as Martin. Michel de Sallaberry never used Irumberry; this name appears only later during his son's efforts to substantiate his noble status; on this subject *see*: Robert La Roque de Roquebrune, "Le voyage d'un Canadien à Paris en 1785," *Nova Francia*, I (1925–26), 15–19. References are sparse and widely scattered but may be found in AN, Col., B, 104, f.36v; C⁸ᴮ, 20; C¹¹ᴬ, 65, f.24; 67, ff.48–48v; 70, ff.125, 168–71; 73, f.412v; 74, f.197; 76, ff.124–24v; 78, f.314; 85, ff.34–34v; 86, ff.160–63, 342–44v; 88, f.106; 117, f.78; 121, f.157v; F²ᴮ, 11 (commerce des colonies), and in AD, Charente-Maritime (La Rochelle), B, 5728, no.1; E, 917 (état civil, Saint-Sauveur de La Rochelle); Gironde (Bordeaux), 6B, 97, 280. J.S.P.]

ANQ, Greffe de C.-H. Du Laurent, 30 juill. 1750; Greffe de J.-N. Pinguet de Vaucour, 13 mai 1735; AP, Famille Salaberry, 1641–1896. Archives paroissiales de

Saint-Vincent (Ciboure, dép. des Pyrénées-Atlantiques, France), Registres des baptêmes, mariages et sépultures, 4 juill. 1704. P.-G. Roy, *Inv. coll. pièces jud. et not.*, I, 105, 110, 141; *Inv. jug. et délib., 1717–1760*, III, IV, V.

SALUSBURY (Salisbury), JOHN, member of the Nova Scotia Council; b. 1 Sept. 1707 at Bach-y-Graig, North Wales, son of Thomas and Lucy Salusbury; d. 18 Dec. 1762 at Offley Place, Hertfordshire, England.

John Salusbury was descended from a prominent Welsh family. He was educated at Whitchurch School (probably in Wales) and Trinity Hall, Cambridge, where he obtained the MA degree in 1728. For several years after his graduation he seems to have led a carefree life in England. Some time before 1737 he returned to Wales and became a captain in the militia, probably through the influence of his cousin, Sir Robert Cotton. He married Sir Robert's sister, Hester, in 1739, and though she brought a small fortune to the marriage, Salusbury, through poor management of the family finances, was unable to keep himself out of debt. Finally, under the patronage of the Earl of Halifax, then head of the Board of Trade, he attempted to re-establish himself financially through a colonial venture. On 21 June 1749 Salusbury arrived at Chebucto (Halifax, N.S.) in the suite of Governor Edward Cornwallis* and was sworn in on 14 July as a member of the new council of Nova Scotia along with Paul MASCARENE, Edward HOW, John GORHAM, and others. As register and receiver of rents, at a salary of 20 shillings per day, he was responsible for parcelling out land in Halifax and its environs and supervising its allocation to settlers.

From the beginning of this venture, however, Salusbury had no interest in the eventual development of the settlement. Since he had come to Nova Scotia for personal reasons he began to look forward to returning to England from the time of his arrival. Having been raised in a comfortable and sophisticated social group and lacking the qualities of the pioneer he quickly became bored and unhappy with the style of life in the colony. He was further distressed by the prospect of a long separation from his wife and his daughter Hester (later Mrs Thrale, the friend and correspondent of Samuel Johnson), whom he desperately wanted to see again. He was constantly apprehensive about the Indians and French who threatened the settlement in its first year. On 5 April 1750 he joined an expedition under Charles LAWRENCE to Chignecto in search of French troops. He finally became so discontented, however, that he urged his wife and

friends in England to seek his recall by Lord Halifax. Expecting it to come at any time he refused to go on the second Chignecto expedition in August. But no news came.

To add to his despair Salusbury had become jealous of his position in the settlement, for changes had been made in the nature of his work which had reduced his status. Some of his associates he openly distrusted; he quarrelled with others – especially the secretary, Hugh Davidson, whom he accused of using his office for personal gain. His entreaties to Governor Cornwallis were rewarded on 6 May 1751 when he was told he would be carrying the first dispatches of the year to England. His departure was deferred several times, however, until he was permitted to sail on 10 August.

In England Salusbury found his personal affairs unchanged. So with the encouragement of Lord Halifax he again set sail for Nova Scotia, arriving on 26 July 1752. This time there was a new governor, Peregrine Thomas HOPSON, whom Salusbury hated and described in his journal as a "poor big man [who] hath only the appearance of what he ought to be." Salusbury noted the increasing influence in the colony of the merchants, led by Joshua Mauger*, "a proud, troublesome, sorry rascal," who "cares not what becomes of [the colony]." He also mentioned the open attacks by the merchants on the partiality of the justices, especially Charles Morris*, and warned that "the business of government can never go on if [the merchants] are always to be humoured."

The functions of the register's office were transferred to the secretary. In April 1753 Salusbury reported that he was "out of the Cabinet" and that the authorities were attempting to force him out of his appointment. In the summer of 1753 he was finally permitted to return to England, his personal affairs unimproved by his years abroad. Only by grants from his brother Thomas were his latter years made secure.

RONALD ROMPKEY

Corpus Christi Church (Bach-y-Graig, North Wales), Records. John Rylands Library (Manchester, Eng.), Eng. MSS, 530–32, 615. PANS, RG 3, Minutes of Nova Scotia Council, 1749–53. *Gentleman's Magazine*, 1762, p.601. [H. L. Thrale], *Thraliana: the diary of Mrs Hester Lynch Thrale (later Mrs Piozzi), 1776–1809*, ed. K. C. Balderston (2nd ed., 2v., Oxford, Eng., 1951). *Alumni Cantabrigienses: a biographical list of all known students, graduates, and holders of office at the University of Cambridge, from the earliest times to 1900*, comp. John and J. A. Venn (2pt., 10v., Cambridge, Eng., 1922–54), pt. I, IV, 7. J. L. Clifford, *Hes-*

Saquima

ter Lynch Piozzi (Mrs Thrale) (Oxford, Eng., 1941). J. G. Adshead, "Hon. John Salusbury, 1707–62," N.S. Hist. Soc. *Coll.*, XXIX (1951), 1–21. T. B. Akins, "The first council," N.S. Hist. Soc. *Coll.*, II (1881), 17–30.

SAQUIMA (Saquin). *See* SAGUIMA

SAUGUAARAM (Laron, Loring, Loron, Sagouarrab, Sagouarrat, Saguaarum, Seguaron), Penobscot Abenaki sachem, warrior, orator; fl. 1724–51 in the vicinity of the Penobscot River, Massachusetts (now Maine).

Sauguaaram first appears in historical records during Dummer's War (1722–27) between the Abenakis and Massachusetts. After the deaths of Mog* and Father Sébastien Rale* at Norridgewock (Narantsouak; now Old Point, Madison, Me.) in 1724 and the second destruction of their own village early in 1725, the Penobscots considered the war lost and accepted Massachusetts' invitation to negotiate a treaty. Although Wenemouet* was Sauguaaram's superior in rank, it was Sauguaaram who spoke for the tribe at the conferences in July and August 1725, November and December 1725, and again in July and August 1726.

The Penobscots' moves for peace were a radical break with the policy of the French and the Canadian Abenakis. To maintain the traditional alliance, Sauguaaram travelled to Canada between conferences, trying unsuccessfully to persuade them to agree to a peace. In the negotiations with the English, Sauguaaram achieved an implicit acceptance by Massachusetts of the presence of Jesuit missionaries among his tribe and by helping improve trade relations between the Penobscots and the English he laid the cornerstone for the subsequent peace. Despite his pleading, however, Massachusetts refused to admit that her settlements had caused the war, nor would she agree to limit them. She also insisted that the ratifying tribes aid her in suppressing future Indian uprisings, and this article became a strong irritant throughout the remaining colonial wars. War weariness, not generous concessions, led Sauguaaram and the Penobscots to accept a tentative agreement.

Sauguaaram repudiated the agreement in January 1726 [N.S.], after Étienne LAUVERJAT, the missionary at Pannawambskek (Panaouamské; Indian Island, Old Town, Me.), interpreted the document to him. He had not intended, the sachem said, to acknowledge the British king or to agree to force the other tribes to submit. Whether there had been a genuine mis-understanding, or whether Sauguaaram's move was a tactic of negotiation, Massachusetts was unwilling to make further concessions. So Sauguaaram acquiesced, and the Penobscots accepted the treaty on 5 Aug. 1726.

Sauguaaram learned a valuable lesson from the treaty negotiations: Massachusetts would not compromise her claims, and the French were hostile to conferences in any case. His solution was to maintain good relations with both colonies. Pleased by his cooperation, Lieutenant Governor William Dummer of Massachusetts called him a "particular Friend" and sent him a gun marked with his totem. Sauguaaram was unusually favoured by the truck master at Fort St George (now Thomaston, Me.) in return for information.

When the treaty that Massachusetts had negotiated with the Penobscots was ratified by all the Abenaki tribes in July 1727, Sauguaaram signed it. He wrote to Governor Charles de BEAUHARNOIS, however, reaffirming his original interpretation of the document. "If, then, anyone should produce any writing that makes me speak otherwise, pay no attention to it," he explained, "for I know not what I am made to say in another language. . . ."

Although eager to keep on good terms with both colonies, Sauguaaram remembered the Penobscots' interests. When Father René-Charles de Breslay* was mistreated in Nova Scotia, Sauguaaram angrily reminded the Massachusetts governor that "as to our Religion, Wee were not to Interrup't one the other in the Injoyment of itt." On the same grounds he refused an offer of Protestant missionaries in 1732, and led his tribe's opposition to English settlements in the Penobscot River region. The dispute over the settlements drove the Penobscots into closer ties with the French, and several sachems surrendered their English commissions to Governor Beauharnois. Sauguaaram himself had never accepted one of these tokens of English favour, and he complained in fact to the Massachusetts governor that they made the Indians "exceeding proud, & they breed mutinies & wont come to Prayers, but do nothing but get drunk."

The Penobscots were still determined to preserve good relations with both English and French, and in accordance with the treaty Sauguaaram spent the summer of 1740 calming the Abenakis of Saint-François, who were angered by Massachusetts' expansion. On his return he exasperated Governor Jonathan Belcher by cautioning Massachusetts to avoid irritating the other Abenaki tribes. "It looks as if you were ready," Belcher told him, "to take up the Hatchet and were directed in it by the French. . . ." "We are a free People," Sauguaaram replied.

Sauguaaram always led the attempt to achieve better trading conditions. He complained to the Massachusetts governor about prices and about the acting truck master at Fort St George. He also frequently asked that the rum trade be more closely regulated because "it interrupts our Prayers & does us Mischeif. . . ."

By the fall of 1744 the Indians of Nova Scotia and the Saint John River had begun open warfare against the English. Governor William Shirley of Massachusetts had hoped to prevent the Abenakis from joining the French, but some of the Penobscots, provoked in part by his demand that they join in suppressing the outbreak, attacked Fort St George in June 1745. Sauguaaram attempted to soothe the English in October, when he and three other Indians brought word that "the Jesuits have told them [the Indians] not to hurt ye English any more. . . ." That night Sauguaaram and his companions were attacked by a scouting party, and only Sauguaaram escaped. He and the remaining Penobscots fled to Canada, where he told Beauharnois that 25 warriors had set out to take revenge on Massachusetts. The Penobscots remained in Canada, sending forays into New England, for the rest of the war. One of Sauguaaram's sons was killed in the conflict, and the sachem was reluctant to make peace. Although he foresaw that "when there is a *French* war we must break again," the Penobscots finally ended their part in King George's War with a treaty signed at Falmouth (Portland, Me.) in October 1749.

The treaty failed almost immediately when a Norridgewock Indian was killed at Wiscasset, Massachusetts (now Maine), in December 1749. You promised us justice, Sauguaaram reminded the lieutenant governor, "so we expect you will realy do it." By June 1750, however, one of the accused Englishmen had been acquitted and the trial of the other two had been postponed. Although the French encouraged the Abenakis to take revenge, Sauguaaram and the Penobscots assured Massachusetts that they desired peace. The final reference to Sauguaaram in Massachusetts documents reveals that in September 1751 he was still working for peace, but all his efforts and those of the Norridgewock sachem NODOGAWERRIMET failed to prevent continued English intrusion into Indian lands.

Sauguaaram's life reflects all the major issues between the Abenakis and Massachusetts. Under his leadership the Penobscots protected their religion, agitated for better trading conditions, opposed new settlements, and balanced their affairs between the demands of New France and New England.

KENNETH M. MORRISON

Mass., Archives, Council records, VIII, IX, XI, XII. Benjamin Coleman, "Some memoirs for the continuation of the history of the troubles of the New-English colonies . . . ," *Mass. Hist. Soc. Coll.*, 1st ser., VI (1799), 108–18. *Coll. de manuscrits relatifs à la N.-F.*, III, 128, 134–36, 140–41, 149–50, 153, 188–90, 263–65. *Correspondence of William Shirley* (Lincoln), I, 253–54, 261. *Documentary history of Maine*, X, XII, XXIII, XXIV. "Indian treaties," Maine Hist. Soc. *Coll.*, 1st ser., III (1853), 377–405, 407–47; IV, 145–67. New Hampshire, *Provincial and state papers, published by the authority of the legislature of New Hampshire*, ed. I. W. Hammond et al. (40v., Manchester, Concord, N.H., 1867–1943), IV. *NYCD* (O'Callaghan and Fernow). PRO, *CSP, Col., 1726–27*, 137, 144, 335, 539, 574; *1727–28*, 573–74; *1730*, 101, 348, 369; *1731*, 120. R. H. Lord et al., *History of the archdiocese of Boston in the various stages of its development, 1604 to 1943* . . . (3v., New York, 1944), II. H. O. Thayer, "The Indian's administration of justice: the sequel to the Wiscasset tragedy," and "A page of Indian history: the Wiscasset tragedy," Maine Hist. Soc. *Coll.*, 2nd ser., X (1899), 185–211, 81–103.

SAUL, THOMAS, supply agent, commissary at Halifax, Nova Scotia; fl. 1750–60.

Thomas Saul came to Nova Scotia in 1749 or 1750 as the agent of William Baker, an important London merchant and government contractor and a close political ally of the Duke of Newcastle. Baker and his cousin Samuel Baker held the contract for victualling the recently captured fortress of Louisbourg, Cape Breton Island. Upon the return of Cape Breton to France in July 1749 [see Peregrine Thomas HOPSON], all of the contractors' provisions were sent to the new English settlement at Halifax. Baker agreed to victual and pay all the troops in Nova Scotia other than Governor Edward Cornwallis*' own regiment, and the immediate supervision of the contract was the job of Thomas Saul.

As Baker's representative, with established channels for the supply of provisions and a ready fund of money, Saul soon became the most reliable source of food and cash in Halifax. In September 1751 Governor Cornwallis turned to him to provide coin to pay the labourers employed on public works. When, at the same time, another contractor who was to supply the settlers failed, it was Saul who provided 224,000 pounds of bread. Unfortunately, as his master's good and faithful servant, he used the urgent necessity of the colony as an occasion to strike a hard bargain and charge twice the market price for the bread.

Schuyler

The Board of Trade, however, forced Baker to adjust the price downward before payment was made. Such occasional sharp dealing did not seem to hurt Saul's position in Halifax. By July 1752 he was employing ten servants, and he soon enjoyed the confidence of the new governor, Peregrine Hopson. Saul supplied food and money to the colony on another occasion when other sources failed and he became the "Commissary of Stores and Provisions" for the province.

Hopson had been enjoined by the Board of Trade to check into the execution of Baker's contract, but apparently found no reason to make an adverse report. Another investigation, under Charles LAWRENCE in 1755, gave Saul a clean bill. This was no surprise, as relations between Saul and Lawrence were close. Lawrence was the major of Warburton's regiment (45th Foot), one of those for which Baker and Saul provided victuals and pay, and there is every reason to believe that, as was common among officers in the 18th century, he already had close financial connections with the regimental agents when he became president of the Nova Scotia Council. In March 1757 an anonymous correspondent wrote to Lord Loudoun [John Campbell], then commander-in-chief of British forces in North America, that Lawrence had diverted thousands of pounds of public money to his own use. He was accused of being "under obligations to Alderman Baker, or rather his Agent Thomas Saul, a villan consumate in iniquity." Saul was charged with giving the soldiers short provisions. Whatever the truth of these and other allegations, Saul could easily gain every possible advantage from his position; with his business and official connections he was virtually immune to effective control, save by those whose interests coincided with his.

The summer of 1757 brought large British forces to Halifax. Saul, who was now deputy paymaster, received £22,000 in coin for paying subsistence money to the troops. By the end of the year he still held over half this amount. Doubtless he followed the common practice and used this balance for private trading, for he was said to have been "the wealthiest and most enterprising merchant" in Halifax. Receiving many favours from above, Saul likely also dispensed them. He assisted Lawrence and perhaps also George Saul – presumably a kinsman – who was commissary for the removal of the Acadians and then went to New York to act as agent for the British contractors Baker and Christopher Kilby. The seemingly endless profits open to Saul and his master could, however, be threatened by a cessation of hostilities in America or a political

upheaval in London. Both occurred in 1760, with the conquest of New France and the death of George II. Baker was no doubt anticipating these events when he terminated his contracts by 1760. In the same year Governor Lawrence died. Saul had been elevated to the governor's council in 1759, but he apparently had no taste for remaining in Halifax in that capacity or as a private trader, for he returned to England at the end of 1760.

Thomas Saul was one of a type increasingly common in the 18th-century British empire. He appears in written records only as an occasional signature on an account or a name in a report. Yet, by virtue of his semi-official position and his control of a sure supply of money, he wielded great power over the lives of soldiers, settlers, and traders in the first decade of settlement at Halifax.

JAMES C. HIPPEN

BM, Add. MSS, 33029. Henry E. Huntington Library (San Marino, Calif.), AB 876, LO 3250. Library of Congress (Washington), Great Britain coll., Army accounts, 1745–75, pp.25, 283–95, 299. PANS, RG 1, 165, pp.83, 139. PRO, AO 17/41, pp.202–7, 214–17; 17/42; T 29/32, p.13; 29/33, pp.224, 310; T 38/373; 38/374, p.194. *Documents relating to currency in Nova Scotia, 1675–1758* (Shortt). "Letter book of John Watts . . . ," N.Y. Hist. Soc. *Coll.*, LXI (1928), 239. *N.S. Archives, I.* PRO, *JTP, 1749/50– 1753.* Bell, *Foreign Protestants.* Murdoch, *History of Nova-Scotia*, II, 373, 391, 394, 398. T. B. Akins, "History of Halifax City," N.S. Hist. Soc. *Coll.*, VIII (1895).

SCHUYLER, JOHANNES (John), military officer, envoy to the Iroquois; b. 5 April 1668 (O.S.) at Albany, New York, the sixth and youngest son of Philip Pieterse Schuyler and Margarita Van Slichtenhorst; d. February 1747 at Albany.

Growing up in Albany, the centre of the fur trade in New York province, John Schuyler became familiar with wilderness living and had frequent contact with the neighbouring Iroquois. War broke out between France and England in 1689, and in February of the following year a French force under Jacques Le Moyne* de Sainte-Hélène attacked Schenectady. That summer Schuyler volunteered to join a colonial expedition against Canada. Troops under the command of Major-General Fitz-John Winthrop were to proceed against Montreal *via* Lake Champlain, while Sir William Phips* sailed up the St Lawrence to Quebec. John and his brother Peter* served with the land forces.

Winthrop led his army to Wood Creek (Rivière du Chicot) at the headwaters of Lake Champlain but, impeded by a shortage of canoes to transport his troops and of provisions to feed them, he made no further progress. John Schuyler volunteered to lead a company into enemy territory, so Winthrop commissioned him captain, supplied him with canoes, arms, and supplies, and sent him off with 29 white and 120 Indian volunteers. He left camp on 13 Aug. 1690 and on his way down Wood Creek met Captain John Sanders Glen, who joined the expedition with 13 white men and five Indians. They paddled northward down Lake Champlain and the Richelieu River, to the vicinity of Fort Chambly. Leaving their canoes, they turned westward and came to Prairie-de-la-Madeleine (Laprairie) on the south bank of the St Lawrence, opposite Montreal. Shortly before their arrival, Governor Frontenac [Buade*] had returned to Montreal with about 1,200 troops he had brought to Prairie-de-la-Madeleine to counter Winthrop's forces. On 23 August Schuyler's men attacked. Although they did not capture the well-defended fort at Prairie-de-la-Madeleine, they took some prisoners and destroyed dwellings, barns, cattle, grain, and hay. They returned to Albany on 30 August, having saved the first colonial expedition against Canada from utter contempt.

Schuyler obtained land at Saratoga (Schuylerville, N.Y.), 20 miles north of Albany, where he built mills and a small fort and accumulated considerable property. Through his friendship with the Iroquois he was able to obtain information on raids planned by the Indians and warn the neighbouring settlers. In 1695 he had married Elizabeth Staats in Albany. Their grandson, Philip John, became one of George Washington's generals.

Between 1703 and 1706 John Schuyler was mayor of Albany, and was later a member of the provincial assembly. He also served in Albany as a justice of the peace, an alderman, a lieutenant of a cavalry company, and, beginning in 1711, a commissioner of Indian affairs. Several English governors used him as a courier to the Iroquois because he was liked and trusted by them. In 1724 Lieutenant Governor William Dummer of Massachusetts appointed him a commissioner to negotiate with the Iroquois. He visited Canada in 1713 and again in 1725 (with William DUDLEY and others) seeking the return of prisoners.

JOHN H. G. PELL

The "Journal of Captain John Schuyler [1690]" is printed in *Documentary history of New-York* (O'Callaghan), II, 160–62. For other primary materials on Schuyler, see: *Calendar of council minutes, 1668–1783* (N.Y. State Lib. *Bull.*, LVIII, Hist., VI, Albany, 1902). Charlevoix, *History* (Shea). "Correspondance échangée entre la cour de France et le gouverneur de Frontenac, pendant sa seconde administration (1689–1699)," APQ *Rapport, 1927–28*, 38–39. *NYCD* (O'Callaghan and Fernow). Coleman, *New England captives*. W. J. Eccles, *Frontenac: the courtier governor* (Toronto, 1959). G. W. Schuyler, *Colonial New York; Philip Schuyler and his family* (2v., New York, 1885).

SCHUYLER, PETER, military officer; b. 1710 in Bergen County, New Jersey, son of Arent Schuyler and Swantie Dyckhuyse; m. to Hester Walter and after her death to Mary ———; had one daughter by his first marriage; d. 7 March 1762 after a long illness at his home near Newark, New Jersey.

On the death of his father in 1730, Peter Schuyler inherited a large house and grounds in Elizabethtown (Elizabeth, N.J.), 787 acres of land, and one-third of the considerable profits from the copper mine his father had developed and operated. Schuyler's estate increased considerably upon his marriage to Hester Walter, the daughter of a rich New York merchant and business associate of his father. On his estate he maintained a park and a garden which the Reverend Andrew Burnaby described in 1760 as containing "a very large collection of citrons, oranges, limes, lemons, balsams of Peru, aloes, pomegranates, and other tropical plants."

In April 1746, amid continuing hostilities between England and France, Governor Lewis Morris of New Jersey received orders from the secretary of state for the southern department, the Duke of Newcastle, to raise troops as part of an English expeditionary force gathering at Albany, New York, for "the immediate reduction of Canada." The governor's council recommended that Peter Schuyler, "a Gentleman . . . of good Estate & Reputation," be given command of the New Jersey forces, known as the "New Jersey Blues," and Schuyler was appointed colonel. Although the campaign envisioned by Newcastle came to nothing, Schuyler gained valuable experience as a commanding officer. The forced idleness at Albany from September 1746 on, the inadequate supplies, and the lack of pay caused discontent amongst all the provincial troops. In the spring of 1747, the president of the New Jersey Council, John Hamilton, received word from Schuyler that the Jersey troops had mutinied and threatened to quit "if they do not Receive his Majesty's Pay that was Promised. . . ." To avoid further trouble, Schuyler used his "own private Creditt to procure money for the Pay of the Jersey

Schuyler

Companys," an action which brought him a reprimand from New York Governor George CLINTON, who was commander of all the troops at Albany; Clinton felt that such generosity encouraged discontent among the other provincial troops. The only military action seen by the Jersey Blues was in relieving the fort at Saratoga which was besieged by the French about the end of June 1747. Schuyler returned to New Jersey in November 1747 and dismissed his troops.

In 1754, with the outbreak of skirmishes leading to the Seven Years' War, Schuyler, as "an Officer of known Courage and Experience," was again appointed to command the Jersey forces. From June 1755 through the end of the year, Schuyler served along the New York-Canada border under General William Shirley. He won the respect of both Shirley and Colonel William Johnson* of New York. In April 1756, Shirley ordered Schuyler's regiment (about 500 men) to Fort Oswego (Chouaguen) to join an already heavy concentration of provincial and British troops. Oswego soon came under attack by forces under MONTCALM and with the death of the fort's commanding officer, James Mercer, a council of officers decided to surrender – a decision Schuyler evidently opposed. According to Montcalm, on 14 August "they gave themselves up as prisoners of war, to the number of 1700, including 80 officers and two English regiments. . . ."

From the fall of Oswego until October 1757, Schuyler was a prisoner of the French. He was taken to Quebec, where he occupied himself with two principal activities: gathering military intelligence, which a fellow prisoner, Joseph Morse, transmitted to British authorities in October 1757, and making himself guardian to other English prisoners. He sent back estimates of the number of troops in Canada, and noted that provisions in the colony were scarce. At his own expense, " this public spirited Gentleman" (as fellow prisoner Robert Eastburn described Schuyler) relieved the plight of many unfortunate prisoners; he loaned money to some and purchased others from their Indian captors. He was a close friend in Quebec of Robert STOBO and was later thanked by the Virginia House of Burgesses "for his unparalleled Tenderness and Humanity" to Stobo and others; subsequently he was reimbursed for some of his expenses. In October Governor Pierre de Rigaud* de Vaudreuil granted Schuyler parole to return to his home "to obtain funds to enable [him] to live in Canada." Schuyler was accorded a hero's welcome, not for his military accomplishments but for his "great Support of many English Prisoners, without whose Assistance several of them would have been reduced to the greatest Extremities."

While on parole, Schuyler complained to William Pitt that he was "Impatient of Confinement, . . . [when my] Country needs [my] best Service." But despite Pitt's concern and the repeated efforts of General James Abercromby*, no exchange could be arranged. In an angry letter to Abercromby in June 1758, Vaudreuil recalled Schuyler, who returned in August authorized to negotiate prisoner exchanges. With the fall of Fort Frontenac (Kingston, Ont.) to the English at the end of August, an exchange was arranged. The fort's commander, Pierre-Jacques Payen* de Noyan, and the garrison were exchanged for Schuyler and 114 persons, including 25 women and children, many of whom Schuyler purchased "out of his own private Purse" from the French or their Indian allies.

During 1759–60 Schuyler was under the orders of General Jeffery Amherst* at Crown Point, New York, and in the Niagara area, and entered Montreal in September 1760 with the conquering English armies. He returned to New Jersey in November 1760 and died in the spring of 1762. A notice in the *Pennsylvania Journal* at the time of his capture aptly summarizes Schuyler's career: he was "a brave and loyal Subject, who despised his own Ease, and all the Delights of an affluent Fortune, for the Service of his Country."

JOHN DAVID KRUGLER

AN, Col., B, 107, f.16. "Abstract of wills on file in the Surrogate's office. . . 1730–1744," N.Y. Hist. Soc. *Coll.*, XXVII (1894), 14–15. *An analytical index to the colonial documents of New Jersey, in the State Paper offices in England*, comp. Henry Stevens, ed. W.A. White (N.J. Hist. Soc. *Coll.*, V, New York, 1858), 202, 204, 205, 214–16, 221. Andrew Burnaby, *Travels through the middle settlements in North-America, in the years 1759 and 1760; with observations upon the state of the colonies* (London, 1775; repr. Ithaca, N.Y., 1960), 70. [Cadwallader Colden], *The letters and papers of Cadwallader Colden. . .* (9v., N.Y. Hist. Soc. *Coll.*, L–LVI (1917–23), LXVII–LXVIII (1934–35), New York, 1918–37), IX, 129. *Correspondence of William Pitt* (Kimball), I, 268–69, 286–87, 315, 325, 332–35, 405; II, 8. *Correspondence of William Shirley* (Lincoln), II, 193–94, 277–78. *Documents relating to the colonial history of the state of New Jersey*, ed. W. A. Whitehead et al. (1st ser., 42v., Newark, 1880–1949), VI–IX, XII, XV–XVII, XIX–XX, XXXIII. [Robert Eastburn], *The dangers and sufferings of Robert Eastburn, and his deliverance from Indian captivity*, ed. J. R. Spears (Cleveland, 1904), 63–64. "Intelligence from Colonel Peter Schuyler of the New Jersey Regiment, taken at Oswego, and now a prisoner at Quebec: sent by Joseph Morse, who left that place October 4, 1757," in *Colonial captivities, marches and journeys*, ed. I. M. Calder

(New York, 1935), 140–42. *Johnson papers* (Sullivan *et al.*). Virginia, *Journal of the House of Burgesses of Virginia*, ed. H. R. McIlwaine and J. P. Kennedy (13v., Richmond, Va., 1905–15), IX, 112. Knox, *Historical journal* (Doughty). "Letter book of John Watts . . . ," N.Y. Hist. Soc. *Coll.*, LXI (1928), 27, 134. *Military affairs in North America, 1748–1765: selected documents from the Cumberland papers in Windsor Castle*, ed. S. M. Pargellis (New York, London, 1936), 189, 218–21, 243. "Montcalm's correspondence," PAC *Report, 1929*, 47. *NYCD* (O'Callaghan and Fernow). *New York Evening Post*, 6 July 1747. *New-York Gazette, or the Weekly Post-Boy*, 12 Dec. 1747. *New-York Mercury*, 2, 30 June, 17 Nov., 8 Dec. 1755; 2 Feb., 22 March, 12 April, 22 July 1756; 4 April, 24 Oct., 28 Nov. 1757; 9 Jan., 3 July, 7 Aug., 27 Nov., 4 Dec. 1758; 16, 30 April 1759; 14 April, 24 Nov. 1760. *The papers of Lewis Morris, governor of the province of New Jersey, from 1738 to 1746* (N.J. Hist. Soc. *Coll.*, IV, New York, 1852), 311–12. *Pennsylvania Gazette* (Philadelphia), 8 May 1755, 1 Dec. 1757, 14 Sept. 1758, 24 May 1759, 27 Nov. 1760. *Pennsylvania Journal, and Weekly Advertiser* (Philadelphia), 1 May 1755; 22 April, 9 Sept. 1756; 17 Nov. 1757; 6 July, 31 Aug. 1758; 16 April 1761; 11 March 1762. *Royal Fort Frontenac* (Preston and Lamontagne).

R. C. Alberts, *The most extraordinary adventures of Major Robert Stobo* (Boston, 1965). E. J. Fisher, *New Jersey as a royal province, 1738 to 1776* (New York, 1911; repr. 1967), 296–97, 326–28, 335–39, 355, 469. Gipson, *British Empire before the American revolution*, VI, VII. G. W. Schuyler, *Colonial New York; Philip Schuyler and his family* (2v., New York, 1885), II, 207–16.

SCOTT, GEORGE, army officer; date and place of birth unknown; d. as the result of a duel fought, probably on 6 Nov. 1767, in Dominica.

George Scott's early days are obscure. He was probably not the George Scott commissioned in the army as early as 1721, who was an officer in the Earl of Rothes' Regiment of Foot (25th Foot), being appointed captain in 1742. Beckles Willson, WOLFE's biographer, appears to have believed that George Scott the subject of this article was a son of a Mrs Scott who was a friend of General Wolfe's mother: Wolfe in 1750 sought support for obtaining preferment in the artillery for a son of Mrs Scott, but without success. It seems unlikely, however, that the son in whom Wolfe rather reluctantly interested himself was George, who in 1750 was already serving as captain-lieutenant in what was shortly to become the 40th Foot, then in Nova Scotia. He had been a captain in the army, as distinct from the regiment, since 1746. In June 1751 he became a captain in the 40th.

Scott appears in the pages of history in the summer of 1753, when he succeeded Colonel Robert Monckton* in the command of Fort Lawrence, on the isthmus of Chignecto a short distance from the French Fort Beauséjour. Some months later he made contact with Thomas Pichon*, a commissary at Beauséjour, who entered into treasonable correspondence with him, betraying much military information. Pichon stated that he had previously met Scott at Louisbourg, Île Royale (Cape Breton Island); what business took Scott there is unknown. Scott relinquished command of Fort Lawrence in the autumn of 1754. Preparations were then being made for an attack on Beauséjour, and he was appointed to command one of the two battalions of Massachusetts troops raised for the purpose, evidently with the provincial rank of lieutenant-colonel. He played a considerable part in the brief siege directed by Monckton which ended with the surrender of Fort Beauséjour by Louis Du Pont* Duchambon de Vergor on 16 June 1755. Although the other Massachusetts battalion, commanded by John Winslow*, was the force chiefly employed in the grim business of the expulsion of the Acadians that followed, Scott's unit was used in destroying villages (notably Memramcook) that might give shelter to refugees or resisters. When Monckton departed in November Scott was left in command in the Chignecto area.

Scott had probably impressed his superiors as a useful commander of light and irregular forces; when the expedition against Louisbourg was planned in 1758 he was given command (with the local or temporary rank of major) of the light infantry unit improvised for the occasion, "a corps of 550 men, chosen as marksmen from the different regiments." General Jeffery Amherst*'s journal indicates that before the army landed Scott made a daring reconnaissance, going ashore with a party and examining the ground at the foot of Gabarus Bay, which Amherst decided after receiving Scott's report was an unsuitable spot for landing. When the actual landing took place at the Anse de la Cormorandière (Kennington Cove) on 8 June [*see* MASCLE de Saint-Julhien], Scott, leading his light infantry, was perhaps the greatest hero of the day. His disreputable acquaintance Pichon, the "spy of Beauséjour," is the authority for the details, describing how Scott maintained a foothold on shore with only five survivors of the initial landing against a much superior French force until reinforced; the anonymous "Journal of the expedition against Louisbourg" in Monckton's papers confirms that he played a vital part. He continued to be active during the siege that followed, fighting under Wolfe as he had in the landing.

After Louisbourg's fall Monckton (who had

589

remained at Halifax) was ordered to destroy the French settlements on the Saint John River, and Scott was placed under him in command of a force of light infantry and rangers. On 11 November Monckton detached Scott to the Petitcodiac River to lay waste the settlements there. These orders were thoroughly executed during the following week, many houses being burned, cattle killed, grain destroyed, and some prisoners taken. Most of the inhabitants fled. Scott was given the rank of major in the army effective 28 Dec. 1758. He remained on the list of the 40th Foot as a captain, and evidently was an absentee company commander in the regiment until his death.

Scott served under Wolfe in the Quebec campaign of 1759. His chief task was a mission of destruction similar to that on the Petitcodiac. After his defeat at Montmorency Wolfe began a systematic devastation of the parishes about Quebec. At the beginning of September he sent Scott with a force said to have been as large as 1,600 men, including all the rangers and some regulars and seamen, to destroy "the Buildings and Harvest of the Enemy on the South Shore." Scott sailed down the St Lawrence to Kamouraska and marched back, burning as he came. On 19 September he reported, "Upon the whole, we marched fifty two Miles, and in that distance, burnt nine hundred and ninty eight good Buildings, two Sloops, two Schooners, Ten Shalloops and several Batteaus and small Craft, took fifteen Prisoners (Six of them Women and five of them Children) kill'd 5 of the Enemy, had One Regular wounded, two of the Rangers kill'd and four more of them wounded." This nasty proceeding meant that Scott and his force were not present for the battle of the Plains on 13 September, in which the rangers might have been very useful.

Nothing has been found concerning Scott's part in the events of the next two years. He was appointed lieutenant-colonel in the army on 11 July 1761. At the end of that year Monckton undertook a large-scale expedition against Martinique. Scott had remained on friendly terms with Monckton, and was godfather to his illegitimate daughter. Scott served in the expedition, again commanding a unit of light infantry, which distinguished itself. Martinique surrendered on 13 Feb. 1762 and Grenada, one of its dependencies, on 5 March. Monckton appointed Scott governor of the latter island. Scott made his will there in December 1764, just before leaving to become lieutenant-governor of Dominica. The will reveals that he had acquired (by means that remain unknown) considerable estates in

Grenada; it also disposes of property in Boston and Nova Scotia. On a date which seems to be 5 Nov. 1767, in Dominica, Scott added to this will an unwitnessed codicil saying that he had been "grossly insulted" by one Alexander Campbell and was determined to "meet him" tomorrow morning. Attached is a certificate by another officer, dated 9 Nov. 1767, that the codicil is in the hand of George Scott, late lieutenant-governor of Dominica. Presumably Scott was killed or mortally wounded in a duel on 6 Nov. 1767.

Scott's will left an annuity to his wife Abigail and provided for her return to New England, of which she was probably a native. They evidently had no children. The will of 1764 leaves legacies to Scott's father, three brothers (one of whom, Joseph, lived in Halifax) and three sisters. A purported miniature of Scott is reproduced in Webster's *Thomas Pichon*; it portrays a sharp and rather unpleasant face.

C. P. STACEY

[Scott's will and codicil are in PRO, Prob. 11/943, f.394. His report on the Petitcodiac operation of 1758 is in PAC, MG 18, M1, 21 and is printed in the calendar, *Northcliffe coll.*; his report on the St Lawrence operation of 1759 is in the same collection but is not printed in full. The collection also contains some documents on the campaign against Martinique. For information on the siege of Louisbourg, *see* Jeffery Amherst, *Journal* (Webster); Pichon, *Lettres et mémoires*; and a journal of the siege in *Gentleman's Magazine*, 1758, pp.384–89. In 1762 (pp.123–27) that magazine also published Monckton's dispatches concerning the campaign in Martinique. C.P.S.]

Army list, 1740; 1756; 1760; 1761; 1763; 1767; 1768. "Diary of John Thomas," N.S. Hist. Soc. *Coll.*, I (1878), 119–40. *Gentleman's Magazine*, 1767, p.525. Brebner, *New England's outpost*. Smythies, *Historical records of the 40th regiment*. Stacey, *Quebec, 1759*. J. C. Webster, *Thomas Pichon, the spy of Beauséjour, an account of his career in Europe and America . . .* (Sackville, N.B., 1937). Beckles Willson, *The life and letters of James Wolfe . . .* (London, 1909).]

SCRIMSHIRE. *See* SKRIMSHER

SEGUARON. *See* SAUGUAARAM

SENEZERGUES DE LA RODDE, ÉTIENNE-GUILLAUME DE, officer in the French regular troops; b. 29 Aug. 1709 at Aurillac, France, son of Louis de Senezergues, governor of Aurillac; d. 14 Sept. 1759.

Étienne-Guillaume de Senezergues entered his father's old regiment, La Sarre, as a supernumerary half-pay lieutenant at the age of 14 and was commissioned an ensign on 1 Oct. 1726, a lieutenant the following year, and captain in 1734. He saw action in Italy during the War of the Polish Succession and campaigned in Germany and Italy in the War of the Austrian Succession. By 1747 he commanded the second battalion of his regiment, the titular lieutenant-colonel being unfit for active service.

When, in 1756, one battalion of the La Sarre was posted to Canada Senezergues, now breveted lieutenant-colonel of the second battalion, was not obliged to go. His patrimony of some 10,000 *livres* a year made him financially independent and his family ardently desired him to remain in France. But he was an ambitious career soldier, sought advancement, and was motivated by a stern sense of duty. Thus he sailed from Brest on 3 April 1756, arriving at Quebec 13 May.

In June his battalion was ordered to Fort Frontenac (Kingston, Ont.) for garrison duty and then took part in the capture of Oswego [*see* MONTCALM]. For his role in this campaign he was awarded a pension of 500 *livres*. In 1757 he distinguished himself at the siege of Fort William Henry (also called Fort George, now Lake George, N.Y.). The Chevalier de Lévis* wrote that although it had not been Senezergues's turn to march, he had volunteered to serve with the advance assault since he was the only lieutenant-colonel fit for such arduous duty. He was awarded a second pension of 500 *livres* after this campaign.

The following year Governor General Vaudreuil [Rigaud*] organized a force of 1,600 men, comprising colonial regular troops, Canadian militia, an élite force of French regulars, and allied Indians, for an assault on Schenectady, New York. Lévis was given the command and again Senezergues offered to accompany him as second in command, an offer that Lévis was glad to accept. No sooner had the expedition left Montreal, however, than it was recalled and sent post-haste to Lake Champlain. Word had been received that Major-General James Abercromby* had massed 25,000 men for an assault on the French forts.

Lévis and Senezergues arrived at Carillon (Ticonderoga, N.Y.) with their relief force of 400 Canadian regulars and militia on the night of 7 July. Montcalm's army was entrenched behind a hastily constructed barricade on the crest of the slope west of the fort. Next day the British attacked in four columns. Senezergues and his battalion on the left flank under Colonel BOURLAMAQUE's command came under heavy assault by two of the columns. When Bourlamaque was severely wounded Senezergues took over the command. Three assaults were beaten back with heavy losses to the British who broke and fled in disorder. In reports to the minister of War both Montcalm and Lévis singled out Senezergues for praise; they urged strongly that he be promoted brigadier without regard for seniority. Montcalm declared that he was the senior officer most often called on for active duty, was better qualified than any of the other battalion commanders to command a corps with dignity, and the only one fit to remain in Canada to command the battalions that might stay in the colony at the end of hostilities. He was duly promoted brigadier on 10 Feb. 1759.

The same year, at the siege of Quebec, Senezergues was again in the thick of the fighting. After the departure of Lévis for the Montreal front on 9 August he became Montcalm's second in command. On 13 September when Montcalm belatedly became aware that the British army was massed on the Plains of Abraham, Senezergues was ordered to hold the Beauport flank until the enemy's intentions became clear, then to bring his battalion to the heights on the far side of Quebec. He and his men thus arrived on the battlefield after a forced march. With hardly a pause for breath they were ordered to charge the left of the enemy line. In that brief fateful clash Senezergues fell, mortally wounded. When the smoke of battle cleared he was taken on board a British warship. He died the next day. On receiving word of the outcome of the battle Colonel Bourlamaque wrote: "We have lost in M. de Senezergues an officer of distinction, as virtuous as he was brave; I am terribly sorry."

W. J. ECCLES

SHA, A¹, 3417, 3498–99, 3540. Doughty and Parmelee, *Siege of Quebec*. "Étienne-Guillaume de Senezergues de la Rodde," APQ *Rapport, 1922–23*, 266–73. *Guerre du Canada: relations et journaux* (Casgrain). *Journal du chevalier de Lévis* (Casgrain). *Lettres de M. de Bourlamaque* (Casgrain). Hozier, *Armorial général de France* (1738–68), I, pt.II. Frégault, *La guerre de la conquête*. Stanley, *New France*.

SERVIAN, JEAN D'ALQUIER DE. *See* ALQUIER

SHIKELLIMY. *See* SWATANA

SHORT, RICHARD, naval officer and topographical draughtsman; fl. before 1754 to after 1766.

Nothing is known of Richard Short's naval career except the vessels in which he served: *Baltimore* (a sloop), *Peregrine* (a sloop built in 1749), *Mermaid* (a frigate, which he appears to have left before she sailed for Nova Scotia in 1754), *Gibral-*

Silvain

tar (a frigate), and four ships of the line, *Leopard* (built in 1756), *Prince of Orange, Dublin* (which returned from the West Indies in 1763), and *Neptune*. After this service at sea he was appointed to the Chatham dockyard, England. Though the list of ships does not indicate extensive service for Short in North America, the *Prince of Orange* brought him there in the fleet accompanying WOLFE's forces in 1759.

With Hervey Smyth* Short was one of the first English military artists to record the Canadian scene. In the days before photography, drawing lessons formed a regular part of the training of officers. Military topographical artists were active throughout the period when British forces were stationed in Canada.

Short is known for two sets of views, which were engraved by various hands after sketches he made in Canada; the engravings were published in London in 1761. One set consists of six views of Halifax. These, including views of the harbour and the Citadel, the governor's house and St Paul's Church, seem to have been engraved after paintings which the marine artist Dominique Serres had made from Short's drawings. The other set, of Quebec, was apparently engraved directly from the drawings. It is entitled (on a rare copy of the wrapper now in the Royal Ontario Museum, Toronto) "Twelve views of the principal buildings in Quebec, from drawings, taken on the spot, at the command of Vice-Admiral [Charles Saunders*] by Richard Short, purser of his majesty's ship the Prince of Orange."

The Quebec views form a unique record of the appearance of that city immediately after the naval bombardment of 1759. But as the original drawings have not come to light, and as the London engraver inevitably altered the scale, perspective, and details of the buildings, the accuracy of representation leaves something to be desired. Thus the little square before the church of Notre-Dame-des-Victoires appears much larger than it is, and the intendant's and bishop's palaces and the Jesuit college somewhat grander than they actually were. Yet the general character of these latter and of other lost buildings of Quebec seems to be conveyed. The interiors of the Jesuit and Recollet churches – our only records of them – are true to what is known of them from documents and from churches of the same period in France. But above all it is the wide extent of war damage that is most striking in the engravings – damage which was all neatly repaired by the time Thomas Davies* and his contemporaries painted Quebec a generation later.

In addition to the above engravings, Short is known for views of naval engagements, engraved as a series by Caroline Watson and published by Boydell in London.

ROBERT H. HUBBARD

ASQ, Album 1G (1761 edition of the 12 engravings of Quebec). Royal Ontario Museum (Toronto), Sigmund Samuel Collection. *Allgemeines Lexikon der bildenken Künstler von der Antike bis zur Gegenwart*, ed. Ulrich Thieme, *et al*. (37v., Leipzig, 1907–50), XXX, 576. "Les estampes de Richard Short," *BRH*, XXIV (1918), 279–80. M. H. Grant, *A dictionary of British landscape painters from the 16th century to the early 20th century* (Leigh-on-Sea, Eng., 1952), 176. J. Russell Harper, *Painting in Canada; a history* (Toronto, 1966), 41, 429, pl.30. Isaac Schomberg, *Naval chronology; or an historical summary of naval and maritime events, from the time of the Romans to the treaty of peace, 1802* (5v., London, 1802). F. St. G. Spendlove, *The face of early Canada; pictures of Canada which have helped to make history* (Toronto, 1958), 8–9, 11–12, pl.3–15, 22–27.

SILVAIN, TIMOTHÉE. *See* SULLIVAN, TIMOTHY

SIMONET (Simmonet) D'ABERGEMONT, JACQUES, forge master and partner in the Saint-Maurice ironworks; b. in Dompierre, in the diocese of Langres, France, son of Jean-Baptiste Simonet and Élisabeth Bériault; m. first, in France, Marie Foissey, and secondly, at Trois-Rivières, Geneviève, daughter of Lambert Boucher* de Grandpré and widow of Charles Hertel de Chambly; buried 21 May 1742 in Trois-Rivières.

Nothing positive is known of Jacques Simonet d'Abergemont's activities in France prior to his arrival in the colony in 1736. A concern with the iron industry was common in Champagne, the area of his birth, in the 18th century, when members of the French gentry or civil service were often deeply involved in this industry.

Maurepas, the minister of Marine, and Gilles Hocquart*, New France's intendant, were primarily responsible for recruiting Simonet to aid in developing the Saint-Maurice ironworks. Both believed that a second forge master, to assist Pierre-François Olivier* de Vézin, the French forge master who had arrived in 1735, would accelerate the establishment of the industry. Simonet, in agreeing to move to New France, made it a condition that he be allowed to participate in the company to be formed; he became a partner of Vézin and the Canadians François-Étienne CUGNET, Ignace Gamelin* the younger, and Thomas-Jacques TASCHEREAU. As well, he was, like Vézin, to receive an annual salary which was to be considered an expense of the company and not taken from profits. Only in Vézin's absence did he act as forge master; his main task was to recruit experienced workers from France, and in this he fulfilled his duties well, so much so that French forge masters complained to Maurepas that he was stealing away their workers, including some who were deeply in debt to them. Like Vézin, Simonet was not above taking advantage of his position: in 1739, at the expense of the government, he brought a son born of his first marriage, Jean-Baptiste, to the colony and employed him at the ironworks. Both father and son, however, appear to have been well thought of by local officials.

In 1739–40 Vézin was in France and Simonet was the *de facto* forge master, albeit with reduced powers; in effect, the supplying of materials for the ironworks, both for construction and for the maintenance of the workers, was put into the hands of a subcontractor. During Vézin's absence attempts were made to set the affairs of the company in better order, its financial position being a cause for great concern. Simonet and Vézin were put on a piece-work stipend, the total of which, however, could not exceed their old annual salary; in Simonet's case, this had been 1,500 *livres* per year, plus room and board of a rather luxurious nature.

Disputes among the partners were constant in late 1741 and the company went bankrupt that year. Simonet took the side of his metropolitan colleague, Vézin, accused of undertakings too ambitious for the resources available, but he never suffered as did Vézin from the barbs of his Canadian associates. Amid the ironworks' difficulties, Simonet made a serious offer to Maurepas to take over the operation of the industry in his own name; he was unable to prove that he had the capital required and his considerate offer was refused. He died soon after. In 1743 the ironworks had to be removed from private hands and reunited to the king's domain; at this time Simonet's indebtedness to the crown, and that of his partners, was cancelled.

Jean-Baptiste Simonet, having a good reputation, had replaced Vézin as forge master in 1741 at the same time as Hocquart made Guillaume Estèbe* his subdelegate to administer the ironworks. The confidence of Hocquart and Maurepas was quickly put to the test: Jean-Baptiste diverted both cash and products to his own pocket. Hocquart arranged for his return to France in 1742.

Jacques Simonet cannot, of course, be held responsible for the behaviour of his son. But, although he had greater probity, he had his own self-seeking tendencies. After the debacle of the bankruptcy, he was unsparing in his criticisms of his ex-partners. While a partner in the Saint-Maurice ironworks he had flirted with the possibility of assisting Louis LEPAGE de Sainte-Claire in establishing an iron industry on Lepage's lands in Terrebonne. Like many others who came to the colony with a specialized knowledge he attempted, though in his case with little success, to acquire all he could, behaviour typical of a metropolitan and even, it must be added, of the citizens of New France.

CAMERON NISH and CLAUDE RICHARD

ANQ, NF, Coll. de pièces jud. et not., 1176. PAC *Report, 1904*, app.K, *passim*. *Dictionnaire national des Canadiens français (1608–1760)* (2v., Montréal, 1958), II. Tanguay, *Dictionnaire*. Sulte, *Mélanges historiques* (Malchelosse), VI. Albert Tessier, *Les forges Saint-Maurice, 1729–1883* (Trois-Rivières, 1952).

SKRIMSHER, SAMUEL (the name is found as **Scrimshire, Skrimshire, Skimisher,** but he signed Skrimsher), HBC employee; son of Samuel Skrimsher and probably a cousin of James ISHAM; d. 18 May 1755.

Aged about 14 Samuel Skrimsher went to Hudson Bay in 1733 to serve as an apprentice at York Fort (York Factory, Man.). Following the expiry of his apprenticeship in 1740, he was employed at the fort as a book-keeper and warehouse-keeper. He served as second under Thomas WHITE (1744–46), James Isham (1746–48), and John NEWTON (1748–50). In August 1749 Newton complained to the London committee of Skrimsher's "Lazy Habit," and Skrimsher was consequently recalled to London by the committee's letter of May 1750. Before the order reached the bay, however, Newton drowned and Skrimsher took over at York. His command was short-lived, for Isham arrived at York on the company's vessel *Prince Rupert* (Capt. George SPURRELL) in August 1750 and assumed charge. Skrimsher took passage by the vessel to London. There he evidently convinced the committee of his worth (perhaps on account of his knowledge of Cree or his having journeyed between York and Churchill), for in the summer of 1751 he returned to the bay, appointed for five years to the charge of Flamborough House. This "small Factory house" had been established in 1749 on the Nelson River to collect provisions for York and to prevent any sea-borne interlopers from ascending the river and intercepting Indians coming to trade at the bay. Skrimsher continued in charge until he died on 18 May 1755, apparently from being struck on the face by a drunken

Smith

Indian. He was buried at York, the inscription on his tomb noting his age at death as 34.

JOAN CRAIG

HBC Arch. A.1/38, pp.268, 270, 324; A.6/6, p.203; A.6/7, pp.45, 150, 188, 217, 276, 282, 325–26, 329; A.6/8, pp.28–29, 132, 135, 231, 237; A.11/114, ff.104–6, 109–9d, 113d, 117, 122d, 129d, 134, 139, 144–45, 184–85; A.16/31, ff.32, 68, 82; B.68/a/2; B.68/a/4; B.68/b/1, ff.8–8d; B.68/b/2; B.239/a/33; B.239/a/39. PRO, Prob. 6/131. HBRS, XII (Rich and Johnson), XXV (Davies and Johnson). Rich, *History of the HBC*, I.

SMITH, FRANCIS, HBC sloopmaster, explorer; fl. 1737–47.

Francis Smith first appears in the records of the Hudson's Bay Company as a second mate on its ship *Seahorse*, which sailed to Hudson Bay in 1737. The next year he became master of the *Churchill* sloop, a position he held at the bay until his return to England in the autumn of 1744. During these years he had made five trading voyages north from Churchill (Man.) in a series of relatively ineffectual attempts to establish trade with the Eskimos of the west coast of Hudson Bay. The only one of his sloop journals that survives gives no indication of any interest in exploration. On his return to England Smith was probably approached by Arthur Dobbs or one of his associates, for in 1746 he was appointed captain of the discovery vessel *California*, which was to accompany William MOOR in the *Dobbs Galley* on a voyage to Hudson Bay in search of the northwest passage.

A feature of the venture was to be the continual quarrels between Moor and Smith. Soon after the ships arrived in Hudson Bay in August 1746 Smith refused to explore the uncharted waters of Rankin Inlet, and the expedition instead headed for York Factory (Man.) to winter at Ten Shilling Creek, about five miles from the HBC post. Here the two captains indulged in acrimonious bickering with each other and with the factor, James ISHAM, who commented ironically on the disunity evident among members of the expedition, "which I imagingd. to be one family." By December Moor and Smith were no longer on speaking terms. In January Smith left the expedition's scurvy-stricken quarters at Ten Shilling Creek to stay at York Factory, and was soon followed by his wife Kitty (the first white woman to winter in Hudson Bay in the 18th century).

On 24 June 1747 the two vessels sailed from York northwards towards the hoped-for passage. Moor and Smith explored independently of each other for much of the time. While Smith remained offshore in the *California* his longboat discovered that Rankin Inlet was a closed body of water (in contrast to its representation on John WIGATE's map of 1746) and that the expedition's new discovery, Chesterfield Inlet, became shallower as the boats followed it inland. At the end of July the ships reached the Wager, where Dobbs had insisted a passage would be found. Moor and Smith, commanding their longboats in person, found that the Wager was a closed bay. As the *California* sailed out of the Wager so many of her crew were ill with scurvy that Smith himself had to take the helm, and when the vessel reached the Orkneys he had to borrow men from a naval ship to help her reach the Thames.

Although the expedition had carried out some useful surveys, particularly in Chesterfield Inlet and the Wager, the strained relations between the two captains resulted in a diffusion of effort, overlapping explorations, and disagreement on the nomenclature of several inlets on the west coast of the bay. The voyage had neither found a northwest passage nor proved conclusively that one did not exist, and the organizing North West Committee expressed grave dissatisfaction with the conduct of both Smith and Moor on the expedition. Unlike Moor, Smith was not called upon to give evidence before the investigating parliamentary committee of 1749, and no trace of his later career has been found.

GLYNDWR WILLIAMS

[The only extant journal of the *Churchill* sloop under Smith's command is that for 1743–44 in HBC Arch. B.42/a/26; it is not an illuminating document. For the discovery voyage of 1746–47 Smith's manuscript log of the *California* gives a terse, seaman's account of events; the original is in the Public Record Office of Northern Ireland (Belfast), D.162/44, and a contemporary copy is in HBC Arch. E.18/2. There are printed accounts of the voyage in Henry Ellis, *A voyage to Hudson's-Bay, by the Dobbs Galley and California, in the years 1746 and 1747, for discovering a north west passage* ... (London, 1748), and in the pseudonymous account by Smith's own clerk, "The Clerk of the California" [Charles Swaine (T. S. Drage)], *An account of a voyage for the discovery of a north-west passage* ... (2v., London, 1748–49). Isham kept copies of the letters exchanged between himself, Moor, and Smith during the wintering at York, and these have been printed in HBRS, XII (Rich and Johnson), 241–308; pages 336–37 contain a brief biographical sketch of Smith. A modern description of the discovery voyage will be found in Williams, *British search for the northwest passage.* G.W.]

SMITH, JOSEPH, HBC labourer, explorer; d. June 1765 en route to York Fort (York Factory, Man.) from the Saskatchewan country.

As Pierre GAULTIER de Varennes et de La Vérendrye, his family, and his successors developed French trade in the west, the Hudson's Bay Company felt increasingly threatened by the "pedlars" in the interior. To meet the challenge, James ISHAM began sending men inland from York Fort. Anthony HENDAY in 1754 was the first to go. In 1756 Joseph Smith, who had come to the bay as a labourer three years before, and Joseph Waggoner, a halfbreed son of Rowland Waggoner*, received orders to accompany Washiabitt, a captain of the Sturgeon Indians (a Cree band), to his home grounds. On 23 Aug. 1756 "the two Josephs," as Isham called them, left York with instructions to distribute presents to the Indians they met in order to encourage them to go down to York to trade. The travellers were to resist should any French traders oppose them, but they were not to seek trouble.

After following the Hayes and Fox rivers to Cross Lake and ascending the Nelson to Little Playgreen Lake and Lac Ouinipigon (Lake Winnipeg), on 31 October they reached Lac Bourbon (Cedar Lake), where they learned that the French post, Fort Bourbon, was unoccupied. Having adapted themselves perfectly to the Indian mode of travel and way of life, they drifted south, passing the Porcupine Hills and Duck Mountain and crossing the Assiniboine River into what is now southwestern Manitoba and southeastern Saskatchewan, where they hunted buffalo. At different times during their winter on the prairies they encountered groups of French traders who were also wintering with the Indians.

In March 1757 Smith, Waggoner, and their companions went north to the Indians' home grounds in the Swan River area. After building canoes they set out for Fort Bourbon, where they found the French in residence and trading. The explorers returned to York by way of Little Playgreen Lake, the Echimamish River, Oxford and Knee lakes, the first Englishmen to travel this route, which later became the standard one from York to the interior. They reported to Isham that they had encountered 20 French traders and that food had been plentiful on the prairies. After spending less than a week at York, they departed with the same Indians on 30 June 1757 and again wintered in the vicinity of the Assiniboine River. They came down to the bay the following spring with 57 canoes.

In 1759 Smith and Anthony Henday went into the Saskatchewan country and returned with a 61-canoe flotilla. Waggoner travelled there the following year, and in 1763 Smith made the journey with an Indian leader named Meesinkeeshick, going by way of the Grass River. He observed that the French posts had been abandoned and that Fort Saint-Louis (near Fort à La Corne, Sask.) had been burned. In 1764 he left for the Saskatchewan once more, accompanied for part of the journey by Isaac Batt*. Smith died on his return journey and the Indian woman with whom he had been travelling brought his personal effects and their child to Governor Ferdinand Jacobs* at York.

Altogether Smith made five inland journeys and Waggoner three. Smith kept journals on his 1756, 1757, and 1763 trips, but it is difficult to pinpoint his routes, for his entries are crude and laconic. The two explorers were certainly the first Englishmen to penetrate the Assiniboine River region, and the first to describe a buffalo pound. Unfortunately for the HBC, their discoveries were not at once followed by the development of a post at Little Playgreen Lake or on the Paskoya (Saskatchewan) River. The masters at York felt that the menace from Montreal was ended by the fall of New France and reasoned that there was no further need for the vigorous policy of inland travel they had promoted since 1754. The travels of Henday, Smith, Waggoner and Batt greatly increased the immediate fur returns at York, but English "pedlars" from Montreal were soon to mount a rivalry more severe and better organized than the French efforts had been. Had an inland post already existed the HBC would have been better prepared to face the fierce competition of its new English rivals.

GEORGE E. THORMAN

HBC Arch. A.5/1, ff.57d, 65d, 73d; A.11/114, ff.109d, 149d, 156d, 159, 197d; A.11/115, ff.2–3d, 7–8, 16, 23d, 37, 52d, 61–61d, 67d, 85, 87d, 97d, 101d. Morton, *History of the Canadian west*. E. E. Rich, *The fur trade and the northwest to 1857* (Toronto, 1967); *History of the HBC*, I.

SOULARD. *See* BAUDRY

SOUPIRAN, SIMON, master surgeon; b. 5 Feb. 1704 at Quebec, son of Simon Soupiran*, surgeon barber, and Marthe Bélanger; d. 16 June 1764 at Quebec.

Simon Soupiran was evidently a man of probity and, trained by his father, he was a capable surgeon, if not a distinguished one. He built on the social foundations laid by his father and became a solid townsman of Quebec. Soupiran lived on Rue de la Fabrique in the city's Upper Town and, to judge from the birth and death records of his children, spent some time in the nearby village of Lorette. On 16 May 1727 at Quebec he had mar-

Southack

ried Marie-Anne Gaultier by whom he had seven children. On 26 June 1736 at Quebec he took a second wife, Marie-Jeanne Avisse, widow of the merchant François Trefflé, *dit* Rottot; they had five children.

Like other surgeons, Simon Soupiran was obliged from time to time to take legal action to have some of his bills paid. When he was taken to court, it was for debts or a trifling matter like a coffee spoon which he had found and kept. Soupiran had other financial ups and downs. He seems to have been a commercial partner of Jean Vidal and their collective property was seized in the late 1720s. His family took in boarders, and Soupiran in 1737 claimed payment from his former mother-in-law for six years' bed and board.

Official recognition of Soupiran's capacity as a surgeon is evident in his occasional appointment to act as an expert by the lower courts at Quebec. In 1754 Soupiran was consulted on the character of Henry HICHÉ before Hiché's appointment to the Conseil Supérieur. He also acted as a reference for Guillaume Guillimin* in 1757. In addition to his private clientele, Soupiran was surgeon to the Ursuline nuns. Simon's son, Charles-Simon, followed his father's profession.

PETER N. MOOGK

ANQ, Greffe de Gilbert Boucault de Godefus, 3 août 1743; Greffe d'Henry Hiché, 3 mai 1729, 24 juin 1736; Greffe de Florent de La Cetière, 16 mai 1727; Greffe de J.-C. Panet, 11 nov. 1750, 18 déc. 1764; NF, Coll. de pièces jud. et not., 801, 825, 885, 899, 1136, 1566, 1883, 1944, 1961, 2140, 2148. PAC, MG 8, B1, 20/1, pp.220–22. "Journal du siège de Québec" (Fauteux), APQ *Rapport, 1920–21*, 180. "Recensement de Québec, 1744" (APQ *Rapport*). P.-G. Roy, *Inv. jug. et délib., 1717–1760*, II, 11, 13, 17; IV, 68, 70, 72, 82; VI, 53. Godbout, "Nos ancêtres," APQ *Rapport, 1951–53*, 544. Ahern, *Notes pour l'histoire de la médecine*, 517–18. "La famille Soupiran," *BRH*, XLI (1935), 135–38, 144–54.

SOUTHACK, CYPRIAN, cartographer, naval commander, member of the Nova Scotia Council; b. 1662 in London, England, son of Cyprian Southack and Elizabeth Oakley; m. Elizabeth Foy, by whom he had 11 children; d. 27 March 1745 (o.s.) in Boston, Massachusetts.

Following in the footsteps of his father, a naval lieutenant under Charles II, Cyprian Southack went to sea. At the age of ten he was present at a battle between Anglo-French and Dutch fleets at Southwold Bay. He went to Boston in 1685, and soon became well known as a cartographer and privateer. He entered the service of the colony of Massachusetts in 1690, when the man-of-war *Mary*, of which he was commander and part-owner, was rented for use in the expedition against Port-Royal (Annapolis Royal, N.S.) under Sir William Phips*. After the capture of Port-Royal, Southack went to Cape Sable Island, where he combatted Indians allied to the French; to Chedabouctou (Guysborough, N.S.), where he reduced Fort Saint-Louis [*see* Charles Duret* de Chevry]; and to Newfoundland, where he raided French outposts. These missions mark the beginning of a long period of employment for Southack by the Massachusetts government.

In March 1692 Southack was sent by the Massachusetts government to the Bay of Fundy (Baie Française), accompanied by Captain John Alden*, to pursue a French privateer – possibly Pierre Maisonnat* – operating in the area. Later that year he was given orders to cruise in Massachusetts Bay and east to Casco (Maine) to protect shipping. In the summer of 1696 he was appointed commander of the first *Province Galley*, a small vessel of ten guns built in 1694 by order of the Massachusetts General Court to deal with French and Indian problems. This vessel was replaced in 1705 by the second *Province Galley*, (16–18 guns), which Southack commanded until 1714.

As commander of these vessels, Southack guarded the coasts and shipping of New England against French incursions, represented Massachusetts in its dealings with the Indians on the northern frontier of the colony, and tried to suppress illegal trade with the French. In 1696 he participated in a futile attack on Governor Joseph Robinau* de Villebon's headquarters on the Saint John River. He took part in other expeditions against Acadia in 1704 and 1707, under Benjamin Church* and John March* respectively, and played a major role in helping to save the settlement of Casco when it was attacked by French forces under Alexandre Leneuf* de La Vallière et de Beaubassin in 1703. In 1710 he commanded the *Province Galley* in the successful expedition against Port-Royal under Francis Nicholson*. During this period he also produced charts of the New England coast, the Saint John River, and the St Lawrence River.

In 1711, probably because of his experience as a map-maker and mariner, Southack was asked to guide the expedition against Quebec under Sir Hovenden Walker* up the St Lawrence. While the fleet was being readied in Boston, Walker was lodged with Southack so that he might avail himself of Southack's knowledge of the route to Quebec. Southack, however, was reluctant to accompany the expedition in spite of Walker's entreaties. Eventually he was sent to Annapolis

Royal to pick up men and supplies. He was supposed to join the fleet en route to Quebec, but was delayed at Annapolis and could not do so. At the conclusion of Queen Anne's War in 1713, Southack was sent to Nova Scotia to notify French privateers of the end of the conflict. His efforts ended with the loss of his sloop, worth £200, to privateers at either Cape Sable Island or Port La Tour. In the next few years he was a member of several government missions. He accompanied Thomas Smart* to Île Royale (Cape Breton Island) in 1718 to confer with Governor Saint-Ovide [MONBETON] about French encroachments on the Canso fishery. In the same year he was in Quebec as a commissioner in an attempt to resolve the disputed boundary of Nova Scotia. Early in 1720 he sought a further appointment as a boundary commissioner and requested a pension in recognition of his services.

In April 1720 Southack was appointed to the first council of Nova Scotia. He attended the first few meetings of the council that year, but then returned to naval service. In August 1721, as commander of the *William Augustus*, he transported Governor Richard PHILIPPS and Paul MASCARENE to Canso. The next spring the *William Augustus* was used for a ten-day survey of the coast north of Canso; it is not known whether Southack himself did the surveying. The survey was resumed later that year, but was disrupted by Indian troubles – possibly by attacks on New England fishing vessels. Southack sailed again in 1723, but the *William Augustus* was laid up later that year. In 1724 Major Lawrence Armstrong* asked for the replacement of Southack and several other absent members of the council.

By 1724 Southack seems to have retired from public service, and may then have confined his activities to his commerical interests, which had been extensive. From being part-owner of a privateering vessel in 1690 he progressed to fishing, and, on at least one occasion, the sale of building materials. Fishing off Nova Scotia, however, was a hazardous undertaking. In 1715 Southack was threatened with the loss of his life by Indians while fishing at Port Roseway (Roseway, N.S.), and he was forced to flee, suffering a loss of £600. In 1718 he had a fishing sloop worth £300 burned by Indians when it went aground. That year he claimed to have lost a total of ten sloops over the years worth £6,000. He was also involved in the fishery at Canso, where he held property in 1725 and probably earlier.

Southack's activities after 1724 are obscure. He seems to have remained active in King's Chapel (Boston) as late as 1739, when he last served as an officer of the church, ending a period of service which began about 1702. In 1733 he was ordered by a committee of Boston selectmen to make improvements in his property to avoid danger to the public. This is not an indication that was impoverished, for when he died in 1745 he left an estate of over £3,600.

DONALD F. CHARD

American Antiquarian Soc. (Worcester, Mass.), Edmonds papers, miscellaneous MSS and letters. "Mass. Archives," II, 639, 643; VII, 141, 148, 163, 198, 336, 345, 382; XI, 430; XXXVI, 6a, 28, 127; XXXVII, 328, 390a; XXXVIIIA, 8, 16–18; LXI, 506; CXIV, 136. Mass. Hist. Soc., Gay papers, N.S., II, 91, 117. PANS, RG 1, 9, no.10; 18, nos.5, 17, 26, 28; 23, nos.1–10. "Journal of Colonel Nicholson at the capture of Annapolis, 1710," N.S. Hist. Soc. Coll., I (1878), 65. Mass. Hist. Soc. Proc., 3rd ser., VII (1914), 154, 155. PRO, CSP, Col., 1689–92 to 1724–25. Walker expedition (Graham). Bibliotheca Americana: a dictionary of books relating to America from its discovery to the present time, ed. Joseph Sabin et al. (29v., New York, 1868–1936), XXII, 341. DAB (biography of Southack; gives some details on his maps). Annals of King's Chapel from the Puritan age of New England to the present day, ed. H. W. Foote et al. (2v., Boston, 1882–96), I, 176, 177, 193, 211, 230, 242, 246, 351, 360, 401; II, 603, 605.

H. M. Chapin, Privateer ships and sailors: the first century of American colonial privateering, 1625–1725 (Toulon, Ill., 1926). S. G. Drake, The history and antiquities of Boston from its settlement in 1630, to the year 1770 (Boston, 1856), 539, 593. H. A. Hill, History of the old South Church (Third Church), Boston, 1669–1884 (2v., Boston, 1890), I, 282. McLennan, Louisbourg. The memorial history of Boston, including Suffolk County, Massachusetts, 1630–1880, ed. Justin Winsor (4v., Boston, 1880–81), II, 104, 541. Murdoch, History of Nova-Scotia, II, 269–71, 307, 357, 363, 404. Privateering and piracy in the colonial period: illustrative documents, ed. J. F. Jameson (New York, 1923), 291. Elizabeth Reynard, The narrow land; folk chronicles of old Cape Cod (Boston, New York, 1934), 239, 241, 244. G. M. Waller, Samuel Vetch, colonial enterpriser (Chapel Hill, N.C., 1960). S. C. Clough, "Notes on Cotton Hill and adjacent estates, 1650–1750," Col. Soc. Mass. Pubs., XX (1920), 266–67. H. C. Hart, "History of Canso, Guysborough County, N.S.," N.S. Hist. Soc. Coll., XXI (1927), 11. Samuel Niles, "A summary historical narrative of the wars of New-England with the French and Indians, in the several parts of the country," Mass. Hist. Soc. Coll., 3rd ser., VI (1837), 249; 4th ser., V (1861), 344. H. S. Tapley, "The Province Galley of Massachusetts Bay, 1694–1716," Essex Institute (Salem, Mass.), Hist. Coll., LVIII (1922), 73–74, 82, 84.

SPAGNIOLINI (Espagnoli, Hispanioli), JEAN-FERNAND, surgeon; b. 1704, son of Domenico Spagniolini and Margherita Tussichi (Toussiqui) of Rome; m. first on 26 Aug. 1733 at Chambly (Que.) to Charlotte Bourloton, secondly on 7 Jan. 1737 at Boucherville (Que.) to Catherine Bénard, *dit* Carignan, and thirdly on 16 Jan. 1745 at Boucherville to Françoise Boucher de Niverville; buried 25 Feb. 1764 at Boucherville.

Spagniolini's life before his first marriage is as yet unknown. Judging from his association with military men, it is likely he had come to Canada with the colonial regular troops and had been a garrison surgeon at Fort Chambly. His wife's family had migrated from Charlesbourg to Chambly *via* Quebec. Charlotte died childless at about the age of 20, a few years after their wedding.

Although Spagniolini had bought an island called "Île à la brisé" in the Bassin de Chambly in July 1736, he moved to Boucherville the following winter. There he married the orphaned daughter of Joseph Bénard, *dit* Carignan. Spagniolini's friends Marien Tailhandier*, *dit* La Baume, a fellow surgeon, and François Garreau, a merchant, acted as witnesses to the marriage contract. Of the children of this union only Marie-Apolline attained maturity; she married François Poudret.

The Spagniolinis lived in comfort at Boucherville, with a paid maidservant. The surgeon travelled throughout the south shore and visited Montreal Island. One record, for August 1736, reports him at the poor-house of the Hôtel-Dieu at Pointe-Saint-Charles to examine a girl who had been struck with a pitchfork when her parents were seeking damages from the owners of a runaway pig. Other records note the surgeon's presence at Verchères and Longue-Pointe.

Early in 1745 Spagniolini married a daughter of Jean-Baptiste BOUCHER de Niverville, seigneur of Chambly, who had sold him "Île à la brisé" in 1736. In the intimidating presence of his future wife's relatives, Spagniolini increased her *préciput* from 500 to 1,000 *livres*. Of their ten children just two escaped death in infancy: Marie-Élisabeth, who married Michel-Joseph Gamelin, and Jean-Baptiste. The Spagniolini name was not perpetuated. His two married daughters left few if any descendants and the fate of the one son is unknown.

PETER N. MOOGK

ANQ-M, Greffe de J.-B. Adhémar, 21 janv. 1751; Greffe d'Antoine Loiseau, 3 janv. 1737, 7, 10 janv. 1745, 4 mars 1746; Greffe de J.-C. Raimbault, 6 juill. 1736; Greffe de François Simonnet, 13 août 1737, 16 sept. 1738; Documents judiciaires, 20 août 1736, 7 mars 1764. É.-Z. Massicotte, "Les chirurgiens de Montréal au XVIIᵉ siècle," *BRH*, XXVII (1921), 41–47; "Chirurgiens, médecins et apothicaires sous le régime français," *BRH*, XXXVIII (1932) 522; "Les chirur-

giens, médecins, etc. de Montréal sous le régime français," APQ *Rapport, 1922–23*, 142. Tanguay, *Dictionnaire*, II, 266, 377, 429; III, 595; IV, 167; VI, 422; VII, 209. Ahern, *Notes pour l'histoire de la médecine*, 520.

SPURRELL, GEORGE, HBC captain and member of the company's London committee; d. October 1770 at Barking, England.

George Spurrell was the longest-serving of the Hudson's Bay Company's ship-captains during the 18th century. He first commanded an HBC ship in 1722, was senior captain by 1727, and continued to take a ship on the annual voyage to Hudson Bay until his retirement in 1756. For this remarkable run of 35 voyages there is no record of serious accident to his ships – a tribute to his professional skill on one of the most taxing trade routes used by British shipping, involving as it did the negotiation on the outward and the homeward passage of the icebound bottleneck of Hudson Strait. During the parliamentary investigation into the company's affairs in 1749, Spurrell revealed that he had never stayed longer than 23 days at an HBC post, and consequently had no first-hand knowledge of the hinterland. Even so, under close questioning he stoutly defended the company's policy of limiting its trading activities to coastal posts in the bay rather than expanding into the interior.

Spurrell was one of the few HBC captains of the period who seems not to have been suspected of private trade by his superiors, and in November 1756 this solid, respectable figure was elected to the governing committee of the company in London. Ex-servants with practical experience of the bay trade rarely found their way to places on the London committee, and the minute books show that Spurrell was invariably entrusted with the manifold problems that the annual voyage to the bay of three or four company ships involved. By this time Spurrell was a man of substance, and in 1756 and 1757 he acquired more than £2,500 worth of company stock, most of which he transferred to his son Joseph, also an HBC captain, when he retired from the committee in 1765.

After his career at sea ended Spurrell had moved his place of residence from Stepney in East London to Barking, where he died in October 1770 leaving Joseph his sole executor.

GLYNDWR WILLIAMS

[Notes on Spurrell's long career are scattered through the company records, particularly in HBC Arch. A.1/120–22 and A.1/34–42. The journals of his voyages to the bay between 1751 and 1755 survive in

C.1/869–73, but they are brief and uninformative. The evidence Spurrell gave before the parliamentary committee in 1749 is noted in E.18/1, ff.198d–203. Records of his stock transactions are in A.43/4–5; and details of his will are in A.44/1, p. 51. G.W.]

STAUNTON, RICHARD, HBC cooper, warehouse-keeper, and factor; fl. 1694–1741.

The date and place of Richard Staunton's birth (and indeed, of his death) are unknown; but in 1694 he was a qualified cooper and was sent to serve as such at York Factory (Man.) by the Hudson's Bay company, at an annual wage of £10. Within a few months of his arrival the post was surrendered to Pierre Le Moyne* d'Iberville although 36 heavy guns were mounted for its defence. The HBC men were promised a passage to England, but they had to spend the winter in the woods, and afterwards suffered much in the journey, being treated as common criminals in the prisons of France. Like Henry Kelsey*, Staunton survived the hardships; he was in London by 1696, was engaged by the company, and was again sent to York, which was recaptured by the English that year. Staunton became a prisoner of the French for a second time when Iberville reappeared in September 1697, fought and sank the man-of-war *Hampshire*, and again took the fort. Once more, Staunton was soon in England and recruited by the HBC, and in 1698 he was ordered to Fort Albany (Ont.).

From the loss of York in 1697 until its reoccupation in 1714 after the treaty of Utrecht, Albany was the only post at the bay in English hands. Staunton served there until 1706, still young enough to claim (later) that he had spent his youth in the company's service. His wages rose steadily, to £40 in 1705, and when he rejoined in 1708, after coming home in 1706, they were £48 a year. All the men at Albany were demanding "very extravagant terms" for remaining to face probable attacks from the French, but Staunton's increases related also to his growing knowledge of the fur trade, and in 1712 he was getting £60 a year as warehouse-keeper at Albany.

With the treaty of Utrecht and the reoccupation of York, Albany lost some of its importance, but it remained the company's main post for opposing the French coureurs de bois from the south. Staunton, made chief factor there in 1714, was instructed to "trade hard" with Indians from the north so that they would take their furs to York, but to entice Indians from the south away from French traders and draw over trade from the Eastmain River. These orders involved delicate variations in the prices paid for furs, but Staunton appears to have given satisfaction, and when he

was recalled in 1715 it was at his own request since a raise in pay had been rejected. In 1716, however, his successor, Thomas McCLIESH, reported that the unruly men at Albany had done what they liked with Staunton.

Staunton was unable to return to the bay until 1716, and was then almost immediately re-engaged for four years at the suggestion of James Knight*. Knight was in charge at York and wanted Staunton as a stand-in for himself if he should go to establish Churchill (Man.) or visit other posts. He described Staunton as the best-qualified man to manage Indians and to understand the trade. Staunton was sent to Churchill in 1718 to be chief trader there, subordinate to York. It was he who was instructed to name the new post Fort Prince of Wales, and he reported on the defences and the extent to which the post might draw trade away from York.

Staunton was a staunch supporter of projects for "discovery to the northward." In 1721 he sent the intrepid traveller Richard NORTON to bring in some Northern and Copper (Yellowknife) Indians who claimed to know where the rumoured copper mine was, and he supported Kelsey's efforts to find a way to the mine, either "by water in Cannoes through the Countrey and not to come Creeping by Land," or by sea-voyages to the north and west. Staunton was still in command in 1722 when John Scroggs* reported that he had found the grisly remains of Knight's search for gold, copper, and the legendary strait of Anian. He had in fact been recalled in 1721, at the end of his contract, but the ship of the year had been unable to call at the post.

When Christopher MIDDLETON took him aboard the *Hannah* in 1722 he called Staunton "a good-natured easy man," but at Churchill the trader had inspired confidence. Staunton was re-engaged that same year and was sent again to command at Albany, where discipline was such a problem that he reported the men as "Sotts to a man." But he supported his predecessor, Joseph Myatt*, who was demoted to deputy at the post, apparently because he had taken an Indian boy into the trading-room and had taught him to read and because he had held aloof from the general debauchery. As previously, Staunton's chief task at Albany was to entice the Indians from the south away from the French by variations in his standard of trade. His contract ran out in 1726 and he retired claiming he had done a good job. Myatt, however, despite Staunton's support for him, claimed that Staunton had exaggerated his success against the French and had not imposed his will on the men.

Between 1726 and 1737 Staunton probably

Stobo

lived in England. He was not again employed by the HBC till he was taken on in 1737 to be chief factor at Moose Factory (Ont.) at £100 a year, with Albany and Eastmain House under his command. Moose had become the centre of opposition to the French, but the post had been burned down in a drunken revel at Christmas 1735, and Staunton faced problems of discipline as well as of trade and defence. Over the four years of his last tour he managed to improve the trade of Moose, and his comments on the "Overplus Trade" (by which the trader sometimes gave the Indians short measure so as to build up a balance of goods, which he used at his discretion), the standard of trade, and "Trust" (which he deplored as a sure way of driving debt-ridden Indians to the French) were shrewd and helpful. With experience of two surrenders to the French at York, he was convinced that a clear field of fire and small-arms provided better defence for Moose than heavy cannon requiring professional gunners, and he sent home the big guns which had been shipped out for its defence. Staunton's control over his own men still seemed weak, however, and his orders for the appointment of George Spence to be master at Albany were defied by the council there in 1741 as Staunton left Hudson Bay for the last time. He was, he said, "glad that your honours can have one to manage your affairs with more prudence and advantage, for I am advanced in Years."

E. E. RICH

HBC Arch. A.6, A.11/2, A.11/43, A.11/114; B.42/a. HBRS, XXV (Davies and Johnson). Morton, *History of the Canadian west*. Rich, *History of the HBC*, I.

STOBO, ROBERT, military officer; b. in Glasgow, Scotland, on 7 Oct. 1726, son of William Stobo, a well-to-do merchant; d. a bachelor 19 June 1770 at Chatham, England.

Robert Stobo studied at the University of Glasgow and then, on the death of his parents, was sent to Virginia at age 16 to learn the trade of a merchant-factor. He settled in Petersburg and on coming of age converted his estate to cash and set himself up in business there. As a friend and distant relative of Governor Robert Dinwiddie, he had access to the governor's palace and spent much of his time in pleasurable pursuits in Williamsburg, the capital city.

Early in April 1754 Dinwiddie sent Colonel George Washington to secure the Forks of the Ohio (present-day Pittsburgh) against the advancing French. Stobo, who had been made a captain on 5 March, followed the small army about a month later in command of a company of Virginia troops. Perhaps because he had acquired a knowledge of military construction, Stobo was named regimental engineer. He rode to the frontier supported by ten personal servants, who were mechanics, and a covered wagon carrying a butt of Madeira wine. In mid-April a French force under Claude-Pierre Pécaudy* de Contrecœur, with Indian allies, had paddled down the Allegheny River, driven off a few dozen English who had started a fort at the forks, and there began to build Fort Duquesne. The killing of Joseph COULON de Villiers de Jumonville by the English on 28 May prompted the French to march south to surround Washington's outnumbered army at his improvised "Fort Necessity" (near Farmington, Pa.). The battle that followed on 3 July marked the start of the last war between the English, French, and Indians in America. In capitulating to the French, Washington turned over two of his captains as a guarantee that 21 French prisoners he had taken several weeks earlier would be returned. The two hostages were the Dutch-born Jacob Van Braam and Robert Stobo.

At Fort Duquesne, Stobo encountered eight members of his regiment who had been taken prisoner by Indians after the battle had ended. Stobo concluded thereby that the terms of the capitulation were "broke" and that he was released from his obligations as a hostage. He drew a scale map of Fort Duquesne and on the back wrote a long letter in which he advised Dinwiddie not to return the French prisoners, and urged that Fort Duquesne be taken that fall. "When we engaged to serve the country," he wrote, "it was expected we were to do it with our lives. Let them not be disappointed. Consider the good of the expedition without the least regard to us. For my part, I would die ten thousand deaths to have the pleasure of possessing this fort but one day, they are so vain of their success at [Fort Necessity], 'tis worse than death to hear them." The letter was safely delivered by a friendly Indian and was given to General Edward Braddock, probably when he arrived at Alexandria, Virginia, the following spring with a large body of British regulars.

Since Dinwiddie refused to return the French prisoners for whom he was being held hostage, Stobo was taken to Quebec. There, under the sponsorship of Paul-Joseph Le Moyne* de Longueuil, he was free to mingle in the best society and even to engage in some trading ventures in concert with Luc de La Corne*, known as La Corne Saint-Luc. Following the defeat of Braddock's army in July 1755, however, the French found Stobo's letter, signature affixed, among the dead general's effects. Stobo and Van Braam were tried by a military court in Montreal, Governor General Pierre de Rigaud* de Vaudreuil presiding, on the charge that they had violated their parole and had spied for the enemy. Stobo fought the charge through a trial that lasted 19 days, but at the end broke down and confessed that he had written the letter in evidence. Van Braam was acquitted of the charge but still held a prisoner. Stobo was sentenced to be beheaded.

The court at Versailles, however, had secretly ordered that the sentence be suspended, perhaps because it was not sure of its legal position in trying and condemning a hostage for an act committed in time of peace. In a 1756 white paper, attributed to the Duc de Choiseul and circulated with *éclat* throughout Europe, Stobo's letter was cited as evidence of British aggression against French territory in the Ohio country. The case became a matter of international controversy.

Stobo, promoted *in absentia* to the rank of major, escaped twice, in May and July 1757, and was captured twice. On his third attempt (1 May 1759), he fled down the St Lawrence in a canoe with eight other American prisoners – four men, a woman, and her three children. Thirty-six days later, after a series of hair-raising escapes and hardships, they sailed triumphantly into Louisbourg, Cape Breton Island, in command of a French schooner, which they had taken in the Baie des Chaleurs, and with two captive French sea captains.

Stobo was received in Louisbourg by Edward WHITMORE who sent him on to serve on General WOLFE's staff. Stobo led the English attack on Pointe-aux-Trembles (Neuville) on 21 July; his "Memoirs" claim that it was he who showed Wolfe the path to the Plains of Abraham at the Anse au Foulon. The evidence is intriguing but inconclusive. In any case, he was not present at the fall of the city, for Wolfe had sent him with dispatches to General Jeffery Amherst* at Crown Point on Lake Champlain. When Amherst decided to delay his invasion of Canada until spring of the following year (1760), Stobo returned to Williamsburg carrying a letter from Amherst recommending his preferment. There he received the accolades of his countrymen, his back pay with interest, a gift of £1,000, and a citation of the House of Burgesses (carried to him by Colonel Washington) containing thanks "for his steady and inviolable attachment to the interest of this country; for his singular bravery and courage exerted on all occasions. . . ."

Stobo chose to seek next a career in the British army. He therefore went to London, where he had an audience with William Pitt and was given, without purchase, a commission as captain in Amherst's own 15th Regiment of Foot. He joined Amherst again at Crown Point and on 11 Sept. 1760, marched at the head of his company into Montreal, the town where he had been condemned to death.

Stobo served in garrison in Montreal and Quebec until the following spring, when he sailed to the Caribbean with General Robert Monckton*'s force and participated in the capture of Martinique and Havana. At the assault on Morro Castle (Cuba) he was struck on the head and seriously wounded by masonry dislodged by a Spanish cannonball. He rejoined his regiment in Quebec in September 1763, but it is not known if he was present during the mutiny of the 15th Foot (18–21 September). In 1767 he bought from the heirs of Jacques-Pierre DANEAU de Muy a seigneury of 69,000 acres called "aux Loutres," on the east shore of Lake Champlain. His title was questioned, however, and neither he nor his heirs ever took possession of the land.

Stobo went to England with his regiment in the summer of 1768 and served in barracks at Chatham. Through the recommendation of a fellow Scot, the novelist Tobias Smollett, he became acquainted with another Scot, the philosopher David Hume. "He seemed to be a man of good sense," Hume wrote to Smollett, "and has surely had the most extraordinary adventures in the world." Suffering from his old head wound, disappointed at lack of promotion, and troubled by his inability to validate his claim to the Lake Champlain lands, Stobo began to drink excessively and his conduct became erratic. On 19 June 1770 in barracks at Chatham, he killed himself with his pistol. His Scots-English relatives effectively concealed the story of his suicide, and the date and manner of his death were a mystery, despite a continuing interest in his career, until 1965.

ROBERT C. ALBERTS

[Stobo's birth is recorded in the General Register Office (Edinburgh), Register of births and baptisms for the City of Glasgow. For a full-length biography of Stobo, with complete documentation of his career, *see*: R. C. Alberts, *The most extraordinary adventures of Major Robert Stobo* (Boston, 1965); Stobo's "Memoirs," which do not seem to have been written by Stobo himself, are discussed on pp.345–49. A manuscript copy of the memoirs, dated 1760, can be found in the Harvard College Library, MS Can 45 (44M-382). The memoirs were first printed in London in 1800: *Memoirs of Major Robert Stobo, of the Virginia regiment*, and were reprinted, with notes by N. B. Craig, Pittsburgh, 1854. *See also*: PRO, Adm 1/307. Wis. State Hist. Soc. (Madison), Draper MSS, 12 U 73–76, 77, 80, 88–89.

For copies of documents concerning Stobo's trial,

Strouds

see: "Procès de Robert Stobo et de Jaco Wambram pour crime de haute trahison," APQ *Rapport, 1922–23*, 299–347. *See also*: "L'évasion de Stobo et de Van Braam de la prison de Québec en mai 1757," *BRH*, XIV (1908), 147–54, 175–82. *Papiers Contrecoeur* (Grenier). [Simon Stevens], *A journal of Lieutenant Simon Stevens . . . with an account of his escape from Quebec . . .* (Boston, 1760). *Westminster Journal, or New Weekly Miscellany* (London), 23 June 1770. R. J. Jones, *A history of the 15th (East Yorkshire) regiment . . .* (Beverly, Eng., 1958). Gilbert Parker, *The seats of the mighty; being the memoirs of Captain Robert Moray . . .* (New York, 1897), is a romanticized account of Stobo's career. R.C.A.].

STROUDS, GILLES WILLIAM (later baptized Louis-Claude-Joseph), entrepreneur; b. *c.* 1712 at London, England, son of William Strouds and Rachel Relind Baionas; buried 5 April 1757 at Quebec.

The Strouds family emigrated from England to Carolina early in the 18th century. In 1738 an affair of honour forced the younger William to flee the justice of the colony to New France. Four years later he abjured his Protestant faith and was baptized in the chapel of the Jesuit college with Gilles Hocquart* serving as his godparent. No doubt at that time he acquired the Christian names, Louis-Claude-Joseph, by which he was identified in the 1744 census of Quebec; he lived then with three servants on Rue de la Montagne. Ten years later, after he had married, he resided on Rue Saint-Jean.

Strouds' major commercial interest appears to have been the Labrador seal fishery. In August 1751 he entered a five-year partnership with Jacques de LAFONTAINE de Belcour to exploit the latter's posts along the north shore of the St Lawrence from the Nontagamion (Nétagamiou) to the Chicataka (Chécatica) rivers and at the Rivière Saint-Augustin, which Lafontaine leased from Charles Cheron. Strouds assumed one-half of the lease on Saint-Augustin and furnished 4,000 *livres* to Lafontaine's son Gilles to outfit two ships with supplies. Lafontaine retained one-eighth interest. Seal hunting must have been successful. In September 1754 Strouds borrowed 2,200 *livres* on future returns to supply victuals, nets, lead, and wages for the schooner *Marie-Louise* in order to hunt seals at Nontagamion; he paid back the loan within a year. Strouds also supplied firewood to Quebec. In 1752 he hired two men for the season to exploit his lighter, *Baleine du Port* (30 to 35 tons), by transporting cordwood from the south shore of the St Lawrence and selling it in Quebec for 40 *sols* per cord. Strouds took one-half of the profits; the two sailors shared the remainder and paid a third

crew-member. Nothing else is known concerning Strouds' business career, but the above account suggests that in true entrepreneurial fashion he sought to use his own and other individuals' capital to exploit market opportunities he observed around him.

On 26 Feb. 1748 Strouds married Marie-Josephte Morisseau at Charlesbourg, near Quebec, and the same year successfully applied to the French crown for letters of naturalization. A child lived only for a few months; in 1751 Strouds purchased from some Acadian Indians a two-year-old boy born of English parents and had him baptized Pierre at Quebec. Gilles William Strouds died at Quebec and, on 5 April 1757, he was buried in the church of the Recollets. Strouds had left sums to be distributed to a servant and to the poor.

JAMES S. PRITCHARD

ANQ, Greffe de C.-H. Du Laurent, 24 févr. 1748; Greffe de J.-C. Panet, 15 mars 1757. *Coll. de manuscrits relatifs à la N.-F.*, III, 419–20. *Inv. de pièces du Labrador* (P.-G. Roy), II, 95–97, 98–99, 104–5, 106, 107. "Recensement de Québec, 1744" (APQ *Rapport*). Tanguay, *Dictionnaire*. "Biographies canadiennes," *BRH*, XX (1914), 375–76.

SULLIVAN, TIMOTHY, known as **Timothée Silvain,** king's physician; b. 1690 or 1696, son of Daniel Sullivan, physician of Cork (Republic of Ireland), and Mary Elizabeth MacCarthy; d. 16 June 1749 in Montreal.

Timothy Sullivan had, by various accounts, lived in Canada since 1717. The only source of information on his earlier career is a contradictory and improbable letter of nobility discovered by Abbé Cyprien Tanguay*. It is likely that Sullivan was the author of this fanciful document.

According to the letter, allegedly written by several Irish peers at Paris in 1736, Timothy Sullivan was "the son of Cornelius Daniel O'Sullivan, Count of Killarney . . . and Lieutenant General in the armies of King James II" and had served "as a Captain of Dragoons in Spain for sixteen years; . . . having left Spain in 1716 by order of the General Staff to recruit men in Ireland for his regiment, he was seized by privateers who took him to New England, from whence he fled to Canada in order to remain a Roman Catholic." At his marriage in January 1720 Sullivan had described himself simply as the 24-year-old son of an Irish physician, though a social or military title would have been an asset in New France. The signatures of the Irish nobles (Fitzjames of Berwick is "Fitzjam de Barwick") appear to be copied from a French history book, possibly from

Sullivan's extensive library. Ægidius Fauteux* uncovered many errors of fact in the letter's text.

Sullivan's marriage and his vanity provided the need for an aristocratic lineage. In 1720 he was a young *parvenu* with money. His bride was an impoverished widow of 38 with six children. She was, nonetheless, Marie-Renée Gaultier de Varennes, daughter of the late governor of Trois-Rivières, René Gaultier* de Varennes, sister of Pierre GAULTIER de Varennes et de La Vérendrye, and former wife of Captain François-Christophe Dufrost de La Gemerais. The wedding was clandestine and was held at Pointe-aux-Trembles (Neuville), far from the bride's home and family. The marriage contract was, contrary to custom, concluded after the marriage. Sullivan's powerful in-laws were undoubtedly mollified when he paid out approximately 20,000 French *livres* in the next three years to cover his wife's accumulated debts. Governor Vaudreuil's wife [Louise-Élisabeth de Joybert*] testified that Sullivan "deprived himself of necessities to raise [his stepchildren] and to give them all the education possible."

Late in 1721 the newlyweds moved from Varennes to Montreal where they eventually made their home on Rue Saint-Paul. Like his father, Sullivan acted as a physician *and* surgeon. Several seigneurs and townspeople of note asked that he be officially named resident physician of the region. Governor Philippe de Rigaud* de Vaudreuil endorsed their petition in September 1723 since Sullivan was a "fine gentleman who has lived in the town [Montreal] for six years, whose probity and competence are well known to me thanks to the large number of remarkable cures he effected there." Sullivan, a devout Roman Catholic, also had the confidence of the clergy.

On 7 March 1724 two letters patent were issued by the French crown: one a certificate of naturalization requested by Sullivan, and the other an official appointment without salary as physician on Montreal Island. Sullivan was to visit the officers and soldiers there "in order to prescribe suitable remedies for them and to carefully oversee their recovery under the orders of Sieur [Michel Sarrazin*]", (king's physician). Sullivan improperly assumed the title "king's physician" on the strength of this commission. In 1727 he complained that Joseph Benoist, surgeon to the troops at Montreal, hindered him in his official duties. Letters sent to the council of Marine by the nuns of the Montreal Hôtel-Dieu, where Sullivan worked from 1725 to 1730, the priests, and high officials of the town supported him in this dispute. Intendant Dupuy* repeated Vaudreuil's

endorsement of Sullivan and added that he was "extremely charitable to the poor, risking his life every day by crossing rivers when the ice is very weak to succour them."

The new governor of Canada, Charles de BEAUHARNOIS, did not share this enthusiasm and in 1727 he wrote that Sullivan "exercises his trade in a somewhat strange manner: he is at once physician, surgeon, and apothecary; he . . . gives remedies that no one recognizes and I believe that one can regard him as an empiricist, never making any formal prescription . . . He is allied to a family that obtained a physician's certificate for him." Favourable testimony from so many others in 1727 and 1728 induced Beauharnois to reserve judgement for six more years. His suggestion that Sarrazin examine the Irishman was not pressed.

When Sullivan went to France in 1734 the governor and Intendant Hocquart* feared that he was after the vacant post of king's physician at Quebec. In October they warned the minister that Sullivan "obtained or rather snatched up a commission as physician at Montreal . . . this foreigner is a very bad physician, in whom no one has confidence . . . He is a charlatan that all sensible people and others have abandoned." Their fear was unwarranted but Sullivan must have learned of their low opinion of him.

The physician, once praised as generous and charitable, became extravagantly vain and ill-tempered. In 1740s he styled himself "Timothée Silvain écuyer, sieur O'Sullivan, Médecin du Roi en ce pays" and probably concocted the letter of nobility at this time. Though he possessed *arrière-fiefs* in the seigneuries of Varennes, Cournoyer, and Plaines and claimed to own others in Belœil and Rouville, he did not add them to his titles. From 1724 to 1731 he had committed assault and battery against three persons. Now that he affected that mark of nobility, the sword, he was particularly dangerous.

In 1737 after mass on Christmas eve Sullivan beat his wife so badly that she feared for her life. Despite promises to clerics, he could not control his rage. On 10 January his wife's brother, La Vérendrye, and a nephew, René Gaultier de Varennes, tried to rescue her. Sullivan held them off with a sword and a poker, boxed his wife, and shouted at all three. Abbé François Chèze* established a truce but even in his presence Sullivan threatened and attacked his wife.

After the fray Sullivan tried unsuccessfully to have the would-be rescuers prosecuted, and his wife petitioned for a legal separation. In a counter-petition Sullivan declared that only the *Officialité* (ecclesiastical court) could separate

Sutherland

him from the wife given him by God. Eventually, and here we must admire Sullivan's power of persuasion and his wife's capacity for forgiveness, the couple was reconciled.

Sullivan's behaviour continued contradictory. After cutting La Vérendrye's finger with a sword on 10 January he stopped to dress the wound before resuming the argument. In February he savagely attacked a court usher, then bandaged the cuts and forced his bleeding victim to drink with him and to embrace him upon leaving. This usher was armed when he delivered another writ but was attacked by Mme Sullivan when he brandished his pistol.

Sullivan's most notorious brawl involved the lieutenant general for civil and criminal affairs in Montreal, Jacques-Joseph GUITON de Monrepos. In December 1742 the magistrate ordered one of Sullivan's houses vacated as a fire hazard. Sullivan went to demand an explanation and as a parting gesture he jabbed Monrepos in the chest with his cane. The court ushers who were ordered to arrest Sullivan wisely sought military reinforcement. The officer on duty was, however, Jacques-René GAULTIER de Varennes and he withheld aid until his brother-in-law escaped from Montreal with his belongings. Monrepos was furious and in October 1743 Intendant Hocquart reported that his relentless legal pursuit of Sullivan, "whose wife is related to the entire colony" had "antagonized many worthy people."

Sullivan retired to Cap de Varennes to undertake the reconstruction of his wife's former home. By 1744 the details of the Monrepos affair reached the minister of Marine, Maurepas, who reprimanded Governor Beauharnois, suspended three officers and cashiered Varennes to preserve, he said, what little discipline remained in the colonial troops. Sullivan remained at Varennes playing the role of "Lord O'Sullivan." He died on 16 June 1749 and was buried the next day near his pew in the Saint-Amable chapel of Montreal's parish church. Without living children, he left his estate to his wife's descendants; half his library went to Marie-Marguerite Dufrost* de Lajemmerais, Mme d'Youville, who disliked him. Sullivan was probably an Irish immigrant to the English colonies who had come to Canada for religious reasons. He was literate, he had an ability to make money and possessed attractive qualities, but his pretensions and passionate temper disgraced him.

PETER N. MOOGK

AN, Col., B, 47, p.116; 50, p.428; 52/1, pp.172–73; 61/1, p.33; C¹¹ᴬ, 45, pp.83–85; 46, p.69; 58, p.40; 61, pp.172–73; 79, pp.270–75, 352–54; F³, 10, pp.328–30; 13, pp.193–96 (PAC transcripts). ANQ, Greffe de J.-É. Dubreuil, 29 janv. 1720; NF, Coll. de pièces jud. et not., 986, 2439; NF, Documents de la juridiction de Montréal, IV, 97v, 120f., 129v; X, 34–36. ANQ-M, Greffe de J.-B. Adhémar, 18 févr. 1733, 5 sept. 1741, 1ᵉʳ sept. 1747; Greffe de L.-C. Danré de Blanzy, 21 avril 1741; Greffe de Jacques David; Greffe de C.-R. Gaudron de Chevremont, 3 avril 1733; Greffe de J.-C. Porlier, 3 mars 1738, 22 déc. 1742; Greffe de J.-C. Raimbault, 10 mars 1732, passim; Greffe de Pierre Raimbault, 22 avril 1720; Greffe de Simon Sanguinet, 30 oct. 1743, passim; Greffe de Nicolas Senet, 19 févr. 1720; Documents judiciaires, 10 oct. 1729; Registres des audiences, 9, f.370; 11, f.124; 12, ff.761v, 851, 893, 960; 13, ff.1145, 1164, 1166v, 1168v.

"Brevet de médecin de l'île de Montréal pour Thimothée Sylvain," BRH, XXXIX (1933), 192. L'île de Montréal en 1731 (A. Roy). "Recensement de Montréal, 1741" (Massicotte). P.-G. Roy, Inv. concessions, IV, 102, 234; V, 170–71; Inv. ins. Cons. souv., 173; Inv. jug. et délib., 1717–1760, III, 62; IV, 131; Inv. ord. int., II, 170; III, 142, 167. Tanguay, Dictionnaire, I, 555–56; III, 235. Ahern, Notes pour l'histoire de la médecine, 523–26. Thomas Guérin, The Gael in New France (Montreal, 1946). [Antoine] Champagne, "Les Gaultier de La Véranderie en France et au Canada et leurs relations par delà l'océan," RHAF, XIII (1959–60), 118–19. É.-M. Faillon, "Le sieur Timothée Sylvain," BRH, VII (1901), 24–27. Ægidius Fauteux, "Un médecin irlandais à Montréal avant la Cession," BRH, XXIII (1917), 303–11, 333–38, 356–72. Albertine Ferland-Angers, "Où habitait La Verendrye?", RHAF, III (1949–50), 622; "Varennes, berceau d'une sainte," RHAF, XIII (1959–60), 4, 12–13, 14, 15. Antoine Roy, "Ce qu'ils lisaient," Cahiers des Dix, XX (1955), 208.

SUTHERLAND, PATRICK, military officer; fl. 1746; d. c. 1766.

After serving at Gibraltar as a captain in the 45th regiment, Patrick Sutherland went to Louisbourg, Cape Breton Island, with that regiment in 1746. He commanded a detachment at Pisiquid (Windsor, N.S.) in 1752. In the spring of 1753, when arrangements were made for the founding of a colony at Merligueche (Lunenburg) and for the transfer there of "foreign Protestants" from Halifax, Governor Peregrine Thomas HOPSON made Captain Sutherland·second in command to Lieutenant-Colonel Charles LAWRENCE during the establishment of the new township and officer commanding at Lunenburg when Lawrence returned to Halifax. Sutherland was appointed lieutenant-colonel of the Lunenburg militia regiment on 10 May 1753 and justice of the peace and *custos rotulorum* for the township of Lunenburg on 26 May.

Except for short intervals Sutherland remained in charge at Lunenburg for about nine years, endeavouring to maintain order, to provide security, and to promote the welfare of the settlers. His initial concern in the summer of 1753 was with the disposition of troops – some 90 regulars and 70 rangers – and with the building and manning of blockhouses. Within a few weeks two blockhouses were built, and work was begun on a palisade to stretch across the neck of the peninsula on which the town stood. The settlers soon took possession of the town lots for which they had drawn shortly before leaving Halifax, and later that year garden lots and farm lots were laid out.

There was dissatisfaction, however, among many of the settlers, frustrated by waiting in Halifax for up to four years before being given their land, and with grievances over the cost of ocean passages and the kinds of goods the government had supplied. It erupted in an armed insurrection in December 1753 [see PETTREQUIN]. Sutherland tried to persuade the settlers to discuss their grievances peaceably, but finally found it necessary to summon troops under Robert Monckton* from Halifax to disarm them.

During the winter of 1754–55 the settlers, who had cleared a considerable amount of land, sustained substantial losses from a cattle distemper. Captain Sutherland applied to the government of Nova Scotia for seed corn for their subsistence, and wheat and oats were purchased for them. As more Lunenburg inhabitants settled on farm lots at a distance from the town, the death-rate at childbirth rose. On Sutherland's suggestion, the council advised in April 1755 that two midwives should be appointed to reside among them.

Victualling was a special concern for Captain Sutherland. The initial one year's rations had been extended for a year. In June 1755 Sutherland reported that "the most deserving here cannot Subsist without the Governments Assistance. . . . I leave you to Judge of my Situation," he added, ". . . there being between Fifteen and Sixteen hundred Souls who have not a mouthfull of Bread, not a Barrel of Flour to Sell, had they money to buy it as they have not. . . ." Through Sutherland's help the settlers obtained victualling for a sufficient time to make progress on their lands. Prospects were so promising by the summer of 1756 that Sutherland established a weekly public market in the town, "for Selling & Buying, all kinds of Goods & Cattle." The farm settlers were still "much intimidated" by Indians, and Sutherland persuaded the council in June 1756 to authorize the construction of two new blockhouses – on the La Hève (La Have) River and between that river and Mahone Bay.

In the spring of 1758 Captain Sutherland was relieved of his duties at Lunenburg so that he could take part in the expedition against Louisbourg, which had been returned to the French in 1749. During the siege he commanded a post at the bottom of the northeast arm of the harbour; a party of Indians and French was repulsed there on 16 July. Following the capture of Louisbourg, Sutherland returned to Lunenburg. After the creation of Lunenburg County in 1759 he was commissioned justice of the peace for the town and county and *custos rotulorum* on 5 March 1760. A month later he was appointed justice of the newly established Inferior Court of Common Pleas for Lunenburg County.

Early in 1761 Sutherland was promoted major in the 77th Regiment of Foot. At the request of General Jeffery Amherst* and the Nova Scotia Council, he remained in Nova Scotia. It was believed he could be useful in the establishment of new settlements. In September 1762 he was in charge of a battalion from Halifax which assisted in the recapture of St John's, Newfoundland, and he commanded the troops sent to take possession of the town's gate. He returned to Halifax in the autumn.

Sutherland was still in Halifax in 1763 and is shown as a major on full pay in the army list of 1766. His name does not appear in the list for 1767, and a note dated 20 Jan. 1768 on a list of commissioned officers in the Lunenburg militia states that he is dead.

CHARLES BRUCE FERGUSSON

PANS, MG 1, 249–50; RG 1, 38A; 134; 163; 164/2, pp.26, 27; 165; 342; 382; 397; RG 3, Minutes of Nova Scotia Council, 1753–63; RG 20. PRO, WO 34/12, 34/13 (mfm in PAC, MG 12, 1365). [William Amherst], *Journal of William Amherst in America, 1758–1760*, ed. J. C. Webster (Frome, London, Eng., 1927). *Army list, 1756; 1761; 1766; 1767*. E. W. H. Fyers, "The loss and recapture of St John's, Newfoundland, in 1762," Society for Army Hist. Research (London), *Journal*, XI (1932), 199, 205. [Charles Lawrence], *Journal and letters of Colonel Charles Lawrence* (PANS *Bull.*, 10, Halifax, 1953). *The recapture of St John's, Newfoundland, in 1762 as described in the journal of Lieut.-Col. William Amherst, commander of the British expeditionary force*, ed. J. C. Webster (privately printed, 1928). Bell, *Foreign Protestants*. M. B. DesBrisay, *History of the county of Lunenburg* (2nd ed., Toronto, 1895). Prowse, *History of Nfld*.

SWANTON, ROBERT, naval officer; d. 11 July 1765, probably in St James' parish, Westminster, London, England.

Robert Swanton was commissioned lieutenant in the Royal Navy on 17 Jan. 1734/35. In January 1743/44 he was in command of the *Astrea* which

Swatana

burned in the Piscataqua River (Me.-N.H.). In August he was made post captain, commanding the *Mary* galley. He may have been unemployed between 1748 and 1756 when Britain was at peace. Following the outbreak of the Seven Years' War he was appointed to the *Prince* and shortly after moved to the *Vanguard*. He was with BOSCAWEN at the capture of Louisbourg, Île Royale (Cape Breton Island) in 1758 and with Admiral Charles Saunders* at Quebec in 1759, but he performed no unusual services in either campaign.

Although Quebec fell in September 1759, Trois-Rivières and Montreal remained in French hands, and the British were anxious to get a fleet into the St Lawrence in the spring before supplies and reinforcements could arrive from France. Swanton and the *Vanguard* reached the Île du Bic on 11 May 1760, accompanied only by the frigate *Diana* (Capt. Alexander Schomberg). He planned to wait there for the rest of his squadron, which had been scattered during the crossing of the Atlantic, but he soon received word from James Murray*, commander at Quebec, that the city was under attack. Lévis*, with some 11,000 men and the support of Jean Vauquelin*'s two frigates, two armed vessels, and collection of small craft was besieging it. Aided by fresh north-easterly winds Swanton reached Quebec on the evening of 15 May, joining the *Lowestoft* (Capt. Joseph Deane), which had arrived a few days before. The next morning the *Lowestoft* and the *Diana* destroyed or routed the French ships while the *Vanguard* enfiladed the French position at Sillery. Lévis hastily raised the siege, abandoning his guns. "One ship of the line and the place [Quebec] would have been ours," lamented the engineer Jean-Nicolas Desandrouins*. The British naval presence was reinforced on 18 May with the arrival of Alexander, Lord COLVILL's squadron, and François-Chenard Giraudais, commanding a small French relief fleet, did not attempt to go up the St Lawrence when he learned that the British had preceded him.

Swanton returned to England in October, unaware that the admiralty had appointed him to relieve Colvill for the winter as commander-in-chief at Halifax. In the spring of 1761 Swanton helped convoy the outward-bound ships of the East India Company. The next year the *Vanguard* was in the fleet that completed the capture of French possessions in the West Indies. Swanton was promoted rear-admiral of the blue on 21 Oct. 1762. He was at Dominica and Antigua the following summer.

Swanton died on 11 July 1765, and was survived by his wife Emma. The administration of his estate indicates that at the time of his death he was a resident of St James' parish, Westminster.

C. H. LITTLE

PRO, Adm. 1/2474; Prob. 6/141. Knox, *Historical journal* (Doughty). *Logs of the conquest* (Wood). PRO, *Calendar of Home Office papers of the reign of George III, 1760 (25 Oct.)–1765*, ed. Joseph Redington (London, 1878), 300. Charnock, *Biographia navalis*, V, 354–58. G.B., Adm., *Commissioned sea officers, 1660–1815*, III. W. L. Clowes *et al.*, *The Royal Navy, a history from the earliest times to the present* (7v., London, 1897–1903), III. Stanley, *New France*.

SWATANA (an abbreviation of **Onkiswathe-tami**, "he causes it to be light for us"; **Ungquate-rughiathe**, cited in one document, is an alternative expression of the same idea; **Shikellimy**, variously spelled, is an Algonkian equivalent), an Oneida chief of the Bear clan, resident near and at Shamokin (now Sunbury, Pa.), an Iroquois supervisor of the Shawnees and a key figure in Indian-English relations; first mentioned in official records in 1728; d. at Shamokin on 6 Dec. 1748.

The naturalist John Bartram, who met Swatana in 1743 and also obtained information from his son, recorded that "*Shickcalamy* . . . was of the six nations, or rather a *Frenchman* born at *Mont-real*, and adopted by the *Oneidoes*, after being taken prisoner." Nothing more is known of his origin, though Indian relatives (presumably by adoption) are mentioned in contemporary records. His children were, like their mother, of the Cayuga nation and the Turtle clan.

The date of Swatana's appointment by the Iroquois to oversee the Shawnees, who had begun before 1700 to settle on the Delaware and Susquehanna rivers, is unknown. His first known residence in Pennsylvania was, until sometime after 1737, adjacent to a Shawnee village about 12 miles north of Shamokin. Swatana's initial visit to Philadelphia was in 1728; soon after, Pennsylvania officials became aware of his official status and possible usefulness to the province. He was invited back to Philadelphia; official condolences were sent on the death of a son in 1729; and "Shekallamy, . . . a trusty good Man & a great Lover of the English," was sent to invite the Six Nations to a council in 1732, at which the gratified chiefs recommended further meetings, to be arranged by Swatana and the Pennsylvania interpreter Conrad Weiser. The negotiations bore fruit in two deeds, dated 11 and 25 Oct. 1736 (signed by "Shekalamy" or "Shykelimy," among others), releasing all claims by the Six

Nations to land in southeastern Pennsylvania. Six years later Swatana participated in another council at Philadelphia when the Six Nations denied that the Delawares had rights to any remaining land in Pennsylvania; subsequently Pennsylvania oriented its Indian policy towards the Iroquois until about 1755, employing Swatana and Weiser as its agents.

By 1742 Swatana had left the Shawnee village, whose residents had migrated westward, and had moved to Shamokin, an important Indian town and trading place and home of the Delaware "king," Allumapees (Sasoonan). Here in September 1744 Weiser supervised the building of a house, 49½ feet long by 17½ wide and roofed with shingles, in which Swatana was host to the Presbyterian missionary David Brainerd, who visited Shamokin twice in 1745, and to a succession of Moravian missionaries, whose mission was established in the town in the latter year. On other occasions, Indian warriors staged their dances in the house.

Swatana's associations with the Moravians had begun in 1742, when Count von Zinzendorf met him at Shamokin and envisioned "King Shikellimy" as one of the agents for conversion of the Indians. The diplomat and the missionaries established a congenial relationship. The missionaries' attention and behaviour pleased the chief, and the blacksmith whom the Moravians maintained at Shamokin after 1747 was a practical help to the Indians. The Moravians considered Swatana a follower but did not baptize him because, as he told them, a priest had baptized him as a child.

In 1737, 1743, and 1745 Swatana journeyed to the Iroquois council fire at Onondaga (near Syracuse, N.Y.) with Weiser, whom the governor of Virginia employed on these occasions to negotiate peace between the Iroquois and their southern enemies, Catawbas and others. In these negotiations Swatana and Weiser did not serve in their usual capacity as representatives of the Six Nations and Pennsylvania, respectively; rather, Swatana appeared as Pennsylvania's sponsor of the Virginia agent, Weiser. On the second of these trips, the ambassadors were accompanied by the cartographer Lewis Evans and John Bartram, who documented the journey in a map published in 1749 and a journal printed in 1751. On the third trip they were accompanied by two Moravian missionaries, Bishop Joseph (Spangenberg) and David Zeisberger*.

In 1747 the Indians at Shamokin suffered severely from malaria. Among the casualties were the Delaware king and several members of Swatana's family, including his wife. Swatana

himself was very sick but recovered with the help (one trusts) of medicine sent by the government and administered by Conrad Weiser. In the spring of 1748 he performed his final service for Pennsylvania, cautioning against too hasty support of the Indians who, led by ORONTONY, had committed hostilities against the French, and warning the colony that the report of a Six Nations declaration of war against the French on this occasion was erroneous. He was well enough by April 1748 to travel to Moravian headquarters at Bethlehem, Pennsylvania, and to Philadelphia, and he paid another visit to Bethlehem in November. On 6 Dec. 1748 he died.

In contemporary accounts Swatana appears as an able and intelligent man, dignified but pleasant, courteous, unruffled, industrious, and dependable. Of the many anecdotes concerning him, one tells how he came to call on the missionaries sometime in 1747 and, finding the smithy idle, asked them if it was Sunday. Assured that it was, he went home, put on his "kingly robes," and then returned to continue his visit. A rare departure from his usual composure was recorded in 1734, when Mme Montour [Elizabeth COUC], who had been employed by Pennsylvania as an Indian interpreter, belittled a party of visiting Oneidas and was denounced by Swatana as "a certain Woman, whose old Age only protects her from being punished for such Falsehoods."

Sometime before his final illness Swatana took a new wife, a Tutelo woman, who returned to her own people after his death. He was also survived by three sons and two daughters. Two sons had previously been killed in raids on the Catawbas. As supervisor of the Shawnees, Swatana was in effect succeeded by another Oneida chief, Scarroyady, resident on the upper Ohio, where most of the Shawnees had resettled. As Pennsylvania's adviser in Indian affairs, Swatana was followed by his oldest son John (John Shikellimy, John Logan) until about 1755, when provincial policy was altered by the Seven Years' War and by William Johnson*'s appointment as superintendent of northern Indians.

WILLIAM A. HUNTER

Moravian Church Archives (Bethlehem, Pa.), Bethlehem Diary; Indian missions, box 121, Shamokin; Personalia, box 225. John Bartram, *Observations on the inhabitants, climate, soil, rivers, productions, animals, and other matters worthy of notice, made by Mr. John Bartram, in his travels from Pensilvania to Onondago, Oswego and the Lake Ontario, in Canada; to which is annex'd a curious account of the cataracts at Niagara, by Mr. Peter Kalm, a Swedish gentleman who travelled there* (London, 1751). Pennsylvania, *Colonial*

Taché

records, III-V. *Pennsylvania archives,* 1st ser., I, II. "Spangenberg's notes of travel to Onondaga in 1745," ed. J. W. Jordan, *Pennsylvania Magazine of History and Biography* (Philadelphia), II (1878), 56–64. Conrad Wiser [*sic*], "Narrative of a journey from Tulpehocken, Pennsylvania, to Onondaga, in 1737 . . .," in H. R. Schoolcraft, *Historical and statistical information respecting the history, condition and prospects of the Indian tribes of the United States* (6v., Philadelphia, 1851–57), IV, 324–41. David Zeisberger, *Zeisberger's Indian dictionary . . .* (Cambridge, Mass., 1887). L. H. Gipson, *Lewis Evans . . .* (Philadelphia, 1939). P. A. W. Wallace, *Conrad Weiser, 1696–1760, friend of colonist and Mohawk* (Philadelphia, London, 1945).

T

TACHÉ (Tachêt), JEAN (Jean-Pascal), merchant and trader, member of the Grand Jury of the district of Quebec, notary; b. 1698 at Garganvilar (dept. of Tarn-et-Garonne), France, son of Étienne Taché, commissary for supplies at Saint-Malo, and Marguerite Dauzet; d. 18 April 1768 in Quebec.

Jean Taché was probably on his first voyage to Canada when he sailed from La Rochelle on 5 June 1727 for Quebec. He was coming to the colony to deal in furs as an associate of the La Rochelle merchant trader Jean-Pierre Lapeyre the younger, with whom he had been in partnership since 1724. Taché was back in France on 15 Dec. 1727. Towards the end of 1730 he settled permanently in the colony, although continuing his commerce with the mother country.

Taché, it seems, was rapidly successful in business and amassed a rather considerable fortune. It is difficult to list completely his activities, for, like many merchant traders in the colony, he diversified his investments enormously. In 1741 he was one of François-Étienne CUGNET's creditors, and in the years following he was the owner of at least three ships, the *Trinité,* the *Émérillon,* and the *Saint-Roch,* that regularly sailed up the Labrador coast seeking cargoes of salt. At the same time he was dealing with merchant traders in Montauban such as the Mariette brothers, and with others in La Rochelle, Denis Goguet for example. Indeed, Taché stayed at the latter's home when he went to France in 1753. He learned that same year that the king was indemnifying him completely for the loss of one of his ships that had been chartered to transport munitions to the posts along the borders of Acadia.

Taché did not confine himself to these activities, but also engaged in the fishing industry. In 1750 the minister, Rouillé, had refused him permission to operate the concession of the Îles de la Madeleine for hunting walrus, but in 1756 he obtained the post of Saint-Modet on the Labrador coast and not that at Gros Mécatina, which went to the former intendant Hocquart*. Nevertheless, through his marriage to Marie-Anne Jolliet de Mingan, Taché received the income paid for the fishing rights to the concessions of Mingan and Gros Mécatina [*see* Pierre RÉVOL]. Moreover, he operated through a lease the post on the Rivière Nontagamion (Nétagamiou), which belonged to Jacques de LAFONTAINE de Belcour and could produce annually about 800 skins and 100 barrels of oil.

From 1750 to 1753 Jean Taché was a militia captain in the government of Quebec. Because he had won his fellow-citizens' confidence, he acted several times as attorney or arbitrator in disputes between merchants. In 1748 he acted as secretary for the merchant traders of Quebec, and in 1753 he became their syndic. He still held this office at the fall of Quebec, and it was in this capacity that, with François DAINE, Jean-Claude Panet*, and other bourgeois and merchants, he signed shortly after 13 Sept. 1759 the petition addressed to Jean-Baptiste-Nicolas-Roch de Ramezay*, the king's lieutenant, asking him to capitulate to save Quebec's citizens from suffering still heavier losses should the British resume bombarding the town.

The capitulation of Quebec and France's subsequent surrender of the colony in 1763 modified considerably Taché's commercial activities. If he kept his interests in the concessions at Mingan and Saint-Modet, he does not seem to have operated them himself. Indeed, on 30 April 1762 he had leased the Saint-Modet post to John Ord, although confirmation of his ownership rights to that post was not given him by James Murray* until 16 May 1763.

Following the ordinance of 17 Sept. 1764 which created the legal system of the new British colony, Jean Taché was among the first Canadians to be called as members of the Grand Jury for the district of Quebec. It was in this capacity that a month later, together with other members of that jury, Canadian or British, he signed the report criticizing certain dispositions of the ordinance of

17 September. On 4 Feb. 1768 Governor Guy Carleton* granted him a commission as a notary. Taché practised his new profession for about two months only; he died on 18 April of that year.

The inventory of his possessions, made on 2 May 1768, shows that Taché did not leave many belongings; only his furniture shows the easy circumstances in which he had once lived. On 27 Aug. 1742, at Quebec, Jean Taché had married Marie-Anne, the daughter of Jean-Baptiste Jolliet* de Mingan and granddaughter of Louis Jolliet*; of this marriage at least ten children were born. Taché's descendants, who included the politicians Jean-Baptiste* and Sir Étienne-Paschal,* the writer Joseph-Charles*, and the archbishop of Saint-Boniface, Manitoba, Alexandre-Antonin*, bore their ancestor's name honourably and took an active part in the development of French-Canadian society during the 19th century.

MICHEL PAQUIN

AN, Col., B, 83, f.35; 91, f.29; 97, ff.33, 48; 99, f.2; 100, f.17v; 102, f.55. ANQ, Greffe de R.-C. Barolet, 25 août 1742; Greffe de J.-C. Panet, 2 mai 1768; Greffe de Jean Taché, 1768; NF, Coll. de pièces jud. et not., 4227 (66 pièces). *Documents relating to Canadian currency during the French period* (Shortt), II, 760–61. *Documents relating to constitutional history, 1759–91* (Shortt and Doughty), I, 180–89. PAC *Report, 1890,* "State papers," 31; *1921,* app.D, 6, 25. "Les 'papiers' La Pause," APQ *Rapport, 1933–34,* 218. "Recensement de Québec, 1744" (APQ *Rapport*). "Requête des négociants et bourgeois de Québec à M. de Ramezay," APQ *Rapport, 1922–23,* 272 (plate). Bonnault, "Le Canada militaire," APQ *Rapport, 1949–51,* 302. Létourneau et Labrèque, "Inventaire de pièces détachées de la Prévôté de Québec," ANQ *Rapport, 1971.* P.-G. Roy, *Inv. contrats de mariage,* VI, 10; *Inv. ord. int.,* II, III; *Inv. testaments,* II, 231. Tanguay, *Dictionnaire.* Nish, *Les bourgeois–gentilshommes.*

TAFFANEL DE LA JONQUIÈRE, JACQUES-PIERRE DE, Marquis de LA JONQUIÈRE, naval officer, governor general of Canada; b. 18 April 1685 at the château of Lasgraïsses near Albi, France, son of Jean de Taffanel de La Jonquière and Catherine de Bonnes; m. in 1721 Marie-Angélique de La Valette; d. 17 March 1752 in Quebec.

Jacques-Pierre de Taffanel de La Jonquière joined the service as a midshipman at Toulon on 1 Sept. 1697. He took part in his first campaigns the following year at Constantinople, then in 1699 in the Levant and in 1701 at Cadiz. In 1702 he sailed on the fireship *Éclair* and distinguished himself under Claude de Forbin in the operations in the Adriatic, where he commanded a sloop, then a felucca, with which he took several prizes and participated in the capture of the town of Aquileia (Italy).

On 1 Jan. 1703 he was promoted sub-lieutenant and remained in the Mediterranean. As second in command of the *Galatée* in 1705 he fought two privateers from Flushing (Neth.) in a five-hour battle in which his commander was killed and one of the enemy ships captured. The following year La Jonquière took part for a time in the operations conducted by the colonial regular troops against the Protestant rebels in the Cévennes mountains, then sailed on the *Fendant* and was on it at the siege of Barcelona, which had just gone over to Archduke Charles (the future Emperor Charles VI) against Philip V of Spain. He was given command of a small galley, the *Thon,* and was attacked during a patrol off Alicante (Spain) by a British ship of 60 guns, forced to surrender, and taken to England as a prisoner. He was quickly exchanged and in 1707 took command of the *Galatée,* on board which he had already distinguished himself, and fought two sharp actions with privateers from Flushing.

In 1708 and 1709 he sailed in the Mediterranean, and in 1710 he made a cruise to Spitzbergen. In 1711 he was commissioned first lieutenant on the *Achille* and took part in René Duguay-Trouin's memorable expedition which ended in the capture and pillage of Rio de Janeiro. On 25 Nov. 1712 La Jonquière was promoted fireship captain, and the following year in command of the *Baron de la Fauche* he sailed to Louisiana and took part in the defence of Pensacola (Fla.). From 1715 to 1719 he waged a long campaign along the west coast of Spanish America and was named lieutenant-commander on his return to France on 20 Feb. 1720.

After six years of land service at Brest, La Jonquière received command in 1727 of the frigate *Thétis,* which was sent to the West Indies with the *Vénus,* commanded by LE PRÉVOST Duquesnel, the future governor of Île Royale. For 18 months they made life difficult for the many pirates and smugglers who were trading clandestinely along the coasts of Martinique and Guadeloupe. La Jonquière was made a captain on 1 Oct. 1731, and in 1733 he received command of the *Rubis,* to escort ships to Canada. The following year he was second in command on the *Éole,* in the squadron commanded by Court de La Bruyère, lieutenant-general of naval forces, which was to cruise off the coasts of North Africa. In 1735 he went on station at Cadiz as commanding officer of the *Ferme,* and in 1738 he was again in command of the *Rubis* serving on the Quebec run.

When war broke out in 1739 between England

and Spain as a result of many different incidents off the coasts of Spanish America, a squadron of 12 ships of the line was fitted out at Brest and sent in September 1740 to the West Indies under the orders of the Marquis d'Antin, lieutenant-general of naval forces. La Jonquière accompanied him as captain of the flagship the *Dauphin Royal*. Upon his return to France La Jonquière was named inspector of the colonial regular troops of the department of Rochefort on 1 May 1741. As tension with England had again worsened, a squadron of 17 ships of the line and four frigates was fitted out at Toulon in 1744 under the orders of Court de La Bruyère, who also took La Jonquière as his flag captain on the *Terrible*. Combined with a Spanish force of 16 ships commanded by Don Juan de Navarro, the fleet fought an indecisive battle on 24 Feb. 1744 off Cap Sicié, near Toulon, against a British squadron commanded by Admiral Thomas Mathews; then it went to cruise off the coasts of Catalonia and finally returned to Toulon. La Jonquière then commanded a division, with which he escorted convoys between Toulon and the island of Malta.

On 1 March 1746 La Jonquière was promoted rear-admiral, and on 19 March he was appointed governor general of New France. While on his way to Canada he participated, as commander of the flagship *Northumberland*, in the disastrous expedition led by the Duc d'Anville [LA ROCHEFOUCAULD] along the coasts of Acadia, and on 30 Sept. 1746, after d'ESTOURMEL attempted suicide, he brought what remained of the squadron back to France. Thus he was not able to go to Quebec to take up his new functions until the following year. For this voyage he was put in command of a division consisting of three frigates and two ships of the line, the 64-gun *Sérieux*, on which he hoisted his colours, and the 50-gun *Diamant*. La Jonquière left from the Île d'Aix on 10 May 1747 and four days later, at about 25 leagues west of Cape Ortegal (Spain), the convoy, which with the merchant ships and the vessels of the Compagnie des Indes comprised 39 vessels, was overtaken by a British squadron of 14 ships of the line and two frigates under the orders of Vice-Admiral George Anson and Rear-Admiral Peter WARREN. It was an unequal match, since the French could line up only 312 guns against 978 for the British. Despite his overwhelming superiority Anson attacked rather uncertainly, which gave the merchant ships time to escape and to reach their destination without further interference. The ships of war lined up for battle. The combat, as bloody as it was stubborn, lasted about five hours and ended in the capture of all the French warships, which

surrendered only when any possibility of resistance had gone. The *Sérieux* had to sustain the assault of five enemy vessels, which killed or wounded 140 of her crew and inflicted so much damage that she was in danger of capsizing with three metres of water in her hold. The *Diamant* was the last to surrender, after being sheared off like a hulk. La Jonquière, who had been wounded, was taken prisoner and reached Portsmouth on 28 May. The court of France then named BARRIN de La Galissonière to occupy temporarily the post of governor general of New France.

When he was liberated by the peace of Aix-la-Chapelle (1748), La Jonquière was at last able to take up his post; he landed at Quebec on 14 Aug. 1749, relieving La Galissonière, who had been recalled to France. The new governor's ideas about the colony were vague, for he had never stayed there for any length of time. On his arrival in Quebec he had some conferences with La Galissonière, and he evidently had high regard for his predecessor's policy, since he tried to continue it in all domains, especially in relations with the Indians. In the two and a half years of his government, La Jonquière had to confront many problems, the most acute of which was obviously the defence of the colony against British encroachments in the region of Acadia and in the interior. Indeed, the peace signed at Aix-la-Chapelle had not settled any of the outstanding problems in North America over the boundaries between the British and French possessions.

During the years 1750 and 1751 commissioners from the two countries [*see* Barrin de La Galissonière; William Shirley] met in Paris to discuss these problems, without any particular results, while on the spot incidents were becoming more frequent, on land and on sea. The Acadians refused to recognize British sovereignty, and continuing his predecessor's policy La Jonquière stuck to his positions, reinforced fortifications – in 1750 he had the fort on the Saint John River restored by Deschamps* de Boishébert – and in October 1751 sent the engineer Gaspard-Joseph CHAUSSEGROS de Léry to France to report to the minister on the situation in that region. At the instigation of the French the Indians harassed the British unceasingly, and La Jonquière could write on 1 May 1751: "It is certain that what the Indians have done against the British at least makes up for what they have done against us." On that same day he issued instructions "to have the Indians patrol Baie Verte continually to keep it open for us, plunder any British ship which runs aground on our territory, [and] hunt the British who are obliged to come into our territory to tow their ships that are going to Beaubassin.'' La Jonquière, who wanted the Acadians to move to French territory, also ordered the Indian bands to incorporate "a few Acadians dressed and made up as Indians,'' in order to compromise the white population further and to provoke violent acts of repression against them by the British, which in the governor's mind should help decide the Acadian families to settle in French territory. In addition, in order to weaken the Acadians' neutrality, La Jonquière did not hesitate to issue an ordinance on 12 April 1751 calling upon them to take the oath of loyalty to the king of France within a week of their arrival in French territory and to join the militia on pain of being considered rebels.

In his instructions dated 1 April 1746 La Jonquière had been advised to keep an eye on British intrigues among the Indians at Sault-Saint-Louis (Caughnawaga, Que.), and to endeavour to destroy the British post at Fort Oswego (Chouaguen), on the south shore of Lake Ontario, which constituted an active smuggling base. The governor general's policy towards the Indian tribes vacillated, however, and he was not successful in using them effectively in the struggle against the British. Fort Rouillé (Toronto) was built in 1750 to compete with Oswego; the post at Detroit was reinforced because of its economic and military importance, and an ordinance on 2 Jan. 1750 accorded numerous advantages to families willing to settle there. But in the Ohio region he failed completely. Posts were improved below the portage at Niagara and at Sault Ste Marie near Lake Superior, but the governor's visit in 1751 to the Iroquois at Sault-Saint-Louis and at Lac des Deux-Montagnes, who received him well with military honours, was of little importance in the struggle against British expansion. In June 1751 Philippe-Thomas CHABERT de Joncaire was sent to the Six Nations to renew the peace treaties concluded in the time of their ancestors with Governor Callière*, and François LEFEBVRE Duplessis Faber negotiated with the Ottawas and endeavoured to prevent them from trading with the English. In addition, through an ordinance issued on 27 Feb. 1751 La Jonquière had authorized Ensign Pierre-Marie Raimbeau de Simblin to establish a fort at Lac de la Carpe to counter British influence in the area south of Hudson Bay. The mission to the Sioux which the governor entrusted to Paul MARIN de La Malgue was aimed at restoring peace between them and the Missouris.

The governor general, who in most cases seems to have been well served by his officers, had great difficulties with Pierre-Joseph CÉLORON de Blainville who, according to the governor, showed obvious ill will in carrying out orders concerning the campaign against the Indians of Rivière à la Roche (Great Miami River, Ohio). But La Jonquière had given him only a small number of troops from Canada and Céloron was not able to recruit Indians "because of the small number of Frenchmen . . . who have arrived from Montreal for this expedition.'' La Jonquière had to send François-Marie Picoté* de Belestre to investigate; Belestre went to France at the end of 1751 to report to the minister. The governor also had a rather sharp dispute with the Jesuits over the Sault-Saint-Louis mission and the missionary Jean-Baptiste TOURNOIS. Three persons from Montreal, Marie-Madeleine, Marie-Anne, and Marguerite Desauniers, had set up in business at the mission around 1726 and were actively engaged in trade, sometimes illicit. La Jonquière expelled them from the colony, as well as Father Tournois, who was suspected of having aided them.

Trade with the *pays d'en haut*, on which two ordinances were published on 29 May 1750, aroused many complaints from certain traders, who claimed that the fur trade was monopolized by "a private company formed of a small number of persons, including officers of the trading posts.'' La Jonquière, who at times seems to have exhibited a certain naïvety, weakly defended the persons concerned, prudently adding: "There is no one in this country who is not secretly motivated by self-interest.'' The governor general himself was not free of it and let himself be drawn by Intendant Bigot* into commercial speculation from which his position should have forced him to abstain. Despite the court's prohibition, he entered into partnership with Bigot, Jacques LEGARDEUR de Saint-Pierre, and Paul Marin de La Malgue to operate the *postes de l'Ouest* and the post at Baie-des-Puants (Green Bay, Wis.), and allowed his secretary, André Grasset de Saint-Sauveur, to proceed freely with his embezzlements. The stir caused by the Tournois-Desauniers affair and the denunciations and complaints sent to Versailles were, in fact, on the point of causing La Jonquière's recall when he died. Exactly what was his role in Bigot's *Grande Société*? It is difficult to determine precisely. Above all it seems that he allowed profits to be made and collected some himself, without playing any role personally in commercial operations.

To meet the British threat the governor general concerned himself with increasing the military forces of the colony. He asked for and obtained the dispatch of recruits whom he mixed in with the experienced soldiers to bring company strengths up to 50; he created a company of gunners, which was raised in 1750, and he went ahead that same year with a general census of the militia, which included about 12,000 men. La Jonquière would have liked to see the post of general officer commanding the troops and militia re-established, and he counted above all for the defence of the country on the Canadians, because the soldiers from France "not being trained since their early youth in getting about in the *pays d'en haut*, still less in Indian warfare, are good only for garrisoning towns." New barracks were built in Montreal and Quebec; work also went on to fortify Quebec, despite opposition from Versailles, which feared that it would attract an attack by the British. A meeting of the inhabitants called by Charles de BEAUHARNOIS and Gilles Hocquart* after the capture of Louisbourg in 1745 had decided on the necessity of fortifying the town, and La Jonquière was not able to oppose the carrying out of this desire.

Peopling the colony worried him, and like his predecessor he would have liked to attract new settlers. "Men are extremely scarce," he wrote the minister on 6 Oct. 1749, "and the war has carried off many of them. The majority have gone to France or the West Indies, where they have remained, and we can only replace them by discharging men from the troops to get married."

As a good sailor La Jonquière concerned himself with improving piloting on the St Lawrence and also wanted to encourage shipbuilding at Quebec. Unfortunately, as a result, it seems, of an error on the part of the builder, René-Nicolas Levasseur*, the ship *Orignal* broke up on the day it was launched and could not be repaired. This accident did not, however, prevent the *Algonkin* from being laid down.

Among the projects which the governor general did not have time to carry out was the creating of a printing house in the colony, which he proposed in October 1751, and the reform of the administration of the Hôpital Général of Montreal, which an ordinance of 15 Oct. 1750 joined with that of Quebec to receive all the old and disabled in Canada and Île Royale. Because of its unrealistic nature this decision, ordered by the minister, provoked vigorous protests, and was not carried out [*see* Marie-Marguerite Dufrost* de Lajemmerais].

La Jonquière proved to be a good administrator in Canada but hesitant in a time of political and economic difficulties. He was certainly a man of great courage, and his naval career, comprised of 29 campaigns and nine combats, is proof of that. It is certain, however, that he liked money and turned out to be regrettably greedy. He was able to see clearly certain problems facing the colony and succeeded partly in following his predecessors' policy, but he lacked firmness in his dealings with the British and the western Indians and showed unpardonable weakness, particularly in his relations with Bigot. Shortly after his death, which occurred on 17 March 1752 after some months of illness, the acting governor, Charles LE MOYNE de Longueuil, and Intendant Bigot could write: "We have missed him very much." These regrets seem to have been shared by the population.

ÉTIENNE TAILLEMITE

AN, Col., B, 89–95; C¹¹ᴬ, 95–97; F³, 69, ff.218ff.; Marine, B¹, 63–64; B², 269, f.33; 324, ff.466, 519; B³, 289, ff.256–57; 312, ff.34–41; 315, f.322; 426, ff.449–530; 446, *passim*; B⁴, 61, ff.101–75; B⁸, 28, ff.693, 822, 851; C¹, 165; 166, p.21. Étienne Taillemite, *Dictionnaire de la marine* (Paris, 1962), 162. Frégault, *François Bigot*; *Le grand marquis*; *La guerre de la conquête*. Lacour-Gayet, *La marine militaire sous Louis XV* (1910). Troude, *Batailles navales de la France*, I, 311–15.

TALBOT, JACQUES, minor cleric, schoolmaster; b. at La Plaine (dept. of Maine-et-Loire), France, and baptized 12 Nov. 1678, son of Jacques Talbot and Mathurine Sylvain; d. 2 Jan. 1756 in Montreal.

Jacques Talbot, who arrived in New France in 1716, went to become a schoolmaster at Montreal, probably replacing Antoine FORGET. The first school, which had been set up for the sons of the settlers by Gabriel Souart* in 1666, was held in the Sulpician seminary in Montreal until 1683, when it was decided to construct a building on a piece of land donated by the parish council of Notre-Dame. In 1686 the "petites écoles" – this was the name given the primary school under the French régime – where teaching was always given free of charge, became independent of the seminary and two men's orders made their appearance: the "Teaching Brothers," also called Rouillé Brothers [*see* Louis-François de La Faye*], who remained under the direction of Saint-Sulpice, and later the Brothers Hospitallers of the Cross and of St Joseph, founded in 1692 by François Charon* de La Barre, who wanted to superintend the Montreal schools. Saint-Sulpice was opposed to the project put forward by the latter and took charge of teaching again, ensuring that they obtained competent teachers from their seminary in Paris; it was thus that Yves Priat, Armand Donay, Jacques-Anne Bœsson, Antoine Forget, Marc-Anselme de Métivier, Jean Girard, and particularly Jacques Talbot came to New France.

Jacques Talbot probably prepared to become a schoolmaster by learning the methods of the founder of the Brothers of the Christian Schools, Jean-Baptiste de La Salle, methods in great vogue at that time among the Sulpicians. For his teaching he made use of school books brought from France: Latin primers, psalters, offices of the Holy Virgin, La Salle's *Devoirs d'un Chrétien envers Dieu* (1703). In 1742, in correspondence with their *confrères* in Paris, the Sulpicians of Montreal requested for Talbot "12 copies of *L'Escole paroissiale* or the manner of teaching children in primary school," a work published in Paris in 1654. This manual of pedagogy remains as evidence of the methods of teaching in use in the 17th century. In sending for 12, Talbot probably intended to distribute them among his colleagues, for, the population of Montreal having grown, the number of schoolmasters likewise had to be increased. By 1693 mention was already being made of a "head master," who was in charge of the "petites écoles," which leads us to think that there was a junior master. Jean Girard, who arrived in Montreal in 1724, taught along with Talbot for several years.

The situation was, however, different in the rest of New France. If the habitants of Montreal were able to profit from schoolmasters trained according to La Salle's methods, the same was not true for the other parishes in the colony. Some of them could only count on the nuns of the Congregation of Notre-Dame or the Ursulines, and on a few missionaries or parish priests who were ready to dispense the rudiments of reading and writing. As for the others, most of the time they had to be content with teachers who had no diploma other than their goodwill, a little education, and a great deal of devotion to the cause of teaching. It was quite sufficient at the time to dispense the teaching laid down by the programme of the "petites écoles": the catechism, reading, writing, and arithmetic, to which were added a few elements of domestic science for the girls. Among these schoolmasters may be mentioned Charles Corvaisier, who is known to have been at Sainte-Anne-de-la-Pérade in 1738–39; Nicolas Datte, at Batiscan in 1721; and Étienne Guillemin, at Beauport in 1750.

As for Jacques Talbot, he taught at Montreal for nearly 40 years and died there on 2 Jan. 1756 at 77 years of age.

LOUIS-PHILIPPE AUDET

AD, Maine-et-Loire (Angers), État civil, La Plaine, 12 nov. 1678. Gauthier, *Sulpitiana*, 267. L.-P. Audet, *Histoire de l'enseignement au Québec, 1608–1971* (2v., Montréal, 1971), I, 136–37, 144–50. Amédée Gosselin, *L'instruction au Canada*. Yves Poutet, "L'auteur de *L'Escole Paroissiale* et quelques usages de son temps (1654)," *Bulletin de la Société des bibliophiles de Guyenne* (Bordeaux), 1963, 4–29 [Poutet establishes decisively that the author of this work is Jacques Batencourt and not Charles Démia. L.-P.A.]; "Une institution franco-canadienne au XVIIIe siècle: les écoles populaires de garçons à Montréal," *Revue d'histoire ecclésiastique* (Louvain), LIX (1964), 52–88, 437–84.

TANAGHRISSON (Deanaghrison, Johonerissa, Tanacharison, Tanahisson, Thanayieson, and, as a title, **the Half King),** a Seneca, a leading person among the Iroquois settled on the upper Ohio River from about 1748; d. 4 Oct. 1754 at Harris's Ferry (Harrisburg, Pa.).

Little is known of Tanaghrisson's early life. Gaspard-Joseph Chaussegros* de Léry wrote that he was a Flathead (Catawba) by birth, but had been captured young and adopted by the Senecas; Philippe-Thomas CHABERT de Joncaire reported that he came from the Lac des Deux-Montagnes and that "he was formerly inclined to the French, but at present he is more than English." His special importance lies in the role he played in events leading to the outbreak of Anglo-French hostility in 1754.

The thrust of English traders like George Croghan into the country between the upper Ohio River and the Great Lakes about 1745 occasioned a realignment of some Indian groups in that area. Following the defection from the French alliance of the Huron chief ORONTONY, segments of his tribe and of the Miamis moved from the borders of the lakes to the branches of the Ohio. Tanaghrisson makes his first documented appearance (as Tanareeco) as one of six signers of a 1747 letter, in Croghan's handwriting, reporting a treaty between the pro-British Mingos and Shawnees and the "Inomey Nation" (Miamis). One of the other "Mingo" signers was an Oneida, Scarroyady, who handled relations between the Iroquois and the Shawnees and was Tanaghrisson's closest associate.

The Iroquois council at Onondaga (near Syracuse, N.Y.) regarded its Ohio settlers, the Mingos, as warriors with no authority to hold formal councils; they had no recognized council fire and no designated speaker (or "king," in then-current usage). However, Pennsylvania's and Virginia's interest in trade and, in Virginia's case, in obtaining land for settlement, encouraged direct dealings with the Ohio Indians rather than with the Onondaga council. In April 1748 Croghan delivered on behalf of Pennsylvania a present of goods to the Ohio Indians, and in September the Indian agent Johann Conrad Weiser

Tanaghrisson

delivered a larger present to which Virginia also contributed. The latter occasion seems to have established Logstown (Ambridge, Pa.) as a council place, and at this same meeting Tanaghrisson is identified as "the half King," a title obviously of English origin (the French equivalent *le demi roi* appears only in translations) and presumably defining his role as that of spokesman for the Iroquois colonists on the Ohio. At this meeting Tanaghrisson and his associates, as "new beginners" in council matters, requested a supply of wampum which was one of the essential evidences of the validity of an Indian treaty. Tanaghrisson was the spokesman at a conference held at Logstown by Croghan in May 1751, and at another in June 1752, when Virginia sought ratification of a land cession.

French military occupation of the upper Ohio, beginning in 1753, brought Tanaghrisson's career to a troubled climax. Persuaded that British friendship and protection assured the greatest benefits to the Ohio Indians, he sought to unite the tribes in opposition to the French presence. Not all of them agreed with him, however, and his support dwindled in the face of determined French action. The Indians made three formal protests: a rather mild one by the Delawares, one by Scarroyady in the name of the Shawnees, and, finally, one by Tanaghrisson himself, whose demand on 3 September that the French withdraw was rejected by the French commander, Paul MARIN de La Malgue. Simultaneously with Tanaghrisson's errand, Scarroyady headed a delegation of Iroquois, Delawares, Shawnees, Hurons, and Miamis to Winchester, in response to a Virginian invitation, and then to Carlisle, Pennsylvania, to seek support. At these meetings both Tanaghrisson and Scarroyady insisted that they were acting not for the Iroquois council but for the warriors on the Ohio.

Tanaghrisson advised the English traders to leave the Ohio. Emboldened perhaps by Marin's death, however, he and two other chiefs (Jeskakake and KAGHSWAGHTANIUNT) accompanied Major George Washington on his trip to Fort de la Rivière au Boeuf (Waterford, Pa.) with a Virginia demand that the French depart. Rebuffed again, Tanaghrisson returned to Logstown on 15 Jan. 1754, escorted by a French detachment under Michel Maray* de La Chauvignerie which set up a temporary post nearby.

In the following month Tanaghrisson joined some Virginians in erecting a fort at the site of Pittsburgh, Pa., and aided them until they surrendered on 18 April to Claude-Pierre Pécaudy* de Contrecœur, who proceeded to build Fort Duquesne there. A Virginia detachment under Washington was dispatched to reassert English authority in the region. On the way the troops were joined by Tanaghrisson, and on 28 May he took part with them in an attack on a party of French near the present Jumonville, Pa. The leader of the French, Joseph COULON de Villiers de Jumonville, was killed, reputedly by Tanaghrisson himself. Washington withdrew a few miles to the Great Meadows (near Farmington, Pa.) and hastily built Fort Necessity in anticipation of French retaliation. On 1 June Tanaghrisson and some 80 to 100 Mingos joined him, but left before he surrendered on 4 July to a French siege. The Indians made their way first to the site of Cumberland, Md., and then to Aughwick (Shirleysburg, Pa.) where Croghan had his trading post.

After summoning Delaware and Shawnee leaders to this place for a conference, Tanaghrisson himself went on to John Harris' post from which he accompanied Conrad Weiser back to Aughwick for a council, 4–6 September, aimed at securing the Delawares and Shawnees in the English interest. The attempt failed: these Indians could not leave the Ohio, and Pennsylvania could not protect them there. Most of the refugee Iroquois remained at Aughwick. About the end of the month, however, Scarroyady brought the Half King and his family, in poor health, to Harris', where Tanaghrisson died on 4 October.

Virginia and Pennsylvania promptly recognized Scarroyady as the new Half King but his journeys to New York to seek help from Sir William Johnson*, the superintendent of northern Indians, left the actual leadership of the group unsettled and, as late as January 1756, a matter of dispute.

The fact that Tanaghrisson and Scarroyady were both in turn referred to as the Half King is helpful in defining the sense of this title; but it has occasioned repeated confusion of Tanaghrisson with his associate and successor (who died at Lancaster, Pennsylvania, in June 1757). Not much is known of Tanaghrisson's family. "Gahickdodon the half King's Son" attended treaty negotiations at Carlisle in January 1756. Two daughters, one of them the Indian wife of a trader, John Owen, remained for a time at Aughwick, where Fort Shirley had been built, but they left in July 1756 with a soldier from the garrison. A daughter-in-law, identified as Nancy, was living on the upper Susquehanna River in this same year.

WILLIAM A. HUNTER

ASQ, Fonds Verreau, 5, no.60, liasse A (papiers Marin). [G.-J. Chaussegros de Léry], "Journal de

Joseph-Gaspard Chaussegros de Léry, lieutenant des troupes, 1754–1755," APQ *Rapport, 1927–28*, 355–429. [Christopher Gist], *Christopher Gist's journals . . .*, ed. W. M. Darlington (Pittsburgh, Pa., 1893), 80–87. *The diaries of George Washington, 1748–1799*, ed. J. C. Fitzpatrick (4v., Boston, New York, 1925), I. *History of Colonel Henry Bouquet and the western frontiers of Pennsylvania, 1747–1764*, ed. M. C. Darlington (n.p., 1920), 41–47. *The history of an expedition against Fort Du Quesne in 1755, under Major-General Edward Braddock . . .*, ed. Winthrop Sargent (Philadelphia, 1855), 378. *Papiers Contrecoeur* (Grenier). Pennsylvania, *Colonial records*, V–VII. Pennsylvania archives, 1st ser., I–II. "The treaty of Logg's Town, 1752," *Virginia Magazine of History and Biography* (Richmond), XIII (1905–6), 143–74. *The writings of George Washington from the original manuscript sources, 1745–1799*, ed. J. C. Fitzpatrick (39v., Washington, [1931–44]), I, 40–80.

TARBELL (Tharbell), JOHN, b. 6 July 1695 in Groton, Massachusetts, the fifth of ten children of Thomas Tarbell and Elizabeth Wood; d. after 1740.

On 20 June 1707 John Tarbell, a younger brother Zachariah (b. 25 Jan. 1699/1700), and an older sister Sarah (b. 29 Sept. 1693) were captured in an Indian raid on Groton during Queen Anne's War. The three children were first taken to their captors' home, the mission and Iroquois settlement at Caughnawaga (Sault-Saint-Louis). Sarah later went to live with the sisters of the Congregation of Notre-Dame in Montreal. John and Zachariah remained at Caughnawaga, where they were adopted into the tribe. They learned the Mohawk language and took up the Mohawk way of life. John became known as Karekowa (Karikohe), and Zachariah was called Torakaron. It is believed that they married daughters of Sakonentsiask and Atawenta, chiefs at Caughnawaga, and that they themselves became chiefs, but this information cannot be verified because the mission's records for the period have been destroyed.

John and Zachariah apparently became fully accustomed to their new situation. Although their elder brother Thomas arranged to have them visit Groton during the winter of 1739 in hope of persuading them to settle there, they decided to return to Caughnawaga. In the following autumn John Tarbell and Henry Rice, also a captive at Caughnawaga, conferred with the governor of Massachusetts and received presents. They visited the Tarbell family in Groton and returned to Caughnawaga by way of Albany, New York. One of the Tarbell brothers is said to have been seen again in Albany in 1744.

About 1755 the mission of St Regis was established on the upper St Lawrence River as a French military outpost and as a place to which Mohawk converts to Catholicism could immigrate from the Mohawk valley. According to oral tradition the Tarbells moved there about 1760. Their descendants make up a substantial portion of the present St Regis Mohawks.

There is no record of the deaths of John and Zachariah Tarbell in the church records of Caughnawaga or St Regis.

JACK A. FRISCH

Vital records of Groton, Massachusetts, to the end of the year 1849 (2v., Salem, Mass., 1926–27), I, 237–41. Caleb Butler, *History of the town of Groton . . .* (Boston, 1848), 96–97, 440. Coleman, *New England captives*. S. A. Green, *Groton during the Indian wars* (Groton, Mass., 1883), 109–24. F. B. Hough, *A history of St. Lawrence and Franklin counties, New York, from the earliest period to the present time* (Albany, 1853), 111–13.

TARIEU DE LA PÉRADE, MARIE-MADELEINE. *See* JARRET DE VERCHÈRES

TARRIDE DUHAGET (Du Haget), ROBERT, officer in the colonial regular troops; b. 1702 or 1703 in Estang (dept. of Gers), France, son of Charles Tarride Duhaget and Antoinette de Saint-Thairau (Saint-Turine, Saint-Chéran); m. 29 Sept. 1737 at Louisbourg, Île Royale (Cape Breton Island), Marguerite, sister of Gabriel Rousseau* de Villejouin; d. 19 Dec. 1757 at Brest, France.

Robert Tarride Duhaget probably began his military service in Rochefort, France, perhaps in 1715. By 1723 he was in Île Royale where he was made second ensign on 9 May. Promoted ensign five years later, he was soon posted to Île Saint-Jean (Prince Edward Island). In 1729 he assumed virtual control of the garrison there when its commander, Jacques d'Espiet* de Pensens, was forced by ill health to remain in Louisbourg. On 1 May 1730 Duhaget became a lieutenant.

From 1731 he served at Louisbourg, then returned to Île Saint-Jean in 1736 as interim commander, a post he held until Louis Du Pont* Duchambon was made permanent commander in 1737. On 1 April 1738 he became assistant garrison adjutant, with a captain's commission, at Louisbourg; exactly a year later he was promoted full captain, with his own company. He led his company in defence of the Queen's bastion during the siege of Louisbourg by New England troops under William PEPPERRELL in 1745. After the fall of the fortress he was sent to France with

Taschereau

the rest of the Île Royale garrison. Early in 1748 he was admitted to the order of Saint-Louis.

The rebuilding of Île Royale's defences became a principal policy consideration when, by the treaty of Aix-la-Chapelle, the island was restored to France in 1748. Duhaget was first assigned to recruiting duties at Brest and Bordeaux, but in 1749 he returned to Île Royale as commander of Port-Toulouse (St Peters). This was, in June 1750, the scene of a mutiny brought on by an altercation between a corporal and the garrison cook about poor food. Wounded during the mutiny, Duhaget was obliged to return to France for treatment.

He had not entirely recovered when in 1751 he returned to Île Royale with the new governor, Jean-Louis de Raymond*. At first impressed by Duhaget, by the fall of 1752 Raymond recommended that he be retired. This recommendation was, however, rejected by Rouillé, the minister of Marine. On 11 July 1753 Duhaget was made major of Louisbourg. Although an object of contempt and ridicule for his fellow officers, he held the post until the autumn of 1757 when, in declining health, he returned to France "to take the waters." He died soon afterwards.

ANDREW RODGER

AN, Col., A, 1, p.5; B, 49/1, pp.198–200, f.246; 54, ff.503–3v; 58, f.130v; 59/2, pp.533–36; 78, ff.396–96v; 88/1, p.197; 88/2, p.280; 91, p.342; 92/1, p.145; 97, p.303; 108/1, p.249; C^{11B}, 7, f.189v; 10, ff.170–71v; 11, ff.41, 170v; 12, ff.265v, 274–75; 14, ff.8v, 119; 15, f.34; 18, ff.52, 57, 310–10v; 20, ff.57v, 271–77v, 318; 23, f.170v; 28, ff.63–63v, 75–78, 83–84, 370–74; 29, ff.45–47v, 104–5, 319–25; 31, ff.15–16v, 226–26v; 32, ff.72v, 322–22v; 33, ff.469–69v, 471–71v, 473–73v; 34, ff.18–19v, 70; 35, ff.139–40, 247–48; 36, f.77; 37, ff.281–82, 283–83v; C^{11C}, 16, pièce 26 (2e sér.); D^{2C}, 3, p.61; 47; 48; 60, ff.6v, 15; 222; E, 151; Section Outre-Mer, G^1, 406/3, p.593; G^2, 193/4, pièce 25; 197, dossier 150; 207, dossier 474, ff.56v–57 (paginated references are to PAC transcripts). *Derniers jours de l'Acadie* (Du Boscq de Beaumont). Fauteux, *Les chevaliers de Saint-Louis*. Harvey, *French régime in P.E.I.*

TASCHEREAU, THOMAS-JACQUES, agent of the treasurers-general of the Marine, councillor in the Conseil Supérieur, seigneur; b. 26 Aug. 1680 at Tours, France, son of Christophe Taschereau, Sieur de Sapaillé, king's councillor, director of the mint and treasurer of the city of Tours, and Renée Boutin; d. 25 Sept. 1749 at Quebec.

Pierre-Georges Roy* claimed that the nobility of the Taschereau family was of long standing. Whether or not that is true, it was of the nobility of the robe, and it had lost a great deal of its prestige by the time its first and only representative to come to Canada, Thomas-Jacques Taschereau, arrived in the country. He was descended from a line of royal or municipal officials whose toponymical surname was Sapaillé; but to Canada he brought the surname Linière, which belonged to another branch of the family in France.

Thomas-Jacques Taschereau, baptized privately at his birth, received public baptismal rites only at the age of 14, and thus was able to sign his baptismal certificate. Almost immediately afterwards he lost his father and mother. Nothing more is known about him until Claude-Thomas Dupuy*, who had been appointed intendant of New France, brought him with him as his private secretary. If he accompanied his master on the same ship to Canada, Taschereau would have left Paris in June 1726, to arrive at Quebec on 18 August.

During his brief stay of two years, Intendant Dupuy was immensely active, and his secretary must not have languished in idleness. But as a result of the trouble which developed after the death of Bishop Saint-Vallier [La Croix*], Dupuy was recalled and returned to France in the autumn of 1728. Taschereau, perhaps counting too much upon the security of his employ, had taken a wife on 17 January of that year; it was time for him to think of marrying, since he was already 48. He married a Canadian girl who belonged to the nobility and who was not yet 20, Marie-Claire, daughter of Joseph de FLEURY de La Gorgendière and grand-daughter of the discoverer Louis Jolliet*. With this responsibility, Taschereau remained some time at Quebec; there, in February 1729, he had his first child, who was buried a few days later, baptized. Then he returned to France, and was there with his wife in February 1732 when he was appointed to succeed Nicolas LANOULLIER de Boisclerc as agent of the treasurers-general of the Marine in Canada. Canon Pierre Hazeur* de L'Orme, in Paris at the time, wrote to his brother Joseph-Thierry HAZEUR: "M. Taschereau has his office as treasurer. He is going back this year with his wife. . . . I think he will do well in that country. We have always been good friends since his return from Canada. As for M. Dupuy and his wife, I have not been to see them at all. If they had both followed Taschereau's advice, they would not be in the situation they are today."

In addition to the office of agent, which bore with it prestige and a relatively lucrative salary, Taschereau received the office of councillor in the Conseil Supérieur, one of the highest responsibilities in the colony, on 1 April 1735. Used to administering public funds, the agent had the idea of speculating on his own account by entering into partnership on 16 Oct. 1736 with François-Étienne CUGNET, Pierre-François Olivier* de Vézin, Jacques SIMONET d'Abergement, and Ignace Gamelin* the younger to exploit the Saint-Maurice ironworks. The lack of experience of the manager of the company, Olivier de Vézin, brought the undertaking to bankruptcy in 1740 and the king, who had advanced the main part of the finances, took it over.

The best known and most lasting achievement of Thomas-Jacques, ancestor of the huge and illustrious Taschereau family of Canada, remains however his contribution to the settling of the seigneury of Sainte-Marie and the development of the Nouvelle-Beauce region. On 23 Sept. 1736 three adjoining seigneuries, all the same size, were granted by Governor Charles de BEAUHARNOIS and Intendant Gilles Hocquart* to Joseph de Fleury de La Gorgendière and his two sons-in-law, Taschereau and Pierre de Rigaud* de Vaudreuil. The seigneuries of Sainte-Marie, Saint-Joseph, and Saint-François were surveyed by Noël BONHOMME, *dit* Beaupré in December 1737. Taschereau received the first grant, which was behind the seigneuries of Lauzon and Jolliet, beginning at the Île au Sapin and consisting of "land with a frontage of 3 leagues and a depth of 2, on both sides of the river called the Sault de la Chaudière."

The settlement of the Beauce region began in 1738 and the three seigneurs carried out in the allotted time the condition set by the authorities that "they build a carriage and cart road which will follow the river" as far as the Île au Sapin. On 2 Aug. 1738 the first native of the Beauce, Joseph-Marie Raymond, son of Étienne Raymond and Marie-Cécile Mignot, was born in the seigneury of Sainte-Marie. In less than two years Taschereau granted 28 pieces of land, thus creating the embryo of a parish; the grants belonging to Fleury de La Gorgendière and Rigaud de Vaudreuil constituted a separate nucleus centred upon the chapel of the seigneury of Saint-Joseph. In the autumn of 1739 the region of Nouvelle-Beauce already had 262 inhabitants.

In the course of one of the earliest surveys on his seigneury Taschereau had had the church site marked out and a piece of land reserved for the parish priest; later, on 25 Feb. 1746, he donated it formally by deed to the bishop of Quebec, who was at the time Pontbriand [DUBREIL]. He did still more for the religious life of his *censitaires*. In 1741 he had ordered from Paris all the articles of worship for the chapel which was at that time installed in the seigneur's home at the place

called "le Domaine," and he had given from his own furnishings a fine painting of the Madonna, chosen as the patron saint of the parish in honour of the lady of the seigneury.

As he was kept in Quebec by his duties as agent and councillor, Taschereau the seigneur must have come only rarely to his seigneury; at no time is his presence mentioned in documents. On 1 July 1745 he entrusted the material organization of his seigneury to an attorney-at-law, Étienne Parent, whom Intendant Hocquart had commissioned the previous year to act as surveyor in Nouvelle-Beauce. From then on the life of the parish and seigneury finally knew its full development.

At his death on 25 Sept. 1749 Thomas-Jacques Taschereau owned one of the two houses that were later to form the site of the bishop's palace in Quebec; his great-grandson, Elzéar-Alexandre Taschereau*, was to become famous in the palace as the first Canadian cardinal. After her husband's death Mme Taschereau was left well enough off, and, despite the long service of her husband, "a very honest man moreover," she was not able to obtain a royal pension. She saw to the education of the eight children who remained of the 14 whom she had borne. Marie-Anne-Louise entered the Ursuline order in Quebec and became superior of the convent; the youngest child, Gabriel-Elzéar*, was the only one to continue the name and became the second seigneur of Sainte-Marie. Taschereau's widow died at Quebec on 19 Feb. 1797, after having lived for several years with her son in the manor-house of Sainte-Marie.

HONORIUS PROVOST

AN, Col., B, 56, f.140v; 58, f.465v; 62, f.20v; 63, f.462v; 64, f.421; 65, ff.413, 423v, 436v; 66, ff.13, 24, 249; 76, ff.44, 86v; 81, f.66; 87, f.26v; 89, f.23; 91, f.30v; C^{11A}, 66, f.249; 92, f.58; 93, ff.29, 193. ANDQ, Registres des baptêmes, mariages et sépultures, 25 sept. 1749. ANQ, Greffe de Jacques Imbert; Greffe de J.-N. Pinguet de Vaucour; AP, Famille Taschereau. ASQ, Fichier des écoliers. PAC, MG 18, H17. "Contrat de concession d'un terrain pour l'église de Saint-Marie, Nouvelle-Beauce," *BRH*, XIII (1907), 372–73. "Lettre du comte de La Galissonière à madame Thomas-Jacques Taschereau," *BRH*, VIII (1902), 328. "Recensement de la Nouvelle-France, 1739" (*Census of Canada*). Gaumond, *Les forges de Saint-Maurice*. Honorius Provost, *Sainte-Marie de la Nouvelle-Beauce: histoire civile* (Québec, 1970); *Sainte-Marie de la Nouvelle-Beauce: histoire religieuse* (Québec, 1967). P.-G. Roy, *La famille Taschereau* (Lévis, Qué., 1901). Henri Têtu, "Le chapitre de la cathédrale de Québec et ses délégués en France," *BRH*, XVI (1910), 206, 226.

TAVERNER, WILLIAM, planter, trader, and

Taverner

surveyor; b. possibly in Bay de Verde, Nfld., about 1680, perhaps the son of William Taverner, a planter; d. probably at Poole, Dorset, England, 7 July 1768.

Information about William Taverner's early life is difficult to find and substantiate. Apparently he was a member of the Taverner family of Poole and Bay de Verde, Nfld. – a moderately well-off group which divided its time between Poole and Newfoundland. From at least 1698 he was owner of a plantation in St John's. A document found in Dorset mentions that another planter's son, John Masters, was apprenticed to William about 1700–1. In 1702 William is mentioned as a planter of Trinity and a trader from Poole to Trinity. It appears that he captained Newfoundland fishing vessels and led a privateering raid on the French fisheries. About 1705 he was able to move his wife Rachel and his family to Poole and to live there himself during the winters. By that time he owned one small vessel, the *William*.

William Taverner and his brother, Abraham, emerge in 1708 as opponents of Major Thomas Lloyd*, commander of the Newfoundland garrison. Abraham, an obscure figure, was Newfoundland agent for the London merchant, James Campbell, who had extensive plantations at Bay de Verde. Campbell was financial agent in London for Captain John Moody* who had been commander of the Newfoundland garrison during Lloyd's absence in 1704–5 and who was an avowed adversary of Lloyd. Although many of the Newfoundland planters tried to keep away from both Lloyd and Moody, William Taverner led a group which, early in 1708, complained about Lloyd's exploitation of the colonists.

By 1712 he began to present memoranda to the Board of Trade on the French possessions in Newfoundland and elsewhere on the Gulf of St Lawrence. Some of his London associates regarded him, by 1713, as an expert on the location, character, and potentialities of the fishery based at Placentia (formerly Plaisance) and extending to southwest Newfoundland, an area ceded to Great Britain by the treaty of Utrecht. Taverner had also been involved in a plan to develop cod fisheries in the Newfoundland manner on the northwest coast of Scotland, a venture by the London fish merchants who found the war interfered with the Newfoundland fishery.

On 21 July 1713 Taverner was commissioned as "Surveyor of such part of the coast of Newfoundland and the Islands adjacent as the French have usually fished upon and wherewith our subjects are at present unacquainted." Frequently consulted by the Board of Trade during the next eight months, he was able to pass on useful information as well as advice about the situation in the newly acquired territories. When Taverner arrived at Placentia on 27 June 1714, Lieutenant-Colonel Moody, who had been designated deputy governor of Placentia, put a ship at his disposal to begin the survey. On 23 July Taverner set out to discover the nature and extent of the outlying French settlements on the island of Saint-Pierre and elsewhere, to report what French ships were fishing, and to carry through a charting operation designed to provide sailing information for English fishermen.

The transition from French to British control was difficult; the French under the supervision of Philippe Pastour* de Costebelle were evacuating the population to Île Royale (Cape Breton Island) and threatening those who remained and took the oath of allegiance that they would be treated as traitors. At Saint-Pierre Taverner had a lively summer trying to impose the oath of allegiance on the French. He had some trouble too with one William Cleeves of Poole over the sale of salt, and was accused by him of charging the French for surveying their plantations, of compounding with French ships which came to trade, and of engaging in trade on his own account, sending home, for example, ten hogsheads of oil to Poole. On 22 Sept. 1714 Taverner returned to Placentia and made a full and interesting report. He thought the possibilities of exploiting the salmon fishery were good and was most optimistic about building up a fur trade, having engaged a Canadian with a knowledge of Indian languages to make contacts for him.

Meantime, back in England, there was some discussion about whether Taverner's appointment should be continued: the fishing ports wished the survey completed, though only the Londoners named Taverner as surveyor, so it may be the accusation made in 1715 that he was appointed to serve sectional interests (those of the Londoners against the Westerners) had some foundation. Many Western merchants protested that Taverner was unqualified for the surveying work. William Cleeves' complaints caused Taverner's wife some anxiety but she put up a spirited defence of her husband and pointed out that his salary of 20 shillings a day had not been paid, so that she was in grave financial difficulties. The arrival in February 1715 of his report together with his "new chart of the islands and harbor of St. Peter's [Saint-Pierre], with the island of Columba and the adjacent rocks," stifled criticism and led to his getting his salary, expenses, and – most important – reappointment. Taverner continued his work in 1715. With his second report was a "new chart or map of Newfoundland from Cape St. Mary's to Cape Lahun [Cape La Hune]," which it was suggested should be published at public expense.

In the winter of 1715–16 Taverner was again in England explaining to the Board of Trade the complex position of the former French coasts. At Placentia Moody had bought foreshore rights from departing French settlers, and Taverner had made similar purchases on Saint-Pierre despite the fact that this action was in direct defiance of the policy of the Committee for Trade and Plantations. Consequently Taverner and Moody deprived the English fishing captains of the free "fishing rooms" – spaces for handling and drying the fish – to which they claimed they were entitled. Taverner maintained that he had protected the handful of French who remained at Saint-Pierre from intimidation by William Cleeves and others, and had left adequate "fishing rooms" free for such vessels as appeared. Taverner seems to have convinced the Board of Trade that the charges against him were exaggerated, it being understood that he might have to make some money to supplement his irregularly paid salary but that he ought not to oppress his countrymen in the process. He returned to Newfoundland on 8 March 1716. In 1718 the Board of Trade reported his services were satisfactory and it seems that in this year he wound up his survey of the former French possessions in Newfoundland and was paid off.

From 1718 to 1725 it seems probable that he fished and traded annually from Poole with the Placentia–Saint-Pierre region. In March 1726 he was involved with other Poole merchants (having apparently cut his links with the Londoners) in a plan to develop the salmon fisheries of southern Newfoundland. He offered to combine a reconnaissance of the fishery, which he was about to make, with a survey of the west and northwest coasts of Newfoundland. He had earlier drawn attention to the continued French and Basque presence on the south coast near Cape Ray, but the west coast was still unknown to the English. He undertook at his former rate of pay to complete a survey in two and half years. This time his plans were supported by both London and Westerners, showing that the value of his earlier work was appreciated by the fishing interests; his plans were also endorsed by the Board of Trade. This second survey, carried out between 1726 and 1728, has not left much in the way of documentation, but as a result he was able to disturb the virtual monopoly held by the Basques on the west coast fishery. He also had begun to engage experimentally in fishing and trade in the area.

By 1729 Taverner was operating on his own account also in the Strait of Belle Isle and met some resistance from Breton fishermen at Cap de Grat (Cape Bauld). At this time he evidently resided in St. John's for part of the summer and his attempt to collect rents from some properties he had earlier held caused trouble. He proposed to sail right round Newfoundland in 1730, hoping for some financial assistance from the government. It is unlikely that he obtained further subsidies, though he continued his trade with the outlying parts of Newfoundland. Taverner made an important report early in 1734, showing that the French sent Indian hunting parties in winter from Île Royale to western Newfoundland, thus prejudicing the English market for furs, and that a settlement of French runaways had grown up at Port aux Basques, which was becoming a centre for illegal trade by the French in fish, oil, and furs. He was anxious that this should be stopped, and suggested he be appointed to do it. His offer was not taken up, but Lord Muskerry, who was going out as governor, was told to instruct the French to leave and to expel them if necessary. It was perhaps thought that Taverner was getting rather old for further services, and indeed he is found in 1739 asking for a gratuity for what he had done.

The outbreak of war with Spain and the growth of friction with France led the fishing interests early in 1740 to raise the question of further fortifications in Newfoundland, and Taverner appeared for the last time before the Board on 14 Feb. 1740 to give his advice. He presented an elaborate review of the fishery 1736–39, showing that it represented a turnover of £227,000 per annum, and employed 8,000 men and 21,500 tons of shipping so that it deserved full protection.

William Taverner was a remarkably regular and persistent trader in the fishery and his ships can be traced back and forward across the Atlantic to the mid-1750s. By this time his son William was also a ship's captain and an agent for some of the Poole merchants trading to Trinity. In 1762 the son was a signatory to a petition concerning the French capture of part of Newfoundland. The father's signature does not appear and one presumes that he was no longer active.

William Taverner did good work in opening up the former French shore in southern Newfoundland to the knowledge of Englishmen, though his surveys were, after 1714, verbal reports rather than sailing charts, and it is not known how efficient a cartographer he was. He also pioneered English trade and fishery in the French areas and was the first to make effective use of the west coast, which Englishmen had avoided.

DAVID B. QUINN

619

Techenet

PRO, CO 326/15 (Ind. 8315), p.13, no.6 (F. A. Assiotti, "List of maps," MS list, 1780, records the chart of Saint-Pierre as published, but no copy of it, nor of the subsequent chart, has been located). PRO, CO 194/10, ff.86, 116; *CSP, Col., 1706–8, 1708–9, 1712–14, 1714–15, 1716–17, 1717–18, 1722–23, 1726–27, 1728–29, 1730, 1734–35; CTP, 1708–14; JTP, 1704–1708/9, 1708/9–1714/15, 1714/15–1718, 1722/23–1728, 1728/29–1734, 1734/35–1741.* A. M. Field, "The development of government in Newfoundland, 1638–1713" (unpublished MA thesis, University of London, 1924). Lounsbury, *British fishery at Nfld.* Keith Matthews, "A history of the west of England–Newfoundland fishery" (unpublished PHD thesis, University of Oxford, 1968). Janet Paterson, "The history of Newfoundland, 1713–63" (unpublished MA thesis, University of London, 1931). J. D. Rogers, *Newfoundland* (C. P. Lucas, *Historical geography of the British colonies (dominions)*, V, pt.IV, Oxford, 1911; 2nd ed., 1931).

TECHENET, Mme. *See* COUC, ELIZABETH

TEE YEE NEEN HO GA ROW (Teoniahigarawe). *See* THEYANOGUIN

TERROUX, JACQUES, silversmith and merchant trader; b. in Geneva, son of François Terroux; fl. 1725–66.

According to his own affirmations Jacques Terroux practised the silversmith's craft before coming to Canada. His name appears for the first time in Canadian documents in 1755. In October of that year he had registered with the Quebec notary Claude Louet the dissolution of a verbal agreement with Louis-Alexandre Picard, a merchant silversmith originally from Paris. During the last years of the French régime Terroux is believed to have taken on a number of apprentices and to have manufactured cheap goods for the fur trade, as well as some works of art. It has not been possible, however, to discover any of his artistic work other than a chalice in the Canadian style preserved in the bishop's palace in Baie-Comeau and believed to be by his hand.

In 1758 or 1759 Terroux travelled to Europe in quest of funds. He went to Amsterdam, where he formed a company to do business in America. In the spring of 1760 he was back at Quebec and was seeking by every means to become rich rapidly, imitating in this the British merchants who had set up businesses in Quebec and Montreal. Between 1760 and 1765 he was putting money in trade with the West Indies, in fishing off the north shore of the St Lawrence, in shipping, in speculation in landed property. He imported goods from England and the West Indies and in return exported iron from the Saint-Maurice ironworks, fish, and furs. Moreover, Terroux advanced

money to several people, including the nuns of the Hôtel-Dieu and the Hôpital Général as well as certain individuals. He also speculated in "Canadian bills," buying payment orders and bills of exchange for a song, to sell them in turn to London suppliers, particularly to Francis Rybot; in all, Terroux succeeded in acquiring 1,333,681 *livres.* He seems to have exceeded his credit with Rybot, since the latter sent a representative, John Jennisson, to Quebec in 1765 to liquidate Terroux's assets. These were sold by a court officer, and once debts were paid 4,680 *livres* remained for the Quebec merchant. He then went to Halifax, Nova Scotia, where he met Joseph Frederick Wallet DesBarres*, a friend of Sir Frederick Haldimand*, the former governor of Trois-Rivières. Terroux borrowed money from Desbarres, after which he disappears from sight.

His will, dated 18 Dec. 1762, included a stipulation for payment of 3,000 *livres tournois* that he "recognized having received from Mademoiselle Louise Loubier." Further on, the trader ordered that whatever remained of his assets after his death be put aside "for the children already born or to be born of me and the said Mademoiselle Loubier for the purpose of paying for their keep, having them educated, having them learn a trade or commerce."

Despite the impressive number of business deals in which he engaged, this rather enigmatic person does not seem to have played a role of prime importance in the economy of New France.

JOSÉ IGARTUA

ANQ, Greffe de Claude Louet, 2 oct. 1755, 17 janv. 1763. Marcel Hamelin, "Jacques Terroux et le commerce entre 1760 et 1765" (unpublished L.ÈS L.(hist.) thesis, Université Laval, Québec, 1961).

TESTU DE LA RICHARDIÈRE, RICHARD, navigator, naval officer, port captain of Quebec; b. 15 April 1681 at L'Ange-Gardien (Que.), son of Pierre Testu Du Tilly, a merchant, and Geneviève Rigault; m. first on 22 July 1709 at Quebec Marie Hurault, and secondly on 17 Oct. 1727 at Quebec Madeleine-Marie-Anne Tarieu de La Pérade; d. 24 Oct. 1741 at Quebec without children.

Nothing is known of Richard Testu de La Richardière's youth. During the 1690s he may have received instruction in navigation and pilotage from Louis Jolliet* and perhaps later from Jean Deshayes*. The intendant, Dupuy*, was later to claim that no officer had more improved the safety of navigation in the St Lawrence River and the training of pilots in the colony.

La Richardière probably went to sea before 1720, when he was reported captain of the *Suzanne* (130 tons) recently purchased by Joseph de FLEURY de La Gorgendière. Three years later La Gorgendière gave him command of a newer ship, the 150-ton *Marguerite*. La Richardière sailed these ships annually between La Rochelle and Quebec until 1726 when, probably owing to the loss of the king's ship *Chameau* in 1725 and to his experience, he was chosen to pilot the king's ship to Quebec. There La Richardière applied for the post of port captain, vacant following the death of Louis Prat*. Intendant Dupuy privately, and then jointly with Governor Charles de BEAUHARNOIS, recommended La Richardière over other applicants. La Richardière obtained the temporary rank of flute captain, perhaps because of his service in the navy in 1726 and 1727, but in 1727 he returned to Quebec as port captain.

Prat had been little more than a harbour master, but La Richardière was given responsibility for navigation in the St Lawrence. He was to sound the shoals and banks in the river each spring after they had been altered by the ice coming downstream. He was to place marker buoys in the channel during the navigation season and to draw them up each fall. Beacons were to be erected on major capes and headlands. The anchorage at Quebec, known as the Cul-de-Sac, was to be kept in a proper state for vessels, and necessary repairs to ships were to be carried out. La Richardière was also to inform himself about the river's shores and the depths of bays and rivers, and to share this knowledge with other ship's masters. He was even required to survey stands of oak and pine in the colony, and the rivers from which to draw down timber, and to be familiar with the problems of stowing timber for sea voyages. Little wonder that in contrast to Prat, who had received 150 *livres,* La Richardière's salary was 500 *livres* annually. In 1728, he was also directed to pilot the king's ships through the passage at the eastern end of Île d'Orléans known as the Traverse at no extra cost to the crown.

With all of these responsibilities it is not surprising that La Richardière never carried out any timber surveys. He once attempted to establish pilotage fees of three *livres* per draft-foot on each merchantman that requested his services, but this proposal was rejected by the minister of Marine who ordered him to negotiate a mutually acceptable fee each time he guided a merchant ship in the river. Later, La Richardière abandoned these claims and devoted more time to improving his knowledge of navigation in the river.

The need was demonstrated in 1729 when the king's ship, *Éléphant*, ran aground on shoals off Cap Brulé. The captain, Louis-Philippe de RIGAUD de Vaudreuil, had not waited for the royal pilot but had pressed on upstream at night and lost his ship as a result. La Richardière and his men worked through September and October raising guns and cargo out of the ruined vessel. As a result Beauharnois and the new intendant, Hocquart*, pressed for La Richardière's promotion to flute captain, but the minister sent only a commendation. A year later the commander of the king's ship also recommended La Richardière: "he is always ready for duty and it would be difficult to replace him." In response to these testaments, in 1731 La Richardière received a bonus of 300 *livres*.

Beginning in 1730, each year one or two pilots from the king's ship were left at Quebec to acquire greater knowledge of the St Lawrence by working over charts during the winter, and they assisted La Richardière in hydrographic surveys downstream the following summer. In the spring of 1731, Pierre Dizet and a crew of five, with La Richardière, made the first of several such voyages. They were not easy. On the first, La Richardière was unable to survey the south shore; "the journey that was carried out this year, in which he lived only on biscuit and salt pork, was equivalent to a voyage of three or four months." The next year the pilot was Jean-Baptiste Garnier. Illness interfered with the voyages of 1733 and 1734 but in 1735 the surveys were resumed. Another pilot, Jean Galochau, piloted the king's ship upstream, leaving La Richardière with greater liberty for his surveys. During the next three or four years the most extensive hydrographic surveying and navigational improvement during the French régime were carried out.

In 1735, La Richardière and a young pilot, Gabriel Pellegrin*, familiarized themselves with the whole length of the river and completed an important survey of the Strait of Belle Isle. Both the governor and the intendant had been worried about the lack of knowledge of the area and recommended that it be considered as an alternate route into the St Lawrence. Up to that time, New France could be blockaded by ships cruising between Newfoundland and Île Royale (Cape Breton Island). Only French fishermen, chiefly from Saint-Malo, made regular use of the Belle Isle waters. La Richardière's voyage to the strait was the longest of its type. His expedition left Quebec in mid-May and returned four months later. A chart and journal containing its observations were sent to the "Dépôt des cartes et plans" at the Marine in Paris where they were added to its growing body of knowledge. Twenty years later, Gabriel Pellegrin returned to these waters when he guided units of the French navy through the strait to France to avoid a British force cruising off the main entrance to the Gulf of St Lawrence [*see* Emmanuel-Auguste de CAHIDEUC].

In 1736, accompanied by the pilot Julien Joly, La Richardière carried out a systematic survey of the islands in the Gulf of St Lawrence. Two years later, he and his assistants covered the south coast of Newfoundland. In 1739 and 1740 they continued to work in the gulf, surveying Île Saint-Jean, Baie des Chaleurs, and the Strait of Canso. To lower costs the intendant began to hire local vessels sailing between Quebec and Louisbourg, Île Royale, to carry La Richardière and his survey party to their destination rather than outfit a special craft.

In the fall of 1736, La Richardière had gone to France. He returned in 1737 with the rank of fireship captain and a salary of 1,000 *livres* annually. Bonuses on top of this amount indicate the regard in which he was held. On the return voyage, La Richardière took up an old idea of establishing navigational aids for the Traverse. Aided by pilots on board the king's ship, 20 members of the crew, and ten Canadian axemen, he cleared a path 100 ft wide and 1,000 ft in length through Île aux Ruaux. In 1739, two large wooden panels were erected on stone foundations at the edge of the St Lawrence at Pointe Saint-Jean and at Saint-François where two low points on Île d'Orléans, normally visible only on clear days, were located. The initial constructions were not high enough and a year later they were extended.

La Richardière's health was not always good. He may not have carried out a major survey in 1741, but he continued to work until his death at Quebec on 24 October; he had returned from piloting the king's ship to La Prairie, Île aux Coudres. Had depression and war not followed his death, La Richardière's program might have been continued, but no working appointment was made until years later. Quebec remained without a port captain until after the treaty of Aix-la-Chapelle. La Richardière's annual surveys were not renewed in the St Lawrence, but the result of the work during the 1730s provided the basis for French navigational charts published two decades later.

JAMES S. PRITCHARD

AN, Col., C¹¹A, 46, p.300; 48, pp.82–83, 261; 50, p.58; 51, pp.103v–4, 106; 52, pp.48–49; 54; 56, pp.14–14v; 59, pp. 117–19; 61, pp.29–30; 65, pp.8–9; 67, pp.5, 7–8; 71, p.20; 75, p.92; 114, pp.55–55v., 300, 326–26v.; Marine, B⁴, 41, pp.5v–6v; C⁷, 319; 4 JJ, 8, nos.41, 46 (PAC transcripts). P.-G. Roy, *Inv. ord. int.*, II, 225–26, 243–44, 291–92. Tanguay, *Dictionnaire*. P.-G. Roy, "Les capitaines de port à Québec," *BRH*, XXXII (1926), 65–78.

TÊTE BLANCHE. *See* GRAY LOCK

THANAYIESON. *See* TANAGHRISSON

THARBELL. *See* TARBELL

THEYANOGUIN (Teoniahigarawe, Tiyanoga, Tee Yee Neen Ho Ga Row or more correctly Deyohninhohhakarawenh, **White Head, Hendrick, King Hendrick,** or after 1750 **Hendrick Peters),** Mohawk warrior, sachem, diplomat, and orator; b. *c.* 1680, probably at or near Westfield, Massachusetts, as a Mahican; d. 8 Sept. 1755 at Lake George (Lac Saint-Sacrement).

At a young age Theyanoguin moved from the Westfield region to Mohawk country and was adopted by the Wolf clan. About 1690 he was converted to Christianity by the Dutch pastor Godfrey Dellius and became a preacher to his fellow Mohawks.

Although the Mohawks had had a treaty of friendship with the English of New York for many years, Jesuit missionaries from New France had also worked among the Iroquois, and a number of Mohawks had gone to live near Montreal at the mission settlement of Caughnawaga (Sault-Saint-Louis). Theyanoguin visited New France in 1697 but as a Protestant he dissuaded other chiefs from settling there.

In 1698 Theyanoguin and another Christian Mohawk accused Dellius and four associates (including Peter Schuyler*) of fraudulently obtaining their signatures on a land deed the previous year. The deed was eventually declared invalid by the governor of New York and Dellius was suspended as a pastor. The case was one of the few in which Iroquois fought land speculators and won.

In 1701 Teganissorens* and other Iroquois leaders signed on behalf of the Confederacy a treaty with New France, guaranteeing Iroquois neutrality in any war between France and England. The War of the Spanish Succession (1701–13), however, brought pressure on the Iroquois from the English to join the fight against the French. Theyanoguin was persuaded to enlist warriors for Colonel Francis Nicholson*'s projected attack on Canada in 1709. The invasion proved abortive.

Nicholson and Peter Schuyler took Theyanoguin and three lesser sachems to London in 1710 when they were promoting another invasion scheme and wanted to draw attention to the importance of Indian support. Presented at the court of Queen Anne, lionized and fêted, the "Four Kings" appealed to the queen for help against the French and for resident missionaries. Their request for religious instruction resulted in the queen's patronage of missions in America and the establishment of a chapel at Fort Hunter (near Amsterdam, N.Y.) in 1711. The Society for the Propagation of the Gospel supplied a missionary and Theyanoguin became his principal ally, serving as a Church of England lay preacher and living near the chapel.

Theyanoguin visited England again in 1740. On this occasion King George II presented him with a court costume – a blue coat with gold lace and a cocked hat. Four years later, wearing such a costume, Theyanoguin was in Boston. One observer called him "Henrique, a bold intrepid fellow" and remarked on his oratorical powers.

When the War of the Austrian Succession spread to North America in 1744, the role of the Iroquois was of major concern to both English and French. The official policy of the Confederacy was still neutrality, but a number of individuals, especially Mohawks, wanted to fight the French. Theyanoguin went to Montreal in the fall of 1746 with a delegation of Mohawks who, after being laden with presents by Governor Charles de BEAUHARNOIS, on their return journey attacked some French carpenters on Île Lamothe (Isle La Motte, Vt.). The Mohawk leader became a marked man for the French. The following spring they sent a raiding party to kidnap him. Theyanoguin, however, was himself leading a large war party, striking at various points along the St Lawrence near Montreal. Although French forces under Louis de LA CORNE and Jacques LEGARDEUR de Saint-Pierre detected and broke up his expedition, he and a few companions reached home safely.

In 1749 the French sent several hundred men under Pierre-Joseph CÉLORON de Blainville to assert their jurisdiction over the Ohio valley, and the expedition encroached on territory that the Iroquois claimed by right of conquest. Theyanoguin unsuccessfully sought help from the English against this invasion of rights. He also informed them that a French agent (one of the Joncaire brothers) was spreading rumours among the Iroquois that the English were planning to destroy the Indians. William Johnson*'s resignation in 1750 from his post as Indian agent for New York seemed to add weight to the rumours, for Johnson was trusted by the Mohawks more than any other colonial official. In June 1753 a delegation of 17 Mohawks led by Theyanoguin confronted Governor George CLINTON and announced that their people were so dissatisfied with their treatment by New York that they were ending the longstanding Mohawk treaty of friendship with the colony. Clinton prevailed on Johnson to accept reappointment. At the Albany congress the following year delegates from seven British colonies tried to gain Indian aid and heard Theyanoguin, as spokesman for some 200 Iroquois who attended, denounce both French and English for encroachment on Indian lands. "Brethren," he said, "The Governor of Virginia and the Governor of Canada are both quarrelling about lands which belong to Us, and such a quarrell as this may end in our destruction; they fight who shall have the land." His answer to the dilemma was to side with the English, but he deplored their reluctance to take action against the French. " 'Tis your fault Brethren that we are not Strengthened by conquest," he said to the English, "for we would have gone and taken Crown Point [Fort Saint-Frédéric] but you hindered us .... Look about your country and see, you have no Fortifications about you, no, not even to this City, 'tis but one Step from Canada hither, and the French may easily come and turn you out of your doors."

At the time of the conference John H. Lÿdius*, acting on behalf of Connecticut speculators, lured Theyanoguin, KARAGHTADIE, and some other Iroquois, one by one, into signing deeds to land in the Wyoming valley (now in eastern Pennsylvania). Pennsylvania, which claimed the lands, appealed to Johnson, and he arranged for Theyanoguin to lead a delegation of 12 sachems to Philadelphia in January 1755. There Theyanoguin repudiated the sale and promised his aid in undoing the speculators' deeds. Before he could lay the case before the Six Nations Council as he had promised, however, he became involved in military preparations for the coming season.

Although still not officially at war with France, the English planned attacks on the Ohio, Niagara, and Lake Champlain fronts for 1755. Johnson was selected to command the expedition against Fort Saint-Frédéric because of his influence with the Indians, who were a key factor in English strategy. Some 300 Indians, mostly Mohawks headed by Theyanoguin, joined Johnson's expedition at its camp on Lake George. While the English and their Indian allies were there, word came that a French force under DIESKAU was approaching and was expected to attack Fort Edward, at the southern end of the portage to the Hudson River. Johnson's council of war proposed sending 500 men to destroy the French boats, which had been left behind at Wood Creek (Rivière du Chicot), and 500 men to relieve Fort Edward. Theyanoguin and his followers, however, refused to participate unless the whole thousand men were sent to Fort Edward. The decision was changed to suit the Indians and the detachment set out, accompanied by Theyanoguin and a number of Indians; but Dieskau had altered his plans and he ambushed the English and Indian detachment on its way to Fort Edward. Theyanoguin called to the Caughnawagas with Dieskau not to assist the French against their Iroquois kinsmen, but to no avail. When his horse was shot from under him, the Mohawk leader was left at a great disadvantage since he was old and corpulent. First reports said that he was at once bayoneted and killed; later accounts revealed that he was not killed at once but was pursued, then stabbed and scalped by a small guard.

Theyanoguin's death was greatly lamented by his nation, and his loss was also deeply felt by the English, for he had been of much assistance to them. Johnson had promised to care for his family, and he paid a pension to Theyanoguin's widow for many years.

MILTON W. HAMILTON

[There are a number of likenesses of Theyanoguin. Several were painted in England in 1710: a full length study, entitled "The Emperor of the Six Nations," by John Verelst, is held by the British Museum, as is a miniature on ivory by Bernard Lens (1682–1740); a third portrait, an oval bust by John Faber, was also painted on this visit. When Theyanoguin was in England in 1740 another portrait was done, and a number of large engravings based on it are extant. An oval aquatint profile of him as an old man is owned by Williams College, Williamstown, Mass. A portrait attributed to William Heine and appearing in H. R. Schoolcraft, *Notes on the Iroquois . . .* (Albany, 1847), and *Information respecting the history, condition and prospects of the Indian tribes of the United States* (6v., Philadelphia, 1851–57), VI, is probably that of another Indian. For further information about portraits and engravings see R. P. Bond, *Queen Anne's American kings* (Oxford, 1952), and R. W. G. Vail, "Portraits of 'the four kings of Canada,' a bibliographical footnote," in *To Dr. R.: essays here collected and published in honor of . . . Dr. A. S. W. Rosenbach . . .* (Philadelphia, 1946), 218–26. M.W.H]

Samuel Blodget, *The battle near Lake George in 1755, a prospective plan . . .* (London, 1756; repr. 1911). [Daniel Claus], "Daniel Claus' narrative of his relations with Sir William Johnson and experiences in the Lake George fight," New York Soc. of Colonial Wars *Pubs.* (New York), A (1896–1907). *Documentary history of New-York* (O'Callaghan). Alexander Hamilton, *Gentleman's progress: the itinerarium of Dr. Alexander Hamilton, 1744*, ed. Carl Bridenbaugh (Chapel Hill, N.C., 1948). *Johnson papers* (Sullivan *et al.*). NYCD (O'Callaghan and Fernow). J. W. Lydekker, *The faithful Mohawks . . .* (Cambridge, Eng., 1938). G. C. Nammack, *Fraud, politics and the dispossession of the Indians; the Iroquois land frontier in the colonial period* (Norman, Okla., 1969). P. A. W. Wallace, *Conrad Weiser, 1696–1760, friend of colonist and Mohawk* (Philadelphia, London, 1945). Malvina Bolus, "Four kings came to dinner with their honours," *Beaver* (Winnipeg), outfit 304 (autumn 1973), 4–11.

THIBAULT, LOUISE. *See* GUYON [Appendix]

THIERRY, FRANÇOIS-NICOLAS DE CHASSIN DE. *See* CHASSIN

THOMPSON, EDWARD, HBC surgeon; fl.*c.* 1725–49.

Before Edward Thompson joined the Hudson's Bay Company in 1737 he had a varied career, serving seven years with a surgeon, four or five years as a journeyman (his trade is not known), and two in the navy as a mate. He spent three years in the company's employ as a surgeon at Moose Factory (Ont.), during which time he seems to have acquired a reputation for garrulous indiscretion. In 1739 the factor, Richard STAUNTON, refused to let him see or sign the general letter to the London committee on the grounds that with him "every thing which is spoake or acted upon all affairs is tould in publick at the Stoves mouth. . . ." In 1740 Thompson was sent home at the expiry of his contract, and during the winter of 1740–41 decided to sail as surgeon with Christopher MIDDLETON on the naval sloop *Furnace*, bound for Hudson Bay in search of the northwest passage. His appointment was approved by the admiralty, "notwithstanding his Qualification is only for a Surgeon's Mate."

The discovery expedition wintered at Churchill (Man.), where the death of ten crewmembers from scurvy and the illness of many others at the semi-derelict "old fort" say little for the professional capabilities and zeal of Thompson who, although he visited the men occasionally, spent most of his time five miles distant with the other officers at the newly built Prince of Wales Fort. Soon after the expedition's return to England in the autumn of 1742 Thompson became one of the first to support Arthur Dobbs' allegations that Middleton had deliberately concealed the existence of a northwest passage. He gave evidence to this effect in May 1743 before the admiralty, and on many occasions thereafter.

Middleton maintained that Dobbs' main witnesses were bribed by money or the offer of posts on a forthcoming private discovery expedition. In 1746 and 1747 Thompson did serve as surgeon and member of council, despite his own poor health, on a venture organized by Dobbs which sailed for Hudson Bay under the command of William MOOR. After that expedition's failure he played a prominent part in the campaign to discredit the HBC. In an affidavit sworn before the attorney general and solicitor general in February 1747/48 he was the most loquacious of Dobbs' witnesses, claiming that the company neglected exploration, expansion, and agriculture in the Hudson Bay area. His evidence in 1749 before the investigating parliamentary committee was equally critical of the company, and in the pamphlet literature that accompanied the campaign against the company he tried to keep alive hopes of a northwest passage by hinting that one lay through Chesterfield Inlet. In the controversies of these years Thompson figures as a vindictive, unscrupulous critic of his former commander, Middleton, and his former employer, the HBC; his reliability as a witness impresses even less than his skill as a doctor.

GLYNDWR WILLIAMS

[Details of Thompson's early years and his role in the attack on Middleton are given in Arthur Dobbs, *Remarks upon Middleton's defence*. Further examples of the evidence Thompson gave against Middleton and the HBC are in: G.B., Parl., *Report from the committee on Hudson's Bay*; House of Commons, *Report relating to the finding a north-west passage* ([London, 1745]); HBC Arch. E.18/1, ff.142–51; and in *Reasons to shew, that there is a great probability of a navigable passage to the Western American Ocean, through Hudson's Streights, and Chesterfield Inlet* (London, 1749). A short biographical sketch of Thompson is in HBRS, XII (Rich and Johnson), 337–38, and the discovery voyages of the period are surveyed in Williams, *British search for the northwest passage*. G.W.]

TIBIERGE, MARIE-CATHERINE, *dite* **de Saint-Joachim,** Hospitaller, superior of the Hôtel-Dieu of Quebec; b. 28 Feb. 1681 at Saint-François, Île d'Orléans, daughter of Hippolyte Tibierge, a merchant, and Renée Hervé (Hervet); d. 27 Nov. 1757 at the Hôtel-Dieu of Quebec.

We know nothing about Marie-Catherine Tibierge's education. She entered the Hôtel-Dieu of Quebec on 7 May 1695, at 14 years of age, and made her profession on 2 March 1697 under the name of Saint-Joachim. In October of that year her sister, Angélique de Sainte-Agnès, who had joined her in the community the previous year, died of purpura, which she had caught while car-

ing for passengers from the *Gironde* who had been stricken with the malady. Mother Saint-Joachim was elected Hospitaller (general directress of the hospital) in 1713, and the following year was again entrusted with the position.

In 1726 Mother Saint-Joachim was elected superior of the Hôtel-Dieu. She must have had the necessary qualifications for this important function, since she was re-elected regularly until her death and held the office as long as the regulations permitted. These allowed a superior's term of office to be prolonged for a second three-year period, after which an interval of three years was required before the holder would again be eligible for election. In 1732, when her second three-year term was completed, Mother Saint-Joachim was replaced by Marie-Andrée REGNARD Duplessis, *dite* de Sainte-Hélène, who was superior until 1738. Mother Saint-Joachim then assumed the office again and occupied it until 1744.

It was during this second period that two events which were memorable for the community took place. First, in 1739 the centenary of the arrival of the Nuns Hospitallers on Canadian soil was celebrated [*see* Marie Guenet*, *dite* de Saint-Ignace]. The festivities, which started on 1 August, were resumed on 18 August and lasted four days in all. During the forty hours' devotion, which began at 4:00 A.M. on 18 August and went on for two days, the inhabitants of Quebec were able to satisfy their thirst for devotion and give the sisters evidence of their attachment by attending in large numbers the religious services which followed one another almost without interruption: masses, vespers, benediction of the Holy Sacrament, sermons by the Jesuits, nothing was lacking. The second noteworthy event was the special ceremony in 1744 by which Bishop Pontbriand [DUBREIL] of Quebec handed over to the community a crucifix which a soldier of the garrison of Montreal, François-Charles HAVARD de Beaufort, known as L'Avocat, had profaned during an alleged séance of sorcery. The crucifix, which is still at the Hôtel-Dieu, became the object of special veneration.

Mother Saint-Joachim again held the office of superior for six years from 1750 to 1756. Her last three-year term of office was saddened by the disastrous fire which entirely consumed the hospital. Scarcely anything could be saved, and the archives were almost completely destroyed. Later it was discovered that the fire had been set in the roof by two sailors who were displeased with the Mother Hospitaller.

On 27 Nov. 1757 Mother Saint-Joachim died "after an illness of two months' duration, contracted while waiting upon the sick." In addition

Tilly

to having been superior and Hospitaller, she had been assistant superior and the sister in charge of the dispensary, although at what period cannot be determined.

JEAN-PIERRE ASSELIN

AHDQ, T 21, 500; Registre des entrées, 7 mai 1695. Juchereau, *Annales* (Jamet). Tanguay, *Dictionnaire*. Casgrain, *Histoire de l'Hôtel-Dieu de Québec*.

TILLY, JEAN-BAPTISTE LEGARDEUR DE. *See* LEGARDEUR

TING. *See* TYNG

TISSERANT DE MONCHARVAUX (Montchervaux), JEAN-BAPTISTE-FRANÇOIS, officer in the colonial regular troops; b. 1696 or 1697 in the parish of Saint-Pierre, diocese of Langres, France, to François Tisserant de Moncharvaux and Marie-Louise de Vienne; m. 3 June 1721 at Quebec to Marie-Thérèse L'Archevêque; m. again in 1737 to Marie-Agnès Chassin at Kaskaskia, (Ill.); d. 14 June 1767 in Paris, France.

Jean-Baptiste Tisserant de Moncharvaux entered the army in 1713 and served in Flanders, where he was wounded. In 1716 he came to Canada as a cadet in the colonial regulars and seems to have spent most, if not all, of the next 13 years here, becoming a cornet in the governor's guards in 1727. He saw action "against English and Indians amid the rigours of winter by land and by water. . . ."

Following his return to France in 1729 he was given a commission in the Louisiana troops. He arrived in New Orleans in March 1731 and was given command at Pointe Coupée (near New Roads, La.). The colony came under a more active administration in July 1731, when it reverted from the Compagnie des Indes to royal government. This change and the appointment of Bienville [LE MOYNE] as governor the next summer brought a revived interest in upper Louisiana. Moncharvaux was sent to the Illinois country with Pierre d'Artaguiette d'Itouralde, the new commandant, who early in 1733 put him in charge of a smaller fort just erected at Cahokia (East St. Louis, Ill.). His wife and three sons left Canada to join him but died in a shipwreck on the way.

In late 1735 or early 1736 Moncharvaux received instructions from d'Artaguiette to bring a force of Illinois Indians south to join in an attack against the powerful Chickasaws, a tribe hated by the French because of its friendship with the English. The Illinois were in their winter hunting grounds, and by the time Moncharvaux brought them to Chickasaw country d'Artaguiette had already been defeated. Moncharvaux's late arrival seems not to have been held against him by the authorities, for in October 1736 he was promoted lieutenant. In 1739 he took part in a more successful French show of force against the Chickasaws. As commandant of a post near the mouth of the Arkansas River in the 1740s he continued to be involved in French manoeuvring against the tribe. He received a captaincy in December 1747.

Having gained the confidence of Pierre de Rigaud* de Vaudreuil, the new governor of Louisiana, Moncharvaux was given command of the 1749 royal convoy, which took goods up the Mississippi to the settlements in the Illinois country. He received the position at a time when the recently arrived financial commissary, Honoré MICHEL de Villebois de La Rouvillière, was determined to keep a closer watch on expenditures. Michel transmitted to the minister of Marine reports of Moncharvaux's drunkenness and peculation, but he and Vaudreuil later wrote in the commandant's defence that the position had traditionally been regarded by officers as a means of supplementing their incomes and that Moncharvaux had been no worse than his predecessors. He had a numerous family and, Vaudreuil noted, his poverty was evidence that he had not engaged in private trade at the posts where he had been stationed.

By late 1751 Moncharvaux was commanding at Kaskaskia; in 1757 he was stationed on the Missouri River, along with his son Jean-Baptiste and four other soldiers. He probably remained in upper Louisiana until 1763 when another officer was sent to replace him at the Arkansas post. Moncharvaux returned to France, perhaps before he learned that the lands for which he had spent a lifetime fighting were being ceded to England and Spain. On the journey he lost most of his goods in two successive shipwrecks. He began receiving a pension of 200 *livres* a year in 1764, and he attempted to improve his financial situation further by taking his brother to court to regain a share in an inheritance. Early in 1767 he entered the Hôtel-Dieu of Paris, where he died in June.

IN COLLABORATION

AN, Marine, C⁷, 213. *Anglo-French boundary disputes, 1749–63* (Pease). *Before Lewis and Clark: documents illustrating the history of the Missouri, 1785–1804*, ed. A. P. Nasatir (2v., St Louis, Mo., 1952), I, 50. [J.-B. Bossu], *Travels in the interior of North America, 1751–1762*, trans. and ed. Seymour Feiler (Norman, Okla., 1962), 70–71. *Illinois on eve of Seven Years' War* (Pease and Jenison). *Mississippi Provincial*

Archives, 1701–1740, French dominion, ed. Dunbar Rowland and A. G. Sanders (2v., Jackson, 1927–29), I. *Old Cahokia: a narrative and documents illustrating the first century of its history*, ed. J. F. McDermott (St Louis, Mo., 1949). Tanguay, *Dictionnaire*. Alvord, *Illinois country*. Belting, *Kaskaskia*. Wilfrid Bovey, "Some notes on Arkansas Post and St Philippe in the Mississippi valley," *RSCT*, 3rd ser., XXXIII (1939), sect.II, 29–47. Stanley Faye, "The Arkansas post of Louisiana: French domination," *Louisiana Historical Quarterly* (New Orleans), XXVI (1943), 633–721.

TIYANOGA. *See* THEYANOGUIN

TOHASWUCHDONIUNTY. *See* KAGHSWAGH-TANIUNT

TONNANCOUR, CHARLES-ANTOINE GODE-FROY DE. *See* GODEFROY

TONTY DE LIETTE (Deliette, Desliettes), CHARLES-HENRI-JOSEPH DE, officer in the Louisiana colonial regular troops; b. 13 May 1697, probably in Montreal, to Alphonse Tonty* and Marie-Anne Picoté de Belestre; d. 9 July 1749 in Montreal.

On 19 March 1720 Charles-Henri-Joseph de Tonty was commissioned lieutenant in the Louisiana colonial regular troops. He was assigned to Pierre d'Artaguiette's company and began two decades of service among the Missouris and Illinois. On 16 Feb. 1722, during a brief visit to Canada, he married Marie-Madeleine Sabourin in Chambly. Their only child, born in April 1723, died at Chambly in infancy. Joseph married Louise Renaud Dubuisson in Montreal on 15 Sept. 1732 and probably took her to Fort de Chartres (near Prairie du Rocher, Ill.) where, according to the 1732 census, he owned a house, two cows, and two pigs. He was second in command under Claude-Antoine de BERMEN de La Martinière at Baie-des-Puants (Green Bay, Wis.) in 1737 and the following year was appointed commandant of the post, a vital link between the Great Lakes and the Mississippi. He served a short term as commandant of Fort Frontenac (Kingston, Ont.) in 1746 and returned to Montreal where he died on 9 July 1749.

Several authors have confused Joseph with his brothers and with his father's cousin. Three of his brothers were militarily active. Alphonse was commissioned ensign in Île Royale (Cape Breton Island) in 1714; he petitioned for a lieutenancy in 1716, to which he was promoted in 1721 in Martinique. He was raised to captain in 1725. Claude-Joseph requested and received a half-pay ensigncy in 1730 while working as an assistant garrison adjutant in Canada. Pierre-Antoine was

killed with several other young officers in the 1736 Chickasaw war. The death date of Joseph's second cousin Pierre-Charles de Liette* was questioned in his biography in volume II of the *DCB*. CHARLEVOIX wrote that de Liette had died in 1721; other sources indicated the death of a de Liette in 1728 or 1729. The possibility of a third de Liette was entertained because documents showed that the de Liette active between 1721 and 1728/29 could not have been Joseph. Subsequent research reveals that Charlevoix was probably mistaken and that Pierre-Charles may have lived until 1728/29. Whatever the case, Joseph did not add the title "de Liette" to his name until after 1729.

C. J. RUSS

AN, Col., B, 35, f.126; 43, ff.47, 272, 345, 351; C¹¹ᴬ, 37, f.196; 51; 52, f.214; C¹³ᴬ, 6, f.332v; 11, ff.89v–96v, 323, 360; D²ᶜ, 47; 222/2, pp.133, 275, 276 (PAC transcripts); E, 42; Marine, C⁷, 324; Section Outre-Mer, G¹, 464/2, p.283 (PAC transcript). ANQ-M, Greffe de J.-C. Porlier, 25 mai 1738; Greffe de Pierre Panet, 3 août 1761. Chicago Historical Society, Otto L. Schmidt collection, II, 248. Charlevoix, *Histoire de la N.-F.* (1744), IV, 235; VI, 165, 168. *Royal Fort Frontenac* (Preston and Lamontagne). Tanguay, *Dictionnaire*. Belting, *Kaskaskia*, 49. Gosselin, *L'Église du Canada jusqu'à la conquête*, III, 317. Kellogg, *French régime*.

TOURNOIS, JEAN-BAPTISTE, priest, Jesuit, missionary; b. 1 Jan. 1710 at Orchies, Flanders (now dept. of Nord, France); d. at his birthplace sometime after 1761.

Jean-Baptiste Tournois entered the Society of Jesus in Tournai (Belgium) on 27 Sept. 1727. He arrived in Quebec in June or July 1741 and almost immediately joined Father Luc-François NAU at the Sault-Saint-Louis (Caughnawaga) mission, where the Desauniers sisters, Marie-Madeleine, Marie-Anne, and Marguerite, had been running a store since 1726. They were suspected of smuggling with the English in Albany, New York, under cover of honest trade with the Indians. The minister of Marine, Maurepas, ordered that their store be closed in 1742; two years later he repeated his order to the colonial authorities.

In 1744 Tournois, who since his arrival had been closing his eyes to this trade, was named superior of the mission, replacing Nau who was returning to France. The new superior did not change his attitude, considering it preferable that the Indians should not have to go to Montreal to buy what they needed, since they easily found brandy there. In 1745 Maurepas ordered the expulsion of the Desauniers from Sault-Saint-Louis and made it clear that the king wished to see these tradeswomen retire to Montreal or

Townsend

Quebec. Two years later the Desauniers were still in business at Sault-Saint-Louis, and Governor La Galissonière [BARRIN] tolerated their presence in the mission during his term of office. Upon the arrival of the new governor, La Jonquière [TAFFANEL], in the autumn of 1749, an inquiry confirmed to his satisfaction the veracity of the accusations against the Desauniers.

Tournois became concerned about this situation and obtained an audience with the governor for his Indians, in the course of which they asserted their right to trade with the English colonies. La Jonquière had no choice but to rebuke the Indians, and they declared that Tournois had told them what to say and that the Desauniers ran the smuggling with the Jesuits. During a visit to the mission Governor La Jonquière ascertained that there was a large quantity of English goods there, and Tournois explained that these goods were much less expensive and of much better quality than French goods. La Jonquière recognized the validity of this argument, but in May 1750 he had Tournois come to Quebec, and a year later forced him to return to France, with the Desauniers sisters, on board the *Chariot Royal*.

The court upheld La Jonquière but reproached him for having publicized the affair too much and above all for not finding a means of persuading the missionary to end the illicit trade at Sault-Saint-Louis. In addition he was blamed for having withdrawn the missionary without consulting Bishop Pontbriand [DUBREIL] and Father Gabriel MARCOL, the Jesuits' superior.

Tournois stayed for two years in Cambrai. In 1753 he went to Valenciennes, and in 1761 he left that city during the events which preceded the suppression of the Society of Jesus in France. He took refuge at Orchies, where he died at an unknown date. Other than the Sault-Saint-Louis incident, Tournois left behind him the memory of a strong-willed man, capable of understanding but also of firmness towards the Indians. His successors were not satisfactory, and in 1754 Governor Duquesne* requested without success that Tournois, the person who had "best directed the Sault-Saint-Louis mission," be sent back to Canada.

JEAN-MARIE LE BLANC

AN, Col., B, 75, f.57v; 78, f.20; 81, ff.32, 41v; 85, f.3; 93, ff.19–20; 94, f.32; 95, f.31; C^{11A}, 95, ff.163–82. *JR* (Thwaites), LXIX, 56–58, 76, 236, 296, 304; LXXI, 174–75. "Les malignités du sieur de Courville," *BRH*, L (1944), 72. E. J. Devine, *Historic Caughnawaga* (Montreal, 1922), 239–40, 248–51. Lanctot, *History of Canada*, III. J.-G. Forbes, "Saint-François-Xavier de Caughnawaga," *BRH*, V (1899), 137.

TOWNSEND, ISAAC, naval officer; b. *c.* 1685; m. Elizabeth Larcum, by whom he had a son and a daughter; d. 21 Nov. 1765 at Greenwich, England.

Isaac Townsend joined the navy in 1696 under the patronage of his uncle Sir Isaac Townsend, longtime Navy Board commissioner resident at Portsmouth, England. He passed his lieutenant's examination on 15 Jan. 1705/6, and was promoted post captain in February 1720. His early service was almost entirely on the Irish station and in home waters. Following the outbreak of war with Spain in 1739, he went to the West Indies as flag captain in the squadron sent to reinforce Admiral Edward Vernon, and he took part in the abortive siege of Cartagena (Colombia) in 1741. He was promoted rear-admiral 23 June 1744.

In reply to pleas from the West Indies for naval protection after Commodore Peter WARREN sailed for Île Royale (Cape Breton Island) in the spring of 1745, the admiralty sent Townsend with a squadron of eight vessels to the Leeward Islands. When he reached Barbados he discovered that the French squadron which had caused such anxiety there had already sailed home. Though he had instructions to organize an attack on the island of St Lucia, he confined his activities to cruising off Martinique, where at the end of October 1745 he intercepted a convoy and took or destroyed more than 30 vessels.

Townsend's association with North America was confined to 1746. In view of the general belief expressed by William Shirley, governor of Massachusetts, and Warren, that the French would attempt the recovery of Louisbourg, the admiralty ordered Townsend to Cape Breton with his squadron. Leaving Antigua in January 1746 he reached Louisbourg harbour only on 9 May; and being senior to Warren he immediately assumed command. His squadron was shortly reinforced by the arrival of Commodore Charles Knowles* (sent as governor of Cape Breton) with two men of war.

Early in June fresh orders reached Townsend to prepare an assault on Quebec that summer. He presided over a council of war which decided that Warren should sail to Boston to help coordinate the preparations among the colonial troops, while Knowles bent his efforts to putting the Louisbourg garrison in a state of readiness. Townsend sent the *Pembroke* to cruise off Newfoundland, the *Kinsale* and the *Albany* to sail up the St Lawrence as far as Anticosti Island, and the *Dover* to warn the garrison at Annapolis Royal, Nova Scotia. In addition the *Shirley* (Capt. ROUS) was sent to Île Saint-Jean (Prince Edward Island) to deliver the terms for its evacuation, and the sloop

Hinchingbroke was sent to cruise eastward along the coast of Cape Breton for early intelligence about the arrival of the anticipated French and English squadrons. When neither squadron appeared in July and August, ships were sent to the St Lawrence, to Newfoundland, and to Annapolis Royal to replace those already there on station. In mid-September, however, news of the appearance of the French in great strength reached Townsend. Seriously outnumbered, he made no attack upon them in their anchorage at Chebucto (Halifax), and La Jonquière [TAF-FANEL] was able to lead them back to France unharmed, after supplying the Acadians with arms and vessels and sending a convoy of merchant ships to Quebec. In November Townsend sailed with the bulk of his squadron to Spithead, and never again served at sea.

In 1754 he was named governor of Greenwich Hospital, the refuge for aged and infirm seamen, at £1,000 *per annum*; and in this capacity became in 1757 the jailer of the unfortunate Admiral John BYNG, whom he treated, in the opinion of some contemporaries and historians alike, with undue severity.

Townsend was twice elected to parliament and represented the borough of Portsmouth from December 1744 to 1754; upon Byng's death he was elected for Rochester, Byng's constituency, and represented it from March 1757 till his own death in 1765. Though listed as a supporter of succeeding ministries, he seems never to have spoken in the house, nor played any sort of active political role.

His prize money earned in 1745 together with his handsome income made Townsend a man of some wealth. He bought an estate at Thorpe in Surrey, and by 1756 had invested some £19,000 in the funds.

JULIAN GWYN

[There is a portrait of Townsend as a young officer by an unidentified artist at Greenwich Hospital. Information on Townsend's life can be found in: PRO, Adm. 1/305; 1/480, ff.139–40, 142, 149–50, 152–53, 164; 2/65; 6/4, f.54; 6/9, f.85; 6/12, ff.103, 173; 6/15, f.325; 6/16, f.325; 50/25; 107/2, f.74. J.G.]

Charnock, *Biographia navalis*, IV, 85. *DNB*. *The history of parliament: the House of Commons 1754–1790*, ed. Lewis Namier and John Brooke (3v., London, 1964), III, 537. Dudley Pope, *At 12 Mr Byng was shot . . .* (London, 1962). H. W. Richmond, *The navy in the War of 1739–48* (3v., Cambridge, Eng., 1920), II, 224–29.

TRÉGURON, MAURICE QUÉRÉ DE. *See* QUÉRÉ

TREMBLAY, HENRI-JEAN. *See* Appendix

TROTTIER, MARGUERITE, *dite* **Saint-Joseph,** sister of the Congregation of Notre-Dame, superior of the community (superior general); b. 21 April 1678 at Batiscan, daughter of Jean-Baptiste Trottier and Geneviève de La Fond; d. 6 Oct. 1744 on the St Lawrence River, opposite Île d'Orléans.

Marguerite Trottier belonged to one of the founding families of Batiscan. When the Jesuits opened their seigneury to settlement in 1666, four brothers by the name of Trottier were among the *censitaires*. They came from Trois-Rivières, where their father, Jules, had settled in 1646 after emigrating from Saint-Martin d'Igé (dept. of Orne) in Le Perche. It has been impossible to find Marguerite's certificate of baptism – in 1678 Batiscan was only a mission served by the Jesuits. This fact explains why Cyprien Tanguay* and the few historians who have spoken of the Trottier family, among them Étienne-Michel Faillon* and Benjamin Sulte*, disagree about Marguerite Trottier's genealogy. But according to the census of 1681 which, it appears, was followed by the *Histoire de la Congrégation de Notre-Dame*, Marguerite was the daughter of Jean-Baptiste Trottier, youngest of the Trottier brothers, and Geneviève de La Fond, daughter of Étienne de La Fond and Marie Boucher, Pierre Boucher*'s sister.

Marguerite became acquainted with the sisters of the Congregation of Notre-Dame in her native village. In 1679 Marguerite Bourgeoys* set up missions at Champlain and Batiscan. But "lacking the resources which were indispensable for living and for giving charity in their turn," the sisters had to withdraw in 1685. Even though their mission had been temporary, it brought the community several recruits. Marguerite and her sister Catherine, who was four years older, were sent to its boarding school in Montreal, then asked to be received into the community. They made their profession in 1694.

Sister Marguerite Trottier immediately left for Château-Richer, where, according to a report made in 1698, she earned the unusual reputation of being a "very good schoolmistress." In August 1698 she was one of the sisters representing the Quebec district called together by Bishop Saint-Vallier [La Croix*] to witness the ceremony of approval of the community's regulations. Sister Trottier then took the vows of poverty, chastity, obedience, and the vow to teach girls. Later she made her profession a perpetual one by taking the vow of permanence in the community. On this occasion she received the name of Saint-Joseph. In 1705 she was called back to Ville-Marie from Château-Richer and was appointed depositary of the community. Since she displayed great aptitude for business matters, she held this office for 17 years until she was elected superior general of the congregation in 1722.

During Sister Saint-Joseph's superiority the first biography of the foundress, Marguerite Bourgeoys, appeared: it was a small volume, 123 pages long, published by Abbé Sylvestre-François-Michel RANSONNET in Avignon in 1728, and entitled *La vie de la sœur Bourgeois.* . . . Although she did not approve, as superior of the institution Sister Saint-Joseph presided over the founding of the mission at Louisbourg, Île Royale (Cape Breton Island), in 1727 by Marguerite ROY, *dite* de la Conception.

After leaving the office of superior, Sister Saint-Joseph was appointed to run the mission at Louisbourg. The task promised to be a difficult one, and an able person was needed to sustain this establishment, the future of which had been endangered by Sister Roy's improvident administration. Bishop Dosquet* chose Sister Trottier because, as he wrote, "she is very capable in temporal matters and is of never-failing virtue."

Sister Saint-Joseph left for Louisbourg in the autumn of 1733 with two companions: her cousin, Sister Saint-Benoît [Marie-Josephte Lefebvre Belle-Isle], and Sister Saint-Arsène [Marie-Marguerite-Daniel ARNAUD]. The sisters soon wrote to their superior, Marie-Élisabeth Guillet, *dite* Sainte-Barbe, that they were not able "to cope with teaching the boarders and day-pupils, especially since they were burdened with housekeeping tasks, being unable to find suitable servants in Louisbourg for their house." Consequently reinforcements were sent them the following year from Ville-Marie: Sister Saint-Placide [Françoise Boucher de Montbrun], Sister Sainte-Gertrude [Marie-Geneviève Hervieux], and a lay sister, Catherine Paré, who was to make her profession at Louisbourg in 1736 under the name of Sister Saint-Louis-des-Anges. Because travelling was so difficult Bishop Dosquet had authorized the sisters to train novices at Louisbourg; he had even granted the sisters the liberty of returning to Montreal when they considered that the institution could get along without them. Thus he authorized a type of institution which was contrary to the spirit of Mother Bourgeoys and to the practice followed up till then in the community [see Marguerite LE MOYNE, *dite* du Saint-Esprit].

The six missionaries lived on the annual pension of 1,500 *livres* which the king had granted Sister Roy. Nevertheless, in the period 1733–40 Sister Saint-Joseph succeeded in reducing from 8,000 to 2,500 *livres* the sisters' debt to Josué DUBOIS Berthelot de Beaucours. Such a reduction implied many sacrifices and labours of all sorts, even though the governor, Saint-Ovide [MONBETON], had assigned the sisters certain fines and the minister, Maurepas, had made them a gift of 3,000 *livres* in 1739. In 1740 the governor of Île Royale, Isaac-Louis de Forant*, who appreciated "the services which the country received from the labours of the teaching sisters" and wanted "to make firm and solid their institution in this colony," set up in favour of the community at Louisbourg an annual allowance for eight places for boarding pupils, intended for daughters of officers on the island. To guarantee this allowance the governor had mortgaged all his belongings. But his sister and sole heir, Mlle Marguerite de Forant, offered to replace the perpetual mortgage with the sum of 32,000 *livres*. When this arrangement was agreed to, the money was "invested with the clergy of France," who by a contract signed 1 June 1742 guaranteed the sisters at Louisbourg an annual income of 1,600 *livres*, all of which the king confirmed by letters patent on 22 Aug. 1742.

Sister Saint-Joseph did not long enjoy M. de Forant's liberality. After 11 years at Louisbourg she was exhausted, and in the autumn of 1744 she was authorized to return to Montreal. But she died at sea, opposite the Île d'Orléans, on 6 Oct. 1744, without having the consolation of setting foot again "in Canada" and of dying in the bosom of her community. She was buried on 8 October in the chapel of Notre-Dame-de-Piété in the church of Notre-Dame de Québec. She had given 54 years of her life to the Congregation of Notre-Dame and to the church in New France.

ANDRÉE DÉSILETS

ACND, La Congrégation de Notre-Dame : son personnel, 1653–1768; Fichier général des sœurs de la Congrégation de Notre-Dame; Plans des lieux de sépulture depuis 1681–CND; Registre des sépultures des sœurs de la Congrégation de Notre-Dame; Registre général des sœurs de la Congrégation de Notre-Dame de Montréal. "Recensement du Canada, 1681" (Sulte). Tanguay, *Dictionnaire*. [Prosper Cloutier], *Histoire de la paroisse de Champlain* (2v., Trois-Rivières, Qué., 1915–17). [É.-M. Faillon], *Mémoire pouvant servir à l'histoire religieuse de la Nouvelle-France* (2v., Paris, 1853). Lemire-Marsolais et Lambert, *Histoire de la Congrégation de Notre-Dame*. Albert Jamet, *Marguerite Bourgeoys, 1620–1700* (2v., Montréal, 1942). Raymond Douville, "Les lents débuts d'une seigneurie des Jésuites," *Cahiers des Dix*, XXV (1960), 249–77.

TROTTIER DESAUNIERS, PIERRE (baptized Antoine-Pierre), merchant and shipowner, syndic of the merchants of Quebec; b. 2 Sept. 1700 in Montreal, son of Pierre Trottier Desauniers, a merchant, and Catherine Charest; went to live in France in 1747.

Pierre Trottier Desauniers was from a well-established business family. His uncle, Étienne Charest, seigneur of Lauson, owned a large business in Quebec, and it was perhaps at his suggestion that Desauniers took up residence there. On 27 Dec. 1723 he married Marguerite Chéron, daughter of a councillor of the Conseil Supérieur, Martin Chéron. The beginnings of Desauniers's career are not known to us, but he seems already well established by 1730, since in that year he sold a two-storey stone house on Rue Sous-le-Fort; the following year he rented three houses belonging to Pierre Perrot* de Rizy, adjutant of the Quebec militia.

Desauniers devoted most of his energies to maritime trade and the fitting-out of ships. In 1733 he owed the Domaine d'Occident 1,365 *livres* in import duties, which suggests a sizable import trade. Around 1732 he had gone into business with his first cousin, François MARTEL de Brouague, in the fishing trade. Martel de Brouague held a large land grant at Baie de Phélypeaux (Brador Bay) on the Labrador coast and supervised the exploitation of it at the site. Desauniers acted as his supplier and attended to the marketing of the products of the Labrador fishery. The business required a large outlay of funds; in 1735 the two men formed a partnership, for which Desauniers put up 100,000 *livres*. As ships were needed to ply between Labrador and Quebec and to promote export trade, Desauniers wanted to launch into shipbuilding in 1737. But faced with the difficulty of finding the necessary wood, he could not execute his plan immediately. In 1739 he began building ships, encountering stiff competition, however, from the royal shipyard for wood and labour. Indeed, the shortage of carpenters had prompted Intendant Hocquart* to assign a certain number of them to the royal shipyard. A few others were free to work for the private shipbuilders, but the intendant required in return that the shipowners train carpenters. In addition to shipbuilding, Desauniers seems to have been interested for a time in the manufacture of fish glue.

In October 1740 Desauniers was chosen as syndic of the merchants of Quebec, an office he held until 1746. This nomination shows clearly the importance of his business concerns and bears witness to the confidence his colleagues had in him. Representing the commercial interests of Quebec, in 1741 Desauniers sent a report to the minister of Marine, Maurepas, asking for card money to be issued instead of bills of exchange, to facilitate retail trade. In another report to Governor Charles de BEAUHARNOIS and Intendant Hocquart he transmitted the complaints of the merchants of Quebec about the competition of the "coast runners" or smugglers, the scarcity of negotiable instruments, and the difficulty of handling them. He also requested contracts for building ships for the king or subsidies for private shipbuilding. In 1744 Desauniers, with Louis CHARLY Saint-Ange, the syndic for Montreal, signed another complaint to the minister of Marine over the difficulties of sea-borne trade in wartime. The syndics asked for escorts between French ports and Quebec, to avoid additional losses of ships.

In 1744 Desauniers's commerce had reached a level sufficient to ensure him a comfortable living. He had four domestic servants to attend his family. Two years earlier he had married his two elder daughters to Étienne Charest and Joseph Dufy Charest, both of them sons of the rich seigneur of Lauson. On his ships Desauniers brought alcohol and general merchandise from France, and he sold the products of the Labrador fishery to the West Indies, from which he brought back tobacco. But the War of the Austrian Succession was to transform this promising career as a colonial merchant.

In 1745 the war on the seas and the English threat increased tenfold the risks in the import trade and caused shipowners to suffer enormous losses. The over-all economic situation became dark for merchants. Only the naval forces of the mother country could protect sea-borne trade, and their successes were irregular. Struck with consternation by the fall of Louisbourg, Île Royale (Cape Breton Island), the military forces at Quebec decided to fortify the town without asking for royal assent. On 12 Aug. 1745 the decision was taken, and Desauniers received the construction contract for the fortifications. He obtained 60,000 *livres* in advance, "to further its prompt execution," and set to work following plans drawn up by Gaspard-Joseph CHAUSSEGROS de Léry. But his expenditures had not been authorized in the budget of the colony, and when Maurepas learned of them in 1746 he ordered that the works be stopped until the colony decided whether it wanted to continue them and pay for the cost, or preferred to give them up. As opinions were divided, it was left to Versailles to decide, and the works were abandoned. Desauniers then wanted to be paid for the construction done, a sum, according to the terms of his contract, amounting to 185,000 *livres*. Hocquart made difficulties for him about the payment of the last 5,000 *livres*. This last sum amounted to a third of Desauniers' profit on the work, a profit which, to begin with, was only about eight per cent. In discouragement the merchant made up his mind to wind up his business and to go to live in France.

On 8 Sept. 1746 he sold his share in the fief of Argentenay (Île d'Orléans) to his partner, Martel de Brouague. On 7 November they dissolved their company and Desauniers withdrew his initial investment of 100,000 *livres*, plus 93,999 *livres* 7 *sols* as his share in the profits since 1735; he was to receive this sum of 193,999 *livres* 7 *sols* in France from the company's funds. In October 1747 he sailed for France with his two sons, Pierre-François and Jacques, and his son-in-law, Joseph Dufy Charest – the three of them returned, it seems, to New France the following year. As his business had not been completely settled when he left the colony, Desauniers was involved in lawsuits heard by the provost court and the Conseil Supérieur in 1750, 1754, and 1755. At that time he was said to be "a merchant of Bordeaux."

Born in Montreal of a bourgeois family, Desauniers had settled in Quebec, the seat of large-scale business, where he had prospered. Following the crisis brought on by the war, he chose to move to the mother country to continue his commercial activities. In so doing he achieved an ambition that was cherished by many colonial merchants in the 18th century.

JOSÉ IGARTUA

AJQ, Registre d'état civil, Notre-Dame de Québec, 27 déc. 1723, 8 févr. 1731. AN, Col., C¹¹ᴬ, 54, ff.235–37; 59, f.388; 67, f.78v; 69, ff.39–43; 70, f.138; 71, ff.125, 142–43; 75, ff.9–13v, 76, 79–80; 78, ff.94–96v; 80, ff.74–75; 82, ff.338–43; 84, ff.6–28, 120–30, 200–5, 218–21, 228–30; 85, ff.76–78, 323–33; 86, ff.283–86; 89, f.12; 94, ff.59–64; 121, f.174. ANQ, Greffe de Jacques Barbel, 4 août 1730, 28 déc. 1735; Greffe de Gilbert Boucault de Godefus, 20 oct. 1742; Greffe de Florent de La Cetière, 26 déc. 1723; NF, Registres du Cons. sup., 1721–1723, ff.90v.–91; 1729, ff.179v–81v; 1735, ff.22–25; 1735–1736, ff.39v–41v, 96–99v, 113v–15; 1739–1740, ff.142v–43; 1741, ff.173v–76v. ANQ-M, Registre d'état civil, Notre-Dame de Montréal, 3 sept. 1700. ASQ, Livres de comptes, C 8, 50, 323; C 10, 24; Polygraphie, XXIV, 36j; XXVII, 3b; XXXV, 22c, 22h; XLVI, 16g. Harvard College Library, bMS Can 1. PAC, MG 8, A2, 33, ff.75–85; 35, ff.87v–89v, 106–7; 37, ff.139v–40, 152v–54v; 40, f.12; A6, 15, ff.427–29. *Inv. de pièces du Labrador* (P.-G. Roy), II, 70–83, 192–93. "Recensemenet de Québec, 1744" (APQ *Rapport*), 104. P.-G. Roy, *Inv. contrats de mariage*, VI, 58; *Inv. jug. et délib.*, III, 76, 92, 103, 107, 109, 116, 118, 122, 164–65, 250, 272, 292, 295, 302; IV, 42, 46, 58, 99, 164, 199, 232; V, 9, 14–15, 157, 164; VI, 25, 34. Tanguay, *Dictionnaire*.

TURC DE CASTELVEYRE, LOUIS, known as **Brother Chrétien**, superior of the Brothers Hospitallers of the Cross and of St Joseph; b. 25 Aug. 1687 at Martigues, France, son of Claude Turc de Castelveyre, provost, and of Marie Bonnel; d. 21 March 1755 at Cap-Français (Cap-Haïtien), Île de Saint-Domingue (Hispaniola).

We know almost nothing of Louis Turc de Castelveyre's youth and education. But the office of provost held by his father and the title of schoolmaster which Turc gave himself when he arrived in New France suggest that he had received the upbringing and schooling of a young bourgeois of the period. In 1719 Louis Turc met François Charon* de La Barre, superior of the Hôpital Général of Montreal, who was making a brief visit to France seeking schoolmasters who would assist him in New France. The superior persuaded Turc to accompany him, and he also took along five other schoolmasters and some workmen for a factory making woven stockings. They travelled on the king's flute the *Chameau*; Charon died on board in July 1719, after having appointed Turc his executor.

Upon his arrival in Montreal Turc became a member of the community of the Hôpital Général under the name of Brother Chrétien. On 17 Sept. 1719, acting, as he believed, in accordance with the founder Charon's views, Bishop Saint-Vallier [La Croix*] named Brother Chrétien superior of the community. Some months later the council of Marine approved this appointment. The colonial authorities, Governor Philippe de Rigaud* de Vaudreuil and Intendant Michel BÉGON, had doubts, however, about Brother Chrétien's ability to administer the Hôpital Général; they wrote that the superior, "although a virtuous man, knows little about directing this house." They even expressed a wish that a responsible person who had nothing to do with the community had been appointed, but since the letters patent of the hospital conferred entire responsibility for administration upon the hospitallers, the governor and intendant were powerless to relieve the superior of his administrative functions.

During his term of office, from 1719 to 1728, Louis Turc met with several administrative and financial disappointments as well as some successes. He had pronounced his provisional vows of religion on 2 Oct. 1722 and, more fortunate than the founder, he received in 1723 approval of the rules that the brothers had been observing since the founding of their community. He made great efforts to provide material support for the Hôpital Général. Thus on 13 Dec. 1719 he renewed the agreement, made on the preceding 15 June by his predecessor, with François Darles and André Souste for running a factory for making woven stockings. But in 1722 Intendant Bégon ordered that this partnership be ended because of the futile quarrels among the partners. As his time was completely taken up with other problems caused by his predecessor's administration, however, Brother Chrétien had not played a great role in this affair. He had undertaken first to pay back the debts contracted by Charon with several French merchants, which Turc estimated at 17,000 *livres*. The superior also set up a trading company which operated in Quebec and Montreal through agents and which he hoped would make a profit. In this way he enabled the Hôpital Général to take in an attractive revenue for the years 1723 and 1724.

Brother Chrétien continued the founder's efforts in education. In the period 1722–24 he recruited some 15 schoolmasters to meet the needs of teaching in New France, for which the Brothers Hospitallers were in part responsible. But the recruits, who had signed on almost blindly, resigned after a few months, for "the Hôpital Général did not supply them with anything for their upkeep." Some returned to France, others settled in the colony. In the hope of remedying this constant lack of teachers, Brother Chrétien worked, during a voyage to France in 1723, at setting up a normal school at La Rochelle. Turning to account the desire of Bishop Étienne de Champflour of La Rochelle who himself wanted competent teachers for the youth of his episcopal city, he offered the services of his community. The hospitallers of Montreal accepted this project officially in 1724, hoping in this way to be able to train teachers in France before bringing them to the colony. To support this common work, Bishop Champflour requested royal consent and endowed the hospitallers of Montreal by testament with a house, garden, and outbuildings, and the sum of 12,000 *livres*.

The administrative and financial methods employed by Brother Chrétien confirmed the doubts that the governor and the intendant had already expressed concerning his managerial abilities. Thus, to settle his predecessor's debt, Brother Chrétien had received from the hospitallers 409 *livres* 9 *sols*, which he used for other purposes; consequently, to settle this debt he had to make use of sums taken from the 3,000 *livres* in annual subsidies intended for the upkeep of the schoolmasters. These transfers of funds made normal financing of the teaching work of the Hôpital Général impossible. He had borrowed 40,000 *livres* to found the normal school in La Rochelle, in the hope that this sum would be returned to him by Bishop Champflour. Bishop Saint-Vallier's consent to the union of the house in La Rochelle with that in Montreal did not reach Brother Chrétien until after Bishop Champflour's death, the project fell through, and Brother Chrétien found himself in a precarious financial situation. In addition, he left unpaid many accounts in France, and he used the royal gratuities intended for education to settle his other transactions – these subsidies the king suspended in 1731. The total of his debts amounted to 53,968 *livres* 9 *sols* 4 *deniers*.

In the face of his numerous creditors' insistence, Brother Chrétien left France in 1725 to go to the French colony on the Île de Saint-Domingue, thinking that he would set up several fishing establishments there. The king then ordered the governor of Saint-Domingue, Charles-Gaspard de Goussé, Chevalier de La Rochalar, to have him arrested and to send him to Quebec to account for the large loans he had contracted in France in the name of the Hôpital Général of Montreal. Brother Chrétien fled to the Spanish part of the island, where he lived for three years. He was finally forced to return to New France. He arrived in July 1728 and retired to the Recollet convent in Quebec. On 17 September the hospitallers removed him from the office of superior of the community.

To settle his numerous debts Brother Chrétien sued the Brothers Hospitallers, who, he claimed, owed him the sum of 54,776 *livres* 8 *sols* 6 *deniers*. He also demanded from one of his agents in the colony, Claude Morillonnet, *dit* Berry, payment for goods he had had sent to him from France. For their part, 39 of his French creditors sued him before the courts of New France for the sum of 29,938 *livres* 9 *sols* 4 *deniers* and demanded subrogation of Brother Chrétien in their favour in the legal proceedings against the hospitallers and the agent Morillonnet. On 22 April 1735, having inspected all the documents pertinent to this financial imbroglio, the Conseil Supérieur finally found the Brothers Hospitallers in debt to their former superior to the amount of 24,940 *livres* 13 *sols* 9 *deniers*. As for Morillonnet, he had been sentenced in a judgement on 10 July 1731 to pay Brother Chrétien 9,073 *livres* 6 *sols* 4 *deniers* and to hand over to him goods valued at 5,188 *livres* 2 *sols* 4 *deniers*.

Although the bankruptcy of the Hôpital Général of Montreal is not to be attributed solely to Brother Chrétien, the fact remains that the expenditures made without the hospitallers' knowledge – if the account book of the Hôpital Général is to be believed – aggravated the already shaky financial situation of that enterprise. In 1735, after all the differences between the hospitallers and his French creditors had been settled, Brother Chrétien requested permission of the authorities of New France to return to Saint-Domingue, where he hoped to set up a brewery, with the idea presumably that its profits would serve to pay off the rest of his creditors.

Louis Turc de Castelveyre then went to Cap-Français. He rented a small house, where he took in some orphans to educate; subsequently he harboured indigent old men. Encouraged by the Jesuits, who were ministering to the northern part of the island, and supported by the alms of rich colonists, Turc de Castelveyre was able at the end of five years to acquire a huge property which he named "La Providence." He then increased the number of boarders, agreeing to lodge emigrants from Europe. When he found himself at the head of a growing organization, Turc de Castelveyre wanted to be relieved of all financial responsibility and presented a petition to the Conseil Supérieur of Cap-Français on 12 Nov. 1740, requesting that administrators be appointed for this hospice and reserving for himself only the right to devote himself to it as a hospitaller. This petition was granted on 5 March 1741.

Louis Turc de Castelveyre spent his days in charitable works until his death on 21 March 1755. Moreau de Saint-Méry has left us the following portrait of the "founder and first director of 'La Providence des Hommes'": "He was a stout man 5 feet 4 inches tall, slightly stooped, broad-shouldered, pug-nosed, his face indicated gentleness and kindness."

IN COLLABORATION WITH
ALBERTINE FERLAND-ANGERS

AAQ, 22 A, Copies de lettres expédiées, II, 325. AN, Col., B, 42, f.44; 44, ff.507, 508; 45, f.111; 46, f.526; 48, f.884; 50, ff.500–1; 51, f.171; 57/2, f.627; C¹¹ᴬ, 39, f.391; 40, f.51; 47, f.271; 107, ff.93ff. ANQ-M, Greffe de J.-B. Adhémar, 25 août 1719; Greffe de J.-C. Raimbault, 17 sept. 1728; Greffe de Pierre Raimbault, 22 sept. 1721. ASGM, Inventaire des biens meubles et immeubles des frères Hospitaliers dits Frères Charon de l'Hôpital Général de Montréal, 4 sept. 1747; Recette et dépense de juin 1718 à septembre 1746; Registre des vêtures, professions, etc. des Frères Charon, 1701–48. ASSM, Cahiers Faillon, 197c (mfm F1).

Édits ord., I, 389. [M.-L.-É.] Moreau de Saint-Méry, *Description topographique, physique, civile, politique et historique de la partie française de l'isle de Saint-Domingue* (2v., Philadelphia, 1897; Blanche Maurel et Étienne Taillemite, édit., Bibliothèque d'histoire coloniale, nouv. sér., 3v., Paris, 1958); *Éloges de M. Turc de Castelveyre* (Paris, 1790). Massicotte, "Inventaire des documents concernant les frères Charon," APQ *Rapport, 1923–24*, 163–201. P.-G. Roy, *Inv. ord. int.*, I, 183, 229–30; II, 104. [É.-M. Faillon], *Vie de Mme d'Youville, fondatrice des Sœurs de la Charité de Villemarie dans l'île de Montréal en Canada* (Villemarie [Montréal], 1852). Albertine Ferland-Angers, *Mère d'Youville* (Montréal, 1945). Amédée Gosselin, *L'instruction au Canada*, 460. Lionel Groulx, *L'enseignement français au Canada* (2v., Montréal, 1931–33), I, 117–18. É.-Z. Massicotte, "Les frères Charon," *BRH*, XXIII (1917), 150ff.

TUTTY, WILLIAM, priest of the Church of England; b. *c.* 1715 in Hertfordshire, England, son of William Tutty and Gruzzel Drew; d. 24 Nov. 1754 in Hertford, England.

William Tutty received his BA from Emmanuel College, Cambridge, in 1737, and his MA in 1741. He was ordained a deacon of the Church of England in 1737 by Bishop Robert Butts of Norwich, on letters dimissory from the bishop of Lincoln. He became a curate and "afternoon lecturer" at the parish of All Saints, Hertford, in 1744, and was ordained a priest by Bishop John Thomas of Lincoln on 18 Dec. 1748.

In April 1749 Tutty was accepted by the Society for the Propagation of the Gospel as a missionary for Nova Scotia; his salary was to be £70 per year. He arrived at Halifax on 21 June with the first settlers for the new colony in the expedition led by Edward Cornwallis*, the governor of Nova Scotia. His first services were held in the open air at the governor's residence (site of the present Province House), and later in Alexander Callendar's warehouse (close to the present St Paul's Church). St Paul's Church was built in 1750 and Tutty preached the first sermon there on 2 September.

During the first months in Halifax, Tutty shared his work with the Reverend William Anwyl, who was appointed a missionary by the SPG about the same time as he. Anwyl was prone to excessive drinking, and became more and more negligent in his work. Tutty observed that "both his actions and Expressions bespeak rather the Boatswain of a Man-of-War than a Minister of the Gospel. . . ." The SPG ordered Anwyl's recall to answer charges about his behaviour, but he died before receiving this order, on 9 Feb. 1750.

From Nova Scotia Tutty wrote about a dozen letters to the SPG, describing in detail the progress of the colony. In the fall and early winter of 1749 he complained about "the perverseness of the settlers and their immorality," and spoke of friction between the settlers from England, who adhered to the Church of England, and those from New England, who were Dissenters, mainly Congregationalists [*see* Aaron CLEVELAND]. By July of 1751, however, Tutty could report to the SPG that "there is perfect harmony at present between the Church of England and the Dissenters. . . . The prejudices which they have conceived against the Church of England seem rather to be softened into a kind of liking. . . ."

Tutty's efforts at reforming some of the older settlers were not too effective, so he turned his attention to "our Chief Hope, the rising generation," for whom he secured a schoolmaster, Edward HALHEAD. He found some difficulty in ministering to the French and Swiss Protestants in the settlement, and recommended in September 1749 that the SPG appoint as his assistant Jean-Baptiste MOREAU, who had also come with the settlers in June. Moreau succeeded Anwyl in June 1750.

The first winter at Halifax was hard for people not used to such a raw climate and by the spring of 1750 the number of settlers had shrunk to 1,900 from the original 3,000. With regular trading between New England and Halifax, every ship that left Halifax for the old colonies carried passengers seeking a more comfortable life there. There were other adverse factors than the weather, as Tutty observed: "There is . . . no proportion between the Baptisms and the Burials; the latter exceed prodigiously occasioned by an inviolable attachment to New England rum, ye most destructive of all destructive spirits." By July 1750, however, with the arrival of more settlers, Tutty reported that the population of Halifax was nearly 3,000 again. He noted in October that new settlers had been located on the other side of Halifax harbour (Dartmouth), thus adding to the difficulties of his office. "The business of this place to a man of the strongest constitution would be laborious enough," he wrote. His own health was "Bad at Best."

As early as August 1749 Tutty had asked for leave to return to England on private business, but he was not able to go until shortly after 18 Oct. 1752, when he wrote his last letter to the SPG from Nova Scotia. His successor in Halifax was John Breynton*, who had arrived in June. On 3 Jan. 1753 Tutty married a widow, Mrs Catherine Hollows, at All Saints Church, Hertford, where he was again employed as an "afternoon lecturer." A daughter was born in November 1753. A year later, on 24 November, Tutty died and was buried in the churchyard of All Saints.

C. E. THOMAS

All Saints Church (Hertford, Eng.), Parish registers. Hertford County Records Office (Hertford, Eng.), Allen index to Hertfordshire marriages. Lincoln (Eng.) Archives Office, Episcopal register 38, f.545. USPG, B, 17, pp.22, 38; 18, pp.1, 4, 223; 19, p.6; 20, p.5 (copies in PANS, USPG mfm, reels 14, 15); Journal of SPG, 1, p.156. *Alumni Cantabrigienses: a biographical list of all known students, graduates and holders of office at the University of Cambridge, from the earliest times to 1900*, comp. John and J. A. Venn (2 pt., 10v., Cambridge, Eng., 1922–54), pt.I. Bell, *Foreign Protestants*. G. W. Hill, "History of St. Paul's Church, Halifax, Nova Scotia," N.S. Hist. Soc. *Coll.*, I (1879), 35–38.

TYNG (Ting), EDWARD, merchant and naval officer; b. 1683 in Falmouth (now Portland, Maine), eldest son of Colonel Edward Tyng* and Elizabeth Clarke; married Elizabeth Parnel, a widow (daughter of Cyprian SOUTHACK), on 8 Jan. 1725 (o.s.); his second wife, Ann Waldo (sister of Samuel WALDO), whom he married on 27 Jan. 1731, bore him six children, only three of whom lived to maturity; d. 7 Sept. 1755 in Boston, Massachusetts.

Edward Tyng went to sea at an early age. He sailed as a merchant seaman and engaged in mercantile pursuits in Boston. In 1736 the General Court of Massachusetts granted him a tract of land on the Merrimack River, in consideration of his father's services and tragic demise in a French prison.

On 16 April 1740 Governor Jonathan Belcher appointed Tyng captain of the batteries and fortifications of Boston, and on 26 August Tyng assumed command of the province's new snow, *Prince of Orange*. For the next two years he cruised the New England coast in search of Spanish and French privateers. In the spring of 1744 Captain Tyng was sent to Annapolis Royal with news of the outbreak of war with France. He returned to Boston on 27 May, carrying 26 women and children refugees, as the Annapolis garrison feared an attack by the French and their Indian allies. In June Tyng set out in search of French privateers off the New England coast. While cruising off Cape Cod he met a French sloop, commanded by Captain Joannis-Galand d'Olobaratz*, and after a 12-hour engagement disabled the smaller vessel and brought it into Boston as a prize. In July he carried reinforcements to Annapolis Royal, breaking the siege of that fortress by Micmac and Malecite Indians. The rest of the year he spent in convoy duty between Boston and the Grand Banks of Newfoundland.

On 27 Jan. 1744/45, Captain Tyng was elevated to the command of a new, larger vessel, the *Massachusetts*. He sailed from Boston on 16 March

Ungquaterughiathe

1745 as commodore of the colonial flotilla of 13 armed and about 90 transport vessels engaged in the expedition against Louisbourg, Île Royale (Cape Breton Island). During this campaign he performed blockade duty and was involved, along with ships commanded by Peter WARREN, in the early stages of the chase that led to the capture of the French man-of-war *Vigilant*, commanded by Alexandre de LA MAISONFORT Du Boisdecourt. He participated in the destruction of Port-Dauphin (Englishtown, N.S.) and in June went to relieve Annapolis Royal which had been briefly besieged by the French and Indians in May. Tyng was still commanding the *Massachusetts* in April 1747.

One of the leading American naval officers of the colonial period, Tyng died in Boston on 7 Sept. 1755, after suffering for six years the effects of a paralytic stroke.

ROBERT L. WAGNER

[Adonijah Bidwell], "Journal of Rev. Adonijah Bidwell," *New Eng. Hist. and Geneal. Register*, XXVII (1873), 153–60. Boston, Registry Dept., *Records* (Whitmore *et al.*), [24], [28]. *Correspondence of William Shirley* (Lincoln), I, 288–89, 305, 311. William Douglass, *A summary, historical and political, of the first planting, progressive improvements, and present state of the British settlements in North-America . . .* (2v., Boston, 1747–52; London, 1755; London, 1760), I, 341–42. *The memorial history of Boston, including Suffolk County, Massachusetts, 1630–1880*, ed. Justin Winsor (4v., Boston, 1880–81), II, 115. "The Pepperrell papers," *Mass. Hist. Soc. Coll.*, 6th ser., X (1899). [William Pepperrell], "The Sir William Pepperrell journal," *American Antiquarian Soc. Proc.* (Worcester, Mass.), new ser., XX (1909–10), 139–76. Timothy Alden, "Memoirs of Edward Tyng, Esq.," *Mass. Hist. Soc. Coll.*, 1st ser., X (1809), 180–83. Calnek, *History of Annapolis* (Savary), 99–101. H. M. Chapin, "New England vessels in the expedition against Louisbourg, 1745," *New Eng. Hist. and Geneal. Register*, LXXVII (1923), 59–71, 95–110. *DAB*. William Goold, *Portland in the past, with historical notes of Old Falmouth* (Portland, Maine, 1886), 247 (portrait of Tyng), 249. Waldo Lincoln, "The province snow 'Prince of Orange,'" *American Antiquarian Soc. Proc.*, new ser., XIV (1900–1), 251–305. McLennan, *Louisbourg*.

U

UNGQUATERUGHIATHE. *See* SWATANA

V

VALLÉE, FRANÇOIS-MADELEINE, surveyor; fl. 1710–42; m. Laurence Casselle in France.

François-Madeleine Vallée was trained in the engineering sciences, including surveying and hydrography. In 1723, by *lettre de cachet*, he was exiled with his family from France to Île Royale (Cape Breton Island), following a period of imprisonment for undetermined misdemeanours. Until 1725 he was forbidden to take gainful employment; instead, the state provided the family with rations. Probably to demonstrate his usefulness, he undertook a critical review of the construction work done at Louisbourg prior to his arrival there. In 1725 François GANET, with the consent of the authorities, appointed Vallée as his agent in Louisbourg. In that capacity Vallée looked after the general contractor's interests until the latter arrived in Louisbourg later that year, including the initial negotiations to settle the claims of the heirs of Michel-Philippe Isabeau*, the previous general contractor.

An attempt in the same year to have Vallée appointed king's surveyor and teacher of mathematics and hydrography to officers' sons failed; he had to wait until July 1731 for his surveyor's licence. Thereafter he was responsible for preparing town plans and survey reports on property concessions in Louisbourg and throughout the colony. He settled boundary differences between owners and on occasion studied all original land titles in order to provide official advice on the current status of various properties. He kept the court up to date on new concessions by providing plans and statements and he was frequently called upon to furnish precise facts respecting properties about to change hands. Vallée's reports and plans are among the best surviving documentary evidence of town planning at Louisbourg.

In 1731 Vallée was expected to live by the fees he could charge for his services. Evidently this arrangement proved most difficult: he was in a "miserable situation" and it was "absolutely impossible" for him and his family to subsist without a salary. No salary was provided, but from 1733 he was given an annual gratuity of 200 *livres*. Vallée also raised 5,500 *livres* by selling his stone house on the corner of Rue Saint-Louis and Rue de France in Louisbourg.

Archival references to Vallée at Louisbourg peter out in 1742. There is some evidence that he may have been allowed leave in France in 1738–39 and that he may have returned there in 1743. He had died by the time a register of officers who had served in the French colonies from 1747 to 1763 was drawn up. He is known to have had one son, Louis-Félix, an artillery officer in Île Royale from 1742 to 1745.

F. J. THORPE

AD, Charente-Maritime (La Rochelle), B, 275, f.6v. AN, Col., B, 47, 48, 49, 55, 58, 61, 63, 68, 69, 74; C^{11B}, 6, 7, 8, 12, 14, 15, 17, 18, 20, 21, 22, 23, 24; D^{2C}, 222; Marine, C^7, 335 (dossier Vallée); Section Outre-Mer, G^1, 407; G^2, 181; G^3, 2038, 2039, 2046; Dépôt des fortifications des colonies, Am. sept., nos.43, 182, 183. McLennan, *Louisbourg*, 335, 351.

VALLETTE DE CHÉVIGNY, MÉDARD-GABRIEL, king's writer, merchant, storekeeper; fl. 1712–1754.

Médard-Gabriel Vallette de Chévigny probably came to New France with the intendant BÉGON late in 1712. For many years Chévigny served as a junior official in the intendant's office. On 25 Nov. 1720 he married at Quebec Marguerite, daughter of Jean-Baptiste MAILLOU, *dit* Desmoulins. In the marriage act Chévigny is described as king's writer and son of Charles Vallette de Chévigny, "king's attorney of rivers and forests at Vitry," and Marie-Anne Deschamps de Fellière, both of Saint-Médard parish, diocese of Orléans, France. Chévigny's career holds great interest, for he probably did as much as anyone to develop the tar and pitch industry in New France. As early as 1724 he accompanied a party sent by Bégon to Baie Saint-Paul to search for masts needed by the French navy, and later in the decade he was placed in charge of 25 soldiers and two sergeants, drawn from the colonial regulars, who worked at the royal tar works at Grande-Anse (seigneury of La Pocatière) on the St Lawrence. Under the impetus of Gilles Hocquart*, who had come to New France as financial commissary in 1729 and was anxious to foster shipbuilding and associated industries, Chévigny began to devote all of his time to tar manufacture.

In 1731 he went to France to learn processes for producing tar, pitch, resin, and turpentine. He returned to Canada in 1732 and before the next summer season distributed copies of his reports to interested habitants. In 1733, however, he was diverted to search for ship timber in the Lake Champlain region. This trip was significant. He advised the minister of Marine, Maurepas, that no trees could be found for ships with a keel length greater than 100 feet. Thus five years before the royal shipyards at Quebec began construction of vessels of larger dimensions a report existed that denied the possibility of success.

Chévigny's own enterprise was not very successful. In late spring 1734, with three soldiers, he began to experiment with the red and white pines in the Baie Saint-Paul area. By the end of the season about 1,000 pounds of dry pitch and resin had been obtained. The climate, however, was too severe. Sap in the white pines only began flowing in July, and the enterprise could not be economic. During the next two seasons Chévigny turned to the southwest, where in the seigneuries of Berthier and Dautré he manufactured pitch and resin on his own account, and instructed interested habitants in procedures. In 1736, although he worked for only part of the summer, he again sent 1,000 pounds of pitch and resin to Quebec whence it went to France for inspection. In 1737 his operations in the pineries of New France were concluded; results may not have met the intendant's expectations or Chévigny may have thought the enterprise a bad business venture. Further development was carried out by Antoine Serindac, a soldier who had worked for Chévigny at Grande-Anse in the 1720s.

On 27 March 1738 Chévigny was sent by Hocquart to Fort Saint-Frédéric (Crown Point, N.Y.) as storekeeper. Two years later he took strong exception to the activities of the fort's commandant François LEFEBVRE Duplessis Faber, who wanted to increase settlement and exploit timber resources. Chévigny objected that Duplessis Faber claimed the right to distribute food and supplies to the garrison and had taken the keys to the storehouses. In 1741 Hocquart recalled both men to Quebec, and it is significant that almost immediately he sent Chévigny back to the fort with a new commandant, François-Antoine PÉCAUDY de Contrecœur. Nevertheless the intendant complained that the storekeeper appeared incapable of presenting well ordered accounts and by 1744 was planning to replace him as soon as possible.

Hereafter Chévigny disappears from view. In 1754 he was identified as a bourgeois of Quebec. The absence of any death notice in the records suggests that he returned to France during the Seven Years' War or after the conquest.

Vallier

Although he had 12 children only one appears to have survived to adolescence.

JAMES S. PRITCHARD

AJQ, Registre d'état civil, Notre-Dame de Québec, 25 nov. 1720. AN, Col., B, 58, f.423; 63, f.472; C¹¹ᴬ, 62, f.265; 74, pp.168–76; 75, pp.362–66, 367; 82, pp.15–20 (PAC transcripts); Marine, C⁷, 334. P.-G. Roy, *Inv. contrats de mariage*, VI, 87; *Inv. jug. et délib.*, *1717–1760*, I, 317, 318, 321; II, 52, 122–25; V, 304; *Inv. ord. int.*, I, 246, 274, 291; II, 20, 26, 163, 184, 199, 241; III, 72. Tanguay, *Dictionnaire*. J.-N. Fauteux, *Essai sur l'industrie*, I, 201; II, 319, 322–26.

VALLIER, FRANÇOIS-ELZÉAR, priest, canon, and theologal of the chapter of Quebec, promoter of the officiality, procurator and superior of the seminary of Quebec, ecclesiastical councillor on the Conseil Supérieur of New France; b. 1707 in the diocese of Apt, France; d. 16 Jan. 1747 in Quebec.

François-Elzéar Vallier landed at Quebec along with Bishop Dosquet*, coadjutor to Louis-François Duplessis de Mornay, bishop of Quebec, and Louis Bertrand* de Latour, dean of the chapter, on 2 Sept. 1729. It was the coadjutor who had urged the directors of the Séminaire des Missions Étrangères in Paris to send him to Canada. When the procurator, Henri-Jean TREMBLAY, announced to his fellow religious of the seminary of Quebec that Vallier was coming, he mentioned specifically that the bishop was counting on using him "for the instruction of the young ecclesiastics as well as the youths who are being educated for that state." M. Vallier, wrote the procurator, "is a very virtuous ecclesiastic, both pious and fitted for studies, of the most gentle disposition, and thus I believe that you will do well to make him a director." Dosquet also had the highest opinion of his protégé. "He has a superior mind," he wrote in 1731, "extraordinary talent for learning, and above all for making himself liked by everyone."

Abbé Vallier, who was only a deacon, received the priesthood on 23 Sept. 1730. But his superiors had not waited for his ordination to entrust to him the teaching of the pupils and seminarists. They could not have made a better choice, since the young priest, reported Dosquet, had "done his philosophy at 12 years of age," and had "taught since his boyhood." According to the bishop his lectures on theology were received "with general applause." Someone so brilliant and endowed with such an agreeable character could not fail to advance more rapidly than usual. In 1732 he was elected a director of the seminary, and the following year he became procurator. The directors in Paris were delighted to see that Vallier had won the confidence and affection of his associates, and on 14 May 1734 they appointed him superior of the seminary of Quebec.

At that time the seminary was going through a critical period. It was bending under the burden of large debts and found itself exposed to the rivalries which were setting Canadian clerics against French. The superior succeeded in surmounting all obstacles, and the happy effects of his administration soon made themselves felt. In 1736 the directors in Paris congratulated their colleagues in Quebec on the "great peacefulness" and "very good understanding" which reigned among them. The financial situation also improved. In 1742 the most pressing debts were paid off, and four years later it was noted in Paris that at the present rate, the seminary of Quebec would in a short time be able to send money to France.

Dosquet and his successor, Bishop Pontbriand [DUBREIL], who arrived in New France in 1741, did not fail to put Vallier's talents to use. Dosquet had him appointed by the king theologal of the chapter on 18 Feb. 1732; he named him superior of the Hôpital Général, a post he held from 1734 to 1740, and chose him as his procurator in 1734 and 1737. Pontbriand appointed him promoter of the officiality on 3 Nov. 1741 and obtained for him the office of ecclesiastical councillor on the Conseil Supérieur of New France in 1743.

In 1739 a serious illness had forced Vallier to seek treatment in his native land. When his fellow ecclesiastics in Quebec expressed to him their fear of never seeing him again, the superior replied that he had absolutely no intention of remaining in France. He saw a single obstacle to his return. This, he wrote, "could come from my superiors, but far from taking measures different from those which your benevolence leads you to desire for me, they are most firmly resolved to send me back as soon as possible." He returned to Canada as promised, in 1741, on the same ship as Pontbriand.

Vallier was to die too early, a victim of his zeal. At the beginning of 1747 many English prisoners, stricken with contagious diseases, were at the Hôtel-Dieu of Quebec. The superior, who knew their language slightly, and some priests from the seminary generously went to their aid. But Vallier had overestimated his strength. On 16 January he died at the Hôtel-Dieu of the fevers which he had caught while giving medical care without regard to himself. His loss was deeply felt at the seminary and in the whole colony, as one can read in the eulogy which his fellow ecclesiastics in the chapter devoted to him in their record of deliberations: "He was endowed with all the virtues and had all the qualities and talents that one can desire in a perfect servant of Jesus Christ. He was gentle and kindly, with a quick and penetrating mind, great judgement, and unparalleled prudence which always caused him to be calm and of equable temperament. Above all, he combined deep humility with great and widespread learning, true mortification and disregard for himself with complete detachment, unlimited charity towards all the afflicted with an untiring zeal for the glory of God and the salvation of souls which was always guided by the spirit of obedience."

NOËL BAILLARGEON

AAQ, 12 A, Registres d'insinuations A; 12 A Registres d'insinuations B; B, Chapitre de la cathédrale de Québec. AN, Col., D²ᶜ, 222/2, p.287 (PAC transcript). ASQ, Brouillard, 1732–1749; Évêques, 179; Lettres, M, 67–112; S, 105; MSS, 12; Polygraphie, IV, 74. Provost, *Le séminaire de Québec: documents et biographies*. P.-G. Roy, *Inv. jug. et délib., 1717–1760*, IV. Gosselin, *L'Église du Canada jusqu'à la conquête*, III. *Mgr de Saint-Vallier et l'Hôpital Général*, 710, 712. Henri Têtu, "Le chapitre de la cathédrale de Québec et ses délégués en France," *BRH*, XIV (1908), 106.

VARENNES, JACQUES-RENÉ GAULTIER DE. *See* GAULTIER

VARENNES ET DE LA VÉRENDRYE, PIERRE GAULTIER DE. *See* GAULTIER

VARLET, DOMINIQUE-MARIE, priest, missionary, vicar general, bishop of Babylon; b. 15 March 1678 in Paris, son of Achille Varlet, Sieur de Verneuil, and Marie Vallée; d. at Rijnwijk (Zeist, Neth.), 14 May 1742.

Dominique-Marie Varlet was the son of an actor. His father, known under the name of Sieur de Verneuil, and his uncle, Charles Varlet, the famous La Grange, collaborator and friend of Molière, had won renown on various Parisian stages before becoming members of the Comédie-Française at its creation in 1680. Little is known about his mother other than that she was the daughter of a Parisian hatter, that she too had been in the theatre, and that she was much younger than her husband. The Varlets had had seven children, only three of whom reached adulthood: Jean-Achille, born in 1681, who died, an attorney in the *parlement* of Paris, in 1720; Marie-Anne, the youngest of the family, who was married to Antoine Olivier, an attorney at the Châtelet; and Dominique-Marie.

The latter had early been destined, it seems, to the ecclesiastical state. He was enrolled in the Séminaire de Saint-Magloire in Paris, which was run by the Oratorians, then in the Collège de Navarre (one of the colleges in the University of Paris), studying in succession for the *baccalauréat* (1701), licentiate, and doctorate in theology (1706). It was at Saint-Magloire that he became acquainted with two well-known Jansenists with whom he became fast friends, Jacques Jubé, the future liturgist, and Jean-Baptiste-Paulin d'Aguesseau, the brother of the chancellor of France, Henri-François d'Aguesseau. Through his father, who on occasion retired to his country home near the famous place of pilgrimage of Mont Valérien, Varlet had already come into contact with the Congrégation des prêtres du Calvaire, with the result that in 1699 he had asked to be admitted and had been accepted as a member of this community. All these circles, which were strongly impregnated with Jansenism, were going to contribute in no small way to determining his future orientation.

In 1706 he was ordained a priest and was immediately assigned to parishes in the Paris suburbs. In 1708 he was parish priest at Conflans-Sainte-Honorine. Three years later, faced with all sorts of difficulties, he went to see the directors of the Séminaire des Missions Étrangères in Paris and asked to be admitted into their society in order to devote himself to the evangelization of pagans, as he had long desired. In 1712 he resigned as parish priest and came to put himself at the disposal of his new superiors. He was then designated to go to restore the mission to the Tamaroas (Cahokia, now East St Louis, Ill.), which had remained practically without a priest since Marc Bergier*'s death in 1707.

Varlet sailed from Port-Louis (dept. of Morbihan) at the end of January 1713 and on 6 June he arrived at Mobile (Mobile Bay, Ala.). Upon his arrival he suffered an attack of dysentery which almost carried him off, and he had to resign himself to staying where he was with his fellow religious, Albert Davion* and François Le Maire, while waiting until more favourable circumstances allowed him to push on to the Illinois country.

His first impressions were on the whole negative. Louisiana, he wrote, was not, as was believed in France, "one of the marvels of the world." Undoubtedly the soil seemed fertile, the forest abounding in game, but for the moment what one beheld was only a "wild, uncultivated" country, which was consequently not very attractive. As for the work of evangelization, the picture that he painted was scarcely more cheering. The missionaries were too few in number, and the difficulties they encountered in their apostolate among amazingly primitive and rough tribes too great.

Varlet resolved to take advantage of an expedition organized at the beginning of 1715 by Lamothe Cadillac [Laumet*], governor of Louisiana – at that time exploration was going on for mines in the upper Mississippi country – to go to Cahokia to establish himself at the Sainte-Famille mission, as the seminary of Paris had asked him to do. That same year he was appointed vicar general to the bishop of Quebec for the Mississippi and Illinois region. He was to remain a little more than two years at Cahokia, devoting the greater part of his time to his Tamaroas, not hesitating to accompany them to their hunting grounds when winter arrived, but encountering the same obstacles as had his predecessor Bergier. In the spring of 1717 he thought of leaving for Quebec. His idea was to go there to recruit a certain number of assistants, but particularly to consolidate his position in the face of claims put forward by the Jesuits, who continued to deplore the presence of priests of the seminary of Quebec in a region that they considered had been reserved for them.

Varlet left Cahokia on 24 March and succeeded in reaching Quebec on 11 September. On 6 October he received from Bishop Saint-Vallier [La Croix*] confirmation of the privileges granted in 1698 for the Tamaroa mission. Taking advantage of the long winter months, he was successful besides in persuading the seminary to give him reinforcements. On 10 May 1718 Goulven Calvarin*, Dominique-Antoine-René Thaumur* de La Source, and Jean-Paul Mercier left for Cahokia. But Varlet himself was never to see the Illinois country again. He was recalled to Paris by his superiors and left Quebec around the beginning of October 1718; he had spent a little more than 13 months in the capital.

On 13 November he was at La Rochelle and a fortnight later in Paris, where he learned of his appointment as coadjutor to the bishop of Babylon, Louis-Marie Pidou de Saint-Olon. On 19 Feb. 1719, in Paris, he was consecrated titular bishop of Ascalon. One of the consecrating prelates was Louis-François Duplessis de Mornay, coadjutor to the bishop of Quebec. On the same day Varlet received letters from the Congregation for the Propagation of the Faith informing him of Bishop Saint-Olon's death and urging him to leave as soon as possible for his bishopric. In his haste he neglected, consciously or not, to call upon the papal nuncio, between whose hands he was supposed, as prescribed by Rome, to pronounce the oath of allegiance to the bull

Unigenitus Dei Filius, which had been proclaimed on 8 Sept. 1713 and which condemned as heretical the 101 Jansenist propositions drawn from the *Réflexions morales sur le Nouveau Testament* (1699 edition) of the Oratorian Pasquier Quesnel. This "oversight" was fatal for him. Upon his arrival in Persia at the beginning of November 1719 he found himself interdicted by a decree of the Congregation for the Propagation of the Faith from all exercise of his religious function. Obliged to retrace his steps, he went to take up his abode in Holland, where he had stayed some months earlier, on his way to his bishopric, and where he counted on being able to work for his justification. It did not take long for circumstances to lead him to identify his cause with that of the Dutch Jansenists. Not content with supporting them in their conflict with Rome, in 1724 he agreed to confer the office of bishop upon Cornelius Steenoven, who had been elected archbishop of Utrecht by the chapter of that city; he thus consecrated the rupture of these Jansenists with the Holy See, at the same time earning the title of "spiritual father" of the so-called Church of Utrecht. In 1723 he became an appellant against the bull *Unigenitus* and remained so until his death, despite the efforts made by François de Montigny, procurator of the Société des Missions Étrangères in Rome, to regularize his situation.

A missionary to the depths of his soul, he remained obsessed all his life by the problem of the salvation of unbelievers. His experience with the Tamaroas had left its mark on him. In 1733, at the height of his quarrels with Rome, he had written: "I still frequently miss the woods of America." Perhaps he secretly wished that he had never left them.

Pierre Hurtubise

D.-M. Varlet, *Apologie de Mgr. l'évêque de Babilone . . .* (Amsterdam, 1724); *Lettre de Mgr. l'évêque de Babylone à Mgr. l'évêque de Montpellier pour servir de réponse à l'ordonnance de M. l'archevêque de Paris . . .* (Utrecht, 1736); *Lettre de Mgr. l'évêque de Babylone à Mgr. l'évêque de Senez, au sujet de la lettre de ce prélat sur les erreurs avancées dans quelques nouveaux écrits* (n.p., 1737); *Lettre de Monsieur l'évesque de Babylone, aux missionnaires du Tonquin* (Utrecht, 1734); *Réponse de Mgr. l'évêque de Babylone à Mgr. l'évesque de Senez . . .* (n.p., 1736); *Seconde apologie de Monseigneur l'évêque de Babilone . . .* (Amsterdam, 1727). C. J. [Steenoven] et D.-M. [Varlet], *Lettre de Mgr. l'archevesque d'Utrecht à Mgr. l'évesque de Babylone à Mgr. l'évesque de Senez, au sujet du jugement rendu à Ambrun contre ce prélat* (n.p., 1728).

AN, LL, 1591. Archives du Vatican, Fonds de la Secrétairerie d'État, Nonciature de France, 234, 389. Archives royales d'Utrecht (Pays-Bas), Fonds Port-Royal d'Ammersfoort, 3797. BN, MSS, Fr. 22832; MSS, NAF, 5398. *Mandements des évêques de Québec* (Têtu et Gagnon), I, 495–96. *Nouvelles Ecclésiastiques; ou Mémoires pour servir à l'histoire de la Constitution Unigenitus* (Paris), 1731, 195; 1735, 15; 1736, 81; 1737, 13; 1742, 105–8, 185–88. Auguste Jal, *Dictionnaire critique de biographie et d'histoire* (Paris, 1867), 726–29. Delanglez, *French Jesuits in Louisiana*, 71–74. Giraud, *Histoire de la Louisiane française*, I, 311. Edmond Préclin, *Les Jansénistes du XVIII* siècle et la Constitution civile du clergé; le développement du richérisme; sa propagation dans le bas clergé 1713–1791* (Paris, 1929). Pierre Hurtubise, "Dominique-Marie Varlet, missionnaire en Nouvelle-France," SCHÉC *Rapport, 1968*, 21–32. B. A. van Cleef, "Dominicus Maria Varlet (1678–1742)," *Internationale Kirchliche Zeitschrift* (Berne), LIII (1963), 78–104, 149–77, 193–225.

[The reader may also consult Gosselin, *L'Église du Canada jusqu'à la conquête*, I, 331–35, and Anselme Rhéaume, "Mgr Dominique-Marie Varlet," *BRH*, III (1897), 18–22, as well as Maximin Deloche's article, "Un missionnaire français en Amérique au XVIII* siècle: contribution à l'histoire de l'établissement des Français en Louisiane," France, Comité des Travaux historiques, *Bulletin de la section de géographie* (Paris), XLV (1930), 39–60, which corrects several of their statements. P.H.]

VAUCOUR, JACQUES-NICOLAS PINGUET DE. *See* PINGUET

VAUDREUIL, JOSEPH-HYACINTHE DE RIGAUD DE. *See* RIGAUD

VAUDREUIL, LOUIS-PHILIPPE DE RIGAUD DE VAUDREUIL, Marquis de. *See* RIGAUD

VAUGHAN, WILLIAM, fishing and lumbering entrepreneur in Maine; b. 12 Sept. 1703 (O.S.) at Portsmouth, New Hampshire, eldest son of George Vaughan*, lieutenant governor of New Hampshire, and Elizabeth Elliot; d. a bachelor 11 Dec. 1746 at Bagshot, England.

After graduating from Harvard College in 1722, William Vaughan was a merchant in Portsmouth; he then became involved in the fishing industry at Matinicus Island (Maine), off Penobscot Bay. Some of his ships also fished off Newfoundland. By 1732, however, Vaughan's commercial interests had shifted to lumbering in the Damariscotta area. At "Damariscotty Falls," where he built a thriving community in the wilderness, Vaughan lived the life of a feudal baron.

In the fall of 1744, soon after war broke out between France and England, Vaughan visited Boston. There he met some of the soldiers who had been captured by the French at Canso, Nova Scotia, in May, taken to Louisbourg, Île Royale (Cape Breton Island), and then exchanged for French prisoners held in Massachusetts [*see* Patrick HERON]. They claimed that Louisbourg could easily be captured by a small New England force. Vaughan, who was concerned about the French and Indian threat to his lumbering business, was taken with the idea and gave his considerable energy and his "daring, enterprising and tenacious mind" to developing it. Always a restless man, he seemed to have become dissatisfied with his life in isolated Maine and to be eager to gain fame and prestige in his new enterprise. By late December 1744, he had come to the conclusion that Louisbourg could be captured by a "force consisting of 1500 raw militia, some scaling ladders, and a few armed craft of New England." Assured of considerable support in eastern Massachusetts for his daring proposal, Vaughan, in January 1744/45, provided Governor William Shirley of Massachusetts with a "regular scheme" to surprise and capture Louisbourg. Later both Vaughan and John Bradstreet* claimed sole authorship of this naïve plan. In all likelihood the original plan placed in Shirley's hands was drafted by Bradstreet and then revised by Vaughan.

Vaughan realized that the plan would never be implemented unless Shirley vigorously endorsed it. But though Shirley was willing to support Vaughan's proposal, the Massachusetts General Court was not. Vaughan was not discouraged by the rebuff; rather he became even more determined to exert pressure on the court to reverse its decision. He therefore persuaded over 100 leading fishing entrepreneurs in Marblehead and over 200 Boston merchants to ask the General Court to organize an expedition against Louisbourg. He also assiduously fanned the dying embers of Shirley's enthusiasm for the plan. On 25 Jan. 1744/45 by a margin of one vote, the General Court resolved to attack Louisbourg.

When the expedition sailed from New England in the early spring under the command of William PEPPERRELL, Vaughan, commissioned as a lieutenant-colonel, had no special command. His offer to lead the expedition had been turned down by Shirley who regarded him as a "whimsical, wild projector." In spite of this disappointment, Vaughan had spent considerable time and energy recruiting scores of volunteers. After the successful landing at Gabarus Bay (Cape Breton Island) on 30 April, Vaughan was ordered by Pepperrell to lead a detachment of 400 or 500 men to drive the French from the northern extremity of Louisbourg harbour. No other officer apparently

Verchères

wanted the job. Vaughan soon lost control of his men, who were far more interested in marauding, and at dawn on 2 May he and only a dozen of them were camped within a quarter mile of the Royal battery which commanded the mouth of the harbour. Observing no sign of life within, but suspecting a French ruse, Vaughan bribed an Indian with a bottle of brandy to investigate. The battery proved to be empty, with its cannon inadequately spiked, and Vaughan proudly took possession of it. His unexpected success exacerbated still further his relations with Pepperrell and his senior officers.

Vaughan remained active throughout the siege, in spite of what he conceived to be his fellow officers' jealousy and slights. He volunteered on 11 May to lead the assault on the Island battery but Pepperrell refused to accept his offer. Having received a similar request from Brigadier-General Samuel WALDO, Pepperrell resolved to reject both offers and to delay the project indefinitely. Vaughan felt rebuffed, but decided to concentrate his attention on building the siege batteries. He directed the digging operation, "continually encouraging the Army to keep up their Spirits wh. were almost cast down through their extraordinary Fatigue & Slavery." On 19 May, undaunted by the fact that he knew nothing about artillery, Vaughan overloaded a 42-pound cannon in the advanced battery, some 220 yards from the west gate of the town. The resulting explosion shattered the cannon, dismounted another, destroyed almost two barrels of powder, and "Killed two men and wounded two more." Vaughan next helped to build the Lighthouse battery on the opposite side of the harbour. This battery, by destroying the Island battery, prepared the way for the surrender of the fortress on 17 June.

Because of his contribution not only to the organization of the expedition, but also to the actual capture of Louisbourg, Vaughan expected to be sent to London with news of the event. It appears, however, that Pepperrell and Commodore Peter WARREN, commander of the British fleet blockading Louisbourg, sought all of the credit and did not want Vaughan to share in the rewards. Vaughan sailed to London in July in an unofficial capacity, but his memorials to the Duke of Newcastle and to George II, requesting among other offices the governorship of Nova Scotia, did not receive a sympathetic hearing. On 11 Dec. 1746 he died of smallpox.

G. A. RAWLYK

New Hampshire Hist. Soc., Vaughan papers, Waldron papers. PRO, CO 5/753. Jeremy Belknap, *The history of New Hampshire* (2nd ed., 3v., Boston, 1813), II, 154–55, 168. William Douglass, *A summary, historical and political, of the first planting, progressive improvements, and present state of the British settlements in North-America . . .* (2v., Boston, 1747–52; London, 1755; London, 1760), I, 348. *Louisbourg journals* (De Forest), 57. "The Pepperrell papers," Mass. Hist. Soc. *Coll.*, 6th ser., X (1899). PRO, *JTP, 1741/42–1749*, 175. Shipton, *Sibley's Harvard graduates*, VII, 128–36. Bell, *Foreign Protestants*. McLennan, *Louisbourg*, 109–66, 360–69. Rawlyk, *Yankees at Louisbourg*; "New England origins of the Louisbourg expedition of 1745," *Dal. Rev.*, XLIV (1964–65), 469–93. William Goold, "Colonel William Vaughan, of Matinicus and Damariscotta," Maine Hist. Soc. *Coll.*, 1st ser., VIII (1881), 293–313.

VERCHÈRES, MARIE-MADELEINE JARRET DE. *See* JARRET

VÉRON DE GRANDMESNIL, ÉTIENNE, clerk in the king's warehouse at Trois-Rivières, merchant, receiver of the admiral of France; b. 19 Dec. 1679 at Trois-Rivières, son of Étienne Véron* de Grandmesnil and Marie-Thérèse Moral de Saint-Quentin; d. 22 April 1743 at Quebec.

Étienne Véron de Grandmesnil spent his childhood and youth at Trois-Rivières. It was there that he married Madeleine, the daughter of Joseph-François Hertel* de La Fresnière, in 1694. At that period Véron was, it seems, clerk in the king's warehouse at Trois-Rivières. Become a widower, he married Marie-Catherine Le Picard in 1713 in Montreal, where he lived until 1715. Then he went to Quebec and set himself up as a merchant in Rue Notre-Dame in Lower Town.

Because few documents remain concerning Véron's activities as a merchant, it is difficult to state exactly what his business was. He is better known to us as a litigant, and a litigant who did not give up easily, remaining in this respect faithful to his Norman ancestry. Through his second marriage, with Marie-Catherine Le Picard, Véron had become brother-in-law to the notary Jacques Barbel*, the husband of Marie-Anne Le Picard; the two were daughters of the merchant Jean Le Picard. At his death in 1714 Le Picard left a property which was rented to the merchant Gabriel Greysac. As he was thinking of moving to Quebec, Véron de Grandmesnil obtained from the Conseil Supérieur an order to Greysac to move out. This was only the prelude to a long dispute which was not settled until 1721. That same year a new quarrel broke out between Véron de Grandmesnil and his young brother-in-law, Joseph Le Picard. Both men claimed the part of the house that the other occupied. In 1725 an ordinance allowed Véron to have first choice, on condition that he paid the other the sum of 117 *livres*. There was also a disagreement over a neighbouring piece of land belonging to Joseph Le Picard, on which he was building. Véron disputed the boundaries of this piece of land, had arbitrators appointed, and attended to having the whole thing surveyed and measured.

At his father's death in 1721 Véron de Grandmesnil took in hand the interests of Lamothe Cadillac [Laumet*], whose secretary Étienne Véron the elder had been for several years. In 1730 Véron the younger, who had become Cadillac's attorney, had an ordinance issued by Gilles Hocquart* concerning the collection of the former governor of Louisiana's assets. This was probably the last time that Véron intervened on Cadillac's behalf, since the latter died that same year.

During his last years Véron de Grandmesnil held the office of receiver of the admiral of France. A document dated 1740 describes Véron in this capacity when he collected the fees owing the admiral of France on the oil and bone from a whale cast up on the sandbanks at Manicouaguen. After his death he was replaced in this office by Denis Goguet.

ROLAND-J. AUGER

Jug. et délib., VI, 856. *Recensement de Québec, 1716* (Beaudet), 39. P.-G. Roy, *Inv. coll. pièces jud. et not.*, I, 76, 122; II, 313, 315, 324, 328, 330; *Inv. jug. et délib., 1717–1760*, I, 84–85, 97, 110–17, 126, 132, 257–62, 284, 297; *Inv. ord. int.*, II, 60, 255, 291; III, 39. J.-E. Roy, *Histoire du notariat*, I, 194, 370. Tanguay, *Dictionnaire*.

VÉRONNEAU, AGATHE, Sister of Charity of the Hôpital Général of Montreal; b. 17 April 1707 at Saint-François-du-Lac, daughter of Louis Véronneau, a merchant, and Marguerite Maugras; d. 20 April 1764 in Montreal.

On 10 Feb. 1746 Agathe Véronneau joined the community of Grey Nuns, which had been founded in 1737 by Marie-Marguerite d'Youville, *née* Dufrost* de Lajemmerais. In the autumn of 1747 the foundress recorded in the new registry of the Hôpital Général of Montreal that the aspirant, Agathe Véronneau, had not yet "been admitted into the society." On 23 Aug. 1749 Sister Véronneau dedicated herself "unreservedly to the service of the poor," and in the letters patent of 1753 she is ranked sixth among the administrators of the Hôpital Général of Montreal.

In 1755 the smallpox epidemic which was raging in the colony spread its ravages to Montreal and the Indian villages at Lac des Deux-Montagnes and Sault Saint-Louis. The women who were stricken by the scourge were taken into the Hôpital Général, because the Hôtel-Dieu was overcrowded by a "prodigious number" of sick persons. This humanitarian gesture by Mme d'Youville was encouraged by Bishop Pontbriand [DUBREIL]. In the first six months of the year 18 deaths were recorded, among them those of 14 Indians. Faced with the urgency of the task Sister Véronneau exerted herself unsparingly on behalf of those who had contracted the infection until her health was seriously endangered by a complication brought on by typhus. Her strong constitution permitted her to get the better of the illness, but unfortunately the violent fever had already affected her mental faculties.

She remained in this state until her death, which occurred on 20 April 1764, and she was buried the following day in the crypt of the church of the Hôpital Général of Montreal.

LAURETTE DUCLOS

ASGM, Dossier: Constitutions, 4; Dossier: Maison mère, doc. 146 (oct. 1747), doc. 202 (3 juin 1753); Mémoires, 10 [Sœur Baby, Julie Casgrain, 1835–1898]; MY/B: Correspondance, doc. 28 (22 sept. 1755); Notices biographiques: 1741–1848, [Mère McMullen, s.g.m.]; Recueil des règles et constitutions à l'usage des Filles séculières administratrices de l'Hôpital Général de Montréal dites Sœurs de la Charité recueillies sur les anciens titres et usages de la communauté, M. Montgolfier, Étienne, p.s.s., 1781, 129; Registre d'admission des pauvres, 1694–1796, 21; Registre des baptêmes de la paroisse de Saint-François-du-Lac; Registre des baptêmes et sépultures de l'Hôpital Général de Montréal, 1725–1759, ff.12, 13; 1759–1776, f.13.

André Chagny, *Un défenseur de la « Nouvelle-France »: François Picquet, « Le Canadien » (1708–1781)* (Montréal, 1913), 237–38. [É.-M. Faillon], *Vie de Mme d'Youville, fondatrice des Sœurs de la Charité de Villemarie dans l'île de Montréal en Canada* (Villemarie [Montréal], 1852), 141–42, 262. Albertine Ferland-Angers, *Mère d'Youville* (Montréal, 1945), 96, 141, 164, 324. Mondoux, *L'Hôtel-Dieu de Montréal*, 300–1.

VERRIER, ÉTIENNE, engineer; b. 4 Jan. 1683 at Aix-en-Provence, France, son of Christophe, master-sculptor (d.1709) and Marguerite Ferrant (Ferran); m. 1709 Hélène Papin, by whom he had at least four children; d. 10 Sept. 1747 at La Rochelle, France.

Admitted into the engineer corps in 1707 at La Rochelle, Étienne Verrier served there and at Rochefort for the next 17 years, except for an expedition in 1720 to the islands of Poulo Condore off the coast of present-day Vietnam. In 1720 he was promoted infantry captain in the Régiment de Navarre and awarded the cross of Saint-Louis. In 1724 the minister of Marine, Maurepas, asked Claude-François Bidal, Marquis d'Asfeld, for Verrier's services as resident chief engineer at Louisbourg, Île Royale (Cape Breton Island), a post he was to hold until the surrender of the fortress to the British in 1745. For one construction season, Verrier worked under the orders of Jean-François de Verville*, director of fortifications. In 1725, upon Verville's transfer to Valenciennes in northern France, the position of director was discontinued and thenceforth Verrier directed the works himself.

During the next 20 years, he completed the landward front of fortification, the Royal and Island batteries, and the chief public buildings of the town; designed the lighthouse and redesigned it after a destructive fire; designed and built the whole harbour front which completed the *enceinte*; and planned and directed the construction of essential works and buildings at Port-Dauphin (Englishtown, N.S.), Port-Toulouse (St Peters, N.S.) and Port-La-Joie (Fort Amherst, P.E.I.). Verrier would have liked to have been made director of fortifications at Louisbourg, or allowed to return to France to seek advancement in the corps. For the latter he had to await the fall of the fortress. He supervised the defensive works of Louisbourg during the Anglo-American siege of 1745 and participated in Louis Du Pont* Duchambon's decision to surrender the fortress to Peter WARREN and William PEPPERRELL. In 1746, after an unsuccessful bid for the directorship of fortifications at La Rochelle, he was named chief engineer of the Île d'Oléron off the west coast of France. He died the following year.

Verrier arrived at Louisbourg with an established reputation as an engineer and an inherited flair for the aesthetic. His approach to the construction of fortifications and public buildings was pragmatic. He dealt through trial and error with the effects of climate and defective building materials: he covered exterior walls with boards to protect them from the alternating frost and thaw; he experimented with proportions in the ingredients of mortar; and he replaced building materials of poor quality wherever possible. If the design was faulty – as in the barracks of the King's bastion – he proposed no expensive new design, but patched up the defects in order to reduce the trouble. He found it politic not to recommend costly improvements to the court and to the senior officers of the engineer corps who could decide his future career.

Verrier was indeed very much aware of politi-

cal realities. Although his views did not always coincide with those of Saint-Ovide [MONBETON], the governor of Île Royale from 1718 to 1739, Verrier avoided confrontations with him. His relations with other officials of the colony, such as the financial commissaries, Jacques-Ange LE NORMANT de Mézy and his son, Sébastien-François-Ange*, and François Bigot*, were calm. He was loyal to his assistants, Jean-Baptiste de Couagne* and Pierre-Jérôme BOUCHER, and to the contractors François GANET and David-Bernard MUIRON. He defended the last two against criticism of shortcomings in their work which he felt were beyond their control. Preferring Ganet to Muiron when the general construction contract came up for renewal in 1737, he recommended Ganet for subsidiary work after Muiron had made the successful bid. Yet he worked well with Muiron. Although the court warned him – as it did most engineers – against financial collusion with contractors, there is nothing to suggest that the warning to Verrier was particularly necessary.

In spite of his political skill, Verrier eventually encountered criticism for his financial management. His chief fault in official eyes was that he underestimated costs. In 1730, for example, he estimated the construction of the lighthouse at 14,000 *livres* but had to revise his estimate to 26,000 in 1731. He estimated at 6,000 *livres* the alterations to his official residence (which originally had not been a dwelling); the cost reached 28,000! The minister of Marine admonished Verrier for rendering some erroneous and incomplete accounts, and slipping back – after ten years at Louisbourg and against official instructions – into Verville's practice of not providing annual statements of work finished. Although Verrier undertook to follow instructions more closely, he steadfastly resisted attempts to have him provide prematurely the final calculations necessary for settling accounts between the crown and the successors of Michel-Philippe Isabeau*, the general contractor from 1720 to 1724. He maintained – successfully – that it was impossible to indicate how much the estate owed the crown and *vice versa* until the work was completed. The necessary *toisé definitif* was submitted in September 1731.

As the senior engineer, Verrier was the key officer of the garrison in the defence of the fortress. He had been trained in the French engineer corps, had had extensive European experience in it, and, by the time of the Anglo-American attack of 1745, had spent 20 years in directing the construction of the permanent defences of Louisbourg. An important part of his training – which admittedly he had had little opportunity to put to the test – comprised the defensive tactics of siegecraft. According to Sébastien Le Prestre de Vauban, by whose precepts French engineers were being trained, the latter "would be wrong to believe that with all the secrets of the art and all the advantages of nature you could make a place impregnable; they can all be taken by an enemy who combines strength and resolution. The defense that I teach . . . certainly cannot hold a fortress invulnerable, but it can contribute greatly to making a siege long and difficult, perhaps until it is lifted by some happy chance." A professional in siegecraft, Verrier faced (until the arrival of John Henry BASTIDE ten days before the surrender) only amateurs in the art. On the surface, therefore, a large share of the responsibility for the fall of Louisbourg rests on his shoulders. However, a balanced view must be taken. French naval strength was insufficient for the protection and supplying of the garrison, and the garrison itself was pitifully small in relation to the attacking force. Neither of these difficulties can be laid at Verrier's door. None of the field defences, however, appear to have increased the effectiveness of the besieged; with the proper quality and quantity of defensive works, a much smaller force than the attackers' might have held on for a considerable time before retiring behind the fortress walls.

Verrier's most serious fault, however, was surely the advice he gave respecting the Royal battery. On 11 May 1745 he voted in council of war for its abandonment without a fight and, as a minority of one, against its demolition. After the siege, he defended his action to Maurepas on the grounds that major alterations, begun on the orders of the late governor, Jean-Baptiste-Louis LE PRÉVOST Duquesnel, while Verrier himself was on leave in France in 1743–44, had not been completed and had left the battery defenceless from the landward side. In particular, the breastwork or epaulements had been demolished to increase the number of embrasures in order to accommodate additional guns brought from the Grave battery. Verrier had written to the minister in November 1744 that the demolition had been unnecessary and the whole operation unwise because of the exposure of the structure. Nevertheless, he had forecast that the work of reconstruction could be finished in the spring of 1745 within a month and a half. His prediction proved over-optimistic, as he admitted after the siege: "in the month of April I was unable to rebuild either the walls of the epaulement or the palisades of the covert way, given that the lime and the ground were frozen that month. The battery being in disorder, it would have meant sac-

rificing almost 200 men . . . [during the siege] and there would have been fewer in Louisbourg."

Roger Wolcott, the Connecticut commander, held a contrary view. Since the gun-swivels were still mounted on the towers of the battery, though the defensive walls were down, he wrote, "two hundred men might hold the battery against five thousand without cannon." One of the besieged held a similar opinion, and the British engineer, Bastide, agreed with it by implication. Presumably behind temporary cover, such as gabions and fascines, and separated from the attackers by a glacis and a ditch ten feet deep and 12 feet wide, the gunners could have held out for some time against infantry attack from the hills to the rear. After that, orderly evacuation of men and armament might have been attempted. Since Verrier had not provided for such an eventuality, he favoured abandonment. Once abandonment had been decided upon, demolition was a logical corollary. Evidently Verrier could not bear the thought of deliberately destroying works which had cost the king so much, which represented such an important part of the chief engineer's own accomplishment, and which might remain French after the war. It is a measure of Verrier's importance to the besieged that his lone vote persuaded Duchambon not to order the battery demolished. On the night of 11 May it was hurriedly abandoned by its commander, François-Nicolas de CHASSIN de Thierry. Fearing that there was too little time to remove the guns or even to spike them properly, the garrison of the battery left it in such a state that the Anglo-Americans under Samuel WALDO were able to use some of its guns and ammunition effectively against the town long before manhandling their own field artillery across the marshes west of the town to Green Hill. The abandonment of the battery must have hastened the fall of the fortress. By 26 June Verrier's reports to the council of war revealed serious damage to the landward defences by enemy bombardment. Persuaded by these reports and by the misery of the besieged civilians, the council of war voted unanimously for capitulation.

Verrier's ability as a military engineer was severely tested by those events of the spring of 1745 (when, incidentally, he was over 60 years of age). There is no question, however, that he deserves to be remembered for his town-planning and architectural achievement. The public buildings of Louisbourg bore witness to the 18th-century French flair for attractive design. The original plans for which Verrier was responsible were over 100 in number and survive in the Archives Nationales, the Bibliothèque Natio-

Verrier

nale, the archives of the Comité technique du Génie, and other Paris repositories. They include several plans of the king's hospital, of the Dauphine gate, of the lighthouse, of the Maurepas gate, and of the king's stores; and a score of plans of the town. Verrier prepared a plan for the parish church that was never built. He was also responsible for a number of plans of buildings and forts at Port-Dauphin, Port-Toulouse, and Port-La-Joie. It was his son, Claude-Étienne*, however, who painted the well-known watercolour view of Louisbourg in 1731. In 1750, Verrier's successors at Louisbourg were still trying to recover from his widow all the plans of Île Royale and its dependencies that he had taken to France with him after the siege.

Verrier spent most of his 21 years at Louisbourg without his wife. She, with their daughter, experimented briefly with life in the colony from 1732 to 1735 but returned because of poor health to La Rochelle. By 1735 he himself was suffering from sciatica as well as from over-exposure to colonial service. In 1743 he took home leave for his health, returning to the colony in the spring of 1744. Throughout most of his stay in Île Royale he had the assistance of his son Claude-Étienne until the latter, admitted to the engineer corps in 1734, was called in 1736 to serve in France. His place was taken at Louisbourg by one of Verrier's other sons, the one known as the "chevalier."

F. J. THORPE

The vast majority of Verrier's maps are to be found in original form in AN, Col., C¹¹ᴬ, 126; Section Outre-Mer, Dépôt des fortifications des colonies, Am. sept.; and CTG, Archives, art.14. There are copies of many of these maps in PAC, National Map Collection.

AD, Bouches-du-Rhône (Aix-en-Provence), État civil, Sainte-Madeleine d'Aix-en-Provence, 4 janv. 1683; Charente-Maritime (La Rochelle), Greffe de Mᵉ Hirvoix, 19 août 1709; État civil, Notre-Dame de La Rochelle, 12 sept. 1747. AN, Col., B, 46–50, 52–55, 57–59, 61, 63–66, 68, 70, 72, 74, 76, 78, 84, 86; C¹¹ᴬ, 126; C¹¹ᴮ, 7–27; C¹¹ᶜ, 11–13, 16; D²ᶜ, 222/2, p.305 (PAC transcript); F¹ᴬ, 23–35; F³, 50; Marine, C⁷, 344 (dossier Verrier); Section Outre-Mer, G³, 2046; Dépôt des fortifications des colonies, Am. sept., nos.150–80, 184–214, 248–53, 264–67, 272–74. Archives maritimes, Port de Rochefort, 1E, 103, 105. CTG, Archives, arts.3, 14; Bibliothèque, mss in fol., 205ᵇ, ff.8–10; 208. PRO, CO 5/44, ff.136–41; 5/900, ff.234–35; WO 55/352B, ff.2–3; 55/1813, ff.10–11v. SHA, Xᵉ, 4, 5; Yᵃ, 183. Sébastien Le Prestre de Vauban, *Mémoire pour servir d'instruction dans la conduite des sièges et dans la défense des places . . .* (Leiden, 1740); trans. and ed. by G. A. Rothrock as *A manual of siegecraft and fortification* (Ann Arbor, Mich., 1968), 131. A.-M. Augoyat, *Aperçu historique sur les fortifications, les ingénieurs et sur le corps du génie en France . . .* (3v., Paris, 1860–64), II, 45. McLennan, *Louisbourg*, 45, 86–87, 102, 150. Association for Preservation Technology *Bull.* ([Ottawa]), IV (1972).

VERRIER, LOUIS-GUILLAUME, lawyer in the *parlement* of Paris, attorney general of the Conseil Supérieur of New France; b. 19 Oct. 1690 in Paris, son of Guillaume Verrier, king's attorney, and Marie-Madeleine Thibault; d. 13 Sept. 1758 in Quebec.

Louis-Guillaume Verrier descended from a family of lawyers – his father and his maternal grandfather had been king's attorneys – and he studied law in Paris. On 8 Aug. 1712, when he was 21, he was admitted to the bar of Paris, where he practised his profession; in 1719 his office was located in Rue Mûrier. When the attorney general of the Conseil Supérieur of New France, Mathieu-Benoît Collet*, died in Quebec on 5 March 1727, Verrier sought the office. On 23 March 1728 the minister, Maurepas, inquired of the attorney general of the *parlement* of Paris about Verrier's capacities for the office he was seeking, and on 20 April Verrier received the appointment. A month later Maurepas informed Governor Charles de BEAUHARNOIS that he was granting a passage on the *Éléphant* for the new attorney general, who landed in New France at the beginning of September.

On 5 Sept. 1728 Étienne Boullard*, the vicar general and parish priest of Quebec, furnished a certificate stating that Verrier had conducted himself as a good Catholic and had been a regular communicant since his arrival in the colony. On 9 September the investigation into the new attorney general's character was held, and on 17 September his commission was registered by the Conseil Supérieur.

At that period the attorney general had to combine with a knowledge of the ordinances and decrees of the Conseil Supérieur perfect mastery of the laws and ordinances of the kingdom, and especially of the customary law of Paris. His duties were to conduct the king's affairs before the Conseil Supérieur and to transmit the council's edicts and ordinances to the king's attorneys of the provost court of Quebec and the royal jurisdictions of Trois-Rivières and Montreal; he supervised the manner in which the attorneys carried out their duties. In addition the attorney general was consulted on points of law, delivered indictments, and formulated conclusions which the Conseil Supérieur generally followed.

Shortly after Verrier's appointment, Governor Beauharnois wrote to Maurepas, "that the council seemed very pleased with the present" which the minister had made it in the person of Verrier. He added that the attorney was "acquainted with his position and very much attached to his duty." Indeed, Verrier paid close attention to the slightest detail of his work as attorney; at the end of October 1728, in accordance with the ordinance of 1717, he required the heirs of the notary Florent de La Cetière* to deposit his minute-book with the registry of the provost court of Quebec. The heirs of a deceased notary had the troublesome habit of considering the notarial deeds as a piece of personal property belonging to the succession. On the same occasion he was able to recover the minute-book of the notary Louis Chambalon*, whose wife had kept it since 1716.

Verrier made his mark in the colony not only by exercising his functions as attorney general, but more by tackling other related tasks. On 25 March 1730, as the result of a royal decree, Maurepas entrusted to Verrier the task of examining all the minute-books of the notaries of the provost court of Quebec. It was, in fact, known that a great number of notarial deeds were badly drawn up [see Florent de La Cetière]. In addition to a general inventory of the documents in the various minute-books, Verrier was to make a complete list of all the errors encountered in the deeds and subsequently to present a report recommending remedies. Choosing the notary Christophe-Hilarion Du Laurent as his recording clerk, the attorney general set to work forthwith. The work promised to be long, since for each register Verrier had to record every deed, note what was faulty, indicate the beginning and end of each minute-book, sort out the papers and put them in order, and on occasion add some biographical details concerning the notary.

On 18 Oct. 1730 Governor Beauharnois and Intendant Hocquart* reported to the minister the work that had been accomplished and requested that Verrier be granted a gratuity in proportion to his work. A year later the governor and the intendant were able to send to France eight reports on the examination of faulty deeds. They had nothing but praise for Verrier and again requested a gratuity for the work he had done and as reimbursement for the payments he had advanced in the performance of this task. The attorney general continued with his work for two whole years. On 7 Feb. 1732 the minister informed Verrier that he was sending him a gratuity of 1,000 *livres* and that he wanted him, in collaboration with the governor and the intendant, to prepare from his report three statements concerning defects in the notarial deeds, marriage contracts, and the levying of fines on notaries who did not respect the required formalities. The councillors François-Étienne Cugnet and Eustache Chartier de Lotbinière were given the responsibility of going over these three statements. They reported to the minister in October 1732, and the following year the king passed laws following their recommendations. Verrier had examined and classified 34 minute-books.

At the end of 1732 Verrier had been given the task of compiling the register of landed property in the colony. The work, whose length sometimes made the minister impatient, was not completed until eight years later. On 4 Oct. 1740 Hocquart informed the minister that Verrier had just delivered to him the seventh and final volume of the register of landed property. As for the gratuity which the authorities had been promising the attorney general since 1738, it was not paid until 6 April 1744, when the minister received the supplement to the register.

The most original aspect of Verrier's work in New France was without doubt his teaching of law. The courses he gave were elementary and amounted to lectures on the ordinances, customary law, and jurisprudence of the period; these courses in law are believed by some to be the first given in North America. Despite Beauharnois's and Hocquart's scepticism and the lack of success the attorney general Collet had met with, Verrier undertook to present such lectures and he gave them free of charge. On 9 Oct. 1733 he could write to the minister that he had no other ambition but to devote every moment of his life unreservedly to the public interest. During the early years of his teaching the candidates were few in number. His first two pupils were Jean-Victor Varin* de La Marre and François Foucault. In 1736 he had three new students: Jacques de Lafontaine de Belcour, Jean-Baptiste Gaillard, and Guillaume Guillimin*. The following year the minister expressed to Verrier his satisfaction at seeing him continue his courses, and the king urged those Canadians who were suited for legal studies to follow the attorney general's teaching, in order to qualify themselves for the office of councillor. Subsequently, thanks to Verrier's remonstrances, the king gave his preference to the attorney's pupils when new appointments were made to the Conseil Supérieur. In 1738 the number of regular students was seven, among them Thomas-Marie Cugnet, the son of the councillor Cugnet. The following year Verrier found himself obliged to increase the number of his courses to two a week; in them he commented upon the substance of the first and second volumes of M. Argou's *Institutions* of French law,

Vézina

and he had his students read the *Ordonnances civiles et criminelles* to familiarize themselves with the form of legal matters. In 1740 René-Ovide Hertel* de Rouville and, in 1742, Jean-François GAULTIER came to join his students. Verrier continued his law lectures beyond 1753, when one of his students was Jacques IMBERT. The attorney general had had to interrupt his courses twice while he travelled to France in 1744–45 and in 1749. The authorities recognized Verrier's work and awarded him several gratuities, which were added to his salary of 600 *livres* per year up till 1751 and 1,000 *livres* after that.

Outside of his legal activities little is known of Louis-Guillaume Verrier's life. A scholar and bibliophile, he had a library of 997 works, a great number of which comprised several volumes. Verrier died a bachelor and intestate on 13 Sept. 1758; his succession was not completely settled until 14 Jan. 1776. He had devoted his life to the law, and he had spared neither time nor money to enable his fellow citizens to acquire a broader knowledge of it. Verrier had not engaged in business, and his emoluments were often insufficient, as he pointed out to the minister on several occasions. His contemporaries and, later, men of law were unanimous in their homage to him; he was a dedicated man, assiduous in his work, honest and unbiased in the execution of his duty.

CLAUDE VACHON

AN, Col., C¹¹ᴬ, 59, p.101; 60, p.97; 71, p.135 (PAC transcripts); E, 385 (dossier Verrier). ANQ, Greffe de J.-B. Decharny, 10 janv. 1759; AP, Louis-Guillaume Verrier, 1730–1759; NF, Ins. Cons. sup., 1728–1758; NF, Registres du Cons. sup., 1728–1758. PAC *Report, 1904*, app.K; *1905*, I, pt.vi. L.-G. Verrier, "Les registres de l'Amirauté de Québec," APQ *Rapport, 1920–21*, 106–31. Edmond Lareau, *Histoire du droit canadien depuis les origines de la colonie jusqu'à nos jours* (2v., Montréal, 1888–89), I. J.-E. Roy, *Histoire du notariat*, I, 300–14. Vachon, *Histoire du notariat*, 29–38. Édouard Fabre-Surveyer, "Louis-Guillaume Verrier (1690–1758)," *RHAF*, VI (1952–53), 159–76.

VÉZINA, CHARLES, wood-carver; b. 25 Jan. 1685 at L'Ange-Gardien, son of François Vézina and Marie Clément; m. on 27 July 1705, in Quebec, Louise Godin (Gaudin), by whom he had nine children; d. 8 Aug. 1755 at Les Écureuils.

At the end of the 17th century few native-born craftsmen were practising the decorative arts in New France. For that reason Bishop Laval* had to bring from France between 1675 and 1680 a group of craftsmen to train carpenters, wood-carvers, masons, and stone-cutters to meet the colony's needs. At that time the school of arts and crafts at Saint-Joachim, the creation of Jean Talon* and Bishop Laval, became the most important centre of apprenticeship in the crafts [*see* Louis Soumande*]. According to a statement by Intendant Jacques de Meulles* in 1685, instruction was given there in "carpentry, wood-carving, painting, gilding, for the decoration of churches, [as well as] masonry work and framework." The proximity of the school at Saint-Joachim and particularly the fact that towards 1700 its members worked on the retable in the church of L'Ange-Gardien suggest that Charles Vézina may have received his training from the craftsmen who worked on his parish church. Vézina was thus to become one of the first Canadian wood-carvers, along with Noël Levasseur*. According to Gérard Morisset* Vézina is supposed to have been one of the most famous disciples of Jacques Leblond* de Latour, a teacher at the Saint-Joachim school. Vézina is even believed to have assumed the headship of this educational establishment in 1705. The almost complete lack of documentation for the institution's development does not permit us, however, to determine whether Charles Vézina received his training there, or what his role was as head of the school at Cap-Tourmente, if indeed he did occupy that office.

Subsequently his career is better known. Indeed, certain account books inform us that in 1707 he worked on the "carving of the altar custodial, the altar gradin, and the frame of the high altar" in the chapel of Notre-Dame-de-Pitié in the church of Notre-Dame de Québec, then in 1708 and 1709 on the retable of the church of Sainte-Anne-du-Petit-Cap (Sainte-Anne de Beaupré). He also did various carvings between 1728 and 1746 at Pointe-aux-Trembles (Neuville), Saint-Pierre on Île d'Orléans, Saint-Augustin de Québec, and especially at Charlesbourg. The account books of the last parish reveal that in the period 1741–46 Vézina carved a retable, a tabernacle, and several other works intended for the decoration of the church choir. Charles Vézina died in 1755 at Les Écureuils, where he had been living for some years.

MICHEL CAUCHON and ANDRÉ JUNEAU

AJQ, Registre d'état civil, L'Ange-Gardien, 26 janv. 1685; Saint-Jean-Baptiste des Écureuils, 9 août 1755. Archives paroissiales de Saint-Charles (Charlesbourg, Qué.), Livres de comptes, I, 1675–1749. IOA, Dossier Charles Vézina, sculpteur. Tanguay, *Dictionnaire*. Gérard Morisset, "Généalogie et petite histoire: École des Arts et Métiers de Saint-Joachim," SGCF *Mémoires*, XVI (1965), 72. Musée du Québec, *Sculp-*

ture traditionnelle du Québec (Québec, 1967), 64, 138. Gérard Morisset, "L'École des Arts et Métiers de Saint-Joachim," *La Patrie* (Montréal), 1er oct. 1950.

VILERMAULA (Villermola), LOUIS-MICHEL DE, Sulpician, parish priest; b. at Charmey (Switzerland); d. March 1757 or 1758 in France.

Louis-Michel de Vilermaula is an enigmatic figure. References to him are cursory and little survives from his own hand beyond entries in church registers and a few documents that he witnessed. He entered the seminary of Saint-Sulpice at Paris on 27 Nov. 1691 and arrived in Canada in July 1697. Evidently he spent some time in Montreal before his appointment in 1702 to the nearby parish of Prairie-de-la-Madeleine (Laprairie). Vilermaula was an energetic parish priest and he promoted the interests of the Jesuits, who were the seigneurs of Prairie-de-la-Madeleine.

In 1704 and 1705 Vilermaula supervised the construction of a stone church at Prairie-de-la-Madeleine (Laprairie) to replace an earlier wooden chapel. The events in the parish during the autumn of 1704 are recorded in three rare letters by Vilermaula, addressed to members of the Society of Jesus in Canada. The construction of a new church strained the resources of the parish, and Vilermaula considered the possibility of completing the church at his own expense. In September 1704 the Jesuits offered the churchwardens of Prairie-de-la-Madeleine 800 *livres* in exchange for the right of patronage. If the Jesuits, as seigneurs, were considered the donors of the stone church they would have the right of presenting their candidate to the bishop for appointment as the parish priest. Vilermaula saw no objections to this arrangement and assured Father Pierre Raffeix*, procurator, that "the affection I have had for the Society [of Jesus] will ensure that I shall support your plan with all my power." Late in October Vilermaula wrote to Father Pierre Cholenec*, superior of the Jesuits in Montreal, that "it would need only a word from your mouth" to obtain the consent of the Baron de Longueuil [Charles Le Moyne*] for the transfer of the right of patronage.

The parishioners of Prairie-de-la-Madeleine however, proved unpredictable. They opposed Father Cholenec and the proposal of the Jesuits. Vilermaula was crestfallen and in November he reported that his parishioners blamed him "for having pushed them with excessive eagerness." It was said, even by the senior churchwarden, that Vilermaula only wanted to get hold of the Jesuits' money to indemnify himself. Vilermaula

advised the Jesuits to follow another course in future "and not to address themselves to a mob of rude and ignorant persons, as has been done, but only to the churchwardens." In any event, the work on the church continued and it was inaugurated in 1705. In the same year Vilermaula was instrumental in establishing a convent at Prairie-de-la-Madeleine for the sisters of the Congregation of Notre-Dame.

On 29 Sept. 1706 Vilermaula became the parish priest of Lachine on Montreal Island and for the next dozen years he remained there. It was said that he had fallen into icy water while crossing the St Lawrence River and because "he became subject to frequent ailments as a consequence of that fall, M. de Belmont [François Vachon*, superior of the Sulpician seminary], made him curé of Lachine." He encouraged the development of the parish with the same zeal and generosity he had shown at Prairie-de-la-Madeleine. He built a new priest's house and in 1712 Gédéon de Catalogne* wrote that at Lachine Vilermaula "has facilitated and contributed to an establishment of the sisters of the Congregation for the education of young girls."

Vilermaula was recalled to France by his superiors in September 1718 and he died in that country in March 1757 or 1758. We know practically nothing about the last four decades of his life. He left the Company of Saint-Sulpice; indeed, according to one anonymous writer, he was expelled "because of his Jansenist sympathies." If this is so, one is forced to remark that Vilermaula's conduct in New France on behalf of the Jesuits made him a very unusual Jansenist.

PETER N. MOOGK

[The author has in his possession a letter written by Louis-Michel de Vilermaula to Pierre Raffeix dated 20 Sept. 1704. ANQ, AP, Samuel Bouvard (Vilermaula à Bouvard, 10 nov. 1704); AP, Pierre Cholenec (Vilermaula à Cholenec, 26 oct. 1704). ANQ-M, Greffe d'Antoine Adhémar, 3 juill. 1705 (notarial acts relating to the establishment of the Sisters of the Congregation of Notre-Dame at Prairie-de-la-Madeleine); Juridiction de Montréal, 4, 10, 21 avril, 23, 28 mai 1711 (feuillets séparés). "Mémoire de Gédéon de Catalogne sur les plans des seigneuries et habitations des gouvernements de Québec, les Trois-Rivières et Montréal," *BRH*, XXI (1915), 267. Allaire, *Dictionnaire*. Ivanhoë Caron, "Liste des prêtres séculiers et religieux qui ont exercé le saint ministère en Nouvelle-France (1691–1699)," *BRH*, XLVII (1941), 296. Gauthier, *Sulpitiana*. Gowans, *Church architecture in New France*, 131. Lemire-Marsolais et Lambert, *Histoire de la Congrégation de Notre-Dame*, II, 113, 144; III, 34, 44, 57–60, 285. *BRH*, IV (1898), 223; this anonymous inquiry about Vilermaula contains valuable information which cannot be completely verified. P.N.M.]

Villebois

VILLEBOIS DE LA ROUVILLIÈRE, HONORÉ MICHEL DE. *See* MICHEL

VILLEBON, CHARLES-RENÉ DEJORDY DE. *See* DEJORDY

VILLERAY, BENJAMIN ROUER DE. *See* ROUER

VILLERMOLA. *See* VILERMAULA

VILLIERS, LOUIS COULON DE. *See* COULON

VILLIERS, NICOLAS-ANTOINE COULON DE. *See* COULON

VILLIERS DE JUMONVILLE, JOSEPH COULON DE. *See* COULON

VINCENT, chief of the Huron Indians at Lorette; fl. 1740–45.

In 1740 the unhappy survivors of the Huron tribe were living at Jeune-Lorette, Lac-des-Deux-Montagnes, and Father Armand de LA RICHARDIE's mission near Detroit. During that year a dispute arose between the Lorette Hurons and those of Lac-des-Deux-Montagnes. Vincent had gone to visit the latter settlement and had asked to see its treasure, 12 strings of wampum (their exact significance is not known) which his tribe had deposited when the village was founded in 1716. Finding that only 2 of the 12 strings remained, Vincent took them away with him. He also declared that the village's fire had been extinguished, a serious statement which seems to have struck a blow at the chiefs' authority.

The Indians at Lac-des-Deux-Montagnes made their grievances known to the governor of New France, Charles de BEAUHARNOIS. Foreseeing that war was going to break out again between France and England, Beauharnois wanted to prevent any internal quarrelling among the Indian allies of France. So he made Vincent take the strings of wampum back to Montreal, to be kept there by the governor, Josué DUBOIS Berthelot de Beaucours, until the dispute was settled. After negotiations it was decided that Vincent should return them. On 12 Aug. 1741 there was a great feast at Lac-des-Deux-Montagnes, and Jean-Baptiste-Nicolas-Roch de Ramezay* came in the name of Governor Beauharnois "to rekindle a new fire," around which the Indians would gather to smoke and discuss their affairs.

Vincent fought in Acadia during the War of the Austrian Succession. In 1745 he was in command of a party of Hurons from Lorette which took part in the capture of a merchant ship at Annapolis Royal, Nova Scotia. William POTE, the captain, was among the prisoners whom the Hurons took back to Quebec, and he described Vincent as "a Verey Subtil Cunning fellow." The Huron chief acted humanely towards the prisoners, refusing, among other things, to give the Micmac women permission to dance about them because, he said, this custom was "Intierly contrary to what is allowed or permitted with us. . . ."

Neither the date nor the circumstances of Vincent's death are known. The name Vincent is famous among the Indians of Lorette. Among those who bore it might be mentioned Nicolas (Tsawouenhouhi*), who was in England from 1824 to 1825 as a delegate to George IV, the two brothers Joseph and Stanislas, who distinguished themselves at the battle of Châteauguay in 1813, Abbé Prosper, who was ordained in 1870, the first Catholic priest from his nation, and finally the painter Tehariolin* (Zacharie Vincent), who died in 1886, the last of his race to speak the language of his ancestors.

RENÉ BÉLANGER

Archives paroissiales de Saint-Ambroise de la Jeune-Lorette (Loretteville, Qué.). *NYCD* (O'Callaghan and Fernow), IX, 1069–70. [William Pote]. *The journal of Captain William Pote, jr., during his captivity in the French and Indian war from May 1745, to August 1747,* ed. J. F. Hurst and Victor Paltsits (New York, 1896). J.-B.-A. Ferland, *Cours d'histoire du Canada (1534–1759)* (2v., Québec, 1882), II, 470. L. St-G. Lindsay, *Notre-Dame de la Jeune-Lorette en la Nouvelle-France . . .* (Montréal, 1900).

VINCENT, ROBERT, priest of the Church of England; b. probably in England; d. Halifax, Nova Scotia, 15 Nov. 1765.

Nothing is known of Robert Vincent's career prior to August 1761, when he was appointed by the Nova Scotia Council, on the recommendation of Lieutenant Governor Jonathan Belcher*, "Minister at Lunenburg [Nova Scotia] at a salary of 70 Pounds, and with 20 Pounds per annum as the Schoolmaster." He was to assist Jean-Baptiste MOREAU, the Church of England minister at St John's Church, who was suffering from ill health. As the salary given Vincent was inadequate, Belcher asked the Society for the Propagation of the Gospel in January 1762 to adopt Vincent as their missionary and schoolmaster at Lunenburg. The appointment was made in March.

Belcher had definite intentions in sending Vincent to a settlement where German was the predominant language. He wanted the settlers' children to learn to speak English, so that in time the use of the German language would wane, and hoped that "Mr Vincent's known abilities and exemplary life [would] render him universally acceptable to the Germans, whose children will by his means, be trained up in the principles of the Established Religion, and many of their parents drawn from their Errors." According to Belcher there were 596 children under the age of 12 in the settlement. As schoolmaster Vincent taught them the church catechism as well as reading, writing, and arithmetic. In writing to the SPG, Belcher also noted that "the General Assembly of the Province has passed a law Establishing the Church of England as the official religion of the Province." This meant that the Germans at Lunenburg could obtain a German-speaking Lutheran minister only if they were prepared to pay him themselves, and this they refused to do. The restriction of financial aid to the Church of England was to cause friction in Lunenburg, off and on, for about the next 60 years.

Shortly after his arrival at Lunenburg, Vincent took on as "assistant schoolmaster" Gottlob Neuman, who had been serving the Germans as schoolmaster since 1760. As Vincent's assistant Neuman received a government allowance of one shilling a day. Vincent could not speak German and made no effort to learn the language. Neuman, for his part, could barely speak English. Vincent's insistence that instruction in the school be conducted entirely in English antagonized the German settlers, who had hired Neuman to instruct their children in the Lutheran doctrines in German.

When he sent his first report to the SPG in January 1763, Vincent stated that there were 300 families in his mission and most of the young people spoke English. It is likely, however, that their vocabulary was quite limited. Vincent appealed to the SPG for a special grant to Neuman as his assistant and by August 1764 a salary of £5 per year had been approved. In November, however, Belcher and Vincent had to appeal to the society for further assistance as the British government had withdrawn Neuman's allowance and suspended paying the rent on Vincent's house.

Vincent had difficulty gaining adherents to the Church of England. The Germans remained determined to follow their Lutheran faith, and in April 1765 Vincent reported that they were "anxious to have a German minister and have prepared timber towards building a Meeting House." The previous September he had complained that "an Enthusiast [Calvinist] has taken to exhorting the Congregation after the services." The Indians of the area Vincent described as "a roving Crew, [who] never remain settled in any Habitation. . . . They are very averse to the Ceremonies of ye Church of England, as they have not that Show which is used in ye Romish Church."

By November 1764 Vincent was beginning to complain of ill health and in March 1765 he offered to give up his salary as schoolmaster, as "violent feavers hath affected my eyes, and I can no longer act as School Superintendent." In June the Reverend John Breynton* of Halifax notified the SPG that "Mr Vincent's health is in a declining state," and recommended that his successor should be able to officiate in English and German. Breynton reported in October that Vincent's health had completely broken down and that he was then in Halifax "on his way home to England, but is too ill to write to the Society."

Vincent's illness prevented a sea voyage at that time and he stayed on in Halifax, where he died of tuberculosis on 15 November. He was buried in the cemetery of St Paul's Church. The SPG made an allowance to his widow while she was in Halifax, and she sailed for England the following summer.

C. E. THOMAS and JOHN ST. JAMES

PANS, RG 1, 164. St Paul's Church (Halifax), Parish registers, 15 Nov. 1765. USPG, B, letters 15, 16, 20, 50, 55, 59, 60, 61, 64, 65, 67, 71, 75, 95 (copies in PANS, USPG mfm, reel 15). Bell, *Foreign Protestants*.

W

WABBICOMMICOT (Wabacumaga, Wapack-camigat, Wapaumagen), Mississauga chief in the Toronto area; fl. 1761; d. 1768.

Like the Iroquois, the Mississaugas lived along the French line of communication with the *pays d'en haut* and the Illinois country. They were, as a result, subjected to similar pressures to ally themselves either with France or with Britain as the two imperial powers struggled for control of the North American interior. Although there were Mississaugas fighting on the French side during the Seven Years' War, at least one chief kept up friendly contact with Sir William Johnson*, the British superintendent of northern

Waldo

Indians. The chief, whose name is not recorded, may perhaps have been Wabbicommicot.

Wabbicommicot is first mentioned by name in British documents in a report of his meeting with Johnson at Fort Niagara (near Youngstown, N.Y.) in July 1761. Prompted by word that the Senecas Kayashoton* and Tahahaiadoris were attempting to stir up the western tribes against the British, Johnson was on his way to Detroit for his first official meeting with the nations formerly allied to the French. At his request Wabbicommicot and some other Mississauga chiefs accompanied him on this delicate mission. At the conference Wabbicommicot welcomed him as "our Brother Warraghiyagey who has brought peace to our Country which was in a treamor, & has fixed our hearts in their proper places which before his arrival were fluttering & knew not where to settle."

Johnson's diplomacy, however, could not offset the British policy of cutting off the supply of ammunition and rum to the Indians. Some French, moreover, were unofficially encouraging Indian discontent. Wabbicommicot reported to an English trader at Toronto in the winter of 1762–63 that Luc de La Corne*, known as La Corne Saint-Luc, had earlier sent a message to the various nations promising that a French fleet would arrive and retake the country. The chief warned the trader that the Indians would go to war against the British in the spring. He disapproved of the policy himself, but although he was "ye Chief Man North & West upon Lake Ontario and so far upon Lake Erie as ye big [Grand] River . . ." he could not dictate to his people.

Late in May 1763 he appeared at Niagara, demanding rum and threatening that he would not be responsible for the consequences if he were refused. This action had clearly been forced on him by pressures within his tribe, for he added the personal opinion that the English were more generous than the French and he warned that trouble was afoot. News soon arrived at Niagara that some Mississaugas had attacked a party of traders at the mouth of the Grand River. More serious still, Detroit was under siege from PONTIAC. Among the Ottawa chief's allies were some Mississaugas from the Rivière à la Tranche (Thames River); it is not clear whether any of Wabbicommicot's warriors were also involved. Johnson believed that Wabbicommicot had "prevented Numbers of his People from Joining against us." In the autumn, the season when Indians began to think of dispersing for their winter hunting, Wabbicommicot travelled to Detroit. He conferred with the commandant, Henry Gladwin*, informing him that the Mississaugas

wanted to end the fighting and that the Ojibwas and Ottawas would also make peace.

Although there was no open warfare in 1764 the year was an uneasy one in Indian-British relations. Wabbicommicot carried messages between Niagara and Detroit on at least one occasion and he was present in September 1764 at the signing of the abortive treaty that Colonel John Bradstreet* negotiated. With a delegation of Mississaugas he visited Johnson Hall (near Amsterdam, N.Y.) in June 1765. On the Indian superintendent's request, he agreed to warn the western nations against further disturbances. "Be assured," he told Johnson, "I shall communicate without delay wt. you desire to ye neighbouring Nations also to Pondiac who I think will pay regard to what I shall Say to him, should he not to Yours." Accompanied by the interpreter Jean-Baptiste de Couagne*, who had lived among the Miamis for many years, Wabbicommicot reached Detroit in mid August and gave the message to Pontiac and his followers, who were in the vicinity.

During the following years the Mississauga chief visited Niagara from time to time, bringing bits of news which were relayed to Johnson. On one of his visits in 1767, he was asked by the fort's commandant to stop the trading that was going on at Toronto (trade with the Indians having been restricted to the garrisoned posts since 1764). Wabbicommicot expressed his personal disapproval of the illicit trading and agreed to attempt again to prevent it, although he had tried unsuccessfully before.

In mid August 1768 four Mississaugas brought Johnson the news "of the death of our chief, and your Friend Wabicomicot. . . ."

JANE E. GRAHAM

PAC, RG 10, A2, 1827, pp.55, 56. *Documentary history of New-York* (O'Callaghan), II, 504–11. "The Gladwin manuscripts," ed. Charles Moore, *Michigan Pioneer Coll.*, XXVII (1896), 647, 652. *Johnson papers* (Sullivan et al.). *NYCD* (O'Callaghan and Fernow), VI, 486; VII, 239, 259. Peckham, *Pontiac*. P. J. Robinson, *Toronto during the French régime . . .* (Toronto, Chicago, 1933).

WALDO, SAMUEL, Massachusetts merchant, land speculator and politician; brigadier-general in the 1745 expedition against Louisbourg; b. 1695 at Boston, son of Jonathan Waldo and Hannah Mason; m. 1722 Lucy Wainwright, by whom he had three sons and two or three daughters; d. 23 May 1759, on the Penobscot River, near present-day Bangor, Maine.

Samuel Waldo's chief commercial interest was land speculation on a grand scale. He had a huge tract of land between the Penobscot and Muscongus rivers (present-day Maine), and there he settled some 40 German-speaking families in 1740. In 1730 Waldo had purchased from John Nelson*, the aged heir of Sir Thomas Temple*, the questionable claim to Sir William Alexander*'s 1621 patent to land in Nova Scotia. Waldo spent much time in London during 1731–32 and again in 1737–38 attempting to validate this claim to virtually all of the land "lying between the River St. Croix and St. Lawrence." During his negotiations he presented to the British authorities, probably in 1738, a perceptively drafted memorial in which he proposed "To begin upon the Immediate settlement of the said Tract of Land by a considerable number of Familys from Switzerland, the Palatinate and other parts adjacent." At least 2,000 "Foreign Protestant" families were to be settled in the colony at Waldo's expense within a period of ten years. Waldo hoped that his settlement would, among other things, neutralize significantly what he conceived to be the growing power of France in North America.

Even though his proposal for Nova Scotia was rejected in 1738, Waldo's interest in that area persisted. In 1740, for example, anticipating a declaration of war between France and Great Britain, he gave the Duke of Newcastle a "Plan for the Reduction of Cape Breton" and of New France. In the following year, the new governor of Massachusetts, William Shirley, one of Waldo's closest friends, was also given a copy of the "Plan." It is not surprising, therefore, that during the winter months of 1744–45, Waldo was among the most enthusiastic Massachusetts proponents of an expedition against Louisbourg, Île Royale (Cape Breton Island). Confronted by serious financial difficulties, he probably saw in the Louisbourg project an excellent opportunity to protect his land investments in northern Maine, then threatened by possible French-Indian assaults, and also to have his claim to much of Nova Scotia finally recognized by the British government. In addition, he realized that a major military expedition would result in the creation of a vast new reservoir of patronage and Waldo was probably eager to benefit fully, financially and otherwise, from such a windfall.

Soon after the decision of the Massachusetts General Court on 25 Jan. 1744/45 (o.s.) to organize an expedition against Louisbourg, Waldo apparently asked Shirley for the post of commander-in-chief. But Waldo lacked the necessary popular appeal and his close association with the governor must have been resented by some members of the General Court. Consequently Shirley rejected Waldo's offer, but not before awarding him a brigadier-general's commission and appointing him second in command to William PEPPERRELL – the commander-in-chief of the Massachusetts troops. Waldo expended a great deal of time and energy in raising volunteers for his 2nd Massachusetts Regiment. According to his own calculation he was responsible for the enlistment of approximately 850 men – over 20 per cent of the total number of New England volunteers.

Soon after landing on Île Royale, Pepperrell ordered Waldo on 2 May to march his regiment to the Grand or Royal battery situated on the northeast shore of the inner harbour, approximately one mile by sea from both the town of Louisbourg and the Island battery. The battery had been captured early that morning by William VAUGHAN, who had found it empty. Waldo's task was to supervise the drilling out of the spiked cannon and to begin the bombardment of the western walls of the fortress. He soon grew tired of the monotony of siege warfare, however, and offered, sometime before 12 May, to lead an assault against the Island battery. With this battery in New England hands, it was expected that Louisbourg would quickly surrender. Pepperrell, who had received a similar offer from William Vaughan, decided to reject both and to delay the assault on the Island battery indefinitely.

Later in May, however, under pressure from Commodore Peter WARREN, commander of the British fleet blockading Louisbourg, Pepperrell changed his mind. He selected Waldo to organize the attack on the Island battery. On 22 May Waldo managed to enlist volunteers who marched to the beach near the Grand battery after sunset and prepared their boats for the assault. Waldo cancelled the raid, however, because there were no officers to lead the men and many volunteers were drunk. Moreover, he observed to Pepperrell, "The night oweing to the moon & the northern lights was not so agreeable." On the following night, which was calm and foggy, Waldo persuaded Arthur NOBLE and John GORHAM to command an expedition of 800 men. By the time the whaleboats neared the battery, however, the two officers had disappeared from view. The 800 volunteers decided to return to the Grand battery. On 26 May Waldo dispatched a force of 400 volunteers against the Island battery. This one reached its target, but the invaders were easily turned back by the French.

After the capture of Louisbourg, Waldo, with other New England officers acting as a council, participated in the governing of the fortress until

Wanduny

Warren's commission as governor finally arrived in the spring of 1746. Waldo returned to Massachusetts to command a proposed expedition against Fort Saint-Frédéric (Crown Point), but it never took place.

In 1749 Waldo became involved in a bitter dispute with Shirley over the settling of the colony's military accounts, and went to London to defend himself. During his sojourn there he had an audience with King George II. On his return to Massachusetts, Waldo continued to be involved in colonial politics and in land speculation. He refused to abandon his claim to Nova Scotia, but it was never recognized in spite of his persistent pleas.

In 1757 he sent to William Pitt a detailed plan for the capture of Louisbourg, which had been returned to the French in 1748. Pitt used Waldo's plan as the basis for his instructions to Major-General Jeffery Amherst* to capture Louisbourg in 1758.

Waldo died of apoplexy on 23 May 1759 while on a military expedition in Maine; he was accompanying Governor Thomas Pownall's force of 400 men in taking possession "of the King's ancient Rights, and establishing the same by setting down a Fort on the Penobscot River."

G. A. RAWLYK

PRO, CO 5/753. *Boston Weekly News-Letter*, 31 May 1759. PAC *Report, 1886*, viii–xii, cli–clvi. "The Pepperrell papers," Mass. Hist. Soc. *Coll.*, 6th ser., X (1899), 3, 4, 6–10, 13, 16, 18–21, 23, 25–33, 36–38, 40–65, 139, 141, 143, 150–51, 154–55, 157, 166, 169, 172, 190, 192, 196, 198, 203, 208, 210, 212–15, 223, 231, 234, 271–72. PRO, *JTP, 1754–58*, 248. Bell, *Foreign Protestants*. McLennan, *Louisbourg*. New Eng. Hist. and Geneal. Register, XVIII (1864), 177. Rawlyk, *Yankees at Louisbourg*. J. A. Schutz, *William Shirley: king's governor of Massachusetts* (Chapel Hill, N.C., 1961). Joseph Williamson, "Brigadier General Samuel Waldo, 1696–1759," Maine Hist. Soc. *Coll.*, 1st ser., IX (1887), 75–93.

WANDUNY. *See* ORONTONY

WAPPISIS (Woodbee, Woudby), a captain of the Home Indians (Crees) at Albany Factory (Fort Albany, Ont.); hanged 21 June 1755.

Wappisis was first mentioned at Albany in 1741. From 1743 to 1753 he received an annual gift of a captain's coat from the Hudson's Bay Company in recognition of his influence among the Indians in the vicinity of the post. The fact that he was several times given presents for his friends the Abitibi Indians indicates that he may previously have been at Moose Factory (Ont.),

which was nearer their territory. Under the slack discipline of George Spence, chief factor at Albany from 1747 to 1753, Wappisis was permitted – contrary to HBC rules – to enter the factory. When Joseph Isbister* replaced Spence in 1753 he alienated Wappisis by withdrawing the privilege.

In 1754 Wappisis and his two sons, Shanap and Snuff the Blanket, were at Henley House (at the junction of the Albany and Kenogami rivers) where William Lamb, the master since 1751, exercised the same loose discipline as Spence had at Albany. He kept Wappisis' daughter and Shanap's wife "at Bed and Board." The Indian men were angered because Lamb refused to share the post's provisions with them also. One December morning Wappisis, his two sons, his son-in-law Annssoet, and two other Indians shot Lamb and two men in the house and waylaid the other two Henley men on their way home from trapping. They then ate the provisions and traded the goods.

Isbister first learned that there had been trouble on 6 March 1755, when an Indian reported Henley abandoned and emptied of goods. The factor concluded that there had been a surprise attack by the French. Wappisis, who had threatened death to anyone who told the truth, boldly came to Albany on 28 May to trade. He told Isbister that Henley had been taken in January, and that he and his sons had subsequently seen some "French Indians" there. Isbister was suspicious because of Wappisis' former behaviour and because of the Home Indians' unwillingness to talk about the incident. His first informant was a woman who had been a prisoner of the Home Indians. Then on 6 June some Indians from Henley arrived at Albany, and one who had lost three children during the winter because he could not obtain provisions at Henley told Isbister that Wappisis had sacked the post.

The next day the factor invited Wappisis "the land pirate" and his two sons into the fort on the pretext of giving them captains' coats. "They came in very gaily," were arrested, and confessed immediately. On 12 June a council of all 24 men at Albany decided that the three should "be hanged untill they are dead, dead, dead for a terour to all the Savage Natives from ever being guilty of the like barbarity in future." Uncertain of the legality of his actions, Isbister asked Thomas WHITE, chief at Moose Factory, for his opinion. White's reply arrived on 21 June: "the sooner they are put out of the way the better . . . had the case been with me they would not have liv'd one hour after their convictions." The three were hanged that afternoon.

The trouble at Henley was the first such incident in the company's history, and there was alarm at Moose and Albany. According to Isbister the Indians at the latter place accepted the executions since they resented the destruction of the inland post; in recalling Isbister at the expiry of his contract in 1756, the London committee claimed that "the Indians are greatly exasperated at the execution of the assasins. . . ." At Albany a story survives of an Indian who made himself master at Henley, traded like a factor, and served himself pancakes every Friday.

GEORGE E. THORMAN

HBC Arch. A.6/9, ff.29–30; A.11/2, ff.165–66, 167–68, 169–69d, 171, 173–74d, 175–76, 182–84; A.11/3, f.6; A.11/43, ff.76, 77–78, 79, 83–83d, 87, 89–89d. HBRS, XXVII (Williams) 253–55. Rich, *History of the HBC*, I.

WARREN, Sir PETER, naval officer, commander of the British squadron at Louisbourg, Île Royale (Cape Breton Island), 1745; b. 1703 or 1704, son of Michael Warren, of Warrenstown, Co. Meath (Republic of Ireland), and of Lady Catherine Plunket, *née* Aylmer, members of old Anglo-Irish families; d. 29 July 1752 in Dublin (Republic of Ireland).

Peter Warren joined the navy at Dublin in 1716 as an ordinary seaman, under the protection of his maternal uncle, Admiral Matthew Aylmer. He was made midshipman in 1719, lieutenant in 1723, and post captain in 1727. His early advancement was hastened by the patronage of Aylmer's son-in-law, Admiral Sir John NORRIS, under whom he served on several occasions. Serving first in the Irish sea, Warren spent most of his career from 1718 either on the North American coast or in the West Indies. Before the outbreak of war with Spain in 1739 he commanded the station ships at Boston, New York, and Charleston, South Carolina, and acquired a good knowledge of the coastal waters as far north as Canso, Nova Scotia, a familiarity with colonial politics, an appetite for investments in colonial land, and a taste for clandestine trade with the French at Louisbourg. Warren's most ambitious investment was the creation of a settlement on the Mohawk frontier (near modern Amsterdam, N.Y.). This was at first under the care of his Irish nephew, William (later Sir William) Johnson*, whom he brought to America in 1738. In July 1731 he had married at New York Susannah, daughter of Stephen DeLancey, a Huguenot, and sister of James, chief justice and lieutenant governor of New York.

Warren's first involvement in the war was at the abortive siege of San Augustin, Florida, in 1740, which he describes as "Ill concerted and worse conducted." From Florida he went to Jamaica and served briefly under Admiral Edward Vernon, who thought him an "active good officer." In August 1742 the admiralty adopted his suggestion for employing some of the North American station ships during the winter in the West Indies, and appointed him to command a small squadron based at Antigua. His principal success with the squadron came in 1744 upon the outbreak of war with France, when numerous French ships were captured. The result was the temporary discomfiture of the enemy, a large increase in his fortune, and some personal publicity at home.

The highlight of Warren's career came in 1745. The Massachusetts General Court, spurred on by Governor William Shirley, decided to attack the great French fortress at Louisbourg, and Warren was asked in January for naval support though he was then at Antigua. At first he felt unable to come to Shirley's aid, but in March he received new orders from the admiralty to take under his command all vessels on the North American coast north of Virginia, and he set sail for New England.

Warren had known the commander of the New England force, William PEPPERRELL, since at least 1736 when he was first stationed at Boston. In 1741 he had stayed for several weeks with Pepperrell in Kittery, Maine, where they had discussed the idea of jointly commanding an attack on Louisbourg. Warren had told the admiralty in 1743 that the capture "of Canada and Cape Bretoon, wou'd be of greater consequence to Great Britain than any other conquest that we may hope to make in a Spanish or French war." His idea had been to capture the fortress with regular British troops and suitable artillery, supported by colonial levies and protected by a properly equipped squadron.

The expedition that Warren's orders now clearly committed him to support fell far short of his expectations and he had real doubts of its prospects for success. The force consisted of some 3,000 undisciplined and untrained colonial troops with arms but no artillery. The supporting squadron under his command, was made up of his own four ships (a ship of the line and three frigates) and a dozen small armed vessels, sloops, and brigantines, the largest of which carried 24 guns. The troops from New England were convoyed to Canso by their own escorts. Warren met them there late in April 1745 and helped to escort them to Louisbourg with part of his squadron.

Warren saw as his prinicipal aim the blockading of the fortress by sea, no easy task on a coast notorious for its fogs. His overriding fear was that the French might attempt to lift the siege with a larger squadron than the one under his command. His second purpose was to cooperate with the New Englanders in formulating a successful plan of assault. He was not officially part of Pepperrell's council of war, which met more or less daily on land, and was almost invariably at sea off the entrance to Louisbourg harbour. However he asked for and welcomed Pepperrell's suggestions for the disposal of the squadron, and felt free to propose to the council plans to expedite the siege. During the seven weeks' siege he actually submitted four plans of attack, each a joint land-sea operation, none of which was ever carried out. Late in May, when the third such plan had been set aside by Pepperrell's council, Warren complained to Pepperrell: "I am sorry no Plan of mine, tho' approv'd of by all my Captains, has been so fortunate, as to meet your approbation, or have any weight with you. I Flatter'd myself, from the little knowledge, I have endeavour'd to acquire, in Military affairs, my advice singly, wou'd have had some Influence, in the Conducting of the present Expedition." He short-temperedly spoke of the indolence of the New England officers, when in fact it was their inexperience that really taxed his patience. His frustration must have been the more intense as he perceived his own lack of naval strength.

Toward the end of May, however, though the New Englanders' morale and strength had declined, Warren's position was greatly strengthened. On the night of 19–20 May (o.s.) his small squadron had taken the *Vigilant* (64 guns), which had tried to relieve the fortress [see Alexandre de La Maisonfort]. Two days later reinforcements began to arrive from England, and by 10 June Warren had six ships of the line and five frigates, mounting 554 guns and carrying 3,585 officers, seamen, and marines. Warren now felt certain that the siege would succeed and persuaded Pepperrell's council to agree to an altered version of his third plan of assault. On 15 June, the eve of the planned attack, Warren addressed the New England troops, saying "He'd Rather Leave his Body at Louisbourg than not take the Citty." Just as the troops and seamen were girding themselves for battle, however, the French sued for peace.

Warren and Pepperrell jointly negotiated the terms of capitulation with the French commander, Louis Du Pont* Duchambon. They agreed that all Frenchmen in the city and the territories under the jurisdiction of the governor of Louisbourg would "have their personal Estates

Secur'd to them and have Liberty to transport themselves and said effects to any part of the French King's Dominions in Europe." Warren reported to the admiralty that although the French had asked that any inhabitant who so wished be allowed to remain at Louisbourg, "wee wou'd by no means agree to it; wee have an example of the Ill Consequence of the French being among us at Annapolis." He had no faith in the ability of the French settlers to live side by side at peace with English families. He shipped most of Cape Breton's population to France in 1745 and planned to repatriate the settlers of Île Saint-Jean (Prince Edward Island), who also came under the terms of capitulation, the following summer. He often suggested that the Acadians be resettled in the more populous southern colonies, believing that, as long as Canada was under French rule, the Acadians could not be trusted to remain loyal British subjects, whether or not they took the oath of allegiance.

The surrender of the fortress of Louisbourg occasioned a sharp though momentary dispute between Warren and Pepperrell, and some historians have accused Warren of trying at this point to steal the glory due to the New Englanders. The argument arose when Warren manœuvred successfully to get the keys of the city from the French governor and post his marines in Louisbourg before the New England troops entered. He was not so much concerned with prestige, though this was by no means unimportant, as with the orderly transfer of power. He feared that the New Englanders, denied the right to take the booty they had hoped for in joining the expeditions, would ransack the town. This falling-out, which has been interpreted as an overt attempt by Warren to assume sole command of the garrison, did not destroy the generally good relations that had characterized Warren's dealings with Pepperrell. Their friendship was real and lasting, as their lengthy correspondence amply testifies.

When news of the fall of Louisbourg reached England, Warren was made a rear-admiral, and a baronetcy was suggested, which he declined on the grounds that he had no son. Much to his consternation, he was also made first British governor of Cape Breton on 1 Sept. 1745. He had no desire to be isolated in the fortress and at once asked to be relieved of the post, preferring to serve at sea. His request was accepted and Commodore Charles Knowles* was sent in May 1746 as his successor. Warren hoped to see a "Civil Government" established on Cape Breton Island as soon as the war was over, believing that few settlers would come as long as military rule survived. Only a large settlement and a proper garrison could protect the island against the French. Warren urged that grants be made free of quit rents, that the fishery be encouraged as the principal source of wealth, and that Louisbourg be declared a free port to stimulate trade. He wanted it also, so long as the war lasted, to become the principal rendezvous where all British trading vessels returning from the American continent and the West Indies could meet to proceed home under convoy of warships.

In letters home Warren frequently spoke of Louisbourg as merely a stepping stone toward the conquest of Canada, which would open to the British alone "the whole Furr and Fish Trade . . . a Source of immense Treasure." He thought at first that an attack on Quebec could be mounted by the spring of 1746, but after discussions with Shirley, who was at Louisbourg from August to December 1745, he felt the plan could only be executed in 1747, for it involved troops not only from England but from all the colonies as far south as North Carolina. The government, however, took up Warren's first suggestion and decided to attack Quebec in the summer of 1746. Warren found this decision completely exasperating. He feared failure and saw both his career ending in ruin and vast expense being laid upon the colonies and England, simply because the scheme, however strategically sound, was projected a year too soon.

As a result of the government's orders, Warren and Pepperrell decided to postpone the repatriation of the French settlers on Île Saint-Jean. Warren left for Boston 6 June 1746 with one ship, the *Chester*, under his command. While in Boston he helped Shirley coordinate plans for the attack on Quebec, and sent out the *Chester* first to scout for a French fleet which was expected soon in North American waters, and then to protect Annapolis which was likely to be a target of any French attack. By the end of August 7,000 men had been raised for the expedition, but Warren thought the force insufficient, even with the support of British regulars. As the weeks passed and English reinforcements failed to appear, Warren knew the plan would have to be delayed until the spring of 1747. He and Shirley proposed an alternative plan for the autumn and winter months: an attack against the French at Fort Saint-Frédéric (Crown Point, N.Y.) on the western shore of Lake Champlain, which had become a base for raids upon the frontiers of New England and New York. Its capture would provide as useful a spring-board for an attack in 1747 on Montreal as Louisbourg would provide for an attack on Quebec. All these plans fell apart when news reached Boston and Louisbourg in September 1746 that the French fleet, commanded by the Duc d'Anville [LA ROCHEFOUCAULD], which had been sent to prevent an attack on Quebec, recapture Louisbourg, and attack Placentia and Annapolis, had arrived on the coast of Nova Scotia. Shirley rushed reinforcements to Annapolis and Warren expected a major sea battle. He remained in Boston in a high state of tension until October when the full story of the disasters suffered by the French reached him; decimated by disease and starvation, they had buried their dead and sailed homeward. Warren thereupon decided to return to England and left on 28 Nov. 1746.

Warren was summoned in January 1747 to advise the Privy Council on the situation in America. His ambitions for an early conquest of Canada had vanished as the government would not be further deflected from its commitment to the war in Europe. Warren now limited his comments to the need to settle Cape Breton and Nova Scotia. He advised the government, as he often had before, to initiate a conciliatory policy toward the Indians of Nova Scotia. He suggested the fortification of Canso, Placentia, and Chebucto (Halifax, where he hoped to see a permanent settlement established), and the retention of a strong squadron of warships at Louisbourg as long as the war lasted. In March 1747 he was placed in command of just such a squadron, but never sailed for America. When the admiralty learned of the French preparations to send yet another fleet to Louisbourg, they decided the home fleet should be strengthened with the ships then under Warren's command. Admiral George Anson, with Warren under him, was ordered to sea with the western squadron and on 3 May they defeated the French in an important battle off Cape Ortegal, Spain [see TAFFANEL de La Jonquière]. As a reward Warren was made a knight companion of the Order of the Bath, and two months later became a vice-admiral. He went to sea again that summer and took many prizes before returning to port in August. Illness prevented him from commanding the squadron again that year but Admiral Edward Hawke, whom Warren had nominated as his successor, secured a second and even more crushing victory over the French in October. So complete was English mastery of the seas that in 1748 neither France nor Spain was able to mount an effective counterstroke. Warren, again in command of the western squadron, fought no major sea battle. The peace preliminaries brought the war to an end and Warren struck his flag on 4 Aug. 1748 for the last time.

Warren now began to devote much time to politics. As early as 1742 he had expressed the ambi-

Warren

tion of becoming governor of New York, and when Lewis Morris died in 1746, Warren had also lobbied for the governorship of New Jersey. He did not confine his political ambitions to America and expressed in 1746 a vague hope of getting into parliament. Shortly after the victory of Cape Ortegal, parliament was suddenly dissolved and Warren, who had earlier agreed to support the government, stood for the City of Westminster, which "invariably returned men of the highest social standing." Election success came easily though it cost him £7,000. He also sought office under Henry and Thomas Pelham (Duke of Newcastle) by bidding for a vacancy on the admiralty board in December 1748. Despite Anson's support, Warren's bid failed. When the next vacancy on the board occurred six months later, Warren was not even considered, for he had alienated his political friends by leading the opposition of many naval officers to certain clauses of a bill to reform the navy. Warren gravitated toward the Earl of Egmont and other supporters of the Prince of Wales, and was listed as an admiralty commissioner in the administration to be formed upon the prince's accession; but the prince died in March 1751. Despite his failure with the Pelhams, Warren warmly supported Newcastle's European system of alliances to counter-balance the power of France, about whose policies he remained deeply suspicious. He was also an advocate of a strong navy as the chief instrument of British policy. In parliament he was one of the best informed members on American affairs, being active in matters relating to colonial trade, currency problems, boundary disputes, and the fisheries.

Warren's income from war prizes amounted to at least £126,000, of which not less than £53,000 came from the prizes taken at Louisbourg. Next to Anson's prize fortune, Warren's was probably the largest ever accumulated before the Seven Years' War. He invested his wealth in land and moneylending in various American colonies, particularly New York, as well as in England and Ireland; in government bonds, especially the 1745 loan; and in the stock of the great trading and insurance companies.

Warren was also something of a philanthropist, his philanthropy being more distinguished by its scope than its size. He subscribed funds for the building of churches in America; in England he was particularly interested in hospitals. Although he was probably raised a Catholic, he was a strong supporter of the Church of England in his later life. In 1749 he was given a commission of £900 for helping the New England governments secure compensation from parliament for some of their expenses in 1745 and 1746, and put most of this sum into a trust for the education of Indian children. In his eyes this was the perfect blending of religion and practical politics, for the Indians would be brought to a "Knowledge of . . . the Glorious Redeemer of the World" and be won over to the "British Interest." He intended to organize a subscription to increase the fund but died before the plan matured.

Warren died suddenly in Dublin on 29 July 1752 "of a most Violent Fever," when it seemed his active talent had only begun to be tapped. His naval career, however distinguished, had achieved nothing memorable, and his brief political career must only have disappointed him and his friends. His fame and fortune brought him to the outer fringes of power, but his lack of strong political allies and his own independent spirit, buoyed up by his considerable wealth, soon isolated him from the centre of political life. His lasting monuments were, curiously, his remarkably perceptive comments on the future course of Anglo-American relations in America, and his large fortune, traces of which survive even today through the marriages of his daughters into the English aristocracy.

Warren was buried in Ireland in the parish of his birth, but the exact site of his grave is unmarked. There is a large, unlovely monument of him in the east transept of Westminster Abbey, carved by Louis-François Roubillac.

JULIAN GWYN

Baker Library, Harvard University, Peter Faneuil letterbook, 1737–39. Bedford Office (London), Woburn MSS H.M.C. no. 8, 4th Duke of Bedford MS letters, X, 94; XVII, 41, 45; XXVI, 68. Boston Public Library, MSS B.11.94; Chamberlain coll. of Hancock MSS, Ch.M.1.10. BM, Add. MSS, 15955, ff.26–27, 141, 149; 15957, ff.147, 152, 152v, 156–58, 160, 191–92, 195–97, 219, 222, 310, 312; Egerton MSS, 929, ff.168–72. Clements Library, George Clinton papers, I, II; Peter Warren papers. Maine Hist. Soc. (Portland), Fogg autograph coll., Warren MSS. "Mass. Archives," I, 296–98; XIII, 245–47; XX, 559–60. Mass. Hist. Soc., Belknap papers, 61.B, 61.C; Louisbourg MSS, V, VI; Pepperrell papers, 71.A, f.193. N.Y. Hist. Soc. (New York), De Lancey papers; J. E. Stillwell coll.; Peter Warren papers, 12; Peter Warren deeds, 3. PRO, Adm. 1/233, f.49; 1/480; 1/2652–1/2655 (Warren's letters); 1/3817; 1/4114, f.23; 2/58, ff.439–44; 2/69, ff.178, 267–68, 269; 2/482, f.196; 2/505, ff.66–67; 33/307; CO 5/36; 5/44, ff.16–22, 31–32, 33–37, 45, 97, 105–14; SP 42/30. Sussex Archaeological Soc. (Lewes, Eng.), Gage papers, America, G/Am/1, G/Am/6, G/Am/21; Hampshire, G/Ah/66 (26); Ireland, G/Ir/2 (70). Some letters between Warren and Pepperrell can be found in the private collection of J. G. Johnson, Sydney, Ohio.

"Biographical memoirs of the late Sir Peter Warren,

K.B., vice-admiral of the red squadron,'' *Navy Chronicle* (London), XII (1804), 257–75. *The correspondence of the colonial governors of Rhode Island, 1723–1775*, ed. G. S. Kimball (2v., Boston, New York, 1902–3), II, 3–8. *Correspondence of William Shirley* (Lincoln). *Dublin Gazette*, 1–4 Aug. 1752. *Gentleman's Magazine*, 1744, 424; 1747, 307; 1752, 285. *Johnson papers* (Sullivan et al.). *The Law papers; correspondence and documents during Jonathan Law's governorship of the colony of Connecticut, 1741–1750* (3v., Conn. Hist. Soc. *Coll.*, XI, XIII, XV, Hartford, 1907–14), I, 248–49; II, 143–47, 288–92. *Leicester House politics, 1750–60, from the papers of John, second Earl of Egmont*, ed. A. N. Newman (Camden Miscellany, XXIII; Camden Fourth Series, VII, London, [1969]). *Louisbourg journals* (De Forest), 185. Mass. Hist. Soc. *Coll.*, 1st ser., I (1792), 36, 46, 48–49. *NYCD* (O'Callaghan and Fernow). *New-York Gazette*, 19–26 July 1731. *The parliamentary history of England from the earliest period to the year 1803*, ed. William Cobbett and John Wright (36v., London, 1806–20), XIV. "The Pepperrell papers," Mass. Hist. Soc. *Coll.*, 6th ser., X (1899), 291–93, 297–98, 305–6, 327–29, 437–45, 475–77, 482–85. *The Yale edition of Horace Walpole's correspondence*, ed. W. S. Lewis et al. (31v. to date, London, New Haven, Conn., 1937–), XX, 16–17, 33.

Charnock, *Biographia navalis*, IV, 184–92. *DAB. DNB. The history of parliament: the House of Commons, 1754–1790*, ed. Lewis Namier and John Brooke (3v., London, 1964), I, 336. *The knights of England: a complete record from the earliest time to the present day of the knights of all the orders of chivalry in England, Scotland, and Ireland, and of knights bachelors*, ed. W. A. Shaw (2v., London, 1906), I, 169. *Annals of King's Chapel from the Puritan age of New England to the present day*, ed. H. W. Foote et al. (2v., Boston, 1882–96), II, 50–51, 63. F. J. Aylmer, *The Aylmers of Ireland* (London, 1931). Julian Gwyn, "The personal fortune of Admiral Sir Peter Warren," (unpublished DPHIL thesis, University of Oxford, 1971). *A history of the parish of Trinity Church in the city of New York*, ed. Morgan Dix (4v., New York, 1898–1906), I, 258. S. N. Katz, *Newcastle's New York; Anglo-American politics, 1732–1753* (Cambridge, Mass., 1968), 220–25. McLennan, *Louisbourg*. Usher Parsons, *The life of Sir William Pepperrell, bart. . . .* (1st ed., Boston, 1855; 2nd ed., Boston, London, 1856). Rawlyk, *Yankees at Louisbourg*. F. V. Recum, *The families of Warren and Johnson of Warrenstown, County Meath* (New York, 1950). H. W. Richmond, *The navy in the War of 1739–1748* (3v., Cambridge, Eng., 1920). J. A. Schutz, *William Shirley: king's governor of Massachusetts* (Chapel Hill, N.C., 1961). Thomas Warren, *A history and genealogy of the Warren family in Normandy, Great Britain and Ireland, France, Holland, Tuscany, United States of America, etc., A.D. 912–1902* ([London], 1902).

WATSON, CHARLES, naval officer; b. 1714, probably in London, England, son of John Watson; m. 1741 to Rebecca Buller; d. 16 Aug. 1757 at Calcutta, India.

Charles Watson entered the navy in 1728 as a volunteer per order (roughly the equivalent of a modern naval cadet) on the *Romney*. He was promoted lieutenant on 23 July 1734 and post captain four years later when he was given command of the *Guarland*, 20 guns. His quick rise through the ranks can probably be attributed to the fact that his uncle, Sir Charles Wager, was first lord of the admiralty.

Watson's first visit to North America was in the summer of 1738, when the *Guarland* was sent to protect the fishery at Canso, Nova Scotia. During the next ten years he served in the Mediterranean and with the squadron guarding the western approaches to the English Channel. He returned to North America in 1748 as rear-admiral of the blue, governor of Newfoundland, and commander-in-chief, Cape Breton, an appointment he evidently owed to the patronage of the Duke of Bedford. The War of the Austrian Succession ended in October 1748, and Watson's main duty became the reduction of the British naval establishment at Louisbourg in preparation for the return of the fortress to France. As governor of Newfoundland he began reconstruction of the magisterial system, revoking the commissions of justices of the peace who were military officers and giving them to civilians. He also attempted to deport Irish and Scots Catholics thought to be disaffected, the presence of large numbers of Catholics having been particularly alarming to the English since the 1745 rising in Scotland.

Watson relinquished his command in 1749, and nothing is known of him for the next five years. In 1754 he was made commander-in-chief, East Indies, and he served in this capacity with great distinction, cooperating with Robert Clive in the British victories of 1756 and 1757. He became vice-admiral of the white in 1757. The climate, however, undermined his health, and he died that year at Calcutta.

C. H. LITTLE

PRO, Adm. 1/480; 1/917; 1/2652; 1/2658; 2/71, ff.448–53; 3/56; 3/61; 107/3; CO 194/12, ff.57–78, 167; 194/13, ff.32–33. Charnock, *Biographia navalis. DNB. G.B., Adm., Commissioned sea officers, 1660–1815*. W. L. Clowes et al., *The Royal Navy, a history from the earliest times to the present* (7v., London, 1897–1903), III. Lounsbury, *British fishery at Nfld*.

WAWATAM, Ojibwa chief at Michilimackinac; fl. 1762–64.

Wawatam is known to history as the man who rescued the trader Alexander Henry* during the Ojibwa uprising at Michilimackinac in 1763. According to Henry's *Travels and adventures*, in

Wawenorrawot

the spring of 1762 Wawatam, inspired by a dream, adopted him as a brother. A year later the Ojibwa, whom Henry described as about 45 years old and "of an excellent character among his nation," came to him visibly disturbed and begged him to accompany him to Sault Ste Marie the next morning. Not understanding Wawatam's hints of impending trouble, the trader delayed departing and was captured when Ojibwas led by Madjeckewiss* and MINWEWEH overthrew the British garrison on 2 June 1763. The other Ojibwas had asked Wawatam to leave the settlement before the uprising because of his friendship for Henry, but he had extracted a promise that the trader would not be harmed. Several days after the attack he returned and with great eloquence and many presents obtained custody of Henry.

Wawatam kept the trader in his family for a year, travelling to the Rivière aux Sables (Big Sable River) on the east coast of Lake Michigan and thence into the northern interior of the lower Michigan peninsula, where they hunted and trapped for furs. In April 1764 Henry went with Wawatam's party to maple sugar grounds near the lakeshore, returning to Michilimackinac later that month. After accompanying Wawatam to Boutchitaouy Bay (St Martin Bay, Mich.) in May to fish and to hunt wild fowl, the trader left for Sault Ste Marie. Henry's account of the activities of Wawatam and his family provides valuable information on aspects of the social organization, material culture, and seasonal round of Ojibwas in the northern Great Lakes region at that time.

Wawatam appears in no other document than the *Travels and Adventures*. In the mid-19th century H. R. Schoolcraft tried to trace him or his family, but learned only a tradition that he had become blind and had died when his lodge at Ottawa Point (near Cross Village, Mich.) burned.

HAROLD HICKERSON

Alexander Henry, *Travels and adventures in Canada and the Indian territories between the years 1760 and 1776*, ed. James Bain (Boston, 1901, repr. Edmonton, 1969). G. I. Quimby, "A year with a Chippewa family, 1763–1764," *Ethnohistory* (Tucson, Ariz.), IX (1962), 217–39.

WAWENORRAWOT (Wawanolewat, Wewonorawed). *See* GRAY LOCK

WEBB, JAMES, naval officer, governor of Newfoundland; b. probably in England; d. 14 May 1761 at Plymouth Sound, England.

James Webb served in the Royal Navy as a volunteer on the *Success* in 1728. He was made a frigate captain in 1746 after distinguishing himself by capturing many French privateers. Early in the Seven Years' War Webb held a series of commands – the *Speedwell, Sunderland, St Albans,* and *Hampton Court* – and again proved effective in hunting down enemy ships. He was appointed governor of Newfoundland and commander of the annual squadron in May 1760, arriving in St John's at the end of June on the *Antelope*. In August he sailed in quest of hostile ships fishing on the French shore, and in Noddy Harbour (near Quirpon, on the northern tip of the island) he quickly captured a French privateer, the *Tavignon*, with 3,600 quintals of fish, and burnt French boats and stages.

Shortly thereafter three Labrador Eskimos captured in the Strait of Belle Isle were brought to Webb, who treated them kindly and took them to Chateau Bay. His gifts to them included "some tallow to eat, it being a delicious dish to them as they are actually Canibals." Subsequently over 20 canoes of Eskimos came to Chateau with whalebone to trade. Webb sealed a pact of friendship with a "King's Son" by the present of an old deck awning. He described Chateau Bay as "one of the best harbours I ever see in my life nor can a ship go in or out the Straits but must be seen from thence," and formally took possession of it for the crown, renaming it York Harbour and carefully charting its many arms.

Newfoundland in 1760 was peaceful and fairly prosperous. A permanent population of some 8,000 persons was mainly settled around the Avalon peninsula; 1,000 persons lived in St John's. In July and September Webb held court there, hearing disputes arising from the fishery. He appointed magistrates and surrogates to administer justice in the outports, tried to suppress illegal trade, confirmed the land titles of several merchants and settlers, and sought a measure of justice for maltreated employees of fish merchants.

Early in November Webb escorted the laden fishing ships to Spanish and Portuguese markets. Webb was thanked by the British traders at Lisbon "for the great care he has taken of the Newfoundland trade this year, expressed to us by every Master of the merchant ships." By mid-February 1761 the *Antelope* was once again at Portsmouth. Webb busied himself refitting his squadron for the 1761 season, but later in February had to consult doctors in London, being "much afflicted with an nervous gouty disorder in my head, and have been so most all the voyage." With country air he was able to rejoin his ship in mid March, and on 1 May reported to the admiralty from Plymouth that he was almost ready to sail. Fourteen days later he was dead.

Webb and his family resided in Plympton, a small market town near Plymouth. He was apparently a man of considerable property, with substantial sums invested in stocks, perhaps the proceeds of prize money won over the years. His property was left to his wife Grace and his only child, a daughter.

James Webb was the right governor for Newfoundland in these times, when the chief need was effective naval protection for the fishery. In 1760 125 British fishing ships, carrying over 3,500 seamen, came to Newfoundland. The English fishermen and the Newfoundland inhabitants together produced over 400,000 quintals of fish, most of it exported to foreign markets. Not a ship was lost from enemy action, and the northern Newfoundland harbours were swept clear of privateers. Webb was not only an able naval commander. He grasped the importance of the northern fisheries and the possibilities of Chateau Bay as a base. His conciliatory overtures to the Eskimos foreshadowed the policies of later governors which brought the Labrador coast and its inhabitants firmly under British control.

WILLIAM H. WHITELEY

PANL, Nfld., Dept. of Colonial Secretary, Letter books, III. PRO, Adm. 1/2665, 1/2666, 2/84, 6/13, 6/17, 36/4884, 51/50; CO 194/15, 195/8, 195/9; Prob. 11/868, f.305. *Lloyd's Evening Post and British Chronicle* (London), 20 May 1761. *London Chronicle*, 16–19, 21–23 May 1761. PRO, *JTP, 1759–1763*. Charnock, *Biographia navalis*, VI. Prowse, *History of Nfld*.

WHITE, RICHARD, HBC clerk and accountant; b. *c*. 1707; fl. 1749.

Richard White joined the Hudson's Bay Company in 1726 and went "to keep the Books at Albany Fort [Fort Albany, Ont.]," first under Joseph Myatt* and then under Joseph Adams*. He made good there, but because he voiced such dissatisfaction with the increase in wages offered when his contract was renewed in 1731 he was recalled to London two years later. By continuing to hold out for higher terms in 1734 he lost the opportunity of returning to Albany as "second." Had he gone to Albany, he would probably have succeeded Adams, who died in 1737. Instead, in 1735 he was apparently obliged by circumstances to accept the company's terms, and he went to Churchill (Man.) as "second." The post's location was grim compared to that of Albany, and from 1736 to 1740 he had to serve under the difficult Richard NORTON. Uneducated himself, Norton no doubt feared being superseded by some ambitious young man who knew how to keep accounts and write letters, and so jealously

did he guard the secrets of his trading methods that he refused to divulge them even to his employers. Not surprisingly, White described the position of "second" as "no more than an empty Title."

Having returned to England in 1740, White went back to Churchill in 1741 as "Supervisor of the Works" at the stone Fort Prince of Wales, which had been under construction for ten years. He held the position under Norton's successor, James ISHAM, and subsequently under Robert PILGRIM. In 1746 he returned to London disappointed, embittered, and with no further hope of employment in Hudson Bay. The quarrelsome Pilgrim had suspended him from duty on the grounds that he was a corrupting influence – one of "the greatest Sotts in Europe" and a "very Dangerous Fellow."

In 1749 White appeared before the parliamentary committee which was investigating the HBC. Though his own inland journeys had been limited to 40 miles up the Albany River in search of timber, he ventured the opinion that "the Countries adjoining to *Hudson's Bay* might be settled and improved." He testified about the company's trade, trading methods, and treatment of the Indians, and about life at the bay in general. Reflecting, no doubt, on his personal experience, he remarked that "the Governors loved to have the sole Management of Affairs; and if any inferior Person should offer to interfere in Matters of that Nature, he is sure to be immediately discharged."

ALICE M. JOHNSON

[White's own account of his service in Hudson Bay is in G.B., Parl., *Report from the committee on Hudson's Bay*, 217–20. References to White at Albany (1726–33) and at Churchill (1735–40) are to be found in HBRS, XXV (Davies and Johnson), which also lists the pertinent sources in the HBC Archives. The correspondence between London and Churchill (HBC Arch. A.6/6, A.6/7, and A.11/13) is the main source of information on the years 1741 to 1746. For background information on the period *see* Rich, *History of the HBC*, I. A.M.J.]

WHITE, THOMAS, HBC sailor and chief factor; fl. 1719–56.

Thomas White sailed for York Fort (York Factory, Man.) in 1719 as a foremast hand for the Hudson's Bay Company. It is not always easy to substantiate the details of his service, since Richard WHITE was also in the company's employ from 1726 to 1746 and some references to "Mr. White" might apply to either man. Thomas White's entire career was marked by reports of his diligence, honesty, and devotion to the company's interests. These qualities earned his promotion to steward of York Fort in 1723, but he was recalled in 1724 when his time expired and actually made the journey home in 1725.

White next emerges in 1731, when he was made second in command and book-keeper at York. The double responsibility was held to be too heavy, however, and the following year he was relieved of his book-keeping duties by James Isham. He remained at York and was directed to manage the post when the chief factor, Thomas McCliesh, went home in 1734. White's integrity was specially praised and he was continued as chief for 1735 and 1736. Anxious to return to England after so long an absence, in 1737 he handed over command to Isham with a report that the post needed substantial repairs, if not complete rebuilding.

In 1741 the London committee called White into their discussions of proposals made by Arthur Dobbs, a noted critic of the HBC, and Christopher Middleton, a former company captain, for the discovery of a northwest passage. White was going to command at York that year, and the committee entrusted him with verbal instructions to Isham, who was posted to Churchill (Man.), regarding the reception of Middleton's expedition. White was also told to divert as much trade as possible to Churchill, where the great stone bastions of Fort Prince of Wales were being erected to create a defensible centre for English trade, but he was nevertheless instructed to proceed with the reconstruction of York Fort. Although White accepted the policy of directing trade to Churchill, his manner of dealing with the Indians was so fair and affable that he was accused by Robert Pilgrim of "enticing" customers from Churchill to York. His reputation as a trader well beloved by Indians lingered long after he had left the post in 1746 to return to England.

In May 1751 White re-entered the company's service and was sent to command at Moose, where Pilgrim had died after a long illness and Robert Temple was in charge temporarily. The men at Moose had a reputation for bad behaviour, trade there had steadily declined, and the buildings had fallen into disrepair. White made steady progress with the rebuilding, but he failed to revitalize business in face of competition from French "pedlars" who traded in the interior, saving the Indians the long journey to the coast. In 1756 he left the country for the last time.

White was above all the conscientious servant. Although the HBC had occasionally elicited information from him, he was not consulted at the policy-making level. When he voiced his opinions he seems to have been unprogressive. He moved the new building at York to the old site, which had been abandoned, and he was apathetic and undistinguished where innovations were concerned. He took his orders and endeavoured to carry them out, and he was honest and fair-minded in an age when such virtues were not universal.

E. E. Rich

HBC Arch. A.6, A.11/43, A.11/114, B.135/a. HBRS, XXV (Davies and Johnson); XXVII (Williams). Rich, *History of the HBC*, I.

WHITE HEAD. *See* Theyanoguin

WHITE THUNDER. *See* Kaghswaghtaniunt

WHITMORE, EDWARD, army officer, governor of Cape Breton Island and the Island of St John (Prince Edward Island); b. *c.* 1694, apparently the son of Captain Arthur Whitmore of York, whose will refers to a son Edward; d. 1761.

Edward Whitmore was commissioned ensign in his father's regiment, the 36th Foot, on 13 March 1710/11 (o.s.); he was promoted lieutenant on 1 June 1723; captain, 1 Nov. 1739; major, 2 July 1747; and lieutenant-colonel, 17 July 1747. On 11 July 1757 he became colonel of the 22nd Foot and was made major-general 19 Feb. 1761.

Whitmore served first in the unsuccessful expedition to Quebec in 1711 under Admiral Hovenden Walker*. Between 1712 and 1714 his regiment occupied the fortress of Dunkerque, France. He saw action in Scotland during the Jacobite uprising of 1715, and from 1718 to 1739 he was stationed in Ireland. Upon the outbreak of war with Spain in 1739 his regiment returned to England and the following year was sent to the West Indies to support Admiral Edward Vernon. Whitmore took part in the unsuccessful attack on Cartagena (Colombia) in 1741 before returning to England in 1743. After war with France was declared in 1744 his regiment served in Flanders, garrisoning Ghent at the time of the battle of Fontenoy (1745). During the Jacobite revolt of 1745 he was sent to Scotland where he fought at Falkirk (1746) and Culloden (1746).

The year 1757 found him in North America commanding the 22nd regiment in Lord Charles Hay's brigade at Halifax, Nova Scotia. The following summer Whitmore, Wolfe, and Lawrence were made local brigadiers in preparation for an attack on Louisbourg. Whitmore commanded the right wing, directed against Pointe Blanche (White Point), when the British landed at the French stronghold in June. During the siege he was in charge of the troops laboriously preparing batteries to destroy the fortifications. Wolfe thought little of him, calling him "a poor, old, sleepy man," but Whitmore's efforts, along with those of the other senior commanders, were altogether successful.

After the capitulation of the fortress, Whitmore was made governor of Cape Breton and the Island of St John with a garrison composed of his own regiment and the 28th, 40th, and 45th Foot. As governor he was responsible for the orderly evacuation to Great Britain and France of the French troops and population in 1758, the support of the expedition to Quebec in 1759, and the demolition of the Louisbourg fortifications in 1760.

He served without complaint in this rather unimportant position, while his fellow officers, both younger and junior, covered themselves with glory in great victories elsewhere in North America and the West Indies. He took leave in December 1761 for the recovery of his health only after being ordered to do so by his commander, Jeffery Amherst*. On his passage from Louisbourg to Boston on 11 Dec. 1761 he was swept overboard and drowned. He was buried in King's Chapel, Boston. His loss was genuinely felt by his fellow officers. Montagu WILMOT wrote: "Those who had the honour to serve under him will have reason to Lament his Loss, the sole Endeavour of this truly amiable Person was to contribute to the happiness of others, even at the risque of his own Disquiet," an opinion which Amherst, who called him "a worthy Good Man," fully shared. Whitmore was survived by a son Edward, who in 1762 was granted power to administer his will, and by a daughter, the wife of a Captain Scott of Greenwich.

JULIAN GWYN

PRO, CO 5/53, ff.172–74; 5/213, ff.151–54; Ind. 5431, p.180; 5436, pp.98–99; WO 4/21, 35; 34/17, Amherst to Whitmore, 11 Oct. 1761; Wilmot to Amherst, 13 Dec. 1761; Amherst to Wilmot, 23 Dec. 1761. *Gentleman's Magazine*, 1767, 525. C. H. S. Sackville, *The manuscripts of Mrs Stopford Sackville of Drayton House, Northamptonshire* (Historical Manuscripts Commission, *Reports*, 9, pt.III, London, 1884), 76. Dalton, *George the first's army*, I, 365; II, 415. *Herald and Genealogist* (London), VI (1871), 682.

WIGATE, JOHN, naval clerk, fl.1741–46.

John Wigate was appointed in the spring of 1741 as clerk of the naval sloop *Furnace*, which sailed in June to Hudson Bay under the command of Christopher MIDDLETON in search of a northwest passage. After the failure of the expedition

Wigate became associated with his fellow crewmembers Edward THOMPSON and John RANKIN in the campaign organized by Arthur Dobbs to discredit Middleton's handling of the expedition. Like the others, Wigate was ready to swear at the admiralty hearings of 1743 that Middleton had falsified his journal and chart of the voyage, and he was perhaps the more ready to do so since nine months after the expedition's return in the autumn of 1742 Wigate had still received no pay as a result of Middleton's insistence that he must first deliver up the accounts of the *Furnace*. Wigate's only distinctive contribution to the controversy over the Middleton expedition was his apparent responsibility for a map issued under his name in 1746 (probably to coincide with the sailing of the private discovery expedition organized by Dobbs). The map summed up in vivid cartographical form Dobbs' main arguments. It showed the west coast of Hudson Bay broken by unexplored inlets, notably Rankin Inlet; and the Wager was firmly marked "Wager Strait," open to the west, and with a tide flowing through it from that direction. Whether Wigate did more than lend his name to Dobbs for the map is questionable; but in any case the honour of composition was a doubtful one, for within a year of the map's publication William MOOR's expedition discovered that both Rankin Inlet and the Wager were closed bays, as Middleton had always maintained.

GLYNDWR WILLIAMS

[The argument between Middleton and Wigate over the accounts of the *Furnace* is set out in PRO, Adm. 2/480, pp.55, 171. References to Wigate's role in the attack on Middleton are to be found in the latter's *A vindication of the conduct of Captain Christopher Middleton . . .* (London, 1743) and in Arthur Dobbs, *Remarks upon Middleton's defence*. Wigate's map was published as *Chart of the seas, straits, &c. thro' which his majesty's sloop "Furnace" pass'd for discovering a passage from Hudson's Bay to the South Sea* (London, 1746); a modern representation of it is given in Williams, *British search for the northwest passage*, 76. G.W.]

WILMOT, MONTAGU, military officer, governor of Nova Scotia; place and date of birth unknown; son of Christopher Wilmot and Anne Montagu; d. 23 May 1766 at Halifax, Nova Scotia.

Montagu Wilmot's father was physician-in-ordinary to George II when he was Prince of Wales, and his mother was a daughter of Edward Montagu, of Horton, Northampton, England, and a sister of George Montagu, 1st Earl of Halifax. Thus Wilmot was a cousin of George Montagu Dunk, 2nd Earl of Halifax, president of

Wilmot

the Board of Trade and secretary of state; Lord Halifax was Wilmot's patron.

Wilmot began his military career in April 1730 as an ensign in the 18th Regiment of Foot (Armstrong's). He was promoted lieutenant in the 5th Regiment of Marines in November 1739, captain in the 15th Foot in April 1741, and major in Lord Halifax's regiment in October 1745. At that time he was transferred to the 29th Foot (Hopson's) and likely joined it at Louisbourg, Cape Breton Island, where the regiment had been sent from Gibraltar to form part of the British garrison at the recently captured fortress. In the summer of 1749, Louisbourg having been restored to France, the regiment was posted to the newly founded settlement at Halifax, Nova Scotia.

Wilmot was promoted lieutenant-colonel in the 45th regiment (Warburton's) in April 1755. In December he was appointed a member of the Nova Scotia Council. After the French success at Fort Oswego (Chouaguen) in August 1756 [see MONTCALM], it was decided to strengthen Fort Cumberland on the Chignecto isthmus of Nova Scotia. On 12 November Wilmot was sent by Governor Charles LAWRENCE to take command of the garrison there, along with 200 soldiers from the Halifax garrison. He was later accused by a trader at Fort Cumberland of illegally paying bounties on French scalps brought there by the Indian rangers of Joseph Gorham*. At the siege of Louisbourg in 1758 Wilmot commanded the 4th brigade, comprised of the 45th and 22nd regiments and the 3rd battalion of the 60th regiment. He remained at Louisbourg for a time after the capture of the fortress, and may have taken part in the recapture of St John's, Newfoundland, from the French in 1761. In the spring of 1762 he was made lieutenant-colonel of the 80th regiment and moved to Quebec.

Wilmot was appointed lieutenant governor of Nova Scotia on 14 March 1763, succeeding Jonathan Belcher*, but did not arrive at Halifax from Quebec until September. That fall Henry Ellis resigned the governorship of Nova Scotia, and in May 1764 Wilmot assumed this office. The province was suffering from heavy debts and deficits when he became governor, for almost the whole British naval and military establishment had been withdrawn from Halifax, and with it the revenue from duties on the sale of liquor. The British parliamentary grant had been drastically reduced in recent years as well. Wilmot was repeatedly warned by the Board of Trade to avoid extravagant expenditures such as those made while Belcher was in office. During Wilmot's régime between 2 1/2 and 3 1/2 million acres of provincial land were granted, unwisely, to local and foreign speculators, although it is unfair to blame Wilmot alone for this activity. A royal proclamation of 7 Oct. 1763 had encouraged settlement in Great Britain's newly conquered possessions of Florida, Quebec, and Nova Scotia – which now included Cape Breton and the Island of St John (Prince Edward Island) – and forbade settlement west of the Appalachians. Wilmot protested that these new instructions, which offered unlimited grants and imposed few responsibilities on the grantees, opened the way for speculation. He delayed making new and large grants to Alexander McNutt*, a major speculator, and appealed to the Board of Trade for more stringent regulations; the board failed to reply. Wilmot finally granted McNutt's request for land in the fall of 1765, but insisted that if some settlers were not placed upon any grant within four years it could be escheated by the crown.

Wilmot has been described by historians as "an easy-going, complaisant soldier," and a "man of weak character . . . poorly fitted for the post of governor." He was remembered in his own day for the stilted and lengthy speeches he delivered on all occasions. In Nova Scotia he suffered from rheumatism and gout which prevented him from signing his name for months, and confined him to his home in winter. Shortly before his death he applied for a year's leave of absence to return to Europe to take "the Bath Waters." He died on 23 May 1766 and was buried in a vault beneath St Paul's Church. His state funeral cost £245 11s. 4d., which the Nova Scotia Assembly refused to pay because of "the distressed Situation of the Province, and the heavy Debt it labours under."

PHYLLIS R. BLAKELEY

Halifax County Court, Papers, Inferior Court of Common Pleas, 1769, John Butler [administrator of estate of Governor Wilmot] v. Joseph Pierpoint. Halifax County Court of Probate, Estate papers, W96. Harvard College Library, MS Sparks 4, Bernard papers, III, 7. Nova Scotia, Dept. of Lands and Forests, Crown Land papers, V, 5, 207; VI, 34, 535, 546, 762; VII, 190. PANS, RG 1, 31, nos.22–56; 37; 41; 42; 163/3, pp.87–90; 164/2, pp.222–38; 165, pp.281–413; 166, p.8; 286, nos.17, 18, 20, 48, 56; 349, nos.9–10; RG 3, Minutes of Nova Scotia Council, 1755–56, 1763–66; F.-J. Audet, "Governors, lieutenant-governors, and administrators of Nova Scotia, 1604–1932" (bound typescript, n.d.). PRO, CO 217/20, ff.215–388; 217/21, ff.1–394 (mfm copies in PAC and PANS); Ind. 5435, 5438. St Paul's Church (Halifax), "Record of burials performed by the clergy of St Paul's Church gathered from loose memoranda, and written up by W. Simms Lee"; Burial records, 1766 (mfm at PANS).

Army list, *1758*, 92. Knox, *Historical journal* (Doughty). Nova Scotia, *A journal of the votes of the*

Lower House of Assembly, for the Province of Nova Scotia [1763–66] (Halifax, [1763–66]). PRO, *JTP, 1759–1763; 1764–1767.* Joseph Foster, *The peerage, baronetage, and knightage of the British empire for 1881* ([London], n.d.), 663. *Record of services of the officers of the 1st and 2nd battalions the Sherwood Foresters, Nottinghamshire and Derbyshire Regiment, 45th and 95th, 1741–1931*, comp. H. C. Wylly (n.p., [1931]). Brebner, *Neutral Yankees.* Murdoch, *History of Nova-Scotia*, II, 321, 431, 432, 437, 439, 441, 443, 460. Margaret Ells, "Clearing the decks for the loyalists," CHA *Report, 1933*, 43–58. J. S. Macdonald, "Richard Bulkeley," N.S. Hist. Soc. *Coll.*, XII (1905), 70–72.

WINNIETT, MARIE-MADELEINE. *See* MAISONNAT

WINNIETT, WILLIAM, military officer, merchant, and settler at Annapolis Royal, Nova Scotia, member of the Nova Scotia Council; b. *c.* 1685; drowned in Boston harbour, Massachusetts, April 1741.

William Winniett is said to have been born in France of Huguenot parents, but this is not certain. In 1710 he accompanied Francis Nicholson* from London as a volunteer in the successful expedition against Port-Royal (Annapolis Royal), serving as ensign, adjutant, and second lieutenant in Walton's New Hampshire regiment. He was a lieutenant in the Annapolis Royal garrison for a time, but resigned his military commission in 1711 to embark upon a career as a merchant-trader. In that year he married Marie-Madeleine MAISONNAT, daughter of Pierre Maisonnat* and Madeleine Bourg.

Winniett had trading connections at Annapolis Royal, the Acadian settlements up the Bay of Fundy, and Canso, selling a variety of provisions, many of which had been transported from Boston. He procured wood for the Annapolis garrison and seems to have been involved in fishing in the 1720s. In June 1722 he was robbed by Indians at Minas, "to ye value of 1,500 pounds, goods & Vessell." Micmac and Malecite Indians attacked Annapolis Royal on 4 July 1724; Winniett testified to the Nova Scotia Council on 16 July that he had learned of the proposed attack at Minas on 1 July, but had been assured by the French that the Annapolis garrison would already have been warned. In 1725 he helped persuade the Nova Scotia Council to restrict trading up the Bay of Fundy to the Annapolis settlers. He supported this policy again in 1727 as a means of making the Acadians more dependent on Annapolis Royal for supplies and less able to support the Indians in their expeditions against the English.

Winniett's relations with the government of Nova Scotia were often strained. In 1714 Governor Nicholson warned Lieutenant Governor Thomas Caulfeild* not to employ Winniett or even allow him to enter the garrison, pointing to the pro-French sentiments of Winniett's wife and relatives. About this time Winniett was also at odds with Captain Lawrence Armstrong*, who sought to exclude him from any dealings with the garrison. Caulfeild, however, defended Winniett and condemned Armstrong's treatment of him. In 1720, after complaining about the establishment of a grain magazine at Annapolis Royal, Winniett was rebuked by the governor and council for behaving towards them in an "insolent, disrespectfull, audacious, contemptuous, and undutiful manner," and was ordered to apologize. His letter of submission restored him to good standing.

In November 1729 Winniett, as "the most Considerable Merchant, and one of ye first British Inhabitants in this Place" was appointed to the Nova Scotia Council, replacing one of two councillors who were sick. With Erasmus James PHILIPPS he drew up in 1730 a scheme for procuring and keeping currency in Nova Scotia. He sought unsuccessfully in 1731 to validate a claim he had to some land east of the Penobscot River (Maine), and thereafter absented himself more and more from council meetings. The conflict between his son-in-law, Alexander COSBY, and Lieutenant Governor Lawrence Armstrong, which resulted in Cosby's withdrawal from the council in 1732, probably affected Winniett as well. About the same time, Henry COPE accused Winniett of informing the Indians at Minas that the government was building a house there as quarters for a company of soldiers. Finally on 9 Jan. 1734 Armstrong suspended Winniett from the council, citing his infrequent attendance and general behaviour. The Lords of Trade refused to uphold Armstrong's action, however, and advised him not to be so strict about the behaviour of councillors when the colony was so young and there were so few civil inhabitants who could sit on council.

Little is known of Winniett's activities from this time until his death in 1741. Paul MASCARENE stated that his widow was left in deplorable circumstances. Winniett had seven sons and six daughters. One son, Joseph*, was a member of the Nova Scotia assembly and a judge. Three of his daughters – Anne, Elizabeth, and Marie-Madeleine – were married to council members: Alexander Cosby, John HANDFIELD, and Edward How, respectively.

CHARLES BRUCE FERGUSSON

Wolfe

BM, Add. mss, 19070, no.2, ff.65–66 (transcript in PAC, MG 21, E5). PAC, Nova Scotia A, 3, p.185. PANS, RG 1, 14, 22, 23, 24; Unpub. papers of N.S. Hist. Soc., A. W. Savary, "Ancestry of General Sir William Fenwick Williams of Kars" (contains notes on the Winniett family). PRO, CO 217/1, ff.62–63, 402; 217/2, ff.25–30, 68, 71, 73, 190; 217/4, ff.8, 17, 19, 128–29, 300; 217/5, ff.66–68; 217/6, ff.117, 208–9; 218/2, f.153.

Boston Gazette, 27 April 1741. *Boston Weekly News-Letter*, 24 April 1741. Knox, *Historical journal* (Doughty). *N. S. Archives, I*; *II*; *III*; *IV*. PRO, *CSP, Col., 1722–23, 1731, 1732, 1734–35, 1735–36*; *JTP, 1714/15–1718*. *The Fulham papers in the Lambeth palace library*, ed. W. W. Manross (Oxford, Eng., 1965), 6. Calnek, *History of Annapolis* (Savary). Murdoch, *History of Nova-Scotia*. Savary, *Supplement to history of Annapolis*. C. J. d'Entremont and H.-J. Hébert, "Parkman's diary and the Acadian exiles in Massachusetts," *French Canadian and Acadian Geneal. Rev.* (Quebec), I (1968), 251, 255–63. "Historical Nova Scotia families," in *Morning Herald* (Halifax), 5 Sept. 1889, and in *Morning Chronicle* (Halifax), 6 Sept. 1889.

WOLFE, JAMES, army officer, commander of the British expedition that took Quebec in 1759; b. 2 Jan. 1727 (N.S.) at Westerham, England; d. 13 Sept. 1759 of wounds received in the battle of the Plains of Abraham. He was the son of Lieutenant-General Edward Wolfe, a respectable but not particularly distinguished officer, and Henrietta Thompson.

James Wolfe was educated in schools at Westerham and at Greenwich, to which the family moved in 1738; in 1740 he was prevented by illness from taking part as a volunteer in the expedition against Cartagena (Colombia), in which his father was a staff officer; and in 1741 he received his first military appointment, as second lieutenant in the 1st Regiment of Marines, of which Edward Wolfe was colonel. He never actually served with the marines, however, and in 1742 exchanged into the 12th Foot as an ensign and went with that regiment to Belgium. The following year, at the age of 16, he underwent his baptism of fire in Bavaria at the battle of Dettingen, and thereafter was promoted lieutenant. In 1744 he was appointed captain in the 4th Foot and in 1745 he returned to England with the army withdrawn to deal with Prince Charles Edward's invasion. In January 1746 he was present at the British defeat at Falkirk, Scotland. He was shortly afterwards made aide-de-camp to Lieutenant-General Henry Hawley. In this capacity he took part in the battle of Culloden (16 April 1746), and may or may not have refused to obey an order from William Augustus, Duke of Cumberland, to shoot a wounded Highlander. In January 1747 he

returned to the continent, where the 4th Foot was serving, and on 2 July was wounded in the battle of Laffeldt (Belgium). Following a period on leave in England he was sent back to the Low Countries as a brigade major. When in 1748 the War of the Austrian Succession ended, he was appointed major in the 20th Foot, then stationed in Scotland. He became acting lieutenant-colonel and in practice commander of the regiment as a result of Edward Cornwallis*' appointment to the governorship of Nova Scotia. While stationed at Glasgow Wolfe studied Latin and mathematics. Most of the next few years he spent in Scotland, the regiment being part of the time engaged in road-building. He was confirmed as lieutenant-colonel in 1750. In 1752 he visited Ireland and that autumn went to Paris, where he stayed six months. Thereafter he rejoined the 20th Foot in Scotland and subsequently moved with it to the south of England.

Wolfe's first active service in the Seven Years' War was as quartermaster-general to the expedition of 1757 against Rochefort on the French Biscay coast. This was a fiasco, nothing effective being even attempted. Wolfe's own part in the affair is not so clear as his biographers indicate; but he seems to have made a reconnaissance and suggested an offensive plan. His evidence before the subsequent inquiry into the conduct of his friend Sir John Mordaunt, the military commander, was naturally restrained; privately he wrote scathingly of the failure to make an attack. His own reputation seems to have profited rather than suffered; immediately after the failure the 2nd battalion of the 20th Foot was converted into a new regiment, the 67th, and he was appointed its colonel. This was the highest substantive rank he was to achieve.

In January 1758 came further evidence that Wolfe was regarded as a particularly valuable soldier. A comparatively junior officer, Colonel Jeffery Amherst*, was promoted major-general and placed in command of an expedition to proceed against Louisbourg, Île Royale (Cape Breton Island). Wolfe was given local rank as "Brigadier in America" and made one of Amherst's three brigade commanders, the others being Charles LAWRENCE, the governor of Nova Scotia, and Edward WHITMORE, who was also already in the American theatre. In February he embarked in Admiral Edward BOSCAWEN's flagship *Princess Amelia*, which reached Halifax only on 9 May. Amherst had not yet arrived. While the force waited for him, training exercises were carried out, and Boscawen and the brigadiers made plans for the landing at Louisbourg. On 28 May the expedition sailed from Halifax without the military commander, but luckily met him just outside the harbour. The fleet and transports anchored in Gabarus Bay, close to Louisbourg, on 2 and 3 June. On the evening of the 2nd, Amherst with Lawrence and Wolfe "reconnoitred the shore as near as we could." Amherst, dissenting from the plan made before his arrival, which provided for landings east of Louisbourg, had decided instead to land to the west of it. According to the author of the anonymous "Journal of the expedition against Louisburg" in Robert Monckton*'s papers – Monckton himself was not present – Wolfe "opposed this Attack in Council"; he nevertheless played a leading part in executing it.

Bad weather postponed the landing until 8 June. Wolfe, with the grenadier companies of the army, the improvised light infantry battalion commanded by Major George SCOTT, the ranger companies, and Fraser's Highlanders, was to make the genuine attack on the left in the Anse de la Cormorandière (Kennington Cove) while Lawrence's brigade made one feint farther east at Pointe Platte (Simon Point) and Whitmore's another, still closer to the town, at White Point. The French had in fact entrenched themselves above the chosen beach, and as soon as the boats came close they opened heavy musketry and artillery fire upon them. Wolfe is said to have signalled the boats to sheer off. A few of them carrying the light infantry nevertheless reached the shore and landed their men in a rocky area just east of the beach, and in spite of the rocks and the surf which damaged or wrecked many boats they were quickly reinforced, Wolfe himself setting a bold example. Seized with panic, the French, led by Jean MASCLE de Saint-Julhien, abandoned their position, and Lawrence's and Whitmore's brigades, moving in behind Wolfe's, landed in their turn. The British force thus got ashore with relatively little loss and was ready to begin siege operations, though these were delayed by continuing bad weather which prevented landing guns and stores.

During the weeks of the siege Wolfe did not command a brigade in the usual sense. The force under him was an *ad hoc* grouping of élite troops, especially light infantry and grenadiers; Amherst at first used this force for a detached task, while Whitmore and Lawrence (who are scarcely mentioned in Amherst's journal or other contemporary accounts) held the line at large. On 12 June Amherst found that the French had evacuated and destroyed the Grand or Royal battery on the north side of the harbour, and the Lighthouse battery on the east side of the entrance. He ordered Wolfe with (according to one version) 1,200 men of the line, four companies of grenadiers, three

ranger companies, and some light infantry to move round the harbour to the Lighthouse Point, with a view to setting up batteries there to silence the Island battery in the harbour mouth and destroy the enemy ships in the harbour; the necessary guns were sent by sea. Wolfe's batteries opened fire against the Island battery and the ships on the night of 19 June, and had silenced the battery by the evening of the 25th. Amherst then instructed Wolfe to come back around the harbour with his artillery (which was replaced in the Lighthouse batteries by naval guns) and to "try to destroy the shipping, and to advance towards the west-gate." From this time Wolfe may be said to have commanded the left or northernmost attack against the fortress. A reference in the contemporaneously published version of Amherst's journal for 3 July to Wolfe "making an advanced work on the right" has misled various writers; Amherst's personal version edited by J. C. Webster* indicates that this was actually done by the engineer Major Patrick Mackellar*. By this time Wolfe's new batteries were firing actively at the ships, and on 6 July the frigate *Aréthuse*, commanded by Jean Vauquelin*, which had greatly impeded the besiegers' progress with her own fire, was forced to leave her position off the lagoon called the Barachois. Wolfe continued to push his batteries closer to the town defences and increasing damage was done to them as well as to the vessels. On 21 July one of his shot set a French ship on fire; the fire spread to two others and all three were destroyed. In the early morning of the 26th a British naval cutting-out force entered the harbour and captured the two remaining French ships. Plans for moving the British ships into the harbour and undertaking a joint assault by army and navy were forestalled when on the same day Governor Drucour [BOSCHENRY] surrendered. Wolfe had undoubtedly shown himself throughout the siege to be an unusually efficient and active officer, and his merits were forcibly brought to the attention of the British government and people by the prompt publication of Amherst's journal and other accounts.

Admiral Boscawen decided, probably wisely, that it was too late in the season to push on the campaign to Quebec. Wolfe had favoured this bold measure, and on 8 August, in a letter to Amherst that seems to verge on the insolent, he urged that in its place "we might make an offensive and a destructive war in the Bay of Fundy and in the Gulf of St. Lawrence. I beg pardon for this freedom, but I cannot look coolly upon the bloody inroads of those hell-hounds the Canadians; and if nothing further is to be done, I must

Wolfe

desire leave to quit the army." Perhaps as a result of this suggestion, Monckton (who had sat out the siege of Louisbourg at Halifax) was sent to destroy the French settlements in the Saint John valley; Lieutenant-Colonel Lord ROLLO to take possession of Île Saint-Jean (Prince Edward Island); and Wolfe, with three battalions convoyed by a naval squadron of nine sail under Sir Charles Hardy, to lay waste the settlements and fishery in the Gulf of St Lawrence. Leaving Louisbourg on 29 August, the squadron anchored off Grande-Grève in Gaspé Bay on 4 September. The affair is described in some detail in the journal of Captain Thomas Bell*, who was evidently already acting as an aide-de-camp to Wolfe and who held this appointment in the Quebec campaign the following year. Most inhabitants of the region had fled into the woods, but some were taken prisoner and attempts were made to use them to negotiate with the fugitives. A detachment in boats was sent to destroy the settlements along the Gulf shore to the southwest and the Baie des Chaleurs. Another made a difficult march along the shore of the St Lawrence to do the same at Mont-Louis. Still another force under Colonel James Murray* was sent to lay waste the settlements on the Miramichi River. Bell claims that much unnecessary suffering was inflicted on the inhabitants of these outlying communities as the result of the navy's extreme anxiety to get out of those waters as quickly as possible, and the seamen's "accustomed rage for plundering." But even at Gaspé, where Wolfe himself was present, "the General gave orders for every thing being burnt," and this was done on 10 and 11 September. At the Miramichi Murray "destroy'd all the Houses & c. & a good Stone Church." Large numbers of "shaloupes" and quantities of supplies of various sorts were burned. Wolfe's force re-embarked on 25 and 26 September and arrived at Louisbourg on the 30th. On that day Wolfe reported to Amherst that his task had been accomplished, writing in terms that might suggest that he had forgotten that he had proposed it: "We have done a great deal of mischief, – spread the terror of His Majesty's arms through the whole gulf; but have added nothing to the reputation of them."

Bell recorded that Wolfe "as soon as he found what a small Game he had to play wanted Sir C. Hardy to go to Quebeck, if not so high as that, to go some way up in order to destroy their Settlements." Hardy, however, had made difficulties. Bell added to his text at a later time the comment, "Had Sir Charles Hardy pursued Gen. Wolfe's advice, Quebeck must certainly have fallen." In fact, Wolfe's idea seems to have been extremely rash, and it is more than doubtful whether the very small force at his disposal could have taken Quebec.

Wolfe at once went back to England; he had understood his return to be the intention of the British army's commander-in-chief, Lord Ligonier, and the state of his health "and other circumstances" made him desire to comply. On arriving in London, however, he found that orders had been sent for him to remain in America. In a letter to William Pitt dated 22 Nov. 1758 he made his apologies and wrote further, "I take the freedom to acquaint you that I have no objection to serving in America, and particularly in the river St. Lawrence, if any operations are carried on there." Whether the mention of the St Lawrence was his own idea, or whether some suggestion had already been made to him on the subject, remains uncertain. A letter he wrote to Amherst (who had now been appointed commander-in-chief in America) on 29 December describes, not too explicitly, the process by which his own share in the next year's campaign was decided. In his first interview with Ligonier, on a date not given, he learned that the plan was to attack on two lines, one by Lake George (Lac Saint-Sacrement), the other by the St Lawrence against Quebec. Wolfe says, "I express'd my desire to go up the River, but to be excused from taking the chief direction of such a weighty enterprise." He then went to Bath, but "in about a week" was called back to London to attend a meeting of "some of the principal Officers of State." During his absence, he says, "Mr. Pitt had named me to the King for the command in the River." It seems quite likely that Ligonier had recommended him. A commission dated 12 Jan. 1759 appointed Wolfe major-general and commander-in-chief of the land forces for the expedition against Quebec. The king's secret instructions dated 5 February directed him at the conclusion of the campaign to put himself "as Brigadier General in North America" under Amherst's command.

Wolfe wrote to his uncle, Major Walter Wolfe, "I am to act a greater part in this business than I wished or desired. The backwardness of some of the older officers has in some measure forced the Government to come down so low." Service in America was not popular. If a junior officer was to get the command, the golden opinions won by Wolfe at Louisbourg made him an obvious choice. In appointing him, however, Pitt was making a considerable gamble; for the young general had never attempted to plan and conduct an independent campaign. And although at Quebec he would technically be under Amherst, he would in fact be an independent commander and Amherst would be unable to assist or advise him. He was given an excellent army, whose core consisted of ten battalions of British regular infantry, all already serving in America. They were below establishment, and Wolfe's force amounted overall to only some 8,500 instead of the 12,000 for which Pitt had planned, but the quality was high. Wolfe moreover was apparently allowed to a large extent to choose his own officers, a point he had tried to insist upon in his dealings with Ligonier. From Louisbourg he had written, "If his Majesty had thought proper to let Carleton come with us as engineer and Delaune and 2 or 3 more for the light Foot, it would have cut the matter much shorter." In 1759 George II was prevailed upon to allow Guy Carleton* to accompany him as deputy quartermaster-general, and Captain William DeLaune of Wolfe's 67th Foot was also in his army. In one important appointment, nevertheless, Wolfe did not get his way. The original intention was that his three brigadiers should be Monckton, Murray, and Ralph Burton, a selection with which he appears to have been happy. At a late stage, however, Burton, a special friend of Wolfe's, was put aside in favour of the Hon. George Townshend*, the eldest son of the 3rd Viscount Townshend. The circumstances remain obscure, but the episode contained the seeds of later trouble. The naval commander was Vice-Admiral Charles Saunders*, an able, self-effacing officer, whose second-in-command was Rear-Admiral Philip Durell (for whom Wolfe seems to have acquired a dislike at Louisbourg), the third naval officer being Rear-Admiral Charles Holmes. The naval force numbered 49 sail, 22 being ships of 50 guns or more.

At the time when Wolfe undertook this great enterprise he was in poor health. He had written in December 1758, "I am in a very bad condition, both with the gravel & Rheumatism, but I had much rather die than decline any kind of service that offers." This combination of disorders, almost certain to render a person irritable and difficult, doubtless contributed to the deterioration of Wolfe's relations with his subordinates as the campaign proceeded. Despite ill health, however, he had been paying his addresses to Katherine Lowther, the daughter of Robert Lowther and afterwards Duchess of Bolton. No letters that passed between them have survived, and it seems uncertain whether there was a formal engagement; but the reference to the lady in Wolfe's will, and one of her own letters after his death, suggest that they intended to marry.

Wolfe sailed from Portsmouth in mid February 1759 in Saunders' flagship *Neptune*. They had a slow passage, and when they arrived off Louisbourg, their planned destination, ice prevented the fleet from entering. They sailed on to Halifax, where they arrived on 30 April. Here, to Wolfe's indignation, they found Durell's squadron still at anchor, though he had been ordered to enter the St Lawrence as early as possible to prevent supplies or reinforcements reaching Quebec. The ice had kept him from acting, but had not kept some 20 vessels from France, almost all supply ships, from getting up the St Lawrence. Without the supplies thus obtained the French would probably not have been able to hold out through the summer. Durell finally sailed from Halifax on 5 May. The army, having been concentrated at Louisbourg, sailed thence for Quebec on 4 June. Durell's force pushed rapidly up the St Lawrence, neither it nor the main body coming on in the rear being seriously delayed by the difficulties of the channel which had been widely feared. Wolfe himself, full of eagerness, went forward as fast as the navy could take him; and on 27 June he landed on the south shore of the Île d'Orléans with the main body of his army and proceeded to reconnoitre the French positions from the west point of the island.

Although there is no evidence that Wolfe had studied Sir William Phips*' campaign of 1690, his intention had evidently been to follow much the same plan used by Phips: to land and encamp on the north shore of the St Lawrence near Beauport, east of Quebec, cross the Saint-Charles River, and attack the city from its weak land side. He also proposed to establish posts on the south side of the St Lawrence opposite Quebec, and suggested in addition that it might be possible to "steal a detachment," land it some miles above the town, and entrench there. His first reconnaissance showed him that the idea of landing on the Beauport shore was impracticable; the French had anticipated him. Montcalm, the French commander, had occupied and fortified that area, and the main French force was encamped there. The first of many tactical reassessments was thus forced upon Wolfe.

Montcalm's army was, in the beginning, nearly twice as large as Wolfe's but in quality it was far inferior, being in great part composed of untrained militia. Wolfe's object throughout was to bring the French to action in the open, and he never had any doubt of the result if he succeeded in doing so. The victory won on the Plains of Abraham is evidence of the soundness of his calculations. The nature of his strategic problem is nowhere better stated than in Wolfe's last letter to his mother (31 Aug. 1759): "My antagonist has

Wolfe

wisely shut himself up in inaccessible entrenchments, so that I cant get at him without spilling a torrent of blood, and that perhaps to little purpose. The Marquiss de Montcalm is at the head of a great number of bad soldiers, and I am at the head of a small number of good ones, that wish for nothing so much as to fight him – but the wary old fellow avoids an action doubtful of the behaviour of his army. People must be of the profession to understand the disadvantages and difficulties we labour under arising from the uncommon natural strength of the country.'' For success Montcalm had only to hold his position through the short campaigning season until the approach of winter would drive the British fleet out of the river. The soundness of his cautious tactics is attested by the frustration which they caused Wolfe. Nevertheless, there was in the French situation an element of weakness that ultimately proved fatal. The orders from the court at Versailles had emphasized the importance of holding at least part of the colony even if Quebec were lost. This meant keeping the army in being, and it could not exist without food. Accordingly the decision had been taken not to store the available supplies in the city; the supply ships that had arrived from France were taken far up the St Lawrence to Batiscan, and the city and the army were provisioned by regular boat or cart convoys from there. Wolfe had only to cut this essential line of communication above Quebec to force Montcalm to come out of his defences and fight to reopen it. It is not to the credit of the British general that he took so long to discover this situation and exploit it.

For two months, while the summer ran away, Wolfe struggled with the problem of bringing the French to battle; his health plagued him (''Sad attack of dysentery,'' he notes on 4 July) and his relations with his senior subordinates got worse and worse. During July there was increasing tension with Townshend; and in the course of the campaign Murray acquired a hatred for Wolfe which he continued to nourish long after the object of it was dead. About Monckton, the second in command, we know less. In August Wolfe was writing him apologizing for what Monckton evidently considered a slight. Monckton's letters to Wolfe seem to have perished. But it is interesting that Monckton was the only one of the three brigadiers who allowed himself to be included in Benjamin West's famous (and highly inaccurate) painting *The death of Wolfe* (1771); and the Monckton family commissioned West to paint a copy of it. These incidents suggest that Monckton was at least less hostile to Wolfe than the other brigadiers. There was trouble also with

Guy Carleton, for whom Wolfe had had particular regard; on 31 July Bell, the general's aide-de-camp, wrote in his diary, ''Colonel Carlton's abominable behaviour to ye General.'' What Carleton had done is unknown.

The progress of Wolfe's planning cannot be described in detail. What seems evident is that he had great difficulty in making up his mind, and that he frequently changed it. On 29 and 30 June he occupied Pointe-Lévy (Lauzon) and on 2 July ordered the construction of batteries opposite Quebec. Thereafter he considered landing a detachment above the city while also putting a brigade ashore just east of the Montmorency River, close to the left flank of the French fortified position, to draw the enemy's attention in that direction. This scheme he shortly abandoned, and on 10 July the troops intended for the upper landing joined the brigade at Montmorency, where the main body of the army was now assembled. On the night of 12 July the guns on the south shore opened fire on Quebec. In the middle of the month Wolfe was actively considering an attack on the Beauport lines; but on the night of the 18th several British vessels got past the city into the upper river, and his attention was diverted to that sector. The 20th was a day of great activity, Wolfe contemplating an attack that night in the area of Saint-Michel, near Sillery. He cancelled it in the afternoon, probably because of visible French reactions to the movement of the ships. Within a few days he was again planning action on the Beauport side. On 31 July, for the first time, he attempted a major attack, just west of the Montmorency. His scheme – which all the brigadiers seem to have disliked – was to seize a small redoubt near the shore in the hope that Montcalm would come out of his entrenchments and attack in the open to recover it. As soon as the operation began it became evident that the redoubt was closer to the entrenchments than Wolfe had thought; it would not be tenable under their fire. On the spot he changed his plan to a frontal assault on the lofty entrenchments. This broke down in a bloody reverse, partly perhaps because the grenadiers who led the attack got out of hand, partly because a tremendous thunderstorm burst at the critical moment, and partly because Wolfe had attacked the French under the only circumstances in which the Canadian militia were formidable. He wisely called off the enterprise after losing over 200 men killed. Characteristically, he had exposed himself recklessly to the French fire, and he was with the rearguard of Murray's and Townshend's brigades as they retired to their camp east of the Montmorency just before the tide made the ford impassable.

The defeat on 31 July put an end for the moment to Wolfe's feverish planning activity. He sent Murray up the river with a detachment to get at the French ships if possible and to open communications with Amherst; Murray did not succeed in either object, but did a certain amount of damage and compelled Montcalm to dispatch a force under Colonel Bougainville* to watch the upper river. Wolfe also began to apply a policy of terror against the outlying parishes, in part it appears in reprisal for attacks on British detachments, in part with a view to bringing pressure on Montcalm "to try the Event of a Battle to prevent the Ravage." Early in September a large party under Major George Scott (who had had a similar command at Louisbourg), including all six of the American ranger companies in the army, was sent to lay waste the south shore from Kamouraska to Pointe-Lévy. Scott later reported that he had burned 998 "good buildings." Before the campaign was over the communities on both shores of the river below Quebec, and on the south shore for some distance above, had been largely destroyed, only churches being spared. Quebec itself had been laid in ruins by the bombardment from the Lévis heights. This policy of devastation had long been in Wolfe's mind. He had written to Amherst during his voyage in the *Neptune*, "If ... we find, that Quebec is not likely to fall into our hands (persevering however to the last moment), I propose to set the Town on fire with Shells, to destroy the Harvest, Houses, and Cattle, both above and below, to send off as many Canadians as possible to Europe, and to leave famine and desolation behind me; belle resolution, and tres chrétienne! but we must teach these scoundrels to make war in a more gentlemanlike manner." If this letter is to be taken literally, Wolfe by September, at least, was seriously contemplating the likelihood that he was not going to take Quebec.

About 19 August Wolfe became so ill that he was forced to take to his bed in his quarters in Montmorency. He was not able to resume his usual activities until nearly the end of the month. On or about 27 August (the document is not dated) he wrote a famous letter to the three brigadiers, asking them in the light of his indisposition to "consult together" and to "consider of the best method of attacking the Enemy." He noted the absence of provisions in Quebec but did not mention the desirability of severing the French supply line. He thought that the army rather than the city should be attacked, and he suggested three possible methods. All were variants of the attack on the Beauport lines which had already failed. One proposed a combination of a frontal attack with a turning movement up the Montmorency, intended to strike the Beauport entrenchments in the rear; a ranger captain and a French deserter had reconnoitred the route. Wolfe's admirers have put strained interpretations upon these projects, suggesting that the general did not really mean them seriously; but there is no evidence whatever that they were not the best plans that Wolfe (who, it must be remembered, was a sick man) was able to produce. The three brigadiers wrote an able and polite reply. They thought the chances of success in an attack on the Beauport side slight, and pointed out that even if it were successful Montcalm would still be able to withdraw across the Saint-Charles and provision Quebec from the ships and magazines above. "We therefore are of Opinion that the most probable method of striking an effectual blow, is to bring the Troops [from Montmorency] to the South Shore, and to direct the Operations above the Town: When we establish ourselves on the North Shore, the French General must fight us on our own Terms; We shall be betwixt him and his provisions, and betwixt him and their Army opposing General Amherst." This paper was supported by a detailed plan for the proposed movements. The brigadiers are known to have had prolonged consultations with Admiral Saunders while drafting these memoranda.

For the first time, it appears, the basic strategic factors had now been stated on paper. The brigadiers' logic was really unanswerable, and Wolfe accepted it. Orders were given for the evacuation of the Montmorency camp. The British army, except for a small force on Île d'Orléans, was concentrated on the south shore, and on 5 and 6 September the main body embarked in the British ships above the town. It apparently would have landed on 9 September in the area on the north shore favoured by the brigadiers, between Saint-Augustin (now Saint-Augustin-de-Québec) and Pointe-aux-Trembles (Neuville), if the weather had not broken; heavy rain caused the operation to be cancelled. And on the 8th or the 9th, or perhaps both, Wolfe "went a reconoitering down the River." For reasons that are still obscure – the decision may well have been based simply on his own observations – he decided to abandon the plan for a descent in the Pointe-aux-Trembles area (which had many advantages, including distance from the main French force and a low and accessible shore). He adopted a far riskier plan, a landing much nearer the town, at the Anse au Foulon (later also called Wolfe's Cove) where a track led up the cliffs. For the oft-repeated story that this track had been pointed out by a French traitor no evidence has ever been adduced.

Wolfe

Although he took Monckton and Townshend with him on another reconnaissance on the 10th, he evidently did not take them fully into his confidence, and on the 12th there was a rather sharp exchange of notes between him and the three brigadiers, in which they complained of being insufficiently informed. It is recorded that after an interview with Monckton that day "Mr. Wolfe said to his own family [his personal staff] that the Brigadiers had brought him up the River and now flinch'd: He did not hesitate to say that two of them were Cowards and one a Villain."

That night the decisive operation was launched, the boats carrying the first "flight" of British troops dropping down with the tide from the ships off Cap-Rouge. Everything depended on achieving surprise, for in the face of serious opposition a landing at the Foulon would be quite impossible. But surprise was achieved. Montcalm's attention was fixed on the Beauport shore, where the boats from the British ships lying in the Quebec Basin staged an effective feint. Bougainville, who was responsible for the whole area above Quebec, was at Cap-Rouge and apparently did not realize what was going on until too late. The French were expecting a provision convoy (though it had in fact been cancelled) and were too easily deceived into believing that the British boats were their own. Wolfe's intention had apparently been to have a picked detachment of men under Captain DeLaune rush the path leading up the cliff; but the tide carried the boats beyond the point planned for the landing, and Lieutenant-Colonel William Howe, commanding Wolfe's provisional light infantry battalion, led several companies of his unit straight up the cliff (an action which seems to have been improvised). They dislodged Louis Du Pont* Duchambon de Vergor's party guarding the path, which offered only slight opposition. This was about four in the morning of 13 September. Wolfe, who had lately written several dispatches and letters reflecting a mood of black pessimism, seems to have found it hard to believe in his own good luck; there is evidence that he sent his adjutant-general, Major Isaac Barré, to stop the landing of the second flight of troops until he was sure that the French were actually not present in strength. Barré, finding the troops ready to land, refrained from delivering the order. Cooperation between the army and navy was admirable throughout the affair, which deserves to be regarded as a classic amphibious operation.

From the time of the landing Wolfe made no mistakes. He chose his ground, formed his battle-line, and confidently awaited the French attack which was certain to come. The mistakes on the Plains of Abraham were Montcalm's. The French general had to attack to open his line of communications; but he should have waited for Bougainville, who was belatedly moving towards the scene of action. Instead he launched his mixed force of Canadians and Frenchmen against Wolfe's solid line of regulars about ten in the morning. His senior artillery officer, Captain Fiacre-François Potot* de Montbeillard, records him as saying, "If we give him [the enemy] time to establish himself, we shall never be able to attack him with the sort of troops we have." The British let the French come close and then with a succession of volleys blew them into ruin and retreat. Montcalm himself was mortally wounded.

Wolfe had again exposed himself, perhaps actually courting death. He first suffered a wound in the hand or wrist, which he disregarded; then, as the British line began to move forward to pursue the French, the general, leading the right, was struck again in the body, many accounts say by two bullets. This injury was fatal, and he lived only a short time. The log of HMS *Lowestoft* records that his body was brought on board at 11 A.M. Though the French army was routed, it was not destroyed. Had Wolfe lived, the victory might have been more complete. As it was, there was a period of uncertainty before Townshend took command (Monckton having been wounded), and most of the French force got away across the Saint-Charles to the Beauport camp. That night it marched around the British and withdrew towards Montreal leaving Quebec to surrender on 18 September. The final conquest of Canada required another year's campaign. Wolfe's body was taken to England accompanied by Captains Bell and DeLaune. He was buried in the family vault at Greenwich alongside his father, who had died in March 1759.

James Wolfe was an excellent regimental officer, a splendidly brave fighting soldier, and so far as one can judge from his short career a competent battlefield commander. He has had many admirers and a great historical reputation. That reputation is not supported, however, by his performance before Quebec, the only occasion when he conducted a campaign as commander-in-chief. He was an ineffective planner, vacillating and uncertain; the campaign is a story of plans made only to be cast aside. He could not get on with his senior subordinates, and the fact that his diary is full of abuse of the navy suggests that he was not a good cooperator. His unpleasant policy of terror and devastation did little to advance his campaign. The one attack undertaken on Wolfe's own motion (that at Montmorency on 31 July) was a costly failure. The final plan which succeeded was basically the brigadiers'; Wolfe's contribution, the actual place of landing, merely added an element of unnecessary risk to the conception and placed the whole operation at the mercy of luck. As it turned out, his luck was extraordinarily good; and this, combined with the efficiency of the British army and navy and the marked inefficiency of the French, produced a famous victory which has remained identified with the name of Wolfe.

C. P. STACEY

[The happenings at Quebec in 1759 were, one might say without exaggeration, stranger than fiction. The final episode – the descent of the dark river, the climb up the cliff, the deaths of the two opposing leaders – had an irresistible appeal to the popular imagination. The result was that from the very beginning the history of the campaign was written in romantic terms, particularly the treatment of the two central figures, who have both been depicted as rather larger than life. Wolfe and Montcalm, neither of whom was really better than a second-rate commander, were raised to the level of legend. There are a good many biographies of Wolfe, all of them in varying degrees works of uncritical laudation. Not all will be mentioned here. The earliest full-length treatment was Robert Wright, *The life of Major-General James Wolfe* . . . (London, 1864). It is still useful, and has served later biographers well. The most valuable of the biographies is Beckles Willson, *The life and letters of James Wolfe* . . . (London, 1909), simply for the documents it contains, even though their text is not always reliable. Of the books called forth by the bicentenary in 1959, Robin Reilly, *The rest to fortune: the life of Major-General James Wolfe* (London, 1960), uses a wider range of sources than some others, including Wolfe's letters to Monckton which were long neglected, but the interpretation is the usual one. *Wolfe: portraiture & genealogy* (Westerham, Eng., 1959) contains J. F. Kerslake, "The likeness of Wolfe," A. R. Wagner, "The genealogy of James Wolfe," and W. W. Shaw-Zambra, "James Wolfe: a chronology." A more critical assessment than the biographers' was that of J. W. Fortescue, who wrote in his *History of the British army* (13v., London, New York, 1899–1930), II, "a brilliant success, however fortunate, is rightly held to cover all errors." E. R. Adair's important and striking paper, "The military reputation of Major-General James Wolfe," CHA *Report, 1936*, 7–31, is somewhat overdone but is damaging to Wolfe. Its interpretation is in curious contrast with that of a book by Professor Adair's late McGill colleague, W. T. Waugh, *James Wolfe, man and soldier* (Montreal, 1928). The writings of W.C.H. Wood, amateur soldier and amateur historian, have had more influence than they deserve; see particularly *The fight for Canada* ("definitive ed.," London, 1905). Parkman, *Montcalm and Wolfe*, still has much value, though Parkman takes liberties with documents and is sometimes over-romantic. Stacey, *Quebec, 1759*, is an attempt at producing a version without preconceptions, based on the contemporary

documents; see also the same author's "Generals and generalship before Quebec, 1759–1760," CHA *Report, 1959*, 1–15. J. M. Hitsman with C. C. J. Bond, "The assault landing at Louisbourg, 1758," *CHR*, XXXV (1954), 314–30, is very useful. A monumental Canadian contribution is Doughty and Parmelee, *Siege of Quebec*. It is partly history, partly documentary collection, and is much more important in the latter than in the former respect; even some of the documents, however, are incomplete. *Correspondence of William Pitt* (Kimball) contains many fundamental documents in accurate texts; enclosures, often more important than the covering letters, are not included. Doughty's edition of Knox, *Historical journal*, is valuable, as is another Champlain Society publication, *Logs of the conquest* (Wood).

Important printed sources for the siege of Louisbourg are the "Journal of the expedition against Louisburg," *Northcliffe coll.*; Jeffery Amherst, *Journal* (Webster); and the contemporary published versions of the Amherst journal (e.g., *Gentleman's Magazine*, 1758, pp.384–89). The contemporary plan of the siege by Samuel Holland, reproduced in [William Amherst], *Journal of William Amherst in America, 1758–1760*, ed. J. C. Webster (Frome and London, Eng., 1927) is enlightening.

Only a selection of manuscript sources can be listed here. Wolfe's personal journal of the Quebec campaign came to light only in 1910. Three versions of it are known; all are in PAC as originals or photocopies. One is a transcript by Captain Thomas Bell, included in his own series of journals (PAC, MG 18, M3, 24). Unfortunately Wolfe destroyed his journal for the period after 16 Aug. 1759. The Bell journal is one of the items in the enormously valuable Northcliffe coll. (PAC, MG 18, M). Others include large groups of Townshend and Monckton papers; among the latter are many letters by Wolfe which are not in Willson. Also in the collection are various important miscellaneous items, including George II's instructions to Wolfe for the Quebec expedition. There are letters from Wolfe in PRO, WO 34/46b, pt.II. Wolfe's dispatches from Quebec are in PRO, CO 5/51. Various important documents are in PRO 30/8, particularly bundles 33, 49, 50, and 98, vol.7.

A significant anonymous narrative of the events at Quebec which internal evidence suggests may have been written by one of Wolfe's aides-de-camp is in Public Record Office of Northern Ireland (Belfast), D.162/77. (*See* C. P. Stacey, "Quebec, 1759: some new documents," *CHR*, XLVII (1966), 344–55, which also discusses some other papers on the campaign that have come to light in recent years.) A source of great value for the whole Quebec campaign is the large map signed by Major Patrick Mackellar, "Plan of the town of Quebec the capital of Canada . . . showing the principal encampments and works of the British army commanded by Major General Wolfe and those of the French army commanded by Lieut. General the Marquis of Montcalm . . .," PAC, National Map coll. In general, it may be said that all the most vital known records of Wolfe's Canadian campaigns are available in the PAC either as originals or as copies.

In the interest of avoiding duplication, sources in

Woodbee

French are omitted from this bibliographical note. They will be found listed in the note in the present volume appended to the biography of the Marquis de Montcalm.

A good deal has been written on the portraiture of Wolfe. See particularly the article by Kerslake, above; J. C. Webster, *Wolfe and the artists* . . . (Toronto, 1930); and A. E. Wolfe-Aylward, *The pictorial life of Wolfe* (Plymouth, Eng., n.d.). These writers devote much attention to posthumous pictures and the few which may or may not have been painted from life, including that attributed to Joseph Highmore which the PAC acquired in 1932. It is surprising that they make so little of the most striking and most authentic portrait in existence, the watercolour signed by George Townshend which, though unfortunately not dated, was presumably painted during the 1759 campaign. It is in the McCord Museum (Montreal) and has frequently been reproduced. On the most famous picture concerning Wolfe, see C. P. Stacey, "Benjamin West and 'The death of Wolfe'," National Gallery of Canada *Bull.* (Ottawa), IV (1966), 1–5. Statues of Wolfe have been erected in England at Westerham and in Greenwich Park. C.P.S.]

WOODBEE (Woudby). *See* WAPPISIS

Y

YVON, YVES PHLEM, *dit. See* **Phlem**

Appendix

GAULTIER (Gautier, Gauthier, or **Gaulthier,** but he signed Gaultier), **JEAN-FRANÇOIS,** physician, naturalist; b. 6 Oct. 1708 at La Croix-Avranchin (dept. of Manche, France), son of René Gaultier and Françoise Colin; d. 10 July 1756 in Quebec. He has sometimes been confused with a contemporary of the same name who lived in Acadia and with a French botanist of the second half of the 18th century.

Little is known about Jean-François Gaultier's childhood and education. Canon Pierre Hazeur* de L'Orme met him in Paris in 1741, and from a letter of 11 May 1741 we know that Gaultier had already studied medicine and had been practising in Paris for six or seven years. After Michel Sarrazin*'s death in 1734 the office of king's physician was vacant for seven years; it was sought by Timothy SULLIVAN and by Hubert-Joseph de LA CROIX. But one of Sarrazin's sons, Joseph-Michel, was a medical student in Paris, and the position was kept open in the expectation of his receiving his degree. He died, however, in 1739. Encouraged by Canon Hazeur and with a recommendation from Henri-Louis Duhamel Du Monceau (1700–82), Gaultier asked for and obtained the position in 1741. He would have Sarrazin's books at his disposal, wrote Hazeur. But the inventory of Mme Sarrazin's property at her death in 1743 shows that she still owned 175 volumes of scientific works.

Gaultier was already favourably known in 1741 to the Jussieus, members of the Académie Royale des Sciences with whom he associated and who held him in high esteem. Antoine de Jussieu (1686–1758) was appointed in 1709 to the chair in botany that had been vacant since the death of Joseph Pitton de Tournefort (1656–1708), the creator of the Genus. Bernard de Jussieu (1699–1777) succeeded Sébastien Vaillant (1669–1722) as administrator of the Jardin du Roi. About 1707 Vaillant had compiled a text of nearly 200 pages, based upon Sarrazin's collections and notes, entitled "Histoire des plantes de Canada," a sort of introductory study of a flora. Thanks to Bernard de Jussieu's kindness no doubt, Gaultier took a copy of this text with him to Quebec, and it was one of his main tools. This manuscript, with marginal notes by Gaultier, has been preserved and is known today as the "Saint-Hyacinthe manuscript."

Gaultier did not go to Canada immediately upon his appointment; he continued studying the treatment of illnesses in some Parisian hospitals for another year. Not until April 1742 did Maurepas, the minister of Marine, advise Governor Charles de BEAUHARNOIS that Gaultier would sail on the *Rubis*. The salary for the position amounted to 800 *livres* per year, at a time when a workman's wages scarcely exceeded one *franc* a day (the *livre* being equivalent to the *franc*). This amount was increased by special gratuities in 1752 and 1753 and by a fur-trading concession in 1749. In addition to his official position Gaultier was the regular physician of the Hôtel-Dieu and the seminary of Quebec.

Upon his arrival in Quebec Gaultier enrolled in the law courses being given by the attorney general, Louis-Guillaume VERRIER, and followed them assiduously, probably with a view to a request he was to make in 1743 to be appointed to the Conseil Supérieur. After a favourable recommendation by Attorney General Verrier and Governor Beauharnois, he was appointed to the council in March 1744 and joined it in October of that year. He served principally as assessor in several cases.

In May 1745 he was elected a corresponding member of the Académie Royale des Sciences. The members of the academy were supposed to live in Paris, but could appoint correspondents outside Paris or abroad. Gaultier was Duhamel Du Monceau's correspondent. The latter was interested in such subjects as meteorology, arboriculture, and agriculture. Gaultier had similar interests, but also contributed to the works of two other members of the academy: Jean-Étienne Guettard (1715–86) and René-Antoine Ferchault de Réaumur (1683–1757).

In 1747 Roland-Michel BARRIN de La Galissonière was appointed temporary governor. He quickly evolved an over-all policy for the colony, not neglecting the natural sciences, in which he was keenly interested. At his request Gaultier prepared a memoir which was distributed to all the commandants of forts, thus creating a network of bases for cataloguing and collecting specimens. The specimens were sent to Quebec, where Gaultier had the task of keeping in touch with and of sending the specimens on to Paris. Library facilities were improved, the garden of the intendant's palace was at the botanist's disposal, and the government financed scientific voyages and other cataloguing expenses.

When Pehr Kalm* came to Quebec in 1749 on a

botanical exploring voyage, he was received as an official guest; all his expenses were paid by the administration, and Gaultier, the foremost naturalist in Canada, served as his guide, organizing botanical expeditions in the region about Quebec and as far as Les Éboulements and visits to the main institutions in the region. Under Gaultier's guidance, Kalm's two months of botanizing excursions in Canada were so fruitful that he compiled from them a "*Flora Canadensis*," which unfortunately remained in manuscript form and has disappeared today, but which Carolus Linnaeus (1707–78) consulted. In recognition of Gaultier's services Kalm dedicated to him the genus *Gaultheria*, which is in fact our wintergreen. This genus comprises about 150 species distributed about Asia, the Pacific, and the Americas. Some 25 or 30 species are used in horticulture as background greenery or plant carpeting. *Gaultheria Shallon*, known in the vernacular as salal, is one of the cut plants preferred for greenery. *Gaultheria procumbens* is one of the three sources of essence and oil of wintergreen, used in pharmacy and confectionery. Later the name of Gaultier gave birth to a small chemical and botanical vocabulary. We have noted: *Gaultnettya*, *Gaulteria*, gaultherase, *Gaultheria*, *Gaultheriae*, Gaultheriaöl, Gaulthérie, gaultheriflora, gaultherifolia, gaultherilin, gaultherin, *gaultherioideae*, gaultheriosidis, gaultheroid, gaultheroline, Gaulthettya, Gaulthiera, Gaulthieria, Gauthiera, Gautiera, Golterya, Gualteria, Gualtieria, Гаультерия. The personal relations between François Bigot* and Gaultier are not explained clearly in documents now extant, but it is known that Gaultier owed him several favours. Gaultier asked for and received the fur-trading and fishing licence for the post at Chateau Bay, on the Labrador coast, in consideration of his services and the smallness of his official salary. He operated this post in partnership with his brothers-in-law. The deed granting the post was delivered to him before the minister's approval had been received. He paid only two beaver pelts and four *livres* a year for the post, the operation of which required a capital of 60,000 *livres*. The government of the colony had only five posts of this sort to grant to private interests whom it wanted to favour. Bigot also requested that Gaultier receive a special gratuity of 500 *livres* for 1752. It was granted, and repeated in 1753. From that time on Gaultier wrote a series of adulatory letters in Bigot's favour, the extravagant style of which cannot help but be surprising, coming from a man of science who lived so close to the intendant. Bigot probably needed such letters to counter the suspicions of profiteering that already hung over him, but why did Gaultier agree to write them? At Bigot's trial three of these letters were filed for the defence.

On 12 March 1752 Gaultier married Madeleine-Marie-Anne (1707–76), the oldest daughter of Pierre-Thomas Tarieu de La Pérade and Marie-Madeleine JARRET de Verchères. She was the widow of Richard TESTU de La Richardière and of Nicolas-Antoine COULON de Villiers. Gaultier declared that he was delighted with his new existence and confided to his correspondent Guettard: "I have finally settled in Canada. . . . I have married a lady of rank. I have reason to be satisfied in every way; my wife has much wit, a fine education, and great ability for running and organizing a house, and she can expect wealth after the death of her father, who is 78. I have just had a house built in Quebec which is large and very liveable. I shall probably not leave it for a good while." The father-in-law would outlive his son-in-law by a year.

His official salary and his income from the fur trade brought Gaultier more money than he needed, to the amount of several thousand *livres* a year, which he tried to dispose of in France by buying properties. In 1756 he sent his agent Larsher four bills of exchange amounting to 3,880 *livres* and asked him to buy some property for him in Normandy. But the agent declined to take the responsibility and insisted that Gaultier come to examine personally any property to be acquired. Gaultier's death prevented him from answering this letter.

Gaultier was first hospitalized at the Hôtel-Dieu in May 1743, then again in July 1756. The *Léopard*, one of the ships in the squadron which brought MONTCALM to Canada, also brought typhus. Nearly 1,000 people were stricken by the malady, and in June 1756 some 300 were hospitalized at the same time. Several nuns hospitallers paid for their devotion with their lives. The same was true of Gaultier, who died on 10 July after being ill for nine days. He was not replaced, for the first person designated to succeed him, the Sieur Chomel, died before coming to Canada; the second one, the Sieur Lebeau, does not seem to have come to Canada, probably because of the war.

Gaultier had agreed to pay the cost of the education of one of his nephews who was studying in Paris. Gaultier's widow instructed Larsher to use the balance of the amounts in his hands to continue the education of the nephew, to whom she sent her husband's medical books. She retired to live in the Ursuline convent in 1774 and died there on 6 Jan. 1776, at 68 years of age.

If Gaultier is fairly well known by the general public, he owes his fame above all to William Kirby*, who made him one of the minor personages in *The Golden Dog*, a novel about society in Bigot's period [*see* Nicolas JACQUIN, *dit* Philibert]. Kirby depicted Gaultier as a rich, generous, learned, and likeable physician and bachelor who was at the same time a highly esteemed conversationalist. This portrait seems to fit the personage. Later in the book Gaultier is presented as an astrologer, which seems less sure.

Philippe-Joseph Aubert* de Gaspé relates in his *Mémoires* (1866) how a certain Gaultier, an officer on the *Capricieuse*, having learned that in earlier times a king's physician by the name of Gaultier had married a Lanaudière, arrived at the home of one of Aubert de Gaspé's aunts, also a Lanaudière, calling her his aunt. His claim was not taken seriously since Gaultier had died without issue. The so-called nephew was reprimanded by the aunt.

Gaultier left the memory of a man who was faithful to his duty and who had a pleasant personality. He was a person of varied talents, who continued Michel Sarrazin's work, studying various fields at once and contributing to several new ones. He left no posterity in this privileged realm of genealogy, and he would be almost forgotten today were it not for the genus of plant that perpetuates his name and for Kirby's novel.

The physician. Since the archives of the Hôtel-Dieu of Quebec were destroyed in a fire in 1755, we know little about Gaultier's medical practice, but his meteorological reports published for the period 1742–49 contain a monthly medical bulletin on the state of health in the colony: the most frequent illnesses in each month, their severity, the most commonly used remedies, the results obtained, and the months (for example May 1744) when few people were ill, or even none (as in September 1744).

Indirectly through these reports we discover the remedies he used: tea, infusions of corn poppy, couch-grass, liquorice, etc.; blood lettings, purgatives, tartar emetic, senna-tea, emulsions, blisters, etc. We also discover his medical theories: like Hippocrates and contrary to Thomas Sydenham, he thought that the great differences of temperature in winter could well cause colds, chest illnesses, and malignant fevers. His mineralogical reports also give us information about the medical use of certain mineral waters, including the sulphur water at Baie-Saint-Paul and Les Éboulements.

Gaultier does not seem to have been inclined towards the clinical and pathological study of maladies, but he noted much about popular medicine among the Canadians and Indians. He tested certain of these practices and no doubt contributed to popularizing some of them and advising against others. Such medical ethnobotany is recorded particularly in an unpublished manuscript to which attention was drawn by Jacques Rousseau* (1905–70) and which was acquired by the Archives Nationales du Québec in 1951. This important manuscript has not been studied systematically, and it is not yet possible to pick out in it all of Gaultier's original contributions. We know that he encouraged the use of wintergreen tea (*Gaultheria*). Jacques Rousseau also pointed out that Gaultier had tested the antiscorbutic properties of the spruce and had recommended the use of spruce beer to cure scurvy. Gérard Filteau credits him also with a treatment for bronchitis.

The meteorologist. In November 1742, at Duhamel's request, Gaultier set up at Quebec the first meteorological station in Canada, and he kept a daily meteorological log, which remained unknown to meteorologists for two centuries. A contemporary of Gaultier, the Sulpician Jean-Marie Castagnac de Pontarion (1723–77), also kept a meteorological log in Montreal in 1749. A second permanent station was not set up in Quebec until 1870. Gaultier's meteorological log goes from 1742 to 1756. Duhamel had part of the monthly tables for the period 1742–49 published in the *Mémoires* of the Académie Royale des Sciences, with a rather brief summary of his comments. These reports constitute the first attempt at quantification in Canadian meteorology. They are obviously modelled on Duhamel's, but with less detail and less care in the findings. The tables comprise five columns: the temperature between seven and eight o'clock in the morning and three and four in the afternoon, the state of the sky, precipitation, and wind direction, all accompanied by comments on derived or dependent phenomena. Gaultier even noted incidentally an earthquake at Quebec on 16–17 May 1744. Meteorology in the 18th century lacked standardization; it was often marred by errors in methodology and limited by its equipment. A critical study of Gaultier's 15 years of meteorology has still to be made; conversion of his figures into Fahrenheit or centigrade might perhaps open up another century of perspective on meteorology in Canada.

Gaultier's meteorological reports to Duhamel Du Monceau were accompanied by valuable commentaries on life in the colony, in particular on the state of agriculture, a sort of precursor of today's *Canadian Plant Disease Survey*. He de-

Gaultier

scribed the 1742 crop as mediocre and the wheat straw as being too short. The year 1743 was a good one for maple sugar, and the farming season got off to a good start, but an invasion of caterpillars in May threatened to destroy everything. Attempts to hold them in check with sulphur proved unsuccessful; on the other hand, a tobacco solution gave good results, except that there was not enough of it. Finally the stands of wheat were blighted with smut and rust, the yield insufficient in quantity and mediocre in quality. But in 1744, 1745, 1746, and 1749 the harvest was abundant and good. He noted down the arrival of the swallows, the start of ploughing and sowing, the flowering of the amelanchiers, lilies, tulips, and narcissuses, the ripening of the first strawberries, the harvest of such crops as hay, oats, barley, wheat, peas, rye, apples, and melons. He kept track of late frosts and floods, of the ice-jam and the breakup. He reported that the "settlers in Canada claim that the winters are no longer as severe as they used to be, which they attribute to the great amount of land that has been cleared."

The manuscript log has come down to us, at least in part, if not perhaps completely. In the record for 1754 we learn that Gaultier had just received from Réaumur a new thermometer which was capable of registering the lowest winter temperatures in Canada; he described the spot where the thermometer had been placed and explained the reasons for the choice of that spot.

The astronomer. Few astronomical observations by Gaultier are known: displays of northern lights, a comet in 1745. He was sent instruments, including a timing pendulum in 1745 and a telescope which he had to share with the Jesuit Joseph-Pierre de Bonnecamps*. A proposal to build an observatory was turned down. Observations which had to be made at some distance from Quebec, such as the eclipse in 1745, were entrusted to others.

The botanist. Because of his own inclination or circumstances, and perhaps primarily because of La Galissonière's support, it was botany which, after meteorology, absorbed most of Gaultier's intellectual effort. This concentration, moreover, was what seems to have been expected of him, and what maintained continuity with Sarrazin's work.

Popular medicine, botanical pharmacopoeia, and the use of woods caught his attention. He contributed to popularizing several products – vegetable, pharmaceutical, and other – among them the maidenhair fern and wintergreen tea. He took an interest in compiling a Canadian botanical vocabulary and prepared several memoirs, of which those on maple sugar and the

making of pitch and resin were published. Three ships, the *Castor, Caribou*, and *Saint-Laurent*, the last one partly of red pine, were built at Quebec on an experimental basis to try out Canadian woods.

Long before Gaultier, Louis Hébert* and Jacques-Philippe Cornuti (1606–51) had begun listing the flora of Canada. Sarrazin made a major contribution to this effort, part of which was recorded in Tournefort's *Institutiones rei herbariae*. But only a small beginning had nevertheless been made. Spurred on by Duhamel and backed up by La Galissonière, Gaultier set himself to this task, studying in particular the ligneous plants, which his predecessors had somewhat neglected. He prepared for Duhamel's use a manuscript of about 400 pages, discovered by Rousseau in 1951, on the plants of Canada. This text, not yet critically studied, is after the manner of Vaillant; it does not repeat Sarrazin's texts but deals primarily with additional species. There is no documentation for this text or for the reasons a copy of it was sent to Duhamel in 1749. Duhamel made copious use of it in preparing his *Traité des arbres et arbustes* and made known several of the new species described by Gaultier. This manuscript was perhaps prepared to be part of the project for an illustrated work in six volumes on the flora of northern America, a project we know of only through an estimate of the costs drawn up around 1754. Duhamel, who was the author of manuals and treatises on some 30 subjects, and probably Bernard de Jussieu too, may have been the originators of this project. It was not followed up, probably because of the war.

In a memoir on pines Gaultier was already making a distinction between the four species of pines in eastern Canada. Duhamel accepted his classification. But Linnaeus knew nothing of it and in 1753 named only one Canadian species in the *Species Plantarum*. Another half-century had to go by before the four species were recognized in binary nomenclature. If it had been published in its time, in the works of the Académie Royale des Sciences, Gaultier's memoir would have advanced science to that extent. But the academicians disposed of their correspondents' texts as they pleased. Gaultier did not complain. Every year he sent Duhamel seeds, bulbs, and slips for the Jardin du Roi and the experimental nursery at the Château de Denainvilliers. The garden of the intendant's palace in Quebec served as a transit nursery. Gaultier also seems to have kept there a permanent collection of Canadian plants, the embryo of a botanical garden. It is not known whether he also sent herbarium specimens. He had already noted the presence of some weeds: in

1743 the *Fagopirum sylvestre* (*Polygonum Convolvulus L.*) and the *Bidens tagetes folio & facie*) had to a great extent squeezed out the wheat in the land sown with wheat; in 1744 he noted that couch-grass (*Agropyron repens*) was overrunning nearly all the lands.

His opinion on vernacular botanical nomenclature is close to ours: "I shall keep the everyday names, Canadian or Indian, which have been given to each of these trees, convinced as I am that this nomenclature has reasonable bases and can be of great service in recognizing the trees and plants that are described." He systematically made a distinction between the vocabulary of the French and that of the Canadians. Thus he wrote under *Carpinus*: "in French *Charme*, and in Canadian *Bois dur.*" Again, under *Citrullus iroqueorum*: "in French and in Canadian *Citrouille iroquoise.*" The term "Canadian" to designate the particular form of French spoken in Canada came naturally to his mind, and it had already been used by Sarrazin. But the term did not take root, and the Canadians refused for a long time still to recognize that their language had sufficient originality to deserve a distinctive epithet.

The mineralogist. One of the regulations of the Académie Royale des Sciences stipulated that a member outside Paris would correspond only with his sponsor. But Gaultier corresponded regularly with Guettard and Réaumur. The administration of the colony was concerned with mineral resources. The mines at Baie-Saint-Paul had already been visited by Hocquart* in 1740; in 1749 the official naturalist, accompanied by Kalm, was sent there to do prospecting. The official report described particularly the outcrops at Rivière du Moulin and the sulphur springs, and also the springs and geological formations at Les Éboulements, Cap aux Oies, and Petite-Rivière.

Guettard was in the process of elaborating a general theory about the distribution of minerals and the structures of the continents. He had already applied his theory in studies on Egypt, France, and Switzerland. Thanks to Gaultier's shipments in 1752, he extended his theory to North America, and in 1756 he published the first geological and mineralogical map of Canada. Along with it were sketches of some fossils. The shipment of samples of minerals to Guettard was perhaps made annually; four at least are known, and often the list of the specimens has also survived: gypsum, talc, copper, ferruginous sands, steatite, slate, limestone, etc., and even some fossils.

The zoologist. Réaumur had sent Gaultier the documentation which enabled him to introduce into Canada techniques for preserving eggs and raising chickens in all seasons, thanks to incubators. These innovations were fortunate for the well-being of the colony and particularly for the diet of the sick. Gaultier sent Réaumur several shipments (perhaps every year or almost every year) of preserved animals, particularly birds, fish, and mammals. Certain shipments were accompanied by memoirs on the habits of these animals. Presumably these samples were added to the royal collections and were used by the zoologists of the time, but there is no record of such use. The author has read several books by Buffon and Cuvier without discovering in them any material credited to, or that could be credited to, Gaultier's contributions in specimens or descriptive memoirs. Gaultier also refers to hunting and fishing activities and reports that at Quebec in 1742, for the first time, "people thought of making holes in the ice to fish for small cod, and this fishing was successful."

Gaultier has been credited with "excellent work in entomology," but we do not know what justifies this compliment; the author has found only the description of some invasions by caterpillars, the techniques used to check them, and a shipment of caterpillars. Details are to be found in the meteorological reports.

The shipping of specimens in 1753 had a sad story, and Réaumur expressed his disappointment. If the collection was limited in size, replied Gaultier, it was because the local correspondents had not sent the promised samples: if the specimens were damaged, it was because the person responsible for packaging them had done his work badly; if the specimens did not bear labels, it was because the same person responsible had left them on his work bench. A fine example of trying to find justification! On the other hand, most of the other shipments were satisfactory and were greatly appreciated.

The man of science. Gaultier's training was not especially scientific, but rather that of a physician of the period. He seems, however, to have prepared himself for the task expected of him; he associated with the Jussieus and Duhamel. Yet his career as a scientist was due more to the accident of the circumstances of his employment than to an insatiable intellectual curiosity.

Gaultier quite naturally continued Sarrazin's work and opened up several fields of research new for the colony. Duhamel had about 115 pages of Gaultier's works published. Kalm and modern authors added another 35 pages of texts which remained of historical interest. Other unpublished works by Gaultier deserve to be published, as Rousseau had planned. His total scientific production seems to have amounted to around

Gaultier

1,500 manuscript pages, about half of which dated from the period of La Galissonière's term as governor and about a tenth of which has been published. His scientific contribution is primarily an indirect one, made through Duhamel, Kalm, and Guettard.

Gaultier has been called a modest scientist, which is true of his character, but his contribution was not modest. He carried out the tasks expected of him; he did not aim at a great work of his own. He sometimes apologized for the fact that certain shipments or works were not as carefully done as could have been desired, but he never complained that his memoirs and manuscripts, numerous and bulky, remained unpublished. He did not attach great importance to his works, he did not boast of his contribution. He was conscious only of doing his duty as a physician and a naturalist to the best of his ability. Compared to that of the modern scientist, Gaultier's published work is varied and its quantity places him in the upper ten per cent.

Gaultier has been compared to Sarrazin, and yet the two men were hardly similar. Sarrazin's motivation came from within him; he chose the subjects of his study, complained of his inadequate equipment, and indulged in recriminations if his reports were not published rapidly. Gaultier resembles rather the average modern scientist, who is capable of an enormous effort in favourable circumstances, such as during La Galissonière's governorship, but who can become almost ineffective if support and stimulus are lacking, as was the case under Bigot, who was preoccupied with personal aggrandizement.

Gaultier's influence on his contemporaries was considerable. He prepared the memoir distributed by the governor to the commandants of the forts asking them to contribute to the cataloguing of natural resources, and he maintained contact with those who actually did, spreading and encouraging interest in science throughout the colony. His shipments to the members of the academy contributed in a way that was often indispensable to their works, such as Guettard's zoological and mineralogical study on North America. Réaumur's development of a thermometer with a longer scale was probably motivated by the need for an instrument better adapted to Canada. Gaultier's contribution to Kalm's work deserves special mention.

The end of a scientific movement. When the smallness of its population is taken into account, the colony's scientific effort was considerable. It was first directed to geographical exploration, then to the cataloguing of languages and ethnography, and very early to the surveying of natural resources. This survey was at first a series of isolated or intermittent efforts by travellers or amateurs such as Louis Hébert. But with Sarrazin this effort was institutionalized, and with Gaultier continuity was established. Collections accumulated: Sarrazin's herbarium seems to have contained some 800 specimens; the garden of the intendant's palace maintained a collection of living plants: scientific libraries were formed – Sarrazin's contained 175 volumes. There were others in Gaultier's home, in the intendant's palace, in the Jesuit seminary, etc. A network of local correspondents was set up; regular correspondence was carried on with the Académie Royale des Sciences and a series of works was published in its *Mémoires*. Canadian plants were introduced into the gardens of Europe, amateurs were encouraged to contribute their share, new species were described, drugs were experimented with and evaluated.

With the Seven Years' War and Gaultier's death in 1756, all disappeared; publication ceased in 1756 and many manuscripts remained unpublished. The collections disappeared, and the libraries were scattered. Thus ended a scientific movement which had become considerable in the 18th century, reaching its culmination with Sarrazin and Gaultier. In many disciplines a century was to go by before there was a rebirth of indigenous activity. And the interruption was so long that the new naturalists had generally forgotten the work of their predecessors and had to start again from the beginning.

BERNARD BOIVIN

Several works by Gaultier have been published, including "Histoire du sucre d'érable" in *Mémoires de mathématique et de physique présentés à l'Académie royale des sciences, par divers sçavans, & lûs dans les assemblées* (11v., Paris, 1750–86), II, 378–92, and "Maniere de retirer le suc résineux du pin, et d'en faire le brai-sec et la résine jaune suivant les pratiques qu'on suit au Canada," published by Duhamel in his *Traité des arbres et arbustes qui se cultivent en France en pleine terre* (2v., Paris, 1755). In addition, Gaultier's "Observations botanico-météorologiques faites à Québec . . .," which was presented before the academy by Duhamel, is published in the *Histoire de l'Académie royale des sciences . . . avec les mémoires de mathématique & de physique . . .* for 1744 (1748), 135–55; 1746 (1751), 88–97; 1747 (1752), 466–88; 1750 (1754), 309ff.; and Guettard's "Mémoire dans lequel on compare le Canada à la Suisse, par rapport à ses minéraux," based on Gaultier's work, appears in the issue for 1752 (1756), 189–220, 323–60, 524–38. Finally, Pehr Kalm, in *En Resa til Norra America* (3v., Stockholm, 1753–61), III, 458–61, reproduces a text by Gaultier.

The American Philosophical Society Library (Philadelphia) holds about 750 pages of notes and memoirs by Gaultier (B, D87, 20, 21, 24, 25). The Archives de l'Académie des Sciences (Paris) has five letters written by him to Réaumur; these have been published in *RSCT*, 3rd ser., XXIV (1930), sect. I, 31–43. The ANQ (AP, Jean-François Gaultier) holds two of Gaultier's manuscripts, bound with a manuscript by Sarrazin entitled "Histoire des plantes de Canada"; there is also a copy of these two manuscripts entitled "Description de plusieurs plantes du Canada." The Archives du séminaire de Saint-Hyacinthe has a manuscript by Sarrazin, "Histoire des plantes de Canada," annotated by Gaultier. The BN, NAF 22253, preserves three letters of Gaultier, deposited in Bigot's dossier, of which copies are held in PAC, MG 7, IA, 3. The Harvard College Library, MS Can 57, M-13, has seven memoirs and manuscripts by Gaultier, as well as three letters addressed to Duhamel. Finally, in the archives of the Muséum d'Histoire naturelle (Paris), vol. 293, there are letters and memoirs of Gaultier, addressed to Guettard; copies are kept in PAC, MG 7, V.

AHDQ, Notes sur messieurs les médecins et chirurgiens, 42. AN, Col., B, 74, f.49; 76, ff.24, 36v; 78, ff.25, 39, 63v; 81, ff.23, 60; 89, ff.25, 41; 91, ff.40, 44, 45; 97, f.29; 105, f.8 (copies at PAC). ANDQ, Registres des baptèmes, mariages et sépultures, 11 juill. 1756. ANQ, Greffe de C.-H. Du Laurent, 4 oct. 1743, 2 mars 1752; NF, Ord. int., 12 juin 1750. Bibliothèque de l'Observatoire de Paris, A.A.7.6, "Observations botanico-météorologiques faites au Canada, par Gaultier de 1742 à 1748." Bibliothèque de l'université de Montréal, Collection Baby, Correspondance, pp. 1385–87, 1440–41, 1454–59 (copies at PAC). Ahern, *Notes pour l'histoire de la médecine*. Frégault, *François Bigot*. William Kirby, *The Golden Dog* (Rouses Point, N.Y., 1877). Roland Lamontagne, *La Galissonière et le Canada* (Montréal, Paris, 1962). Arthur Vallée, *Un biologiste canadien: Michel Sarrazin, 1659–1735, sa vie, ses travaux et son temps* (Québec, 1927), 66–72. Jacques Rousseau, "Anneda et l'arbre de vie," *RHAF*, VIII (1954–55), 171–212; "Le mémoire de La Galissonière aux naturalistes canadiens de 1749," *Le naturaliste canadien* (Québec), 93 (1966), 669–81; "Michel Sarrazin, Jean-François Gaultier et l'étude prélinnéenne de la flore canadienne," *Colloque international du C.N.R.S.* (Paris), LXIII (1957), 149–57.

GUYON, LOUISE (Thibault, Damours de Freneuse), baptized 1 May 1668 on Île d'Orléans, daughter of Simon Guyon and Louise Racine; d. sometime after 1711.

Louise Guyon lost her parents when she was young, and married her first husband, Charles Thibault, at Château-Richer on 10 April 1684. He died 17 months later, and on 1 Oct. 1686, at Quebec, she married Mathieu Damours* de Freneuse; at the same time her older sister, Marguerite, married Louis Damours* de Chauffours, Mathieu's brother. Louise's marriage introduced her into one of the first families of Canada; her father-in-law Mathieu Damours* de Chauffours, was a councillor of the Conseil Souverain, and four of the sons owned seigneuries in Acadia. Mathieu, Louise's husband, had obtained two leagues of land on the Saint John River between Jemseg and Naxouat (Nashwaak, N.B.). The couple settled there in 1686, and for ten years attended to developing their domain. The 1695 census informs us that they owned 30 acres of land under cultivation, as well as a herd of livestock and that they harvested 200 bushels of grain. They also engaged in the fur trade with the Indians.

In 1696 Mathieu Damours went to Quebec to replace his father, who had died the previous year, on the Conseil Souverain. Intending to settle in the capital, he rented out his seigneury and went back to get his wife and five children; he died before he could return to Quebec. Mme Damours de Freneuse remained for a few years on the Saint John River, trying to put her finances in order. An order from the king granted the office which her husband had held on the Conseil Souverain to the Sieur Denis Riverin* on the condition that he pay 1,000 *livres* to the family.

In 1700 the seat of the government of Acadia was transferred to Port-Royal (Annapolis Royal, N.S.), and Fort Saint-Joseph (Naxouat), where Governor Joseph Robinau* de Villebon resided, was demolished. As its inhabitants were left without defence, they moved to Port-Royal; Mme de Freneuse went to live there around 1702 with her sister and brother-in-law Louis Damours de Chauffours. The new governor, Jacques-François de Monbeton* de Brouillan, and the officers welcomed warmly this young widow of 34 years of age, mother of five children, and took into the garrison her three oldest sons, whose ages varied from 10 to 15 years. Simon-Pierre Denys* de Bonaventure, the king's lieutenant, extended the courtesy to the point of sheltering her in his home until she acquired a house not far from the fort. M. de Bonaventure probably went a little beyond the bounds of gallantry, for a child was born the following year who was named Antoine and whose baptism, which took place on 6 Nov. 1703, appears in the parish records of Port-Royal. From then on this liaison kept tongues wagging at Port-Royal and took on the dimensions of an affair of state in official correspondence. The lieutenant general for justice in Acadia, Mathieu de Goutin*, along with the missionaries Félix Pain and Patrice René, denounced the scandal. Bishop Saint-Vallier [La Croix*] of Quebec asked that the woman be sent away, and Pontchartrain, the minister of Marine, ordered her to be sent to Canada or to the Saint

Guyon

John River. But Bonaventure put up a vigorous defence, affirming that simple charity had guided his conduct. He demanded an inquiry and, in a chivalrous gesture, offered to leave himself rather than see exiled this unfortunate woman, who, in addition to keeping her five children, had just taken in two orphaned nieces. Brouillan, the governor, also took up Mme de Freneuse's defence and was satisfied with removing her temporarily from Port-Royal.

Thereupon Brouillan died, in September 1705, and Bonaventure took over his duties temporarily while waiting to become governor in name – it was an office he greatly desired. Probably in order not to hinder this promotion, Mme de Freneuse left for La Rochelle, France. But on 22 May 1706 the court named Daniel d'Auger* de Subercase governor, and the minister told Bonaventure flatly that the scandal he had caused had prevented the king from appointing him. His virtuous majesty could indeed keep mistresses, but did not stand for them among his officers.

Mme de Freneuse returned to Port-Royal. A new storm now broke; this time it was victims of Bonaventure's authority who complained of him. Despite the minister's orders Subercase temporized and contented himself with sending the lady off to the upper part of the Rivière Dauphin (Annapolis River). In 1707, after changing her mind several times, Bonaventure's legal wife, Jeanne Jannière, finally came to live in Acadia. There ensued temporarily a period of calm, but the lovers still saw each other. Goutin continued sending his dispatches to the court, the bishop of Quebec returned to the charge, and Father Patrice René went to France to complain to the minister. Upon learning that he had not yet been obeyed, the minister became angry: he blamed Subercase, giving him a formal order from the king to send Mme de Freneuse away, and told Bonaventure that if by the time the ships departed she had not left, he would be cashiered and deprived of his post. Subercase complied with the order and Mme de Freneuse left for Quebec in the summer of 1708 escorted by Charles-Joseph Amiot* de Vincelotte. In 1710 Bonaventure returned to France after the British capture of Port-Royal and he died at Rochefort in 1711.

In the course of that year Mme de Freneuse returned to Port-Royal (renamed Annapolis Royal) with a pass from Philippe de Rigaud* de Vaudreuil, the governor of New France. She crossed the Baie Française (Bay of Fundy) in a canoe in the heart of winter, alone with her youngest son and an Indian. The acting English governor of Annapolis Royal, Sir Charles Hobby*,

allowed her to stay there, but Paul MASCARENE claimed that she was acting as a spy for the French government. Certainly Mme de Freneuse would have had several valid reasons for returning to Acadia, if only because of the many relatives she had there and to see to the possessions she had had to leave in haste behind her at the Saint John River and at Annapolis Royal. On the other hand, we know that the court of France was seriously thinking of retaking Annapolis Royal. Already Denys de Bonaventure had drawn up at Rochefort a detailed plan to this end, and it is possible that Mme de Freneuse collaborated in this plan by supplying Vaudreuil with information on the English forces at Annapolis Royal. According to Mascarene, two of her sons may have taken part in June 1711 in the attack at Bloody Creek (near Bridgetown, N.S.), where 30 English soldiers perished. They are then supposed to have returned to Annapolis Royal to conduct their mother to a safe place.

After that Mme de Freneuse drops from sight. She must have lived some time at Quebec, then have gone back to France, for we find some of her children living at La Rochelle in 1727; two of her sons had naval careers. An American novelist has written a questionable novel about Mme de Freneuse. What need is there of adding imaginary episodes to the ardent and courageous life of this woman, the heroine of a true romance filled with adventure and passion?

RENÉ BAUDRY

AN, Col., B, 15, f.69; 20, f.80v; 23–33; C¹¹A, 29; C¹¹D, 4–6; 7, ff.100ff.; Section Outre-Mer, G¹, 466, pièces 10, 17, 20, 22, 24 (recensements de l'Acadie). "Correspondance de Vaudreuil," APQ *Rapport, 1939–40,* 427. Archange Godbout et R.-J. Auger, "Familles venues de La Rochelle en Canada," ANQ *Rapport, 1970,* 193, 206. *Jug. et délib.,* III, 436; IV, 43. J. C. Webster, *Acadia at the end of the seventeenth century: letters, journals and memoirs of Joseph Robineau de Villebon, commandant in Acadia, 1690–1700, and other contemporary documents* (N. B. Museum, Monographic ser., I, Saint John, N. B., 1934). Tanguay, *Dictionnaire,* I, 294, 565.

E. S. M. Eaton, *Quietly my captain waits* (New York, London, 1940). Murdoch, *History of Nova-Scotia,* I, 268, 302. W. O. Raymond, *Glimpses of the past; history of the River St. John, A.D. 1604–1784* (St John, N.B., 1905), 73–74. Pierre Daviault, "Mme de Freneuse et M. de Bonaventure," *RSCT,* 3rd ser., XXXV (1941), sect.I, 37–56. W. F. Ganong, "Lease of the seigniory of Freneuse on the St. John in 1696," *Acadiensis* ([Saint John, N.B.]), I (1901), 121–25. P.-G. Roy, "Mathieu Damours de Chauffours," *Les petites choses de notre histoire* (7 sér., Lévis, Québec, 1919–44), 6e sér., 68–78; "Mathieu Damours de Freneuse," *BRH,* XXXII (1926), 577–82.

TREMBLAY, HENRI-JEAN, priest, missionary, procurator of the seminary of Quebec in Paris, director of the Séminaire des Missions Étrangères in Paris; b. 1664, probably at Lagny (Lagny-sur-Marne), France; d. in Paris, 9 July 1740, and not in 1741 or 1747, as certain authors have maintained.

Henri-Jean Tremblay entered the Séminaire des Missions Étrangères in Paris in 1686 and received the subdiaconate there the following year. His superiors were planning to send him to the missions in the Orient, but Bishop Laval*, who also had his eye on him, succeeded at the last moment in getting him for his seminary in Quebec and had him leave immediately for Canada. In a letter dated 9 June 1687 the prelate informed the officials of the seminary that M. Tremblay was the only recruit they would receive that year. But this candidate was a choice one, who possessed "charm and submissiveness, good judgement, a firm and generous mind." "He is wise and prudent," continued the founder of the seminary, "capable, as far as I can judge, of observing secrecy and someone in whom you may have confidence"; in short "the best-tempered mind of all the persons who have come forward in more than two years." The directors were therefore urged to "take care to train and lead M. Tremblay in the ways of virtue not as a simple missionary to be in charge of a parish," but with a view to admitting him "into the body of the seminary," of which, without the shadow of a doubt, he would soon become one of the firmest supports. Bishop Laval recommended, however, that the new arrival be spared until he "becomes accustomed to the atmosphere of the country and catches the spirit of the seminary." When his apprenticeship was completed, he could then be put at the head of the Petit Séminaire, which it was "of the greatest importance to maintain in a spirit of grace."

Whether Abbé Tremblay was put in charge of the pupils shortly after his arrival is not known; in any event it is certain his superiors were not long in discovering that he possessed all the qualities of an excellent businessman. When Bishop Saint-Vallier [La Croix*] had conferred the diaconate upon him on 30 Nov. 1688 and the priesthood on 18 December, the superior, Henri de Bernières*, and his colleagues did not hesitate an instant in appointing their young *confrère* a director and bursar of the seminary. The bishop of Quebec, however, had also noticed his talents. After trying to attach Tremblay to himself, he called upon him to serve the parish of Saint-Pierre, on Île d'Orléans. Henri-Jean Tremblay took up this unexpected act of obedience will-ingly and went to his post at the beginning of November 1689. He stayed there three years. But it was his last post in Canada. In 1692 Bishop Laval and the directors decided to make him procurator of the seminary and chapter of Quebec in Paris, an office which had remained vacant since the death of Jean Dudouyt* in 1688. As Bishop Saint-Vallier had not raised any objections, the procurator sailed for France in the autumn.

Tremblay had not accepted his appointment without some apprehension, and during the early years of his administration he was often tempted, he said, to "discard this meanness which taking care of temporal matters brings with it and which weakens so greatly one's fervour for God's business." On several occasions he begged to be replaced and to be allowed to devote himself to some humble mission in Canada or Acadia. But the procurator did his job so competently and with such exemplary zeal, that the founder and the officials of the seminary of Quebec took good care not to transfer him. Besides, the directors of the Missions Étrangères in Paris would not have allowed a collaborator who had become indispensable to them to leave. After electing him a director in 1694, they put him in 1697 in charge of the office of procurator of the seminary itself and of all the missions in Asia. In 1736 his colleagues chose him, despite his age and infirmities, to be assistant superior and renewed his term of office in 1739.

Although Tremblay was closely attached to his fellow religious in Paris, the seminary of Quebec nevertheless remained his preference. "I beg of you," he wrote to M. de Bernières in 1694, "to consider me still as one of the members of the seminary, filled with the desire to be useful to it and to serve the entire mission in Canada." Not only the founder of the seminary of Quebec and its directors, but also the other members of the community, parish priests and missionaries in Louisiana and Acadia, seminarists and even pupils, profited greatly from the complete availability of the devoted procurator [see François Charon* de La Barre]. Each autumn he received voluminous mail from Canada which he endeavoured to answer with the greatest attention. Tremblay forgot no one, and his vigilance extended to the smallest detail. He discharged bills of exchange to the best of his ability, paid bills, saw personally in Paris, or through his agents in Caen and Châteauroux, to the purchase of supplies and other goods of all sorts that he had been asked for and then looked after their delivery to La Rochelle. The procurator did not limit himself to this role as intermediary: he was also capable of giving advice or opinions to everybody

Tremblay

or again of commenting upon the latest news with a pertinency that demonstrated the sureness of his judgement and his knowledge of men and events [see Goulven Calvarin*; Albert Davion*; François Dupré*]. When he felt obliged to do so in the interest of correspondents, even if they were Bishop Laval and the officials of the seminary, Tremblay did not fail to increase, invariably with respect and charity, his remonstrances and admonitions [see Nicolas Foucault*].

The procurator of the seminary was a conscientious administrator, and he had made a practice of foreseeing the future prudently and of taking appropriate measures in all matters to assure the preservation of the work of the seminary in Quebec. His fellow ecclesiastics in Quebec seemed to him, on the contrary, to be carrying out their undertakings without any forethought, and to be spending their income as if it were inexhaustible [see Jean-Baptiste Gaultier* de Varennes]. How many times he blamed them for admitting too many pupils without charge, or again for "always having the trowel in their hands at the seminary, at La Canardière, Saint-Michel, and Île Jésus"! To his great disappointment Tremblay was not successful in convincing the directors to change their conduct [see Jean-François Buisson* de Saint-Cosme (1660–1712)]. When the directors had written him one day that their accounts were difficult to make up, he retorted sharply: "Do you know mine?" That was in 1707, and the list of those who were taxing the procurator's devotion and ability had grown considerably longer in the preceding years. In case the superiors had forgotten, Tremblay undertook to remind them. He had to run the affairs of the seminary in Paris, of the seminary and chapter in Quebec, of the benefices, abbeys, and priories in Normandy, Touraine, and Berry which were attached to them, of all the missions, those in the east as well as the west, and finally of the Hôtel-Dieu and the Hôpital Général of Quebec. And even then he spared his correspondents the enumeration of private accounts which he could not avoid looking after, such as those of Bishop Laval and his family, for example, or those of friends and acquaintances in Paris and in the provinces. Every year more than 70,000 *livres* thus passed through his hands. "If all that," concluded the procurator, "seems to you easier to keep in order than the receipts and expenditures for a year of the seminary and chapter of Quebec, then I am quite lost!"

Despite the little effect that his vehement objurgations had, Tremblay never let himself become disheartened. "I am not easily discouraged," he wrote to Bishop Laval, "and although I speak strongly to Your Excellency and to our gentlemen, I do not give up in despair." He was indeed convinced that the seminary of Quebec was truly God's work, as he wrote to Abbé Louis Ango* Des Maizerets in 1696. "Every day I see new proof," he added, and "that is what sustains me in the difficulties and vexations my position entails." The confidence which the superiors of the seminary showed in him contributed in no small measure to comfort him. Bishop Laval in particular held him in high esteem and had no secrets from him. For his part the procurator held "our former dear prelate" in great veneration. Although he disapproved of the founder's fondness, to his mind exaggerated, for fine stone buildings, Tremblay did not often dare reprimand him directly. He preferred to leave that to his *confrères*: "He is so kind," he wrote to M. Des Maizerets, "that he will always listen to reason when it is presented to him gently." Tremblay moreover fought with the utmost energy all those who threatened to divert the seminary of Quebec from its vocation. Bishop Saint-Vallier, who intended to reduce the institution founded by his predecessor to the sole role of training young clerics, was to encounter in the procurator an indomitable opponent. So did the Jesuits when in 1698 they opposed the presence of priests of the seminary of Quebec in the Mississippi country [see Jean-François Buisson* de Saint-Cosme (1667–1706)]. Henri-Jean Tremblay defended with no less fervour the thesis sustained by the Société des Missions Étrangères against the Society of Jesus in the affair of the "Chinese Rites." On this subject, several of his letters constitute unequivocal evidence of the acts of violence, at least verbal, which this deplorable quarrel provoked in ecclesiastical circles in the 18th century.

The crushing task which Tremblay assumed could not fail, however, to undermine his health. Already during his stay in Canada he had suffered a hernia, an accident that was frequent at the time and which was attributed to the use of snowshoes. In 1706 other infirmities came on top of this first one. "You will learn," he told his confidant, Abbé Charles de Glandelet*, "of the affliction which God has sent me by giving me the gout at 42 years of age. . . . This year I have become a man full of inflammations and infirmities." His condition continued to grow worse. In 1712 it was necessary to give him an assistant as procurator of the missions: François de MONTIGNY, a former missionary in the Mississippi country and in China. Some years later his sight began to grow weak. With a cataract in his left eye and having become almost blind in 1728, Henri-Jean Tremblay reluctantly handed over the administration of his affairs to M. de Montigny. A successful operation in 1732 gave him back the use of his eyes, to the great joy of his associates and of his fellow ecclesiastics in Quebec. But he had never been able to get over his gout. It was this malady which brought on his death on 9 July 1740.

In announcing his death to Quebec the directors of the seminary in Paris stressed that with Abbé Henri-Jean Tremblay disappeared "the oldest member of our whole body and even of all the missionaries in Canada." For its part the seminary of Quebec lost in its former procurator the last survivor of the period of its founders and indisputably one of its most remarkable benefactors.

NOËL BAILLARGEON

[The principal manuscript sources are Abbé Henri-Jean Tremblay's letters, which are preserved at the ASQ. In addition to a certain number of reports and statements of accounts, there are in it about a hundred letters, sometimes 100 pages or so in length. One may also consult at the ASQ the correspondence between the Séminaire des Missions Étrangères in Paris on the one hand and Bishop Laval and the directors of the seminary of Quebec on the other. *See also*: AAQ, 12 A, Registres d'insinuations A, *passim*, and ANQ, Copies d'archives d'autres dépôts, Paroisses, Saint-Pierre, île d'Orléans. N.B.]

Provost, *Le séminaire de Québec: documents et biographies*, 202, 429. Adrien Launay, *Mémorial de la Société des Missions étrangères* (2v., Paris, 1912–16), II, 609.

GENERAL BIBLIOGRAPHY AND
LIST OF ABBREVIATIONS

List of Abbreviations

AAQ   Archives de l'archidiocèse de Québec
ACAM   Archives de la chancellerie de l'archevêché de Montréal
ACND   Archives de la Congrégation de Notre-Dame, Montréal
AD   Archives départementales, France
AHDQ   Archives de l'Hôtel-Dieu de Québec
AHGQ   Archives de l'Hôpital Général de Québec
AHSJ   Archives générales des Religieuses hospitalières de Saint-Joseph, Montréal
AJM   Archives judiciaires de Montréal
AJQ   Archives judiciaires de Québec
AJTR   Archives judiciaires de Trois-Rivières
AMUQ   Archives du monastère des Ursulines de Québec
AN   Archives nationales, Paris
ANDM   Archives paroissiales de Notre-Dame de Montréal
ANDQ   Archives paroissiales de Notre-Dame de Québec
ANQ   Archives nationales du Québec
ANQ-M   Archives nationales du Québec, dépôt de Montréal
APQ   Archives de la province de Québec
AQ   Archives du Québec
ARSI   Archivum Romanum Societatis Iesu, Rome
ASGM   Archives des sœurs Grises, Montréal
ASJCF   Archives de la Compagnie de Jésus, province du Canada français
ASQ   Archives du séminaire de Québec
ASSM   Archives du séminaire de Saint-Sulpice, Montréal
BM   British Museum, London
BN   Bibliothèque nationale, Paris

BRH   *Le Bulletin des recherches historiques*
CCHA   Canadian Catholic Historical Association
CHA   Canadian Historical Association
CHR   *Canadian Historical Review*
CTG   Comité technique du Génie, Paris
DAB   *Dictionary of American biography*
DBF   *Dictionnaire de biographie française*
DCB   *Dictionary of Canadian biography*
DNB   *Dictionary of national biography*
DPL   Detroit Public Library
HBC   Hudson's Bay Company
HBRS   Hudson's Bay Record Society
IOA   L'Inventaire des œuvres d'art, Québec
JR   *Jesuit relations and allied documents*
NYCD   *Documents relative to the colonial history of the state of New-York*
PAC   Public Archives of Canada
PANL   Public Archives of Newfoundland and Labrador
PANS   Public Archives of Nova Scotia
PRO   Public Record Office, London
RHAF   *Revue d'histoire de l'Amérique française*
RSCT   Royal Society of Canada *Proceedings and Transactions*
RUL   *La Revue de l'université Laval*
SCHÉC   Société canadienne d'histoire de l'Église catholique
SGCF   Société généalogique canadienne-française
SHA   Service historique de l'Armée, Paris
SHM   Société historique de Montréal
SHQ   Société historique de Québec
SHS   Société historique du Saguenay
USPG   United Society for the Propagation of the Gospel, London

General Bibliography

The General Bibliography is based on the sources most frequently cited in individual bibliographies in volume III. It should not be regarded as providing a complete list of background materials for the history of Canada in the 18th century.

Section I provides a description of the principal archival sources used for this volume and is divided by country. Section II contains printed primary sources: documents and printed works of the 18th century which may be regarded as contemporary sources. Section III includes various dictionaries, nominal lists, indexes, and inventories of documents. Section IV contains secondary works of the 19th and 20th centuries, including a number of general histories, and theses. Section V describes the principal journals and the publications of various societies which contain material on the 18th century.

I. ARCHIVES AND MANUSCRIPT SOURCES

CANADA

ARCHIVES DE LA CHANCELLERIE DE L'ARCHE-VÊCHÉ DE MONTRÉAL. This archives, which contains documents dating to 1896 inclusively, consists of photographs, maps, 634 registers in 17 series (including, in particular, the correspondence of the bishops of Montreal), and some 500,000 dossiers containing unbound items relating to dioceses, clergy, laity, institutions, missions, religious communities, etc. For a description of the archives see: *RHAF*, XIX (1965–66), 652–55; SCHÉC *Rapport, 1963*, 69–70. There is a detailed inventory of a number of registers and dossiers in *RHAF*, XIX (1965–66), 655–64; XX (1966–67), 146–66, 669–700; XXIV (1970–71), 111–42.

ARCHIVES DE LA COMPAGNIE DE JÉSUS, PROVINCE DU CANADA FRANÇAIS, Saint-Jérôme, Terrebonne. Founded in 1844 by Father Félix Martin*, the archives was originally housed in the Collège Sainte-Marie, Montreal, and known by the initials ACSM. In 1968 the records were moved to the noviciate of the province of French Canada at Saint-Jérôme, and are now identified by the initials ASJCF. Richly endowed in the year of its foundation by a valuable gift from the community of the Hôtel-Dieu of Quebec, which had preserved some of the records (1635–1800) of the old Jesuit college in Quebec, the archives contains numerous documents, both originals and copies, concerning the history of the Jesuit missions in New France, Canada, and the United States, as well as documents relating to the history of the Catholic Church in Canada [see: ARCHIVES DU COLLÈGE SAINTE-MARIE, *DCB*, I, 686].

Documents from the following sections were used in the preparation of volume III:

The section which consists of 140 metal boxes containing approximately 6,800 numbered documents (personal papers and correspondence, both originals and copies) and the Fonds Bernier and Fonds Baraga, which are not yet numbered:
1–5,343: Fonds général
5,344–5,565: Fonds Guérin
6,000–6,800: Fonds Prud'homme

Fonds Rochemonteix: 28 notebooks of documentation, numbered 4,001 to 4,028, which were used by Camille de Rochemonteix in the preparation of *Les Jésuites et la N.-F. au XVIIe siècle* and *Les Jésuites et la N.-F. au XVIIIe siècle* [see section IV].

The section of original manuscripts written by Jesuit missionaries:
Abbé Maillard, "Livre de prières en langue micmaque avec traduction française en regard"

Séries A-1 à 20, B-1 à 24: correspondence, diaries, papers relating to various Jesuit missions, colleges, retreat houses, and residences in Canada

689

Série BO: papers left by the Jesuit fathers
Série D: papers left by the Jesuit fathers at the time of their deaths
Cahier des vœux
Extraits des catalogues

ARCHIVES DE LA CONGRÉGATION DE NOTRE-DAME, Montréal. In the process of being catalogued.

The principal documents used in the preparation of volume III:
La Congrégation de Notre-Dame: son personnel, 1653–1768. 2v.
Fichier général des sœurs de la Congrégation de Notre-Dame
Nominations, la Congrégation de Notre-Dame et son personnel
Plan des lieux de sépulture depuis 1681-CND
Registre des sépultures des sœurs de la Congrégation de Notre-Dame
Registre général des sœurs de la Congrégation de Notre-Dame de Montréal

ARCHIVES DE L'ARCHIDIOCÈSE DE QUÉBEC. Contains about 1,060 feet of documents, an analytical card file for all documents prior to 1930, and a six-volume general index to the official registers of the archdiocese from 1659 to the present. There is a guide to this archives in SCHÉC *Rapport, 1934–35*, 65–73.

Series used in the preparation of volume III:
A: Évêques et archevêques de Québec
12A: Registres des insinuations ecclésiastiques
20A: Lettres manuscrites des évêques de Québec
22 A: Copies de lettres expédiées
B: Chapitre de la cathédrale de Québec
10 B: Registre des délibérations
11 B: Correspondance
C: Secrétairerie et chancellerie
CB: Structures de direction
1 CB: Vicaires généraux
CD: Discipline diocésaine
42 CD: Abjurations
61 CD: Notre-Dame de Québec
69 CD: Visites pastorales
CM: Église universelle
91 CM: France
CN: Église canadienne
312 CN: Nouvelle-Écosse
T: Fonds privés. Manuscrits amérindiens
Manuscrits Maillard
W: Copies d'archives étrangères
1W: Église du Canada

ARCHIVES DE L'HÔPITAL GÉNÉRAL DE QUÉBEC. The following documents have been used in the preparation of volume III:
Actes capitulaires. 1699–1941. (This series also contains the Registre des entrées et des dots, 1699–1860.)
Actes de profession et contrats de dot. 1717–1845.
"Annales." 3v., 1693–1793.
Cahiers divers, notices, éloges funèbres, circulaires, notes diverses. 1v., 1727–1952.
Divers extraits de nos annales et autres notes diverses. 1v., 1686–1866.
Livres de comptes. 4v., 1693–1760.
"La vie de Mongr. Jean-Baptiste de La Croix de Chevrières de St Vallier, second évêque de Québec." (This manuscript dates from about 1850.)

ARCHIVES DE L'HÔTEL-DIEU DE QUÉBEC. This repository contains about 200 feet of documents concerning the establishment, government, and administration of the Hôtel-Dieu of Quebec (hospital and convent). For a description of the archives, now being reorganized, *see*: Claire Gagnon et François Rousseau, "Deux inventaires des archives de l'Hôtel-Dieu de Québec," *Archives, 73-1* (Québec), 62–82.

The principal documents used in the preparation of volume III:
Registre des malades, I–IV. 1689–1804.
Registre des comptes du monastère, I–VIII. 1691–1824.
Registre des comptes de l'hôpital, I–IV. 1665–1826.
Registre d'entrées, vêtures, et professions des sœurs de chœurs et des sœurs converses (in the process of being catalogued). 7v., 1646–1825.
Jeanne-Françoise Juchereau de La Ferté de Saint-Ignace, "Histoire abrégée de l'établissement de l'Hôtel-Dieu de Québec." This manuscript, written by Marie-Andrée REGNARD Duplessis de Sainte-Hélène, has been published under the title *Les annales de l'Hôtel-Dieu de Québec, 1636–1716* [*see* section II, JUCHEREAU].

ARCHIVES DES FRANCISCAINS, Montréal. This repository contains copies of documents concerning the Recollets in Canada, 1615–1849. These copies, collected by Fathers Odoric-Marie Jouve and Archange Godbout, are handwritten and not easily legible, and have not been entirely classified. There are two sections where the classification work is more advanced: the biographical dossiers of the Recollets and the dossiers of the parishes where they worked. The biographical dossiers have been used in the preparation of volume III.

ARCHIVES DES SŒURS GRISES, Montréal. The documents which were at the Hôpital Général of Montreal when Mme d'Youville [Dufrost*] became administratrix there in 1747 make up the Fonds "Charon" and are the source of this archival repository. Subsequently the items necessary for the general administration of the community were added. The classification for this repository is alphabetical for the dossiers and chronological within each dossier. The archives contains thousands of documents, the earliest dating from 1663, and about 300 maps and plans.

The principal documents used in the preparation of volume III:
Dossiers
  Constitutions
  Lettres patentes
  Maison mère
MY/B
  Correspondance
Mémoires
  10 [Sœur Baby. Julie Casgrain, 1835–1898]
Notices biographiques
  1741–1848 [Mère McMullen, s.g.m.]
Recette et dépense de juin 1718 à septembre 1746
Recueil des règles et constitutions à l'usage des filles séculières administratrices de l'Hôpital Général de Montréal dites Sœurs de la Charité recueillies sur les anciens titres et usages de la communauté, M. Montgolfier, Étienne, p.s.s., 1694–1796
Registre d'admission des pauvres. 1694–1796.
Registre des baptêmes et sépultures de l'Hôpital Général de Montréal. 1725–1776.
Registre des baptêmes de la paroisse de Saint-François-du-Lac
Registre des sépultures. 1725–1759.
Registre des vêtures, professions, etc. des frères Charon. 1701–1748.

ARCHIVES DU MONASTÈRE DES URSULINES DE QUÉBEC. In the process of being catalogued.
The following documents were used in the preparation of volume III:
Actes d'élection des supérieures. 1788–1941.
Actes des assemblées capitulaires. 1686–1802.
Actes des professions et des sépultures. 1688–1781.
"Annales," I. 1639–1822.
Cahier du P. Ragueneau, copié par Jacques Bigot, s.j., et dédié à M. S.-Benoît
Charlotte Daneau de Muy, dite de Sainte-Hélène, "Abrégé de la vie de Mme la comtesse de Pontbriand"
Entrées, vêtures, professions et décès des religieuses, I. 1647–1861.
Fonds des pères jésuites
  Lettres du père Charles-Michel Mésaiger
Lettre autographe de M. S.-Pierre, 18 juin 1699
Livre des entrées et sorties des filles françaises et sauvages. 1641–1720.
Registre de l'examen canonique des novices, I. 1689–1807.
Registre des entrées des pensionnaires. 1704–1761, 1719–1838.

ARCHIVES DU SÉMINAIRE DE QUÉBEC. One of the most important archival repositories in North America. The records date from the founding of the seminary in 1663, but Mgr Thomas-Étienne Hamel* and Mgr Amédée Gosselin* may be considered to have founded the ASQ at the end of the 19th and the beginning of the 20th century. ASQ contains some 1,172 feet of documents (seminary and private papers, the oldest dating from 1636 and the majority from 1675 to 1950), 2,000 maps, and 160 feet of engravings and photographs.

Documents used in the preparation of volume III include:
Brouillard. 2v., 1705–1753.
Carton Laverdière. 1 carton.
Chapitre. 1 carton containing 340 items, 1666–1785.
Documents Faribault. 1 carton containing 70 items.
Évêques. 1 carton containing 330 items, 1626–1860.
Fichier des écoliers
Fonds Casgrain
Fonds Verreau. Includes the Fonds Viger and is therefore frequently called Viger-Verreau. The collections of Abbé H.-A.-J.-B. Verreau* and Jacques Viger* consist in the main of about a hundred cartons, several notebooks, and the series of Viger's manuscript volumes entitled "Ma Saberdache" (see: Fernand Ouellet, "Inventaire de la Saberdache de Jacques Viger," APQ Rapport, 1955–57, 31–176).
Grand livre de délibération, 1734–1736
Lettres, M, 171 items; N, 181 items; O, 157 items; P, 100 items; R, 190 items; S, 188 items; T, 156 items
Livres de comptes, C 8, 1730–1747; C 10, 1730–1735
Manuscrits, 2, "Annales du petit séminaire"; 12, Grand Livre, 1730–1747; 71–a–1, J.-F. Le Sueur, "Catechismus prolixus de Baptismo et dissertatio christiana de justifica-

tione ... apud Uanbanakaeos Nanransua-kos, 1730''; 176, Charles Plante, ''Éloges funèbres de Mgr de St-Vallier''; 196, Maillard, ''La Religion'' (a poem with explanatory notes); 436–37, A.-É. Gosselin, ''Prêtres du séminaire de Québec (notices), du début à nos jours''; 457, 466–67, ''Annales du petit séminaire''

Missions. 2 cartons (numbering continuous).

Paroisse de Québec. 1 carton containing 101 items, 1652–1877.

Plumitif

Polygraphie. 248 cartons.

Registre des copies de tous les titres du séminaire de Québec. 1710–1754. [Registre A.]

Seigneuries, XIII, île Jésus

Séminaire. 204 cartons.

ARCHIVES DU SÉMINAIRE DE SAINT-SULPICE, Montréal. An important archival repository for the history of the Montreal region under the French régime; on his departure in 1665 Paul de Chomedey* de Maisonneuve left there the greater part of his papers, dating from 1642. The repository, divided into 49 sections, contains 190 feet of documents for the years 1586–1950, and about 1,200 maps and plans.

The following sections were most useful in the preparation of volume III:

Cahiers Faillon. 24 notebooks containing copies of documents (1677–1834) made under the direction of É.-M. Faillon*, with a view to continuing the writing of his *Histoire de la colonie française en Canada* (3v., Villemarie [Montréal], 1865–66).

Catalogue historique et chronologique des prêtres du séminaire de Montréal. 1 notebook.

Joseph-Vincent Quiblier, ''Notes sur le séminaire de Montréal, 1847'' (typescript)

Section de la correspondance générale. 49 cartons, 1670–1928.

Section de la seigneurie du Lac-des-Deux-Montagnes. 69 cartons, 1717–1936.

Section des associations et des communautés. 5 drawers and 18 cartons, in part not classified, 1659–1900.

Section des biographies. 88 items arranged in alphabetical order, 1657–1926.

Section des cartes et plans. About 1,200 items.

Section des concessions de terre et d'emplacement de l'île de Montréal. 25 drawers (5,000 documents), 1648–1854.

Section des manuscrits indiens. 10 cartons, 1660–1880.

Section des titres de propriété du séminaire de Montréal. 1 drawer, 1636–1840.

Section prédication. 8 double drawers, 1724–1940.

ARCHIVES GÉNÉRALES DES RELIGIEUSES HOSPITALIÈRES DE SAINT-JOSEPH, Montréal. This archival repository contains about 200 feet of manuscripts and 250 maps and plans for the period 1589–1900. These documents relate particularly to the administration of the community and of the hospital. There is a well defined system of classification for pre-1760 documents, completed as the preparation of volume III of the *DCB* was drawing to a close. For a description of the archives *see*: ''Cadre de classement des documents antérieurs à 1760'' (manuscript guide available at AHSJ); Jacques Ducharme, ''Historique des archives de l'Hôtel-Dieu de Montréal et des Religieuses hospitalières de Saint-Joseph,'' in *L'Hôtel-Dieu de Montréal (1642–1973)* (Cahiers du Québec, 13, Montréal, 1973).

The principal documents used in volume III of the *DCB*:

Annales de sœur Marie Morin. 1697–1725.

Annales de sœur Véronique Cuillerier. 1725–1747.

Déclarations de nos anciennes mères pour constater la profession et le décès de nos sœurs

Marie Morin, ''Histoire simple et véritable de l'établissement des Religieuses hospitalières de Saint-Joseph en l'île de Montréal, dite à présent Ville-Marie, en Canada, de l'année 1659 . . . .'' Published as *Annales de l'Hôtel-Dieu de Montréal* [*see* section II, MORIN].

ARCHIVES JUDICIAIRES. The repositories of the judicial archives are to be found in the chief towns of the various judicial districts of Quebec. They preserve the registers of births, deaths, and marriages and numerous documents relating to the judicial affairs of their districts, as well as the *greffes* of the notaries and surveyors who practised there.

Documents from the archives of the following districts were particularly useful in the preparation of volume III:

Beauce (Saint-Joseph-de-Beauce). (*See*: ''Inventaire sommaire des archives judiciaires conservées au palais de justice de Saint-Joseph, district de Beauce,'' APQ *Rapport, 1921–22*, 388–90.)

Registre d'état civil
Saint-Joseph-de-Beauce

Montréal. (For pre-1900 documents *see* section I, ANQ, Montréal.)

Québec. (For the *greffes* of notaries *see* section
I, ANQ, Québec.)
Registre d'état civil
Fort Beauharnois-de-la-Pointe-à-la-Che-
velure
L'Ange-Gardien
Notre-Dame de Québec
Notre-Dame-de-Miséricorde-de-Beauport
Saint-Jean-Baptiste-des-Écureuils
Rimouski
Registre d'état civil
Saint-Germain
Trois-Rivières. (*See*: J.-B.-M. Barthe, "Inven-
taire sommaire des archives conservées au
palais de justice des Trois-Rivières," APQ
Rapport, 1920–21, 328–49.)
Greffes de: J.-B. Badeau, 1770–1796
Nicolas Duclos, 1751–1769
Louis Pillard, 1736–1767
A.-B. Pollet, 1730–1754
J.-B. Pottier, 1699–1711
Pierre Poulain, 1711–1720
H.-O. Pressé, 1735–1746
Registre d'état civil
Bécancour
Champlain
Immaculée-Conception de Trois-Rivières
Notre-Dame de Trois-Rivières
Sainte-Geneviève-de-Batiscan
Grand voyer
Registre des procès-verbaux

ARCHIVES NATIONALES DU QUÉBEC. At the conquest, articles 43, 44, and 45 of the capitulation
of Montréal – contrary to the custom of international law at that time – permitted the administrators of New France to take back to France documents relating to the government of the colony.
Only records having a legal value for individuals
were to remain in the country, and these were to
suffer many misfortunes before the office of the
Archives de la province de Québec – now the
Archives nationales du Québec – was created in
1920 [*see*: Gilles Héon, "Bref historique des
Archives du Québec," ANQ *Rapport, 1970*,
13–25]. Some 3,300 feet of documents are preserved there today (official and private papers,
originals and copies), the majority for the period
1663–1867. In 1968 the ANQ published an *État
général des archives publiques et privées* and
established a new system of classification.
　The following documents were used in the
preparation of volume III:
Greffes de: Jacques Barbel, 1703–1740
R.-C. Barolet, 1731–1761
Nicolas Boisseau, 1731–1744

Gilbert Boucault de Godefus,
1736–1756
Louis Chambalon, 1692–1716
J.-B. Choret, 1730–1755
Antoine Crespin, 1750–1782
J.-É. Dubreuil, 1708–1739
C.-H. Du Laurent, 1734–1760
François Genaple de Bellefonds,
1682–1709
Henry Hiché, 1725–1736
Jacques de Horné, dit Laneu-
ville, 1701–1730
Jacques Imbert, 1740–1749
Étienne Jeanneau, 1674–1743
Florent de La Cetière, 1702–
1728
P.-A.-F. Lanoullier Des
Granges, 1749–1760
Jean de Latour, 1736–1741
Claude Louet, 1718–1737
J.-C. Louet, 1738–1767
Abel Michon, 1709–1749
J.-C. Panet, 1745–1775
N.-C. Pinguet de Bellevue,
1749–1751
J.-N. Pinguet de Vaucour,
1726–1748
François Rageot, 1709–1753
Pierre Rivet Cavelier, 1709–1719
Guillaume Roger, 1694–1702
J.-A. Saillant, 1750–1776
Simon Sanguinet, 1748–1771
Jean Taché, 1768

AP: Archives privées. In the process of being
classified according to a numerical system.
NF: Nouvelle-France
Arrêts du Conseil d'état du roi, 1663–1753.
9v.
Aveux et dénombrements, 1723–1758. 5v.
Collection de pièces judiciaires et notariales,
1638–1759. 125v.
Cours seigneuriales, 1662–1760. 1v.
Documents de la juridiction de Montréal,
1675–1705. 1 carton.
Documents de la juridiction des Trois-
Rivières, 1646–1759. 20v.
Documents de la Prévôté de Québec,
1668–1759. 17v.
Dossiers du Conseil supérieur, 1663–1759.
11v.
Foi et hommage, 1667–1759. 5v.
Insinuations de la Prévôté de Québec,
1667–1863. 207 boxes.
Insinuations du Conseil supérieur, 1663–
1758. 10v.
Ordonnances des intendants, 1666–1760.
46v.

Procès-verbaux des grands voyers, 1668–1780. 9v.

Registres de la Prévoté de Québec, 1666–1759. 113v.

Registres d'intendance, 1672–1759. 4v.

Registres divers et pièces détachées du Conseil supérieur, 1663–1760. 5v.

Registres du Conseil supérieur, 1663–1760. 69v.

Taxes de dépens du Conseil supérieur, 1703–1759. 10 cartons.

QBC: Québec et Bas-Canada

  Cours de justice, 1760–1880. 67v.

    Chambres des milices. Montréal, 1760–1764. 6v.

    Conseil militaire. Québec, 1760–1764. 6v.

Copies d'archives d'autres dépôts

  Canada

    Paroisses. Saint-Pierre, île d'Orléans, 1679–1708.

  France

    Manuscrits relatifs à l'histoire de la Nouvelle-France. 3e série: manuscrits relatifs à l'histoire de la Nouvelle-France, 1713–1731. 7v.

  Archives de la Guerre

    "Inventaire analytique des Archives de la Guerre concernant le Canada (1755–1760)," compilé par Jehan-Éric Labignette et Louise Dechêne.

ANQ, Montréal. On 21 Sept. 1971 the ANQ took possession of a repository in Montreal where it preserves pre-1900 documents formerly kept at AJM. In the individual bibliographies we have used the old AJM system of classification, whose series titles appear here in square brackets. For further information, consult "État sommaire des Archives nationales du Québec à Montréal," ANQ *Rapport, 1972*, 1–29.

Series cited in volume III include:

Greffes de: Antoine Adhémar, 1668–1714

    J.-B. Adhémar, 1714–1754

    Guillaume Barette, 1709–1744

    Bénigne Basset Des Lauriers, 1657–1699

    Hilaire Bourgine, 1685–1690

    François Comparet, 1736–1755

    C.-F. Coron, 1734–1767

    François Coron, 1721–1732

    L.-C. Danré de Blanzy, 1738–1760

    Jacques David, 1719–1726

    Antoine Foucher, 1746–1800

    C.-R. Gaudron de Chevremont, 1732–1739

    N.-A. Guillet de Chaumont, 1727–1752

    F.-M. Lepailleur, 1733–1739

    Michel Lepailleur, 1703–1732

    Antoine Loiseau, 1730–1760

    Claude Maugue, 1677–1696

    Cyr de Monmerqué, 1731–1765

    Michel Moreau, 1681–1698

    Pierre Panet, 1755–1778

    J.-C. Porlier, 1733–1744

    J.-C. Raimbault, 1727–1737

    Pierre Raimbault, 1697–1727

    Simon Sanguinet, 1734–1747

    Nicolas Senet, 1704–1731

    François Simonet, 1737–1778

    Marien Tailhandier, dit La Beaume, 1699–1730

    J.-B. Tétro, 1712–1728

État civil [Registre d'état civil]

  Catholique:

    Chambly

    Laprairie

    Notre-Dame de Montréal

    Saint-Laurent

Documents judiciaires

  Pièces détachées de documents surtout à caractère judiciaire, classées par ordre chronologique [Documents judiciaires], 1677–1760. 163v.

  Dossiers sur divers procès célèbres [Procès fameux], 1660–1756. 5v.

  Bailliage. Juridiction de Montréal [Registre du bailliage], 1665–1687. 2 registers.

  Registres des audiences, 1687–1760. 30 registers.

Procès-verbaux d'arpenteurs

  Procès-verbaux divers [Arpentage], 1663–1913. 4v.

Inventaires, clôtures d'inventaires et successions

  Inventaires et clôtures d'inventaires [Clôtures d'inventaires], 1665–*c*. 1760. 9v.

Arrêts, ordonnances et mandements

  Ordonnances (especially those of the governors of Montreal; also some ordinances of intendants and certain pastoral letters of bishops) [Documents divers], 1653–1765. 7v.

ARCHIVES PAROISSIALES. Contain in particular the registers of births, marriages, and deaths, of which copies are kept in the judicial archives of the district, and the parish account books.

The following documents from parish archives have been consulted in the preparation of volume III:

Notre-Dame-de-Foy (Sainte-Foy, Québec)

  Registres des baptêmes, mariages et sépultures

Notre-Dame de Montréal
  Livres de comptes, 1724–1735
  Registres des baptêmes, mariages et sépultures
Notre-Dame de Québec
  Livres de comptes, 1709–1724
  Registres des baptêmes, mariages et sépultures
Saint-Ambroise (Loretteville, Québec)
  Registres des baptêmes, mariages et sépultures
Saint-Charles (Charlesbourg, Québec)
  Livres de comptes, I, 1675–1749
Saint-Charles (Lachenaie, Québec)
  Livres de comptes, I, 1725–1739
Sainte-Anne (Beaupré, Québec)
  Registres des baptêmes, mariages et sépultures
Sainte-Anne (La Pérade, Québec)
  Registres des baptêmes, mariages et sépultures
Sainte-Anne (Varennes, Québec)
  Livres de comptes, I, 1725–1729
Sainte-Geneviève (Berthier, Québec)
  Livres de comptes, I–II
Sainte-Geneviève (Pierrefonds, Québec)
  Livres de comptes, I
Saint-Étienne (Beaumont, Québec)
  Livres de comptes, I
Saint-François-de-Sales (Laval, Québec)
  Livres de comptes, I
Saint-François-de-Sales (Neuville, Québec)
  Livres de comptes, I
  Registres des baptêmes, mariages et sépultures
Saint-François-de-Sales (Saint-François, île d'Orléans)
  Livres de comptes, I
  Registres des baptêmes, mariages et sépultures
Saint-François-Xavier (Verchères, Québec)
  Livres de comptes, I
Saint-Louis (Lotbinière, Québec)
  Registres des baptêmes, mariages et sépultures
Saint-Pierre (Saint-Pierre, île d'Orléans)
  Livres de comptes

L'INVENTAIRE DES ŒUVRES D'ART, Québec. In 1940 Gérard Morisset* established the Service de l'Inventaire des œuvres d'art for the purpose of recording and locating works of art. In taking over responsibility for this work in the same year, the government of Quebec gave recognition to a project which had been conducted personally by Morisset for more than ten years. Aided by a staff which he had trained himself, until 1967 Morisset photographed articles of silver, works of architecture, and paintings, searched parish account books, newspapers, and notarial registers, and accumulated many thousands of documents on artisans and their work. This impressive collection (about 70,000 photographs, 40,000 biographical cards, 20,000 slides, and 5,000 old photographs) had already acquired an archival value as the result of the disappearance of a number of the works of art. The conservation and processing of the collection was undertaken by the Ministère des Affaires culturelles in 1970. In collaboration with the Centre de documentation de l'université Laval, the documents were studied, reclassified according to geographical location, and described in a manner which allows researchers to identify quickly the title, the symbolic content, and the technical features of each work. The collection is open to all researchers upon application to the Ministère des Affaires culturelles.

PUBLIC ARCHIVES OF CANADA, Ottawa. In 1873 the government of Canada commissioned Douglas Brymner and Abbé H.-A.-J.-B. Verreau* to investigate the holdings of English and French archives with a view to copying documents concerning the early history of Canada. The work of transcribing and microfilming such manuscripts, and of collecting original materials, has proceeded since that time.

Many unpublished finding aids are available only in the archives. The following *Preliminary inventories* and *Inventories* to manuscript and record groups used in the preparation of volume III have been published by the manuscript division:

General inventory, manuscripts, I (1971). MG 1–MG 10.
General inventory, manuscripts, IV (1972). MG 22–MG 25.
Manuscript group 11, Public Record Office, London, Colonial Office papers (1961)
Manuscript group 17, religious archives (1967)
Manuscript group 18, pre-conquest papers (1964)
Manuscript group 19, fur trade and Indians, 1763–1867 (1954)
Manuscript group 21, transcripts from papers in the British Museum (1955)
Manuscript group 30, twentieth century manuscripts (1966)
Record group 1, Executive Council, Canada, 1764–1867 (1953)
Record group 4, civil and provincial secretaries' offices, Canada East, 1760–1867 (1953)

Record group 10, Indian affairs (1951) Unpublished "addenda" for the above inventories are available for consultation at the PAC. Also available is the unpublished provisional inventory, "Manuscript group 36, finding aids to sources in other archival repositories." Revised inventories to record groups 1 and 4 are in preparation.

See also: "Guides to calendars of series and collections in the Public Archives," PAC *Report, 1949*, 451–59; H.P. Beers, *The French & British in the old Northwest: a bibliographical guide to archive and manuscript sources* (Detroit, 1964) and *The French in North America: a bibliographical guide to French archives, reproductions, and research missions* (Baton Rouge, 1957).

The following collections were found useful in the preparation of volume III:

MG 6: Archives départementales, municipales, maritimes et de bibliothèques (France)
  A: Archives départementales
    2: Charente-Maritime (La Rochelle). Transcriptions, 1599–1786; microfilm, 1616–1787.
MG 7: Bibliothèques de Paris
  I: Bibliothèque nationale
    A: Département des manuscrits
      3: Nouvelles acquisitions françaises. Transcriptions, 1510–1889; microfilm, 1660–1889; photocopies, 1619–86.
  II: Bibliothèque de l'Arsenal. Transcriptions, 1673–1772.
  V: Bibliothèque du Muśee d'histoire naturelle. Transcriptions, 1749–55.
MG 8: Documents relatifs à la Nouvelle-France et au Québec (XVIIᵉ–XXᵉ siècles)
  A: Documents généraux
    2: Jugements et délibérations du Conseil supérieur. Transcriptions, 1717–59.
    6: Ordonnances des intendants. Transcriptions, 1705–60.
    14: Conseil supérieur: matières civiles. Transcriptions, 1682–1712.
  B: District de Québec
    1: Registres de la Prévôté de Québec. Transcriptions, 1666–1759.
    3: Prévôté: pièces diverses. Transcriptions, 1689–1746.
    6: Successions, tutelles et émancipations. Transcriptions, 1639–1736.
  C: District de Montréal
    3: Répertoire de greffes de notaires. Transcriptions, 1648–1842; photocopies, 1740–1814.

4: Index des contrats de mariage. Transcriptions, 1650–1839.
  E: Régime militaire
    6: Chambre de milice de Montréal. Transcriptions, 1760–64.
  F: Documents relatifs aux seigneuries et autres lieux
    50: Livaudière. Transcriptions, 1733–54.
  G: Archives paroissiales
    24: Québec. Transcriptions, 1621–1847.
MG 9: Provincial, local, and territorial records
  B: Nova Scotia
    8: Church records
    9: Local records
MG 11: Public Record Office, London: Colonial Office papers
  Nova Scotia A: Correspondence. Transcripts and photocopies, 1603–1840. Up to 1801 this series is a composite of transcripts from various sources in Great Britain, especially the PRO. By the time that the work of transcription had reached 1802 the PRO had established the CO 217 series. For the period 1802–31 Nova Scotia A consists of transcripts from CO 217, and for the period 1831–40 of photocopies from the same series. Documents for the period covered by volume III are calendared in PAC *Report, 1894*.
  Nova Scotia B: Minutes of the Executive Council. Transcripts, 1720–85. A composite series taken principally from sources which are now part of PRO, CO 217 or CO 220. Documents for the period covered by volume III are calendared in PAC *Report, 1949*.
MG 17: Religious archives
  A: Église catholique
    3: Séminaire des Missions étrangères, Paris. Transcriptions, 1640–1851.
  D: Moravian Brethren
    1: Moravian Brethren. Originals, 1827–1955; transcripts, 1752, 1770–79; microfilm, 1749–1944.
MG 18: Pre-conquest papers
  F: Acadia and Newfoundland
    10: Morris, Charles. Photocopies, [1748].
    12: Pichon, Thomas. Transcripts, 1750–62; photocopies, 1754–55.
    13: Lawrence, Charles. Photocopies, 1754–55; typewritten copies, 1747–61.
    20: Chalmers collection. Photocopies, 1755–1817.
    23: Holdsworth, Arthur. Originals, 1730–73.
    24: Keen, William. Original, 1736.
  H: New France

13: Denys, famille. Original, 1710; transcriptions, 1655–1787; microfilm, 1654–1870; photocopies, 1658, 1724.

17: Taschereau, famille. Originaux, 1707–1874.

28: Morin, Pierre-Louis. Originaux, 1836–84; transcriptions, 1504–1763.

J: Memoirs and travel

8: Boucault, Nicolas-Gaspard, Originaux, 1754; photocopies, 1728, 1738.

L: British officers

1: Colvill(e), Alexander, Baron. Photocopies, 1732–64.

4: Amherst family. Microfilm, 1758–63; transcripts, 1758–1836; photocopies, 1758–1854.

M: Northcliffe collection [*see also* section II]

Series 1: Robert Monckton papers. Originals, transcripts, and printed papers, 1742–1834.

Series 3: Separate items. Originals, transcripts, and printed items, 1683–1799.

N: Military and naval documents

8: New England troops, muster rolls of. Originals, 1760; transcripts, 1710–60.

13: Beaujeu, Louis Liénard de. Photocopie, 1747.

15: Seven Years' War. Originals, 1758–60; transcripts, 1754–59.

16: Louisbourg: 1758 campaign. Originals, 1758; transcripts, 1757.

30: Hopson, Peregrine Thomas. Originals, 1752–58.

O: Miscellaneous

6: Couagne, famille. Originaux, 1761–69.

9: Hancock, Thomas and John. Microfilm, 1744–83.

MG 19: Fur trade and Indians

F: Indians

1: Claus family. Originals, 1755–1886.

MG 21: Transcripts from papers in the British Museum

E: Nova Scotia

5: Add. MSS 19069–76. Papers relating to Nova Scotia collected by Dr Andrew Brown. Transcripts, Add. MSS 19069–74; photocopies, Add. MSS 19075–76.

H: Military and naval

10: The King's topographical collection, CXIX, 107B. Report by J. H. Bastide on the fortifications of Newfoundland. Photocopy, 1750.

MG 23: Late eighteenth century papers

C: Nova Scotia

16: How, Edward. Transcripts, 1744–90.

GII: Quebec and Lower Canada: political figures

1: Murray, James. Originals, 1757–78; transcripts, 1734–92; photocopies, 1765–93.

2: Collier, John and family. Transcripts, 1723–79.

19: Monk family. Originals, 1735–1888.

GIII: Quebec and Lower Canada: merchants and settlers

25: Antiquarian and Numismatic Society of Montreal. Microfilm, 1712–1930.

28: Guy, Pierre, père et fils. Microfilm, 1739–79.

MG 24: Nineteenth century pre-confederation papers

L: Miscellaneous

3: Collection Baby. Originaux, 1871, 1879; transcriptions, 1629–1907; microfilm, 1691, 1740–1836.

MG 30: Twentieth century manuscripts

D: Education and cultural development

58: Roy, Pierre-Georges. Originaux, *c*.1915–23; photocopie, 1917.

62: Audet, Francis Joseph. Originaux, 1907–42.

RG 1: Executive Council of Canada, 1764–1867

E: State records

1: Minute books (state matters). Originals, 1764–1867; certified typed copies, 1764–91.

RG 4: Civil and provincial secretaries' offices, Quebec, Lower Canada and Canada East

A: Civil secretary's correspondence, 1760–1841

1: S series. Originals, 1760–1840.

RG 10: Indian affairs records

A: Administration records of the imperial government, 1677–1860

2: Records of the superintendent's office. Originals, 1755–1830.

3: Records of the military. Originals, 1677–1841.

National Map Collection. A separate division within the PAC since 1908, the National Map Collection has assembled much of the cartographic record of Canada, both archival and current, as well as architectural and engineering drawings of national interest. For the period 1700–1800 over 2,000 maps, charts, plans, atlases, drawings, and related cartographical materials have been acquired, touching upon the exploration of the country, the settlement of the land, the evolution of political boundaries, and urban development. These include original and printed items as well as many photocopies of materials, the originals of which are in other archives, mainly French and British.

PUBLIC ARCHIVES OF NOVA SCOTIA, Halifax. Founded in 1857 when the Nova Scotian government decided to preserve and arrange "the ancient records and documents illustrative of the History and progress of Society in this province," thus establishing the first provincial archives in Canada. The present fireproof building was officially opened on 14 Jan. 1931, and records were transferred from various government departments. The archives also contains court papers, municipal records, family and business papers, collections of societies such as the Nova Scotia Historical Society, community and church records, microfilm copies of deeds and wills from county registries and courts of probate, and a collection of Nova Scotian newspapers. For further information *see*: C. B. Fergusson, *The Public Archives of Nova Scotia* (PANS *Bull.*, 19, Halifax, 1963). For a further description of the collections cited in volume III see: *Catalogue or list of manuscript documents, arranged, bound and catalogued under the direction of the commissioner of public records . . .* (Halifax, 1877; 2nd ed., 1886). Available for use at PANS are sections of an "Inventory of manuscripts" which is now being compiled for publication in 1975.

Materials used in the preparation of volume III include:

MG 1: Papers of families and individuals

109–11: Winthrop Bell, "Register of Lunenburg settlers." Originals.

472–74: Edward How family. Originals.

RG 1: Miscellaneous government documents which had been arranged in bound volumes

7: Annapolis Royal, N.S. – Letters and other documents from governors Nicholson and Philipps at Annapolis Royal to Secretary of State and Plantations Office, 1712–25. Transcripts.

8: Annapolis Royal, N.S. – Letters and orders relating to affairs of Annapolis Royal, 6 June 1711–October 1713, while under the government of Colonel Samuel Vetch. Transcripts.

9: Annapolis Royal, N.S. – Government at Annapolis Royal, including memorials of Captain Paul Mascarene, 1713, 1714, 1720–25; private letter book and journal of Governor Paul Mascarene, 1742–53; also letters from and to Mascarene, Governor William Shirley, and others, as well as other papers, 1710–53. Transcripts.

12: Nova Scotia – Documents relating to Nova Scotia and its connection with the government of Massachusetts Bay, 1725–44, including journal of proceedings of conference held by governors of Massachusetts, New Hampshire, and New York with eastern Indians at Casco Bay, 1725. Transcripts.

13: Nova Scotia – Papers from Public Record Office, London, regarding Nova Scotia, 1745–50. Transcripts.

13¹/₂: Nova Scotia – Papers from Public Record Office, London, regarding Nova Scotia, 1745–49. Transcripts.

14: Annapolis Royal, N.S. – Letters written by governors R. Philipps, Paul Mascarene, Lawrence Armstrong, and others to the Board of Trade and Secretary of State, to French deputies and others, 2 Jan. 1719–8 June 1742. Contemporary copies. Published in abstract in *N.S. Archives, II* [see section II].

17: Annapolis Royal, N.S. – Dispatches from governors of Nova Scotia to Secretary of State, 1720–48. Transcripts.

18: Annapolis Royal, N.S. – Dispatches from governors of Nova Scotia to Board of Trade and Plantations, February 1715/16–April 1749. Transcripts.

21: Annapolis Royal, N.S. – Commission and letter book, 1742–49. Original.

23: Annapolis Royal, N.S. – Minutes of H.M. Council at Annapolis Royal, September 1720–1732. Transcripts.

26: Annapolis Royal, N.S. – Register of baptisms, marriages, and burials at Annapolis Royal, 1702–28. Original, in French.

37: Nova Scotia – Dispatches from governors of Nova Scotia to Board of Trade and Plantations, 26 Oct. 1760–25 Nov. 1781. Transcripts.

134: Nova Scotia–Dispatches and letters of governors and secretaries of Nova Scotia and other colonies in North America, including several documents relating to the Acadians, and to the French governors of Cape Breton, November 1753–June 1755. Original, known as "Inland letter-book."

163: Nova Scotia commission and order book, July 1749–Nov. 1759. Original.

163/1: 14 July 1749–23 Sept. 1752

163/2: 3 Aug. 1752–27 Oct. 1753

163/3: 2 Nov. 1753–13 Nov. 1759

164: Nova Scotia commission book, 1749–66. Original.

164/1: May 1749–29 July 1752

164/2: 4 May 1752–4 June 1766

165: Nova Scotia commission and order book, 1759–66. Original.

206: Nova Scotia minutes of Council concerning intestate and insolvent estates, 4 March 1761–19 Feb. 1781. Originals.

342: Nova Scotia – Papers connected with crown prosecutions for treason, murder, etc., 1749–79, and also concerning the Lunenburg riots of 1753. Originals.

382: Lunenburg, N.S. – Documents relative to the settlement of the town, 1751–99, 1828. Originals.

492: Nova Scotia court of vice-admiralty, record of proceedings and some commissions and letters of marque, June 1751–November 1756. Originals.

RG 3: Minutes of Nova Scotia Council, 1750–66. Originals and transcripts.

FRANCE

ARCHIVES DÉPARTEMENTALES. The departmental archives of France contain valuable information on many figures belonging to early Canadian history. For lists of analytical inventories *see*: France, Direction des Archives, *État des inventaires des archives nationales, départementales, communales et hospitalières au 1er janvier 1937* (Paris, 1938); *Supplément, 1937–54* [by R.-H. Bautier] (Paris, 1955); *Catalogue des inventaires, répertoires, guides de recherche et autres instruments de travail des archives départementales, communales et hospitalières . . . à la date du 31 décembre 1961* (Paris, 1962). For copies of documents in the PAC see: *General inventory, manuscripts, I* (Ottawa, 1971), 87–99. There is a uniform system of classification for all departmental archives. A list of the various series may be found in *DCB*, II, 683–84.

Series cited in volume III:

B: Cours et juridictions

E: Titres de famille, états civils, notaires [*États civils* are often more complete in municipal archives.]

The archives of the following departments have been consulted:

Alpes-Maritimes	Loire-Atlantique
Ardennes	Maine-et-Loire
Bouches-du-Rhône	Nord
Charente-Maritime	Puy-de-Dôme
Côte-d'Or	Seine-Maritime
Eure	Tarn-et-Garonne
Gironde	Var
Haute-Vienne	Vendée
Haut-Rhin	Vienne
Ille-et-Vilaine	Yonne
Landes	Yvelines

ARCHIVES DU MINISTÈRE DES ARMÉES, Paris:

INSPECTION DU GÉNIE. The Dépôt des fortifications was for a long time subject to the authority of the Ministère de la Guerre; in 1791, however, it was placed under the Direction des officiers du Génie, and later the Comité technique du Génie. The governing authority is now the Inspection du Génie. The aim of the establishment has always been to create a collection illustrating the art of fortification by the accumulation of memoirs, maps and plans, and printed works.

There are two repositories:

Archives du Génie. Situated at the Château de Vincennes, this archives originally included 23 articles. A certain number have been turned over to other archives, notably article 9 (Colonies françaises), which is now in AN, Section Outre-mer, Dépôt des fortifications des colonies, and article 16 (Cartes), which has passed to the BN. There remain, however, several *registres* or cartons which contain information on former French colonies.

Articles used in the preparation of volume III include:

Article 3: Personnel

Article 8: Place française

Article 14: Places étrangères: Amérique septentrionale, possessions anglaises, États-Unis, Louisbourg, île Royale . . .

Article 15: Histoire militaire, campagnes et sièges

Bibliothèque du Génie, 39, rue de Bellechasse. The library contains both manuscript items, dating from the middle of the 17th century, and printed works. The manuscripts are catalogued in France, Ministère de la Guerre, *Catalogue général des manuscrits des bibliothèques publiques de France: bibliothèques de la Guerre* (Paris, 1911).

Manuscript items used in the preparation of volume III include:

mss in 4°, 66: Collection Lafitte (mémoires divers sur les sièges et campagnes)

mss in fol., 205b: "Registres des lettres écrites de rapport au service des fortifications de l'Isle Royale et du Canada." 1750–55.

mss in fol., 208: "Estat alphabétique des ingénieurs du Roi en 1743 où sont marqués les apointements qu'ils avoient en 1717 et les grades et augmentations qui leur ont été accordés depuis." The list stops at the letter V, which is incomplete.

mss in fol., 208c: État des ingénieurs du roi. 1683–1777.

mss in fol., 210f: contains a manuscript account of Louis FRANQUET's journey to Île Saint-Jean, Baie-Verte, Beauséjour, Fort Gaspereau, and Port-Toulouse in 1751; several letters (with maps and plans) from

Franquet to Noël de Régemortes, dated from Louisbourg in 1751; and a manuscript account of François-Claude-Victor GRILLOT de Poilly's survey of Île Royale in 1757.

SERVICE HISTORIQUE DE L'ARMÉE. This archival group was officially formed in 1688; the earliest volumes date from 1631. Now housed at the Pavillon du Roi, Château de Vincennes, the archives were, before 1919, referred to as the Archives de la Guerre. The organization of the archives is described in Madeleine Lenoir, "La documentation historique militaire en France," *Revue de défense nationale* (Paris), numéro hors série (décembre 1952); J.-E. Roy, *Rapport sur les archives de France* [*see* section III]. The archives consists of two separate collections, the historical archives and the administrative archives. A manuscript inventory is available at PAC: Louise Dechêne, "Inventaire analytique des documents relatifs à l'histoire du Canada conservés en France au Service historique de l'Armée."

The following series from the two collections were used in the preparation of volume III:

Archives historiques

A: Archives antérieures à 1789

A¹: Correspondance générale, opérations militaires. Inventoried in France, Archives de la Guerre, *Inventaire sommaire des archives historiques (archives anciennes: correspondance)...*, Félix Brun, comp. (Paris, 1898).

A³: Fonds divers
Mémoires historiques et reconnaissances militaires. Inventoried in Louis Tuetey, *Catalogue général des manuscrits des bibliothèques publiques de France: Archives de la Guerre* (3v., Paris, 1910–12).
Mémoires historiques. Comprising diaries of campaigns, accounts of battles and sieges. (The Reconnaissances militaires are mostly documents of a topographic nature. Also included in the series are more than 1,100 articles relating to military administration.)

Archives administratives

X: Corps des troupes
Xᵉ: Génie: administration des corps et écoles, bâtiments (à l'exclusion des travaux) (1715–1870)
Xⁱ: Troupes coloniales (1770–1830)
Y: Documents individuels
Yᵃ: Mémoires et projets
Yᵇ: Contrôles "officiers." Classified only for the years 1715–90.
Yᵈ: Dossiers individuels. Not yet classified.

Y⁴ᵈ: Brigadiers
Sub-series Xᵉ, Xⁱ, Yᵇ, and Yᵈ are inventoried in France, Archives de la Guerre, *Inventaire des archives conservées au Service historique de l'État-major de l'Armée, château de Vincennes (archives modernes)* (2ᵉ éd., rev. et complétée par M.-A. Fabre *et al.*, Paris, 1954).

ARCHIVES NATIONALES, Paris. The Archives nationales was founded in 1789 to accommodate the original papers of the Constituent Assembly. The papers of the pre-revolutionary administration were added later. The basic inventories are: France, Direction des Archives, *Inventaire sommaire et tableau méthodique des fonds conservés aux Archives nationales, 1ʳᵉ partie, régime antérieur à 1789* (Paris, 1871); *État sommaire par séries des documents conservés aux Archives nationales* (Paris, 1891); *Catalogue des manuscrits conservés aux Archives nationales* (Paris, 1892). Guides to finding aids are: France, Direction des Archives, *État des inventaires des archives nationales, départementales, communales et hospitalières au 1ᵉʳ janvier 1937* (Paris, 1938), and *Supplément, 1937–54* [by R.-H. Bautier] (Paris, 1955); Gilles Héon, "Fonds intéressant le Canada conservés en France: quelques instruments de recherche," *Archives, 73-1* (Québec), 40–50. J.-E. Roy, *Rapport sur les archives de France* [*see* section III], and H. P. Beers, *The French in North America: a bibliographical guide to French archives, reproductions, and research missions* (Baton Rouge, 1957), give sketches of the history and organization of the archives. For copies in the PAC of documents in the Archives nationales see: *General inventory, manuscripts, I* (Ottawa, 1971), 5–48.

The basic classification of the Archives nationales is as follows:

I: Section ancienne (which includes the Fonds des Colonies and the Fonds de la Marine)
II: Service des Sceaux
III: Section moderne
IV: Section contemporaine
V: Section Outre-mer
VI: Département des activités scientifiques, culturelles, et techniques

The following material from sections I, V, and VI was used in the preparation of volume III:

I: Section ancienne
G: Administration financière, etc.
G⁵: Amirauté et conseil des prises, 1675–1758
L: "Monuments" ecclésiastiques
LL: Registres
M: Mélanges

Fonds des Colonies. These records date from 1458 and consist largely of pre-1815 documents, although some material up to 1898 is included. Eventually they will be integrated with the Section Outre-mer [*q.v.*]. Colbert established the distinction between papers relating to the Marine and those concerning the colonies and also laid down the major series in the Fonds des Colonies. These series and the many later sub-divisions of series are described in Étienne Taillemite, "Les archives des colonies françaises aux Archives nationales," *Gazette des Archives* (Paris), XLVI (1964), 93–116. For copies of manuscripts in the PAC see: *General inventory, manuscripts, I,* 5–16.

A: Actes du pouvoir souverain, 1669–1782. Royal edicts and ordinances, proclamations of the Conseil d'État, etc.

B: Correspondance envoyée, 1663–1815. Dispatches of the king, the minister of Marine, and the Conseil d'État to officials in the colonies. For the 17th and 18th centuries *see* the following calendars: Étienne Taillemite, *Inventaire analytique de la correspondance générale avec les colonies, départ, série B (déposée aux Archives nationales), I, registres 1 à 37 (1654–1715)* (Paris, 1959), and PAC *Report, 1899,* Supp., 245–548; *Report, 1904,* App. K, 1–312; *Report, 1905, I,* pt. VI, 3–446.

C: Correspondance générale, lettres reçues. Letters from officials in the colonies to the king and to the minister of Marine and some drafts of documents sent to the colonies.

C^2: Inde, 1664–1808

C^8: Martinique

C^{8A}: 1663–1815. For an analysis of this series *see*: Étienne Taillemite, *Inventaire de la série Colonies C^{8A}, Martinique (correspondance à l'arrivée)* (2v., Paris, 1967–71). [Articles 1 to 121.]

C^{8B}: 1635–1789

C^9: Saint-Domingue

C^{9A}: 1664–1789

C^{11}: Canada et colonies d'Amérique du Nord

C^{11A}: Canada, 1458–1784. A calendar of documents is published in PAC *Report, 1885,* xxix–lxxix; *Report, 1886,* xxxix–cl; *Report, 1887,* cxl–ccxxxix. *See also*: Parker, *Guide,* 227ff [*see* section III]. An unpublished index for this series exists at the PAC.

C^{11B}: Île Royale, 1712–62. Volumes 1–38 are calendared in Parker, *Guide,* 241–45, and PAC *Report, 1887,* cclxxxii–cccxciv.

C^{11C}: Amérique du Nord, 1661–1898. Papers concerning Newfoundland, Îles de la Madeleine, Île Royale, and Gaspé. Calendared in Parker, *Guide,* 246, and PAC *Report, 1887,* cccxciv–cccxcviii. An unpublished index to C^{11B} and C^{11C} is available at the Fortress of Louisbourg and on microfilm at the PAC.

C^{11D}: Acadie, 1603–1788. Calendared in Parker, *Guide,* 238–40, and PAC *Report, 1887,* ccxxxix–cclxiii.

C^{11E}: Canada, divers, 1651–1818. Letters etc. dealing with boundary disputes. Calendared in Parker, *Guide,* 240–41, and PAC *Report, 1887,* cclxiii–cclxxxii.

C^{11G}: Correspondance Raudot-Pontchartrain, Domaine d'Occident et île Royale, 1677–1758. Calendared in Parker, *Guide,* 246–48, and PAC *Report, 1889,* Supp., 201–44.

C^{13}: Louisiane

C^{13A}: 1678–1803

C^{13B}: 1699–1803

C^{13C}: 1673–1782

D: Matricules des troupes

D^{2C}: Troupes des colonies, 1627–1885. Selected volumes are calendared in PAC *Report, 1905, I,* pt. VI, 508–18. The following volume was particularly useful:

222: Alphabet Laffilard. Service records of officers who served in the colonies before 1740.

D^{2D}: Personnel militaire et civil, 1685–1789

E: Personnel individuel

F: Documents divers

F^1: Commerce aux colonies

F^{1A}: Fonds des colonies, 1670–1789. Financial documents.

F^2: Commerce aux colonies

F^{2B}: Commerce des colonies, 1663–1790

F^{2C}: Colonies en général, 1704–89

F^3: Collection Moreau de Saint-Méry, 1540–1806. Seventeenth-, 18th- and 19th-century originals, and copies of documents in the C^{11A} and B series and of others that have since disappeared. Papers relating to Canada, Louisiana, Île Royale, Saint-Pierre, and Miquelon have been copied and microfilmed by the PAC. Calendared in PAC *Report, 1899*, Supp., 39–191; *Report, 1905*, I, pt. VI, 447–505; Parker, *Guide*, 249–53.

F⁵ᴬ: Missions religieuses, 1639–1808. Inventoried in Albert Mirot, *Inventaire général des documents relatifs aux missions religieuses conservés aux Archives nationales* (Paris, s.d.), and PAC *Report, 1899*, Supp., 192–200.

Fonds de la Marine. After the formation of the Marine under Colbert, papers relating to the navy and to colonial affairs were collected in the Fonds de la Marine. In 1884 the Fonds des Colonies were separated from the Marine. The material in the Fonds de la Marine extends to 1870. For descriptions of the archives *see*: Didier Neuville, *État sommaire des Archives de la Marine antérieures à la Révolution* (Paris, 1898); J.-E. Roy, *Rapport sur les archives de France*, 157–243; Étienne Taillemite, *Les archives anciennes de la Marine* (Académie de Marine, Paris, [1961]). For copies of manuscripts in the PAC see: *General inventory, manuscripts, I*, 24–30.

A: Actes du pouvoir souverain, 1558–1790

B: Service général. Inventoried in Didier Neuville *et al.*, *Inventaire des Archives de la Marine, série B: service général* (8v., Paris, 1885–1963).

B¹: Décisions, 1686–1786. Reports prepared for the council of the Marine, the king, the minister of Marine, and the Conseil d'État.

B²: Correspondance, lettres envoyées, 1662–1789. The kings' and ministers' orders to the department of the Marine, military commanders, and intendants of the Marine in French ports.

B³: Correspondance, lettres reçues, 1660–1789. Correspondence received by the minister from the ports of France and from various authorities. For a name and subject index to this and the two preceding series *see*: Étienne Taillemite *et al.*, *Tables des noms de lieux, de personnes, de matières et de navires, sous-série B¹, B² et B³* (Paris, 1969).

B⁴: Campagnes, 1640–1789. Material relating to naval campaigns.

C: Personnel

C¹: Officiers militaires de la Marine, 1400–1789. "Revues Laffilard" and "Alphabets Laffilard" are contained in volumes 105–7, 151, 153–55, 157, 160–61.

C²: Officiers civils de la Marine, 1663–1770

C⁶: Rôles d'équipage, 1668–1792

C⁷: Personnel individuel, 1651–1789

G: Mémoires et documents divers

Dépôt du service central hydrographique (formerly Archives du service hydrographique)

1 JJ: Correspondance du directeur du service central hydrographique, 1643–1909

4 JJ: Journaux de bord, [1594]–1789, 1815–71. For an analysis of this subseries *see*: Georges Bourgin et Étienne Taillemite, *Inventaire des archives de la Marine, service hydrographique, sous-série 4 JJ (journaux de bord)* ... (Paris, 1963).

V: Section Outre-mer. The Section Outre-mer came into being on 1 Jan. 1961 when the Ministère de la France d'Outre-mer ceased to exist. This section preserves post-1815 documents relating to the colonies; pre-1815 material remains in the Section ancienne as the Fonds des Colonies [*q.v.*]. Two important series dealing with the earlier period are, however, to be found in the Section Outre-mer and were of use in the preparation of volume III. For copies of manuscripts in the PAC see: *General inventory, manuscripts, I*, 31–48.

Dépôt des fortifications des colonies. This series contains technical reports, maps, reports on discoveries, fisheries, commerce, and military campaigns, as well as papers on the Compagnie des Indes. Series Amérique septentrionale and Louisiane were used in the preparation of volume III. Another series, Saint-Pierre et Miquelon, concerns North America. A manuscript inventory of the various series is available at the AN. *See*: PAC *Report, 1905*, I, pt. III, 3–43; J.-E. Roy, *Rapport sur les archives de France*, 535–59.

G: Dépôt des papiers publics des colonies

G¹: Registres d'état civil, recensements et documents divers

406–9: État civil de Louisbourg, 1722–58

410: État civil de l'île Royale, 1715–57

411: État civil de l'île Saint-Jean, 1721–44, 1749–58

412: État civil de la Louisiane, 1720–34

413: État civil de Saint-Pierre et Miquelon, 1763–89

459: Réfugiés, 1781–89. Lists of French inhabitants of North America who took refuge in France or in the French colonies.

462: Concessions du Canada, de l'île Royale et de l'île Saint-Jean, 1670–1760

464: Louisiane, 1706–37. General correspondence, lists of passengers who embarked for Louisiana, censuses, etc.

465: Concessions de la Louisiane, 1696–1881

466: Recensements de l'Acadie, de l'île Royale et de l'île Saint-Jean, 1671–1758, et des pièces relatives aux concessions de l'île Royale.

467: Recensements de Terre-Neuve, de Saint-Pierre et de Miquelon, 1671–1784

G²: Greffes des tribunaux

178–83, 185, 188–89, 190–93: Conseil supérieur de Louisbourg, 1678, 1711–58

196–99, 202–7, 209: Bailliage de Louisbourg, 1733–58

212: Bailliage de Louisbourg, 1756–57; Conseil de Louisbourg, 1749–56

213, 215: Conseil supérieur et contrôle de la Marine à Québec, 1666–1758

G³: Notariat

7–8, 2037–39, 2041–47, 2055–58: Louisbourg, 1715–58

VI: Département des activités scientifiques, culturelles, et techniques

AQ: Archives d'entreprises. Inventoried in Bertrand Gille, *État sommaire des archives d'entreprises conservées aux Archives nationales (série AQ)* (1v. to date, Paris, 1957). [Covering 1AQ to 64AQ.]

62 AQ: Papiers Du Gard

Minutier central des notaires de Paris et du département de la Seine

BIBLIOTHÈQUE NATIONALE, Paris. The holdings of the BN are based on the collections of the Bibliothèque du Roi, founded by Charles V; collections seized during the revolution (the libraries of *émigrés* and Paris convents) were added later. From the time of François I copyright has assured it all works printed or published in French territory.

Since 1721 the Bibliothèque nationale has been divided into departments on the basis of the nature of the documents kept: Cartes et plans, Estampes, Imprimés, Manuscrits, Médailles, Musique, Périodiques. For biographical research on Canada the most important is the manuscript department, consisting of documents classified by language as well as independent collections. The French manuscripts are the most numerous and are divided among the Fonds français (Fr.), the Nouvelles acquisitions françaises (NAF), and

the Clairambault, Colbert (Cinq-cents and Mélanges), Joly de Fleury, and Moreau collections. For a description of the BN *see*: J.-E. Roy, *Rapport sur les archives de France* [*see* section III]; W. G. Leland *et al.*, *Guide to materials for American history in the libraries and archives of Paris . . .* (Carnegie Institution of Washington Pubs., 392, 2v., Washington, 1932–43), I: *Libraries*. *See also* the following catalogues to the French manuscripts (alphabetical indexes are available): J.-A. Taschereau *et al.*, *Catalogue des manuscrits français* (5v., Paris, 1868–1902) [Fr. 1–6170]; H.-A. Omont *et al.*, *Catalogue général des manuscrits français* (13v., Paris, 1895–1918) [Fr. 6171-33264; NAF 1-11353, 20001-2811]; BN, Dép. des MSS, *Nouvelles acquisitions françaises, 1946–1957* (Paris, 1967) [NAF 13005-4061, 24219-5100]; Philippe Lauer, *Catalogue des manuscrits de la collection Clairambault* (3v., Paris, 1923–32); C.-G.-M. Bourel de La Roncière, *Catalogue des manuscrits de la collection des Cinq cents de Colbert* (Paris, 1908); C.-G.-M. Bourel de La Roncière et P.-M. Bondois, *Catalogue des manuscrits de la collection des Mélanges de Colbert* (2v., Paris, 1920–22); Auguste Molinier, *Inventaire sommaire de la collection Joly de Fleury* (Paris, 1881); H.-A. Omont, *Inventaire des manuscrits de la collection Moreau* (Paris, 1891). For other guides to the Manuscrits and for catalogues to other departments see: *Les catalogues imprimés de la Bibliothèque nationale: liste établie en 1943 suivie d'un supplément (1944–1952)* (Paris, 1953); *Catalogues et publications en vente* (Paris, 1973). A revised guide to the catalogues is under way; *Les catalogues du département des Imprimés* appeared in 1970; "Les catalogues du département des Manuscrits" will be published shortly.

COMITÉ TECHNIQUE DU GÉNIE. *See* ARCHIVES DU MINISTÈRE DES ARMÉES, INSPECTION DU GÉNIE

GREAT BRITAIN

BRITISH MUSEUM, London. In 1753 the British Museum was established as the repository for the Sloane collection of manuscripts, which were numbered from 1 to 4100. Since that time many collections have been acquired and variously designated. Used in the preparation of volume III were the Egerton, Sloane, and Additional manuscripts and the King's topographical collection. For a brief guide to catalogues of the manuscript collections *see*: T. C. Skeat, "The catalogues of the British Museum, 2: Manuscripts," *Journal of Documentation* (London), VII (1951), 18–60; revised as *British Museum: the catalogues of the manuscript collections* (London, 1962). For copies in the PAC of documents from the British Museum see: *Preliminary inventory, manuscript group 21 ...* (Ottawa, 1955).

Add. MSS 15955–57: Private and official correspondence of George, Lord Anson, 1744–62

Add. MSS 19069–76: Papers relating to Nova Scotia collected by Dr Andrew Brown

19070: Paul Mascarene papers, 1713–46/47

19071: Papers relating to Nova Scotia, 1720–91

Add. MSS 21631–60: Henry Bouquet papers, 1757–65

Add. MSS 21661–892: Official correspondence and papers of Sir Frederick Haldimand, 1758–85

21661: Correspondence mainly with Sir Jeffery Amherst on military affairs, 1758–77

21662: Correspondence with Thomas Gage on military affairs, I: Three Rivers, in Lower Canada, 1758–66

21670: Correspondence with Sir William Johnson and Guy Johnson, together with other papers relating to Indian affairs, 1759–74

21679: Correspondence mainly with military agents in New York and London, 1765–78

21687: Miscellaneous papers, regimental returns, etc., relating to troops in North America, 1756–76

21728: Miscellaneous correspondence, 1757–68

Add. MSS 23780–830: Original despatches and letters of Thomas Robinson [later Baron Grantham], 1730–50

23830: October 1748–July 1750

Add. MSS 28126–57: Papers of Sir John Norris, 1703–46

Add. MSS 32686–992: Official correspondence of Thomas Lekham Holles, Duke of Newcastle, 1697–1768

32709: Home correspondence, October–December 1746

32713: Home correspondence, September–December 1747

32716: Home correspondence, August–September 1748

32733: Home correspondence, October–December 1753

32736: Home correspondence, July–September 1754

Add. MSS 33028–30: Papers relating to Ameri-

can and West Indian colonies which passed through the Duke of Newcastle's hands, 1701–68 (with a few of later date, to 1802)

33029: 1744–58

Add. MSS 35349–36278: Hardwicke papers

35870: Minutes of cabinet and privy council, 1733–66

35909: Papers relating to the American plantations, 1710–58

35915: Papers relating to Canada and Newfoundland, 1766–73

Egerton MSS

929: Miscellaneous letters and papers chiefly addressed to Charles Montagu [later Earl of Halifax]

3324–508: Leeds papers

3401–97: Papers of Robert Darcy, 4th Earl of Holdernesse

Sloane MSS

3607: Correspondence and orders of Samuel Vetch, 1711–13

The King's topographical collection comprises the map collection of King George III, purchased in 1828. It includes "many important contemporary MS surveys of the North American colonies and theatres of war in America." The K. Top. collection was supplemented in 1968 by the collection of maps formed by Field Marshal Lord Amherst, many of which relate to the Seven Years' War in North America. The relevant part of it is numbered Add. MSS 57701–10.

HUDSON'S BAY COMPANY ARCHIVES, London. The HBC archives comprises over 30,000 volumes and files of records dating from the founding of the company in 1670. The archives as constituted at present was established in 1932, and the work of organization proceeded thereafter [*see* R. H. G. Leveson Gower, "The archives of the Hudson's Bay Company," *Beaver* (Winnipeg), outfit 264 (December 1933), 40–42, 64; Joan Craig, "Three hundred years of records," *Beaver*, outfit 301 (autumn 1970), 65-70]. A publishing programme was undertaken by the Hudson's Bay Record Society [*see* section II], and in 1949 the HBC and PAC arranged jointly to microfilm the records. In 1974 the original records will move to Winnipeg, where they will form part of the Manitoba Provincial Archives. Information on the PAC copies is found in PAC *Report, 1950*, 13–14; *1952*, 16–18; *1953–54*, 21–22; *1955–58*, 44–46.

Documents from the following categories were used in the preparation of volume III:

Section A: London office records

A.1/: Minute books of the governor and committee

A.2/: General Court minute books

A.5/: London outward correspondence books – general

A.6/: London outward correspondence books – HBC official

A.11/: Correspondence from HBC factories to governor and committee

A.15/: Grand journals

A.16/: Officers' and servants' ledgers

A.43/: Transfer books (books of assignments of stock)

A.44/: Register books of wills and administrations

Section B: North America trading post records

B.3/a: Albany journals

B.3/b: Albany correspondence

B.3/d: Albany account books

B.42/a: Churchill records

B.42/d: Churchill account books

B.59/a: Eastmain journals

B.68/a: Flamborough House journals

B.68/b: Flamborough House correspondence books

B.86/a: Henley journals

B.135/a: Moose journals

B.182/a: Richmond journals

B.239/a: York journals

B.239/b: York correspondence books

Section C: Records of ships owned or chartered by the HBC

C.1/: Ships' logs

C.2/: Seamen's wages books

Section E: Records of a varied nature, mainly originating from Canada, which do not belong in sections such as B (post records)

E.2/: "Observations on Hudson's Bay." Pieces 1-3 are by James Isham, 4-13 by Andrew Graham.

E.18/1: Parliamentary select committee of enquiry on state and condition of countries adjoining Hudson's Bay, held in 1749 – miscellaneous papers, 1733–49

E.18/2: Parliamentary select committee of enquiry on state and condition of countries adjoining Hudson's Bay, held in 1749 – log of *California*, 1746–47

Section G: Maps, both manuscript and published (not including maps which are attached to journals or other documents)

G.1/: Manuscript charts

PUBLIC RECORD OFFICE, London. For an introduction to the contents and arrangement of these archives see: *Guide to the contents of the Public Record Office* (3v., London, 1963–68). Since 1969 the holdings of the PRO have been divided between two repositories, Chancery Lane and Portugal Street. Of the series cited in volume III, CO 5, CO 110, CO 194, and CO 217 are to be found at Chancery Lane; the remainder are at Portugal Street. Lists of additions to the archives since 1966 are available at both repositories. For copies of Colonial Office documents available at the PAC see: *Preliminary inventory, manuscript group 11 . . .* (Ottawa, 1961).

The documentary series cited in volume III include:

Admiralty

Accounting departments

Registers

Adm. 25: Officers, half pay (1693–1836)

Ships' musters

Adm. 36: Series I (1688–1808)

Ships' pay books

Adm. 33: Treasurer's. Series I (1669–1778)

Admiralty and secretariat

Adm. 1: Papers (1660-1951)

Adm. 2: Out-letters (1656–1859)

Adm. 3: Minutes (1657–1881)

Log books

Adm. 50: Admirals' journals (1702–1916)

Adm. 51: Captains' logs (1669–1852)

Adm. 52: Masters' logs (1672–1840)

Registers, returns and certificates

Adm. 6: Various (1673–1859)

Adm. 7: Miscellanea (1563–1871)

Adm. 8: List books (1673–1893)

Greenwich Hospital

Miscellanea

Adm. 80: Various (1639–1957)

Navy Board

Adm. 107: Passing certificates (1691–1848)

Colonial Office. [*See*: R. B. Pugh, *The records of the Colonial and Dominions offices* (PRO handbooks, 3, London, 1964).]

America and West Indies

CO 5: Original correspondence ([1606]–1807)

Guadeloupe

CO 110: Original correspondence, etc. (1758–1816)

Newfoundland

CO 194: Original correspondence (1696–1922)

CO 195: Entry books (1623–1867)

Nova Scotia and Cape Breton

CO 217: Original correspondence (1710/11–1867)

CO 218: Entry books (1710–1867)

Colonies, general
CO 325: Miscellanea (1744–1858)
Court of King's (Queen's) Bench
Plea Side
KB 122: Plea or judgement rolls (1702–1875)
Exchequer and Audit Department
AO 17: Absorbed departments (1580–1867)
High Court of Admiralty
Instance and prize courts
HCA 32: Prize papers (1661–1855)
Index (available for various classes)
Prerogative Court of Canterbury (formerly held at Somerset House)
Prob. 6: Act books: administrations (1559–1858)
Prob. 11: Registered copy, wills (1384–1858)
Privy Council Office
PC 2: Registers (1540–1957)
Public Record Office
Documents acquired by gift, deposit or purchase
PRO 30/8: Chatham papers
State Paper Office
Domestic
SP 42: Naval (1689–1782)
SP 43: Regencies (1716–1760)
Treasury
Accounts
T 38: Departmental (1558–1881)
Minutes
T 29: Minute books (1667–1870)
War Office
Correspondence
WO 1: In-letters (1732–1868)
WO 4: Out-letters: secretary-at-war (1684–1861)
Returns
WO 12: Muster books and pay lists: general (1732–1878)
WO 25: Registers, various (1660–1938)
Private Collections
WO 34: Amherst papers (1712–1784)
Ordnance Office
WO 55: Miscellanea (1568–1923)
Judge Advocate General's Office
Courts martial
WO 71: Proceedings (1668–1956)

UNITED SOCIETY FOR THE PROPAGATION OF THE GOSPEL, London. Formed in 1965, the USPG is responsible for continuing work formerly carried on by the Society for the Propagation of the Gospel in Foreign Parts (incorporated by royal char-ter, 1701) and the Universities' Mission to Central Africa (founded, 1857). The archives is in the process of reorganizing and reclassifying some material. Thus classifications used by Canadian archives holding USPG microfilm do not always correspond to those of the archives itself. Indexes are available at USPG, however, and most dated references are easily transferred. For copies of USPG archives documents in the PAC see: *Preliminary inventory, manuscript group 17* ... (Ottawa, 1967).

Documents from the following groups were used in preparing this volume:
A: Contemporary copies of letters received, 1701–38
B: Original letters received from the American colonies, the West Indies, Newfoundland, Nova Scotia, 1701–86
Journal of proceedings of the Society for the Propagation of the Gospel. Comprises bound and indexed volumes of the proceedings of the general meetings held in London from 1701, and four appendices, A, B, C, D (1701–1860) of which the first two cover the eighteenth century.

UNITED STATES

DETROIT PUBLIC LIBRARY, Burton Historical Collection, Detroit, Mich. Founded on the private library of Clarence Monroe Burton the collection concentrates on the history of Detroit and Michigan from the 17th century to the present. The collection contains personal papers, business records, church records, books, pamphlets, newspapers, maps, pictures, etc. Its holdings are listed in *The national union catalog of manuscript collections...* (Ann Arbor and Washington, 1962–).

Materials used in volume III include:
Macdonald (George Fortune) papers
Porteous (John) papers
Registres des baptêmes, mariages et sépultures de Sainte-Anne (Detroit, Mich.), 2 Feb. 1704–30 Dec. 1848. 5 vols. in 7. Manuscript copy.
Christian Denissen. [Genealogy of the French families of Detroit.] 26 vols. Typescript, n.d.

HARVARD UNIVERSITY LIBRARY, Cambridge, Mass. Founded in 1638 it now contains more than 8,800,000 volumes. The Canadian history and literature shelflist of its central research collection in the Widener Library, published in 1968

(*Widener Library shelflist, 20. . .*), lists 12,712 volumes and 1,078 pamphlets. The library of Francis Parkman* was received by bequest in 1894. Rare books and manuscripts, most of them not listed in the *Shelflist*, are housed in the Houghton Library, adjacent to the Widener. Manuscripts are traditionally cited under the heading, Harvard College Library.

The following collections were used in the preparation of volume III:

MS Can 1: the Chadenat collection of documents bearing on the history of the French in Canada, 3 boxes

MS Can 3: alphabetical file of autograph letters and documents

MS Can 39: "Reflexions sur la contestation," 1728

MS Can 45: Robert Stobo's memoirs, 1760

MS Can 62: documents concerning the British army in Canada, 1744–45

MS Sparks 4: papers of Governor Francis Bernard, 12 vols.

Pepperrell papers

MASSACHUSETTS HISTORICAL SOCIETY, Boston, Mass. Founded in 1791 it is the oldest historical society in the United States. About half the holdings of the society are manuscripts and transcriptions. For further information *see*: S. T. Riley, *The Massachusetts Historical Society, 1791–1959* (Boston, 1959); "The manuscript collections of the Massachusetts Historical Society: a brief listing," *M.H.S. Miscellany*, 5 (December 1958); *Catalog of manuscripts of the Massachusetts Historical Society* (7v., Boston, 1969).

The following collections were used in the preparation of volume III:

Belknap papers

Louisbourg MSS

Mascarene family papers

Miscellaneous Large collection

Pepperrell papers

Waldo papers

Winslow papers

MASSACHUSETTS, SECRETARY OF THE COMMONWEALTH'S OFFICE, ARCHIVES, Boston, Mass. This archives contains primarily the records of the General Court of Massachusetts from the 17th century until the present day. For copies of documents in the PAC see: *Preliminary inventory, manuscript group 18 . . .* (Ottawa, 1964).

The following series of documents are of interest for 17th- and 18th-century Canadian history:

"Massachusetts Archives." This is the title usually given to the 326 volumes of legislative records rearranged in the 19th century by J. B. Felt and his successor according to subject. Excellent name card-indexes have been prepared for about 55 volumes on such subjects as colonial affairs (including letters received and sent to other North American and West Indian colonies), commerce, depositions, foreign affairs, judicial and pecuniary matters, and maritime records.

Executive records of the Council (called Council Records), about 150 vols. For the 17th and 18th centuries, the records cover 1650–56, 1686–87, and 1692 on.

Legislative records of the Council (called Court Records). These records cover the period 1692–1780. The first five volumes of the Court Records (binder's title) are *Records of the governor and company of the Massachusetts Bay in New England* (Boston, 1853–54), which covers the period 1628–86.

Military records. These records consist of petitions, orders, receipts, and muster rolls for the period 1643–1788.

J. B. Poore's transcripts from French archives, from the discovery of America to 1780, 10 vols. Copies of these copies were published by the Quebec legislature as *Coll. de manuscrits relatifs à la N.-F.* [*See* section II; *see also* H. P. Beers, *The French in North America: a bibliographical guide to French archives, reproductions, and research missions* (Baton Rouge, 1957), 153–56.]

WILLIAM L. CLEMENTS LIBRARY, University of Michigan, Ann Arbor. The Clements Library houses source materials on America from 1493 to 1860. Its manuscript collections are concentrated in the years 1740 to 1840, and several of these collections concern the British side of the American revolution. These items are catalogued, and brief descriptions appear in *The national union catalog of manuscript collections . . .* (Ann Arbor and Washington, 1962–), and *Guide to the manuscript collections in the William L. Clements Library*, comp. W. S. Ewing (2nd ed., Ann Arbor, 1953).

The main documents used in volume III include:

George Clinton papers

Thomas Gage papers:
    American series
    Supplementary accounts

Peter Warren papers

Louisbourg papers

II. PRINTED PRIMARY SOURCES

[AMHERST, JEFFERY.] *The journal of Jeffery Amherst, recording the military career of General Amherst in America from 1758 to 1763.* Edited with introduction and notes by John Clarence Webster. (Canadian historical studies. . . .) Toronto and Chicago, 1931.

Anglo-French boundary disputes in the west, 1749–1763. Edited with introduction and notes by Theodore Calvin Pease. (Illinois State Historical Library *Collections*, XXVII, French series, II.) Springfield, Ill., 1937.

ARCHIVES NATIONALES DU QUÉBEC, Québec et Montréal.

PUBLICATIONS

APQ, AQ, and ANQ *Rapports.* Documents from the ANQ – as well as from other archives – have been published in the *Rapport de l'archiviste de la province de Québec.* Volumes correspond to the fiscal years for 1920–21 to 1948–49 and 1959–60; those for the years 1949–51 to 1957–59 include two years; no volumes were published for 1961 or 1962, but publication was resumed in 1963 as the AQ *Rapport*; the title ANQ *Rapport* dates from 1970. There is an index to the contents of the first 42 volumes: *Table des matières des rapports des Archives du Québec, tomes 1 à 42 (1920–1964)* (1965).

L'île de Montréal en 1731 (A. Roy).

Inv. de pièces du Labrador (P.-G. Roy).

Inv. des papiers de Léry (P.-G. Roy).

Lettres de noblesse (P.-G. Roy).

ARCHIVES DU SÉMINAIRE DE QUÉBEC, Québec.

PUBLICATIONS

I: *Papiers Contrecœur* (Grenier).

II: Provost, *Le séminaire de Québec: documents et biographies.*

"Aveu et dénombrement de messire Louis Normand, prêtre du séminaire de Saint-Sulpice de Montréal, au nom et comme fondé de procuration de messire Charles-Maurice Le Pelletier, supérieur du séminaire de Saint-Sulpice de Paris, pour la seigneurie de l'île de Montréal (1731)," APQ *Rapport, 1941–42*, 1–163.

BORNIER, PHILIPPE. *Conférences des ordonnances de Louis XIV, roi de France et de Navarre, avec les anciennes ordonnances du royaume, le droit écrit & les arrêts. . . .* Nouvelle édition. 2 vols. Paris, 1737.

BOSTON, MASS., REGISTRY DEPARTMENT

PUBLICATIONS

Records relating to the early history of Boston. Edited by William Henry Whitmore *et al.* 39 vols. Boston, 1876–1909.

Numbers used in volume III include:

[6]: *Roxbury land and church records.* 1881.

[12]: *Boston records, 1729–1742.* 1885.

[13]: *Records of Boston selectmen, 1716–1736.* 1885.

[15]: *Records of Boston selectmen, 1736–1742.* 1886.

[19]: *Selectmen's minutes, 1754–1763.* 1887.

[24]: *Boston births, 1700–1800.* 1894.

[28]: *Boston marriages, 1700–1751.* 1898.

[34]: F. S. Drake, *The town of Roxbury.* 1905.

Boston Evening-Post, Boston, Mass. Published from 18 Aug. 1735 to 24 April 1775. Weekly.

Boston News-Letter, Boston, Mass. Published from 24 April 1704 to [29 Feb. 1776]. Weekly, except for the last eight months of 1709 when it was not published. Title varies. *See:* C. S. Brigham, *History and bibliography of American newspapers, 1690–1820* (American Antiquarian Soc. pub., 2v., Worcester, Mass., 1947).

[BOUGAINVILLE, LOUIS-ANTOINE DE.] *Adventure in the wilderness: the American journals of Louis Antoine de Bougainville, 1756–1760.* Translated and edited by Edward Pierce Hamilton. Norman, Okla., 1964.

——— "Le journal de M. de Bougainville," Amédée Gosselin, édit., APQ *Rapport, 1923–24*, 202–393.

"Cadillac papers." See: *Michigan Pioneer Collections.*

CENSUSES. *See* RECENSEMENTS

CHAMPLAIN SOCIETY. "Founded in 1905, with headquarters in Toronto, for the purpose of publishing rare and inaccessible materials relating to the history of Canada. Its publications are issued only to elected members, limited in number. . . ."

PUBLICATIONS

III: *Documents relating to seigniorial tenure* (Munro).

IV: *Logs of the conquest* (Wood).

V: Le Clercq, *New relation of Gaspesia* (Ganong).

VIII, IX, X: Knox, *Historical journal* (Doughty).

XVI: *Journals and letters of La Vérendrye* (Burpee).

XXXII: *Walker expedition* (Graham).

CHAMPLAIN SOCIETY. ONTARIO SERIES. The Champlain Society was invited by the Ontario government to prepare and publish a series of documentary volumes "to preserve in printed form . . . a representative selection of the more interesting and significant records of the past. . . .'' This series is sold through normal publishing channels.

PUBLICATIONS

II: *Royal Fort Frontenac* (Preston and Lamontagne).

IV: *Windsor border region* (Lajeunesse).

CHARLEVOIX, [PIERRE-FRANÇOIS-XAVIER] DE. *Histoire et description générale de la Nouvelle France, avec le Journal historique d'un voyage fait par ordre du roi dans l'Amérique septentrionale.* 3 vols.; another edition 6 vols. Paris, 1744.

CHARLEVOIX, PIERRE-FRANÇOIS-XAVIER DE. *History and general description of New France.* Translated and edited, with notes, by John Gilmary Shea. 6 vols. New York, 1866–72; reprinted Chicago, 1962.

[CHAUSSEGROS DE LÉRY, GASPARD-JOSEPH.] ''Journal de Joseph-Gaspard Chaussegros de Léry, lieutenant des troupes, 1754–1755,'' APQ *Rapport, 1926–27,* 348–71; *1927–28,* 355–429.

''Church and state papers for the years 1759 to 1786, being a compendium of documents relating to the establishment of certain churches in the province of Quebec,'' ed. A. R. Kelley, APQ *Rapport, 1948–49,* 293–340.

Collection de documents inédits sur le Canada et l'Amérique, publiés par ''Le Canada-français.'' 3 vols. Québec, 1888–90.

Collection de manuscrits contenant lettres, mémoires, et autres documents historiques relatifs à la Nouvelle-France. . . . 4 vols. Québec, 1883–85. [*See* section I, MASSACHUSETTS, SECRETARY OF THE COMMONWEALTH'S OFFICE, ARCHIVES.]

Collection des manuscrits du maréchal de Lévis. Henri-Raymond Casgrain, éditeur. 12 vols. Montréal et Québec, 1889–95.

[I]: *Journal des campagnes du chevalier de Lévis.*

[II]: *Lettres du chevalier de Lévis.*

[III]: *Lettres de la cour de Versailles.*

[IV] *Lettres et pièces militaires.*

[V]: *Lettres de M. de Bourlamaque.*

[VI]: *Lettres du marquis de Montcalm.*

[VII]: *Journal du marquis de Montcalm.*

[VIII]: *Lettres du marquis de Vaudreuil.*

[IX]: *Lettres de l'intendant Bigot.*

[X]: *Lettres de divers particuliers.*

[XI]: *Guerre du Canada: relations et journaux.*

[XII]: *Table analytique de la collection des manuscrits du maréchal de Lévis.*

CONNECTICUT HISTORICAL SOCIETY, Hartford, Conn.

PUBLICATIONS

Collections. 30 vols., in progress. 1860–19 .
The papers of Thomas Fitch, Jonathan Law, William Pitkin, and George Wyllys, governors of Connecticut, have been published in the *Collections* and were used in the preparation of volume III.

''La correspondance de madame Bégon, 1748–1753,'' Claude de Bonnault, édit., APQ *Rapport, 1934–35,* 1–277.

''Correspondance entre M. de Vaudreuil et la cour,'' APQ *Rapport, 1938–39,* 12–179; *1939–40,* 355–463; *1942–43,* 399–443; *1946–47,* 371–460; *1947–48,* 135–339.

Correspondence of William Pitt, when secretary of state, with colonial governors and military and naval commissioners in America. Edited by Gertrude Selwyn Kimball. 2 vols. New York and London, 1906.

Correspondence of William Shirley, governor of Massachusetts and military commander in America, 1731–1760. Edited by Charles Henry Lincoln. 2 vols. New York, 1912.

The critical period, 1763–1765. Edited with introduction and notes by Clarence Walworth Alvord and Clarence Edwin Carter. (Illinois State Historical Library *Collections,* X, British series, I.) Springfield, Ill., 1915.

Découvertes et établissements des Français dans l'ouest et dans le sud de l'Amérique septentrionale . . . mémoires et documents inédits. [1614–1754.] Pierre Margry, éditeur. 6 vols. Paris, 1879–88. Documents reproduced here should be checked against the originals. Copies of an English translation of this work, completed in 1914, are in the possession of the Burton Historical Collection (Detroit Public Library), the Michigan Historical Commission (Lansing), and the University of Chicago.

Les derniers jours de l'Acadie (1748–1758), correspondances et mémoires: extraits du portefeuille de M. Le Courtois de Surlaville, lieutenant-général des armées du roi, ancien major des troupes de l'île Royale. Gaston Du Boscq de Beaumont, éditeur. Paris, 1899.

DESROSIERS, LOUIS-ADÉLARD. ''Correspondance de cinq vicaires généraux avec les évêques de Québec, 1761–1816,'' APQ *Rapport, 1947–48,* 71–133.

DOBBS, ARTHUR. *Remarks upon Capt. Middleton's defence: wherein his conduct during his late voyage for discovering a passage from Hudson's-Bay to the South-Sea is impartially examin'd. . . .* London, 1744.

Documentary history of the state of Maine. Edited by William Willis *et al.* (Maine Historical Society *Collections,* 2nd series.) 24 vols.

Portland, Maine, 1869–1916. Not to be confused with Maine Historical Society *Collections and Proceedings* [*q.v.*].

The documentary history of the state of New-York. Edited by Edmund Bailey O'Callaghan. 4 vols. Albany, 1850–51.

Documents relating to Canadian currency, exchange and finance during the French period. Selected and edited with notes and introduction by Adam Shortt. (PAC, Board of historical publications.) 2 vols. Ottawa, 1925.

Documents relating to currency, exchange and finance in Nova Scotia, with prefatory documents, 1675–1758. Selected by Adam Shortt, completed with an introduction by Victor Kenneth Johnston, and revised and edited by Gustave Lanctot. (PAC, Board of historical publications.) Ottawa, 1933.

Documents relating to the constitutional history of Canada. . . . Edited by Adam Shortt, Arthur George Doughty *et al.* (PAC publication.) 3 vols. Ottawa, 1907–35.
  I : *1759–1791*. 2nd edition. (PAC, Board of historical publications.) 1918.

Documents relating to the seigniorial tenure in Canada, 1598–1854. Edited with an introduction and notes by William Bennett Munro. (Champlain Society publications, III.) Toronto, 1908.

Documents relative to the colonial history of the state of New-York; procured in Holland, England and France, by John Romeyn Brodhead . . . . Edited by Edmund Bailey O'Callaghan and Berthold Fernow. 15 vols. Albany, 1856–87.

Édits, ordonnances royaux, déclarations et arrêts du Conseil d'état du roi concernant le Canada. [II]: *Arrêts et réglements du Conseil supérieur de Québec, et ordonnances et jugements des intendants du Canada*. [III]: *Complément des ordonnances et jugements des gouverneurs et intendants du Canada, précédé des commissions des dits gouverneurs et intendants et des différents officiers civils et de justice*. . . . 3 vols. Québec, 1854–56.

Extraits des archives des ministères de la Marine et de la Guerre à Paris; Canada, correspondance générale: MM. Duquesne et Vaudreuil, gouverneurs-généraux, 1755–1760. Henri-Raymond Casgrain, éditeur. Québec, 1890.

[Franquet, Louis.] *Voyages et mémoires sur le Canada par Franquet*. (Institut canadien de Québec publication.) Québec, 1889. Also published in Institut canadien de Québec *Annuaire*, 13 (1889), 31–240.

The French regime in Wisconsin: I, 1634–1727. Edited by Reuben Gold Thwaites. (Wisconsin State Historical Society *Collections*, XVI.) Madison, 1902.

The French regime in Wisconsin: II, 1727–1748. Edited by Reuben Gold Thwaites. (Wisconsin State Historical Society *Collections*, XVII.) Madison, 1906.

"The French regime in Wisconsin, 1743–1760," ed. R. G. Thwaites, Wis. State Hist. Soc. *Coll.*, XVIII (1908), 1–222.

Gaultier de La Vérendrye. See: *Journals and letters*. . . .

Gentleman's Magazine: or, monthly intelligencer, London. Published from January 1731 to September 1907. Monthly. Title varies: *Gentleman's Magazine: and historical chronicle* from 1736 to 1833 and from July 1856 to May 1868. Volume numbering irregular.

Great Britain, Parliament, House of Commons. *Report from the committee appointed to inquire into the state and condition of the countries adjoining to Hudson's Bay, and of the trade carried on there*. London, 1749.
——*Report relating to the finding a north-west passage*. London, 1745.

Guerre du Canada: relations et journaux de différentes expéditions faites durant les années 1755–56–57–58–59–60. Henri-Raymond Casgrain, éditeur. (*Collection des manuscrits du maréchal de Lévis*, [XI].) Québec, 1895.

"Historical records of the Church of England in the diocese of Quebec," ed. A. R. Kelley, APQ *Rapport, 1946–47*, 179–298.

Hudson's Bay Record Society. Initiated in 1938 by the Hudson's Bay Company after classification of its London archives, begun in 1932, had progressed to the point where publication was feasible. Membership in the society is limited.

PUBLICATIONS

General editor for vols. I–XXII, Edwin Ernest Rich; for vols. XXIII–XXV, Kenneth Gordon Davies; for vols. XXVI–XXVII, Glyndwr Williams. 27 vols. to date. Vols. I–XII issued in association with the Champlain Society, Toronto.

XII: *James Isham's observations on Hudsons Bay, 1743, and notes and observations on a book entitled "A voyage to Hudsons Bay in the Dobbs Galley," 1749*. Edited by Edwin Ernest Rich and Alice Margaret Johnson. London, 1949; reprinted Nendeln, Liechtenstein, 1968.

XXI, XXII: Rich, *History of the HBC*. [See section IV.]

XXIV: *Northern Quebec and Labrador journals and correspondence, 1819–35*. Edited by Kenneth Gordon Davies and Alice Margaret Johnson, with an introduction by Glyndwr Williams. London, 1963.

XXV: *Letters from Hudson Bay, 1703–40.* Edited by Kenneth Gordon Davies and Alice Margaret Johnson, with an introduction by Richard Glover. London, 1965.

XXVII: [Graham, Andrew.] *Andrew Graham's observations on Hudson's Bay, 1767–91.* Edited by Glyndwr Williams, with an introduction by Richard Glover. London, 1969.

HUTCHINSON, THOMAS. *The history of the colony and province of Massachusetts-Bay.* Edited from the author's own copies of vols. I and II and his manuscript of vol. III, with a memoir and additional notes, by Lawrence Shaw Mayo. 3 vols. Cambridge, Mass., 1936. [For earlier editions see: *DCB*, II, 692.]

L'île de Montréal en 1731: aveu et dénombrement des messieurs de Saint-Sulpice, seigneurs de Montréal. Antoine Roy, éditeur. (APQ publication.) Québec, 1943.

Illinois on the eve of the Seven Years' War, 1747–1755. Edited with an introduction and notes by Theodore Calvin Pease and Ernestine Jenison. (Illinois State Historical Library *Collections*, XXIX, French series, III.) Springfield, Ill., 1936.

ILLINOIS STATE HISTORICAL LIBRARY, Springfield, Ill.

PUBLICATIONS

Collections. 35 vols. to date. 1903–

    X: *Critical period, 1763–65* (Alvord and Carter).

    XI: *New régime, 1765–67* (Alvord and Carter).

    XVI: *Trade and politics, 1767–69* (Alvord and Carter).

    XXVII: *Anglo-French boundary disputes, 1749–63* (Pease).

    XXIX: *Illinois on eve of Seven Years' War* (Pease and Jenison).

"Indian treaties," Maine Hist. Soc. *Coll.*, 1st ser., III (1853), 359–447.

Inventaire de pièces sur la côte de Labrador conservées aux Archives de la province de Québec. Pierre-Georges Roy, éditeur. (APQ publication.) 2 vols. Québec, 1940–42.

Inventaire des papiers de Léry conservés aux Archives de la province de Québec. Pierre-Georges Roy, éditeur. (APQ publication.) 3 vols. Québec, 1939–40.

The Jesuit relations and allied documents: travels and explorations of the Jesuit missionaries in New France, 1610–1791, the original French, Latin, and Italian texts, with English translations and notes. . . . Edited by Reuben Gold Thwaites. 73 vols., including 2 index vols. Cleveland, 1896–1901; facsimile reproduction, 73 vols. in 36, New York, 1959. [For a discussion of the *Relations* see: *DCB*, I, 455–57.]

Johnson papers (Sullivan *et al*). See: *The papers of Sir William Johnson.*

Journal des campagnes du chevalier de Lévis en Canada de 1756 à 1760. Henri-Raymond Casgrain, éditeur. (*Collection des manuscrits du maréchal de Lévis*, [I].) Montréal, 1889.

Journal du marquis de Montcalm durant ses campagnes en Canada de 1756 à 1759. Henri-Raymond Casgrain, éditeur. (*Collection des manuscrits du maréchal de Lévis*, [VII].) Québec, 1895.

"Journal du siège de Québec du 10 mai au 18 septembre 1759 . . . ," Ægidius Fauteux, édit., APQ *Rapport, 1920–21*, 137–241.

Journals and letters of Pierre Gaultier de Varennes de La Vérendrye and his sons, with correspondence between the governors of Canada and the French court, touching the search for the Western Sea. Edited with introduction and notes by Lawrence Johnstone Burpee. (Champlain Society publications, XVI.) Toronto, 1927.

JUCHEREAU [DE LA FERTÉ] DE SAINT-IGNACE, JEANNE-FRANÇOISE, ET MARIE-ANDRÉE [REGNARD] DUPLESSIS DE SAINTE-HÉLÈNE. *Les annales de l'Hôtel-Dieu de Québec, 1636–1716.* Albert Jamet, éditeur. Québec et Montréal, 1939. The original work was dictated to Mother Duplessis [REGNARD] by Mother Juchereau*, and was printed in Montauban, France, in 1751 by Louis Bertrand* de Latour, as *Histoire de l'Hôtel-Dieu de Québec.*

Jugements et délibérations du Conseil souverain de la Nouvelle-France. [1663–1716.] 6 vols. Québec, 1885–91. *Index* par Pierre-Georges Roy. (APQ publication.) Québec, 1940.

KNOX, JOHN. *An historical journal of the campaigns in North America for the years 1757, 1758, 1759, and 1760.* Edited with introduction, appendix, and index by Arthur George Doughty. (Champlain Society publications, VIII, IX, X.) 3 vols. Toronto, 1914–16.

LA VÉRENDRYE, GAULTIER DE. See: *Journals and letters. . . .*

LE CLERCQ, CHRESTIEN. *New relation of Gaspesia, with the customs and religion of the Gaspesian Indians.* Translated and edited, with a reprint of the original, by William Francis Ganong. (Champlain Society publications, V.) Toronto, 1910.

Lettre d'un habitant de Louisbourg. . . . See: *Louisbourg in 1745* (Wrong).

Lettres de divers particuliers au chevalier de Lévis. Henri-Raymond Casgrain, éditeur. (*Collection des manuscrits du maréchal de Lévis*, [X].) Québec, 1895.

"Les lettres de Doreil," APQ *Rapport, 1944–45*, 1–171.

Lettres de la cour de Versailles au baron de Dieskau, au marquis de Montcalm et au chevalier de Lévis. Henri-Raymond Casgrain, éditeur. (*Collection des manuscrits du maréchal de Lévis*, [III].) Québec, 1890.

Lettres de l'intendant Bigot au chevalier de Lévis. Henri-Raymond Casgrain, éditeur. (*Collection des manuscrits du maréchal de Lévis*, [IX].) Québec, 1895.

Lettres de M. de Bourlamaque au chevalier de Lévis. Henri-Raymond Casgrain, éditeur. (*Collection des manuscrits du maréchal de Lévis*, [V].) Québec, 1891.

Lettres de noblesse, généalogies, érections de comtés et baronnies insinuées par le Conseil souverain de la Nouvelle-France. Pierre-Georges Roy, éditeur. (APQ publication.) 2 vols. Beauceville, Qué., 1920.

Lettres du chevalier de Lévis concernant la guerre du Canada (1756–1760). Henri-Raymond Casgrain, éditeur. (*Collection des manuscrits du maréchal de Lévis*, [II].) Montréal, 1889.

Lettres du marquis de Montcalm au chevalier de Lévis. Henri-Raymond Casgrain, éditeur. (*Collection des manuscrits du maréchal de Lévis*, [VI].) Québec, 1894.

Lettres du marquis de Vaudreuil au chevalier de Lévis. Henri-Raymond Casgrain, éditeur. (*Collection des manuscrits du maréchal de Lévis*, [VIII].) Québec, 1895.

"Lettres et mémoires de l'abbé de L'Isle-Dieu," APQ *Rapport, 1935–36*, 275–410; *1936–37*, 331–459; *1937–38*, 147–253.

Lettres et pièces militaires, instructions, ordres, mémoires, plans de campagne et de défense, 1756–1760. Henri-Raymond Casgrain, éditeur. (*Collection des manuscrits du maréchal de Lévis*, [IV].) Québec, 1891.

LITERARY AND HISTORICAL SOCIETY OF QUEBEC/SOCIÉTÉ LITTÉRAIRE ET HISTORIQUE DE QUÉBEC. The oldest historical society in Canada, founded 6 Jan. 1824 in Quebec.

PUBLICATIONS

The most useful of its publications is its collection, Historical Documents. This collection consists of 12 vols. in 9 series (1838–1915), later numbered consecutively by the society D.1, D.2, etc., irrespective of the fact that the first series contains 4 vols. and the remaining 8 series only 1 vol. each. For this and other collections see: *Index to the archival publications . . . 1824–1924* (Quebec, 1923).

[D.1]: *Mémoires sur le Canada, depuis 1749 jusqu'à 1760.*

[D.4]: *Mémoire du sieur de Ramezay.*

The logs of the conquest of Canada. Edited with an introduction by William Wood. (Champlain Society publications, IV.) Toronto, 1909.

Louisbourg in 1745: the anonymous "Lettre d'un habitant de Louisbourg" (Cape Breton), containing a narrative by an eye-witness of the siege in 1745. Edited and translated by George McKinnon Wrong. (University of Toronto studies, History, 2nd series, I.) Toronto, 1897; reprinted 1901. The original letter was printed surreptitiously in France in 1745 under the title *Lettre d'un habitant de Louisbourg, contenant une relation éxacte et circonstanciée de la prise de l'Isle-Royale, par les Anglais.* It bore a fictitious Quebec imprint.

Louisbourg journals, 1745. Edited by Louis Effingham De Forest. (Society of Colonial Wars in the State of New York publications, 44.) New York, 1932.

MAINE HISTORICAL SOCIETY, Portland, Maine

PUBLICATIONS

Collections. 1st series. 9 vols. and index. 1831–91.

Collections and Proceedings. 2nd series. 10 vols. 1890–99.

Documentary history of the state of Maine.

Province and court records of Maine.

Mandements, lettres pastorales et circulaires des évêques de Québec. 18 vols. to date. Québec, 1887–19 . The first six volumes were edited by Henri Têtu and Charles-Octave Gagnon; no editors are given for later volumes. Volume numbering is peculiar: [1re série], I–IV; nouvelle série [2e série], I–V; nouvelle série [3e série], I–III; a second set of cumulative volume numbers begins with vol. V of the nouvelle série [2e série].

MASSACHUSETTS HISTORICAL SOCIETY, Boston, Mass.

PUBLICATIONS

Collections. 7 series of 10 vols. each plus 10 vols. to date. 1792–19 .

Proceedings. 3 series of 20 vols. each plus index volumes for each series and an additional 23 vols. to date. 1859–19 .

Shipton, *Sibley's Harvard graduates.* [*See* section III.]

As a guide to contents and indexes see: *Handbook of the publications and photostats, 1792–1935* (1937).

"Mémoire du Canada," APQ *Rapport, 1924–25*, 96–198.

Mémoire du sieur de Ramezay, commandant à Québec, au sujet de la reddition de cette ville le 18ᵉ septembre 1759. . . . (Literary and Historical Society of Quebec, Historical Documents, 1st series, [D.4].) Québec, 1861. The "Mémoire du sieur de Ramezay . . . ," with accompanying documents, forms the second part of the compilation.

Mémoires sur le Canada, depuis 1749 jusqu'à 1760. . . . (Literary and Historical Society of Quebec, Historical Documents, 1st series, [D.1].) Quebec, 1838; reprinted 1873.

Michigan Pioneer Collections. 40 vols. 1874–1929. To avoid confusion the Michigan Historical Commission, Department of State, Lansing, has standardized the citation for these volumes, which were originally published by various historical agencies and under various titles. Volumes are traditionally cited by their spine dates. The following volumes were particularly useful for volume III:
XXXIII, XXXIV: containing "Cadillac papers." 1903, 1904.

MORIN, MARIE. *Annales de l'Hôtel-Dieu de Montréal.* Ægidius Fauteux *et al.*, éditeurs. (Société historique de Montréal, Mémoires, XII.) Montréal, 1921. An incomplete and inaccurate edition of the manuscript in AHSJ, "Histoire simple et véritable . . ." [*see* section I].

NAVY RECORDS SOCIETY, London, Eng. Founded in 1893 "for the purpose of rendering accessible the sources of [Britain's] naval history."
PUBLICATIONS
XCIV: *Walker expedition* (Graham).

The new régime, 1765–1767. Edited with an introduction and notes by Clarence Walworth Alvord and Clarence Edwin Carter. (Illinois State Historical Library *Collections*, XI, British series, II.) Springfield, Ill., 1916.

NEW-YORK HISTORICAL SOCIETY, New York.
PUBLICATIONS
Collections. 1st series. 5 vols. 1811–30.
2nd series. 4 vols. 1841–59.
John Watts de Peyster publication fund series. 82 vols. to date. 1868–19 . Subtitle varies: vols. 1–35, Publication fund series.
The last series was used in volume III.

The Northcliffe collection. . . . (PAC publication.) Ottawa, 1926.

[*Nova Scotia Archives, I:*] *Selections from the public documents of the province of Nova Scotia.* Edited by Thomas Beamish Akins. (PANS publication.) Halifax, 1869.

Nova Scotia Archives, II: a calendar of two letter-books and one commission-book in the possession of the government of Nova Scotia, 1713–1741. Edited by Archibald McKellar MacMechan. (PANS publication.) Halifax, 1900.

—— *III: original minutes of His Majesty's council at Annapolis Royal, 1720–1739.* Edited by Archibald McKellar MacMechan. (PANS publication.) Halifax, 1908.

—— *IV: minutes of His Majesty's council at Annapolis Royal, 1736–1749.* Edited by Charles Bruce Fergusson. (PANS publication.) Halifax, 1967.

NOVA SCOTIA HISTORICAL SOCIETY, Halifax, N.S.
PUBLICATIONS
Collections. [*See also* section V.]
III, IV: contain [Winslow], "Journal."

The papers of Sir William Johnson. Edited by James Sullivan *et al.* (New York State, Division of archives and history publication.) 14 vols., including *General index.* Albany, 1921–65.

Papiers Contrecœur et autres documents concernant le conflit anglo-français sur l'Ohio de 1745 à 1756. Fernand Grenier, éditeur. (ASQ publications, I.) Québec, 1952.

PENHALLOW, SAMUEL. *The history of the wars of New-England, with the eastern Indians.* . . . Boston, 1726. Reprinted in 1824 in New Hampshire Historical Society *Collections*, I, and in 1859, with a memoir and notes, in Cincinnati, Ohio.

Pennsylvania archives. . . . Edited by Samuel Hazard *et al.* 9 series [with varying subtitles and varying numbers of vols.]. Philadelphia and Harrisburg, 1852–1935. As a guide to contents and indexes *see*: H. H. Eddy, *Guide to the published archives of Pennsylvania covering the 138 volumes of colonial records and Pennsylvania archives series I–IX* (Harrisburg, 1949).

[PENNSYLVANIA. *Colonial Records.*] *Minutes of the provincial council of Pennsylvania, from the organization to the termination of the proprietary government.* [1683–1775.] 10 vols. Philadelphia and Harrisburg, 1851–52.

[PICHON, THOMAS.] *Lettres et mémoires pour servir à l'histoire naturelle, civile et politique du Cap Breton, depuis son établissement jusqu'à la reprise de cette isle par les Anglois en 1758.* La Haye, Pays-Bas, 1760. An English translation was published in London in the same year under the title *Genuine letters and memoirs, relating to the natural, civil, and commercial history of the islands of Cape Bre-*

ton, and Saint John, from the first settlement there, to the taking of Louisburg by the English, in 1758 . . . ; the original French has been reprinted, [East Ardsley, Eng.] and [New York], 1966.

"Procès-verbaux du procureur général Collet sur le district des paroisses de la Nouvelle-France . . . ," Ivanhoë Caron, édit., APQ Rapport, 1921–22, 262–380.

Province and court records of Maine. [1636–1718.] Edited by Charles Thornton Libby et al. (Maine Historical Society publication.) 5 vols., in progress. Portland, Maine, 1928– .

PROVOST, HONORIUS. Le séminaire de Québec: documents et biographies. (ASQ publications, II.) Québec, 1964.

PUBLIC ARCHIVES OF CANADA, Ottawa.

BOARD OF HISTORICAL PUBLICATIONS
Documents relating to Canadian currency during the French period (Shortt).
Documents relating to constitutional history, 1759–91 (Shortt and Doughty; 1918).
Documents relating to currency in Nova Scotia, 1675–1758 (Shortt).
NUMBERED PUBLICATIONS. [See section III.]
OTHER PUBLICATIONS. [See also section III.]
Documents relating to constitutional history, 1759–91 (Shortt and Doughty).
Reports and Rapports. 1881–19 . Published annually until 1952; irregularly thereafter.

PUBLIC ARCHIVES OF NOVA SCOTIA, Halifax, N.S.
PUBLICATIONS
N.S. Archives, I.
N.S. Archives, II.
N.S. Archives, III.
N.S. Archives, IV.

PUBLIC RECORD OFFICE, London, Eng.
PUBLICATIONS
The following calendars contain information on events in or affecting Canada in the 17th and 18th centuries, and were used in the preparation of volume III:

Acts of the Privy Council of England: colonial series. [1613–1783.] Edited by William Lawson Grant and James Munro. 6 vols. Hereford and London, 1908–12.

Calendar of state papers, colonial series, America and West Indies. . . . [1574–1738.] Edited by William Noel Sainsbury et al. 44 vols., in progress. London, 1860–19

Calendar of Treasury papers. . . . [1556–1728.] Edited by Joseph Redington. 6 vols. London, 1868–89.

Journal of the commissioners for Trade and Plantations. . . . [1704–82.] 14 vols. London, 1920–38.

Quebec Gazette/La Gazette de Québec, Quebec. Published from 21 June 1764 to 30 Oct. 1874. Frequency of publication varies. The paper was originally bilingual; after 30 April 1832 separate French and English editions appeared. With the issue of 29 Oct. 1842 the French edition was discontinued. See: André Beaulieu et Jean Hamelin, La presse québécoise: des origines à nos jours (1v. to date, Québec, 1973).

RECENSEMENTS
CANADA
1681: Sulte, Hist. des Can. fr., V, 53–92. [See section IV.]
1716: Recensement de la ville de Québec pour 1716. Louis Beaudet, éditeur. Québec, 1887.
1739: Census of Canada . . . Recensements du Canada (5v., Ottawa, 1873–78), IV, 60.
1741: "Un recensement inédit de Montréal, en 1741," É.-Z. Massicotte, édit., RSCT, 3rd ser., XV (1921), sect. I, 1–61.
1744: "Le recensement de Québec, en 1744," APQ Rapport, 1939–40, 1–154.
1762: "Le recensement du gouvernement de Québec en 1762," Amédée Gosselin, édit., APQ Rapport, 1925–26, 1–143.
TERRE-NEUVE ET PLAISANCE
1687, 1691, 1693, 1694, 1704: "Recensement de Terre-Neuve, 1687 à 1704," F.-D. Thibodeau, édit., SGCF Mémoires, XIII (1962), 204–8, 244–55.
See also: Canada, Bureau of Statistics, Demography branch, Chronological list of Canadian censuses (Ottawa, 1942).
Since the printed versions of the censuses are not always accurate it is preferable to consult the originals. See section I, ARCHIVES NATIONALES, Section Outre-mer, série G.

Royal Fort Frontenac. Texts selected and translated by Richard Arthur Preston; edited with introduction and notes by Léopold Lamontagne. (Champlain Society publications, Ontario series, II.) Toronto, 1958.

Trade and politics, 1767–1769. Edited with introduction and notes by Clarence Walworth Alvord and Clarence Edwin Carter. (Illinois State Historical Library Collections, XVI, British series, III.) Springfield, Ill., 1921.

TRUDEL, MARCEL. Atlas historique du Canada français: des origines à 1867. Québec, 1961.

—— Atlas de la Nouvelle-France/An atlas of New France. Québec, 1968. Described by the author as "a complete revision of our Atlas historique du Canada français. . . ."

The Walker expedition to Quebec, 1711. Edited with an introduction by Gerald Sandford Graham. (Champlain Society publications,

XXXII; Navy Records Society publications, XCIV.) Toronto and London, 1953.

The Windsor border region, Canada's southernmost frontier. . . . Edited with an introduction by Ernest Joseph Lajeunesse. (Champlain Society publications, Ontario series, IV.) Toronto, 1960.

[WINSLOW, JOHN.] "Journal of Colonel John Winslow of the provincial troops, while engaged in removing the Acadian French inhabitants from Grand Pré, and the neighbouring settlements, in the autumn of the year 1755," N.S. Hist. Soc. *Coll.*, III (1883), 71–196;

". . . while engaged in the siege of Fort Beauséjour, in the summer and autumn of 1755," N.S. Hist. Soc. *Coll.*, IV (1885), 113–246.

WISCONSIN STATE HISTORICAL SOCIETY, Madison, Wis.

PUBLICATIONS

Collections. 31 vols. 1855–1931.

　XVI: *French regime in Wis., 1634–1727* (Thwaites)

　XVII: *French regime in Wis., 1727–48* (Thwaites)

　XVIII: "French regime in Wis., 1743–60" (Thwaites)

III. REFERENCE WORKS

ALLAIRE, JEAN-BAPTISTE-ARTHUR. *Dictionnaire biographique du clergé canadien-francais.* 6 vols. Montréal, 1910–34.

ARCHIVES NATIONALES DU QUÉBEC, Québec et Montréal.

　PUBLICATIONS. [*See also* section II.]

　P.-G. Roy, *Inv. coll. pièces jud. et not.*

　——— *Inv. concessions.*

　——— *Inv. contrats de mariage.*

　——— *Inv. ins. Cons. souv.*

　——— *Inv. ins. Prév. Québec.*

　——— *Inv. jug. et délib., 1717–1760.*

　——— *Inv. ord. int.*

　——— *Inv. procès-verbaux des grands voyers.*

　——— *Inv. testaments.*

　P.-G. Roy et al., *Inv. greffes not.*

Army list. See: GREAT BRITAIN, WAR OFFICE, *A list.* . . .

AUBERT DE LA CHESNAYE-DESBOIS, FRANÇOIS-ALEXANDRE, ET ——— BADIER. *Dictionnaire de la noblesse, contenant les généalogies, l'histoire & la chronologie des familles nobles de la France. . . .* 2ᵉ édition. 15 vols. Paris, 1770–86; 3ᵉ édition, 19 vols., 1863–76. The first edition of this work, written by La Chesnaye-Desbois alone, is entitled *Dictionnaire généalogique, héraldique, chronologique et historique . . .* (7v., Paris, 1757–65).

A bibliography of Canadiana, being items in the Public Library of Toronto, Canada, relating to the early history and development of Canada. Edited by Frances Maria Staton and Marie Tremaine, with an introduction by George Herbert Locke. Toronto, 1934.

A bibliography of Canadiana: first supplement. Edited by Gertrude Mabel Boyle and Marjorie Colbeck, with an introduction by Henry Cummings Campbell. Toronto, 1959.

Biographie universelle, ancienne et moderne. . . .

Joseph-François et Louis-Gabriel Michaud, éditeurs. 85 vols. Paris, 1811–62; nouvelle édition, Louis-Gabriel Michaud et Eugène-Ernest Desplaces, édit., 45 vols., 1854–65; reprinted Graz, Austria, 1966.

BONNAULT, CLAUDE DE. "Le Canada militaire: état provisoire des officiers de milice de 1641 à 1760," APQ *Rapport, 1949–51*, 261–527.

BURKE, JOHN. *A genealogical and heraldic dictionary of the peerage and baronetage of the United Kingdom.* London, 1826; 105th edition, revised and enlarged, edited by Peter Townend, 1970.

CARON, IVANHOË. "Inventaire des documents concernant l'Église du Canada sous le régime français," APQ *Rapport, 1939–40*, 155–354; *1940–41*, 333–473; *1941–42*, 179–298.

CHARLAND, PAUL-VICTOR. "Notre-Dame de Québec: le nécrologe de la crypte ou les inhumations dans cette église depuis 1652," *BRH*, XX (1914), 137–51, 169–81, 205–17, 237–51, 269–80, 301–13, 333–47.

CHARNOCK, JOHN. *Biographia navalis: or, impartial memoirs of the lives and characters of officers of the navy of Great Britain, from the year 1660 to the present time; drawn from the most authentic sources, and disposed in a chronological arrangement.* 6 vols. London, 1794–98.

[COKAYNE, GEORGE EDWARD.] *Complete peerage of England, Scotland, Ireland, Great Britain and the United Kingdom, extant, extinct, or dormant. . . .* 8 vols. London and Exeter, Eng., 1887–98; new edition, revised and enlarged, edited by Vicary Gibbs et al., 13 vols. in 14, London, 1910–59.

Dictionary of American biography [to 1928]. Edited by Allen Johnson and Dumas Malone. 20 vols. and index. New York, 1928–37. 3 supplements [to 1945]. New York, 1944–73. New edition, comprising 22 vols. in 11. New York, 1959. *Concise DAB*. New York, 1964. In progress.

Dictionary of national biography [to 1900]. Edited by Leslie Stephen and Sidney Lee. 63 vols.; supplement, 3 vols.; index and epitome. London, 1885–1903. 6 supplements [to 1960]. London, 1912–70. *Concise DNB*. 2 vols. London, 1952–61. In progress. *Corrections and additions to the "Dictionary of national biography"*. . . . (University of London, Institute of historical research publication.) Boston, Mass., 1966.

Dictionnaire de biographie française. Jules Balteau *et al*., éditeurs. 13 vols. to date. Paris, 1933– . "A" to "Féréol" included.

Encyclopedia Canadiana. John Everett Robbins, editor-in-chief. 10 vols. Ottawa, 1957–58.

English army lists and commission registers, 1661–1714. Edited by Charles Dalton. 6 vols. London, 1892–1904.

FAUTEUX, ÆGIDIUS. *Les chevaliers de Saint-Louis en Canada*. Montréal, 1940.

GAREAU, JEAN-BAPTISTE. "La Prévôté de Québec, ses officiers, ses registres," APQ *Rapport, 1943–44*, 51–146.

GAUTHIER, HENRI. *Sulpitiana*. 1re édition. s.l., 1912; 2e édition, Montréal, 1926.

GODBOUT, ARCHANGE. "Nos ancêtres aux XVIIe siècle," APQ *Rapport, 1951–53*, 447–544; *1953–55*, 443–536; *1955–57*, 377–489; *1957–59*, 381–440; *1959–60*, 275–354; AQ *Rapport, 1965*, 145–81. "A" to "Brassard" included. The last instalment includes notes by R.-J. Auger.

GREAT BRITAIN, ADMIRALTY. *The commissioned sea officers of the Royal Navy, 1660–1815*. Editing begun by David B. Smith; project continued by the Royal Naval College in cooperation with the National Maritime Museum. 3 vols. [n.p., 1954?]

GREAT BRITAIN, WAR OFFICE. *A list of the general and field officers as they rank in the army*. . . . [London, 1754–1868.] The first known official army list was published in 1740 and has been reprinted as *The army list of 1740 . . . with a complete index of names and of regiments* (Soc. for Army Hist. Research, Special no., III, Sheffield, Eng., 1931).

Handbook of American Indians north of Mexico. Edited by Frederick Webb Hodge. (Smithsonian Institution, Bureau of American Ethnology *Bulletin*, 30.) 2 vols. Washington, 1907–10; reprinted New York, 1965. The Canadian material in this work has been revised and republished as an appendix to the tenth report of the Geographic Board of Canada, entitled *Handbook of Indians of Canada* (Ottawa, 1913).

HOZIER, LOUIS-PIERRE D', ET ANTOINE-MARIE D'HOZIER DE SÉRIGNY. *Armorial général, ou Registres de la noblesse de France*. 1re édition. 6 registres en 10 vols. Paris, 1738–68; 2e édition, 7 registres en 13 vols., 1865–1908; 3e édition, 7 registres en 13 vols., 1970.

LABRÈQUE, LUCILE. "Inventaire de pièces détachées de cours de justice de la Nouvelle-France (1638–1760)," ANQ *Rapport, 1971*, 5-50.

LA CHESNAYE-DESBOIS. *See* AUBERT

LEBŒUF, JOSEPH-AIMÉ-ARTHUR. *Complément au dictionnaire généalogique Tanguay*. (Société généalogique canadienne-française publications, 2, 4, 6.) 3 séries [3 vols.]. Montréal, 1957–64.

LE JEUNE, LOUIS-MARIE. *Dictionnaire général de biographie, histoire, littérature, agriculture, commerce, industrie et des arts, sciences, mœurs, coutumes, institutions politiques et religieuses du Canada*. 2 vols. Ottawa, 1931.

LÉTOURNEAU, HUBERT, ET LUCILE LABRÈQUE. "Inventaire de pièces détachées de la Prévôté de Québec (1668–1759)," ANQ *Rapport, 1971*, 51–413.

MARION, MARCEL. *Dictionnaire des institutions de la France aux XVIIe et XVIIIe siècles*. Paris, 1923; reprinted 1968.

MASSICOTTE, ÉDOUARD-ZOTIQUE. "Inventaire des documents et des imprimés concernant la communauté des frères Charon et l'Hôpital Général de Montréal sous le régime français. . . ," APQ *Rapport, 1923–24*, 163–201.

—— "Répertoire des engagements pour l'Ouest conservés dans les Archives judiciaires de Montréal. . . ," APQ *Rapport, 1929–30*, 191–466; *1930–31*, 353–453; *1931–32*, 243–365; *1932–33*, 245–304.

[MÉLANÇON, ARTHUR.] *Liste des missionaires-jésuites: Nouvelle-France et Louisiane, 1611–1800*. Montréal, 1929.

"Les notaires au Canada sous le régime français," APQ *Rapport, 1921–22*, 1–58. Contains biographies of nearly 200 notaries.

PARKER, DAVID WILLSON. *A guide to the documents in the manuscript room at the Public Archives of Canada*. (PAC publications, 10.) Ottawa, 1914.

Place-names and places of Nova Scotia. With an introduction by Charles Bruce Fergusson. (PANS publication, Nova Scotia series, III.) Halifax, 1967.

PUBLIC ARCHIVES OF CANADA NUMBERED PUBLICATIONS

1: *Index to reports of Canadian archives from 1872 to 1908.* Ottawa, 1909.

6: J.-E. Roy, *Rapport sur les archives de France.*

10: Parker, *Guide.*

OTHER PUBLICATIONS [*See also* section II.]

Inventories of holdings in the manuscript division. [*See* section I.]

Union list of manuscripts (Gordon *et al.*).

ROY, JOSEPH-EDMOND. *Rapport sur les archives de France relatives à l'histoire du Canada.* (PAC publications, 6.) Ottawa, 1911.

ROY, PIERRE-GEORGES. *Inventaire des concessions en fief et seigneurie, fois et hommages et aveux et dénombrements, conservés aux Archives de la province de Québec.* (APQ publication.) 6 vols. Beauceville, Qué., 1927–29.

—— *Inventaire des contrats de mariage du régime français conservés aux Archives judiciaires de Québec.* (APQ publication.) 6 vols. Québec, 1937–38.

—— *Inventaire des insinuations de la Prévôté de Québec.* (APQ publication.) 3 vols. Beauceville, Qué., et Québec, 1936–39.

—— *Inventaire des insinuations du Conseil souverain de la Nouvelle-France.* (APQ publication.) Beauceville, Qué., 1921.

—— *Inventaire des jugements et délibérations du Conseil supérieur de la Nouvelle-France de 1717 à 1760.* (APQ publication.) 7 vols. Beauceville, Qué., 1932–35.

—— *Inventaire des ordonnances des intendants de la Nouvelle-France conservées aux Archives provinciales de Québec.* (APQ publication.) 4 vols. Beauceville, Qué., 1919.

—— *Inventaire des procès-verbaux des grands voyers conservés aux Archives de la province de Québec.* (APQ publication.) 6 vols. Beauceville, Qué., 1923–32.

—— *Inventaire des testaments, donations et inventaires du régime français conservés aux Archives judiciaires de Québec.* (APQ publication.) 3 vols. Québec, 1941.

—— *Inventaire d'une collection de pièces judiciaires, notariales, etc., etc., conservées aux Archives judiciaires de Québec.* (APQ publication.) 2 vols. Beauceville, Qué., 1917.

—— *Les officiers d'état-major des gouvernements de Québec, Montréal et Trois-Rivières sous le régime français.* Lévis, Qué., 1919.

ROY, PIERRE-GEORGES, *et al. Inventaire des greffes des notaires du régime français.* (APQ publication.) 23 vols., in progress. Québec, 1943– . Vols. I-II prepared by P.-G. and Antoine Roy; vols. III-XIX by Antoine Roy.

SEDGWICK, RICHARD [ROMNEY]. *The history of parliament: the House of Commons, 1715–1754.* 2 vols. London, 1970.

SHIPTON, CLIFFORD KENYON. *Sibley's Harvard graduates. . . .* (Massachusetts Historical Society publication.) 13 vols., in progress. Cambridge, Mass., and Boston, 1933– . A continuation of Sibley, *infra*, the volumes are numbered consecutively from it. Vols. IV-XVI include graduates of the years 1690–1767.

SIBLEY, JOHN LANGDON. *Biographical sketches of graduates of Harvard University, in Cambridge, Massachusetts.* 3 vols. Cambridge, 1873–85. Includes graduates of the years 1642–89.

TAILLEMITE, ÉTIENNE. *Inventaire analytique de la correspondance générale avec les colonies, départ, série B (déposée aux Archives nationales), I, registres 1 à 37 (1654–1715).* (Ministère de la France d'Outre-mer, Service des archives, publication.) Paris, 1959.

TANGUAY, CYPRIEN. *Dictionnaire généalogique des familles canadiennes depuis la fondation de la colonie jusqu'à nos jours.* 7 vols. [Montréal], 1871–90. *Complément. . .* par J.-A.-A. Lebœuf [*q.v.*].

—— *Répertoire général du clergé canadien par ordre chronologique depuis la fondation de la colonie jusqu'à nos jours.* Québec, 1868.

Union list of manuscripts in Canadian repositories. Edited by Robert S. Gordon *et al.* (PAC publication.) Ottawa, 1968.

VACHON, ANDRÉ. "Inventaire critique des notaires royaux des gouvernements de Québec, Montréal et Trois-Rivières (1663–1764)," *RHAF*, IX (1955–56), 423–38, 546–61; X (1956–57), 93–103, 257–62, 381–90; XI (1957–58), 93–106, 270–76, 400–6.

WALLACE, WILLIAM STEWART. *The Macmillan dictionary of Canadian biography.* 3rd edition, revised and enlarged. London, 1963. First published in Toronto in 1926 as *The dictionary of Canadian biography.*

WATTERS, REGINALD EYRE. *A checklist of Canadian literature and background materials, 1628–1960. . . .* 2nd edition, revised and enlarged. Toronto and Buffalo, 1972.

IV. STUDIES (BOOKS AND THESES)

AHERN, MICHAEL-JOSEPH ET GEORGE. *Notes pour servir à l'histoire de la médecine dans le Bas-Canada depuis la fondation de Québec jusqu'au commencement du XIXe siècle.* Québec, 1923.

ALVORD, CLARENCE WALWORTH. *The Illinois*

country, 1673–1818. (Centennial history of Illinois, I.) Springfield, Ill., 1920; Chicago, 1922; reprinted (The American west, [I]), Chicago, 1965.

ARSENAULT, BONA. *Histoire et généalogie des Acadiens.* 2 vols. Québec, [1965].

BELL, WINTHROP PICKARD. *The "foreign Protestants" and the settlement of Nova Scotia: the history of a piece of arrested British colonial policy in the eighteenth century.* Toronto, 1961.

BELTING, NATALIA MAREE. *Kaskaskia under the French régime.* (University of Illinois studies in the social sciences, XXIX, no. 3.) Urbana, Ill., 1948.

BREBNER, JOHN BARTLET. *The neutral Yankees of Nova Scotia, a marginal colony during the revolutionary years.* New York, 1937; reprinted, with an introduction by William Stewart MacNutt (Carleton library, 45), Toronto and Montreal, 1969.

—— *New England's outpost: Acadia before the conquest of Canada.* (Columbia University studies in history, economics and public law, 293.) New York and London, 1927.

BRUNET, MICHEL. *Les Canadiens après la conquête, 1759–1775: de la Révolution canadienne à la Révolution américaine.* (Collection Fleur de lys.) Montréal, 1969.

CALNEK, WILLIAM ARTHUR. *History of the county of Annapolis, including old Port Royal and Acadia, with memoirs of its representatives in the provincial parliament, and biographical and genealogical sketches of its early English settlers and their families.* Edited and completed by Alfred William Savary. Toronto, 1897; reprinted (Canadiana reprint series, 30), Belleville, Ont., 1972. *Supplement . . . by A. W. Savary [q.v.].*

CASGRAIN, HENRI-RAYMOND. *Histoire de l'Hôtel-Dieu de Québec.* Québec, 1878.

—— *L'île Saint-Jean – île du Prince-Édouard sous le régime français: une seconde Acadie.* Québec, 1894.

—— *Les Sulpiciens et les prêtres des Missions-Étrangères en Acadie (1676–1762).* Québec, 1897.

—— *Un pèlerinage au pays d'Évangéline.* Québec, 1887; 2ᵉ édition, 1888.

CHAMPAGNE, ANTOINE. *Les La Vérendrye et le poste de l'Ouest.* (Cahiers de l'institut d'histoire, 12.) Québec, 1968.

—— *Nouvelles études sur les La Vérendrye et le poste de l'Ouest.* (Cahiers de l'institut d'histoire, 17.) Québec, 1971.

CHARLAND, THOMAS-MARIE. *Histoire des Abénakis d'Odanak (1675–1937).* Montréal, 1964.

[CIMON], ADÈLE, DITE DE SAINTE-MARIE, ET CATHERINE [BURKE], DITE DE SAINT-THOMAS. *Les Ursulines de Québec, depuis leur établissement jusqu'à nos jours.* 4 vols. Québec, 1863–66; 2ᵉ édition, 1866–78.

CLARK, ANDREW HILL. *Acadia: the geography of early Nova Scotia to 1760.* Madison, 1968.

COLEMAN, EMMA LEWIS. *New England captives carried to Canada between 1677 and 1760 during the French and Indian wars.* 2 vols. Portland, Maine, 1925.

CORBETT, JULIAN STAFFORD. *England in the Seven Years' War: a study in combined strategy.* 2 vols. London, 1907; 2nd edition, 1918.

D'ALLAIRE, MICHELINE. *L'Hôpital-Général de Québec, 1692–1764.* (Collection Fleur de lys.) Montréal, 1971.

DALTON, CHARLES. *George the first's army, 1714–1727.* 2 vols. London, 1910–12.

DELANGLEZ, JEAN. *The French Jesuits in lower Louisiana (1700–1763).* New Orleans, 1935.

DOUGHTY, ARTHUR GEORGE, AND GEORGE WILLIAM PARMELEE. *The siege of Quebec and the battle of the Plains of Abraham.* 6 vols. Quebec, 1901. The last three volumes of this work consist of documents.

DUBÉ, JEAN-CLAUDE. *Claude-Thomas Dupuy, intendant de la Nouvelle-France, 1678–1738.* (Collection Fleur de lys.) Montréal et Paris, 1969.

ECCLES, WILLIAM JOHN. *The Canadian frontier, 1534–1760.* (Histories of the American frontier.) New York, 1969.

—— *France in America.* New York, 1972.

FAUTEUX, JOSEPH-NOËL. *Essai sur l'industrie au Canada sous le régime français.* 2 vols. Québec, 1927.

FRÉGAULT, GUY. *La civilisation de la Nouvelle-France (1713–1744).* Montréal, 1944; 2ᵉ édition (Collection du Nénuphar), 1969.

—— *Le XVIIIᵉ siècle canadien: études.* (Collection Constantes, 16.) Montréal, 1968; reprinted (Collection H.), 1970.

—— *François Bigot, administrateur français.* (Études de l'Institut d'histoire de l'Amérique française.) 2 vols. [Montréal], 1948.

—— *Le grand marquis: Pierre de Rigaud de Vaudreuil et la Louisiane.* (Études de l'Institut d'histoire de l'Amérique française.) Montréal et Paris, 1952; 2ᵉ édition (Collection Fleur de lys), 1962.

—— *La guerre de la conquête, 1754–1760.* (Collection Fleur de lys.) Montréal et Paris, 1955; reprinted as vol. IX of *Histoire de la Nouvelle-France,* Marcel Trudel, directeur général, [1966]; translated as *Canada: the war of the conquest* by M. M. Cameron (Toronto, 1969).

GAUMOND, MICHEL. *Les forges de Saint-Maurice*. (Société historique de Québec, Textes, 2.) Québec, 1968.

GIPSON, LAWRENCE HENRY. *The British empire before the American revolution*. . . . 15 vols. Caldwell, Idaho, and New York, 1936–70.

GIRAUD, MARCEL. *Histoire de la Louisiane française*. 3 vols. to date. Paris, 1953– .
I: *Le règne de Louis XIV (1698–1715)*. 1953.
II: *Années de transition (1715–1717)*. 1958.
III: *L'époque de John Law (1717–1720)*. 1966.

GOSSELIN, AMÉDÉE. *L'instruction au Canada sous le régime français (1635–1760)*. Québec, 1911.

GOSSELIN, AUGUSTE [-HONORÉ]. *L'Église du Canada après la conquête*. 2 vols. Québec, 1916–17.
I: *1760–1775*.
II: *1775–1789*.
———— *L'Église du Canada depuis monseigneur de Laval jusqu'à la conquête*. 3 vols. Québec, 1911–14.

GOWANS, ALAN [WILBERT]. *Church architecture in New France*. Toronto, 1955.

HAMELIN, JEAN. *Économie et société en Nouvelle-France*. (Cahiers de l'institut d'histoire, 3.) [Québec, 1960]; reprinted 1970.

HARRIS, RICHARD COLEBROOK. *The seigneurial system in early Canada: a geographical study*. Madison, 1966.

HARVEY, DANIEL COBB. *The French régime in Prince Edward Island*. New Haven, Conn., and London, 1926.

HILLER, JAMES K. "The foundation and the early years of the Moravian mission in Labrador, 1752–1805." Unpublished MA thesis for Memorial University of Newfoundland. St John's, 1967.

[*L'Hôpital Général de Montréal*]: *L'Hôpital Général des Sœurs de la Charité (sœurs grises) depuis sa fondation jusqu'à nos jours*. 3 vols. to date. Montréal, 1916– .

HUDSON'S BAY RECORD SOCIETY PUBLICATIONS. [*See also* section II.]
XXI, XXII: Rich, *History of the HBC*.

JENNESS, DIAMOND. *The Indians of Canada*. (National Museum of Canada *Bulletin*, 65, Anthropological series, 15.) Ottawa, 1932; 5th edition, 1960.

JOHNSON, MICHELINE DUMONT. *Apôtres ou agitateurs: la France missionnaire en Acadie*. (Collection 1760.) Trois-Rivières, Qué., 1970.

JOUVE, ODORIC-MARIE. *Les Franciscains et le Canada: aux Trois-Rivières*. Paris, 1934.

KELLOGG, LOUISE PHELPS. *The French régime in Wisconsin and the northwest*. (Wisconsin State Historical Society publication.) Madison, 1925; reprinted New York, 1968.

KENNETT, LEE. *The French armies in the Seven Years' War: a study in military organization and administration*. Durham, N.C., 1967.

LACHANCE, ANDRÉ. *Le bourreau au Canada sous le régime français*. (Société historique de Québec, Cahiers d'histoire, 18.) Québec, 1966.

LACOUR-GAYET, GEORGES. *La marine militaire de la France sous le règne de Louis XV*. Paris, 1902; 2e édition, revue et augmentée, 1910.

LA MORANDIÈRE, CHARLES DE. *Histoire de la pêche française de la morue dans l'Amérique septentrionale*. . . . 3 vols. Paris, 1962–66.
I, II: *(Des origines à 1789)*.
III: *(De la Révolution à nos jours)*.

LANCTOT, GUSTAVE. *Histoire du Canada....* 3 vols. Montréal, 1959–64.
[I]: *Des origines au régime royal*.
[II]: *Du régime royal au traité d'Utrecht, 1663–1713*.
[III]: *Du traité d'Utrecht au traité de Paris, 1713–1763*.
Translated as *A History of Canada* by Josephine Hambleton and M. M. Cameron (3v., Toronto and Cambridge, Mass., 1963–65).

LANGDON, JOHN EMERSON. *Canadian silversmiths, 1700–1900*. Toronto, 1966.

LAUVRIÈRE, ÉMILE. *La tragédie d'un peuple: histoire du peuple acadien de ses origines à nos jours*. 2 vols. Paris, 1922; nouvelle édition révisée, 1924.

[LEMIRE-MARSOLAIS, DARIE-AURÉLIE, DITE SAINTE-HENRIETTE] ET THÉRÈSE LAMBERT, DITE SAINTE-MARIE-MÉDIATRICE. *Histoire de la Congrégation de Notre-Dame de Montréal*. 11 vols. (numbered I-X) and an index to date. Montréal, 1910– . Before her death in 1917 Sister Sainte-Henriette had completed nine volumes of her history as well as an index; only two volumes were published, in 1910. In 1941 her complete work was published and the first two volumes reissued. The index was published in 1969 along with two volumes covering the period 1855–1900, written by Sister Thérèse Lambert.

LOUNSBURY, RALPH GREENLEE. *The British fishery at Newfoundland, 1634–1763*. (Yale historical publications, Miscellany, XXVII.) New Haven, Conn., and London, 1934.

McLENNAN, JOHN STEWART. *Louisbourg from its foundation to its fall, 1713–1758*. London, 1918; reprinted, without appendices, Sydney, N.S., 1957.

MacNutt, William Stewart. *The Atlantic provinces: the emergence of colonial society, 1712–1857*. (Canadian centenary series, 9.) Toronto, 1965.

Mathieu, Jacques. *La construction navale royale à Québec, 1739–1759*. (Société historique de Québec, Cahiers d'histoire, 23.) Québec, 1971.

Military affairs in North America, 1748–1765: selected documents from the Cumberland papers in Windsor Castle. Edited by Stanley McCrory Pargellis. New York and London, 1936; reprinted [Hamden, Conn.], 1969.

[Mondoux, Maria.] *L'Hôtel-Dieu, premier hôpital de Montréal . . . 1642–1763*. Montréal, 1942.

Monseigneur de Saint-Vallier et l'Hôpital Général de Québec: histoire du monastère de Notre-Dame des Anges. . . . Québec, 1882.

Morisset, Gérard. *Coup d'œil sur les arts en Nouvelle-France*. Québec, 1941.

Morton, Arthur Silver. *A history of the Canadian west to 1870–71, being a history of Rupert's Land (the Hudson's Bay Company's territory) and of the North-West Territory (including the Pacific slope)*. London, [1939]; 2nd edition, edited by Lewis Gwynne Thomas, Toronto, 1973.

Murdoch, Beamish. *A history of Nova-Scotia, or Acadie*. 3 vols. Halifax, 1865–67.

Neatby, Hilda. *Quebec: the revolutionary age, 1760–1791*. (Canadian centenary series, 6.) Toronto, 1966.

Nish, Cameron. *Les bourgeois-gentilshommes de la Nouvelle-France, 1729–1748*. (Histoire économique et sociale du Canada français.) Montréal et Paris, 1968.

O'Neill, Charles Edwards. *Church and state in French colonial Louisiana: policy and politics to 1732*. New Haven, Conn., and London, 1966.

Parkman, Francis. *France and England in North America: a series of historical narratives*. 8 parts. Boston, 1851–92. Many editions of each of the parts have been published. Parts used in volume III, with dates of first editions:
5th: *Count Frontenac and New France under Louis XIV*. 1877.
6th: *A half-century of conflict*. 2 vols. 1892.
7th: *Montcalm and Wolfe*. 2 vols. 1884.
For a summary of the various editions of Parkman's works see: *The Parkman reader . . .*, ed. S. E. Morison (Boston and Toronto, 1955).

Peckham, Howard Henry. *Pontiac and the Indian uprising*. Princeton, 1947; reprinted Chicago, 1961.

Prowse, Daniel Woodley. *A history of Newfoundland from the English, colonial, and foreign records*. London and New York, 1895; 2nd edition, London, 1896; reprint of 1st edition (Canadiana reprint series, 33), Belleville, Ont., 1972.

Rawlyk, George Alexander. *Yankees at Louisbourg*. (University of Maine *Bulletin*, 69, no.19 (13 April 1967); University of Maine studies, 2nd series, 85.) Orono, Maine, 1967.

Rich, Edwin Ernest. *The history of the Hudson's Bay Company, 1670–1870*. (Hudson's Bay Record Society publications, XXI, XXII.) 2 vols. London, 1958–59; another edition, 3 vols., Toronto, 1960. A copy of this work available in the PAC contains notes and bibliographical material omitted from the printed version.

Richard, Édouard. *Acadie: reconstitution d'un chapitre perdu de l'histoire d'Amérique*. Henri D'Arles [Marie-Joseph-Henri-Athanase Beaudé], éditeur. 3 vols. Québec et Boston, Mass., 1916–21.
I: *Depuis les origines jusqu'à la paix d'Aix-la-Chapelle*.
II: *Depuis la paix d'Aix-la-Chapelle jusqu'à la déportation*.
III: *La déportation et au-delà*.

Rochemonteix, Camille de. *Les Jésuites et la Nouvelle-France au XVIIe siècle. . . .* 3 vols. Paris, 1895–96.
———— *Les Jésuites et la Nouvelle-France au XVIIIe siècle. . . .* 2 vols. Paris, 1906.

Roy, Joseph-Edmond. *Histoire du notariat au Canada depuis la fondation de la colonie jusqu'à nos jours*. 4 vols. Lévis, Qué., 1899–1902.

Roy, Pierre-Georges. *Bigot et sa bande et l'affaire du Canada*. Lévis, Qué., 1950.
———— *Fils de Québec*. 4 vols. Lévis, Qué., 1933.
————*Hommes et choses du fort Saint-Frédéric*. Montréal, 1946.
———— *La ville de Québec sous le régime français*. (APQ publication.) 2 vols. Québec, 1930.

Savary, Alfred William. *Supplement to the history of the county of Annapolis. . . .* Toronto, 1913; reprinted (Canadiana reprint series, 63), Belleville, Ont., 1973. [*See* Calnek.]

Smythies, Raymond Henry Raymond. *Historical records of the 40th (2nd Somersetshire) regiment, now 1st battalion the Prince of Wales's volunteers (South Lancashire regiment), from its formation, in 1717, to 1893*. Devonport, Eng., 1894.

STACEY, CHARLES PERRY. *Quebec, 1759: the siege and the battle.* Toronto, 1959.

STANLEY, GEORGE FRANCIS GILMAN. *New France: the last phase, 1744–1760.* (Canadian centenary series, 5.) Toronto, 1968.

SULTE, BENJAMIN. *Histoire des Canadiens-français, 1608–1880.* . . . 8 vols. Montréal, 1882–84.

—— *Mélanges historiques.* . . . Gérard Malchelosse, éditeur. 21 vols. Montréal, 1918–34. This series is a mixture of volumes of articles and monographs.

TRAQUAIR, RAMSAY. *The old silver of Quebec.* Toronto, 1940.

TROUDE, ORÉSIME [-JOACHIM]. *Batailles navales de la France.* 4 vols. Paris, 1867–68.

TRUDEL, MARCEL. *L'Église canadienne sous le régime militaire, 1759–1764.* 2 vols. Québec, 1956–57.

—— *L'esclavage au Canada français: histoire et conditions de l'esclavage.* Québec, 1960.

Les Ursulines de Québec. See [CIMON].

VACHON, ANDRÉ. *Histoire du notariat canadien, 1621–1960.* Québec, 1962.

WILLIAMS, GLYNDWR. *The British search for the northwest passage in the eighteenth century.* (Royal Commonwealth Society, Imperial Studies series, XXIV.) London, 1962.

V: JOURNALS AND STUDIES (ARTICLES)

Le Bulletin des recherches historiques. Published usually in Lévis. Journal of archaeology, history, biography, bibliography, numismatology, etc. Founded by Pierre-Georges Roy* as the organ of the Société des études historiques, the *BRH* became the journal of the APQ (later the AQ, now the ANQ) in March 1923. Published monthly from 1895, it became a quarterly in 1949. After 1956 it was published irregularly. I (1895)–LXX (1968). *Index*: I (1895)–XXXI (1925). 4 vols. Beauceville, Qué., 1925–26. For subsequent years see the manuscript index in the ANQ.

Les Cahiers des Dix. Montréal et Québec. Annual review published by "Les Dix," a group of historians who formed a legal association on 6 Aug. 1935. I (1936)– .

Le Canada français. Québec. First series: *Le Canada-français*, journal published irregularly under the direction of a committee of professors of Université Laval. Concerned with religion, philosophy, history, fine arts, science and letters. I (1888)–IV (1891), with index in IV. *Coll. doc. inédits Canada et Amérique* [*see* section II], which contains many documents on Acadia, appeared in connection with *Le Canada-français*, vols. I-III, as a separately paginated supplement. Second series: incorporated *Parler français* and *La Nouvelle-France*. Publication of Université Laval and journal of the Société du Parler français au Canada. I (1918–19)–XXXIII (1945–46). Renamed *La Revue de l'université Laval* [*q.v.*].

CANADIAN CATHOLIC HISTORICAL ASSOCIATION/SOCIÉTÉ CANADIENNE D'HISTOIRE DE L'ÉGLISE CATHOLIQUE, Ottawa. A bilingual society, founded 3 June 1933, it has published simultaneously each year (except for 1933–34) a *Rapport* in French and a *Report* in English, of which the contents are entirely different. 1933-34– . *Index*: 1933-34–1958. Title varies: *Study Sessions/Sessions d'étude* from 1966.

CANADIAN HISTORICAL ASSOCIATION/SOCIÉTÉ HISTORIQUE DU CANADA, Ottawa. The association, founded in 1922, continues the work of the Historic Landmarks Association of Canada (1915–21). Its aims are "to encourage historical research and public interest in history; to promote the preservation of historic sites and buildings, documents, relics, and other significant heirlooms of the past; to publish historical studies and documents as circumstances may permit." Publications include *Annual Report*, 1922– (title varies: *Historical Papers/Communications historiques* from 1966), and historical booklets, issued irregularly. *Index* to annual reports: 1922–51; 1952–68.

Canadian Historical Review. Toronto. Quarterly. I (1920)– . *Index*: I (1920)–X (1929); XI (1930)–XX (1939); XXI (1940)–XXX (1949). Université Laval has published an index for later volumes: *Canadian Historical Review, 1950–1964: index des articles et des comptes rendus de volumes*, René Hardy, comp. (Québec, 1969). Each issue includes a current bibliography of publications in English and French, a continuation of the annual *Review of Historical Publications relating to Canada* (I (for 1895–96)–XXII (for 1917–18); *Index*: I–X; XI–XX).

Dalhousie Review. Halifax. Quarterly publication of Dalhousie University. I (1921–22)– .

GANONG, WILLIAM FRANCIS. "A monograph of

historic sites in the province of New Brunswick," *RSCT*, 2nd ser., V (1899), sect. II, 213–357.

Mississippi Valley Historical Review. Cedar Rapids, Iowa, and Lincoln, Neb. Quarterly publication of the Mississippi Valley Historical Association. Succeeded by the *Journal of American History*. I (1914–15)–L (1963–64). *Index*: I-L.

New-England Historical and Genealogical Register. Boston. Quarterly publication of the New England Historic Genealogical Society. I (1847)– . The title *New-England Historical & Genealogical Register and Antiquarian Journal* was used in 1869–73. Separate index volumes of places, genealogies and pedigrees, testators, persons, and subjects have been published.

Nova Francia. Paris. Published every two months. Organ of the Société d'histoire du Canada, founded in France in 1924. I (1925–26)–VII (1932).

NOVA SCOTIA HISTORICAL SOCIETY, Halifax. Publishes *Collections*. Issued irregularly. I (1878)– . The title *Report and Collections* was used in 1878 and 1882–83.

Revue canadienne. Montréal. Monthly. [Ire série]: I (1864)–LIII (1907) (vols. XVII (1881)–XXIII (1887) called nouv. sér. [2e sér.], I–VII; vols. XXIV (1888)–XXVIII (1892) called 3e sér., I–[V]). Nouvelle série: I (1908)–XXVII (1922). Indexes. The numbering of this journal is imprecise.

La Revue de l'université Laval. Québec. Monthly. Publication of the university and organ of the Société du Parler français au Canada. I (1946–47)–XXI (1966). A continuation of the review *Le Canada français*, it was succeeded in 1968 by *Études littéraires*.

Revue d'histoire de l'Amérique française. Montréal. Quarterly publication of the Institut d'histoire de l'Amérique française. Founded by Canon Lionel Groulx*. I (1947–48)– . *Index*: I (1947–48)–X (1956–57); XI (1957–58)–XX (1966–67).

ROYAL SOCIETY OF CANADA/SOCIÉTÉ ROYALE DU CANADA, Ottawa. Under the patronage of the Marquess of Lorne [John Douglas Sutherland Campbell*], the society was formed in 1882 for the encouragement of literature and science in Canada. Originally it was composed of four sections, two for literature and two for sciences. Publishes *Proceedings and Transactions/Mémoires et comptes rendus*, of which sections I and II include historical articles. Annual. First series: I (1882–83)–XII (1894). Second series: I (1895)–XII (1906). Third series: I (1907)–LVI (1962). Fourth series: I (1963)– . Indexes.

SOCIÉTÉ GÉNÉALOGIQUE CANADIENNE-FRANÇAISE, Montréal. Founded on the initiative of Father Archange Godbout, 3 Sept. 1943. Publishes *Mémoires*. Originally biannual, now quarterly. I (1944–45)– .

TÊTU, HENRI. "Le chapitre de la cathédrale de Québec et ses délégués en France: lettres des chanoines Pierre Hazeur de L'Orme et Jean-Marie de la Corne, 1723–1773," *BRH*, XIII (1907), 225–43, 257–83, 289–308, 321–38, 353–61; XIV (1908), 3–22, 33–40, 65–79, 97–109, 129–46, 161–75, 193–208, 225–39, 257–70, 289–98, 321–37, 353–64; XV (1909), 3–16, 33–48, 65–79, 97–111, 129–42, 161–76, 193–211, 225–41, 257–74, 289–301, 321–28, 353–60; XVI (1910), 3–10, 33–44, 65–75, 97–109, 129–41, 161–75, 193–206, 225–40, 257–74, 289–302, 321–30, 353–64.

ZOLTVANY, YVES FRANÇOIS. "New France and the west, 1701–1713," *CHR*, XLVI (1965), 301–22.

Contributors

ADAMS, BLAINE. Secondary school teacher, Silverthorn C. I., Etobicoke, Ontario.
François-Joseph Cailly. Jean-Baptiste-Louis Le Prévost Duquesnel.

ALBERTS, ROBERT C. Writer; contributing editor, *American Heritage Magazine*, New York, U.S.A.
Robert Stobo.

ARMOUR, DAVID ARTHUR. Assistant superintendent, Mackinac Island State Park Commission, Michigan, U.S.A.
Jean-Baptiste Amiot. James Gorrell. Louis Liénard de Beaujeu. Claude Marin de La Perrière. Minweweh. Johannes Rooseboom.

ASSELIN, JEAN-PIERRE. Assistant à l'édition, *Dictionnaire biographique du Canada / Dictionary of Canadian Biography*, Les Presses de l'université Laval, Québec, Québec.
Jean-Félix Récher. Marie-Andrée Regnard Duplessis, dite de Sainte-Hélène. Philippe-René Robinau de Portneuf. Pierre Robinau de Portneuf. Marie-Catherine Tibierge, dite de Saint-Joachim.

AUDET, LOUIS-PHILIPPE. Professeur à la retraite, Sillery, Québec.
Joseph Des Landes. Antoine Forget. Michel Guignas. Jean-Baptiste Guyart de Fleury. Jacques Talbot.

AUGER, ROLAND-J. Responsable de la section de généalogie, Archives nationales du Québec, Québec.
Noël Bonhomme, dit Beaupré. Jean Boucher de Montbrun. Jean-Baptiste Boucher de Niverville. Jacques-Joseph Cheval, dit Saint-Jacques, and dit Chevalier. François de Galiffet de Caffin. Jean-Baptiste Gastineau Duplessis. François Perrault. Joseph Riverin. Étienne Véron de Grandmesnil.

BAILEY, ALFRED GOLDSWORTHY. Professor emeritus of history, University of New Brunswick, Fredericton, New Brunswick.
Samuel Moody.

BAILLARGEON, NOËL, PTRE. Historien, Séminaire de Québec, Québec.
Jacques-François Forget Duverger. Joachim Fornel. Joseph-Thierry Hazeur. Jean Lyon de Saint-Ferréol. Jean-Paul Mercier. François de Montigny. Henri-Jean Tremblay. François-Elzéar Vallier.

BATES, GEORGE E., Jr. Professor of history, Winona State College, Winona, Minnesota, U.S.A.
John Barnard.

†BAUDRY, RENÉ. Représentant des Archives publiques du Canada en France, Paris, France.
Louise Guyon.

BÉLANGER, HERVÉ. Agent de recherche et de planification socio-économique, Montréal, Québec.
Martin Descouts. Nicolas Deslongrais.

BÉLANGER, RENÉ, P.D. Écrivain, Québec, Québec.
Vincent.

BERNIER, HÉLÈNE. Chargée de cours, Université de Sherbrooke, Québec.
Marie-Anne-Véronique Cuillerier. Françoise Gaudé. Anne-Françoise Leduc, dite Saint-Joseph.

BIRON, HERVÉ. Éditeur du *Journal des débats*, Assemblée nationale du Québec, Québec.
Pierre Poulin.

BLAIS, MARIE-CÉLINE. Chargée de recherche, *Dictionnaire biographique du Canada / Dictionary of Canadian Biography*, Les Presses de l'université Laval, Québec, Québec.
Yves Phlem, dit Yvon.

BLAKELEY, PHYLLIS R. Assistant provincial archivist, Public Archives of Nova Scotia, Halifax, Nova Scotia.
Silvanus Cobb. Robert Denison. Leonard Lockman. James Monk. Montagu Wilmot.

BOISSONNAULT, CHARLES-MARIE. Écrivain, Québec.
Jean-Jard Boispineau.

BOIVIN BERNARD. Institut de recherches sur les végétaux, Ministère de l'Agriculture du Canada, Ottawa, Ontario.
Jean-François Gaultier.

BORINS, EDWARD H. Manager, David Mirvish Books on Art, Toronto, Ontario.
Claude-Antoine de Bermen de La Martinière.

BOWSFIELD, HARTWELL. Lecturer in history, York University, Downsview, Ontario.
Joseph La France.

BUFFET, F. M. Vicar of Ipplepen, Newton Abbot, Devonshire, England.
John Fordyce. Henry Jones.

BUMSTED, J. M. Associate professor of history, Simon Fraser University, Burnaby, B.C.
Otis Little.

CAMERON, WENDY. Historian, Toronto, Ontario.
Peregrine Thomas Hopson.

CAMPEAU, LUCIEN, S.J. Professeur agrégé d'histoire, Université de Montréal, Québec.
Pierre de Mareuil. Charles-Michel Mésaiger. Luc-François Nau. Jean-Baptiste de Saint-Pé.

CAUCHON, MICHEL. Conservateur, Inventaire des œuvres d'art du Québec, Québec.
Gilles Bolvin. Michel Cotton. Jean-Baptiste Deschevery, dit Maisonbasse. Jacques Gadois, dit Mauger. Paul-Raymond Jourdain, dit Labrosse. Jean-François Landron. Pierre-Gabriel Le Prévost. Pierre-Noël Levasseur. Paul Mallepart de Grand Maison, dit Beaucour. Jacques Pagé, dit Carcy. Roland Paradis. Charles Vézina. [In collaboration with A. Juneau.]

CERBELAUD SALAGNAC, GEORGES. Directeur littéraire des Éditions Tequi, Paris, France.
Joseph d'Abbadie de Saint-Castin.

CONTRIBUTORS

CHAMPAGNE, ANTOINE. Professeur à la retraite, Winnipeg, Manitoba.
Charles-René Dejordy de Villebon. Louis-Joseph Gaultier de La Vérendrye. Pierre Gaultier de La Vérendrye (fils).

CHAPUT, DONALD. Senior curator of history, Natural History Museum, Los Angeles, California, U.S.A.
Jacques Campot. Louis-Césaire Dagneau Douville de Quindre. Jacques Legardeur de Saint-Pierre. Mikinak.

CHARD, DONALD F. Lecturer in history, St Mary's University, Halifax, Nova Scotia.
John Bushell. Bartholomew Green. Thomas Kilby. Cyprian Southack.

CHARLAND, THOMAS-M., O.P. Bibliothécaire et archiviste, Couvent des Dominicains, Montréal, Québec.
Atecouando. Étienne Lauverjat. Jacques-François Le Sueur.

CHEVRETTE, LOUIS A. Archiviste, Division des manuscrits, Archives publiques du Canada, Ottawa, Ontario.
Pontiac.

CHIASSON, ANSELME, O.F.M. CAP. Archiviste, Centre d'études acadiennes, Université de Moncton, Nouveau-Brunswick.
Patrice René.

COLEMAN, MARGARET I. Formerly research historian, National Historic Sites Service, Department of Indian Affairs and Northern Development, Ottawa, Ontario.
Jean-Pierre Roma.

COSSETTE, JOSEPH, S.J. Archiviste, Archives de la Compagnie de Jésus, Saint-Jérôme (Prévost), Québec.
Jean-Baptiste Chardon. Claude-Godefroy Coquart. Jean-Baptiste Duparc. Pierre de Lauzon. Gabriel Marcol.

CÔTÉ, ANDRÉ. Professeur d'histoire, Université du Québec à Chicoutimi, Québec.
Jacques-Quintin de La Bretonnière. Marie. François-Antoine Pécaudy de Contrecœur.

CRAIG, JOAN. Formerly archivist, Hudson's Bay Company, London, England.
John Newton. Robert Pilgrim. Samuel Skrimsher.

CROWLEY, TERENCE ALLAN. Lecturer in history, University of Guelph, Ontario.
Jean Delaborde. Jacques-Ange Le Normant de Mézy. Louis Levasseur. Jacques-Philippe-Urbain Rondeau. Antoine Sabatier.

D'ALLAIRE, MICHELINE. Professeur agrégé d'histoire, Université d'Ottawa, Ontario.
Marie-Joseph Juchereau Duchesnay, dite de l'Enfant-Jésus. Marie-Thérèse Langlois, dite de Saint-Jean-Baptiste. Marie-Charlotte de Ramezay, dite de Saint-Claude de la Croix.

DANIELL, JERE ROGERS. Associate professor of history, Dartmouth College, New Hampshire, U.S.A.
George Mitchell.

DANSEREAU, ANTONIO, P.S.S. Archiviste, Collège de Montréal, Québec.
Joseph Dargent. Antoine Déat. Élie Depéret.

Hamon Guen. Pierre Le Sueur. Louis Normant Du Faradon. Maurice Quéré de Tréguron.

DAY, GORDON M. Eastern Canada Ethnologist and Head, Research Section, National Museum of Man, National Museums of Canada, Ottawa, Ontario.
Glossary of Indian Tribal Names. *Gray Lock.*

DECHÊNE, LOUISE. Professeur adjoint d'histoire, McGill University, Montréal, Québec.
André Carrerot. Philippe Carrerot. Alexis Lemoine, dit Monière.

DÉSILETS, ANDRÉE. Directeur, Département d'histoire, Université de Sherbrooke, Québec.
Marie-Marguerite-Daniel Arnaud, dite Saint-Arsène. Marie-Madeleine de La Corne de Chaptes, dite du Saint-Sacrement. Marie-Angélique Lefebvre Angers, dite Saint-Simon. Marguerite Le Moyne de Sainte-Marie, dite du Saint-Esprit. Lydia Longley, dite Sainte-Madeleine. Marguerite Roy, dite de la Conception. Marguerite Trottier, dite Saint-Joseph.

DESLOGES, YVON. Historien, Service des lieux historiques nationaux, Ministère des Affaires indiennes et du Nord canadien, Ottawa, Ontario.
Benjamin Rouer de Villeray.

DESPATIE, AIMÉ. Directeur, *La Revue de Terrebonne*, Terrebonne, Québec.
Louis Lepage de Sainte-Claire.

DE VILLE, WINSTON. Executive director, Polyanthos, Inc., Connecticut, New Jersey, U.S.A.
Louis Juchereau de Saint-Denis [in collaboration].

DOUGLAS, W. A. B. Director, Directorate of history, National Defence Headquarters, Ottawa, Ontario.
Edward Boscawen. Alexander Colvill. Philip Durell. Charles Holmes. John Rous.

DOUVILLE, RAYMOND. Trois-Rivières, Québec.
Charles Alavoine. André Arnoux.

DUBÉ, JEAN-CLAUDE. Professeur agrégé d'histoire, Université d'Ottawa, Ontario.
Pierre André de Leigne. François de Beauharnois de La Chaussaye. Louis Rouer d'Artigny.

DUCLOS, LAURETTE, S.G.M. Archiviste, Archives des sœurs Grises de Montréal, Pierrefonds, Québec.
Agathe Véronneau.

DUPONT, JEAN-CLAUDE. Professeur d'ethnologie historique, Université Laval, Québec, Québec.
Jean-Baptiste Baudry, dit Saint-Martin. Nicolas Jacquin, dit Philibert.

DUPRÉ, CÉLINE. Agent culturel, Office de la langue française, Ministère de l'Éducation du Québec, Québec.
Marie-Élisabeth Rocbert de La Morandière.

ECCLES, W. J. Professor of history, University of Toronto, Ontario.
Introductory essay: *The French forces in North America during the Seven Years' War. Pierre-Joseph Céloron de Blainville. Louis Coulon de Villiers. Nicolas-Antoine Coulon de Villiers. Joseph Coulon de Villiers de Jumonville. Paul Marin de La Malgue. Louis-Joseph de Montcalm. Étienne-Guillaume de Senezergues de La Rodde.*

EINHORN, ARTHUR. Associate professor of anthropology, Jefferson Community College, Watertown, New York, U.S.A.

Glossary of Indian Tribal Names. *Gawèhe. Kak8enthiony. Ononwarogo.*

ENTREMONT, CLARENCE J. D'. Aumônier, Our Lady's Haven, Fairhaven, Massachusetts, U.S.A.
Alexandre Bourg, dit *Belle-Humeur. Joseph Brossard,* dit *Beausoleil.*

FAIRCHILD, BYRON. Formerly chief, Special Studies Branch, Historical Office, Department of State, Washington, D.C., U.S.A.
Sir William Pepperrell.

FENTON, WILLIAM N. Research professor of anthropology, State University of New York, Albany, New York, U.S.A.
Joseph-François Lafitau.

FERGUSSON, CHARLES BRUCE. Archivist, Public Archives of Nova Scotia, Halifax, Nova Scotia; associate professor of history, Dalhousie University, Halifax, Nova Scotia.
Sir Danvers Osborn. Patrick Sutherland. William Winniett.

FERLAND, MADELEINE D. Professeur agrégé, Université Laval, Québec, Québec.
Agathe de Saint-Père.

†FERLAND-ANGERS, ALBERTINE. Sorel, Québec.
Louis Turc de Castelveyre, dit *Frère Chrétien* [in collaboration].

FINGARD, JUDITH. Associate professor of history, Dalhousie University, Halifax, Nova Scotia.
Jean-Baptiste Moreau.

FLEURENT, MAURICE. Professeur d'histoire, Université du Québec à Trois-Rivières, Québec.
Pierre Dizy de Montplaisir.

FLINN, JOHN F. Professor of French, University College, University of Toronto, Ontario.
Translator of French biographies into English.

FORTIER, JOHN. Director of research, Fortress of Louisbourg, National Historic Park (Department of Indian Affairs and Northern Development), Nova Scotia.
Augustin de Boschenry de Drucour. Charles Des Herbiers de La Ralière. Jean Mascle de Saint-Julhien.

FORTIN-MORISSET, CATHERINE. Assistante de recherche, Département de biologie, Université Laval, Québec, Québec.
Jean-Baptiste Gosselin. Catherine Jérémie, dit *Lamontagne. Hubert-Joseph de La Croix.*

FRISCH, JACK A. Associate professor of anthropology, Washington State University, Pullman, Wash., U.S.A.
John Tarbell.

GAGNÉ, ARMAND. Directeur, Archives de l'archidiocèse de Québec, Québec.
Eustache Chartier de Lotbinière. Charles Plante. Pierre-Joseph Resche.

GARIÉPY, RAYMOND. Sous-ministre adjoint, Ministère des Affaires culturelles du Québec, Québec.
Louis-Gaspard Dufournel. Joseph Navières.

GILLESPIE, BERYL C. Graduate student of anthropology, University of Iowa, Iowa City, Iowa, U.S.A.
Glossary of Indian Tribal Names.

GODFREY, MICHAEL, R.N. (RETD). Record agent, East Molesey, Surrey, England.

Hugh Bonfoy. John Byng. Richard Dorrill. Edward Falkingham. Fitzroy Henry Lee. Sir John Norris.

GODFREY, WILLIAM G. Assistant professor of history, Mount Allison University, Sackville, New Brunswick.
Christopher Aldridge (Sr). Christopher Aldridge (Jr). John Henry Bastide. Otho Hamilton. John Handfield. Erasmus James Philipps.

GRAHAM, DOMINICK STUART. Associate professor of history, University of New Brunswick, Fredericton, New Brunswick.
Charles Lawrence.

GRAHAM, JANE E. Supervisory editor, *Dictionary of Canadian Biography / Dictionnaire biographique du Canada,* University of Toronto Press, Ontario.
John Lottridge. Wabbicommicot.

GRIMARD, JACQUES. Étudiant, VIᵉ section, École Pratique des Hautes Études, Paris, France.
Jean Jeantot.

GWYN, JULIAN. Associate professor of history, University of Ottawa, Ontario.
Charles Hay. Isaac Townsend. Sir Peter Warren. Edward Whitmore.

HAMILTON, MILTON W. Formerly acting state historian, New York, U.S.A.
Theyanoguin.

HAMILTON, WILLIAM B. Associate professor of history, University of Western Ontario, London, Ontario.
John Collier. Edward Halhead.

HAY, DOUGLAS. Assistant professor of history, Memorial University of Newfoundland, St John's, Newfoundland.
Glossary of Indian Tribal Names.

HAYNE, DAVID M. Second general editor, *Dictionary of Canadian Biography / Dictionnaire biographique du Canada,* 1965–69; professor of French, University College, University of Toronto, Ontario.
Pierre-François-Xavier de Charlevoix.

HÉBERT, HECTOR J., S.J. Centre d'études acadiennes, Université de Moncton, Nouveau-Brunswick.
Marie-Madeleine Maisonnat.

HELM, JUNE. Professor of anthropology, University of Iowa, Iowa City, Iowa, U.S.A.
Glossary of Indian Tribal Names.

HICKERSON, HAROLD. Professor of anthropology, Simon Fraser University, Burnaby, British Columbia.
Glossary of Indian Tribal Names. *La Colle. Wawatam.*

HIPPEN, JAMES C. Associate professor of history, Luther College, Decorah, Iowa, U.S.A.
Thomas Saul.

HODY, MAUD H. Writer, Moncton, New Brunswick.
Michel Chartier.

HORTON, DONALD J. Assistant professor of history, University of Waterloo, Ontario.
Claude-Michel Bégon de La Cour. Louis Denys de La Ronde [in collaboration with B. Pothier]. *François Foucault. François Foucher. Jean-Eustache Lanoullier de Boisclerc. Jean de Laporte*

725

de Lalanne. Honoré Michel de Villebois de La Rouvillière. Nicolas-Marie Renaud d'Avène Des Méloizes. Étienne Rocbert de La Morandière.

HUBBARD, ROBERT HAMILTON. Chief curator, National Gallery of Canada, Ottawa, Ontario.
Richard Short.

HUMPHREYS, JOHN. Researcher, Amnesty International, London, England.
Robert Elliot. Alexander Murray. Andrew Rollo.

HUNTER, WILLIAM A. Chief, Division of history, Pennsylvania Historical and Museum Commission, Harrisburg, Pennsylvania, U.S.A.
Glossary of Indian Tribal Names. *Elizabeth Couc. Kaghswaghtaniunt. Orontony. Swatana. Tanaghrisson.*

HURTUBISE, PIERRE. Directeur, Centre de recherche, Université Saint-Paul, Ottawa, Ontario.
Dominique-Marie Varlet.

HUTCHESON, MAUD M. Research assistant, Centre for Reformation and Renaissance Studies, Victoria University, Toronto, Ontario.
Aaron Cleveland. John Pattin.

IGARTUA, JOSÉ. Lecturer, University of Western Ontario, London, Ontario.
Jean-Baptiste Amiot. René de Couagne. Pierre Guy. Louis-François Hervieux. François Martel de Brouague. Barthélemy Martin. Joseph Rouffio. Jacques Terroux. Pierre Trottier Desauniers.

JENNINGS, FRANCIS. Chairman, Department of history, Cedar Crest College, Allentown, Pennsylvania, U.S.A.
Peter Bisaillon.

JOHNSON, ALICE M. Formerly archivist, Hudson's Bay Company, London, England.
Robert Evison. Thomas McCliesh. Richard Norton. Richard White.

JOHNSON, MICHELINE D. Professeur d'histoire, Université de Sherbrooke, Québec.
Joseph Aubery. Étienne Bâtard. Claude-Jean-Baptiste Chauvreulx. Jean-Baptiste Cope. Henri Daudin. Justinien Durand. Jean-Baptiste de Gay Desenclaves. Pierre de La Chasse. Charles de La Goudalie. Paul Laurent. Pierre Maillard. Jean Manach. Jacques Padanuques.

JOHNSTON, BASIL H. Lecturer in American Indian history, Royal Ontario Museum, Toronto, Ont.
Glossary of Indian Tribal Names.

JONES, FREDERICK. Lecturer in history, Bournemouth College of Technology, Bournemouth, England.
Robert Kilpatrick. William Peaseley.

JUNEAU, ANDRÉ. Adjoint au directeur et conservateur de l'art traditionnel, Musée du Québec, Québec.
Gilles Bolvin. Michel Cotton. Jean-Baptiste Deschevery, dit *Maisonbasse. Jacques Gadois,* dit *Mauger. Paul-Raymond Jourdain,* dit *Labrosse. Jean-François Landron. Pierre-Gabriel Le Prévost. Pierre-Noël Levasseur. Paul Mallepart de Grand Maison,* dit *Beaucour. Jacques Pagé,* dit *Carcy. Roland Paradis. Charles Vézina.* [In collaboration with M. Cauchon.]

KALLMANN, HELMUT. Chief, Music Division, National Library of Canada, Ottawa, Ontario.

Charles-François Coron.

KELSAY, ISABEL T. Freelance historian, Glen Mills, Pennsylvania, U.S.A.
Karaghtadie.

KELSEY, HARRY. Chief curator of history, Los Angeles County Museum of Natural History, Los Angeles, California, U.S.A.
Donald Campbell. Jean-Baptiste Chapoton. Jean-Baptiste Chevalier. Sir Robert Davers. John Jamet. Michipichy. Charles Robertson.

KIDD, KENNETH E. Professor of anthropology, Trent University, Peterborough, Ontario.
Kisensik.

KRAUSE, ERIC R. Historian, Fortress of Louisbourg, National Historic Park (Department of Indian Affairs and Northern Development), Nova Scotia.
François-Marie de Goutin.

KRUGLER, JOHN DAVID. Assistant professor of history, Marquette University, Milwaukee, Wisconsin, U.S.A.
John Gorham. Peter Schuyler.

LACHANCE, ANDRÉ. Professeur d'histoire, Université de Sherbrooke, Québec.
Michel Bénard. Jean Corolère. Jean Corpron. Thérèse de Couagne. Charles-Paul Denys de Saint-Simon. Jacques-Joseph Guiton de Monrepos. François-Charles Havard de Beaufort, known as *L'Avocat. Henry Hiché. Jacques Imbert. Charles Le Moyne de Longueuil. Mathieu Léveillé. Jean-François Malhiot. François Maurin. Joseph Nouchet. Joseph-Étienne Nouchet. Jean-Baptiste-Ignace Perthuis. François-Louis Poulin de Courval. Louis-Jean Poulin de Courval. Charles-Denis Regnard Duplessis de Morampont. Louis-Jacques-Charles Renaud Dubuisson.*

LACOURCIÈRE, LUC. Directeur, Archives de folklore, Université Laval, Québec, Québec.
Marie-Josephte Corriveau, known as *La Corriveau.*

LAHAISE, ROBERT. Professeur d'histoire, Université du Québec à Montréal, Québec.
Pierre Claverie. Joseph Durocher.

LAJEUNESSE, ERNEST J. Associate pastor, Assumption Church, Windsor, Ontario.
Louis Gervaise. Armand de La Richardie.

LANGDON, JOHN E. Chairman, Ontario Heritage Foundation, Toronto, Ontario.
Paul Lambert, dit *Saint-Paul.*

LAPOINTE, GABRIELLE, O.S.U. Monastère des Ursulines, Québec, Québec.
Geneviève Boucher, dite *de Saint-Pierre. Charlotte Daneau de Muy,* dite *de Sainte-Hélène. Marie-Anne Davis,* dite *de Saint-Benoît.*

LAVALLÉE, JEAN-GUY. Professeur d'histoire, Université de Sherbrooke, Québec.
René-Jean Allenou de Lavillangevin. Henri-Marie Dubreil de Pontbriand.

LEBLANC, JEAN-MARIE. Représentant des Archives publiques du Canada en France, Paris, France.
Louis de Bonne de Missègle. François Mounier. Jean-Baptiste Tournois.

LEE, DAVID. Historian, National Historic Sites Service, Department of Indian Affairs and Northern Development, Ottawa, Ontario.

Paul Bécart de Granville et de Fonville. Jean-Pierre Daniélou. Jean-François Lefebvre de Bellefeuille.

LE GOFF, TIMOTHY J. A. Assistant professor of history, York University, Downsview, Ontario.

Michel Daccarrette (d. 1745). Michel Daccarrette (d. 1767). Jean-Baptiste Lannelongue. François Milly.

LITTLE, CHARLES HERBERT. Formerly chief editor, Royal Commission on Pilotage, Ottawa, Ontario.

Robert Swanton. Charles Watson.

MACBEATH, GEORGE. Historical resources administrator, Province of New Brunswick, Fredericton, New Brunswick.

William Pote.

MACLEOD, MALCOLM. Associate professor of history, Nova Scotia Teachers College, Truro, N.S.

Philippe-Thomas Chabert de Joncaire. Jacques-Pierre Daneau de Muy. Daniel-Hyacinthe-Marie Liénard de Beaujeu. Claude-Nicolas de Lorimier de La Rivière. Paul Perrault.

MACNUTT, WILLIAM STEWART. Professor of history, University of New Brunswick, Fredericton, New Brunswick.

John Gyles.

MATHIEU, JACQUES. Professeur d'histoire, Université Laval, Québec, Québec.

François Daine.

MATTHEWS, KEITH. Chairman, Maritime history group, Memorial University of Newfoundland, St John's, Newfoundland.

William Keen.

MAUDE, MARY McD. Executive editor, *Dictionary of Canadian Biography / Dictionnaire biographique du Canada*, University of Toronto Press, Ontario.

Robert Potier Dubuisson.

MILNE, ALEXANDER TAYLOR. Formerly secretary and librarian, Institute of Historical Research, University of London, England.

Peter Frederick Haldimand.

MIQUELON, DALE. Assistant professor of history, University of Saskatchewan, Saskatoon, Saskatchewan.

Louis Bazil. Léon Fautoux. Louis Fornel. François Havy. Jean Lefebvre. Pierre de Lestage. Bernard Paris.

MOODY, BARRY M. Lecturer in history, Acadia University, Wolfville, Nova Scotia.

John Adams. Alexander Cosby. Benjamin Goldthwait. François Mangeant, dit Saint-Germain. Arthur Noble.

MOOGK, PETER N. Assistant professor of history, University of British Columbia, Vancouver, British Columbia.

Jean Brunet, dit La Sablonnière. David Corbin. Nicolas Dasilva, dit Portugais. Girard-Guillaume Deguise, dit Flamand. Antoine-Bertrand Forestier. Dominique Janson, dit Lapalme. Jordain Lajus. Jean-Baptiste Lozeau. Jean-Baptiste Maillou, dit Desmoulins. Edme Moreau. Jean-Louis Plessy, dit Bélair. Pierre Pouchot. Simon Soupiran. Jean-Fernand Spagniolini. Timothy Sullivan, known as Timothée Silvain. Louis-Michel de Vilermaula.

MOREL, ANDRÉ. Professeur titulaire de droit, Université de Montréal, Québec.

Nicolas-Gaspard Boucault.

MORRISON, KENNETH M. Graduate student in history, University of Maine, Orono, Maine, U.S.A.

Nodogawerrimet. Sauguaaram.

NASATIR, ABRAHAM P. Professor of history, California State University, San Diego, California, U.S.A.

Pierre-Antoine Mallet.

NEATBY, HILDA. Formerly professor of history, Queen's University, Kingston, Ontario.

Ralph Burton. Benjamin Price.

NISH, CAMERON. Associate professor of history, Sir George Williams University, Montreal, Quebec.

François-Étienne Cugnet. Jean-Urbain Martel de Belleville [in collaboration with C. Richard]. Jacques Simonet d'Abergemont [with C. Richard].

O'NEILL, CHARLES EDWARDS. Professor of history, Loyola University, New Orleans, Louisiana, U.S.A.

Michel Baudouin. Nicolas-Ignace de Beaubois. Jean-Baptiste Le Moyne de Bienville.

PAQUIN, MICHEL. Adjoint au directeur des recherches, *Dictionnaire biographique du Canada / Dictionary of Canadian Biography*, Les Presses de l'université Laval, Québec, Québec.

Jean-Baptiste Adhémar. Jean d'Alquier de Servian. Louise-Catherine André de Leigne. Claude Barolet. Gervais Baudoin. Gilbert Boucault de Godefus. Luc Callet. Toussaint Cartier. Justinien Constantin. Louis-Claude Danré de Blanzy. Christophe-Hilarion Du Laurent. Marguerite Duplessis. Simon Foucault. René Gaschet. Valérien Gaufin. Nicolas-Auguste Guillet de Chaumont. Gervais Hodiesne. Jean-Michel Houdin. Maurice Imbault. Étienne Jeanneau. François Margane de Lavaltrie. Pierre. Jacques-Nicolas Pinguet de Vaucour. Arnould-Balthazar Pollet. Hyacinthe-Olivier Pressé. Pierre Révol. Ambroise Rouillard. Jean Taché.

PELL, JOHN H. G. Chairman, New York State American Revolution Bicentennial Commission; president, Fort Ticonderoga Association, New York, U.S.A.

Johannes Schuyler.

PINCOMBE, CHARLES ALEXANDER. Civic archivist, Moncton, New Brunswick.

Edward How.

POTHIER, BERNARD. Historian, Canadian War Museum, National Museums of Canada, Ottawa, Ontario.

François-Nicolas de Chassin de Thierry. Louis Denys de La Ronde [in collaboration with D. Horton]. Joseph Du Pont Duvivier. Joseph-Nicolas Gautier, dit Bellair. Joseph Lartigue. Joseph Leblanc, dit Le Maigre. François Le Coutre de Bourville. Joseph de Monbeton de Brouillan, dit Saint-Ovide. Pierre Morpain. Félix Pain. Barthélemy Petitpas.

PRITCHARD, JAMES S. Assistant professor of history, Queen's University, Kingston, Ontario.

Bernard Cardeneau. Pierre Constantin. Jacques Kanon. Jean-Baptiste Legardeur de Tilly. François Lemaître, dit Jugon. Pierre Lupien, dit Baron. Abel Olivier. Jean-Baptiste Pommereau. Louis-Pierre

Poulin de Courval Cressé. Michel de Sallaberry. Gilles William Strouds. Richard Testu de La Richardière. Médard-Gabriel Vallette de Chévigny.

PROULX, JEAN-PIERRE. Historien, Service des lieux historiques nationaux, Ministère des Affaires indiennes et du Nord canadien, Ottawa, Ontario.

Pierre-Benoît Payen de Noyan.

PROVOST, HONORIUS, PTRE. Archiviste, Séminaire de Québec, Québec.

Jean-Charles Chevalier. Charles-Antoine Godefroy de Tonnancour. Sylvestre-François-Michel Ransonnet. Thomas-Jacques Taschereau.

QUESNEL, YVES. Éclusier, Voie maritime du Saint-Laurent, La Salle, Québec.

Pierre Gamelin Maugras. Jean-Baptiste Le Comte Dupré. Jean-Baptiste Neveu. Charles Nolan Lamarque.

QUINN, DAVID BEERS. Andrew Geddes and John Rankin professor of modern history, University of Liverpool, England.

William Taverner.

RAWLYK, GEORGE A. Professor of history, Queen's University, Kingston, Ontario.

Patrick Heron. William Vaughan. Samuel Waldo.

RICH, EDWIN ERNEST. Formerly master, St Catharine's College; emeritus Vere Harmsworth professor of imperial and naval history, University of Cambridge, England.

James Isham. Richard Staunton. Thomas White.

RICHARD, CLAUDE. Étudiant gradué en histoire, Université de Montréal, Québec.

Jean-Urbain Martel de Belleville. Jacques Simonet d'Abergemont. [In collaboration with C. Nish.]

RILEY, BARBARA. Historian, National Museum of Man, National Museums of Canada, Ottawa, Ontario.

Jean Claparède. Guillaume Delort.

RODGER, ANDREW. Ownership analyst, Canadian Radio and Television Commission, Ottawa, Ontario.

Claude-Élisabeth Denys de Bonnaventure. Joseph de Fleury de La Gorgendière. Robert Tarride Duhaget.

ROMPKEY, RONALD G. Senior English master, St Michael's University School, Victoria, British Columbia.

Johann Burghard Erad. Jean Pettrequin. John Salusbury.

RUSS, CHRISTOPHER J. Senior teacher of history, United Talmud Torahs School Board of Montreal, Quebec.

Gaspard Adhémar de Lantagnac. Paul d'Ailleboust de Périgny. Louis Aubert de La Chesnaye. René Boucher de La Perrière. Josué Dubois Berthelot de Beaucours. Zacharie-François Hertel de La Fresnière. Etienne Hertel de Saint-François. Louis de La Corne. François-Josué de La Corne Dubreuil. Jean-Baptiste de Lamorinie. François Lefebvre Duplessis Faber. René Legardeur de Beauvais. Charles Legardeur de Croisille. François-Marie Le Marchand de Lignery. Jean-Baptiste Levrault de Langis Montegron. Daniel Migeon de La Gauchetière. Jacques

de Noyon. Jacques-Hugues Péan de Livaudière. Jean-Baptiste de Saint-Ours Deschaillons. Charles-Henri-Joseph Tonty de Liette.

ST. JAMES, JOHN. Formerly manuscript editor, *Dictionary of Canadian Biography/Dictionnaire biographique du Canada*, University of Toronto Press, Toronto, Ontario.

Robert Vincent. [In collaboration with C. E. Thomas.]

SEINEKE, KATHRINE WAGNER. Writer, El Granada, California, U.S.A.

Antoine Giard. Jean-François Mercier.

SMITH, DONALD B. Graduate student in history, University of Toronto, Ontario.

Glossary of Indian Tribal Names. Kinousaki. Saguima.

STACEY, CHARLES P. Professor of history, University of Toronto, Ontario.

Introductory essay: The British forces in North America during the Seven Years' War. François-Charles de Bourlamaque. William DeLaune. George Scott. James Wolfe.

STANDEN, S. DALE. Assistant professor of history, Lady Eaton College, Trent University, Peterborough, Ontario.

Jean-Charles d'Arnaud. Charles de Beauharnois de La Boische. Louis Charly Saint-Ange. Charles-René Gaudron de Chevremont. Jacques-René Gaultier de Varennes. Jacques de Lafontaine de Belcour. Nicolas Lanoullier de Boisclerc. Nicolas-Joseph de Noyelles de Fleurimont.

†STEARNS, RAYMOND P. Professor of history, University of Illinois at Urbana, Champaign, Illinois, U.S.A.

Joseph Kellogg.

STEELE, IAN K. Associate professor of history, University of Western Ontario, London, Ontario.

William Eyre. John Forbes.

STEWART, ALICE R. Professor of history, University of Maine, Orono, Maine, U.S.A.

Jeremiah Moulton.

SUTHERLAND, MAXWELL. Assistant chief (history), Research Division, National Historical Sites Service, Department of Indian Affairs and Northern Development, Ottawa, Ontario.

Paul Mascarene. Richard Philipps.

TAILLEMITE, ÉTIENNE. Conservateur en chef, Section ancienne, Archives nationales, Paris, France.

Roland-Michel Barrin de La Galissonière. Louis-Joseph Beaussier de Lisle. Emmanuel-Auguste de Cahideuc Dubois de La Motte. Constantin-Louis d'Estourmel. Alexandre de La Maisonfort Du Boisdecourt. Jean-Baptiste-Louis-Frédéric de La Rochefoucauld de Roye. Charles Latouche MacCarthy. Joseph-Hyacinthe de Rigaud de Vaudreuil. Louis-Philippe de Rigaud de Vaudreuil. Jacques-Pierre de Taffanel de La Jonquière.

THIBAULT, H. PAUL. Historien, Service des lieux historiques nationaux, Ministère des Affaires indiennes et du Nord canadien, Ottawa, Ontario.

Charles-Joseph d'Ailleboust. Michel de Gannes de Falaise.

CONTRIBUTORS

THOMAS, CHRISTMAS EDWARD. Research assistant, Public Archives of Nova Scotia, Halifax, Nova Scotia.
Henry Cope. William Tutty. Robert Vincent [in collaboration with J. St. James].

THORMAN, GEORGE E. Principal, Parkside Collegiate, St Thomas, Ontario.
George Clark. Robinson Crusoe. William Isbister. Joseph Smith. Wappisis.

THORPE, FREDERICK J. Chief, History division, National Museum of Man, National Museums of Canada, Ottawa, Ontario.
Gratien d'Arrigrand. Pierre-Jérôme Boucher. Gaspard-Joseph Chaussegros de Léry. Louis Franquet. François Ganet. François-Claude-Victor Grillot de Poilly. Jean-Claude-Henri de Lombard de Combles. David-Bernard Muiron. François-Madeleine Vallée. Étienne Verrier.

TRIGGER, BRUCE G. Professor of anthropology, McGill University, Montreal, Quebec.
Glossary of Indian Tribal Names.

TURNBULL, JAMES R. Lecturer in history, University of Manitoba, Winnipeg, Manitoba.
Paul-Louis Dazemard de Lusignan. Jean-Armand Dieskau. André Doreil. François-Xavier de Saint-Ours.

VACHON, ANDRÉ. Conservateur, Archives nationales du Québec, Québec.
Marie-Madeleine Jarret de Verchères. Louis Pillard.

VACHON, CLAUDE. Documentaliste, Fédération des commissions scolaires catholiques du Québec, Sainte-Foy, Québec.
Louis-Guillaume Verrier.

WAGNER, ROBERT L. Librarian, Free Library of Philadelphia, Pennsylvania, U.S.A.
Robert Hale. Edward Tyng.

WALLE, DENNIS F. Graduate student of history, University of Illinois, Urbana, Illinois, U.S.A.
George Clinton. William Dudley.

WHITELEY, WILLIAM H. Associate professor of history, Memorial University of Newfoundland, St John's, Newfoundland.
Daniel Bayne. John Christian Erhardt. Francis Lucas. James Webb.

WILLIAMS, GLYNDWR. Reader in history, Queen Mary College, University of London, England.
John Bean. William Coats. John Longland. Christopher Middleton. Thomas Mitchell. William Moor. John Potts. John Rankin. Joseph Robson. Francis Smith. George Spurrell. Edward Thompson. John Wigate.

WILSON, CLIFFORD P. Formerly assistant director, National Museum of Canada, Ottawa, Ontario.
Anthony Henday.

ZOLTVANY, YVES F. Associate professor of history, University of Western Ontario, London, Ontario.
Michel Bégon de La Picardière. Pierre Gaultier de Varennes et de La Vérendrye.

Index

Included in the index are the names of persons mentioned in volume III. They are listed by their family names, with titles and first names following. Wives are entered under their maiden names with their married names in parentheses. Persons who appear in incomplete citations in the text are fully identified when possible. An asterisk indicates that the person has received a biography in a volume already published, or will probably receive one in a subsequent volume. A death date or last floruit date refers the reader to the volume in which the biography will be found. Numerals in bold face indicate the pages on which a biography appears. Titles, nicknames, variant spellings, married and religious names are fully cross-referenced.

ABBADIE, Jean-Jacques-Blaise d', 527
Abbadie* de Saint-Castin, Bernard-Anselme d', Baron de Saint-Castin (1689–1720), xxxix, 3, 330
Abbadie* de Saint-Castin, Jean-Vincent d', Baron de Saint-Castin (1652–1707), xxxix, 3
Abbadie de Saint-Castin, Joseph d', Baron de Saint-Castin, xxxii, **3**, 359
Abbadie de Saint-Castin, Marie-Anselme d', Baronne de Saint-Castin (Bourbon), 3
Abbadie de Saint-Castin, Marie-Josephe (Anastasie?) d' (Le Borgne de Belle-Isle), 567
Abbadie de Saint-Castin, Marie-Mathilde d', Baronne de Saint-Castin. *See* Pidianske
Abel, Olivier. *See* Olivier
Abercromby*, James (1706–81), xxv, xxviii, xxix, 85, 273, 462, 535, 588, 591
Abergemont. *See* Simonet
Acaret. *See* Daccarrette
Acosta, José de, 337
Adams, Avis (wife of John Sr), 3
Adams, John, Sr, 3
Adams, John, **3–4**, 143, 437, 517
Adams*, Joseph (d. 1737), 415, 661
Adams, Sir Thomas, 411
Adhémar, Catherine. *See* Lepailleur de Laferté
Adhémar, Catherine. *See* Moreau
Adhémar, Jean-Baptiste, **4–5**, 271
Adhémar de Lantagnac, Anne. *See* Rigaud de Vaudreuil
Adhémar de Lantagnac, Anne (La Barre), 5
Adhémar de Lantagnac, Antoine, 5
Adhémar de Lantagnac, Gaspard, **5**, 550
Adhémar de Lantagnac, Geneviève-Françoise. *See* Martin de Lino
Adhémar de Lantagnac, Jeanne-Antoinette. *See* Truchi
Adhémar de Lantagnac, Pierre, 5
Adhémar de Lantagnac, Pierre-Gaspard-Antoine, 5
Adhémar* de Saint-Martin, Antoine (d. 1714), 4, 505
Adhémar de Saint-Martin, Michelle. *See* Cusson
Adoucourt. *See* Souart
Agemantan. *See* Argimault
Aguesseau, Henri-François d', 491, 639
Aguesseau, Jean-Baptiste-Paulin d', 639
Aigremont. *See* Clairambault

Aiguillon, Duc d'. *See* Vignerot
Ailleboust, Charles-Joseph d', **5–7**, 236
Ailleboust, Françoise-Charlotte d'. *See* Alavoine
Ailleboust, Marie-Josephte d'. *See* Bertrand
Ailleboust d'Argenteuil, Marie-Louise d'. *See* Denys de La Ronde
Ailleboust* d'Argenteuil, Pierre d' (1659–1711), 5, 7
Ailleboust de Coulonge et d'Argentenay, Marie-Barbe d'. *See* Boullongne
Ailleboust de Manthet, Louise-Catherine d' (Charly Saint-Ange), 110
Ailleboust de Manthet, Madeleine d' (Jarret de Verchères; Levrault de Langis Montegron), 399
Ailleboust de Périgny, Madeleine-Louise d'. *See* Margane de Lavaltrie
Ailleboust de Périgny, Paul d', **7**
Ailleboust de Périgny, Thérèse d' (Hertel de Moncours), 7
Ailleboust de Saint-Vilmé, Hector-Pierre d', 6
Ailleboust Des Muceaux, Catherine d'. *See* Legardeur de Repentigny
Ailleboust* Des Muceaux, Charles-Joseph d' (d. 1700), 7
Ailleboust Des Muceaux, Félicité d' (Guillet de Chaumont), 270
Ailleboust* Des Muceaux, Jean-Baptiste d' (1666–1730), 270
Alavoine, Charles (father), 7
Alavoine, Charles, 6, **7–8**, 430
Alavoine, Françoise-Charlotte (Ailleboust; Guyon, Marquise de Diziers), 6
Alavoine, Marie-Anne. *See* Lefebvre, *dit* Laciseraye
Alavoine, Marie-Françoise (Chevalier), 121
Alavoine, Marie-Thérèse. *See* Macard
Alby, Comte d'. *See* Sartine
Alden*, John (d. 1701/2), 7, 596
Aldridge, Christopher, Sr, **8–9**, 10, 297
Aldridge, Christopher, Jr, **9–10**, 324
Aldridge, Christopher (III), 10
Aldridge, Martha (wife of CHRISTOPHER JR), 10
Alexander*, Sir William (d. 1640), 652
Algimou, 358
Allain, Louis, 254
Allain, Marguerite. *See* Bourg
Allain, Marie (Gautier), 254

740

769

771